C O N T E N T S

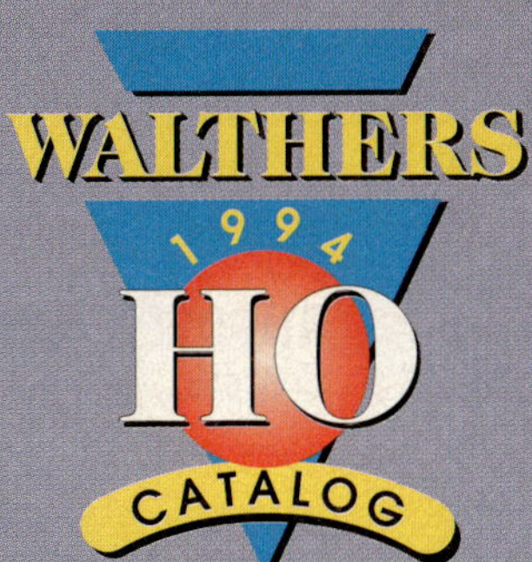

Dear Hobbyist,

Welcome to Walthers 1994 HO Scale Catalog. With its numerous changes and improvements, you'll find this latest edition is easier and more fun to use. Many of these came directly from your ideas and comments.

One of the most important is our all-new Manufacturer's Index. This handy reference lists each line in the catalog by name, and specifies the sections where products are featured. Our standard index is also included to provide detailed information. We've color-coded the edges of each page so you can find sections right away. Page numbers have been moved to the outside edge, so it's much easier to locate an item once you've found it in either index.

As part of our long-range plans to implement more of your ideas, we've completely redesigned the Locomotives, Freight Cars and Cornerstone Series® pages. These new sections are more exciting to read and feature a variety of photos and special features, along with complete part number and price information.

You'll also find that those fabulous "Magic" photos are now featured in various sections of the catalog, where they can be reproduced in a larger format. This really shows off the fine craftsmanship of the builders and photographers.

We've also updated all of the information on our vendors, and added 33 new lines in this year's book. In fact, we've added so much, that at 928 pages, this is our biggest HO Catalog to date!

As always, this is really YOUR catalog, so please feel free to drop us a line with your comments and suggestions.

Happy modeling!

Phil Walthers

WALTHERS

P.O. BOX 18676 MILWAUKEE, WI 53218
(414) 527-0770

PRINTED IN USA

ISBN 0-941952-38-X

Pacific Rail Products
PRP

Pentrex

Plastruct

PERMACRAFT PRODUCTS

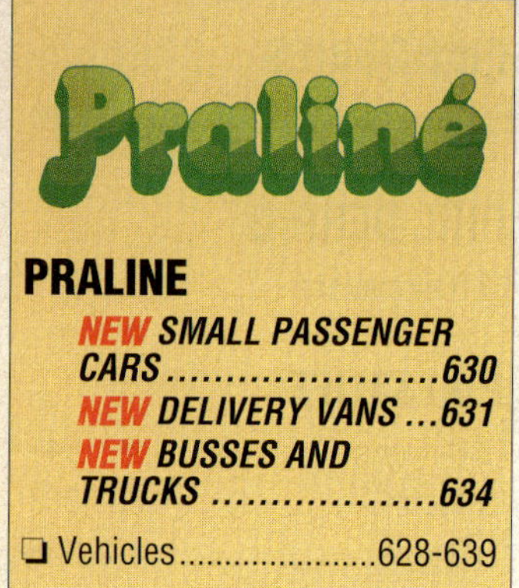

PRALINE

NEW SMALL PASSENGER CARS **630**
NEW DELIVERY VANS ...**631**
NEW BUSSES AND TRUCKS **634**
❏ Vehicles.................628-639

PRE SIZE MODEL SPECIALTIES

NEW BRIDGE ABUTMENTS/PIERS......**324**
NEW FX WEATHERING MATERIALS **308**
NEW CULVERTS **531**

❏ Pigments 308
❏ Retaining Walls 325
❏ Structures......................531
❏ Tunnel Portals 324

PRECISION INVESTMENT ASSOCIATES
❏ Parts........................829-831
❏ Couplers 224
❏ Figures............................585
❏ Trucks.............................236

PRECISION MASTERS
❏ Couplers 224

PRECISION SCALE
❏ Books 890
❏ Couplers 224
❏ Figures............................563
❏ Freight Cars 182
❏ Lighting/Electrical 693
❏ Locomotives 81
❏ Parts........................834-859
❏ Passenger Cars 214
❏ Scratch Building Supplies 775
❏ Track...............................256
❏ Trucks.......................237-240

PREISER
❏ Brick 303
❏ Circus 355-362
❏ Circus Tents 358
❏ Figures......................576-585
❏ Roadway 327
❏ Scenery 339
❏ Scenic Accessories 348
❏ Trees 287
❏ Vehicles 640-647

PRESTYPE
❏ Chalk 309

Q

Q CAR CO
❏ Parts 860
❏ Structures 471
❏ Traction...........................85

QUADRANT PRESS
❏ Books 891

QUALITY PRODUCTS
❏ Lighting/Electrical 696-697

R

R & RF
❏ Roadway 327
❏ Roadbed 265
❏ Yardsheet.........................346

RAIL LINE
❏ Couplers 229
❏ Freight Cars 177

RAIL POWER
❏ Locomotives 78
❏ Parts 782

RAILROAD AVENUE
❏ Books 892
❏ Structures 555
❏ Railroadiana 909-923
❏ Rail-Scenes 318
❏ Rail Truck 670

RAILWAY ASSOCIATES
❏ Structures 553

RAINTREE
❏ Locomotives 79
❏ Structures 560

RARITAN VALLEY
SNOW TO GO **292**
RIP/RAP **292**
❏ Ground Cover...................292

REID, GIL
❏ Art Prints 914-915

RIBBONRAIL
❏ Cleaner............................718
❏ Engine Cradle 728
❏ Freight Cars 182
❏ Lighting/Electrical 698
❏ Motors 701
❏ Track...............................259

RIETZE
❏ Vehicles 653

RIVAROSSI
❏ Locomotives 58-59
❏ Passenger Cars: See INTERNATIONAL HOBBY

RIX PRODUCTS

NEW HIGHWAY OVERPASS **534**
RIX RAX.....................**258**
MAXWELL AVENUE HOMES..................**534**

❏ Couplers 229
❏ Lighting/Electrical 682
❏ Structures 534
❏ Telephone Poles................349
❏ Throttle 707
❏ Track...............................258

ROBART
❏ Paint Shaker.....................727
❏ Tools 741

ROBB LTD
❏ Books 890

ROCO

ROCO LINE TRACK **249**

❏ Ballast.............................297
❏ Books 890
❏ Catalog............................165
❏ Circus Cars 352
❏ Cleaners 718
❏ Couplers 229
❏ Figures 562
❏ Freight Cars 163-165
❏ Lighting/Electrical 698
❏ Locomotives 62-73
❏ Minitanks 654-661
❏ Motors 701
❏ Paint 728
❏ Parts 812
❏ Passenger Cars...........190-198
❏ Signals & Detection 280
❏ Structures 556
❏ Track 249,260-263
❏ Traction....................72,84
❏ Trees 287
❏ Vehicles 648-653
❏ Wrench 745

ROUNDHOUSE
❏ Couplers 229
❏ Freight Cars 152-161
❏ Locomotives 60-61
❏ Parts 793
❏ Passenger Cars...........212-213
❏ Structures 491
❏ Trucks..............................241

S

SALFORD CONSULTING
❏ Video 904-905

SATELLITE CITY
❏ Adhesives 717

SCALE SCENICS
❏ Lighting/Electrical 699
❏ Parts 863
❏ Scratch Building Supplies ..777
❏ Solder 719
❏ Vehicles 661

W

WABASH VALLEY

WAHL

WAHL CLIPPER CORP.

WALKER MODELS

WB VIDEO

WEEKEND CHIEF

WELDBOND

WESTERFIELD

WESTERN RAIL PRODUCTS

WESTON

WHEEL WORKS

WHISTLES UNLIMITED

WALTHERS

WHITEGROUND MODEL WORKS

WHITEGROUND MODELS
THE SHOP SERIES KITS **558**

WIKING

WILLIAMS BROS

WINCHESTER STATION

WIRE WORKS

WOODLAND SCENICS

XYZ

X-ACTO

YE OLD HUFF -N- PUFF

Calls of coyotes and crickets mix in the warm summer air. We're standing across the tracks from the Lomax Lumber Camp for this spectacular shot. Bob Boudreau used a double exposure, featuring his HO Scale module and the actual moon, to create this unusual view.
Models and photos by Bob Boudreau

GLOSSARY*

Section gangs, like this CB&Q crew, rode the rails on handcars to replace rotted ties, tamp loose spikes and tighten bolts. As a memento of their shared sense of responsibility they struck this pose in the 1870s. Their foreman's solemn little daughter is in the place of honor. — *Photo courtesy Burlington Northern Railroad*

—A—

AAR The full-size railroad's trade group, the Association of American Railroads, that establishes their standards for equipment and safety.

ACC Alphacyanoacrylate. Extremely fast-setting glue that cures upon exposure to moisture in the air. Best for bonding non-porous surfaces. Extreme caution should be used as ACC will bond skin or eyes instantly.

ABS plastic A polymeric material made of acrylonitrile-butadiene-styrene. Harder and more resistant than styrene.

airbrush Small spray tool for fine-spray application of paints and stains with compressed air.

articulated A steam locomotive with two separate sets of drivers, rods and cylinders beneath a single boiler. Usually one set of drivers, rods and cylinders is pivoted so it can swing from side-to-side around curves while the boiler remains rigidly attached to the rear set of drivers, rods and cylinders.

—B—

back saw Fine toothed saw with reinforcing strap along top (back) of blade. Also called razor saw.

bad order The term the real railroads use to describe a malfunctioning part.

balsa Lightest modeling wood; 7-10 lbs./ft. Easily crushed and broken.

basswood (American Linden) Light weight, close-grained wood used for many modeling projects. Harder than balsa; has a tendency to raise a fuzz when painted or stained.

big hook The wrecking crane.

block A section of track that is electrically isolated from the adjoining sections for multiple-train operation or to prevent short circuits.

board and batten siding Vertical wooden planking with small wooden strips (battens) nailed over the seams between planks.

bolster The portion of a railroad freight or passenger car that runs across the underbody of the car to connect the trucks' pivot points to the body of the car. Sometimes used to describe all the cross members, including the ends, of a car's underframe.

branch A portion of a real railroad that branches off from the main line to reach a town or industry or to connect with another railroad.

Bristol board Heavy duty paper board with soft surface. Sold in thickness based on weight—10 lb., 20 lb.

bumper A device placed at the stub end of a track siding so cars or locomotives do not derail.

butt joint Wood joint where the end of one board is butted or glued directly to the second board.

—C—

caboose The rolling office and living quarters for the crew of a freight train. Sometimes called crummy, bobber or way car.

caliper Precision measuring tool for determining small dimensions between two jaws.

cardstock General term for all laminated paper sheet material; usually cut with razor knife.

casting Making copies of an original by means of a mold and some free-flowing material such as plaster or resin plastics.

catenary Overhead trolley wires, usually used by prototype interurbans (electric-powered locomotives and self-propelled cars) with diamond-shaped current pick up devices on the roofs called pantographs.

coaling station Any building where coal for steam locomotives is stored and shoveled or dumped through chutes into the locomotives' tenders. When the storage bins are elevated and the coal hoisted by conveyor belts or buckets, the structure is usually called a coaling tower. When the elevated storage bins are reached by a trestle so the coal can be dumped from the cars or shoveled right into the storage bins, the structure is usually called a coaling trestle.

corner board Trim on outside corner of wood frame building. Siding fits tight against corner boards.

cornice Horizontal molding or trim which crowns or finishes a wall.

coursed rubble Masonry wall made from random sized stones in crude rows (courses) with small stones filling the gaps. Farm foundations.

craft train kits Also called "craftsman" style kits, they are designed for the experienced modeler. These kits consist of unpainted wood, metal or plastic parts often accompanied by decals. Instruction sheets usually include assembly drawings or templates.

creosote Oily liquid from coal tars used to waterproof wooden beams and piers. Simulated with black and gray paints.

cribbing Framework of wood, concrete or metal beams filled with stones or earth to act as retaining wall or support for a structure.

crossing When two tracks cross each other, as in the center of a one-level figure-eight-style model railroad.

crossover The pair of switches that allow trains to travel from one parallel track to the adjacent one on double-track systems.

cut When the railroad has to dig or blast through a hill or mountain to maintain a level roadbed. Also, a few cars coupled together.

—D—

D.P.D.T. (Double pole, double throw) An electrical slide or toggle-type switch that is used for reversing the flow of current to the tracks by wiring across the back of the switch. Some types have an "off" position midway in their throw and these "Center-off D.P.D.T." switches are often used for wiring model railroads to allow two-train and two-throttle operation.

dental plaster Hard casting plaster used for molding.

die cast Casting process where molten metal or other liquid is forced into a mold.

diorama Small scene or portion of a scene usually modeled in great detail. Used by modelers lacking room for a complete layout.

double hung window Window with two sliding sashes that move vertically next to each other.

draft gear The box under the ends of a prototype car or locomotive (and on most models) where the coupler is spring-mounted to center it and to help absorb shocks and bumps.

dry brushing Process of rubbing paint only on the surface of a material without any flowing of the paint. A brush is dipped in just a little paint, the excess wiped off, and the nearly "dry brush" is used to rub pigment on an object. Used for weathering.

—E—

easy-to-build kits These kits feature very simple construction with few parts and step-by-step instructions. Most of these kits are pre-painted or molded in appropriate colors. They usually require only several basic tools such as screwdriver and modeling knife.

*This glossary combines material from *Model Railroad Structures from A to Z* by Carstens Publications Inc. and *The HO Model Railroading Handbook* by Robert Schleicher, published by Chilton Book Company. Reprinted with permission.

elevation   1) Drawing showing one side only of a structure. 2) Vertical distance above an established level or grade.

epoxy   Two-part (hardener and resin) thermosetting adhesive. Very resistant to chemical attack. Good for bonding nonporous materials such as plastic to metal.

escutcheon pins   Small pins or nails for ornamental fasteners. Originally used to attach keyhole plates.

—F—

fascia   Board nailed vertically to the end of roof rafters; sometimes used for gutter support.

fiddle yard   A hidden track or series of tracks used by modelers to make up or break down trains, lifting the equipment by hand.

fill   When the prototype railroad has to haul dirt to fill in a valley to bring the roadbed level up to that of the nearest trackage.

flange   The portion of any railroad wheel that guides that wheel down the rails. The flange extends around the circumference of each railroad wheel as its largest diameter.

flash   Small thin sections of casting material that has oozed out between mold sections.

frog   The point where the track rails actually cross at every switch and rail/rail crossing.

—G—

gap   A break in the rails to electrically isolate some portion of the track from another to prevent short circuits or to allow for multiple-train operation on the same stretch of track.

gauge   The spacing of the rails as measured from the inside of one rail head to the next. The "standard gauge" for most American railroads is 4 feet 8-1/2 inches; this distance was also once the standard center-to-center spacing for wagon wheels. Narrow gauge is any track spacing less than standard. Common examples are 3 ft., 2 ft., and 1 meter gauges. Gauge and scale may be combined in a short-hand notation. On3 means O scale (1/4" = 1'0") with a 3'0" space between the rails. HOn2-1/2 means an HO scale model (3.5mm=1'0") but the rails are spaced 2'6" apart.

gauze   A thin, open-weave fabric; can be cloth or wire. Used for support in molds and castings.

grab iron   The steel hand rails on the sides, ends and roofs of rolling stock.

grade: The angled rise or fall of the track so it can pass over another track or so it can follow the rising or falling contour of the land.

grain   The direction and arrangement of fibers in wood, cardstock or stratified stone.

gypsum   Common chemical calcium sulfate used to make plaster of Paris.

—H—

head-end cars   The cars that are normally coupled to the front of a passenger train, including express refrigerator, baggage and mail cars.

helper   The locomotive that is added to a train to supply extra power that may be needed to surmount a steep grade.

hostler   Men who service and sometimes move locomotives from one servicing facility to another to prepare the locomotive for the engineer.

hotbox   A bearing that has become overheated from lack of lubrication.

Hydrocal   Trade name of U.S. Gypsum Corporation for a very hard, dense plaster. Much stronger than plaster of Paris or patching plaster.

—I—

interchange   A section of track or several tracks where one railroad connects with another so trains or individual cars can move from one railroad to the next.

interlocking   A system of mechanical or electrical controls so only one train can move through a junction of two or more tracks like a crossing or yard throat.

interurban   Prototype railroads and railroad cars that were self-propelled with electrical power pick-up from an overhead wire, catenary, or from a third rail suspended alongside the track. The cars ran from city-to-city as well as inside the city limits and hence the name. (See also trolley and traction.)

—JK—

journal   The end of a railroad car or locomotive axle that actually serves or rides-in the bearing that supports the load.

keystone   A wedged shape stone at the top of an arch which holds the other pieces in place.

kingpin   The pivot point for a freight or passenger car truck where it connects to the bolster.

kitbash   To combine parts from two or more kits to produce a model different from both. Sometimes called cross-kitting, customizing or converting.

—L—

LCL   Less-than-carload lot; freight shipments that are too small to require an entire car.

lap joint   Wood joint where two boards are joined, each being cut to one half their normal thickness.

lintel   Structural element across the top of a window. Stone or concrete in stone structure. Does not show in modern buildings because of siding cover.

—M—

main line   The most heavily trafficked routes of the railroad.

maintenance-of-way   (MOW) The rolling stock or structures that are directly associated with maintaining the railroad or with repairing and righting wrecked trains.

modules   1) Small sections of model railroads designed for portability. Can be joined with other modules to form operating layouts. 2) Repeating patterns or designs.

mortise and tenon joint   Wood joint where a hole is cut into one board and the second is cut down in a tooth fashion to slide into the hole.

motor tool   Hand held motor driven drill with exchangeable collets. Can be used with drills, saws, grinders, sanding discs and other cutting and milling tools.

muntin   Framing to hold panes of a window in place. Also called *glazing bar*.

—NOP—

NMRA   National Model Railroad Association.

narrow gauge   Railroads that were built with their rails spaced closer than the 4-feet 1/2-inch standard gauge. Two-foot and three-foot spacings between the rail heads were the most common in this country, particularly in the 1880-1900 period.

nut, bolt and washing casting (NBW)   Simulating the end of rod showing the protruding threaded rod with the usual washer and locking nut.

parting line   Demarcation or mark where two-part molds join.

peddler freight   A freight train that switches cars at most towns along its route from terminal to terminal. Also called a way freight.

piggyback   The modern railroads' special flatcar service to transport highway trailers. Sometimes called TOFC.

pike   Short for turnpike or refers to a layout and general railroad scene.

pilaster   A pier or decorative column, not a supporting member. May have base, shaft and capital as part of the wall itself.

points   The portions of a switch that move to change the track's route from the main line to a siding. The point where the rails actually cross is called the "frog" part of the switch.

prototype   The term used to describe the full version that any model is supposed to duplicate.

Pullman   The passenger cars that were owned and operated by the Pullman company, usually sleeping cars, diners, or parlor cars. Sometimes used to describe any sleeping car.

—R—

r-t-r Abbreviation for ready-to-run.

rail joiner The pieces of metal that join two lengths of rail together. They slide onto the ends of the rail on a model railroad; they are bolted to the rails on the prototype.

razor saw Very fine tooth miniature type of backsaw with a ribbed reinforcement on the top to stiffen the saw.

reefer The insulated cars, cooled by either ice in bunkers fed through hatches on the roof or, in modern times, by mechanical refrigeration units.

resin High molecular weight organic type chemical which will harden under the appropriate conditions. Generally not water soluble.

right of way The property and the track owned by the railroad.

—S—

scale A proportion in size. The most common scales are:

Scale		Proportion
G	1/2″ = 1 ft.	1:24
1	3/8″ = 1 ft.	1:32
O	1/4″ = 1 ft.	1:48
HO	3.5mm = 1 ft.	1:87.1
S	3/16″ = 1 ft.	1:64
TT	1/10″ = 1 ft.	1:120
N	1.9mm = 1 ft.	1:160
Z	1.38mm = 1 ft.	1:220

scale lumber Small pieces of wood cut to same exact scale proportions as commercial building material; e.g. O scale 2 × 4, 1 × 10; HO scale 2 × 12, 4 × 4.

schedule A portion of a timetable listing authorized movements of a regular train.

scratchbuilding Make a model or item from basic materials such as wood, paper and plastic without the use of a kit. Engineering drawings are optional and commercial castings such as windows and doors may be used.

scribe To cut or scratch or mark or line. Scribed material has lines cut into it to resemble board joints.

selective compression Reducing the overall size of a building, retaining the basic design elements.

sill Horizontal piece directly below a window, usually angled downward slightly to remove the water.

snowshed The protective buildings that cover the track, usually in mountain areas, so deep snow and drifts won't cover the tracks themselves.

solder Mixtures of metal which melt at varying temperatures with different degrees of hardness.

Solder	Melting Point	Strength
Silver Solder	high	high
Lead-Tin(40-60)	medium	medium
Cerro (Bismuth Solders)	low (about 212°F)	low

SPDT Abbreviation for Single Pole, Double Throw electrical switch.

spot The switching maneuver whereby a freight or passenger car is moved to a desired position on a track.

Strathmore Commercial name of high quality hard surface cardstock or paper material. Supplied in various thicknesses based on plies; 1-ply, 2-ply, 3-ply, etc. Cuts very cleanly with sharp razor or knife. Also see Bristol board.

stripwood General term for small pieces of wood cut to exact dimensions as 1/32 × 1/16. Also includes scale lumber which are reproductions of actual lumber sizes in various scales; HO 2 × 4, O 2 × 10. Lengths range from actual 12″ to 2′4″ depending on supplier.

styrene A polymeric plastic material available in thin sheets that are easily cut by scoring and breaking along the score.

superelevation Banking the tracks in a curve so the trains can travel at some designated speed with a minimum of load on the outer wheels and rails and with a minimum of sway.

Super Glue See ACC

super scale Any train or accessory larger than O Scale. This includes 1 Scale (1/32) and G Scale (1/24).

switch Usually used to refer to the portion of the railroad track that allows the trains to change routes, but also used for electrical switches on model railroads, such as D.P.D.T. or S.P.S.T. switches. Track switches are sometimes call ''turnouts'' to avoid this confusion.

switch machine The electrical solenoid-type devices that move the track switch from one route to another to allow remote-controlled operation of trains over diverging trackage.

—T—

talgo Model railroad trucks with the couplers mounted to them so the couplers swivel with the trucks to allow operation of longer cars on tighter radius curves. Talgo trucks can, however, cause derailments when pushing or backing a long train.

tangent Straight sections of trackage.

tank engine A steam locomotive without a tender where the coal or fuel oil is carried in a bunker behind the cab and the water in a tank over the top of the boiler. Often used for switching on the prototype and on model railroads.

tender The car just behind most steam locomotives that carried the water, coal, wood or fuel oil.

throat The point where the yard trackage begins to diverge into the multiple tracks for storage and switching.

timetable The authorized movements of regular trains and engines which prescribe class, superiority and direction for a regular train. Schedules and special instructions covering operation of trains are provided for the crew.

traction The term used to describe all prototype locomotives and self-powered cars like trolleys and interurbans that operated by electrical power.

transistor throttle An electrical speed control for model railroad layouts that is used in place of the more common wire-bound rheostat to provide infinitely better and smoother slow speed and starting control for locomotives.

transition curve A length of track where any curve joins a tangent with gradually diminishing radius to ease the sudden transition of straight-to-curve for smoother operation and to help prevent derailments of extra-length cars that are caused by coupler bind in such areas of trackage. Also called an easement.

trolley Self-propelled, electric-powered cars that ran almost exclusively in city streets as opposed to the interurbans that ran through the country between cities and towns.

truck The sprung frame and four (or more) wheels under each end of most railroad freight and passenger cars.

turnout Where two diverging tracks join; also called a switch.

turntable A rotating steel or wooden bridge to turn locomotives or cars and/or to position them to align with the tracks in the engine house or round house.

—V—

vestibule The enclosed area, usually in both ends of a passenger car, where patrons enter the car from the station platform and where they walk to move from one car to the next.

—W—

way freight See peddler freight.

weathering Process of painting, staining or coloring to show aging, use or effects of weather on a model.

white glue A polymer suspension in water. Sold under a variety of commercial names—Elmer's, Ambroid, etc. Some forms may be sanded. Others peel rather than sand.

wye A track switch where both diverging routes curve away in opposite directions from the single straight track. Also, the triangular-shaped track (in plan view) where trains can be reversed.

SAFETY FIRST

WARNING -- HAZARDOUS PRODUCTS

We certainly don't have to tell any adult who has spent a week of evenings turning one of our kits into a work of art that these things should be kept out of the reach of children. Common sense and the amount of time and effort spent on the finished product make it fairly obvious that little fingers can turn your pride and joy ''back into a kit'' in less time than it will take to wipe the tears from your eyes.
There are also some less obvious points that need to be made.

THE PRODUCTS WE SELL ARE NOT TOYS

While we enthusiastically recommend Model Railroading as a Family Hobby, we expect you to work at it together. Adults must impart a respect for the tools, materials, and craftsmanship that goes into a finished effort, be it a single kit, a diorama, or a complete layout. Only after this has been done should a younger member of the family be allowed to work unsupervised on the railroad. (This is one of the big differences between ''Ready-to-Run'' and ''Craft Train Kits''.) Generalizing is difficult, but one rule is always important:

START WITH THE DIRECTIONS on the packages, cans and bottles, and follow whatever precautions are indicated. Next, read the assembly instructions that come with the kit.

YOU MAY BE EXPOSED TO SPECIFIC HAZARDS in three categories: **TOXIC** (poisons), **MECHANICAL** (including heat), and **ELECTRICAL**. The following list is not complete, but does point out some of the more general hazards to be aware of.

TOXIC CHEMICALS

Before anything else, read the warning on the label. Where adequate ventilation is required, be sure you have a large room with open windows or doors and an exhaust fan. Wearing a respirator is also extremely important. And don't forget to exhaust fumes from the room **AFTER** you are finished working! Eye protection is also a good idea with any toxic material, and of course **NO SMOKING**. Following are some specific chemical hazards:

METHYL ALCOHOL - Extremely poisonous when ingested or absorbed through the skin. Causes severe nervous system toxicity, especially blindness. Used as solvent in shellac and varnish and some paint removers.

TEFLON - Harmful when smoking or near fire or flame. Heated Teflon produces fumes that can cause congestion of the lungs.

1,1,1, TRICHLOROETHANE - A carbon tetra-chloride substitute that is much safer but still very toxic. Can cause fatal heart disturbances.

TRICHLOROETHYLENE - Can cause severe central nervous system depression and damage to the heart muscle.

PETROLEUM HYDROCARBONS - (Petroleum Distillates) May produce depression, coma, or convulsions, as well as pulmonary irritation. Avoid aspiration into the lungs. Do not induce vomiting.

TOLUOL - (Toluene) Depresses the nervous system and may cause bone marrow destruction. (This is the risk found in glue sniffing).

XYLENE - Produces the same problems as Toluol. Examples of products containing Toluol or Xylene are certain lubricants and cleaning fluids, dull coating spray, plastic cements, matte finish spray, and some thinners and paints.

MODEL LOCOMOTIVE SMOKE - is usually composed of volatile oils that are harmful or fatal if swallowed. Do not induce vomiting.

EPOXY CEMENTS - The ''hardener'' is very irritating to the skin. Wash off immediately.

INSTANT GLUES - Certain new ''super glues'' such as the cyanacrylates, adhere skin to skin or an object to the skin so that only surgery will break the bond. Use eye protection with any liquid glue.

ACETONE - (Including Isopropyl and Isobutyl Acetates) As little as fifty grams can be fatal. Produces skin and mucous membrane irritation and central nervous system depression. Contained is some cements. Use with adequate ventilation (1000 parts per million maximum allowable concentration).

GASOLINE - Intensely flammable and explosive. One cup can lift one ton 1000 feet instantly. Use a non-flammable cleaning agent instead.

CARBON TETRACHLORIDE - DO NOT USE UNDER ANY CIRCUMSTANCES! Ingesting 1/10 to 1/6 of an ounce is fatal! A concentration of 1.5 grams in the air of a room 10 x 10 x 8 feet square, equals 10 parts per million is the maximum allowable concentration. It injures all the cells of the body, especially the liver and kidneys.

SOLDERING FLUX - Some contain hydrochloric acid and sometimes oxalic acid. These substances are extremely irritating to the skin and mucous membranes on contact or inhalation.

MECHANICAL AND HEAT HAZARDS

Understand and appreciate the sophisticated nature of the materials furnished. Die castings, punched metal parts, wire forms, strips and shapes, and even plastic parts may have sharp edges and points which can cause cuts and punctures. They should be kept away from children. Knives, files, drills and other power tools are capable of doing severe damage. The edge of a 1'' wheel rotating at 30,000 rpm is moving at 90 mph. Make sure you wear eye protection and keep your fingers clear. Do not wear a necktie, loose clothing, long hair or jewelry that could become caught in a whirling tool. Also be aware of the heat generated and transmitted when working with power tools. Screwdrivers should be squared up occasionally to repair rounded edges. Replace or file off ''burred'' screw heads. Soldering irons, torches and hot knives represent both fire and heat hazards. Protect against burns and be careful of any fumes released due to the heat. Always work in a well ventilated area.

ELECTRICAL HAZARDS

The prime safety factor is the **PROPER GROUNDING** of electrical tools. Proper grounding will send stray current to the ground instead of through you! But remember, tools with ground wires are useless unless the receptacle is properly grounded. Make sure your three-pronged receptacles are correctly grounded. (Adapters are useless unless the pigtail is grounded.) A person can be paralyzed by a current of 10 milliamps, pushed by enough volts. This shock, long continued, can cause asphyxiation, heart fatigue and death. It takes only 50 milliamps to produce cardiac arrest, and the normal household fuse is 15 amps; 300 times that needed to stop your heart. An expensive but almost foolproof appliance for your work area is a ''Ground Fault Circuit Interrupter''. Most of these devices shut off the power after they sense a current leak as small as 5 milliamps. On the layout remember that even though trains run on 12-18 volts, power packs plug into 110 volt sockets and that can kill you. Again, proper grounding is of the utmost importance. When you are doing wiring or repair work, make sure the power pack is unplugged.

PRACTICE GOOD HABITS

Do not breathe dusts and oversprays — wear a respirator in a well ventilated room when doing any painting or using chemicals. Avoid inhaling lead fumes (as in soldering) and wash your hands after working with lead parts. Clean up and dispose of lead filings carefully, especially if you are working on the kitchen table! Above all, be sure to keep all lead parts well out of the reach of toddlers. (Lead compounds have been banned in paint and similar products. Lead is a very dangerous substance if it gets into your system.) Keep all flammable and explosive materials away from fire and heat. Be careful so no unexpected spark could ignite a burning inferno!

So, be careful. Properly used, hobby products can relieve tension, help you enjoy leisure time, develop manual dexterity, provide satisfaction, be a life-time of enjoyment, help curb delinquency, fill idle hours, provide meaning and purpose to retirement, help you earn a living, and keep us all from going crazy from government regulations, but they do demand your **RESPECT AS WELL AS YOUR APPRECIATION.**

(Adapted from an April 1976 MODEL RAILROADER feature by Dr. W. T. Watkins, Jr., M.D.)

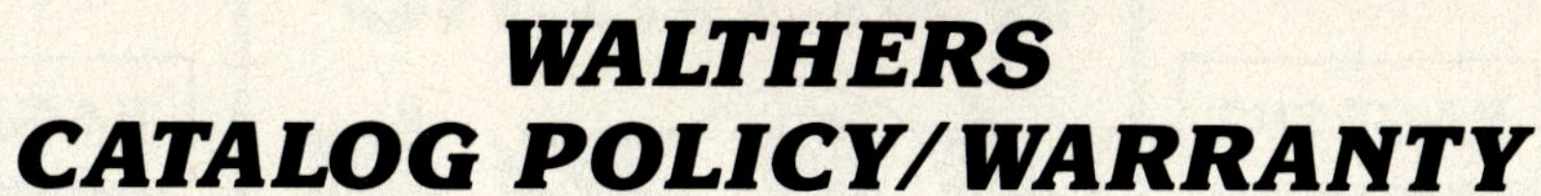

WALTHERS
CATALOG POLICY/WARRANTY

WALTHERS CATALOG POLICY

We realize the average dealer cannot stock everything shown in this catalog, and that it is necessary for you (and your dealer) to rely on us to accurately describe items which may be special ordered from this catalog. We try to describe each item correctly; however, if it is not what you expected, your dealer can return it to us. If it is clearly our mistake, we will pay return transportation; otherwise, your dealer must pay the return transportation.

PRICES

All prices are subject to change without notice. All items are invoiced at prices in effect at the time of shipment.

IMPORTANT

There are certain things which are beyond our control; therefore: 1) All items are offered subject to availability at time of shipment. 2) We reserve the right to correct errors, change prices, and modify designs without notice and without obligation to previous purchasers. If you do not like the "correction" or "change," they may be returned by your dealer.

WARRANTIES

As a prospective purchaser of materials offered in this catalog, you benefit from three separate warranties, as follows:
(1) The warranty offered by the manufacturer
(2) The warranty we extend to our dealers
(3) The warranty offered by the dealer to you, the purchaser

Some warranties are better than others, and we recommend that you inquire before you buy.

WALTHERS LIMITED WARRANTY

We will replace any Walthers part which is defective when received by you, or which is lost or damaged by you during assembly. We reserve the right to ask you to send the defective or damaged part back to us; however, DO NOT send it back until we ask for it, as we will not be responsible for this shipping cost. If the part was defective, we will pay transportation costs to send you a new part. If you are asking for replacement because the part was lost or damaged during assembly, we ask you to pay the transportation costs and to send us a stamped, self-addressed envelope (or sufficient postage) to send the part to you. This warranty applies to the original purchaser only, with a time limit of 90 days. We reserve the right to request proof of purchase; however, in order to save time, please write to us directly regarding replacement or repair, and DO NOT RETURN MERCHANDISE UNLESS REQUESTED. Since our designs are subject to change without notice, we must also reserve the right to make reasonable substitution or refund, if the item requested is no longer available. If refund is made, it will be sent through your dealer.

OTHER MANUFACTURERS WARRANTIES

Each manufacturer establishes his own warranty policy. Detailed information may be included with merchandise, or can be obtained from the manufacturer. In most cases, the manufacturer requires that parts be returned to the factory, frequently accompanied by proof of purchase. Under Federal Regulations, these are "Limited" Warranties. If you have problems with other manufacturers' warranties, we will try to help. However, DO NOT send merchandise back to us unless we request it.

DEALER WARRANTIES AND POLICIES

Each dealer establishes his own policy regarding returns, credits and refunds. We suggest you find out what these are, in advance, as some dealers are unable or unwilling to take the time and spend the money to return merchandise to us, or to the factory. We, in turn, cannot accept responsibility for merchandise sent to us without authorization.

KITS VS ASSEMBLY

Unless stated otherwise, the merchandise offered is in KIT FORM for assembly by the hobbyist. If you feel that you are unable to put it together, this is reason for return under our Catalog policy, but it is important to do this before attempting assembly of the kit. We normally will not accept the return of parts that have been worked on or are otherwise in unsalable condition. Also, we do not have an assembly service.

Brought to you by the graphic arts crew...

Lance Burton, Sandy Ellington, Sharon Hettinger, Allen Neuwirth, Arlene Ramthun, Mary Spilger, Todd Thornberry and Jim Zehner.

With help from . . . Peter Abbott, Kim Benson, Lisa Bergman, Kaci Christensen, Mark Hintz, Dennis Koller, Renee Newman, John Pradarelli, Ian Rotondi, Laurie Sanheim, Cynthia Turman and Wayne Wallschlager.

. . . And *SPECIAL* thanks to everyone in Data Processing, the General Office, Maintenance, Manufacturing, Merchandising, Sales and the Warehouse for the "behind the scenes" work they do to make this catalog possible.

WALTHERS '94 New Items

ADAM'S RIBS
You can almost smell the hickory smoke coming from this handsome restaurant, one of several new buildings in our Mainstreet USA Collection.

PAGE 112

PULLMAN-STANDARD PS2CD 4427 COVERED HOPPER
Built especially for the grain industry and still going strong, this is the first time these cars have been available in plastic!

PAGE 373

GRAIN BIN ETC.
Superdetail your new ADM Grain Elevator or farm operation with the new Grain Bins, Conveyor and Dryer kits from the Cornerstone Series®.

We're proud to present the latest new products from Walthers. Our selection of exciting models for steam- and diesel-era operations continues to grow, with new additions to our popular line of easy-to-build freight cars, Cornerstone Series® structures and accessories, Magnuson models vehicles, American Circus Series™ wagons and accessories and much, much more. Be sure to check with your Dealer each month, too, for other exciting new Walthers products which will be released throughout the coming year!

You'll also find dozens of new items in the various sections of this catalog from over 300 suppliers and manufacturers whose products are available from Walthers.

Your hobby Dealer can provide more information about these products and will be happy to answer any additional questions.

KEEP UP-TO-DATE WITH CRAFT TRAIN NEWS

Update your catalog and get the latest new product information each month with "Craft Train News." This special newsletter is available from your Dealer each month and provides a complete listing of new products which are in stock and ready for delivery.

You'll also find timely information on newly announced products, special events and other interesting hobby news.

PAGE 589

YARD TRACTOR
Pick-up or spot high-cube containers and trailers with this version of the Ottawa Yard Tractor, listed in the Intermodal section of Walthers freight cars.

PAGE 97

MI-JACK TRANSLIFT CRANE
Lift trailers or containers with this incredible new kit, one of many exciting new Intermodal cars and accessories listed in the Freight Car section.

PAGE 589

LINE TRUCK
Repair crews will be ready for any inspection or emergency with this rig, one of many new Magnuson vehicles.

PAGE 371

HIGH VOLTAGE TRANSMISSION TOWERS
A great scenery detail for a modern layout, especially with the new Transmission Wire. Look for these and many more new accessories, listed with the Cornerstone Series® kits.

PAGE 370

NORTHERN LIGHT & POWER
Generate new business for your railroad with this powerhouse! It's one of the many all-new industries joining the Cornerstone Series® this year.

FAST TRACK VIDEO
Bring the latest railroad action into your living room, with this all-new quarterly video magazine.

PAGE 897

BACHMANN
Direct from ''Chocolate Town USA'' comes this superb set, with loco and freight cars painted for your favorite Hershey chocolates.

PAGE 47

CM SHOPS
Keep your layout in top shape with the track maintenance equipment from Custom Finishing, including this new Pandrol-Jackson Rail Flaw Detection Vehicle.

PAGE 137

VOLLMER FIREHOUSE
Protect citizens and property with this classic station, ideal for a small town or suburban setting.

PAGE 448

'94 New Items

Here is a brief overview of the NEW products and NEW manufacturers added to ''Walthers 1994 HO Catalog''! For complete details on these new items, see the listing on the page indicated. In addition to the sections just listed, be sure to see the Locomotive-Traction, Passenger Cars, Couplers-Trucks, Track, Signals & Detection, Scenery, Circus, Figures, Lighting-Electrical-Motors, Power-Sound-Smoke, Adhesives-Cleaners-Lubricants, Paint & Supplies, Tools, Scratchbuilding Supplies, Parts, Books & Railroadiana sections for more new items.

NOTES ON AVAILABILITY OF "NEW PRODUCTS"

We have worked closely with each manufacturer to provide up-to-date delivery information on the products listed in this catalog. However, because many items are announced several months ahead of their delivery, some items will not be available at the time this catalog is published. For your convenience, we have included those items that we feel will be released and available during the life of this catalog. In some cases, items which will be released in 1994 are marked with an expected delivery date. Other items not listed in this catalog, but which have been announced, will be stocked as soon as they are available.

To get the latest information on new products available from Walthers, ask to see the Stock Advisory Service™ or Craft Train News at your Dealer. Each provides the latest monthly updates on new products, current prices and expected delivery dates.

NEW MANUFACTURERS

A-West
Accurate Lighting
American Limited Models
American Model Builders, Inc.
City Classics:
  (Short Discount)
Conway incentives:
  (Short Discount)
Creative Custom Craft
Depots by John:
  (Short Discount)
Design Preservation:
  (Short Discount)
Fast Track
Fine Scale Miniatures
Guts, Gravel & Glory
H & M Productions
Industrial Heritage
  Scale Models
Intermountain Railroad
  Supply: (Short Discount)
J. L. Innovative Design
Mini-Highways
P. H. Hobbies
Plano

Rail Power Products:
  (Short Discount)
Raritan Vally Scenic
Scale Works Models
Small World
Sun Coast Models
Superior Promotions, Inc.
Train Station Products
Wahl Clipper Corporation
Western Rail Products
Whistles Unlimited
Winchester Station
Wire Works
State Tool & Die
CS Design
Market Identity

PAGE 51

LIFE-LIKE
Put new modelers on the right track with this 120 piece starter set that's complete with track, loco, cars, signs and more.

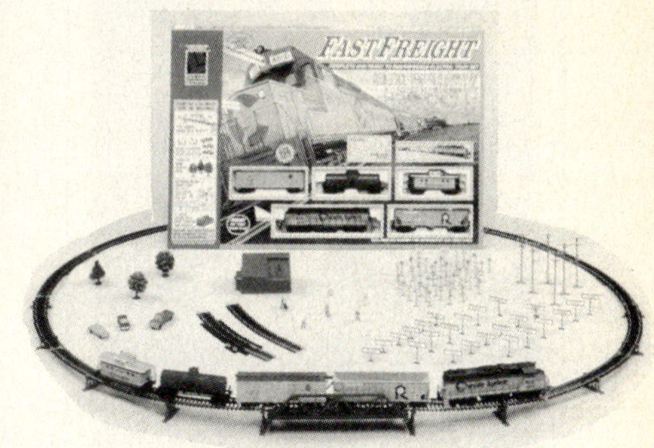

PAGE 367

FALLER ROLLER COASTER
This WORKING model captures all the color and motion of a real roller coaster in a limited-edition model.

PAGE 433

FALLER SWIMMING POOL
You've got to see this one to believe it as HO Scale swimmers actually MOVE through real water!

PAGE 624

KIBRI
KALMAR TRANSPORTER
An outstanding model, that will stand out in your intermodal terminal or highway scene.

THREE GENERATIONS OF SERVICE TO MODEL RAILROADERS

The Walthers company was started in 1932 as the result of one man's dream—Bill Walthers dreamed of being his own boss while creating products for others to enjoy. The first products were accessories and controls for improving Lionel Standard gauge layouts, but O and HO kits and supplies were quickly added.

In 1946, after serving 3 years in the Navy during World War II, Bruce Walthers joined the company. In 1958, when Bill retired, Bruce became president and CEO. Two years later, the company established a "full line" wholesale division to distribute other manufacturers products.

Phil Walthers began his training in the family business while he was still in high school, joining the company full time in 1972, after 2 years experience with a Chicago engineering firm. Phil became a third generation president and CEO in 1984.

From 1932 until 1958, Wm. K. Walthers Inc. rented space in two large warehouse buildings. In 1958, this historic building at 1245 N. Water St. was purchased, making it the first real "home" of Walthers trains. In 1983, Magnuson produced a model of this building, modestly hoping that all HO modelers will want to have one on their layout.

When in Milwaukee, you are invited to visit our plant and showroom. Attractions include: tours of the building, layouts and historical displays.

This view of the Warehouse shows just a few of the over 50,000 products stocked at Walthers.

In Shipping and Receiving, each order is checked and items are carefully packaged before being sent to Dealers.

The air is cold , sharpening the smell of diesel exhaust on this quiet Sunday. A pair of Katy SD40-2's, resplendent in "John Deere" green and yellow wait the call to duty which will come tomorrow morning. This scene combines the talents of Carter Osborne and Virgil Young, of Amarillo, Texas. Virgil scratchbuilt the Car Masters shed, basing it on a prototype which once stood in the BN yard at Amarillo. Carter stated with Athearn locos and rebuilt them with numerous detail parts to match Katy practice.

Photo by Carter Osborne.

WALTHERS ™

Highly detailed and ready-to-run, these engines are great for any HO Scale switching assignment. Best of all, they run as great as they look! Under the detailed plastic body is a skew-wound, five-pole motor with dual flywheels. Electrical pickup is through all eight wheels for smoother running. And with the cast metal frame, each engine WEIGHS OVER ONE POUND for super pulling performance. Putting them to work on your railroad is easy, they're available prepainted in 12 different roadnames, each with two different engine numbers. And for do-it-your-selfers, there's an undecorated version too.

CONRAIL
932-1353 #8461 (blue, white)

932-1354 #8593 (blue, white)

CHICAGO & NORTH WESTERN
932-1359 #1212 (yellow, green)

SOUTHERN PACIFIC
932-1358 #1004 "Bloody Nose" (gray, red, white)

LIMITED QUANITY AVAILABLE

UNDECORATED
932-1350 (molded in light gray, not shown)

Archer Daniels Midland

Cargill

LIMITED-RUN GRAIN ELEVATOR SW1 LOCOS

Many grain elevators own and operate SW1's to handle switching chores around their plants. These models finished in special paint schemes, based on actual prototypes. They're perfect for use with our new Cornerstone Series® ADM Grain Elevator (933-3022) and accessories, which are listed in the Structures section.

Choose from the new Archer Daniels Midland #69 or the Cargill #1004, or get one of each for your collection!

932-1362 Archer Daniels Midland #69 (yellow, blue, white) *NEW*
932-1363 Cargill #1004 (white, black) *NEW*

"ADM" and the ADM logo are trademarks of Archer Daniels Midland, used with permission.

"Cargill" and the Cargill logo are trademarks of Cargill, used with permission.

The rain has held this long, but these look like the last shots of the day. And we're in luck too, as the second unit is one of those brand new GP30's we've been hearing so much about! Its a hot summer day in 1963 as an SD9 pounds the diamond on Karl Erk's module in West Milford, New Jersey. The lead unit is a repainted Athearn model, will the EMD demo is a Bachmann loco. The tower is from Atlas, while Karl scratchbuilt the elevator and processing plant behind the tracks.

Models and Photo by Karl Erk

WALTHERS™

EMD SW1 SWITCHER

AFFORDABLY PRICED AT JUST $79.98 EACH

In 1939, Electro-Motive Corporation launched one of its most successful diesels, the SW1. When new, they were generally assigned to industrial switching or big city yards where smoke from steam locos presented problems. As newer and more powerful switchers arrived, they were bumped to lighter duties. Many were reassigned to branch lines where poor track and slow speeds were easily handled by the lightweight SW1. As retirements began, many shortline operators found them an ideal choice for their first diesels. Lumber companies, sand and gravel pits, steel mills and other heavy industries also used "retired" SW1's. Some remained in service to appear on the rosters of such modern roads as the Burlington Northern and Conrail!

On your layout, the SW1 is right at home from 1939 to the present day. Although their numbers are dwindling, many are still in use as industrial switchers, and a handful remain in service with large railroads.

Walthers HO Scale model is a superb replica, with a highly detailed plastic body, add-on handrails, cab interior, window "glass" and other details. Inside, there's a rugged Mashima can motor with a flywheel, and a unique Roco drive that powers both trucks. Eight-wheel electrical pick-up and an operating headlight are standard equipment, along with a die-cast metal frame that brings the weight of the loco to 11 ounces!

The fabulous SW1 is available prepainted in eight authentic schemes, and there's an undecorated version so you can create a custom model.

PENNSYLVANIA
932-1351 #5987 (Brunswick green, gold)
932-1352 #5993 (Brunswick green, gold)

BURLINGTON NORTHERN
932-1355 #93 (green, black, white)
932-1356 #97 (green, black, white)

MILWAUKEE ROAD
932-1360 #877 (orange, black, white)

NEW YORK CENTRAL
932-1357 #580 (black, white)

CHESSIE SYSTEM
932-1361 #8401 (yellow, orange, blue)

"Should'a been here in the winter of '77-78 when they had to bring up the rotary from Kansas City" says our engineer. His story reminds us that this is only the first blast of winter in the upper midwest, but it does seem to have started early. Rocketing towards Chicago, our hot intermodal train is making good time behind a trio of Overland Models brass imports. Ken Patterson painted and photographed the locos on a module constructed for the Midwest Valley Modeler's layout.

Models and Photo by Ken Patterson

WALTHERS™

Highly detailed and ready-to-run, these engines are great for any HO Scale switching assignment. Best of all, they run as great as they look! Under the detailed plastic body is a skew-wound, five-pole motor with dual flywheels. Electrical pickup is through all eight wheels for smoother running. And with the cast metal frame, each engine WEIGHS OVER ONE POUND for super pulling performance. Putting them to work on your railroad is easy, they're available prepainted in 12 different roadnames, each with two different engine numbers. And for do-it-your-selfers, there's an undecorated version too.

FAIRBANKS-MORSE H10/12-44

NEW LOWER PRICE - NOW JUST $74.98 EACH!
Was $84.98 in '93 Catalog!

MILWAUKEE ROAD
932-1303 #728 (orange, black with red, white herald)

932-1304 #750 (orange, black with red, white herald)

Rear view of cab

UNDECORATED
932-1300 (molded in light gray, not shown)

PENNSYLVANIA
932-1301 #5980 (Brunswick green with dulux gold lettering)

932-1302 #9086 (Brunswick green with dulux gold lettering)

SANTA FE
932-1305 #503 "Zebra Stripe" (black, silver)

932-1306 #516 "Zebra Stripe" (black, silver)

CENTRAL OF NEW JERSEY
932-1309 #9700 "Miss Liberty" Herald (Baltimore & Ohio blue, yellow)

932-1310 #9703 "Miss Liberty" Herald (Baltimore & Ohio blue, yellow)

NICKEL PLATE ROAD
932-1307 #125 (black with large yellow stripes at front and rear)

932-1308 #131 (black with large yellow stripes at front and rear)

CANADIAN NATIONAL
932-1311 #1640 (olive green, gold)

932-1312 #1658 (olive green, gold)

Introduced in 1944, the H10-44 marked Fairbanks-Morse entry to the locomotive business. Introduced as a 1,000 horsepower switcher and later upgraded to 1200 horsepower, they were know for their pulling power. Railroads large and small rostered these brutes, and some were in operation until the late 80's.

WALTHERS™

NEW YORK CENTRAL
932-1315 #8305 "Cigar Band" Herald (white sill)

932-1316 #8324" Cigar Band" Herald (white sill)

CHICAGO & NORTH WESTERN
932-1313 "Route of the Streamliners" #1054 (green, yellow)

932-1314 "Route of the Streamliners" #1057 (green, yellow)

UNION PACIFIC
932-1317 #1303 "Route of the Streamliners" (yellow)

932-1318 #1304 "Route of the Streamliners" (yellow)

SOUTHERN PACIFIC
932-1321 #1486 "Tiger Stripe" Scheme (black)

932-1322 #1490 "Tiger Stripe" Scheme (black)

WABASH
932-1319 #380 (black with yellow stripes)

932-1320 #381 (black with yellow stripes)

FRISCO
932-1323 #276 (red, white)

932-1324 #278 (red, white)

CUSTOM FINISHING

BUILD A LATER MODEL H12-44 WITH THIS CONVERSION KIT

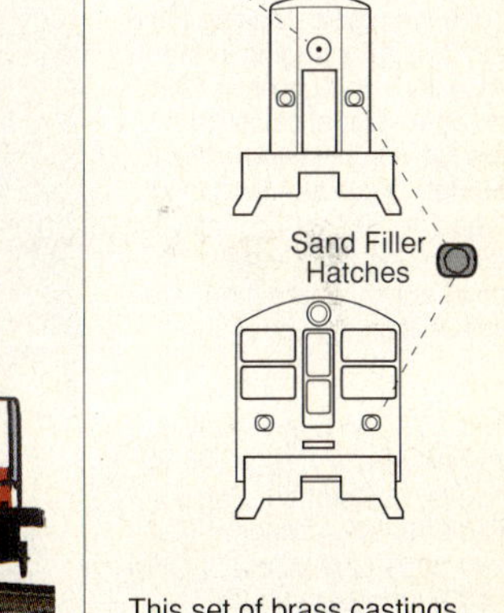

This set of brass castings includes a new nose, sand fillers, and headlights (which accept 1.5V bulbs and MV lens #159, both sold separately) as used on these later units. The illustrated instruction sheet covers the basic body modifications and the installation of the new parts

In September of 1952, F-M changed the styling of the H12-44. The cab overhang was removed, the sloped nose was changed slightly, the headlight was lowered and new sand fillers were installed. Production of this body style continued through February of 1953.

247-264 Fairbanks-Morse H 12-44 Conversion Kit 8.79

ATLAS
MODEL RAILROAD CO., INC.

Working way freights, switching yards or racing along in passenger service, these rugged Atlas engines will be at home on any layout! Featuring prepainted and lettered plastic bodies, the detailed, ready-to-run models include twin flywheels with can motors for smooth operation at all speeds. Heavy cast metal frames and all-wheel drive provide excellent tractive effort and pulling power.

ALCO LOCOS

ALCO S-2

An early builder and designer of diesel locos, Alco introduced the S2 in 1940 and continued production until June of 1950. Over 1300 were sold, making it the most popular engine in the Alco line. In August of 1950, an almost identical model, the S4 was unveiled.   Both models could be found in all types of yard service, as well as working for private companies, where there are still units in service today.

ALCO S-4

150-8077 Southern Pacific #1346 (black, orange) 98.95
150-8078 Southern Pacific #1362 (black, orange) 99.95
150-8083 Gulf Mobile & Ohio #1006 (maroon) 99.95
150-8084 Gulf Mobile & Ohio #1010 (maroon) 99.95
150-8085 Canadian Pacific #7015 (maroon, gray) 104.95
NEW
150-8086 Canadian Pacific #7024 (maroon, gray) 104.95
NEW
150-8087 Boston & Maine #1261 (black, red) 104.95
NEW
150-8088 Boston & Maine #1264 (black, red) 104.95
NEW
150-8070 Undecorated 98.95

ALCO S-4
150-8285 Pennsylvania #8431 (Brunswick green) 98.95
150-8286 Pennsylvania #8434 (Brunswick green) 98.95
150-8288 Southern #6075 99.95
150-8289 Santa Fe #1502 (black, aluminum) 104.95
NEW
150-8290 Santa Fe #1536 (black, aluminum) 104.95
NEW
150-8270 Undecorated 104.95

ALCO C424 PHASE I ea 99.95 *NEW*
150-8061 Erie Lackawanna #2401 (black, yellow)
150-8062 Erie Lackawanna #2409 (black, yellow)
150-8063 Conrail #2491 (blue)
150-8064 Conrail #2497 (blue)
150-8055 Undecorated

ALCO RSD-4/5 ea 99.95
150-8171 Pennsylvania #8451 (Brunswick green)

Limited Quantities Available ea 99.95
150-8170 Pennsylvania #8446 (Brunswick green)
150-8173 Santa Fe #2158 (black)

ALCO C424 PHASE II ea 99.95 *NEW*
150-8051 Canadian National #3205 (black, orange)
150-8052 Canadian National #3219 (black, orange)
150-8053 Burlington Northern #4240 (green, black)
150-8054 Burlington Northern #4244 (green, black)
150-8050 Undecorated

ALCO RS-11 ea 99.95
150-8186 Seaboard Coast Line #1205 (black, yellow)
150-8187 Seaboard Coast Line #1208 (black, yellow)

ALCO C425 ea 99.95 *NEW*
150-8038 New Haven #2553 (black, orange)
150-8039 New Haven #2557 (black, orange)
150-8040 British Columbia Railway #805 (light green, dark green)
150-8041 British Columbia Railway #812 (light green, dark green)
150-8042 Norfolk & Western #1001 (black, white)
150-8043 Norfolk & Western #1006 (black, white)
150-8030 Undecorated

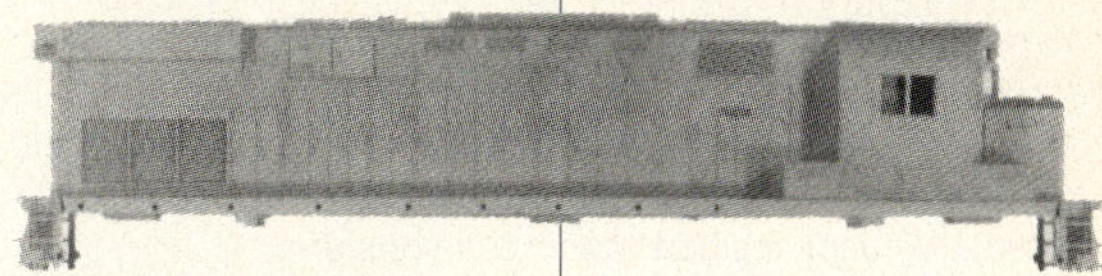

UNDECORATED SHELLS

Bodies are molded in gray plastic and are complete with window "glass," add-on details and full set of handrails, which are molded in black engineering plastic.

150-707210 RS-3, RSD4/5 12.00
150-709210 RS-11, RSD-12 12.00
150-803210 C424/C425 12.50
150-805210 C424 Phase 2 12.50
150-805225 C424, Phase 1 13.00
150-810211 RS-1 9.25

ALCO C425

INFORMATION STATION

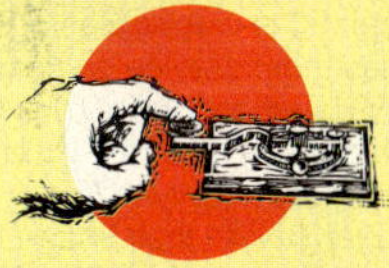

Steam locos have long been identified by the number of wheels. But an eight-wheel engine on one road might be an engine with eight drivers, or one with a four-wheel lead truck and four drivers.

In December of 1900, the American Engineer and Railroad Journal ran an article by Fredric M. Whyte detailing his system of identifying locos by using numerals to indicate lead, driving and trailing wheels.

With the Whyte system, our "eight-wheelers" would be an 0-8-0 and a 4-4-0.

The American Locomotive Company (ALCo) adopted the system in 1903 and within a few years, it was used throughout the railroad industry.

EMD LOCOS

EMD FP7 ea 109.95
150-8328 Soo Line #504A nondynamic, with dual headlights (maroon, yellow)
150-8329 Soo Line #505A nondynamic, with dual headlights (maroon, yellow)
150-8301 Undecorated, nondynamic, with dual headlight
150-8302 Undecorated, dynamic, with single headlight

Limited Quantities Available
150-8300 Undecorated, dynamic, with single headlight 109.95

EMD FP7
Roadname shown
not available

All models are ready-to-run (hood units require installation of handrails which are included) with prepainted and lettered styrene bodies and metal underframes. All wheels are powered and engines feature flywheel drive where noted. All locos include horn-hook couplers.
We have worked closely with this manufacturer to provide accurate availability information at the time this catalog was published. Items listed in blue ink may not be available at all times. Please see you dealer for current delivery information.

EMD F7

One of the all-time great locos, the F7 was an upgrade of earlier F unit models. Packing 1500 horsepower, they were built in A (with control cab) and B (cabless booster) unit configurations, so they could be MU-'ed. Many were fitted with water tanks and steam generators for use in passenger service. Nearly 2400 were purchased for use in the US, Canada and Mexico, and some remained in service until the 1980's.

Our models shown here depict the classic Santa Fe passenger service engines in silver, red and yellow "warbonnet" colors. Pulling flagship trains like "The Super Chief," their image became world-famous. This colorful scheme is offered on both powered and dummy versions of A and B units, which are listed below.

POWERED WITH FLYWHEELS ea 26.50 (unless noted)
140-3201 Santa Fe Passenger (war bonnet-red, yellow, silver)
140-3203 Santa Fe Freight (blue, yellow)
140-3205 Pennsylvania Passenger (maroon, yellow)
140-3207 Pennsylvania Freight (green, yellow)
140-3209 Southern Pacific (red, gray)
140-3211 Burlington Northern (cascade green, black, white)
140-3213 Union Pacific (gray, yellow)
140-3215 Rio Grande (black, yellow, silver)
140-3217 Milwaukee Road (gray, yellow)
140-3219 Baltimore & Ohio (blue, black, gray)
140-3221 New Haven (red, white, black)
140-3225 Canadian National (green, yellow, black)
149-3227 Chesapeake & Ohio (blue, yellow)
140-3229 Northern Pacific (green, yellow, red)
140-3231 Chicago & North Western (green, yellow)
140-3233 Amtrak
140-3235 Southern Pacific "Daylight" (red, orange)
140-3237 Canadian Pacific (red, white, black)
140-3241 Black Widow 30.50 **NEW**
140-3223 Undecorated

EMD F7A

POWERED - STANDARD ea 22.00 (unless noted)
140-3101 Santa Fe Passenger (war bonnet-red, yellow, silver)
140-3103 Santa Fe Freight (blue, yellow)
140-3107 Pennsylvania Freight (green, yellow)
140-3109 Southern Pacific (red, gray)
140-3111 Burlington Northern (cascade green, black, white)
140-3113 Union Pacific (gray, yellow)
140-3117 Milwaukee Road (gray, yellow)
140-3119 Baltimore & Ohio (blue, black, gray)
140-3125 Canadian National (green, yellow, black)
149-3127 Chesapeake & Ohio (blue, yellow)
140-3129 Northern Pacific (green, yellow, red)
140-3131 Chicago & North Western (green, yellow)
140-3135 Southern Pacific "Daylight" (red, orange)
140-3141 Black Widow 26.00 **NEW**
140-3123 Undecorated
140-3105 Pennsylvania Passenger (maroon, yellow)
140-3115 Rio Grande (black, yellow, silver)
140-3133 Amtrak
140-3137 Canadian Pacific (red, white, black)

EMD F7B

POWERED WITH FLYWHEELS ea 26.50 (unless noted)
140-3202 Santa Fe Passenger (warbonnet red, yellow, silver)
140-3204 Santa Fe Freight (blue with yellow stripe)
140-3206 Pennsylvania Passenger (tuscan with yellow stripe)
140-3208 Pennsylvania Freight (olive with yellow stripes)
140-3210 Southern Pacific (gray, red)
140-3212 Burlington Northern (green and white with black roof)
140-3214 Union Pacific (yellow with gray roof and red stripes)
140-3216 Rio Grande (aluminum, yellow with black stripes)
140-3218 Milwaukee Road (gray with orange and yellow band)
140-3220 Baltimore & Ohio (black, blue, gray with gold stripes)
140-3222 New Haven (black, orange, white)
140-3226 Canadian National (green and gray with black roof and yellow stripe)
140-3228 Chesapeake & Ohio (blue, yellow)
140-3230 Northern Pacific (green, yellow with red stripe)
140-3232 Chicago & North Western (green, yellow)
140-3234 Amtrak (silver with black roof)
140-3236 Southern Pacific "Daylight" (red, orange)
140-3237 Canadian Pacific (red, white, black)
140-3238 CP Rail (red with silver stripe) **NEW**
140-3242 Black Widow 30.50 **NEW**
140-3224 Undecorated

EMD F7A

DUMMY ea 11.00 (unless noted)
140-3001 Santa Fe Passenger (silver, red)
140-3003 Santa Fe Freight (blue, yellow)
140-3005 Pennsylvania Passenger (maroon, yellow)
140-3007 Pennsylvania Freight (green, yellow)
140-3009 Southern Pacific (red, gray)
140-3011 Burlington Northern (green)
140-3013 Union Pacific (yellow)
140-3015 Rio Grande (aluminum, yellow with black stripes)
140-3017 Milwaukee Road (gray)
140-3019 Baltimore & Ohio (blue, black, gray)
140-3021 New Haven (black, orange, white)
140-3025 Canadian National (green, yellow, black)
140-3027 Chesapeake & Ohio (blue, gold, silver)
140-3029 Northern Pacific (green, yellow)
140-3031 Chicago & North Western (green, yellow)
140-3033 Amtrak (silver with black roof)
140-3035 Southern Pacific "Daylight" (red, orange)
140-3037 Canadian Pacific (red, white, black)
140-3041 Black Widow 15.25 **NEW**
140-3023 Undecorated (black)

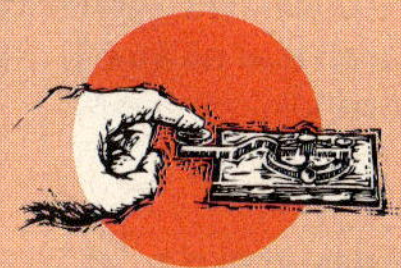

EMD GP9

WITH FLYWHEELS - POWERED ea 26.00
(unless noted)
140-3152 Baltimore & Ohio (blue, black, gray)
140-3153 Southern Pacific (red, gray)
140-3154 Union Pacific (yellow, gray)
140-3155 Chicago, Burlington & Quincy (red, white, gray)
140-3156 Santa Fe Freight (blue, yellow)
140-3157 Great Northern (orange, green)
140-3159 Milwaukee Road (black, orange)
140-3160 Conrail (blue) *NEW*
140-3161 Canadian National (red, black, white) *NEW*
140-3162 Black Widow 30.00 *NEW*
140-3151 Undecorated (black)

DUMMY ea 13.00
(unless noted)
140-3052 Baltimore & Ohio (blue, black, gray)
140-3053 Southern Pacific (red, gray)
140-3054 Union Pacific (yellow, gray)
140-3055 Chicago, Burlington & Quincy (red, white, gray)
140-3056 Santa Fe Freight (blue, yellow)
140-3057 Great Northern (orange, green)
140-3059 Milwaukee Road (black, orange)
140-3060 Conrail (blue)
140-3061 Canadian National (black, red, white) *NEW*
140-3062 Black Widow 30.00 *NEW*
140-3051 Undecorated (black)

EMD F7B

DUMMY ea 11.00
(unless noted)
140-3002 Santa Fe Passenger (silver, red)
140-3004 Santa Fe Freight (blue, yellow)
140-3006 Pennsylvania Passenger (maroon, yellow)
140-3008 Pennsylvania Freight (green, yellow)
140-3010 Southern Pacific (red, gray)
140-3012 Burlington Northern (green)
140-3014 Union Pacific (yellow)
140-3016 Rio Grande (gold, silver)
140-3018 Milwaukee Road (gray)
140-3020 Baltimore & Ohio (blue, black, gray)
140-3022 New Haven (black, orange, white)
140-3026 Canadian National (green, yellow, black)
140-3028 Chesapeake & Ohio (blue, gold, silver)
140-3030 Northern Pacific (green, yellow)
140-3032 Chicago & North Western (green, yellow)
140-3034 Amtrak (silver with black roof)
140-3036 Southern Pacific "Daylight" (black, red, orange)
140-3038 Canadian Pacific (red, white, black)
140-3042 Black Widow 15.25 *NEW*
140-3024 Undecorated (black)

F7A SINGLE HEADLIGHT - POWERED WITH FLYWHEEL
140-3239 Undecorated 26.50

F7A SINGLE HEADLIGHT - STANDARD
140-3139 Undecorated 20.00

F7A SINGLE HEADLIGHT - DUMMY
140-3039 Undecorated 11.00

F7A SINGLE HEADLIGHT - SHELL ONLY
140-30390 Undecorated 3.00

"Dress Up" your F-7 and F-9 A & B Units with this Super-Detailing Kit by Walthers

Kit contains clear plastic windshield, windows and port holes, pre-formed wire grab irons and two clear plastic headlight lenses. Packed with placement diagram and instructions, designed especially for Athearn F units.

DIESEL DRESS-UP KIT
933-822 (51 pieces) 4.98

EMD GP35

WITH FLYWHEELS - POWERED ea 26.00
140-4201 Atlantic Coast Line (black, yellow)
140-4202 Baltimore & Ohio (blue, yellow)
140-4203 Chicago, Burlington & Quincy (red, white, gray)
140-4204 Illinois Central (black, white)
140-4205 Santa Fe Freight (blue, yellow)
140-4206 Southern Pacific (red, gray)
140-4207 Erie Lackawanna (gray, maroon, yellow)
140-4208 Chessie System (orange, yellow, blue)
140-4209 Soo (red, white)
140-4200 Undecorated (black)

DUMMY ea 10.00 (unless noted)
140-4221 Atlantic Coast Line (black, yellow)
140-4222 Baltimore & Ohio (blue, yellow)
140-4223 Chicago, Burlington & Quincy (red, white, gray)
140-4224 Illinois Central (black, white)
140-4225 Santa Fe Freight (blue, yellow)
140-4226 Southern Pacific (red, gray)
140-4227 Erie Lackawanna (gray, maroon, yellow) 13.00
140-4228 Chessie System (orange, yellow, blue)
140-4229 Soo (red, white)
140-4220 Undecorated (black)

INFORMATION STATION

As the steam versus diesel debates grew in the late 40's, tests were conducted to find out which was better. Many claims were made for the diesels' superior performance, but results showed that modern steamers performed at about the same level.

But diesels won hands down in maintenance. They could go hundreds of miles daily, requiring nothing more than a quick inspection or refueling. This meant much lower operating costs and a higher rate of availability.

With fewer moving parts, diesels were usually easier to repair. Some estimates figured a typical steamer spent half its working life in a roundhouse for repairs and inspections. With diesels, parts could be purchased from the builder, rather than custom-made in the railroads' shops.

And, diesels were cheaper to run. At the time, diesel fuel sold for pennies per gallon, while a ton of coal was quite expensive.

All models are ready-to-run (hood units require installation of handrails which are included) with prepainted and lettered styrene bodies and metal underframes. All wheels are powered and engines feature flywheel drive where noted. All locos include horn-hook couplers.

We have worked closely with this manufacturer to provide accurate availability information at the time this catalog was published. Items listed in blue ink may not be available at all times. Please see you dealer for current delivery information.

EMD GP38-2

WITH FLYWHEELS- POWERED ea 30.50
140-4601 Burlington Northern (green, black)
140-4602 Conrail (big sky blue)
140-4603 Illinois Central Gulf (gray, orange, red)
140-4604 Seaboard System (gray)
140-4605 Missouri Pacific (blue, white)
140-4606 Milwaukee Road (black, orange)
140-4607 Norfolk Southern (black)
140-4608 Santa Fe (blue, yellow)
140-4609 Soo Line (white, red, black)
140-4610 Southern Pacific (gray, red)
140-4611 Union Pacific (gray, yellow)
140-4613 Burlington Northern (cascade green, white) *NEW*
140-4614 Canadian Pacific (cascade green, white) *NEW*
140-4612 Undecorated, Nondynamic (black)
140-4600 Undecorated, Dynamic (black)

DUMMY ea 15.25
140-4651 Burlington Northern (green, black)
140-4652 Conrail (big sky blue)
140-4653 Illinois Central Gulf (gray, orange, red)
140-4654 Seaboard System (gray)
140-4655 Missouri Pacific (blue, white)
140-4656 Milwaukee Road (black, orange)
140-4657 Norfolk Southern (black)
140-4658 Santa Fe (blue, yellow)
140-4659 Soo Line (white, red, black)
140-4660 Southern Pacific (gray, red)
140-4661 Union Pacific (gray, yellow)
140-4663 Burlington Northern (cascade green, white) *NEW*
140-4664 Canadian Pacific (cascade green, white) *NEW*
140-4662 Undecorated, Nondynamic (black)
140-4650 Undecorated, Dynamic (black)

EMD GP40-2

WITH DYNAMIC BRAKES POWERED ea 33.00
140-4702 Burlington Northern (green, white)
140-4703 Conrail (blue, white)
140-4704 CSX Transportation (blue, gray)
140-4705 Rio Grande (black, orange)
140-4706 Seaboard System (red, yellow, gray)
140-4707 Southern Pacific (red, gray, white)
140-4708 Southern Pacific '91 (red, gray, white)
140-4709 Burlington Northern (cascade green, white) *NEW*
140-4700 Undecorated (black)

DUMMY ea 16.50
140-4722 Burlington Northern (green, white)
140-4723 Conrail (blue, white)
140-4724 CSX Transportation (blue, gray)
140-4725 Rio Grande (black, orange)
140-4726 Seaboard System (red, yellow, gray)
140-4727 Southern Pacific (red, gray, white)
140-4728 Southern Pacific '91
140-4729 Burlington Northern (cascade green, white) *NEW*
140-4720 Undecorated (black)

EMD GP40-2 NONDYNAMIC POWERED
140-4701 Undecorated 33.00

DUMMY
140-4721 Undecorated 16.50

EMD SD9

WITH FLYWHEELS - POWERED ea 27.50 (unless noted)
140-3801 Santa Fe (yellow, blue)
140-3802 Burlington Northern (green, black, white)
140-3803 Milwaukee Road (orange, black)
140-3804 Pennsylvania (black, yellow)
140-3805 Southern Pacific (gray, red)
140-3806 Union Pacific (yellow, gray)
140-3807 Black Widow 31.50 *NEW*
140-3800 Undecorated (black)

DUMMY ea 11.00 (unless noted)
140-3821 Santa Fe (blue, yellow)
140-3822 Burlington Northern (green, black, white)
140-3823 Milwaukee Road (orange, black)
140-3824 Pennsylvania (black, yellow)
140-3825 Southern Pacific (gray, red)
140-3826 Union Pacific (yellow, gray)
140-3827 Black Widow 15.75 *NEW*
140-3820 Undecorated (black)

EMD DD40

2 MOTORS ea 38.50
140-4281 Baltimore & Ohio
140-4282 Chicago, Burlington & Quincy
140-4283 GM Demo
140-4284 Pennsylvania
140-4285 Union Pacific
140-4286 Southern Pacific
140-4280 Undecorated

1 MOTOR ea 30.25
140-4242 Chicago, Burlington & Quincy
140-4244 Pennsylvania
140-4240 Undecorated
140-4243 GM Demo
140-4245 Union Pacific
140-4246 Southern Pacific

DUMMY ea 16.50
140-4261 Baltimore & Ohio
140-4262 Chicago, Burlington & Quincy
140-4263 GM Demo
140-4260 Undecorated

EMD F45

WITH FLYWHEELS - POWERED ea 27.50
140-3601 Santa Fe Freight (blue, yellow)
140-3602 Great Northern (gray, blue, white)
140-3603 Burlington Northern (green, black, white)
140-3600 Undecorated

DUMMY ea 11.00
140-3611 Santa Fe Freight (blue, yellow)
140-3612 Great Northern (gray, blue, white)
140-3613 Burlington Northern (green, black, white)
140-3610 Undecorated

EMD FP45

WITH FLYWHEELS - POWERED ea 27.50

140-3621 Santa Fe (silver, red)
140-3622 Milwaukee Road (yellow, gray)
140-3623 Baltimore & Ohio (blue, yellow)
140-3624 Amtrak (black, silver, red)
140-3620 Undecorated (black)

DUMMY ea 13.75

140-3631 Santa Fe (silver, red)
140-3632 Milwaukee Road (yellow, gray)
140-3633 Baltimore & Ohio (blue, yellow)
140-3634 Amtrak (black, silver, red)
140-3630 Undecorated (black)

EMD SDP40

WITH FLYWHEELS - POWERED ea 27.50

140-4101 Baltimore & Ohio (blue, yellow)
140-4102 Chicago & North Western (green, yellow)
140-4103 New Haven (black, orange, white)
140-4104 New York Central (black, white)
140-4105 Santa Fe Freight (blue, yellow)
140-4106 Southern Pacific (gray, red)
140-4107 Santa Fe Passenger (war bonnet-red, yellow, silver)
140-4108 Great Northern (blue)
140-4100 Undecorated (black)

DUMMY ea 13.75

140-4121 Baltimore & Ohio (blue, yellow)
140-4122 Chicago & North Western (green, yellow)
140-4124 New York Central (black, white)
140-4125 Santa Fe Freight (blue, yellow)
140-4126 Southern Pacific (gray, red)
140-4127 Santa Fe Passenger (war bonnet-red, yellow, silver)
140-4128 Great Northern (blue)
140-4120 Undecorated (black)

EMD SD45

WITH FLYWHEELS - POWERED ea 27.50 (unless noted)

140-4161 Seaboard Air Line (red, black, yellow)
140-4162 Southern Pacific (gray, red)
140-4163 Union Pacific (gray, yellow)
140-4164 Chicago, Burlington & Quincy (gray, red, white)
140-4165 Santa Fe Freight (blue, yellow)
140-4166 Pennsylvania (black, yellow)
140-4167 GM Demo (blue, white)
140-4168 Conrail (blue, white) 25.00 *NEW*
140-4160 Undecorated (black)

DUMMY ea 13.75

140-4181 Seaboard Air Line (red, black, yellow)
140-4182 Southern Pacific
140-4183 Union Pacific (gray, yellow)
140-4184 Chicago, Burlington & Quincy (gray, red, white)
140-4185 Santa Fe Freight (blue, yellow)
140-4186 Pennsylvania (black, yellow)
140-4187 GM Demo (blue, white)
140-4180 Undecorated (black)

EMD SW7 "COW"

WITH FLYWHEELS - POWERED ea 25.50

140-4002 Burlington Northern (green, black)
140-4003 Illinois Central (black, white)
140-4004 Southern (black, white)
140-4005 Santa Fe Freight (blue, yellow)
140-4007 Union Pacific (gray, yellow)
140-4008 Pennsylvania (black, yellow)
140-4009 Baltimore & Ohio (blue, white)
140-4010 Conrail (blue) *NEW*
140-4011 Canadian Pacific (red) *NEW*
140-4012 Canadian National (red, black, white) *NEW*
140-4001 Undecorated (black)
140-4006 Southern Pacific (red, gray)

DUMMY ea 12.75

140-4052 Burlington Northern (green, black)
140-4053 Illinois Central (black, white)
140-4054 Southern (black, white)
140-4055 Santa Fe Freight (blue, yellow)
140-4056 Southern Pacific (red, gray)
140-4057 Union Pacific (gray, yellow)
140-4058 Pennsylvania (black, yellow)
140-4059 Baltimore & Ohio (blue, white)
140-4060 Conrail (blue) *NEW*
140-4061 Canadian Pacific (red) *NEW*
140-4062 Canadian National (red, black, white) *NEW*
140-4051 Undecorated (black)

EMD SW7 "CALF"

WITH FLYWHEELS - POWERED ea 25.50

140-4027 Burlington Northern (green, black)
140-4028 Illinois Central (black)
140-4029 Southern (black, white)
140-4030 Santa Fe Freight (blue, yellow)
140-4031 Southern Pacific (red, gray)
140-4032 Union Pacific (gray, yellow)
140-4033 Pennsylvania (black, yellow)
140-4034 Baltimore & Ohio (blue, white)
140-4035 Conrail (blue) *NEW*
140-4036 Canadian Pacific (red) *NEW*
140-4037 Canadian National (black, red) *NEW*
140-4026 Undecorated (black)

DUMMY ea 12.75

140-4077 Burlington Northern (green, black)
140-4078 Illinois Central (black)
140-4079 Southern (black, white)
140-4080 Santa Fe Freight (blue, yellow)
140-4081 Southern Pacific (red, gray)
140-4082 Union Pacific (gray, yellow)
140-4083 Pennsylvania (black, yellow)
140-4084 Baltimore & Ohio (blue, white)
140-4085 Conrail (blue) *NEW*
140-4086 Canadian Pacific (red) *NEW*
140-4087 Canadian National (black, red) *NEW*
140-4076 Undecorated (black)

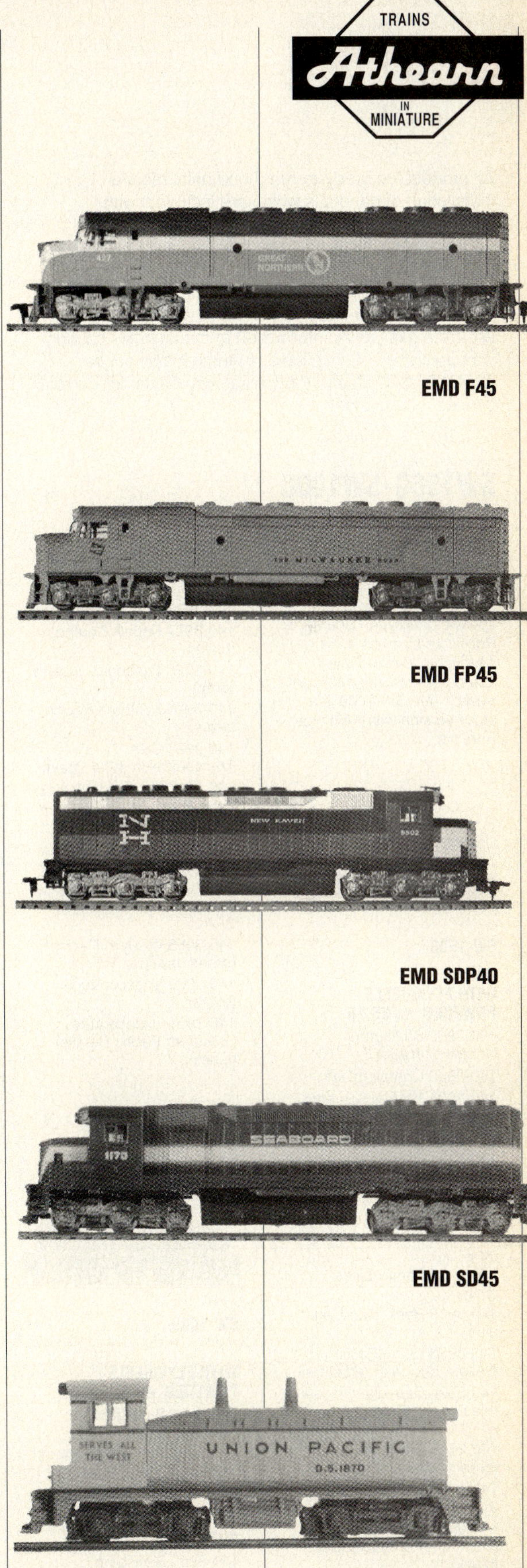

All models are ready-to-run (hood units require installation of handrails which are included) with prepainted and lettered styrene bodies and metal underframes. All wheels are powered and engines feature flywheel drive where noted. All locos include horn-hook couplers.

We have worked closely with this manufacturer to provide accurate availability information at the time this catalog was published. Items listed in blue ink may not be available at all times. Please see you dealer for current delivery information.

SW1500 - SW1000

The SW-1500 is available in two versions: Stock with Flexicoil trucks, or with AAR type A trucks to match a specific prototype. Southern Pacific version has extra headlights, cab-mounted numberboards and Flexicoil trucks. The SW-1000 is a stock version with AAR type A trucks.

SW-1500

WITH FLYWHEELS - POWERED ea 35.75
140-3902 Burlington Northern (green)
140-3903 Conrail (blue)
140-3904 Norfolk Southern (black)
140-3905 Seaboard System (gray)
140-3906 Southern Pacific (green)
140-3907 CSX Transportation (blue, gray)
140-3908 Family Lines (gray)
140-3909 Rock Island (light blue)
140-3933 Union Pacific (yellow, gray with red stripe)
140-3934 Canadian National (black, red, white, yellow) *NEW*
140-3935 Western Pacific (green, orange) *NEW*
140-3900 Undecorated (black)
140-3901 Undecorated (Southern Pacific Details) (black)

DUMMY ea 18.00
140-3922 Burlington Northern (green)
140-3923 Conrail (blue)
140-3924 Norfolk Southern (black)
140-3925 Seaboard System (gray)
140-3926 Southern Pacific (green)
140-3927 CSX Transportation (blue, gray)
140-3928 Family Lines (gray)
140-3929 Rock Island (light blue)
140-3953 Union Pacific (yellow, gray with red stripe)
140-3954 Canadian National (black, red, white, yellow) *NEW*
140-3955 Western Pacific (green, orange) *NEW*
140-3920 Undecorated (black)
140-3921 Undecorated (Southern Pacific Details) (black)

SW-1000

WITH FLYWHEELS - POWERED ea 32.50
140-3931 Burlington Northern (green)
140-3932 Rio Grande (black)
140-3930 Undecorated (black)

DUMMY ea 16.25
140-3951 Burlington Northern (green)
140-3952 Rio Grande (black)
140-3950 Undecorated (black)

EMD GP50

WITH FLYWHEELS - POWERED ea 30.50
140-4628 Chicago & North Western (yellow, green)
140-4629 Missouri Pacific (dark blue)
140-4630 Norfolk Southern (black)
140-4631 Santa Fe (yellow, blue)
140-4632 Union Pacific (gray, yellow)
140-4633 Burlington Northern (cascade green, black)
140-4634 Burlington Northern (cascade green, white) *NEW*
140-4626 Undecorated With Dynamics (black)
140-4627 Undecorated Less Dynamics (black)

DUMMY ea 15.25
140-4678 Chicago & North Western (yellow, green)
140-4679 Missouri Pacific (dark blue)
140-4680 Norfolk Southern (black)
140-4681 Santa Fe (yellow, blue)
140-4682 Union Pacific (gray, yellow)
140-4683 Burlington Northern (cascade green, black)
140-4684 Burlington Northern (cascade green, white) *NEW*
140-4676 Undecorated With Dynamics (black)
140-4677 Undecorated Less Dynamics (black)

FM TRAINMASTER

POWERED ea 27.50 (unless noted)
140-4302 Milwaukee Road (orange, black)
140-4303 Chicago North Western (green, yellow)
140-4304 Norfolk & Western (dark blue)
140-4305 Pennsylvania (black)
140-4306 Santa Fe (blue, yellow)
140-4307 Southern Pacific (gray, red)
140-4308 Black Widow 31.50 *NEW*
140-4300 Undecorated
140-4301 Undecorated (Southern Pacific Details)

DUMMY ea 13.75
140-4322 Milwaukee Road (orange, black)
140-4323 Chicago North Western (green, yellow)
140-4324 Norfolk & Western (dark blue)
140-4325 Pennsylvania (black)
140-4326 Santa Fe (blue, yellow)
140-4327 Southern Pacific (gray, red)
140-4328 Black Widow 15.75 *NEW*
140-4321 Undecorated (Southern Pacific Details)
140-4320 Undecorated

GENERAL ELECTRIC

GE U28B

WITH FLYWHEELS - POWERED ea 26.50
140-3401 Burlington Northern (green, black)
140-3402 Norfolk & Western (blue)
140-3403 Western Pacific (silver, orange, gold)
140-3400 Undecorated (black)

DUMMY ea 10.00
140-3411 Burlington Northern (green, black)
140-3412 Norfolk & Western (blue)
140-3413 Western Pacific (silver, orange, gold)
140-3410 Undecorated (black)

GE U30B

WITH FLYWHEELS - POWERED ea 26.50
140-3441 Chicago, Burlington & Quincy (gray, red, white)
140-3442 Illinois Central (white, orange)
140-3440 Undecorated (black)
140-3443 Santa Fe Freight (yellow, blue)
140-3444 Chessie System (orange, yellow, blue)

DUMMY ea 13.25
140-3451 Chicago, Burlington & Quincy (gray, red, white)
140-3452 Illinois Central (white, orange)
140-3453 Santa Fe Freight (yellow, blue)
140-3454 Chessie System (orange, yellow, blue)
140-3450 Undecorated (black)

GE U28C

WITH FLYWHEELS - POWERED ea 27.50
140-3421 Southern Pacific (red, gray)
140-3423 Penn Central (black, white)
140-3422 Union Pacific (gray, yellow)
140-3420 Undecorated (black)

DUMMY ea 11.00
140-3431 Southern Pacific (red, gray)
140-3432 Union Pacific (gray, yellow)
140-3433 Penn Central (black, white)
140-3430 Undecorated (black)

GE U30C

WITH FLYWHEELS - POWERED ea 27.50
140-3461 Chesapeake & Ohio (blue, yellow)
140-3462 Milwaukee Road (orange, black)
140-3463 Pennsylvania (black, yellow)
140-3460 Undecorated (black)

DUMMY ea 11.00
140-3471 Chesapeake & Ohio (blue, yellow)
140-3472 Milwaukee Road (orange, black)
140-3473 Pennsylvania (black, yellow)
140-3470 Undecorated (black)

GE U33B

WITH FLYWHEELS - POWERED ea 26.50
140-3481 Rock Island (red)
140-3482 New York Central (black)
140-3483 Seaboard Coast Line (black)
140-3480 Undecorated

DUMMY ea 10.00
140-3491 Rock Island (red)
140-3492 New York Central (black)
140-3493 Seaboard Coast Line (black)
140-3490 Undecorated

INFORMATION STATION

Many EMD model designations are shorthand for the type of loco:

SC: Six hundred horsepower - Cast frame

SW: Six hundred horsepower - Welded frame

NW: Nine hundred horsepower, Welded frame

TR: Transfer service

BL: Branchline

DD/DDX: Double-Diesel and/or Double-Diesel Experimental (two-engined units, essentially a pair of SD40's in a single body, built for UP)

F: Freight

FP: Passenger service F unit, with large water tank for steam generator.

B or B Unit: cabless Booster locomotive

GP: General Purpose (often pronounced "geep") 4 axle unit

SD: Special Duty - six axle unit

SDP: Special Duty - Passenger (equipped with steam boiler)

EMD GP50

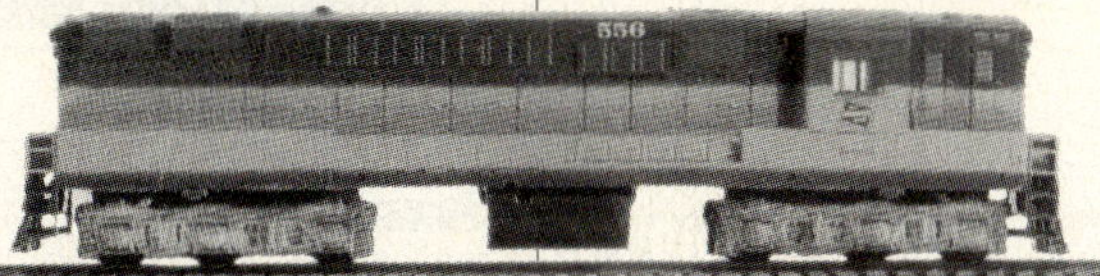

FM TRAINMASTER

GE U28 B

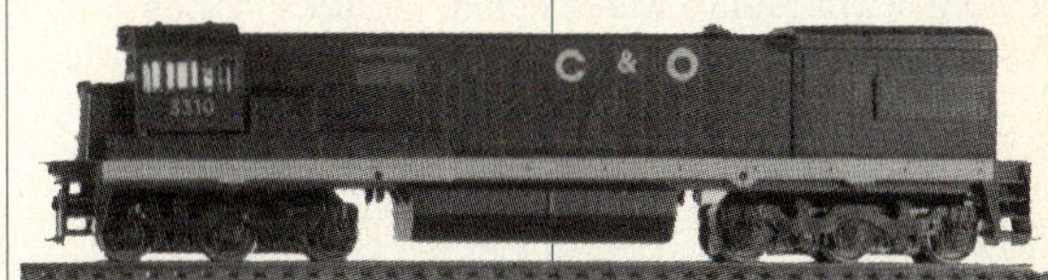

GE U28 C

GE U30 C

GE U33 B

GE U33C

WITH FLYWHEELS - POWERED ea 27.50
140-3501 Santa Fe Freight (blue, yellow)
140-3502 Great Northern (blue, gray, white)
140-3503 Southern Pacific (red, gray)
140-3500 Undecorated (black)

DUMMY ea 11.00
(unless noted)
140-3511 Santa Fe Freight (blue, yellow) 13.75
140-3512 Great Northern (blue, gray, white)
140-3513 Southern Pacific (red, gray)
140-3510 Undecorated (black)

BALDWIN S12

WITH FLYWHEELS - POWERED ea 25.50
140-3701 Santa Fe (blue, yellow)
140-3702 Baltimore & Ohio (blue, yellow)
140-3703 Erie-Lackawanna (gray, brown, gold)
140-3705 Milwaukee Road (orange, black)
140-3706 New York Central (black, white)
140-3707 Pennsylvania (black, yellow)
140-3708 Southern Pacific (red, gray)
140-3700 Undecorated (black)
140-3704 Great Northern (orange, green)

DUMMY ea 12.75
140-3721 Santa Fe (blue, yellow)
140-3723 Erie-Lackawanna (gray, brown, gold)
140-3724 Great Northern (orange, green)
140-3725 Milwaukee Road (orange, black)
140-3726 New York Central (black, white)
140-3727 Pennsylvania (black, yellow)
140-3728 Southern Pacific (red, gray)
140-3720 Undecorated (black)
140-3722 Baltimore & Ohio (blue, yellow)

ALCO PA1

WITH FLYWHEELS - POWERED ea 38.50
140-3302 Baltimore & Ohio (blue, black, gray)
140-3303 New York Central (white, gray)
140-3304 Pennsylvania (maroon, yellow)
140-3305 Santa Fe (warbonnet red, yellow, silver)
140-3306 Southern Pacific "Daylight" (red, orange)
140-3307 Union Pacific (yellow, gray)
140-3308 Delaware & Hudson (yellow, blue, silver)
140-3309 Erie Lackawanna (gray, yellow, maroon)
140-3310 Nickel Plate (blue, white)
140-3301 Undecorated (black)

DUMMY ea 17.50
140-3322 Baltimore & Ohio (blue, black, gray)
140-3323 New York Central (white, gray)
140-3324 Pennsylvania (maroon, yellow)
140-3325 Santa Fe (warbonnet red, yellow, silver)
140-3326 Southern Pacific "Daylight" (red, orange)
140-3328 Delaware & Hudson (yellow, blue, silver)
140-3329 Erie Lackawanna (gray, yellow, maroon)
140-3330 Nickel Plate (blue, white)
140-3321 Undecorated (black)
140-3327 Union Pacific (yellow, gray)

ALCO PB1

WITH FLYWHEELS - POWERED ea 38.50
140-3342 Baltimore & Ohio (blue, black, gray)
140-3343 New York Central (white, gray)
140-3344 Pennsylvania (maroon, yellow)
140-3345 Santa Fe (warbonnet red, yellow, silver)
140-3346 Southern Pacific "Daylight" (red, orange)
140-3347 Union Pacific (yellow, gray)
140-3348 Delaware & Hudson (yellow, blue, silver)
140-3349 Erie Lackawanna (gray, yellow, maroon)
140-3350 Nickel Plate (blue, white)
140-3341 Undecorated (black)

DUMMY ea 19.25
140-3362 Baltimore & Ohio (blue, black, gray)
140-3363 New York Central (white, gray)
140-3364 Pennsylvania (maroon, yellow)
140-3366 Southern Pacific "Daylight" (red, orange)
140-3368 Delaware & Hudson (yellow, blue, silver)
140-3369 Erie Lackawanna (gray, yellow, maroon)
140-3370 Nickel Plate (blue, white)
140-3361 Undecorated (black)
140-3365 Santa Fe (warbonnet red, yellow, silver)
140-3367 Union Pacific (yellow, gray)

All models are ready-to-run (hood units require installation of handrails which are included) with prepainted and lettered styrene bodies and metal underframes. All wheels are powered and engines feature flywheel drive where noted. All locos include horn-hook couplers.

We have worked closely with this manufacturer to provide accurate availability information at the time this catalog was published. Items listed in blue ink may not be available at all times. Please see you dealer for current delivery information.

SD 40-2

ALCO PA1

ALCO PB1

SD40T-2 "TUNNEL MOTOR"

POWERED ea 38.50

140-4501 Southern Pacific (gray, red) This version includes the extra headlights and the long "nose."

140-4502 Cotton Belt (gray, red, white)
140-4503 Rio Grande (black, orange) This is the standard design with medium length nose and front "porch."

140-4500 Undecorated, Southern Pacific Details (black)
140-4504 Undecorated, Rio Grande Details (black)

DUMMY ea 19.25

140-4551 Southern Pacific (gray, red) This version includes the extra headlights and the long "nose."

140-4552 Cotton Belt (gray, red, white)
140-4553 Rio Grande (black, orange) This is the standard design with medium length nose and front "porch."

140-4550 Undecorated, Southern Pacific Details (black)
140-4554 Undecorated, Rio Grande Details (black)

SD40-2

WITH TWIN FLYWHEELS - POWERED ea 36.00

140-4401 Santa Fe (blue, yellow)
140-4402 Baltimore & Ohio, Chessie (blue, orange, yellow)
140-4403 Burlington Northern (green, black)
140-4404 Conrail (big sky blue)
140-4405 Louisville & Nashville, Family Lines System (gray, yellow, red)
140-4406 Norfolk & Western (black, white)
140-4407 Soo Line (white, red, black)
140-4408 Union Pacific (yellow, gray, red)
140-4410 Rock Island (orange, white, yellow)
140-4411 Missouri Pacific (blue, white)
140-4412 Canadian Pacific (orange)
140-4413 SPSF Santa Fe (black, red, yellow)
140-4414 Burlington Northern (cascade green, white) **NEW**
140-4400 Undecorated (black)
140-4409 Undecorated, Non-Dynamic (black)

DUMMY ea 18.00

140-4451 Santa Fe (blue, yellow)
140-4452 Baltimore & Ohio, Chessie (blue, orange, yellow)
140-4453 Burlington Northern (green, black)
140-4454 Conrail (big sky blue)
140-4455 Louisville & Nashville, FAMILY LINES SYSTEM (gray, yellow, red)
140-4456 Norfolk & Western (black, white)
140-4457 Soo Line (white, red, black)
140-4458 Union Pacific (yellow, gray, red)
140-4460 Rock Island (orange, white, yellow)
140-4461 Missouri Pacific (blue, white)
140-4462 Canadian Pacific (orange)
140-4463 SPSF Santa Fe (black, red, yellow)
140-4464 Burlington Northern (cascade green, white) **NEW**
140-4450 Undecorated (black)
140-4459 Undecorated, Non-Dynamic (black)

BUDD RDC

BUDD RDC-1

POWERED ea 20.00
140-2171 Santa Fe (silver)
140-2172 New Haven (silver)
140-2173 Baltimore & Ohio (silver)
140-2170 Undecorated

DUMMY ea 11.00
140-2071 Santa Fe (silver)
140-2072 New Haven (silver)
140-2073 Baltimore & Ohio (silver)
140-2070 Undecorated

BUDD RDC-3

POWERED ea 20.00
140-2176 Santa Fe (silver)
140-2177 New Haven (silver)
140-2178 Baltimore & Ohio (silver)
140-2175 Undecorated

DUMMY ea 11.00
140-2077 New Haven (silver)
140-2078 Baltimore & Ohio (silver)
140-2075 Undecorated

HUSTLER

POWERED ea 16.50
140-2991 Black
140-2992 Red
140-2993 Silver
140-2994 Yellow
140-2995 Bronze
140-2997 Rio Grande

If you've got 40 bucks, you can buy a bell or headlight! But that's a lot of money in 1953, so we'll have to take pictures from the edge of the scrap yard and call it even. Using parts from an old Monogram (out of production) model kit, Dave Roeder built this steam-era scene, depicting a Frisco engine meeting the scrapper's torch.

Model and Photo by Dave Roeder

These HO Scale locos feature numerous separate detail parts, working headlight and authentic paint schemes. Most roadnames are offered with at least two different unit numbers, so it's easy to have several engines from your favorite roads. Each is ready to run and produced as a limited-run model.

GE DASH 8-40C WIDE CAB ea 59.95 *NEW*

160-86002 Union Pacific #9372
160-86003 Union Pacific #9404
160-86004 Union Pacific #9456

160-86005 Santa Fe #802
160-86006 Santa Fe #834
160-86007 Santa Fe #854
160-86008 Conrail #6058
160-86009 Conrail #6062
160-86010 Conrail #6082

160-86011 CSX #7652
160-86012 CSX #7664
160-86013 CSX #7738
160-86001 Undecorated

FAIRBANKS-MORSE H16-44 DIESEL ea 59.95 *NEW*

Features see-through metal fan grills (with fans visible underneath) and see-through safety-tread front and rear pilot steps.

160-81202 Santa Fe #3014
160-81203 Santa Fe #3019
160-81204 Baltimore & Ohio #926
160-81205 Baltimore & Ohio #929
160-81206 Pennsylvania #8809

160-81207 Pennsylvania #8815
160-81208 Canadian Pacific #8552
160-81209 Canadian Pacific #8554
160-81210 Virginia & Truckee #32
160-81211 Virginia & Truckee #38
160-81201 Undecorated

4-6-2 K-4 CLASSIC STEAM ea 99.95 *NEW*

160-84001 Pennsylvania #5404

160-84002 Pennsylvania #5425

GE 70 TON SWITCHERS ea 45.00

160-81104 Southern Pacific #5108 (orange, black)
160-81107 Family Lines/Louisville & Nashville #98 (gray)
160-81108 Family Lines/Louisville & Nashville #99 (gray)

LIMITED QUANTITIES AVAILABLE

160-81103 Southern Pacific #5103 (orange, black) 45.00

EMD GP-30 DIESEL ea 49.95

160-82010 Union Pacific #731 (armor yellow, gray)
160-82011 Union Pacific #844 (armor yellow, gray)
160-82012 Baltimore & Ohio "Sunburst" #6904 (dark blue)
160-82013 Baltimore & Ohio #6954 (dark blue)
160-82014 Pennsylvania #2204 (Brunswick blue)
160-82015 Pennsylvania #2218 (Brunswick blue)
160-82016 Nickel Plate Road #902 (black, yellow)
160-82017 Nickel Plate Road #908 (black, yellow)
160-82018 Canadian Pacific #8200 (gray, maroon)
160-82019 Canadian Pacific #8201 (gray, maroon)
160-82849 Undecorated

GE DASH 8-40C ea 59.95 *NEW*

160-85011 Union Pacific #9194
160-85012 Conrail #6032
160-85013 Conrail #6038
160-85014 Conrail #6044
160-85015 Chicago & North Western #8508
160-85016 Chicago & North Western #8514
160-85017 Chicago & North Western #8526
160-85018 Norfolk Southern #8668

160-85019 CSX #7563
160-85020 CSX #7584
160-85021 CSX #7598
160-85001 Undecorated

EMD F40PH ea 59.95 *NEW*

160-87015 Amtrak #208
160-87016 Amtrak #214
160-87017 Amtrak #227
160-87018 Amtrak #242
160-87019 Amtrak #318

160-87020 Amtrak #332
160-87021 VIA #6404
160-87022 VIA #6425
160-87001 Undecorated

STEAM LOCOMOTIVES

BACHMANN PLUS

Bachmann Plus series engines feature an all-metal chassis with additional weight, worm gear and flywheel drive, five-pole motor and a new idler gear box.

4-4-0 AMERICAN ea 54.00

160-51001 Union Pacific #119

160-51024 Central Pacific "Jupiter"

HO Scale Locomotives are ready-to-run and feature prepainted and lettered plastic bodies, operating headlights and horn-hook couplers.
We have worked closely with this manufacturer to provide accurate availability information at the time this catalog was published. Items listed in blue ink may not be available at all times. Please see your dealer for current delivery information.

BACHMANN PLUS 4-8-4 WITH SMOKE

With plenty of power for freight or passenger trains, the 4-8-4 was one of the most popular dual-service engines in North America.

160-31301 Southern Pacific Daylight, GS-4 #4449 129.95
160-31305 New York Central, Niagara 129.95

160-31320 Santa Fe, Northern 99.95
160-31315 Norfolk & Western, Class J 99.95

USRA 0-6-0 & VANDERBILT TENDER

160-50701 Union Pacific Greyhound

4-8-4 NORTHERN WITH SMOKE

160-58016 Chicago Burlington & Quincy 100.00

USRA 0-6-0 SWITCHER WITH SMOKE ea 40.00

160-50602 Santa Fe
160-50614 Pennsylvania, With Slope Tender

BACHMANN PLUS 2-8-0 CONSOLIDATION WITH SMOKE ea 79.95

160-31401 Santa Fe
160-31402 Reading

160-31403 Great Northern

USRA 0-6-0 AND SHORT HAUL TENDER ea 40.00

160-50440 Smokey

Mountain Express, with Short Haul Tender

2-8-2 MIKADO WITH SMOKE ea 80.00

160-54501 Union Pacific

160-54512 Baltimore & Ohio

2-6-2 PRAIRIE WITH SMOKE ea 54.00

160-51501 Union Pacific

160-51520 New York Central

STEAM LOCOMOTIVES ACCESSORIES

160-99993 Smoke Fluid 2 1/4 fl oz 2.00

The temperature is rising fast now that the sun is up, and it's going to be a scorcher out on the Illinois prairies today. A CB&Q freight ho'ds the siding and the conversation in the cab swings to the impending merger of "the Q" with GN and NP. This scene of early 70's railroading is the work of Ron Furto of Crest Hill, Illinois. The U28C is an old AHM, reworked with see-through screens from a Stewart Hobbies loco. The GP35 is from Kato and both units were redone with various details.

Models and Photo by Ron Furto

EMD DD40X

HO Scale Locomotives are ready-to-run and feature prepainted and lettered plastic bodies, operating headlights and horn-hook couplers.

We have worked closely with this manufacturer to provide accurate availability information at the time this catalog was published. Items listed in blue ink may not be available at all times. Please see your dealer for current delivery information.

BACHMANN PLUS EMD F7B
ea 39.95

BACHMANN PLUS EMD F7A
ea 39.95

DIESEL LOCOMOTIVES

BACHMANN PLUS
Bachmann Plus diesels feature five-pole, skew wound motors, dual flywheels, helical cut gears, metal chassis and eight-wheel drive.

BACHMANN PLUS GE B23-7 ea 39.95

EMD GP50 ea 34.00 (unless noted)

EMD SD40-2
160-67023 Seaboard System (gray) 42.00

EMD GP40 ea 32.00
160-63503 Burlington Northern (green, silver)
160-63618 CSX, With Caboose (gray, blue)

EMD F9 ea 25.00
(unless noted)
160-61618 CSX, With Caboose (gray, blue) 28.00

PLASSER EM80C GEOMETRY/TRACK CLEANING DIESEL ea 30.00

BACHMANN PLUS EMD GP35 ea 29.95 *NEW*

LIMITED QUANTITIES AVAILABLE

160-61501 Union Pacific (armor yellow, gray)
160-61502 Santa Fe (red, silver)

EMD GP18
160-67500 Assortment pkg (12) 480.00

GE 35 TON SWITCHER
160-68000 Assortment pkg (12) 240.00

GE U36B ea 32.00
160-64002 Santa Fe (red, silver)
160-64009 Chessie System/Chesapeake & Ohio (blue, orange, yellow)

EMD DD40X
Comes with a blinking warning light.

160-66501 Union Pacific (armor yellow, gray) 55.00

BACHMANN PLUS GE B23-7 ea 39.95
160-31102 Union Pacific #124 (armor yellow, gray)
160-31103 Union Pacific #156 (armor yellow, gray)
160-31104 Santa Fe #6380 (blue, yellow)
160-31105 Santa Fe #6410 (blue, yellow)
160-31106 Conrail #1991 (blue)
160-31107 Conrail #2001 (blue)
160-31108 Chessie System/Chesapeake & Ohio #8238 (blue, yellow, orange)
160-31109 Chessie System/Chesapeake & Ohio #8256 (blue, yellow, orange)
160-31101 Undecorated

BACHMANN PLUS EMD F7A ea 39.95
160-31203 Union Pacific #1468 (armor yellow, gray)
160-31204 Union Pacific #1470 (armor yellow, gray)
160-31207 Great Northern #316A (orange, green)
160-31208 Great Northern #311A (orange, green)
160-31211 Baltimore & Ohio #231 (blue, black, gray)
160-31212 Baltimore & Ohio #251 (blue, black, gray)
160-31215 Pennsylvania #9651A (Brunswick green)

160-31216 Pennsylvania #9656A (Brunswick green)
160-31219 New York Central #1711 (gray, black)
160-31220 New York Central #1873 (gray, black)
160-31201 Undecorated

BACHMANN PLUS EMD F7B ea 39.95
160-31205 Union Pacific #1476B (armor yellow, gray)
160-31206 Union Pacific #1492B (armor yellow, gray)
160-31209 Great Northern #313B (orange, green)
160-31210 Great Northern #314B (orange, green)
160-31213 Baltimore & Ohio #231X (blue, black, gray)
160-31214 Baltimore & Ohio #251X (blue, black, gray)
160-31217 Pennsylvania #9648B (Brunswick green)
160-31218 Pennsylvania #9666B (Brunswick green)
160-31221 New York Central #2443 (gray, black)
160-31222 New York Central #2457 (gray, black)
160-31202 Undecorated

BACHMANN PLUS EMD GP35 ea 29.95 *NEW*
160-11502 Union Pacific #749
160-11503 Union Pacific #763
160-11504 Santa Fe #2894
160-11505 Santa Fe #2949
160-11506 Conrail #2271
160-11507 Conrail #2324
160-11508 Great Northern #3018
160-11509 Great Northern #3024
160-11510 Pennsylvania #2262
160-11511 Pennsylvania #2320
160-11512 Canadian Pacific #5017
160-11513 Canadian Pacific #5025
160-11514 CSX #4404
160-11515 CSX #4418
160-11501 Undecorated

EMD GP50 ea 34.00
(unless noted)
160-61200 Assortment pkg (12) 408.00
160-61202 Santa Fe (red, silver)
160-61228 Erie Lackawanna (gray, maroon, yellow)
160-61201 Union Pacific

LIMITED QUANTITIES AVAILABLE

160-61203 Burlington Northern (green, silver)

PLASSER EM80C GEOMETRY/TRACK CLEANING DIESEL ea 30.00
Features reversing headlight and blinking warning light.

160-62500 Assortment pkg (12) 360.00 *NEW*
160-62501 Union Pacific (armor yellow)
160-62505 Amtrak (red, white, blue)

TRAIN SETS

Ready-to-run train sets feature prepainted and lettered plastic bodies, include loco with operating headlight, track, UL listed power pack, rerailer and instructions.

OLD TIMER PASSENGER

THE AMERICAN

GOLDEN SPIKE

SMOKEY MOUNTAIN EXPRESS

OVERLAND LIMITED

EMPIRE BUILDER

OLD TIMER FREIGHT

LIGHTNING EXPRESS

TORNADO

THUNDER CHEIF

160-276 The Old Timer Union Pacific Passenger set 86.50
Includes 4-4-0 American loco with tender, 2 old time coach cars, old time combine, and 36" circle of track.

160-370 The American set 90.50
Includes USRA 0-6-0 steam locomotive with Vanderbilt-type tender, 42' 3-dome tank car, 41' wood stock car, 51' mechanical steel reefer, 42' open quad offset hopper, off-center caboose, 17-piece bridge and trestle set, 24-piece railroad and street sign set, 24 telephone poles, 12 HO Scale figures, 36" x 63" track layout with plug-in terminal re-railer track, 11 pieces curved track, and 6 pieces straight track.

160-175 Golden Spike Union Pacific set 80.50
Includes EMD GP40 diesel locomotive, flat car with logs, 51' box car, gondola, 56' all-door box car, caboose, blinking bridge and trestle set, railroad and street signs, 36 figures, 24 telephone poles, and 87" x 40" over and under track layout.

160-182 Smokey Mountain Express set 76.75
Includes 0-6-0 steam locomotive and short haul tender, plug door box car, flat car with logs, three dome tank car, steel off-center caboose, 45" x 36" oval track set with plug-in terminal rerailer track, 11 pieces of curved track and 2 pieces straight track, 17 piece bridge and trestle set, 12 telephone poles, 24 railroad and street signs, and 12 piece figure set.

160-250 Overland Limited Union Pacific set 148.50
Includes 4-8-4 loco with tender, 3-dome tank car, two piece 51' plug door box cars, 41' wood stock car, 51' cylindrical hopper, 56' center-flow hopper, quad hopper, caboose and an 87" x 40" figure-8 track.

160-495 McKinley Explorer Passenger set 100.00
Includes GP40 diesel locomotive, 4 full dome passenger cars, 36" x 54" oval track.

160-510 Chocolate Town USA set 100.00 *NEW*
Includes B23-7 loco, Mr. Goodbar reefer, Hershey's Milk Chocolate wood reefer, Reese's Pieces open quad hopper, "Whatchamacallit" plug door box car, Hershey syrup single dome tank car, Hershey Kisses steel off-center caboose, Hershey train station, Hershey dairy barn and 63" x 36" oval track set.

160-340 Empire Builder Union Pacific set 101.50
Includes GP18 diesel locomotive, 42' 3-dome tank car, 42'steel gondola, 42' open quad offset hopper, 41' wood stock car, two 51' steel plug door box cars, 36' wide vision caboose, blinking bridge and trestle set, crossing gate, railroad and street signs, telephone poles and 87" x 40" over and under track layout.

160-275 The Old Timer Central Pacific Freight set 86.50
Includes 4-4-0 American loco with tender, box car, gondola, flat car, caboose and 36" circle of track.

KING OF THE RAIL TRAIN SETS
King of the Rail train sets all include an F9 diesel locomotive with a bright silver cLustra Chrome finish and operating headlight, prepainted and lettered freight cars, track, UL listed power pack, rerailer and instructions.

160-503 Lightning Express set 62.75
Includes F9 diesel locomotive with Lustra Chrome finish, 42' open quad hopper, 51' plug door box car, gondola, single dome tank car, wood stock car, caboose, 54" x 36" oval track set with plug-in terminal rerailer track, 11 pieces of curved track, 4 pieces straight track, 17 piece bridge and trestle set, 24 telephone poles, 24 railroad and street signs, and 48 piece figure set.

160-502 Tornado set 46.25
Includes F9 diesel locomotive with Lustra Chrome finish, gondola, 42' open quad hopper, 51' plug door box car, caboose, 45" x 36" oval track set with plug-in terminal rerailer track, 11 pieces of curved track, 2 pieces straight track, 17 piece bridge and trestle set, 12 telephone poles, 24 railroad and street signs, and 12 piece figure set.

160-501 Thunder Chief set 40.50
Includes F9 diesel locomotive with Lustra Chrome finish, 42' open quad hopper, 51' plug door box car, caboose, 36" circle track with plug-in terminal rerailer, 11 pieces of curved track, 12 telephone poles, 24 railroad and street signs, and 12 piece figure set.

These HO Scale, ready-to-run locomotives are offered in several paint schemes and most feature two different unit numbers. Each loco has a can motor, flywheels and truck assemblies geared for low speeds.

DIESEL LOCOS

EMD SD24 ea 69.98
223-151051 Union Pacific #448 (yellow, gray)
223-151054 Burlington Northern #6254 (cascade green, black)
223-151055 Southern #2504 (black)
223-151056 Southern #2519 (black)
223-151057 Chicago & North Western #6224 (green, yellow)
223-151058 Chicago & North Western #6228 (green, yellow)
223-151059 Pennsylvania #7634 (black)

223-151053 Burlington Northern #6243

EMD E7, DUMMY ea 35.98
223-152205 Pennsylvania #5872 (brown, yellow)
223-152210 Baltimore & Ohio #1430 (dark blue, yellow)
223-152215 New York Central #4030 (gray, white)
223-152220 Southern Pacific #2922 (gray, red)
223-152225 Southern Pacific #6002 (gray, red)
223-152230 Amtrak #369 (silver, black, red)

223-152405 Chesapeake & Ohio #4522 (blue, gray, yellow)
223-152410 Union Pacific #927A (yellow, gray)
223-152415 Milwaukee Road #16B (yellow, gray, red)
223-152420 Wabash #1002 (blue, yellow)
223-152425 Norfolk & Western #1016 (blue, yellow)
223-152435 Chicago & North Western #50089 (yellow, green)
223-152200 Undecorated
223-152400 Undecorated

EMD E7, POWERED ea 89.98
223-152110 Pennsylvania #5840 (tuscan, single stripe and large lettering)
223-152111 Pennsylvania #5856 (tuscan, single stripe and large lettering)
223-152120 Baltimore & Ohio #1415 (dark blue, yellow)
223-152121 Baltimore & Ohio #1423 (dark blue, yellow)

223-152130 New York Central #4000 (gray, white)
223-152131 New York Central #4011 (gray, white)
223-152140 Southern #2905 (green, gray)
223-152141 Southern #2916 (green, gray)
223-152150 Southern Pacific #2150 (gray, red)
223-152151 Southern Pacific #6001 (gray, red)

223-152160 Amtrak #353 (black, silver, red)
223-152161 Amtrak #357 (black, silver, red)
223-152310 Chesapeake & Ohio #4520 (blue, yellow, gray)
223-152311 Chesapeake & Ohio #4521 (blue, yellow, gray)
223-152320 Union Pacific #930A (yellow, gray)

223-152321 Union Pacific #931A (yellow, gray)
223-152330 Milwaukee Road #16A (yellow, gray, red)
223-152331 Milwaukee Road #17A (yellow, gray, red)
223-152340 Wabash #1001 (blue, yellow)
223-152341 Wabash #1001A (blue, yellow)

223-152350 Norfolk & Western #1001 (blue, yellow)
223-152351 Norfolk & Western #1002 (blue, yellow)
223-152370 Chicago & North Western #5008A (yellow, green) NEW
223-152371 Chicago & North Western #5009A (yellow, green) NEW
223-152300 Undecorated

EMD SD35 ea 69.98
223-152051 Pennsylvania #6004 (black)
223-152052 Pennsylvania #6027 (black)
223-152053 Norfolk & Western #1506 (black)
223-152054 Norfolk & Western #1524 (black)
223-152055 Southern Pacific #4702 (gray, red)
223-152056 Southern Pacific #4709 (gray, red)
223-152057 Chesapeake & Ohio #7421 (dark blue, yellow)
223-152058 Chesapeake & Ohio #7424 (dark blue, yellow)
223-152059 Cotton Belt #2963 (gray, red)
223-152060 Cotton Belt #2965 (gray, red)
223-152061 Conrail #6012 (blue)
223-152062 Conrail #6015 (blue)
223-152063 Seaboard System #6587 (gray, yellow)
223-152064 Seaboard System #6592 (gray, yellow)
223-152050 Undecorated

EMD GP38 ea 59.98
223-152002 Burlington Northern #2075 (cascade green)
223-152003 Illinois Central #9521 (black, globe herald)
223-152004 Illinois Central #9534 (black, globe herald)
223-152005 Conrail #7659 (blue)
223-152006 Conrail #7684 (blue)
223-152000 Undecorated
223-152001 Burlington Northern #2073 (cascade green)

EMD GP40 ea 69.98
(unless noted)
223-151002 Santa Fe #3781 (blue, yellow)
223-151003 CSX Transportation #6503 (gray, blue)
223-151005 Union Pacific #620 (gray, yellow)
223-151006 Union Pacific #622 (gray, yellow)
223-151007 Conrail #3188 (blue, white)
223-151008 Conrail #3192 (blue, white)
223-151009 Southern Pacific #4705 (gray, red) 59.98

223-151010 Southern Pacific #4712 (gray, red) 59.98
223-151011 Cotton Belt #7601 (gray, red)
233-151012 Cotton Belt #7606 (gray, red)
233-151014 Rio Grande #3064 (black, orange)
223-151015 Rio Grande #3083 (black, orange)
223-151016 Burlington Northern #3080 (cascade green, white front scheme)
223-151017 Burlington Northern #3075 (cascade green, white front scheme)
223-151019 Wisconsin Central #3003 (maroon, yellow) 74.98
223-151020 CSX Transportation #4067 (blue, gray with yellow nose) 74.98
223-151022 Southern Pacific #7130 (gray, red)
223-151023 Southern Pacific #7129 (gray, red)
223-151024 Western Maryland (red, white) 74.98
223-151025 Western Maryland (red, white) 74.98
223-151026 Royal American #301 (silver, red, yellow stripes) 74.98
223-151007 Soo Line #4403 (red)

223-152008 Soo Line #4410 (red)
223-152012 Pennsylvania #2312 (black)
223-152013 Pennsylvania #2341 (black)
223-152014 Wabash #540 (blue, yellow)
223-152015 Wabash #543 (blue, yellow)
223-152016 Canadian Pacific #3022 (red, white, black)
223-152017 Canadian Pacific #3031 (red, white, black)
223-152018 Baltimore & Ohio #3802 (dark blue, yellow)
223-152019 Baltimore & Ohio #3837 (dark blue, yellow)
223-152020 Conrail #7752 (blue - white side sill)
223-152021 Conrail #7783 (blue - white side sill)
223-152022 Milwaukee Road 74.98 (orange, black)
223-152023 Milwaukee Road 74.98 (orange, black)
223-151013 Undecorated
223-152009 Undecorated (cream)

223-151021 CSX Transportation #4073 (blue, gray, yellow nose) 74.98
223-151027 Royal American #307 (red, silver, yellow stripes) 74.98

Limited Quantities Available
223-152010 Missouri Pacific #2002 69.98 (blue, white)

EMD GP38 HIGH HOOD
ea 74.98 (unless noted)
223-153002 Norfolk Southern #2743 (black)
223-153003 Norfolk Southern #2762 (black)
223-153004 Norfolk & Western #4112 (black)
223-153005 Norfolk & Western #4155 (black)
223-153006 Pennsylvania #2381 (black)
223-153007 Pennsylvania #2385 (black)
223-153000 Undecorated 64.98

STEAM LOCOS

2-6-0 MOGUL ea 69.98
348-510 Santa Fe (black)
348-511 Pennsylvania (black)
348-512 Southern Pacific (black)
348-513 Mogul Southern
348-515 Baltimore & Ohio
348-516 Chicago & North Western (black)

0-4-0T DOCKSIDE ea 39.98
NEW
348-471 Pennsylvania (black)
348-472 Baltimore & Ohio (black)
348-473 Undecorated (black)

0-4-0 SWITCHER ea 17.98
348-8000 Canadian National
348-8001 Canadian Pacific (black)
348-8002 Santa Fe (tuscan, black)
348-8003 Southern
348-8004 Union Pacific (black)
348-8005 Pennsylvania (black)

0-4-0 OLD TIMER ea 17.98
348-8006 Santa Fe (red, black)
348-8007 Southern (green, black)
348-8008 Pennsylvania (black)
348-8009 Denver, South Park & Pacific (blue, black, brown)
348-8010 Virginia & Truckee (red)
348-8011 Virginia & Truckee (grey)

2-8-2 MIKADO ea 69.98
NEW
With flywheel and Mabuchi can motor.
348-9450 Santa Fe (black, silver, red roof)
348-9456 Pennsylvania (black, red roof)
348-9458 Louisville & Nashville (black, silver, red roof)
348-9463 Western Maryland
348-9464 Reading
348-9465 Southern Pacific (black)
348-9466 New York Central
348-9467 Nickel Plate Road
348-9468 Frisco
348-9469 Milwaukee
348-9470 Erie
348-9471 Baltimore & Ohio
348-9472 New Haven

348-518 New York Central (black)
348-519 Mogul Central of Georgia (black, brown)
348-521 Mogul Texas Pacific (black)
348-522 Illinois Central (black)

348-9473 Lackawanna
348-9474 Burlington
348-9475 Canadian Pacific

2-8-2 MIKADO ea 69.98
348-9350 Santa Fe
348-9351 Southern (green)
348-9352 Southern Pacific (black, brown, orange)
348-9353 Chesapeake & Ohio (black)
348-9354 Chessie (blue, orange, gold)
348-9355 Great Northern (olive green, black)
348-9356 Pennsylvania (olive green, black)
348-9359 Canadian National (black)
348-9360 Chicago & North Western
348-9361 Union Pacific (black)

4-6-2 PACIFIC ea 69.98
NEW
With flywheel and Mabuchi can motor.
348-9700 Santa Fe
348-9701 Southern Railway
348-9703 Chesapeake & Ohio (black)
348-9705 Great Northern
348-9706 Pennsylvania
348-9708 Louisville & Nashville
348-9713 Western Maryland
348-9714 Reading
348-9715 South Pacific (black)
348-9716 New York Central
348-9717 Nickel Plate Road
348-9718 Frisco
348-9719 Milwaukee
348-9720 Erie
348-9721 Baltimore & Ohio
348-9722 New Haven
348-9723 Lackawanna
348-9724 Burlington
348-9725 Canadian Pacific
348-9712 Undecorated

4-6-2 PACIFIC ea 69.98
348-9400 Santa Fe (black)
348-9401 Southern (green, black)

348-9402 Southern Pacific
348-9403 Chesapeake & Ohio (black)
348-9404 Chessie (blue, orange, gold)
348-9405 Great Northern (olive green, black)
348-9406 Pennsylvania
348-9407 Atlantic Coast Line
348-9408 Louisville & Nashville
348-9409 Canadian National (black)
348-9410 Chicago & North Western (black)
348-9411 Union Pacific

DIESEL LOCOMOTIVES

SD40 DIESEL ea 34.98
348-350 Santa Fe (black, gold)
348-352 Canadian Pacific (red)
348-353 Canadian National (black, red, white)
348-354 Atlantic Coast Line (black)
348-355 Northern Alberta Railway
348-356 Quebec, North Shore & Labrador
348-357 Southern Pacific (gray)
348-358 Burlington Northern (cascade green, black)
348-359 Chicago & North Western (green, gold, black)
348-360 Conrail (bright blue)
348-361 Western Maryland (orange, white)
348-362 Union Pacific (gray, orange, red)
348-363 Chessie B&O (blue, orange, gold)
348-364 Chessie C&O (blue, orange, gold)
348-366 Southern (green, white)
348-367 Pennsylvania (black)
348-368 Algoma Central Railway (gray, maroon)

MDT SWITCHER ea 19.98
NEW
348-480 Santa Fe
348-481 Pennsylvania (silver)
348-482 Baltimore & Ohio (blue)
348-483 Reading
348-484 Illinois Central
348-485 Penn Central (black)
348-486 Union Pacific
348-487 New Haven

CENTER CAB DIESEL ea 19.98 *NEW*
348-500 General Electric (black, orange, silver)
348-501 Union Pacific
348-502 Santa Fe
348-503 Burlington Northern
348-504 Soo Line
348-505 Milwaukee Road (black, orange)

International Hobby Corp.

IHC locos are ready-to-run. The plastic and die cast bodies are prepainted and lettered. Steam locos feature working valve gear. All locos have working headlight and horn-hook couplers.

348-506 Pennsylvania
348-507 Southern Pacific

EMD E8A POWERED & A DUMMY ea 68.49
Designed for passenger service, the first E8's were delivered in 1949. In later years, they served in commuter and freight service. Sets include two A units; one powered with working headlight and one dummy. Units are painted in the same color schemes as IHC passenger equipment, listed in the Passenger Cars section.)
348-1925 New York Central (light gray)
348-1926 Santa Fe (silver, red)
348-1927 Northern Pacific (olive green)
348-1928 Baltimore & Ohio (dark blue, gray)
348-1929 Illinois Central (dark brown , orange)
348-1930 Chicago & Alton (red, maroon)
348-1931 Pennsylvania (tuscan red)
348-1932 Union Pacific (yellow)
348-1933 Southern Pacific (daylight-orange, red)
348-1934 Amtrak (silver, red, blue)
348-1935 Erie (2-tone green)
348-1936 Kansas City Southern (black, yellow, red)
348-1937 Rock Island (red, yellow)
348-1938 Frisco (deep red, gold)
348-1939 Canadian Pacific (black, wine red)
348-1940 Milwaukee (yellow, gray)
348-1941 Gulf, Mobile & Ohio (red, maroon)
348-1942 New Jersey Transit (black, silver)
348-1943 Florida East Coast (yellow, red)
348-1944 Richmond, Fredricksburg & Potomac (dark blue, gray)
348-1945 Atlantic Coast Line (purple, silver)
348-1946 Southern (green, white)
348-1947 Lackawanna (maroon, gray, black)
348-1948 Missouri Pacific "Colorado Eagle" (blue, gray)
348-1949 Chessie System (blue, yellow, gray)
348-1950 Burlington Northern (green, white)
348-1951 Milwaukee Road (maroon, orange)
348-1952 Great Northern

(brown, orange, green)
348-1953 Pennsylvania (green)
348-1954 VIA (yellow, blue w/yellow lettering)
348-1955 New Haven (black, orange, white)
348-1956 Monon (red, gray)
348-1957 Denver & Rio Grande (yellow, black)
348-1958 Norfolk & Western (maroon, gold)
348-1959 Southern Pacific "Golden State" (red, silver)
348-1960 Wabash (blue, silver)
348-1961 Delaware & Hudson (silver, blue)
348-1962 Chicago & North Western (yellow, green)
348-1963 Lehigh & Valley Jersey (red, black stripes)
348-1964 Jersey Central (blue, orange)
348-1965 Reading (black, green, yellow stripe)
348-1967 Louisville & Nashville (blue, tan, orange)
348-1966 Undecorated

FM DIESEL ea 29.98
A powered and A dummy set.
348-377577 Pennsylvania NEW (green)
348-378578 Southern Pacific (gray, red) *NEW*
348-379579 Lackawanna (gray, maroon) *NEW*
348-380580 Santa Fe (silver, red)
348-381581 Union Pacific (orange, red)
348-382582 Illinois Central *NEW*
348-384584 Northern Pacific (olive green, black)
348-385585 Baltimore & Ohio (blue, gray, black) *NEW*
348-386586 Pennsylvania (tuscan red)
348-390590 Canadian National
348-391591 New York Central (gray, black)
348-394594 Seaboard System (black, orange) *NEW*
348-395595 Louisville & Nashville (gray, orange) *NEW*
348-396596 Soo Line (white, red) *NEW*
348-397597 Burlington Northern (gray, white)
348-398598 Chesapeake & Ohio (royal blue, silver) *NEW*
348-399599 Southern (green, white) *NEW*

LIFE-LIKE®

These HO Scale steam and diesel locos feature detailed plastic bodies, which are painted. All models have operating headlights and horn-hook couplers.

STEAM LOCOS

Classic steam locos from the "Golden Era" of railroading, ideal for light service and switching.

OLD TIME TEA KETTLE
433-8300 Baltimore & Ohio (black, maroon) 24.00

0-4-0 SWITCHER WITH TENDER ea 29.00
433-8344 Pennsylvania (black)
433-8394 Union Pacific (black)

ALL PURPOSE MAINTENANCE KIT

This kit includes: track cleaner, track brite, oil gun, grease gun and electrical tester.

433-8629 Maintenance Kit 11.00

INFORMATION STATION

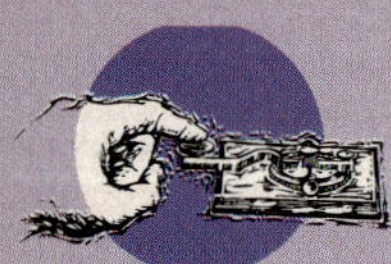

Unlike steam locos, diesels could be operated comfortably in either forward or reverse. With a steamer, there was a clear understanding of front and rear, but with early diesels it was hard to tell.

As road switchers appeared, the problem was compounded. Now, there was an obvious cab, but the engine could still be operated in either direction. Most railroads designated that the long hood end of these units was to be run facing forward for safety.

A rule was finally passed stating that all diesels must have a small letter "F" on the side sill, designating the FRONT of the loco. This is still done today!

0-4-0T DOCKSIDE ea 24.00
433-8301 Baltimore & Ohio (black)
433-8302 Santa Fe (black) magnets and more.

F40PH ea 32.00
433-8241 Amtrak
433-8243 Massachusetts Bay Transit Authority (black, red, silver)
433-8264 Nortran Suburban Transit (blue, silver, white)

F40PH WITH CABOOSE ea 32.00
The caboose has the same roadname as the loco.

433-8675 Burlington Northern (green, black, white)
433-8676 Union Pacific
433-8677 Rock Island
433-8678 Amtrak **NEW**
e.

DIESEL LOCOS

PROTO 2000 SERIES EMD GP18 DIESEL LOCOS
LIMITED RUN
These models feature over 100 hand-applied, precision-molded parts. Details include functional drop steps and cab doors, laser-printed decoration, molded screens and movable shutters, 5-pole skew-wound motor, dual flywheels, all wheel-drive and pickup, powerful aristropic magnets and more.

PROTO 2000 SERIES-BL2
LIMITED RUN
433-8356 Western Maryland (Speedlettering) #82 64.95

LIMITED QUANTITIES AVAILABLE
433-8355 Florida East Coast 64.95

ALCO-FA2 ea 80.00
LIMITED RUN
433-8324 Demo #1602A (dark green, yellow)
433-8325 Demo #1602D (dark green, yellow)
433-8327 Louisville & Nashville #355 (black, cream)
433-8328 Louisville & Nashville #356 (black, cream)
433-8336 Chicago & North Western #4103A (dark green, yellow)

433-8337 Chicago & North Western #4104A (dark green, yellow)
433-8383 Undecorated - Dual Headlight
433-8318 Ann Arbor #52A (gray, dark blue, white)

HIGH NOSE NONDYNAMIC ea 70.00
LIMITED RUN
433-8139 Chicago & North Western #1777 (dark green, yellow)
433-8140 Chicago & North Western #1778 (dark green, yellow)
433-8142 Southern #177

GP38-2 WITH CABOOSE ea 32.00
LIMITED RUN
Set includes loco and caboose with same roadname.

433-8679 Chessie System (black, orange, yellow)
433-8668 Seaboard Coast Line Family Lines
433-8663 Atchison, Topeka, Santa Fe

EMD FP45
LIMITED RUN
433-8323 Baltimore & Ohio 42.00
433-8322 Pennsylvania (black) 42.00

THIRD SERIES HIGH NOSE NONDYNAMIC ea 70.00
LIMITED RUN
433-8845 Norfolk & Western #2702 (black)
433-8846 Norfolk & Western #2706 (black)

HIGH NOSE WITH DYNAMIC BRAKES ea 70.00
LIMITED RUN
433-8143 Lehigh Valley #302 (dark maroon)
433-8144 Lehigh Valley #303 (dark maroon)
433-8145 Burlington Northern #1994 (green, black, white)
433-8146 Burlington Northern #1996 (green, black, white)
433-8147 Norfolk & Western #918 (black)
433-8148 Norfolk & Western #923 (black)

F7A WITH CABOOSE ea 32.00
LIMITED RUN
Set includes loco and caboose with same roadname.

433-8667 Chessie (black, orange, yellow)
433-8669 Southern Pacific (orange, red)
433-8672 Amtrak (black, silver, blue)
433-8686 Burlington Northern (green, white, silver)
433-8666 Santa Fe (silver, red)
433-8674 Southern (green)

ALCO-FB2 DUMMY ea 40
LIMITED RUN
433-8326 Demo #1602B (dark green, yellow)
433-8338 Chicago & North Western #4103B (dark green, yellow)

THIRD SERIES LOW NOSE NONDYNAMIC ea 70.00
LIMITED RUN
433-8155 Illinois Central #9423 (black, white stripe)
433-8159 Missouri Pacific #413 (dark blue)
433-8161 Missouri Pacific

#480 (dark blue)
433-8162 Norfolk Southern #2 (Original, gray, black)
433-8164 Norfolk Southern

#4 (Original, gray, black)
433-8167 Toledo, Peoria & Western #600 (orange, white)
433-8168 Louisville & Nashville #902 (gray, yellow)
433-8169 Louisville & Nashville #904 (gray, yellow)
433-8854 Undecorated

TRAIN SETS

Start your model railroading fun right away with these complete HO Scale train sets. Each includes a ready-to-run loco with working headlight and freight cars, all equipped with horn-hook couplers. Sets are complete with track and lots of accessories, plus a UL. listed power pack with forward and reverse, and a terminal rerailer.

433-8760 Chessie System Fast Freight 70.00
NEW

Includes a GP38-2 diesel locomotive with working headlight, 4 freight cars including deluxe 100 Ton hopper and 8 wheel caboose, 17 piece bridge and trestle set, 6 utility poles, 43 signs, 24 authentic BURMA SHAVE® signs, 3 trees, 6 figures, 2 automobiles, 1 pickup truck, hook-up wires, extra couplers and rail joiners, illustrated instructions, and a 45" x 36" track oval.

433-8770 Pennsylvania Trail Blazer 70.00

Includes an 0-4-0 steam locomotive with tender car, 3 freight cars and caboose, signal bridge, 43 signs, 12 utility poles, and a 45" x 36" oval of track.

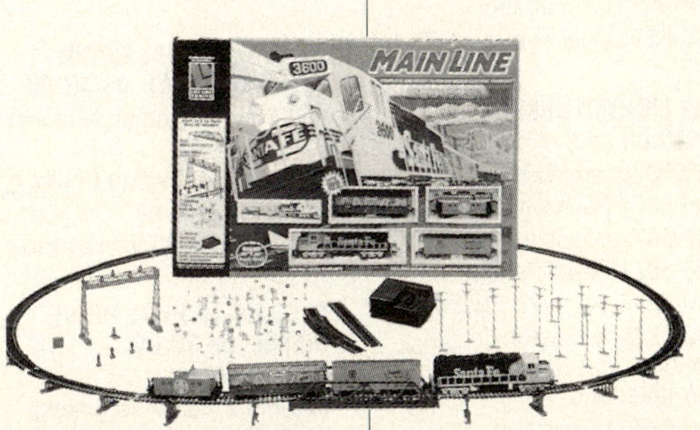

433-8744 Santa Fe Main Line 60.00

Includes a GP38-2 diesel locomotive, 2 freight cars and caboose, bridge and trestle set, 43 signs, 6 utility poles and a 45" x 36" oval track.

433-8766 Santa Fe Thundering Rails 80.00
NEW (not shown)

Includes a GP38-2 diesel locomotive with working headlight, 6 freight cars and 8 wheel caboose, operating blinking bridge, 17 piece trestle set, signal bridge with trackside accessories, 67 signs, 6 utility poles, 24 authentic BURMA SHAVE® signs, hook-up wires, extra couplers and rail joiners, illustrated instructions and a 45" x 45" track layout.

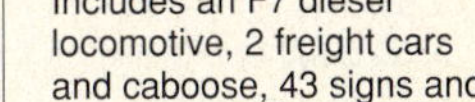

433-8739 Santa Fe Super Chief 55.00

Includes an F7 diesel locomotive, 2 freight cars and caboose, 43 signs and a 36" circle of track.

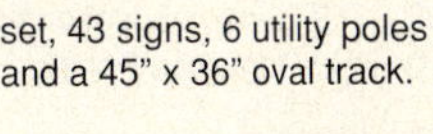

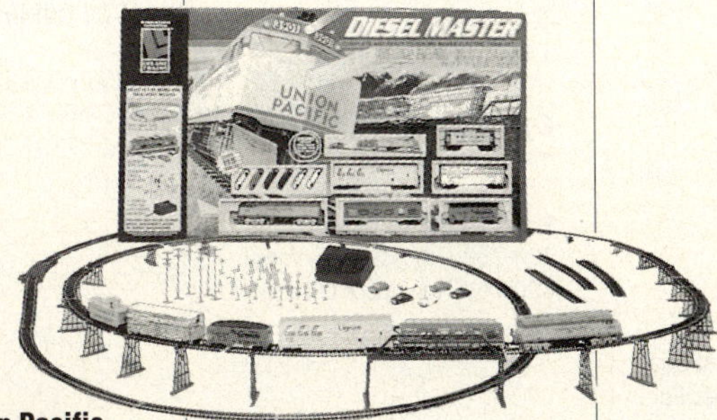

433-8740 Union Pacific Diesel Master 90.00

Includes a GP38-2 diesel locomotive, 4 freight cars and caboose, 6 autos, 43 signs, 6 utility poles and a 48" x 49" double oval over-under track.

433-8727 Santa Fe Heavy Hauler 100.00

Includes two GP38-2 diesel locomotives (one is unpowered), 4 freight cars and caboose, bridge and 36 piece trestle set, 67 signs, 6 utility poles, trees, automobiles, figures and a 84" x 36" over-under figure track.

These HO Scale locos feature a prepainted and lettered plastic shell and die cast chassis. All models are ready-to-run and include horn-hook couplers and RP25 wheels. E units and SD40's have flywheel drive.

We have worked closely with this manufacturer to provide accurate availability information at the time this catalog was published. Items listed in blue ink may not be available at all times. Please see your dealer for current delivery information.

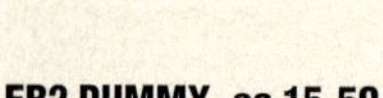

ALCO FA2

STEAM LOCOS

4-6-2 PACIFIC WITH TENDER ea 85.00
This twin-lighted loco includes "Puff-of-Smoke" unit.

490-6639 Southern Pacific (red)
490-6643 Santa Fe

0-4-0 LOCOMOTIVE WITH TENDER ea 33.00 *NEW*
490-6632 Canadian National
490-6633 Canadian Pacific
490-6634 Santa Fe
490-6635 Pennsylvania
490-6636 Southern

2-8-0 CONSOLIDATION ea 79.99 *NEW*
490-6550 Southern Pacific
490-6551 Pennsylvania
490-6552 Great Northern
490-6553 Chicago, Burlington & Quincy
490-6554 Canadian Pacific
490-6555 Canadian National
490-6556 Santa Fe
490-6557 Baltimore & Ohio
490-6558 Burlington Northern
490-6559 Grand Canyon
490-6560 Norfolk & Western
490-6561 Northern Pacific
490-6562 Massachusetts & Pennsylvania
490-6563 Rio Grande

DIESEL LOCOS

ALCO FA2 POWERED & B DUMMY ea 93.50
(unless noted)
8-wheel drive. "A" units feature operating headlight. (Some model magazines suggest it's a cross between an FA1-1 and an FA2-2.)

490-891 Santa Fe (silver, red)
490-892 Burlington Northern (green, silver)
490-893 Pennsylvania (brown) 75.00 *NEW*

FA2 DUAL LIGHTED LOCOMOTIVE ea 33.00 *NEW*
490-6800 Santa Fe
490-6801 Pennsylvania
490-6802 Chessie
490-6803 Union Pacific
490-6804 Southern Pacific
490-6805 Burlington Northern
490-6806 Amtrak
490-6807 Conrail
490-6808 Southern Railway
490-6809 Canadian National
490-6810 Canadian Pacific

FA2 LIGHTED DUMMY ea 19.78 (unless noted) *NEW*
490-850 Santa Fe
490-852 Central Pacific
490-849 Undecorated
490-859 Undecorated 18.68

FA2 LIGHTED DUMMY ea 15.50 *NEW*
490-6870 Santa Fe
490-6871 Pennsylvania
490-6872 Chessie
490-6873 Union Pacific
490-6874 Southern Pacific
490-6875 Burlington Northern
490-6876 Amtrak
490-6877 Conrail
490-6878 Southern Railway
490-6879 Canadian National
490-6880 Canadian Pacific

FB2 B UNIT POWERED ea 82.50 *NEW*
490-840 Santa Fe
490-842 Pennsylvania
490-844 Union Pacific
490-845 Burlington Northern

FB2 DUMMY ea 15.50 *NEW*
490-6850 Santa Fe
490-6851 Pennsylvania
490-6852 Chessie
490-6853 Union Pacific
490-6854 Southern Pacific
490-6855 Burlington Northern
490-6856 Amtrak
490-6857 Conrail
490-6858 Southern Railway
490-6859 Canadian National
490-6860 Canadian Pacific

FB2 B UNIT DUMMY ea 18.68 *NEW*
490-860 Santa Fe
490-861 Pennsylvania
490-863 Union Pacific
490-864 Burlington Northern

ALCO RS-2 DUAL DRIVE LIGHTED DIESEL ea 35.00
490-6841 Canadian National (black)
490-6842 Canadian Pacific
490-6845 Conrail
490-6846 Southern Railway

ALCO RS-11 DUAL DRIVE DIESEL ea 36.00
(unless noted)
490-6692 Santa Fe (black, yellow)
490-6695 Southern Railway (green, white)
490-6697 Chessie 33.00
490-6699 Burlington Northern (green, black)

ALCO 1000 POWERED ea 33.00
490-6832 Santa Fe
490-6833 Union Pacific
490-6835 Amtrak

DDT PLYMOUTH INDUSTRIAL DIESEL ea 25.00 *NEW*
490-6669 Burlington Northern
490-6670 Santa Fe
490-6673 Canadian National
490-6674 Canadian Pacific
490-6676 Amtrak
490-6678 Chessie
490-6679 Conrail

ALCO C430 DUAL DRIVE LIGHTED DIESEL ea 37.00
490-6770 Canadian National (red, black, white)
490-6771 Canadian Pacific
490-6772 Santa Fe
490-6774 Burlington Northern (green, black)
490-6775 Missouri - Kansas - Texas (green)

EMD SW-1 POWERED ea 33.00
490-6821 Canadian Pacific 30.00 *NEW*
490-6822 Canadian National 33.00 *NEW*
490-6823 Santa Fe
490-6825 Southern Railway
490-6826 Burlington Northern
490-6827 Amtrak (silver, black)

A-B-A 2 POWER UNITS WITH DUMMY ea 79.98 *NEW*
490-56203 Santa Fe
490-56223 Southern Pacific
490-56253 Burlington Northern

BALDWIN "SHARK NOSE" DIESELS
A & B SET ea 93.50 *NEW*
490-791 Santa Fe
490-792 New York Central
490-795 Canadian National

LIGHTED DUMMY ea 19.78 *NEW*
490-730 Santa Fe
490-731 Pennsylvania
490-733 Canadian National
490-729 Undecorated

B UNIT DUMMY ea 17.58 (unless noted) *NEW*
490-750 Santa Fe
490-753 Canadian National
490-754 New York Central

EMD F3A LIGHTED, POWERED ea 36.00
8-wheel drive, 8 wheel pick-up, metal chassis.

490-6732 Union Pacific
490-6735 Canadian National (black, red, white)
490-6736 Canadian Pacific
490-6737 Burlington Northern (green, black)
490-6738 Amtrak

EMD F3A LIGHTED DUMMY
490-6731 Santa Fe (silver, red) 15.50

PORTER HUSTLER - LIGHTED ea 24.95 *NEW*
490-6705 Santa Fe
490-6706 Burlington Northern
490-6707 Southern Railway
490-6708 Southern Pacific

F9A DIESEL WITH SINGLE HEADLIGHT ea 24.00 *NEW*
490-6612 Canadian Pacific
490-6613 Canadian National

EMD GP-9 LIGHTED, POWERED ea 37.00
490-6752 Conrail
490-6754 Canadian National
490-6750 Santa Fe
490-6751 Southern Railway
490-6755 Burlington Northern
490-67501 Santa Fe (red, silver)

LOCO DUMMIES ea 11.00 *NEW*
490-66024 Canadian Pacific
490-66074 Santa Fe
490-77104 Rock Island

TRAIN SETS

ORIENT EXPRESS

model power

SILVER STAR

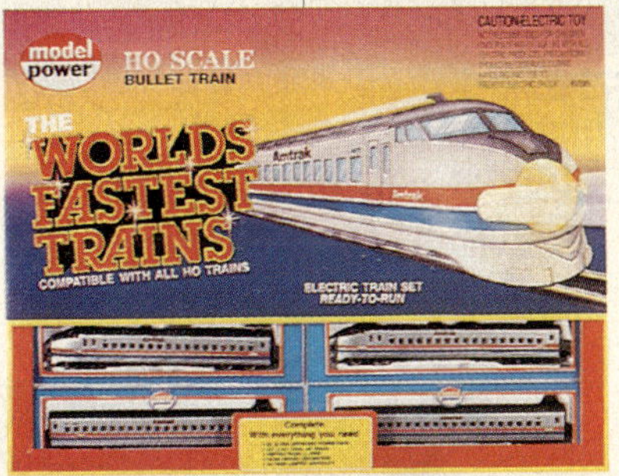

AMTRAK BULLET

PACIFIC PRINCE

TRAIN SETS *NEW*

490-1024 Li'l Donkey 46.00
490-1025 The Champ 47.00
490-1031 Santa 66.00
490-1035 Pride Of The Line 50.00
490-1038 The Orient Express 435.00
490-1045 Northern Star TBA
490-1046 Tuxedo Junction 83.00
490-1050 Super Brute 90.00
490-1061 Double Diesel Train Set 108.00
490-1065 Midnight Express 75.00
490-1068 Golden Spike II 99.00
490-1073 Smokin' Joe 85.00
490-1095 World's Fastest Amtrak 55.00
490-521205 Der Adler 239.00

BLUE EAGLE

490-1049 Blue Eagle 65.00
This set includes a SW-1 or Alco 1000 loco (lighted), 3 cars, circle of track, power pack, hook up wire and instructions.

GOLDEN SPIKE II

490-1051 Golden Spike II 108.00
This set includes a lighted GP9 with metal chassis, 8 wheel drive, 8 wheel pick-up, 5 cars, blinking bridge with piers, figure 8 over and under track layout (4'x8'), 7 piece signal bridge, 40 piece building set, power pack, hook up wire and instructions.

PRESIDENTIAL SPECIAL TRAIN SETS ea 125.00
NEW

490-1009 Southern Pacific
490-1011 Baltimore & Ohio
490-1012 Santa Fe
490-1013 Canadian Pacific
490-1014 Canadian National
490-1015 Central Pacific
490-1016 CNR
490-1019 Erie

THE WORLD'S FASTEST TRAINS

490-1063 Silver Star 67.00
Includes: lighted diesel loco, 2 freight cars, caboose, 40 piece pop-out building set, 22 piece poles and accessories, circle of track, power pack, hook-up wire and instructions.

CHRISTMAS SET

490-1093 Christmas Set (not illustrated) 89.00

AMTRAK BULLET

490-1084 Amtrak Bullet 80.00
This set includes 1 powered loco, 1 unpowered loco, 2 passenger cars, 45 x 36" oval of track, heavy duty power pack with circuit breaker, hook-up wire and instructions.

PACIFIC PRINCE

490-1090 Pacific Prince 125.00
This set includes a 4-6-2 USRA Pacific lighted locomotive with smoke, 5 freight cars, 45 x 36" (114 x 92 cm) oval of track, power pack, hook-up wire and instructions.

ORIENT EXPRESS

490-1092 Official Deluxe Orient Express 199.00
This set includes equipment based on the equipment of the actual Orient Express, including a lighted steam loco with tender, 2 coach cars, 1 dining car, 1 sleeper, a 2nd Class Coach, oval of track and power pack.

MISCELLANEOUS

490-6630 'Lil Tugger Steam Loco 25.00 *NEW*
490-6665 FP45 25.00 *NEW*
490-6720 2-6-0 Loco with Tender 35.00 *NEW*
490-7630 0-4-0 with Caboose 27.96 *NEW*
490-7720 Rolling Thunder 2-6-0 with Caboose 28.50
490-673031 F3A Powered and Dummy Lighted 52.50 *NEW*
490-763038 F3 and Caboose 41.98 *NEW*
490-763070 0-4-0 With Caboose 27.96 *NEW*
490-763236 Shifter/Tender and Caboose 38.98 *NEW*
490-766999 DDT and Caboose 30.98 *NEW*
490-769099 RS11 and Caboose 41.98 *NEW*

MANTUA

HO Scale ready-to-run steam locomotives are powered and have prepainted and lettered die cast and plastic bodies. All have operating headlights and smoke units (unless noted), moving metal bells, wire handrails and include horn-hook couplers.

We have worked closely with this manufacturer to provide accurate availability information at the time this catalog was published. Items listed in blue ink may not be available at all times. Please see your dealer for current delivery information.

STEAM LOCOMOTIVES

0-4-0 SHIFTER
455-362081 Canadian National 85.99

0-6-0 TANK SWITCHER
455-361059 Leetonia & Cherry Valley 78.99

4-4-2 CAMELBACK ATLANTIC ea 195.99
NEW
455-378241 Pennsylvania

2-6-6-2 TANK MALLET
455-365157 Rayonier 270.99
Includes oil conversion tank, 33" spoked plastic wheels, lead and trailing trucks with interval bearings, metal spark arrestor and smokestack.

0-6-0 SWITCHER
455-376164 Baltimore & Ohio #386 (black) 141.99
NEW
Includes operating headlight and back-up light , coal pusher - less smoke unit.

0-8-0 EIGHT WHEEL SWITCHER
455-368145 Wabash 115.99

2-8-2 LIGHT MIKADO
455-383070 Nickel Plate Road 237.99 *NEW*
Includes operating back-up light.

2-8-2 MIKADO
455-386040 Southern 254.99
NEW

2-8-4 BERKSHIRE S-4
455-385098 Erie (black) 237.99 *NEW*
Includes pilot, whistle, modified power drive, numberboard under headlight and operating back-up light.

2-6-6-2 LOGGER
455-373125 Booth Kelly Lumber 193.99

4-6-0 ROGERS
455-363006 Central Pacific 108.99
455-377165 Clinchfield #16 (black) 181.99 *NEW*
Includes headlight and back-up light, whistle, and handrails.

0-6-0T LITTLE SIX KIT
Limited Quantities Available
455-502 Undecorated 55.00

0-8-0 SWITCHER ea 223.99
NEW
455-380070 Nickel Plate Road
455-387004 Northern Pacific (black)
Includes coal pusher, builders plate and operating back-up light.

0-4-0 SHIFTER
455-375163 Santa Fe #318 (black) 132.99 *NEW*
Includes operating headlight and back-up light - less smoke unit.

COAL HAULER

MOUNTAIN SUPPLY TRAIN

F-7 A-B-A

0-8-0 SWITCHER

MANTUA

BONUS PACKS

These specially grouped engines and cars are not available anywhere else in the Mantua line.

PASSENGER TRAIN
455-629390 Pennsylvania 128.99 **NEW**

Includes 4-6-0 American loco with 1890 style combine and coach.

COAL HAULER

Limited Quantities Available

455-627030 Pennsylvania 41.99
Includes GP-20 diesel and 2 hoppers with coal loads.

455-630030 Erie Lackawanna 51.99 **NEW**
Includes GP-20 diesel, 2 hoppers with coal loads, and a 36' Erie Lackawanna caboose.

CONSTRUCTION SUPPLY TRAIN
455-628012 Frisco 185.99
Includes light Mikado loco and two 41' flat cars loaded with culvert pipes.

MOUNTAIN SUPPLY TRAIN
455-631389 Reading 180.99 **NEW**
Includes a B8a Camelback

DIESELS

switcher loco and tender, with two flatcars carrying crate loads.

EMD F7 A-B-A sets
Includes two powered A units and a non-powered B unit. The rear A unit is wired to operate in reverse.

455-413032 Amtrak, Single A Unit Only (silver, blue, red) 32.00
455-415058 Rock Island 76.99
455-415170 Pennsylvania 81.99 **NEW**

EMD GP20
455-414063 Burlington Northern (cascade green) 37.99 **NEW**
455-414073 Missouri Pacific (dark blue) 35.49
455-414900 Super Bowl Express 45.99

0-10-0 TEN WHEEL SWITCHER
455-367086 Alton Southern 183.99

4-4-0 AMERICAN
455-369240 Rock Island & Peoria #305 (silver, black, brown) 181.99 **NEW**

4-6-2 HEAVY PACIFIC
455-382064 Chicago & North Western "400" 223.99 **NEW**

Includes whistle, coal pusher, pilot, numberboard under headlight, "400" logos on side of engine and operating back-up light.

4-6-4 HEAVY HUDSON
455-384037 Boston & Albany 237.99 **NEW**

Includes whistle, numberboard under headlight, operating back-up light and black nickel plated wheels.

MANTUA

HO Scale ready-to-run steam locomotives are powered and have prepainted and lettered die cast and plastic bodies. All have operating headlights and smoke units (unless noted), moving metal bells, wire handrails and include horn-hook couplers.

We have worked closely with this manufacturer to provide accurate availability information at the time this catalog was published. Items listed in blue ink may not be available at all times. Please see your dealer for current delivery information.

TRAIN SETS

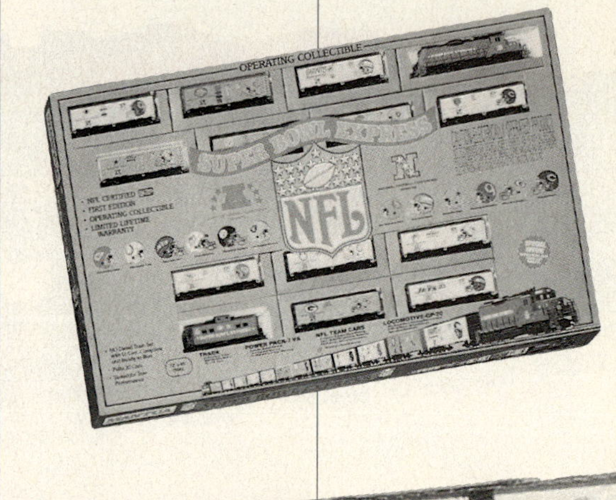

READY-TO-RUN TENDERS

**READY-TO-RUN TENDERS
LONG HAUL TENDER**
455-713000 Undecorated
23.99
455-749000 Undecorated,
With Operating Backup Light
35.49 *NEW*

VANDERBILT TENDER
455-712000 Undecorated
23.99
455-748000 Undecorated,
With Operating Backup Light
35.49 *NEW*

PENNSYLVANIA TENDER
455-746000 With Operating
Backup Light (black) 35.49

STEAM TRAIN SETS

455-934390 The Old Timer
132.99 *NEW*
Includes steam locomotive with operating headlight, tender with wood load, water car with three tanks, log car with logs, stock car with opening doors, flat car with crates, and a caboose with smoke stack and metal handrails. Less track and power pack.

455-935391 Western and Atlantic Special 132.99 *NEW*
Includes steam loco with operating headlight, tender with wood load, stock car with opening doors, water car with three tanks, box car with opening doors, combination , and coach with window detail, metal handrails and frame supports. Less track and power pack.

455-936304 High Country Rail Runner 169.99 *NEW*
Includes an 0-6-0 steam loco with operating headlight, tender with coal load and metal handrails, a 32' hopper with coal load, a 40' wood sided reefer, a single dome tank car with metal handrails, 41' steel reefer, gondola with coal load, 41' steel sided box car with opening doors, and a caboose with smoke stack and handrails. Less track and power pack.

DIESEL TRAIN SETS
455-921414 Super Bowl Express '92 (red) 222.99
This edition has been updated and includes the winner of the Super Bowl . Each car is boldly painted in team colors and features an exact replica of the official team helmet and logo, along with the National or American Conference letter and winning Super Bowl in Roman numerals. The locomotive and matching caboose are decorated with the official NFL symbol and colors.

Set includes NFL Super Bowl GP-20 diesel locomotive with eight wheel drive and operating headlight, NFL Super Bowl Caboose, NFL Team cars featuring 12 Super Bowl winning team cars (weighted for stability), nickel silver track with rerailer to make 72" x 45" oval, and UL listed power pack.

SUPER BOWL WINNERS
NATIONAL FOOTBALL CONFERENCE
Chicago Bears
Dallas Cowboys
Green Bay Packers
New York Giants
San Francisco 49ers
Washington Redskins

AMERICAN FOOTBALL CONFERENCE
Indianapolis Colts
Kansas City Chiefs
Los Angeles Raiders
Miami Dolphins
New York Jets
Pittsburgh Steelers

455-931414 Reading Freight Express 55.49 *NEW*
Includes a GP-20 diesel loco with eight wheel drive, GD-500 can motor and operating headlight, a single dome tank car, boxcar with opening doors, gondola with coal load, and caboose with smoke stack and handrails. Less track and power pack.

455-932414 Conrail Heavy Hauler 55.49 *NEW*
Includes a GP-20 diesel loco with eight wheel drive, GD-500 can motor and operating headlight, a gondola with coal load, boxcar with opening doors, single dome tank car with metal handrails, and caboose with smoke stack and handrails. Less track and power pack.

455-933413 Amtrak Record Breaker Express (silver, blue, red) 89.99 *NEW*
Includes an Amtrak F7A powered diesel with eight wheel drive, GD-500 can motor and operating headlight, two unpowered F7B diesel locos, a boxcar with operating doors, a flatcar with crate load, a reefer, a single dome tank car with metal handrails, and a 36' caboose with smoke stack and handrails. Less track and power pack.

MANTUA

Couple more inches and the table will be aligned, allowing #12 to head out to her waiting train. One of the bigger locos on the Bicci & Onri, this 2-4-4-2 is a United brass import. The turntable is a modified Atlas unit, which now features a scratchbuilt gallows frame.   Built by Michael Terry, this little B&O can be seen on display at the real B&O Railroad museum in Ellicott City, Maryland.
Model and Photo by Michael Terry

RIVAROSSI

Bring back the era of the great steam locos with these models on your roster Each ready-to-run model is highly detailed and painted in an authentic scheme. A powerful three-pole motor and worm gear drive insure smooth performance, and a working headlight is standard equipment.

THREE TRUCK HEISLER

HEISLER LOCOMOTIVES

With sharp curves, steep grades and some of the roughest trackwork ever built, the logging industry presented special challenges to locomotive builders. In 1891, Charles Heisler unveiled an all-new style of loco, especially suited to this type of service. The cylinders were mounted on the boiler and drove a large drive shaft that ran beneath the loco. This was connected to gearboxes on one axle of each truck. Small side rods transferred the power to each wheel. This extremely flexible design allowed the engine to negotiate curves as tight as 50' and provided superb pulling power.   In 1906 a three-truck version was introduced, which offered a substantial increase in pulling power, without sacrificing performance, although it did require a slightly larger turning radius.

Since the gears were enclosed and protected from dust, Heislers were highly favored by the mining industry as well.

Both versions of these HO models are based on prototype locos and are highly detailed. Like the real engines, their flexible drive trains allow them to run on rough track and require only a 15" minimum radius. The model includes hook-loop couplers, which can be replaced with Kadee #6 couplers, sold separately.

TWO-TRUCK HEISLER
NEW
635-1568 Salmon Creek Company #4 189.99

THREE-TRUCK HEISLER
NEW
635-1569 Ohio Match Company #1 199.99

LOGGING BUGGY **NEW**
635-2349 28' Logging Buggy 17.00
This car is typical of the rough-and-ready equipment made by logging companies in their own shops. Each car is complete with a load of logs, real chain tie-downs and hook-loop couplers. They're ideal for use with either the Two- or Three-Truck Heisler locos.

LOGGING BUGGY

TWO-TRUCK HEISLER

STEAM LOCOMOTIVES

SOUTHERN PACIFIC 4-8-8-2 CAB FORWARD

RIVAROSSI

SOUTHERN PACIFIC 4-8-8-2 CAB FORWARD ea 264.99 *NEW*

635-1570 #4257
635-1571 #4270
The miles of tunnels and snow sheds on Southern Pacific's route across the Sierra Nevada mountains were a major hazard to steam engine crews. Ventilation was poor at best and when bigger engines came into use, conditions become intolerable. To combat this, SP ordered 4-8-8-2's from Baldwin with their cabs on the front of the loco. In all, 195 were built (in different classes) and served until the end of the steam era.

4-6-2 STREAMLINED PACIFIC *NEW*

635-1579 Lehigh Valley "John Wilkes" 199.99
The Lehigh Valley joined the streamlining craze in June of 1939 with all-new equipment for the "John Wilkes." Racing between Pittston/Wilkes-Barre and New York City, this streamlined Pacific kept this important train on schedule! This model is finsihed in the classic black with red and white stripping.

4-6-4 STREAMLINED HUDSON *NEW*

635-1580 Milwaukee Road F-7 #100 "Hiawatha" Scheme 199.99
For many years, travelers between Chicago and the Twin Cities had their choice of three fast streamliners: Burlington's "Zephyr," Chicago & North Western's "400" and the Milwaukee Road "Hiawatha." In late 1938, the first of the class F7 streamlined Hudsons entered service on the route. Between Milwaukee and Chicago, they often rolled along between 90 and 100 mph every day! The model will be finished in gray, with orange and red stripping.

UNION PACIFIC FEF 4-8-4 ea 199.99 *NEW*

Between 1937 and 1944, some 45 locos of class FEF were delivered to the Union Pacific. These high-stepping Northerns were used on the road's major passenger trains before being bumped to freight duty in the 50's. The 844 was among the last in service and was set aside for preservation. Later renumbered as #8444, the engine became one of the all-time great fan trip locos and continues to delight railfans around the world.

These HO Scale models are offered in three distinct versions. There's engine #841, which matches the as-built appearance of the class in 1944. For fantrip service in modern times, there are two versions equipped with smoke deflectors (which were first applied in 1946): #8444 in black, or the 8444 in the classic "greyhound" scheme of two-tone gray, as the engine appears today. All models feature the correct centipede tender.

635-1528 #8444 w/"Elephant Ear" smoke deflectors (black)
635-1572 #8444 ("Greyhound" Scheme - two-tone gray)
635-1578 #841 As-built in 1944

These HO Scale craft train locomotive kits feature a die cast zinc boiler and underframe, molded plastic cab and tender, and illustrated instructions. Box cab diesels are ready-to-run. The Saddle tanker, 0-6-0, box cab and Alco RS3 diesel kits feature molded plastic bodies and zinc underframes.

We have worked closely with this manufacturer to provide accurate availability information at the time this catalog was published. Items listed in blue ink may not be available at all times. Please see you dealer for current delivery information.

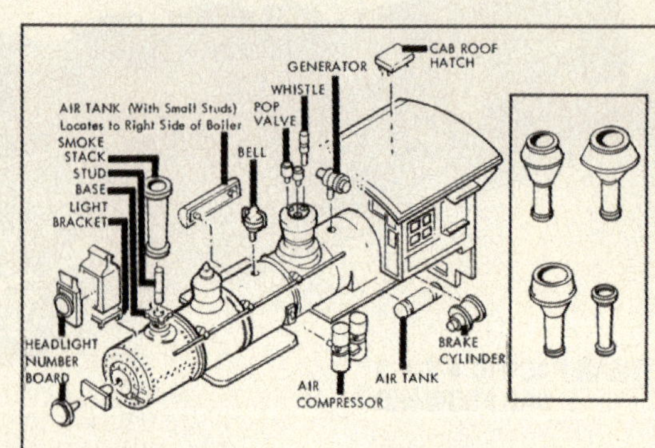

STEAM LOCOMOTIVES

2-6-2 PRAIRIE

2-6-2 PRAIRIE

2-6-0- OLD TIMER

2-6-0- OLD TIMER

2-8-0 OLD TIMER

2-8-0 OLD TIMER

ALCO RS-3 (READY-TO-RUN)
ea **69.00** (unless noted)
Features new power mechanism, and detailed body, which is painted and lettered in appropriate color schemes. Includes separate sideframes with add-on details, and wire handrails.

480-2381 Western Maryland (black, yellow)
480-2382 Santa Fe (black, white)
480-2383 New York Central (black, white, red)
480-2384 Canadian National (black, white)
480-2385 Southern Pacific (black, red)
480-2386 Union Pacific (yellow, gray) 75.00
480-2387 Chicago & North Western (yellow, green) 75.00
480-2388 Pennsylvania (green, yellow)
480-2389 Burlington Northern (cascade green, black, white) 75.00

ALCO RS3 POWERED ea **39.98**
480-2354 Delaware & Hudson
480-2360 Louisville & Nashville
480-2365 Canadian National
480-2369 Conrail (blue)
480-2370 Pacific Electric (black, orange)
480-2350 Undecorated
480-2352 St Louis Southwestern

Limited Quantities Available
480-2356 Soo Line (black, yellow)

0-6-0T SADDLE TANKER KIT
ea **34.50** (unless noted)
480-421 Southern Pacific (NM&SP)
480-422 Santa Fe
480-425 Union Pacific
480-426 Weyerhaeuser
480-420 Undecorated 29.00

DETAILING SET

LOCO DETAILING SET
This set includes molded plastic detail parts, less cab and boiler.

480-2980 Baldwin Steam Loco Detailing Set pkg (26 pieces) 2.75
480-2981 Shay Loco Detailing Pack 5.25

SHAY LOCOMOTIVE ea **69.98** (unless noted)
Kits are powered and undecorated, and include a 12V in-line motor. Frame and boiler are cast in zamac metal, cab and tender are molded in plastic.

STANDARD GAUGE
480-360 Class B 2-Truck 59.98
480-370 Class C 3-Truck

NARROW GAUGE
480-380 Class B 2-Truck HOn3 59.98
480-390 Class C 3-Truck HOn3
480-361 Class B 2-Truck Rio Grande

0-6-0 LOCO KIT ea 39.98 (unless noted)
480-411 Southern Pacific
480-412 Union Pacific
480-410 Undecorated 35.00

2-6-0 OLD TIMER ea 69.98 (unless noted)
480-495 Illinois Central
480-496 Colorado & Southern
480-490 Undecorated 59.98
480-491 Baltimore & Ohio

2-6-0 STANDARD ea 59.98
480-510 Undecorated

2-8-0 OLD TIMER ea 69.98 (unless noted)
480-481 Southern Pacific
480-486 Maryland & Pennsylvania
480-480 Undecorated 59.98
480-482 Santa Fe
480-483 Pennsylvania
480-484 Union Pacific
480-485 Rio Grande

SHAY LOCOMOTIVE STANDARD GAUGE

CLIMAX 2-TRUCK CLASS "B" KIT ea 29.98 (unless noted)

"Old Timer" Logging Complex 2-truck locos are prepainted and lettered.

480-1510 Dummy, Battle Mountain 10.00
The instructions cover how to convert the Climax to HOn3 or to run on N Scale track. Modeler will have to do some kitbashing and purchase small boiler (or scratch build one). Includes undecorated plastic body and trucks, less metal underframe.

480-2770 Undecorated 26.50
480-2771 Undecorated (brown, maroon, with gold and black lettering)
480-2773 Moose Jaws - Saskatchewan Lumber Company (light and dark green, with white, red and black lettering)
480-2774 Rio Grande

0-6-0 SWITCHER ea 39.98 (unless noted)
This kit includes slope back tender.

480-411 Southern Pacific
480-412 Union Pacific
480-410 Undecorated 35.00

2-8-0 CONSOLIDATION ea 69.98 (unless noted)
480-315 Rio Grande
480-461 Southern Pacific With Vanderbilt Tender
480-460 Undecorated, Harriman With Vanderbilt Tender 59.95

2-6-2 PRAIRIE KIT ea 69.98 (unless noted)
480-443 Southern Pacific Harriman/Vanderbilt
480-451 Pennsylvania With Coal Tender
480-442 Undecorated, Harriman Type Boiler & Vanderbilt Tender 59.98

TRACK CLEANING CAR

TRACK CLEANER KIT
This track cleaner works without fluid! Spring loaded plungers have flat sanding discs which ride on rail tops and clean track. (Undecorated)

480-2796 Dummy 9.50
480-2799 Accessory Kit 2.98
This kit converts the Roundhouse box cab diesel to a track cleaner. Complete kit with instructions.

480-2805 Undecorated 29.98
480-2835 Replacement Disc pkg (12) 1.00

3-in-1 HOn3 STATIC STEAM
This unpowered kit features one molded plastic saddle tanker body, plastic detail parts, metal "outside frame" chassis with two sets of steam cylinders, counter weights and main rods. Unassembled drivers consist of brass rims, steel axles, molded centers, plus screws. Includes instructions to build one of the following: 2-4-4-0T, 0-8-0T (logging type), or 0-8-0T (plantation type).

480-1550 3-in-1 HOn3 Static Steam Articulated Kit 19.98

2-8-0 BALDWIN, HOn3 ea 59.98 (unless noted)
480-472 Outside Frame, Undecorated
480-473 Inside Frame, Undecorated
480-474 Outside Frame, Rio Grande 69.98

4-4-2 ATLANTIC KIT ea 69.98 (unless noted)
480-436 Pennsylvania With Coal Tender
480-429 Southern Pacific, Harriman With Vanderbilt Tender
480-428 Undecorated, Harriman Type Boiler And Vanderbilt Tender 59.98

BOX CAB DIESEL KIT ea 29.98 (unless noted)
This kit features molded plastic body and zinc underframe.

480-2814 Ford
480-2815 Union Pacific
480-2810 Undecorated 26.50

4-6-0 TEN WHEELER KIT ea 69.98 (unless noted)
480-455 Undecorated, Harriman Type Boiler And Vanderbilt Tender 59.98
480-453 Pennsylvania With Coal Tender
480-456 Southern Pacific, Harriman Type Boiler And Vanderbilt Tender

TENDER ea 15.00
Tender kits feature black

TENDERS

plastic bodies with die cast zamac underframes. Tenders are undecorated (unless noted) and include trucks.

480-400 Slope Back

404

405

(switcher)
480-401 Oil (Santa Fe type)
480-402 Coal (Pennsylvania type)
480-403 Vanderbilt - This kit is convertible to either coal or oil.
480-404 "Old Timer" coal
480-405 Rio Grande HOn3

Roco

Imported from Austria by Walthers

These engines feature authentically painted and lettered plastic bodies with die-cast frames, metal gears and European-style couplers. Many have operating, reversing headlights and include multiple locomotive numbers. All Roco engines operate on 2-rail D.C. (unless otherwise indicated). Engines with pantographs can also be powered from overhead catenary. Many models are also available equipped for 3-rail AC operation.

625-43410

625-43203

625-43218

625-43270

625-43263

625-43427

625-43257

625-43514

GERMAN STATE RAILWAY (COMPANY)

CLASS 57 0-10-0
625-43230 Era II 203.49

CLASS 58 2-10-0
625-43203 Era II 187.99

CLASS 74 2-6-0T
Formerly class T12 locomotives of the Prussian State Railways, these engines were acquired by the German State Railways (Company) and later added to the locomotive fleets of the German State and German Federal Railways.

625-43270 Era II 176.49

CLASS 01 4-6-2
625-43243 Era II 209.49

CLASS 18 4-6-2
625-43218 Era II 258.99

CLASS 44 2-10-0 ea 210.49
From 1926 through 1949, about 2,000 of these locomotives were put into heavy freight train service. After World War II, many of these engines were acquired by other railway administrations, including the French National Railways and the Austrian Federal Railways.

625-43263 Era II
625-43262 Era III-IV

CLASS 98 0-4-4-0 MALLET
NEW
625-43282 Era II 235.99

CLASS E71 ELECTRIC
27 of these locos, nicknamed "Baby Crocodiles," were built between 1914 and 1921 for branchline service in central Germany.

625-43514 Era II (green) 174.99

CLASS E44 ELECTRIC
Built between 1931 and 1934, these locomotives were used in freight and passenger service on the Freilassing-Berchtesgaden route in southern Bavaria.

625-43410 Era II (gray) 130.99 **LIMITED RUN**

CLASS 98 0-4-0T
This "Glassbox" locomotive was one of 22 0-4-0T engines obtained by the German State Railway (Company) from the Royal Bavarian State Railway. Used in branchline service, the loco ran into the 1950's.

625-43257 Era II 132.49

CLASS E91 ELECTRIC
Used in freight service, these engines were purchased by the Prussian and Bavarian State Railways, as well as the German State Railway (Company). The engines were so successful that 17 of the units were reconditioned by the German Federal Railways after World War II and used in switching service.

625-43427 Era II (gray) 169.49 **LIMITED RUN**

GERMAN FEDERAL RAILWAYS

Between 1919 and 1925, a total of 2,589 locomotives of this typically Prussian design (0-10-0) were built. The engines were used for years in freight and switching service by the DB, finally being retired from duty in 1968.

CLASS 57 0-10-0
625-43220 Era III 203.49

CLASS 74 2-6-0T
625-43271 Era III 176.49

CLASS 01 4-6-2
Two hundred thirty-one locos of this class were put in service between 1925 and 1938 for hauling express passenger trains. They were used by the DB in scheduled service until 1973.

625-43240 Era III-IV 209.49

CLASS 23 2-6-2
Over 100 engines of this type were constructed by the DB between 1950 and 1959 for heavy passenger service. They were used in scheduled service until 1975. This model is available in two versions: a standard production version lettered for engine 23 058, or a special limited-run museum edition model based on loco 23 105, the last steam loco of any class built for the DB (December 4, 1959), which is now on display at the Nuremberg Traffic Museum. The museum edition model includes a 96-page book on the history of the loco.

625-43248 Museum Edition 262.99
625-43249 Era III-IV 209.49

CLASS 50 2-10-0
625-43288 Era III 273.99

CLASS 42 2-8-2
625-43244 Era IV, Oil Tender 231.49

CLASS 80 0-6-0T
A total of 39 locos of this type were placed in service between 1928 and '29. The DB kept them in operation until 1963, with some lasting until 1978 on industrial roads. Some class 80 locos are still in use today on museum railways.

625-43208 Era III 99.49

CLASS 98 0-4-0T
Now on exhibit at the Nuremberg Traffic Museum, the prototype for this "Glassbox" replica was originally built for the Royal Bavarian Railway in the early 1900's.

625-43255 Era III 132.49

CLASS E18 ELECTRIC
Built by AEG, the class E18 electrics were the most powerful single-frame locomotives running on German rails when introduced in 1935. In 1984, almost 50 years later, the final E18's were retired from service. This model is available in a standard production version, or a special limited-run museum edition decorated in as-delivered colors for engine E18 08, now restored and operating in fan trip service on German and Austrian rails. A special book tracing the history of the engine is also included with the museum edition model.

625-43660 Museum Edition (gray) 213.49
625-43981 Museum Edition, AC 3-Rail (gray) 259.99
625-43659 Era III (blue) 176.49
625-43972 Era III, AC 3-Rail (blue) 222.99

CLASS E32 ELECTRIC
625-43917 Era III, AC 3-Rail (green) 214.99

CLASS E41 ELECTRIC ea 222.99 (unless noted)
625-43637 Era III (green) 175.99 *NEW*
625-43957 Era III, AC 3-Rail (green) *NEW*
625-43636 Era III (blue) 176.49
625-43956 Era III, AC 3-Rail (blue)

CLASS E44 ELECTRIC
625-43404 Era III (green) 126.99

CLASS E445 ELECTRIC
625-43405 Era III (green) 126.99

625-43220

625-43405

625-43660

625-43255

625-43240

625-43248

625-43271

625-43288

625-43208

625-43404

625-43917

EUROPEAN RAILROADS

B	Belgian National Railways
BBO	Federal Railways of Austria (until 1956)
CFL	Luxembourg National Railways
DB	German Federal Railways
DRG	German State Railway (Company) (until 1945)
DR	German State Railway (after 1945)
DSB	Danish State Railways
FS	Italian State Railways
NS	Netherlands State Railways
NSB	Norwegian State Railways
OBB	Austrian Federal Railways
SJ	Swedish State Railways
SBB	Swiss Federal Railways
SNCF	French National Railways

Roco

Imported from Austria and marketed by Walthers

GERMAN FEDERAL RAILWAYS

CLASS E50 ELECTRIC
625-43584 Era III (green)
165.99

CLASS 103 ELECTRIC
ea 164.49
625-43619 Era V (red)
625-43442 Era IV (red, beige)

CLASS 110 ELECTRIC *NEW*
625-43392 Era IV (blue)
182.49
625-43990 Era IV, AC 3-Rail (blue) 228.99

CLASS 111 ELECTRIC
Since 1974, over 220 of these locos have been built to handle heavy passenger and freight assignments.

625-43413 Era IV-V (blue, beige) 122.49
625-43412 Era V (red) 130.99
625-43414 Era IV-V (light gray, orange) 125.49

CLASS 114 ELECTRIC
625-43448 Era IV (beige, red) 114.99

CLASS 140 ELECTRIC *NEW*
625-43421 Era IV (green)
125.49
625-43388 Era IV (gray)
182.49
625-43991 Era IV, AC 3-Rail (gray) 228.99

CLASS 150 ELECTRIC
625-43585 Era IV (green)
175.99
625-43924 Era IV, AC 3-Rail (green) 222.49

CLASS 151 ELECTRIC *NEW*
625-43380 Era V (red)
169.49

CLASS 181 ELECTRIC TBA
NEW
625-43692 Era IV, "Lorraine" (beige, blue) **LIMITED RUN**
625-43984 Era IV, "Lorraine," AC 3-Rail (beige, blue) **LIMITED RUN**
625-43690 Era IV (blue)
625-43985 Era IV, AC 3-Rail (blue)

CLASS 1189 ELECTRIC
Nine locomotives of this type were placed in express passenger service in 1929 on the Arlberg line. As a result of their articulated construction, they were nicknamed "Crocodiles." Thanks to restoration efforts, four of the locomotives have been preserved.

CLASS 194 ELECTRIC
625-43483 Era IV DB (green)
199.49

CLASS V60 DIESEL
625-43620 Era III (red) 145.99
625-43959 Era III, AC 3-Rail (red)192.99

CLASS V100 DIESEL
625-43644 Era III (red) 130.99
625-43964 Era III, AC 3-Rail (red) 177.49

CLASS V200 DIESEL
625-43522 Era III (red, gray)
136.49
625-43928 Era III, AC 3-Rail (red, gray) 183.49

CLASS 211 DIESEL *NEW*
625-43648 Era IV (blue) 133.49
625-43989 Era IV, AC 3-Rail (blue) 180.49

625-43413

CLASS 215 DIESEL
The first locomotives of this class were obtained by the DB in 1968. Before 1968 and 1972, 145 locos were built for use in both passenger and freight service.

625-43600 Era V (red, gray)
106.49 *NEW*
625-43417 Era IV (red, gray)
102.99

CLASS 220 DIESEL
625-43523 Era IV (red, gray)
136.49

CLASS 290 DIESEL
625-43458 Era V (red)
105.99

CLASS 335 DIESEL
The first Kof III locomotives were placed in service in 1959. Currently there are over 570 class 335 diesels on the DB roster, handling light switching and work train assignments.

625-43437 Era V (red) 88.49

CLASS 360 DIESEL
625-43621 Era IV (blue)
149.99

CLASS 361 DIESEL
625-43960 Era V, AC 3-Rail (red) 195.49

GERMAN STATE RAILWAYS

CLASS 74 2-6-0T
625-43275 Era III 176.49

CLASS 01 4-6-2
625-43239 Era IV 209.49

CLASS 50 2-10-0 *NEW*
625-43293 Era IV 280.99

CLASS 112 ELECTRIC
625-43681 Era V (red)
182.49
625-43979 Era V, AC 3-Rail (red) 228.99

CLASS 143 ELECTRIC
625-43683 Era V, "S-Bahn" (white, orange, yellow)
187.99 *NEW*
625-43992 Era V, "S-Bahn," AC 3-Rail (white, orange, yellow) 234.49 *NEW*
625-43680 Era V (maroon)
182.49
625-43978 Era V, AC 3-Rail (maroon) 228.99

625-43619

625-43522

625-43585

625-43584

Imported from Austria by Walthers

AUSTRIAN FEDERAL RAILWAYS

CLASS 688 0-4-0T
At the end of World War II, this former Bavarian "Glassbox" engine was found in the Tyrol Railway Station. Secured by the Austrian Federal Railways, the loco was assigned to the Vienna Western Terminal, where it handled switching duties into the late 1950's.

625-43258 Era III 123.99

OBB Austrian
625-43447 Era IV (orange) 202.49

CLASS 50 2-10-0 NEW
625-43289 Era III-IV 280.99

150th ANNIVERSARY SET
This special "Jubilee" set cele-

LIMITED QUANTITIES AVAILABLE

brates the 150th anniversary of the Austrian Railways. The set includes a powered class 2045 diesel and class 1670 electric loco, painted in "as-delivered" colors to match the prototypes, which have been restored for fantrip service.

625-43027 Anniversary Loco Set 245.99 **LIMITED RUN**

CLASS 1141 ELECTRIC
ea 178.99 (unless noted)
625-43640 Era III-IV (green)
625-43962 Era III-IV, AC 3-Rail (green) 225.99
625-43641 Era IV (orange)
625-43963 Era IV, AC 3-Rail (orange) 225.99

CLASS 1044 ELECTRIC
625-43658 Era IV (orange) 152.99
625-43971 Era IV, AC 3-Rail (orange) 199.49

CLASS 1110 ELECTRIC
625-43516 Era III-IV (green) 146.99
625-43628 Era V (orange) 155.99

CLASS 1020 ELECTRIC
Acquired after World War II, these former German engines were used in all types of service. A few class 1020 engines are still in operation, generally being called on in doubleheader or helper service on routes with steep grades.

625-43485 Era IV-V (orange) 202.49

625-43523

625-43275

625-43620

625-43437

625-43621

625-43644

625-43640

625-43027

625-43616

Imported from Austria by Walthers

625-43538

625-43290

625-43485

625-43655

625-43512

625-43447

625-43647

625-43200

625-43434

625-43507

625-43629

AUSTRIAN FEDERAL RAILWAYS

CLASS 1045 ELECTRIC
ea 132.49 (unless noted)
Built between 1927 and 1929, these mixed-traffic locomotives were the first to feature individual axles with Bo-Bo wheel arrangements. Three engines remain on the roster, used for switching duties or an occasional branchline assignment.

625-43701 Era IV-V (green) 145.99 *NEW*
625-43530 Era III-IV (green)
625-43533 Era IV (red)

CLASS 1189 ELECTRIC
Nine locomotives of this type were placed in express passenger service in 1929 on the Arlberg line. As a result of their articulated construction, they were nicknamed "Crocodiles." Thanks to restoration efforts, four of the locomotives have been preserved.

625-43447 Era IV (orange) 202.49

CLASS 1018 ELECTRIC
625-43434 Era IV (orange) 177.49

CLASS 2045 DIESEL
625-43702 Era IV-V (orange) 135.49 *NEW*
625-43553 Era IV (orange) 133.49

CLASS 2048 DIESEL
625-43647 Era V (red) 138.49
625-43983 Era V, AC 3-Rail (red) 184.99

SWISS FEDERAL RAILWAYS

CLASS C5/6 2-10-0
The heaviest steam locos on the roster of the Swiss Federal Railways, the engines of the C 5/6 class were designed primarily for the steep grades of the Gotthard line. Nicknamed "Elephants," the engines were in service until the mid-1960's.

625-43200 Era II-III, Coal Tender 206.49
625-43201 Era III, Oil Tender 205.99

CLASS Be4/6 II ELECTRIC
ea 181.99 (unless noted)
A total of 40 locos of this class were purchased between 1920 and 1923 for express passenger service on the Gotthard line. Today only two locos exist as museum locomotives and are used occasionally for charter trains.

625-43507 Era II-III (green)
625-43925 Era II-III, AC 3-Rail (green) 228.49
625-43508 Era II (brown)
625-43926 Era II, AC 3-Rail (brown) 228.49

CLASS Ce6/8 II ELECTRIC
ea 291.99 (unless noted)
The Gotthard line was the domain of the class Ce6/8 II "Crocodiles," built between 1920 and 1922. 33 units in all were constructed, with 13 being rebuilt in the 1940's with larger motors for increased horsepower. The Era II models are based on engine 14253, now an operational museum locomotive.

625-43538 Era III (green)
625-43940 Era III, AC 3-Rail (green) 338.49
625-43539 Era II (brown)
625-43941 Era II, AC 3-Rail (brown) 338.49

CLASS Re4/4 IV ELECTRIC
ea151.49 (unless noted)
In 1978, the SBB ordered four test engines for its Re4/4 IV class (#10101-10104). To easily identify the locomotives during testing, each was decorated in a different paint scheme. After extensive preliminary tests, all of the engines were finished in the "Bahn 2000" livery.

625-43512 Era IV-V, "Bahn 2000" (red)
625-43921 Era IV-V, #10101, AC 3-Rail (gray, red) 198.49
625-43493 Era IV-V, #10102 (white, red)
625-43922 Era IV-V, #10103, AC 3-Rail (red) 198.49
625-43494 Era IV-V, #10104 (red)

CLASS Ee3/3 ELECTRIC
625-43529 Era III-IV (brown) 155.99
625-43936 Era III-IV, AC 3-Rail (brown) 199.99
625-43528 Era IV-V (red) 163.99
625-43939 Era IV-V, AC 3-Rail (red) 210.49

CLASS Am4/4 DIESEL
625-43580 Era IV (red) 141.49
625-43929 Era IV, AC 3-Rail (red) 188.49

CLASS 460 ELECTRIC
625-43655 Era V (red) 211.99
625-43970 Era V, AC 3-Rail (red) 258.99

CLASS Ae6/6 ELECTRIC
A total of 118 class Ae6/6 locos were put into service between 1952 and 1966, succeeding the famed "Crocodiles." These multipurpose locos are still used in passenger as well as heavy freight train service. Beginning in 1985, the engines were repainted in the standard SBB red livery.

625-43696 Era IV-V (green) TBA *NEW*
625-43986 Era IV-V, AC 3-Rail (green) TBA *NEW*
625-43536 Era V (red) 146.99
625-43938 Era V, AC 3-Rail (red) 192.99

LIMITED QUANTITIES AVAILABLE
625-43937 Era III-IV, AC 3-Rail (green) 165.99

ITALIAN STATE RAILWAYS

CLASS 880 2-6-0 *NEW*
625-43277 Era III TBA

CLASS E645 ELECTRIC
625-43612 Era IV (olive green) 203.49

CLASS E626 ELECTRIC
625-43501 Era III-IV (olive green) 143.49

625-43277

625-43232

625-43629

625-43559

625-43670

625-43465

625-43580

625-43623

625-43675

625-43474

625-43467

625-43480

625-43501

625-43593

625-43615

625-43624

RO CO *Roco*
Imported from Austria by Walthers

CLASS E636 ELECTRIC
From 1940 to 1942, 108 of these locomotives were purchased by the FS for freight and passenger assignments. Due to motive power shortages after World War II, additional orders were placed for these engines between 1952 and 1962, bringing the total number of class E636 locos to 459.

625-43613 Era V (white, red) 217.49 **NEW**
625-43605 Era III-IV (olive green) 195.49

CLASS D345 DIESEL
625-43614 Era IV (green, brown) 129.99

FRENCH NATIONAL RAILWAYS

CLASS 050B 0-10-0
625-43232 Era III-IV 206.49

CLASS 150Z 4-6-2

Left in France by Germany after World War II, these former class 50 locomotives of the German Federal Railways were stationed in Alsace.

625-43290 Era III 291.99

CLASS BB300 ELECTRIC
625-43474 Era III-IV (dark green) 125.49

CLASS BB4600 ELECTRIC
625-43578 Era III-IV (dark green) 132.49

CLASS BB9300 ELECTRIC
625-43560 Era IV (green) 176.49

CLASS BB15000 ELECTRIC
625-43510 Era IV (gray, maroon, orange) 147.49

CLASS BB20000 ELECTRIC
The first two engines of this advanced French locomotive class were delivered in 1984. These "dual current" engines with thyristor-controlled synchronized motors are the first representatives of a future French standard locomotive.

625-43487 Era IV "Sybic" (white, blue, orange) 142.99

CLASS BB22200 ELECTRIC
625-43480 Era III-IV (light gray, orange) 138.99

CLASS Y8000 DIESEL
625-43475 Era IV (orange, gray) 75.99

CLASS BB63000 DIESEL-ELECTRIC
625-43467 Era IV (orange, gray) 136.49

NETHERLANDS STATE RAILWAYS

CLASS 59 2-6-0
625-43274 Era III 180.49

CLASS 1000 ELECTRIC
Introduced in 1948, these engines worked in passenger and freight service before being retired in 1982. The prototype for this model is engine 1010, which was restored for the 150th anniversary of the Netherlands State Railways.

625-43615 Era III-IV, Anniversary Loco (blue) 176.49

CLASS 1100 ELECTRIC
625-43465 Era III-IV (blue) 116.99

CLASS 1600 ELECTRIC
These locos, built by the French manufacturer Alstholm, are used by the NS in express passenger service.

625-43675 Era IV-V (yellow, gray) 149.99

CLASS 200/300 DIESEL
625-43678 Era IV-V (yellow, gray) TBA **NEW**
625-43677 Era IV (yellow, gray) 89.49

CLASS 500/600 DIESEL
625-43398 Era IV-V (yellow, gray) TBA **NEW**

CLASS 2200/2300 DIESEL-ELECTRIC
625-43673 Era IV (yellow, gray) 118.49

BELGIAN NATIONAL RAILWAYS

CLASS 20 ELECTRIC
625-43670 Era IV-V (blue-green, yellow) 210.49
625-43974 Era IV-V, AC 3-Rail (blue-green, yellow) 257.49

CLASS 80 DIESEL
625-43623 Era IV-V (green, yellow) 153.49

CLASS 62 DIESEL
625-43592 Era IV-V (green, yellow) 132.49
625-43548 Era IV (blue, yellow) 106.99

SWEDISH STATE RAILWAYS

CLASS Rc5 ELECTRIC
The most recent of the successful Rc series, the Rc5 electrics were introduced in 1982.

625-43629 Era V (blue, red, gray) 178.99

NORWEGIAN STATE RAILWAYS

CLASS EL16 ELECTRIC
Between 1977 and 1984, 17 of these engines were built for the mountain lines originating out of Oslo. The locos are assigned to both passenger and freight service, and feature snowplows and sharply slanted cab windows to battle snow and ice.

625-43559 Era IV-V (red, black) 198.49
625-43933 Era IV-V, AC 3-Rail (red, black) 244.99

CLASS Di5 DIESEL
625-43624 Era IV (yellow, red) 153.49

625-31010

Imported from Austria by Walthers

PASSENGER TRAIN SET

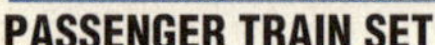

PASSENGER TRAIN SET

ANNIVERSARY SET

COMMUTER TRAIN SET

TRAIN SETS

Expand your layout or collection with Roco train sets! Each year, Roco produces special limited-run sets, featuring specially painted and numbered models or unique cars and/or locos. Perfect for operation or display, the sets feature fully assembled, ready-to-run models with prepainted and lettered plastic bodies. Many locomotives in the sets have operating, reversing headlights and include multiple locomotive numbers. All Roco engines operate on 2-rail D.C. (unless otherwise indicated). Engines with pantographs can also be powered from overhead catenary. Sets are less track and powerpack (unless noted).

GERMAN STATE RAILWAY (COMPANY)

PASSENGER TRAIN SET

This limited-edition set of a German State Railway (Company) express passenger train includes a class E44 locomotive, a type C4i36 3rd class coach, a type BC4i-37 2nd/3rd class coach, a type B4i-30 2nd class coach and a type Pw4i-34 baggage car.

A type B4i-29a 2nd class coach (#625-14255) and a type C4i-33h 3rd class coach (#625-

FREIGHT TRAIN SET

14256), produced by Sachsen-modelle, are available separately to complement this set.

625-43032 Era II 297.49
LIMITED RUN

GERMAN FEDERAL RAILWAYS

WORK TRAIN SET

This set includes a class 333 diesel locomotive, a kitchen-lounge car, a shower car, a sleeper, a foreman's car and a section of ROCO-LINE track to display the set.

625-41084 Era IV 187.99
LIMITED RUN

SWISS FEDERAL RAILWAYS

FREIGHT TRAIN SET

This limited-edition set features a Swiss Federal Railways Be6/8 II "Crocodile"

locomotive, a type Gs box car and a type Tgpps hopper, plus an Italian State Railways box car, a German Federal Railways gondola and a VTG tank car.

LIMITED QUANTITIES AVAILABLE

625-43966 Era III, AC 3-Rail 329.99 **LIMITED RUN**

COMMUTER TRAIN SET

Known as the "Sulgen Shuttles," these Swiss passenger trains are still in operation today, powered by De4/4 railcars that were built in the late 1920's and upgraded between 1966 and '71. The limited-edition set comes with a powered and dummy class De4/4 railcar, a type II AB 1st/2nd class coach and a type II B 2nd class coach.

LIMITED QUANTITIES AVAILABLE

625-43920 Era IV, AC 3-Rail 339.99 **LIMITED RUN**

ANNIVERSARY SET
LIMITED RUN

A tribute to 70 years of electric traction on the Gotthard line, this set consists of a Ce6/8 II "Crocodile" locomotive, a type AB4 1st/2nd class coach, a type BC4 2nd/3rd class coach and a C4 3rd class coach.

625-43023 Era II 328.99
625-43982 Era II, AC 3-Rail 368.99

FRENCH NATIONAL RAILWAYS

"CAPITOLE" PASSENGER TRAIN SET *NEW*

This set includes a class BB9200 electric loco, a type A9 and A7D coach and a type VRu restaurant car.

625-43044 Era IV TBA

AUSTRIAN FEDERAL RAILWAYS

MARIAZELL RAILWAY SET

Among the most famous of Europe's narrow gauge lines, the Mariazell Railway was Austria's first electric railway. Located in the beautiful mountain region of central Austria, the line was constructed between 1896 and 1907 and electrified in 1911. At that time, 16 class 1099 locos were placed in service. From 1959 to 1962, the engines were upgraded and still remain in operation today, pulling express trains through the popular vacation area.

This set includes a class 1099 locomotive, a type AB 1st/2nd class coach, a type B 2nd class coach and a type BD 2nd class combine. Each is finished in modern colors and is compatible with all other HOe models. An informational booklet about the Mariazell Railway is also included.

625-31010 Era III/IV 214.99

DIESEL INDUSTRIAL SET

STEAM INDUSTRIAL SET

ROCO *Roco*
Imported from Austria by Walthers

625-33201   625-33205   625-34520   625-32210   625-32211

MINE CARS 625-34500   625-34501   625-34502   625-34503   625-34504   625-34506   625-34507

Expand your Mariazell train set with these models, finished in original or modern "Jaffa" colors. "Jaffa" coaches feature different numbers than the cars included in the Mariazell Railway Set.

MARIAZELL "JAFFA" PASSENGER COACHES ea 32.99
625-34000 Era IV, Type AB 1st/2nd Class
625-34001 Era IV, Type B 2nd Class
625-34002 Era IV, Type BD 2nd Class Combine

MARIAZELL "ORIGINAL" PASSENGER COACHES ea 31.49
625-34003 Era III-IV, Type AB 1st/2nd Class
625-34004 Era III-IV, Type B 2nd Class
625-34005 Era III-IV, Type BD 2nd Class Combine

MARIAZELL FREIGHT CARS ea 22.99 (unless noted)
625-34520 Type OOm Gondola, Era III-IV

625-34521 Type SSm Flat Car, Era III-IV
625-34522 Type GGm Box Car, Era III-IV 25.99
625-34524 Type GGm Bicycle Box Car, Era IV-V 25.99
Roco offers a complete selection of industrial narrow gauge rolling stock and locomotives. Each ready-to-run model features a detailed plastic body and is finished in authentic colors. HOe narrow gauge track and turnouts (with a gauge of 9 mm) are also available. Track products use correctly scaled and spaced HO ties.

NARROW GAUGE INDUSTRIAL RAILROADS

Narrow gauge railroads represent an interesting chapter in railroad history. Developed to move bulky freight over short distances, they were common in mining and logging operations. Where space was a problem, narrow gauge was often chosen for its smaller size. A right-of-way could be constructed in a fraction of the

space needed for a highway or conventional railroad. Today, many of the world's narrow gauge lines remain in operation, both as common carriers and as museum roads.

DIESEL INDUSTRIAL SET
This kit includes a diesel locomotive (#33205), two wood gondolas (#34503), two timber cars (#34502), two dump cars (#34500), a shed building kit and an oval of Roco HOe narrow gauge track.

625-31004 105.99

STEAM INDUSTRIAL SET
This kit comes with a steam locomotive (#33201 in different livery), two coal cars (#34505), two mine cars (#34506), a shed building kit and an oval of Roco HOe narrow gauge track.

625-31005 101.99

LOCOMOTIVES
625-33201 Steam (black, green) 61.99
625-33205 Diesel (dark green) 55.99

MINE CARS ea 6.49
625-34500 Dump Car
625-34501 Cement Car
625-34502 Timber Car
625-34503 Wood Gondola
625-34504 Bulkhead Flat Car
625-34505 Coal Car
625-34506 Mine Car
625-34507 Flat Car

HOe TRACK

Roco HOe narrow gauge track products are exactly to prototype in type, size and spacing of ties. The track "gauge" is 9 mm (N Scale), but it is HO "scale."

DEALERS: MUST Order Dealer Pack Of 24.
625-32200 28" Flexible Track (730 mm) 4.49
625-32201 28" Flexible Track, Temporary Ties (730 mm) 4.49
625-32202 5-3/8" Straight (134 mm) pkg (12) 19.49
625-32203 2" Straight (48 mm) pkg (12) 19.49

625-32204 30° Curved pkg (12) 19.49
625-32205 15° Curved pkg (12) 19.49

REMOTE CONTROL TURNOUT SET
Modeled after temporary turnouts used by industrial railroads, this set includes a left- and right-hand turnout with a diverging track angle of 24°.

625-32402 41.99

MANUAL TURNOUT SET
This set includes a left-hand and right-hand 15° manual turnout.

625-32410 25.99

FILL-IN TIES pkg (24) ea 7.49
625-32210 Standard Track
625-32211 Temporary Track

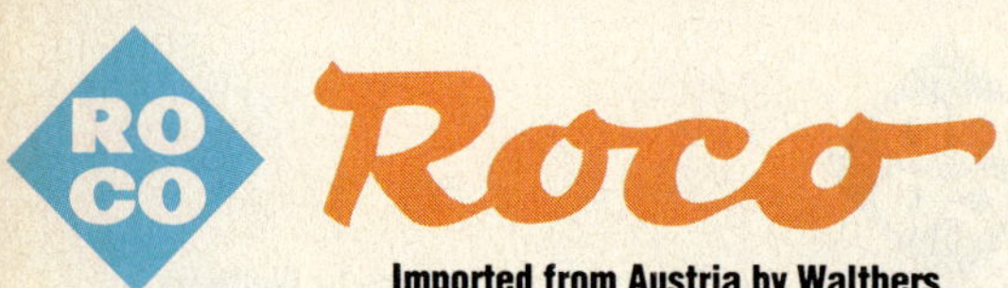

Imported from Austria by Walthers

These models are authentically painted and lettered with plastic bodies and die-cast metal frames, metal gears and European-style couplers. Many have operating, reversing headlights and interior lighting. Models with pantographs may be powered from overhead caternary or track. All models operate on 2-rail D.C. (unless otherwise indicated).

GERMAN STATE RAILWAY (COMPANY)

CLASS eIT1130 COMMUTER RAILCAR TBA *NEW*
625-43007 3-Unit Set, Era II (maroon, cream)
LIMITED RUN
625-43910 3-Unit Set, Era II, AC 3-Rail (maroon, cream)
LIMITED RUN

GERMAN FEDERAL RAILWAYS

CLASS VT98/VS98 "CHIEMGAU RAILWAY" DIESEL RAILCAR
625-43040 Powered & Trailer Car, Era V (sky blue, light green, gray) 187.49
LIMITED RUN

CLASS VT98/VS98 DIESEL RAILCAR
625-43945 Powered & Trailer Car, Era III, AC 3-Rail (red) 183.99
625-43946 Class VM98 Center Car, Era III, AC 3-Rail (red) 43.99
625-43019 Class VM98 Center Car, Era III (red) 43.99

CLASS 798/998 DIESEL RAILCAR
625-43045 Powered & Trailer Car, Era IV-V (red) 167.99
625-43046 Center Car, Era IV-V (red) 53.99
625-43969 Center Car, Era IV-V, AC 3-Rail (red) 53.99

CLASS VT11 "TEE" MULTIPLE-UNIT TRAIN
625-43903 3-Unit Supplement Set, Era III, AC 3-Rail (red, cream) 108.99

CLASS BR628/928 DIESEL RAILCAR
625-43022 Powered & Trailer Car, Era V (sky blue, light green, gray) 235.49
625-43949 Powered & Trailer Car, Era V, AC 3-Rail (sky blue, light green, gray) 281.99

CLASS VT601 "INTERCITY" MULTIPLE-UNIT TRAIN
LIMITED RUN
625-43904 4-Unit Set, Era IV, AC 3-Rail (red, cream) 144.99

CLASS Bxf 796 "S-BAHN" COACH

LIMITED QUANTITIES AVAILABLE

625-44672 2nd Class Driving Trailer, Era IV (orange, gray) 64.99

CLASS ET491 "GLASS TRAIN" ELECTRIC RAILCAR ea 255.99 (unless noted)
During the 1930's, the German State Railway ordered five of these unique sight-seeing cars for excursion service. The cars were designed with extra windows for better views of the countryside, leading to the name "glass trains." Two electric and three diesel-hydraulic units were built, but only a single railcar remains in excursion service. Today, the car is often seen on fan trips in Germany, Austria and Switzerland. Because of the differences in catenary, a single Swiss pantograph was installed for operation in that country.

625-43527 Era IV-V (blue, white) 209.49
625-43932 Era IV-V, AC 3-Rail (blue, white)
625-43930 Era IV, AC 3-Rail (powder blue, gray)

CLASS ET420 SUBURBAN MULTIPLE-UNIT TRAIN
625-43002 Era IV (blue,

625-43051

625-43007

625-43013

625-34016

625-43045

625-43046

625-43527

625-43053

625-43052

Roco
RO CO
Imported from Austria by Walthers

625-43051

625-43052

625-43930

625-43033

AUSTRIAN FEDERAL RAILWAYS

CLASS 5081 DIESEL RAILCAR

625-43051 Powered & Trailer Car, Era IV (blue, silver) 171.99

625-43052 Center Car, Era IV (blue, silver) 57.99

625-43020 Powered & Trailer Car, Era III-IV (blue, silver) 162.99

625-43947 Powered & Trailer Car, Era III-IV, AC 3-Rail (blue, silver) 218.99

625-43948 Center Car, Era III-IV, AC 3-Rail (blue, silver) 57.99

CLASS 4010 "TRANSALPIN" MULTIPLE-UNIT TRAIN TBA
NEW

625-43894 3-Unit Set, Era III-IV, AC 3-Rail (blue, white)

SPECIAL ORDER ONLY

These items must be specially ordered from the manufacturer. You will be notified upon receipt of merchandise.

GERMAN FEDERAL RAILWAYS

CLASS EB85 COACH

625-44250 2nd Class, Era IV (maroon) 19.49

AUSTRIAN FEDERAL RAILWAYS

CLASS 4010 "TRANSALPIN" MULTIPLE-UNIT TRAIN TBA
NEW

625-43053 3-Unit Set, Era III-IV (blue, white)

625-43054 3-Unit Supplement Set, ERA III-IV (blue, white)

FRENCH NATIONAL RAILWAYS

CLASS X2700/XR7700 "TEE" DIESEL RAILCAR

625-43033 Powered & Trailer Car, Era III-IV (red, cream) 261.49

GERMAN STATE RAILWAY

CLASS BR601 "MAX LIEBERMANN" MULTIPLE-UNIT TRAIN LIMITED RUN

625-43013 4-Unit Set, Era V (red, cream) 294.49

625-43902 4-Unit Set, Era V, AC 3-Rail (red, cream) 341.49

625-43016 3-Unit Supplement Set, Era V (red, cream) 132.49

625-43905 3-Unit Supplement Set, Era V, AC 3-Rail (red, cream) 132.49

SWISS FEDERAL RAILWAYS

CLASS De4/4 ELECTRIC BAGGAGE RAILCAR

625-43630 Era II-III (green) 181.99

625-43950 Era II-III, AC 3-Rail (green) 228.49

CLASS Fe4/4 ELECTRIC BAGGAGE RAILCAR

625-43951 Era II, AC 3-Rail (sky blue, white) 217.99
LIMITED RUN

BRAWA

These HO Scale locos are die cast, painted metal (unless otherwise noted). They are powered by a three-pole motor, with all-wheel electrical pickup. Engines include add-on details and three styles of couplers. AC Locos are designed for use with Marklin equipment.

186-400

186-484

186-490

186-471

186-482

SPECIAL ORDER ONLY

These items must be specially ordered from the manufacturer. You will be notified upon receipt of merchandise.

DIESEL

CLASS 119/219 DIESEL
186-400 DC Powered 230.49
NEW
186-430 AC Powered TBA
NEW

SWITCHERS

KOFII DIESEL SWITCHER
Built in 1932, over 1900 were used by the DRG and the DB at large stations, shops and private industries. Locos are available in DRG or DB colors, with 12 decals for lettering styles used from the 1930's to the present.

MODERN, POWERED
186-470 DC (red) 227.49
186-472 AC (red) 336.99
186-484 DC (red) 227.49
186-485 AC (red) 336.99
186-486 DC Industrial (black) 240.99
186-487 AC Industrial (black) 350.49
186-48401 S-O-B KOFII DB, DC (orange) 264.99
186-48501 S-O-B KOFII DB, AC (orange) 376.99

KOI DIESEL SWITCHER

Introduced in 1933, 262 of these tiny switchers were built for the German State Railways. By 1971, 35 were still in service with the Federal Railways. The models feature die cast zinc body, finished in black with red underframe.
186-490 DB, DC Powered (black) 227.49
186-491 DB, DC Powered (red) 227.49
186-492 DR, DC Powered (black) 227.49
186-495 DB, AC Powered (black) 336.99
186-496 DB, AC Powered (red) 336.99
186-497 DR, AC Powered (red) 336.99

OLD SWITCHER
186-471 DC Powered (black) 227.49
186-473 AC Powered (black) 336.99

BATTERY-POWERED SWITCHER

In 1955, the DB built two battery-powered KOF II locos for use inside warehouses.
186-482 DC Powered (red) 227.49
186-483 AC Powered (red) 336.99

Limited Quantities Available
186-466 Robot Switcher (blue) 65.99
Remote-control industrial switcher, built by Vollert. Loco features flywheel drive for slow speed operation. Die cast metal body in blue enamel finish. Model is equipped with hook coupler for use with Roco or Trix models. Length over buffers approximately 3 1/2".

MOTORS

186-9716 Motor With Worm Gear 19.99
This is for all KOI locomotives.

186-9717 Motor 109.99
This is for 0-4-OT Glass locomotives.

"The west siding switch is lined and locked for the main, and you have permission to depart, over." " Roger dispatcher, #43 with engine #6655 west has permission to pass signal displaying stop indication and proceed. . . ." A trio of Wisconsin Central locos dig in and start pulling as they depart Burkardt Yard. Set in the midwest, this layout is the work of Merlin, Mark and Marvin Preussler from Sheboygan, Wisconsin. The lead SD45 features a Rail Power shell on a Kato chassis, trailed by a Kato GP35 and an Overland Models brass SDL39.

Photo by Marv Preussler

A steady hand at the throttle, a light touch on the airbrake and 100 loads of coal trail obediently behind the matched Alco FA's of the Lehigh & New England. Captured on their way across the Lehigh Gap Bridge, the locos are the work of Jim Hertzog of Coopersburg, Pennsylvania. Both A units feature Model Power shells mounted on drive units from Atlas RS3's.

Models and Photo by Jim Hertzog

STEWART HOBBIES, INC.

These HO Scale, easy-to-build kits feature a plastic body and a zamac die cast frame. Units are equipped with Athearn trucks, motor, flywheels, and drive train; F-units and others as noted, include Kato motor. F units include couplers, all others are less couplers.

ALCO RS-3 PHASE 2A

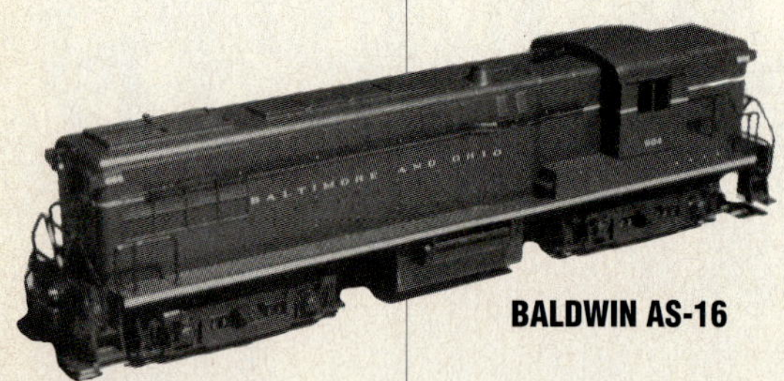

BALDWIN

BALDWIN AS-16

EMD

EMD F3PA PHASE I

BALDWIN AS-16 WITH KATO DRIVE ea 75.00
(unless noted)
Upgraded AS-16 diesels feature a Kato drive.

691-4401 Western Maryland #175 (black)
691-4402 Western Maryland #176 (black)
691-4403 Pennsylvania-Reading Seashore Lines #6000 (black)
691-4404 Pennsylvania-Reading Seashore Lines #6013 (black)
691-4999 Power Chassis 65.00
691-4400 Undecorated

BALDWIN AS-16 ea 45.00
(unless noted)
Coupler pockets on metal frame will accept Kadee or horn-hook couplers.

691-4100 Baltimore & Ohio (dark blue)
691-4160 Nickel Plate Road (black)
691-4170 Soo Line (black)
691-4180 Missouri - Kansas - Texas (orange)
691-4000 Undecorated, powered (gray)
691-4050 Undecorated, dummy 23.00

BALDWIN AS-616
691-6000 Undecorated (gray) 49.95

BALDWIN RS-12 ea 75.00
NEW
Baldwin introduced its light road switcher in 1946, with the 1,000 horsepower DRS-4-4-10. In 1951, the model was upgraded with a new 1,200 horsepower prime mover and redesignated as the RS12. Externally, the two models were identical and could be found in yard or light freight service. A few RS12's lasted into the early 80's.

691-4502 Pennsylvania (black)
691-4504 New York Central (black)
691-4505 Central of New Jersey (dark green)
691-4506 Penn Central (black)
691-4507 Canadian Pacific
691-4500 Undecorated

EMD F3A PHASE I Dual Headlights ea 99.00
691-8040 Undecorated

Limited Quantities Available
691-8050 Santa Fe
691-8070 Chicago & North Western (black, yellow)

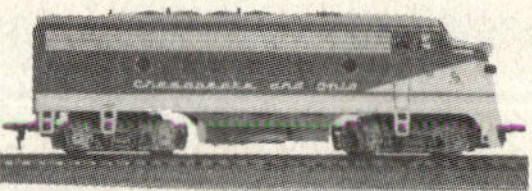

EMD F3A PHASE II Single Headlight ea 99.00
691-8110 Pennsylvania (black)
691-8120 New York Central (black)
691-8130 Baltimore & Ohio (black)
691-8100 Undecorated

EMD F3A PHASE II Dual Headlights ea 99.00
691-8510 Union Pacific
691-8500 Undecorated

Limited Quantities Available
691-8520 Western Pacific 99.00

691-8530 Rock Island (red, black)

EMD F3A PHASE II LATE Dual Headlights ea 99.00
691-8240 Southern Pacific
691-8230 Undecorated

EMD F3A PHASE IV Single Headlight ea 99.00
691-8410 Lehigh Valley (red)
691-8420 Baltimore & Ohio (black)
691-8430 Reading (black)
691-8440 Pennsylvania (black)
691-8460 Erie (black, yellow)
691-8400 Undecorated

Limited Quantities Available
691-8450 Santa Fe (dark blue, yellow) 99.00

EMD F3B PHASE I
691-8035 Southern, dummy (green) 45.00

EMD F3B PHASE II
691-8135 Baltimore & Ohio, dummy 45.00

EMD F7A PHASE II Dual Headlights ea 99.00
691-9220 Chesapeake & Ohio (dark blue, yellow)
691-9240 Southern Pacific, Black Widow
691-9210 Undecorated

ALCO RS-3 PHASE 2A
Features horizontal box filters in side doors.

691-2000 Undecorated, powered (gray) 39.95
691-2050 Undecorated, dummy (gray) 21.95

ALCO RS-3 PHASE 3
Features vertical box filters in side doors.

691-3000 Undecorated, powered (gray) 39.95
691-3050 Undecorated, dummy (gray) 21.95

ALCO RS-3 PHASE 1B
ea 39.95 (unless noted)
Features punched louvers in side doors.

691-1110 New York Central (black)
691-1130 Delaware & Hudson (blue)
691-1140 Chicago & North Western (yellow)
691-1150 Rock Island (mineral red)
691-1000 Undecorated, powered
691-1050 Undecorated, dummy 24.40

AMERICAN LIMITED

HO SCALE (1/87) DIAPHRAGM *NEW*
147-9900 for Stewart F-Units pair 4.49
Make your Stewart F Units look their best, with this set of diaphragms. Includes alignment spacers and works with close coupling adapter.

GENERAL ELECTRIC

EMD F3A PHASE II LATE

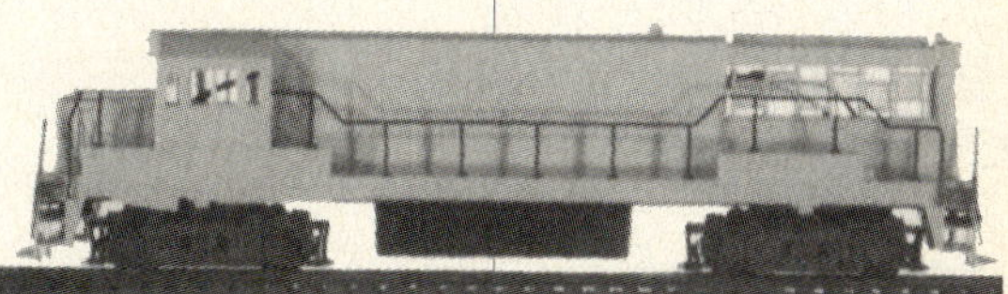

GE U25B PHASE IV

EMD F7B PHASE I LATE (POWERED) ea 89.00
691-9141 New York Central (black, gray)
691-9151 Western Maryland (black)

Limited Quantities Available
691-9121 Pennsylvania (black) 89.00
691-9191 Rio Grande (black, yellow) 89.00

EMD F9
691-9330 Burlington Northern (cascade green) 89.00

EMD FTA SINGLE LIGHT
ea TBA *NEW*
691-5014 New York Central
691-5016 Santa Fe
691-5000 Undecorated

EMD FTA SINGLE LIGHT LARGE SIDE PANELS TBA
NEW
691-5001 Undecorated

EMD FTA DOUBLE LIGHT TBA *NEW*
691-5002 Undecorated

EMD FTA DOUBLE LIGHT LARGE SIDE PANELS TBA
NEW
691-5003 Undecorated

EMD FTB DUMMY ea TBA
NEW
691-5015 New York Central
691-5017 Santa Fe
691-5004 Undecorated, unpowered
691-5005 Undecorated, 5 port holes
691-5999 Undecorated, powered

EMD FTA ELECTRO MOTIVE
ea TBA *NEW*
691-5012 Demo
691-5013 Demo, unpowered

GE U25B

GE U25B PHASE II
691-7160 Conrail (blue) 69.95

GE U25B ea 54.99
691-7110 Santa Fe (dark blue, yellow)
691-7120 Chesapeake & Ohio
691-7140 New York Central
691-7000 Undecorated

GE U25B PHASE III
691-7476 Undecorated Shell 15.00
691-7477 Weight Set pkg (6) 4.00

GE U25B PHASE IV ea 69.95
691-7510 Southern Pacific (gray)
691-7540 Conrail (blue)
691-7550 Pennsylvania (black)
691-7999 U25B Power Chassis 59.00
691-7400 Undecorated

GE U25B PHASE IV/U28B PHASE I
691-7475 Undecorated Shell 15.00

POWERED CHASSIS
691-8999 F3A Power Chassis 59.00

Grandt Line

These HO Scale kits contain injection molded, black plastic parts and nonmagnetic wheelsets. They will accept Kadee couplers. Powered kits include Mabuchi Motor and Grandt Line gears with 80:1 reduction.

25 TON LOCOMOTIVES

POWERED GE 25 TON INDUSTRIAL LOCOS ea 35.00
Small switchers like this are owned and operated by many types of heavy industries including steel mills, cement plants, grain elevators and more. This model accepts Kadee #714 (narrow gauge) or #711 (standard gauge) couplers.

300-7090 HOn3
300-7091 HO

23 TON BOX CAB DIESELS
Early box cab diesels were found in many large cities, where smoke from steam locos and tight clearances created problems. In later years, they were often sold to on-line industries for use as plant switchers.

POWERED ea 35.00
300-7088 Narrow Gauge
300-7089 Standard Gauge

UNPOWERED ea 17.50
300-5114 Narrow Gauge
300-5127 Standard Gauge

POWERED GE 25 TON INDUSTRIAL LOCOMOTIVE

23 TON BOX CAB DIESEL

INFORMATION STATION

Steam locos needed frequent refueling, which was usually done before and after each run.

Terminals were equipped with a coaling tower, which fed coal by gravity into the tender. A water tower or water crane was also nearby. Dry sand for traction was often supplied from a tower on the coaling dock, or the nearby sand house. If oil was used for fuel, an oil storage tank and filler would be on hand. Coal burners had to have accumulations of ash and unburned coal (clinkers) removed from the fire box. This was done over the ash pit.

Steamers were designed to run in one direction and had to be turned after each trip. This was usually done on a turntable, but some locations had loops or wyes. Engine were usually stored overnight in a roundhouse, where light repairs could be done under cover.

Keystone Locomotive Works

These HO Scale craft train kits are unpainted metal, and include trucks.

LOCOMOTIVES

SHAY ea 43.95
395-105 20 Ton Class A, HO
395-1053 20 Ton Class A, HOn3
Based on engine #31 of the Kelly Island Lime & Transport Co. this model includes an optional oil bunker and wood burning or shotgun stacks. The unpowered model can be made operational with a North West Shortline Shay powering kit, sold separately. Model is less couplers.

GE 44 TON DIESEL
395-108 Powered Loco 89.95
This loco includes an assembled chassis with North West Shortline gears and a Sagami motor. Electrical pickup is through all eight nickel-silver wheels.

Brass etched hoods, cast metal cab, pilots and details are included and the model and can be built as Phase III or Phase IV loco. This kit accepts Kadee couplers and can be adapted to constant lighting, both sold separately.

CAB INTERIORS

CAB INTERIORS ea 9.98
Add a realistic touch to your next model with these interior kits. Adaptable to powered or dummy units, kits feature plastic and metal parts, with complete instructions.

395-3301 "F" Unit

395-3302 EMD SW and NW SWITCHER
This fits Athearn SW-7 as well as other diesels.

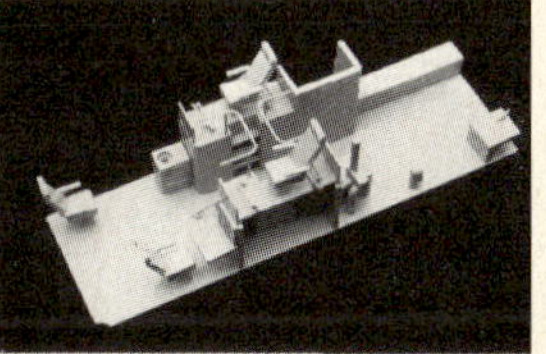

395-3304 EMD 1st Generation GP/SD
This fits the following models GP-7, 9, 18, 20, & SD-7, 9, 18, 24.

395-3305 EMD 2nd Generation GP/SD

This fits the following models 40-2, 38-2, 35, 40 & 50 and can also be modified to fit Bachmann GP-30.

395-3309 "E" Unit

There's a full days work ahead for the Coal Belt Railroad.   As the morning shift reports in, the first order of business is to fill the waiting tenders. Under a cloud of coal dust, the Autumn Park terminal comes to life on the layout of Bill Henderson of Florence Park, Alabama. The camelback locos are modified Mantua and Custom Brass products. A couple of Life-Like figures are on hand to supervise.

Models and Photo by Bill Henderson

These HO Scale easy-to-build kit is a one-piece plastic body shell.

CONVERSION BODY SHELLS

EMD FT CONVERSION BODY SHELLS ea 17.98

705-4101 A Unit
Improved reproduction of AHM shell; fits Athearn or Hobbytown drives with minor modifications.

705-4102 B Unit
Can be modified to fit various drives.

HIGHLINERS

The following are HO Scale easy-to-build kits.

F UNIT BODY SHELL KITS

Body shell kits can build any version of the F3, F5, F7 or F9 diesel and are available as A (with cab) and B (cabless booster) units. They are for use with powered or unpowered Athearn F7 diesels.

These kits include molded plastic detail parts, cast and sheet metal pilots, nose doors with and without headlight, three styles of number boards, four versions of the dynamic brake hatch, five pairs of side panel inserts, windshields with and without rim beading, flush-mount porthole, cab window "glass," photoetched brass fan grills, windshield wipers, wind wings and cab step foot guards.

328-1002 B Unit 27.95
328-1004 B Unit With Screens 35.95

F3 WIRE SCREENING

These self adhesive, thin brass screens simulate the "chicken wire" applied over air intakes on prototype F3's.

328-10020 B Unit 8.00

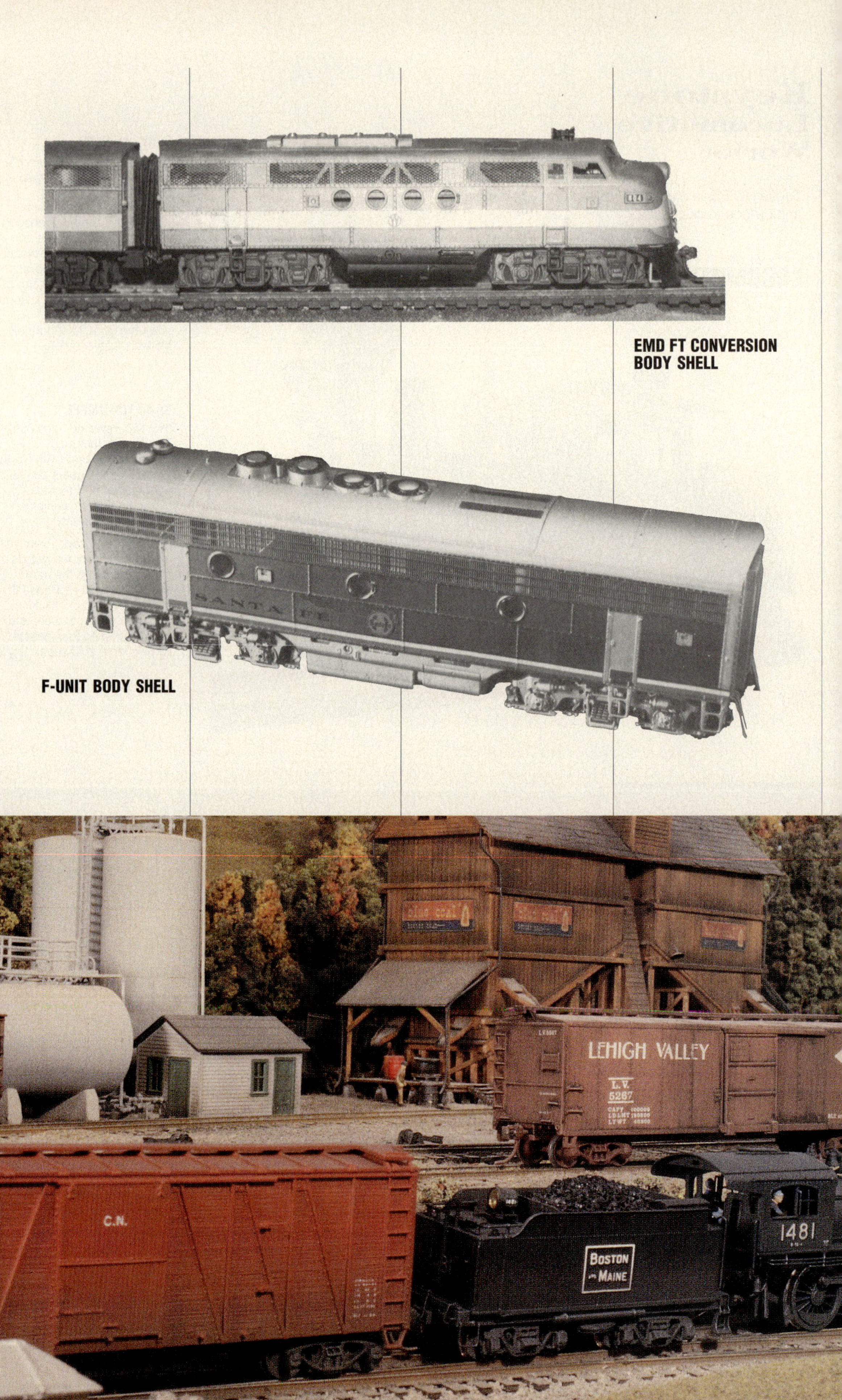

EMD FT CONVERSION BODY SHELL

F-UNIT BODY SHELL

YE OLDE HUFF-N-PUFF

NON-POWERED LOCO

792-1050 Climax Locomotive 21.00
This undecorated dummy locomotive kit consists of wood floor, sides and roof with plastic and metal detail parts.

HOn3 MINE TRAIN SET

Details include drawbars, dummy front and rear lights, horn, operator and a NWSL drive unit with can motor and driven wheelsets. Mine cars are side dumping type with link and pin couplers. Sets include loco and three cars.

792-1500 Unpowered 28.50
792-1501 Unpowered 48.50
This kit also includes 12 trolley poles, wire and hangers.

792-1502 Overhead Powered 82.50
This kit also includes 12 trolley poles, wire, hangers and undumping ramp.

792-1503 2-Rail Powered 82.50
This kit also includes 12 trolley poles, wire, hangers and undumping ramp.

792-1505 Extra Mine Hopper kit 6.50
792-1506 HOn3 Track Extension Set 11.50
This kit measures approximately 36" Code 70 track, has 6 trolley poles, 6 hangers and wire.

MINE TRAIN SET

CLIMAX LOCOMOTIVE

MASTER CREATIONS

These HO Scale craft train locomotive kits feature zinc cadmium castings, plated drivers, and completely illustrated instuctions.

SUPER DETAIL KIT

Limited Quantities Available
464-542 Universal Valve Gear Set 34.95
This is for 2-8-4 or 2-10-4 Arbour Models.

TENDER

Limited Quantities Available
464-534 Pennsylvania 18.95

WALKER MODEL SERVICE

This is a HO Scale cast metal craft train kit.

SHAY CONVERSION BOILER

Cast alloy boiler will backdate the MDC Shay prior to 1915. Boiler is straight version with a fluted steam and sand dome with removable hatch and cast number boards.

786-5019 Conversion Boiler 12.95

UNPOWERED KITS ea 17.95
These kits are of cast metal construction.

786-5203 Mack Switcher

This is less couplers.
786-5205 Kerosene Loco
This is less the figure shown in photo.

It's all downhill from here, and those firemen could certainly stand a break.

With the worst of the grade behind them, doubleheaded Boston & Maine steamers roll past our vantage point on Bill McChesney's;s layout in Schenectady, New York. Powering this heavy freight are a pair of imported brass models which Bill painted and weathered. A mix of Accurail and Walthers freight cars can also be seen.

Models and Photo by Bill McChesney

CLEAR CASE
by Hotchkiss Manufacturing

Protect your investment in your favorite models by using Clear Case HO Scale display cases. These cases feature a base constructed of rich grain solid oak, with a mitered edge to ensure a dust-free enclosure. The cover is crystal clear acrylic. The result is a display case that makes the hobbyist's model a museum masterpiece. The interior dimension of the cover is 2-3/4" wide by 3-1/4" high.

DISPLAY CASES

The interior dimensions are shown.

248-8710 10-5/8" Long 24.95
248-8716 16-1/2" Long 36.95
248-8722 22" Long 45.95

SPECIAL ORDER ONLY

These items must be specially ordered from the manufacturer. You will be notified upon receipt of merchandise.

MULTI-SHELF DISPLAY CASE

248-1322 5" Deep x 23-1/2" Wide x 29-1/2" High 263.95
NEW
This case has 8 shelves and measures 2-3/4" Deep x 21-1/2" Wide x 3" High

248-1336 5" Deep x 37-1/2" Wide x 27-1/2" High 395.95
NEW
This case has 8 shelves which measures 2-3/4" Deep x 35-1/2" Wide x 3" High

KADEE

LOCO DRIVER CLEANER

No special wiring is needed to operate. Cleans corrosion from loco driver treads to improve electrical conductivity.

380-236 Speedi-Driver Cleaner Brush 7.95

RAIL POWER PRODUCTS

INFORMATION STATION

**LOCOMOTIVE SHELL KITS
ea 14.00** (unless noted)
NEW

These undecorated body shells are an excellent starting point for custom models of many different locos. Each shell is molded in light gray plastic, and includes a variety of add-on details. Bodies can be mounted on Rail Power frames, (listed in Parts) or Overland Models chassis and will fit Athearn frames and drive trains with minor modification (all sold separately). Kits are unpowered and are supplied less trucks, frames, (unless noted) handrails and couplers. Frames are diecast metal.

60-1001 C32-8 Shell 12.00
60-1002 C30-7 Shell
60-1003 SD-60 Shell
60-1004 B23-7 Shell
60-1005 CF-7 Angle (Topeka style) Cab Shell
60-1006 CF-7 Round Cab Shell
60-1007 Dash 8-40B Complete Dummy Kit 26.00
Includes body shell, frame, add-on details, handrails and trucks.
60-1008 Dash 8-40B Shell
60-1009 SD-45 Shell
60-1010 GP-35 Dynamic Shell
60-1011 GP-35 Nondynamic Shell
60-1012 Dash 8-40CW Shell
60-1013 Dash 8-40CW Shell/Chassis 23.00
60-1014 CF-7 Round Cab Shell/Chassis 23.00
60-1015 CF-7 Angle Cab Shell/Chassis 23.00
60-1016 Dash 8-40CW Santa Fe "Gull Wing" Cab Shell

60-1017 Dash 8-40CW Santa Fe "Gull Wing" Cab Shell/Chassis 23.00
60-1019 SD60M Shell/Chassis 23.00
60-1022 SD7/9 Dynamic Shell
60-1023 SD7/9 Nondynamic Shell

PAINTED SHELLS ea 38.00
NEW
Dash 8-40CW shells custom painted by Track One. Numbered shells are decorated with various unit numbers, unnumbered shells are painted and lettered but do not have a number.

60-1020 Union Pacific, numbered (armor yellow, gray)
60-1026 Union Pacific, no number (armor yellow, gray)
60-1027 CSX, numbered (blue, gray, yellow)
60-1028 CSX, no number (blue, gray, yellow)

CUSTOM RAILWAY SUPPLY

BRASS LOCO FRAME

212-1055 Brass Loco Frame pair 23.50
Loco frames can be used to make a PRR Q-1 or a Free Lance 2-10-4, by using Bowser T-1 800 wheels.

THE LOCO FRAMES ARE KITBASHING ITEMS INTENDED FOR THE EXPERIENCED MODELER.

PRECISION SCALE COMPANY

DETAIL KITS

INTERIOR DETAIL KITS
These sets include an assortment of brass parts such as seats, throttle stands and more to model a detailed locomotive cab interior.

585-3702 Rio Grande C-16/17 37.00
585-3704 Rio Grande C-18/19 38.00
585-3706 Rio Grande K-27 34.00
585-3708 Rio Grande K-28 33.00
585-3710 Rio Grande K-36 28.00
585-3714 Small Steam Loco 30.00
585-3716 Large Steam Loco 45.00
585-3720 Interior Detection Kit AC-6 Cab forward 26.00
585-3744 Rio Grande C-21 33.00
585-3765 EMD Cab, Late 18.75

COMPLETE DETAIL KITS
These complete kits include numerous brass castings to detail the cab interior, boiler and tender.

585-3701 Rio Grande C-16/17 86.00
585-3703 Rio Grande C-18/19 90.00
585-3705 Rio Grande K-27 98.00
585-3707 Rio Grande K-28 108.00
585-3709 Rio Grande K-36 96.00
585-3711 Rio Grande K-37 88.00
585-3713 Small Steam Loco 70.00
585-3715 Large Steam Loco 108.00
585-3719 Shay Class B 27T 34.00
585-3717 2-8-0 Roundhouse Loco TBA
585-3721 Interior Detection Kit AM-2 Cab forward 25.00

With just enough time to park and race to the edge of this overpass, we're rewarded with this fine shoot of a CP "red barn" screaming along with a freight. These distinctive SD40-2F locos are seen on all types of CP trains, so Bob Boudreau knew he had to have one for his HO Scale collection. The model was built from a Rail Power SD60 shell, with a Smokey Valley (now Train Station Products) cab and rides on an Athearn chassis.

Models and Photo by Bob Boudreau.

WALTHERS™

Add Mass Transit Service to Your Modern Layout with these Models

Operate modern intercity passenger service with Walthers Rapid Transit Cars. Based on equipment of the Bay Area Rapid Transit (BART) system in San Francisco and the METRO system in Washington, D.C. these models are a great way to add new operations to your layout.

Each easy-to-build kit features an injection molded styrene body. All cars are prepainted in silver and METRO cars feature the correct metallic brown trim. Sharp decal lettering provides the colorful logos and car numbers, and METRO cars include decals for the red, white and blue stripe.

Each kit also includes separately molded underbody details, diaphragms and tinted window "glass." BART cars have separately molded grab irons.,

Powered models are driven by an under-floor mounted, self-contained power truck.

BAY AREA RAPID TRANSIT

Each kit also includes separately molded underbody details, diaphragms and tinted window "glass." BART cars have separately molded grab irons.,

In operation since September of 1972, the system serves Oakland and San Francisco, as well as nearby suburbs. BART has its own right-of-way with no grade crossings or crossovers. At present, 34 stations are served by a fleet of 447 cars,

932-6030 A Unit Powered ea 34.95
932-6031 A Unit Dummy ea 19.95
932-6032 B Unit Dummy ea 19.95

WASHINGTON D.C. METRO

Serving the District of Columbia and suburbs in Maryland and Virginia, the first four miles of the METRO system opened in March of 1976. Currently, 103 miles are in operation, serving 83 stations with a fleet of 660 cars.

932-6035 Powered ea 34.95
932-6036 Dummy ea 19.95

International Hobby Corp.™

These models are HO Scale and are ready to run.

BOEING LRV

This model is based on the Light Rail Vehicle, built by Boeing and now in service with several mass transit systems around the country. The model is powered, has a prepainted and lettered plastic body, and Rapido style couplers.

348-9385 Boston 39.95
348-9386 Frisco 29.98 (cream)

GG-1

PENNSYLVANIA GG-1 ea 69.98
These electric locos were used throughout the Pennsy's electrified district and served in both freight and high-speed passenger service. Each model is ready to run, with a prepainted body, detailed pantographs and working headlight.

348-9300 PRR (red)
348-9301 PRR (green)
348-9302 PRR #4880 (silver)

BRILL TROLLEY

BRILL TROLLEY ea 27.98
These four-wheel cars were common on many big city streetcar lines. Models are prepainted and ready to run.

348-9381 PTC
348-9382 Connecticut Company
348-9383 United Transit Lines
348-9384 Downtown

PANTOGRAPHS

348-600 Westinghouse (pair) 19.98 **NEW**
Used on Pennsylvania GG-1, P-5, D1, L6 and MP54s.

BOEING LRV

BOEING TROLLEY

BRAWA

These HO Scale models ride on rubber tires, are powered and illuminated. Buses feature prepainted plastic bodies, in red, blue or yellow. Both standard or articulated types are available. Buses are available in sets with poles and wire or separately. Buses require 12-16V AC or DC power supply. AC power supply needs a rectifier, but both require a 6150 speed controller. Minuimum radius: 8" with poles on inside of curve. Maximum Grade: 30%

TROLLEYBUSES

Trolleybuses replaced streetcars in many cities and are still a familiar sight in some areas. These buses draw power from overhead electrical wires providing quiet, non-polluting transportation.

The minimum road dimensions are as follows: road width; approximately 2", standard bus (1-way street); width at corners, Artic or Standard bus pulling trailer: 2-1/2" width at corners (2-way street), approximately 5".

BACHMANN

These models are ready to run and feature prepainted and lettered plastic bodies, operating headlights and horn-hook couplers (unless noted).

CABLE CAR

SAN FRANCISCO CABLE CAR ea 32.00
160-60541 Powell & Hyde (brown, maroon, light blue)
160-60542 Powell & Mason

TROLLEY

BRILL TROLLEY CAR ea 20.00 (unless noted)
160-61047 Mainstreet
160-61048 36 Yellow

COMMITTEE CAR

PRESIDENT'S COMMITTEE CAR - STREAMLINED TROLLEY ea 24.00
160-62945 Philadelphia Transportation Company (dark green, tan) 24.00
160-62946 7407 National City Lines (yellow, cream) 24.00

HERSHEY TROLLEYS ea 22.00 NEW
These Brill streetcars are finished in several paint schemes for Hershey, Pennsylvania, better known as "Chocolate Town USA™ ."
160-61037 Hershey™ #7, (Chocolate brown)
160-61039 Hershey™ #9, (Chocolate Brown w/cream trim)

186-6100 Trolleybus Powered 114.99
The poles measure approximately 3-1/2" high.
186-6102 Standard Trolleybus (orange, white) Set 195.49
This ready to run set includes standard power car and trailer, 8 poles, two power supply poles and 20 sections of wire, each about 10" (25cm) long. Transformer not included.
186-6103 Articulated Trolleybus (blue, white) Set 190.99
Ready to run set includes articulated trolleybus, 8 poles, two power supply poles and 20 sections of wire, each 10" (25cm) long. A transformer is not included.
186-6104 Articulated Trolleybus (yellow, white) 134.49
This trolleybus measures approximately 7-3/4".
186-6106 Trolleybus Trailer 24.99
This trolleybus trailer measures approximately 5".

ACCESSORIES

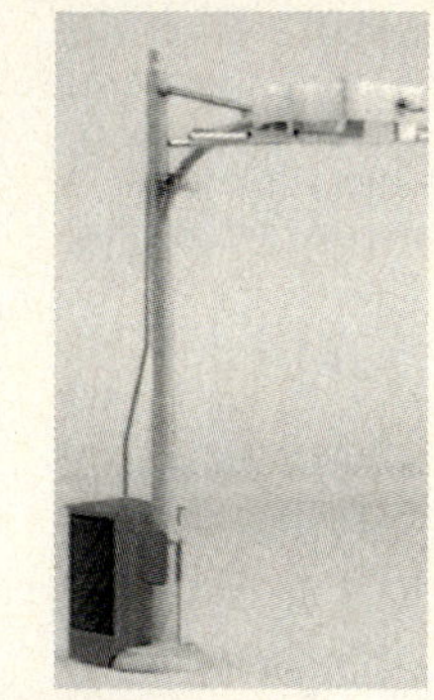

OVERHEAD ELECTRIC SWITCH
186-6101 T Bus Trolley Pole 10.49
These poles are used with buses 6100 or 6104.
186-6111 Overhead Mast 5.99
186-6112 Overhead Power Mast 12.49
186-6120 Overhead Electric Switch 37.99
186-6127 Insulating Mast 6.99
186-6148 Overhead Reversing Loop 24.99
186-6117 Crossing 10.49
186-6115 Overhead Wires pkg (20) 8.99
186-6143 Wire Connector Sleeves pkg (10) 6.49

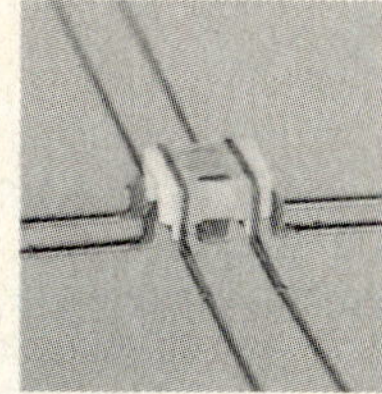

CROSSING

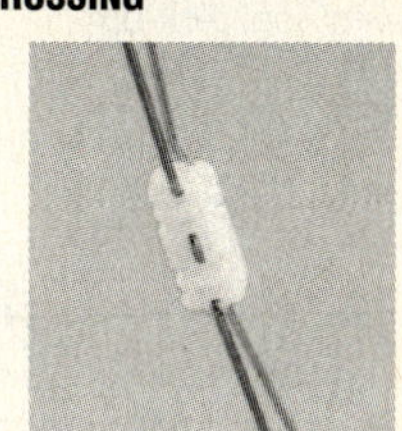

OVERHEAD WIRE CROSSING
186-6144 Insulating Connector Sleeves 4.49
186-6140 Overhead Wire Crossing 8.49
These are for use between train and trolleybus wires.
186-6126 Contact Switch Pole 7.99
186-6133 Rubber Tires pkg (10) 5.99
These tires will fit numbers 6100 and 6104.
186-60 Trolley Bus Catalog English/German Text 17.49
This catalog contains 39, 8-1/2 x 11" pages of illustrations and color photos pertaining to the operations, maintenance and circuits for the Brawa Trolleybus.

SAN FRANSISCO CABLE CAR

PRESIDENTS COMMITTEE CAR

Roco

Imported from Austria by Walthers
These authentically painted and lettered plastic models feature die cast zinc frames, metal gears, European style couplers and headlights. Models may be operated from overhead catenary or 2-rail electrical pick-up.

TRAMWAYS

In Europe, where the costs of owning and maintaining an automobile are high, tramways are an important means of public transportation in metropolitan areas. Roco tramways give any layout a modern image and will introduce you to the fun of traction modeling. The cars are exactingly detailed with full interior, realistic trucks and pantograph. Separate detail parts such as windshield wipers, external rear view mirrors, antennas and decals are also included. These tramways can negotiate curves of about seven inches (180mm) radius.

625-43191 8-Axle, Cologne Public Transit System 151.49
This eight-axle streetcar of the Cologne Public Transit System features a large advertising area.

625-43189 8-Axle, NSB (white) kit 116.99 NEW
625-43190 8-Axle, NSB with billboard advertising (blue) 151.49 _NEW_

Heck, there's no reason why anyone would even want to own a car when they can ride the North Shore! line. Here we see a pair of the big "Greenliners" meet in the city streets on the Little "Q" Model Railroad Club in Aurora, Illinois. This joint project features cars owned by Mike Bezin and painted by Dave Hanks, which were shot by George Griesmann.

Photo by George Griesmann.

Q-CAR COMPANY

These HO Scale craft train kits have one-piece cast epoxy body shells. They will accept Bowser or NorthWest Short Line power and trailer trucks. Kits are less trucks, floors, finishing details and couplers.

We have worked closely with this manufacturer to provide accurate availability information at the time this catalog was published. Items listed in blue ink may not be available at all times. Please see your dealer for current delivery information.

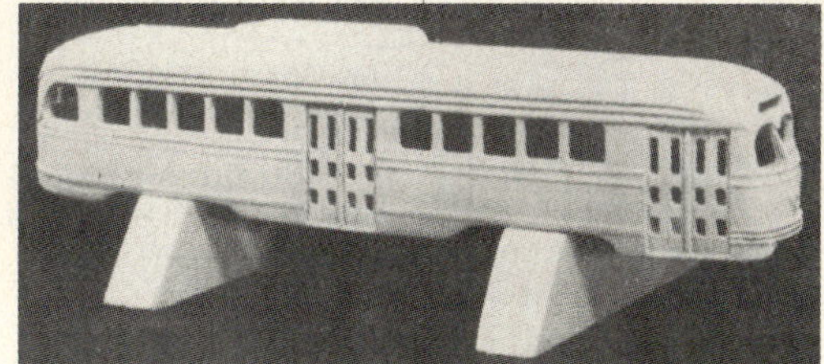

PCC CAR

BMT STANDARD CAR

BMT

BMT STANDARD CARS ea 43.05
Brooklyn-Manhattan Transit (BMT Lines) built these "Standard" subway cars from 1914 to 1924, and they served until 1972.

608-100 Monitor Roof
This is series 2600-2899, 4000-4049; built 1920 until 1924

608-101 Streamlined Roof
This is series 2000-2599; built 1914 until 1919.

STILLWELL COACH

608-104 New York, Westchester & Boston 45.95
Built in the 1920s, these cars were based on the Erie Railroad Stillwell coach. Modified for electric service, the cars had both conventional and subway-style center doors for loading and unloading passengers. Fifty were owned by the New Haven and leased to the Westchester. Following its abandonment in 1937, they were rebuilt as coaches for suburban service.

IND R1-9 CAR

The R1-9 series cars were built for the Independent Division of the New York City Transit System. A total of 1,399 were built between 1930 and 1940 and served into the mid-70s. Ten have been preserved in the Metropolitan Transit Authority Museum. One found its way to the Branford Trolley Museum in Connecticut.

608-102 R1-9 Subway Car 45.50

608-103 Chicago Rapid Transit #4000 44.20

IND R1-9 CAR

PCC CARS ea 40.40
As an answer to bus competition, the PCC (President's Conference Car) was developed. Sleek, and streamlined, the first were built for the Brooklyn & Queens Transit in 1936. The Brooklyn PCCs lasted until the end of streetcar service on October 31, 1956. PCCs, continued to operate in Boston, Philadelphia, Pittsburgh, Cleveland, Toronto, San Francisco and Mexico City.

608-501 Brooklyn & Queens Transit
This is series 1001-1099; built 1936.

608-502 St. Louis Public Service
This is series 1500-1599. The St Louis PCC was the first of several orders to the St Louis Car Company for its home city. They served from 1940 until 1961.

BROOKLYN CLARK CAR
PCC Car number 1000 was the first true PCC built and was the only PCC built by Clark Equipment Company. Clark remained in the PCC program as the main supplier of trucks. Number 1000 also had the distinction of being the only riveted all-aluminum PCC and the first to have standee windows. It served on the BQ&T until October 1956 and has been preserved at the New York Trolley Museum in Kingston, New York.

608-503 Clark Built 45.00

MODEL TRACTION SUPPLY COMPANY

These HO Scale craft train kits have epoxy bodies.

RAIL GRINDER CAR

505-8 CTA 79.95
This is a one piece body.

WOOD MULTIPLE UNIT

505-7 PRSL 39.95

PCC CAR

505-9 Brooklyn #1000 Body Kit 65.00
This model features a one-piece primed body and a metal floor.

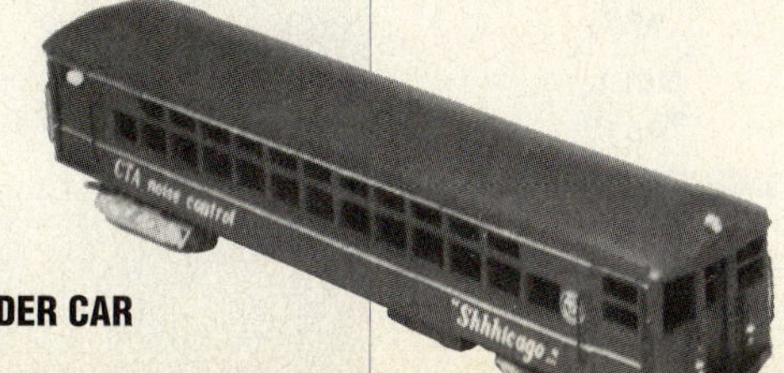

WOOD MULTIPLE UNIT

RAIL GRINDER CAR

FUNARO & CAMERLENGO

43' BOX TRAILER

This HO Scale kit consists of thin flexible styro-urethane castings with details cast in place, strip-wood, wire and instructions. This kit does not include decals, trucks or couplers.

279-4400 Cincinnati & Lake Erie 22.99

TOMAR INDUSTRIES

Drumheads were used for many years on the last car of interurbans, making it easy for passengers to find their train in a terminal. The lighted sign was also useful for advertising , especially after dark. These kits are complete with cast and machined drum housing, 1.5 volt micro-miniature lamp, full color sign, light diffuser, diodes, hookup wire and complete instructions.

INTERURBANS

CHICAGO SOUTH SHORE & SOUTH BEND
081-1540 Herald (round) 9.95

1535

1536

CINCINNATI & LAKE ERIE
081-1535 Fleeting Sun (rectangular) 9.95
081-1536 Valley Queen (rectangular) 9.95

1500

1501

1502

SACRAMENTO NORTHERN ea 9.95
081-1500 Comet (round)
081-1501 Meteor (round)
081-1502 Sacramento Valley Limited (round)

1505

1506

SACRAMENTO SHORT LINE ea 9.95
081-1505 The Comet (round)
081-1506 The Meteor (round)

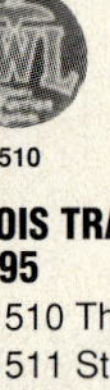

ILLINOIS TERMINAL RAILROAD
081-1525 Illinois Terminal Railroad Company (rectangular) 9.95

1510

1511

ILLINOIS TRACTION SYSTEM ea 9.95
081-1510 The Owl (round)
081-1511 St Louis/Peoria Limited (round)

1515

1516

1517

NORTH SHORE LINE ea 9.95
081-1515 Gold Coast Limited (round)
081-1516 The Eastern Limited (round) 9.95
081-1517 Prairie State Special (round)

THE MILWAUKEE ELECTRIC RAILWAY & LIGHT COMPANY
081-1530 Land O'Lakes Limited (round) 9.95

LEHIGH VALLEY TRANSIT
081-1550 Liberty Bell Route (round) 9.95

ACCESSORIES

081-801 Constant Intensity Light Source 2.95
This kit contains a 14 volt ballast lamp, four diodes and hook-up wire. It will power a 1.5 volt lamp from track power.

081-802 Micro Miniature Slide Switch pkg (2) 2.50
This is a 1.5 volt pen light cell switch.

END OF TRAIN DEVICE
This kit simulates the flashing units used in place of a caboose on freight trains. Kits include a metal casting with a permanently installed lens, 1.5 volt lamp installed in casting, electronic flasher unit, AA battery holder, (less battery) and instructions.

081-806 End of Train Device 10.95
This kit has a red face and an amber lens.

081-822 End of Train Device 10.95
This kit has a red face and a red lens.

ADLAKE MARKER LIGHTS
Markers indicate the rear of a train and were mounted on cabooses or observation cars. The kit includes two brass markers with lenses installed, 1.5v lamps and instructions.

081-807 Adlake Marker Lights pkg (2) 10.45
These lights are green and red as used by most roads.

081-809 Adlake Marker Lights 10.45
These lights are yellow and red, as used by some roads.

081-813 Red Tail Light Kit 2.50
This kit includes an 1.5 volt red lamp and instructions.

081-812 Battery Hook-up Kit 2.95
This kit includes a battery holder and switch to be mounted inside your car (less battery).

081-816 Ballast Bulb pkg (2) 1.39
This bulb can be used with drumhead kits and #801 to keep heat down inside of cars.

081-818 Lamp for #807 pkg (2) 5.45
081-819 Lamp for #806 pkg (2) 3.45

VOLLMER

Complete catenary system is designed to provide overhead power or can be used for non-operating catenary with standard track power. Based on German Railways prototypes, equipment can be adapted for any model railroad.

All wiring is made from chrome-nickel steel for improved conductivity. Masts are molded in break-resistant plastic to prevent short-circuits. Each is approximately 3-7/8" tall (97 mm) and provides a wire height of about 3" (76mm).

CATENARY WIRE

770-1011 Contact Wire 16" 2.49
770-1310 Cross Span With Accessories (310mm long) 10.99
770-1315 Bridging Section pkg (5) 13.49
Used between two bridges.
770-1316 Bridging Section pkg (5) 10.49
770-1320 Insulating Unit (1") pkg (5) 18.49
770-1331 3.9" pkg (10) 23.49
For radii under 280mm
770-1335 5.5" Long (140mm) pkg (10) 25.99
For radii over 10.10" (280mm)

770-1339 1.95 x 7.4" (190mm) pkg (10) 27.49
For radii over 437mm
770-1343 Contact Wire 15.8" pkg (10) 32.49
770-1345 For Loco Shed 5750 pkg (2) 7.49
770-1347 For Loco Shed 5752 pkg (2) 9.99
770-1349 For Loco Shed 5760 pkg (2) 9.99
770-1351 For Bridge 2506 pkg (2) 9.99

CATENARY MAST

770-1300 Mast With Short Arm pkg (10) 39.99
770-1301 Mast With Long Arm pkg (10) 39.99
770-1304 Terminal/Feeder pkg (5) 33.99
770-1308 Tower Mast pkg (10) 58.49
770-1311 Registration For Tower Mast pkg (10) 34.99
770-1314 Mast Bracket pkg (10) 19.99
For use with #1300 and #1301.
770-4021 Mast Base .99

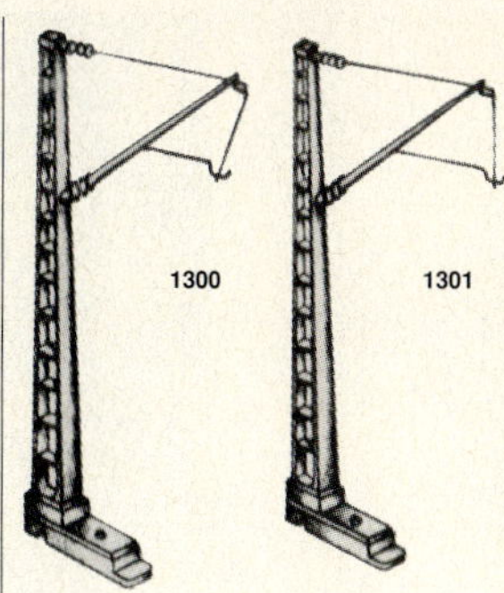
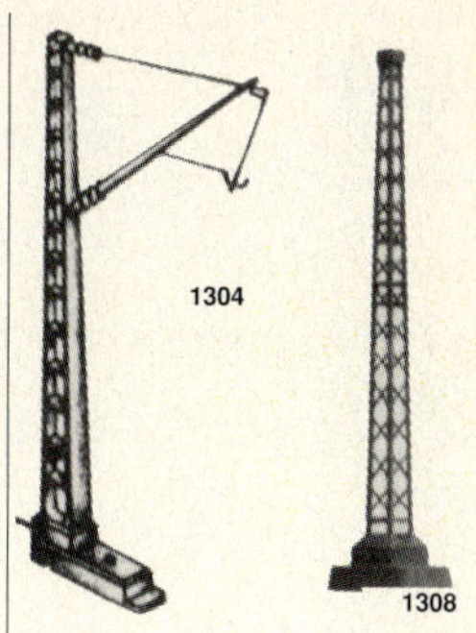

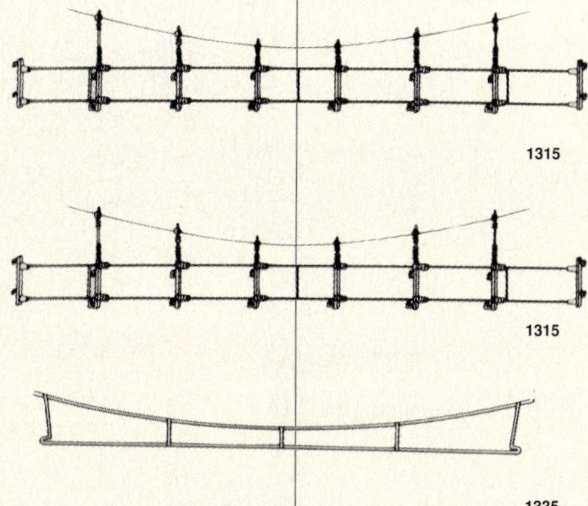

OVERHEAD SET

770-1390 HO Overhead Set 134.49
This set includes 9 #1300, 10 #1301, 1 #1304, 18# 1335 and 2 contact wires (15.6" long)

The Electroliner wheels out on to the main, enroute to a downtown station stop. Once clear of the city limits, the streamliner will be hard to catch as she flies to Milwaukee. It's hard to believe the North Shore has been gone for 30 years when you see this shot from the Little "Q" model Railroad Club layout in Aurora, Illinois. Mike Bezin's equipment was used for the scene and the cars were painted by Dave Hanks.

Photo by George Griesmann

TAPERED TROLLEY POLES

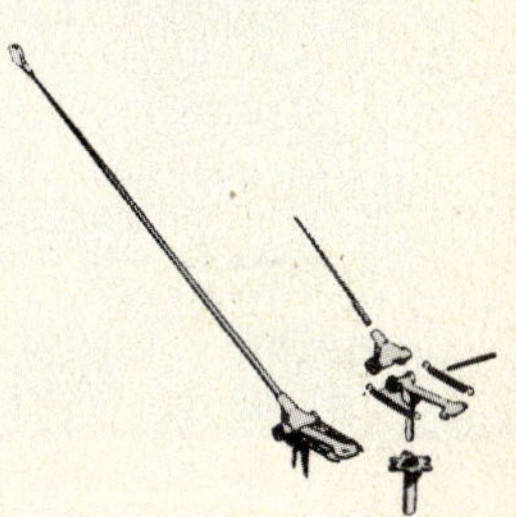

585-31563 Poles Only (pair) 2.75
585-31564 With Shoes (pair) 7.50
585-31565 With Wheels (pair) 7.50

Keeping a steamer lubricated is no mean task, but it's especially tough with the extra hardware on a big articulated. At virtually every stop, the engineer will swing down and "oil around" while the fireman watches for the signal to depart. This handsome hauler was rebuilt for service on Bill Henderson's Coal Belt Railroad and started life as a Mantua loco.

Models and Photo by Bill Henderson

North Powder Paper uses and receives dozens of freight cars each day. Here , a cut of wood chip cars is being spotted by a pair of leased SP 70 tonners. This is one of several busy industries on the Mount Hood Model Engineers layout . And this really is a PAPER mill; it's built from old cereal boxes! The locos are Bachmann Spectrum units which have been weighted, while the wood chip cars were scratchbuilt. You can admire this layout in person during the 1994 NMRA convention, held August 15 - 20, 1994 at Portland, Oregon.

Photo by Joe Brugger

WALTHERS™

1993 SHOWMANSHIP AWARD CAR

YOU CAN'T BUY IT, BUT YOU CAN EARN ONE FOR YOUR CLUB

Each year clubs and other organizations host hundreds of mall shows, layout tours and other programs that bring the fun and excitement of model railroading to the public.

To acknowledge and thank these groups, Walthers Award Program was created in 1980. This annual event is marked by the presentation of an extremely limited-run car, with special paint and lettering.

If you belong to a club or other non-profit group that hosts an open house or show, you can qualify for this special car. The information is available at no charge, simply request item #949-755 by writing to:

Attn: Award Car Information
c/o **Walthers**
5601 W. Florist Ave.
Milwaukee, WI 53218

Information on planning your show is also available. In order to qualify, a group must host a public show which involves advance planning and publicity.

WALTHERS™

Heading in with a cabin car in tow, this Conrail B23-7 is about to get a much needed rest. The loco has put in some hard hours, kicking up a little dust in the process. A Rail Power Products shell was the starting point for this model by Ed Sanicky. Ed used photos of the actual #1966 to add the numerous details, along with the grit and grime to his model!
Photo by W. Terry Stuart

FREIGHT CAR ACCESSORIES

The annual York Haven open house is quite an event for local residents. And local railfans have spread the word up and down the coast, insuring a great turnout. Several members of the fleet are on display, but once the sun sets and the last visitor is gone, it will be business as usual. The President of The York Haven is John Klotz, from Stratford, Connecticut, who proudly arranged this display of custom painted locos from his collection.
Photo by John Klotz

Modernize your freight car fleet! Modern freight cars look their best with the cushion car coupler pocket kit. Easy to install, the kit simulates the end-of-car cushioning devices used on box cars, auto racks, cabooses and other types of cars. The longer draft gear increases the distance between cars for a more realistic appearance.

When freight cars couple at speeds over five miles per hour, they can hit with enough force to severely damage loads. End-of-car cushioning equipment absorbs this force before it can be transmitted to the load. Cars with cushioning equipment carry easily damaged loads like glass, newsprint, automobiles, canned food, and appliances.

Both new and rebuilt older cars are equipped with these devices.

Underframe mounted cushioning devices for freight cars first appeared in the early 1960s. As fuel conservation and car weight became important factors in the 1970s, railroads began using end-of-car cushioning systems which were less expensive and lighter than the underframe units.

The Walthers Cushion Car Coupler Pocket Kit is molded in rust colored styrene and can easily be painted to match your favorite prototype. Assembly drawings and detailed instructions make this modeling project easy and fun for beginners or experienced modelers alike.

Like the prototype, these detail parts can be used on flat cars, box cars, auto racks and cabooses to make your models more realistic. Parts to modify four cars and complete step-by-step instructions are included. Horn hook or Kadee #5 couplers work well with this kit

CUSHION CAR COUPLER POCKET
933-1030 Cushion Car Coupler Pocket Kit pkg (4 pair) 3.98

HORN HOOK COUPLERS
Standard replacement fits all Walthers kits. Molded in Delrin® plastic.

941-1282 X2F Horn Hook Couplers pkg (12) 1.98

WALTHERS™

Walthers HO Scale kits feature detailed styrene parts and are designed for easy construction with basic hobby tools. Each car is prepainted and lettered in an authentic scheme that includes end reporting marks. All kits are complete with instructions, weights, trucks with nonmagnetic brass axles and horn-hook couplers.

INTERMODAL SECTION

Some historians trace the start of railroad intermodal service to 1872, when William Coup loaded circus wagons on flat cars to move his show faster. In 1884, the Long Island Railroad hauled loaded farm wagons to market in New York city. By the early 20's, the New York Central was using small containers for some freight shipments. In 1926, the North Shore line began hauling tiny highway trailers on special flat cars between Milwaukee and Chicago. On July 7, 1936, the Chicago Great Western began what many consider the first true intermodal service, hauling another company's trailers on specially modified flat cars.

In the 1950's, the piggyback revolution began, with virtually every large railroad handling trailers-on-flat-cars. Pennsy introduced Truc-Train Service and 75' flats capable of carrying two trailers.

In the 60's, standardized car designs, containers, 89' flat cars and 40' trailers appeared on the nation's rails.

In the 70's and 80's new fuel-saving car designs, articulated cars, double-stacks, domestic service containers, fluid containers and larger trailers were introduced.

Today, intermodal service continues to expand, with innovative car designs, faster schedules and dedicated service trains.

And best of all, with Walthers selection of kits and accessories, it's possible to model the history of intermodal from the 1950's to the present!

FLAT CARS

GSC "COMMONWEALTH" 53' 6" FLAT CAR

One of the most common flat cars converted for piggyback service in the 1950's, these steel cars were considered strong enough to withstand the strain of carrying trailers. Their 53-6" length was ideal for the 32' and 35' trailers then in use. When fitted for piggyback service, the cars were equipped with a hitch and rub rails, numerous tie-downs and bridge plates. In later years, a new hitch replaced the tie-downs, and the cars remained in piggyback service into the 1960's.

This kit is the correct length and includes early and late piggyback hitches, plus parts for bulkhead and standard versions. They're perfect for use on any layout from the 1950s to the present. Vehicles, lumber and other loads are listed elsewhere in this catalog.

INCLUDES PARTS TO BUILD FOUR WAYS:

* EARLY PIGGYBACK

* LATER PIGGYBACK

* BULKHEAD

* STANDARD FLAT CAR

53' 6" GENERAL STEEL "COMMONWEALTH" FLAT CARS ea 9.98

932-3751 Pennsylvania (oxide red)
932-3752 Union Pacific (armor yellow)
932-3753 Rio Grande (black)
932-3754 Santa Fe (red)
932-3755 Soo Line (white)
932-3756 Burlington Northern (cascade green)
932-3750 Undecorated

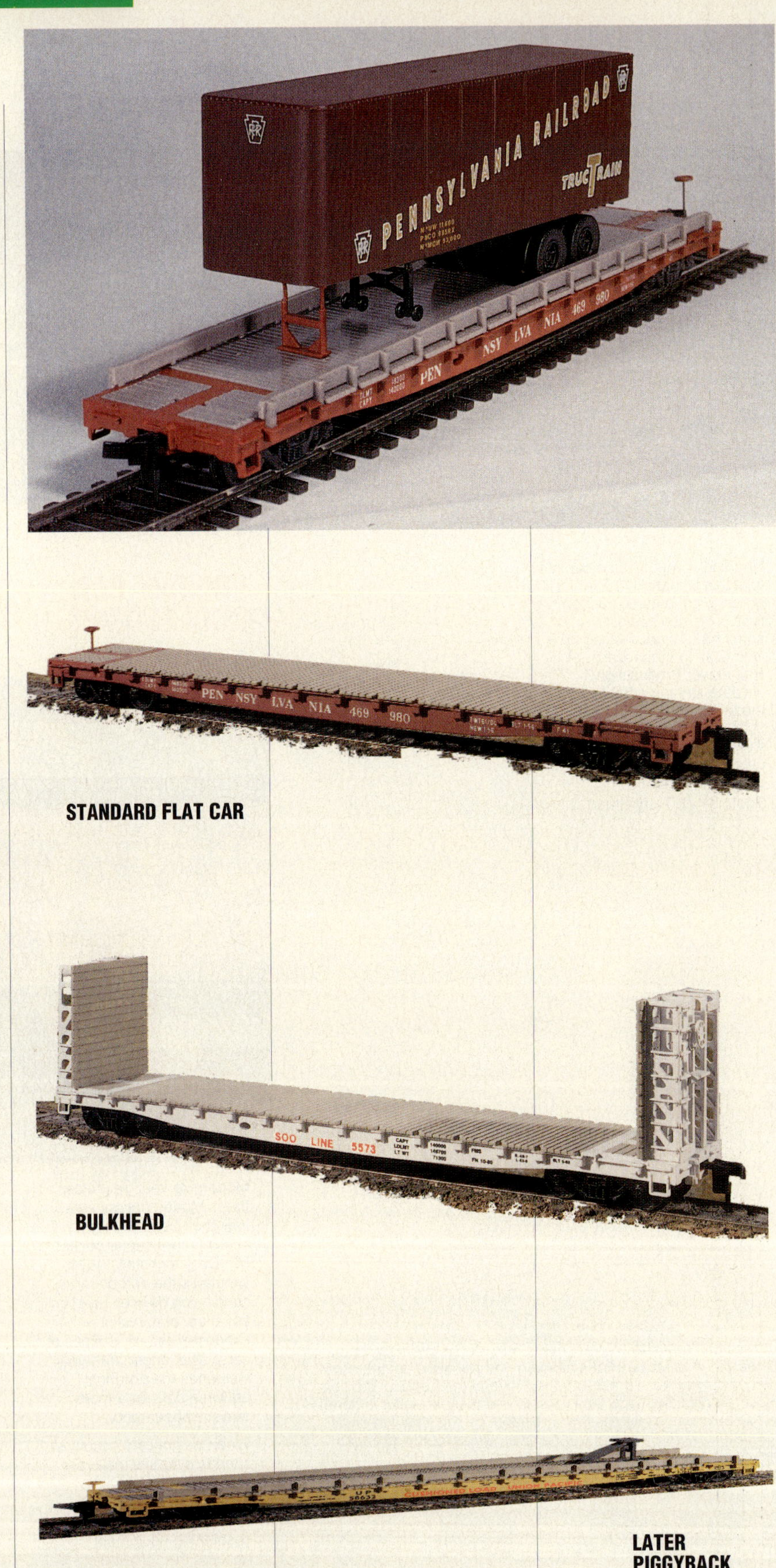

STANDARD FLAT CAR

BULKHEAD

LATER PIGGYBACK

75' PIGGYBACK FLAT CAR

In 1954, the Pennsylvania revolutionized piggyback service with 75' flat cars capable of carrying two 35' trailers. In the late 50's, these cars were some of the first to use a folding fifth wheel to support and hold the trailer, replacing elaborate load restraints.

Trailer Train began operations in 1956, with the Pennsylvania cars as the backbone of their fleet. In the 60s, cars for trailer service were painted tuscan red with TTX reporting marks, while some were reclassified ATTX and converted to general purpose cars with tie downs but no trailer hitches. Some ATTX cars are still in service and are frequently used for moving agricultural implements.

WALTHERS ™

75' PIGGYBACK FLAT CAR
ea 9.98

932-3951 Trailer Train (tuscan red)
932-3952 Erie (black)
932-3953 Pennsylvania (tuscan red)
932-3954 Wabash (black)
932-3955 Southern Pacific (box car red)
932-3956 Chicago, Burlington & Quincy (box car red)

932-3957 TTX, Modern (yellow)
932-3958 ATTX, Modern (yellow)
932-3959 TTX, 1960s (tuscan red)
932-3960 ATTX, 1960s (tuscan red)
932-3950 Undecorated

32' VAN TRAILER ea 3.49

In the 1950's, piggyback service was used for LCL shipments traveling a short distance. Trailers ranged from 20 to 35' long and many were painted to promote piggyback service. The 32' outside braced trailer was among the most common, due its ability to withstand the stresses of being shipped by train. These trailers are perfect for loading the GSC or 75' Piggyback Flats and are prepainted in authentic schemes. These kits require only minor assembly and each package includes one trailer.

933-1601 Erie (aluminum)
933-1602 Pennsylvania (tuscan red)
933-1603 Wabash (royal blue)
933-1604 Cooper-Jarret (aluminum)
933-1605 Santa Fe (aluminum)
933-1606 Southern Pacific (aluminum)
933-1607 Mid States (aluminum)

933-1608 Illinois-California Express (aluminum)
933-1609 Chicago, Burlington & Quincy
933-1610 Baltimore & Ohio (blue)
933-1611 Nickel Plate Road (dark blue)
933-1612 Chesapeake & Ohio (aluminum)
933-1613 Carolina (aluminum)
933-1614 GI Truck (white)
933-1615 Gateway (white)
933-1616 Pacific Intermountain Express (white)
933-1617 Roadway (aluminum)
933-1618 Preston 151 Line (aluminum)
933-1619 Ringsby (aluminum)
933-1620 Glendenning (maroon)
933-1621 Western Pacific (aluminum)
933-1622 Western Maryland (oxide red)
933-1623 Frisco (yellow)
933-1624 Soo Line (orange)
933-1600 Undecorated

40' TRAILERS ea 3.98

With changes in weight and length regulations, trucking companies quickly moved up to 40' trailers in the 1960's. Railroads were obliged to follow suit and began introducing larger cars, like the F89F, capable of carrying two of these trailers. These models are prepainted in authentic schemes and require only minor assembly.

933-1651 New York Central (aluminum)
933-1652 Milwaukee Road (orange)
933-1653 Seaboard Air Line ("Razorback" logo - aluminum)
933-1654 Campbell Express ("Humpin' to Please" - aluminum)
933-1655 Railway Express Agency (dark green)
933-1656 Clipper Express (white)
933-1657 Illinois Central Gulf (aluminum)
933-1658 Union Pacific (aluminum)
933-1659 Vermont Railway (aluminum)

933-1660 US Mail (white)
933-1661 AVAILCO (aluminum)
933-1662 XTRA (aluminum)
933-1663 Santa Fe (aluminum)
933-1664 Pennsylvania (tuscan red)
933-1665 Northern Pacific (white)
933-1666 Time DC (white)
933-1667 Iowa Beef (white)
933-1668 A&P (aluminum)

Expected Delivery - Late 1993:

933-1669 Navajo *NEW*
933-1670 Seaboard *NEW*
933-1671 Chicago & North Western *NEW*
933-1672 Strick *NEW*
933-1673 Union Pacific - "We Can Handle It" *NEW*
933-1674 Illinois Central (New scheme) *NEW*
933-1675 Southern
933-1676 TransAmerica
933-1650 Undecorated

INFORMATION STATION

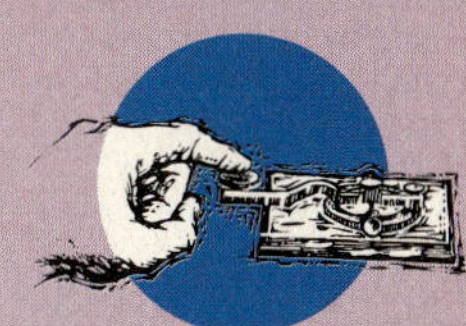

Loading highway trailers on flat cars was a pretty radical idea in the 1950's. Railroads took no chances with the unproved technology. Using the chain, binder and screwjack system invented by the Chicago Great Western in the 30's, nearly every road modified the design to meet their own requirements. So much so, that a typical car had 40 tie-downs!

A loaded trailer was chained at each corner as well as front and rear. A pair of screwjacks held the nose and the wheels were chocked. And the process had to be repeated for every trailer on the train.

WALTHERS™

Walthers HO Scale kits feature detailed styrene parts and are designed for easy construction with basic hobby tools. Each car is prepainted and lettered in an authentic scheme that includes end reporting marks. All kits are complete with instructions, weights, trucks with nonmagnetic brass axles and horn-hook couplers.

FLAT CARS

FLAT CAR ACCESSORIES

933-1024 TOFC Trailer Hitch pkg (6) 3.98
Based on an American Car & Foundry (ACF) prototype, this realistic hitch is adaptable to most piggyback flat cars. Easy-to-build plastic kit includes parts for 6 hitches.

439-303 Piggyback Ramp 4.98
"Circus-style" loading ramps (So called because trailers were loaded on flat cars like circus wagons.) appeared in yards, at sidings, near freight houses and in many small towns during the 50's and 60's. This one-piece, urethane casting includes a bridge plate, and is ready to paint and install.

F89F 89' "CHANNEL-SIDE" FLAT CAR *NEW*

Expected Delivery - Late 1993
Introduced in the 1960's and still going strong, these cars were purchased by many railroads and TTX for trailer-on-flat-car service. They're easily identified from similar flat cars by their steel channel sides. As trailer sizes increased, these cars were rebuilt into various "new" types. Our kit can be built in three versions: Standard, Twin 45 and Triple 28 using the hitches and other parts which are included.

These cars use the same proven underframe design found on our Enclosed Auto Carriers so they can be operated on small layouts with tight radius curves. Each kit also has a nearly full-length weight to improve tracking and performance.

F89F FLAT CARS ea 11.98
932-4951 TTX - Standard (Elephant style loading)
932-4952 TTX - "Twin 45"
932-4953 TTX - "Triple 28"
932-4954 Union Pacific
932-4955 Southern Pacific
932-4956 Santa Fe
932-4950 Undecorated

PIGGYBACK RAMP

F89 FLAT CARS PROTOTYPE PHOTO

WALTHERS™

SPINE CARS

FIVE-UNIT ALL-PURPOSE SPINE CARS ea 39.98
NEW
Expected Delivery - Fall 1993

Working with the railroads to determine their changing requirements, Trailer Train introduced the All-Purpose Spine Car in 1988. Equipped to carry containers and trailers at the same time, each of the five units has collapsible hitches and container locks. Trailers from 28 to 48' long, or 40, 45 or 48' containers can be carried. The end (A&B) units have additional locks to carry a pair of 20' containers. Brake wheels are installed on each end unit, reducing the rigging needed to activate the hand brakes. Today, these all-purpose cars are state-of-the-art equipment, and can be seen running in general freights, or with other types of intermodal equipment.

This new model features a prepainted and lettered diecast metal body for improved performance. Add-on brake gear hitches, container pedestals and other plastic details are included so the model can carry trailers or containers like the prototypes.

FIVE-UNIT ALL-PURPOSE SPINE CARS ea 39.98
NEW
932-3931 TTX
932-3932 Burlington Northern
932-3933 Santa Fe
932-3934 Union Pacific
932-3935 Conrail
932-3930 Undecorated

XTRA

TRANSAMERICA

OVERNITE

SCHNEIDER

48' STOUGHTON SEMI TRAILERS ea 4.98 *NEW*

Expected Delivery - Fall 1993
Some of the most common trailers on the road or the rails are the 48' Stoughton Semi Trailers. Available for the first time, these easy-to-build kits come decorated in eight popular roadnames, which are seen on intermodal trains throughout the US.

933-1901 XTRA Intermodal (white)
933-1902 Overnite (white)
933-1903 Conrail Mercury (white)
933-1904 JB Hunt (white)
933-1905 TransAmerica (white)
933-1906 Schneider (white)
933-1907 Strick Lease (white)
933-1908 Tip Lease (white)
933-1900 Undecorated

CONRAIL

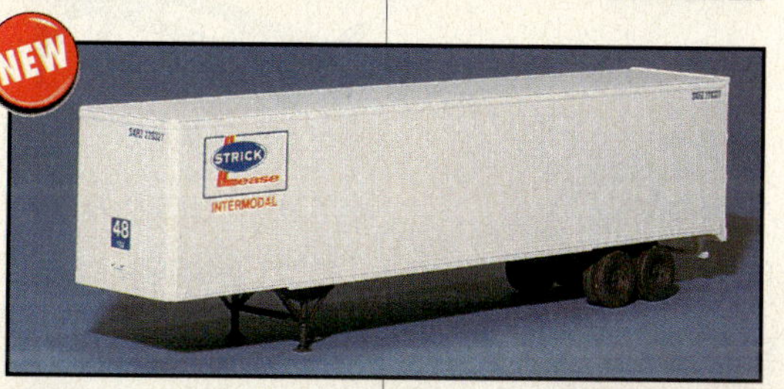

STRICK LEASE

JB HUNT

TIP LEASE

WALTHERS™

Walthers HO Scale kits feature detailed styrene parts and are designed for easy construction with basic hobby tools. Each car is prepainted and lettered in an authentic scheme that includes end reporting marks. All kits are complete with instructions, weights, trucks with nonmagnetic brass axles and horn-hook couplers.

STANDARD

HI CAB

EXTENDIBLE CONTAINER CHASSIS

WELL CARS

FIVE-UNIT ARTICULATED WELL CARS ea 39.98
NEW

Thrall introduced a new five-unit articulated well car in 1983, equipped with interbox connectors (IBCs) to lock containers on the car using the four corner castings. By the late 1980's, longer 45 and 48' containers were in service, and the design was again reworked to accommodate these heavier loads in the middle wells. The latest version (which is the prototype of this kit) has additional reinforcements and IBCs to carry everything from a pair of 20 footers up to a single 48' container in any of the wells.

These kits are designed for easy assembly, with five prepainted and lettered "bodies" to make a complete car. Lots of add-on details are included.

FIVE-UNIT ARTICULATED WELL CARS ea 39.98
NEW

932-3971 TTX - Old Scheme (gold)
932-3972 TTX - American President Lines
932-3973 TTX - Burlington Northern
932-3974 Santa Fe
932-3970 Undecorated

Expected Delivery - Early 1994:

932-3975 TTX - Latest Scheme
932-3976 Canadian National
932-3977 APL Liner Train
932-3978 Southern Pacific
932-3979 K-Line

STAND-ALONE WELL CARS

Stand-alone Well Cars entered service in the early 90's as larger and heavier containers came into use. With a truck at each end, they have a larger carrying capacity and are easier to maintain than articulated cars. Some owners run them with drawbars as three, four or five "unit cars." These cars are being used for heavy shipments such as the movement of garbage and some foreign shipments moving in 20' containers.

STAND-ALONE WELL CARS
932-3901 TTX single unit (new TTX yellow) 9.98
932-3902 TTX three-pack (new TTX yellow) 27.98
932-3903 TTX Original "TT" logo four-pack (new TTX yellow) 36.98
932-3904 Canadian National single unit (blue) 9.98
932-3905 Canadian National five-unit car (blue) 44.98
Prototype consists of five stand-alone cars, connected by drawbars.
932-3900 Undecorated single unit 9.98

OTTAWA YARD TRACTORS
pkg (2) 7.98

Make fast work of moving trailers or containers around your terminal or large industry with these small tractors. The kits feature one-piece resin cabs with details molded in place. Separate frames, hitches and wheels are included, along with instructions and colorful decals.

439- 941 Standard
439-948 Hi-Cab
Expected Delivery - Fall 1993

This variation has a taller cab with additional windows, making it easier for a driver to pick up taller containers and trailers.

933-3110 EXTENDIBLE CONTAINER CHASSIS
pkg (2) 8.98

When containers arrive for delivery, they're usually reloaded on extendible chassis. And on occasion, you may see a container being handled as a regular trailer on a flat car, still riding on its chassis. This easy-to-build kit can be adjusted from 40 to 48' scale feet, and looks great behind the Magnuson semi tractors you'll find in Vehicles.

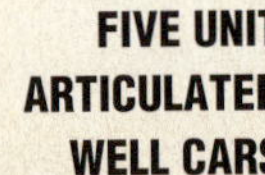

FIVE UNIT ARTICULATED WELL CARS

WALTHERS™

STAND-ALONE WELL CARS

This all-new kit will be the star of your intermodal terminal! The Translift Crane is a dual purpose machine used by many railroads, that can lift trailers or containers. It's wide enough to straddle two rows of trailers or containers parked side by side and the intermodal car, making short work of loading or unloading.

Many parts on the model are adjustable to simulate a working crane. Magnets are included to hold containers securely, (container requires Metal Plate Set 933-3134, sold separately) without gluing. Decals and complete instructions are included.

CONTAINER CRANES
933-3122 MI-JACK TRANSLIFT INTERMODAL CRANE ea 21.98 *NEW*

Expected Delivery - Fall 1993

Translift and MI-Jack are trademarks of Mi-Jack Products, used with permission.

933-3134 METAL PLATE SET ea 2.98
Expected Delivery - Early 1994:

Modify your containers for use with the Mi-Jack Crane in minutes. Set includes metal plates which mount inside containers, so they can be held on the crane without gluing. (24 plates- enough for 12 containers)

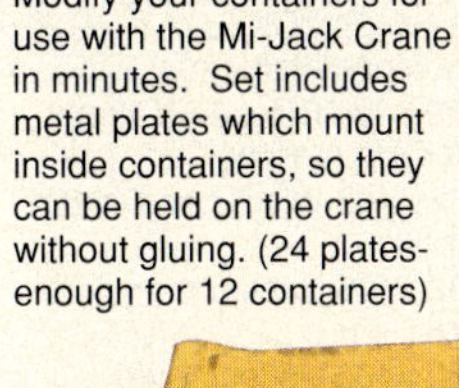

933-3109 KALMAR CONTAINER CRANE ea 15.98
To speed loading and unloading of containers, railroads use these self-propelled giants. These mobile cranes are used for side loading or unloading and are especially well suited to smaller terminals. The model is molded in a realistic safety yellow, and includes decals and instructions.

KALMAR CONTAINER CRANE

CONTAINERS

The container has become the international symbol of modern freight shipments. Walthers containers, available in the three most common prototype lengths of 20, 40 and 48', are great loads for any modern intermodal car and a must for realistic terminal scenes. Each package includes one prepainted and assembled container, ready to use on your layout.

20' RIBBED SIDE CONTAINERS ea 2.98
933-1751 Maersk
933-1752 K-Line
933-1753 Hanjin
933-1754 Evergreen
933-1755 Genstar
933-1756 OOCL
933-1757 Mitsui OSK
933-1758 Triton
933-1759 Nedlloyd *NEW*
933-1760 GELCO *NEW*
933-1761 CP Ships *NEW*
933-1762 CAST *NEW*
933-1763 American President Lines (APL) *NEW*
933-1764 Flexi-Van *NEW*
933-1750 Undecorated

40' HIGH CUBE CONTAINERS ea 2.98
933-1701 Maersk
933-1702 American President Lines
933-1703 Evergreen
933-1704 K-Line
933-1705 Hapag-Lloyd
933-1706 Matson
933-1707 ITEL
933-1708 CAST
933-1709 CP Ship
933-1710 OOCL
933-1711 Hyundai
933-1712 Hanjin
933-1713 TransAmerica
933-1714 Genstar
933-1715 XTRA
933-1716 Tropical
933-1700 Undecorated

48' STOUGHTON SMOOTH-SIDE CONTAINER ea 3.98
933-1801 Canadian Pacific/US Service
933-1802 Canadian National Laser
933-1803 Burlington Northern America
933-1804 Conrail Mercury
933-1805 Norfolk Southern
933-1806 American President Lines (APL)
933-1807 Conquest
933-1808 Genstar
933-1809 CSX Transportation/SL *NEW*
933-1810 XTRA *NEW*
933-1811 Santa Fe *NEW*
933-1812 Southern Pacific *NEW,*
933-1813 Union Pacific/Genstar *NEW*
933-1814 ITEL *NEW*
933-1800 Undecorated

REFRIGERATED CONTAINERS ea 3.49
Expected Delivery - Early 1994

These all-new containers represent the latest in perishable shipping technology. Equipped with a "picture frame" refrigeration unit that draws its power from a separate generator, these containers are lighter and can carry more than other containers of this type. These easy-to-build kits are prepainted and lettered.

933-1851 K- Line
933-1852 Sealand
933-1853 TransAmerica
933-1854 Evergreen
933-1855 Maersk
933-1856 APL
933-1857 Dole
933-1858 Del Monte
933-1850 Undecorated

WALTHERS™

Walthers HO Scale kits feature detailed styrene parts and are designed for easy construction with basic hobby tools. Each car is prepainted and lettered in an authentic scheme that includes end reporting marks. All kits are complete with instructions, weights, trucks with nonmagnetic brass axles and horn-hook couplers.

COVERED HOPPERS

Since their introduction in the late 19th century, the covered hopper has become increasingly important. Protecting cargo from dirt, insects, moisture and other contaminants, they're ideal for shipping powdered or granular materials in bulk.

The cars were first built in large numbers in the 1920's, primarily for cement service, and were fairly common by the 1940's, when the first Airslide® hopper appeared.

In the 1950's, larger capacity cars like the PS2 were introduced. During this period, covered hoppers began replacing box cars for many types of loads. Today, they are the most widely used car type on the nation's rails and whether railroad owned or leased from a private firm, they often sport colorful paint jobs.

Walthers easy-to-build kits are based on several popular prototypes, with prepainted and lettered bodies.

84' PAIRED AIRSLIDE® HOPPERS ea 19.98 *NEW*

Faced with s surplus of Single-Bay cars in the mid 80's, GATX began converting them into 84' Paired Airslides. Connected by a drawbar, they are handled as a single car and can deliver a large payload.

Each kit includes two complete sets of parts and is finished in an authentic scheme.

932-4681 Union Pacific (gray)
932-4682 Missouri Pacific (gray)
932-4683 Burlington Northern (cascade green)
932-4684 Soo Line (gray)
932-4685 GATX (powder blue)

AIRSLIDE® COVERED HOPPER

Developed in the late 40's for cement service, the Airslide Covered Hopper began to appear in large numbers after 1954. These air-tight cars kept loads clean and dry, while a special fabric liner simplified unloading. Thousands are still in use today, hauling food products, chemicals and other powdered materials.

Walthers offers three popular versions of these cars. Each easy-to-build kit has a one-piece body, with numerous add-on details like loading hatches with separate securing clamps, a see-through roofwalk, brake gear and more.

("Airslide" is a registered trademark of General American Transportation Company.)

39' SINGLE-BAY AIRSLIDE® COVERED HOPPERS 9.98

The Single-Bay Airslide remains in widespread service and has been popular with railroads and private owners for almost 40 years.

These kits have the end framing molded in place, for fast and easy construction.

932-4601 Soo Line (white)
932-4602 Santa Fe (brown)
932-4603 Burlington Northern (cascade green)
932-4604 Baltimore & Ohio (gray)
932-4605 Golden Loaf Flour (white)
932-4606 Multi-Foods (gray)
932-4607 Union Pacific (gray)
932-4610 Southern Railway (gray)
932-4612 Pillsbury (gray)
932-4600 Undecorated

37' CEMENT SERVICE COVERED HOPPERS ea 9.98 *NEW*

In the early 1980's, Greenville Steel Car Company introduced a new hopper for powdered materials. Cement proved to be too heavy for the car, so a slightly smaller version was created for cement service. This smaller car was also sold as a general purpose covered hopper, and can be found carrying plastic pellets, roofing granules, flour, grain and more.

This kit has a one-piece body with end ladders molded in place, separate hatches, a thin profile roofwalk and other add-on details.

932-5401 Union Pacific (gray)
932-5402 Burlington Northern (gray)
932-5403 CSX Transportation (gray)
932-5404 Chicago & North Western (yellow)
932-5405 Wisconsin Central (gray)
932-5406 Santa Fe (mineral red)
932-5400 Undecorated

WALTHERS™

50' AIRSLIDE® COVERED HOPPER ea 9.98

In the early 1960s, demand for larger cars capable of carrying heavier loads led to the development of a 100 ton capacity, 50' Airslide® hopper.

932-3651 Southern Railway (gray)
932-3652 Chessie System/Chesapeake & Ohio (yellow)
932-3653 Milwaukee Road (yellow)
932-3657 GATX General American Transportation Company (gray)
932-3658 Missouri-Kansas-Texas (red)
932-3659 ADM Milling (gray)
932-3660 Santa Fe (brown)
932-3665 Burlington Northern (cascade green)

932-3667 Wonder Bread (gray)
932-3668 Chicago & North Western (yellow)
932-3669 Great Northern (blue, white)
932-3670 Norfolk & Western (gray)
932-3671 CSX Transportation (cream)
932-3673 Illinois Central Gulf (orange)
932-3676 Rio Grande (orange)
932-3650 Undecorated

Limited Quantities Available

932-3655 Union Pacific (gray)

PULLMAN-STANDARD PS2 CENTER DISCHARGE HOPPERS ea

With their assembly line manufacturing, Pullman-Standard was able to modify its PS2 hopper to meet the needs of many customers. In the 1960's a new version was introduced for the grain industry. The new car was fitted with a trough-style roof hatch for faster loading and retained the proven center discharge for fast unloading. Immensely popular, the cars were purchased by dozens of railroads and private firms, and many are still going strong.

This all-new kit features a superbly detailed body, separate roofwalk, brake gear and hatches, plus a variety of authentic paint schemes.

PULLMAN-STANDARD PS2 CENTER DISCHARGE HOPPERS ea 9.98

932-5701 Union Pacific (gray)
932-5702 Burlington Northern (cascade green)
932-5703 Chicago & North Western (new yellow)
932-5704 Pillsbury (light gray)
932-5705 Cargill (mint green)
932-5706 Continental Grain (white)
932-5700 Undecorated

UNION PACIFIC

PILLSBURY

BURLINGTON NORTHERN

CARGIL

CHICAGO & NORTH WESTERN

CONTINENTAL GRAIN

WALHERS ™

Walthers HO Scale kits feature detailed styrene parts and are designed for easy construction with basic hobby tools. Each car is prepainted and lettered in an authentic scheme that includes end reporting marks. All kits are complete with instructions, weights, trucks with nonmagnetic brass axles and horn-hook couplers.

HOPPERS

Open top hoppers transport a wide variety of bulk materials including coal, sand, ore, gravel and even sugar beets which do not require protection from the weather.

Since hoppers are subject to rough loads and handling, they are some of the strongest cars built. Two body styles are common and both offer certain advantages. The offset side car has a smooth exterior and is a bit wider, increasing the carrying capacity. Ribbed side cars are better able to withstand the stress of rotary car dumps and their smooth interior allows for faster unloading.

Hoppers were among the earliest types of freight cars and many design changes have occurred over the years.

As new coal fields opened in the western US during the early 1960s, it was discovered that coal from this region had a lower density. Since the coal weighed less, more could be carried and many railroads and shippers began purchasing the new 100 ton quadruple bay (quad) hoppers. Today, cars of this type are the backbone of many railroads' hopper fleets. They can be seen throughout the country, usually in unit trains, bringing coal to power plants and other customers.

Serving all types of industries, your new hopper cars will be right at home with The Northern Light and Power Powerhouse (933-3021) the New River Mining Company (933-3017) or the O.L. King & Sons Coal Yard (933- 3015) which are illustrated in the Structures section.

49' 100T QUAD HOPPERS ea 9.98

As new clean air standards were mandated in the 1970s, coal-fired power plants around the country found themselves in need of clean-burning, low sulfur coal. The vast deposits in the western US met this criteria and demand skyrocketed. New rail lines were built to serve the coal field and orders for 100 ton cars poured in.   For the finishing touch, fill your hoppers with Magnuson Coal Loads (439-536) designed for use with these kits.

932-4901 Burlington Northern (black)
932-4902 Union Pacific (black)
932-4903 Rio Grande (black)
932-4904 Chicago & North Western (black)
932-4905 Family Lines/Louisville & Nashville (black)
932-4906 CSX Transportation (black)
932-4900 Undecorated (black)

49' 100T QUAD HOPPERS 6-PACKS 49.98 NEW

It's easy to add unit train service to your layout with these new six-packs!

These cars feature DIFFERENT numbers, in the same roadnames as the individual cars.

932-4931 Burlington Northern (black)
932-4932 Union Pacific (black)
932-4933 Rio Grande (black)
932-4934 Chicago & North Western (black)
932-4935 Family Lines/Louisville & Nashville (black)
932-4936 CSX Transportation (black)

36' 50 TON OFFSET SIDE TWIN HOPPER

36' 50 TON RIBBED SIDE TWIN HOPPER

49' 100 TON QUAD HOPPER

36' WOOD CHIP HOPPER

36' 50 TON HOPPER

Introduced in 1948, this car is very similar to earlier two-bay hoppers used by many railroads. And, cars of this style are still in Maintenance-of-Way service on many lines, hauling ballast.

36' 50 TON OFFSET SIDE TWIN HOPPER ea 6.98

932-2951 Baltimore & Ohio (black)
932-2952 Chesapeake & Ohio (black)
932-2957 Data Only (black)
932-2963 Pennsylvania (tuscan)
932-2950 Undecorated

36' 50 TON RIBBED SIDE TWIN HOPPER ea 6.98

932-3001 Reading (black)
932-3015 Union Pacific (box car red)
932-3019 Norfolk & Western
932-3000 Undecorated

36' WOOD CHIP HOPPER

With the introduction of larger hoppers in the late 1950s, many older two-bay cars were rebuilt for new jobs. Many cars, especially on eastern roads where hoppers were plentiful, were rebuilt for wood chip service.

Because wood chips are much lighter than coal or stone, a car can carry a greater amount without being overloaded. The sides are extended with steel panels, increasing the carrying capacity. Many industries receive rail shipments of the chips, which are used to make paper, building materials, chemicals or plastics and are sometimes used as fuel.

36' WOOD CHIP HOPPER ea 6.98

932-3051 Western Maryland (box car red)
932-3052 Louisville & Nashville (black)
932-3053 Baltimore & Ohio (black)
932-3054 Southern (box car red)
932-3062 Northern Pacific (black)
932-3050 Undecorated

WALTHERS™

FLAT CARS

Flat cars haul large, heavy loads such as machinery, vehicles and building materials that are difficult to load in box cars. With no loading restrictions, flat cars are ideal for oversize loads. When loads are longer than the assigned car, flats are coupled at each end to act as idlers. Special cars with depressed center sections are used to carry tall items, such as transformers.

To extend the life of older flats many are fitted with special equipment such as bulkhead ends, which prevent end to end shifting of loads. Lumber and other building products are usually carried on these cars.

The first auto racks appeared in the 1960s, as conversions for piggyback flats. Although successful, vehicles were exposed to weather and were easy targets for vandals. To combat this, metal panels were installed between the braces, a roof was added and doors installed at each end. Today, these enclosed cars are in service all over the country, delivering new autos and trucks to regional distribution centers.

Be sure to check the selection of loads at the ends of the Freight Car section, or ideas on detailing your new cars.

42' FLAT CAR WITH STAKES ea 6.98

This all-purpose flat is perfect for the steam- or early diesel-era and includes a set of side stakes.

932-2601 Southern Pacific (box car red)
932-2603 Great Northern (tuscan)
932-2605 Santa Fe (box car red)
932-2607 Union Pacific (yellow)
932-2600 Undecorated

42' BULKHEAD FLAT CARS ea 6.98

A great way to move lumber or other building materials, these kits feature prepainted bulkheads to match the basic car body.

932-2901 Boston & Maine (black)
932-2902 Maine Central (yellow)
932-2905 Kansas City Southern (black)
932-2909 Southern Pacific (box car red)
932-2900 Undecorated

ENCLOSED AUTO CARRIER

Walthers Enclosed Auto Carrier produces a great looking model with a minimum of effort. The one-piece body (The flat car portion of the model, end doors and superstructure are molded as a single unit, similar to a box car kit.) comes prepainted and lettered in the correct colors. Separate side panel sections are prepainted and lettered to match the prototypes, along with a separate roof that's painted aluminum. The cars are the proper 89' length and include a special swinging (radial) coupler mounting to improve operation on curves. (Minimum track radius 22", however, we recommend 24" or larger for best performance.)

89' ENCLOSED AUTO CARRIERS ea 14.98

932-4801 Rio Grande (orange, yellow)
932-4802 Canadian Pacific (tuscan red, yellow)
932-4803 Conrail (tuscan red, yellow)
932-4804 Grand Trunk Western (blue with blue panels)
932-4805 Missouri-Kansas-Texas (green, yellow)
932-4806 Chicago & North Western (yellow)
932-4807 Southern Pacific (tuscan red)
932-4808 Union Pacific (armor yellow)
932-4809 CSX Transportation (yellow, new TTX color)
932-4810 Burlington Northern (cascade green)
932-4811 Milwaukee Road (yellow)
932-4812 Santa Fe "Q for Quality" (brown)
932-4800 Undecorated

AUTO CARRIER ACCESSORIES ea 8.98

Complement your new auto carrier service with these easy-to-build kits:

933-3107 Automotive Billboards

This set includes 12 full-color signs for a variety of cars, and three billboard structures.

933-3108 Auto Unloading Ramp

This model simulates the adjustable loading and unloading ramps used at auto plants and distribution centers.

DEPRESSED CENTER, FOUR-TRUCK FLAT CAR ea 12.98
NEW
Expected Delivery - Early 1994:

Railroads are called upon to move all kinds of loads, many of which are big and heavy. When presented with this type of lading, a depressed center flat car is often used. As the name implies, the center is lower than the ends, to provide additional clearance for the load when moving under bridges or other obstructions. To spread the weight, and increase the carrying capacity of the car, additional trucks may be used, such as the four-truck design which serves as the prototype for this kit. It's similar to cars used by many roads, and has been carefully engineered so it can operate on almost any size layout.

932-5631 TTX
932-5632 Burlington Northern
932-5633 Department of Defense
932-5634 Union Pacific
932-5635 Southern Pacific
932-5636 General Electric Company
932-5637 Chicago & North Western
932-5638 Norfolk & Western
932-5639 Conrail
932-5630 Undecorated

89' ENCLOSED AUTO CARRIER

42' BULKHEAD FLAT CAR

AUTOMOTIVE BILLBOARDS

AUTO UNLOADING RAMP

WALTHERS™

Walthers HO Scale kits feature detailed styrene parts and are designed for easy construction with basic hobby tools. Each car is prepainted and lettered in an authentic scheme that includes end reporting marks. All kits are complete with instructions, weights, trucks with nonmagnetic brass axles and horn-hook couplers.

40' WOOD REEFERS

1910-1925 ERA 40' WOOD REEFERS WITH WOOD ENDS ea 9.98

1910-1925 ERA 40' WOOD REEFERS WITH DREADNAUGHT ENDS ea 9.98

1910-1925 ERA 40' WOOD BODIED REEFERS WITH WOOD ENDS ea 9.98

With their bright paint and "billboard" lettering, these early reefers were some of the most colorful in service. Walthers models are noted for their crisp, authentic lettering and fine details.

932-2414 Schlitz (mustard)
932-2428 Swift (red)
932-2464 Pabst Blue Ribbon (yellow)
932-2467 Coors (white)
932-2471 Blatz/Old Heidelberg (yellow)
932-2472 Carling Breweries (black)
932-2473 Puritan Malt (yellow)
932-2474 Genesee (white, brown)
932-2476 P Ballantine & Sons (yellow)
932-2477 Worthington Creamery & Produce (yellow)
932-2478 Wescott & Winks Dairy Dispatch (yellow)

932-2479 Carnation (white)
932-2480 Van Camps Milk (white)
932-2481 Nestle's (white)
932-2482 Borden's Eagle Brand Milk (yellow)
932-2483 Superior Buttermilk (yellow)
932-2484 Brook Hill Farm Dairy (white)
932-2400 Undecorated

1925-1950 ERA 40' WOOD BODIED REEFERS WITH DREADNAUGHT ENDS ea 9.98

In late years, wooden cars were upgraded with more durable dreadnaught steel end. These were less likely to be damaged if the load shifted.

932-2356 Jerpe Dairy (white)
932-2357 Cotton County Poultry & Egg Company (white)
932-2358 Peter Fox Sons Company Deluxe Brand Poultry (white)
932-2359 National Produce Co. (white)
932-2300 Undecorated

40' ALL-STEEL REEFER

40' ALL-STEEL REEFERS ea 9.98

In the early 1940s, new insulation materials were developed that could economically keep an all-steel car cool. Reefers with steel sides were more durable and required fewer repairs than wood sheathed cars, some lasted in service into the early 1970's.

932-2501 Southern Pacific/Union Pacific (yellow)
932-2505 Railway Express Agency (dark green)
932-2512 Pacific Fruit Express (silver)
932-2541 Bangor & Aroostook "State of Maine" (red, white, blue)
932-2500 Undecorated

WALTHERS™

Meet the Arcticar™, the refrigerated rail car of the future. First built in 1992, these cars use carbon dioxide vapor and "snow" to keep their loads frozen in transit. Designed to meet the needs of high-volume purchasers and producers of frozen foods, this big car measuers 76' over the couplers and stands nearly 17' tall. They're now hard at work hauling frozen juice, meat, potatoes, poultry and more. Like the classic reefers of the steam era, they're finished in bold colorful schemes!

FRUIT GROWERS EXPRESS STYLE RBL INSULATED BOX CAR

FRUIT GROWERS EXPRESS RBL INSULATED BOX CARS ea 9.98

Palletized shipments of perishables led to the introduction of this class in the early 1960s. The interior is fitted with restraints, which hold the loads securely and protect them against damage caused by slack action. To speed loading times, 10'6" plug doors are used, providing easier access for forklifts. These cars also carry electronic items, furniture, paper and machinery.

932-4751 Fruit Growers Express/Seaboard Coast Line "Solid Gold" (yellow)
932-4752 Chessie System/Western Maryland (yellow)
932-4753 Union Pacific (yellow)
932-4754 Rio Grande (orange)
932-4755 Conrail (yellow)
932-4756 Burlington Northern (cascade green)
932-4750 Undecorated

40' PLUG DOOR REEFERS

40' PLUG DOOR REEFER ea 9.98

By the late 1950s, ice-cooled, steel reefers were being rebuilt with plug doors. Larger than conventional doors, they made loading and unloading much easier.

932-3301 Pacific Fruit Express (Union Pacific/Southern Pacific Heralds) (orange)
932-3305 Rio Grande (orange, silver)
932-3300 Undecorated

ARCTICAR™ REFRIGERATED BOX CARS

CRYO-TRANS

MCCAIN

UNIVERSAL FOODS

ARCTICAR™ REFRIGERATED BOX CARS ea 11.98 NEW

932-5451 Arcticar™/GATX Demonstrator (white)
932-5452 Simplot (white)
932-5453 McCain (white)

932-5454 Carnation (white)
932-5455 Cryo-Trans (white)

932-5456 Universal Frozen Foods (white)
932-5450 Undecorated

WALTHERS ™

Walthers HO Scale kits feature detailed styrene parts and are designed for easy construction with basic hobby tools. Each car is prepainted and lettered in an authentic scheme that includes end reporting marks. All kits are complete with instructions, weights, trucks with nonmagnetic brass axles and horn-hook couplers.

MAINTENENCE OF WAY EQUIPMENT

WORK TRAIN SET #1

Keep your railroad running smoothly with these Maintenance-of-Way cars. Each six-car set includes a 42' bunk car, 42' kitchen car, 42' tool and engineering car, 30' blacksmith car, 40' storage box car, and a 42' work flat car.

**WORK TRAIN SET #1
ea 44.98**

932-84 Maintenance-of-Way (gray)

932-85 Southern Pacific (box car red)

932-86 Rio Grande (gray)

932-87 Santa Fe (silver)

932-88 Pennsylvania (yellow)

932-90 Union Pacific (silver)

40' Storage Box Car

42' Bunk Car

42' Kitchen Car

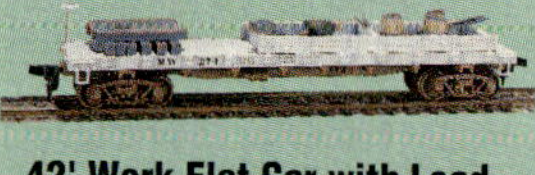

42' Tool & Engineering Car

42' Work Flat Car with Load

30' Blacksmith Car

ADDITIONAL WORK CARS (Undecorated) ea 7.98 (unless noted)

932-3100 40' Storage Box Car

932-5520 42' Bunk Car (gray)

932-5530 42' Kitchen Car (tan)

932-5540 42' Tool & Engineering Car (tan)

932-5560 42' Work Flat Car with Load (brown)

932-5580 30' Blacksmith Car (black) 8.98

MOW GONDOLA

932-5620 40' Steel Gondola MOW with Load 7.98

This specially painted 40' gondola, includes a one-piece Magnuson scrap load and makes a terrific detail for yard or engine terminal scenes.

932-5620 40' Steel Gondola MOW with Load 7.98

CRANES

25 TON CRANE ea 8.98

Used by railroads, these versatile cranes are also operated by all types of private industries.

932-5610 Vulcan Steel

932-5611 Brownhoist (black)

932-5612 Electric Company

932-5613 Knapp Railroad Construction (yellow)

932-5614 Purdy Salvage (red, black)

932-5615 Saginaw Dock

932-5500 Undecorated

WALTHERS™

WORK TRAIN SET #2

Expand your Maintenance fleet with this set of six cars built specifically for work train service. Prepainted and lettered to match Work Train Set #1, each set comes with a 25 ton crane, 42' crane tender, 42' work flat car, Hart gondola, 42' rail and tie car and a 42' work caboose.

WORK TRAIN SET #2 ea 44.98

932-92 Maintenance-of-Way (gray)
932-93 Southern Pacific (box car red)
932-94 Rio Grande (gray)
932-95 Santa Fe (silver)
932-96 Pennsylvania (yellow)
932-98 Union Pacific (silver)

42' Crane Tender

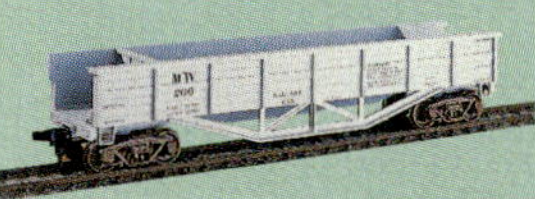

Hart Gondola

42' Work Flat Car with Load

42' Rail and Tie Car

42' Transfer/Work Caboose

ADDITIONAL WORK CARS (Undecorated) ea 7.98

932-5510 42' Crane Tender
932-5550 Hart Gondola
932-5560 42' Work Flat Car with Load
932-5600 42' Rail and Tie Car
932-5800 42' Transfer/Work Caboose

SCALE TEST CAR

prototype photograph

SCALE TEST CARS ea 7.98 *NEW*

Expected Delivery - Spring 1994

Railroads bill for their services based on the weight of the commodity shipped. This means they and their customers must have accurate scales to determine the weight of loaded and empty cars. Periodic inspections are done using a scale test car. Measuring just 13' long, these tiny cars have a verified weight anywhere from 20 to 50 tons to activate the scales. Because of their small size, they are moved at slow speed and coupled at the rear of the train. Some roads now ship them aboard flat cars to move them faster.

A must for steam- or diesel-era layouts, these all-new, plastic cars feature easy construction and include a weight so they can be moved in trains like the prototypes. The cars are prepainted in several schemes and include add-on details.

932-5651 Pennsylvania
932-5652 Milwaukee Road
932-5653 Conrail
932-5654 Chicago & North Western
932-5655 Union Pacific
932-5656 Santa Fe
932-5657 Burlington Northern
932-5658 Southern Pacific
932-5659 New York Central
932-5660 Rio Grande
932-5661 New Haven
932-5650 Undecorated

INFORMATION STATION

Keeping structures, bridges and track in good repair is the responsibility of the Maintenance-of-Way (MOW) department. These jobs require a variety of specialized equipment, much of which is rebuilt from "retired" freight cars.

To keep costs down, virtually any kind of car is used. As a result, you may still see old wood freight cars or 40' box cars on modern railroads.

Since these cars often no longer meet certain safety requirements, they can not be interchanged with another railroad. To identify their new role, they are repainted in a special color scheme and lettered as MOW equipment.

With 13 different cars to choose, from Walthers has MOW equipment that will be right at home on your railroad, no matter what era you model!

WALTHERS™

Walthers HO Scale kits feature detailed styrene parts and are designed for easy construction with basic hobby tools. Each car is prepainted and lettered in an authentic scheme that includes end reporting marks. All kits are complete with instructions, weights, trucks with nonmagnetic brass axles and horn-hook couplers.

GONDOLAS

Perhaps the most versatile freight car, gondolas carry a wide range of heavy and unusual loads. They come in all sizes from 40' up to huge 65' mill gondolas that carry large steel products. There are also low side gons for easier loading and high side gondolas used for pulpwood, ore service and stone. Many can be equipped with special equipment and used for hauling other types of loads such as steel coils.

All-steel construction has long been standard for gondolas, because of the rough service and constant exposure to the elements. As a result, these cars survive many years of revenue service despite their beat-up appearance..

55' CUSHION COIL CAR

Among the unusual loads moved by railroads are large steel coils used to make automobile bodies, appliances and other products. Because of their size (6 to 10' in diameter) and weight, coils are more easily shipped by rail than by truck.

Classified as both gondolas and flat cars, coil cars feature a "V" shaped cradle in place of the usual floor. Adjustable retainers hold the coils in place and a cushion underframe helps prevent end-to-end load shifting. Removable hoods protect the coils from the weather.

55' CUSHION COIL CARS
ea 9.98

932-3854 Detroit, Toledo & Ironton (black, yellow)
932-3857 Chicago & North Western (green, yellow)
932-3858 Elgin, Joliet & Eastern (orange, black)
932-3860 Erie Lackawanna (black)
932-3861 Union Pacific
932-3864 Milwaukee Road (black, yellow)
932-3865 Illinois Central Gulf (red, black)
932-3866 Reading (green)
932-3867 Grand Trunk Western (blue)
932-3868 Southern Pacific (brown)
932-3869 New York Central (green)

932-3870 CSX Transportation (yellow, black)
932-3871 Iowa Interstate (black)
932-3872 Missouri Pacific (brown)
932-3873 Norfolk Southern (black)
932-3874 Bessemer & Lake Erie (orange, gray)
932-3875 Penn Central (green)
932-3850 Undecorated

Limited Quantities Available

932-3852 Norfolk & Western
932-3859 Conrail (brown)
932-3862 Baltimore & Ohio

Walthers Cushion Coil Cars are packed with detail from top to bottom! The underframe includes a simulated cushioning device, wire brake line, plus separate brake cylinder, reservoir and triple valve details.

40' ALL-STEEL GONDOLA
The most common style of gondola is the fixed end, solid bottom car with low sides, which is the prototype for this series of Walthers kits. These cars are easy to load and are preferred for shipping smaller steel shapes, scrap metal, pipes, poles and other heavy materials.

40' ALL-STEEL GONDOLAS
ea 6.98 (unless noted)
932-3804 Rio Grande (black)
932-3806 Pennsylvania (tuscan)
932-3800 Undecorated

Limited Quantities Available

932-3808 Elgin, Joliet & Eastern (black) 6.98

CSX

PENN CENTRAL

**CHICAGO AND
NORTH WESTERN**

MISSOURI PACIFIC

ELGIN, JOLIET & EASTERN

**BESSEMER AND
LAKE ERIE**

IOWA INTERSTATE

COIL CAR HOODS

Add variety to steel service cars or detail your mill scene with these Round and Corrugated Coil Car Hoods. Matching the styles commonly seen on prototype equipment, these parts are designed for use with Walthers Coil Cars (3850 series) or MDC Gondolas (1680 series).

Basic kits include a pair of unpainted hoods. For big projects, sets of six hoods are available. All kits include add-on stacking braces and instructions.

ROUND

661-1012	Set of 2	3.79
661-1016	Set of 6	9.95

CORRUGATED

661-2012	Set of 2	4.25
661-2016	Set of 6	11.95

COIL CAR ACCESSORIES

**933-1499 Steel Coil Loads
pkg (12 coils) 4.98**
Load your Walthers or other steel service cars with this kit! Injection molded parts capture the look of the huge coils but are easy to build. Parts for 12 coils in two sizes are included.

**COIL CAR HOODS
pkg (7) 6.98**
Once unloaded, coil cars seldom get their original hoods back. This results in some colorful combinations, which you can model with this set of seven assorted kits, They're identical to those found in various Walthers Coil Car kits, and are complete with stacking braces.

WALTHERS™

Walthers HO Scale kits feature detailed styrene parts and are designed for easy construction with basic hobby tools. Each car is prepainted and lettered in an authentic scheme that includes end reporting marks. All kits are complete with instructions, weights, trucks with nonmagnetic brass axles and horn-hook couplers.

FUNNEL-FLOW® TANK CAR

Developed in the 1960's by Union Tank Car, the Funnel-Flow® carries all types of liquids and slurries which can be unloaded by gravity. The funnel-shaped tank is slightly lower in the middle than at the ends, on both the top and bottom. The slope forces the contents towards the bottom of the car for faster unloading and more of the load is removed.

Available in several lengths, these cars are found at all types of industries, and are often fitted with heater coils so the contents can be reheated for faster unloading. The kits feature the distinctive funnel-shaped body, with a variety of safety valves, manways and other add-on details to match prototype cars.

30' FUNNEL-FLOW® TANK CARS ea 9.98

932-5101 UTLX Union Tank Car Line (black)
932-5102 GATX General American Transportation Company (black)
932-5103 DOW Dow Chemical (white)
932-5104 AESX Staley Chemical (white)
932-5105 ECUX Exxon Chemical Americas
932-5100 Undecorated

40' FUNNEL-FLOW® TANK CARS ea 9.98

932-5151 UTLX Union Tank Car Line (black)
932-5152 Georgia Kaolin Company (gray)
932-5153 Tru-Sweet Corn Syrup (black)
932-5154 ADM Corn Sweeteners (black)
932-5155 Amaizo Corn Syrup (black)
932-5156 Ontario Carbonate
932-5157 GATX General American Transportation Company (black)
932-5158 Anglo-American Clays (white)
932-5159 JM Huber (white)
932-5160 Corn Products (mustard)
932-5161 Cargill Corn Syrup (black)
932-5163 Nord Kaolin (white)
932-5150 Undecorated
("Funnel-Flow" is a registered trademark of Union Tank Car.)

65' TANK CARS

65' PROPANE TANK CAR
ea 10.98

Some of the biggest tankers are the 65' cars that carry compressed gases such as propane and anhydrous ammonia. These cars can be found at oil refineries (propane is obtained from crude oil, refinery gases and natural gas), regional propane distributors or any large industry that requires bulk shipments of propane. Anhydrous ammonia is used as fertilizer and is distributed at Farmer's co-ops.

Put your new propane tank cars to work serving the Central Gas & Supply Company or the ADM Grain Elevator, which you'll find in the Structures section. 932-5251 UTLX Union Tank Car Line (black)932-5252 PROX Procor Limited (black)

932-5253 TXPX Texas Petrochemicals Corporation (blue)
932-5254 CITX PLM Railcar Management Services Canada Limited (black)
932-5255 NATX Aeron CPC (white)
932-5256 GATX General American Transportation Company (black)
932-5250 Undecorated

65' ANHYDROUS AMMONIA TANK CAR ea 10.98

932-5257 UTLX Union Tank Car Line (black)
932-5258 GATX General American Transportation Company (white)
932-5259 RTMX Terra Chemicals (dark green)
932-5260 PLMX PLM International (black)
932-5261 BADX Baden Investment Company (white)
932-5262 CHVX Chevron USA Incorporated (black)

WALTHERS™

54' FUNNEL-FLOW® TANK CAR

10,000 GALLON TANK CAR

54' FUNNEL-FLOW® TANK CARS ea 9.98

Responding to requests from petroleum producers for a larger capacity car, a 54' Funnel-Flow® design was unveiled in 1967. These new cars incorporated the sloped body for easier unloading and had a capacity of 23,000 gallons.

Cars of this type are still very popular with petroleum shippers and the design is also used in general service to transport hundreds of different liquids. As a result, these cars can be found at both producing and receiving industries.

If you're planning to use these cars in petroleum service, be sure to see the Cornerstone Series® North Island Refinery, Interstate Fuel & Oil and other accessories in the Structures section.

932-5201 UTLX Union Tank Car Line (black)
932-5202 NATX Celotex (black)
932-5203 Procor (white)
932-5204 CGTX Incorporated (white)
932-5205 TGOX US Rail Services Inc. (tan)
932-5206 RAIX Rail America Ltd. (blue)
932-5207 Clark (black)
932-5208 Sunoco (black)
932-5209 Exxon (black)
932-5210 Citgo (black)
932-5211 Conoco (black)
932-5212 UTLX "Excellent Quality" (blue)
932-5200 Undecorated
("Funnel-Flow" is a registered trademark of Union Tank Car.)

INFORMATION STATION

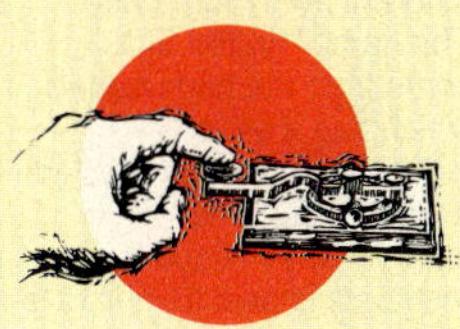

One of the first railroad "tank cars" appeared in 1865. Consisting of two large wooden tanks mounted on a flat car, it was used to carry oil. Horizontal tanks appeared on flat cars by 1868, and a steel tank was introduced in the 1870's. By 1890, all-steel tank cars were in service.

Standardized designs appeared in the early 1900's and remained in use for many years. Although petroleum continued to be the primary commodity shipped in tank cars, within a few decades, the food and chemical industries were also major customers.

The move to larger freight cars during the 1950's and 60's also occurred as new types of industrial materials and chemicals were coming into use. New tank cars appeared that could carry larger loads. Many were built with special linings and loading/unloading equipment, creating a customized car to best suit the needs of the shipper.

During the 1970's, the increasing numbers of hazardous materials being shipped by train led to new safety regulations and further changes in tank car design.

Walthers offers an assortment of tank cars which are prepainted and lettered in authentic schemes, making them ideal for layouts set in the steam-to-diesel-era, the 1960's and the present day.

10,000 GALLON STEAM/DIESEL TANK CARS ea 9.98

This model is typical of uninsulated, nonpressurized cars with a capacity of 10,000 gallons, as built in the 1930's for general service. These cars were used well into the 1960's, carrying fuel oils, vegetable oils and various chemical products. Some roads still use them in maintenance service.

932-5001 UTLX Union Tank Car Line (black)
932-5002 Conoco (aluminum)
932-5003 Phillips (black)
932-5004 Sinclair (black)
932-5005 Shell (black)
932-5006 Southern Pacific (black)
932-5007 GATX General American Transportation Company (black)
932-5008 Humble Oil (aluminum)
932-5009 Texaco (aluminum)
932-5010 Dow Chemical (aluminum)
932-5011 Gulf Oil (black)

932-5012 Arogas (aluminum)
932-5013 Santa Fe (black) *NEW*
932-5014 SHPX Shippers Car Line (black) *NEW*
932-5015 Union 76 (powder blue) *NEW*
932-5016 Standard Oil (aluminum) *NEW*
932-5017 Deep Rock (black) *NEW*
932-5018 Cities Service (green) *NEW*
932-5099 Interstate Fuel & Oil (aluminum) *NEW*
932-5000 Undecorated

WALTHERS ™

Walthers HO Scale kits feature detailed styrene parts and are designed for easy construction with basic hobby tools. Each car is prepainted and lettered in an authentic scheme that includes end reporting marks. All kits are complete with instructions, weights, trucks with nonmagentic brass axles and horn-hook couplers.

50' WAFFLE BOX CAR

40' PSI BOX CAR

40' STOCK CAR W/SLATTED
Roadname Shown Not Available

BOX CARS

To protect cargo from the weather, an ingenious mechanic erected a small structure on a flat car. Looking large a large box, the design became known as a box car, although on some lines they were called house cars, since the structure resembled a small dwelling.

Railroads built hundreds of thousands of these cars over the years. Their simple design and ability to haul virtually any kind of load without modifications made them the most commonly used type of freight car

Steel parts were first used for bracing during the 1920's and within a few years all-steel cars were being built. Steel cars were stronger and less likely to be damaged than wooden equipment. Although more expensive to construct, the longer service life and lower maintenance costs quickly proved the steel cars superior.

As covered hoppers began taking over much of the bulk traffic (grain, flour, sugar etc.) in the 1960's, the number of box cars in service began to drop. Box cars slowly became more specialized and were fitted with load restraints, underframe cushioning and other equipment to better meet the needs of shippers. Today, they are still an important part of any modern freight car fleet.

50' WAFFLE BOX 3 PACKS
ea 19.98 *NEW*
Add more cars from your favorite line to your collection with these three-packs. Each includes a prepainted and lettered car from the same line, but with a different number.

932-94701 Baltimore & Ohio (box car red)
932-94702 Chessie System/Chesapeake & Ohio (royal blue)
932-94703 Chicago & North Western (box car red)
932-94704 Seaboard System (black)
932-94705 Maine Central (yellow)
932-94706 Rock Island (box car red)
932-94707 Family Lines/Louisville & Nashville (box car red)
932-94708 Illinois Terminal (yellow)
932-94709 Rio Grande (orange)
932-94710 Chattahoochee Industrial Railroad (gray)
932-94711 Green Bay & Western (yellow)
932-94712 Southern Railway

50' WAFFLE SIDE BOX CAR
In 1965, a new 50' box car appeared that was radically different from other cars. The name "Waffle Side" came from the body panels, which had a series of indentations that resembled a waffle iron. The indentations housed load restraints known as belt rails, which created a smooth interior so that the car could be used for almost any commodity. These cars also had an increased carrying capacity and larger door openings, which allowed easy access by fork lifts and other equipment for faster loading and unloading.

50' WAFFLE-SIDE BOX CARS
ea 9.98
932-4701 Baltimore & Ohio (box car red)
932-4702 Chessie Syctom/Chocapoako & Ohio (royal blue)
932-4703 Chicago & North Western (box car red)
932-4704 Seaboard System (black)
932-4705 Maine Central (yellow)
932-4706 Rock Island (box car red)
932-4707 Family Lines/Louisville & Nashville (box car red)
932-4708 Illinois Terminal (yellow)
932-4709 Rio Grande (orange)
932-4710 Chattahoochee Industrial Railroad (gray)
932-4711 Green Bay & Western (yellow)
932-4712 Southern Railway (box car red)
932-4700 Undecorate(box car red)

PS-1 40' BOX CAR
Introduced in 1947, the PS-1 was one of the first freight cars to be built "assembly line" fashion and body panels were welded rather than riveted. The distinctive ends and side panels gave the cars a unique appearance. Over 100,000 cars saw service on 78 railroads. As a testimony to their popularity, the PS-1 remained in production until 1963.

Walthers PS-1 kits include three styles of working doors (Pullman Standard, Youngstown and Superior), a correct scale underframe and Bettendorf trucks.

40' PS-1 BOX CARS **ea 9.98**
932-3701 New York Central (box car red)
932-3703 Nickel Plate Road (oxide red)
932-3705 Santa Fe (box car red)
932-3706 Union Pacific (oxide red)
932-3716 New York Central "Pacemaker" (red, gray)
932-3700 Undecorated

WALTHERS™

40' STOCK CAR

Similar in design and construction to a box car, the stock car was used from the

from the mid 1800s until the late 1950s to transport livestock from ranch to market. The cars are easily identified by the open, slatted sides which provide ventilation for the animals in shipment.

Shippers usually sent their own men to care for the stock while in transit and these "drovers" rode in the caboose with the train crew. Since large shipments often required 10 or more men, this led to the development of the Drover's Caboose to accommodate these additional passengers.

40' STOCK CAR WITH SLATTED OPEN ENDS

932-3350 Undecorated 6.98
Create custom equipment for your favorite railroad, using this kit and Walthers decals. See your dealer for more information.

X-29 40' STEEL BOX CAR ea 6.98

932-2051 Pennsylvania (tuscan)
932-2053 Central of New Jersey (dark green)
932-2050 Undecorated

40' SINGLE SHEATHED BOX CAR

Single sheathed cars were the first tom make use of steel bracing, but retained a wooden wall. During World War II, the design was revived to conserve steel and thousands were built, some as late as 1945. It was not uncommon to see them in revenue service through the 1960s.

Roadname Shown
Not Available

X-29 40' STEEL BOX CAR

40' OUTSIDE BRACED SINGLE SHEATHED BOX CAR WITH BRACED ENDS

932-2650 Undecorated 6.98
Create custom equipment for your favorite railroad, using this kit and Walthers decals. See your dealer for more information.

40' STEEL BOX CAR

One of the first all-steel cars to gain widespread popularity was the X-29, built by the Pennsylvania Railroad. With minor changes, this became the basis for the American Railroad Association (ARA) steel box car. This marked the first time that a car design was copied by several railroads. The lessons learned in the X-29 laid the foundation for all subsequent box car design and construction.

WALTHERS™

Walthers HO Scale kits feature detailed styrene parts and are designed for easy construction with basic hobby tools. Each car is prepainted and lettered in an authentic scheme that includes end reporting marks. All kits are complete with instructions, weights, trucks with nonmagnetic brass axles and horn-hook couplers.

FREIGHT CAR MULTI-PACKS

Limited Run Sets
Add colorful cars to your collection or operations with these limited run sets from Walthers. Each includes easy-to-build Walthers freight car kits, which have been custom painted by Walthers in unique roadnames. Each car in the multi-pack has its own number and single cars (sorry, no choice of car number) are also available for many roadnames.

932-9106 ADM PS-2 COVERED HOPPER
ea 29.98 *NEW*
Includes large ADM logos, printed on plastic side panels.

CORN SYRUP TANK CAR SET
932-9094 Three-pack with different numbers 29.98
Includes cars from Clinton Corn Products, Union Starch and A.E. Staley.

CSX TRANSPORTATION 50' WAFFLE BOX CARS
932-9102 Three-pack with different numbers 29.98 *NEW*
Includes two CSX and one CSXT (SBD) car in blue.

A.E. STALEY TANK CARS
932-9104 40' FUNNEL-FLOW TANK CARS NEW 29.98
Includes 30, 40 and 54' cars.

WALTHERS™

CHICAGO & NORTH WESTERN 24' ORE CARS (Roundhouse kit)

932-9053 Individual car (dark green) 9.98

Limited Quantities Available
932-9052 Four-pack with different numbers (dark green) 29.98 (Roundhouse kit)

CHICAGO & NORTH WESTERN 40' PS-1 BOX CARS

932-9108 Three-pack with different numbers 29.98 **NEW**

Includes two C&NW and one Omaha car with "400" slogans.

932-9118 ADM 54' FUNNEL-FLOW® TANK CARS pkg(3) 29.98 NEW

Expected Delivery - Early 1994
The prototypes of these cars are used to haul ethanol.

NEBRASKA CO-OP 54' COVERED HOPPERS

932-9060 Three-pack with different numbers 29.98

UTLX 40' TANK CAR

932-9096 Three-pack with different numbers 29.98

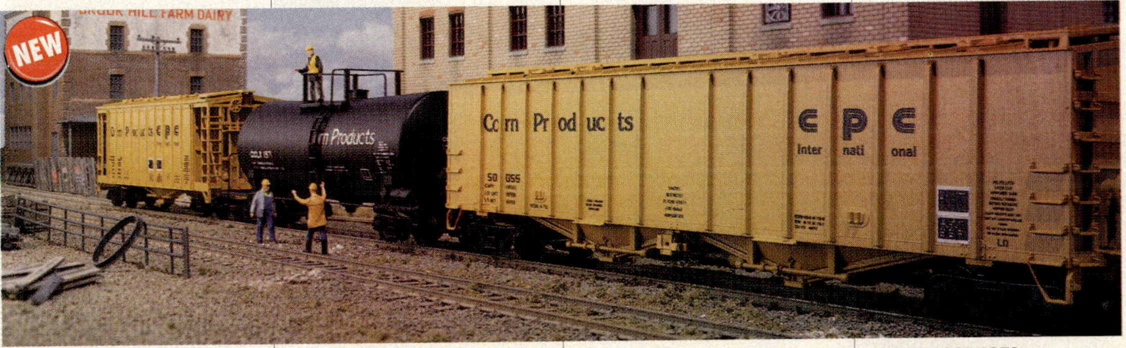

CORN PRODUCTS

932-9100 Includes 40' Tank Car, 39' Single Bay Airslide and 50' Airslide Covered Hopper 29.98 **NEW**

932-9110 40' REEFERS - COLD STORAGE NAMES   (3 pack) ea 29.98 NEW
Includes three different cars, in colorful schemes.

932-9112 RIB TWIN HOPPER, NORTHERN LIGHT & POWER ea 19.98 NEW

Includes three cars painted in green with different numbers, ideal for serving the new Northern Light & Power Powerhouse.

932-9114 ILLINOIS CENTRAL - ILLINOIS CENTRAL GULF 50' WAFFLE BOX (3 schemes) ea 29.98 NEW
Expected Delivery - Late 1993

932-9116 GOLDEN WEST SERVICE 50' AIRSLIDE® COVERED HOPPER pkg(3) 29.98 NEW
Expected Delivery - Late 1993

Latest style with blue body and multi-color lettering.

932-9120 65' LPG TANK CARS pkg(3) 29.98 NEW
Expected Delivery - Early 1994

Three new roadnames, perfect for use with the North Island Refinery, or Central Gas & Supply kits.

932-9122 NORFOLK SOUTHERN 50' WAFFLE BOX CARS pkg(3) 29.98 NEW

Expected Delivery - Spring 1994

932-9124 DELAWARE & HUDSON 40' PS-1 BOX CARS pkg(3) 29.98 NEW

Expected Delivery - Spring 1994

CORN PRODUCTS CORPORATION 54' COVERED HOPPERS

932-9056 Three-pack with different numbers 29.98
932-9057 Individual car 9.98

WISCONSIN CENTRAL 35' CEMENT COVERED HOPPERS

932-9065 Individual cars 10.98

Limited Quantities Available
932-9064 Three-pack with different numbers 32.98

CHICAGO & NORTH WESTERN 50' AIRSLIDE® COVERED HOPPERS

932-9098 Three-pack with different numbers 29.98
Includes cars painted gray, dark green and Zito yellow.

WALTHERS ™

Walthers HO Scale kits feature detailed styrene parts and are designed for easy construction with basic hobby tools. Each car is prepainted and lettered in an authentic scheme that includes end reporting marks. All kits are complete with instructions, weights, trucks with nonmagnetic brass axles and horn-hook couplers.

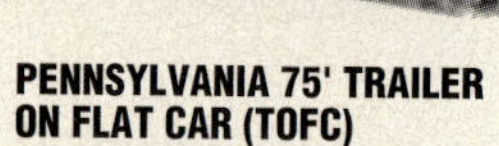

CANADIAN PACIFIC 55' CUSHION COIL CAR
932-9086 Three-pack with different numbers 29.98
932-9087 Individual car 9.98

FREIGHT CAR MULTI-PACKS

Limited Run Sets

Add colorful cars to your collection or operations with these limited run sets from Walthers. Each includes easy-to-build Walthers freight car kits, which have been custom painted by Walthers in unique roadnames. Each car in the multi-pack has its own number and single cars (sorry, no choice of car number) are also available for many roadnames.

PENNSYLVANIA 75' TRAILER ON FLAT CAR (TOFC)
932-9078 Three-pack with different numbers 29.98

40' CANNERY REEFERS

Limited Quantities Available
932-9092 Three-pack with different numbers 29.98
Includes cars in three

BRACH'S 39' AIRSLIDE® COVERED HOPPERS
932-9068 Three-pack with different numbers 29.98

WALTHERS™

SEABOARD COAST LINE 50' WAFFLE BOX
932-9090 Three-pack with different numbers 29.98
NEW

GULF 35' TANK CAR
932-9070 Three-pack with different numbers 29.98

PEABODY 36' TWIN HOPPER
932-9082 Three-pack with different numbers 29.98
932-9083 Individual car 9.98

A. E. STALEY 50' AIRSLIDE® COVERED HOPPERS
932-9072 Three-pack with different numbers 29.98
932-9073 Individual car 9.98

These easy-to-build HO scale kits are prepainted and lettered, molded in styrene, and weighted. They can be assembled with a screwdriver, and come complete with horn-hook couplers and Delrin trucks.

We have worked closely with the manufacturer to provide accurate availability information at the time this catalog was published. Items listed in blue ink may not be available at all times. Please see your dealer for current delivery information.

BOX CARS

40' STEAM ERA ea 4.00

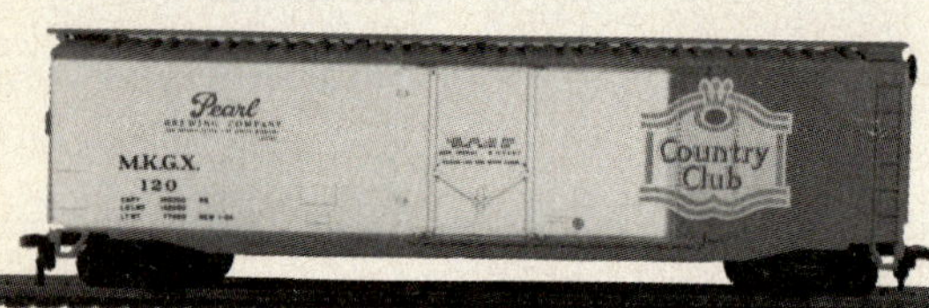

50' PLUG DOOR ea 4.25

40' STEAM ERA ea 4.00
140-5001 Atlantic Coast Line (box car red)
140-5002 Chicago, Burlington & Quincy (box car red)
140-5003 Chicago & North Western (box car red)
140-5004 Seaboard Air Line (box car red)
140-5005 Canadian Pacific (box car red)
140-5006 Gulf Mobile & Ohio (box car red)
140-5007 Great Northern (box car red)
140-5008 Delaware, Lackawanna & Western (box car red)
140-5009 New Haven (box car red)
140-5010 Northern Pacific (box car red)
140-5011 Southern Pacific (box car red)
140-5012 Union Pacific (box car red)
140-5013 Santa Fe El Capitain (box car red)
140-5014 Santa Fe Grand

Canyon (box car red)
140-5015 Santa Fe Scout (box car red)
140-5016 Santa Fe Chief (box car red)
140-5017 Santa Fe Super Chief (box car red)
140-5018 Sante Fe San Francisco Chief (box car red)

50' PLUG DOOR ea 4.25
140-1323 Western Pacific (tuscan red)
140-1326 Rock Island (tuscan red)
140-1330 Milwaukee Road (orange, black)
140-1332 Pearl Brewery
140-1335 Soo Line
140-1361 Green Bay & Western (yellow)
140-1329 Undecorated (black)
140-1322 Illinois Central
140-1324 Missouri-Kansas-Texas (red)
140-1325 Santa Fe
140-1327 Penn Central
140-1362 American Refrigerator Transit (orange)

40' HI CUBE, OUTSIDE BRACED ea 4.50 NEW
140-1951 Baltimore & Ohio
140-1952 St. Louis Southwestern
140-1953 Great Northern
140-1954 Penn Central
140-1955 Seaboard Coast Line
140-1956 Southern Pacific
140-1950 Undecorated

40' HI CUBE PLUG DOOR ea 4.50 NEW
140-1961 Chicago, Burlington & Quincy
140-1962 Illinois Central
140-1963 Milwaukee Road
140-1964 Rio Grande
140-1965 Santa Fe
140-1966 Union Pacific
140-1960 Undecorated

40' WOOD BOX CAR ea 4.00
140-5231 Santa Fe
140-5232 Erie
140-5233 Great Northern
140-5234 Southern Railway System
140-5235 Southern Pacific
140-5236 Western Pacific
140-5230 Undecorated

40' GRAIN LOADING ea 4.25
140-2093 Northern Pacific
140-2096 Union Pacific
140-2090 Undecorated (black)
140-2091 Chicago, Burlington & Quincy (red)
140-2092 Great Northern (big sky blue)
140-2094 Santa Fe (red)
140-2095 Soo Line (brown)

40' SINGLE DOOR ea 4.00
140-1201 Gulf Mobile & Ohio (caboose red)
140-1204 Great Northern (big sky blue)
140-1205 Southern Pacific (box car red)
140-1206 Penn Central

(Penn Central Green)
140-1207 Illinois Central (box car red)
140-1209 Canadian National (box car red)
140-1210 Norfolk & Western (tuscan red)

50"ACF OUTSIDE BRACED ea 4.50

Successive runs of this car will have different numbers.

140-5521 Railbox (yellow)
140-5520 Undecorated (black)

50' PLUG DOOR, STEEL SIDE BOX CAR ea 4.25
140-5273 Evans
140-5278 Richmond Fredericksburg & Potomac
140-5271 Hamms Beer
140-5272 Evergreen

140-5274 Dresser
140-5275 Abbott Lab
140-5276 Volclay
140-5277 EELX

50' STEEL SINGLE DOOR ea 4.25

140-5055 Sante Fe San Francisco Chief (box car red)
140-5057 New York Central (box car red)
140-5058 Northern Pacific (box car red)
140-5060 Southern (box car red)
140-5061 Southern Pacific (box car red)

140-5050 Undecorated (black)
140-5051 Santa Fe Super Chief (box car red)
140-5052 Santa Fe El Capitain
140-5053 Santa Fe Grand Canyon (box car red)
140-5054 Santa Fe Chief (box car red)

140-5056 Santa Fe Texas Chief (box car red)
140-5059 Pennsylvannia (box car red)
140-5062 Union Pacific (box car red)

140-1211 Grand Trunk Western (box car red)
140-1212 Akron, Canton & Youngstown (yellow)
140-1213 Ontario Northland (dark green)
140-1214 Vermont Railway (dark green)
140-1221 Santa Fe Shock Control (caboose red)
140-1223 Great Northern (turquoise)
140-1200 Undecorated (black)

50' PLUG DOOR, OUTSIDE BRACED ea 4.25

140-1337 Baltimore & Ohio
140-1339 Great Northern (big sky blue)
140-1342 Union Pacific
140-1343 Lehigh Valley (white)
140-1344 Santa Fe (caboose red)
140-1345 Southern Railway System (tuscan red)
140-1346 Kansas City Southern (caboose red)
140-1336 Undecorated (black)

50' PLUG DOOR, OUTSIDE BRACED RIB ea 4.25

140-5281 Rohm-Haas (black, white)
140-5283 Borg-Warner (white)
140-5284 Nestles (blue, white)

50' DOUBLE DOOR RAILBOX ea 5.00

140-5071 Union Pacific of Oregon
140-5072 Arcata
140-5073 Prineville
140-5074 Southern Pacific
140-5075 Burlington Northern

140-5076 Yreka
140-5077 Western Pacific
140-5078 McCloud
140-5079 Milwaukee Road
140-5080 Longview, Portland & Northern

140-5082 Camino, Placerville & Lake Tahoe
140-5070 Undecorated
140-5081 Galveston

86' HI CUBE 8-DOOR ea 5.50 *NEW*

140-1986 Southern Pacific
140-1987 Baltimore & Ohio
140-1988 Grand Trunk Western
140-1989 Missouri Pacific
140-1990 New York Central
140-1991 Pennsylvania RR
140-1985 Undecorated

50' DOUBLE DOOR AUTO CAR STEAM ERA ea 4.25

140-5031 Kansas City Southern
140-5032 St. Louis Southwestern (box car red)
140-5033 Missouri-Kansas-Texas
140-5036 Union Pacific (box car red)
140-5037 Rock Island (box car red)
140-5038 Pennsylvannia (box car red)
140-5039 Rio Grande (box car red)
140-5040 Chicago, Burlington & Quincy
140-5041 Seaboard Air Line
140-5042 Pere Marquette
140-5034 Santa Fe Express Service (pullman green)
140-5035 Southern Pacific (box car red)

50' DOUBLE DOOR AUTO CAR ea 4.25

140-1305 Seaboard Coast Line (box car red)
140-1306 Chicago & Eastern Illinois
140-1315 Southern Pacific Hydro-Cushion (box car red)
140-1317 Santa Fe (red)
140-1319 Union Pacific (reefer yellow)
140-1309 Undecorated (black)
140-1307 Detroit & Toledo Shoreline
140-1308 Norfolk & Southern (light gray)
140-1310 Chicago, Burlington & Quincy (red)
140-1311 Great Northern (red)
140-1316 New York Central (Penn Central green)

86' HI CUBE 4-DOOR ea 5.50 *NEW*

140-1975 Santa Fe
140-1976 Union Pacific
140-1977 Chicago, Burlington & Quincy
140-1978 Detroit, Toledo & Irontown

140-1979 Wabash
140-1980 Norfolk & Western
140-1974 Undecorated

These easy-to-build HO scale kits are prepainted and lettered, molded in styrene, and weighted. They can be assembled with a screwdriver, and come complete with horn-hook couplers and Delrin trucks. We have worked closely with the manufacturer to provide accurate availability information at the time this catalog was published. Items listed in blue ink may not be available at all times. Please see your dealer for current delivery information.

54' PS 3-BAY COVERED ea 4.50

HOPPERS

55' ACF COVERED HOPPER ea 4.75

140-1901 ACF Demo
140-1902 Dow Chemical
140-1903 DuPont (red)
140-1904 Enjay (white)
140-1907 Gulf Oil (light gray-green)
140-1908 New York Central
140-1909 Coop Fertilizers (white)
140-1910 Shell Oil

140-1911 Southern Pacific
140-1912 Union Pacific
140-1913 Diamond Plastic (light gray-green)
140-1914 United Carbon (black)
140-1915 Santa Fe (mineral brown)
140-1916 Tenneco
140-1917 Borg-Warner

140-1918 St. Louis Southwestern (light gray-green)
140-1919 Firestone (light gray-green)
140-1920 Chevron (light gray-green)
140-1921 Union Carbide (light gray-green)
140-1922 Stauffer Chemical (light gray-green)

140-1923 Chicago, Burlington & Quincy (light gray-green)
140-1924 Sinclair Kopper (light gray-green)
140-1900 Undecorated (black)
140-1906 Grace

54' PS 3-BAY COVERED ea 4.50

140-5300 Undecorated (black)
140-5301 Santa Fe (box car red)
140-5302 Chicago, Burlington & Quincy (dark gray-green)
140-5303 Cargill (yellow)
140-5304 CO-OP
140-5305 Missouri-Kansas-Texas
140-5306 Milwaukee Road (reefer yellow)
140-5307 Northern Pacific
140-5308 Pillsbury (light gray-green)
140-5309 Rio Grande (light green)
140-5310 Rock Island
140-5311 Soo Line
140-5312 Union Pacific

34' TWIN, COMPOSITE ea 4.00

140-5421 Santa Fe (box car red)
140-5422 Chicago, Burlington & Quincy (box car red)
140-5423 Lehigh Valley (box car red)
140-5424 Southern (box car red)
140-5426 Union Pacific (tuscan red)
140-5420 Undecorated (black)
140-5425 Southern Pacific (box car red)

34' OFFSET SIDE, TWIN ea 4.00

140-5401 Santa Fe (box car red)
140-5402 Canadian Pacific (box car red)
140-5403 Erie Lackawanna (black)
140-5404 St. Louis San Francisco (box car red)
140-5405 Great Northern (tuscan red)
140-5406 Milwaukee Road (box car red)
140-5400 Undecorated (black)
140-5407 Undecorated, Flat End (black)

40' QUAD ea 4.00

140-1750 Lehigh Valley (box car red)
140-1751 Elgin, Joliet & Eastern (black)
140-1753 Baltimore & Ohio (black)
140-1754 Chicago, Burlington & Quincy (red)
140-1756 Peabody (yellow)

140-1758 Santa Fe (box car red)
140-1759 Illinois Central (black)
140-1760 Seaboard Coast Line (box car red)
140-1749 Undecorated (black)
140-1752 Boston & Maine (light blue)
140-1757 Western Maryland (gray)

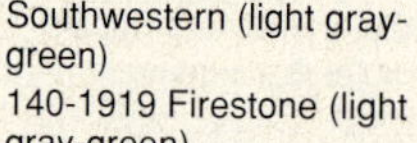

34' TWIN, RIBBED SIDE ea 4.00

140-5441 Baltimore & Ohio (black)
140-5442 Delaware & Hudson (box car red)
140-5443 New York Central (box car red)
140-5444 Norfolk & Western (black)

140-5445 Pennsylvania (tuscan red)
140-5446 Virginian (black)
140-5440 Undecorated, Peaked End (black)
140-5447 Undecorated, Flat End (black)

GONDOLAS

50' GONDOLA ea 4.00

140-1643 Great Northern (green)
140-1644 Union Pacific (box car red)
140-1645 Erie Lackawanna (black)

140-1646 Soo Line (white)
140-1648 Chicago, Burlington & Quincy (red)
140-1647 Undecorated (black)

50' GONDOLA W/CANISTERS ea 4.25

140-1653 Erie Lackawanna

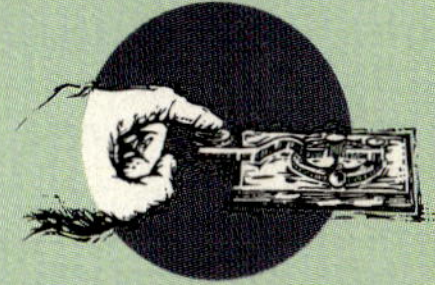

50' FROZEN FOOD CAR ea 4.75

140-1676 Norfolk & Western

50' COVERED GONDOLA ea 4.25

140-1660 Southern Railway System
140-1661 Chicago, Burlington & Quincy

140-1664 Chicago & Eastern Illinois
140-1665 Southern Pacific

INFORMATION STATION

Moving loads of freight by rail is a complex business, and it's essential to keep track of every car at all times. Today, this is a computerized operation, but some of the time-honored methods have been adapted.

One of these is the way bill, a preprinted form that includes specific information one each load and car in a train or yard. The way bill stays with the car from begining to end and and is also used for billing purposes. Each lists the type of car, its reporting marks, type of load, the shipper and their city, the destination city and the specific customer, information on how the car is being routed (a list of which railroads will move the car between cities) and the charges for the services.   Empty cars get their own shortened version, while unit trains carrying a single commodity to one customer, may need only one way bill

Pride of the traffic department and the paint shop, the Poco Valley showcases its new dedicated LCL train for the local newspapers. A pair of new F9's, built from Tyco shells and Kato drives, are on hand, along with a string of Athearn box cars. Builder Ken Nelson of Scotia, New York, painted and lettered all of the equipment.

Models and Photo by Ken Nelson

These easy-to-build HO scale kits are prepainted and lettered, molded in styrene, and weighted. They can be assembled with a screwdriver, and come complete with horn-hook couplers and Delrin trucks.
We have worked closely with the manufacturer to provide accurate availability information at the time this catalog was published. Items listed in blue ink may not be available at all times. Please see your dealer for current delivery information.

FLAT CARS

Oh sure, the crew took quite a ribbing about doing a "bang-up" job with today's mine run. Like their full-scale counterparts, model freight cars come in all shapes and sizes, but thankfully, they don't carry the same kinds of loads! This scene features scratchbuilt equipment, pulled by brass North West Shortline Shay, on Fred Gill's HOn3 Diamond Valley Lines, located in his home in Winston Hills, Australia. Models and Photo by Fred Gill

40' FLAT CAR W/STAKES ea 4.00

86' ALL PURPOSE FLAT CAR ea 4.75

50' FLAT CAR W/STAKES ea 4.00

86' PIGGY BACK FLAT ea 4.75

WELL CARS

These all-new kits model some of the most popular intermodal cars now in service. Designed for fast and easy construction, both the five-unit articulated cars and the stand-alone versions are prepainted and lettered in several exciting roadnames.

GWF10 HUSKY STACK
ea 7.50 (unless noted)
NEW
140-5901 Trailer Train (yellow)
140-5902 TTX (yellow)
140-5903 Greenbrier Leasing Corporation (red)
140-5904 Burlington Northern (red)
140-5905 Coe Rail (red)
140-5906 Burlington Northern pkg (3) 18.00
140-5900 Undecorated

CONTAINER WELL
ea TBA NEW
140-5911 Trailer Train (yellow)
140-5912 TTX (yellow)
140-5913 APC (yellow)
140-5914 Greenbrier Leasing Corporation/APC (red)
140-5915 Burlington Northern (yellow)
140-5916 Burlington Northern (red)
140-5917 CSX Transportation (blue)
140-5918 Santa Fe (red)
140-5919 Southern Pacific (Ely red)
140-5920 Southern Pacific (light red)
140-5910 Undecorated

50' FLAT CAR W/STAKES
ea 4.00
140-1398 Southern Pacific
140-1400 Santa Fe
140-1401 Milwaukee Road (box car red)
140-1399 Undecorated (black)

40' FLAT CAR W/STAKES
ea 4.00
140-1347 Rio Grande
140-1348 Southern Pacific (box car red)
140-1350 Pennsylvania (box car red)
140-1351 Union Pacific (box car red)
140-1358 Rock Island
140-1349 Undecorated (black)

86' PIGGY BACK FLAT
ea 4.75
140-2001 Trailer Train
140-2002 Pacific Fruit Express
140-2003 NAFX
140-2004 Great Northern Big Sky
140-2005 Santa Fe
140-2006 Southern Pacific
140-2000 Undecorated (black)

86' ALL PURPOSE FLAT CAR
ea 4.75
140-2016 Trailer Train
140-2018 St. Louis Southwestern
140-2019 Pacific Fruit Express
140-2020 Southern Pacific
140-2021 Union Pacific
140-2015 Undecorated (black)
140-2017 Chesapeake & Ohio (black, yellow)

IMPACK CARS

IMPACK PIGGYBACK END ea 6.00

IMPACK PIGGYBACK INTERMEDIATE ea 9.00

In the 1970's the Santa Fe built an experimental series of light-weight intermodal cars to save fuel on long runs. The result was the "Fuel-Foiler," a ten-unit, articulated car that could carry trailers up to 48' long. The design was purchased by Itel, a major builder of specialized freight cars, in the 1980's. Renamed the Impack, the cars were custom-built in three, four, five, eight and ten unit configurations. These Impack Cars will look great in your intermodal fleet, and fit any size layout.

By combining a pair of end units and several intermediate units, you can match the configurations run by your favorite road. Each "car" includes numerous add-on details, plus short wheelbase trucks with 28" wheels. The five-unit Itel car modeled here was built from kit #140-5553 End Units and #140-5563 Intermediate Units. Loading your cars is easy with trailers from Athearn and other manufacturers listed in "Vehicles."

**IMPACK PIGGYBACK END
pkg(2) 6.00**
140-5551 Burlington Northern
140-5552 St. Louis
Southwestern
140-5553 Itel
140-5554 Santa Fe
140-5555 Southern Pacific
140-5550 Undecorated
140-5556 Trailer Train

**IMPACK PIGGYBACK
INTERMEDIATE pkg(3) 9.00**
140-5561 Burlington Northern
140-5562 St. Louis
Southwestern
140-5563 Itel
140-5564 Santa Fe
140-5565 Southern Pacific
140-5560 Undecorated
140-5566 Trailer Train

These easy-to-build HO scale kits are prepainted and lettered, molded in styrene, and weighted. They can be assembled with a screwdriver, and come complete with horn-hook couplers and Delrin trucks. We have worked closely with the manufacturer to provide accurate availability information at the time this catalog was published. Items listed in blue ink may not be available at all times. Please see your dealer for current delivery information.

INFORMATION STATION

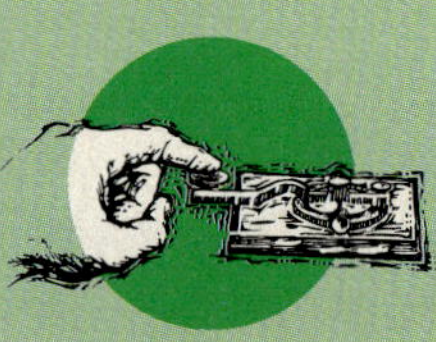

The word "caboose" may have origins in both Dutch ("kabius") and German ("Kabuse") and was originally used in reference to a small room or hut. The word later became a nautical term, describing a small house on the deck of a ship where cooking was done.

The first American car we might recognize as a caboose appeared on the Auburn & Syracuse in the 1840's. Conductor Nat Williams outfitted an old box car with a variety of tools, lanterns, flags and other equipment. With a barrel for a desk and a wooden box for a chair, he used the car as a rolling office.

Known as conductor's cars, the idea soon spread. The first reference to these cars as "cabooses" appeared in the late 1850's in reference to cars operated by the Buffalo, Corning & New York.

The basic duties of the caboose as a rolling office and home-away-from-home for the crew, remained unchanged for many decades. The design however, evolved from a haphazard conversion to a custom-built car. Most roads constructed their own, giving them a unique styling. Wood construction was predominant until the 40's, when the first all-steel cars began to appear. The interior design also remained about the same, with lockers for equipment, a few bunks that doubled as seats and a stove for cooking and heating. In later years, toilets, electric lights, train radios and air conditioning were installed in some cars.

Finally, most sources agree the plural is cabooses, not cabeese. But that's another story.

CABOOSES

29' WIDE VISION

34' CUPOLA

37' BAY WINDOW

29' WIDE VISION ea 4.50

140-5361 Burlington Northern (white)
140-5362 Chesapeake & Ohio
140-5364 Illinois Central
140-5365 Penn Central
140-5367 Santa Fe (caboose red)
140-5368 Union Pacific
140-5369 Chessie System (yellow)
140-5370 Soo Line
140-5360 Undecorated (black)
140-5366 Rock Island (caboose red)

34' CUPOLA ea 4.50

140-1250 Santa Fe
140-1251 Southern Pacific (box car red)
140-1252 Union Pacific (yellow)
140-1253 Pennsylvania (box car red)
140-1255 Baltimore & Ohio (caboose red)
140-1256 Milwaukee Road
140-1259 New Haven
140-1260 Great Northern (box car red)
140-1262 Canadian National (caboose red)
140-1266 Northern Pacific
140-1267 Chicago & North Western (tuscan red)
140-1268 New York Central (box car red)
140-1269 Santa Fe (caboose red)
140-1249 Undecorated (black)
140-1254 Chicago, Burlington and Quincy
140-1258 Rio Grande (yellow)
140-1265 Chesapeake & Ohio

37' BAY WINDOW ea 4.50

140-1286 Santa Fe (box car red)
140-1287 Baltimore & Ohio (blue)
140-1288 Chicago, Burlington & Quincy (silver)
140-1289 Chicago & North Western
140-1290 New Haven
140-1292 Pennsylvania (tuscan red)
140-1293 Southern Pacific (box car red)
140-1285 Undecorated (black)

Robins and redwing blackbirds not withstanding, it's got to be spring if tankers of anhydrous ammonia are moving. Starting with a Walthers 54' Funnel-Flow® tank car, Mark Hills of Des Moines, Iowa, added a modified Plano walkway, brass wire and Athearn diesel handrail stanchions to this model. A trip through the paint shop was completed with the application of decals from Islington Station and Microscale. Mark used artist's oils to weather the model, and these colors were blended with a bit of airbrushing.

Models and Photo by Mark Hills

REEFERS

50' MECHANICAL

57' MECHANICAL

50' PLUG DOOR OUTSIDE BRACED

MOW EQUIPMENT

ROTARY SNOW PLOW ea 8.25

140-1195 Canadian National
140-1196 Great Northern
140-1197 New York Central

140-1198 Union Pacific
140-1194 Undecorated

200 TON CRANE ea 8.00

140-1701 Pennsylvania (black)
140-1702 Santa Fe (black)
140-1699 Undecorated

140-1700 Union Pacific (red, black)

50' MECHANICAL ea 4.25

140-1620 Milwaukee Road
140-1623 Burlington Refrigerator Express
140-1627 Pacific Fruit Express
140-1629 Safeway
140-1630 Santa Fe
140-1624 Undecorated

57' MECHANICAL ea 4.75

140-5462 Santa Fe (reefer orange)
140-5463 Bangor & Aroostock (reefer orange)
140-5465 Union Pacific Fruit Express
140-5467 Pacific Fruit Express - Union Pacific
140-5460 Undecorated (black)
140-5461 American Refrigerator Transit (red)
140-5464 Burlington Refrigerator Express - Burlington Route (reefer yellow)
140-5466 Western Fruit Express (reefer yellow)

50' PLUG DOOR OUTSIDE BRACED ea 4.25

140-1633 Fruit Growers Express (yellow)
140-1631 Undecorated (black)
140-1632 Chicago, Burlington & Quincy (yellow)
140-1634 Great Northern (yellow)
140-1636 Pacific Fruit Express (orange)
140-1637 Santa Fe

40' ICE BUNKER ea 4.00

140-1601 Pacific Fruit Express (reefer orange)
140-1602 Carnation
140-1603 Blatz (reefer yellow)
140-1604 Canadian National (gray)
140-1605 Santa Fe, Chief (reefer orange)
140-1609 Railway Express Agency (green)
140-1610 Chicago, Burlington & Quincy
140-1615 Bangor & Aroostock (orange)
140-1599 Undecorated (black)

40' ICE BUNKER, WOOD ea 4.00

140-5201 Baby Ruth (red)
140-5202 Canada Dry (reefer yellow)
140-5203 Coors Beer (reefer yellow)
140-5204 Crisco
140-5205 Kraft (silver, blue)
140-5206 Mars, Snickers
140-5207 Morrell (reefer orange)
140-5208 Old Dutch Cleanser (reefer yellow)
140-5209 Oscar Mayer
140-5210 Pluto Water
140-5211 Schlitz (reefer yellow)
140-5212 Swift (reefer orange)
140-5213 Soo Line (reefer orange)
140-5214 Pacific Fruit Express-Western Pacific (reefer yellow)
140-5215 Chicago & North Western
140-5216 Western Fruit Express-Great Northern (reefer yellow)
140-5217 Burlington Refrigerator Express (yellow)
140-5218 Fruit Growers Express (reefer yellow)
140-5200 Undecorated (black)

40' ICE BUNKER, STEAM ERA ea 4.00

140-5020 Santa Fe, Grand Canyon (reefer orange)
140-5021 Santa Fe, Scout
140-5022 Santa Fe, Chief (reefer orange)
140-5024 Santa Fe, Texas Chief (reefer orange)
140-5025 Merchants
140-5026 Illinois Central (yellow)
140-5027 Burlington Refrigerator Express (yellow)
140-5029 American Refrigerator Transit
140-5030 Pacific Fruit Express (reefer orange)
140-5019 Santa Fe, El Capitan (reefer orange)
140-5023 Santa Fe, Super Chief (reefer orange)
140-5028 Northern Pacific (reefer orange)

50' EXPRESS ea 4.50

140-5331 Santa Fe dark brown)
140-5332 Great Northern (dark brown)
140-5335 Pacififc Fruit Express (dark brown)
140-5341 Hood (dark brown)
140-5343 Sheffield (dark brown)
140-5345 General American (dark brown)
140-5346 Abbott (dark brown)
140-5330 Undecorated (black)

These easy-to-build HO scale kits are prepainted and lettered, molded in styrene, and weighted. They can be assembled with a screwdriver, and come complete with horn-hook couplers and Delrin trucks.
We have worked closely with the manufacturer to provide accurate availability information at the time this catalog was published. Items listed in blue ink may not be available at all times. Please see your dealer for current delivery information.

VANS

25' VAN ea 8.25
140-1426 Baltimore & Ohio

140-1429 International Forward

40' VAN ea 5.50
140-5163 Northern Pacific

140-5171 Seaboard Coast Line
140-5151 Undecorated

STOCK CARS

40' DOUBLE DECK ea 4.00
Double deck stock cars are used to ship sheep, goats and pigs.

140-1771 Great Northern
140-1772 Rock Island (box car red)
140-1773 Texas & Pacific
140-1776 Santa Fe (box car red)
140-1777 Rio Grande (black)
140-1779 Union Pacific
140-1774 Undecorated (black)

TANK CARS

40' SINGLE DOME

40' THREE DOME

40' CHEMICAL

40' SINGLE DOME ea 4.00
140-1571 Conoco (silver)
140-1572 Phillips Petroleum (black)
140-1574 Santa Fe (black)
140-1575 Southern Pacific (yellow)
140-1577 Baltimore & Ohio (black)
140-1578 Southern Pacific (silver)
140-1579 Firestone (light green, black)
140-1570 Undecorated (black)

40' THREE DOME ea 4.00
140-1500 Shell (yellow)
140-1501 Texaco (silver)
140-1504 Union Oil (dark blue)
140-1506 Koppers (black)
140-1507 Ethyl Corporation (light gray-green)
140-1499 Undecorated (black)
140-1503 Mobil Gas (red)

40' PICKLE CAR ea 4.50
140-1475 Heinz w/Tank
140-1476 Heinz

40' CHEMICAL ea 4.25
140-1550 Gulf Oil (orange)
140-1551 Michigan Alky
140-1552 Dow Chemical (blue)
140-1553 Dupont (silver)
140-1557 Hooker (orange)
140-1558 Staley (gray)
140-1549 Undecorated (black)

62' TANK ea 4.50
140-1522 Chicago, Burlington & Quincy
140-1526 Union Pacific
140-1527 North American Car Corporation
140-1528 San Angelo Tank Car (yellow)
140-1529 ACF Industries
140-1530 Conslidated Gas
140-1520 Undecorated (black)
140-1524 General Dynamics

INFORMATION STATION

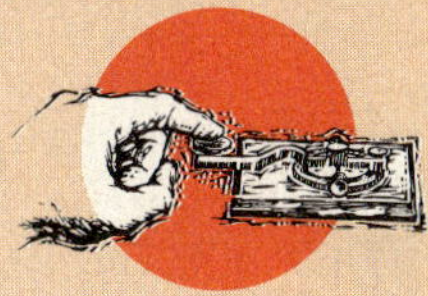

GBW, DRGW, FGE, BN, NS, CSX. No, they're not a secret code. Each railroad and private company has a shorthand identification in the form of a two, three or four letter combination, called a reporting mark.

Assigned by the Association of American Railroads, they're usually based on the company's initials. For example, CNW indicates a car owned by the Chicago & North Western. This mark is applied to all of the company's equipment used in interchange service.

This simplifies paperwork, but care must be taken to avoid errors: a car marked OPIX belongs to the Occidental Chemical Corporation, while a car marked OPSX belongs to the Public Service Company of Oklahoma.

Each car is numbered and similar cars are usually numbered as a series. This makes it possible to identify one from another, much like license plates on autos. Standards determine the size and placement of the lettering. A large mark and number are applied to the left on both sides of the car. Small versions of the same marks are applied on each end, in the upper right hand corner.

Railroads and leasing companies may use more than one reporting mark to identify cars owned by divisions or trust groups, or cars acquired during mergers. Some, like Trailer Train indicate the car type by the first letter, followed by their ID, as in QTTX. Many roads once used an ampersand, as in CB&Q, but this was dropped when computers came into use, and the new mark became CBQ.

To keep track of the hundreds of marks in use, The Official Railway Equipment Register is published quarterly. This lists all cars in service, by railroad and by number, along with information on size and capacity.

All brakes are released and everything is o.k. as the car man gives us a highball. Apparently something needs fixing up the line and the blacksmith is tagging along for our ride over Carl Cascone's pike in Northport, New York. The old tankers are from Roundhouse and have been weathered to show their age. Carl isn't sure who originally made his blacksmith car (it's pretty close to the current version from Walthers) which has been upgraded with add-on details.

Models and Photo by
Carl Cascone

ACCURAIL

These easy-to-build HO Scale plastic car kits feature a one-piece body with details molded in place. Decorated models feature authentic paint and lettering schemes with end reporting marks. In addition, the trucks feature nonmagnetic axles, and the coupler pockets accept Kadee #5 couplers. Another special detail of these Accurail kits is that they have exceptionally free rolling wheels.

Waiting for the local switcher, these hard-working freight cars make a great addition to any steam- or early diesel-era layout . Each is designed for easy construction and finished in authentic schemes. (Some items shown are preproduction models.)

BOX CARS

40' STEEL DOUBLE DOOR BOX CAR ea 7.98

112-3001 Santa Fe (dark tuscan)
112-3002 Baltimore & Ohio (light tuscan)
112-3003 Burlington Northern (cascade green)
112-3004 Canadian National (dark tuscan)
112-3005 Chicago & North Western (maroon tuscan)
112-3006 Chicago, Burlington & Quincy (maroon tuscan)
112-3007 Great Northern (scarlet)
112-3008 New York Central (dark tuscan)
112-3009 Pennsylvania (light tuscan)
112-3010 Union Pacific (light tuscan)
112-3011 Wabash (maroon tuscan)
112-3012 Canadian Pacific (dark tuscan)
112-3013 Cotton Belt (maroon tuscan)
112-3014 Southern Pacific (dark tuscan)
112-3015 Seaboard (light tuscan)
112-3016 Frisco (light tuscan)
112-3017 Milwaukee Road (dark tuscan)
112-3018 Mopac (maroon tuscan)
112-3019 Southern Railway (light tuscan)
112-3020 Atlantic Coast Line (maroon tuscan)
112-3021 Northern Pacific (dark tuscan)
112-3022 Norfolk & Western (dark tuscan)
112-3000 Undecorated (black)

40' AAR STEEL BOX CAR (POST WAR) ea 7.98

The following three items (1500 series) are limited run items:

112-1506 Gulf, Mobile & Ohio (green) *NEW*
112-1508 Chicago & Eastern Illinois (box car red, white) *NEW*

Limited Quantities Available
112-1501 Rock Island, "The Rock" (light blue) 7.98

112-3201 Santa Fe (dark tuscan)
112-3202 Chesapeake & Ohio (maroon tuscan)
112-3203 Northern Pacific (cascade green)

112-3204 Pennsylvania (light tuscan)
112-3205 Union Pacific (light tuscan)
112-3206 New York Central (New York Central Jade)
112-3207 Rio Grande (dark tuscan)
112-3208 Canadian Pacific (dark tuscan)
112-3209 Southern Pacific (dark tuscan)
112-3210 Chicago & North Western (dark tuscan)
112-3211 Missouri - Kansas - Texas (dark tuscan)
112-3212 Grand Trunk Western (GTW blue)
112-3213 Southern Railway (light tuscan)
112-3214 Canadian National (dark tuscan)
112-3215 Great Northern (maroon tuscan)

112-3216 Chicago, Burlington & Quincy (scarlet)
112-3217 Baltimore & Ohio (light tuscan)
112-3218 Soo Line (light tuscan)
112-3219 Burlington Northern (cascade green)

112-3220 Frisco (light tuscan)
112-3221 Nickel Plate Road (light tuscan)
112-3222 Rock Island (dark tuscan)
112-3223 Illinois Central (maroon tuscan)
112-3224 Western Pacific (maroon tuscan) *NEW*
112-3298 Data (dark tuscan) *NEW*
112-3299 Data (light tuscan) *NEW*
112-3200 Undecorated (black)

Limited Quantities Available
112-3306 Union Pacific 3-pack 23.98

This item (3300 series) is a limited run.
112-3310 Great Northern 3-pack 23.98 *NEW*

40' WOOD OUTSIDE BRACED BOX CAR (WOOD DOOR & ENDS) ea 8.98

One look and you'd swear these cars were really made of wood! Actually, the kits have a one-piece styrene body with superb wood grain detail, along with a detailed underframe, doors and other parts. Typical of cars built by many roads during the steam-era, the models are prepainted and lettered in a wide selection of period schemes.

112-4001 Western Pacific (maroon tuscan)
112-4002 Chicago, Burlington & Quincy (light tuscan)
112-4003 Canadian National (light tuscan)
112-4004 Milwaukee Road (dark tuscan)
112-4005 Maine Central (maroon tuscan)
112-4006 Texas & New Orleans (dark tuscan)
112-4007 Norfolk & Western (box car red)
112-4008 Grand Trunk Western (tuscan)
112-4009 Rutland
112-4098 Data (dark red) *NEW*
112-4099 Data (red) *NEW*
112-4000 Undecorated

BOX CARS

40' WOOD OUTSIDE BRACED BOX CAR (STEEL ENDS & WOOD DOOR) ea 8.98

112-4201 Southern Pacific (dark tuscan)
112-4202 Delaware & Hudson (maroon tuscan)
112-4203 Missouri - Kansas - Texas (light tuscan)
112-4204 Canadian Pacific (dark tuscan)
112-4205 Chicago & North Western (maroon tuscan)
112-4206 Ann Arbor (light tuscan)
112-4207 Canadian National (light tuscan)
112-4208 Pennsylvania (tuscan)
112-4209 New York Central (dark tuscan)
112-4210 Baltimore & Ohio
112-4211 Erie
112-4212 Clinchfield
112-4213 Western Maryland
112-4214 Chicago, Burlington & Quincy
112-4200 Undecorated (black)

40' WOOD OUTSIDE BRACED BOX CAR (STEEL ENDS & DOORS) ea 8.98

112-4401 Santa Fe (dark tuscan)
112-4402 Pennsylvania (light tuscan)
112-4403 Northern Pacific (maroon tuscan)
112-4404 Mopac (light tuscan)
112-4405 Reading (dark tuscan) *NEW*
112-4498 Data (maroon tuscan)
112-4499 Data (light tuscan)
112-4400 Undecorated (black)

The following item (1500 series) is a limited run item:

40' WOOD OUTSIDE BRACED BOX CAR

112-1509 Pacific Electric (tuscan) 8.98 *NEW*

HOPPERS

47' ACF 3-BAY CENTER FLOW HOPPER ea 9.98
NEW

All new tooling will be used for the following 2000 series cars. These cars are 47 cubic feet and were "Plate B" cars used on a large number of railroads.

112-2001 Data (dark gray)
112-2002 Santa Fe (brown)
112-2003 New York Central (light gray)
112-2004 Wisconsin Central Limited (putty)
112-2005 Union Pacific (gray)
112-2006 Chicago & North Western (green)
112-2007 Milwaukee Road (gray)
112-2008 Southern Pacific (gray)
112-2009 Illinois Central Gulf (gray)
112-2010 Great Northern (green)
112-2011 Western Pacific (light gray)
112-2012 Missouri Pacific (gray)
112-2013 Conrail (brown)
112-2014 Grand Trunk Western (blue)
112-2015 Burlington Northern (cascade green)
112-2016 Pennsylvania (gray)
112-2017 Chicago, Burlington & Quincy (gray)
112-2018 Soo Line (white)
112-2019 Baltimore & Ohio (gray)
112-2000 Undecorated

GONDOLAS

50' MILL GONDOLA

112-1105 Burlington Northern (black, white) 9.95
112-1106 Burlington Northern pkg (2) 19.90

HOPPERS

47' ACF 3-BAY CENTER FLOW HOPPER

112-1044 International Mineral & Chemical (light green) pkg (2) 19.90
112-1049 General Chemical (gray, blue, black) 9.95
112-1056 Conrail 3 (box car red) pkg (2) 19.90
112-1062 Soo Line (white) pkg (2) 19.90

Limited Quantities Available

112-1042 Illinois Central Gulf (gray, black, white) pkg (2) 19.90
112-1046 Western Pacific (gray) pkg (2) 19.90
112-1048 Elders Grain (red) pkg (2) 19.90
112-1053 Englehard Minerals & Chemicals (gray, red) 9.95
112-1054 Englehard pkg (2) 19.90
112-1100 GTA Grain Marketing (light gray with red & black graphics) pkg (2) 19.90

47' ACF 3-BAY CENTER FLOW HOPPER

Accurate Finishing Inc.

We offer limited run cars which add color and variety to your freight car collection with this line of kits! Each HO Scale model is an easy-to-build kit (from various manufacturers), prepainted and lettered in authentic colors. Cars are complete with trucks and horn-hook couplers. Two different car numbers in all packages of two.

BOX CARS

40' PS-1 BOX CAR

112-1023 Texas Mexican (red, white) 9.95
112-1024 Texas Mexican pkg (2) 19.90

54' COVERED HOPPERS ea 9.95 (unless noted)

112-1085 Norfolk & Western (gray) *NEW*
112-1089 Union Pacific (gray)
112-1099 GTA Grain (gray)
112-1097 Penn Central (jade green with black & white graphics) 9.95

A-LINE
A division of PROTO POWER WEST

These easy-to-build HO Scale kits are based on contemporary intermodal equipment used by many roads. They include injection molded parts which are unpainted, trucks, weights and step-by-step instructions. Kits are less couplers, but accept horn-hook or Kadee styles.

HUSKY STACK DECALS

CONTAINERS

RIBBED SIDE CONTAINERS

Used by APL, Maersk, Sea Land and others, these containers are seen around the world. These kits feature a one-piece body with separate floor and stacking pins. Undecorated containers are molded in silver styrene. Painted containers are ready for decals, which are available separately.

116-25101 40' Painted (silver) pkg (2) 7.95 **NEW**
116-25201 45' Painted (silver) pkg (2) 7.95 **NEW**
116-25100 40' Undecorated pkg (2) 7.50
116-25200 45' Undecorated pkg (2) 7.50

CONTAINER DECALS ea 4.50

Each set includes detailed lettering diagram and color photo of container.

116-25800 APL 40'/45'
116-25801 Maersk 20'/40' (original)
116-25802 Sea Land 40'
116-25803 Maersk 40'/45' (new)
116-25804 Burlington Northern America 48'
116-25805 APC 48'
116-25806 APC 53'
116-25807 ITEL/Burlington Northern/ITEL 48'
116-25808 Santa Fe 45'/48'/53'
116-25809 CSX/CSL 48'
116-25810 XTRA 48'
116-25811 Southern Pacific 48'
116-25812 Canadian National Intermodal 48' **NEW**
116-25813 Canadian Pacific Intermodal 48' **NEW**
116-25814 Burlington Northern America Special 48' **NEW**
116-25815 Conrail Mercury 48' **NEW**
116-25816 Conrail Mercury 53' **NEW**
116-25817 Con-Quest 48' **NEW**

SMOOTH SIDE CONTAINERS ea pkg (2) 11.50 (unless noted)

Used by APL/APC, CSX/CSL, ITEL, XTRA, Burlington Northern, Santa Fe, Southern Pacific, Canadian National, Canadian Pacific, Conrail, Genstar, Con-Way and others. Based on a Monon prototype, these are the most common domestic containers in use today. Each kit features a one-piece body with separate roof and stacking pins. The undecorated containers are molded in white styrene. The painted containers are ready for decals, which are available separately. Decorated containers are ready to run.

116-25301 48' Santa Fe pkg (2)
116-25303 48' APL pkg (2) **NEW**
116-25304 48' Painted (white) pkg (2) TBA **NEW**
116-25300 48' Undecorated pkg (2) 7.50
116-25401 53' Santa Fe pkg (2)
116-25402 53' APC pkg (2)
116-25404 53' Painted (white) pkg (2) TBA **NEW**
116-25400 53' Undecorated pkg (2) 7.50

CORRUGATED CONTAINERS ea pkg (2) 5.95 (unless noted) **NEW**

Used by NYK, Mitsui, OSK, YS Line, OOCL, Triton, Hyundai, Matson, IEA, Evergreen, CGM, Transamerica, Maersk and others. Each kit features the "beveled" style of corrugation, 2-logo panel or all corrugated sides, smooth or corrugated doors, see-through forklift pockets, corrugated roofs and one-piece body with separate floor, stacking pins, vents and door bars. Undecorated containers are molded in gray styrene. Painted containers are ready for decals, which are available separately.

116-25500 20' Undecorated 2-logo panel sides/smooth doors
116-25501 20' Orange 2-logo panel sides/smooth doors TBA
116-25510 20' Undecorated 2-logo panel sides/corrugated doors
116-25511 20' Silver 2-logo panel sides/corrugated doors TBA
116-25520 20' Undecorated 2-logo corrugated sides/smooth doors
116-25521 20' Brown 2-logo corrugated sides/smooth doors TBA
116-25530 20' Undecorated 2-logo corrugated sides/corrugated doors
116-25531 20' Silver 2-logo corrugated sides/corrugated doors TBA

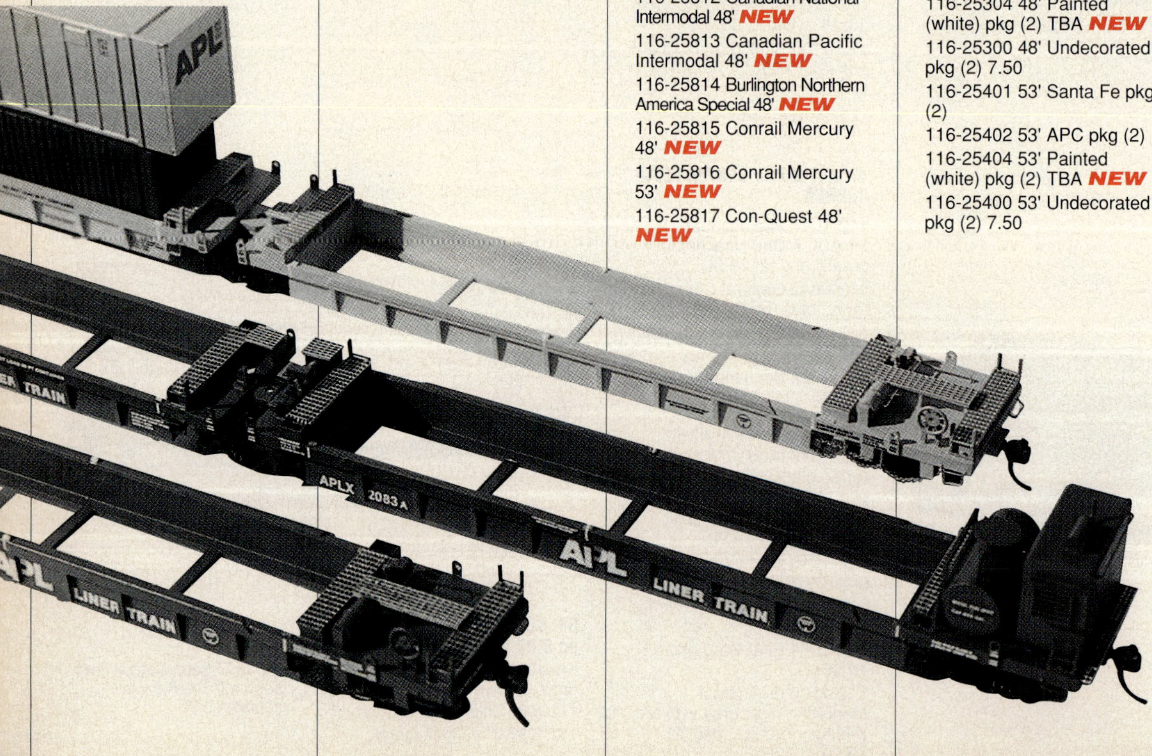

Racing containers east and west, double stack cars are the backbone of the railroad's intermodal fleets. The modular design of each series allows you to build longer or shorter cars to fit your operation, and add-on details, containers, and decals are available separately.

DOUBLE STACK CONTAINER CARS

40' & 45' THRALL DOUBLE STACK CAR

These five-unit cars are used by American President Lines/APC and Trailer Train/TTX. The 40' and 45' units can carry two 20' or one 40' or 45' container on the bottom, and a 40', 45', 48' or 53' container on the top (depending on the kit). The cars are packaged as either: two end units, two center units, or a five-unit set (prototypical). The end and center unit kits can be combined to build shorter cars for small layouts.

116-26100 40' End Units, Undecorated pkg (2) 20.95
116-26102 40' Mid Units, Undecorated pkg (2) 19.95
116-26103 40' 5-Unit Set, Undecorated 46.95
116-26104 45' Mid Units, Undecorated pkg (2) 20.95
116-26105 40'/45' 5-Unit Set, Undecorated 47.95
This kit includes two 40' end units and three 45' mid units.

116-26900 Thrall Extra-Detail Kit 8.80

GUNDERSON "TWIN-STACK" DOUBLE STACK CAR

These five-unit cars are used by Trailer Train, Santa Fe, Southern Pacific, Burlington Northern, Conrail, Soo Line, Sea Land (NYSW & CSX) and others. Units can carry two 20' or one 40' container on the bottom, and a 40', 45' or 48' container on top. The cars are packaged as either: two end units, two center units, or a five-unit set (prototypical). The end and center unit kits can be combined to build shorter cars for small layouts.

116-27100 40' End Units, Undecorated pkg (2) 22.95
116-27102 40' Mid Units, Undecorated pkg (2) 21.95
116-27103 5-Unit Set, Undecorated 49.95
116-27900 Twin Stack Extra-Detail Kit 5.80

GUNDERSON "HUSKY-STACK"™ DOUBLE STACK CAR

This single-unit, 48' well car is used by Trailer Train/TTX, Burlington Northern, Greenbrier Leasing, Coe Rail and others. The car can carry either two 20' or one 40', 45' or 48' container on the bottom, and a 40', 45', 48' or 53' container on top.

116-27200 Husky-Stack™, Undecorated 8.95

DECALS

THRALL CAR DECALS ea 4.50

Each set includes complete decals for one 5-unit set and detailed lettering diagram.

116-26700 APL/APC (blue or red car)
116-26701 Trailer Train (yellow car)

TWIN-STACK CAR DECALS ea 4.50

Each set includes complete decals for one 5-unit set and detailed lettering diagram.

116-27700 TTX/SP (yellow car)
116-27701 TTX/Santa Fe (yellow car)
116-27702 TTX/Burlington Northern (yellow car)
116-27703 Southern Pacific (red car)

116-27704 Santa Fe (red car)
116-27705 Sea Land (red car)
116-27706 Burlington Northern (cascade green car) **NEW**
116-27707 Soo Line (red car) **NEW**
116-27708 Conrail (box car red) **NEW**

HUSKY-STACK™ DECALS ea 4.50

Each set includes detailed lettering diagram and color photo of car.

116-27800 TTX (enough to do 4-single cars)
116-27805 Burlington Northern (enough to do 2-single and 1-3 unit)
116-27806 GBRX/Burlington Northern **NEW**
116-27807 CRLE/GBRX **NEW**

FLAT CARS

85' FLAT CAR WITH END WEIGHT

Commonly used for intermodal service, this flat car kit includes an undecorated Athearn body with trucks. The custom weights improve performance and simplify installing body-mounted couplers.

116-13202 Flat Car, Undecorated 10.95

These HO Scale ready-to-run cars are prepainted and lettered, and include trucks and horn-hook couplers.

We have worked closely with this manufacturer to provide accurate availability information at the time this catalog was published. Items listed in blue ink may not be available at all times. Please see your dealer for current delivery information.

OPERATING CARS

LOG CAR
160-46203 Log Car (yellow) 18.00

250 TON CRANE & 51' FLOODLIGHT CAR
160-46103 Erie Lackawanna (black, box car red) 20.00
160-46105 Amtrak (orange) 20.00
160-46311 Union Pacific Floodlight Car only (yellow, silver) 12.00
160-46313 Erie Lackawanna Floodlight Car only 12.00
160-46315 Amtrak Floodlight Car only (orange) 12.00
160-46101 Union Pacific (yellow) 20.00

250 TON CRANE & 51' BOOM CAR ea 18.00
160-46111 Union Pacific (yellow)
160-46115 Amtrak (orange)
160-46213 Erie Lackawanna (black, box car red)

GANDY DANCER HAND CAR
160-46202 Powered 20.00
Shown 1/2 actual size.
(yellow, red, green)

ACTION CABOOSE
160-46206 Santa Fe (caboose red, yellow) 15.00

89' TRI-LEVEL TRANS-PORTER ea 16.00
This transporter includes 15 autos.

160-46002 Santa Fe (caboose red, white)
160-46032 Penn Central (green, white)

52' DEPRESSED CENTER FLAT CAR
160-71300 USAF with missile (black) 6.50

27' ORE CAR ea 4.00
160-77501 Union Pacific (box car red)
160-77541 Chicago & North Western (caboose red)
160-77542 Norfolk & Western (black)
160-77543 Duluth, Missabe & Iron Range

36' WIDE VISION CABOOSE ea 5.00
160-70701 Union Pacific (armor yellow, red)
160-70702 Santa Fe (caboose red, yellow)
160-70709 Chessie (yellow, caboose red)
160-70716 Burlington Northern (silver)
160-70728 Erie Lackawanna (caboose red)

GANDY DANCER HAND CAR

ACTION CABOOSE

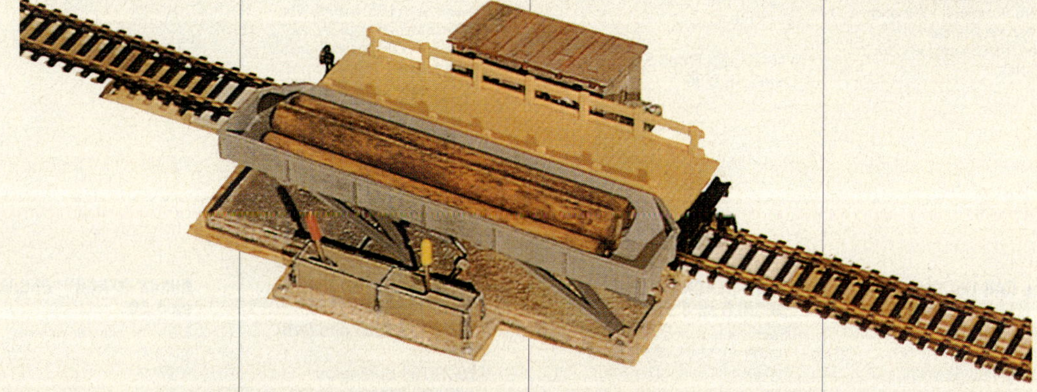

LOG CAR

89' TRI LEVEL TRANSPORTER

250 TON CRANE & 51' FLOODLIGHT CAR

OLD TIMERS

"OLDTIMERS" are scaled authentically from prototypes in use on Western Railroads circa 1860.

51' PICKLE CAR
160-79941 Heinz (brown, yellow) 6.00

34' GONDOLA ea 6.00
160-72501 Union Pacific (black, caboose red)
160-72524 Central Pacific (black, caboose red)

34' BOX CAR ea 6.00
160-72301 Union Pacific (caboose red, black)
160-72324 Central Pacific (green, yellow)

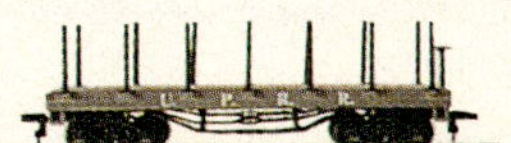

34' FLAT CAR WITH STAKES ea 6.00
160-72401 Union Pacific (gray)
160-72424 Central Pacific (caboose red)

51' VINEGAR TANK CAR
160-79942 Heinz (brown, yellow) 6.00

FREIGHT CAR ASSORTMENT
160-76936 pkg (36) 120.00
This assortment includes a variety of box, tank, refrigerator and hopper cars.

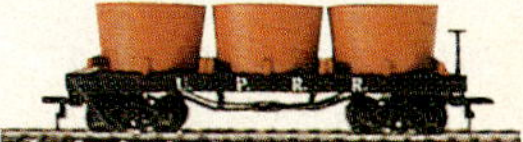

34' WATER TANK CAR ea 6.00
160-72601 Union Pacific (caboose red, black)
160-72624 Central Pacific (caboose red, gray)

21' 4-WHEEL CABOOSE ea 6.00
160-72701 Union Pacific (yellow)
160-72724 Central Pacific (caboose red, black)

Listen closely and you'll hear the timbers groan as a heavy cut of logs rolls onto this tall trestle. It's a long way down and crews on the Tall Pine Railroad pay close attention to the five mph speed limit on this part of the railroad! This dramatic trestle was built and photographed by Angelo Battistella of Trieste, Italy. The Shay is a Model Die Casting kit, while the Kadee cars sport a load of handmade logs.

Models and Photo by Angelo Battistella.

C M SHOPS, INC.

These easy-to build HO Scale plastic car kits are prepainted and lettered, and include weights, trucks and horn-hook couplers.
We have worked closely with this manufacturer to provide accurate availability information at the time this catalog was published. Items listed in blue ink may not be available at all times. Please see your dealer for current delivery information.

GONDOLAS

52' COVERED GONDOLA

50' GONDOLA

50' COVERED GONDOLA

These covered gondolas are an economical car for both model and prototype railroads. With their covers in place, the cars are used to carry steel coils which are protected from the weather. If business is slow, the covers can be removed and the car used as a standard gondola. This model comes prepainted and requires only minor assembly

50' COVERED GONDOLA ea 8.50
012-118 Baltimore & Ohio (black)
012-119 Chesapeake & Ohio
012-117 Nickel Plate Road
012-138 Chicago & North Western

50' GONDOLA ea 7.95
012-129 Pennsylvania
012-139 Reading
012-148 Pittsburgh & Lake Erie
012-149 Detroit, Toledo & Ironton (black)
012-160 Baltimore & Ohio/Chessie (black)
012-171 Rutland
012-184 Conrail (box car red)
012-210 Delaware & Hudson (black)

CABOOSES

WIDE VISION CABOOSE

BAY WINDOW CABOOSE *NEW*

BOX CARS

50' PLUG DOOR STEEL BOX CAR

40' BOX CAR

50' SINGLE DOOR STEEL BOX CAR

50' DOUBLE DOOR BOX CAR

50' PLUG DOOR STEEL BOX CAR ea 8.50
012-105 Chessie/Baltimore & Ohio
012-113 Providence & Worcester
012-134 Boston & Maine
012-143 Santa Fe
012-145 Chicago Great Western (dark tuscan)
012-147 Chessie System/Chesapeake & Ohio (yellow)
012-166 New Haven (red, black)
012-177 Chesapeake & Ohio (yellow, blue)
012-181 Maine Central (yellow, green)
012-182 Texas & Pacific (orange)
012-196 Northern Pacific
012-203 Candian Pacific, "Newsprint" (tuscan)
012-224 Conrail (tuscan)
012-225 Canadian National (tuscan)
012-269 Chicago & Illinois Midland *NEW*

40' BOX CAR ea 7.95
012-101 Erie Lackawanna
012-103 Norfolk & Western (black)
012-106 Illinois Central Gulf (orange)
012-111 Canadian National
012-161 Lehigh Valley (green)
012-188 Erie (tuscan)
012-190 New York Central
012-191 Union Pacific
012-192 Southern Railway
012-193 Frisco
012-194 Lackawanna
012-195 Cotton Belt
012-208 Buffalo Creek
012-209 Great Northern (jade green)
012-211 Lehigh Valley (white)
012-216 Baltimore & Ohio
012-217 Indiana Harbor Belt
012-254 Grand Trunk Western "Maple Leaf" (tuscan)

C M SHOPS, INC.

WIDE VISION CABOOSE
ea 9.95

012-256 Conrail
012-257 Rio Grande
012-258 Delaware & Hudson (red, black)
012-259 Spokane, Portland & Seattle (red, silver)
012-260 Seaboard Air Line (red, black)
012-261 Canadian National (red, black)

BAY WINDOW CABOOSE
ea 9.95 *NEW*

012-263 Burlington Northern (cascade green, yellow) 9.95

50' SINGLE DOOR STEEL BOX CAR ea 8.50 (unless noted)

012-108 Chicago & North Western (box car red)
012-115 Grand Trunk Western
012-121 Burlington Northern
012-123 Southern Pacific "DF"
012-126 Southern Railway
012-130 Chessie System/Western Maryland (blue)
012-133 Conrail (tuscan)
012-137 Illinois Central Gulf (orange)
012-151 Atlantic Coast Line
012-165 Delaware, Lackawanna & Western
012-176 Louisville & Nashville
012-179 Wabash (tuscan)
012-226 Delaware & Hudson "I Love New York" 10.95
012-246 Seaboard Coast/Line Family Lines (tuscan) 9.50
012-218 Gulf, Mobile & Ohio

50' DOUBLE DOOR BOX CAR ea 8.50

012-120 Erie (tuscan, black)
012-197 Union Pacific
012-215 New York Central "Early Bird"
012-198 Candian National

50' RAILBOX-TYPE BOX CAR ea 8.95 (Not Shown)

012-212 Bangor & Aroostook
012-213 Norfolk & Western (dark tuscan)
012-214 Chicago & North Western "Employee Owned"

HOPPERS

55' ACF CENTERFLO COVERED HOPPER ea 9.50

012-127 Arco Polymers (dark blue)
012-128 Hercules
012-186 Conrail
012-189 Soo Line (white)
012-204 Erie Lackawanna (light gray)
012-205 El Rexene (gray)
012-206 Chessie System/Baltimore & Ohio (yellow)
012-207 Chicago & North Western (yellow)
012-219 Burlington Northern (cascade green)
012-228 Chessie System (1 ea: Baltimore & Ohio, Chesapeake & Ohio and Western Maryland) pkg(3) 29.95
012-229 Robintech (gray)
012-240 New York Central
012-241 Baltimore & Ohio (gray)
012-242 Chesapeake & Ohio (gray)
012-243 Pennsylvania (gray)
012-244 Great Northern (gray)
012-245 Cotton Belt (gray)
012-247 Grand Trunk Western (gray)
012-248 Norfolk & Western (gray)
012-249 Louisville & Nashville (blue)
012-250 Grand Trunk Western (blue)
012-265 Rock Island, "The Rock" *NEW*
012-266 Union Pacific (white) *NEW*
012-267 E.C.C. America *NEW*
012-268 Burlington Northern (1991)(cascade green) *NEW*

54' PULLMAN STANDARD RIBSIDE COVERED HOPPER ea 9.50

012-124 Delaware & Hudson (red)
012-187 Conrail
012-200 Chicago & North Western (yellow)
012-201 Chessie System/Baltimore & Ohio
012-202 Missouri-Kansas-Texas
012-220 Burlington Northern 9.50
012-221 Soo Line (white)
012-222 Transportation Corporation of America (red, white)
012-223 Union Pacific "Sugar" (white)
012-230 Norfolk & Western (dark gray)
012-231 Frito-Lay (gray)
012-232 Union Pacific (gray)
012-233 New York Central (light gray)
012-234 Erie Lackawanna (light gray)
012-235 Southern Railway (gray)
012-236 Illinois Central
012-237 Illinois Central Gulf
012-238 Rio Grande
012-239 Great Northern (blue)
012-251 Seaboard System (cream)
012-252 Louisville & Nashville/Family Lines (cream)
012-253 Penn Central (jade green)
012-255 Burlington Northern (cascade green)
012-262 Chicago & North Western "Employee Owned" (gray) *NEW*
012-264 Rock Island, "The Rock" *NEW*

HOPPER LOADS

These hopper and gondola loads are cast plastic. They will also fit AHM, Tyco & Bachmann cars with some modification.

COAL
012-3101 Athearn Twin, single "hump" contour pkg (2) 2.50
012-3102 Athearn Twin, double "hump" contour pkg (2) 2.50
012-3104 Athearn Quad pkg (2) 3.00
012-3108 Roundhouse Triple pkg (2) 3.00
012-3110 Roundhouse Thrall pkg (2) 3.50
012-3112 McKean Triple pkg (2) 3.50
012-3114 Roundhouse Bathtub pkg (2) 3.50
012-3116 Walthers/TMI Twin pkg (2) 3.50
012-3118 MDC Ortner pkg (2) 3.50

GRAVEL
012-3106 Athearn Twin pkg (2) 2.50
012-3107 Athearn Quad pkg (2) 3.00
012-3109 Roundhouse Triple pkg (2) 3.00
012-3119 Walthers/TMI Twin pkg (2) 3.50

ORE
012-3105 MDC 21' Ore Car pkg (2) 2.50
012-3115 MDC Modern 26' Gondola pkg (2) 3.50

SAND
012-3113 Athearn 50' Gondola pkg (2) 3.50

WOOD CHIP
012-3117 Walthers/TMI 36' Hopper pkg (2) 3.50

REEFER

57' MECHANICAL REEFER
012-227 Pacific Fruit Express (white) 9.50

TANK CAR

62' TANK CAR
012-174 Publicker (black) 8.95

These HO Scale easy-to-build kits are prepainted and lettered and include trucks and horn-hook couplers. We have worked closely with this manufacturer to provide accurate availability information at the time this catalog was published. Items listed in blue ink may not be available at all times. Please see your dealer for current delivery information.

40' AIRSLIDE COVERED HOPPER

BOX CARS

OLD TIME BOX CAR ea 7.98
(unless noted)
223-123 40' Oldie Trailer Assortment pkg (12) 143.76 **NEW**
223-136 Oldtime box car Assortment #1 95.76 **NEW**
223-520101 Rio Grande
223-520102 Pennsylvania
223-520103 Atlantic Coast Line
223-520104 Chicago & Illinois Midland (yellow)
223-520105 Union Pacific
223-520106 Maintenance-Of-Way (gray)
223-520107 Norfolk & Western (tuscan)
223-520108 Santa Fe (tuscan)
223-520109 Seaboard Air Line (tuscan)
223-520110 Southern Pacific (tuscan)
223-520111 Nashville, Chattanooga & St. Louis (tuscan)
223-520112 Florida East Coast (tuscan)
223-520100 Undecorated

40' PS-1 BOX CAR
ea 5.98, pkg (unless noted)
These kits include separate weights and feature working Pullman Standard panel doors. The underframe has been modified and will accept body-mounted horn-hook or Kadee #5 couplers.

223-9405 Southern
223-9406 Soo Line
223-9407 Data Only (tuscan)
223-9408 Data Only (red)
223-9409 Data Only (oxide red)
223-9410 Grand Trunk Western (tuscan)
223-9411 Union Pacific
223-9412 Missouri-Kansas-Texas (tuscan)
223-9413 Boston & Maine
223-9414 Green Bay & Western
223-9415 Louisville & Nashville
223-9416 Chesapeake & Ohio (tuscan)
223-9417 Milwaukee Road (tuscan)
223-9418 Western Pacific (tuscan, orange)
223-9419 Pittsburgh & West Virginia (black)
223-9420 Great Northern (jade green)
223-9421 Delaware & Hudson (black)
223-9422 Baltimore & Ohio (blue)
223-9423 Illinois Central (orange)
223-9424 Erie Lackawanna (gray)
223-9425 Norfolk & Western (blue)
223-9426 Western Maryland (box car red)
223-9427 Florida East Coast (blue)
223-9428 Rio Grande
223-9400 Undecorated
223-9401 Santa Fe
223-9402 Southern Pacific
223-9403 Baltimore & Ohio
223-9404 Conrail

40' PS-1 BOX CAR 3-PACKS
Three-packs include three prepainted cars, each with a different number. Kits feature printed end lettering, brass 36" wheels and "sprung" roller bearing trucks.

223-940101 Pennsylvania #1 pkg (3) 23.98
223-940102 Pennsylvania #2 pkg (3) 23.98
223-940201 Santa Fe #1 pkg (3) 23.98
223-940202 Santa Fe #2 pkg (3) 23.98
223-940301 New York Central #1 pkg (3) 23.98
223-940302 New York Central #2 pkg (3) 23.98
223-940401 Chicago & North Western #1 pkg (3) 23.98
223-940402 Chicago & North Western #2 pkg (3) 23.98
223-940501 Southern Pacific #1 pkg (3) 23.98
223-940502 Southern Pacific #2 pkg (3) 23.98
223-940601 Bangor & Aroostook #1 pkg (3) 23.98
223-940602 Bangor & Aroostook #2 pkg (3) 23.98
223-940701 Baltimore & Ohio pkg (3) 17.98
223-940801 Conrail pkg (3) 17.98
223-940901 Union Pacific pkg (3) 17.98
223-941001 Rio Grande pkg (3) 17.98

40' PS-1 INSULATED BOX CAR ea 5.98
223-9451 Chicago, Burlington & Quincy
223-9452 Union Pacific TBA
223-9453 Canadian Pacific
223-9454 Miller
223-9455 Evergreen
223-9456 Conrail
223-9457 Data (red)
223-9458 Railway Express Agency
223-9459 Food Growers Express (tuscan, yellow)
223-9461 Rio Grande
223-9462 Pacific Fruit Express
223-9463 Hormel
223-9464 Thermal Ice (silver)
223-9465 New York Central Express (REA green)
223-9466 American Refrigerator (tuscan, yellow)
223-9467 Detroit, Toledo & Ironton
223-9468 Canadian National (tuscan)
223-9469 Southern Pacific (REA green)
223-9450 Undecorated

60' GREENVILLE BOX CAR
ea 8.98 (unless noted)
223-9603 Union Pacific (oxide red)
223-9606 Burlington Northern
223-9607 Data (red)
223-9608 Detroit, Toledo & Ironton (drab green)
223-9609 Chicago & North Western
223-9610 New York Central
223-9611 Western Pacific (box car red)
223-9612 Norfolk & Western
223-9613 Southern Railway System
223-9615 Illinois Central Gulf
223-9616 Pennsylvania
223-9617 Missouri Pacific (box car red)
223-9618 Data (oxide red)
223-9619 Data (box car red)
223-55301 Union Pacific #1 (box car red) 9.98
223-55302 Union Pacific #2 (box car red) 9.98
223-55401 Chessie #1 9.98
223-55402 Chessie #2 9.98
223-9600 Undecorated 9.98
223-9630 Undecorated 9.98
223-9601 Santa Fe (red)
223-9602 Conrail (box car red)
223-9604 Southern Pacific
223-9605 Chessie

REEFERS

40' WOOD REEFER
223-187 Assortment pkg (12) 75.00
223-135100 Undecorated 6.25 **NEW**

HOPPERS

40' AIRSLIDE COVERED HOPPER ea 9.49
223-9701 Santa Fe (dark gray)
223-9702 Pennsylvania (original, gray)
223-9703 Southern Pacific (gray, black)
223-9704 Western Maryland
223-9705 Revere Sugar (black)
223-9706 Firestone (black, red)
223-9707 Canadian Donut (gray)
223-9708 Bond Baking (gray)
223-9715 Conrail (oxide red)
223-9751 Santa Fe #2 (dark gray)
223-9752 Pennsylvania (modern)
223-9765 Conrail #2 **NEW**
223-19704 Southern Pacific #2 **NEW**
223-9750 Undecorated

40' AIRSLIDE COVERED HOPPER ASSORTMENTS ea 113.88
223-166 Santa Fe pkg(12)
223-167 Pennsylvania pkg (12)
223-174 Southern Pacific pkg (12) **NEW**
223-175 Assortment pkg (12) **NEW**

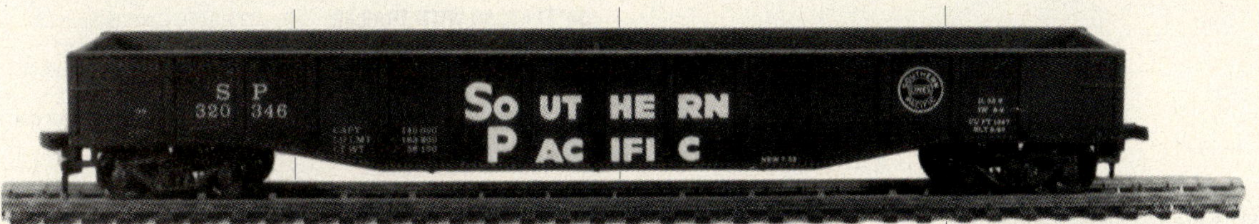

GREENVILLE 12 PANEL HOPPER ea 5.98

223-9301 Data (red)
223-9304 Southern Railway System
223-9308 Santa Fe
223-9313 Frisco (box car red)
223-9314 Illinois Central
223-9315 Pennsylvania
223-9316 Seaboard Coast Line
223-9317 Chattahoochee Industrial
223-9318 Soo Line
223-9319 Western Pacific
223-9351 Data (red)
223-9352 Baltimore & Ohio
223-9354 Western Maryland
223-9357 Norfolk & Western
223-9320 Undecorated
223-9300 Data (black)
223-9302 Chessie
223-9303 Conrail
223-9305 Southern Pacific
223-9306 Burlington Northern
223-9307 Rio Grande
223-9309 Union Pacific
223-9310 Norfolk & Western
223-9311 Chicago & North Western
223-9312 Chesapeake & Ohio

47' PS-2 COVERED HOPPER ea 7.98

These kits will accept body mounted couplers. Some kits include add-on lettering panels that mount over the ribs and simulate the sheet metal plates used on the prototypes.

223-9502 Southern Pacific
223-9503 Santa Fe
223-9505 Southern Railway System
223-9507 Data (light gray)
223-9508 Data (dark gray)
223-9509 Maintenance-Of-Way Data (gray)

223-9512 Baltimore & Ohio
223-9516 Cotton Belt (dark gray)
223-9517 Chicago, Burlington & Quincy
223-9518 Norfolk & Western
223-9519 Elgin, Joliet & Eastern (gray)
223-9520 CSX Transportation
223-9521 Western Pacific (dark gray)
223-9522 Pennsylvania (gray)
223-9523 Jack Frost Cane Sugar (blue, white)
223-9524 Great Western Malt (gray, green)
223-9525 BakeLite Plastics (red, white)
223-9526 New York Central (light gray)
223-9527 Chicago & North Western
223-9528 Great Northern
223-9529 Florida Tile (light gray)
223-9530 Warps Plastic (yellow)
223-9531 Lehigh Valley (white)
223-9532 Chicago & North Western (dark green)
223-9533 Atlantic Coast Line (yellow)
223-9534 Sutton Co-Op (blue)
223-9500 Undecorated
223-9501 Union Pacific
223-9504 Conrail
223-9506 Rio Grande
223-9513 Milwaukee Road
223-9514 Soo Line
223-9515 Burlington Northern

100 TON 12 PANEL HOPPER 12-PACKS ea 71.76

223-500 Burlington Northern pkg (12)
223-502 Norfolk Southern pkg (12)
223-504 Chessie pkg (12)
223-505 Union Pacific pkg (12)
223-506 Norfolk & Western pkg (12)
223-507 Chicago & North Western pkg (12)

GREENVILLE 12 PANEL HOPPER 3-PACKS

Three-packs include three prepainted cars, each with a different number. Kits feature printed end lettering, brass 36" wheels and "sprung" roller bearing trucks.

223-930101 Rio Grande #1 pkg (3) 23.98
223-930102 Rio Grande #2 pkg (3) 23.98
223-930201 Conrail #1 pkg (3) 23.98
223-930202 Conrail #2 pkg (3) 23.98

100 TON 15 PANEL HOPPER ea 5.98

223-9350 Data (black)
223-9353 Detroit, Toledo & Ironton
223-9355 Santa Fe
223-9360 Erie Lackawanna
223-9361 Delaware & Hudson
223-9362 Northern Pacific
223-9363 Chicago, Burlington & Quincy
223-9364 New York Central
223-9358 Undecorated (black)

47' PS-2 COVERED HOPPER ASSORTMENT

Three-packs include three prepainted cars, each with a different number. Kits feature printed end lettering, brass 36" wheels and "sprung" roller bearing trucks.

54' MILL GONDOLA

223-950001 Cement de Mexico #1 pkg (3) 29.98
223-950002 Cement de Mexico #2 pkg (3) 29.98
223-950101 Union Pacific #1 pkg (3) 29.98
223-950102 Union Pacific #2 pkg (3) 29.98
223-950201 Erie Lackawanna #1 pkg (3) 29.98
223-950202 Erie Lackawanna #2 pkg (3) 29.98
223-950301 Southern Pacific pkg (3) 23.98
223-950401 Santa Fe pkg (3) 23.98
223-950501 Conrail pkg (3) 23.98
223-950601 Baltimore & Ohio pkg (3) 23.98

40' AIRSLIDE COVERED HOPPER ea 9.49

223-9709 ATL Sugar
223-9711 Diamond Chemicals
223-9712 American Chemical Products
223-9713 Chicago, Burlington & Quincy
223-9714 Nickel Plate Road
223-9716 Norfolk & Western

42' COVERED HOPPER

223-1768 Southern Pacific 5.98 *NEW*

GONDOLAS

54' MILL GONDOLA ea 5.98 (unless noted)

223-9006 Wabash (black)
223-9010 Southern Pacific (Modern)
223-77 Assortment #3 71.76
223-8408 Milwaukee, Racine & Troy (box car red)
223-9001 Chicago & North Western (Chinese red)
223-9002 Union Pacific
223-9003 Pennsylvania
223-9004 Southern Pacific (box car red)
223-9005 Santa Fe
223-9007 Conrail
223-9008 CSX Transportation
223-9009 Santa Fe (modern)
223-9011 Burlington Northern
223-9012 Rio Grande
223-9013 Pittsburgh & Lake Erie
223-9014 Chesapeake & Ohio
223-9015 Louisville & Nashville
223-9016 Missouri Pacific
223-9017 Norfolk & Western (black)
223-9018 Southern Pacific (box car red)
223-9019 Cotton Belt (box car red)
223-9020 Santa Fe (Modern)
223-9021 Union Pacific (Modern)
223-9022 Southern Railway System
223-9023 Milwaukee Road
223-9024 Delaware & Hudson
223-9025 Data (black)
223-9026 Data (red)
223-9000 Undecorated

54' MILL GONDOLA W/LOAD ea 7.98

223-9028 Alaska Railroad
223-9029 Wisconsin Central
223-9030 Florida East Coast
223-9031 Central Railroad of New Jersey (olive green)

GREENVILLE 12-PANEL HOPPER

These HO Scale easy-to-build kits are prepainted and lettered and include trucks and horn-hook couplers.
We have worked closely with this manufacturer to provide accurate availability information at the time this catalog was published. Items listed in blue ink may not be available at all times. Please see your dealer for current delivery information.

54' PULPWOOD FLATCAR

54' FLATCAR WITH CABLE LOAD

FLATCARS

45' FLATCAR WITH 45' TRAILER ea 10.98
(unless noted) *NEW*
223-165 pkg (12) 131.76
223-9172 Alaska Railroad (blue), Lynden Transport (white)
223-9173 Illinois Central Gulf (black, silver)
223-9174 Burlington Northern (green, white)

54' FLATCAR WITH CABLE LOAD ea 5.98
223-9251 Southern Pacific (box car red)
223-9252 Trailer Train
223-9253 Burlington Northern
223-9254 Illinois Central Gulf (orange)
223-9256 Union Pacific
223-9257 Santa Fe (red)
223-9258 Rio Grande (orange)
223-9259 Conrail (box car red)
223-9260 CSX Transportation
223-9261 Southern Railway
223-9262 Family Lines
223-9255 Norfolk & Western
223-9250 Undecorated

54' PULPWOOD FLATCAR ea 7.98
Each kit includes a one-piece removable pulpwood load.
223-9204 Burlington Northern (cascade green)
223-9206 Ontario Northland (blue)
223-9207 Great Northern
223-9208 Norfolk & Western (black)
223-9201 Santa Fe (red)
223-9202 TTX
223-9203 Soo Line (white)
223-9205 Southern Railway System

54' FLATCAR WITH TRAILER ea 9.98 (unless noted)
223-160 45' Modern Trailer pkg (12) 131.76
223-178 40' Trailer pkg (12) 131.76
223-9155 Wabash (black, blue)
223-9157 Illinois Central (box car red, orange, brown)
223-9158 Santa Fe
223-9167 Nitrol 10.98
223-9168 Conrail (box car red), Crab Orchard (silver) 10.98
223-9169 Southern Railway System (box car red), Texas Mexican (white) 10.98
223-9170 Union Pacific (oxide red), Cornucopia (silver) 10.98
223-9175 Trailer Train (yellow), Preferred Pool (white) 10.98 *NEW*
223-9276 Trailer Train (yellow), UPS (silver)
223-9277 Rio Grande (black, gray)
223-9278 Chicago & North Western (black, white)
223-9279 Southern Pacific
223-9280 Southern Railway
223-9281 Illinois Central
223-9282 Norfolk & Western
223-9283 Royal American Shows
223-9284 w/Royal American 40' Trailer 10.98
223-9285 w/Royal American Rib Trailer 10.98
223-9286 w/Royal American 28' Trailer 10.98
223-9287 w/Royal American Tanker 10.98
223-9150 Undecorated
223-9171 Undecorated 10.98
223-115 Flatcar/Trailer Assortment pkg (12) 119.76
223-9151 Pennsylvania
223-9152 Western Pacific
223-9153 Union Pacific
223-9154 Pacific Fruit Express
223-9156 Great Northern

54' FLATCAR WITH OLD TIME TRAILER ea 9.98
223-9159 New York Central
223-9161 Seaboard Coast Line (box car red, silver)
223-9163 Florida East Coast (box car red), Seaboard (silver, red)
223-9165 Chicago & North Western
223-9166 Rio Grande (black), Navajo (silver, blue)
223-9160 Southern Pacific
223-9162 Northern Pacific
223-9164 Baltimore & Ohio

54' FLATCAR WITH CONTAINER ea 9.98
223-9176 Trailer Train/Dole (yellow, white)
223-9177 Canadian Pacific/CP Ships (box car red, green)

223-9178 Conrail/Spanish Line (box car red, blue)
223-9179 Santa Fe/Maersk (box car red, silver)
223-9180 Chessie/American President Lines (black, silver)
223-9181 Soo Line/Hanjin (white, light blue)

54' BULKHEAD FLATCAR ea 7.98
223-9209 Chicago & North Western (dark green)
223-9200 Undecorated

COIL CARS

54' COIL CAR ea 10.98 (unless noted)
223-177 Assortment pkg (12) 131.76
223-9051 Santa Fe
223-9052 Norfolk Southern (black)
223-9053 Chessie System (dark blue)
223-9054 Conrail (box car red)
223-9055 Pennsylvania
223-9056 New York Central (black)
223-9057 Detroit, Toledo & Ironton
223-9050 Undecorated
223-9059 Undecorated, Flat covered

FUEL FOILERS ea 14.98 (unless noted)
223-2901 Santa Fe - 4 Section
223-2903 Santa Fe - 3 Mid 12.98
223-2904 TTX - 4 Section
223-2906 Southern Pacific - 4 Section
223-2907 Southern Pacific - 3 Mid 12.98
223-2900 Undecorated - 4 Section
223-2902 Undecorated - 3 Mid 12.98
223-2908 Conrail - 4 Section
223-2909 Conrail - 3 Mid 12.98
223-2910 ITEL - Section
223-2911 ITEL - 3 Mid 12.98

INFORMATION STATION

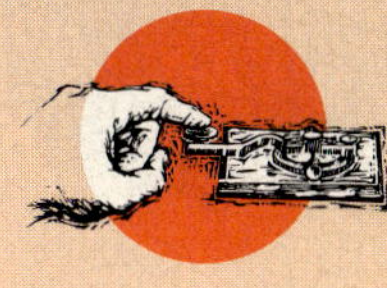

For almost 150 years, railroad car wheels were made of cast iron. Dozens of companies supplied wheels, and many railroads cast their own. Their most distinguishing features were the cooling fins on the back. These dissipated heat after the casting process, so the wheel cooled evenly.

But as car weights approached and then exceeded 70 tons, failures of cast iron wheels increased. Higher speeds and greater braking pressures caused burning, which weakened the metal. Longer cars also put more steering strain on the wheels, causing flanges to wear more rapidly.

Cast steel wheels were required on all new or rebuilt cars after January 1, 1958. On January 1, 1969, the use of cast iron wheels on cars in interchange service was prohibited.

During the course of a typical year, many railroads experience seasonal traffic peaks or rushes. This is especially common in agricultural areas, where grain and fruit must be moved to distant markets. During these periods, trains move day and night, and normally quiet areas come alive with activity.

Planning for the event goes on year 'round and involves every department. An adequate supply of cars, such as covered hoppers or reefers must be available, along with sufficient motive power.

Most of these trains will run as extras (trains not listed in a regular schedule) so additional crews must be on hand too.

Custom Finishing

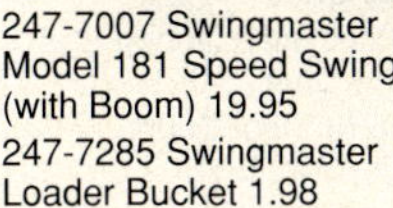

These HO Scale kits feature detailed brass and white metal parts, and include rotating, insulated wheel.

MAINTENANCE OF WAY EQUIPMENT

BURRO CRANE

247-7000 Burro Model 40 Crane (12-1/2 Ton) 34.95
The boom in this kit is made of etched brass. The kit can be built so that the cab rotates.

247-7008 Burro Model 50 (20 Ton) TBA

BURRO CRANE ACCESSORIES

247-7282 Clamshell Bucket kit 14.95
This 1/2 cubic yard bucket includes brass castings and can be assembled to operate.

247-7283 Crane Accessories 4.98
This set of brass castings includes a 39" nonoperating magnet, hoistblock, hook and railtongs.

247-7800 Burro Crane Decals 4.95
247-70001 Boom Only 8.99

TRACK MAINTENANCE EQUIPMENT

247-7001 Fairmont Tie Handler 19.95
The kit cab be assembled so the cab rotates.

247-7801 Faimont Decal Set 4.95
247-7002 Fairmont Rail Spot Grinder 31.95
247-7003 Permaquip (Fairmont) 19.95
This welders vehicle's side shutter panels operate and may be left open to show interior detail (sold separately).

247-7284 Permaquip Welders Vehicle Interior 3.29
The details in this kit include a welder console, V6 style engine, and hoist winches.

247-7803 Permaquip Decal Set 4.95
247-7004 Permaquip Permaclipper (Fairmont) TBA
This kit is a rail fastener system for welded rail.

247-7005 Nordco Nordberg Spike Puller 19.95
247-7006 Nordco Nordberg Hydra-Hammer (Rail Spiker) 19.95

247-7007 Swingmaster Model 181 Speed Swing (with Boom) 19.95
247-7285 Swingmaster Loader Bucket 1.98

247-7009 Hy-Rail Guide Wheels for Light Duty Vehicles 1.98 NEW
247-7010 Pyke Utility Crane (1 ton capacity) 29.95 NEW
247-7011 Pyke Model M Ballast Regulator TBA NEW
247-7012 Tamper Model STM Switch Tamping Machine 44.95 NEW
247-7013 Pyke On Track Brush Cutter TBA NEW
247-7014 Tamper MK III Rail Alignment/Tamper Machine 39.95 NEW
247-7015 Pyke 18 Ton Rail Crane TBA NEW
247-7016 Rail Maintenance Equipment Flat Car Loading Ramp 8.95 NEW
247-7017 Pyke Model M Snow Clearing Machine TBA NEW
247-7018 Nordberg Anchor Applicator TBA NEW
247-7019 Nordberg Model C Scarifier/Tie Inserter TBA NEW
247-7020 Fairmont Heavy Duty Gang Car with Trailer 15.95 NEW
247-7220 Trailer for Gang Car Extra 4.95 NEW
247-7021 Pandrol - Jackson Model 6700 Production/Switch Tamper TBA NEW
247-7022 Knox Kershaw Ballast Regulator TBA NEW
247-7023 Pandrol - Jackson Ultrasonic Flaw Detection Vehicle TBA NEW
247-7024 160 psi Compressor TBA NEW

PYKE BALLAST REGUATOR

SWINGMASTER MODEL 181 SPEED SWING WITH BOOM

FAIRMONT RAIL SPOT GRINDER

FUNARO & CAMERLENGO

These kits consist of thin flexible styro-urethane castings with details (cast in place), stripwood, wire and instructions. Cars do not have couplers or trucks. Decorated kits include decals.

We have worked closely with this manufacturer to provide accurate availability information at the time this catalog was published. Items listed in blue ink may not be available at all times. Please see your dealer for current delivery information.

BOX CARS

BOX CARS 1890's BOX CAR
279-3800 Undecorated 22.99

BOX CAR ea pkg (2) 26.99
(unless noted)
279-1003 C&K, HOn3
279-1004 C&K, HOn2-1/2
279-1005 East Broad Top Steel Box Car, HOn3 22.99
279-5101 East Broad Top Box Car, HOn3, #73 19.99
NEW

**27' BOX CAR
ea pkg (2) 29.99**
279-5040 Sandy River & Rangely Lake, HOn3
279-5041 Sandy River & Rangely Lake, 2.5 Wood Version, HOn2-1/2

**34' BOX CAR ea 23.99
NEW**
279-5110 NY Ontario & Western, as built
279-5111 NY Ontario & Western, upgraded

**36' DS WOOD BOX CAR
ea 23.99**
279-1006 Northern Pacific
279-5120 Ulster & Delaware
NEW

**36' TRUSS ROD BOX CAR
WITH HUTCHINS ENDS**
279-3201 NY Ontario & Western 23.99
279-3200 Undecorated 22.99

**36' SOUTHERN WOOD BOX
CAR WITH HUTCHINS ENDS**
279-3130 Undecorated 22.99

**36' DELAWARE & HUDSON
WOOD BOX CAR**
The following kits include decals. ea 23.99 (unless noted)
279-3405 Rebuilt Z-Bar Ends
279-3406 Reverse Hutchins Ends
279-3407 3-Pack 55.99
279-3409 Converted to Sand Service
The following kits do not include decals. ea 22.99 (unless noted)
279-3400 Burnett Ends
279-3401 Rebuilt Z-Bar Ends
279-3402 Reverse Hutchins Ends
279-3403 3-Pack 49.99
279-3408 Converted to Sand Service

**36' RE-BUILT BOX CAR,
NEW HAVEN ea 23.99
NEW**
279-5090 Steel Door and Ends
279-5091 Wood Door, Braced Ends
279-5092 Steel Door, Braced Ends

**40' WOOD BOX CAR WITH
TRUSS ROD UNDERFRAME**
279-3701 Great Northern 23.99
279-3070 Undecorated 19.99

**40' WOOD BOX CAR WITH
STEEL UNDERFRAME**
279-3060 Undecorated 22.99

**40' BOSTON & MAINE XM-1
SINGLE SHEATHED BOX CAR
ea 24.99 NEW**
Each kit includes decals and Tichy trucks.
279-6000 Flat Pullman Roof
279-6001 Rib Outside Carline Roof

**40' USRA DOUBLE
SHEATHED BOX CAR**
279-3059 Missouri Pacific 23.99
279-3050 Undecorated 22.99

**40' 1-1/2 DOOR AUTO BOX
CAR MILWAUKEE ROAD**
279-3301 Milwaukee Road 23.99

**WABASH 40' SINGLE
SHEATHED AUTO CAR WITH
RADIAL ROOF**
The following kits include decals. ea 23.99
279-3504 Wood Doors & Murphy Ends
279-3505 Steel Doors, End Loading Door
279-3506 Steel Doors, 3/3/3 Dreadnaught Ends
The following kits do not include decals. ea 22.99
279-3501 Steel Doors, End Loading Door
279-3502 Steel Doors, 3/3/3 Dreadnaught Ends

GONDOLAS

50' "BATTLESHIP" GONDOLA

**DELAWARE & HUDSON
TRUSS ROD COMPOSITE
GONDOLA**
279-4600 Height 3'2", Length 36' Less Decals 22.99
279-4601 Height 3'2", Length 36' With Decals 23.99

**DELAWARE & HUDSON
COMPOSITE GONDOLA**
279-4620 Height 3', Length 33' Less Decals 22.99
279-4621 Height 3', Length 33' With Decals 23.99
279-4631 Height 3'8", Length 33' With Decals 23.99
279-4640 Extended Sides, Height 4'6", Length 33' Less Decals 22.99
279-4641 Extended Sides, Height 4'6", Length 33' With Decals 23.99

40' COMPOSITE GONDOLA
279-1021 Baltimore & Ohio 23.99
279-1022 Undecorated 22.99

**"GR" COMPOSITE
GONDOLA pkg (2) 29.99**
279-5000 Pennsylvania
279-5001 Long Island

TANK CARS

MILK TANK CAR ea 23.99
(unless noted)
279-1010 Borden's, white lettering
279-1011 Borden's, yellow lettering
279-1012 Borden's, black lettering
279-1013 Borden's/Chemical Division
279-1009 Undecorated 22.99

**40' LOW SIDE STEEL
GONDOLA ea 23.99
NEW**
279-5080 Atlantic Coast Line

**50' "BATTLESHIP"
GONDOLA**
279-2071 Virginian 23.99
279-2070 Undecorated 22.99

FLAT CARS

**Flat Car pkg (2) 29.99
NEW**
279-5100 East Broad Top, HOn3

HOPPERS

STEEL HOPPER *NEW*
279-5102 East Broad Top #800, as-built 23.99

34' WOOD HOPPER
279-2081 Ontario & Western Style, with decals 23.99
279-2080 Ontario & Western Style, Undecorated 22.99

34' PENNSY COVERED HOPPER ea 23.99
(unless noted)
279-30010 H35A (white lettering)
279-30040 H30A (black steam era)
279-30001 Undecorated 23.99

40' HORIZONTAL RIB HOPPER *NEW*
279-5050 Erie/NY Susquehanna & Western 23.99

52' PENNSY COVERED HOPPER
279-2094 H32 (black steam era) 23.99
279-2090 Undecorated 22.99

DELAWARE & HUDSON COMPOSITE TWIN HOPPER
The following kits include decals. ea 23.99
279-3083 As-Built
The following kits do not include decals. ea 22.99
(unless noted)
279-3090 Modernized
279-3093 Modernized pkg (3) 55.99

DELAWARE & HUDSON COMPOSITE TRIPLE HOPPER
279-3112 40' Wood 23.99
279-3110 Undecorated 22.99

DELAWARE & HUDSON QUAD HOPPER
279-3122 with Decals 23.99
279-3120 less Decals 22.99

READING CHANNEL SIDE HOPPER ea 22.99
(unless noted)
279-1020 Circa 1913 with Decals 23.99
279-10191 Circa 1904 less Decals
279-10201 Circa 1913 less Decals
279-1019 Circa 1904 with Decals 23.99

SPECIAL ORDER ONLY

These items must be specially ordered from the manufacturer. You will be notified upon receipt of merchandise.

52' PENNSY COVERED HOPPER ea 23.99
279-2091 H32 (white lettering)
279-2092 H32 (black lettering)

DELAWARE & HUDSON COMPOSITE TWIN HOPPER
The following kits include decals. ea 23.99
279-3092 Modernized
279-3102 Modernized, Peaked End
The following kits do not include decals. ea 22.99
279-3081 As-Built
279-3100 Modernized, with Peak Ends

REEFERS

36' CANADIAN NATIONAL 8-HATCH REEFER ea 23.99 *NEW*
279-5130 Dreadnaught Ends
279-5131 Improved Dreadnaught Ends
279-5132 Plug Door

37' WOOD REFRIGERATOR ea 23.99 (unless noted)
279-3603 Wilson 1940-1960
279-3605 Kahn's
279-3606 Patrick Cudahy
279-3607 Oscar Mayers
279-3608 American Refrigerator Transit
279-3609 Hormel
279-3600 Undecorated 22.99

40' OUTSIDE BRACED REEFER
279-1015 Reading 23.99
279-10151 Undecorated 22.99

40' GPEX WOOD MILK REEFER ea 23.99
279-1042 Borden's, Billboard
279-1045 Hoods, Billboard
279-1047 Nestles
279-1048 Borden's (gold)
279-4200 Renken's Billboard Lettering

NEW YORK, ONTARIO & WESTERN MILK CAR
279-1091 New York, Ontario & Western 23.99
279-1090 Undecorated, New York, Ontario & Western Style 22.99

40' GREENVILLE MILK CAR ea 23.99
279-2050 Boston & Maine
279-2051 Erie

40' STEEL MILK REEFER ea 23.99 (unless noted)
279-1031 Hoods
279-5020 Boston & Maine, with Viking roof
279-5021 Erie, with Viking roof
279-1030 GPEX Undecorated 22.99
279-5022 Undecorated, with Viking roof 22.99

40' GPEX STEEL MILK REEFER, ROUND FLOOR ea 23.99
279-3021 HP Hoods & Sons
279-3022 Borden's
279-3023 Milky Way

40' TWIN TANK MILK CAR ea 29.99 (unless noted) *NEW*
279-5060 Borden's, Fishbelly Side
279-5061 Bell, Fishbelly Side
279-5062 Borden's, Fishbelly Center
279-5064 Tank Only, Borden's pkg (2) 9.99
279-5065 Tank Only, Bell pkg (2) 9.99

50' GPEX STEEL MILK REEFER, ROUND FLOOR ea 23.99
279-1081 Hoods
279-1082 Borden's

50' GPEX MILK REEFER WITH NARROW DOOR ea 23.99 ((unless noted)
279-1053 Eversweet Orange Juice
279-1054 Baker's Chocolate
279-1050 Undecorated 22.99
Each undecorated kit includes alphabet set decals.
279-1055 HP Hoods & Sons

50' GPEX WOOD MILK REEFER WITH WIDE DOOR ea 23.99 (unless noted)
279-1062 Borden's 22.99
279-1063 United Farms
279-1064 Hoods
279-1065 Sheffield Farms
279-1066 United 22.99
279-1060 Undecorated 22.99

50' DELAWARE & HUDSON STYLE WOOD MILK REEFER
279-2001 Delaware & Hudson 23.99
279-2000 Undecorated 22.99

50' WOOD MILK REEFER WITH FOUR DOORS
279-2060 Undecorated 22.99

50' WOOD MILK REEFER WITH NARROW LETTERBOARD ea 23.99 (unless noted)
279-2021 Rutland, New York Central/Rutland Style
279-2022 New York Central, New York Central/Rutland Style
279-2020 Undecorated 22.99

50' WOOD REEFER WITH WIDE LETTERBOARD
279-2010 Undecorated, New York Central/Rutland Style 22.99
279-2012 New York Central, New York Central/Rutland Style 23.99

50' EXPRESS REEFER WITH HIGH ARCH ROOF
279-1070 Undecorated 22.99

50' TRUSS ROD WOOD REEFER WITH WIDE LETTERBOARD ea 23.99
(unless noted)
279-3031 Rutland
279-3032 New York Central
279-3030 Undecorated 22.99

50' TRUSS ROD WOOD REEFER WITH NARROW LETTERBOARD ea 23.99
(unless noted)
279-3041 Rutland
279-3042 New York Central
279-3040 Undecorated 22.99

FUNARO & CAMERLENGO

SPECIAL ORDER ONLY

These items must be specially ordered from the manufacturer. You will be notified upon receipt of merchandise.

37' WOOD REFRIGERATOR
279-3602 Wilson 1920-1940 23.99

40' GPEX WOOD MILK REEFER ea 23.99
(unless noted)
279-1041 Sheffield Farms, Billboard
279-1044 Abbot's Milk, Billboard
279-1040 Undecorated 22.99

40' GREENVILLE MILK CAR
279-2052 Undecorated 22.99

40' STEEL MILK REEFER
279-1034 Milky Way 23.99

40' GPEX STEEL MILK REEFER, ROUND FLOOR
279-3024 Baker's Chocolate 23.99
279-3020 Undecorated 22.99

CABOOSES

CABOOSES ea 22.99
279-501 Long Island N52A, Original
279-502 Long Island N52A, Rebuilt
279-503 Long Island Class N22A
279-504 Long Island/New York, Ontario & Western Class N52B
279-505 Long Island Class N22B Bay Window
279-506 Southern, Wood
279-1001 Rio Grande Short Wood, HOn3
279-1002 Rio Grande Short Wood, HOn2-1/2
279-5030 Sandy River & Rangely Lakes, HOn3
279-5031 Sandy River & Rangely Lakes, HOn2/HOn2-1/2

GLOOR·CRAFT MODELS

These HO Scale craft train kits feature polished scale basswood precut parts, color coded stripwood, metal castings, step-by-step instructions and full size drawings. These kits do not include trucks and couplers.

We have worked closely with this manufacturer to provide accurate availability information at the time this catalog was published. Items listed in blue ink may not be available at all times. Please see you dealer for current delivery information.

FLAT CARS

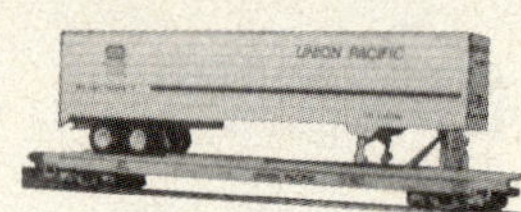

50' PIGGYBACK WITH 45' TRAILER
288-3208 Undecorated, Flat 25.95

60' BULKHEAD WITH LOAD
288-3202 TTX 21.95

TRANSPORTS

50' AUTO TRANSPORT
288-3004 Pennsylvania, X41A 23.95
288-3005 Santa Fe, Fe27 23.95

MAINTENANCE OF WAY

MAINTENANCE-OF-WAY CARS
Maintenance-of-Way cars are often old coaches or freight cars which have been specially rebuilt for their new use.

288-3600 Flanger with Plow, Undecorated 18.95
288-3601 55' Payroll Car 22.95

BOX CARS

40' VERTICAL RIB BOX CAR
288-3001 Rio Grande XML 21.95

50' GRAIN LOADING BOX CAR
288-3002 Chicago, Burlington & Quincy DR 23.95

70' LUMBER BOX CAR
288-3003 "Hello Dolly" 26.95

HOn3 BOX CAR
288-3501 East Broad Top #170 18.95

50' CANSTOCK BOX CAR
288-3012 Baltimore & Ohio XL 25.95

60' INSULATED BOX CAR
288-3000 Chicago, Burlington & Quincy 25.95

50' GRAIN LOADING BOX CAR

HOn3 BOX CAR

70' LUMBER CAR

HOPPERS

2-BAY HOPPER
288-3502 East Broad Top, HOn3 17.95

34' COMPOSITE 2-BAY HOPPER
288-3400 Nickel Plate Road, 50T 18.95

34' COVERED 2-BAY HOPPER ea 18.95
288-3401 70-Ton
288-3402 100-Ton

3-BAY HOPPER
288-3503 East Broad Top, HOn3 17.95

32' 3-BAY HOPPER
288-3403 Pennsylvania, H31 17.95

34' COMPOSITE 2-BAY HOPPER

3-BAY HOPPER

AUTO RACKS

89' BI-LEVEL AUTO RACK
288-3200 TTX 22.95

89' TRI-LEVEL AUTO RACK
288-3201 TTX 25.95

GONDOLAS

HOn3 GONDOLA
288-3504 East Broad Top, No. 346 12.95

CABOOSES

WOOD CABOOSE

REEFERS

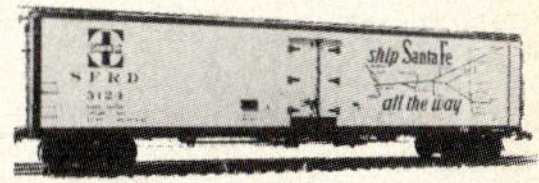

36' WOOD REEFER
288-3020 Olympia Beer 22.95

50' WOOD REEFER
288-3009 Santa Fe, R37 19.95

WOOD CABOOSE ea 20.95 (unless noted)
288-3102 Nickel Plate Road, 1000 Series
288-3103 32' Norfolk & Western
288-3105 Union Pacific, CA-1 21.95
288-3106 30' Chesapeake & Ohio 19.95
288-3107 30' Baltimore & Ohio, I-1

288-3108 30' Baltimore & Ohio, I-5
288-3109 37' Baltimore & Ohio, Bay Window, I-16 21.95
288-3110 Pittsburgh & Lake Erie, Standard
288-3111 New York Central Class 19000
288-3112 35' Santa Fe 21.95
288-3113 29' Northern Pacific 22.95

288-3114 30' Delaware & Hudson
288-3115 32' Erie
288-3116 35' Canadian National
288-3500 East Broad Top, No. 27/28 HOn3 18.95
288-3506 32' Rio Grande, HOn3 19.95

PENNSYLVANIA CABOOSE
288-3101 Class N6B 20.95
288-3104 Class ND Caboose with 33" wheels 21.95
288-3100 Class N6A 20.95

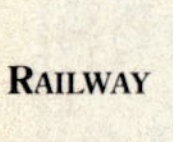

INTERMOUNTAIN

RAILWAY COMPANY

WHERE DETAIL MAKES THE DIFFERENCE

NEW

These easy-to-build styrene kits have numerous add-on parts. Each is complete with trucks and step-by-step instructions, but does not include weights or couplers. Coupler pockets will accept Kadee #5 couplers. The cars are prepainted and lettered, and each roadname is offered with multiple car numbers. So you can have several cars in your fleet, subsequent production runs feature new numbers. New roadnames are released monthly, please see your Dealer for the latest releases.

CYLINDRICAL HOPPER

REEFERS

59' 4-BAY CYLINDRICAL HOPPERS

Introduced in 1972, these cylindrical hoppers are commonly known as "Canadian grain cars." Almost 20,000 were built for grain service throughout Canada and the cars are frequent visitors to the US.

CANADIAN WHEAT BOARD - CANADA CARS (bright red)
ea 14.50 *NEW*

85-107 CNWX 7th Number
85-108 CNWX 8th Number
85-109 CNWX 9th Number
85-110 CNWX 10th Number
85-111 CNWX 11th Number
85-112 CNWX 12th Number

CANADIAN WHEAT BOARD - CANADA CARS (bright red)
ea 14.50 *NEW*

85-207 CPWX 7th Number
85-208 CPWX 8th Number
85-209 CPWX 9th Number
85-210 CPWX 10th Number
85-211 CPWX 11th Number
85-212 CPWX 12th Number

ALBERTA "HERITAGE FUND" (Early Scheme)
ea 14.50 *NEW*

85-301 CP Rail (ALPX) 1st Number
85-302 CP Rail (ALPX) 2nd Number
85-303 CP Rail (ALPX) 3rd Number
85-304 CP Rail (ALPX) 4th Number
85-305 CP Rail (ALPX) 5th Number
85-306 CP Rail (ALPX) 6th Number

ALBERTA "HERITAGE FUND" (Early Scheme)
ea 14.50 *NEW*

85-401 Canadian National (ALNX) 1st Number
85-402 Canadian National (ALNX) 2nd Number
85-403 Canadian National (ALNX) 3rd Number
85-404 Canadian National (ALNX) 4th Number
85-405 Canadian National (ALNX) 5th Number
85-406 Canadian National (ALNX) 6th Number

PILLSBURY
ea 15.95 *NEW*

These cars are blue with white lettering and logo.

85-501 1st Number
85-502 2nd Number
85-503 3rd Number
85-504 4th Number
85-505 5th Number
85-506 6th Number

CANADIAN NATIONAL "WET NOODLE" **ea 15.95** *NEW*

Cars in this series are painted gray with red lettering.

85-601 1st Number
85-602 2nd Number
85-603 3rd Number
85-604 4th Number
85-605 5th Number
85-606 6th Number
85-607 7th Number
85-608 8th Number
85-609 9th Number
85-610 10th Number
85-611 11th Number
85-612 12th Number

CP RAIL **ea 15.95** *NEW*

These hoppers are painted in the new all-black scheme with white lettering.

85-701 1st Number
85-702 2nd Number
85-703 3rd Number
85-704 4th Number
85-705 5th Number
85-706 6th Number
85-707 7th Number
85-708 8th Number
85-709 9th Number
85-710 10th Number
85-711 11th Number
85-712 12th Number

SCOULAR GRAIN HOPPER
ea 15.95 *NEW*

These hoppers are yellow-gold with black, brown and green lettering.

85-800 1st Number
85-802 2nd Number
85-803 3rd Number
85-804 4th Number
85-805 5th Number
85-806 6th Number
85-807 7th Number
85-808 8th Number
85-809 9th Number
85-810 10th Number
85-811 11th Number
85-812 12th Number

FARMLAND CO-OP
ea 15.95 *NEW*

These hoppers are gray with a red, white and black herald.

85-901 1st Number
85-902 2nd Number
85-903 3rd Number
85-904 4th Number
85-905 5th Number
85-906 6th Number
85-907 7th Number
85-908 8th Number
85-909 9th Number
85-910 10th Number
85-911 11th Number
85-912 12th Number

KOPPEL INC.
ea 15.95 *NEW*

These hoppers are dark blue with yellow herald and reporting marks.

85-1001 1st Number
85-1002 2nd Number
85-1003 3rd Number
85-1004 4th Number
85-1005 5th Number
85-1006 6th Number
85-1007 7th Number
85-1008 8th Number
85-1009 9th Number
85-1010 10th Number
85-1011 11th Number
85-1012 12th Number

ALBERTA "HERITAGE FUND" ("Take a Break" Scheme)
ea 15.95 *NEW*

These hoppers are bright blue with yellow lettering.

85-1101 CP Rail (APLX) 1st Number
85-1102 CP Rail (APLX) 2nd Number
85-1103 CP Rail (APLX) 3rd Number
85-1104 CP Rail (APLX) 4th Number
85-1105 CP Rail (APLX) 5th Number
85-1106 CP Rail (APLX) 6th Number

ALBERTA "HERITAGE FUND" ("Take a Break" Scheme)
ea 15.95 *NEW*

These hoppers are bright blue with yellow lettering.

85-1201 Canadian National (ALNX) 1st Number
85-1202 Canadian National (ALNX) 2nd Number
85-1203 Canadian National (ALNX) 3rd Number
85-1204 Canadian National (ALNX) 4th Number
85-1205 Canadian National (ALNX) 5th Number
85-1206 Canadian National (ALNX) 6th Number

GTA GRAIN MARKETING
ea 15.95 *NEW*

These hoppers are gray with red and black heralds.

85-1401 1st Number
85-1402 2nd Number
85-1403 3rd Number
85-1404 4th Number
85-1405 5th Number
85-1406 6th Number
85-1407 7th Number
85-1408 8th Number
85-1409 9th Number
85-1410 10th Number
85-1411 11th Number
85-1412 12th Number

SANTA FE
ea 15.95 *NEW*

These hoppers are tuscan red with white lettering.

85-1701 1st Number
85-1702 2nd Number
85-1703 3rd Number
85-1704 4th Number
85-1705 5th Number
85-1706 6th Number
85-1707 7th Number
85-1708 8th Number
85-1709 9th Number
85-1710 10th Number
85-1711 11th Number
85-1712 12th Number

MILWAUKEE ROAD
ea 15.95 *NEW*

These cars are gray with black lettering.

85-2001 1st Number
85-2002 2nd Number
85-2003 3rd Number
85-2004 4th Number
85-2005 5th Number
85-2006 6th Number
85-2007 7th Number
85-2008 8th Number
85-2009 9th Number
85-2010 10th Number
85-2011 11th Number
85-2012 12th Number

PS 4750 HOPPER

HONEYMEAD ea 15.95
NEW

These cars are painted gray with the Honeymead logo in brown.

85-2101 1st Number
85-2102 2nd Number
85-2103 3rd Number
85-2104 4th Number
85-2105 5th Number
85-2106 6th Number
85-2107 7th Number
85-2108 8th Number
85-2109 9th Number
85-2110 10th Number
85-2111 11th Number
85-2112 12th Number

UNDECORATED
85-1 Undecorated 11.50
NEW

PULLMAN STANDARD CENTER DISCHARGE 4750 HOPPER

Introduced in the early 70's by Pullman-Standard, 30 railroads and some 120 private firms have purchased these cars. Several builders have also constructed similar three-bay hoppers with a 4,750 cubic-foot capacity.

UNION PACIFIC
ea 14.95 **NEW**

These hoppers are gray with black lettering and full-color herald.

85-10001 1st Number
85-10002 2nd Number
85-10003 3rd Number
85-10004 4th Number
85-10005 5th Number
85-10006 6th Number
85-10007 7th Number
85-10008 8th Number
85-10009 9th Number
85-10010 10th Number
85-10011 11th Number
85-10012 12th Number

BURLINGTON NORTHERN
ea 14.95 **NEW**

These hoppers are finished in the latest cascade green and white scheme.

85-10101 1st Number
85-10102 2nd Number
85-10103 3rd Number
85-10104 4th Number
85-10105 5th Number
85-10106 6th Number
85-10107 7th Number
85-10108 8th Number
85-10109 9th Number
85-10110 10th Number
85-10111 11th Number
85-10112 12th Number

KANSAS CITY SOUTHERN
ea 14.95 **NEW**

These cars are brown with white lettering.

85-10201 1st Number
85-10202 2nd Number
85-10203 3rd Number
85-10204 4th Number
85-10205 5th Number
85-10206 6th Number
85-10207 7th Number
85-10208 8th Number
85-10209 9th Number
85-10210 10th Number
85-10211 11th Number
85-10212 12th Number

CHICAGO & NORTH WESTERN ea 14.95 **NEW**

These cars are painted dark green with white and yellow lettering, and feature the "Employee Owned" herald in red, white and black.

85-10301 1st Number
85-10302 2nd Number
85-10303 3rd Number
85-10304 4th Number
85-10305 5th Number
85-10306 6th Number
85-10307 7th Number
85-10308 8th Number
85-10309 9th Number
85-10310 10th Number
85-10311 11th Number
85-10312 12th Number

SOO LINE
ea 14.95 **NEW**

This series of cars is finished in white with black and green lettering and the yellow wheat sheaf emblem.

85-10401 1st Number
85-10402 2nd Number
85-10403 3rd Number
85-10404 4th Number
85-10405 5th Number
85-10406 6th Number
85-10407 7th Number
85-10408 8th Number
85-10409 9th Number
85-10410 10th Number
85-10411 11th Number
85-10412 12th Number

UNDECORATED PS2CD 4750 CUBIC FEET HOPPER **NEW**
85-10000 Undecorated 10.95

40' AAR BOX CARS CHICAGO, BURLINGTON & QUINCY (Chinese red)
ea 13.95 **NEW**

85-20001 1st Number
85-20002 2nd Number
85-20003 3rd Number
85-20004 4th Number

GREAT NORTHERN (brown, white, black)
ea 13.95 **NEW**

85-20101 1st Number
85-20102 2nd Number
85-20103 3rd Number
85-20104 4th Number
85-20105 5th Number
85-20106 6th Number

MISCELLANEOUS
85-2 Barber 100 Ton Truck pkg (2) 1.75 **NEW**

Late summer and the grain rush is on. From the plains and the prairies, train after train of covered hoppers make their way across the Chicago Heights Central. This busy urban scene was built by Bill Butt of Chicago Heights, Illinois, and includes Magnuson and Design Preservation structures. Those are the line's new SD60M's on the point, with a string of Custom Rail hoppers in tow.

Photo by Phillip Serviss

McKean

These HO Scale easy-to-build plastic car kits are prepainted and lettered, and have trucks with 28", 33" or 36" wheels. They feature Kadee compatible dummy couplers, and weights are included.

We have worked closely with the manufacturer to provide accurate availability information at the time this catalog was published. Items listed in blue ink may not be available at all times. Please see your dealer for current delivery information.

BOX CARS

40' PS-1 BOX CAR WITH DOUBLE DOORS

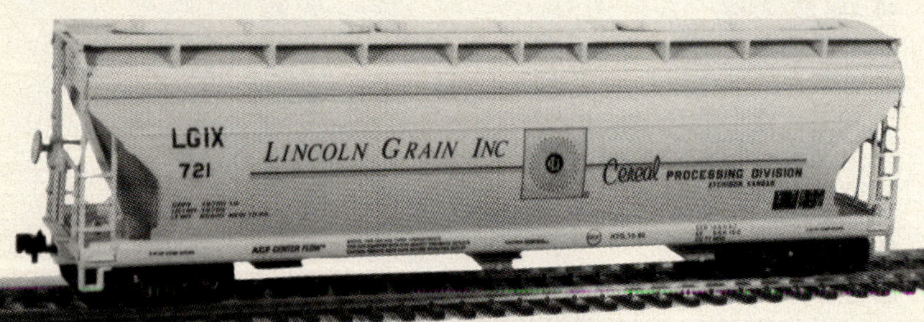

47' ACF GRAIN CAR ea 9.95

50' DOUBLE PLUG DOOR BOX CAR

50' ACF RIVET-SIDE DOUBLE-DOOR BOX CAR ea 9.95 *NEW*

457-3001 Nickel Plate Road (tuscan)
457-3002 Rock Island (tuscan)
457-3003 New York Central (brown)
457-3004 Gulf Mobile & Ohio (tuscan)
457-3000 Undecorated

40' BOX CAR WITH MOLDED DETAILS ea 7.95

457-451 Southern Pacific T&NO (tuscan) *NEW*
457-452 Pennsylvania *NEW*
457-450 Undecorated

40' BOX CAR WITH DOUBLE DOORS ea 8.95

Limited Quantities Available

457-306 Baltimore & Ohio (brown)
457-309 Pennsylvania (brown)

40' PS-1 BOX CAR WITH DOUBLE DOORS ea 8.95

457-776 Northern Pacific (tuscan)
457-777 Burlington Northern (cascade green)
457-778 Milwaukee Road
457-780 Soo Line (brown)
457-775 Undecorated
457-779 Seaboard

50' DOUBLE PLUG DOOR BOX CAR ea 9.95 (unless noted)

457-1101 Northwest Hardwoods (orange)
457-1102 Georgia Pacific (blue)
457-1103 Boise Cascade (green)
457-1104 USLX (red)
457-1105 Evans Product Co (blue) pkg (3) 39.95
457-1106 Magobar (orange)
457-1100 Undecorated

50' BOX CAR WITH DOUBLE DOORS ea 9.95

457-10004 Triangle Pacific (red)
457-10009 Southern Pacific (brown)

40' ACF BOX CAR WITH DOUBLE DOORS 3-PACKS

Limited Quantities Available

457-10015 Pennsylvania (brown) pkg (3) 24.98

47' ACF GRAIN CAR listings

457-1601 Data Only (gray)
457-1602 Baltimore & Ohio (gray)
457-1603 Southern Pacific (gray)
457-1604 Detroit, Toledo & Ironton (gray)
457-1605 Pennsylvania (gray)
457-1606 Seaboard Coast Line (yellow)
457-1608 CSX Transportation (yellow)
457-1609 Southern Railway System

457-1610 Louisville & Nashville (sky blue)
457-1611 St Louis South Western (gray)
457-1613 Missouri & Pacific (gray)
457-1614 Chicago & North Western (yellow)
457-1615 Lincoln Grain Cereal (gray) *NEW*
457-1616 Burlington Northern (cascade green) *NEW*
457-1617 Golden West Service (CRLE) *NEW*

457-1618 Golden West Service (GVSR) *NEW*
457-1619 Soo Line (grain of wheat)
457-1620 Union Pacific (gray)
457-1621 Western Pacific (gray)
457-1623 Simpson Paper Co (tan)
457-1600 Undecorated
457-1607 FMC Chemicals

40' PS-1 BOX CAR WITH 8' DOOR ea 7.95

The master series of HO freight car kits features a one-piece body construction with 8' door.

457-701 Delaware & Hudson (box car red)
457-702 Chicago & North Western (box car red)
457-703 Baltimore & Ohio (box car red)
457-705 Milwaukee Road
457-706 Illinois Central Gulf (reefer orange)
457-707 Chesapeake & Ohio (brown)
457-708 Norfolk & Western (black)
457-709 Southern Railway (brown)
457-710 Seaboard Air Lines
457-711 Soo Line (box car red)
457-712 Data Only (box car red)
457-713 St Louis South Western (box car red)
457-714 Union Pacific (box car red)
457-715 Missouri Pacific (box car red)
457-716 Erie (box car red)
457-718 Detroit, Toledo & Ironton (box car red)
457-733 Central of Georgia (box car red)
457-735 Seaboard Coast Line (box car red)
457-736 Louisville & Nashville
457-737 Central of Georgia (brown) *NEW*
457-700 Undecorated
457-704 Chicago, Rock Island & Pacific
457-717 Nickel Plate Road
457-731 Pennsylvania (box car red)
457-732 Frisco

50' OUTSIDE BRACED BOX CAR WITH MODERN "RAILBOX" ENDS

40' PS-1 BOX CAR WITH 6' DOOR ea 7.95

457-719 Santa Fe (box car red)
457-722 Colorado & Southern (box car red)
457-723 Burlington Northern (cascade green)
457-725 Minneapolis & St Louis (dark blue)
457-726 Monon (box car red)
457-727 New York Central (box car red)
457-729 Richmond, Fredericksburg & Potomac (box car red)
457-734 Canadian National (brown)
457-749 Undecorated
457-720 Chicago Great Western
457-721 Canadian Pacific
457-724 Gulf, Mobile & Ohio (red)
457-728 Pittsburgh & Lake Erie (jade)
457-730 Western Pacific (box car red)

50' OUTSIDE BRACED BOX CAR WITH MODERN "RAILBOX" ENDS ea 9.95 (unless noted)

These kits include plug and sliding door.

457-902 Missouri Pacific (brown)
457-904 Chicago & North Western (brown)
457-905 Canadian National (brown)
457-906 Norfolk & Southern (orange)
457-907 Bangor & Aroostook
457-909 Maine Central (orange)
457-911 Golden West Service (GVSR) (blue) *NEW*
457-10007 Grand Trunk (light blue) 10.95
457-900 Undecorated
457-901 Kansas City Southern (rust)
457-903 Seaboard Coast Line (black)
457-908 Chessie
457-910 Rock Island

50' OUTSIDE BRACED BOX CAR WITH DREADNAUGHT ENDS ea 9.95

These kits include plug and sliding door.

457-802 Conrail (tuscan)
457-803 Santa Fe (tuscan)
457-805 Union Pacific (tuscan)
457-808 Montana Rail Link (dark blue)
457-810 Soo Line (white)
457-800 Undecorated
457-801 Burlington Northern (cascade green)
457-804 Rock Island
457-806 Kansas City Southern
457-807 Illinois Central Gulf
457-809 Great Northern
457-811 Chessie - CSX

40' BOX CAR WITH MOLDED DETAILS STEAM ERA ea 7.95

457-401 Union Pacific *NEW*
457-402 Maine Central *NEW*
457-404 Baltimore & Ohio *NEW*
457-405 Santa Fe (brown) *NEW*
457-400 Undecorated

50' ACF BOX CARS WITH DOUBLE DOORS

Limited Quantities Available

457-10017 Rio Grande (orange) 9.95

McKean

These HO Scale easy-to-build plastic car kits are prepainted and lettered, and have trucks with 28", 33" or 36" wheels. They feature Kadee compatible dummy couplers, and weights are included.

We have worked closely with this manufacturer to provide accurate availability information at the time this catalog was published. Items listed in blue ink may not be available at all times. Please see your dealer for current delivery information.

LUMBER CARS

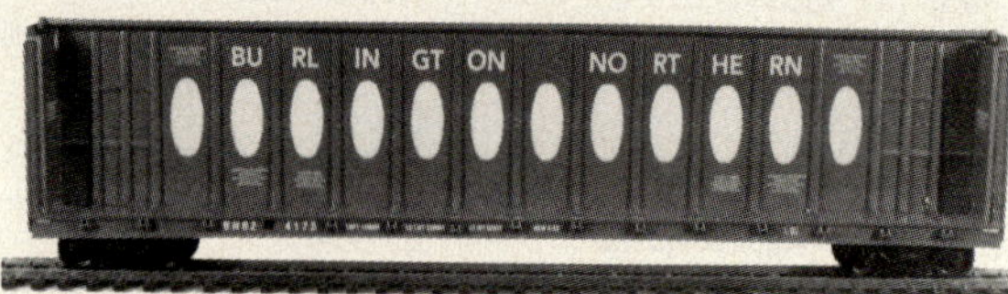

63' THRALL LUMBER CAR WITH OPERA CENTERBEAM ea 12.95

457-1701 Burlington Northern (cascade green)
457-1702 Milwaukee Road (mustard)
457-1703 Union Pacific
457-1704 Western Pacific (black)
457-1705 British Columbia Railway (olive green)
457-1706 Trailer Train (yellow)
457-1700 Undecorated

FLAT CARS

50' TOFC FLAT CAR WITH TRAILER

50' TOFC FLAT CAR WITH TRAILER ea 9.95

457-1201 Southern (brown)
457-1202 Union Pacific
457-1203 Santa Fe
457-1204 Canadian Pacific (red)
457-1205 Canadian National (black)
457-1200 Undecorated

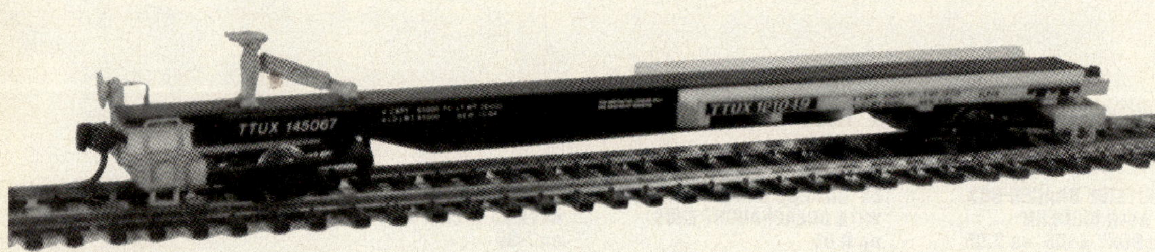

50' FRONT RUNNER

**50' FRONT RUNNER
ea pkg (2) 9.95**
(unless noted)
457-601 TTX (gold)
457-611 TTX w/Metal Wheels pkg (4) 21.95
457-600 Undecorated
457-610 Undecorated pkg (4) 19.95
457-620 TTX/Trans America (white)
457-650 Undecorated/Undecorated **NEW**
457-621 TTX/Santa Fe w/45' Trailer

**50' TOFC FLAT CAR
ea pkg (2) 9.95**
457-1001 Union Pacific (mustard)
457-1002 Santa Fe (white)
457-1003 Southern Railway (brown)
457-1004 Canadian Pacific
457-1005 Grand Trunk Western (dark blue)
457-1006 Canadian National (black)
457-1007 Chicago & North Western
457-1008 Norfolk Southern (black)
457-1009 Seaboard Coast Line (black)
457-1010 TTX (gold)
457-1011 Missouri - Kansas - Texas (gold)
457-1012 Canadian Pacific **NEW**
457-1013 Chicago & North Western XTRA **NEW**
457-1000 Undecorated

50' TOFC FLAT CAR

McKean

63' THRALL LUMBER CAR WITH OPEN CENTERBEAM ea 12.95

Railroads move a wide range of building materials, and many use these special Centerbeam Flat Cars to haul wrapped lumber. The centerbeam makes the car stronger and it can carry a much heavier load than a conventional bulkhead flat. Spacers on the deck allow for fast loading or unloading with a forklift. They also tip the load inward, helping to prevent shifting while the car is in motion, or tipping during loading and unloading. A series of tie-downs and ratchetrs are located on each side of the car to help hold the load securely.

These kits are packed with detail, and come prepainted and lettered for many of the railroads who own and operate them. To model a loaded car, be sure to see the Jaeger Lumber load kits, listed elsewhere in this section.

457-1751 Burlington Northern (cascade green)
457-1752 CSX Transportation (red)
457-1753 Union Pacific (mustard)
457-1754 Canadian Pacific (mineral red)
457-1755 Trailer Train (yellow)
457-1750 Undecorated

74' THRALL LUMBER CAR WITH OPERA CENTERBEAM ea 14.95

457-1901 Burlington Northern (cascade green)
457-1902 Union Pacific (tuscan)
457-1903 TTX (TTX yellow)
457-1904 Hampton Lumber (red, white)
457-1900 Undecorated

74' THRALL LUMBER CAR WITH OPEN CENTERBEAM ea 14.95

457-1951 Burlington Northern (cascade green)
457-1952 Union Pacific (tuscan)
457-1953 TTX (TTX yellow)
457-1954 McCloud River (blue, white)
457-1950 Undecorated TBA

HOPPERS

62' ACF GRANULES HOPPER ea 10.95

457-1501 ACFX (gray)
457-1502 ACF Demo (gray)
457-1503 Dependable Feed Service
457-1504 Norchem (gray)
457-1505 Arco Polymers
457-1506 Polysar Resins **NEW**
457-1507 Rocor Resins **NEW**
457-1508 ADM Corn Sweeteners **NEW**
457-1509 J.M. Huber Corp. **NEW**
457-1510 W.R. Grace Company **NEW**
457-1511 Rexall Chemical **NEW**
457-1512 Plaskon Products **NEW**
457-1513 Sinclair Koppers (gray) **NEW**
457-1514 Engelhard Minerals & Chemicals (silver) **NEW**
457-1515 Amoco Chemical (silver) **NEW**
457-1516 North American (silver) **NEW**
457-1517 American Hoechst Plastics (silver) **NEW**
457-1518 Burlington **NEW**
457-1519 Continental Grain **NEW**
457-1520 Stauffer Chemical (gray) **NEW**
457-1500 Undecorated

62' GRANULES COVERED HOPPER CAR ea 10.95

457-1550 Alathion
457-1552 Chemplex (gray)
457-1555 Santa Fe **NEW**
457-1551 ADM Corn Sweeteners
457-1553 CPC Greene (yellow)
457-1554 El Rexene (gray)

34' 2-BAY COVERED HOPPER ea 9.95

457-1301 Rio Grande (gray)
457-1303 Corning Glass **NEW**
457-1305 Southern Pacific (gray)
457-1306 Chicago & Eastern Illinois (gray)
457-1308 Western Maryland (gray)
457-1309 Southern Railway (gray)
457-1316 Great Northern (gray)
457-1317 Chicago & North Western (green)
457-1318 Chicago & North Western (yellow)
457-1319 Data Only (gray)
457-1324 Monon
457-1300 Undecorated

62' GRANULES COVERED HOPPER CAR

62' ACF GRANULES HOPPER

34' 2-BAY COVERED HOPPER

These HO Scale ready-to-run cars are prepainted and lettered.

We have worked closely with this manufacturer to provide accurate availability information at the time this catalog was published. Items listed in blue ink may not be available at all times. Please see your dealer for current delivery information.

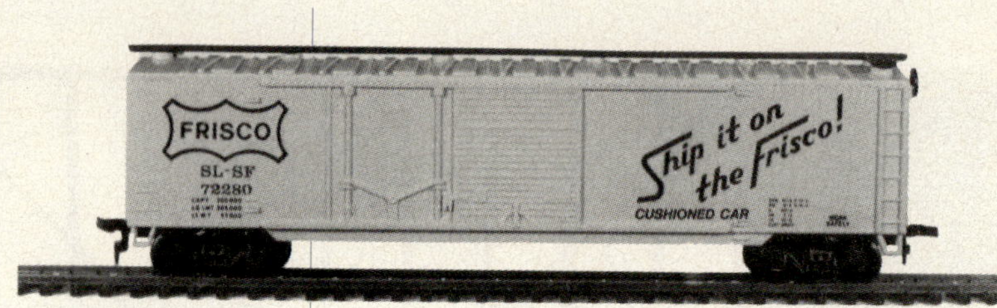

50' PD/SD BOX CAR

BOX CARS

40' SLIDING DOOR BOX CAR
ea 5.98

490-7970 Baltimore & Ohio Sentinel (silver, blue)
490-7971 Great Northern

490-7972 Central of Georgia (silver, purple)
490-7974 Southern Pacific (brown)

40' WOOD DD BOX CAR

40' SINGLE DOOR STEEL BOX CAR

50' BOX CAR

50' PD/SD BOX CAR ea 5.98
490-9031 Western Pacific (silver)
490-9034 Illinois Central Gulf (orange)
490-9036 Conrail (blue)
490-9037 Frisco (yellow)
490-9039 Santa Fe

40' BOX CARS ea 5.98
(unless noted) *NEW*
490-3706 Southern Pacific Overnight
490-7973 Timken
490-7976 Lifesaver
490-80051 Napa Parts 4.98
490-80052 Champion 4.98

40' WOOD DD BOX CAR
490-9002 Great Northern (sky blue) 4.98

40' SINGLE DOOR STEEL BOX CAR ea 4.98
490-8001 Conrail
490-8002 Baby Ruth (orange)
490-8003 Maine Central (bright orange)

50' BOX CAR ea 5.98
490-8040 Grand Trunk Western
490-8041 Burlington Northern (cascade green)
490-8042 Canadian National
490-8043 Canadian Pacific
490-8044 General Electric

The last express train has left for the day and the first cars for the evening shift have been spotted. Less-than-Carload-Lot merchandise is still a primary source of traffic for the Madison Railroad, built by Martin Pollizotto of East Islip, New York. The freight terminal is from Walthers Cornerstone Series® and the cars are Accurail kits. Those pesky weeds along the tracks were made from rope fibers. Models and Photo by Martin Pollizotto.

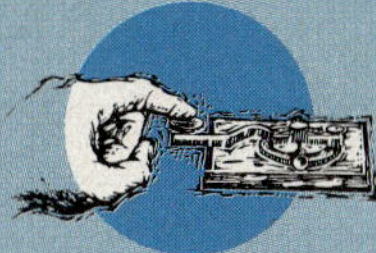

INFORMATION STATION

Every freight train has the same basic job of moving loaded or empty cars between shippers. Not every train does the same kind of work, so most are classified by the traffic they handle.

Priority Freights move time-sensitive or priority traffic. In the steam-era, highly perishable loads like strawberries and meat were carried at top speed in solid trains of reefers. Today's intermodal trains fall into this category, carrying domestic and international loads that must be delivered on time.

General Freights handle lower priority traffic that isn't time-sensitive.   They also ferry cars between yards, where they may be reclassified into other trains. Typical loads include chemicals, lumber and steel products.

Drag Freights were common in the steam era and still exist. These slower trains handle high tonnage loads that do not have to be moved quickly. In the steam-era, most coal trains were drag freights, while today, ballast or stone and other heavy items can be seen.

Unit Trains provide efficient service to customers needing or producing large quantities of a single item. Modern coal and grain trains are common examples, and some lines now run unit trains of taconite pellets and garbage.

The Wayfreight is the most often modeled, as it moves short consists of cars from yards to local customers and back again.

HOPPERS

36' 2-BAY HOPPER ea 4.98
490-8060 Dixie
490-8061 Western Maryland
490-8062 Frisco
490-8063 Pennsylvania
490-8064 Southern Pacific

36' 2-BAY COVERED HOPPER ea 4.98
490-8080 Norfolk & Western (gray)
490-8081 Portland Cement (gray)
490-8082 Ontario Northland (blue)
490-8083 Jack Frost Cane Sugar (gray, blue)
490-8084 Granite Rock (orange)

40' 3-BAY HOPPER ea 4.98
(unless noted)
490-8050 Santa Fe (red)
490-8051 Penn Central (blue, green)
490-6931 Rio Grande (orange)
490-6932 Illinois Central Gulf
490-8052 Canadian National 3.98

51' CYLINDRICAL COVERED HOPPER ea 6.98
490-9501 Canadian (brown)
490-9502 Canadian (silver)
490-9509 Wheat Bread
490-9513 Canada Red
490-9514 Saskatchewan
490-9515 Alberta
490-9516 Winnipeg
490-9517 Canadian Pacific

COAL LOADS
490-4020 Coal Loads pkg(2) .98

36' 2-BAY COVERED HOPPER

40' 3-BAY HOPPER

51' CYLINDRICAL COVERED HOPPER

ARMED FORCES

AIR FORCE ea 9.98
(unless noted) *NEW*
490-91611 Searchlight Command Center Car
490-91621 Tank Buster Q-Car
490-91641 Launcher Car with Missiles
490-91651 Caboose 4.98
490-91661 Tank Car 5.98

ARMY ea 9.98 *NEW*
490-9160 Flat Car with Tank
490-9162 Q-Car
490-9163 Big Cannon
490-9164 Exploding Car
490-9180 Base with Launcher (olive drab)

STOCK CARS

40' STOCK CAR ea 4.98
490-8010 Great Northern
490-8011 Santa Fe
490-8013 Missouri - Kansas - Texas (yellow)
490-8014 Canadian National
490-8015 Burlington Northern
490-8016 Louisville & Nashville

These HO Scale ready-to-run cars are prepainted and lettered.

We have worked closely with this manufacturer to provide accurate availability information at the time this catalog was published. Items listed in blue ink may not be available at all times. Please see your dealer for current delivery information.

REEFERS

REEFERS 50' THERMO-KING REEFER ea 5.98
490-9053 Railway Express Agency (green)
490-9054 Burlington Northern (cascade green)
490-9057 Olympia Beer

40' WOOD REEFER
490-3719 Maine Potatoes 5.98

FLAT CARS

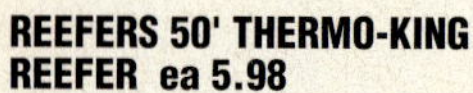

50' FLAT CAR WITH TRAILER

40' DEPRESSED CENTER FLAT CAR
490-8220 Safety with Light 7.98

40' FLAT CAR ea 4.98
490-8140 Santa Fe
490-8141 Pennsy

50' FLAT CAR WITH TRAILER ea 6.98
490-6910 Santa Fe (silver)
490-6911 Union Pacific with Consolidated Freightways
490-6912 Burlington Northern (cascade green)
490-6913 Santa Fe, Old
490-6914 Penn Central with Conrail

40' FLAT CAR WITH TWIN REMOVABLE TANKS ea 5.98 NEW
490-8160 Citi Service
490-8161 Gulf
490-8162 Sonoma Wine
490-8163 Water Car

40' FLAT WITH LUMBER
490-8210 Burlington Northern 5.98 NEW

Rocketing through central Illinois, Santa Fe is making sure that this intermodal traffic is going to arrive on time! The country module was built by the Midwest Valley Modelers, based out of the St. Louis area. Those are member Ken Patterson's Overland Models brass locos in command, pulling a Custom Rail Flat car loaded with McKean trailers.

Photo by Ken Patterson

CABOOSES

40' WORK CABOOSE

Wooden cabooses were used well into the 1950's by many railroads, so this handsome model is right at home behind your favorite steam or early diesel power. The one-piece body is nicely detailed, and the car is offered in a variety of paint and lettering schemes.

36' BAY WINDOW CABOOSE ea 4.98 *NEW*
490-8240 Safety
490-8241 Santa Fe
490-8242 Conrail
490-8243 Pennsylvania
490-8244 Southern Railway
490-8245 Burlington Northern
490-8246 Canadian National
490-8247 Southern Pacific

40' WORK CABOOSE WITH TANK ea 5.98 *NEW*
490-8181 Amtrak
490-8182 Weed Control
490-8180 Undecorated

32' WOOD CABOOSE ea 5.98
490-9141 Pennsylvania
490-9142 Baltimore & Ohio (caboose red)
490-9145 Southern (green)
490-9147 Canadian Pacific
490-9148 Canadian National (orange)

36' CABOOSE ea 5.98
(unless noted)
490-9121 Conrail
490-9123 Santa Fe (caboose red)
490-9125 Red Safety (red)
490-9127 Canadian Pacific Rail
490-9128 Canadian National
490-9165 Army 4.98

40' WORK CABOOSE
490-8200 Safety First (silver) 5.98

40' WORK CABOOSE WITH CRANE ea 5.98 *NEW*
490-8191 Santa Fe
490-8190 Undecorated

TANK CARS

40' TANK CAR

CHEMICAL TANK CARS ea 5.98 *NEW*
490-8101 Tank-Train
490-8102 Kodak
490-8103 Shell
490-8104 Hudson Bay
490-8105 Exxon
490-8106 Texaco
490-8107 Baker's Chocolate

38' HIGH CAPACITY TANK CAR "FAT ALBERT" ea 4.98
490-9023 Gulf Refining (silver)
490-9025 Celanese Chemicals (lime green)
490-9027 Shamrock
490-9028 Dow Chemical (royal blue)
490-9030 Union Starch (red)

40' TANK CAR ea 4.98
490-6920 Texaco (silver)
490-6921 Dupont (yellow, olive green)
490-6922 Union 76 (royal blue)
490-6923 Hooker (black)
490-8030 Dow Chemical (powder blue)
490-8031 Tootsie Roll (dark brown)
490-8032 Cities Service Oils (green)
490-8033 Michigan Alkali Co

50' HEATED TANK CAR ea 5.98
490-9081 Exxon
490-9083 Shell
490-9084 Tank Train

86' TANK CAR
490-7010 Burlington Northern 1.98 *NEW*

MAINTENANCE OF WAY

WORK CAR WITH CRANE
490-3161 Undecorated 24.95 *NEW*

200 TON CRANE
490-91612 Canadian National 15.95

GONDOLAS

GONDOLAS40' GONDOLA ea 4.98
490-8501 Southern Pacific
490-8502 Pennsy
490-8503 Southern
490-8504 Canadian National
490-8506 Soo Line

These easy-to-build HO Scale kits one-piece plastic bodies. They are prepainted and lettered for a variety of railroads. Trucks, couplers and weights are included.
We have worked closely with the manufacturer to provide accurate availability information at the time this catalog was published. Items listed in blue ink may not be available at all times. Please see you dealer for current delivery information.

BOX CARS

36' BOX CAR ea 5.98 (unless noted)
These kits include operating doors.

480-3061 Southern Pacific (tuscan)
480-3062 Santa Fe (tuscan)
480-3063 Colorado & Midland (tuscan)
480-3064 Tonopah & Tidewater (tuscan)
480-3065 Pennsylvania (tuscan)
480-3066 Northern Pacific (tuscan)

480-3067 Baltimore & Ohio (tuscan)
480-3202 Illinois Traction (green)
480-3203 Illinois Traction - Express
480-3204 Illinois Traction (red)
480-3060 Undecorated 5.50
480-3000 Colorado & Southern
480-3103 Union Pacific
480-3104 Western Union
480-3119 Devils Gulch

36' BILLBOARD BOX CAR ea 5.75 (unless noted)

480-3021 Standard Wagons (box car red)
480-3022 Lindsay Brothers (green)

480-3023 Ball Glass Jar Company (box car red)
480-3024 NK Fairbanks (box car red)

480-3025 Hercules Powder Company (gray)
480-3020 Undecorated 5.25

40' ROUND TOP BOX CAR ea 5.25 (unless noted)

40' HORIZONTAL RIB BOX CAR ea 5.25 (unless noted)

40' ROUND TOP BOX CAR ea 5.25 (unless noted)
These kits include operating doors.

480-1081 Pennsylvania (tuscan)
480-1083 Norfolk & Western (tuscan)
480-1084 Seaboard Air Line (tuscan)
480-1087 Northern Pacific (brown)
480-1088 Baltimore & Ohio (REA blue)
480-1089 Baltimore & Ohio
480-1080 Undecorated 4.75
480-1082 Bessemer & Lake Erie (tuscan)
480-1085 Baltimore & Ohio (tuscan)
480-1086 Santa Fe

40' HORIZONTAL RIB BOX CAR ea 5.25 (unless noted)
These kits include operating doors.

480-1021 Milwaukee Road Olympian (tuscan)
480-1022 Milwaukee Road Hiawatha (tuscan)
480-1023 Chicago, Milwaukee, St. Paul & Pacific Olympian (tuscan)
480-1024 Chicago, Milwaukee, St. Paul & Pacific Hiawatha (tuscan)
480-1025 Western Pacific (orange)
480-1020 Undecorated 4.75

40' AAR BOX CAR ea 5.25 (unless noted)

480-751 Norfolk & Western pkg(12) 63.00
480-1041 Burlington Northern (Burlington Northern cascade green)
480-1042 Pennsylvania (box car red)
480-1044 Union Pacific (box car red)
480-1047 Great Northern (silver)
480-1048 Rio Grande (white)

480-1049 Canadian National (tuscan)
480-1050 Southern Pacific "Overnight" (black)
480-1053 Baltimore & Ohio (dark blue)
480-1056 Canadian Pacific (tuscan gloss)
480-1062 Canadian Pacific "CP Rail" (red) 6.25
480-1063 Ontario Northern (blue) 5.50

480-1064 British Columbia Railway (olive green) 5.98
480-1066 Canadian National (box car red) 5.98
480-1067 New York Central 5.98
480-1068 Baltimore & Ohio (box car red)
480-1069 Western Pacific (tuscan)
480-1070 Chesapeake & Ohio "Progress" (box car red)
480-1071 Southern Pacific "Overnight" (silver)

480-1072 Chesapeake & Ohio "REA" (green)
480-1073 Soo Line (tuscan)
480-1074 Frisco (tuscan)
480-1075 Western Pacific "Feather" (orange)
480-1076 Erie Lackawanna (mineral red)
480-1077 Santa Fe (mineral red)
480-1078 Western Maryland, Speed Lettering (tuscan)
480-1079 Western Maryland (tuscan)

480-2041 New York Central "Early Bird" (mineral red)
480-2042 Pittsburgh & Lake Erie (mineral red)
480-2043 Pittsburgh & Lake Erie (jade green)
480-2044 Peoria & Eastern (mineral red)
480-2045 Missouri - Kansas - Texas
480-1040 Undecorated 4.75

50' PULLMAN STANDARD
ea 5.75 (unless noted)

480-1901 Frisco (tuscan)
480-1902 Milwaukee Road (box car red)
480-1903 Louisville & Nashville (box car red)
480-1904 Southern (tuscan)

480-1906 Boston & Maine (blue)
480-1907 Chicago & North Western/Rock Island (white)
480-1908 South Branch Valley (yellow)
480-1909 Texas-Mexican Railway

480-1910 Ann Arbor Railway System (orange)
480-1912 St Mary's Railroad (white)
480-1913 Lamoille Valley (yellow)
480-1914 Alabama State Docks (yellow)

480-1915 CSX Transportation/Seaboard System (blue)
480-1900 Undecorated 5.25
480-1905 Chicago & North Western (box car red)
480-1911 New Orleans Public (orange)

50' FLAT TOP HI CUBE ea 5.75 (unless noted)

These kits have single plug doors.

480-811 Golden West Service pkg(12) 78.00
NEW
480-1761 Union Pacific (tuscan) 6.50
480-1762 Erie Lackawanna (blue)
480-1763 Seaboard Coast Line (black)

480-1764 Burlington Northern (cascade green)
480-1765 Santa Fe (black, red)
480-1766 Southern Pacific (box car red)
480-1767 Golden West Service
480-1760 Undecorated 5.25

50' RIBBED SIDE FLAT TOP HI CUBE ea 5.75 (unless noted)

These kits have single plug doors.
480-1821 Santa Fe (red, black)
480-1822 Conrail (tuscan)
480-1824 Southern Pacific (box car red)
480-1825 Ontario Northern (dark blue)

480-1826 Chesapeake & Ohio (black)
480-1827 Soo Line (white, red door)
480-1828 Frisco (beige)
480-1820 Undecorated 5.25

50' FLAT TOP (WAFFLE SIDE) ea 5.75 (unless noted)

480-1801 Seaboard Coast Line (box car red)
480-1802 Louisville & Nashville
480-1803 Delaware & Hudson (reefer yellow)
480-1804 Southern Pacific (box car red)
480-1805 Burlington Northern (cascade green)

480-1806 Chessie (Chesapeake & Ohio) (royal blue)
480-1807 Union Pacific/Rock Island (blue)
480-1808 Frisco (beige)
480-1800 Undecorated 5.25

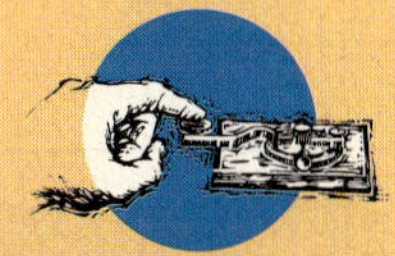

These are easy-to-build HO Scale Kits with one-piece plastic bodies. They are prepainted and lettered for a variety of railroads. Trucks, couplers and weights are included. We have worked closely with this manufacturer to provide accurate availability information at the time this catalog was published. Items listed in blue ink may not be available at all times. Please see your dealer for current delivery information.

BOX CARS

50' FMC SINGLE DOOR BOX
ea 5.75 (unless noted)
This is a ribbed side box car.

480-776 Golden West pkg(12) 102.00
480-1953 Warwick Railway (dark green)
480-1954 Ashley Drew & Northern (green)
480-1955 Providence & Worcester (red)
480-1956 Lake Erie Franklin & Clarion (yellow)
480-1958 Sabine River (red)
480-1959 Savannah State Docks (blue)
480-1960 Marinette, Tomahawk & Western (green)
480-1961 Meridian & Bigbee (blue)
480-1962 Bath & Hammondsport (tuscan)
480-1963 Port Huron & Detroit (blue)
480-1964 Seaboard (black)
480-1965 Seaboard (red)

480-1966 CSX Transportation (blue)
480-1967 Norfolk Southern 9.50
480-1973 Railbox (yellow) 9.50
480-1976 Railbox - Burlington Northern (yellow) 9.50
480-1977 Railbox - Santa Fe (yellow) 9.50
480-1978 Railbox - Seaboard (yellow) 9.50
480-1950 Undecorated 5.25
480-1952 Maine Central (yellow)
480-1974 Railbox - Southern Pacific (yellow) 9.50
480-1975 Railbox - Southern (yellow) 9.50
480-1979 Railbox - Richmond, Fredricksburg & Potomac (yellow) 9.50

Limited Quantities Available
480-781 Montana Rail Link pkg(12) 102.00

50' FMC DOUBLE DOOR OFFSET ea 6.50 (unless noted)
480-3641 Union Pacific 7.50
480-3642 East St Louis Junction (yellow)
480-3643 Columbia & Cowlitz (blue)
480-3644 Pend Oreille Valley (blue)
480-3645 Oregon, Pacific & Eastern (blue)
480-3646 Galveston Wharves (orange)
480-3647 Yreka Western (blue)
480-3640 Undecorated 5.75

40' MODERN BOX CAR
ea 4.98 (unless noted)
480-1101 Southern Pacific (box car red)
480-1102 Soo Line (box car red)
480-1103 Burlington Northern (Burlington Northern cascade green)
480-1104 Canadian Pacific (tuscan) 5.50
480-1105 Southern (box car red)
480-1106 Santa Fe (box car red)
480-1107 Erie Lackawanna (tuscan)
480-1100 Undecorated 4.50

50' FMC DOUBLE DOOR BOX
ea 5.75 (unless noted)
480-1981 Western Pacific (mineral red)
480-1982 Amador Central (sky blue)
480-1983 Chicago & North Western (box car red)
480-1984 Milwaukee (blue)
480-1985 Cotton Belt (St Louis Southwestern) (box car red)
480-1986 Southern Pacific (box car red)
480-1987 Seattle & North Coast (dark green)
480-1988 Longview Piedmont & Northern (orange)
480-1989 McCloud River (white)
480-1993 British Columbia Railway (green)

480-1994 Burlington Northern (cascade green)
480-1995 Chesapeake & Ohio (blue)
480-1980 Undecorated 5.25

50' FLAT TOP HI CUBE
ea 5.75 (unless noted)
These kits have double plug doors.

480-1782 Southern Pacific (box car red) 6.25
480-1783 Santa Fe (black, red)
480-1784 Conrail (tuscan)
480-1785 Norfolk & Western (black)
480-1786 Western Pacific (tuscan)
480-1787 Union Pacific Automated (silver, yellow) 9.25
480-1780 Undecorated 5.25

50' FMC DOUBLE DOOR BOX
ea 5.75 (unless noted)

50' FLAT TOP HI CUBE
ea 5.75 (unless noted)

50' FMC PLUG DOOR BOX
ea 6.50 (unless noted)

50' FMC PLUG DOOR BOX
ea 6.50 (unless noted)
480-3622 Grand Trunk Western
480-3623 Burlington Northern (cascade green)
480-3625 Minnesota, Dakota & Western (green, white)
480-3626 Canadian Pacific (green)
480-3627 Soo Line (black) 7.50
480-3628 Soo Line (red) 7.50
480-3629 Rio Grande 7.50
480-3620 Undecorated 5.75
480-3621 Santa Fe (red)
480-3624 Milwaukee Road (tuscan)

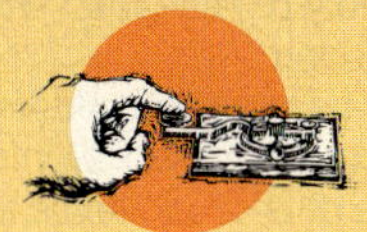

INFORMATION STATION

Each time a freight car pulls into a yard, it's given a visual inspection. Walking down each side of the train, inspectors check the couplers (for chips, cracks or worn spots) frame, (including cushioning devices, inside of wheels and axles)

end ladders, crossover steps and all mounting brackets, brake shoes, wheel flanges and truck springs.

To experienced eyes, loose bolts, a streak of grease, newly rusted or shiny metal may indicate a part that needs attention. If a defect is found, the car is "bad ordered" with a special tack card indicating the type of repair needed.

Small repairs are done onsight. A more extensive job may require the car be removed from the train and taken to the repair-In-place (rip) track. Here, heavier work that may require welding, cutting, lifting or other more time-consuming work can be done with the appropriate equipment. If the job is extensive, but the defect won't prevent safe operation of the car, it may be placarded with a special tag, and returned empty to its owner for repairs.

50' BOX CAR ea 5.25 (unless noted)

480-1199 Conrail (box car red)
480-1202 Illinois Central (orange)
480-1203 Canadian National (box car red)
480-1207 Seaboard Coast Line
480-1209 Wabash (red)
480-1210 Pennsylvania Railroad/Railway Express Agency (olive)
480-1211 Union Pacific (box car red)
480-1212 Great Northern (orange, green)
480-1215 Southern (brown)
480-1216 Southern Pacific (red, gray)
480-1220 Western Pacific (orange) 5.75
480-1221 Western Pacific (mineral red) 6.25
480-1222 Santa Fe, Modern (box car red) 6.25
480-1223 Erie Lackawanna (box car red) 6.25
480-1200 Undecorated 4.50
480-1219 Union Pacific/MAP 9.25

50' PLUG DOOR ea 5.25 (unless noted)

480-1251 Burlington Northern (Burlington Northern cascade green)
480-1255 Union Pacific
480-1256 Union Pacific (silver, yellow, black letters) 9.25
480-1257 Union Pacific (silver, yellow, red letters) 9.25
480-1261 Railway Express Agency
480-1262 Rock Island "Modern" (blue)
480-1263 Canadian Pacific (green, new styling lettering) 7.50
480-1264 Canadian Pacific (insulated) 7.50
480-1265 British Columbia Railway 7.50
480-1266 Pacific Great Eastern 7.50
480-1267 Frisco (blue)
480-1268 Frisco (tuscan)
480-1269 Union Pacific/MAP (yellow) 9.25
480-1271 Western Pacific (mineral red) 6.25
480-1272 Tidewater South (mineral red)
480-1273 Santa Fe, Modern (mineral red)
 480-1250 Undecorated 4.50

50' FMC PLUG DOOR BOX ea 6.25 *NEW*

480-7726 Southern Pacific Large Circle DF Logo "Hydra-Cushion for Fragile Freight" Logo (mineral red)
480-7727 Southern Pacific (mineral red) "Hydra-Cushion for Fragile Freight" Logo
480-7728 Southern Pacific (mineral red) "Hydra-Cushion" Logo
480-7729 Southern Pacific (mineral red) "Cushion Car" Logo
480-7730 Cotton Belt (mineral red) "Hydra-Cushion for Fragile Freight" Logo
480-7731 Cotton Belt (mineral red) "Hydra-Cushion" Logo

40' TRUSS SIDE BOX CAR ea 5.25 (unless noted)

480-1031 Santa Fe (tuscan)
480-1032 Seaboard Air Line (tuscan)
480-1033 Chicago, Burlington & Quincy (tuscan)
480-1034 Southern Pacific (tuscan)
480-1035 Nickel Plate Road (box car red)
480-1036 Erie Lackawanna (box car red)
480-1030 Undecorated 4.75

50' FMC 1½ DOOR BOX ea 5.75 (unless noted)

These kits include combination door-sliders and plug door.

480-788 Railbox pkg(12) 107.40
480-1931 Railbox (yellow) 9.50
480-1932 Seaboard Coast Line (box car red)
480-1933 Missouri Pacific (box car red)
480-1934 Minnesota Dakota & Western (white, green door)
480-1935 Burlington Northern (cascade green)
480-1936 British Columbia Railway (light green) 6.75
480-1937 Union Pacific (tuscan) 6.50
480-1944 Railbox (Canadian National) (yellow) 9.50
480-1930 Undecorated 5.25

50' FMC 1½ DOOR BOX ea 5.57 (unless noted)

These are easy-to-build HO Scale Kits with one-piece plastic bodies. They are prepainted and lettered for a variety of railroads. Trucks, couplers and weights are included.

We have worked closely with this manufacturer to provide accurate availability information at the time this catalog was published. Items listed in blue ink may not be available at all times. Please see your dealer for current delivery information.

ORE CARS

26' RECTANGULAR SIDE ORE CAR ea 4.25 (unless noted)

26' TAPER SIDE ORE CAR ea 4.25 (unless noted)

26' LOW SIDE ORE CAR ea 5.95 (unless noted)

26' RECTANGULAR SIDE ORE CAR ea 4.25 (unless noted)
480-1322 Bessemer & Lake Erie (brown) 5.25
480-1323 Duluth, Missabe & Iron Range (brown) 5.25
480-1324 Rio Grande (silver) 5.25
480-1417 Canadian National (silver)
480-1418 Ontario Northern (Ontario Northern blue)
480-1420 Great Northern
480-1421 Duluth, Missabe & Iron Range (tuscan)
480-1422 Canadian National (tuscan)
480-1423 Milwaukee Road (tuscan)
480-1424 Union Pacific (tuscan)
480-1425 Great Northern (big sky blue)
480-1426 Penn Central (green)
480-1427 Baltimore & Ohio (tuscan)
480-1428 Santa Fe (tuscan)
480-1429 Union Pacific (silver)
480-1402 Undecorated 3.75

26' TAPER SIDE ORE CAR ea 4.25 (unless noted)
480-1405 Rio Grande (black)
480-1406 Canadian Pacific (tuscan)
480-1407 Canadian National (tuscan)
480-1408 Chesapeake & Ohio (black)
480-1409 Pennsylvania (tuscan)
480-1410 Great Northern (tuscan)
480-1411 Soo Line (tuscan)
480-1412 Chicago & North Western (tuscan)
480-1413 Lake Superior & Ishpeming (tuscan)
480-1414 Southern Pacific (tuscan)
480-1415 Burlington Northern (Burlington Northern cascade green)
480-1401 Undecorated 3.75

26' LOW SIDE ORE CAR ea 5.95 (unless noted)
480-1712 Southern Pacific
480-1713 Union Pacific
480-1714 Canadian Pacific 6.75
480-1715 Pennsylvania
480-1711 Undecorated 4.50

HOPPERS

50' 5-BAY RAPID DISCHARGE CAR ea 5.25 (unless noted)

48' RIB BALLAST HOPPER ea 5.25 (unless noted)

35' 2-BAY COVERED HOPPER ea 6.75 (unless noted)

40' 3-BAY RIB SIDE HOPPER ea 5.25 (unless noted)

50' 5-BAY RAPID DISCHARGE CAR ea 5.25 (unless noted)
480-1721 Santa Fe (box car red)
480-1723 US Steel - Cumberland Mine (light blue)
480-1727 Chesapeake & Ohio (black)
480-1728 Southern (box car red)
480-1735 Seaboard Coast Line (black)
480-1736 Norfolk & Western (black)
480-1720 Undecorated 4.75
480-1724 Black Mesa & Lake Powell (dark blue)
480-1726 Colorado Springs (black)

48' RIB BALLAST HOPPER ea 5.25 (unless noted)
480-1561 Union Pacific MOW (green)
480-1562 Pittsburgh & Lake Erie (black)
480-1563 New York Central (black)
480-1564 Rio Grande
480-1560 Undecorated 4.75

35' 2-BAY COVERED HOPPER ea 6.75 (unless noted)
480-762 Norfolk & Western pkg(12) 102.00
480-1431 Pennsylvania
480-1432 Union Pacific (gray)
480-1435 Southern Pacific
480-1436 Milwaukee Road (gray)
480-1437 Haliburton (red, white)
480-1441 Great Northern (big sky blue)
480-1443 Burlington Northern (cascade green)
480-1444 Rock Island "Modern" (blue)
480-1445 Conrail (box car red)
480-1446 Chesapeake & Ohio (black)
480-1447 Soo Line (tuscan)
480-1448 Erie Lackawanna (gray)
480-1465 Nickel Plate Road (black)
480-1466 Wabash (black)
480-1467 Ann Arbor (gray)
480-1430 Undecorated 6.25
480-1468 Lehigh Valley (gray)
480-1469 Western Maryland (gray)

40' 3-BAY RIB SIDE HOPPER ea 5.25 (unless noted)
480-1486 Western Maryland (black)
480-1488 Pennsylvania (tuscan)
480-1489 Virginian (black)
480-1490 Norfolk & Western (black)
480-1493 Rio Grande (black)
480-1494 Union Pacific (tuscan)
480-1495 Chesapeake & Ohio (black)
480-1496 Baltimore & Ohio (black)
480-1498 Burlington Northern (black)
480-1531 Erie Lackawanna (black, yellow)
480-1532 Seaboard (black)
480-1533 Missouri - Kansas - Texas (red)
480-1535 CSX Transportation (black)
480-1537 Southern (mineral red)
480-1538 Pennsylvania (black)
480-1539 Chicago & North Western
480-1540 CSX Transportation/Chesapeake & Ohio (black)
480-1541 Chicago, Burlington & Quincy (black)
480-1542 Norfolk Southern (black)
480-1543 New York Central (black)
480-1485 Undecorated 4.75
480-3220 Rio Grande 5.75

50' FMC 3-BAY COVERED HOPPER ea 7.98 (unless noted)

When the grain rush starts, you'll see plenty of these distinctive covered hoppers in every train. Introduced in the early 1980's, these 100 ton capacity cars are being used by many railroads and private companies.   The large carrying capacity (4,750 cubic feet) makes them an ideal choice for grain and many other loads. The highly detailed body has the unique horizontal stiffening ridge that makes both the prototype and the model stand out from other hoppers. The low-profile roofwalk is nicely detailed, adding to the overall realism of the finished car. Prepainted and lettered for a variety of roadnames, Including the Model Die Casting version shown, (480-7725) this easy-to-build kit is a great addition to your modern layout.

480-3521 Burlington Northern (cascade green, white)
480-3522 Rio Grande (orange)
480-3525 Western Pacific (gray) *NEW*
480-3526 Percival Grain *NEW*
480-3527 Mid Iowa (medium blue, white) *NEW*
480-3528 Val-Hi Supply (cascade green, white) *NEW*
480-3529 Arthur Farms (yellow, black) *NEW*
480-3530 Klemme Co-op (pink, black) *NEW*

480-3531 Farnhamville, Iowa (pink, black) *NEW*
480-3532 NAHX (gray w/red FMC logo) *NEW*
480-3533 Cook Industries (gray, blue logo) *NEW*
480-3534 XTRA (gray, red logo) *NEW*
480-3535 Procor (gray, blue logo) *NEW*
480-7725 Roundhouse (red)
480-3520 Undecorated 7.50
480-3523 Chicago & North Western (green) 8.98
480-3524 Chicago & North Western (yellow) 8.98

STOCK CARS

36' STOCK CAR ea 5.98 (unless noted)

480-3261 Rio Grande (black)
480-3263 Great Northern (box car red)
480-3264 Pennsylvania (box car red)
480-3265 Santa Fe (box car red)
480-3266 New York Central (black)
480-3268 Colorado Midland (black)
480-3260 Undecorated 5.50
480-3014 Rio Grande
480-3200 Colorado & Southern

40' OFFSET BALLAST HOPPER ea 5.25 (unless noted)

480-1581 Union Pacific, "Be Specific" (mineral red)
480-1582 Union Pacific, "Streamliner" (mineral red)
480-1583 Union Pacific (mineral red)
480-1584 Rio Grande (black)
480-1585 Southern (black)
480-1586 Southern (red)
480-1580 Undecorated 4.75

40' 3-BAY OFFSET SIDE HOPPER ea 5.25 (unless noted)

480-772 Bessemer & Lake Erie pkg(12) 63.00
480-1611 Erie (black)
480-1612 Illinois Central (black)
480-1613 Nickel Plate Road (black)
480-1614 Canadian Pacific (box car red) 5.50
480-1615 New York Central (black)
480-1616 Missouri Pacific (black)

480-1617 Canadian National (box car red)
480-1618 Bessemer & Lake Erie (brown)
480-1619 Baltimore & Ohio (black)
480-1620 Soo Line (mineral red)
480-1621 Chicago, Burlington & Quincy (red)
480-1610 Undecorated 4.75

HANDCAR

These kits are molded plastic.
480-2976 Handcar Kit (black) pkg(2)3.50

These are easy-to-build HO Scale Kits with one-piece plastic bodies. They are prepainted and lettered for a variety of railroads. Trucks, couplers and weights are included. We have worked closely with this manufacturer to provide accurate availability information at the time this catalog was published. Items listed in blue ink may not be available at all times. Please see your dealer for current delivery information.

3 IN-1 CAR KITS

BATTLE MOUNTAIN THEME KIT

"Battle Mountain" represents America's "silver mining boom," from the 1870s to 1930's. "Battle Mountain" was located on the Central Pacific (later Southern Pacific) line between Elko & Reno, Nevada. "Battle Mountain" was also the northern terminus of the narrow gauge "Nevada Central Railroad" which supplied the silver town of Austin.

480-1507 Fire Fighting Train Set pkg (3) 12.00
This kit includes a water tank car, chemical tank car and a tower car.

480-1509 Log Car & Building Set 10.00
This kit includes three 36' log cars and one building.

480-1510 Climax Mine Loco (Dummy) 10.00
This kit feature molded body, detailing parts, HO & HOn3 trucks, 30' flat car body, less boiler and metal underframe.

480-1514 "Austin City" Street Scene 12.00
This kit is a molded two story stone building, 8½ x 4¼".

SHANTY TOWN THEME KIT

When "Steam was King," the railroads needed plenty of men, and they needed places to live. Wherever the steam loco stopped for water you could find a small telegraph station, coal or oil loading facility and a "section gang's living quarters."

480-1504 Wayside Station 12.00
This kit includes two 36' wood style box car kits and a molded single story brick freight station, less details. The station measures 8½ x 5 x 2".

480-1505 Gandy Dancer's Quarters 12.00
This kit includes one ea: 36' Overton coach, 36' reefer car kit and a molded single story stone building which measures 4½ x 6 x 2".

3 in -1 Kits represent the use of more than one kit which can be combined with "partner" kits, to establish an overall theme. Not all 3-in-1 Kits contain 3 individual kits. Kit-bashing and the purchase of some details from other manufacturers is necessary. Rolling stock kits come undecorated, complete with trucks and couplers.

3 IN-1 CAR KIT

This kit includes three 26' metal log car kits and detailing parts, less logs.

480-1501 21' Wood Chip Car Set pkg(3) 10.00
This kit includes three one car kits and gondola sides, less load.

480-1502 MOW "Shorty" Flat Car Set pkg(3) 10.00
This kit includes three 26' shorty flat car kits with gondola sides, less load.

480-1503 MOW Passenger Car Set pkg (3) 12.00
This kit includes three 30' wood style molded work cars, MW Supply, MW Bunk, MW Repair, less details.

480-1515 Rotary Snowplow & Tender 12.00

480-1516 Jordan Spreader & Snow Crab 12.00
This kit also includes one flanger car.

480-1517 Snow Dozer & MW Flanger 12.00
This kit also includes one flat car push plow.

480-1518 "Galloping Goose" Diesel Conversion Dummy 12.00
This kit includes one ea: box car, diesel body and details, and 4 wheel lead truck, less diesel truck.

480-1506 Telegraph Office & Service Facility 12.00
This kit includes one ea: 26' tank car, 30' Shorty flat car kit and a molded single story brick telegraph office, less figures and details. The building measures 8½ x 6 x 3¼".

VICTORIA SQUARE THEME KIT

Victoria Square represents a mythical place and is appropriate on layouts from early 1900 right up to today's most modern period. Included in this theme are cable car terminal buildings and a model of the popular "Victoria Station" restaurants.

480-1511 Victoria Station 12.00
This kit includes a molded single story brick station, molded metal style box car and a modern style caboose. The station measures 8 x 8 x 2".

480-1512 Cable House & Passenger Car 12.00
This kit includes a 1-story brick building, two molded style old timer passenger car kits with cable car instructions. It measures 5 x 2½ x 4".

480-1500 26' Log Car Set pkg(3) 8.50

FLAT CARS

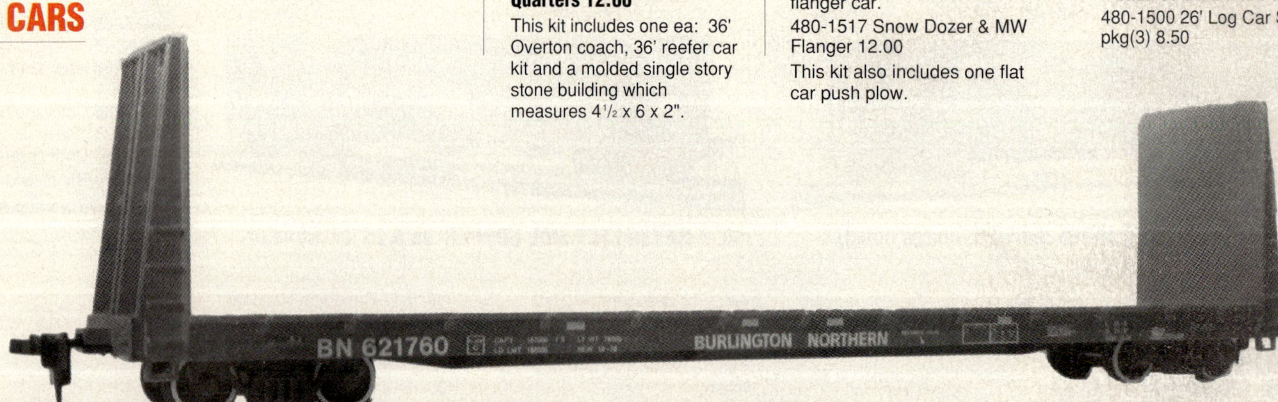

60' BULKHEAD FLAT CAR ea 5.75 (unless noted)

480-1301 Trailer Train (yellow)
480-1302 Burlington Northern (Burlington Northern cascade green)
480-1303 Canadian Pacific (red)

480-1306 St Louis Southwestern "Cotton Belt" (red)
480-1308 Soo Line (white)
480-1309 Frisco
480-1310 Union Pacific (yellow)
480-1311 Santa Fe (red)
480-1314 British Columbia Railway (olive)

480-1316 Missouri Pacific (box car red)
480-1317 Kansas City Southern (box car red)
480-1318 Oregon, Pacific & Eastern (orange)
480-3259 Golden West Service (blue) 7.25
480-1300 Undecorated 5.50

480-1307 Milwaukee Road (yellow)
480-1312 Western Pacific (black)
480-1315 Southern Pacific (box car red)
480-1319 Longview, Portland & Northern (orange)

REEFERS

36' REFRIGERATOR ea 5.98 (unless noted)

36' BILLBOARD REEFER ea 8.25 (unless noted)

50' EXPRESS REEFER ea 7.25 (unless noted)

36' REFRIGERATOR ea 5.98 (unless noted)
480-3161 Pennsylvania (reefer yellow)
480-3162 Pacific Fruit Express (reefer orange)
480-3163 Santa Fe (reefer orange)
480-3164 Canadian Pacific (orange)
480-3165 Chicago, Milwaukee & St. Paul (green)
480-3166 Illinois Central (reefer yellow)
480-3167 Erie (reefer yellow)
480-3168 Houston & Texas Central (green)
480-3169 Lehigh Valley (olive green)
480-3201 Illinois Traction
480-3160 Undecorated 5.50

480-3107 Union Pacific
480-3110 Colorado & Southern
480-3012 Rio Grande
480-3120 Devil's Gulch & Hellengone

36' BILLBOARD REEFER ea 8.25 (unless noted)
480-817 Assortment pkg(12) 99.00 *NEW*
480-3123 Pabst Beer (yellow)
480-3124 Miller High Life Beer (white)
480-3126 Roberts Meats (yellow)
480-3127 Schlitz Beer (white)
480-3130 Columbia Soup (red) *NEW*
480-3135 Bull Frog Beer (orange)

480-3137 Budweiser Beer (white) 9.00
480-3138 Heinz 57 Varieties (yellow) 9.50
480-3146 Cracker Jack (orange) *NEW*
480-3149 Hershey (brown) *NEW*
480-3150 Old Dutch Cleanser (yellow) *NEW*

36' VENTILATED REEFER
480-3040 Undecorated 5.25
480-3013 Rio Grande 5.75

TANK CARS

50' TANK TRAIN

480-1391 Tank Train (black) 8.50

480-1390 Undecorated 7.98

50' TANK CAR ea 8.50 (unless noted)
480-770 ADM Corn Sweetener pkg(12) 114.00
480-1373 General American Transport (black)
480-3251 ADM Corn Sweetener (white) 10.50
480-8442 Santa Fe (black) 6.25

480-8443 Burlington Northern 6.25
480-8444 Southern Pacific 6.25
480-1370 Undecorated 7.98
480-1374 Southern Pacific (black)
480-1375 Sunoco

50' EXPRESS REEFER ea 7.25 (unless noted)
480-3605 Pennsylvania
480-3608 Central Vermont (silver)
480-3610 Railway Express Agency (green)
380-3612 Chateau Martin Wines (burgundy)
480-6116 Canadian National
480-6117 Canadian Pacific
480-3600 Undecorated 6.75
480-6113 Pennsylvania (passenger)
480-6114 Union Pacific (passenger)

28' MODERN TANK CAR ea 7.25 (unless noted)
480-748 GATX (white) pkg(12) 87.00
480-766 UTLX (white) pkg(12) 87.00
480-3301 GATX (black)
480-3302 Hooker
480-3304 GATX (white) 7.25
480-3300 Undecorated 6.75

26' TANK CAR ea 7.25 (unless noted)
480-3109 Gorre & Daphetid
480-3361 Pennsylvania (black)
480-3362 Santa Fe (black)
480-3363 Southern Pacific (black)
480-3364 Sun Oil (black)
480-3365 Union Pacific (black)
480-3366 Union Tank Line (black)
480-3371 Battle Mountain Liquid Gold (burgundy)
480-3360 Undecorated 6.75

26' BILLBOARD TANK CAR ea 7.25 (Not Shown)
480-779 Gramps pkg(12) 82.50
480-3367 Conoco (black)
480-3368 Zerolene (silver)
480-3369 Standard Oil (black)
480-3372 RPM Motor Oil (silver)
480-3370 Gramps (black)

30' FLAT CAR ea 5.25 (unless noted)

480-1453 Milwaukee Road (black)
480-1454 Pennsylvania (box car red)
480-1455 Southern Pacific (box car red)

480-1456 Union Pacific (box car red)
480-1457 Santa Fe (box car red)
480-1458 Baltimore & Ohio (black)

480-1459 Canadian National (box car red)
480-1460 New York Central (black)
480-1450 Undecorated 4.75

60' FLAT CAR ea 5.50 (unless noted) (Not Shown)
480-1281 Trailer Train (yellow)
480-1282 Soo Line (white)
480-1283 Southern Pacific (red)
480-1284 Santa Fe (red)
480-1285 Missouri Pacific (red)

480-1286 Union Pacific (yellow)
480-1287 Southern (red)
480-1288 Frisco (yellow)
480-1280 Undecorated 4.98 (black)

These are easy-to-build HO Scale Kits with one-piece plastic bodies. They are prepainted and lettered for a variety of railroads. Trucks, couplers and weights are included.

We have worked closely with this manufacturer to provide accurate availability information at the time this catalog was published. Items listed in blue ink may not be available at all times. Please see your dealer for current delivery information.

MODERN CABOOSES

30' 3-WINDOW ea 7.98 (unless noted)

26' 2-WINDOW ea 7.98 (unless noted)

26' 4-WINDOW ea 7.98 (unless noted)

GONDOLAS

50' HIGH SIDE GONDOLA (THRALL) ea 6.25 (unless noted)

50' HIGH SIDE GONDOLA (THRALL) ea 6.25
(unless noted)
480-813 Union Pacific pkg(12) 75.00 **NEW**
480-1642 Wisconsin Electric (ochre, black)
480-1643 Union Pacific (black, yellow)
480-1644 Rio Grande (black, orange)
480-1645 Burlington Northern (black)
480-1650 Canadian Pacific (orange)
480-1652 Santa Fe (black, yellow) 6.25
480-1640 Undecorated 4.75

**50' MILL GONDOLA
ea 5.25** (unless noted)
480-1692 Delaware & Hudson (black)
480-1682 Elgin, Joilet & Eastern (black)
480-1683 Illinois Terminal (yellow)
480-1684 Soo Line (box car red)
480-1685 Missouri Pacific (box car red)
480-1686 Milwaukee Road
480-1687 Chicago & North Western (black)
480-1688 Kansas City Southern
480-1689 Philadelphia Bethlehem & New England (orange)
480-1690 Maine Central (green)
480-1691 Boston & Maine (orange)
480-1693 Norfolk & Western (blue)
480-1694 Frisco (box car red)
480-1696 CSX Transportation/Seaboard System
480-1698 Baltimore & Ohio/Railgon (black, yellow) 6.25
480-1680 Undecorated 4.75
480-1681 Railgon (black, yellow) 6.25

40' GONDOLA ea 5.25

40' OVAL - END GONDOLA

50' MILL GONDOLA ea 5.25 (unless noted)

**40' GONDOLA
ea 5.25** (unless noted)
480-1342 Santa Fe (tuscan)
480-1343 Southern Pacific (tuscan)
480-1344 Union Pacific
480-1345 Pennsylvania (tuscan)
480-1346 New York Central (black)
480-1350 Burlington Northern
480-1353 Canadian Pacific (tuscan)
480-1354 Canadian National (black)
480-1356 British Columbia Railway (olive) 6.25
480-1359 Erie (black)
480-1340 Undecorated 4.75

50' BATHTUB GONDOLA ea 5.25 (unless noted)
480-1662 Union Pacific (yellow, black)
480-1660 Undecorated 4.75
480-1661 Chessie System (Chesapeake & Ohio) (yellow, black)
480-1665 Burlington Northern (black)
480-1666 Rio Grande (orange, black)

40' OVAL - END GONDOLA
480-815 Chesapeake & Ohio pkg(12) 63.00 **NEW**
480-1331 Chesapeake & Ohio (black) 5.25 **NEW**

26' GONDOLA - HIGH SIDE
480-1701 Undecorated 4.50

30' 3-WINDOW ea 7.98
(unless noted)
480-3492 Ontario Northland (yellow, blue)
480-3493 Grand Trunk Western (black, orange)
480-3495 Chicago, Burlington & Quincy (silver)
490-3496 Rio Grande
480-3497 Santa Fe
480-3491 Undecorated 7.50

26' 4-WINDOW ea 7.98
(unless noted)
480-3481 Southern Pacific (box car red)
480-3483 Great Northern
480-3484 Great Northern (big sky blue)
480-3485 Union Pacific (reefer yellow)
480-3487 Southern Pacific "Overland" (silver)
480-3488 Erie Lackawanna
480-3480 Undecorated 7.50
480-3486 Santa Fe (caboose red)

26' 2-WINDOW ea 7.98
(unless noted)
480-3471 Pennsylvania (caboose red)
480-3472 AMTRAK (gold, blue)
480-3473 Burlington Northern (cascade green)
480-3475 Baltimore & Ohio (caboose red)

480-3478 Rock Island (light blue)
480-3479 Conrail (blue)
480-3511 Chesapeake & Ohio (red)
480-3470 Undecorated 7.50

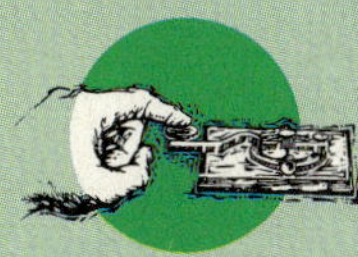

INFORMATION STATION

In any passing freight train, you'll see cars from several different railroads. This interchange of equipment allows all of the available cars to be used as one large pool. A complex series of regulations governs how this is done. One of these, the Car Service and Per Diem Act is an agreement between the nation's railroads that spells out the rules under which the freight cars are operated.

Under the act, each railroad pays a daily fee (per diem) for the use of cars from another line.   There's also a penalty for cars kept longer than 30 days.   This encourages the quick return of cars, and makes economic sense for a railroad to maintain its own cars for use by on-line shippers.

Lets say our local furniture factory on the Norfolk Southern just received a Burlington Northern box car loaded with lumber. This "foreign" BN car is now empty and ready to be returned.   Under the rules of interchange, this car has to be returned to or routed in the direction of its "home" road, in this case the nearest BN connection.

This same factory has two car-loads of furniture ready for shipment to a customer in Minneapolis. Although we could send two NS cars to be loaded, we're paying for the time the BN car is on our line, so it's to our advantage to return it as quickly as possible. With a load, we can generate revenue by billing the factory for transporting their products. And since Seattle is in the direction of "home" for the BN car, loading and returning it also satisfies this portion of the rules.

At the same time, we have an empty NS car available, so our local wayfreight will spot it for loading. Both cars will be routed back to the BN. Once there, our car becomes the "foreigner" and the BN will pay us the per diem charge.

This generates a considerable volume of work for the clerks who must keep accurate records of our cars, as well as those from other roads, which will be used for payment and billing purposes.

OLD TIMER CABOOSES

30' 3-WINDOW STANDARD ea 7.98 (unless noted)

30' SMALL SIDE DOOR ea 8.00 (unless noted)

30' OPEN END SIDE DOOR ea 7.98 (unless noted)

30' BLIND END SIDE DOOR ea 7.98 (unless noted)

30' OUTSIDE BRACED ea 7.98 (unless noted)

30' 3-WINDOW STANDARD
ea 7.98 (unless noted)
480-3441 Rio Grande (caboose red)
480-3442 Northern Pacific (caboose red)
480-3443 Pennsylvania
480-3444 Wabash (caboose red)
480-3445 Southern Pacific (caboose red)
480-3447 Canadian National (orange)
480-3448 Great Northern (caboose red)
480-3440 Undecorated 7.50

30' SMALL SIDE DOOR
ea 8.00 (unless noted)
480-3401 Union Pacific (box car red)
480-3400 Undecorated 7.50
480-3402 Atlantic Coast Line (box car red)
480-3403 Chicago, Burlington & Quincy (box car red)
480-3404 Lehigh Valley (tuscan)

30' OPEN END SIDE DOOR
ea 7.98 (unless noted)
480-3431 Baltimore & Ohio (caboose red)
480-3432 Colorado & Midland (caboose red)
480-3433 St. Louis Southwestern
480-3434 Southern Pacific (caboose red)
480-3403 Undecorated 7.50

30' BLIND END SIDE DOOR
ea 7.98 (unless noted)
480-3421 Santa Fe (tuscan)
480-3422 Erie (box car red)
480-3423 Illinois Central (box car red)
480-3420 Undecorated 7.50

30' OUTSIDE BRACED
ea 7.98 (unless noted)
480-3463 Western Pacific (silver, orange)
480-3461 Missouri - Kansas - Texas (reefer yellow)
480-3462 Rock Island (box car red)
480-3464 Norfolk & Western (tuscan)
480-3460 Undecorated 7.50

30' DROVER CABOOSE
480-3767 Rio Grande (yellow) 7.98
480-3760 Undecorated 7.50

MANTUA

These HO Scale, ready-to-run cars are prepainted and lettered, and include trucks and couplers.

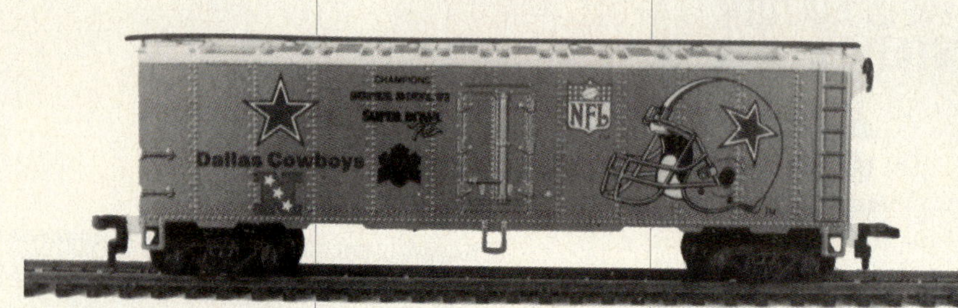

NFL FREIGHT CARS

REEFERS

40' WOODSIDE REEFER
455-739054 Northern Refrigerator (yellow) 9.49

41' WOODSIDE REEFER
455-739148 Baby Ruth 9.25

BOOM TENDER
455-744032 Amtrak 12.99 (orange, black)

Limited Quantities Available

FLOODLIGHT CAR
455-745022 New York Central (gray) 25.49

CABOOSE

OLD TIME ea 9.99
455-725006 Central Pacific (red)
455-725085 Rock Island & Peoria (tuscan)
455-725025 Baltimore & Ohio (caboose red)

36' CABOOSE ea 9.99
455-726003 Union Pacific (orange)
455-726012 Frisco (red)
455-726022 New York Central (Jade Green)
455-726030 Erie Lackawanna
455-726061 Great Northern (caboose red)
455-726087 Chicago & Illinois Midland (dark green)
455-726088 Midland Valley (brown)
455-726172 Conrail (bright blue) *NEW*
455-726173 Reading (green, yellow) *NEW*
455-726174 Radio Dispatch (bright red) *NEW*

BOBBER CABOOSE
455-736084 New York Central & Hudson River Railroad (red) 9.99

GONDOLAS

43' GONDOLA WITH LOAD
455-731053 Maine Central (black) 9.99

BOX CARS

41' STEEL BOX CAR
455-734012 Frisco (beige) 9.99

VALUE PACK

These packs are only available as sets, and feature consecutive car numbers.

43' GONDOLA
455-624055 Rail Gon (black, yellow) pkg (4) 37.99

BOX CAR
455-632022 New York Central System pkg (4) 37.99 *NEW*
Includes cars in P&LE, (tuscan) "Pacemaker," (red & gray) "Early Bird Service" (tuscan) and Jade Green schemes.

41' STEEL BOX CAR
455-625056 Rail Box (yellow) pkg (4) 37.99

40' WOODSIDE REEFER
455-633242 US Railroads (yellow) pkg (4) 37.99 *NEW*
Includes Great Northern Western Fruit Express, Minneapolis & St. Louis, North Western Refrigerator Line (C&NW) and American Refrigerator Transit (with MP and Wabash heralds) cars.

FLATCAR
455-634747 Louisville & Nashville (red, gray) pkg (2) 37.99 *NEW*
Set includes two flat cars with different numbers, loaded with pipe.

NFL FREIGHT CARS
ea 18.49 (unless noted)
These ready-to-run cars are painted in team colors and feature an exact replica of the official team helmet and logo.
455-726900 Super Bowl Express Caboose (red) *NEW*
455-733901 San Francisco 49er's (bronze, red) 17.99
455-733902 Chicago Bears (white, black)

Limited Quantities Available
455-733903 Cincinnati Bengals (white, black)
455-733905 Denver Broncos (white, orange)
455-733906 Cleveland Browns (white, brown)
455-733907 Tampa Bay Buccaneers (white, orange)
455-733908 Phoenix Cardinals
455-733909 San Diego Chargers (white, blue)
455-733910 Kansas City Chiefs (white, red)
455-733911 Indianapolis Colts
455-733913 Miami Dolphins (white, green)
455-733916 New York Giants
455-733917 Detroit Lions (silver, blue)
455-733918 New York Jets (white, green)
455-733919 Houston Oilers (white, red)
455-733920 Green Bay Packers (gold, green)
455-733921 New England Patriots (white, red)
455-733922 Los Angeles Raiders (silver, black)
455-733923 Los Angeles Rams (yellow, blue)
455-733924 New Orleans Saints (bronze, black)
455-733925 Seattle Seahawks (silver, blue)
455-733927 Minnesota Vikings (white, purple)
455-733928 Washington Redskins (white, red)
455-733929 Dallas Cowboys XXVII Super Bowl Winner (silver, white) *NEW*

FLOODLIGHT CAR

40' WOODSIDE REEFER

43' GONDOLA

41' STEEL BOX CAR

Roco

Imported from Austria by Walthers

Roco models are prepainted and lettered in authentic period schemes. Each car is fully assembled and ready-to-run with NEM style couplers (unless noted).

EUROPEAN ROADNAMES

SNCB	Belgian State Railways
B	Belgian National Railways
BBO	Federal Railways of Austria (before 1950)
OBB	Austrian Federal Railways (after 1950)
DSB	Danish State Railways
SNCF	French National Railways
DB	German Federal Railways (after 1949)
DRG (DR)	German State Railways (least common era, 1945)
FS	Italian State Railways
CFL	Luxembourg National Railways
NS	Netherlands State Railways
NSB	Norwegian State Railways
RENFE	Spanish State Railways
SJ	Swedish State Railways
SBB	Swiss Federal Railways
JZ	Railways of Yugoslavia

EUROPEAN PROTOTYPES FROM ROCO

HO scale ready-to-run models have prepainted and lettered plastic bodies and include trucks and NEM couplers.

33' BARREL ROOF OUTSIDE BRACED WOOD BOX CAR
625-46059 SNCF 10.49

33' BARREL ROOF OUTSIDE BRACED BOX CAR
625-46014 DB, Steel (box car red) 11.99

30' WOOD BOX CAR
625-46001 DB (box car red) 11.99
625-46052 DB Lowenbrau 12.99 *NEW*

34' BARREL ROOF OUTSIDE BRACED WOOD BOX CAR
625-46015 DRG, Beer Reefer (white)12.99
625-46016 DB (box car red) 11.99
625-46021 OBB 11.99

35' OUTSIDE BRACED WOOD BOX CAR
625-46103 DRG 17.99
625-46105 DB (box car red) 19.49
625-46254 SBB 19.99
625-46448 SNCF (brown) 21.49

35' BOX CAR GMS-54
625-46256 DB, With Brakeman's Platform (box car red) 21.49
625-46259 DB, Converted Crew Car 20.99

35' OUTSIDE BRACED VENTILATED BOX CAR
625-46266 DB 20.99

35' BARREL ROOF BOX CAR
With moveable side doors.
625-46274 FS, Ventilation (box car red)
625-46282 OBB/B, Ventilation (tuscan)
625-46412 OBB/G, Ventilation (tuscan)

39' VENTILATED BOX CAR
625-46444 SNCF 21.49
625-46501 SSB TBA *NEW*

35' BARREL ROOF OUTSIDE BRACED STEEL BOX CAR
625-46407 DB, Class 252 16.49
625-46408 DB, Class 254 21.49
625-46417 OBB/Bahn Express 19.99

45' STAKE WAGON
625-46309 NS "Heineken Beer" Class Kbs (green) 23.99

46' ALL DOOR BOX CAR
625-46428 OBB (brown, silver) 22.99
625-46451 SJ (silver, brown) 19.99
625-46456 SJ Class Hbi KKS (blue, silver) 22.99

48' ALL-DOOR BOX CAR ea 18.99
625-46170 SBB (silver)
625-46171 SBB, Ribbed (silver)

MOVABLE SIDEWALL VAN
625-46399 SBB "Ovomaltine" 20.49

46' BOX CAR
625-46210 DB, Taes 891 (box car red) 21.99
Roof moves sideways

46' OUTSIDE BRACED STEEL BOX CAR ea 21.49
625-46415 OBB
625-46416 SNCF

59' BOX CAR ea 26.49
625-46222 Bromberg (box car red) *NEW*
625-46230 DB, GGths43 (box car red)
625-46231 OBB

STOCK CARS

35' STOCK CARS
625-46035 DB, For Sheep (tuscan) 12.99

REEFERS

MECHANICAL REEFER
625-16060 MK4 (blue) 29.99 *NEW*

35' REEFER
625-46047 DB, Tk20 (white) 12.49
625-46234 DB Interfrigo 19.99 *NEW*
625-46401 For Dry Ice Transportation (white) 21.49

48' CLOSED RIB REEFER
625-46403 DB "Transthermos" 20.49

48' RIBBED REEFER
625-46442 SNCF (white) 19.99
625-46404 DB (gray) 19.49

REFRIGERATOR VAN

625-46235 DB Class T38 19.99

GONDOLAS

GONDOLA TBA *NEW*
625-16062 DB
625-16064 SBB
625-16066 NS

GONDOLA
625-46090 DB Omm 37 10.49 *NEW*

27' GONDOLA ea 10.99
625-46011 DB, Low Side
625-46043 DB, High Side
625-46046 SNCF, High Side (box car red)
625-46056 OBB (box car red)

30' GONDOLA
625-46039 DB (box car red) 10.99

31' GONDOLA
625-46280 DRG With Brakeman's Cabin (box car red) 16.49
625-46277 DRG With Hinged Cover And Brakeman's Cabin (box car red) 18.49

33' GONDOLA
625-46010 DB (box car red) 10.99
625-46278 DB, With Brakeman's Cabin (box car red) 16.49

HOPPERS

23' SIDEDUMP HOPPER
625-46128 DB "Talbot" (box car red) 20.49
625-46129 OBB 18.99
625-46130 DRG, "Stuttgart" (box car red) 20.49

32' SIDEDUMP HOPPER
625-46132 DB "Talbot" (box car red) 23.99
625-46133 OBB 23.99
625-46248 NS-BL (blue) 27.49
625-46431 RENFE (box car red) 25.49
625-46432 SNCF (box car red) 28.49
625-46433 DR TBA *NEW*
625-46438 DB 26.99 *NEW*

30' COVERED HOPPER ea 25.49 (unless noted)
625-46420 DB (box car red)
625-46422 OBB 23.99
625-46430 SNCF (box car red)

GARBAGE DUMP CAR
625-46345 "Vam Compost" (green) 28.99 *NEW*

36' COVERED HOPPER
625-46391 SBB/GY 23.99

40' 8 WHEEL HOPPER
625-46239 DB oot 42 (box car red) 28.99
625-46242 DRG (box car red) 27.99

49' 12 WHEEL HOPPER ea 31.49
625-46250 DB/Peine & Salzgitter (box car red)
625-46251 DB (box car red)

62' COVERED HOPPER
625-46195 DB/VTG 28.99

RO CO Roco

Imported from Austria by Walthers

Roco models are prepainted and lettered in authentic period schemes. Each car is fully assembled and ready-to-run with NEM style couplers (unless noted).

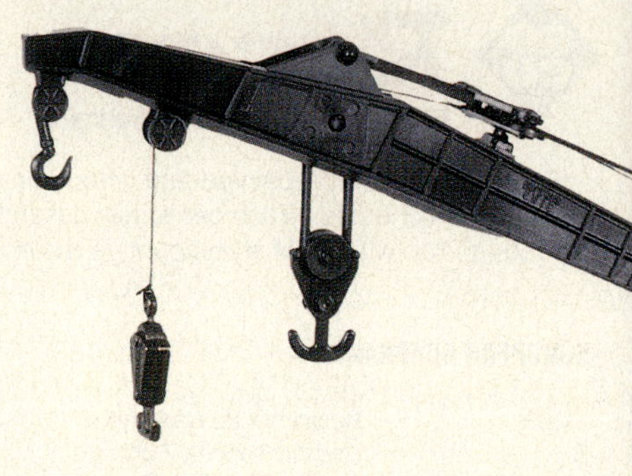

HOPPER SETS

GRAVEL HOPPERS
625-44037 NS Sidedump Hopper - Set of 3 74.99
Set of three Netherlands State Railways gravel hoppers.

625-44074 DB TBA *NEW*
Includes three multi-section Side Dump Hoppers with different numbers.

GRAVEL HOPPERS
625-44075 4-Wheel Gravel Cars - Set of 3 81.99 *NEW*
Set of three Netherlands State Railways gravel hoppers.

MOW EQUIPMENT

CRANE AND JIB CAR
625-46331 DB 33.98

35' MOW BOX CAR
625-34525 OBB HOe 25.99 *NEW*

FLAT CARS

35' STAKED FLAT CAR
625-46029 OBB (box car red) 12.49
625-46031 DB 12.99

35' HEAVY DUTY FLAT CAR
625-46385 DR 19.99
625-46386 OBB 17.49

35' DEPRESSED CENTER WELL FLAT CAR
625-46380 DB (box car red, black) 19.99

36' STAKED FLAT CAR
625-46482 DB With Brakeman's Platform 23.49 *NEW*

40' FLAT CAR
625-46369 SBB, With two 20' Containers 33.99
625-46483 OBB With Steyr 680 Truck 28.49 *NEW*

45' STAKED FLAT CAR
625-46313 OBB 20.99
625-46315 SNCF 20.99
625-46320 NS, Two Containers 26.99
625-46322 SNCF With 20' Container TBA *NEW*
625-46480 DB, Class R10 (box car red) 28.49
625-46481 DB, Class R10 With Brakeman's Cabin (box car red) 23.49
625-46490 DB, "Cologne", Class SS15 34.49

49' CUSHION FLAT CAR
625-46110 DB (black) 17.49

54' PIGGYBACK FLAT CAR
625-46361 OBB/Panalpina 39.99
625-46371 SBB/Jacky Maeder 41.99

54' FLAT CAR WITH CONTAINER ea 41.99
(unless noted)
625-46356 DB/Schenker With Lettered Trailer (box car red) 37.98
625-46372 OBB/LKW Augustin 39.49
625-46373 DB/Danzas
625-46374 SNCF/Guyon (gray, bright blue)
625-46377 SNCF With Regular Flatbed (gray, white, green) *NEW*
625-46378 DB With 2-20' Container (brown, silver, gray) *NEW*
625-46379 OBB With 2 Flatbeds 44.49 *NEW*

FLAT CARS TBA *NEW*
625-1905 With Tractors
625-46530 ACTS Container Flatcar With Three Garbage Containers

CONTAINERS FOR FLAT CARS
625-40060 Containers (red, gray) pkg (2) 9.49
625-46520 Twin Flat Cars With Six Spherical Containers TBA *NEW*

54' PIGGYBACK FLAT CAR
625-46365 HU Pack 39.99

COWL CARS
39' COWL CAR ea 20.99
625-44076 39' Flat Standard DP 2-Cars 43.49 *NEW*
625-46284 DB, Telescoping (box car red)
625-46292 FS, Telescoping (box car red, gray)
625-46293 39' SSB HOn3 22.99 *NEW*

49' TELESCOPING COWL CAR
625-46286 DB (box car red) 22.99

COVERED METAL CAR
625-46220 NS 25.49

39' COIL CAR
With 5 sheet metal coils.
625-46304 SNCB (box car red) 22.49

TANK CARS

29' TANK CAR (220hl) ea 18.99 (unless noted)
625-46071 DB/DEA (silver, black)
625-46143 DB/VTG
625-46146 SNCF/OMV (black, gray) 17.49
625-46174 NS 17.49

29' TANK CAR (300hl) ea 18.99
625-46070 DB/BP (green)
625-46137 DB/VTG (black, gray)

47' TANK CAR
625-46072 DB/EVA, 220hl (black, white, orange) 29.49
625-46186 DB/ARAL, 600hl 22.99
625-46188 DB/VTG, 400hl (gray) 23.99
625-46200 DB/EC 29.99
625-46197 OBB/OMV (black, gray) 25.99

51' TANK CAR (880hl)
625-46191 VTG 26.49
625-46194 Esso 24.99

BEER TANK CAR THREE-PACK
Set of three beer tank cars with sloping tank, in different schemes as operated by "Dortmunder" union.

625-44049 Dortmunder 70.49

59' TANK CAR
625-46204 DB/Petro Chem 200 (black, cream, orange) 33.49

TANK CAR
625-16040 Caltex Tank Car With Brakeman's Cabin 24.49 NEW

TANK CAR SETS *NEW*
625-14108 DB Assorted 78.49
625-44070 SSB TBA
625-44073 DB 88OHL Tank 3-Set 99.49

MISCELLANEOUS CARS

66' FERRY CAR
625-46272 DB/VTG (silver, blue) 25.99

49' RUBBISH CAR
625-46229 NS/Vam Compost (green) 25.99

SILO WAGONS ea 26.99
625-44055 28' DB Eva Set 81.49 *NEW*
625-46469 DB, Kds 54
625-46471 DB, Kds 56 (gray)

AUTO TRANSPORTER
625-1900 DB With Vehicles (forest green) (Limited Run) 89.99
625-46460 DB (forest green) 39.99
625-46461 OBB (orange) 39.99
625-46462 OBB (red) 41.99
625-46465 DB, Class DDm 915 (green) 41.99

MAIL CAR
625-46281 NS 23.49

FREIGHT WAGON THREE-PACK
This three-pack has two silo cars class Kds 54 and Kds 56, and one bulk side dump hopper wagon Tds 39.

625-44048 Quarzwerke Set Era V 75.99

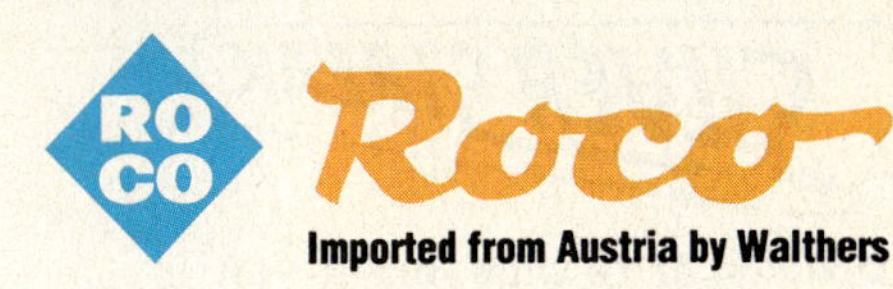

ROCO
Imported from Austria by Walthers

200 T CRANE

AMERICAN PROTOTYPES FROM ROCO

When a heavy transformer shifts, it takes special equipment to straighten things out. A call for the "big hook" and the load will soon be safely on its way. Big jobs require special equipment. Your HO railroad will be ready with the 200 ton cranes from Roco! HO scale ready-to-run models have prepainted and lettered plastic bodies and include six wheel Buckeye trucks with RP25 metal wheels and horn-hook couplers.

200 TON CRANE ea 19.99
Painted and lettered to match Walthers Work Train Cars, the Roco Crane will be the star of your Maintenance Department! Based on a Bucyrus Erie prototype, this 20 ton diesel-powered crane is right at home from the 50's to the present. The model features moveable boom with retractable hook.

625-48681 Maintenance-of-Way (gray, black)
625-48682 Southern Pacific (tuscan, black)
625-48684 Santa Fe (gray, black)
625-48685 Pennsylvania (yellow, black)
625-48693 Milwaukee Road (black)
625-48695 Chicago, Burlington & Quincy
625-48680 Undecorated

TRACK CLEANING CAR

Clean track is essential to your layout, but out-of-scale hands can't reach everywhere. Roco Track Cleaning Cars go where the track goes. Rails are cleaned quickly and easily in hard-to-reach spots, in tunnels, beneath catenary and next to delicate scenery. Just couple a Roco track cleaner into your train and start cleaning! As the car is pulled, the soft-abrasive pad wipes away grime without scratching rail surfaces. The track cleaner is mounted on a 40' insulated box car, lettered for the Burlington Northern/Western Fruit Express. A European style car with NEM couplers and decorated for Roco, is also available.

625-47900 Burlington Northern (yellow) 17.99
625-46400 Roco (European style car, orange) 29.99

625-40019 Replacement Wiper 8.99
For use with either #46400 or #40019.

TRACK CLEANING CAR

NEW 1993/94 HO ROCO CATALOG

DISCOVER THE WORLD WITH YOUR VERY OWN 1993 ROCO CATALOG

NEW LOWER PRICE - NOW JUST $8.99

Get your copy of the Roco Catalog and discover the fun of model railroading with a European flavor! With a complete listing of motive power, passenger equipment and freight cars from 14 different countries, there's plenty of variety. And every

page has full-color photos, detailed prototype history and information that provides hours of fascinating reading.Plus there's a complete listing of track, electrical accessories, narrow gauge equipment and train sets that will introduce you to the complete Roco line.

Best of all, we've lowered the price to $8.99 - a $2.00 savings from last year!

80193 1993/94 HO ROCO Catalog **NEW**

Division of Ye Olde Huff-N-Puff

These kits feature prepainted and lettered scribed wood sides. They include one piece molded styrene ends and cast metal detail parts, less trucks and couplers. Cars are lettered for the "Classic Age of Steam".

BOX CARS

BOX CARS 36' DS WOOD BOX CAR ea 15.50
(unless noted)
792-240 Chesapeake & Ohio (box car red)
792-241 Delaware & Hudson (box car red)
792-242 Nickel Plate Road (box car red)
792-243 New Haven (box car red)
792-244 Piedmont & Northern (box car red)
792-245 Toronto, Hamilton & Buffalo (box car red)
792-239 Undecorated 14.00

40' BOX CAR ea 15.50
(unless noted)
792-252 Union Pacific (box car red)
792-253 Central of Georgia (box car red)
792-254 Minneapolis & St Louis (light green)
792-255 Frisco (box car red)
792-256 Rock Island, "Rocket Freight" (box car red)
792-257 Rio Grande, "Cookie Box" (reefer white)
792-258 Minneapolis & St Louis (caboose red)
792-259 Great Northern (box car red)
792-260 Texas & Pacific (box car red)
792-261 Pere Marquette (box car red)
792-262 Rio Grande (box car red)
792-263 Pittsburgh & Lake Erie, "New York Central" (box car red)
793-264 SLGW, Saltair (green, orange)
792-265 St Louis & South Western, "Cotton Belt" (box car red)
792-266 Missouri - Kansas - Texas (reefer yellow)
792-251 Undecorated 14.00

40' DOUBLE DOOR BOX CAR ea 16.00 (unless noted)
792-291 Southern (box car red)
792-292 Rio Grande (box car red)
792-293 Great Northern (caboose red)
792-290 Undecorated 14.50

40' BOX CAR WITH TRUSS ROD
792-274 Northern Pacific (box car red) 16.00
792-275 Undecorated 14.50

50' DOUBLE DOOR BOX CAR ea 16.00 (unless noted)
792-282 Rock Island (box car red) 16.50
792-283 Santa Fe (box car red)
792-284 Union Pacific (box car red)
792-285 Milwaukee Road (box car red)
792-286 Wabash (box car red)
792-287 Southern Pacific/Texas & New Orleans (reefer yellow)
792-281 Undecorated (box car red) 15.00

GONDOLAS

40' HART GONDOLA ea 14.50
792-162 Southern Pacific (box car red)
792-163 Missouri - Kansas - Texas (reefer yellow)
792-164 Northern Pacific (black)
792-165 Rio Grande (black)
792-166 Chicago & North Western (box car red)
792-167 Western Pacific (reefer yellow)
792-168 Michigan Central (box car red)
792-169 Hocking Valley (box car red)
792-161 Undecorated

WORK CARS

40' WORK CARS WITH TRUSS ROD ea 16.50 (unless noted)
792-323 Bunk Car
792-324 Commissary Car
792-325 Engineering
792-326 MOW Gondola 14.50
792-327 Boom
792-328 Caboose Supply Car 17.00

CABOOSES

37' DROVER CABOOSE
792-342 Missouri Pacific 19.50

34' CABOOSE COMBINATION ea 17.50
792-344 Santa Fe
792-345 Chicago, Burlington & Quincy
792-346 Sierra
792-347 Pacific Lumber
792-343 Undecorated

STANDARD CABOOSE ea 18.50
(unless noted)
792-144 Southern Pacific, Bay Window (box car red)
792-145 30' Southern Pacific (box car red)
792-146 36' Union Pacific (reefer yellow)
792-147 28' Baltimore & Ohio (caboose red)
792-148 24' Great Northern (caboose red)
792-149 30' Southern Pacific (silver)
792-150 Milwaukee Road, Bay Window (silver)
792-151 Chicago, Burlington & Quincy 16.50
792-152 Chicago & North Western 16.50
792-153 Chesapeake & Ohio 16.50
792-154 Missouri - Kansas - Texas
792-302 28' Undecorated 17.00
792-303 30' Undecorated, Bay Window 17.00

TRUSS ROD CABOOSE ea 19.50 (unless noted)
792-317 Erie (caboose red)
792-318 Santa Fe (box car red)
792-319 Southern (caboose red)
792-320 30' Undecorated 18.00

4-WHEEL WOOD CABOOSE ea 17.50 (unless noted)
792-132 Belt Railway of Chicago (yellow)
792-133 Delaware, Lackawanna & Western (box car red)
792-134 Maryland & Pennsylvania (red)
792-135 Western Maryland (caboose red)
792-136 Pennsylvania (box car red)
792-137 New York Central (box car red)
792-138 Lehigh & New England (caboose red)
792-139 Baltimore & Ohio (caboose red)
792-140 Milwaukee Road CM&StP (box car red)
792-141 Reading (caboose red)
792-142 Great Northern (caboose red)
792-143 Southern (caboose red)
792-131 Undecorated 16.00

REEFERS

40' REFRIGERATOR CAR ea 15.50 (unless noted)
792-424 Northern Pacific (reefer yellow)
792-425 Southern Pacific/Union Pacific (orange)
792-426 Green Bay & Western (gray)
792-427 Wabash (reefer yellow)
792-428 Swift Premium (caboose red)
792-429 Burlington (reefer yellow)
792-430 Southern Pacific/Union Pacific (orange)
792-431 Union Pacific Ice (orange)
792-432 Chicago & North Western (reefer yellow)
792-433 Bangor & Aroostook, Maine Potatoes (reefer white)
792-435 Chicago & North Western (yellow)
792-436 Grand Union (green)
792-437 Baby Ruth (yellow)
792-438 Wescott & Winks (yellow)
792-439 Edelweiss (yellow)
792-440 Pacific Fruit Express (orange)
792-443 Santa Fe, Grand Canyon (reefer orange)
792-444 Santa Fe, Chief West (reefer orange)
792-445 Santa Fe, Super Chief (reefer orange)
792-446 Santa Fe, El Capitan (reefer orange)
792-447 Santa Fe, Scout (reefer orange)
792-448 Santa Fe, Texas Chief (reefer orange)
792-449 Santa Fe, San Fan Chief (reefer orange)
792-423 Undecorated 14.00

40' REFRIGERATOR WITH TRUSS ROD ea 16.00 (unless noted)
792-54 Great Northern (reefer yellow)
792-55 Colorado Southern (reefer orange)
792-53 Undecorated 14.50

40' MECHANICAL REEFER
792-401 North Western 16.50
792-402 Undecorated 15.00

INFORMATION STATION

Captive and assigned service cars are common on railroads. The idea is great for model operations, especially on smaller layouts, where the same car may be seen at every operating session.

If you've seen the same freight car at a local industry several times, it's likely to be in "captive" service. In such a case, the car is probably carrying the same load on each trip and is returned empty to the producer for more materials. The car is in essence "captured" as it makes the trip over and over.

Assigned service cars operate in a similar manner. However they are usually marked that they are assigned to a specific type of load and must be returned empty.

STEWART HOBBIES, INC.

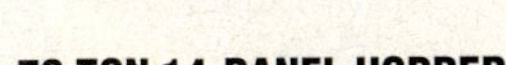

These HO Scale easy-to-build plastic kits feature one-piece, pre-painted and lettered bodies. They include trucks and weights, and the coupler pockets accept Kadee couplers.

HOPPERS

55 TON TWO-BAY FISHBELLY HOPPER ea 9.98

691-10106 Western Maryland #10932 (oxide red)
691-10107 Western Maryland #10933 (oxide red)
691-10108 Reading #80080 (black)
691-10109 Reading #80131 (black)
691-10110 Reading #80262 (black)
691-10111 Central of New Jersey #67009 (black)
691-10112 Central of New Jersey #67114 (black)
691-10113 Central of New Jersey #67224 (black)
691-10114 Delaware & Hudson #5374 (black)
691-10115 Delaware & Hudson #5611 (black)
691-10116 Delaware & Hudson #5774 (black)

70 TON 14-PANEL HOPPER

691-10117 Lehigh Valley #25018 (box car red)
691-10118 Lehigh Valley #25104 (box car red)
691-10119 Lehigh Valley #25218 (box car red)
691-10175 Norfolk & Western #38044 (black) *NEW*
691-10176 Norfolk & Western #38262 (black) *NEW*
691-10177 Norfolk & Western #38288 (black) *NEW*
691-10100 Undecorated
691-10174 Undecorated, peaked end *NEW*

Limited Quantities Available

691-10103 Western Maryland #10912 (oxide red)
691-10105 Western Maryland #10931 (oxide red)

70 TON 14-PANEL HOPPER ea 9.98

691-10001 New York Central #905035 (black)
691-10002 Rio Grande #17341 (black)
691-10003 Western Maryland #80293 (oxide red)
691-10004 Santa Fe #80000 (box car red)
691-10005 Data (black)
691-10007 Erie Lackawanna #32256 (black)
691-10010 Clinchfield Railroad #54332
691-10013 Chessie System
691-10015 New York Central #905031 (black)
691-10016 New York Central #905038 (black)
691-10205 Pennsylvania #670122 (black) *NEW*
691-10206 Pennsylvania #668567 (black) *NEW*
691-10207 Data (black) *NEW*

691-10208 Rio Grande *NEW*
691-10209 Rio Grande *NEW*
691-10210 Rio Grande *NEW*
691-10211 Erie Lackawanna #33460 (black) *NEW*
691-10212 Erie Lackawanna #33482 (black) *NEW*
691-10213 Erie Lackawanna #33508 (black) *NEW*
691-10214 Pittsburgh & Lake Erie *NEW*
691-10215 Pittsburgh & Lake Erie *NEW*
691-10216 Pittsburgh & Lake Erie *NEW*
691-10217 Western Maryland *NEW*
691-10218 Western Maryland *NEW*
691-10219 Western Maryland *NEW*
691-10220 Conrail *NEW*

691-10221 Conrail *NEW*
691-10222 Conrail *NEW*
691-10000 Undecorated
691-10200 Undecorated, H-39 *NEW*

Limited Quantities Available

691-10008 Erie Lackawanna #32389 (black)
691-10012 Chessie System #13985
691-10017 New York Central #905042 (black)
691-10204 Pennsylvania #669902 (black) *NEW*

This Rio Grande caboose is as fancy as any passenger car and finished in the same color scheme! Bringing up the markers in style, this steel car was built by Peter Theodore from Paramus, New Jersey. The model is an Overland Models brass import, painted with Scalecoat and Floquil colors. Decal lettering from Champ and Microscale was used to finish the caboose as it would have looked in the mid 60's.

TICHY TRAIN GROUP

These easy-to-build HO Scale kits feature unpainted plastic parts, separate ladders and grab irons. They also include underbody details, and the coupler pockets accept horn-hook couplers or Kadee couplers.

We have worked closely with the manufacturer to provide accurate availability information at the time this catalog was published. Items listed in blue ink may not be available at all times. Please see you dealer for current delivery information.

BOX CARS

40' SINGLE SHEATHED BOX CAR
293-4026 USRA, Pennsylvania 14.50
293-4028 USRA, Rebuilt 14.50
This kit features steel sides and AB type brake gear.

293-4032 USRA, Rebuilt 14.50
This kit features steel sides.

293-6026 USRA, Wood Box pkg (6) 74.98
293-6028 USRA, Rebuilt 6 Pack 74.98
This kit features steel sides and AB type brake gear.

293-6032 USRA, Rebuilt pkg (6) 74.98
This kit features steel sides.

293-40324 USRA, Rebuilt with decals 16.50
293-60284 Same as 6028, with decals 87.00293-60324 USRA, Georgia with decals pkg (6) 86.98

X-29 BOX CAR *NEW*
293-1021 Pennsylvania 10.50
293-1020 Undecorated 9.50

MK-26 BOX CAR *NEW*
293-1031 Baltimore & Ohio 10.50
293-1030 Undecorated 9.50

HOPPERS

36' 2-BAY HOPPER
293-4029 USRA, Wabash 14.50
This kit features panel sides.

293-6027 USRA, pkg (6) 74.98
293-6029 USRA, Wabash pkg (6) 74.98
This kit features panel sides.

293-9029 USRA, with decals 2.50 *NEW*
293-40284 USRA, with decals 16.50 *NEW*
This kit features steel sides.

293-40294 USRA, with decals 16.50
293-60294 USRA, Wabash pkg (6) with decals 87.00
293-4027 USRA, Undecorated 14.50

CONVERSION HOPPERS
293-4030 USRA, Delaware & Hudson Cement Conversion 14.50
293-4031 Panel Hopper, Anderson Grain Conversion 18.50
293-40304 USRA, Delaware & Hudson Cement Conversion with decals16.50293-60304 USRA, Cement Conversion with decals pkg (6) 86.98
293-6030 USRA, Delaware & Hudson Cement Conversion pkg (6) 75.00
293-6031 Panel Hopper, Andersen Grain Conversion pkg (6) 96.00

120T BROWNHOIST CRANE

120T BROWNHOIST CRANE

Ready to go on a moment's notice, the 120 Ton Capacity Crane was an important piece of maintenance equipment for any railroad. The kit is based on a Brownhoist prototype, many of which lasted well into the diesel era. This detailed model has over 200 parts and features a working boom plus heavy-duty trucks. Complete instructions are included.

293-4010 Undecorated

CONVERSION HOPPERS

FLAT CARS

293-3010 Scale Wheelset pkg (96) 9.50
These wheelsets are non-operating, and are for use with #4023.

293-4021 40' 50 Ton Steel 8.95
This flat car was built by AC&F in 1928. Features include molded deck, straight side sills, detailed underframe and complete brake rigging.

293-6021 50 Ton Steel pkg (6) 46.00

293-4023 40' Wheel Flat Car, Undecorated 14.50

53' GSC COMMONWEALTH FLAT CAR ea 9.00
(unless noted)
293-1001 Pennsylvania
293-1002 Wabash
293-1003 Soo Line
293-1004 Union Pacific
293-1000 Undecorated 8.00

BULKHEAD FLAT ea 9.50
(unless noted)
For handling building materials and other loads, bulkheads were later added to many of these cars.

293-1011 Pennsylvania
293-1012 Wabash
293-1013 Soo Line
293-1014 Union Pacific
293-1010 Undecorated 8.50

36' TANK CAR

40' PFE WOOD REEFER

40' WHEEL FLAT CAR

20' WOOD ORE CAR

TANK CARS

36' TANK CAR
Represents the industry standard from 1920 through the 1960s.
293-4020 USRA 10,000 Gallon 14.50
50" single dome tank car includes underbody detail, separate tank straps and trucks.

293-4025 USRA 10,000 Gallon 14.50
This kit features a 60" dome

293-6020 USRA Tank pkg (6) 75.00
293-6025 USRA Tank pkg (6) 75.00

6' UTILITY CAR

293-4011 Handcar/Pushcar pkg (12) 9.50
This kit contains six handcars with optional side benches and six pushcars or material cars.

GONDOLAS

293-4033 USRA Composite 14.50
293-6033 USRA Composite pkg (6) 75.00

BOOM CARS

293-4022 40' Boom Car 14.50
With crane tender, this kit features toolbox underframe, deck cabins, toolboxes and many accessory tools and detail parts to customize the design.

293-6022 Boom Car pkg (6) 74.98

REEFERS

40' PFE WOOD REEFER
293-4024 Class R-404 14.50
This kit features a detailed underbody, hatches and doors.

293-6024 Class R-404 pkg (6) 74.98

ORE CARS

20' WOOD ORE CAR
A replica of a CM&StP prototype. Based on drawings from the 1906 Car Builders Dictionary. Enough material to build two cars.

293-4012 21' Wood Ore Car pkg (2) 14.50
293-6012 Ore Car pkg (6) 74.98

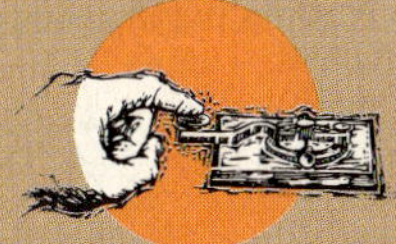

INFORMATION STATION

You may know how much fun it is to listen to railroad radio operators with a scanner. But it may surprise you that railroads have been experimenting with radio for almost 90 years! One of the first tasks took place on the Lackawanna in 1914, when a wireless telephone was used between a train and stations up to 50 miles away.

Testing continued into the 1920's with pure radio and carrier systems. Although both worked well, lack of available radio frequencies and the costs of the carrier system limited their usefulness. By 1930, the Federal Communications Commission revoked licenses issued for railroad use. But years of testing proved that crews could work better and faster, thereby saving money. The railroads were sold on using radio and experimental licenses were issued so testing could continue.

In the 1940's, the introduction of Frequency Modulation (FM) and new equipment, such as the walkie talkie, solved many of the early problems. On December 31, 1945, the FCC established the Railroad Radio Service and assigned a portion of the very high-band for railroad use.

Today, railroads use frequencies between 160.215 and 161.565 megahertz. Most have two or three channels for road and yard operations, with other channels for maintenance, security and shop operators.

(Remember, laws on the use of scanners vary so check with your local authorities.)

Westerfield specializes in cars from 1895 to 1930, the "golden age" of railroading. HO scale craft train kits feature unpainted ultra-thin impact-resistant castings with detail parts. Prototypical custom decals included in the decorated kits. Trucks and couplers not included.

BOX CARS

36' XL BOX CAR ea 25.00
(unless noted)
The first steel underframe box car, with over 37,000 built by the Pennsylvania Railroad between 1901 and 1912. They lasted into the late 1930s.

783-1300 Pennsylvania
783-1301 Empire Line
783-1302 Union Line
783-1303 Anchor Line **NEW**
783-1305 Adams Express
783-1306 PCC & St. Louis **NEW**
783-1307 Cleveland, Akron & Columbus **NEW**
783-1308 Long Island
783-1309 Vandalia Line **NEW**
783-1310 New York Philadelphia & Norfolk 26.00
783-1304 Undecorated, as built 24.00

36' MODERN XL BOX CAR
Beginning in 1911, the cars were modernized with the addition of iron roofs and safety appliances.

783-1351 Pennsylvania 25.00
783-1352 Maryland & Pennsylvania 24.00
783-1350 Undecorated 24.00

36 XM VENTILATED BOX CAR
783-2754 Pennsylvania 26.00

36' COMPOSITE Bx-W/X/Y/Z BOX CAR
ea. 25.00 (unless noted)
Built between 1910 and 1915, these four classes represent the last truss rod cars built for the Santa Fe. Almost 9,500 cars were built and some lasted into the 1950s. Decals included for all eras.

783-1400 Bx-Z Undecorated 24.00
783-1401 Bx-Z Santa Fe
783-4001 Bx-W Santa Fe
783-4021 Bx-X Santa Fe
783-4031 Bx-Y Santa Fe
783-4000 Bx-W Undecorated 24.00

36' FOWLER PATENT BOX CAR ea 25.00
(unless noted)
A number of roads ordered the cars with 6' wide doors. Some of these cars were built as late as 1923.

783-4301 Canadian National, 1923 production
783-4302 Erie/Susquehanna, 1917 production
783-4303 Erie/Wells Fargo Express Service (green)
783-4304 Grand Trunk, US assigned cars
783-4305 Nashville Chattanooga & St. Louis
783-4306 Erie/Susquehanna, 1913 production
783-4307 Grand Trunk, 1912 production
783-4308 Grand Trunk, 1913 production, steel roof
783-4309 Grand Trunk, 1913 production, wood roof
783-4310 Grand Trunk, 1918 production
783-4352 Erie/Susquehanna, modernized
783-4354 Grand Trunk Western, modernized
783-4355 Nashville Chattanooga & St. Louis
783-4357 Canadian National, 1912 production
783-4358 Canadian National, 1913 production, steel roof
783-4359 Canadian National, 1913 production, modernized
783-4360 Canadian National, 1918 production
783-4350 Undecorated Modern 24.00

36' COMPOSITE SOUTHERN BOX CAR ea 25.00
(unless noted)
Built in 1922-28, almost 15,000 cars ran the rails, making them the last truss rod cars produced in quantity. Several variations were made during production with four sets of unusual ends. The kit includes decals for all known lettering styles.

783-4101 Southern, Hutchins End
783-4102 Southern, T-Brace End
783-4103 Southern, Late Hutchins End
783-4104 Mobile & Ohio, T-Brace End
783-4105 Southern, Murphy End
783-4100 Undecorated, Hutchins End 24.00
The cars were rebuilt in the late 1930s, many lasting into the late 1950s. Southern sold about 100 to the Atlantic & Danville in 1949.

783-4151 Southern/Atlantic & Danville, Hutchins End
783-4153 Southern/Atlantic & Danville, Late Hutchins End
783-4154 Mobile & Ohio, T-Brace End
783-4155 Southern/Atlantic & Danville, Murphy End
783-4150 Undecorated, T-Brace End 24.00

40' FOWLER PATENT BOX CAR ea. 25.00
(unless noted)
Chicago & North Western ordered 8,500 true Fowler box cars for itself and its Omaha subsidiary in 1914-15. They made up 20% of the box car fleet on delivery and 38% in 1940. The cars were upgraded periodically; separate details in the kit allow all versions to be modeled. Modernized version has side bulge plates and Camel door rollers. The cars lasted until 1970.

783-4401 Chicago & North Western, original 24.00
783-4402 Chicago St. Paul Minneapolis & Omaha, original 23.00
783-4451 Chicago & North Western, modernized 25.00
783-4452 Chicago St. Paul Minneapolis & Omaha, modernized 25.00
783-4400 Undecorated, original 24.00
783-4450 Undecorated, modernized 24.00

50' FOWLER CLONE BOX CAR

40' BOX CAR

40' FOWLER PATENT BOX CAR

36' MARYLAND & PENNSYLVANIA MODERN XL BOX CAR
Pennsylvania gave four XL box cars to the Maryland & Pennsylvania to replace wrecked cars. Extensively rebuilt in the 1940s, they served in MOW service until the 1950s. Kit can be built with either left or right hand door.

783-3551 Maryland & Pennsylvania 25.00
783-3550 Undecorated 24.00

40' FOWLER CLONE BOX CAR ea 25.00 (unless noted)
American car builders copied the Canadian car but with distinctive differences for Rio Grande and Rock Island, delivering 7,000 cars between 1913-15. Each version listed below is physically different.

783-6401 Rock Island, 1913 WSC&F
783-6402 Rock Island, 1915 Bettendorf
783-6403 Rio Grande, as built
783-6404 Rock Island, 1915 Pullman
783-6405 Rock Island, 1915 Haskell & Barker
783-6453 Rio Grande, rebuilt
783-6463 Rio Grande, AB brakes
783-6400 Undecorated, 1915 Pullman 24.00
783-6450 Undecorated, Rio Grande rebuilt 24.00

40' BOX CAR ea 25.00
(unless noted)
About 16,000 cars were built between 1922 and 1926 for the New York Central and its subsidiaries. Cars were given new doors in the 1940s but otherwise remained unchanged into the 1960s. Kit supplies both types of doors to model either period.

783-2901 New York Central
783-2902 Boston & Albany
783-2903 Big Four
783-2904 Michigan Central
783-2905 Cincinnati Northern
783-2906 Peoria & Eastern
783-2900 Undecorated 24.00
In 1927 the design was revised to add early Dreadnaught ends. 3,500 cars were built for New York Central and its subsidiaries.

783-2951 New York Central
783-2950 Undecorated 24.00

40' USRA SS BOX CAR
ea 25.00 (unless noted)
The USRA designed and ordered 25,000 single sheathed 50 ton box cars in 1918. At least 5,000 were originally lettered for the Federal Equipment Trust but by 1920 all were assigned to about two dozen roads.

783-3301 Federal Equipment Trust
783-3302 Central of New Jersey
783-3303 Chesapeake & Ohio
783-3304 Chicago & North Western
783-3305 New York Central
783-3306 Pennsylvania
783-3307 Southern Pacific
783-3308 Baltimore & Ohio
783-3309 Delaware & Hudson
783-3310 Philadelphia & Reading/Reading Co
783-3312 Michigan Central/Pittsburgh McKeesport & Youghiogheny
783-3313 Grand Rapids & Indiana/New York Philadelphia & Norfolk
783-3314 Erie
783-3315 Norfolk & Western
783-3300 Undecorated 24.00
783-3311 Chicago, Milwaukee & St. Paul

40' COMPOSITE BX-3/6 BOX CAR
ea 25.00 (unless noted)
Distinctive plate steel doors and panel sides identify the Bx-3 and the identical Bx-6. 5,000 were delivered between 1923-25.

783-3601 Santa Fe
These cars were rebuilt with AB brakes, power handbrakes and corrugated doors, lasting into the late 1960s.

783-3651 Santa Fe
783-3600 Undecorated 24.00
783-3650 Undecorated 24.00

40' USRA DS BOX CAR
ea 25.00 (unless noted)
Over 25,000 cars were designed and ordered in 1918. Some twenty railroads used these cars, some of which were in service until the 1950s.

783-3801 Santa Fe
783-3802 Atlantic Coast Line
783-3803 Boston & Maine, original
783-3804 Chicago & Eastern Illinois
783-3805 Chicago & North Western
783-3807 Missouri Pacific
783-3808 New York Central
783-3809 Rock Island
783-3810 St Louis San Francisco

783-3811 Chicago Burlington & Quincy
783-3812 Chicago St Paul Minneapolis & Omaha
783-3813 Delaware Lackawanna & Western
783-3815 Great Northern
783-3817 Big Four/Toledo & Ohio Central
783-3818 Northwestern Pacific
783-3819 Spokane Portland & Seattle
783-3820 Wabash
783-3853 Boston & Maine, modernized
783-3855 Great Northern, modernized
783-3858 Northwestern Pacific, original
783-3800 Undecorated 24.00

40' HARRIMAN B-50-1 BOX CAR
ea 25.00 (unless noted)
The Harriman roads adopted a 40 foot fishbelly underframe for their house cars in 1902. From that date until about 1912 most box, refrigerator and stock cars were built on this frame. The Illinois Central, Chicago & Alton, Southern Pacific, Union Pacific, and their subsidiaries ran more than 15,000 of the B-50-1 box cars. The first Pacific Fruit Express cars were 6,600 of the companion R-30-1 design. All kits contain two sets of end and details to model either pre- or post-Safety Appliances Act (1911) prototypes.

783-1701 Southern Pacific & subsidiaries
783-1702 Union Pacific & subsidiaries
783-1703 Illinois Central
783-1704 Southern Pacific/Central Pacific (Ogden Route)
783-1705 Oregon & California (Shasta Route)
783-1706 Houston & Texas Central
783-1707 Chicago & Alton
783-1700 Undecorated 24.00

40' COMPOSITE BX-11\12\13 BOX CAR
ea 25.00 (unless noted)
In 1929-31 Santa Fe ordered 6,600 cars in three similar classes, differing in roofs and minor details.

783-4601 Bx11 Santa Fe 26.00
783-4701 Bx12 Santa Fe 26.00
783-4801 Bx13 Santa Fe 26.00
783-4600 Bx11 Undecorated
783-4700 Bx12 Undecorated
783-4800 Bx13 Undecorated 24.00

40' COMPOSITE M-15 BOX CAR
ea 25.00 (unless noted)
Baltimore & Ohio designed its standard M-15 box car in 1910. Between then and 1924 it constantly improved the design with various end, roof and door combinations. Earlier cars were rebuilt to 1920s standards. The result was a total of nine classes comprising 12,000 cars, some of which lasted as long as the 1960s.

783-5002 Baltimore & Ohio M-15E – reverse Murphy end
783-5003 Baltimore & Ohio M-15D – USRA alt steel end
783-5005 Baltimore & Ohio M-15H – indestructible end

50' B-50-20 BOX CAR
ea 27.00 (unless noted)
Converted from the Union Pacific A-50-6 auto car in 1934-40, the cars sported three different lettering styles until retirement in the 1960s. They were modernized with AB brakes in the 1950s.

783-5901 Union Pacific, as rebuilt
783-5951 Union Pacific, AB brakes
783-5900 Undecorated 26.00

AUTO CARS

40' AUTO CAR
Michigan Central had 4,000 double door versions of the standard 40' NYC box car.

783-3001 Michigan Central 25.00
783-3000 Undecorated 24.00

40' SS AUTO CAR
Built in 1924-26, this car is an example of composite construction. Car features radial roof and reverse-corrugation Murphy ends.

783-1901 Missouri Pacific 26.00
783-1900 Undecorated 25.00

40' DS AUTO CAR
The companion double-sheathed car was built at the same period for a closely allied railroad.

783-2001 Texas & Pacific 26.00
783-2000 Undecorated 25.00

50' AUTO CAR ea 26.00
(unless noted)
Built in 1925-27, cars were equipped with both solid and door ends. Kit allows either variation to be modeled. Door end cars remained substantially unchanged into the early 1960s.

783-2801 Great Northern 27.00
783-2800 Undecorated
In 1940-41 the solid end cars were converted to single doors and were equipped with power hand brakes and ladders. They lasted until 1970.

783-2851 Great Northern 27.00
783-2850 Undecorated
In the 1950s the cars were given heavier bracing and AB brakes.

783-2852 Great Northern, final version 27.00

50' A-50-4 AUTO CAR
ea 27.00 (unless noted)
Built in 1914, this car was the first all-steel house car mass-produced for UP. As delivered, the cars had radial roofs and full A end doors. Between 1928 and 1930 the cars were given peaked roofs. Later they were given power hand brakes. During World War II many were leased to Grand Trunk Western. They lasted into the early 1950s.

783-1101 Union Pacific, original
783-1151 Union Pacific/Grand Trunk Western, modernized
783-1100 Undecorated, original 26.00

50' A-50-6 AUTO CAR
ea 27.00 (unless noted)
Union Pacific's follow-up to the A-50-4, it differed because of a small lumber door in the A end, peaked roof and lack of stringer pockets on the sides. Most cars were converted to B-50-20 box cars but some lasted as auto cars into the 1950s. During World War II the auto cars were leased to New York Central.

783-5801 Union Pacific, original
783-5851 Union Pacific/New York Central, modern
783-5800 Undecorated 26.00

REEFERS

34' HEINZ REEFER ea 25.00
(unless noted)
These colorful cars were built in the 1890s. They were repainted in the early 1900s and rebuilt later in the decade. All versions include three styles of doors and two types of end sills.

783-3901 Pickle Refrigerator line (white)
783-3902 Baked Beans (brown)
783-3903 Apple Butter (brown)
783-3904 Tomato Ketchup (yellow)\
783-3905 India Relish
783-3906 Euchred Figs
783-3907 Food Products
783-3908 Pure Malt Vinegar
783-3900 Undecorated 23.00
The cars were modernized in the teens with wider doors, steel strapping and safety appliances. Lettering covers two different paint schemes.

783-3951 Heinz 57, modernized
783-3950 Undecorated, modernized 23.00

36' RF REEFER ea 25.00
(unless noted)
As the companion to the XL box car, over 3,000 RF's ran between 1902 and the early 1930s. Many were leased to Fruit Growers Express in 1922. The modernized version is offered. Decals include appropriate striping.

783-2751 Pennsylvania, four billboards
783-2752 Pennsylvania American Railway Express/Adams Express 26.00
783-2753 Fruit Growers Express
783-2750 Undecorated 24.00

Westerfield specializes in cars from 1895 to 1930, the "golden age" of railroading. HO scale craft train kits feature unpainted ultra-thin impact-resistant castings with detail parts. Prototypical custom decals included in the decorated kits. Trucks and couplers not included.

We have worked closely with this manufacturer to provide accurate availability information at the time this catalog was published. Items listed in blue ink may not be available at all times. Please see your dealer for current delivery information.

GONDOLAS

46' G22/G22A/G22B GONDOLA ea 24.00
(unless noted)
4,000 G22 and 2,250 G22A gondolas were built in 1915-1917. The G22 had drop bottom doors and fixed end. The G22A had a solid floor and drop ends. The G22 as built lasted into the 19 50s.

783-1251 Pennsylvania, as-built
783-1250 Undecorated, as-built 23.00
Most G22 cars were rebuilt in the 1930s to remove the drop bottom doors. Two sets of ends are included in the rebuilt kit so that the G22 rebuilt, the G22A as-built, and the G22B may be modeled. All kits include Pennsylvania KD brakes, lift bars, and brake wheels.

783-1201 Pennsylvania, rebuilt G22A/B
783-1200 Undecorated, rebuilt G22A/B 23.00

CONTAINERS FOR G22s
Many G22s were modified to class G22B for less-than-carload container service. Class HB1A containers are offered separately to modify the kit. Decals are included in the container kits.

783-1290 HB1A Container, 1 carload PRR 16.00
783-1291 HB1A Container, 1 container PRR 4.00

40' COMPOSITE GONDOLA ea 24.00 (unless noted)
The Chicago Milwaukee & St Paul (Milwaukee Road) built 7,000 of these drop-bottom gons in the early 1920s; they lasted until about 1950. The doors and door hardware are faithfully reproduced on the model.

783-2501 Milwaukee Road
783-2500 Undecorated 23.00

41' GRA GONDOLA ea 25.00
(unless noted)
A stretched version of the 37' GR class, Pennsylvania received them beginning in 1907. About 10,000 were

put in service and they lasted into the 1960s. As-built model contains decals suitable through the 1940s.

783-4502 Pennsylvania, post-1911 version
783-4500 Undecorated 24.00
783-4501 Pennsylvania, pre-1911 version
The gondolas were modified in numerous ways over the years. They lasted into the 1960s. Modernized kit contains AB brakes.

783-4550 Undecorated, modern 24.00
783-4551 Pennsylvania, modernized
783-4552 Pennsylvania, no stake pockets

REEFERS

40' COMPOSITE IE-X REEFER ea 25.00
In 1952, 76 Bx-3/6 box cars were converted to ice service reefers. From 1951 to 1953, 45 cars were rebuilt for salt service.

783-3701 Santa Fe, ice
783-3702 Santa Fe, salt

40' AC&F TYPE I REEFER ea 26.00 (unless noted)
A standard design from 1911 on, it was gradually improved through the 1920s. A variety of modifications and billboards are offered. Kit features fully detailed ice hatches.

783-6001 Union Refrigerator Transit Co/Bananas 1911-on
783-6002 Great Northern/Western Fruit Express 1920-1930 25.00
783-6003 American Refrigerator Transit 1911-1920
783-6501 American Refrigerator Transit 1912-1930s, no side sill

40' AC&F TYPE II REEFER ea 26.00 (unless noted)
In 1922, AC&F revised its standard design to enlarge and modernize the door, add ladders and more modern roof hatches. Hundreds of billboards were painted on the cars. Dozens of decals and dry transfers are available specifically for this car from other manufacturers. See the Walthers decal catalog.

42' AC&F TYPE IC REEFER ea 26.00
(unless noted)
A stretched version of the 40' AC&F car, it was delivered in 1915 with the "bananas" billboard. In 1926 the cars were repainted in at least ten billboards for which Walthers has specially revised decals.

783-2601 Union Refrigerator Transit Co/Bananas
783-2602 Union Refrigerator Transit Co/Milwaukee Road 1922-30s
783-2600 Undecorated 24.00

WALTHERS DECALS
These Walthers decal sets have been revised and are designed for use with the Westerfield 2600 series Billboard Reefer.

934-1104 Atlantic & Pacific 2.98
934-1110 Carnation Milk 2.98
934-1111 Carnation Flaked Wheat 2.98
934-1154 Mobil gas horse 2.98
934-1167 Pabst-ett 2.98
934-1177 Phenix Cheese 2.98
934-1201 Blatz/Old Heidelburg 2.98
934-1214 Milky Way 2.98
934-1502 Van Camp's 2.98

783-6601 Union Refrigerator Transit Co/Milwaukee Road 1922-30s
783-6602 North Western 1926-1950s
783-6603 Union Refrigerator Transit Co/Erie 1934-1940s
783-6604 Union Refrigerator Transit Co/Milwaukee Road 1934-1940s
783-6605 BPDX Bordens NEW
783-6606 CIPX College Inn NEW
783-6652 North Western modernized NEW
783-6600 Undecorated 24.00

40' COMPOSITE IE-X REEFER
783-3700 Undecorated 24.00

40' HARRIMAN R-30-1 REEFER ea 25.00
(unless noted)
Built on the same frame as the B-50-1, this reefer was the first of 6,500 placed in service by Pacific Fruit Express in 1906.

783-1801 Pacific Fruit Express
783-1802 Pacific Fruit Express (green)
783-1800 Undecorated 24.00

40' AC&F TYPE III REEFERS ea 26.00 (unless noted)
In 1927, AC&F again revised the design to add the USRA reefer underbody and again improve the roof hatches. North Western retained the earlier hatches. Slight changes were also made to the sides and ends, requiring a kit entirely different from the type II kits above.

783-6701 Union Refrigerator Transit Co/Milwaukee Road 1927-30s
783-6702 North Western 1927-50s
783-6703 NWX Tracy NEW
783-6704 Union Refrigerator Transit Co/Milwaukee Road 1934-40s
783-6752 North Western modernized NEW
783-6700 Undecorated 24.00

G22 CONTAINERS

GOLDEN AGE LINE
WESTERFIELD

40' HARRIMAN R-30-4/5/6 REEFER

ea 25.00 (unless noted)
The second major series of Pacific Fruit Express cars, three different classes comprising over 6,600 cars, were delivered between 1909 and 1913. The R-30-4 had standard ice hatches, the -5 and -6 had ventilators. R-30-6 had more modern door latches. R-30-4 and -5 were delivered before the Safety Appliances Act of 1911 and are modeled both pre- and post-1911.

783-4901 R-30-6 Pacific Fruit Express
783-4902 R-30-4 Pacific Fruit Express, as delivered
783-4903 R-30-5 Pacific Fruit Express, as delivered
783-4952 R-30-4 Pacific Fruit Express, safety appliances
783-4953 R-30-5 Pacific Fruit Express, safety appliances
783-4900 R-30-6 Undecorated 24.00

HOPPERS

30' HP HOPPER
The Norfolk & Western built 11,000 cars in 1910-11. The cars became the mainstay of their coal fleet for many years. The last cars were scrapped in 1959.

783-1601 Norfolk & Western 24.00
783-1600 Undecorated 23.00

33' GLA HOPPER CAR
ea 24.00 (unless noted)
Successor to the famous GL hopper, almost 30,000 were built between 1904 and 1911, becoming the standard of the railroad. Rebuilt in the teens to add safety appliances, many lasted into the late 1960s and some are still around today.

783-5701 Pennsylvania, as built
783-5751 Pennsylvania, rebuilt
783-5700 Undecorated, as built 23.00
783-5750 Undecorated, rebuilt 23.00

46' GONDOLA

31' PRESSED STEEL CAR CO TWIN HOPPER ea 24.00
(unless noted)
Pressed Steel Car Co sold thousands of a generic version of the GL to many railroads. It differed in length, side stake spacing and door hardware from the GL. Each roadname has specific detail parts to exactly match that prototype.

783-2401 New York Central and Subsidiaries
783-2402 Union Pacific and Subsidiaries
783-2400 Undecorated 23.00

33' GL/GLC TWIN HOPPER
ea 24.00 (unless noted)
An enlarged version of the first all-steel hopper design, over 20,000 were ordered by the Pennsy between 1898 and 1903 for itself and its subsidiaries. The GL went through nemerous rebuildings, lasting into the 1960s. Original GL and 1920s GLc rebuilt are offered with decals to model any period to 1940.

783-2301 GL Pennsylvania
783-2302 GL Berwind-White
783-2303 GL Keystone Coal & Coke
783-2304 GL Penn Coal Gas
783-2305 GL Westmoreland
783-2351 GLc Pennsylvania
783-2300 GL Undecorated 23.00
783-2350 GLc Undecorated 23.00

40' W-1 HOPPER ea 25.00
(unless noted)
Based on the Pennsylvania's H21A hopper and built from 1910-11, W-1 hoppers remained in service until the 1950s. The 1923 rebuilt includes original door locks and the wine door locks applied in the 1930s.

783-3151 Baltimore & Ohio
783-3150 Undecorated 24.00

40' H21A HOPPER ea 25.00
(unless noted)
Between 1909 and 1917 over 36,000 cars were built for Pennsylvania and its subsidiaries. It was the first quad hopper to be built in quantity. Although a rebuilding program started in 1926, some cars ran essentially as-built through World War II.

783-3201 Pennsylvania, 1911-1926
783-3202 Pennsylvania, 1927-1940s
783-3200 Undecorated 24.00

39' USRA 70 TON HOPPER
ea 25.00 (unless noted)
Built in 1923-25 to the USRA standard, many lasted into the early 60s. Over 19,000 were built for the two major railroads and subsidiaries. The USRA cars were rebuilt in 1937-39 to add a third saw-tooth hopper and AB brakes. Chesapeake & Ohio added both flat plate and dreadnaught radial ends.

783-2101 Chesapeake & Ohio
783-2103 New York Central
783-2104 Pittsburgh & Lake Erie
783-2151 Chesapeake & Ohio, Flat Plate Radial Ends
783-2152 Chesapeake & Ohio, Dreadnaught Radial Ends
783-2153 New York Central
783-2154 Pittsburgh & Lake Erie/Pittsburgh McKeesport & Youghiogheny
783-2100 Undecorated 24.00
783-2150 Undecorated, New York Central end 24.00

40' MODERN H21A HOPPER
ea 25.00 (unless noted)
Pennsylvania began replacing the clamshell hoppers with sawtooth ones in 1926. The program took 20 years. Beginning in 1941 AB brakes were added.

783-3251 Pennsylvania, 1927-1940s
783-3252 Pennsylvania, AB brakes
783-3250 Undecorated, K brakes 24.00

46' NORFOLK AND WESTERN
ea 30.00 *NEW*
Built in 1917 to test high capacity design, this one-of-a-king giant lasted until 1941. A limited run to mark the tenth anniversary of Westerfield, the kit includes Pilcher sideframes and bolsters, a commemorative pin an higher detail/complexity.

783-5101 Norfolk and Western

ORE CARS

22' PRESSED STEEL CAR CO ORE CAR
ea 29.00 (unless noted)
These were the first ore cars made entirely of steel and were delivered around 1900. Safety appliances were added around 1914. Great Northern cars were equipped with unique side walkways and these cars were later sold to many western roads.

783-3401 Great Northern pkg(2)
783-3402 Algoma Central/Lake Champlain & Moriah pkg(2)
783-3451 Great Northern pkg (2)
783-3452 Yosemite Valley/Sierra pkg(2)
783-3400 Undecorated pkg(2) 27.00
783-3450 Undecorated pkg(2) 27.00

TANK CARS

36' "COFFIN" PICKLE TANK CAR
ea 25.00 (unless noted)
Built between 1903 and 1912, these cars were used in captive service between salting stations and packing plants. The coffin cars are extremely colorful and add variety to the freight mix.

783-2201 CF Claussen & Sons
783-2202 HJ Heinz, 1907
783-2203 HJ Heinz, 1902
783-2200 Undecorated 24.00

STOCK CARS

36' HARRIMAN STD STOCK CARS ea 27.00 (unless noted)
Between 1905 and 1927, Union Pacific and Southern Pacific and their subsidiaries received about 6,200 stock cars of similar design, but in five distinct classes. Many of the cars lasted into the 1950s. The three kits listed model each of the classes.

783-5201 S-40-4 Southern Pacific and subsidiaries
783-5202 S-40-4 Union Pacific and subsidiaries
783-5301 S-40-6 Southern Pacific and subsidiaries
783-5302 S-40-6 Union Pacific and subsidiaries
783-5401 S-40-8/9/10 Southern Pacific and subsidiaries
783-5200 S-40-4 Undecorated 26.00
783-5300 S-40-6 Undecorated 26.00
783-5400 S-40-8/9/10 Undecorated 26.00

36' FOWLER PATENT STOCK CAR
ea 27.00 (unless noted)
Over 6,000 were rebuilt from Fowler box cars between 1919 and 1949. The major Canadian Stock car for over 30 years, some lasted into the 1980's. Original kits have K-brakes; modern have AB brakes.

783-4201 Canadian National, 5' door, original
783-4202 Canadian Pacific, 2-brace, original
783-4203 Canadian National, 6' door, original
783-4205 Canadian Pacific, 2-brace, original
783-4251 Canadian National, 5' door, modern
783-4252 Canadian Pacific, 5' door, 3-brace, modern
783-4253 Canadian National, 6' door, modern
783-4254 Canadian National, steel roof, 1949
783-4200 Undecorated, CP 4-brace, original 26.00
783-4250 Undecorated, CN steel roof, original 26.00

Ye Olde Huff-N-Puff

Ye Olde Huff-N-Puff features wood and metal HO Scale craft train kits. The decorated kits in this line include pre-painted and lettered sides. All kits feature scale wood siding, metal castings, and sliding doors on some models. Instructions are included. Kits do not include trucks and couplers.

OLD TIME CARS

34' TRUSS ROD BOX CAR
792-501 Bellefonte Central (dark green) 15.00
792-502 Undecorated 13.50

60' LCL TRUSS ROD BOX CAR
792-321 Northern Pacific (box car red) 17.00
792-322 Undecorated 15.50

36' TRUSS ROD REEFER
792-52 Pittsburgh & Shawmut 13.50

37' TRUSS ROD GONDOLA
792-352 Undecorated 12.50

36' TRUSS ROD FLAT CAR ea 10.00 (unless noted)
792-121 Great Northern (box car red)
792-122 Southern Pacific (black)
792-123 New York Central (black)
792-124 Western Pacific (black)
792-125 Santa Fe (black)
792-126 Pennsylvania (box car red)
792-127 Erie (box car red)
792-129 Northern Pacific (black)
792-128 Undecorated 9.00

37' TRUSS ROD FLAT CAR
792-351 Undecorated 11.50

29' TANK CAR ea 12.50
792-380 Steel Tank (unpainted)
792-381 Wood Tank (unpainted)

37' TRUSS ROD COKE CAR
792-353 Undecorated 13.50

OIL VAT CAR
792-354 Oil Vat Car 12.00

TRUSS ROD BARREL CAR
792-370 Barrel Car less Barrels 11.00

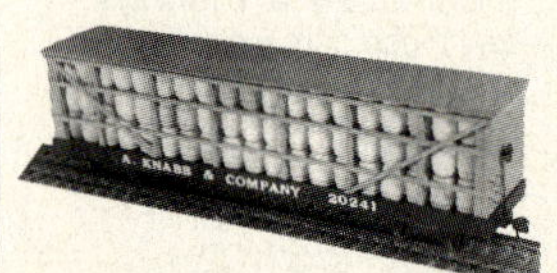

TRUSS ROD BARREL CAR
792-371 Barrel Car with 108 barrels 17.00

HOn3 OLD TIME CARS

30' TRUSS ROD GONDOLA
792-452 Victor Gold Mining Company (yellow, black lettering) 13.00
792-451 Undecorated 12.00

30' TRUSS ROD FLAT CAR
792-450 Undecorated 10.00

STEAM ERA CARS

50' SINGLE DOOR BOX CAR ea 15.50
792-176 Milwaukee Road (box car red)
792-178 Baltimore & Ohio (box car red)
792-177 Undecorated 14.00

50' DOUBLE DOOR BOX CAR ea 15.50 (unless noted)
792-276 Santa Fe (tuscan red)
792-277 Pennsylvania (Auto) (box car red)
792-278 Undecorated 14.00
792-279 Wabash (box car red)
792-280 Southern Pacific (box car red)

BOX CARS

36' BOX CAR ea 14.50 (unless noted)
792-202 Baltimore & Ohio, Globe (box car red)
792-204 NK Fairbanks (dark green)
792-205 Wells Fargo Express (box car red)
792-210 Saginaw, Tuscola & Huron (box car red)
792-217 Minnesota & St Paul (box car red)
792-218 Ft Worth (box car red)
792-222 Pittsburgh & Shawmut 13.50
792-225 Union Line Penn (box car red)
792-226 PRR Union Line (box car red)
792-227 Pennsylvania (box car red)
792-228 GW Dispatch (box car red)
792-236 Baltimore & Ohio (box car red)
792-237 Undecorated 13.00
792-223 Overland Dispatch (box car red)
792-229 Southern Pacific (box car red)

40' BOX CAR ea 14.50 (unless noted)
792-201 Standard Wagons (box car red)
792-203 Rome Watertown (box car red)
792-206 Minnesota Mining - 3M (caboose red)
792-207 Chicago, Burlington & Quincy (box car red)
792-208 Big Four (box car red)
792-209 Oregon Short Line (box car red)
792-211 Detroit, Mackinac & Marquette (box car red)
792-212 Fort Dodge Line (tuscan red)
792-213 Western Maryland (box car red)
792-214 Chicago & North Western (box car red)
792-215 Pennsylvania (box car red)
792-216 Bessemer & Lake Erie (reefer orange)
792-219 Chicago & Rock Island (box car red)
792-220 Soo Line (tuscan red)
792-221 Hocking Valley (box car red)
792-230 Penn State (dark blue)
792-233 Penn Furnace Foundry (reefer orange)
792-234 Mennonite Committee (reefer gray)
792-235 Louisville & Nashville (box car red)
792-231 Undecorated 13.00
792-224 PRR Empire Line (box car red)
792-232 West Indies Fruit (box car red)

WORK CAR

21' 4 WHEEL CABOOSE

WORK CARS

WORK CAR ea 16.00 (unless noted)
All cars are undecorated unless noted.

792-330 Bunk
792-331 Kitchen
792-332 Mess
792-333 Recreation
792-334 Supply

792-335 Boom
792-340 Clearance Car 18.50
792-341 28' Crane 20.00 This kit includes trucks.

792-349 Tool & Water 15.00
792-350 50' Fire 15.50

Ye Olde Huff-N-Puff

REEFERS

36' REEFER ea 14.50
(unless noted)
792-1 Armour (reefer yellow)
792-2 Armour (Oldie) (reefer yellow)
792-3 Armour Bacon (reefer yellow)
792-4 Armour Butter (reefer yellow)
792-6 Armour Lard (reefer yellow)
792-7 Blatz Beer (reefer yellow)
792-8 Budweiser Beer (dark green)
792-10 Carnation Milk (reefer yellow)
792-12 Crazy Water Crystals (reefer yellow)
792-13 Dubuque (reefer yellow)
792-14 Fred Miller (reefer yellow)
792-15 Great Northern (reefer yellow)
792-17 Kahn's (reefer yellow)
792-19 Mathieson Dry Ice (silver)
792-21 Mobile & Ohio (reefer orange)
792-22 Morrell (reefer yellow)
792-23 Old Log Brew (reefer yellow)
792-24 Oppenheimer (light green)
792-25 Pabst Beer (reefer yellow)
792-26 Pluto Water (reefer yellow)
792-27 Rath Packing (reefer yellow)
792-29 Swift (reefer yellow)
792-31 Tiffany (reefer yellow)
792-32 Yakima Valley (reefer yellow)
792-35 Old Dutch Cleanser (reefer yellow)
792-37 Addison & Pennsylvania (reefer yellow)
792-38 John Gund Brewing (reefer yellow)
792-39 Fruit Growers Express (reefer yellow)
792-40 Western RFP Lines (reefer yellow)
792-45 Schlitz Beer (reefer yellow)
792-48 Heinz Ketchup (reefer yellow)
792-49 Old Heidelberg (reefer yellow)
792-51 Undecorated 13.00
792-9 Booth Storage (dark green)
792-11 Carnation Wheat (reefer yellow)
792-16 Hormel (reefer yellow)
792-18 Kingan's (reefer yellow)
792-34 New York Central Early Bird (reefer orange)
792-43 Central of New Jersey (reefer yellow)
792-44 Happy Valley (reefer yellow)

40' REEFER ea 14.50
(unless noted)
792-20 Michigan Alkali (silver) 14.50
792-33 Penn State (reefer white)
792-47 E&A Opler (reefer gray)
792-50 Hershey Chocolate (roof brown)
792-36 Undecorated 14.00

50' REEFER
792-70 Pacific Fruit Express (yellow) 15.50
792-71 Western Fruit Express (yellow) 15.50
792-72 Undecorated 14.00

50' REEFER - ROUND ROOF
792-80 Old Frothingslosh (white) 15.50

**50' EXPRESS REEFER - ROUND ROOF
ea 15.50** (unless noted)
792-78 Illinois Central (green)
792-79 Pennsylvania (tuscan)
792-83 Railway Express (green)
792-84 Milwaukee Road (orange)
792-86 Western Dairy (green) 16.00
792-87 Pacific Fruit Express (green)
792-88 Northern Pacific (green) 16.00
792-90 Borden's (green)
792-81 Undecorated 14.50
792-82 Dairymen's League (white)
792-85 Hoods (green)
792-89 Missouri Pacific (green)

36' REEFER ea 14.50
792-5 Armour Ham (reefer yellow)
792-28 St Louis Southwestern (reefer yellow)
792-30 Swift (Oldie) (reefer yellow)
792-41 Westcott & Winks (reefer yellow)
792-42 Wilson Car Lines (reefer yellow)
792-46 Wolf Packing (reefer yellow)

40' STOCK CARS

GONDOLAS

40' GONDOLA ea 13.50
(unless noted)
792-155 Pennsylvania (box car red)
792-156 Missouri - Kansas - Texas (black)
792-157 Monon (black)
792-159 Soo Line (box car red)
792-160 Southern Railway (silver)
792-158 Undecorated 12.00

4-DOOR OPEN PULPWOOD GONDOLA
792-91 Pulpwood Gondola 17.50

46' THRALL HIGH-SIDE GONDOLA
792-300 Undecorated 14.50
792-301 3-in-1 36.00
This kit contains enough material for 3 complete cars

TANK CARS

PICKLE TANK CAR ea 13.00
792-503 Budlong (maroon)
792-504 Monarch (maroon)
792-506 Libby (black)
792-507 Lutz & Schramm (gray)
792-508 Harbauer (black)
792-505 Undecorated

STOCK CARS

40' STOCK CAR
792-400 Undecorated Open Top 12.00

CABOOSES

21' 4-WHEEL CABOOSE
Sideframes and wheelsets are included.

792-314 Cupola, Undecorated 14.50
792-315 Plain Roof, Undecorated 14.50
792-316 Honey Bobber, Undecorated 12.00

CABOOSE ea 15.50
(unless noted)
792-310 Side Door, Undecorated
792-311 Bay Window, Undecorated
792-312 Drover, Undecorated
792-313 Transfer, Undecorated 13.00

RACK CARS

42' RACK CAR ea 11.50
792-105 Atlantic Coast Line (black)
792-106 Missouri Pacific (black)
792-108 Seaboard Air Line (tuscan red)
792-109 Wabash (black) 11.50
792-107 Undecorated 10.50

FLAT CARS

FLAT CAR ea 10.50
792-110 50' Undecorated Fishbelly
792-120 40' Undecorated

POULTRY CARS

40' POULTRY CAR
792-392 Stentz Palace (black, olive green) 17.00
792-393 Leghorn 17.00
792-391 Undecorated 15.00

CAR SHOP

These HO Scale craft train kits are etched on brass sheet which is sheared and bent to facilitate assembly. Features include wire, soft metal or brass end platforms, brass structural shapes and detail castings. Canadian cars include CDS dry transfer lettering. These kits do not include trucks, couplers or underbody details.

SPECIAL ORDER ONLY

These items must be specially ordered from the manufacturer. You will be notified upon receipt of merchandise.

BRASS CABOOSE

ea 38.00 (unless noted)

227-207 Canadian Pacific ea 40.00
This car features a steel, offset cupola circa 1949.

227-101 Delaware, Lackawanna & Western
35.00
#755 Series
227-103 USRA wood center
This is a standard, 8-wheel car.
227-104 Canadian National wood
This car features a cupola style offset.
227-106 Canadian Pacific
This car features a cupola style wood offset.
227-108 Pennsylvania N-6-b Wood
This is an all brass kit which includes end platforms.
227-202 Wheeling & Lake Erie/Nickel Plate Road/Norfolk & Western
This car features a 700 series steel center cupola.
227-203 New Haven/Boston & Maine/Chicago Great Western/Penn Central/Conrail
This car features a cupola style steel welded center.

227-204 Nickle Plate Road/Norfolk & Western
This car is a 451 series steel bay window caboose.
227-207 Canadian Pacific
40.00
227-10420 Canadian National Wood Transfer Van
36.00
This car does not have a cupola.
227-10423 Canadian National Caboose Style #2
This car features an offset cupola and a wide side window.

BRASS TENDER WRAP

This etched brass piece, which is sheared and bent, is wrapped around to form tender sides.

This car uses a 6-wheel Buckeye truck under coal bunker and a 4-wheel under tank, which is not included.

227-16 Tender, Nickel Plate Road prototype 45.00

EXPRESS CAR

227-205 Canadian Pacific Steel Silk ea 40.00

CENTRAL VALLEY

STOCK CAR KIT

This easy-to-build HO Scale kit features highly detailed plastic parts and includes a one-piece body with separate details and a detailed underframe.

After the round-up, ship your livestock to market in this detailed car. Based on a Northern Pacific prototype, it's typical of stock cars used by many western roads.
210-1001 Stock Car Kit 9.85

WALKER

These kits feature white metal and wood detail parts. They do not include trucks and couplers

LOG CAR

786-5000 28' Open Frame pkg (2) 11.95

WEED SPRAYER

Weeds and underbrush have always created problems for railroads with low traffic densities. Allowed to grow unchecked, weeds eventually encumber the running surface of the rails, and derailments can result. This car is of a free-lance design.
786-5014 Weed Sprayer 11.95

ORE CAR

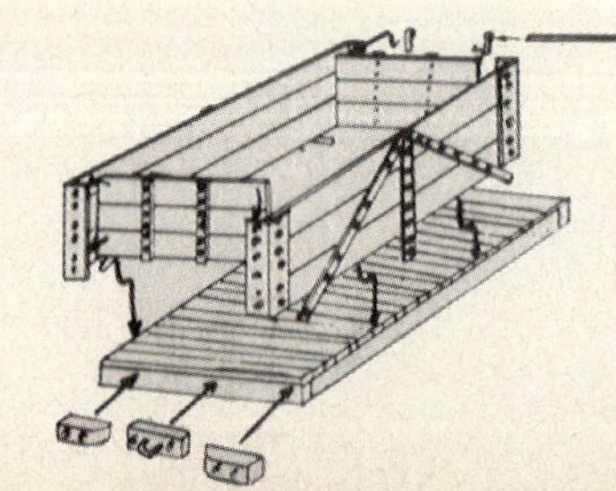

786-5005 Old Time Ore Car pkg (3) 25.95

EASTERN CAR WORKS

These kits feature prepainted and lettered, molded plastic parts. The cars are Kadee coupler compatible (less couplers), and include trucks.

HOPPERS

70 TON ACF COVERED HOPPER
117-2000 Undecorated 7.95

35' 70 TON ACF/M&K BALLAST HOPPER
117-2200 MOW Undecorated 7.95

35' 70 TON ENTERPRISE COVERED HOPPER ea 8.95
117-2020 New York Central
117-2021 Canadian National

GATC 40' SINGLE BAY AIRSLIDE™ HOPPER
117-2600 Undecorated 7.95

GONDOLAS

65' MILL GONDOLA ea 6.95
117-3000 Pensylvania G-26 Undecorated
117-3010 Ann Arbor 70 Ton Undecorated

CABOOSE

Caboose Reading TBA
NEW
117-4000 Northeastern

These HO Scale Craft Train Kits feature metal and plastic parts, as well as sprung metal trucks. Kadee couplers are also included.

LOGGING CABOOSE KIT

380-104 Red Kit 16.95
Keep timber trains moving safely with this caboose, typical, of the home-made equipment on many logging lines. One-piece plastic molded body with removable roof. Includes #4 MagneMatic® couplers.

LOGGING TRUCK KIT

380-107 Logging Trucks Kit 15.95
This kit includes two pairs of #4 couplers, but does not include logs.

Kadee® is a Registered Trademark
Magne-Matic® is a Registered Trademark

LOGGING CAR KIT

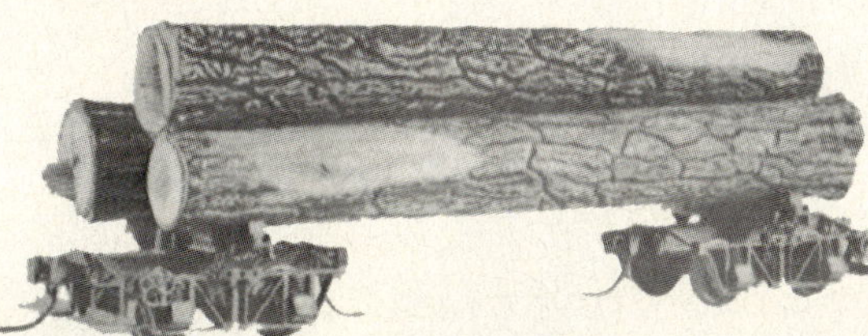

380-101 Disconnect Log Car Kit 17.95
Old-time disconnect logging trucks have been in use for over 70 years and are still being used today. This kit includes two pairs of #4 couplers.

380-102 Skeleton Log Car Kit 21.95
This kit includes one pair of #4 couplers.

380-103 Truss Log Car Kit 27.95
This kit includes one pair of #4 Magne-Matic® couplers with insulated draft gear.

RAIL LINE

These HOn3 kits are based on Rio Grande prototypes. They feature injection molded bodies, separate grab wires and other details. They also include dummy couplers, but do not come with trucks and decals.

NARROW GAUGE CARS

The dimensions for the sliding side doors are taken from the prototype.
620-130 Rio Grande 3000 Series Box Car - As Rebuilt 13.95

620-131 Rio Grande 30' Idler Flat Car 6700 Series 10.95

This prototypical design features sliding doors, adjustable end doors and molded details.
620-132 Rio Grande Stock Car 13.95

TAURUS

These kits feature scale lumber and plastic and metal detail parts. They do not include trucks and couplers.

TANK CAR

707-306 Conoco Tank Car C.O.N.X.5 HOn3 13.95 (not illustrated) **NEW**

REEFERS

40' DOUBLE SHEATHED REEFERS ea 12.95
707-303 Pacific Fruit Express/Southern Pacific Herald on other side
707-304 Chicago, Rock Island & Pacific

STOCK CAR

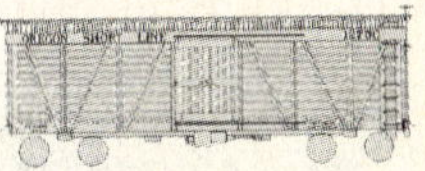

This kit includes brass detail parts and decals.
707-300 Oregon Short Line 12.95

ORE CAR

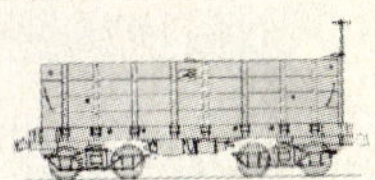

20' WOOD ORE CAR
707-305 Undecorated pkg (2) 13.95

INFORMATION STATION

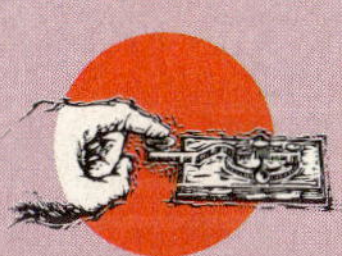

What kind of freight cars are "right" for your railroad? It depends on the industries you serve, both on- and off-line, as well as the time period you've chosen.

If you model a specific railroad and time frame, you can check The Official Equipment Registers, found in some larger libraries. These books list all of the cars in interchange service by railroad and private owner.

They won't indicate the exact types of loads, but a road with more hoppers than box cars for example, will give you some idea of the traffic on that line.

Since most of your operations will be confined to the industries on your layout, think about what types of cars they need, to receive both raw materials and ship finished goods. A commercial bakery might receive tank car loads of corn syrup and cooking oil, and Airslide® covered hoppers (modern-era) or box cars (steam-era) of flour and sugar. Baked goods might be shipped out in insulated box cars or reefers.

These items may be delivered in cars from your road, or shipped across country in the cars of another line.

Your freight car fleet can also suggest that industries exist beyond the confines of your layout. You may not have room to model a Gary steel mill, but your railroad might handle a unit train of taconite pellets headed there, and then return the empties to the mine in Minnesota. And there may be an appliance factory on your line who has coils of steel from the mill delivered by rail.

These HOn3 and HO Scale craft train kits include wood and cardstock parts with plastic and metal details. Kits includes decals and trucks, but are less couplers.

SNOW PLOW

ROTARY SNOW PLOW ea 74.95

Meet winter head-on with this rugged rotary plow. The kit is based on Rotary "OM" which was built by Cooke and delivered to the Rio Grande narrow gauge in 1889. The same design was also used by many standard gauge roads. Kits include wood, metal, plastic and cardstock parts, plus decals and complete instructions.

DRAG FLANGERS

DECALS

HAND CAR

MINE CAR

254-30 Rotary Snowplow (HOn3)
Includes decals for Rio Grande OM
254-31 Rotary Snowplow (HO)
Includes decals for Southern Pacific, Union Pacific, Canadian Pacific, Soo Line and Great Northern.

DRAG FLANGERS
254-42 Rio Grande Southern #02 Drag Flanger (HOn3) 49.95
254-51 Rio Grande Southern #01 Drag Flanger (HOn3) 28.95

DECALS
254-126 Rio Grande Southern Drag Flanger #1 (HOn3) 1.00

Set includes numbers and data for use with kits #42 and 51 as shown above, printed in gray.

HAND CAR
Taken directly from Rio Grande plans, this kit consists of detail castings, brass wire and scale lumber.
254-12 Rio Grande Hand Car (HO) 6.95
254-22 Rio Grande Hand Car (HOn3) 7.95
254-14 Hand Car Wheels pkg (4) 1.95
These wheels are for use with #12 and #22.

MINE CAR
254-43 I8" Gauge 3.25

DIAMOND SCALE CONST.

These are HO Scale craft train kits.

WOOD CHIP CAR

WOOD CHIP CAR 16.95
This unpainted wood and metal kit is based on 354200 series roll-dump chip cars built by Southern Pacific. This kit includes decals, but does not include trucks and couplers.

239-13 60' Wood Chip Car

These easy-to-build HO Scale kits feature highly detailed plastic parts, as well as separate ladders and grab irons. Underbody details and trucks are included, and coupler pockets accept horn-hook or Kadee couplers Step-by-step instructions are also included.

GONDOLAS

40' GENERAL SERVICE SUGAR BEET GONDOLA ea 21.95

For almost half a century, these gondolas have been used in sugar beet service on the Southern Pacific. Detailed kits include side panel extensions to match the prototype wood or plywood conversions. As Shown

229-201 Wood Extensions
Not Illustrated
229-202 Plywood Extensions

40' GENERAL SERVICE GONDOLA ea 18.95 May be built with drop doors open or closed. Decals are not included.
229-200 Composite Sides
229-220 Steel Sides

Most of the line is open following yesterday's storm. There are still a few drifts to battle, and those dark clouds are a stern reminder that winter is far from over. Modified from a Tri-Ang kit (out of production) the plow is a regular visitor each winter on Bob Boudreau's Fundy Northern Railroad

Keystone Locomotive Works

All items are HO Scale craft train kits.

LUMBER CARS

395-104 Barnhart Log Loader 32.95

This kit is designed for use with Keystone, Alexander and Model Engineering Works log buggies. It includes a cast body with interior/exterior wood planking, interior details with boiler and steam engine, and a brass chain for the drive mechanism. The kit also features a corrugated metal roof, boom and cable.

DETAILS WEST

These easy-to-build HO Scale kits feature one-piece plastic bodies with separate ladders and brake gear. They also include a non-operating detailed Hydro-Cushion Underframe and Delrin® trucks.

50' INSULATED SINGLE PLUG DOOR BOX CAR
ea 7.95 (unless noted)
Fruit Growers Express Series

235-701 Southern (yellow)
235-702 Burlington Northern (cascade green)
235-703 Louisville & Nashville (yellow) 5.25
235-704 Conrail (yellow)
235-706 Norfolk & Western (yellow)
235-708 Southern Pacific (box car red) (food load)
235-709 Norfolk & Western (modern) (black)
235-710 Green Bay & Western (yellow)
235-711 Solid Gold (yellow)
235-712 Erie Lackawanna (blue, white)
235-700 Undecorated

50' INSULATED SMOOTH SINGLE PLUG DOOR BOX
ea 7.95 (unless noted)
235-801 Santa Fe
235-802 Soo Line
235-803 Boston & Maine (light blue)
235-804 Rock Island 5.75
235-806 Providence & Worcester 5.75
235-800 Undecorated 5.75

395-106 Grasse River Logging Caboose #2 15.95
This kit is approximately 21 scale feet in length. It features a cast metal frame, cupola, ends, windows, steps and details. The sides, floor, and roof pieces are all wooden. Trucks are also included.

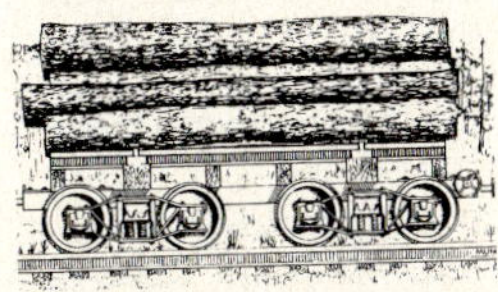

395-100 Log Buggie pkg (2) 9.95
This kit, modeled after a Grasse River prototype, includes a pressure cast body, brass rails for loader to run on, brass chain, cast brake cylinders and brake wheel. Trucks, couplers, and logs are not included. Kit accepts horn hook or Kadee couplers.

395-103 HOn3 Log Car pkg (2) 9.95
This car, a typical 29' log car, is short enough for small layouts, and includes pressure cast body, separate cheese block castings and brake parts. Trucks and couplers are not included. Kit accepts 380-714 couplers.

395-107 Climax Log Car pkg (2) 9.95
This kit assembles to any length from 20' to 45'. It features an all in one cast metal end, with bunk and cheese blocks. The wood center beam can be cut to desired length. Also included are cast metal bunk straps, NBW detail and additional details. This kit does not include logs, trucks and couplers.

CABOOSE INTERIOR

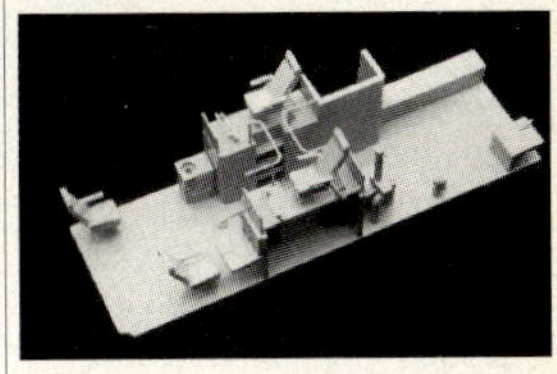

395-3501 Wide Vision 12.98
This interior fits Athearn, Bachmann, and AHM.

LOGGING TRUCK
395-30 Grasse River Logging pkg (2) 2.95
This is an all metal kit.

50' INSULATED SINGLE PLUG DOOR BOX CAR

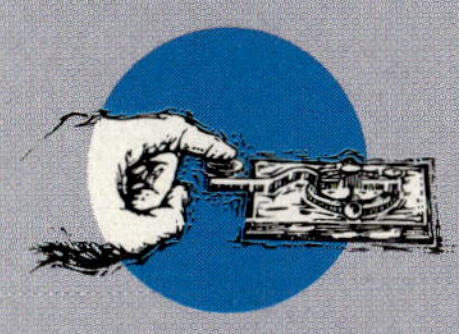

INFORMATION STATION

Freight car doors have undergone numerous changes over the years.

Like the cars themselves, the first doors were made of wood. Subjected to rough handling and exposed to the elements, they required frequent repair and replacement. All-steel cars likewise had steel doors. Through the years, there were numerous types available.

In the 1950's the tight-fitting plug door that kept out dirt and moisture was introduced. First used on reefers and uninsulated box cars, they were later applied to standard box cars as well. In the 60's, the use of forklifts to move palletized shipments led to 10' wide doors, with special pockets so a forklift could open and close the door.

MASTER CREATIONS

These HOn3 narrow gauge craft train kits contain molded plastic parts and lead weights. Archbar trucks and Kadee HOn3 automatic couplers are also included, unless otherwise noted.

BOX CARS

24' BOX CAR, CC
464-403 Undecorated 14.95
This kit does not include trucks and couplers.

464-404 Undecorated 21.95

27' WOOD BOX CAR, DSP&P
464-413 Undecorated 14.95
This kit does not include trucks and couplers.

464-414 Undecorated 21.95

REEFERS

27' WOOD REEFER, DSP&P
464-405 Undecorated 14.95
This kit does not include trucks and couplers.

464-406 Undecorated 21.95

ORE CARS

18 TON ORE CAR, SP&M
464-401 Undecorated 13.95
This kit does not include trucks and couplers.

464-402 Undecorated 19.95

FLAT CARS

26' FLAT/GONDOLA, DSP&P
464-407 Undecorated 14.95
This kit does not include trucks and couplers.

464-408 Undecorated 21.95

EXCURSION CAR

EXCURSION CAR, CC
464-409 Undecorated 14.95
This kit does not include trucks and couplers.

464-410 Undecorated 21.95

GRANDT LINE.

These easy-to-build craft train kits are in HOn3 and HOn30 Scale.

BOX CARS

30' WOOD BOX CAR
300-5226 Colorado & Southern, HOn3 18.00

REEFERS

30' REEFER
300-5231 Colorado & Southern/Rio Grande Southern, HOn3 18.00

DUMP CAR

The prototype of these cars ran on the "Baby Railroad"; a two foot Borax mine road in Death Valley, California.

Easy-to-build Koppel 3-1/2 yard, 4 wheel gable bottom dump car. All plastic construction with silver-colored Delrin wheels and brass axles.

300-5147 HOn3 Dump Car pkg (2) 6.50
300-5148 HOn3 Dump Car pkg (2) 6.50

HOn3 Rio Grande Car

These Craft Train Kits consist of detailed black styrene parts, underbody detail, brake gear and necessary wire parts. Decals, plans, dummy couplers and trucks are included.

300-5186 30' Flat Car 14.95
300-5187 30' Wheel & Tie Car 18.95
300-5188 30' Drop Bottom Gondola 26.95

This drop bottom gondola features over 200 parts.

GONDOLAS

30' STEEL UNDERFRAME GONDOLA
300-5214 Colorado & Southern, HOn3 18.00

CABOOSES

30' CABOOSE
300-5235 Colorado & Southern, HOn3 kit 18.00

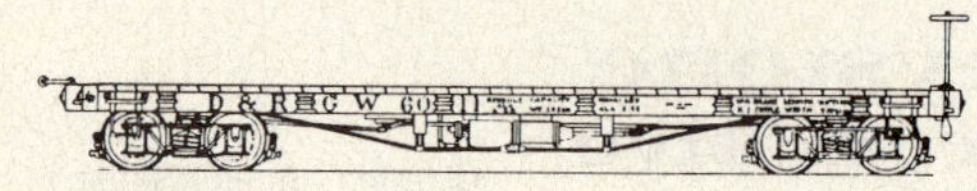

30' FLAT CAR

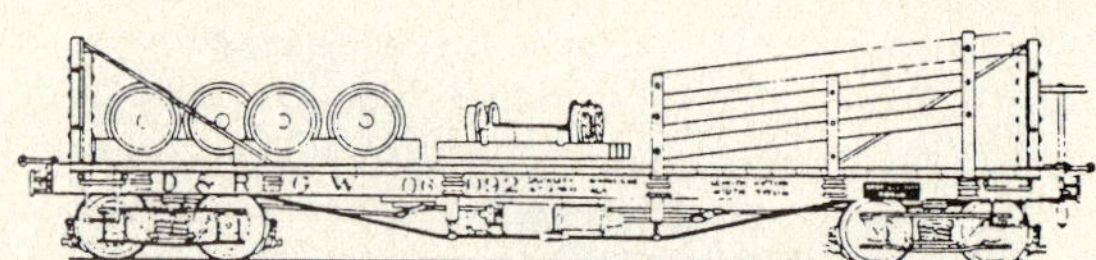

30' WHEEL & TIE CAR

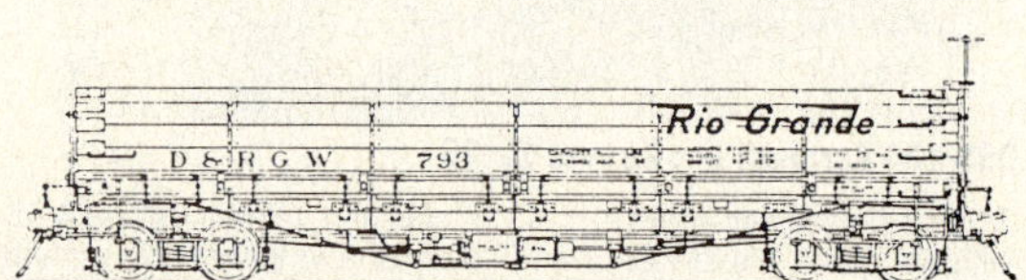

30' DROP BOTTOM GONDOLA

DUMP CAR

Emptied of it's load of flour, a Santa Fe Airslide® heads out to repeat the cycle. These cars often wind up in "captive" service, carrying the same type of load between a single producer and consumer. Most likely, the car brought in materials for the Ragu Spaghetti plant. Built by Jim Senese of Walnut Creek, California, the car is seen passing Stockton tower, scratchbuilt by Gene Caxton.
Model and Photo by Jim Senesea

INTERNATIONAL HOBBY CORPORATION

These ready-to-run cars are prepainted and lettered in a variety of roadnames and include Talgo trucks with horn-hook couplers.

TRACK CLEANING CAR

TRACK CLEANING CAR
ea 14.98
It's a caboose AND a track cleaning car all in one, the perfect way to clean your track whenever you run a train.

348-4355 Union Pacific
348-4356 Santa Fe (caboose red)
348-4357 Pennsylvania (tuscan)
348-4358 Chicago & North Western (yellow)
348-4359 Baltimore & Ohio (gold)
348-4368 New York Central (aqua)
348-4369 Southern Railway System
348-4398 Replacement Pads pkg (6) 2.98

SOUND CARS

STEAM SOUND CAR
ea 19.98
This car requires a 9V battery, which is sold separately.

348-4300 Union Pacific (gold, brown)
348-4301 Santa Fe (brown)
348-4302 Pennsylvania (black, brown)
348-4304 New York Central
348-4305 Southern Pacific (brown)

ASSORTMENTS

FREIGHT CAR ASSORTMENTS
ea pkg (12) 59.76 *NEW*
348-1500 Single Dome Tank Car
348-1550 50' Reefers, Assorted Roadnames
348-1600 50' Box Car
348-1650 50' Box Cars, Assorted Roadnames
348-1700 40' Double Door Box Car
348-1750 40' Reefer
348-1800 50' Stock Car
348-1850 50' Gondola
348-1900 50' Hopper
348-2600 36' Excended Vision Caboose
348-26501 40' Hopper

TRACK CLEANING CAR

STEAM SOUND CAR

N-WAY

These HO scale kits are all metal and are less trucks, couplers and trailers.

535-751 Fuel Foiler Lead Unit, Last Unit & 4 Intermediate Units 14.95
535-752 4 Intermediate Units 10.95
When this kit is added to kit #535-751, it will make a full 10-Pack.
535-753 Lead Units & Last Unit Only 5.95
When this kit is added to kit #535-751, it makes two 4-packs.

LIFE-LIKE

CABOOSES

PROTO-2000 CABOOSE, LIMITED RUN ea 25.00
These center cupola cabooses were a familar sight , especially in the northeastern US. The models require only minor assembly and feature opening doors, interior and working light. Separate grab irons, flush mounted "glass" and underbody details are installed on the models, which are prepainted in a variety of schemes.

433-8230 Western Maryland #1891 (black, white, red)
433-8231 Lehigh & New England #580 (red)
433-8272 South Branch Valley #1892 (red, silver)

433-8280 Chicago & North Western #10809 (yellow, green)
433-8281 Rock Island #17604 (red, black)
433-8282 Chessie System/Western Maryland #1828 (yellow, silver)
433-8283 Belfast & Moosehead Lake #28 (red)
433-8284 Penn Central #18423 (jade green, black)
433-8286 Ashley, Drew & Northern #17 (black, red)
433-8244 Undecorated

Limited Quantities Available

433-8271 Chesapeake & Ohio #90353 (yellow, silver)

These HO Scale, ready-to-run, appropriately colored plastic cars feature working doors, trucks, and horn-hook couplers.

50' BI-LEVEL AUTO RACK
433-8089 TTX flat (yellow)/Santa Fe rack (red), with 6 cars 12.50

PROTO 2000 CABOOSE

FREIGHT CAR ASSORTMENT
433-8451 Deluxe 36 pieces 216.00
This assortment includes 36 cars: 10 each 50' Flat Car with Containers (TTX with American President Lines and Sealand Containers) and 60' Thrall All-Door Box Car (Delson Lumber and Green Bay & Western) and eight each of 100 ton Hoppers (Reading, Rock Island)

and 50' Hi-Roof Box Car (Richmond Fredricksburg & Potomac and Erie Lackawanna).
433-8467 48 pieces 264.00
This assortment includes three each of the roadnames listed (48 cars total):

Wood Brace Box Cars, (Great Northern, Chicago & Illinois MIdland) Steel Box Car, (Linde Gas,

Chessie) Covered Hopper, (Burlington, Erie) Tank Car, (Conoco, DuPont) Reefer, (Armour Ham & Bacon, Oscar Meyer) Gondola, (Southern Pacific, Baltimore & Ohio) Stock Car (Katy, New Yrok Central) Coal Hopper (Lousiville & Nashville, Reading)

RIBBONRAIL
by Earl Eshleman
(formerly Wallace Metal Products)

These ready-to-run track cleaning cars are in HO scale.

PRECISION SCALE Co.

TRACK CLEANING CAR

TRACK CLEANING CAR

Cleans the running rail for improved electrical contact. Cars are equipped with rubber blocks impregnated with silicon-abrasive. This ready-to-run brass car includes trucks, but does not include couplers.

170-6 for standard 2-rail track 29.95

170-7 for Marklin track 29.95 Precision Scale Co. Freight Listing

These HO Scale craft train kits consist of unpainted brass, plastic and wood parts. Some include decals. We have worked closely with the manufacturer to provide accurate availability information at the time this catalog was published. Items listed in blue ink may not be available at all times. Please see your dealer for current delivery information.

CABOOSES

585-10049 Bay Window, All Brass 29.95
585-10069 23', Rio Grande 25.50

FLAT CARS

The following kits are HO and HOn3 Scale, and are made of brass.

585-31277 Flat Car - HO 5.50
585-31278 Flat Car - HOn3 5.50
585-37001 Bulkhead, 6500 Series 27.75

TANK CARS

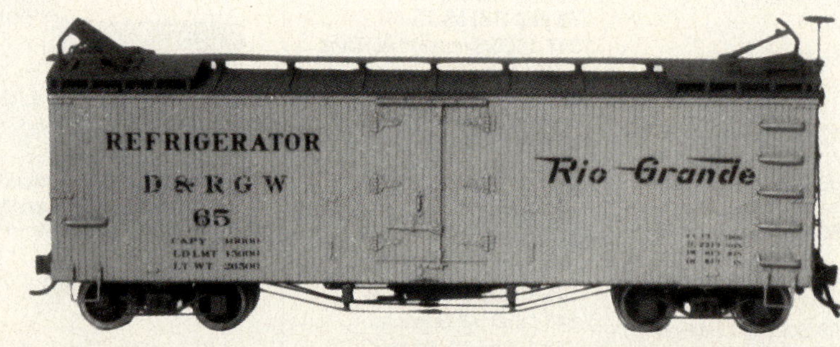

TANK CAR

The following Tank car kits are HOn3 Scale, unpainted plastic kits. They include

UTLX and Gramps decals.
585-604 UTLX, Plastic Trucks 21.95

585-606 UTLX, Brass Trucks 23.75

REEFERS

The following kits are HOn3 Scale, and include decals.

585-607 Rio Grande, Plastic Trucks 21.95
585-608 Rio Grande, Brass Trucks 23.75
585-10081 NCNG, Scribed 21.50
585-10080 NCNG, Wood Grain 21.50

MISCELLANEOUS

585-9739 HO/HOn3 Freight & Passenger Car Illustrations 6.95

ORE CAR

The following kit is HOn3 Scale, and consists of brass and wood parts.

585-73 Side Dump 21.95

CABOOSES

585-68 Caboose, 4 wheel 22.50 *NEW*
585-69 Caboose, 8 wheel 25.50 *NEW*

A steady stream of black diamonds feed the fires of the power plant at Electric, Pennsylvania. And a steady stream of Coal Belt hoppers bring in the fuel. This is one of many customers along Bill Henderson's Coal Belt Railroad. Set in 1910, Bill's equipment includes these extensively modified Life-Like hoppers. The loco is a Key Imports brass model, with a crew of Life-Like figures.

Models and Photo by Bill Henderson

The Wheel Works

These HOn3 craft train kits feature metal and plastic parts.

LUMBER CARS

"TIMBER GANG"

These HO Scale craft train kits consist of metal castings and include electrical wire for hydraulic lines where appropriate.

778-92037 Fairmont Speeder 5.95
This non-operating kit is composed of metal castings.

778-92097 Fairmont Spike Puller 5.95
The prototype of this unit is used to pull spikes from bad ties.

778-92098 Fairmont Tie Shear 9.50
The prototype of this machine cuts bad ties in half, for faster removal.

778-92099 Kershaw Tie Crane 11.50
This small crane is used to lift new ties and put them in place.

778-92100 Track Equipment Set 27.95
This set includes one each of #37, 97, 98 & 99.

LOG CAR

778-90058 Denver & Rio Grande Western / New Mexico 10.95
This kit features a cast metal body and is less trucks and couplers.

GONDOLAS

778-90112 High Side - Denver & Rio Grande Western HOn3 11.95

778-90114 Pipe Gondola - Denver & Rio Grande Western HOn3 11.95

FLAT CARS

778-90050 Westside Lumber Company HOn3 10.95
The car body is a one-piece metal casting, so no extra weight is needed. All add-on details are also cast metal.

778-90053 Westside Lumber Company - Aged Deck HOn3 10.95
This kit is identical to #90050, but has a weathered deck with rotten boards.

778-90116 Idler Flat Car - Denver & Rio Grande Western HOn3 10.95

CABOOSE

778-90055 Westside Lumber Company HOn3 13.95
This all-plastic kit is less trucks and couplers.

TRANSPORT VEHICLES

ROADRAILER® TRANSPORT VEHICLE

Now in use on some major railroads, the Roadrailer can be operated as a truck trailer or rail car using the retractable running gear. A special coupler is used so that Roadrailers are run as unit trains. Kits include unpainted plastic and metal parts.

778-90101 Van Trailer 13.95
Designed to run on rails, but can be modified for highway use with some scratchbuilding.

778-90102 AdaptaRailer® 14.95
This unit is used as an idler between the loco and other Roadrailer units. It has a standard coupler at the front, and the special Roadrailer coupler at the rear.

GONDOLA

FAIRMOUNT SPEEDER

FAIRMOUNT TIE SHEER

Jaeger

HO Scale easy to build freight car load kits include coated paper, 22 small blocks, banding, spacers and instructions.

PIPE LOADS

BUILDING PRODUCTS LOAD

50' FLAT CAR LUMBER LOAD

LOADS

50' FLAT CAR LUMBER LOAD KIT ea 5.95

347-100 Boise Cascade
347-200 Bulkley Valley
347-300 Edward Hines
347-400 Georgia-Pacific
347-500 Pack River
347-600 Weyerhauser
347-700 Babine
347-800 Idapine Mills
347-900 Louisiana-Pacific
347-1000 Modoc
347-1100 St Regis
347-1200 West Fraser
347-1300 Bennett Lumber
347-1400 Collins Pine
347-1500 High Cascade
347-1600 International Paper
347-1700 Keystone
347-1800 Potlatch
347-1900 Weldwood

60' FLAT CAR LUMBER LOAD ea 12.95

347-4000 ATCO Lumber Ltd
347-4100 Canfor
347-4200 Carrier Western Spruce
347-4300 Champion
347-4400 Crown Zellerbach
347-4500 Evans Products
347-4600 Grand Prairie
347-4700 Hines
347-4800 Northwood
347-4900 Pope & Talbot
347-5000 Publishers Forest Products
347-5100 Roseburg
347-5200 Simpson
347-5300 Washington Idaho
347-5400 Weyerhauser Building Products
347-5500 Clearwater Forest Industries
347-5600 Great West Timber
347-5700 Hanel Lumber Company
347-5800 Sierra Pacific
347-5900 Slocan
347-6000 Weyerhauser Lumber

CENTERBEAM LUMBER LOAD ea 11.95

Each kit contains blocks, printing, banding, and wood strips to completely fill one car.

347-7000 Boise Cascade
347-7100 MacMillan Boedel
347-7200 Quadra Wood Products
347-7300 Rustad Brothers
347-7400 Snow Mountain
347-7500 Weyerhauser
347-7600 Jacobson Brothers
347-7700 Millar West
347-7800 Plum Creek
347-7900 Ranger
347-8000 Georgia-Pacific *NEW*
347-8100 Idaho Timber *NEW*
347-8200 Potlatch *NEW*

BUILDING PRODUCT LOAD ea 8.95

Ready to run loads fit Roundhouse 60' Bulkhead flat cars.

347-3100 Evans Products
347-3200 Gold Bond Products
347-3300 Johns-Manville
347-3400 Masonite
347-3500 Plum Creek
347-3600 US Gypsum
347-3000 Undecorated Product Load (black) 8.95

PIPE LOADS

These pipe loads include material to build two complete loads, with wood bracing and straps. Loads are designed for Athearn 40 or 50' flats, or MDC gondolas, and can be adapted to other cars.

347-2400 Corrugated 14.95
For 40-50' flat cars or gondolas
347-2900 Aluminum 11.95
For 40-50' gondolas

UTILITY POLE LOAD

Two complete loads for gondolas or bulkhead flat cars are included.

347-2300 Natural 6.95
347-2350 Dark Brown 8.95

MISCELLANEOUS LOAD

347-2500 Heavy Timbers Load 14.95
Four assembled, stained and banded bundles of timbers are included.

347-2600 Aluminum Ingot Load 5.95
Two complete loads for gondolas or bulkhead flat cars are included.

347-2700 Rail 5.95
This fits all gondolas at least 40' long.

347-2800 Cable Reel 5.95
This load contains 12 assembled reels and will fit 50' gondolas.

MISCELLANEOUS

FREIGHT PLATFORM/LOADING DOCK ACCESSORY KIT

347-2200 Accessory Kit pkg (47 items) 9.95
Kit include pallets, barrels, cable reels, drums, crates, bottle cases and sacks.

FREIGHT CAR PLACARDS

347-2100 Placards pkg (400) 1.00
The placard notices apply to placard boards on freight car sides. Lettering shown is 3 times actual size.

SIGNODE GRAIN DOORS

347-2000 Grain Doors (red lettering) pkg (24) 1.00
Signode grain doors are the makeshift 'doors' used on grain carrying box cars. Six sheets are enough for twenty-four 40' box car doors.

JAY BEE

INTERIOR LIGHTING KIT

This HO Scale unit is fully assembled and ready to install with no soldering required.

369-157 for Athearn caboose 18.50

ELECTRICAL PICKUP

This HO Scale easy-to-build converts Athearn freight truck and includes metal wheelsets.

369-1533 for Athearn 6.50

LOADS

BH MODELS

All of the following kits are HO Scale and feature injection molded parts. Basic assembly instructions are included.

INGOT BUGGIES *NEW*
159-601 pkg (3) 9.95
159-602 pkg (9) 28.00
These tiny two-axle cars carry ingot molds inside the steel mill. Kits include wheel sets with nonmagnetic brass axles and can be fitted with horn-hook or Kadee couplers.

INGOT BUGGIES AND MOLDS *NEW*
159-603 pkg (6) 24.95
Includes parts for six complete ingot buggies and molds.

INGOT MOLDS FREIGHT CAR LOAD
159-1001 Ingot Molds 2.99
These large molds are used to transport molten steel within the mill complex. They can also be loaded aboard gondolas to carry molten steel from the furnace to another facility. Kit includes two molds, two stools, four lugs and two keys, all made of injection molded styrene. These are for use with #601 and #602 Ingot Buggies.

JV MODELS

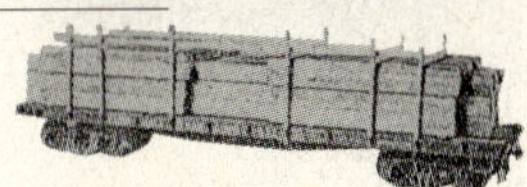

LUMBER LOAD
345-2010 Triple Kit pkg (3) 19.95
This HO Scale easy-to-build kit includes wooden loads for three 40-60' flat or gondola cars, braces and stake posts, incorporating removable design for more operating possibilities.

WHITE GROUND

These HOn3 Scale plaster loads are for Hallmark, Quality Craft and Car Shops hoppers.

HOPPER LOADS
pkg (6) ea 9.95
771-5012 Ganister Rock
771-5013 Mine Run Coal
771-5014 Processed Coal

CHOOCH

All loads featured are prepainted and weathered polyurethane castings. They are for use with Athearn and MDC cars.

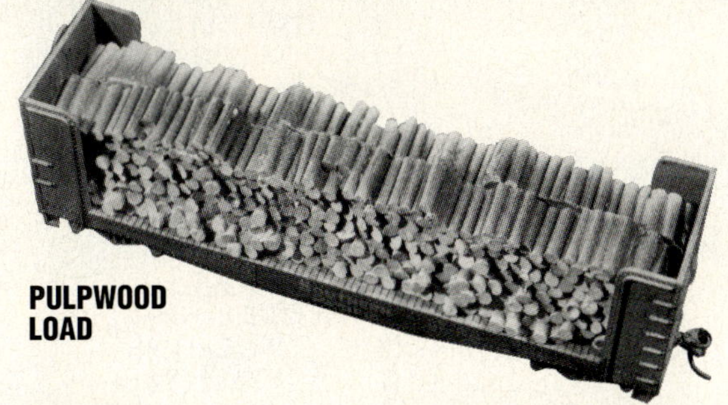

PULPWOOD LOAD

JUNK LOAD
pkg (2) ea 5.99
214-7052 50' Gondola Junk for Athearn #1647 cars
214-7072 50' Gondola Auto Junk for Athearn #1647 cars
214-7077 40' Gondola Machinery for MDC #1340 cars
214-7079 50' Gondola Junk for MDC #1680 cars

SCRAP LOAD
pkg (2) ea 5.99
214-7053 50' Gondola Scrap

for Athearn #1647 cars
214-7069 50' Gondola Scrap for MDC #1680 cars

COAL LOAD pkg (2) ea 5.99
214-7056 40' Quad Hopper Coal for Athearn #1749 cars
214-7057 34' Hopper Coal for Athearn #5400 cars
214-7059 50' Coal for MDC #1640 Thrall Cars
214-7063 40' Hopper Coal for MDC #1485 cars
214-7065 50' Coal for MDC Bathtub Gondolas

STEWART PRODUCTS

These HO Scale craft train kits are unpainted metal kits.

683-201 Clamshell Bucket Kit 9.95
This operating bucket is for use with any HO crane and can be constructed as an oiperating model. Kit includes complete instructions.

FLAT CAR LOADS
683-203 Air-Cooled Transformer 6.95
683-204 Turbine Gear & Blocking 6.95
683-205 Diesel Generator 6.95
683-209 Ship Propellers pkg (4) 6.95
This package includes two 4 blade and two 3 blade propellers.
683-210 Steel Coils pkg (6) 6.95
683-216 Refinery Pressure Tank 9.95
683-217 Tank Extension Section pkg (4) 5.95

ACCESSORIES

NOCH

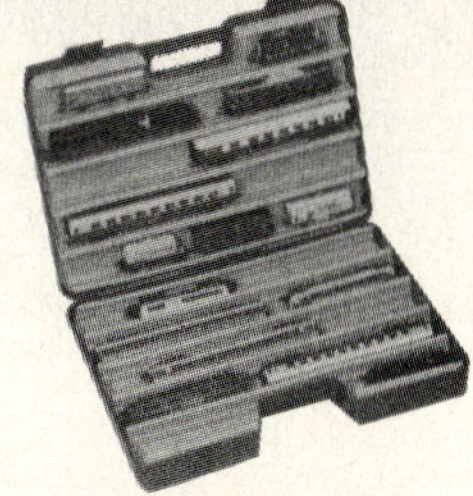

Imported from Germany by WALTHERS
This item is designed for use with HO Scale models.

STORAGE SUITCASE
528-8800 20x14" 259.99

MOUNTAINS

The inside dimensions are: 16x5-1/2x3-1/2".

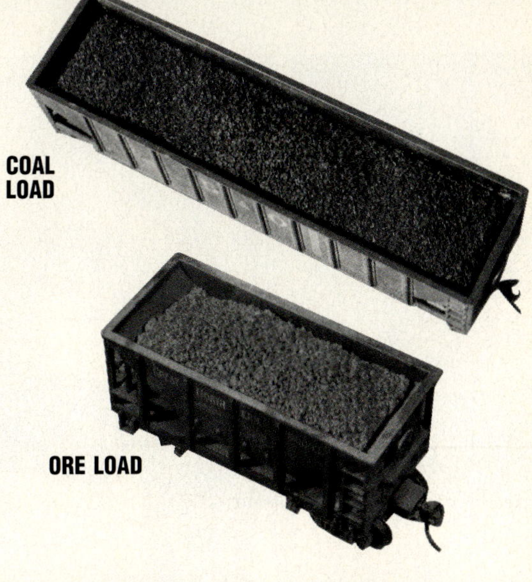

COAL LOAD

ORE LOAD

214-7071 for MDC Ortner Cars

PULPWOOD LOAD
214-7058 for Athearn Cars pkg(2) 5.99

ORE LOAD

214-7088 Ore Load for MDC #1401 cars pkg (4) 7.99

LUMBER & MACHINERY LOAD
214-7086 Banded Lumber pkg (4) 7.99
214-7087 Covered Machinery pkg (6) 7.99

CRATE LOAD
214-7085 Flat Car Crates pkg (2) 9.99

KIBRI

Imported from Germany by WALTHERS

DISPLAY CASES
These finished hardwood display cases include plastic backing and either clear glass doors or a plastic protective cover. (Dimensions shown are approximate.)

405-12000 5 Shelves, Plastic Cover 14 x 14.5 x 2" 42.99
405-12002 5 Shelves, Plastic Cover 28 x 14.5 x 2" 87.99
405-12012 3 Shelves, Glass Doors 82 x 11 x 3" 331.49
405-12020 For Marklin 182.99
405-12048 Display Case 40 x 25 x 3" 168.99 *NEW*

DISPLAY CASE
473-850 Collector's Display Case 35.98
This case features a rock background fashioned of high density plastic foam in a natural oak satin finish. The roadbed and grassy embankment are hand finished in natural acrylic colors. A 16" of HO trackis included for mounting your model. The model shown is not included.

TOMAR

These HO Scale metal shoes are for electrical pickup.

081-804 Shoes for Passenger Cars and Cabooses pkg (4) 2.95
081-805 Shoes for Locos pkg (4) 2.95

With their own switcher down for lengthy repairs, the Grey Steel Works has leased an S-2 from CP Rail. Fresh from the shops, the Atlas unit was built by Allan Speight of Welsford, New Brunswick, Canada. Grey Steel Works was scratchbuilt by Ted Grey.

Photo by Allan Speight

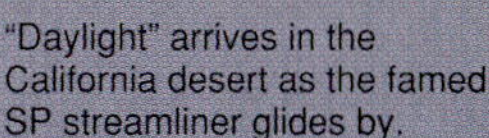

"Daylight" arrives in the California desert as the famed SP streamliner glides by.

A pair of steamers hold the sidings, waiting their call for the freights that will follow the passenger train to Los Angeles. It's February, 1946 in this scene on Angelo Battistella's layout, where he showcases some of his imported brass motive power and equipment. Brawa structural shapes and bulbs were used to build the signal bridge, while the trackwork is Shinohara Code 70. Angelo has done a beautiful job capturing the flavor of western railroading. although he lives in Trieste, Italy!

Models and Photo by Angelo Battistella

ALL ABOARD AMTRAK

6011

6001

Commuters board the "red eye" back to suburbia. This consist is made up of cars from the Amfleet 1 series, the first car built to Amtrak specifications. Budd Manufacturing Company began producing these modern streamliners in the mid 70's.

Realistic HO reproductions of these Amfleet cars are now available from Walthers. Put hustle and bustle into your cityscape with commuter scenes like this one.

Get into training the Amtrak way. Modeling modern rail travel adds a new dimension of excitement to your pike.

These easy-to-build Amfleet Coaches and Food Service cars feature injection molded styrene bodies: prepainted in authentic red, white and blue on silver. Sharp decal lettering is included for the Amtrak logo, car designation and numbers. Also included are trucks, smoke tinted window inserts, separate grab irons, horn-hook couplers (will accept Kadee) and full under body details.

85' AMFLEET I AMTRAK

932-6002	Coach, Phase I	**NEW**	15.98
932-6012	Food Service, Phase I	**NEW**	15.98
932-6001	Coach, Phase II		15.98
932-6011	Food Service, Phase II		15.98
932-6003	Coach, Phase III	**NEW**	15.98
932-6013	Food Service, Phase III	**NEW**	15.98

6001

6011

"Fly by rail" on board Amfleet, reaching lightning speeds up to 120 mph, 10,000 hp on demand is supplied by this big, powerful General Electric E-60 CP. Faithfully reproduced in HO Scale, its smooth and rivetless Monocoque body is framed by Walther's Instant Horizons™ Country to Eastern Foothills background scene.

Lush pine forests stretch for miles in a sea of green, as passengers relish the scenic view from the Amcafe. The Amfleet Food Service Car can be lettered for any of the following: Amdinette, Amclub, Amlounge or Amcafe. Our eye-opening scenery was created with Walthers Ponderosa Pine Trees™ and an Instant Horizons™ Tall Timber background scene.

What better place to rest and recuperate after a long day of railfanning! This exclusive hotel regularly hosts visiting railfan groups from the United States. Klaus Becker of Gefrees, Germany, constructed the ''Hotel California'' and added lots of details to finish the modular scene.

Model by Klaus Becker

The Diamond Valley M-O-W sprayer and crew are all set for fighting weeds. Of course, when they start depends on the foreman finishing his discussion with the Track Supervisor! Like many shortlines, the DV relies on home-made equipment to keep things running. The section car is scratchbuilt from styrene and detailed with Jordan, MV Products, Central Valley and other parts. A Precision Scale Company MDS truck provides power. The shed was also scratchbuilt by owner Fred Gill of Baulkham Hills, New South Wales, Australia.

Models and Photo by Fred Gill

Business isn't what it used to be, but a wayfreight still makes its rounds twice a week on this branch line. A Spectrum GE 70 tonner is the usual motive power, while a variety of freight cars, including this Ulrich (out of production) gondola can be seen. Gerry Gilliland also scratchbuilt the freight station and the outhouse on this 2 x 4′ module.

Models and Photo by Gerry Gilliland

ROCO — Roco
Imported from Austria by WALTHERS

HO SCALE   READY-TO-RUN
Roco passenger cars feature exact paint and lettering schemes, detailed interiors, diaphragms, European style couplers and blackened brass wheels. Coaches are made to exact scale length except as noted. Cars marked with an asterisk (*) are not scale length.

GERMAN STATE RAILWAY

4-WHEELED COACH ERA III

625-44227 Coach DR   14.49

38' BRANCH LINE COACH ERA I/II

625-44821 3rd Class CLBay IIa DRG   29.99
625-44822 2nd Class Coach   **NEW**   29.99
           Era IIIB DB

625-44825 3rd Class CLBay 06 DRG   29.99
625-44826 2nd Class Coach   **NEW**   29.99
           Era IIIB DB

625-44551 3rd Class type C4i-36   35.99
           Supplementary coach to 43032

625-44829 Luggage Van Pwl Bay   32.49
           02 DRG
625-44830 Baggage Era IIIB DB **NEW**   32.49

625-44833 2nd Class/Mail Coach   29.99
           BPostl Bay 01 DRG
625-44834 1st Class Coach   **NEW**   29.99
           Era IIIB DB

EXPRESS COACH   **NEW**

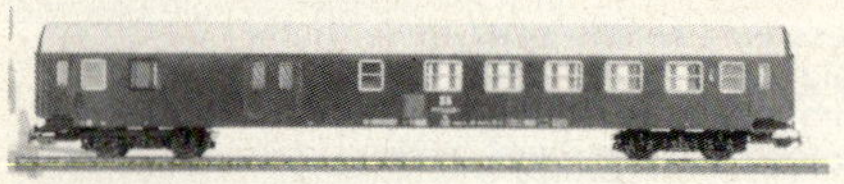

625-14330 2nd Class Baggage   43.49
           DR BDmse

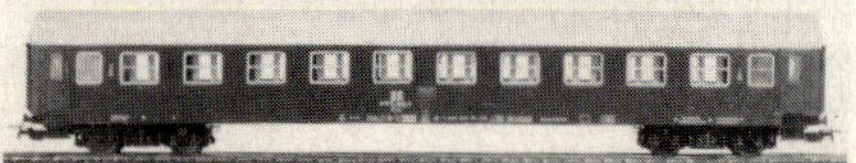

625-14333 2nd Class Coach DR Bme   43.49
625-14342 2nd Class Coach DR BCme   43.49

625-14336 1st Class Coach DR Ame   43.49
625-14339 1st/2nd Cl Coach DR ABme   43.49

RECONDITIONED COACHES   **NEW**

625-14365 Diner WRge   (red) 33.49

625-14368 2nd Class Coach Bghwe   34.99
625-14370 2nd Cl Baggage DR DBghwe   34.99

LUXURY COACHES   **NEW**

625-14005 Luxury Coach Set   153.99
           4-Unit Set, part of the former GDR Government era IV.

OLD TIME COACH w/BRAKEMAN'S CABIN

625-44508 43' 1st Class DR   32.99

625-44510 39' Mail DR   32.99

SPECIAL SETS ERA III/IV

625-44025 Thunderboxes Coach   83.99
           Set DR   Includes 4 coaches
625-44026 Additional Coach for 44025   19.99

625-44027 Fast Train Coach Set DR   151.49
           Includes 4 coaches
625-44028 Additional Coach for 44027   38.49

625-44030 Additional Coach for 44029   28.49

625-44863 Additional Coach   **NEW**   42.49
           for #43048

SPECIAL SETS ERA III/IV/V

625-14006 Express City   **NEW**   172.99
           Coach-Munich
   Includes two 2nd class coaches, one 1st class coach
   and one reconditioned restaurant car.
625-14335 2nd Class DR LR   **NEW**   45.99
           Additional coach to #14006

625-44020 S-Bahn "Toshiba"   209.99
           Coach Set DB
           Includes 3 coaches

625-44033 InterRegion Set Coach Set DB   98.49
           Includes 3 coaches
625-44034 Additional Coach for 44033   33.49

41' OLD TIME COACH

625-44511 3rd Class DR   32.99

625-44526 2nd Class DR   32.99

ROCO — *Roco*
Imported from Austria by WALTHERS

HO SCALE   READY-TO-RUN
Roco passenger cars feature exact paint and lettering schemes, detailed interiors, diaphragms, European style couplers and blackened brass wheels. Coaches are made to exact scale length except as noted. Cars marked with an asterisk (*) are not scale length.

41' OLD TIME COACH (continued)

625-44505 41' 3rd class DR   32.99

GERMAN FEDERAL RAILWAYS

625-44047 Coach Set DB 6-wheel rebuilt (Includes four coaches)   **NEW** 81.49

(not illustrated)
625-44053 Rebuilt Coach Set DB Limited Run   111.49

PRUSSIAN COMPARTMENT COACH
Very large numbers of the 6-wheel Prussian compartment coaches were in use. Their period of utilization was from the beginning of this century until the 60's.

625-44255 40' DB, Post   23.49
e-p/10 Mail Coach

625-44223 2nd Class DB   14.49

46' "THUNDERBOX"
Following the creation of the German State Railways in 1920, plans were made for a series of standard passenger car designs. The first "standard" cars were built of wood, but steel cars with wooden roofs soon followed. These cars were modified several times to reduce high maintenance costs. This eventually prompted the change to riveted, all-steel construction and interchangeable parts.

Nicknamed for their sometimes rough and noisy ride, the all-steel cars came to be known as "Thunderboxes". They were used throughout Germany and remained in revenue service until the 1950's.

625-44201 2nd Class, Bie-28 DB   23.99

625-44211 1st/2nd Class, DB ABiw-28   23.99

625-44212 1st Class, Aie-29 DB   23.99

625-44222 Baggage, Pwi-28 DB   24.99

BAVARIAN BRANCHLINE ERA II

625-44800 2nd Class Coach   28.49
625-44801 3rd Class   28.49
625-44804 Baggage & Postal   28.49
625-44805 Mail Car   28.49
625-44808 Baggage Van   28.49
625-44809 Luggage Car   31.49

BAVARIAN BRANCHLINE ERA III

625-44828 Baggage   32.49

625-44832 Mail   29.99

■ LIMITED QUANTITIES AVAILABLE ■

625-44824 Coach, 3rd Class, CL06 546 27.99

BAVARIAN BRANCHLINE ERA I
625-44014 Coach Set   119.99
2 passenger coaches 3rd class, 1 luggage van and 1 postal van

625-44858 2nd Class Coach   42.49
Class B3i Bay 99a Era 111b

HO SCALE   READY-TO-RUN

Roco passenger cars feature exact paint and lettering schemes, detailed interiors, diaphragms, European style couplers and blackened brass wheels. Coaches are made to exact scale length except as noted. Cars marked with an asterisk (*) are not scale length.

Roco — Imported from Austria by WALTHERS

BAVARIAN BRANCHLINE ERA I (cont)

625-44865 1st/2nd Class Coach   42.49
Class ex BC3i Bay 07, Era 111b

625-14327 1st/2nd Class Coach **NEW** 33.49
DB BC4i pr23

TEN-POOL COACHES ERA IV

625-44841 Sleeping Car, DB   47.99

EXPRESS LUGGAGE VAN ERA IV

625-44750 DB Type DM902   48.99
625-14322 Baggage Car DB   **NEW** 34.99
c-Pwi 31a

BAGGAGE

625-16061 DB CI-PW 07   **NEW**   29.99

REBUILT COACH

During the 50's, the German Federal Railways instituted a large scale rebuilding program to produce a large number of new passenger coaches using the chassis of older, no longer suitable passenger coaches (including some of the old provincial railway coaches).

625-44252 44' 2nd Class, B3yge-54   23.49

625-44254 44' 2nd Class, BD3yge-54   23.49
w/baggage compartment
625-44253 44' 1st/2nd Class,   22.99
AB3yge-54

FAST TRAIN COACH

625-14263 86' Coach LR   **NEW** 40.49
"Deutsche Weinstrabe"

625-44546 70' 2nd Class   **NEW** 38.99
Coach Bye
625-44547 67' 1st/2nd Class **NEW** 38.99
Coach DB
625-44548 70' 1st Class DB   **NEW** 38.99
625-44549 70' Baggage DB   **NEW** 38.99

625-14008 Coach Set DB 4-car **NEW** 151.49
Includes 4 fast train coaches.

625-44550 1st & 2nd Class Coach   35.99

625-44556 70' Baggage Car   38.99

625-44680 2nd Class Combine, DB   39.99

625-44681 86' 1st/2nd Class Coach, DB 39.99
625-44743 86' Coach, 2nd Class   44.99
625-44749 Combine, 2nd Class   48.99

625-44552 1 & 2nd Class Coach, DB   38.99
625-44554 1st Class, DB   38.99

HALF DINING CAR ERA III/IV

625-44745 Class ART4um-65, DB   55.49

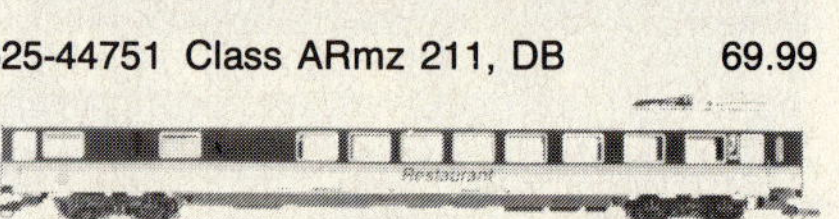

625-44751 Class ARmz 211, DB   69.99

625-44757 79' Class ARmz 211 **NEW** 69.99

THE "PIKE" COACH

The German State Railways (DRG) placed the first standardized express coaches of the classes A40, AB40, and C40 in service during the time period from 1922 until 1925. Some coaches were rebuilt during the 50's, i.e. the class C40-22 into B40-22, later on the AB40-23 was converted into B40-23/58. Both classes remained in service until the end of the 70's.

625-44454 70' DB, Mail Post 4u-b/20   31.49
625-44439 67' 2nd Class, B4uwe-22/53 31.49
625-44452 67' 2nd Class, Sleeper   31.49
WLB4u-21d
625-44450 67' 1st/2nd Class, AB4u-23a 31.49
625-44444 67' 1st Class, A4ue-23   31.49

625-44449 65' Baggage Pw4u-23D4u-23 31.49

BOGIES REBUILT COACH

625-44370 64' 2nd Class Fast Train   30.99
BDyg531 w/Baggage Compartment

HO SCALE   READY-TO-RUN

Roco passenger cars feature exact paint and lettering schemes, detailed interiors, diaphragms, European style couplers and blackened brass wheels. Coaches are made to exact scale length except as noted. Cars marked with an asterisk (*) are not scale length.

Imported from Austria by WALTHERS

BOGIES REBUILT COACH (cont)

625-44363 64' 2nd Class Fast Train 30.99
    Byg515

625-44367 64' 1st/2nd Class Fast Train 30.99
    AByg503

TEE AND IC COACH

These comfortable passenger train coaches are primarily used in Intercity and TEE operation. They may run at speeds up to 200 km/h.

625-44752 2nd Class DB Bm 234 **NEW** 46.99
625-44753 1st Class DB Am 203 **NEW** 46.99
625-44754 1st/2nd Class DB **NEW** 46.99
    ABm 225
625-44755 2nd Class Baggage **NEW** 46.99
    DB BDms 273
625-44756 Baggage DB, Dm902 **NEW** 46.99

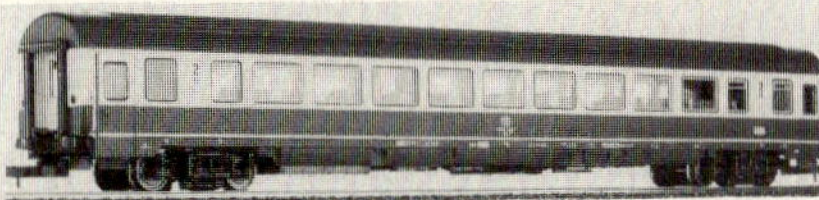

625-44651 2nd Class Coach, DB + 42.49

625-44653 86' 1st Class Avmz207 42.49
625-44303 75' 1st Class Avmz207* 27.99

625-44404 75' 1st Class Compartment, 32.49
    Avumz111/Avmz111*

625-44405 75' 1st Class Open Interior, 29.99
    Apumz121/Apmz121*

625-44301 75' 2nd Class Btmz/292* 27.99
625-44536 64' C4uwe, 3rd Class 26.99

75' "SILVERFISH" PUSH-PULL TRAIN

By 1975, over 5,000 of these push-pull traffic coaches were in service on the DB. The natural aluminum coloring and textured pattern on the body resulted in the nickname "Silverfish".

Push-pull trains like the "Silverfish" are common in suburban and commuter service. Using a single locomotive for power, the train can be operated from the engine cab or remotely controlled from a special coach equipped with a cab at the "rear". This eliminated the need to turn the train at the end of the run. **(1:100)**

Suitable locos (625-43421, 43413 and 43414) for these cars will be found in the Locomotive section.

625-44380 86' 2nd Class **NEW** (grn) 30.99
    Coach DB Bm 234
625-44381 86' 1st Class **NEW** (blue) 30.99
    Coach DB Am 203
625-44382 86' Baggage DB **NEW** 30.99
    D4um-60

625-44400 2nd Cl, BDnrzt740* 54.99

625-44403 1st/2nd Cl, ABnb* 29.99

625-44402 2nd Class, Bnb719* 29.99

COMPOSITE

625-44742 Coach 1st/2nd Class (green) 44.99
625-44748 Coach (cream, blue) 48.99
    1st/2nd Class

75' EXPRESS COACH

625-44390 2nd Class (ylw,blue) 30.99
    Bum234/Bm234*
625-44391 1st Class (ylw,blue) 30.99
    Aum203/Am203*

625-44900 75' Str Coach DB **NEW** TBA
    Touropa BCM 241

prototype photo

625-44744 Luggage Pw4um60 DB 44.99

625-44399 DBP, Mail Post m-a/56* 30.99

625-44740 BUM 234, 2nd Class 44.99
625-44741 AUM 203, 1st Class 44.99

625-44641 1st/2nd Class Coach 42.49
    Class ABvmz 227

75' SUBURBAN COACH

625-44245 2nd Class Coach 69.49

625-44246 2nd Class Coach 40.99

625-44247 1st/2nd Class Coach 40.99

625-44683 86' Str 2nd Class **NEW** 48.99
    Coach DB Bym 421
625-44684 86' 1st/2nd Class **NEW** 48.99
    Coach DB ABym 411
625-44685 2nd Class Str **NEW** 62.99
    Baggage DB

HO SCALE   READY-TO-RUN

Roco passenger cars feature exact paint and lettering schemes, detailed interiors, diaphragms, European style couplers and blackened brass wheels. Coaches are made to exact scale length except as noted. Cars marked with an asterisk (*) are not scale length.

Imported from Austria by WALTHERS

75' EXPRESS COACH (cont)

625-44674	75' 1st/2nd Class Coach DB n ABx 791 **NEW**	43.49
625-44675	75' 2nd Class Coach DB new Bx 794 **NEW**	43.49

625-44676	75' 1st Class Str Coach DB new w/driver's compartment **NEW**	68.99
625-44678	2nd Class Coach DB **NEW**	55.99

STREAMLINE

625-44780	75' 1st Class, DB	31.99
625-44782	75' 2nd Class, DB	33.49
625-44784	75' Diner, DB	49.99
625-44746	86' BM 235, 2nd Class	45.99
625-44747	86' AM 203, 1st Class	48.99
625-44410	78' Diner, DB	39.99

75' INTERCITY

625-44789	75' 2nd Class Coach DB Bvmz 185 **NEW**	TBA

625-44790	75' 1st Class Coach DB Avmz 107 **NEW**	TBA

625-44785	Bpmz 291.2 2nd Class Coach	45.49
625-44786	BM235 2nd Class Coach	53.49

86' INTERCITY

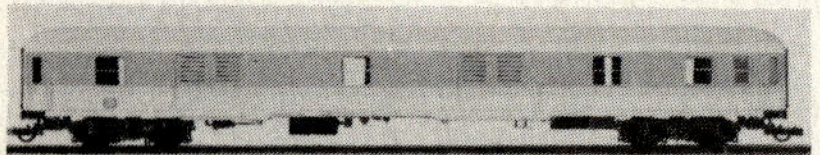

625-44787	Baggage DMS 902	53.49
625-44788	2nd Class Coach BDm 273	53.49

AUSTRIAN FEDERAL RAILWAYS

OLD TIME COACH

Formerly Prussian compartment coaches of the BBO. Coaches, as well as locomotives, changed owners as a result of two World Wars. Even formerly "Royal" Prussian coaches came into the "Imperial" Austria.

625-44505	41' 3rd Class w/brakeman's cabin	32.99

70' STANDARD

625-44576	2nd Class Coach, OBB	37.99

625-44573	1st/2nd Class Coach, OBB	37.99

625-44574	Baggage, OBB	37.99

625-44578	2nd Class Coach, OBB	37.99

EXPRESS EUROFIMA

625-44644	1st/2nd Class Coach	42.49
625-44645	OBB 1st/2nd cl ABmoz	42.49

625-44668	Coach, 2nd Class	42.49
625-44647	Dining Car	47.49
625-44648	Coach, 2nd Class	47.49

625-44317	Dining Car (Scale 1:100)	33.49
625-44315	Coach, 1st Cl (Scale 1:100)	30.49
625-44316	Coach, 2nd Cl (Scale 1:100)	30.49

78' DOMESTIC SERVICE COACHES, ERA V

625-44850	2nd Class Bmpz, OBB	53.49

625-44851	1st Class, Ampz 2, OBB	53.49

625-44852	1st & 2nd Class, Ampz OBB	53.49

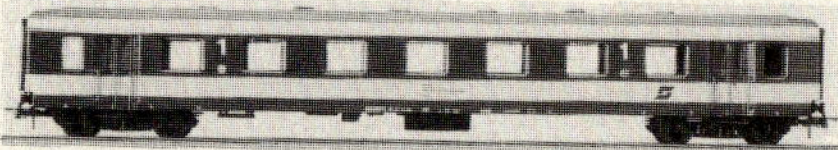

625-44853	2nd Class/Baggage Coach BDmpsz	53.49
625-44854	2nd Class Dining OBB **NEW**	56.49

625-44487	OBB 1-Cl APZ	37.99
625-44488	OBB 2-Cl BPZ	37.99
625-44489	Baggage OBB 2-Cl BDP	37.99

SLEEPING CAR, ERA IV

625-44843	"Ten" Sleeping Car, OBB	47.99

EUROFIMA COACH

These comfortable coaches are primarily used in international service.

625-44665	86' 1st Class, Amoz	42.49
625-44663	86' 2nd Class Combine	44.99
625-44666	86' 2nd Class, Bmoz	42.49
625-44312	75' Efima Restaurant*	26.99

SWISS FEDERAL RAILWAYS

OLD TIMERS

625-44466	67' 3rd Class Express	29.49

After the 2nd class coaches were taken out of service a few remaining coaches were rebuilt in 1975 to their original 3rd class configuration. They are still in use today for special events as part of "old-timer" trains (e.g. with loco Be 4/6, model 43507/43508 or C5/6, model 43200).

Roco — Imported from Austria by WALTHERS

HO SCALE   READY-TO-RUN
Roco passenger cars feature exact paint and lettering schemes, detailed interiors, diaphragms, European style couplers and blackened brass wheels. Coaches are made to exact scale length except as noted. Cars marked with an asterisk (*) are not scale length.

STANDARD COACH

625-44334	60' Baggage	(green/white)	33.49
625-44333	60' Baggage	(green)	30.49
526-44331	60' Baggage **Ltd Qty**	(blue)	19.99

625-44471 81' EW-1V 1st Class, SBB   35.99

625-44472 81' EW-1V 2nd Class, SBB   35.99

625-44473 86' Diner   44.99

625-44324 81' 2nd Class Express   30.49

625-44336 Express Teddy Coach Era IV   42.99

625-44438 Mail SBB CI-II Z   30.49

625-44329 81' 1st Class SBB-IV   30.49

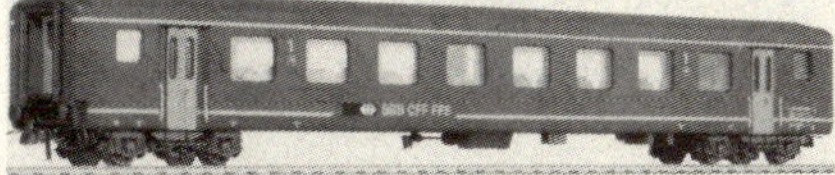

625-44341 Coach SBB 1st Class 2A   27.99

81' STREAMLINE COACH

625-44323	2nd Class, SBB		23.99
625-44337	1st/2nd Class, SBB		33.49

625-44338	1st/2nd Class, SBB		36.99
625-44339	1st/2nd Class, SBB		26.99

87' COACH   *NEW*

625-44883	1st Class, SBB		TBA
625-44884	2nd Class, SBB		TBA

55' SEETAL COACH

625-44730	1st/2nd Class, SBB		43.99
625-44731	2nd Class, SBB		43.99

EUROFIMA COACH

625-44655 86' 1st Class Express, Am19 42.49

prototype photo

625-44769 1st Class Coach SSB "Sight-Seeing"   *NEW* TBA

prototype photo

625-44770 2nd Class Express   48.99

prototype photo

625-44771 1st Class Expres Type Apm   48.99

DANISH STATE RAILWAYS

625-44417 75' 2nd Class Coach   28.99

ITALIAN STATE RAILWAYS

69' "DESIGN 3000"

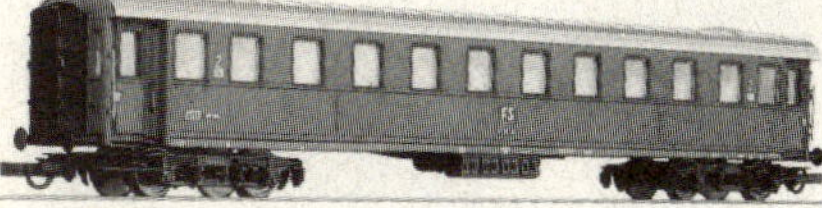

625-44704	3rd Class	(green)	37.99
625-44706	2nd Class	(brown)	37.99

625-44707	2nd Class	(gray)	47.49
625-44708	1st Cl, Design 10.000	(grn)	37.99
625-44710	1st Cl, Design 10.000	(gray)	47.49
625-44711	1/2 Cl, Dsgn 10.000	(gray)	47.49
625-44712	1/2 Cl, Design 10.000	(brn)	37.99

"DESIGN 2000" COACH

625-44703 69' 1st Class   (gray) 47.49

83' COACH   *NEW*

625-44847 FS U-Hansa Sleeping Car   (blue) 47.99

EUROFIMA COACH

625-44656	86' 1st Class		39.99
625-44660	86' 2nd Class		39.99
625-44636	1st Class Era IV/V		42.49
625-44637	2nd Class Era IV/V		42.49

EXPRESS COACHES

625-44772	1st Class Coach FS	*NEW*	50.49
625-44773	1st/2nd Class Coach FS	*NEW*	50.49
625-44774	2nd Class Coach FS	*NEW*	50.49

625-44736	1st Class, Am		58.99
625-44737	1st/2nd Class, ABm		58.99
625-44738	2nd Class, Bm		58.99

HO SCALE   READY-TO-RUN
Roco passenger cars feature exact paint and lettering schemes, detailed interiors, diaphragms, European style couplers and blackened brass wheels. Coaches are made to exact scale length except as noted. Cars marked with an asterisk (*) are not scale length.

EXPRESS COACHES (cont)

625-44697 Mail Van (gray) 47.49
Class U2 1300 FS

CENTO-PORTE

625-44691 2nd Class, FS (gray) 55.99
625-44775 1st/2nd Class (gray) TBA
Era IV

NORWEGIAN STATE RAILWAYS

625-44267 64' 3rd Class Coach 32.49
625-44268 64' 2nd Class Coach 32.49

NETHERLANDS STATE RAILWAYS

625-44261 64' Str 3rd Class NSB 32.49

"PLAN D" COACH

625-44242 74' 1st Class 37.99
625-44243 74' 2nd Class Dining 37.99

625-44244 74' 2nd Class 37.99

INTER-CITY COACH

625-44287 2nd Class NS/IC* (blue,ylw) 36.99
625-44289 74' Std, 3rd Class (blue) 29.99

EXPRESS COACH, ERA IV

625-44297 73' Diner NS cl-Plan D

625-44385 1st Class, A6000 29.99

BELGIAN STATE RAILWAYS

EUROFIMA COACH

625-44657 86' 1st Class Express 42.49
625-44661 86' 2nd Class 42.99
625-44350 86' 1st Class 56.49
625-44351 86' 2nd Class 56.49

SPANISH STATE RAILWAYS

86' EUROFIMA COACH

625-44462 75' Baggage 24.99

625-44463 75' 2nd Class, RENFE* 24.99

LUXEMBERG NATIONAL RAILWAYS

75' STREAMLINE COACH

625-44423 1st/2nd Class 29.99
625-44424 2nd Class 26.99

NEW 39.99

625-44290 Dining Car 32.99

81' UIC COACH

625-44598 2nd Class 32.99
625-44529 2nd/3rd Class, Type B3C5 39.49

COACH SET **NEW**

625-44031 Thunderbox 104.49
Includes four "Thunderboxes", one former 1st class coach, one 1st/2nd class coach, one 2nd class coach and one baggage wagon.

See also: FREIGHT CARS, COUPLERS, LOCOMOTIVES-TRACTION, PARTS, MINI-TANKS, SCENERY, VEHICLES, CIRCUS, CLEANERS, LIGHTING-ELECTRICAL-MOTORS, TOOLS, MULTIPLE-UNIT, BOOKS, SIGNALS & DETECTION, TOOLS, and FIGURES for additional ROCO items.

Imported from Austria by WALTHERS

HO SCALE   READY-TO-RUN

Roco passenger cars feature exact paint and lettering schemes, detailed interiors, diaphragms, European style couplers and blackened brass wheels. Coaches are made to exact scale length except as noted. Cars marked with an asterisk (*) are not scale length.

ORIENT EXPRESS

625-44050 U-Hansa Set **(Limited Run)**   182.99
4 Sleeping cars of U-Hansa design in CIWLT livery with raised nameplate, as used throughout all of Europe.

HUNGARIAN STATE RAILWAYS

86' STREAMLINE COACH

NEW

625-44497 2nd Class Coach Eurocity   TBA

625-44498 1st/2nd Class Coach Eurocity   TBA

FRENCH NATIONAL RAILWAYS

EXPRESS COACH

625-44642 1st/2nd Class, SNCF   42.49

81' STANDARD CAR

625-44608 Couchette Coach   32.99
           2nd Class

77' STANDARD COACH

■ **LIMITED QUANTITIES AVAILABLE** ■

625-44634 1st/2nd Class   23.99

75' CORAIL COACH

625-44273 2nd Class SNCF-b   32.49

EUROFIMA EXPRESS COACH

625-44308 1st Class*   (orange) 27.99
625-44667 Coach 1st Class   42.49

80' UIC-Y EXPRESS COACH

625-44602 2nd Class SNCF   32.99
625-44609 2nd Class, Era IV B10 SNCF   32.99
625-44610 1st Class SNCF   26.99
625-44611 1st Class SNCF (gray/green)   32.99
625-44613 2nd Class SNCF/Wasteel   34.49
625-44614 1st Class SNCF (gray/green)   35.49
625-44618 Diner BDymf 457   **NEW**   TBA
           SNCF

SWEDISH STATE RAILWAYS

86' STREAMLINE COACH

625-44726 2nd Class, Type A7 SJ   47.49

LIGHTING KITS

Lighting sets contain all parts required for installation. Some sets are almost completely pre-assembled and may be installed very quickly. A requirement for satisfactory operation of interior lighting are clean rails and wheels. The rail cleaning van "ROCO Clean" and the cleaning spray "ROCO Cleaner", are the ideal solution for obtaining clean rails and wheels.

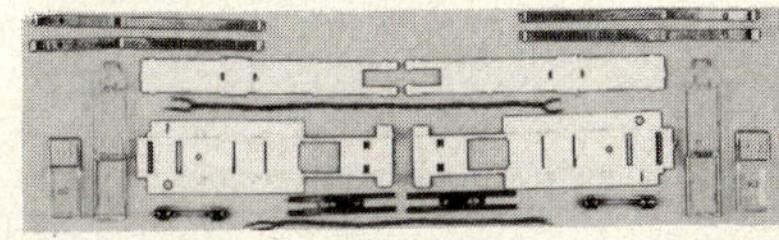

625-40301 for #44409   11.99
625-40300 8-wheel Short Coaches   10.99
625-40302 for Modern Coaches   10.99
625-40303 for 4-wheel Coaches   9.49

625-40306 for Commuter Coach   11.99
625-40305 for Commuter Baggage   11.99
625-40307 for Prussian Car   11.99
625-40308 for Modern Long Coach   11.99
625-40310 for WURTT Coaches   11.99
625-40311 for FS Coaches   11.99

What a great way to start your Pacific vacation, with a long-distance ride on Amtrak! Slowing for the station stop at Ocean View Bay, today's train is led by one of the colorful new GE 8-32BHW locos. Gary Hoover of Florissant, Missouri, created this seaside town for his Missouri, Kansas & Quincy. The GE was built from a Railpower shell, while the trailing F40 is reworked Life-Like model. The Superliners are from Con-Cor and the nearby town includes Kibri and Campbell structures.

Models and Photo by D. Gary Hoover

Grandt Line

HO SCALE
(1/87)

Parts are injection molded styrene plastic.

D&RGW Pass Car
Stove with Stack
300-5008   kit 1.50

Coach Seats (Narrow Gauge)
Wood End
300-5048   pkg(12) 2.50

Coach Seats (Standard Gauge)
with 2 Wood Ends
300-5049   pkg(12) 2.75

See also: PARTS Section for the entire line of GRANDT LINE HO Super Detail parts.

FUNARO & CAMERLENGO

HO CRAFT TRAIN KITS

Craft Train Kits consist of thin flexible styro-urethane castings with details cast in place, stripwood, wire and instructions. Cars are less trucks and couplers.

LONG ISLAND

| 279-5010 | "Ping-Pong" Coach | 29.99 |
| 279-5011 | "Ping Pong" Combine | 29.99 |

279-102   MU "World's Fair" Coach   29.99

279-103   Double Deck Coach   29.99

ERIE

279-201   Stillwell Coach   29.99

| 279-202 | Stillwell Combine | 29.99 |

NEW YORK CENTRAL   *NEW*

| 279-5070 | Standard Coach | 29.99 |

NEW YORK, ONTARIO & WESTERN

279-301	Coach	29.99
279-302	Combine	29.99
279-3001	Coach & Combine	set 58.99
279-303	Baggage	29.99
279-304	Railway Post Office	29.99
279-3002	Baggage & RPO	set 58.99
279-306	Osgood Bradley Coach	29.99

NYO&W/SP/SSW (By Special Order Only.)

| 279-309 | Observation Car | 29.99 |

READING

| 279-601 | Arch Roof Coach | 29.99 |

DELAWARE, LACKAWANNA & WESTERN

| 279-401 | Boonton Coach | 29.99 |

CENTRAL OF NEW JERSEY

| 279-701 | Clerestory Roof Coach | 29.99 |

NEW HAVEN

| 279-308 | Osgood Bradley Coach | 29.99 |

MA&PA

279-4001	Wood Coach	29.99
	(By Special Order Only.)	
279-4002	Wood RPO	29.99
	(By Special Order Only.)	
279-4003	Wood Baggage	29.99
279-4004	Coach, RPO & Baggage	set 80.99

HO SCALE (1/87) EASY-TO-BUILD KITS

Kits are easy to assemble. Molded plastic bodies are prepainted and lettered. Complete with horn-hook couplers and Delrin trucks with metal and plastic wheels.

CAR COLORS: Standard cars are Pullman Green except B&O which are gray & blue. Streamline cars are painted silver (aluminum) with appropriate trim colors, except for SP Daylight cars (red & orange with silver striping), Northern Pacific (green & yellow with red striping) and PRR (maroon).

We have worked closely with this manufacturer to provide accurate availability information at the time this catalog was published. Items listed in *blue ink* may not be available at all times. Please see your dealer for current delivery information.

72' STREAMLINE

BAGGAGE   each 7.25

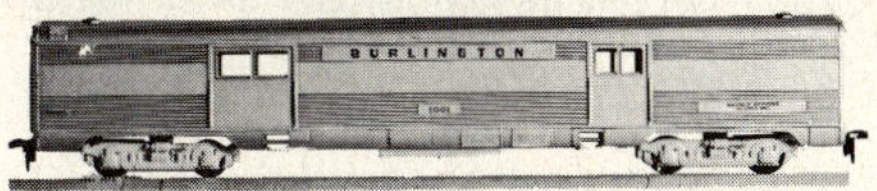

140-1781 Atchison, Topeka & Santa Fe
140-1782 Pennsylvania
140-1783 Chicago, Burlington & Quincy
140-1784 New Haven
140-1785 Baltimore & Ohio
140-1786 Northern Pacific
140-1787 New York Central
140-1788 Southern Pacific "Daylight"
140-1789 Amtrak
140-1780 Undecorated

DINER   each 7.25

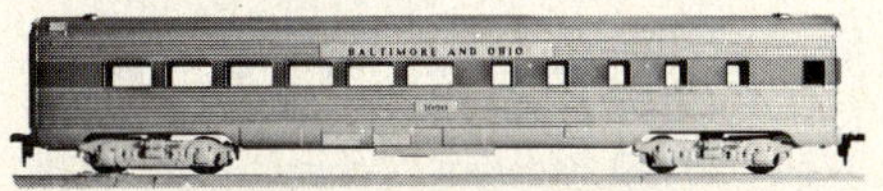

140-1791 Atchison, Topeka & Santa Fe
140-1792 Pennsylvania
140-1793 Chicago, Burlington & Quincy
140-1794 New Haven
140-1795 Baltimore & Ohio
140-1797 New York Central
140-1798 Southern Pacific "Daylight"
140-1799 Amtrak
140-1790 Undecorated
140-1796 Northern Pacific

RAILWAY POST OFFICE   each 7.25

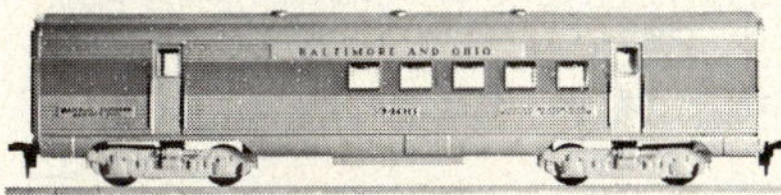

140-1801 Atchison, Topeka & Santa Fe
140-1802 Pennsylvania
140-1803 Chicago, Burlington & Quincy
140-1808 Southern Pacific "Daylight"
140-1800 Undecorated
140-1804 New Haven
140-1805 Baltimore & Ohio
140-1806 Northern Pacific
140-1807 New York Central
140-1809 Amtrak

COACH   each 7.25

140-1811 Atchison, Topeka & Santa Fe
140-1812 Pennsylvania
140-1813 Chicago, Burlington & Quincy
140-1814 New Haven
140-1815 Baltimore & Ohio
140-1816 Northern Pacific
140-1817 New York Central
140-1818 Southern Pacific "Daylight"
140-1819 Amtrak
140-1810 Undecorated

VISTA DOME   each 7.25

140-1821 Atchison, Topeka & Santa Fe
140-1822 Pennsylvania
140-1823 Chicago, Burlington & Quincy
140-1824 New Haven
140-1825 Baltimore & Ohio
140-1826 Northern Pacific

140-1827 NYC
140-1828 SP "Daylight"
140-1829 Amtrak
140-1820 Undec

OBSERVATION   each 7.25

140-1831 Atchison, Topeka & Santa Fe
140-1832 Pennsylvania
140-1833 Chicago, Burlington & Quincy
140-1834 New Haven
140-1835 Baltimore & Ohio
140-1836 Northern Pacific
140-1837 New York Central
140-1838 Southern Pacific "Daylight"
140-1839 Amtrak
140-1830 Undecorated

STANDARD

67' RAILWAY POST OFFICE   ea 7.25

140-1843 Southern Pacific
140-1840 Undecorated
140-1841 Atchison, Topeka & Santa Fe
140-1842 New York Central
140-1845 Baltimore & Ohio

70' COACH   each 7.25
Arch Roof

140-1851 Atchison, Topeka & Santa Fe
140-1852 New York Central
140-1853 Southern Pacific
140-1855 Baltimore & Ohio
140-1850 Undecorated

70' COACH   each 7.25
Clerestory Roof

140-1856 Atchison, Topeka & Santa Fe
140-1857 New York Central
140-1858 Southern Pacific
140-1859 Baltimore & Ohio
140-1854 Undecorated

70' PULLMAN   each 7.25

140-1863 Southern Pacific
140-1860 Undecorated
140-1861 Atchison, Topeka & Santa Fe
140-1862 New York Central
140-1865 Baltimore & Ohio

70' OBSERVATION   each 7.25

140-1875 Baltimore & Ohio
140-1870 Undecorated

140-1871 Atchison, Topeka & Santa Fe
140-1872 New York Central
140-1873 Southern Pacific

70' BAGGAGE   each 7.25

140-1882 New York Central
140-1881 Atchison, Topeka & Santa Fe
140-1883 Southern Pacific
140-1885 Baltimore & Ohio
140-1880 Undecorated

70' DINER   each 7.25

140-1891 Atchison, Topeka & Santa Fe
140-1892 New York Central
140-1893 Southern Pacific
140-1895 Baltimore & Ohio
140-1890 Undecorated

LIGHTING KITS

140-90200 for Streamline (4 wheel truck)   1.00
140-90201 for Standard (6 wheel truck)   1.00

HO SCALE (1/87) CRAFT TRAIN KITS

50' PULLMAN TROOP CARS
Styrene with weights. Will accept Kadee #5 couplers.

Items listed in *blue ink* may not be available at all times. Please see your dealer for current delivery information.

Sleeper
197-45020
15.00

prototype photo

prototype photo

197-45021 Kitchen   15.00
(not illustrated)
197-45022 REA Converted Sleeper   20.00
(Baggage Door)

BRASS CAR SIDES

HO SCALE (1/87)

See PARTS section for doors and car ends

PASSENGER CAR SIDES

Photoetched brass sides for streamlined passenger cars. Etched door outline, grab iron holes and other surface features. Designed to be used with either the Basic or Deluxe Body Kit, or as an overlay on Rivarossi, Con-Cor or Bachmann plastic car bodies. Construction and prototype information is supplied with car sides. Sides are undecorated.

COACH

173-1 Chicago & North Western "400" 26.75
C&NW 3431-3476, also GN, NP and CB&Q

173-2 Milwaukee Road 25.75
1948 Hiawatha, 480-497, 535-551 and 600-661

173-4 Northern Pacific North Coast Ltd 25.75
56 seats, 588-599. Also CB&Q, SP&S

173-12 Great Northern Empire Builder 26.75
48 seats, 1215-1231, CB&Q, SP&S 350

173-14 Great Northern Empire Builder 26.75
60 seats, 1209-1214

173-20 Great Northern Empire Builder 26.75
NP North Coast Ltd
Budd Dome Coach
GN 1320-1331, NP 549-556, CB&Q, SP&S.
To overlay Con-Cor Budd Dome Coach.

173-30 NP NCL/Mainstreeter 25.75
56 seats, NP 500-517, SP&S 301-306

173-31 Union Pacific "Challenger" 26.75
48 seats, UP 5331-5365

173-32 PRR "Jeffersonian" P-85BR 26.75
4100-4169, 4068-4091

173-39 Canadian National CCF Coaches 26.75
CN 5437-5654.

173-40 UP/C&NW ACF 44-Seat Coaches 26.75
UP 5450-87, C&NW 3477-82 (SP, GN, GTW, ATK)

173-44 Illinois Central Streamlined 26.75
56 seats. IC received 27 lightweight coaches (IC 2614-2640) from Pullman-Standard in early 1947 in Lot #6766 and Plan #7531. Assigned to the *City of New Orleans, Daylight, Land O'Corn, Green Diamond* and pool service. Feature end skirts. To overlay Rivarossi car bodies.

173-45 C&O/D&RGW P-S NEW 26.75
Plan 7600
52 seats. Original skirting. D&H, SAL, C&NW, SP, NKP, Amtrak. Use Evergreen 4526 & 4527 siding for fluting.

173-46 C&O/D&RGW P-S NEW 26.75
Plan 7600
52 seats. Partial skirting. D&H, SAL, C&NW, SP, NKP, Amtrak. Use Evergreen 4526 & 4527 siding for fluting.

PARLOR/LOUNGE

173-3 Milwaukee 1948 Hiawatha 25.75
Valley Series Parlor Car 190-197

173-27 GN Empire Builder 26.75
GN 1390-95 "View" Great Dome Lounge
To overlay Bachmann Full Dome Coach.

173-36 Union Pacific Observation 28.75
Dome Lounge
UP 9000-14, Tail End Version

173-10 GN Empire Builder Ranch 26.75
Lounge Coffee Shop
1240-1245

173-19 NP-NCL "Traveler's Rest" 25.75
494-499

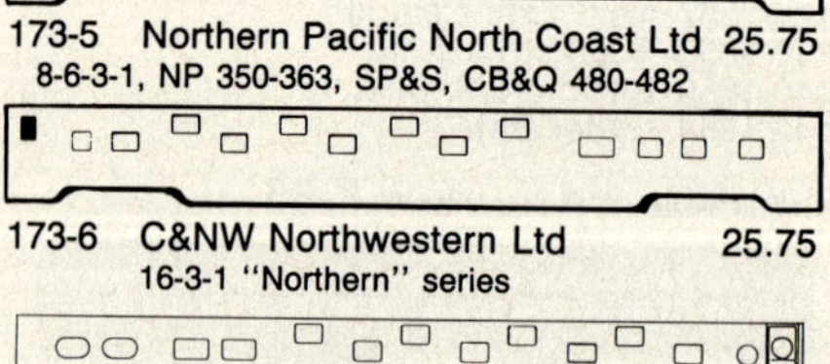

173-26 Union Pacific Mid-Train 28.75
Dome Lounge
UP 9000-9014, Auto Train

PULLMAN

173-5 Northern Pacific North Coast Ltd 25.75
8-6-3-1, NP 350-363, SP&S, CB&Q 480-482

173-6 C&NW Northwestern Ltd 25.75
16-3-1 "Northern" series

173-7 MILW Pioneer Ltd "Raymond" 25.75
16-4 Milwaukee 27-30

173-8 MILW Pioneer Limited "River" 25.75
8-6-4 Milwaukee 19-26

173-9 PS "American" 4099 26.75
6-6-4 UP, SP, CN&W, AT&SF, Erie, MP, IC and CRIP

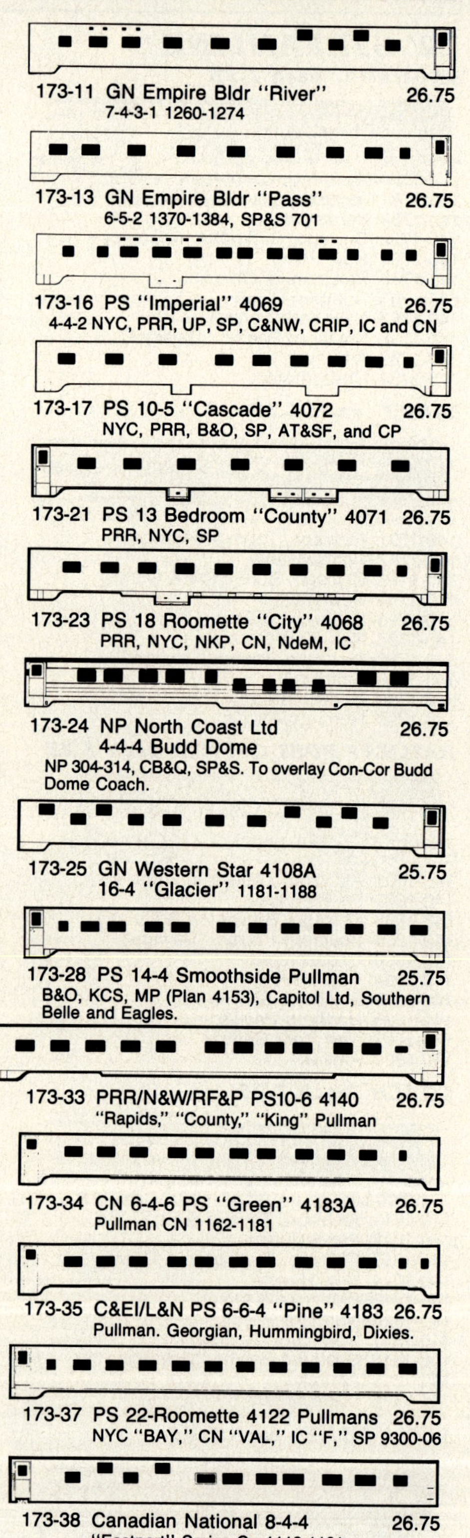

173-11 GN Empire Bldr "River" 26.75
7-4-3-1 1260-1274

173-13 GN Empire Bldr "Pass" 26.75
6-5-2 1370-1384, SP&S 701

173-16 PS "Imperial" 4069 26.75
4-4-2 NYC, PRR, UP, SP, C&NW, CRIP, IC and CN

173-17 PS 10-5 "Cascade" 4072 26.75
NYC, PRR, B&O, SP, AT&SF, and CP

173-21 PS 13 Bedroom "County" 4071 26.75
PRR, NYC, SP

173-23 PS 18 Roomette "City" 4068 26.75
PRR, NYC, NKP, CN, NdeM, IC

173-24 NP North Coast Ltd 26.75
4-4-4 Budd Dome
NP 304-314, CB&Q, SP&S. To overlay Con-Cor Budd Dome Coach.

173-25 GN Western Star 4108A 25.75
16-4 "Glacier" 1181-1188

173-28 PS 14-4 Smoothside Pullman 25.75
B&O, KCS, MP (Plan 4153), Capitol Ltd, Southern Belle and Eagles.

173-33 PRR/N&W/RF&P PS10-6 4140 26.75
"Rapids," "County," "King" Pullman

173-34 CN 6-4-6 PS "Green" 4183A 26.75
Pullman CN 1162-1181

173-35 C&EI/L&N PS 6-6-4 "Pine" 4183 26.75
Pullman. Georgian, Hummingbird, Dixies.

173-37 PS 22-Roomette 4122 Pullmans 26.75
NYC "BAY," CN "VAL," IC "F," SP 9300-06

173-38 Canadian National 8-4-4 26.75
"Eastport" Series Cn 1110-1161

173-41 IC/B&O PS 10-6 Pullman 4167 26.75
IC "C" Series, B&O 7040-49

BRASS CAR SIDES

PASSENGER CAR SIDES

Photoetched brass sides for streamlined passenger cars. Etched door outline, grab iron holes and other surface features. Designed to be used with either the Basic or Deluxe Body Kit, or as an overlay on Rivarossi, Con-Cor or Bachmann plastic car bodies. Construction and prototype information is supplied with car sides. Sides are undecorated.

DINER

173-15 GN Empire Builder "Lake" 26.75
    1250-1255

173-22 Union Pacific Dome 26.75
    8000-8009, Auto-Train 800-808. To overlay Rivarossi Vista Dome Coach.

173-29 NP North Coast Limited 25.75
    NP 459-463, CB&Q 468 Budd Diner. To overlay Con-Cor Budd 10-6/Sleeper.

BAGGAGE/DORM

173-18 GN Empire Builder 1200-1205 26.75

173-43 GN/UP/C&NW ACF 32.75
    Baggage Mail
    GN 37-44, UP 5900-02, C&NW 8225-26

BODY KITS

173-101 Basic Body Kit 9.25
Includes cast lead alloy ends, scale-width milled basswood roof, floor, and centersill for one car. Use with all non-dome brass side sets. Some cutting required, instructions included. Less trucks and couplers.

173-102 Deluxe Body Kit 17.75
Includes lost-wax brass ends, heavy copper-clad pc board floor, milled basswood roof for one car. Use with all non-dome brass side sets. Some cutting required. Instructions included. Less trucks and couplers.

CONVERSION TABLE
The following sets of sides are designed to be applied directly to RTR plastic cars without the need to shorten the plastic body. Some trimming of plastic around windows is required.

Rivarossi 1930 85′ Coach or Sleeper:
    173-10-15, 18, 19, 25, 28, 30-35, 37, 38, 40, 41, 43, 44, 45, 46

Rivarossi Vista Dome Coach: 173-22, 26, 36

Bachmann Full Dome Coach: 173-27

Con-Cor Budd Dome Coach: 173-20, 173-24

Con-Cor Budd Sleeper: 173-29

HO EASY-TO-BUILD KITS
Kits feature prepainted and lettered molded plastic parts. Cars are compatible with Kadee draft gear (not included) & feature trucks with RP-25 36″ Delrin wheel sets. Less couplers.

P-70 SERIES HEAVYWEIGHTS
All cars feature 6-wheel trucks unless noted.

80′ STANDARD COACH

117-1030 Undecorated 23.95
117-1031 Undecorated, 4-wheel truck 22.95

80′ STANDARD P-70 FBR ARCH ROOF COACH

117-1120 Undecorated 23.95
117-1121 Undecorated, 4-wheel truck 22.95
117-1122 Undecorated, 4-wheel Pennsy 23.95

80′ P-70 FBR CLERESTORY ROOF COACH
117-1123 Undecorated 23.95
117-1124 Undecorated, 4-wheel Common 22.95
117-1125 Undecorated, 4-wheel Pennsy 22.95

80′ P-70 FAR LOW ARCH ROOF COACH
117-1141 Undecorated, 4-wheel Pennsy 24.95

78′ STANDARD PB-70 COMBINE

117-1001 Undecorated 23.95

80′ Z-74 BUSINESS/OBSERVATION CAR
with Clerestory roof

117-1100 Undecorated 23.95
117-1101 Undecorated, 4-whl common 22.95

PS LIGHTWEIGHTS
BAGGAGE/LOUNGE

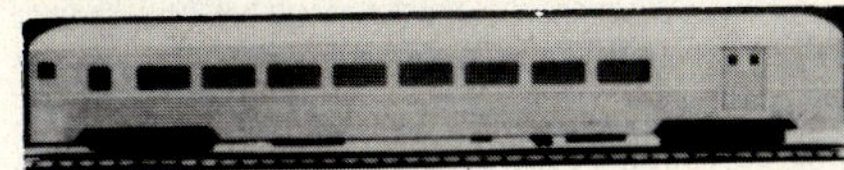

117-1311 Stainless Steel Undecorated 19.95

COACH

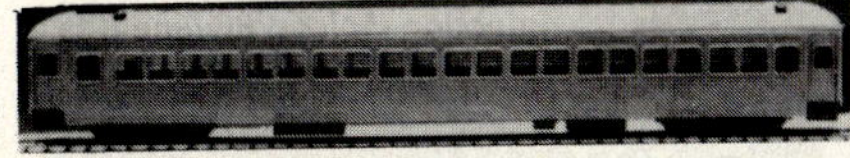

117-1300 Osgood Bradley 84-seat 19.95
    Commuter, Undecorated

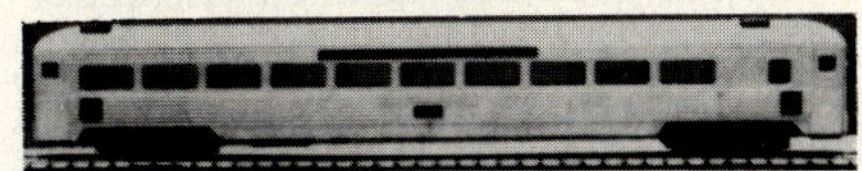

117-1310 Stainless Steel Commuter, 19.95
    Undecorated

SLEEPER **NEW**
117-1330 Stainless Steel 4-4-2 19.95
117-1331 Stainless Steel 6-6-4 19.95

85′ PS STREAMLINES
RPO-BAGGAGE

117-1201 Undecorated 14.95

DINER

117-1203 Undecorated 14.95

COACH

117-1202 Undecorated 14.95

DORMITORY-LOUNGE

117-1204 Undecorated 14.95

SLEEPER

117-1205 6-6-4 Undecorated 14.95

117-1206 4-4-2 Undecorated 14.95

117-1208 7-4-3-1 Undecorated 14.95

OBSERVATION

117-1207 Undecorated 14.95

CUSTOM RAILWAY SUPPLY

DIAPHRAGM
HO SCALE (1/87)

WW II era operating diaphragm kit features brass full width buffer plates and cloth bellows.

(Can be used with Walthers Diaphragm 933-429)

212-1056 Streamline Passenger ea 4.95
    Full Width Diaphragms

HO SCALE (1/87) EASY-TO-BUILD KITS

Kits are easy to assemble. Molded plastic bodies are prepainted and lettered. Complete w/horn-hook couplers and trucks w/metal wheels. Cars are painted silver (aluminum) except where noted.

AMERICAN VINTAGE SETS

1880's era cars sold only in sets of four (two coaches, full baggage car and combine).

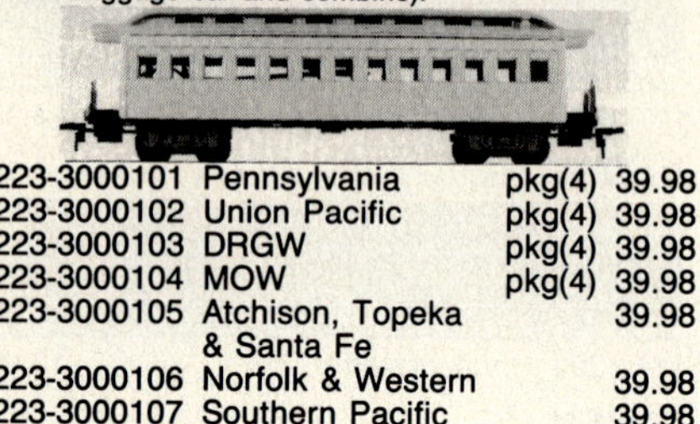

223-3000101	Pennsylvania	pkg(4)	39.98
223-3000102	Union Pacific	pkg(4)	39.98
223-3000103	DRGW	pkg(4)	39.98
223-3000104	MOW	pkg(4)	39.98
223-3000105	Atchison, Topeka & Santa Fe		39.98
223-3000106	Norfolk & Western		39.98
223-3000107	Southern Pacific		39.98
223-3000100	Undecorated	pkg(4)	39.98

SUPERLINERS

85' COMBINE

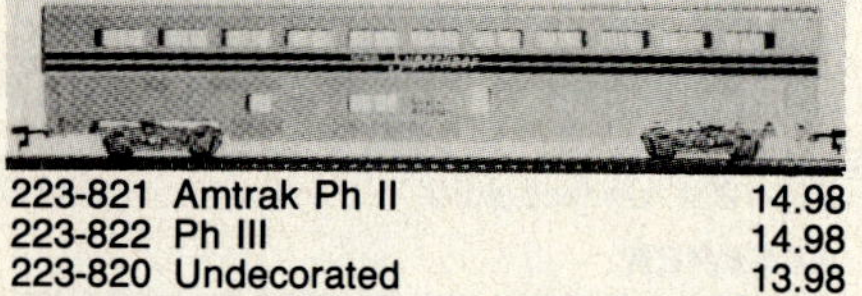

223-821	Amtrak Ph II	14.98
223-822	Ph III	14.98
223-820	Undecorated	13.98

85' DINER

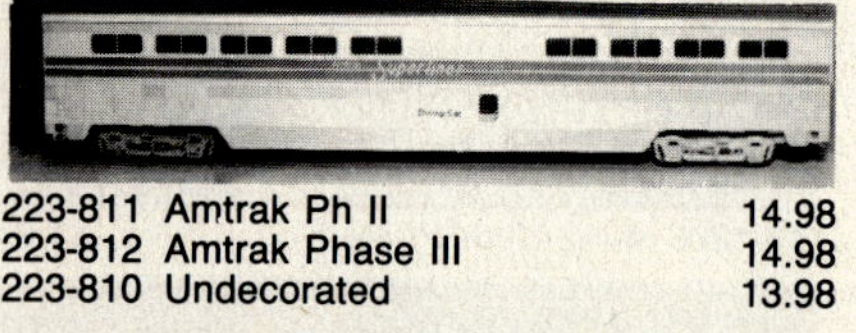

223-811	Amtrak Ph II	14.98
223-812	Amtrak Phase III	14.98
223-810	Undecorated	13.98

85' LOUNGE/CAFE

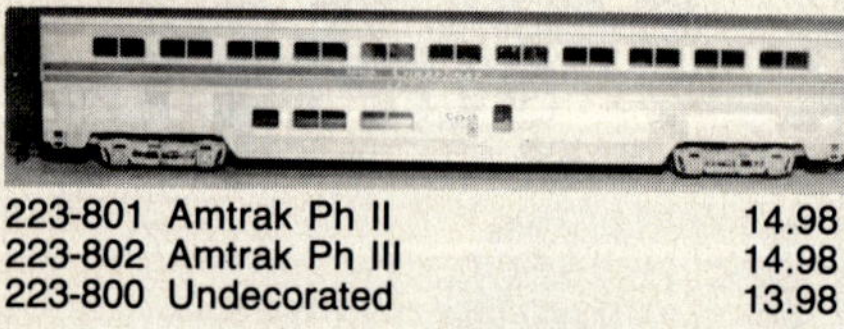

223-841	Amtrak Ph II	14.98
223-842	Amtrak Ph III	14.98
223-840	Undecorated	13.98

85' COACH

223-801	Amtrak Ph II	14.98
223-802	Amtrak Ph III	14.98
223-800	Undecorated	13.98

85' SLEEPER

223-831	Amtrak Ph II	14.98
223-832	Amtrak Ph III	14.98
223-830	Undecorated	13.98

STREAMLINE

60' MATERIAL HANDLING CARS "EXPRESS BOX CARS"

In the mid-1980's, the Thrall Mfg Company built several 60' box car-type cars designed to run with high-speed passenger Amtrak trains. Amtrak owns a total of 74 of these cars and is now having 80 additional cars built for their fleet. These cars can be found at the head of almost all Amtrak trains carrying mail, express packages and passenger baggage. Most trains will have up to three between the locomotive and first passenger car.

223-871	Amtrak	12.98
223-11041	Union Pacific	12.98
223-11042	SP Daylight	12.98
223-11044	Southern Crescent	12.98
223-11045	Pennsylvania	12.98
223-11047	Norfolk & Western	12.98
223-11048	Royal American	12.98
223-11049	Milwaukee Road	12.98
223-11050	Santa Fe	12.98
223-11051	Norfolk Southern	12.98
223-11052	Via Rail	12.98
223-11053	New York Central	12.98
223-11054	Southern Pacific Lark	12.98
223-870	Undecorated	12.98

Three packs; each car has a different road number.

223-90603	Amtrak	pkg(3)	38.94
223-90604	REA	pkg(3)	38.94
223-87003	Undecorated	pkg(3)	38.94

72' MATERIAL HANDLERS CAR

223-11043	Great Northern Empire	TBA
223-11055	Overland	12.98

70' BAGGAGE

223-746	California Zepher	13.98
223-7501	Union Pacific (yellow,gray)	15.98
223-7506	Southern	12.98
223-7507	SP Daylight (red,orange)	15.98

72' RAILWAY POST OFFICE

223-921	Union Pacific	12.98
223-922	Southern Pacific Daylight	12.98
223-923	Great Northern Empire	TBA
223-924	Southern Crescent	12.98
223-925	Pennsylvania	12.98
223-926	Amtrak Phase 2	12.98
223-927	Norfolk & Western	12.98
223-928	Royal American	12.98
223-929	Milwaukee Road	12.98
223-930	Santa Fe Flyer	12.98
223-931	Norfolk Southern	12.98
223-932	Via Rail	12.98
223-933	New York Central	12.98
223-934	Southern Pacific Lark	12.98
223-935	Overland Mail	12.98
223-920	Undecorated	12.98

72' BAGGAGE

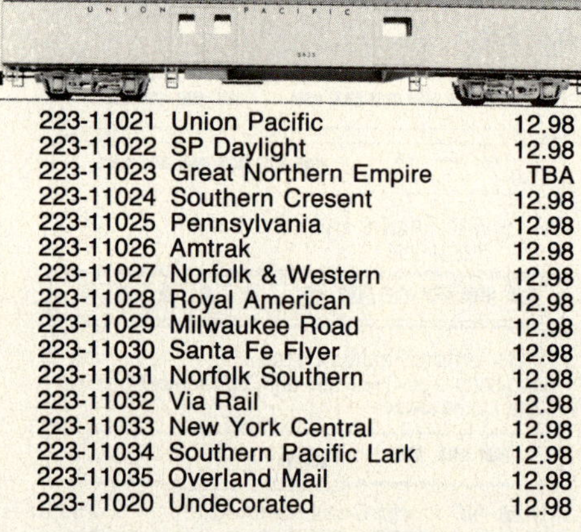

223-11021	Union Pacific	12.98
223-11022	SP Daylight	12.98
223-11023	Great Northern Empire	TBA
223-11024	Southern Cresent	12.98
223-11025	Pennsylvania	12.98
223-11026	Amtrak	12.98
223-11027	Norfolk & Western	12.98
223-11028	Royal American	12.98
223-11029	Milwaukee Road	12.98
223-11030	Santa Fe Flyer	12.98
223-11031	Norfolk Southern	12.98
223-11032	Via Rail	12.98
223-11033	New York Central	12.98
223-11034	Southern Pacific Lark	12.98
223-11035	Overland Mail	12.98
223-11020	Undecorated	12.98

72' DINER

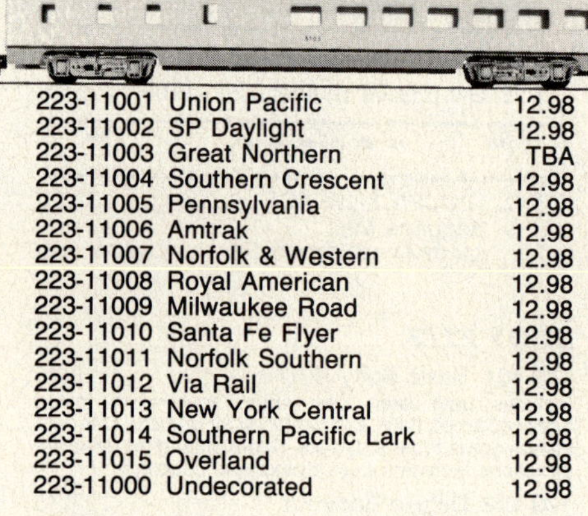

223-11001	Union Pacific	12.98
223-11002	SP Daylight	12.98
223-11003	Great Northern	TBA
223-11004	Southern Crescent	12.98
223-11005	Pennsylvania	12.98
223-11006	Amtrak	12.98
223-11007	Norfolk & Western	12.98
223-11008	Royal American	12.98
223-11009	Milwaukee Road	12.98
223-11010	Santa Fe Flyer	12.98
223-11011	Norfolk Southern	12.98
223-11012	Via Rail	12.98
223-11013	New York Central	12.98
223-11014	Southern Pacific Lark	12.98
223-11015	Overland	12.98
223-11000	Undecorated	12.98

72' COACH

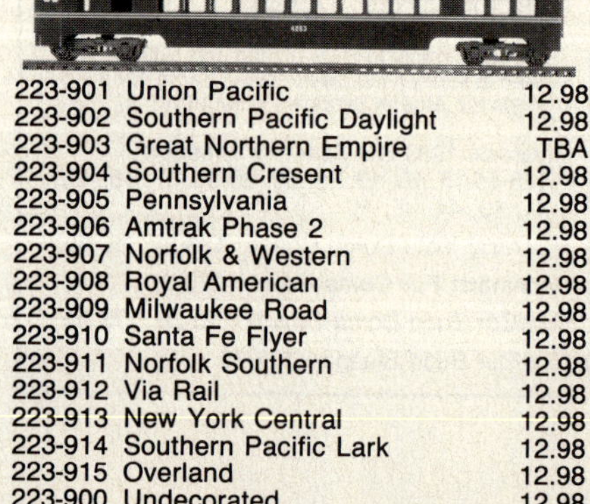

223-901	Union Pacific	12.98
223-902	Southern Pacific Daylight	12.98
223-903	Great Northern Empire	TBA
223-904	Southern Cresent	12.98
223-905	Pennsylvania	12.98
223-906	Amtrak Phase 2	12.98
223-907	Norfolk & Western	12.98
223-908	Royal American	12.98
223-909	Milwaukee Road	12.98
223-910	Santa Fe Flyer	12.98
223-911	Norfolk Southern	12.98
223-912	Via Rail	12.98
223-913	New York Central	12.98
223-914	Southern Pacific Lark	12.98
223-915	Overland	12.98
223-900	Undecorated	12.98

CON-COR

HO SCALE (1/87) EASY-TO-BUILD KITS

Kits are easy to assemble. Molded plastic bodies are prepainted and lettered. Complete w/horn-hook couplers and trucks w/metal wheels. Cars are painted silver (aluminum) except where noted.

72' SLEEPER

223-981	Union Pacific	12.98
223-982	SP Daylight	12.98
223-983	Great Northern Empire	TBA
223-984	Southern Crescent	12.98
223-985	Pennsylvania	12.98
223-986	Amtrak	12.98
223-987	Norfolk & Western	12.98
223-988	Royal American	12.98
223-989	Milwaukee Road	12.98
223-990	Santa Fe Flyer	12.98
223-991	Norfolk Southern	12.98
223-992	Via Rail	12.98
223-993	New York Central	12.98
223-994	Southern Pacific Lark	12.98
223-995	Overland	12.98
223-980	Undecorated	12.98

72' DOME

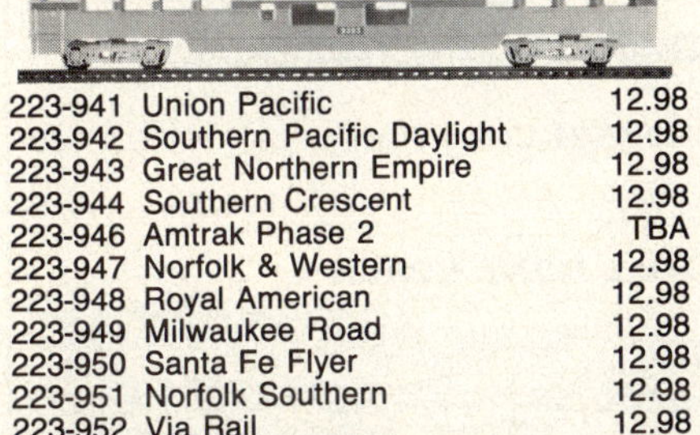

223-941	Union Pacific	12.98
223-942	Southern Pacific Daylight	12.98
223-943	Great Northern Empire	12.98
223-944	Southern Crescent	12.98
223-946	Amtrak Phase 2	TBA
223-947	Norfolk & Western	12.98
223-948	Royal American	12.98
223-949	Milwaukee Road	12.98
223-950	Santa Fe Flyer	12.98
223-951	Norfolk Southern	12.98
223-952	Via Rail	12.98
223-953	New York Central	12.98
223-954	Southern Pacific Lark	12.98
223-955	Overland Vista	12.98
223-940	Undecorated	12.98

72' OBSERVATION CAR

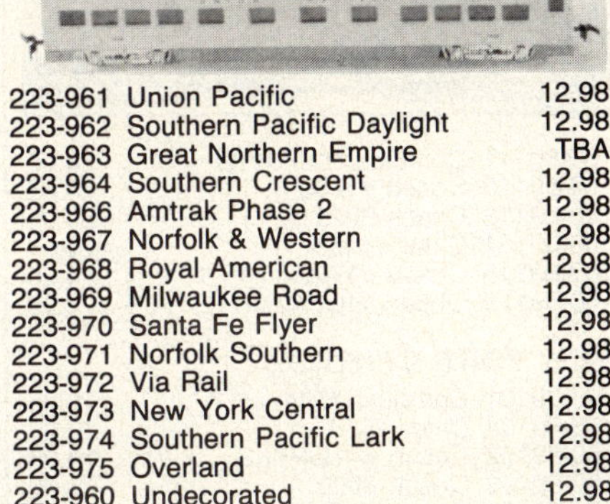

223-961	Union Pacific	12.98
223-962	Southern Pacific Daylight	12.98
223-963	Great Northern Empire	TBA
223-964	Southern Crescent	12.98
223-966	Amtrak Phase 2	12.98
223-967	Norfolk & Western	12.98
223-968	Royal American	12.98
223-969	Milwaukee Road	12.98
223-970	Santa Fe Flyer	12.98
223-971	Norfolk Southern	12.98
223-972	Via Rail	12.98
223-973	New York Central	12.98
223-974	Southern Pacific Lark	12.98
223-975	Overland	12.98
223-960	Undecorated	12.98

75' COACH

223-705	New York Central	13.98
223-17106	Southern	13.98

75' DOME

223-715	New York Central	13.98
223-17206	Southern	13.98

75' BAGGAGE

223-745	New York Central	13.98
223-17506	Southern	13.98

75' DINER

223-725	New York Central	13.98
223-17306	Southern	13.98

75' OBSERVATION

223-735	New York Central	13.98
223-17406	Southern	13.98

75' SLEEPER

223-755	New York Central	13.98
223-17606	Southern Railwau	13.98

75' BUDD DOME

223-785	New York Central	13.98
223-17906	Southern	13.98

75' PULLMAN

223-795	New York Central	13.98
223-18006	Southern	13.98

72' PASSENGER CAR SETS

223-90001	Asst UP **NEW**	pkg(12)	103.84
223-90002	Southern **NEW** Pacific Day	pkg(12)	103.84
223-90004	Southern Cresent **NEW**		103.84
223-90006	Amtrak A	pkg(8)	103.84
223-90007	Norfolk & **NEW** Western	pkg(12)	103.84
223-90009	Milwaukee **NEW** Road	pkg(8)	103.84
223-90010	Santa Fe A	pkg(8)	103.84
223-90013	New York Central	pkg(8)	103.84
223-90014	Southern Pacific Lark	pkg(8)	103.84
223-90015	Overland Pass	pkg(12)	103.84
223-90021	Asst UP **NEW**	pkg(12)	103.84
223-90022	Southern Pacific Day	pkg(8)	103.84
223-90041	Southern Crescent		103.84
223-90061	Amtrak Phase 2	pkg(12)	103.84
223-90071	Norfolk & **NEW** Western	pkg(12)	103.84
223-90091	Asst Milw **NEW**	pkg(8)	103.84
223-90113	Asst New York Central		103.84
223-90110	Santa Fe B	pkg(8)	103.84
223-90114	Southern Pacific Lark #2	pkg(12)	103.84
223-90115	Overland Pass B	pkg(12)	103.84

85' DINER

223-722	ATSF		13.98
223-723	Pennsylvania		13.98
223-726	California Zepher		13.98
223-7301	UP	(yellow,gray)	15.98
223-7302	GN	(orange,green)	15.98
223-7305	Amtrak		16.98
223-7306	Southen		12.98
223-7307	SP Daylight	(red,orange)	15.98
223-721	Undecorated		13.98

85' BAGGAGE

223-742	ATSF	13.98
223-743	Pennsylvania	13.98
223-7502	Great Northern	15.98
223-7505	Amtrak	16.98
223-741	Undecorated	13.98

85' COACH

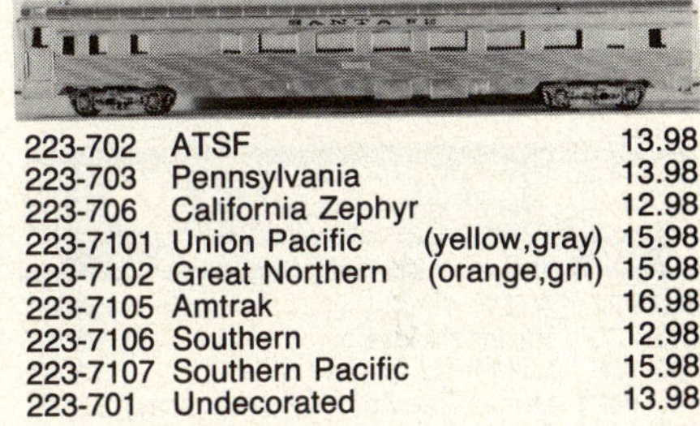

223-702	ATSF		13.98
223-703	Pennsylvania		13.98
223-706	California Zephyr		12.98
223-7101	Union Pacific	(yellow,gray)	15.98
223-7102	Great Northern	(orange,grn)	15.98
223-7105	Amtrak		16.98
223-7106	Southern		12.98
223-7107	Southern Pacific		15.98
223-701	Undecorated		13.98

85' BUDD SLUMBERCOACH

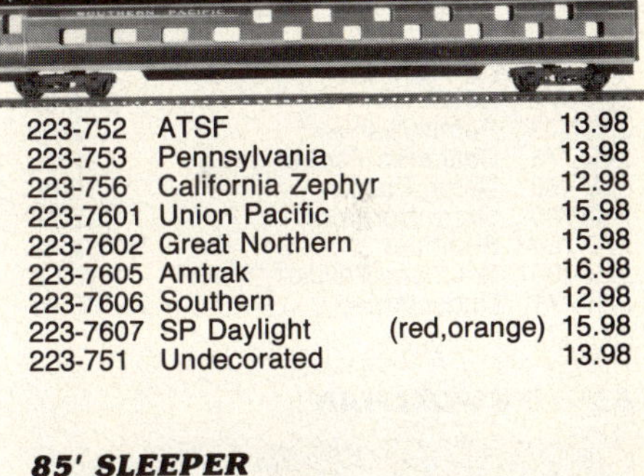

223-752	ATSF		13.98
223-753	Pennsylvania		13.98
223-756	California Zephyr		12.98
223-7601	Union Pacific		15.98
223-7602	Great Northern		15.98
223-7605	Amtrak		16.98
223-7606	Southern		12.98
223-7607	SP Daylight	(red,orange)	15.98
223-751	Undecorated		13.98

85' SLEEPER

223-761	Undecorated	13.98

85' 10-6 PULLMAN SLEEPER

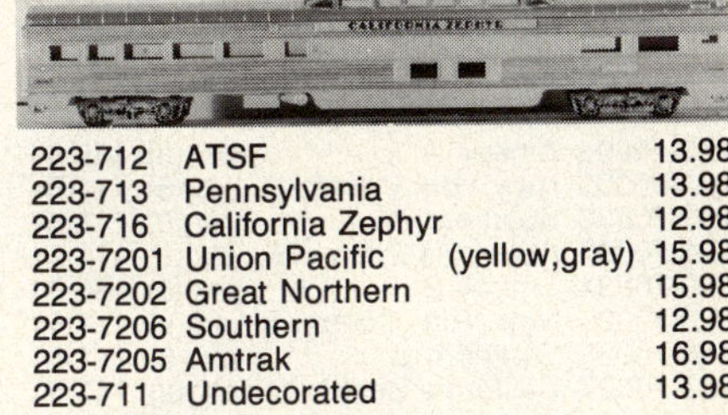

223-791	Undecorated	13.98

85' DOME

223-712	ATSF		13.98
223-713	Pennsylvania		13.98
223-716	California Zephyr		12.98
223-7201	Union Pacific	(yellow,gray)	15.98
223-7202	Great Northern		15.98
223-7206	Southern		12.98
223-7205	Amtrak		16.98
223-711	Undecorated		13.98

HO SCALE (1/87)
EASY-TO-BUILD KITS

85' BUDD DOME

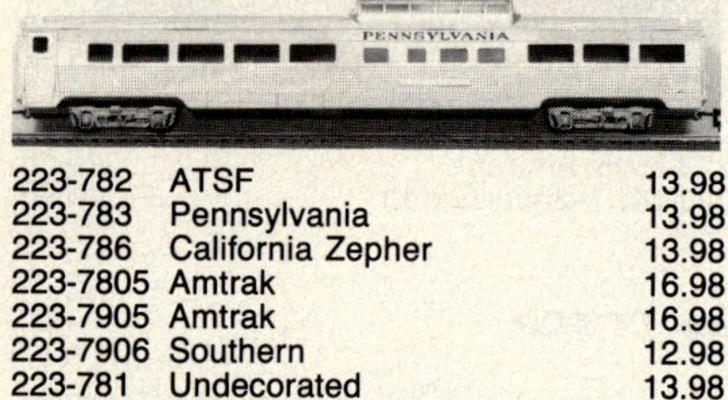

223-782	ATSF	13.98
223-783	Pennsylvania	13.98
223-786	California Zepher	13.98
223-7805	Amtrak	16.98
223-7905	Amtrak	16.98
223-7906	Southern	12.98
223-781	Undecorated	13.98

85' OBSERVATION

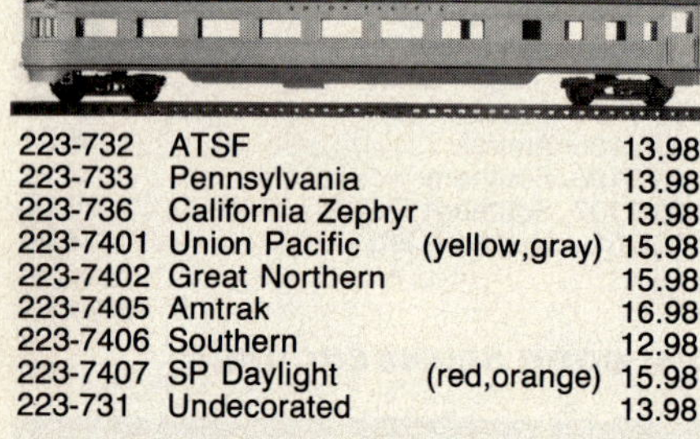

223-732	ATSF		13.98
223-733	Pennsylvania		13.98
223-736	California Zephyr		13.98
223-7401	Union Pacific	(yellow,gray)	15.98
223-7402	Great Northern		15.98
223-7405	Amtrak		16.98
223-7406	Southern		12.98
223-7407	SP Daylight	(red,orange)	15.98
223-731	Undecorated		13.98

85' DOME-OBSERVATION

223-772	ATSF	12.98
223-773	Pennsylvania	12.98
223-776	California Zepher	12.98
223-7801	Union Pacific	15.98
223-7802	Great Northern	15.98
223-7806	Southern	12.98
223-7807	Southern Pacific	15.98
223-771	Undecorated	12.98

85' 10-6 PULLMAN

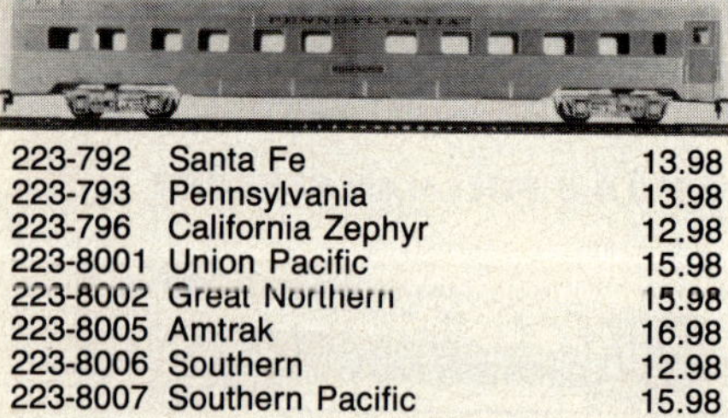

223-792	Santa Fe	13.98
223-793	Pennsylvania	13.98
223-796	California Zephyr	12.98
223-8001	Union Pacific	15.98
223-8002	Great Northern	15.98
223-8005	Amtrak	16.98
223-8006	Southern	12.98
223-8007	Southern Pacific	15.98

85' PASSENGER CAR SETS

Sets include 2 each coach, baggage, dome and observation cars.

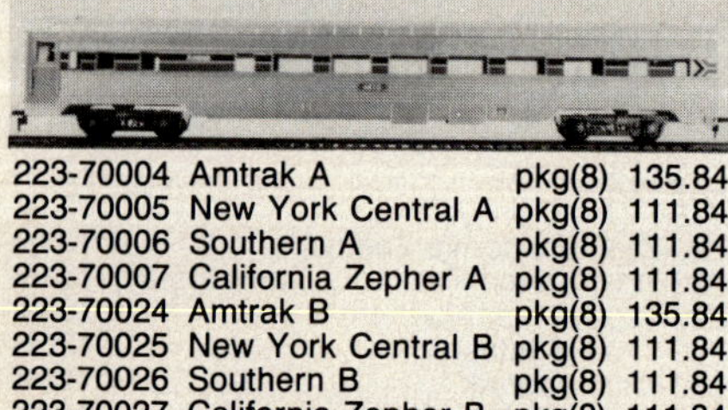

223-70004	Amtrak A	pkg(8)	135.84
223-70005	New York Central A	pkg(8)	111.84
223-70006	Southern A	pkg(8)	111.84
223-70007	California Zepher A	pkg(8)	111.84
223-70024	Amtrak B	pkg(8)	135.84
223-70025	New York Central B	pkg(8)	111.84
223-70026	Southern B	pkg(8)	111.84
223-70027	California Zepher B	pkg(8)	111.84

HO SCALE READY-TO-RUN

Ready-to-Run passenger cars feature molded plastic bodies; prepainted and lettered. Complete with trucks and horn-hook couplers.

OLD TIMER

"Old Timers" are prototypes of cars used on Western Railroads circa 1860.

47' COMBINE

160-72801	Union Pacific	7.00	160-72824 Central Pacific	7.00

47' COACH

160-72901	Union Pacific	7.00	160-72924 Central Pacific	7.00

85' AMFLEET

COACH

160-72205	Amtrak, lighted	16.00

FULL DOME COACH

160-71705	Amtrak, less lighting	14.00

Spectrum

(Division of Bachmann)

HO READY-TO-RUN

HEAVYWEIGHTS

BALTIMORE & OHIO

89044

160-89041	Combine #1447		19.95
160-89044	Diner Molly Pitcher		19.95
160-89042	Coach #5480	LTD QTY	19.95
160-89043	Coach #5482	LTD QTY	19.95
160-89045	Coach #5489		19.95
160-89046	Observation #900		19.95

GREAT NORTHERN ▬ LTD QTY ▬

160-89031	Combine #574	19.95
160-89034	Diner #1032/Minnesota	19.95
160-89032	Coach #961	19.95
160-89033	Coach #967	19.95
160-89035	Coach #958	19.95
160-89036	Observation #A10	19.95

PENNSYLVANIA

89115 **NEW**

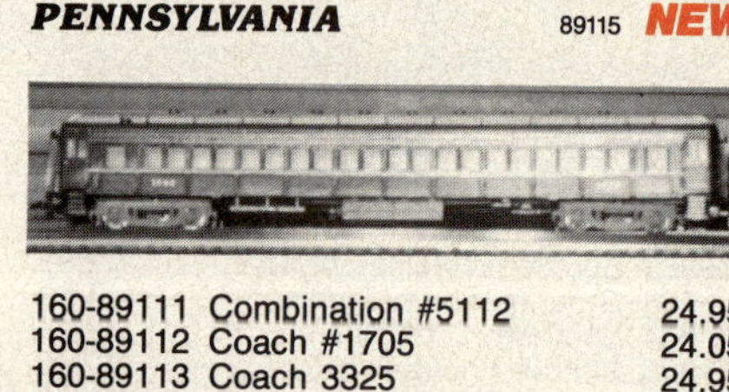

160-89111	Combination #5112	24.95
160-89112	Coach #1705	24.05
160-89113	Coach 3325	24.95
160-89114	Diner #4493	24.95
160-89115	Coach #1700	24.95
160-89116	Observation #7507	24.95

NEW YORK CENTRAL

160-89101	Combine #304	19.95
160-89104	Diner #636	19.95
160-89102	Coach #412/P&LE	19.95
160-89103	Coach #809	19.95
160-89105	Coach #964	19.95
160-89106	Observation Detroit	19.95

UNION PACIFIC ▬ LTD QTY ▬

160-89021	Combine #2514	19.95
160-89024	Diner #4051	19.95
160-89022	Coach #1086	19.95
160-89023	Coach #1114	19.95
160-89025	Coach #1128	19.95
160-89026	Observation #1505	19.95

International Hobby Corp.

HO SCALE
(1/87)
READY-TO-RUN

Ready-to-Run cars are correct scale length (85′, unless noted) and are prepainted. Heavyweights feature six-wheel Talgo trucks with horn-hook couplers; streamlines feature four-wheel. Most passenger car sets contain 8 cars; although the number of cars and type may vary.

HEAVYWEIGHTS — 1920

BALTIMORE & OHIO
(dark blue, gray)   6560

348-6560	Baggage Express	14.98
348-2808	72′ RPO Baggage	14.98
348-6048	Baggage	14.98
348-2767	Combine	14.98
348-2769	Diner	14.98
348-2790	Coach	14.98
348-2768	Pullman	14.98
348-2823	Duplex Sleeper	14.98
348-2770	Observation	14.98
348-9100	Passenger Set	119.98

BALTIMORE & OHIO
(dark green)   2692

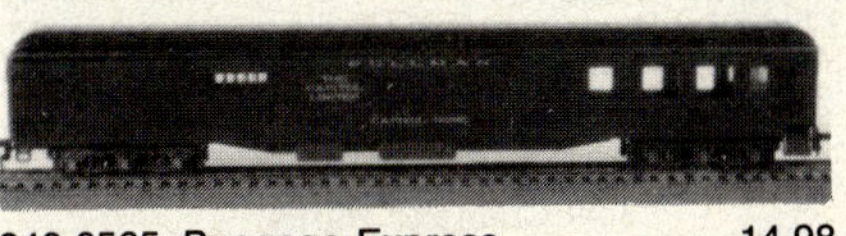

348-6565	Baggage Express	14.98
348-2696	72′ RPO Baggage	14.98
348-2692	Combine	14.98
348-2694	Diner	14.98
348-2792	Coach	14.98
348-2693	Pullman "Lincoln"	14.98
348-2697	Pullman "Washington"	14.98
348-2793	Duplex Sleeper	14.98
348-2695	Observation	14.98
348-9101	Passenger Set	119.98

BALTIMORE & OHIO "NATIONAL LTD"
(dark blue, gray)   6513

348-6555	Baggage Express	14.98
348-6508	72′ RPO Baggage	14.98
348-6511	Diner	14.98
348-6510	Coach	14.98
348-6512	Pullman	14.98
348-6513	Duplex Sleeper	14.98
348-6514	Observation	14.98
348-9102	Passenger Set	119.98

CANADIAN NATIONAL
(black, green)   2651

348-6546	Baggage Express	14.98
348-6593	72′ RPO Baggage	14.98
348-2649	Combine	14.98
348-2651	Diner	14.98
348-2811	Coach	14.98
348-6041	Coach	14.98
348-2650	Pullman	14.98
348-6592	Duplex Sleeper	14.98
348-2652	Observation	14.98
348-9103	Passenger Set	119.98

CANADIAN PACIFIC
(black, wine red)   2810

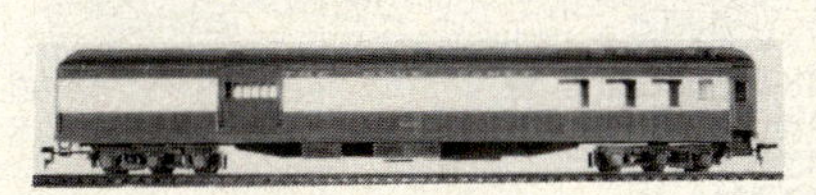

348-6547	Baggage Express	14.98
348-6525	72′ RPO Baggage	14.98
348-2629	Combine	14.98
348-2631	Diner	14.98
348-2810	Coach	14.98
348-2630	Pullman	14.98
348-6542	Duplex Sleeper	14.98
348-2632	Observation	14.98
348-9104	Passenger Set	119.98

CENTRAL OF NEW JERSEY "BLUE COMET"
(blue, cream)   2644

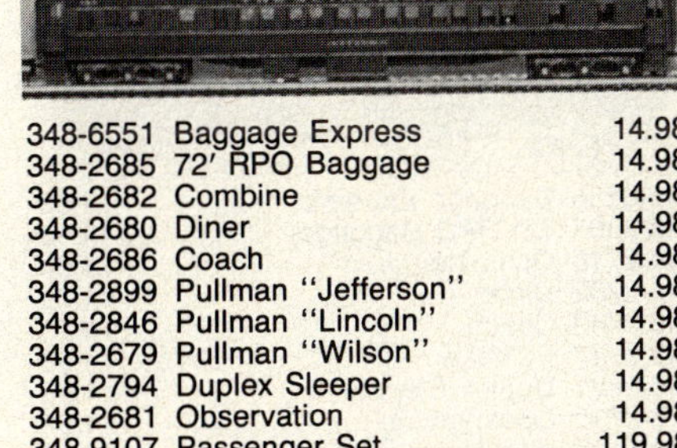

348-6002	Baggage Express	14.98
348-2730	72′ RPO Baggage	14.98
348-2644	Combine	14.98
348-2645	Diner	14.98
348-2648	Coach	14.98
348-2646	Pullman	14.98
348-2729	Duplex Sleeper	14.98
348-2647	Observation	14.98
348-9105	Passenger Set	119.98

CHESAPEAKE & OHIO
(blue, yellow, gray)   2953

348-6549	Baggage Express	14.98
348-2837	72′ RPO Baggage #114	14.98
348-6043	72′ RPO Baggage #117	14.98
348-2828	Combine	14.98
348-2835	Diner	14.98
348-2957	Coach	14.98
348-6044	Coach #206	14.98
348-2833	Pullman	14.98
348-2953	Duplex Sleeper	14.98
348-2830	Observation	14.98
348-9106	Passenger Set	119.98

CHICAGO & ALTON "ALTON LTD"
(red, maroon)   2899

348-6551	Baggage Express	14.98
348-2685	72′ RPO Baggage	14.98
348-2682	Combine	14.98
348-2680	Diner	14.98
348-2686	Coach	14.98
348-2899	Pullman "Jefferson"	14.98
348-2846	Pullman "Lincoln"	14.98
348-2679	Pullman "Wilson"	14.98
348-2794	Duplex Sleeper	14.98
348-2681	Observation	14.98
348-9107	Passenger Set	119.98

CHICAGO, MILWAUKEE & ST. PAUL "THE OLYMPIAN"
(orange, brown, black)   6016

348-6016	Baggage Express	14.98
348-6017	72′ RPO Baggage	14.98
348-6019	Diner	14.98
348-6018	Pullman	14.98
348-6020	Observation	14.98

DELAWARE & HUDSON
(gray, dark green)   6502

348-6554	Baggage Express	14.98
348-6501	72′ RPO Baggage	14.98
348-6502	Combine	14.98
348-6504	Diner	14.98
348-6503	Coach	14.98
348-6506	Duplex Sleeper	14.98
348-6505	Pullman	14.98
348-6507	Observation	14.98
348-9108	Passenger Set	119.98

DENVER & RIO GRANDE WESTERN
(yellow, black)   6575

348-6568	Baggage Express	14.98
348-6569	72′ RPO Baggage	14.98
348-6570	Combine	14.98
348-6572	Diner	14.98
348-6571	Coach	14.98
348-6573	Pullman	14.98
348-6574	Duplex Sleeper	14.98
348-6575	Observation	14.98
348-9154	Passenger Set	119.98

LACKAWANNA
(Pullman Green)   2784

348-6003	Baggage Express	14.98
348-2784	72′ RPO Baggage	14.98
348-2831	Combine	14.98
348-2836	Diner	14.98
348-2834	Coach	14.98
348-2839	Pullman	14.98
348-2841	Duplex Sleeper	14.98
348-2842	Observation	14.98
348-9109	Passenger Set	119.98

LEHIGH VALLEY
(Pullman Green)   6007

348-6007	Baggage Express	14.98
348-2320	72′ RPO Baggage	14.98
348-2321	Combine	14.98
348-2323	Diner	14.98
348-2322	Coach	14.98
348-2324	Pullman	14.98
348-2325	Duplex Sleeper	14.98
348-2326	Observation	14.98
348-9110	Passenger Set	119.98

International Hobby Corp.

HO SCALE (1/87) READY-TO-RUN

Ready-to-Run cars are correct scale length (85′, unless noted) and are prepainted. Heavyweights feature six-wheel Talgo trucks with horn-hook couplers; streamlines feature four-wheel. Most passenger car sets contain 8 cars; although the number of cars and type may vary.

LEHIGH VALLEY (cont)
(tuscan red) — 2385

348-2381	Combine	14.98
348-2380	72′ RPO Baggage	14.98
348-2383	Diner	14.98
348-2382	Coach	14.98
348-2384	Pullman	14.98
348-2385	Duplex Sleeper	14.98
348-2386	Observation	14.98
348-9111	Passenger Set	119.98

LONG ISLAND
(gray,orange) — 6073

348-6073	Coach	14.98
348-6074	Observation	14.98

MILWAUKEE ROAD
(orange,brown,black) — 2845

348-6550	Baggage Express	14.98
348-2847	72′ RPO Baggage	14.98
348-2838	Combine	14.98
348-2845	Diner	14.98
348-2958	Coach	14.98
348-2843	Pullman	14.98
348-6045	Duplex Sleeper	14.98
348-2954	Duplex Sleeper	14.98
348-2840	Observation	14.98
348-9112	Passenger Set	119.98

MISSOURI PACIFIC
(blue,gray) — 6025

348-6024	Baggage Express	14.98
348-6025	72′ RPO Baggage	14.98
348-6026	Combine	14.98
348-6028	Diner	14.98
348-6027	Coach	14.98
348-6029	Pullman	14.98
348-6030	Duplex Sleeper	14.98
348-6031	Observation	14.98
348-9060	Passenger Set	119.98

NEW HAVEN
(black,orange) — 2787

348-6548	Baggage Express	14.98
348-2809	72′ RPO Baggage	14.98
348-2785	Combine	14.98
348-2787	Diner	14.98
348-2791	Coach	14.98
348-2786	Pullman	14.98
348-2822	Duplex Sleeper	14.98
348-2788	Observation	14.98
348-9113	Passenger Set	119.98

NEW YORK CENTRAL
(pullman green) — 2728

348-6561	Baggage Express	14.98
348-2395	72′ RPO Baggage	14.98
348-2672	Combine	14.98
348-2673	Diner	14.98
348-2737	Coach	14.98
348-2674	Pullman	14.98
348-2728	Duplex Sleeper	14.98
348-2675	Observation	14.98
348-9114	Passenger Set	119.98

NEW YORK CENTRAL "MOTOR QUEEN TRAIN"
(brown,fawn,gold) — 6011

348-6008	Combine	14.98
348-6010	Diner	14.98
348-6009	Coach	14.98
348-6011	Observation	14.98

PENNSYLVANIA
(tuscan,black) — 2725

348-6567	Baggage Express	14.98
348-2806	72′ RPO Baggage	14.98
348-2723	Combine	14.98
348-2726	Diner	14.98
348-2738	Coach	14.98
348-2724	Pullman	14.98
348-6046	Pullman	14.98
348-6612	Pullman, "Lambs Club"	14.98
348-2820	Duplex Sleeper	14.98
348-2725	Observation	14.98
348-6615	Observation, "The Lady Bird Special"	14.98
348-9115	Passenger Set	119.98

PENNSYLVANIA WORK TRAIN
(yellow) — 2951

348-6004	Baggage Express	14.98
348-2951	Diner	14.98
348-2950	Pullman	14.98
348-2952	Duplex Sleeper	14.98
348-9116	Passenger Set	44.94

SANTA FE
(dark green) — 2717

348-6566	Baggage Express	14.98
348-2807	72′ RPO Baggage	14.98
348-2716	Combine	14.98
348-2732	Diner	14.98
348-2743	Coach	14.98
348-2717	Pullman	14.98
348-2821	Duplex Sleeper	14.98
348-2718	Observation	14.98
348-9118	Passenger Set	119.98

SOUTHERN RAILWAY
(2-tone green,black) — 2388

348-6553	Baggage Express	14.98
348-2387	72′ RPO Baggage	14.98
348-2388	Combine	14.98
348-2390	Diner	14.98
348-2389	Coach	14.98
348-2391	Pullman	14.98
348-2392	Duplex Sleeper	14.98
348-2393	Observation	14.98
348-9119	Passenger Set	119.98

SOUTHERN "CRESENT"
(2-tone green) — 2864

348-6564	Baggage Express	14.98
348-2894	72′ RPO Baggage	14.98
348-2889	Combine	14.98
348-2864	Diner	14.98
348-2876	Coach	14.98
348-2881	Pullman	14.98
348-2896	Duplex Sleeper	14.98
348-2887	Observation, "Joel Chandler Harris"	14.98
248-9120	Passenger Set	119.98

SOUTHERN PACIFIC
(Pullman Green) — 2867

348-6563	Baggage Express	14.98
348-2783	72′ RPO Baggage	14.98
348-2829	Combine	14.98
348-2867	Diner	14.98
348-2866	Coach	14.98
348-2882	Pullman	14.98
348-2883	Duplex Sleeper	14.98
348-2832	Observation	14.98
348-9121	Passenger Set	119.98

UNION PACIFIC
(yellow) — 6552

348-6552	Baggage Express	14.98
348-2373	72′ RPO Baggage	14.98
348-2374	Combine	14.98
348-2376	Diner	14.98
348-2375	Coach	14.98
348-2377	Pullman	14.98
348-2378	Duplex Sleeper	14.98
348-2379	Observation	14.98
348-9123	Passenger Set	119.98

UNION PACIFIC "OVERLAND"
(2-tone gray) — 2688

348-6562	Baggage Express	14.98
348-2789	72′ RPO Baggage	14.98
348-2690	Combine	14.98
348-2656	Diner	14.98
348-2688	Coach	14.98
348-2691	Pullman	14.98
348-2844	Duplex Sleeper	14.98
348-2657	Observation	14.98
348-9122	Passenger Set	119.98

International Hobby Corp.

HO SCALE (1/87) READY-TO-RUN

Ready-to-Run cars are correct scale length (85', unless noted) and are prepainted. Heavyweights feature six-wheel Talgo trucks with horn-hook couplers; streamlines feature four-wheel. Most passenger car sets contain 8 cars; although the number of cars and type may vary.

WABASH
(blue,silver)   2613

348-6001	Baggage Express	14.98
348-2612	72' RPO Baggage	14.98
348-2609	Combine	14.98
348-2610	Diner	14.98
348-2611	Coach	14.98
348-2607	Pullman	14.98
348-2613	Duplex Sleeper	14.98
348-2608	Observation	14.98
348-9124	Passenger Set	119.98

UNDECORATED
(black)

348-6596	Baggage Express	12.98
348-6597	72' RPO Baggage	12.98
348-6598	Combine	12.98
348-6600	Diner	12.98
348-6599	Coach	12.98
348-6601	Pullman	12.98
348-6602	Duplex Sleeper	12.98
348-6603	Observation	12.98

STREAMLINERS — 1930

AMTRAK
(silver,red,blue)   2985

348-2986	Baggage	14.98
348-2983	72' RPO	14.98
348-2875	Diner	14.98
348-2984	Coach	14.98
348-2987	Vista Dome	14.98
348-2981	Roomette Sleeper	14.98
348-2985	Duplex Sleeper	14.98
348-2982	Observation	14.98
348-9125	Passenger Set	119.98

BALTIMORE & OHIO
(dark blue,gray)   2777

348-2827	Baggage Express	14.98
348-2774	72' RPO	14.98
348-2819	Diner	14.98
348-2776	Coach	14.98
348-2777	Vista Dome	14.98
348-2771	Roomette Sleeper	14.98
348-2803	Duplex Sleeper	14.98
348-2772	Observation	14.98
348-9126	Passenger Set	119.98

BALTIMORE & OHIO "NATIONAL LTD"
(dark blue,gray)   6517

348-6509	Combine	14.98
348-6515	Coach	14.98
348-6517	Diner	14.98
348-6516	Duplex Sleeper	14.98
348-6518	Observation	14.98
348-9127	Passenger Set	19.98

BURLINGTON NORTHERN
(green,white)   2955

348-2955	Baggage	14.98
348-2851	72' RPO	14.98
348-2756	Diner	14.98
348-2853	Coach	14.98
348-2852	Vista Dome	14.98
348-2850	Roomette Sleeper	14.98
348-2848	Duplex Sleeper	14.98
348-2849	Observation	14.98
348-9128	Passenger Set	119.98

CANADIAN NATIONAL
(black,gray)   2615

348-6595	Baggage	14.98
348-2614	72' RPO	14.98
348-6545	Diner	14.98
348-6047	Coach	14.98
348-6543	Coach	14.98
348-2991	Vista Dome	14.98
348-2615	Roomette Sleeper	14.98
348-6544	Duplex Sleeper	14.98
348-2616	Observation	14.98
348-9150	Passenger Set	119.98

CANADIAN "VIA"
(yellow,blue)   **NEW**   6034

348-6032	Baggage	14.98
348-6033	72' RPO	14.98
348-6038	Diner	14.98
348-6034	Coach	14.98
348-6036	Vista Dome	14.98
348-6035	Roomette Sleeper	14.98
348-6037	Duplex Sleeper	14.98
348-6039	Observation	14.98
348-9151	Passenger Set	119.98

CHICAGO & NORTH WESTERN
(yellow,green)   2602

348-2603	Baggage Express	14.98
348-2605	72' RPO	14.98
348-2890	Diner	14.98
348-2601	Coach	14.98
348-2606	Vista Dome	14.98
348-26001	Roomette Sleeper	14.98
348-2604	Duplex Sleeper	14.98
348-2602	Observation	14.98
348-9129	Passenger Set	14.98

DENVER & RIO GRANDE WESTERN
(yellow,black)   2620

348-2626	Baggage Express	14.98
348-2622	72' RPO	14.98
348-2893	Diner	14.98
348-2623	Coach	14.98
348-2624	Vista Dome	14.98
348-2620	Roomette Sleeper	14.98
348-2625	Duplex Sleeper	14.98
348-2621	Observation	14.98
348-9130	Passenger Set	119.98

EAST WIND
(yellow,silver)   5632

348-5632	Baggage	14.98
348-5631	Diner	14.98
348-5633	Coach	14.98
348-5634	Observation	14.98

ERIE
(2-tone green)   2353

348-2350	Baggage	14.98
348-2351	72' RPO	14.98
348-2355	Diner	14.98
348-2352	Coach	14.98
348-6040	Coach #2714	14.98
348-2353	Roomette	14.98
348-2354	Duplex Sleeper "Spirit of Youngstown"	14.98
348-2341	Duplex Sleeper "Pride of Youngstown"	14.98
348-2356	Observation	14.98
348-9131	Passenger Set	119.98

GREAT NORTHERN
(brown,orange,gold)

348-2665	Baggage	14.98
348-2666	72' RPO	14.98
348-2892	Diner	14.98
348-2668	Coach	14.98
348-2671	Vista Dome	14.98
348-2667	Roomette Sleeper	14.98
348-2669	Duplex Sleeper	14.98
348-2670	Observation	14.98
348-9133	Passenger Set	119.98

(sky blue)

348-6534	Baggage	14.98
348-6535	72' RPO	14.98
348-6540	Diner	14.98
348-6536	Coach	14.98
348-6538	Vista Dome	14.98
348-6537	Roomette Sleeper	14.98
348-6539	Duplex Sleeper	14.98
348-6541	Observation	14.98
348-9134	Passenger Set	119.98

GULF, MOBILE & OHIO
(red,maroon)   2366

348-2365	Baggage	14.98
348-2366	72' RPO	14.98
348-2372	Diner	14.98
348-2367	Coach	14.98
348-2369	Vista Dome	14.98
348-2368	Roomette Sleeper	14.98
348-2370	Duplex Sleeper	14.98
348-2371	Observation	14.98
348-9135	Passenger Set	119.98

ILLINOIS CENTRAL
(dark brown,orange)   2860

348-2884	Baggage	14.98
348-2860	72' RPO	14.98
348-2815	Diner	14.98
348-2879	Coach	14.98
348-2872	Vista Dome	14.98
348-2870	Roomette Sleeper	14.98
348-2862	Duplex Sleeper	14.98
348-2868	Observation	14.98
348-9136	Passenger Set	119.98

International Hobby Corp.

HO SCALE (1/87) READY-TO-RUN

Ready-to-Run cars are correct scale length (85', unless noted) and are prepainted. Heavyweights feature six-wheel Talgo trucks with horn-hook couplers; streamlines feature four-wheel. Most passenger car sets contain 8 cars; although the number of cars and type may vary.

KANSAS CITY SOUTHERN
(black, yellow, red)   2330

348-2327	Baggage	14.98
348-2328	72' RPO	14.98
348-2333	Diner	14.98
348-2329	Coach	14.98
348-2331	Vista Dome	14.98
348-2330	Roomette Sleeper	14.98
348-2332	Duplex Sleeper	14.98
348-2334	Observation	14.98
348-9137	Passenger Set	119.98

LACKAWANNA
(maroon, gray)   2979

348-2980	Baggage	14.98
348-2977	72' RPO	14.98
348-2757	Diner	14.98
348-2978	Coach	14.98
348-2874	Vista Dome	14.98
348-2975	Sleeper	14.98
348-2979	Duplex Sleeper	14.98
348-2976	Observation	14.98
348-9138	Passenger Set	119.98

LOUISVILLE & NASHVILLE
(dark blue)   6057

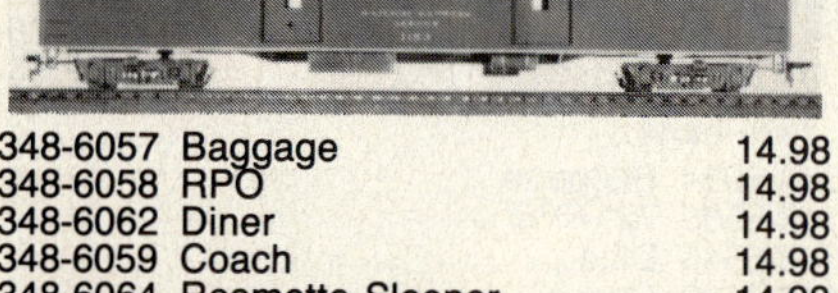

348-6057	Baggage	14.98
348-6058	RPO	14.98
348-6062	Diner	14.98
348-6059	Coach	14.98
348-6064	Roomette Sleeper	14.98
348-6061	Duplex Sleeper	14.98
348-6063	Tail Car	14.98
348-9157	Passenger Set	119.98

MISSOURI PACIFIC "GOLDEN EAGLE"
(blue, gray)   2749

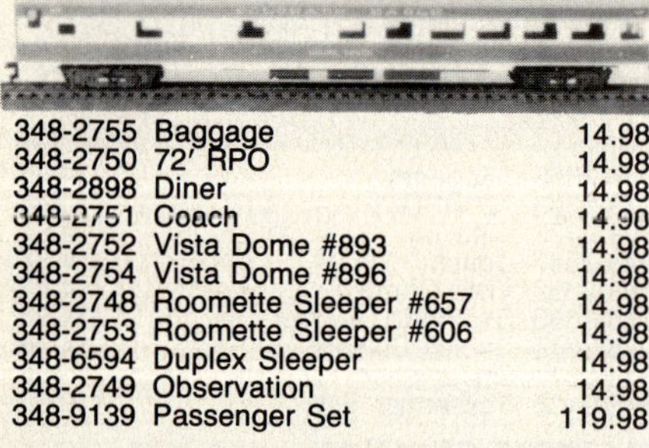

348-2755	Baggage	14.98
348-2750	72' RPO	14.98
348-2898	Diner	14.98
348-2751	Coach	14.90
348-2752	Vista Dome #893	14.98
348-2754	Vista Dome #896	14.98
348-2748	Roomette Sleeper #657	14.98
348-2753	Roomette Sleeper #606	14.98
348-6594	Duplex Sleeper	14.98
348-2749	Observation	14.98
348-9139	Passenger Set	119.98

NEW JERSEY TRANSIT
(silver, blue, purple)   6519

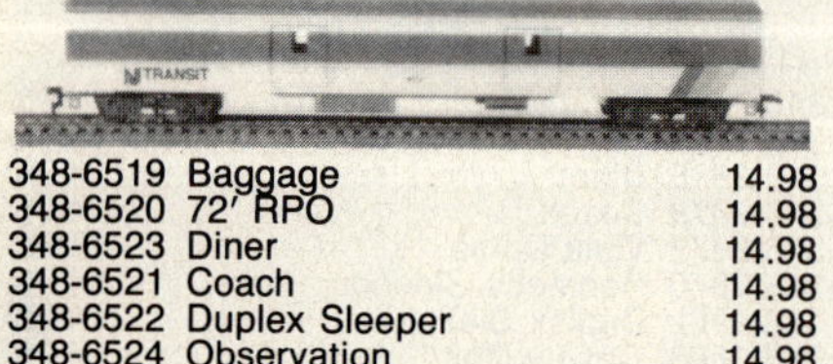

348-6519	Baggage	14.98
348-6520	72' RPO	14.98
348-6523	Diner	14.98
348-6521	Coach	14.98
348-6522	Duplex Sleeper	14.98
348-6524	Observation	14.98
348-9140	Passenger Set	119.98

NEW YORK CENTRAL
(2-tone gray, multi-stripe, light gray)   2708

348-2707	Baggage	14.98
348-2708	72' RPO	14.98
348-2813	Diner	14.98
348-2710	Coach	14.98
348-2687	Vista Dome	14.98
348-2709	Roomette Sleeper	14.98
348-2711	Duplex Sleeper	14.98
348-2712	Observation	14.98
348-9141	Passenger Set	119.98

NEW YORK CENTRAL
(dark gray, solid stripe)

348-6049	Baggage	14.98
348-6050	RPO	14.98
348-6055	Diner	14.98
348-6051	Coach	14.98
348-6053	Vista Dome	14.98
348-6052	Roomette	14.98
348-6054	Duplex Sleeper	14.98
348-6056	Tail Car	14.98
348-9156	Passenger Set	119.98

NORFOLK & WESTERN "THE PAWHATTAN ARROW"
(maroon, gold)   2891

348-2658	Baggage	14.98
348-2659	72' RPO	14.98
348-2891	Diner	14.98
348-2661	Coach	14.98
348-2664	Vista Dome	14.98
348-2660	Roomette Sleeper	14.98
348-2662	Duplex Sleeper	14.98
348-2663	Observation	14.98
348-9142	Passenger Set	119.98

NORTHERN PACIFIC "NORTH COAST LTD"
(green, olive, gray)   2973

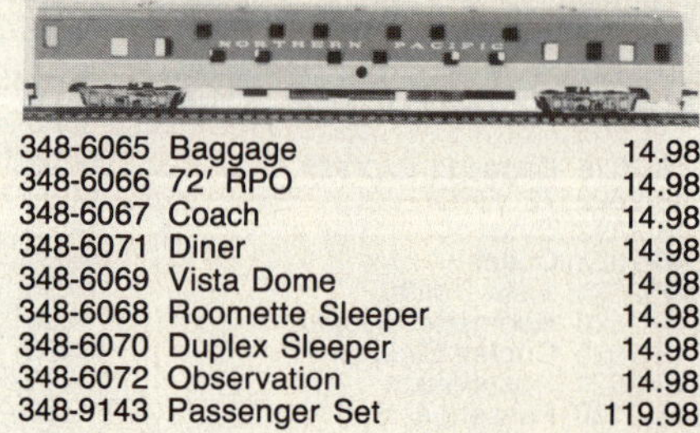

348-2825	Baggage	14.98
348-2773	72' RPO	14.98
348-2817	Diner	14.98
348-2775	Coach	14.98
348-2764	Vista Dome	14.98
348-2765	Roomette Sleeper	14.98
348-2804	Duplex Sleeper	14.98
348-2766	Observation	14.98
348-9155	Passenger Set	119.98

NORTHERN PACIFIC
(2-tone green)   6070

348-6065	Baggage	14.98
348-6066	72' RPO	14.98
348-6067	Coach	14.98
348-6071	Diner	14.98
348-6069	Vista Dome	14.98
348-6068	Roomette Sleeper	14.98
348-6070	Duplex Sleeper	14.98
348-6072	Observation	14.98
348-9143	Passenger Set	119.98

PENNSYLVANIA
(tuscan)   6616

348-2824	Baggage	14.98
348-2741	72' RPO	14.98
348-2816	Diner	14.98
348-2761	Coach	14.98
348-2795	Vista Dome	14.98
348-2746	Roomette Sleeper	14.98
348-6616	Roomette Sleeper "Colonial House"	14.98
348-6617	Roomette, "Imperial Loch"	14.98
348-6618	Roomette, "Imperial Park"	14.98
348-6619	Roomette, "Buffalo Rapids"	14.98
348-2802	Duplex Sleeper	14.98
348-6613	Pullman, "Blue Rapids"	14.98
348-2745	Observation	14.98
348-2747	Observation "Mountain View"	14.98
348-9144	Passenger Set	119.98

RICHMOND, FREDRICKSBURG & POTOMAC
(purple, 2-tone gray)

348-6584	Baggage	14.98
348-6585	72' RPO	14.98
348-6590	Diner	14.98
348-6586	Coach	14.98
348-6588	Vista Dome	14.98
348-6587	Roomette Sleeper	14.98
348-6589	Duplex Sleeper	14.98
348-6591	Observation	14.98
348-9152	Passenger Set	119.98

ROCK ISLAND
(red, gray, yellow)   6578

348-6576	Baggage	14.98
348-6577	72' RPO	14.98
348-6582	Diner	14.98
348-6578	Coach	14.98
348-6580	Vista Dome	14.98
348-6579	Roomette Sleeper	14.98
348-6581	Duplex Sleeper	14.98
348-6583	Observation	14.98
348-9153	Passenger Set	119.98

ROCK ISLAND "GOLDEN STATE"
(red, silver)   6526

348-6526	Baggage	14.98
348-6527	72' RPO	14.98
348-6502	Diner	14.90
348-6528	Chair Coach	14.98
348-6529	Roomette Sleeper	14.98
348-6530	Vista Dome	14.98
348-6531	Duplex Sleeper	14.98
348-6533	Observation	14.98
348-9132	Passenger Set	119.98

SANTA FE "SUPER CHIEF"
(blue, silver)   2635

348-2640	Baggage	14.98
348-2636	72' RPO	14.98
348-2812	Diner #1488	14.98
348-6042	Diner #1486	14.98
348-2637	Coach	14.98
348-2638	Vista Dome #893	14.98
348-2634	Roomette Sleeper #657	14.98
348-2639	Duplex Sleeper	14.98
348-2635	Observation	14.98
348-9145	Passenger Set	119.98

International Hobby Corp.

HO SCALE (1/87) READY-TO-RUN

Ready-to-Run cars are correct scale length (85', unless noted) and are prepainted. Heavyweights feature six-wheel Talgo trucks with horn-hook couplers; streamlines feature four-wheel. Most passenger car sets contain 8 cars; although the number of cars and type may vary.

SOUTHERN PACIFIC "DAYLIGHT"
(orange,red) 2956

348-2956	Baggage	14.98
348-2857	72' RPO	14.98
348-2394	Diner	14.98
348-2859	Coach	14.98
348-2858	Vista Dome #893	14.98
348-2856	Roomette Sleeper #657	14.98
348-2854	Duplex Sleeper	14.98
348-2855	Observation	14.98
348-9146	Passenger Set	119.98

SOUTHERN PACIFIC
(silver,red) 2362

348-2357	Baggage	14.98
348-2358	72' RPO Baggage	14.98
348-2364	Diner	14.98
348-2359	Coach	14.98
348-2361	Vista Dome	14.98
348-2360	Roomette Sleeper	14.98
348-2342	Duplex Sleeper "Golden Flake"	14.98
348-2362	Duplex Sleeper "Golden Down"	14.98
348-2363	Observation	14.98
348-9147	Passenger Set	119.98

UNION PACIFIC
(yellow,gray) 2805

348-2826	Baggage	14.98
348-2760	72' RPO	14.98
348-2818	Diner	14.98
348-2762	Coach	14.98
348-2763	Vista Dome	14.98
348-2758	Roomette Sleeper	14.98
348-2805	Duplex Sleeper	14.98
348-2759	Observation	14.98
348-9149	Passenger Set	119.98

UNION PACIFIC "OVERLAND"
(2-tone gray) 2654

348-2641	Baggage	14.98
348-2653	72' RPO	14.98
348-2814	Diner	14.98
348-2654	Coach	14.98
348-2642	Roomette Sleeper	14.98
348-2689	Vista Dome	14.98
348-2655	Duplex Sleeper	14.98
348-2643	Observation	14.98
348-9148	Passenger Set	119.98

UNDECORATED
(black) 6605

348-6604	Baggage	12.98
348-6605	72' RPO	12.98
348-6610	Diner	12.98
348-6606	Coach	12.98
348-6608	Vista Dome	12.98
348-6607	Roomette Sleeper	12.98
348-6609	Duplex Sleeper	12.98
348-6611	Observation	12.98

BUDD STREAMLINERS — 1940

AMTRAK
(silver,red,blue) 6620

348-6620	Diner	14.98
348-6621	Coach	14.98
348-6622	Roomette	14.98
348-6623	Observation	14.98

ATLANTIC COASTLINE
(silver,purple)

348-6631	Coach	14.98
348-6632	Roomette Sleeper	14.98
348-6633	Observation	14.98

BALTIMORE & OHIO
(silver,blue,gray) 6641

348-6640	Diner	14.98
348-6641	Coach	14.98
348-6642	Roomette Sleeper	14.98
348-6643	Observation	14.98

BOSTON & MAINE
(silver) 6840

348-6840	Diner	14.98
348-6841	Coach	14.98
348-6842	Roomette	14.98
348-6843	Observation	14.98

BURLINGTON
6652

348-6650	Diner	14.98
348-6651	Coach	14.98
348-6652	Roomette	14.98
348-6653	Observation	14.98

CALIFORNIA ZEPHYR
(silver) 6661

348-6660	Diner	14.98
348-6661	Coach	14.98
348-6662	Roomette Sleeper	14.98
348-6663	Observation	14.98

CANADIAN PACIFIC
(silver,purple) 6670

348-6670	Diner	14.98
348-6671	Coach	14.98
348-6672	Roomette	14.98
348-6673	Observation	14.98

CHESAPEAKE & OHIO
(silver,blue,yellow,black) 6681

348-6680	Diner	14.98
348-6681	Coach	14.98
348-6682	Roomette	14.98
348-6683	Observation	14.98

CHESAPEAKE & OHIO PERE MARQUETTE

348-6740	Diner	14.98
348-6741	Coach	14.98
348-6742	Roomette	14.98
348-6743	Observation	14.98

FLORIDA EAST COAST
(red,silver) 6693

348-6690	Diner	14.98
348-6691	Coach	14.98
348-6692	Roomette	14.98
348-6693	Observation	14.98

FRISCO
(red,silver) 6703

348-6700	Diner	14.98
348-6701	Coach	14.98
348-6702	Roomette	14.98
348-6703	Observation	14.98

LOUISVILLE & NASHVILLE
(silver) 6851

348-6850	Diner	14.98
348-6851	Coach	14.98
348-6852	Roomette	14.98
348-6853	Observation	14.98

NEW YORK CENTRAL
(silver) 6712

348-6710	Diner	14.98
348-6711	Coach	14.98
348-6712	Roomette	14.98
348-6713	Observation	14.98

NYC "EMPIRE STATE EXPRESS"
Prepainted and lettered corrugated side panels.
(silver) 6557

348-6556	Diner	14.98
348-6557	Coach	14.98
348-6558	Roomette	14.98
348-6559	Observation	14.98

International Hobby Corp.
HO SCALE (1/87) READY-TO-RUN

Ready-to-Run cars are correct scale length (85', unless noted) and are prepainted. Heavyweights feature six-wheel Talgo trucks with horn-hook couplers; streamlines feature four-wheel. Most passenger car sets contain 8 cars; although the number of cars and type may vary.

PENNSYLVANIA "FLEET OF MODERNIZATION"
(2-tone, tuscan)   6862

348-6860	Diner	14.98
348-6861	Coach	14.98
348-6862	Roomette	14.98
348-6863	Observation	14.98

PENNSYLVANIA "CONGRESSIONAL"
(silver, brown)   6733

348-6730	Diner	14.98
348-6731	Coach	14.98
348-6732	Roomette	14.98
348-6614	Pullman "John Hancock"	14.98
348-6733	Observation	14.98

READING
(silver)

348-6750	Diner	14.98
348-6751	Coach	14.98
348-6752	Roomette	14.98
348-6753	Observation	14.98

ROCK ISLAND
(silver, red)   6761

348-6760	Diner	14.98
348-6761	Coach	14.98
348-6762	Roomette	14.98
348-6763	Observation	14.98

SANTA FE
(silver)   6773

348-6770	Diner	14.98
348-6771	Coach	14.98
348-6772	Roomette	14.98
348-6773	Observation	14.98

SEABOARD
(silver)   6783

348-6780	Diner	14.98
348-6781	Coach	14.98
348-6782	Roomette	14.98
348-6783	Observation	14.98

SOUTHERN PACIFIC
(silver, red)   6790

348-6790	Diner	14.98
348-6791	Coach	14.98
348-6792	Roomette	14.98
348-6793	Observation	14.98

SOUTHERN
(silver)   6801

348-6800	Diner	14.98
348-6801	Coach	14.98
348-6802	Roomette	14.98
348-6803	Observation	14.98

TEXAS SPECIAL
(silver)   6810

348-6810	Diner	14.98
348-6811	Coach	14.98
348-6812	Roomette	14.98
348-6813	Observation	14.98

UNION PACIFIC
(yellow, gray)   6822

348-6820	Diner	14.98
348-6821	Coach	14.98
348-6822	Roomette	14.98
348-6823	Observation	14.98

WABASH

348-6830	Diner	14.98
348-6831	Coach	14.98
348-6832	Roomette	14.98
348-6833	Observation	14.98

ACCESSORIES
PASSENGER CAR INTERIORS
Easy-to-install, one-piece molded plastic, unpainted.

HEAVYWEIGHT   83172

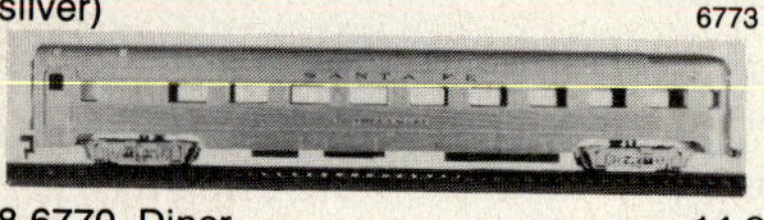

348-9009	Baggage	4.98
348-85822	Heavyweight Diner	4.98
348-9005	Coach	4.98
348-83152	Combine	2.98
348-83162	Pullman	4.98
348-83172	Observation	4.98

STREAMLINE

348-20977	Diner	4.98
348-20140	Chair Coach	4.98
348-9648	Vista Dome	5.98
348-9052	Roomette Sleeper	4.98
348-9051	Observation	4.98

DIAPHRAGMS
Plastic diaphragm for use with all Passenger cars.

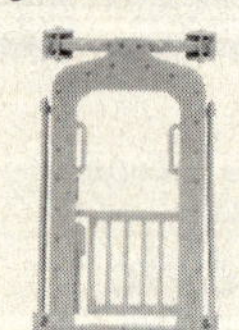

348-6060
pair 3.98

WALTHERS
HO SCALE (1/87)

LIGHTING KITS

There is nothing quite as impressive as a train of passenger cars, complete with lights, winding over a darkened layout. Install one and you'll agree that interior details provide the final touch of realism to your layout.

IMPORTANT: To get electrical contact, you MUST use metal wheels on metal axles, insulated on one side only. If car body is metal, truck must be insulated from body. You cannot pick up electrical current with plastic wheels or with wheels insulated on both sides. One car equipped for pickup can be used to light an entire train by using feeder wires.

CAR LIGHTING KITS

Easily installed, these insulated sockets can be cemented directly to metal, plastic or wood roof. Milk white tubular bulbs fit snugly out of the way of interior details, give uniform diffuse lighting over a large area. Wired as directed, bulbs give realistic illumination lasting for hundreds and hundreds of hours. Kits contain bulbs, sockets and wiring diagrams.

| 933-717 | Standard Kit, 2 Bulbs | 5.98 |

Two 942-352 16v bulbs included

| 933-963 | Lighting Kit, 1 Bulb | 3.98 |

The interior details of this car are highlighted by combining standard and deluxe lighting kits.

Use GOO® to attach socket to underside of roof.

SERIES WIRING DIAGRAM FOR 933-717 2-BULB KIT

Uses 942-352 16v bulbs for best results on track voltages ranging from 10v to 24v AC or DC.

ACCESSORIES

DIAPHRAGMS

Diaphragm
933-429   pr 2.98
folded bellows
w/vinyl striker plate

Black Rubber
Diaphragm
933-977   pr 2.98

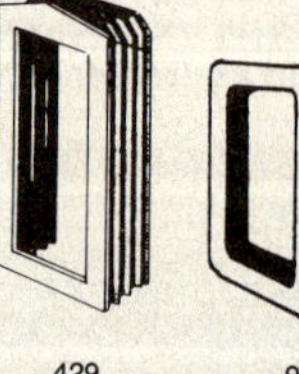
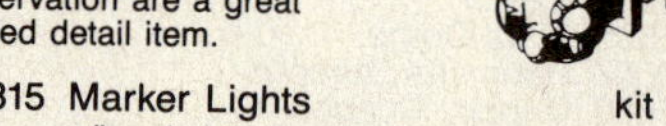

MARKER LIGHT KITS
Marker lamps for your observation are a great added detail item.

| 933-815 | Marker Lights | kit 2.98 |

w/bracket & Jewels

MANTUA

HO SCALE READY-TO-RUN
Aluminum bodies have illuminated interior with die cast highly detailed trucks.

VINTAGE CARS
Super-detailed reproductions of old time cars. Features planking, window frames and doors in high relief, and decorated in bright colors with contrasting lettering. Steps, platforms and undergear are in black.

1860 COMBINE
455-718020	Pennsylvania **LTD QTY**	8.25
455-718044	Western & Atlantic	8.25

STREAMLINE CARS
PENNSYLVANIA CONGRESSIONAL LTD **NEW**

455-224171 Diner Car #4624 66.99

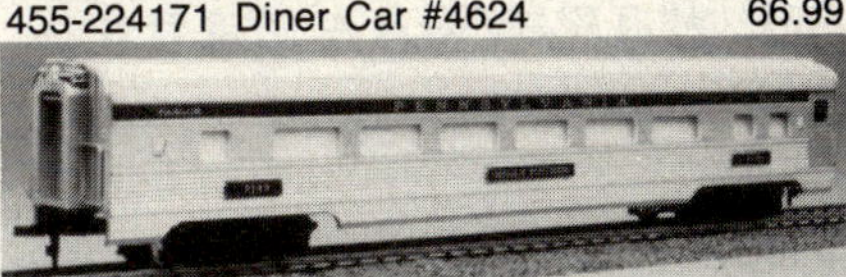
455-223171 Molly Pitcher Coach Car 66.99

455-223180 Betsy Ross Coach Car 66.99

455-225171 Thomas A. Edison Conference Car 66.99

455-226171 Alexander Hamilton Observation Car 77.99

ROCK ISLAND & PACIFIC GOLDEN STATE LTD.

455-224058 Golden Banquet Dining Car 66.99

455-224240 Golden Goblet Tavern Car **NEW** 66.99

455-225240 Golden Outlook Lounge Car **NEW** 66.99

455-223058 Golden Bell Coach Car 66.99

455-225058 Golden Locket Room Car 66.99

455-226058 Golden Vista Observation Car 77.99

Keil-Line Models

HO SCALE (1/87) CRAFT TRAIN KITS
85' BI-LEVEL COACHES

382-700	C&NW	25.95

Kits contain wood roof and floor sections, pre-lettered and painted plastic sides, cast metal ends, doors, trucks and details and dry transfer car numbers and ventilater grill. Includes RP25NS wheels and axles. Coupler pocket mounting permits cars to operate around tight radius. Use either Horn Hook or Kadee couplers.

382-701	C&NW Cab	25.95

Same as #700.

382-708	SP (gray)	26.95

Same as #700 plus: Dry transfer name. Extra dry transfer silver lettering and stripes are included to make either two-tone gray (1955), or the newer all-gray scheme.

382-709	RTA	26.95
382-710	RTA Cab	26.95
382-715	SP (two-tone gray)	26.95

Same as #708.

N.J. International

HO SCALE (1/87) CRAFT TRAIN KITS

All brass kits are designed to be soldered or glued together. Each kit includes enough material for one car, with all etching, punching and forming already completed. Includes centersill, bolsters and Kadee compatible coupler mounting pads. Less trucks, couplers and underbody detail.

P70 HEAVYWEIGHT COACHES

prototype photo

525-877178	Long Island, 1930 Era	227.14
525-877179	Long Island, 1950 Era	227.14

POC70R OBSERVATION CARS
525-877176	PRR, 1940 Era	198.59

D70CR TWO CAR COUPLET PENNSYLVANIA

prototype photo

525-877471	1939 Diner-Ktn-Dorm	342.78
525-877472	1939 Diner-Ktn-Lunch	342.78
525-877474	1943 Diner-Ktn-Lunch	342.78

A sunny Monday morning finds GE 44 Tonner #4 at the fuel pumps. Bob Boudreau repainted the Bachmann Spectrum Series loco for his Lomax Lumber Company. The logging camp features a Welding Shop built from a Railroad Avenue kit and numerous scratchbuilt structures. Completing the scene are vehicles from Wheel Works, Tyco and Woodland Scenics. *Models and Photo by Bob Boudreau*

HO SCALE (1/87) EASY-TO-BUILD KITS

Model Die Casting "Roundhouse" kits are easy to assemble. Molded plastic bodies are prepainted and lettered. Kits come complete with underbody details, trucks and couplers.

30' OVERTON CAR

COACH   each 7.98

480-3702	Denver & Rio Grande Western	
480-3704	Northern Pacific	(grn,silver)
480-3705	Central Pacific RR	(pullman grn)
480-3706	Pennsylvania RR	(maroon,cream)
480-3707	D&RGW (Silverton)	
480-3708	Sierra Railroad	
480-3709	Baltimore and Ohio	
480-3710	Virginia & Truckee	(grn,ylw)
480-3700	Undecorated	each 7.50

COMBINE   each 7.98

480-3715	Sierra RR	
480-3716	Baltimore & Ohio	(blue,cream)
480-3717	Virginia & Truckee	(grn,ylw)
480-3722	D&RGW	(cream,red)
480-3723	Union Pacific	(Pullman Grn,cream)
480-3724	Northern Pacific	(grn,silver)
480-3725	Central Pacific	(pull grn,cream)
480-3726	Pennsylvania	(maroon,cream)
480-3720	Undecorated	each 7.50

BUSINESS   each 7.98

480-3727	D&RGW (Silverton)	(blk,ylw)
480-3728	Sierra RR	
480-3729	Baltimore & Ohio	
480-3732	D&RGW	(cream,red)
480-3733	Union Pacific	(Pullman Grn,cream)
480-3734	Northern Pacific	(grn,silver)
480-3735	Central Pacific	(pull grn,cream)
480-3736	Pennsylvania	(maroon,cream)
480-3737	Virginia & Truckee	(grn,ylw)
480-3730	Undecorated	each 7.50

BAGGAGE   each 7.98

480-3742	D&RGW	(cream,red)

480-3744	Northern Pacific	(grn,silver)
480-3745	Central Pacific	(pull grn,cream)
480-3746	Pennsylvania	(maroon,cream)
480-3747	D&RGW (Silverton)	(blk,ylw)
480-3748	Sierra RR	
480-3749	Baltimore & Ohio	
480-3750	Virginia & Truckee	
480-3740	Undecorated	each 7.50

SOUTHERN PACIFIC "DAYLIGHT OVERTON CARS   each 7.98 NEW
(Painted daylight red & orange,silver)

480-7732	Coach
480-7733	Combination
480-7734	Business
480-7735	Baggage

ASSORTMENTS   NEW
(Includes three each Coach, Combine, Business & Observation.)

480-819	Virginia & Truckee	pkg(12) 95.76
480-821	SP "Daylight" (red,orange,silver)	pkg(12) 95.76

50' PULLMAN CAR

Kits are prepainted, lettered and feature separate attaching hardware, hidden metal underbody weight, Delrin four wheel Pullman talgo trucks and couplers.

COACH   each 7.98

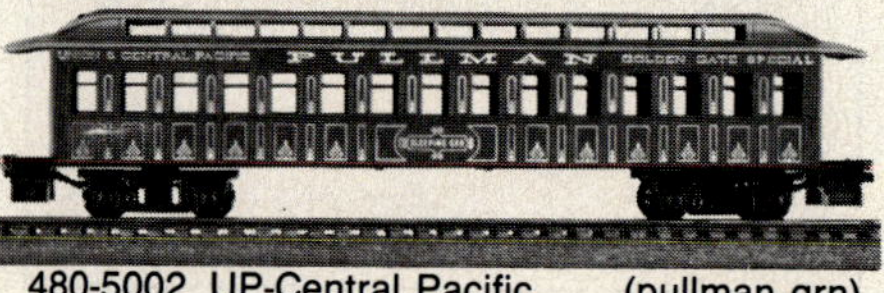

480-5002	UP-Central Pacific	(pullman grn)
480-5006	Pennsylvania	(maroon)
480-5007	Virginia & Truckee	(green,yellow)
480-5009	Baltimore & Ohio	(blue,cream)
480-5001	Undecorated	each 7.50

BAGGAGE   each 7.98

480-5020	Baltimore & Ohio	(blue,cream)
480-5022	UP-Central Pacific	(pullman grn)
480-5026	Pennsylvania	(maroon)
480-5027	Virginia & Truckee	(green,yellow)
480-5021	Undecorated	each 7.50

COMBINATION   each 7.98

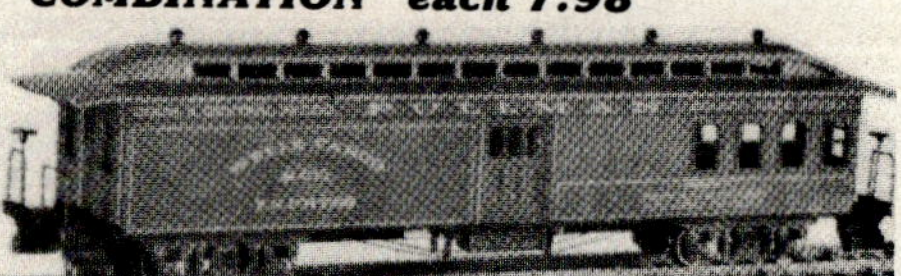

480-5060	UP-Central Pacific	(pull grn)

480-5061	Pennsylvania	(maroon)
480-5062	Virginia & Truckee	(green,yellow)
480-5065	Baltimore & Ohio	(blue,cream)
480-5035	Undecorated	each 7.50

BUSINESS CAR   each 7.98

480-5067	Pennsylvania	(maroon)
480-5068	Virginia & Truckee	(grn,ylw)
480-5071	Baltimore & Ohio	
480-5045	Undecorated	each 7.50

60' HARRIMAN CARS

RPO   each 8.50

480-6123	Pennsylvania	(tuscan,black)
480-6124	Union Pacific	(yellow,brown)
480-6126	Canadian National	(lt gray,black)
480-6127	Canadian Pacific	(maroon,black)
480-5980	Undecorated	each 7.98

BAGGAGE   each 8.50

480-6133	Pennsylvania	(tuscan,black)
480-6134	Union Pacific	(yellow,brown)
480-6136	Canadian National	(lt gray,black)
480-6137	Canadian Pacific	
480-6020	Undecorated	each 7.98

COMBINATION   each 8.50

480-6143	Pennsylvania	(tuscan,black)
480-6144	Union Pacific	(yellow,brown)
480-6146	Canadian National	(lt gray,black)
480-6147	Canadian Pacific	
480-5990	Undecorated	each 7.98

DINER   each 8.50

480-6153	Pennsylvania	(tuscan,black)
480-6154	Union Pacific	(yellow,brown)
480-6156	Canadian National	(lt gray,black)
480-6157	Canadian Pacific	(maroon,black)

HO SCALE (1/87) EASY-TO-BUILD KITS

Model Die Casting "Roundhouse" kits are easy to assemble. Molded plastic bodies are prepainted and lettered. Kits come complete with underbody details, trucks and couplers.

OBSERVATION   each 8.50

480-6163	Pennsylvania	(tuscan,black)
480-6166	Canadian National	(lt gray,black)
480-6167	Canadian Pacific	(maroon,black)
480-6164	Union Pacific	
480-6000	Undecorated	each 7.98

COACH   each 8.50

480-6173	Pennsylvania	(tuscan,black)
480-6174	Union Pacific	(yellow,brown)
480-6176	Canadian National	(lt gray,black)
480-6177	Canadian Pacific	(maroon,black)
480-6010	Undecorated	each 7.98

60' HARRIMAN CAR SETS

Sets include one each: Express Reefer, RPO, Baggage, Combination, Diner and Observation kits.

480-6103	Pennsylvania	pkg(6) 49.75
480-6104	Union Pacific	pkg(6) 47.50
480-6106	Canadian National	pkg(6) 47.25
480-6107	Canadian Pacific	pkg(6) 47.25

80' PULLMAN PALACE CARS, UNDECORATED

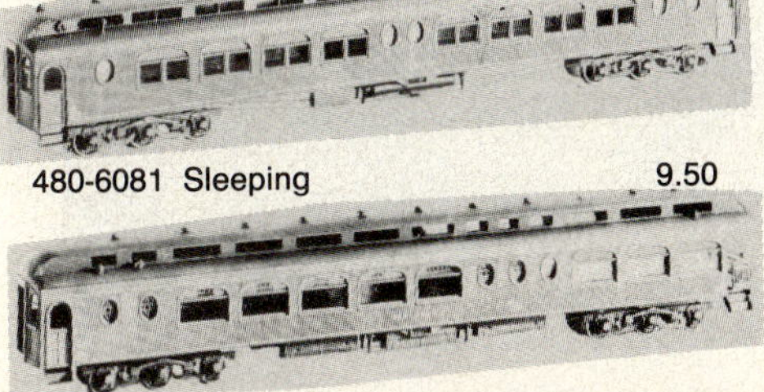

480-6081	Sleeping	9.50
480-6082	Observation	9.50
480-6083	Combination	9.50
480-6084	Dining	9.50

50' CLERESTORY OVERLAND SERIES
BUSINESS CAR

480-5231	Denver & Rio Grande Western	7.98
480-5230	Undecorated	7.50

SLEEPER

480-5251	D&RGW	7.98
480-5250	Undecorated	7.50

BAGGAGE CAR

480-5211	D&RGW	7.98
480-5210	Undecorated	7.50

MAIL CAR

480-5201	D&RGW	7.98
480-5200	Undecorated	7.50

ACCESSORIES

480-2999	50' Clerestory Roof	2.25

The local is getting closer, as we can hear him whistling for the logging road. It will be a few minutes before the train arrives at the Horseshoe Meadows depot, but a Jordan baggage wagon and several Preiser figures are already on the platform. After several years in On3, Chris Comport of Arlington, Texas, recently began building HO Scale dioramas using craftsman kits. Chris shortened the Evergreen Hill Designs depot and added a scratchbuilt retaining wall to keep things from sliding away.

Models and Photo by Chris Comport

Throttles set in run eight, a Canadian National freight roars past our vantage point. The lead GP38-2 is a reworked Athearn unit, featuring a Canadian Prototype Replicas (now out of production) Safety Cab. The head-end power was painted in Floquil colors and sports Accu-Cals lettering in this scene on Bob Boudreau's module.

Models and Photo by Bob Boudreau

Upgrading and rebuilding kept many passenger cars in service for years. For modelers, rebuilding cars with new parts makes it possible to create unique equipment. This prize-winning Pullman was rebuilt from an International Hobby Corporation car, by Don Valentine of Newbury, Vermont. New windows, air conditioning ducts and underbody parts from New England Rail Service were used in the conversion. The complete selection is listed in the Parts section.

*Photo by Lou Sassi,
courtesy New England Rail Service*

The strident blast of airhorns announces the departure of the Milwaukee wayfreight. The modified Athearn unit is just about done with it's work on this diorama built by John Harbeck of Cedarburg, Wisconsin. While numerous Magnuson buildings fill the foreground, the city skyline was modeled with Instant Horizons™ scenes.

Models and Photo by John Harbeck

TOMAR INDUSTRIES

HO SCALE (1/87) CRAFT TRAIN KITS

LIGHTED DRUMHEAD KITS each 9.95
DOUBLE KITS each 15.45

TOMAR kits are complete with cast and machined drum housing, 1.5 volt micro-miniature lamp, full color train sign, light diffuser, 4 diodes, hookup wire and complete instructions and illustrations. Double kits contain all parts for only one car but with two tailsigns. (Only a few roads used double tailsigns, such as kit #179 for the CB&Q Railroad).

TYPICAL APPLICATIONS

Rectangular housing mounted on streamlined observation car.

Round drumhead mounted on observation platform railings. (Also may use rectangular housing).

HW— Used on Heavyweight Trains (Older style heavy steel or wood cars)

LW— Used on Lightweight Trains (New style lightweight streamlined cars)

HOUSING STYLES & SHAPES

PENNSY KEYSTONE

SQUARE

SHORT ROUND DRUMHEAD

Used on observation car railings, tailgates and streamlined cars.

RECTANGULAR

(Horizontal mounting) Used on all types of tail end cars.

RECTANGULAR

(Vertical mounting) Used on all types of tail end cars.

ALASKA

Herald NG (HW round)
081-91

Herald (LW round)
081-89

ALGOMA CENTRAL

Algoma Central (HW round)
081-90

AMTRAK

129
770
771

081-129 Amtrak (LW rect)
081-770 Pere Marquette (LW rect)
081-771 Panama Ltd (LW rect)

772
774

081-772 Carolinian (LW rect)
081-773 Lake Shore Ltd (LW rect)
081-774 Abraham Lincoln (LW rect)

ATCHISON, TOPEKA & SANTA FE

97
100
118
101
95

081-97 Tulsan (LW round)
081-100 California Ltd (HW round)
081-118 California Ltd, Scout (HW round)
081-101 Chief (LW or HW round)
081-95 Chief (yellow) (LW round)

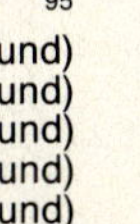

102
98
103
104
105

081-102 El Capitan (LW round)
081-98 El Capitan (yellow) (LW round)
081-103 X-Fare Deluxe (HW round)
081-104 Grand Canyon (HW round)
081-105 Ranger (HW round)

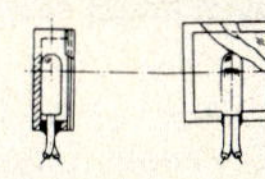
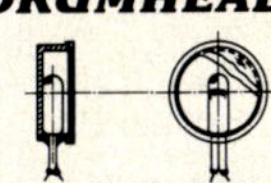
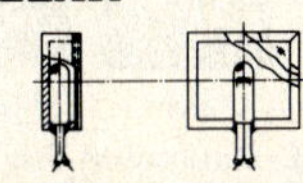
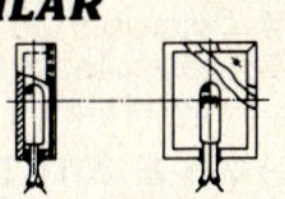

96
99
106
107
117

081-96 Ranger (LW round)
081-99 San Diegan (blue) (LW round)
081-106 San Diegan (LW round)
081-107 Super Chief (LW round)
081-117 Super Chief (purple) (LW round)

108
109
110
111
112

081-108 Conquistador (LW round)
081-109 Kansas City Chief (LW round)
081-110 San Francisco Chief (LW round)
081-111 Texas Chief (LW round)
081-112 Chicagoan (LW round)

113
114
115
116
119

081-113 Kansas Cityan (LW round)
081-114 Golden Gate (LW round)
081-115 Grand Canyon (LW round)
081-116 Super Chief/El Capitan (LW round)
081-119 Scout (1937) (HW round)

600
601
602
603
604

081-600 Oil Flyer (LW round)
081-601 El Pasoan (LW round)
081-602 Scout (LW round)
081-603 Herald (LW round)
081-604 Herald (HW square)

605
606
607
608
609

081-605 Chicago-KC-Flyer (HW round)
081-606 Texas Chief, Dallas (HW round)
081-607 Texas Chief, FW-H-G (HW round)
081-608 Valley Flyer (LW round)
081-609 Navajo **NEW** (HW round)

ATLANTIC COAST LINE

120
121
122
123
124

081-120 Florida Special (HW round)
081-121 The Champion (LW rect)
081-122 Florida Special (HW rect)
081-123 Gulf Coast Ltd (HW round)
081-124 Herald **NEW** (round)

BALTIMORE & OHIO

130
131
132
133
134

081-130 Capitol Ltd (HW round)
081-131 Capitol Ltd (LW rect)
081-132 Cincinnatian (LW rect)
081-133 Columbian (HW round)
081-134 National Ltd (HW round)

135
136
137
138
139

081-135 Royal Blue (LW round)
081-136 Shenandoah (LW round)
081-137 Capitol Ltd, 1929 (HW round)
081-138 National Ltd, 1929 (HW round)
081-139 Royal Blue (white) (LW rect)

720
721
722

081-720 Royal Blue (blue) (LW square)
081-721 National Ltd (LW rect)
081-722 Columbian (LW square)

723
724
725

081-723 Great Lakes (HW round)
081-724 Cinncinnatian (HW round)
081-725 Diplomat (HW round)

726
727
728

081-726 Royal Blue (HW round)
081-727 Baltimore Special (HW round)
081-728 Ambassador (HW round)

BOSTON & MAINE

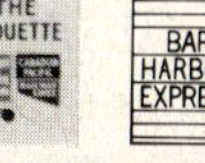

140
141
142
143
220

081-140 Alouette (HW round)
081-141 Minuteman (HW rect)
081-142 Flying Yankee (HW rect)
081-143 Alouette (HW rect)

CANADIAN NATIONAL

150
151

081-150 CNR w/Maple Leaf (HW square)
081-151 Herald (HW square)

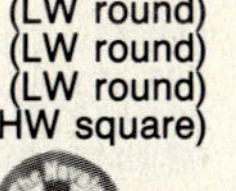

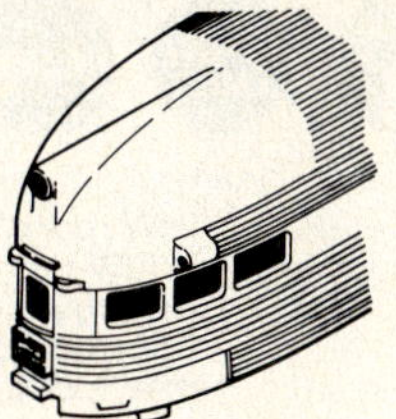
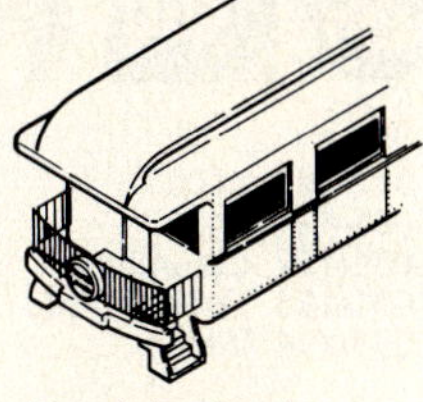

TOMAR INDUSTRIES

HO SCALE (1/87) CRAFT TRAIN KITS

LIGHTED DRUMHEAD KITS each 9.95
DOUBLE KITS each 15.45

TOMAR kits are complete with cast and machined drum housing, 1.5 volt micro-miniature lamp, full color train sign, light diffuser, 4 diodes, hookup wire and complete instructions and illustrations. Double kits contain all parts for only one car but with two tailsigns. (Only a few roads used double tailsigns, such as kit #179 for the CB&Q Railroad).

CANADIAN NATIONAL (continued)

152 153 154

081-152	Herald	(LW rect)
081-153	The Continental	(LW rect)
081-154	Ocean Ltd	(HW rect)

CANADIAN PACIFIC

160 161 162 163

081-160	Alouette	(HW round)
081-161	Herald	(HW square)
081-162	Shield w/Beaver	(HW rect)
081-163	Plain Shield w/Beaver	(HW rect)

164 165 166 167 168

081-164	Canadian (1968)	(LW square)
081-165	Dominion	(LW rect)
081-166	Canadian (1955)	(LW rect)
081-167	Alouette	(HW rect)
081-168	The Mountaineer	(HW round)

169 920 921 922 923

081-169	Empress	(HW round)
081-920	Expo Ltd	(LW rect)
081-921	Trans-Canada Ltd	(HW rect)
081-922	Canadian Shield	(HW rect)
081-923	Le Quebec	(LW rect)

CENTRAL NEW JERSEY

Herald
(HW rect)
081-440

Blue Comet
(HW round)
081-260

CHESAPEAKE & OHIO

170 171 172 173

081-170	C&O for Progress	(HW round)
081-171	C&O Lines	(HW square)
081-172	Flying Virginian	(HW square)
081-173	George Washington	(HW round)

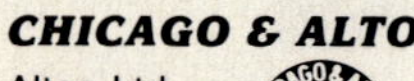  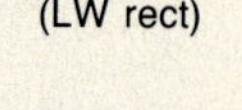
174 175 176

081-174	George Washington Portrait	(HW round)
081-175	The Sportsman	(HW square)
081-176	Chessie	(LW rect)

CHICAGO & ALTON

Alton Ltd
(HW round)
081-93

CHICAGO, BURLINGTON & QUINCY

177 178 179 180 181

081-177	Pioneer Zephyr	(LW rect)
081-178	Kansas City Zephyr (Double Kit)	(LW rect)
081-179	Burlington & Denver Zephyr (Double Kit)	(LW rect)
081-180	Advance Texas Zephyr	(HW rect)
081-181	Buffalo Bill	(HW rect)

        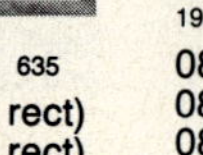  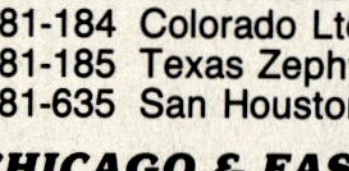
182 183 184 185 635

081-182	Burlington Route	(HW round)
081-183	California Zephyr	(LW rect)
081-184	Colorado Ltd	(HW rect)
081-185	Texas Zephyr	(HW rect)
081-635	San Houston Zephyr **NEW**	(LW rect)

CHICAGO & EASTERN ILLINOIS

    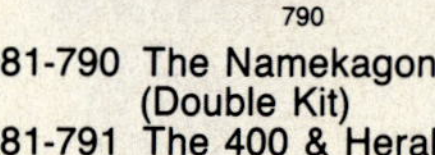
186 187 500 501 502

081-186	Cardinal	(HW round)
081-187	Dixieland	(HW round)
081-500	Dixie Flager	(LW rect)
081-501	Dixie Mail	(HW round)
081-502	Dixie Flyer	(HW round)

    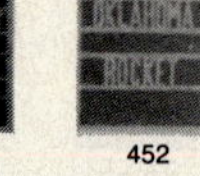
503 504 505 506

081-503	Dixie Ltd	(HW round)
081-504	Dixie Express	(HW round)
081-505	Silent Knight	(HW round)
081-506	Zipper	(HW round)

CHICAGO & GREAT WESTERN

Corn Belt Route
(HW round)
081-189

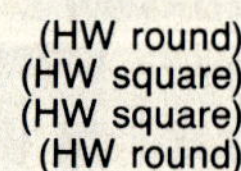

CHICAGO, INDIANAPOLIS & LOUISVILLE

410 411 412 413

081-410	The Hoosier Line	(HW round)
081-411	Monon Special	(HW round)
081-412	The Hoosier	(LW rect)
081-413	The Tippecanoe	(LW rect)

414 415 416

081-414	Throughbred	(HW round)
081-415	Herald	(HW round)
081-416	Red Devil	(HW round)

CHICAGO & NORTH WESTERN

190 191 192 193 194

081-190	"400"	(HW round)
081-191	"400"	(LW rect)
081-192	Columbine	(HW round)
081-193	Overland Ltd	(HW round)
081-194	Viking	(HW round)

195 196 197 198 199

081-195	San Fran Overland Ltd	(HW round)
081-196	"49er"	(LW rect)
081-197	Herald	(HW round)
081-198	NW Ltd	(HW round)
081-199	Flambeau	(HW round)

790 791

081-790	The Namekagon (Double Kit)	(LW rect)
081-791	The 400 & Herald (Double Kit)	(HW round)

CHICAGO, ROCK ISLAND & PACIFIC

450 451 452 453 454

081-450	Twin Star Rocket	(LW rect)
081-451	Corn Belt Rocket	(LW rect)
081-452	Oklahoma Rocket	(LW rect)
081-453	Golden State	(LW rect)
081-454	Golden State	(HW round)

455 456 457 458 459

081-455	Apache	(HW round)
081-456	Rocky Mountain Ltd	(HW round)
081-457	Choctaw Rocket	(LW rect)
081-458	Golden Rocket	(LW rect)
081-459	Arizona Ltd	(LW rect)

730 731 732

081-730	The Rocket	(LW round)
081-731	Texas Rocket	(LW rect)
081-732	Rocket	(LW round)

733 734 735

081-733	Quad City Rocket	(LW round)
081-734	RI, Route of the Rocket	(LW round)
081-735	Zephyr Rocket	(LW rect)

TOMAR INDUSTRIES

HO SCALE (1/87) CRAFT TRAIN KITS

LIGHTED DRUMHEAD KITS each 9.95
DOUBLE KITS each 15.45

TOMAR kits are complete with cast and machined drum housing, 1.5 volt micro-miniature lamp, full color train sign, light diffuser, 4 diodes, hookup wire and complete instructions and illustrations. Double kits contain all parts for only one car but with two tailsigns. (Only a few roads used double tailsigns, such as kit #179 for the CB&Q Railroad.)

CRI&P (continued)

736   737   738

081-736 Rocky Mountain Rocket   (LW rect)
081-737 Golden State   (LW square)
081-738 Rocky Mountain Limited   (HW rect)

CMstP&P (MILW)

200   201   202   203   204

081-200 Olympian   (HW round)
081-201 Pioneer Ltd   (HW round)
081-202 Sioux   (HW round)
081-203 Southwest Ltd   (HW round)
081-204 Columbian w/MILW   (HW round)

205   206   207   208   209

081-205 Olympian w/MILW   (HW round)
081-206 Olympian Hiawatha   (HW round)
081-207 Pacific Express w/MILW   (HW round)
081-208 Varsity w/MILW   (HW round)
081-209 Arrow w/MILW   (HW round)

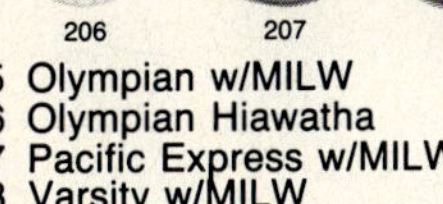 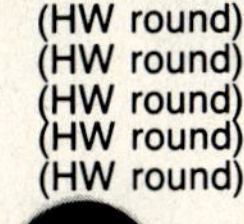

570   571   572   573

081-570 Pioneer Ltd w/MILW   (HW round)
081-571 Marquette w/MILW   (HW round)
081-572 Chippewa w/MILW   (HW round)
081-573 Omaha Chicago Limited   (LW round)

COLORADO & MIDLAND

Pikes Peak Route
(HW round)
081-210

COTTON BELT

Lone Star Trains
(HW rect)
081-700

DELAWARE & HUDSON

220   221   222   223

081-220 Bar Harbor Express   (LW rect)
081-221 Champlaine   (LW rect)
081-222 D&H Shield   (HW round)
081-223 Laurentian   (LW rect)

224   225   226

081-224 Montreal Ltd   (LW rect)
081-225 Plain Shield   (HW round)
081-226 Adirondack   (LW round)

DELAWARE, LACKAWANNA & WESTERN

227   228

081-227 Phoebe Snow, Double Kit   (LW rect)
081-228 Phoebe Snow   (HW round)

229   473   474

081-229 Lackawanna Limited   (HW rect)
081-473 Sussex County Express   (HW round)
081-474 Lackawanna Ltd   (HW round)

DENVER & RIO GRANDE WESTERN

(Narrow Gauge & Standard Gauge)

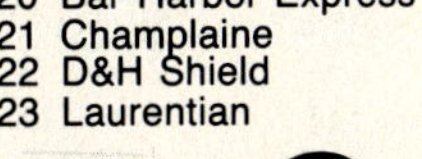

230   231   232   233

081-230 California Zephyr   (LW rect)
081-231 Panoramic   (HW round)
081-232 Prospector   (LW round)
081-233 San Juan   (NG round)

234   235   236   237

081-234 Scenic Lines   (HW round)
081-235 Scenic Ltd   (HW round)
081-236 Shavano   (NG round)
081-237 The Royal Gorge   (LW round)

DULUTH, MISSABE & IRON RANGE

Herald
(HW round)
081-215

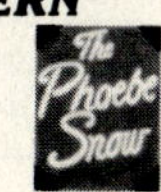

EAST BROAD TOP

Herald, Narrow Gauge
(rectangular)
081-149

ERIE

240   241   242

081-240 Erie Ltd   (HW rect)
081-241 Herald   (HW square)
081-242 Pacific Express   (HW square)

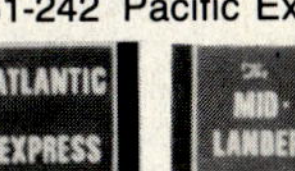   

243   244   568   569

081-243 Atlantic Express   (HW square)
081-244 The Midlander   (HW square)
081-568 Erie Limited   (HW square)
081-569 Herald   (HW round)

FLORIDA EAST COAST

550   551   552

081-550 Florida East Coast Ltd   (HW round)
081-551 Miamian   (HW round)
081-552 Herald   (HW round)

GRAND TRUNK WESTERN

 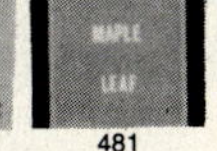  

480   481   482   483

081-480 International   (HW rect)
081-481 Maple Leaf   (HW square)
081-482 La Salle   (HW square)
081-483 Inter-City Ltd   (HW square)

GREAT NORTHERN

250   251   252   253   254

081-250 Cascadian   (HW rect)
081-251 Empire Builder, Goat   (HW square)
081-252 Empire Builder, Neon   (LW square)
081-253 Herald   (HW round)
081-254 Orient Ltd, Red Dot   (HW rect)

255   256   262   263   495

081-255 Orient Ltd, Goat   (HW rect)
081-256 Western Star   (LW square)
081-262 Badger   (LW rect)
081-263 Gopher   (LW rect)
081-264 Badger/Gopher
  Double Kit   (LWrect)
081-495 The Red   **NEW** (LW square)
  River Neon

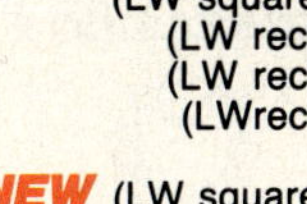

490   491   492   493   494

081-490 Oriental Limited, Double Kit   (HW rect)
081-491 Empire Builder   (HW square)
081-492 International Ltd   (HW rect)
081-493 International Ltd   (LW square)
081-494 Herald   (HW square)

GREEN BAY WESTERN

Green Bay Route
(HW round)
081-685

GULF, MOBILE & NORTHERN

760   761

081-760 The Rebel   (LW rect)
081-761 Road of Service   (HW round)

GULF, MOBILE & OHIO

257   258   259

081-257 Abe Lincoln   (LW square)
081-258 Alton Ltd   (HW round)
081-259 Ann Rutledge   (LW rect)

540   541   542   543

081-540 Abraham Lincoln   (LW square)
081-541 Gulf Coast Rebel   (LW round)
081-542 St Tammany Special   (HW round)
081-543 Rebel   (LW square)

TOMAR INDUSTRIES

HO SCALE (1/87) CRAFT TRAIN KITS

**LIGHTED DRUMHEAD KITS each 9.95
DOUBLE KITS each 15.45**

TOMAR kits are complete with cast and machined drum housing, 1.5 volt micro-miniature lamp, full color train sign, light diffuser, 4 diodes, hookup wire and complete instructions and illustrations. Double kits contain all parts for only one car but with two tailsigns. (Only a few roads used double tailsigns, such as kit #179 for the CB&Q Railroad).

ILLINOIS CENTRAL

245   246   247   248   249

081-245	Panama Ltd	(HW rect)
081-246	City of New Orleans	(LW rect)
081-247	Seminole	(HW square)
081-248	Daylight	(LW square)
081-249	Night Diamond	(HW rect)

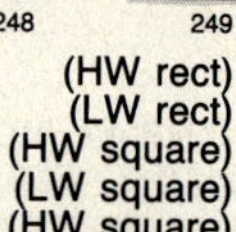 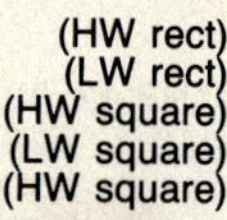 

900   901   902

081-900	Green Diamond	(HW square)
081-901	Herald	(LW rect)
081-902	Panama Ltd	(LW rect)

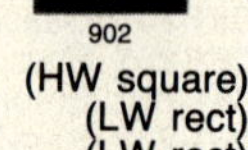 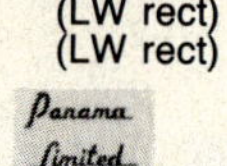  

903   904   905

081-903	Daylight	(LW rect)
081-904	City of Miami	(LW rect)
081-905	Panama Limited	(LW square)

KANSAS CITY SOUTHERN

405   406   407

081-405	Flying Crow	(HW round)
081-406	Southern Belle	(LW rect)
081-407	Herald	(LW rect)

LAKE ERIE & FRANKLIN & CLARION

Herald (rect)
081-559

LEHIGH & NEW ENGLAND

Herald (HW round)
081-265

LEHIGH VALLEY

460   461   462

081-460	Black Herald	(HW rect)
081-461	Black Diamond, Double Kit	(HW rect)
081-462	Black Diamond	(HW round)

LONG ISLAND

750   751   752

081-750	Sunrise Special	(HW keys)
081-751	Sundowner	(HW rect)
081-752	Cannonball	(HW square)

LOUISANA & ARKANSAS

716   717

081-716	Hustler	(HW rect)
081-717	Shreveporter	(HW rect)

LOUISVILLE & NASHVILLE

261   640   641

081-261	Pan-American	(HW round)
081-640	Humming Bird	(LW rect)
081-641	Herald	(HW round)

MICHIGAN CENTRAL

Niagra Falls Deluxe (HW square)
081-449

MISSOURI-KANSAS-TEXAS

    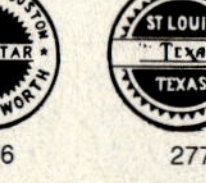 

530   531   532   533   534

081-530	Texas Special, Double Kit	(HW rect)
081-531	Texas Special (red)	(LW rect)
081-532	Texas Special (white)	(LW rect)
081-533	Katy Flyer	(HW square)
081-534	Herald	(HW rect)

MISSOURI & ARKANSAS

Herald (HW round)
081-715

MISSOURI PACIFIC

273   274   275   276   277

081-273	Sunshine Special	(HW rect)
081-274	Texas Eagle	(LW rect)
081-275	Herald	(HW round)
081-276	The Star	(HW round)
081-277	The Texan	(HW round)

660   661   662   663   664

081-660	The Orleanean	(HW round)
081-661	Hot Springs Special	(HW rect)
081-662	Delta Eagle	(LW rect)
081-663	The Westerner	(LW rect)
081-664	Kay See Flyer	(HW rect)

665   667   668   669

081-665	Sunshine Special	(HW round)
081-667	Royal Gorge	(HW square)
081-668	Royal Gorge	(HW round)
081-669	Texan	(LW rect)

NDEM

(LW Square)
081-995

NEW YORK, NEW HAVEN & HARTFORD

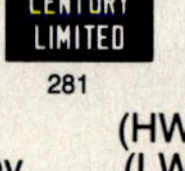

270   271   272

Yankee Clippers (HW rect) 081-270	Merchants Ltd (LW rect) 081-271	Herald (square) 081-272 **NEW**

NEW YORK CENTRAL

278   279   280   281   282

081-278	Pacemaker	(HW rect)
081-279	James Whitcomb Riley	(LW rect)
081-280	20th Century Ltd	(HW rect)
081-281	20th Century Scroll	(HW rect)
081-282	20th Century Ltd	(LW rect)

283   284   285   286

081-283	Empire State Express	(HW rect)
081-284	New England States	(LW rect)
081-285	Pacemaker	(LW rect)
081-286	Twilight Ltd	(LW rect)

  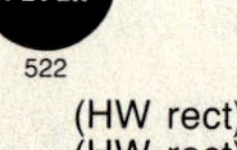

287   288   289

081-287	Wolverine	(HW rect)
081-288	Commodore Vanderbilt	(HW rect)
081-289	Advance 20th Century	(HW rect)

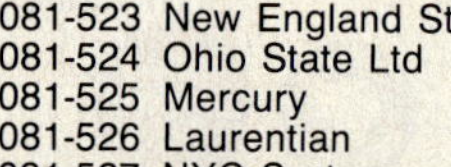 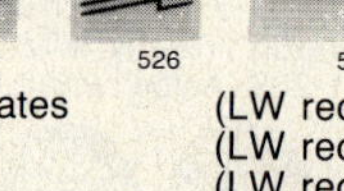

520   521   522

081-520	Knickerbocker	(HW rect)
081-521	The Michigan	(HW rect)
081-522	Cleveland Flyer	(HW round)

 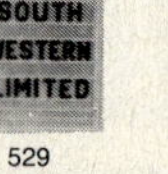  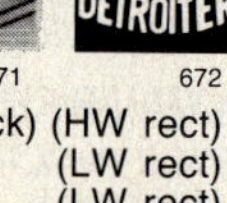

523   524   525   526   527

081-523	New England States	(LW rect)
081-524	Ohio State Ltd	(LW rect)
081-525	Mercury	(LW rect)
081-526	Laurentian	(LW rect)
081-527	NYC System	(LW rect)

528   529   670   671   672

081-528	NYC System (black)	(LW rect)
081-529	South Western Ltd	(LW rect)
081-670	James Whitcomb Riley	(LW rect)
081-671	Commodore Vanderbilt	(LW rect)
081-672	Detroiter	(HW rect)

  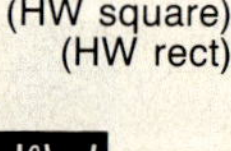

673   674   675   676

081-673	Southwestern Ltd	(HW rect)
081-674	Lake Shore Ltd	(HW rect)
081-675	Empire State Express	(HW round)
081-676	Motor Queen **NEW**	(square)

NICKEL PLATE

296   298   299

081-296	Nickel Plate Ltd	(HW rect)
081-298	Herald	(HW square)
081-299	Herald	(HW rect)

NORFOLK & WESTERN

290   291   292

081-290	Cavalier	(LW rect)
081-291	Herald	(HW round)
081-292	Herald	(HW rect)

293   294   295

081-293	Pocahontas	(LW rect)
081-294	Powhatan Arrow	(LW rect)
081-295	Banner Blue	(LW rect)

TOMAR INDUSTRIES

HO SCALE (1/87) CRAFT TRAIN KITS

LIGHTED DRUMHEAD KITS each 9.95
DOUBLE KITS each 15.45

TOMAR kits are complete with cast and machined drum housing, 1.5 volt micro-miniature lamp, full color train sign, light diffuser, 4 diodes, hookup wire and complete instructions and illustrations. Double kits contain all parts for only one car but with two tailsigns. (Only a few roads used double tailsigns, such as kit #179 for the CB&Q Railroad).

NORTHERN PACIFIC

300   301   302

081-300	North Coast Ltd	
081-301	North Coast Ltd	(LW rect)
081-302	Herald	(HW round)

303   304   305

081-303	Puget Sound Ltd	(HW round)
081-304	Yellowstone Comet	(HW round)
081-305	Yellowstone Park	(HW round)

NORTHWESTERN PACIFIC

| Herald (HW round) 081-780 | Redwood Empire Route (HW round) 081-781 |

ONTARIO NORTHLAND

Shield (LW rect) 081-269

PENNSYLVANIA

310   311   312   313   314

081-310	Broadway Ltd	(HW keys)
081-311	Broadway Ltd	(LW keys)
081-312	Cincinnati Ltd	(HW keys)
081-313	General	(HW keys)
081-314	Golden Arrow	(HW keys)

315   316   317   318   319

081-315	Jeffersonion	(LW keys)
081-316	Liberty Ltd	(LW keys)
081-317	Manhattan Ltd	(HW keys)
081-318	Pennsylvania Ltd	(HW keys)
081-319	Rainbow	(HW keys)

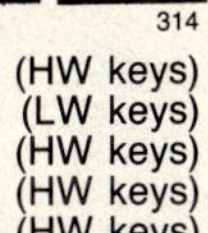 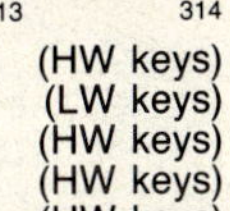 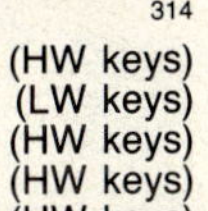
320   321   322   323

081-320	Senator	(LW keys)
081-321	South Wind	(LW keys)
081-322	Spirit of St Louis	(HW keys)
081-323	Congressional	(LW keys)

324   325   326   580

081-324	Trail Blazer	(LW keys)
081-325	Statesman	(HW keys)
081-326	Representative	(HW keys)
081-580	Pittsburger	(HW keys)

  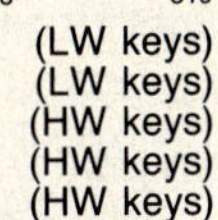
581   582   583   584

081-581	Congressional	(HW keys)
081-582	President	(HW keys)
081-583	Liberty Ltd Chicago	(HW keys)
081-584	Red Bird	(LW keys)

585   586   945   946

081-585	Spirit of St Louis	(HW keys)
081-586	Detroit Arrow	(HW keys)
081-945	Herald	(round)
081-946	Trail Blazer **NEW**	(LW keys)

587   588   589   590   591

081-587	Pennsylvania Special	(HW keys)
081-588	Herald	(LW keys)
081-589	The Red Arrow	(HW keys)
081-590	The Steeler	(HW keys)
081-591	The Clevelander	(HW keys)

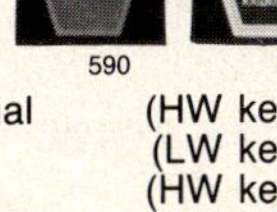
592   593   594   595

081-592	The Southland	(HW keys)
081-593	Buckeye Ltd	(HW keys)
081-594	The Senator	(HW keys)
081-595	Gotham Ltd	(HW keys)

596   597   598   599

081-596	The Metropolitan	(HW keys)
081-597	The St Louisan	(HW keys)
081-598	The American	(HW keys)
081-599	St Louis Express	(HW keys)

PERE MARQUETTE

327   445

| 081-327 | Resort Special | (HW round) |
| 081-445 | Pere Marquette (Double Kit) | (LW round) |

READING

 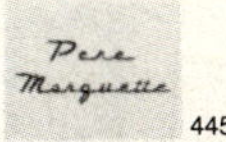
560   561

| Herald (LW rect) 081-560 | | Iron Horse Ramble (HW round) 081-561 |

RICHMOND, FREDERICKSBURG & POTOMAC

Old Dominion (HW round) 081-475

RUTLAND

Mount Royal (HW rect) 081-710

ST LOUIS—SAN FRANCISCO

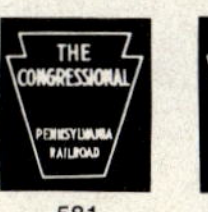  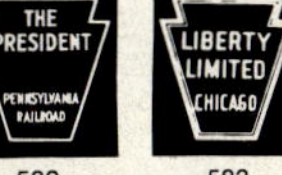 
328   329   510   511   512

081-328	Firefly	(HW round)
081-329	Meteor	(HW round)
081-511	5000 Mile Service	(HW round)
081-511	Will Rogers	(HW round)
081-512	Lead Belt Special	(HW round)

SAN DIEGO & ARIZONA

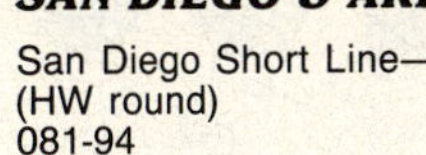

San Diego Short Line—Herald (HW round) 081-94

SEABOARD AIR LINE

362   363   364   365

081-362	Silver Meteor	(LW square)
081-363	Orange Blossom	(LW square)
081-364	Herald	(HW round)
081-365	Silver Comet	(LW square)

SEABOARD COAST LINE

Herald (LW round) 081-690

SIERRA

748   749

| 081-748 | Preserving Yesterday for Tommorow | (HW round) |
| 081-749 | Herald | (HW round) |

SOO LINE

420   421   422   423

081-420	Twin-City—Seattle	(HW round)
081-421	Soo-Spokane-Portland (Train Deluxe)	(HW round)
081-422	Herald	(HW rect)
081-423	The Mountaineer	(HW round)

SOUTHERN

350   351   352   353

081-350	Crescent Ltd	(LW rect)
081-351	Crescent	(LW rect)
081-352	Queen Crescent Ltd	(HW round)
081-353	Herald	(HW round)

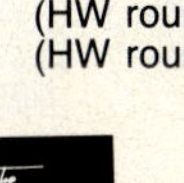
354   355   356

081-354	Carolina Special	(HW rect)
081-355	Royal Palm	(HW round)
081-356	Southerner	(LW rect)

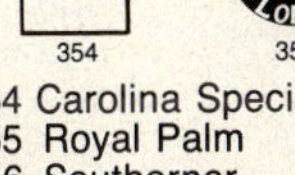 
357   358   359   910

081-357	Tennessean (Double Kit)	(LW rect)
081-358	Royal Palm	(HW rect)
081-359	Memphis Special	(HW rect)
081-910	Crescent-Sunset Ltd	(HW round)

TOMAR INDUSTRIES

HO SCALE (1/87) CRAFT TRAIN KITS

LIGHTED DRUMHEAD KITS each 9.95
DOUBLE KITS each 15.45

TOMAR kits are complete with cast and machined drum housing, 1.5 volt micro-miniature lamp, full color train sign, light diffuser, 4 diodes, hookup wire and complete instructions and illustrations. Double kits contain all parts for only one car but with two tailsigns. (Only a few roads used double tailsigns, such as kit #179 for the CB&Q Railroad).

SOUTHERN PACIFIC

330   331   332   333   334

081-330	Cascade	(HW round)
081-331	Daylight Ltd	(HW round)
081-332	Daylight	(LW rect)
081-333	Daylight	(HW round)
081-334	Del Monte	(HW round)

335   430   336   337

081-335	Golden State	(HW round)
081-430	Golden State	(LW rect)
081-336	Lark	(LW rect)
081-337	Oregonian	(HW round)

338   339   340   935

081-338	Overland Ltd	(HW round)
081-339	Owl (Photo)	(HW round)
081-340	San Joaquin	(LW rect)
081-935	Sunbeam	**NEW** (LW square)

341   342   343   344

081-341	Shasta	(HW round)
081-342	Sunbeam	(LW rect)
081-343	Sunset Ltd	(HW round)
081-344	San Fran Overland Ltd	(HW round)

345   346   347   348   349

081-345	West Coast	(HW round)
081-346	Sunset Ltd	(LW rect)
081-347	Sunbeam	(HW round)
081-348	Pacific Ltd	(HW round)
081-349	''49er''	(LW rect)

431   432   433   434

081-431	Herald	(LW round)
081-432	Owl	(HW round)
081-433	Apache	(HW round)
081-434	Argonaut	(HW round)

   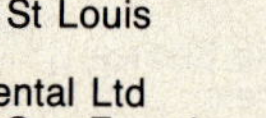 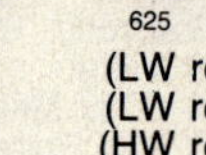
435   436   437   438   439

081-435	Imperial	(HW round)
081-436	Crescent/Sunset	(HW round)
081-437	Golden State	(LW square)
081-438	Klamath	(HW round)
081-439	Sun-Tan Special	(HW round)

930   931   932   933   934

081-930	St Louis Express	(HW round)
081-931	Golden Coast Ltd	(HW round)
081-932	Cascade	(LW rect)
081-933	Lark	(LW rect)
081-934	Shasta Ltd.	(HW round)

SPOKANE, PORTLAND & SEATTLE

  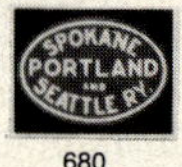
360   361   680

081-360	Columbia River Express	(HW rect)
081-361	Empire Builder	(HW square)
081-680	Herald	(HW rect)

TEXAS & PACIFIC

Herald (LW rect)
081-297

TEXAS STATE

Herald (LW round)
081-709

UNION PACIFIC

370   371   372   373   374

081-370	Cheyenne	(LW square)
081-371	City of Los Angeles	(LW square)
081-372	City of San Francisco	(LW round)
081-373	City of Los Angeles	(LW round)
081-374	Columbine	(LW round)

375   376   377   378   379

081-375	Denver Ltd	(HW round)
081-376	Los Angeles Ltd	(HW round)
081-377	LA Ltd, Flower	(HW round)
081-378	Overland Ltd	(HW round)
081-379	Portland Rose	(HW round)

380   381   382   383   384

081-380	SF Overland Ltd	(HW round)
081-381	''49er''	(LW rect)
081-382	City of Denver	(HW square)
081-383	City of Denver	(LW round)
081-384	City of Las Vegas	(LW round)

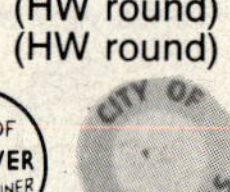
385   386   387

081-385	Old Timer	(LW round)
081-386	Pony Express	(HW round)
081-387	Challenger	(HW round)

388   389   620   621

081-388	Streamline Challenger	(LW round)
081-389	Streamline	(LW round)
081-620	City of Portland	(LW round)
081-621	Adios	(LW round)

622   623   624   625

081-622	City of St Louis	(LW round)
081-623	Herald	(LW round)
081-624	Continental Ltd	(HW round)
081-625	City of San Francisco	(LW square)

VIA

Herald (LW rect)
081-470

VIRGINIA & TRUCKEE

Herald (round)
081-214

WABASH

390   391   392   393   394

081-390	Wabash Cannonball	(HW round)
081-391	Bluebird	(LW rect)
081-392	Banner Blue	(HW round)
081-393	City of St Louis	(LW rect)
081-394	City of Kansas City	(LW rect)

395   396   397   398   399

081-395	Banner Ltd	(HW round)
081-396	Kansas City-Omaha-Des Moines Limited	(HW round)
081-397	The Midnight	(HW round)
081-398	Detroit-St Louis Ltd	(HW round)
081-399	Kansas City-Pacific Coast Ltd	(HW round)

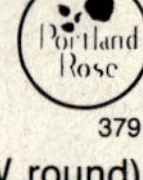
650   651   652   653   654

081-650	Banner Blue	(LW rect)
081-651	Detroit—St Louis Ltd	(LW round)
081-652	Midnight	(LW round)
081-653	City of St Louis	(LW round)
081-654	Blue Bird—Cannon Ball	(LW square)

WESTERN MARYLAND

Fast Freight Lines (HW round)
081-479

WESTERN PACIFIC

400   401

081-400	California Zephyr	(LW rect)
081-401	Scenic Ltd	(HW round)

WHITE PASS & YUKON

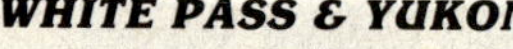
Herald (HW round)
081-92

MISCELLANEOUS

990   991   992   993   966   994

081-990	Clown	(round)
081-991	Freedom Train	(LW square)
081-992	Santa Claus	(round)
081-993	Hot Dog Special	(round)
081-994	Chessie Steam Special	(square)
081-996	Circus Parade Ltd	(round)

TOMAR INDUSTRIES

ACCESSORIES

BATTERY POWER HOOK-UP KIT
Battery holder & switch to be mounted inside your car (less battery).

081-812 Battery Hook-up Kit   2.95

PICK-UP SHOES
Metal shoes for electrical pickup

081-804 for Passenger Cars	pkg(4)	2.95
081-805 for Locos	pkg(4)	2.95
081-814 for Passenger & Caboose	pkg(8)	2.25
081-815 for Locomotive only	pkg(8)	2.25

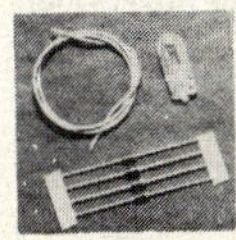
801

802

081-801 Constant Intensity Light Source 2.95
Contains 14v ballast lamp, four diodes and hook-up wire. Will power a 1.5v lamp from track power.

081-802 Micro Miniature   pkg(2) 2.50
Slide Switch
1.5v penlight cell switch

816

806

807

081-816 Ballast Bulb   pkg(2) 1.39
Use with drumhead kits and #801 to keep heat down inside cars.

081-806 End of Train Device   10.95
Red face, amber lens. Includes metal casting with permanently installed amber lens, 1.5v lamp installed in casting, electronic flasher unit, AA battery holder (less battery) and instructions.

081-822 End of Train Device   **NEW** 10.95
Red face, red lens.

081-819 1.5v Lamps   pkg(2) 3.45
Replacement bulbs for #806 end of train device.

081-807 Adlake Marker Lights   10.45
Green, green, red. Can be installed on cabooses or observation cars. Includes two brass markers with lenses installed, 1-1/2v lamp and instructions.

081-809 Adlake Marker Lights   **NEW** 10.45
Yellow, yellow, red

081-818 1.5v Lamps   pkg(2) 5.45
Replacement bulbs for #807 Adlake marker light and all drumheads.

081-813 Red Tail Light Kit   2.50
Includes 1.5v red lamp and instructions.

JEWELS-PEARL PLATE #9   **NEW**
081-56 Clear	pkg(12)	1.50
081-57 Red	pkg(12)	1.50
081-58 Green	pkg(12)	1.50
081-59 Yellow	pkg(12)	1.50

081-820 Drumhead Kit   **NEW** pkg(2) 3.50
Replacement Lamp

See also: TRACTION, FREIGHT CARS, SIGNALS & DETECTION UNITS and TRACK for more TOMAR INDUSTRIES products.

LIFE-LIKE®

60' HEAVYWEIGHT CAR

COACH

433-8023 Baltimore & Ohio		10.25
433-8043 Southern		10.25
433-8063 Pennsylvania		10.25

STANDARD PULLMAN

433-8032 New York Central		10.25
433-8062 Pennsylvania		10.25

COMBINE

433-8020 Baltimore & Ohio		10.25
433-8030 New York Central		10.25
433-8050 Union Pacific		10.25
433-8060 Pennsylvania		10.25

DINING CAR

433-8021 Baltimore & Ohio		10.25
433-8031 New York Central		10.25
433-8051 Union Pacific		10.25
433-8061 Pennsylvania		10.25

OBSERVATION

433-8024 Baltimore & Ohio		10.25
433-8054 Union Pacific		10.25
433-8064 Pennsylvania		10.25

60' LIGHTED STREAMLINE CAR

AMTRAK

433-8079 Coach   13.50

433-8077 Observation   13.50

HO SCALE (1/87) READY-TO-RUN
Ready-to-Run appropriately colored plastic cars include trucks and couplers.

433-8078 Full Dome   13.50

433-8091 Vista Dome   13.50

433-8090 Diner   13.50

PASSENGER CAR ASSORTMENTS
(By Special Order Only.)
Includes 3 each of the 60' Amtrak Lighted Streamline cars.

433-8076   pkg(12) 162.00
Includes 2 each of Combine, Dining, Observation, 3 each of Pullman and Coach in the appropriate roadnames.

433-8081 Pennsylvania Railroad	123.00
433-8084 New York Central	123.00
433-8085 Baltimore & Ohio	123.00

American Limited
Models

HO SCALE 1/87
DIAPHRAGM   **NEW**

Operating passenger car diaphragms are injection molded plastic kits and are accurate models of the specific prototype. Sprung to hold together in turns, down to 24″ radius — no minimum radius limitation. They do not interfere with operation of most couplers. All kits are in pairs, enough for one car.

147-9000 Streamline Cars   pair 3.95
ACF style can be modified to look like Pullman or Budd diaphragm. Fit directly on Athearn Streamliners.

147-9100 Athearn Standard   pair 3.95
Heavyweight Cars

147-9200 Rivarossi & other   pair 3.95
Heavyweight Cars

model power

HO SCALE READY-TO-RUN
Plastic, prepainted and lettered cars.

HARRIMAN CARS
67' COACH

490-9901	Southern Pacific	13.98
490-9902	Southern	13.98
490-9903	Baltimore & Ohio	13.98
490-9904	AT&SF	13.98
490-9907	Canadian Pacific	13.98
490-9908	Canadian National	13.98
490-9909	Pennsylvania	13.98
490-9910	Erie Lackawanna	13.98

67' OBSERVATION CAR

490-9911	Southern Pacific	14.98
490-9912	Southern	14.98
490-9915	Canadian Pacific (modern)	14.98
490-9917	Canadian Pacific	14.98
490-9919	Penn	14.98
490-9920	Erie Lackawanna	14.98
490-9900	Undecorated	14.98

COACH SET — *NEW*
490-99014	Coach set	56.92

Includes 3 Coaches & 1 Observation Car

BUDD CARS — *NEW*
AMTRAK
8800

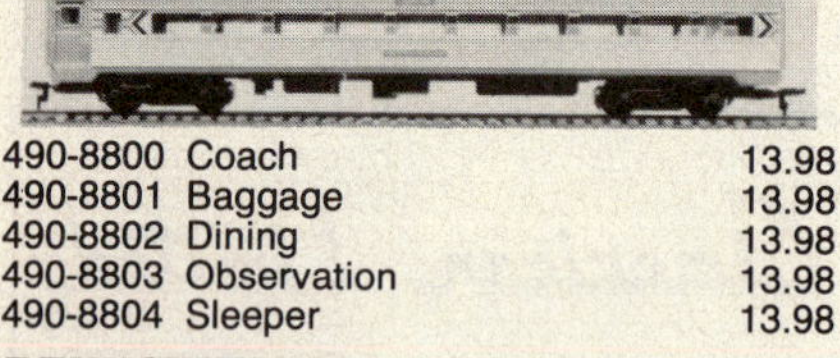

490-8800	Coach	13.98
490-8801	Baggage	13.98
490-8802	Dining	13.98
490-8803	Observation	13.98
490-8804	Sleeper	13.98

PENNSYLVANIA
8811

490-8810	Coach	13.98
490-8811	Baggage	13.98
490-8812	Dining	13.98
490-8813	Observation	13.98
490-8814	Sleeper	13.98

SOUTHERN PACIFIC
8822

490-8820	Coach	13.98
490-8821	Baggage	13.98
490-8822	Dining	13.98
490-8823	Observation	13.98
490-8824	Sleeper	13.98

UNDECORATED
8833

490-8830	Coach	13.98
490-8831	Baggage	13.98
490-8832	Dining	13.98
490-8833	Observation	13.98
490-8834	Sleeper	13.98

CANADIAN NATIONAL
8840

490-8840	Coach	13.98
490-8841	Baggage	13.98
490-8842	Dining	13.98
490-8843	Observation	13.98
490-8844	Sleeper	13.98

CANADIAN PACIFIC

490-8850	Coach	13.98
490-8851	Baggage	13.98
490-8852	Dining	13.98
490-8853	Observation	13.98
490-8854	Sleeper	13.98

SANTA FE

490-8860	Coach	13.98
490-8861	Baggage	13.98
490-8862	Dining	13.98
490-8863	Observation	13.98
490-8864	Sleeper	13.98

Jay-Bee

■ INTERIOR LIGHTING KITS ■

Kits fit most popular brands of passenger cars and come fully assembled, ready to install. No soldering is required.

369-150	for Rivarossi 1920 Series	21.75
369-151	for Rivarossi 1930/40 Series	18.75
369-154	for Con-Cor Budd	12.75
369-155	for Con-Cor Superliner	13.50
369-156	for Con-Cor 72' Budd	12.75
369-158	"EOT" Flasher	16.50
369-159	for Athearn	11.75
369-1501	for Rivarossi 72' 1920 Baggage Car	20.75
396-1511	for Rivarossi 72' 1930 Series	17.75

BRAWA
Imported from Germany by WALTHERS
HO READY-TO-RUN
BAVARIAN STATE RAILWAY

186-816 King Ludwig II Parlor Car 1307.49
This distinctive car was one of the four built for King Ludwig II of Bavaria and the Royal Court in 1862. The set was rebuilt and extended to seven cars in 1891. Today, this parlor car is displayed in the Transportation Museum at Nuremberg.

Based on the modernized (1891) version, this brass model features a complete interior, separately molded trim pieces, sprung trucks, plus authentic paint and lettering.

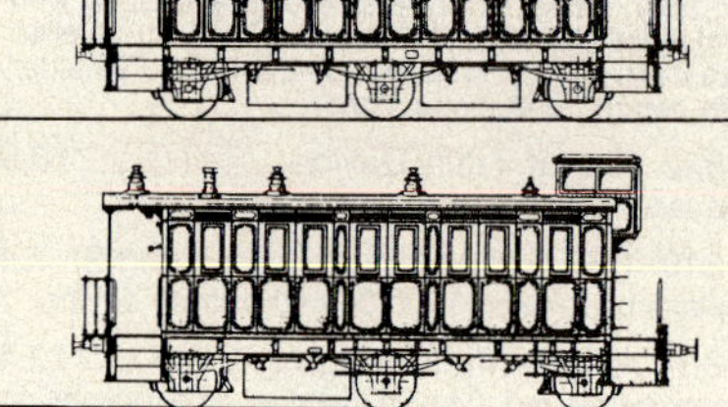

186-815 Royal Train   **3840.49**
Complete four-car train with Platform Observation Car, Royal Parlor, Attendent's Coach and Train Heating Car.

We're in luck, the Bollstown & Oilsmell is running their Baldwin S12 this morning! With a highway alongside the yard, we should be able to get plenty of views of this rare shortline switcher. Like many shortlines, the B&O uses a variety of older power, including this Athearn model, rebuilt with a strobe light and the road's current paint scheme. The venerable caboose is a Silver Streak kit, and a crew of Preiser people are keeping things running. Alf Bossaers of Lichtenvoorde, the Netherlands, photographed his models on a small diorama, which he also constructed.

Models and Photo by Alf Bossaers

Athearn

HO SCALE (1/87)

HORN-HOOK COUPLERS

140-90601	Regular Horn-Hook pkg(8) Style	1.00
140-90602	Snap-on Coupler pkg(12) Cover Plates, Metal	.75
140-90606	Snap-on Coupler pkg(12) Plates, Plastic	.75

Alexander scale models

HO SCALE (1/87)

COUPLERS

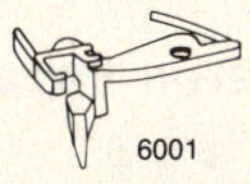
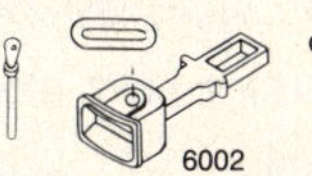

6001   6002

120-6001	Plastic	pair .60
120-6002	Link & Pin	pair 1.50

Die cast, with turned brass pins, formed brass link. Fits NMRA universal coupler pocket.

COUPLER POCKETS

Screw Mounting
120-6003   pair .75

Pin Mounting
120-6004   pair .75

CENTRAL VALLEY

HO SCALE (1/87) NEW

"UN-DEE"© UNCOUPLER

210-3001 "Un-Dee"© Uncoupler   9.95

Unique open shape allows heavyweight passenger cars with narrow diaphragms to be uncoupled within arms reach or, under hidden conditions, such as the 4th or 5th track of crowded classification yard. Incorporates two movable miniature super magnets.

CAL-SCALE

HO SCALE (1/87)

Cal-Scale parts are lost brass wax castings.

DUMMY COUPLERS

Standard
190-292
pair 2.75

Standard "E"
190-302
pair 2.55

WALTHERS

MODERNIZE YOUR FREIGHT CAR FLEET

Modern freight cars look their best with the Cushion Car Coupler Pocket kit! Easy to install, the kit simulates end-of-car cushioning devices used on box cars, auto racks cabooses and other types of cars. The longer draft gear increases the distance between cars for a more realistic appearance. Parts to modify four cars and complete step-by-step instructions are included. Horn hook or Kadee #5 couplers work well with this kit.

Freight cars coupled at speeds over five mph can hit with enough force to severely damage loads. End-of-car cushioning devices absorb the impact and are used on freight cars that carry automobiles, glass, canned goods, paper and other fragile loads.

933-1030   Cushion Car Coupler Pocket Kit   pkg(8) 3.98

HORN-HOOK COUPLERS

941-1282 Horn-Hook Couplers   pkg(12) 1.98
Standard replacement fits all Walthers kits. Molded in Delrin® plastic.

Jay-Bee

HO SCALE (1/87)
COUPLER MOUNTING PADS

For better handling of long HO Scale passenger cars, replace the Talgo couplers with these body-mounted coupler mounting pads. For Rivarossi, Athearn or Con-Cor cars.

When used with the proper size wheels, these pads provide correct coupler heights. Each mounting pad is adjustable so cars can be spaced close together or apart when coupled. Parts to convert three cars are included in each pack.

RIVAROSSI

369-110	1920's Baggage	2.75
369-111	1920 Cars	2.75
369-112	1930 Cars	2.75
369-117	Budd Cars	2.75

ATHEARN

369-113	Streamline	2.75
369-114	Heavyweight	2.75

CON-COR

369-115	Budd Cars	2.75
369-116	Superliners	2.75

BACHMANN

369-118	Spectrum	3.25

Grandt Line

HO, HOn3 SCALE (1/87)

Injection molded black plastic, except where noted.

DUMMY COUPLERS

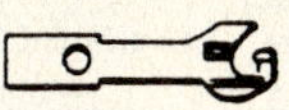

Plastic
300-5003   pkg(10) 1.75

COUPLER POCKETS

for D&RGW Box Car,
300-5006   pkg(4) 1.75

Brass
300-6006   pair 2.75

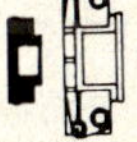

for D&RGW 30' Refrigerator
300-5044   pkg(4) 1.75

for D&RGW Drop Bottom Gondola
300-5047   pkg(4) 1.75

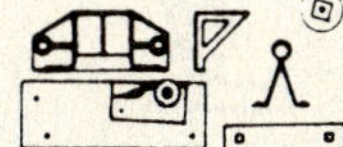

for D&RGW High Side Gondola w/End Detail
300-5086
pkg(2 sets) 1.50

PORTER COUPLER

300-158 8-ton   NEW 1.65

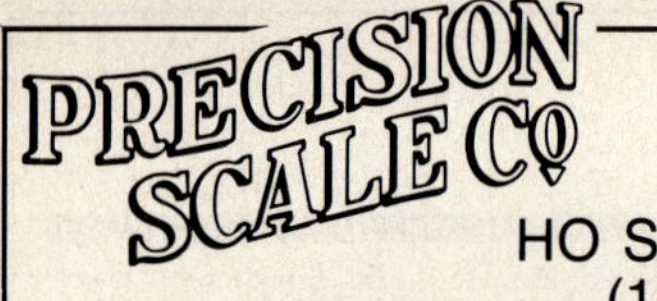
PRECISION SCALE Co.
HO SCALE (1/87)

Lost wax brass castings, unless noted.
Illustrations are approximately full size.

COUPLERS

Dummy for Link &
Pin Pocket
585-3468   pr 1.75

SP Pilot
w/Dummy Coupler
585-3269   ea 2.00

Long Shank
585-31169   pr 2.00

Short Swing
585-31172   pr 1.75

HOn3 Long Shank
585-31171   pr 2.00

Automatic Ramp
Operating
585-31173   pr 3.00

3-Prong
Short Shank
585-31166   pr 1.75

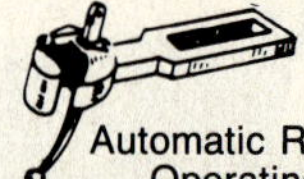
2-Prong
Short Shank
585-31167   pr 1.75

Short Shank
Dummy with Hole
585-31168   pr 1.75

HOn3 for
Side Dump Ore Car
585-3587   pr 2.25

Large Radius, w/Bracket
585-31175   pair 2.75
traction or pass car

Traction
NMRA Type
585-31174   pr 2.25

AAR Common,
Operating
585-32048   pr 3.00

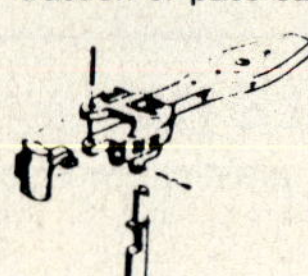
(not illustrated)
585-31170 Coupler Dummy   pkg(2) 2.00

LINK & PIN

Link & Pin
D&RGW HOn3
585-3060   pr 1.75

Link & Pin
Draw Bar
585-31177   ea 1.75

Link & Pin Shay
585-3132   pr 2.00

(not illustrated)
C-16 Original
585-31178   pr 1.75

Link & Pin Shank,
HOn3 for
Side Dump Ore Car
585-3574   pr 1.75

Link & Pin
Extended Knuckle
Dummy
585-3141   pr 2.00

COUPLER POCKETS

SP Loco Type
585-3217   pr 2.00
(By Special Order Only.)

D&RGW Stock &
Steel Box Cars
585-3354   pr 1.75
585-3496 pkg(4) 3.00
Plastic
585-3497 pkg(4) 2.00

HO/HOn3 Three Level
585-31574   pr 1.75
(By Special Order Only.)

Freight & Pass Car
585-31181   pr 1.50

Old Style
Freight Car
585-31180   pr 1.75
(By Special Order Only.)

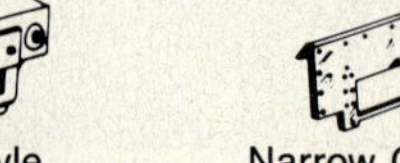
Narrow Gauge
Flat Car
585-3111   pr 2.75
Plastic
585-31645
pkg(4)   1.75

Alco Front
585-3901   pr 1.75
fits Kadee HOn3

C-16 Intermediate
HOn3
585-31631   pr 1.75

Long, Use with
Kadee Coupler
585-3524   pr 1.75
(By Special Order Only.)

Short, Use with
Kadee Coupler
585-3525   pr 1.75
(By Special Order Only.)

Wabash Coupler
Pocket & Plate
585-31179   ea 2.00

Striking Plates
for #31175 Coupler
585-31176   pr 1.50

Common Std.
Pennsy Cast Steel
with Drop Coupler
585-3477   ea 5.25

Universal Draft Gear,
Freight Car
585-31215   pkg(4) 2.75

Delrin
585-31216   pkg(2) 2.25

HOn3
585-3475
pkg(4) 2.75

HOn3
Plastic
585-3476
pkg(4) 1.75

Stubby
585-31575
pair 1.75

COUPLER LIFT BAR BRACKETS

Brass
585-39119
pkg(10) 2.25

Plastic
585-39120
pkg(10) 1.75

HOn3
585-3339
pkg(6) 1.75

EMD, brass
585-39077
pkg(5) 2.00

EMD, plastic
585-39078
pkg(10) 1.50

PIA
PRECISION INVESTMENT ASSOCIATES, INC.
HO SCALE (1/87)

Lost wax brass castings.

COUPLERS

Dummy, Short Shank
063-27   each 1.79
fits pocket #26

Extended Knuckle
for CP-5
063-60   pkg(2) 1.95

COUPLER POCKETS

26
59

063-26 Standard Fits Most Pilots   pair 1.98
063-59 Logging, 3 Pocket Type   pair 2.25

COUPLER LIFT STANCHION

57
58

063-57 Strap Iron Type   pkg(4) 2.25
063-58 Modern Type   pkg(4) 2.25

Precision Masters Inc.
HOn3 SCALE (1/87)

COUPLERS
Plastic dummy knuckle couplers for use on all
types of HOn3 cars. Can be mounted for normal
or close-coupling. Includes mounting instructions.

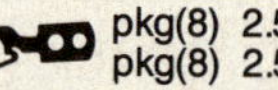
584-1060 Black   pkg(8) 2.50
584-1065 Rust   pkg(8) 2.50

WASHERS
584-1250 Height Adjustment   pkg(12) 1.10
.013" (6pcs), .039" (6pcs)

WESTERN RAIL PRODUCTS   NEW
HO SCALE (1/87)

UNCOUPLERS

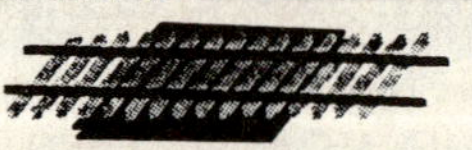
757-201 Magnetic Uncoupler   (each) 1.95

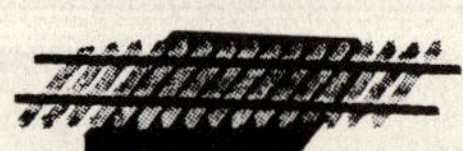
Delayed Magnetic Uncoupler
757-202   (each) 2.95

HO & HOn3
(1/87) SCALE

SEE INFORMATION SHEETS (NEXT TWO PAGES)
FOR AID IN ADAPTING AND INSTALLING COUPLERS

Kadee® is a Registered Trademark.
Magne-matic® is a Registered Trademark.

The Kadee® COUPLING AND UNCOUPLING SYSTEM!

COUPLERS

Couplers are part of the "Delayed Action Series" using delayed magnetic uncoupling.

COUPLER SHANK TYPES

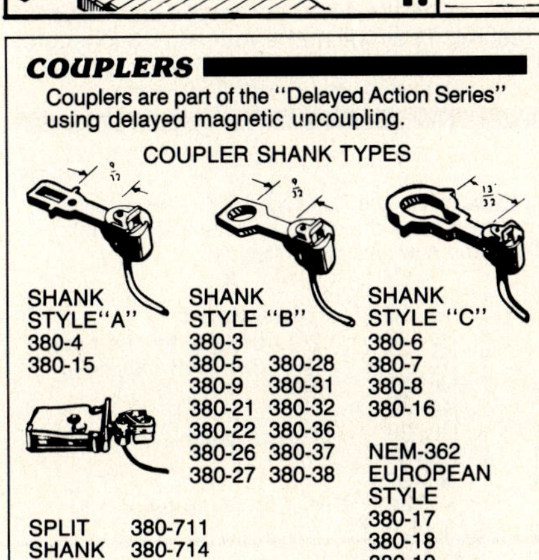

SHANK STYLE"A"	SHANK STYLE "B"		SHANK STYLE "C"
380-4	380-3		380-6
380-15	380-5	380-28	380-7
	380-9	380-31	380-8
	380-21	380-32	380-16
	380-22	380-36	
	380-26	380-37	NEM-362
	380-27	380-38	EUROPEAN STYLE
			380-17
SPLIT	380-711		380-18
SHANK	380-714		380-19
STYLE			380-20

380-3	#5 coupler & draft gear box, fully assembled	2 pr	5.25
380-4	Metal coupler & draft gear box for Ulrich hoppers and gondolas	2 pr	2.95
380-5	Universal metal coupler w/plastic gear box	2 pr	2.95

for Walthers. Athearn and Silver Streak, Golden Spike, some Ulrich.

380-6	13/32" long with compression centering springs	2 pr	3.30
380-7	1/4" long w/compression centering springs, offset	2 pr	3.30
380-8	5/16" long w/compression centering springs	2 pr	3.30
380-9	for Talgo type trucks	2 pr	3.30
380-15	#4 Couplers w/B-38 thin plastic gearbox	2 pr	3.30

This coupler features low height and width draft gear for hard-to-fit applications, draft gear is insulating.

380-16	with Draft Gear #6 coupler with #7 gearbox	2 pr	3.30

for some European Cars or equipment with buffer beams.

380-21	#5 box, .392" short longest underset shank	2 pr	3.75

for low mountings w/assorted adapters for Talgo-truck conversions

380-22	#5 box, .277" short overset shank	2 pr	3.75

for high and tight mountings w/assorted adapters for Talgo-truck conversions

380-26	#5 style box, .392" shank	2 pr	3.75

w/assorted adapters for Talgo-truck conversions

380-27	#5 box, .277" underset shank	2 pr	3.75

for low mountings, w/assorted adapters for Talgo-truck conversions

380-28	#5 style box, .287" shank	2 pr	3.75

w/assorted adapters for Talgo-truck conversions

380-32	w/Draft Gear		3.30
380-17	European, NEM-362 Short	2 pr	3.95
380-18	European, NEM-362 Med	2 pr	3.95
380-19	European, NEM-362 Long	2 pr	3.95
380-20	European, NEM-362 Ex-Long	2 pr	3.95
380-711	with Draft Gear "Old Timer" (3/4 HO size)	2 pr	2.95
380-714	HOn3 Couplers	2 pr	2.95

ACCESSORIES

MAGNE-MATIC® UNCOUPLERS

380-312	Non-Delayed	pkg(2)	4.65
380-321	Delayed	pkg(2)	4.45
380-709	HOn3	pkg(2)	4.65

321

PERMANENT MAGNET

Magnet is under the track.

380-308	Super-Magnet	ea	3.90

MAGNE-ELECTRIC UNCOUPLERS

Delayed action, Thru-the-Track

380-307	HO Magne-Electric		8.50
380-708	HOn3 Magne-Electric		8.90

708

ASSEMBLY JIG

Coupler Assembly Jig allows you to load and unload couplers with ease.

380-701	for #4 & #5 & #9	7.95
380-703	for #6, #7 & #8	7.95
380-702	for #714 & 711	7.95

KNUCKLE SPRINGS

380-622	For K, MK, Delayed Action Couplers	pkg(12)	.98

CENTERING SPRINGS

380-623	for 380-4	pkg(12)	.98
330-634	for 380-5 delayed	pkg(12)	1.35
380-621	Torsion Springs for 30 Series Gear Boxes	pkg(12)	1.60
380-635	for 380-6, 380-7, 380-8 & 380-16	pkg(12)	.98
380-636	coiled, for 380-711 380-714	pkg(12)	1.10
380-620	Centering Springs	pkg(20)	2.00
380-36	#26 Torsion Spring Gear		3.30
380-37	#27 Torsion Spring Gear		3.30
380-38	#28 Torsion Spring Gear		3.30
380-621	Torsion Spring Gear Box	pkg(12)	1.60

COUPLERS TOOLS

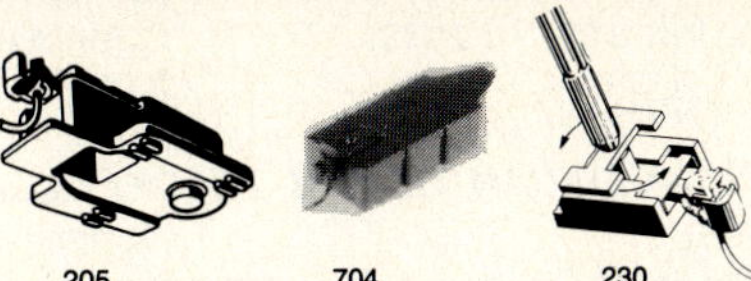

205   704   230

380-230	Adapter Insertion Pic	ea	2.25

For use with #21, #22, #26, #27 & #28 Talgo-truck adapter kits. Pic will set adapter into spring and coupler holes.

380-205	Coupler Height Gauge		3.90

For use with #26, #27 & #28. Talgo-truck adapter kits. Pic will set adapter into spring and coupler holes. Gauges coupler height, trip pin height, trackage.

380-704	Coupler Height Gauge HOn3		5.95

Gauges coupler height, trip pin height, trackage

380-235	Spring "Pic"		1.80

Crowned tip grips miniature springs such as used in couplers and trucks.

(not illustrated)

380-334	Uncoupler Gluing Jig		2.55

for installing #312 & #321 uncouplers in track.

380-246	Tap & Drills for HO Coupler Mounting		5.05

2-56 tap, #50 & #43 drills

380-780	Tap & Drills for HOn3 Coupler Mounting		5.05

0-80 tap, #55 & #52 drills

380-204	Min Space Adapter	NEW	2.65
380-237	Trip Pin Pliers		10.95
380-1020	Tweezers		3.50
380-1059	Tap and Drill		5.05

MOUNTING SCREWS

380-400	0-48 x 1/8	NEW		3.95
380-402	1/4"	NEW	pkg(24)	3.95
380-403	3/8"	NEW	pkg(24)	3.95

COUPLER DRAFT GEAR BOXES

Draft gear boxes with covers only.

380-228		pkg(20)	2.50

For K-4, MK-4 and 380-4 Couplers. Centering springs and dowels not included.

380-232	Plastic	pkg(20)	2.50

For K-10, MI-5 & -10 and 380.5. Couplers and centering springs not included.

380-211	Draft Gear Shims	pkg(40)	1.60

MISCELLANEOUS

Greas-Em
380-231
tube 1.95

A dry lubricant for couplers.

CONVERSION BOLSTERS

Each package contains two conversion bolsters and one pair of couplers. For Central Valley and AHM, Passenger Trucks.

380-505	for AHM 6-wheel passenger trucks	3.30

adjusts to different car lengths

380-506	for CV 4-wheel passenger trucks	3.30

adjusts to different car lengths

380-507	for CV 6-wheel passenger trucks	3.30
380-508	for AHM 4-wheel passenger trucks	3.30

COUPLER TEST KIT

380-13	Test Kit	18.95

Contains one each: HO couplers #4, #5, #6, #7, #8, #9, #21, #22, #26, #27, #28, #31, #32, #36, #37, #38, #711. Uncouplers #308, #321.

COUPLER CONVERSION

To get closer spacing between units.

380-450	Fits Stewart F Units	pkg(2)	4.95

HO COUPLER ADAPTATION LIST

SPECIFY MANUFACTURER #380 WHEN ORDERING.   SEE PRECEDING PAGE FOR PRICES.

Kadee® is a registered Trademark.
Magnematic® is a registered Trademark.
Reprinted courtesy Kadee Quality Products

ACKNOWLEDGEMENT

We wish to thank all of the manufacturers and distributors, and in some cases model railroaders, for their help in making up this list. Without them it would have been difficult.

This list is designed to help the model railroader in his selection of the right Kadee Coupler for his particular brand of car or locomotive. In most cases, we actually performed the conversion ourselves. Used were basic modeler's hand tools. You will note that this list contains only recommendations for our delayed-action type couplers which are the latest development in Magne-Matic coupling and uncoupling in the model railroad industry. They were designed as delayed action types, but can be operated as non-delayed simply by selecting the proper uncoupler.

We recommend that our couplers be used within their own draft gear whenever possible—they naturally perform best in the housing designed for them. However, there are situations encountered on certain models that make it necessary to alter the Kadee draft gear box, or use the

Kadee coupler and spring in the cast-on draft gear box of the car or locomotive. If common sense is used, alterations can be made without seriously affecting the coupler action. The main things to remember are:

1. The draft gear must not be weakened to where it collapses and binds against the coupler or spring.
2. Do not trim away draft gear box at any point where the coupler pivots or is supported.

To assist you in mounting Kadee Couplers to cars or locos on this list, or figuring out ones that aren't on the list, we recommend our Coupler Height Gauge and Coupler Test Kit. They will make your work a lot easier and help you to maintain proper standards throughout your railroad.

COUPLER HEIGHT GAUGE

Coupler Height Gauge
380-205   3.90

(1) gauges coupler height from rail
(2) gauges trip pin height from rail
(3) gauges trackage
(4) movable dowel "feels" for magnetic uncoupler to determine its correct height
(5) uncoupler height is indicated by sight or touch as dowel registers height at top of gauge

instructions enclosed

COUPLER TEST KIT

380-13 Coupler Test Kit   18.95

Coupler Test Kit contains Delayed-Action Couplers and adaptation sheet to show you what coupler will fit what makes of locos and cars. There are also magnetic uncouplers so you can see first hand how well our system works.

CONTENTS:

I. HO Couplers		II. Uncouplers
1 No. 4 (MKD-4)	1 No. 22	1 308 (under the ties)
1 No. 5 (MKD-5 & 10)	1 No. 26	1 321 (between rails)
1 No. 6 (MKD-6)	1 No. 27	
1 No. 7 (MKD-7)	1 No. 28	
1 No. 8 (MKD-8)	1 No. 31	
1 No. 9 (MKD-9)	1 No. 32	III. Adaptation List
1 No. 711 (MKD-11)	1 No. 36	
1 No. 21	1 No. 37	IV. Loco Adaptation List
	1 No. 38	

AHM (RIVAROSSI)

STEAM LOCOMOTIVES

	COUPLER #
0-4-0 Dockside (early model)	5
0-4-0T Dockside (early model)	8,6
0-4-0 Dockside (late model)	27
0-4-0T Dockside (late model)	7
0-4-0 Shifter	5
0-4-0 Switcher w/tender	27
0-4-0 Switcher	7,6
0-4-0 Switcher class 16-a (shifter	5
0-6-0 Switcher	7,6
0-8-0 Switcher	7,6
0-8-0	27
2-4-0 Bowker (tender only)	27
2-8-4 Berkshire/Rivarossi	5
2-8-8-2 USRA Mallet	28
2-10-2 Santa Fe Class Pilot	27
2-10-2 Santa Fe Class Tender	5
4-4-0 Genoa or Reno	27
4-6-2 Heavy Pacific Pilot	6 or 7
4-6-2 Heavy Pacific Tender	5
4-6-4 J3a Hudson Pilot	26
4-4-4 J3a Hudson Tender	5
4-8-2 Cab Forward AHM/Rivarossi	
Pilot	28
Tender	5
4-8-8-4 Big Boy Pilot	7
4-8-8-4 Big Boy Tender	5
Heisler	28

DIESEL LOCOMOTIVES

	COUPLER #
BL-2 Front	28
BL-2 Rear	27
Alco RS-2	5
EMD E-8 & E-9 AHM/Rivarossi	
Front	26
Rear	27
EMD GP-18	27
Fairbanks/Morse 'C' Liner	26
GE U25C (with #7 gear box)	28
GG1	38
Krauss-Maffi (L5051)	5
Plymouth MDT 0-4-0 Switcher	27
Whitcome Switcher	?
Most New Diesels (mfr's suggest)	27

ROLLING STOCK (CARS)

Caboose (plastic)	5
Freight Cars	5
Freight Trucks	27
Gondolas	5
Hoppers (open and covered)	5
Old Time 4-wheel Passenger Trucks	508
Old Time Gondolas Truck	26
Old Time Freight Cars	503
Old Time Gondolas Body	5
Sleeping Car (NEM 362)	18
4-Wheel Passenger Trucks	506,508
6-Wheel Passenger Trucks	505,506

Note: Most AHM Cars (hoppers, box cars, reefers, cabooses, flats, etc.) use #5 for body mounting.

AMBROID

ROLLING STOCK (CARS)

	COUPLER #
Freight & Passenger Cars	5

ALCO

DIESEL LOCOMOTIVES

	COUPLER #
DL-640, DL-600 B	5
DL-701, DL-721	6
C-420, C-630	5
C-643 DH	6
RS-18 MLW	6
GE E-44, U-25B	5
Baldwin RF-16A, RF-16B	5
EMD SD-45	6

AMERICAN FLYER

ROLLING STOCK (CARS)

	COUPLER #
Box Car (plastic) Gilbert	5
Flat Car (metal)	5

ATT (AMERICAN TRAIN & TRACK)

DIESEL

	COUPLER #
Alco 415	5
Plymouth DDT Switcher	7

ROLLING STOCK

Box Car (truck mount)	27
Coach (old time)	8
Flat Car (3 container)	508
Ore Car	502,503
Passenger Cars	7
Pulpwood Car	8
Reefers (truck mount)	27

ARISTO CRAFT

STEAM LOCOMOTIVES

	COUPLER #
4-4-0 Thomas Rogers (tender only)	5

ATHEARN

STEAM LOCOMOTIVES

	COUPLER #
0-4-2 Tank Loco	5
0-6-0 Tank Loco	5
4-6-2 Pacific Pilot	7

DIESEL LOCOMOTIVES

Alco H 24-66 (Trainmaster)	37
Alco PA-1	37
Baldwin S-12	27
Budd RDC	5
EMD DD40	5
EMD F-7	27
EMD F-7 (late model)	27
EMD F-7A SP	37
EMD F-7B	37
EMD F-45 PWR RTR	38
EMD FP-45 PWR RTR	38
EMD GP-9 PWR	38
EMD GP-30	8
EMD GP-35 PWR SP	38
EMD GP-38-2	38
EMD GP-40-2 SP	38
EMD GP-50 PWR UP	38
EMD SD-9 PWR UP	37
EMD SD-40	37
EMD SD-40-2 SF	37
EMD SD-40T-2 PWR SP	37
EMD SD-45	37
EMD SD P-40	27
EMD SW-1000	37
EMD SW-1500	5,28
GE U28C	28
GE U33C	5
Hustler Switcher	5
S-12 PWR RTR	27

Note: Most Athearn Diesels can utilize the #5 coupler and spring in cast-on draft gear box. Spring can be sparingly glued in with Walthers Goo®.

ROLLING STOCK (CARS)

Box Car (high cube)	5
Chemical Cars & Gondolas	5
Flat Cars	5
Freight Cars (metal)	4
Freight Cars (plastic)	5
Hoppers	28
Streamlined Passenger Cars	
Small radius	26
Large radius	28
Tank Cars	5
Piggyback Car	32
PB-1	5
TOFC	5
Work Caboose	27
200 Ton Crane	5

ATLAS

DIESEL LOCOMOTIVES

	COUPLER #
Alco B-B Century 3's 425 & 426	5
Alco C-425	5

ATLAS (continued)

DIESEL LOCOMOTIVES — COUPLER #

Alco RS-1	5
Alco RS-3	5,38
Model Railroader Magazine says	8
Alco RSD-4/5	5,38
Alco RSD-12	5
Alco S-2	27
Alco S-4	38
EMD F-3	37
EMD F-7	37
EMD F7A Front	4
EMD F7A Rear	28
EMD FP-7 Austria	37
EMD FP-7 Japan & Kato	38
EMD GP 7	5
EMD GP-38	37
EMD GP-40	37
EMD SD-9	37
EMD SD-24	27
EMD SD-35	37

BACHMANN

STEAM LOCOMOTIVES — COUPLER #

4-4-0 Jupiter w/tender (tender only)	28
BLT Proto 2000	32

DIESEL LOCOMOTIVES — COUPLER #

Budd 85' Electric Coach	5
EMD F-9	28,37
EMD F45 PH	27,37
EMD FP-45	27
EMD GP-40	28
EMD SD 40-2	27
F-9A, GP-40	7
GE E-60-CP Electric AMTRAK	38
GE U-36-B	37

ROLLING STOCK (CARS) — COUPLER #

All Cars	5
Box Cars (talgo mounted)	38
(body mounted)	5
Box Car "Old Time" (talgo mounted)	37
(body mounted)	5,38
Fleet Coach Passenger Car	38
Gondola (talgo mounted)	37
(body mounted)	5,38
Grain Car (talgo mounted)	37
(body mounted)	5,38
Ore Car (talgo mounted)	37
(body mounted)	5,38
Reefer	38
Wide Vision Caboose	37

BACHMANN SPECTRUM

STEAM LOCOMOTIVES — COUPLER #

4-6-2 K4 Pacific	4
Tender Only	37

DIESEL LOCOMOTIVES — COUPLER #

Dash 8-40C	5
EMD GP-30	37
GE 44 Tonner	37,38
Factory suggests all others	5
GE 70 Tonner SP	21

ROLLING STOCK (CARS) — COUPLER #

Spectrum Observation Car	
OB's end	27,38
Front end	28,37
Non Observation Passenger Car	27

BACHMANN PLUS

DIESEL LOCOMOTIVES — COUPLER #

B 23-7	5

BALBOA-TRAIN MASTERS

ROLLING STOCK (CARS) — COUPLER #

Freight Cars	5

BOWSER

STEAM LOCOMOTIVES — COUPLER #

2-8-2 Mikado Loco (pilot only)	8
2-10-0	5
4-4-2	5
4-6-2 Pacific	5
4-6-6-4 Pilot	6
4-6-6-4 Tender	5
4-8-2 USRA Heavy Mountain	6
4-8-2 PRR	8
High Side Tender	5
Long Haul Tender	8
Low Side Tender (formerly Penn Line)	
Used with 4-4-2 & 2-8-0	5
Semi-Vanderbilt Tender for K-11	
Pacific & Challenger	5
T-7 Tender	5

BRASS CAR SIDES

ROLLING STOCK (CARS) — COUPLER #

Basic HO Passenger Car	5

CAMPBELL

ROLLING STOCK (CARS) — COUPLER #

32' Flatcar	5

CENTRAL VALLEY

ROLLING STOCK (CARS) — COUPLER #

Freight Cars, Cabooses	5
4 Wheel Passenger Trucks	506
6 Wheel Passenger Trucks	507

CON-COR

ROLLING STOCK (CARS) — COUPLER #

Amtrak Superliners	27
Amtrak Phase III Coach-Baggage	508
Box Cars	27
EMD SW-7	8
H 700 Streamlined Coaches	27
Streamlined Passenger Cars	
Small radius	26
Large radius	28
Streamlined Passenger Car	37
Amtrak Mail Car (looks like box car)	5

COX

DIESEL LOCOMOTIVES — COUPLER #

Hustler	5

CROWN

ROLLING STOCK (CARS) — COUPLER #

Freight Cars	5

CUSTOM RAIL

ROLLING STOCK (CARS) — COUPLER #

Piggy Back TOFC	5

DETAILS WEST

ROLLING STOCK (CARS) — COUPLER #

BC-600 Series Cars	5
Door Box Cars	5

FLEISHMAN

DIESEL LOCOMOTIVES — COUPLER #

Baldwin Switcher	8
O-C-O Steeple (Nem-362)	37

FRONT RANGE

DIESEL LOCOMOTIVES — COUPLER #

EMD GP-9 PWD	38
EMD GP-9 PWD Phase III	5,28

ROLLING STOCK (CARS) — COUPLER #

Front Runner/TRLR #4148	5
TOFC #4105	27

GEM

STEAM LOCOMOTIVES — COUPLER #

0-4-0 Camelback	6

GLOOR CRAFT MODELS

STEAM LOCOMOTIVES — COUPLER #

0-6-0 Switcher, metal	4
0-6-0T Switcher, metal	4
2-6-2 Prairie, metal	4
2-6-2 Prairie & 4-6-0 Ten Wheeler, plastic & metal	9
4-4-2 Atlantic, metal	4

DIESEL LOCOMOTIVES — COUPLER #

Old-time Box Cab Diesel	5

ROLLING STOCK (CARS) — COUPLER #

All Rolling Stock	5
Stock Cars, Reefers, Ore Cars, Gondolas	5
Vanderbilt & Square Type Oil Tenders, plastic & metal	5
30' Flatcars	4
50' Pullman Passenger & Harriman Cars	5
80' Pullman Palace Cars	505,507

GRANDT

ALL PRODUCTS
See instructions in kits. All accept Kadee's®

HI BALLER

ROLLING STOCK (CARS) — COUPLER #

Old Time Passenger Cars	4

HOBBY LINE

STEAM LOCOMOTIVES — COUPLER #

Saddle Tank Switcher (plastic)	28

ROLLING STOCK (CARS) — COUPLER

Box Cars	28
Freight Cars (plastic)	4(?)

HOBBY TOWN

DIESEL LOCOMOTIVES — COUPLER #

Power Chassis for:	
Athearn GP-30 & GP-9	8
TYCO GP-20	8
1600 HP Units	6

IMWX

ROLLING STOCK (CARS) — COUPLER #

Box Cars	5

KATO

DIESEL LOCOMOTIVES — COUPLER #

EMD GP-35	5,38
EMD GP-35 Phase 1a (in #5 gear box)	27
SD-40	38

KEN KIDDER

STEAM LOCOMOTIVES — COUPLER #

0-4-0 Tank	8

LIFE-LIKE

STEAM LOCOMOTIVES — COUPLER #

0-4-0 Switcher	27
0-4-0 Tank	28

DIESEL LOCOMOTIVES — COUPLER #

Alco FA-2 Proto 2000 Front	36
FA-2 Proto 2000 Rear	38
BL-2 Diesel	28
EMD F-7 Front	38
EMD F-7 Rear	27
EMD F-7 B	28
EMD F-40-PH	28
EMD GP-9	27
EMD GP-35	27
EMD GP-38-2	28
FB-2	38

ROLLING STOCK (CARS) — COUPLER #

Box Cars (single door)	28
Box Cars (old style)	28
Caboose	28
Coach Car	28
Coal Car (hopper) w/#521 wheels	5
Container Car	28
Crane Car	28
Diner Car	28
Gondola (talgo mounted)	27
(body mounted)	5
Hopper	28
Observation Car	26
Reefer	28
Searchlight Car	28
Tank Car	28
Vista Dome	27

LIMA

DIESEL LOCOMOTIVES — COUPLER #

Alco C-420	26

LINDBERG

DIESEL LOCOMOTIVES — COUPLER #

EMD SW 600 Switcher	5

ROLLING STOCK (CARS) — COUPLER #

Freight Car (plastic)	5
Passenger Cars	5

LIONEL

DIESEL LOCOMOTIVES — COUPLER #

'A' Unit	7
'B' Unit	8

ROLLING STOCK (CARS) — COUPLER #

Old Lionel Cars	7

MANTUA

STEAM LOCOMOTIVES — COUPLER #

0-4-0	27
0-4-0 Switcher	7
0-4-0 Camel Back	27
2-8-2 Camel Back Front	4
2-8-2 Camel Back Rear	27
2-8-2 Camel Back Pilot	15
2-8-2 Camel Back Tender	27
2-6-6-2	5
4-6-2 Pacific (tender only)	27
Logging Tank Locomotive	22
Mallet Logger Front	22
Mallet Logger Rear	28
Mantua Tender	8
Slope Back Tender	7

MANTUA (continued)

DIESEL LOCOMOTIVES	COUPLER #
EMD F7A (powered) Now by Atlas	
Front	4
Rear	28

ROLLING STOCK (CARS)	COUPLER #
Amtrak Baggage #221-32 (metal car)	28

MARX

DIESEL LOCOMOTIVES	COUPLER #
EMD F-7	8

ROLLING STOCK (CARS)	COUPLER #
Freight Cars	5

McKEAN

ROLLING STOCK (CARS)	COUPLER #
Box Cars	5

MDC

STEAM LOCOMOTIVES	COUPLER #
Yard Hog (all metal) w/RA box	28
0-6-0 Switcher	4
2-6-2 Plastic & Metal Kit	9
2-6-2 Older Metal Kit	5
2-8-0 Old Time Consolidation	5,8
4-4-2 Older Metal Kit	5
4-6-0 Plastic & metal kit	9
Vanderbuilt & Square Oil Tenders	5

DIESEL LOCOMOTIVES	COUPLER #
Alco RS-3	5

ROLLING STOCK (CARS)	COUPLER #
36' Log Cars	5
Metal Freight Cars (Roundhouse)	5
MOW Fire Cars #1507	5
Ore Car Tapered Sides	5
50' Plug Door	5
50' Sleeping Car	5

MEHANO

ROLLING STOCK (CARS)	COUPLER #
Hoppers	28

MICRO-ENGINEERING

ROLLING STOCK (CARS)	COUPLER #
90-050 Westside Flat	714
90-053 Westside Flat w/Rotted Board	714
90-055 Westside Caboose	714
90-058 Log Car	714

ROLLING STOCK (CARS)	COUPLER #
90-102 Adapte-Railer	5
90-112 D&RGW High Side Gondola	714
90-114 D&RGW Gondola	714
90-116 D&RGW	714

MODEL ENGINEERING WORKS

DIESEL LOCOMOTIVES	COUPLER #
44 Tonner w/RA Box	5

ROLLING STOCK (CARS)	COUPLER #
Caboose w/RA Box	5
Air Dump Car w/RA Box	5
Log Buggie w/RA Box	5

MODEL POWER

DIESEL LOCOMOTIVES	COUPLER #
Baldwin Shark Nose A & B Units	27
EMD E-7 Front	36
Rear	38
or both	36
EMD E-8	27
EMD E-9	27
FA-1 or FB-1 (powered)	7

ROLLING STOCK (CARS)	COUPLER #
Box Car New Haven (body mounted)	5
(truck mounted)	28
Streamlined Diner	37
Streamlined Passenger Car	5

NEW ENGLAND RAIL SERVICE

	COUPLER #
All Locos	5

NORTHWEST SHORT LINE

	COUPLER #
All HO Products	5
12 Ton and 15 Ton Climax's	714

STEAM LOCOMOTIVES	COUPLER #
HO 12/15T Climax, 18T Shay	711

O.K. HERKIMER

ROLLING STOCK (CARS)	COUPLER #
Streamlined 4-Wheel Passenger Truck	506

PENN LINE

STEAM LOCOMOTIVES	COUPLER #
4-4-4-4 T-1 w/RA Box	5

DIESEL LOCOMOTIVES	COUPLER #
GG-1	5

ROLLING STOCK (CARS)	COUPLER #
Freight Cars	5
Passenger Cars	5

PFM

	COUPLER #
All Products in HO	5
All Steam Locomotives	5
All Diesel Locomotives	6
HOn3 Locomotives	714

QUALITY CRAFT MODELS

	COUPLER #
All Cars and Locos	804,805

RAILWORKS

	COUPLER #
All Brass Imports	5

REVELL

STEAM LOCOMOTIVES	COUPLER #
0-6-0 Switcher	8

ROLLING STOCK (CARS)	COUPLER #
Freight Cars (plastic)	5

RIVAROSSI (AHM)

STEAM LOCOMOTIVES	COUPLER #
0-4-0 Dockside Pilot	8
0-4-0 Dockside Rear	6
0-8-0 Switcher Pilot	5
0-8-0 Switcher Tender	27
2-8-4 Berkshire/AHM	5

DIESEL LOCOMOTIVES	COUPLER #
EMD E-8	
Front	26
Rear	27

ROLLING STOCK (CARS)	COUPLER #
Passenger Cars	26

ROCO

ROLLING STOCK (CARS)	COUPLER #
200 Ton Crane	31
Passenger Cars SNCF (NEM-362)	18
DB (NEM-362)	20

ROUNDHOUSE

ROLLING STOCK (CARS)	COUPLER #
Box Cars	5
Bulkhead Flat Cars	5
Caboose	4
Hoppers	4
200 Ton Flat Car	4

RSO

DIESEL LOCOMOTIVES	COUPLER #
RSD-12 (#20 draft gear box)	28

SCOTIA SCALE MODELS

ROLLING STOCK (CARS)	COUPLER #
36' x 40' HO Freight Cars	5
36' Boom & Wheel Cars	5
HO Russel Log Cars	711
HOn3 Cars	714

STEWART

DIESEL LOCOMOTIVES	COUPLER #
Alco RS-3	(?)
EMD F3 (A & B)	450
EMD F7A Phase 1 Late (#450)	32
Tiger Valley	5
or with Snow Plow	6

ROLLING STOCK (CARS)	COUPLER #
Fishbelly Two Bay Hopper	5
Tripple Bay Hopper	5

TENSHODO

STEAM LOCOMOTIVES	COUPLER #
0-6-0 Tank Loco - Zamek Metal	
Instructions same as Varney 0-4-0.	5

DIESEL LOCOMOTIVES	COUPLER #
EMD GP-9	6

ROLLING STOCK (CARS)	COUPLER #
Passenger Cars	5

TIGER VALLEY

	COUPLER #
All Diesels	5
or with snow plow	6

TRAIN MINIATURES

DIESEL LOCOMOTIVES	COUPLER #
Alco FA-1 Pilot	6
Alco FA-1 Rear	8
Alco FB-1 Dummy	8

ROLLING STOCK (CARS)	COUPLER #
40' Freight and Work Cars	5

Note: Some cars have cast-on draft gear boxes that are too narrow for #5 springs. Solution: cut away portion of draft gear box walls or cut away entirely and install #5 draft gear box.

TYCO

STEAM LOCOMOTIVES	COUPLER #
0-4-0 Booster or Shifter Pilot	7
0-4-0 Booster or Shifter Rear	5
0-6-0 Big Six or Tank Lit'l 6 Pilot	7
0-6-0 Big Six or Tank Lit'l 6 Rear	5
0-8-0 Chattanooga #1261 Pilot	4
0-8-0 Chattanooga #1261 Tender	27
2-6-2 Prairie	7
2-8-2 Prairie	5
4-4-0 General (tender only)	5
4-6-2 Pacific	8

DIESEL LOCOMOTIVES	COUPLER #
EMD F-9 A & B Units	8
EMD GP-20	9
Plymouth Industrial Switcher	5

ROLLING STOCK (CARS)	COUPLER #
Box Car (Billboard)	27
Caboose (4-Wheel)	5
Caboose (8-Wheel)	5
Truck	9
Body	5
Freight Cars (plastic)	5
Freight Trucks - TYCO/Mantua Delrin	5,9
Hopper 54' Covered	27
Hopper Operating Truck	9
Hopper Operating Body	5
Horse Car Circa 1860	9
Passenger Streamlined Combine	5
Passenger - Brass 1890 Era	8
Passenger Streamlined Coach	9

ULRICH

ROLLING STOCK (CARS) (CARS)	COUPLER #
Standard & Triple Hoppers	4
40' Flatcars	4
Gondolas, Track Cleaner	5
Offset Side Hopper	5

Note: All hopper cars can use #5 couplers. A hollow tube over square peg in cast-on draft gear box is helpful.

VAN HOBBIES MODELS

Canadian Models Sold by PFM-All HO 5

VARNEY

STEAM LOCOMOTIVES	COUPLER #
0-4-0 Dockside (metal) Pilot	8
0-4-0 Dockside (metal) Rear	7
0-4-0 Dockside (plastic)	5
4-6-0 Casey jones	5

DIESEL LOCOMOTIVES	COUPLER #
Alco S-1 (actually EMD NW-1)	5
EMD F-7 A and B Units	5

ROLLING STOCK (CARS)	COUPLER #
Box Car	5
Freight Cars (plastic)	5
Ore Car	7

WALTHERS

DIESEL LOCOMOTIVES	COUPLER #
H12-44 (Austria Roco)	5

ROLLING STOCK (CARS)	COUPLER #
Auto Carrier	5
Box Car Cushion Underframe	5
Double Stack Cars	5
Golden Spike Cars	5
Passenger Cars & Traction	16,6
Silver Streak Cars	5
Tank Cars	5
40' Plastic Freight & Work Cars	5

WESTERFIELD

ROLLING STOCK (CARS)	COUPLER #
All Car Kits	5

Kadee® is a Registered Trademark.
Magnematic® is a Registered Trademark.

Roco
RO CO
Imported from Austria by WALTHERS

HO SCALE (1/87)
Couplers are injection molded plastic.

ROUNDHOUSE
Products

HO, HOn3 SCALE (1/87)

DUMMY COUPLERS
Molded in precolored plastic.

480-2972	HO	pkg(12) 1.50
480-2973	HOn³	pkg(12) 1.25

DELAY CLOSE COUPLERS

The ROCO close-couplings are not merely a "shortened" coupling. A specially designed steering mechanism takes care that the ends of locomotives and coaches separate sufficiently while traversing curves so that the buffers do not become entangled. While running on straight track the separation between coaches reduces itself realistically. This permits the model railway operator to run trains in a realistic manner.

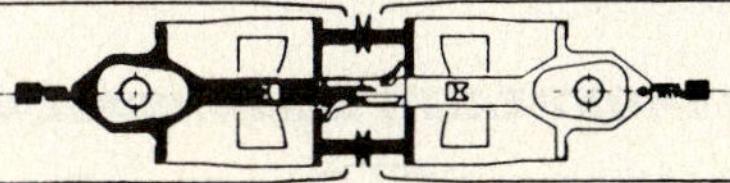

This is the way two close-coupled coaches look from below after removal of the trucks. On straight track the buffers plates will be close together as in the prototype.

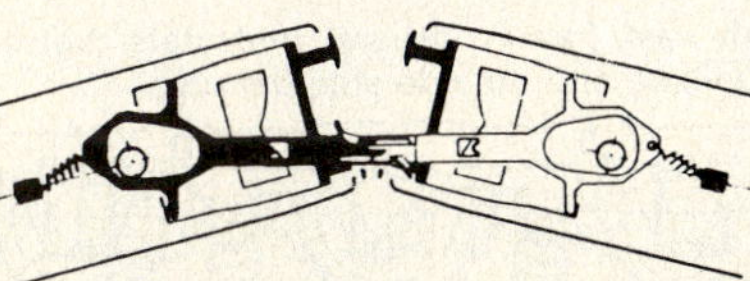

As soon as the coaches enter a curve and form an angle between each other the visible shafts push the coaches apart. The separation is increased in the same proportion as the curve is tightened. While running straight the coaches are again pulled together by means of the gull winged grooves in the coach floors.

625-40274	for 2-axle Box Cars	2.99
625-40287	Adjustable Height pkg(2)	3.49

Fits NEM standard coupler pockets on Roco or other cars. Height can be adjusted up or down for correct alignment between couplers.

625-40326	for 4-axle Pass Cars	pair 3.49
625-40201	for #46106-41107	each 1.99
625-40202	for #46176-46180	each 1.99
625-40203	for #44360-44461	each 1.99
625-40221	for Roewa Cars	each 2.99
625-40233	for #46250-46251	each 2.49
625-40243	for Freight Cars	each 2.49
625-40244	for Fleischmann Freight Cars	each 2.49
625-40248	for #43213	1.99
625-40272	for #43512-43513	pair 2.99
625-40273	Close Coupler	pair 2.99
625-40276	for #40256	pair 2.99
625-40277	for #40257	pair 2.99
625-40279	for #40261	pair 2.99
625-40280	for Fleischmann	pair 2.99
625-40281	for TRIX	pair 2.99
625-40282	Close Coupler	pair 2.99
625-40286	for Ade	each 2.99
625-40292	Uncouplers, Undertrack Mount	12.49
625-40329	for Long Frt Cars	pair 2.99
625-40330	Close Coupler	pair 2.99
625-40332	for 2-axle Flat Cars	pair 2.99
625-40334	Close Coupler	pair 2.99
625-40335	for #46227-46229	pair 2.99
625-40337	Close Coupler	pair 2.99
625-40338	Close Coupler	pair 2.99
625-40341	Retrofit Set	each 5.49
625-40372	for 2-Axle Boxcar pkg(12)	19.99
625-40343	for Small Freight pkg(12)	16.99
625-40344	for Large Freight pkg(12)	16.99
625-40350	Couplers Standard	pkg(12) TBA
625-40351	Couplers Adjustable	pkg(12) TBA

CLOSE COUPLER MULTI-PACKS

625-40270	Delayed Coupler	pkg(4)	2.99
625-40220	Coupler	pkg(4)	2.49
625-40271	Delayed Coupler	pkg(50)	23.99

TRACTION TIRES

625-85602	for Locos, large steam	pkg(10) 3.99

43200, 43208, 43212, 43210, 43213, 43220, 43223, 43224, 43225, 43231, 43233, 43234, 43235, 43206, 43241, 43242, 43243, 43215, 43214, 43260, 43261, 43263, 43265, 43266, 43004, 43449, 43450, 43451, 43452, 43453, 43454, 43457, 43459, 43461, 43462, 43468, 43469, 43011, 43498, 43017

WHEELSETS
Insulated and non-insulated wheel sets.

625-40189	For Flat Wagon Saads 704,7.5 diam.	3.49

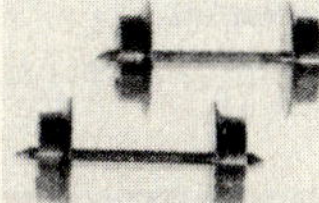

Insulated, 11mm
625-40198 pair 3.49
one side only

625-40264	RP-25 36" Steel Wheels	pr 4.49
625-40196	3-Rail AC	pair 3.49

for freight cars, fits all Roco except, 46330, 46331, 46176, 46177 and 46178

625-40195	3-Rail AC	pair 3.49

for passenger cars, fits coaches 46330, 46331, 46176, 46178, 46121, 44326, 44327, 44328, 44329 and 44330

625-40192	Wheelset	pair 4.49
625-40194	9mm diameter	pair 3.49
625-40266	31" RP-25	pair 4.49
625-40267	Wheelsets RP25	pair 5.49

LIFE-LIKE®

HO SCALE (1/87)
Black molded plastic.

HORN-HOOK COUPLERS

Horn-Hook Coupler
433-1433
pkg(2 pair) 3.00

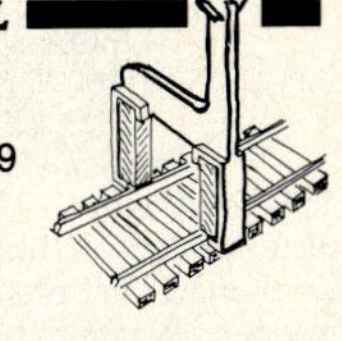
Rix Products

HO SCALE (1/87)

UNCOUPLING TOOL

Rix Uncoupling Tool
628-14   2.99
When inserted between two cars (with Kadee couplers), the tool will cause the couplers to open immediately.

RAIL LINE

HO SCALE (1/87)

COUPLERS
Molded in black nylon.

620-101	Magnetic w/Draft Gear	pkg(4)	2.50
620-106	Regular w/Draft Gear	pkg(4)	2.00
620-107	Regular less Draft Gear	pkg(4)	1.20

620-115	HOn3 "Sharon"	pkg(3 pair)	1.00

non-operating, styrene, 3/32" hole

620-116	HOn3 "Sharon"	pkg(3 pair)	1.00

non-operating, long shank

UNCOUPLERS

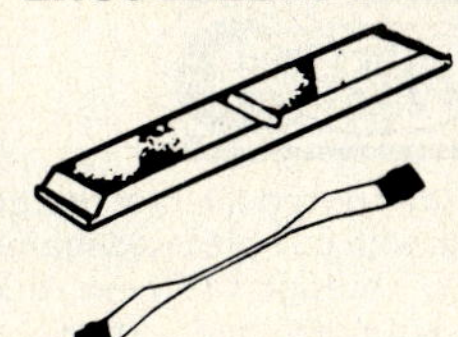

Magnet for #101
620-102
pkg(2) 3.00

Stationary Ramp
620-112
pkg(2) 1.20

---

model power

NEW

COUPLERS

490-96002	Standard	1.98
490-97002	Heavyweight	1.98

Just as freight cars and passenger cars have changed through the years, so have the wheel sets, known as trucks, on which the cars ride. The need to provide a safer, smoother ride for freight and passengers has produced a wide range of designs, many of which are identified with a specific era in railroad history.

The correct style of trucks makes your models more accurate and helps set the time period of your layout.

FREIGHT TRUCKS

ARCH BAR

1860's through 1925. Sideframes, bolsters and other parts were bolted together, but stress often weakened the bolts, resulting in derailments and wrecks. Banned from interchange service in 1938, but frequently used on maintenance equipment after that time.

LEAF SPRING ARCH BAR

Variation on the Arch Bar design, fitted with leaf springs for a smoother ride. Used on tenders and cabooses.

ANDREWS

Developed in the 1920's, cast steel side frame, which used the bolt-in journals from Arch Bar trucks. Used into the 1950's and can still be seen on work equipment.

FOX

Commonly used at the turn-of-the-century, this pressed steel truck was used on all types of cars and some loco tenders. Rare by 1930.

BETTENDORF

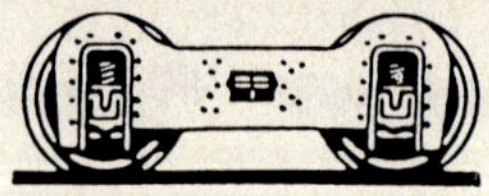

In 1903, Bettendorf introduced the first design of a new style of truck with one-piece sideframe and integral bolsters. Through the years, this truck, which was stronger and offered a smoother ride than most, became standard equipment under all types of freight equipment.

BETTENDORF SWING MOTION

Fitted with leaf springs for a smoother ride, this truck was commonly used under cabooses.

BARBER STABILIZED

Freight cars such as express reefers or merchandise service cars which operated in passenger trains, needed trucks capable of higher speeds. This is just one of many different types which were used.

VULCAN

A fairly common design, used with freight cars.

ROLLER BEARING

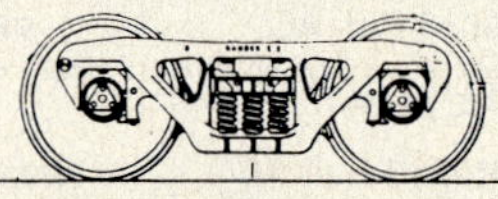

To meet the increased needs of bigger, heavier freight cars, the roller bearing truck was introduced in the early 50's. As roller bearings are less likely to burn out than the older friction bearings, these trucks are now mandatory on all new freight cars and are often seen under rebuilt or upgraded cars.

BUCKEYE FRICTION/ROLLER BEARING TRUCKS

Railroads commonly move large and heavy loads. Special flat cars, gondolas, wreck cranes and other cars are often fitted with heavy-duty trucks with friction or roller bearings. These trucks generally feature six wheels.

COMMONWEALTH

As steam locomotives got bigger, their appetite for fuel and water also increased. Larger tenders, capable of carrying tons of coal, or several thousands of gallons of oil and water, were built. The six-wheel Commonwealth truck became common under many tenders in the late steam era and was used under some heavy duty freight cars.

PASSENGER TRUCKS

Through the years, the development and use of new materials of trucks for passenger cars generally followed the same trends as freight car trucks. The major development of passenger car trucks was the use of the longer wheelbase, which provided a smoother ride. In later years, as cars grew in size and weight, six-wheel trucks became common.

In the 1930's and late 40's when lightweight and streamlined equipment was first introduced, many of the new trains rode on four-wheel trucks. Through experiments, these were greatly refined from early designs and some very distinctive trucks were produced with unique shock absorber, frame, spring and brake gear arrangements.

COMMONWEALTH

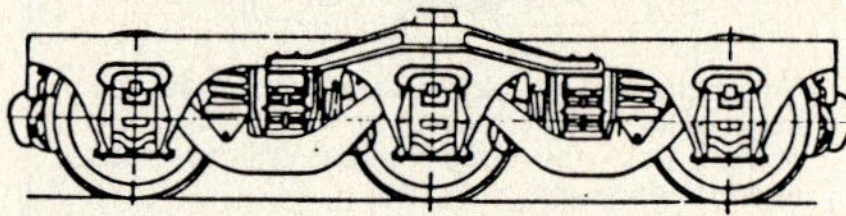

With cast frame, integral pedestals, bottom equalized and outside side bearing.

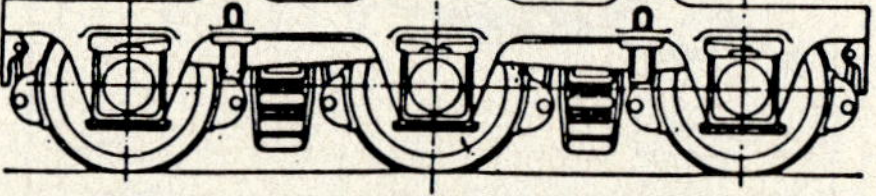

With cast side frame, integral pedestals, straight equalized, inside side bearings, roller bearings.

OLD STYLE COMMONWEALTH

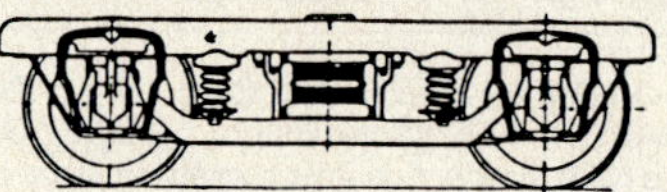

With cast frame, separate pedestals, bottom equalized.

HARLAN

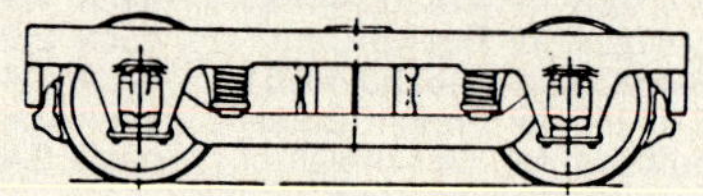

With riveted frame, bottom equalized.

PENNSYLVANIA RAILROAD

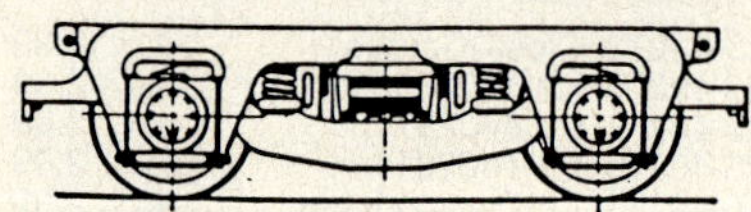

With cast frame, integral pedestals, bottom equalized and roller bearings.

UNION PACIFIC RAILROAD

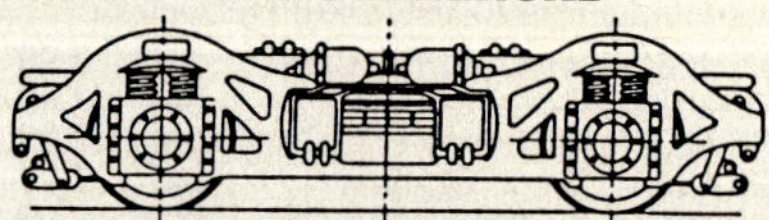

Built for streamliner "Challenger", cast frame with roller bearings.

COMMONWEALTH STREAMLINE

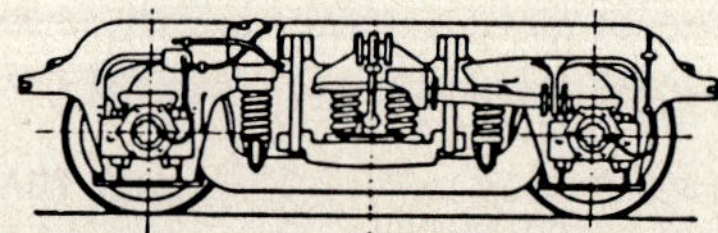

With cast frame, all coil springs, roller bearings, with outside swing hanger.

Items listed in *blue ink* may not be available at all times. Please see your dealer for current delivery information.

HO READY-TO-RUN

Trucks come assembled and ready-to-run. Illustrations are approximately 3/4 actual size. See also — Parts section for more Athearn truck related items, such as gear parts, drive assemblies, etc. Parts are available *only* for current production items.

LOCOMOTIVE TRUCKS

The following Athearn trucks have drive or partial drive mechanisms (or mountings) attached. With some cutting and refabricating of bolsters, these trucks can be used for other manufacturer's products. Sideframes are either Delrin or metal. Power trucks have metal wheels while dummies have Delrin wheels.

For PA1/PB1
140-33233	Front Dummy	each	3.00
140-33234	Rear Dummy	each	3.00

For PB1
140-33236	Front Power	each	4.50

For GE U28B, U30B and U33B
140-34022	Rear Power	each	3.00
140-34021	Front Power	each	3.00
140-34023	Front & Rear Dummy	pair	2.00

For GE U28C, U30C and U33C
140-34213	Rear Power	each	4.50

For SW-1500
140-39021	Front Power	each	2.00
140-39022	Rear Power	each	3.50
140-39023	Dummy	each	2.50

For SW-7/1000
140-41022	Front/Rear Dummy	each	2.00

For F7/GP
140-42010	Front Power	each	3.50
140-42020	Rear Power	each	3.50

For GP50/38-2
140-46010	Front Power	each	4.50
140-46020	Rear Power	each	4.50

For H24-66
140-43016	Front Power	each	4.50
140-43017	Rear Power	each	4.50

For SD9
140-38019	Front Power	each	4.50
140-38020	Rear Power	each	4.50
140-38021	Front Dummy	each	2.25
140-38022	Rear Dummy	each	2.25

For SD40-2
140-44011	Front Power	each	4.50
140-44012	Rear Power	each	4.50
140-44021	Front Dummy	each	3.00
140-44022	Rear Dummy	each	3.00

For SD40/45 F-FP
140-40024	Front Power	each	4.50
140-40025	Rear Power	each	4.50
140-40034	Front/Rear Dummy	each	2.25

For RDC
140-90457	Rear, Power	each	1.50
140-90565	Insulation, Large	pkg(6)	1.20
140-90566	Insulation, Small	pkg(6)	1.20

SIDEFRAMES

140-42009	Blomberg "B"	pkg(4)	2.00
140-45036	for SD40-2		2.00
140-46036	Blomberg "M"	pair	2.00

BLOMBERG TRUCKS

Molded plastic Blomberg trucks have sideframes with arch contour, individual brake cylinders with brake levers and separate outside swing hangers (less worm housing).

140-42011	Geared	pair	7.00
140-46011	Front & Rear Power	each	7.00
140-90459	Dummy 'B'	pair	3.30
140-90469	Dummy 'M'	pair	3.30

FREIGHT TRUCKS

Trucks have RP-25 Delrin wheels.

Hyatt Roller Bearing
140-90399 pair 1.25

Bettendorf
140-90400 pair 1.25

140-90396	28' Impact		TBA
140-90397	Caboose Roller Bearing	pair	1.00
140-90398	Timken Roller Bearing, Working	pair	1.25
140-90407	6-Wheel Buckeye	each	1.75

PASSENGER TRUCKS

Trucks have RP-25 metal wheels.

140-90379	Pick-up Wiper 4-wheel	(6)	1.20
140-90380	Pick-up Wiper 6-wheel	(6)	1.20
140-90411	Streamline Talgo	pair	2.00
140-90413	6-Wheel Talgo	pair	1.90

WHEEL ASSEMBLIES

140-40019	40" Drive Wheels	pkg(2)	1.50
140-40023	Geared Drive Whls	pkg(2)	1.20
140-45034	40" Wheelset w/Bearing	pkg(4)	1.00
140-90501	33" Delrin	pkg(4)	.98
140-90502	36" Plastic Wheelset	pkg(6)	.90
140-90504	36" Metal	pkg(4)	1.00
140-90513	33" Plastic Timken	pkg(4)	1.20

Custom Finishing

Easy-to-build modern freight and passenger car trucks feature brass parts, springs and NorthWest Short Line wheelsets.

PASSENGER CAR

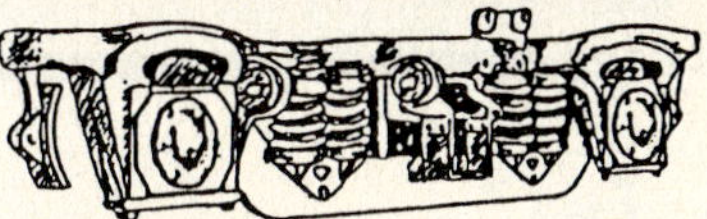

247-185	GSC 41-N/41-ND	pair 23.95

Less details

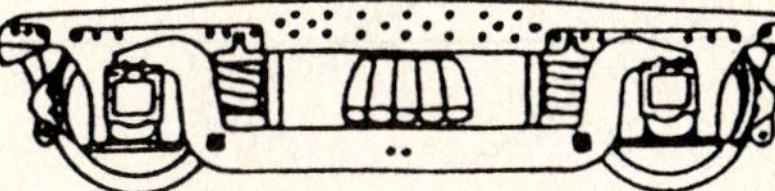

247-244	Standard Motor Car NWSL	pair 10.95

White metal, wheels unsprung.

ROLLER BEARING

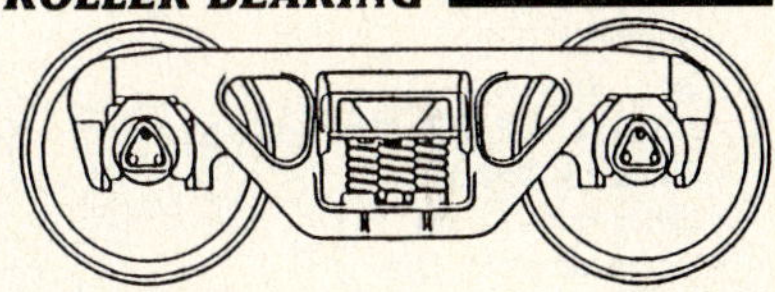

247-177	70 Ton	pair	19.89
247-218	100 Ton	pair	20.95

TRUCK SPRING

247-132   pkg(8) 2.09
Replacement springs fit many HO Scale trucks. Measure .150 long by .090" diameter.

247-180   pkg(12) 2.09
Measure .130 by .060" diameter.

247-227 Truck Spring   pkg(12) 2.09
.250 long by .164" diameter, both ends flat.

ACCESSORIES FOR GSC 41-N/41-ND

Each pkg. contains enough parts for 1 pair trucks.

247-186	12 x 10 Brake Cylinder w/Stack Adjustor	pkg(4)	7.59
247-187	Monroe Shock	pkg(4)	2.19
247-188	Houde Shock	pkg(4)	2.19
247-189	Hyatt Bearing Caps	pkg(8)	2.69
247-190	Timken Bearing Caps, Round	pkg(8)	2.69
247-191	Timken Bearing Caps	pkg(8)	2.69
247-216	SKE Bearing Caps	pkg(8)	2.69
247-217	Decelostat Caps	pkg(4)	1.59

ORIENTAL limited

HO READY-TO-RUN

All metal castings.

LOCOMOTIVE TRUCK

Commonwealth Two-Wheel Delta Type
541-131   5.00
for 2-8-2/4-6-2

prototype photo

Ernst Manufacturing Inc.

HO SCALE (1/87)

Gearing kits for Athearn 4-axle, 6-axle and SD40-2 diesel trucks.

GEARS

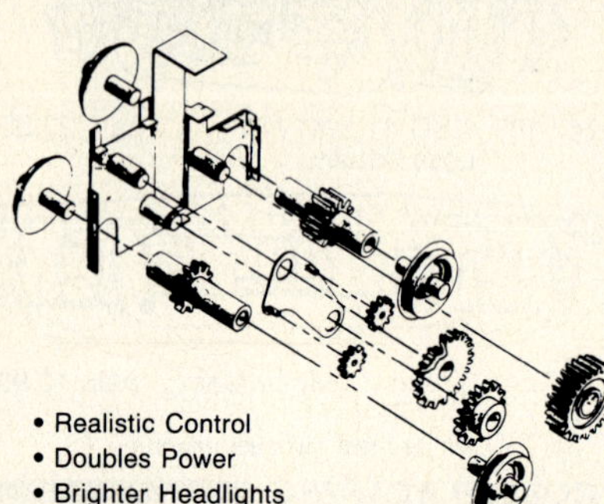

- Realistic Control
- Doubles Power
- Brighter Headlights
- Durability
- Self-Lubricating
- Slower Low Speed (32:1 gearing)
- Smoother Operation
- Motor Runs Cooler
- Increased Motor Life
- Triple Reduction

259-44 Gearing Kit MKII 7.98
for 4-axle Trucks
F7, A & B, GP9, GP35, U28B, U30B, U33B, S12, SW1500 Cow and SW1500 Calf.

259-6 Super Gearing for 6-axle 7.98
EMD-SD9, F45, SDP40, SD45, U28C, U33C, Trainmaster, Alco PA1 and PB1 (Alcos require modeling skill).

259-66 Gearing Kit for SD40-2 7.98
Converts 12:1 ratio of the stock SD40-2 to a 32:1 gear ratio. Greater pulling power, slower speed and less current draw.

259-2 Gearing Kit for Hustler 11.98
Provides a 36:1 gear ratio with two 1/2" flywheels. Includes two flywheels, brass worms and gearboxes with all gears necessary.

259-3 Gearing Kit for RDC 11.98
Provides a 12:1 gear ratio with a large flywheel for smoother operation. Includes a gearbox, geared axle pieces, worm gears, 1" flywheel and added components.

LIFE-LIKE®

HO SCALE (1/87) READY-TO-RUN

Ready-to-Run, molded plastic trucks with couplers.

FREIGHT TRUCKS

433-1435 Bettendorf   pair 3.00

Grandt Line

HOn3 SCALE (1/87) READY-TO-RUN

Trucks and wheelsets are molded in Delrin, unless noted.

BETTENDORF
With metal wheels. Used by C&S, RGS and WP&Y.

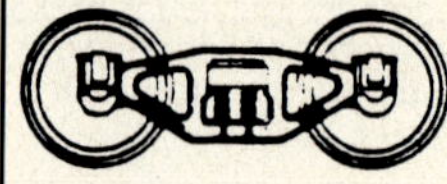

54" Wheelbase
300-5120   pr 4.50

D&RGW ANDREWS HOn3
With metal wheels.

300-5144 4'8" Wheelbase (brown) pr 4.50
300-5145 4'8" Wheelbase (black) pr 4.50

D&RGW ARCHBAR
With metal wheels.

4'8" Wheelbase (brown)
300-5159   pr 4.50

SR&RL ARCHBAR HOn2-1/2
With silver Delrin wheels.

300-5146 4' Wheelbase pr 4.50
(black, gray)

D&RGW FREIGHT CAR
With nickel plated brass wheels.

3'7" Wheelbase (brown)
300-5110   pr 4.50

3'7" Wheelbase (black)
300-5111   pr 4.50

PASSENGER CAR HOn3
With metal wheels.
300-5182 HOn3   pair 9.00

WHEELSETS

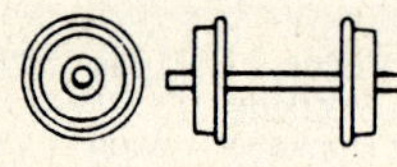

26" Non-magnetic Metal, Hon3
300-5132
pkg(2 pair) 3.00

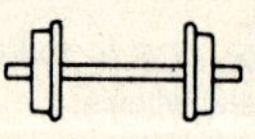

20" Brass Axle HOn3
300-5141
pkg(2 pair) 2.00
silver Delrin wheels

300-5142 20" Brass Axle pkg(2 pair) 2.00
HOn30
silver Delrin wheels

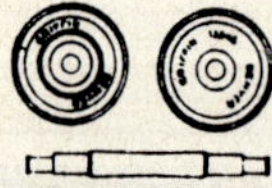

Griffen-Denver 26" Wheelsets, Non-operating
300-5055
pkg(4 pair) 2.75

(not illustrated)
300-7092 HOn3 Wheelsets   10.50
from 23 ton box cab
(includes 1 plain, 1 geared axle)

300-7093 HO Wheelsets   10.50
from 23 ton box cab
(Includes 1 plain, 1 geared axle)

GLOOR·CRAFT MODELS

HO READY-TO-RUN

FREIGHT TRUCKS
Sideframes are metal and fully equalized, black Delrin 33" wheels (unless noted) and RP-25 contour.

Bettendorf
288-801 pr 4.25

Bettendorf with 36" wheels
288-805 pr 4.25

Arch Bar
288-804 pr 4.25

Roller Bearing
288-800 pr 4.25

Roller Bearing with 36" wheels
288-803 pr 4.25

Andrews
288-802 pr 4.25

(not illustrated)
288-807 Wheel Set 33"   pkg(4) 2.25
288-808 Wheel Set 36"   pkg(4) 2.25

CAL-SCALE

HO SCALE (1/87) CRAFT TRAIN KITS

Kits consist of brass castings.

LOCOMOTIVE TRUCKS

190-2000 USRA   each 14.25
includes opening journal lids

TENDER TRUCKS

4-Wheel USRA
190-311 pr 19.95

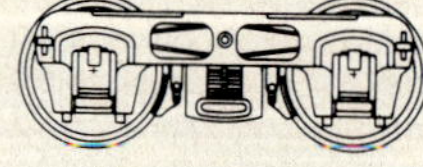

Andrews
190-310 pr 19.95

HO SCALE (1/87)

Kadee offers two styles of trucks, Talgo style (with couplers and coupler pockets mounted on truck) and standard style (does not include couplers and coupler pockets). All trucks feature blackened non-magnetic metal side frames and wheels with Delrin axles. Cannot be used for car lighting unless wipers are used on wheels.

BETTENDORF TRUCKS

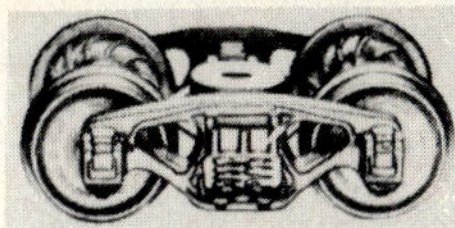

Double Truss, Standard
380-500   pr 5.75

Double Truss, Talgo
380-502   pr 8.00
with #4 couplers mounted

(not illustrated)
380-511   less coupler   5.75
380-512   w/coupler   8.00

ARCH BAR TRUCKS

Standard Style
380-501   pr 5.75

Talgo Style
380-503   pr 8.00
with #4 couplers mounted

#503:

ASF CAST TRUCKS

Andrews, Standard
380-509   pr 5.75

380-510   Andrews, Talgo   pair 8.00
with #4 couplers mounted

LOGGING TRUCKS

Two trucks come in each kit, without logs. Also included are two pairs of #4 Magne-Matic couplers.

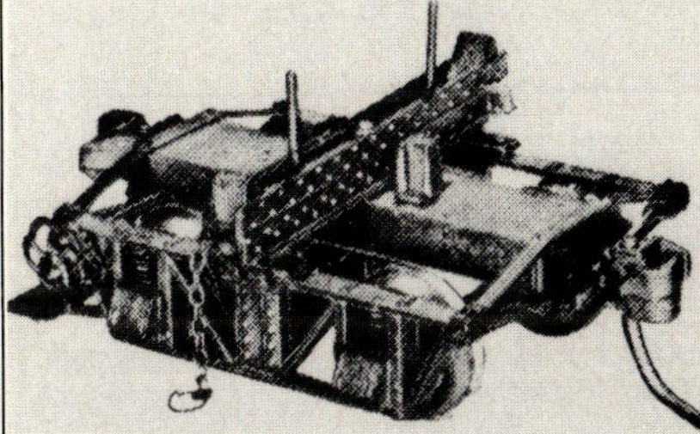

380-107   Disconnect Logging Trucks pr 15.35

ROLLERBEARING TRUCKS

380-513   without couplers   1 pr 5.75
380-514   with couplers   1 pr 8.00

VULCAN TRUCKS

380-515   without coupler   5.75
380-516   with coupler   5.75

HOn3 TRUCK ASSEMBLIES

Kits include body and truck bolsters, sideframes, spring planks, wheel sets, truck bushings and track springs.

380-716   3'7"   pkg(2)   7.95

380-717   4'6"   pkg(2)   7.95

(not illustrated)
380-715   HOn3   3.95

CONVERSION BOLSTERS

Each package contains two conversion bolsters and one pair of #5 couplers. For Central Valley and AHM passenger trucks.

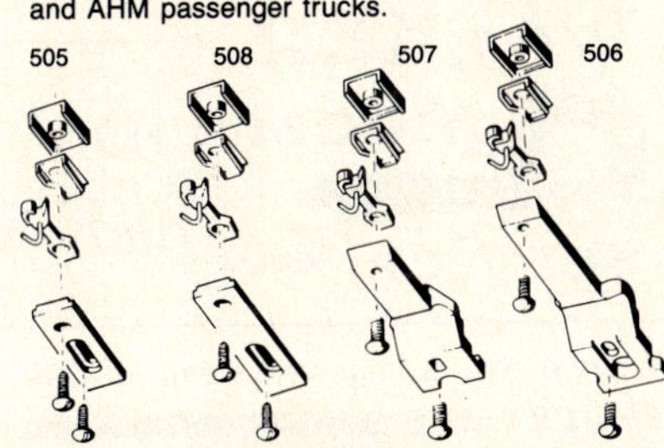

380-505   For AHM 6 Wheel   pair 3.30
Passenger Trucks
Adjusts to different car lengths.

380-506   For CV 4 Wheel   pair 3.30
Passenger Trucks
Adjusts to different car lengths.

380-507   For CV 6 Wheel   pair 3.30
Passenger Trucks

380-508   For AHM 4 Wheel   pair 3.30
Passenger Trucks

WHEELSETS

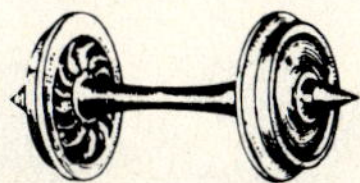

RP-25 contour, tapered axles, ribbed back and founding data on wheels (unless noted).

380-520   For Freight Cars   pkg(12) 7.20
with 33" wheels, smooth back
380-521   For Passenger Cars   pkg(12) 9.00
with 36" wheels
380-522   For Passenger **NEW** pkg(12) 9.00
Cars with 36" wheels, smooth back
380-523   For Freight **NEW**   pkg(12) 7.20
Cars with 33" wheels
380-524   For Freight **NEW**   pkg(12) 7.20
Cars with 28" wheels, smooth back

FIBER WASHERS

Truck spacer washers for adjusting car height or coupler height.

380-208   Truck Spacer Washers   pkg(48) 2.30
.015" thick, red only
380-209   Truck Spacer Washers   pkg(48) 2.30
.010" thick, gray only

PLASTIC SCREWS

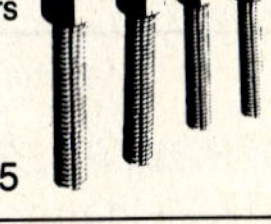

Uses include mounting metal trucks to metal underframes with fiber washers in between. 2-5/16" x 1/2" long.

Delrin Insulating Roundhead Screws
380-256   pkg(12) 1.65

TRUCK SPRINGS

380-624   HOn3   pkg(12)   .98
380-637   HO   pkg(18) 1.95

Keil-Line Models
HO SCALE (1/87)
CRAFT TRAIN KITS

FREIGHT TRUCKS

Kit contains three pair of all metal construction sprung trucks less wheelsets. For use with Kadee wheelsets.
382-8721 Bettendorf   pkg(3 pair) 5.95
382-8722 Timken   pkg(3 pair) 5.95

PASSENGER TRUCKS

382-8701 CNW/RI Smooth   pkg(2) 6.95
382-8703 MILW/RI Ribbed pkg(2) 6.95

Keystone Locomotive Works

HO SCALE (1/87)
ALL-METAL TRUCK KITS

FREIGHT

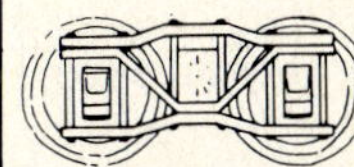

Grasse River Logging
395-30   pair 2.95
kit

PASSENGER

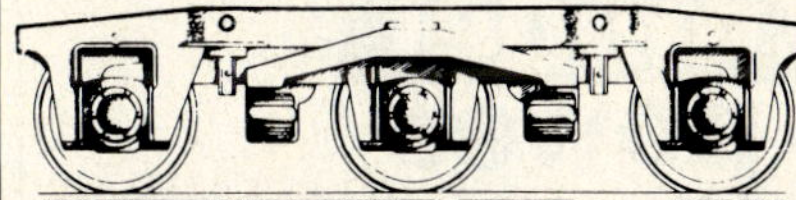

395-9   PRR 6-Wheel   pair 9.25
Pre-assembled, NorthWest Short Line nickel-silver wheelsets.

SHAY

395-28   Complete Truck   pair 7.95

McKean

HO READY-TO-RUN

TRUCKS

Easy to build kits include plastic sideframes and wheels, metal axles.

457-17 Bettendorf   pair 1.50
457-18 70 Ton   pair 1.50
457-23 Bettendorf Trucks   ea 1.50
      Flat Bolster
457-24 70 Ton Trucks   ea 1.50
      Flat Bolster
457-25 100 Ton Trucks   ea 1.50
      Flat Bolster

WHEELSETS

457-44 Plastic 33'   pkg(8) 1.25
457-46 36" Delrin **NEW**   pkg(8) 1.25

COUPLERS

457-41 Standard Dummy, Long   pair 1.95
457-42 Standard Dummy, Short   pair 1.95
457-43 Standard Dummy, Slotted   pair 1.95

International Hobby Corp.

HO SCALE (1/87)

PASSENGER TRUCKS

Super free-wheeling

348-4240 Black   pair 19.98
348-4241 Silver   pair 19.98
348-4242 Truck Adapter   3.98

DIAPHRAGMS

348-6060 Rivarossi Detailed   pair 2.98

WHEEL SETS

Metal, insulated-one side, replaces plastic Rivarossi wheel sets.
348-4254 31" RP25   pkg(12) 12.98
348-4255 31" RP25   pkg(36) 35.98

model power **NEW**

TRUCKS

490-94002 RP25   1.98
490-95002 Standard   1.98

STEWART PRODUCTS

HO SCALE (1/87)

VINYL TRACTION TIRES

Vinyl tires increase pulling power and give a smoother ride with less bounce. (These tires can only be used on wheels that had traction tires on them originally. Wheels must be grooved to accept tires.)

683-505 Super Traction Tires   pkg(20) 5.95
683-510 AHM Small Steam   pkg(18) 5.95
    fits AHM GG-1, 0-8-0 Switcher, 2-8-8-2 Mallet
683-511 AHM Medium Steam   pkg(18) 5.95
    fits AHM Mikado, Berkshire, Bowker, Challenger, Reno
683-512 AHM Large Steam   pkg(18) 5.95
    fits AHM Hudson, Heavy Pacific
683-513 AHM Steam   pkg(18) 5.95
    Assortment
includes six each of #510, 511 and 512

TRACTION TIRE TOOL

For easy application of traction tires.

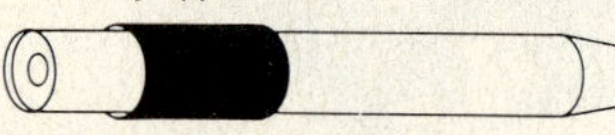

683-504 Traction Tire Tool   9.95
    with ten traction tires

WALKER Model service
HO SCALE (1/87)

White metal castings with Delrin wheels

TRUCKS

PSC
Arch Bar
786-5301
pair 5.50

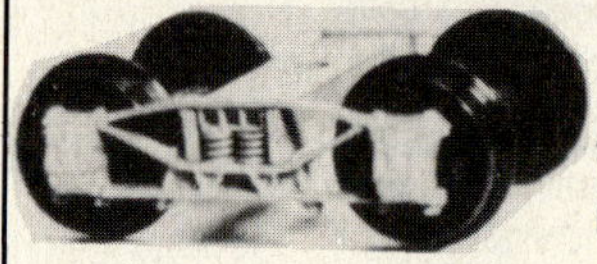

PRR
70 Ton
786-5302
pair 5.50

Swing
Motion
786-5303
pair 5.50
5' wheel
base

Arch
Bar
786-5304
pair 5.50
5' wheel
base

TRAIN STATION PRODUCTS
DIVISION OF QUALITY-WRIGHT CORPORATION

HO SCALE (1/87)

These detailed plastic parts can be combined with other manufacturers' products to create customized or superdetailed cars. Molded in Delrin®.

PASSENGER TRUCKS

732-410 Superliner less Wheels   pkg(2) 7.95

732-411 Superliner   pkg(2) TBA
    w/Brass Wheels
732-412 Superliner   pkg(6) 21.95
    less Wheels
Fits Con-Cor and other Superliner passenger cars. Accepts Con-Cor, Kadee and Jay-Bee 36" wheelsets. Coupler pocket accepts Kadee No 5 couplers.

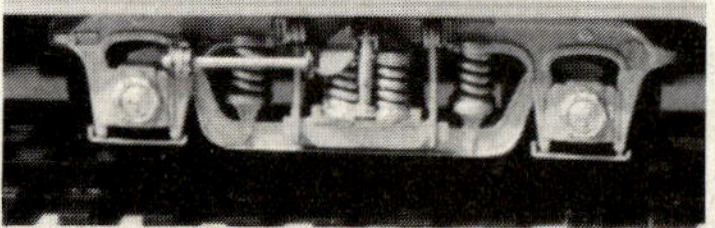

732-414 Outside Swing Hanger pkg(2) 8.95
    less Wheels
732-416 Outside Swing Hanger pkg(6) 23.95
    less Wheels
Fits Rivarossi, Con-Cor, Athearn, AHM and other passenger cars. Accepts Kadee, Con-Cor and Jay-Bee 36" wheel sets. Coupler pocket accepts Kadee No 5 couplers.
732-402 Mounting Screws   pkg(12) 4.95
    For attaching passenger car trucks to Con-Cor, AHM or Rivarossi passenger cars. Non-magnetic, stainless steel screws.

STEWART HOBBIES, INC.

HO CRAFT TRAIN KITS

Commonwealth trucks with plastic sideframes, including cylinders, brake arms and rods, less worm and housing.

LOCO TRUCKS

691-6076 AS-616 Commonwealth pr 19.00
691-6077 AS-616   2 pair 5.00
    Commonwealth
    sideframes only

NorthWest Short Line

HO SCALE (1/87)

POWER TRUCKS
- Flea II
- 4-Wheel PDT
- 6-Wheel PDT
- Worm Kit

WHEELSETS
- Shouldered
- Flush
- Blunt
- Pointed

POWER TRUCKS

Will power almost any model—from steam loco-motive boosters to passenger cars. Leaves loco or car bodies open and empty for sound systems or control equipment.

FLEA II

Flea II is a miniature drive unit that can be gauged from 9.0mm to On3. Includes a Sagami Can Motor and HO Gauge 33"/88 wheelset (design of Flea II permits easy change-out of wheelsets).

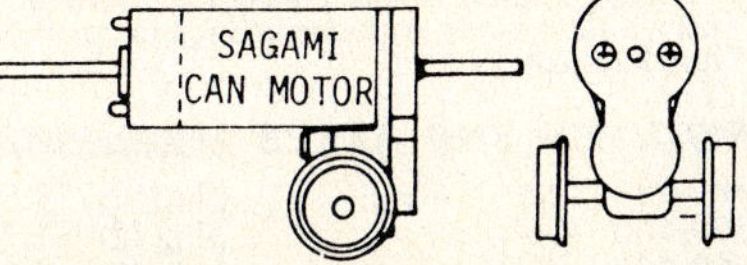

053-2056	Flea II Power Truck	39.95

Sagami motor: 12v DC can type #122039, 41 scale mph

053-2066	Flea II Power Truck	42.95

Sagami motor: 12v DC can type #122539, 30 scale mph

053-2076	Auxiliary Gearbox	6.50

15:1 ratio (less geared wheelset). Provides easy powering of models, quality performance in a minimum space and permits flexibility.

4-WHEEL PDT

The PDT (Pretty Darn Tiny) power truck com-bines the best features of the Sagami can motor plus NWSL gear reduction design that provides more power, slower speed, smoother operation, quiet running and long life bearings in a versatile unit. These units are based on the Sagami 1200 and 1225 size system.

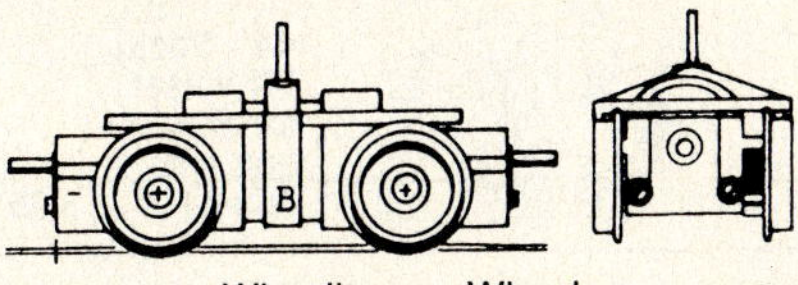

	Wheelbase	Wheel	
053-70014	5'6"	26"	54.95
053-70114	6'	26"	54.95
053-70124	6'	33"	54.95
053-70224	6'6"	33"	49.95
053-70234	6'6"	36"	49.95
053-70314	7'	33"	49.95
053-70324	7'	36"	49.95
053-70334	7'	40"	49.95
053-70514	8'	26"	49.95
053-70524	8'	36"	49.95
053-70534	8'	40"	49.95
053-70624	8'6"	36"	49.95
	for Athearn RDC		
053-70734	9'	40"	49.95
053-70804	13'3"	42"	49.95
	for Athearn Hustler		

6-WHEEL PDT

Center axle is unpowered and can be set for EMD 6-wheel truck style either centered or off-centered. Trucks include NWSL/110 nickel-plated brass wheels that provide power con-tact and stay clean. The PDT power truck is self-operating with accessible wiring for simplified power control or lighting.

	Wheelbase	Wheel	
053-70824	13'7"	40"	54.95
	for SD40-2, SD-9, SD-45		
053-70834	14'	36"	54.95
	for E Units		
053-70844	15'6"		54.95
	for Alcos		

WORM KIT

Worm replacement kit for GSB, KMT vertical motor style power truck mechanism. Provides a steel worm plus spacer to adapt the worm to the original wormgear. Truck disassembly not required.

053-3286	GSB/Kumata Power Truck Worm Kit	4.25

UNPOWERED TENDER TRUCKS

053-4605	Baldwin HOn3	pair 3.95

SIDEFRAME

053-4325	Brill 77EI	pkg(4) 4.50

BRASS WHEELSETS & WHEELS

Non-magnetic wheelsets with nickel-plated wheels (insulated on one side only for electrical pick-up), 3/32" axle, 1/16" journal on shouldered style.
110 are standard HO thread.
88 is finescale HO and HOn3

FLEA II GEARED WHEELSETS

Wheelsets have a shoulder style axle, except for 053-20196, which is flush.

053-20016	33"	NWSL/110 regular	3.95
053-20026	36"	NWSL/110 regular	3.95
053-20036	40"	NWSL/110 regular	3.95
053-20046	42"	NWSL/110 regular	3.95
053-20056	26"	NWSL/110 regular	3.95
053-20086	26"	NWSL/88 narrow	3.95
053-20096	33"	NWSL/88 narrow	3.95
053-20106	36"	NWSL/88 narrow	3.95
053-20186	26"	NWSL/88 HOn3	3.95
053-20196	26"	NWSL/88 HOn3	3.95
053-20236	3/32"	Geared Axle	3.50

BRASS REPLACEMENT WHEELSET

For AHM E8 Unit EMD diesel. Allows for closer to scale flanges. Includes six wheelsets, two are geared to match original model.

053-71834	Replacement Wheelset	pkg(6)	12.95

BLUNT STYLE END

053-71094	40" NWSL-110B	pkg(6)	5.95
053-71104	42" NWSL-110B	pkg(6)	5.95

POINTED CONE STYLE ENDS

053-71164	30" NWSL-110P	pkg(4)	3.95
053-71174	33" NWSL-110P	pkg(4)	3.95
053-71184	36" NWSL-110P	pkg(6)	5.95
053-71194	40" NWSL-110P	pkg(6)	5.95
053-71204	42" NWSL-110P	pkg(6)	5.95
053-72174	33" NWSL-88P	pkg(4)	3.95
053-72184	36" NWSL-88P	pkg(6)	5.95
053-71394	40"	pkg(6)	6.95
	for geared Athearn, metal sideframe		
053-71404	42"	pkg(6)	6.95
	for geared Athearn, metal sideframe		
053-71804	36" P F/KLW 44T	pkg(4)	10.00
053-71814	36" F F/KLW 44T	pkg(4)	10.00
053-71824	33" P F/KLW 44T	pkg(4)	10.00
053-71154	28" NWSL-110P	pkg(4)	3.95
053-72154	28" NWSL-88P	pkg(4)	3.95
053-73124	24" NWSL-88P	pkg(4)	3.95
053-73134	26" NWSL-88P	pkg(4)	3.95
053-73154	28" NWSL-88P	pkg(4)	3.95
053-73164	30" NWSL-88P	pkg(4)	3.95
053-71414	40" Inside Frame	pkg(6)	6.95
	for Athearn, plastic sideframe		
053-71424	42" Inside Frame	pkg(6)	6.95
	for Athearn, plastic sideframe		
053-72394	40" Outside Frame for Geared Athearn	pkg(6)	6.95
053-72414	40" Inside Frame for Geared Athearn	pkg(6)	6.95
053-71364	38" NP-110P *NEW*	pkg(4)	3.95
053-71434	36" Brass		6.95
053-71814	36" F/KLW 44T4		10.00
053-72364	38" NP 88P *NEW*	pkg(4)	3.95
053-73124	24" HOn3-P88	pkg(4)	3.95
053-74424	40" Rapido Replacement		15.95
053-171154	28" 110P Weathered	pkg(4)	3.95
053-171174	33" x 110 pt Axle	pkg(4)	3.95

POINTED CONE STYLE ENDS (cont)

053-171184	36" x 110 pt Axle	pkg(4)	5.95
053-171364	38" 110P *NEW* Weathered	pkg(4)	3.95
053-172364	38" 88P *NEW* Weathered	pkg(4)	3.95

SHOULDERED STYLE

053-71034	26" NWSL-110s	pkg(4)	3.95
053-71054	28" NWSL-110s	pkg(4)	3.95
053-71064	30" NWSL-110s	pkg(4)	3.95
053-71074	33" NWSL-110s	pkg(4)	3.95
053-71084	36" NWSL-110s	pkg(6)	5.95
053-71314	40" NWSL-110s	pkg(6)	5.95
053-71324	42" NWSL-110s	pkg(6)	5.95
053-73024	24" NWSL-88s	pkg(4)	3.95
053-73034	26" NWSL-88s	pkg(4)	3.95
053-72054	28" NWSL-88s	pkg(4)	3.95
053-72074	33" NWSL-88s	pkg(4)	3.95
053-72084	36" NWSL-88s	pkg(6)	5.95

FLUSH END STYLE

053-71234	26" NWSL-110F	pkg(4)	3.95
053-71244	26" NWSL-110F PCC	pkg(4)	3.95
053-71254	28" NWSL-110F	pkg(4)	3.95
053-71294	40" NWSL-110F	pkg(6)	5.95
053-71304	42" NWSL-110F	pkg(6)	5.95
053-72244	26" NWSL-88F	pkg(4)	3.95
053-72254	28" NWSL-88F	pkg(4)	3.95
053-73224	24" NWSL-88F	pkg(4)	3.95
053-73234	26" NWSL-88F	pkg(4)	3.95
053-176174	33"	pkg(4)	3.95
053-176184	36"	pkg(4)	5.95

Pia
PRECISION INVESTMENT ASSOCIATES, INC.

HO SCALE (1/87)
Kits consist of brass castings, unless noted.

PASSENGER

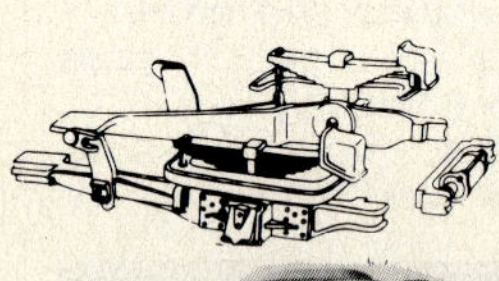

063-130	HOn3 w/Bolsters,	pair	12.00
063-129	HOn3 w/Bolsters,	pair	7.75
	Pads and Plastic Wheels		

LOCOMOTIVE TRAILING

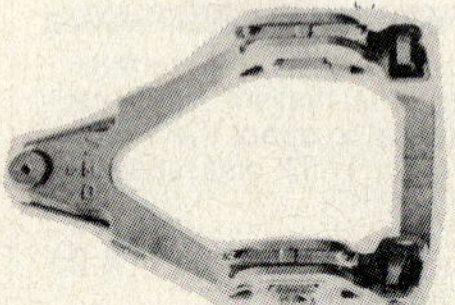

USRA Heavy Two Wheel Trailing Truck (less wheels) kit pkg(3 pcs)
063-46   9.95

Delta Trailing Truck Commonwealth (less wheels) kit pkg(7 pcs)
063-45   9.98

(not illustrated)
063-101 Booster Engine   9.98
Complete for 45 trailing truck

DIESEL

063-162	Ulitmate Type B, Blomberg	pair	39.95
063-163	Ultimate Type M, Blomberg	pair	39.95

TENDER

(Tender Truck Kits Include: 4 sideframes & 2 bolsters, unless otherwise noted.)

063-181	Andrews Bar WP 2-6-6-2	6.95
063-182	Arch Bar, NP Style	6.98
063-183	Six Wheel, NYC H106 14 pcs	14.95
063-184	Commonwealth Rutland	6.95
063-185	Andrews, Std, GN01	6.95
063-186	Southern Pacific	6.95

SIDEFRAMES & WHEELS

063-43 Hi-Speed Tender   pkg(4) 6.98
Truck Sideframe

063-44 Truck Sideframe   6.95
Archbar NP Y1

063-86 Tender Truck   pkg(4) 6.98
Sideframes, Arch Bar Type

SIDEFRAMES & WHEELS (cont)

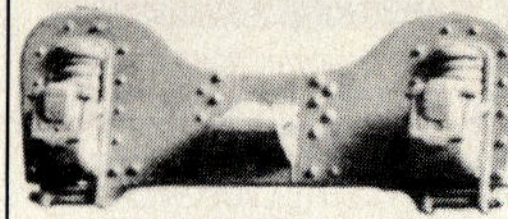

Tender, Sideframe Fox Patent
063-148
pkg(4) 6.98

44″ Spoked Wheelset for #063-45 and #46
063-51   3.95

OLD PULLMAN

HO SCALE (1/87)

Assembled trucks with needle-point non-magnetic axles and sprung Delrin sideframes and bolsters. ''Black Label'' trucks have precision-made NMRA RP-25 black nickel-plated brass wheelsets. ''Red Label'' trucks feature Walthers RP-25 plastic wheels.

FREIGHT CAR TRUCKS

Bettendorf 50-Ton AAR — 1940/1950 Era
536-40001 Black Label 33″ Wheels pr 5.25
536-40081 Red Label 33″ Wheels pr 2.50

Andrews — 1930-1939 Era
536-40011 Black Label 33″ Wheels pr 5.25
536-40061 Red Label 33″ Wheels pr 2.50

Timken Roller Bearing 1955-Present
536-40021 Black Label 33″ Wheels pr 5.25
536-40091 Red Label 33″ Wheels pr 2.50

Timken Roller Bearing 1955-Present
536-40031 Black Label 36″ Wheels pr 5.25

Jay-Bee

HO SCALE (1/87)
METAL WHEELSETS & AXLES

All wheelsets are brass with blacknickel plating (unless noted) and are RP25 contour, .110 tread.

ATHEARN DIESEL

369-100	36″ Wheels w/1/2″ Axle	pkg(12)	6.50
369-101	42″ Wheels w/1/2″ Axle	pkg(8)	4.50
369-102	40″ Solid Nickel Silver Wheels w/1/2″ Axle	pkg(8)	7.45

For use in newer Athearn diesels with molded plastic sideframes. Includes enough to convert one four-axle loco.

POINTED END AXLES

369-98	38″	pkg(12)	12.50
369-106	36″	pkg(12)	11.75
369-107	28″	pkg(8)	7.50
369-108	33″	pkg(12)	11.50
369-109	40″	pkg(4)	3.90
369-988	(4) 33″ & (8) 38″	pkg(12)	11.90

For Walthers Double Stack

SHOULDER END AXLES

369-1012	42″	pkg(4)	3.90
369-1062	36″	pkg(4)	3.90
369-1072	28″	pkg(4)	3.90
369-1082	33″	pkg(4)	3.90
369-1092	40″	pkg(4)	3.90

BLUNT END AXLES

369-1011	42″	pkg(4)	3.90
369-1061	36″	pkg(4)	3.90
369-1081	33″	pkg(4)	3.90
369-1091	40″	pkg(4)	3.90

AXLES & MOLDED PLASTIC WHEELS

369-103 36″, for Rivarossi pkg(24) 4.95
Passenger
For use on 1920 and 1930 series models. Enough wheels to convert two heavyweight or three lightweight cars.

369-105 Nonmagnetic Axles pkg(24) 3.25
for Athearn and MCD Freight Cars, 33″ Wheels, Brass

N.J. International

HO SCALE (1/87)

TRUCKS

525-266	PRR Dauphin	8.99
525-269	4-Wheel Tender w/Booster	13.99

PRECISION SCALE Co.

HO SCALE (1/87) CRAFT TRAIN KITS

Truck kits are lost wax brass castings, unless noted, or unless obviously excepted (springs, screws, etc.). All kits are HO Scale, standard gauge, unless noted. Illustrations are not to scale.

+ (PLUS SIGN) = SPECIAL ORDER ONLY ITEMS

STEAM LOCOMOTIVE TRUCKS

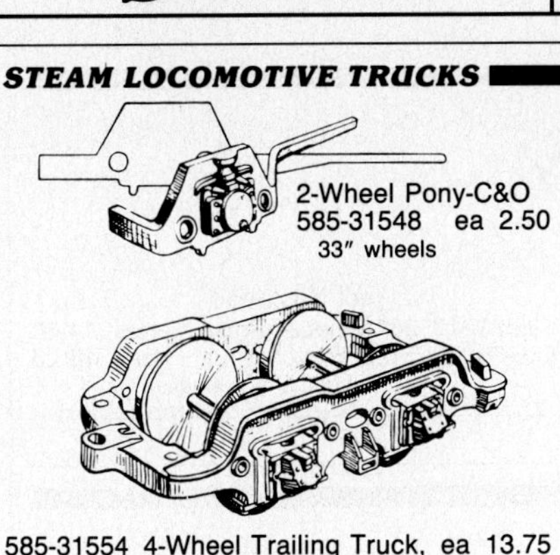

2-Wheel Pony-C&O
585-31548   ea 2.50
33" wheels

585-31554 4-Wheel Trailing Truck, ea 13.75
Plain Journals
40" wheels, 5'6" wheelbase

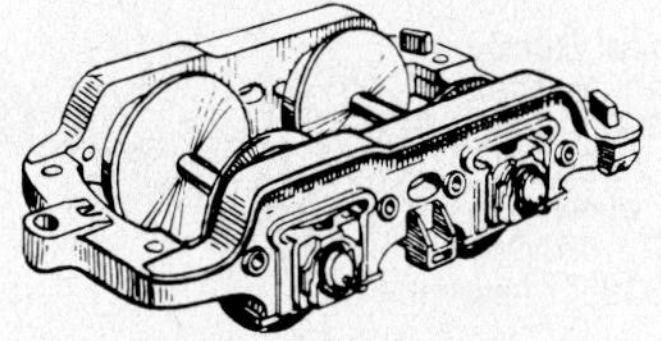

585-31555 4-Wheel Trailing Truck, ea 13.75
Roller Bearing
40" wheels, 5'6" wheelbase

585-31557 Delta Trailing Trucks,   ea 13.50
Roller Journals & Booster Engine
45" spoked wheels, required

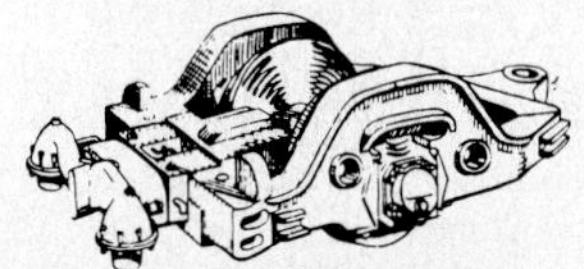

585-31556 Delta Trailing Trucks,   ea 13.50
Plain Bearings & Booster Engine
45" spoked wheels, required

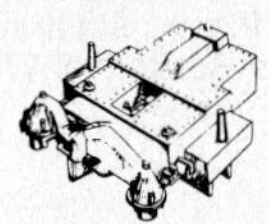

585-3334 Franklin Booster   18.00

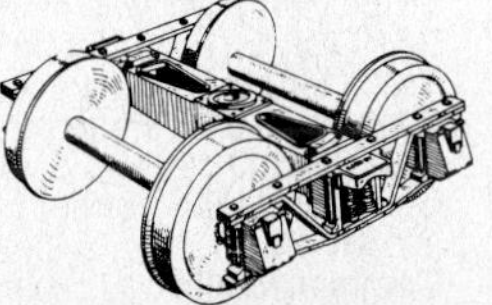

585-30251 Archbar w/26" Wheels   9.75
HOn3, assembled

(not illustrated)
585-3823 HOn3 Lead Truck, Brill,   4.00
Less Wheels

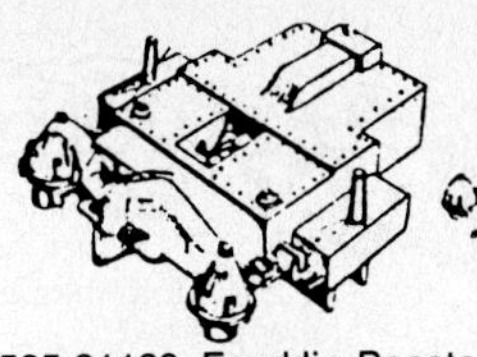

585-31139 Franklin Booster Engine   ea 4.00
for Trailing Truck
585-31660 Plastic   **NEW** each 2.50

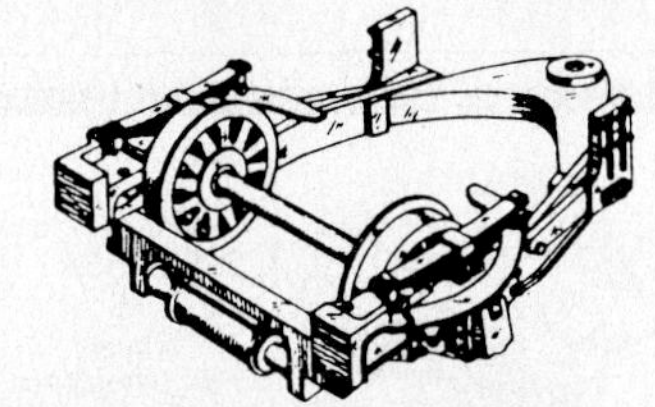

585-31010 Hodges Trailing Truck,   ea 12.25
Northern Pacific, 42" Wheels

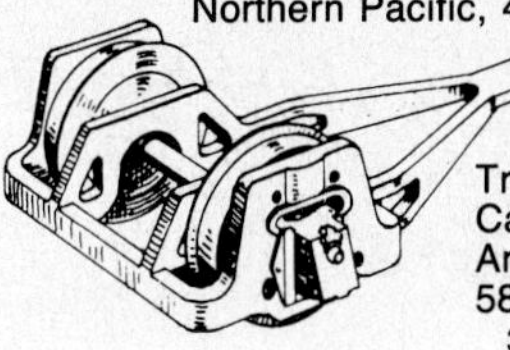

Trailing Truck for Cab Foward Articulated
585-31553 ea 6.75
36" wheels

Pilot Truck, HOn3
585-31543   ea 3.50
20" wheels

Lead Truck HOn3
D&RGW C-16
585-31550   ea 6.00
24" wheels

Lead Truck
585-31544 26" Spoked Wheels   8.00
585-31545 33" Spoked Wheels   8.00
585-31546 36" Spoked Wheels   8.00
585-31547 40" Spoked Wheels   8.00

Brill Lead Truck
585-31812   ea 4.50
20" Wheels

C-16 Lead Truck
Frame HOn3
585-31784 + ea 2.75
Plastic
585-31785   1.75

Dockside Switcher
Lead Truck
585-31813   ea 4.50
26" wheels

26" Wheels
585-31810   ea 7.75
33" Wheels
585-31811   ea 7.75

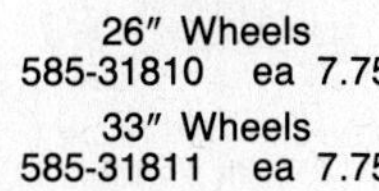

Mantua Booster
Electrical Pick-up
585-31549
each 6.75
26" wheels

HOn3 Baldwin Lead
Truck C-class
D&RGW
585-3133 each 3.00
less wheels

D&RGW Lead Truck
K-27
585-3010 each 3.00
less wheels

D&RGW Lead Truck
K-28, 36, 37
585-3178 each 3.25
less wheels

Lead Truck for Cab
Forward Articulated
585-31552
each 7.50
33" wheels,
7'3" wheelbase

DIESEL LOCOMOTIVE TRUCKS

585-39031 Early Blomberg-C   pr 16.75
36" wheels, 14' wheelbase
585-39030 Early Blomberg-B for   pr 13.25
EMD F3, FT, GP7
40" wheels, 9' wheelbase

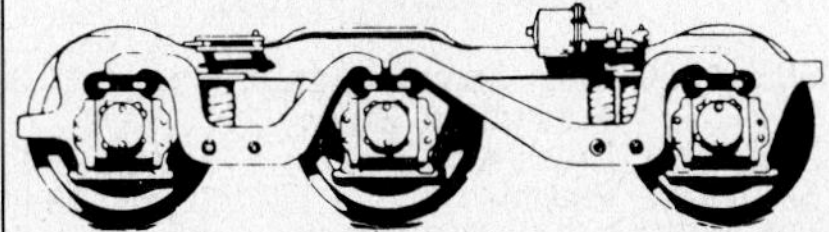

585-3954 6-Whl Trk for Alco Diesel pr 16.50
40" wheels, 12'6" wheelbase
585-3955 Plastic   pair 13.25

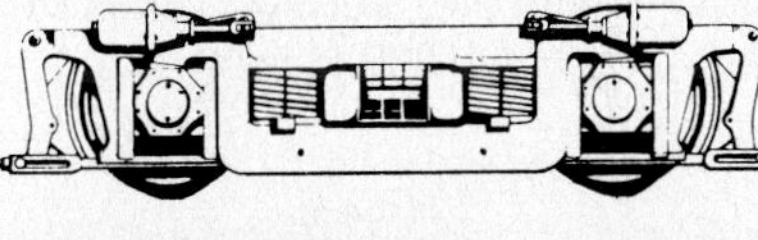

585-39026 Alco B Trucks   pair 14.85
40" wheels, 9'0" wheelbase

585-39027 Alco B Zamac   pair 8.25
40" wheels, 9'0" wheelbase

585-39032 Alco 6-Wheel Trucks pair 20.25
40" wheels, 15'9" wheelbase

PRECISION SCALE Co.

HO SCALE
(1/87)
CRAFT TRAIN
KITS

We have worked closely with this manufacturer to provide accurate availability information at the time this catalog was published. Items listed in *blue ink* may not be available at all times. Please see your dealer for current delivery information
+ (PLUS SIGN) = SPECIAL ORDER ONLY ITEMS.

DIESEL LOCOMOTIVE TRUCKS (continued)

585-39025 Alco Switcher Trucks   pr 13.75
Blunt Trucks with Wheels +
40″ wheels, 8′ wheelbase

EMD Intermediate
Blomberg-B
585-39028   pair 13.25
40″ wheels, 9′ wheelbase

(not illustrated)
585-33217 36″ Wheels, Brass Kit pair 14.50
585-39029 EMD Switcher   pair 13.25
40″ wheel, 8′ wheelbase

TENDER TRUCKS

Light Arch Bar Truck
for Modern Tender
HOn3, D&RGW C-16
585-31540 pair 7.50
26″ wheels

Simplex
Tender Truck, HOn3
585-31551   pr 8.25
26″ wheels
4′9″ wheelbase

Arch Bar Truck
for Wabash Tender
585-31542   pr 10.50
33″ wheels,
5′6″ wheelbase,
includes brake shoes

585-315421 Assembled   12.75

Andrews Leaf Spring,
with Wheels
585-31651   pr 9.75
33″ wheels
5′4″ wheelbase
Assembled
585-316511 *NEW* 12.25

585-31541 4-Wheel Truck for
Commonwealth Tender
33″ wheels, 6′ wheelbase   pr 8.75

■ LTD QUANTITIES AVAILABLE ■
585-315411 Assembled   10.00

585-3197 Heavy Duty, Buckeye   pr 14.50
Tender Timkin Bearings
36″ wheels, 9′6″ wheelbase

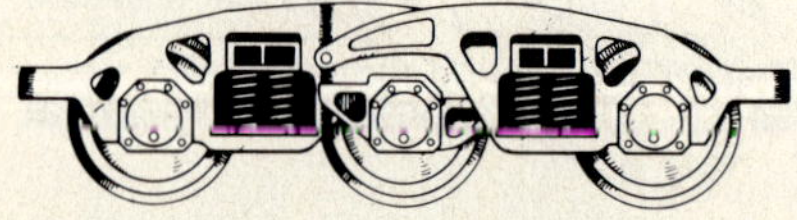

585-33206 Commonwealth Std   13.25
36″, Brass Kit 8′ wheelbase
585-33207 Plastic   8.25
585-33208 Assembled, Brass   16.75
585-33209 Bolster for #33206 pair 2.50
585-33210 Bolster, Plastic   pair 1.50

4-Wheel Truck
585-31539
kit 7.75
40″ wheels
7′6″ wheelbase

585-31537 10-Wheel Truck   kit 20.25
40″ wheels, 20′3″ wheelbase

Franklin Tender
with Booster Engine,
Less Wheels
585-31814 ea 14.50
5′9″ wheelbase

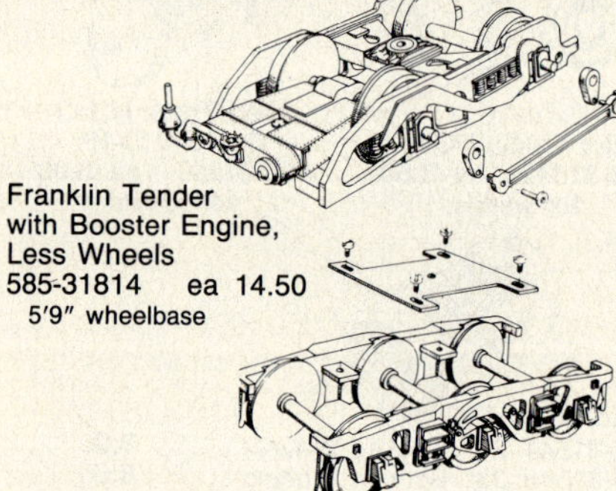

Buckeye 6-Wheel,
Plain Journals
585-3397   pair 13.50
33″ wheels, 9′10″ wheelbase

585-33971 Assembled   17.50

Same as #3397 but
w/Plastic Sideframes,
Bolsters and Wheels
585-31815   pair 7.75

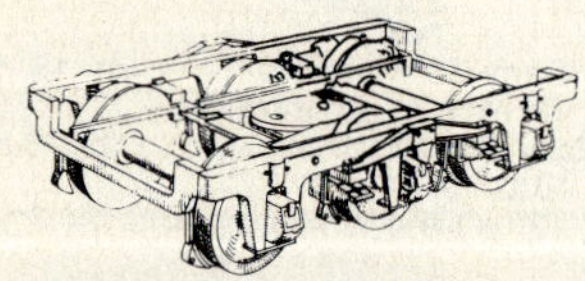

585-33250 242A Commonwealth   21.25
Assembled, Brass
585-33251 Brass Kit   pair 14.50
585-33252 Plastic   pair 10.50
585-33257 3-Axle, 36″, 10′-6″ wheelbase 14.50
585-33258 Plastic, 2426 Cast *NEW* kit 10.50
Steel Bottom, 10′-6″ wheelbase
585-33259 3-Axle, 36″, Assembled   21.25

6-Wheel Buckeye
Timkin Journals
585-3399
pair 13.50
33″ wheels,
9′10″ wheelbase
585-33991 Assembled   17.50

585-3127 Commonwealth Tender, pr 13.75
Long
33″ wheels, 105″ wheelbase
585-31271 Assembled   15.75
585-31646 Same as #3127 but   pair 7.75
with Plastic Sideframes,
Brass Bolsters & Wheels

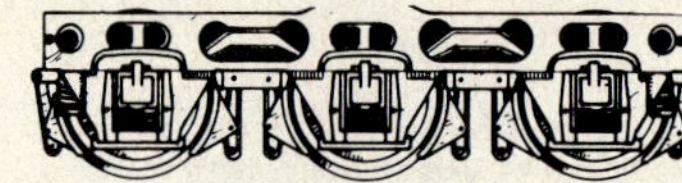

585-3186 Commonwealth   pair 13.75
Tender, Short
33″ wheels, 105″ wheelbase
585-331861 Commonwealth,   15.75
Short Assembled
585-31657 Same as #3186 but   pair 7.75
with Plastic Sideframes,
Brass Bolsters & Wheels

(not illustrated)
585-31827 Early C-16 Tender   pair 7.50
Truck HOn3 26″ whls 4′ wheelbase
585-31907 D&RGW K-27 Tender pair 8.00
Truck HOn3 26″ whls 5′ wheelbase
585-31908 D&RGW K-28 Tender pair 8.00
Truck HOn3 26″ whls 5′ wheelbase
585-31926 Commonwealth Tender pr 16.75
36″ wheels
585-31925 Commonwealth   pair 16.75
Roller Bearing 36″ wheels
585-32116 Commonwealth asmb pr 14.00
Symington
585-33262 Commonwealth Late   14.50
3-Axle +
585-33263 Plastic   10.50
585-33264 Assembled   21.25

PRECISION SCALE CO

HO SCALE (1/87) CRAFT TRAIN KITS

Truck kits are lost wax brass castings, unless noted, or unless obviously excepted (springs, screws, etc.). All kits are HO Scale, standard gauge, unless noted. Illustrations are not to scale.

+ (PLUS SIGN) = SPECIAL ORDER ONLY ITEMS

FREIGHT CAR TRUCKS

Arch Bar, RGS/C&S HOn3
585-3491   pr 7.50
26" wheels

585-3492   Same as #3491   4.50
with Delrin sideframes

HOn3 Arch Bar
585-3025   pr 7.75
26" wheels, 3'7" wheelbase

585-31902   Plastic   pair 4.50

(not illustrated)
585-33114   Beam End UP/SP +   pkg(4) 2.50
585-33115   Beam End UP/SP pls +   pkg(4) 1.50
585-33274   PRR 33" wheels +   asmb 14.25

West Side Logging Truck, HOn3
585-31780   pr 6.75
26" wheels, 4' wheelbase
585-31781   Plastic   pair 4.50
585-317801   Assembled   9.50

Diamond Arch Bar HOn3
585-31778   pair 7.50
26" wheels, 4'6" wheelbase
585-31779   Same as #31778   pair 4.50
with plastic sideframes

Short Arch Bar D&RGW HOn3
585-31786   pair 7.75
26" wheels, 3'7" wheelbase
585-31787   Same as #31876   pair 4.50
with plastic sideframes

West Side, Coil Sprung Logging Truck HOn3
585-31782   pair 6.75
26" wheels, 4' wheelbase
585-31783   Same as #31782   pair 4.50
with plastic sideframes
585-317821   Same as #31782, Asmb.   21.25

HOn3 D&RGW American Steel and Foundry with Wheels
585-3026   pr 8.00
26" wheels, 4'11" wheelbase
585-30261   Assembled   9.75
585-31640   Same as #3026   pair 6.75
with Delrin sideframes, brass bolsters and wheels

SP Thielsen, HOn3
585-31788   pair 7.50
26" wheels, 4'6" wheelbase
585-31808   Same as #31788   pair 4.50
with plastic sideframes

AS&F Andrews, HOn3, D&RGW
585-3527   pr 7.50
26" wheels, 4'-8" wheelbase
585-3528   Same as #3527   pair 4.50
with plastic sideframes

PASSENGER TRUCKS

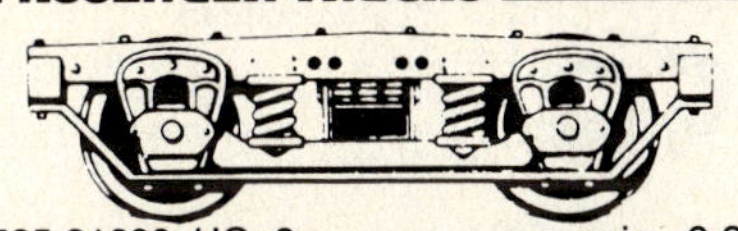

585-31600   pair 9.25
26" RP-25 wheels, 5' wheelbase
585-31876   Same as #31600   pair 4.50
with plastic sideframes

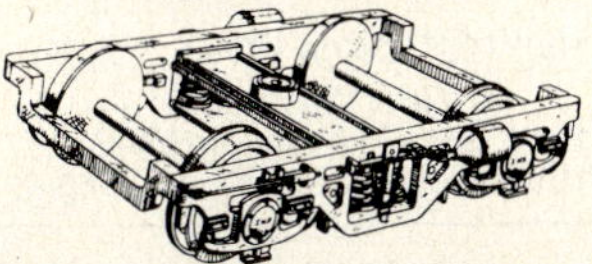

585-33100   4-Wheel, 36", 9' wheelbase   18.75
585-33101   4-Wheel, Plastic, 36"   9.75
585-331001   Assembled   **NEW** 21.25
(not illustrated)
585-33122   Harriman 2-axle asmb pr   15.75
585-33116   UP Chair, 36" wheel   18.75
585-33117   UP Chair, Plastic 36" whl   9.75
585-33154   Hvy Pullman 36" wheel   14.50
585-33155   Hvy Pullman, Plastic   10.50
    36" wheel
585-33177   WB, 36" wheels   11.75
585-33178   3-Axle, 36" wheels   asmb 21.25
585-33179   PRR, 4-Wheel   asmb 14.50
585-33185   Budd Class, 36"   asmb 16.95
585-33218   Hvy Pullman, Late, Plastic 10.50
    36" wheels, 10'6" wheelbase
585-33219   Hvy Plmn 6-Wheel asmb 21.50
585-33220   Hvy Pullman 3-Axle   14.75
585-33221   Hvy Plmn 3-Axle, Plastic 10.75
585-33222   Hvy Plmn Late   asmb 21.50
    36" wheels, 10'6" wheelbase
585-33223   Hvy Pullman, Early   14.75
585-33224   Hvy Plmn, Early, Plastic 10.75
    10' wheelbase
585-33225   Hvy Pullman, Early asmb 21.50
    10' wheelbase, brass
585-33226   Stabilizer for #33220 pkg(4) 2.25
585-33227   Stabilizer for #33220 pkg(4) 1.75
    Plastic +

TRACTION TRUCKS

All traction trucks have 36" S-4 wheels and 7' wheelbase.

585-31560   Baldwin 84-30   pair 10.25

585-31559   Baldwin 84-35 AA   pair 10.25

585-31561   Standard C-80-P   pair 11.25

585-31558   Brill 27-MCB-3   pair 11.25

POWER TRUCKS

MINIATURE DRIVE SYSTEMS (MDS) are self-contained power trucks.

MDS #3

Design for PSC SD-EMD 40 series diesel. These six wheel under the floor units allow the freedom of adding sound, carrier system, extra weights or interior details. With very little frame modification these units can be adapted to existing Athearn units or older brass imports. Self contained, pick-up is totally internal. Supplied tabs that mount on top of the truck body provide you with electrical connections for headlights or other electrical use.

585-39096   Flexcoil 3-Axle   pair 41.00
Power Unit
less sideframes

585-39097   Flexcoil 3-Axle   pair 43.50
Power Unit
with plastic sideframes, slack adjustors, brake cylinders and shock absorbers

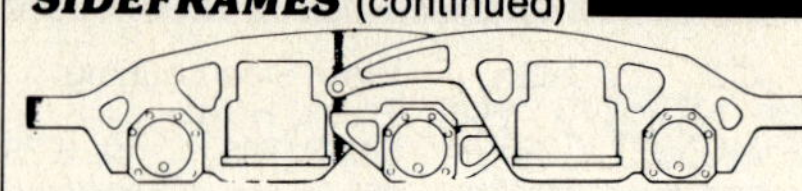

PRECISION SCALE Co

HO SCALE (1/87) CRAFT TRAIN KITS

We have worked closely with this manufacturer to provide accurate availability information at the time this catalog was published. Items listed in *blue ink* may not be available at all times. Please see your dealer for current delivery information

+ (PLUS SIGN) = SPECIAL ORDER ONLY ITEMS.

POWER TRUCKS (continued)

585-39098 HT-C 3-Axle Power Unit +   pair 41.00
less sideframes

585-39099 HT-C 3-Axle Power Unit   pair 43.50
with plastic sideframes, slack adjustors, brake cylinders and shock absorbers

SIDEFRAMES

585-39000 EMD SD 2nd Generation HT-C 6-Wheel 3-Axle   pkg(4) 14.75
with slack adjuster, brake cyliner and shock absorber.

585-39001 Same as #39000   pkg(4) 7.50
plastic

585-39094 3-Axle w/Brake Cylinder +   14.75
585-39095 3-Axle w/Brake Cylinder, plastic   7.50

585-39107 w/Adjustable cylinder & shock   pkg(4) 13.75

585-39108 w/Adjustable cylinder & shock, plastic   pkg(4) 7.50

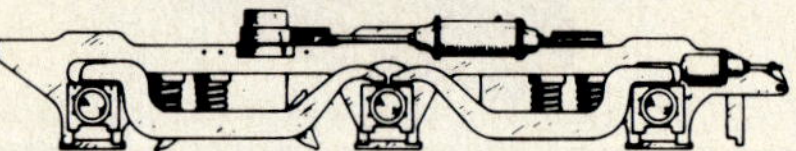

585-3398 Modern 6-Wheel   pkg(4) 5.25
Buckeye side frames with Timkin roller bearings, for #3399. 9'10" wheelbase

585-3902 Alco Front w/Flanger Actuator, HOn3   pr 7.00
11' wheelbase

585-3003 Alco Rear, HOn3   pair 7.00
11' wheelbase

585-3395 Modern 6-Wheel Buckeye with Plain Bearings for #3397   pkg(4) 5.00
9'10" wheelbase

585-3396 Same as #3395 +   pkg(4) 2.50
plastic

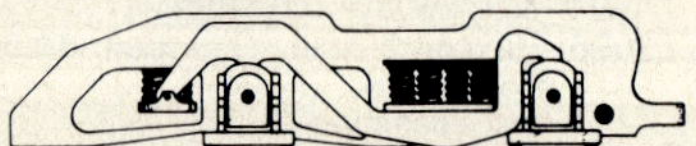

585-3300 Franklin Tender (3 pc kit) w/Bolster for Booster Engine   8.00
for #3334

SIDEFRAMES (continued)

585-3196 Heavy Duty Buckeye Tender   pkg(4) 6.75
with Timkin bearings, 9'6" wheelbase

585-31650 Bolsters for #3197   pair 4.50

585-31647 Commonwealth Tender, Long, Plastic   pkg(4) 2.50

585-3187 Commonwealth Tender, Short   pkg(4) 4.50
585-31649 Same as #3187   pkg(4) 2.50
plastic

585-3530 8-Wheel Tender Pennsy   pkg(4) 7.00
13'6" wheelbase

585-3531 Same as #3530   pkg(4) 3.50
plastic

Side Ore Dump Car, HOn3
585-3568   pr 3.50

SP Theilsen Freight
585-31789 +   pkg(4) 3.50
for #31788

585-31809 Plastic   pkg(4) 2.00

Logging for #31780
585-31828   pkg(4) 3.50
4' wheelbase

585-31829 Same as #31828   pkg(4) 2.00
plastic

Logging for #31782
585-31830   pkg(4) 3.50
4' wheelbase

585-31831 Same as #31830   pkg(4) 2.00
plastic

Diaphragm Arch Bar for #31779
585-31878   pkg(4) 2.00
plastic

585-31877 Sideframe Diameter Archbar +   pkg(4) 3.50

(not illustrated)
585-31538 4-wheel for #31539   pair 4.50
585-31536 10-wheel for #31537 +   pair 11.00
585-31746 D&RGW K-28 HOn3   pkg(4) 4.00

SIDEFRAMES (continued)

585-3253 for #3025 Truck   pkg(4) 3.50
585-3254 for #31902 Truck, Plastic   pkg(4) 2.00
585-3462 SP GS-5 +   pkg(4) 6.50
585-33102 UP/SP/C&NW   pkg(4) 8.75
585-33118 UP Chair   pkg(4) 8.75
585-33119 UP Chair, Plastic   pkg(4) 4.00
585-33152 Sideframe   pkg(4) 6.00
585-33153 Spring Bar   pkg(4) 2.50
585-33204 NYCRT Type +   pkg(4) 5.00
585-33205 NYCRT Type, + Plastic   pkg(4) 3.50

WHEELSETS

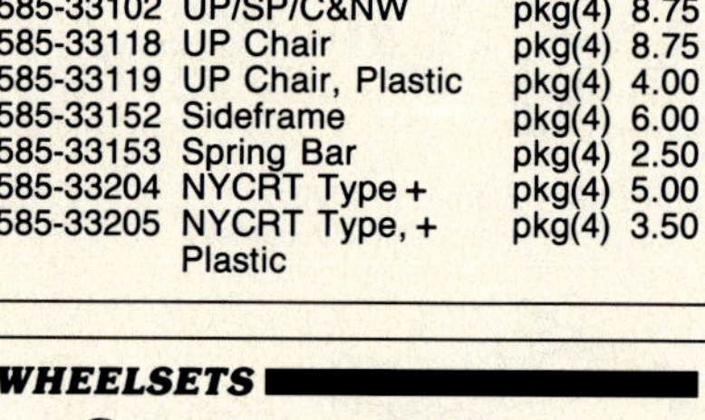

33" Blunt
585-3279   pkg(4) 4.25
insulated one side, plated

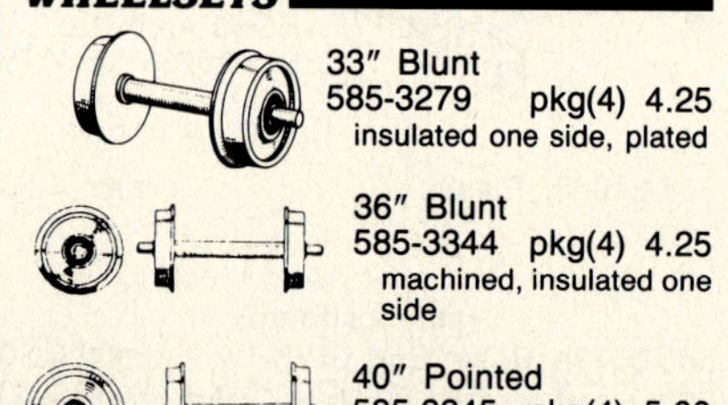

36" Blunt
585-3344   pkg(4) 4.25
machined, insulated one side

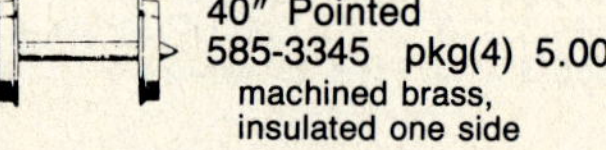

40" Pointed
585-3345   pkg(4) 5.00
machined brass, insulated one side

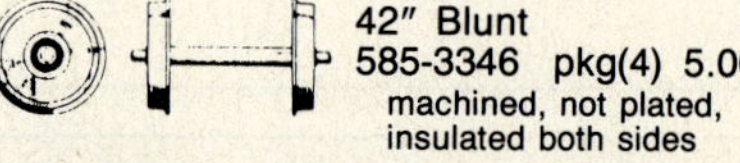

42" Blunt
585-3346   pkg(4) 5.00
machined, not plated, insulated both sides

26" HOn3, Pointed
585-3240   pkg(4) 5.25
plastic centers, machined, plated rims, axle ends ins, 2 sides

20" Delrin, HOn3
585-31006   pkg(4) 4.00

585-31007 20" Delrin HOn3   pkg(4) 4.00
(not illustrated)
585-31011 26" Point Axle, HOn3   5.25
585-31987 Flush Axle, 20" +   pkg(4) 4.00

"The sides are of card stock scribed to simulate the simulated wood sheathing on the metal sides of the prototype."

Cartoon courtesy of *Model Railroader* Magazine.

ROUNDHOUSE Products

HO SCALE (1/87) READY-TO-RUN

Assembled trucks with one piece molded Delrin frame, RP-25 Delrin wheels and steel needle-point axles.

FREIGHT TRUCKS

Bettendorf
480-2923 pr 1.50

480-2903 Bettendorf Tender pair 3.75
metal wheels

Arch Bar
480-2922
pair 1.50

480-2902 Arch Bar Tender pair 3.75
metal wheels

HOn3 Arch Bar
480-2917
pair 3.50

480-2928 HOn3 Arch Bar pair 3.75
metal wheels

Roller Bearing
480-2925
pair 1.50

Modern
Roller Bearing
480-2918
pair 1.50

Heavy Duty
Roller Bearing
480-2919
pair 1.50

LOCOMOTIVE TRUCKS

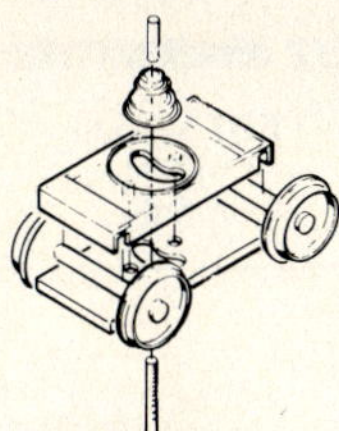

4-Wheel Lead Truck
480-2860 kit 2.75

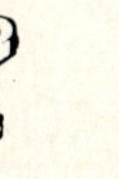

SF 2-Wheel Trailing
480-2863 kit 3.50

2-Wheel Lead Truck
480-2861 kit 1.75

2-Wheel Trailing Truck
480-2864 kit 1.75

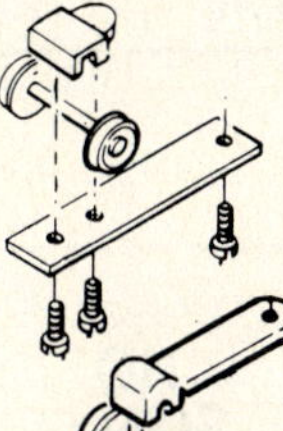

2-Wheel Lead Truck
480-2865 kit 1.75

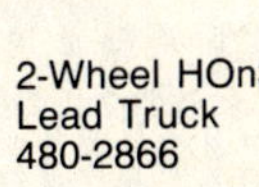

2-Wheel HOn3
Lead Truck
480-2866 kit 2.50

(not illustrated)
480-2862 PRR 2-Wheel Trailing kit 3.50

TENDER TRUCKS

Fox
480-2904
pair 3.75
metal wheels
Fox
480-2924
pair 1.50
plastic wheels

PASSENGER TRUCKS

480-2931 6-Wheel Pullman pair 2.00

480-2937 4-Wheel Pullman pair 1.75
talgo truck

480-2936 Wood Beam Passenger pair 1.75

480-2933 Pennsy Roller bearing pair 1.75

480-2934 Challenger pair 1.75

480-2935 Commonwealth pair 1.75

(not illustrated)
480-2929 4-Wheel HOn3 3.75

ACCESSORY KIT

480-2930 Long Throw pkg(3 sets) 1.50
Toggle Coupler Arm/Bolster

We have worked closely with these manufacturers to provide accurate availability information at the time this catalog was published. Items listed in *blue ink* may not be available at all times. Please see your dealer for current delivery information

EASTERN CAR WORKS

HO SCALE EASY-TO-BUILD KITS

PASSENGER TRUCKS
All plastic parts

117-9000	For 36" Wheels	pkg(2)	4.00
117-9001	2D-P5 Pennsy 4 Wheel	pkg(2)	4.00
117-9002	Commonwealth 4 Wheel	pkg(2)	4.00
117-9003	Pullman Standard 4 Wheel Lightweight	pkg(2)	4.00
117-9004	Commonwealth 4 Wheel Spring Bolster	pkg(2)	4.00
117-9005	Pullman Standard	NEW	4.00
117-9006	Taylor	NEW	TBA
117-9011	3D-P1, 3D-P7 Pennsy 6 Wheel	pkg(2)	4.00

FREIGHT TRUCKS NEW

117-9050	33" Axle Sets	pkg(4)	1.50
117-9051	Barber-Bettendorf Caboose		2.00
117-9052	Taylor 70 ton Caboose/Freight		2.00
117-9053	Bettendorf Friction Bearing		2.00
117-9054	Barber S-2		2.00
117-9055	Birdsboro/Andrews Caboose/Freight		2.00
117-9056	Bettendorf Roller Bearing Conversion		2.00
117-9057	Pyle-National B-1		2.00
117-9070	33" Axle Sets	pkg(6)	2.00
117-9071	Commonwealth Integral Pedestal		4.00

WALTHERS

HO SCALE (1/87)

Walthers offers a selection of plastic and metal trucks, suitable for use on all types of freight and passenger equipment. Trucks are available as kits or assembled where noted.

FREIGHT TRUCKS

RIGID PLASTIC

- One-piece, rigid sideframe
- Molded in black Delrin® plastic
- Non-magnetic brass axles
- RP25 wheel contour

Bettendorf
933-1012
pair 1.98

Arch Bar
933-1010
pair 1.98

"T" Section
933-1011
pair 1.98

Roller Bearing
933-1013
pair 1.98

SPRUNG PLASTIC

- Easy-to-Assemble
- Black colored sideframes, bolsters & wheels
- Sprung and equalized
- Brass non-magnetic axles

Bettendorf
933-1001
pair 3.49

Diamond Arch Bar
933-1002
pair 3.49

Roller Bearing
933-1005
pair 3.49

Andrews
933-1004
pair 3.49

"T" Section
Bettendorf
933-1003
pair 3.49

WHEELSETS

with non-magnetic brass axles

BRASS

933-383	36"	pkg(4) 5.98
933-870	33"	pkg(4) 5.98

BLACK PLASTIC

933-1006	33"	pkg(12) 3.49

HOn3 SCALE (1/87)

Delrin sideframes and wheels with brass axles.

FREIGHT TRUCK KIT

EBT Vulcan
771-5001
pair 5.00

HO READY TO RUN

223-99220	Freight, 33" brass	2.79
223-99221	Freight, 36" brass	2.79

TICHY TRAIN GROUP

HO SCALE (1/87)

FREIGHT TRUCKS

Heavy-duty trucks have a 5'6" wheel base and include wheelsets. Trucks are paintable styrene with nylon bearings, separate journal lids and spring plank with brake shoes.

ARCH BAR

293-3002	Kit	pair	2.95
293-3022	100T Kit	pair	2.95
293-3035	Assembled	(10pr)	14.50

ANDREWS

293-3012	Kit	pair	2.95
293-3016	Kit	(10pr)	15.50
293-3026	Assembled	pair	2.95
293-3027	Assembled	(10pr)	15.50

BETTENDORF

293-3008	Kit	pair	2.95
293-3014	Kit	(10pr)	14.50
293-3024	Assembled	pair	2.95
293-3025	Assembled	(10pr)	14.50
293-3049	1 coil, 1 Leaf Spring	pair	2.95
293-3050	1 coil, 1 Leaf Spring	(10pr)	15.50
293-3051	Caboose Truck (Leaf Springs)	pair	2.95
293-3052	Caboose Truck (Leaf Springs)	(10pr)	15.50

ROLLER BEARING

293-3009	Kit	pair	2.95
293-3036	Assembled	(10pr)	14.50

WHEELSET

293-3004	33" Non-operating	8 sets	1.50
293-3010	Scale	pkg(96)	9.50

Non-operating, for use with #4023

ASF RIDE CONTROL TRUCK

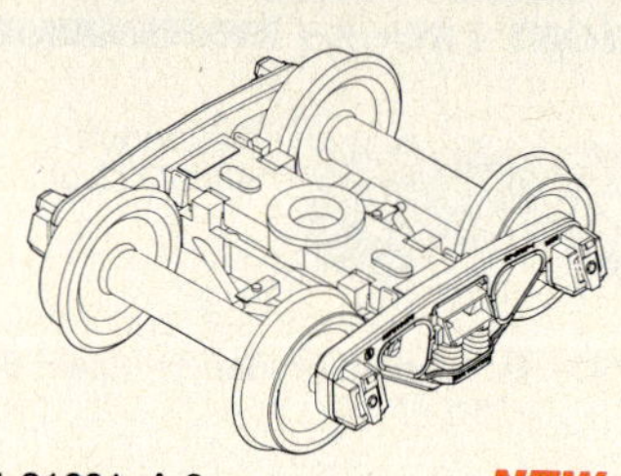

381-31601 A-3   NEW 4.98

Tenshodo

HO SCALE (1/87)

GT-1 SERIES

36" disc wheels

724-131	9' Wheelbase	56.99
724-126	7-1/2' Wheelbase	56.99
724-1245	7' Wheelbase	56.99
724-1285	8' Wheelbase	56.99

39" spoked wheels

724-13119	9' Wheelbase	58.99
724-128519	8' Wheelbase	58.99

WB SERIES

36" disc wheels

724-31	9' Wheelbase	32.99
724-245	7' Wheelbase	32.99
724-262	7-1/2' Wheelbase	32.99
724-287	8' Wheelbase	32.99

36" spoked wheels

724-24519	7' Wheelbase	35.99
	(By Special Order Only.)	
724-26219	7-1/2' Wheelbase	35.99

39" spoked wheels

724-3119	9' Wheelbase	35.99

39" stainless steel disc wheels

724-31194	9' Wheelbase	35.99

WALTHERS

Made exclusively by Shinohara for WALTHERS

CODE 83
HO TRACK

GET THE PROTOTYPE LOOK WITH CODE 83 TRACK

Your railroad looks its best with the Code 83 system! The correctly scaled rail gives your rolling stock and accessories that massive, more realistic appearance. Now you can get the look of Code 83 without handlaying track.

Made exclusively by Shinohara for Walthers, the Code 83 system is designed for operation! Prototypical ''all-rail'' frogs and rail are made of nickel silver. The turnouts are route selective with track power controlled by the turnout setting.

The system includes flex track, standard, curved, wye and 3-way turnouts, a double crossover, double slips, crossings, rail and rail joiners.

Make your entire layout more realistic with the growing Code 83 system!

•A COMPLETE AND EXPANDING TRACK SYSTEM

Everything needed to build an entire layout! Choose from flex track, several sizes of turnouts, bulk rail and rail joiners. Many new additions are planned throughout the coming year and will be announced in Craft Train News.

•REALISTIC DETAIL

Code 83 simulates 132 pound mainline rail used by many railroads, correct proportion for HO Scale.

Thin profile ties are molded in dark brown with fine woodgrain detail.

•EASY TO USE

Fully assembled, ready to install. Can be combined with Code 100 for realistic variety of rail sizes on the same layout.

Turnouts are route selective, power is controlled by turnout setting.

Prototypical ''all-rail'' frogs and rail made of nickel silver for best conductivity.

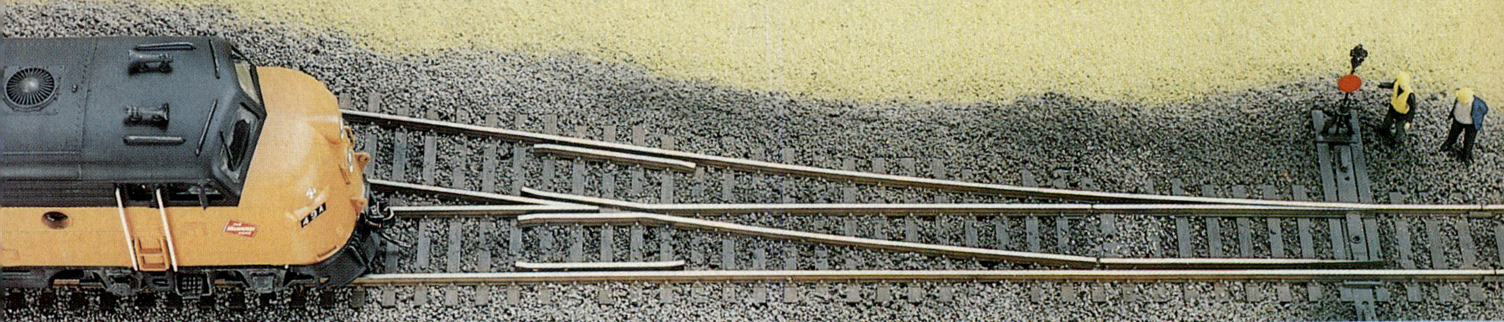

The correctly proportioned Code 83 rail of this #6 turnout gives the loco a larger, more realistic appearance.

TRACK PLANNING TEMPLATE   SCALE 3/4″ = 1′

To help you plan your layout, cut out and rearrange the illustrations provided.

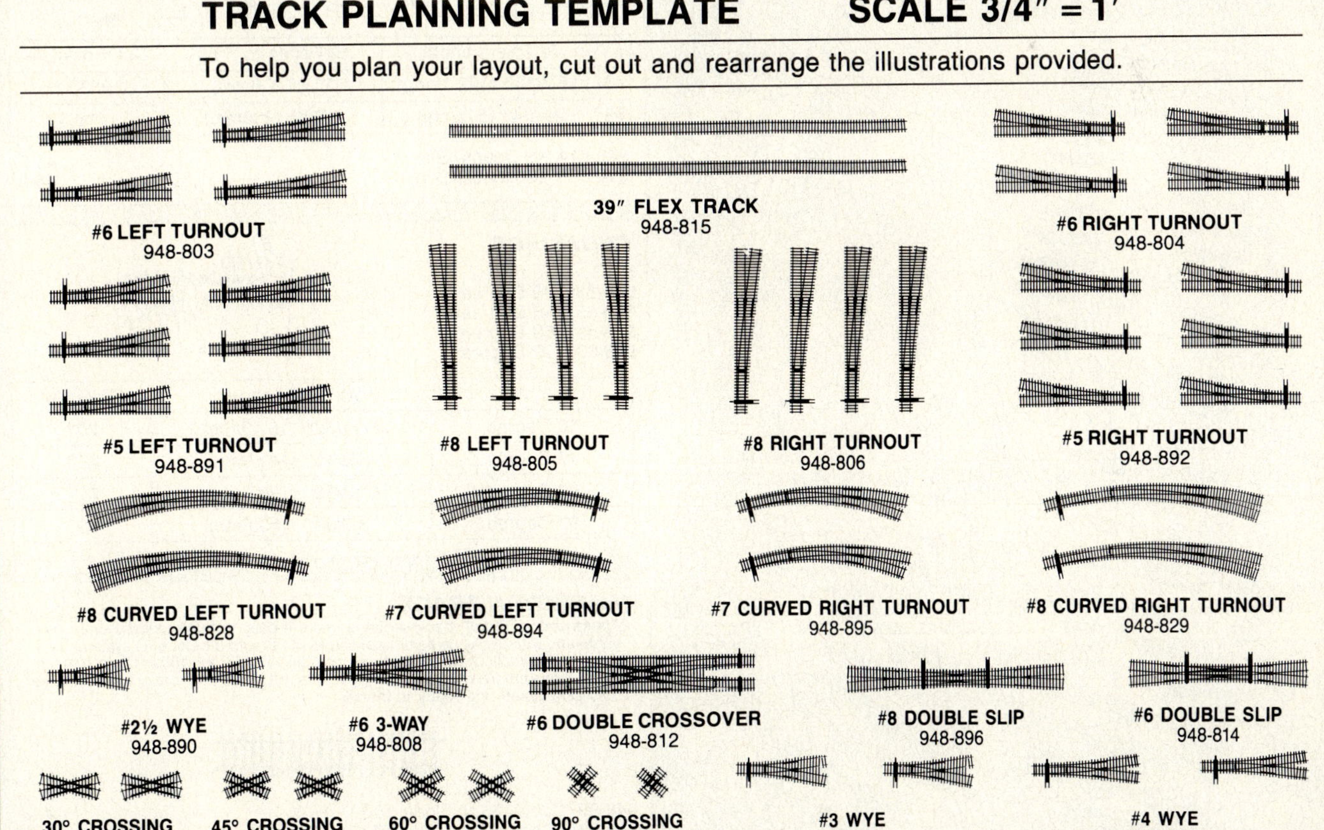

WALTHERS

Made exclusively by Shinohara for **WALTHERS**

CODE 83 HO TRACK

- **A COMPLETE TRACK SYSTEM**
- **REALISTIC DETAIL**
- **EASY TO USE**

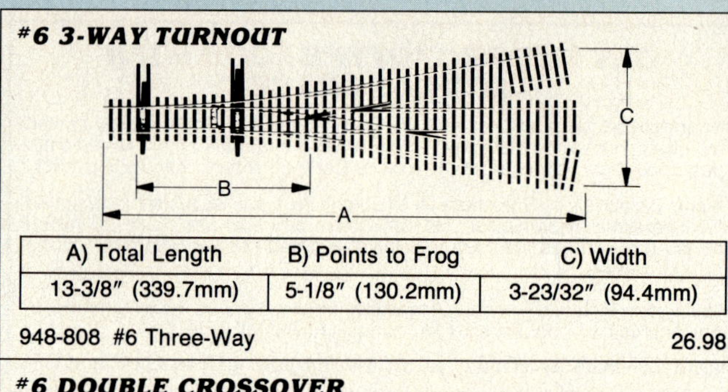

#6 3-WAY TURNOUT

A) Total Length	B) Points to Frog	C) Width
13-3/8″ (339.7mm)	5-1/8″ (130.2mm)	3-23/32″ (94.4mm)

948-808 #6 Three-Way   26.98

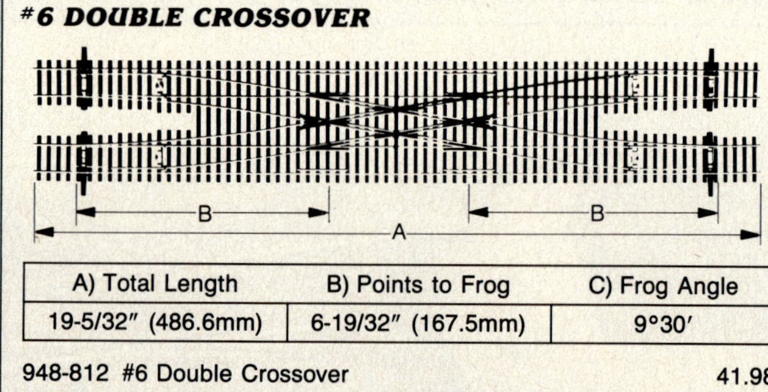

#6 DOUBLE CROSSOVER

A) Total Length	B) Points to Frog	C) Frog Angle
19-5/32″ (486.6mm)	6-19/32″ (167.5mm)	9°30′

948-812 #6 Double Crossover   41.98

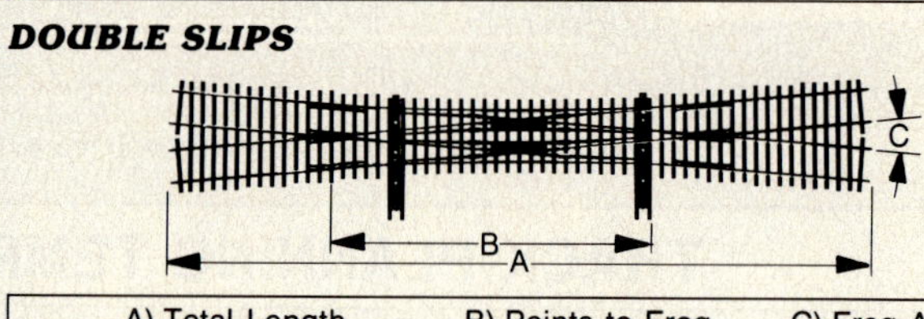

DOUBLE SLIPS

	A) Total Length	B) Points to Frog	C) Frog Angle
#6	15-7/16″ (392.1mm)	7″ (177.8mm)	9°30′
#8	20-1/4″ (515mm)	7-7/8″ (200mm)	7°9′

948-814 #6 Double Slip   41.98
948-896 #8 Double Slip   46.98

CROSSINGS

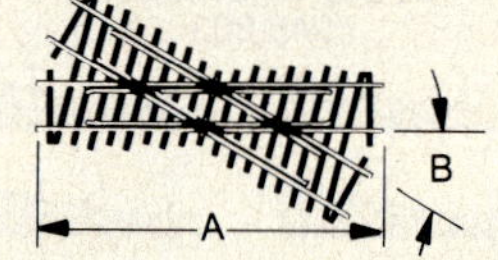

948-830	30 Degree	13.98
948-831	45 Degree	13.98
948-832	60 Degree	13.98
948-833	90 Degree	13.98

	A) Total Length	B) Angle
30 Degree	6-11/32″ (161.5mm)	30°
45 Degree	5-9/16″ (141.9mm)	45°
60 Degree	4-13/16″ (123.0mm)	60°
90 Degree	3-7/32″ (82.0mm)	90°

TRANSITION TRACK

These special 6 inch track sections make it easy to build realistic mainlines, yards and sidings, by using different sizes of rail with the Code 83 system! Each piece has a small section of Code 83, combined with Code 100 or Code 70 track, to provide a smooth transition between the rail sizes. The straight sections are fully assembled and ready to install.

948-897 Code 83 to Code 100   4.98
948-898 Code 83 to Code 70   4.98

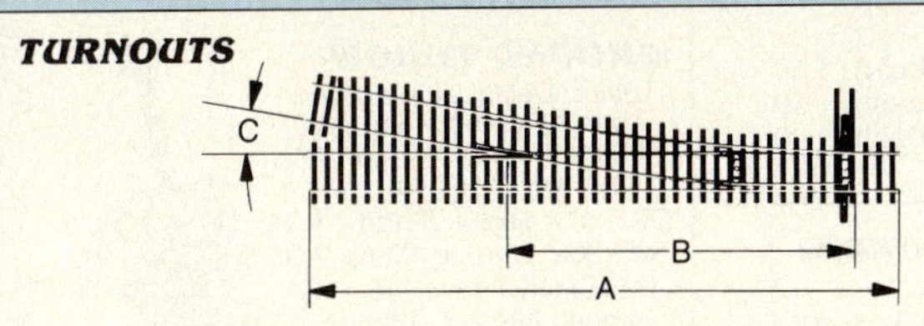

WALTHERS

Made exclusively by Shinohara for *WALTHERS*

CODE 83 HO TRACK
- **A COMPLETE TRACK SYSTEM**
- **REALISTIC DETAIL**
- **EASY TO USE**

TURNOUTS

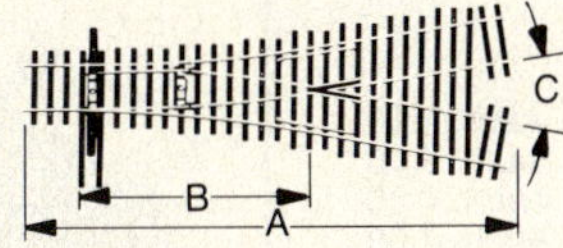

	A) Total Length	B) Points to Frog	C) Frog Angle
#5	10-3/8″ (263.5mm)	5-21/32″ (143.7mm)	11°26′
#6	11-5/6″ (287.3mm)	6-9/16″ (166.7mm)	9°32′
#8	13-7/8″ (352.4mm)	8-1/32″ (204.0mm)	7°9′

948-891 #5 Left Hand   13.98
948-892 #5 Right Hand   13.98
948-803 #6 Left Hand   13.98
948-804 #6 Right Hand   13.98
948-805 #8 Left Hand   14.98
948-806 #8 Right Hand   14.98

WYE TURNOUTS

	A) Total Length	B) Points to Frog	C) Frog Angle
#2½	7-3/16″ (182.6mm)	3-19/32″ (91.3mm)	22°54′
#3	7-7/8″ (200.0mm)	3-3/4″ (95.2mm)	19°5′
#4	9-23/32″ (247.8mm)	5-5/16″ (134.9mm)	14°15′

948-890 #2-1/2 (Matches #5 Turnouts)   13.98
948-893 #3 (Matches #6 Turnouts)   13.98
948-807 #4 (Matches #8 Turnouts)   13.98

CURVED TURNOUTS

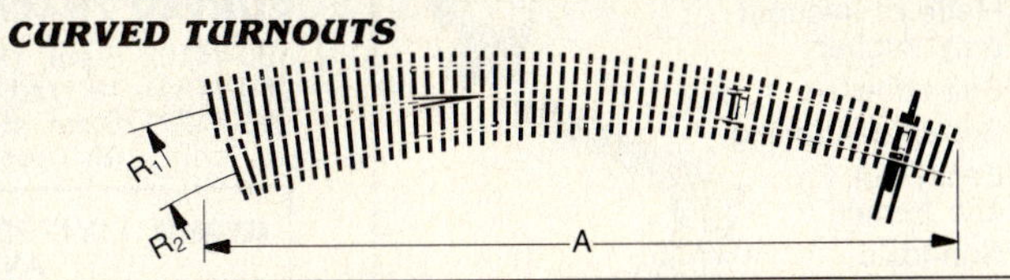

	A) Total Length	R_1) Inside Radius	R_2) Outside Radius
#6½	12-25/32″ (324.6mm)	20″ (508mm)	24″ (609.6mm)
#7	14-31/32″ (380.2mm)	24″ (609.6mm)	28″ (711.2mm)
#7½	17-7/32″ (437.4mm)	28″ (711.2mm)	32″ (812.8mm)
#8	19″ (482.6mm)	32″ (812.8mm)	36″ (914.4mm)

948-826 #6-1/2 Left Hand, 20/24″ Radii   23.98
948-827 #6-1/2 Right Hand, 20/24″ Radii   23.98
948-894 #7 Left Hand, 24/28″ Radii   23.98
948-895 #7 Right Hand, 24/28″ Radii   23.98
948-888 #7-1/2 Left Hand, 28/32″ Radii   23.98
948-889 #7-1/2 Right Hand, 28/32″   23.98
948-828 #8 Left Hand, 32/36″ Radii   23.98
948-829 #8 Right Hand, 32/36″ Radii   23.98

FLEX TRACK

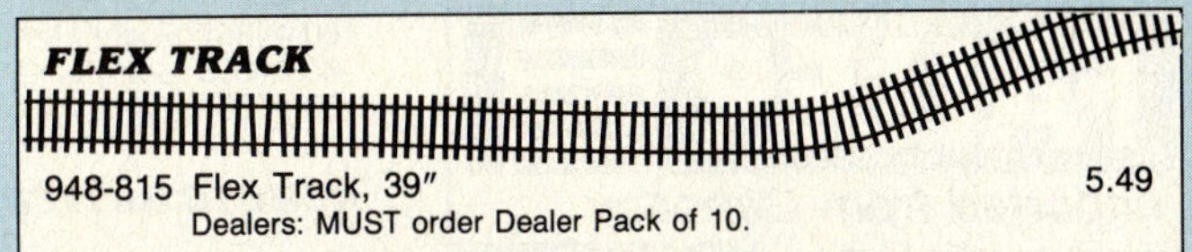

948-815 Flex Track, 39″   5.49
Dealers: MUST order Dealer Pack of 10.

CODE 83 ACCESSORIES   CODE 70 SPIKES

948-841 Rail Joiners pkg(50) 5.98   947-645 Spikes   pkg(70) 6.98
948-870 Rail 100′   62.98   .024 x 3/8″, 9/16 oz

AMI
Instant Roadbed

''Gandy Dancer's Delight''

- Made of uncured butyl rubber
- Self-adhesive
- Sound deadening
- Easily cut and formed
- Non-toxic

Just press realistic appearing Instant Roadbed onto a clean surface, then press track into it to complete layout. Can be used with any scale.

(2" x 1/8" x 30' roll, black)
(5.08cm x 3.175mm x 9.144m)

128-30	Instant Roadbed	pkg(30')	11.95
128-18	Insta Base	**NEW**	3.50

Track laying projects in any scale will take only a few minutes with the Insta Base roadbed.

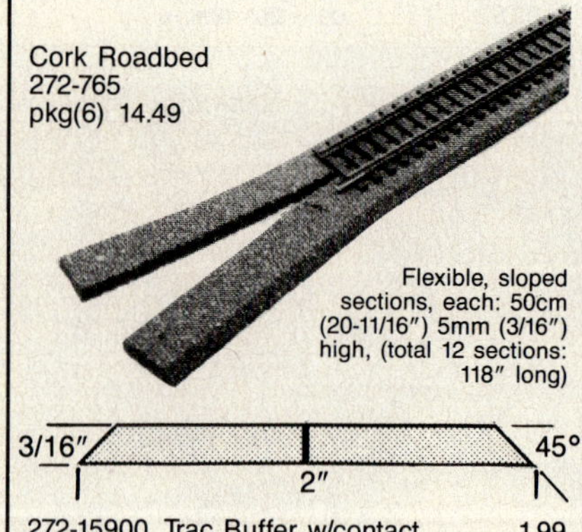

FALLER

Imported from Germany and marketed by **WALTHERS**

HO SCALE (1/87)

Cork Roadbed
272-765
pkg(6)   14.49

Flexible, sloped sections, each: 50cm (20-11/16") 5mm (3/16") high, (total 12 sections: 118" long)

3/16"   2"   45°

272-15900	Trac Buffer w/contact	1.99

MIL-SCALE
Products

Ties are unstained, precut wood.

HO TIES

477-1	Regular	pkg(1000)	8.95
477-2	Switch	pkg(250)	5.95
477-3	Double Long	pkg(250)	6.95

HOn3 TIES

477-4	Regular	pkg(1000)	8.95
477-5	Switch	pkg(250)	5.95
477-6	Double Long	pkg(250)	6.95

BACHMANN
QUALITY SINCE 1833

HO SCALE (1/87)

CURVED TRACK

160-44102	Steel, 18" radius	pkg(4)	1.50
160-44201	18" radius	each	.50
160-44221	Steel, 18" radius	each	.40

(By Special Order Only.)

LIMITED QUANTITIES AVAILABLE

160-44101	Brass, 18" radius	pkg(4)	2.00

STRAIGHT TRACK

160-44112	Steel, 9"	pkg(4)	1.50
160-44120	Terminal, 9"	each	3.25
160-44211	9" Straight	each	.50
160-44231	Steel 9"	each	.40

(By Special Order Only.)

FLEX TRACK

160-44312	36", Steel	each	1.50

MANUAL SWITCH

160-44351	Left Hand, Brass	each	5.00
160-44352	Right Hand, Brass	each	5.00
160-44353	Left Hand, Steel	each	4.00
160-44354	Right Hand, Steel	each	4.00

REMOTE SWITCH

160-44365	Left Hand, Steel	each	5.50
160-44366	Right Hand, Steel	each	5.50

CROSSING

160-44355	30 Degree	each	4.50
160-44358	90 Degree	each	4.50

MISCELLANEOUS

160-44329	Rerailer, 9" Straight	each	3.50
160-99991	Track Cleaner **NEW**	8oz	2.50

LIMITED QUANTITIES AVAILABLE

160-44332	Rail Joiners	pkg(48)	1.25

CENTRAL VALLEY

HO SCALE (1/87)

FLEXIBLE TIES

Made of injection molded, black plastic styrene.

Branchline 210-2002	pkg(50)	24.98

CABOOSE INDUSTRIES

HO SCALE (1/87)

GROUND THROW

Black Delrin with external cam for strength and maximum throw. Molded on pin for direct mounting.

097-101	Rigid Stand	1.84
097-202	Sprung Stand	2.30

Maximum travel for HO ground throw is .190".

shown approximately actual size

097-109	Rigid Stand	3.09
097-210	Sprung Stand	3.25

w/operating target. Maximum travel for HO ground throw is .190".

shown approximately 3/4 actual size

GROUND THROW w/CONTACTS   **NEW**

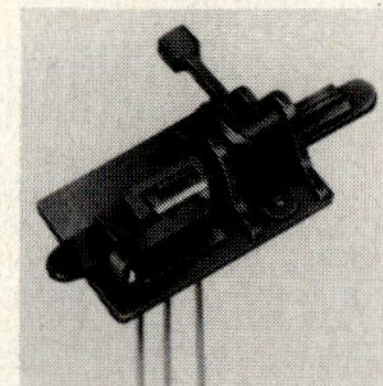

Models have .165" travel and include materials to assemble one low-current ''C'' contact set. Can be mounted above or below the bench work.

Available with round or blade pins (blade pins are for use with Atlas/Roco Code 83 switches).

097-111	Round Pin Rigid	3.19
097-212	Round Pin Sprung	3.65
097-113	Blade Pin Rigid	3.19
097-214	Blade Pin Sprung	3.65

SHORT POINT TRAVEL GROUND THROW

Maximum travel for HO Scale is .135". N Scale ground throws can be used for HO Scale.

097-105	Rigid Stand	1.94
097-206	Sprung Stand	2.45

SWITCH STAND

Operating high level switch stand is made of Delrin and is supplied with six paintable, bondable ABS targets, including a lantern and square diamond. Manual targets can be made to operate from electric switch machine below the table.

097-103	Rigid Stand	4.08
097-204	Sprung Stand	4.65

shown approximately 3/4 actual size

ARNOLD

Imported from Germany & marketed by WALTHERS

HO SCALE (1/87) **NEW**

125-1910 Track Nails   pkg(500) 5.49

125-1920 Flat Head Screws pkg(50) 6.49

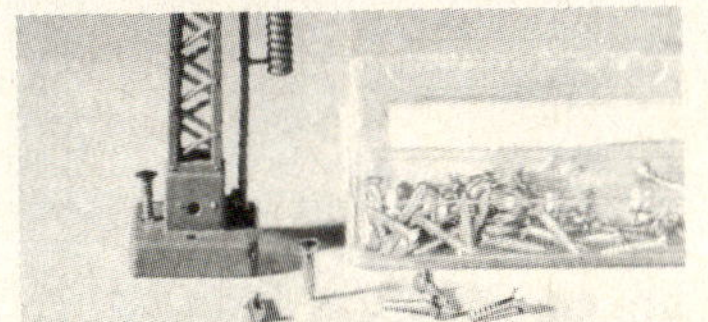

125-7100 Rail Joiners   pkg(2) 5.49

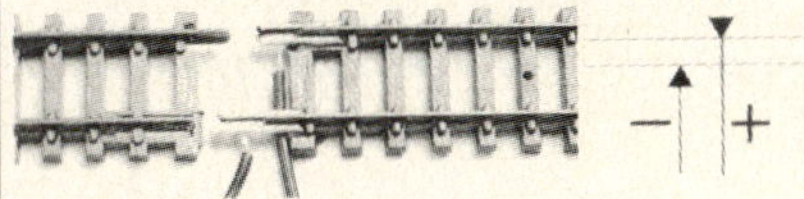

125-7110 Track Clips   pkg(10) 11.99

KAPPLER MILL & LUMBER CO.

SCALE TIES

Ties are made of unstained sugar pine. Dimensions are in prototype inches.

REGULAR TIES
385-51 HOn3 5 x 7″ x 6′   pkg(1000) 9.95
385-52 HOn3 5 x 7″ x 6′6″   pkg(1000) 9.95
385-53 HO 7 x 9″ x 8′   pkg(1000) 10.95
385-54 HO 7 x 9″ x 8′6″   pkg(1000) 10.95

SWITCH TIES
385-59 HOn3 5 X 7″ X 12′   pkg(500) 9.95
385-60 HO 7 x 9″ x 16′   pkg(500) 10.95

BRIDGE & TRESTLE TIES
385-69 HO/HOn3 8 x 8″ x 10′ pkg(500) 10.95

KONTOUR CROSS TIES
Kontour Cross Ties are about 1/2 the thickness of regular scale ties in order to use less ballast.

385-72 HOn3 4 x 7″ x 6′   pkg(1000) 9.95
385-73 HOn3 4 x 7″ x 6′6″   pkg(1000) 9.95
385-74 HO 4 x 9″ x 8′   pkg(1000) 10.95
385-75 HO 4 x 9″ x 8′6″   pkg(1000) 10.95

KONTOUR SWITCH TIES
385-84 HOn3 4 x 7″ x 12′   pkg(500) 9.95
385-85 HO 4 x 9″ x 16′   pkg(500) 10.95

CTT, Inc.

Designing and planning your next layout will be easy with this new line of track and accessory templates plus Layout Design sheets. All items are calibrated to a 1″ = 12″ scale.

HO SCALE TEMPLATES

Templates are molded in tough, see-through plastic with outlines for curves, crossings, turn-outs and other track.

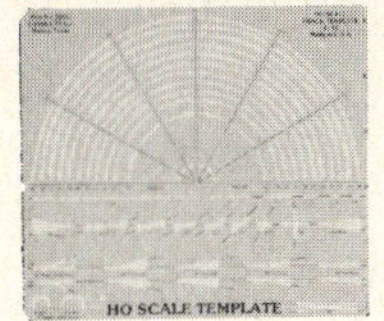

233-5000 Template Only   10.50
233-5003 Template & Paper   kit   13.95

SCALE RULER

12″ clear plastic. Includes scale feet, inches, full-size inch, millimeter, decimal and metric conversion table.

233-9072 1/72   2.89
233-9087 1/87   2.89

LAYOUT DESIGN PAPER

The Design Sheets feature a 1″ square grid pattern, printed in light gray, and are available for 9x16′, or 16x23′ rooms. (Sheets can be overlapped for larger areas.)

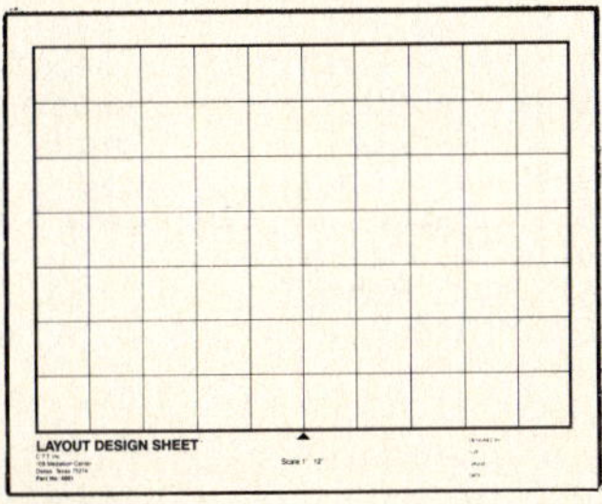

233-4000 Paper Kit   3.95
233-4001 Ffor 7 x 10′   .25
233-4002 For 9x16′   .75
233-4003 For 16x23′   2.00

Sequoia SCALE MODELS
HO SCALE

All items are metal or plastic castings.

SWITCH STANDS
non-operating

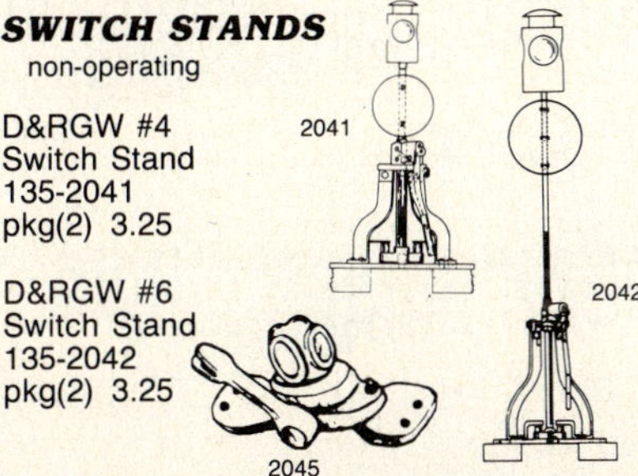

D&RGW #4 Switch Stand
135-2041 pkg(2) 3.25

D&RGW #6 Switch Stand
135-2042 pkg(2) 3.25

135-2045 Low Ramapo Switch Stand ea 2.75
with red/green jewels

135-2046 Low Ramapo Switch Stand ea 2.75
with red/amber jewels

Mountains in Minutes™
I.S.L.E. LABORATORIES
HO SCALE (1/87)

BRIDGES

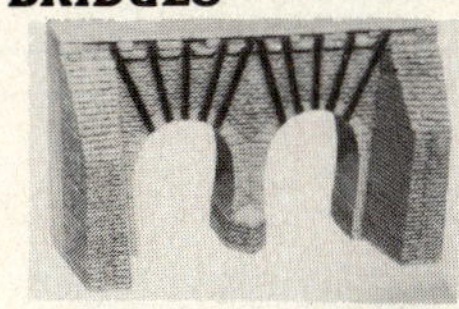

Cross-Over Bridge/Tunnel
473-828 13.59

473-827 Multi-Scale Viaduct   19.98
(8 x 21″   20 x 44 cm, can be used with HO, O and N Scales.)

473-826 Multi-Scale Arch Bridge   11.98
(1-3/4 x 11-7/8″   4.5 x 30 cm, can be used for HO and N scales.)

SCALE SHOPS
HO SCALE (1/87)

TURNOUT MACHINE

Slow motion, motorized, screw type switch machines. Each includes one pair of contacts and switch linkage. Available fully assembled and in kit form and bulk packs.

649-1040 Switch Machine assembled 12.98
649-1030 Switch Machine   kit 6.98
Easy-to-build kit assembles in six steps. Includes cut-out contacts, diodes and complete assembly, wiring and installation instructions.

Switch Machine Bulk Packs (Kits only)
649-1006 Kit   pkg(6) 38.95
649-1012 Kit   pkg(12) 69.98

ACCESSORIES
649-4080 Switch Machine   pkg(2)   .79
          Extra Contacts
649-4082 Switch Machine   pkg(12) 4.29
          Contacts
649-4085 Switch Machine   pkg(50) 16.79
          Contacts
649-6010 Switch Machine   pkg(2)   1.98
          Linkage

ATLAS MODEL RAILROAD CO., INC.

HO SCALE (1/87)

CODE 100 TRACK & ACCESSORIES

NOTE: 15 or 18" Radius Curved Snap Track takes 12 full sections to make a circle. 22" Radius Track requires 16.

BRASS TRACK

FLEX TRACK

150-104	3' on plastic ties	each	2.40
150-105	3' on plastic ties	pkg(5)	12.00

STRAIGHT SNAP-TRACK

150-21	9"	pkg(6)	2.80
150-19	9"	each	.44
150-22	6"	pkg(4)	1.52
150-23	3"	pkg(4)	1.52
150-25	1-1/2"	pkg(4)	1.52
150-47	Assortment	set	1.52

Two each of the following: 3/4", 1", 1-1/4", 1-1/2", 2", 2-1/2" plus 24 rail joiners.

CURVED SNAP-TRACK

150-31	15" Radius	pkg(6)	2.82
150-17	15" Radius **NEW**	each	.44
150-32	1/2-15" Radius	pkg(4)	1.52
150-33	18" Radius	pkg(6)	2.80
150-20	18" Radius **NEW**	each	.44

(By Special Order Only.)

150-34	1/2-18" Radius	pkg(4)	1.52
150-35	1/3-18" Radius	pkg(4)	1.52
150-36	22" Radius	pkg(6)	2.80
150-18	22" Radius **NEW**	each	.44

TERMINAL SNAP-TRACK

150-40	9" Straight		2.03
150-45	18" Radius		2.03

SNAP-SWITCH (TURNOUT)

18" Radius

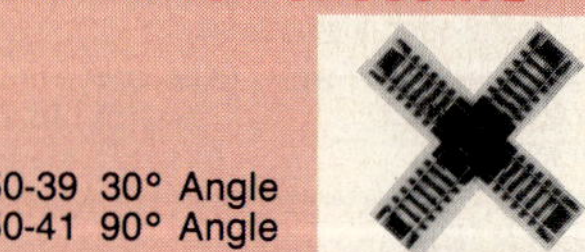

150-50	Left, Remote Control		9.68
150-51	Right, Remote Control		9.68
150-60	Left, Manual		5.85
150-61	Right, Manual		5.85

SNAP-TRACK CROSSING

150-39	30° Angle		4.28
150-41	90° Angle		4.28

CUSTOM-LINE CROSSING

150-140	12-1/2°, use w/#4 turnout		4.46
150-141	19°, use with #6 turnout		4.28
150-142	25°, use with #4 turnout		4.28
150-143	30°		4.28
150-144	45°		4.28
150-145	60°		4.28

CUSTOM-LINE MARK III TURNOUT

150-240	Wye		7.20
150-241	#4, Left		7.20
150-242	#4, Right		7.20
150-243	#6, Left		7.20
150-244	#6, Right		7.20

NICKEL SILVER TRACK

SUPER FLEX TRACK

150-168	3' on black ties	each	2.50
150-178	3' on black ties	pkg(5)	12.50
150-16822	3' on brown ties	each	2.75

STRAIGHT SNAP-TRACK

150-150	9"	each	.60
150-821	9"	pkg(6)	3.75
150-822	6"	pkg(4)	2.00
150-823	3"	pkg(4)	2.00
150-825	1-1/2" **NEW**	pkg(4)	2.00
150-847	Assortment	set	2.40

Two each of the following: 3/4", 1", 1-1/4", 1-1/2", 2", 2-1/2" plus 24 rail joiners.

CURVED SNAP-TRACK

150-151	15" Radius	each	.60
150-152	18" Radius	each	.60
150-153	22" Radius	each	.60
150-831	15" Radius	pkg(6)	3.75
150-832	1/2-15" Radius	pkg(4)	2.00
150-833	18" Radius	pkg(6)	3.75
150-834	1/2-18" Radius	pkg(4)	2.00
150-835	1/3-18" Radius	pkg(4)	2.00
150-836	22" Radius	pkg(6)	3.75

TERMINAL SNAP-TRACK

150-840	9" Straight	each	2.40
150-845	18" Radius	each	2.40

SNAP SWITCHES (TURNOUTS)

150-850	Left, Remote Control		11.00
150-851	Right, Remote Control		11.00
150-860	Left, Manual		7.00
150-861	Right, Manual		7.00

CUSTOM-LINE MARK III TURNOUT

Black Ties

150-280	Wye		8.25
150-281	#4, Left		8.25

150-282	#4, Right		8.25
150-283	#6, Left		8.25

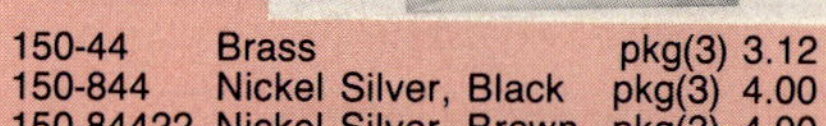

150-284	#6, Right		8.25

Brown Ties

150-28022	Wye		8.25
150-28122	#4, Left		8.25
150-28222	#4, Right		8.25
150-28322	#6, Left		8.25
150-28422	#6, Right		8.25

SNAP-TRACK CROSSING

150-839	30°		5.00

CUSTOM-LINE CROSSINGS

Black

150-171	19°	5.00	150-174	45°	5.00
150-172	25°	5.00	150-175	60°	5.00
150-173	30°	5.00	150-176	90°	5.00
150-177	12-1/2°	5.50			

Brown

150-17122	19°		5.00
150-17222	25°		5.00
150-17322	30°		5.00
150-17422	45°		5.00
150-17522	60°		5.00
150-17622	90°		5.00
150-17722	12-1/2°		5.50

STARTER SET

150-48	Nickel Silver Snap-Track	25.95

Set includes: 5-9" straight track, 12-18" radius curved track, 2 bumpers, 2 1/3-18" radius curved track, 2 wired terminal joiners, 2 left hand manual "snap-switches", 1 rerailer section & 48 rail joiners.

MISCELLANEOUS

BUMPER

150-43	Brass	pkg(2)	1.52
150-843	Nickel Silver, Black	pkg(2)	2.00
150-84322	Nickel Silver, Brown	pkg(2)	2.00

RERAILER

150-44	Brass	pkg(3)	3.12
150-844	Nickel Silver, Black	pkg(3)	4.00
150-84422	Nickel Silver, Brown	pkg(3)	4.00

UNCOUPLER

150-49	Dead End, Brass		2.03
150-849	Dead End, Nickel Silver		2.40

TRACK ACCESSORIES

MODELER'S SUPER SAW

150-400	Snap Saw	1.95

TRACK NAILS

"HO" & "N" Gauge. #19 x 1/2" long, round head, black oxidized steel.

150-2540	Track Nails	pkg(2oz)	2.50

RAIL

3' Sections, 33 per Package

150-101	Brass, Code 100	pkg(99')	26.00
150-102	NS, 36" L, Cd 100	pkg(99')	27.00

TERMINAL JOINER

Dealers: MUST order Dealer packs of 24.

150-842	Nickel Silver	each	1.60
150-42	Brass	each	1.60

RAIL JOINER

Dealers: MUST order Dealer packs of 6.

150-54	Brass	pkg(48)	1.50
150-55	Plastic	pkg(24)	.90
150-170	NS	pkg(48)	1.50

ROADBED

150-111	Desert Tan-3' Section	1.50

ATLAS MODEL RAILROAD CO., INC.

HO SCALE (1/87)

ELECTRICAL ACCESSORIES
BRIDGES
CODE 83 TRACK & ACCESSORIES

ELECTRICAL ACCESSORIES

SWITCH MACHINE

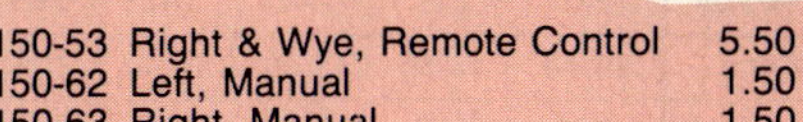

Remote Control, Left
150-52   5.50

150-53 Right & Wye, Remote Control   5.50
150-62 Left, Manual   1.50
150-63 Right, Manual   1.50

for Under Table
Installation
150-65   5.50

SWITCH CONTROL BOX

Switch Control Box
150-56   2.50

WIRING ACCESSORIES

150-200 Snap Relay   6.75
Feeds control panel lamps and allows selective power control (i.e. frogs & signals.)

150-205 Connector   5.25
Three SPST on-off switches in parallel. Use to control power to sidings, accessories, etc. Can be coupled together in any number.

150-210 Twin   5.25
Two DPDT switches in parallel. Useful for reversing section and turntable control on single-cab layouts, etc.

150-215 Selector   5.25
Four single-pole, double-throw switches provide two-cab operation for four blocks. May be coupled together in any number for control of additional blocks without inter-switch wiring. Can be used as area selectors for four-cab operation. Can be used with #220.

150-220 Controller   5.25
Simple way to wire and control reversing loops, wyes and turntables. Has reversing switches for two mainline cabs plus a switch, selectable for either cab, for directional control on reversing loops, etc. Can be used with #215.

BRIDGES

TRUSS

65' Pony
150-86   kit 10.00
Brass 9" long

65' Pony
150-886 kit 10.25
Nickel Silver 9" long

65' Deck
150-884 kit 4.00
Nickel Silver 9" long

65' Warren
150-83   kit 3.25
Brass 9" long

65' Warren
150-883 kit 4.00
Nickel Silver 9" long

65' Deck
150-84   kit 3.75
Brass 9" long

CHORD

Curved
150-87   kit 16.00
Brass 18" long

Curved
150-887 kit 16.50
Nickel Silver 18" long

GIRDER

150-85   65' Thru Plate   3.75
Brass, assembled

150-885 65' Thru Plate   4.00
Nickel-silver, assembled

MISCELLANEOUS

150-81   3" Bridge Pier   pkg(4) 2.50
150-82   Pier Girder   pkg(4) 2.00
150-80   Pier Set   9.95
Includes 46 stone masonry piers graduated in height, one pier girder and snap-in shims.

CODE 83 TRACK & ACCESSORIES

Made in USA

SUPER FLEX TRACK

150-500 3' on brown ties   each 3.50
150-501 3' on black ties   each 3.00

RAIL JOINERS Dealers must order pkg(6)

150-550 Nickel Silver   pkg(48) 1.75

TRANSITION JOINERS Dealers: pkg(6)

150-551 Nickel Silver   pkg(12) 1.75

TURNOUTS

Nickel silver, brown ties only

150-505 #6 Left Hand   9.95
150-506 #6 Right Hand   9.95

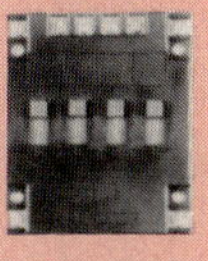

Imported from Austria by **ATLAS**
HO SCALE CODE 83 TRACK & ACCESSORIES

Roco-Line Track System makes it easy to create realistic looking track with less work. Each piece is fully assembled with Code 83 nickel silver rail and features detailed plastic ties which are not marred by track nail holes. The nail holes are partially open on the underside of the ties and can be easily opened as needed. Equipment fitted with RP25 or NEM Standard 311 wheels are compatible with the track.

CROSSINGS

150-919 30°   7.50
159-926 15°   22.00

FLEX-TRACK

Approximate length each section: 37"

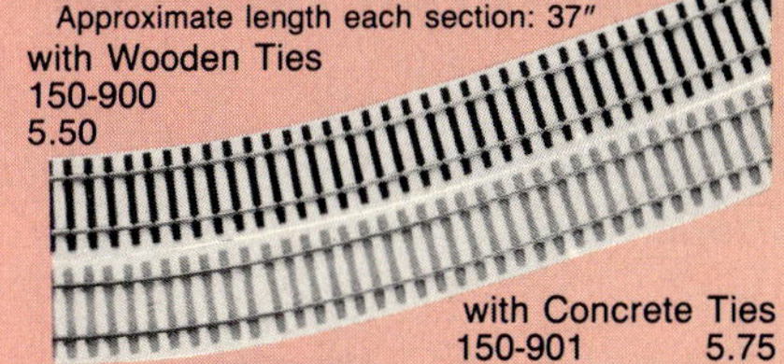

with Wooden Ties
150-900
5.50

with Concrete Ties
150-901   5.75

STRAIGHT TRACK

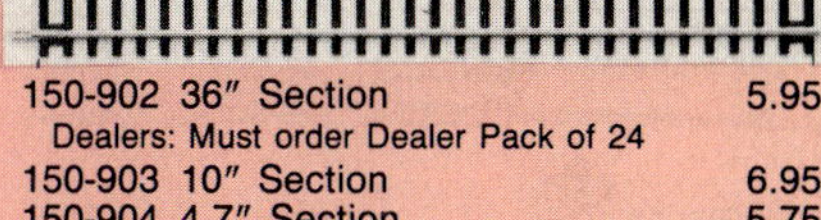

150-902 36" Section   5.95
Dealers: Must order Dealer Pack of 24
150-903 10" Section   6.95
150-904 4.7" Section   5.75
150-905 4.5" Section   5.75
150-924 2.5" Section   5.50

CURVED TRACK

150-906 14.1" Radius-30°   pkg(4) 6.95
150-907 16.5" Radius-30°   pkg(4) 7.50
150-908 18.9" Radius-30°   pkg(4) 7.75
150-909 21.4" Radius-30°   pkg(4) 8.75
150-910 35" Radius-15°   pkg(4) 8.25
150-911 77.2" Radius-5°   pkg(4) 7.25

TURNOUTS

150-912 Left Hand-15°   17.50
150-913 Right Hand-15°   17.50

150-915 Curved Left-30°   17.50
150-916 Curved Right-30°   17.50
150-917 Left Hand-10°   19.95
150-918 Right Hand-10°   19.95

150-914 Single Slip Switch-15°   27.98
150-925 Single Slip Switch-10°   34.50
150-927 3-Way Turnout 15°   42.75

RAIL JOINERS

DEALERS: Must order dealer pack of 6.

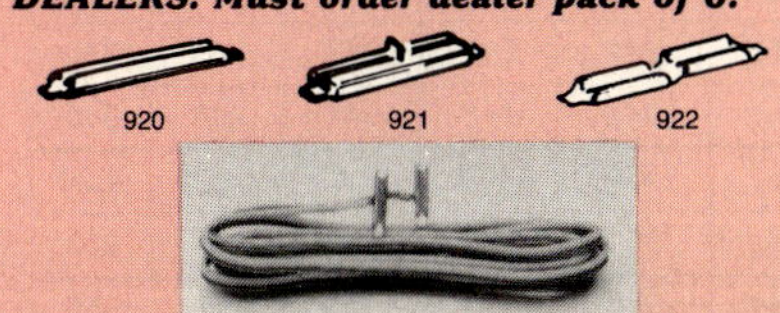

150-920 Standard-steel   pkg(12) 2.75
150-921 Insulated   pkg(12) 2.75
150-922 Code 83 to 100   pkg(12) 2.75
         Conversion Rail Joiners
Use to make the transition from track with Code 83 to Code 100 rail. Ideal for use where sidings join the mainline.
150-923 Joiner with Wire Leads   3.75
Preassembled railjoiners with wire leads.

BK Enterprises
QUALITY TRACK PRODUCTS

HO & HOn3 turnout kits, assembled turnouts, crossings and profile ties.

Specify manufacturer #180 when ordering BK ENTERPRISES.

NICKEL SILVER TURNOUT

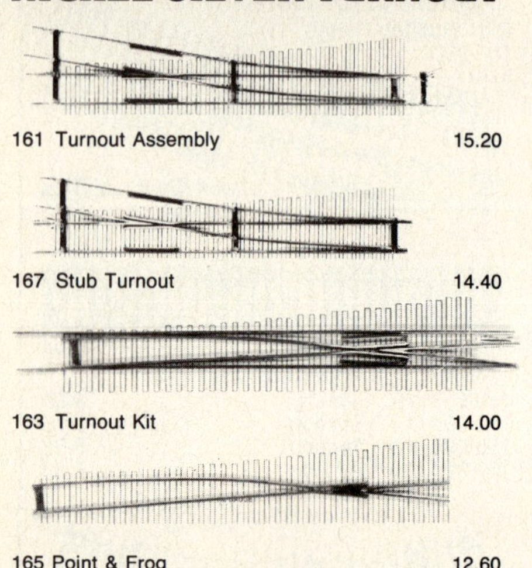

161 Turnout Assembly — 15.20

167 Stub Turnout — 14.40

163 Turnout Kit — 14.00

165 Point & Frog — 12.60

160 Frog Only 8.00

HO CODE 55 TURNOUT

55	Turnout Assembly	Stub Turnout	Turnout Kit	Point & Frog
Price	**14.80**	**14.00**	**13.60**	**12.20**
#4 Right	2341	2347	2343	2345
#4 Left	2342	2348	2344	2346
Price	**15.20**	**14.40**	**14.00**	**12.60**
#5 Right	2351	2357	2353	2355
#5 Left	2352	2358	2354	2356
Price	**15.60**	**14.80**	**14.40**	**13.00**
#6 Right	2361	2367	2363	2365
#6 Left	2362	2368	2364	2366
Price	**14.80**	**14.00**	**13.60**	**12.20**
Wye #2½	2391	2397	2393	2395
Wye #4	2392	2398	2394	2396

HOn3 CODE 55 TURNOUT

55	Turnout Assembly	Stub Turnout	Turnout Kit	Point & Frog	Frog only
Price	**14.40**	**13.60**	**13.20**	**11.80**	**8.20**
#4 Right	941	947	943	945	940
#4 Left	942	948	944	946	940
Price	**14.80**	**14.00**	**13.60**	**12.20**	**8.20**
#5 Right	951	957	953	955	950
#5 Left	952	958	954	956	950
Price	**15.20**	**14.40**	**14.00**	**12.60**	**8.40**
#6 Right	961	967	963	965	960
#6 Left	962	968	964	966	960
Price	**14.40**	**13.60**	**13.20**	**11.80**	**8.20**
Wye #2½	991	997	993	995	990
Wye #4	992	998	994	996	980 9.40

HO CODE 70 TURNOUT

70	Turnout Assembly	Stub Turnout	Turnout Kit	Point & Frog	Frog only
Price	**13.80**	**13.00**	**12.60**	**11.20**	**7.60**
#4 Right	741	747	743	745	740
#4 Left	742	748	744	746	740
Price	**14.20**	**13.40**	**13.00**	**11.60**	**7.60**
#5 Right	751	757	753	755	750
#5 Left	752	758	754	756	750
Price	**14.60**	**13.80**	**13.40**	**12.00**	**7.80**
#6 Right	761	767	763	765	760
#6 Left	762	768	764	766	760
Price	**15.20**	**14.40**	**14.00**	**12.60**	**8.20**
#8 Right	781	787	783	785	780
#8 Left	782	788	784	786	780
Price	**13.80**	**13.00**	**12.60**	**11.20**	**7.60**
Wye #2½	791	797	793	795	790
Wye #4	792	798	794	796	

HOn3 CODE 70 TURNOUT

70	Turnout Assembly	Stub Turnout	Turnout Kit	Point & Frog	Frog only
Price	**13.40**	**12.60**	**12.20**	**10.80**	**7.60**
#4 Right	841	847	843	845	840
#4 Left	842	848	844	846	840
Price	**13.80**	**13.00**	**12.60**	**11.20**	**7.60**
#5 Right	851	857	853	855	850
#5 Left	852	858	854	856	850
Price	**14.20**	**13.40**	**13.00**	**11.60**	**7.80**
#6 Right	861	867	863	865	860
#6 Left	862	868	864	866	860
Price					**8.20**
#8 Right					880
#8 Left					880
Price	**13.40**	**12.60**	**12.20**	**10.80**	**7.60**
Wye #2½	891	897	893	895	890
Wye #4	892	898	894	896	

HO CODE 83 TURNOUT

83	Turnout Assembly	Stub Turnout	Turnout Kit	Point & Frog	Frog only
Price	**14.00**	**13.20**	**12.80**	**11.40**	**7.80**
#4 Right	241	247	243	245	240
#4 Left	242	248	244	246	240
Price	**14.40**	**13.60**	**13.20**	**11.80**	**7.80**
#5 Right	251	257	253	255	250
#5 Left	252	258	254	256	250
Price	**14.80**	**14.00**	**13.60**	**12.20**	**8.00**
#6 Right	261	267	263	265	260
#6 Left	262	268	264	266	260
Price	**15.60**	**14.80**	**14.40**	**13.00**	**8.40**
#8 Right	281	287	283	285	280
#8 Left	282	288	284	286	280
Price	**14.00**	**13.20**	**12.80**	**11.40**	**7.80**
Wye #2½	291	297	293	295	290
Wye #4	292	298	294	296	

HO CODE 100 TURNOUT

100	Turnout Assembly	Stub Turnout	Turnout Kit	Point & Frog	Frog only
Price	**14.40**	**13.60**	**13.20**	**11.80**	**7.80**
#4 Right	141	147	143	145	140
#4 Left	142	148	144	146	140
Price	**14.80**	**14.00**	**13.60**	**12.20**	**7.80**
#5 Right	151	157	153	155	150
#5 Left	152	158	154	156	150
Price	**15.20**	**14.40**	**14.00**	**12.60**	**8.00**
#6 Right	161	167	163	165	160
#6 Left	162	168	164	166	160
Price	**15.60**	**14.80**	**14.40**	**13.00**	**8.20**
#7 Right	171	177	173	175	170
#7 Left	172	178	174	176	170
Price	**16.00**	**15.20**	**14.80**	**13.40**	**8.40**
#8 Right	181	187	183	185	180
#8 Left	182	188	184	186	180
Price	**17.00**	**16.20**	**15.80**	**14.40**	**8.60**
#10 Right	111	117	113	115	110
#10 Left	112	118	114	116	110
Price	**14.40**	**13.60**	**13.20**	**11.80**	**7.80**
Wye #2½	191	197	193	195	190
Wye #4	192	198	194	196	

TRANSITION RAIL

Connects two different size rails.

180-31 for Code 40 to 55	pkg(2)	6.00
180-32 for Code 55 to 70	pkg(2)	6.00
180-33 for Code 70 to 83	pkg(2)	6.00
180-34 for Code 83 to 100	pkg(2)	6.00

HO CROSSINGS

	90°	70°	60°	45°	30°	Price
Code 70	731	738	732	733	734	**35.00**
Code 83	231		232	233	234	**35.00**
Code 100	131		132	133	134	**35.00**

	28°	Price	19°	14°	Price
Code 70	735	**35.00**	736	737	**40.00**
Code 83	235	**35.00**	236	237	**40.00**
Code 100	135	**35.00**	136	137	**40.00**

CURVED TURNOUTS

Code 70 suitable for HO & HOn3. Code 83 & 100 suitable for HO.

Price	30.00	27.00	**Price**	28.00	**Price**	28.00
#6 Right Code 70	825	725	#6 Right Code 83	225	#6 Right Code 100	125
#6 Left Code 70	826	726	#6 Left Code 100	226	#6 Left Code 100	126
Price		29.00	**Price**	30.00	**Price**	30.00
#8 Right Code 70		727	#8 Right Code 83	227	#8 Right Code 100	127
#8 Left Code 70		728	#8 Left Code 83	228	#8 Left Code 100	128

BK Enterprises
QUALITY TRACK PRODUCTS

DUAL GAUGE TURNOUTS HO/HOn3

	Code 83	Code 70
Price	40.00	38.00
Right Hand Narrow on Right	2211	7211
Right Hand Narrow on Left	2212	7212
Left Hand Narrow on Right	2221	7221
Left Hand Narrow on Left	2222	7222

3 WAY TURNOUTS

180-129	Code 100	35.00
180-229	Code 83	35.00
180-729	Code 70	34.00

PROFILE TIES

GAUGE	HO			
STAIN	Gray	Brown	Black	Plain
Price	9.40	9.40	9.40	8.80
Regular pkg	11 (1200)	13 (1200)	15 (1200)	17 (1200)
Switch pkg	12 (700)	14 (700)	16 (700)	18 (700)

GAUGE	HOn3			
STAIN	Gray	Brown	Black	Plain
Price	9.40	9.40	9.40	8.80
Regular pkg	25 (1200)	19 (1200)	21 (1200)	23 (1200)
Switch pkg	26 (700)	20 (700)	22 (700)	24 (700)

CAR WEIGHTS

180-37	1/2 ounce	pkg(8)	4.60
180-38	1 ounce	pkg(8)	7.20

EARL R. ESHLEMAN

TURNOUT LINKAGE

Designed for under-the-table operation of turnouts with choke-rod or switch machine. Fits any gauge.

257-1	3/4" max thickness	2.00
257-2	1-3/8" max thickness	2.00
257-3	1-7/8" max thickness	2.00
257-4	1-7/8" max thickness w/spring	2.15

for manual applications

Turnout Link Drilling Jig
257-10
1.25

DIAMOND SCALE CONST.

STEEL GIRDER TURNTABLE

Turntable bridge is a wood frame with injection molded detail overlay on side frames. Bridge can be lifted out of pit for maintenance.

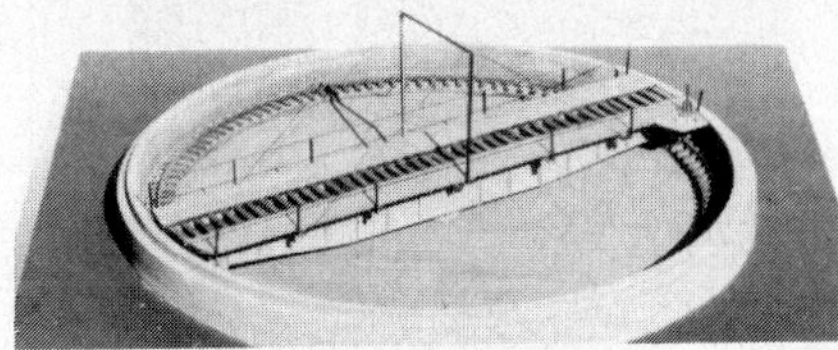

239-65	65', 8-3/4" rail length	96.50
239-75	75', 10-1/8" rail length, includes metal cab and arch	97.50

239-901	90', 12-1/2" rail length	101.50
239-1051	105', 14-5/8" rail length	102.50
239-1201	120', 16-1/2" rail length	106.50
239-1341	134', 18-1/2" rail length	108.50

STEEL TRUSS TURNTABLE

Center shaft has steel out-of-reach arms welded on to apply turning pressure to bridge. Bridge can be removed from the pit for maintenance.

239-90	90', 12-1/2" rail length	139.50
239-115	115', 15-7/8" rail length	149.75
239-135	135', 18-3/4" rail length	153.75

TIMBER TRUSS TURNTABLE

for standard and narrow gauge

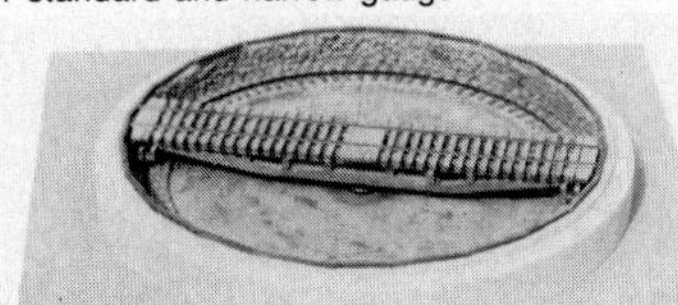

239-51	51', 7" rail length	88.75
239-60	60', 8-1/4" rail length	89.75

GALLOWS TURNTABLE

for standard and narrow gauge.

239-56	56', 7-11/16" rail length	92.75

TURNTABLE MOTOR & GEAR BOX

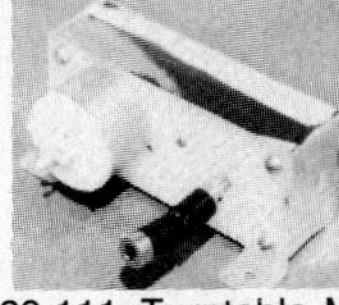

Designed to operate all Diamond Scale turntables through the 3/16" steel worm shaft supplied in each turntable kit. Attaches to underside of pit and requires indexing kit to achieve total automatic operation. Reversing switch included.

239-111	Turntable Motor & Gear Box Kit	49.50

OPERATING TURNTABLE HO CRAFT TRAIN KITS

Kits are constructed of scale basswood, metal castings, oil lite bronze bearings, nylon gears, steel shafting, and a reconstituted wood composition product that forms the pit walls and bottom.

You can determine which of your locos will fit on which turntable by referring to bridge rail length listed with each item.

TURNTABLE ARCH

Arches are installed at mid-table upon which feeder wires are connected to insure good electrical connections.

Round Top
239-101
kit 16.95

Angle Top
239-102
kit 16.95

TURNTABLE INDEXING KIT

Designed to control the operation of the motor to stop turntable in correct rail alignment at track selected. Operator selects track, determines direction of bridge rotation and starts unit with push of a button. Turntable turns until it is within 3/4" of selected track, then automatically slows until alignment is made.

Kit consists of prewired electronic board, six track sensors, twelve-position rotary selector switch, switch knob, two push buttons and control rotor.

239-110	for 105' and Under Turntables N and Sn3 Scales	90.25
239-114	for 115' & over Turntables	90.25

A.J. FRICKO COMPANY

"making toy trains run like real trains"

TRACK & MOTOR CLEANER

Universal track and motor cleaner for layouts & locos.

Use one drop per rail per 4 x 8' area. Remains effective for 1 year. Cleano will protect against rust even in damp basements.

274-8 Cleano   30ml 19.95

EVERGREEN HILL designs
HO SCALE (1/87)

SWITCH STAND

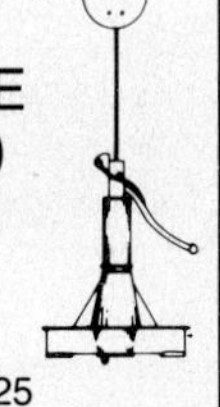

Non-operating, cast white metal kit.
261-620 Sierra Switch Stand 2.25

Campbell Scale Models

HO SCALE (1/87)

Smooth-milled roadbed from soft pine for ease in track laying and for soundproofing.

Bridge and trestle kits feature precision-cut wood with templates and complete instructions.

BRIDGES

TRESTLE

200-301   50' Ballasted Deck Pile   12.30
(less ties)   6-7/8 x 3"   17.3 x 7.6 cm

200-302   50' Open Deck Pile   12.30
(ties included)   6-7/8 x 3"   17.3 x 7.6 cm

200-303   70' Curved   22.00
(ties included)   15-1/4 x 1-3/8"   38.7 x 3.4 cm

200-304   110' Tall Curved   29.30
(ties included)   15-1/4 x 1-3/8"   38.7 x 3.4 cm

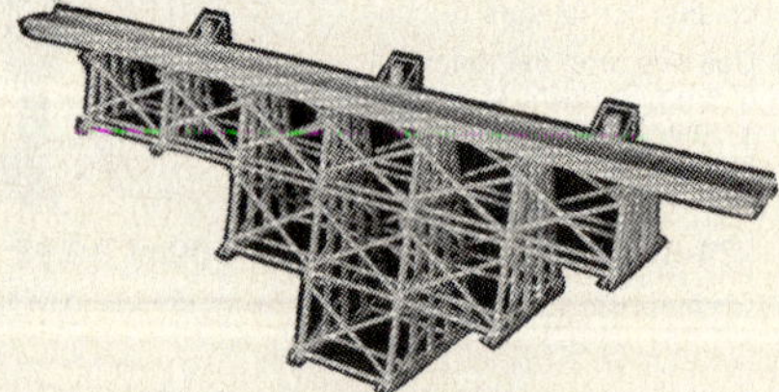

200-751   Tall Timber (144-216')   30.50
(includes ties: 20-29")   50.8-73.6 cm

COVERED

200-306   Covered   45.10
(ties included)   14-21/32 x 3-1/4"   37.2 x 8.2 cm

TIMBER

200-761   50' Deck   30.50
(ties included)   14"   35.6 cm

200-762   70' Thru Bridge   30.50
(ties included)   14 x 3-3/4"   35.5 x 9.5 cm

GIRDER

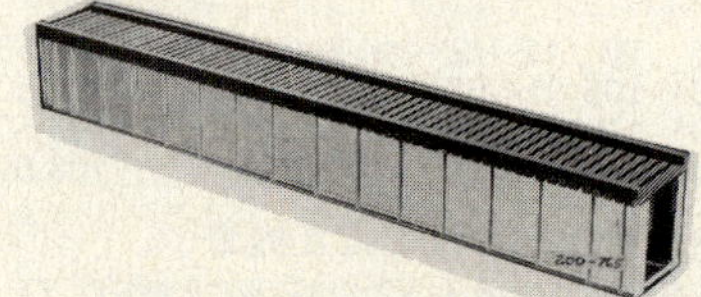

200-765   70' Deck Plate   22.80
(ties included)   9-5/8 x 1-3/8"   24.4 x 3.4 cm

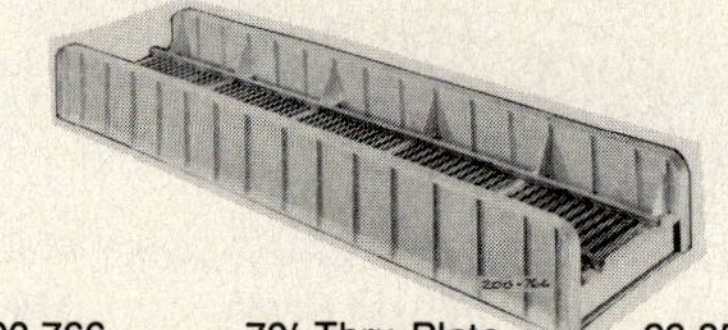

200-766   70' Thru Plate   23.85
(ties included)   9-5/8 x 2-1/2"   24.4 x 5.2 cm

TRUSS

200-305   Howe   38.50
(ties included)   14-1/2 x 3-1/8"   36.8 x 7.6 cm

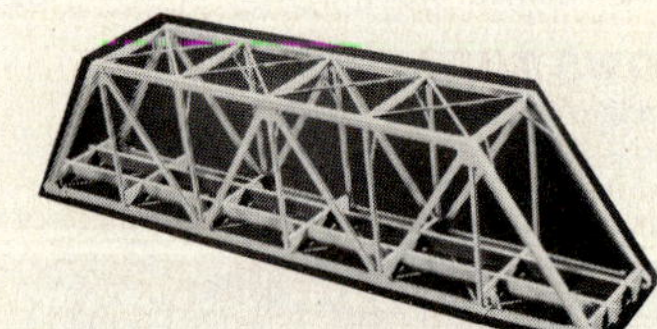

200-763   125' Single Track   30.50
(less ties)   17-1/4 x 3-3/4"   35.5 x 9.5 cm

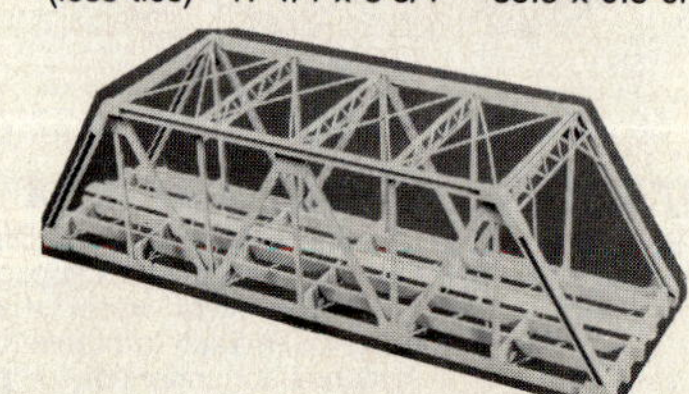

200-764   125' Double Track   32.80
(less ties)   14-1/8 x 3-3/8"   35.8 x 8.5 cm

MISCELLANEOUS

PROFILE TIES

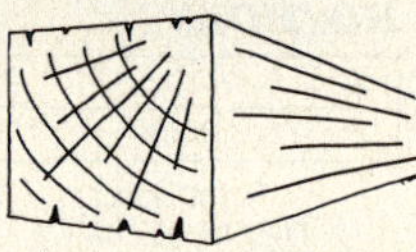

Standard
200-796   pkg(1000)   8.00

200-797	Turnout & Crossover	pkg(250)	8.00
200-798	Bridge	pkg(500)	8.00
200-799	Narrow Gauge	pkg(1000)	8.00

BALLAST

200-790	Light Gray	3.50
200-791	Dark Gray	3.50
200-792	Cinder	3.50
200-793	Decomposed Granite	3.50
200-794	Iron Ore	3.50
200-795	Coal Load	3.50

TEST LIGHT

Set it on the track. If power is on, it lights up. Works with any gauge. In green, red or amber.

200-550   Track Test Light   each 4.25
(Dealer Pack: 6 per card)

CUSTOM RAILWAY SUPPLY

HO SCALE (1/87)

TRACK PLANNING TEMPLATE

Metal track planning template. 1/8th actual HO size. Use with graph paper ruled 8 squares per inch.

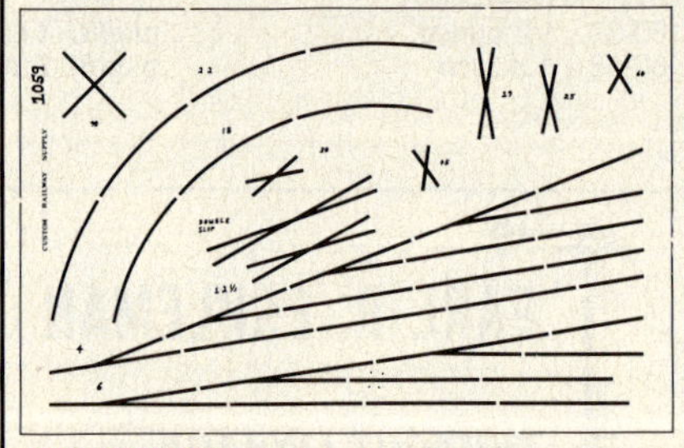

212-1059   Track Planning Template   9.95

Circuitron

Electronics for Model Railroads

THE TORTOISE™ SWITCH MACHINE

Easy-to-Mount switch machine features low current drain and prototypical slow motion action (3 seconds to complete throw).

The Tortoise™
800-6000   14.95

HIGHBALL PRODUCTS

BALLAST *pkg(1 lb) 3.30*

	N	★ HO	O
Limestone	330-120	330-220	330-320
Light Gray	330-121	330-221	330-321
Dark Gray	330-122	330-222	330-322
Black	330-123	330-223	330-323
Cinder	330-124	330-224	330-324
Brown	330-125	330-225	330-325

DIRT

330-510   Real Dirt   12oz 5.50
Specially processed for model scenery.

GRAVEL

330-520   Real Gravel   16oz 5.50

Grandt Line

HO SCALE (1/87)

SWITCH STAND
3-Position, Heavy Cast Iron
Black Styrene with Jewels
300-5061   kit 1.50

RAIL CLIPS
Dummy
300-5155   pkg(55) 1.75

Kadee ®   HO SCALE (1/87)

"QUICKIE" PANEL SWITCHES
Single pole, single throw, button switches for uncouplers, turnout motors, etc. 16 volts AC or DC
1 amp.

380-160   Amber   pkg(3) 3.45
380-161   Green   pkg(3) 3.45
380-162   Red   pkg(3) 3.45

TRACK GAUGE
"Flip-over" multi-purpose gauge.

380-341   Code 70 & 100 2.15
380-342   Code 55, 66 & 70 2.15
    HOn3

TRACK SPIKE   *NEW*

380-372   Code 70   pkg(4000) 6.15
380-392   Code 100   pkg(4000) 6.15

Kadee® is a Registered Trademark.
Magne-Matic® is a Registered Trademark.

- TRACK
- TURNOUTS
- SWITCHES

UNITRACK SYSTEM

Modular track system, with attached plastic roadbed.
Track sections interlock for easy assembly.

STRAIGHT TRACK
Dealers: MUST order Dealer Pack of 10

381-2120   4-1/2"   each 2.60
381-2150   9-3/4"   each 2.80

CURVED TRACK
Dealers: MUST order Dealer Pack of 10

381-2210   21-5/8" Radius 22.5°   each 2.80
381-2220   24" Radius 22.5°   each 2.80
381-2240   28-3/4" Radius 22.5°   each 3.30
381-2250   31-1/8" Radius 22.5°   each 3.60

FEEDER TRACK

381-2151   9.7"L   each 5.00

TURNOUTS

381-2850   Left Hand #4   each 44.00
381-2851   Right Hand #4   each 44.00
381-2860   Left Hand #6   each 53.00
    Can have live or insulated frogs.
381-2861   Right Hand #6   each 53.00
    Can have live or insulated frogs.

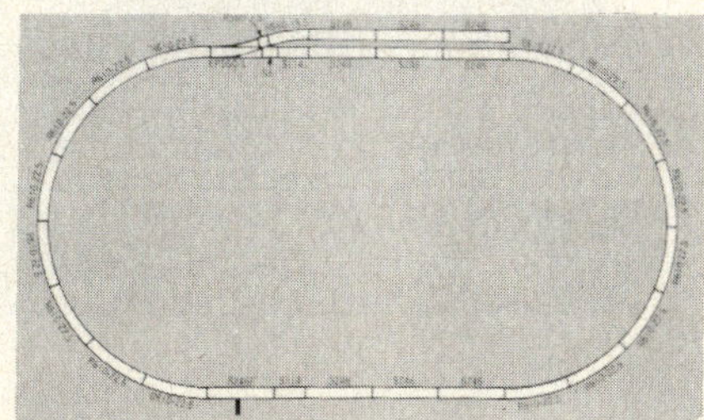

381-3101   Unitrack Set   132.00
Includes complete oval of track with straight and
curves, one turnout, turnout adaptor and adaptor
cord. Fits in area of 7'.9" x 4'4".

ACCESSORIES

381-24815   Uni-Joiner,   pkg(20) 5.25
    Rail Joiners
381-24816   Insulated Unijoiners   pkg(20) 5.25
381-24818   Terminal Joiner   TBA

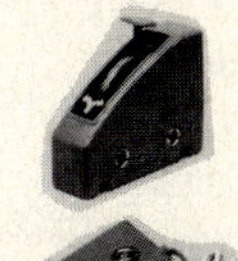
Turnout
Control Switch
381-20500   7.75

DC Converter
381-20504   6.50

3-Way
Extension Cord
381-24827   5.25

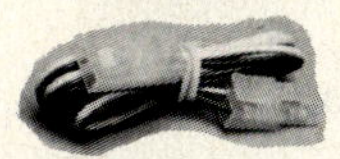
DC
Extension Cord
381-24825   3.25

381-24826   AC Extension Cord   3.25

Adaptor Cord
381-2501   3.25

Bumper
381-5101   pkg(2) 11.75

Signal Power
Supply
381-20601   23.50

Signal Extension
Cord
381-20602   3.25

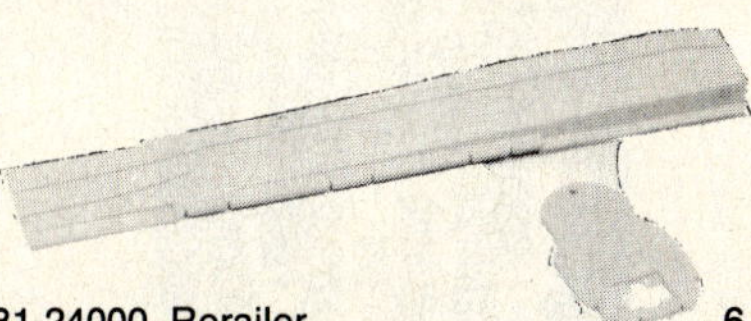

381-24000   Rerailer   6.50

(not illustrated)
381-24830   Connector Switch   (green) 3.50
381-24831   Selector Switch   (red) 3.75
381-24832   Reverse Switch   (blue) 4.00

381-22060   KC-I Controller   *NEW* TBA

381-22080   KM-1 Main   *NEW* TBA
    Power Supply
381-30703   Red Epoch-DC   *NEW* TBA

TRACK AND ACCESSORIES

TRACK   *NEW*

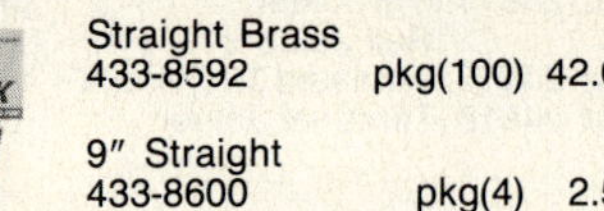

Straight Brass
433-8592   pkg(100)   42.00

9" Straight
433-8600   pkg(4)   2.50

Curved Radius
433-8601   pkg(4)   2.50

Flex Track 3' Brass
433-8632   pkg(25)   58.75

Flex Track 3'
433-8656   pkg(5)   11.75

BUMPERS   *NEW*

Lighted
433-8638
pkg(2)   3.50

ROADBED   *NEW*

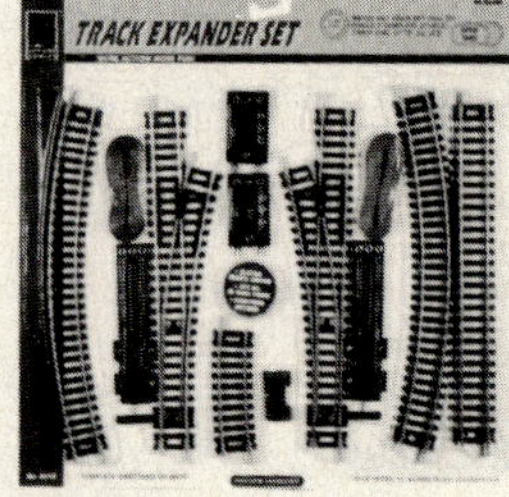

433-8627   Cork   pkg(5)   8.50

TRACK EXPANDER SETS   *NEW*

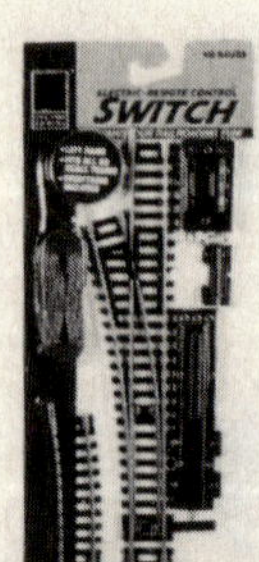

433-8650   Brass   24.50
433-8651   Figure 8   14.00

SWITCHES   *NEW*

Remote Control
Right Hand
433-8604   9.50

Remote Control
Left Hand
433-8605   9.50

MISCELLANEOUS

433-8620   90' Crossing   *NEW*   4.25
433-8621   Rerailer   *NEW*   3.00

NAILS/SCREWS/SPIKES

1/2" Track Nails
433-1405
pkg(20 grams)   3.00

1/2" Track Screws
433-1404
pkg(24)   3.00

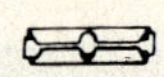

HO Spikes
433-1407
pkg(20 grams)   3.00

3/4" Track Nails
for Cork
433-1434
pkg(20 grams)   3.00

CODE 100 RAIL JOINERS

Brass
433-1408
pkg(24)   3.00

Alexander scale models

MINE EQUIPMENT

18" GAUGE
120-9802   Straight Track   pkg(4)   .95
120-9803   Curved Track   pkg(4)   .95

2' GAUGE
120-2801   Latrine Car   each   2.25
120-2804   Straight Track   pkg(4)   1.00
120-2805   Curved Track   pkg(4)   1.00

MISCELLANEOUS

Timber Car
120-9805
kit   3.00

Yard Air
Connection
120-305
pkg(3)   1.75

(not illustrated)
120-9804   Mine Track Kick Switch   pkg(2)   1.25

Looks like most people are beating the heat by staying indoors this afternoon. This quaint village scene is part of the Antwerp Model Railroad Association layout, located in Antwerp, Belgium. Typical details like the cobblestone streets, Wiking vehicles and an ornate Brawa street lamp capture the rural flavor of the village. Structures from Faller, Vollmer, Pola and Kibri fill the square.
Photo by Alf Bossaers

Micro Engineering Company

HO, HOn3 and HOn2-1/2 Flex Trak,™ nickel silver rail and track accessories.

FLEX TRAK™
Flex Trak™ features scale size ties, tie plates and spikes, irregular tie spacing, natural brown tie color and nickel silver rail. 3′ lengths.

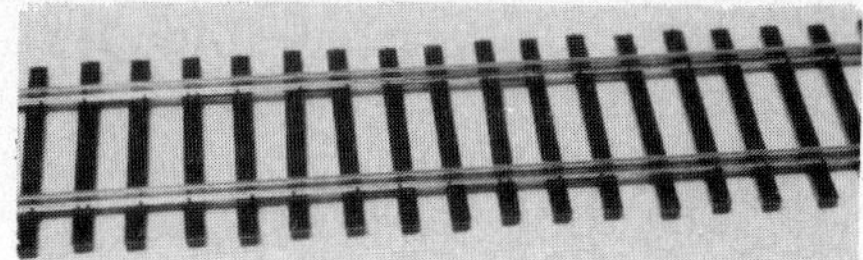

255-10102	Code 100	pkg(6)	24.65
255-10104	Code 83	pkg(6)	23.15
255-10106	Code 70	pkg(6)	23.15
255-10108	Code 55	pkg(6)	23.15

WEATHERED FLEX-TRAK™
255-12102	Code 100	pkg(6)	25.75
255-12104	Code 83	pkg(6)	24.25
255-12106	Code 70	pkg(6)	24.25
255-12108	Code 55	pkg(6)	24.25

HOn3
WEATHERED FLEX TRAK™
255-12110	Code 70 Dual	pkg(6)	30.25
255-12112	Code 55 Dual	pkg(6)	28.95
255-12114	Code 70	pkg(6)	24.25
255-12116	Code 55	pkg(6)	22.95
255-12118	Code 40	pkg(6)	22.95

DUAL GAUGE FLEX TRAK™
Three rail track for combined standard and narrow gauge operations.

255-10110	Code 70	pkg(6)	28.95
255-10112	Code 55	pkg(6)	27.75

NARROW GAUGE HOn3 FLEX TRAK™
255-10114	Code 70	pkg(6)	23.15
255-10116	Code 55	pkg(6)	21.95
255-10118	Code 40	pkg(6)	21.95

HOn2-1/2 (HOe) FLEX TRAK™
255-10120	Code 55	pkg(6)	21.95

HOn2-1/2
WEATHERED FLEX TRAK™
255-12120	Code 55	pkg(6)	22.95

BRIDGE FLEX TRAK™
Flex Trak™ with bridge tie dimensions and spacing. Scale size ties, tie plates and spikes. Natural brown tie color and nickel silver rail. 7″ lengths.

255-11101	Code 83	pkg(2)	4.35
255-11102	Code 55, HOn3	pkg(2)	4.35

WEATHERED RAIL
Preblackened nickel silver rail sections. 3′ lengths.

255-16100	Code 100	pkg(33)	42.95
255-16083	Code 83	pkg(33)	37.15
255-16070	Code 70	pkg(33)	34.25
255-16055	Code 55	pkg(33)	29.95

NICKEL SILVER RAIL
Three feet lengths.

255-17100	Code 100	pkg(33)	39.95
255-17083	Code 83	pkg(33)	34.50
255-17070	Code 70	pkg(33)	31.75
255-17055	Code 55	pkg(33)	27.50

GIRDER RAIL
Prototype was used for street trackage.

255-17107	Code 100	pkg(17)	39.95

RAIL JOINERS
Low profile, nickel silver, slip-on type joiners.

255-26148	Code 148	pkg(50)	3.50
255-26100	Code 100	pkg(48)	3.50
255-26083	Code 83	pkg(50)	5.25
255-26070	Code 70	pkg(50)	4.95
255-26055	Code 55	pkg(50)	4.95

SPIKES
Blackened metal.

255-30102	1/2″	pkg(500)	5.65
255-30103	3/8″	pkg(12,000)	95.00
255-30104	3/8″	pkg(800)	6.95
255-30105	1/4″	pkg(15,000)	77.00
255-30106	1/4″	pkg(1000)	5.95

WEATHERED TIES
Full profile scale ties, stained and weathered brown.

255-36101	Ties	pkg(1000)	7.85
255-36102	Turnout	pkg(250)	4.95
255-36103	Hon3 Ties	pkg(1000)	6.80
255-36104	HOn3 Turnout	pkg(250)	4.35
255-36107	Low Profile	pkg(1000)	7.85
255-36108	Turnout, Low	pkg(250)	4.95

TIES
Full profile scale ties in natural wood.

255-37101	Ties	pkg(1000)	6.95
255-37102	Turnout	pkg(250)	4.35
255-37103	Ties, HOn3	pkg(1000)	5.95
255-37104	Turnout, HOn3	pkg(250)	3.95
255-37107	Low Profile	pkg(1000)	6.95
255-37108	Turnout, Low	pkg(250)	4.35

TRACK GAUGES

3-point, die-cast metal track gauge keeps rails aligned when hand-laying track.

255-42101	Code 100	2.95
255-42102	Code 83	2.95
255-42103	Code 70	2.95
255-42104	Code 55	2.95
255-42105	Code 70 HOn3	2.95
255-42106	Code 55 HOn3	2.95
255-42107	Code 40 HOn3	2.95

TRACK TOOLS

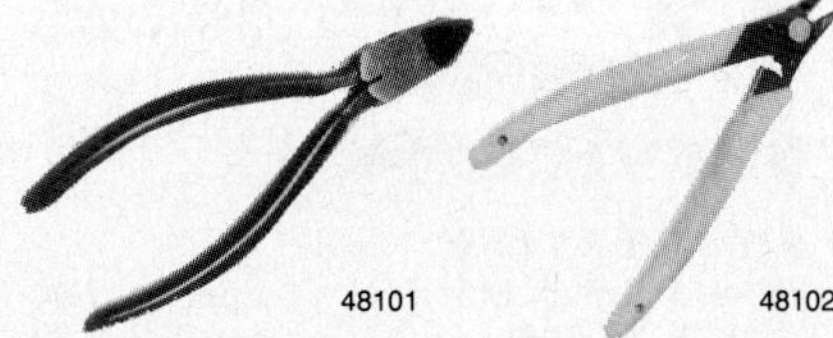

255-48101	Rail Cutter, Heavy Duty	21.95
255-48102	Rail Nipper, Light Duty	10.95

TRACK TOOL

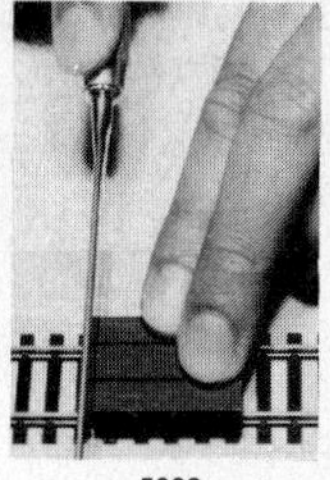

479-5001	HO	2.96
479-5003	HO & HOn3	2.96

Square cuts flex track on straightaways and curves without tie separation, helps locate misaligned rail joints and straightens used flex track in seconds.

479-5002	Parallel, HO & HOn3	2.96

Allows uniform spacing maintenance on straightaways and curves while laying parallel tracks with HO or HOn3 track.

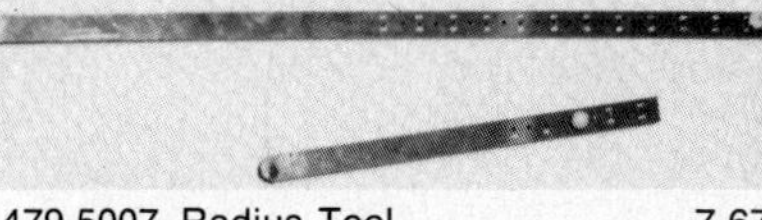

479-5007	Radius Tool	7.67

Set contains two units—short unit will swing a radius from 7 to 11″, long unit 11 to 23″.

SOLDER TOOL
Tool holds rail alignment for soldering rail joint.

479-5005	HO	2.96
479-5006	HOn3	2.96

BALLAST SPREADER
479-5008	HO	8.93

TRACK TOOL SET
Set contains one each—track tool, parallel tool, soldering tool, ballast spreader.

479-5012	HO	16.81
479-5013	HOn3	16.81
479-5014	Assortment	302.58

Contains 6 track tool sets each of N-HO-HOn3. Dealers special order only.

FLEX TRACK ALIGNMENT TOOL
8″ section will keep rail straight during construction of hand-laid mainlines, sidings and yard tracks.

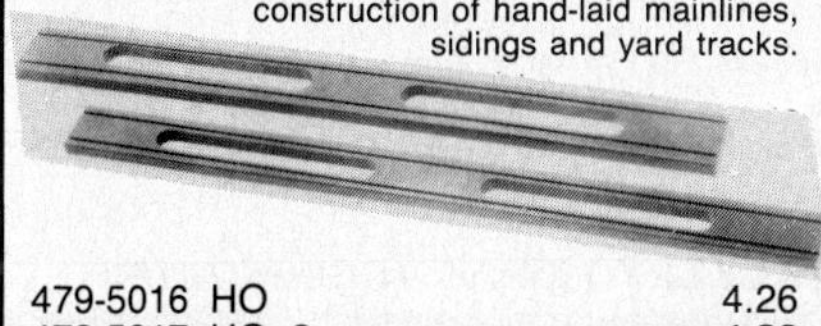

479-5016	HO	4.26
479-5017	HOn3	4.26

MAY 1, 1971

Today IN RAILROAD HISTORY

Amtrak begins operating interstate passenger trains on 22 United States railroads. Southern, Rio Grande and Rock Island do not join and continue operating their own trains.

N.J. International

HO SCALE (1/87)

SWITCH MACHINE & ACCESSORIES

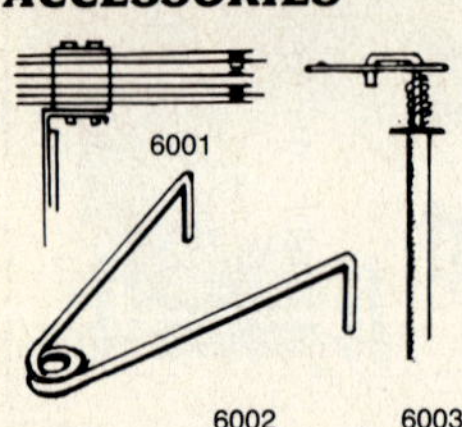

525-6000	Twin Coil Switch Machine		11.95
525-6001	Extra Contacts	pkg(2)	3.79
525-6002	Throw Springs	pkg(2)	.99
525-6003	Under Table Mounting Kit	pkg(2)	3.99
525-6004	Switch Machine Wiring Connector		3.99

SWITCH STANDS

525-1911	Star	7.95
525-1912	Branch Line	7.95
525-1913	Main Line	7.95
525-1914	Low Ramapo	7.95
525-1915	High Ramapo	7.95

HARTEL™ TROLLEY TRACK SYSTEM

In road modular trolley track system features molded styrene sections with nickel silver rail.

Right Hand Parallel
525-48044
pkg(2) 7.99

Left Hand Parallel
525-48043
pkg(2) 7.99

(not illustrated)

525-48012	Section w/Reed Switch	each	7.99
525-48010	Straight, 5-1/2″ long	pkg(4)	18.99
525-48011	Straight, 3″ long	pkg(4)	16.99
525-48020	7.26″ r x 22.5 d	pkg(4)	13.99
525-48021	9.04″ r x 22.5 d	pkg(4)	16.99
525-48040	LH Switch	pkg(2)	49.99
525-48041	RH Switch	pkg(2)	49.99
525-48045	Left Hand Turnout	pkg(2)	8.99
525-48046	Right Hand Turnout	pkg(2)	8.99
525-48101	Street Plates, Asphalt	pkg(4)	9.99
525-48091	Connector Plate	pkg(25)	2.99
525-48100	Street Plates, Cobblestone	pkg(4)	9.99
525-48200	Street Plates, Universal Cobblestone	pkg(4)	9.99
525-48201	Street Plates, Universal Asphalt	pkg(4)	9.99

TROLLEY TRACK ACCESSORIES

525-44020	Track Power Contact, 1-rail	**NEW**	3.99
525-44090	Track Power Contact, 2-rail	**NEW**	3.99
525-48050	Median for #48010	pkg(10)	9.99
525-48051	Median for #48011	pkg(10)	9.99
525-48052	Curved Median	pkg(10)	8.99
525-48092	Rail Joiners	pkg(25)	3.99

See also: SIGNALS, SCENERY, FIGURES, and BOOKS for more NJ INT'L products.

Peerless Industries

HO SCALE (1/87)

AUTOMATIC REVERSING UNIT

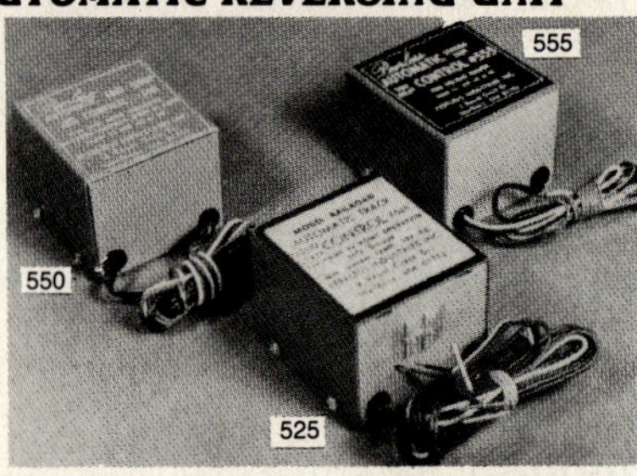

Solid State electronic equipment automatically reverses train direction without the need for track switches, optical sensors, special lights or other devices. Completely assembled in a small aluminum case, with color-coded wires factory soldered to nickel silver rail joiners for simple track hook up. Operates on any 12 volt DC power supply. Can be used:

- for automatic single or multi-track point to point operation.
- for a wall or bookcase mini-layout or display track for your favorite locomotive.
- for a test or break-in track.

564-525	Reverse Control less track	65.95

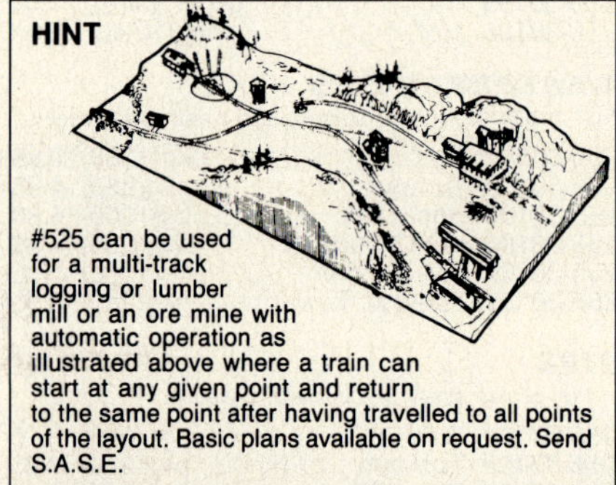

HINT

#525 can be used for a multi-track logging or lumber mill or an ore mine with automatic operation as illustrated above where a train can start at any given point and return to the same point after having travelled to all points of the layout. Basic plans available on request. Send S.A.S.E.

AUTOMATIC TRAIN STOP CONTROL

For use with Peerless #525 & #535. Provides automatic delayed stops at the end points of your reversing section. Delay is adjustable for 1 to 30 seconds. Takes only a few minutes to install. Operates from any 12 volt DC power supply.

564-550	Automatic Train Stop	69.95

AUTOMATIC INTERMEDIATE TRAIN STOP

Train will make automatic stops at intermediate points such as a station, watertower, etc. Train will stop-delay-start automatically. Delay time is adjustable from 1 to 30 seconds. Operates from any 12 volt DC power supply.

564-555	Automatic Intermediate Train Stop	69.95

WALKER Model service

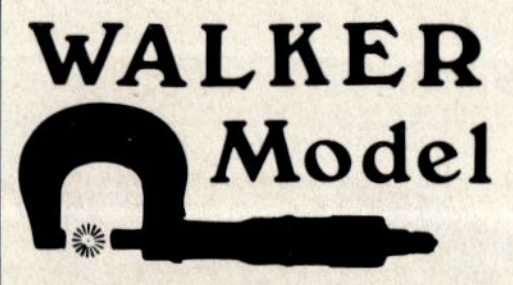

HO GROUND THROWS

Cast metal detail parts.

SWITCH STAND

786-818	Switch Stand	pkg(2)	1.50
786-819	w/Lamp	pkg(2)	2.25
786-820	w/Lamp & Jewels	pkg(2)	3.75
786-920	Lamps	pkg(12)	2.20

PRECISION SCALE CO. TOP TRACK

HO SCALE (1/87)

Top Track features nickel silver flexible rails on appropriately colored plastic ties. Track length of 36″, scale 9′ ties.

NICKEL SILVER FLEXIBLE TRACK

Dealers: MUST order packages of 6 each.

585-4925	Code 100	3.60
585-4927	Code 83	3.60
585-4931	Code 83, HOn3	4.10
585-4932	Code 83, Mainline HOn3	3.60
585-4929	Code 70	3.60

SUPER ELEVATED CURVED FLEXIBLE TRACK

One rail is super-elevated .040″ and gauge widened to maximum specifications to allow long wheelbase locomotives to negotiate sharper curves.

Dealers: MUST order packages of 6 each.

585-4926	Code 100	3.95
585-4928	Code 83	3.95
585-4930	Code 70	3.95

TRACK ACCESSORIES

RAIL JOINER

585-4972	Code 172, Delrin with tieplate (By Special Order Only.)	pkg(150)	2.75
585-4973	Code 40, Delrin with tieplate	pkg(40)	3.50
585-321	Code 70	pkg(24)	2.00

TRACK GAUGE

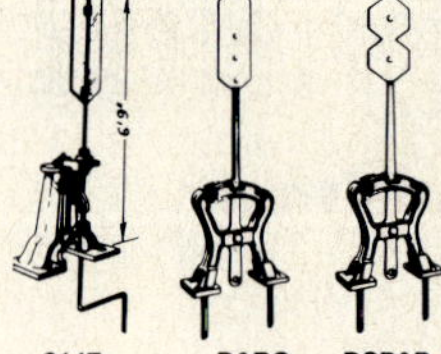

585-4956	Code 100	3.75
585-4958	Code 70	3.75
585-4955	Code 70 HO-HOn3	3.75
585-4954	Code 40 HOn3	3.75

WORKING HARP SWITCH STAND KITS

	Switch Stand, brass 585-31471		4.00
	Switch Stand, plastic 585-31841	ea	3.50
	DSP&P, brass 585-31472		4.00
	DSP&P, plastic 585-31473	pkg(2)	3.50
585-31474	DR&G, brass		4.00
585-31475	D&RG, plastic	pkg(2)	3.50

TOMAR INDUSTRIES

HO SCALE (1/87)

HAYES WHEEL STOP

Cast white metal "stops" protect your spur ends. They won't come off when bumped by a car. Used on heavy or lightweight service.

081-803	Hayes Wheel Stop Type SF	pkg(4) 1.50

HAYES BUMPING POST

Assembled post mounted on track w/insulated rail joiners.

081-808	Bumping Post	3.45

PECO

HO SCALE (1/87)

Imported from Great Britain by **WALTHERS**

Peco offers a large selection of track and accessories including turnouts, switch machines and flex track with simulated wooden or concrete ties. Rail is made of nickel silver for excellent conductivity. Turnouts do not match NMRA standards. Dimensions are shown with individual listings.

BULK RAIL

Simulate the wide variety of rail sizes found on mainlines and sidings with these packs of bulk rail. Each is made of nickel silver for realistic appearance and improved electrical conductivity.

552-4000	Code 60	7.49
552-4002	Code 75	8.99
552-4003	Code 80	8.99
552-4004	Code 100	10.49
552-4008	Code 250	42.99

FLEX TRACK

Each piece measures 36" long and features nickel silver rail.

Dealers: MUST order Dealer Pack of 25.

Concrete Ties, Code 100
552-1162   4.49
Simulates modern concrete ties being tested on some railroads.

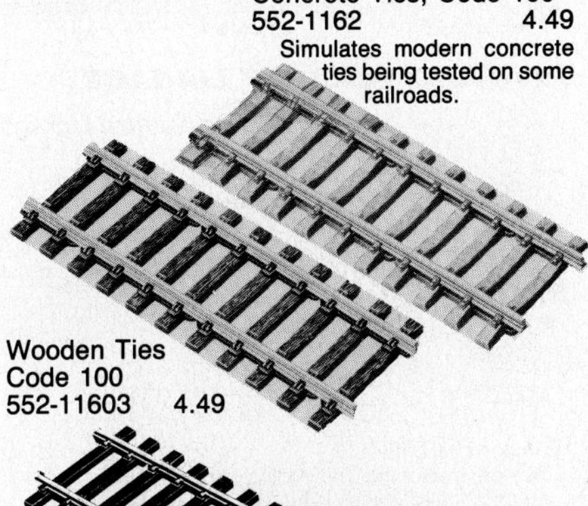

Wooden Ties
Code 100
552-11603   4.49

Wooden Ties
Code 75
552-1163   4.49

#5 DOUBLE SLIP SWITCH

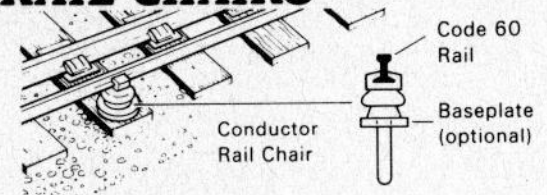

Code 100
Nickel Silver Rail
552-1046   43.99
Matches Long Crossing #1050.
Angle: 12°, Length: 250 mm (9-13/16")

CROSSINGS

Short 24 Degree
Code 100
552-1049   11.99
Approximate length: 5" (127 mm)
Angle: 24°

Long 12 Degree
Code 100
552-1050   13.49
Approximate length: 10" (250mm)
Angle: 12°

RAIL JOINERS

Dealers: MUST order Dealer Pack of 12.

552-10	Nickel Silver, Code 100	2.49
552-11	Insulated-Nylon, Code 100	2.49
552-1164	Insulated-Nylon, Code 75	2.99
552-1165	Nickel Silver, Code 75	2.99

CONDUCTOR RAIL CHAIRS

Code 60 Rail
552-4009
5.99

TURNOUTS

WYE TURNOUTS

Nominal Radius: 610 mm (24"), Angle: 24°
Length: 148 mm (5-13/16") with code 100 rail.

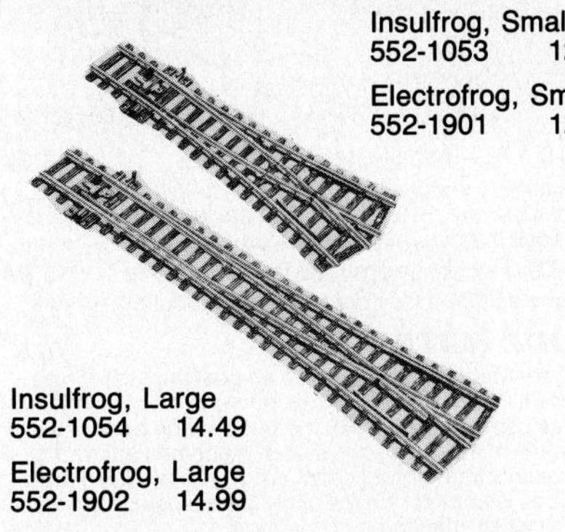

Insulfrog, Small
552-1053   12.99

Electrofrog, Small
552-1901   12.49

Insulfrog, Large
552-1054   14.49

Electrofrog, Large
552-1902   14.99

SMALL TURNOUTS

Nominal Radius: 610 mm (24"), Angle: 12°
Length: 185 mm (7-9/32") with code 75 rail.

Left Hand Insulfrog
552-1048   12.49

Left Hand Electrofrog
552-1904   12.99

Right Hand Insulfrog
552-1047   12.49

Right Hand Electrofrog
552-1903   12.99

With code 75 rail

Right Hand Electrofrog
Small Radius
552-1916   12.99

Left Hand Electrofrog
Small Radius
552-1917   12.99

MEDIUM TURNOUTS

Nominal Radius: 914 mm (36"), Angle: 12°
Length: 219 mm (8-5/8") with code 100 rail.

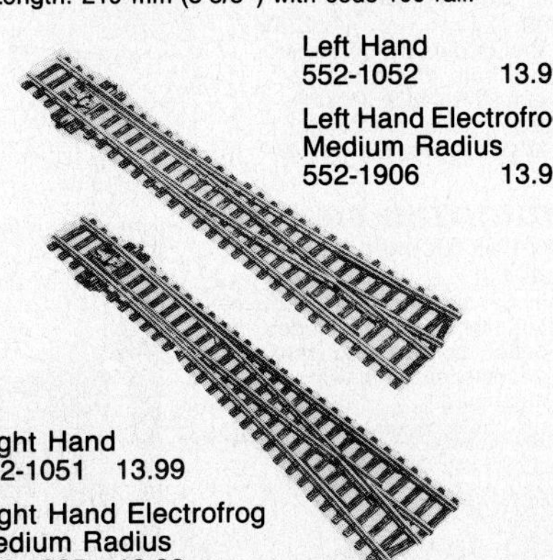

Left Hand
552-1052   13.99

Left Hand Electrofrog
Medium Radius
552-1906   13.99

Right Hand
552-1051   13.99

Right Hand Electrofrog
Medium Radius
552-1905   13.99

With code 75 rail

Right Hand Electrofrog
552-1912   15.49

Left Hand Electrofrog
552-1913   15.49

LARGE TURNOUTS

Nominal Radius: 1524mm (60"), Angle 12°
Length: 258mm (10-5/32") with code 100 rail.

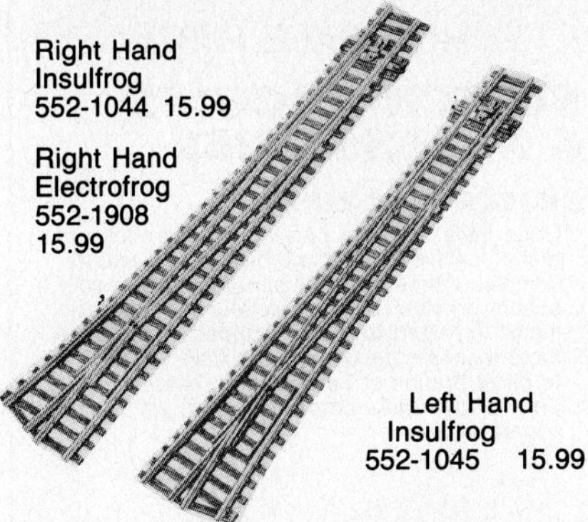

Right Hand
Insulfrog
552-1044 15.99

Right Hand
Electrofrog
552-1908
15.99

Left Hand
Insulfrog
552-1045   15.99

Left Hand
Insulfrog
552-1045   15.99

with code 75 rail

Right Hand
Electrofrog
552-1914   16.49

Left hand
Electrofrog,
552-1915   16.49

UNIVERSAL CURVED DOUBLE RADIUS TURNOUTS

with code 100 rail

Nominal Radii: Outside: 1524mm (60")
Inside: 762mm (30") Length: 256mm (10-5/32")

Right Hand
Insulfrog
552-1042 16.49

Right Hand
Electrofrog
552-1910 16.99

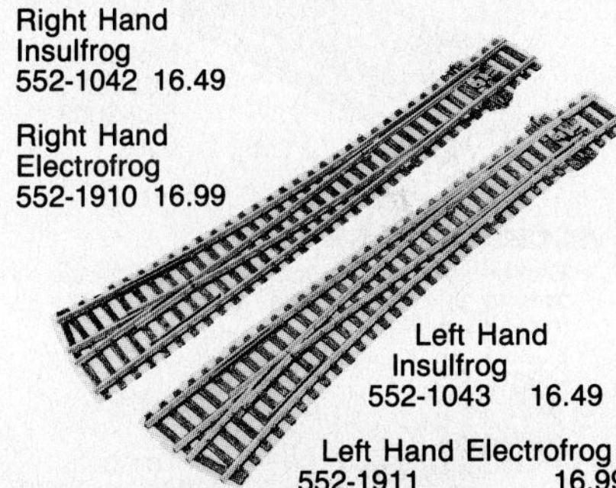

Left Hand
Insulfrog
552-1043   16.49

Left Hand Electrofrog
552-1911   16.99
Stats. same as RH

CURVED SETRACK DOUBLE RADIUS TURNOUTS

552-6242	Insulfrog Right Hand	16.49
552-6243	Insulfrog Left Hand	16.49

3-WAY TURNOUTS

Nominal Radius: 914mm (36")
Angle: 12" Length: 220mm (8-21/32")

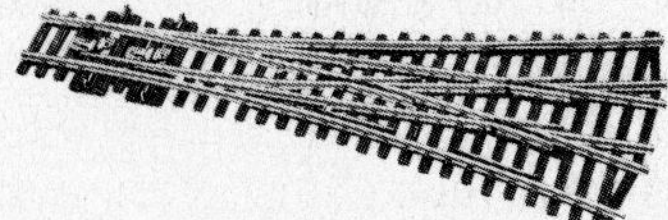

552-1055	Medium Radius	33.99
552-1907	Medium Radius Electrofrog	34.99

PECO

Imported from Great Britain by WALTHERS

HO SCALE (1/87)

SWITCH MACHINE & ACCESSORIES

SWITCH MACHINE

Units install directly beneath the turnout and make positive contact without linkage or other complex connections. Just cut a hole in your benchwork deep enought to clear the motor and install. An extension pin is included to mount the motor beneath the benchwork. Can be adapted to other brands of turnouts with extension pin (included) and motor adapter, available separately.

Switch Machine
552-3010
6.99

MOTOR ADAPTER

Allows mounting of the switch machine on the benchwork, along side of the turnout. Can be adapted for use with various makes of turnouts.

Motor Adapter
552-3003
2.49

ACCESSORY SWITCH

Can be used with switch machine to control turnout polarity, operate signals or other trackside devices.

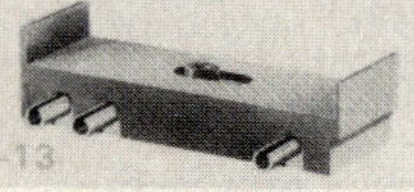

Accessory Switch for Turnouts
552-3013   3.49

HOe (HOn 2-1/2) NARROW GAUGE TRACK

Items are fully assembled and ready to use with code 80 nickel silver rail.

FLEX TRACK

Features randomly spaced wooden ties.

Dealers: MUST order Dealer Pack of 25.

552-500 36" Nickel Silver   4.99

TURNOUTS

12" radius.

552-491	Right Hand	11.99
552-492	Left Hand	11.99
552-497	Wye (18" radius)	11.99

Rix Products

SWITCH MACHINE

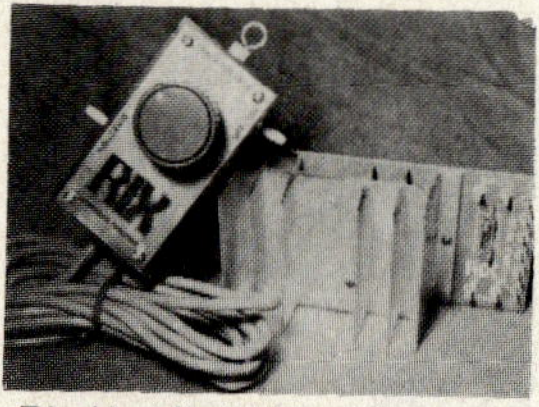

628-4   Rix T-C Switch Machine   6.59
Controls turnouts from above or below the layout. Includes two SPDT add on sets of contacts and needed hardware. Operates on 6-32 volts.

628-15 Rix Economy Switch Machine   5.99
Same as 628-4 less contacts and mounting screws.

DIODE MATRIX   NEW

Diode Matrix board makes it possible to control several switch machines at once so that an entire route can be aligned with the push of one button. Will work with most twin coil switch machines and motor drives, including Hankscraft and Tortoise. Use 1 amp diodes with motor drives and 3 amp diodes with twin coil switch machines.

628-50	RIX Diode Matrix Board	9.95
628-52	RIX 1K Resistors	pkg(12) 1.20
628-51	One Amp Diode	pkg(14) 2.99
628-53	Three Amp Diode	pkg(14) 3.99

ACCESSORIES

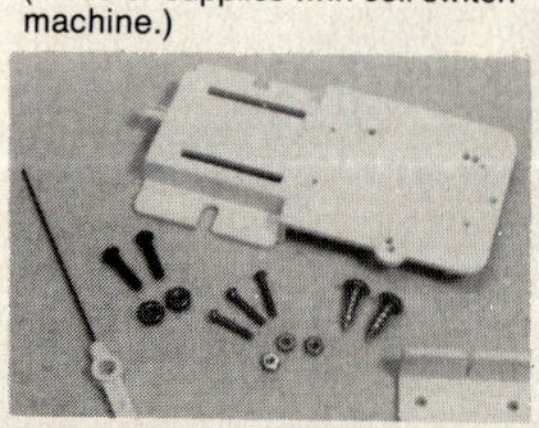

628-8   Rix Handheld Throttle   79.95
Stay cool throttle includes automatic circuit breaker, track voltage lamp, eyelet for hanging, P.C. board mounting rack and 12' cord. 4 amps, 6-24 volts.

Rix Momentary Contact Push Buttons
628-16   pkg(4) 3.49
Buttons are complete with mounting nut and soldering terminals. For controlling switch machines. 125 volts, 3 amps.

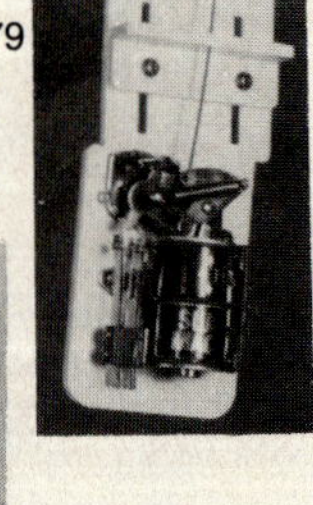

SWITCH STAND KIT

Rix Shorty Type, 2'
628-13   3.49
Works directly off throw bar from any type turnout. 90° rotation. Includes switch ties, throw bar, target, linkage & housing.

MOUNTING BRACKET

Rix-Rax Mounting Bracket
628-1   2.79
Under layout bracket, completely adjustable and includes nuts, bolts, screws and throw rod. (Modeler supplies twin coil switch machine.)

628-5 Rix-Rax Flat Mounting Bracket Kit 2.79
Under-layout mounting bracket, works with most any switch machine for flat mounting.

HO SCALE (1/87)

Switch machines & accessories, switch stand kit, mounting bracket, turnout linkage and rail it.

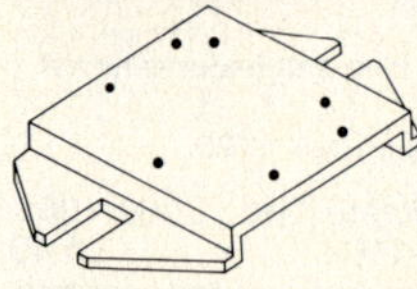

628-21 Rix-Rax II   2.79
Under layout mounting bracket complete with press-on linkage to motor shaft, adjustable stop blocks to limit the force on the switch points, mounting holes for most brands of adjustable limit switches and all hardware. Designed for use with the Hanscraft Display Motor, works with all scales.

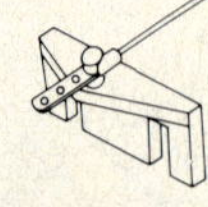

Rix Adjusto Pad
628-7   1.99
For mounting switch machine above or below layout. Adjustable and interchangeable. Includes wood & switch machine screws.

PIVOTING TURNOUT LINKAGE

Rix Pivoting Turnout Linkage
628-6   1.99
For controlling turnout from underneath layout.

RAIL IT

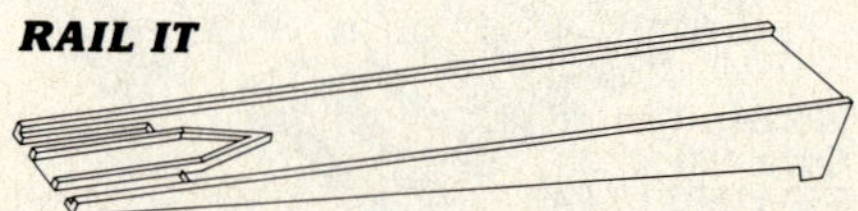

628-2   Rix-Rail-It   2.19
Set on track and roll rolling stock down ramp—automatically places wheels on track. Works with code 70, 83 and 100 track.

NOCH

Imported from Germany by WALTHERS

HO SCALE (1/87)

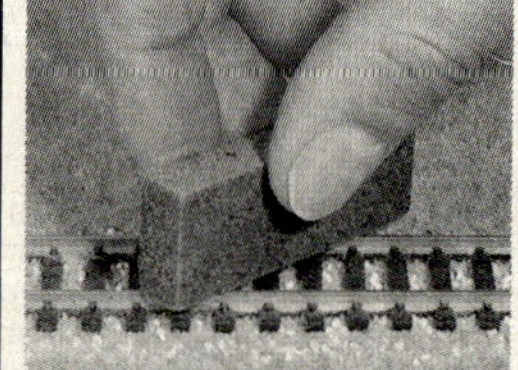

Track Cleaning Block
528-5014 6.99

(not illustrated)
528-5103 Contact Switch (Automatic) 27.49

RIBBONRAIL
by Earl Eshleman

HO SCALE (1/87)

- Upson Board Roadbed
- Track Alignment Gauges
- Track Cleaners

ROADBED

Precut Upson board pieces feature beveled edges. Easy to spike into and sound-deadening.

24" SECTIONS

170-9010	Straight	pkg(4)	4.60
170-9020	Flexible	pkg(4)	6.80
170-9030	Double Track	pkg(4)	8.80

TURNOUT SECTIONS

170-9041	#4 Right Hand	pkg(4)	8.00
170-9042	#4 Left Hand	pkg(4)	8.00
170-9061	#6 Right Hand	pkg(4)	8.80
170-9062	#6 Left Hand	pkg(4)	8.80
170-9081	#8 Right Hand	pkg(4)	9.60
170-9082	#8 Left Hand	pkg(4)	9.60

CURVED SECTIONS

FOR COMPLETE CIRCLE — 8 PIECES

170-9150	15"	pkg(4)	4.00
170-9160	16"	pkg(4)	4.16
170-9170	17"	pkg(4)	4.32
170-9180	18"	pkg(4)	4.48
170-9190	19"	pkg(4)	4.64
170-9200	20"	pkg(4)	4.80
170-9210	21"	pkg(4)	4.96
170-9215	21.5"	pkg(4)	5.04
170-9220	22"	pkg(4)	5.12
170-9230	23"	pkg(4)	5.28
170-9240	24"	pkg(4)	5.44
170-9250	25"	pkg(4)	5.60
170-9260	26"	pkg(4)	5.76
170-9270	27"	pkg(4)	5.92
170-9280	28"	pkg(4)	6.08
170-9290	29"	pkg(4)	6.24

FOR COMPLETE CIRCLE — 12 PIECES

170-9300	30"	pkg(4)	4.80
170-9310	31"	pkg(4)	4.96
170-9320	32"	pkg(4)	5.12
170-9330	33"	pkg(4)	5.28
170-9340	34"	pkg(4)	5.44
170-9350	35"	pkg(4)	5.60
170-9360	36"	pkg(4)	5.76
170-9370	37"	pkg(4)	5.92
170-9380	38"	pkg(4)	6.08
170-9390	39"	pkg(4)	6.24
170-9400	40"	pkg(4)	6.40
170-9410	41"	pkg(4)	6.56
170-9420	42"	pkg(4)	6.72
170-9430	43"	pkg(4)	6.88
170-9440	44"	pkg(4)	7.04
170-9450	45"	pkg(4)	7.20
170-9460	46"	pkg(4)	7.36
170-9470	47"	pkg(4)	7.52
170-9480	48"	pkg(4)	7.68

TRACK ALIGNMENT GAUGES

Slide between rails to correctly gauge rails.
Helps in laying, spiking and joining rail. Precision machined to NMRA (S-2 Feb 63) standards.

RADIUS GAUGE

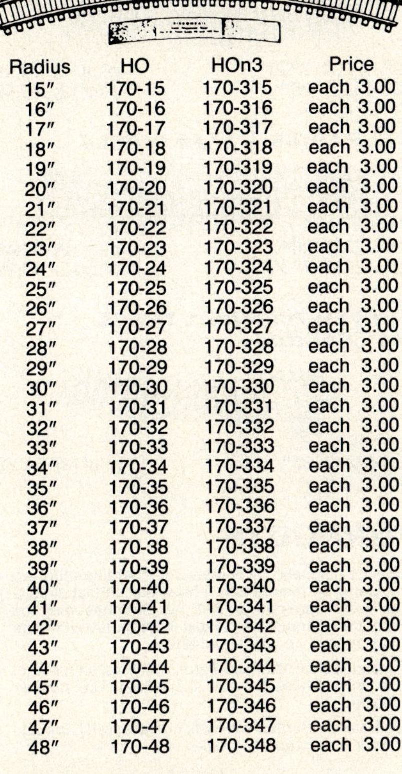

Radius	HO	HOn3	Price
15"	170-15	170-315	each 3.00
16"	170-16	170-316	each 3.00
17"	170-17	170-317	each 3.00
18"	170-18	170-318	each 3.00
19"	170-19	170-319	each 3.00
20"	170-20	170-320	each 3.00
21"	170-21	170-321	each 3.00
22"	170-22	170-322	each 3.00
23"	170-23	170-323	each 3.00
24"	170-24	170-324	each 3.00
25"	170-25	170-325	each 3.00
26"	170-26	170-326	each 3.00
27"	170-27	170-327	each 3.00
28"	170-28	170-328	each 3.00
29"	170-29	170-329	each 3.00
30"	170-30	170-330	each 3.00
31"	170-31	170-331	each 3.00
32"	170-32	170-332	each 3.00
33"	170-33	170-333	each 3.00
34"	170-34	170-334	each 3.00
35"	170-35	170-335	each 3.00
36"	170-36	170-336	each 3.00
37"	170-37	170-337	each 3.00
38"	170-38	170-338	each 3.00
39"	170-39	170-339	each 3.00
40"	170-40	170-340	each 3.00
41"	170-41	170-341	each 3.00
42"	170-42	170-342	each 3.00
43"	170-43	170-343	each 3.00
44"	170-44	170-344	each 3.00
45"	170-45	170-345	each 3.00
46"	170-46	170-346	each 3.00
47"	170-47	170-347	each 3.00
48"	170-48	170-348	each 3.00

STRAIGHT GAUGE

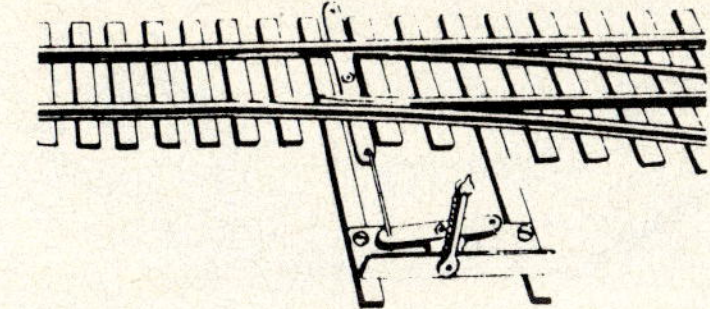

170-5	HO, 5"		3.00
170-305	HOn3, 5"		3.00
170-10	HO, 10"		3.50
170-310	HOn3, 10"		3.50

GROUND THROW

Assembled, all metal construction, includes linkage and universal mounting for either side. Operating 3/8" maximum throw.

170-9	Compact Manual	pkg(2)	4.50

MICRO MATIC TRACK GAUGE

Used to check for correct spacing between rails. Helps to eliminate derailments.

170-8	Micro Matic Track Gauge	9.95

TRACK CLEANING

BLOCK

Abrasive block for cleaning rail and wheels.(1 x 3 x 1/4").

170-11	Track Cleaning Block	3.75
170-12	Track Cleaning Block w/handle	4.75

CAR

Cleans the running rails for improved electrical contact. Cars are equipped with rubber blocks impregnated with silacone-abrasive. Ready-to-Run brass car, includes trucks, less couplers.

170-6	for standard 2-rail track	29.95
170-7	for Marklin track	29.95

Finishing **SELLEY** Touches

HO SCALE (1/87)

Assembled details are unpainted metal castings.

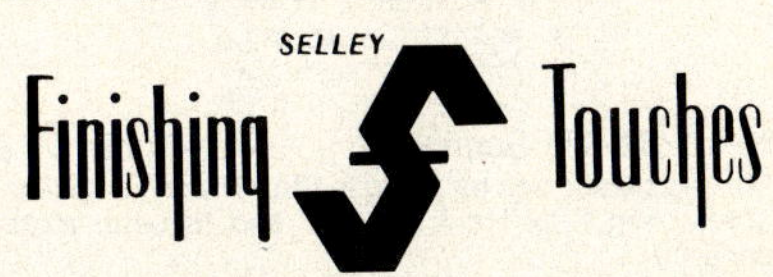

675-677	Hayes Wheel Stops	pkg(6) 1.25

SUPERIOR HOBBY PRODUCTS

Rough sawn basswood lumber.

+ (PLUS SIGN) = SPECIAL ORDER ONLY ITEMS

We have worked closely with this manufacturer to provide accurate availability information at the time this catalog was published. Items listed in *blue ink* may not be available at all times. Please see your dealer for current delivery information.

SCALE TIES

REGULAR TIES

697-780	HOn3 5 x 7" x 6'	pkg(1000)	5.49

(By Special Order Only.)

697-781	HO 7 x 9" x 8'	pkg(1000)	5.49

(By Special Order Only.)

697-785	HOn3 Weathered	pkg(1000)	6.95
697-786	HO Weathered	pkg(1000)	6.95

(By Special Order Only.)

SWITCH TIES

697-782	HOn3	pkg(500)	5.49

(By Special Order Only.)

697-783	HO	pkg(500)	5.49

(By Special Order Only.)

697-787	HOn3 5 x 7" Weathered	pkg(500)	6.95
697-788	HO 7 x 9" x 6' Weathered	pkg(500)	6.95

BRIDGE & TRESTLE

697-784		pkg(300)	5.49

(By Special Order Only.)

697-789	8 x 10"	pkg(300)	6.95

(By Special Order Only.)

Roco
Imported from Austria
by WALTHERS

HO SCALE CODE 100 TRACK

Roco offers modelers a wide selection of track and accessories, including turnouts, flex-track and pre-ballasted roadbed. Rail is Code 100 and is made of nickel silver for excellent electrical conductivity.

FLEX TRACK

Two types of flex-track are available: very flexible for tight curves; and semi-rigid for straight tracks or slight curves. **Dealers must buy a dealer pack of 24.**

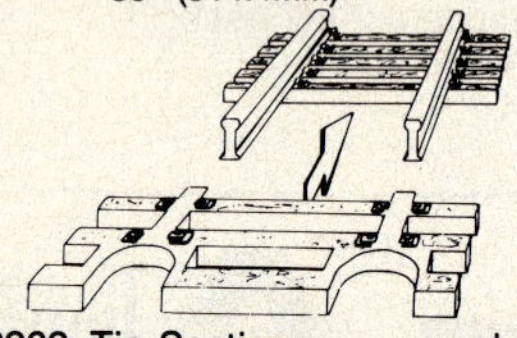

625-42200	Very Flexible	114.49
	38.5″ (970mm)	
625-42201	Semi Rigid	101.99
	36″ (914.4mm)	

625-42262	Tie Sections	pkg(24)	7.99

Molded plastic ties for filling in Flex-Track. Simplifies connecting Flex-Track to itself and to other track sections.

STRAIGHT TRACK

Nickel Silver

625-42202	9″ (228.6mm)	pkg(12)	20.49
625-42203	8″ (204mm)	pkg(12)	20.49
625-42204	3.3″ (85mm)	pkg(12)	37.99
625-42206	2.2″ (57mm)	pkg(12)	18.99
625-42207	2″ (51mm)	pkg(12)	18.99
625-42208	1.1″ (29mm)	pkg(24)	37.99
625-42209	1″ (26.5mm)	pkg(24)	37.99
625-42211	.9″ (24.5mm)	pkg(24)	37.99
625-42213	.2″ (6mm)	pkg(24)	37.99
625-42210	1″ (26.5mm)	pkg(24)	37.99
625-42212	25/32″	pkg(24)	37.99

UNCOUPLING TRACK

625-42261	4.5″ (1143mm)	17.99
	for Close Coupling	

TRACK SECTION W/DIODE

Section w/Direction Controlling Diode
625-42260   3.49

CURVED TRACK

10″ RADIUS – 1/6 CIRCLE

625-42221	60°	pkg(12)	20.49

14″ RADIUS – 1/12 CIRCLE

625-42222	30°	pkg(12)	20.49
625-42232	12°10′	pkg(12)	18.99
625-42242	7°30′	pkg(12)	18.99

17″ RADIUS – 1/12 CIRCLE

625-42223	30°	pkg(12)	20.49
625-42233	12°10′	pkg(24)	37.99
625-42243	7°30′	pkg(12)	18.99

19″ RADIUS – 1/12 CIRCLE

625-42234	7°30′	pkg(12)	18.99
625-42224	30°	pkg(12)	22.49

21″ RADIUS – 1/12 CIRCLE

625-42225	30°	pkg(12)	22.49
625-42235	7°30′	pkg(12)	18.99

CURVED TERMINAL TRACK (14″ RADIUS)

625-42252	30°	pkg(12)	34.99

TURNOUTS

Electro-magnetically operated standard turnouts are actuated by motors which have disconnect circuits to avoid burn-out of coil. All switches may be operated manually. Available in under layout mounting, remote control and manual.

Because European standards don't match those of the United States, turnouts approximate U.S. number shown.

* Polarized turnouts include contact switch to route power to appropriate track.

#4 REMOTE

Straight track 9″ (228.6mm), radius of diverging track 28″ (700mm), turn-off angle 12°50′

625-42302	Left & Right	55.49

#4 CURVED TURNOUT

Turnout includes all track illustrated.

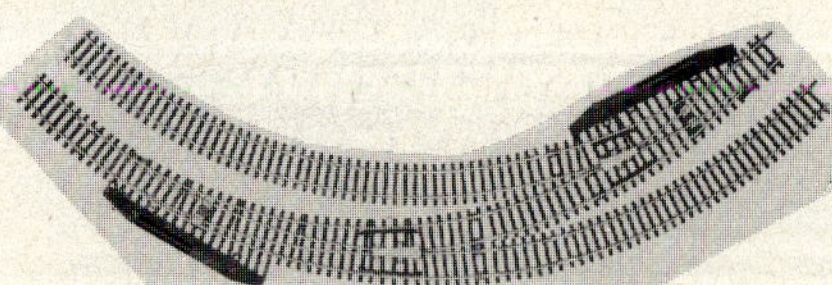

625-42324	Remote, Left	77.49
625-42325	Remote, Right	77.49

#4-WAY REMOTE

Straight track 9″ (226mm), radius of diverging track 28″ (700mm), turn-off angle 12°50′.

625-42318	Unpolarized	51.49

#4 DOUBLE SLIPSWITCH

Length of tracks 9″ (228.6mm), crossing angle 12°50′.

625-42320	Remote	55.99

#10 DOUBLE SLIPSWITCH

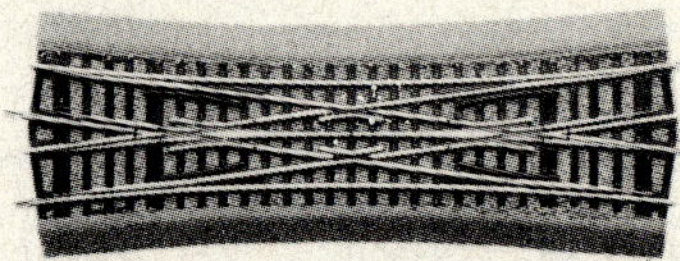

625-42594	w/Roadbed	72.99

#6 UNDER LAYOUT OPERATION

625-42360	Left & Right	31.99

CROSSINGS

625-42270	13°	12.49
625-42271	90°	12.49

STYROPLAST ROADBED

ROCO offers you track underlay pre-formed out of Styroplast. The ballast is already provided therein. For each piece of track there exists a matching underlay. The Styroplast Underlay offers a practical and fast alternative to individual ballasting. Furthermore, it is an accurate representation of the DB ballasted roadbed.

625-42701	Fits 42202	1.99

fits when shortened: 42203, 42204, 42205, 42206, 42207, 42208, 42209, 42211 & 42213.

625-42704	16″ fits 42223	2.49

fits when shortened: 42233 & 42243

625-42705	18″ fits 42224	2.49

fits when shortened: 42234

625-42708	Fits 42318 & 42319	4.99

ROCO
Imported from Austria
by WALTHERS

HO SCALE CODE 100 & CODE 83 TRACK
Roco offers modelers a wide selection of track and accessories, including turnouts, flex-track and pre-ballasted roadbed.

STYROPLAST ROADBED (continued)

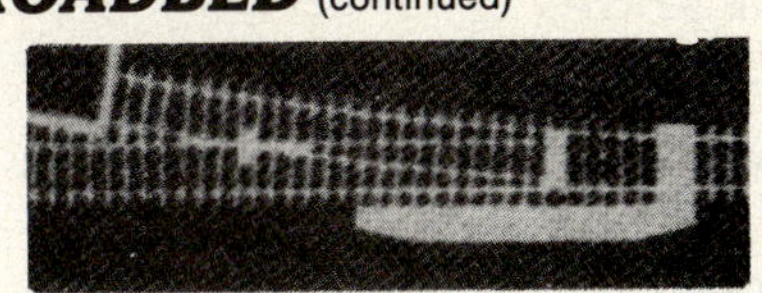

625-42709	Fits #6 Turnouts: 42355, 42351, 42363 & 42359	4.99
625-42710	Fits #6 Turnouts: 42357, 42361, 42365 & 42353	4.99
625-42713	Fits #6 Turnouts: 42371, 42367, 42379 & 42375	4.99
625-42714	Fits #6 Turnouts: 42369, 42381, 42373 & 42377	4.99
625-42717	Fits #6 Turnouts: 42382, 42385, 42383 & 42384	4.99
625-42719	Fits #4 Turnouts: 42301, 42313, 42305 & 42309	4.99
625-42720	Fits #4 Turnouts: 42303, 42315, 42307 & 42311	4.99

625-42723	Fits 42320 & 42321	4.99

625-42724	Fits 42270	4.99

625-42728	Fits 42324	13.99
625-42729	for #42325	each 13.99

STYROPLAST ACCESSORIES

625-42730	Bulk Material ballasted	2.49

SWITCH MACHINES

625-10010	Left	15.99

twin coil drive and power-disconnect after actuation, single-pole

625-10011	Right	15.99

twin coil drive and power-disconnect after actuation, single-pole

625-10015	Conversion Set	7.99

converts to under layout mounting

625-10014	Underfloor Operation Conversion Kit	6.49

Left hand, fits turnout motor #10008 and 10010.

625-10016	Underfloor Operation Conversion Kit	6.49

TRACK ACCESSORIES

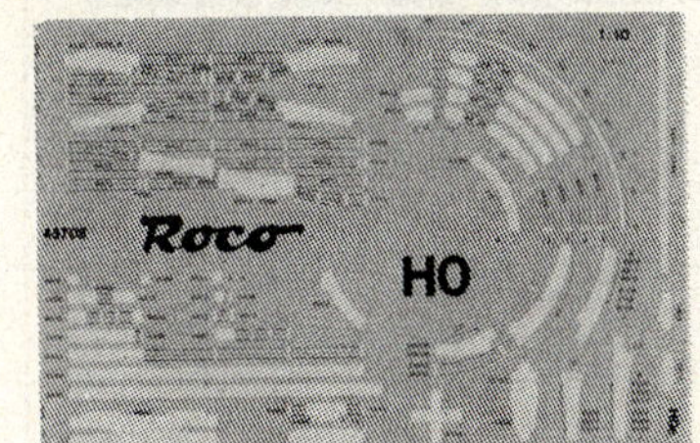

625-40008	Track Template	15.99

(By Special Order Only.)

Bumper Kit
625-42267   3.49

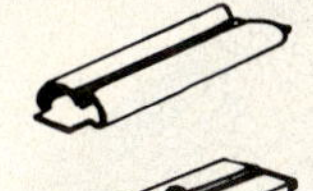

1/2" Track Nails
625-10000
pkg(400)   4.49

POLARIZING SET

625-40289	Polarizing Set	3.49

RAIL JOINERS

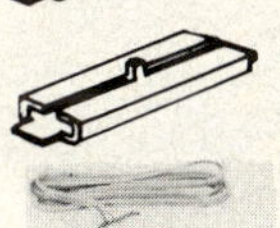

Nickel Silver
Non-Insulated
625-42263
pkg(30) 3.49

Insulated
625-42264
pkg(24) 3.49

Non-Insulated
625-42265   3.49
w/connecting cable set

(not illustrated)

625-42256	Magnet for #42255	each 9.49

TRACK CLEANING

625-46400	Roco Cleaning Car	29.99
625-40019	Replacement Wiper for 46400 & 47900	8.99

Track Cleaner
625-10002   8.49
for removing dirt & oil deposits

BRIDGES

Curved
Girder
625-40081
24.49
Length:
18"   45.7 cm

Straight Girder
625-40080   12.49
Length 9"   23 cm

TRACK WITH ROADBED CODE 83 TRACK
Roco-Line Track System makes it easy to create realistic looking track with less work. Each piece is fully assembled with Code 83 nickel silver rail and realistic plastic ties.

STRAIGHT SECTIONS

625-42506	36" Straight	69.49
625-42510	9" Section	18.49
625-42511	4.7" Section	16.99
625-42512	4.5" Section	16.99
625-42513	2.5" Section	14.99
625-42518	4.5" with FDR Contact Relay	16.99
625-42519	4.5" with Uncoupler	20.99
625-42520	Terminal Track Section	6.99

With wire leads for easy hook up to powerpack.

FLEX TRACK

625-42400	36.2" Flex	114.49

CURVED TRACK

625-42426	24" Radius	**NEW** TBA
625-42522	14.1" Radius × 30°	19.99
625-42523	16.5" Radius × 30°	19.99
625-42524	18.9" Radius × 30°	23.99
625-42525	21.4" Radius × 30°	25.99
625-42527	32.5" Radius × 15° w/roadbed	25.99
625-42528	Curve 35" Radius × 15 Dia	25.99

Reverse curve for #4 turnouts.

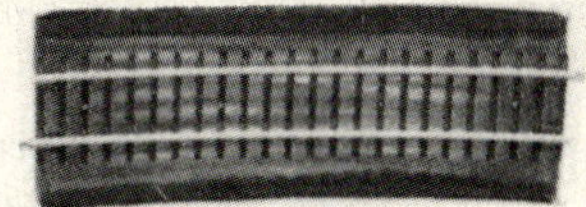

625-42530	Curve 77.2" Radius × 5 Dia	21.49

Two pieces form a reverse curve for #6 turnouts.

MANUAL TURNOUTS
Manually controlled turnouts with preformed roadbed sections. Can be fitted with motor #42620 for remote control.

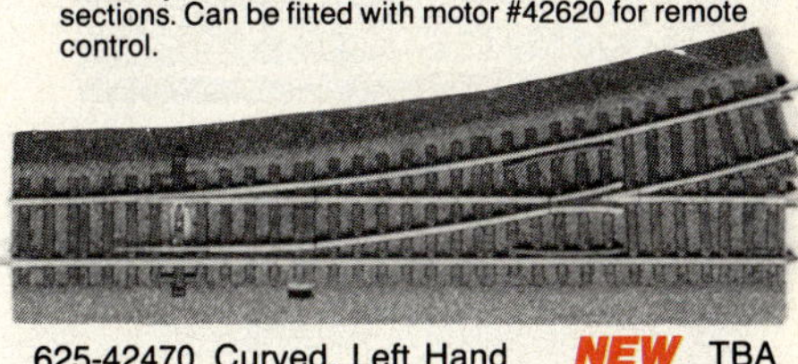

625-42470	Curved, Left Hand	**NEW** TBA
625-42471	Curved, Right Hand	**NEW** TBA
625-42532	#4 Left Hand	24.99
625-42533	#4 Right Hand	24.99

625-42546	#4 15 Degree Single Slip	48.49

(not illustrated)

625-42594	Double Slip, 10°	72.99

(By Special Order Only.)

Roco

RO CO

Imported from Austria
by **WALTHERS**

HO SCALE
(1/87)

CODE 83 TRACK & ACCESSORIES

Roco-Line Track System makes it easy to create realistic looking track with less work. Each piece is fully assembled with Code 83 nickel silver rail and realistic plastic ties. For faster construction, all items are available with premolded roadbed. Equipment fitted with RP25 or NEM Standard 311 wheels are compatible with the track.

ROCO LINE

ROCO-LINE WITH ROADBED: This series of track products and accessories comes complete with a unique two-piece roadbed system. The top piece duplicates the ballasted right-of-way, with realistic size and colored "stones," (molded in light gray, but easily painted to match your favorite prototype) plus a sloping edge. Underneath is the plastic core which locks with other sections to provide a rigid track assembly, that's strong enough to use for temporary operations. The space underneath can also be used for routing wires.

625-42549 Lefthand, double slip turnout,
      manual control w/roadbed   64.99

625-42557 #4 Right Hand Curved   27.49
625-42556 #4 Left Hand Curved   27.49
14" inside radius, 16-1/2" outside radius

625-42569 #8 Right Hand Curved   59.99
625-42568 #8 Left Hand Curved   59.99
32.5" inside radius, 35" outside radius

#6 Left Hand Turnout
625-42580 13.6" Length x 10°   37.49

#6 Right Hand Turnout
625-42581 13.6" Length x 10°   37.49

Three-Way 15°
625-42543
63.99

CROSSINGS

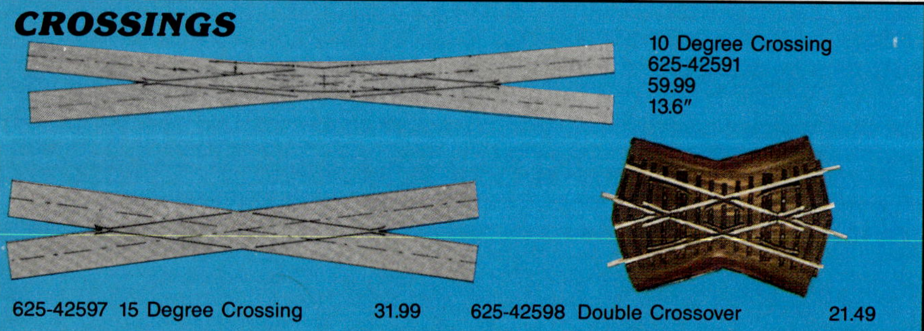

10 Degree Crossing
625-42591
59.99
13.6"

625-42597 15 Degree Crossing   31.99

625-42598 Double Crossover   21.49

ACCESSORIES

TIE STRIPS
Use to fill gap at the end of flex track sections, or when cutting rail.

625-42600 Wooden Ties pkg(12) 2.99
625-42601 Concrete Ties pkg(12) 3.49
625-42605 Reed Relay   7.99
Wooden tie with built-in reed switch, for activating electrical accessories.

Track Bumper
625-42608
3.99

RAIL JOINERS

42610   42611   42612

625-42610 Standard-steel   pkg(24) 3.49
625-42611 Insulated   pkg(12) 3.49
625-42612 Code 83 to 100   pkg(12) 3.49
Conversion Rail Joiners
Use for transition from track with Code 83 to Code 100 rail. Ideal for use where sidings join mainline.
625-42613 Joiner with Wire Leads   3.99
Preassembled railjoiners with wire leads.

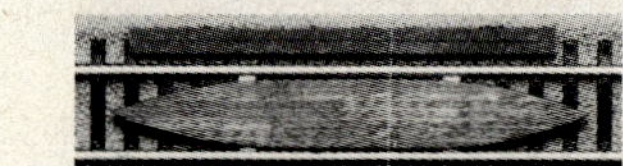

625-42609 Rerailing Set   3.99

Roadbed Filler Piece 14.2"
625-42650 pkg(12) 11.49
Sloped side pieces for Roco Line roadbed sections.

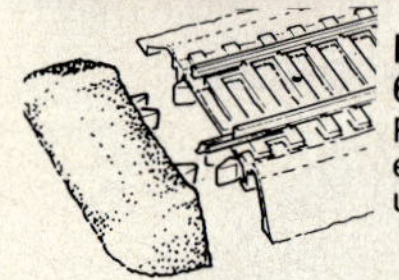

Roadbed End Piece
625-42651 pkg(6) 6.49
Realistic, rounded piece fits on end of roadbed section. Ideal for use on sidings or display tracks.

625-42652 Ballast Gravel   3.99
Matches size and color of molded roadbed sections.
625-42653 Ballast Filler Plate   14.49

FLEXIBLE ROADBED
For use with flex track section.
625-42660 for #42400 w/Wooden Ties   11.99
625-42661 for #42401 w/Concrete Ties   11.99

SWITCH MACHINES

LIMITED QUANTITIES AVAIL

625-42620 Roadbed Switch Machine   17.49
Low profile switch machine for mounting under Roco-Line roadbed sections. Prewired, easy to install, machine features end of stroke power disconnect.

625-10030 Universal Underfloor Motor   25.99
Designed for mounting under benchwork, fits all Roco-Line and can be adapted to other track systems. Prewired, easy to install, machine features end of stroke disconnect.

ROCO
Imported from Austria by WALTHERS

HO SCALE (1/87)

ACCESSORIES (continued)

STANDARD SWITCH MACHINES

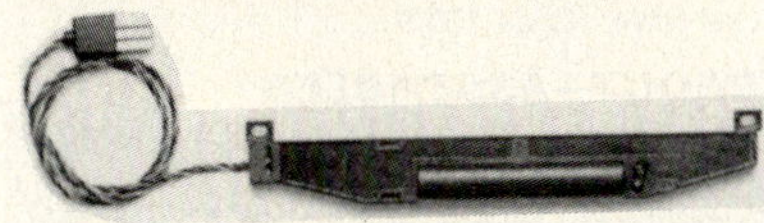

625-40295 Left Hand Turnout 19.99
625-40296 Right Hand Turnout 19.99
Fits all Roco turnouts and mounts on switch, above the benchwork. Prewired, easy to install, machine features end of stroke power disconnect.

MANUAL CONTROLS
625-40297 Left Hand Turnout 5.49
625-40298 Right Hand Turnout 5.49
Manual controls fit all Roco turnouts and make it easier to open or close the switch. Ideal for fiddle yards or other trackage where remote control is not needed.

625-40293 Switch Lamps 10.49
Based on lamps used by the German Federal Railways, the lanterns indicate if the turnout is open or closed. Fits motor #10030.

625-10001 Track Nails pkg(500) 4.99
Correct length for mounting Roco-Line track and roadbed to benchwork.

TRACK SETS

Expand the basic oval of Roco-Line track, included with starter train sets, into a model railroad with these track sets. A variety of track pieces that add more operating possibilities, such as turnouts, curves and more included.

625-41078 Starter Set DB A,B,C **NEW** 266.99

625-42011 Passing Siding Expansion Set 70.49
Add a passing siding to your mainline and automatic uncoupling with this set. Includes one #4 right hand turnout, one #4 right hand curved turnout, a manually operated uncoupler and one 4.5″ straight section.

625-42012 Double Track Expansion Set 127.49
Build a double track mainline and add an extra siding to your operations with this set. Includes 10 straight sections, one 4.5″ straight section, one track bumper, 10 curve sections, one #4 right hand turnout, one #4 left hand turnout, one #4 left hand curved turnout and replacement roadbed wedges.

625-42010 Industrial Siding Expansion Set 61.99
Add an industrial siding and lengthen the basic oval with this set. Includes one #4 left hand turnout, 13 straight sections and one track bumper.

625-42013 Crossover Extension Set 108.99
Add a crossover in station or yard area and convert single track spur to double track. Includes one 10″ straight section, one 4.5″ straight section, one track bumper, one #4 left hand turnout and one #4 right hand turnout.

625-42001 Track Set Large 2719.99
625-42004 Track Set D 89.99

U.S. DISTRIBUTOR
MIDWEST PRODUCTS COMPANY

HO SCALE (1/87)

CORK ROADBED

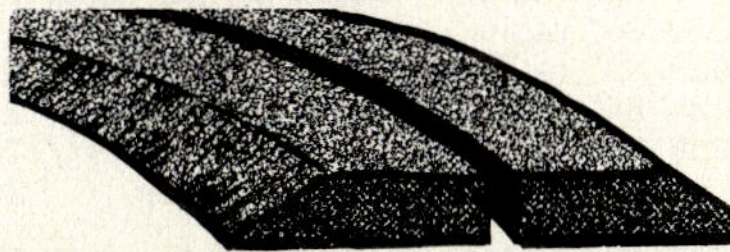

472-3013 3′ Section 1.00
Dealers: MUST order box of 25 of above 3′ sections.
472-3015 3′ Section pkg(5) 7.00

CORKSHEET PACK
472-3014 Corksheet ea 3.00
Sheet stock can be used on switches, sidings, yards and loading areas. Each sheet is 5mm x 5 x 36″.
Dealers: MUST order dealer pack of 9 sheets.

model power

HO SCALE (1/87)

FLEXIBLE TRACK

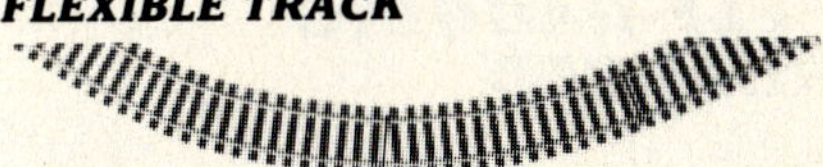

490-105 Super Flex, 3′ 2.59
Code 100 nickel silver rail.

CURVED TRACK
490-3344 18″ Long pkg(4) 2.50
Code 100 nickel silver

TERMINAL TRACK
490-4044 Curved 9″ Long 1.45
Code 100 nickel silver

AUTOMATIC TURNOUT
Nickel silver turnouts include electric switch machine and black plastic ties.

490-170 #6 Left 29.98
490-171 #6 Right 29.98

490-180 Left, 18/22″ curved 29.98
490-181 Right, 18/22″ curved 29.98

490-189 #6 Double Slip 45.00

490-198 #6 3-Way 59.95
(not illustrated)
490-5044 Left Switch - Remote 9.98
490-5144 Right Switch - Remote 9.98

CORK ROADBED
Each section of cork roadbed is 36″ (91.44cm) long unless noted.
490-4311 Single Track pkg(25) 25.00
490-4315 Single Track pkg(5) 7.50
490-4316 Switch Block, 9″ long pkg(2) 3.25
490-4317 Switch Block, 9″ long pkg(20) 30.00

RAIL JOINERS
490-125 Nickel Silver pkg(24) 1.30

MAGNETIC NAIL TOOL
490-5312 Magnetic Nail Tool 2.98

TRACK NAILS
490-220 Long 1.98
490-244 Spike L-Shaped 1.98
490-245 Short 1.98

CLEANING BLOCK
Contains pumice stone.
490-250 Cleaning Block 1.98

TRACK LIGHTED BUMPER
490-8744 Code 100 Nickel Silver pkg(2) 2.49

Tru-Scale Models

HO SCALE (1/87)

Delivery of products has been slow, with delays between production runs. As a result, some items shown are not in stock.

TRU-SWITCH
Brings added realism, offering a good, long, smooth ride with a simple true-to-prototype look; made in all popular variations. Hi-Speed switches are available in kit form.

SELF-GAUGING ROADBED

STRAIGHT

730-1201 1' Straight   1.10 per pc pkg(5)
Dealers: MUST order full packages

CROSSOVER

730-1975 #8 Crossover   3.40 per pc pkg(6)
Dealers: MUST order full packages of 6

TURNOUT

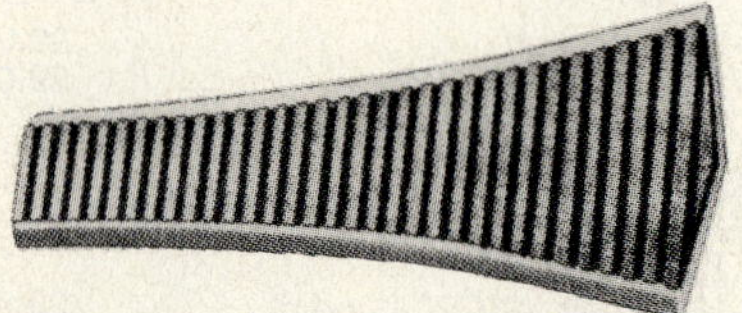

730-1950 Wye Switch   4.00 per pc pkg(6)
730-1951 #4 Right   3.40 per pc pkg(6)
730-1952 #4 Left   3.40 per pc pkg(6)
730-1953 #6 Right   3.60 per pc pkg(6)
730-1954 #6 Left   3.60 per pc pkg(6)
730-1955 #8 Right   3.80 per pc pkg(6)
730-1956 #8 Left   3.80 per pc pkg(6)
Dealers: MUST order Dealer pack of 6

PLAIN ROADBED

CIRCLE

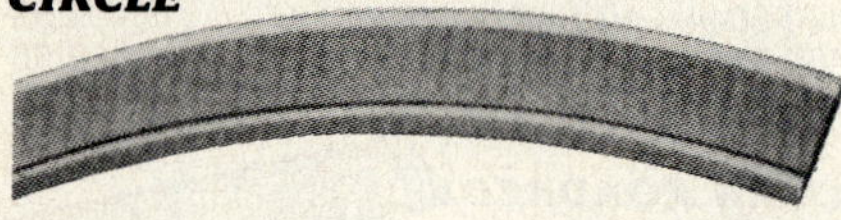

730-1316 16" radius   1.80 per pc pkg(8)
730-1318 18" radius   1.90 per pc pkg(8)
730-1320 20" radius   2.05 per pc pkg(8)
730-1322 22" radius   2.20 per pc pkg(8)
730-1324 24" radius   2.35 per pc pkg(8)
730-1326 26" radius   2.55 per pc pkg(8)
730-1328 28" radius   2.75 per pc pkg(8)
Dealers: MUST order full packages of 8

730-1330 30" radius   2.05 per pc pkg(12)
730-1332 32" radius   2.15 per pc pkg(12)
730-1334 34" radius   2.25 per pc pkg(12)
730-1336 36" radius   2.35 per pc pkg(12)
Dealers: MUST order full packages of 12

730-1306 16 to 26" radius asst pkg(6) 14.00
730-1307 26 to 36" radius asst pkg(6) 15.40
730-1308 36 to 48" radius asst pkg(6) 18.60
Dealers: MUST order Dealer pack of 6

(By Special Order Only)
730-1338 38" radius   2.30 per pc pkg(12)
730-1340 40" radius   2.45 per pc pkg(12)
730-1342 42" radius   2.60 per pc pkg(12)
730-1344 44" radius   2.75 per pc pkg(12)
730-1346 46" radius   2.90 per pc pkg(12)
730-1348 48" radius   3.30 per pc pkg(12)
Dealers: MUST order full packages of 12

STRAIGHT

730-1301 1'   1.00 per pc pkg(6)
730-1302 2'   1.85 per pc pkg(10)
730-1303 3'   2.40 per pc pkg(18)
730-1304 2' Super-flex   3.00 per pc pkg(18)
730-1305 Bulk Pack (random lengths-20') 18.00
Dealers: MUST order full packages

TURNOUT
less ties.

730-1350 Wye Switch   3.40 per pc pkg(6)
730-1351 #4 Right   3.00 per pc pkg(6)
730-1352 #4 Left   3.00 per pc pkg(6)
730-1353 #6 Right   3.20 per pc pkg(6)
730-1354 #6 Left   3.20 per pc pkg(6)
730-1355 #8 Right   3.40 per pc pkg(6)
730-1356 #8 Left   3.40 per pc pkg(6)
730-1375 #8 Crossover   2.90 per pc pkg(6)
Dealers: MUST order full packages of 6

MILLED ROADBED
Wood ties, for use with Code 70 or 83

STRAIGHT
730-1901 1'   1.10 per pc   pkg(6)
730-1902 2'   2.10 per pc   pkg(8)
730-1903 3'   4.15 per pc   pkg(12)
730-1904 2' Super-flex   3.40 per pc   pkg(8)
730-1905 Bulk Pack   16.80   pkg(16)
Dealers: MUST order full packages

CIRCLE
730-1916 16" radius   2.20 per pc   pkg(8)
730-1918 18" radius   2.35 per pc   pkg(12)
730-1920 20" radius   2.50 per pc   pkg(12)
730-1922 22" radius   2.65 per pc   pkg(12)
730-1924 24" radius   2.80 per pc   pkg(12)
730-1926 26" radius   2.95 per pc   pkg(12)
730-1928 28" radius   3.10 per pc   pkg(12)
730-1930 30" radius   2.50 per pc   pkg(12)
730-1932 32" radius   2.65 per pc   pkg(12)
730-1934 34" radius   2.80 per pc   pkg(12)
730-1936 36" radius   2.95 per pc   pkg(12)
Dealers: MUST order full packages

730-1906 16 to 26" radius assortment   15.60
730-1907 26 to 36" radius assortment   17.00
730-1908 38 to 48" radius assortment   21.00

(By Special Order Only)
730-1938 38" radius   2.45 per pc pkg(12)
730-1940 40" radius   2.60 per pc pkg(12)
730-1942 42" radius   2.75 per pc pkg(12)
730-1944 44" radius   2.90 per pc pkg(12)
730-1946 46" radius   3.05 per pc pkg(12)
730-1948 48" radius   3.20 per pc pkg(12)
Dealers: MUST order Dealer pack of 12

READY-TRACK
Nickel Silver, Code 100 Rail.

TURNOUT—ASSEMBLED

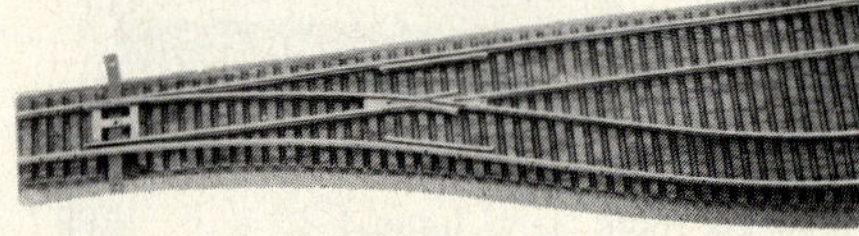

730-1150 Wye Switch   25.00
730-1153 #6 Single Right   23.00
730-1154 #6 Single Left   23.00
730-1155 #8 Single Right   24.00
730-1156 #8 Single Left   24.00

TURNOUT—KIT
730-1450 Wye Switch   10.00
730-1451 #4 Single Right   10.00
730-1452 #4 Single Left   10.00
730-1453 #6 Single Right   11.00
730-1454 #6 Single Left   11.00
730-1455 #8 Single Right   12.00
730-1456 #8 Single Left   12.00
730-1457 #4 Double Right   32.00
730-1458 #4 Double Left   28.00

CROSSING
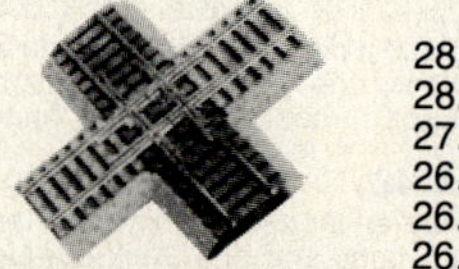
730-1190 14°   28.00
730-1191 19°   28.00
730-1192 28°   27.00
730-1193 45°   26.00
730-1194 60°   26.00
730-1195 90°   26.00

CROSSOVER
less Motors

730-1172 #4 Single Left   33.00
730-1173 #6 Single Right   35.00
730-1174 #6 Single Left   35.00
730-1175 #8 Single Right   37.00
730-1176 #8 Single Left   37.00

LIMITED QUANTITIES AVAILABLE
730-1471 #4 Right   kit 14.60
730-1472 #4 Left   kit 14.60

STRAIGHT

730-1101 1'   3.20
Dealers: MUST order full packages of 4
730-1180 Rerailer (12" long)   13.00
730-1102 2'   5.40 per pc pkg(6)
730-1104 2' Super-flex   9.60 per pc pkg(6)
Dealers: MUST order full packages of 6
730-1103 3'   7.60
Dealers: MUST order full packages of 12
730-1115 Modular Track   10.00
Consists of one 41" straight Ready-Track, one 9" straight and one 9" Atlas straight track.
730-1116 Modular Track   10.00
with S Connect

READY-TRACK (continued)
CIRCLE

730-1118	18″ radius	3.40 per pc	pkg(8)
730-1120	20″ radius	3.80 per pc	pkg(8)
730-1122	22″ radius	4.20 per pc	pkg(8)
730-1124	24″ radius	4.60 per pc	pkg(8)
730-1126	26″ radius	5.00 per pc	pkg(8)
730-1128	28″ radius	5.40 per pc	pkg(8)

Dealers: MUST order full packages of 8

730-1130	30″ radius	3.80 per pc	pkg(12)
730-1132	32″ radius	4.20 per pc	pkg(12)
730-1134	34″ radius	4.60 per pc	pkg(12)
730-1136	36″ radius	5.00 per pc	pkg(12)

Dealers: MUST order full packages of 12

(By Special Order Only)

730-1138	38″ radius	4.80 per pc	pkg(12)
730-1140	40″ radius	5.10 per pc	pkg(12)
730-1142	42″ radius	5.50 per pc	pkg(12)
730-1144	44″ radius	5.90 per pc	pkg(12)
730-1146	46″ radius	6.30 per pc	pkg(12)
730-1148	48″ radius	6.70 per pc	pkg(12)

Dealers MUST order full packages of 12

HOn3 PLAIN ROADBED
Less ties

TURNOUT

730-1650	Wye Switch	3.40 per pc	pkg(6)
730-1651	#4 Right	3.00 per pc	pkg(6)
730-1652	#4 Left	3.00 per pc	pkg(6)
730-1653	#6 Right	3.20 per pc	pkg(6)
730-1654	#6 Left	3.20 per pc	pkg(6)
730-1655	#8 Right +	3.40 per pc	pkg(6)
730-1656	#8 Left +	3.40 per pc	pkg(6)
730-1675	#8 Crossover	2.85 per pc	pkg(6)

Dealers: MUST order full packages of 6

STRAIGHT

730-1601	1′	1.00 per pc	pkg(8)
730-1602	2′	1.55 per pc	pkg(12)
730-1603	3′	2.10 per pc	pkg(22)
730-1604	2′ Super-flex	2.60 per pc	pkg(12)

Dealers: MUST order full packages

730-1605	Bulk Pack +	18.60

CIRCLE

730-1612	12″ radius	1.55 per pc	pkg(8)
730-1614	14″ radius	1.80 per pc	pkg(8)
730-1616	16″ radius	1.80 per pc	pkg(8)
730-1618	18″ radius	1.90 per pc	pkg(8)
730-1620	20″ radius	2.05 per pc	pkg(8)
730-1622	22″ radius	2.20 per pc	pkg(8)
730-1624	24″ radius	2.35 per pc	pkg(8)
730-1626	26″ radius	2.55 per pc	pkg(8)
730-1628	28″ radius	2.75 per pc	pkg(8)

Dealers: MUST order full packages of 8

730-1630	30″ radius +	24.50	pkg(12)

Dealers: MUST order full packages of 12

730-1606	16 to 26″ radius assortment +	14.00
730-1607	26 to 36″ radius assortment	15.40

TEST CAR

730-1420	Track Laying Test Car	11.00

Delivery of products has been slow, with delays between production runs. As a result, some items shown are not in stock.

HO SCALE TRU-SWITCH
Brings added realism, offering a good, long, smooth ride with a simple true-to-prototype look; made in all popular variations. Hi-Speed switches are available in kit form.

+ (PLUS SIGN) = SPECIAL ORDER ONLY ITEMS

730-1421	Track Laying Test Car, HOn3	11.00

Clear plastic, allowing to see problems with laying of track, switches and crossovers. Fully sprung trucks allow ''feeling'' the conditions of the rail by keeping fingers on the car.

ACCESSORIES

CAST FROG

730-1412	Wye	pkg(2)	4.00
730-1413	#4	pkg(2)	4.00
730-1414	#6	pkg(2)	4.00
730-1415	#8	pkg(2)	4.00

RAIL JOINERS

730-1446	Rail Joiners	pkg(50)	3.60

Code 100, nickel silver

RERAILER

Rerailer Kit

730-1480		7.00

True-to-prototype look. Kit consists of two rerailer points as shown in circle illustration at right.

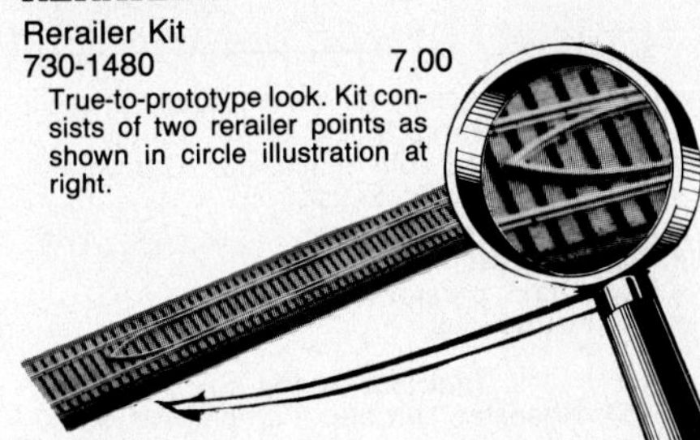

YARD ITEMS

Bumper, Tie
730-2001		10.00

Bumper, Rail
730-2002		11.00

730-2008	Uncoupler Track w/Kadee ramp	13.00

Grade Crossing
730-2010		12.00

MISCELLANEOUS

730-1443	Spikes, Code 100	pkg (500)	5.00
730-1416	Bridge Stock, 6″		6.00
730-1417	Bridge Stock, 12″		8.00
730-1418	Bridge Stock, 18″ +		10.00
730-1419	Super-Elevation Wedge	pkg(10)	5.00
730-1440	HO Test Track +		32.00

WALTHERS
TRACK ACCESSORIES
SPIKES

For Fine Track Work in all Gauges. Highest quality, ebonized, .028 square shank with clean corner, fine points, precision heads. Illustrated actual size.

Number	Length	Pkg	Price	Qty*
945-3571	9/32″	13/16 oz	8.98	600
945-3411	3/8″	1 oz	8.98	575
945-3421	7/16″	1-1/8 oz	8.98	550
945-3431	1/2″	1-1/8 oz	8.98	500

*Quantity approximate.

TRACK CLEANER

"Bright Boy" Track Cleaner
949-521	each	3.98

Keeps rails and wheels clean and bright.

WELDBOND
"its concentrated"

All around wood glue, ballast cement, sealer, hardener, weather-proofer and more.

For ballast cement; mix one part Weldbond with two parts water.

797-125	4oz	2.98
797-185	8oz	4.35
797-795	1/2 gallon	19.45
797-1395	1 gallon	32.50

A Weldbond application book is available at no charge. Please send a stamped self-addressed envelope to Walthers.

R. & R. F., Inc.
HO SCALE (1/87)

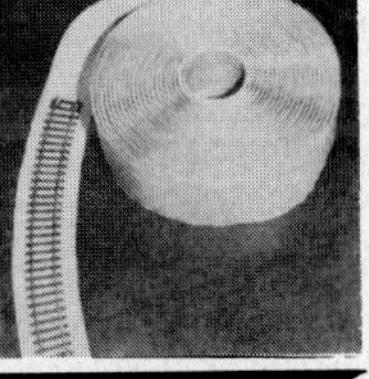

ROADBED
Pliable cork filled compound for easy application. Tapered to a natural realistic appearance. Press into place on a dust free surface. No ballast or spikes needed. 2″ x 30′ roll.

approximate size and shape

624-101	Flexible Roadbed	(gray)	11.95
624-102	Flexible Roadbed	(black)	11.95

B HOBBY L PRODUCTS

HO SCALE (1/87)

Fiber Optic Signals, LED Signals, Block Controls, Fiber Optics, and Capacitor Discharge Unit.

FIBER OPTIC SIGNAL

HO Scale signals utilizing fiber optics to transmit the light from the base mounted bulbs to the proper indications.

Plastic and metal construction. Fully assembled, wired and ready to install.

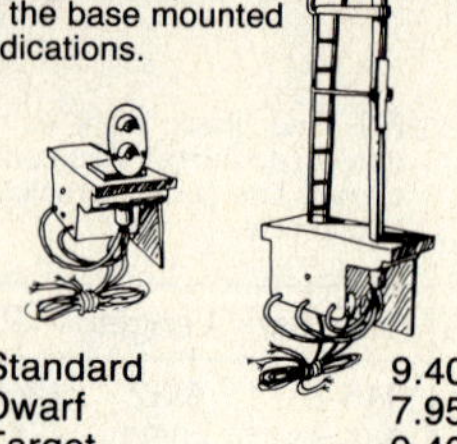

183-221	Two Light Standard	9.40
183-222	Two Light Dwarf	7.95
183-223	Two Light Target	9.40
183-231	Three Light Standard	10.50
183-232	Three Light Dwarf	8.90
183-233	Three Light Target	9.95

LED SIGNAL

Light emitting diode signals completely assembled and ready to be installed.

183-224	Two Light Standard	10.25
183-225	Two Light Dwarf	9.75
183-226	Two Light Target	10.25
183-234	Three Light Standard	11.25
183-235	Three Light Dwarf	11.00
183-236	Three Light Target	14.95
	(By Special Order Only.)	

DIODES

183-261	Diodes	pkg(5)	2.50

LED LENSES

183-250	Small (red), 3/32" lens	pkg(4)	3.50
183-251	Small (grn), 3/32" lens	pkg(4)	3.50
183-252	Small (ylw), 3/32" lens	pkg(4)	3.50
183-253	Regular T-1 (red)	pkg(4)	3.50
183-254	Regular T-1 (green)	pkg(4)	3.50
183-255	Regular T-1 (yellow)	pkg(4)	3.50

RESISTOR

183-260	Drop 560 ohms	2.00

PANEL TRAIN CONTROL

- Electronic controls for train operation.
- For S, HO, & N Scale
- Panels 9" wide X 2, 4, 6, & 8" high.
- All on 9 x 4" panels unless stated.
- Brushed metal finish with black lettering.
- Each unit can be used with other units or your current electronic components.
- Color code wires for installation.
- Full instructions with each unit.

Throttle, 2 Amp
183-450 84.50

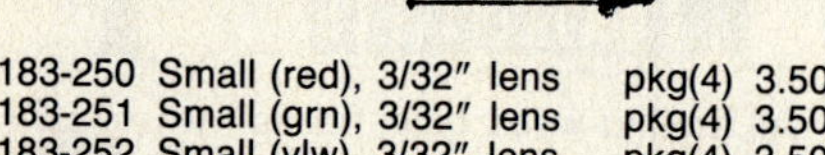

- Full 2 amps of power.
- Circuit breaker.
- Overload indicator.
- Power switch.
- Reverse Switch.
- Direction indicator light.
- Transistor control.

DC Power Supply
183-460 2 Amp 63.75

- 12 volts at 2 amps.
- Circuit breaker.
- Overload Indicator.
- Power source for auto blocks listed below.
- Use for any DC accessories.
- Color coded wires for installation
- Full instructions.

183-462 Power Supply **NEW** 55.00
2 amp 12 volts

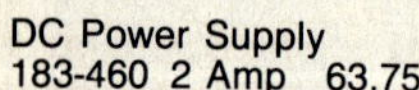

Hand Held Throttle
183-458 2 amp **NEW** 54.95

- Works from any 16 volt unfiltered DC power (see #461).
- 10 ft cable with plug.
- Exceptional slowspeed control.
- Circuit breaker.
- Reverse switch
- Full instructions

Switcher Transistor Throttle
183-452
NEW 75.00

- 1 amp of power.
- Slow switching speed control.
- Circuit breaker protected.
- Overload indicator.
- Power switch.
- Reverse switch.
- Direction indicator light.
- Full instructions.

Hand Held Throttle Base
183-461
NEW 59.95

- Designed specially for the handheld throttle, but can serve as DC power supply.
- Full 2 amps 16 volts unfiltered DC power.
- Circuit breaker protected.
- Overload indicator light.
- Power switch.
- Power on indicator light.
- Full instructions.

(not illustrated)

183-451 Rheostat Throttle, 2 amp **NEW** 95.50
- Full 2 amps of power.
- Circuit breaker protected.
- Overload indicator.
- Power switch.
- Reverse switch.
- Direction indicator light.
- Rheostat speed control.
- Full instructions.

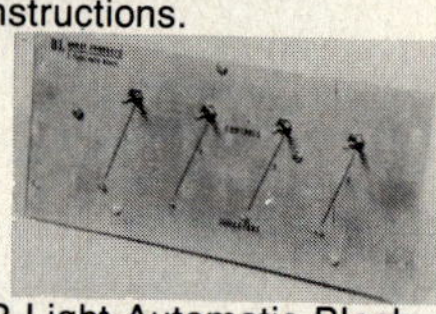

183-464 2 Light Automatic Block 164.00
- Four blocks are included.
- Use present track and signals.
- Use regular or led signals.
- Each block can be controlled from panel.
- Occupancy indicator light for each block.
- Each block has two open switches to run accessories in that block. One can be used for the BL sound system to be developed soon.
- Train will stop on red and precede on green.
- Color coded wires for installation.
- Full instructions.
- Use Harness Wire item No 473 or your wire to run from panel to track.

Wiring Harness
183-473 **NEW** 15.00
25' of color coded wire. Simplifies installation of #464.

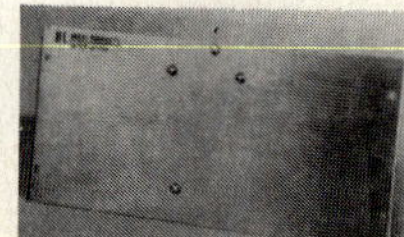

Panel Switch-A-Roo
183-468 35.00
- This is the same capacitor discharge unit we list as No. 300, but installed on a 9x4" panel.

183-470	Blank Panel (2x9")	3.50
183-471	Blank Panel (4x9")	7.00
183-472	Blank Panel (6x9")	10.50

- The above panels are blank. Can be easily drilled for toggle switches for accessories.
- Can also be used for layout diagram.

TRAIN LOCATOR INDICATOR **NEW**

183-465 Train Locator Indicator 78.99
For use with Panel Train Control. Keep track of your trains even when you cannot see them. Full instructions for wiring included.

TRAIN REVERSE KIT **NEW**

183-466 Train Reverse Kit 29.00
Can be installed on any length of track to allow the train to reverse itself. Just turn on the throttle and the train will run continuously.

FIBER OPTICS

183-700	Fiber Optic Assortment	4.00
	5 ft each of 10, 20, 30 mil fiber	
183-701	100 ft—10 mil fiber	6.00
183-702	30 ft—20 mil fiber	5.50
183-703	15 ft—30 mil fiber	5.00
183-704	15 ft—40 mil fiber	6.25
183-711	Clear Fiber w/Light Source*	4.75
183-712	Green Fiber w/Light Source*	4.75
183-713	Red Fiber w/Light Source*	4.75
183-714	Yellow Fiber w/Light Source*	4.75

* w/2 ft each of 20 and 30 mil optic fiber

183-720	Fiber Optic Auto Light	kit 6.25

1 red and 1 clear bulb, 3 ft each of 20 and 30 mil fiber optic material

183-721	Fiber Optic Flasher Light	kit 6.25

w/2 red bulbs

ACCESSORIES

CAPACITOR DISCHARGE UNIT

Used with switch machines, the "Switch-a-Roo" stores electric current, building up voltage to 25v, to operate many switch machines at once.

Switch-a-Roo
183-3000   29.00

BH MODELS

HO SCALE (1/87) **NEW**

CROSSBUCKS & MILEPOSTS

All parts are molded in white plastic, with decals provided for the lettering. Includes complete instructions covering assembly and installation.

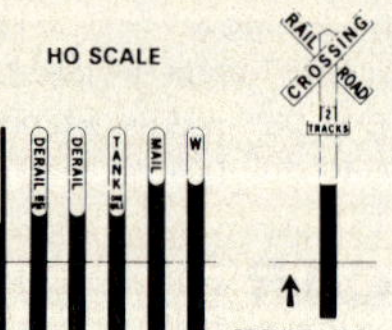

159-402	Crossbucks (4) & Mileposts (20)	9.95
159-403	Crossbucks (8) & Mileposts (40)	17.50

BRAWA

HO SCALE (1/87)

Imported from Germany by WALTHERS

Brawa signals are made of brass (except as noted) in exact HO Scale. Each is a fully assembled, working model of a European prototype. The line features models of all signals used by the German Federal Railways (DB) and decals, where appropriate, to identify the signal type. The Brawa Signal Manual provides detailed information on wiring and operation of a model signal system.

Signals equipped with bulbs or LEDs can be wired to AC or DC transformers with a maximum output of 10 to 16V. For longer bulb life, 10 to 12V is recommended. When properly installed, the miniature bulbs in Brawa Color-Light signals can burn up to 5,000 hours.

Brawa relays 2760 or 2761 feature matching color-coded wiring and are designed for use with these signals and accessories.

SEMAPHORE STOP SIGNAL

Semaphore signals were a common sight during the steam era and are still in widespread service today in Europe. The moving signal arm adds realistic action to a layout, while providing a visual indication of the route setting. Approx 4″ high.

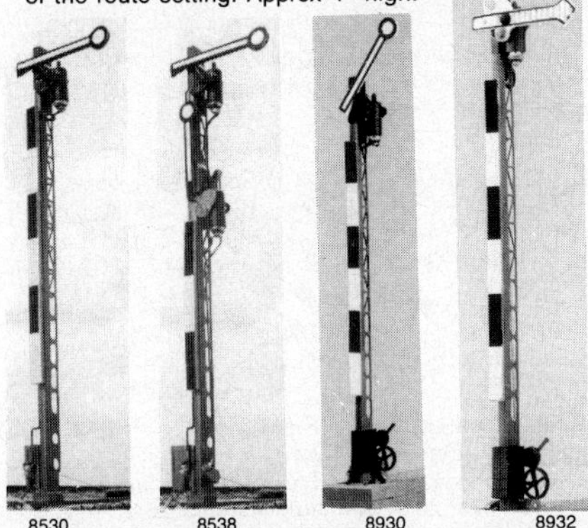

186-8530 Home Signal 1-Arm 59.49
w/Memory 2 position
186-8538 Home Signal 2-Arm 77.49
w/Memory 3 position
186-8930 Single Arm (red,green lights) 45.49
186-8932 Bavarian Railroad prototype 45.49
Single arm, green/red lights, fixed blue light in "track closed" position. Approx 4″ high.

(not illustrated)
186-8534 Advance Signal Arm 77.49
w/Memory 2 Position
186-8535 Advance Signal w/Memory 77.49
3 Position

DISTANT SIGNAL

Distant signals give train crews advance warning of the next signal aspect. Signals are approx 3″ high.

186-8536 Distant Semaphore 84.99
w/Memory
186-8934 Movable Disk 54.99
Lights change from double yellow to double green.
186-8933 Movable Disk Display 43.49
illuminated; approx 2-1/2″ high

LED COLOR LIGHT SIGNAL

Brawa LED (Light-Emiting Diode) color-light signals are exact HO Scale. The signals can be used to display all the aspects used by the prototype. Signals are based on DB (German Federal Railways) designs and are about 21 scale feet tall.

The high intensity of the miniature LED's makes these signals easy to see under any lighting conditions. The signals have a built-in resistor for use with any AC or DC 14-16 V power supply. The low current draw (15mA from 14V supply) allows use of Brawa LED signals with transistor or integrated circuits.

To install Brawa LED signals on benchwork, drill a 23/64″ (9mm) hole and simply press into place.

Brawa relays 2760 or 2761 feature matching color-coded wiring and are designed for use with these signals and accessories.

LED COLOR LIGHT SIGNAL

Signals are approx 3.3″ high, unless noted.

186-8831 Home 50.99
4 LED's, 14-16V
186-8832 Home and Distant 82.99
8 LED's, 14-16V AC or DC

186-8834 Starting and Distant 89.49
w/track closed; 10 LED's, 14-16V AC or DC
186-8835 Block 46.99
2 LED's, 14-16V. Prototype automatic block signals are located at the start of each track block and are operated by passing trains.

Distant signals give train crews advance warning of the next signal aspect.
186-8836 Block and Distant 78.99
6 LED's, 14-16V AC or DC

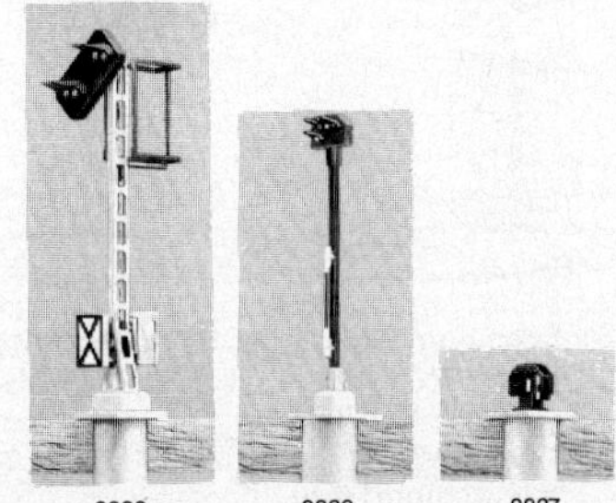

186-8838 Distant 50.99
4 LED's, 14-16V AC or DCAC or DC
186-8839 Track blocked; signal, raised. 50.99
4 LED's 14-16V. Head: 4.8 x 7.2 x 1.8mm
186-8837 Track blocked; signal, dwarf. 46.99
4 LED's, 14-16V. Head: 4.8 x 7.2 x 1.8mm

COLOR LIGHT SIGNAL

Most European State and private railways have begun replacing semaphores with color-light signals which display a variety of aspects.

Signals are approx 3 1/2″ high, unless noted.

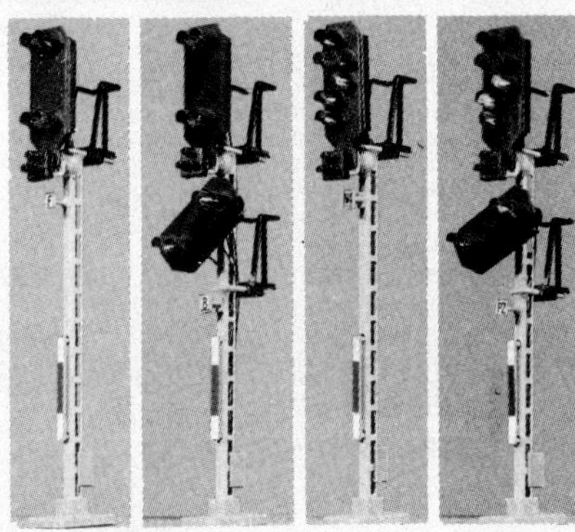

186-8801 Home 30.49
w/plain base, 14V
186-8802 Home and Distant 51.99
w/plain base; 14V supply
186-8803 Starting and Track Blocked 41.49
w/plain base; 14V supply
186-8804 Starting; Distant and Track 62.49
Blocked
w/plain base, 14V supply

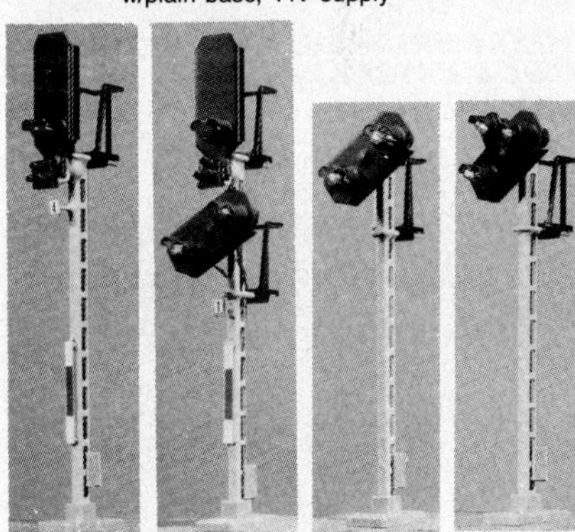

186-8805 Automatic Block Signal 24.99
w/plain base; 14V supply
186-8806 Automatic Block and Distant 46.49
w/plain base; 14V supply
186-8808 Distant 30.49
w/plain base; approx 3″ high; 14V supply
186-8817 Distant w/Marker Light 24.49
w/plain base; approx 3″ high, 14V supply

ADDITIONAL SIGNALS

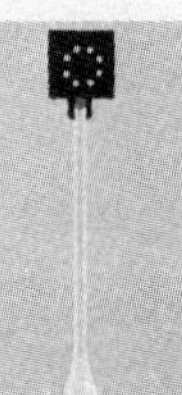

186-8816 Departure ZP9 34.49
Tells the loco crew to start; green light; light gray mast.

BRAWA

HO SCALE (1/87)

Imported from Germany by WALTHERS

Brawa signals are made of brass (except as noted) in exact HO Scale. Each is a fully assembled, working model of a European prototype. The line features models of all signals used by the German Federal Railways (DB) and decals, where appropriate, to identify the signal type. The Brawa Signal Manual provides detailed information on wiring and operation of a model signal system.

Signals equipped with bulbs or LEDs can be wired to AC or DC transformers with a maximum output of 10 to 16V. For longer bulb life, 10 to 12V is recommended. When properly installed, the miniature bulbs in Brawa Color-Light signals can burn up to 5,000 hours.

Brawa relays 2760 or 2761 feature matching color-coded wiring and are designed for use with these signals and accessories.

ADDITIONAL SIGNALS (continued)

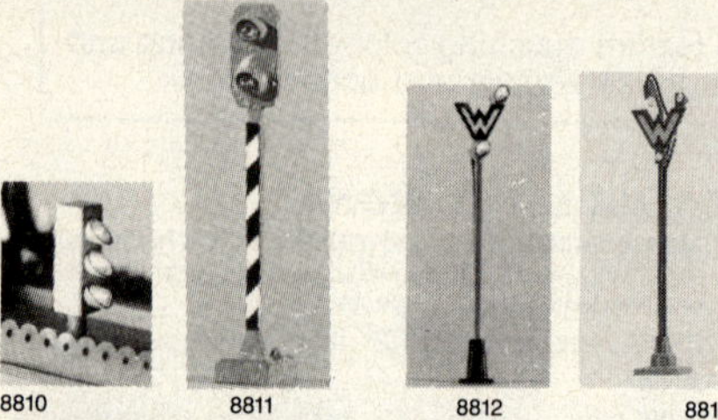

8810 8811 8812 8813

186-8810 Brake Test Signal 18.99
Installed at stations, signal indicates if train brakes are working properly. On the prototype, each lamp is illuminated separately and indicates, Top only: apply brakes, Center and Bottom: release brakes, All lamps lit: brakes operating properly. May be wired for prototypical operation. Finished in light gray; approx .8" high (22mm).

186-8811 Flashing Warning 17.99
anthracite gray, approx 2" high

186-8812 Wait Signal 20.99

186-8813 Wait Signal w/Three Lights 11.49
approximately 2" high

TRACK BLOCKED SIGNAL

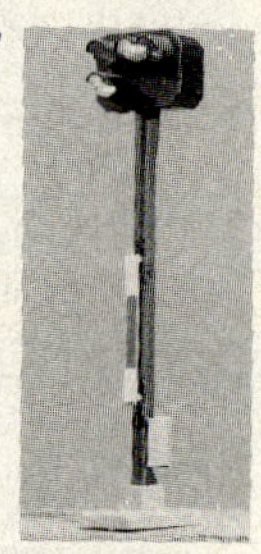

186-8809 Raised Dwarf 30.49
14V supply, w/plain base; approx 2-1/2" high

8809

SIGNAL BRIDGES, CANTILEVER MAST & CATENARY LIGHT

Brawa signal bridges and cantilever masts do not include cages or signals. Individual signals (8822, 8823, 8825) include cages, which can be glued on the bridge with plastic cement.

186-8621 Signal Bridge 15.49
less signals; approx 5 x 7"

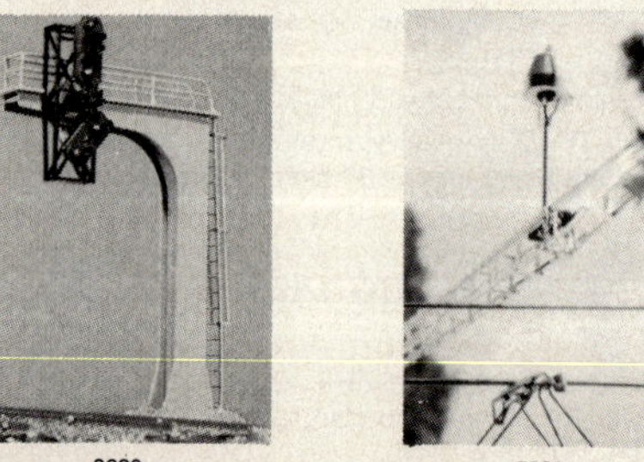

8620 5531

186-8620 Cantilever Signal Mast 10.99
less signals; approx 4-1/4" x 3" high

186-5531 Cantenary Light, Swiss NEW 7.99

8822 8825

186-8822 Home 40.49
w/cage and head, 4 bulbs, 14V supply

186-8825 Distant 24.49
w/cage and head, 4 bulbs, 14V supply

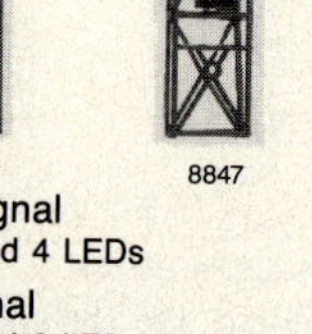

8845 8846 8847 8848

186-8845 Entry Signal 36.49
w/cage and 4 LEDs

186-8846 Exit Signal 43.99
w/cage and 6 LEDs

186-8847 Block Signal 33.99
w/cage and 2 LEDs

186-8848 Advance Signal 40.99
w/cage and 4 LEDs

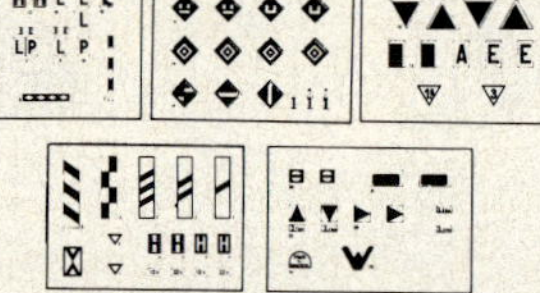

186-8618 Advance Warning Signs Set 10.49
Set includes all types of trackside signs used by the DB with descriptions of each. Posts are molded in black plastic, signs are printed in full color with self-adhesive backing.

HIGHWAY CROSSING

On lesser traveled roads, railroads often install crossing signals in place of gates. Brawa crossing signals are made of brass, except where noted and feature red LEDs. Crossing signals can be operated automatically with relay 2760, and track contacts.

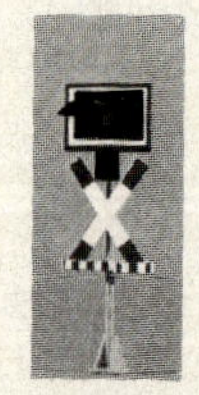

6131 / 6128 6130 / 6129

186-6131 Crossing Signal Set pkg(4) 44.99
Includes 4 of #6128 (plastic) Crossing Signals w/alternating electronic flashing unit.

186-6128 Crossing Signal w/Flashing Light each 8.49
German prototype w/LED and resistor for 14V AC supply. Black plastic; height 1-1/2" (42mm).

186-6130 Crossing Signal w/Guard Ring each 13.49
LED and resistor for 14V AC supply. Mast colored light gray. Height approx. 1-1/2" (35mm). Replacement LED #3296.

186-6129 Crossing Signal Set pkg(4) 64.99
Includes 4 of #6130 crossing signals and alternating electronic flasher unit.

186-5579 Sequential Flashing Barricade Set 59.49
Set includes six upright barricades with yellow LEDs, which flash in sequence. Electronic flasher unit for use with 10-16V output AC or DC transformers is also included.

186-5586 Barricade Set 49.99
Set of 2 barricades (each with 3 yellow LEDs), two road signs with self-adhesive labels and electronic control unit for use with 10-16V output AC or DC transformers. Up to 6 barricades can be operated from one control unit.

186-5585 Electronic Flasher Unit 25.99
For use with Brawa highway barricades, or adaptable to other projects. Unit will flash up to 18 LED's in rapid succession. For use with 10-16V output AC or DC transformers.

CROSSING GATE

Brawa Crossing Gate 1196 is gear-driven and may be operated by pushbutton, or automatically by passing trains. A resistor is included to adjust opening and closing speeds. For more realism, bell 1141 may be installed to give an audible warning when the gates close. Automatic operation when connected to drive unit.

The drive unit has automatic shut-off, with color-coded wire leads to install Bell 1141 and working Crossing Signals 6128. Measures about 2-3/4 x 1 x 7/16" (68 x 24 x 10mm). Unit can be mounted on or under benchwork. The unit requires a power supply of 14-16V DC (use of Bridge Rectifier 2185 required for AC operation).

Brawa crossing gates are supplied as individual units. Since there is not mechanical link between gates, they may be separated by any number of tracks. Complete installation and operating instructions are included.

Brawa relay 2762 features matching color-coded wiring and is designed for use with crossing signals. This control relay can be used with single or double track crossings.

186-1194 Slow Moving Crossing Gate 256.99

186-1191 Full Width Crossing Gate w/Barrier (NON-OPERATING) 22.99
Includes two gates.

BRAWA

Imported from Germany by WALTHERS

HO SCALE (1/87)

Model lights add realistic atmosphere to a layout, especially in "night" scenes. Brawa offers a variety of old-fashioned and modern lighting, suitable for use in any era.

All Brawa lights are made of brass (with plastic parts where appropriate), fully assembled, and ready to install. Lamps can be powered from any AC or DC transformer with a maximum output of 16V.

TELEGRAPH POLES

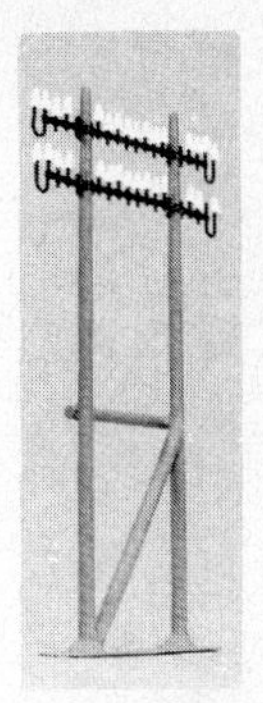
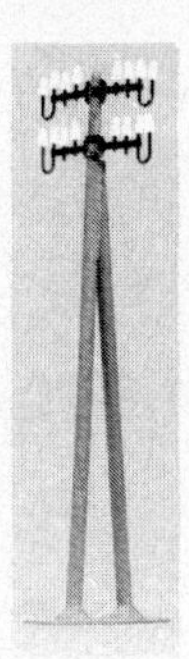
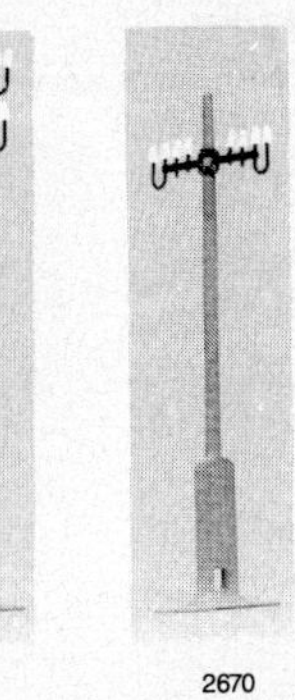

2668   2669   2670

186-2668 Double-Poles   pkg(3) 23.99
approx 3-1/4" high

186-2669 Poles w/Support   pkg(3) 16.99
approx 3-1/4" high

186-2670 Poles   pkg(3) 15.49
approx 3" high

OVERHEAD POWER LINES

Suitable for use in HO or N Scale, towers are made of metal. Approximate height 4" (100mm).

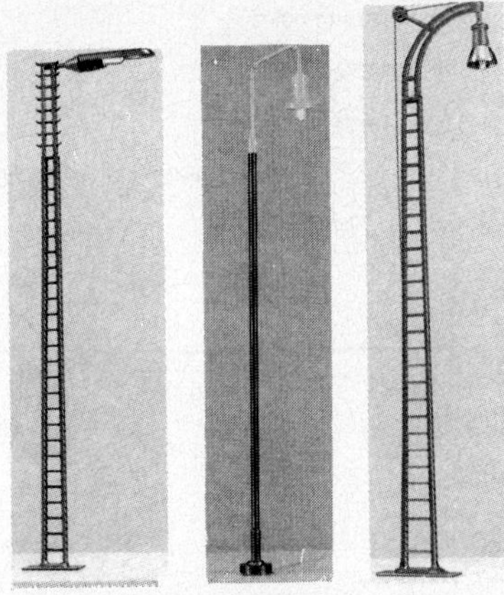

186-2658 High Tension Tower   each 16.99

186-2659 High Tension Tower Set   pkg(4) 69.99
Includes 4 overhead towers with top sections, wires, warning globes and tension springs.

STATION LIGHT

Model light adds realistic atmosphere to a layout, especially in "night" scenes. Brawa offers a variety of old-fashioned and modern lighting, suitable for use in any era.

All Brawa lights are made of brass (with plastic parts where appropriate), fully-assembled and ready to install. Lamps can be powered from any AC or DC transformer with a maximum output of 16V.

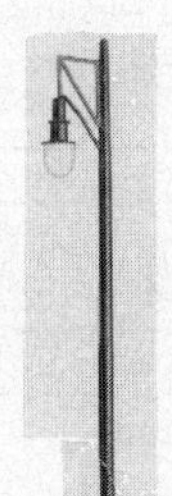

Aachen Station Light
186-5274   10.49

5274

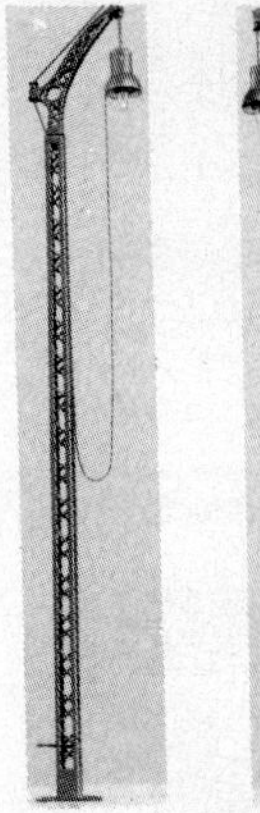
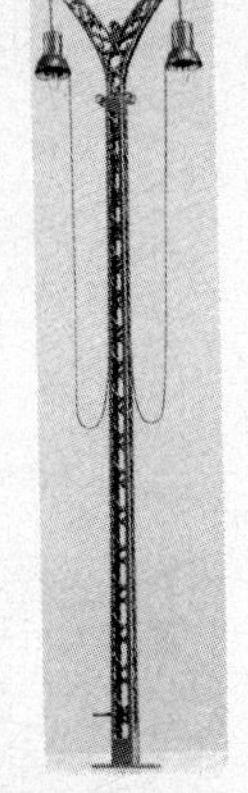
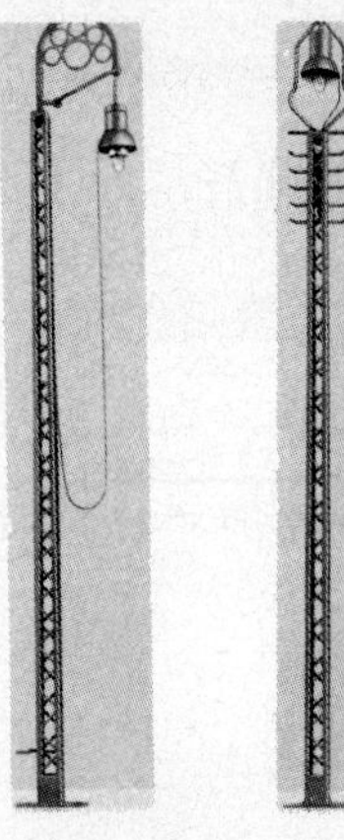

5518   5451   5506

186-5518 Festoon Bulb   12.99
Olive green. Approx 5" high

186-5451 Tall Station Light   9.99

186-5506 Ladder Mast Light   12.99
Olive green, modern flat pattern, 6" high

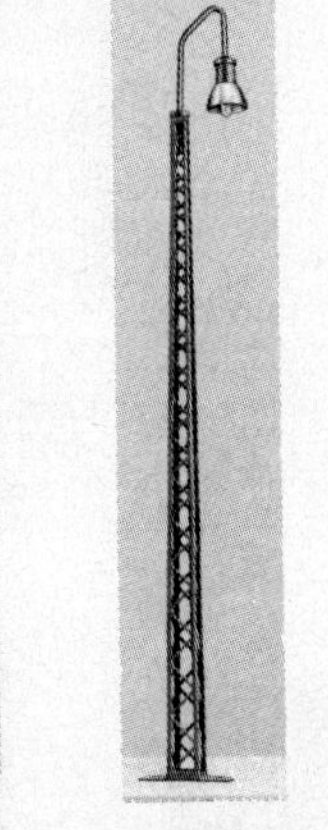

5509   5505

186-5509 Slim Lattice Mast Light   13.49
Olive green, rectangular section mast, approx 6" high

186-5505 Lattice Mast Light   12.99
Olive green, slim retangular section mast, approx 6" high

LATTICE MAST LIGHT

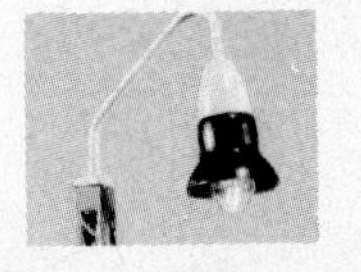

5534   5535

186-5534 Add-on Light   (lt gry/blk) 7.49
for catenary towers

186-5535 Twin Add-on Light   (black) 12.99
for HO catenary towers, fits Vollmer, Marklin and Sommerfeld towers

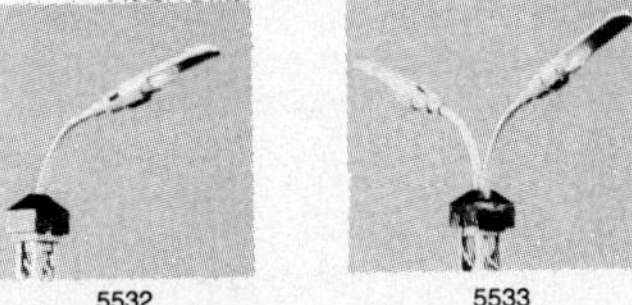

5519   5520   5521   5522

186-5519 Single Arm   (olive green) 19.99
approx 6" high

186-5520 2-Curved-Arm   (olive green) 26.49
approx 5-1/2"

186-5521 Curved-arm   (olive green) 19.99
approx 5-1/2"

186-5522 Lattice Mast Light   (olive grn) 19.99
w/Ring
approx 5-1/2"

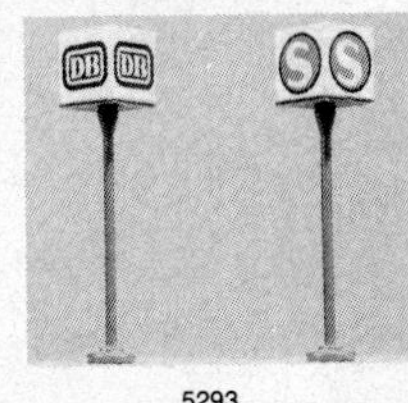

5532   5533

186-5532 Single Add-on Light   (gray) 7.49
w/Festoon Bulb
for HO catenary towers, fits Vollmer, Marklin and Sommerfeld towers

186-5533 Twin Add-on Light   (gray) 12.99
for HO catenary towers, fits Vollmer, Marklin and Sommerfeld towers

PLATFORM ACCESSORIES

5292   5293

186-5292 Train Arrival, illuminated   24.49
post dark gray, frame red; approx 2" high

186-5293 "DB" or "S BAHN" Sign   7.99
Includes decals for both signs and one illuminated sign, approx 2" tall (45mm); gray mast.

See also: PARTS, LOCOMOTIVES, LIGHTING & ELECTRICAL, STRUCTURES, SCENERY, SCRATCH-BUILDING and TRACTION sections for additional BRAWA items.

BRAWA

HO SCALE (1/87)

Imported from Germany by WALTHERS

Model lights add realistic atmosphere to a layout, especially in "night" scenes. Brawa offers a variety of old-fashioned and modern lighting, suitable for use in any era.

All Brawa lights are made of brass (with plastic parts where appropriate), fully assembled, and ready to install. Lamps can be powered from any AC or DC transformer with a maximum output of 16V.

PLATFORM ACCESSORIES (continued)

5537

5536

186-5537　Modern Platform Light　　7.49
　　approx .16 x .2 x .8" high
186-5536　Platform Light　(black)　6.99
　　Installs under roof

5538

5295

186-5538　Car Arrival Signs　　7.49
Indicates where reserved seat or through cars will stop at station platforms. Illuminated, installs under platform roof. Includes decals "A" to "E"; approx 1/2" x 1/2".

186-5295　U-BAHN Sign　　7.49
　　illuminated, hanging mount

PLATFORM LIGHT

Lights are approx 3" high, unless otherwise noted.

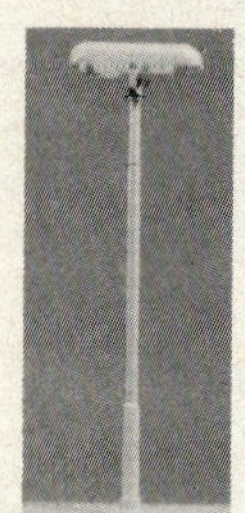
5499

5501

186-5499　Light Gray　　each　9.99
186-5501　Light Gray　　each　9.99

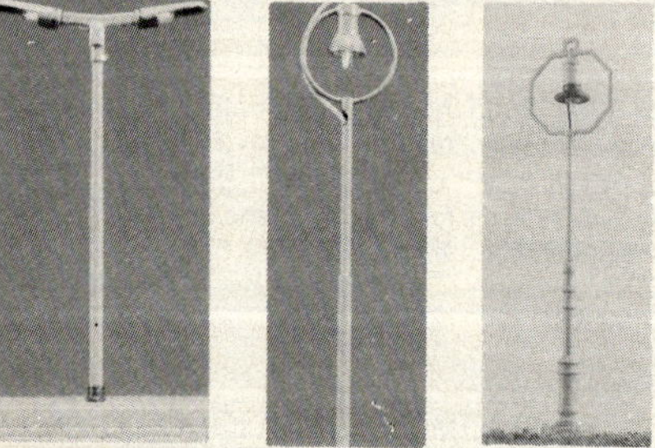
5502　　5504　　5456

186-5502　Double-Arm　(light gray)　ea　14.99
186-5504　Ring-Post Light　(light gray)　ea　9.99
　　approx 3-1/2" high
186-5456　Octagon Post City Light　　12.49

LARGE LIGHT

Lights are light gray in color.

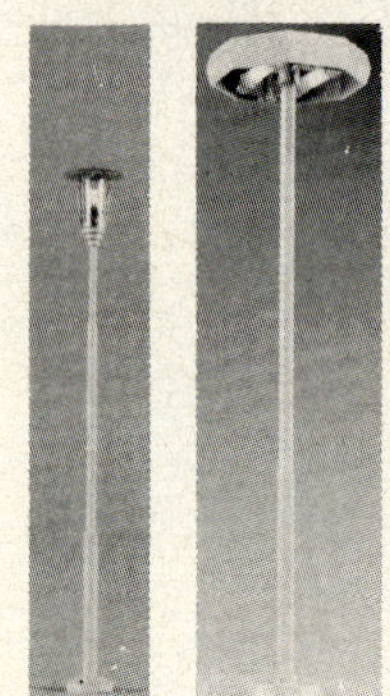
5050　　5517

Station Light
186-5050　　8.99
approx 4-1/2" high

Large-Area Light
"Stuttgart" Model
186-5517　　15.99
2 bulbs, approx 6" high

PARK LIGHTING—SUSPENDED

5230

Park Light
186-5230　(blk)　8.49
approx 2" high

5320

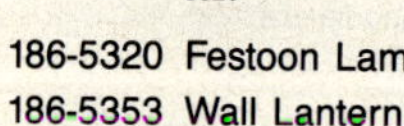
5353

186-5320　Festoon Lamp　(gray)　7.99
186-5353　Wall Lantern　(black)　9.49

5090　　5001　　5240

186-5090　Park Lantern　　8.49
　　approx 2-1/2"
186-5001　Park Lamp　　7.99
186-5240　Street Light　　8.49
　　black, approx 2-1/2" high
186-5901　Lighting Set　　48.99
　　3 each of #5240 and #5450

STREET LIGHTS AND WALL LANTERNS

STATION

Historic models, approx 3-1/2" high; green in color, except as noted.

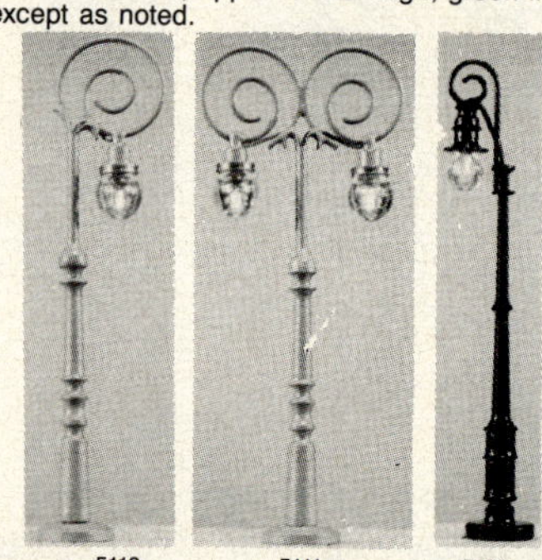
5110　　5111　　5176

186-5110　Single-Arm　　16.99
186-5111　Double-Arm　　22.99
186-5176　"Berlin Stettiner Station"　(blk)　15.49
　　approx 3" high

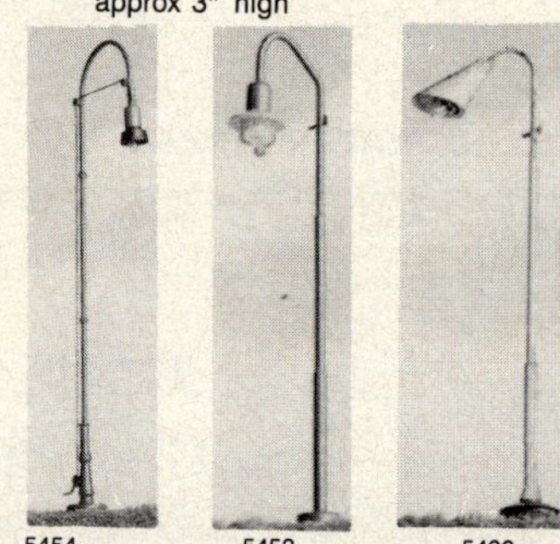
5454　　5453　　5496

186-5454　Loco Shed　　each　14.99
186-5453　Forecourt　　each　9.99
186-5496　Rail Crossing/Working Light　ea　9.99

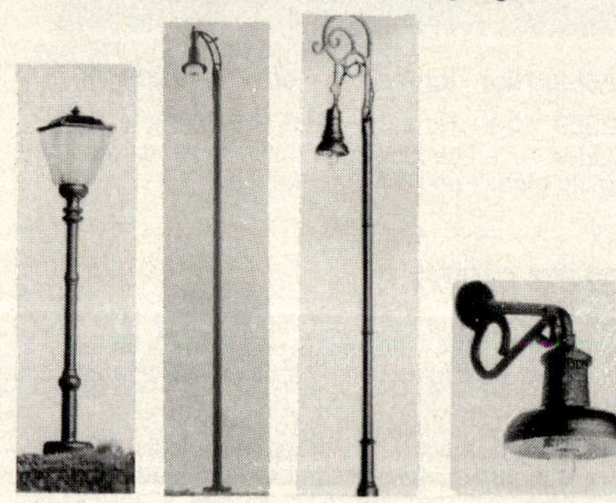
5498　　5276　　5527　　5358

186-5498　Bavarian, Platform Light　　9.99
186-5276　Wooden Pole Light Birkenau　　10.99
186-5527　Frankfurt Loco Shed　　10.49
186-5358　Wall Mounted Light　　8.49

BRAWA

HO SCALE (1/87)

Imported from Germany by WALTHERS

Model lights add realistic atmosphere to a layout, especially in "night" scenes. Brawa offers a variety of old-fashioned and modern lighting, suitable for use in any era.

All Brawa lights are made of brass (with plastic parts where appropriate), fully assembled, and ready to install. Lamps can be powered from any AC or DC transformer with a maximum output of 16V.

STREET LIGHTS AND WALL LANTERNS (continued)

STREET

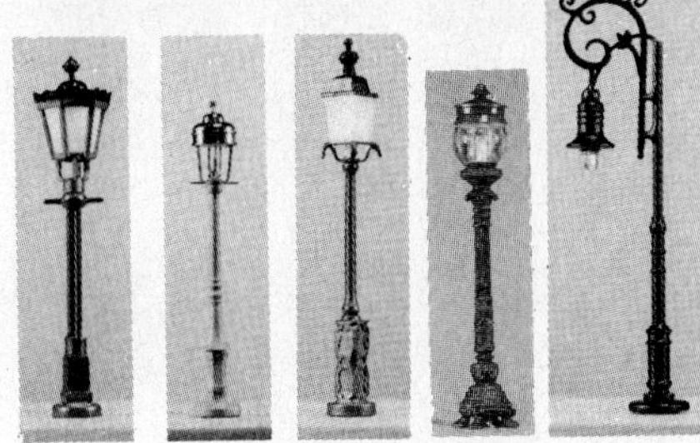

5000   5010   5011   5012   5175

186-5000 Old Street Lamp (dk green) 12.99
approx 2-1/2"

186-5010 Gas Lamp (green) 11.99
approx 2" high

186-5011 Street Light (dark green) 13.99
approx 2-1/2" high

186-5012 Park or Street Lamp (dk brn) 21.49
approx 2" high

186-5175 "Waiblingen" Light w/shade (blk) 13.99
approx 2-1/2" high

186-5903 Lighting Set 63.99
3 ea of #5175 and of #5526

5352   5354   5356   5357

186-5352 Wall Lantern (black) 9.49

186-5354 "Waiblingen" Wall Lantern (blk) 10.49
w/shade

186-5356 "Baden-Baden" Wall (black) 10.49
Lantern w/shade

186-5357 "Nuremburg" Wall Lantern (blk) 10.49
w/shade

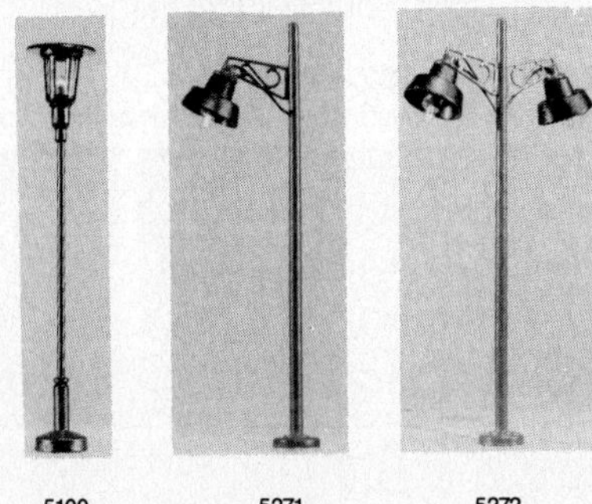

5100   5271   5272

186-5100 Park Light (black) 8.49
approx 3" high

186-5271 Wooden-post Lamp, 1-arm (brn) 11.99
approx 3" high

186-5272 Wooden-post Lamp, 2-arm (brn) 17.49
approx 3" high

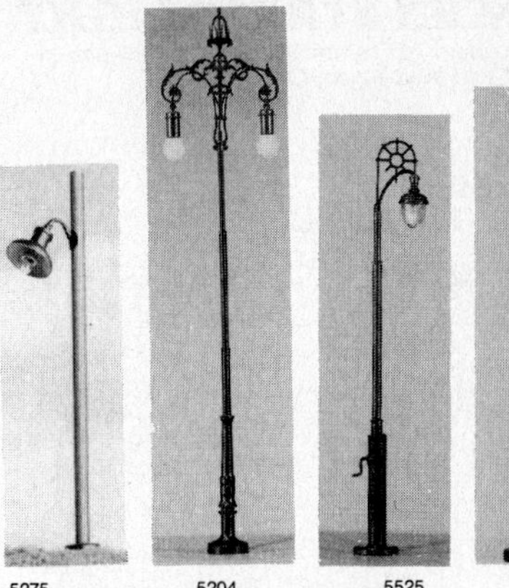

5275   5204   5525   5273

186-5275 Wooden Mast w/Light 9.49
186-5204 Koln Boulevard Light 22.99
186-5525 Munich Street Light 13.49
186-5273 Tall Goose-Neck 11.49

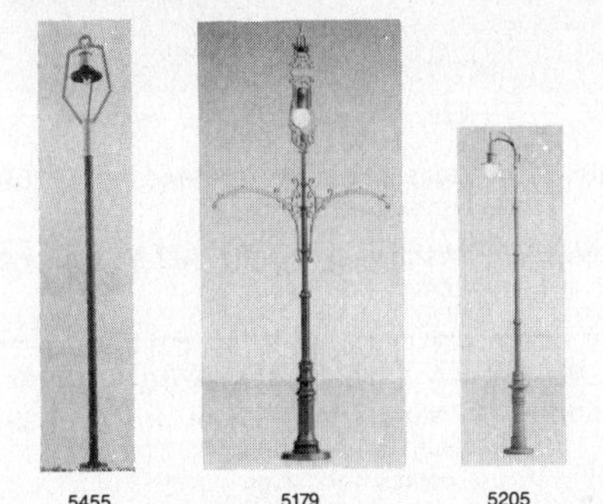

5455   5179   5205

186-5455 Angular Post Platform Light 10.49

186-5179 Koln Boulevard Light w/Arms 21.49
6-1/4" high

186-5205 Munich Boulevard Light 13.49
4-3/4" high

GAS LAMP

5180   5190   5200   5202

186-5180 Gas Lamp, 2-1/2" high (black) 9.49
186-5190 Gas Lamp, 2" high (black) 9.49
186-5200 Old Gas Lamp, 2" high (black) 9.49
186-5202 Gas Lantern (black) 12.99
"Hamburger" Post, approx 2" high

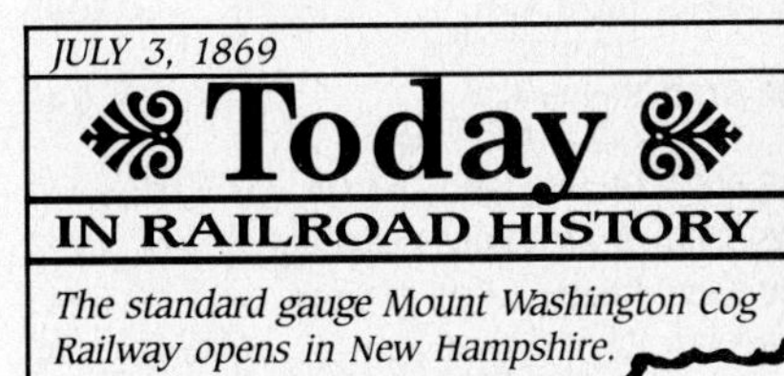

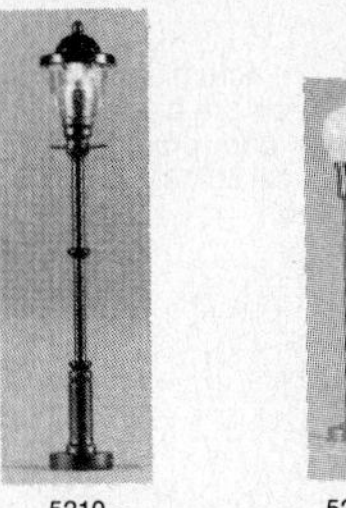
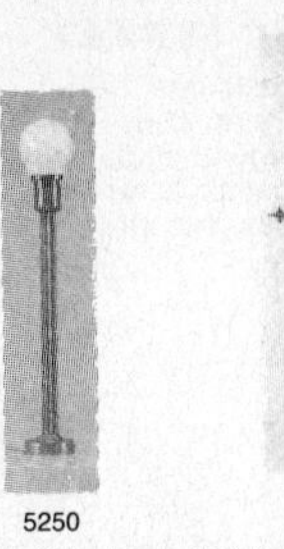

5210   5250   5203

186-5203 Gas Lantern "Stuttgart" (dk grn) 18.99
4" high

186-5210 Street Lamp, 2-1/2" high (blk) 8.49

186-5250 Park w/globe, approx 2" (lt gray) 8.49

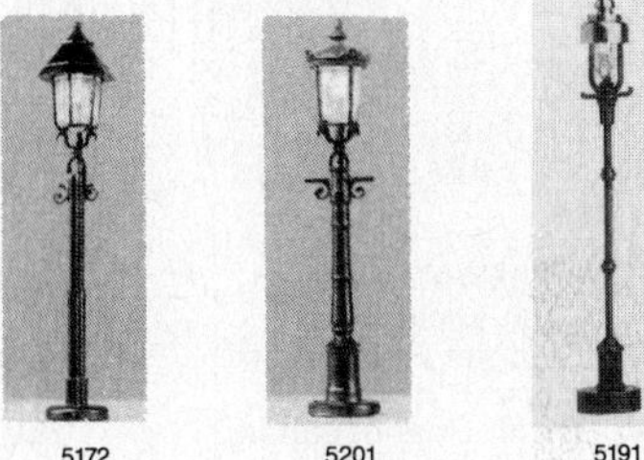

5172   5201   5191

186-5172 "Nuremberg" Street Lamp (blk) 13.49
approx 2" high

186-5201 "Baden-Baden" Gas Lamp (blk) 13.99
approx 2" high

186-5191 Gas Lantern, 2" high 10.49

HISTORIC PARK LIGHT

Lights are appoximately 3.3" high and are dark green in color, unless noted.

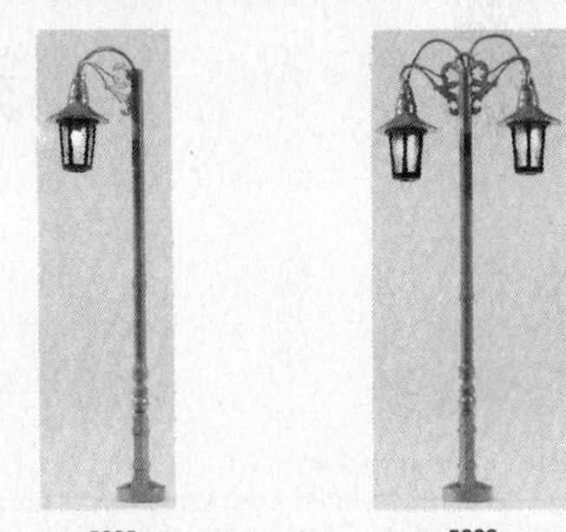

5225   5222

186-5225 Single Arm 16.99
186-5222 Double Arm 22.99

5226   5223   5173

186-5226 Double Arm 22.99
approx 3-1/2" high

186-5223 Triple Arm 28.99
approx 3-1/2" high

186-5173 "Nuremberg" Light (black) 33.49
4 arm; approx 2-1/2" high

BRAWA

HO SCALE (1/87)

Imported from Germany by WALTHERS

Model lights add realistic atmosphere to a layout, especially in "night" scenes. Brawa offers a variety of old-fashioned and modern lighting, suitable for use in any era.

All Brawa lights are made of brass (with plastic parts where appropriate), fully assembled, and ready to install. Lamps can be powered from any AC or DC transformer with a maximum output of 16V.

HISTORIC STREET

These models are based on actual lamps from various German cities. The lamps are being restored to their original appearance and provide an interesting contrast to modern street lighting. Lights are black in color, except as noted.

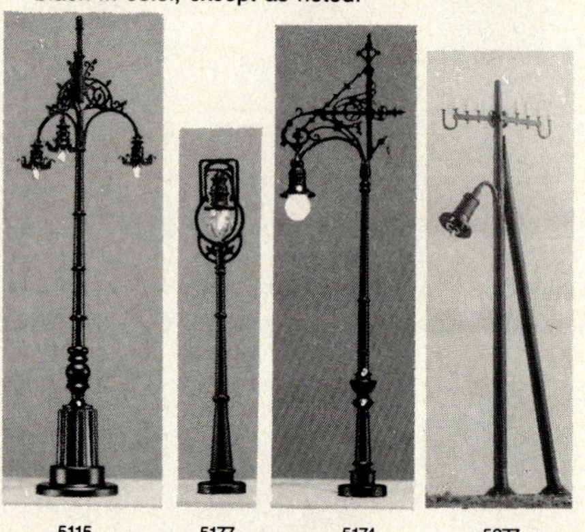

5115 · 5177 · 5174 · 5277

186-5115 "Frankfurt" Model — 39.99
  3 arm; approx 6" high
186-5177 "Cologne Rhine Bank" — 16.49
  approx 3" high
186-5174 "Berlin Charlottenberg" — 18.99
  approx 4-1/2" high
186-5277 Telegraph Pole w/Light — 12.99

PARK LIGHTING FROM BADEN-BADEN

Located in southwest Germany, the traditional spa at Baden-Baden is illuminated by these unique lamps. These brass models are replicas of the originals. Lights are approx 3" high with 6 light fittings.

5224 · 5228 · 5220

186-5224 Candelabra #1 — 71.49
  Standard version, cast brass post, etched brass arms, turned brass shades. Base brown, post black.
186-5228 Candelabra #2 — 101.49
  Super-detailed version with engraved post. Made from centrifugal brass castings throughout. Base brown, post black brushed finish.
186-5220 Candelabra Lantern (black) — 25.99
  3 arm; approx 3-1/2"
Lamps feature marble-finish plastic bases and are based on prototypes that were used in Berlin and Nuremburg.

5171

186-5171 Candelabra Lantern (black) — 39.49
  5 arm; approx 3-1/2"

MODERN STREET LIGHT

These modern lamps are based on prototypes in Stuttgart and Waiblingen, Germany.

TOWN SQUARE

Lights are light gray in color

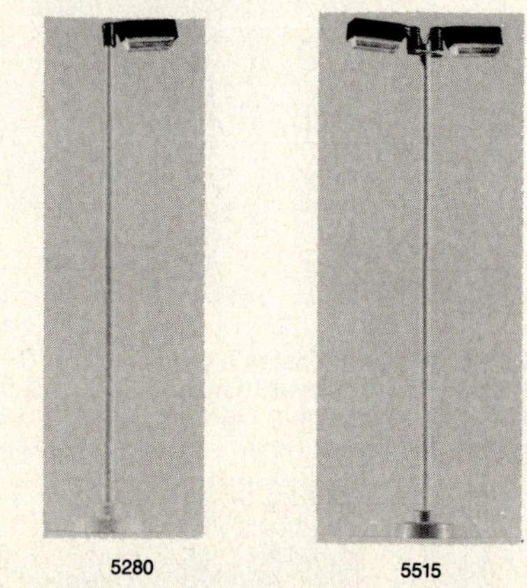

5280 · 5515

186-5280 Light w/rectangular head — 8.99
  approx 4-1/2" high
186-5515 "Waiblingen" Model w/2 heads — 14.99
  approx 4-1/2" high

■ **LIMITED QUANTITIES AVAILABLE** ■

186-5516 "Waiblingen" Model — 19.99
  with 4 heads
  approx 4-1/2" high

CANTILEVER-MAST

Lights are light gray in color.

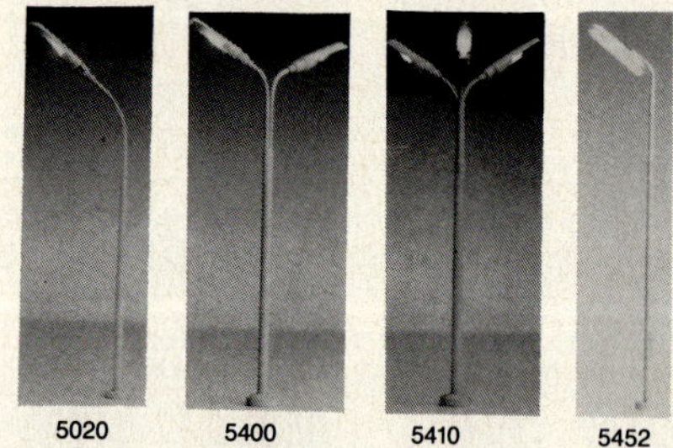

5020 · 5400 · 5410 · 5452

186-5020 Single Arm — 8.49
  approx 4" high
186-5400 Double Arm — 14.49
  approx 4-1/2" high
186-5902 Lighting Set — 44.99
  3 ea of #5020 and #5090
186-5410 Triple Arm — 20.99
  approx 5" high
186-5452 Single Arm — 9.49
  approx 4-1/2" high
186-5005 Street Light, Urbach — **NEW** 10.49
186-5006 Street Light, Talfingen — **NEW** 9.49
186-5458 Station Light, 165mm — **NEW** 9.49
186-5459 Old Time Station Light, 165mm — **NEW** 11.49

FLOOD AND SPOT

Floodlights are olive green in color and pivot horizontally and vertically.

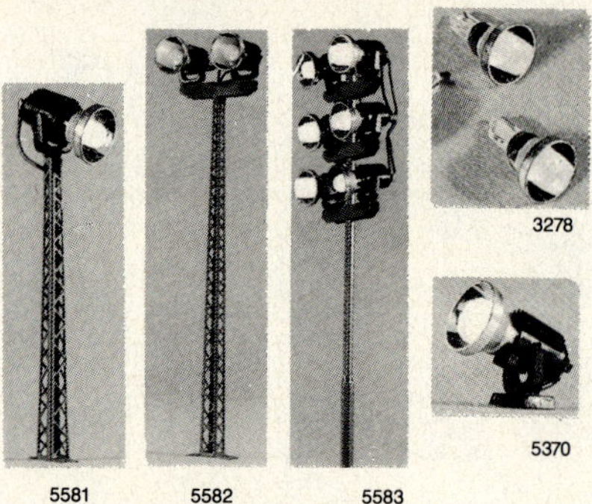

3278 · 5370

5581 · 5582 · 5583

186-5581 Single Lattice Mast — 13.99
  approx 3" high
186-5582 Double Latice Mast — 25.99
  approx 5-1/2"
186-5583 Hexagon Mast — 51.99
  6 lights, very intense lighting effect; approx 6" high
186-3278 Spare Bulb — pkg(2) 8.49
  with reflector, for 14-16V supply
186-5370 Spotlight (black) — 11.99
  approx dimensions .7 x .6 x .5"; pivots vertically

LATTICE-MAST

Lights are approx 5" high and are dark gray in color.

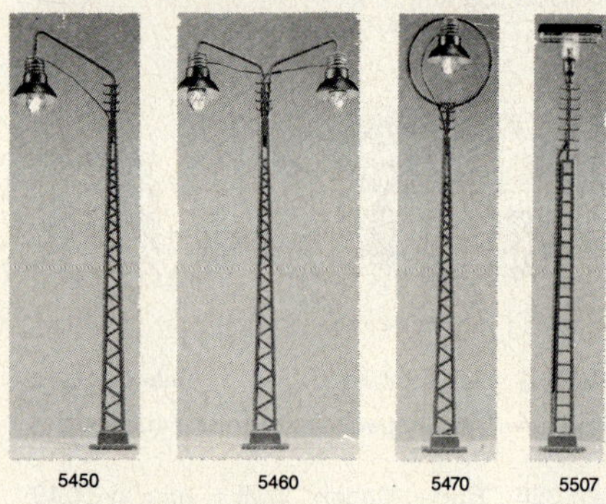

5450 · 5460 · 5470 · 5507

186-5450 Single Arm — 9.49
186-5460 Double Arm — 12.99
186-5470 Lattice-Mast Light w/Ring — 9.49
186-5507 Festoon Light — 12.99
  Modern flat mast pattern

CURVED-MAST

Lights are light gray in color and contain a 5mm bulb.

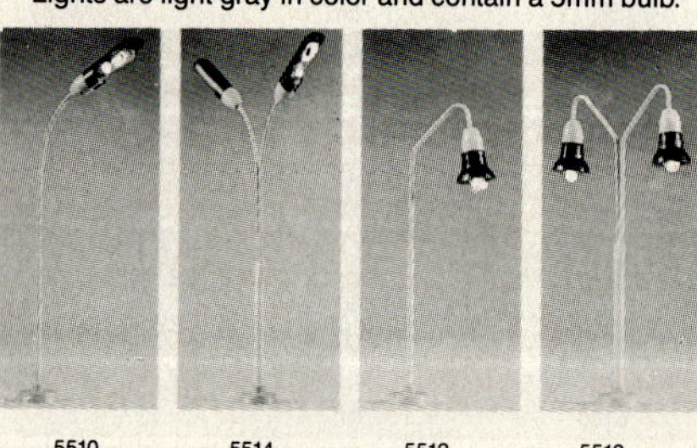

5510 · 5514 · 5512 · 5513

186-5510 Single Arm — approx 5" high — 7.99
186-5514 Cantilever-Mast Light Double Arm — approx 5" high — 12.49
186-5512 Curved-Arm; Single approx 4" — 7.99
186-5513 Curved Double Arm Light — 12.49
  approx 5" high

BRAWA
HO SCALE (1/87)
Imported from Germany by WALTHERS

Model lights add realistic atmosphere to a layout, especially in "night" scenes. Brawa offers a variety of old-fashioned and modern lighting, suitable for use in any era. All Brawa lights are made of brass (with plastic parts where appropriate), fully assembled, and ready to install. Lamps can be powered from any AC or DC transformer with a maximum output of 16V.

CLOCK-ILLUMINATED

Old Wall Clock
186-5361   14.49
Prototype in Baden-Baden, hands are adjustable; black.

5291   5761

186-5291 Train Destination Sign   25.99
w/twin-dial clock, adjustable signboards. Approx 1-1/2″ high; green.

186-5761 Column with Clock   24.99
Advertisements internally lit, clock hands are adjustable; Approx 1-1/2″ high

5340   5360   5362   5366

186-5340 Station Yard Clock   13.99
(also used at loco shops), olive green; approx 3″ high

186-5360 Station Clock   25.99
Adjustable hands, dark green; Approx 2-3/4″ high

186-5362 "Baden-Baden" Clock   34.99
3 dials with adjustable hands; black. Approx 2-1/2″

186-5366 "Berlin Stettin Station" Clock   28.99
Brass dial, adjustable hands, black; approx 3″ high

5260   5290   5294

186-5260 Platform Clock   8.49
Concrete-gray post; approx 2″ high

186-5290 Platform Clock   24.49
w/train direction indicators, light gray post; approx 2″

186-5294 Illuminated Clock   16.49
w/Advertising Cube
Can display advertising or DB/S Bahn symbol, included. Approx 2-1/8″ high, dark gray post.

5261   5365

186-5261 Wall or Platform Clock   8.49
Horizontal or vertical mounting. Black arm, red frame. Frame diameter approx 1/2″.

■ LIMITED QUANTITIES AVAILABLE ■
186-5365 Electronic Digital Clock   116.99
Red LED display in 24 hour "military" time with casing for adapting to model buildings. Clock displays standard time or can be adjusted to show 6x and 12x "fast" time. Complete set with control unit. Casing measures 3/4 x 1″ (19 x 28 mm), requires approximately 1/4 x 1″ (8 x 23 mm) for installation.

5368   5495

186-5368 Clock   19.99
mounted on a lattice mast

186-5495 Station Light w/Clock   14.49

■ LIMITED QUANTITIES AVAILABLE ■

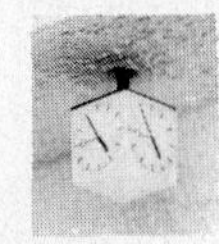

186-5367 Station Clock   7.99
hanging mount

186-5369 Station Clock   7.99
side mount

MODEL RAILROAD QUARTZ CLOCK
These working "models" feature an adjustable Swiss quartz movement. Clocks are powered by a standard "penlight" AA battery.

Model Railroad Clock
186-5363   119.99
Red second hand; analog display, Includes battery holder for standard 1.5V dry-cell battery (not included). Size approx 1 x 1″.

Traditional Church/Town Hall Clock
186-5364   119.99
Blue/black/gold dial with gold hands. Frame printed blue and brown. Dial .6″, frame .8 x 1″.

WARNING BELL
Gives station personnel advance warning of approaching trains.

1197   1198

186-1197 DR/DB Green & Black   12.49
186-1198 DR/DB Gray & Black   12.49

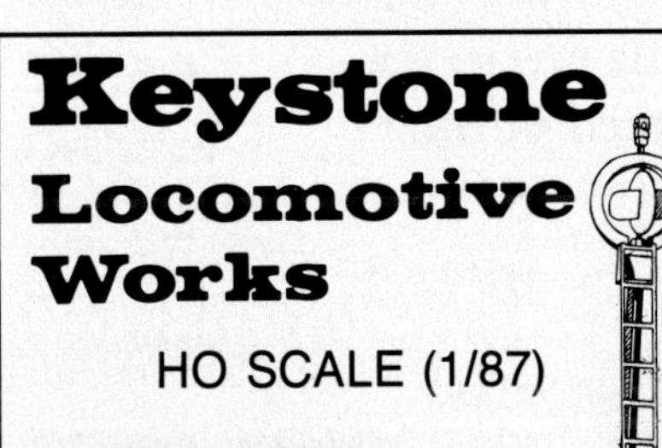

Keystone Locomotive Works
HO SCALE (1/87)

NON-OPERATING BLOCK SIGNAL

Old Time Banjo Block Signal Kit
395-13   pkg(2) 5.95
Kit contains metal pressure castings, brass rod and wire. Illustration not to scale.

HO SCALE SIGNAL KITS

Each signal includes an assortment of Number and ID plates and can be fully illuminated using an LED or incandescent light source. Kit includes fibre optics. Detailed white metal castings. Illustrations are not to scale.

SEARCHLIGHT SIGNAL

Fiber optics included with searchlight signal kits.

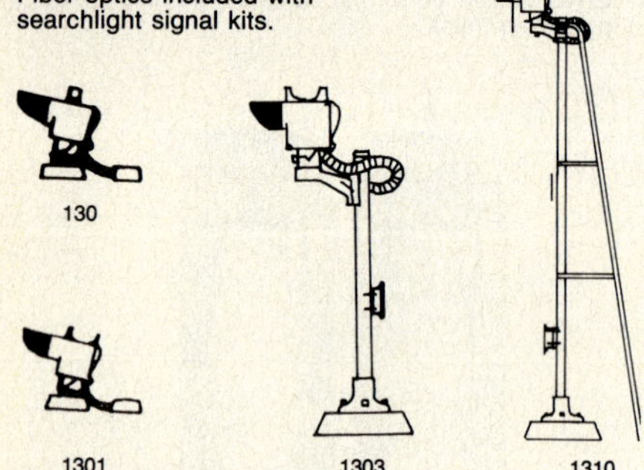

130		
1301	1303	1310

215-130	Dwarf Type SA, working	2.75
215-1301	Dwarf Type SA **NEW**	TBA
215-1303	Siding Signal Low	5.00
215-1310	w/Footrest & Ladder	7.25

WIG-WAG SIGNAL

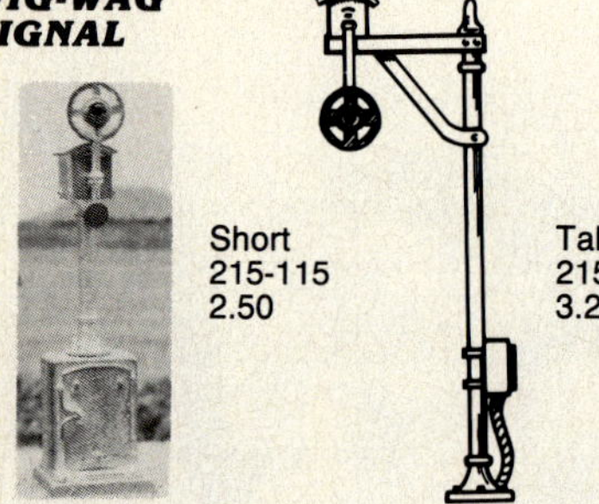

Short	Tall
215-115	215-116
2.50	3.25

RELAY & BLOCK INDICATOR

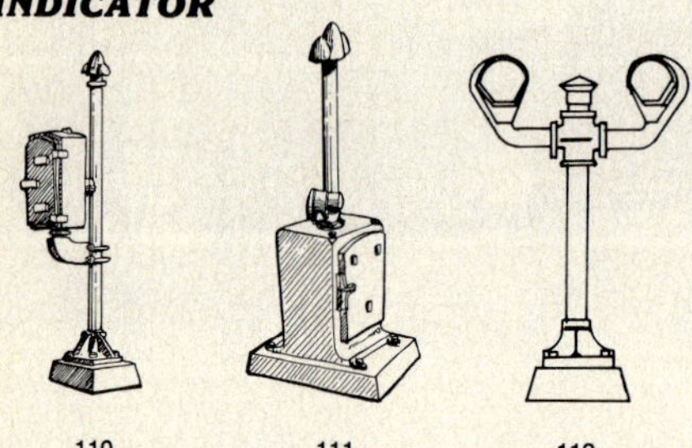

110	111	112

215-110	Pole Relay	pkg(3)	1.75
215-111	Ground Relay Box and Mast	pkg(3)	2.50
215-112	Block Indicator	pkg(4)	1.75

SWITCH MOTOR

Switch Motor		
215-135	pkg(2)	2.75

ACCESSORIES

215-113	Trackside Battery Box	pkg(6)	1.75

FIBER OPTICS

For installation in signal kits.

215-10	.010 Diameter	pkg(12′)	1.50
215-20	.020 Diameter	pkg(12′)	1.75
215-30	.030 Diameter	pkg(12′)	2.50
215-40	.040 Diameter	pkg(6′)	2.25
215-50	.050 Diameter	pkg(6′)	2.75
215-60	.060 Diameter	pkg(6′)	4.00

JACKETED MULTI-FIBER, FIBER OPTIC BUNDLE

215-87	.087 16 Fibers of .010 dia	pkg(4′)	5.50
215-117	.117 32 Fibers of .010 dia	pkg(4′)	5.75
215-140	.140 19 Fibers of .020 dia	pkg(3′)	4.50

See also: PARTS for additional CENTURY products.

DIAMOND SCALE CONST.

NON-OPERATING YARD LIGHT

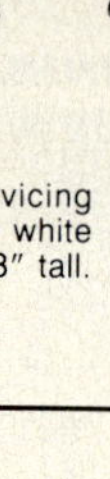

Yard Light Pole
239-404   pkg(4) 2.35
Used for workmen servicing equipment at night. Cast white metal, non-operating, 1-5/8″ tall.

Folks in New England made good use of their natural resources, constructing many buildings from native stone. This close-up view of Railway Design Associates "Hermanson Woolen Mill" was made by Mike Tylick using a pinhole lens. From this angle you can rally appreciate the detail of the wall castings, which were painted with latex and watercolors to bring out the texture. Other details from Fine Scale Miniatures, Woodland Scenics, Preiser and a few scratch-built pieces complete the building and the scene.
Model and Photo by Michael Tylick

CIRCUITRON products constructed on printed circuit boards are designed to mount by snapping them into a section of CIRCUITRON's PCMT (Printed Circuit Mounting Track). Solid State integrated circuit technology. Connections to any CIRCUITRON printed circuit board can be made using .110" female solderless connectors or by soldering the leads directly to the terminals on the board. Complete instructions are included. One year limited warranty.

DETECTION SYSTEMS

Detection is the ability to determine when a piece of rolling stock is at a given location. Circuitron uses the opto-electronic detection method. Tiny opto-sensors are mounted between the rails where they will be shaded from ambient room light by a passing train. The shaded opto-sensor then activates the appropriate circuitry for the given application. The system is independent of track power, and no modifications to rolling stock are necessary. The opto-sensors supplied with Circuitron products are small enough to fit between the ties in HO scale and may be ballasted over in most cases. The circuitry is extremely sensitive and will operate properly under very low levels of room light.

PCMT PRINTED CIRCUIT MOUNTING TRACK

This plastic assembly provides simple, snap-in mounting of all Circuitron printed circuit boards. Can be mounted using screws, adhesive, or double-backed tape. After PCMT is mounted, circuit boards are simply snapped into the track. Holds the printed circuit boards firmly, yet they are easily removed for service.

800-9506 PCMT—6 inch   4.50

BLOCK OCCUPANCY DETECTORS

Provides positive indication whenever a section of a layout is occupied by any piece of rolling stock. Operates on a photo-electric principle. Any piece of rolling stock entering the block activates logic circuitry on the circuit board. No modifications to rolling stock necessary. Completely bi-directional. Also contains all the necessary circuitry to power two-color block signals at each end of the protected block. No additional driver boards or relays are necessary. Requires a 6-20 volt DC input. Independent of track power. May be used with any AC or DC track power. Compatible with radio or carrier control systems.

800-5501 Block Occupancy Detector, BD-1   29.95

BLOCK SIGNAL DRIVERS   **NEW**

The SD-1 provides all the logic and output drivers to control any 3 lamp, 3 color Block Signal. Will power LED or incandescent lamp type signals. LED type requires common positive (anode) connection of all LEDs. Detection circuits (such as BD-1) are needed for a minimum of 3 blocks to display all three aspects. 10-18 volts DC input.

SD-1 Tri-Color Signal Driver
800-5510   10.95

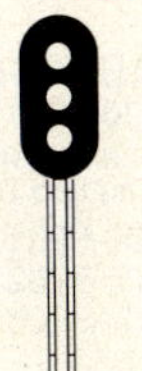

Capable of driving any single target by-color LED type signal to red, green and amber aspects. Will not drive 3 lamp signals. Amber hue fully adjustable. May be controlled by 3 position switch or automatically by detection circuits such as BD-1 (minimum of 3 blocks required). 10-18 volts AC or DC (DC required shown used with detection circuits).

SD-3 Tri-Color LED Signal Driver
800-5530   14.95

BLOCK SIGNALS   **NEW**

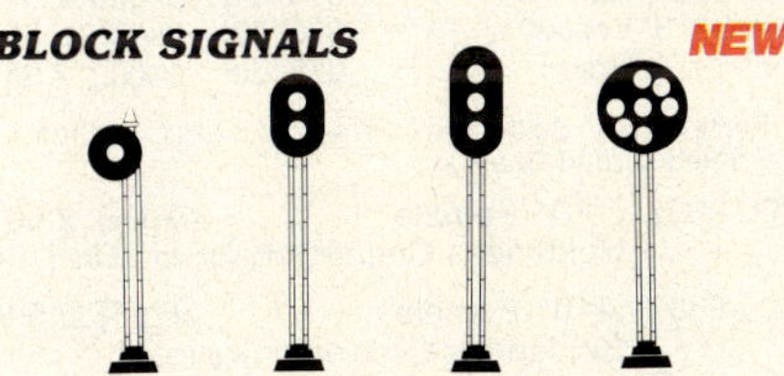

8101   8102   8103   8107

Block Signals require detection circuits for automatic operation. For 3-color signalling, a minimum of 4 blocks should be used. All signals (except 8102) also require Signal Driver circuits for 3-aspect automatic operation. However, all signals can display 2 aspects (red/green) without additional driver circuits when driven by Circuitron BD-1,800-5501.

800-8101 Single Searchlight, Bi-color   19.95
LED will display all 3 aspects when used with 800-5530 Signal Driver Circuit

800-8102 2 aspect, Type D Color   14.95
Light Signal

800-8103 3 aspect, Type D Color   15.95
Light Signal

800-8107 7 lamp, PRR Position Light   25.95
Signal (all amber)

Note: Both 8103 and 8107 require 800-5510, SD-1 Signal Driver Circuit for automatic 3-color signalling.

ROLLING STOCK DETECTOR

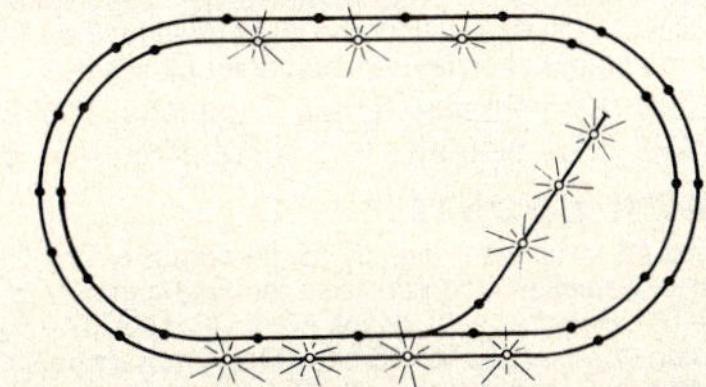

An ideal system for spotting a train or piece of rolling stock in hidden location. Supplied with four opto-sensors which are to be mounted between rails wherever it is desired to detect a train. If it is desired, a number of DT-4 circuit boards can be utilized with the opto-sensors spaced at set intervals along the track. With indicator lamps mounted on the control panel, the progress of a train can be observed even when it is hidden from view. Constructed on a 3 x 3" printed circuit board and requires a 10-18 volt DC power source (not included). Independent of track power. May be used with any AC or DC track power. Compatible with radio or carrier control systems.

800-5204 DT-4 Rolling Stock Detector   32.95

AUTOMATIC REVERSE CIRCUITS

The AR-1 and AR-2 will consistently reverse direction whenever the first piece of rolling stock covers one of the Opto-Sensors. Some applications for the AR-1 might be for test track, a window display, a mine train or for automatic reverse loop operation. AR-1 may be used on carrier control layouts for reverse loops wherever automatic operation as a replacement for a cross-wired DPDT switch is desired. Pushbuttons can also be connected to the AR-1 to provide manual reversing at any time. Constructed on a 3 x 3" printed circuit board.

800-5400 AR-1 Auto Reverse Circuit   38.95

The AR-2 incorporates an adjustable time delay that will stop the train at each Opto-Sensor for a set period of time before reversing direction. This time delay is continuously variable from .1 second to over 1 minute. In addition, a terminal is provided for external activation of the time delay circuitry without reversing direction. This terminal can be connected to panel pushbutton or a detection unit to permit stops at any point. The AR-2 requires a filtered and regulated 12 volt DC power supply (not included).

800-5401 AR-2 Automatic Reverse   49.95
with Adjustable Delay

AUTOMATIC SLOWDOWN

Provides automatic train speed reduction within a section of track. Bi-directional and may be used with AC or DC track power. Output is continuously variable between 1/4 and 3/4 of the input voltage.

AS-1 Automatic Slowdown Circuit
800-5601   15.95

TIME DELAY

Designed to be used in conjunction with one of Circuitron's Detection units and provides an adjustable delay period with a self-contained relay on the output. The TD-1 can be used to "make" a circuit for the time period, or to "break" a circuit for the time period. The time delay period can be adjusted from 0 to over 1 minute in length. Requires a 12 volt DC power supply.

One useful application of the TD-1 is to provide automatic train stopping at a station, etc.

800-5602 TD-1 Time Delay Circuit   20.95

GRADE CROSSINGS

FL-2 Alternating Flasher
800-5102   15.95
- 2 x 3" Printed Circuit Board
- 10-18 volt AC or DC input
- Will power bulbs or LEDs
- Control terminal for Connecting Detection Unit
- 230 MA Output

800-5122 FL-2HD Alternating Flasher   17.95
Identical operation to the standard FL-2 but the outputs are capable of flashing a maximum of 500 ma per side. Adaptable for all scales.

800-5103 FL-3 Alternating Flasher   26.95
w/Three Independent Outputs
- Provides independent control of up to three separate grade crossings
- Three outputs can be connected together to make a heavy-duty flasher
- Three control terminals for use with Detection units
- 3 x 3" printed circuit board
- 10-18 volts AC or DC input
- Will power bulbs or LEDs

800-5201 DT-1 Detection Unit   26.95
- Utilizes tiny Opto-Sensors mounted between rails
- Completely bi-directional
- Detects track polarity and activates only the sensors in the direction of travel
- Turns off after last car clears crossing
- 2 x 3" Printed Circuit Board
- "On" whenever an Opto-Sensor in the proper direction is covered
- Sensitivity controls for adjusting to varying room lighting
- 4 Opto-Sensors included
- Output can control flasher, bells, gates
- 10-18 volt DC input

800-5202 DT-2 Logic Grade Crossing   39.95
Detection Unit
- Completely bi-directional
- Totally independent of train length
- Utilizes only 4 Opto-Sensors (included)
- Detects short trains, even between sensors
- 3 x 4" Printed Circuit Board
- 10-18 volt AC or DC input

800-5203 DT-3 Grade Crossing Detection 20.95
Single Direction
- Uses Opto-Electronic Detection, will operate properly with any length train
- Completely independent of track power
- Use with any scale
- Controls flashers, bells, etc.
- Output has current capacity of 250 ma
- Requires 10-18 volt AC or DC input

800-5250 DF-1 Grade Crossing Detector 29.95
with Flasher
A single direction grade crossing detector with alternating flasher on one circuit board. Utilizes Circuitron's Opto-Electronic Detection and will provide accurate grade crossing action for a single loco, or a 100 car train. Independent of track power and may be used with all scales. Can power two 250 ma loads (5 grain-of-wheat lamps or 10 LEDs per side). 10-18V AC or DC input.

BELL RINGER CIRCUITS

Can be connected to any Circuitron Detection Unit and will simulate the ringing bell at grade crossings. Bell Ringer circuitry allows for adjustment of ring rate and strike force (volume). Use with 10-18 volt AC or DC.

800-5700 BR-1 with Bell   39.95
800-5702 BR-2 less Bell   24.95

Circuitron
Electronics for Model Railroads

CIRCUITRON products constructed on printed circuit boards are designed to mount by snapping them into a section of CIRCUITRON's PCMT (Printed Circuit Mounting Track). Solid State integrated circuit technology. Connections to any CIRCUITRON printed circuit board can be made using .110" female solderless connectors or by soldering the leads directly to the terminals on the board. Complete instructions are included. One year limited warranty.

We have worked closely with this manufacturer to provide accurate availability information at the time this catalog was published. Items listed in *blue ink* may not be available at all times. Please see your dealer for current delivery information.

SIGNALS   NEW

Scale height signals are completely assembled, wired and painted, ready to install. All signals use long-life Light Emitting Diodes which emit pure colors and no heat. No filters or bulb dye to change color over time. Signals must be powered from a DC power source. Appropriate current limiting resistors are included for 12 volt operation.

800-8001   Operating Crossing   2/ 24.95
Flasher Signals, 2 Track
Includes signs for 1 and 3 tracks.

800-8200   Non-Operating post mounted   6.95
Traffic Light

800-8201   3-color, functional post   13.95
mounted Traffic Light
See 800-5802, TL-1, for automatic sequencer.

HIDDEN ACCESSORY SWITCHES

To provide a completely hidden switch for controlling Strobe Flashers, marker lights or other rolling stock electrical accessories. Reed Switch Kits are turned on and off simply by bringing an external magnet up to the outside of the locomotive or car body. No external projections to detract from the appearance of the model. Kits contain a subminiature reed switch and a tiny bias magnet.

800-9101   RS-1 Reed Switch Kit   4.95
requires adjustment before mounting

800-9102   RS-2 Reed Switch Kit   6.95
requires no adjustment

800-9100   External Magnet for   1.50
#9101 & #9102

800-9103   Sub-miniature Slide   pkg(2) 2.95
Switch

AUTOMATIC TURNOUT CONTROL

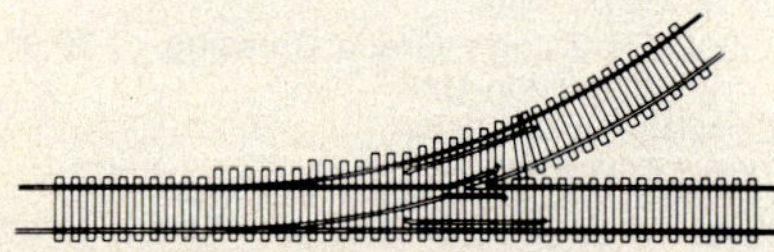

Designed to provide automatic activation of a dual-coil switch machine when used in conjunction with one of Circuitron's Detection Units (the DT-4 is ideal). Provides a momentary pulse to the switch machine coil when the output of the detection units is first activated. This short, high current pulse protects the switch machine from burnout. Can be used to control both directions of a turnout. The TC-1 requires a 10-18 volt AC or DC input. The higher the voltage input, the greater the output power. Recycle time on each side is a second or two.

800-5605   TC-1 Automatic Turnout Control 25.95

TURNOUT DIRECTION ALTERNATOR

Designed to provide automatic alternation of turnout direction when used in conjunction with a Circuitron Detection Unit (DT-4 is ideal). The first time the output of the detection system turns on, the TC-2 will provide a momentary pulse to one coil of the switch machine, throwing the turnout in the one direction. The next time the output of the detection system turns on, the TC-2 will provide a momentary pulse to the coil of the switch machine, throwing the turnout in the other direction, and so on. In this way, a train can be made to travel alternate routes around a layout, automatically. Requires a 10-18 volt AC or DC input for proper operation.

800-5606   TC-2 Turnout Direction   27.95
Alternator

AUTOMATIC TORTOISE CONTROLS

800-5615   Automatic Tortoise Control,   16.95
TC-3

Provides automatic activation of the Circuitron Tortoise switch machine when used in conjunction with one of Circuitron's detection units. Has two inputs; When one input is activated (grounded) the Tortoise will be driven one way, when the other input is activated, the Tortoise will be driven the other way. Only momentary inputs are required, can be used for pushbutton or matrix control. Requires 12-18 volt DC.

800-5616   Tortoise Direction Alternator, TC-4 17.95
Similar function to 800-5606, but output is designed to drive the Tortoise switch machine. Requires 12-18 volt DC.

LT-1, LT-2, LOGIC TRANSLATOR CIRCUITS

Interface circuits that allow CIRCUITRON products to function with other manufacturer's products that do not follow current electronic industry standards. Both boards have 4 independent inverter circuits on the one board.

LT-1 — Converts the grounded (-) output of any CIRCUITRON product to a positive voltage. Requires a DC power source and the positive (+) output of the LT-1 will be the same voltage as the source powering the board. 250 ma output capacity.

LT-2 — Takes a positive (+) output signal from an external source (alternate manufacturer's product) and converts it to the grounded (-) signal required by CIRCUITRON products "Control" or "Trigger" input terminals. The same DC power source being used to power the CIRCUITRON products should be used for the LT-2. 250 ma output capacity. Adaptable for all scales.

800-5271   LT-1 Positive Logic Translator   8.95
800-5272   LT-2 Negative Logic Translator   8.95

POWER BOOSTER

Designed to connect directly to the output of any Circuitron Detection Unit and raise the load capacity to 1 amp DC. Requires a 10-18 volt AC or DC input. The output can only be used for DC circuits and provides a connection to Common (ground). The PB-1 will present a negligible loading effect on the detection unit it is connected to as input to the control terminal of the PB-1 is only on the order of a few milliamperes. In this way, the output of the detection unit can also be used to control other devices. Up to 50 PB-1's could be controlled by the output from one Circuitron Detection Unit.

800-5603   PB-1 Power Booster   11.95

EXTERNAL RELAY

A single pole, double throw, 2 amp relay mounted on a circuit board with all necessary driver circuitry to enable it to be directly connected to the output of any Circuitron Detection Unit. Provides high current, bi-directional contacts that can be used for train control. Ideal for use with one of Circuitron's Block Occupancy Detectors to control power to the blocks in an automatic train control setup. Requires a 12 volt DC power supply for proper operation.

800-5604   ER-1 External Relay SPDT   12.95
The Circuitron ER-2 is double pole, double throw version of ER-1. All other specifications are the same.

800-5624   ER-2 External Relay DPDT   18.95

POWER SUPPLIES

Most Circuitron accessories are designed to operate off AC or DC supplies, but best performance will be achieved when a DC supply is used. A section of PCMT is supplied with both the PS-1 and PS-2. PS-1: A highly filtered AC to DC converter. Maximum load capacity of 1 amp, and maximum input voltage of 22 volts AC. Output is not regulated; thus output voltage will vary depending upon input voltage and output load. (Requires transformer or power pack for AC input).

PS-2: Filtered and fully regulated AC to DC converter which will provide a 1 amp output at a constant 12 volts DC independent of input voltage and output load. The PS-2 has a maximum input of 18 volts AC. (Requires transformer or power pack for AC input).

PS-2A; A self-contained AC to DC converter with an adjustable voltage regulated output. The output voltage can be adjusted anywhere between 1.25 and 12.00 volts DC. Maximum continuous current output of the PS-2A is in excess of one amp. The PS-2A is ideal for powering any low current DC accessories including 1.5 bolt micro-lamps. Ahe AC or unfiltered DC input to the PS-2A should be about 5-6 volts higher than the desired regulated output voltage to allow maximum current output. The input voltage may be as high as 22 volts, but this may result in reduced current available at the output, particularly at lower voltage settings.

800-5301   PS-1 Filtered AC to DC Converter 13.95
800-5302   PS-2 Filtered & Regulated   22.95
AC to DC Converter
800-5305   PS-2A Adjustable Converter &   24.95
Regulator
800-9601   Inline Fuse Holder   2.00

TRACK POWER ADAPTERS

This miniature voltage regulator can power any Circuitron Strobe Flasher from track power. Can be used as a constant lighting kit in unpowered rolling stock. Sufficient to power any number of Circuitron Strobe Flashers if desired, or power two 1.5 volt grain of wheat or rice lamps connected in series. Bi-directional, output will be present if train is moving forward or backward. May be used with AC track power, although slightly irregular flashing may occur. The TP-1 measures 0.3 x 0.3 x 0.8".

800-2001   TP-1 Track Power Adapter   8.95

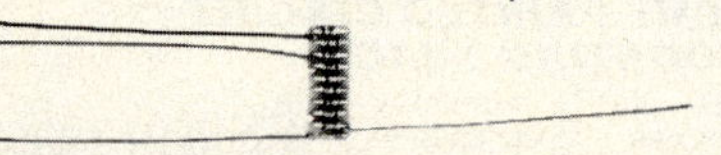

For powering the ML-1 Mars Light and Strobe. Has output that provides directional constant lighting; fits most HO locos, maximum 1 amp.

800-2002   TP-2 Track Power Adapter   9.95

Adjustable output (1.5 or 3.0v DC), for constant lighting source in unpowered cars. Powers Mars Flasher with low current can motors. Works with all forms of track power. Maximum 1/2 amp.

800-2003   TP-3 Track Power Adapter   14.95

SNAPPER, SWITCH MACHINE POWER SUPPLY

Designed to provide positive power to all dual-coil switch machines. Provides protection from burnout due to stuck pushbuttons, short circuits, etc. Operates off accessory terminals of power pack, or any 25 volt or less transformer. With a 24 volt input, it will activate between 5 and 10 switch machine coils simultaneously if they are connected to the same control. Recycle time is instantaneous. A section of Printed Circuit Mounting Track (PCMT) is included.

800-5303   SNAPPER Switch Machine   24.95
Power Supply
800-9350   3 Amp Diode for   pkg(2) 1.50
Matrix Control

ACCESSORIES

800-9351   1 amp Diode   pkg(6) 1.50
Opto-Sensors (.185" diameter) for use with all Circuitron Detection Circuits

800-9201   1 Opto-Sensor   each   3.95
800-9202   2 Opto-Sensors   pkg(2)   7.50
800-9206   6 Opto-Sensors   pkg(6)   19.95

Light Emitting Diodes (Super Bright)

Number	Color	Dia.	Pkg	Price
800-9301	Orange	.125"dia	pkg(2)	2.95
800-9302	Red	.125"dia	pkg(2)	2.95
800-9303	Yellow	.125"dia	pkg(2)	2.95
800-9304	Green	.125"dia	pkg(2)	2.95
800-9306	Red/Grn Bi-Color	.125"dia	ea	2.95
800-9311	Orange	.200"dia	pkg(2)	2.95
800-9312	Red	.200"dia	pkg(2)	2.95
800-9313	Yellow	.200"dia	pkg(2)	2.95
800-9314	Green	.200"dia	pkg(2)	2.95
800-9316	Red/Grn	.200"dia	ea	2.95
800-9321	Orange	.075"dia	pkg(2)	2.95
800-9322	Red	.075"dia	pkg(2)	2.95
800-9323	Yellow	.075"dia	pkg(2)	2.95
800-9324	Green	.075"dia	pkg(2)	2.95

Female .110" Solderless Connectors for all Circuitron Printed Circuit Boards

800-9602   .110" Female   pkg(6) 2.50
Solderless Connector, Non-Insulated
800-9603   .110" Female   pkg(6) 2.50
Solderless Connector, Insulated

CATALOG

800-9999   Catalog & Application Book   4.00

HO SCALE (1/87)

Easy-to-Assemble and assembled signals are prepainted plastic parts with preassembled components.

OPERATING ACCESSORIES

433-8203 Operating Switchman kit 16.25
w/Lighted Building
HO Scale Switchman emerges automatically from lighted shack as train nears, goes inside after last car passes. 9″ brass straight track included.

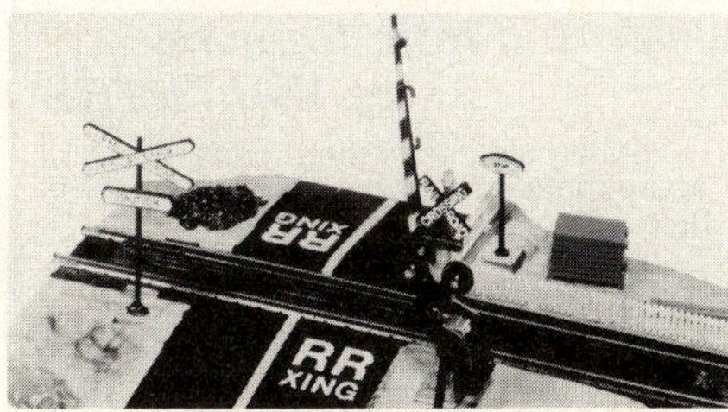

433-8209 Operating Crossing Gate kit 10.25
Gate lowers automatically as train nears, raises after last car crosses. 9″ brass straight track included.

SIGNAL

Operating signals include switches, wire and are self standing.

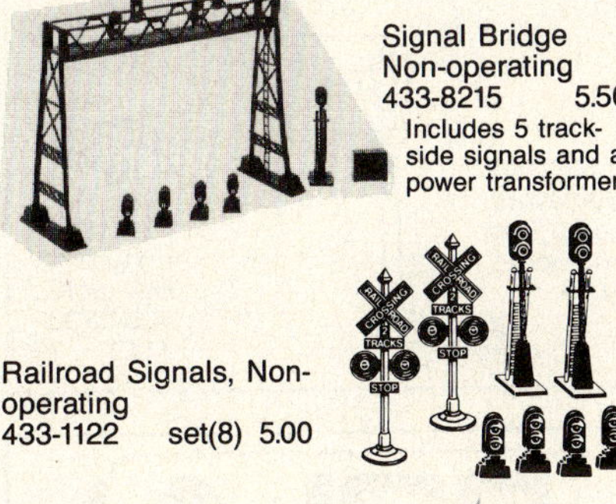

Signal Bridge
Non-operating
433-8215 5.50
Includes 5 track-side signals and a power transformer.

Railroad Signals, Non-operating
433-1122 set(8) 5.00

Operating Railroad Signal
433-1207 each 7.00

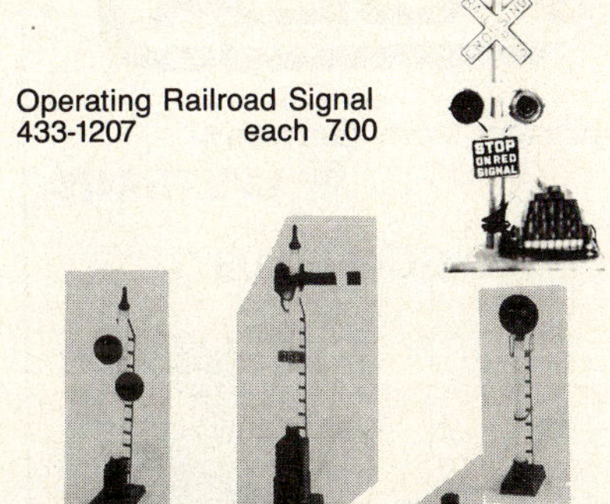

433-1262 Operating 2-Light Target 10.00
red/green
433-1261 Non-operating Light Semaphore 10.00
433-1263 Operating 3-Light Target 10.00
red/amber/green

OPERATING SIGNALS ASSORTMENT

433-1270 240.00
Includes 8 each of 1261, 1262, & 1263.
(By Special Order Only.)

LIGHT-UPS

Working lights are assembled.

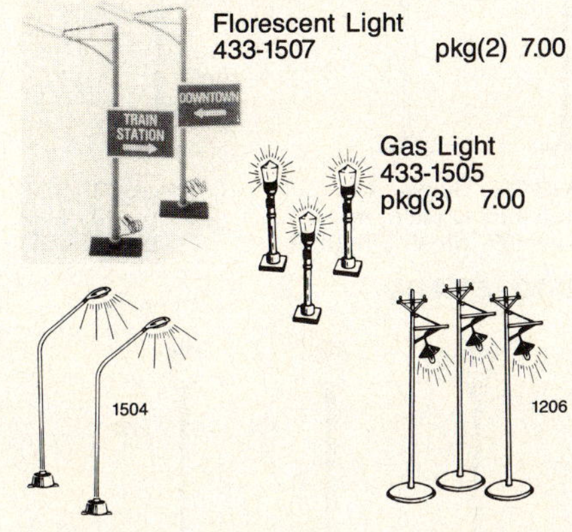

Florescent Light
433-1507 pkg(2) 7.00

Gas Light
433-1505
pkg(3) 7.00

433-1206 Light Pole pkg(3) 7.00
433-1504 Expressway Light pkg(2) 7.00

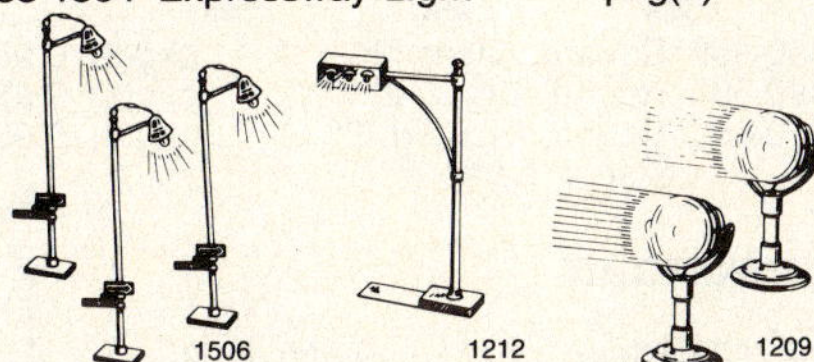

433-1506 Highway Light pkg(3) 7.00
433-1212 Blinking Traffic Light each 7.00
433-1209 Spot Lights pkg(2) 7.00
Double action swivels up and down and turns 360°

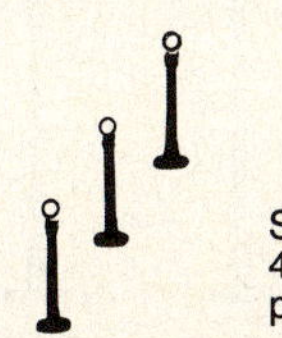

Street Lights
433-1208
pkg(3) 7.00

272-1655 with Switch pkg(2) 71.49
Micro-processor controlled traffic light electronics can operate four traffic lights. 12-16V AC/DC.

272-1656 less Switch pkg(2) 37.49
for use with operating switch in #272-1655.

HO SCALE (1/87)

Precolored plastic signals & traffic signs are non-operating (unless noted).

Block Signals
160-42101
pkg(4) 2.95

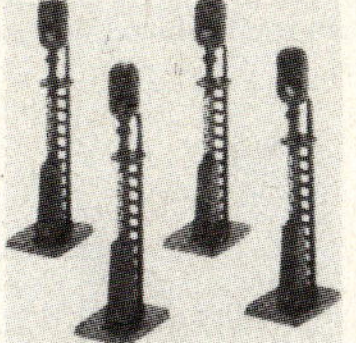

Railroad & Street Signs
160-42204
pkg(24) 4.00

Traffic Lights & Signs
160-42207
pkg(12) 4.00

Signal Bridge
160-45134 4.00

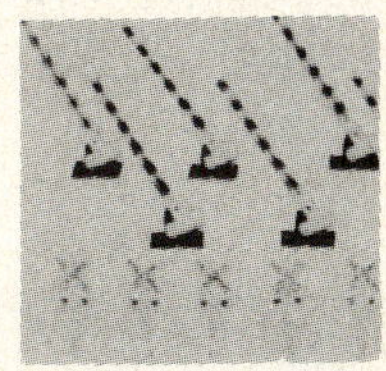

Crossing Signals & Gates (6 each)
160-42200
pkg(12) 4.00

		(not illustrated)	
160-42421	Lighted Crossing Signal	pkg(2)	9.95
160-42422	Lighted 2 Light Signal	pkg(2)	9.95
160-42423	Lighted 3 Light Signal	pkg(2)	9.95
160-42424	Lighted Target Signal	pkg(2)	9.95

SEMAPHORE

160-42432 Semaphore 9.95
160-42434 Three-Light Warning Signal 9.95

GRADE CROSSING

160-46214 Operating w/Light 25.00
160-42208 Non-operating 4.00

Dual Crossing Gate
160-46220 12.00

model power

HO SCALE (1/87)
Assembled signals and lights are operating, handcrafted brass, unless noted.

SIGNALS

BLOCK
490-1451 Block Signals   pkg(6) 4.98
Molded gray plastic; three green and three red signal lights and two relay cabinets. Non-operating.

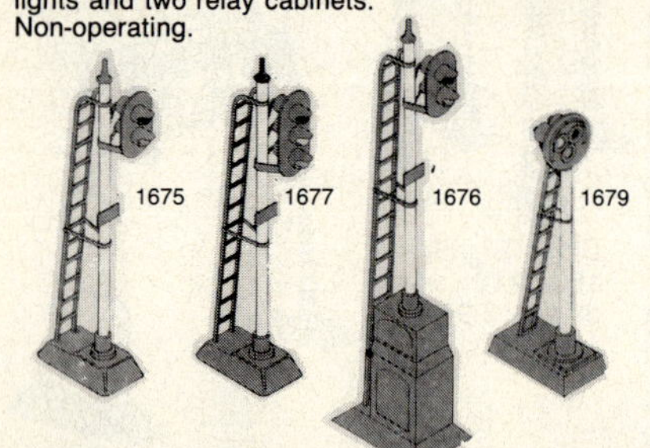

490-1675 2 Indication   8.98
490-1676 2 Indication with Relay   8.98
490-1677 3 Indication   8.98
490-1679 3 Indication   8.98

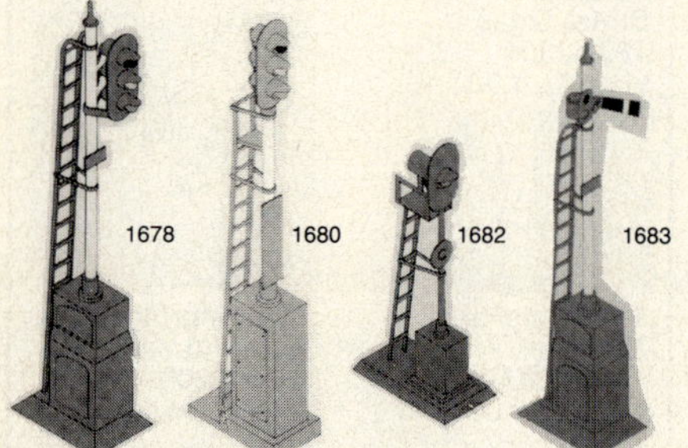

490-1678 3 Indication with Relay   8.98
490-1680 3-Indication   8.98
490-1682 2 Color with Relay   8.98

CROSSING

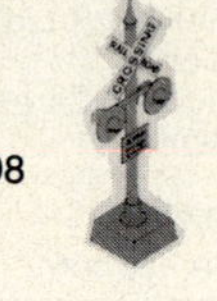

Crossing
490-1681
pkg(2) 8.98

LIGHTS

TRAFFIC
Includes 4-way slide switch and red, green & amber bulbs. Painted and prewired.

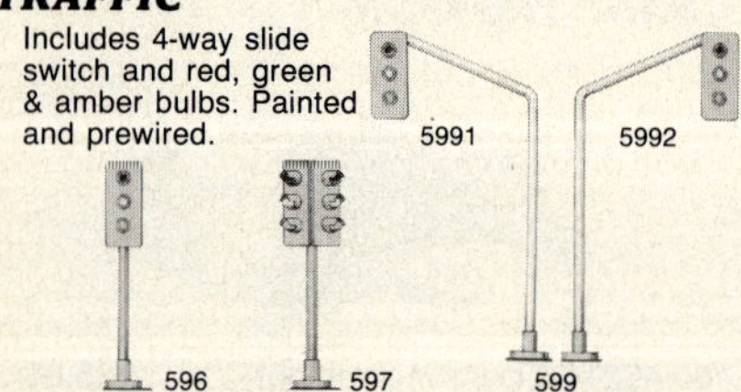

490-596   2-3 Way   each   9.98
490-597   1-6 Way   each   9.98
490-599   Left & Right   pkg(2) 12.98
490-5991 Left   each   6.98
490-5992 Right   each   6.98
(not illustrated)
490-5961 1-3 Way   each   6.98
(By Special Order Only.)

GAS
Clear, Small
1-1/2"
490-493   pkg(3) 6.98
Frosted, Small
1-1/2"
490-494   pkg(3) 6.98

HIGHWAY

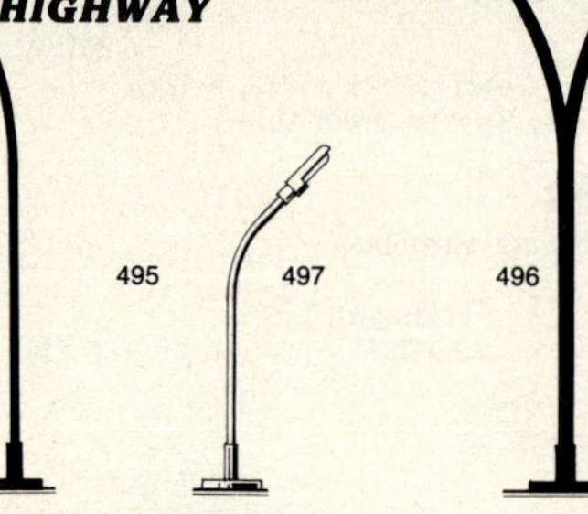

490-495   Single, 4"   pkg(3) 6.98
490-496   Double, 4"   pkg(2) 6.98
490-497   Small Single, 2-1/4"   pkg(3) 6.98

BOULEVARD

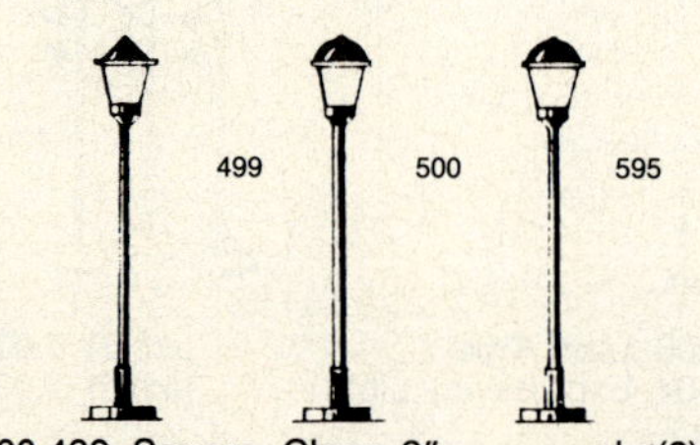

490-499   Square, Clear, 2"   pkg(3) 6.98
490-500   Round, Clear, 2"   pkg(3) 6.98
490-595   Round, Frosted, 2"   pkg(3) 6.98
          Station Lamp

SUBURBAN

490-593   Clear, 1-1/2"   pkg(3) 6.98
490-594   Frosted, 1-1/2" pkg(3) 6.98

MISCELLANEOUS

Globe Post Lamp, 2"
490-498   pkg(3) 6.98
Lighted Clock,
2-Sided
490-598   pkg(2) 6.98

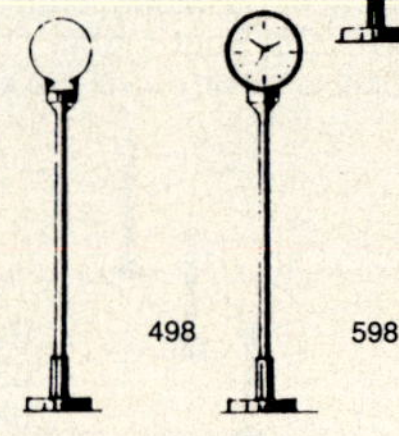

490-602 Building Interior Lighting Kit   9.00

490-603 Building Exterior/Lamp Post   9.00

CROSSINGS

GATE
490-1   Reverse Shuttle Unit   **NEW** 33.20
490-4161 Dual Auto   6.98

Master Creations

HO SCALE (1/87)
Non-operating, cast metal lamp post.

Undecorated
464-732   each 1.00

---

kibri
HO SCALE (1/87)

Imported from Germany by WALTHERS

Operating streetlamps are constructed of appropriately colored plastic and include bulb and wiring.

FLORESCENT LAMP

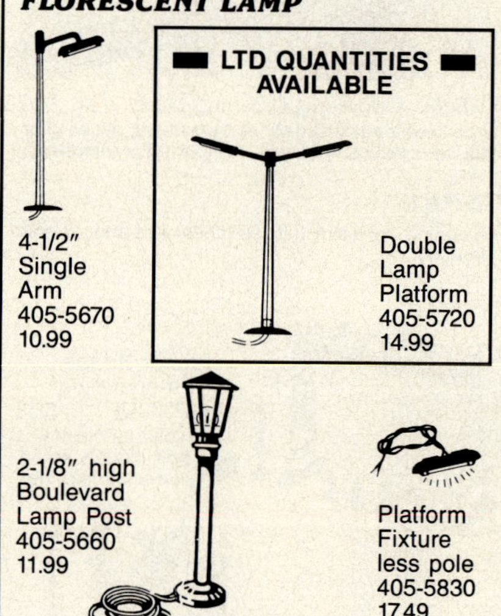

4-1/2"
Single
Arm
405-5670
10.99

Double
Lamp
Platform
405-5720
14.99

2-1/8" high
Boulevard
Lamp Post
405-5660
11.99

Platform
Fixture
less pole
405-5830
17.49

POLA

Imported from Germany by WALTHERS

HO SCALE (1/87)

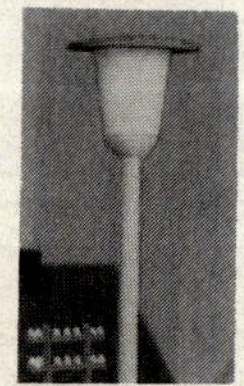

STREET LAMP
Operating; plastic construction. Each includes 2 street lamps and 6 telegraph poles. 14-19V.

578-70 Street Lamp Set   6.49

N.J. International

HO SCALE (1/87)

OPERATING SIGNALS

Signals are of brass construction, assembled, painted and wired with bulbs (unless noted).

BLOCK SIGNALS

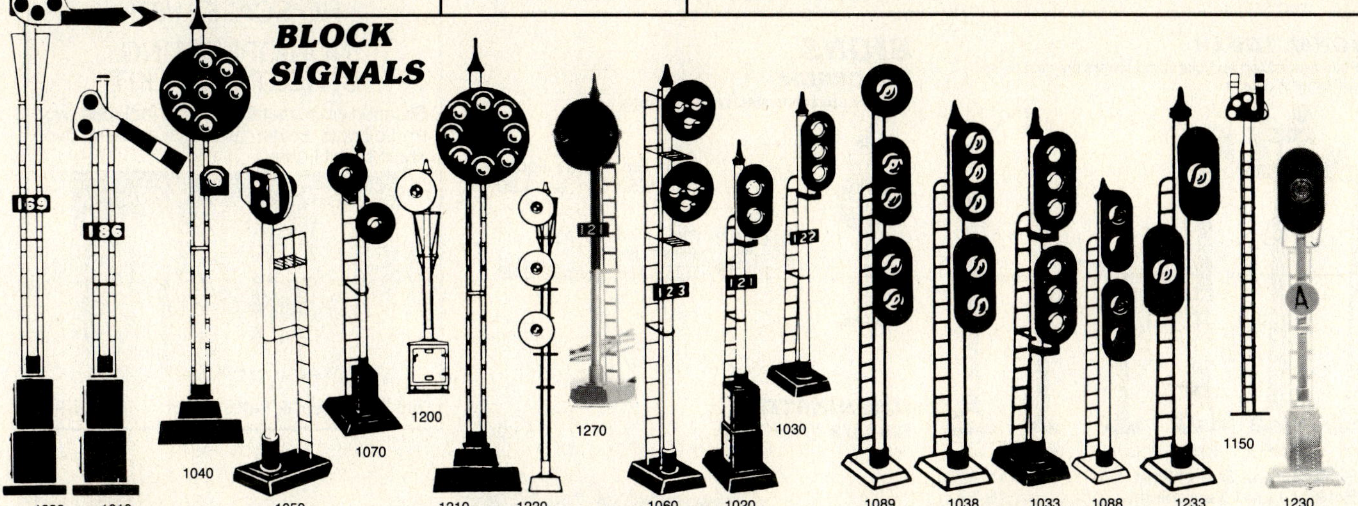

SEMAPHORE
525-1000	3 Light	32.99
525-1010	2 Light	28.99

TARGET
525-1040	8 Light, PRR	32.99
525-1050	3 Light, Hooded	17.99
525-1070	1 Light, Double	17.99
525-1200	1 Light w/Relay Base	22.99
525-1210	8 Light, B&O	29.99
525-1220	3 Light	17.99

CROSSING & SOUND SYSTEMS
525-8021	Sound Module	29.99
525-8119	Sound – Flasher with Signal	54.99

This module is to flash crossing signal lamps alternately at a rate of 80-90 times per minute. Can be joined with a signal system for automatic operation. (Max 200 mA.)

525-8219	Sound-Flasher w/N Signal	54.99
525-8022	Flasher – Sound Module	37.99

(By Special Order Only.)

CROSSING FLASHER
Designed for 12-16v operation on both AC or DC current. It will alternately light up two GOW or GOR bulbs or any similar loads. The two lights will flash at a realistic rate of 80 times per minute.

Flasher Unit Only
525-8020
18.99

(see diagram for item #1090)

HIGHWAY CROSSING SIGNAL

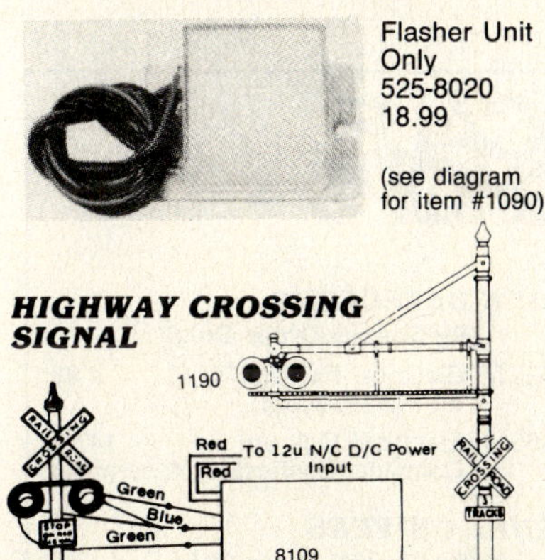

525-1090	Cross Buck	14.49
525-8109	#1090 w/Flasher Unit #8020	31.99
525-1190	Over-Road Crossing Signal	32.99

(middle column signals)
525-1270		2 Light, N&W	16.99
525-1280		3 Light, Triple	32.99
525-1060		3 Light, Double	28.99
525-10411		Pennsylvania	25.95

SINGLE BOARD
525-1020	2 Light w/Relay Base	16.99
525-1023	3 Light w/Relay Base	15.99
525-1031	3 Light, black	15.99
525-1032	3 Light, silver	15.99
525-1081	2 Light, black	14.99
525-1082	2 Light, silver	14.99

525-1160	Cross Buck w/Gate	**NEW** TBA
525-1170	Automatic Crossing Gates, red and white	27.95
525-1171	Automatic Crossing Gates, black and white	27.95
525-1240	RR Crossing Warning Sign	pkg(2) 5.99
525-1260	Crossbucks	pkg(2) 5.99

SIGNAL SYSTEMS

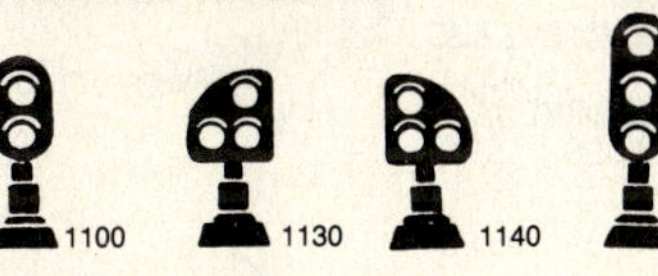

Easy to install signal system allows one control module to light up to four 50ma 12v DC bulbs at one time, in any combination. Activated by sensors, installs without rail gaps or blocks.

2-LIGHT SYSTEM
Red-green
525-8300	Signal Module w/Sensor	29.99
525-8318	Signal System w/HO Signal	43.99

3-LIGHT SYSTEM
Red-amber-green
525-8330	Signal Module w/2 Sensors	45.99
525-8331	w/HO Signal	55.99

ACTIVATING SENSORS
525-8301	CDS Sensor	each 3.59
525-8306	CDS Sensor	pkg(6) 19.99

MISCELLANEOUS

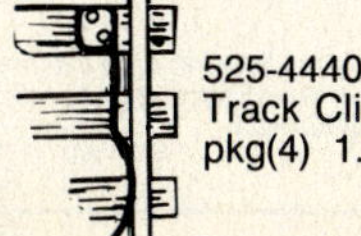

525-1820	Relay Box pkg(2)	4.99
525-4440	Track Clips pkg(4)	1.99

DOUBLE BOARD
525-1089	1 Target, 2 Light	37.99
525-1038	3 Light over 2 Light	27.99
525-1033	3 Light over 3 Light	27.99
525-1088	2 Light over 2 Light	24.99
525-1233	1 Light over 1 Light	37.99

MISCELLANEOUS
525-1150	Train Order Board	21.99
525-1230	1 Light Board w/Base	19.99
525-9060	Signal LED, red pkg(3)	3.59
525-9061	Signal LED, yellow pkg(3)	3.59
525-9062	Signal LED, green pkg(3)	3.59
525-1887	Ladders, Standard-Brass pkg(2)	3.99

GROUND SIGNAL
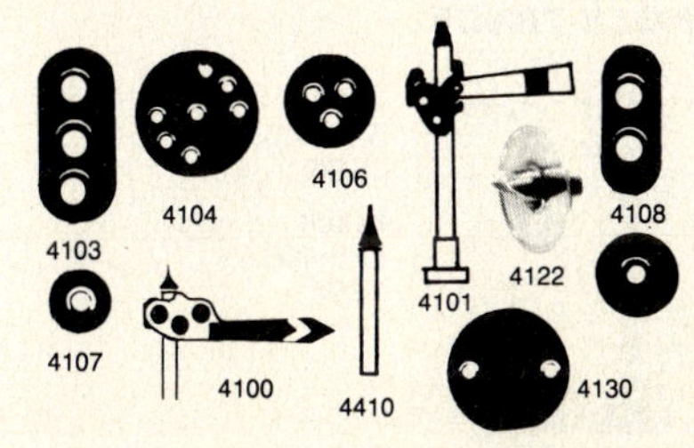

525-1100	2 Light	8.99
525-1110	3 Light	7.99
525-1130	3 Light, Left Hand	9.99
525-1140	3 Light, Right Hand	9.99

SIGNAL DISC HEADS

Use Signal Disc Heads on signal bridges and for making combination signals (brass construction).

525-4101	2 Light Semaphore	4.99
525-4100	3 Light Semaphore	5.99
525-4104	8 Light Target, PRR	3.49
525-4106	3 Light Target	1.99
525-4107	1 Light Small Target	1.59
525-4122	1 Light Large Target	1.59
525-4130	2 Light Large Target	1.59
525-4103	3 Light Board	1.99
525-4108	2 Light Board	1.99
525-4410	Signal Mounting Stem pkg(4)	2.99

N.J. International

HO SCALE (1/87)

OPERATING SIGNALS, SIGNS & LIGHTS

Signals and signs are of brass construction, assembled, painted and wired with bulbs (unless noted). Street lights are appropriately colored plastic, assembled and wired with bulbs.

SIGNAL TOWER

Fully assembled and operating towers are cast plastic with metal details.

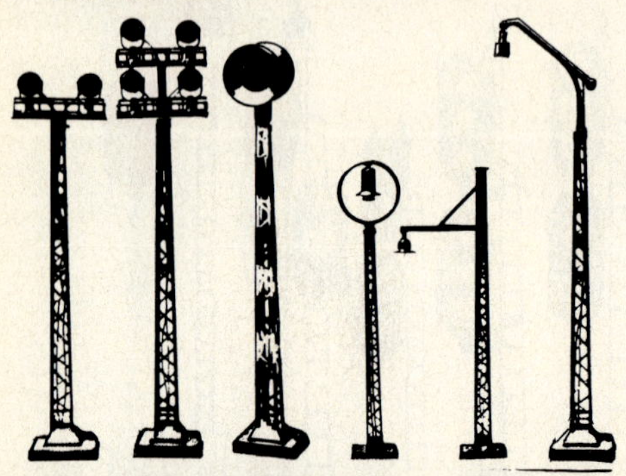

1972 1973 1974 1976 1977 1975

525-1972	Twin Searchlight	11.99
525-1973	Quad Searchlight	16.99
525-1974	Microwave	10.99
525-1975	Yard Tower Light	10.99
525-1976	Yard Tower Light Loop (steel)	9.99
525-1977	Yard Light	9.99

SIGNAL BRIDGE **NEW**

Easy-assemble plastic kit with scale handrails, open walkways and platforms, plus prototypical square bar construction.

525-4006 Double-Track "I-Beam" Type   12.95

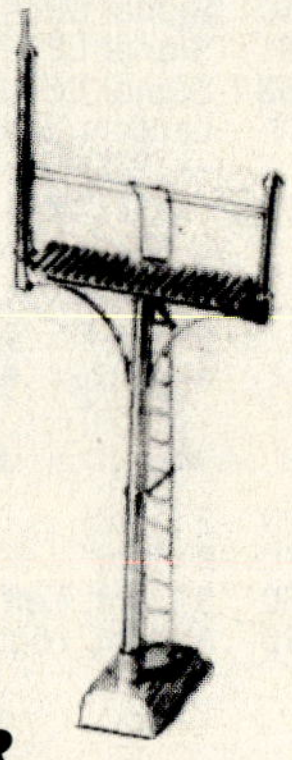

VERTICAL SIGNAL BRIDGES

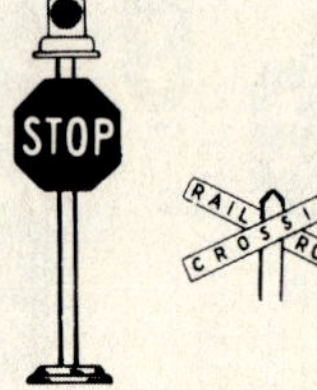

Assembled
525-4030   15.99
Kit
525-4039   8.99

SHORT BRIDGE

525-6179 Short   3.99

CANTILEVER SIGNAL BRIDGE

Injection-molded plastic kits

SINGLE TRACK

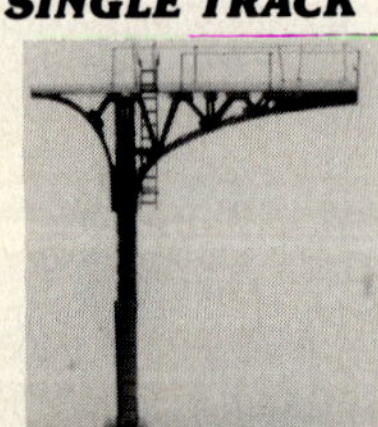

Silver
525-4001
10.95

Black
525-4002
10.95

DOUBLE TRACK

Silver
525-4003
11.95

Black
525-4004
11.95

SIGNS

TRACKSIDE

Signs are prepainted brass castings.

Stop Sign w/red light
525-1250   ea 8.99

RR Crossing Sign
(less posts)
525-4126   pkg(3) 2.99

1250

ILLUMINATED

525-1979 "A&P" Sign   5.99

STREET LIGHTS

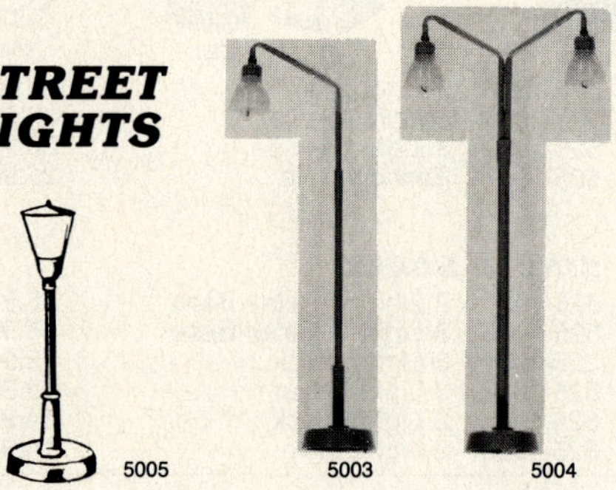

5005   5003   5004

525-5005	Street Light	6.99
525-5003	Single Arm	9.99
525-5004	Double Arm	13.99
525-1980	Gas Street Lamp pkg(3)	6.99

BOULEVARD LAMP

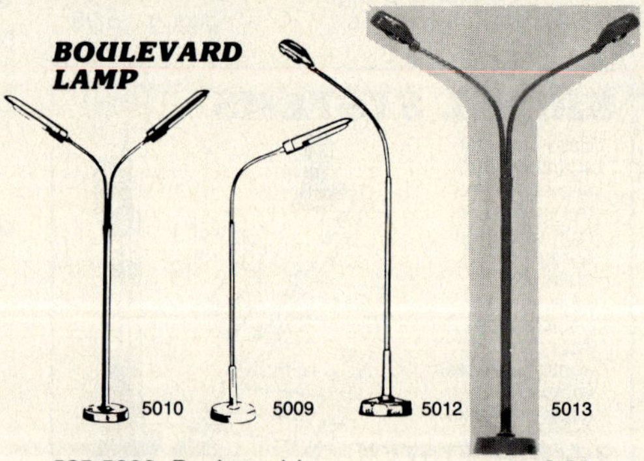

5010   5009   5012   5013

525-5009	Boulevard Lamp	9.99
525-5010	Double Arm	10.99
525-5012	Tall	6.99
525-5013	Tall, Double Arm	10.99

TRAFFIC SIGNAL

Plastic and metal construction, wired for illumination. Yellow light flashes.

Traffic Signal
525-1978
9.99

Items listed in *blue ink* may not be available at all times. Please see your dealer for current delivery information.

WOODLAND SCENICS

HO SCALE (1/87)
NON-OPERATING STREET LIGHT KIT

Detailed white metal castings. Includes two traffic lights, seven tall single arm and two short street lights.

785-248 Street & Traffic Lights   5.98

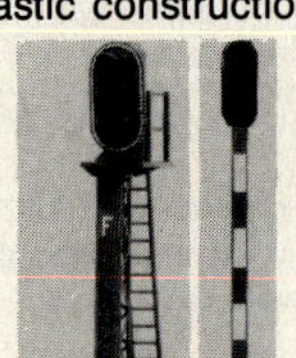

Roco

Imported from Austria by WALTHERS

HO SCALE (1/87)

Operating, assembled signals feature pre-colored plastic construction and easy installation.

Light
625-40021
16.99
SNCF Style

2 Light Distant
625-40020
12.49

SCALE SHOPS

HO SCALE (1/87)

BLOCK DETECTORS

(By Special Order Only)

649-5510	Electrical Pick up, on Panel/Layout	4.98
649-5511	Electrical Pick up, Computer Connection, Assembled	14.98

SIGNAL DRIVERS

(By Special Order Only)

LED or Light, Red-Green-Yellow, one wire to track.

649-5610	2 Signal	kit	3.98
649-5611	2 Signal	assembled	13.98

"N"-WAY PRODUCTS

HO SCALE (1/87)

OPERATING SIGNALS

CROSSING SIGNAL

Typical of many railroad standard crossing signals. Can be operated manually, mechanically or automatically by the Track Detection Kit listed. The Flasher is powered by two 9 volt batteries or the Power Supply Kit listed and will operate up to six signals at one time. Signals can only be used with the approved flasher.

535-151 With Flasher   pkg(2) 19.95
535-152 Signals Only   pkg(2) 14.95
535-155 Two Directions pkg(2) 24.95

Same as #151, except each signal has two crossbucks and lights that flash in both directions.

BOULEVARD CROSSING

Stylized overhead "flashing" signal. Because of the number of lights on the signals, additional flashing crossing signals should not be used with this unit's flasher. The flasher is powered by two 9 volt batteries or the Power Supply Kit listed.

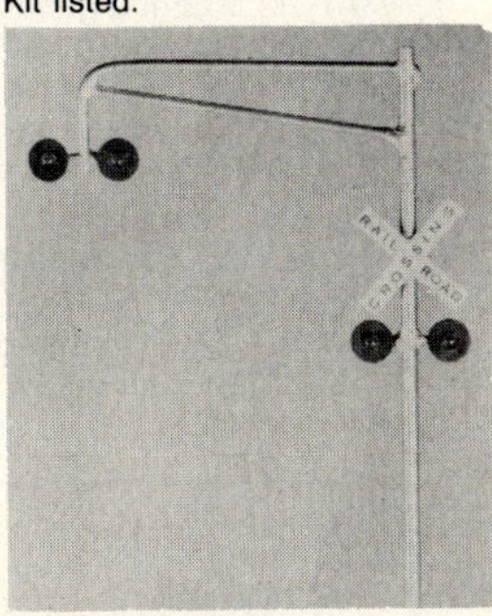

Boulevard Crossing
535-251
pkg(2) 24.95

RAILROAD CROSSING BELL

3″ bell provides a loud, clear tone to be used with warning signals. Kit requires assembly of 110 volt components (included). Bell will operate in conjunction with the train detector, #535-400.

535-191   Railroad Crossing Bell   19.95

SEARCHLIGHT SIGNAL

These signals are used to indicate location and condition of manual or automatic blocks. #351 shines either green or red. #352 shows either both reds on for stop or no light for go. Power supply must be 12 volt DC supply. Dropping resistors, brass ladder stock included.

535-351 Green-Red pkg(2) 12.95
535-352 Red-Red   pkg(2) 8.95
535-353 Red   pkg(2) 7.95

535-354 Green-Yellow-Red   pkg(2) 14.95
Each color is separately controlled.

POWER SUPPLY KIT

This kit will eliminate the two 9 volt batteries necessary to power the "N"-Way "Flashing" Crossing Signals. One power supply kit will power 4 sets of signals. This kit will also power the "N"-Way Train Detection Kit. Requires 110 volts input.

535-425 Power Supply Kit   12.95

MANHOLE COVER/FIRE HYDRANDT

535-855 Manhole Cover/Fire   pkg(5) 1.95
         Hydrandt

TRAIN DETECTION KIT

This kit will operate all "N"-Way signals and other signals in N or HO. It will make two complete detection units that will activate signals at two locations anywhere on your layout. Magnets are used to activate reed switches you mount in the tracks. This kit requires soldering skills. Magnets, reed switches and wiring instructions included. (Semi-automatic).

Can also be used for automatic block control. Be advised that automatic block control requires extensive technical knowledge and a number of Track Detection Kits.

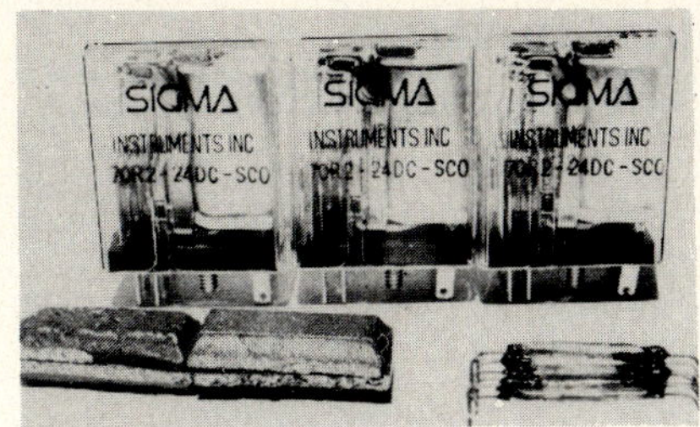

535-400 Train Detection Kit   12.95

TOMAR INDUSTRIES

HO SCALE (1/87)

Assembled signals are painted and wired with bulbs or LEDs and feature brass construction. Complete instructions included. Illustrations not to scale.

SWITCH STAND

Switch Stand
081-851   11.45

Finished in black with red and green lenses, red & white target blades. Illuminated with 1.5v bulb, rotates 360 degrees.

90° Operator
081-848   5.95

Assembled, links switch-machine to switchstand, indexes to 90°.

BLOCK SIGNAL

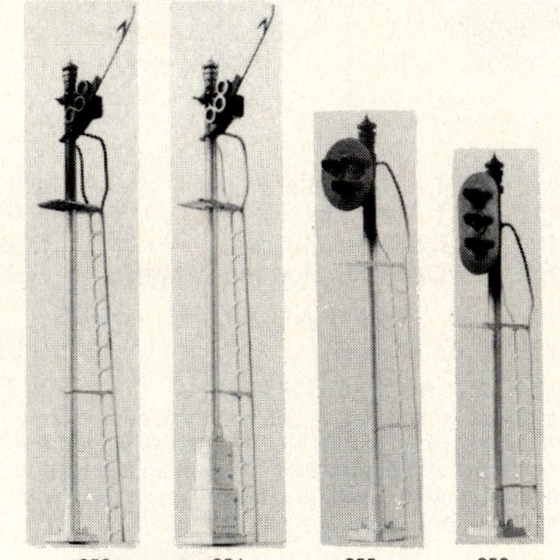

853   854   855   856

081-853 3-position Semaphore   19.45
         1.5v bulb

081-854 3-position Semaphore   20.95
         w/relay box for base, 1.5v bulb

081-849 Operating Mechanism   24.95
         for Semaphore #853 & 854

Allows three position stop of semaphore arm. Uses Switchman motor for slow motion operation. Includes instructions and mounting screws.

081-855 Target with LEDs   16.95

STREET LIGHTS

Gas Street Lights
535-851
pkg(5) 19.95
Turn of the century style, yellow light

FLICKERING FLAMES

Flickering Flames can be used to simulate fires in buildings, sheds and homes. This hearth lighting unit is a solid state device made to flash two sets of dual LED's to simulate the flames. Requires 12 volt transformer.

535-901 Flickering Flames Kit   19.95

DWARF SIGNAL

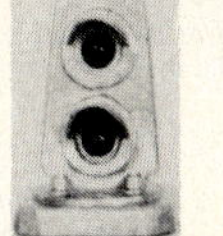

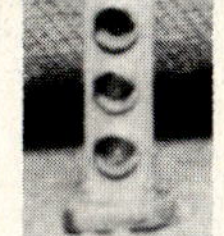

Two Light
081-852   7.45
Green over red with black finish

Three Light
081-850   9.45
Red, yellow and green LED's

FLASHER UNIT

NEW

081-823
9.95

VERTICAL SIGNAL

Two Light w/LED's
081-857   15.45

Three Light w/LED's
081-856   16.95

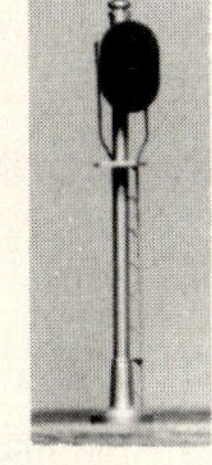

857

SEARCHLIGHT SIGNAL

3 color from one LED.

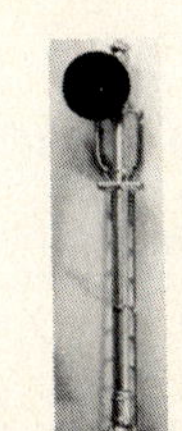

Single Head
081-858
each
22.95

Double Head
081-859
each
30.45

See also: PASSENGER CARS, TRACTION, FREIGHT CARS and TRACK sections for additional TOMAR products.

OREGON RAIL SUPPLY

HO SCALE (1/87)
Flexible system of signal heads, LEDs and accessories can be used to create a variety of working signals. All parts are molded in black styrene and can be illuminated using LEDs or fiber optics.

SIGNAL BRIDGE

Signal Bridge
538-101 12.95
Chesapeake & Ohio prototype at Peach Creek, West Virginia. Can be installed on single or double track and includes wire handrails and assembly instructions.

Union Pacific/ D&RGW
538-99
kit 19.95
Includes hooded UP targets, LED's and resistors.

(not illustrated)
538-129 Single Searchlite Unit NEW 12.95
2 complete targets with LED's and for mounting on signal bridge.

"SEARCHLIGHT" SIGNAL LIGHT TARGETS
Each set includes three heads with brackets and finales. Introduced in 1920's and still in use on many railroads.

538-102	Single	pkg(3) 3.95
538-103	Double	pkg(3) 4.50
538-104	Triple	pkg(3) 4.50

"POSITION LIGHT" SIGNAL HEADS
Models are based on signal heads used by specific roads and their affiliates. Each includes accessories. Commonly used by eastern railroads, these signals were introduced in 1915 and use lights in various positions to prevent misreading signals.

538-105	Pennsylvania/N&W	pkg(6) 7.95
538-106	Baltimore & Ohio	pkg(3) 5.95
538-107	NYC/Rock Island	pkg(3) 4.50

SAMPLER SET
Includes one of each type of signal head, with bases, walkway grating, brackets and more.

538-108 Sampler Kit 7.95

LIGHT EMITTING DIODES
Correctly sized for press fit in signal heads.

538-109	Green	.088 square	pkg(3) 2.95
538-110	Red	.088 square	pkg(3) 2.95
538-111	Yellow	.088 square	pkg(3) 2.95

(not illustrated)
538-126 Red/Green NEW pkg(2) 4.95
3mm diameter (1/8"). LED's change color when polarity is reversed.

CROSSBUCKS
Kit includes two each of 60 and 90 degree crossbucks. White styrene.

538-112 Railroad Crossbucks pkg(4) 4.95

SIGNAL LIGHTS

538-122	1 Dwarf	8.95
538-123	2 Dwarf	7.50

Two single-light dwarf signals with two-color LED's that turn red or green depending on polarity.

BLOCK SIGNALS
Each kit builds a complete signal, with target, mast, ladder, base and finale. Small LED's and resistors also included.

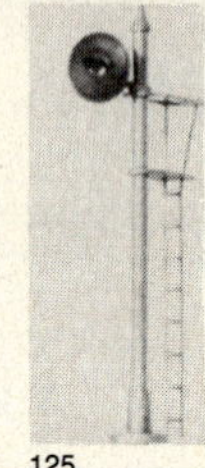

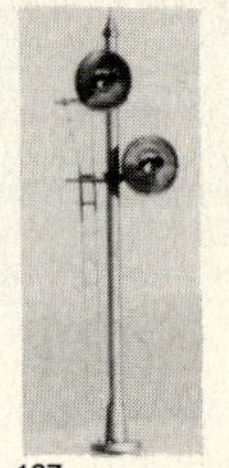

125   127

538-125	Single	**NEW**	9.95
538-127	2 Target Single	**NEW**	15.95
538-128	3 Color Single	**NEW**	34.95
538-303	3 Color Driver Circuit	**NEW**	27.95

Circuit used in #128. Converts any 2 color LED signal to 3 color with a simple wiring change. Circuit will operate on an input voltage range of 9 to 15 volts DC.

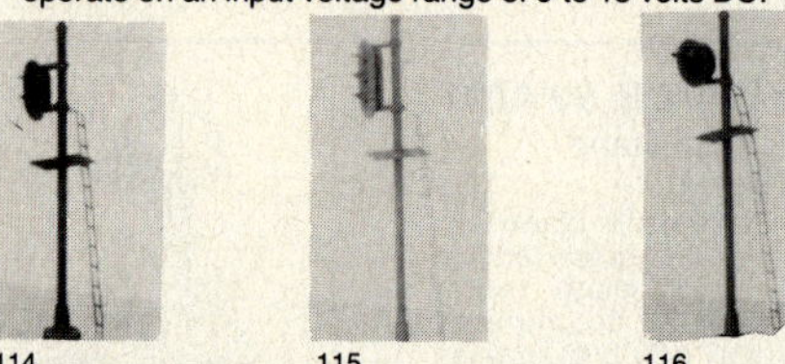

114   115   116

538-114	Two Light	6.95
538-115	Three Light	7.95
538-116	Three Light-Circular	7.95

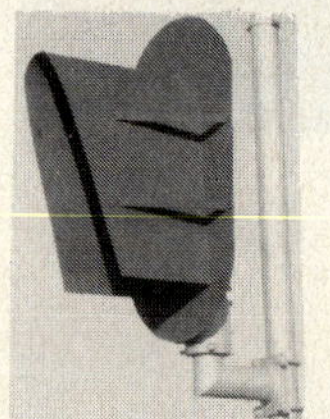

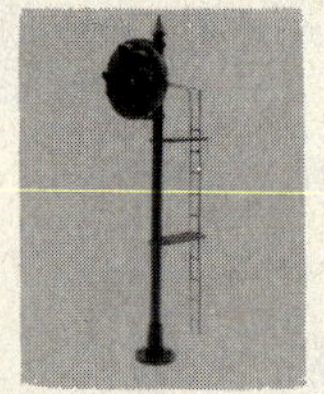

121   117

538-117	PRR Intermediate	15.95
538-118	PRR Absolute	15.95
538-120	UP/D&RGW Hooded	8.95
538-121	UP/D&RGW Hooded Target	5.95

(not illustrated)
538-119	B&O Absolute	19.95
538-124	Diode Logic Board	4.95

This device is required to operate the Pennsylvania style signals, #117 and 118. The unit activates the center lamp and is designed to be used between a detection system and the signal. Assembled with logic circuit and resistor to drive the signal.

CROSSING FLASHERS
Crossing Flasher
538-113 pkg(2) 15.98
Easy-to-build with targets, crossbucks, base, mast, red LED's and decals.

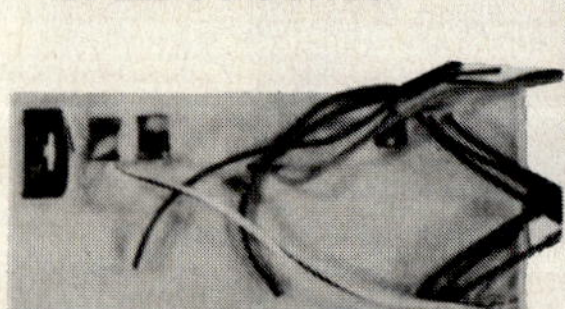

538-301 Detector/Flasher Circuit NEW 34.95
Senses the approach of trains from either direction to start crossing flashers (available separately). Each unit powers up to 8 LED's and installs in a few minutes. Requires two 9-volt batteries.

Switchmaster

Division of Builders-In-Scale

SWITCH MACHINE

Switch Machine
169-1001
14.95

169-1006 Switch Machine pkg(6) 86.00
Slow motion switch machine operates on 12V DC. Provides positive rail contact. Mounting diagram and linkage included. Can be used in all scales.

169-1101 Power Routing Contact 2.98
Adds a boost of power for "lazy" turnout points.

ACCESSORIES
169-1102 Panel Lighting Basic Kit 1.89
Includes two pairs of LEDs (red and green), resistors and instructions.

169-1103 Panel Lighting Dual Color 2.98
One pair LEDs (green and red) with resistors.

169-1104 Signal Kit .79
Converts power from switch machine #1001 for use with signals.

169-1105 LED Mounting Ring pkg(6) 1.29
Mounting rings for use with LEDs in #1001 and #1002.

MODEL MASTERPIECES LTD

HO SCALE (1/87)
NON-OPERATING SIGNALS

Unpainted metal castings shown actual size.

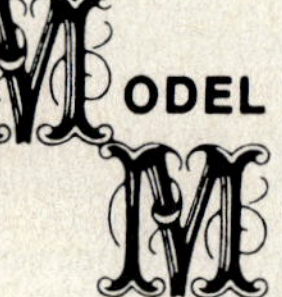

3 Position
Upper Quadrant
485-384
pkg(2 sets)
2.25

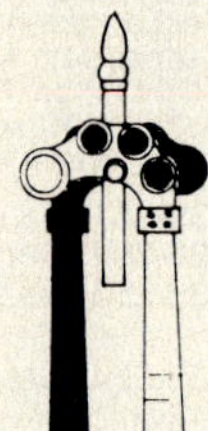

3 Position
Lower Quadrant
485-302
pkg(4) 2.00

Wabash Valley

HO SCALE SIGNAL PARTS
Die cast metal unless noted.

SEMAPHORE BLADE
Includes lamp housing and colored lenses.

■ LTD QTY AVAILABLE ■

772-683 Round End each 1.50

TRAIN TRONICS

- Automatic Reversing Circuit
- Automatic Turnout Control
- Grade Crossing Flasher
- Crossing Control with Bell
- Switches
- Chase Lights
- Progressive Light Kits

AUTOMATIC REVERSING CIRCUIT

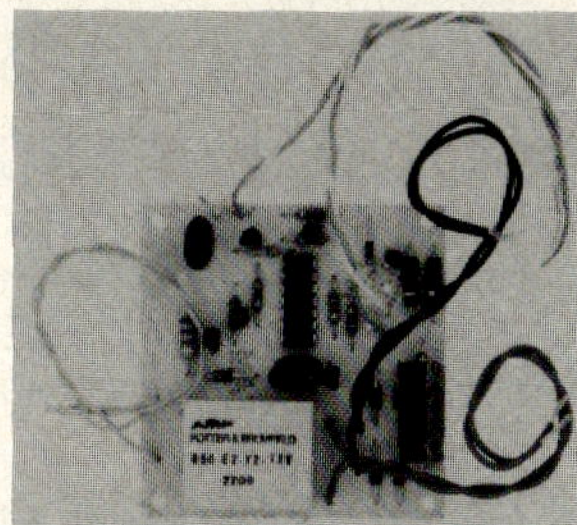

723-601 Automatic Reversing Circuit   36.95
Solid state automatic reversing of your locomotives on any predetermined length of track can be accomplished with this kit. Track reversing length can be adjusted by the placement of the magnetic sensors. No need to replace existing trackage. Works with any type of rail power.

AUTOMATIC TURNOUT CONTROL

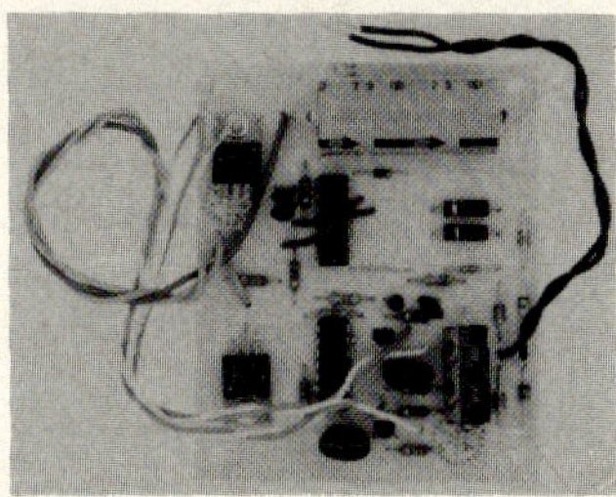

723-602 Automatic Turnout Control   32.95
Can alternate your locomotives route of travel through the layout, and throw two turnouts simultaneously.

When used in conjuction with the #601 Automatic Reversing Circuit, it incorporates all of its features, plus permitting reverse operation on alternate sidings and automatic reverse loops.

SWITCHES

723-406 Reed Switch & Magnet   pkg(2) 5.95
Provides momentary switch that is activated by magnets placed on bottom of train. Use to operate various track detection systems, controls and signals.

723-407 Pushbutton   pkg(4) 5.95
SPST—normally open, momentary, mounts in 5/16″ hole.

GRADE CROSSING FLASHER

Signal Flasher
723-501   14.95

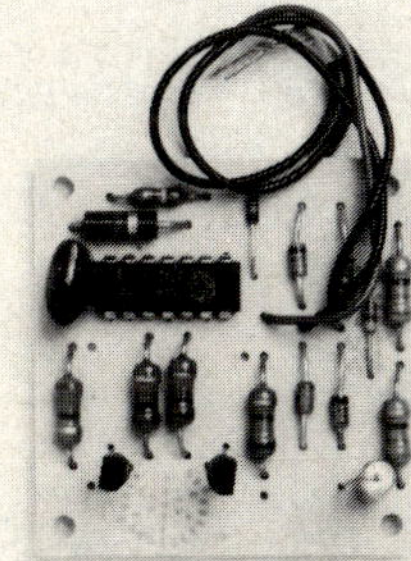

Solid state crossing flasher module for use with Train Tronics #505 bulb or #510 LED crossing signals.

Operates on 6 to 16 volts AC or DC 2″ circuit board. This unit will run several sets of crossing signals with the proper switching set up.

723-502 Crossing Activator   19.95
Connects to #501 Flasher for realistic operation. Crossing signals turn on as train approaches crossing and remain flashing until train has passed. Placement of sensors on track allows operation in either direction. Includes built and tested solid state printed circuit, magnets and magnet sensors.

CROSSING SIGNAL

Crossing Signal (Bulb)
723-505   pkg(2) 8.95
Use in conjunction with #501 Signal Flasher for true signal action. 2-1/4″ high.

Crossing Signal (LED)
723-510   pkg(2) 8.95
Use in conjunction with #501 Signal Flasher for true signal action. 2-1/4″ high.

CROSSING CONTROL WITH BELL

723-515 Crossing Control w/Bell   29.95
Allows for crossing signals and electronic bell to be turned off and on automatically as train enters and leaves crossing area. This unit is bi-directional and comes complete with track detector, crossing flasher, electronic bell and speaker. This unit for LED crossing signals only. (#723-510 suggested crossing signals).

CHASE LIGHT

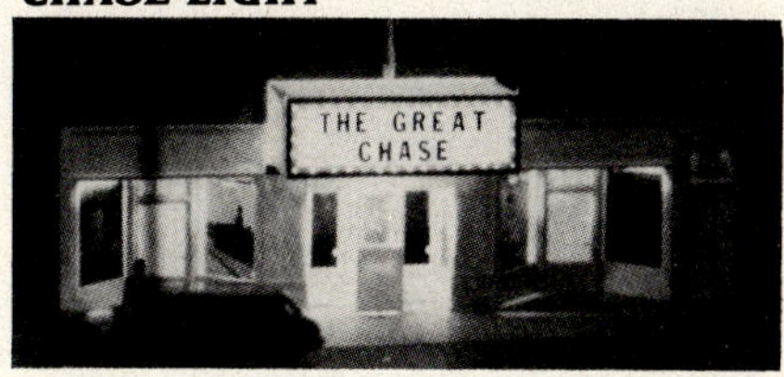

723-201 Sign Border Chase Light Kit   29.95
Kit includes all materials needed to add an action light marquee to movie theater, car dealership, restaurant, taverns, etc. Tiny tips of light, via fiber optics, chase around the sign to provide light action to the building and model city. The kit comes complete with sign material, prebuilt circuit board, and enough fiber optics to build a 36 light sign. Use 12-16 volt DC power supply (not included). Completed sign operates either in a chasing mode or alternating mode; your selection at the push of a button. To expand the kit to 72 lights, use #723-401 fiber optic kit.

PROGRESSIVE LIGHT KIT

723-205 Progressive Light Kit   39.95
Up to nine lights turn on in sequence, one at a time. When all bulbs are illuminated they turn off and repeat the sequence. Use it as a sign to identify factories, banks, motels, restaurants and many other structures. Kit is complete with all prebuilt electronics, plastic sign front, stick-on letters and all parts necessary to assemble sign.

International Hobby Corp.

CROSSING GATES

348-422300 Assorted   pkg(12) 3.98
            Railroad Crossings
    Contains 6 grade crossings and 6 one-lane crossings.

SIGNALS   NEW

348-4422 3 Aspect	pkg(12)	2.98
348-4423 3 Aspect Triangular	pkg(12)	2.98
348-4424 3 A Sun Bonnet	pkg(12)	2.98

UTAH PACIFIC
MODEL RAILROAD PRODUCTS
HO OPERATING SIGNALS & LIGHTS

MARKER LIGHT
Marker light kit comes with bulbs as shown.
Marker Light Kit
1.5 Volt

755-64   pair 10.45

SWITCH STAND
Non-Illuminated
755-89   5.95
    assembled

SWITCH STAND LANTERN
755-86   3.00
Consist of one lantern casting and four jewels; two red and two green.

ILLUMINATED LANTERN
Illuminated Lantern
755-95 1.5 Volt   kit 7.95

Illustration is approximately 3 times actual size.

JEWELS
755-56 Clear	pkg(12)	1.50
755-57 Red	pkg(12)	1.50
755-58 Green	pkg(12)	1.50
755-59 Yellow	pkg(12)	1.50

Tru-Scale Models

HO SCALE (1/87)

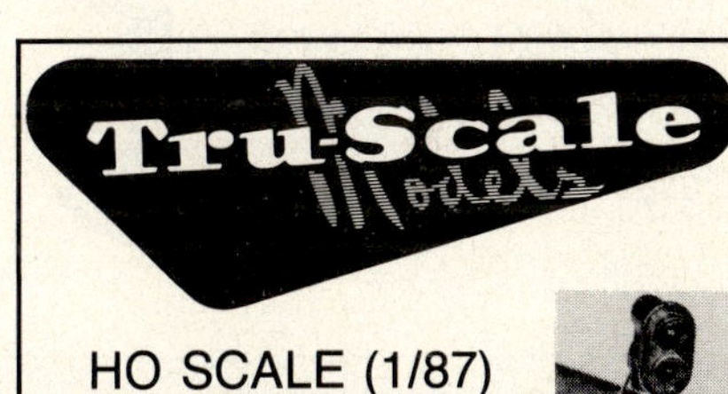

ASSEMBLED SIGNAL
Wired with electrical binding posts for use with any signal control system. Red and green 12-16 volt pea bulbs are installed.

Two-Color Signal
730-1410   10.60
730-1409 Dwarf Signal   8.40   1410

HO SCALE (1/87)

SIGNAL BRIDGES   NEW
348-5011 Pennsylvania	pkg(12)	19.98
348-5012 Baltimore & Ohio	pkg(12)	19.98
348-5013 Norfolk & Western	pkg(12)	19.98
348-5014 Union Pacific/	pkg(12)	19.98
Denver & Rio Grande		

BLINKING BEACONS   NEW
348-5200 Light Red	9.98
348-5201 Light Yellow	9.98

WALTHERS

HO SCALE CRAFT TRAIN KITS

Signals are die cast metal. Special signal ladders are brass.

DWARF UNITS

Single castings require no assembly or painting. Bulbs have 6″ pigtails, color coded for ease in installation.

753	692	651

933-753 Two Indication   4.29
933-692 Single Indication w/Base   3.29
933-651 Two Indication w/Base   4.29

NOTE: Signals include appropriately colored grain-o-wheat bulbs. LEDs (light emitting diodes) also can be used.

DIFFERENT WAYS TO USE DWARFS

Dwarf signals are normally used to control the movement of trains in yards, but because of their realistic size, ease of application and low cost, Walthers Dwarfs lend themselves to a variety of uses on a model railroad. They can be used for city stop lights, pillar signals, bridge signals, headlights and tail signs, mine, factory or stadium floodlights, or for control panel indicators. They may also be combined to make triangular and taller units.

WARNING SIGNAL

As with all Walthers signals, this warning signal is designed for realistic operation.

Raised letters on the die cast signs are prepainted. Kit includes 12v bulbs with 6″ color coded pigtails.

Highway Warning Signal
933-597   7.98

GROUND UNIT

The Walthers Ground Units come in kit form requiring simple assembly, but the finished items are well worth the effort. Kit includes 12v bulb with 6″ color coded pigtails and new brass ladders.

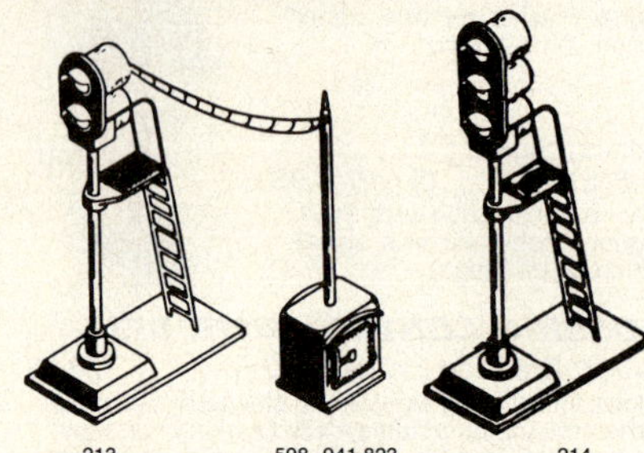

213	598, 941-823	214

933-213 2-Indication Ground Unit   each 5.29
933-214 3-Indication Ground Unit   each 6.29

OLD TIME STREET LAMP

These operating lamps can be used in scenes from the 1920s to the present for lighting streets, boulevards or station platforms. Lamps are fully assembled, unpainted brass with plastic globes.

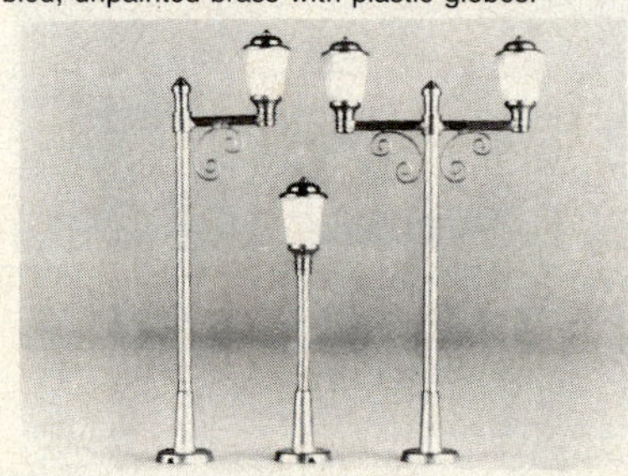

933-939   2-1/4″ tall, 12v bulb   pkg(2) 5.29
933-1022 Single Arm, 18v bulb   each 5.29
          (25 scale feet tall)
933-1023 Double Arm, 18v bulb   each 6.98
          (25 scale feet tall)

INFORMATION STATION
SIGNALS AND SLANG

Fixed railroad signals were introduced around 1832. Consisting of a large post with an arm facing the tracks, the device had a red and a white ball mounted on ropes. With the white ball raised, the track was clear. When the train had passed, the red ball was raised part way and indicated stop. From this, the term "highball" (used to mean proceed or run fast) was introduced.

When rail lines began crossing each other, the gate signal was introduced to protect the junction. The first train to arrive swung the gate over the opposing track and went on its way. At night a red lantern was attached. Trainmen soon began referring to this as a "clear board" or "red board" and the terms are still used today.

TRIGOR™

The Track Section That Operates Signals, Protects Blocks . . . Automatically

Trigor is the equivalent of a standard 9″ section of Atlas Snap Track. It can be placed anywhere in the track layout where it is desired to have a signal or control point. It is attached in the usual manner to adjoining sections of track by the clips provided. Trigor must be mounted loosely so it is free to flex up and down when a train passes over it. This flexing action operates SPDT contacts which control signals and other devices. Trigor uses track power, so all you need to do is connect your signals to the Trigor contacts.

Trigor handles the whole job—it is ready to slip right in with the Atlas track on your layout or to replace a 9″ section of ANY HO train set track you may be using.

933-690 Trigor, brass rail   5.98
933-691 Trigor, nickel silver   5.98

To curve Trigor track, cut through the web between the ties under the outside rail and bend gently to desired radius.

Complete, ready for your signals
• No relays
• Low cost
• No gadgets on car or loco
• Completely automatic

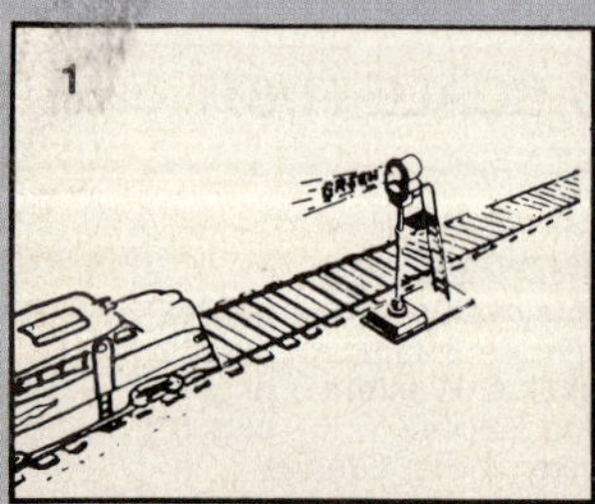

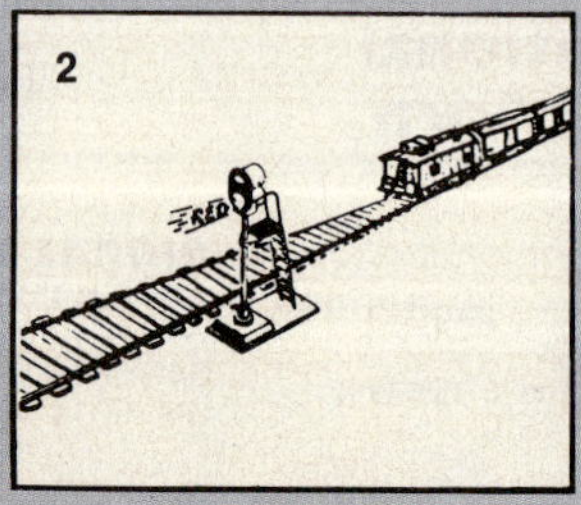

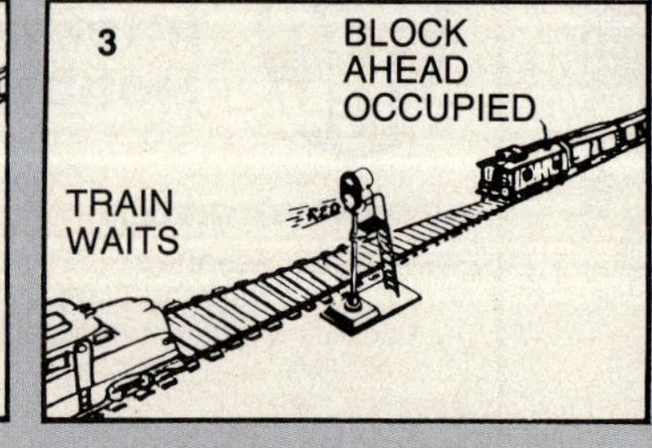

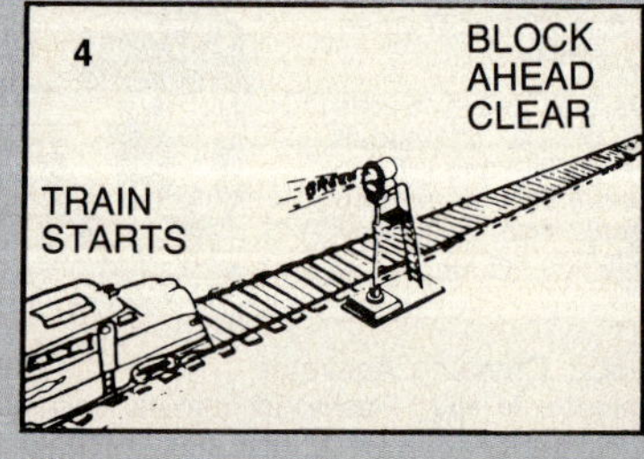

(1) (2) Signal Lights change automatically as train passes.   (3) (4) Approaching train stops, waits until block ahead is clear, then proceeds.

TREES, HEDGES & SHRUBS

ASSEMBLED TREES

Trees and shrubs can be used in various scales. Each is fully assembled, (unless noted), with realistic foliage colors. Dimensions shown is approximate height.

FALLER *Imported from Germany & marketed by* **WALTHERS**

DECIDUOUS

A

B

C

D

J

K

L

M

N

O

P

Q

R

F

G

H

I

A	272-1412	Small 2-1/2"	pkg(4)	5.49
B	272-1410	Large 5-1/4"	pkg(3)	5.99
	272-1413	Small 2-1/2"	pkg(4)	5.49
	272-1415	1-3/4" Mini	pkg(5)	5.49
	272-1416	Med 4-1/4" 11 cm	pkg(4)	7.49
	272-1451	Mountain Maple 8-3/4" 22 cm	each	16.49
	272-1453	Large, 5-1/2"	pkg(2)	7.49
	272-1470	Trees 5" 13 cm	pkg(14)	19.49

FRUIT

C	272-1400	Large 4-1/2"	pkg(3)	5.99
	272-1401	Medium 3-1/4"	pkg(3)	5.99
	272-1402	Small 2-1/2"	pkg(3)	5.99
D	272-1403	Apple 3-1/4"	pkg(3)	5.99
E	272-1406	Cherry **NEW**	pkg(3)	5.99
F	272-1407	Small 2-1/3"	pkg(4)	5.99
G	272-1408	Medium 4-1/4"	pkg(3)	6.99
H	272-1409	Apple 4-1/2"	pkg(2)	12.49

AUTUMN

| I | 272-1405 | 3", 8 cm | pkg(3) | 5.99 |
| | 272-1461 | 4-3/4", 12 cm | pkg(2) | 5.99 |

OAK

| J | 272-1450 | Large Oak 6-5/8" | each | 7.49 |

WEEPING WILLOW

| K | 272-1424 | Medium 3-7/8" | pkg(2) | 7.49 |

BIRCH

L	272-1420	Medium 5-1/4"	pkg(3)	5.99
	272-1423	3-1/2"	pkg(4)	5.99
	272-1457	6-3/4"	each	7.49
	272-1456	Assorted 4-1/2"	pkg(3)	6.49
	272-1422	Medium 4-1/4"	pkg(4)	7.49

BEECH

| M | 272-1452 | Cooper 4-3/4" | pkg(2) | 5.99 |
| | 272-1454 | 7" 18 cm | pkg(2) | 7.49 |

PINE

| N | 272-1436 | Medium 4" | pkg(3) | 5.99 |

POPLAR

O	272-1425	Large 5-1/4"	pkg(3)	5.99
	272-1426	White 5-1/2"	pkg(4)	7.49
	272-1459	Medium 5-1/4"	pkg(3)	7.49
	272-1460	Black, Medium	pkg(4)	7.49

FLOWERING

P	272-1429	Small 2"	pkg(3)	5.99
	272-1427	Large 4-3/4"	pkg(3)	5.99
Q	272-1404	Medium 4-1/4"	pkg(3)	5.99
	272-1475	Forsythias **NEW** Yellow Flowers	pkg(6)	5.99

CHESTNUT

| R | 272-1463 | Large 6-3/4" | each | 7.49 |

BUSHES (shrubs) **NEW**

| | 272-1476 | Bush w/red flowers | pkg(6) | 5.99 |
| | 272-1477 | Bush w/blue flowers | pkg(6) | 5.99 |

EVERGREENS

A

B

C

D   E   F

G

H

I

D	272-1435	Tall Spruce 6-1/2"	pkg(8)	6.49
	272-1434	Small Fir 2"	pkg(5)	6.49
	272-1431	Medium Fir 3-3/4"	pkg(4)	6.49
	272-1430	Large Fir 5-1/2"	pkg(3)	6.49
	272-1441	Nordic Pine 5-1/4"	pkg(3)	6.99
	272-1462	Nordic, 3" 8 cm	pkg(4)	7.49

COLORADO SPRUCE **NEW**

| E | 272-1480 | | pkg(6) | 5.99 |
| | 272-1481 | | pkg(12) | 6.99 |

PINE ASSORTMENT

F	272-1319	1 ea: 2 & 6"	pkg(6) kit	13.99
G	272-1318	4 ea: 1-1/4 & 5-1/2"	kit	12.49
	272-1444	3 ea: 2 & 4-1/2"	pkg(6)	11.49
	272-1439	5 ea: 3-1/2, 4-3/4 & 6"	pkg(15)	11.49
H	272-1440	10 1-1/4, 2 & 2-3/4"	pkg(30)	11.99
I	272-1464	Fir, asst	pkg(50)	20.49
	272-1465	Fir, asst	pkg(25)	15.99

BLUE SPRUCE

| A | 272-1432 | Blue Spruce | pkg(3) | 6.49 |
| | | One medium 4-1/2" and two large 5-1/2" | | |

LARCH

| B | 272-1437 | Assorted 4-1/2" | pkg(3) | 6.49 |
| | 272-1438 | Small 3-1/2" | pkg(4) | 6.49 |

PINE

| C | 272-1433 | Large Fir 4-1/2" | pkg(3) | 6.49 |

A

B

HEDGES

A	272-1446	Large 6.5"	pkg(2)	4.99
	272-1449	Small 19"	pkg(2)	4.99
B	272-1447	Small 4.0"	pkg(3)	4.99
	272-1448	Medium 19"	pkg(2)	4.99
		(not illustrated)		
	272-1466	Flowering, White 14 x 1.4 cm	pkg(2)	4.99

LTD QTY AVAILABLE

| | 272-1468 | Flowering, White 10 x 1 cm | pkg(2) | 4.99 |

BUSHES

| | 272-1445 | 1-1/4" | pkg(4) | 5.49 |

TREES, HEDGES & SHRUBS

A·M·S·I — LANDSCAPE MATERIALS
SCALE MODEL SUPPLIES

BIG TREE KIT
Tree is approximately 18" high with a 12" spread. Kit includes green cloth wire, putty powder, green covering material, ground foam and instruction book.

137-50	Big Tree Kit	22.50
137-26	Big Tree Putty Powder 8 oz	3.99
137-30	Big Tree Wire Kit #24	8.25

TREE COVER MATERIAL
6 x 9" pad is enough for several trees. Non-magnetic, flexible mesh material unless noted.

137-1	Green, painted steel wool	3.49
137-2	Green	3.99
137-3	Brown	3.99

HEDGE MATERIAL
Black nylon foam pad of various thicknesses can be cut in any shape and covered with foam to look like trimmed hedges or bushes.

137-100	5 x 5 x 1/4"	pkg(2)	3.99
137-200	5 x 5 x 1/2"	each	3.99
137-350	5 x 5 x 1"	each	4.49
137-80100	1 x 2" *NEW*	pkg(2)	13.49
137-80101	1 x 1" *NEW*	pkg(4)	13.49
137-80110	1/2 x 1" *NEW*	pkg(4)	11.99
137-80111	1/2 x 1/2" *NEW*	pkg(4)	11.99
137-80120	1/4 x 1/2" *NEW*	pkg(4)	10.99
137-80121	1/4 x 1/4" *NEW*	pkg(4)	10.99

FLOWERING VINE *NEW*

137-90670	17.99

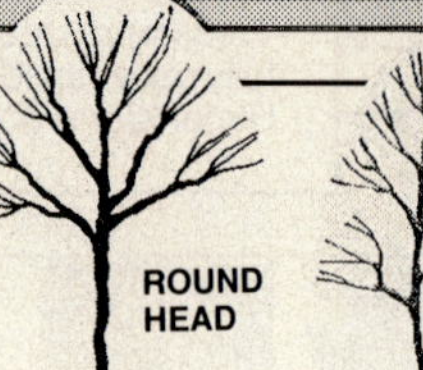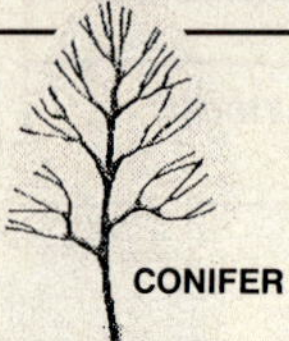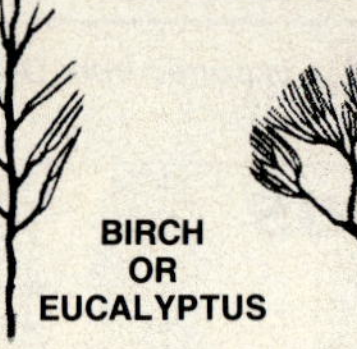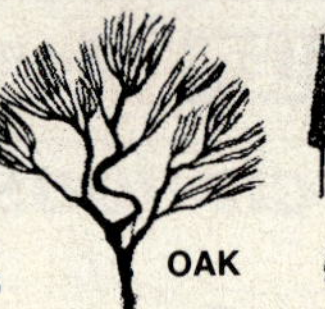

TREE STRUCTURE KIT
Kits consist of metal structures packaged flat, ready to articulate to make finished trees (less flocking material).

Order No	Tree Type	Height	HO ft	Spread	Qty	Price
137-102	Oak, Round	5-1/2"	44'	4-1/4"	1	3.99
137-103	Conifer, Monterey Pine	7-1/2"	56'	3-1/2"	1	3.99
137-104	Redwood	7-1/2"	56'	1-3/4"	1	3.99
137-90604	Redwood	7-1/2"	54'		6	12.99
137-105	Oak	4"	34'	5"	1	3.99
137-90618	Oak	4"	29"		6	9.98
137-106	Round Head	4-1/2"	40'	4"	1	3.99
137-107	Elm	3-1/2"	25'	3"	2	3.99
137-109	Conifer, Monterey Pine	5-1/2"	44'	2-1/2"	1	3.99
137-90610	Redwood	5-1/2"	40'		6	9.98
137-110	Redwood	5"	44'	1-1/2	2	3.99
137-90612	Birch, Eucalyptus	5"	36'		4	7.99
137-112	Birch, Eucalyptus	4-1/2"	33'	1-1/2"	2	3.99
137-90616	Elm	5"	36'		6	13.98
137-116	Elm, Round Head	4-1/2"	36'	2-1/2"	1	3.99
137-117	Conifer, Monterey Pine	3"	22'	1-1/2"	3	3.99
137-90620	Pine	3"	22'		8	6.98
137-118	Round Head	3-1/4"	24'	2-1/2"	2	3.99
137-119	Round Head	2-3/4"	18'	2-1/2"	3	3.99
137-120	Conifer, Monterey Pine	3"	20'	1"	3	3.99
137-124	Birch, Eucalyptus	3"	17'	1"	3	3.99
137-125	Redwood	3-1/2"	22'	1-1/4"	2	3.99
137-129	Conifer, Monterey Pine	1-1/2"	9'	1"	5	3.99
137-132	Round Head	1-1/2"	14'	1"	5	3.99
137-134	Oak, Round Head	2"	12'	1-1/4"	6	3.99
137-135	Oak, Round Head	1-1/4"	9'	1"	6	3.99

SOLID STRUCTURES — small painted gray cast metal trees. (By Special Order Only.)

Order No	Tree Type	Height	HO ft	Spread	Qty	Price
137-140	Conifer	1/2"	4'	1/8"	10	3.99
137-141	Conifer	3/4"	6'	3/16"	8	3.99
137-142	Conifer	1-1/8"	8'	1/4"	8	3.99
137-143	Conifer	1-3/8"	10'	3/8"	6	3.99
137-144	Conifer	1-5/8"	12'	1/2"	4	3.99
137-145	Monterey Pine	1"	7'	3/8"	6	3.99
137-146	Round Head	5/8"	4'	3/16"	8	3.99
137-147	Round Head	3/4"	6'	5/16"	6	3.99
137-148	Round Head	1"	9'	1/2"	5	3.99

Mountains in Minutes
I.S.L.E. LABORATORIES

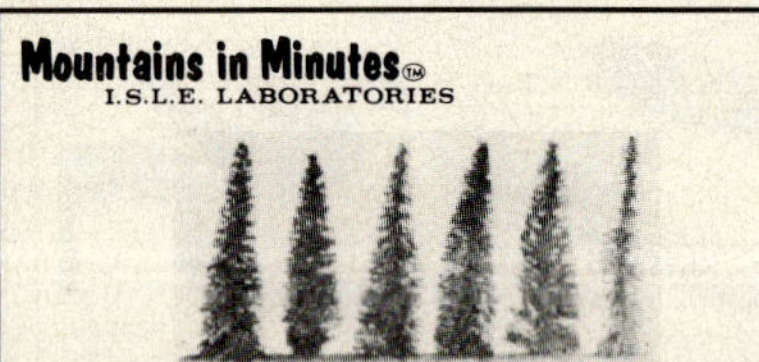

SPRUCE TREES

473-302	Spruce Tree, 4-1/4"	pkg(6)	3.98
473-303	Spruce Tree, 3"	pkg(10)	3.98

Campbell Scale Models

PINE TREE KIT
Pine Tree Kit, with instructions and enough material for five trees. (N, HO, S and O Scales.)

200-100 pkg(5) 17.50

Heki

338-301	1.5-3.5"	*NEW*	pkg(40)	19.99
338-302	2" - 3.5"	*NEW*	pkg(40)	19.99
338-303	2.5" - 4"	*NEW*	pkg(30)	19.99
338-304	3"-5"	*NEW*	pkg(24)	19.99
338-305	2.5-5.5"	*NEW*		19.99
338-308	4-7"	*NEW*	pkg(12)	19.99

ASSORTED TREES
Assortments includes Shade, Birch, Cedar Oak, Ash, Maple, Evergreen, Juniper, Fir, Forest Pine and Hedgerows. Can be used in any scale.

1-1/2 to 3" high			
338-201		pkg(50)	29.99
1 to 3" high			
338-202		pkg(50)	29.99
1 to 4" high			
338-203		pkg(40)	29.99
2 to 5" high			
338-204		pkg(40)	29.99
4-1/2 to 6-1/2" high			
338-205		pkg 20)	29.99

FLOCKED PINES

338-206	2 to 3-1/2"		pkg(40)	29.99
338-207	4-7"		pkg(20)	29.99
338-306	2-3.5"	*NEW*	pkg(30)	19.99
338-307	4-7"	*NEW*	pkg(12)	19.99
338-309	1.5-3"	*NEW*	pkg(100)	19.99

model power

Items listed in *blue ink* may not be available at all times.

TREES

TREES, HEDGES & SHRUBS

Customcraft

NEW

EZ-TREES™

For any scale. Ready to use.
Free standing or glue in place.

EVERGREEN

153-1082	4″	pkg(6)	5.99
153-1085	6″	pkg(3)	7.99
153-1089	8″	pkg(2)	6.99

BLUE SPRUCE

153-1081	4″	pkg(6)	5.99
153-1086	6″	pkg(3)	7.99
153-1090	8″	pkg(2)	6.99

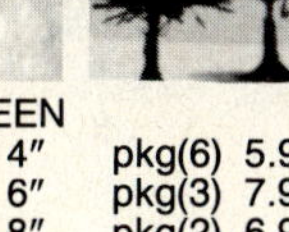

kibri — Imported from Germany by WALTHERS

Trees are assembled, ready to install.

TREES

A	405-6282	Dec 8-1/2″	(2)	17.49
B	405-6288	Fir 4-6″	(15)	40.99
C	405-6320	Larch 5-7/8″	(3)	15.49
D	405-6312	Pine 3-7/8″	(3)	11.99
	405-6314	Pine **NEW**	(3)	12.99
E	405-6318	Pine 2-4″	(10)	16.99
F	405-6316	Pine 8-7/8″	(2)	15.49
G	405-6310	Pine 2-3/8″	(4)	10.49
H	405-7920	Pine, Assort	(20)	15.49
I	405-7922	Fir, Assort 2-3″	(15)	31.49

HEDGES

J	Green Bushes 5-1/8″			
	405-6322	(3)	9.99
K	Flowering Hedges 5-1/8″			
	405-6324	(3)	8.99
L	405-7930	Hedges 4-3/4″	(4)	11.49

FLOCKING MATERIAL

pkg (1/2 oz)

405-5983	Medium Green	1.49
405-5989	Medium Gray	1.99
405-5990	Mixed	1.99

A   B   C   D

E   F   G   H

I   J   K   L

Preiser — Imported from Germany by WALTHERS

Trees are easy-to-assemble appropriately colored plastic.

590-18600	Palm Trees	pkg(4) 12.99

LIFE-LIKE

Trees are assembled self-standing, appropriately colored trees. (Size are approximate.)

EVERGREENS

433-1326	2″	pkg(4)	6.00
433-1012	Winter 3″	pkg(4)	6.00
433-1022	3″	pkg(4)	6.00
433-1003	4″	pkg(4)	6.00
433-1008	Winter, Large	pkg(2)	6.00
433-1051	Winter, 8-1/2″	pkg(2)	10.50
433-1010	Blue Spruce, 5-1/2″	pkg(2)	6.00
433-1011	Fir, 5-1/2″	pkg(2)	6.00
433-1053	6-1/2″	pkg(2)	10.50

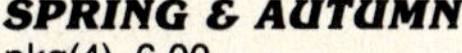

SPRING & AUTUMN

pkg(4) 6.00

433-1021	Autumn, 3″	
433-1002	Autumn, 4″	
433-1006	Spring, 4″	

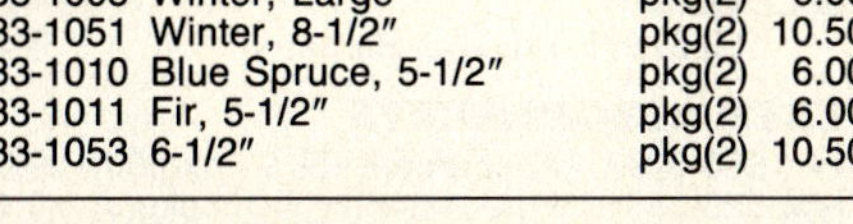

DECIDUOUS

433-1325	Shade, 2″	pkg(4)	6.00
433-1020	Shade, 3″	pkg(4)	6.00
433-1001	Shade, 4″	pkg(4)	6.00
433-1015	Shade, 5-1/2″	pkg(2)	6.00
433-1004	White Birch, 4″	pkg(4)	6.00
433-1005	Poplar, 4″	pkg(4)	6.00
433-1013	Redwood, 5-1/2″	pkg(2)	6.00
433-1052	Oak, 6-1/2″	pkg(2)	10.50

FRUITS & FLOWERS

433-1023	Apple, 3″	pkg(4)	6.00
433-1024	Orange, 3″	pkg(4)	6.00

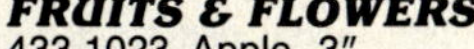

TREE ASSORTMENT   **NEW**

433-1029	36 pieces	216.00

N.J. International

TREES

Mountain Topper™ trees are ready-to-use, self-standing appropriately colored trees.

FRUIT

525-6716	Small Mixed	pkg(4)	5.49
525-6726	Mixed	pkg(4)	5.99

EVERGREEN

525-6473	w/Snow (mixed)	**NEW**	pkg(15)	6.79
525-6779	w/Snow 7-1/2″		pkg(2)	5.99
525-6781	w/Snow 9″		pkg(2)	6.79
525-6742	Small-Large		pkg(15)	5.99
525-6751	Medium		pkg(10)	7.99
525-6758	Small	**NEW**	pkg(10)	4.99
525-6760	Extra-Small		pkg(12)	4.99
525-6780	Medium		pkg(2)	5.99
525-6784	Mixed		pkg(50)	35.99
525-6787	Large Mixed		pkg(100)	59.99

ASSORTED

525-6706	Small	pkg(5)	4.79
525-6707	2-1/4 x 3″ Mixed Fruit Trees	pkg(10)	8.99
525-6708	Medium	pkg(5)	4.99

LICHEN

525-6701	Medium		pkg(4)	4.99
525-6702	Small	**NEW**	pkg(4)	4.79
525-6785	Mixed		pkg(25)	27.99
525-6786	Mixed		pkg(50)	54.99

GREEN HEDGE ROWS

Ready-to-use, appropriately colored hedges.

525-6711	Small 40″ Long	4.99
525-6712	Large 5″ Long	pkg(4) 3.79

Roco — Imported from Austria and marketed by WALTHERS

TREES

Plastic, snap-together tree kit makes up to 8 trees. Also includes woods-man and mushrooms.

625-40090	Pine Trees	pkg(8) 10.49

TREES, HEDGES & SHRUBS

TREES

DECIDUOUS

A	528-2153	Blooming Bushes 1-3/4"	pkg(2)	4.99
B	528-2155	Fruit, Green 3"		4.49
C	528-2157	Fruit, Blooming 3"		4.49
D	528-2158	Cherry 3"		4.49
E	528-2160	Pear, Green 4"		5.49
F	528-2161	Pear, Blooming 4"		5.49
G	528-2164	Birch, 4"		5.49
H	528-2167	Poplar, 7"		6.49
I	528-2170	Maple 3-3/4"		5.49
J	528-2172	Beech 5"		7.49
K	528-2174	Elm 5-1/2"		7.49
L	528-2176	Oak 6-1/4"		9.99
M	528-2178	Lime, 7-1/4"		9.99
N	528-2180	Chestnut, 7-3/4"		10.99
O	528-2227	Green Pear, 4"	each	2.49
P	528-2228	Blossoming Pear 4"	ea	2.49
Q	528-2362	Maple 6.3"	each	13.99
R	528-2274	Red Oak, 7-3/4"	each	6.99
S	528-2276	Linden, 7"	each	6.49
T	528-2277	Horse-Chestnut 7-3/4"	each	6.49
U	528-2279	Ash, 8"	each	6.49

(By Special Order Only.)

V	528-2353	Beech 5-3/4"	each	16.49
W	528-2355	Elm, 5-1/2"	each	16.49
X	528-2365	Oak, 7-3/4"	each	19.99
Y	528-2571	Oak, 5-3/4"	each	6.99
Z	528-2575	Beech 4-3/4"	pkg(2)	8.49
A A	528-2599	Sycamore 7"	pkg(2)	13.49
B B	528-2642	Juniper 2"	pkg(20)	30.49
C C	528-21710	Nut 5-1/2"	NEW	7.49
DD	528-21750	Alder 5-7/8"	NEW	9.99
EE	528-23250	Beech	NEW	64.49
	528-23290	Oak Summer	NEW	64.49
	528-23330	Alder Summer	NEW	64.49
FF	528-23260	Beech Autumn	NEW	64.49
	528-23300	Oak Autumn	NEW	64.49
	528-23340	Alder Autumn	NEW	64.49
GG	528-25540	Apple	NEW pkg(3)	7.49
HH	528-25560	Elm	NEW pkg(2)	9.99

(not illustrated)

528-2168	Poplar Tree 4-3/4"		5.49
528-2583	Poplar Tree 4-3/4"	NEW pkg(5)	11.49
528-2350	Fruit, 5"	each	16.49
528-2358	Birch, 4.3"	each	13.99
528-2361	Poplar, 7"	each	16.49
528-2570	Chestnut, 7"	each	8.49
528-2574	Elm, 5"	pkg(2)	10.49
528-2579	Plum, 3-1/4"	pkg(2)	7.49
528-2588	Autumn 3"	pkg(3)	8.49
528-2599	Sycamore, 7.1"	pkg(2)	13.49

FIR

II	528-2424	2.3"	pkg(20)	28.49
	528-2425	3.5"	pkg(20)	33.99
	528-2426	5.1"	pkg(20)	43.99
	528-2427	7"	pkg(20)	59.99
JJ	528-23400	Fir	NEW pkg(3)	35.99
KK	528-25610	Fir	NEW pkg(4)	7.99

(not illustrated)

528-2364	Pine, 6.7"	each	16.49
528-2593	Blue Fir	pkg(3)	7.49
528-2247	Spruce, 7"	each	5.49
528-2363	Pine, 5.5"	each	13.99
528-2258	Weathered Pines, 9"	ea	9.49

HEDGES

	528-22070	Privet & Barberry	NEW 6.49

TREE ASSORTMENTS

LL	528-3272	Assortment Kit	pkg(50)	29.99
MM	528-2564	Pine Assort	pkg(5)	9.49
NN	528-2582	Deciduous Assort	pkg(5)	11.99
OO	528-2380	Large	pkg(5)	49.99
	528-2382	Medium	pkg(5)	22.99
PP	528-2385	Deciduous	pkg(2)	22.99
	528-2386	Deciduous	pkg(3)	25.99
QQ	528-2551	Assorted Fruit	pkg(5)	11.99
RR	528-2552	Red Oak/Pear	pkg(4)	10.99
SS	528-2555	Beech/Fruit	pkg(5)	11.99
TT	528-2550	3.2" w/Chinese Lantern		22.99

(not illustrated)

528-952	Deco Assortment	pkg(6)	11.99
528-2206	Hedge Privet 20"	pkg(2)	6.49
528-2351	Bushes Filigran Asst	pkg(4)	16.49
528-2560	Spruce Assort	pkg(5)	7.49
528-2562	Spruce	pkg(4)	8.99
528-2566	Pine Assortment	pkg(4)	10.99
528-2567	Fir	pkg(3)	6.99
528-2569	Fir 6-8" Assort	pkg(4)	10.49
528-2572	Maple/2 Deciduous	pkg(3)	7.49
528-2573	Elm/2 Fruit	pkg(3)	9.99
528-2576	Birch Pine Willow 3-5"		10.49
528-2587	Trees/Bush Assort	pkg(4)	8.49
528-2591	Willow 2"	pkg(3)	8.99
528-2643	Fir 4-8"	pkg(20)	43.99
528-2652	Fir, 3/4"	pkg(25)	14.99
528-2646	Fir, 3/4"	pkg(8)	13.99
528-23830	Tree w/asstd foliage	NEW pkg(12)	18.49

TREES, HEDGES & SHRUBS

REALISTIC TREES

READY MADE

Each tree is hand crafted, individually shaped and uniquely foliated. No two trees are exactly the same. Use the selection guide below to determine the variety of trees to make your layout or diorama more authentic . . . quickly and easily.

GREEN DECIDUOUS

B	785-1001	¾" - 1¼"	Medium Green	pkg(8)	4.98
B	785-1002	1¼" - 2"	Medium Green	pkg(5)	4.98
A	785-1003	2" - 3"	Light Green	pkg(4)	5.49
B	785-1004	2" - 3"	Medium Green	pkg(4)	5.49
C	785-1005	2" - 3"	Dark Green	pkg(4)	5.49
A	785-1006	3" - 4"	Light Green	pkg(3)	5.98
B	785-1007	3" - 4"	Medium Green	pkg(3)	5.98
C	785-1008	3" - 4"	Dark Green	pkg(3)	5.98
A	785-1009	4" - 5"	Light Green	pkg(3)	6.49
B	785-1010	4" - 5"	Medium Green	pkg(3)	6.49
C	785-1011	4" - 5"	Dark Green	pkg(3)	6.49
A	785-1012	5" - 6"	Light Green	pkg(2)	5.98
B	785-1013	5" - 6"	Medium Green	pkg(2)	5.98
C	785-1014	5" - 6"	Dark Green	pkg(2)	5.98
A	785-1015	6" - 7"	Light Green	pkg(2)	6.98
B	785-1016	6" - 7"	Medium Green	pkg(2)	6.98
C	785-1017	6" - 7"	Dark Green	pkg(2)	6.98
B	785-1018	7" - 8"	Medium Green	pkg(2)	8.98
B	785-1019	8" - 9"	Medium Green	pkg(2)	10.98

FALL DECIDUOUS

E	785-1040	1¼" - 3"	Fall Mix	pkg(9)	9.98
E	785-1041	3" - 5"	Fall Mix	pkg(6)	11.98

CONIFERS

D	785-1060	2¼" - 4"	Conifer Green	pkg(5)	5.98
D	785-1061	4" - 6"	Conifer Green	pkg(4)	5.98
D	785-1062	6" - 7"	Conifer Green	pkg(3)	6.49
D	785-1063	7" - 8"	Conifer Green	pkg(3)	7.98

KIT FORM

Now! Bulk kits for economy on forested layouts. New patented clump-foliage and bendable plastic trunks (at room temperature!) make Realistic Tree Kits easy for the beginner to duplicate craftsman quality in just two quick steps (shown below).

GREEN DECIDUOUS

ABC	785-1101	¾" - 3"	Lt., Med., Dk. Green	pkg(36)	11.98
ABC	785-1102	3" - 5"	Lt., Med., Dk. Green	pkg(14)	11.98
ABC	785-1103	5" - 7"	Lt., Med., Dk. Green	pkg (7)	11.98

CONIFERS

D	785-1104	2 ½" - 4"	Conifer Green	pkg(42)	11.98
D	785-1105	4" - 6"	Conifer Green	pkg(24)	11.98
D	785-1106	6" - 8"	Conifer Green	pkg(16)	11.98

Realistic Trees, either Ready Made or Kit Form, lend instant authenticity to a layout or diorama. Natural colors and realistic textures duplicate nature and blend perfectly with other Woodland Scenics landscaping products.

COLOR GUIDE

TWO EASY STEPS . . . HANDMADE QUALITY

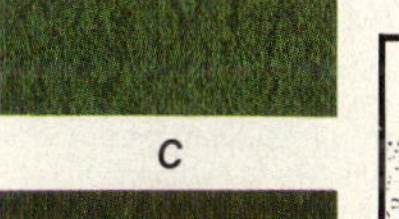
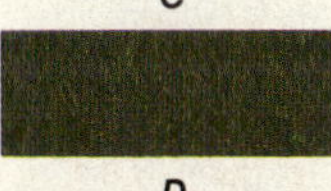
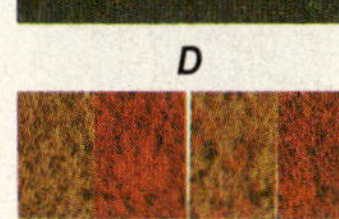

A

B

C

D

E

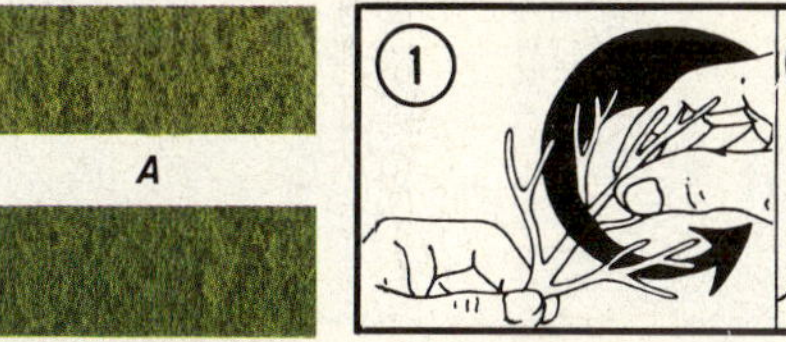

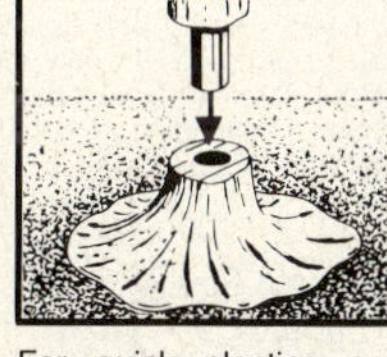

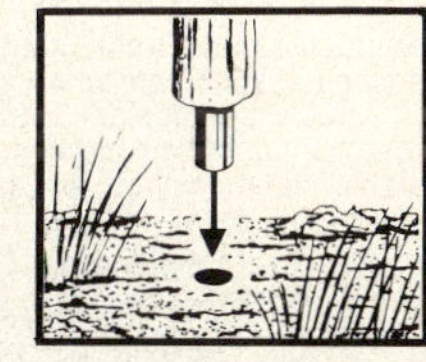

TREES, HEDGES & SHRUBS

TREES
Cast Metal

A	785-11 Forked Trunk 2-1/4″	pkg(4)	3.98
B	785-12 Ornamental 2-1/2″	pkg(5)	3.98
C	785-13 Straight Trunk 2-1/2″	pkg(5)	3.98
D	785-14 Softwood Pine 3-1/4″	pkg(5)	3.98
	785-20 Columnar Pine 4-1/2″	pkg(4)	3.98
E	785-18 Double Fork 3-1/2″	pkg(2)	3.98
F	785-19 Shade Tree 4″	pkg(2)	3.98
G	785-17 Shag Bark 3-1/2″	pkg(3)	3.98
H	785-21 Gnarled 4-1/2″	pkg(2)	3.98

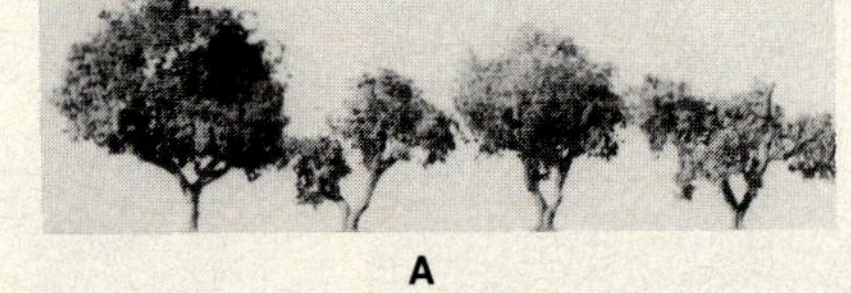

A

B

C

D

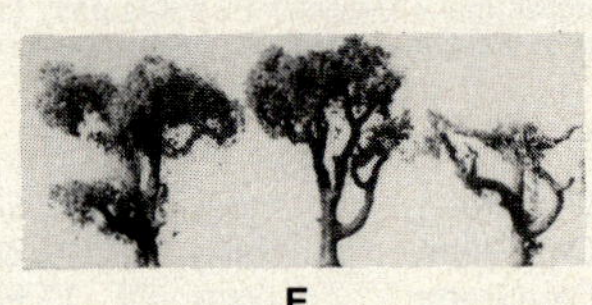

E

F

G

H

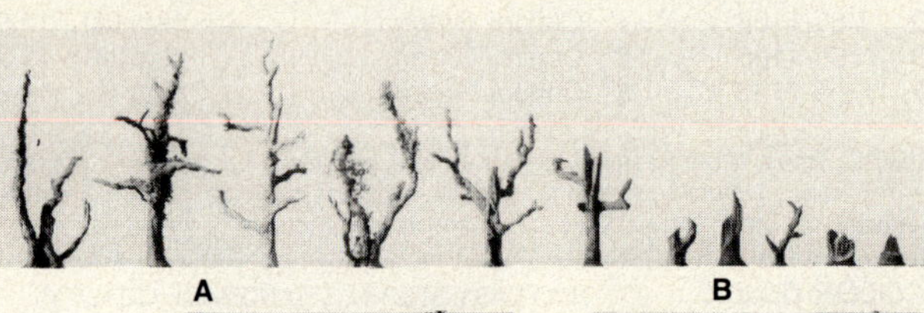

A   B

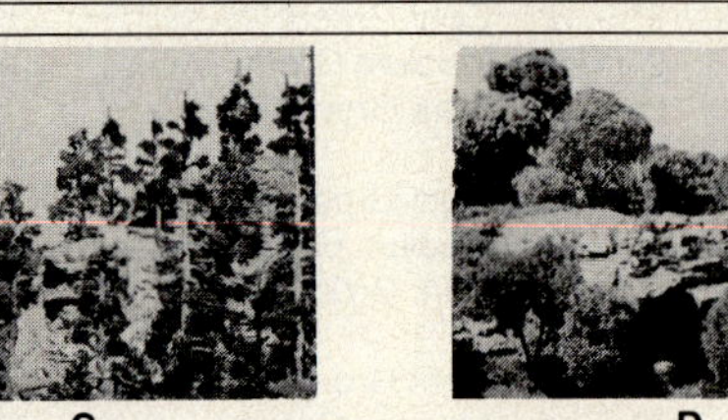

C   D

E

F

G

H

LANDSCAPE KITS & SCENIC MATERIAL

Bendable metal trunks that are easily altered and an extremely versatile foliage system can be combined to produce virtually any shape, size or species of tree or plant. Bark texture detailing allows highlight painting and weathering, without highly developed artistic talent. Contains two to five bendable metal castings and pre-colored foliage.

A	785-22 Dead Trees	pkg(5)	3.98
B	785-31 Cut Stumps	pkg(14)	1.98
C	785-27 Pine Forest, approx 2-4 inches tall	pkg(24)	8.98
D	785-28 Hardwood Forest, approx 2-4 inches tall	pkg(24)	8.98
E	785-23 Pine Trees, approx 6-9 inches tall	pkg(5)	7.98
F	785-25 Hardwood Trees, approx 5-1/2 to 6-1/2 inches tall	pkg(3)	7.98
G	785-26 Big Old Trees, approx 7 to 7-1/2 inches tall	pkg(2)	7.98

H Hedge Row Scene
785-24   each 7.98
24-30 inches long
Contains: 18 trees,
6 bushes,
3 colors foliage,
2 colors turf

Complete Landscape Kit
785-926   18.49
Contains: 18 trunks (2″-4″ tall)
3 packs foliage, 7 stumps,
2 packs green blend turf
3 packs accent turf

(not illustrated)

785-32 Broken Stumps   pkg(14) 1.98

REFERENCE MANUAL
785-100   1.50
Explains landscaping and terrain materials, details and scenic structures.

TREES, HEDGES & SHRUBS

Plastruct

Assembled assorted trees. Additional coloring may be added with ground foam or lichen.

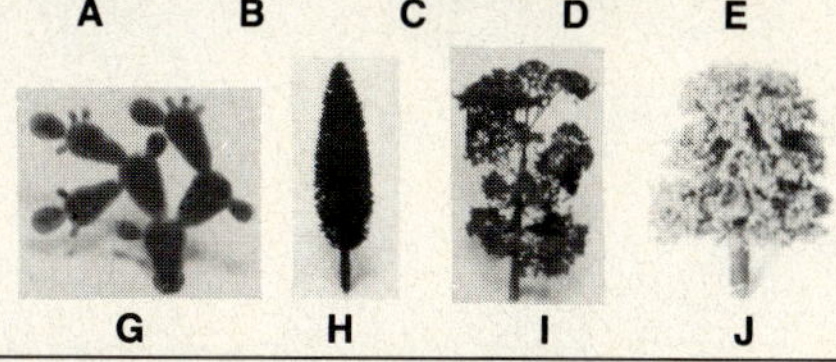

A B C D E F

G H I J

A ARMATURES

570-9730	1-1/4"	pkg(5) 5.95
570-9750	2"	pkg(5) 6.95
570-9775	3"	pkg(5) 7.95
570-9700	4"	pkg(4) 7.95

B BLOSSOMED TREES

570-9203	Red	pkg(5) 2.95
570-9204	Violet	pkg(5) 2.95
570-9205	Yellow	pkg(5) 2.95
570-9206	White	pkg(5) 2.95

C BUSH

570-12435	1"	pkg(6) 3.95

D SAGUARO CACTUS

570-9625	1/2"	pkg(5) 6.95
570-9650	3/4"	pkg(5) 8.95
570-9600	1"	pkg(4) 9.95
570-9640	2"	pkg(2) 9.95

E FIR

570-9407	1/2"	pkg(5) 5.95
570-9411	7/8"	pkg(5) 6.95
570-9420	1-1/4"	pkg(5) 6.95
570-9445	2"	pkg(5) 7.95
570-9450	2-7/16"	pkg(5) 9.95
570-9490	4"	pkg(4) 11.95

F PALM TREES

570-9507	7/8"	pkg(5) 6.95
570-9511	1-3/4"	pkg(5) 7.95
570-9538	1-3/8"	pkg(2) 9.95
570-9555	2-1/4"	pkg(2) 12.95

570-9500	3-5/8"	pkg(2) 13.95
570-9550	6"	each 14.95

G PRICKLY PEAR CACTUS

570-9604	18 Pods	pkg(3) 2.49

H POPLAR

570-9307	1/4"	pkg(5) 6.95
570-9311	1/2"	pkg(5) 6.95
570-9320	1-1/4"	pkg(5) 7.95
570-9345	2"	pkg(5) 7.95
570-9350	2-5/8"	pkg(5) 9.95
570-9390	4"	pkg(4) 11.95

I PRO SYCAMORE

570-9906	1/4"	pkg(5) 7.00
570-9912	1/2"	pkg(5) 11.25
570-9919	3/4"	pkg(5) 14.00
570-9925	1"	pkg(4) 16.00
570-9938	1-1/2"	pkg(4) 19.00
570-9950	2"	pkg(3) 19.00
570-9960	2-1/2"	pkg(2) 13.00
570-9975	3"	each 9.00
570-9985	3-1/2"	each 10.00

J DECIDUOUS ELMS

570-9207	1/4"	pkg(5) 5.95
570-9211	1/2"	pkg(5) 6.95
570-9218	1"	pkg(5) 6.95
570-9220	1-1/4"	pkg(5) 7.95
570-9230	1-3/8"	pkg(5) 8.95
570-9238	1-1/2"	pkg(5) 9.95
570-9245	2"	pkg(5) 8.95
570-9250	2-1/4"	pkg(4) 9.95
570-9270	2-3/4"	pkg(4) 9.95
570-9290	3-1/2"	pkg(3) 10.95

WHITE GROUND MODEL WORKS

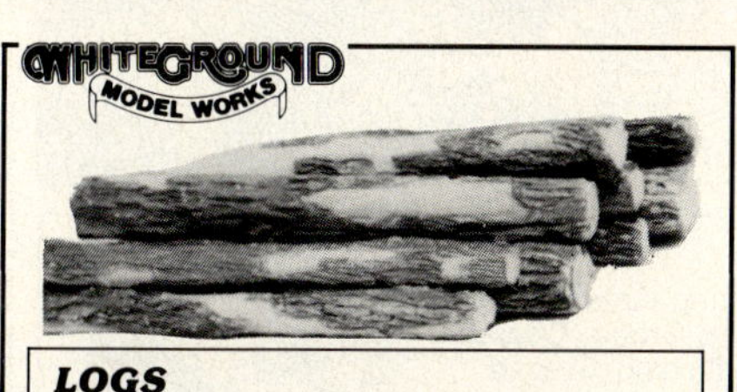

LOGS

Molded plaster unless noted.

771-5004	Logs on Land	pkg(12) 8.00
771-5005	Floating Logs	pkg(12) 6.00

TRAINS of TEXAS

TREES

Bulk Caspia Material
226-103   5.95

Keil-Line Models

Cactus are metal castings.

CACTUS

382-8774	Small Saguaro	pkg(5) 3.99
382-8775	Medium Saguaro	pkg(2) 3.99
382-8776	Large Saguaro	pkg(2) 4.99
382-8777	Medium Tall	pkg(2) 3.99

MLR MFG CO

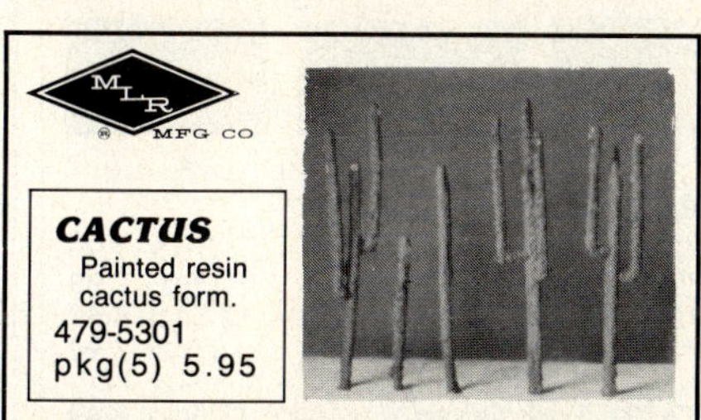

CACTUS

Painted resin cactus form.
479-5301
pkg(5) 5.95

SUPERIOR HOBBY PRODUCTS

Natural bark appearance.

TREES

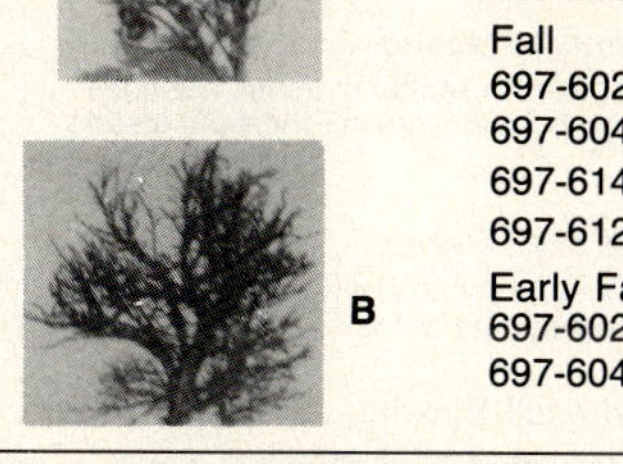

A	697-602	Deciduous 2 to 4"		2.98
B	697-601	Dead 2 to 4"		2.25
	Autumn			
A	697-6021	N-HO	NEW	3.25
	697-6041	HO-S	NEW	5.98
	697-6061	S-O	NEW	10.98
	Fall			
B	697-6026	N-HO (ylw)	NEW	3.25
	697-6046	HO-S (ylw)	NEW	5.98
	697-6145	Ylw-Orn 18-24	NEW	24.95
	697-61256	Foliage (ylw)	NEW	17.95
	Early Fall Trees			
	697-60256	N-HO	NEW	3.25
	697-60456	HO-S	NEW	5.98

STUMPS & LOGS

697-607	Small pkg(24)	1.80
697-608	Large pkg(12)	1.80
697-610	Extra Large each	1.80
697-609	Assorted pkg(18)	1.80

Assorted Logs
697-600
pkg(18)   2.75
(By Special Order Only.)

Vintage Reproductions

FELLOWS KITS FLOCKING MATERIAL

766-717	Flowers, Color #1 (Rd, Ylw, Pale Bl)	6.00
766-718	Fowers, Colors #2 (Orn, Med Bl, Lav)	6.00

LOG & TREE BARK

Kit consists of six wooden dowels (2-5/8" L x 5/8" dia) "rusty" scale cable 2 ft L x .012" dia) and double length bark wrapper stock.

766-3	Logging Load Kit	(brn) 8.00
766-774	Tree Bark Wrapper 22 x 36"	(dk brn) 6.00

"BUNNY TAILS"

Fiber material for modeling tall grass, weeds and sagebrush.

697-401	Grass	(green) 1.89
697-402	Sagebrush	(brown) 1.89
697-403	Beige	1.89

GRASS & GROUND COVER

FALLER

Imported from Germany & marketed by **WALTHERS**

FLOCK 1.99 *NEW*

272-756 Spring Green, Fine
272-757 Dark Green, Fine

272-758 Spring Green, Medium
272-759 Dark Green, Medium

272-760 Spring Green, Coarse
272-761 Dark Green, Coarse
272-762 Multicolor, Coarse

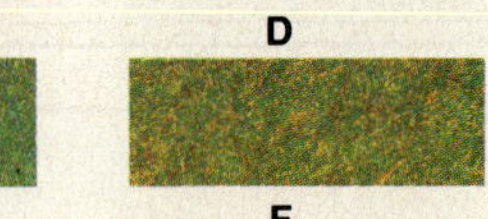

SCATTER MATERIAL

For realistic outside decor   pkg(1 oz)

A	272-702	Spring Green	1.49
B	272-703	Forest Green	1.49
C	272-707	Yellow	1.49
D	272-710	Meadow Green	1.49
E	272-725	Grass Fiber	3.99
F	272-726	Grass, Dark Green	3.99
G	272-716	Marsh Reeds	6.99
H	272-718	Green Foam	7.99
I	272-717	Flower Decor	6.49
J	272-730	Lichen, 5 assorted colors	6.49
	272-727	Brown, Dark *NEW*	3.99

(not illustrated)

272-700 Scatter Material Assortment 10.49
Contains 10 colors: 3 shades of green, 2 shades of brown, and one of each: gray, red, black, blue and yellow.

272-698 Scenery Material Assortment 8.99
Contains: 6 shades of scatter material, 2 shades of fibers (brown & green), green lichon and green flocks.

272-502 Hydrozell Powder 120 grams 4.99
Colored compound for landscaping. 40 grams each: brown, gray and ochre.

272-503 Hydrozell Powder 120 grams 4.99
Uncolored compound for landscaping.

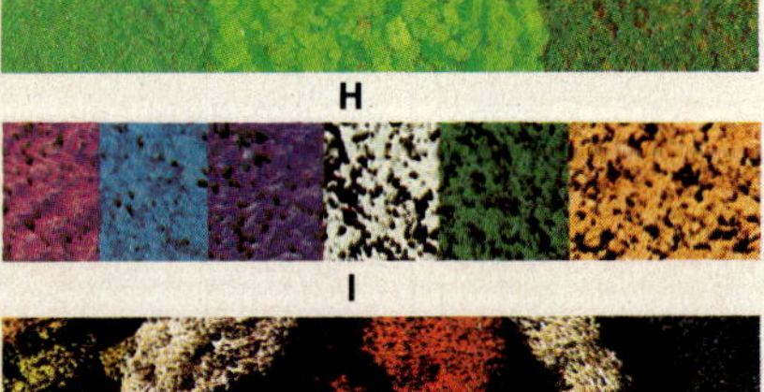

GROUND MATS

272-766	Light Green, 100 x 75 cm	9.49
272-770	Dark Green, 100 x 75 cm	9.49
272-773	Dark Green, 100 x 250 cm	29.99
272-775	Flowering Meadow, 100 x 75 cm	18.49
272-777	Flowering Meadow, 100 x 150 cm	29.99

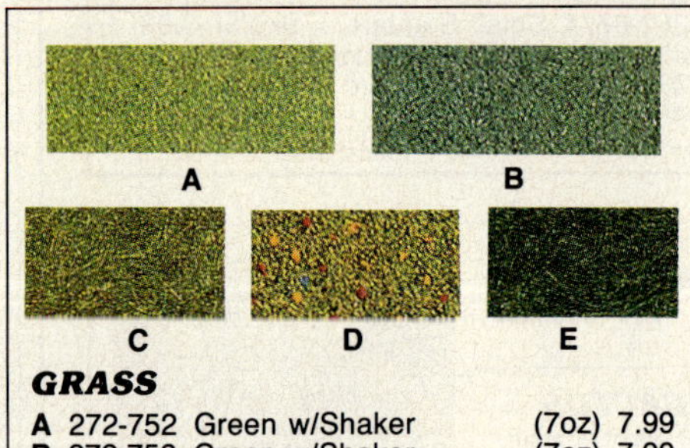

GRASS

A	272-752	Green w/Shaker	(7oz)	7.99
B	272-753	Green w/Shaker	(7oz)	7.99
C	272-736	Light Green *NEW*	(3.5oz)	6.49
D	272-754	Meadow Flowers w/Shaker	(7oz)	7.99
E	272-737	Dark Green *NEW*	(3.5oz)	6.49

model power

GRASS MAT
490-172 Velour 54 x 99"   15.98
LICHEN
490-1430 Green   4.98
GRASS & GROUND COVER
490-1431 Mixed Colors *NEW*   4.98

Raritan Valley Scenic Accents

Use adhesive (white glue, matte medium, etc.) on area to be covered (not included).

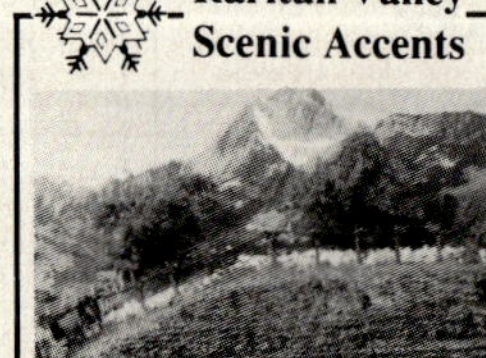

RIP-RAP *NEW*
Build a stone fence, foundation, use as river bank material, around mines, etc.

Large (O-G)
617-104   8oz 3.29

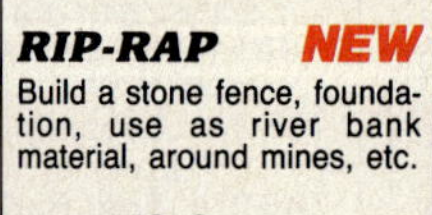

SNOW *NEW*
Let it snow on your layout, or diorama, etc. Synthetic, nonconductive.
Dry Powder
617-101   8oz 3.50
Granular
617-102   8oz 3.50

GRASS & GROUND COVER

Heki

LICHEN
338-401	Light Green	5 oz	7.99
338-402	Dark Green	5 oz	7.99
338-403	Assorted Colors	5 oz	7.99
338-601	Light Green	10 oz	14.99
338-602	Dark Green	10 oz	14.99
338-603	Assorted Colors	10 oz	14.99

kibri

LICHEN
405-5971	Light Green	pkg(1 oz)	2.99
405-5972	Medium Green	pkg(1 oz)	2.99
405-5973	Medium Gray	pkg(1 oz)	2.99
405-5974	Red Brown	pkg(1 oz)	2.99
405-5975	Medium Ochre	pkg(1 oz)	2.99
405-5976	Mixture	pkg(1 oz)	2.99
405-5977	Large Green	pkg(2 oz)	5.99
405-5978	Large Mixed	pkg(2 oz)	5.99

■ LTD QTY AVAILABLE ■

GRASS pkg(2-1/2 oz)
405-5903	Medium Yellow	2.49

HIGHBALL PRODUCTS

GRASS   (4 oz pkgs)   3.99 each
330-160	Grass-Green (Regular)
330-161	Grass-Lt Green (Regular)
330-162	Grass-Green (Fine)
330-163	Grass-Lt Green (Fine)
330-164	Grass-Moss Green (Regular)

Labelle industries

LICHEN
430-5001	Light Green	1-1/2 oz	1.99
430-5002	Dark Green	1-1/2 oz	1.99
430-5003	Gray	1-1/2 oz	1.99
430-5004	Fall Red	1-1/2 oz	1.99
430-5005	Fall Yellow	1-1/2 oz	1.99
430-5006	Mixed Colors	1-1/2 oz	1.99
430-5007	Sunset Orange	1-1/2 oz	1.99
430-5101	Light Green	4 oz	4.99
430-5102	Dark Green	4 oz	4.99
430-5103	Gray	4 oz	4.99
430-5104	Fall Red	4 oz	4.99
430-5105	Fall Yellow	4 oz	4.99
430-5106	Mixed Colors	4 oz	4.99
430-5107	Sunset Orange	4 oz	4.99

LIFE-LIKE

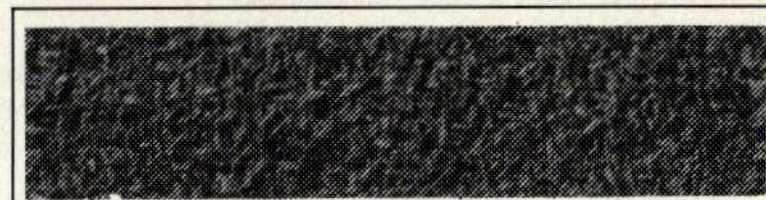

GRASS MATS

Quick & easy to use mats can be modified or removed when landscaping progresses. Paper backing for easy cutting.
* Realistic textures
* Bright, pure colors
* non magnetic flocking
* Completely reusable

433-1151	Grass Mat 50 x 33"		4.25
433-1156	Grass Mat 50 x 99"		9.00

Dealers MUST order Dealer Pack of 12

LANDSCAPING MATERIAL
Lichen, Mixed
433-1064		3-1/2 oz	10.00
433-1065	Lichen, Green	3-1/2 oz	10.00
433-1107	Grass	7 oz	3.75
433-1108	Economy Grass	16 oz	5.25

LICHEN
433-1060	Mixed	6.00
433-1061	Green	6.00

▲ NOCH
Imported from Germany by WALTHERS

GRASS MAT
Synthetic, 3-dimensional mat is 24 x 48"
528-10	Assorted	pkg(10)	99.49
528-24	Meadow		10.49
528-28	Autumn Meadow		10.49
528-624	Assorted Scenery Mats		12.99
528-618	Arable Field		13.49
	8-1/2 x 9-1/2" 21.5 x 24 cm		
528-620	Stubble Field		9.49
	12-1/2 x 9-1/2" 32 x 22 cm		
580-625	Moor Pond		20.49
580-619	Dandelioin Meadow		9.49
580-621	Corn/Poppy		9.49
528-833	Flowering		2.49

SNOW MAT

39 x 30"
528-18
9.99

SEA MAT   **NEW**
528-6085   20.49

TERRAIN MAT SURFACER   **NEW**
528-60920   7.49

STATIC GRASS
528-831	Light Green	pkg(3/8 oz)	2.49
528-5019	Light Green	pkg(100g)	8.99
528-811	Light Green w/Dispenser		7.99
528-832	Dark Green	pkg(3/8 oz)	2.49
528-5020	Dark Green	pkg(100g)	8.99
528-812	Dark Green w/Dispenser		7.99
528-834	Brown	pkg(3/8 oz)	2.49
528-810	Dispenser Only		3.99

GRASS APPLIER
Applies electrostatically charged grass to scenic areas. For use with 12-16v transformer (not included.)

Turbostat Grass Applier
528-5018   130.49

LICHEN
528-850	Stone Gray	pkg(7/8 oz)	4.49
528-8621	Light & Dark Green		5.49

■ LTD QTY AVAILABLE ■
528-853	Fall Colors	pkg(7/8 oz)	4.49

GROUND COVER   **NEW**
528-6410	Assorted Color	8.99

FOLIAGE
528-801	Light Green		3.99
528-802	Medium Green		3.99
528-804	Yellow		3.99
528-805	Fir Needles		3.99
528-957	Assorted	pkg(6)	11.99
528-6420	Assorted Colors **NEW**		8.99

SCATTER MATERIAL
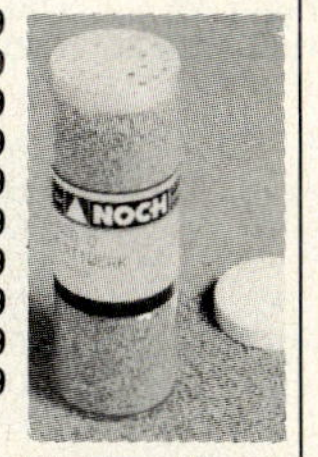
528-806	Leaves, Autumn	3.99
528-820	Flower Meadow	3.99
528-821	Light Green	3.99
528-822	Dark Green	3.99
528-824	Brown	3.99
528-825	Alp	3.99
528-826	Gray	3.99
528-827	Forest Ground	3.99
528-8350	Forest **NEW**	3.49
528-8360	Stoney **NEW**	3.49
	Mountain Meadow	

N.J. International

FLOCK
525-6851	Light Green	1 oz	1.99
525-6852	Dark Green	1 oz	1.99
525-6853	Brown/Weeds	1 oz	1.99

LICHEN
525-6763	Dark Green	10 oz	14.99
525-6770	Mixed	10 oz	14.99
525-6790	Dark Green	2.2 lbs	49.99
525-6862	Light Green	1 oz	1.99
525-6863	Dark Green	1 oz	1.99
525-6867	Gray	1 oz	1.99
525-6868	Yellow	1 oz	1.99
525-6869	Fall Rust	1 oz	1.99
525-6870	Mixed Colors	1 oz	1.99
525-6962	Light Green	2.5 oz	3.99
525-6963	Dark Green	2.5 oz	3.99
525-6969	Fall Rust	2.5 oz	3.99
525-6970	Mixed	2.5 oz	3.99

BALLAST
525-6886	Medium Brown	9 oz	.99

GROUND CORK   **NEW**
525-6887	Fine Light	2 oz	1.99
525-6888	Fine Dark	2 oz	1.99
525-6889	Coarse Dark	2 oz	1.99

GRASS & GROUND COVER

VISTA SCENIC HOBBY PRODUCTS

PINE SCENTED LICHEN

Lichen can be used to model trees, bushes or shrubs in any scale. Nine colors from summer greens to autumn reds are available. All colors are available in bulk packs of 17.5 oz (500 gm) or 2.1 oz (60 gm) packages.

2.1 oz 4.50		17.5 oz 28.50	
767-500	Light Green	767-5000	Light Green
767-501	Dark Green	767-5010	Dark Green
767-502	Mixed Colors	767-5020	Mixed Colors
767-503	Autumn	767-5030	Autumn
767-504	Olive Green	767-5040	Olive Green
767-505	Gray	767-5050	Gray
767-506	June Green	767-5060	June Green
767-507	Forest Green	767-5070	Forest Green
767-508	Fall Browns	767-5080	Fall Browns

SCENIC GRASS

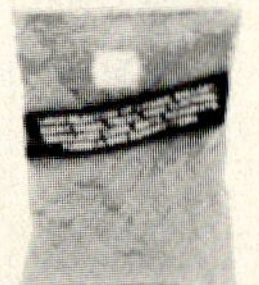

Medium grade sawdust dyed to simulate various types of grass, ground cover and earth. Use in a variety of scales and layout applications by mixing two or more colors, or by additional sieving. Covers approximately 2500 sq cm (400 sq inches)

2.6 oz (75 grams) packages 2.25

767-300	Light Green	767-306	Rusty Brown
767-301	Medium Green	767-307	Medium Brown
767-302	Dark Green	767-308	Light Brown
767-303	Grass with Flowers	767-309	Tan (Natural, Undyed)
767-304	Brown Earth Mix	767-310	Black
767-305	Yellow		

STATIC GRASS

Rayon fibers, only a few thousandths of an inch in thickness, produce a surface that has a velvet smooth texture. Suitable for use on smaller scale models such as HO, N, and Z. Use to decorate tunnels, rock-cuts, lakes and trees.

1.0 oz (30 grams) packages

767-360	Light Green	3.25
767-361	Dark Green	3.25
767-362	Brown	3.25
767-363	Yellow	3.25
767-364	Red	3.25
767-370	Sea Blue (Blended)	4.25
767-371	Desert Sand (Blended)	4.25
767-372	Terra Brown (Blended)	4.25
767-373	Meadow Green (Blended)	4.25

vintage Reproductions

GROUND COVER

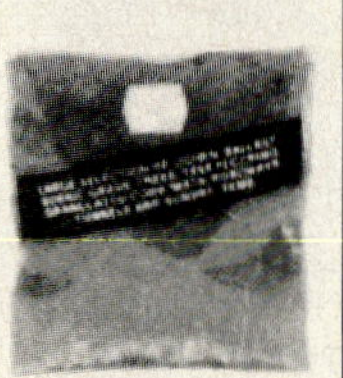

Each flexible, refillable bellow dispenser contains 30cc of blended synthetic fiber material. Kits Include four bellows filled with different shades of material.

766-701	1/32" L Summer Assort	8.50
766-704	1/32" L Winter Assort	8.50
766-705	1/32" Needles & Brwn Bark	8.50
766-710	1/32" Evergreen Ground	4.00
	Litter Needles	
766-713	Scale Soot Bellows	3.25
766-796	Evergreen Ground Litter (brown) 250cc	5.00
766-797	Evergreen Ground Litter (rusty) 250cc	5.00
766-803	Evergreen Needles (olive/green) 250cc	5.00
766-804	Evergreen Needles (blue/green) 250cc	5.00
766-805	Evergreen Needles (yellow/green) 250cc	5.00
766-806	Evergreen Needles (blue spruce) 250cc	5.00

BULK GRASS **NEW**

766-784	Light Tawny Green	5.00
766-785	Light Yellow-Green	5.00
766-786	Light Meadow Green	5.00
766-787	Dark Meadow Green	5.00
766-792	Light Buff	5.00
766-793	Light Golden Brown	5.00
766-794	Medium Golden Brown	5.00
766-795	Russet	5.00

A·M·S·I SCALE MODEL SUPPLIES

FLOWER FOAM PACKS   2 oz 8.49

137-800   Spring Color Pack 1/2oz of each: white, canary, bluebell & coral
137-820   Fall Color pack 1/2oz of each: red, gold, orange, plum
137-830   Summer Color Pack 1/2oz of each: fuchsia, delphinium, rose, violet

FLOWER COLORS GROUND FOAM   0.5 oz 2.49

137-10801	White	137-10813	Calico Rose
137-10802	Canary	137-10821	Maple Red
137-10803	Bluebell	137-10822	Fall Orange
137-10804	Salmon Pink	137-10823	Aspen Gold
137-10805	Pink Raspberry	137-10824	Plum
137-10810	Fuchsia	137-10825	Cherry Red
137-10811	Delphinium	137-10826	Purple
137-10812	Violet		

TEXTURES   pkg(1oz) 3.99

Premixed in combination shades of green; ready to apply as foliage, grass or ground cover.

137-1109	Lawn	137-309	Ground Cover
137-1206	Light Tree		
137-1207	Medium Tree	137-205	Medium Dark Tree
137-1208	Dark Tree		

FLEX-TURF   6.99

Ground foam texture on cloth backing material. 12 x 24".

137-1010	Turf Green	137-1030	Topsoil Brown
137-1020	Gravel Gray	137-1040	Hillside Tan

TERRAIN BRUSH   6.99

Topographical relief material for landscaped models. 12 x 12".

137-2010	Sage Brush	137-2030	Riverbank Brush
137-2020	High Mountain Brush	137-2040	Hill Country Brush

FLEX MAT   42.35

137-1002   48 x 54 x 1/2"   42.35

GROUND FOAM

Soft foam material is used for grass, ground cover, trees, shrubs & flowers. Fine grade is used for grass or small scale models. Medium grade is used for large scale ground cover or foliage. Coarse grade can simulate small shrubs or mass small tree plantings.

Use prefix #137 when ordering ground foam

	REGULAR 1oz 3.99			ECONOMY 5oz 16.00		
	FINE	MEDIUM	COARSE	FINE	MEDIUM	COARSE
Apple Green	611	612	613	6115	6125	6135
Spring Green	401	402	403	4015	4025	4035
Yellow Green	411	412	413	4115	4125	4135
Ochre Green	421	422	423	4215	4225	4235
Olive Green	431	432	433	4315	4325	4335
Grass Green	441	442	443	4415	4425	4435
Conifer Green	451	452	453	4515	4525	4535
Leaf Green	541	542	543	5415	5425	5435
Spruce Green	551	552	553	5515	5525	5535
Eucalyptus	561	562	563	5615	5625	5635
Dirt Brown	461	462	463	4615	4625	4635
Gray Green	471	472	473	4715	4725	4735
Black Forest	481	482	483	4815	4825	4835
Straw	491	492	493	4915	4925	4935
Plum	501	502	503	5015	5025	5035
Aspen Gold	511	512	513	5115	5125	5135
Fall Orange	521	522	523	5215	5225	5235
Maple Red	531	532	533	5315	5325	5335
Dust	571	572	573	5715	5725	5735
Top Soil	581	582	583	5815	5825	5835
Gravel Gray	591	592	593	5915	5925	5935
Coal Black	601	602	603	6015	6025	6035
Jungle Green	10621	10622	10623			

GRASS & GROUND COVER

WOODLAND SCENICS

COLOR GUIDE
The color swatches are to help in choosing color selection. Not all are true texture representations. See the 785-100 Woodland Scenics Reference Manual for authentic depictions.

A   P
B   Q
C   R
D   S
E   T
F   U
G   V
H   W
I   AA
J   BB
K   CC
L   DD
M   EE
N   FF
O   GG

The ultimate in model scenery realism is created by blending authentic colors of scenery material in various textures to depict nature. The different groups of ground cover products provide you with the various textures you'll need in representative natural hues. These realistic colors are formulated to blend in a variety of combinations and are monitored continuously to meet high quality standards. This assures you of color compatibility from one product to the next and consistency of color from one purchase to the next. Simple instructions are on each package with an overview of all product instructions in the 785-100 Woodland Scenics Reference Manual.

Turf is a ground foam material for modeling grass, dead grass, earth and soil. Three grades and eight realistic colors provide a wide range of combinations and textures for all seasons. Turf colors are formulated to blend with all other Woodland Scenics products for maximum realism.

BLENDED TURF
A	785-49 Green Blend		45 cu in	4.49
B	785-50 Earth Blend		45 cu in	4.49

FINE TURF
G	785-41 Soil		18 cu in	2.29
H	785-42 Earth		18 cu in	2.29
C	785-43 Yellow Grass		18 cu in	2.29
D	785-44 Burnt Grass		18 cu in	2.29
E	785-45 Green Grass		18 cu in	2.29
F	785-46 Weeds		18 cu in	2.29

COARSE TURF
I	785-60 Earth		18 cu in	2.29
C	785-61 Yellow Grass		18 cu in	2.29
D	785-62 Burnt Grass		18 cu in	2.29
J	785-63 Light Green		18 cu in	2.29
K	785-64 Medium Green		18 cu in	2.29
L	785-65 Dark Green		18 cu in	2.29

EXTRA COARSE TURF
C	785-34 Yellow Grass		18 cu in	2.29
D	785-35 Burnt Grass		18 cu in	2.29
J	785-36 Light Green		18 cu in	2.29
K	785-37 Medium Green		18 cu in	2.29
L	785-38 Dark Green		18 cu in	2.29
GG	785-39 Conifer Green		18 cu in	2.29

LICHEN
P	785-161 Spring Green		1-½qts	3.98
Q	785-162 Light Green		1-½qts	3.98
R	785-163 Medium Green		1-½qts	3.98
S	785-164 Dark Green		1-½qts	3.98
T	785-165 Autumn Mix		1-½qts	3.98
U	785-166 Natural		1-½qts	3.98
V	785-167 Light Green Mix		3qts	7.98
W	785-168 Dark Green Mix		3qts	7.98

FIELD GRASS
AA	785-171 Natural Straw		1.98
BB	785-172 Harvest Gold		1.98
CC	785-173 Light Green		1.98
DD	785-174 Medium Green		1.98

FOLIAGE
M	785-51 Light Green		60 sq in	2.79
N	785-52 Medium Green		60 sq in	2.79
O	785-53 Dark Green		60 sq in	2.79
GG	785-54 Conifer Green		60 sq in	2.79
EE	785-55 Early Fall		60 sq in	2.79
FF	785-56 Late Fall		60 sq in	2.79

FOLIAGE CLUSTERS
M	785-57 Light Green		45 cu in	3.98
N	785-58 Medium Green		45 cu in	3.98
O	785-59 Dark Green		45 cu in	3.98

GROUND COVER/MISCELLANEOUS
785-47	Fruit (Orange and Red)	2.29
785-48	Flowers (4 Colors)	2.29
785-178	Poly Fiber (Green)	1.49

ACCESSORIES
785-191	Scenic Cement	4.49
785-192	Scenic Sprayer	2.98
785-193	Scenic Sifter	2.98
785-100	Reference Manual	1.25

DIRT, GRAVEL & BALLAST

FALLER
Imported from Germany & marketed by WALTHERS

SCATTER MATERIAL
For realistic outside decor pkg(1 oz)

A	272-704	Plowed Field	1.49
B	272-705	Sand Brown	1.49
C	272-706	Ballast Gray	1.49
D	272-720	Gravel Brown	2.99
E	272-721	Brown/Gray	2.99
F	272-723	Coal	2.99
G	272-722	Gravel, Stone Gray	2.99
H	272-715	Assorted Rocks	7.99

(not illustrated)

272-740	Slate, Natural	1.99
272-743	Slate, Gray	1.99
272-744	Quartz	1.99
272-747	Beach Pebble, Beige	1.99

BALLAST

272-731	Track **NEW** 10.5oz Dark Brown	4.99
272-751	Track pkg(24 oz)	11.49
272-778	Mat (gray, 100x75 cm)	7.99

VOLLMER

Imported from Germany & marketed by WALTHERS

GRAVEL
770-5240   4.49

COAL
770-5224   4.49

STONE SHEET
12 x 8"
770-6012
pkg(5) 32.99

12 x 4"
770-6013
pkg(5) 19.99

WALL

770-6039	Gneiss	10 x 5"	pkg(10) 13.99
770-6040	Granite	10 x 5"	pkg(10) 13.99

WOODLAND SCENICS

BALLAST
pkg(7 oz) 2.29

Volume, not weight, determines how far a bag of ballast will spread. Woodland Scenics standard bag of ballast contains 12 fluid ounces (volume) and only weighs 7 oz, but is equivalent to approximately 20 oz (weight) of stone ballast.

	Colors	Fine	Medium	Coarse
A	Iron Ore	785-70	785-77	785-84
B	Dark Brown	785-71	785-78	785-85
C	Brown	785-72	785-79	785-86
D	Buff	785-73	785-80	785-87
E	Light Gray	785-74	785-81	785-88
F	Gray	785-75	785-82	785-89
G	Cinders	785-76	785-83	785-90
	785-91 Dry Ballast Cement			2.79
I	785-94 Blended Medium Gray			4.49

COAL (9 cubic inches)

H	785-92	Mine Run Coal Unsorted	2.29
H	785-93	Lump Coal	2.29

Chunks 4" or greater in diameter

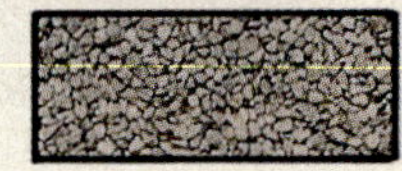

DIRT

785-41	Soil	2.29
785-42	Earth	2.29
785-50	Blended Turf-Earth	4.49

SCALE	FINE	MEDIUM	COARSE
N	1½"-5"	5"-8"	8"-16"
HO	¾"-2½"	2½"-4"	4"-8"
O	⅜"-1¼"	1¼"-2"	2"-4"

Ballast Reference Chart

SCALE	N	HO	O
B-92	0"-12"	0"-6"	0"-3"
B-93	8"-20"	4"-10"	2"-5"

Coal Reference Chart

kibri
Imported from Germany by WALTHERS

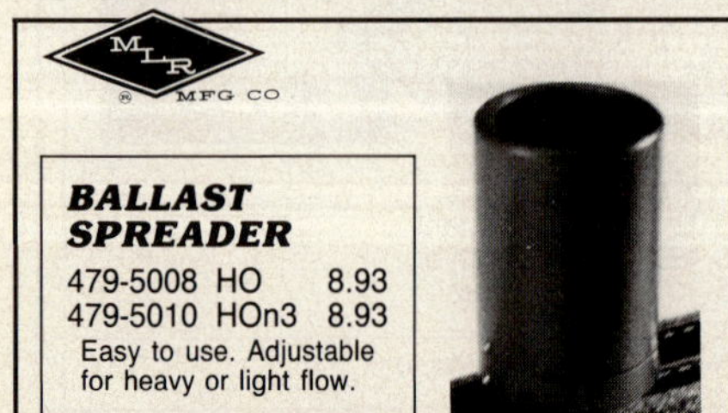

BALLAST
pkg(7-1/2 oz)

405-5891	White	2.49
405-5893	Brown	2.49
405-5894	Black	2.49
405-5895	Natural Cork	2.49

MLR MFG CO

BALLAST SPREADER

479-5008	HO	8.93
479-5010	HOn3	8.93

Easy to use. Adjustable for heavy or light flow.

SUPERIOR HOBBY PRODUCTS

QUARTZ AND GRANITE
These are the genuine item, crushed and sifted for model railroads. Use around mines, quarries or as car loads. NOTE: These items may be magnetic. If used for ballast, we suggest running a magnet over the rocks to remove any magnetic material.

Quartz-Ore
697-300   8 oz   3.50

LIFE-LIKE

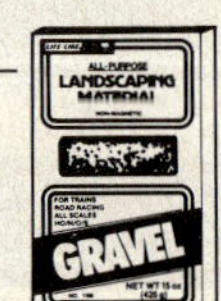

BALLAST

433-1104	Ballast White	15 oz	2.80
433-1105	Coal	15 oz	2.80
433-1106	Gravel	15 oz	2.80
433-1109	Earth	7 oz	3.75
433-1111	Economy Earth	16 oz	5.25

LANDSCAPING CEMENT

Clean, Non-toxic non-flammable adhesive. Dries hard & clean on almost an surface. Resealable can. 1 pint.

Landscaping Cement
433-1403   5.00

DIRT, GRAVEL & BALLAST

Campbell Scale Models

BALLAST
7 ounces
200-790	Light Gray	ea	3.50
200-791	Dark Gray	ea	3.50
200-793	Decomposed Granite	ea	3.50
200-792	Cinder	ea	3.50
200-794	Iron Ore	ea	3.50

COAL
200-795	Coal Load	3.50

Roco

Imported from Austria & marketed by WALTHERS

BALLAST
625-42652	Ballast	3.99
625-42653	Ballast Filler Plate	14.49

HIGHBALL PRODUCTS

COAL
(HO Scale dimensions)
330-130	Stoker 1-3″	14oz	5.50
330-131	Egg 2-5″	14oz	5.50
330-132	Lump over 6″	14oz	5.50
330-134	Coal Dust	5oz	5.95

SAWDUST
330-400	Sawdust Pack	each	11.95
	(Five assorted packs of sawdust)		

DIRT
330-510	Real Dirt	12oz	5.50
	Specially processed for model scenery.		

GRAVEL
330-520	Real Gravel	16oz	5.50

BALLAST
1 pound package of ballast
330-220	Limestone	each	3.30
330-221	Light Gray	each	3.30
330-222	Dark Gray	each	3.30
330-223	Black	each	3.30
330-224	Cinder	each	3.30
330-225	Brown	each	3.30

EARTH
330-170	Light Brown (Reg)	3oz	3.99
330-171	Light Brown (Fine)	3oz	3.99
330-172	Dark Brown (Reg)	3oz	3.99
330-173	Dark Brown (Fine)	3oz	3.99
330-174	Top Soil	3oz	3.99
330-175	Red	3oz	3.99

NOCH

Imported from Germany by WALTHERS

BALLAST
528-849	Gray, Coarse	1.4oz	1.99
528-935	Brown, Fine	17oz	4.99
528-936	Gray, Fine	17oz	4.99

A	B	C	D	E

NATURAL STONE
A	528-922	Fine, Mixed	pkg(16oz)	4.99	
B	528-926	Med, Mixed	pkg(16oz)	4.99	
C	528-930	Coarse, Red	pkg(16oz)	4.99	
	528-931	Med, Beige		4.99	
	528-932	Coarse Pink		4.99	
	528-921	Fine, Rust	pkg(16oz)	4.99	
	528-928	Med, Multi Colored		4.99	
D	528-9230	Crushed		**NEW** 4.99	
E	528-9240	Lime		**NEW** 4.99	

Plastruct **NEW**

GRAVEL
	Extra Fine 570-12850	4oz	1.49
	Fine 570-12851	8oz	1.49
570-12855	Super Fine	8oz	1.49

BALLAST
570-12871	Super Fine Black	8oz	1.49

Once, they seemed alive. Breathing smoke and fire, they raced the winds across the praries. Now they lie dead and cold, and the only fire they will ever feel again is the scrapper's torch. Chunks of engine #1064 will soon be headed for the mills in a battered gon that looks like it's seen better days too. Dave Roeder of St. Louis, Missouri, built this scene of a Frisco engine meeting its end on his home layout. The various loco parts are from Monogram plastic engine kits, (out of production) along with a variety of commercial details and hand-made items. Plenty of weathering was applied to finish the scene. *Models and Photo by Dave Roeder*

ROCKS & MOLDING MATERIALS

FALLER

Imported from Germany and marketed by WALTHERS

ROCK CASTINGS
Polyurethane rigid foam with filler compound and flocking material. 19 x 10" sheet.

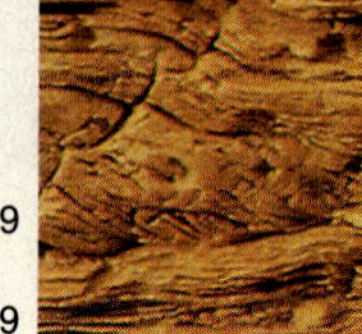

Sand Stone
272-798   14.99

Granite
272-797   14.99

ROCK ASSORTMENT
Quarry walls, rugged mountain passes, or mine scenes are just a few places to use these realistic rocks! Each is made from rigid foam and can easily be blended with your scenery.

272-799   Assorted Rocks   11.49

CHEMCO RESIN CRAFTS

CASTING RESIN
Water-clear, less catalyst. Shelf-life of approximately nine months, can be extended if stored at cool temperatures.

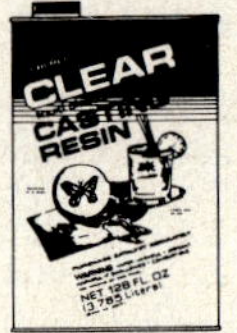

207-175	16oz	8.99
207-183	32oz	14.79
207-191 **NEW**	1gal	43.99

CATALYST
Hardner (turns liquid resin into a solid) for use with #175 and #183.

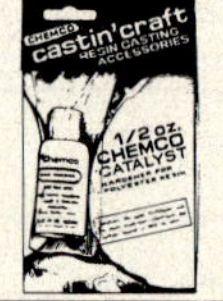

207-46388   1/2oz   2.49

TRANSPARENT DYE
Add for see-through color in casting resin.

207-46434	Blue	1/2oz	2.99
207-46469	Green	1/2oz	2.99
207-46418	Pearl	1/2oz	2.99
207-46493	Amber	1/2oz	2.99

MOLD BUILDER
Liquid latex rubber for mold making.

207-779   16 oz 7.99

AMACO
American Art Clay Co., Inc.

A.I.M. PRODUCTS
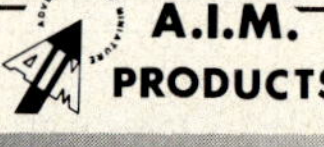

POUND OF ROCKS
Assorted rock castings sold by the pound, usually about 9 castings per package.

110-500   Rocks (16 oz net, min)   4.50

MOLDING MATERIALS
126-41810   Instant   pkg(1 lb)   5.39
           Papier Mache

Dry powder mixes with water, ready to use in 15 to 20 minutes. Material is nontoxic and dries white. Can be painted with any type of paint when dry.

126-41821	Sculpta-Mold	pkg(3lb) 5.39
126-41822	Sculpta-Mold	pkg(25lb) 36.75
126-41823	Sculpta-Mold	pkg(50lb) 68.25

White, nontoxic powder material mixes with water, sets in 30 minutes without shrinking. Clings to most clean surfaces and can be applied over forms without fear of cracking. Finished material is lightweight yet durable. May be cut, carved, sawed or sanded.

126-53301   Crea-Stone   pkg(5 lb) 15.69

Dry powder mixes with water to make castings or moldings. Can be sculpted and carved for long periods if kept moist. Drys rock-hard with rough granite texture and color.

126-75541   Mix-A-Mold   pkg(8 oz) 8.09

Nontoxic material for creating original molds of 3-D objects. Picks up every detail of original item. Powder mixes with water and molds are ready in two minutes. Can be used with Sculpta-Mold, Crea-Stone, plaster or other casting materials.

NOCH
Imported from Germany by WALTHERS

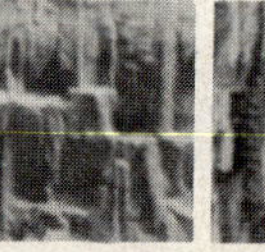 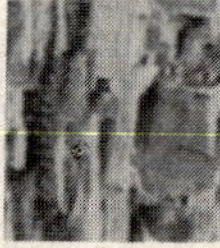 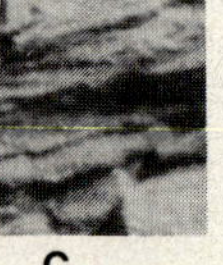

A   **B**   **C**

FORMATION
Flat mountain rock sides formed from appropriately colored plastic. 10-5/8 x 5-1/8" 27 x 13 cm.

A	528-6078	Slate	pkg(5)	15.49
B	528-6079	Granite	pkg(5)	15.49
C	528-6080	Multi-Colored Sandstone	pkg(5)	15.49

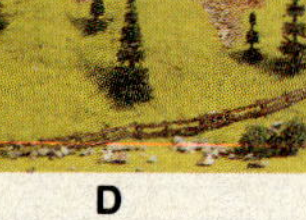

D

E

D	528-593	11-3/4 x 7"		33.49
E	528-6082	Rocky Wall	pkg(2)	17.49

CORK
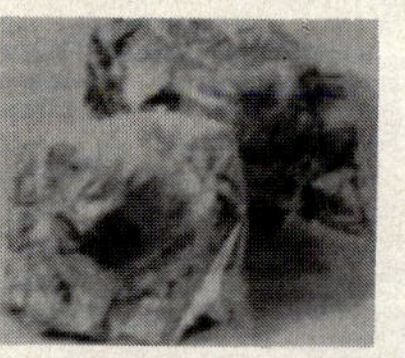

Small
528-881   6.49
pkg(80 grams)

Large
528-882   11.99
pkg(180 grams)

GRANITE ROCK PLATE

Rock plates can be used in a scattered fashion or continuous to form a wall.

528-5847   Granite Panel   16.49
       13 x 6-3/4" 33 x 17 cm

LIFE-LIKE
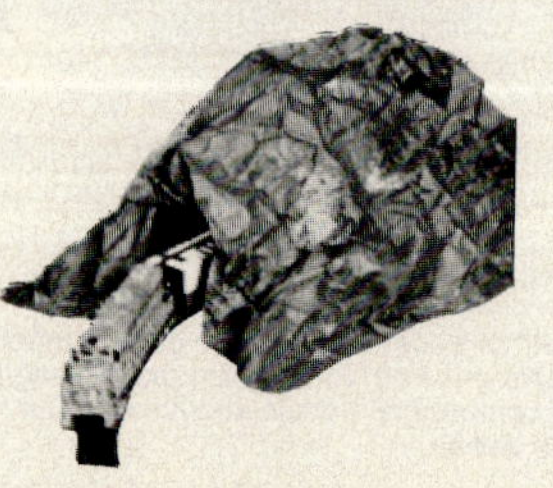

MOUNTAIN PAPER
Ready-to-use mountain paper can be used to create mountains, tunnels and scenes. Easy-to-shape, just wet it, shape it; place it.
- Realistic color
- Reuseable
- 24 x 72"

433-1157   Mountain Paper   5.00

kibri
Imported from Germany by WALTHERS

ASSORTED ROCKS
ANY SCALE
Illustration approximately 1/3 full scale.

405-4112   pkg(10) 21.49
gray molded plastic

ROCKS & MOLDING MATERIALS

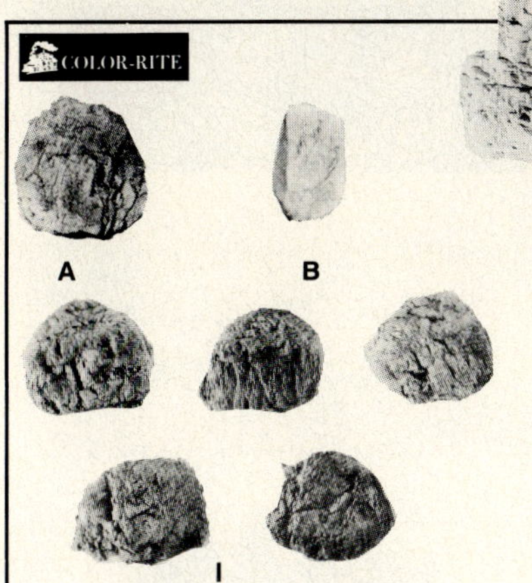

 C

 D

 E

 F

 G

H

A

B

I

ROCK MOLDS

Made of a soft rubber-like vinyl. Each mold will allow unlimited casting variations with finger and thumb pressure. You can use the same mold side by side without the appearance of repetition. Almost indestructible, will not lose detail with use.

A	211-802	3-1/2″ x 3-1/2″	3.69
B	211-803	6″ x 2-1/2″	3.69
C	211-804	4″ x 4-1/4″	3.69
D	211-805	8″ x 3-1/2″	3.69

E	211-806	4-1/4″ x 2-1/2″	3.69
F	211-807	4-3/4″ x 3-1/2″	3.69
G	211-808	6-1/2″ x 4-1/4″	3.69
H	211-809	5″ x 3-1/2″	3.69
I	211-810	5 Mold Set (Large)	27.95

Molds are 6 × 6-1/2″ to 6-1/2 × 8″ in area and about 1/2″ to 3/4″ deep.

211-801 8 Mold Set 27.95
Includes ''A-H''

ACTIVA PRODUCTS, INC.

CELLUCLAY

A clean, instant papier machine for sculpting scenery, etc.

142-100 1 lb 4.50

RIGID WRAP

Plaster cloth wrap; moisten with water and form mountains, hills, etc. Sets in five minutes. Follows any curve or crease. Non-toxic.

142-230 4 x 180″ 3.50

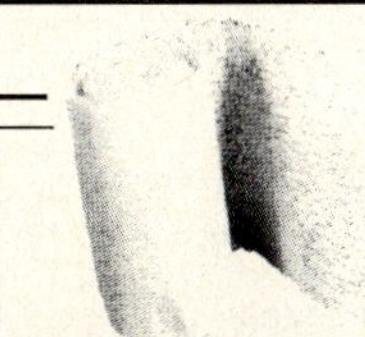

ART PLASTER

Plaster for casting figures in molds or free form sculpting

142-225 5 lb 6.50

INSTAMOLD

Ready-to-use, molds in 2 minutes. Non-toxic, mixes with water, use with wax, plaster, resin, Permastone™. Makes up to 3/4 gallon.

142-250 12 oz 7.00

LANDSCAPING KIT

Contains:
6 rolls of plaster cloth-Rigid Wrap
2 lbs of Papier Mache - Celluclay
1 pkg mold making compound - Instamold
1 pkg of casting compound - Permastone™
4 ozs resin glue - Se-cur-ir
1 modeling tool
Full instructions

142-177 27.95

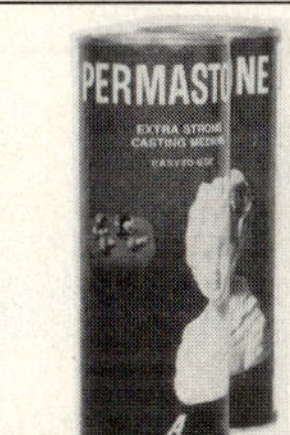

PERMASTONE

Mix with water to make extra-hard castings. Damaged castings are easilty repaired.

142-350 28 oz 4.50

PERMACRAFT PRODUCTS

PERMA-SCENE MODELING COMPOUND

Mixes with water and can be spread with a spatula, teaspoon or with your hands. It can be applied over wood, any type of screen, cardboard, foil or styrofoam. When dry, any type of paint can be applied for different effects.

- Perma Scene
- Natural Earth Color
- Odorless
- Non-Toxic
- Crack Resistant
- Featherweight

557-101 pkg(12oz) 3.99
557-102 pkg(22oz) 6.49

ACCESSORIES

557-400	Scene-Stick Adhesive	2oz	2.49
557-500	Scene-Six Colors of Tint	3/4oz	8.99
557-600	Scene-Stone		2.99
557-601	Scene-Rock		2.99

Creative Customcraft NEW

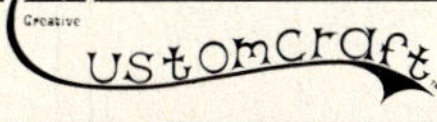

MODELING COMPOUND

FASTFILL™
153-124 8oz 4.99
Ultralight, fast drying, non-shrinking filler.

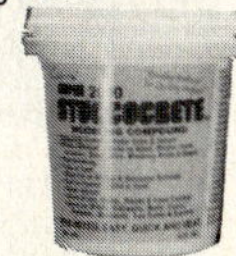

STUCCOCRETE™
153-519 16oz 9.99
Concrete mortar color and texture. Strong adhesion, non-shrinking compound.

MODELER'S ASPHALT™
153-523 16oz 9.99
For flat black color and texture. Strong adhesion, non-shrinking compound.

SPRAYLOCK 2000™
153-82629 11oz 10.99
All purpose spray adhesive. Temporary or permanent bonds. Works fast, dries clear. Safe on painted or unpainted surfaces, foam products, and grass mats. Perfect for Instant Horizons & Instant Buildings.

Plastruct

SCENIC ROCK

Coarse
8oz 1.49
570-12811 Marble
570-12812 Beige
570-12813 Concrete
570-12814 Light Gray
570-12815 Dark Gray

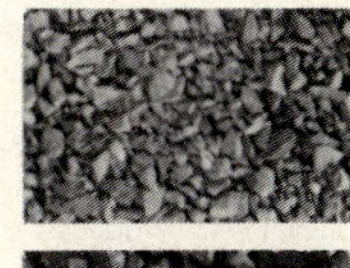

Medium
8oz 1.49
570-12821 Marble
570-12822 Beige
570-12823 Concrete
570-12824 Light Gray
570-12825 Dark Gray

Landscape Boulders
570-12882
pkg(2) 1.95

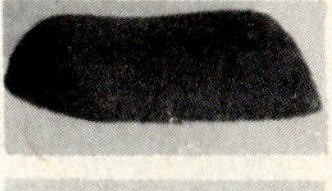

Natural Boulders
570-12883
pkg(3) 1.95

Rock Assortments
570-12852
4oz 1.49

ROCKS & MOLDING MATERIALS

Mountains in Minutes®
I.S.L.E. LABORATORIES

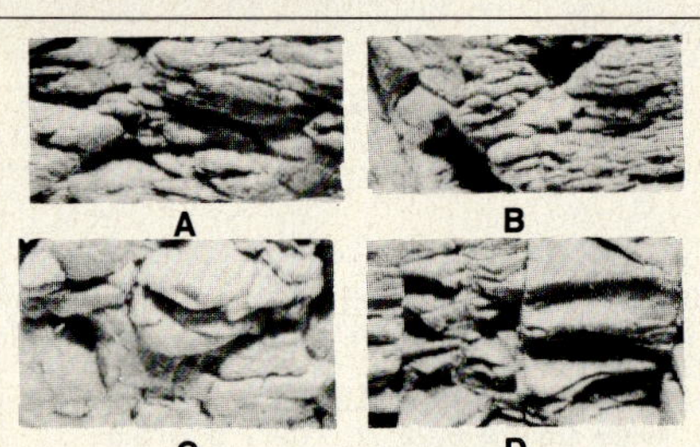

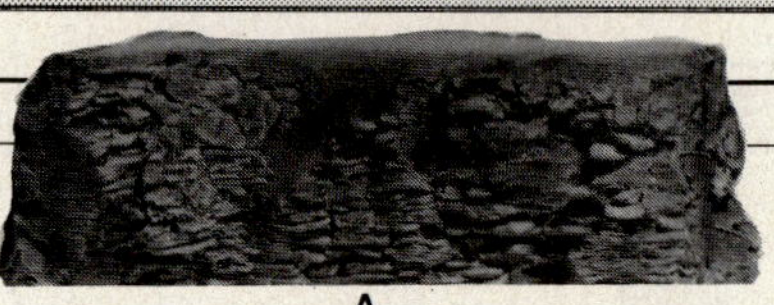

A

NATURAL ROCK CASTINGS

Foam duplicates of actual rock formations. Use as models to produce your own duplicate castings (using Mountains in Minutes materials) or cut them out and fit them right into your layout. Each casting comes complete with instructions and painting tips.
(All natural rock castings 12″ × 12″)
(30.5 × 30.5 cm)

A	473-804	Colorado Red Rock	12.98
B	473-801	Agawa Canyon Wall	12.98
C	473-803	Royal Gorge	12.98
D	473-802	Kittanning Slope	12.98

(not illustrated)

473-501	Rock Canyon Wall	12.98
473-502	Rock Embankment Wall	12.98
473-503	Flexrock Rock Gorge **NEW**	12.98

ROCK FORMATIONS

A 473-820 Multi-Scale Embankment   12.98
     15 × 6-1/2″ 38 × 16 cm
Easily cut with serrated knife or modeling knife. Paint with enamels, oils or water base acrylics. (Lacquer base paints may cause cracking.)

B 473-860 Multi-Scale Mountain - medium   34.98
   * Premolded rigid foam mountain in variable color and detail of natural rock.
   * Templates provided for easy carving of optional size tunnel openings.
   * Approximate size: 10″ × 18″ × 20″.
     (254 × 470 × 508 mm)

C 473-880 Multi-Scale Mountain-Front   59.98

(not illustrated)

473-855 Multi-Scale Mountain-Small   14.98

ACCESSORIES

473-701	Model Landscape Kit		35.98
473-702	''Part A'' Polyfoam Refill	qt	16.49
473-703	''Part B'' Polyfoam Refill	qt	16.49
473-704	Latex Mold Compound	qt	15.98
473-705	Latex Mold Compound	pt	8.49
473-706	Mold Release Comp.	2oz	1.98
473-350	Mini Centrifugal Pump		12.98

Operates on 12 v DC, pumping rate one pint per minute. Uses: Model waterfalls, fountains and displays.

B

C

CRAFT CAST

473-900 Craft Cast Expanding   17.98
     Foam Resin

(1 pt each: Polyfoam ''A'' & B'') Expands up to 30 times amount of original material. Forms rigid foam that can be stained, carved, sanded or molded.

SUPERIOR
HOBBY PRODUCTS

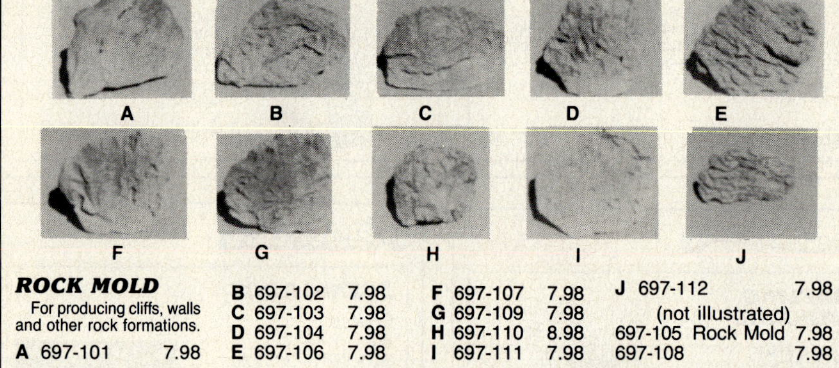

ROCK MOLD

For producing cliffs, walls and other rock formations.

A	697-101	7.98					
B	697-102	7.98	F	697-107	7.98	J	697-112 7.98
C	697-103	7.98	G	697-109	7.98		(not illustrated)
D	697-104	7.98	H	697-110	8.98	697-105 Rock Mold	7.98
E	697-106	7.98	I	697-111	7.98	697-108	7.98

ROCK MOLD POCKET

Duplicates rock outcropping of mountain tops, etc. Produces a ''3-D'' casting with texture on all sides.

A	697-113	9.98
B	697-116	9.98
C	697-117	9.98
D	697-114	9.98
E	697-115	9.98
F	697-118	9.98

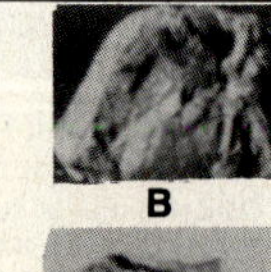
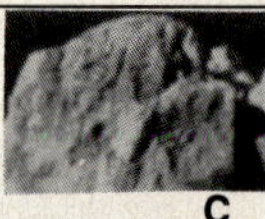
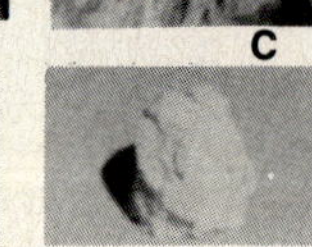

MOLD RELEASE AGENT

Simplifies removal of finished castings from rock molds, compatible with latex used in Superior molds.

Mold Release Agent
697-200   4oz 3.89

LATEX MOLD MATERIAL

Liquid rubber for making your own models.

697-201	8oz	6.89
687-202	16oz	9.89
697-203	32oz	18.98

PLASTER AND CASTINGS   **NEW**

697-9201	Hydrocal Plaster	8lb	11.97
697-9202	Dental Casting Plaster	3lb	5.97
697-9203	Hydrocal Plaster	3lb	5.97
697-9204	Dental Casting Plaster	8lb	11.97

Vintage Reproductions

GRANITE ROCK DUSTER

Use with rubber molds and plaster castings to create a ''glint of granite''. One bellow kit contains duster blend to be puffed onto wet mold before filling.

766-722	Granite Duster	3.00
766-775	Granite Duster (bulk 250cc)	5.50

FOOLS GOLD

A single bellows filled with pale yellow, sparkling ''fools'' gold.

766-721	''Fools'' Gold	3.00

EXTRA DISPENSER

A disposable/refillable bellows syringe ideal for dusting powder, ground covers, ballast, flocking fibers, liquids & glue.

Dispenser for Liquids
766-702   pkg(2) 2.00
Liquid dispenser has a small opening in the nozzle for liquids and glues to flow out.

Dispenser for Dry Materials
766-709   pkg(2) 2.00
Dispenser for dry material has a wider opening in the nozzle to allow particles through.

EYEBOLTS/PADEYES

3/16″ Height, .055″ Diameter

766-359	Cast	2.50
766-360	Machined	2.50
766-361	Eyepin—0.7″ Dia Hole—	2.00
	.029″ Wire	
766-363	Stone Sheathing— pkg(6)	3.50
	Marble & Slate Paper	

ROCKS & MOLDING MATERIALS

ROCK MOLD CASTINGS
Detail cast plaster.

A 226-114 5 × 6″	6.95	
B 226-113 6 × 9″	6.95	
C 226-115 6 × 8″	6.95	
D 226-116 6 × 6-1/2″	6.95	
E 226-117 6 × 7″	6.95	
F 226-118 7 × 6-1/4″	6.95	
G 226-119 8-1/2 × 6″	6.95	

WOODLAND SCENICS — NEW

TERRAIN SHELL SUPPLIES
785-1201	Lightwt Hydrocal	1/2 gal	6.98
785-1202	Mold-a-Scene Pl	1/2 gal	6.98
785-1203	Plaster Cloth	10 sq ft	6.98
785-1204	Latex Rubber	16 oz vol	9.49
785-1205	Flex Paste	16 oz vol	9.98

ROCK MOLDS
5″ x 7″
785-1230	Outcroppings	4.98
785-1231	Surface Rocks	4.98
785-1232	Boulders	4.98
785-1233	Embankments	4.98
785-1234	Random Rock	4.98
785-1235	Laced Face Rock	4.98
785-1236	Classic Rock	4.98
785-1237	Wind Rock	4.98
785-1238	Weathered Rock	4.98
785-1239	Strata Stone	4.98
785-1240	Rock Mass	4.98
785-1241	Layered Rock	4.98

5″ x 10-1/2″
785-1242	Washed Rock	5.98
785-1243	Base Rock	5.98
785-1244	Facet Rock	5.98

TUNNEL LINER FORM
Cast realistic rock walls and ceilings for single or double track tunnel.

785-1250	2.98

TALUS (ROCK DEBRIS)
785-1270	Fine Buff	2.29
785-1271	Medium Buff	2.29
785-1272	Coarse Buff	2.29
785-1273	Extra Coarse Buff	2.29
785-1274	Fine Brown	2.29
785-1275	Medium Brown	2.29
785-1276	Coarse Brown	2.29
785-1277	Extra Coarse Brown	2.29
785-1278	Fine Gray	2.29
785-1279	Medium Gray	2.29
785-1280	Coarse Gray	2.29
785-1281	Extra Coarse Gray	2.29
785-1282	Fine Natural	2.29
785-1283	Medium Natural	2.29
785-1284	Coarse Natural	2.29
785-1285	Extra Coarse Natural.	2.29

Build a complete scene by combining these items with products from Woodland Scenics Terrain System.

HIGHBALL PRODUCTS

SCENIC ROCK
(1 lb pkgs) 4.79 each

330-150 Sand-White	330-153 Iron Ore
330-151 Stone	330-154 Sand-Brown

INSTA-ROCK

INSTA-ROCK

Towering mountains, deep canyons or weathered stone outcroppings are easy to build for your layout, module or diorama when you use Insta-Rock!

This material is a nontoxic blend of compounds which you just mix with water and apply in a 1/4″ layer. The material will follow the contours of your scenery forms and can be spread on to produce cliffs. Extra material can be applied and shaped with a pallette knife to simulate weathered rock formations. Average working time is about 25 to 30 minutes and the material will dry completely in two to five days, depending on temperature and humidity. As it dries, the material takes on a natural granite color which can be used as is or blended with earth-tone spray paints. Insta-Rock may be used in Rock Molds.

When dry, Insta-Rock is strong, lightweight and fireproof, so it's ideal for use on display layouts or modules which are frequently moved.

354-768238	1 pound, 10 ounces	3.98
354-768249	8 pounds, 12 ounces	17.98

Passengers and passersby await the arrival of a DTS local. Like small towns everywhere, train time is something of a social occasion, and folks don't seem to mind if the train is late. This father-and-son layout is the work of Donald and Tom Staton (from whom the DTS takes its name) of Jordan, New York. A Timberline station (out of production) occupies the foreground, while additional Timberline false-front buildings line Main Street. Rocky's Tap is a Woodland Scenics kit.
Photo by Tom Staton

STONE & BRICK MATERIALS

FALLER
Imported from Germany & marketed by **WALTHERS**

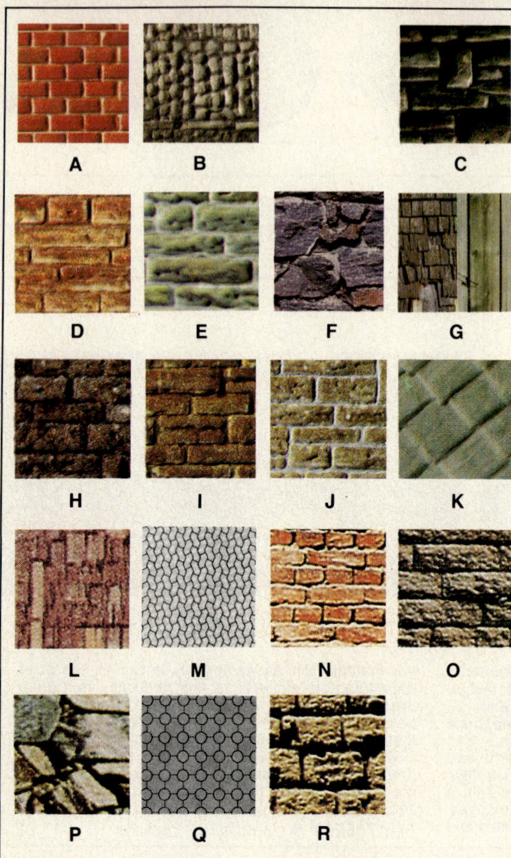

SCENERY PANELS
Ea 1.49

Embossed panels are pre-printed in appropriate colors. Panels measure: 9-7/8 x 4-7/8" 25 x 12.5 cm

Dealers: MUST order Dealer Pack (10)

A	272-608	Red Brick
B	272-601	Cobblestone
C	272-604	Cut Stone Brown
D	272-605	Cut Stone Yellow
E	272-606	Cut Stone Gray
F	272-610	Natural Stone
G	272-612	Shingles & Board
H	272-614	Cut Stone Brown
I	272-615	Cut Stone Yellow
J	272-616	Cut Stone Gray
K	272-623	Roof Tile Slate
L	272-613	Cut Stone Red
M	272-600	Sidewalk Material
N	272-607	Glazed Brick
O	272-617	Cut Stone Basalt
P	272-618	Cut Stone Slate
Q	272-619	Ornamental Pavement
R	272-620	Cut Stone Limestone

ROOF TILE
272-596   6.49

Brown plastic roofing material includes 2 sheets ridge tiles and down pipes.

Campbell Scale Models

PLASTIC STONE
200-810 Clear   5-3/8 x 17-1/4"   ea 8.00

AIM MODELS

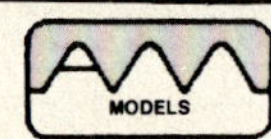

STONES
129-502   1.98

Stones are molded in various colors. Enough stones to cover an area of 10 square inches. Various shapes.

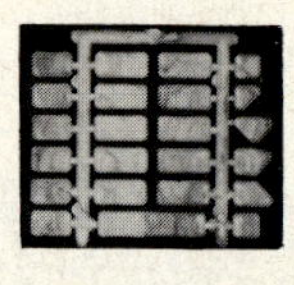

WHITEGROUND MODEL WORKS

TAR PAPER
771-50031	Black	2.00
771-50032	Red	2.00
771-50033	Green	2.00
771-50034	Blue	2.00
771-50035	Brown	2.00

SCALE WORKS MODELS

MORTAR 2oz. 3.89   **NEW**

For all brick & stone mortar lines. Can be applied to any material. Clean up with warm water.

644-10	Weathered White
644-20	Concrete Gray
644-30	Light Gray
644-40	Light Sand
644-50	Red
644-60	Tar Black

NOCH
Imported from Germany by **WALTHERS**

STONE SHEETS
9 x 6" plastic sheets, unless noted.

528-5751	Granite		1.49
528-5752	Dolomite		1.49
528-5753	Basalt		1.49
528-5754	Green Slate		1.49
528-5755	Brick		1.49
528-5756	Square Stone		1.49
528-5757	Sandstone		1.49
528-5770	Granite, 26 x 6"	pkg(5)	5.49
528-5771	Dolomite, 26 x 6"	pkg(5)	5.49
528-5772	Basalt, 26 x 6"	pkg(5)	5.49
528-5773	Brick, 26 x 6"	pkg(5)	5.49

NATURAL STONE

528-917	Sand	4.99
528-918	Fine & Coarse	4.99
528-919	Fine, Colored	4.49
528-921	Fine, Rust 16oz	4.99
528-923	Fine, Red	4.49
528-924	Medium, red	4.49
528-927	Medium, green	4.49
528-928	Med, Multi Color	4.99
528-950	Assorted pkg(6)	11.99
528-9230	Crushed **NEW**	4.99
528-9240	Lime **NEW**	4.99

Plastruct

BRICK, ROCK & STONE SHEETS

7" x 12" Patterned Sheets Vacuum Formed from .030 Styrene Plastic. All Ho Scale or Equivalent.

Coursed Stone 570-10061 pkg(3) 11.85

Rock Embankment 570-10068 pkg(3) 11.85

Random Stone 570-10073 pkg(3) 11.85

Field Stone 570-10076 pkg(3) 11.85

Rough Brick 570-10091 pkg(3) 11.85

Concrete Block 570-10103 pkg(3) 11.85

Diamond Plate 570-10145 pkg(3) 11.85 **(By Special Order Only.)**

Coursed Stone 570-10064 pkg(3) 11.85

Stucco 570-10070 pkg(3) 11.85

Field Stone 570-10074 pkg(3) 11.85

Dressed Stone 570-10082 pkg(3) 11.85

Brick 570-10097 pkg(3) 11.85

Sidewalks & Curbs 570-10160 pkg(3) 11.85

STONE & BRICK MATERIALS

VOLLMER

Imported by Germany & marketed by **WALTHERS**

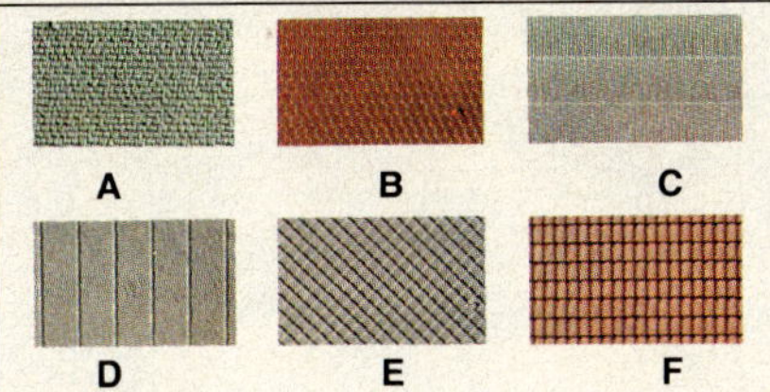

ROOFING

Each plastic sheet measures 4-1/2 x 8-1/2".

A	770-6025	Wood Shingles	pkg(5) 24.49
B	770-6026	Red Tile	pkg(5) 24.49
C	770-6027	Corrugated Iron	pkg(5) 24.49
D	770-6029	Tar Paper	pkg(5) 24.49
E	770-6030	Slate	pkg(5) 24.49
F	770-6032	Tile	pkg(5) 24.49

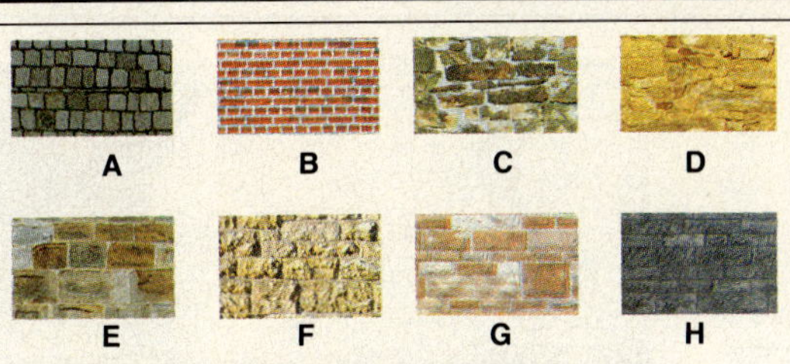

STONE PATTERN EMBOSSED PAPER

Embossed paper can be used as pavement or buildings. Less adhesive. 10 x 5"   25 x 12.5cm

A	Cobblestone	770-6041	pkg(10) 13.99
B	Red Brick	770-6042	pkg(10) 13.99
C	Brown Stone	770-6043	pkg(10) 13.99
D	Buff Sandstone	77-6044	pkg(10) 13.99
E	Gray Sandstone	770-6045	pkg(10) 13.99
F	Marble	770-6046	pkg(10) 13.99
G	Red Sandstone	770-6047	pkg(10) 13.99
H	Granite	770-6048	pkg(10) 13.99

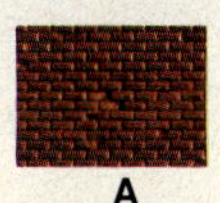
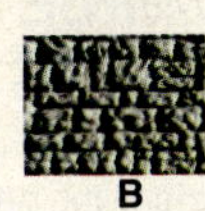

WALL SECTIONS

Cut stone wall sections are printed on self-adhesive vinyl.

Brick and stone wall sections are molded of appropriately colored styrene plastic. 4-1/2 x 8-1/2".

A	Red Brick	770-6028	pkg(5) 24.49
B	Rough Stone	770-6031	pkg(5) 24.49

kibri

Imported from Germany by **WALTHERS**

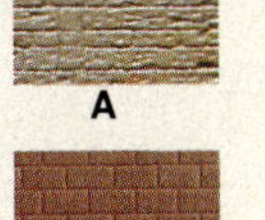

STONE, BRICK, SIDEWALK

Stone, brick and sidewalk sheets are molded in appropriately colored plastic. Each sheet is 8 x 4-3/4". Illustrations approximately 2/3 full scale.

A	Cut Stone	405-4119 (beige)	4.49
B	Smooth Cut Stone	405-4145 (beige)	4.49
C	Natural	405-4121 (gray)	4.49
D	Brick	405-4122 (red)	4.49
		405-4147 (brown)	4.49
E	Sidewalk	405-4123 (light gray)	4.49
F	Cobblestone	405-4124	4.49
G	Cobblestone with grooves for track	405-4125	4.49

Wall sections are printed in full color on cardstock. Natural Stone, Roof Sections and Assorted Rocks are molded in appropriately colored plastic. 5-1/8 x 6-3/4". Illustrations approximately 2/3 full scale.

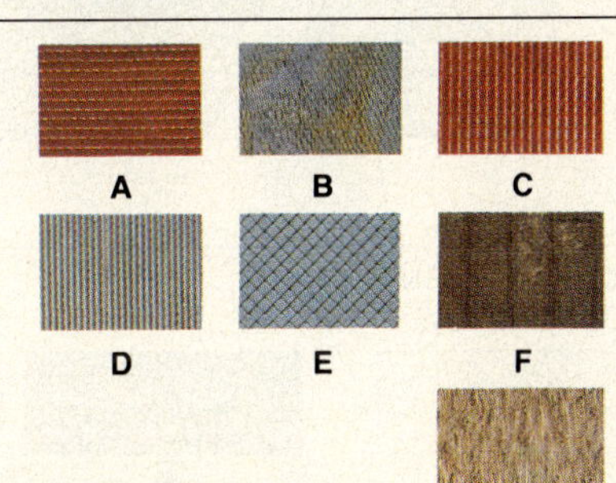

ROOF SECTIONS

Roof sections are molded in appropriately colored plastic. Each sheet is 8 x 4-3/4".

A	405-4140	Flat Tile (red)	each 4.49
B	405-4141	Shingle (gray)	each 4.49
C	405-4142	Round Tile (red)	each 4.49
D	405-4143	Corrugated Metal (light gray)	each 4.49
E	405-4144	Slate Tile	each 4.49
F	405-4116	Tile (brown)	each 4.49
G	405-4139	Thatched (tan)	each 4.49

PAVEMENT

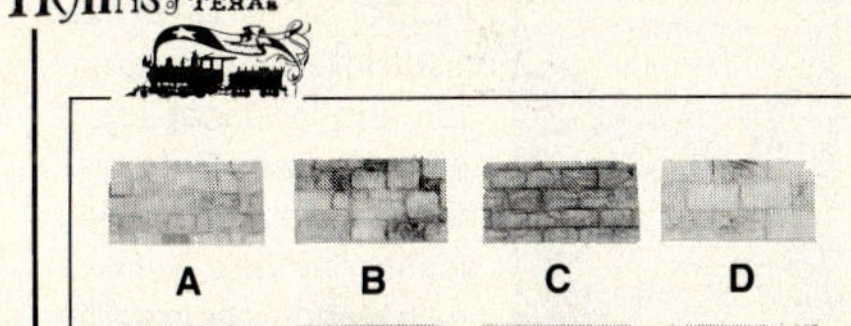

A	405-4127	Paving for Dock-side Crane	4.49
B	405-4128	Concrete Slab (5 x 8")	4.49

WALL SECTIONS

A	Uneven Stone Pattern Tan/Green	405-4150	1.49
B	Even Stone Pattern-Gray	405-4151	1.49
C	405-4155 Red Brick		1.49
D	Random Cut Stone, plastic sheet	405-4120 HO	4.49
E	Cut Stone, plastic sheet	405-4118	4.49

TRAINS of TEXAS

A	B	C	D
E	F	G	H

STONE SHEETS
CAST PLASTER

A	226-552	Random Cut, small 4-3/8 x 7-3/4"	ea 6.95
B	226-553	Random Cut, large 5 x 7-3/4"	ea 6.95
C	226-554	Even Cut, small 5 x 7-3/4"	ea 6.95
D	226-555	Even Cut, large 5-1/2 x 7-3/4"	ea 6.95
E	226-556	Random Cut, smooth 7-5/8 x 5-1/2"	ea 6.95
F	226-557	Random Field, small 7-5/8" x 5"	ea 6.95
G	226-558	Brick 7-5/8 x 5"	ea 6.95
H	226-559	Cast Masonry 7-7/8 x 5"	6.95

MISCELLANEOUS

226-524	Pallisade **NEW** 10 x 4-1/2"	each 13.95
226-523	Cobblestone 4-5/8 x 7-3/4"	pkg(2) 13.95
226-520	Small Log Wall 4-1/2 x 1"	pkg(6) 13.95
226-521	Large Log Wall 6-1/8 x 1-3/4"	pkg(3) 13.95

Preiser

Imported from Germany by **WALTHERS**

PLASTIC SHEET

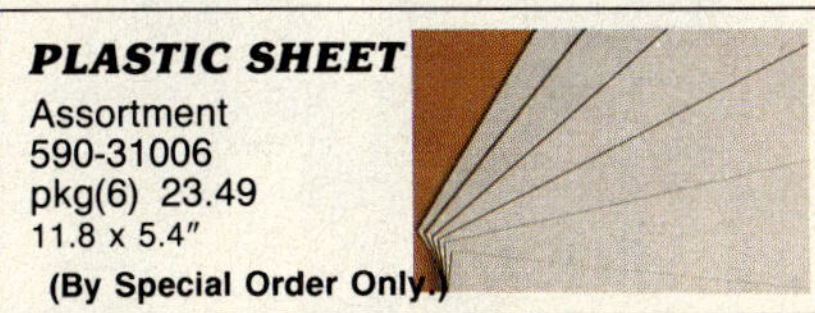

Assortment
590-31006
pkg(6) 23.49
11.8 x 5.4"
(By Special Order Only.)

PAVING

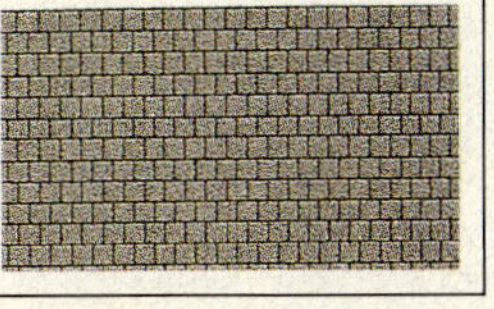

Flagstone Paving Blocks
590-18142 7.99
190 x 480 x 3 mm

TERRAIN

THE COMPLETE TERRAIN SYSTEM

Woodland Scenics Terrain Products are a complete system for beginners and crafts-man modelers alike. The Terrain System has all the products needed to make earth contour models that reflect any type of terrain. The system includes Lightweight Hydrocal, Mold-A-Scene, Plaster Cloth, E-Z Water, Flex Paste, Latex Rubber, Tunnel Portals, Retaining Walls, Culverts, Talus, Tunnel Liner Form, Earth Color Liquid Pigments, Scenic Sprayer, Rock Molds and The Scenery Manual. Each product has easy to follow instructions. The Terrain System is the way, the Woodland Scenics Way.

THE SCENERY MANUAL

"Terrain and Landscape Modeling the Woodland Scenics Way" is an illustrated start-to-finish guide to terrain construction and landscaping. It is full of basics for beginners and secrets of skilled scenery modelers. Easy to do techniques are fully explained.

785-1207   The Scenery Manual $4.98

SCENIC SPRAYER

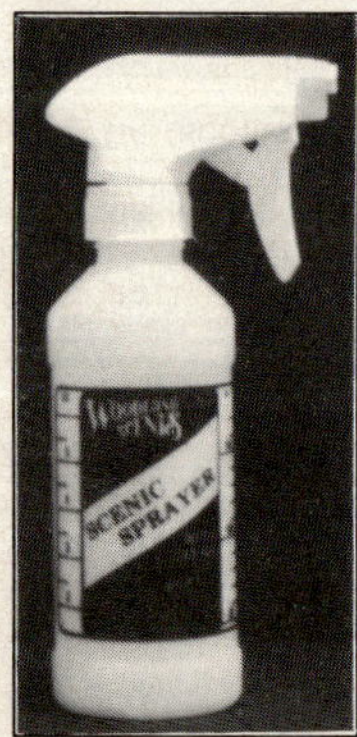

The Scenic Sprayer comes with a long siphon tube and spray head that fits the Scenic Cement bottle. Nozzle is adjustable from a very fine mist to a steady stream. May be used to spray water, diluted Earth Color Liquid Pigments, and Scenic Cement.

785-192   Scenic Sprayer $2.98

LIQUID PIGMENT COLOR GUIDE

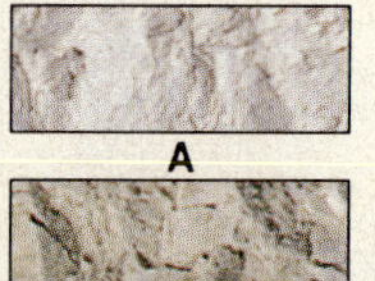

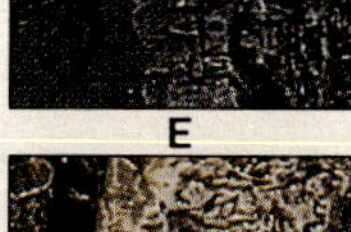

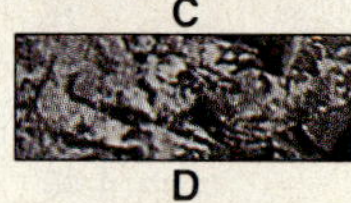

UNDERCOAT

LIQUID PIGMENTS

A	785-1216	White	4 oz.	$3.98
B	785-1217	Concrete	4 oz.	$3.98
C	785-1218	Stone Gray	4 oz.	$3.98
D	785-1219	Slate Gray	4 oz	$3.98
E	785-1220	Black	4 oz.	$3.98
F	785-1221	Raw Umber	4 oz.	$3.98
G	785-1222	Burnt Umber	4 oz.	$3.98
H	785-1223	Yellow Ocher	4 oz.	$3.98

UNDERCOATS

I	785-1228	Green Undercoat	8 oz.	$4.98
J	785-1229	Earth Undercoat	8 oz.	$4.98

ASSORTMENT

K	785-1215	Earth Color Kit	$14.98

EARTH COLOR KIT   785-1215

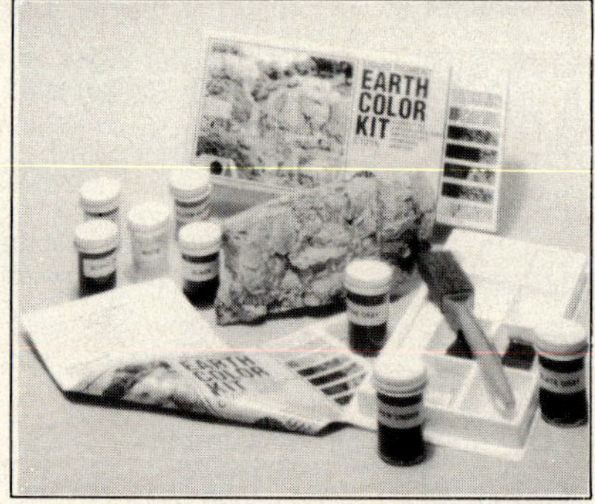

A simple system for staining rocks and terrain. A new technique for rock, terrain, portal, culvert, concrete, asphalt, grass undercoat and earth undercoat that anyone can do. Water soluble colors can be diluted and blended in limitless combinations. Start with the Earth Color Kit that includes instructions, applicator, palette and eight colors. Individual colors available separately.

LIQUID PIGMENTS

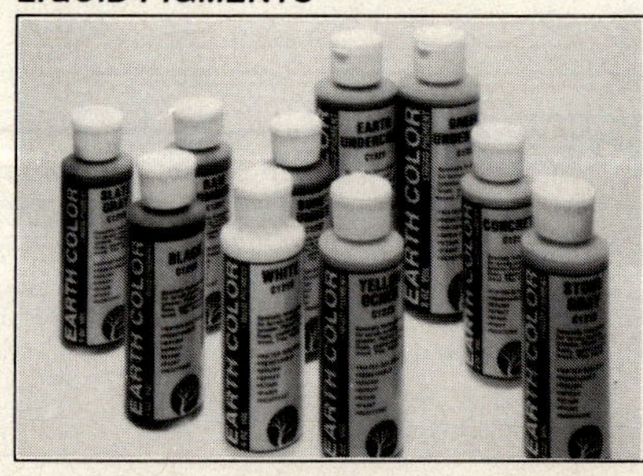

TERRAIN

WOODLAND SCENICS

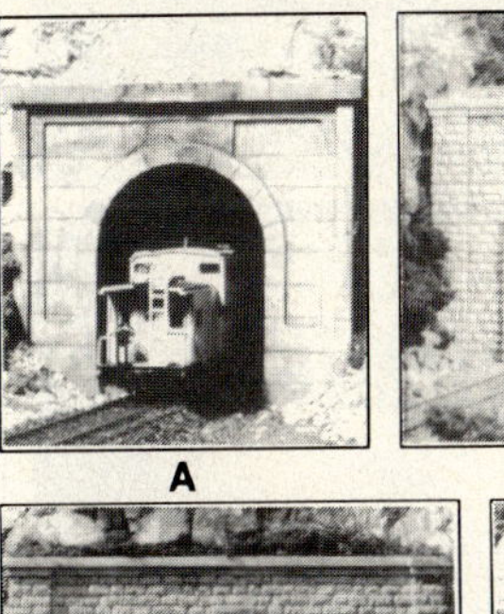

A   B   E   G

F   D   C   I

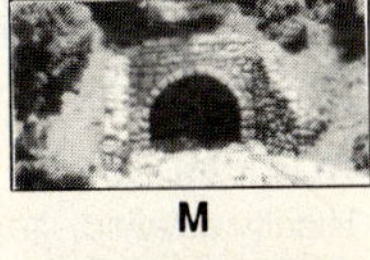

J   M   K   H
    N   L

NEW

E-Z WATER

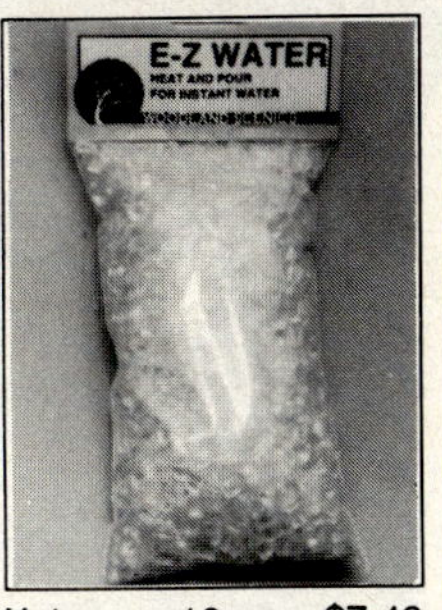

This heat activated water modeling material has been developed for the special needs of the scenery modeler. Melt on stove and pour.

785-1206   E-Z Water   16 oz. $7.49

TUNNEL LINER

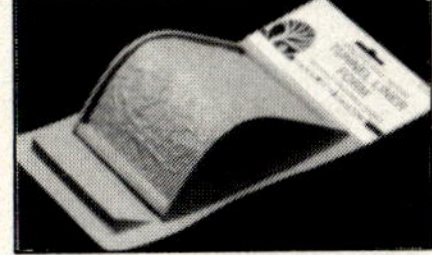

You cast realistic rock walls and ceilings for single or double track tunnel.

785-1250   Tunnel Liner Form $2.98

TALUS

Natural rock debris usually occurs in nature…near rock faces and rock outcroppings…near culverts and portals…and in creeks and ditches. For super detailing add talus to models in appropriate areas with white glue. Intermix grades, blend shades, and even stain your own to match your rock castings with Woodland Scenics Earth Colors.

FOUR COLORS

Buff

Brown

Gray

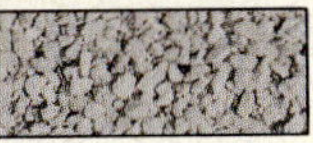

Natural

FOUR GRADES

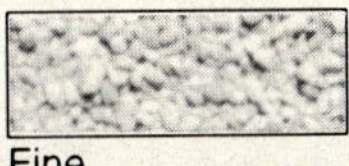

Fine

Medium

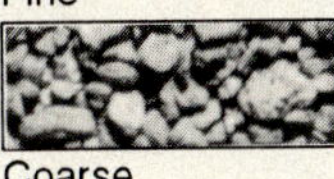

Coarse

Extra Coarse

PORTALS and WALLS

Tunnel Portals and Retaining Walls are high density Hydrocal castings that are easy to stain with Earth Color Liquid Pigments and are available in concrete, cut stone, random stone and timber styles. Portals contain one per package. Double portals are available in concrete and cut stone styles. Retaining Walls come three sections per package. Each section can be used alone or installed adjacent to another in an endless chain fashion. They can be installed at varying heights to accommodate the adjoining terrain.

CULVERTS

Culverts are also high density Hydrocal castings and are available in four styles. There are two culverts per package.

TUNNEL PORTALS

A	785-1252	Concrete	Sing.	$5.98
B	785-1253	Cut Stone	Sing.	$5.98
C	785-1254	Timber	Sing.	$5.98
D	785-1255	Random Stone	Sing.	$5.98
E	785-1256	Concrete	Dbl.	$6.49
F	785-1257	Cut Stone	Dbl.	$6.49

RETAINING WALLS

G	785-1258	Concrete	3 ea.	$5.98
H	785-1259	Cut Stone	3 ea.	$5.98
I	785-1260	Timber	3 ea.	$5.98
J	785-1261	Random Stone	3 ea.	$5.98

CULVERTS

K	785-1262	Concrete	2 ea.	$5.49
L	785-1263	Masonry Arch	2 ea.	$5.49
M	785-1264	Random Stone	2 ea.	$5.49
N	785-1265	Timber	2 ea.	$5.49

TALUS (ROCK DEBRIS)

785-1270	Fine Buff	$2.29
785-1271	Medium Buff	$2.29
785-1272	Coarse Buff	$2.29
785-1273	Extra Coarse Buff	$2.29
785-1274	Fine Brown	$2.29
785-1275	Medium Brown	$2.29
785-1276	Coarse Brown	$2.29
785-1277	Extra Coarse Brown	$2.29
785-1278	Fine Gray	$2.29
785-1279	Medium Gray	$2.29
785-1280	Coarse Gray	$2.29
785-1281	Extra Coarse Gray	$2.29
785-1282	Fine Natural	$2.29
785-1283	Medium Natural	$2.29
785-1284	Coarse Natural	$2.29
785-1285	Extra Coarse Natural	$2.29

TERRAIN

NEW

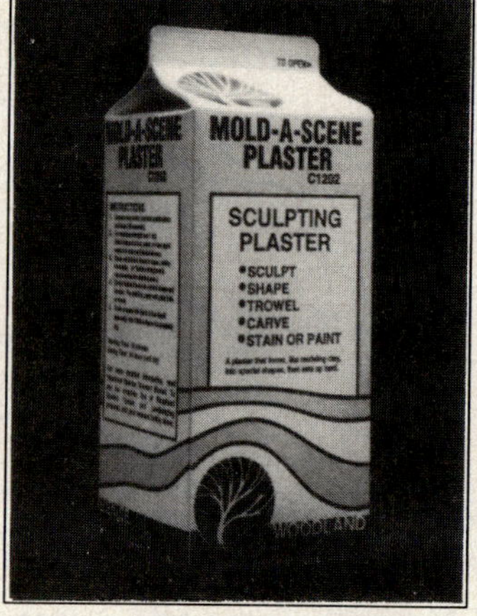

LIGHTWEIGHT HYDROCAL*

A specially formulated new Lightweight Hydrocal for terrain model builders. Lightweight Hydrocal is nearly half the weight of Hydrocal, goes almost twice as far and is the tough, quick setting product.

MOLD-A-SCENE PLASTER

Mold-A-Scene is a plaster material that can be shaped without a mold like modeling clay. Its longer setting time allows a scenery modeler to add terrain contours to new or existing scenery. Add a terrace to a hillside, a dam for a pond or lake, or a grade crossing...in just minutes! It dries overnight. It is excellent for dioramas, layouts and models, as well as volcanoes and other school projects.
* Hydrocal is a product of U.S. Gypsum.

PLASTER CLOTH

Woodland Scenics Plaster Cloth is the simple, convenient, and lightweight way to create a durable terrain shell or base. Just wad newspaper and stack to form the desired shape. Dip Plaster Cloth in water, lay it over the newspaper and allow to dry. It is a quick, no mix, no mess lightweight scenery base.

FLEX PASTE

Use as a flexible, noncracking coating over Styrofoam or as a road base for concrete or asphalt modeling.

LATEX RUBBER

Make your own rock molds with this ready-to-use Latex Rubber. It is formulated to reproduce fine detail and to be durable.

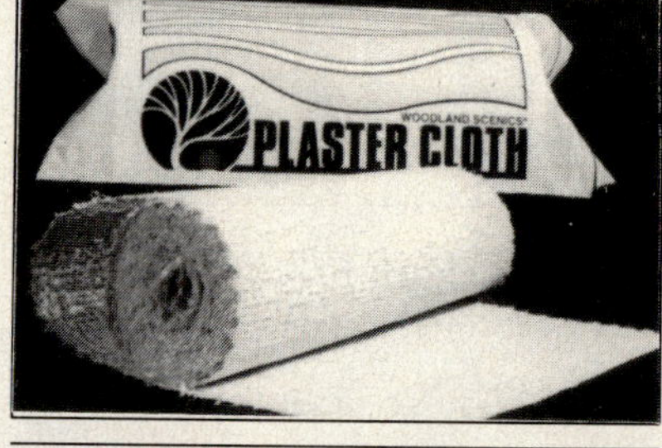

TERRAIN SHELL SUPPLIES

785-1201	Lightwt Hydrocal	1/2 gal.	$6.98
785-1202	Mold-A-Scene Pl.	1/2 gal.	$6.98
785-1203	Plaster Cloth	10 sq. ft.	$6.98
785-1205	Flex Paste	16 oz. vol.	$9.98
785-1204	Latex Rubber	16 oz. vol	$9.49

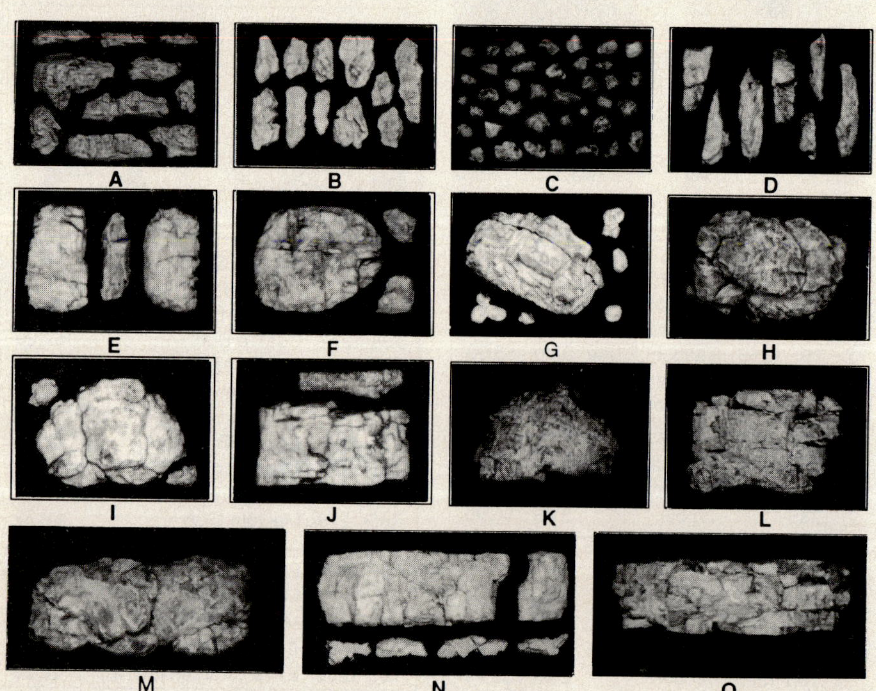

ROCK MOLDS

Highly detailed, flexible, and durable rock molds. Use to cast small boulders, rock outcroppings, top rocks for fields and creeks, or make entire rock faces by combining castings produced with these molds.

5" x 7" MOLDS

A	785-1230	Outcroppings	$4.98
B	785-1231	Surface Rocks	$4.98
C	785-1232	Boulders	$4.98
D	785-1233	Embankments	$4.98
E	785-1234	Random Rock	$4.98
F	785-1235	Laced Face Rock	$4.98
G	785-1236	Classic Rock	$4.98
H	785-1237	Wind Rock	$4.98
I	785-1238	Weathered Rock	$4.98
J	785-1239	Strata Stone	$4.98
K	785-1240	Rock Mass	$4.98
L	785-1241	Layered Rock	$4.98

5" x 10 1/2" MOLDS

M	785-1242	Washed Rock	$5.98
N	785-1243	Base Rock	$5.98
O	785-1244	Facet Rock	$5.98

WATER

QIK WATER KIT

Qik-water Kit consists of a thin, versatile film. Can be crumpled to give wave & ripple textures to the surface. Kit includes: Qik-water film 27 x 72″, sample wavy swatch, polyester foam matrix ''button-paks'' with material to resemble barnacle and foam sparkle, and instructions.

766-328 Med Blue/Green   20.00
766-719 Supplementary Kit   5.00
  Contains 2 bellows w/barnacles and foam sparkle and polyfiber pad for special effects.

RIVER KITS

Add color sparkle, depth, foam, and froth to your fast moving rivers and streams. A 6 bellows kit containing 5 shades of sparkling particulate tints - plus clear foam sparkle. Includes instructions. Use with clear silicone resins and acrylic artist mediums.

766-720 White Water-Wild River   20.00
  has various muddy or dark water shades.
766-724 Up a Lazy River   20.00
  has various blue water shades.

WILD RIVER MINI WATER KIT

Two bellows kit. One shade of color, plus polyfoam, and one white for foam.

766-776 Aqua   7.50
766-777 Sea Green   7.50
766-778 Medium Blue   7.50
766-779 Icy Blue   7.50
766-780 Sky Blue (By Special Order Only.)   7.50
766-798 Rusty/Cedar   7.50
766-799 Muddy Brown   7.50
766-800 Dog Days Green   7.50
         (By Special Order Only.)
766-801 Steel Gry (By Special Order Only.)   7.50
766-802 Soft Black   7.50

COLOR-RITE

WATERFALL KIT

62′ high by 26′ wide (HO Scale). A soft, heat sensitive plastic composition that can altered to fit almost any application. Can be cut with a plain pocket knife. Hot water easily changes the shape. Waterfall is semi-transparent allowing you to spray the back of it to the color of the water that's in the area you are modeling.

211-701 Waterfall 4.25

LAKE & RIVER KIT

Contains wax for the base and a high gloss finish coat that will not affect the wax. Realistic water without the danger and smell. Covers about 300 sq in

211-702   8.50

WOODLAND SCENICS

E-Z WATER   *NEW*

This heat activated water modeling material has been developed for the special needs of the scenery modeler. Melt on stove and pour.

785-1206   16 oz 7.49
  Build a complete scene by combining this item with products from Woodland Scenics Terrain System.

Plastruct

PLASTIC WATER SHEETS
7 x 12″ Plastic patterned sheets.

CALM   pkg(2) 11.90
570-14602 Blue
570-14612 Clear *NEW*

AGITATED pkg(2) 13.90
570-14603 Blue
570-14613 Clear *NEW*

CHOPPY   pkg(2) 15.90
570-14604 Blue
570-14614 Clear *NEW*

Mountains in Minutes
I.S.l E. LABORATORIES

LAKE STREAM & FALLS KIT

Operating Lake Stream and Falls features a long lasting water pump that sends water over the falls and down stream into the lake. Includes water tinting color and spruce trees. Use with all scales. Size: approximately 28 x 20 x 8″.

473-890   69.98
473-895 Waterfall Planter   219.98

FALLER

Imported from Germany and marketed by WALTHERS

LAKE CONSTRUCTION KIT
Includes rippled plastic sheet and blue landscaped paper.

272-791   8.49

WATER VARNISH

To create realistic model water surfaces, rivers and lakes. Includes complete instructions.

272-508   500g 40.99

WATER PUMP w/ ACCESSORIES
Contains 12-16v AC electric pump, 90 cm PVC hose and two connecting pieces. Detailed instructions included.

272-627   25.49

NOCH

Imported from Germany by WALTHERS

RIVER SET
528-6086 Wild Water Set   9.49
  Includes multi-colored pebbles and 1 bottle each: blue paint and transparent blue gloss.

CHEMCO
RESIN CRAFTS

Decoupage resins, such as Ultra-Glo, do not produce odors and heat associated with polyester, are nonflammable. Transparent dyes can be mixed with the resin to produce different ''colors'' of water.

POLYMER COATINGS
Simply mix, measure and pour to create realistic water in any scale! Dries to a hard, high-gloss finish. Set includes decoupage resin and hardener, plus complete instructions.

ULTRA-GLO

207-27   8 oz   7.99
207-35   16 oz 13.49

ENVIROTEX LITE
32 oz
207-2032
           21.99

MIXING CUP SET

Include 6 mixing cups, stirring paddles and 3 craft brushes.

207-1013   3.99

COLOR PIGMENTS

PRE-SIZE MODEL SPECIALTIES

NEW

FX™ Weathering Materials produce realistic effects on builders scenery, and rolling stock. Sticks well, and does not require any clear coating. Liquid effects are water based and may be removed with soap and water. Packed in 1/2 oz. jars.

POWDERS

Dealers: MUST buy a Dealer Pack of 6.

483-900	Black	1.50
483-901	White	1.50
483-902	Light Grey	1.50
483-903	Dark Grey	1.50
483-504	Red Dirt	1.50
483-505	Desert Tan	1.50
483-506	Desert Pink	1.50
483-907	Light Brown	1.50
483-908	Dark Brown	1.50
483-973	Light Green Moss	1.50
483-974	Dark Green Moss	1.50

LIQUID EFFECTS

483-930	Light Rust	1.50
483-931	Medium Rust	1.50
483-932	Dark Rust	1.50
483-933	Weathered Rubber	1.50
483-970	Oil	1.50
483-971	Grease	1.50
483-972	Fuel Stain	1.50
483-975	Hydraulic Fluid	1.50

PACKAGED SETS

483-550	9 Jar Set 900-908	10.50
483-951	Aging Set 930, 931, 932, 933	4.75
483-552	Petroleum Set 970, 971, 972, 975	4.75
483-958	Shading 900, 901, 902, 903	4.75

WOODLAND SCENICS

NEW

LIQUID PIGMENTS

785-1216	White	4oz	3.98
785-1217	Concrete	4oz	3.98
785-1218	Stone Gray	4oz	3.98
785-1219	Slate Gray	40z	3.98
785-1220	Black	4oz	3.98
785-1221	Raw Umber	4oz	3.98
785-1222	Burnt Umber	4oz	3.98
785-1223	Yellow Ocher	4oz	3.98

UNDERCOATS

785-1228	Green Undercoat	8oz	4.98
785-1229	Earth Undercoat	8oz	4.98

ASSORTMENT

785-1215	Earth Color Kit	14.98

Build a complete scene by combining these items with products from Woodland Scenics Terrain System.

A-West

NEW

WEATHER-IT

Ages unpainted wood. Not a paint or a stain. Also for old paint effects & realistic plaster "concrete".

158-1	4oz	4.98

BLACKEN-IT

Works on most metals, not a paint. Conducts electricity, can be soldered.

158-2	4oz	4.98

PATINA-IT

Produces shades of blue/green on copper, brass and bronze. Not a paint. Also for Corrode-It technique on white metal, producing a pewter-gray/black patina.

158-4	4oz	4.98

Lacking money but not imagination and spare parts, the crew of the Cliffside Railroad constructed this engine house. What's even more amazing is that this model is based on a real structure, an abandoned cotton gin, located outside of Jim Scancarelli's hometown of Charlotte, North Carolina. After shooting several rolls of film, Jim built his model almost board for board. And yes, the prototype has since collapsed!

Model and Photo by Jim Scancarelli

There are still some regular steam assignments on the West Hoosic Division, but for how long is anyone's guess. Capturing the action along Connecticut Creek. Lou Sassi photographed a Key Import brass loco, which was painted by Bill McChesney. The box car is from McKean, while the bridge was scratchbuilt from Kappler lumber.

Photo by Lou Sassi

COLOR PIGMENTS

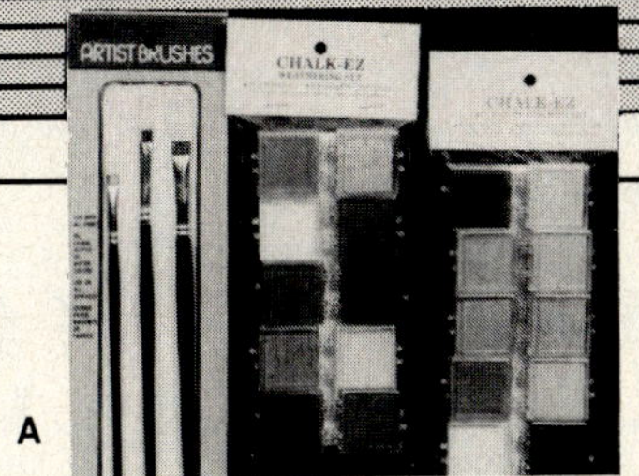

hobby helpers

CHALK-EZ

Easily applied with fingertip or a cotton swab. For best results, apply desired color or blended shade and dust lightly with a flat artist's brush. If project is to be handled heavily, we suggest you seal it with a flattener such as Testors Dullcote. In cake form.

Many desirable shades may be achieved by blending colors. If desired effect is not achieved with first application, Chalk-EZ is easily removed with water.

099-103	Light Brown	1 oz 1.08	099-114	Light Blue	1 oz 1.08
099-104	Grey	1 oz 1.08	099-115	Red-Orange	1 oz 1.08
099-106	White	1 oz 1.08	099-116	Yellow-Green	1 oz 1.08
099-107	Black	1 oz 1.08			
099-108	Rust	1 oz 1.08	099-117	Turquoise	1 oz 1.08
099-109	Yellow	1 oz 1.08	099-118	Amber/Light Rust	1 oz 1.08
099-110	Blue	1 oz 1.08			
099-111	Red	1 oz 1.08	099-119	Yellow-Orange	1 oz 1.08
099-112	Green	1 oz 1.08			
099-113	Orange	1 oz 1.08	099-120	Dark-Green	1 oz 1.08

WEATHERING SETS

A 099-301 Master Set — 13.67
Set includes both #101 and 102 powder sets. In cake form.

(not illustrated)

099-101 For Railroad Equipment — each 6.99
Set of ten one ounce chalks: brown, light brown, black, white, grey, red, yellow, rust, blue and green. In cake form.

099-102 For Buildings and Scenery — each 6.99
Set of ten one ounce chalks include: orange, red orange, light rust, yellow orange, yellow green, turquoise, light blue, dark green, white and black. In cake form.

SUPERIOR HOBBY PRODUCTS — STAIN

Water-based, nontoxic powdered stains for coloring rock castings. Can be mixed directly with plaster or with water to make "paint" for coloring rocks, structures etc.

697-501	White	1.80	697-509	Red	1.80	697-517	Aqua Blue	1.80
697-502	Black	1.80	697-510	Orange	1.80	697-518	Mud	1.80
697-503	Blue	1.80	697-511	Green	1.80	697-519	Cloud White	1.80
697-504	Yellow	1.80	697-512	Brown	1.80	697-520	Rust	1.80
697-505	Burnt Sienna	1.80	697-513	Rock Gray	1.80	697-521	Iron Ore Red	1.80
697-506	Burnt Umber	1.80	697-514	Rock Tan	1.80	697-522	Clay Red	1.80
697-507	Raw Sienna	1.80	697-515	Rock Red	1.80	697-523	Clay Gray	1.80
697-508	Raw Umber	1.80	697-516	Moss Green	1.80	697-524	Burnt Orange	1.80

COLOR-RITE

PURE PAINT PIGMENTS

According to "Scenery for Model Railroads" (Kalmach #400-12008), Pure Paint Pigments are the only coloring recommended for mixing with plaster for "zip-texturing" or hardshell scenicking.

211-301	Chrome Green	3 oz	3.25
211-302	Chrome Yellow	3 oz	3.25
211-303	Burnt Sienna	3 oz	3.25
211-304	Raw Sienna	3 oz	3.25
211-305	Burnt Umber	3 oz	3.25
211-306	Raw Umber	3 oz	3.25

ROCK & EARTH STAINS

Acrylic base stains for re-creating Nature's coloring on exposed rock.

211-402	Yellow Ochre	4 oz	2.25
211-403	Burnt Sienna	4 oz	2.25
211-404	Raw Sienna	4 oz	2.25
211-405	Burnt Umber	4 oz	2.25
211-406	Raw Umber	4 oz	2.25
211-407	Lamp Black	4 oz	2.25
211-408	Ultra-Marine Blue	4 oz	2.25
211-401	#402-#408 Assortment	each	13.95

prestype, inc.

Create unique weathering, highlights, shadows and other special effects on your models and scenery with shading cakes. The chalk-like material is formulated for easy application on most surfaces, including plaster, wood, metal, ceramics, paper and more. Special combinations can be created by blending colors, or using them with other forms of weathering. Can be applied with a cotton ball or cotton swab and sealed with flat or gloss finishes. Each one ounce color comes in a plastic container for easy storage and identification.

562-5619	Yellow	each .75
562-5621	Red	each .75

SHADING CAKES

562-5615	Royal Blue	each .75
562-5616	Turquoise	each .75

■ LIMITED QUANTITIES ■

562-5613	Light Blue	each .75

Shoving hard on the caboose, a pair of Hudson, Delaware & Ohio RS-1's fight their way to the top of the grade outside of Gilberton, Pennsylvania. The RS-1's have just arrived on the property, according to builder Chris Carfaro of Decatur, Georgia, and are finished in the road's early paint scheme. The rugged mountain scenery is located on the Model Railroad Club Inc. layout in Union City, New Jersey.

Models and Photo by Chris Carfaro

INSTANT HORIZONS™ AND INSTANT BUILDINGS.©...

- *Create a Unique Backdrop that's Perfect for Your Layout*
- *Adds Depth and Distance to any Layout*
- *Smooth Transition from Actual Scenery to Printed Backdrop*
- *Identify the Time and Place of Your Layout*
- *Easily Mixed and Matched*
- *Easy to Use, Includes Complete Instructions*

. . .*YOUR COMPLETE BACKGROUND MODELING SYSTEM*

Instant Buildings© plus Instant Horizons™ provide a complete system for modeling backgrounds! The printed "buildings" and scenes expand your perception of distance, adding miles of scenery to your layout. The buildings are placed in the limited space between actual structures and the Instant Horizons™ scenes. This smooths the transition from foreground objects (3-D) to the printed, two-dimensional backdrop.

On the following pages, you'll find more ideas for adding Instant Horizons™ and Instant Buildings© to your layout!

USING INSTANT HORIZONS™ AND INSTANT BUILDINGS©

Here are some suggestions for adding Instant Buildings© and Instant Horizons™ to your layout. You may also find other ways, so feel free to experiment and have fun! Instant Horizons™ and Instant Buildings© are easily added to layouts that are "finished" or still under construction. Complete instructions for assembly and mounting are included in each set.

Instant Buildings© and Instant Horizons™ are easily adapted to dioramas and modules! A small project like this is a great way to experiment with the scenes. ►

Put more scenery in less space with Instant Buildings© and Instant Horizons™! Both can be placed within inches of other models or the edge of your layout. ►

Where space is limited, create a unique backdrop for your layout by gluing Instant Buildings© directly to Instant Horizons™. This can also be done to hide the seams between scenes. ►

◄ For a 3-D effect, Instant Buildings© can be layered by arranging them in tiers. Elevating the structures at the rear adds depth to the entire scene.

◄ To add more depth to the structures, mount them on a sheet of styrofoam. Small angles and openings can be cut out using a hot wire cutter.

◄ For a quick change photo backdrop, or more layout variety, assemble Instant Buildings© but do not glue them to your layout. The scene can be changed over and over again.

Instant Buildings© smooth the transition from actual scenery to printed backdrop, making your entire layout more realistic.

Using Instant Buildings© with Instant Horizons™ expands your perception of distance, adding miles of scenery to your layout. ►

By blending 3-D scenery with Instant Horizons™, the same scene can be used several times on your layout. Covering different portions of the scene avoids repetition. ►

◄ Instant Buildings© and Instant Horizons™ can set the time and place of your layout. They're perfect for every era and are easily mixed and matched.

◄ From tiny modules to entire rooms, Instant Horizons™ and Instant Buildings© make any layout look bigger.

INSTANT HORIZONS ™

Manufactured by
Wm. K. *WALTHERS* Inc.
Scenes Measure 24 x 36"   each 7.95

949-703 Mountain to Desert Transition

949-705 Drywash Desert

949-706 Saguaro Desert

949-707 Desert to Country Transition

949-709 Prairie/Grain Elevator

949-710 Whistle Stop

INSTANT HORIZONS™

Manufactured by
Wm. K. *WALTHERS* Inc.

Scenes Measure 24 x 36"   each 7.95

949-708 Country to Desert Transition

949-704 Desert to Mountain Transition

949-702 Tall Timber

949-701 Sierra Boomtown (Gold Rush)

949-715 Eastern Foothills

949-717 City to Country Transition

INSTANT HORIZONS™

Manufactured by Wm. K. WALTHERS Inc.

Scenes Measure 24 x 36″   each 7.95

949-716 Country to City Transition

949-714 Country to Eastern Foothills

949-712 Hotel/Business

949-711 Freight Yards

949-713 The Docks

MATCHING INSTANT HORIZONS™ WITH INSTANT BUILDINGS ©

Although Instant Buildings can be used with any Instant Horizons scene, here are some suggestions for matching the Buildings to the Backgrounds:

949-722 Back Street Structures
Use with: 949-711 Freight Yards, 949-712 Hotel/Business, 949-713 The Docks

949-723 Old West Frontier
Use with: 949-703 Mountain to Desert, 949-705 Dry Wash Desert, 949-706 Saquaro Desert, 949-707 Desert to Country, 949-701 Sierra Boomtown, 949-702 Tall Timber

949-724 Industrial District
Use with: 949-711 Freight Yards, 949-712 Hotel/Business, 949-713 The Docks

949-725 Main Street Stores
Use with: 949-709 Prairie/Grain Elevator, 949-710 Whistle Stop, 949-711 Freight Yards, 949-712 Hotel/Business

Instant Buildings ©

Manufactured by
Wm. K. **WALTHERS** Inc.
each 4.95

Instant Building illustrations are shown about 3/16 actual size. Some sets include additional details (not illustrated).

Old West Frontier *949-723*

Back Street Structures *949-722*

Instant Buildings©

Manufactured by
Wm. K. *WALTHERS* Inc.
each 4.95

Main Street Stores *949-725*

Industrial District *949-724*

FREE HOW-TO BROCHURE

Learn how to create a unique background for your layout using Instant Horizons and Instant Buildings, with these FREE brochures! Tips on mounting scenes, blending with existing scenery plus examples of how Instant Buildings and Instant Horizons can be used on your layout are all included. Lots of colorful illustrations and photos will give you lots of modeling ideas! To order, clearly print your name/address, specify part number 949-10474 and submit $.87 postage to:

WALTHERS
Consumer Services
P.O. Box 18676
Milwaukee, WI 53218

Instant Horizons/Instant Buildings Brochures
949-10474   N/C

BACKGROUND SCENES

VOLLMER

*Imported from Germany & marketed by **WALTHERS***

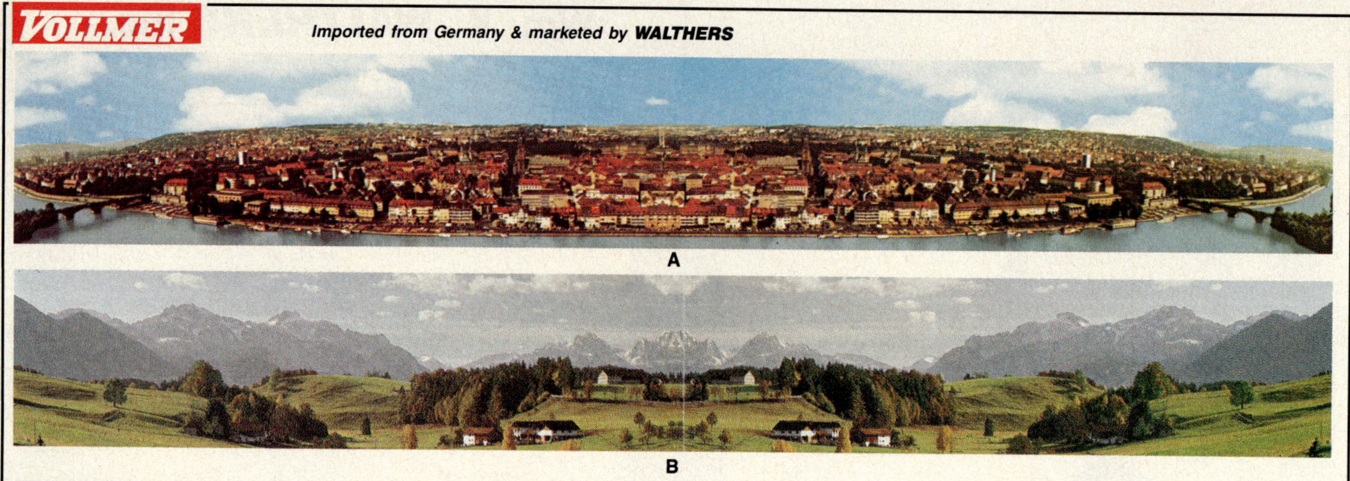

A

B

BACKGROUND SCENES

A Scenic Background
770-6100   26.99
(3 sections) 140 long x 30" high

B Foothills & Mountains Scene
770-6110   26.49
(2 sections) 112 x 20" 280 x 50 cm

(not illustrated)
770-6112 Background Clouds   21.49
270 x 50 cm

DETAIL ASSOCIATES

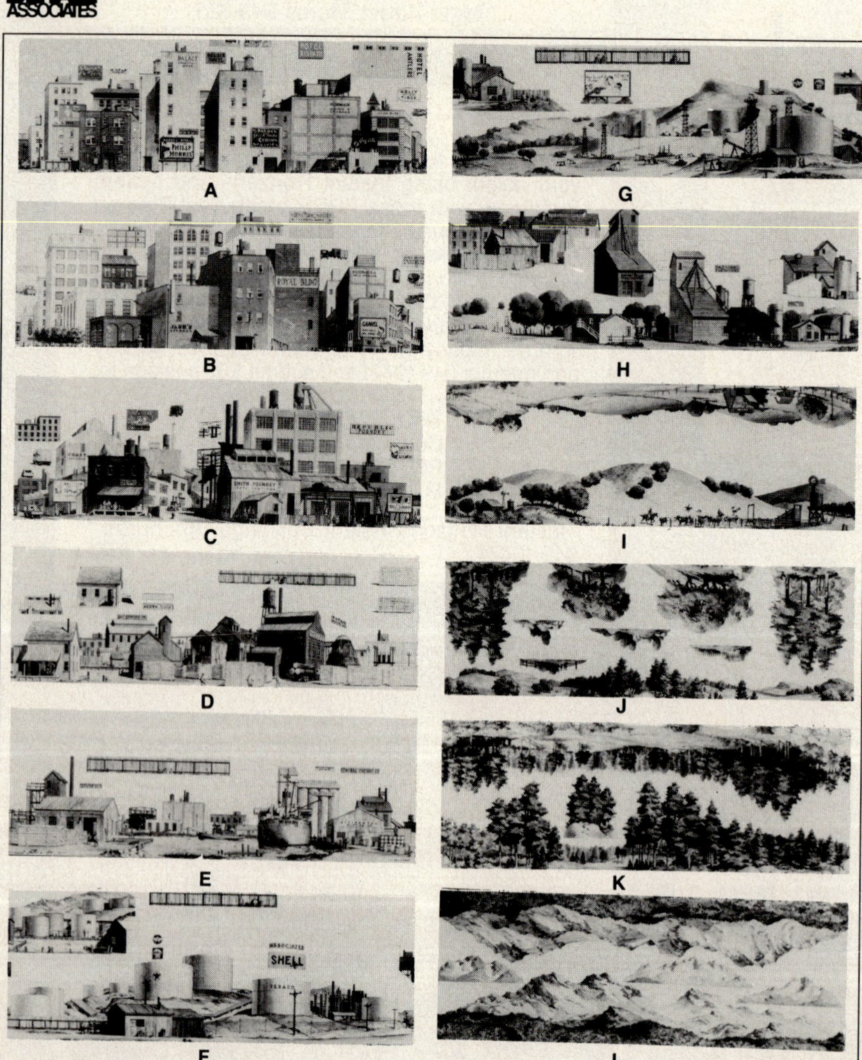

A

B

C

D

E

F

G

H

I

J

K

L

RAIL SCENES

A system of painted modules that link in unique ways to form a continuous backdrop for model railroads. The various modules of the system can be jointed together in any order the modeler wishes, creating the type of backdrop best suited to the layout. Each module is 8-1/2" x 22".

RAIL-SCENE   Each 6.98

A 229-7501 City
B 229-7502 Downtown
C 229-7503 Industrial District
D 229-7504 Lumber Yard
E 229-7505 Estuary
F 229-7506 Tank Farm
G 229-7507 Oil Fields
H 229-7508 Farm Town
I 229-7509 Land
J 229-7510 Woods
K 229-7511 Forest
L 229-7512 Mountains

INSTRUCTION MANUAL

Modular Backdrop System Manual
229-7550   each 4.98
38 page illustrated booklet contains instructions for creating a personalized backdrop; showing possible module combinations and suggestions for adding optional details. (11 x 8-1/2")

BACKGROUND SCENES

The air conditioners are getting a real workout this afternoon. You can almost feel the heat coming off the right-of-way in this scene by Bill Baker of Rochester, New York. Bill hand painted the background scene (his first!) and used a variety of materials to capture the look of the desert southwest. *Models and Photo by Bill Baker*

new london industries

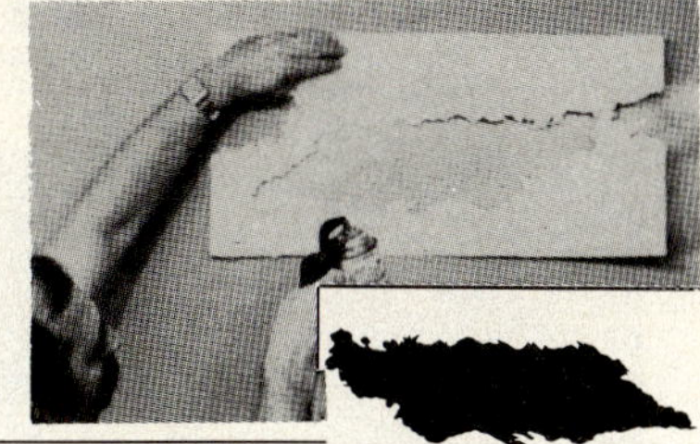

BACKGROUND STENCILS

Create a unique background scene for your layout! Stencils are cut from heavy cardstock and can be used over and over. May be used for various scales. Includes instructions.

519-1	The Clouds	9.98
519-2	The Mountains	9.98
519-3	The City	9.98
519-4	The Details **NEW** pkg(2)	9.98

(Fine-cut cloud Stencils)
Ideal for adding extra detail to 519-1 & for smaller scales near the horizon line.

FALLER *Imported from Germany & marketed by* **WALTHERS**

A

B

C

D

BACKGROUND SCENES

Each scene is a full color photo.

A 272-514 "Schwarzwald-Baar" 25.99
4 sections totaling 152 x 25"

B 272-515 "Lowenstein" 20.49
3 sections totaling 9'8" x 17-3/4"

C 272-516 "Oberstdorf" 20.49
3 sections totaling 9'8" x 17-3/4"

D 272-517 Oberstdorf Expander Scene 20.49
Three part expander scene can be combined with #516 to measure 5.8 meters.

E 272-512 "Neuschwanstein" 19.99
2 sections, totaling 12' x 3.3'

F 272-513 "Karwendelgebirge" 19.99
2 sections, totaling 12' x 3.3'

E

F

TUNNELS & BRIDGE ABUTMENTS

A.I.M. PRODUCTS

A.I.M. Products are cast in high density plaster to give maximum strength and stain absorption. This process is exclusive with A.I.M. Products. Includes complete installation and staining instructions.

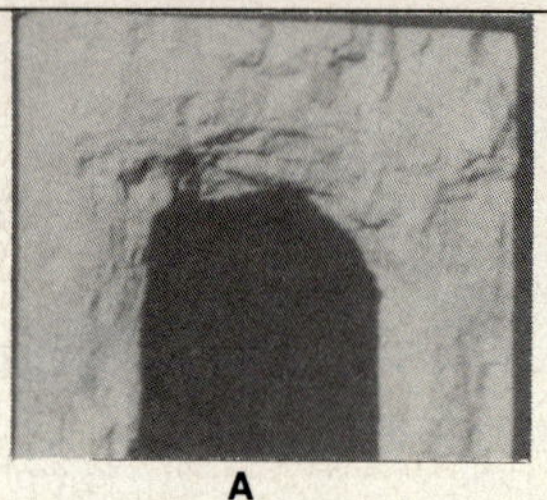

A

B

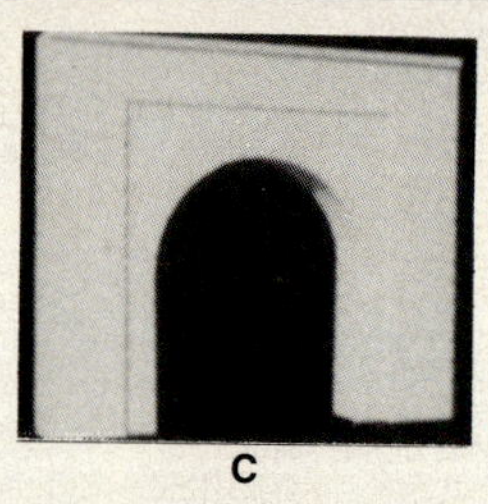

C

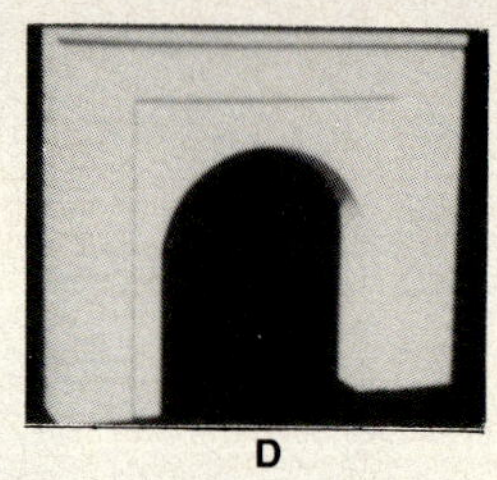

D

E

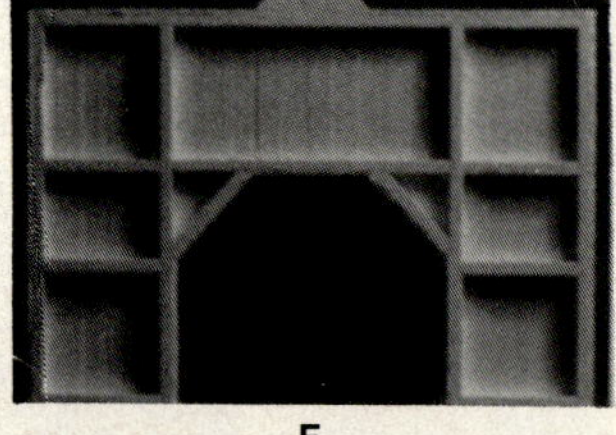

F

SINGLE TRACK TUNNEL PORTALS

Overall Height 36'9"   Overall Width 43"   Overall Thickness 7"

A Blasted Rock 110-109	each 5.25	(not illustrated)	
B Cut Stone 110-110	each 5.25	Poured Concrete 110-128	each 5.25
C Groove Face 110-116	each 5.25	Blasted Rock 110-120 HOn3 43-1/2 x 37"	5.25
D Plain Face 110-117	each 5.25	Random Stone 110-112	each 6.25
E Concrete Lined 110-119	each 5.25	Eroded Limestone 110-130	each 5.25
F Wood Outside Braced 110-121	each 5.45	Granite Gingerbread 110-131	each 5.25
		Modern Concrete 110-133	each 5.25

DOUBLE TRACK TUNNEL PORTALS

Overall Height 40"
Overall Width - at Base 53"
Overall Thickness 8"

110-111	Cut Stone	each 6.25
110-113	Random Stone	each 6.25
110-129	Poured Concrete	each 6.25

(not illustrated)

110-132	Granite Face	each 6.25
110-134	Concrete	each 6.25

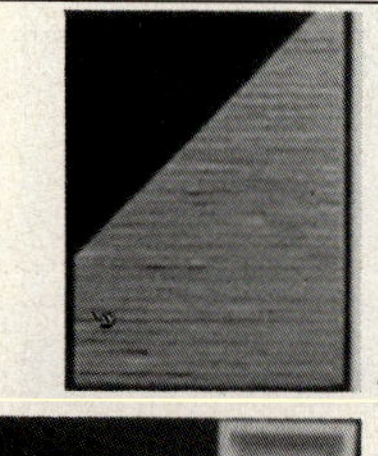

A

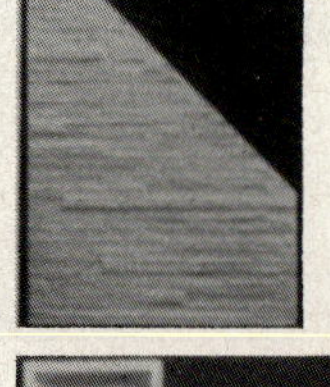

B

C

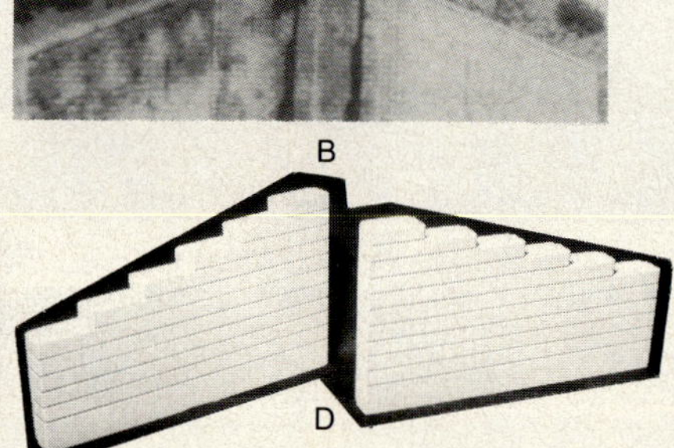

D

ABUTMENT WINGS

Height - High End 26'6"   Height - Low End 15'   Width 41'6"   Thickness 5'9"

A	110-126 Poured Concrete	pair 6.25	
B	110-102 Cut Stone	pair 6.25	(not illustrated)
C	110-123 Wood Outside Braced	pair 6.25	
D	110-115 Poured Concrete	pair 6.25	
	110-103 Fieldstone		pair 6.25
	110-105 Random Stone		pair 6.25

A

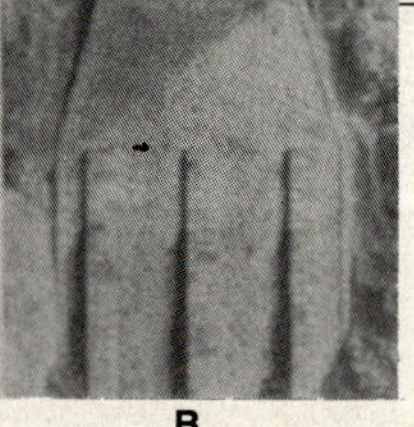

B

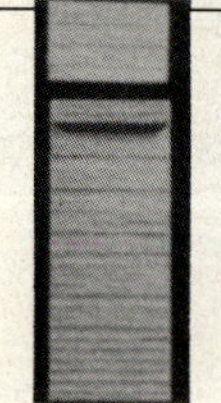

C

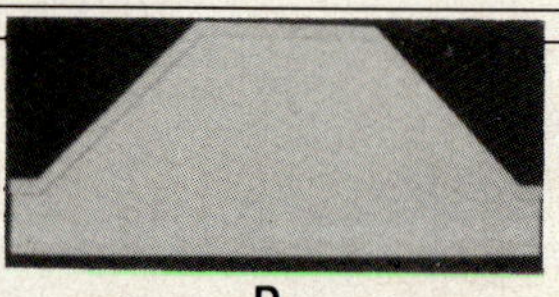

D

Numbers 110-124 and 125 are designed to fit Micro-Engineering structures, numbers 255-501, 502, 503, 504, 507, and 508.

BRIDGE ABUTMENTS

Overall Height 41'6"
Width at Base 29'6"
Overall Thickness 5'9"

A	110-100	Cut Stone	pair 6.25
B	110-101	Fieldstone	pair 6.25
C	110-124	Poured Concrete	pkg(2) 6.25
D	110-118	Concrete	pkg(2) 6.25
		(not illustrated)	
	110-104	Random Stone	pair 6.25

WOODLAND SCENICS

TUNNEL PORTALS   NEW

Build a complete scene by combining these items with products from Woodland Scenics Terrain System.

785-1252	Concrete Single	5.98
785-1253	Cut Stone Single	5.98
785-1254	Timber Single	5.98
785-1255	Random Stone Single	5.98
785-1256	Concrete Double	6.49
785-1257	Cut Stone Double	6.49

model power

Items listed in *blue ink* may not be available at all times. Please see your dealer for current delivery information.

TUNNEL

Styrene tunnels molded in brown with flocking and some lichen applied for ground cover.

490-373	Straight	8.98
490-1324	Curved Corner *NEW*	19.98

TUNNELS & BRIDGE ABUTMENTS

All scenery items are painted and weathered polyurethane castings.

A   **B**   **C**   **D**

DOUBLE TUNNEL PORTALS

A 214-7004 Outside Braced Timber   7.99
7 × 4-1/2" 17.8 × 10.8 cm
B 214-7010 Early Concrete   7.99
6-7/8 × 4-5/8" 17.5 × 11.8 cm

C 214-7015 Cut Stone   7.99
6-3/8 × 4-7/8" 16.5 × 12.4 cm
D 214-7019 Random Stone   7.99
6-1/4 × 4-5/8" 15.9 × 11.8 cm

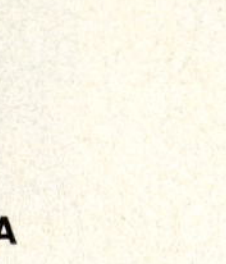
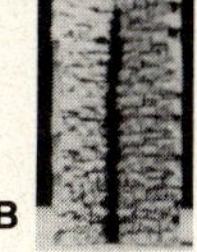

A   **B**

STONE CORNERS

A Cut Stone, Inside
214-7046 (for 7017)   pkg(2) 9.99
B Random Stone, Inside
214-7048 (for 7021)   pkg(2) 9.99

(not illustrated)
Cut Stone, Outside
214-7047 (for 7017)   pkg(2) 9.99
Random Stone, Outside
214-7049 (for 7021)   pkg(2) 9.99

BRIDGE ABUTMENTS

A 214-7027 Single Track Stone   6.99
2-3/4 × 3-3/4" 1.8 × 9.5 cm
B 214-7039 Cut Stone   pkg(2) 14.99
4-1/4 × 3-7/8" 10.8 × 9.9 cm
C 214-7028 Double Track Stone   7.99
4-5/8 × 3-3/4" 1.8 × 9.5 cm

A   **B**   **C**

BRIDGE PIERS

Cut Stone
214-7040
9.99
5 × 3-1/8"
12.8 × 8 cm

DOUBLE TUNNEL PORTAL

214-7023 Modern Concrete each 7.99
6-1/4 × 4-1/4" 15.9 × 10.8 cm

A   **B**   **C**   **D**   **E**   **F**

TUNNEL PORTALS & WING WALLS

A Outside Braced Timber Portal
214-7001 4-1/2 × 4-1/2" 11.4 × 11.4 cm 6.99
B Outside Braced Timber Walls
214-7005   pr 8.99
(for 7001 & 7004) 4-1/8 × 4-1/8" 10.5 × 10.5 cm
C Cut Stone Portal
214-7014   4-1/4 × 4-3/8"   6.99

D 214-7016 Cut Stone Walls   pr 8.99
(for 7014 & 7015) 4-3/4 × 4-7/8" 12 × 12.4 cm
E 214-7020 Random Stone Wall   pr 8.99
(for 7018 & 7019) 4-1/2 × 4-7/8" 11.4 × 12.4 cm
F 214-7018 Random Stone Portal   6.99
4-1/2 × 5" 11.4 × 12.5 cm

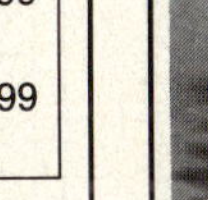

A   **B**   **C**   **D**

SINGLE TUNNEL PORTALS

A 214-7002 Wood Sheathed   6.99
4-3/4 × 4-1/2" 12 × 11.4 cm
B 214-7003 "1901" Concrete   6.99
4-3/4 × 4-1/2" 12 × 11.4 cm

C 214-7022 Modern Concrete   6.99
3-7/8 × 4-1/4" 9.9 × 10.8 cm
D 214-7041 Blasted Rock   7.99
5-1/8 × 5" 13.4 × 12.7 cm

STONE CULVERTS

214-7033 Random Stone   pkg(2) 8.99
7-5/8 × 1-7/8" 19.5 × 4.8 cm

TIMBER TUNNEL PORTAL KIT
Use as Mine Portal in "O Scale".

200-351   11-1/2"W × 5"H   each 12.30

TUNNELS & BRIDGE ABUTMENTS

Mountains in Minutes
I.S.L.E. LABORATORIES

A

B

C

D

E

TUNNEL PORTALS

Tunnel Portals molded in rigid plastic foam.

These foam plastic portals come in two-tone, golden brown and burnt umber finish. The "Brick Portal" is surrounded by a mixture of boulders and stratified rock. The rough hewn "Cut Stone Portal" is set back into a sheer rock wall. The "Wolfe's Cover Portal" is a scale model of a Canadian Pacific portal of concrete with wooden snow doors, also surrounded with stratified rock. The "Hoosac Tunnel Portal" will accommodate double track.

A	473-101	Brick Portal	5.79
B	473-102	Cut Stone Portal	5.79
C	473-103	Wolfe's Cove Portal	5.79
D	473-104	The Hoosac, West Face	5.79
E	473-105	Tunnel Portal Box Style	6.98

(not illustrated)
473-201 Dual Scale: Double-N, Single-HO   5.79

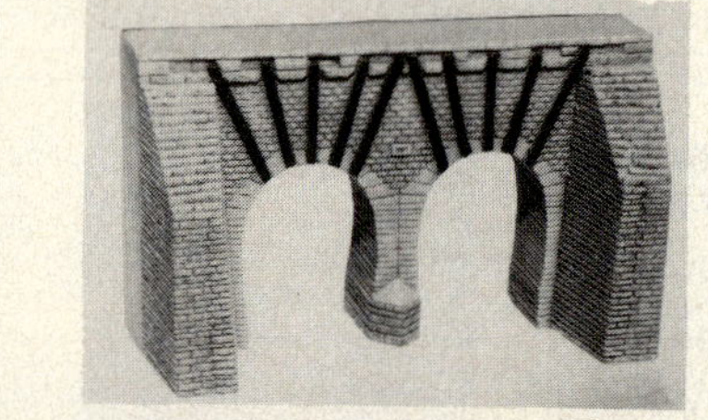
A

B

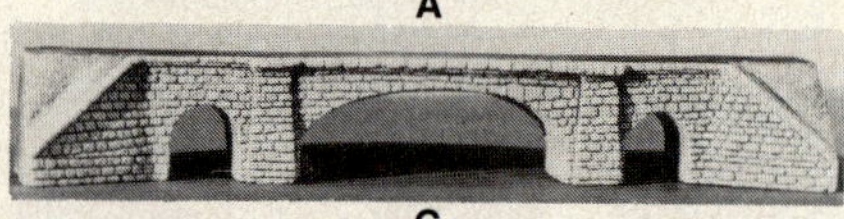
C

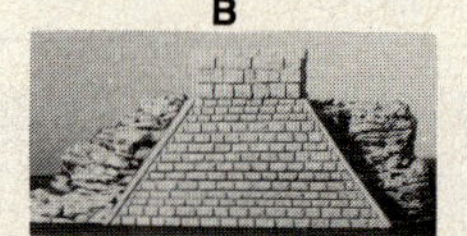
D

BRIDGES

A	473-828	Cross-over Bridge/Tunnel	13.59
B	473-827	Multi Scale Viaduct	19.98
		(O, HO, N) 8 × 21" 20 × 44 cm	
C	473-826	Multi Scale Arch Bridges	11.98
		(HO, N) 1-3/4 × 11-7/8" 4.5 × 30 cm	
D	473-825	Bridge Abutments pkg(2)	6.98
		3-1/2 × 8-3/4" 9 × 22.5 cm	

CULVERT

Culverts are molded in rigid plastic foam.

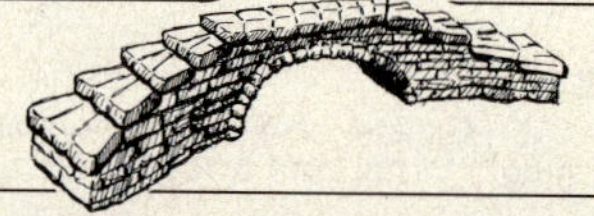

473-204 Culverts   pkg(2)   5.99
(Approx 4-1/8 × 7/8 × 3/4"
105 × 22 × 19 mm)

WHITEGROUND MODEL WORKS

A

B

TUNNEL PORTALS

A	771-5015	Rocky Ridge HOn3	8.95
B	771-5016	Sideling Wall HOn3	10.95
	(not illustrated)		
	771-5010	Portal	8.95

BRIDGE PIER

711-5011 50" 1 Track   8.95
(By Special Order Only.)

POLA   *Imported from Germany by WALTHERS*

STONE TUNNEL PORTAL

Molded plastic with approach walls.

Wide top surface of the walls make installation much easier.

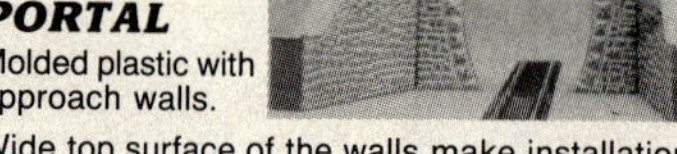

578-586   pkg(2)   8.99

BH MODELS

CULVERT

Add realistic detail wherever your right-of-way crosses creeks or streams with this culvert kit. Detailed plastic parts simulate cut stone construction and each kit includes one pair of culverts and sidewalls. Arch measures 20' wide and 15' tall.

159-401 Stone Culvert   pkg(2)   9.00
w/Sidewalls

SCENERY HINTS

HOW DO I ADD SCENERY TO MY LAYOUT?

Scenery adds the ultimate touch of realism to any layout, module or diorama. Even the finest models will look out of place on bare plywood or benchwork, because the sense of reality is lost. Scenery construction is surprisingly easy, and requires no special skills or tools. Using the materials in this section, it's easy to start landscaping your layout!

1. Start by reading some of the "How-to-do-it" books listed in this Catalog. These books will explain the different construction methods and materials available for building scenery.

2. Plan the type of scenery you want for your layout. If you model a specific railroad or region, you may wish to research your prototype. This can also determine the type of structures, rolling stock and equipment you'll want for your layout in the future.

3. Start small. Working on a small section of your layout will help build confidence. Work in stages, completely finishing a small section before starting the next. (This makes it easier to start over if your first efforts don't turn out quite right!)

4. Learn by doing. Most of the "tried and true" scenery construction methods were first developed by experimentation. You may find ways of doing things that are easier and produce more satisfying results.

5. Study the prototype. Do a little railfanning and observe how your favorite real railroad does things. Be sure to observe little things, like piles of junk, weeds, stacks of ties and other details that fill a scene. Small elements like these make any model scene more convincing!

6. Finish your scenery with Instant Horizons™ background scenes. These printed backdrops increase your perception of distance, adding miles of scenery and more realism to your layout.

TUNNELS & BRIDGE ABUTMENTS

NOCH

Imported from Germany by **WALTHERS**

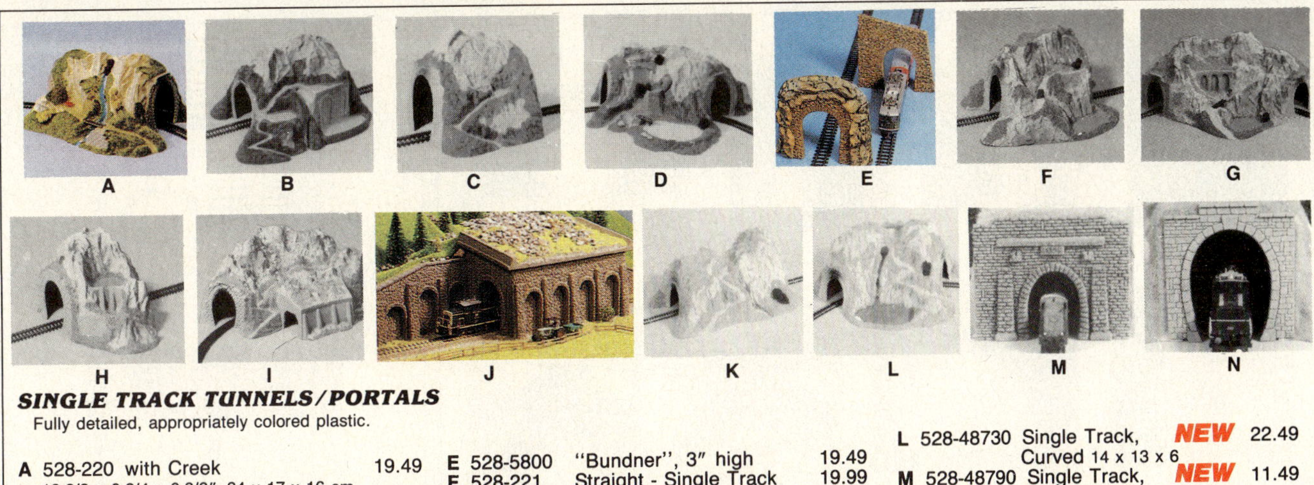

A B C D E F G

H I J K L M N

SINGLE TRACK TUNNELS/PORTALS
Fully detailed, appropriately colored plastic.

A	528-220	with Creek	19.49
	13-3/8 x 6-3/4 x 6-3/8" 34 x 17 x 16 cm		
B	528-225	Straight	16.49
	13-3/8 x 9-1/2 x 7-1/2" 34 x 24 x 19 cm		
C	528-212	Single Track	9.99
	7 x 6-1/2 x 6-3/4" 18 x 16.5 x 17 cm		
D	528-508	with Pond	28.99
	17-3/4 x 17-1/2 x 6-3/4" 45 x 44 x 17 cm		

E	528-5800	"Bundner", 3" high	19.49
F	528-221	Straight - Single Track	19.99
G	528-512	Curved - Single Track	28.99
H	528-211	Straight & Curved	11.99
I	528-522	Curved w/Straight	28.99
J	528-5834	Avalanche Tunnel pkg(6)	58.99
K	528-48670	Single Track, Straight 12 x 7 x 5 *NEW*	15.99

L	528-48730	Single Track, Curved 14 x 13 x 6 *NEW*	22.49
M	528-48790	Single Track, 2 Entrances *NEW*	11.49
N	528-60030	Single Track, 2 Entrances *NEW*	3.49
	(not illustrated)		
	528-3464	Single Track, Straight w/Park *NEW*	14.49

A B C

DOUBLE TRACK TUNNEL/PORTALS

A	528-518	Curved	28.99
B	528-5803	"Arlberg", Double Track	11.49
C	528-596	Double Track Tunnel Portals	96.99
D	528-48800	Double Track, 2 Entrances *NEW*	11.49
E	528-60040	Double Track, Double Entrance *NEW*	5.49
	(not illustrated)		
	528-5804	Two Track Ice	14.49

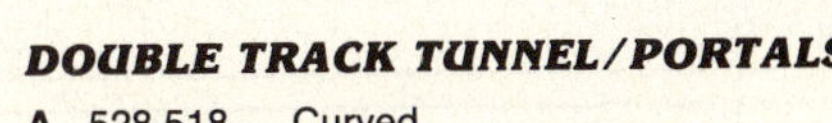

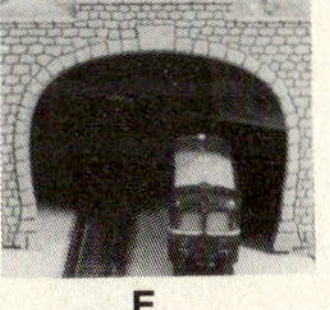

D E A B

Think your guidance counselor noticed you scheduled all of your classes on this side of the building? You'll only have a few moments to study the passing F units as they leave Evansville, on Rick Rideout's L&N Henderson Subdivision. Reitz High is scratchbuilt from posterboard and Holgate and Reynolds brick material. The F's are old Hallmark brass imports. A variety of Rix products compliment the scene on Rick's layout in Evansville, Indiana.

Models and Photo by Rick Rideout

C D

STRUCTURAMA
Constructed foam material. Less figures, structures and scenic material.

A	528-555	Simplon Tunnel **LTD QTY**	69.99
B	528-560	Arlberg Tunnel	96.99
C	528-590	Quarry	32.99
D	528-595	Landscaped Tunnel Entrance	57.99
E	528-5940	Rock Wall (red) *NEW*	37.49
	37 x 25 cm		
	(not illustrated)		
	528-565	Gotthard Tunnel	96.99
	528-58460	Rock *NEW*	17.49
	528-5848	Rocky Plate	17.49
	(partly grassed)		17.49

E

TUNNELS & BRIDGE ABUTMENTS

FALLER
Imported from Germany & marketed by **WALTHERS**

(A)

A

(A)

B

C

D

E

F

A

B

C

TUNNEL PORTALS

Tunnel portal kits are pre-colored plastic. Kits include numbered instructions.

A 272-557 Loreley Tunnel — pkg(2) 24.99
B 272-561 1-Track — pkg(2) 3.99
  Low Steam Era
C 272-563 1-Track, High for — pkg(2) 3.99
  Catenary Operation
  8.5 cm clearance
D 272-565 2-Track for Steam & — pkg(2) 4.99
  Catenary Operation
  10 cm clearance
E 272-559 Steam Operation — 6.49
  9/9.8 cm clearance
F 272-558 1 Track, Low Steam Era — 4.99
  7.2 cm clearance

TUNNEL ACCESSORIES

A 272-540 Structural Sections, asst 7.49
B 272-550 Tunnel Facing Strips 8.49
C 272-624 Tunnel Wall Card 11.49

PRE-SIZE MODEL SPECIALTIES

SINGLE DECK BRIDGE ABUTMENTS   *NEW*

483-140 4' Timber with Rock Base	pair 8.95	
483-141 15' Timber	pair 14.00	
483-142 30' Random Stone	pair 14.00	
483-143 30' Cut Stone	pair 14.00	
483-144 30' Old Concrete	pair 14.00	
483-145 30' Smooth Concrete	pair 12.00	

LIFE-LIKE

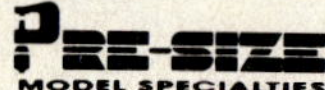

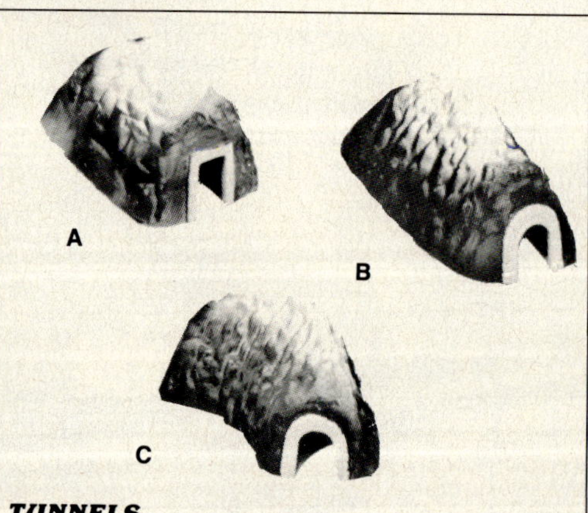
A

B

C

TUNNELS

Tunnels are light weight durable LiFoam®, realistic colors.

A 433-1304 Straight — 4.00
B 433-1305 Large Straight — *NEW* 7.35
C 433-1306 Curved — *NEW* 9.00

kibri
Imported from Germany by **WALTHERS**

TUNNELS

405-4414 Single Track Tunnel
  16.99

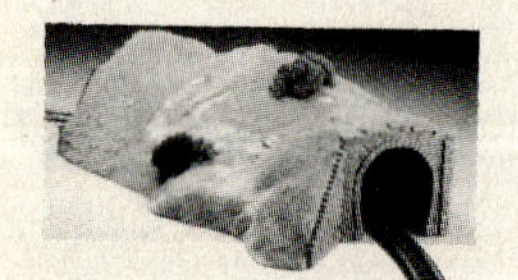

TUNNEL PORTALS

A 405-4101 Single Track 2-3/4" pkg(2) 6.49
B 405-4102 Single Track 3-7/8" each 5.99
C 405-4104 Double Track 4-1/8" each 5.99

(not illustrated)
405-4103 #4102 w/Tunnel Tube 7.49
405-4105 #4104 w/Tunnel Tube 8.49

A

B

C

WALLS

PRE-SIZE MODEL SPECIALTIES

Tunnel portals and accessories made of an odorless urethane casting in a natural "smokey gray" color, which can be used as is or painted.

CUT STONE CONSTRUCTION

Single Tunnel Portal		
483-105		5.10
Double Tunnel Portal		
483-106		5.60
Tunnel Abutment		
483-109	pkg(2)	6.00
Retaining Wall		
483-112		4.35

CONCRETE CONSTRUCTION

Single Tunnel Portal		
483-113		5.10
Double Tunnel Portal		
483-114		5.60
Tunnel Abutment		
483-115	pkg(2)	6.00
Retaining Wall		
483-116		3.35

RANDOM STONE CONSTRUCTION

Single Tunnel Portal		
483-103		5.10
Double Tunnel Portal		
483-104		5.60
Tunnel Abutment		
483-108	pkg(2)	6.00
Retaining Wall		
483-111		4.35

TIMBER CONSTRUCTION

483-101	Single Tunnel Portal	5.10
483-102	Double Tunnel Portal	5.60
Tunnel Abutment		
483-107	pkg(2)	6.00
483-110	Retaining Wall	4.00

BLASTED ROCK   *NEW*

483-117	Square	5.25
483-118	Round	5.25
483-119	Smooth Square	5.25
483-120	Smooth Round	5.25

BRAWA

Imported from Germany by **WALTHERS**

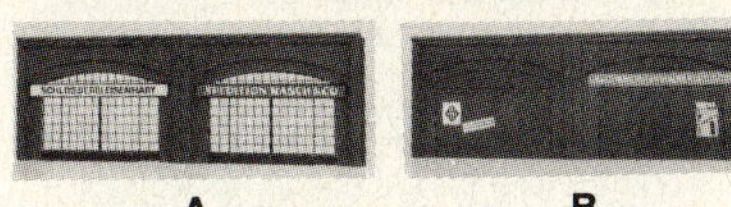

A   B

ARCADE WALL

Additional wall section for use with 186-2880.

Arch w/Recessed Recess		
186-2881	pkg(2)	13.99
Arch w/Enclosed Windows		
186-2882	pkg(2)	13.99

VIADUCT

Plastic kits are molded in appropriate colors.

186-2880	"Berlin Stadbahn"	14.99
	Railroad Arches w/Shops	

Kit, with 2 arch sections; approx size 3 × 8-1/2". Arches are approx 4-1/4" long.

RETAINING WALLS

Each has 2 sheets.

186-2860	Arched Retaining Wall	4.49
	each with 6 arches, gray	
186-2865	Arched Retaining Wall	4.49
	each with 4 arches, gray	
186-2866	Arched Retaining Wall	4.49
	each with 4 arches, brick red	

NOCH

Imported from Germany by **WALTHERS**

A   B   C   D

E   F   G   H

WALLS, ARCADES & RETAINERS

A	528-5816	Stone Wall	8.99
		9-1/2 × 5-1/4"	
B	528-5819	Wall Ledge	11.49
		14-3/8" 36.5 cm	
C	528-5818	Brick Wall	8.99
		9-1/2 × 5-1/4" 24 × 13 cm	
D	528-5824	Brick Arcades	11.49
		14-3/8 × 4-1/4" 36.5 × 10.5 cm	
E	528-5806	Wing	pkg(2) 16.49
		Arcade Wall	
F	528-5808	Tunnel	pkg(2) 21.99
		Portal - Single Track	
G	528-5809	Rock	each 20.49
		Arcades	
H	528-5815	Retaining	each 16.49
		Wall w/Rock	

(not illustrated)

528-5817	Stone Arcade (24 × 13 cm)	8.99
528-5855	Concrete Wall	7.49
528-5856	Dutch Brick	6.99
528-5858	Wooden Wall	7.49
528-5859	Wooden Slab Wall	7.49
528-5821	Shoreline Support	7.99
528-5822	Brick Wall	8.99
528-5825	Quarry Stone Wall	8.99
528-5826	Quarry Stone	each 11.99
	Arcade Wall	
528-5827	Quarry Stone	pkg(4) 20.49
	Arcade Tunnel	
528-5828	10 x 5"	14.49
	(By Special Order Only.)	
528-5832	Ashlar Facing Wall	8.99
528-5833	Ashlar Facing Arcades	11.49

kibri

Imported from Germany by **WALTHERS**

AVALANCHE WALL SECTION

8" length HO

405-4110	each	5.49

STAIRWAY

Molded of appropriately colored plastic. Includes a large stair, side walls, and ending plates.

528-5807	Stone Stairway	9.99

WALLS

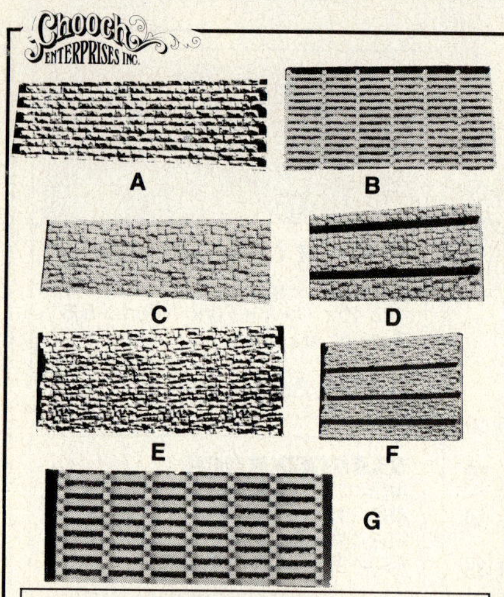

CHOOCH ENTERPRISES INC.

A
B
C
D
E
F
G

RETAINING WALLS

A 214-7017 Cut Stone — 7.99
8 x 3-5/8" 20.3 x 9.2 cm
#7017 & #7021 have parts that interconnect for continued walls.

B Timber Piled Cribbing Small
214-7025 — 8.99
7 x 4-1/8" 17.8 x 10.5 cm

C 214-7035 Sandstone — 7.99
8 x 3-5/8" 20.3 x 9.2 cm

D 214-7036 Sandstone Low — 7.99
6-3/4 x 5-1/4" 17.3 x 13.4 cm

E 214-7021 Random Stone — 7.99
8 x 3-3/4" 20.3 x 9.5 cm

F 214-7034 Random Stone — 7.99
8 x 5" 20.4 x 12.6 cm

G 214-7026 Timber Piled Cribbing, Large — 8.99
7 x 4-1/4 17.8 x 10.5 cm

A.I.M. PRODUCTS

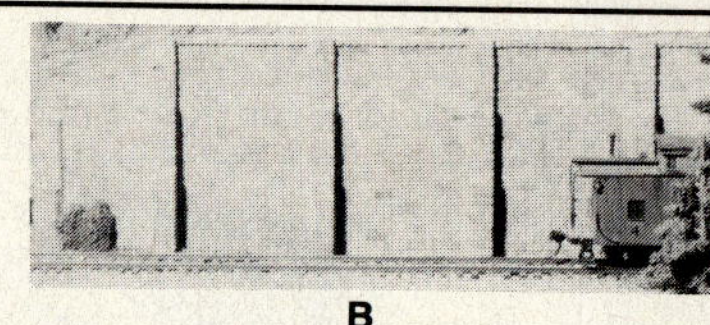

A
B
C

RETAINING WALLS

Overall Height 25'6"   Overall Width 40'9"   Overall Thickness 5'9"

A Wood Outside Braced 110-122	pair 6.25	
B Cut Stone 110-106	pair 6.25	(not illustrated)
C Poured Concrete 110-114	pair 6.25	110-107 Field Stone — pair 6.25
		110-108 Random Stone — pair 6.25

MODEL MASTERPIECES LTD

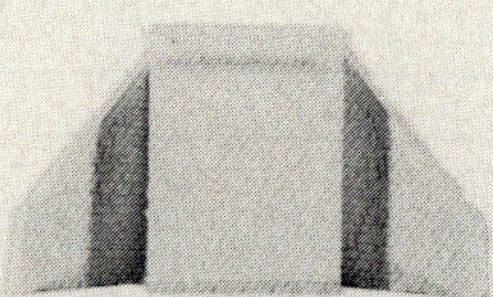

RETAINING WALL & PIERS

Cast dental stone bridge wall and pier sets are designed to match the steel truss bridge from CENTRAL VALLEY & the brass pin truss bridge from OVERLAND MODELS.

Retaining wall set includes recessed center bridge support sections, angle top wing walls, cast metal bridge expansion shoes. A hidden pivot allows wing wall placement at any angle.

Center pier set includes one center pier with bridge shoes.

485-133 Concrete Retaining Wall — 9.50
485-134 Stone Retaining wall — 9.50
485-135 Concrete Center Pier — 4.00
485-136 Stone Bridge Center Pier — 4.00

Mountains in Minutes
I.S.L.E. LABORATORIES

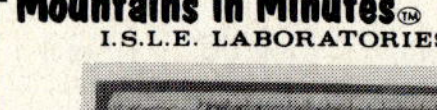
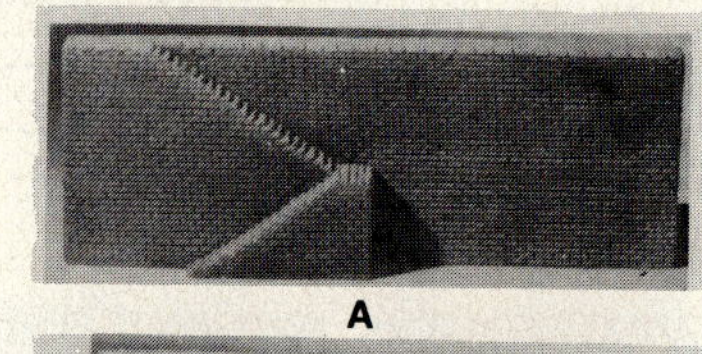

A

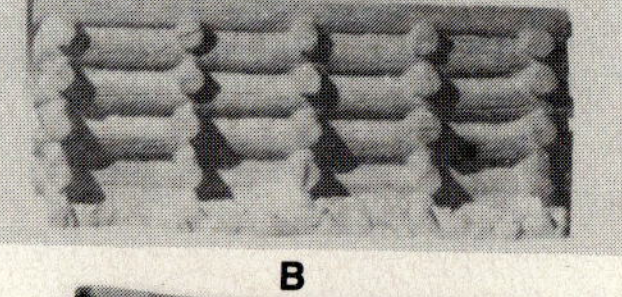

B

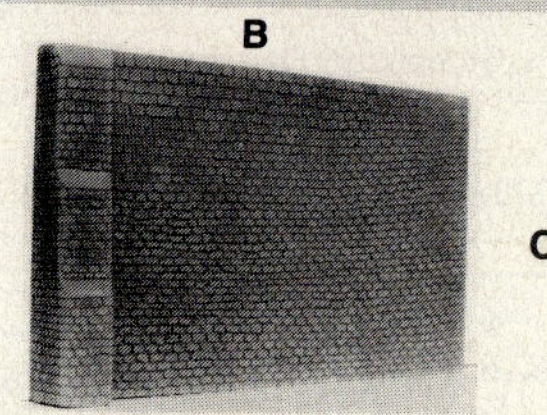

C

RETAINERS & WALLS

A 473-821 Cut Stone Wall w/Staircase — 5.98
B 473-822 Log Cribbing — 5.98
Used for reinforcing embankments or holding steep banks. 8" long × 3-1/2" high.
C 473-824 Cut Stone Wall — 6.98

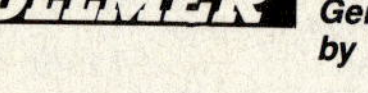

N.J. International

525-6198 Brick Wall — 2.99

VOLLMER *Imported from Germany & marketed by WALTHERS*

RETAINING WALL

770-4508 Kit   pkg(5) 24.99

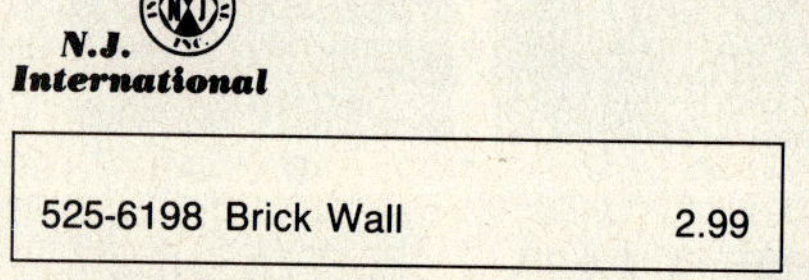

NEW

WOODLAND SCENICS

RETAINING WALLS

785-1258 Concrete — 3 each 5.98
785-1259 Cut Stone — 3 each 5.98
785-1260 Timber — 3 each 5.98
785-1261 Random Stone — 3 each 5.98
Build a complete scene by combining these items with products from Woodland Scenics Terrain System.

As the years went by, the weeds got taller, the rust got thicker and no one had any idea what to do with this old bus chassis. But as passenger traffic increased on the Nevada Southern, Burk Shields rebuilt the model for use as the line's #2 railcar. This "before" shot features a cut down Roskopf bus, covered with an aluminum foil tarp. The weeds are made from macrame rope, and the engine shed is also scratch built. *Models and Photo by Burk Shields*

ROADS & ACCESSORIES

Plastruct

STREET LIGHTS

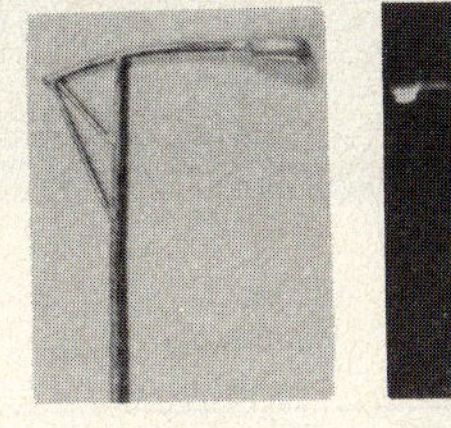 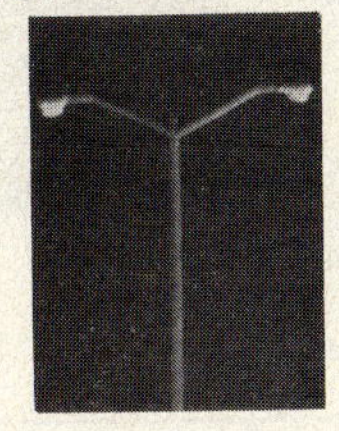 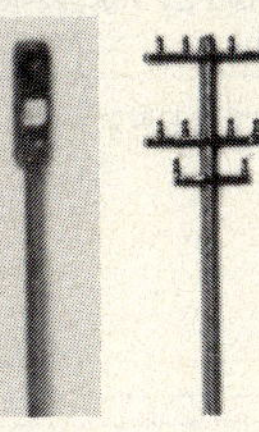 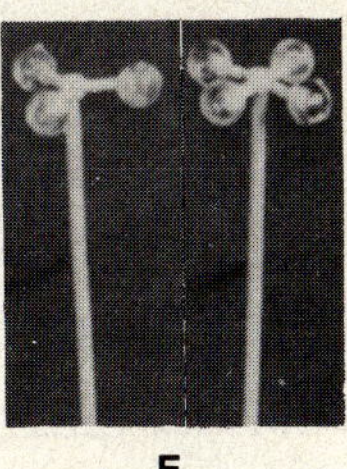 

	A	B	C	D	E	F

A 570-18100 Single pkg(2) 6.00
B 570-18510 Double pkg(4) 3.25
C 570-19610 Traffic Signal pkg(5) 3.50
D 570-19310 Telephone Pole pkg(10) 5.50

E 570-18310 3 Shere pkg(5) 9.95
  570-18410 4 Sphere pkg(5) 9.95
F 570-18810 1800's Style pkg(4) 3.25

PAVEMENT

	G	H	I	J

G 570-12911 Paper Asphalt each 3.25
  11-3/4" x 26-3/4"
H 570-12912 Paper Concrete each 3.25
  11-3/4" x 26-3/4"

I 570-12902 Asphalt Flex Matt ea 13.95
  12" x 24"
I 570-1022 Asphalt Roadway Kit ea 16.95
J 570-12903 Concrete Flex Matt ea 13.95
J 570-1023 Concrete Roadway Kit ea 16.95

Preiser

ORIGINAL

Imported from Germany by WALTHERS

COBBLESTONE ROADWAY

''Straight'' brick type
A 590-18131 Section for Sidewalks, Square Cobble ea 9.99
  190 x 480 x 2mm Stones in a scalloped pattern.
B 590-18120 Flexible Cobble St, SL ea 8.99
  70 x 950 x 2mm Stones laid in a line.
C 590-18130 Flexible Cobbled Street 70 x 950 x 2mm ea 8.99

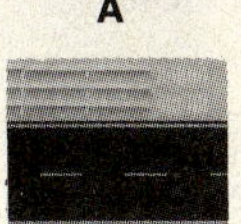 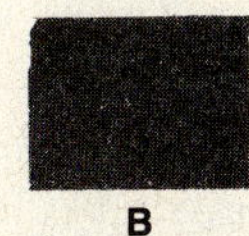 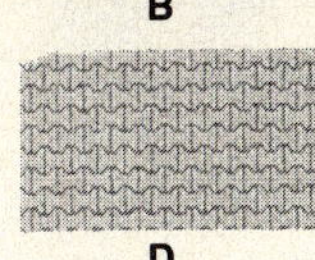

 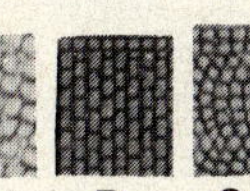

ROADS & PARKING AREAS

A Flexible Roadway & Accessories 6.49
  590-18115
  2 × 40 × 5/64" (50 × 950 × 2 mm)
B 590-18101 Black Top Surface 7.99
  7-1/2 × 19 × 5/64" (190 × 480 × 2mm)
C Flexible HO Roadway & Accessories 8.99
  (20 side markers, 6 crash barriers)
  590-18100
  2-3/4 × 37-1/2 × 5/64" (70 × 950 × 2mm)
D Cobblestone Pavement Material 7.99
  590-18141
  7-1/2 × 19 × 3/32" (20 × 48 × .03 cm)

  (not illustrated)
590-18102 Curved **NEW** pkg(3) 9.99
  Pavement
590-18140 Pavement Square Block 7.99

ROADWAY MARKINGS & SIGNS

Made of flexible gray foam than can be bent to
any road configuration.

A Curbstone Set pkg(38 pcs) 7.99
  590-18200
B Guard Rail Set pkg (40 pcs) 7.99
  590-18202
C Sign Assortment pkg(40) 9.99
  590-18203

FALLER

*Imported from Germany &
marketed by WALTHERS*

ROADWAY MARKINGS

272-591 Roadway Markings 8.49
  self-adhesive rub on transfers
  (not illustrated)
272-650 2-Lane Flexible **NEW** 5.49
  Roadway w/Markings
272-651 2-Lane Flexible **NEW** 4.49
  Roadway w/o Markings
272-1677 Junction **NEW** 20.99
  Branch Off

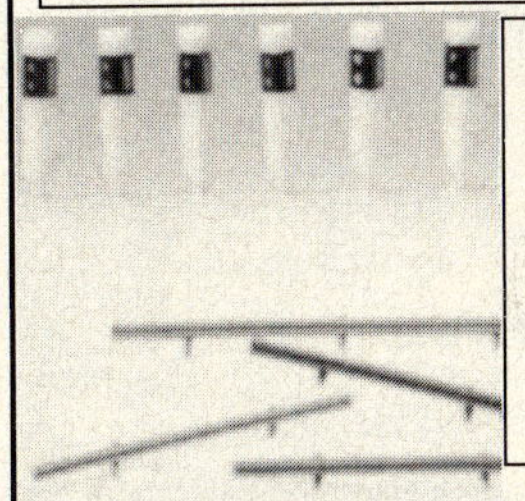

CRASH BARRIERS

Crash Barriers
272-592 8.49

Plastic construction. Includes 80cm of barriers and 32 marker posts.

SMALLTOWN, U.S.A.

SIDEWALKS

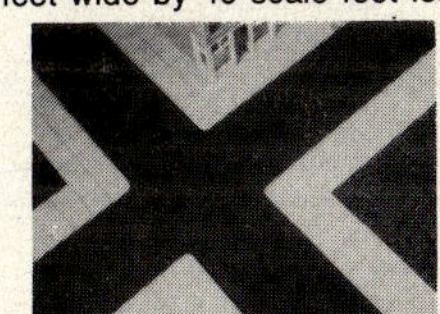

Finish your city scene with these plastic sidewalk sections. Each piece measures 10 scale feet wide by 40 scale feet long.

699-7000 City Sidewalks pkg(6) 2.75

kibri

Imported from Germany by WALTHERS

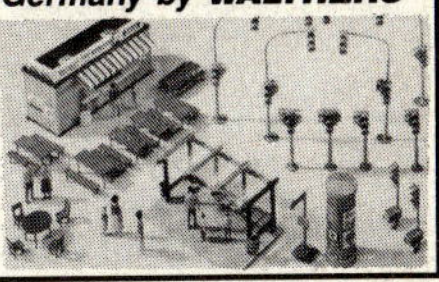

CITY STREETS
Assortment
405-8102 16.49

R. & R. F., Inc.

ROAD CROSSING

Black rubber crossing can be nailed, glued or adhered with R&RF Gravel Bed.
624-420 Flexible Road Crossing 3.40

ROADWAY

3" x 10' roll of flexible rubber material. Press tacky surface into place with fingertips - conceals seams and joints.
624-301 Instant Highway, gray roll 6.40
624-303 Instant Blacktop, black roll 6.40

ROADS & ACCESSORIES

Pikestuff

HIGHWAY GUARDRAIL
Kits include plastic molded parts with illustrated instructions.

541-3	Guardrail		1.15
541-12	Highway Guardrail	pkg(3)	2.50
541-13	Highway Guardrail	pkg(6)	4.00

PARKING BARRIER
Concrete
541-1016
pkg(12) 1.25

VOLLMER

Imported from Germany &
marketed by **WALTHERS**

COBBLESTONE STREET
adhesive paper

6 x 39" Strip
770-6023   15.49

3 x 78" Strip
770-6024   14.49

A   B

NOCH
Imported from Germany by **WALTHERS**

  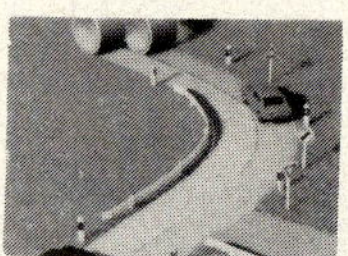    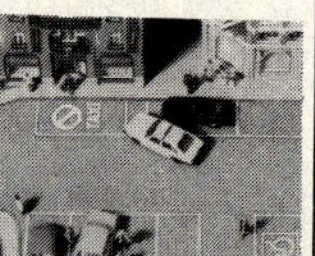

A   B   C   D   E   F   G

PAVEMENT

A Flexible Road, black
528-6041   39 × 1"   each 7.49

B Flexible Highway, gray
528-6049   pkg(2) 10.99
1/2" wide to create 4 lanes.

C Flexible Roadway, gray
528-6050   39 × 1"   pkg(2) 7.49

D Street Intersection
528-6042   pkg(2) 7.49
8 x 3-7/8" 20.5 x 10 cm

E Paved Courtyard Cobblestone
528-6046   pkg(2) 7.49
8 x 3-7/8" 20.5 x 10 cm

F 528-5854 Cobblestone Panel   7.49
Road pave panel: 3-1/2 x 6-3/4" 9 x 17.1 cm

H   I

J   K

G 528-6055   Parking Lot, gray 4 x 8" 10 x 20.3 cm   pkg(2) 8.49
Adhesive backed with printed parking spaces. Includes 4 silver plastic parking meters.

H 528-48570 Paved Square 8 x 3-7/8"   **NEW** pkg(2) 8.49
I 528-60451 Flexible Bike Path   7.49
J 528-60481 Flexible Gravel Road   5.99
K 528-60531 Flexible Foil w/Garden Paving   8.49

(not illustrated)

528-6047	Highway	pkg(2) 8.99
528-6060	Country Road	pkg(2) 8.99
528-6053	Flexible Roadway Paving Station 8 x 4"	pkg(2) 8.49
528-6061	Flexible Roadway, Country	9.99
528-6062	Flexible Roadway, Pavement	5.99
528-6063	Flexible Roadway, Garden	5.49

mini HIGHWAYS — NEW

Division of Leisuretime Products

RAILROAD CROSSING & INTERSECTIONS

Thin, precut material with realistic black/brown color to recreate roads and highways. Will lie flat without adhesives, but can be glued for permanent scenery.

406-201	Straight Passing Zone (9ft)	4.99
406-203	Curved Roadway	4.99
406-205	RR Crossing & Intersection	4.99

WOODLAND SCENICS — NEW

CULVERTS

785-1262	Concrete	2 each	5.49
785-1263	Masonry Arch	2 each	5.49
785-1264	Random Stone	2 each	5.49
785-1265	Timber	2 each	5.49

Build a complete scene by combining these items with products from Woodland Scenics Terrain System.

VISTA SCENIC HOBBY PRODUCTS

When ordering, use Manufacturer #767.   **NEW**

ROADWAYS

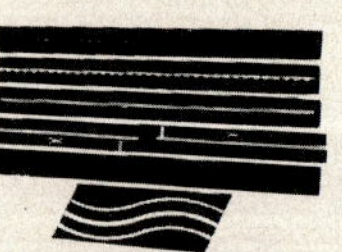

Create realistic highways, roads, streets, parking lots and more with these roadway sections made from foam material. Feature self adhesive backing that sticks to most surfaces. Available in either gray or black road surface colors. All sections are 30" in length except curves, which are 14."

5.50 each

Road surface color	Gray	Black	Gray	Black
Markings color	Yellow	Yellow	White	White
Two lane passing	800	810	820	830
One lane passing	801	811	821	831
No passing	802	812	822	832
Curve	803	813	823	833
RR crosswalk	804	814	824	834
Unmarked	805	815		

FENCES

FALLER
Imported from Germany and marketed by WALTHERS

A

B

D

C

G

F

E

FENCES
A 272-525 Garden & Field   9.99
B 272-527 Black   pkg(10) 9.49
C 272-523 Wrought Iron pkg(24) 11.49
Assorted fences and matching gates.
D Metal Industrial Fencing
272-520   11.49
Includes fine mesh, concrete posts, corner posts, entry door and moveable, wide sliding door. 41" (105 cm) total length.

E 272-524 Fencing   pkg(8) 8.49
7" (18 cm) sections
F Fencing with Gate
272-528   pkg(6) 6.49
G Iron Railing
272-529   pkg(6) 8.49
(not illustrated)
272-522 Railing Fence pkg(8) 11.49
plastic, each 18 cm long

VOLLMER
Imported from Germany & marketed by WALTHERS

RAILING
Hand Railings
770-5000
pkg(20) 7.49
90 mm long

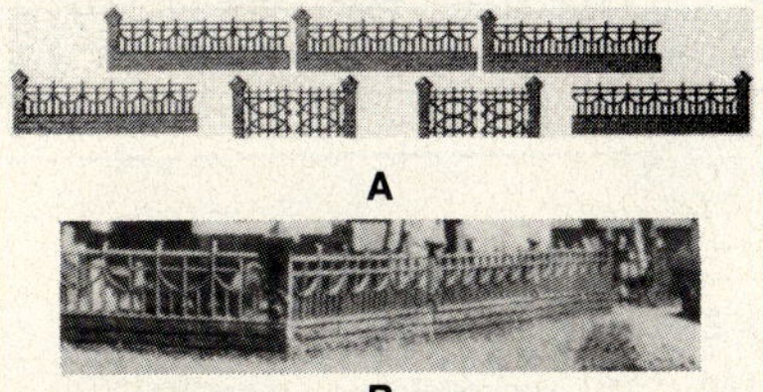

A

B

FENCING
770-5009 Chain Link Fencing   9.99
(6 frames—150 mm long, 1 meter wite mesh, 2 gates)
770-5133 Ornate Fencing   8.49
approximately 39" long

BRAWA
Imported from Germany by WALTHERS

ETCHED FENCES
186-3611 Wrought Iron Garden   23.99
Fence-Large
With 4 drop-in gates; black finish. 6 × 4".

186-3631 Wrought Iron Garden   14.99
Fence-Small
With 4 drop-in gates; black finish. 3 × 2".

186-3608 5 Garden Fences   20.49
w/Gate, Large
3-1/4 × 4-3/4"

186-3628 5 Garden Fences   12.49
w/Gate, Small
2 × 3". (total length approx 26")

ALLOY FORMS, INC.

FENCES
Chain Link Fence Kit
119-2009   14.95
200 Scale feet of detailed prototype chain link fence contains 200 feet of top rail, 14 fence contains 200 feet of top rail, 14 fence posts, 4 corner posts, left and right gate posts and two 8 foot swinging gates. Brass castings with aluminum fencing material and barbed wire.

AM MODELS

FENCE
Board Fence
129-503   1.98

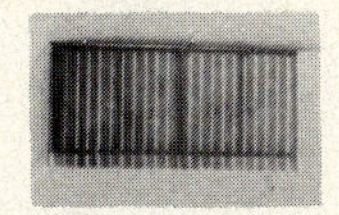

CUSTOM RAILWAY SUPPLY

A

B

GATES AND PANELS
212-1066 Wrought Iron Gate   3.95
and Panel
212-1065 Wrought Iron Gate   3.95

MERTEN
Imported from Germany by WALTHERS

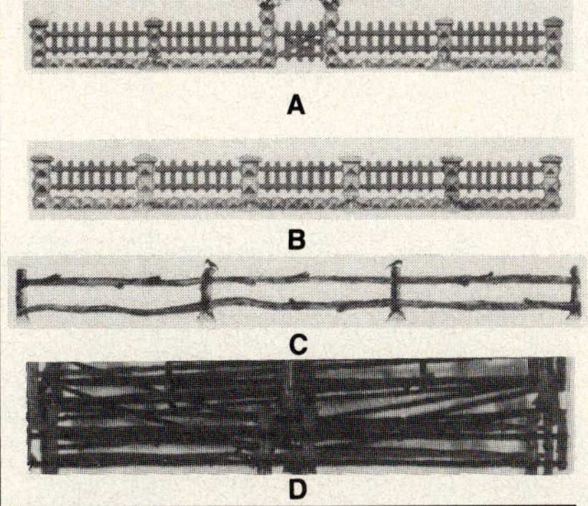

A

B

C

D

FENCES
A 447-91   Garden Fence w/Gate 2.49
B 447-92   Garden Fence   2.49
C 447-399 Rustic Fence w/Birds 2.49
D 447-2418 Fence   pkg(44") 7.49
w/Gate, (113 cm)

kibri
Imported from Germany by WALTHERS

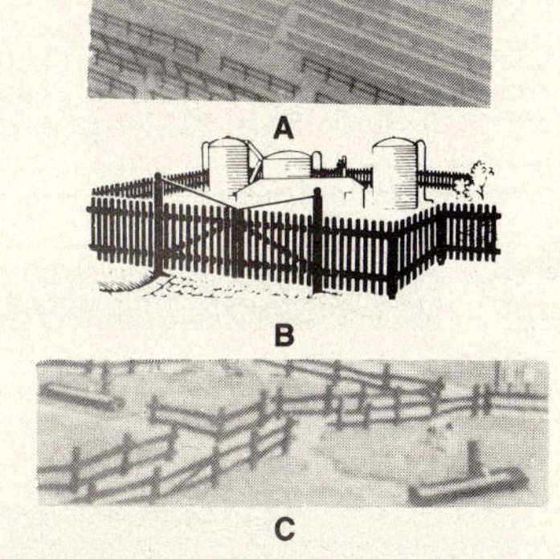

A

B

C

FENCING
A 405-9356 Fence   10.99
B 405-9353 Picket w/Gate   10.49
total length 33"
C 405-8008 Cattle   9.49
w/water trough & accessories

FENCES

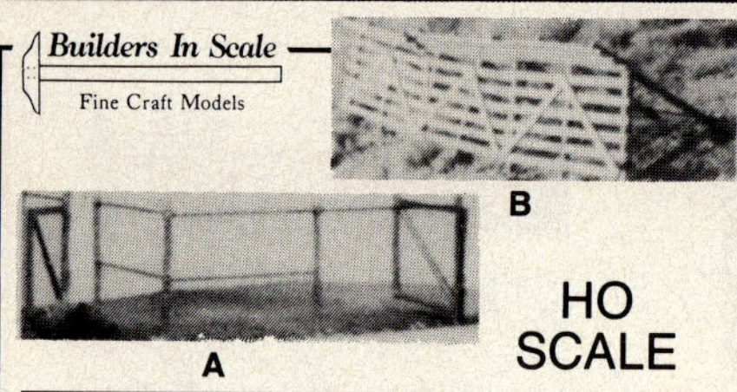

Builders In Scale
Fine Craft Models

B

A

HO SCALE

FENCES

A 169-604 Chain Link Fence   kit 6.98
Includes 150" of chain link material, cast metal posts, corner posts, gates and gate posts.

B 169-608 UP Snow Fence   kit 9.98
2 part metal castings, 8 snow fences (128')

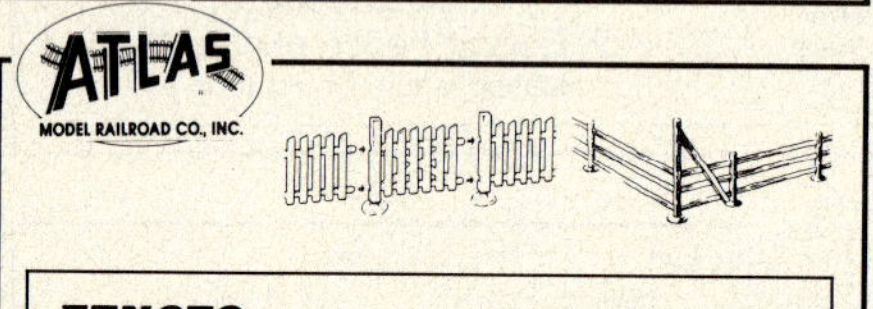

ATLAS MODEL RAILROAD CO., INC.

FENCES

Parts are molded of styrene in appropriate colors.

150-776 Picket Fence & Gate-White 2.75
150-777 Rustic Fence & Gate-Brown 2.75

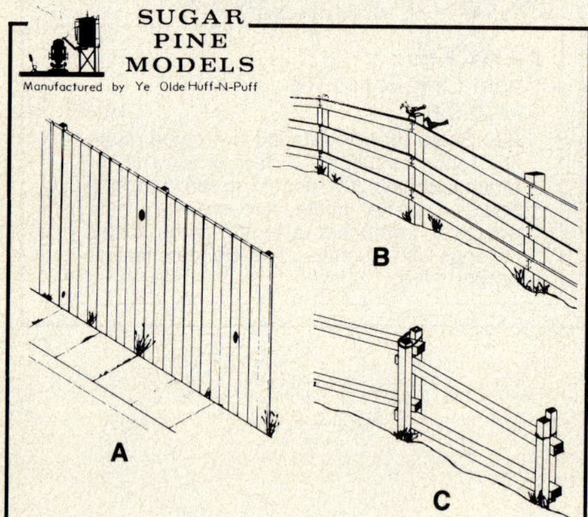

SUGAR PINE MODELS
Manufactured by Ye Olde Huff-N-Puff

B

A

C

FENCES

HO Scale, easy to build kits.
Kits include pre-cut wood and templates for fast construction.

A 685-1108 Plank Style, 16" long   4.00
B 685-1109 Cattle Style, 16" long   3.50
C 685-1110 Rustic Style, 35" long   3.50

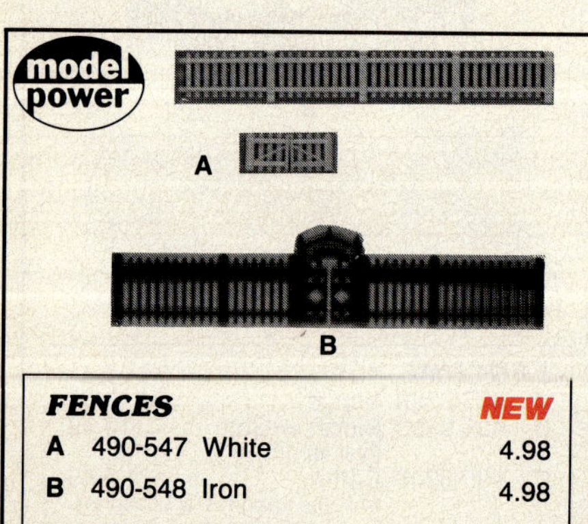

model power

A

B

FENCES   *NEW*

A 490-547 White   4.98
B 490-548 Iron   4.98

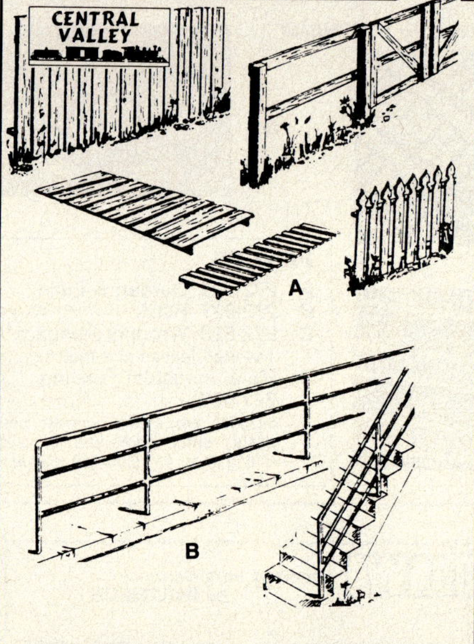

A

B

FENCES, LADDERS & STAIRS

A Fencing and Handrail Assortment
210-1601   each 4.95
B Ladders, Stairs & Railways
210-1602   each 4.95

N.J. International

FENCING

525-6188 Spearpoint   2.99

Plastruct

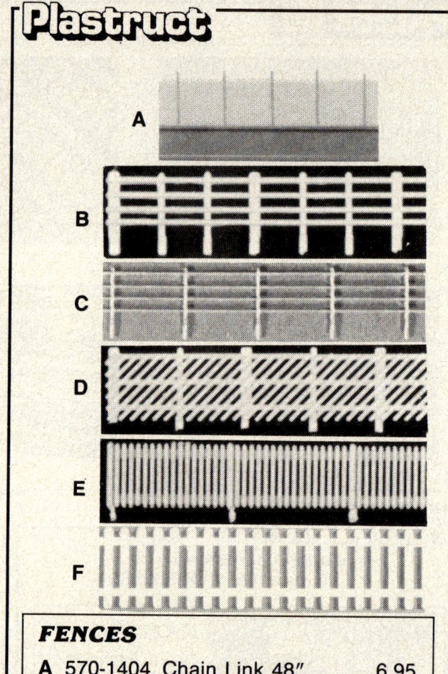

A

B

C

D

E

F

FENCES

A 570-1404 Chain Link 48"   6.95
B 570-1414 4 Bar Horizontal 20"   4.95
C 570-1415 4 Bar Ranch 9-1/2"   8.95
D 570-1424 Diagonal Picket 20"   4.95
E 570-1434 Vertical Picket 20"   4.95
F 570-1454 Ranch Picket 28"   4.95

BACHMANN QUALITY SINCE 1833

FENCE

160-42100 Picket Fence   pkg(24) 2.95

Bet there's more than one railfan who brings the family to the resort town of Ocean View Bay. This line of the Missouri, Kansas & Quincy skims the Pacific coast, and there's a constant parade of Intermodal traffic. Hightailing it for the midwest, this hotshot is pulled by a Rail Power loco, decorated for Gary Hoover's home road, in Florissant, Missouri. The swingbridge was rebuilt from a Bowser kit, while the lighthouse is a Blue Jacket kit.

Models and Photo by Gary Hoover

WALTHERS · *ADD LIFE TO YOUR LAYOUT*

Walthers Sign Kit makes it easy for shoppers to find bargains! The set adds realism to any storefront and is easy to assemble.

Signs Bring Scenes to Life

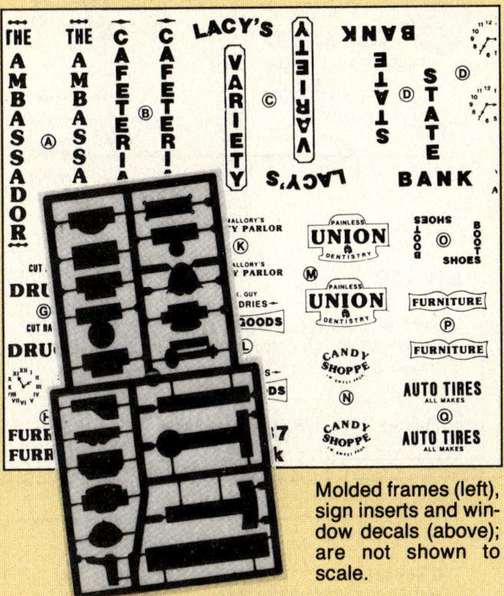

Molded frames (left), sign inserts and window decals (above); are not shown to scale.

A busy day begins on Main Street as proprietors unlock their doors. Signs on each building identify products and services offered to residents and commuters alike. The magic words, "On Sale" attract the bargain hunters.

Turn your HO buildings into a bustling, busy town with Walthers Sign kit. Kit contains 54 different signs—20 moulded frames with 24 different inserts, plus 30 window decals for different kinds of shops, offices, products and services. "Sale", "For Rent", "Closed", etc., are included. One package will bring an entire HO Main Street to Life.

941-3136 Walthers Sign Kit   5.98

Walthers Decals Add Life

The final touch to your layout can be a magical one when you use Walthers decals. "A Breath of Life" (not to mention true realism) is easily achieved with the wide variety of decals that Walthers manufactures. Decaling your layout adds a unique look and Walthers decals offer limitless possibilities.

GRAFFITI, SCRIBBLINGS

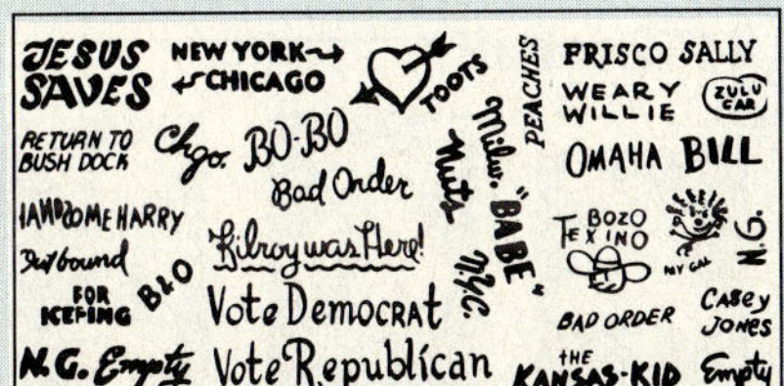

You can add realism to your railroad by adding these decals to your rolling stock, structures, locos, bridges or rock formations.

934-701070 Graffiti (white)   3.98
934-701080 Graffiti (black)   3.98

Listed below are some of Walthers Accessory Decals.

FIRE ENGINE DATA

ENGINE	ENGINE	ENGINE
LADDER	LADDER	SALVAGE
RESCUE	COMBINATION	HIGH PRESSURE

934-1495 Fire Engine Names (gold) 3.98

STARS

Red, white and blue stars are shown actual size.

Your basic all around star. Ideal for bicentennial units such as the white stars on frame edge and in stripes. Why, you could conceivably make up an entire flag using just stars. Each set includes two sheets of each color.

934-706870 Stars (red,white,blue)   3.98

PLAIN DECAL PAPER

For people who are interested in making their own decals, Walthers has available plain decal paper—coated with wet transfer glue, lacquered and ready for printing, painting or drawing upon. This is the same high quality paper that is used in making all the latest Walthers decals.

934-706820 Plain Decal Paper   3.98
Four 6 x 9" sheets per package. Larger sheets for your convenience.

VENETIAN BLINDS

934-701180 Venetian Blinds,   set 3.98
            w/tapes (silver)
934-701190 Venetian Blinds   set 3.98
            w/tapes (dulux)

SIGNS

CRESCENT STATION

SIGNS

Over 425 different signs printed on sturdy cardstock in full color, black and white and brown and white. Signs are shown actual size.

513-550 HO 1/87 Scale Sign Kit   2.95

C-THRU

DRY TRANSFERS

A   470-1001   Railroad Sheet #1, Black   1.50
B   470-1002   Railroad Sheet #2, Black   1.50

Plastruct

BILLBOARDS

570-1013   pkg(4)   9.95
Scratch-built kit contains enough material to construct four modern, steel billboards, including posters.

WHITEGROUND MODEL WORKS

Special Order only

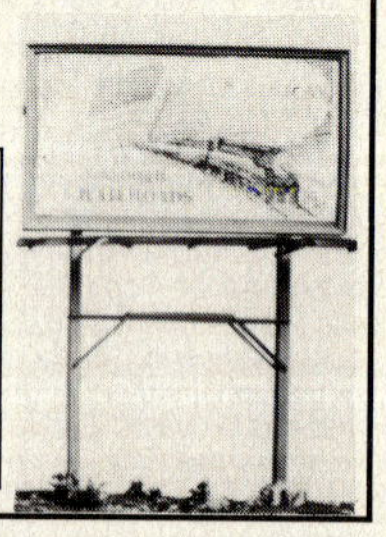
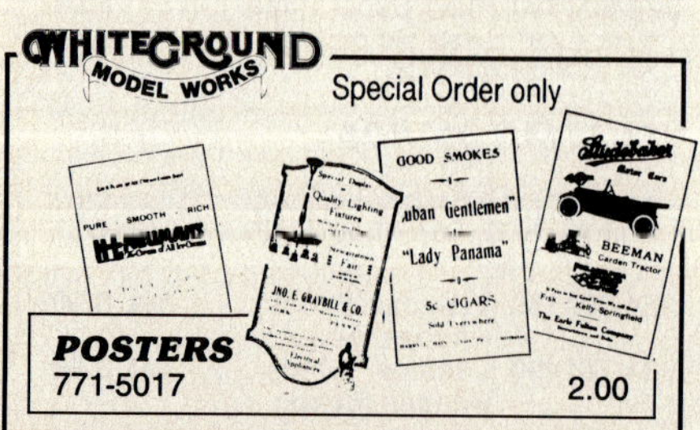

POSTERS

771-5017   2.00

BRAWA

Imported from Germany by WALTHERS

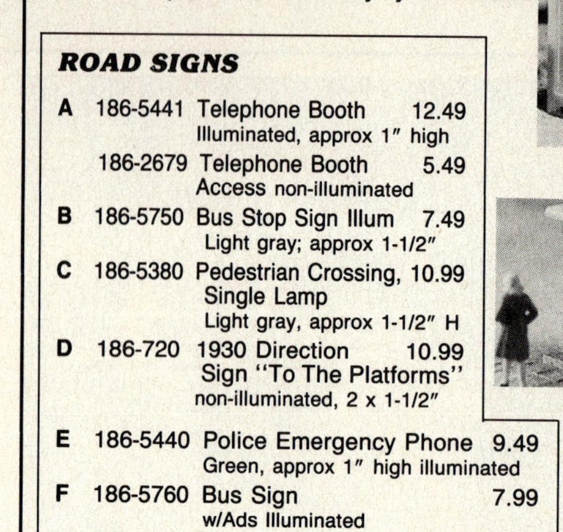

ROAD SIGNS

A   186-5441   Telephone Booth   12.49
      Illuminated, approx 1″ high
      186-2679   Telephone Booth   5.49
      Access non-illuminated
B   186-5750   Bus Stop Sign Illum   7.49
      Light gray; approx 1-1/2″
C   186-5380   Pedestrian Crossing, 10.99
      Single Lamp
      Light gray, approx 1-1/2″ H
D   186-720   1930 Direction   10.99
      Sign ''To The Platforms''
      non-illuminated, 2 x 1-1/2″
E   186-5440   Police Emergency Phone   9.49
      Green, approx 1″ high illuminated
F   186-5760   Bus Sign   7.99
      w/Ads Illuminated
G   186-5444   Telephone Booth   **NEW**   12.49
H   186-5445   Telephone Stand   **NEW**   11.49
      Booth (yellow)

      (not illustrated)
186-3600   Tavern Signs, Large   20.49
      3-3/4 x 6″
186-3620   Tavern Signs, Small   12.49
      2-1/2 x 4″

Country Trains

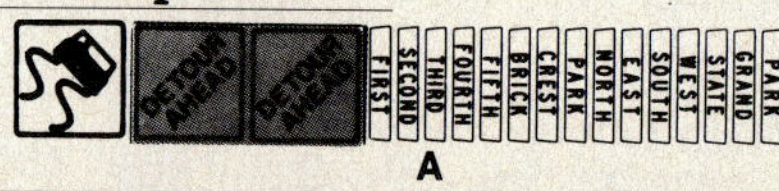

ROAD SIGNS   Each set 1.50

Signs are printed in appropriate colors on glossy, coated cardboard. Four sets are available and each set has two sheets. Illustrations are approximately 2/3 actual size.

A   203-1   Street Corner & Road Signs & construction (110 signs)
B   203-2   Highway Signs (56 Signs)
C   203-4   RR Track & Crossbucks (86 signs)
D   203-3   Speed Limit, RR Crossing, Stop, & Warning (72 signs)

      (not illustrated)
203-5   Road Decals RR,   pkg(28)   2.98
      Stop, Center Line
203-6   Road Decals, RR   pkg(18)   2.98
203-92   Decal RR Ca Graffiti   1.98

International Hobby Corp.

STREET/TRAFFIC SIGNS

Street & Traffic
348-422307   pkg(12)   3.98

---

kibri   *Imported from Germany by WALTHERS*

SIGN/BUILDING LETTERING

20 sheets of full color transfers.

405-8090   Railroad Line Lettering   16.49
405-8094   DB Advertising Signs   pkg(150)   13.99

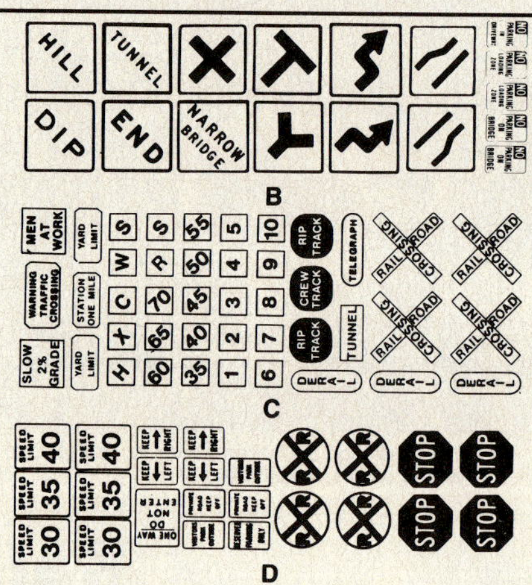

FALLER   *Imported from Germany & marketed by WALTHERS*

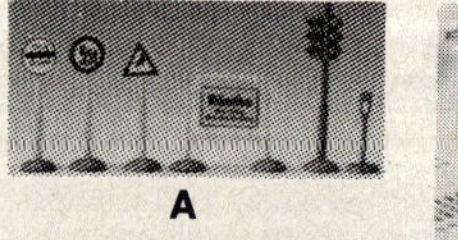
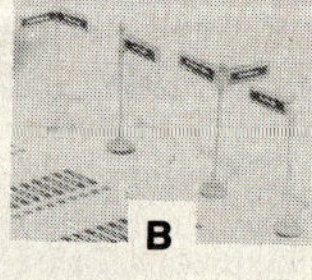

TRAFFIC SIGNS

A   272-578   Traffic   pkg(150)   15.99
B   272-579   Road Sign Set   12.49

Pikestuff

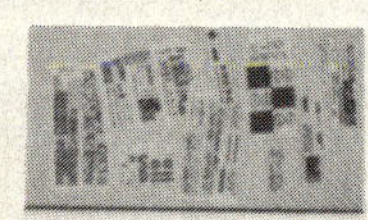
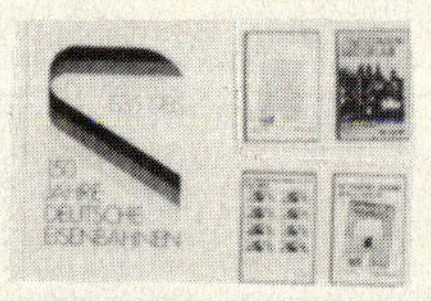

CROSSBUCKS

541-1017   Crossbucks   pkg(4)   2.50
Includes plastic molded parts, decals and assembly instructions.

SIGNS

Vintage Reproductions

We have worked closely with this manufacturer to provide accurate availability information at the time this catalog was published. Items listed in *blue ink* may not be available at all times. Please see your dealer for current delivery information.

RAILWAY SIGNS

COLORADO MIDLAND CROSSBUCKS

Prototype is Colorado Midland Terminal sign. Includes drawings and templates.

766-102 Railway Crossing   pkg(24) 3.50

CMR TICKET OFFICE

Buena Buena, Colorado, wall sign. Set contains several sizes. White.

766-105 Any Scale   4.00

SIMULATED METAL SIGNS

Reproduction on thin adhesive-backed glossy photo emulsion. Cut around sign, peel away backing and attach to base, or fold over for two sided signs.

766-202 Round Railroad Crossing Warning Signs HO Scale	pkg(24)	2.75
766-205 Western Union Old Style HO	pkg(36)	2.75
766-208 Western Union New Style HO	pkg(36)	2.75
766-228 Railway Express Agency	pkg(18)	2.75
766-211 Railway Express Rectangular Depot	pkg(24)	2.75
766-214 REA Diamond Depot Signs		3.00
prototype from New Hampshire, red and white.		
766-215 Street Stop Signs (red, white)	pkg(24)	2.75
766-216 Street Stop Signs (yellow, black)	pkg(24)	2.75
766-225 Railroad Crossing Crossbucks HO Scale		2.75

Sign Assortments
Contains 2 each of all signs listed above.

766-221 Metal Sign Sampler HO Scale 3.25

DEPOT SIGNS

Assorted train arrival-departure boards with train names, numbers, times, messages. Includes office roundhouse signs. 3 colors available.

766-106 White		4.00
766-107 Yellow		4.00
766-108 Green		4.00
766-110 Economy Pack (#106-108)		11.00

RTR CROSSING CROSSBUCK

Dry Transfer
766-159 HO Scale   3.00

LEGACY SIGNS

Dry transfer signs for windows, walls, fences, false fronts, vehicles, etc. Seven colors available. Each set is entirely different. Sets include both single and two-color signs. Can be converted to regular decal by applying to plain decal paper, not included.

Each set contains two 3 x 5-1/2" transfer sheets & instruction folder. Non-distorting or curling transfer sheet.

766-111	Red-Gold	set	6.75
766-112	Black-White	set	6.75
766-113	Black-Yellow	set	6.75
(By Special Order Only.)			
766-114	Red-White	set	6.75
766-115	Blue-Gold		6.75
776-116	Blue-Yellow		6.75
766-117	Economy Pack (#111-116)		35.00
766-118	Red-Black		6.75
766-119	Black-Gold		6.75
766-120	Red-Gold		6.75
(By Special Order Only.)			
766-121	Yellow-Black		6.75
766-122	Green-Yellow	set	6.75
766-123	Green-Black	set	6.75
766-124	Economy Six-Pak		35.00
(1 each: Sets 118-123)			

EXPRESS SIGNS

766-109 Adams Express   4.00

BILLBOARD & BUILDING SIGNS

Project sets include dry transfers, HO Scale photograph or drawing, parts list and construction notes with suggestions to build a structure with bold lettering.

A Whimsical Billboards St #1
766-131   All Scales 4.00

B Whimsical Billboards Set #2
766-151   All Scales 4.00

C The Ute Pass Paint Co.
766-132   10.00

D Eureka Horseshoeing and Plow Work
766-133   4.00

E Sanborn's Antiques
766-154   4.00

F Esso Gas Station
766-137   4.00

G Imperial Laundry
766-135   4.00

H Mail Pouch - Barn
766-139   4.00

I Mogollan's General Store
766-140   3.50

J "Beech-Nut in Glass Jars" Barn
766-144   4.00

K Victors "Mail Pouch" - Wall, 2 Story
766-145   4.00

L The Oasis Saloon
766-147   4.00

M "Railroad Mills Snuff" - Farm Silo
766-149   4.00

N Oshkosh B'Gosh Overalls - Farm Silo
766-150   4.00

O Rouselle Motor Co.
766-152   4.00

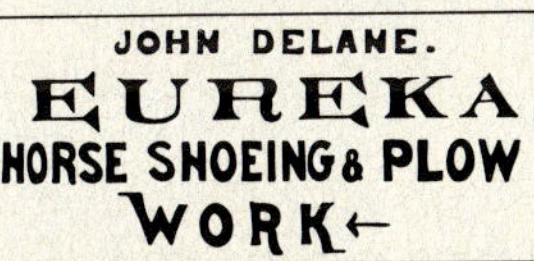

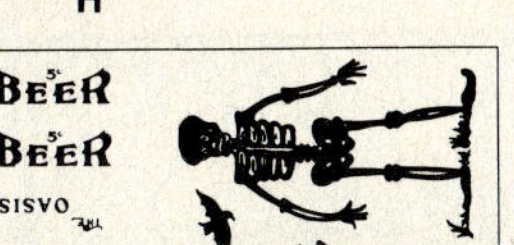

(not illustrated)

Blackhawks "Bull Durham"-Machine Shop
766-125   4.50

Winthrops "Bull Durham"-Barn
766-126   4.00

Georgetowns "Bull Durham"-Fence
766-127   4.00

Last Chance Livery & Feed Stable
766-128   4.00

Diamond Springs Hillside Water Tank
766-130   4.50

(By Special Order Only.)

Lucky Strike Barn
766-142   4.00

Golden Garter Tavern
766-156   4.00

BURNISHING TOOL

766-313 for Dry Transfers   6.50
1-1/2" curved blade machinists burnisher with smooth curved back for wide areas & very fine tip for small details.

SIGNS

A

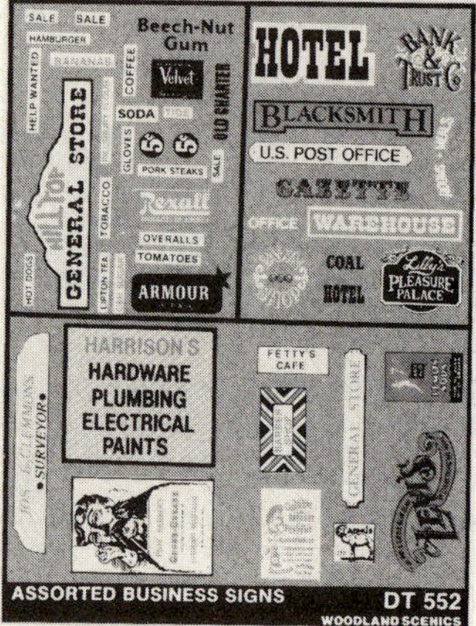

B

HO SCALE TRANSFERS

Full color dry transfers can be applied to a smooth or textured surfaces of wood, metal, paint, plastic, etc., by positioning the sign in the desired area, rubbing gently on the back and peeling away the carrier sheet. One 4 × 5″ sheet per package.

A 785-551 Tavern, Gas Station & Commercial — 4.98

B 785-552 Assorted Business Signs — 4.98
C 785-553 Depot, REA & Advertising — 4.98
D 785-555 Road, Product, & Burma Shave — 4.98
E 785-556 Assorted Logos & Advertising — 4.98
F 785-557 Data/Warning Labels & Commercials — 4.98

G 785-558 Railroad Heralds — 4.98
H 785-560 Crate Labels & Warnings — 4.98
I 785-561 1960's Signs & Posters — 4.98
J 785-563 1940's Signs & Posters — 4.98

(not illustrated)

785-600 Dry Transfer Burnisher — 2.98

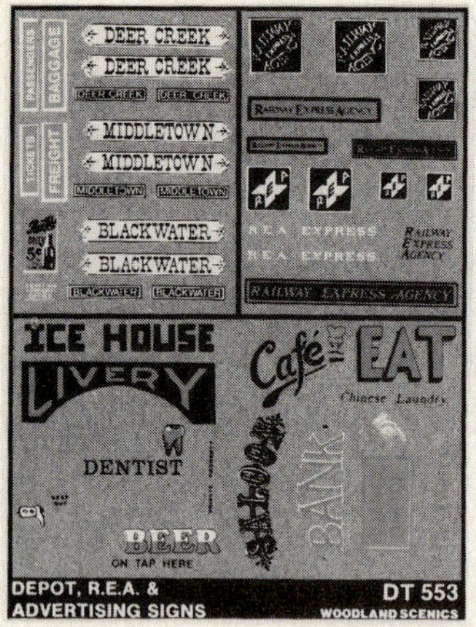

C

D

E

F

(The following are panels G, H, I, J across the bottom of the page)

G

H

I

J

SIGNS

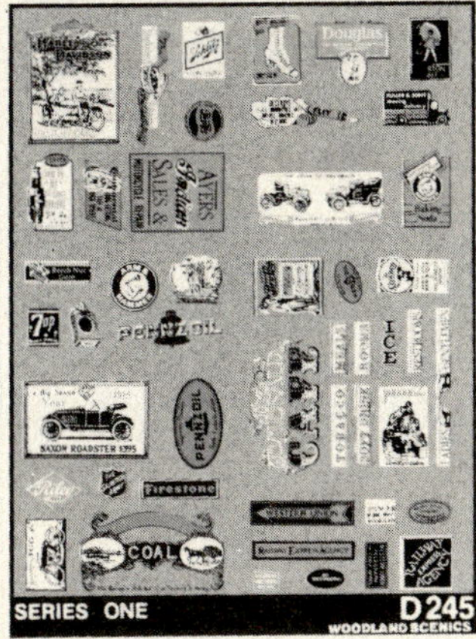

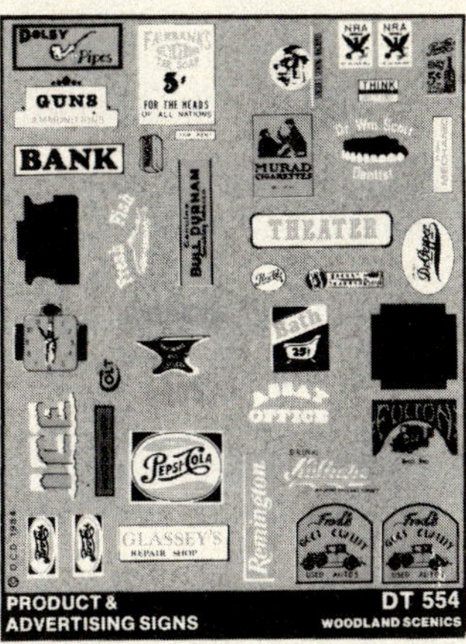

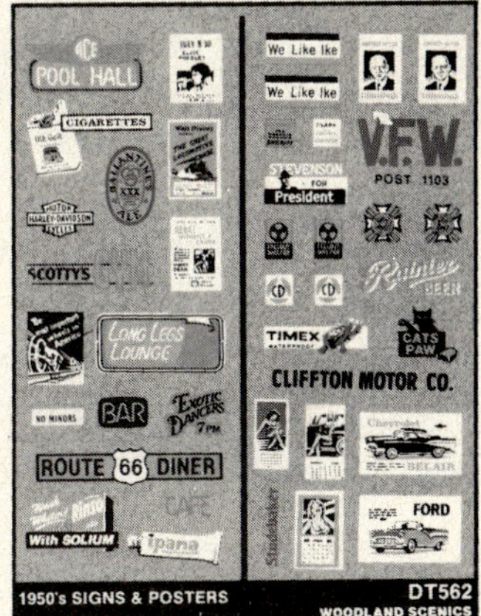

K   L   M   N

HO SCALE TRANSFERS (continued)

K	785-245 Series One	4.98
L	785-554 Product & Advertising Signs	4.98
M	785-559 Standard Oil & Business	4.98
N	785-562 1950's Signs & Posters	4.98

NEW

These N Scale transfers can be used as small signs for HO Scale. $4.98 each.

O	785-570 Product Logos	
P	785-571 Railroad Signs	
Q	785-572 Business Signs	
R	785-573 Signs & Posters	
S	785-574 Service Station Signs	

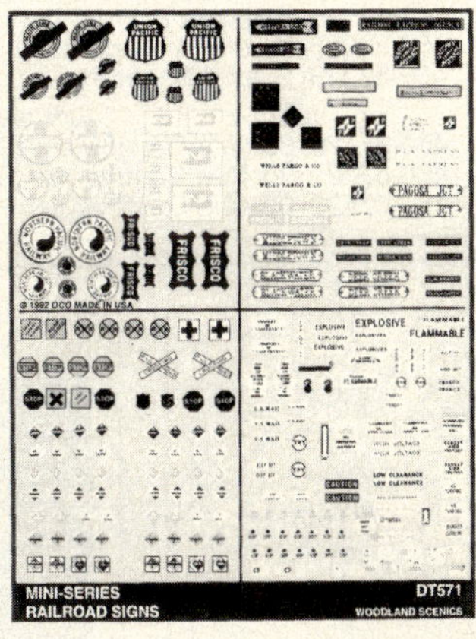

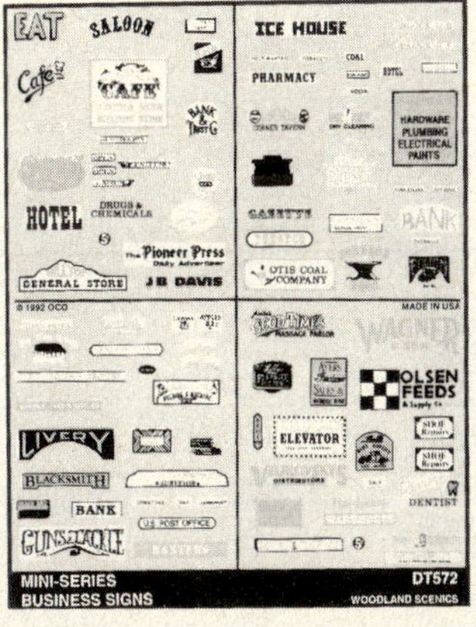

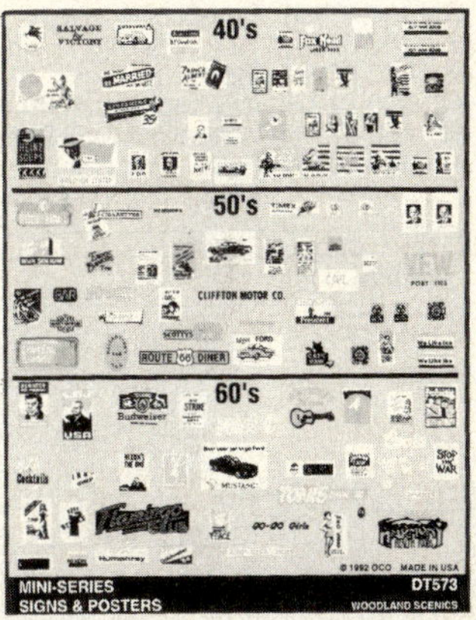

O   P   Q   R

S

In this eastern community there's a main line rather than a Main Street! Jeff Riley of Pittsburgh, Pennsylvania, based this area of his layout on the actual town of Thurmond, West Virginia. The businesses are scratchbuilt, while a "Grandma's House" is also visible. The homes on the hill are N Scale structures, to give an illusion of distance. The Kanawha & Western coal drag is pulled by a brass import.

Models and Photo by C.J. Riley

SIGNS

MICROSCALE DECALS

A

B

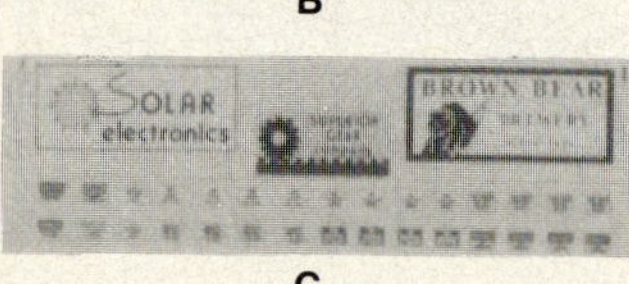

C

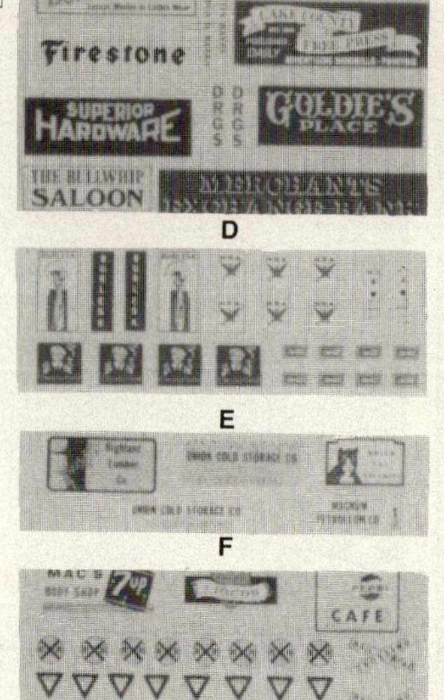

D

E

F

G

H

I

J

K

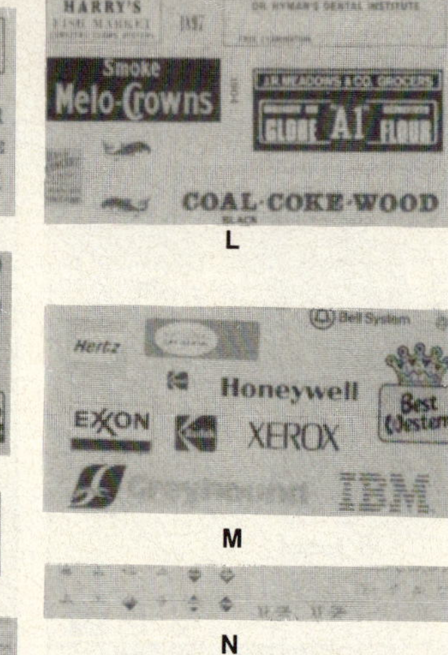

L

M

N

O

DECAL SIGNS

These full-color decal signs can be applied directly to smooth, glossy, painted building walls or can be applied to separate styrene signboards fastened to the building. Signs without a color background can be mounted on a board of any color.

A variety of different business titles are provided, along with a number of personal names, so you can make whatever combinations you like. Illustrations are not actual size. 5 × 7.5″ sheets. **Each packet is 4.00.**

A	460-87162	Western Cowtown Signs 1850-1900
B	460-87166	Rural Farming Community 1880-1920
C	460-87273	Signs for Industry
		chemical/steel/typical heavy industry
D	460-87163	Small Town Signs 1850-1910 farming communities
E	460-87287	1930 Era Signs with Window Markings
F	460-87289	Industrial Signs #2
G	460-87275	City Signs for Streets & Buildings
H	460-87164	Western Town Signs 1840-1900
I	460-87197	Early 20th Century Signs 1900-1930
		billboards & private business

J	460-87245	Neon Lettering	
K	460-87206	Railroad Way Signs	
L	460-87165	Industrial Town & City 1895-1920	
M	460-87198	Late 20th Century Signs 1950-1978	
		billboards & private business	
N	460-87228	Graffiti & Placards	
O	460-87243	Graffiti Sheet #2	
		(not illustrated)	
	460-87420	30/40's Commercial Signs #1	4.00
	460-87421	30/40's Commercial Signs #2	4.00
	460-87422	30/40's Commercial Signs #3	4.00

model power

A

B

C

LIGHTED BILLBOARDS

A 490-700 Billboards pkg(2) 6.98
B 490-703 Blinking Billboard 26.98
Contains 28 LED running lite bulbs, Blinker control and is pre-wired.
C 490-701 Running **NEW** ea 26.98
Contains 28 LED running lite bulbs. Use for Movie Theater #421 (see Structures - Model Power).

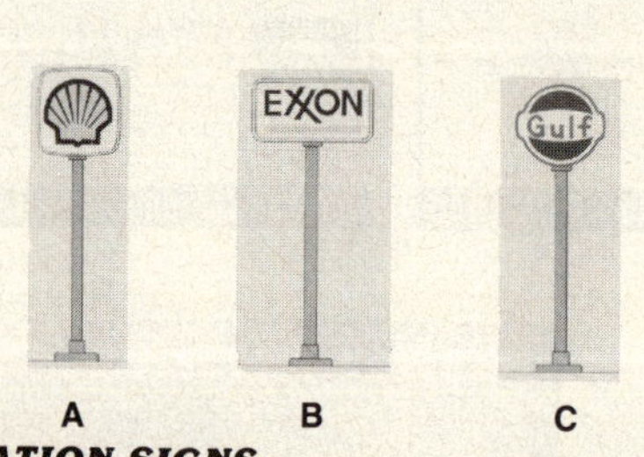

A   **B**   **C**

STATION SIGNS

Illuminated, brass parts.
A 490-704 Shell   pkg(2) 6.98
B 490-705 Exxon   pkg(2) 6.98
C 490-706 Gulf   pkg(2) 6.98

Finishing Touches

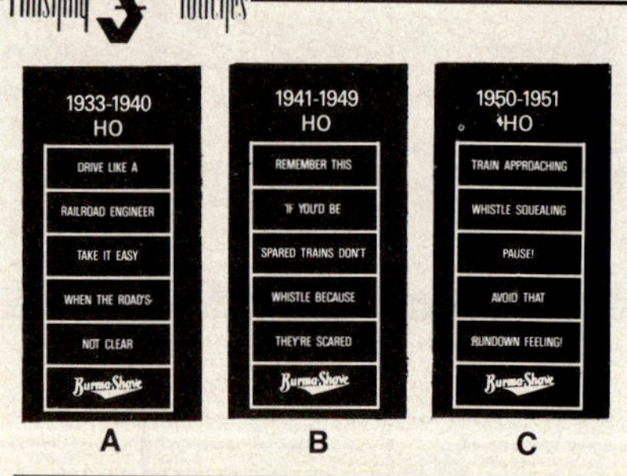

A   **B**   **C**

BURMA SHAVE SIGNS

A 675-6281 Burma Shave 30's 2.95
B 675-6282 Burma Shave 40's 2.95
C 675-6283 Burma Shave 50's 2.95

A

SCENERY ACCESSORIES

A 490-702 1924-1940's pkg(8) 5.98
Movie Poster Assortment
B 490-7021 1940-1960 Movie pkg(8) 6.98
Poster Assortment

(not illustrated)
490-1454 Road & Rail Signs pkg(24) 4.98
Assorted signs made of molded white plastic with black lettering.

B

SIGNS

BILLBOARDS   Kits include 12 full-color signs, three easy-to-assemble billboards and non-illuminated light fixtures. All of the plastic parts are molded in color. Rounding out the kits are complete instructions with tips for adding signs to existing scenery.

933-3116 Roadside Billboards #4 Petroleum Signs   8.98

Roadside Billboards #1 Steam/Diesel Era Signs 933-3103 8.98

Roadside Billboards #2 Food Signs 933-3106 pkg(3) 8.98

Roadside Billboards #3 Automotive Signs 933-3107 8.98

(not illustrated)
933-3133 Plain Billboard   **NEW** pkg(2) 4.98

That just might be Joe Friday restoring law and order to the streets of Los Angeles. Woody Langley models the Pacific Electric of the early 40's and has filled his layout with detailed scenes like this. The patrol car is a Crescent Station (Formerly Mountain States Model Works) kit, fitted with a GRS Micro-Liting™ warning light. "Rocky's" was built from a Woodland Scenics kit. The PE freight motor is a Suydam brass model, fitted with constant lighting.
Models and Photo by Woody Langley

SIGNS

JL Innovative Design — NEW

BILLBOARDS-AUTO/BUS/RAIL THEMES

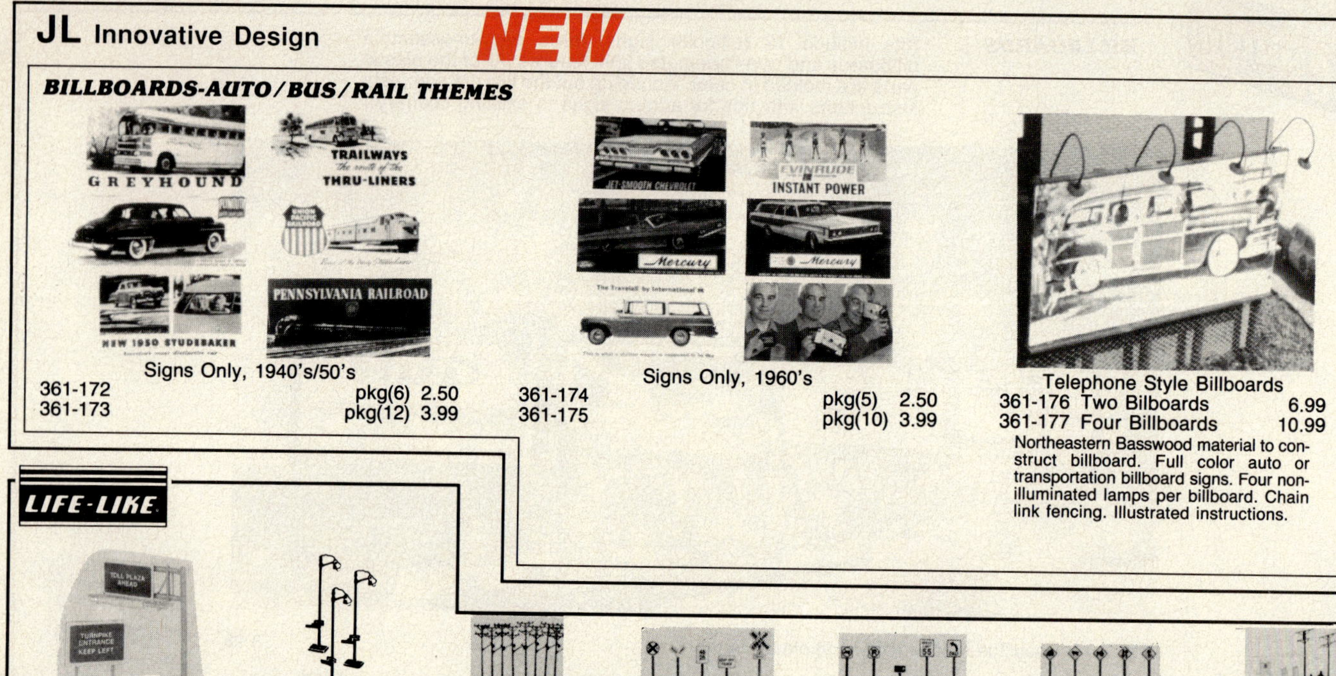

Signs Only, 1940's/50's

361-172   pkg(6) 2.50
361-173   pkg(12) 3.99

Signs Only, 1960's

361-174   pkg(5) 2.50
361-175   pkg(10) 3.99

Telephone Style Billboards

361-176 Two Bilboards   6.99
361-177 Four Billboards   10.99

Northeastern Basswood material to construct billboard. Full color auto or transportation billboard signs. Four non-illuminated lamps per billboard. Chain link fencing. Illustrated instructions.

LIFE-LIKE

A   **B**   **A**   **B**   **C**   **D**   **E**

LIGHT UPS

Appropriately colored plastic, working HO Scale lights are ready-to-use.

A 433-1218 Overhead Road Signs pkg(3) 7.00
B 433-1506 Highway Lights   pkg(3) 7.00

ACCESSORIES

Appropriately colored, molded plastic.

A 433-1113 Telephone Poles   pkg(12) 5.00
B 433-1125 Railroad Signs   pkg(19) 5.00
C 433-1126 Street & Highway Signs   pkg(24) 5.00

D 433-1131 Road Signs   pkg(24) 5.00
E 433-1112 City Sidewalks   5.00 (not illustrated)

433-1196 Scenic Assortment   **NEW**   pkg(24) 120.00
433-1633 Burma Shave Signs   **NEW**   pkg(24) 5.00

DEPOTS BY JOHN — NEW

CUSTOM BUILT STRUCTURES IN SCALE

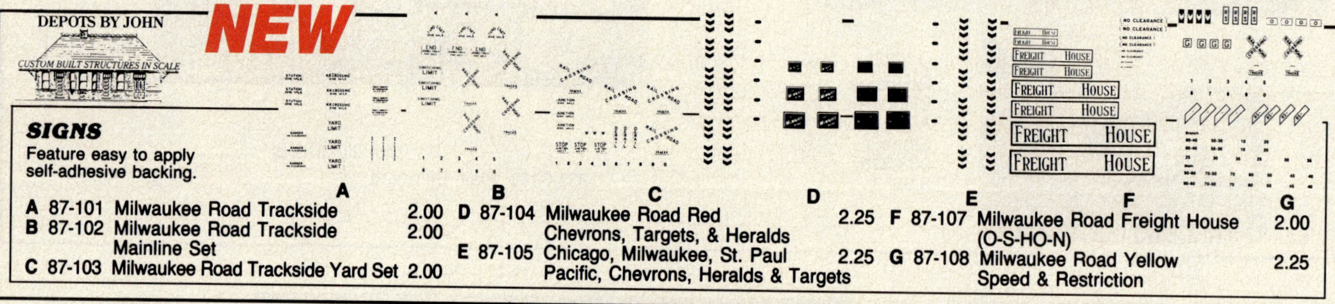

SIGNS

Feature easy to apply self-adhesive backing.

A 87-101 Milwaukee Road Trackside   2.00
B 87-102 Milwaukee Road Trackside Mainline Set   2.00
C 87-103 Milwaukee Road Trackside Yard Set 2.00
D 87-104 Milwaukee Road Red Chevrons, Targets, & Heralds   2.25
E 87-105 Chicago, Milwaukee, St. Paul Pacific, Chevrons, Heralds & Targets   2.25
F 87-107 Milwaukee Road Freight House (O-S-HO-N)   2.00
G 87-108 Milwaukee Road Yellow Speed & Restriction   2.25

The operator has a clearance card and waybills ready as a Delaware & Hudson caboose hop prepares to head down a branchline. An Atlas C424 (now out of production) leads the Athearn caboose past a Tyco tower. Utility poles from Walthers Cornerstone Series® and various scenery materials complete this realistic scene, built by Ron Furto of Crest Hill, Illinois.

Models and Photo by Ron Furto

MINI SCENES

NOCH — *Imported from Germany by WALTHERS*

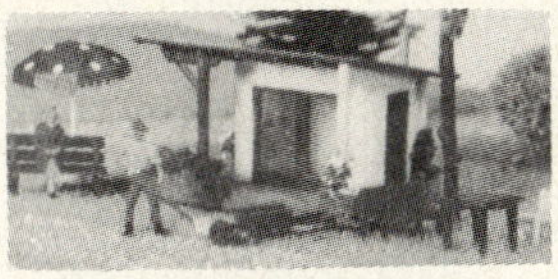

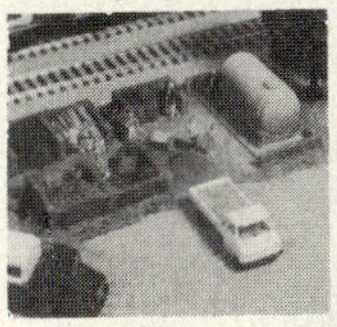

SCENIC DETAILS & FIGURE SETS

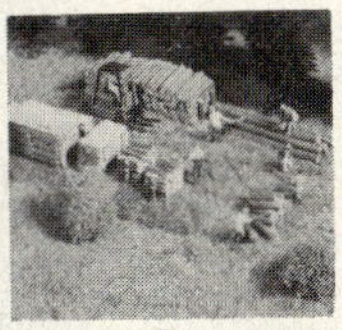

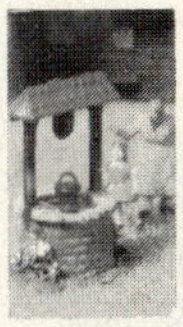

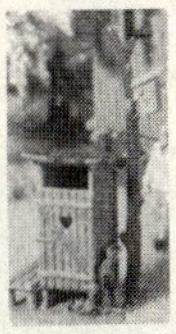

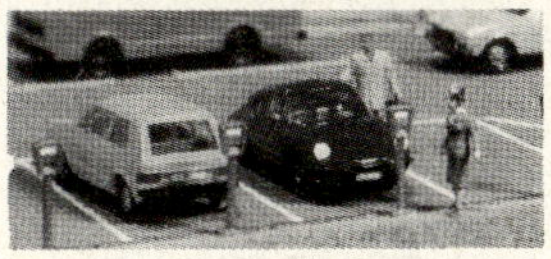

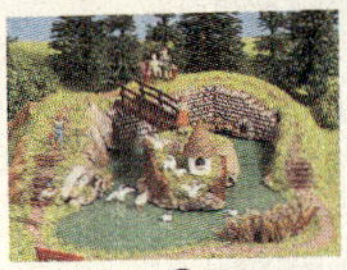

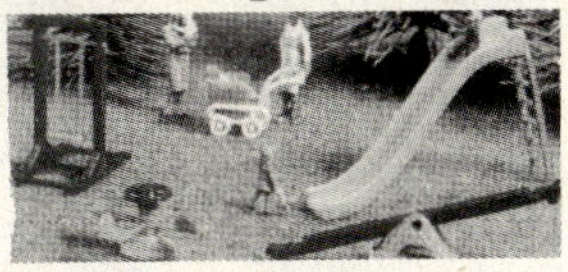

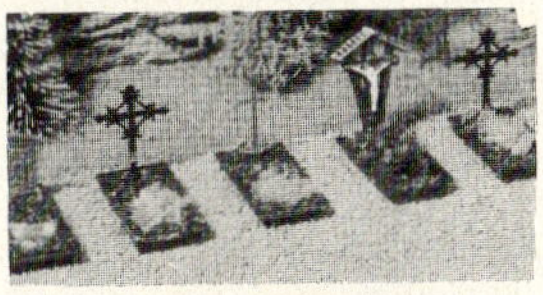

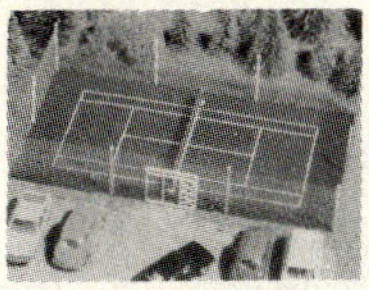

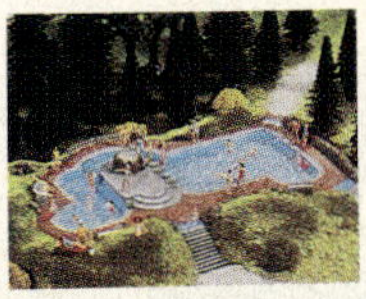

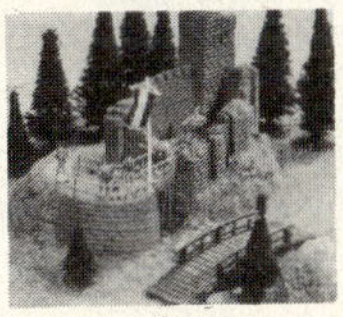

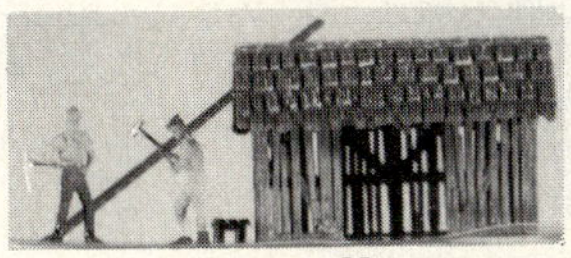

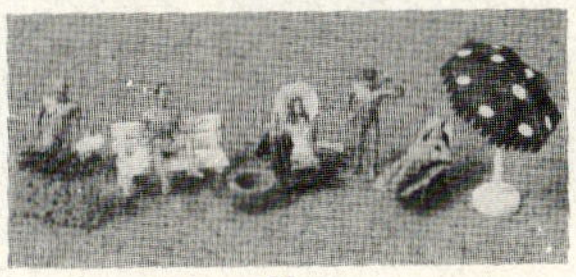

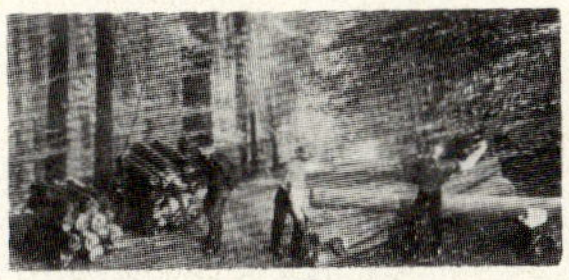

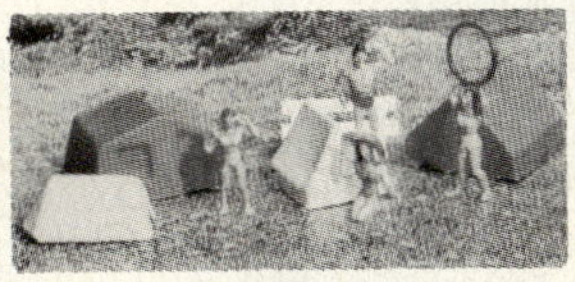

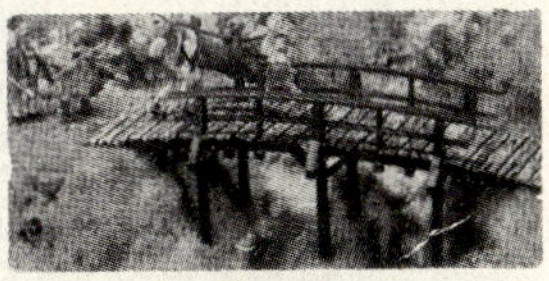

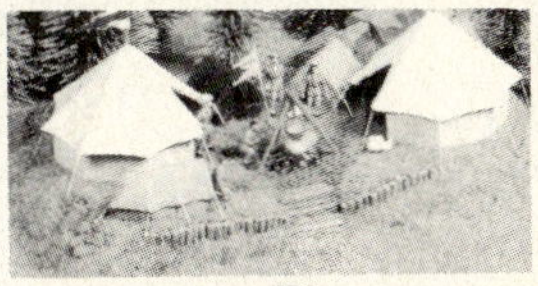

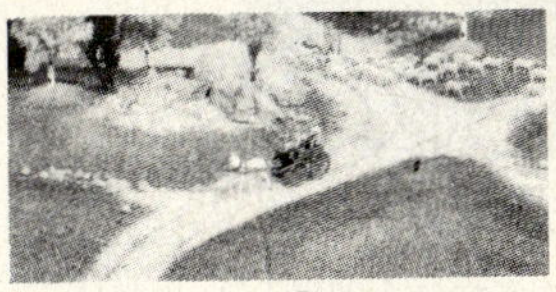

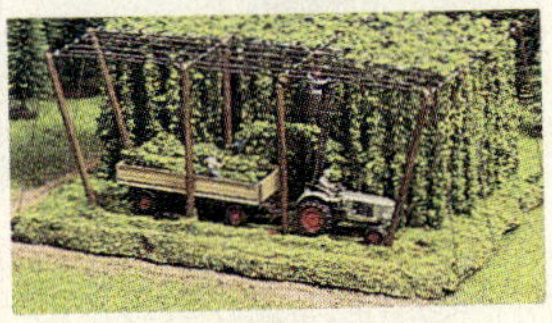

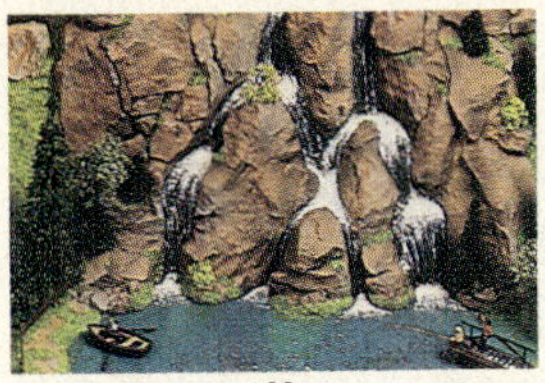

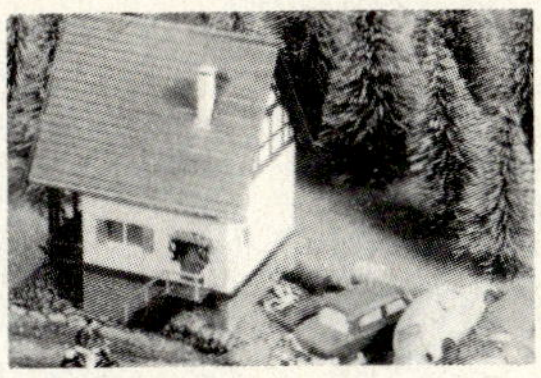

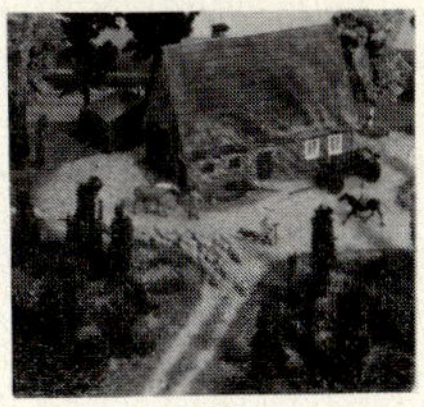

Put life in your layout with this assortment of figures and accessories! Each item is prepainted, ready to install.

A	528-1188	Garden House w/Figures and Accessories	19.49
B	528-614	Coal Dealer	18.99
C	528-616	Wood Piles	18.99
D	528-1090	Well	5.99
E	528-1091	Outdoor Privy	5.99
F	528-1101	Parking Meters pkg(16)	5.99
G	528-627	Garden Pond 8-1/4 x 6-1/4"	27.99
H	528-1158	Playground Equipment	12.99
I	528-1134	Graves pkg(5)	9.99
J	528-6058	Tennis Court w/Fence	12.99
K	528-601	Swimming Pool	42.99
L	528-605	Castle Ruin	22.99
M	528-1189	Quarry Assortment	19.49
N	528-1191	Back Yard Pool Scene	19.49
O	528-1136	Cutters Scene	9.99
P	528-1170	Campers and Tents	16.49
Q	528-1097	Wild Water Scene w/Bridge	5.99
R	528-610	Camp	24.99
S	528-623	Moorland	9.49
T	528-626	Hop Harvest	44.99
U	528-591	Waterfall	33.99
V	528-608	Car Dump	22.99
W	528-628	House Kit 15-3/4 x 11-3/4" **(By Special Order Only.)**	38.99

(not illustrated)

528-1165	Table Tennis Scene **(By Special Order Only.)**	16.49
528-6059	Soccer Field w/Goals & Flags	32.99
528-609	Birchwood Farm	36.99
528-611	Gravel Works	32.99

DIORAMA SCENES

528-600	Graveyard	47.99
528-602	Playground	29.99
528-603	Roadworks	19.99

GRS Micro Liting

CAMP KIT WITH WORKING FIRE

296-2000 Hobo Camp Kit   32.95

Kit includes detailed scene casting, two painted hobo figures, two soft metal unpainted bedroll castings, painted soft metal tote-stick, FM-1 Micro Flamemaker™ lamp kit, complete instructions for wiring, installation and painting.

Preiser — *Imported from Germany by WALTHERS*

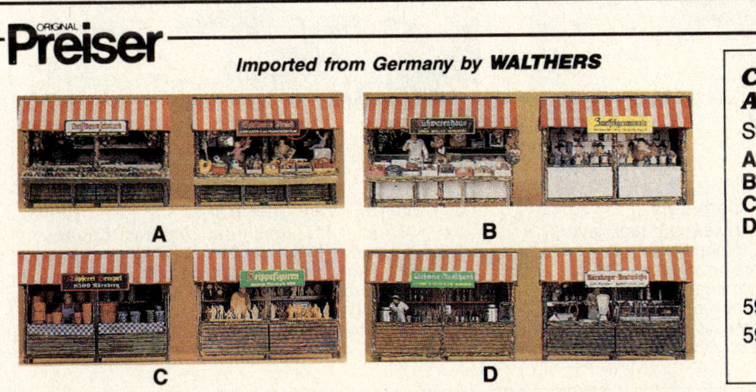

CHRISTMAS FAIR ACCESSORIES

Stalls

A	590-17523	#1	(2)	16.49
B	590-17524	#2	(2)	16.49
C	590-17525	#3	(2)	16.49
D	590-17526	#4	(2)	16.49

(not illustrated)

590-17527	Christmas Trees		9.99
590-17528	Booths- Porcelain Household	(2)	16.49

ACCURATE LIGHTING — *NEW*

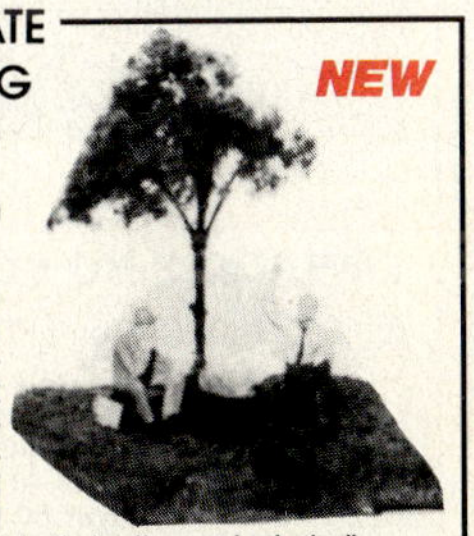

Bums in Paradise
144-90000   28.95

Two hobos sitting around a fire. Flickering fire unit (also separately) is powered by an FM radio headset jack (radio not included).

144-90010 Campfire Simulation Unit   11.95

MINI SCENES

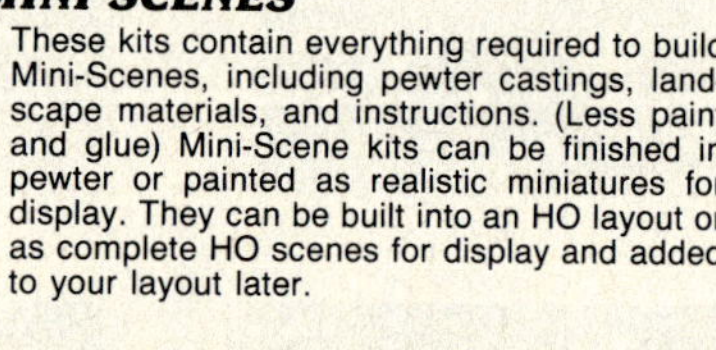

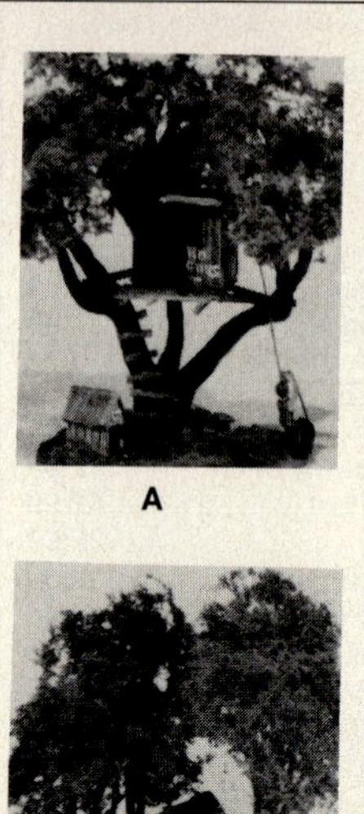

A   B   C   D

MINI SCENES

These kits contain everything required to build Mini-Scenes, including pewter castings, landscape materials, and instructions. (Less paint and glue) Mini-Scene kits can be finished in pewter or painted as realistic miniatures for display. They can be built into an HO layout or as complete HO scenes for display and added to your layout later.

A	785-107	Tommy's Treehouse	8.98
B	785-111	Floyd's Barber Shop	8.98
C	785-105	The Sign Painter	8.98
D	785-106	The Tack Shed	8.98
E	785-108	Outhouse Mischief	8.98
F	785-104	The Hunter	8.98
G	785-110	Saturday Night Bath	8.98
H	785-112	Tractor Pit Stop	8.98
I	785-101	Abandoned Log Cabin	8.98
J	785-102	Moonshine Still	8.98
K	785-103	The Windmill	8.98
L	785-109	Ernie's Fruit Stand	8.98

E   F   G   H

I   J   K   L

A   B   C

COMPLETE HO SCALE SCENE KITS

A 785-130 Smiley's Tow Service   18.49
(7 × 9") Includes: basswood building, basswood fence, seven trees (with two colors for foliage), four different colors of grass and soil, three colors of foliage for bushes and weeds, and over 60 white metal castings including tires, concrete blocks, fuel tanks, oil drums, firewood, mail box, man and several other assorted pieces including junk pile.

B 785-131 Maple Leaf Cemetery   18.49
(8 × 11" Includes: basswood tool shed, basswood fence rail, eight trees (with two colors of foliage), four colors of grass and soil, two colors of foliage for bushes and weeds, and over 40 white metal castings including stone fence posts, stone walls, gates, two men, a central monument and 28 tombstones with names.

C 785-132 Memorial Park   18.49
(8 × 14") Includes: Shelter house, basswood fence, nine trees (with two colors of foliage), four colors of grass and soil, two colors of foliage for bushes and weeds, and over 40 white metal castings including Bar B-Q ovens, tire swing, teeter-totter, picnic tables, people, trash cans and park sign.

LAYOUT FORMS

kibri
Imported from Germany by **WALTHERS**

SCENIC LAYOUT FORMS

The layout forms and the layout form extensions are vacuum formed of heavy plastic which has been decorated with grass, roadways, etc., and mounted on a wooden frame. Layout forms include bridges, piers and other indicated accessories in kit form, less structures, track, scenery or train sets. Assembly required. Recommended for experienced modelers.

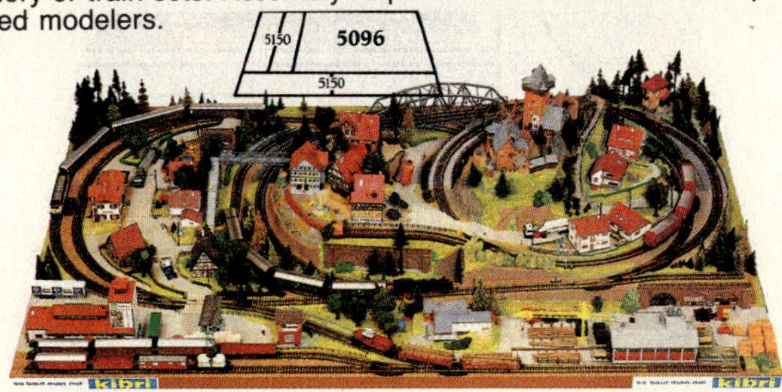

405-5096 The GAU Layout Form 399.99
59 x 39" 150 x 100 cm
Comprised of 3 Kibri railway bridges, base including brook and scenery.

405-5130 Wendelstein Layout Form 599.99
79 x 39" 200 x 100 cm
Includes 2 Kibri railway bridges, tunnel & base, road or brook bridges.

450-5106 Chiemgau Layout 349.99
59 x 39" 168 x 108 cm
Includes 3 railway bridges, 1 bascule bridge and 1 tunnel.

405-5108 Seebruck Layout Form 249.99
49 x 39" 125 x 100 cm
Includes 1 viaduct, 3 straight arch bridges, 8 curved arch bridges and 1 tunnel.

EXTENSION UNITS *NEW*

405-5150	39 x 10" 100 x 25 cm	75.99
405-5152	20 x 10" 50 x 25 cm	22.99
405-5154	31 x 24" 80 x 60 cm	59.99
405-5156	9 x 9" 25 x 25 cm	18.99
405-5158	39 x 19.5" 100 x 50 cm	70.99

405-5134 Hunsruck Layout Form 599.99
79 x 39" 200 x 100 cm
Includes 8 railway bridges, 8 piers and more.

405-5104 Emmental Layout Form w/Tunnel 349.99
59 x 39" 150 x 100 cm
Includes 4 railway bridges, 1 brook crossing and 1 tunnel.

405-5102 Grevaslvas Layout Form 369.99
59 x 39 x 70" 150 x 100 x 24 cm
Includes 7 railway bridges, 1 road bridge, 3 piers and more.

405-5136 Ortenstein Layout Form *NEW* 417.99
78 x 49" 200 x 125 cm
Includes 3 bridges, 2 ramps, 15 straight arch bridges and 38 curved arch bridges.

BASEBOARD CONTROL PANEL

405-5090	Legs and Brackets	pkg(4)	64.99
	Length 22-3/4" 68 cm		
405-5093	Layout Legs	pkg(2)	50.99
405-5091	Control Panel		25.49
	19-5/8" x 7-7/8 x 2-3/8"		
405-5148	Mounting Bolts	pkg(6)	5.49
	1/8 x 2" 5 x 50 cm		

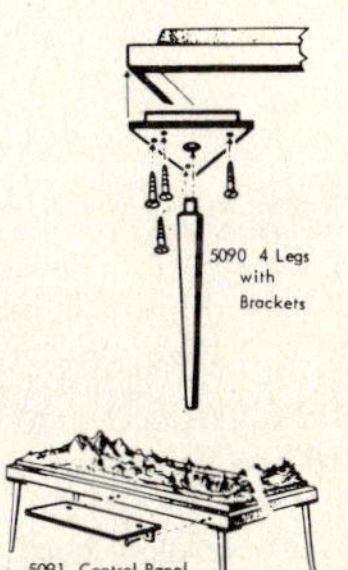

LAYOUT FORMS

NOCH — *Imported from Germany by* **WALTHERS**

Weisengrund Layout
Layouts consist of wooden base with vacuum formed plastic terrain, plus precolored roadways, paths and grass. (less trees, bridges, structures, rolling stock and track).

528-6170	Weisengrund Layout Form	131.99

47 x 78 x 12" 120 x 200 x 30 cm

Terra Forms
Terra-Form layout kit includes all scenery material to detail the Noch layout forms. Set is complete with cardboard and plastic supports for mountains, covering material, static grass, dispenser, adhesive and more. Can be adapted to any layout.

528-9081	Klausenhohe Layout	219.99

69 x 50 cm

Forms:
- Assembly Required
- Recommended for experienced modelers

528-6190	Immenstadt Layout	529.99

Complete kit with all necessary material for construction of a model train set in size 250 x 140cm.

528-6191	Immenstadt Baseboard	239.99
528-6192	Leutkirch Layout	**NEW** 487.99

Complete kit with all necessary material for construction of a model train set in size 220 x 120 cm.

528-6193	Leutkirch Baseboard	208.49
528-9927	Engadin Layout 55 x 87"	963.99

SPECIAL ORDER ITEMS

528-8020	"Spessart"	2113.99
528-8160	"Waldberg"	256.99
528-8161	Universal	781.49
528-8198	Front Extension 78.7 x 7.8"	163.99
528-9913	Right Mountain Extension 47 x 55"	350.49
528-9914	Darbor Extension 47 x 71"	558.99
528-99101	Front Extension 16 x 87"	89.99
528-99121	Left Front Extension 16 x 39"	46.49
528-99131	Right Front Extension 16 x 47"	50.49

POLA

DIORAMA SETS
All parts of these dioramas (especially the facades and the roofs) have been weathered to varying degrees. Also included are road signs, hydrants, etc. Less figures and cars.

578-101	School Road	kit 82.99

19-1/2" x 11" 50 x 29 cm

Includes town house with cinema on ground floor, two-story house of local plumber and primary school building where fire has broken out.

578-102	Wide Road	kit 89.99

20-1/2 x 11-1/2" 52 x 29.5 cm

Includes two-story building with archway leading to workshop of auto mechanic, grocer stand, 3-story townhouse with butcher shop (includes two ceiling lights (16v); and a townhouse with a milkbar on the ground level.

Small ● World, Inc.  NEW

LAYOUT KIT

94-10	Layout Kit	180.00

Add your own track trains and scenery for a self contained layout that can be set up anywhere. Layout measures 80 x 65" (comes in 2 halves, 65 x 40"), weighs 40 lbs with a basic loop length of 50', a minimum radius of 18" and a maximum grade of 3%. Pieces are precut, interlocking - uses no glue. Material can be cut with a utility knife.

APRIL 28, 1869

❦ Today ❦
IN RAILROAD HISTORY

A new record for the most track laid in a single day is set by a Central Pacific construction crew. By 7:00 p.m. the 4,000 man crew has constructed 10 miles, 56 feet of new trackage.

MISCELLANEOUS

FALLER   *Imported from Germany & marketed by* **WALTHERS**

WINTER SCENEMAKING SET

272-735 Winter Scenemaking Set   35.99
Set includes enough material to completely cover an area about 39-1/4 × 39-1/4″ (100 × 100 cm) or three to four houses and some trees. Comes complete with detailed instructions, six trees, spatula and large and small icicles.

A

B

C

D

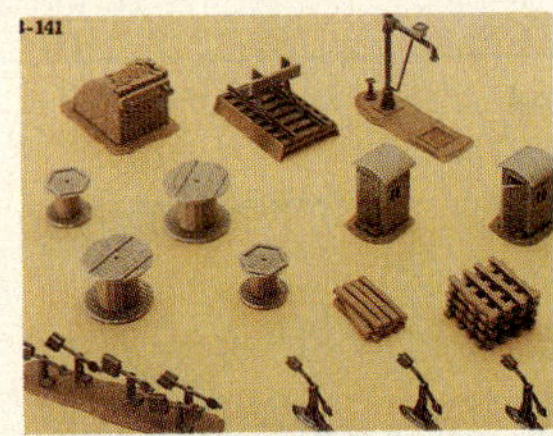

E

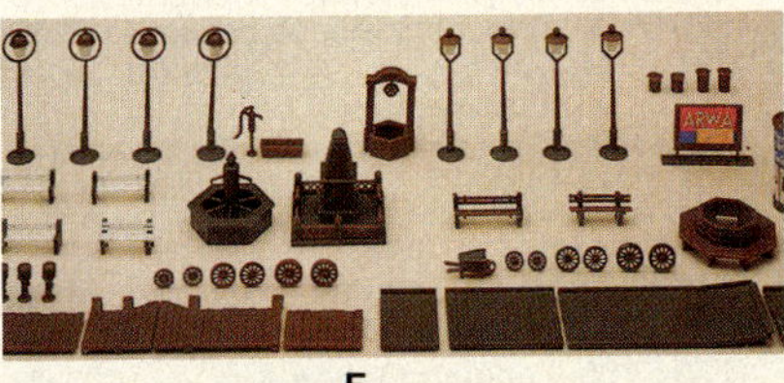

F

G

ACCESSORIES

A   272-573   Picnic Accessories   12.49
      Includes two of the following: tables, benches, stools, fountain and wood pile.

B   272-576   Playground Equipment   11.49

C   272-575   Barbecue Site   16.99
      Includes wooden hut with benches, tables and stools, open and stone fireplaces and pile of firewood. A smoke generator can be fitted into the stone fireplace.

D   272-582   Market Stands & Carts   14.99

E   272-141   Trackside Accessories   16.99

F   272-580   Park Accessories   18.99

G   272-142   Trackside Accessories   17.99
      4 gas containers, telephone hut, switch box, shanty and planks.

H   272-570   Tables & Chairs, assorted   4.99

I   272-574   Benches   pkg(20) 4.99

J   272-597   Roof Set Accessories   6.49
      9-3/4 × 4-7/8   25 × 12.5 cm

H

I

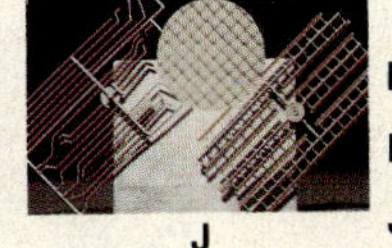

J

MISCELLANEOUS

FALLER — *Imported from Germany & marketed by* **WALTHERS**

Marklin
Hot Air
Balloon
272-1004
29.49
NEW

HOT-AIR BALLOONS

Europe
272-1003   29.49
Easy-to-assemble
kit features special
Europe logo.

Lufthansa Hot-Air
Balloon (yellow)
(Balloon Only)
29.49

VOLLMER — *Imported from Germany & marketed by* **WALTHERS**

A

B   C

D

E

F

G   H   I   J   K

ACCESSORIES

A	770-5021	Structural Shapes	7.49
B	770-5742	Bicycle Stands pkg(3)	13.99
C	770-5136	Turnout Scenic Accessories	8.49
D	770-3761	Town pkg(28)	15.49
		Square Items	

Set of 28 "downtown" details including 2 cobblestone sheets (16 x 24cm), litter bins, water
pumps, parking meters, police and fire alarm
boxes plus other details.

E	770-6524	Water Column	6.49
		60 x 24 x 72mm	
F	770-5705	Loading Gauge &	11.99
		Water Spout	
		Gauge: 2-3/4 x 1/2 x 2-1/2"	
		Column: 2-1/2 x 1 x 3"	
G	770-5241	Brick Piles & Pipe	5.49
H	770-5242	Wooden Cases pkg(10)	5.49
		11.5 x 7 x 7mm	
I	770-5243	Bales tied w/rope pkg(10)	5.49
		11.5 x 7 x 7mm	
J	770-5142	Round Tables	7.49
		& Chairs	
K	770-5143	Rectangular Tables	7.49
		& Chairs	

MISCELLANEOUS

Imported from Germany & marketed by WALTHERS

SCENIC MODELING BOOK

272-840 Scenic Modeling Made Easy   11.99

English text, introductory to scenic modeling. Covers initial considerations, tools and materials, first steps, mountain building, rock design, water, assembling structures, backgrounds, laying track, ballasting, bridges and viaducts, winter landscaping, dioramas and electrical tips. Over 120 color illustrations, softcover, 35 pages, 8-1/4 × 11-1/2.

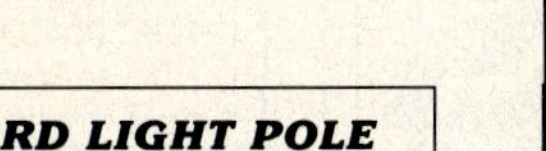
DIAMOND SCALE CONST.

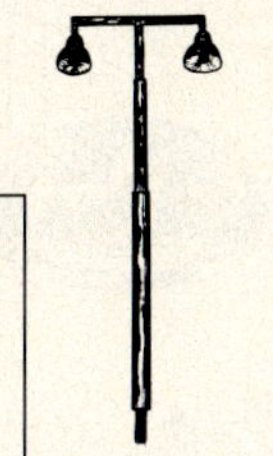

YARD LIGHT POLE

239-404   pkg(4) 2.35

Yard lights were needed for workmen servicing equipment at night. Cast white metal, 1-5/8″ tall.

Alexander scale models

TOMBSTONES

120-1603 Tombstones,   pkg(12) 1.25
         Assorted, Metal Castings
120-9808 Pick & Shovel   2pair .59

BRAWA

Imported from Germany & marketed by WALTHERS

A

B

C

D

E

F

G

H

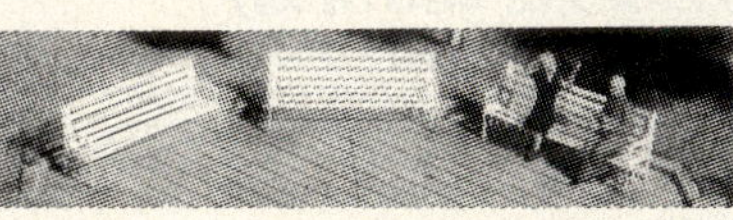
I

J

K

L

M

N

ACCESSORIES

A	186-705	Railway Repair Shop Accessories	96.99
B	186-706	Railway Repair Shop Details pkg(80)	154.99
C	186-5910	Bus Stop Set pkg(13)	70.99
D	186-5911	Park Set pkg(10)	50.49
E	186-5442	Phone Booth	12.49
F	186-671	Scrap Metal Bins & Yard Junk	31.99

Three storage bins for storing scrap metal, etc. Kit consists of cast metal and precut wood parts. Measures approx 1-3/4 × 5-1/4″.

G	186-2654	Railroad Telephone Shanty	5.99

Approx 1 x 3/4″.

H	186-2650	Signal Telephone Box	3.99

Approx size 1/4 × 1/4″; height 3/4″.

I	186-3609	6 Park Benches, Large	20.49
		2-1/2 x 3-3/4″	
	186-3629	6 Park Benches, Small	12.49
J	186-2652	Distance Posts pkg(10)	5.49

Prototypes are spaced 100 meters apart. Approx size 1 × 2 × 5″.

K	186-2653	Switch Heater	11.49

Prototypes prevent switch points from freezing. 2 tanks, width approx 3-3/4″.

L	186-3630	Boulevard-Style Garden Furniture-Small 1-1/4 × 2″	12.49
	186-3610	Boulevanrd-Style Garden Furniture-Large	20.49

To build eight chairs, two benches and two tables. 2-1/2 x 3-3/4″.

M	186-675	Fuel Pump	19.99
N	186-5762	Train or Bus Passenger Shelter	22.99

Illuminated; complete model (less figures and poster column). Approx 1 x 3 x 1-1/2″

ETCHED BRASS DETAILS

Scenic details are etched from 0.20 and 0.30 brass sheets.

186-3600	Tavern Signs, Large	3-3/4 × 6″	20.49
186-3620	Tavern Signs, Small	2-1/2 × 4″	12.49
186-3604	Antennas and Clocks, Large	4 × 5-1/2″	20.49
186-3612	Fine Mesh Screen-Brass	6 × 4″, black finish	23.99
186-3613	Fine Mesh Screen	nickel silver	26.99

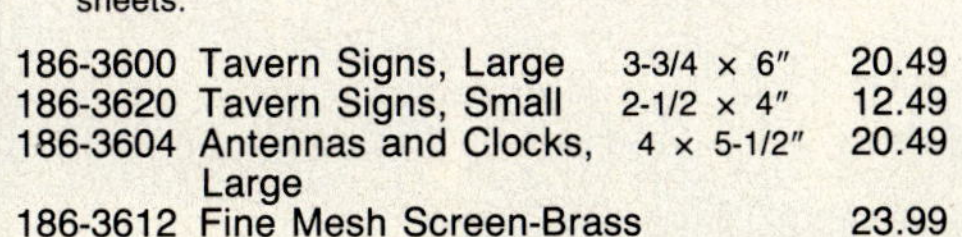

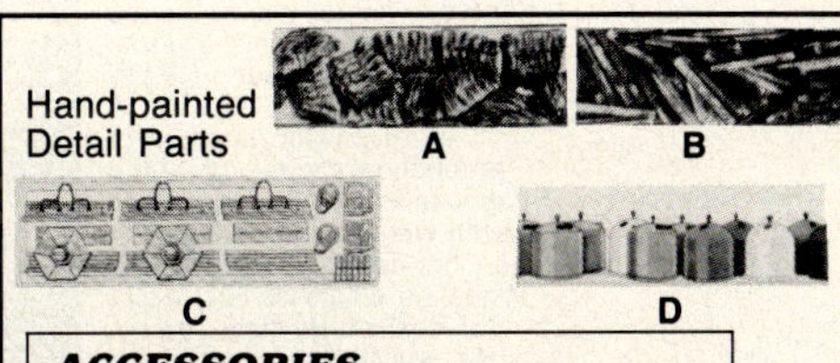

Hand-painted Detail Parts

A

B

C

D

ACCESSORIES

A	447-932	Grain Stacks pkg(12)	7.49
B	447-933	Railroad Ties pkg(150)	7.49
C	447-2491	Benches, assorted	7.49
D	447-2521	*NEW* pkg(12)	7.49
		Recyclable Containers	

MISCELLANEOUS

WOODLAND SCENICS

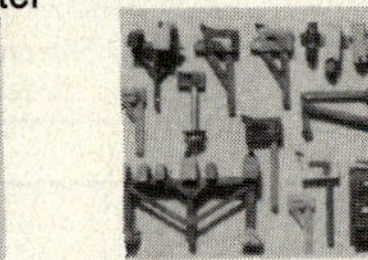

ACCESSORIES

785-127 Glass Display Dome w/Base each 5.98
Dealers: MUST order Dealer Pack of 4.

(not illustrated)
785-1207 The Scenery Manual **NEW** 4.98
Build a complete scene by combining this item with products from Woodland Scenics Terrain System.

785-191 Scenic Cement 4.49
785-192 Scenic Sprayer 2.98
785-193 Scenic Sifter 2.98

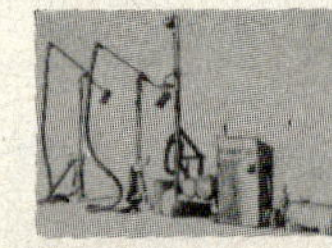

Tombstones
785-201 pkg(20) 3.98

Assorted Mailboxes
785-206 pkg(17) 3.98

3 Asst Fuel Stands
785-212 5.98

Rural Sawmill
785-243 6.98

Vending Machines
785-230 pkg(8) 5.98

Diesel Fuel Facility
785-232 5.98

Aeromotor Windmill
785-209 5.98

Steam Engine
& Hammermill
785-229 5.98

Trackside Junk
785-202 3.98

Assorted Junk
785-205 pkg(10) 3.98

Industrial Junk
785-225 3.98

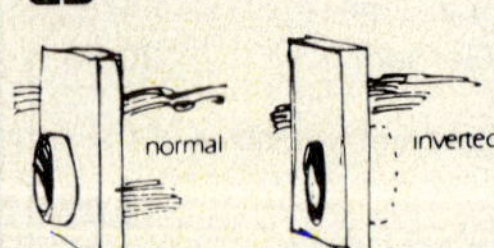

Crates, Barrels & Sacks
785-203 3.98

Assorted Skids
785-204 pkg(15) 3.98

CS DESIGN, INC. **NEW**

155-7001 Scale Crete™ 11.95
Ready to use latex material for modeling various paving materials. Covers approx 6 sq ft x 1/16" thickness.

155-7004 Asphalt Paint 4.00
Cover Scale Crete™ and make it look like asphalt. Water soluble.

kibri

Imported from Germany by **WALTHERS**

A

B

ACCESSORIES

A Platform Trolley Assortment
405-9561 Pre-Assembled 32.49
B Backyard Assortment
405-8100 16.49
(not illustrated)
Platform Trolley Assortment Kit
405-9560 20.49

N.J. International

ACCESSORIES

525-6172	Crates & Barrels	pkg(16)	2.99
525-6177	Steel Drums	pkg(6)	2.99
525-6173	Bicycles	pkg(6)	2.99
525-6174	Baggage	pkg(14)	2.99
525-6175	Sacks of Freight	pkg(12)	2.99
525-6176	BMW Motorcycle	pkg(3)	2.99
525-6178	Modern Station Baggage	each	2.99

CRESCENT STATION

TELEPHONE BOOTH KIT

Kit includes three solid acrylic rectangular blocks. Phone booth details are printed on pressure sensitive adhesive film which is "wrapped" around the acrylic block (no adhesive or solvents are necessary). Exterior details such as roof & roof sign are made of cardstock and should be glued on.

513-566 Phone Booth pkg(3) 3.95

Pikestuff

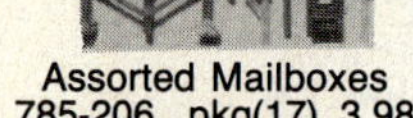

CONCRETE CULVERTS

541-2 Concrete Culverts pr 1.00
Molded grey plastic culverts to be used as a bridge type culvert, or at the base of a hill (emptying into a creek, river or drainage ditch).

R. & R. F., Inc.

UNIVERSAL YARDSHEET

6" x 6" sheets, use in rail yards, for switches, loading areas and sidings. Can be used as substitute to glue as a base for scenery.

624-602 Black pkg(6) 6.95

An early winter snowfall adds extra charm to the photo session for this year's CE&W annual report cover. The MP15 is a Con-Cor (now out of production) model, while the caboose is an Athearn model. Both were custom painted in the Charleston, Eagle Ridge & Wheeling colors by Bob Adler of Kenilworth, New Jersey. His son Bob Jr. painted the snowy mountain scene used as a backdrop.
Models and Photo by Bob Adler

MISCELLANEOUS

Master Creations

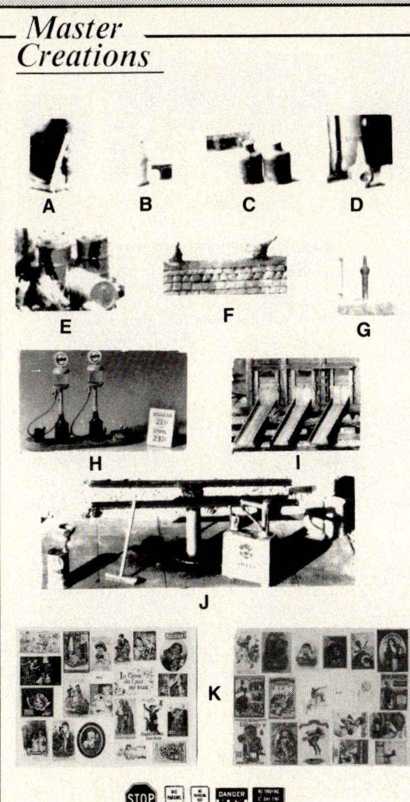

ACCESSORIES
HO Scale (1/87). Parts are unpainted metal castings, unless noted.

A	464-790	Pick Axe	pkg(2) 1.00
B	464-730	Five Gallon Can	pkg(6) 1.00
C	464-720	Jug	pkg(6) 1.00
D	464-714	Hand Lantern	pkg(2) 1.00
E	464-760	55 Gallon Drum	pkg(4) 1.25
F	464-750	Pigeon	pkg(6) 1.25
G	464-740	Lightning Rod	pkg(6) 1.00
H	464-772	Gas Pump Island Set	7.95

Includes urethane island, two pumps, oil bottles, water can and decals.

I	464-792	Mine Chute Assembly	2.25
J	464-774	Gas Station Detail Set	19.95

Contains a complete set of three color decals, two oil bunkers with crank arms, filler pipe stand and vapor vents for two large underground storage tanks, air compressor, innertube test tank, concrete lub pad, pump island, vehicle lift, two pumps and other detail.

K COLOR POSTERS   each 1.95

464-906 Set #1	464-910 Set #3
464-908 Set #2	464-912 Set #4

L   464-914   OSHA/Street Signs color, 2 sets   1.00

(not illustrated)

Franz Falk Brewery Billboard

464-916	22'6" x 14'6"	1.00
464-918	42'6" x 27'	2.95
464-752	Chickens	pkg(4) 1.00
464-754	Skunk	1.00
464-756	Pierce Arrow Engine	1.50
464-758	Automobile Transmission	1.50
464-799	Leaning Sack	1.00
464-924	Victorian Wallpaper **NEW**	1.95
464-7030	Coca Cola **NEW** Button Sign	pkg(2) 1.00

model power

ACCESSORIES
490-1452	Telephone Poles set(12)	4.98

Molded brown plastic, single pole set includes 12 poles, 2 with transformers and phone boxes.

490-1454	Road & **NEW** Rail Signs	pkg(24) 4.98
490-1339	Park **NEW** Scenes	pkg(20) 7.98
490-5710	Park Scenes	pkg(6) 7.98
490-5712	Winter Scenes	pkg(6) 3.98

CHRISTMAS TREE

4", Lighted w/Flashing GOW Bulbs

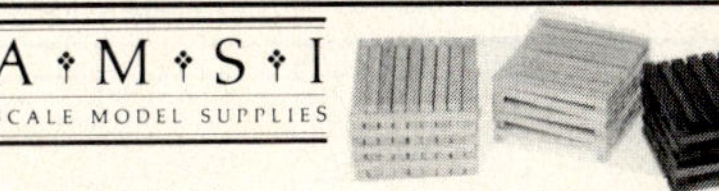

490-600
7.98

WHITEGROUND MODEL WORKS

ICE BLOCKS
771-5006	Ice Blocks	pkg(12) 2.00

A · M · S · I
SCALE MODEL SUPPLIES

SNOW
137-900	Snow	1/2 lb 3.99

Non-metallic powder you can sift on your layout.

PARK BENCHES   NEW
137-90500	Kit	10.49
137-90501	Ornate	15.49
137-90502	Kit 1/2"	9.99
137-90503	Kit Ornate 1/2"	11.99
137-90504	Kit 1/4"	9.99

WESTON MINI-FIGURE CO.
a division of *Campbell Scale Models*

ACCESSORIES
A	780-1605	Concrete Bridge	5.25
		w/road markers & mail boxes	
B	780-1600	Rowboat w/oars & oarlocks 2"L x 3/4"W	3.00
C	780-1604	Windmill	4.00
D	780-1606	Stone Bridge	5.25
		w/road markers & mail boxes	

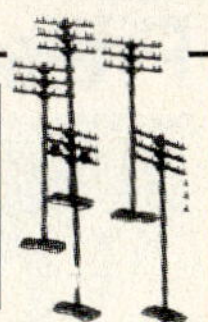
BACHMANN QUALITY SINCE 1933

ACCESSORIES
Telephone Poles
160-42102
pkg(12)   4.00

LIGHTING   Operating
160-42411	Lamp Post	pkg(2)	7.95
160-42412	Modern Street Lights	pkg(2)	7.95
160-42414	Billboard	pkg(2)	7.95
160-42431	Service Station	pkg(2)	9.95
160-42433	Traffic Lights	pkg(2)	9.95
160-42420	Signal Assort	pkg(36)	358.20
	(By Special Order Only.)		
160-42410	Assortment	pkg(36)	286.20
	(By Special Order Only.)		

Vintage Reproductions

SNOW
Ultra realistic sparkling snows blended from various plastics. Micro-sparkle are microscopic irridescent flakes for added sparkle effects.

766-711	3 Bellows Set		6.50
	w/cold/dry, wet/fluffy & slushy snows (w/Micro-Sparkle)		
766-771	Fluffy Wet Snow	(300cc)	6.50
	(w/Micro-Sparkle)		
766-772	Cold Dry Snow	(300cc)	6.50
	(w/Micro-Sparkle)		
766-773	Slushy Snow	(300cc)	6.50
	(w/Micro-Sparkle)		
766-812	Fluffy Wet Snow	(300cc)	6.50
766-813	Cold Dry Snow	(300cc)	6.50
766-814	Slushy Blend	(300cc)	6.50
766-815	1 Bellows	(300cc)	3.50
	Shimmering Ice Flakes Kit		
766-816	Shimmering Ice Flakes		6.50
766-817	Snub Nose "Puff-n-Pak"		2.00
	Dispenser Only		

GLOWING MATERIAL
766-326	Glo-Light	sheet each	4.00

Glow-in-the-dark 3 × 6" vinyl sheet is a yellow-green light with adhesive backing. Good for background lighting or for any dry transfer signs or control panels.

DUST
766-712	Puff-n-Glo Dust	5.50

Glow-in-the dark powder pigment with "puff-n-pak" bellows syringe can be dusted on or mixed with clear paint.

Tru-Scale

STACKED TIES
HO Scale stacked wood ties to be used as scenic detail.

730-2005	Treated	pkg(2) 9.00
730-2006	Untreated	pkg(2) 8.40

Campbell Scale Models

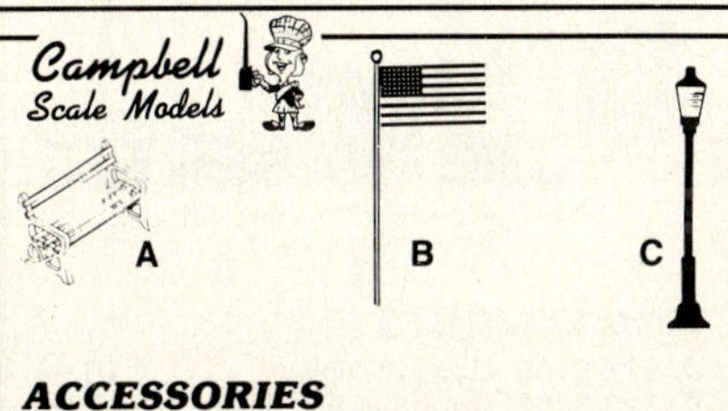

ACCESSORIES
A	200-930	Park Bench Sides	pkg(4) 2.00
		(includes plastic slats)	
B	200-931	Flagpole & Flag	Set 2.00
		(plastic & paper)	
C	200-928	Street Lamps	pkg(3) 2.00

MISCELLANEOUS

Preiser
Imported from Germany by WALTHERS

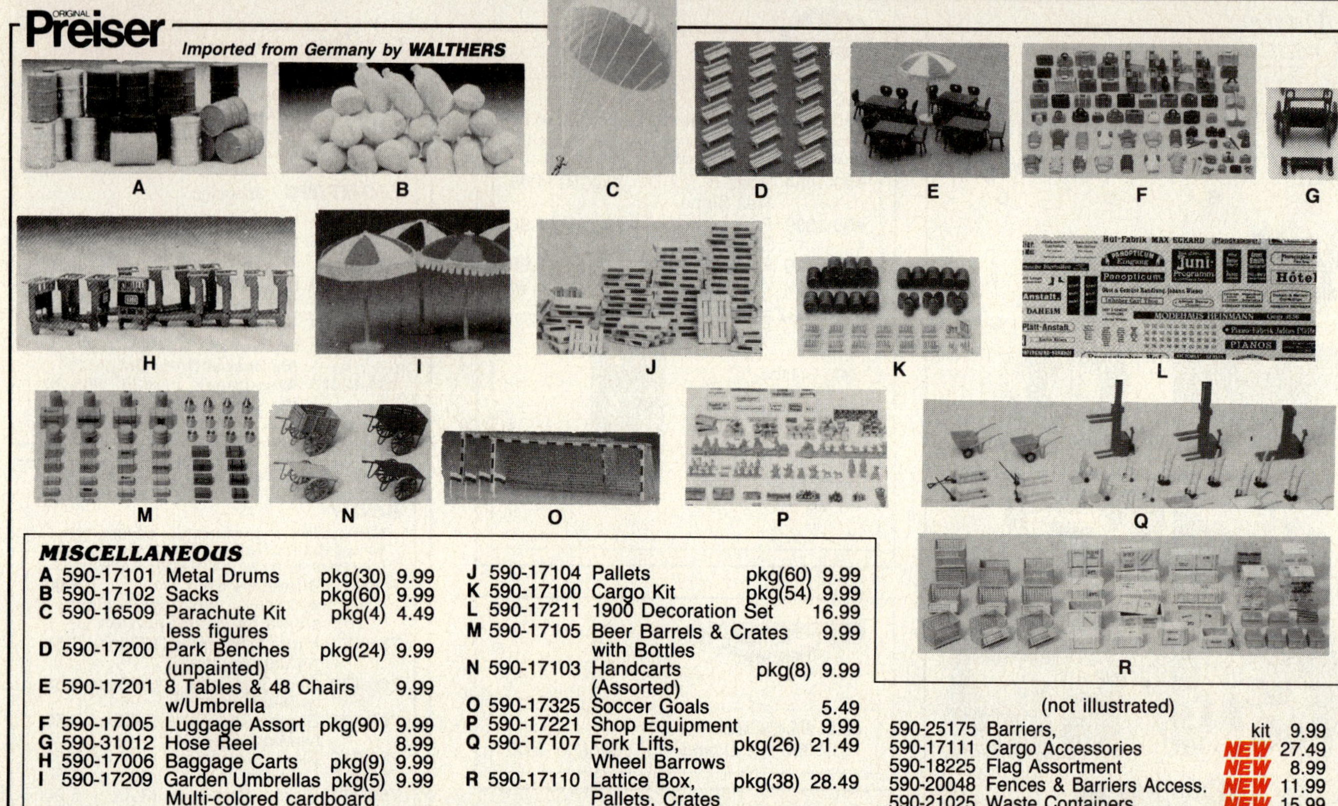

MISCELLANEOUS

A	590-17101	Metal Drums	pkg(30)	9.99
B	590-17102	Sacks	pkg(60)	9.99
C	590-16509	Parachute Kit less figures	pkg(4)	4.49
D	590-17200	Park Benches (unpainted)	pkg(24)	9.99
E	590-17201	8 Tables & 48 Chairs w/Umbrella		9.99
F	590-17005	Luggage Assort	pkg(90)	9.99
G	590-31012	Hose Reel		8.99
H	590-17006	Baggage Carts	pkg(9)	9.99
I	590-17209	Garden Umbrellas Multi-colored cardboard	pkg(5)	9.99
J	590-17104	Pallets	pkg(60)	9.99
K	590-17100	Cargo Kit	pkg(54)	9.99
L	590-17211	1900 Decoration Set		16.99
M	590-17105	Beer Barrels & Crates with Bottles		9.99
N	590-17103	Handcarts (Assorted)	pkg(8)	9.99
O	590-17325	Soccer Goals		5.49
P	590-17221	Shop Equipment		9.99
Q	590-17107	Fork Lifts, Wheel Barrows	pkg(26)	21.49
R	590-17110	Lattice Box, Pallets, Crates	pkg(38)	28.49

(not illustrated)

590-25175	Barriers,	kit	9.99
590-17111	Cargo Accessories	**NEW**	27.49
590-18225	Flag Assortment	**NEW**	8.99
590-20048	Fences & Barriers Access.	**NEW**	11.99
590-21025	Waste Containers	**NEW**	15.99

NOCH
Imported from West Germany by WALTHERS

ROOFING MATERIAL

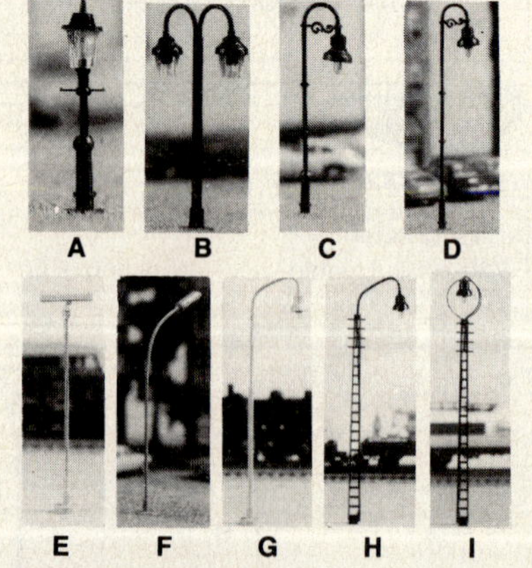

A	528-5850	Tile	7.49

LTD QTY AVAILABLE

B	528-5851	Corrugated	7.49

STREETLIGHTS

A	528-5105	Gas, 2" high	10.99
B	528-5107	Double 2-3/4" high	18.99
C	528-5109	Curved 2-1/2" high	12.49
D	528-5110	Curved 3-1/3" high	11.99
E	528-5112	Platform 3-1/3" high	9.99
F	528-5114	Whip Light 4-1/3" high	10.49
G	528-5116	Curved, 5" high **Limited Qty**	10.99
H	528-5118	Lattice Mast 5-1/3" high	16.99
I	528-5120	Circle 5-1/3" high	16.99

TRAFFIC **NEW**

A	528-60521	Assorted Signs	11.99
B	528-60511	Traffic Accessories	7.99

ACCESSORIES

528-5830	Platform w/Ramps	each	26.99
528-6097	Landscape Fleece (39 x 29")		18.49
528-6120	Glue Set for roads (colored)		9.49
528-6123	Glue Set for Walls (colored)		21.49
528-875	Powdered Snow pkg(150g)		7.49
528-1100	Freight Load Assort		5.99
528-1102	Assorted Luggage		8.49
528-6114	Glue Neutral		9.49
528-6116	Glue Spray		32.99
528-612	Playground		21.49
528-615	Municipal Park		19.99
528-617	Picnic Site		24.99

IHC International Hobby Corp.

KWIK KITS **NEW**

348-4550	Crossbucks	pkg(2)	2.98
348-4551	RR Assortment	pkg(5)	3.49
348-4552	Rural Assortment	pkg(9)	3.98
348-4553	City Assortment	pkg(17)	3.98

MISCELLANEOUS

348-4408 Rooftop & Street Access. 2.98
Contains a fire hydrant, skylight, clothes line w/hanging wash, pedestal base, step railings, chaise lounge, park bench & more.

348-4410	Flags	pkg(66)	6.98

Contains US & States

348-422309	Park Assortment	3.98

Chooch Enterprises Inc.

JUNK PILES
Junk piles are pre-painted cast polyurethane.

214-7128	Automotive	9.99
214-7129	Railroad	9.99

RR TIES
Prepainted cast polyurethane

214-7191
pkg(6) 5.99

MISCELLANEOUS

Plastruct

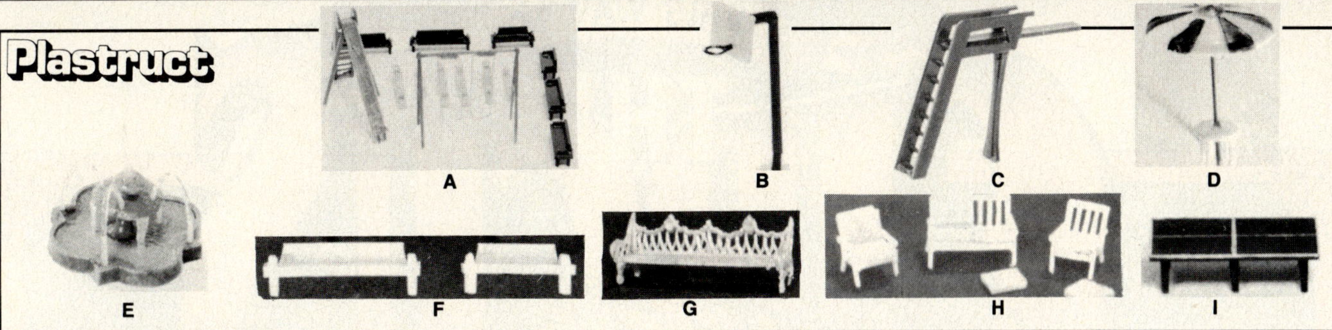

A   B   C   D

E   F   G   H   I

OUTDOOR FURNITURE

A	570-43510	Playground Set	each 7.95	E	570-42603	1″ Fountain-Square	each 4.95
B	570-43810	Basketball Set	pkg(2) 2.25	F	570-41210	Park Bench Set	pkg(5) 2.25
C	570-43310	Diving Board	each 2.25	G	570-41110	1800's Park Bench	pkg(2) 4.50
D	570-42210	Umbrella Tables	pkg(3) 3.50	H	570-41310	Patio Lounge Chair Set	pkg(3) 4.50
E	570-42503	1″ Fountain-Hexagon	each 4.95	I	570-43110	Ping Pong Table	each 2.25

ATLAS MODEL RAILROAD CO., INC.

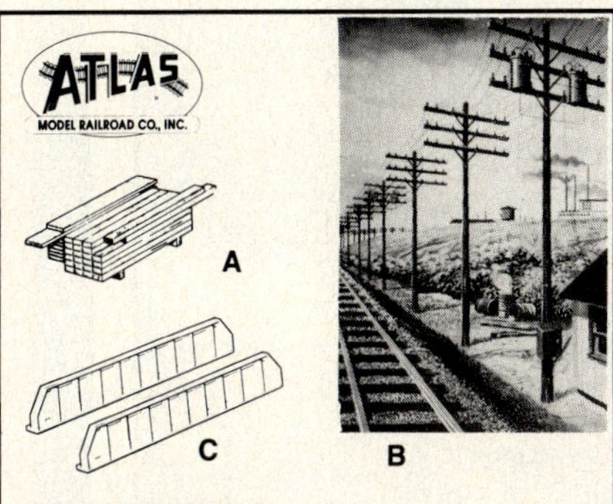

A

C   B

ACCESSORIES
Parts are molded of styrene in appropriate colors.

A	150-791	Mill Lumber Pack	2.75
B	150-775	Telephone Pack pkg(12)	2.75
C	150-790	Flat Car Girder Load pkg(4)	2.25

Builders In Scale
Fine Craft Models

SNOW
Create a permanent snow scene with marbel dust. Sprinkle over plaster that has been brushed with water and matte medium.
169-252 Snow   8 oz 3.29

Rix Products

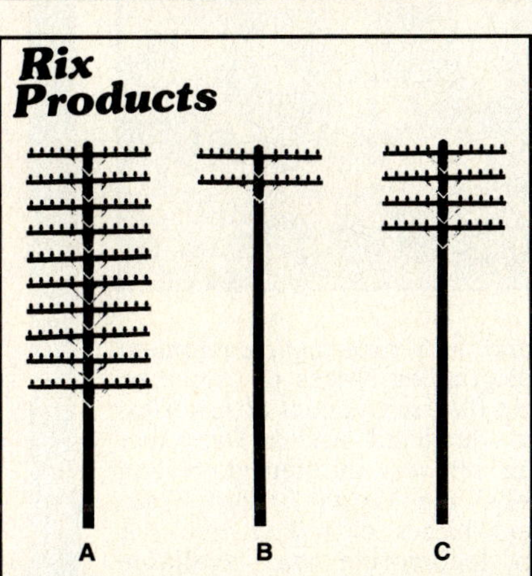

A   B   C

Poles are two piece construction. Any number of Crossarms can be added to the poles. Notches are provided in the poles for easy assembly of the crossarms. Molded in realistic colors.

RAILROAD TELEPHONE POLES

	628-30	Only 30′ & 40′	pkg(36)	3.99
A	628-31	Crossarms	pkg(72)	3.99
B	628-32	2 Arm	pkg(18)	3.99
C	628-34	4 Arm	pkg(12)	3.99
	628-40	Only 40′	pkg(36)	3.99

N.J. International

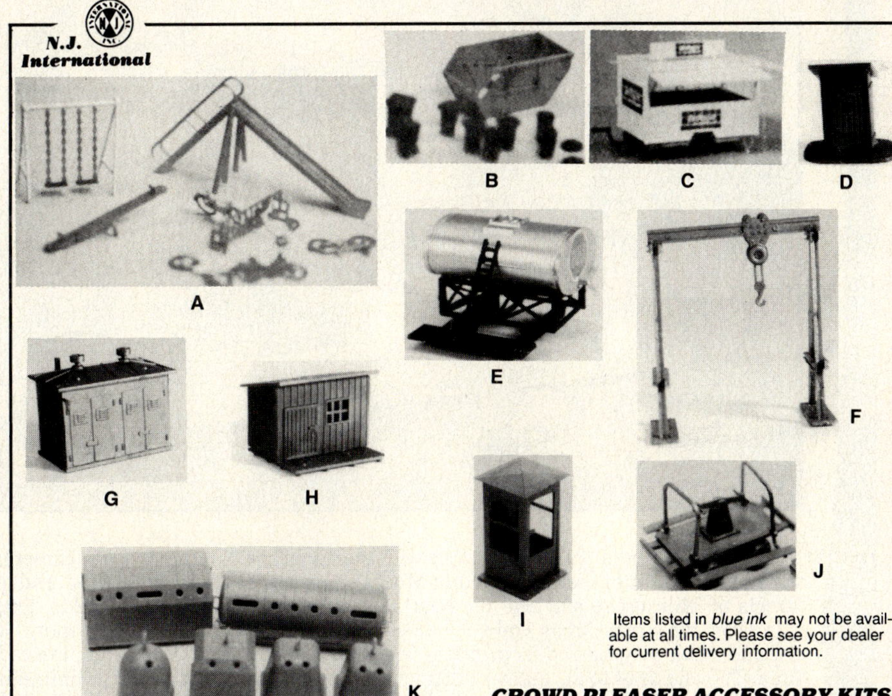

A

B   C   D

E

F

G   H

I   J

K

Items listed in *blue ink* may not be available at all times. Please see your dealer for current delivery information.

CROWD PLEASER ACCESSORY KITS

A	525-6196	Play Yard Set		2.99
B	525-6197	Garbage Dumpster & Cans		2.99
C	525-6199	Concession Trailer		4.99
D	525-6183	Outhouse	pkg(2)	2.99
E	525-6184	Oil Tank w/Stand		3.99
F	525-6185	Gantry Crane		2.99
G	525-6186	Signal Cabinet	pkg(2)	3.99
H	525-6187	Tool Shed		3.99
I	525-6189	Telephone Booth	pkg(2)	2.99
J	525-6190	Hand Car	pkg(2)	3.99
K	525-6195	Environmental Containers	pkg(5)	3.99
		(not illustrated)		
	525-6180	Umbrella/Table/Stool Asst		2.99
	525-1185	Ladder	pkg(3)	2.99

HELJAN

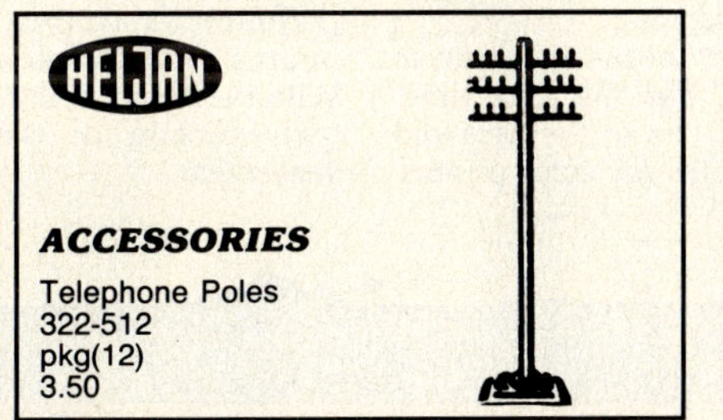

ACCESSORIES

Telephone Poles
322-512
pkg(12)
3.50

THIS WAY TO THE CIRCUS

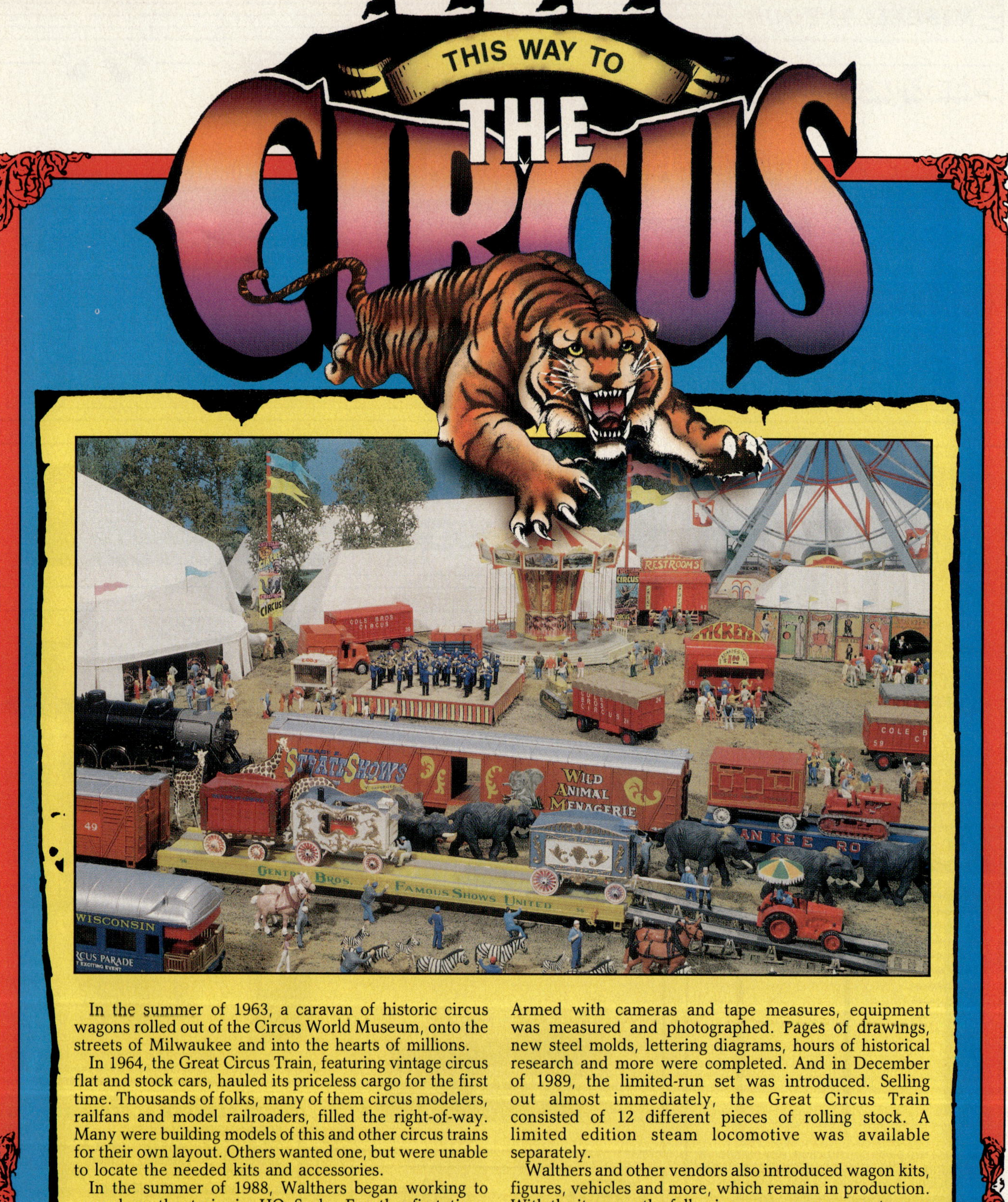

In the summer of 1963, a caravan of historic circus wagons rolled out of the Circus World Museum, onto the streets of Milwaukee and into the hearts of millions.

In 1964, the Great Circus Train, featuring vintage circus flat and stock cars, hauled its priceless cargo for the first time. Thousands of folks, many of them circus modelers, railfans and model railroaders, filled the right-of-way. Many were building models of this and other circus trains for their own layout. Others wanted one, but were unable to locate the needed kits and accessories.

In the summer of 1988, Walthers began working to reproduce the train in HO Scale. For the first time, modelers would have easy-to-build kits of the cars and equipment. Phone calls turned up 60's era color photos.

Armed with cameras and tape measures, equipment was measured and photographed. Pages of drawings, new steel molds, lettering diagrams, hours of historical research and more were completed. And in December of 1989, the limited-run set was introduced. Selling out almost immediately, the Great Circus Train consisted of 12 different pieces of rolling stock. A limited edition steam locomotive was available separately.

Walthers and other vendors also introduced wagon kits, figures, vehicles and more, which remain in production. With the items on the following pages, you can create your own version of the magnificent railroad shows of yesteryear.

CAPTURE THE COLOR AND EXCITEMENT OF A CARNIVAL ON THE MOVE

The night sky explodes with color. Music and laughter reverberate along the midway. Kids of every age test their strength and skill at various games. Smells of hot dogs and popcorn drift on the summer breeze. Lines of riders wait their turn to try the thrilling assortment of rides. At midnight, it's all over. Trucks and tractors roar to life, spotting wagons for loading. Wrenches clang onto steel bolts as an army of workers begin the tear-down. Within minutes, the first wagons disappear down the dark streets, headed for the railroad yard and the waiting train.

Some of America's biggest and best-loved carnivals still moved to their next show by train, long after circuses had switched to trucks. Now, you can add the color and excitement of a carnival on the move to your HO Scale layout, with Carnival Trains from Walthers.

For years, Royal American thrilled generations of carnival and fairgoers with its magnificent "Mile-Long Midway." Based in Tampa, Florida, the show rolled across the United States aboard a train of seventy-two cars (for Canadian tours, ten more were added).

This limited run set includes seven cars finished in silver with the "Royal American Shows" name emblazoned in red on the sides. The set includes six Warren flat cars, as used by the show, plus a stock car (used as a storage and equipment car). The kits are designed for easy construction.

Limited Run
Royal American Shows/
Carnival Train
932-900   64.98

Each summer, hundreds of thousands of visitors are thrilled by "America's Brightest Midway" on the James E Strates Show. Based in Orlando, Florida, this carnival is the last that moves by rail, a tradition dating back to 1935 when the first five flat cars were purchased. Today, the job requires a train of 58 cars (48 flats and 10 sleepers), which cover more than 7,000 miles through the eastern United States each season!

Now, you can add the color and excitement of this great amusement enterprise to your Ho Scale layout with the James E Strates Carnival Train from Walthers. This set commemorates the years when the show traveled aboard former circus rail cars and includes seven easy-to-build kits.

The highlight of the set is the equipment car (a converted elephant car, now owned by the Circus World Museum), which is a miniature masterpiece, decorated with 10 different colors and a striking portrait of a hippo. Rounding out the set are three Mount Vernon and three Warren Flat Cars, all finished in bright orange with red and blue lettering, plus data in white.

LIMITED RUN
932-901   James E Strates Carnival Train   69.98
Includes prepainted equipment car, 3 Mount Vernon & 3 Warren Flats.

WALTHERS

DOUBLE-LENGTH FLATCARS

These double-length flat, stock and elephant cars are undecorated, ready for you to paint and letter. Each is a miniature masterpiece in HO Scale, recreating equipment once used in every circus and carnival.

Each is an easy-to-build kit with trucks and horn-hook couplers, so you can create an entire circus train in a few evenings. The one-piece plastic bodies are packed with detail, but we also include "extras" like a full-underbody, separate brake gear and "wooden" flooring for the flat cars.

And to add the finishing touch, each kit includes our Circus Alphabet and Number decal set, printed in red. (Flat car kits include two sheets of decals). This set includes a complete alphabet and numbers, plus key words such as "Circus, Shows, Combined, Bros, Wild Animal", and much, much, more!

932-4400 72' Warren Flat Car pkg(2) 19.98

932-4450 72' Mt Vernon Flat Car pkg(2) 19.98

932-4500 72' Elephant Car 14.98

932-4550 72' Stock Car 14.98

Roco

Imported from Austria by WALTHERS

625-44009 Krone Circus Box Car Set (for animals) 142.99
Includes three ventilated box cars and one Elephant Car.

625-44008 Krone Circus Flat Car Set 172.99
Includes four cars and eight Preiser wagons.

625-44017 Circus Set #4 w/Vehicle NEW 239.49
Includes four stake flat cars w/Krone vehicles and wagons.

1625-44016 DB Krone Circus Set 202.99
Includes 4 stake flat cars with Krone vehicles and wagons.

International Hobby Corp.

348-2704 85' Pullman (yellow, red, silver) 14.98

Royal American Shows passenger cars. Ready-to-run with trucks and horn-hook couplers.

(not illustrated)
348-2705 85' Diner 14.98
348-9117 Passenger Set 44.94

348-2706 85' Observation 14.98

WALTHERS

WAGONS

Walthers wagons are typical of equipment on circuses large and small. Kits feature a one-piece resin body (unless noted), with details cast in place and a plastic underframe with separate wheels. Decals for several shows and complete instructions are included.

Circus Trunk Wagon
933-1360 8.98

Circus Power Plant Wagon
933-1361 8.98

Circus Canvas Wagon
933-1362 8.98

Circus Ticket Wagon
933-1363 9.98

Circus Office Wagon
933-1371 9.98

Circus Commissary Wagon
933-1370 9.98 ▼

933-1369 Circus Pole Wagon 12.98

NEW

TIM McCOY WAGONS

(not illustrated)
933-1392 14' Plank 9.98
933-1393 21' Chair 9.98
933-1394 14' Light 9.98

933-1365 Circus Plank/Jack Wagon 12.98

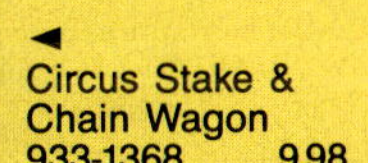
Circus Chair Wagon
933-1364 9.98

Circus Stake & Chain Wagon
933-1368 9.98

933-1366 Circus Wardrobe Wagon 10.98
Injection-molded body

WALTHERS

WAGONS (continued)

Circus Hippo ▶
Cage Wagon
933-1367
9.98
Injection-molded body

933-1377   20' Seat Wagon   9.98

933-1382   Generator/Baggage Wagon   8.98

933-1385   Ringling Stake Driver   9.98

◀
Charging
Tiger Tableau
933-1381   9.98

▶
19' Equipment
Wagon
933-1389
8.98

933-1378   19' Storage Van   8.98

933-1384   Lion's Bride Tableau   10.98   Mother Goose Tableau   Cole Brothers Una-Fon
                                              933-1386   10.98 933-1387   9.98

TRAILERS

933-1376   Concession Trailers #2   9.98

933-1373   Concession Trailer #1   9.98

RAMPS

Load or unload your circus train with this all-plastic kit which includes
two ramps and graduated stringers.

933-1375 Run Kit (Ramps)   4.98

prototype photo

WAGONS

Krone Equipment Wagon NEW
590-21009   10.99

Animal Wagon-Open
590-21019   Krone 15.99

**Krone Baggage
Wagon w/Windows**
590-21017   15.49

Animal Wagon-Closed
590-21018   15.99

Baggage Wagon
590-21016   Krone 15.49

MAN Tractor
590-21001   Krone 20.49

Krone Office Wagon
590-21007   10.99

Krone Changing Wagon NEW
590-21008   10.99

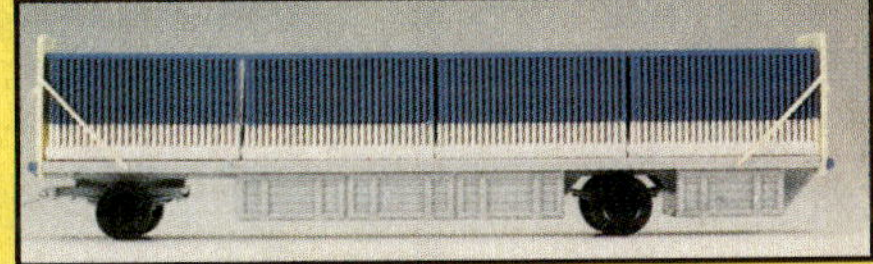
590-21022   Krone Equipment Caravan   18.49

Caravan Wagon
590-21015   Krone 15.99

Krone Open Wagon NEW
590-21010   12.49

590-24681   Baggage & Caravan Wagons   27.49

590-24680   MB 710 w/Baggage Wagon   31.99

590-20005   Caravan   pkg(3) 28.49

590-20006   Equipment Caravan   pkg(4) 28.49

590-20007   Animal Wagon   pkg(3) 28.49

Equipment Caravan
590-21023   Krone 15.99

Equipment Wagon
590-21020   Krone 15.99

Krone
Equipment
Caravan
590-21021
15.99

3 Arch Cage
590-22103
19.99
3 Arch Cage
w/Figure
590-22153
24.99

2 Arch Cage
590-22102
19.99
2 Arch Cage
w/Figure
590-22152
24.99

Gollmar
w/Driver & Horse
590-22151
29.99
Gollmar Wagon
590-22101
21.99

ORIGINAL Preiser

Imported from Germany by WALTHERS

WAGONS (continued)

590-22100	Barnes	13.99
590-22150	w/Driver & Horses	19.99

(not illustrated)

590-20008	Equipment Caravan	**NEW**	28.49
	(unlettered)		
590-21024	Caravan w/Mast	**NEW**	23.49
590-21026	Equipment Caravan	**NEW**	15.99

These items By Special Order Only

590-22105	Baggage Wagon less Horses	15.49
590-22106	Mirror Bandwagon less Horses	25.99
590-22107	2 Arch Cage Wagon less Horses	20.99
590-22108	3 Arch Cage Wagon less Horses	20.99
590-22155	Baggage Wagon w/2 Horses	23.49
590-22156	Mirror Bandwagon w/2 Horses	32.49
590-22157	2 Arch Cage Wagon w/2 Horses	28.49
590-22158	3 Arch Cage Wagon w/2 Horses	28.49

TRAILERS

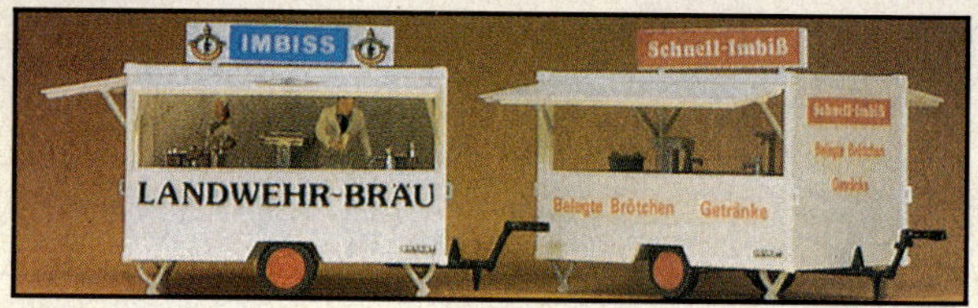

590-24676	Sales Trailer	pkg(2) 12.49

CAGE FENCES ►

For detailing animal tents and other uses. Molded in white and gray styrene.

590-20047	8.99

TRAIN CARS ►

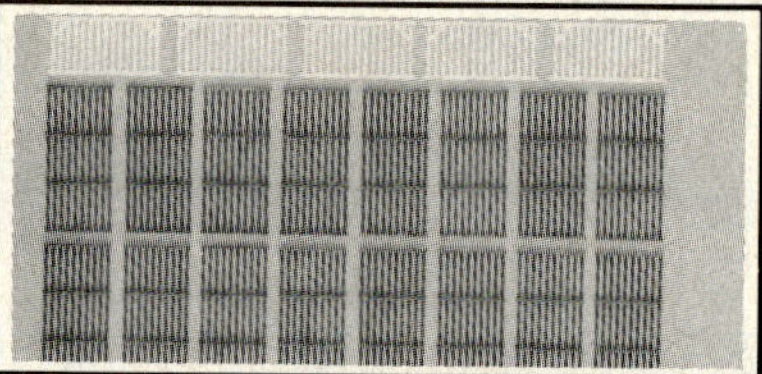

Elephant Car Krone

590-21151	81.49

RAINTREE PRODUCTS INTERNATIONAL, INC.

HO SCALE 1/87

CIRCUS WAGONS

Add the finishing detail to your showgrounds with these detailed plastic wagon kits. Kits are undecorated.

◄ Small Animal/Dog Wagon
705-4202   12.98

Parade Billboard Wagon
Semi-Craftsmen Plastic Kit
705-4203   12.98 ►

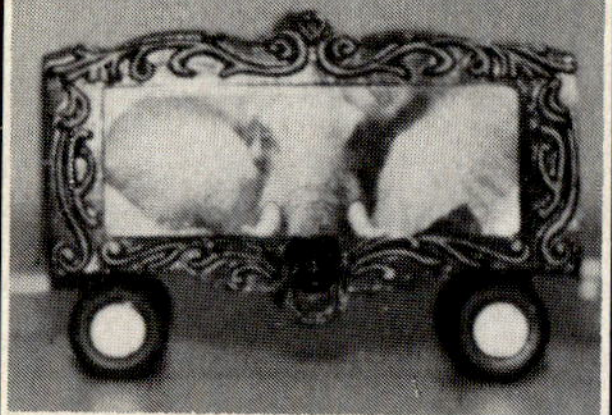

Cook House Wagon
705-4204   15.98 ►

Cage Wagon/Spoke Wheel
705-4205   15.98

► Parade/Billboard Wagon
705-4203   11.98
Same as 4201 but cast pneumatic wheels instead of wagon wheels. (Mural is for display only.)

(not illustrated)

Cage Wagon
w/Pneumatic Wheels
705-4206   15.98

Footboard **NEW**
705-16001   pkg(2) 1.98

Brake Assembly **NEW**
705-16002   pkg(2) 1.98

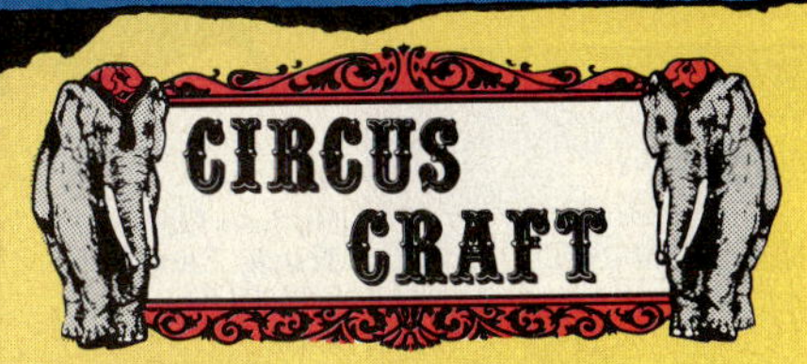
CIRCUS CRAFT

FIGURES

PAINTED
Plastic, seated.
220-1021 Men	pkg(6)	2.75
220-1022 Women	pkg(6)	2.75

UNPAINTED
Men/Women, seated.
220-1020	pkg(24)	2.25
220-1025	pkg(102)	7.50

WHEELS
1/8" Scale. Can be used with HO Scale.

WAGON

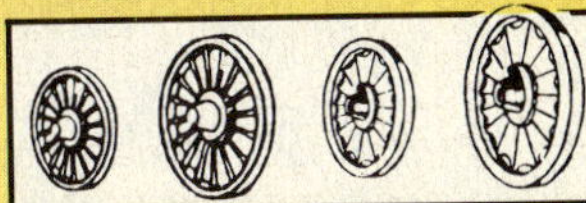

220-220 Sunburst 36 & 48" pkg(2) .50
(2 each of 36" and 48")
220-221 Baggage, 76 & 48" pkg(2) .50
(2 each of 76" and 48")

TRUCK
220-226 pkg(12) 1.50

CIRCUS CARS

Craft Train Kits consist of precut wood, unpainted plastic wheels and hardware.

ELEPHANT CARS
220-161	72' Slatted Sides	7.25
220-162	72' Solid Sides	7.25

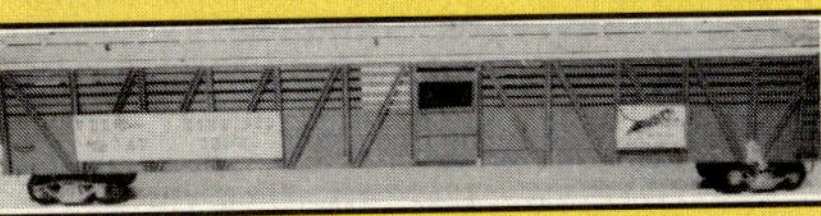

HORSE CARS
220-163	72' Horse Car	7.25

FLAT CARS
220-164	72' Mt Vernon	4.25
220-165	72' Warren	4.25

WAGONS
Craft Train Kits consists of precut wood, unpainted plastic wheels and hardware.

Side Show Canvas Wagon
220-17   3.75

Goliath Wagon
220-18   3.75

20' Folding Seat Wagon
220-1   3.75
30' Folding Seat Wagon
220-2   3.75

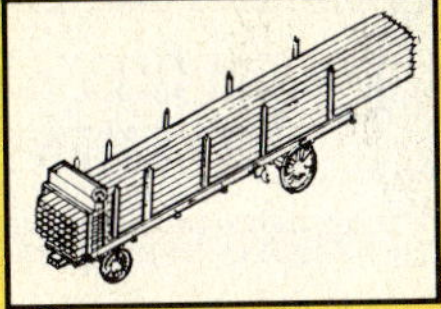
Quarter Pole Wagon w/Poles
220-19   4.75

Dining Department Wagon
220-15   3.75

Commissary Wagon
220-16   3.75

Barnes Dog Wagon
220-23   3.75

Hot Dog Wagon
220-24   3.75

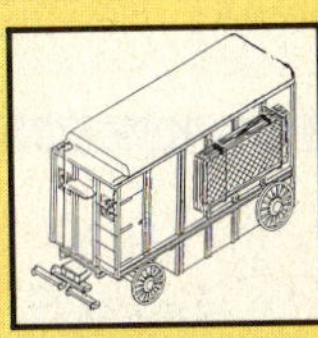
Giraffe Companion Wagon
220-26
4.50

Giraffe Wagon
220-20
4.25

Lion Cage Wagon
220-25
4.50

Cookhouse Water/ Equipment Wagon
220-27
4.25
NEW

JORDAN
HIGHWAY MINIATURES

HO SCALE 1/87

VEHICLES
Model is molded of high impact polystyrene in appropriate colors and requires only minimum painting.

360-232 Mack Water Truck   6.95
less driver

360-235 1913 Popcorn   6.95
Wagon w/Horse

WALTHERS

Human Cannon Truck, Zacchini
933-1379
9.98

TRUCKS & TRACTORS

◄ Circus Sound Truck
933-1374   8.98

Rocket Car ►
933-1383   8.98

CHASSIS
(not illustrated)
933-1390 Barnes   4.98
933-1391 Gollmar   4.98

GEM CITY AMUSEMENTS

TENTS
Kits are made of fabric and come complete with precut poles, braided "rope" and brass eyelets. Instructions with diagrams and placement templates are also included.

(not illustrated)

294-8901 Full Circus Set   179.95
Includes a Big Top, Entrance Marque, Menagerie and Side Show tents. To help set things up, a video tape of instructions is included.

294-8903 Accessory Tents   99.95
Four accessory tents with hip and gable roofs. These tents can be used for the cookhouse, horse tents, dining tent, dressing table and more.

294-8902 Big Top and Entrance Marque   pkg(2) 99.95
For building a smaller circus scene or diorama, which includes a Big Top and Entrance Marque.

ORIGINAL Preiser
Imported from Germany by WALTHERS

CIRCUS TENT w/ACCESSORIES

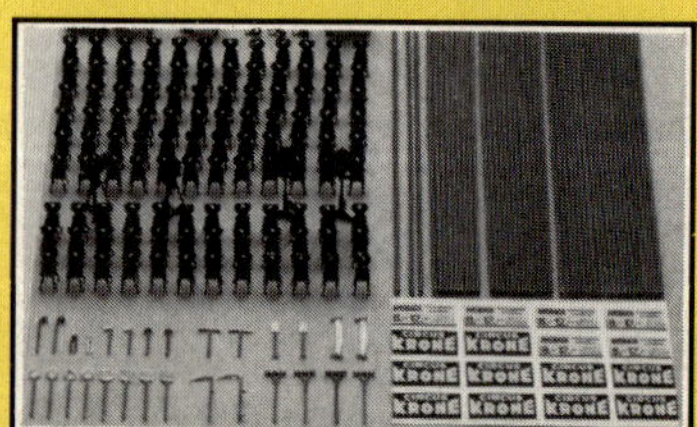

◄ Accessories for Krone Circus Tent
590-21048
23.49
NEW

(not illustrated)
590-21045 Krone Main Tent 38 x 15 x 9.5   **NEW** 166.99

CON-COR

HO SCALE 1/87

NEW

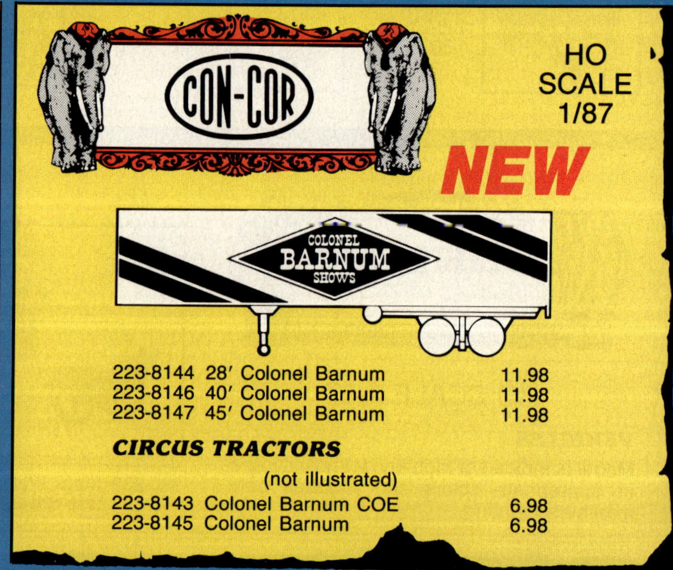

223-8144 28' Colonel Barnum   11.98
223-8146 40' Colonel Barnum   11.98
223-8147 45' Colonel Barnum   11.98

CIRCUS TRACTORS
(not illustrated)
223-8143 Colonel Barnum COE   6.98
223-8145 Colonel Barnum   6.98

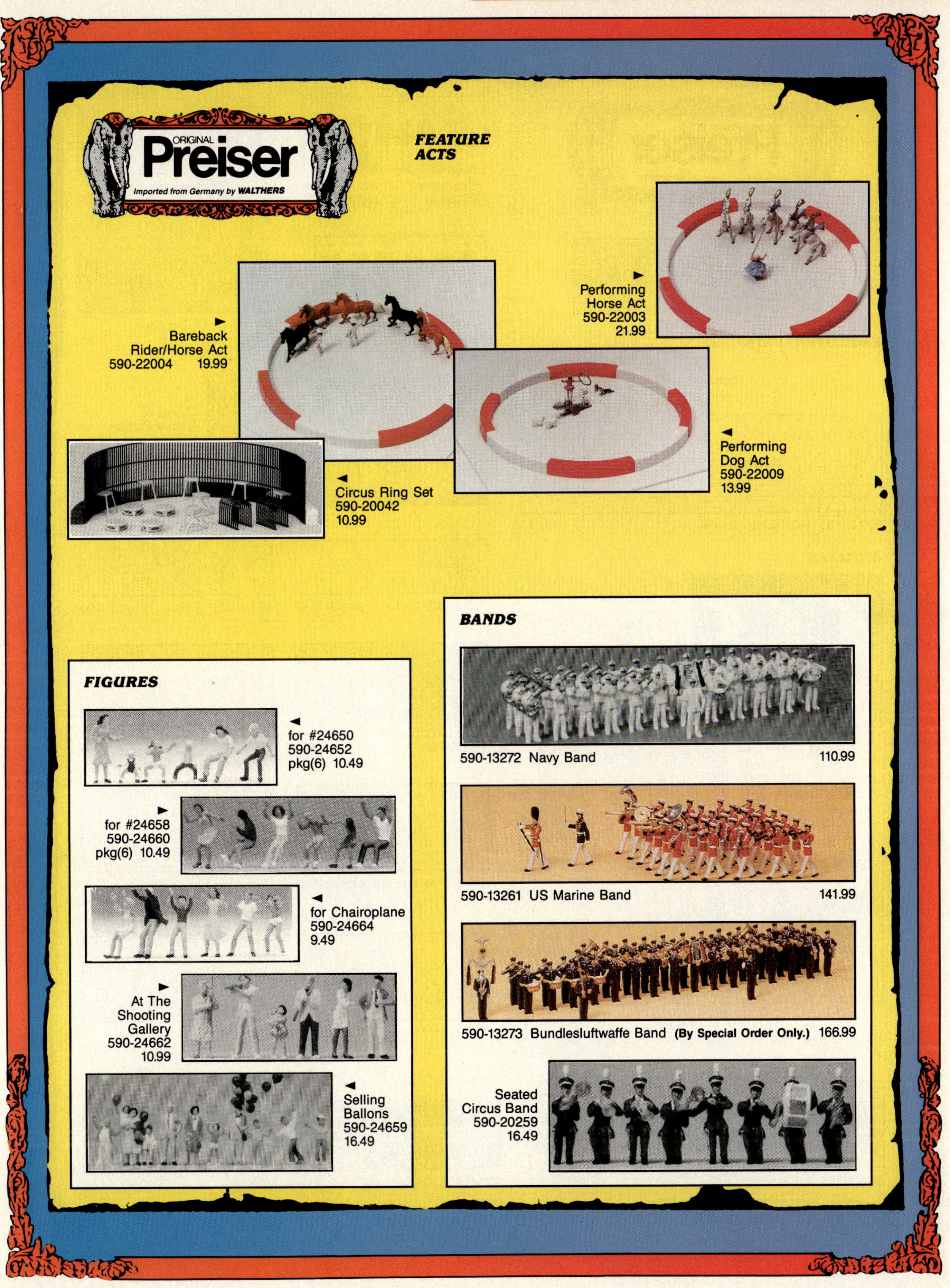

FEATURE ACTS

Performing
Horse Act
590-22003
21.99

Bareback
Rider/Horse Act
590-22004   19.99

Performing
Dog Act
590-22009
13.99

Circus Ring Set
590-20042
10.99

FIGURES

for #24650
590-24652
pkg(6) 10.49

for #24658
590-24660
pkg(6) 10.49

for Chairoplane
590-24664
9.49

At The
Shooting
Gallery
590-24662
10.99

Selling
Ballons
590-24659
16.49

BANDS

590-13272   Navy Band   110.99

590-13261   US Marine Band   141.99

590-13273   Bundlesluftwaffe Band (By Special Order Only.)   166.99

Seated
Circus Band
590-20259
16.49

ORIGINAL **Preiser**
Imported from Germany by WALTHERS

PERFORMERS

590-20254
pkg(8) 23.49

EMPLOYEE/PATRONS

590-10109
pkg (6) 10.99

590-24661 Selling Ice Cream   21.49

ANIMALS

Dressed Up Horses
590-20382
pkg(6) 16.49

Camels
590-20383
pkg(6) 12.49

Draught Horses for Carriage-and-Four (light hair)
590-30153   16.49

(not illustrated)
Draught Horses for Carriage-and-Four (dark hair)
590-30154   16.49

590-20391 Buffalos   pkg(4) 12.49

Ringmaster, Clowns, Ushers
590-22001   pkg(6) 14.99

Circus Ring Personnel
590-22007   pkg(6) 9.99

Girls w/Monkeys
590-20257   10.99

Clowns
590-20258   23.49

Group of Circus Parade Riders
590-22011
pkg(3) 16.49

590-20379 Lions   pkg(3) 8.99

590-20380 Tigers   pkg(3) 8.99

Performing Lions
590-20381   pkg(3) 8.99

Reindeer
590-20394   pkg(6) 13.49

590-20389 Llamas pkg(3) 8.99

Kangaroos
590-20392   pkg(3) 8.9

90-20388 Monkeys   8.99

Sea Lions w/Tamer
590-20260   10.49

590-16338 Unpainted Circus & Zoo Animals   pkg(50) 21.49

ORIGINAL **Preiser**
Imported from Germany by **WALTHERS**

Weight Lifter,
Sword Swallower,
Stilt Walker
NEW
590-24656
23.49

590-20250 Circus Performers #1 **NEW** 12.49

▶
At the
Sweet Stand
590-24663
NEW
11.99

MERTEN
Imported from Germany by **WALTHERS**

ANIMALS

▶
4 Horses with
Harness & Rider
447-2426 7.49

AFRICAN ELEPHANTS

447-748	Family	pkg(3) 7.49
447-749	Bull	2.49
447-750	Cow	2.49
447-751	Baby	.99

INDIAN ELEPHANTS

447-752	Family	pkg(3) 7.49
447-753	Cow	2.49
447-754	Bull	2.49
447-755	Baby	.99

AFRICAN RHINOCEROS

447-756 Family pkg(3) 7.49

INDIAN RHINOCEROS

447-760 Family pkg(3) 7.49

WALTHERS

ANIMALS

Visitors to your circus will thrill to the Super Elephant Set
which includes a prepainted Preiser handler and eight
elephants (two bulls, four cows in two different poses and
two babies) molded in gray vinyl.

933-1380 Super Elephant Set (8 elephants plus handler) 11.98

CIRCUS DECALS

ORIGINAL **Preiser**
Imported from Germany by WALTHERS

Krone
590-30649
12.49

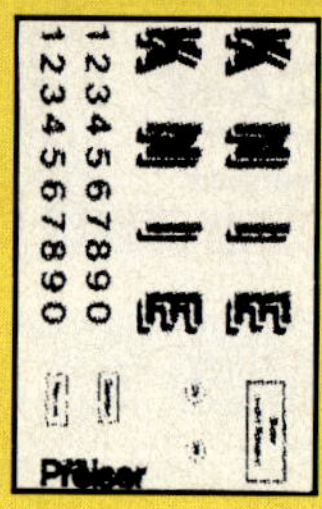

Knie
590-20078
NEW
13.49

Sarrasani
590-20076
13.49

(not illustrated)
590-21049 Krone   13.49
590-22110 Decal set—American Circus   17.99

SWINGS

590-24658   20.49

RIDE

Kiddie Ferris Wheel
590-24654   23.49

CIRCUS TRUCKS

590-21150 Krone   19.49

Hanomog R55 (white)
590-24679   16.49

GAME BOOTHS

590-24650 Merry-Go-Round 23.49

590-24692 Fun Fair Stall "Toys"   33.99

(not illustrated)
Gingerbread Booth
590-24690 **NEW** 33.99

590-24693 Fun Fair Stall "China"   33.99

Fun Fair Stall
"Shooting Gallery"
509-24694   33.99

Fun Fair Stall
"Hot Dogs"
509-24691   32.49

RIDES

Customize your midway with these easy-to-build plastic kits. Models are molded in colors and include full-color printed signs. Each can be built as a working model, using motorizing kit #5115, sold separately.

348-5128 Kiddie Motorcycle Ride   19.98
Motorcycle tubs go up and down.

348-5127 Kiddie Boat Ride   19.98
Boat tubs go around, up & down.

348-5111 Carousel   17.98
Many parks and fair grounds once boasted an elegant carousel! This model is about 9″ in diameter with two rows of horses and chair cars. When fitted with the motorizing kit, available separately, the horses will move up and down!

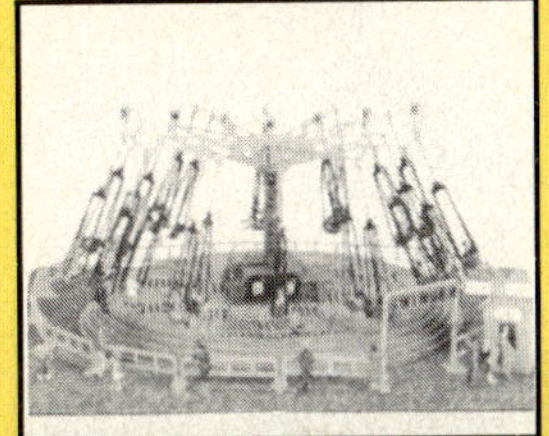

348-5117 Falling Star 19.98
This ride really has its ups and downs! The platform rises and falls like the real thing.

348-5119 The Tunder Bolt   19.98
Like a bolt from the blue, the cars on this ride roar around the track. Molded in seven colors, with 85 full-color printed signs!

348-5118 Sea Dragon 19.98
Ahoy matey! Carnival goers will be thrilled as the colorful ship sweeps back and forth across the midway.

348-5113 Swinger   14.98
Loads of twirling fun! As hanging seats spin out and up, the faster the ride turns. Great fun.

BOOTHS

Weight Guessing Game & Baseball Bulls-eye
348-5123   12.98
Two great models in one.

348-5124 Octopus   17.98
8 gyrating arms each have a tub at the end.

348-5125 Spider   19.98
6 gyrating arms, each with twin tubs.

(not illustrated)

348-4407	Carnival Rail/Ticket Office	2.98
348-5198	Battery Box and Harness	3.98
348-5115	Motorizing Kit for Rides	4.98

348-5190 Deluxe Motor Unit   *NEW* 6.98
For use with #5124 & #5125; uses 12V DC power supply

Concession Booths #1
348-5121   12.98
Shooting Gallery, Dart and Balloon Game and Birthday Game.

Concession Booths #2
348-5122   12.98
King Kong Hoop Toss, Barney's Basketball Game and Spinning Wheel Game.

Concession Booths #3
348-5129   12.98
Kentucky Derby, Ring a Bottle and Frog Pond.

Concession Booths #4
348-5130   12.98
Big Mouth Pig, Squirt Gun & Milk Can Toss.

CARNIVAL & CIRCUS BACKGROUNDS

348-5310 Country Carnival   7.98
Full color w/rides, band gazebo, concession stands, hot air balloon, plane w/parachuters falling and more. 36 x 24″.

348-5311 Country Circus   7.98
Full color w/circus tent, animals, hot air balloon, plane pulling sign & more. 36 x 24″.

RIDE

Skywheel Double Ferris Wheel
348-5112
17.98
Rounding out the carnival accessories is the Skywalker, a double Ferris Wheel with two rows of seats. When motorized, the seats rotate in opposite directions and will stand about 12″ tall.

Ferris Wheel
348-5110
12.98
NEW
An exciting, operable model. Molded in 5 colors, easy and fun to build. Start your Carnival!

Corkey's Carnival Caravan

Caravans include 8-wheel drive locomotive, caboose, carousel box car, ferris wheel box car, terminal rerailer, clown figures, ferris wheel kit, UL approved, self-resetting power pack & instructions.

348-400	Corkey's Flyer w/Oval of Track	69.98
348-410	Corkey's Carney	85.98
	Tiger Box Car, 7′ Oval of Track, Carousel Kit & 3 Concession Booth Kits	
348-420	King Corkey	129.98

Tiger Box Car, Spider Box Car, Elongated Figure 8 Track, Carousel Kit, Swinger Kit, Sky Wheel Kit, 12 Concession Booth Kits, Automatic Twin-Arm and Operating Crossing Gate

348-8851 Assorted Clowns   6.98

348-8853 Hobo Clowns   **NEW** 6.98

SNACK SHACKS

This exciting selection includes performers, clowns, animals, roustabouts, side show people and more. Each is a metal casting.

CIRCUS TOWN

SNACK STANDS

196-251	Popcorn Stand	4.98
196-252	Lemonade Stand	4.98
196-253	Ice Cream Stand	4.98
196-257	Hot Dog Stand	4.98
196-258	Snow Cone Stand	4.98
196-259	Cotton Candy Stand	4.98

PERFORMING ANIMALS

196-205	Jumbo the Elephant	4.98
196-227	Ring Horse	12.92
196-231	Mount Elephant	4.98
196-232	Baby Elephant	2.98
196-234	Dancing Horse	2.98
196-239	Elephant Ride	2.98

ROUSTABOUTS

196-241	George Game/Ride Operator	1.98
196-242	Chris Game Operator	1.98
196-243	Cathie Game Operator	1.98
196-244	Standing Customer Dave	1.98
196-245	Set-Up Man Marty	1.98
196-246	Ticket Taker Elisa	1.98
196-249	High Striker Bernie	6.98
196-254	Food Server	1.98
196-260	Half Man Butch **NEW**	1.98

PERFORMERS

196-226	Animal Trainer - Female	1.98
196-212	Trapeze Act	2.98

196-213	Tightrope Walker	1.98
196-214	Human Cannonball	4.98
196-217	Animal Rider	3.98
196-223	"The Web" Rope Twirler	3.98

CLOWNS

196-237	Program Clown	1.98
196-248	Stanchion	1.98

SIDE SHOW PEOPLE

196-219	Siamese twins	6.98

MISCELLANEOUS

196-255	Young Boy	1.98
196-256	Young Girl w/Small Boy	2.98

FALLER

Imported from Germany and marketed by *WALTHERS*

SHOWMANS TRAILER

272-1030 w/Accessories   27.49
272-1031 Home   23.99

RIDES

FERRIS WHEEL ▶

Complete Ferris Wheel
272-1   149.99

Ferris Wheel
272-310   75.99
The star attraction of fairs and carnivals, kit can be built as a static or operating, illuminated model. Operating model requires #629, two #314 bulb sets (available separately) and light set #313.

Electric Motor for #310
272-629   20.99

Bulb Set for #310
272-314   each 13.49

Lighting Set for #310
272-313   35.49

◀ Chairoplane
272-315   56.49
7-7/8" 20 cm diameter. Operating, includes motor and light.

Tea Cup Merry-Go- ▶ Round, Motorized
272-326   53.49
Board these turning tea cups and now the fun begins. Suitable only for those not liable to dizziness. With motor (12-16 Va.c.) Less figures.

◀ Merry-Go-Round
272-316   33.49
Can be motorized with Faller motor #629. Less motor and figures.

Bumper Cars ▶ w/12-16 VAC driving mechanism
272-328   74.99
Six cars move over the running surface, three cars without any function are parked on the side of the carriage-way. 18.5 x 20.1 cm

◀ Jupiter Roundabout
272-319   45.49
Rocket ships climb and dive as this powered ride rotates. Includes motor and can be illuminated with 2 bulbs #272-671 (sold separately).

Swingboats w/Motor ▶
272-318   45.49
This colorful ride includes a motor to produce back and forth motion and can be fitted with flashing lights, using bulb #272-671 (sold separately).

◀ Inflatable Booth
272-327   12.99
Everybody knows them...the inflatables highly popular with children for endless fun. Less figures.

"Octopus" Carousel ▶
272-317 **LTD QTY** 41.99
The colorful gondolas rise and fall on the arms of the "Octopus" as the rounda bout rotates. Includes Faller motor #629, less figures.

BOOTHS & CONCESSION STANDS

Bratwurst Stand
272-446   **NEW** 26.99
11.8 x 8.3 x 6.9 cm

272-447 Snack Bar   **NEW** 26.99
11.8 x 8.3 x 8.4 cm

Snack Bar Accessories
272-448   **NEW** 11.49

(not illustrated)
Amusement Park
Brochure
272-839   TBA
NEW

Midway
Booths
272-320
pkg(2)   14.99
3-3/4 x 1-1/4"
9.6 x 3.2 cm

272-321   Concession Booths   pkg(2) 14.99
3-3/4 x 1-1/4"   9.6 x 3.2 cm

Fun Fair
Stands
272-322
pkg(2)   15.49
3-5/8 x 1-3/4"
9.4 x 4.6 cm
Includes a
flower stand and
sweet shop.

272-445 Fun Fair Stands   12.99
1-3/4 x 1-1/2", 2 x 1-1/2",   4.5 x 3.8 cm, 5.0 x 3.8 cm
Includes silhouette specialist and a game booth. Less figures.

Potato Concession
Booth
272-442   19.99
4-3/4 x 2-1/2", 12 x 6.5 cm
Everything that can be
made from a potato is
sold here! Less figures.

RIDES

272-441 Roundabout   **NEW** 41.99
Merry-go-round w/six gondolas. Includes motor
#62912. 16 vac.

Break-Dance
Roundabout
272-440
59.99
7-1/2 x 8"
19.5 x 20.5 cm
16 colorful
gondolas on
four rotary
tables,
complete with
motor #272-629
(12-16V). Less
figures.

NEW ROLLER COASTER

272-450   Big Dipper   220.99
Fully functional, entrance and passenger areas with safety grills, intricate uprights and supports. Also includes fairground noise unit, two transport bed trailers w/stanchions, and lighting.
60 x 41.8 x 41 cm

SHOWS

272-443 Shark Show   24.99
6 x 4-1/4", 15.5 x 11.2 cm
Step right up and see the greatest mobile sea show. Less figures.

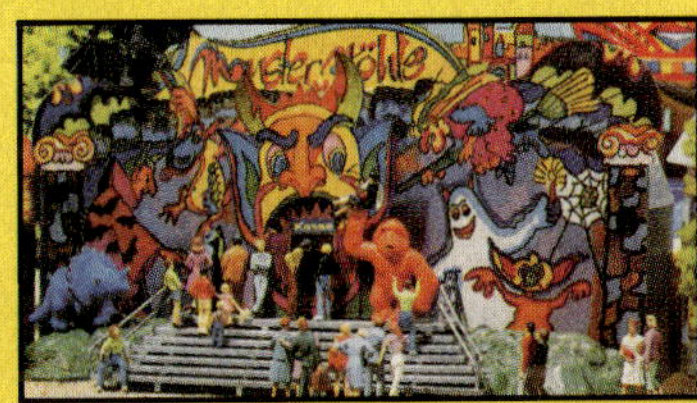

272-444 Monster Cave   17.49
Includes colorful front decoration strips and "scary" accessories. Less figures.

VIEWING TOWER

Viewing Tower "Rust"
272-325
66.49
9 x 7"   22.8 x 18 cm
Platform is raised to the top (powered by Faller motor #629) and then slowly lowered. Motor included.

BOOKS

Carstens
PUBLICATIONS, INC.

CIRCUS TRAINS, TRUCKS AND MODELS

205-70   12.95

Discover the fun of modeling a railroad or truck circus with this historic and informative book. Photos of prototype equipment and operations, plus an up-to-date listing of available circus kits make this a valuable reference for any circus library.

DOVER PUBLICATIONS

THE GREAT CIRCUS PARADE IN PICTURES

241-26201   9.95

Contains 183 rare and unusual photographs and posters (10 in full color) of the great circus street parades so popular at the turn of the century. With captions. Softcover, 127 pages, 8-3/8 x 9-1/4".

AMERICAN CIRCUS POSTERS

241-23693   9.95

Features reproductions of original posters from 1890 through 1940, highlights unusual acts, wild animals, performers and more. Softcover, 48 pages, 10-1/4 x 14-1/4".

CUT & ASSEMBLE CIRCUS PARADE

241-24861   5.95

Includes band, horses, wild animals, wagons and more.

VOLLMER
Imported from Germany and marketed by WALTHERS

A 770-3623 Tent   26.99
18 x 12 x 8.5 cm
Take a break from a day at the fair under the cool shade of this colorful tent. Add some appropriate figures and details to turn it into a dining tent, exhibit hall or beer garden.

B 770-3622 Roundabout Fair Ride 37.99
18.5 x 16 x 11.2 cm
Round and around in a swirl of color and motion, you can build this colorful roundabout as a static model, or add motor #4200 (available separately) for a working ride!

C 770-3625 Fair Booths pkg(2) 14.49
You're a winner every time with these games of luck and skill! The kit includes parts to build a toy lottery and a plant lottery. Full color panels make these eyecatching models for any miniature midway.

D 770-3620 Swingboat Ride 39.99
18 x 11.6 x 13.2 cm
Ahoy mates, this swingboat ride will be a popular attraction on any midway! The kit can be built for display, or powered with motor #4200 (available separately) to animate your scene.

E 770-3627 Ghost Train w/Ghost 41.99
20 x 11.5 x 10 cm
Add thrills and chills to your model midway with this haunted house ride! For added excitement, there's a special electronic sound unit that produces eerie noises. 7-3/4 x 4-1/2 x 3-7/8"

770-4200 Motorizing Kit each 26.99
for Rides

F 770-3626 Fair Assortment 104.99
Build a midway in miniature with this set of four kits, perfect for a carnival, county fair or amusement park. Try your luck at either of the two game booths in kit #3625. Then it's on to a thrilling ride aboard the Swingboats, #3620 or the Roundabout, #3622. Finally, relax out of the sun under tent #3623, all included in this set.

Mining companies. Cement plants. Coal dealers. Grain elevators. Heavy industry is an important customer for America's railroads. From the refineries of Texas to the dairy plants of New York and the grain elevators of Kansas, railroads are the arteries that carry the lifeblood of our growing, industrialized nation.

For more than 100 years, heavy industry and railroading have gone hand in hand. Some say railroads were the most important development of the industrial revolution. Many towns and industries were created by the presence of the railroads. Today, industry still relies heavily on the railroads, who are embracing new technologies and methods to meet the changing needs of industrial shippers.

With the Cornerstone Series®, you can model a variety of industries that count on the railroads to move their products, whether your layout is set in the steam or diesel era. These industries give you a reason for your model railroad, providing new business that adds interest and excitment to your operations.

Each kit is a detailed model of an authentic industry, ready to start generating revenue for your model railroad. The kits have been carefully engineered to capture the realism of the prototypes they represent, in sizes that work on most layouts.

The easy-to-build kits feature detailed styrene parts that are molded in colors, plus add-on details, full-color decal signs and illustrated instructions. For added fun, Cornerstone Series accessories are available to customize each building. To model a complete operation, Walthers freight cars and Magnuson Models vehicles are also available for each type of industry.

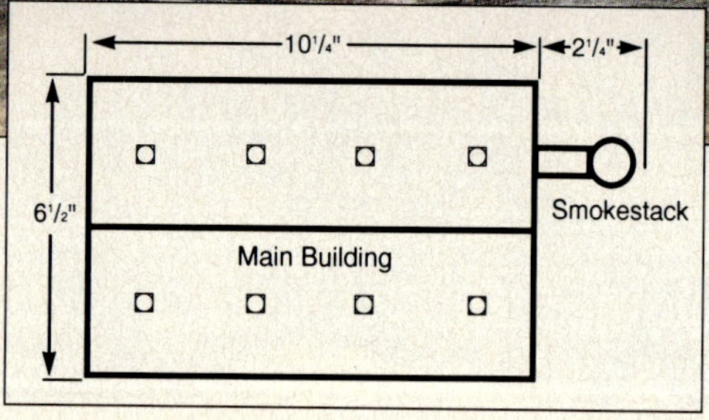

NORTHERN LIGHT & POWER POWERHOUSE

Generate new revenue for your steam- or diesel-era railroad with Northern Light & Power. This detailed model is similar to power stations operated by utility companies, private industries and institutions, as well as streetcar or interurban lines. The easy-to-build kit features a brick main building, large smokestack, coal dump pit, separate doors, roof and windows, clear window "glass" and complete instructions. Decal signs and a special billboard sign decal are also included.

933 3021 29.98

ACCESSORIES

NORTHERN LIGHT & POWER INTERIOR

Superdetail your powerhouse with this interior kit, complete with boiler walls, generators and turbines. (Also shown: Overhead Traveling Crane, 933-3102, $10.98, available separately.) From the Cornerstone Series.

933-3130 9.98

HIGH-VOLTAGE TRANSMISSION TOWERS

Carrying high-voltage current from the powerhouse to the substation, these tall towers will add realism to your railroad's skyline. The set includes four easy-to-build towers with molded-on eyelets for stringing "wire." From the Cornerstone Series.

933-3121 14.98

TRANSMISSION WIRE

Don't worry about adding high-voltage lines to your layout; this nifty rubber wire bounces back when bumped! Package includes 80' of material to superdetail your Transmission Towers. From the Cornerstone Series.

933-3127 6.98

49' QUAD HOPPER SIX-PACKS

Model a unit train in under 90 minutes? It's possible - with Walthers Quad Hopper Six-Packs. Each features cars decorated in the same roadname, but with different numbers. Plus, car numbers are different from earlier releases in the same schemes. Don't forget to fill up your new cars with Magnuson Models Coal Loads (439-563, $4.49), available separately.

CHAIN-LINK FENCE

Where there's an electric plant, there's chain-link fence. Lots of it. This terrific kit comes with styrene parts for poles, gates and other details, plus a separate piece of chain-link material. From the Cornerstone Series.

933-3125 9.98

<table>
<tr><td colspan="2">DIMENSIONS</td></tr>
<tr><td>Length:</td><td>8"</td></tr>
<tr><td>Width:</td><td>12-7/8"</td></tr>
<tr><td>Height:</td><td>6-3/8"</td></tr>
</table>

NORTHERN LIGHT & POWER SUBSTATION

This model's a must for an authentic electrical operation. Installations like the Northern Light & Power Substation are used to lower the current of high voltage before routing it to residential and commercial customers. This kit includes all the details of the prototype, from the transformers and steel framework to the chain-link fencing around the facility. Warning sign decals and a billboard sign decal for use with the Cornerstone Series Basic Billboards are also included.
933-3025 24.98

ELECTRIC UTILITY POLE SET

This electric pole set includes 24 easy-to-assemble power poles, transformers, insulators, nonilluminated street lights and realistic "wire." From the Cornerstone Series.
933-3101 9.98

BASIC BILLBOARDS

This set includes two regular Cornerstone Series billboards (without signs) that can be decorated with the special billboard decal included with the Northern Light & Power Powerhouse and Substation kits.
933-3133 (2) 4.98

TRANSFORMER

High-tonnage equipment like this transformer is just the ticket for a flat car load, or a detail around the Northern Light & Power plant or substation. From the Cornerstone Series.
933-3126 9.98

75' DEPRESSED-CENTER, FOUR-TRUCK FLAT CARS

These modern cars move all types of loads, especially large transformers for installations like the Northern Light & Power Substation. For more information on these Walthers models, see the Freight Cars section.

1982 LINE TRUCK

When the call goes out to make repairs, your crew will be ready with this 1982 model Line Truck. The kit features a popular cab style, along with a special body and full-color decals. From Magnuson Models.
439-942 7.98

NEW

ADM GRAIN ELEVATOR

They say there are usually three things in a small town in rural America: a gas station, a grocery store and a grain elevator. Patterned after the concrete elevators found in small towns and the central facilities in larger complexes, this authentically detailed kit includes an elevator, eight storage silos, dust bins, a head house and loading and unloading sheds for rail cars and trucks. Full-color decal signs, ADM logos and a billboard sign decal are also included.
933-3022 29.98

ACCESSORIES

ADD-ON SILOS

Not all grain elevators are created equal. Some are downright huge. This kit allows you to expand your elevator with the same set of concrete silos found in the ADM Grain Elevator kit. Additional sections for the corrugated metal headhouse are also included. Dimensions: 9 x 4-3/4 x 9". From the Cornerstone Series.
933-3023 19.98

PS-2CD COVERED HOPPERS

Introduced in the 1960's, the high-capacity PS-2 Center Discharge Covered Hopper was built especially for the grain industry. Purchased by dozens of railroads and private owners, many are still going strong today. Look in the Freight Cars Section for more information on these cars.

65' TANK CARS

Deliver propane and anhydrous ammonia to your grain elevator complex with Walthers 65' Propane Tank Cars. See the Freight Cars section for a complete list of roadnames.

TRACKMOBILE

Small, self-propelled units that run on roads or rails, these powerful haulers are used as switch engines around heavy industries. This kit features a resin body and is offered in powered and unpowered versions. From Magnuson Models.
POWERED
439-953 39.98
UNPOWERED
439-952 19.98

FARM VEHICLES

Here's everything you need to get the grain out of the fields and over to the elevator. From Magnuson Models.
GRAIN TRUCK
439-947 7.98
COMBINE
439-948 7.98
TRACTOR
439-949 7.98
GRAVITY BOX WAGON
439-950 7.98

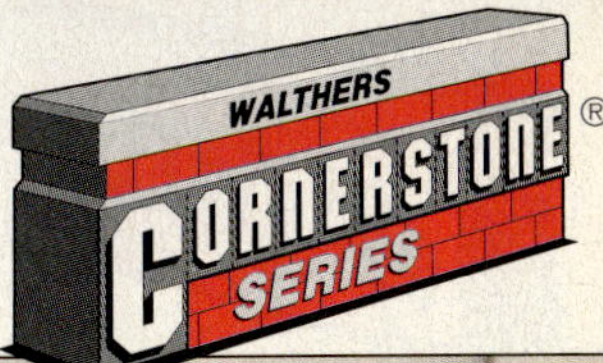

ADM SCALEHOUSE

When receiving or shipping grain at a grain elevator, the incoming trucks and hoppers must first be weighed at the scalehouse. The ADM Scalehouse serves as the office for the ADM Grain Elevator complex and includes details for both truck and rail car scales, separate doors and windows (bay windows are included on each side of the building), vents and a chimney. ADM decals, signs and a billboard decal sign are also provided.
933-3027 19.98

DIMENSIONS	
Length:	5-7/8"
Width:	3-7/8"
Height:	1-7/8"

ACCESSORIES

LIMITED-EDITION SW-1 SWITCH ENGINES

Many ADM facilities have their own switchers to move hoppers. This limited-edition model is finished in yellow with the blue and white ADM logo. A Cargill version is also available, finished in white with black underframe and black Cargill logo.

ADM
932-1362 79.98
CARGILL
932-1363 79.98

SCALE TEST CARS

On a scale of 1 to 10, our scale test cars are a 10! In order to insure the accuracy of railroad scales, most lines maintain these small cars. See the Freight Cars section for additional details on these cars.

GRAIN HANDLING EQUIPMENT

Drying and storing grain are important functions of a grain elevator complex. With these kits, you can model the complete operation! From the Cornerstone Series.

GRAIN BIN
933-3123 14.98
GRAIN CONVEYOR
933-3124 14.98
GRAIN DRYER
933-3128 9.98

(not shown)
PROPANE/AMMONIA TANKS
933-3129 (2) 10.98
This kit includes the same tanks that are in the Central Gas & Supply kit, plus piping and decals for both types of gases.

FLOUR MILL

Flour mills have changed dramatically since the water-powered mills of the 1800's. Today's mills are much larger in size and scope, producing enormous quantities of flour and other milled grains. This model represents a modern concrete mill, which would receive grain from facilities like the ADM Grain Elevator. The kit features truck and rail loading facilities, blowers, vents, separate doors and windows, full-color decal signs and a billboard sign decal.
933-3026 24.98

DIMENSIONS	
Length:	9-5/8"
Width:	5-5/8"
Height:	9"

ACCESSORIES

AIRSLIDE COVERED HOPPERS

Simulate loads-in/empties-out traffic at your mill with Walthers Airslide® Covered Hoppers. For a complete listing of available roadnames, see the Freight Cars section.

BASIC BILLBOARDS

Watch business pick up when you advertise your mill on these billboards. The kit includes parts for two billboards (without signs), that can be decorated with the decal sign included with the flour mill kit. From the Cornerstone Series.
933-3133 2/4.98

ADD-ON SILOS

Many flour mills have storage silos to hold grain before it's processed. This kit includes parts to build a set of eight concrete silos that will turn your mill into a major flour producer. Dimensions: 9 x 4-3/4 x 9". From the Cornerstone Series.
933-3023 19.98

VAN TRUCK

This truck really delivers! The modern box van comes equipped with a detailed cab, separate body and colorful decals. From Magnuson Models.
439-951 7.98

FREIGHT LOAD SET

Put the finishing touches on your mill with this selection of pallets, crates, sacks, machinery, barrels, hand trucks and ladders. From Faller.
272-588 8.49

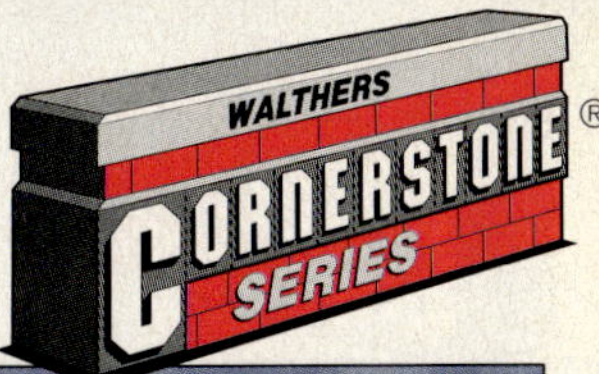

R.J. FROST ICE & STORAGE

The destination for produce from all corners of the country, R.J. Frost Ice & Storage is typical of cold storage plants used to hold perishable fruits, vegetables and meats on their way to local markets. With its roof-top refrigeration unit, fire escape and rail and truck loading platforms, the simulated concrete structure fits perfectly into a steam- or diesel-era industrial district. Other details include separate windows and doors, full-color decal signs and a billboard sign decal.
933-3020   29.98

ACCESSORIES

ARCTICAR™ REFRIGERATED BOX CARS

These ultra-modern cars are designed especially to meet the needs of the frozen food industry. And like old-time reefers, they're being painted in flashy schemes for a variety of private companies. You'll find more information on these Walthers cars in the Freight Cars section.

BASIC BILLBOARDS

Use the special billboard decal sign included in the R.J. Frost Ice & Storage kit with these billboards to advertise your new cold storage business. The kit includes parts for two billboards, without signs. From the Cornerstone Series.
933-3133   4.98

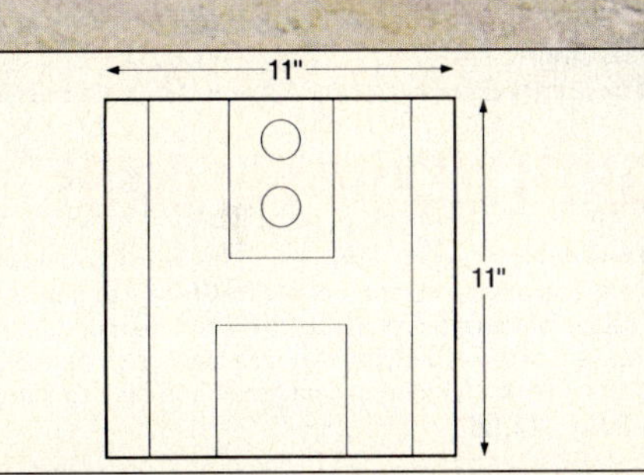

CAB-OVER REEFER TRUCK

Ready to make local deliveries of frozen foods, this model features a popular style cab that has been in use for over 30 years! An all-new reefer body with a nose-mounted refrigeration unit, and full-color decals complete the kit. From Magnuson Models.
439-943   7.98

WOOD & STEEL REEFERS

Create an authentic steam-era scene around R.J. Frost Ice & Storage with Walthers Wood-Bodied and All-Steel Reefers, available in a variety of unique roadnames. For a complete listing of these cars, see the Freight Cars section.

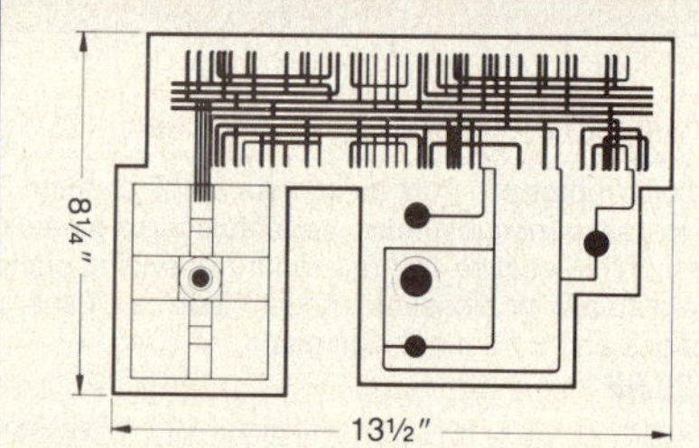

NORTH ISLAND REFINERY

Day and night, crude oil from around the world arrives at the North Island Refinery. Railroads are vital to refinery operations, from the fleet of switchers that moves cars around the complex to the mainline freights that hustle the finished products to distant markets. The North Island Refinery is carefully designed to capture the realism of the prototype, in a size that works on most layouts. The superdetailed kit includes a main fractioning tower, furnace, piping group and heat exchangers, vacuum pipe still and decal warning signs.
933-3013 29.98

ACCESSORIES

OIL STORAGE TANKS

Used to store oil and other petroleum products, these tanks are a common sight at oil refineries and terminals. Kits include one-piece styrene tank bodies, spiral access ladders, safety railing, outlet valves and decal warning signs. From the Cornerstone Series.

575,000 GALLON HORIZONTAL OIL STORAGE TANK
933-3120 19.98
(7-1/2" diameter by 4" tall)

500,000 GALLON VERTICAL OIL STORAGE TANK
933-3115 19.98
(6" diameter by 6-1/4" tall)

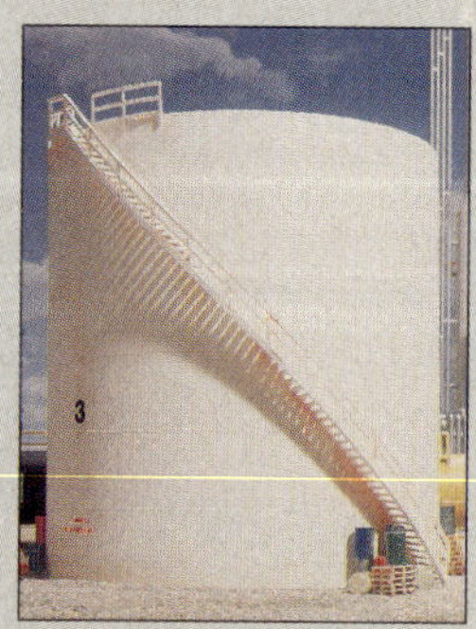

PETROLEUM BILLBOARDS

Advertise the products produced by your refinery with this set of three billboards, complete with 12 full-color signs. From the Cornerstone Series.
933-3116 8.98

REFINERY PIPING KIT

Kit includes overhead supports, angles and other fixtures. Modular design allows for many possible configurations to fit your refinery complex. From the Cornerstone Series.
933-3114 7.98

OIL TANK DECALS

Promote your favorite oil brand with this set of 10 full-color oil company logos, for use with oil storage tanks #3115 and #3120. From the Cornerstone Series.
933-3117 4.98

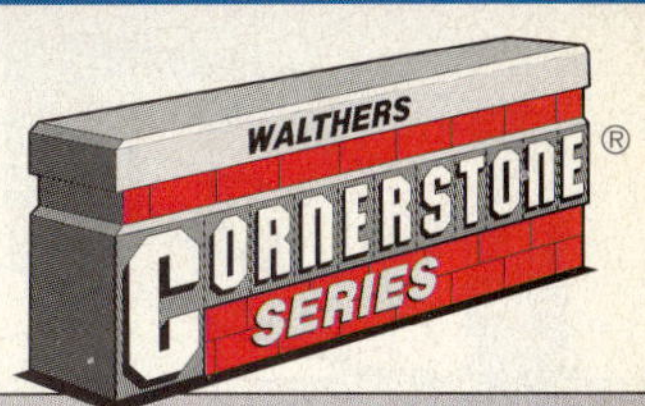

INTERSTATE FUEL & OIL

Since the 1920's, bulk oil distributors have been important trackside customers for every railroad. At home in big cities or country towns, dealerships like this one distribute fuel oil, gasoline and other petroleum products locally. This kit is typical of nearly all complexes, with horizontal and vertical storage tanks, above-ground piping, a pump house with header stand to unload tank cars, a truck loading rack and a corrugated metal office/warehouse building. Like the prototypes, the various pieces can be arranged to fit available space. A gas pump, oil drums and other details are also provided.
933-3006 24.98

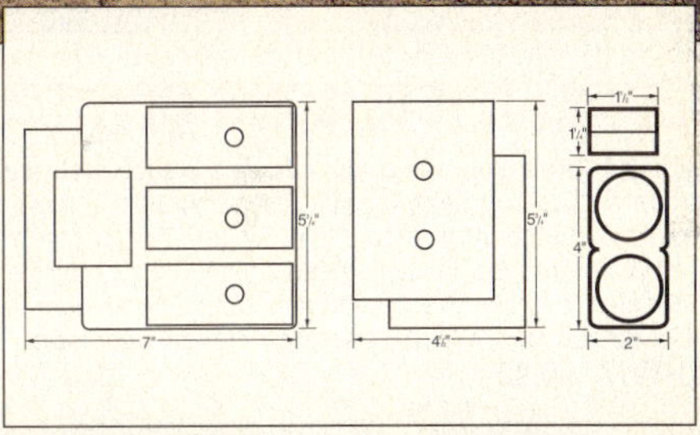

ACCESSORIES

OIL LOADING PLATFORM

This detailed kit simulates a typical tank car loading platform which serves two tracks. Complete with piping, nozzles, platforms and stairway, safety sign decals, nonworking light fixtures and more. Illustration shows two kits combined to build a longer platform. From the Cornerstone Series.
933-3104 11.98

TANK CARS

Meet the increased demand for petroleum shipments on your layout with Walthers Tank Cars. Choose from old-time 36' Tank Cars, or modern Funnel-Flow®Tank Cars in a variety of sizes.

VEHICLES

Detail your oil distributorship or refinery by adding a custom truck to your company vehicle fleet. From Magnuson Models.

CREW CAB PICKUP TRUCK	439-933	7.98
TANK TRUCK	439-921	7.98
MACK OIL TRUCK	439-930	7.98

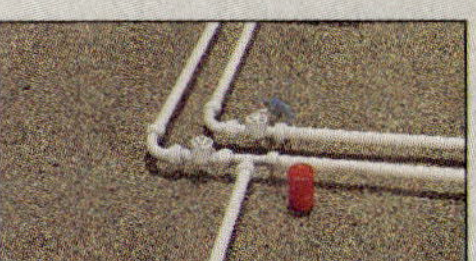

PIPING KIT

Here's an easy way to model supply lines used to bring oil and other materials to and from the platforms. The kit includes a variety of angles, elbows, tees, straight pipes, valves and more. From the Cornerstone Series.
933-3105 4.98

OIL DRUM & FIGURE SET

This set includes 36 plastic drums to simulate all types of chemical and petroleum products. Three painted workmen figures and a hand truck are also included. From the Cornerstone Series.
933-3100 9.98

NEW RIVER MINING COMPANY

Loading 100-car unit trains with coal is a big job that requires heavy facilities like the New River Mining Company. The prototype for this tipple was built in the early 1950's and is typical of loading facilities found in all parts of the country. A conveyor system brings coal from the mine to the tipple, where it's crushed and screened before being loaded into waiting hopper cars or trucks. The finished model is packed with detail, but is modeled in a size that fits most layouts. The kit comes complete with a tipple building, truck loading facility, enclosed conveyors, plus separate windows and doors.

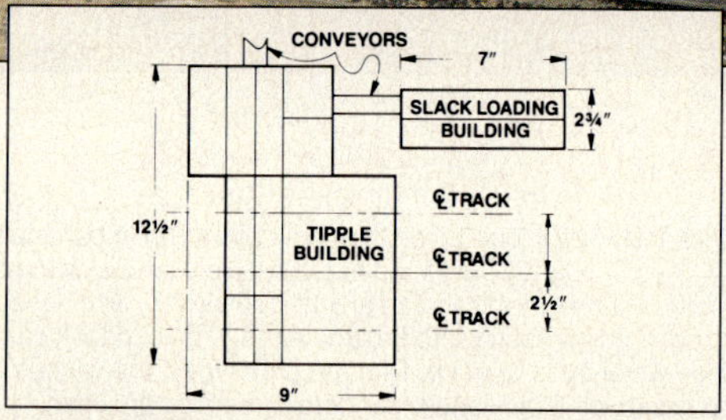

933-3017 29.98

ACCESSORIES

TWIN & QUAD HOPPERS

Serve on-line coal customers with Walthers 100-Ton Quad Hoppers, 50-Ton Twin Hoppers and limited-edition 3-packs. For more information, see the Freight Cars section.

FRONT-END LOADER

Pick up spills, load trucks or shove an occasional car with this rugged Front-End Loader. The easy-to-build plastic kit is molded in colors and includes decals. From the Cornerstone Series.

933-3118 14.98

COAL & ACCESSORIES

See the Scenery section for coal, ground cover and other details to put the finishing touches on your mining company scene.

HEAVY-DUTY COAL TRUCK

This tough truck is perfect for moving coal from mine to loader. A detailed resin cab and bed, cast-metal wheels and decals are all included. From Magnuson Models.

439-936 7.98

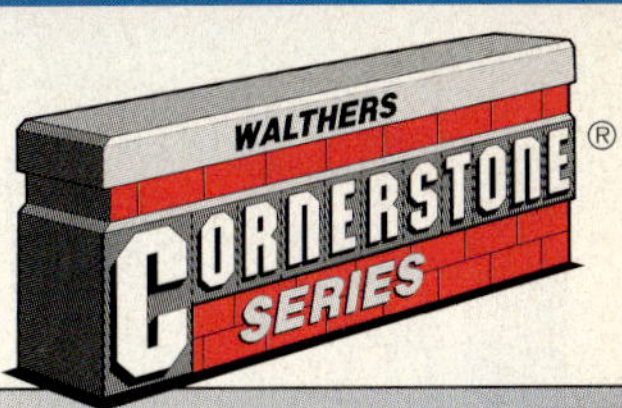

O.L. KING & SONS COAL YARD

Back when just about everyone had a coal furnace, the coal yard was one of the most important businesses in any city. Coal dealers received hoppers of coal direct from the mines, and then made deliveries by truck or wagon to homes, stores and small industries. To facilitate the unloading of freight cars, an elevated trestle, like the one included with this kit, was favored by most dealers. Many coal companies also sold building materials, ice and other items to keep a steady income when coal was not in demand, so some facilities are still in use today as storage buildings. The kit comes complete with a brick office, fencing, shed and decals.

933-3015 17.98

ACCESSORIES

DIAMOND T COAL TRUCK

Deliver coal to local customers with the Diamond T Coal Truck. The kit includes a resin body, frame and cab, metal wheels and decals. From Magnuson Models.

439-932 7.98

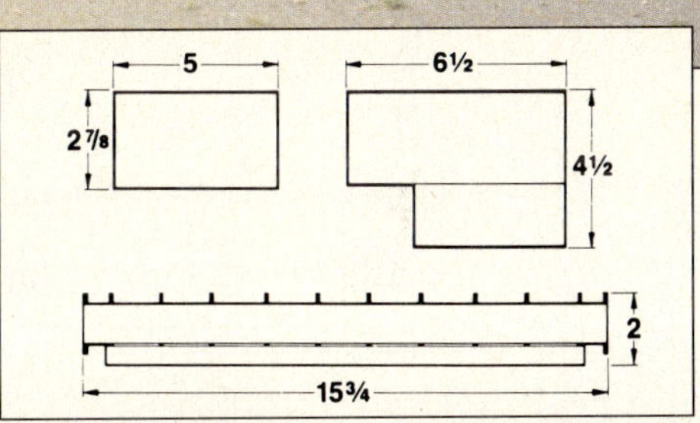

36' 50-TON HOPPERS

Move coal direct from the mine to the coal yard with Walthers 50-Ton Two-Bay Hoppers, available in a variety of roadnames, including a special limited run of Peabody Short Line cars. See the Freight Cars section for more details.

WORKMEN FIGURE SET

Bring your coal yard to life with this set of six prepainted figures, molded in various poses. From Preiser.

590-10036 8.99

COAL & ACCESSORIES

See the Scenery section for coal, ground cover and other details to finish your coal yard scene.

STEAM/DIESEL ERA BILLBOARDS

These billboards make great roof-top details for buildings like O.L. King & Sons. This set includes three billboards, plus 12 full-color signs from the 1950's and 60's. From the Cornerstone Series.

933-3103 8.98

MEDUSA CEMENT COMPANY

Hoppers full of powdered cement arrive at the Medusa Cement Company, ready to be unloaded into giant storage silos before being transported to local customers. Cement distribution plants are vital to the construction industry, providing the bulk cement used to make concrete. This kit makes a great addition to a growing industrial district, with its eight tall storage silos, conveyor tower and rail car unloading shed. Other details include separate roll-up doors on the ends of the building for truck loading, plus a variety of separate roof-top details, including piping, railing and dust collectors. To create a larger structure, use the Cornerstone Series Add-On Silos (933-3023).

933-3019 29.98

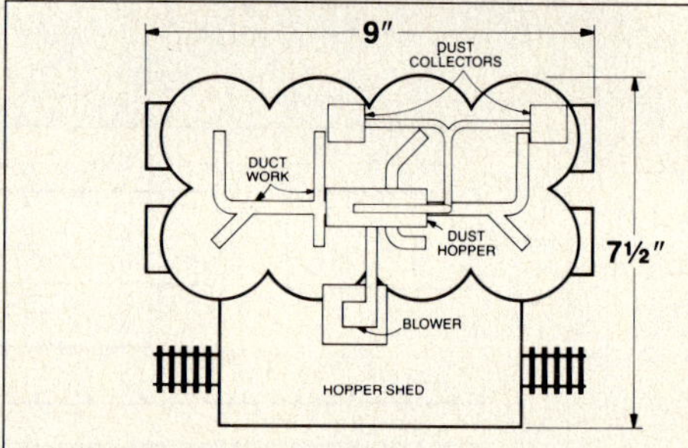

ACCESSORIES

HOPPERS & BOX CARS

Deliver bulk cement in Walthers Two-Bay Cement Covered Hoppers. To ship out bagged cement, use Walthers 40' Steel Box Cars, available in a number of styles and roadnames.

CHAIN-LINK FENCE

Secure the area around your cement company with this chain-link fence kit. Includes styrene parts for poles, gates and other details, plus a separate piece of chain-link material. From the Cornerstone Series.

933-3125 9.98

CEMENT TRUCK

Serve local cement customers with this custom cement truck! The kit features a detailed resin body and cab, cast-metal wheels and decals. From Magnuson Models.

439-938 9.98

ELECTRIC UTILITY POLE SET

Facilities like Medusa Cement need a steady supply of electricity for conveyors, dust collectors, lighting and more. This set includes 24 easy-to-assemble power poles, tranformers, insulators, nonilluminated street lights and realistic "wire." From the Cornerstone Series.

933-3101 9.98

ALLIED RAIL REBUILDERS

As more and more railroads turn to private firms for repair and maintenance work, companies like Allied Rail Rebuilders have become common sights across the country. Performing everything from paint jobs to complete rebuilds, these shops are often housed in older buildings that have been refurbished to meet the needs of the new owners. Allied Rail Rebuilders captures the realism of these prototypes in a size that works on most layouts, and comes with an EMD 567 prime mover, separate roof vents, interior trusses and doors and windows. With appropriate details, it can also be used for other types of heavy industry.

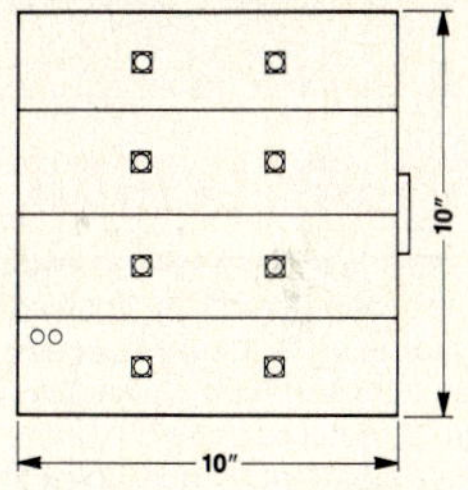

933-3016   24.98

ACCESSORIES

GENERAL STEEL CASTINGS "COMMONWEALTH" FLAT CARS

Finally, a correct version of this widely used flat car! Perfect for layouts from the 1950's to today, the easy-to-build Walthers model is four kits in one - parts are included to build a standard car, early or late piggyback version, or a bulkhead flat. See the Freight Cars section for complete details on these cars.

WORKMEN FIGURE SET

With the rebuilding business booming, you'll need plenty of employees on your payroll. This set includes six prepainted figures, molded in various poses. From Preiser.

590-10036   9.99

EMD 567 PRIME MOVER

From 1938 to 1966, the 567 was used in all types of EMD locos, from switchers to high-speed passenger power. Many are being rebuilt and still going strong today. This styrene kit is easy to build, and makes a great detail out on the shop floor or as a flat car load. From the Cornerstone Series.

933-3119   3.98

OIL DRUM & FIGURE SET

A facility like Allied Rail Rebuilders gets everything from lube oil to paint in 55-gallon drums. This set includes 36 drums and three painted figures, plus a hand truck. From the Cornerstone Series.

933-3100   9.98

FLATBED TRUCK

Haul machinery and other supplies aboard this rugged flatbed! The kit includes a resin cab. frame and flatbed, cast-metal wheels and decals. From Magnuson Models.

439-935   7.98

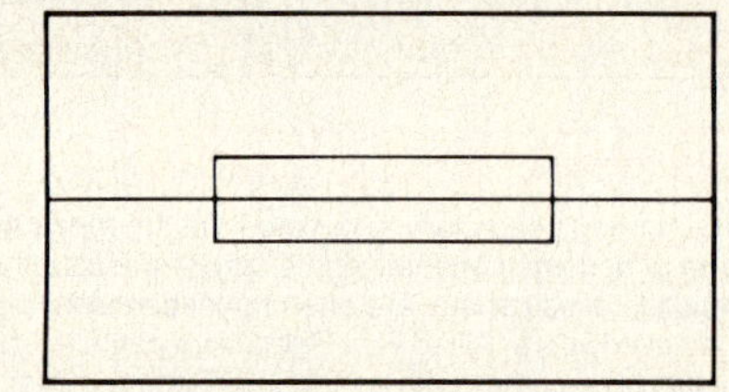

AMERICAN MILLWORK COMPANY

The roar of power tools and the smell of sawdust fill the air at the busy American Millwork Company. Producing building materials and wood products, businesses like this one are important customers for railroads. This brick factory building is typical of structures built since the early 1900's to house all types of small industries, and many are still in use today. The large windows allow plenty of natural lighting and make it easy to showcase interior details. The kit features separate doors and windows, a loading dock and overhead crane to handle freight shipments, a roof-mounted dust collector, plus four different end panels.
933-3008 24.98

12¾ x 7 x 5½"

ACCESSORIES

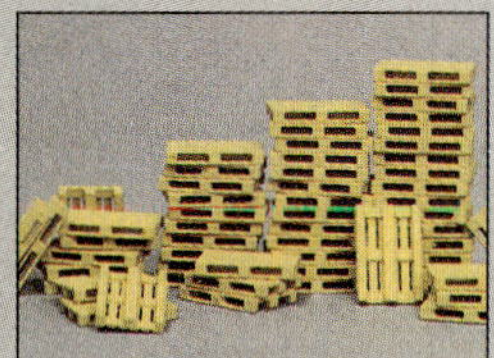

PALLETS

Pallets are a common sight around any millwork. This set includes 60 one-piece pallets molded in a realistic wood color. From Preiser.
590-17104 9.99

40' BOX CARS

Transport raw materials and finished products produced by your millwork in Walthers 40' Box Cars. Available in a variety of body styles and roadnames, the models are ideal for steam- or diesel-era scenes. See the Freight Cars section for complete details on these cars.

DELIVERY TRUCK

Heavy loads won't be a problem for this box delivery truck. The kit features a resin body, cast-metal wheels and decals for the American Millwork Company and other businesses. From Magnuson Models.
439-926 7.98

FREIGHT LOAD SET

Here's everything you need to superdetail your millwork in one set! Includes pallets, crates, machinery (band saw, table saw, joiner, drill presses), barrels, hand trucks, ladders and more. Over 140 pieces. From Faller.
272-588 8.49

LUMBER SET

Rough-cut wood, finished boards, stacked lumber - all ready to be cut, planed and sanded at your millwork. From Faller.
272-589 8.49

CENTRAL GAS & SUPPLY

Propane distribution facilities are common throughout the country, receiving bulk shipments by rail and truck. Because propane can be converted to a liquid under pressure and low temperature, it is easily shipped by rail. Propane or "bottled gas" has a variety of uses, including heating homes and industries, and powering trucks and buses. Besides propane, facilities like this also handle anhydrous ammonia, which is used in agriculture as a fertilizer. This kit is similar to dealerships served by railroads from coast to coast, with an office, tanks and other details that can be arranged to fit available space on your layout. For added realism, smaller tanks and bottles are also included.

933-3011 19.98

ACCESSORIES

65' TANK CARS

Deliver bulk shipments of propane or anhydrous ammonia with Walthers 65' Tank Cars. For more information on these models, see the Freight Cars section.

CHAIN-LINK FENCE

Fence in propane bottles and tanks with this kit, which includes styrene parts for poles, gates and other details, plus a separate piece of chain-link material. From the Cornerstone Series.

933-3125 9.98

DELIVERY TANK TRUCK

To make local propane and anhydrous ammonia deliveries, build a fleet of Delivery Tank Trucks! This kit features a resin cab, one-piece tank body and decals. From Magnuson Models.

439-934 7.98

LPG DECAL SET

This set features additional lettering to customize the storage tanks in the Central Gas & Supply kit, along with the Magnuson Models Delivery Tank Truck. Names include AmeriGas, Thermogas, Suburban Propane and more. From the Cornerstone Series.

933-3111 4.98

ANHYDROUS AMMONIA DECAL SET

Turn Central Gas & Supply into an anhydrous ammonia dealership wtih this custom decal set. Features lettering for storage tanks and the Magnuson Models Delivery Tank Truck. From the Cornerstone Series.

933-3112 4.98

GOLDEN VALLEY CANNING COMPANY

Railroads play a big part in putting food on the tables of Americans each and every day. Canned and frozen foods move in bulk from regional operations like the Golden Valley Canning Company to cities around the country, where they are transported to local stores for sale. Canneries can be found in small towns and large cities, producing everything from fruits and vegetables to meats, jellies and sauces. This kit comes with everything needed to create an authentic steam- or diesel-era cannery, including a main canning building, boiler house, smokestack, steam pipes, roof-top water tank and separate windows and doors.

933-3018 24.98

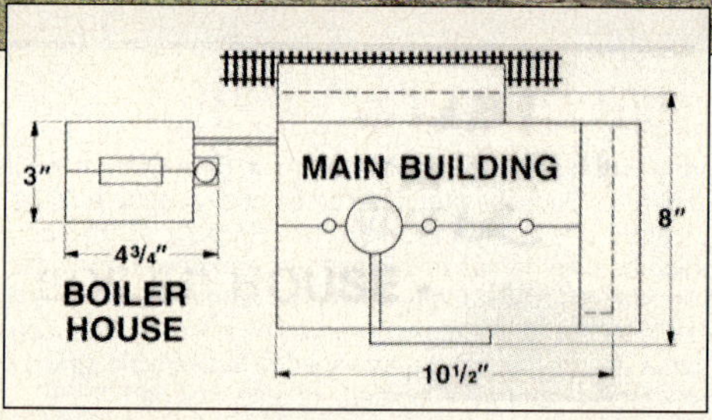

ACCESSORIES

BOX CARS & REEFERS

Walthers offers a variety of freight cars to model the operations of a busy canning facility. 40' Wood or Steel Reefers and Box Cars are perfect for steam-era scenes. For a modern plant, Walthers 50' RBL Insulated Box Cars will be right at home rolling in and out of your cannery siding

STAKE TRUCK

Hauling fruit and vegetables from field to factory, stake trucks are common around farms and canneries. This kit includes a resin body, cast-metal wheels and decals. From Magnuson Models.

439-937 7.98

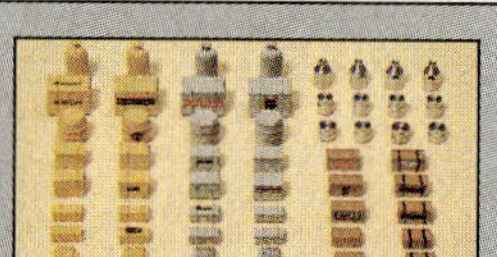

CARGO SET

Great for freight car loads or interior or exterior details, this set includes boxes, barrels, sacks, milk cans, labels and more. From Preiser.

590-17100 9.99

FREIGHT LOAD SET WITH FORKLIFT

No cannery is complete without this kit, which includes pallet jacks, a forklift, oil drums, pallets, boxes and carts. From Kibri.

405-9458 18.49

PALLETS

Stack boxes of canned and frozen goods produced by your cannery on these dturdy pallets. This set includes 60 pallets, molded in a realistic wood color. From Preiser.

590-17104 9.99

BROOK HILL FARM DAIRY

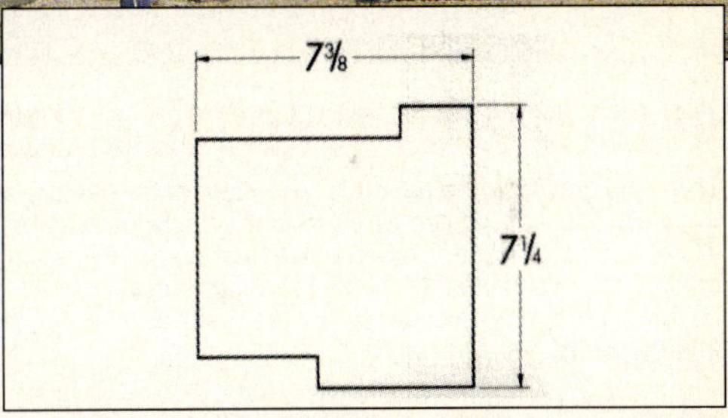

Dairy plants like Brook Hill Farm can still be seen along many railroad lines, receiving raw milk by rail and from local farms. The dairies produce milk, cream and other products, which are then shipped by rail and truck to nearby cities. This kit is based on a structure which once stood near Genesee Depot, Wisconsin, on the Milwaukee Road line. The sturdy three-story building comes with loading docks, large brick smokestack, roof-top elevator housing and other details. Adaptable to many eras, it can easily be converted to other types of manufacturing plants, too.

933-3010 24.98

ACCESSORIES

DAIRY REEFERS

To move products in and out of your new dairy, look in the Freight Cars section for Walthers 40' Wood-Bodied Reefers, specially lettered for Borden's, Carnation Milk, Brook Hill Farm Dairy and other popular dairy brands.

ELECTRIC UTILITY POLE SET

Electricity is vital to a dairy's operations. This electric pole set includes 24 easy-to-assemble power poles, transformers, insulators, nonilluminated street lights and realistic "wire." From the Cornerstone Series.

933-3101 9.98

DAIRY & FOOD BILLBOARDS

These billboards offer a great way to advertise the products your dairy produces. The kit includes full-color signs for twelve different food and dairy products, three easy-to-assemble billboards and nonilluminated light fixtures. From the Cornerstone Series.

933-3106 8.98

DIVCO MILK TRUCK

Handle local milk deliveries with the Divco Milk Truck kit, which includes parts for two trucks, plus full-color decals for different dairies.

439-917 7.98

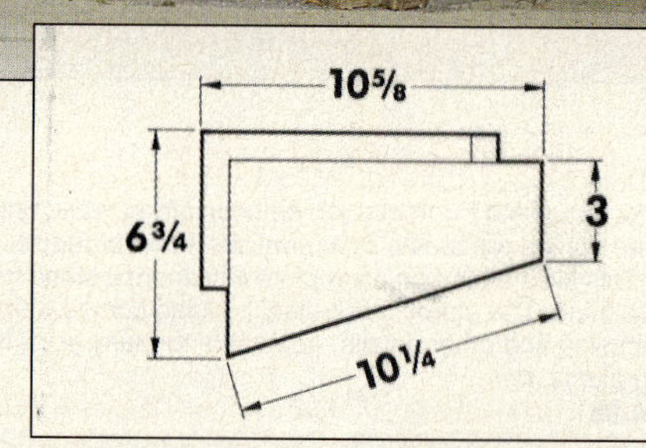

RELIABLE WAREHOUSE & STORAGE

The rapid growth of the railroads at the turn of the century attracted many industries to America's right-of-ways. Businesses located as close to the tracks as possible, often building on oddly shaped lots. Reliable Warehouse & Storage is representative of these unique structures, which are still common in most cities and towns. The triangular-shaped building is ideally suited for layout corners or diverging tracks, and features a roof-top water tower, access stairway, chimney and loading dock.

933-3014 24.98

ACCESSORIES

BOX CARS & REEFERS

See the Freight Cars section for a complete selection of rolling stock to serve Reliable Warehouse & Storage, including Walthers 40' Steel Box Cars, Waffle-Side Box Cars and more.

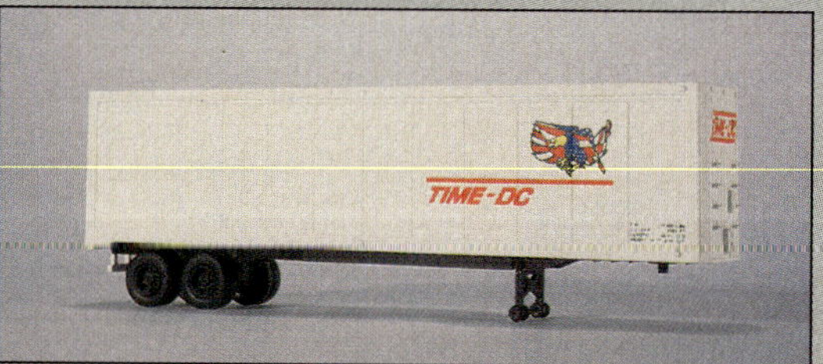

SEMI TRACTORS & TRAILERS

To deliver shipments to local customers, assemble a fleet of Magnuson Models Semi Tractors and Walthers 32, 40' and 48' Trailers.

FREIGHT LOAD SET WITH FORKLIFT

Superdetailing your new structure is easy with this kit, which includes pallet jacks, a forklift, oil drums, pallets, boxes and carts. From Kibri.

405-9458 18.49

WORKMEN FIGURE SET

Make your scene come to life with this set of six prepainted figures, molded in various poses. From Preiser.

590-10036 9.99

WATER STREET FREIGHT TERMINAL

Freight shipments are waiting for local deliveries on the siding at the Water Street Freight Terminal. Freight terminals were once essential to railroad operations, handling less-than-carload lot (lcl) freight shipments. Loads arrived in box cars or refrigerated cars and were transferred to a fleet of trucks for local delivery. Each railroad serving a community had its own freight terminal, usually located near the main passenger station or classification yard. This detailed structure features a large office building, freight house with loading docks to service freight cars and trucks, plus an assortment of crates, barrels and pallets.

933-3009 24.98

ACCESSORIES

40' BOX CARS & REEFERS

To handle increased freight traffic on your layout, see the Freight Cars section for a complete selection of box cars and reefers available from Walthers, including a 40' All-Steel Reefer lettered for Railway Express Agency.

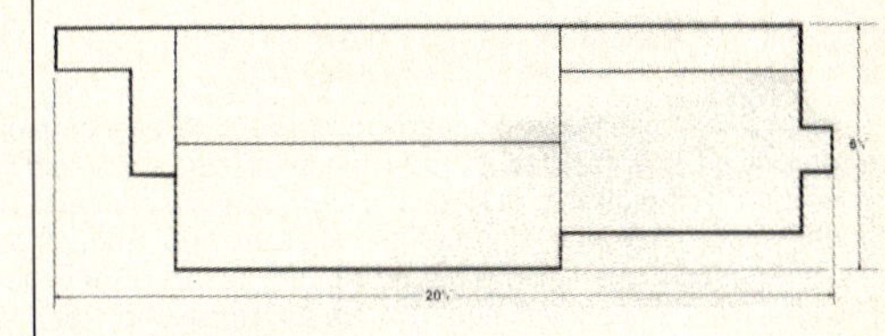

REA DELIVERY TRUCK

You'll need plenty of delivery trucks to service local freight customers. This kit features a one-piece body with details molded in place and separate metal wheels. Decals, including the colorful REA logos, are also provided. From Magnuson Models.

439-923 7.98

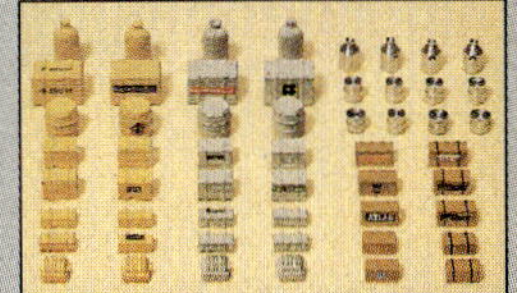

CARGO SET

Keep your freight terminal full with this assortment of boxes, barrels, sacks, milk cans, labels and more. From Preiser.

590-17100 9.99

FREIGHT LOAD SET WITH FORKLIFT

Load up on details for your freight house with this kit, which includes pallet jacks, a forklift, oil drums, pallets, boxes and carts. From Kibri.

405-9458 18.49

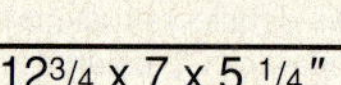

2-STALL ENGINE HOUSE

Typical of engine houses used by many railroads to serve their motive power, this authentic brick engine house is modeled after facilities constructed in the steam era and still in use today. Inside, inspections and light repairs are completed on all types of locos and freight cars. This kit is detailed with moveable doors, oil drums, driver tires, separate windows and a pillar crane. Enough parts are included to extend one track completely through the building. Engines or cars up to 11-5/8" long can be stored inside. For a bigger repair shop, several kits can be combined to serve as a main shop for a shortline or industrial road.
933-3007 24.98

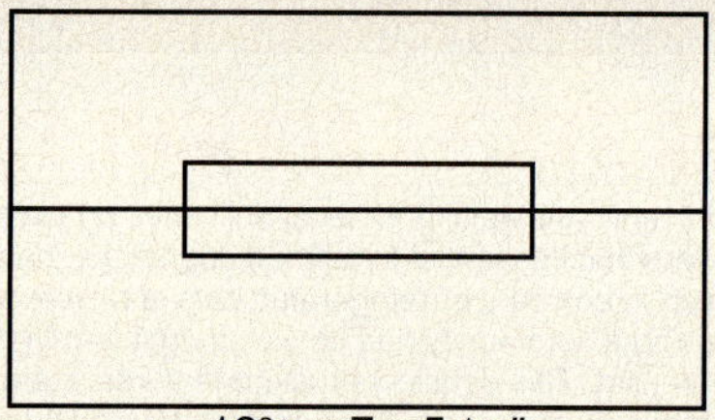

12³/₄ x 7 x 5 ¹/₄"

ACCESSORIES

OVERHEAD TRAVELING CRANE

Heavy overhead cranes like this one were often installed inside engine houses or just outside to lift traction motors, prime movers, car underframes or scrap. This kit includes a positionable bridge and trolley, operator's cab, hook and electro-magnet. From the Cornerstone Series.
933-3102 10.98

PANEL TRUCK

Keep your mechanical department ready for the road with this Panel Truck! The kit features parts for two trucks, including resin bodies, cast-metal wheels and ladders, plus decals for maintenance-of-way, public utilities and more. From Magnuson Models.
439-928 7.98

FIGURES

No engine house scene is complete without figures, like the popular Railroad Crew (590-10017, 9.99) and Railroad Employees (590-10018, 9.99) figure sets. From Preiser.

40' STEEL GONDOLA

This limited-edition gondola comes lettered for maintenance-of-way service and includes a custom scrap load. You'll find additional Walthers Gondolas listed in the Freight Cars section.
932-5620 7.98

DOUBLE-TRACK TRUSS BRIDGE

The truss-type bridge is among the most common used for railroad construction. Early designs date back to the 1820's, when all-wood construction was the standard. As trains and locomotives became heavier, cast-iron parts were used with the wooden trusses. Wrought iron was later used for its added strength, and with the development of the Bessemer process in 1855, steel bridges could be constructed. This model is based on a simple two-track truss bridge, typical of steel bridges found on railroads throughout North America. The kit includes trusses, chords and bridge shoes, plus safety sign and graffiti decals.

933-3012   21.98

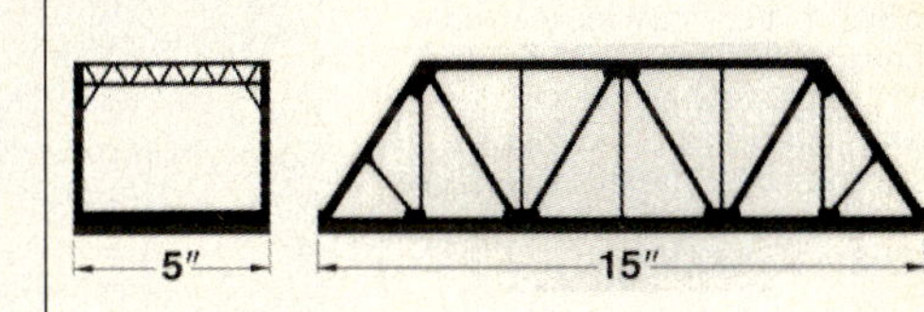

ACCESSORIES

WING WALLS

For realistic detail, you can add these Wing Walls, which simulate the retaining walls used with abutments on many bridges. The kit includes two one-piece resin wings, each measuring 3-3/8" high and 3-3/4" wide at the base. From Magnuson Models.

439-560   4.49

BRIDGE ABUTMENT

This abutment makes bridge installation a snap. Matching the width of the bridge, the one-piece casting is 3-3/8" high, allowing enough clearance for trains to be run underneath. One kit is required to do each end of the bridge. From Magnuson Models.

439-558   6.98

BRIDGE TRACK

Roll trains across your new truss bridge with the Code 83 Bridge Track. Designed especially for this bridge, the single track section features nickel-silver rails, bridge ties and inside guard rails with Code 70 rail. Length: 19-11/16". From Walthers.

948-899   14.98

BRIDGE PIER

To create a longer bridge, additional bridge kits can be combined to produce a longer span, which can be supported with this Bridge Pier. The one-piece casting has a height of 3-3/8" (matching the height of the Bridge Abutment and Wings), a base width of 5-3/8" and a thickness of approximately 1-1/8" at the base. (Not pictured).

439-559   11.98

OVERHEAD TRAVELING CRANE

Since the early 1900's, overhead traveling cranes have been used wherever heavy equipment or materials need to be moved over an extensive area. This kit represents a heavy-duty crane with a capacity of approximately 25 tons, which could be used at manufacturing plants, scrapyards, steel mills and railroad shops. Separate I beams and supports give the model a rugged look, and the bridge and covered motor housing can be positioned to create a custom scene. An operator's cab with window "glass," hoist hooks and an electromagnet are also included. Cranes like this one are ideal for handling steel coil loads in conjunction with Walthers 55' Cushion Coil Cars, which are featured in the Freight Cars section.
933-3102   10.98

DUST COLLECTOR KIT

Easily spotted on the rooftops of all types of industrial buildings, dust collectors are a must for keeping shops and equipment clean. This easy-to-build styrene kit includes parts for two dust collectors with handling pipes, molded in a realistic gray color.
933-3113   4.98

ELECTRIC UTILITY POLE SET

Seen along railroads and highways across the country, utility poles have been used to carry electricity to homes, businesses and factories since the early 1900's. Unlike phone poles, which are smaller, power poles stand about 30 to 35' tall and have a tapered shape. This kit includes parts for 24 poles, plus four residential and four insulated transformers, extra insulators, crossarms, eight street lights (nonilluminated), and for those who want a superdetailed scene, a roll of fine nylon thread for "wire."
933-3101   9.98

WELCOME TO MAIN STREET USA

Every town has a Main Street USA. And everyone has memories of the "Main Street" in his or her hometown. It may be the ice cream parlor where you had your first triple-scoop cone, or the dime store that you rode your bike to on Saturdays for baseball cards. Now you can recapture the excitement and nostalgia of Main Street on your layout with the "Main Street USA" collection from the Cornerstone Series.

Each kit is easy to build, with styrene parts molded in colors, styrene roof and molded styrene parts (replacing cast-metal details formerly in some kits). Trim, windows and doors are molded in place for easy assembly. Plus, new decals for each kit include a number of business names, so you can model several versions of the same kit.

MERCHANT'S ROW I

City modeling made easy! This kit brings together five different stores in one structure, at a dynamite price.
Dimensions: 11 x 5 x 4"
933-3028 24.98

INTERSTATE FUEL & OIL GAS STATION

Deliver fuel from Interstate Fuel & Oil to this gas station, bearing the same name as the Cornerstone Series bulk oil distributor. The model comes with a covered service island with pumps, highway sign, service bays and air pump.
Dimensions: 9-1/4 x 7-3/4 x 1-3/4"
933-3035 9.98

WESTERN AVENUE FIRE STATION

A superdetailer's delight! This new kit is similar to stations throughout the country that were built in the early 1900's and later upgraded for use with more modern equipment. Includes a special set of fire station decals.
Dimensions: 4-1/4 x 6-3/4 x 5-3/4"
933-3037   9.98

ADAM'S RIBS RESTAURANT

From the turn of the century to the present, small buildings like this have been an integral part of many neighborhoods. The kit is ideal for any busy street corner and includes a distinctive corner tower/entry way.
Dimensions: 5-1/2 x 3 x 6"
933-3034   9.98

NEIGHBORHOOD FOOD MART

This double store-front can be home to one large or two small businesses. The kit fits city or small town scenes and includes various sheds and a base plate.
Dimensions: 5 x 8-1/4 x 4"
933-3033   9.98

WHITE TOWER RESTAURANT

Can we take your order for this classic hamburger stand? The original White Tower Restaurants were built in the 1930's, springing up from Boston to Los Angeles.
Dimensions: 4-5/8 x 3 x 2-7/8"
933-3030   14.98

DON'S SHOE STORE

Here's a building with a lot of sole! Graceful curved windows and a recessed doorway make Don's Shoe Store a favorite for downtown districts.
Dimensions: 2-1/2 x 3-1/2 x 3-3/8"
933-3000   9.98

GEMINI BUILDING

It's a modeling twin bill - two duplicate storefronts make up the marvelous Gemini Building. Complete with chimney, the kit will look great in any steam- or diesel-era city scene.
Dimensions: 4-1/4 x 3-5/8 x 3-3/8"
933-3001   9.98

BILL'S GLASS SHOP

This three-story brick building has plenty of space for a growing HO Scale business. The upper floors can be rented out for additional offices or apartments.
Dimensions: 3 x 4 x 4-3/8"
933-3002   9.98

WALLSCHLAGER MOTORS

You can almost hear the salesman hawking those new cars down at Wallschlager Motors. You'll love the large windows of this building, which are great for showing off interior details.
Dimensions: 5-1/4 x 5 x 3-1/2"
933-3004   9.98

LEVIATHAN MANUFACTURING

Good things come in small packages - like Leviathan Manufacturing. This sturdy little building has a roll-up door molded in place and includes ventilators for the roof.
Dimensions: 3-1/2 x 1-5/8 x 2-1/2"
933-3003   9.98

UNITED TRUCKING TRANSFER TERMINAL

Fill up those small spaces with this attractive freight terminal. The kit has roll-up doors molded into the sidewalls to serve box cars or trucks.
Dimensions: 2-5/8 x 6 x 3-3/8"
933-3005   9.98

Magnuson Models ™
Manufactured by
Wm. K. WALTHERS, Inc.

HO SCALE (1/87)
CRAFT TRAIN KITS

These cast resin structures are suitable for any era layout. Kits are composed of one piece wall sections (for ease of assembly), with detailed architectural components already cast in place. Complete instructions are included.

VICTORIA FALLS SERIES

Victoria Falls Hotel
439-505   49.98
9-1/4 × 4-1/2″   23.5 × 11.4 cm
Check out the fine detail on the Victoria Falls Hotel! The classically designed hotel with ornate trim detail offers a good night's rest to salesmen, train personnel and other business-men traveling through Victoria Falls.

FIRE YOUR IMAGINATION WITH MAGNUSON

Pride of the Victoria Falls Fire Department, this charming structure is typical of fire stations built in the late 19th century. With minor remodeling to accom-odate modern apparatus, similar prototypes are still serving their com-munities.

439-547   6-3/4 × 4-3/8″   16.8 × 11.2 cm   39.98

WATER DEPARTMENT

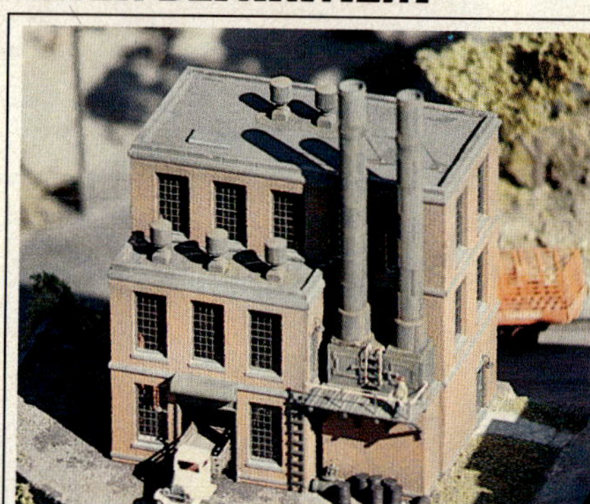

This three story brick public utilities build-ing of the 30's and 40's includes a small two story brick annex, twin boiler-plate stacks, silk-screened windows and cast metal plat-form supports, stan-chions, ladder, lampshades, ven-tilators and more.

439-527   49.98
4-1/2 × 5-3/4″
11.4 × 14.8 cm

Wischer's Washer Company
439-523   49.98
5-1/8 × 9-1/4″
13.2 × 23.5 cm
Wischer's Washer Company is a perfect building for any HO industrial scene! The rugged brick building contains a water tower, roof stairwell shed, large chimney, stone steps and cast metal platforms, stairs, ladders and hoist pulley.

Freight Station/ REA Office
439-515   49.98
11 × 6-1/4″   28 × 16 cm

MERCHANT'S ROW MAKES YOUR CITY GROW

Each kit is highly detailed, with all door and window frames cast in place. A variety of extra details such as chimneys, downspouts, sidewalks and more are included in each kit. Less figures, signs and vehicles.

439-545   Merchant's Row 3   9 × 5″   22 × 12.8 cm   49.98
These three stores can be used to model a small street scene, or combined with kits 1 and 2 to model a complete city block.

439-534   Merchant's Row   11 × 5″   28 × 12.6 cm   49.98
This easy-to-build kit brings you five different stores in on structure, with a detailed one-piece roof.

Magnuson Models ™
Manufactured by **Wm. K. WALTHERS, Inc.**

HO SCALE (1/87) CRAFT TRAIN KITS

These cast resin structures are suitable for any era layout. Kits are composed of one piece wall sections (for ease of assembly), with detailed architectural components already cast in place. Complete instructions are included.

CITY BUILDINGS

FILL YOUR LAYOUT WITH MODEL RAILROADING HISTORY!

Walthers Trains   Hotel

Badger Brush Co Factory

Add a little model railroading history to your layout with "1245 North Water Street"!

Built as double stores in 1890, this Victorian structure may have been a "hotel" during the Mayor Rose "anything goes" administration in Milwaukee.

Walthers purchased the building in 1958, and from 1958 through 1969, it was the home of Walthers trains and the birthplace of Walthers wholesale business.

In 1969, the building was sold to the Yellow Cab Company in Milwaukee. In the interim, it was rented to the "Theatre X", an experimental theatre group sponsored by the University of Wisconsin-Milwaukee.

The fading sign, "Home of Walthers Model Trains" is still visible on the south side of the building.

The easy-to-build structure features fully detailed, one-piece polyester castings with all the architectural components cast in place, including large bay windows. A decal sheet featuring signs for "Walthers Model Trains", "E. Water St. Hotel", "H2O Street Theatre" & "Badger Brush Company" is also included.

An illustrated booklet is provided with the kit and describes the building's colorful history.

439-542   1245 N Water Street   49.98

CANDY FACTORY

439-556   Brach's Candy Factory   49.98
10 x 5-1/8 x 7"   25.4 x 13 x 17.8 cm

You'll need extra sidings to handle the business this impressive factory building will generate on your layout. It's a great destination for loads of sugar in Airslide® hoppers or corn syrup in Funnel-Flow® tankers, too! Window frames, doors and other details are molded in place and the kit has a one-piece roof for faster, easy construction. Full-color sign decals and printed acetate windows are also provided.

POWERHOUSES

The Edison Street Powerhouse
439-550   39.98
4 x 8"   10 x 20 cm

Generating steam and electricity, powerhouses were commonly located near factories and railroad shops. This one-story building includes a large one-piece smokestack (with no seam to hide!), that stands 9-1/2" tall.

(not illustrated)
439-303 Piggyback Ramp   4.98
439-301 Sidewalks   pkg(4) 7.95
9-1/2 x 1"

Powerhouse
439-519
59.98
12-1/2 × 13"
31.8 × 33 cm

HO SCALE (1/87)   EASY-TO-BUILD KITS

Kits consist of prototypically colored plastic parts, printed signs and details where applicable, and fully illustrated, step-by-step detailed instructions.

STATIONS & PLATFORMS

STATION "POSTHALDE"

This half-timbered station building is ideal for that rural branch line. The model is from the "Junior" series and is designed for easy construction.

272-1252   29.99

272-181   Covered Platform   17.99
13 x 3-1/2"   33.8 x 9.2 cm
Platform with passenger exit.
Suitable for all track.

272-189   Covered Platform   14.99
11-1/2 x 2-1/4"   29.5 x 5.3 cm
Covered platform with track lowering. Suitable for all track.

STATION "THALBACH"

Finish your small town in minutes with this fully assembled station building. Model is complete with freight shed and loading dock.

272-1212   34.49

FALLER

Imported from Germany and marketed by WALTHERS

HO SCALE (1/87)   EASY-TO-BUILD KITS

Kits consist of prototypically colored plastic parts, printed signs and details where applicable, and fully illustrated, step-by-step detailed instructions.

STATIONS & PLATFORMS

"BONN" PASSENGER STATION

This classic station is typical of those found in large cities around the world and is based on the prototype at Bonn, West Germany. To complete the scene, add several Passenger Station Canopy kits (272-180), which are patterned after the actual Bonn train shed.

272-113	27-1/2 x 6-1/4"	70 x 16 cm	94.99

272-190	Roofed Platform	11.99
	7-1/8 x 2-7/8" 18 x 7.2 cm	

272-188 Glass Train Shed w/Accessories 21.49
19-1/4 x 2-1/8"   48.8 x 5.3 cm

272-180	Passenger Station Canopy, Bonn	34.99
	11-7/8 x 7" 30.2 x 17.8 cm	
272-183	Platform Lighting for #180	13.49

"MITTELSTADT" PASSENGER STATION

This nicely sized passenger depot is ideal for the larger town or city. It can easily be adapted to a layout or module. Just add a Faller platform and other accessories for a superdetailed scene!

272-115	17-1/2 x 6-1/4"	44.6 x 16 cm	59.99

HO SCALE (1/87)   EASY-TO-BUILD KITS

Kits consist of prototypically colored plastic parts, printed signs and details where applicable, and fully illustrated, step-by-step detailed instructions.

STATIONS & PLATFORMS (continued)

OLD FREIGHT HOUSE

A must for any station scene, the freight house received small shipments of freight for local customers. This detailed brick building is easily adapted to American layouts by leaving off some of the trim.

272-153   43.99
13-7/8 x 5-7/8″
35.3 x 14.8 cm

272-91   Wayside Station   10.49
4-7/8 x 3-3/16″   12.4 x 8.1 cm

272-154   Freight Depot   21.49
8-1/4 x 3-7/16″   21 x 8.8 cm

272-155   Freight Station   18.99
7-9/16 x 4-1/4″   19.2 x 10.8 cm

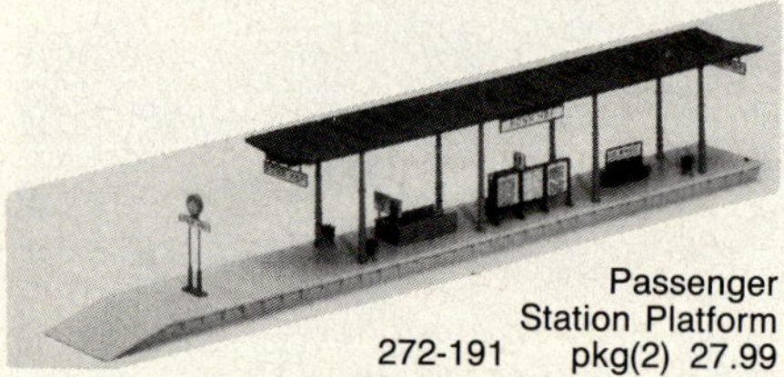

Passenger Station Platform
272-191   pkg(2) 27.99
11-7/8 x 1-7/8″   30.2 x 4.8 cm

LIMITED QUANTITIES AVAILABLE

"LENGMOOS" PASSENGER STATION

Bring rail service to a small town on your layout with this simple station! Constructed of stucco and wood siding, the Alpine style station includes a covered platform and freight shed.

272-100   41.99
12 x 6-7/8″   30.6 x 17.5 cm

"FRIEDRICHSHOHE" PASSENGER STATION
with Covered Platfrom and Built-on Freight Depot

This depot is typical of structures built to serve larger towns. The building features a passenger waiting room, a freight station and living quarters for the agent.

272-110   16 x 6″   40.7 x 15.6 cm   45.99

FALLER

Imported from Germany and marketed by **WALTHERS**

HO SCALE (1/87)   EASY-TO-BUILD KITS

Kits consist of prototypically colored plastic parts, printed signs and details where applicable, and fully illustrated, step-by-step detailed instructions.

STATIONS & PLATFORMS (continued)

MAINLINE STATION

This distinctive station will brighten any mainline setting. The model features lots of details, including flower boxes! A matching freight station (#272-155) is available separately for building a complete station scene.

272-112   41.99
10 x 5"   25.5 x 13 cm

272-1109   Covered Platform   19.49
10-3/16 x 1-15/16"   26 x 5 cm

This covered platform is the perfect addition to a growing station! The model is based on a typical platform seen throughout Europe.

"Talheim" Rural Station
272-105   26.99
9-7/16 x 4-1/2"
23.9 x 11.5 cm

272-187   Glass Covered Platform   14.99
19-1/4 x 2-1/8"   48.8 x 5.3 cm

"Altenstein" Station & Platform
272-102   33.99
shed has sliding doors
18-1/8 x 5-1/8"
46 x 13 cm

272-186   "Radolfzell' Passenger Bridge   22.99
9-3/16 x 8-3/4"   23.4 x 22.4 cm

272-92   Country Station   16.99
8 x 4-1/8"   20.3 x 10.4 cm

272-98   Alterode Station   28.99
11-5/8 x 5-1/4"   29.7 x 13.5 cm

FALLER

Imported from Germany and marketed by WALTHERS

HO SCALE (1/87)   EASY-TO-BUILD KITS

Kits consist of prototypically colored plastic parts, printed signs and details where applicable, and fully illustrated, step-by-step detailed instructions.

STATIONS & PLATFORMS (continued)

ST. JULIEN STATION
The clean lines of this modern station make it perfect for any city! A larger structure can be built by adding the annex buildings, 272-1102, available separately.

272-1101   7-7/8 x 4"   20.5 x 20 cm   35.49

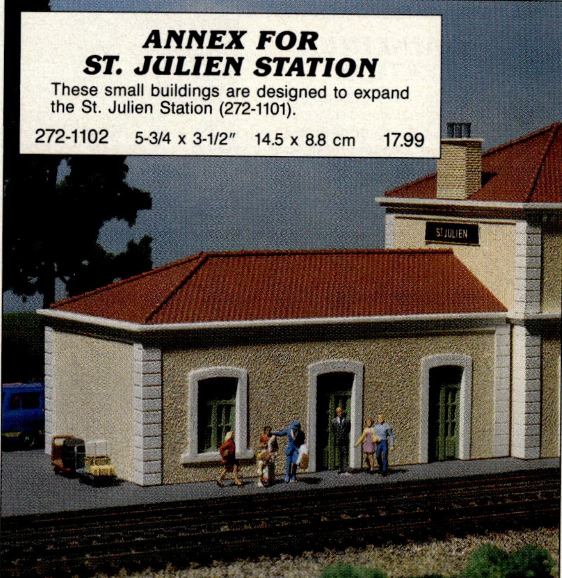

ANNEX FOR ST. JULIEN STATION
These small buildings are designed to expand the St. Julien Station (272-1101).

272-1102   5-3/4 x 3-1/2"   14.5 x 8.8 cm   17.99

272-1110   Public Shelter   4-1/2 x 2"   11.6 x 5 cm   13.49

272-107   Rural Station "Guglingen"   39.99
12-1/16 x 5-1/4"   30.8 x 13.5 cm

272-104   "Kirchbach" Station   26.99
10-3/8 x 4"   26.5 x 10.3 cm

272-192   Roofed Platform w/Accessories   11.99
17-3/4 x 1-7/8"   45 x 4.8 cm

272-182   Platform Accessories   14.99
Kit includes newsstand, hut, lamps, signs, benches, fountains, clocks, fences and many other parts.

FALLER

Imported from Germany and marketed by WALTHERS

HO SCALE (1/87)   EASY-TO-BUILD KITS

Kits consist of prototypically colored plastic parts, printed signs and details where applicable, and fully illustrated, step-by-step detailed instructions.

YARD & EQUIPMENT FACILITIES

TWO-STALL ENGINE HOUSE

For use as electric or diesel engine shed. Motor not included for mechanical door operation. Manual operation is possible.

| 272-156 | 15-3/4 x 6-3/4 x 5-1/8"   40 x 17.2 x 13 cm | 45.99 |

SMALL SIGNAL BOX

A small signal box which can be installed between tracks.

| 272-123 | 5-3/8 x 1-7/8 x 4-7/16   13.6 x 4.7 x 11.3 cm | *NEW* 22.49 |

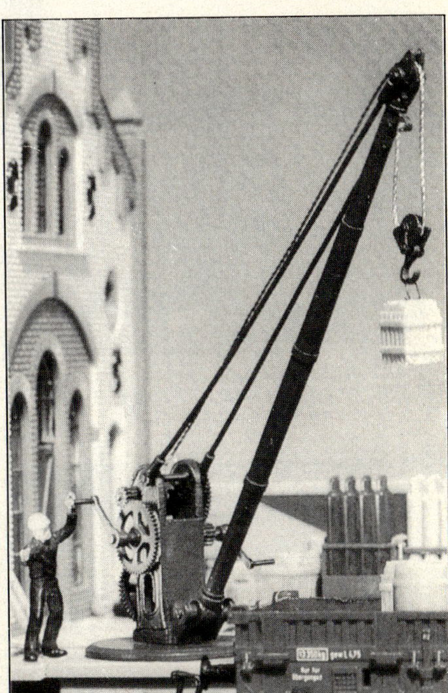

LOADING CRANE

Not operational.

| 272-129 | *NEW* 9.49 |

FALLER

Imported from Germany and marketed by WALTHERS

HO SCALE (1/87)   EASY-TO-BUILD KITS

Kits consist of prototypically colored plastic parts, printed signs and details where applicable, and fully illustrated, step-by-step detailed instructions.

YARD & EQUIPMENT FACILITIES (continued)

Engine Driver's Cabin
272-133   1-1/4 x 1-1/8"   3.2 x 3 cm   12.49

Gantry Crane (less motor)
272-163   9 x 3-1/2"   23 x 9 cm   39.99

272-157   **Diesel Fuel Facility**   27.99
8-7/8 x 4-7/8"   22.5 x 12.4 cm

272-145   **Diesel Oil Facility**   11.99
4-1/8 x 1-3/8"   10.5 x 3.5 cm

Inspection Pits
272-136   pkg(2) 22.99
13-1/2 x 5-3/4"
34.4 x 14.7 cm
Includes molded on rails, base plate with slag pit, slag wagon and slag barrow.

Freight Load
272-588   8.49

272-948   **Oil Tank**   11.99
3-3/4 x 1-11/16"   9.6 x 4.3 cm
with Gasoline Pumps and Hoses

Container Gantry Crane (dummy crane)
272-130   7-7/8 x 5-1/4"   20.2 x 13.5 cm   27.49
Two containers are included in kit

Small Shed
272-151   15.49
4-3/4 x 3"   12 x 7.6 cm

272-147   **Small Coaling Station**   19.99
8-1/8 x 3-1/8"   20.7 x 8 cm

272-635   **Drive Motor for #147**   11.99
momentary contact, turns 90°

272-164   **Overhead Crane**   15.99
5-3/8 x 1-1/4"   13.7 x 3 cm

HEATING & POWER PLANT

Power small cities on your layout with this Heating and Power plant! Always ready for coal shipments from your HO Scale railroad, the kit includes a brick boiler house and power station. For added realism, the smoke-stack can be fitted with Seuthe Steam generator #667-7 (listed in the Sound & Smoke section of this catalog).

272-982   40.49
9 x 8-1/4"   23 x 21 cm

FALLER

Imported from Germany and marketed by **WALTHERS**

HO SCALE (1/87)   EASY-TO-BUILD KITS

Kits consist of prototypically colored plastic parts, printed signs and details where applicable, and fully illustrated, step-by-step detailed instructions.

YARD & EQUIPMENT FACILITIES (continued)

GANTRY CRANE

Give heavy loads a lift with this big Gantry Crane! The kit can be built with a hook, a clamshell bucket or logging hooks. The crane cab can be rotated 360 degrees, use motor 272-629 (available separately) for remote control, or manually.

272-162   13-3/8 x 2-1/4"   34 x 5.8 cm   38.49

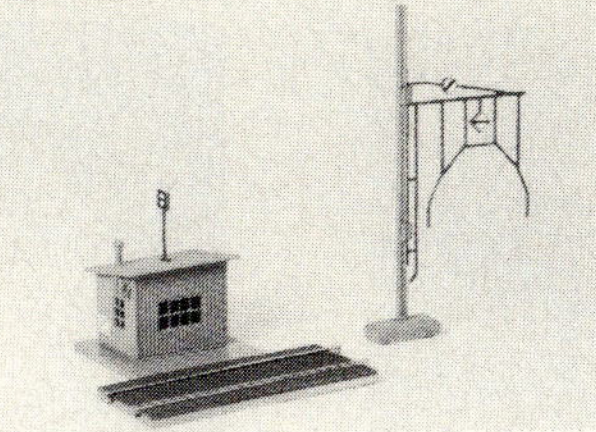

Rail Weight Bridge & Loading Gauge
272-134   12.49
3-1/4 x 3" 8.5 x 8 cm   1 x 1/2" 2.4 x 1 cm

Mittelstadt
Signal Tower
272-120   17.99
3-3/16 x 2-1/2"
8.4 x 6.4 cm

■ **LIMITED QUANTITIES AVAILABLE** ■

Signal Tower
272-121   7.49
2-3/4 x 2-1/16"
6.9 x 5.3 cm

272-167   Double Silo   21.49
3 x 6"   7.8 x 14.8 cm

272-146   Sanding Facility   21.49
6 x 2-1/8"   15.5 x 5.5 cm
1-1/2 x 1-1/2"   3.7 x 3.7 cm
Includes sanding tower, hopper sand store and sand.

Sand for #146
272-719   pkg(1oz) 2.99

272-149   Cinder Removal Facility   41.49
13-1/2 x 5-3/4"   34.4 x 14.7 cm

Includes a hoist, two swivel water cranes, two slag hoppers, base plate with slag pit, slag wagon and slag wheel barrow.

272-973   Operations Building   28.49
6-1/8 x 5-7/8"   15.5 x 14.8 cm

BACK SHOP

This shop building is perfect for heavy repairs to locos or cars. The brick structure features three stalls, large smokestack and lots of details. For a bigger repair shop, just combine a few kits!

272-159   10-3/8 x 6"   26.6 x 15 cm   38.49

FALLER

Imported from Germany and marketed by WALTHERS

HO SCALE (1/87) EASY-TO-BUILD KITS

Kits consist of prototypically colored plastic parts, printed signs and details where applicable, and fully illustrated, step-by-step detailed instructions.

YARD & EQUIPMENT FACILITIES (continued)

272-140 | Three Trackside Huts | 11.99

272-947 | Wooden Hut | 12.49
4-3/8 x 2-7/8" 11.1 x 7.2 cm

FREIGHT HOUSE

Freight houses could be found in every large yard to handle small freight shipments. Combine several of these kits and build a larger, unique structure for your layout!

272-150 | 9-3/4 x 5-5/8" 24.8 x 14.4 cm | 38.49

272-161 | 2-Stall Enginehouse | 37.49
8-1/4 x 6-1/8" 21 x 15.7 cm

(not illustrated)
272-945 | Mine Head w/Winch House | 43.99

COALING STATION

Perfect for loading coal, ore, gravel or stone, this detailed coaling tower can easily be adapted to mining operations. The kit is complete with a large gantry crane, equipped with a clamshell bucket.

272-148 | 13-3/8 x 10-3/4" 34 x 27.4 cm | 64.99

Gatekeeper's House
272-132 | 11.99
3-7/8 x 2-15/16" 9.8 x 7.5 cm

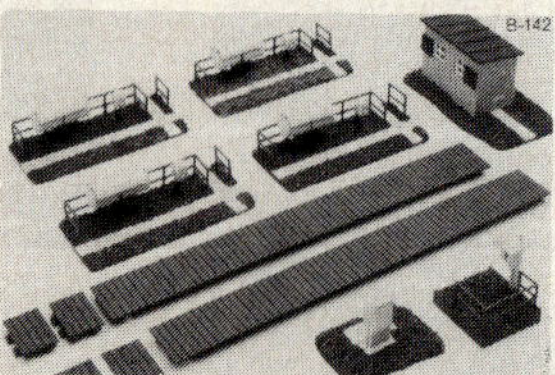

Trackside Accessories
272-142 | 17.99
Includes four gas containers to thaw up the points, hut, switch box, shanty and plank.

272-144 | Water Tower | 16.99
3-7/16 x 3-7/16" 8.7 x 8.7 cm

FALLER

Imported from Germany and marketed by **WALTHERS**

HO SCALE (1/87)   EASY-TO-BUILD KITS

Kits consist of prototypically colored plastic parts, printed signs and details where applicable, and fully illustrated, step-by-step detailed instructions.

YARD & EQUIPMENT FACILITIES (continued)

"DUDERSTADT" ENGINEHOUSE

This three-stall engine house is perfect for shortlines, or as part of a larger engine terminal. Locos up to 11" can be stored inside. The working doors can be opened or closed by hand.

272-160   12-1/4 x 7-1/4"   31 x 18.5 cm   52.49

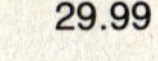

272-125   Overhead Signal Tower   29.99
7 x 6-5/8"   18 x 17 cm

272-126   Signal Tower   24.99
8-1/4 x 3-1/4"   21 x 8.4 cm

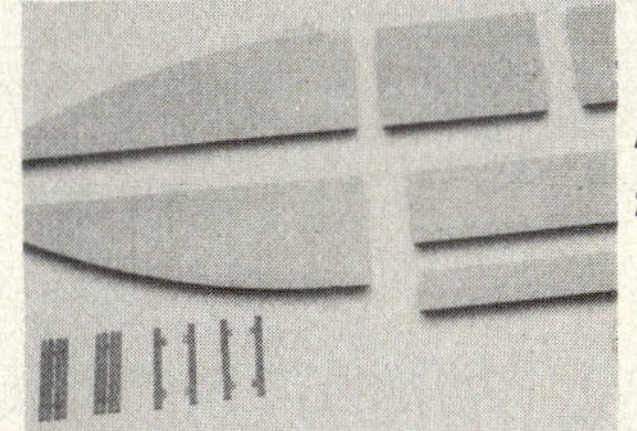

Assorted Level Platforms
272-184 14.99

272-630   Crossing w/Warning Lights   27.99

272-137   Swivel Water Spout   pkg(2) 11.49
3 x 9/16"   7.8 x 1.5 cm
Includes external heater device and two gulley covers.

COMPRESSOR HOUSING & ACCESSORIES

This small facility is used to clean flues and fireboxes on steam locos. It can easily be adapted to diesel era layouts too! A shed with compressor, sand blasting frame and fire cleaning tools with rack are included.

272-139   24.99
3-5/8 x 2-1/8"   9.4 x 5.6 cm
3 x 3-5/8"   7.6 x 9.3 cm

272-143   Water Tower   21.49
radius: 3-7/8"   10 cm
height: 9-1/2"   24.2 cm

Sanding Tower
272-138   12.49
1-3/8 x 1-3/8"   3.7 x 3.7 cm
Includes hopper and ramp.

FALLER

HO SCALE (1/87) EASY-TO-BUILD KITS
Kits consist of prototypically colored plastic parts, printed signs and details where applicable, and fully illustrated, step-by-step detailed instructions.

Imported from Germany and marketed by
WALTHERS

RURAL BUILDINGS

BLACK FOREST SAWMILL
You can almost smell the fresh sawdust around this busy mill! The rustic structure can easily be adapted to many time periods. For extra realism, an electric motor is included in kit 272-230 to power the saw and water wheel.

272-230	with Motor	58.49
272-227	less Motor	39.99

9-1/16 x 6-1/4″   23 x 16 cm

RURAL FIRE STATION
This small fire house will be the pride of your volunteer department! The building features two apparatus bays and a rooftop hose drying tower.

272-268   19.99
5-1/8 x 4″   13 x 10 cm

272-294   Log Barn   10.99
4-3/16 x 2-1/4″   10.6 x 5.7 cm

272-288   Timber Yard   12.49
5-1/8 x 3-1/2″   13 x 9 cm

272-936   "Alsfeld" Town Hall   35.49
4-3/8 x 4-1/16″   11.1 x 10.3 cm
Includes four turrets, arcades and many details.

272-283   Black Forest Farmhouse   21.49
4-7/8 x 4-7/8″   12.5 x 12.5 cm

■ **LIMITED QUANTITIES AVAILABLE** ■

272-353   Agricultural Warehouse   19.99
5-1/8 x 2-3/8″   13.2 x 6 cm

FALLER

Imported from Germany and marketed by WALTHERS

HO SCALE (1/87)   EASY-TO-BUILD KITS
Kits consist of prototypically colored plastic parts, printed signs and details where applicable, and fully illustrated, step-by-step detailed instructions.

RURAL BUILDINGS (continued)

OLD BLACKSMITH SHOP
This blacksmith shop is ready for business! An important business in horse and buggy days, many still survive as welding and metal repair shops. The kit includes a large stamping hammer which can be powered with electric motor 272-269, available separately.

272-266	5-3/4 x 3-13/16" 14.7 x 9.7 cm	38.49

272-228	Black Forest Gristmill, Dummy	22.99
	9-3/8 x 5" 24 x 13 cm	

272-589	Lumber Assortment	8.49

TOWN HALL
This ornate town hall is loaded with architectural features! Four turrets, arcades and other details not included.

272-930	28.99
5-5/16 x 4-1/16"	
13.5 x 10.3 cm	

272-364	Villa	40.49
	7 x 5-3/4" 17.5 x 14.5 cm	

Hunter's Lookout

272-290	11.49
1-9/16 x 1-3/16" 4 x 3 cm	

272-276	Farm Building w/Details	32.49
6-3/8 x 3-7/8" 16.2 x 9.8 cm	3-3/4 x 2-1/16" 9.6 x 5.3 cm	
5-3/8 x 3-7/8" 13.7 x 9.8 cm		

Grain Store w/Accessories

272-333	13.99
3-1/2 x 3-1/8" 9 x 8 cm	

Gutach Valley Farmhouse

272-289	30.49
5-3/4 x 4-15/16" 14.6 x 12.6 cm	

FALLER

Imported from Germany and marketed by **WALTHERS**

HO SCALE (1/87)   EASY-TO-BUILD KITS

Kits consist of prototypically colored plastic parts, printed signs and details where applicable, and fully illustrated, step-by-step detailed instructions.

RURAL BUILDINGS (continued)

ALPINE FARM HOUSE

This charming farmhouse will be right at home in a rugged mountain setting. Built to withstand harsh Alpine winters, it features a stucco first floor with wooden siding on the upper floors.

272-331   5-1/8 x 4-3/8″   13 x 11 cm   32.49

272-385   Hunter's Lodge "Falkeneck"   41.99
7-3/8 x 5-1/4″   18.8 x 13.4 cm
Includes wooden draw-bridge and walkway.

Log Cabin
272-299 9.99
3-1/4 x 30″
8.2 x 7.6 cm

Forest
Log Cabin
272-293 10.99
3-7/16 x 2″
8.7 x 5.1 cm

272-332   Alpine Blacksmith   32.49
7-1/4 x 4-1/2″   18.5 x 11.5 cm

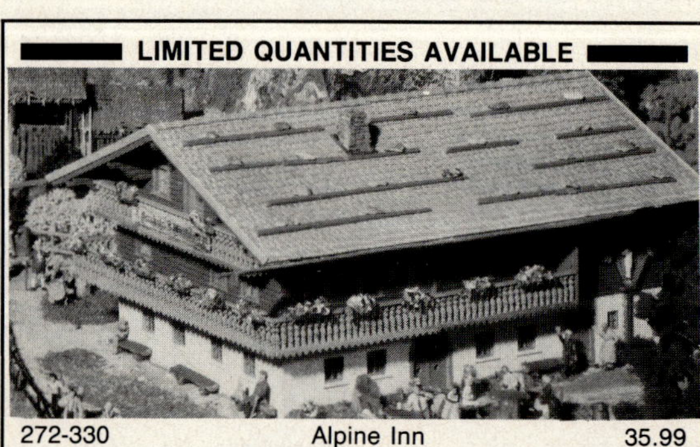

272-330   Alpine Inn   35.99
7-1/4 x 4-3/8″   18.5 x 11 cm

WATERMILL

Nearly every small village once had a stone mill. Powered by a stream, the waterwheel turned the millstone to grind grain into flour. This charming kit includes an electronic pump to circulate real water which turns the wheel! (Also available without the pump.)

272-225   with Pump   48.49
272-226   less Pump   26.99
9-1/2 x 5-1/8″   24 x 13 cm

FALLER

Imported from Germany and marketed by WALTHERS

HO SCALE (1/87)   EASY-TO-BUILD KITS

Kits consist of prototypically colored plastic parts, printed signs and details where applicable, and fully illustrated, step-by-step detailed instructions.

RURAL BUILDINGS (continued)

272-370   Farm   8-3/4 x 13-1/4″   22.5 x 34 cm   **NEW** 61.99
Includes 1/2-timber farmhouse, shed for sheep, barn, pigsty with fence, dog house and dung cart.

272-371   Lower-Saxon Farmhouse **NEW** 32.49
4-1/4 x 7″   11 x 17.5 cm

HOUSES

272-303   House Under Construction   17.99
4-11/16 x 3-1/2″   12 x 9 cm

272-215   Timbered House w/Garage   14.99
4-7/8 x 2-13/16″   12.6 x 6.2 cm

272-214   Detached House   14.99
3-1/2 x 2-13/16″   9.1 x 7.2 cm

HALF-TIMBERED HOUSE

Loaded with old-world charm, this detailed home captures the look of traditional timber and stucco construction, used for all types of European structures.

272-272   26.49
4-7/8 x 4-7/8″
12.5 x 12.5 cm

It's one of those bitter cold, clear nights when the frost goes right into your bones. But there's a fire burning nicely in the old stove on the railbus, and time for a last cup of coffee and donut before pulling out into the night. Serving passengers on the Fundy Northern, this kitbashed railbus combines parts from a MDC coach, a Jordan Mack truck and the drive from a Bachmann trolley. The scene was built by Bob Boudreau of Saint John, New Brunswick, Canada.
Models and Photo by Bob Boudreau

FALLER

Imported from Germany and marketed by WALTHERS

HO SCALE (1/87)   EASY-TO-BUILD KITS

Kits consist of prototypically colored plastic parts, printed signs and details where applicable, and fully illustrated, step-by-step detailed instructions.

HOUSES (continued)

TOWN HOUSE w/PASSAGE SHOPS

Entrance to hair salon and pub, both of which are located on the ground floor of this building.

272-421   3-3/4 x 6-1/2"   9.7 x 16.5 cm   **NEW**   28.99

TWO TOWN HOUSES w/SHOP

Two timbered multi-story houses w/windows. A butcher shop is located on the ground floor of one of the houses.

272-418   4-3/4 x 5-7/8"   12.0 x 14.9 cm   **NEW**   34.49

Townhouse w/Stationer's House **NEW**
272-419   3-3/4 x 5-7/8"   9.7 x 14.9 cm   20.99

Multi-story House w/Antique Shop **NEW**
272-422   3-3/4 x 6-1/2"   9.7 x 16.5 cm   29.49

Timbered House **NEW**
272-423   3-3/4 x 5-7/8"   9.7 x 14.9 cm   22.99

FALLER

Imported from Germany and marketed by WALTHERS

HO SCALE (1/87)   EASY-TO-BUILD KITS

Kits consist of prototypically colored plastic parts, printed signs and details where applicable, and fully illustrated, step-by-step detailed instructions.

HOUSES (continued)

HOUSE "FLAIR"

This handsome home is sure to be a focal point of any HO subdivision. It's complete with a winter garden, patio, upper balcony and a carport.

272-392	7 x 6 x 3-3/4"	17.8 x 15.3 x 9.5 cm	32.49

272-924   5-Story Townhouse   41.49
3-3/4 x 3-5/8 x 10"   9.6 x 9.2 x 25.5 cm
Shops are located on ground floor. The height of house is variable by taking out 1 or 2 stories. Several models can be joined to make additional variations.

272-393   House "Rustica"   29.99
5 x 4-3/4"   12.8 x 12 cm
The majority of the building material of the original house is wood. Has overhanging roof, a built-on winter garden and a balcony.

HOUSE "DURER"

Reproduction of the Albrecht Durer house in Nuremberg. Elaborate half-timber and roof construction.

272-932   5-1/2 x 4-1/4"   14 x 10.5 cm   41.99

FALLER

Imported from Germany and marketed by WALTHERS

HO SCALE (1/87) EASY-TO-BUILD KITS

Kits consist of prototypically colored plastic parts, printed signs and details where applicable, and fully illustrated, step-by-step detailed instructions.

HOUSES (continued)

272-1209 White Plaster w/Tile Roof **14.49**
(pre-assembled)
3-5/8 x 3-3/8"   9.3 x 8.6 cm

272-1208 Brick/Timbered House **14.49**
(pre-assembled)
3-5/8 x 3-3/8"   9.3 x 8.6 cm

FARMHOUSE

Typical of rural homes built during the late nineteenth and early twentieth centuries, homes like these can still be seen today in rural areas of the United States. This two-story farmhouse is based on an American prototype built with clapboard siding, a covered front porch and outside cellar entrance. Just add Preiser figures and Magnuson vehicles to create a complete scene!

272-1130   **19.99**

272-1255 Detached House **13.99**
9-1/2 x 8-1/2" 24.5 x 22.5 cm

272-1257 Half-Timbered House **13.99**
9-1/2 x 8-1/2" 24.5 x 22.5 cm

272-1256 Clinker-Built House **13.99**
9-1/2 x 8-1/2" 24.5 x 22.5 cm

272-1205 Beige Plaster House **14.49**
(pre-assembled)
3-5/8 x 3-3/8"   9.3 x 8.6 cm

272-1206 Red Brick House **14.49**
(preassembled)
3-5/8 x 3-3/8"   9.3 x 8.6 cm

272-1207 Stucco Timbered House **14.49**
(preassembled)
3-5/8 x 3-3/8"   9.3 x 8.6 cm

HO SCALE (1/87)   EASY-TO-BUILD KITS

Kits consist of prototypically colored plastic parts, printed signs and details where applicable, and fully illustrated, step-by-step detailed instructions.

HOUSES (continued)

272-209   House with Balcony   11.49
4 x 3-3/4"   10.1 x 9.5 cm

VILLAGE INN

This charming inn is the perfect place to hold a wedding reception or other celebration! The building is complete with an outdoor bandstand plus tables and chairs.

272-269   20.99
5-5/8 x 5-5/8"   14.5 x 14.5 cm

272-200   House with Dormer   9.99
3-17/32 x 3-1/8"   9 x 8 cm

272-204   Chalet with Porch   9.99
3-15/16 x 3-1/4"   10 x 8.3 cm

272-416   Half-Timbered House   22.49
2-1/4 x 3"   2.34 x 3.12 cm

COUNTRY HOUSE & GARAGE

Here's a handsome home that looks great in any HO suburb! Perfect for the commuter, the house includes a separate two car garage.

272-270   Includes detached double garage   26.49
8-7/8 x 5-1/2"   22.6 x 14 cm

272-590   Cottages   pkg(4) 17.49

FALLER
Imported from Germany and marketed by WALTHERS

HO SCALE (1/87) EASY-TO-BUILD KITS
Kits consist of prototypically colored plastic parts, printed signs and details where applicable, and fully illustrated, step-by-step detailed instructions.

HOUSES (continued)

TUDOR COUNTRY VILLA
This ornate villa makes an elegant home in country or city scenes. The kit is complete with a balcony and other details.

272-292 19.49
4-3/4 x 4-3/8" 12 x 11.2 cm

272-205 1-1/2 Story House 11.49
5-3/16 x 3-1/4" 13.2 x 8.3 cm

272-206 Chalet with Patio 6.49
5-1/8 x 3-1/2" 13 x 9 cm

MONASTERY INN
This eye-catching building will be a welcome rest for weary travelers. The three-story building features stucco and timber construction.

272-352 4-5/16 x 3-1/8" 11 x 8 cm 26.99

272-277 Half-Timbered Chalet 12.99
4-1/2 x 3-3/8" 11.5 x 8.7 cm

Structure #352 can be combined flush with #353 Agricultural Warehouse. The roof features special grooving.

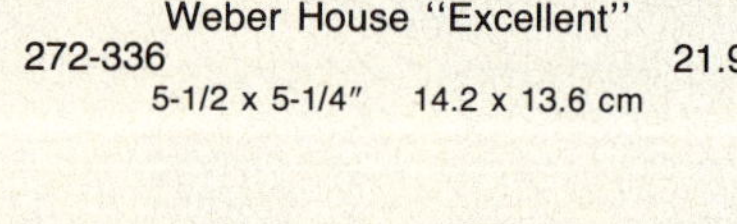

Weber House "Excellent"
272-336 21.99
5-1/2 x 5-1/4" 14.2 x 13.6 cm

Weber House "Noblesse"
272-337 29.99
5-1/2 x 5-1/4" 14.2 x 13.6 cm

FALLER

Imported from Germany and marketed by WALTHERS

HO SCALE (1/87) EASY-TO-BUILD KITS

Kits consist of prototypically colored plastic parts, printed signs and details where applicable, and fully illustrated, step-by-step detailed instructions.

HOUSES (continued)

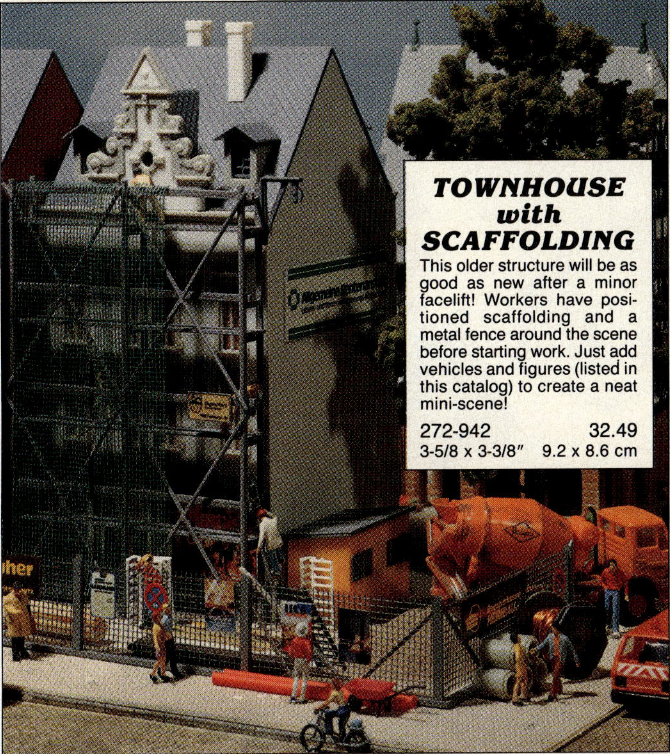

TOWNHOUSE with SCAFFOLDING

This older structure will be as good as new after a minor facelift! Workers have positioned scaffolding and a metal fence around the scene before starting work. Just add vehicles and figures (listed in this catalog) to create a neat mini-scene!

272-942   32.49
3-5/8 x 3-3/8″   9.2 x 8.6 cm

BOATHOUSE & BOAT

This attractive structure will add realism to a lake shore resort, summer camp, or marina! The kit is complete with a row boat.

272-284   9.99
3-5/8 x 2-23/32″   9.2 x 6.9 cm

272-246   House Under Construction   10.99
2-15/16 x 2-3/4″   7.5 x 7.1 cm

Small Mountain Chalet
272-297   13.49
4-11/16 x 3-7/8″
11.9 x 9.9 cm

272-308   "Moosgrund" Duplex House   27.49
5-1/2 x 5-1/2″   16.5 x 14 cm

272-298   Alpine Villa   22.99
4-3/4 x 5-1/8″   12 x 13 cm

1-1/2 Story Half-Timbered House
272-218   5-1/4 x 4-7/8″   13.3 x 12.3 cm   19.99

272-249   Chalet   12.49
3-3/4 x 3-3/8″   9.6 x 8.6 cm

FALLER

Imported from Germany and marketed by WALTHERS

HO SCALE (1/87)   EASY-TO-BUILD KITS

Kits consist of prototypically colored plastic parts, printed signs and details where applicable, and fully illustrated, step-by-step detailed instructions.

HOUSES (continued)

272-306   Two Terraced Housed   29.99
5-5/16 x 5-7/8"   16.2 x 15.2 cm

Creating a realistic rural scene on your layout is easy with buildings like the Faller Parsonage and Rural Fire Station, which can be found throughout the Structures section.

BASIC VILLAGE SET

Here's everything you need to build a small village in one complete set! Including three Cape Cod homes and a small church, the set also features an assortment of fir trees and a playground which is detailed with teeter-totters, a swing set and more.

272-255   56.99

272-304   Brick House w/Balcony, Patio & Lighting   22.99

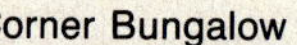

272-302   Corner Bungalow   22.99

272-256   Guest House   22.99
4-1/2 x 4-1/8"   11.6 x 10.6 cm

272-338   Modern Cape Cod Home   21.99

Modern w/Covered Balcony & Roof Lights
272-339   21.99

FALLER

Imported from Germany and marketed by
WALTHERS

HO SCALE (1/87)   EASY-TO-BUILD KITS

Kits consist of prototypically colored plastic parts, printed signs and details where applicable, and fully illustrated, step-by-step detailed instructions.

HOUSES (continued)

SINGLE FAMILY HOME "ERLENSEE"

This attractive single-family home looks great in any HO neighborhood. The model is nicely detailed, with wooden shutters and a roofed terrace on the second floor. A separate one-car garage is also included.

272-300   21.49
6 x 5-3/8"   15 x 13.6 cm

272-367   Suburban Duplex, Yellow 28.99
5-9/16 x 5-1/4"   14.2 x 13.6 cm

272-360   Duplex with Shed Roof 28.99
5-9/16 x 5-1/4"   14.2 x 13.6 cm

272-369   Suburban Duplex, Red Brick 28.99
5-9/16 x 5-1/4"   14.2 x 13.6 cm

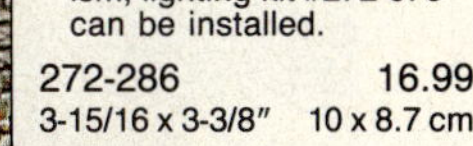

GUEST HOUSE "ROSEL"

HO travelers can always find a vacancy at this charming inn! Nearly every room has its own balcony for a view of the scenery. For more realism, lighting kit #272-670 can be installed.

272-286   16.99
3-15/16 x 3-3/8"   10 x 8.7 cm

272-280   House   19.99
4-5/8 x 4-1/2"   11.7 x 11.5 cm
Includes storks's nest

FALLER

Imported from Germany and marketed by **WALTHERS**

HO SCALE (1/87)   EASY-TO-BUILD KITS
Kits consist of prototypically colored plastic parts, printed signs and details where applicable, and fully illustrated, step-by-step detailed instructions.

HOUSES (continued)

Half-Timbered House w/Shop
272-938   27.49
4-3/8 x 3-3/4"   11 x 9.5 cm

272-939   Half-Timbered House   38.49
4-3/16 x 3-3/8"   10.7 x 8.8 cm

272-250   Country House with Dormer   14.99
4-1/4 x 4-3/4"   10.8 x 12.2 cm

272-586   Garages   pkg(2) 11.49

272-305   Single Family Home "Wiesental"   22.99
6 x 5-3/8"   15 x 13.6 cm

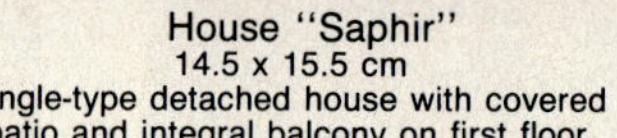

272-394   House "Saphir"   21.99
14.5 x 15.5 cm
Angle-type detached house with covered patio and integral balcony on first floor.

CITY BUILDINGS

CITY HALL with FIRE STATION

This beautiful structure combines the City Hall and Fire Station into a single building. Three apparatus bays are provided to showcase your fire equipment. A large hose drying tower rounds out the structure.

272-901   75.99
10-3/8 x 9-1/2"   26.3 x 24.2 cm

SCHOOL HOUSE

This detailed school house gets an A+ for realism! Two bike racks with bicycles, playground equipment and garbage bins are all included to finish the scene!

272-902   45.49
9-5/8 x 6-1/8"   24.5 x 15.7 cm

FALLER

Imported from Germany and marketed by WALTHERS

HO SCALE (1/87) EASY-TO-BUILD KITS

Kits consist of prototypically colored plastic parts, printed signs and details where applicable, and fully illustrated, step-by-step detailed instructions.

CITY BUILDINGS (continued)

TOWN HALL

Bring your city square to life with this impressive model. Production will be very limited, and each kit includes a special numbered certificate of authenticity. Working features include an actual clock for the tower, plus a special mechanism with moving figures and realistic bell chimes. Working lights and other accessories are also provided to complete the building.

272-400   125.49

DISTRICT COURT

This ornate building makes a fitting monument to the cultural heritage of your model city. It includes a number of details and accessories to complement its design.

272-420   57.49

272-356   Post Office w/Accessories   38.49
6-3/4 x 6-3/8″   2-1/4 x 1″
17.2 x 17.4   5.7 x 2.7 cm

FALLER

Imported from Germany and marketed by WALTHERS

HO SCALE (1/87)   EASY-TO-BUILD KITS

Kits consist of prototypically colored plastic parts, printed signs and details where applicable, and fully illustrated, step-by-step detailed instructions.

CITY BUILDINGS (continued)

HOTEL SONNE

Dress up any corner of your downtown with this superb model! The four story building is designed especially for a corner location and can be used with other Faller buildings to create a complete city scene!

272-927   Corner Building   32.99
4-1/16 x 4-1/16"   10.4 x 10.4 cm

"Krone" Inn w/Beer Garden
272-415   27.49
4-1/2 x 5"   11.6 x 13 cm

Pharmacy Shop w/Multi-Story House
272-417   29.49
4-1/2 x 3-3/4"   11.6 x 9.6 cm

Shell Gas Station
272-217   14.99
4-3/4 x 4-3/8"   12 x 11 cm

272-904   Forestry Office   34.99
6-1/8 x 6-1/8"   15.7 x 15.7 cm   4-5/8 x 2-3/4"   11.9 x 7 cm
With extra buildings for vehicles or storage.

272-135   Newsstands   12.49
round: 2-3/4 x 1-9/16"   7 x 4 cm
square: 1-15/16 x 1-15/16"   5 x 5 cm

City Gate "St Martin's"
272-922   41.99
4-3/8 x 3"   11.2 x 7.8 cm

Mittelstadt Apartments
272-926   pkg(2) 40.49
5-5/8 x 3-1/8"   14.5 x 8 cm

HO SCALE (1/87)   EASY-TO-BUILD KITS

Kits consist of prototypically colored plastic parts, printed signs and details where applicable, and fully illustrated, step-by-step detailed instructions.

CITY BUILDINGS (continued)

"ROMERBERG" ROWHOUSES

This detailed kit is based on an actual street in Frankfurt, Germany. These ornate buildings date back to the 15th century and were restored in 1983. The kit is complete with six different structures. Special plastic sheets to simulate half-timber construction are included, so the finished buildings can be used in various time periods.

272-911   98.49
  14 x 3-1/8"   35.5 x 8 cm
  Includes six structures
  from #912, #913, and #914.

272-258   Delicatessen   20.99
  4-1/2 x 3-3/4"   11.6 c 9.6 cm
  Includes choice of saddle or hip roof and wall with gate.

272-211   Post Office with Bus Shelter   14.99
  8-11/16 x 3-7/8"   22 x 10 cm

SCHILLERSTRASSE CITY BLOCK

Build a better business district with this complete kit! The set combines two large corner buildings with two adjoining structures for the middle of the block. The modular construction makes it possible to arrange the buildings in different combinations to fit available space. A variety of finishing details, including ground foam "flowers" are included to complete a realistic scene.

272-925   15-1/4 x 4-1/4"   38.9 x 11 cm   98.49
  Set contains two corner buildings and two adjoining buildings.

FALLER

Imported from Germany and marketed by WALTHERS

HO SCALE (1/87)   EASY-TO-BUILD KITS

Kits consist of prototypically colored plastic parts, printed signs and details where applicable, and fully illustrated, step-by-step detailed instructions.

CITY BUILDINGS (continued)

CORNER DRUG STORE

Corner the market on unique buildings with this corner drugstore! Complete with a drug store on the first floor and apartments on the second and third floors, the colorful building is designed especially for a corner location on your layout.

272-929   32.99
4-1/16 x 4-1/16"
10.4 x 10.4 cm

Small Food Stand
272-212   11.49
3-1/8 x 3"   8 x 7.7 cm

"The Sun" Travel Agency
272-928   28.49
3-5/8 x 3-3/8"   9.2 x 8.6 cm
Connects with structure kits #927 and #929 to create a city street.

4-Face Clock Tower w/Newsstand
272-583   17.99
2 x 2"   5.2 x 5.2 cm
Prototype pre-war Frankfurt

272-585   Town Accessories   14.99

HOTEL/RESTAURANT

This hotel will be a favorite with HO travelers! First floor features a side entrance and large front window. Structure is designed so several can be combined to build a larger, unique building.

272-1120   35.49
4-3/8 x 4-3/8"   11.3 x 11.3 cm

Engel & Greif Rowhouses
272-912   38.49
3-5/8 x 2-3/4"   9.2 x 7 cm

Wilder & Dachsberg Rowhouses
272-913   38.49
5-3/8 x 2-3/4"   13.8 x 7.1 cm

Grober & Kleiner Rowhouses
272-914   38.49
4-13/16 x 3-1/8"   2.3 x 8 cm

■ LIMITED QUANTITIES ■ AVAILABLE

272-1121 5-Story Townhouse 40.49
3-3/4 x 3-9/16"   9.6 x 9.2 cm
Ideal for housing HO tenants, the historic five-story structure includes a barber shop on the first floor.

FALLER

Imported from Germany and marketed by
WALTHERS

HO SCALE (1/87)   EASY-TO-BUILD KITS

Kits consist of prototypically colored plastic parts, printed signs and details where applicable, and fully illustrated, step-by-step detailed instructions.

CHURCHES

VILLAGE CHURCH
This medium sized church is perfect for smaller towns and cities. The kit features a single bell tower which can be built with a spire or "onion" dome.

272-241   47.99
9-5/16 x 5"   24 x 12.9 cm

Mountain Chapel
272-243   10.99
2-3/4 x 2-3/4"   7.1 x 7.1 cm

Small Village Church   272-236   14.99
4-3/4 x 2-3/4"   12 x 5.5 cm

272-238   Church   21.99
5-13/16 x 3-1/2"   14.8 x 8.8 cm

VILLAGE CHURCH
Nestled in a small village, this tiny church puts big detail in a small space. The building has a single bell tower, with a traditional steeple.

272-240   20.99
4-3/4 x 4"   12 x 10.2 cm

Large City Church w/2 Steeples
272-351   11-1/8 x 5-3/4"   28.3 x 14.9 cm   69.99

272-234   Chapel   9.99
2 x 2-3/8"   5 x 6 cm

FALLER

Imported from Germany and marketed by WALTHERS

HO SCALE (1/87)   EASY-TO-BUILD KITS
Kits consist of prototypically colored plastic parts, printed signs and details where applicable, and fully illustrated, step-by-step detailed instructions.

BUSINESSES

272-345   Gas Station w/Service Bay   24.99
15.8 x 9.6 cm

272-411   Corner House w/Toy Shop   21.99
8.4 x 6.4 cm

272-346   Gas Pumps w/Service Bay   11.49
12.3 x 6.3 cm

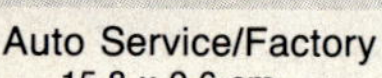
272-946   Auto Service/Factory   17.49
15.8 x 9.6 cm

MERCEDES-BENZ DEALERSHIP

Modern 2-story dealership with showroom and parts store located on ground level. Office and information rooms and living area on upper floor. Can be illuminated with bulbs (272-671), rotating turntables in showroom and roof emblem can be motorized with Faller motor (272-671 and 272-629, not included).
272-344   58.49
9-1/4 x 7-1/2", 6 x 3-3/4"
23.7 x 19.7 cm,   15.5 x 9.5 cm

Railway Hotel "Eschwege"
272-378   30.49
6-1/4 x 4-1/2"   16 x 11.8 cm
Includes flats for railway officials, facilities for small domestic animals, workshop and cellar rooms.

Railway Hotel "Schonheide"
272-379
30.49
6-1/4 x 4-1/2"
16 x 11.8 cm

FALLER

Imported from Germany and marketed by WALTHERS

HO SCALE (1/87)   EASY-TO-BUILD KITS

Kits consist of prototypically colored plastic parts, printed signs and details where applicable, and fully illustrated, step-by-step detailed instructions.

BUSINESSES (continued)

Ford Cargo Truck
272-343   23.99

MINI MARKET

Don't forget to pick up a few groceries on the way home! Shopping will be easy in this modern mini-mart which features a complete interior with shelves, merchandise and cash registers. For added realism, the sign on the roof can be made to rotate with motor #629 and the building can be illuminated with lighting set #671, both sold separately.

272-342   7-3/4 x 7-3/4"   19.8 x 19.8 cm   32.49

272-412   Building w/Shop   32.99
3-5/16 x 2-1/2"   8.4 x 6.4 cm

272-413   House w/Wine Shop   24.99
3-1/2 x 2-15/16"   9.1 x 7.5 cm

272-340   City Cafe & Cake Shop   33.49
7-5/8 x 5"   19.5 x 12.8 cm

272-937   Hotel Romantic **NEW**   45.49
5-1/2 x 5-1/8"   14 x 13 cm

272-414   2 Flats w/Lower Shops   37.49
3-5/16 x 2-1/2"   8.4 x 6.4 cm
3-1/2 x 3"   9.1 x 7.5 cm

272-365   Office Building   38.49
6-7/8 x 6"   17.5 x 15.3 cm

FALLER

Imported from Germany and marketed by **WALTHERS**

HO SCALE (1/87)   EASY-TO-BUILD KITS

Kits consist of prototypically colored plastic parts, printed signs and details where applicable, and fully illustrated, step-by-step detailed instructions.

INDUSTRIAL BUILDINGS

CEMENT WORKS

This detailed cement plant makes a great trackside industry! Similar plants are found by themselves, or as part of a large gravel pit. The plant mixes and loads cement into waiting trucks. The building is complete with storage silos, a loading elevator, walkways and an attached office.

272-950	32.49
8-1/8 x 3" 20.7 x 9 cm	

272-265   **Old Brick Factory Building**   33.49
9-1/16 x 7-1/4"   23 x 18.5 cm
Includes side wing, outhouses and conveyor system.

272-940   **City Gas Works**   23.99
5-3/8 x 4-1/2"   13.7 x 11.5 cm

OLD TIME FACTORY

From steam era to the diesel age, this old factory building can be used in many time periods. The three buildings can be built as individual structures, or combined into one large building. A covered loading ramp and large smokestack (which can be fitted with a smoke generator) are included.

272-980   20-1/8 x 6-7/8"   51.2 x 17.3 cm   64.99

FALLER

Imported from Germany and marketed by WALTHERS

HO SCALE (1/87)   EASY-TO-BUILD KITS

Kits consist of prototypically colored plastic parts, printed signs and details where applicable, and fully illustrated, step-by-step detailed instructions.

INDUSTRIAL (continued)

BREWERY

This small brewery will be the toast of your industrial district! The large windows on the brew house show the interior details, including realistically colored copper kettles.

272-960   35.49
6-15/16 x 6-1/2"
17.6 x 16.5 cm

MINEHEAD w/WINCH HOUSE

Powering underground conveyors, the winch house is an essential part of any mining operation. The kit is complete with a minehead building and can be used with the mine kits available from various manufacturers. For extra realism, the winch can be powered with an electric motor (272-629, available separately).

272-945   43.99
10-1/4 x 6-7/8"   26 x 17.5 cm

272-193   Gravel Tipple   26.99
5-3/4 x 2-15/16"   14.5 x 7.5 cm

(not illustrated)

272-640   Flickering Light   34.49
simulates arc welding

272-629   18 RPM Motor 16V AC   20.99

272-195   Motorized Conveyor Belt   41.99
8-3/8 x 3-3/8"   21.5 x 8.7 cm

272-196   Conveyor Belt w/Load Belt   51.99
9-1/4 x 7-1/2"   23.5 x 19 cm

272-165   Oil Pump & Shed   23.99
7 x 3-3/4"   17 x 9.5 cm, less motor

FREIGHT WAREHOUSE "DISCHINGER"

Start a modern industrial park on your layout with this contemporary building that's based on an actual structure. Modular construction makes it easy to build a custom structure to fit your available space.

272-983   41.99
14-3/4 x 7-1/4 x 5"
37.2 x 18.5 x 12.9 cm

HO SCALE (1/87)   EASY-TO-BUILD KITS

Kits consist of prototypically colored plastic parts, printed signs and details where applicable, and fully illustrated, step-by-step detailed instructions.

BRIDGES & VIADUCTS

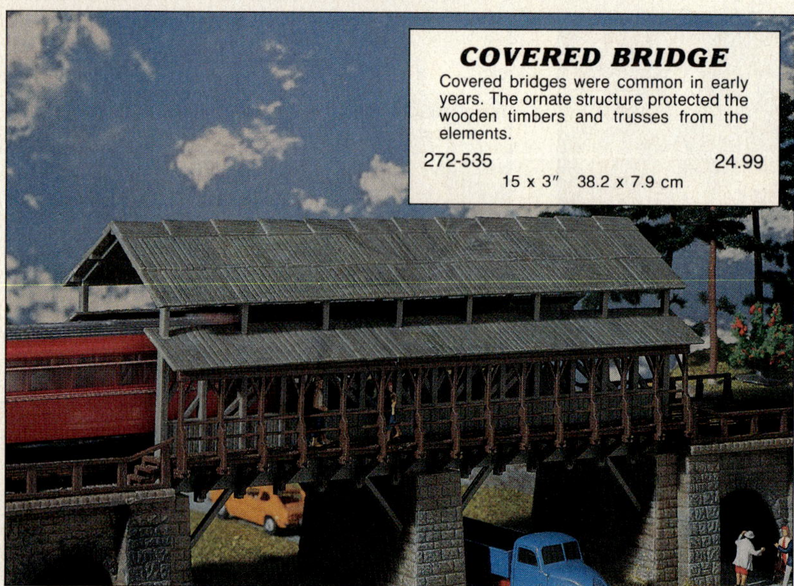

COVERED BRIDGE

Covered bridges were common in early years. The ornate structure protected the wooden timbers and trusses from the elements.

272-535	24.99
15 x 3″ 38.2 x 7.9 cm	

272-531	Arch Bridge	13.99
	7″ 18 cm	

272-534	Girder Bridge	12.49
	7″ 18 cm	

272-178	2-Track Steel Foot Bridge	14.99
	9-1/8 x 7″ 23.3 x 17.8 cm	

ARCH BRIDGE

This detailed bridge looks super on any mainline! It can easily be used with other Faller bridges to cross wide rivers or valleys.

272-536	14-1/4 x 2-1/2″ 36 x 6.5 cm	20.49

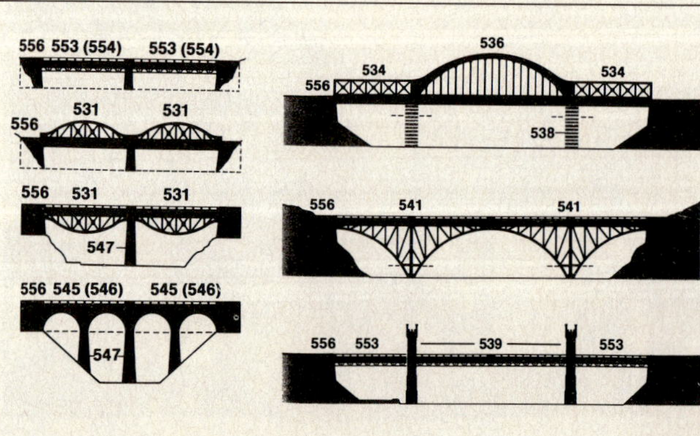

272-545	Straight Stone Viaduct	11.49
	7-1/16″ 18 cm	

272-546	Curved Stone Viaduct	11.49
	7″ 18 cm	
	30°, approximate 14″ radius	

FALLER

Imported from Germany and marketed by WALTHERS

HO SCALE (1/87)   EASY-TO-BUILD KITS

Kits consist of prototypically colored plastic parts, printed signs and details where applicable, and fully illustrated, step-by-step detailed instructions.

BRIDGES & VIADUCTS (continued)

4-TRACK CONCRETE FOOT BRIDGE

This modern pedestrian bridge will be a great addition to a yard or industrial area. The basic kit will cross four tracks and additional kits can be combined to build a longer bridge.

272-179   18.99
13-1/8 x 7-5/8" 33 x 19.5 cm

DECK ARCH BRIDGE

This modern steel bridge is typical of railroad designs used around the world. Detailed steel work and girders highlight this single track bridge.

272-541   14-1/4 x 2-1/2" 36 x 6.5 cm   18.99

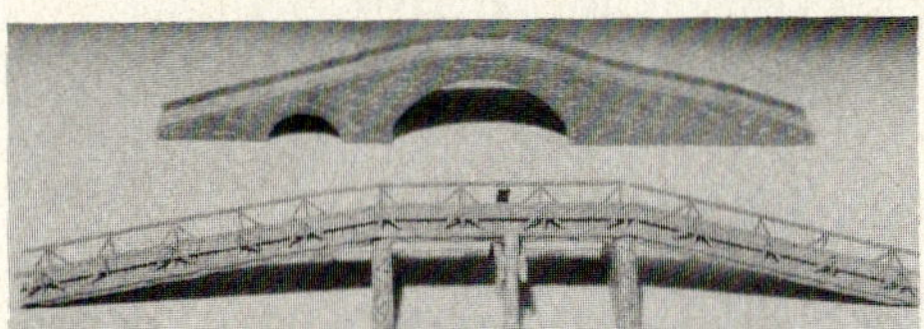

272-537   **Small Foot Bridges**   pkg(2) 11.99
8-5/8 x 7/8" 22 x 2.2 cm
10 x 2-1/8" 25.6 x 5.5 cm

272-530   **Trestle Set**   21.49
Includes approach ramp for all track types.

Viaduct Piers
272-547
pkg(3) 13.99
4-3/4" high
for #'s 531, 534, 545 and 546

Stone Bridge Abutment Set
272-556   15.49
for #'s 553, 554, 531, 534 and 536

Viaduct Piers
272-549 pkg(6) 12.99
1-7/8" long
for #'s 545 and 546

272-543   **Up & Over Bridge Set**   45.99
Includes straight and curved track beds and piers.

272-548   **Circle Set for #543**   48.99

Concrete Bridge Piers
272-538   pkg(18) 14.99
for #'s 534, 536 and 541

High Piers for #543
272-544   pkg(6) 8.49

STONE ARCH BRIDGE

Several bridges can be built and interconnected with each other.

272-533   30.49
14 x 1-3/4" 36 x 4.4 cm

272-552   **Trackbed, curved**   7.49
R42, 4cm

FALLER

Imported from Germany and marketed by WALTHERS

HO SCALE (1/87)   EASY-TO-BUILD KITS

Kits consist of prototypically colored plastic parts, printed signs and details where applicable, and fully illustrated, step-by-step detailed instructions.

BRIDGES & VIADUCTS (continued)

ROADWAY BRIDGE
272-532   30.49
14-1/8" 36cm long

272-553   Straight Bridge Section   7.49
7" 18 cm

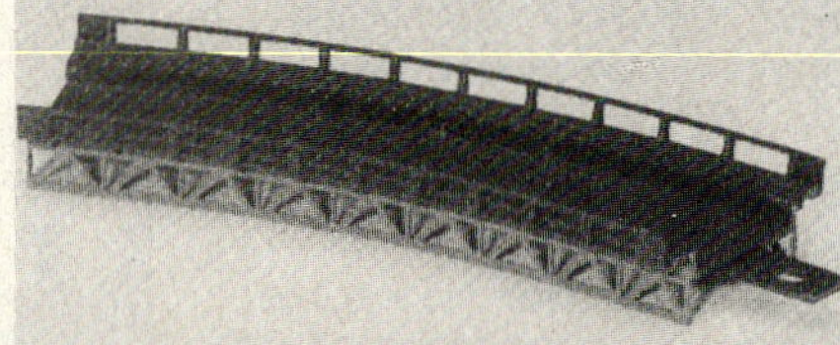

272-554   Curved Bridge Section   7.49
7" 18 cm
30", approximate 14" radius

CROSSING GATES

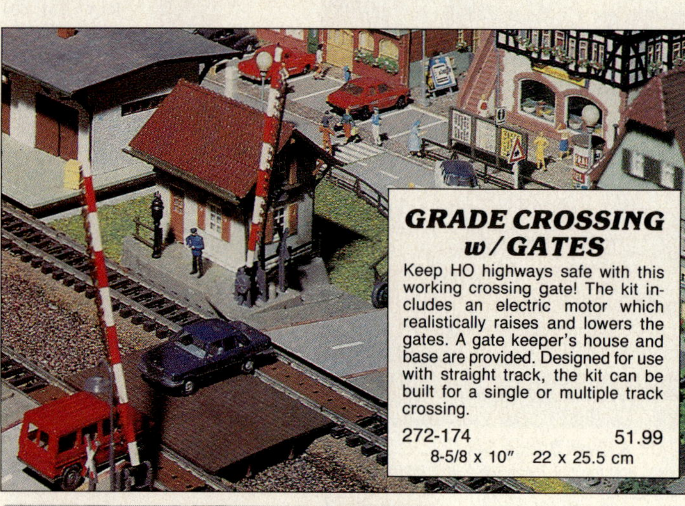

GRADE CROSSING w/GATES

Keep HO highways safe with this working crossing gate! The kit includes an electric motor which realistically raises and lowers the gates. A gate keeper's house and base are provided. Designed for use with straight track, the kit can be built for a single or multiple track crossing.

272-174   51.99
8-5/8 x 10"   22 x 25.5 cm

Railway Bridge, Double Track
272-542   28.99
15-1/4 x 6"
40 x 15.5 cm
Clearance Height
3-1/4", 8.3 cm

Curved Grade Crossing w/Gates
272-172   14.99
7-1/2 x 6-5/16"
19 x 16 cm

Curved Grade Crossing w/Gates (Dummy)
272-173   14.99
5-7/8 x 5-11/16"   15 x 14.5 cm

MISCELLANEOUS

Small Grade Crossing w/Gates
272-170   11.99
5-1/8 x 4-3/4"   13 x 12 cm

272-253   Garden Center   32.49
Includes house, 3 greenhouses,
2 hot beds, straw mats and accessories.

HO SCALE (1/87)   EASY-TO-BUILD KITS
Kits consist of prototypically colored plastic parts, printed signs and details where applicable, and fully illustrated, step-by-step detailed instructions.

MISCELLANEOUS

LARGE GREENHOUSE
This detailed greenhouse is perfect for modeling a nursery or floral shop in your HO community! The kit is complete with three greenhouse buildings and planting beds. The basic kit can be expanded with the Small Greenhouse (272-213) to build a larger scene.

272-254   5 Buildings   24.99
9-1/16 x 4-5/32"   23 x 11 cm

272-213   Small Greenhouse   16.49
3-5/8 x 1-7/8"   9.2 x 4.7 cm   2-3/4 x 1-5/8"   7.1 x 4.2 cm

OLD CASTLE "LICHTENSTEIN"
This imposing castle is specially designed for use as a backdrop building. The finished model is slightly smaller than HO Scale, so it will not overwhelm surrounding scenery.

272-245   28.99
5-1/4 x 2-15/16"   13.3 x 7.5 cm

Castle Tower
Ruins
272-285   15.99
5-11/16 x 3-1/8"
14.5 x 8 cm

Observation
Tower
272-291   12.99
4-1/2 x 2-1/2"
11.5 x 6.5 cm

2 Bicycle Stands
& 16 Bikes
272-584   15.49
2-1/4 x 1-1/8"   5.9 x 2.7 cm
2 x 5/8"   5.1 x 1.7 cm

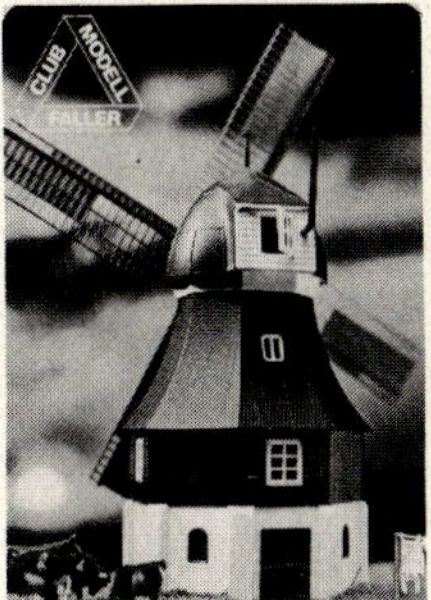

Windmill w/Motor
272-233   41.99

Holland Windmill
with Motor
272-231   48.49
8-1/16 x 6-1/2"
20.5 x 16.5 cm
Includes 12-16 volt
motor.

Fountain w/Figure
272-581   8.49
1-5/8 x 1-5/8"
4.3 x 4.3 cm
non-operating

272-232 Ornamental Fountain 12.49
4-1/2 x 4-5/16"   11.5 x 11 cm

FALLER

Imported from Germany and marketed by WALTHERS

HO SCALE (1/87)   EASY-TO-BUILD KITS

Kits consist of prototypically colored plastic parts, printed signs and details where applicable, and fully illustrated, step-by-step detailed instructions.

MISCELLANEOUS (continued)

SKATING RINK WITH MOTOR AND FIGURES

The skaters offered by Preiser can now do their free skating exercises on the skating surface to perfection. It comes complete with six Preiser figures and driving mechanism (12—16V, AC)

272-382	67.99
8-1/2 x 6-3/4″ 22 x 17.5 cm	

Wind Power Station Less Motor
272-166   18.99
2-3/4 x 5-1/8″   7 x 13 cm
Can be made working by using motor #272-629 for propelling the rotor blades.

BAND STAND PAVILLION "LAHR"

Dance the night away with this Band Stand Pavillion kit! Ideal for creating a unique atmosphere on your layout, the entertaining model is based on the turn-of-century Lahr Pavillion in Lahr, Germany. The colorful kit features an authentically detailed music pavillion, rotating dance floor less motor and chairs.

272-381   Band Stand & Music Pavillion "Lahr"   7-7/8 x 4-3/4″   20 x 12.2 cm   15.49

272-577   Adventure Playground   12.99

PAVILLION

272-355   8-5/8 x 6-1/8″   22 x 15.8 cm   29.49

FALLER

Imported from Germany and marketed by WALTHERS

HO SCALE (1/87)   EASY-TO-BUILD KITS

Kits consist of prototypically colored plastic parts, printed signs and details where applicable, and fully illustrated, step-by-step detailed instructions.

MISCELLANEOUS

SWIMMING POOL

This pool offers super bathing fun. When filled with water swimmers (included) circle the pool. Complete with propellent, changing cabin and diving board.

272-383   39 x 27 x 6 cm   **NEW** 74.99

OBSERVATION TOWER "BREND"

A narrow, two-story observation tower in natural stonework, external stairway in lower area and observation platform above.

272-386   20.99
5.2 x 28 cm

CITY CLASSICS

HO SCALE (1/87) EASY-TO-BUILD

NEW

Kits consist of injection molded plastic parts, styrene roof material, clear window glazing and easy-to-follow instructions.

CITY BUILDINGS

Grant Street Iron Front
195-101   13.98
5-1/4 x 3-1/2"
13.4 x 8.9 cm

Penn Avenue Tile Front
195-102   13.98
5-1/4 x 3-1/2"
13.4 x 8.9 cm

Baum Boulevard Art Deco Building
195-105   13.98
5-1/4 x 3-1/2"
13.4 x 8.9 cm

East Ohio Street Building
195-106   13.98
5-1/4 x 3-1/2"
13.4 x 8.9 cm

Smallman Street Warehouse
195-103   18.98
8-1/2 x 6"
21.6 x 15.2 cm

2-Story Add-on for #103
195-104   10.98

Carson Street Rail/ Truck Terminal
195-107   8.98
8-1/2 x 6"   21.6 x 15.2 cm

(not illustrated)
1940's Gas Station
195-108   TBA

BUILDING COMPONENTS FOR SMALLMAN STREET WAREHOUSE KIT

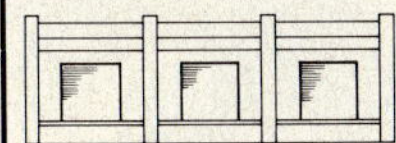

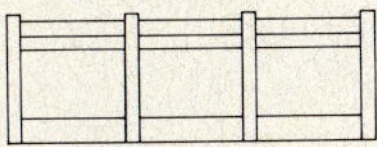

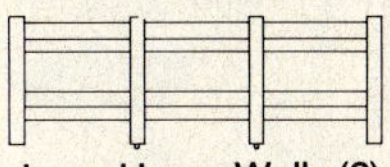

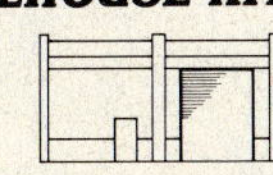

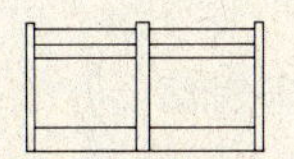

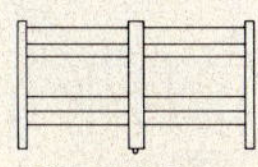

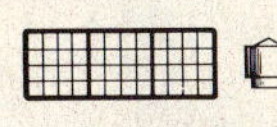

Long Lower Walls (2) w/Doors
195-201   3.50

Long Lower Walls (2) less Doors
195-202   3.50

Long Upper Walls (2) w/Windows
195-203   3.50

Short Lower Walls (2) w/Doors
195-204   3.50

Short Lower Walls (2) less Doors
195-205   3.50

Short Upper Walls (2) w/Windows
109-206   3.50

10 Factory Windows 2 Roof Vents
105-207   3.50

VOLLMER

Imported from Germany and marketed by WALTHERS

HO SCALE (1/87)   EASY-TO-BUILD KITS
These easy-to-build structures feature injection molded styrene plastic parts. Each piece is molded in a realistic color, so no painting is needed. For easier assembly, all parts are numbered and co-ordinated with the instruction sheets. Construction time will vary with the size of the kit.

STATIONS & PLATFORMS

BADEN-BADEN STATION
This beautiful building is typical of large stations built at the turn-of-the-century. Its classic design is ideal for American or European theme layouts. The numerous windows invite interior detailing and lighting for spectacular night scenes! Matching platforms (770-3559) are available for modeling the complete station scene.

770-3560   30-3/4 x 6-1/4 x 7-7/8"   78 x 16 x 20 cm   97.99

PLATFORM W/COVER
This ornate platform is based on prototypes at Baden-Baden. Its classic design is perfect for passenger service from the steam era to modern Amtrak. Printed signs, benches, a newsstand and two non-operating lamps are included. Several can be combined to build a longer platform.

770-3559   40-1/8 x 1-7/8 x 2-5/8"   102 x 4.8 x 6.6 cm   39.49

770-3541   Large Covered Platform   **NEW** 48.99
8.40 x 8.0 cm

770-3515   Swiss Darligen Station   46.49
13-1/2 x 5-1/4"   34.5 x 13.5 cm

770-3539   Station Platform Neuffen   10.49
17-1/8 x 1-3/8 x 3-1/8"   43.6 x 3.5 x 8 cm

770-5748   Storage Racks   pkg(3) 14.49
2-1/4 x 3/4"   6 x 2.1 cm

VOLLMER

Imported from Germany and marketed *by* **WALTHERS**

HO SCALE (1/87)   EASY-TO-BUILD KITS

These easy-to-build structures feature injection molded styrene plastic parts. Each piece is molded in a realistic color, so no painting is needed. For easier assembly, all parts are numbered and co-ordinated with the instruction sheets. Construction time will vary with the size of the kit.

STATIONS & PLATFORMS (continued)

PASSENGER STATION NEUFFEN

This branchline station is loaded with charm and interesting details. It combines a freight house, ticket window and living quarters into one building! Based on an actual German station at Neuffen, it gives any scene a rural flavor.

770-3510   58.99
16-1/8 x 5-3/8 x 5-1/2"
41 x 13.5 x 16.5 cm

NORDSTADT STATION

Serving a suburb or city, this medium-size station is ideal for layouts or modules.

770-3561   55.99
21-1/4 x 6-1/4 x 6-1/4"   54 x 16 x 16 cm

770-3525   Schonwies Station   30.99
9-7/8 x 5-1/8 x 3"   25 x 12.8 x 7.8 cm

770-3532   Covered Platform   25.99
24-1/4 x 1-7/8 x 2-3/4"   61.5 x 4.8 x 7 cm

770-3538   Passenger Platform   35.99
43-1/8 x 1-7/8 x 2-3/4"   109.5 x 4.8 x 7 cm

MAY 25, 1865

❧ Today ❧
IN RAILROAD HISTORY

The first steel railroad rails made with the new Bessemer process are completed at the North Chicago Rolling Mill.

VOLLMER

Imported from Germany and marketed
by WALTHERS

HO SCALE (1/87)   EASY-TO-BUILD KITS

These easy-to-build structures feature injection molded styrene plastic parts. Each piece is molded in a realistic color, so no painting is needed. For easier assembly, all parts are numbered and co-ordinated with the instruction sheets. Construction time will vary with the size of the kit.

STATIONS & PLATFORMS (continued)

STATION "REITH"

770-3530   10-3/4 x 6-1/2"   27 x 16.5 cm   39.49

770-3534   Covered Platform   22.99
14-5/8 x 1-7/8 x 2-3/4"   37 x 4.8 x 7 cm

770-3537   Covered Platform   18.99
14-5/8 x 1-3/8 x 2-5/8"   37 x 3.4 x 6.7 cm

Modern Covered Platform, Large
770-3541   31-1/2 x 3-1/8"   84 x 8 cm   48.99

Modern Covered Platform, Small
770-3542   11 x 3-1/8"   28 x 8 cm   24.49

YARD & EQUIPMENT FACILITIES

SIX STALL ROUNDHOUSE

Showcase your motive power in this impressive roundhouse! A must for steam era layouts, many still survive and service diesels today. The kit is large enough to capture the flavor of the prototype, yet small enough to fit any layout. Additional kits can be combined to build a larger structure, even a complete circle! With a 15 degree angle between bays, the roundhouse can be used with a variety of turntables. Locos up to 11-3/8" long can be stored inside.

770-5758   16-1/8 x 35 x 5-1/8"   41 x 89 x 13 cm   134.99

770-5754   Three Stall Roundhouse   13 x 19-5/8 x 4-7/8"   33 x 50 x 12 cm   88.49

770-5255   Roof Support for #5754   4.49   770-5256   Extension Parts for #5754   7.49
Modifies six stall roundhouse for use with Fleischmann turntable.   Modifies roundhouse for use with Marklin turntable.

VOLLMER
Imported from Germany and marketed *by* **WALTHERS**

HO SCALE (1/87)   EASY-TO-BUILD KITS
These easy-to-build structures feature injection molded styrene plastic parts. Each piece is molded in a realistic color, so no painting is needed. For easier assembly, all parts are numbered and co-ordinated with the instruction sheets. Construction time will vary with the size of the kit.

YARD AND EQUIPMENT FACILITIES (continued)

770-5750   Single Engine Shed   28.99
6-1/8 x 4-7/8 x 3-1/2"   15.5 x 12.5 x 9 cm

770-5761   KOF Engine Shed   17.49
2-3/4 x 1-5/8"   6.7 x 4 cm

770-5760   Operating Diesel 2-Stall Shed   53.99
13 x 5-7/8 x 3-7/8"   33 x 15 x 10 cm

2 STALL ENGINE SHED
This small engine shed is well suited to shortline operations. Use with steam and diesel locos, or electrics using catenary section (770-1347) and base frame (770-5253).

770-5752   12 x 7-5/8 x 3-1/2"   30.5 x 19.5 x 9 cm   54.99
770-5253   Base Frame for #5752   pkg(2) 8.49

770-5603   Railway Workshop   15.49
4-3/8 x 2-1/4 x 2-1/4"   11 x 5.8 x 5.8 cm

770-5721   Scale House   10.49
1-3/4 x 1-3/8 x 1-3/4"   4.5 x 3.5 x 4.6 cm

770-5604   Warehouse   19.99
6-1/4 x 4 x 2-1/2"   16 x 10 x 6.5 cm

770-5743   Corrugated Huts   pkg(3) 15.49
2-1/16 x 1-1/16 x 1-5/16"   5.2 x 2.8 x 3.3cm

FREIGHT WAREHOUSE
Expand your yard or industrial park with this modern structure. Opening freight doors make interior detailing easy! Just add loads and figures for a neat mini-scene on your layout.

770-5706   34.99
11-1/8 x 4-1/8 x 4-1/8"   28.5 x 10.5 x 10.5 cm

VOLLMER

Imported from Germany and marketed by WALTHERS

HO SCALE (1/87)   EASY-TO-BUILD KITS

These easy-to-build structures feature injection molded styrene plastic parts. Each piece is molded in a realistic color, so no painting is needed. For easier assembly, all parts are numbered and co-ordinated with the instruction sheets. Construction time will vary with the size of the kit.

YARD & EQUIPMENT FACILITIES (continued)

770-5747   **Engine Cleaning Plant**   18.99
4-7/8 x 1-3/16"   12.5 x 3.2 cm

770-5739   **Signal Tower-Double Track**   26.49
7-1/2 x 2-3/4 x 5-1/8"   19.2 x 7 x 13 cm

770-5737   **Interlocking Tower**   15.49
3-1/2 x 2 x 3-3/8"   9 x 5 x 8.5 cm

770-5749   **Maintenance Yard**   118.49
Includes #'s 5704, 5719, 5740, 5741, 5743, 5747 and 6524.

FREIGHT STATION

Found in every town and major yards, freight stations served industries without sidings. Vollmer loads, listed in the Scenery section, are perfect for detailing this kit.

770-5715   15 x 5-1/8 x 5-3/8"   38 x 13 x 13.5 cm   42.99

770-5740   **Sanding Tower**   27.99
3-1/8 x 2-3/4 x 5-15/16"   8 x 7 x 15.2 cm

770-5741   **Cinder Conveyor**   23.49
2-9/16 x 1-9/16 x 4-3/16"   6.5 x 4 x 10.6 cm

770-5719   **Coal Bunker**   24.49
5-1/8 x 2-3/8 x 2-1/2"   13 x 6 x 6.5 cm

VOLLMER

Imported from Germany and marketed by WALTHERS

HO SCALE (1/87)   EASY-TO-BUILD KITS

These easy-to-build structures feature injection molded styrene plastic parts. Each piece is molded in a realistic color, so no painting is needed. For easier assembly, all parts are numbered and co-ordinated with the instruction sheets. Construction time will vary with the size of the kit.

YARD & EQUIPMENT FACILITIES (continued)

COALING STATION
(Electronically Operated)

This working coaling tower adds action to your loco servicing area! Just push a button and coal drops into waiting tenders. The kit can also be used to load hoppers at a mine or gravel pit!

770-5722   72.99
    4-1/2 x 4-1/2 x 2-3/4"   11.5 x 11.5 x 7 cm

770-3558   Service Platform   10.49
    35-1/4 x 1-1/8 x 1/4"   89.5 x 2.8 x .6 cm

770-5730   Crossing Shanty   15.49
    4-3/8 x 2-3/8 x 3"   11 x 6.1 x 7.5 cm

FREIGHT SHED w/CRANE & RAMP

This busy freight shed will be a good customer for any railroad! A large platform, detailed loading crane and opening doors are all included. A few extra figures and details will bring the finished model to life!

770-5701   11-3/8 x 3-7/8 x 3-1/2"   29 x 10 x 9cm   32.99

770-5731   Interlocking Yard Tower   19.99
    5-1/8 x 2 x 5-1/8"   13 x 5 x 13 cm

VOLLMER
Imported from Germany and marketed **by WALTHERS**

HO SCALE (1/87)   EASY-TO-BUILD KITS
These easy-to-build structures feature injection molded styrene plastic parts. Each piece is molded in a realistic color, so no painting is needed. For easier assembly, all parts are numbered and co-ordinated with the instruction sheets. Construction time will vary with the size of the kit.

YARD & EQUIPMENT FACILITIES (continued)

Ornate
Water Tower
770-5704
29.99
3-5/8 x 3-5/8"
9 x 9 cm

Yard Tower
770-5733
16.99
3-1/8 x 2-1/4 x 4-3/8"
8 x 5.7 x 11 cm

SWITCH TOWER
The prototype for this classic switch tower is still used by the DB, and is located in Wiesbaden, Germany.

770-5736   27.99
6 x 3-5/8"
15.2 x 9 cm

RURAL BUILDINGS

ALPINE DAIRY WITH COW
Start a new business venture in a rural area of your layout with this small dairy. The building could also be used as a cheese or butter factory, whose finished products are sold to passing tourists. A large blue cow figure is included for a roadside sign that's sure to attract attention. A number of small details, including milk cans, are also provided.

770-3707   7-1½ x 5-7/8 x 3-1/2"   18.5 x 15 x 9.1 cm   46.49

770-3706   Alpine Restaurant   37.99
7 x 5-7/8 x 4"
17.8 x 15 x 11.5 cm

770-3708   Alpine Lodge   15.49

VOLLMER
Imported from Germany and marketed *by WALTHERS*

HO SCALE (1/87)   EASY-TO-BUILD KITS
These easy-to-build structures feature injection molded styrene plastic parts. Each piece is molded in a realistic color, so no painting is needed. For easier assembly, all parts are numbered and co-ordinated with the instruction sheets. Construction time will vary with the size of the kit.

RURAL BUILDINGS

Hunters Raised Hide-Away
770-3795   **NEW**   9.49
1-3/16 x 1-3/16"   3 x 3 cm

Station Restaurant **NEW**
770-3663   42.99
7-3/4 x 4-3/4"   19.8 x 12 cm

Garden Center
770-3644
27.99
NEW

Summer Garden House
770-3643
16.99
NEW

Kindergarten
770-3664
43.49
5-5/16 x 4-3/4"
13.5 x 12 cm
NEW

Hayloft
770-3794
13.99
2 x 2"
5 x 5 cm
NEW

VOLLMER

Imported from Germany and marketed
by WALTHERS

HO SCALE (1/87)   EASY-TO-BUILD KITS
These easy-to-build structures feature injection molded styrene plastic parts. Each piece is molded in a realistic color, so no painting is needed. For easier assembly, all parts are numbered and co-ordinated with the instruction sheets. Construction time will vary with the size of the kit.

RURAL BUILDINGS (continued)

VILLAGE INN RATHSKELLER
HO travelers will enjoy a restful night at this Village Inn. A center of activity in any small town, a few extra details can convert the kit into an "Old World" restaurant for a city scene!

770-3754   34.49
4-3/4 x 4-3/4 x 5-3/4"   12 x 12 x 14.5 cm

COMPLETE FARMSTEAD
Here's everything you'll need to start farming . . . in one complete kit! This set includes a Farmhouse, Barn, Stable, Accessory Set (well, pump, rubbish dump and duck house), Bake House, plus stone walls and gates. The kits can be arranged in various ways to fit your available space.

770-3737   Includes one each #3725, 3727, 3726, 3733 and 3729,   with walls and gates.   124.49

770-3733   Smokehouse   13.99
2-3/8 x 2-1/8 x 3"

770-3729   Farmyard Accessories   15.49
Includes well, pump, rubbish dumps and duck house.

770-4114 Smoke Generator for #3729   26.99

770-3727   Barn   29.99
5-1/2 x 3-3/4"   14 x 9.6 cm

770-3726   Stable w/Pigeon Loft   29.99
5-1/2 x 3-1/8"   14 x 8 cm

770-3680   Winery Festival   33.99
6-1/4 x 5-1/2"   16 x 14 cm
Includes an outdoor serving area with benches, wine press and wooden storage barrel.

VOLLMER

Imported from Germany and marketed by WALTHERS

HO SCALE (1/87)   EASY-TO-BUILD KITS

These easy-to-build structures feature injection molded styrene plastic parts. Each piece is molded in a realistic color, so no painting is needed. For easier assembly, all parts are numbered and co-ordinated with the instruction sheets. Construction time will vary with the size of the kit.

RURAL BUILDINGS (continued)

770-3705 Alpine House/Farm 43.99
7-1/4 x 5 x 3-1/2"   18.5 x 12.8 x 9.2 cm

770-3732 Vintner's Lodge 28.99
4-3/4 x 3-1/2 x 5-3/4"   12 x 9 x 14.5 cm

770-3730 Farmhouse 27.99
4 x 3 x 4-7/8"   10.3 x 7.5 x 12.5 cm

770-3731 House w/Barn 27.99
4-7/8 x 2-3/4 x 4-3/4"   12.5 x 7 x 12 cm

SAWMILL

This attractive model can be used in almost any era! With its attached country home and large water wheel, it will make a great mini-diorama on your layout. For more realism, the wheel can be powered with motor 770-4200.

770-3793   56.99
8-7/8 x 8-1/8 x 4-1/8"
22.5 x 20.5 x 10.5 cm

770-4200 Sawmill Motor 26.99
for #3793, 12V DC

FORESTER'S HOUSE

Nestled in the woods, this handsome kit can serve as a house or hunting lodge.

770-3792   36.49
5-1/2 x 4-1/2 x 5"   14 x 11.5 x 12.5 cm

Tanner's House
770-3734
27.99
4-3/8 x 3-3/4"
11 x 8.5 x 12 cm

■ LIMITED QUANTITIES AVAILABLE ■

770-3685 Coach House 27.99
4-1/2 x 4-5/16" 11.4 x 11 cm

(not illustrated)
770-3735 Timbered Village 130.49
Set includes #'s 3730, 3734, 3750 and 3769.

VOLLMER

Imported from Germany and marketed by WALTHERS

HO SCALE (1/87)   EASY-TO-BUILD KITS

These easy-to-build structures feature injection molded styrene plastic parts. Each piece is molded in a realistic color, so no painting is needed. For easier assembly, all parts are numbered and co-ordinated with the instruction sheets. Construction time will vary with the size of the kit.

HOUSES

HOUSE ON FIRE

There's trouble in the neighborhood! This kit can be the beginning of an exciting mini-scene for your layout! The structure is realistically detailed with a burned out roof and exposed trusses. You can build the model with the fire under control, or for extra action, a smoke generator (770-4113) can be installed. Emergency vehicles, figures and other details to complete the scene can be found in the appropriate sections of the catalog.

770-3728   37.99
    4-3/4 x 3-1/2 x 5-3/4"   12 x 9 x 14.5 cm
770-4113 Smoke Generator for #3728 & 3729 20.99

770-3723   House w/Shop   22.99
  6-7/8 x 4-3/8 x 3"   17.5 11 x 7.5 cm

770-3691   House Under Construction   35.99
  6-7/8 x 5-1/2"   17.5 x 14 cm

770-3718   House w/Garage   19.99
  4-1/2 x 4-3/4 x 3-1/2"   11.5 x 12 x 8.8 cm

770-3724   House w/Bakery   22.99
  4-3/4 x 4-3/4 x 3-1/8"   12 x 12 x 8 cm
  4-3/4 x 3 x 2-1/8"   12 x 7.5 x 5.5 cm

Gate Keeper's House
770-3529
41.99
5-1/4 x 3-3/4"
13.2 x 9.5 cm

770-3690   Scaffolding Kit   11.99

Merchant's House
770-3740
32.99
4 x 3-3/8 x 5-3/4"
10 x 8.5 x 14.5 cm

See also: SCENERY; LIGHTING, ELECTRICAL & MOTORS; CIR-CUS; SIGNALS & DETECTION; and BOOKS for additional VOLLMER items.

VOLLMER

Imported from Germany and marketed by WALTHERS

HO SCALE (1/87)   EASY-TO-BUILD KITS

These easy-to-build structures feature injection molded styrene plastic parts. Each piece is molded in a realistic color, so no painting is needed. For easier assembly, all parts are numbered and co-ordinated with the instruction sheets. Construction time will vary with the size of the kit.

HOUSES (continued)

770-3702   Alpine House-Chalet Style   19.99
6-1/8 x 4-3/8 x 3"   15.5 x 11 x 7.5 cm

770-3714   Cottage   19.99
7-1/2 x 6-1/8 x 3-1/8"   19 x 15.5 x 8 cm

770-3703   Alpine Chalet   19.99
4-7/8 x 4-3/8 x 3"   12.5 x 11 x 7.5 cm

BUNGALOW

Enjoy quiet residential living! All brick construction and a new shingle roof make this an ideal starter home. The finished building requires a very small lot, so it's perfect for any neighborhood.

770-3719   19.99
5-1/8 x 4-3/4 x 2-7/8"
13 x 12 x 7.3 cm

770-3701   Mountain Cottage   19.99
4-3/4 x 5-3/8 x 3"   12 x 13.5 x 7.5 cm

770-3700   2-Story House   19.99
7-1/2 x 5-1/2 x 3-1/8"   19 x 14 x 8 cm

RANCH STYLE HOUSE

Homes like this are a common sight in the suburbs. The kit features simulated stone and stucco construction with a tile roof. For the interior decorator, printed curtains are included.

770-3712   5-7/8 x 4-3/8 x 2-1/2"   15 x 11 x 6.5 cm   19.99

VOLLMER

Imported from Germany and marketed by WALTHERS

HO SCALE (1/87)   EASY-TO-BUILD KITS

These easy-to-build structures feature injection molded styrene plastic parts. Each piece is molded in a realistic color, so no painting is needed. For easier assembly, all parts are numbered and co-ordinated with the instruction sheets. Construction time will vary with the size of the kit.

HOUSES (continued)

770-3757   3-Door Garage   14.99
4-3/8 x 2-3/4 x 1-3/4"   11 x 7 x 4.5 cm

770-3711   Lake Shore House   24.99
7-5/8 x 4-3/4 x 3-3/8"
19.5 x 12 x 8.5 cm

770-3713   Country House   19.99
5-1/8 x 5-1/8 x 2-3/4"   13 x 13 x 7 cm

CITY BUILDINGS

770-3781   Restaurant   45.99
6-1/16 x 4-11/16"   15.5 x 12 cm

770-3782   City Hotel   44.99
5-3/8 x 5-1/16"   13.8 x 13 cm

MODERN PARKING STRUCTURE

This modern structure will be easy to "park" on your layout! The kit has the large, realistic appearance of downtown structures, yet it's perfect for modeling a city scene in a small area. To start your scene, the kit includes a Wiking auto, decorated with the Vollmer logo! Just add vehicles, figures and other accessories (which you'll find elsewhere in this Catalog) for a great mini-diorama!

770-3802   15 x 7-1/2 x 6-3/4"   38.5 x 19 x 17 cm   58.99

770-3783   Coffee Shop   45.99
6-5/8 x 4-11/16"   17 x 12 cm

Private Hotel
770-3774   40.99
4-1/8 x 3-3/4 x 8-1/4"
10.4 x 9.6 x 21 cm

Classic Style Building w/Cafe
770-3770   40.99
4-3/4 x 4 x 7-3/4"
12 x 10 x 19.6 cm

Public Record Office
770-3773   40.99
4-3/8 x 7 x 8"
11 x 10.8 x 20.5 cm

VOLLMER

Imported from Germany and marketed
by WALTHERS

HO SCALE (1/87)   EASY-TO-BUILD KITS

These easy-to-build structures feature injection molded styrene plastic parts. Each piece is molded in a realistic color, so no painting is needed. For easier assembly, all parts are numbered and co-ordinated with the instruction sheets. Construction time will vary with the size of the kit.

CITY BUILDINGS (continued)

770-3776   Sanitorium   92.99
11-5/8 x 3-3/4 x 8-1/4″   29.6 x 9.6 x 21 cm

770-3841   Photo Shop   32.99
4 x 3-3/8 x 5-1/2″   10.5 x 8.5 x 14 cm

CITY HALL

With its ornate clock tower and solid, stone construction, this handsome public office will be a showpiece in any large city.

770-3760   71.49
7-1/8 x 4-3/4 x 11-1/4″   18 x 12 x 28.5 cm

MANSION

This large structure will add realism to your downtown area. It's perfect for a big city apartment building or townhouse.

770-3775   92.99
12-3/8 x 4-1/4 x 8-1/16″
31.5 x 10.8 x 20.5 cm

CASTLE HOTEL

770-3777   8 x 4-1/2″   20.5 x 12 cm   58.99

770-3772   4-Story Hotel   40.99
4-3/8 x 3-3/4 x 8-3/4″
11 x 9.5 x 22 cm

City Council Office Building
770-3750   4-3/4 x 4-1/2 x 5-1/8″   35.99
12 x 11.5 x 13 cm

HO SCALE (1/87)   EASY-TO-BUILD KITS

These easy-to-build structures feature injection molded styrene plastic parts. Each piece is molded in a realistic color, so no painting is needed. For easier assembly, all parts are numbered and co-ordinated with the instruction sheets. Construction time will vary with the size of the kit.

CITY BUILDINGS (continued)

FIRE STATION

Practice makes perfect, for the next alarm just might be the one where you put your life on the line. Much to the delight of some passers-by, the chief has the crew putting on quite a show in front of the station. As one of the most important buildings in any town, this Fire Station is perfect for protecting a small town or suburb. Reflecting the needs of a modern community, the station has five apparatus bays that can hold a variety of equipment, as well as upstairs living quarters. Topped off by the traditional hose tower, the finished model makes a proud addition to your layout. You'll find a well-trained crew ready to go on duty in the Figures section, and a complete line up of emergency equipment in Vehicles.

770-3767   29 x 12 cm   11-7/16 x 4-3/4"   58.49

770-3681   Luigi's Pizzeria   41.99
7 x 4-1/2 x 5"   18 x 11.5 x 12.8 cm

Farm Equipment Repair Shop
770-3682   39.99
6-3/8 x 4-3/4 x 4-3/4"   15.8 x 12 x 12 cm

770-3683   Candy Shop   41.99
5-3/4 x 5 x 4-3/4"   14.7 x 12.8 x 12 cm

BICYCLE SHOP

Make bicycling a popular pastime in your model community with this handsome store. The large display windows show off the detailed interior provided with the kit, and working lights are included for evening hours.

770-3710   7 x 5-7/8 x 3-1/2"   17.8 x 15 x 8.8 cm   39.99

REGISTRY OFFICE

Many a city hall building was based on a classic European design and some are still in use today. To add action to your finished model, this kit includes a bride and groom, plus a special electronic unit to provide music for the happy couple. A bakery and drug store occupy shops on the first floor.

770-3844   8 x 4-3/4 x 7-3/8"   20.5 x 12 x 19 cm   69.99

VOLLMER

Imported from Germany and marketed by WALTHERS

HO SCALE (1/87)   EASY-TO-BUILD KITS

These easy-to-build structures feature injection molded styrene plastic parts. Each piece is molded in a realistic color, so no painting is needed. For easier assembly, all parts are numbered and co-ordinated with the instruction sheets. Construction time will vary with the size of the kit.

CITY BUILDINGS (continued)

SET OF THREE APARTMENTS
Model a complete city block or housing complex with this set of three structures! The "kit" includes one each of #3777, 3778 and 3779. The structures can be arranged to fit your available space.

770-3780   91.99

Ornamental Fountain
770-3758   13.99
2-1/8 x 2-1/8 x 5-3/4"
5.5 x 5.5 x 14.5 cm

Public Restrooms
770-3762   13.49
2 x 2 x 2-3/8"
5.1 x 5.1 x 6cm

770-3749   Old Time Store   32.99
4-1/8 x 3-3/8 x 5-1/2"   10.5 x 8.5 x 14 cm

Modern Office Building
770-3800
41.99
5-1/2" x 5-1/2 x 7-7/8"
14 x 14 x 20 cm

(not illustrated)

Fire Station Detail Set
770-5746   13.49
Details for fire stations or vehicles. Set includes hydrants, hose reels, tools, air bottles, road signs, pylons and more.

4-STORY BANK BUILDING
This Bank Building adds interest to any downtown scene! Its small size and corner location save valuable layout space. The design lends itself to kitbashing or conversion to match American architectural styles.

770-3771   40.99
4-1/8 x 3-5/8 x 7-3/4"
10.5 x 9.3 x 19.7 cm

Fire Station w/Tower
770-3752
35.99
4-3/4 x 4-3/4 x 8-5/8"
12 x 12 x 22 cm

VOLLMER

Imported from Germany and marketed by **WALTHERS**

HO SCALE (1/87)   EASY-TO-BUILD KITS

These easy-to-build structures feature injection molded styrene plastic parts. Each piece is molded in a realistic color, so no painting is needed. For easier assembly, all parts are numbered and co-ordinated with the instruction sheets. Construction time will vary with the size of the kit.

CITY BUILDINGS (continued)

Modern Apartment Building
770-3801   41.99
6 x 4-9/16 x 7-7/8"   15.2 x 11.5 x 20 cm

VARIOUS SHOPS

This set of shops will add interest to your city skyline! The set includes a coffee shop, rest-aurant and city hotel. The versatile five-story struc-tures can be ar-ranged in a variety of ways to fit your layout's city scene.

770-3785   110.99
(includes #3781, 3782 and 3783)

BUILDING SET

These classic shops are an ideal way to rebuild your down-town business dis-trict! Many cities are preserving their cul-tural heritage by restoring older build-ings to their original appearance and re-novating them for new businesses. This complete kit in-cludes three build-ings: a Jewelry Shop (#3840), Book Store (#3841) and Photo Studio (#3842), all with working lights.

770-3843   88.49

CHURCHES

770-3840   Jewelry Shop   30.99
3-3/8 x 3-3/8 x 4-7/8"
8.5 x 8.5 x 12.5 cm

770-3842   Bookstore   32.99
3-7/8 x 3-3/8 x 5-5/8"
10 x 8.5 x 14.5

770-3709   St Andrew   41.99
7-1/4 x 5-1/2"   18.5 x 14 cm

VOLLMER

Imported from Germany and marketed by WALTHERS

HO SCALE (1/87)   EASY-TO-BUILD KITS

These easy-to-build structures feature injection molded styrene plastic parts. Each piece is molded in a realistic color, so no painting is needed. For easier assembly, all parts are numbered and co-ordinated with the instruction sheets. Construction time will vary with the size of the kit.

CHURCHES (continued)

CATHEDRAL

Built between 1853 and 1855, the prototype of this beautiful cathedral still stands in Germany. Its period architecture is similar to buildings found in many cities throughout the world. For extra realism, full-color stained glass "windows", printed on translucent paper, are included. For a slightly larger and more detailed scene, the Cathedral Steps (770-3738) which measure 16-1/2 x 7-7/8 x 1/2" can be added.

770-3739   83.99
11-3/4 x 5-3/8 x 15-3/4"   30 x 13.5 x 40 cm

770-3738   Cathedral Steps   16.49

DITZINGEN CHURCH

This medium-sized church will be right at home in a quiet country town. The building features stucco and stone construction, with a tall clock tower and steeple.

770-3769   50.99
9-1/2 x 6-1/8"   23.5 x 15.5 cm

INDUSTRIAL

770-5624   Overhead Crane   32.99
10 x 4-3/4 x 6-1/2"   25.5 x 12 x 16.5 cm

770-5728   Shanty   15.49
3-1/2 x 2-3/4 x 1-3/4"   9 x 7 x 4.5 cm

770-5607   Modern Truck Depot   39.99
10-5/8 x 5-15/16 x 4-3/8"   27 x 15 x 10.5 cm

770-5612   Workshop   18.99
5-1/8 x 2-3/4 x 4-3/8"   13 x 7 x 11 cm

770-5614   Substation or Annex Office   12.99
2-3/8 x 2-3/4 x 2-3/4"   6 x 7 x 7 cm

770-5610   2-Story Factory Building   24.49
5-1/8 x 2-3/4 x 5-1/8"   13 x 7 x 13 cm

VOLLMER

Imported from Germany and marketed
by WALTHERS

HO SCALE (1/87)   EASY-TO-BUILD KITS

These easy-to-build structures feature injection molded styrene plastic parts. Each piece is molded in a realistic color, so no painting is needed. For easier assembly, all parts are numbered and co-ordinated with the instruction sheets. Construction time will vary with the size of the kit.

INDUSTRIAL (continued)

OIL REFINERY

This impressive refinery packs lots of detail into a small space. Several can be combined to build a larger complex.

770-5525   48.49
5-7/8 x 3-7/8 x 9-1/4"
15 x 10 x 23.5 cm

GAS STORAGE TANK

Gas storage facilities are found in the industrial heart of larger cities. This highly detailed kit is big in detail but small in size. Several can be used to make a large complex.

770-5725   46.99
8-1/4 x 7-1/4 x 5-3/4"
21 x 18.5 x 14.5 cm

A great accessory for use with Walthers "North Island Refinery" #933-3013 featured in the Cornerstone Series® listing in this catalog.

Gas Storage Tank
770-5526   18.99
4-3/4 x 4-3/4 x 4-1/2"

770-5602 Boiler House 18.99
5-1/8 x 2-3/4 x 5-1/8"
18 x 11.5 x 7 cm

Smoke Stack Only
770-6017   6.49

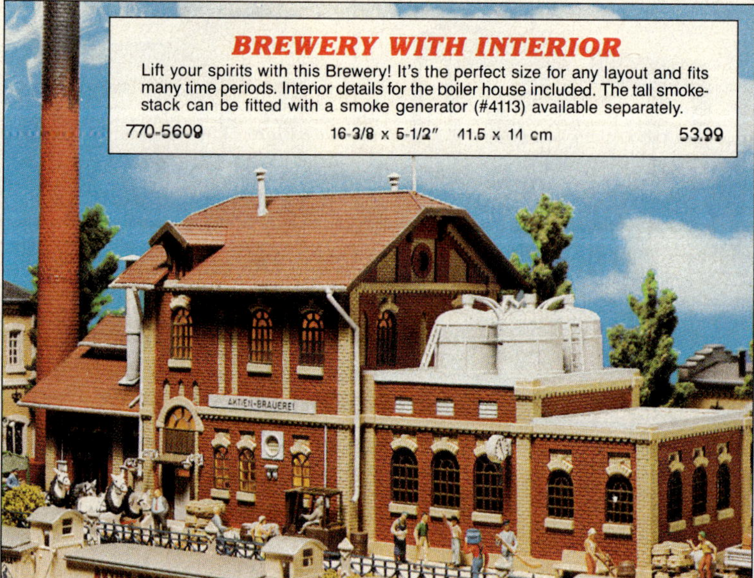

BREWERY WITH INTERIOR

Lift your spirits with this Brewery! It's the perfect size for any layout and fits many time periods. Interior details for the boiler house included. The tall smoke-stack can be fitted with a smoke generator (#4113) available separately.

770-5609   16-3/8 x 5-1/2"   41.5 x 14 cm   53.99

VOLLMER

Imported from Germany and marketed
by **WALTHERS**

HO SCALE (1/87)   EASY-TO-BUILD KITS

These easy-to-build structures feature injection molded styrene plastic parts. Each piece is molded in a realistic color, so no painting is needed. For easier assembly, all parts are numbered and co-ordinated with the instruction sheets. Construction time will vary with the size of the kit.

INDUSTRIAL (continued)

770-5723   Gravel Loader   72.99
11 x 4-3/8 x 5-7/8"   28 x 11 x 15 cm
(electric, operating)

770-5520   Storage Tank-Triple   18.49
3-3/8 x 2-3/8 x 3"

CONVEYOR KIT

This new kit is ideal for mines, gravel pits, and other bulk loading industries. The kit includes an electric motor and can be used to actually load hoppers or trucks. (It's also a perfect accessory to the Coaling Station, 770-5722) In case of a break down, a replacement conveyor belt (770-4611) is available separately.

| 770-4601 | 7-1/8 x 4 x 6-3/4"   18 x 10 x 17 cm | 83.99 |
| 770-4611 | Conveyor Belt for #4601 | 9.49 |

770-5608   Factory Under Demolition   45.99
13-3/8 x 5-1/2 x 11-7/8"

770-5527   Oil Loading Platform   18.99
13-3/8 x 1-7/8 x 3"

MODERN TRUCK TERMINAL

Keep on trucking with this modern terminal building! A natural for today's busy industrial areas, the kit features five loading docks, an attached office and printed signs.

770-5605   12-3/16 x 8"   31 x 20 cm   46.49

VOLLMER

Imported from Germany and marketed
by WALTHERS

HO SCALE (1/87)   EASY-TO-BUILD KITS
These easy-to-build structures feature injection molded styrene plastic parts. Each piece is molded in a realistic color, so no painting is needed. For easier assembly, all parts are numbered and co-ordinated with the instruction sheets. Construction time will vary with the size of the kit.

BUSINESSES

VILLAGE STREET
Start your street scene with this set of three structure kits, which includes a Police Station, Blacksmith and Liquor Store. Includes one each #3693, 3696 and 3697.
770-3699   117.99

Blacksmith
770-3696
35.99
6-1/2 x 5-1/2"
16.5 x 14 cm

SUPERMARKET
Don't forget to pick up some milk, eggs and this new kit on your way home from work. This structure features a ground floor converted to a supermarket, while the upper floors can be rented out as apartments. The model includes an interior for the first floor and working lights.
770-3660   16.8 x 14 cm   41.99

770-5744   Gas Station   25.99
             3-3/8 x 4 x 1-3/4"   8.5 x 10 x 4.3 cm
770-5745   Pump Islands Only   pkg(3) 15.49

Market Accessories
770-5140   13.49

Babyland Store
            12 x 11.5 cm   39.49
770-3661
Includes interior details, working lights, a stork and her nest.

770-3694   Boutique   40.99
      7-1/2 x 5-5/16"   19 x 13.5 cm

Ferrari
Station
770-5606
64.99
20 x 14.8 cm

770-3698   Market Street   116.99
Includes 1 each 3692, 3694, 3695

LIQUOR STORE
This new building will be the toast of your HO neighborhood! It's ornate design makes it an eye-catching building for any street scene. A handy loading dock makes it easy to load beer and wine barrels.
770-3697   44.49
8-1/16 x 5-1/8"   20.5 x 13 cm

VOLLMER
Imported from Germany and marketed
by WALTHERS

HO SCALE (1/87)   EASY-TO-BUILD KITS
These easy-to-build structures feature injection molded styrene plastic parts. Each piece is molded in a realistic color, so no painting is needed. For easier assembly, all parts are numbered and co-ordinated with the instruction sheets. Construction time will vary with the size of the kit.

BUSINESSES (continued)

770-3747   Old Time Drug Store   27.49
3-3/8 x 3-3/8 x 4-7/8" 8.5 x 8.5 x 12.5 cm

770-3722   Butcher's Shop w/Garage   22.99
4-5/8 x 3-3/8 x 4" 11.8 x 8.5 x 10.2 cm

770-3632   Burger King   **NEW** 46.49
7-7/8 x 5-3/4" 20 x 14.8 cm

Travel Agency
770-3662
37.49
7 x 4-1/4"
18 x 11.5 cm

770-5135   Food Stand   10.49

770-3666   Bikers Shop   **NEW** 39.49
16 x 10.5 cm

THE BLACK FOREST CLINIC
This big building will be a real star on your layout! The prototype is the setting for the West German TV soap opera, "Black Forest Clinic" and appears in the opening of each episode.

770-3790   85.99
11-5/8 x 7-5/8 x 7-7/8" 29.5 x 19.5 x 20 cm

770-3667   Hairdresser Shop   **NEW** 39.59

770-3736   Adler Inn w/Beer Garden   39.49
8-1/4 x 5-1/8" 21 x 13 cm

VOLLMER

Imported from Germany and marketed by WALTHERS

HO SCALE (1/87)   EASY-TO-BUILD KITS

These easy-to-build structures feature injection molded styrene plastic parts. Each piece is molded in a realistic color, so no painting is needed. For easier assembly, all parts are numbered and co-ordinated with the instruction sheets. Construction time will vary with the size of the kit.

CITY BUILDINGS (continued)

MODERN FIRE STATION

Don't be ''alarmed'', this large firehouse fits any city scene! Three structures (main building, lobby/office and six-story hose tower) are included and can be arranged in a variety of ways. The large glass doors can be opened to display engines parked inside. (See the Vehicles Section for a complete listing of fire fighting vehicles. Engine and figures available separately.)

770-3759   1-1/4 x 5-7/8"   3.2 x 15 cm   54.49

POST OFFICE

Put your stamp of approval on this ornate Post Office! With its classic architecture, it can easily be converted to a school, library or other public building by adding appropriate details and figures.

770-3765   8-1/4 x 6-1/2"   21 x 16.6 cm   70.49

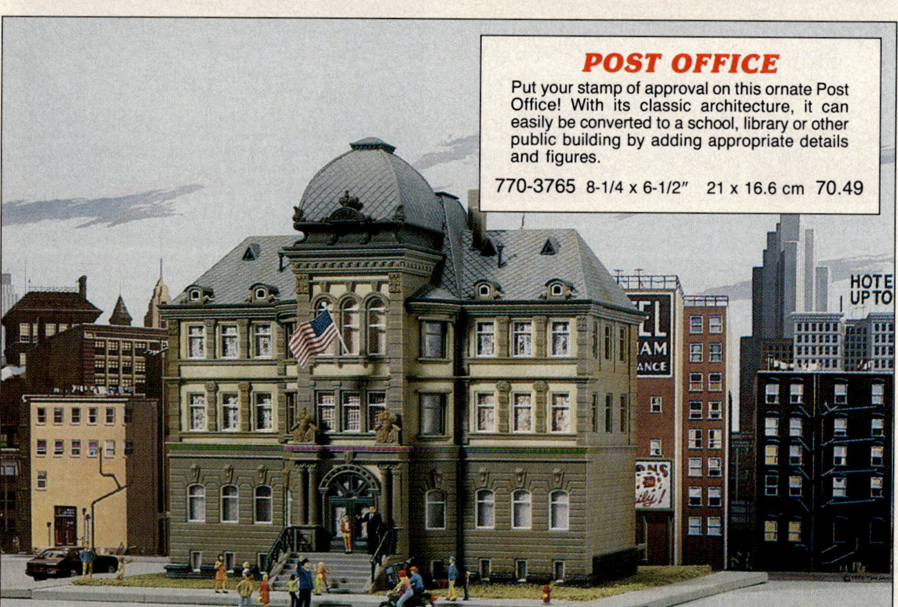

770-3751   5-Stall Fire Station   58.99
11-3/8 x 4-3/4 x 8-5/8"   29 x 12 x 22 cm

770-3753   Road Garage   30.99
6-3/4 x 4-3/4 x 5-1/2"   17 x 12 x 14 cm

770-3756   Maintenance Depot   27.99
5-1/2 x 3-1/8 x 6-5/8"   14 x 8 x 17 cm

770-3748   Old Time Post Office   32.99
4 x 4-3/4 x 7-1/2"   10 x 12 x 19 cm

770-3755   Rural Police Headquarters   58.99
10-5/8 x 5-1/2 x 6-5/8"   27 x 14 x 17 cm

VOLLMER

Imported from Germany and marketed
by WALTHERS

HO SCALE (1/87)   EASY-TO-BUILD KITS

These easy-to-build structures feature injection molded styrene plastic parts. Each piece is molded in a realistic color, so no painting is needed. For easier assembly, all parts are numbered and co-ordinated with the instruction sheets. Construction time will vary with the size of the kit.

BRIDGES AND VIADUCTS

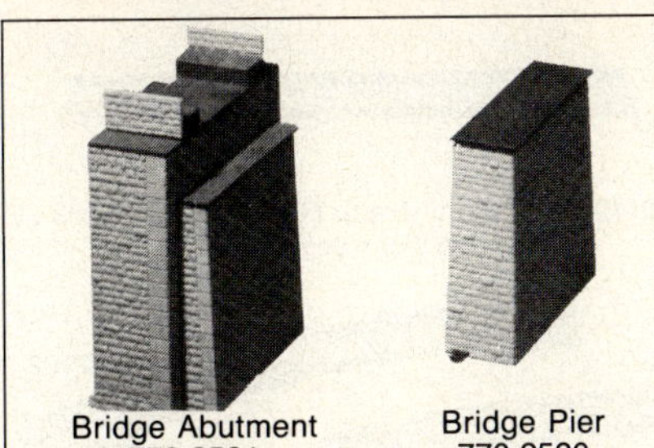

Bridge Abutment
770-2531
pair 16.99
3-5/8 x 1-1/4 x 3-3/4"
9.2 x 3.2 x 9.6 cm

Bridge Pier
770-2530
each 8.49
3-1/8 x 1-1/8 x 3"
8 x 3 x 7.7 cm

770-2508   Arched Bridge   **NEW** 37.49
26 x 6.3 x 9.5 cm

CURVED DECK BRIDGE

Curved bridge deck with two supports. Length: 14-3/4" 37.6 cm, Radius: 29-7/8" 76 cm.

770-2507   14.49

770-2506   Box Truss Bridge   32.99
14-1/8 x 3 x 4-3/8"   36 x 7.5 x 11.2 cm
770-1351   Catenary for #2506   pkg(2) 9.99

770-2505   Truss Bridge   22.99
10-5/8 x 3 x 2-1/4"   27 x 7.5 x 5.8 cm

770-2511   Steel Truss Bridge-Straight   15.99
7-1/8" 18 cm long

CURVED GIRDER BRIDGE

This detailed bridge is designed for use on curves. Can be used with Curved Deck Bridges #2507 and #4515.

770-2510   15.99
7-3/8" 13.8 cm long   29-7/8" 76 cm diameter

VOLLMER

Imported from Germany and marketed by WALTHERS

HO SCALE (1/87)   EASY-TO-BUILD KITS

These easy-to-build structures feature injection molded styrene plastic parts. Each piece is molded in a realistic color, so no painting is needed. For easier assembly, all parts are numbered and co-ordinated with the instruction sheets. Construction time will vary with the size of the kit.

BRIDGES & VIADUCTS (continued)

FOOT BRIDGE

HO Scale pedestrians can cross tracks, highways or other obstacles safely on this foot bridge. Standing 5″ tall, there's plenty of clearance for most freight and passenger cars. Kitbashers will find lots of ways to build unique variations of the basic model.

770-5709   10 x 8-1/4″   25 x 21 cm   24.49

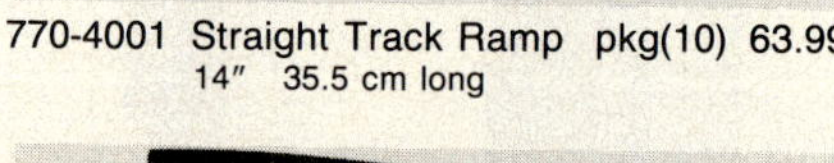

770-4001   Straight Track Ramp   pkg(10) 63.99
    14″   35.5 cm long

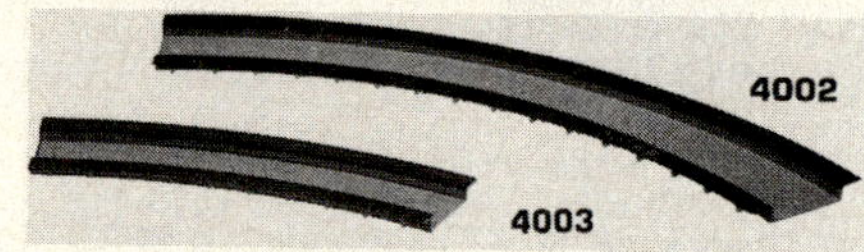

Curved Track Ramp
770-4002   15″ Radius   pkg(10) 63.99
770-4003   18″ Radius   pkg(10) 53.99

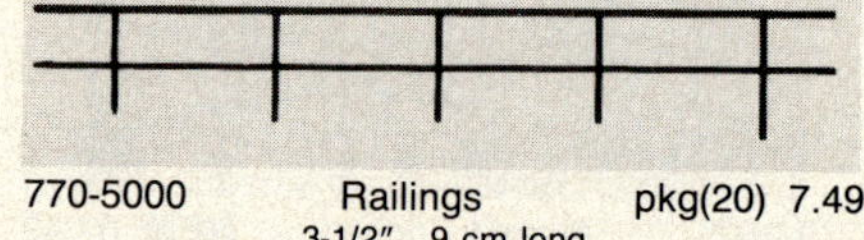

770-5000   Railings   pkg(20) 7.49
    3-1/2″   9 cm long

(not illustrated)

770-4507   Pier & Ramp Starter Set   62.49
    Includes 3 straight track beds #4001, 3 curved trackbeds #4002, 2 piers #4004, 8 top sections #1002, and bases #4005 & #4006, and 16 screws.

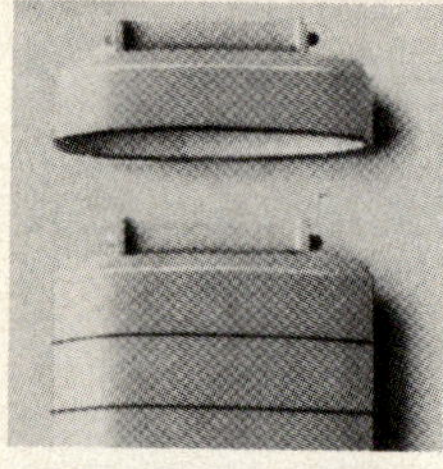

Bridge Pier Units
770-4016
pkg(20) 19.49
    3/8″   1 cm high
    Can be stacked to fit
    various heights.

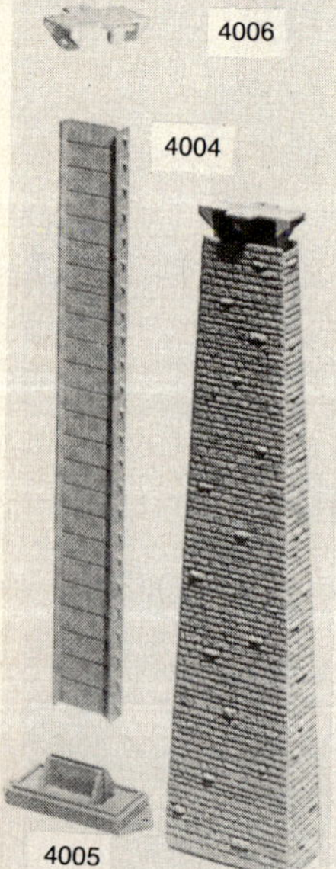

Piers
770-4004
pkg(10) 23.99
    9-1/2″   24 cm high
    Used to support track
    ramps. May be cut to
    shorter lengths.

Base Plate
770-4005
pkg(20) 45.99
    Used to support piers,
    #4004.

Top Section
770-4006
pkg(20) 28.99
    Used to secure ramps
    to piers. Includes 40
    mounting screws.

Pier ''Dressing''
770-4512
pkg(5) 35.99
    Plastic stone for #4004.

(not illustrated)
Unloading Ramp
770-4011   8.49

STONE ARCH BRIDGE-STRAIGHT

Whether modern diesel or classic steam, this bridge will fit into any era! Small enough to compliment every layout, the kit draws attention without overweling the scene.
770-2509   32.99
    14-1/8 x 2-3/8 x 4-1/8″   36 x 6 x 10.5 cm

VOLLMER
Imported from Germany and marketed *by WALTHERS*

HO SCALE (1/87) EASY-TO-BUILD KITS

These easy-to-build structures feature injection molded styrene plastic parts. Each piece is molded in a realistic color, so no painting is needed. For easier assembly, all parts are numbered and coordinated with the instruction sheets. Construction time will vary with the size of the kit.

MISCELLANEOUS

CASTLE WITH GHOST

This castle with ghost will add some spirit to your layout! Featuring realistic stone walls and watch towers, the structure will bring old world charm to your layout.

770-3910   153.49
13-3/4 x 11-3/4″
35 x 30 cm

City Walls for Castle
770-3903   41.99
13-3/4 x 5-7/8″
35 x 15 cm

770-3911 Ghost 15.49

770-3901   Towergate   39.49
10-3/16 x 2-1/2″ 26 x 6.3 cm

770-3630   Windmill   37.49
Less motor, 19 x 9 cm

770-3665   Playground *NEW*   7.99

OLD LADIES MILL

Legend has it that if an old lady slips while coming down the chute of this historic windmill, she'll arrive at the bottom as a young girl! Bring a bit of the legend to your layout with this handsome kit, based on an actual structure located along the route between Stuttgart and Heilbron, Germany.

770-3628   68.99

	(not illustrated)	
770-9254	House Anemone	15.99
770-9300	Mountain Village 5 building set	85.49

A M Models

HO SCALE (1/87) EASY-TO-BUILD KITS

Molded in appropriately colored plastic.

"JENNYSVILLE" YARD FACILITIES

101   102   104

129-101   Trackside Shanty   1.50
5/8 x 3/4"   1.5 x 2 cm

129-102   Shanty   1 x 1"   2.5 x 2.5 cm   2.98
Prototype can be found in Hudsonville, Michigan, next to the C&O tracks.

129-104   Freight Station   3.50
1-1/2 x 2-1/16"   4 x 5.2 cm

129-105   Tower   3.50
1 x 1-1/2"   2.5 x 4 cm

Freight Platform
129-107   2-1/4 x 5-1/2"   2.98

"WILLIAMSBURG" YARD FACILITIES

Workshed
129-106
5.98
1-1/2 x 4-3/4"

Freight Station
129-108   5.98
2-1/2 x 2-1/4"

Bunkhouse
129-109   3.50
2-1/4 x 5-1/2"

Long Freight Station
129-110
5.98

Williamsburg Yard Office
129-103
3.50
1-1/2 x 2-1/16"   4 x 5.2 cm

Hamelton Freight Station
129-111
9.98

BRIDGES

Simple Beam, Bridge
129-301
1.98
4 x 1-9/16"
10 x 4 cm, 4" tall

129-302   Short Trestle Bridge   3.50
2-1/4 x 1-1/4"   5.7 x 3.2 cm

Alexander scale models

HO CRAFT TRAIN KITS

Kit features precision cut wood, metal castings and diecut roof and floor parts.

YARD & EQUIPMENT FACILITIES

NYC Fairbanks-Morse Coaling Station
120-7200   16.00
2-1/2 x 3-1/4"
6.4 x 8.3 cm

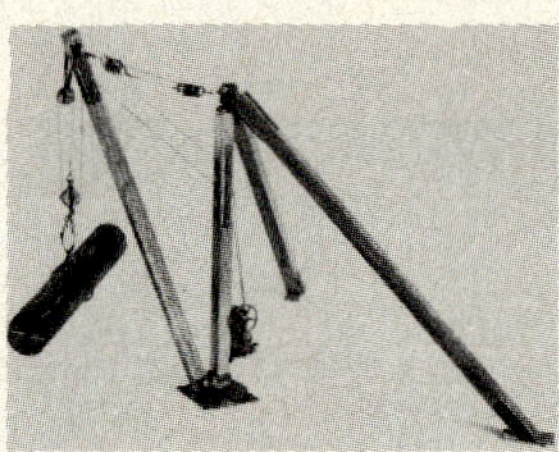

Stiff Leg Derrick
120-7514
8.50

Loading Rack
120-7445
4.00

Brownhoist Little Hook
120-7519
7.75

Oil Drilling Rig
120-7488
19.95

TAURUS PRODUCTS

HO SCALE CRAFT TRAIN KITS

Kits feature die cut wood walls, plastic, etched brass or cast metal details and templates.

"Roll Away" Cattle Loading Ramp
707-200   5-7/8 x 1"   15 x 2.5 cm   12.95
Prototype was in Yorba Linda, California.
Features "working" roll-away ramp and code 40 rail.

Daley Bros Pipe & Supply Co
707-201   3-1/2 x 7"   9 x 17.8 cm   19.95
Includes fence and scale pipe.

Tomahawk Post Office
707-202   24.95
3-1/2 x 3-1/4"
9 x 8.2 cm

Chooch ENTERPRISES INC. ™

HO SCALE (1/87) EASY-TO-BUILD KITS

Kits feature easy polyurethane construction with stripwood, plastic and cast metal details. Walls feature casting of stone and wood grain.

YARD & EQUIPMENT FACILITIES

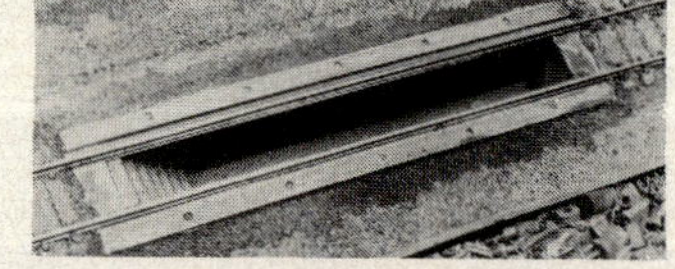

214-9019   40' Loco Inspection Pit   8.99
6 x 1-1/2"   15.3 x 13.8 cm

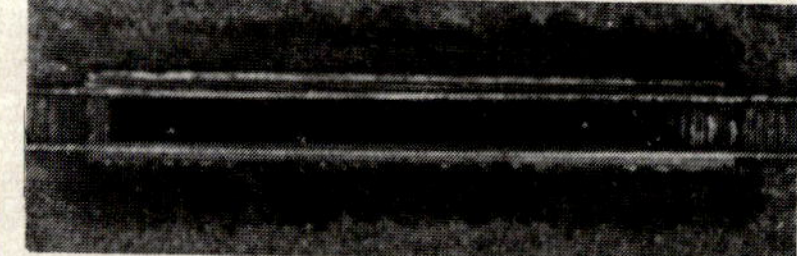

214-9020   60' Loco Inspection Pit   9.99
8-1/4 x 1-1/4"   21 x 3.2 cm

AMERICAN MODEL BUILDERS, INC.

NEW

HO CRAFT TRAIN KITS

Laser kits feature styrene, wood and similar materials which have been cut to a precise shape and size using a computer-controlled laser. These pieces are highly detailed and assemble much like those in injection molded kits.

STATIONS & PLATFORMS

Farber Station
152-111
TBA

Cumbres Station
152-112
45.95

Freight House
152-701
29.95

YARD & EQUIPMENT FACILITIES

Tool & Hand Car House
152-114   TBA

Coal Shed
152-201   4.25

Hose House
152-202
4.95

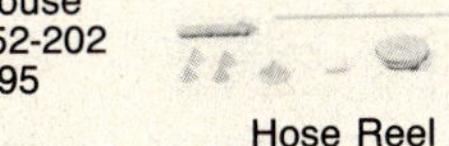

Hose Reel
152-203   2.00

Telephone Booths
152-113
pkg(2) TBA
(not illustrated)

152-204   Oil & Lamp Box   3.95
152-702   Interlocking Tower   29.95

RURAL BUILDINGS   PIER

Country Grain Elevator
152-110   39.95

Cut Stone Pier
152-210 18'   6.95
152-211 18' (2) 12.95
152-212 47'   12.95

Builders In Scale
Fine Craft Models

YARD AND EQUIPMENT FACILITY

Scale House
169-610   22.98
3-1/2 x 3-1/2"   9 x 9 cm
(w/truck pad)
3-1/2 x 9"   9 x 23 cm
(w/rail pad)

Includes a 10' x 10' building, detailed casting of the scale mechanism, "concrete" foundation and separate scale platforms for rail or truck. Rail platform includes non-operating ground throws and additional rails. Over 25 detail castings are included. Brass etched cemetary fence and sign.
(By Special Order Only.)

CITY BUILDINGS

Pitkin City Hall
169-10   89.95
6 x 8"   15 x 20 cm

Includes stone walls, clapboard siding & white metal detail parts. City Hall, Grange, School and Church signs also included. Brass etched cemetary fence and sign.
(By Special Order Only.)

BUSINESSES

Double Stationary Boiler
169-607   16.98
Cast hydrocal brick boiler block and apron, white metal detail parts. 2" x 1-5/8".

CG&T Hose Company
169-605   32.98
2-3/4 x 5"   7 x 12.7 cm

Flybinyte Construction Company
169-603   18.98
4 x 4"   10 x 10 cm
Small job site trailer and 3-man housing cabin on skids. Prototype 1930's. Laser cut wood.

Pump & Boiler House
169-602   24.98
3-1/2 x 3" 8.8 x 7.5 cm
Includes cast plaster stonework foundation and over 25 detail castings. Laser cut wood.

TRACKSIDE SHED

169-601   Trackside Shed   14.98
2 x 4"   5 x 10 cm
Includes aluminum ribbed seam roofing and siding material, over 20 metal detail castings and handcar track.

HO SCALE (1/87) CRAFT TRAIN KITS

Kits feature wood construction with metal details and architectural plans.

HOUSE

169-606   "630 Elm Street"   42.98
Includes precast brick walls, stone foundation with period details (coal door, ash door in fireplace, clapboard gables, venetian blinds). A separate garage and over 60 cast metal details (flower boxes, dog house, old bathtub, clothesline poles, swing set) are also included.

MISCELLANEOUS

■ LTD QUANTITIES AVAILABLE ■
169-9   Tidewater Wharf   135.00
Includes lighthouse, sailmaker's shop, a drydock and other small structures. Detail parts and color signs are also included. Limited run.

Columbia Valley Model

HO CRAFT TRAIN KITS

Kits include diecut siding material, scale lumber, Grandt Line plastic doors and windows and cast metal detail parts.

Johnson Motor Service   19.95
4-1/8 x 2"   10.5 x 5 cm

Victorian Cottage   216-8703   29.49
4 x 3-1/8"   10 x 8 cm

1940-50s Gas Pumps
216-187   pkg(2) 3.95

216-8702 House 28.49
3-1/2 x 5"   9 x 12.7 cm
Turn of the Century

Butler® Bins
216-8704
pkg(2) 13.95

HO SCALE (1/87) EASY-TO-BUILD KITS

Start a construction boom on your layout with the Atlas line of trackside structures and accessories! Based on authentic American prototypes, the kits are molded in realistically colored styrene. The kits also include easy-to-follow instructions, decals and printed window glazing where appropriate.

STATIONS & PLATFORMS

150-706   Passenger Station   8.00
4-1/16 x 8-7/8" 10.3 x 22.5 cm

Station Platform
150-707
pkg(2)
3.75
each:
2-1/8 x 3-1/8"
5.4 x 8 cm

BRIDGES & PIERS

Bridges feature brass rail unless noted.

150-80   Pier Set   9.95
Includes 46 stone masonry piers, graduated in height, 1 pier girder; snap-in shims.

130' Curved Cord
18" 45.7 cm
150-87   Brass   16.00
150-887   Nickel Silver   16.50

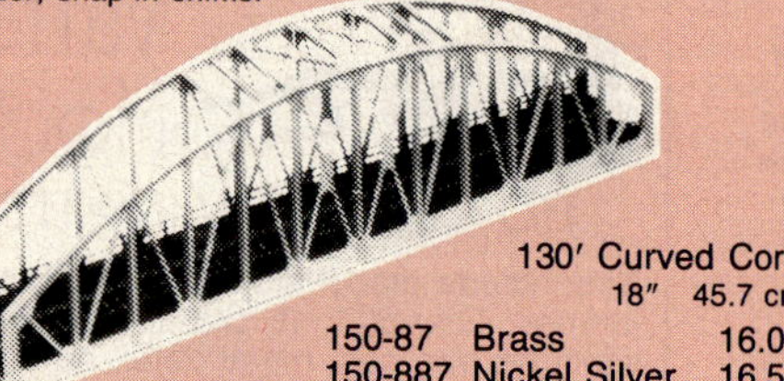

150-85   65' Thru Plate Girder   3.75
9 x 2-5/8" 23 x 6.5 cm brass (assembled)

150-885   65' Thru Plate Girder   4.00
9 x 2-5/8" 23 x 6.5 cm (nickel silver, assembled)

BUSINESSES

Refreshment Stand
150-715   4.50
3-1/2 x 4-1/4" 9 x 10.7 cm

YARD & EQUIPMENT FACILITIES

Elevated Gate Tower
150-701   4.75
1-3/8 x 2" 3.5 x 5 cm

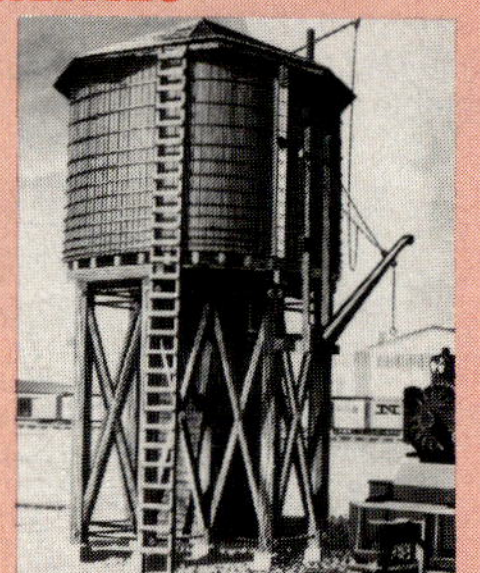

Water Tower
150-703   6.00
3-1/4 x 3-1/4" 8.2 x 8.2

150-704 Signal Tower   6.00
2-5/8 x 5-1/2" 6.5 x 14 cm

Telephone Shanty & Pole
150-705   3.25
1-3/8 x 3-1/16" 3.5 x 7.7 cm

65' Manual Turntable
9" Brass 23cm diam.
150-302   16.75

65' Manual Turntable
Nickel Silver
150-303   17.00

Trackside Shanty
150-702   4.75
2-1/4 x 3-1/8" 5.7 x 8 cm

Turntable Drive Unit
150-304
19.95
NEW

65' Warren Truss
9" 23 cm
150-83   Brass   3.75
150-883   Nickel Silver   4.00

65' Deck Truss
9" 23 cm
150-84   Brass   3.75
150-884   Nickel Silver   4.00

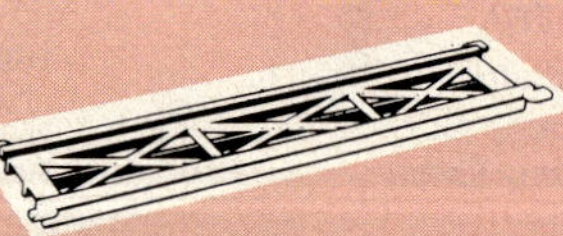

65'
Pony Truss
9" 23 cm
150-86   Brass   10.00
150-886   Nickel Silver   10.25

150-82   Pier Girder   pkg(4) 2.00

Bridge Pier
150-81   pkg(4) 2.50
3" 7.5 cm

150-750   Lumber Yard & Office   7.50
3-3/4 x 8-5/8" 9.5 x 22 cm

150-760   Roadside Restaurant   7.75
5-5/8 x 9-5/8" 14.3 x 24.5 cm

ATLAS
MODEL RAILROAD CO., INC.

HO SCALE (1/87) EASY-TO-BUILD KITS

Construct a complete city scene on your layout with these structure kits. The easy-to-build plastic buildings are molded in colors and can easily be superdetailed with some detail painting and weathering.

HOUSES

150-600   Ranch House   11.50
7-1/2 x 4" 19.2 x 10.1 cm

150-601   Colonial House   11.50
6 x 4" 15.3 x 10.1 cm

150-602   Historic House   11.50
5-1/2 x 4" 14 x 10.2 cm

150-603   Cape Cod House   11.50
7-1/2 x 4-1/4" 19.2 x 10.9 cm

150-604   Split Level House   11.50
4 x 7" 10.1 x 17.7 cm

POOL

150-605   Swimming Pool   7.50
2-1/4" 5 x 10.1 cm

CITY BUILDINGS

150-607   School   14.50
7 x 4-1/4" 17 x 10.8 cm

Municipal Building
150-609   14.50
7 x 6-1/4"
17.5 x 15.6 cm

150-608   Firehouse   14.50
7 x 8-1/4" 17 x 20.9 cm

150-610   Mini-Mall   14.50
8-1/4 x 5-7/8" 21.2 x 14.8 cm

A.I.M. PRODUCTS

HO CRAFT TRAIN KITS

Forks Creek Station
110-602   21.95
4 x 5" 12 x 17 cm
Kit consists of 7 unpainted urethane castings, metal train order board, station sign board and Grandt line castings. Prototype in Colorado.

CENTRAL VALLEY

HO SCALE (1/87) EASY-TO-BUILD KITS

RIGID PRATT TRUSS BRIDGE

Kit includes molded black plastic parts and two steel bands to reinforce lower girders.

150 foot, HO single track bridge features a removable upper truss, premolded bridge ties and extra long girder components. (Ties will accept code 70 or 83 rail, or be easily modified for code 100 rail.)

150' Rigid Truss Bridge
210-1902   33.95
20-5/8" 52.5 cm

PLATE GIRDER BRIDGE

72 foot, one-piece floor frame, injection molded styrene and molded bridge tie sections.

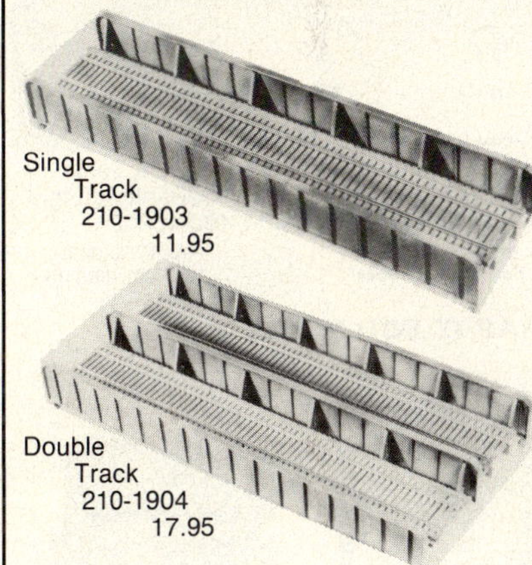

Single Track
210-1903
11.95

Double Track
210-1904
17.95

DETAIL KITS

210-19025	Box Girder Sections	pkg(30)	9.85
210-190210	Bridge Tie Sections	pkg(10)	9.85

OREGON RAIL SUPPLY

HO SCALE (1/87) EASY-TO-BUILD KIT

Plastic kits are molded in color

538-501   Menomonee Falls Depot   44.95
16 x 5" 40.6 x 12.7 cm

HO SCALE
(1/87)
EASY-TO-BUILD
KITS

• Plasticville Kits — "snap-fit" precolored plastic buildings

PLASTICVILLE KITS

Kits feature precolored, plastic "snap-fit" assembly.

STATIONS & PLATFORMS

160-45171   Freight   6.00
2-3/8" x 4-3/4"   12.1 x 6 cm

160-45173   Suburban   6.00
1-7/8" x 5-1/2"   14 x 4.8 cm

Depot
w/Operating Fork Lift
160-46205   20.00
preassembled
5 x 9"   12.7 x 22.9 cm

Passenger w/Light
160-46217   15.00
preassembled
5-3/8" x 9-3/8"   13.7 x 23.8 cm

Freight w/Light
160-46216   15.00
preassembled
5-1/2" x 9-1/2"   14 x 24.1 cm

Platform
160-45194   7.00
2-1/8 x 7"   5.5 x 18 cm

Steam Whistle
Remote
160-46209
18.00

(not illustrated)
Frankford Junction
160-35108   19.95

YARD & EQUIPMENT FACILITIES

Oil Tank
w/Diesel Horn
160-46208   18.00
4-3/4" diameter
12.1 cm diameter

Oil Tank
w/Blinking Light
160-46212   12.00
4-3/4" diameter
12.1 cm diameter

Coaling Station
160-45211 7.50
3-3/8 x 3"
8.6 x 7.6 cm

Water Tank
160-45153 5.00
3-1/4" diameter
8.2 cm diameter

Switch Tower
160-45132 4.00
1-5/8" square
4.2 cm square

Coaling & Sand Complex
160-35111   19.95
4-3/8 x 4-7/8"
11 x 12.5 cm

SNAP-IT BUILDINGS

Gravel Loader
160-45511   5.95
3-1/8 x 3-1/8"   8 x 8 cm

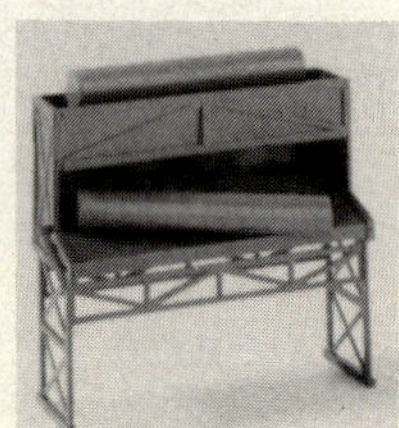

Pipe Loader
160-45512   5.95
1-3/4 x 4-1/2"   4.3 x 11.4 cm

160-45513   Log Loader   5.95
1-1/2 x 9"   23 x 4 cm

Barrel Loader
160-45514   5.95
2-3/8 x 4"   6 x 10.2 cm

(not illustrated)
160-35112 Diesel Fueling Rack **NEW** 14.95
160-35113 Diesel Sanding Rack **NEW** 19.95
160-35114 Diesel Sand Tower **NEW** 12.95

RURAL BUILDINGS

Farm Building w/Animals
160-45152   5.00

160-45151   Barn   5.00
2-1/2 x 3-1/2"   6.4 x 9 cm

HOUSES

160-45432 Contemporary 9.00
2-7/8 x 8-3/4"   7.3 x 22.3 cm

House Under Construction
160-45191   7.00
2-7/8 x 5-1/4"   7.3 x 13 cm

160-45213   Split Level 7.50
2-7/8 x 6-1/8"   7.3 x 15.5 cm

160-45154   Ranch   5.00
2-1/4 x 5-1/2"   5.7 x 14 cm

Cape Cod
160-45131   4.00
1-7/8 x 3"
4.8 x 7.5 cm

(not illustrated)
160-35122 Historical Towne House   17.95

| HO SCALE (1/87) EASY-TO-BUILD KITS | • Plasticville Kits — "snap-fit" precolored plastic buildings |

BUSINESSES

Randy's Candy & Gray's Gifts
160-35101   19.95
8 x 8-15/16"   20.4 x 22.8 cm

Jack's Variety & Ice Cream Parlor
160-35102   19.95
8-3/4 x 9-13/16"   22.4 x 25 cm

160-35103 Lyric Theatre 19.95
9 x 9-3/16"   23 x 23 cm

Murray's Drugs
160-35104   19.95
6-5/8 x 6-1/4"   16.8 x 15.8 cm

Motel
w/Swimming Pool
160-45214   7.50
4-1/8 x 12-3/4"   10.5 x 32.4 cm

160-45174   Gas Station   9.00

160-45141 Super Market 4.00
2-1/8 x 4-5/8"   5.5 x 11.8 cm

160-45142 5 & 10 Store 4.00
2-1/8 x 4-5/8"   5.5 x 11.8 cm

(not illustrated)
Drive-In Hamburger Stand
160-45434   9.00
Texaco Station 1930's
160-35106   19.95
Mike's Feed & Seed
160-35107   19.95
160-35121   Grand Hotel   17.95
Bob's Bicycle Shop
160-35123   17.95

Toy & Hobby Shop
160-45431   9.00
3-3/8 x 5-7/8"   8.6 x 15 cm

Hardware Store
160-45143   4.00
2-1/8 x 4-5/8"   5.5 x 11.8 cm

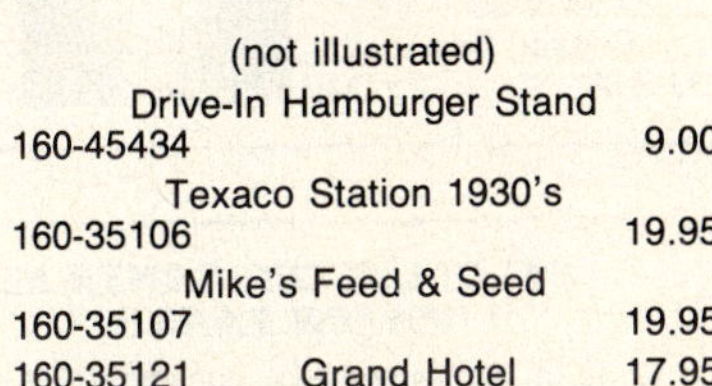

160-45144   Post Office   4.00
2-1/8 x 4-5/8"   5.5 x 11.8 cm

BRIDGES

Includes track mounted on bridge

Trestle
w/Blinking
Light
160-46221
pkg(18pc)
12.00
9 x 2-3/8 x 3"
22.9 x 6 x 7.6 cm

Trestle w/Blinking Light
160-46222   pkg(34pc) 14.00

Trestle
160-46225   pkg(17pc) 7.00

Signal Bridge
160-45134   4.00

Pedestrian
Foot Bridge
160-45172
6.00

Trestle
160-46226
pkg(33pc)
10.00

MISCELLANEOUS

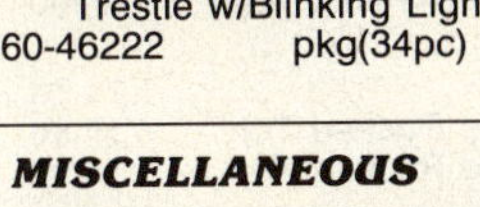

School House
160-45133   4.00
6 x 7-1/8"
15.3 x 4.8 cm

Cathedral
160-45192
7.00

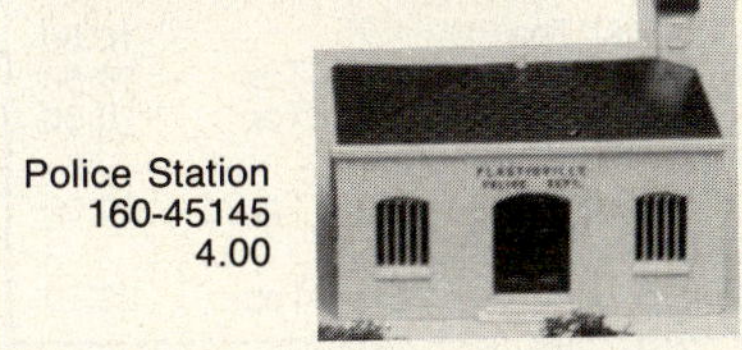

Police Station
160-45145
4.00

(not illustrated)
160-35105   Community Hall   19.95

BH MODELS

HO SCALE (1/87) EASY-TO-BUILD KITS

These easy-to-build storage tanks and other structures add realistic detail to industrial and railroad scenes. Tank and Grain Bin kits consist of individual 1/4 round sections, which are "stacked" to simulate plate steel construction. Each is offered in a variety of styles to meet your space requirements. All kits are molded in color and include instructions.

CORRUGATED GRAIN BINS

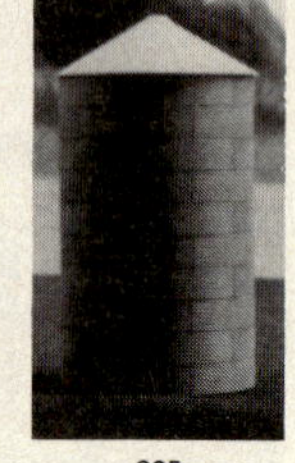

Corrugated metal storage bins can be found at co-ops, elevators and farms storing all types of edible and seed grains. Kits are molded in silver and are available in 26 or 37' heights. Taller bins can be built with the add-on sections in kit #004.

159-304	24 x 26'	15.00
159-305	24 x 37'	18.00
159-4	Grain Bin Extensions	3.50

Includes three rows of bands, for use with #304 or 305.

304 305

GALVANIZED OIL OR WATER TANKS

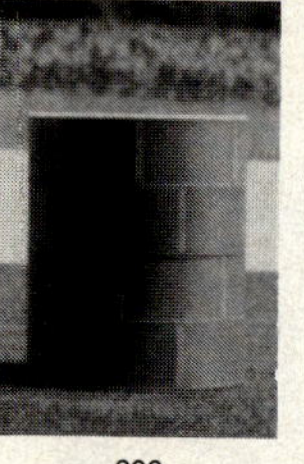

These kits feature parts molded in silver, to simulate galvanized steel components. Kits include ladder.

24 x 28' TANK
159-306	Flat Top	14.00
159-311	Peaked Top	17.00

24 x 43' TANK
159-309	Flat Top	17.00
159-314	Peaked Top	20.00

24 x 60' WATER
159-310	Flat Top	20.50
159-315	Peaked Top	23.50

306 311

BLACK OIL OR WATER TANKS

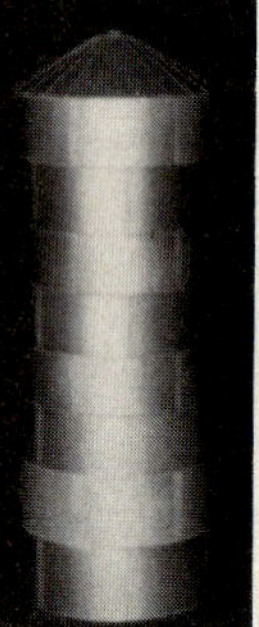

These kits feature parts molded in black, to simulate galvanized steel components. Kits include ladder.

24 x 28' Flat Top
159-328 14.00

24 x 42' Flat Top
159-330 16.50

24 x 60' Peaked Top
159-332 23.00

GRAIN ELEVATOR PIPING KIT

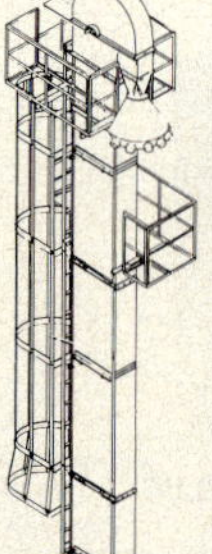

NEW

Includes various pipes, safety cage ladders, grain head and other details. Can be used to detail Grain Bins (304, 305 sold separately) or adapted to other models. Molded in silver-gray styrene. Can be made any height up to 120' in 10' increments.

Grain Elevator - Piping Kit
159-407
29.95

QUONSET HUTS

Developed during WWII, these prefab metal structures were adapted to many types of agricultural, industrial and commercial buildings in later years. They can still be found in use in many areas. Kit includes polystyrene parts for two structures, each measuring 24 x 26 x 12'. Door and window openings are cut out.

159-501 Quonset Huts pkg(2) 17.50

24' DIAMETER SANTA FE WATER TANKS

Based on prototype design constructed at various locations along the Santa Fe. Kits #301 and 302 are molded in black and can be built as a 29, 43 or 60' tall tank. Kit #303 includes parts for two tanks measuring 24 x 28'.

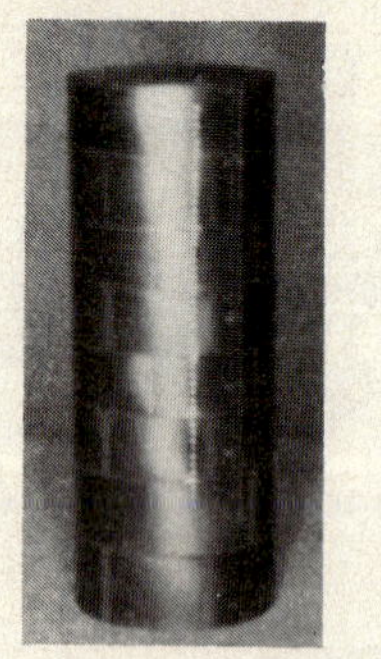

301 302

Flat Top
159-301 20.00

Peaked Top
159-302 23.00

Double Tank Kit — Flat Tops
159-303
pkg(2) 20.00

24' DIAMETER GALVANIZED WATER TANKS

Kits are molded in silver and include a ladder.

FLAT TOP	15 DEGREE PEAKED TOP	30 DEGREE PEAKED TOP
	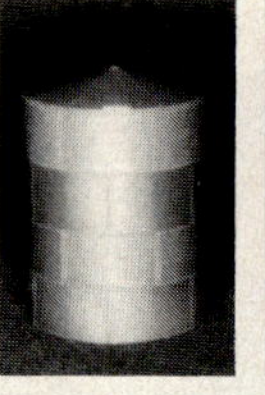	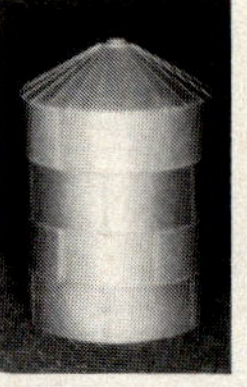
334	335	336

28' TALL
159-316	30 Degree Peaked Top	17.00

29' TALL
159-307	Flat Top	14.50
159-312	15 Degree Peaked Top	17.50
159-317	30 Degree Peaked Top	17.50

31-1/2' TALL
159-334	Flat Top	15.00
159-335	15 Degree Peaked Top	18.50
159-336	30 Degree Peaked Top	18.50

35' TALL
159-340	Flat Top	15.50
159-341	15 Degree Peaked Top	19.00
159-342	30 Degree Peaked Top	19.00

42' TALL
159-308	Flat Top	16.50
159-313	15 Degree Peaked Top	19.50
159-318	30 Degree Peaked Top	19.50

43' TALL
159-319	30 Degree Peaked Top	20.00

60' TALL
159-333	30 Degree Peaked Top	23.50

24' DIAMETER BLACK WATER TANKS

Kits are molded in black and include a ladder.

FLAT TOP	15 DEGREE PEAKED TOP	30 DEGREE PEAKED TOP
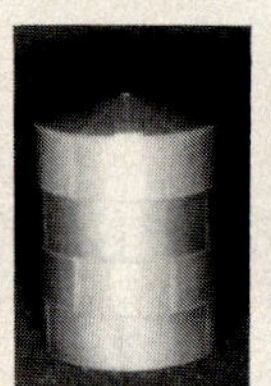	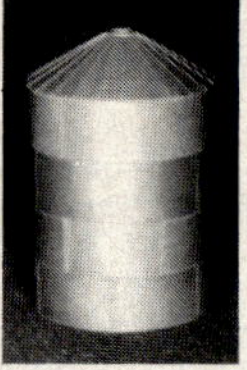	
337	338	339

28' TALL
159-324	15 Degree Peaked Top	17.00
159-320	30 Degree Peaked Top	17.50

29' TALL
159-329	Flat Top	14.50
159-325	15 Degree Peaked Top	17.50
159-321	30 Degree Peaked Top	17.50

31-1/2' TALL
159-337	Flat Top	15.00
159-338	15 Degree Peaked Top	18.50
159-339	30 Degree Peaked Top	18.50

35' TALL
159-343	Flat Top	15.50
159-344	15 Degree Peaked Roof	19.00
159-345	30 Degree Peaked Roof	19.00

42' TALL
159-330	Flat Top	16.50
156-326	15 Degree Peaked Top	19.50
159-322	30 Degree Peaked Top	19.50

43' TALL
159-331	Flat Top	17.00
159-327	15 Degree Peaked Top	20.00
159-323	30 Degree Peaked Top	20.00

BRAWA

HO SCALE (1/87)

Imported from Germany by WALTHERS

Brawa Structures include metal and plastic parts, requiring only minor assembly and installation. Cableways do not include station buildings which are required to finish scenes as shown.

PLATFORM EDGE

186-2869 Platform Edges   7.99
Set includes 4 straight sections, each approx 8-5/16″ long, 4 ramps, each approx 3″ long and 2 transition straight sections, each approx 2″ long. Brawa building material sheets can be used for the platform surface (not included).

YARD FACILITIES

Designed especially for Brawa KOFII engines, this structure will hold other small locomotives. The kit consists of precut wood parts.

186-701 Single Stall Engine Shed   163.99
w/Interior
Includes one set of 186-703, 22 unpainted metal castings for interior.

186-702 Single Stall Engine Shed   119.99
same as 701 less interior

186-703 Engine Shed Interior   49.99
Designed for use with the Brawa engine shed (701 and 702), this set includes 22 unpainted metal castings including workbenches with tools, stove, air compressor, carts, bench grinder, vise and more.

186-712 Branchline Coaling Tower   65.49

Water Crane
186-678
26.99

See also: LOCOMOTIVES,
TRACTION,
SCENERY, VEHICLES and
BOOKS sections for additional
BRAWA items.

CONTAINER TERMINAL

These modern piggyback cranes are used to load and unload containers or semi-trailers from flat cars. This working model is wide enough for three HO tracks, or two tracks and a roadway.

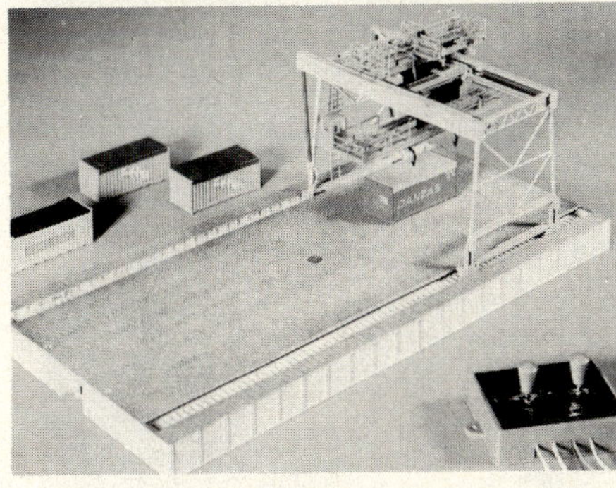

186-1162 Container Terminal Set   298.49
Complete set includes Crane 1161, control unit 1156, loading platform 1170 and four containers. For use with 14-16V DC power supply, requires use of Bridge Rectifier 2185 for use with AC power.

186-1170 Loading Platform   108.49
Die cast zinc base sides and toothed rack-rail provide extra strength. Includes electric drive, for use with Brawa Crane #1161. Measures 16 x 8 x 1″ (400 x 200 x 25 mm). For use with 14-16V DC power supply, requires use of Bridge Rectifier #2185 for use with AC power.

186-1161 Container Crane   146.49
Designed for use with Loading Platform #1170, crane measures approx 7 x 4-1/2 x 5-1/2″ (180 x 110 x 140 mm). Two separate motors control lifting and travel on platform. For use with 14-16V DC power supply, requires use of Bridge Rectifier #2185 for use with AC power.

186-1156 Control Unit   46.99
For use with Platform #1170 and Crane #1161. Moves crane up, down and side to side, also controls travel on platform. For use with 14-16V DC power supply, requires use of Bridge Rectifier #2185 for use with AC power.

186-1163 Container Set   pkg(2) 15.99
Two ACL and two Sea Train containers for use with #1162.

BRIDGE

186-1210 Lattice Girder Bridge   354.49
Prototype stands in the Black Forest. All-brass kit consists of precut, formed and soldered parts. Assembly requires no special tools or skills. Measures approx 18 x 2-1/2 x 3″. Deck width adjustable from 2-1/2 to about 2-3/4″.

TRANSFER TABLE

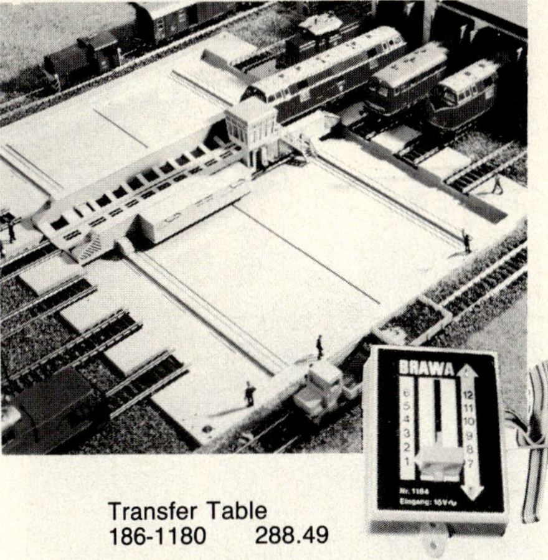

Transfer Table
186-1180   288.49

Used to move equipment at engine and car shops where turntables are not required. Based on an actual prototype, the model will hold locomotives approx 11-1/2″ (290mm) long. The table can serve up to 11 tracks (6 per side with one approach track) and is designed for use with two-rail DC locomotives. Use with Marklin 3-rail AC requires center conductor (Marklin system), Marklin M-Rail requires adapter #2191.

Includes control unit #1184, base and transfer table. Measures approx 14-3/4″ x 17 x 1/2″ (372 x 427 x 15 mm). For use with 14-16V DC power supply, requires use of Bridge Rectifier #2185 for use with AC power.

186-1184 Motor for #1180   *NEW* 61.49

CABLEWAY

Brawa cableways are working models, complete with drive cable, cable stations and "cars," less speed control and structures. Systems can be expanded to any length using additional pylons and cable, available separately. Speed can be adjusted using Brawa 6149 or 6150 controllers. All sets comply with VDE standards for radio and TV interference.

186-6200 Nebelhornbahn Cableway Set   147.49
Opened on June 11, 1930, the "Nebelhornbahn" cableway is over three miles long and climbs over 300 feet from station to station. On the model, the cars are illuminated and stop automatically for a few seconds at each station. As one car descends, the other climbs the hill.

Includes valley and summit cable stations (less structures), 2 cars, center pylon (approx 11″ high) and drive cables. For use with 14-16V AC power supply.

186-6201 Station Buildings   36.99
Set of two structure kits for use with 6200 cableway set. Summit station is approx 6-1/2 x 5″, valley station is approx 6-1/4 x 5″.

BRAWA

HO SCALE (1/87)
Brawa Structures include metal and plastic parts, requiring only minor assembly and installation. Cableways do not include station buildings which are required to finish scenes as shown.

Imported from Germany by WALTHERS

CABLEWAY (continued)

186-6231	Tower Bottom for #6200	10.49
186-6232	Tower Middle for #6200	4.99
186-6233	Tower Top for #6200	9.49
186-6241	Drive Support Cables 39", for #6200	7.99
186-6253	Cableway w/Motor	60.99

186-6280 Kanzelwandbahn Cableway Set 147.49
Built in 1954-55 from Riezlen in the Kleinwalsertal Valley to the summit of the Grundkopf, this cableway climbs almost 600 feet in about a mile-and-a-half.

Set includes valley and summit cable stations (less structures), 6 cars, center pylon (approx 7-3/4" high) and drive cables. For use with 14-16V DC power supply, requires use of Bridge Rectifier #2185 for use with AC power.

186-6290 Station Buildings 31.99
Set of two structure kits for use with #6280 cableway set. Summit station is approx 5 x 7-1/2", valley station is approx 4-1/2 x 6".

186-6283	Center Pylon	each 22.99
186-6292	Spare Drive Cable	5.99

Approx length, 11 yards; for cableways, #6210, #6270 or #6560.

186-9712	Motor for Cableways	28.99
186-6281	Extra Cabin w/Figure	10.49

186-6210 Mineral Cableway Set 126.49
These systems carry stone from quarries to rock crushers or railroad loading points. Consists of valley and summit cable stations, center pylon (approx 3" high), 6 dumper skips and drive cable. For use with 14-16V DC power supply, requires use of Bridge Rectifier #2185 for use with AC power.

186-6211 Station Buildings 25.99
Set of two structure kits for use with #6210 Mineral Cableway. Summit station is approx 3 x 5", valley station is approx 6 x 5".

186-6212	Center Pylon	each 13.49
186-6213	Extra Dumper Skip	7.99
6214	Summit Station Clp	53.49
6560	Schavinsland Cableway Set	135.49
6570	Schavinsland Building Set	34.99

CHAIR LIFT

186-6270 Chair Lift Set 135.49
Skiers get a quick ride to the top of any hill aboard this chair lift. Consists of summit and valley cable stations, support mast (approx 2-3/4" high), 6 chair units and drive cable. For use with 14-16V DC power supply, requires use of Bridge Rectifier #2185 for use with AC power.

186-6271 Station Buildings 20.49
Set of two structure kits for use with #6271 Chair Lift. Summit station is approx 3 x 3", valley station is approx 4 x 4".

186-6272	Support Mast	each 13.49
186-6273	Extra Chair w/Figure	9.49

FUNICULAR
Based on a prototype in Stuttgart, Germany, similar funicular railways are used around the world.

Sets include 2 passenger cars, 4 straight track sections with built-in rollers, 1 passing loop (Abt system), a drive motor with automatic stop action and drive cable. Car length is approx 4". Track section is approx 8" long, passing loop is approx 16" long.

186-6309	Funicular Set-Brown Cars	205.99
186-6310	Funicular Set-Red Cars	205.99
186-6311	Set of Buildings	38.99

(Summit/Valley stations) Summit is approx 3-1/4 x 9". Valley is approx 5 x 7-1/2".

186-6312	Straight Track	pkg(2) 7.99
186-6320	Reel of Cable (13')	each 6.49

HO SCALE (1/87) CRAFT TRAIN KITS

Kits consist of detailed cast plaster walls, (unless noted) with beveled corners to simplify assembly. All doors and windows are cast in place, with stripwood included for the window sash material.

INDUSTRIAL

1   6   7

231-1	Salida Coal Co	29.95

3-3/4 x 8-3/4" 9.5 x 22 cm
Includes dry transfers for Salida Coal Company signs. Prototype still stands in Salida, Colorado.

231-6	70' Square Brick Chimney	8.49
231-7	70' Octagonal Brick Chimney	8.49

231-2	Salida Coal Bins	16.50

2-1/2 x 10-1/2" 6 x 26.5 cm
All wood kit includes plastic details.

Salida Machine Shop
231-3   22.50
3-1/4 x 3-1/4"
9 x 9 cm
Prototype in Salida, CO

Dynamite Igloos
231-4   pkg(3) 14.95
each: 2-1/2 x 1-3/4"
6.4 x 4.5 cm
Solid Hydrocal casting.

BUSINESSES

Menard Wool & Mohair
231-8   34.95
3-1/2 x 7-1/2"
9 x 18.5 cm
Injection molded windows. Prototype in Menard, Texas.

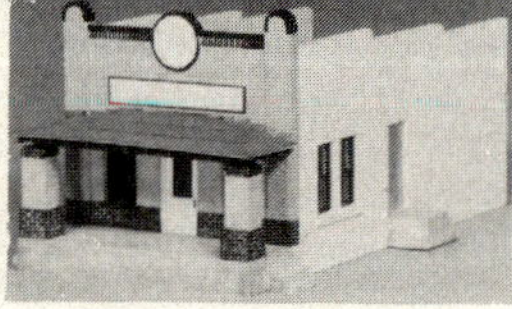

Alamosa Oil Service
231-9   29.95
4-1/2 x 5" 12 x 13 cm
Injection molded windows. Prototype in Alamosa, CO

Blacksmith Shop
231-14   19.95
4 x 4" 10 x 10 cm
Injection molded windows. All wood kit. Pre-weathered wood.

California Model Company

HO SCALE (1/87) CRAFT TRAIN KITS

Kits feature two types of construction:
- **Wood and Matboard**
  Matboard is printed and/or embossed to represent brick, concrete block, board and bat, clapboard or stucco.
- **Corrugated Metal** buildings require soldering skills.

★ Indicates items that are corrugated metal.

Kits include all detail parts. Interior and lighting kits are available for some models.

STATIONS

700-504　Standard Station　9.95
4 x 6"　10 x 15.3 cm

Main Street Station
700-73　24.75
10 x 12"　25.5 x 30.5 cm

700-503　Modern Station　6.95
4-1/2 x 7"　11.5 x 8 cm

Wells Fargo Station
700-86　8.25
3-1/2 x 5"　9 x 12.8 cm

Combination Town Depot
700-7001　Orange　32.95
700-7002　Gray　32.95
700-7003　Red　32.95
6 x 12-1/2"　15.3 x 32 cm

1887 Passenger Depot　19.95
700-5021　Orange　700-5023　Red
700-5022　Gray
5-1/2 x 8"　14 x 20.5 cm

1886 Freight Station　13.75
700-5111　Orange
700-5112　Gray
700-5113　Red
5-1/4 x 6"　13.5 x 15.3 cm

(not illustrated)
700-602　Station Detail　kit 5.95

YARD & EQUIPMENT FACILITIES

★ 700-8　3-Stall　Roundhouse　28.50
12 x 12"　30.5 x 30.5 cm

★ 700-8241　Extra Stall　7.50
for #8

★ 700-8243　3 Extra　18.25
Stalls for #8

Diesel House w/Interior
700-522
24.75
6-1/2 x 16-1/2"
16.5 x 42 cm

2-Stall Engine House
★ 700-9　19.50
5 x 14"　12.8 x 35.5 cm

Yard Tower, Modern
700-80
15.50
2 x 2"
5 x 5 cm

3-Track Car Barn
★ 700-20　22.95
17 x 16"　18 x 40.5 cm

Interlocking Tower & Shed
700-61　11.50
2 x 2"　5 x 5 cm

1870 Water Tank　6.75
700-5361　Orange
700-5362　Gray
700-5363　Red
2 x 3-3/8"　5 x 8.5 cm

HOUSES

700-574　Old Town Homes　pkg(3) 18.95
3-3/4 x 1-3/4"　9.5 x 4.5 cm
3-1/2 x 5"　9 x 12.8 cm
3-1/2 x 5"　9 x 12.8 cm

The Brown Bungalow
700-576　15.75
5-3/8 x 4"　13.7 x 10 cm

Dr Whyte's House
700-577　18.25
5-1/2 x 5-1/4"　14 x 13.4 cm

700-572　Old Town Lodgings　15.75
3-1/4 x 4"　8.3 x 10 cm
4 x 4-7/8"　10 x 12.5 cm

California Model Company

HO SCALE (1/87) CRAFT TRAIN KITS

Kits feature two types of construction:
- **Wood and Matboard**
  Matboard is printed and/or embossed to represent brick, concrete block, board and bat, clapboard or stucco.
- **Corrugated Metal buildings require soldering skills.**

★ Indicates items that are corrugated metal.

Kits include all detail parts. Interior and lighting kits are available for some models.

INDUSTRIAL

700-563   Lumber Yard, Complete   35.25
     8-1/2 x 16" 21.5 x 40.5 cm area

700-561   Lumber Rack & Office Only   14.25
700-562   Lumber Co Store & Shed Only   15.75
700-564   Lumber Company Office Only   4.75
700-565   16' Scale Lumber   pkg(210) 4.75

700-88   Bekins Storage Warehouse   28.95
   Mat, 5-3/4 x 15" 14.2 x 38 cm

700-566   Union Ice Company   25.25
   Mat
building: 6-3/4 x 8" 17.2 x 20.5 cm
platform: 1-1/2 x 16" 4 x 40.5 cm

American Chemical & Potash Co & Annex
★ 700-22 Plant   6 x 14" 35.5 cm   30.75
★ 700-23 Annex   6 x 14" 35.5 cm   35.25

Swift Meat Packing Plant
700-85   mat   19.95
   4 x 8" 10 x 20.5 cm

★ 700-19   Pacific Foundry   13.95
   5 x 8" 12.8 x 20.5 cm

Sunkist Citrus Exchange
700-83   13.75
   "stucco" mat board
   4-1/2 x 6-1/2" 11.5 x 16.5 cm

Grand Junction Box Works
700-81   12.50
   5 x 10" 12.8 x 25.5 cm
   board & batt embossed matboard

Purina Chows Feed Mill
700-82   mat   19.95
   5 x 9" 12.8 x 23 cm

Central Mfg Co Factory
700-541   14.25
   4-1/2 x 10" 11.5 x 25.5 cm

Grain Elevator
★ 700-12   21.25
   5 x 5" 12.8 x 12.8 cm

★ 700-7   Warehouse   17.50
   4-1/2 x 12" 11.5 x 30.5 cm

Power Sub-Station
700-66   20.95
   4-1/4 x 8-1/4" 10.8 x 21 cm

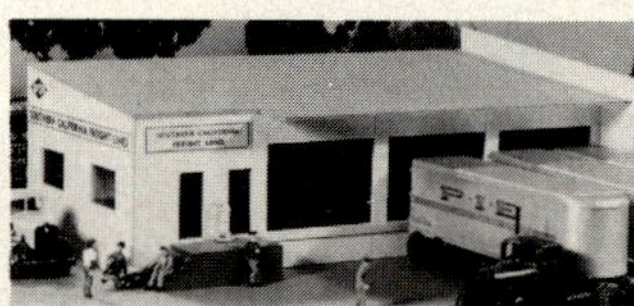

Rail-Truck Terminal
700-542   14.25
   5 x 9" 12.8 x 23 cm

Mail Pouch Tobacco Barn
700-87   mat   6.75
   4-1/2 x 5" 11.5 x 12.8 cm

Industrial Office Bldg
★ 700-16   8.75
   3 x 6" 7.5 x 15.3 cm

Electronics Plant
700-74   14.75
   5-1/4 x 11" 13.5 x 28 cm

Northside Tool & Die Company
700-25   12.50
   6 x 7" 15.3 x 18 cm

Modern Industry
700-543   mat   14.25
   5 x 11-1/4" 12.8 x 28.5 cm

★ 700-1   Furniture Factory   17.50
   4-1/2 x 12" 11.5 x 30.5 cm

California Model Company

HO CRAFT TRAIN KITS

Kits feature two types of construction:
- **Wood and Matboard**
  Matboard is printed and/or embossed to represent brick, concrete block, board and bat, clapboard or stucco.
- **Corrugated Metal** buildings require soldering skills.

★ Indicates items that are corrugated metal.

Kits include all detail parts. Interior and lighting kits are available for some models.

MINES

Red Lake Hillside Mine
★ 700-6   12.50
for hillside construction
5 x 7" 12.8 x 17.8 cm

Wyoming Coal Mine
★ 700-24   28.95
5 x 10" 12.8 x 25.5 cm

Mining Company Mill
★ 700-18   9.95
4 x 6" 10 x 15.3 cm

Black Bart Mine & Shaft
★ 700-5   9.95
3 x 7" 7.5 x 18 cm

Mining Hoist House
★ 700-17   9.95
3 x 5" 7.5 x 12.8 cm

Buckhorn Mine Ore Plant
★ 700-4   23.25
6 x 16" 15.3 x 40.5 cm

BUSINESSES

700-571   **Old Town Buildings**   pkg(3) 25.25
2-1/4 x 4" 5.7 x 10 cm
5-3/4 x 5" 14.7 x 12.8 cm
4-1/4 x 5-1/2" 10.8 x 14 cm

700-573   **Old Town Business Block**   19.95
3-7/8 x 2-1/2" 9.8 x 6.5 cm
3-7/8 x 3-5/8" 9.8 x 9.2 cm

Ed's Market
700-76   mat   19.95
with interior & lights
5-1/2 x 6" 14 x 15.6 cm

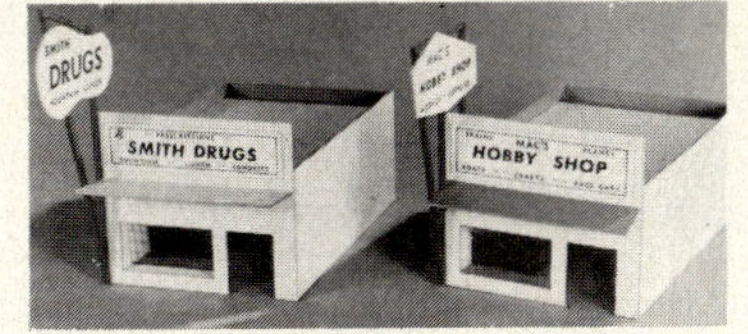

Modern Stores
700-552   pkg(2) 6.75
each: 3-1/2 x 5" 9 x 12.8 cm

Triangle Cafe
700-75   24.75
with interior & lights
4 x 5-1/2" 10 x 14 cm

Your Hobby Shop
700-71   15.50
5-1/2 x 6" 14 x 15.3 cm
Illuminated Sign for #71
700-7112   2.95

Curio Shop
700-575   15.75
3-1/4" 8.3 x 10 cm

CENTENNIAL MODELS

HO SCALE (1/87) CRAFT TRAIN KITS

Kits feature Northeastern lumber, plastic parts and step-by-step instructions.

INDUSTRIAL

198-102   Hercules Mining Co.   44.95

198-103   Silver Belle Mine   44.95
Based on the prototype in Ophir, Colorado.

Baker Tank
198-101   24.95

Silverton Engine House
198-105   (two-stall)   34.95

(not illustrated)

198-104	Water Tank	29.95
198-106	Coal Creek Coal	*NEW* 49.95
198-107	Depot/Warehouse	*NEW* 39.96
198-108	Stanley Mine	*NEW* 49.95
198-109	Redundant & Redundant Mfg	*NEW* 49.95

Q-CAR COMPANY

HO CRAFT TRAIN KIT

Kit features metal castings and a one piece roof. Complete instructions included.

Crossing Shanty
608-8000   8.80
3/4 x 1" 2 x 2.6 cm

Campbell Scale Models

HO SCALE (1/87) CRAFT TRAIN KITS

Kits feature precision-cut wood, "profile shingles", molded plastic windows and doors, vents, signs, corrugated aluminum siding, etc. as needed. Each kit includes templates and complete instructions.

STATIONS & PLATFORMS

Skull Valley Station
200-367   50.10
3-7/8 x 10-1/4"   9.52 x 26.3 cm

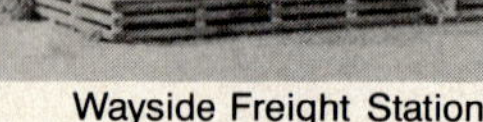

Wayside Freight Station
200-361   30.25
2-7/8 x 6-5/8"   7.62 x 16.8 cm

Passenger Shelter
200-362   25.00
2 x 9-7/8"   4.5 x 24.8 cm

Large Freight Station
200-447   54.60
5-3/4 x 10-5/8"   14.6 x 27 cm
SP Coast Railroad prototype.

Kiowa Junction Station
200-423   45.00
2-7/8 x 7-1/2"   7.3 x 19.2 cm
Prototype in Junction, KS

(not illustrated)

Freight Platform
200-785   pkg(2)   9.50
1-3/8 x 6-7/8"   2.8 x 17.7 cm
plus ramps

Passenger Platform
200-786   pkg(3)   7.00
1-3/32 x 6-7/8"   2.8 x 17.7 cm

LCL Freight Station
200-353   25.00
3-1/2 x 7"   8.9 x 17.8 cm (includes ramp)
Prototypes were built to receive and dispatch small shipments thus the name "Less than Car Load" or LCL Station.

Freight House & Passenger Station
200-442   3-1/16 x 3-3/8"   7.8 x 8.6 cm   24.75
1-5/8 x 1-5/8"   4.2 x 3 cm

YARD & EQUIPMENT FACILITIES

Shed Under Construction & Double Handcar House
200-368   25.00
shed: 2-1/2 x 5-1/4"   6.3 x 13.3 cm
double: 3-1/8 x 3-7/8"   7.9 x 9.8 cm

Supply Shed & Single Handcar House
200-370   25.00
shed: 2-1/2 x 5-1/4"   6.3 x 13.3 cm
house: 2 x 3-7/8"   5 x 10.1 cm

BEGINNER KITS

These kits are designed to introduce modelers to Craft Train Kit construction. The buildings feature simple design and fewer parts, making them ideal for beginners.

Kits include precut wood with plastic castings for the windows and details. Complete step-by-step instructions make construction fast and easy.

Portable Bunkhouse "A"
200-230   6.35
1-1/4 x 3"   3.2 x 7.7 cm

Portable Bunkhouse "B"
200-231   7.00
1-1/4 x 3"   3.2 x 7.7 cm

Freight Storage Shed
200-427   26.45
3-5/8 x 4-5/8"   9.3 x 11.9 cm

Windy Gulch Engine House
200-389   54.90
3 x 12"   7.6 x 30.4 cm

Branch Line Water Tank & Tool House
200-372   25.00
tank: 2 x 3-1/2"   5 x 9 cm
tool house: 1-1/2 x 3.8 cm square

200-358   Sand House   33.35
3 x 8"   7.6 x 20.3 cm

Kiowa Trackside Details #2
200-426   3-9/16 x 6"   9 x 15.2 cm   26.45

Kiowa Trackside Details #1
200-425   26.45

Square Water Tower
200-421   24.75
3 x 3-1/4"   7.5 x 8.5 cm

Northern Water Tank
200-376   38.50
4" sq   10.1 cm sq

Kiowa Tower
200-424   34.95
2-5/16 x 6-1/8"   13.5 x 15.5 cm

Water Tank
200-356   38.50
4' sq   10.1 cm sq

Coaling Station
200-357   48.10
5 x 6"   12.7 x 15.2 cm

Campbell Scale Models

HO SCALE (1/87) CRAFT TRAIN KITS

Kits feature precision-cut wood, "profile shingles", molded plastic windows and doors, vents, signs, corrugated aluminum siding, etc. as needed. Each kit includes templates and complete instructions.

NORM'S LANDING

The "Norm's Landing" complex, pictured above, consists of the following three kits: #'s 392, 396 and 397.

200-392   Fishing Pier   45.00
pier: 7-1/2 x 10"   19 x 25.4 cm
ramp: 2-1/2 x 10"   6.3 x 25.4 cm
float: 4 x 7-1/8"   10.1 x 18 cm

200-396   Boat Shop   45.00
3-1/2 x 6-1/4"   8.9 x 15.8 cm

200-397   Ice House & Cafe   43.75
ice house: 2-1/2 x 4-1/4"   6.3 x 10.8 cm
cafe: 3-1/2" square   8.9 cm square

RURAL BUILDINGS

200-382   Barn   34.10
4-1/8 x 6-3/4"   10.4 x 17.1 cm

Farm House
200-381   25.00
3-1/2 x 4-1/2"   8.8 x 10.7 cm

Grain Storage Bin
200-449   36.30
3-5/8 x 7-1/2"   9.2 x 18.5 cm

200-437   Stockpens w/Double Chutes   25.00
10-1/2 x 1"   26.7 x 27.9 cm

200-781   Cattle Loading Pens   11.50
7-7/8 x 5-3/4"   20.3 x 14.6 cm

HOUSES

200-387   Gran'Ma's House   55.40
house: 5 x 5-1/4"   12.7 x 13.3 cm
garage: 2-1/2 x 1-3/4"   6.3 x 4.5 cm

Back View   Front View

200-413   Carstens' Flop House   71.35
3-3/4 x 6"   9.5 x 15.2 cm

Abandoned House
200-393
30.00
4 x 4-1/2"
10.1 x 10.8 cm

Picken's Place
200-395
30.00
4 x 4-1/2"
10.1 x 10.8 cm

CITY BUILDINGS

Doctor's Office
200-398   45.00
3-5/8 x 5"   9.5 x 12.7 cm

Sheriff's Office
200-364   25.00
3-1/2 x 5"   8.9 x 12.7 cm

Iowa School House
200-369
38.50
2-3/4 x 4-1/2"
7 x 10.8 cm

Community Church
200-359
48.15
3-1/4 x 7-5/8"
8.3 x 19.3 cm
with "stained" glass windows.

1875 Fire House
200-355
25.00
2-3/4 x 3-5/8"
7 x 9.2 cm

Post Office
200-446   23.60
2-1/2 x 5-7/8"
6.5 x 15 cm

Breckenridge Fire House
200-441   52.55
5 x 6-1/4"   13 x 16 cm
prototype in Breckenridge, CO, until 1941

Campbell Scale Models

HO SCALE (1/87) CRAFT TRAIN KITS

Kits feature precision-cut wood, "profile shingles", molded plastic windows and doors, vents, signs, corrugated aluminum siding, etc. as needed. Each kit includes templates and complete instructions.

INDUSTRIAL

Saez Sash & Door Machine Shop,
200-417   Shed & Hopper   67.15
6 x 12″   15.6 x 27.9 cm

Seebold & Sons Manufacturing
200-377   Company   38.50

200-386   Quick's Coal   60.40
yard: 3 x 8″   7.6 x 20.3 cm
office: 2 x 3-1/2″   5 x 8.9 cm

Timber Oil Derrick
200-354   33.35
3-3/4 x 9″   9.5 x 22.8 cm

200-444   Iron Foundry   41.25
4-3/8 x 9-5/8″   11.1 x 24.5 cm

200-452 Popo-Agie Canning Co 72.00
4-3/4 x 14-3/8″   12 x 36.5 cm

200-457 The Paint Factory 47.85
6-1/2 x 11-1/8″   16.5 x 28.2 cm

Ore Bin
200-438
30.75
3-7/8 x 3″
9.9 x 7.7 cm

Saez Sash & Door Mill House
200-416   & Loft   63.80
5-5/8 x 10″   14.3 x 25.4 cm

200-399   Talc Plant   71.50
7-3/8 x 12-3/4″   18.6 x 32.4 cm

200-385   Bret's Brewery   54.60
5-1/2 x 10-1/2″   13.9 x 26.6 cm

Grain Elevator
200-384
48.00
3-1/2 x 10-1/2″
8.9 x 26.6 cm

200-459 Kohler Distributing Co 47.85
13-1/2 x 8-3/4″   34.4 x 22.3 cm

200-458   Barnett Plastic Co   47.85
11″ square   26.6 cm square

200-439   King's Cannery   68.50
6-3/4 x 12-1/2″   17.2 x 31.8 cm
Santa Fe prototype Irvine, California

200-374   Grist Mill   38.50
3-1/4 x 4-1/2″   8.3 x 10.8 cm

Frederick J Hamilton Dinghies Ltd
200-394 3-3/4 x 8-3/4″   9.5 x 22.1 cm 55.00
includes two rowboats

Ayres Chair Factory
200-391   6-3/4 x 7-1/4″   54.90
17.1 x 18.4 cm

Cordage Works
200-455   41.25
5-3/8 x 6-3/8″   13.6 x 16.1 cm

Ten Stamp Mill
200-428
33.10
7-7/8 x 7-1/4″
20 x 18.5 cm

200-451   Tilt-Up Building #1   39.90
8-3/4 x 11″   22.2 x 27.8 cm

Richmond Barrel Manufacturing Company
200-422   45.00
3-1/4 x 6-5/8″
8.3 x 16.8 cm

Corrugated Warehouse
200-373   25.00
3 x 5-3/4″
7.6 x 14.6 cm

Campbell Scale Models

HO SCALE (1/87) CRAFT TRAIN KITS

Kits feature precision-cut wood, "profile shingles", molded plastic windows and doors, vents, signs, corrugated aluminum siding, etc. as needed. Each kit includes templates and complete instructions.

BUSINESSES

200-365 Kee Ling Laundry & Cigar Store 38.50
cigar store: 2-11/16 x 3-3/16" 7 x 8.3 cm
shelter: 2 x 9-7/8" 5 x 25.4 cm

200-379 Produce House 48.10
4 x 16" 10.1 x 40.6 cm

200-363 Campbell Supply Company 38.50
4 x 10" 10.1 x 25.4 cm

W T Stephenson Drug Company & Barber Shop
200-366 38.50
drug co: 3-1/2 x 3-3/16" 8.9 x 17.8 cm
barber: 2-3/8 x 3" 5.8 x 8.9 cm

200-460 Towers Flowers 71.40
3-1/2 x 10" 9 x 25.5 cm

200-400 M E Nelson Livestock Company 43.75
7-1/2 x 14" 19 x 35.5 cm

200-419 Montgomery Feed & Seed 63.80
3-1/4 x 9" 8.3 x 22.8 cm

200-420 Santangelo Fruit Co 60.15
4-7/8 x 9-1/2" 12.4 x 23.5 cm

200-411 Schrock's Meat Co 71.50
3-11/16 x 11-1/16" 9.8 x 28.1 cm

J Brice Produce Warehouse
200-435 41.75
7-1/2 x 4-3/8" 19 x 11.2 cm

200-443 Cabinet Makers Shop 39.90
5 x 7-3/8" 12.7 x 18.7 cm

200-418 Farm Co-Op Creamery 53.00
9-1/2 x 5-5/8" 24.2 x 14.3 cm

200-454 City Transfer 39.90
13-3/4 x 6-1/2" 35 x 16.5 cm

Assay Office/Clothing Store
200-431 29.00
3-3/4 x 4-7/8" 9.6 x 12.5 cm

Marjorie's Millinery
200-390 30.00
3-1/8 x 2-7/8" 7.9 x 7.3 cm

Matthew's Mercantile
200-371 38.50
3 x 3-1/2" 7.6 x 8.9 cm

DeWitt's Depository
200-412 48.10
3 x 7" 7.6 x 17.7 cm

Sherry's Scarlet Slipper
200-378 Saloon 48.10
saloon: 4-1/4" sq 10.8 cm sq
frame: 2-1/8 x 4" 5.3 x 10.1 cm

Columbia Gazette Office
200-380 25.00
4 x 5" 10.1 x 12.7 cm

The Blacksmith Shop
200-461
24.75
3 x 5-1/8"
7.7 x 13 cm

Grocery Warehouse
200-436
38.50
7-3/8 x 4-1/4"
18.7 x 10.8 cm

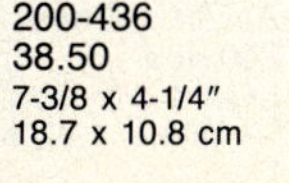

Donna's Diner
200-432 30.20
4-3/16 x 1-3/8" 10.7 x 3.5 cm

Campbell Scale Models

HO SCALE (1/87) CRAFT TRAIN KITS

Kits feature precision-cut wood, "profile shingles", molded plastic windows and doors, vents, signs, corrugated aluminum siding, etc. as needed. Each kit includes templates and complete instructions.

BUSINESSES (continued)

Susannah's Frocks
200-375   38.50
3-1/4 x 4"   8.3 x 10.1 cm

Tobacco Shop
200-434   23.85
2-3/4 x 3-7/8"   7 x 9.9 cm

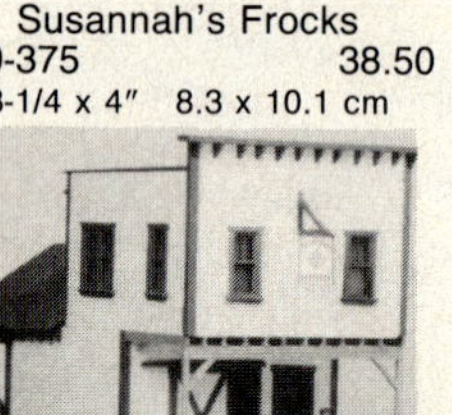

Gunsmith Shop
200-456   30.50
3-1/4 x 5-5/8"   8.2 x 14.4 cm

Carriage Works
200-430   38.50
3-3/4 x 4-3/4"   9.6 x 12.1 cm

MISCELLANEOUS

200-440   Water Treatment Plant   29.90
5 x 6-1/2"   12.7 x 16.5 cm

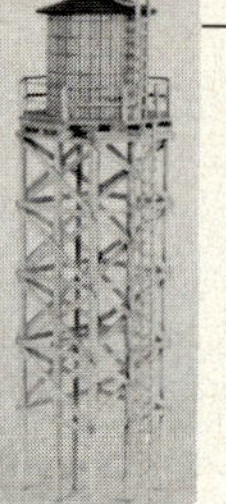

Water Tower
200-453   24.25
1-5/8" square
4.2 cm square

Pump House
200-360   24.15
2-3/4 x 3-1/4"
6.9 x 7.6 cm

200-307   Wharf   41.75
22-3/8 x 5-1/4"   56.6 x 13.3 cm

Summer Bandstand
200-383   30.00
3-1/2 x 3-1/2"   8.8 x 8.8 cm

QUINCY MODULE

The Quincy Railroad is a three-mile line owned by the di Giorgio Fruit Company. Located in California's Feather River country, it connects the agricultural community of Quincy with the Western Pacific at Quincy Junction. The map portrays the layout of the Quincy Railroad at Quincy.

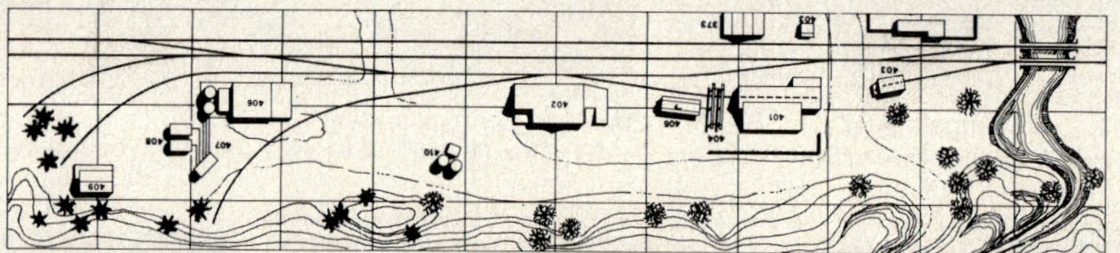

18' Horizontal Tanks
200-407   pkg(2) 18.50
each: 3-3/4 x 1-5/8"   9.5 x 4 cm

200-404   Traveling Crane   23.15
1-5/8 x 6-1/8"   4 x 15.6 cm

200-401   Engine House   60.00
6-3/4 x 11"   17.2 x 28 cm

200-402   Quincy Station   63.75
5-1/8 x 12"   13.1 x 30.6 cm

24' Horizontal Tanks
200-408   pkg(2) 18.50
each: 3-3/4 x 1-5/8"   9.5 x 4 cm

Oil Warehouse & Office
200-406   38.50
4-1/8 x 8-1/4"   10.5 x 21 cm

Loading Tanks
200-410   25.00
4-1/8 x 2-1/8"   10.5 x 5.5 cm
vertical tanks
w/small loading rack

200-409   Oil Compound House   27.60
4 x 5-1/2"   10.2 x 14 cm (including dock)

Auxiliary Sheds & Signs
200-403   25.00
Shed: 2 x 3"   5.1 x 7.7 cm
Ice House: 1-3/4 square   4.5 cm square

Fuel Oil Dock
200-405   each: 3 x 1-5/8"   7.5 x 4 cm   38.50

Campbell Scale Models

HO SCALE (1/87) CRAFT TRAIN KITS

Kits feature precision-cut wood, "profile shingles", molded plastic windows and doors, vents, signs, corrugated aluminum siding, etc. as needed. Each kit includes templates and complete instructions.

BRIDGES & TRESTLES (Bridges and trestles include ties unless noted).

Howe Truss Bridge
200-305   38.50
14-1/2 × 3-1/8″   36.8 × 7.6 cm

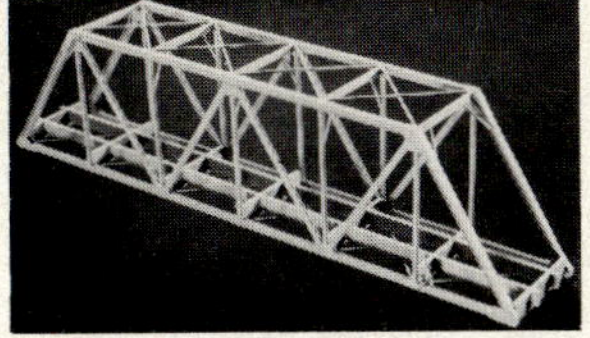

125′ Single Track Truss Bridge
200-763   (less ties)   30.50
17-1/4 × 3″   40.2 × 7.6 cm

125′ Double Track Truss Bridge
200-764   32.80
4-1/8 × 3-3/8″   35.8 × 8.5 cm

70′ Curved Trestle
200-303   22.00
15-1/4 × 1-3/8″   38.7 × 3.5 cm

50′ Open Deck Pile Trestle
200-302   12.30
6-7/8 × 3″   17.3 × 7.6 cm

50′ Ballasted Deck Pile Trestle
200-301   (less ties)   12.30
6-7/8 × 3″   17.3 × 7.6 cm

144-216′ Tall Timber Trestle
200-751   30.50
20 × 29″   50.8 × 73.6 cm

110′ Tall Curved Trestle
200-304   29.30
15-1/4 × 1-3/8″   38.7 × 3.5 cm

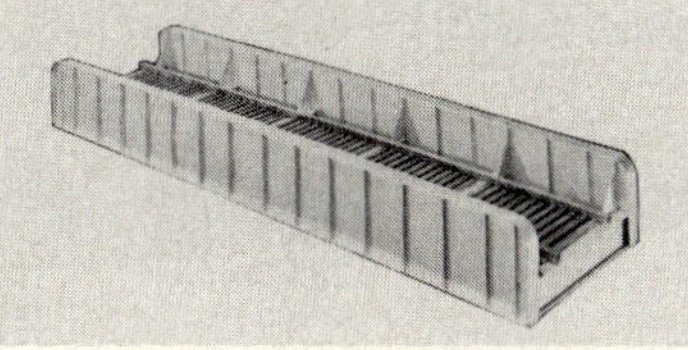

70′ Thru Plate Girder Bridge
200-766   23.85
9-5/8 × 2-1/2″   24.4 × 5.2 cm

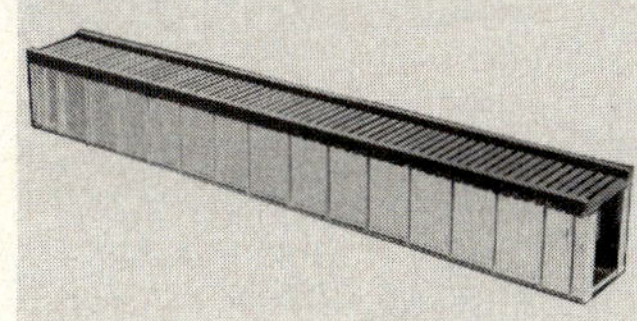

70′ Deck Plate Girder Bridge
200-765   22.80
9-5/8 × 1-3/8″   24.4 × 3.5 cm

50′ Deck Timber Bridge
200-761   30.50
14″   35.5 cm

70′ Thru Timber Bridge
200-762   30.50
14 × 3-3/4″   35.5 × 9.5 cm

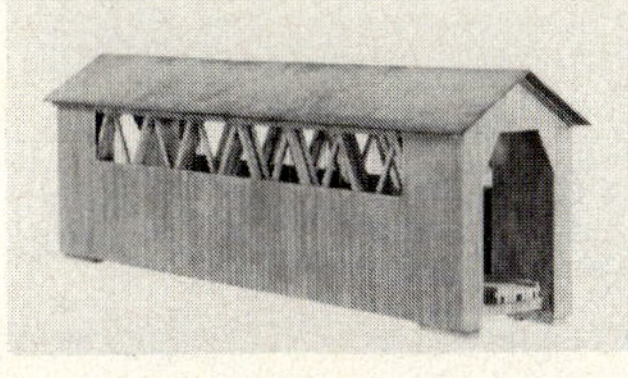

200-306   **Covered Bridge**   45.10
14-5/8 × 3-1/4″   37.2 × 8.2 cm

MINES

200-388   **Silver Spur Mine**   53.55
shaft house: 4-1/2 × 6-1/2″   10.8 × 16.5 cm
tunnel & tipple: 1-3/4 × 3-3/4″   4.5 × 9.5 cm

200-433   **Idaho Springs Mine**   29.00
main structure: 3 × 3-3/8″   7.7 × 8.6 cm
trestle: 12-1/2″   31.8 cm

200-352   **Mine Head Frame**   25.00
3-3/4 × 11-1/2″   9.5 × 29.2 cm

200-429   **Red Mountain Mine**   55.30

CRESCENT STATION

HO SCALE (1/87) CRAFT TRAIN KITS

Telephone Booth Kit
513-566   pkg(3) 3.95
3/8 × 3/8″   1 × 1 cm
Kit includes three solid acrylic rectangular blocks. Phone booth details are printed on pressure sensitive adhesive film which is "wrapped" around the acrylic block (no adhesive or solvents are necessary). Exterior details such as roof and sign are made of cardstock.

513-553   **Gas Station & Garage**   26.95
4-1/8 × 2-3/4″   10.5 × 7 cm
Kit features die cut roof and walls, with metal siding, cardstock signs, window acetate, stripwood, oil drum and an oil bunker. Also includes two gas pumps, 1935 Ford Sedan and telephone booth.

{ CLASSIC MINIATURES }
Division of Taurus Products

HO SCALE (1/87) CRAFT TRAIN KITS

Wood kits feature template construction, Kappler and North-eastern lumber, roofing material, plastic and metal cast details.

STATIONS

Forks Creek Station
225-35　24.95
2-3/4 x 5-1/2"　7 x 14 cm

SP Sparks Depot
225-16　24.95
5 x 6-1/2"　12.5 x 6.5 cm

Mount Princeton Station
225-36
18.95
2-3/4 x 4"
7 x 10.25 cm

YARD FACILITY

225-29　**SP Engine House**　23.95
2-3/4 x 8-1/2"　7 x 21.5 cm
Prototype built in 1883 for the Carson & Colorado. Will accept most HOn3 locos.

BUSINESSES

Silver Plume Store
225-11　17.95
2-1/4 x 4-1/2"　5.5 x 11.5 cm
Silver Plume, CO circa 1883

Work's Hardware
225-19　36.95
4-1/2 x 7"　10.4 x 17.8 cm
Telluride CO circa 1890

Wells Fargo & Co Office
225-7　16.95
3 x 6-1/2"　7.5 x 16.5 cm
Prototype built in Columbia, CA in 1857 to handle express service, still stands today.

Bank Building
225-18
16.95
3-1/2 x 4-1/2"
9 x 11.5 cm
circa 1900

General Store
225-4
19.95
3-3/4 x 5"
9.5 x 12.5 cm
Sutter Creek CA circa 1897

Grand Central Gold Mine
225-37
24.95

Montezuma Post Office
225-38
24.95

MISCELLANEOUS

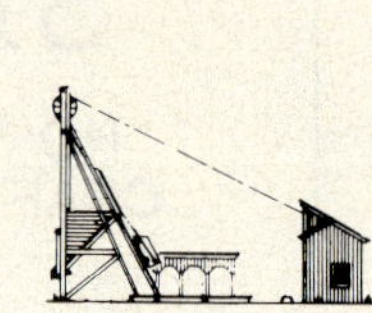

Nevada Fire Station
225-17　19.95
3 x 6-1/2"　7.6 x 16.5 cm
Nevada City, CA circa 1861

Lucky Mine
225-13　19.95

Masonic Lodge
225-8　18.95
3-3/4 x 8"
9.5 x 20.5 cm
Los Angeles, CA circa 1858

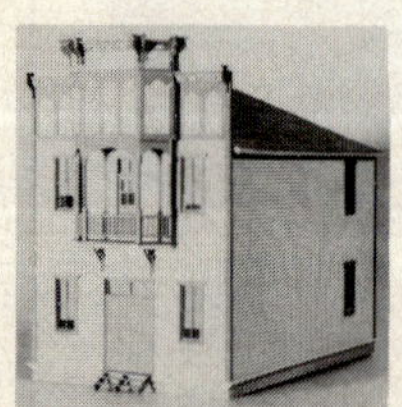

Fraternity Hall
225-1　18.95
3-1/2 x 5-1/2"　9 x 14 cm
Elkhorn, MT circa 1890

Virginia City Ore Bin
225-10　16.95
Virginia City, Nevada

(not illustrated)
Bodie Church
225-21　**NEW**　23.95

HOUSES

225-9　Mine House　28.95
5 x 6-1/2"　12.7 x 16.5 cm
Mojave, CA circa 1890

225-14　Red Light District　pkg(5) 16.95
2-1/2 x 11"　6.5 x 28 cm total length

Gold Hill House
225-24　23.95
4-1/2 x 5"　11.5 x 12.5 cm
Gold Hill, Nevada, circa 1881

Leadville House
225-2　32.95
4 x 6"　10 x 15 cm
Leadville, CO, circa 1900

Queen Anne Cottage
225-3　29.95
3-3/4 x 5"　9.5 x 12.5 cm
Arcadia, CA, circa 1890

Winters Mansion
225-12　32.95
5-1/2 x 7"　14 x 18 cm

Columbia Miners Cabin
225-39　17.95
2 x 3-3/4"　5 x 9.5 cm

HO SCALE (1/87) EASY-TO-BUILD KITS

NEW

Kits include precolored plastic parts and step-by-step instructions.

STATIONS

Small Town Station
222-9001   10.98

Freight & Maintenance Shed
222-9022   10.98

Shed Engine Crew
222-9033   5.98

YARD & EQUIPMENT FACILITIES

Engine House, 2-stall
222-9028   10.98

222-9029   Sandhouse & Fuel Facility   10.98

Yardmaster's Office
222-9032   5.98

(not illustrated)
222-9002 Trackside Bldgs 10.98

BUSINESSES

Summer Stock Theater
222-9035   10.98

Superior Bakery
222-9037   10.98

Weekly Herald Print Shop
222-9038   10.98

222-9051   Ma's Place   12.98

Hardware Store
222-9053   15.98

INDUSTRIAL

222-1702   Coal Mine   15.50

Edison Electric Station
222-1703   14.50

Butane Gas Dist. Center
222-1704   15.50

222-9052   Stockyards   16.98

Warehouse Transfer
222-9058   15.98

Welding Shop
222-9059   12.98

Electric Sub-Station
222-9060   12.98

Cambria Iron Works
222-9054   29.98

Cambria Boiler House
222-9055   12.98

(not illustrated)
Cambria Storage Tanks
222-9056   11.98
Cambria Accessory Pack
222-9057   9.98

RURAL

Rural Schoolhouse
222-9036   10.98
(not continued)
Farm House
222-9003   10.98
Barn & Yard Buildings
222-9015   10.98

HOUSES

Suburban Home
222-9034   10.98

Aunt Millie's House
222-9050   12.98

ASSORTMENTS

222-600   Assorted Buildings   182.00
1 each: 1702, 1703 and 1704

HO SCALE • REALISTIC COLOR • STYRENE PLASTIC

DPM's complete modular wall system allows you to build structures suited to your size and style requirements. Use your own design or DPM's. Build what you want and need. Exotic tools and special skills are not required. Also, excellent for "kit-bashing"!

NEW

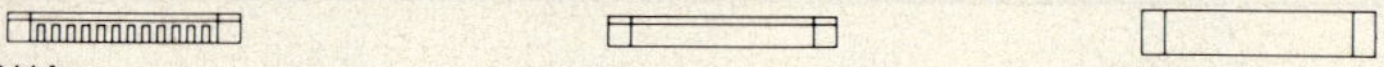

243-30114
CORNICE (8 PER PACKAGE)

243-30117
CORNICE (8 PER PACKAGE)

243-30115
LOADING DOCK WALLS
(8 PER PACKAGE)

CORNICES AND LOADING DOCK WALLS

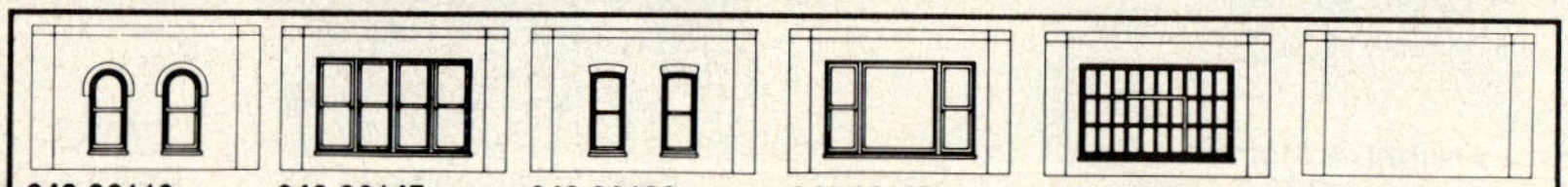

243-30112 243-30147 243-30130 243-30167 243-30175 243-30113

6 SINGLE-STORY WALL SECTIONS (1 7/8"H/ 4.7 cm.)

243-30108 243-30144 243-30138 243-30164 243-30174 243-30111

243-30109 243-30139

243-30110 243-30137

243-30118
4-STORY POWERHOUSE WINDOW

10 TWO-STORY WALL SECTIONS (3 11/16"H/ 9.4 cm.)

243-30103 243-30143 243-30133 243-30163 243-30173 243-30104

243-30105 243-30142 243-30134 243-30162 243-30172

243-30101 243-30141 243-30136 243-30161 243-30171

243-30102 243-30131 243-30132

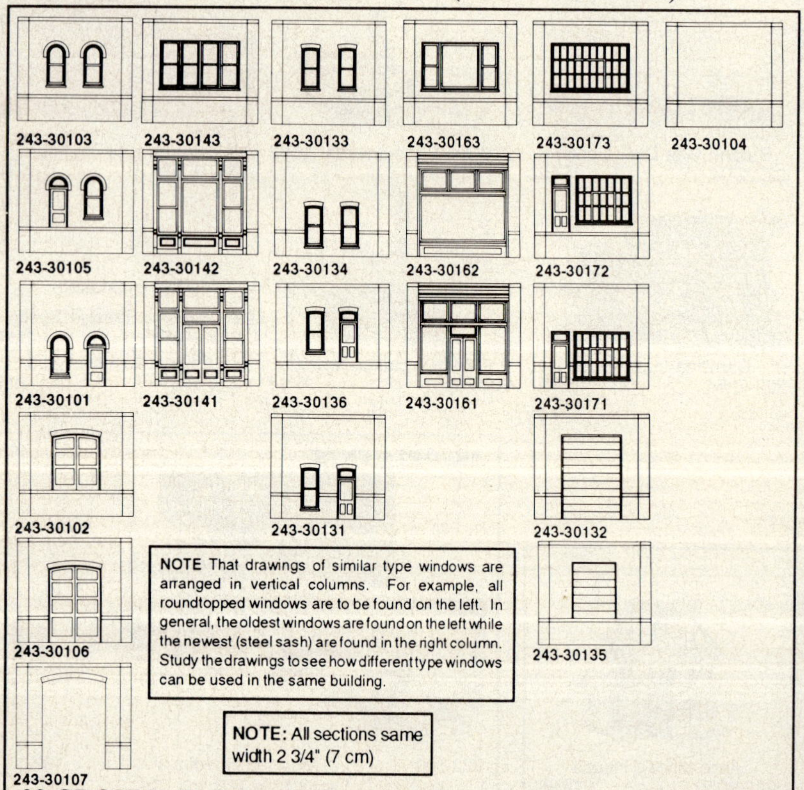

NOTE That drawings of similar type windows are arranged in vertical columns. For example, all roundtopped windows are to be found on the left. In general, the oldest windows are found on the left while the newest (steel sash) are found in the right column. Study the drawings to see how different type windows can be used in the same building.

243-30106 243-30135

243-30107

NOTE: All sections same width 2 3/4" (7 cm)

22 GROUND FLOOR WALL SECTIONS (2 3/4"H/ 7 cm.)

THE MODULAR SYSTEM

Create buildings of any size, shape, or height. A one-story building uses ground floor parts plus cornice. Use ground floor parts topped with single-story upper floor sections and cornice for two stories. For three stories use ground floor parts, two-story upper floor sections, plus cornice. Repeat to desired height. All sections are the same width 2 3/4" (7 cm). Use any plastic cement.

Each parts package contains 4 wall sections that are alike, plus pilasters to join them together side by side and to form corners. The packages include doors, windows, and clear window sheets. Cornice and Loading Dock packages each contain 8 sections. Powerhouse Window includes two windows and required walls.

243-30101 THRU 243-30175 .... 4/PKG $3.98

EXCEPTIONS

243-30104, 243-30107
243-30111, 243-30113 .... 4/PKG $2.98
243-30114, 243-30115, 243-30117 .... 8/PKG $2.98

EXPLODED VIEW

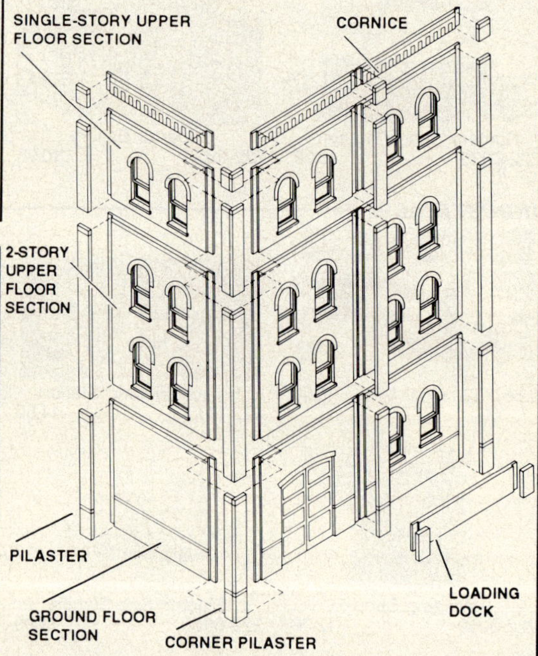

PLANNING PACKET

Planning Packets contain full size drawings of all wall components. Make several photo copies, cut them out and tape together on cardboard to pre-plan your structure and determine exactly what you need.

243-30191 Planning Packet 98¢

DESIGN PRESERVATION MODELS

HO SCALE • REALISTIC COLOR • STYRENE PLASTIC

DPM's complete modular wall system allows you to build structures suited to your size and style requirements. Use your own design or DPM's. Build what you want and need. Exotic tools and special skills are not required. Also, excellent for "kit-bashing"!

NOTE: MODULAR KITS 243-351 THRU 243-355 ARE 33% TO 55% HIGHER IF PURCHASED AS INDIVIDUAL COMPONENTS.

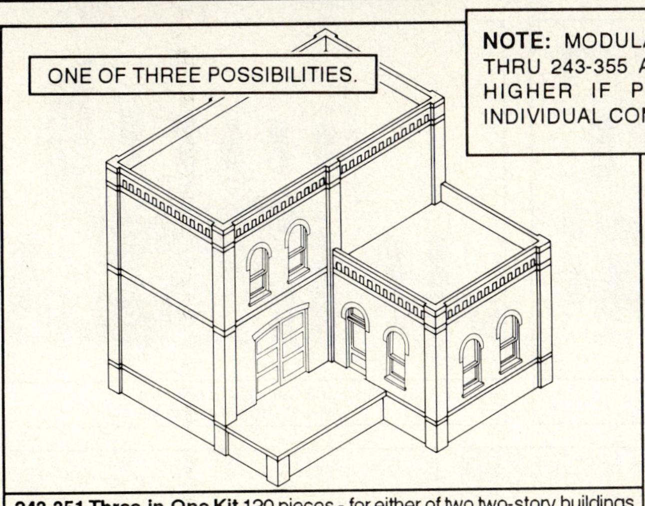

243-351 Three-in-One Kit 120 pieces - for either of two two-story buildings up to 8 1/2" x 6", or a 23" long 3-D background "flat" $13.98

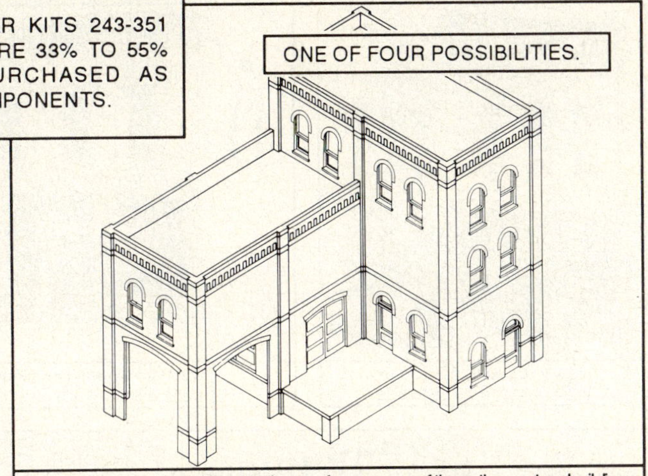

243-352 Four-in-One Kit 175 pieces - for any one of three three-story buildings up to 7 1/2" x 8 1/2", or a 17" long 3-D background "flat" $19.98

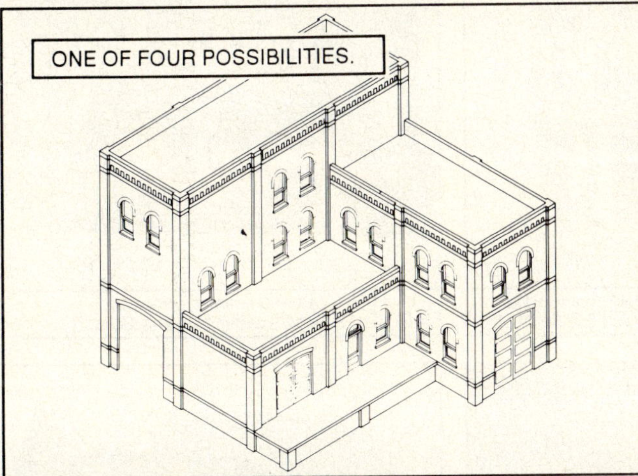

243-353 Four-in-One Kit 213 pieces - for one of three three-story buildings up to 11 1/2" x 8 1/2", or a 20" long 3-D background "flat" $24.98

243-355 Tera Surplus Window Whse - A big industrial/warehouse structure with a small footprint. 8 3/4" x 11 1/2" (22 x 29 cm) $29.98

243-354 Fedups Freight Co. A shipping and receiving center for an action oriented focal point. 19 3/4" x 8 3/4" (50 x 22 cm) $29.98

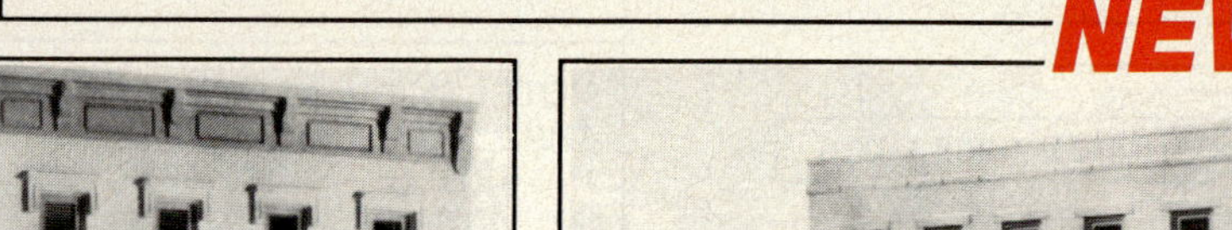

HO SCALE • EASY TO BUILD • STYRENE PLASTIC

Series 1 Structure Kits are molded in a single color with architectural details already in place. Sheet styrene roof material, clear styrene for windows and complete instructions are included. Simply assemble with any model cement and paint. (Figures & vehicles not included.)

NEW

243-101 Kelly's Saloon
2 3/4" x 4" (7 x 10 cm) $8.98

243-102 Roberts Dry Goods
4 1/2" x 3 5/8" (11 x 9 cm) $8.98

243-103 Cutting's Scissor Co.
7 1/4" x 3" (18 x 8 cm) $9.98

243-104 B. Moore Catalog/Showroom
4 7/8" x 5" (12 x 13 cm) $9.98

243-105 Skip's Chicken and Ribs
2 3/4" x 4 1/8" (7 x 11 cm) $8.98

243-106 Laube's Linen Mill
6 3/4" x 3 3/8" (17 x 9 cm) $9.98

CITY LIFE

The hustle and bustle of American life is portrayed on Seymour Block. Stroll down the sidewalk to lunch at M.T. Arms Hotel. Shop at the Front Street Building. Withdraw some cash, yours of course, from First National Bank. End your day with a browse through Pam's Pet Store.

243-107 Freight Depot
5 3/4" x 4 3/4" (15 x 12 cm) $9.98

243-108 Goodfellows Hall
6 1/4" x 4 1/2" (16 x 11 cm) $9.98

DESIGN PRESERVATION MODELS

HO SCALE • EASY TO BUILD • STYRENE PLASTIC

Series 1 Structure Kits are molded in a single color with architectural details already in place. Sheet styrene roof material, clear styrene for windows and complete instructions are included. Simply assemble with any model cement and paint. (Figures & vehicles not included.)

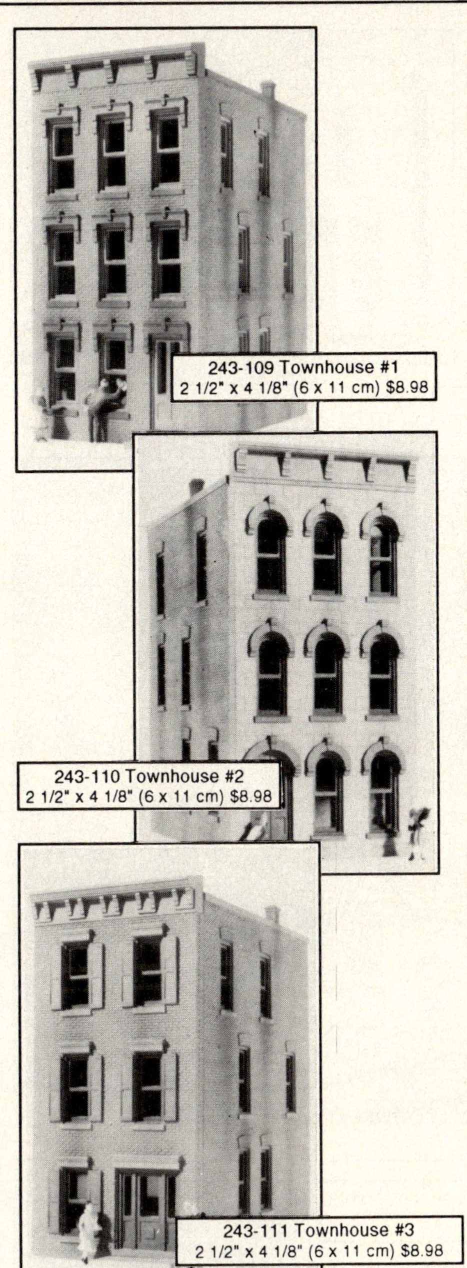

243-109 Townhouse #1
2 1/2" x 4 1/8" (6 x 11 cm) $8.98

243-110 Townhouse #2
2 1/2" x 4 1/8" (6 x 11 cm) $8.98

243-111 Townhouse #3
2 1/2" x 4 1/8" (6 x 11 cm) $8.98

Carol's Corner Cafe • Goodfellows Hall

Modular Building • C. Smith Packing Hse. • Cutting's Scissor Co.

243-113 Carol's Corner Cafe
2 3/4" x 4 1/8" (7 x 11 cm) $9.98

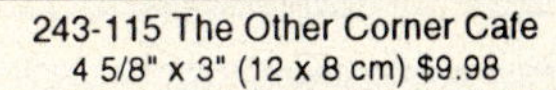

243-115 The Other Corner Cafe
4 5/8" x 3" (12 x 8 cm) $9.98

243-112 City Cab Co.
6 1/8" x 5 3/4" (16 x 15 cm) $9.98

243-114 Townhouse Flats/ 3 Fronts
Ea. 2 1/2" x 4 7/8" (6 x 12 cm) $8.98

243-116 Carr's Parts
4 3/4" x 3 3/4" (12 x 9 cm) $9.98

DESIGN PRESERVATION MODELS

HO SCALE • EASY TO BUILD • STYRENE PLASTIC

Series 1 Structure Kits are molded in a single color with architectural details already in place. Sheet styrene roof material, clear styrene for windows and complete instructions are included. Simply assemble with any model cement and paint. (Figures & vehicles not included.)

NEW

243-117 JC Nickels
6 3/4" x 4" (17 x 10 cm) $9.98

243-118 1st National Bank
3 1/4" x 4 1/2" (8 x 11 cm) $9.98

243-120 Front Street Bldg.
6" x 4" (15 x 10 cm) $9.98

243-121 Seymour Block
7 1/4" x 3" (18 x 8 cm) $10.98

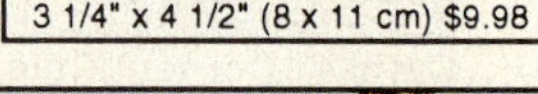

URBAN DETAIL

243-119 M.T. Arms Hotel
8" x 2 3/4" (20 x 7 cm) $17.98

SERIES 2 STRUCTURE KITS

Series 2 Kits have walls molded in one color with separate door, window, and other detail parts in a second color. Sheet styrene roof material, clear styrene for windows and complete instructions are included.

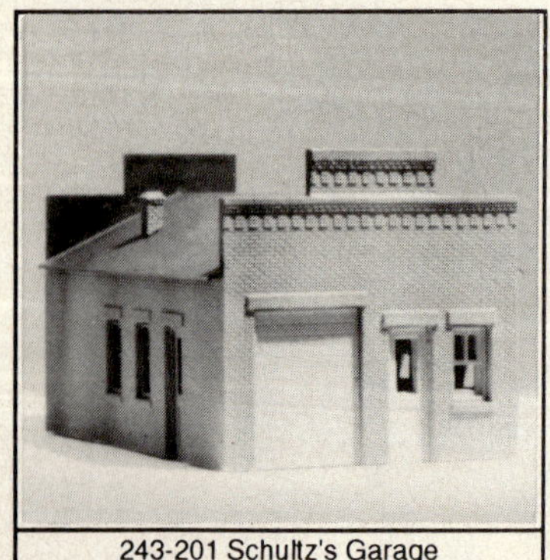
243-201 Schultz's Garage
3" x 5" (8 x 13 cm) $8.98

243-202 Pam's Pet Shop
2 1/8" x 2 7/8" (5 x 7 cm) $8.98

243-203 C. Smith Packing Hse.
5 3/8" x 4 3/4" (14 x 12 cm) $9.98

243-204 Walker Bldg.
3 1/8" x 4 1/2" (8 x 11 cm) $9.98

HO CRAFT TRAIN KITS

BRIDGE

EVERGREEN HILL designs

261-504   Straight Trestle   19.95
3-1/8 x 11-1/8" 8 x 28.3 cm

261-514   HOn3 Wood Trestle   21.95
3-1/8 x 11-1/8" 8 x 28.3 cm

BUSINESSES

261-203   Ash Drugs   39.95
4 x 6-1/2"   10.2 x 16.5 cm
Includes business, home, garage, doghouse
and materials for soda fountain counter, stools
and tables.

261-206   30s Gas Station   35.95
3 x 4"   7.5 x 10.2 cm
Includes two gas pumps, tires, vise, grinder, lube cans,
oxygen and act bottles, and 18 tools.

The end is in sight for the Chicago, Missouri & Western, but trains will still run for a few more days. One of the last freights over the former GM&O track in southern Illinois is shown here behind two GP40's. Wayne Grossklaus of Crest Hill, Illinois, constructed the engines using Atlas (out of production) and Con-Cor GP40's. The lead unit utilizes the factory UP paint job, but portions were painted out and new decals added to match the prototype. Wayne repainted the trailing unit in the WP scheme and superdetailed both locos.

▼ *Photo by Ron Furto*

Rebuilt to save money during the Depression, the Boston & Maine should get many useful years of service from this 2-6-0. Assigned to the West Hoosac Division, she's waiting for her crew and the day's first assignment. Photographed in the yards at Adams, the steamer is a regular on Lou Sassi's home layout in Charlton, New York. George Micklus of Milford, Connecticut, painted the Overland Models loco.

Photo by Lou Sassi

DIAMOND SCALE CONST.

HO SCALE (1/87)

CRAFT TRAIN KITS
Kits feature wood and dental stone cast on hardboard base construction (unless noted) with metal and plastic details.

DIESEL SERVICE FACILITY
Large modern diesel facility provides sand, fuel, lube, oil, treated and untreated water, grease, air supplies, inspection and minor repairs.

#'s 600 & 601 shown

239-600   Diesel Fuel Facility   49.95
Two-track kit: 6-1/2 x 20-1/2" 16.5 x 52 cm

239-601   Diesel Sanding Towers   47.95
Includes four sanding towers with connecting catwalk. Towers may be mounted between two tracks or combined with kit #600. 18 x 15-1/2", 45.7 x 14 cm.

WOOD CHIP LOADER
Chips are loaded into cars through tubes to overhead hopper with revolving wig-wag. To insure even loading, car is slowly pulled to loader by winch and cable.

239-14   Wood Chip Loader   20.95
Includes winch shed and package of wood chips.

ASH PIT
Wood and coal burning locos generated considerable ash residue in their fire box. To remove the ash, the ash pans were dumped and the fire raked. Ash pits had to be constructed to receive the hot ashes and clinkers to prevent burning up the wood cross ties. Most ash pits were constructed of concrete or brick.

239-414   Ash Pit   16.95
4-1/2 x 12" 11.5 x 30.5 cm

65' INSPECTION PIT
Concrete pits between rails made inspection and repair of running gear much easier. Commonly located on the inbound engine terminal tracks so that gear could be inspected before the engine moved to the engine house.

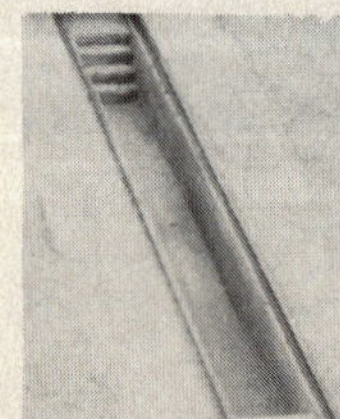

Inspection Pit
239-420   12.95
4-1/2 x 11-1/2"
11.5 x 29.3 cm

WASH PLATFORM
When steam locos arrived at the terminal from a run, they were cleaned to allow a thorough inspection. In all but the largest facilities, the washing area was a simple affair accomplished with a mixture of cleaning solution, steam and water applied under pressure by a workman using a hose. A metal grate or wood platform on both sides of the track provided for sure footing.

239-407   Wash Platform   12.75
scribed planking 2 x 12"   5 x 30.5 cm

COALING TOWER
Coaling towers came in all shapes and sizes and were used to refuel steam locos. Though most often associated with yards or terminals, smaller towers were also constructed in towns and at junctions to serve locos on the road. Coal was delivered in hoppers and dumped into an underground storage bin. From the bin, a hoist lifted the coal into the tower. As the firemen opened the chutes on the bottom, gravity moved the coal down into the waiting tender. At most locations, a water tank or column and sand house were also nearby.

Ogle Two Track Coaling Tower
239-406   64.50
Kit includes a pre-assembled tank and handrail stanchions in brass with plastic construction and white metal details.

WALKING BEAM OIL PUMP
Metal casting on a wood surface.

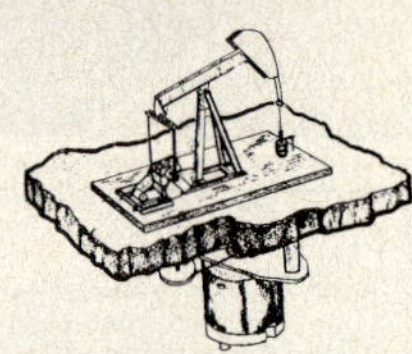

239-401 Kit less Motor   19.95

MISCELLANEOUS
Cast white metal.

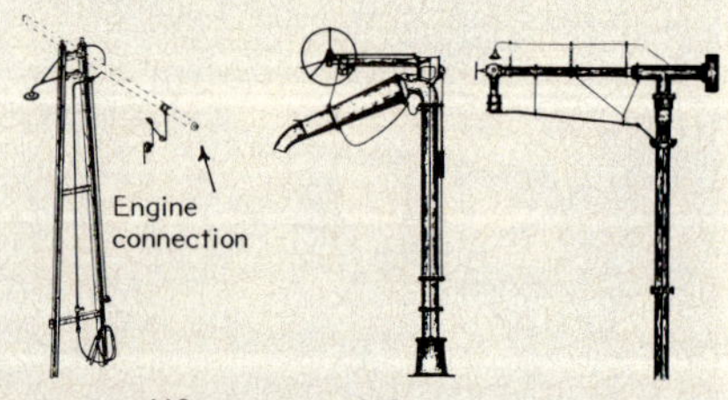

239-410 Roundhouse/Engine Terminal Utility Pole   pkg(2) 15.95
239-412 Water Column   kit 11.95
239-417 Water Column   assembled 29.50
Used by SP, CB&Q and D&RGW.
239-413 Oil Column   kit 8.95
239-418 Oil Column   assembled 15.95

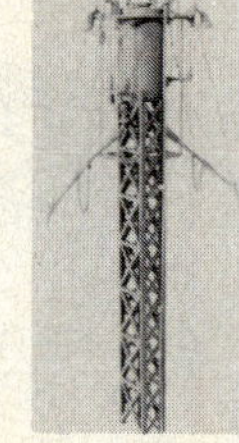

Steel Sanding Tower Kit
239-416   19.95
SP&S prototype at Spokane, WA.

TURNTABLE
Turntables are constructed of scale basswood, metal casting, oil lite bronze bearings, nylon gears, steel shafting, and a reconstituted wood composition product that forms the pit walls and bottom. Bridge can be lifted out of pit for maintenance.

You can figure out which of your locos will fit on which turntable by refering to bridge rail length listed with each item.

STEEL GIRDER
Turntable bridge is a wood frame with injection molded detail overlay on side frames.

single span girders

239-65 65', 8-3/4" rail length   96.50
239-75 75', 10-1/8" rail length   97.50
Twin span girder turntable include metal cap and arch.

239-901   90', 12-1/2" rail length   101.50
239-1051 105', 14-5/8" rail length   102.50
239-1201 120', 16-1/2" rail length   106.50
239-1341 134', 18-1/2" rail length   108.50

STEEL TRUSS
Steel truss bridge center shaft has steel out-of-reach arms welded on to apply turning pressure to bridge.

239-90   90', 12-1/2" rail length   139.50
239-115   115',15 -7/8" rail length   149.75
239-135   135', 18-3/4" rail length   153.75

TIMBER TRUSS
For standard and narrow gauge.

239-51 51', 7" rail length   88.75
239-60 60', 8-1/4" rail length   89.75

DIAMOND SCALE CONST.
HO CRAFT TRAIN KITS

Kits feature wood and dental stone cast on hardboard base construction (unless noted) with metal and plastic details.

GALLOW

For standard and narrow gauge.

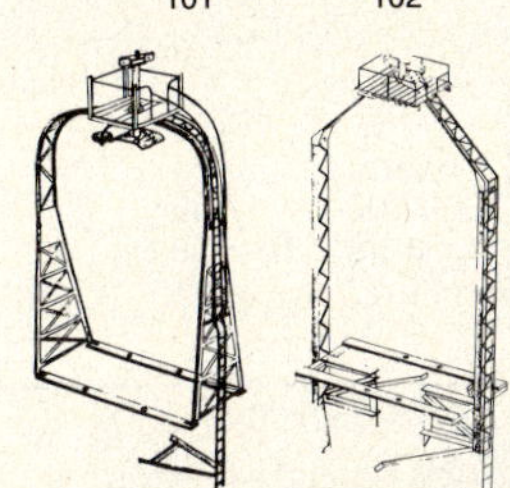

239-56 56′, 7-11/16″ rail length 92.75

TURNTABLE ACCESSORIES

TURNTABLE ARCHES

For installation at mid-table and includes wires for electrical connection.

101   102

Round Top
239-101 16.95

Angle Top
239-102 16.95

MOTOR & GEAR BOX

Specifically designed to operate all Diamond Scale turntables through the 3/16″ steel worm shaft supplied in each kit. Attaches to underside of pit and requires indexing kit (#s 110 or 114) to achieve total automatic operation. Reversing switch included.

Motor &
Gear Box
239-111
49.50

INDEXING KIT

Designed to control the operation of the motor to stop turntable in correct rail alignment at track selected. Operator selects track, determines direction of bridge rotation and starts unit with push of a button. Turntable turns until it comes within 3/4″ of selected track, then automatically slows until final alignment is made.

Kit includes prewired electronic board, six track sensors, 12-position rotary selector switch, switch knob, two push buttons and control rotor.

239-110 for Turntables 105′ and under 90.25
239-114 for Turntables 115′ to 135′ 90.25

See also: POWER SUPPLIES, TRACK, FREIGHT CARS, SIGNALS & DETECTION UNITS and SCENERY for additional DIAMOND SCALE items.

HO SCALE (1/87) CRAFT TRAIN KITS

Kits contain scale lumber, metal castings, signs and instructions.

YARD EQUIPMENT & FACILITIES

HOn3 Handcar Shed
254-29 2 x 3″ 5x 7.7 cm 19.95
HO Handcar Shed
254-32 2 x 3″ 5 x 7.7 cm 19.95
Both handcar sheds include handcars.

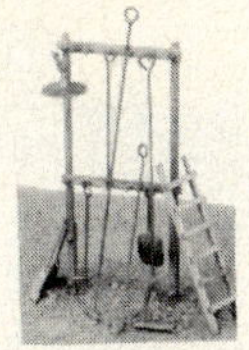

Cleanout
Rack
254-39 4.95
3/4 x 1/16″ 2 x .2 cm

Ashpit
254-40 19.95
3-3/4 x 2-5/8″
9.5 x 6.7 cm

Coal Loader
254-41 14.95
5-1/8 x 1-5/8″ 9.5 x 6.7 cm

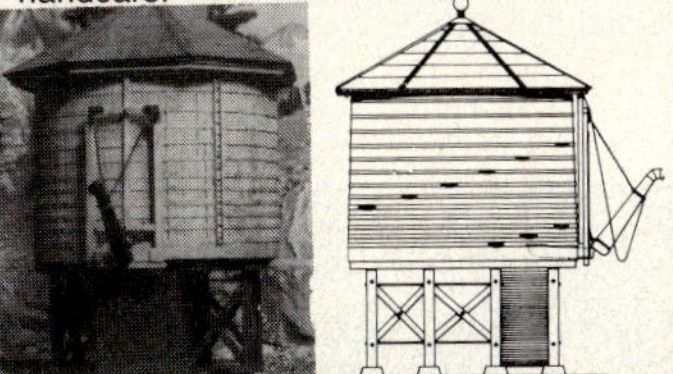
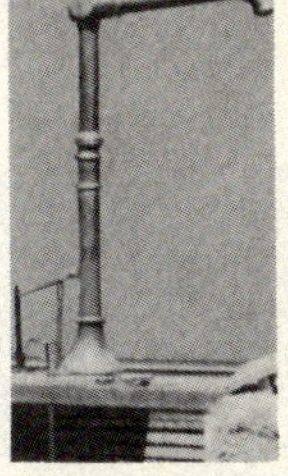

59   67

D&RGW Water Tank
254-59   HOn3 49.95
4-1/4 x 4-1/2″ 11 x 11.5 cm
Standard Water Tank
254-67   HO 49.95
4-1/4 x 4-1/2″ 11 x 11.5 cm
Easy assembly. Wood construction. Plastic and white metal detail parts.

(not illustrated)
254-66 Extra Spout Kit 3.95
For #59 & #67
1-1/2 x 5/8″ 4 x 1.7 cm

Water Crane
254-17 8.95
7/8 x 1-5/8″
2.3 x 4.2 cm

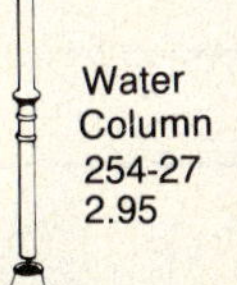

Q&TL Water Tank
254-28 13.00

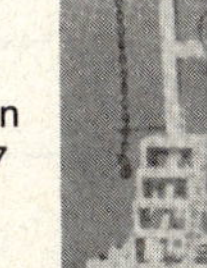

Water
Column
254-27
2.95

RGS Trout Lake
Water Tank
254-119
49.95
3-3/4″ dia 9.5 cm

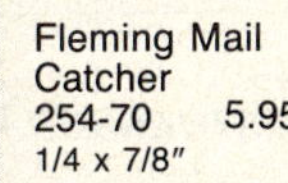

Fleming Mail
Catcher
254-70 5.95
1/4 x 7/8″
.7 x 2.3 cm

STATION

254-19   Palms Station 39.95
4 x 6″

BUSINESSES

The Newspaper Office
254-56 17.95
3-5/8 x 3-1/2″ 9.2 x 9 cm
Easy-to-assemble. Includes die-cut walls, plastic windows and doors & white metal detail parts.

Columbine Cafe
254-118 49.95
Includes curtains, cast metal tables, chairs. Choice of three dry transfer names for cafe. Dozens of interior details. **(By Special Order Only.)**

INDUSTRIAL

Jib Crane
254-68 9.95
2-3/4 x 3/4″ 7 x 2 cm

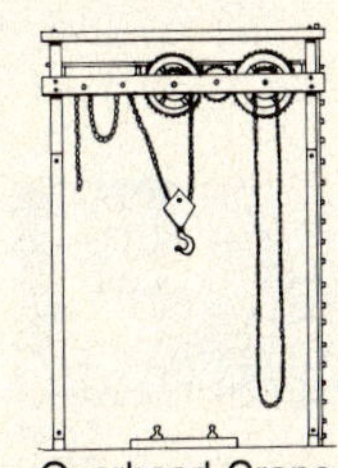

Overhead Crane
254-72 8.95
2-3/4 x 3″ 7 x 7.7 cm

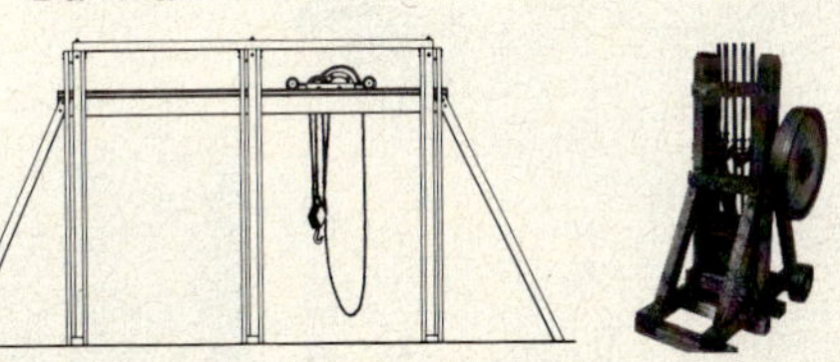
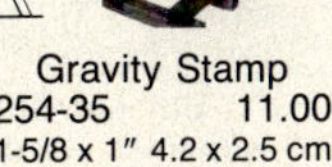

Travelling Crane
254-73 12.95
4-1/2 x 3-5/8″
11.5 x 9.2 cm

Gravity Stamp
254-35 11.00
1-5/8 x 1″ 4.2 x 2.5 cm

OUTHOUSES

Goose/Gander Outhouses
254-120 10.95
Two outhouses w/Trout Station signs.

DYNA-MODEL PRODUCTS COMPANY

HO SCALE (1/87) CRAFT TRAIN KITS

Structures feature milled die cut basswood, fully formed plastic shingle roofing and cast metal windows and doors. Details shown in illustrations are included, unless noted. Some kits can be constructed with removable roof and/or side. Most kits are available with either painted or unpainted accessories.

STATIONS AND PLATFORMS

Small Passenger
260-1 6 x 2-3/4" 15.5 x 7 cm 17.95
less people & benches

Passenger with Tower
260-2 6 x 3-5/8" 15.5 x 9.3 cm 17.95
less people and benches

260-100 Small Freight 17.95

260-101 Large Freight 18.95

260-1011 w/painted accessories 33.95
4 x 8-1/2" 10 x 21.5 cm

HOUSES

Mrs O'Malley's Place
260-312 unpainted 17.95
260-3121 painted 28.95
3-34 x 2-1/2" 9.5 x 6.5 cm

Mabel's Boarding House for Railroad Men 19.95
260-314
260-3141 with painted accessories 35.00
5-3/16 x 5-3/16" 13.5 x 13.5 cm

Two Small Houses
260-310 17.95
260-3101 with painted accessories 30.95
each: 3-5/8 x 3-3/4" 9.3 x 9.5 cm

Shanty
260-306 17.95
4 x 3-3/8" 10 x 8.5 cm

BUSINESSES

260-304 Grist Mill & Feed Store 17.95
260-3041 w/painted accessories 34.95
6-1/2 x 4-3/4" 16.5 x 12 cm

260-305 Plumbing Supply 18.95
260-3051 w/painted accessories 34.95
6 x 5" 15.5 x 12.8 cm; less pick-up truck

260-307 Slaughter House 20.95
260-3071 with painted accessories (8 x 6") 20.5 x 15.3 cm) 40.95
260-4001 Holding Pens with painted Herefords 22.95
260-4002 Holding Pens w/painted Herefords, Pigs/Sheep 22.95
9-3/4 x 4-3/4" 25 x 12 cm

260-303 Barber Shop & Pool Room 17.95
260-3031 with painted accessories 34.95
2-7/8 x 4-3/16" 7.3 x 10.7 cm

260-302 Blacksmith Shop 16.95
260-3021 with painted accessories 33.95
3-1/2 x 3-1/2" 9 x 9 cm; less team of horses

260-300 Shoemaker Shop 17.95
260-3001 w/painted accessories 34.95
4 x 2-1/2" 10 x 6.5 cm

260-301 Butcher Shop 17.95
260-3011 w/painted accessories 34.95
4-5/8 x 2-5/8" 11.8 x 6.7 cm

Grocery Store
260-308 18.95
5-1/2 x 3-3/16"
14 x 8.1 cm

w/painted accessories
260-3081 33.95

News Stand
w/painted accessories
260-3161 7.95

DYNA-MODEL PRODUCTS COMPANY

Structures feature milled die cut basswood, fully formed plastic shingle roofing and cast metal windows and doors.

RURAL BUILDINGS

Small Barn
260-309   12.95
with painted accessories
260-3091   20.95
4-1/2 x 4-3/8"
11.5 x 11.2 cm

260-311   Livery Stable   24.95
260-3111   with painted accessories   38.95
4 x 7"   10 x 18 cm

260-313   MacDougal's Farm House   17.95
260-3131   with painted accessories   30.95
4-3/4 x 3-1/8"   12 x 8 cm

260-4011   Corral w/painted Horses   17.95
3-1/2 x 5-1/2"   9 x 14 cm

Outdoor Privy
w/painted accessories
260-3151   7.95
7/8 x 7/8"   2.2 x 2.2 cm

MISCELLANEOUS

Country Church
260-317   18.95
w/painted accessories
260-3171   28.95

260-99   Dyna-Model Catalog   1.00

DOVER PUBLICATIONS

HO EASY-TO-BUILD KITS

CUT & ASSEMBLE BUILDINGS

Full-color buildings printed on cardboard stock, with illustrations.

241-24754   Early American Seaport   5.95
(11 buildings)

241-23536   Early New England Village   6.95
(12 Buildings)

241-24589   Old Time Farm   5.95
(9 Buildings)

241-23849   Victorian Houses   6.95
(4 Buildings)

241-23736   Western Frontier Town   6.95
(10 Buildings)

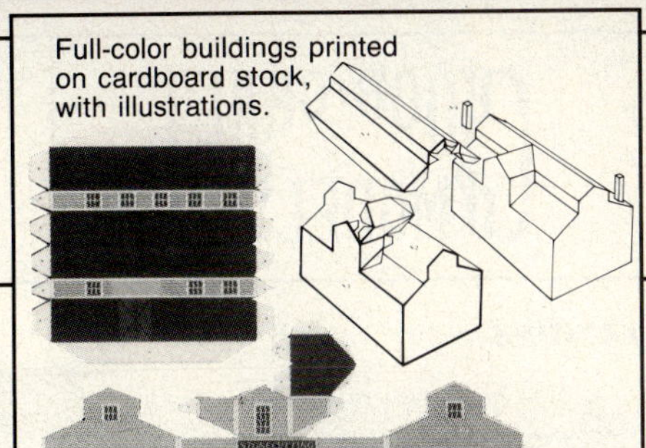

241-24473   1920's Main Street   5.95

241-24663   Caernavon Castle in Wales   6.95

241-25097   Victorian Seaside Resort   6.95
(9 Buildings)

241-25635   Greenfield Village   5.95

241-26150   House of Gables   3.95

GLOOR-CRAFT MODELS

HO SCALE (1/87)

CRAFT TRAIN KITS

Kits feature basswood, precut parts, color coded stripwood, metal castings, step-by-step instructions and full size drawings.

We have worked closely with this manufacturer to provide accurate availability information at the time this catalog was published. Items listed in *blue ink* may not be available at all times. Please see your dealer for current delivery information.

STATIONS

288-4007   Freight House   20.95
9 x 3-1/2"   23 x 9 cm

288-4012   Small Freight   18.95
2-3/4 x 4"   7 x 10 cm

Haydenton Covered
288-4002   38.95
11-1/2 x 5"   29.3 x 12.7 cm

Marlington Station
288-4021   50.95

YARD & EQUIPMENT FACILITIES

PRR Interlocking Tower
288-4004   32.95
2 x 3-1/4"   5 x 8.3 cm
Mount Union Pennsylvania Tower

Elevated Gate Tower
288-4011   16.95
1-1/4 x 1-3/4"
3.2 x 4.5 cm

Lineside Section House
288-4013   16.95
2-1/4 x 2-3/4"   5.7 x 7 cm

Watchman's Shanty
288-4014   18.95
2-1/8 x 3-1/8"   5 x 8 cm

Coaling Tower
288-4001   43.95
5 x 7"   12.7 x 18 cm

Yardmaster's Office
288-4010   11.95
4 x 2-1/2"   10.2 x 6.4 cm

288-4005   Single Stall Engine House   38.95
15-1/2 x 6-1/2"   39.4 x 16.5 cm

288-4015   Tool & Supply Shed   26.95
3-3/8 x 7"   8.6 x 17.8 cm

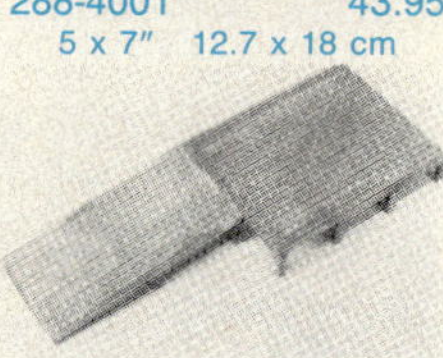

Loading Platform
288-4022   14.95
2-7/8 x 7"   7.3 x 17.8 cm

BUSINESSES

288-4024   Lumber Storage Rack   20.95
2-1/2 x 7"   6.6 x 17.8 cm

288-4023 Cash & Carry Lumber Co 54.95
space varies with arrangement

288-4031   Chuck's Hardware   23.95
4-1/2 x 5-1/2"   11.5 x 14 cm

Roger's Plumbing & Heating
288-4016   6 x 7   15.3 x 17.8 cm   31.95
Clapboard siding and metal roof. Includes lean-to shanty plus a 2-color sign.

H Gluth Feed Co
288-4017   30.95
8-1/2 x 7"   21.6 x 21.6 cm

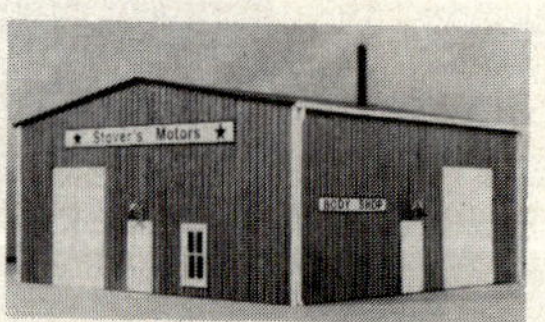

Stover's Motors
288-4025   23.95
5-3/4 x 5-3/4"   14.6 x 14.6 cm

Bryan's Family Supply
288-4008   30.95
6 x 7"   15.3 x 17.8 cm

Store & Warehouse
288-4003   37.95
12 x 4"   30.5 x 10.2 cm

Midwestern Grain Elevator
288-4009   58.95
5 x 16"   12.8 x 47 cm

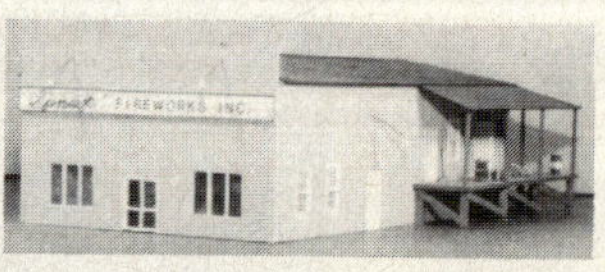

Sunset Fireworks Inc
288-4026   22.95
10-1/2 x 7"   26.8 x 17.8 cm

National Box Factory
288-4027   35.95
7-1/2 x 11-1/4"   19 x 28.6 cm

GLOOR·CRAFT MODELS

HO SCALE (1/87) CRAFT TRAIN KITS

Kits feature basswood, precut parts, color coded stripwood, metal castings, step-by-step instructions and full size drawings.

BUSINESS (continued)

288-4035   Diesel Service Facility   32.95
12 x 10-1/4"   35 x 26 cm

5&10 Store
288-442
20.95

Farmer's
Trust
Bank
288-443
24.95

MISCELLANEOUS

288-4039   85' Covered Bridge   31.95
12 x 4"   30.5 x 10.2 cm

288-4006   Old Style House   27.95
7-1/2 x 5"   19 x 12.7 cm

288-4038   65' Plate Girder   11.95
9 x 2"   23 x 5 cm
Accepts 9" piece of Atlas track.

HO SCALE (1/87) CRAFT TRAIN KITS

Kits are molded plastic, undecorated & some require modification and components from other manufacturers.

STATION & YARD FACILITIES

Victoria Station Restaurant
480-1511   12.00
8 x 8 x 2"   20.4 x 20.4 x 5cm
w/metal box car & modern caboose

Wayside Station
480-1504   12.00
8-1/2 x 5 x 2"   21.5 x 12.7 x 5cm
with two box cars (less details)
21.5 x 10.8 x 10.2cm

Victoria Cable House &
Passenger Car Kits
480-1512   12.00
5 x 2-1/2 x 4"
12.7 x 6.4 x 10.2 cm
w/two old timer style
passenger car kits.

480-1505   Wayside Shanty   12.00
"Grandy Dancer's Quarters" kit includes one Overton 36' old time passenger car and one 36' old time wooden style reefer.

Victoria Shop & Barn Kit
480-1513   12.00

CITY BUILDINGS

480-1514 Battle Mountain Street Scene 12.00
each: 4-1/4 x 2-1/8"   10.8 x 5.4 cm
"Sazerac's Saloon and Nevada Central's Office"

Wayside Telegraph Office & Service
480-1506   4 x 2"   10.2 x 5 cm   12.00
Kit includes one flat car (used as a loading ramp), gondola sides (used as coaling bin) and one tank car which is turned into an oiling facility.

HOUSES

(not illustrated)
480-1526 1-Story Brick House   4.25

Stone
1-Story House
480-1525   4.25
4-1/2 x 2-1/2"
11.5 x 6.4 cm

INDUSTRIAL HERITAGE
SCALE MODELS
NEW

HO SCALE EASY-TO-BUILD

Precut styrene walls, Grandt Line windows, instructions, signs and prototype history included.

356-101   Truck Dump Tipple   80.00
Prototype near Amsterdam, Ohio.

365-201   Retail Coal Dealer   70.00
Prototype near Nichols, New York

Guts, Gravel & Glory
LGG
Scenic Railroad Supplies

HO SCALE
(1/87)
CRAFT TRAIN
KITS

NEW

Kits are made of Hydrocal® castings. Parts are made of industrial grade rubber. Grandt Line windows and wood parts are included.

STATIONS & PLATFORMS

McCartney's Mill Engine House
308-125   6-3/8 x 11"   24.95

Brakeman's Shack
308-153 1-1/2 x 3-5/8" 10.95

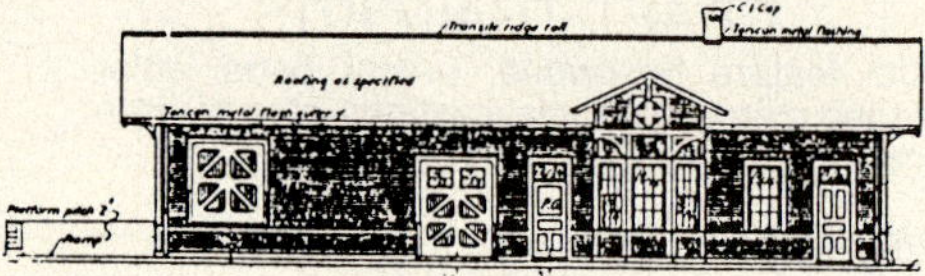
308-155   Santa Fe Station   49.95

RURAL BUILDINGS

J. Hall Feed & Silage
308-136   29.95
3-1/2 x 4-3/4"

Reeds Crib & Carriage
308-137   7 x 16-1/2"   54.95

Welch's Dairy & Feed Mill
308-168   39.95

Burkholt's Ten Stamp Mill
308-132   24.95
3-3/4 x 9"

Grimes Mill Complex
308-146   14 x 10"   109.95

(not illustrated)

308-121 Howard Farm Barn	10.95
308-123 Martin's Pole Barn	6.95
308-160 Farmer's Sod House	8.95

HOUSES (not illustrated)

308-103 Migrant Workers' Rooms	6.95
308-114 Cromwell's Cabin	8.95
308-118 Bueerman's Cottage	8.95

BUSINESSES

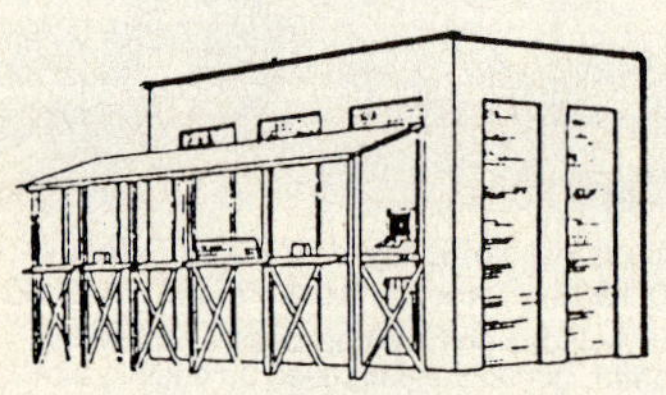
S. Kaulman Ice Plant
308-135   6-1/2 x 11-1/2"   29.95

Lawrence Liquor
308-138   89.95

Ed Smith Cabinetmaker
308-139   5 x 9-1/2"   29.95

CITY BUILDINGS

Tater Hill School
308-141   5-7/16 x 8-3/4"   49.95

(not illustrated)
Clairmont Texas Jail
308-110   11.95

Cliff's Auto Works
308-145   5-1/4 x 6-1/2"   39.95

(not illustrated)

308-102	Paynes Clock Works	6.95
308-104	Wu Tang Laundry & Drugs	8.95
308-105	Ertner's Feed & Grain	14.95
308-106	J. Lott Welding & Blacksmith	8.95
308-108	Lyon Bank	24.95
308-109	Rediger's Storage	8.95
308-112	Mott's Mining Supply	6.95
308-116	Paquette Hardware	10.95
308-122	Wisby's Grocery	8.95
308-124	Duland's Repair Shed	5.95
308-126	D'Orsey Gas Station w/Pit, 1930s	19.95
308-127	Grease Pit for Gas Station, 1930s	5.95
308-128	Baker's Pool Hall	10.95
308-129	Culbertson's Fuel & Solvent	12.95
308-130	Burrus Livery	10.95
308-131	Orr's Broken Butt Cafe	9.95
308-140	Copeland Leather	35.95
308-142	Lyle Lard & Lubricants	25.95
308-143	H. Smith Wagon Works	16.95
308-144	Pop Dudek's FAncy Produce	16.95
308-147	Slick's Plumbing	19.95
308-148	Tinner's Wheat Co.	29.95
308-149	Clark's Fur & Hide Co.	19.95
308-150	Gandy's Wire & Fence	19.95

Lord's Hotel
308-151
49.95

308-169   Fairy's Machine Shop   35.95

Guts, Gravel & Glory
GGG
Scenic Railroad Supplies

HO SCALE (1/87) CRAFT TRAIN KITS

NEW

Kits are made of Hydrocal® castings. Parts are made of industrial grade rubber. Grandt Line windows and wood parts are included.

BUSINESS (continued)   (not illustrated)

308-161	Wally's Hot Dog Haven	8.95
308-162	Kyle's Koffee Shoppe	8.95
308-163	Robbie's Burger Roost	8.95
308-164	Route 66 Eateries	(set of 3) 24.95
308-170	Tye's Saddle Shop	14.95
308-171	Brent's Powder & Shot	19.95
308-172	Greer's Butcher Shop	14.95

MISCELLANEOUS   (not illustrated)

308-101	Edward's Place		5.95
308-111	Shotgun House		9.95
308-113	Three Little Johns	pkg(3)	7.95
308-115	Schacht's Shack (dog house)		10.95
308-117	Prichett Mountain Tattle		8.95

INDUSTRIAL

308-167   Clear Grit Mine   99.95

Fanny Rawlin's Mine
308-157   7 x 12″   59.95

Simmon's Power Plant
308-154   39.95

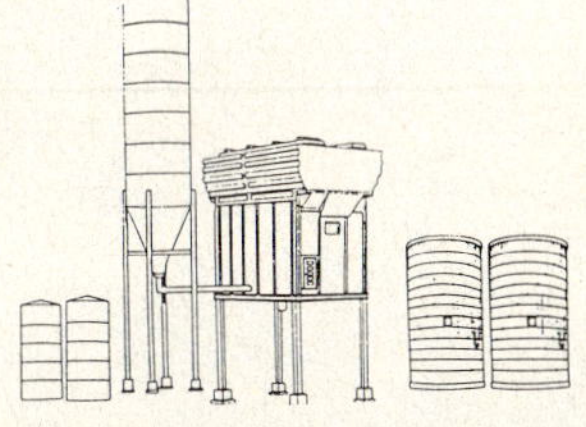

Cement Plant Complex
308-152   49.95

(not illustrated)
308-156   Miner's Half Dugout   8.98

With a recent heat wave, the woods along the Diamond Valley Line have become tinder dry, making the threat of fire all too real. Fresh from the shops and waiting for the auxiliary water car and caboose is the line's new fire fighting car. Fred Gill of Baulkham Hills, New South Wales, Australia, scratch-built the model from Kappler Lumber. A Precision Scale pump and Central Valley ladders, plus a coat of bright Floquil red, completed the job.
Model and Photo by Fred Gill

Time was when it would take several stock trains to serve this branch. But by the time this shot was made in the late 50s, the Union Pacific trains were almost history. Bill Baker combined a pair of Athearn geeps, which were painted by Bob Morley, and an AHM (now discontinued) cowboy figure to recreate this bit of Americana.
Models and Photo by Bill Baker

HO SCALE (1/87) EASY-TO-BUILD KITS

These Easy-to-Build kits consist of prototypically precolored plastic parts and complete instructions. Kits are European prototypes. With minor modifications most can easily be Americanized.

Made exclusively for **WALTHERS** *by Heljan*

YARD EQUIPMENT

3-STALL ROUNDHOUSE

During the steam era, the roundhouse was an essential part of every engine terminal and many are still in use today. This kit is typical of structures found on large or small lines and includes parts for three stalls. For a larger facility, an add-on kit (#803) is available.

322-802   39 x 40 x 12 cm   34.98

WALTHERS

TURNTABLE DRIVE

1 rpm Motor, Bracket and mounting hardware. For use with Heljan #322-804 HO Scale and Cornerstone #933-3203 N Scale Turntables.

942-472   Turntable Drive   24.98

322-803   3-Stall Add-On (for Roundhouse #802)   34.98
Includes three extra stalls and a rear extension to hold locomotives up to 19-1/4" in length.

322-804   Manual Turntable   29.98
Turntables date from the earliest days of railroading and are used to turn locomotives so they face the right way to pull a train. Kit is typical of a steam era turntable but many are used to turn diesels today.

INDUSTRIAL

GRAIN ELEVATOR

Used to store all types of edible grains, this kit is typical of a modern grain elevator, with most of the facility constructed of concrete. Kit includes large storage tanks, an office and elevator.

322-806   19.98

BRIDGE

TIMBER TRESTLE

Larger trestle used for main or branchline operations. Molded in dark brown plastic. Its modular design can be used to arrange the various pieces to fit your scenery.

322-174   19.98

HO SCALE (1/87) EASY-TO-BUILD KITS

These Easy-to-Build kits consist of prototypically precolored plastic parts and complete instructions. Kits are European prototypes. With minor modifications most can easily be Americanized.

Brewery Complex made exclusively for **WALTHERS** by Heljan

BREWERY COMPLEX

When new cultures came to America, they brought many old traditions and skills, including the art of brewing beer. Many a town could boast of it's local brewery, and railroads were vital to the success of the business.

This superb kit includes four structures, which you can arrange to fit your layout, and create a custom brewery complex. There's the large malt house with separate tower, the bottling plant and a cooling tower. Plus, there's a brick smokestack, separate windows and doors and more. Be sure to see the Freight Car section for colorful billboard reefers and other cars to serve your new industry.

322-690 44.99

HOUSES & COTTAGES

Hans Christian Andersen House
322-220 7.75
4-5/16 x 4" 11 x 10 cm

Street Houses
322-155 pkg(2) 10.25
3-3/8 x 2" 8.5 x 5 cm

Half-Timbered House
322-203 6.75
5-1/2 x 3" 14 x 7.5 cm

House Against City Wall
322-1797 15.50
4-1/2 x 3-3/8" 11.5 x 8.5 cm

322-1798 **Downtown House** 16.50
4-1/2 x 3-1/2" 11.5 x 9 cm

2-Story Alpine House w/Balcony
322-1791 5-1/2 x 4-5/16" 14 x 11 cm 14.50

322-1706 **Double House** 12.98
8-1/4 x 7-1/2" 21 x 19 cm

HELJAN

HO SCALE (1/87) EASY-TO-BUILD KITS

These Easy-to-Build kits consist of prototypically precolored plastic parts and complete instructions. Kits are European prototypes. With minor modifications most can easily be Americanized.

FARM & FARMHOUSE

Barn House
322-139   12.25
5-1/8 x 4-1/8"   13 x 10.5 cm

Swedish Farm Building
372-137
18.98
10-5/8 x 5-15/16"
27 x 15 cm

CITY HALL

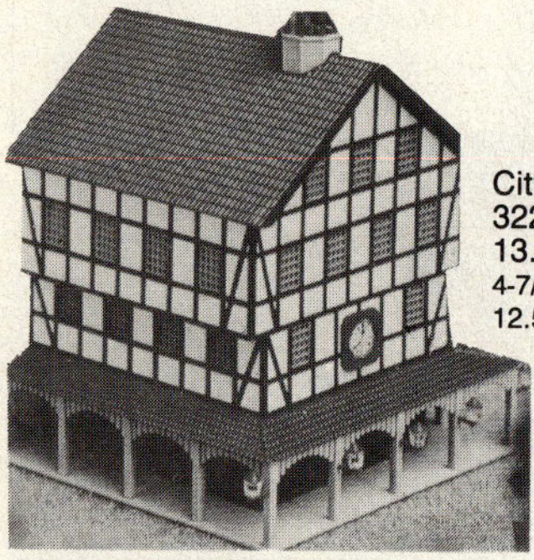

City Hall
322-1788
13.75
4-7/8 x 4-3/4"
12.5 x 12 cm

YARD EQUIPMENT

Canadian Wooden Water Tank
322-1001
11.50
4" square
10 cm square
Includes extra trackside spigot

Modern Freight Warehouse
322-145   15 x 9-13/16"   38 x 25 cm   22.25

INDUSTRIAL

Blacksmith Shop
322-210   5-1/8 x 2-3/4"   13 x 7 cm   7.25

MISCELLANEOUS

322-714   Wayside (British)   9.98

Dairy Plant
322-207
14.50
7-1/8 x 4-3/4"
18 x 12 cm

STATIONS & PLATFORMS

322-712	G.W.R. Station	21.98
322-715	British Pedestrian Overpass	7.75

Swedish Church
322-136   12.25
9-7/8 x 3"   25 x 7.5 cm

Goods Depot (British)
322-717
12.98
11-7/16 x 7-5/16"
29 x 8.5 cm

HO SCALE (1/87) EASY-TO-BUILD KITS

These Easy-to-Build kits consist of prototypically precolored plastic parts and complete instructions. Kits are European prototypes. With minor modifications most can easily be Americanized.

BUSINESSES

2 Story Pub
322-1784   10.49
7-1/16 x 5-7/8"   18 x 15 cm

Drug Store
322-461   7.25
2-3/4 x 6-5/16"   7 x 16 cm

Corner Bank Building & Shops
322-903
14.50
8-1/4 x 6-1/4"
21 x 16 cm

Bar & Beauty Salon w/Apartments
322-465   9.98
4 x 2-1/2"   10 x 6.5 cm

322-206   Danish Roadside Inn   12.50
7-1/8 x 4-1/8"   18 x 10.5 cm

322-208   General Store   14.98
6-3/4 x 4-3/4"   17 x 12 cm

NORTH AMERICAN STRUCTURES

STATION

Glendale Heights Suburban
322-815
14.50
8-1/2 x 5-1/2"
21.7 x 14 cm

HOUSES & COTTAGES

322-1772   Tract House   6.75
4 x 3-5/16"   10 x 8.5 cm

Small Tract House
322-216   4.75

MISCELLANEOUS

Tucson Silver Mine
322-1721   11.98
7-1/16 x 10-3/8 x 4-1/16"
18 x 26.5 x 10.5 cm

Chalet-Type Hotel
322-1787   9.25
4-7/8 x 3-5/16"   12.5 x 8.5 cm

(not illustrated)
322-713   Country Church   12.50

YARD & EQUIPMENT FACILITIES

322-1767   Coaling Station   15.98
7-1/16 x 4"   18 x 10 cm

International Hobby Corp.

HO SCALE (1/87) EASY-TO-BUILD KITS

Easy-to-build kits feature precolored molded plastic construction and include base and concrete sidewalks, trim details and clear plastic windows (unless noted).

BROWNSTONE BUILDINGS

Fill up an entire city block on your layout with this series of Brownstone Buildings! Uniquely designed to create rows of realistic structures, the three-story brick and stone mansions are superdetailed with bay windows, front stairs with railings, simulated plaster trim, concrete sidewalks and window "glass."

POLYBAG KITS

348-19	Abercrombie Mansion	5.98
348-20	Reagan Mansion	5.98
348-21	Morgan Mansion	5.98
348-22	Carrington Mansion	5.98
348-23	Mellon Mansion	5.98

BOXED KITS

348-10019	The Abercrombie	12.98
348-10020	The Reagan	12.98
348-10021	The Morgan	12.98
348-10022	The Carrington	12.98
348-10023	The Mellon	12.98
348-10083	5-Pack Brownstone Kits	each 34.98

VICTORIAN HOME

1001 1002 1003 1004 1005

348-1001	Kavanaugh	12.98	348-1004	Painted Lady	12.98
348-1002	Queen Ann	12.98	348-1005	Victorian	12.98
348-1003	Steiner	12.98	348-10091	1 each of #1001-1005	34.98

COLONIAL HOME

1007 1008 1009 10010 10011

348-1007	Huntington	12.98	348-10010	Pullman	12.98
348-1008	Vanderbilt	12.98	348-10011	Baldwin	12.98
348-1009	Stevenson	12.98	348-10089	Colonial House Assort pkg(5)	34.98

STORES

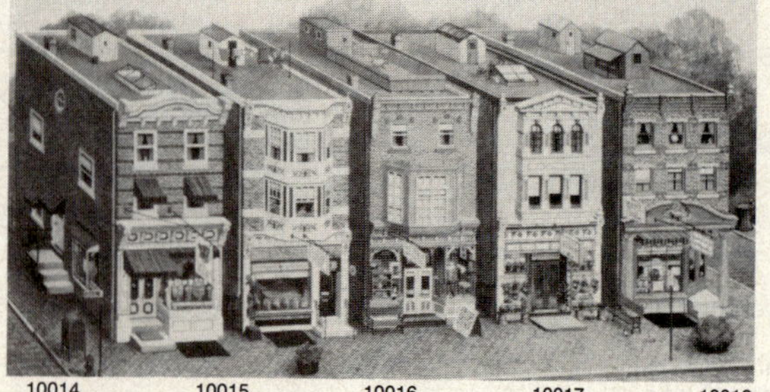

10014 10015 10016 10017 10018

348-10014	Second Hand Rose	12.98	348-10015	The South Street Smoke Shop (includes wooden indian)	12.98
348-10016	Rita's Antiques (includes roof-top shed)	12.98	348-10017	O'Weed's Greenery (includes window displays)	12.98
348-10018	Grant Cary's Apothecary	12.98	348-10090	Store Front House Assort pkg(5)	34.98

10044 10045 10046 10047 10048

348-10044	Fast Photo	6.98	348-10047	Cards & Unusual Gifts	6.98
348-10045	Charisma Dress Shop	6.98	348-10048	Health Aids	6.98
348-10046	Dino's Pizza Parlor	6.98			

348-100100 Shopping Center Assortment **NEW** 19.98
Includes 1 each: 10044, 10045, 10046, 10047 & 10048.

STATIONS & PLATFORMS

Mainline Station
348-3502 11.98

Freight Station
348-3510 11.98

Rico Station
348-807 15.98

Freight Station w/Loading Platform
348-3505 9.98

International Hobby Corp.

HO SCALE (1/87) EASY-TO-BUILD KITS

Easy-to-build kits feature precolored molded plastic construction and include base and concrete sidewalks, trim details and clear plastic windows (unless noted).

INDUSTRIAL

650 Ton Coal Bunker
348-5000   39.98

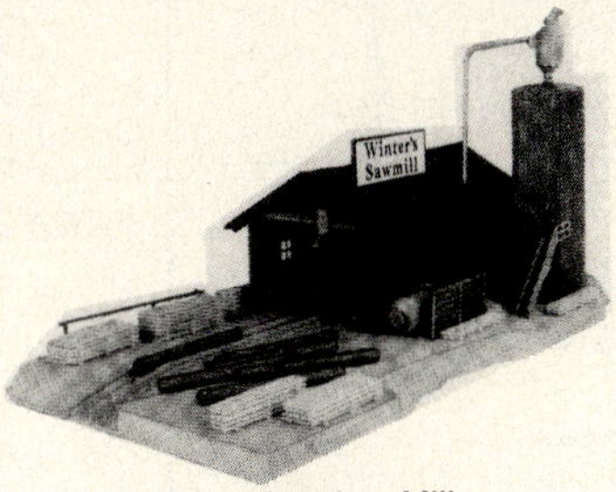

Lumber Mill
348-709   14.98

BRIDGE

Water Bridge
348-5006
8.98

Factory w/Loading Silos
348-3503   11.98

Windmill Pumping Station
348-706   9.98

348 4108 Texaco Station 6.98

RURAL BUILDING

348-812   Barn w/Silo   12.98

BUSINESSES

Store & Auto Repair
348-3504   11.98

Herald Star Newspaper
348-806   13.98

Luigi's Restaurant
348-810   12.98

General Store &
Billiards Parlor
348-3508   6.98

Service Station
348-3509   9.98

Endoline's
Funeral Home
348-707   13.98

Ice Cream Parlor &
Boarding House
348-3507   6.98

County Court House
348-805   16.98

YOUR TOWN USA

348-10025   1st National Bank   14.98
348-10026   Legal & Prof Office   14.98

Old Time Gas Station
348-712   9.98

CITY BUILDING

Store Front
Apartment Building
348-708   12.98

Colonial Church
348-804   15.98

Fire House w/2 Engines
348-808   13.98

Village in a Bag
348-1100   4.98

International Hobby Corp.

HO EASY-TO-BUILD KITS

Easy-to-build kits feature precolored molded plastic construction and include base and concrete sidewalks, trim details and clear plastic windows (unless noted).

SNAP-EAZE SERIES

"SNAP-EAZE" kits feature snap-together construction, no glue required.

RURAL BUILDINGS

Country Barn
348-4100   6.98

School House
348-4104   6.98

Country Church
348-4105   6.98

STATION & YARD FACILITIES

Switch Tower
348-4102   6.98

Rural Freight/Psgr Station
348-4101   6.98

Locomotive Maintenance Building
348-4103   6.98

HOUSES

American Farm House
348-4107   6.98

Society House
348-809   12.98

3 Houses Under Construction
348-711   12.98

2 Suburb House
348-4106   6.98

MASTERPIECE SERIES

Easy-to-Build kits. (Construction time varies with kit size).

YARD & EQUIPMENT FACILITIES

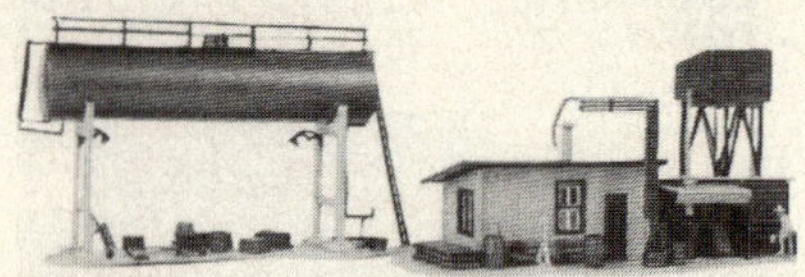
348-3506   Sand & Fueling Depot   11.98

Mainline Tool Shed & Water Tower
348-705   9.98

348-3500   Two Stall Engine House   11.98

Railroad Yard Buildings
348-3501   11.98

Interlocking Tower
348-602   14.98

Sand Tower
348-5005
7.98

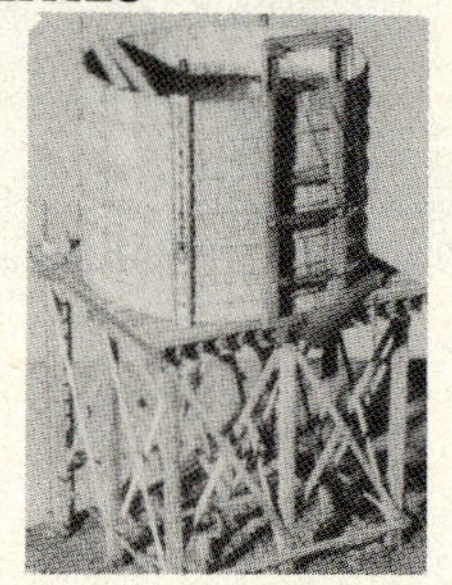

DETAIL ASSOCIATES

HO SCALE (1/87) CRAFT TRAIN KITS

Kits feature diecut milled wood siding, Grandt Line plastic details, templates and instructions.

YARD FACILITIES

Ponderosa Water Tank
229-7004   3 x 4-1/2"   7 x 11 cm   22.00

(not illustrated)
229-7001   Branchline Roadhouse   40.00

229-7002   Extra Stall for Roundhouse   8.00
             3-1/2 x 9"   9 x 23 cm

MODEL TRACTION SUPPLY COMPANY

Trolley Shelter
505-6000   7.95
1 x 1-1/2"   2.6 x 3.8 cm
All metal kit builds into a typical wood passenger shelter used by a trolley or interurban line.

Heading up the Boston & Maine freight is a brass import 2-8-0. This rural scene is the work of Bill McChesney from Schenectady, New York.
Photo by Chris McChesney

NEW
JL Innovative Design
HO CRAFT TRAIN KITS

Features precut Northeastern siding and Kappler stripwood. Includes illustrated instructions.

YARD FACILITIES
Rocky Valley Falls Water Tower
361-111   17.95

INDUSTRIAL

361-121   Hubermill Warehouse   28.95

361-151   Dunn Processing   42.95

BUSINESSES

Vals
Hamburgers
361-131
23.95

LaBosky's
Motorcycle
Repair
361-141
26.95

361-161   Vic's Alignment   22.95

361-171   Pickard Motors   39.95

361-101   JL Inc. Boatworks   34.95

MIL-SCALE Products

HO CRAFT TRAIN KITS
Kits include precut basswood parts and styrene details.

STATIONS & YARD FACILITIES

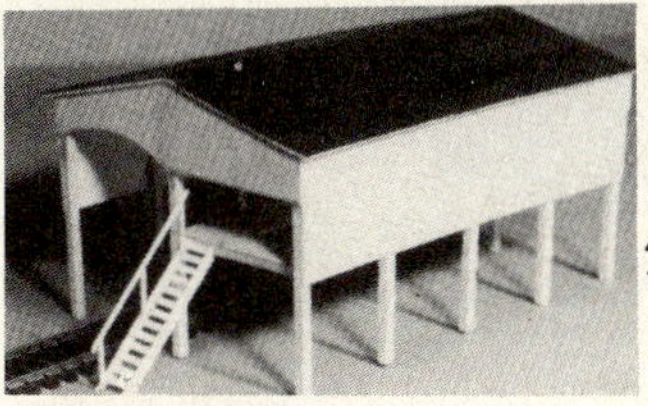

Car Repair
Shed
4-1/8 x 3-3/4"
10.5 x 9.5 cm

477-60   Scribe Siding   17.95
477-61   Board/Batten Siding   17.95
477-62   Corrugated Siding   17.95

Flagstop Station
2 x 3-1/2"   5 x 9 cm

Kit includes printed station names and material for extra platform.

477-10   Clapboard Siding   8.95
477-11   Board/Batten   8.95
          Siding

BRIDGES

60' Concrete
Trestle
Add-on Units
8-1/4" long
21 cm long

477-101   Single Track   8.95
477-103   Double Track   11.95

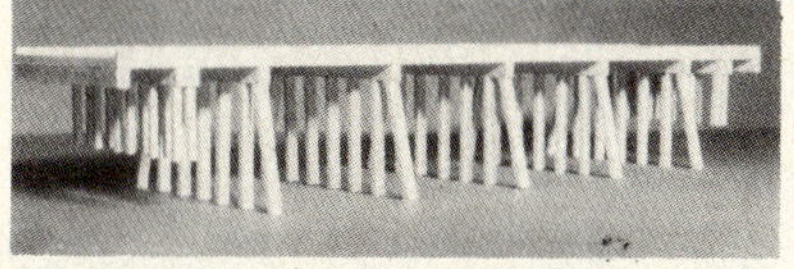

60' Concrete Trestle
8-1/4 x 2-1/2"   21 x 6.3 cm

477-100   Single Track   8.95
477-102   Double Track   11.95

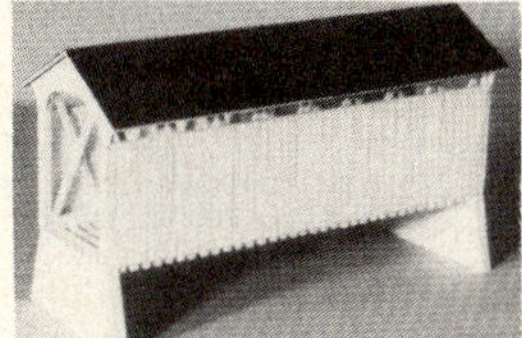

65' Covered
Bridge
477-80   23.95
9"   23 cm

65' WOOD TURNTABLE

477-50   Gallows Type, HO   9" 23 cm   10.95
477-51   Gallows Type, HOn3   9" 23 cm   10.95

477-52   A-Frame Type, HO   10.95
477-53   A-Frame Type, HOn3   10.95
477-601   Turntable Mounting Kit   8.95

MISCELLANEOUS

477-90   Jacobs Coal Co   18.95
3 x 9"   7.6 x 23 cm
Includes pre-painted and silk screened side wall sign.

110' Snow Shed
15"   38 cm

Single Track
477-40   22.95

Double Track
477-41   25.95

Grandt Line
HO SCALE (1/87) EASY-TO-BUILD KIT

Injection molded, styrene plastic kits.

Second Class
Saloon
300-5900   14.95
4-3/4 x 3-1/8"
12 x 8 cm

East Terrible Mill/Mine NEW
300-5901   24.95

JV MODELS
SCALE KITS FOR THE DISCERNING MODELER

CRAFT TRAIN KITS
All kits feature Northeastern Scale Lumber, metal and/or plastic castings, full size templates and detailed instructions.

YARD AND EQUIPMENT FACILITIES

Mainline Wood Water Tower
345-2013   24.95   **NEW**
124,000 gallon capacity scale 28 x 56'. Easily modified for narrow gauge.

Branchline Wood Water Tower
345-2012   22.95   **NEW**
60,000 gallon capacity, scale 22 x 42'. Easily modified for narrow gauge.

Haliburton Engine House
345-2024   **NEW**   31.95
Built in 1878 for the Victoria Railway, kit features Grandt Line details, diagrams, scenery details and color photo. Scale 23 x 79'.

Burnt River Milling Co.
345-2019   **NEW**   29.95
Includes shaft tower ore & ore bins, hoist house, scenery details and wood for embankment. Can be made to operate. Scale 23 x 15'.

Section Tool House
345-2005   15.95
2 x 4-1/8"   4.5 x 9.5 cm
Northern Pacific prototype builds two structures. Includes cast doors and windows. Less figures.

Motor Car House
345-2006   15.95
2 x 4-1/8"   4.5 x 9.5 cm
Northern Pacific prototype builds two structures. Includes cast doors and windows. Less figures.

345-2008   Sand Tower & Drying House   24.95
5-3/8 x 6-1/8"   13.5 x 15.3 cm
Northern Pacific prototype. Double track sanding tower will service two locos at one time. Includes grass, earth, sand, metal spouts and counter balances.

RURAL BUILDING

Gabled Roof Dairy Barn
345-2001   27.95
5-1/4 x 10-1/2"
13.3 x 26.5 cm
Wisconsin prototype, build as a 72 or 84' barn. Strip profile shingles included.

BRIDGES   **NEW**

345-2014   Wood Timber Trestle   26.95
Includes diagrams, color photo & bridge ties. Builds up to 18" long & 18" high. Can be combined for longer spans.

345-2016   Curved Wood Trestle   34.95
Includes diagrams, color photo & bridge ties. Builds up to 36" long & 18" high. Can be combined for longer spans. Can be built to any radius straight or an "S" curve.

MISCELLANEOUS

Roadside Fruit Stand
345-2004   11.95
2 x 2-3/4"   4.5 x 6.4 cm
Scaled from prototype plans. Includes metal castings of produce stand accessories.

Small Boat Landing
345-2003   14.95
2-3/4 x 7-1/4"   7 x 18.2 cm
Includes corrugated aluminum roofing and cast metal boat.

Forest Ranger Tower
345-2002   21.95
3 x 3"   7.5 x 7.5 cm
Includes strip profile shingles and cast stairs.

345-2011   Bunkhouses   NEW   pkg(2) 16.95
Includes windows and doors. Scale 10 x 20'. Use with log scenes or for trackside buildings.

345-2020   Watson's Siding   NEW   30.95
Derelict village includes general store, freight station blacksmith's shop, sheds & fences. Scale 40 x 30'.

STATIONS   **NEW**

345-2025   Victoria Station   26.95
Includes scenery items and color photo.

KATO
PRECISION RAILROAD MODELS

PLATFORM   NEW

381-23113   One Side End #2   5.00

Finishing SELLEY Touches

HO EASY-TO-BUILD
Kits feature cast metal construction.

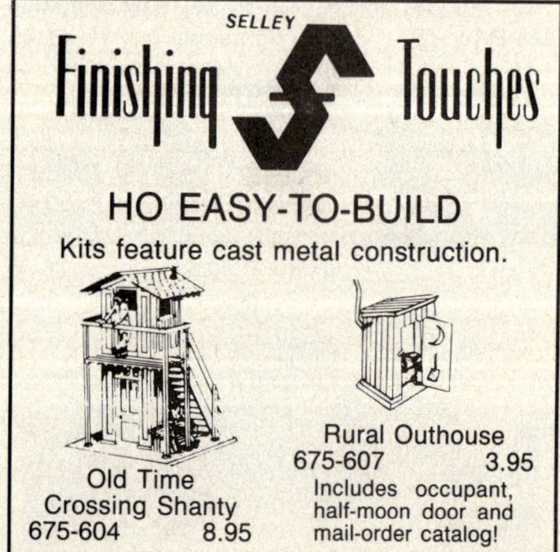

Old Time Crossing Shanty
675-604   8.95

Rural Outhouse
675-607   3.95
Includes occupant, half-moon door and mail-order catalog!

Keystone Locomotive Works

INDUSTRIAL

■ LIMITED QUANTITIES AVAILABLE ■

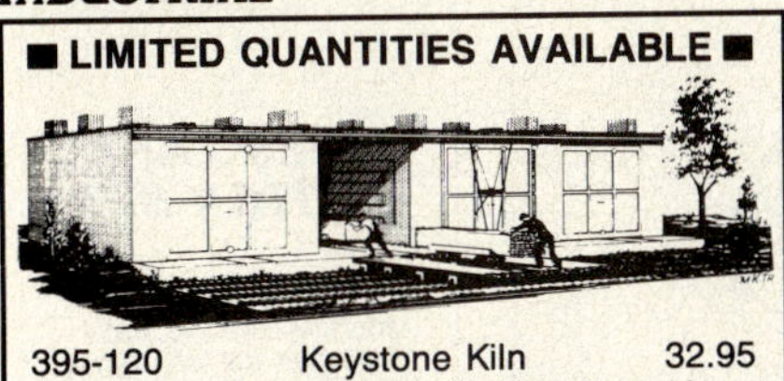

395-120 Keystone Kiln **32.95**
Injection molded styrene kit. Transfer tables included on each side. 7 x 7" 18 x 18 cm.

395-125 Company Store **21.95**
4-1/4 x 7-1/4" 10.8 x 18.5 cm
Typical of logging, mining and farming communities.

395-133 Logging Engine Shop **34.95**
6 x 9-1/2" 15.3 x 23.6 cm

395-122 Company Houses pkg(3) **19.95**
2-3/4 x 6-1/2" 7 x 16.7 cm each
Adaptable to level surfaces or hillside construction. Patterned after Cass, West Virginia prototype.

395-111 Danby Saw Mill **24.95**
7 x 7" 18 x 18 cm
Includes logs, bark, steam engine, separate boiler, tools, log carriage, cistern water supply, and outhouse.

PLATFORM SHELTER

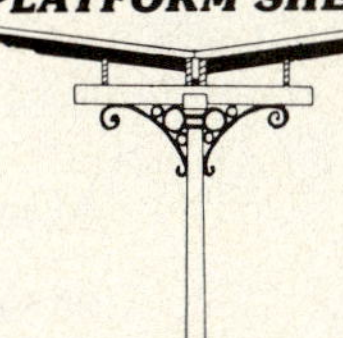

Milton, PA Station Platform Passenger Shelter
395-117 **13.95**
130 scale feet long. Used on many railroads including the PRR, B&O, C&O and NYC.

HO SCALE (1/87) CRAFT TRAIN KITS

Kits contain wood pieces, injection molded styrene parts and cast metal details.

(not illustrated)

395-124 Kindling Wood Factory **48.95**
3 x 3" 7.6 x 7.6 cm 7 x 4" 18 x 10.3 cm
Double building kit consisting of sawing building connected to Kindling drying building.

395-126 Flatwheel Hotel & Saloon **34.95**
5-1/2 x 8-1/2" 14 x 21.8 cm
False front, sloped roof, porch on three sides.

MUIR MODELS

HO CRAFT TRAIN KITS

Feature Kappler stripwood and die cut board & batten siding, Grandt Line plastic castings, Sequoia white metal castings, redesigned instructions & drawings and painting and weathering suggestions.

YARD & EQUIPMENT FACILITIES

Double Logging Cover Water Tanks
517-41 **24.95**
2-1/2 x 4-1/2"
6 x 11 cm

D&RGW Coaling Bin
517-28 **21.95**
(By Special Order Only.)

Cincinnati Yard Tower
517-83 **19.95**
3-1/4 square 8.3 cm

BODIE CITY COMPLEX

Miners Hall
517-122 **22.95**
3-1/2 x 3-1/2" 9 x 9 cm

City Morgue
517-124 **23.95**

HO EASY-TO-BUILD KITS

NEW

WATER TANKS

Injection molded styrene, for easy assembly, and representing common styles of municipal and industrial tanks, suitable for use in many eras.

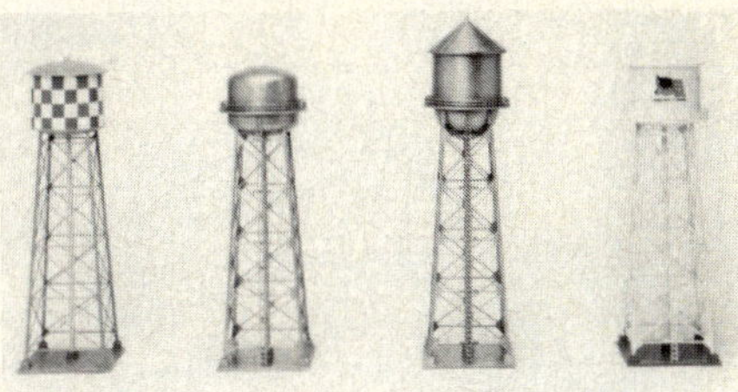

| 125 | 126 | 127 | 128 |

411-125 70′ ERA 1960 Water Tank kit **14.95**
411-126 66′ Ellipsoidal Water Tank kit **16.95**
411-127 74′ ERA 1900 Water Tank kit **16.95**
411-128 69′ ERA 1930 Water Tank kit **16.95**
411-1000 Asst. Water Tanks pkg(12) **167.50**

INDUSTRIAL

411-104 Three Stall Roundhouse **59.95**
15-1/2" x 8-1/2"
Front 16-1/2" Back 5"
American all brick, detailed 20 windows, 3 smoke stacks, detailed doors.

411-105 One Stall Roundhouse **16.95**
Additional stall for 104.

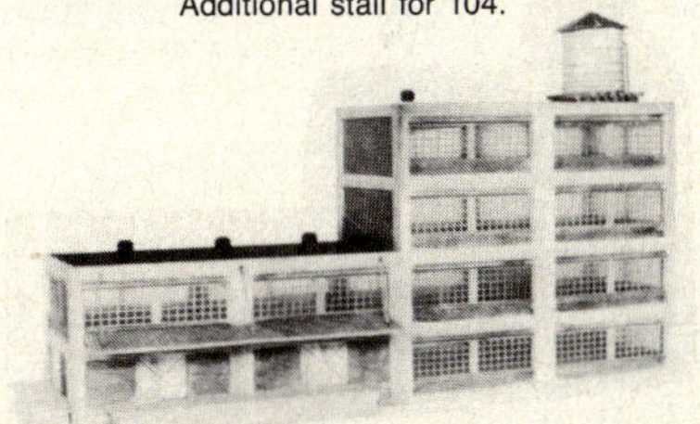

411-108 Global Transfer Company **59.95**
19" x 5" x 11"
Concrete structure with brick walls, 60 detailed windows, loading platform, rooftop water tank.

■ LIMITED QUANTITIES AVAILABLE ■

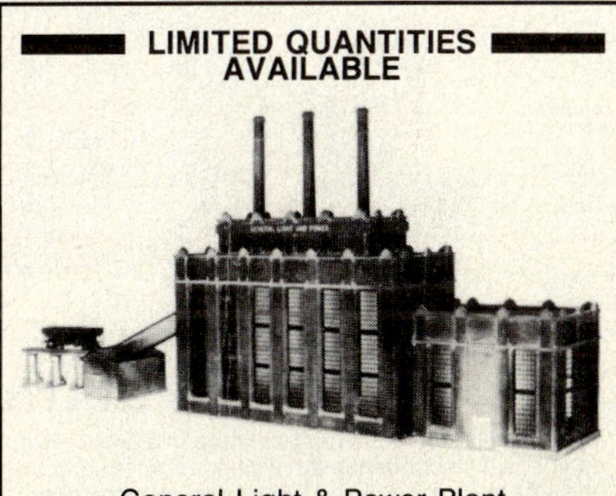

General Light & Power Plant
411-107 6-1/2" x 23-1/2" **89.95**
Early 1900 coal burning electric generating power plant.

kibri
Imported from Germany
by WALTHERS

HO SCALE (1/87) EASY-TO-BUILD KITS

Kits consist of a large range of European prototypes. With minor modifications most can be easily Americanized. Parts are injection molded plastic castings, appropriately colored. Numbered part 'sprues' coordinated with the simple plans allow for easy construction by the modeler.

STATIONS & PLATFORMS

405-9517   Osterheide Station   32.49
7-3/4 x 5-1/2" 19.5 x 14 cm

KONIGSMOOR STATION
405-9515   9-3/4 x 6-1/8" 25 x 15.5 cm   29.99

"ALTES LAND" STATION SET

Creating an entire country town is easy with this set of rustic buildings! Perfect for detailing along a branchline or shortline, the set includes four timber and brick houses (one each of kits #405-8241, 8242, 8243 and 8244), and the "Konigsmoor" Station (#405-9515).

405-8245   106.99

405-9498   Old Time Station   44.99
13-3/8 x 4-3/4" 34 x 12 cm

405-9462   Freight House w/Loading Dock   51.49
18-1/2 x 5-1/2" 47 x 14 cm

405-9528   Lagenthal Station Set   123.99
Consists of #8195, 8196, 8198 & 9504

405-9533   Station Frasdorf   39.99
12-1/4 x 7-1/4" 31.5 x 18.5 cm

SURAWA STATION

Here's a station that's right at home in a small town. It's based on a Swiss prototype, which combines the waiting room, freight house, and living quarters for the agent into one structure. Lots of extra details, including flower boxes, benches and more are provided to complete your station scene.

405-9519   13-1/4 x 5-1/2" 33.5 x 14 cm   38.49

(not illustrated)

405-9495   Station Set Furka   69.49
Includes #'s 8008, 8046, 8048, 8049 and 9493
405-9531   Station Set Alpenland   90.49
Includes #'s 8040, 8044, 8058 and 9533

kibri
Imported from Germany by WALTHERS

HO SCALE (1/87) EASY-TO-BUILD KITS

Kits consist of a large range of European prototypes. With minor modifications most can be easily Americanized. Parts are injection molded plastic castings, appropriately colored. Numbered part 'sprues' coordinated with the simple plans allow for easy construction by the modeler.

STATIONS & PLATFORMS (continued)

405-9494   Old Brick Station   22.99
7-1/2 x 4-1/4"   19.5 x 11 cm

FELDAFING STATION
Built in the 1860's, this impressive station is still in use today! The model is highly detailed and can be used in various time periods.

405-9530   10-1/4 x 3"   25.6 x 7.6 cm   59.99

Station "Kottenforst"
405-9500   46.49
12 x 8"   30 x 20 cm

Station "Calw"
405-9518   62.99
21-5/8 x 6-1/4"   55 x 16 cm

405-9504   Langenthal Station   35.99
17-1/8 x 5-1/2"   43 x 14 cm

REICHELSHEIM STATION
This two-story station is typical of small town depots. The kit includes the attached freight shed.

405-9492   29.99
9-1/2 x 5-1/2"   24 x 14 cm

405-9532   Altkirchen Station   51.49
15-1/2 x 8"   39 x 20 cm

405-9544   Platform Altbach   29.99
2 x 2-3/8"   5 x 6 cm   47-5/8 x 2-1/8"   121.5 x 5.5 cm

405-9502   Brick Station "Eschbronn"   44.99
13-3/8 x 5-1/8"   34 x 13 cm

405-8186   Station Set "Reichelsheim"   63.99
Consists of 8180, 8182, 8184 & 9492

kibri
Imported from Germany
by WALTHERS

HO SCALE (1/87) EASY-TO-BUILD KITS

Kits consist of a large range of European prototypes. With minor modifications most can be easily Americanized. Parts are injection molded plastic castings, appropriately colored. Numbered part 'sprues' coordinated with the simple plans allow for easy construction by the modeler.

STATIONS & PLATFORMS (continued)

PLATFORM "DETMOLD"
Here's a platform that's perfect for your small town or big city stations! It's right at home in the steam or diesel era and several can be combined to build longer platforms.

405-9554   36.49
47-5/8 x 2-1/8″   121.5 x 5.5 cm

405-9508   Station "Blausee"   36.99
13-1/2 x 4-3/4″   34 x 12 cm

405-9550   Station Platform   27.49
47-5/8 x 1-1/2″   121.5 x 3.8 cm

405-9535   Station Achenmuhle   22.99
7-3/4 x 5-3/4″   20 x 15 cm

405-9493   Railway Station Stop   21.49
5-1/2 x 3-1/2″   14 x 9 cm

Platform Extension for #9544
405-9538   9.99
7.2″   18 cm

Platform Extension for #9554
405-9539   9.99
7.2″   18 cm

Platform Extension & Details for #9542, #9544, #9554
405-9540   9.99
7.2″   18 cm

Platform Extension for #9550
405-9551   8.99
7.2″   18 cm

BONN STATION
Based on the Bonn Station in Germany, this realistically detailed model is ideal for use on American or European layouts. The station kit also includes two simulated "glass" train sheds to protect your passengers and trains from inclement weather!

405-9524   w/2 Train Sheds   155.99
station: 19-3/8 x 10″   99 x 25.5 cm   sheds: 33-1/2 x 17-1/4″   86 x 44 cm

405-9506   Station "Oberried" (Alpine)   46.49
22-7/9 x 6-1/4″   55.5 x 16 cm

kibri
Imported from Germany by WALTHERS

HO SCALE (1/87) EASY-TO-BUILD KITS

Kits consist of a large range of European prototypes. With minor modifications most can be easily Americanized. Parts are injection molded plastic castings, appropriately colored. Numbered part 'sprues' coordinated with the simple plans allow for easy construction by the modeler.

YARD & EQUIPMENT FACILITIES

TRAIN SHED BONN, GERMANY
Train sheds were an important part of stations in large cities. This kit is based on the prototype at Bonn, Germany and is ideal for use with the Bonn Station kit (#405-9524) or other large stations.

405-9522   17 x 8-5/8"   43 x 22 cm   42.99

SIGNAL TOWER "BEISLINGEN / STEIGE"
Control yard operations from this modern building! The structure features an attached office and interior details for the tower.

405-9478   5-3/4 x 3-1/2"   14.5 x 9 cm   27.99

405-9418   Steam Loco Sand Facility   25.99
5-1/2 x 2-3/4"   14 x 7 cm
2-3/4 x 3-3/8"   7 x 8.5 cm

405-9450   3-Track Diesel Shed   48.99
13-3/8 x 4-7/8"   34 x 17.5 cm

Coal Merchant's Yard with Accessories
405-9442   10-5/8 x 6"   27 x 15 cm   45.99

Coaling Station w/Crane
405-9420   48.99
15-1/2 x 5-1/2"   39.5 x 14 cm

405-9452   Roundhouse Engine Shed   51.49
Includes 3-stall brick roundhouse for small steam or diesel up to 9-1/2" (24 cm) long. Engines up to 8" can be turned on hand-operated turntable. 9-3/8 x 15-1/4"   24 x 39 cm.

405-9454   Single Stall Add-On Shed   11.49
3-1/2 x 6-1/8"   9 x 15.5 cm

405-9456   Manual Turntable   11.49
8 x 8"   20.5 x 20.5 cm

405-9430   Diesel Oil Station   12.99
4-3/4 x 3-7/8"   12 x 10 cm

405-9422   Water Column   pkg(2) 21.49
3-3/8 x 7/8"   8.5 x 2 cm

405-9434   Coaling Storage   25.49
9-1/2 x 3-7/8"   24 x 6 cm

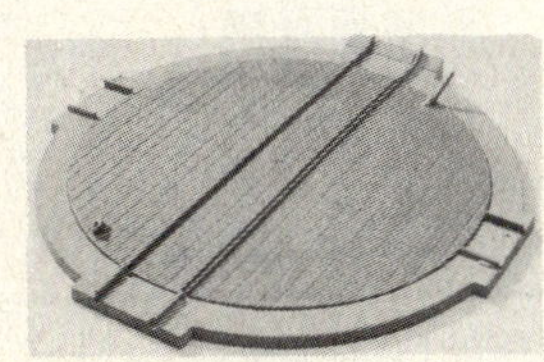

405-4130 Turntable   6.99
4-3/4 x 4-3/4"   12 x 12 cm

405-9474   Signal Box Ottbergen   25.99
8-1/2 x 2-1/4"   22 x 6 cm

kibri
Imported from Germany by WALTHERS

HO SCALE (1/87) EASY-TO-BUILD KITS

Kits consist of a large range of European prototypes. With minor modifications most can be easily Americanized. Parts are injection molded plastic castings, appropriately colored. Numbered part 'sprues' coordinated with the simple plans allow for easy construction by the modeler.

YARD & EQUIPMENT FACILITIES (continued)

SINGLE STALL ENGINE HOUSE
This single stall engine house is a perfect shelter for a branchline loco or local switcher. Many are used today to store maintenance equipment.
405-9436
29.99
7-7/8 x 4-3/4"
20 x 12 cm

GANTRY CRANE
This heavy crane is perfect for industrial areas served by road or rail. Prototypes move large or bulky loads from trucks to freight cars.
405-9602   5-1/8 x 2"   13 x 5 cm   29.99

Signal Tower "Marbach"
405-9487   22.99
4-3/4 x 2-1/8"   12 x 5.5 cm

Colbe Signal Tower
405-9488   26.99
6-1/2 x 2-3/4"   16.5 x 7 cm

Locomotive Repair Shed
405-9438   38.49
10-1/4 x 5-7/8"   26 x 15 cm

Freight House "Eschbronn"
405-9466   20.49
7-5/16 x 4-3/4"   18.5 x 12 cm

Railroad Signal Tower
405-9472   40.49
11 x 3-7/8"   28 x 10 cm

Shed-Schenker
405-9468   27.99

405-9470   Tie Bumper   5.99
2-1/8 x 1-3/4"   5.5 x 4.5 cm

Firehouse "Goldbach"
405-8032   31.99
5-1/4 x 4-5/8"   13 x 11.5cm

CITY BUILDINGS

405-8400   Period Town Hall "Urach"   46.49
5-3/4 x 4-1/8 x 7-7/8"   14.5 x 10.5 x 20 cm

City House w/Balcony
405-8286   32.49
3-1/2 x 5-1/4"   9 x 13.5 cm

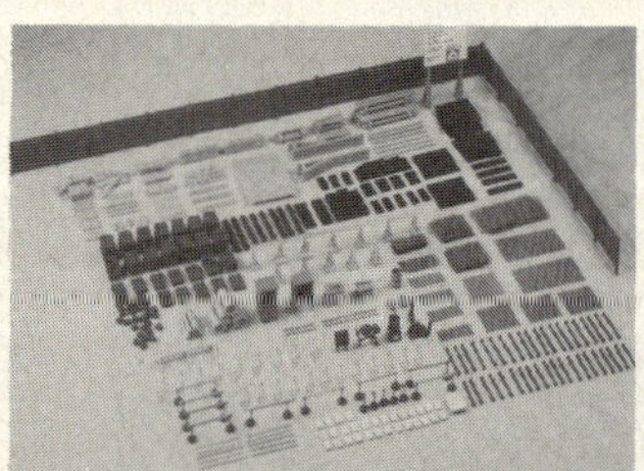

Skyscraper Site Accessories
405-8226   38.49

Inn with Beer Garden
405-8196   39.99
8-7/8 x 6-7/8"   22.5 x 17.5 cm

kibri
Imported from Germany
by *WALTHERS*

HO SCALE
(1/87)
EASY-TO-BUILD
KITS

Kits consist of a large range of European prototypes. With minor modifications most can be easily Americanized. Parts are injection molded plastic castings, appropriately colored. Numbered part 'sprues' coordinated with the simple plans allow for easy construction by the modeler.

CITY BUILDINGS

MODERN APARTMENT BUILDING
These attractive apartments add a city look to any scene. The first floor features small shops, so the structure can be used in a business district or suburb.

405-8222	39.99
9 x 4-1/2 x 5-1/2" 23 x 11.5 x 14 cm	

405-8416	Town Hall	40.49
	6 x 5" 15.5 x 13 cm	

Railway Post Office
405-8199   27.49
5-1/8 x 4-3/4"   13 x 12 cm

SKYSCRAPER UNDER CONSTRUCTION

Perfect for a scale city under construction, this kit comes complete with fencing, cement mixer, piles of construction material and other details. For added realism, superdetail the scene with a construction crane (#405-10202) featured in this section, or a variety of Kibri construction vehicles highlighted in the Vehicles section of this catalog.

405-8224   66.49
8 x 7-1/4"   20 x 18 cm

Munderkingen Post Office
405-8198   39.99
9-1/4 x 4-5/8 x 6-1/4"
23.5 x 11 x 16 cm

kibri
Imported from Germany
by WALTHERS

HO SCALE (1/87) EASY-TO-BUILD KITS	Kits consist of a large range of European prototypes. With minor modifications most can be easily Americanized. Parts are injection molded plastic castings, appropriately colored. Numbered part 'sprues' coordinated with the simple plans allow for easy construction by the modeler.

CITY BUILDINGS (continued)

405-8239   Meeting Hall/Barn   32.49
7-1/4 x 5-1/2" 18.5 x 14 cm

City Gate Tower "Chatenoois"
405-8470   25.99
3-1/2 x 2-3/8"
9 x 6 cm

405-8034   Fire Station   45.99
Includes fire engine and figures.

MODERN OFFICE BUILDING
405-8220   7-7/8 x 7-1/8" 20 x 18 cm   48.99

■ **LIMITED QUANTITES AVAILABLE** ■

Black Forest Guest House
405-8212   45.49

Historic Old Building
405-8410   24.99
4-3/8 x 2-3/4 x 4-1/8" 11 x 7 x 20.5 cm

Craftman's House
405-8210   34.49
7-1/8 x 5-1/2" 18 x 14 cm

405-8380   City Hall "Leer"   68.49
11-3/4 x 9 x 13-3/4" 30 x 22.5 x 35 cm

See also: VEHICLES & SCENERY for additional KIBRI items.

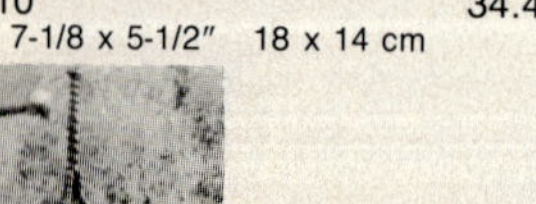

Fountain
405-8412   11.99
3-1/8 x 3-1/8 x 3"
8 x 8 x 7.5 cm

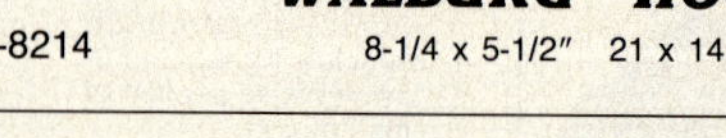

"WALBURG" HOUSE
405-8214   8-1/4 x 5-1/2" 21 x 14 cm   50.99

GARAGES

405-8136   28.99
12-5/8 x 4-3/8" 32 x 11 cm
Garage for eight trucks

kibri
Imported from Germany by WALTHERS

HO SCALE (1/87) EASY-TO-BUILD KITS

Kits consist of a large range of European prototypes. With minor modifications most can be easily Americanized. Parts are injection molded plastic castings, appropriately colored. Numbered part 'sprues' coordinated with the simple plans allow for easy construction by the modeler.

INDUSTRIAL

COMPLETE FACTORY COMPLEX

Consists of one of #9784, 9786, 9788, 9790 and two of 9792.

405-9798   166.49
1-1/8 x 1-1/8
3 x 3 cm

FACTORY BUILDING

This factory includes blower housing, pallets, oil drums and more.

405-9788   63.99
11-5/8 x 10-3/16"
27 x 25 cm

Factory Annex Building
405-9786
42.99
13 x 6-5/8"
28 x 17 cm

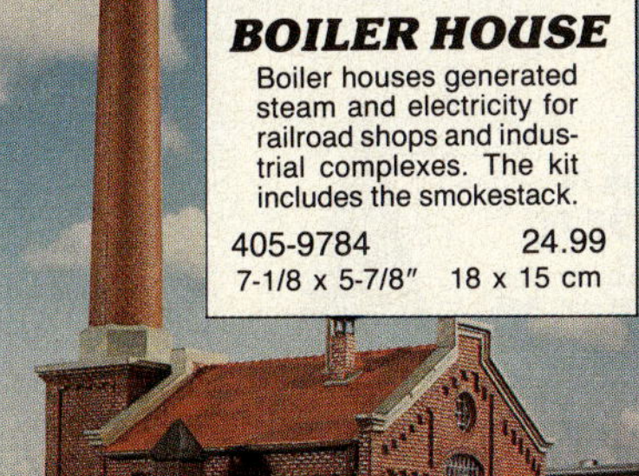

BOILER HOUSE

Boiler houses generated steam and electricity for railroad shops and industrial complexes. The kit includes the smokestack.

405-9784   24.99
7-1/8 x 5-7/8"   18 x 15 cm

405-9960   Sawmill with Interior   68.49
23-5/8 x 6-3/4"   60 x 17 cm

405-9962   Timber Yard with Crane   22.99
10-1/4 x 5-5/16"   26 x 13.5 cm

405-9790   Warehouse Annex   29.99
8-7/16 x 4-3/8"   21.5 x 11 cm

Single Storage Tank
405-9806   32.49
7 x 5-1/2"   18 x 14 cm

Double Storage Tank
405-9808   45.99
10-1/4 x 6"   26 x 15 cm

Truck Fill Tank Station
405-9440   25.99
6-1/4 x 3-7/8"   16 x 10 cm

kibri
Imported from Germany
by WALTHERS

HO SCALE
(1/87)
EASY-TO-BUILD
KITS

Kits consist of a large range of European prototypes. With minor modifications most can be easily Americanized. Parts are injection molded plastic castings, appropriately colored. Numbered part 'sprues' coordinated with the simple plans allow for easy construction by the modeler.

INDUSTRIAL (continued)

Six Containers/Mobile Offices
405-11970   pkg(6) 17.49
2-3/4 x 1-1/8"   6.9 x 2.8 cm

Cement Silo
405-10000
pkg(2) 7.99
1-1/8 x 1-1/8"
3 x 3 cm

WAREHOUSE BUILDING
This small kit can be used to store raw materials, or house a small manufacturing plant. The large roll-up door can accomodate freight cars or trucks.
405-9782   9-1/2 x 5"   24 x 12.5 cm   29.99

Small
Butane Tank
405-9912
29.99
5-1/2 x 4-3/4"
14 x 12 cm

Transformer
Station
405-8131
15.49
1-3/4 x 1-9/16"
4.5 x 4 cm

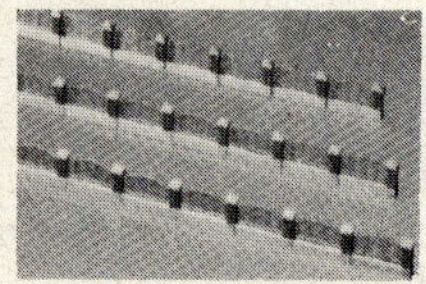

Industrial Fences
w/Gate
405-9792   17.49

CONSTRUCTION CRANE
These tall cranes can be found on construction sights around the world. To fit your building needs, the height can be adjusted from 10 to 22".
405-10202   45.99

405-9804   Truck Fill Pumps   29.99
7 x 3-1/2"   18 x 9 cm

405-9460   Warehouse   39.99
11-1/2 x 4-3/4"   29 x 12 cm

CHURCHES

Bell Tape & Speaker Set
405-9762   29.99
Actual taping of church bells for #9760. Six minutes on each side.

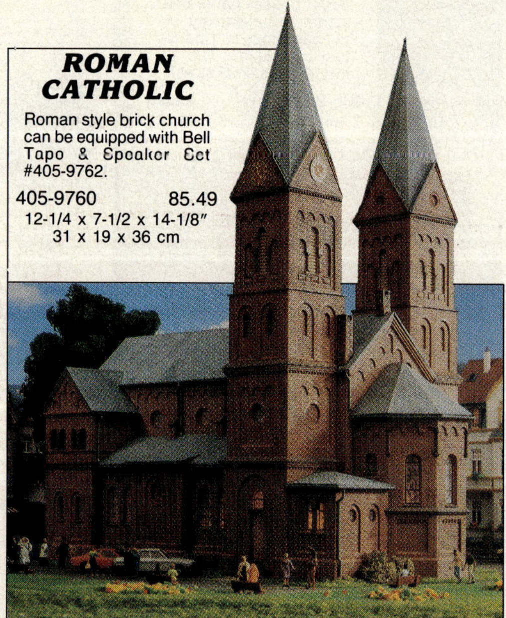

ROMAN CATHOLIC
Roman style brick church can be equipped with Bell Tape & Speaker Set #405-9762.
405-9760   85.49
12-1/4 x 7-1/2 x 14-1/8"
31 x 19 x 36 cm

Village Church "Sertig"
405-8006   22.99
5-1/8 x 4-3/8 x 6-1/2"
13 x 11 x 15 cm

Miniature
"Kuehtzagl" Chapel
405-9781   9.99
2 x 1-5/8"
5 x 4 cm

Outdoor Chapel w/Accessories
405-9780   20.49
2-3/8 x 2-3/8 x 3-7/8"
6 x 6 x 10 cm

kibri
Imported from Germany by WALTHERS

HO SCALE (1/87) EASY-TO-BUILD KITS

Kits consist of a large range of European prototypes. With minor modifications most can be easily Americanized. Parts are injection molded plastic castings, appropriately colored. Numbered part 'sprues' coordinated with the simple plans allow for easy construction by the modeler.

CHURCHES (continued)

AUMENAO CHURCH
This stylish church fits big city or small town locations. The kit features rought stone construction with a tall steeple and covered entryway.

405-9774 42.99
9-1/2 x 6-3/4" 24 x 17 cm

Swiss Alpine Chapel
405-8020 25.99
6-5/8 x 4-3/4 x 7-1/8" 17 x 12 x 18 cm

405-9772 Village Church 35.99
8-7/8 x 5-3/4 x 11" 22 x 14.5 x 28 cm

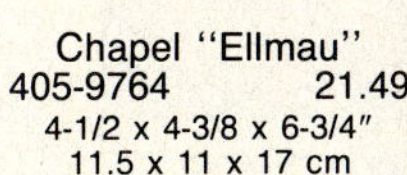

Chapel ''Ellmau''
405-9764 21.49
4-1/2 x 4-3/8 x 6-3/4"
11.5 x 11 x 17 cm

HOUSES

405-8440 405-8442 405-8444 405-8446

405-8440	Timber Market 3-3/4 x 3-3/4" 9.5 x 9.5 cm	38.49
405-8442	Timber Guest House 4 x 3-3/4" 10 x 9.5 cm	38.49
405-8444	Timber w/2 Shops 2-3/4 x 3-1/2" 7 x 9 cm 1-3/4 x 3-3/4" 4.5 x 9.5 cm	38.49
405-8446	Timber w/Shops 4-5/8 x 3-3/4" 4.5 x 9.5 cm	35.99
405-8448	Half Timbered Houses Includes #8840, 8442, 8444 and 8446	127.49

''AN DER KUSTE'' HOUSE SET

405-8228 Includes #'s 8230, 8232, 8236 & 8254 90.49

kibri
Imported from Germany by WALTHERS

HO SCALE (1/87) EASY-TO-BUILD KITS

Kits consist of a large range of European prototypes. With minor modifications most can be easily Americanized. Parts are injection molded plastic castings, appropriately colored. Numbered part 'sprues' coordinated with the simple plans allow for easy construction by the modeler.

HOUSES (continued)

STUCCO HOUSE WITH BAY WINDOWS
This attractive home features an enclosed side entry way and a large bay window. Shutters, printed paper curtains and a TV aerial are all included.
405-8206   5-1/8 x 4-1/2"   13 x 11 cm   21.49

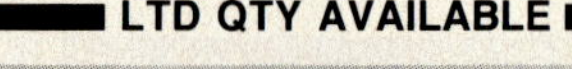

Railroad Worker's House and Outbuilding
405-8194   5-1/8 x 2-3/8"   13 x 6 cm   32.49
7 x 5-1/2"   17.6 x 14 cm

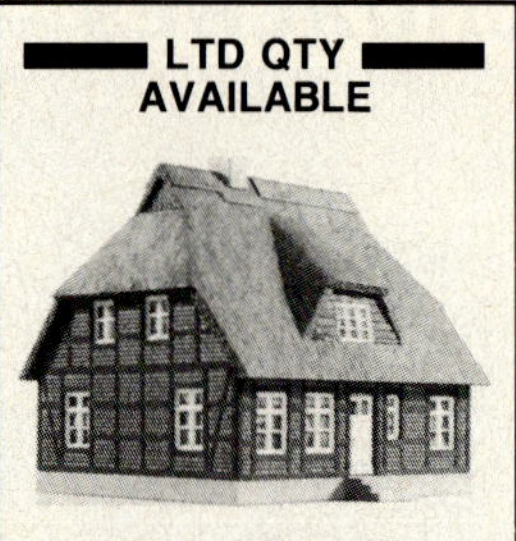

House Heike
405-8232   20.49
3-7/8 x 3-1/2"   10 x 9 cm

House Frisian
405-8236   22.99
6-3/4 x 3-3/4"   17 x 9.5 cm

Single Family House
405-8062   12.99
4-1/8 x 3-3/4"   10.5 x 9.5 cm

Single Family House
405-8180   13.99
5-1/2 x 4-3/4 x 4"   14 x 12 x 10 cm

405-8080   Stone House   16.49
4-3/8 x 3-3/4 x 3-1/2"   11 x 9.5 x 9 cm

Stucco House with Porch
405-8162   20.49
5-1/4 x 5-1/4"   13 x 13 cm

405-8084   House w/Garage   21.49
5-3/4 x 4-3/4 x 3"   14.5 x 12 x 7.5 cm

Stucco House with Addition
405-8168   20.49
4.8 x 4.4"   12 x 11 cm

Stucco House with Balcony
405-8204   21.49
5.6 x 3.4"   14 x 10 cm

Stucco House with Gas Station
405-8202   27.49
6 x 4.4"   15 x 11 cm

Stucco House with Gable
405-8164   20.49
4.8 x 4.4"   12 x 11 cm

Stucco House w/Windows
405-8166   20.49
4.8 x 4.4"   12 x 11 cm

Stucco House with Garage
405-8200   21.49
5.2 x 4"   13 x 10 cm
2.7 x 1.3"
6.9 x 3.4 cm

Stucco House w/Mansard Roof
405-8160   16.99
4.8 x 4.4"
12 x 11 cm

Country House with Timbering
405-8184   13.99
5-1/2 x 4-3/4 x 4"
14 x 12 x 10 cm

kibri
Imported from Germany by WALTHERS

HO SCALE (1/87) EASY-TO-BUILD KITS

Kits consist of a large range of European prototypes. With minor modifications most can be easily Americanized. Parts are injection molded plastic castings, appropriately colored. Numbered part 'sprues' coordinated with the simple plans allow for easy construction by the modeler.

HOUSES (continued)

Station "Oberwald"
405-8046   22.99
4-1/4 x 3-1/4   11 x 8.5 cm

Town House "Stade"
405-8376   32.49
4-1/8 x 4-1/8 x 7-1/2"
10.5 x 10.5 x 19 cm

COUNTRY HOUSE
Here's a home that's ideal for the growing HO family! The structure features two floors and will fit into a medium sized lot in any HO city.
405-8182   13.99
5-1/2 x 4-3/4 x 4"   14 x 12 x 10 cm

HOUSE "BICHLBERG"
405-8058   5-1/2 x 4-1/4   14 x 11 cm   27.99

Bottrop House (2 Buildings)
405-8190   22.99
6-1/2 x 5-1/8 x 4-1/2"   6.5 x 13 x 11.5 cm
4-1/4 x 2-5/8 x 2-1/2"   11 x 6 x 6.5 cm

Bottrop House w/Workshop
405-8192   22.99
6-1/2 x 5-1/8 x 4-1/2"   6.5 x 13 x 11.5 cm
4-1/4 x 2-5/8 x 2-1/2"   11 x 6 x 6.5 cm

City House with Alley
405-8352   29.99
3-1/2 x 4 x 6-1/8"   9 x 10 x 15.5 cm

City House with Work Shop
405-8354   29.99
4 x 4 x 6"   10 x 10 x 15 cm

City House with Balcony
405-8356   29.99
3-1/8 x 4 x 6-3/4"   8 x 10 x 17 cm

City House with Grocery Store
405-8358   29.99
4 x 4 x 6"   10 x 10 x 15 cm

kibri
Imported from Germany by WALTHERS

HO SCALE (1/87) EASY-TO-BUILD KITS

Kits consist of a large range of European prototypes. With minor modifications most can be easily Americanized. Parts are injection molded plastic castings, appropriately colored. Numbered part 'sprues' coordinated with the simple plans allow for easy construction by the modeler.

HOUSES (continued)

405-8048 House "Furka" 22.99
4-1/4 x 3-1/4" 11 x 8.5 cm

Timbered Cottage with Garden
405-8432 19.99
4-3/4 x 4-3/8 x 4-3/8" 12 x 11 x 11 cm

405-8452	Half-Timbered House w/gate	33.99	405-8458	Statue w/Fountain 8.99
	14 x 13, 15 x 16 cm			6 x 6 x 7 cm
405-8454	Half-Timbered House w/recess	33.99	405-8460	Half-Timbered Corner House 36.99
	15 x 10 x 20 cm			15 x 13, 5 x 16 cm
405-8456	Half-Timbered House w/market	32.49	405-8462	"Odenwald" Half-Timbered Set 128.49
	10, 5 x 8 x 16, 5 cm			(Includes all of the above #'s)

Timbered Cottage
405-8430 20.49
4-1/8 x 3-1/2 x 3-7/8" 10.5 x 9 x 10 cm

City House "Gernsbach"
405-8378 40.99
4-1/4 x 4-3/4 x 9-1/2"
11 x 12 x 24 cm

Corner City Home Bonn
405-8280 42.99
5-1/4 x 5-1/4 x 7-1/16"

City Home w/Bay Window Bonn
405-8282 32.49
3-7/8 x 5-1/4 x 6-5/8"

City Home w/Lawn Bonn
405-8284 32.49
3-1/8 x 5-1/4 x 7-1/16"
8 x 13.5 x 18 cm

Country Estate Home
405-9534 34.49
8-3/8 x 8" 20 x 21 cm

Timber & Brick, On the Weser
405-8241 20.49
3-7/8 x 3-5/8"
10 x 9 cm

Timber & Brick, Jork
405-8242 21.49
3-7/8 x 3-5/8"
10 x 9 cm

Timber & Brick, Niederelbe
405-8244 25.99
6-7/8 x 3-7/8"
17.5 x 10 cm

Period Style Dwelling
405-8402 32.49
4-1/2 x 3-3/8 x 5-1/8" 11.5 x 8.5 x 13 cm

Timber & Brick, Borstel
405-8243 25.99
5-1/8 x 3-5/8"
13 x 9.5 cm

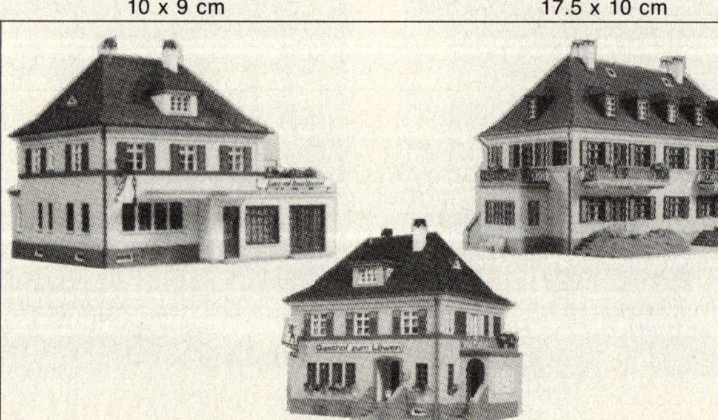

405-8216 House Set (Includes #'s 8208, 8210 and 8212) **93.99**

kibri
Imported from Germany
by WALTHERS

HO SCALE
(1/87)
EASY-TO-BUILD
KITS

Kits consist of a large range of European prototypes. With minor modifications most can be easily Americanized. Parts are injection molded plastic castings, appropriately colored. Numbered part 'sprues' coordinated with the simple plans allow for easy construction by the modeler.

BUSINESSES

ESSO GAS STATION

"Fill-up" empty layout space with this modern service station! The kit includes gas pumps, service islands, a tire rack and authentic Esso signs.

405-8252   29.99
7-7/8 x 3-1/8 x 1-3/4"
19.5 x 8 x 4.5 cm

405-8350   Large City Corner Hotel   42.99
6-1/8 x 6-1/8 x 6-1/4"   15.5 x 15.5 x 16 cm

405-8372   Publishing House   32.49
4-3/4 x 4-3/4 x 6-3/4"   12 x 12 x 17.5 cm

405-8408   Historic Inn "Zur Post"   29.99
3-7/8 x 3-1/8 x 5-1/2"   10 x 8 x 14 cm

405-8434   The White Horse Inn   27.99
3-7/8 x 3-7/8"   10 x 10 cm

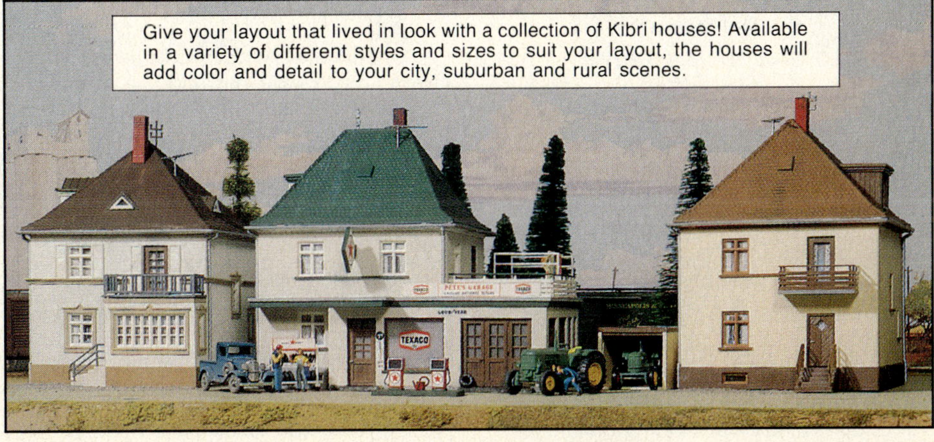

Give your layout that lived in look with a collection of Kibri houses! Available in a variety of different styles and sizes to suit your layout, the houses will add color and detail to your city, suburban and rural scenes.

kibri
Imported from Germany by WALTHERS

HO SCALE (1/87) EASY-TO-BUILD KITS

Kits consist of a large range of European prototypes. With minor modifications most can be easily Americanized. Parts are injection molded plastic castings, appropriately colored. Numbered part 'sprues' coordinated with the simple plans allow for easy construction by the modeler.

RURAL BUILDINGS

CASTLE "FALKENSTEIN"
Built in the 13th century, this castle was restored in 1905 and remains a favorite with tourists. The model is nicely detailed, with rough stone and timber construction.

405-9010   89.99
18-7/8 x 11 x 13"
48 x 28 x 33 cm

Large & Small Hay Barns
405-8007   13.99
2-3/4 x 2-5/8 x 1-5/8" 7 x 6.5 x 4 cm
2-1/8 x 2 x 1-3/8" 5.5 x 5 x 3.5 cm

Chalet "Brienz"
405-8040   22.99
4-3/4 x 3-1/2 x 2-3/4" 12 x 9 x 7 cm

405-9489   Emmental Set   106.99
Set includes one each of #9490, 8024, 8026, 8028 and 8008.

Chalet "Seeblick"
405-8001   16.49
3-3/8 x 3-1/8 x 2" 8.5 x 8 x 5 cm

Chalet "Edelweiss"
405-8002   18.49
4-3/8 x 3-3/8 x 2-3/4" 11 x 8.5 x 7 cm

405-8003   Alpine Store & Inn   20.49
4-3/4 x 3-3/8 x 3-1/2" 12 x 8.5 x 9 cm

405-8004   Chalet "Sonnenhalde"   21.49
4-3/4 x 4-3/4 x 3-3/8" 12 x 12 x 8.5 cm

405-8052   Farm in Tyrol   32.49
6-3/4 x 5-1/8 x 4-1/4" 17 x 13 x 11 cm

405-8050   Farm "Simmental"   39.99
7-7/8 x 5-1/2 x 3-1/2" 20 x 14 x 9 cm

405-8042   Chalet "Sigriswil"   25.49
5-3/8 x 3-7/8 x 3-1/2" 13.5 x 10 x 9 cm

405-8009   Complete Village, 6 Buildings   75.99
Set includes one each of #8001, 8002, 8004, 8006, 8007 and 8008.

HEIMSBACH CHEESE DAIRY
With its old-world styling, this small cheese plant also makes an attractive retail store! Cheese shops like this are common in Wisconsin, just add some tourists and cars out front for a super mini-scene.
405-8024   7-1/4 x 4-7/8" 18 x 12 cm   29.99

kibri

Imported from Germany
by WALTHERS

HO SCALE
(1/87)
EASY-TO-BUILD
KITS

Kits consist of a large range of European prototypes. With minor modifications most can be easily Americanized. Parts are injection molded plastic castings, appropriately colored. Numbered part 'sprues' coordinated with the simple plans allow for easy construction by the modeler.

RURAL BUILDINGS (continued)

STORE HOUSE GRAINARY WITH LOFT

Detail a farm scene with this ornate and truly different building! This detailed kit simulates the detailed wood construction of a Swiss prototype.

405-8028 22.99
4-1/4 x 4-1/4 x 4-3/8" 10.5 x 10.5 x 11 cm

CHALET IN TYROL

Nestled in the high mountains, this modern home is based on similar structures found in Switzerland. The kit features a variety of detail parts, including shutters, a balcony and more.

405-8044 4-3/4 x 4" 12 x 10 cm 25.49

405-8054 Farmhouse from Emmental 55.49
7-1/4 x 11-3/8" 18.5 x 29 cm

405-8056 Guest House Three Bears 51.49
7-1/2 x 5-7/8" 19 x 15 cm

405-7044 "Branzoll" Castle w/Mountain 50.99
13-3/8 x 11 x 9" 34 x 28 x 23 cm
(N Scale, can be used as background structure)

405-8010 Swiss Village Grevasalvas 118.49
Set includes one each of #8012, 8014, 8016, 8018,
8020 and 8022

School House
w/Thatch Roof
405-8238
34.49
5-7/8 x 5-3/8
15 x 13.5 cm

Country Cottage
& Stable
405-9482
20.49
5-1/8 x 4-3/8"
13 x 11 x 8.5 cm

Swiss Alpine House "Palue"
405-8012 22.99
6-5/8 x 4-3/4 x 3" 17 x 12 x 7.5 cm

Swiss Alpine House "Sils"
405-8018 22.99
6-1/4 x 5-1/8 x 4" 16 x 13 x 10 cm

Swiss Alpine Stable
405-8022 w/Accessories 22.99
5-7/8 x 4-1/4 x 3-1/8" 15 x 11 x 8 cm

The wood smoke and the hot coffee both smell pretty good on this chilly morning. It'll be a while before the boiler has enough steam to run the mill, so we'd better enjoy this quiet moment while we can. You can almost smell the fresh-cut lumber in this realistic scene, built by Gerry Gilliland of Saint John, New Brunswick, Canada. The sawmill is a Fine-Scale Miniatures kit (out of production) and is served by Roundhouse and Kadee log cars. Workers on the morning shift are from Campbell and SS Ltd.

Models and Photo by Gerry Gilliland

kibri
Imported from Germany
by WALTHERS

HO SCALE (1/87) EASY-TO-BUILD KITS

Kits consist of a large range of European prototypes. With minor modifications most can be easily Americanized. Parts are injection molded plastic castings, appropriately colored. Numbered part 'sprues' coordinated with the simple plans allow for easy construction by the modeler.

RURAL BUILDINGS (continued)

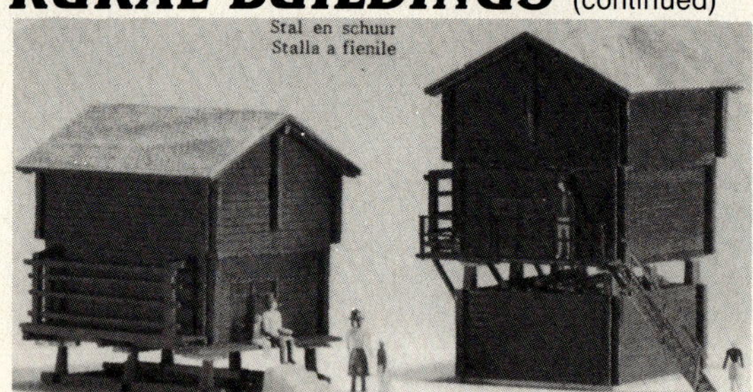

405-8049   Barn and Hayloft   22.99
2-1/4 x 1-3/4" 6.5 x 5.5 cm   2-1/4 x 1-3/4" 6.5 x 5.5 cm

Half Timber House, Tecklenberg
405-8130   27.49
5-1/8 x 4-1/2" 13 x 11.5 cm

■ LIMITED QUANTITIES AVAILABLE ■

HALF TIMBER HOUSE "MUNSTERLAND"

This charming home is perfect for country settings or city suburbs. It features detailed plastic parts to simulate the traditional half-timber and stucco construction.
405-8128   5.5 x 3-3/8" 14 x 10 cm   25.99

Half Timber House/Tile Roof
405-8124   20.49
3-7/8 x 3-6/4"   10 x 9 cm

Swiss Alpine House "Fextal"
405-8014   22.99
6-1/8 x 5-7/8 x 3-1/2" 15.5 x 15 x 9 cm

Half Timber House w/Hip Roof
405-8126   20.49
3-7/8 x 3-6/8"   10 x 9 cm

Swiss Alpine House "Steinbock"
405-8016   22.99
6-1/4 x 5-7/8 x 3-3/4" 16 x 15 x 9.5 cm

HALF-TIMBERED VILLAGE SET w/STATION

Includes #'s 8124, 8126, 8128, 8130, 8131 and 9517.

405-8132   127.49

kibri
Imported from Germany by WALTHERS

HO SCALE (1/87) EASY-TO-BUILD KITS

Kits consist of a large range of European prototypes. With minor modifications most can be easily Americanized. Parts are injection molded plastic castings, appropriately colored. Numbered part 'sprues' coordinated with the simple plans allow for easy construction by the modeler.

BRIDGES

405-8256   Drawbridge Potshausen   32.49
7-3/4 x 3-1/2" 19.5 x 9 cm

Pier with Support and Base
405-9615   4.99
4.4" 11 cm high

Foot Bridge
405-9606   11.99
5-3/4 x 2-1/2"
14.6 x 6.5 cm

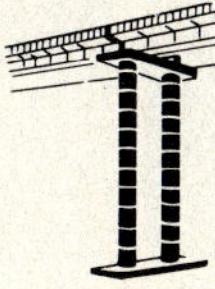

Middle Bridge Pier
405-9690   9.49
3-1/8" 8 cm high

LARGE TRUSS BRIDGE
This big bridge is typical of railroad bridges found around the world. Lattice girder work, plenty of rivets and heavy I beams give the finished model a realistic appearance.

405-9696   17-3/4 x 3-1/8 x 4-1/2" 45 x 8 x 11.5 cm   45.99

405-9648   Arched Retaining Wall   18.49
12" 30 cm

405-9644   Stone Viaduct   21.49
16-1/2" radius x 45°

405-9612   Footbridge   27.99
9 x 7-7/8 x 4-3/4" 23 x 20 x 12 cm

405-9610   Flexible Bridge   49.49
58.2" 14.5 cm

Steel Bridge, Curved 14" Radius
405-9682   11 x 2-3/4 x 1-1/8" 28.2 x 7 x 3 cm   19.49

Stone Viaduct
405-9642   14" radius x 45°   18.49

STRAIGHT STONE ARCH BRIDGE
This handsome stone arch bridge is perfect for steam or diesel era layouts! The kit also includes angled ''ice breaking'' ends for the piers, for use in colder climates!

405-9640   13-3/4 x 3-1/4" 34 x 8 cm   20.49

405-9680   Steel Bridge, Straight   17.49
10-5/8 x 2-3/4 x 1-1/8" 27 x 7 x 3 cm

405-9620   Single Section Flexible Bridge   8.99
7-1/4" 18.5 cm

kibri
Imported from Germany by WALTHERS

HO SCALE (1/87) EASY-TO-BUILD KITS

Kits consist of a large range of European prototypes. With minor modifications most can be easily Americanized. Parts are injection molded plastic castings, appropriately colored. Numbered part 'sprues' coordinated with the simple plans allow for easy construction by the modeler.

BRIDGES (continued)

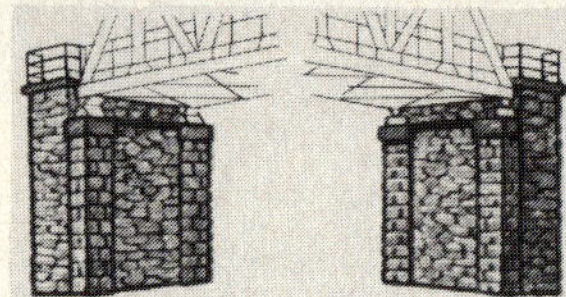

BridgeEnd Piers
405-9691
21.49
pkg(2)
4" 10 cm high

405-9694   Girder Bridge   27.49
10-3/4 x 3-1/8 x 3" 27.5 x 7.5 cm

405-9630 Truss Bridge   31.99
15" long
15 x 2.6" 38.5 x 6.5 cm

Stone Viaduct Piers
405-9646   pkg(4) 14.49
4" 10 cm high

405-9664   Viaduct Curved Kit   41.99

405-9698   Bridge, Deck Truss   32.49

405-9652   Stone Multi-Arch Viaduct   22.99

Viaduct Curved R14
405-9662   6.49

Viaduct Straight
405-9656   6.49

Stone Arch Viaduct
405-9650   12-3/4 x 2-1/2"   33.6 x 7 cm   22.99

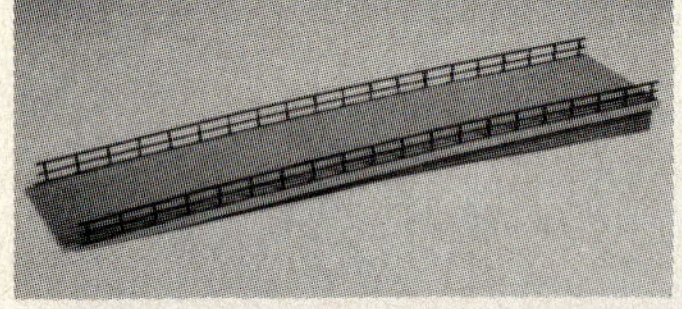

Starting Ramp 11.8"
405-9654   6.49

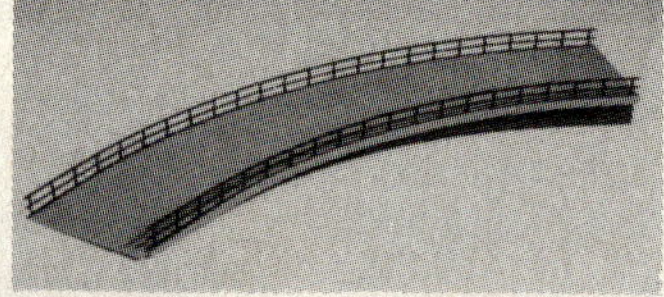

Starting Ramp R14 13.7"
405-9660   6.49

DIORAMAS

Dockside Crane
405-8510   49.49

405-8516   Wharfside Diorama   107.49
15-1/4 x 14-3/16"   40 x 36 cm
(By Special Order Only.)

405-9658   Viaduct Kit Staight 48.4"   41.99

Paving for Dock-Side Crane
405-4127 4.49
7-7/8 x 4-3/4"
20 x 12 cm

kibri
Imported from Germany by WALTHERS

| HO SCALE (1/87) EASY-TO-BUILD KITS | Kits consist of a large range of European prototypes. With minor modifications most can be easily Americanized. Parts are injection molded plastic castings, appropriately colored. Numbered part 'sprues' coordinated with the simple plans allow for easy construction by the modeler. |

DIORAMAS (continued) — SPECIAL ORDER ONLY —

Diorama Set Pontoon Bridge
405-8268 58.49
15-1/4 x 14-3/16"
40 x 36 cm

Wharf Diorama
Includes boat, bridge house and tractor trailer.
405-8262
99.99
12-5/8 x 12-5/8"
32 x 32 cm

Yacht Harbour
405-8267   67.49
15-1/4 x 14-3/16"   40 x 36 cm

Wharf Diorama
Includes boat, lighthouse, kiosk, harbor crane and buffer stop.
405-8264
79.49
12-5/8 x 12-5/8"
32 x 32 cm

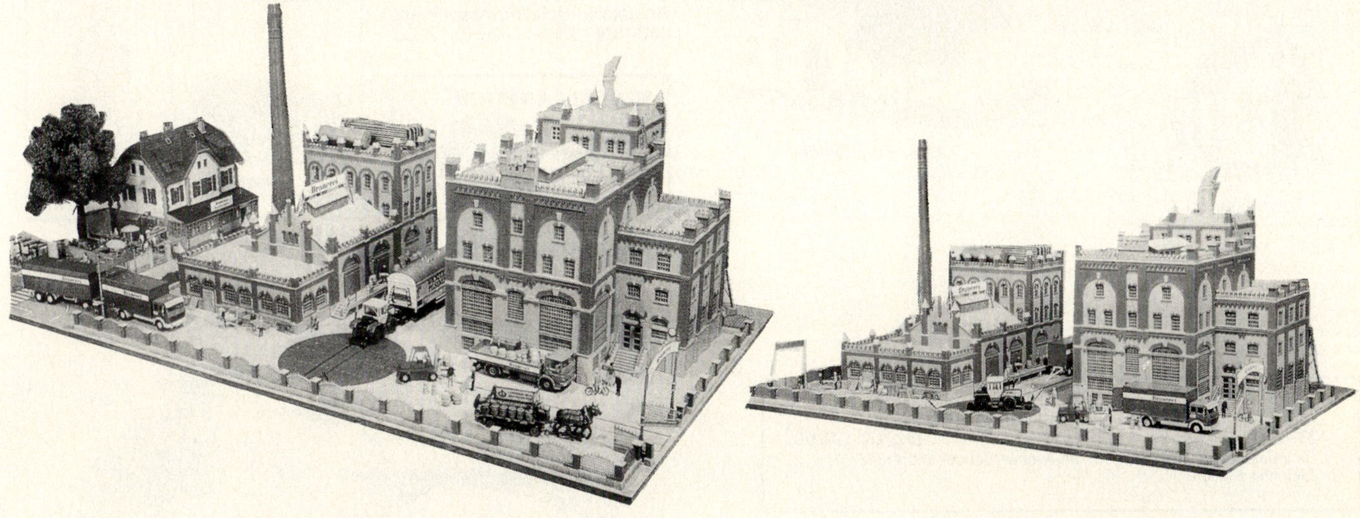

Diorama ''Brauerei''—Large
405-9794   83 x 40 cm   **NEW** 254.49

Diorama ''Brauerei''—Small
405-9796   28 x 30 cm   **NEW** 161.49

HO SCALE (1/87) EASY-TO-BUILD KITS

Easy-to-Assemble, appropriately colored, molded plastic parts. Details are hand painted.

YARD AND EQUIPMENT FACILITIES

433-1345   Engine House   11.50

Operating Logging Mill
433-8201   28.00
Includes dump car, logs and log pond.

Flashing Light Storage Tank
433-8205   10.25
w/blinking light & grafitti decals

Lighted Yard Tower
433-8208   10.25
modern tower w/working light

Operating Coal Tipple w/Hopper Car
433-8200   16.25
Includes hopper car, removable overflow tray, ramps and coal.

Operating Gravel Unloader w/Dump Car
433-8204   12.50
Includes dump car & gravel.

Trackside Shanties
433-1348   6.50
Includes one of each: Line Shack (2 x 2-1/4″ 5.1 x 5.9 cm), Switchman's Shanty (1-5/8 x 2-1/8″ 4 x 5.5 cm) and Whistle Stop (2 x 2-1/4″ 5.1 x 5.9 cm).

CITY BUILDINGS

Union Avenue School
433-1343   20.00

Woodlawn Police Station
433-1382   10.00
6-1/4 x 8-3/8″ 15.9 x 21.3 cm

Hampden Fire Engine House #46
433-1390   10.00
6-1/4 x 8-3/8″ 15.9 x 21.3 cm

Town Church
433-1350   6.50
5 x 6″ 12.8 x 15.3 cm

U.S. Post Office
433-1332   13.00

(not ilustrated)
433-1360   Drive-in Bank   10.00
Hometown Building Assortment
433-1379   **NEW**   pkg(12) 20.00

MISCELLANEOUS
House Lighting Kit
433-1200
each 3.00

HOUSES

Western Homestead
433-1338   11.50

BRIDGES & VIADUCTS

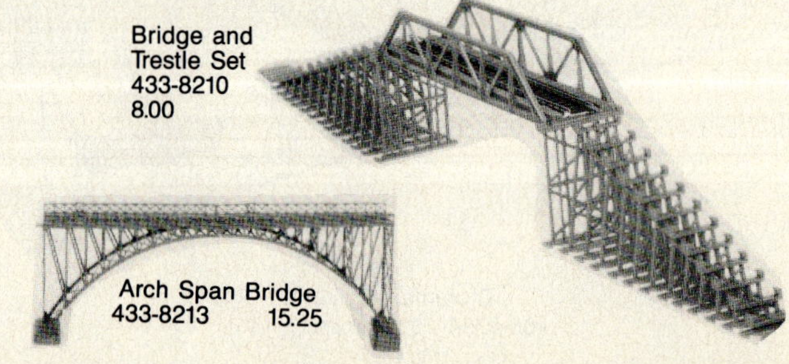

Bridge and Trestle Set
433-8210
8.00

Arch Span Bridge
433-8213   15.25

Municipal Building Assortment   **NEW**
433-1387   pkg(12) 240.00
Includes 6 each of #1343 - Union Avenue School and #1342 Mainline Station.

LIFE-LIKE®

HO SCALE (1/87) EASY-TO-BUILD KITS

Easy-to-assemble, appropriately colored, molded plastic parts. Details are hand painted.

BUSINESSES

Plumbing Supply Company
433-1357   10.00
3-7/8 x 6"   9.9 x 15.3 cm

Car Wash
433-1361   10.00

General Store
433-1351   6.50

Fruit Market
433-1358   10.00

Kentucky Fried Chicken Drive-In
433-1394   10.00

(not illustrated)
433-1359   Contemporary Diner   10.00

Belvedere Downtown Hotel
433-1339   11.50

INDUSTRIAL

433-1344   36th Street Warehouse   20.00

Mt Vernon Manufacturing Co
433-1337   11.50
Includes one freight station and one passenger platform. Can be joined together.

433-1355   **Fairhaven Brewery**   20.00
Features exceptional interior & exterior detail-with realistic shipping and receiving area. The large front window gives view of the vats inside.

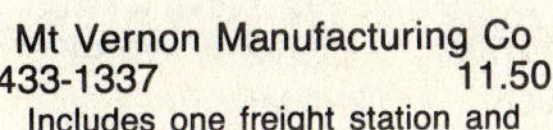

Kustom Kabinet Co
433-1365   13.00

Farmer's Grain & Field
433-1365   13.00

Greenspring Creamery
433-1367   13.00

WS Engineering
433-1364   13.00

STATIONS & PLATFORMS

Train Station
433-1347   6.50
2 x 11-5/8"
5.1 x 29.5 cm

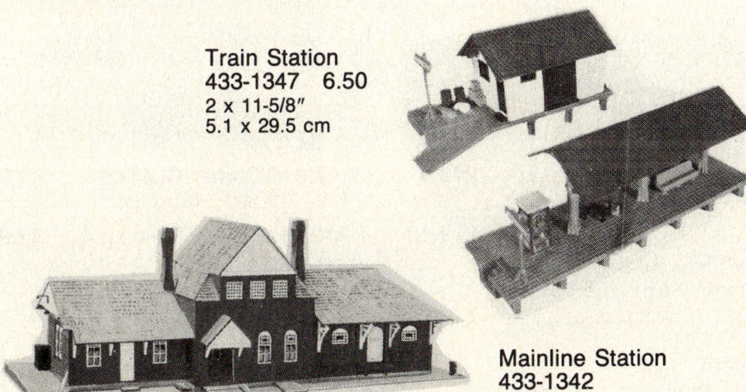

Mainline Station
433-1342
20.00

ASSORTMENT PACKAGES
(By Special Order Only.)

Trackside Buildings
433-1392   pkg(12) 78.00
Includes 2 each of Handcar depot, Train Station, Trackside Shanties, Oil Company, Town, Church and General Store.

Industrial Buildings
433-1368   pkg(12) 156.00
Includes 3 each of WS Engineering Company, Kustom Kabinet Company, Farmer's Grain & Feed, and Greenspring Creamery.

Old Town Buildings
433-1395   pkg(12) 138.00
Includes 4 of each Mt. Vernon Manufacturing, Western homestead, Belvedere downtown hotel, 3-Story rooming house, and Engine house.

Business Buildings
433-1399   pkg(12) 120.00
Includes 3 each of Fruit Market, Contemporary Diner, Drive in Bank and Car Wash.

Operating Accessories, Assortment
433-8731   *NEW* 454.75
Includes two each—8201, 8203, 8205; three each—8200, 8204; six each—8089, 8208; twelve each—8209.

Master Creations

HO SCALE CRAFT TRAIN KITS

Kits include cast metal parts, precision cut bass wood and complete instructions.

BUSINESSES

Fanny Schwann's Confectionary
464-75   **NEW**   199.95

464-1400   Flagstop at Slapout   **NEW**   19.95

(not illustrated)
464-1405   Pickles Gap Mercantile   **NEW**   TBA
464-1410   Cleator Gas Station   TBA
464-1415   Ninty Nine Bank   TBA

LIMITED RUN KITS

Kits feature tabbed construction, hundreds of laser-cut parts, perforated nail holes, computer-controlled lighting, metal castings.

464-70   Cooley's Old Rose Mine   199.95

Cartoon courtesy of *Model Railroader* Magazine.

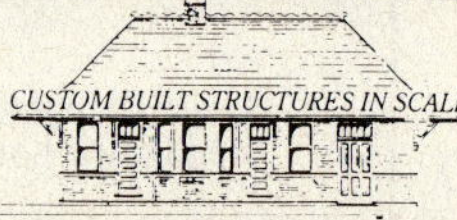

DEPOTS BY JOHN

Easy-to-build. Detailed, urethane and plastic parts, stripwood and illustrated instructions.

Milwaukee Rd Speeder Shed
87-106   8.95

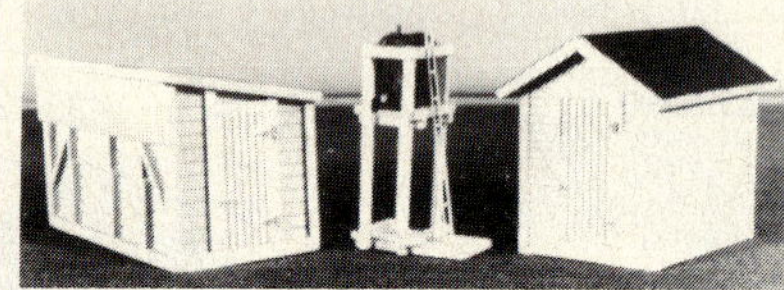

Replica of trackside sheds used by the Milwaukee Road for decades to store speeders, tools and suplies.
Include information on 4 different shed color schemes used by the road from the 1920's to the 1980's.

Trackside Utility Buildings
87-113   pkg(3) 17.95

Includes an outside braced wood/coal shed, a small tool shed, and an elevated fuel oil tank. Typically found near many town depots and section gang houses.

Fairbanks Morse Scale House
87-114   8.95

Railroads often weighed cars to make sure they were not overloaded, or to check the empty weight of the car after major repairs. This six-sided scalehouse is typical of those found on many railroads.

Manned Crossing Gate Tower
87-115   19.95

Design was used by the Milwaukee Road to control crossing gates in busy areas. Prototype was located at 70th and State Streets in Wauwatosa, Wisconsin. Includes a telephone box on the east side and a small walk-in maintenance shed.

FUNARO & CAMERLENGO

STATIONS

Rushland Station w/Asphalt Roof
279-4   2-1/4 x 4-1/2″   5.5 x 11.5 cm   26.99

Rushland Station w/Slate Roof
279-8   2-1/4 x 4-1/2″   5.5 x 11.5 cm   26.99

(not illustrated)
279-11   Art Deco Center Block   36.99
6-1/16 x 2-1/4″   15.5 x 5.7 cm

FUNARO & CAMERLENGO

HO CRAFT TRAIN KITS

Craft Train Kits feature thin flexible styrourethane castings with architectural details cast in place, stripwood and wire.

HOUSES

Sears Catalog Home
279-1   49.99
4-1/4 x 4-1/4″
10.7 x 10.7 cm

D&H Company House
279-14   As-built   29.99
2-5/8 x 4-3/4″   6.7 x 12.2 cm

D&H Company House
279-15 Modernized   29.99
2-5/8 x 4-3/4″   6.7 x 12.2 cm

Gulf Summit Cottage
279-2   15.99
2-1/4 x 2″   5.7 x 5 cm

Company House
279-6   15.99
3-3/4 x 3-5/8″
9.5 x 9.2 cm

Company President's
279-5   Home 26.99
5 x 4-5/16″   12.7 x 11 cm

BUSINESSES

Old Time Gas Station
279-3   15.99
1-1/2 x 1-1/2″
3.8 x 3.8 cm

Island Creek Store
279-7   49.99
6 x 6″   15.3 x 15.3 cm

279-9   Art Deco Corner Building   42.99
6-1/4 x 3-1/2″   16 x 9 cm

279-10   Art Deco Front Building   42.99
6-1/4 x 4-1/2″   16 x 11.5 cm

Art Deco Store
279-12   9.99
2-1/4 x 2-1/4″
5.7 x 5.7 cm

Micro Engineering Company

HO SCALE (1/87)

EASY-TO-BUILD KITS
Injection molded, precolored styrene kits.

OLD TIME BUILDINGS
False front buildings include plastic windows and doors and white metal details.

Hay & Grain Store
255-70600   9.95
2-3/4 x 5"   7 x 12.8 cm
with storage shed & boardwalk

Krukow Hardware
255-70601   9.95
2-3/4 x 4-1/4"   7 x 10.8 cm
with outhouse & boardwalk

255-70603   Building Fronts/Boardwalks   15.95
8-1/4 x 1"   21 x 2.5 cm

Zang's Saloon
255-70602   9.50
2-3/4 x 3-1/2"
7 x 8.8 cm
w/outhouse & boardwalk

255-70604   Groger's Grocery   9.95
5 x 5"   12.8 x 12.8 cm
includes signs, awning, shed and clutter parts

(not illustrated)
Outhouse
255-80172
1.95

MODERN BUILDINGS
Injection molded styrene kits feature precolored parts. Choice of various door and window locations. Includes steps, sidewalks, pallets and ventilators.

255-55004   Murphy Manufacturing   11.95
4-1/4 x 9-1/2"   10.8 x 24 cm

255-55005   Trans World Truck Terminal   13.95
4-1/4 x 13-1/2"   10.8 x 34.2 cm

255-55006   Petroff Plumbing Supply   13.95
8-3/8 x 9-1/2"   21.1 x 24 cm

TIMBER TUNNEL LINING

Timber Tunnel Lining
255-60500   10.95
28 arches, 4 sets of panels, enough for 2-4 tunnels (99 scale feet); straight or curved.

CITY VIADUCTS
Includes HO Code 83 Flex-Trak™ side and cross girders and girder lateral, girder X, lattice, and strap X bracings.

255-75509   90' Single Track   16.95
255-75510   90' Double Track   26.95
255-75511   150' Single Track   26.95
255-75512   150' Double Track   41.95
255-80168   Viaduct Tower   4.50
3-1/2" high

TALL VIADUCT
Includes Code 83 Flex-Trak™, girders, lateral and cross braces, legs and leg bracing. Can be built straight or curved.

255-75514   150' Viaduct, HO   31.95
255-75516   150' Viaduct, HOn3   31.95

Viaduct Tower
255-80169   6.50
10" high

DECK PLATE GIRDER BRIDGES
Includes bridge shoes, "X" and lateral bracing. Designed to fit with A.I.M. Products kits #'s 124 and 125. Includes track unless noted.

255-75507   50' Ballasted Deck,   6.50
7 x 1-13/16"   18 x 4.5 cm
(less track and ballast)

255-75508   30' Ballasted Deck   5.95
4-1/8 x 1-13/16"   10.5 x 4.5 cm
(less track and ballast)

255-75501   50' Code 83 HO   6.50
7 x 1-3/8"   18 x 3.5 cm

255-75502   30' Code 83 HO   5.95
4-1/8 x 1-3/8"   10.5 x 3.5 cm

255-75503   50' Code 55 HOn3   6.50
7 x 1-3/8"   18 x 3.5 cm

255-75504   30' Code 55 HOn3   5.95
4-1/8 x 1-3/8"   10.5 x 3.5 cm

THRU GIRDER BRIDGES
Injection-molded plastic kits come complete with Code 83 Bridge Flex-Trak and a "concrete" trough or troughs which allow the bridge to be built with either an open or ballasted deck.

50' Single Track
255-75520   8.95

50' Double Track
255-75521   13.95

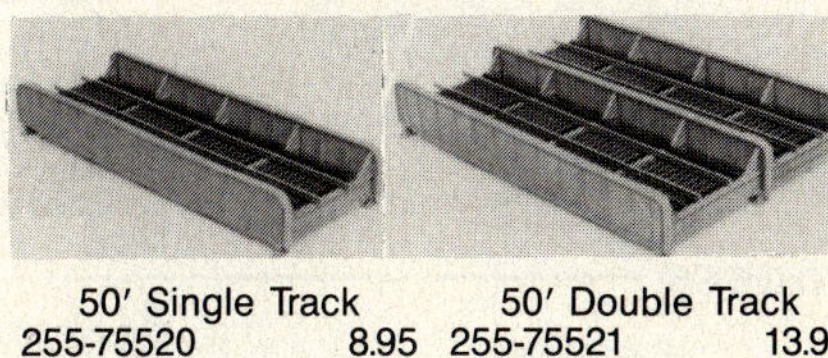

100' Two-span Single Track (includes center support legs)
255-75522   15.95

100' Two-span Double Track (includes center support legs)
255-75523   25.95

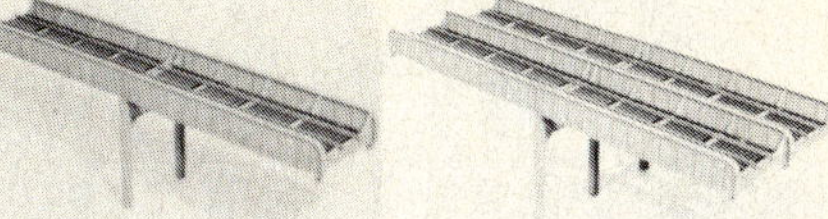

Bridge Support
255-80175
NEW 6.95

(not illustrated)
255-75530   110' Three-span bridge   **NEW** 18.95
255-75532   160' Four-span bridge   **NEW** 27.95
255-48105   Girder Curving Tool   28.95

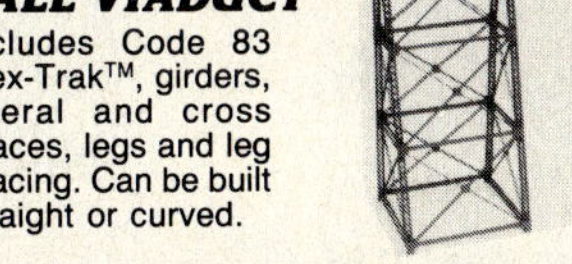

model power

HO SCALE (1/87) EASY-TO-BUILD KITS

Kits include precolored plastic parts and step-by-step instructions. 500 series are built-up structures.

STATIONS & PLATFORMS

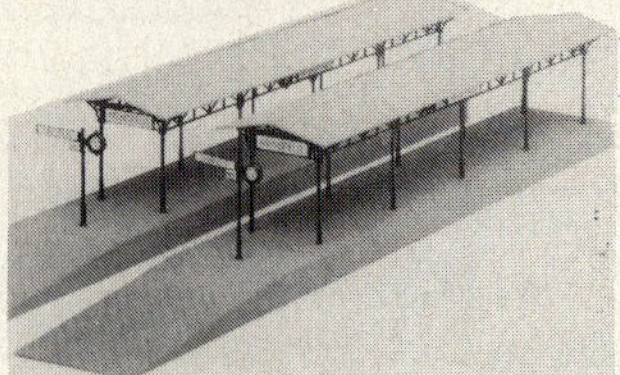

Small Freight Station
490-404   9.00
6-3/4 x 3-3/4" 17 x 7 cm

2-Story Railroad Station
490-480   15.00
9-1/2 x 5" 24 x 12.5 cm

Two Station Platforms
490-478   pkg(2) 15.00
each: 2 x 14" 5.5 x 36 cm

Whistle Stop Station
490-444   10.00

Railroad Platforms
490-612   pkg(4) 10.98
1 x 6-1/2" x 2.5 x 16.5 cm

Silverado Station
490-605   14.00
4-1/4 x 6-1/2" 11 x 16 cm

Chester Station
490-454   15.00
4 x 7-3/4" 11 x 9.7 cm

Port Chester Station
490-542   16.50
5-3/8 x 12-3/8" 13.7 x 31.6 cm

BUILT-UP BUILDINGS
w/light & hand painted figures
490-616 Station Platform   11.98
490-630 Water Tower   9.98
490-631 Search Tower   9.98

YARD & EQUIPMENT FACILITIES

Blue Coal Depot
490-453   16.50
4 x 6-1/2" 10.2 x 16.5 cm

490-424   **Rail Crane**   10.00
3 x 9-1/2" 7.7 x 24 cm

Water Tank w/Shed
490-428   13.00
tank: 3-1/2 x 4" 9 x 10.4 cm
shed: 1-3/3 x 2" 4.5 x 5.4 cm

Coaling Station
490-410   15.00
6 x 6" 15.3 x 15.3 cm

490-407   **Lumber Yard**   15.00
4 x 6" 10 x 15 cm

Railroad Signal Bridge
490-419   5.50
4 x 5-1/2" 10.2 x 14 cm

490-408   **Trackside Maintenance**   11.98
Storage Shed: 1-3/4 x 2" 4.5 x 5.1 cm
Transformer Box: 1-1/4 x 2" 3.2 x 5.1 cm
Shed w/Extension: 3 x 8" 7.6 x 20.3 cm

Twin Loco Shed
490-611   17.98
10 x 6-13/16" 25.7 x 17.4 cm

Interlocking Tower
490-481   11.98

HOUSES

Rooming House
490-426   14.98
6-1/4 x 6-1/2" 16 x 16.5 cm

Farm House
490-433   14.98
3 x 7" 7.7 x 17.7 cm

Burned Town House
490-466   15.00
2-3/4 x 6" 7 x 15 cm

Cape Cod House
490-479   pkg(2) 15.00
3-3/4 x 5" 9.5 x 12.5 cm

House w/Garage
490-425   12.00
4 x 6-3/4" 10 x 14.5 cm

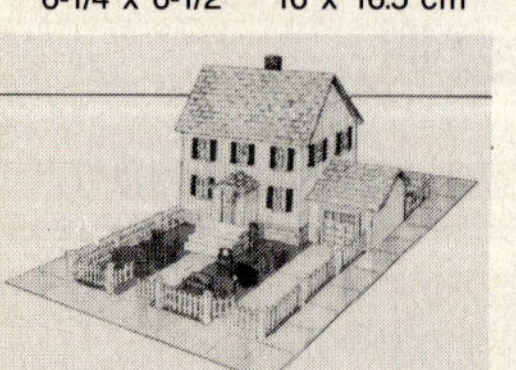

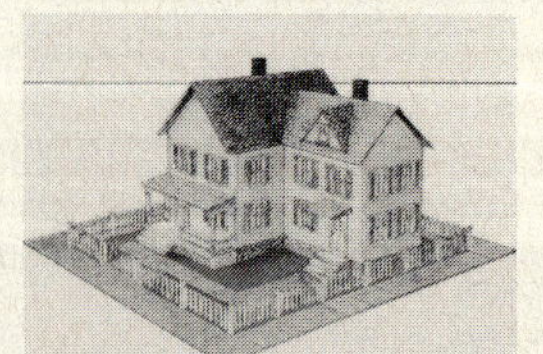

Moving In House
490-484   12.98
7-1/2 x 9" 19 x 23 cm

Grandma's House
490-487   12.98
7-1/2 x 9" 19 x 23 cm

Grabitski House
490-485   12.98
7-1/2 x 9" 19 x 23 cm

Sullivan House
490-488   12.98
7-1/2 x 9" 19 x 23 cm

Jordan's House
490-590   14.98
3-1/2 x 6-3/4" 8.9 x 17.1 cm

model power

HO SCALE
(1/87)
EASY-TO-BUILD
KITS

Kits include precolored plastic parts and step-by-step instructions.
500 series are built-up structures.

HOUSES (continued)

Digger's House
490-489   12.98
7-1/2 x 9"   19 x 23 cm

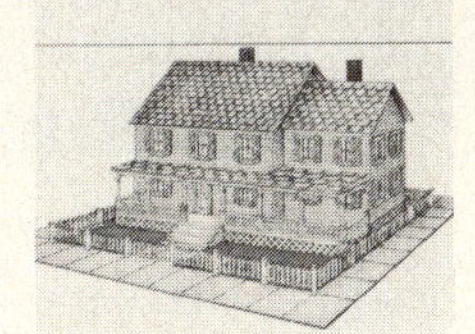

Bella's Farm House
490-490   12.98
7-1/2 x 9"   19 x 23 cm

Haunted House
490-486   12.98
7-1/2 x 9"   19 x 23 cm

Delta
Fraternity House
490-456   15.00
3-1/2 x 7"   9 x 17.5 cm

Simpson's House
490-589 w/Figures 14.98
4-1/2 x 4-7/8"   11.4 x 12.4 cm

Building Under Demolition
490-469   16.50
4-1/2 x 8-1/2"   11.5 x 21 cm

Urban Renewal Project
490-420   16.50
4-1/2 x 9-1/4"   11.4 x 23.5 cm

490-601   Barn   12.98
4-5/16 x 5-1/2"   11 x 14 cm

Modern House
490-606   11.98
5 x 3-1/4"   12.7 x 8.2 cm

Kennedy's House
490-588 w/Figures 14.98
5 x 4-7/8"   12.7 x 12.4 cm

2-Story House
490-609   14.98
3-3/8 x 4-3/8"   8.6 x 11.1 cm

Sinatra's House
490-584   w/Figures   14.98
2-5/8 x 5-1/2"   6.7 x 14 cm

Mr. Roger's House
490-585   w/Figures   14.98
4 x 4-1/2"   10.2 x 11.4 cm

Haunted House
w/Figures
490-586   14.98
3-5/8 x 4"   9.2 x 10.2 cm

Grandma Moses' House
590-587 w/Figures 14.98
4 x 5-1/2"   10.2 x 14 cm

CITY BUILDINGS

490-470   IRS on Fire   38.50
5-1/4 x 7-1/2"   13 x 19.2 cm

Little Red School House
490-604   14.00
3-1/2 x 5-1/2"   8.9 x 14 cm

Fire House w/2 Engines
490-409   14.98
4-1/2 x 5-1/4"   11.5 x 13.5 cm

St. Mary's Hospital
490-446   25.00
5-7/8 x 11-1/8"
14.9 x 28.2 cm

43rd Precinct
490-447   20.00
5-3/4 x 11-1/4"   14.6 x 28.5 cm

CHURCHES

490-613   Church   12.98
7-1/2 x 9"   19 x 22.9 cm

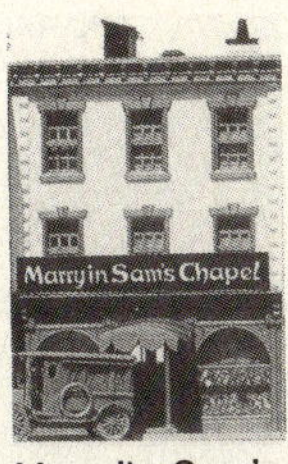

Marry'in Sam's
Chapel
490-457   15.00
3-1/2 x 7"
8.8 x 17.8 cm

Church
490-482   15.00
4-1/2 x 8"
11.5 x 20 cm

(not illustrated)
Built-up Church
w/Lite & Figures
490-582 *NEW* 14.98

BUSINESSES

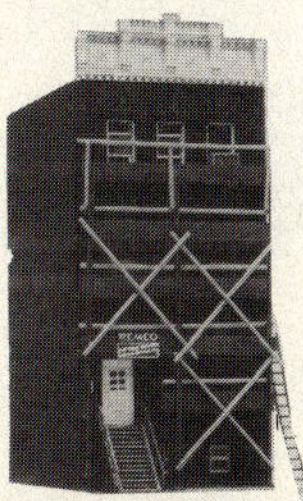

Rileys Building
Renovation
490-468   15.00
2-3/4 x 6"   7 x 15 cm

Building on Fire
490-449   16.50
2-3/4 x 6"   7 x 15.2 cm

model power

HO SCALE (1/87) EASY-TO-BUILD KITS

Kits include precolored plastic parts and step-by-step instructions. 500 series are built-up structures.

BUSINESSES (continued)

Interstate Freight
490-411   13.98
3-1/2 x 7″   8.4 x 18 cm

Western Union Office
490-452   16.50
4-1/2 x 6-1/2″   11.5 x 16.5 cm

Assayer's Office
490-405   7.50
2-1/4 x 3″   5.7 x 7.7 cm

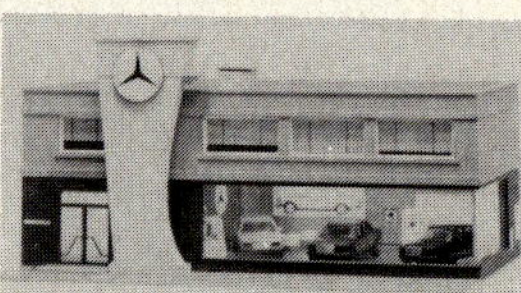

Mercedes Car Agency
490-429   17.98
5-1/4 x 8-1/2″   13.3 x 21.6 cm

Real Estate Office
490-442   12.00
3-7/8 x 4-1/2″   10 x 12 cm

Nick's Pickles
490-471   15.00
3-1/2 x 6″
9 x 15.2 cm

Sneed's Feeds & Tools
490-474   15.00
3-1/2 x 6″   9 x 15.2 cm

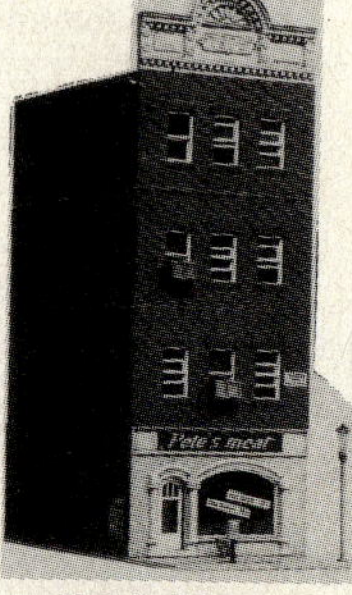

Pete's Meats
490-473   15.00
3-1/2 x 6″
7 x 15.2 cm

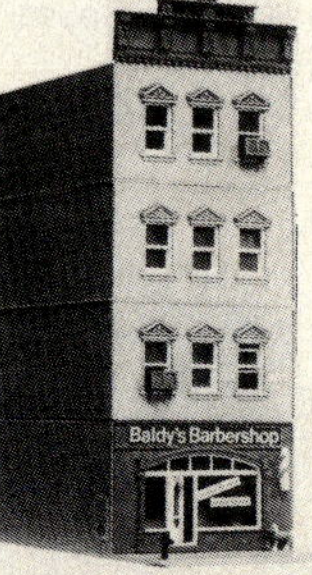

Baldy's Barber
490-472   15.00
2-3/4 x 6″

Jimmy's Barber Shop
490-462   15.00
3-1/2 x 6″
9 x 15.2 cm

Ace Hardware
490-461   15.00
3-1/2 x 7″
9 x 17.7 cm

George's Grocery
490-463   15.00
3-1/2 x 6″
9 x 15.2 cm

Jan's Ice Cream Parlor
490-475
14.00
7 x 4-1/4″
18 x 11 cm
hand-weathered

Annie's Antiques
490-464
16.50
3-1/2 x 6″
9 x 15.2 cm

Billy's Auto Body
490-414   13.98
5 x 6″   12.5 x 15.4 cm

Bob's Hot Dog Stand
490-441   12.00
2-1/2 x 4-1/4″   6.5 x 10.8 cm

Movie House
490-421
19.95
5-1/2 x 7″
14 x 7.7 cm

490-483   **Bobby's Garage**   16.98
9 x 4-3/4″   22.5 x 12 cm
includes advertising signs

490-477   **Globe News & Printing**   15.00
6-3/4 x 9-1/4″   17 x 23.5 cm
hand-weathered

490-476   **Micky's Fruit Stand**   15.00
5 x 5″   12.5 x 12.5 cm
hand-weathered

490-543   **Robert Shaw Wine & Cheese**   11.00
3-3/8 x 7-3/8″   8.6 x 18.9 cm

490-544   **Luigi's La Trotteria**   11.00
3-3/8 x 7-3/8″   8.6 x 18.9 cm

490-545   **Cathy's Flower Shop**   11.00
3-3/8 x 7-3/8″   8.6 x 18.9 cm

490-546   **Spotless Dry Cleaners**   11.00
3-3/8 x 7-3/8″   8.6 x 18.9 cm

Administration Office & Factory Complex
490-610   18.00
Office: 3-1/8 x 7-13/16″   7.9 x 19.9 cm
Factory: 3-13/16 x 7-7/8″   9.7 x 20 cm

Thru-Way Truckstop
490-607   14.98
6 x 6-3/4″   15.2 x 17.1 cm

490-445   **Citibank**   16.50
3-5/8 x 8-1/4″   9.2 x 21 cm

Lenny's Clam Box
490-608   14.98
5-1/2 x 6-13/16″   14 x 17.4 cm

model power

HO SCALE (1/87) EASY-TO-BUILD KITS

Kits include precolored plastic parts and step-by-step instructions.

INDUSTRIAL

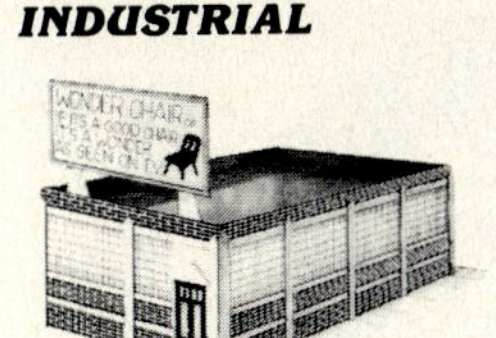

Wonder Chair Factory
490-458   14.00

Averill Gold Refining Co
490-423   11.00
7-1/2 x 4-1/2"
19 x 11.5 cm

490-443 Power Station 6.50

Burlington Mills Factory
490-455   15.00
3-1/2 x 7"   9 x 17.8 cm

490-465   Heinz Pickle Factory   19.50
5-1/2" x 12"   14 x 30.5 cm

490-416 City Power Station No 15 **NEW** 15.00

490-418   Builders Depot   **NEW** 14.98

490-415   Pure Water Supply Co **NEW** 14.98

490-417   Natural Gas Supply   **NEW** 12.98

(not illustrated)
490-79   Trestle Bridge 15pc Set **NEW** 3.98
490-99   Over & Under Pier Set **NEW** 5.98
490-102   Truss Bridge **NEW** 3.98
490-106   Girder Bridge **NEW** 3.98
490-111   Blinking Bridge **NEW** 4.98
490-112   High Trestle Bridge **NEW** 7.98

Pacific Rail Products

Kits feature precision-cut wood, plastic and metal detail parts, windows and doors, vents, etc., corrugated aluminum roof, as needed. Each kit includes templates, complete instructions, and painting and weathering suggestions.

NEW

Prototype Photo

544-801	Packing Shed Kit	45.95
544-802	Packing Shed w/Office Kit	59.95

PRE-SIZE MODEL SPECIALTIES

HO SCALE (1/87)

NEW

CULVERTS

483-122	Random Stone, 48"	pkg(2)	5.95
483-123	Cut Stone, 8' Arch	pkg(2)	5.95
483-124	Concrete, 8' Arch	pkg(2)	5.95
483-125	Concrete, 36" Double Pipe	pkg(2)	5.95
483-126	Concrete, 2—6' Rectangular	pkg(2)	5.95
483-127	Wall w/20' Single Bridge		8.95
483-128	Wall w/20' Double Bridge		10.95

BRIDGES w/PIERS

483-130	33' Random Stone	10.50
483-131	33' Cut Stone	10.50
483-132	30' Old Concrete	10.00
483-133	35' Smooth Concrete	8.95

NOCH

Imported from Germany
by **WALTHERS**

HO EASY-TO-BUILD KITS

All structures are molded in appropriately colored plastic.

RURAL BUILDINGS

Mountain Chapel
528-6480   5.99

Mountain Lodge
528-6481   5.99

Forest Cabin
528-6484   5.99

Lookout Post/Access
528-6490   5.99

528-6485   Weekend House   5.99

BRIDGES

Single track bridges are molded in appropriately colored plastic.

528-2132   Thru Truss   22.99
14 x 2-1/4"   35.6 x 5.7 cm

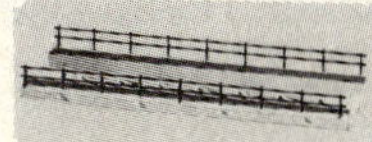

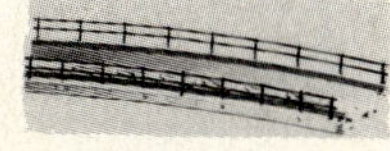

Straight Steel
528-2134   9.99
7 x 2-1/4"
17.8 x 5.7 cm

Curved Steel
528-2135   10.99
7 x 2-1/4"
17.8 x 5.7 cm

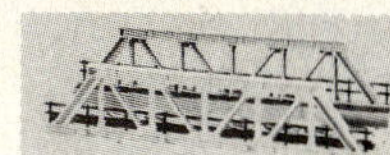

Truss
528-2133   11.99
7 x 2-1/4"   17.8 x 5.7 cm
(By Special Order Only.)

528-11050   Small   **NEW** pkg(4) 8.49

(not illustrated)
528-3961   Bridge   112.99
for layout form #8161 (see Scenery)

MODEL MASTERPIECES LTD

HO SCALE (1/87) CRAFT TRAIN KITS

Craft Train kits are wood construction with plastic and metal detail parts, doors, windows, etc. Buildings with stone walls are cast in Dental Stone.

BUSINESSES

The Gazette
485-111   26.00
4-1/2 x 6-1/2"

Cimarron Supply Company
485-112   40.00
4-1/2 x 6-1/2"

Photo shows #'s 111 and 112.

Brazelton Building
485-137   45.00
Two-story meeting hall with stone front, based on structure in Cripple Creek. Features double door inset entry way with coin store trim and hip style metal roof.

(not illustrated)
485-155   Modern Shopping Annex   12.50

BRIDGES & PIERS

485-128   6' Concrete Pier Trestle   13.75
Includes abutments, piers, wood ties and stringers.

485-126   34' Twin Deck Bridge   17.00

MISCELLANEOUS

Piggyback Ramp
485-153   8.50

Flat Unloading Ramp
485-154   pkg(2) 6.25

INDUSTRIAL

Colorado Midland Sandhouse
485-105   16.00
5-1/2 x 2-1/2"

485-151 City Coal Company   19.00

YARD & EQUIPMENT FACILITIES

D&RGW/ RGS 52' Gallow Turntable HO/HOn3
485-115   40.00

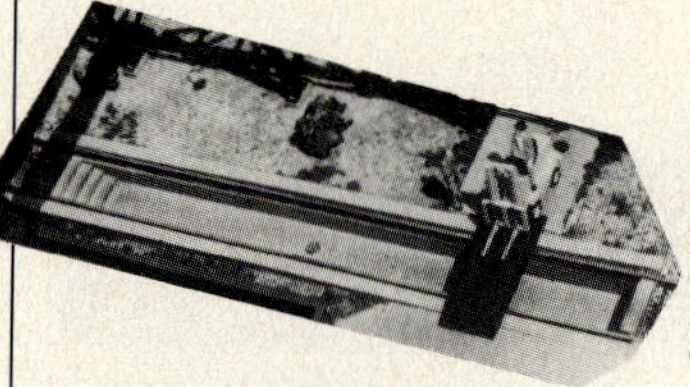

Concrete Inspection Pit
485-132   pkg(2)
8.50

Yard Office & Track Scale
485-152   15.00

Photo shows #'s 140, 141 and 142

Modern Diesel House & Repair Shop
485-140   80 x 57 x 45'   73.50
Based on D&RGW diesel house near Denver, Colorado. Features 2 tracks on raised pylons with four levels of inspection pits, ramps and platforms. Less office and supply building.

Diesel House & Repair Shop Extension
485-141   57 x 76 x 45'   69.00

485-142   Diesel House Office   26.25
25 x 25' w/ramp

(not illustrated)
485-120   65' Turntable HO/HOn3   48.50
Durango, Colorado D&RGW prototype. Use with manual or powered turntable turning arrangement.

Fetching a couple of empty pulpwood cars from the local paper mill, the crew of CN local should have no trouble getting home in time for supper. It's a beautiful day in northern Quebec, where George Dutka set this scene on his layout in London, Ontario, Canada. The engine was reworked from an Athearn GP9, while the caboose was scratchbuilt. Like their prototypes, the wood chip cars were rebuilt from box cars. George used a pair of Front Range (now McKean) kits for the models.

Models and Photo by George Dutka

Mountains in Minutes™
I.S.L.E. LABORATORIES

BUSINESSES

473-407   Taylor's Garage   11.98
12-1/4 x 5″   31.2 x 12.7 cm

Bank Building
473-402
8.98
4 x 2-1/2″
10 x 6.5 cm

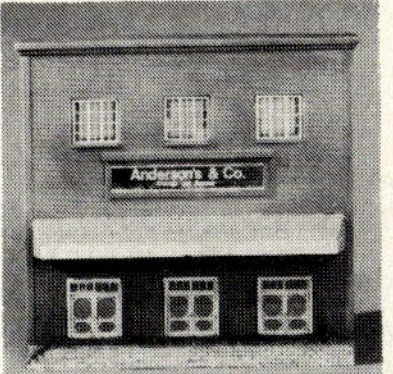

Warehouse
473-404   8.98
7-1/4 x 2-1/8″
18.5 x 5.5 cm

General Store
473-401   8.98
7-1/2 x 1-3/8″   19 x 3.5 cm

INDUSTRIAL

473-408   Factory   11.98
12 x 5″   30.5 x 12.7 cm

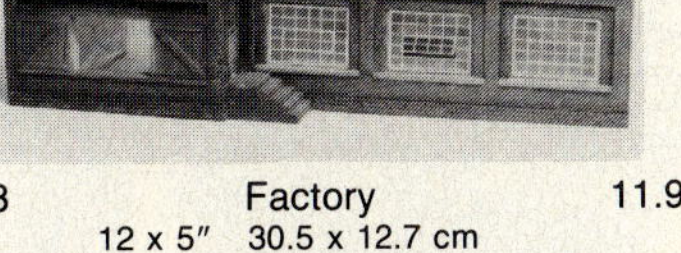

473-406   Rock Brewery   12.98
14-1/4 x 4-1/2″   36.3 x 11.5 cm

MISCELLANEOUS

Victorian Mansion
473-409   12.98
4-1/2 x 3-1/2″
11.5 x 9 cm

Grain Elevator
473-405   11.98
11 x 1-3/4″   28 x 4.5 cm

Memorial Hall
473-403   8.98
7 x 2″   18 x 5 cm

HO SCALE (1/87) EASY-TO-USE FRONTS
The "Old Hometown Series" fronts feature unpainted, precast, rigid foam plastic fronts. Printed windows and signs are included.

473-410   Freight Station   16.98
12-1/2 x 7″   13.7 x 17.7

MASTER RAIL MODELS

HO (1/87) EASY-TO-BUILD
Injection molded plastic with an aluminum center core.

GIRDER DECK BRIDGE

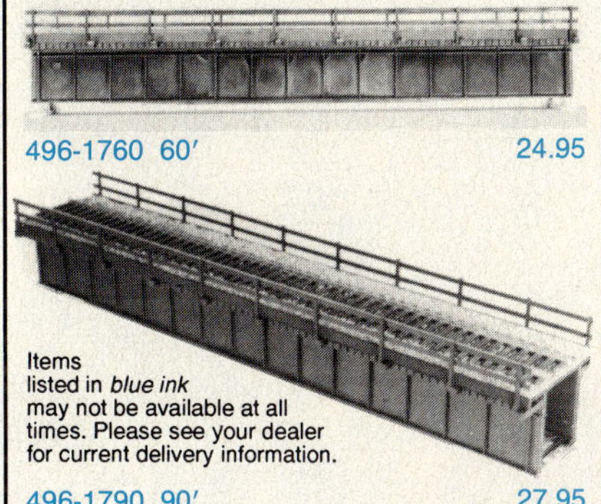

496-1760 60′   **24.95**

Items listed in *blue ink* may not be available at all times. Please see your dealer for current delivery information.

496-1790 90′   **27.95**

(not illustrated)
496-1703 Large Bridge   pkg(4) 4.95
Pedestal
496-1704 Fire Extinguisher   pkg(5) 4.49

TICHY TRAIN GROUP
HO SCALE (1/87) EASY-TO-BUILD KITS

Kits are injection molded styrene.

YARD & EQUIPMENT FACILITIES

400T Concrete Coaling Tower
293-7010   135.00
Tower spans two tracks and services a third. Includes separate coal shed with raised track, sand drying house, and equipment shed.

Steel Water Tank 100,000 gallons
293-7012
29.50
NEW

293-7011   Handcar Shed   9.50

N.J. International INC.

YARD & EQUIPMENT FACILITIES

HO SCALE (1/87)
Trackside accessories feature assembled or brass construction, unless noted otherwise.

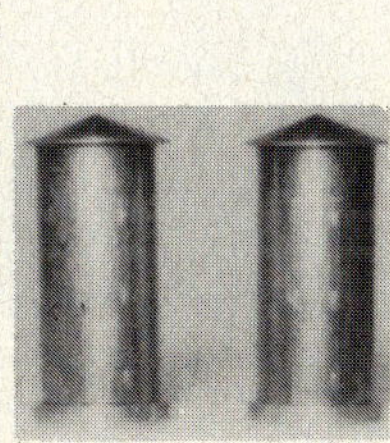

Line Shed
525-1800
pkg(2) 5.99
each: 1/2″ dia
1.3 cm

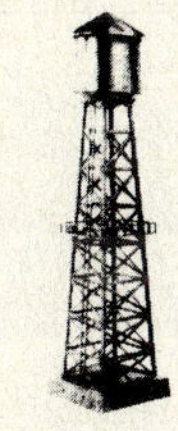

Water Tower
525-1971
7.49
2x2″ 5x5 cm
Easy-to-build
plastic kit

Oil Derrick
525-1970
7.49
2x2″ 5x5 cm
Easy-to-build
plastic kit

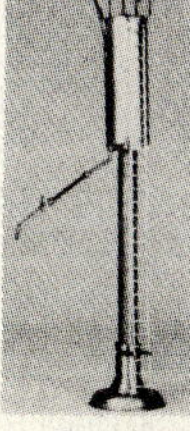

Sanding Tower
525-1700
25.99
1″ dia
2.6 cm

(not illustrated)
68′ Maintenance Platform
525-4020   *NEW* 16.95

102′ Maintenance Platform
525-4021   *NEW* 21.95

136′ Maintenance Platform
525-4022   *NEW* 26.95

68′ Etched Walkway
525-4024   *NEW* 4.99

Rix Products

HO SCALE (1/87) EASY-TO-BUILD KITS

Kits are injection molded styrene, featuring white weatherboard walls, red brick foundations, brown asphalt roofing and clear windows.

"MAXWELL AVENUE" HOUSES

One Story House
628-201   8.95
3 x 3-7/8"
7.7 x 9.9 cm

w/Side Porch
628-203   9.95
3-1/2 x 3-7/8"
9 x 9.9 cm

w/Front Porch
628-202   9.95
3 x 4-3/8"
7.7 x 11.2 cm

(not illustrated)

628-204   Porch Kit 1/2 x 1"   1.3 x 2.5 cm   4.99
Features brick porch, steps, doors, porch floor, gable & porch roof.

RIX HIGHWAY OVERPASS

The Rix Highway overpass represents concrete bridges built back in the 30s and 40s which are still standing today. The overpass comes molded in concrete color.

628-100	Highway Pier	NEW	3.99
628-101	50' Highway Overpass	NEW	5.99
628-102	50' Highway Overpass w/Pier	NEW	9.95
618-103	150' Highway Overpass w/4 piers	NEW	29.95
	(3 overpass kits w/4 piers)		

Work never stops at this busy refinery, and powerful flood lights turn night into day for the second and third shift crew. Over in the rail yards, a long string of tankers are about to move out. Built from a pair of Walthers Cornerstone Series® kits and a Heljan LPG storage facility, this impressive night scene is the work of Mike Osborn of Newhall, California. Mirrors add depth to the scene, which is framed by Roundhouse and Walthers freight cars.
Photo by Darryl Enault

Plastruct

HO SCALE (1/87)

CRAFT TRAIN KITS
Kits feature plastic parts and include plans.

YARD & EQUIPMENT FACILITIES

Welded Steel Water Tank
570-1009   21.95
3-1/2" dia   9 cm dia
100,000 gallon used during
the last days of steam.

Twin Lamp
Posts
570-1012
pkg(2)   5.95
6-1/4" high
Non-operating

Sand Tower
570-1011   9.95
1 x 6-3/4"   2.5 x 17.2 cm
Includes material for concrete
slabs, walkways, etc.

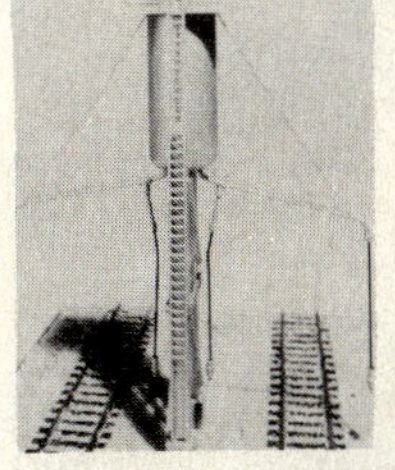

570-1010   Service Platforms   pkg(2)   12.95
3-1/2 x 1"   9 x 2.5 cm

570-1008   Petro/Chemical Refinery   69.95
20 x 24"   51 x 70 cm

570-1015   570-1016   570-1017

570-1015   Oil Storage Tank   13.95
For expanding your refinery, tank farm or bulk oil
distribution center.
570-1016   Utility Water Tower   15.95
A must for all modern trail layouts.
570-1017   Propane Storage Tank   9.95
An outstanding component for your trackside bulk oil
distribution center.

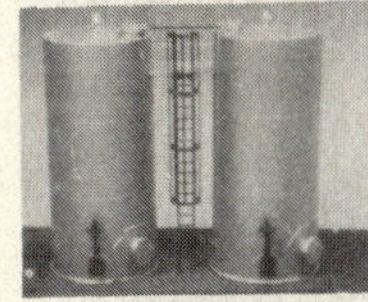

570-1018   570-1005

570-1018   Side by Side Vertical Tank   23.95
Use as chemical tanks or silos.
570-1005   Electrical Towers & Oil Well   19.95
Contains enough material to build either one Oil Well
or one each of the Transmission Towers.

Twin Bulk Oil Storage Tanks
570-1014   **NEW**   15.95

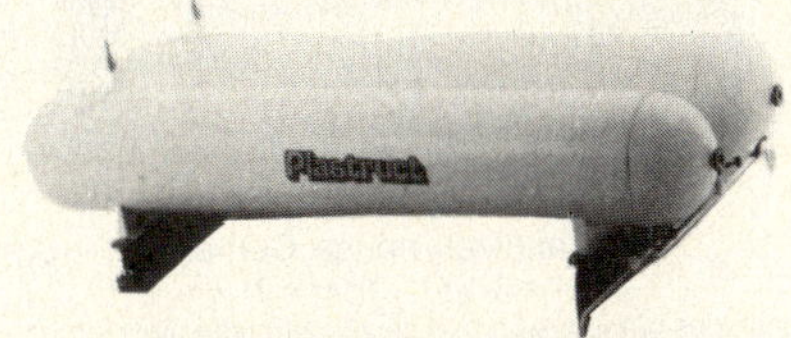

Twin LP Gas Storage Tanks
570-1019   **NEW**   16.95

570-1025   Silos and Grain Elevators   **NEW**   44.95

570-1026   Spherical Storage Tank   **NEW**   17.95

External
Floating
Roof Tank
570-1027
31.95
NEW

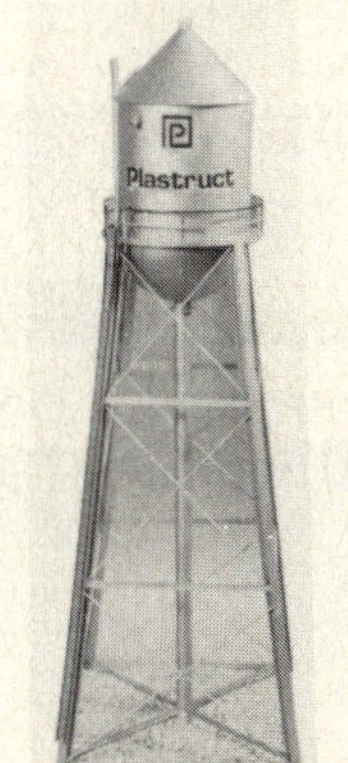

Cone Roof
Elevated
Water Tank
570-1028
19.95
NEW

(not illustrated)
Cage and Ladder Set
570-1704   **NEW**   2.95

MISCELLANEOUS

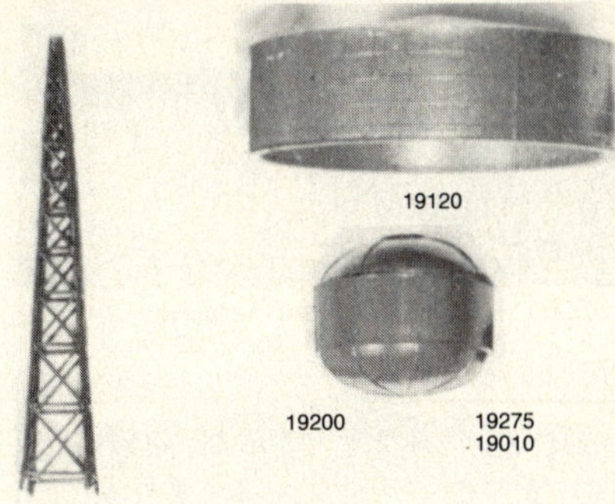

19120

19200   19275
               19010

19135
19155

570-19135   3-1/2" Tower   each   3.95
570-19155   5-1/2" Tower   each   3.95
570-19120   2" Oil Tank   pkg(2)   2.95
570-19200   1" Water Tank   pkg(2)   2.95
570-19275   1-3/4" Water Tank each   2.95
570-19010   Gas Pump   pkg(3)   2.95

BRIDGE

570-1007   Old Time Moving Bridge   22.95
24" long   13-1/2" wide over piers
70 cm long   34.5 cm wide over piers
Opens horizontally using a central pivoting system.

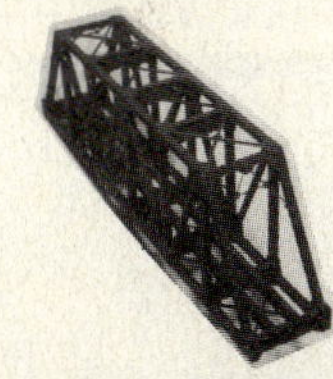

570-1002   Truss Bridge   19.95
The "Grandfather" of Bridges, for the more
sophisticated scratchbuilder.

570-1001   Simple Span Bridge   14.95
Contains enough material for both bridges.

PLAN BOOKS

570-11   Concrete Bridges   1.50
570-12   Tress Bridges   1.50
570-13   Gravel Loading Facility   1.50
570-14   Transfer Dock   1.50
570-15   Oil Well & Electrical
         Transmission Tower (Double Plan)
570-16   Skyscraper Framing   1.50
570-17   Old Time Moving Bridge,
         Swing Span
570-18   Refinery   5.95
570-19   Water Tank & Spout   1.50

Pikestuff

HO SCALE (1/87) CRAFT TRAIN KITS

Kits feature molded plastic parts with plastic doors and windows. All wall sections are molded without windows or door openings, enabling you to add them where you want. Kit can be kitbashed or combined with more kits to create a larger structure.

BUSINESSES

541-5001   Motor Freight Terminal   9.95
4-3/16 x 11-1/8"   10.5 x 28 cm

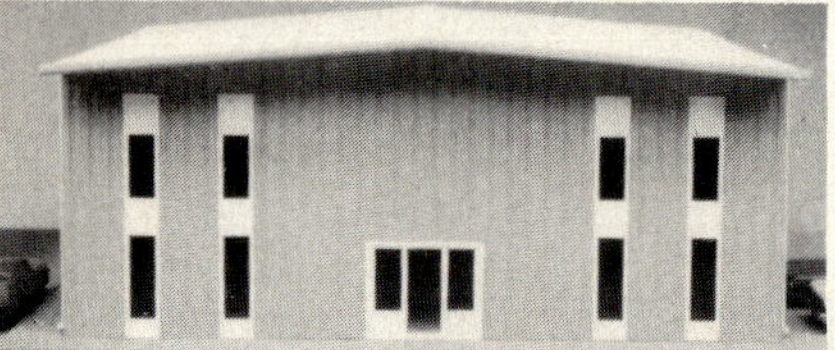
541-5002 Modern 2-Story Office Building   8.45

541-4   Pre-Fab Metal Building   11.95
4-1/8 x 8-1/4"   10.8 x 21 cm

541-9   Auto Repair Shop   14.95
3-1/2 x 8-1/4"   9 x 21 cm

541-16   Yard Office   6.95
Includes material to build one of three heights; 12', 18', 22' x 40' scale feet.

Diamond Tool & Engineering Co
541-18   5-1/2 x 8-1/4"   14 x 21 cm   10.95

541-20   Tri-Star Industries   12.95
9-5/8 x 8-1/4"   24.5 x 21 cm

541-100   Rail/Truck Transfer Facility   17.95

541-7   Retail/Warehouse Center   16.95
4-1/4 x 8-1/4"   10.8 x 21 cm
Includes outdoor sign and decals for a variety of stores.

541-10   Distribution Center   11.95
9-5/8 x 5-1/2"   24.5 x 14 cm

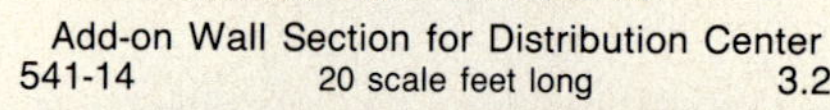
Add-on Wall Section for Distribution Center
541-14   20 scale feet long   3.25

541-15   Shop w/Add on Office   18.95
70 x 80 scale feet

541-11   Add-on Office Showroom   5.50

541-5003   Tire Shack   6.45

541-5004   Trucker/Railroad Motel   12.50

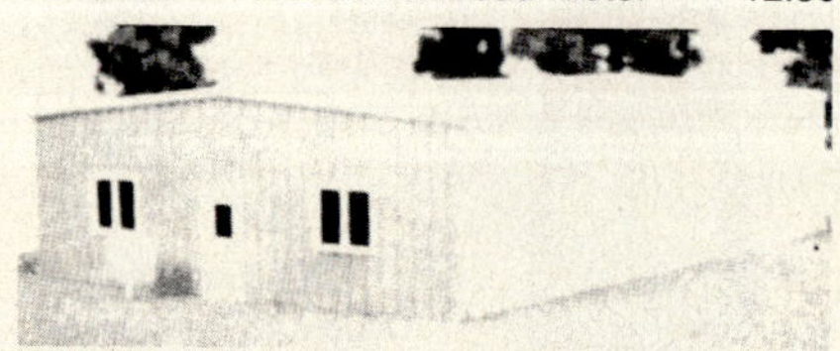
541-5005   Multi-Purpose Steel Building   9.25

541-5006 Contractors Building   9.95

541-101   Machine Tool Center   **NEW** 15.95
Includes one each: Smalltown, USA Hardware Kit, Smalltown, USA Sidewalks Kit, Three Size Yard Office and Loading Docks.

541-102   UIK Plastics   **NEW** 17.95
Includes a factory that's 70' wide 60' deep, plus an attached two-story office that measures 50' wide by 40' deep. Modular construction allows the building to be shortened in 20' intervals for a custom fit. All wall sections are molded in ''Monsoon Green'' so no painting is needed. And, six concrete parking barriers are included for the employee lot.

CITY BUILDING

541-19   Fire Station   9.95

YARD & EQUIPMENT FACILITIES

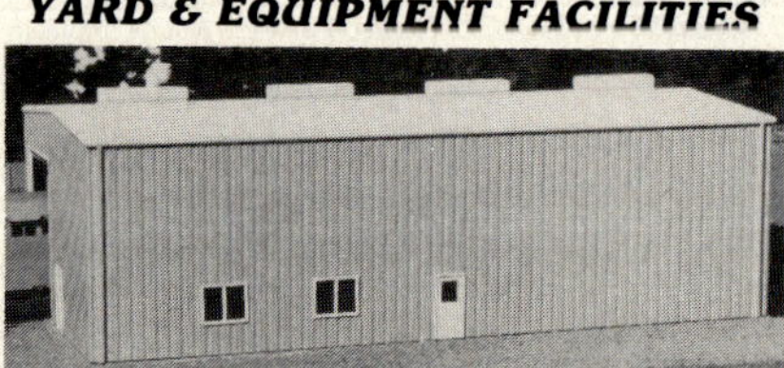
541-8 Modern 1 or 2 Stall Engine House 14.95
5-1/2 x 11"   14 x 28 cm

541-5   Small Yard Office   3.95
1-5/8 x 1-1/4"   4.2 x 3.2 cm

Pikestuff

HO SCALE (1/87) CRAFT TRAIN KITS

Kits feature molded plastic parts with plastic doors and windows. All wall sections are molded without windows or door openings, enabling you to add them where you want. Kit can be kitbashed or combined with more kits to create a larger structure.

YARD & EQUIPMENT FACILITIES (continued)

541-6   Wood Handcar Shed   2.95
1-5/8 x 1-1/4″   4.2 x 3.2 cm

541-5000 Modern Small Engine House   8.25
4-3/16 x 8-5/16″   10.5 x 21 cm

MISCELLANEOUS

541-17   Loading Docks & Ramp   3.25
Includes load ramp and four modular docks, each scale 40′ long, 10′ wide and 5′3″ tall.

Vintage Reproductions

HO CRAFT TRAIN KITS

Diamond Springs Water Tank
766-1   4″   18.00
Horizontal tank built on a trestle. Includes basswood, hardwood dowels, pre-blackened wire & chain and dry transfer.

Alpine Coaling Platform
766-2   pkg(2) 9.00
2-1/4 x 4-1/2″
Comprised of basswood strips and plastic nuts and bolts.

SUNCOAST MODELS — NEW

HO SCALE (1/87) CRAFT TRAIN KITS

Kits feature precut, color coded wood, cast window frames, construction board, roofing, aluminum siding and sheet brass where needed, plus illustrated instructions.

Icing Platform
690-3020
39.95
18 x 4″
45.6 x 10.2 cm

Icing Platform Extension Kit
690-30201
19.95

690-3030   Freight Station   32.95

Yard Office
690-3040
32.95

690-3050   Logging Camp   32.95
8-1/2 x 11″   21.5 x 28 cm

Modern Grain Elevator
690-3060
44.95

Grain Elevator Extension Kit
690-30601
19.95

FM Automatic Coaling Station
690-3080
24.95

Winchester Station — NEW

HO SCALE (1/87) CRAFT TRAIN KITS

Kits feature either Simucrete or polyurethane construction, injection molded parts and details.

INDUSTRIAL

Standard Concrete Sand Tower
763-101   24.98

50-Ton "Teaspoon" Coal Dock
763-102   32.98

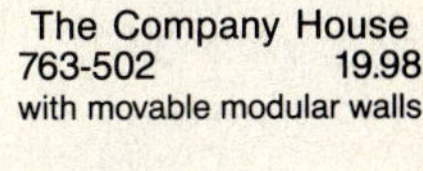

The Royalty Coal & Coke Co Coke Ovens
763-501   4.98

(not illustrated)
The Company House
763-502   19.98
with movable modular walls

300-Ton Coal Dock
763-103   TBA

"Train 711, for New Ritus, Clunkneyville and Chicago arriving on Track One."

Cartoon courtesy of *Model Railroader* Magazine.

MARCH 19, 1918

❖ Today ❖
IN RAILROAD HISTORY

Congress passes the Standard Time Act, making the four time zones adopted by the railroads in 1883, the official time for the United States.

POLA
Imported from Germany
by **WALTHERS**

HO SCALE
(1/87)
EASY-TO-BUILD
KITS

Easy-to-build plastic kits have European prototypes — most can be Americanized with minor modifications. Parts are injection-molded, appropriately colored plastic. Instructions included.

STATIONS AND PLATFORMS

"BAD DUERKHEIM" STATION

For busy passenger routes on your railroad, you'll want this large passenger station to handle the traffic! Modeled after a station built around the turn-of-the-century, the sandstone and plaster structure includes a covered platform and outside steps in front of the main entrance.

578-654   19-1/2 x 8-3/4 x 6-1/2"   50 x 22.5 x 16.5 cm   118.99

578-2011   Hofheim Covered Platform   9.49

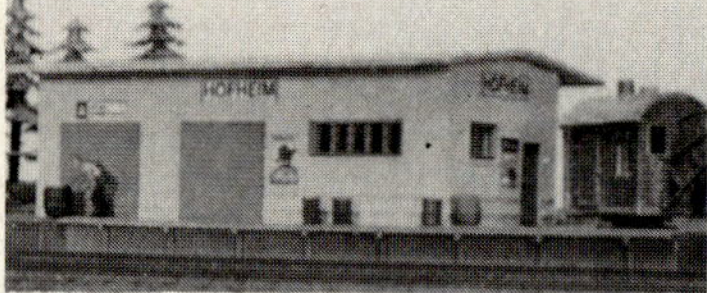

578-2012   Hofheim Freight Shed   8.99

578-818   Border Post   **NEW** 34.99

"BAYWA" STORAGE DEPOT

To handle freight shipments in and out of your small town, use this storage depot! Authentically detailed with half-timbered construction and a broken stone base, the preweathered depot features a roof with overhang, loading ramps and a fence with opening gate.

578-843   9 x 7"   23 x 18.5 cm   52.99

See also: LIGHTING & ELECTRICAL, SCENERY, PARTS and BOOKS for additional POLA items.

"NEUFELD" STATION

Framed with two small natural stone annexes, this station is similar to many structures built during the steam era and still in use today. Other details include movable windows and doors, a hip roof and preweathered parts.

578-663   13-3/4 x 5-3/4"   35 x 14.5 cm   37.99

POLA®
Imported from Germany by WALTHERS

HO SCALE (1/87) EASY-TO-BUILD KITS

Easy-to-build plastic kits have European prototypes — most can be Americanized with minor modifications. Parts are injection-molded, appropriately colored plastic. Instructions included.

STATIONS AND PLATFORMS (continued)

STORAGE DEPOT RAIFFEISEN

Complete with freight details and a specially painted and lettered truck, this small storage depot will be right at home on steam or diesel era layouts!

578-662	6-1/2 x 4-1/2" 16.5 x 11 cm	37.99

"MARMAGNE" STATION

This station will be a regular stop for your freight and passenger trains! Typical of small stations found throughout southern Europe, the building includes a main station building and detachable storage depot.

578-743	17-3/4 x 4-3/4" 45 x 12 cm	42.99

578-655   "Flirsch" Passenger Station   **(By Special Order Only.)**   37.99
13-1/4 x 6-1/4" 34.7 x 15.5 cm

578-555   Old Style Covered Platform   16.49
22-5/8 x 2-1/8" 57.5 x 5.5 cm

578-1005   Passenger Platform   13.49
14-1/4 x 2-1/4" 36 x 5.6 cm

578-740   Susch Passenger Station   39.99
13-1/8 x 5-3/4" 33.5 x 15 cm

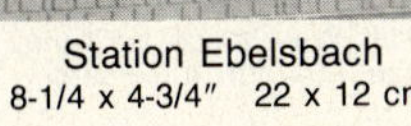

578-604   Station Ebelsbach   14.99
8-1/4 x 4-3/4" 22 x 12 cm

578-2010   Hofheim Passenger Station   9.99

POLA®
Imported from Germany by WALTHERS

HO SCALE (1/87) EASY-TO-BUILD KITS

Easy-to-build plastic kits have European prototypes — most can be Americanized with minor modifications. Parts are injection-molded, appropriately colored plastic. Instructions included.

STATIONS AND PLATFORMS (continued)

"UNTERSTETTEN" STATION
578-652   29.99
16 x 5-1/4"   40.5 x 13.5 cm
(By Special Order Only.)

TRAM STOP
578-676   **NEW** 20.49
17-5/16 x 2"   44 x 5.1 cm

578-650   St Niklaus Station   33.99
12-3/8 x 5"   31 x 12.7 cm
This old-time station will be right at home on steam era pikes! The model is complete with an attached waiting room and an outhouse. Swiss prototype, ideal for narrow gauge.

578-551   Niedlingen Station   19.49
9-3/4 x 4-3/4"   24.5 x 12 cm
This stucco city station features a clock tower and a covered platform.

578-1000   Waldbrunn Station   19.49
9-5/8 x 5"   24 x 12.5 cm
Includes a covered platform, which can be enlarged with platform kit #1005. **(By Special Order Only.)**

578-2052   Station Set   59.99
Includes: Station, Warehouse w/Crane, Switch Tower, Keeper's Cottage, Platform & Cement

See also: SCENERY, PARTS and BOOKS for additional POLA items.

POLA
Imported from Germany by WALTHERS

HO SCALE (1/87) EASY-TO-BUILD KITS

Easy-to-build plastic kits have European prototypes — most can be Americanized with minor modifications. Parts are injection-molded, appropriately colored plastic. Instructions included.

YARD AND EQUIPMENT FACILITIES

578-155   Coal Merchant Schmidt   25.99
7-1/8 x 4-5/16″   18 x 11 cm

578-601   Rustic Engine House   23.99
9-1/2″ long   24 cm

578-602   Track Maintenance Building   11.99
8 x 3″   20.5 x 7.5 cm
Incudes a handcar shed with handcar, too shed and relay box

578-600   1-Stall Engine Houe   19.49
11-1/8 x 5-1/8″   28.5 x 13 cm

578-702   Sand House-Loader   10.49
9-1/4 x 4″   23.5 x 10 cm
Kit includes a drying house, timber bunker with one-piece sand pile and a tower.

578-561   Coal Loader   9.99
7-1/4 x 2″   18 x 5.5 cm
Includes travelling crane, loading bucket and water crane.

TWO-STALL ENGINE HOUSE

Small engine houses like this could be found on many branch and mainline railroads. The kit has moveable doors and holds locos or cars up to 11-5/8″. Several kits can be combined to create a unique building for a large terminal.
578-1020   13 x 6-7/8″   32.3 x 17.2 cm   21.99

Coaling Tower
578-704   15.99
6-1/4 x 6″   16 x 15 cm
Includes coal buckets, machinery house and coal chute.

Large Travelling Crane w/Crane Rails
578-705   15.99
3-5/8 x 2-5/8″
9.3 x 6.7 cm

Signal Tower (Brick)
578-512   11.99
4-5/16 x 2-3/4″
11 x 7 cm

SHUNTING SHED "FREILASSING"

Shed is divided into five stands, each holding a loco up to 32 cm in length; each stand is at a 7.5 degree angle. Doors are operated by special mechanism: engines driving in close the doors, engines driving out open them automatically.
578-670   20-1/2 x 13-3/4″   52 x 35 cm   134.49

POLA
Imported from Germany by WALTHERS

HO SCALE (1/87) EASY-TO-BUILD KITS

Easy-to-build plastic kits have European prototypes — most can be Americanized with minor modifications. Parts are injection-molded, appropriately colored plastic. Instructions included.

YARD AND EQUIPMENT FACILITIES
(continued)

Hofheim Signal Tower
578-2013   6.99

Baywa Grain Elevator
578-844   47.99
9-1/2 x 7-3/4"   24 x 19.5 cm

578-847   Baywa Coal Depot   **NEW** 38.99
8-5/16 x 5-1/8"   21 x 13 cm

COAL STOCK YARD
There's a lot of work to be done at the coal stock yard. This is the place where the engines are fed. Coal is delivered at the top level and then shoveled down to keep the wheels in motion.

578-671   10-3/16 x 6-11/16"   26 x 17 cm   **NEW** 58.99

RURAL BUILDINGS

OLD SMITHY
This village smithy is housed in an old barn and comes complete with anvil, grind stone, forge and other accessories. Just add some animals and figures to finish the scene!

578-569   9.99
5-1/2 x 4-5/16"
14 x 11 cm

578-810   Farmhouse w/Barn   34.99
11-1/4 x 7-3/4"   28.5 x 19.5 cm

Narrow Gauge Lorry Shed Engine House
578-511   4-1/4 x 3-1/8"   10.5 x 8 cm   11.99

(not illustrated)
578-2053   Village Set   pkg(5) 49.99

506   507

ALBERT HEIJN RURAL HOUSE
4-1/2 x 4-1/2"   11.8 x 11.4 cm
578-506   22.49

O. SIMON RURAL HOUSE
3-3/4 x 3-1/3"   9.3 x 8.5 cm
578-507   22.49

POLA
Imported from Germany by WALTHERS

HO SCALE (1/87) EASY-TO-BUILD KITS

Easy-to-build plastic kits have European prototypes — most can be Americanized with minor modifications. Parts are injection-molded, appropriately colored plastic. Instructions included.

HOUSES

House "Roentgen"
578-627   12.99
6-1/4 x 4-1/2"   16.3 x 11.6 cm

House w/Lean-to Shed
578-502   7.99
3-1/4 x 4-1/4"   8.6 x 8.6 cm

1-Story w/Converted Attic
578-2014   7.99

578-503   House w/Pool   7.99
4-1/4 x 8"   10.6 x 20.5 cm

578-1043   House w/Shop   14.99

578-150   House on Fire (w/Interior)   33.99
5-5/8 x 4-1/2"   14.3 xx 11.4 cm

578-2015   Farm House   6.99

578-153   House Under Construction   33.99

RESIDENTIAL HOUSE

Enjoy a fireside chat after dinner in this romantic house situated on the canal.

578-749   7-1/2 x 3-1/2"   19 x 9 cm   **NEW** 31.49

CHURCHES

578-1030   Church   19.49
8-1/8 x 4-3/8"

Small Country Chapel
578-2017   6.49

578-631   Cemetery Chapel   36.49
5-3/4 x 4-1/4"   14.5 x 11 cm

House "Jugendstil"
5-1/4 x 4"   13.6 x 10 cm
578-178   37.99

POLA
Imported from Germany
by **WALTHERS**

HO SCALE
(1/87)
EASY-TO-BUILD
KITS

Easy-to-build plastic kits have European prototypes — most can be Americanized with minor modifications. Parts are injection-molded, appropriately colored plastic. Instructions included.

CITY BUILDINGS

TRAM TERMINAL "DRESDEN"

The tram terminal has doors at the front that open and close and its modular construction makes it possible to extend it both in length and in breadth. It is also possible to fit it into less spacious areas by restricting the size of the construction. In the four-track tram shed, there is even room for eight-axled articulated trams with a maximum length of 35 cm.

578-675   88.49
14-1/3 x 12″   36.2 x 30.4 cm

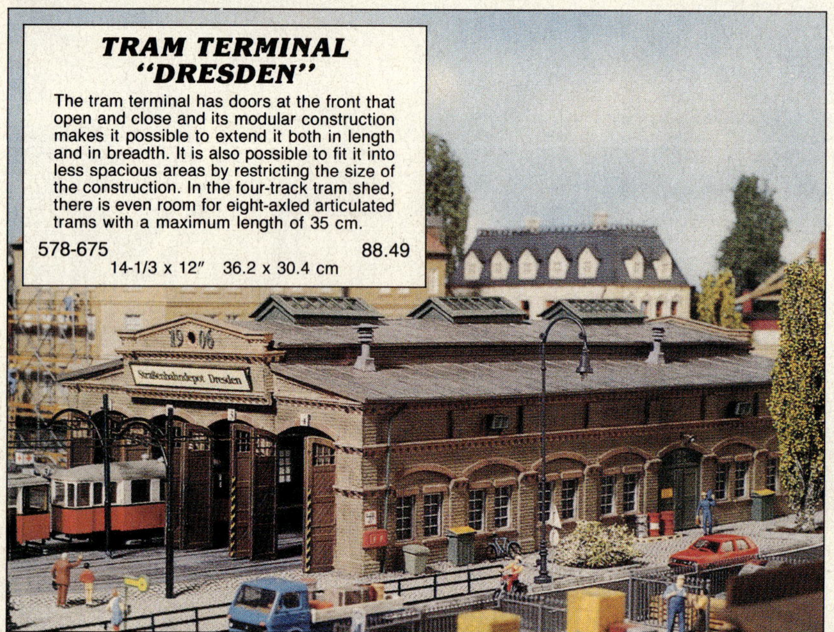

Warehouse
"Lubeck"
578-747
38.99
5-1/2 x 3-1/2″
14.2 x 9 cm
17th century model.
opening and closing
doors.

LTD QUANTITIES AVAILABLE

578-166   Apartment Bldg Under Demolition   37.99

KINDERGARTEN

This set comes complete with tables, stools, shelves, matching bus, and six children, a Mommy and a teacher.

578-400   9-13/16 x 9-3/8″   25 x 24 cm   **NEW** 109.49

PEKING RESTAURANT

What about a Chinese meal? There's never a wait at this inviting Chinese restaurant built in the Hanseatic style.

578-748   7-1/2 x 4-5/16″   19 x 11 cm   **NEW** 37.49

POLA®
Imported from Germany by WALTHERS

HO SCALE (1/87) EASY-TO-BUILD KITS

Easy-to-build plastic kits have European prototypes — most can be Americanized with minor modifications. Parts are injection-molded, appropriately colored plastic. Instructions included.

CITY BUILDINGS (continued)

PRIMARY SCHOOL BUILDING

This large school building will add ''class'' to any scene! The walls of the structure are lightly weathered. The kit also includes printed children's drawings for the windows.

578-169	7-3/4 x 5-3/8"	19.5 x 13.5 cm	35.99

HOSPITAL

This hospital will give your layout a healthy dose of detail! Based on a turn-of-the-century building converted into a hospital, the structure is detailed with sandstone walls, an entrance drive for ambulances, canopied porch, opening doors and windows, a parking lot and more.

578-192	11-1/2 x 11"	29.5 x 28.5 cm	47.49

MUNICIPAL GARAGE

Keep your fleet on the road with this handsome HO Scale garage! The doors can be left open to display vehicles parked inside. To start your scene, a truck is included!

578-180	6-7/8 x 9-3/8"	17 x 23.5 cm	35.99

City Gate w/Interior Light
578-152   36.99
6-1/4 x 6" 16 x 15.5 cm

Clubhouse ''Blue & White''
578-632   30.99
8-1/4 x 5-1/2" 21 x 14 cm

Apartment Building w/Theatre
578-167   39.99
5-1/4 x 6-5/8" 13.5 x 17 cm

CENTRAL FIRE STATION

578-196	13.6 x 10"	34.6 x 25.5 cm	80.99

POLA®
Imported from Germany
by **WALTHERS**

HO SCALE
(1/87)
EASY-TO-BUILD
KITS

Easy-to-build plastic kits have European prototypes — most can be Americanized with minor modifications. Parts are injection-molded, appropriately colored plastic. Instructions included.

CITY BUILDINGS (continued)

578-817   Police Station   36.99
8.5 x 5.3"   21.6 x 13.5 cm
Includes flower tubs and bicycle rack.

LIMITED QUANTITIES AVAILABLE

Townhouse Under Construction
578-154   31.49
5-1/4 x 6-5/8"   13.5 x 17 cm

Townhouse w/City Buildings
578-190   47.49
5-5/8 x 5"   14.5 x 12.7 cm

Burning IRS Office
578-160   57.99
7-3/4 x 5-5/16"   19.5 x 13.3. cm

Corner Pub Under Repair
578-177   39.99
8-3/8 x 7-5/8"   21 x 19 cm

Corner Town House
578-184   39.99
8-1/2 x 6"   21.2 x 15 cm

Art Nouveau House
578-182   39.99
7 x 5"   17.5 x 12.5 cm

EMBASSY
Here's a kit that won't be foreign to your layout! Featuring stately window ornamentation and a large courtyard, the Embassy comes complete with flag emblems for various countries, including Austria, Germany, Canada, the United States, Russia, Switzerland, Italy, France and more.
578-641   9-1/2 x 5-1/2"   24 x 14 cm   25.99

BUSINESSES

Townhouse w/Wine Bar
578-187   39.99
7-3/8 x 4-1/8"   19 x 10.7 cm

Pharmacy/Rococo Building
578-181   38.99
3-3/8 x 7-1/2"   8.7 x 19 cm

Toy Shop/Apartments
578-110   33.99
5-7/8 x 4-7/8"   14.5 x 12.5 cm

LIMITED QUANTITIES AVAILABLE

578-185   Hotel Ross   34.99
5-1/4 x 4-7/8"   13.5 x 12.5 cm

POLA®
Imported from Germany
by WALTHERS

HO SCALE
(1/87)
EASY-TO-BUILD
KITS

Easy-to-build plastic kits have European prototypes — most can be Americanized with minor modifications. Parts are injection-molded, appropriately colored plastic. Instructions included.

BUSINESSES (continued)

Beate's Health Store
578-158   35.99
7 x 4-1/4" 18 x 11 cm
Includes canopies, fruit and vegetable crates, flower boxes and rubbish bins.

Hairdressing Salon
578-188   42.99
5-3/16 x 4-7/8" 13.6 x 12.5 cm
Includes shop fittings, lighting and flower boxes.

Hussel Chocolate Shop
578-189   38.99
7-1/2 x 4-1/4" 19 x 10.8 cm

Paradise Bar
578-191   46.99
7-5/16 x 4-7/8" 18.3 x 12.5 cm

Auto Garage w/Apartments
578-165   39.99
5-1/4 x 6-5/8" 13.5 x 17 cm

Butcher Shop w/Apartments
578-168   33.99
5-3/4 x 4-7/8" 14.5 x 12.7 cm

Plumbing Shop & Apartments
578-164   37.99
5-1/4 x 6-5/8" 13.5 x 17 cm

The Milkbar
578-176   33.99
7-1/8 x 4-3/8" 18 x 11.4 cm

"EDELMANN" ANTIQUE SHOP

Here's a structure that's as collectible as the antiques it sells! This 3-story town house with antique shop is detailed with a bay window in the rear, large wooden doors and ornate window trim. Fencing for the back of the building is also included.

578-186   38.99
7-1/2 x 3-3/16" 19 x 8.6 cm

"RENNER" DRIVING SCHOOL

You'll want to steer clear of this building when driving school is in session! Ideal for a city street corner on your layout, the brick building includes a first floor driving school, rooftop porch, bay windows and an attached outbuilding in the rear.

578-183   42.99
7 x 4-7/8" 18 x 12.5 cm

LIMITED QUANTITIES AVAILABLE

"CHEZ RENE" BISTRO

Enjoy outdoor dining at its finest at the "Chez Rene" Bistro! Featuring a bistro on the first floor and townhouses on the second and third floors, the finely detailed building includes a covered garden restaurant complete with tables, chairs and sun umbrellas.

578-179   8-7/8 x 4-5/8 x 6-5/8" 22.7 x 12 x 17 cm   33.99

| POLA® | HO SCALE | Easy-to-build plastic kits have European prototypes — most can |
| Imported from Germany by WALTHERS | (1/87) EASY-TO-BUILD KITS | be Americanized with minor modifications. Parts are injection-molded, appropriately colored plastic. Instructions included. |

BUSINESSES (continued)

CAFE BUILDING with OUTDOOR TABLE

Take a break in this attractive cafe! The building is complete with an open terrace, umbrellas, tables and stools. Just add a few customers for a realistic scene!

578-577   15.99
5-3/4 x 5-1/4"
14.5 x 13.2 cm

Baden-Baden Casino
578-680
71.49
8-3/4 x 10"
22.7 x 25.6 cm

Pinball Amusements
578-193   48.49
Includes six gambling machines billard table, bar w/bar stools.
5.35 x 4.92"   13.6 x 12.5 cm

Flashing Lights for #193
578-82   40.99
Illuminates gambling machines, must be put in before 193 is assembled.
14-17V AC/DC.

Combination Shop/Home (Brick)
578-535   9.49
4-3/4 x 3-7/8"   12 x 10 cm

Real Estate Agency
578-327   23.49
3-1/2 x 2-13/16"   9 x 7 cm

1930's Gas Station
578-159   16.99
7-7/8 x 4-7/8"   20 x 12.7 cm

Modern Gas Station
578-568   13.99
6-1/4 x 5-1/2"   16 x 14 cm

Delicatessen
578-578   12.49
4-1/2 x 3-3/4"   11.5 x 9.5 cm

Mercedes Auto Showroom
578-161   43.99
8-1/2 x 5-3/16"   21.5 x 13.2 cm

Hennig Tobacco Goods
578-194   53.49
7.7 x 6.7"   19.6 x 17.1 cm

Dombrowsky Electrics
578-195   47.49
5.5 x 4.92"   13.6 x 12.5 cm

744   745

Heinz Herbs & Spices
578-744
38.99
7.4 x 4.3"
18.9 x 10.9 cm

Simon's Pub
578-745
38.99
7.4 x 3.35"
18.9 x 8.5 cm

Bay-Wa Building Materials Store
578-845
9.4 x8"   24 x 20.5 cm   41.49

POLA
Imported from Germany
by WALTHERS

HO SCALE
(1/87)
EASY-TO-BUILD
KITS

Easy-to-build plastic kits have European prototypes — most can be Americanized with minor modifications. Parts are injection-molded, appropriately colored plastic. Instructions included.

BUSINESSES (continued)

"THE SHOT TOWER" HOTEL
(Limited Edition)

The original of this model is found in the old town of Schweinfurt. It was erected between 1611 and 1614 in the form of a building with two wings and a tower. In 1818 a shot factory was set up. The Renaissance tower was converted to a shot tower where hot lead was poured through a sieve at the top of the tower. The lead cooled during the free fall inside the tower and was collected at the bottom in solid form. The tower, which was destroyed during the second World War was renovated in 1988-1990. Kit features movable doors, interior lighting, interior accessories, elaborate interior courtyard, specially painted Preiser hotel staff figures and Praline Cadillac with special painting and printing. Each model is hand numbered and includes a certificate of authenticity.

578-825   8-3/4 x 6-3/4"   22 x 17.5 cm   134.49

578-111   Pizzeria Alfredo   47.99
5-3/4 x 5"   14.5 x 12.5 cm
Includes interior lighting and decor.

"CHRIST'S" JEWELER'S

A three-story corner townhouse with renovated, plastered facade. On the ground floor, "Christ's" Jewelers is featured with a marble floor and interior lighting. Also included is a glass showcase with displays of jewelry; mirrors and pictures on the wall, flower arrangements, etc.

578-112   8-1/3 x 7-1/2"   21 x 19 cm   47.99

"SCHMITT'S" BAKERY

Two town houses built in the Rococo style with ornamented facade, wooden bay windows and small shops on the ground floor. The roofs of both houses join together at the rear. The resulting construction of the model with an angle of 45 degrees at the corner makes it possible to combine several models to make a circular street with a central courtyard.

578-113   7-3/4 x 6-3/4"   19.6 x 17 cm   52.49

POLA®
Imported from Germany by **WALTHERS**

| HO SCALE (1/87) EASY-TO-BUILD KITS | Easy-to-build plastic kits have European prototypes — most can be Americanized with minor modifications. Parts are injection-molded, appropriately colored plastic. Instructions included. |

BUSINESSES (continued)

JOURNAL COFFEE HOUSE

Limited edition of 2,000 models world-wide. Numbered by hand with certificate.
— coloring aged
— set of specially painted Preiser figures (wedding scene)
— wedding coach
— movable doors
— interior fittings (chairs, tables, bars, wallpaper, carpet, pictures)
— window with printed design (decorations and names)
— awnings
— variable construction for use with varying ground plans
— illumination

The high spot of your layout; a model that will delight you with its many unusual extra features:

A set of Preiser figures — wedding scene, the right coach to go with it as well as painted coffee house windows, awnings, a complete set of interior fittings consisting of tables and chairs, wall paper, even little pictures to go on the wall. The building itself is impressive with its lovely large windows on the ground floor giving a good view of the raised interior of the coffee house. The crowning feature: the side sections of the house are constructed in such a way that you can choose various angles for the corner of your row of town houses from approximately 75 to 135 degrees.

| 578-824 | 7.48 x 7.28 x 7.28″ | 19 x 18.5 cm | 134.49 |

Snack Bar
578-630   13.99
3-1/8 x 3-1/8″   7.8 x 7.8 cm

LIMITED EDITION CASTLE

Sightseers of all ages will love touring this majestic Castle! Ideal for use as a background structure for HO Scale scenes, the limited edition N Scale castle comes complete with interior lighting, working gates and a hand numbered certificate. For added detail, a specially painted Wiking tour bus and a set of Preiser tourist figures are also included.

| 578-823 | | 108.99 |
| 11-1/2 x 8-1/4″ | 29.5 x 21 cm | |

| 578-665 | Computer 2000 | 40.49 |

8-1/2 x 5-1/3″   21.6 x 13.5 cm
Details include shelves, computers, monitors, and office equipment.

| 578-664 | Towing Service | 38.99 |

7-1/3 x 4-1/2″   18.5 x 11.5 cm
Includes lorry towing vehicle.

POLA®
Imported from Germany by WALTHERS

HO SCALE (1/87) EASY-TO-BUILD KITS

Easy-to-build plastic kits have European prototypes — most can be Americanized with minor modifications. Parts are injection-molded, appropriately colored plastic. Instructions included.

INDUSTRIAL BUILDINGS

Brinkmann Warehouse
578-746   38.99
5.6 x 3.5″   14.2 x 9 cm

Lauertal Dam
578-619   41.49
15 x 8.5″   38.2 x 21.5 cm

Power Station
578-617   48.49
7.3 x 4.5″   18.5 x 12.5 cm

GALVANIZING WORKS

This factory building will be a boon to your industrial district! The brick building with tall smoke stack is detailed with a loading dock, ventilation ducts, air conditioning units, crates, barrels, pallets and lamps. To complete the scene, add Factory Hall #841 and Storage Tanks #842 (shown at left).

578-840   9-3/8 x 6-5/8″ 24 x 17 cm   49.49

578-618   **Transformer Station**   44.99
12.2 x 3.5″   31 x 9 cm

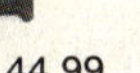

578-813 **Brick Pickle Factory** 12.49
6-1/8 x 4-3/4″   15.6 x 12 cm

578-854   **Town Gas Cylinder**   49.49
6-1/2 x 7-3/4″   16.3 x 17 cm

578-841   **Factory Hall**   14.99
4-1/2 x 3-7/8″   11.5 x 10 cm

578-842 **Storage Tanks** pkg(2) 12.99
3-3/4 x 2″   9.5 x 5.5 cm

OLD STYLE BREWERY

This detailed factory can be used for just about any sort of manufacturing! Its medium size fits almost any layout, without overwhelming the scene! Extra details include a large square smokestack and a covered loading platform.

578-806   13 x 5-3/4″   33 x 14.5 cm   26.99

Schenker Truck Depot
578-816 7-1/4 x 4-1/2″   18.5 x 11.5 cm 13.49
Send local deliveries safely on their way from this busy truck terminal. Doors can be raised so trucks can be parked inside.

POLA
Imported from Germany by **WALTHERS**

HO SCALE
(1/87)
EASY-TO-BUILD
KITS

Easy-to-build plastic kits have European prototypes — most can be Americanized with minor modifications. Parts are injection-molded, appropriately colored plastic. Instructions included.

INDUSTRIAL BUILDINGS (continued)

"BAYWA" AGRICULTURAL MACHINERY WORKSHOP
Includes bike stands, scrap, diesel tank and fencing.

578-846   44.49
4-1/3 x 4-1/3"
11 x 11 cm

578-855   Chimney   22.49
2-1/2 x 1-3/4" 6.5 x 4.5 cm   32 cm high.

BRIDGES

Small Bridge
w/Shed &
Trees
578-2019   7.99

Steel Arched
578-620   12.49
14" 36 cm
Kit builds into a detailed single track bridge, can be used in steam or diesel era.

GIRDER BRIDGE
This small bridge is typical of all-steel bridges constructed by many railroads. Kibashers will find the design ideal for a custom bridge!

578-622   7" 18 cm   6.49

CANAL BRIDGE
The original of this beautifully detailed draw-bridge can be found at one of the numerous Canals in the Netherlands. Moving parts of the kit allow setting up very realistic scenes, e.g. as if the bridge was half way up. A set of two kits of this model span larger waterways and rivers.

578-614   5 x 2" 13 x 5.6 cm   26.49

578-621   Railway/Roadway   28.49
13 x 8-5/8" 33.5 x 22.5 cm

HO SCALE 1/87 CRAFT TRAIN KITS

Based on historic railroad structures, these craftsman kits feature detailed castings molded in polyurethane. Kits also include Grandt Line windows and doors, strip styrene, and plastic and cast-metal detail parts (as noted).

INDUSTRIAL

Hermanson Woolen Mill
619-2003   130.00
13 x 8″   33 x 20 cm
Quarried stone mill includes clock tower, wood loading dock, canal retaining wall, Mack truck, cast-metal palettes, barrels, and more.

Buzzard's Bay Tower
619-2000   40.00
3 x 4″   7.6 x 10.2 cm
Simulated concrete structure with Central Valley injection-molded plastic railings and steps, and cast-metal details.

619-2015 J&J Tool Company 120.00
Simulated cut stone and brick construction, suitable for many uses and time periods.

STATIONS

619-2016   Brookfield Station   60.00

(not illustrated)
Palm Springs Station
619-2018   70.00   **NEW**

Owl Creek Station
619-2017
90.00

With a clear signal and long string of empties, the engineer of this L&N freight wastes no time accelerating out of Springfield, Tennessee. Those hard-working SD40's were rebuilt from Athearn locos and repowered with A-Line Can motors. Several Rix Maxwell Avenue homes occupy the neighborhood beyond the tracks, and the overpass is a Micro Engineering bridge. This is one of several daily trains serving Rick Rideout's L&N Henderson Subdivision, located in Evansville, Indiana. *Models and Photo by Rick Rideout*

HO SCALE (1/87) EASY-TO-BUILD KITS

These kits make it easy to build a custom business district. Each series of buildings share a common front wall, which can be painted and detailed for variety. Side walls feature different window and door locations, so the finished models can be used on right or left corners, or in the middle of a block.

Small enough to fit most layouts, the structures can also be used in various time periods by adding appropriate signs and other details (sold separately). Each easy-to-build kit features plastic parts molded in appropriate colors.

BUSINESSES

Kevin's Toy Store
699-6021   6.95
4-3/4 x 2-3/4"   11.9 x 6.9cm

Bonnie B. Boutique
699-6022   6.95
4-3/4 x 2-3/4"   11.9 x 6.9cm
Left Hand Corner Building

Hal's Hobbies
699-6023   6.95
4-3/4 x 2-3/4"   11.9 x 6.9cm
Right Hand Corner Building

Buck's Book Shop
699-6024   6.95
4-3/4 x 2-3/4"   11.9 x 6.9cm

Freytag's Furnace Co.
699-6025   6.95
4-3/4 x 2-3/4"   11.9 x 6.9cm

Tina's Tart Shop
699-6000   6.95
4 x 4-1/8"   10 x 10.3cm

Mike's Market
699-6001   6.95
4-3/4 x 2-3/4"   11.9 x 6.9cm

Tony's Gym
699-6002   6.95
4-3/4 x 2-3/4"   11.9 x 6.9cm

Jessica's Salon
699-6003   6.95
4-3/4" x 2-3/4   11.9 x 6.9cm

Madelene's Deli
699-6004   6.95
4-3/4" x 2-3/4   11.9 x 6.9cm

Dime Store & Office
699-6005   6.95
4 x 4-1/8"   10 x 10.3cm

Hardware Store
699-6006   6.95
4 x 4-1/8"   10 x 10.3cm

Cab Company
699-6007   6.95
10 x 10.3 cm

Freight Office
699-6008   6.95
4 x 4-1/8"   10 x 10.3cm

Florist's Shop
699-6016   6.95
4-1/8 x 4-1/8"   10.5 x 10.5 cm

John's Place
699-6011   6.95
2-3/4 x 5"   7 x 12.8 cm
Left Hand Corner Building

Helen's Country Kitchen
699-6012   6.95
2-3/4 x 5"   7 x 12.8 cm
Right Hand Corner Building

Family Shoe Store
699-6013   6.95
2-3/4 x 5"   7 x 12.8 cm

Old Indian Tobacco Shop
699-6014   6.95
2-3/4 x 5"   7 x 12.8 cm

Drug Store
699-6017   6.95
4-1/8 x 4-1/8"   10.5 x 10.5 cm

Parcel Delivery Service
699-6018   6.95
4-1/8 x 4-1/8"   10.5 x 10.5 cm

Cycle Repair Shop
699-6019   6.95
4-1/8 x 4-1/8"   10.5 x 10.5 cm

699-6015   **Furniture Showroom**   9.95
9-1/2 x 4-1/8"   24.2 x 10.5 cm

SMALLTOWN, U.S.A.

HO SCALE (1/87) EASY-TO-BUILD KITS

BUSINESSES (continued)

Roy's Fix-It Shop
699-6009   6.95
4-3/4 x 2-3/4" 11.9 x 6.9 cm

Sally's Antiques
699-6010   6.95
4-3/4 x 2-3/4" 11.9 x 6.9 cm

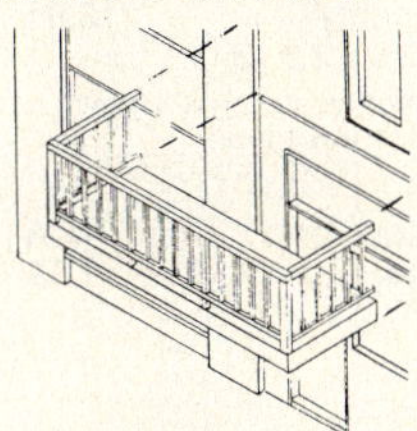

Balcony Kit
699-6
          1.25

(not illustrated)
Appliance Mart
699-6020   9.45
5-1/4 x 5"
13.4 x 12.8 cm

20' STORE FRONTS
699-1 Recessed Entry   1.25
699-2 Flush Entry   1.25
699-3 Corner   1.75

Sequoia SCALE MODELS

HO CRAFT TRAIN KITS

Kits include stripwood and metal castings.

Items listed in *blue ink* may not be available at all times. Please see your dealer for current delivery information.

STATIONS

Branch Line
Passenger Station
135-4005   4.95
1-1/2 x 2"   4 x 5 cm

YARD AND EQUIPMENT FACILITIES

56' SP Gallows
Turntable, HOn3
135-4008   29.95
7-3/4 x 2"   19.7 x 5 cm

65' SP Gallows
Turntable, HO
135-4009   29.95
9 x 2-1/2"   23 x 6.5 cm

BUSINESSES

Ron's Electrical
Supply
135-4020   36.95
4 x 4-7/8"   10.2 x 15 cm

RAILROAD AVE. MODEL WORKS LTD

HO CRAFT TRAIN KIT

Kit features color-coded stripwood, plastic and urethane parts. Grandt details.

STATION

Freight Station
613-9   24.95
7-3/8 x 3-3/8" 18.7 x 8.7 cm.
Includes one piece loading platform.
Perfect for use with any station.

YARD EQUIPMENT

Residential/Commercial
Water Tower
613-16   24.95
Model features resin castings and can be built as an open or closed tank.

BUSINESSES

Hotel   224.95
613-10
Features Grandt Line gingerbread trim, windows, doors and highly detailed resin walls.

Wickett's Mill   189.95
613-12
Includes a main building, log entrance building, dolly on rails, green chain structure and saw entrance building.

The Blue-Bird Cafe
613-1   36.95
3-3/8 x 3-1/2" 8.4 x 8.75cm
Two businesses, restaurant and shoe repair, signs, garage.

(not illustrated)
613-2   The Mill   69.95

Store for Rent
613-8   29.95
Features detailed cast resin parts. Prototype stands in Telluride, Colorado.

(not illustrated)
Branscomb Store
613-14   TBA
(By Special Order Only.)

INDUSTRIAL

Wickett's Lumber Co.
Engine House
613-15   119.95
Includes superdetailed interior walls. Consists of resin parts.

Stump City Log Camp
613-11   19.95
Includes four bunkhouses on skids, typical of structures used in many logging operations.

MISCELLANEOUS

Shake Shingle Roof
613-2001   pkg(2) 5.95
5 x 4-1/2"
Easy alternative to shingle strips. Finished in brown.

HOUSES

613-4   The House   29.95
3-1/2 x 4-1/4"   9 x 11 cm
Includes garage.

Railroad Avenue Houses
613-13   pkg(2) 44.95

(not illustrated)
613-5   The Derelict 24.95

Silverton Green Street House
613-7   29.95
Swaybacked roof, can be built with or without shed at rear of structure.

SMOKY MOUNTAIN MODEL WORKS

HO SCALE (1/87)

Capture the realistic detail found along the right-of-way with this line of authentic trackside structures. Kits feature ready-to-assemble Evergreen styrene walls and structural shapes, Grandt Line castings and complete instructions with detailed drawings, prototype history, photos and painting tips.

YARD & EQUIPMENT FACILITIES

664-8900 Prince Coal Company 29.95
1-5/8 x 4-1/2"   4.1 x 11.4 cm
1-7/8 x 10 x 1-1/2"   4.8 x 25.5 x 3.8 cm
You'll have a warm spot in your heart for this detailed kit! Typical of small town coal dealers, Prince Coal is complete with a trestle (for unloading hopper loads of coal) plus a main office building with an attached truck scale.

Trestle Extension
664-8901   14.95
1-7/8 x 10 x 1-1/2"
4.8 x 25.5 x 3.8 cm
For a larger installation, use this kit to extend the length of the trestle included in the Prince Coal Company kit (#8900).

Track Dump Ramp
with operating tailgate
664-8902   16.95
NEW
Styrene - Easy to build kit includes: Precut trestle bents, Evergreen styrene strips and sheet, Grandt Line castings, Rix products telephone pole w/crossarms, detailed instructions, photos and drawings.

664-8702 Hand Car Shed 14.95
1-5/8 x 3-1/2"   4.1 x 8.9 cm
Every section gang needs a place to store their handcars (or motorcars), tools and supplies. Whether located along the mainline, branch or in the yard, this mini-diorama kit is an attention getter! Comes complete with operating hinged doors or fixed sliding door, Tichy's handcar and pushcar and a Rix phone pole with crossarms.

Swing Gate w/Shanty
664-8703   NEW   14.95
Whether protecting a diamond, an interchange with another railroad or the entrance to an industry, this kit provides an eye-catching, operating mini-scene. Comes complete with watchman's shanty, gate, decals and a Rix phone pole. Gate swings manually but can be remotely controlled by adding a rotary motor and limit switches or pushbuttons.

664-8700 Yard Shanty 6.95
1-1/8 x 1-1/8"   2.8 x 2.8 cm
This small structure is a great way to add a crossing watchman's shanty, or a phone shanty for crews to any yard scene. Model includes Grandt Line Windows, doors, smokestack and lamp with reflector. A Rix phone pole is also included.

664-8701 Double Yard Shanty 12.95
1-1/8 x 1-1/8"   2.8 x 2.8 cm
Double the detail with this money saving kit, which includes two of #8700 for one low price!

664-8000 Branchline Water Tank   NEW   TBA
664-8001 Branchline Water Tank HOn3   NEW   TBA

ROCO
Imported from Austria by WALTHERS

HO SCALE (1/87)

Easy-to-build, precolored plastic kits.

BRIDGES

SAND FACILITY
Facilities like this provide clean, dry sand for steam and diesel locos. Includes tower, sand house and bin.
625-40105   15.49

Curved Girder
625-40081   24.49
Length 18"   45.7 cm

Straight Girder Bridge
625-40080   12.49
Length 9"   23 cm

Bridge Piers Set
625-40082   pkg(2) 9.99
1-1/2 x 5"   3.8 x 12.7 cm
3-3/4" high 9.5 cm high

Watering Spout
625-40104   7.99
3 x 3-3/4"   7.7 x 2 cm

SUGAR PINE MODELS
Manufactured by Ye Olde Huff-N-Puff

HO CRAFT TRAIN KITS
Kits feature stripwood with plastic doors, windows and detail parts, plus various roofing materials (where called for) and complete instructions.

YARD & EQUIPMENT FACILITIES

Twin Stall Engine House
685-1107   23.50
5-1/2 x 10" 14 x 25.5 cm

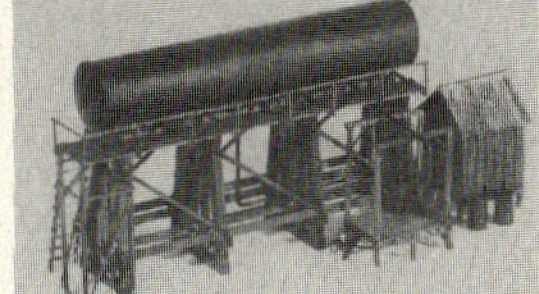

Oil Loading Facility
685-1105   18.50
2-1/2 x 7" 6.5 x 18 cm

Branch Line Water Tank
685-1112
15.50
2 x 2"
5 x 5 cm

Sandhouse
685-1114   19.50
1-1/2 x 7" 4 x 18 cm

MISCELLANEOUS

Farm Style Water Tank
685-1111   20.50
2-3/4 x 2-3/4" 7 x 7 cm

Court House
685-1102   17.50
3-3/4 x 4-1/2"
9.5 x 11.5 cm

Firehouse (Alpine Hose)
685-1103   21.50
3 x 7" 7.5 x 17.8 cm
prototype in Georgetown, Colorado

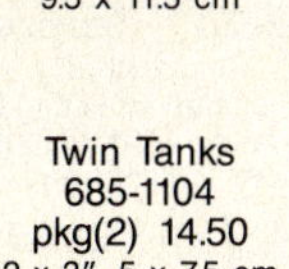

Twin Tanks
685-1104
pkg(2) 14.50
2 x 3" 5 x 7.5 cm

BUSINESSES

Sam's Supply Store
685-1100   14.50
3-3/4 x 5" 9.5 x 12.7 cm
w/loading dock

Smelter Works
685-1101   14.50
3-3/4 x 4-1/2" 9.5 x 11.5 cm
w/loading dock

BRIDGE

Covered Auto Bridge
685-1113   20.50
3 x 9-1/2" 7.5 x 24 cm

Ye Olde Huff-N-Puff

HO CRAFT TRAIN KITS
Wood kits include metal and/or plastic detail parts and instructions.

INDUSTRIAL

Ye Olde Work Shop
792-1001   15.00
3 x 4-1/2"
7.7 x 11.5 cm

STATION & YARD FACILITIES
Unpainted and unlettered kits.

792-1003   792-1004

792-1003 Caboose Way Station   17.50
792-1004 Box Car Way Station   17.50

792-1002   The Drake Oil Well   26.00
3-1/2 x 5-1/2" 8.9 x 14 cm
World's first oil well, near Titusville, Pennsylvania.

HO CRAFT TRAIN KITS
Kits include Kappler wood and Grandt Line castings.

BUSINESS

Blackhawk Blacksmith Shop
226-320   69.95
5 x 9-1/2" 12.7 x 24.2 cm
Features hydrocal wall with cast metal, plastic and wood details.

INDUSTRIAL

Beehive Coke Oven
226-260   pkg(3) 18.95
1-3/4" dia 4.5 cm dia
load ramp: 3-1/4 x 1-1/8"
8.3 x 2.9 cm
Converts coal to coke. Colorado prototype of early days of steel making.

Rundown Beehive Coke Ovens
226-264
pkg(2) 13.95
1-3/4" dia
4.5 cm dia

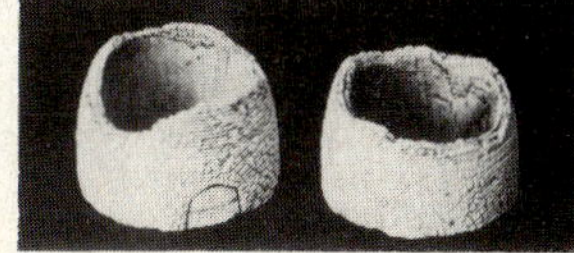

226-266   Coke Oven Ruins   14.95
Features brick-by-brick master and two different hollow castings.

(not illustrated)
226-454   Iron City Mill   **NEW** 129.95

BRIDGES

47' Hermosa Creek Bridge, HOn3
226-205   6-1/2" 16.5 cm   16.95

prototype photo

226-208   63' Howe Truss Bridge   24.95
8-5/8" 22 cm

226-215   32' Wood Trestle   16.95
4-3/8" 11.2 cm

We have worked closely with this manufacturer to provide accurate availability information at the time this catalog was published. Items listed in *blue ink* may not be available at all times. Please see your dealer for current delivery information.

HO CRAFT TRAIN KITS

Kits feature wood construction with molded plastic parts, hydrocal castings, corrugated or paper shingle roofing and complete instructions.

STATIONS

Coles Station, EBT
771-2
19.95

Three Springs Station, EBT
771-14
27.95

YARD & EQUIPMENT FACILITIES

Enclosed Water Tower, EBT
771-3   27.45
3 x 4″   7.5 x 10.2 cm
Prototype in Saltillo, Penn.

Loco & Machine Shop
771-8   27.95
6 x8 ″   15.3 x 20.5 cm

The Car Shop
771-10   29.95
6 x 10″   15.3 x 25.5 cm

Sanding Tower, EBT
771-1   21.95
2 x 6″   5 x 15.3 cm
Prototype Orbisonia, Penn.

Timber Transfer Crane, EBT
771-5   27.45
4 x 10″   10.2 x 15.3 cm
Prototype Mt Union, Penn.

Coaling Dock, EBT
771-4   32.95
4 x 12″   10.2 x 31 cm
Prototype Orbisonia, Penn.

INDUSTRIAL

Three Springs
Ore Tipple
771-6   30.75
2 x 8″   5 x 20.5 cm
Prototype stood at
Three Springs, PA

Astan Ice Company
771-12   32.95
4 x 6″   10.2 x 15.6 cm

771-7 Foundry & Pattern House   31.90
4 x 14″   10.2 x 36 cm
Modeled after the house on the EBT yard
in Orbisonia, Pennsylvania

The Boiler House
771-9   29.95
3 x 4″   7.5 x 10.2 cm

Drying Kiln
771-13   29.99

Wooster Gas Warehouse
771-11   31.95
3 x 6″   7.5 x 15.6 cm

BACKDROP STRUCTURES

Features front and small side walls for building 3-dimensional background buildings.

771-5007   Geiser Manufacturing   4.95
771-5008   Zarfo's & Burg Building   6.95

771-5009   Fox Piano Building   6.95

WILLIAMS
BROS. INC.

HO SCALE (1/87) EASY-TO-BUILD KITS

Molded from high-impact styrene.

Milk Stop Kit
782-502
20.95
6-1/4 x 4-1/2 x 2-5/8″
Features metal roofing, plastic windows, doors and milk cans.

782-500   Loading Facility   20.95
3-3/4 x 5-5/8″   9.6 x 14.2 cm
Simulated stud and beam structure. Corrugated metal covering, 5 frame windows and floor. Includes porch, steps and foundation.

782-501   Storage Tank Kit   pkg(3) 23.95
each: 2 x 4-3/4″   5.2 x 12 cm
Includes mounting bases, ladder and walkway, loading platform, pipelines, pumps and fittings. Less vehicles and figures.

(not illustrated)
782-620 Pipelines & Fittings   6.45
Includes piping, valves, els, tees, unions and pumps.

PATAL
HO SCALE (1/87) EASY-TO-BUILD KIT

■ **LIMITED QUANTITIES AVAILABLE** ■
Easy-to-build kit is molded in realistic colors, so only detail painting and weathering are needed.

CITY BUILDINGS

Police Station/
City Hall
549-3090   13.50
6-11/16 x 6-5/16″
17 x 16 cm

WOODLAND SCENICS

HO SCALE (1/87) EASY-TO-BUILD KITS

These easy-to-assemble kits contain unpainted white metal castings and complete instructions.

STATION & YARD FACILITIES

785-231 Trackside Scale 5.98

785-239 Flag Depot 9.98

Branchline Water Tower
785-241 8.98

785-222 Ticket Office 9.98

RURAL BUILDINGS

Ice House
785-219 9.98

785-213 Smokehouse 6.98

3 Outhouses & Man
785-214 6.98

Chicken Coop
785-215 6.98

Tool Shed
785-216 6.98

BUSINESSES

Doctor's Office & Shoe Repair
785-224 9.98

Daniel's Outfitters
785-220 9.98

Tucker Bros Machine Shop
785-240 9.98

Rocky's Tavern
785-238 9.98

Gas Station
785-223 9.98

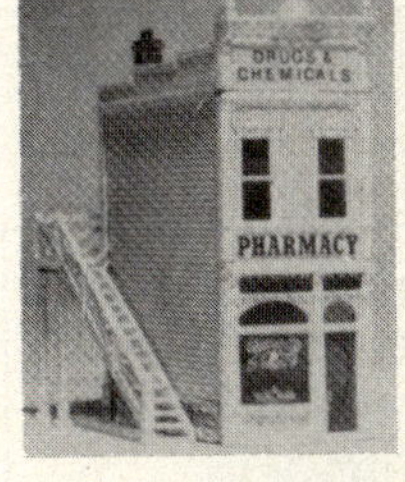

Pharmacy
785-221
9.98

Smiley's Tow Service
785-130 18.49
7 x 9"
Includes basswood building, fence, trees, grass and soil, foliage for bushes and weeds and over 60 white metal castings, including junk pile.

MISCELLANEOUS

Gazebo
785-236
6.98

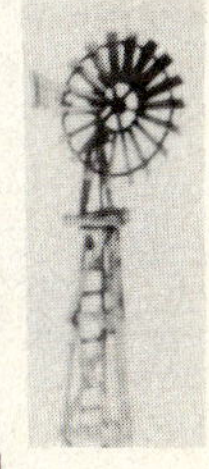

Aermotor
Windmill
785-209
5.98

WOODLAND SCENICS

HO SCALE (1/87) EASY-TO-BUILD KITS

These easy-to-assemble kits contain unpainted white metal castings and complete instructions.

TRACKSIDE SCENES

Trackside scenes contain structure kits of metal castings and turf accessories to complete landscaping up to 200 square inches.

785-151 Possum Hollow   15.98

785-152 Caboose & Sand Facility 15.98

785-153 Otis Coal Company   19.98

785-154 Tie & Plank Mill   19.98

Spectrum

(Division of Bachmann)

HO EASY-TO-BUILD
All plastic kit

HOUSE

160-88001 Catalog House   19.95

STEWART PRODUCTS

YARD & EQUIPMENT FACILITIES

Diesel Oil Storage Tank Center & Pump House
683-107   14.95
1-1/4 x 4"
3.2 x 10.2 cm

Watchman's Shanty
683-108   8.95
1-1/4 x 1-1/2"   3.2 x 3.8 cm
Includes figure & super details.

Yard Diesel Service Facility
683-211   41.95
Includes inspection pit (9" 23 cm long), crane hoist, steam cleaner, oil tank and pump shelter, flood light & talk back speaker.

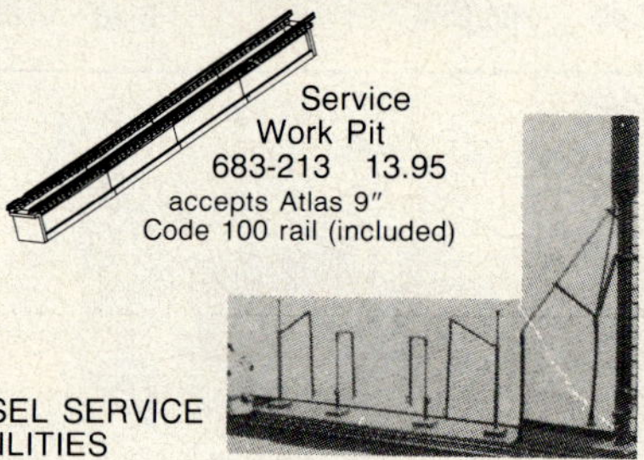

Service Work Pit
683-213   13.95
accepts Atlas 9"
Code 100 rail (included)

DIESEL SERVICE FACILITIES

683-101	Water Column	6.95
	1/2 x 3/4" 1.3 x 2 cm	
683-100	Fuel Column	6.95
	1/2 x 1-1/2" 1.3 x 3.8 cm	
683-102	Sand Tower	13.95
	3/4 x 3-1/2" 2 x 9 cm	
683-103	Sand, Fuel & Water Column	19.95

(not illustrated)

683-215	Oil Pump and Shelter	9.95
683-218	Diesel Oil Storage Tank	9.95

HOUSES

3-Bedroom House Under Construction
683-602   23.95
6-1/8 x 3-1/2" 15.6 x 9 cm

2-Car Garage Under Construction
683-603   11.95
3-1/2 x 3-1/2"   9 x 9 cm

MISCELLANEOUS
CAR WASHERS

683-104	2 Brush	12.95
	1 x 1-1/2" 2.5 x 3.9 cm	
683-105	4 Brush	17.95
	1 x 2-1/2" 2.5 x 6.4 cm	
683-106	6 Brush	22.95
	1 x 3-1/2" 2.5 x 9 cm	
	swing arms are movable	

105

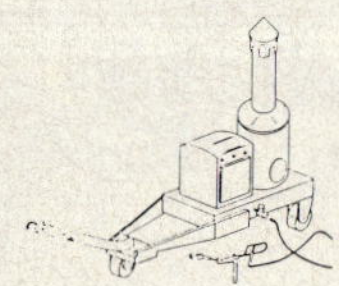

Portable Steam Cleaner
683-212   6.95

HO CRAFT TRAIN KITS

All metal kits consist of die cast, stamped and formed parts, wire tubing, etc. where applicable. Complete instructions included.

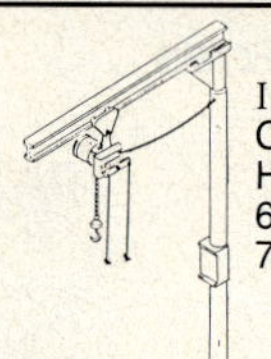

I Beam Crane Hoist
683-214
7.95

(not illustrated)
Building Under Construction
683-601   26.95

LYTLER AND LYTLER

HO SCALE (1/87) CRAFT TRAIN KITS

Kits feature molded plastic siding and soft metal detail castings.

DD Badger Ironfront
435-7704   43.98
11-1/4 x 3-7/16"
28.6 x 8.6 cm
All metal. Facade only.

Chicago Saloon
435-7703   20.98
7-1/4 x 3-3/8 x 4-5/8"
18.4 x 8.5 x 11.75 cm

RAINTREE PRODUCTS INTERNATIONAL, INC.

HOn³ SCALE (1/87)

TRESTLE BENTS
Fully assembled, stained and ready to install. All-wood construction. N Scale kits. Easily adaptable to HOn³

DOUBLE TRACK

102   103

705-101	79' High	4.98
705-102	61' High	4.49
705-103	40' High	3.98
705-104	20' High	3.49

SINGLE TRACK

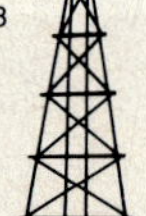

108   105

705-105	11' High	pkg(2) 2.98
705-106	22' High	pkg(2) 3.49
705-107	31' High	pkg(2) 3.98
705-108	45' High	pkg(2) 4.49

HO SCALE (1/87)
Hand-painted plastic figures in lifelike poses.

RR PERSONNEL

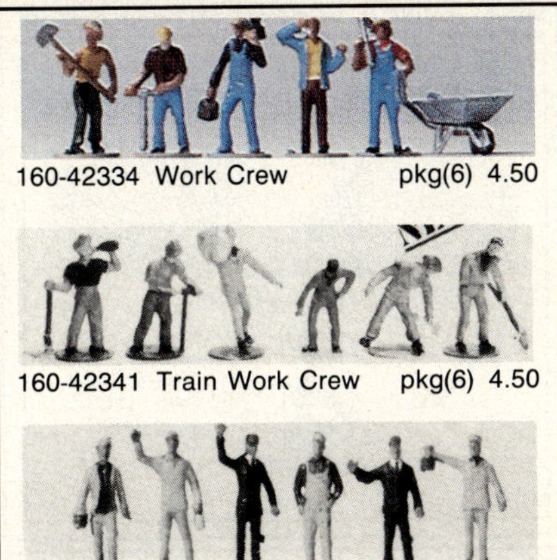

160-42334 Work Crew   pkg(6) 4.50

160-42341 Train Work Crew   pkg(6) 4.50

160-42333 Train Crew   pkg(6) 4.50

PASSENGERS

160-42342 Sitting   pkg(6) 4.50
           Passengers

160-42330 Waiting   pkg(6) 4.50
           Passengers

PEDESTRIANS

160-42339 People at   pkg(6) 4.50
           Leisure

160-42331 Sitting People   pkg(6) 4.50

160-42332 Standing People   pkg(6) 4.50

ANIMALS

Cows &
Horses
160-42201
pkg(12)   4.00

MISCELLANEOUS

160-42335 Old West People   pkg(6) 4.50

160-42209 Park Items   4.00

See also: FREIGHT CARS, TRACK, LOCOMOTIVES, PASSENGER CARS, SCENERY, VEHICLES and STRUCTURES for additional BACHMANN items.

HO SCALE (1/87)
Hand painted plastic figures & accessories.

RR PERSONNEL

490-5700 Track Laying Crew pkg(6) 3.98

490-5701 Work Crew   pkg(6) 3.98

490-5704 Train Crew   pkg(6) 3.98

          (not illustrated)
490-5709 Station Crew   pkg(6) 3.98

HO SCALE (1/87)
Hand painted plastic figures & accessories.

PASSENGERS

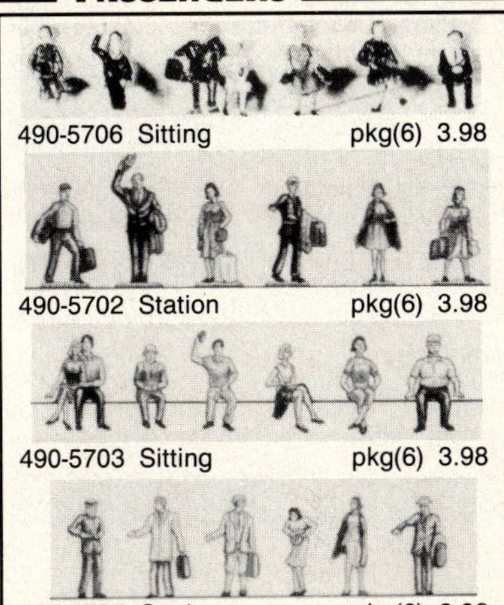

490-5706 Sitting   pkg(6) 3.98

490-5702 Station   pkg(6) 3.98

490-5703 Sitting   pkg(6) 3.98

490-5707 Station   pkg(6) 3.98

PEDESTRIANS

490-5705 Town People   pkg(6) 3.98

490-5708 Standing   pkg(6) 3.98

FIRE FIGHTERS

490-9811 Firemen & Accessories   3.98
Includes six fire fighters, two ladders, and 10 fire fighting accessories.

          (not illustrated)
490-9810 w/Accessories   1.98
          Undecorated

HUNTERS

490-5711 Hunters   pkg(6) 3.98

ACTION

490-5698 Commando   pkg(6) 3.98

490-5699 US Combat   pkg(6) 3.98
          Infantry Figures

DYNA-MODEL PRODUCTS COMPANY

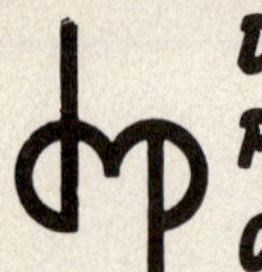

HO SCALE (1/87)
Metal cast figures are hand painted.

CATTLE

Milk Cows
260-15101 Painted   pkg(5) 7.50
260-1510 Unpainted   pkg(5) 5.50

Steers
260-15081 Painted   pkg(6) 7.95
260-1508 Unpainted   pkg(6) 5.95

Beef Cows
260-15091 Painted   pkg(5) 7.50
260-1509 Unpainted   pkg(5) 5.50

Bull & Four Calves
260-15111 Painted   7.50
260-1511 Unpainted   pkg(5) 5.50

Longhorns
260-15121 Painted   pkg(3) 5.95
260-1512 Unpainted   pkg(3) 4.50

HORSES, MULES & BURROS

Horses
260-15071 Painted   pkg(3) 6.50
260-1507 Unpainted   pkg(3) 4.50

Saddled Horses with Hitching Post
260-15011 Painted   pkg(3) 5.50
260-1501 Unpainted   pkg(3) 3.50

Burros
260-15161 Painted   pkg(4) 6.95
260-1516 Unpainted   pkg(4) 3.50

Prospector & Three Pack Burros
260-15171 Painted   pkg(3) 7.50
260-1517 Unpainted   pkg(3) 4.50

HORSES, MULES & BURROS (continued)

Mules
260-15151 Painted   pkg(3) 6.50
260-1515 Unpainted   pkg(3) 4.50

Mule Team
260-15141 Painted   pkg(2) 7.50
260-1514 Unpainted   pkg(2) 4.95

PIGS

Pigs
260-15041 Painted   pkg(4) 5.50
260-1504 Unpainted   pkg(4) 3.50

Sow & Six Piglets
260-15051 Painted   pkg(7) 5.50
260-1505 Unpainted   pkg(7) 3.50

DOGS & CATS

Dog Assortment
Includes one each: Doberman, Shepherd, Spaniel & Dachshund.
260-15001 Painted   pkg(4) 4.50
260-1500 Unpainted   pkg(4) 2.50

Dog & Six Fire Hydrants
260-15131 Painted   pkg(7) 4.50
260-1513 Unpainted   pkg(7) 2.50

Cats
260-15061 Painted   pkg(6) 4.50
260-1506 Unpainted   pkg(6) 2.50

SHEEP

260-15031 Painted   pkg(6) 5.50
260-1503 Unpainted   pkg(6) 3.50

ROOSTER & HENS

Rooster & Hens
260-15021 Painted   pkg(13) 4.50
260-1502 Unpainted   pkg(13) 2.50

Alexander scale models
HO SCALE

Unpainted metal casting.

Items listed in *blue ink* may not be available at all times. Please see your dealer for current delivery information.

MINER

120-9809 "Mike" the Miner   1.50

Prospector Pete
120-9810
2.00

ATLAS
MODEL RAILROAD CO., INC.

HO SCALE (1/87)
Unpainted plastic Figures.

FIGURES

150-793 Assorted Figures pkg(24) 2.75

ANIMALS

150-778 Cows & Horses   pkg(12) 2.75
black & brown plastic

150-779 Sheep   12 white, 1 black   2.75

ROCO
Imported from Austria
by WALTHERS

HO SCALE (1/87)

PAINTED FIGURES

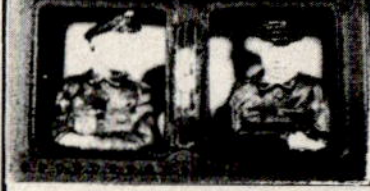

Loco Crew
Engineer & Fireman
625-40001 pkg(6) 5.99
Plastic

LIFE-LIKE®

HO SCALE (1/87)
Handpainted, plastic figures.

PEDESTRIANS

433-1123 Standing   pkg(6) 5.00

433-1128 Walking   pkg(8) 5.00

433-1119 City   pkg(7) 5.00

433-1129 Towns   pkg(8) 5.00

433-1124 Sitting   pkg(6) 5.00
includes 2 park benches

WORKERS

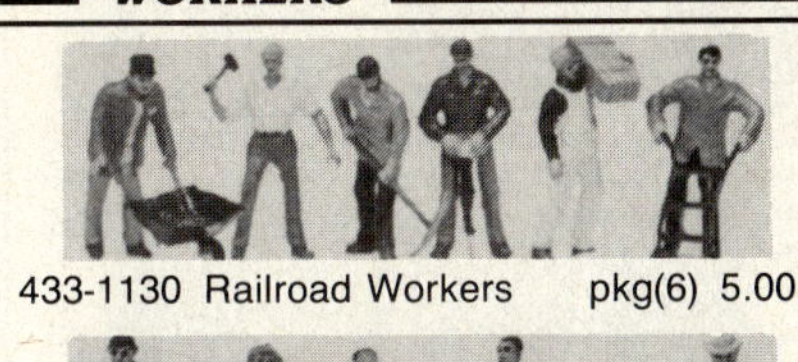

433-1130 Railroad Workers pkg(6) 5.00

433-1127 Farm People   pkg(6) 5.00

ANIMALS

433-1118 Barnyard Animals pkg(7) 5.00
w/four, 3-1/4" fence sections.

MISCELLANEOUS ▪ NEW

433-1184 Figure Assort   pkg(24) 120.00
(By Special Order Only.)

433-1194 Figure and   pkg(48) 240.00
Scenic Assortment
(By Special Order Only.)

Master Creations

HO SCALE (1/87)
Unpainted cast metal figures, (unless noted).

MEN AT WORK

Tom	Fred	Bill	Ted
464-300	464-302	464-304	464-306
ea 1.75	ea 1.75	ea 1.75	ea 1.75

John   Jim
w/movable arm   w/movable arm
464-308   ea 2.00   464-310   ea 2.00

Joe   Logan
PA Truck Driver   Kneeling
464-318   ea 1.75   464-320   ea 1.75

(not illustrated)
464-312 Valdean   1.75
464-314 Arley, Lifting   1.75
464-316 Tyrel, Walking   1.75

ANIMALS

Pigeons
464-750   pkg(6) 1.25

464-752 Chickens   pkg(4) 1.00
464-754 Skunk   each   1.00
painted, black w/white stripe

---

kibri
Imported from Germany
by WALTHERS

HO SCALE (1/87)
Pre-painted plastic figures can be converted to different poses.

ANIMALS

Wildlife
405-6620
pkg(6)   9.99

405-6630 Farmer & Wife   14.99
w/Animals

PEOPLE ASSORTMENTS

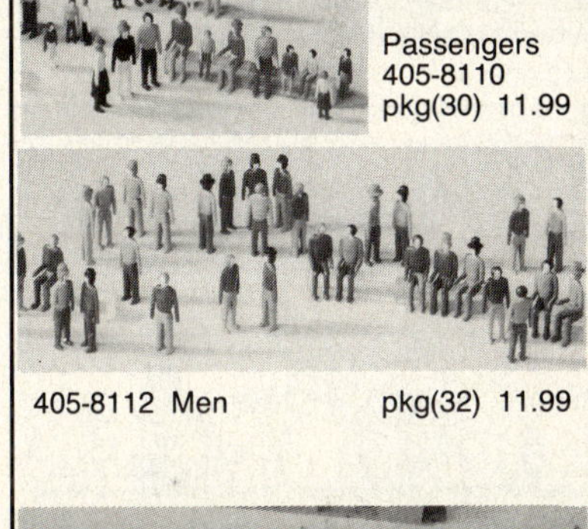

Passengers
405-8110
pkg(30)   11.99

405-8112 Men   pkg(32) 11.99

405-8114 Seated Passengers   11.99

PRECISION SCALE CO.

HO SCALE (1/87)
Figures are unpainted and cast in brass.

RR PERSONNEL

Engineer   Brakeman
585-5863 ea 2.25   585-5864 ea 2.25

585-31281 Set; one each   3.50
5863 & 5864

MERTEN

HO SCALE
(1/87)

Merten figures are hand-painted plastic.

Imported from Germany by **WALTHERS**

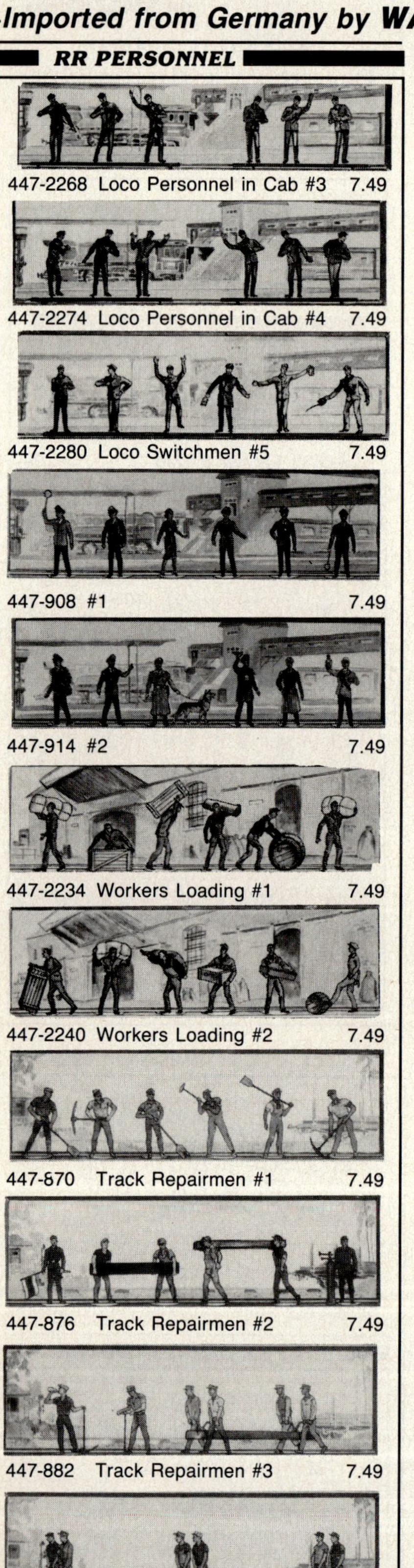

RR PERSONNEL

447-2268 Loco Personnel in Cab #3   7.49

447-2274 Loco Personnel in Cab #4   7.49

447-2280 Loco Switchmen #5   7.49

447-908 #1   7.49

447-914 #2   7.49

447-2234 Workers Loading #1   7.49

447-2240 Workers Loading #2   7.49

447-670 Track Repairmen #1   7.49

447-876 Track Repairmen #2   7.49

447-882 Track Repairmen #3   7.49

447-886 Track Repairmen #4   7.49

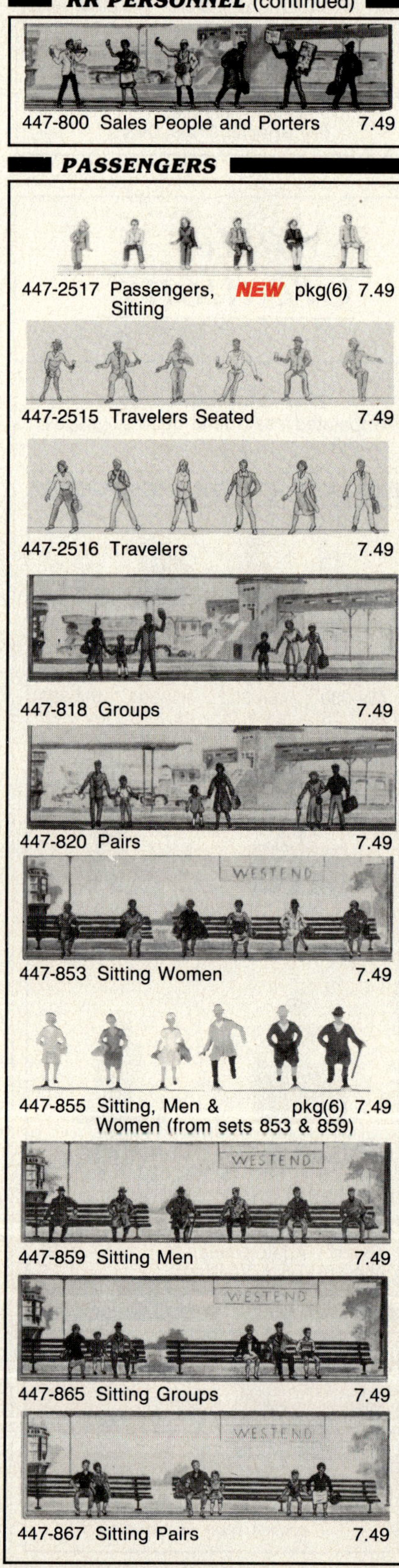

RR PERSONNEL (continued)

447-800 Sales People and Porters   7.49

PASSENGERS

447-2517 Passengers, **NEW** pkg(6) 7.49
Sitting

447-2515 Travelers Seated   7.49

447-2516 Travelers   7.49

447-818 Groups   7.49

447-820 Pairs   7.49

447-853 Sitting Women   7.49

447-855 Sitting, Men &   pkg(6) 7.49
Women (from sets 853 & 859)

447-859 Sitting Men   7.49

447-865 Sitting Groups   7.49

447-867 Sitting Pairs   7.49

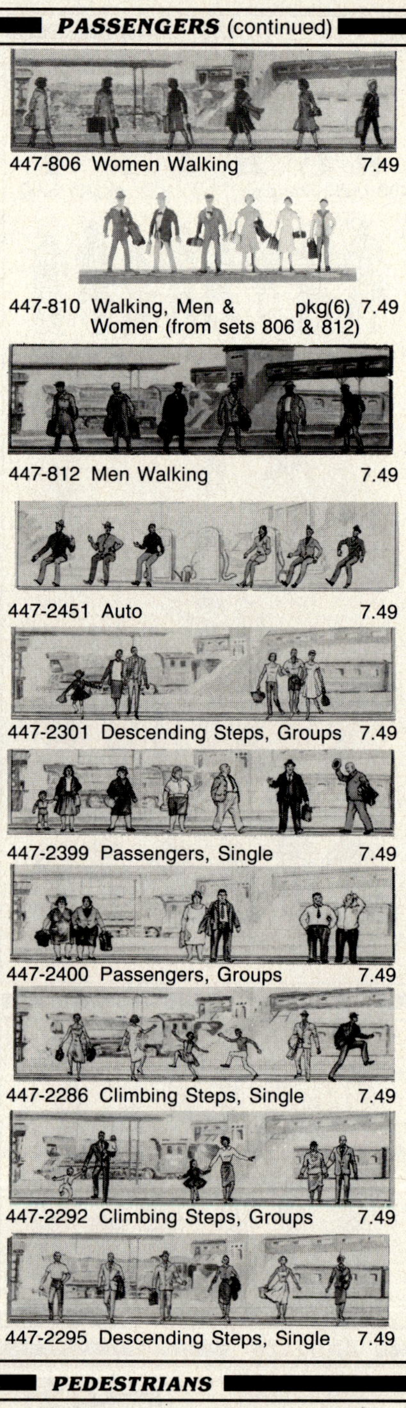

PASSENGERS (continued)

447-806 Women Walking   7.49

447-810 Walking, Men &   pkg(6) 7.49
Women (from sets 806 & 812)

447-812 Men Walking   7.49

447-2451 Auto   7.49

447-2301 Descending Steps, Groups   7.49

447-2399 Passengers, Single   7.49

447-2400 Passengers, Groups   7.49

447-2286 Climbing Steps, Single   7.49

447-2292 Climbing Steps, Groups   7.49

447-2295 Descending Steps, Single   7.49

PEDESTRIANS

447-2520 Passers-by   **NEW** pkg(6) 7.49
Throwing away recyclable
paper & glass

447-2180 #1   7.49

MERTEN

HO SCALE (1/87)

Merten figures are hand-painted plastic.

Imported from Germany by **WALTHERS**

PEDESTRIANS (cont)

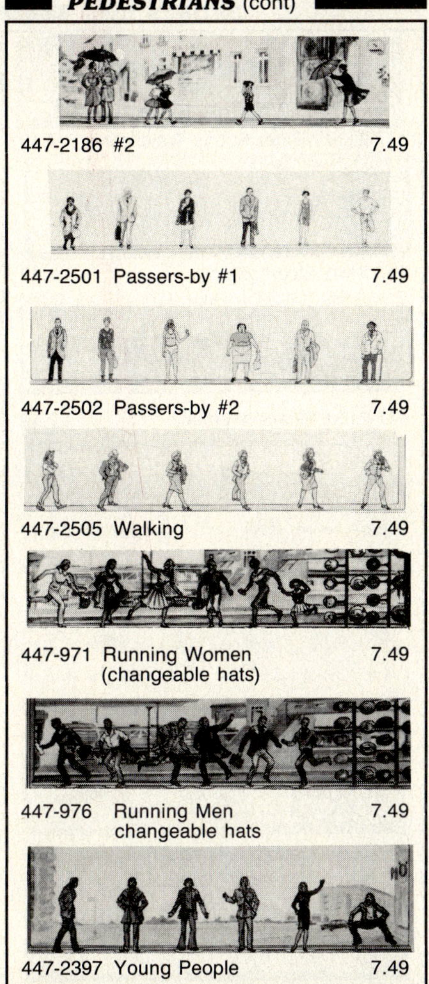

447-2186 #2 7.49

447-2501 Passers-by #1 7.49

447-2502 Passers-by #2 7.49

447-2505 Walking 7.49

447-971 Running Women (changeable hats) 7.49

447-976 Running Men changeable hats 7.49

447-2397 Young People 7.49

CHILDREN

447-2191 School Children 7.49

447-2197 Playing 7.49

447-2454 with Playground Equipment #1 7.49

447-2455 with Playground Equipment #2 7.49

PEOPLE WORKING

447-896 Farm Workers 7.49

447-902 Harvesters 7.49

447-920 Harvest Workers #1 7.49

447-926 Harvest Workers #2 7.49

447-2458 Market Stand and Vendors 7.49

447-2331 Auto Mechanics 7.49

447-2203 Ice Cream Vendor & Customers 7.49

447-2209 Organ Grinder & People 7.49

447-2258 Tradesmen 7.49

447-2264 Street Cleaners and Carts 7.49

447-2313 Street Salesmen & Shoppers 7.49

PEOPLE WORKING (cont)

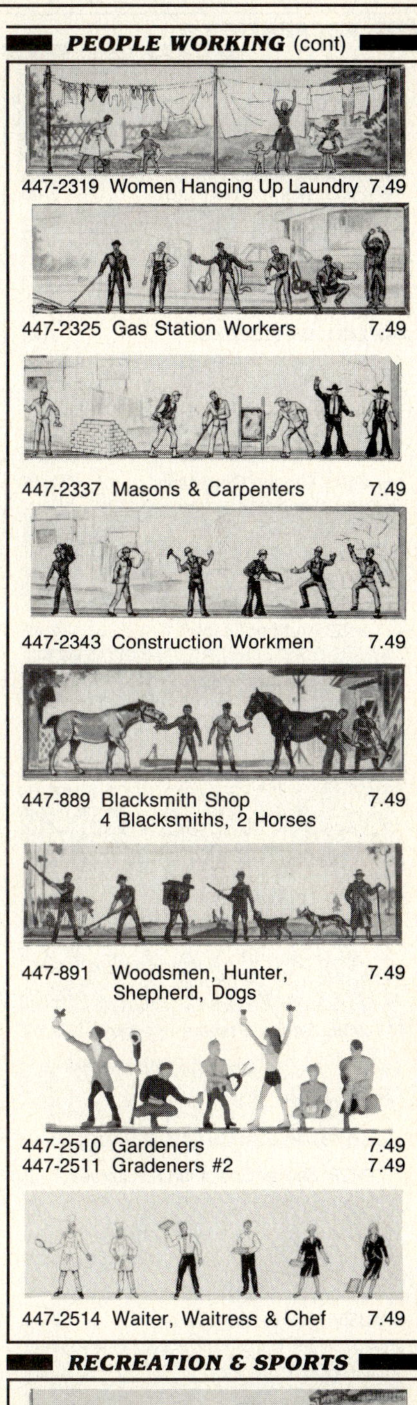

447-2319 Women Hanging Up Laundry 7.49

447-2325 Gas Station Workers 7.49

447-2337 Masons & Carpenters 7.49

447-2343 Construction Workmen 7.49

447-889 Blacksmith Shop 4 Blacksmiths, 2 Horses 7.49

447-891 Woodsmen, Hunter, Shepherd, Dogs 7.49

447-2510 Gardeners 7.49
447-2511 Gradeners #2 7.49

447-2514 Waiter, Waitress & Chef 7.49

RECREATION & SPORTS

447-2174 Musicians on the Beach 7.49

447-2349 Men Running 7.49

MERTEN

HO SCALE (1/87)

Imported from Germany by WALTHERS

Merten figures are hand-painted plastic.

We have worked closely with this manufacturer to provide accurate availability information at the time this catalog was published. Items listed in *blue ink* may not be available at all times. Please see your dealer for current delivery information.

RECREATION & SPORTS (cont)

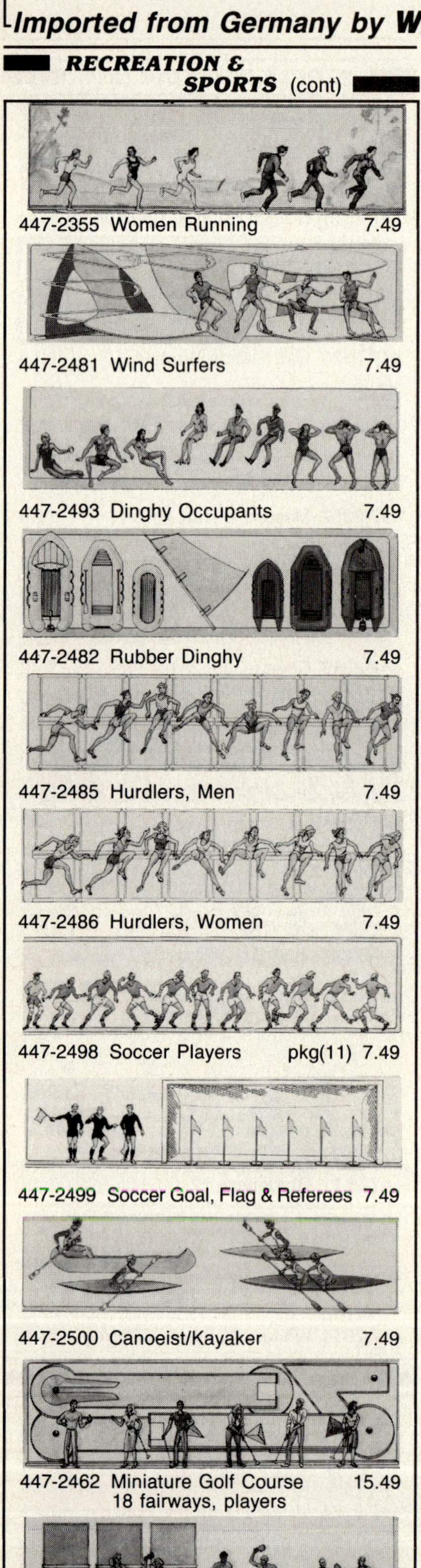

447-2355 Women Running 7.49

447-2481 Wind Surfers 7.49

447-2493 Dinghy Occupants 7.49

447-2482 Rubber Dinghy 7.49

447-2485 Hurdlers, Men 7.49

447-2486 Hurdlers, Women 7.49

447-2498 Soccer Players pkg(11) 7.49

447-2499 Soccer Goal, Flag & Referees 7.49

447-2500 Canoeist/Kayaker 7.49

447-2462 Miniature Golf Course 15.49
18 fairways, players

447-2465 Ping Pong tables & players 7.49

RECREATION & SPORTS (cont)

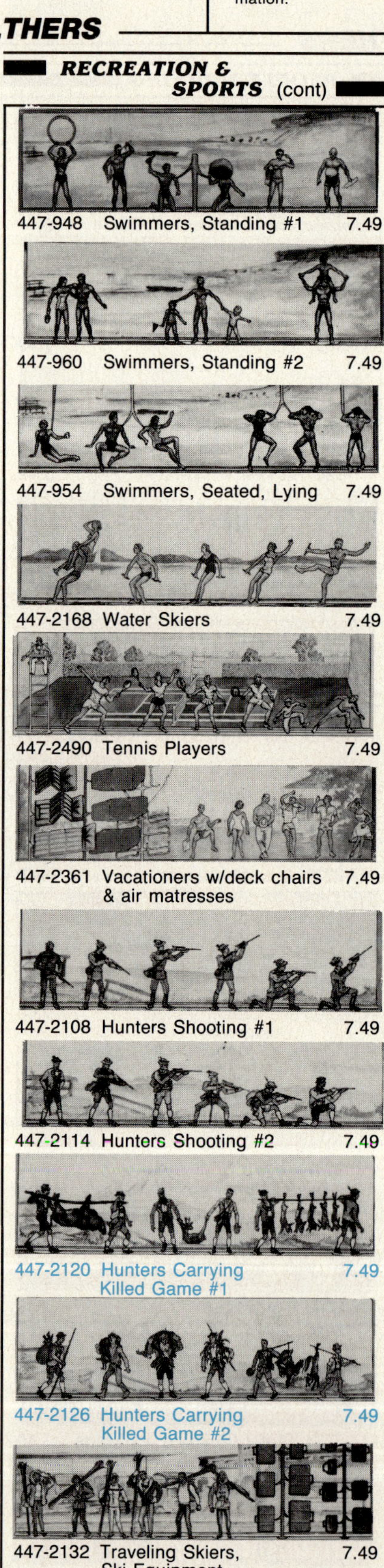

447-948 Swimmers, Standing #1 7.49

447-960 Swimmers, Standing #2 7.49

447-954 Swimmers, Seated, Lying 7.49

447-2168 Water Skiers 7.49

447-2490 Tennis Players 7.49

447-2361 Vacationers w/deck chairs 7.49
& air matresses

447-2108 Hunters Shooting #1 7.49

447-2114 Hunters Shooting #2 7.49

447-2120 Hunters Carrying 7.49
Killed Game #1

447-2126 Hunters Carrying 7.49
Killed Game #2

447-2132 Traveling Skiers, 7.49
Ski Equipment

RECREATION & SPORTS (cont)

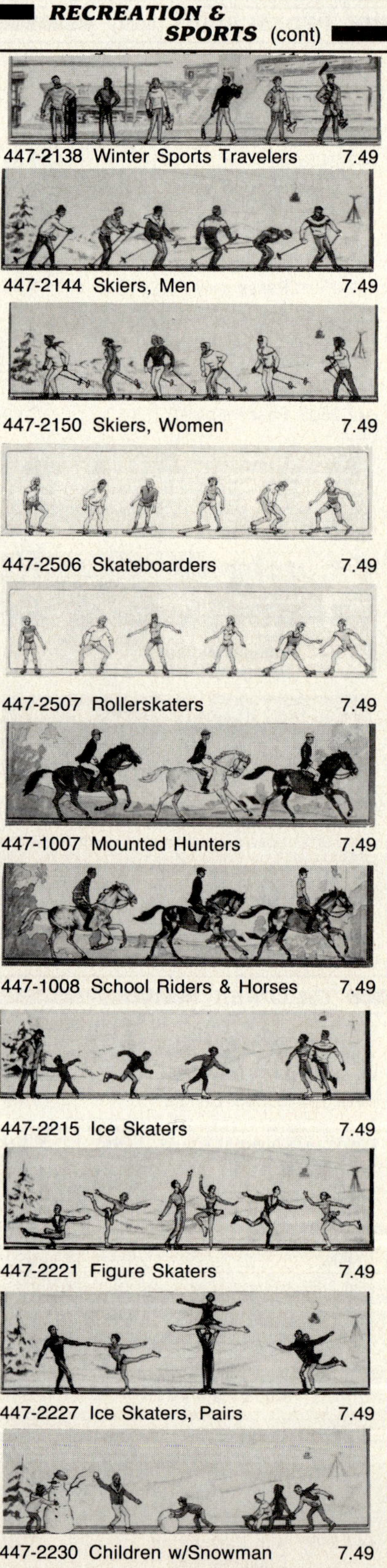

447-2138 Winter Sports Travelers 7.49

447-2144 Skiers, Men 7.49

447-2150 Skiers, Women 7.49

447-2506 Skateboarders 7.49

447-2507 Rollerskaters 7.49

447-1007 Mounted Hunters 7.49

447-1008 School Riders & Horses 7.49

447-2215 Ice Skaters 7.49

447-2221 Figure Skaters 7.49

447-2227 Ice Skaters, Pairs 7.49

447-2230 Children w/Snowman 7.49

MERTEN

HO SCALE (1/87)

Merten figures are hand-painted plastic.

Imported from Germany by **WALTHERS**

RECREATION & SPORTS (cont)

447-1006   Jockeys w/Horses   7.49

(not illustrated)

447-2512   Divers   7.49
447-2513   Divers w/Boat   7.49

POLICE & FIREFIGHTERS

447-2246   Policemen   7.49

447-2252   Traffic Policemen   7.49
(not illustrated)
447-2250   Mixed Policemen   pkg(6) 7.49
(from sets 2246 & 2252)

447-2503   Ambulance   (red)   15.49
w/Attendants
447-2504   Ambulance   (yellow)   15.49
w/Attendants

447-2371   German Fireman #1   7.49

447-2377   German Fireman #2   7.49

447-2508   German Fire Dept. #1   7.49

447-2509   German Fire Dept. #2   7.49

447-2383   USA Firemen #1   7.49

POLICE & FIREFIGHTERS (cont)

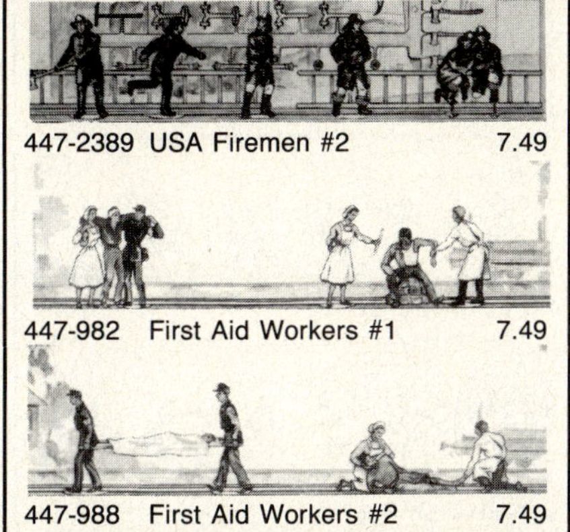

447-2389   USA Firemen #2   7.49

447-982   First Aid Workers #1   7.49

447-988   First Aid Workers #2   7.49

MILITARY

447-936   Sailors In Navy Blue #1   7.49
447-937   Sailors In White #1   7.49
447-938   Sailors In White & Blue #1   7.49

447-939   Sailors In Navy Blue #2   7.49
447-940   Sailors in White #2   7.49
447-941   Sailors in White & Blue #2   7.49

447-942   Sailors in Navy Blue #3   7.49
447-943   Sailors in White   7.49
447-944   Sailors in White & Blue #3   7.49

447-945   Sailors Waving In Navy Blue   7.49
447-946   Sailors Waving In White   7.49
447-947   Sailors Waving In White & Blue   7.49

447-1009   Military Riders   7.49

MISCELLANEOUS

447-2398   Partying People   7.49

MISCELLANEOUS (cont)

447-963   Wedding Group   7.49

447-967   Wedding Guests   7.49

447-2303   9 Elves, 1 Deer   7.49
447-1993   Merten 1993 Catalog   5.99

OLD TIME

447-2156   Oldtime People #1   7.49

447-2162   Oldtime People #2   7.49

COWBOYS & INDIANS

447-788   Indians and Cowboys, Fighting #1   7.49

447-794   Indians and Cowboys, Fighting #2   7.49

447-2441   Cowboys on Foot, Fighting #1   7.49
447-2440   Indians on Foot, Fighting   7.49

447-2448   Mounted Gauchos,   pkg(3) 7.49
Fighting, 3 Gauchos, 3 Horses,
6 Sombreros

MERTEN

HO SCALE (1/87)

Imported from Germany by **WALTHERS**

Merten figures are hand-painted plastic.

We have worked closely with this manufacturer to provide accurate availability information at the time this catalog was published. Items listed in *blue ink* may not be available at all times. Please see your dealer for current delivery information.

COWBOYS & INDIANS (cont)

447-2442 Gauchos on Foot, Fighting, #2   7.49

447-2446 Mounted Indians, Fighting 7.49
3 Indians, 3 Horses, 4 Headdresses

447-2447 Mounted Cowboys, Fighting 7.49
3 Cowboys, 3 Horses, 8 Hats

PIRATES

447-2024 Pirates #1   7.49

447-2025 Pirates #2   7.49

KNIGHTS

447-2015 on Foot #2   7.49

447-2016 on Horses #1   7.49

447-2017 on Horses #2   7.49

447-2018 on Horses #3   7.49

447-2019 on Horses #4   7.49

KNIGHTS (cont)

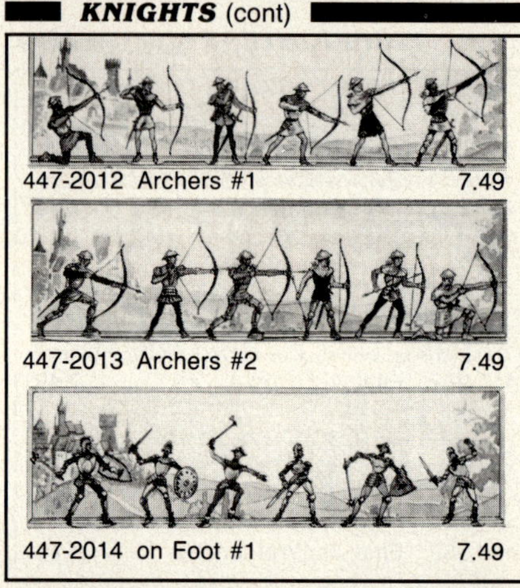

447-2012 Archers #1   7.49

447-2013 Archers #2   7.49

447-2014 on Foot #1   7.49

FARM ANIMALS SETS

447-2409 Work Horses   7.49

447-2408 Show Colts   7.49

447-2426 4 Horses w/Harness & Rider 7.49

447-1001 Cattle and Horses   9.99

447-1002 Farm Animals, Lying   9.99

447-2407 Cows   7.49

447-2403 Shepherd, Sheep   7.49

FARM ANIMALS SETS (continued)

447-1005 Pigs, Sheep & Goats   9.99

447-2406 Herdsmen, Pigs, Goats   7.49

447-724   Geese and Ducks on Land   7.49

447-736   Geese and Ducks, Swimming   7.49

447-764   Storks with Nest in Cartwheel   7.49

FARM ANIMALS INDIVIDUAL

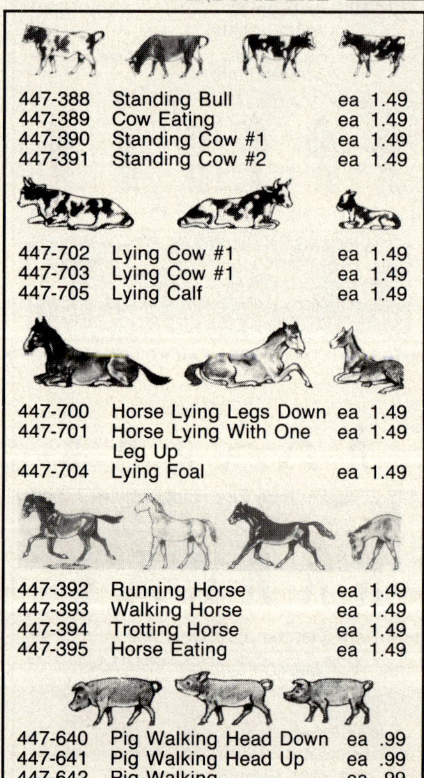

447-388	Standing Bull	ea 1.49
447-389	Cow Eating	ea 1.49
447-390	Standing Cow #1	ea 1.49
447-391	Standing Cow #2	ea 1.49
447-702	Lying Cow #1	ea 1.49
447-703	Lying Cow #1	ea 1.49
447-705	Lying Calf	ea 1.49
447-700	Horse Lying Legs Down	ea 1.49
447-701	Horse Lying With One Leg Up	ea 1.49
447-704	Lying Foal	ea 1.49
447-392	Running Horse	ea 1.49
447-393	Walking Horse	ea 1.49
447-394	Trotting Horse	ea 1.49
447-395	Horse Eating	ea 1.49
447-640	Pig Walking Head Down	ea .99
447-641	Pig Walking Head Up	ea .99
447-642	Pig Walking	ea .99

MERTEN

HO SCALE (1/87)

Merten figures are hand-painted plastic.

Imported from Germany by WALTHERS

FARM ANIMALS
INDIVIDUAL (cont)

447-707	Lying Ram	ea .99
447-649	Sheep Walking Head Up	ea .99
447-650	Sheep Walking Head Down	ea .99
447-651	Walking Sheep #1	ea .99
447-652	Walking Sheep #2	ea .99

447-706	Lying Billy Goat	ea .99
447-659	Walking Goat	ea .99
447-660	Climbing Goat	ea .99
447-661	Goat Walking Head Up	ea .99
447-662	Goat Walking Head Down	ea .99

DOGS & CATS

447-2466 Dogs & Cats 7.49

447-2467 Hunting Hounds w/Fox 7.49

FOREST ANIMALS SET

447-1003 Forest Animals 9.99

447-1004 Deer 9.99

447-2410 Red Stags 7.49

447-2411 Fallow Deer 7.49

FOREST ANIMALS
SET (cont)

447-2414 Deer, Wild Boar 7.49

447-2417 Mountain Goats 7.49

FOREST ANIMALS
INDIVIDUALS

447-715	Fighting Red Stag	ea 1.49
447-716	Leaping Red Stag	ea 1.49
447-717	Lying Red Stag	ea 1.49

447-718	Fallow Deer Stag	ea .99
447-719	Fallow Deer Doe	ea .99
447-720	Roe Deer Stag	ea .99
447-721	Roe Deer Doe	ea .99
447-722	Walking Wild Boar	ea .99
447-723	Wild Boar Head Down	ea .99

447-708	Red Doe Eating	ea .99
447-709	Walking Red Doe	ea .99
447-710	Running Red Doe	ea .99

447-711	Leaping Red Doe	ea .99
447-712	Lying Red Doe	ea .99
447-713	Walking Red Stag	ea .99
447-714	Bellowing Red Stag	ea .99

ZOO ANIMALS

447-748 African Elephant Family 7.49

447-756 African Rhinoceros Family 7.49

ZOO ANIMALS

447-760 Indian Rhinoceros Family 7.49

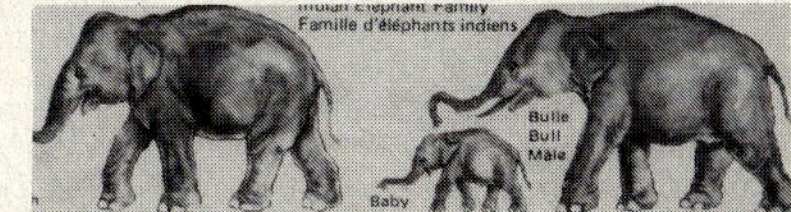

447-749	African Elephant Bull	ea 2.49
447-750	African Elephant Cow	ea 2.49
447-751	African Elephant Baby	ea .99

447-752	Indian Elephant Family	pkg(3) 7.49
447-753	Indian Elephant Cow	ea 1.99
447-754	Indian Elephant Bull	ea 1.99
447-755	Indian Elephant Baby	ea .99

WESTON
MINI-FIGURE CO.

a division of *Campbell Scale Models*

HO SCALE (1/87)
Animals are unpainted plastic.

ANIMALS

780-1404 Cattle pkg(12) 6.85

HELJAN

HO SCALE (1/87)
Hand-painted, plastic figures.

RR PERSONNEL

322-9952 RR Personnel pkg(12) 6.98
 & Townspeople, Set #1

322-9953 RR Personnel pkg(12) 6.98
 & Townspeople, Set #2

MINI METAL

HO SCALE (1/87)

Add some "model citizens" to your HO Scale layout, module or diorama with these period figures! Each is a detailed metal casting that's handpainted in realistic colors, ready to add life to your model railroad. Many sets include accessories or several figures that add extra detail to the scene.

The conductor checks his watch as a couple shares a tender goodbye. The last passengers climb aboard and departure time is fast approaching.

Strike up the band, the cadets are on parade! Led by their colorguard, the long gray lines are an inspiring sight on any main street.

PEOPLE IN THE PARK

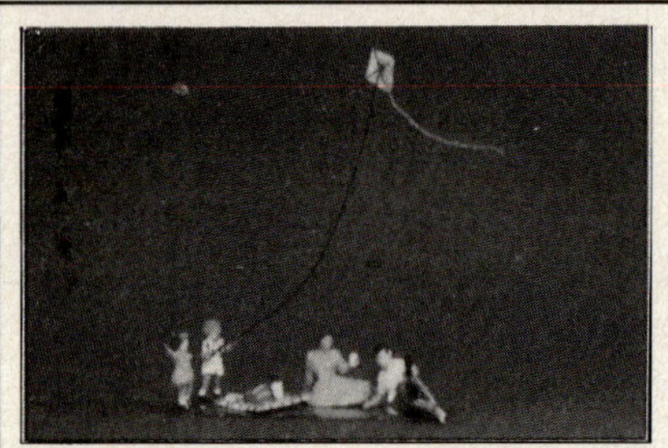

494-56 Family Picnic pkg(5) 12.25

(not illustrated)
494-65 Old Couple & Pigeons pkg(3) 11.50

POLICEMEN

18 19

494-18 1940's with Motorcycle pkg(2) 8.00
494-19 1980's with Motorcycle pkg(2) 8.00

1940's, Seated
494-36 2.25

1980's, Seated
494-37 2.25

36 37

494-58 Policeman on Beat pkg(2) 4.25
494-59 Policeman & Small Girl pkg(2) 4.25

(not illustrated)
494-96 State Trooper 3.90

TEENAGERS

494-21 At the Jukebox pkg(3) 8.00
set of two figures with jukebox
494-22 Bobbysoxers pkg(3) 5.75

494-47 Male Teenagers pkg(3) 5.75
494-48 Pinball Machine pkg(2) 8.00
and Player

(not illustrated)
494-66 Cook & 2 Waitresses pkg(3) 8.00
494-67 Soda Jerk, Cook pkg(4) 10.25
& 2 Car Hops

MISCELLANEOUS

494-63 Telegraph Operator, each 8.00
Seated
494-64 Telegraph Operator, each 8.00
Standing
494-84 Clark Gable & Press pkg(3) 8.00
494-85 Rita Hayworth & pkg(3) 8.00
Press
494-87 Humphrey Bogart & pkg(3) 8.00
Press
494-88 Betty Grable & Press pkg(3) 8.00

494-78 Hunter w/Dogs pkg(3) 3.60
494-42 Baggage Dolly pkg(2) 4.25

MILITARY

10 11

494-10 Colorguard pkg(4) 10.25
494-11 Colorguard Leader each 3.25

494-35 Military Cadets in pkg(4) 9.50
Dress Uniform

12 13

494-12 Sailors on Leave pkg(4) 8.00
494-13 Naval Officers pkg(2) 4.25

14 15 16

494-14 Soldiers on Leave pkg(4) 7.50
494-15 Army Officer pkg(2) 4.25
494-16 Marine with Girlfriend pkg(2) 4.25

SOME PEOPLE STILL THINK RAILROADS GOT LAND FOR FREE

Railroaders are frequently shocked to hear or read of some remark, especially if made by an elected representative, to the effect that America's railroads have been the beneficiaries of munificent gifts of land by the federal government and that, consequently, the railroads are under a tremendous obligation to the country.

Newspapers across the country every now and then come to the defense of the nation's railroads with an editorial which presents the railroad's side of the story. And it needs to be repeated.

The Association of American Railroads periodically distributes copies of its pamphlet titled "The Great Land Grant Myth" in an effort to set the facts straight.

It is true that, after attempts at public sale found no takers, some land was granted to a few railroads, as an inducement to the railroads to lay tracks in undeveloped country in the hope that settlers and commerce would follow.

The government deeded to the railroads alternate sections of land along the rights of way of the railroads receiving land grants, then doubled the price of the remaining sections which were sold to settlers attracted by the railroads.

But to the railroads the land was not free. The government required compensation in the form of reduced rates for government passengers, freight and mail. By the time these reduced rates were terminated on Oct.1, 1946, the repayment by the railroads amounted to $1.25 billion, nearly one thousand times the original value of the land which was set at $1.26 million.

Back in 1859, Charles Russell Lowell wrote, "It may be found that even with the most liberal construction of the grant, the government has not been so 'munificent' as sharp."

Yet, only 8 percent of the national railroad mileage was constructed with the aid of land grants; and there are still people who believe that most of America's railroads owe the public an everlasting debt for lands which they took from the public domain at no cost to themselves, many years ago.

The Association of American Railroads contends that "The United States Government has taken every reasonable precaution to guard against financial loss."

The railroads also believe this policy should be followed in all the government's dealings with other forms of transportation.

HO SCALE (1/87)

Molded in appropriately colored plastic w/painted details.

■ MILITARY

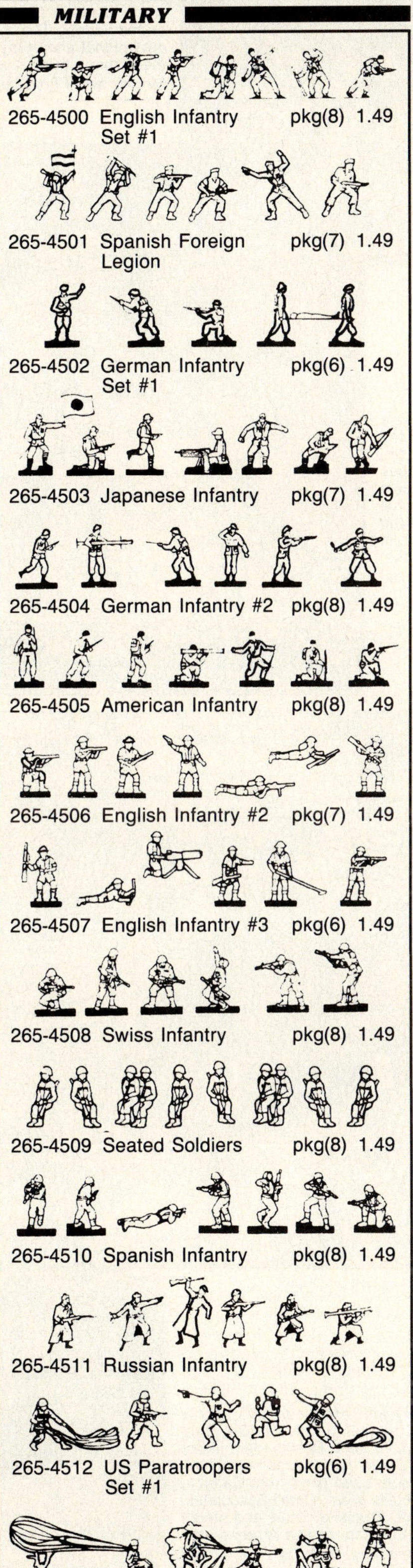

265-4500	English Infantry Set #1	pkg(8) 1.49
265-4501	Spanish Foreign Legion	pkg(7) 1.49
265-4502	German Infantry Set #1	pkg(6) 1.49
265-4503	Japanese Infantry	pkg(7) 1.49
265-4504	German Infantry #2	pkg(8) 1.49
265-4505	American Infantry	pkg(8) 1.49
265-4506	English Infantry #2	pkg(7) 1.49
265-4507	English Infantry #3	pkg(6) 1.49
265-4508	Swiss Infantry	pkg(8) 1.49
265-4509	Seated Soldiers	pkg(8) 1.49
265-4510	Spanish Infantry	pkg(8) 1.49
265-4511	Russian Infantry	pkg(8) 1.49
265-4512	US Paratroopers Set #1	pkg(6) 1.49
265-4513	US Paratroopers Set #2	pkg(4) 1.49

■ MILITARY (continued)

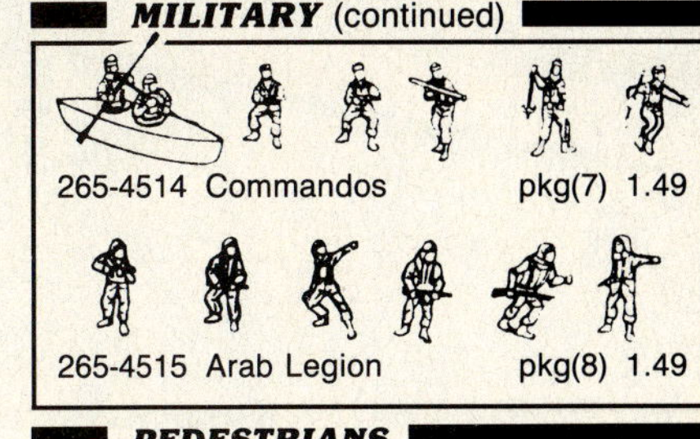

265-4514	Commandos	pkg(7) 1.49
265-4515	Arab Legion	pkg(8) 1.49

■ PEDESTRIANS

265-2201	Assorted	pkg(7) 1.99

(By Special Order Only.)

■ FIGURES w/VEHICLES

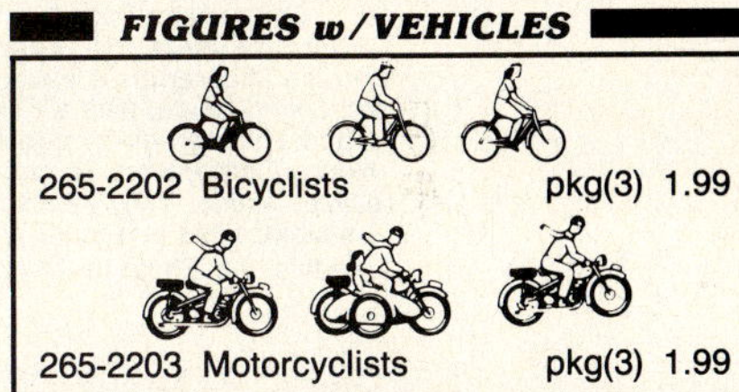

265-2202	Bicyclists	pkg(3) 1.99
265-2203	Motorcyclists	pkg(3) 1.99

HO SCALE (1/87)

Figures are molded in plastic, fully painted and include one engineer and one fireman per set.

■ ENGINEER & FIREMAN ■

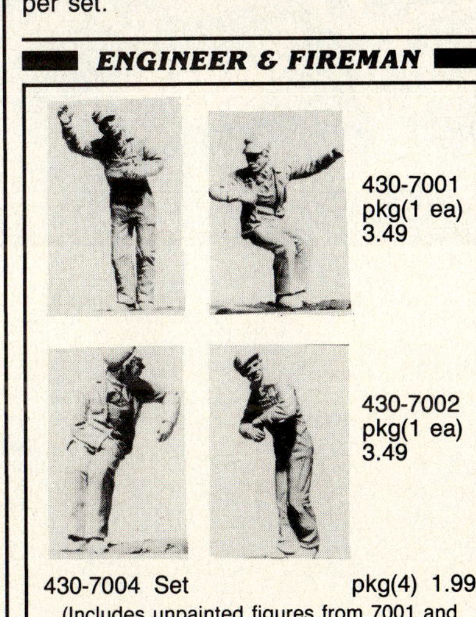

	430-7001 pkg(1 ea) 3.49
	430-7002 pkg(1 ea) 3.49
430-7004 Set	pkg(4) 1.99

(Includes unpainted figures from 7001 and 7002)

''Everybody plays, everybody wins!'' Or so they tell you, but if games aren't your style, there's still lots to do on this busy midway. Smithbridge Amusement Park is the work of Tony Dicanzio of Drexel Hill, Pennsylvania. Almost 1000 figures from Merten and Preiser populate this HO Scale attraction, many of which Tony painted himself for added variety. The numerous rides are operational and many structures, like these game booths, were scratchbuilt.
Models and Photo by Tony Dicanzio

Here's another look at the Smithbridge Amusement Park, built by Tony Dicanzio of Drexel Hill, Pennsylvania. Along the Midway are a Faller Octopus and Swing Boats, plus a Ferris wheel and Thunderbolt from International Hobby Corporation. To complete the realistic scene, Tony also scratchbuilt several rides and other attractions.
Models and Photo by Tony Dicanzio

Of course you've heard of railroad firemen, but this isn't their usual job description. The local volunteers made quick work of this smokey fire on Bob Boudreau's module. The plow is a Northeastern kit (now out of production) that was actually burned with a torch to simulate the fire damage! The pride of the Moosehead Lake Fire Department is a Jordan Ahrens Fox, with a crew of Preiser figures.
Model and Photo by Bob Boudreau

Heavy with intermodal and priority traffic for the gulf, a Katy SD40-2 roars past our photo spot. Resplendent in the ''John Deere'' paint scheme, builder Rick Groom used parts from Cannon, Details West, Detail Associates, PIA, Precision Scale and others to complete this Athearn unit.
Models and Photo by Rick Groom

N.J. International

HO SCALE (1/87)

Crowd Pleasers ™ hand-painted plastic figures.

We have worked closely with this manufacturer to provide accurate availability information at the time this catalog was published. Items listed in *blue ink* may not be available at all times. Please see your dealer for current delivery information.

RR PERSONNEL

525-6100	Standing Engineer	2.99
525-6101	Conductor	2.99
525-6102	Fireman	2.99
525-6103	Oiler	2.99

525-6104	Red Cap w/Cart	2.99
525-6105	Seated Engineer	2.99
525-6106	Walking Engineer	2.99
525-6109	Seated Engineer w/Pipe	2.99

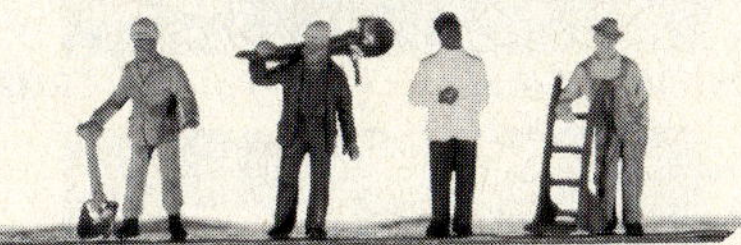

525-6115	Track Worker #1	2.99
525-6116	Track Worker #2	2.99
525-6117	Porter	2.99
525-6127	Freight Handler w/Cart	2.99

525-6118	Railroad Cop	2.99
525-6162	Track Inspector #1	2.99
525-6163	Track Worker #3	2.99

525-6164	Track Worker #4	2.99
525-6165	Track Inspector #2	2.99
525-6170	Railroad People pkg(18) (Unpainted)	4.99

PEDESTRIANS

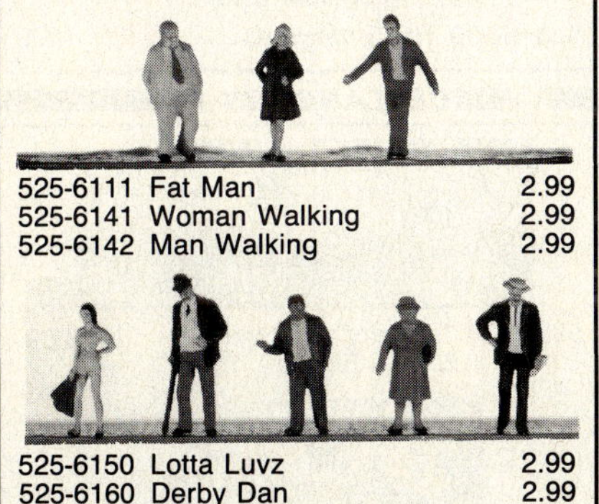

525-6111	Fat Man	2.99
525-6141	Woman Walking	2.99
525-6142	Man Walking	2.99
525-6150	Lotta Luvz	2.99
525-6160	Derby Dan	2.99
525-6154	Man Waving	2.99
525-6152	Matildi Matronly	2.99
525-6159	Smythington Ship	2.99

PEDESTRIANS (cont)

525-6113	Beer Belly	2.99
525-6156	Herb the Salesman	2.99
525-6157	Tenascious Tilley	2.99

525-6161	Fastideous Phineas	2.99
525-6119	News Boy	2.99
525-6121	Bent Ben—Old Man	2.99
525-6128	Man Reading Paper	2.99

525-6132	Dashing Dan	2.99
525-6131	Girl Hitchhiker	2.99
525-6171	Assorted People pkg(18) (Unpainted)	4.99
525-6192	Seated Couple (The Lovers)	4.79
525-6166	Teenage Girl	2.99

PASSENGERS

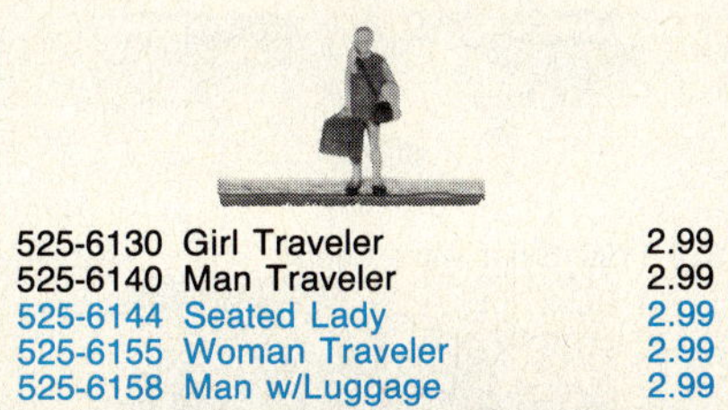

525-6130	Girl Traveler	2.99
525-6140	Man Traveler	2.99
525-6144	Seated Lady	2.99
525-6155	Woman Traveler	2.99
525-6158	Man w/Luggage	2.99

WORKERS

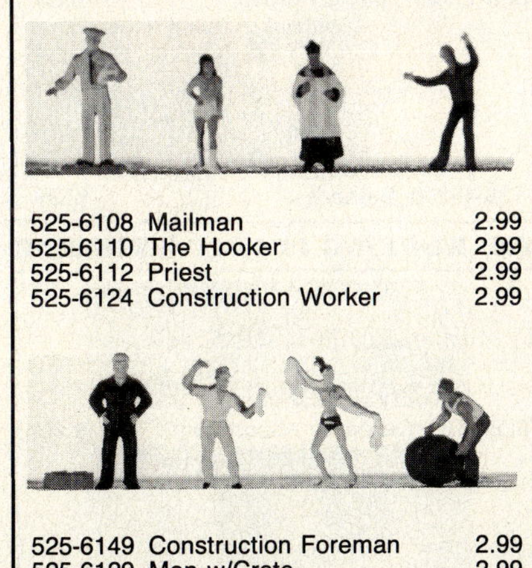

525-6108	Mailman	2.99
525-6110	The Hooker	2.99
525-6112	Priest	2.99
525-6124	Construction Worker	2.99
525-6149	Construction Foreman	2.99
525-6129	Man w/Crate	2.99
525-6125	Go-Go Dancer	2.99
525-6147	Man Rolling Barrel	2.99

WORKERS (cont)

525-6143	Millie the Maid	2.99
525-6145	Joe the Waiter	2.99
525-6146	The Ice Cream Man	2.99

POLICE & MILITARY

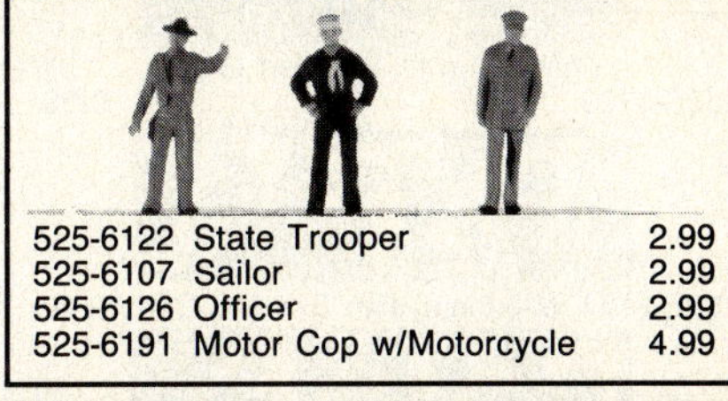

525-6122	State Trooper	2.99
525-6107	Sailor	2.99
525-6126	Officer	2.99
525-6191	Motor Cop w/Motorcycle	4.99

ANIMALS

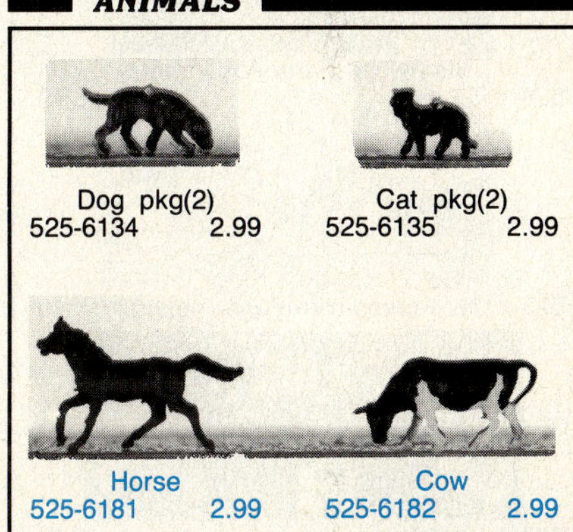

Dog pkg(2)		Cat pkg(2)	
525-6134	2.99	525-6135	2.99

Horse		Cow	
525-6181	2.99	525-6182	2.99

MISCELLANEOUS

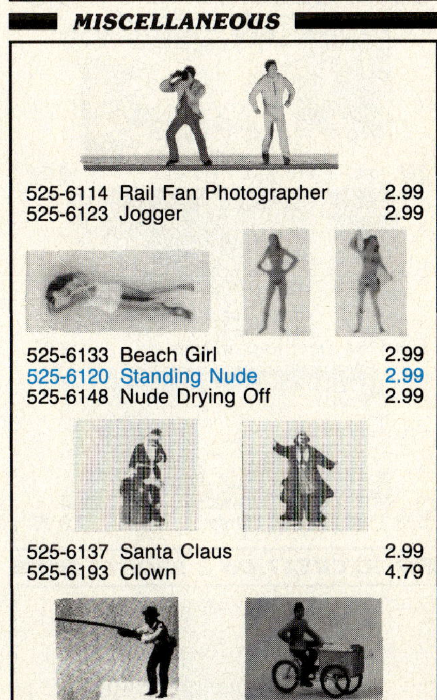

525-6114	Rail Fan Photographer	2.99
525-6123	Jogger	2.99
525-6133	Beach Girl	2.99
525-6120	Standing Nude	2.99
525-6148	Nude Drying Off	2.99
525-6137	Santa Claus	2.99
525-6193	Clown	4.79
525-6139	Gone Fishing	2.99
525-6194	Good Humor Man & Cart	4.79

NOCH
HO SCALE (1/87)

Figures are hand-painted plastic.

Imported from Germany by WALTHERS

FARMERS & ANIMALS

Herder with Sheep, Goats & Dogs
528-1177   16.49

Farmers with Stacked Grain
528-1139   9.99

528-1174   Milkmaid with Cows & Calf   16.49

Birchwood Farm Assortment
528-1180   19.49

528-1175   Horses with Fence   pkg(5)   16.49

528-1140   Geese w/Hut   9.99

528-1143   Farm yard Figures   12.99

528-1184   Deer Park w/Animals   18.99

528-1186   Farrier, Horses & Hut   18.99

RECREATION & SPORTS

528-1164   Tennis Players   pkg(6)   16.49

RECREATION & SPORTS (continued)

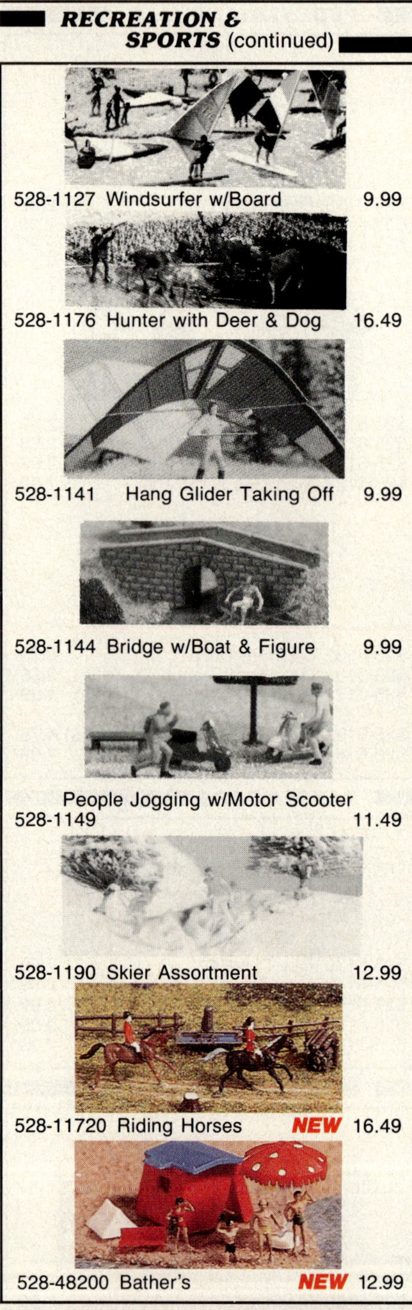

528-1127   Windsurfer w/Board   9.99

528-1176   Hunter with Deer & Dog   16.49

528-1141   Hang Glider Taking Off   9.99

528-1144   Bridge w/Boat & Figure   9.99

People Jogging w/Motor Scooter
528-1149   11.49

528-1190   Skier Assortment   12.99

528-11720   Riding Horses   **NEW**   16.49

528-48200   Bather's   **NEW**   12.99

WORKING PEOPLE

528-1133   Gardener Assortment   9.99

528-1148   Bratwurst Stand   12.99

WORKING PEOPLE (continued)

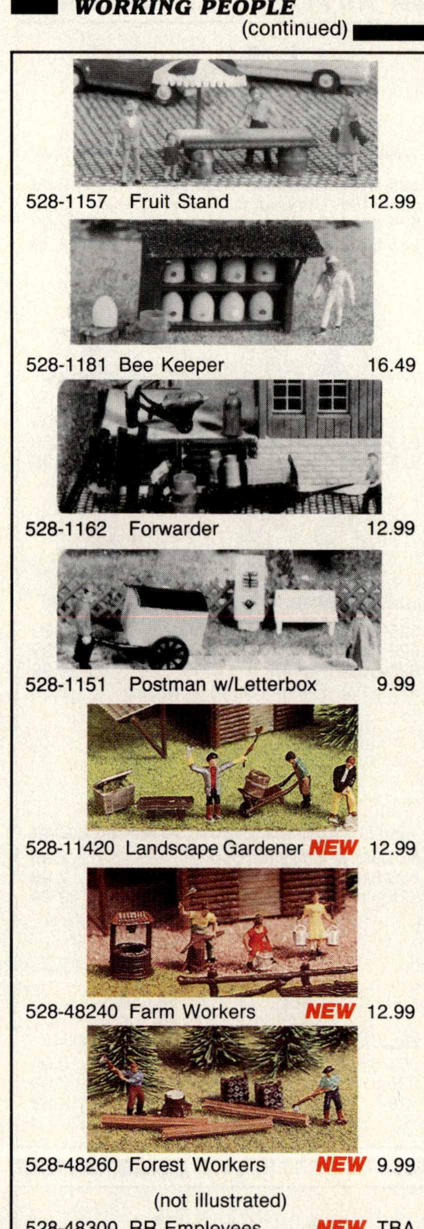

528-1157   Fruit Stand   12.99

528-1181   Bee Keeper   16.49

528-1162   Forwarder   12.99

528-1151   Postman w/Letterbox   9.99

528-11420   Landscape Gardener   **NEW**   12.99

528-48240   Farm Workers   **NEW**   12.99

528-48260   Forest Workers   **NEW**   9.99

(not illustrated)
528-48300   RR Employees   **NEW**   TBA

MISCELLANEOUS

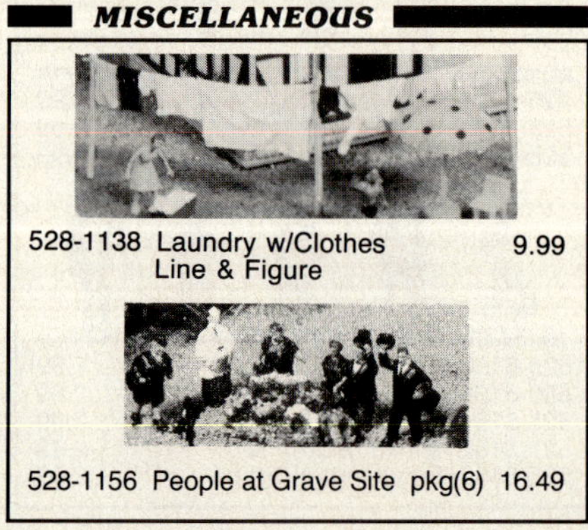

528-1138   Laundry w/Clothes Line & Figure   9.99

528-1156   People at Grave Site   pkg(6)   16.49

NOCH
Imported from Germany by WALTHERS

MISCELLANEOUS (cont)

528-1187 Lumberman w/Wagon 12.99

528-1152 Street Accident 12.99

528-1167 Wood Pile/Fowl/Maiden 12.99

528-1163 Post Office w/Cart & Figures 16.49

528-1166 Figures at RailwayStation 16.49

583-1169 Figures at Market Place 16.49

528-1160 Ice Cream Man & Children 16.49

528-11611 In the Rain **NEW** 16.49

528-11710 In Winter **NEW** 16.49

528-48250 Chasing Deer **NEW** 12.99

528-48320 Travelers **NEW** 16.49

(not illustrated)
528-11621 Construction Worker w/Hut 12.99

LYTLER AND LYTLER

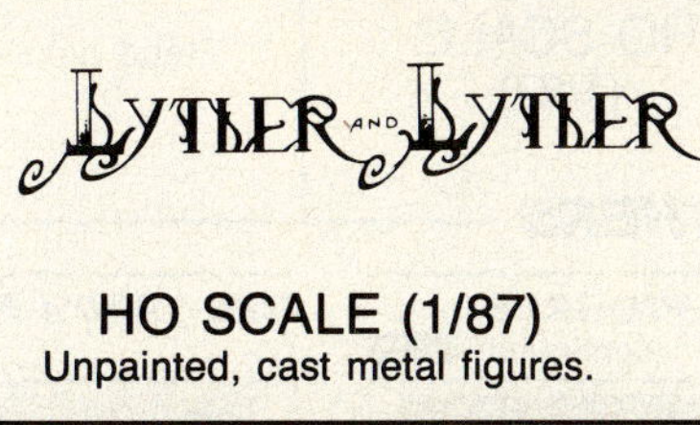

HO SCALE (1/87)
Unpainted, cast metal figures.

VICTORIAN FIGURES

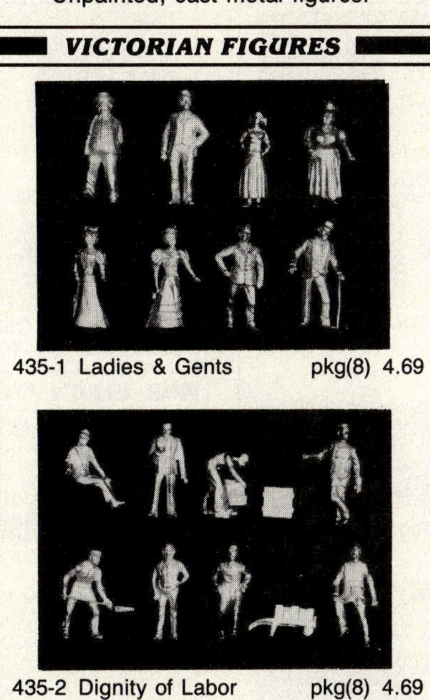

435-1 Ladies & Gents pkg(8) 4.69

435-2 Dignity of Labor pkg(8) 4.69

435-3 Larimer Street Merchants pkg(8) 4.69

Rowboat with 2 Figures
435-4 4.69
Includes two people dressed in Gay Nineties garb.

435-5 "4th of July" Set pkg(8) 4.69
Includes cigar-store Indian

435-6 Breadwinners & Losers pkg(8) 4.69

Heavy spring rains have undermined some of the pilings along the Fundy Northern right-of way. The road's ancient pile driver has been fired up and will soon be heard throughout the valley. This scratchbuilt model is the work of Bob Boudreau, and rides on a pair of Kadee Disconnect Logging Trucks. The well-trained crew are Weston and Lytler & Lytler figures.

Model and Photo by Bob Boudreau

ORIGINAL Preiser
HO SCALE (1/87)
Hand painted, lightweight plastic figures in life like poses.

Imported from Germany by **WALTHERS**

1900's FIGURES

Passers-by Wearing Winter Clothes
590-12197   11.99

590-12193 At the Grocer's 12.49

590-12199 At the Milk Truck 12.49

Standing Cyclists
590-12129   13.49

Prussian RR Personnel
590-12130   11.99

Passers-by & Police
590-12131   10.99

Family Walking
590-12132   11.99

Passengers, Men
590-12133   11.99

Bavarian RR Personnel
590-12134   11.99

1900's FIGURES
(continued)

590-12135 People Bathing 11.99

Passengers, Sitting on Coach
590-12136   11.99

People, Sitting on Platform
590-12137   11.99

Travelers & Passers-by
590-12138   11.99

590-12139 Passers-by   11.99

590-12196 Wilhelm II Era 11.99

590-12102 Firemen   10.49

590-12176 Passers-by   11.99

Passers-by Wearing Winter Clothes
590-12184   11.99

1900's FIGURES
(continued)

People at the Christmas Fair
590-12195   11.99

Postal Officials
590-12198   pkg(5) 12.49

1920's FIGURES

Walking Travelers
590-12445   10.99

Standing Passers-by
590-12446   10.99

590-12448 Passengers   10.99

Pilots & Passenger Standing
590-12408   10.49

Flight Controllers, Ground People
590-12409   10.49

1930's FIGURES

Industrialist/Guests
590-12439   10.99

Prussian Police #1
590-12440   12.49

1930's FIGURES
(continued)

Prussian Police #2
590-12441   12.49

Prussian Police #3
590-12442   12.49

Passengers & Police
590-12483   10.99

Passengers/People & Bikes
590-12484   11.99

Passengers, Men and Women
590-12443   10.49

Passengers, Sitting
590-12444   10.49

RAILROAD PERSONNEL

1989 RR Personnel
590-10236   10.49

590-14011 Station Personnel 7.99

US Personnel & Policeman
590-10018   9.99

ORIGINAL Preiser
HO SCALE (1/87)
Hand painted, lightweight plastic figures in life like poses.

Imported from Germany by **WALTHERS**

RAILROAD PERSONNEL (cont)

Italian RR Workers
590-10238   11.99

590-10031 Track Workers 9.99

Road Construction Workers
590-10030   9.99

Track Gang with Tools
590-10033   9.99

Track Workers with Ties
590-10034   9.99

Construction Crew
590-10035   10.49

Station Personnel
590-10082   10.99

French Train Crewmen
590-10086   10.49

Belgian Railway Personnel
590-10244   13.49

RAILROAD PERSONNEL (cont)

Netherlands RR Personnel
590-10213   13.49

Railway Workers
590-10245   10.49

590-10010 10 RR Workers 9.99

11 Railway Personnel
590-10011   NEW   9.99

12 Station Personnel #2
590-10012   10.49

Japanese RR Personnel
590-10019   NEW   10.49

Swiss Track Workers
590-10224   NEW   23.49

1925 RR Personnel
590-12447   10.99

RR Personnel DB
590-14012   NEW   7.99

RAILROAD PERSONNEL (cont)

Railway Yard Workers
590-14013   NEW   7.99

Steam Engine Crew
590-14014   NEW   7.99

Track Workers
590-14033   NEW   7.99

Railway Shunters
590-14105   NEW   7.99

1989 Train Personnel
590-10237   NEW   10.49

PASSENGERS

Railfans, Standing
590-10026   9.99

Seated on Benches
590-10027   10.49

590-10028 Arriving   10.49

590-10029 Departing   10.49

PASSENGERS (continued)

590-10115 Standing   10.49

590-10123 Teens, Walking 10.49

590-10124 Walking   10.49

Travelers with Luggage
590-10281   10.49

20 Passengers
590-10020   NEW   9.99

590-10114 Waiting   10.49

590-10103 Seated Diners 9.99

Railway, Seated
590-10298   NEW   9.99

Passengers
590-14020   NEW   7.99

590-14028 Arriving NEW 7.99

ORIGINAL Preiser

HO SCALE (1/87)

Hand painted, lightweight plastic figures in life like poses.

Imported from Germany by **WALTHERS**

PASSENGERS (continued)

Travelers Standing
590-14029 **NEW** 7.99

Passengers
590-14104 **NEW** 7.99

Teenage Passengers
590-14123 **NEW** 7.99

48 Seated w/Cargo
590-14400 **NEW** 41.99

24 Standing/Walking
590-14401 **NEW** 23.49

PEOPLE WORKING

Different Professions
590-10014 9.99

Harvest Workers
590-10045 12.49

590-46 Gardeners #1 8.49

Crane Operators
590-10037 9.99

PEOPLE WORKING (cont)

Truck Drivers Standing
590-10036 9.99

590-10038 Truck Drivers 9.99

Farm Workers #1
590-10040 10.49

Farm Workers #2
590-10044 10.99

590-10042 Lumberjacks 10.49

Women Hanging Laundry
590-10050 10.49

Housewives Working
590-10059 10.99

Woman w/Wash Lines
590-55 7.49

Flower Stand w/2 Customers
590-10056 11.99

PEOPLE WORKING (cont)

590-10062 TV/Movie Crew 10.99

590-10089 Photographers 10.99

Delivery Men w/Loads
590-10016 **NEW** 10.49

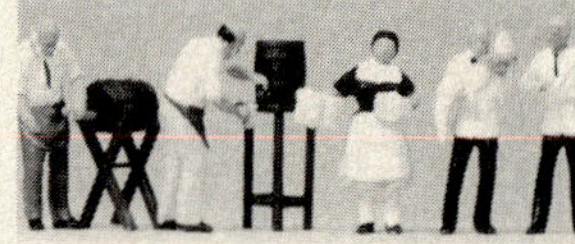

Innkeeper/Writer/Waitress
590-10210 12.49

Farm Workers
590-10295 **NEW** 12.49

Delivery Men w/Loads #2
590-14016 **NEW** 7.99

Road Workers
590-14030 **NEW** 7.99

Farm Workers
590-14040 **NEW** 7.99

Women Hanging Laundry
590-14050 **NEW** 7.99

PEOPLE WORKING (cont)

590-10105 Steeplejacks 10.49

Artists/Models/Nudes
590-10106 10.99

Doctor/Patient/Bathers
590-10108 10.99

590-10243 Craftsmen 13.49

German Postal Workers
590-10248 10.99

Cattle Traders
590-10048 12.49

Balloon Pilots
590-10253 8.99

Delivery Men
590-10255 11.99

Stock Workers
590-10294 16.49

ORIGINAL Preiser
HO SCALE (1/87)
Hand painted, lightweight plastic figures in life like poses.

Imported from Germany by WALTHERS

PEOPLE WORKING (continued)

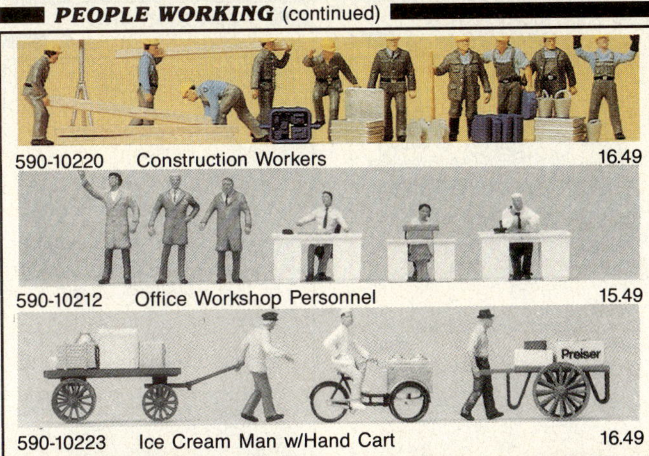

| 590-10220 | Construction Workers | 16.49 |

590-10212 Office Workshop Personnel 15.49

590-10223 Ice Cream Man w/Hand Cart 16.49

SPECTATORS

590-10025 Seated **NEW** 8.99

Spectators #1
590-10301 **NEW** 9.99

Spectators #2
590-10302 **NEW** 10.99

590-14025 Seated **NEW** 7.99

Seated Persons
590-14095 **NEW** 7.99

Seated Youths
590-10297 **NEW** 9.99

(not illustrated)
At Car Race
590-10063 **NEW** 8.99

VENDORS

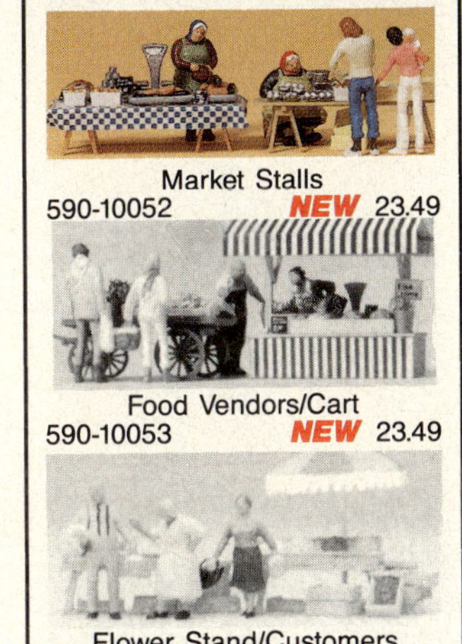

Market Stalls
590-10052 **NEW** 23.49

Food Vendors/Cart
590-10053 **NEW** 23.49

Flower Stand/Customers
590-10056 11.99

RECREATION & SPORTS

590-10315 Skaters 10.99

590-10211 On the Beach 9.99

Spectators Applauding
590-10216 10.99

590-10070 Bathers, Standing 8.99

RECREATION & SPORTS (cont)

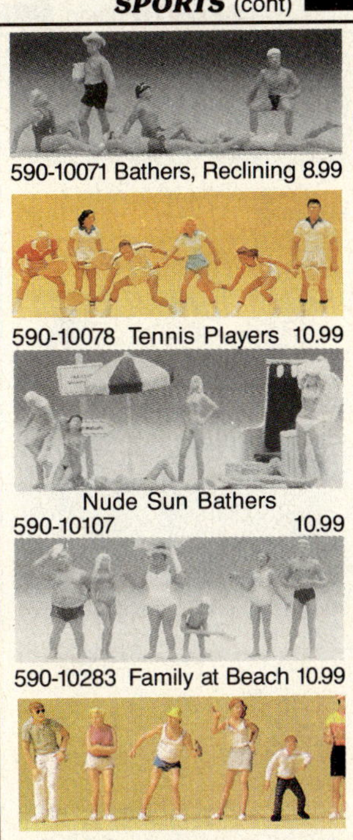

590-10071 Bathers, Reclining 8.99

590-10078 Tennis Players 10.99

Nude Sun Bathers
590-10107 10.99

590-10283 Family at Beach 10.99

590-10259 Spectators 9.99

Wanderers/Hikers
590-10290 10.49

CYCLE RACERS

Team A—Yellow
590-25000 9.99

Team B—White
590-25001 9.99

Team C—Blue
590-25002 9.99

Team D—Red, Yellow
590-25003 9.99

RECREATION & SPORTS (cont)

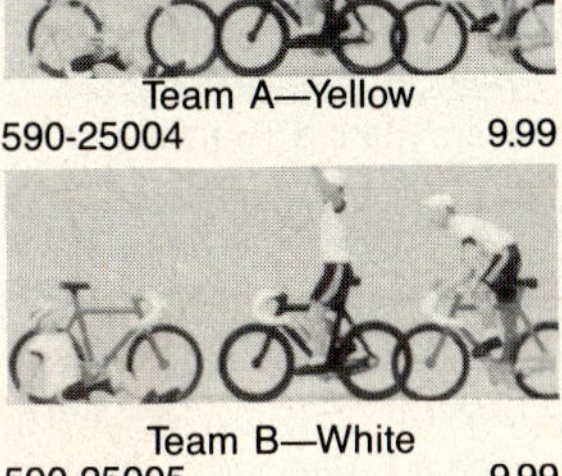

Team A—Yellow
590-25004 9.99

Team B—White
590-25005 9.99

Team C—Blue
590-25006 9.99

Team D—Red, Yellow
590-25007 9.99

Team F—Blue, Black
590-25008 9.99

Team F—Blue, Green
590-25009 9.99

590-10316 Skiers 11.99

590-10282 Family in Garden 11.99

590-10072 Family w/Boats 9.99

590-10073 Barbeque Scene 10.99

Preiser
ORIGINAL

HO SCALE (1/87)

Imported from Germany by **WALTHERS**

Hand painted, lightweight plastic figures in life like poses.

RECREATION & SPORTS (cont)

Rollerskaters & Skateboarders
590-10074   9.99

Joggers & Badminton Players
590-10076   9.99

590-10110   Boys & Girls   10.49

590-10077   Men Fishing   10.99

3 Cyclists w/BMW
590-10080   23.49

3 Cyclists with Hercules
590-10081   16.49

3 Mopeds with Riders
590-10125   16.49

590-10075   Soccer Team   pkg(12) 16.49

590-10091   Bike Riders w/Bikes   13.49

RECREATION & SPORTS (cont)

Motorbikes with Riders
590-10126   16.49

Couples Dancing
590-10120   10.49

590-10241   Folk Dancers   11.99

590-10314   Figure Skaters   10.99

Bavarian Folk Dancers
590-10240   11.99

Mountain Climbers
590-10190   10.99

590-10113   Hikers   10.99

RECREATION & SPORTS (cont)

590-10104   Cyclists—BGS 23.49

Cross Country Skiers
590-10312   10.99

Down Hill Skiers
590-10313   10.99

Spectators
590-25100   pkg(36) 41.99

Golfers
590-10231   11.99

Racing Bicycles
590-25086   kit 11.99

Motor Bikes & Rider Set
590-10128   16.49

PEDESTRIANS

Passers-by & British Policemen
590-10171   10.99

590-10180   Couples Seated 10.49

PEDESTRIANS (continued)

590-10181   School Children 10.49

590-10183   Children   10.49

590-10054   Couples Walking 9.49

Women & Children on Benches
590-10051   9.99

Drivers and Passengers
590-10090   10.49

590-10117   Standing   10.49

590-10118   Walking   10.49

Standing Japanese
590-10119   10.49

590-10096   Seated #2   10.49

590-10097   Seated #3   10.49

ORIGINAL Preiser
Imported from Germany by WALTHERS

HO SCALE (1/87)

Hand painted, lightweight plastic figures in life like poses.

PEDESTRIANS (continued)

590-10258 Girls 10.49

Family with Photographer
590-10278 10.49

590-10279 Family in City 10.49

590-10280 Alpine Family 10.49

Bus Driver & Swiss Passengers
590-12449 10.99

590-10121 Shopping 10.49

Passers-by
590-14125 7.99

Walking Passers-by
590-10116 10.49

Family Walking
590-10284 10.49

590-10095 Seated 10.49

PEDESTRIANS (continued)

590-10291 Teenagers 10.49

590-10122 Group of Girls 10.49

22 Passers-by
590-10022 **NEW** 9.99

Group of Women
590-10024 **NEW** 9.99

Young Travelers
590-10296 **NEW** 15.49

Women & Children
590-12194 **NEW** 11.99

Passers-by
590-14022 **NEW** 7.99

Seated Persons #1
590-14101 **NEW** 7.99

(not illustrated)
Farmer's Family
590-12407 **NEW** 11.99

PEDESTRIANS (continued)

Seated Persons #2
590-14103 **NEW** 7.99

590-14124 Passers-by **NEW** 7.99

24 Passers-by Standing/Walking
590-14401 **NEW** 23.49

36 Passers-by Standing/Walking
590-14402 **NEW** 33.99

POLICE & FIREFIGHTERS

Austrian Firemen
590-10230 12.49

Firemen in Protective Clothing
590-10214 10.49

Firemen Standing In Uniform
590-10217 10.49

590-10065 Bank Robbers 9.99

590-10066 Police w/Cycle 13.49

590-10101 Emergency Team 8.99

POLICE & FIREFIGHTERS (cont)

French Firemen Modern Helmet
590-10232 12.49

Firemen w/Beret
590-10229 10.49

Firemen in Action
590-10242 10.99

French Police w/Motorcycles
590-10191 13.49

590-10064 Traffic Police 10.99

Motorcycle Police
590-10175 12.49

Rescue Workers w/Boat
590-10246 16.49

Railway Police
590-10247 10.49

Swiss Police on Motorcycle
590-226 19.99

Belgian Police
590-10292 9.99

ORIGINAL Preiser

HO SCALE (1/87)

Hand painted, lightweight plastic figures in life like poses.

Imported from Germany by **WALTHERS**

POLICE & FIREFIGHTERS (cont)

Belgian Constables
590-10293   9.99

Italian Police w/Cycles
590-10174   10.99

Fireman Walking
590-10218   10.49

French Firemen
590-10233   **NEW** 12.49

Firemen #1
590-14200   **NEW** 7.99

Firemen #2
590-14201   **NEW** 7.99

Firemen #3
590-14202   **NEW** 7.99

Firemen #4
590-14203   **NEW** 7.99

Firemen #5
590-14204   **NEW** 7.99

Firemen #6
590-14205   **NEW** 7.99

POLICE & FIREFIGHTERS (cont)

Firemen #7
590-14206   **NEW** 7.99

Firemen Seated
590-14207   **NEW** 7.99

Motorcycle Police
590-25101   **NEW** 21.99

German Police
590-25107   **NEW** 16.99

French Police
590-25108   **NEW** 16.99

MILITARY

German Officers
Standing in Uniform
590-10227   10.49

German Officers w/Berets
590-10228   10.49

Group of Officials
590-10215   12.49

CHRISTMAS FAIR

Santa Claus & Visitors
590-10185   12.49

CHRISTMAS FAIR (continued)

590-10186   People   12.49

590-10189   Children   11.99

590-10187   Tree Shoppers   12.49

590-10188   Teenagers   11.99

WEDDING GROUP

590-10057   Protestant   10.49
590-10058   Catholic   10.49

590-14057   Protestant   **NEW** 7.99

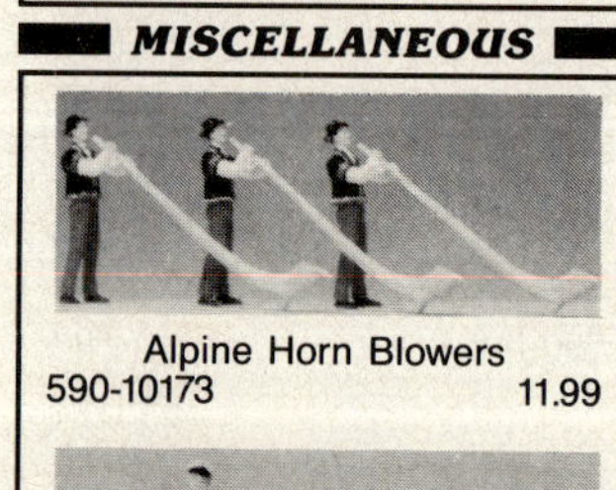

590-14058   Catholic   **NEW** 7.99

MISCELLANEOUS

Alpine Horn Blowers
590-10173   11.99

Family w/Boats
590-10072   9.99

MISCELLANEOUS (continued)

Jockeys & Horses
590-10303   **NEW** 12.49

Farmer's Market
590-10304   **NEW** 16.49

Fair Musicians
590-24653   **NEW** 16.49

Franciscan Friars
590-10198   11.99

Party Goers
590-10111   11.99

Boy Scouts
590-10260   10.99

(not illustrated)
Cowboy Riding Longhorns
590-10159   **NEW** 13.49

BANDS

Military Band
590-13262   178.99

590-10203   Bavarian #1   13.49

West Germany, Standing
590-13270   141.99

ORIGINAL Preiser

HO SCALE (1/87)

Hand painted, lightweight plastic figures in life like poses.

Imported from Germany by **WALTHERS**

BANDS (continued)

590-10112 Jazz 12.49

590-10206 Tyrolean #1 13.49

590-10202 Bavarian 13.49

590-10207 Tyrolean #2 13.49

590-10250 Bavarian Band 23.49

590-13263 Bavarian Band Set 141.99

590-13261 US Marine Band 141.99

590-13272 Navy Band 110.99

590-13273 Bundlesluftwaffe Band Limited Edition 166.99
(By Special Order Only.)

UNPAINTED FIGURE SETS (all figures may not be shown)

590-16337 Passengers & Passers-By pkg(120) 21.49

590-16339 Firemen pkg(60) 10.99

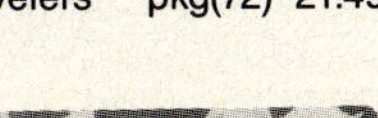

590-16334 1900's RR Personnel, Passers-by/Travelers pkg(72) 21.49

Truckers & Car Drivers
590-16335 pkg(24) 8.99

USA Figures
590-16336 pkg(45) 9.99

590-16332 Cyclists pkg(18) 8.99

590-16300 Nude Models & Artists with Room Scene pkg(18) 9.99

590-16325 Railroad Personnel & Travelers pkg(120) 21.49

590-16326 Trades People pkg(120) 21.49

590-16327 Figures & Animals pkg(120) 21.49

ORIGINAL Preiser
HO SCALE (1/87)

Imported from Germany by **WALTHERS**

Hand painted, lightweight plastic figures in life like poses.

ECONOMY SET: The 14000 series of Preiser figures is identical to other sets, but has less detailed paint schemes. Economy set is marked with a star (★).

■ UNPAINTED FIGURE SETS (continued)
(all figures may not be shown)

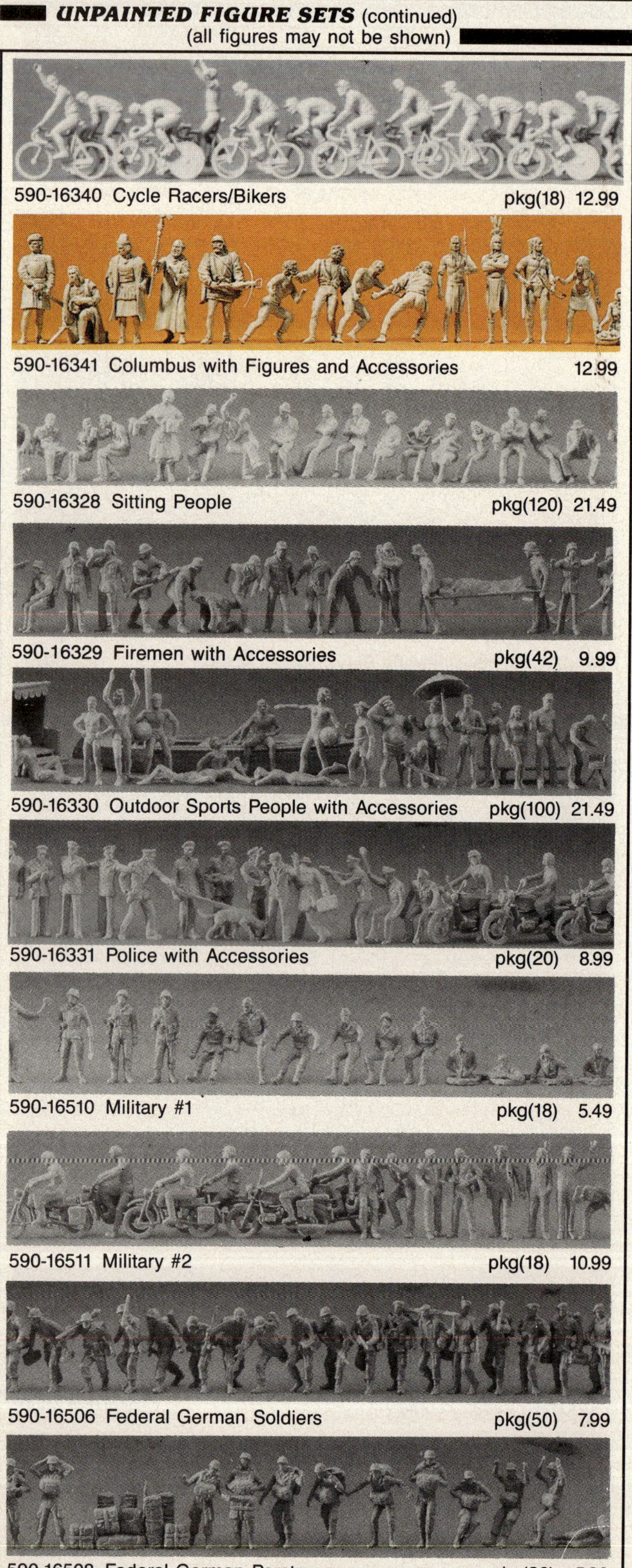

590-16340 Cycle Racers/Bikers pkg(18) 12.99

590-16341 Columbus with Figures and Accessories 12.99

590-16328 Sitting People pkg(120) 21.49

590-16329 Firemen with Accessories pkg(42) 9.99

590-16330 Outdoor Sports People with Accessories pkg(100) 21.49

590-16331 Police with Accessories pkg(20) 8.99

590-16510 Military #1 pkg(18) 5.49

590-16511 Military #2 pkg(18) 10.99

590-16506 Federal German Soldiers pkg(50) 7.99

590-16508 Federal German Paratroopers pkg(30) 5.99

■ FARM ANIMALS ■

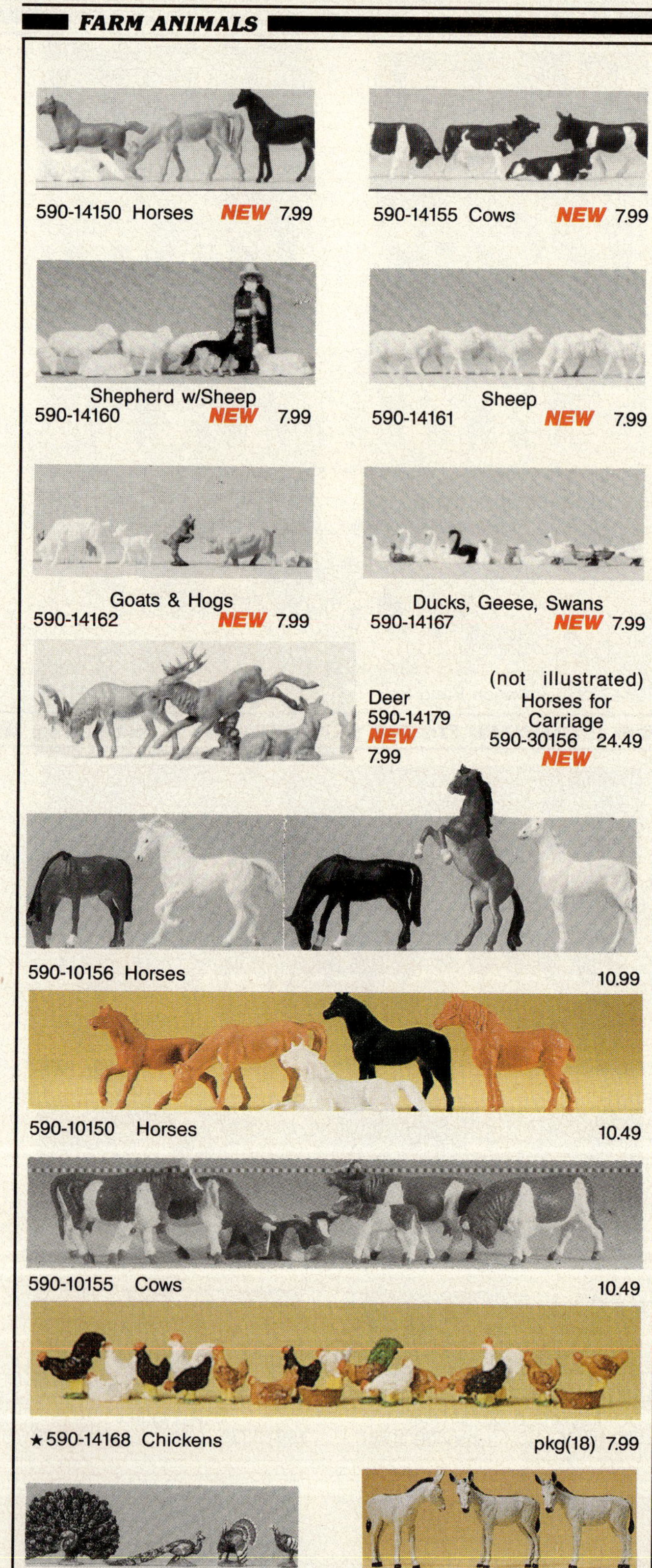

590-14150 Horses **NEW** 7.99

590-14155 Cows **NEW** 7.99

Shepherd w/Sheep 590-14160 **NEW** 7.99

Sheep 590-14161 **NEW** 7.99

Goats & Hogs 590-14162 **NEW** 7.99

Ducks, Geese, Swans 590-14167 **NEW** 7.99

Deer 590-14179 **NEW** 7.99

(not illustrated) Horses for Carriage 590-30156 24.49 **NEW**

590-10156 Horses 10.99

590-10150 Horses 10.49

590-10155 Cows 10.49

★590-14168 Chickens pkg(18) 7.99

590-10166 Turkey/Peacock 10.99

590-10151 Donkeys 8.99

ORIGINAL Preiser

HO SCALE (1/87)

Hand painted, lightweight plastic figures in life like poses.

ECONOMY SET: The 14000 series of Preiser figures is identical to other sets, but has less detailed paint schemes. Economy set is marked with a star (★).

Imported from Germany by **WALTHERS**

FOREST ANIMALS

590-10179 Stags & Does 10.49

DOGS & CATS

Dogs & Cats
★ 590-14165 pkg(12) 7.99

ZOO ANIMALS

590-20379 Lions 8.99

590-20383 Camels 11.49

590-20380 Tigers 8.99

ZOO ANIMALS
(continued)

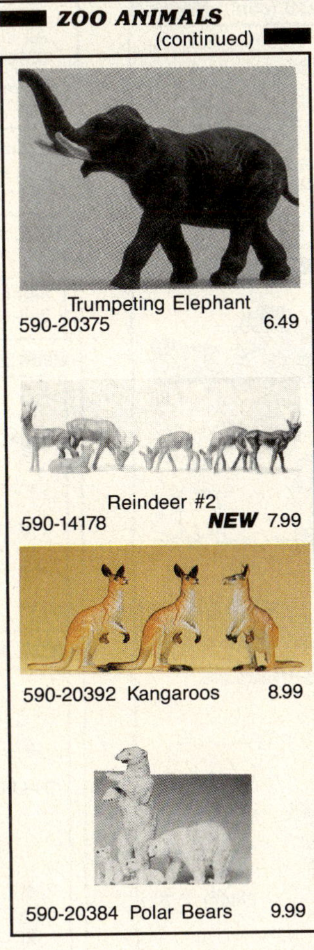

Trumpeting Elephant
590-20375 6.49

Reindeer #2
590-14178 **NEW** 7.99

590-20392 Kangaroos 8.99

590-20384 Polar Bears 9.99

ZOO ANIMALS
(continued)

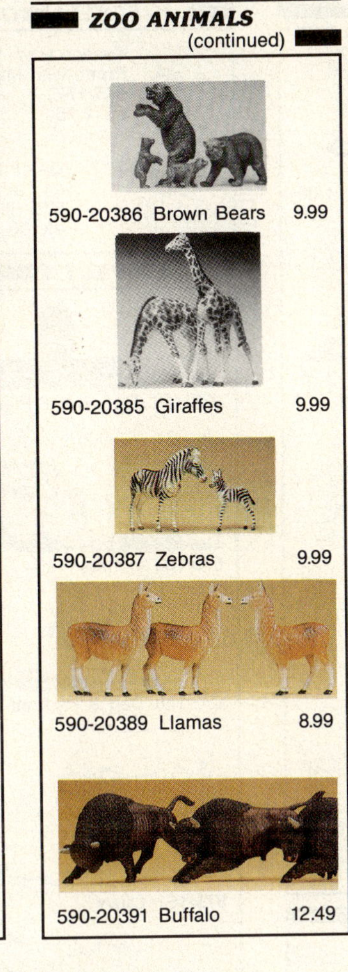

590-20386 Brown Bears 9.99

590-20385 Giraffes 9.99

590-20387 Zebras 9.99

590-20389 Llamas 8.99

590-20391 Buffalo 12.49

ZOO ANIMALS
(continued)

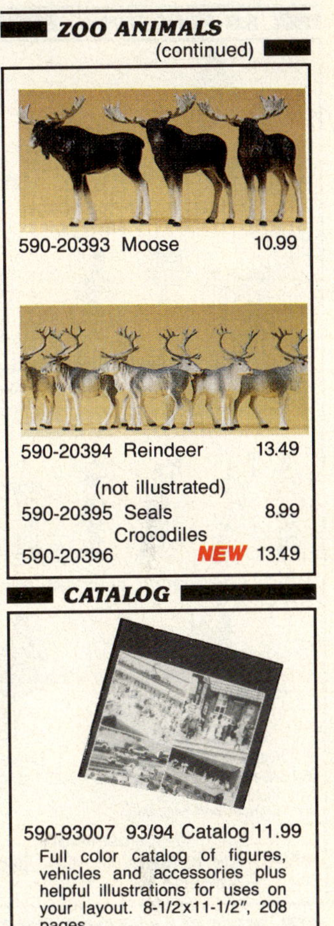

590-20393 Moose 10.99

590-20394 Reindeer 13.49

(not illustrated)
590-20395 Seals 8.99
Crocodiles
590-20396 **NEW** 13.49

CATALOG

590-93007 93/94 Catalog 11.99
Full color catalog of figures, vehicles and accessories plus helpful illustrations for uses on your layout. 8-1/2 x 11-1/2", 208 pages.

WOODLAND SCENICS

HO SCALE (1/87)
Unpainted soft-metal castings.

CATS & DOGS

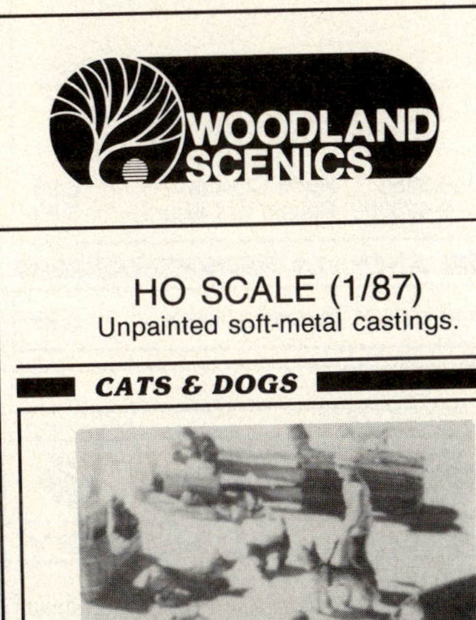

785-226 Assorted Cats & Dogs w/Man 3.98

FARMER

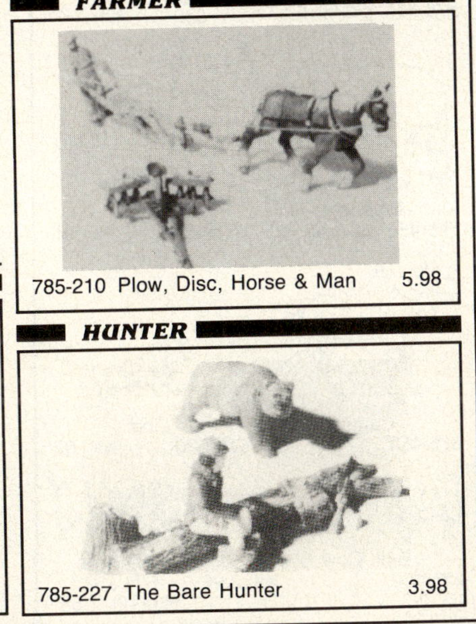

785-210 Plow, Disc, Horse & Man 5.98

HUNTER

785-227 The Bare Hunter 3.98

pia PRECISION INVESTMENT ASSOCIATES

HO SCALE (1/87)
Unpainted lost wax brass castings.

RR PERSONNEL

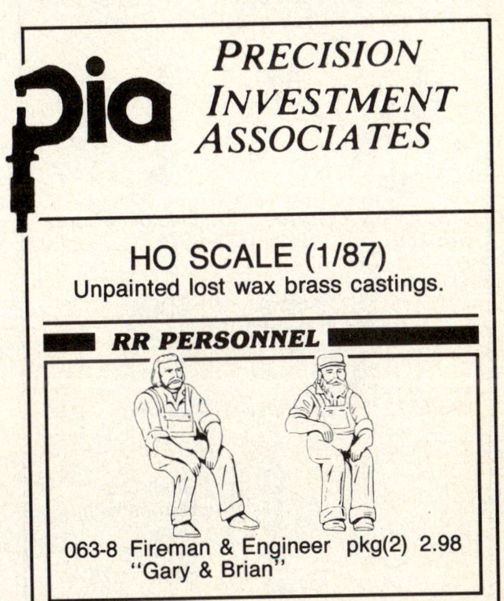

063-8 Fireman & Engineer pkg(2) 2.98
"Gary & Brian"

Finishing *SELLEY* Touches

International Hobby Corp.

HO SCALE (1/87)
Figures are unpainted metal, cast in realistic poses.

HO SCALE (1/87)
All figures are hand-painted plastic, unless noted.

RR PERSONNEL

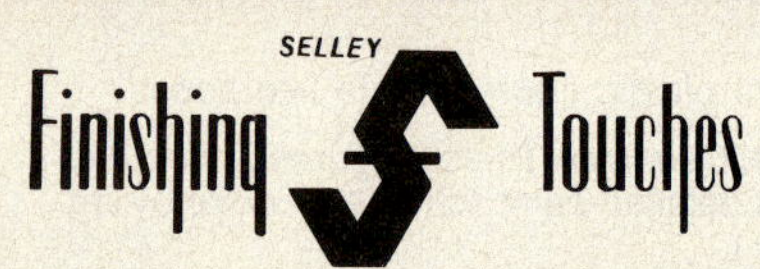

701   139

675-139   Man with Wheelbarrow   1.00
675-701   Handcar Man   .60

675-289   Road Gang Working   pkg(5) 3.95
Includes five figures, tools, ''Men Working'' sign and barricade.

675-294   Brakeman, crewman   pkg(6) 1.30

Diesel Train Crew   Drivers
675-647   1.20   675-231 pkg(3) 1.20
Includes engineer, fireman and brakeman.

(not illustrated)
675-81   Steam train,   *NEW*   pkg(3) 1.20
    crewmen

MISCELLANEOUS

675-662   Hobos & Dogs   pkg(5) 1.75
Includes four different figures and a dog.

Cowboys & 2 Horses   Prospector w/Burro
675-160   2.25   675-6571   2.50

675-6572   Prospector with 2 Burros   2.95

Shell Gas Pumps with Man
675-175
each   1.75

MISCELLANEOUS (cont)

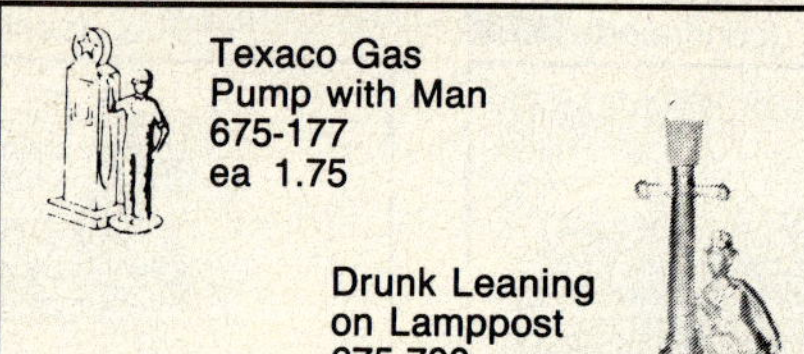

Texaco Gas Pump with Man
675-177
ea 1.75

Drunk Leaning on Lamppost
675-700
ea .80

ANIMALS

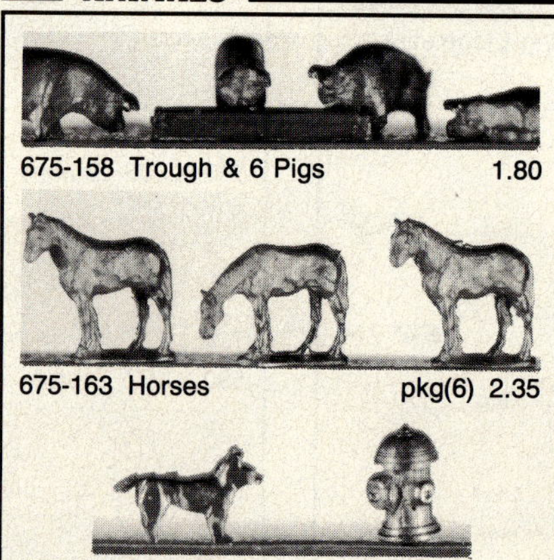

675-158   Trough & 6 Pigs   1.80

675-163   Horses   pkg(6) 2.35

675-178   Dog & Hydrant   .95

675-161   Cows   pkg(6) 2.00

675-454   Horse & Colt   ea 1.25

Elephant   Giraffe
675-456   ea .95   675-457   ea .95

Camel   Lion
675-458   ea .95   675-520   ea .95

Bull, Cow & Calf   Chickens
675-162   ea 2.00   675-297 pkg(12) 1.65

RR PERSONNEL

348-423303	Train Crew	3.98
348-423304	Work Crew	3.98
348-423311	Train Working Crew	3.98

PASSENGERS

348-423301	Sitting Figures	3.98
348-423302	Standing Figures	3.98
348-423312	Sitting Passengers	3.98

FIREMEN

348-4260   Three w/Hose,   pkg(6) 6.49
    Three w/Ax
348-4261   Six Firemen,   pkg(11) 6.49
    Two Extinguishers, Stretcher, Bullhorn, Ax and Hose

MISCELLANEOUS

348-8851   Assorted Clowns   pkg(6) 6.98

348-8852   Winter People   *NEW*   6.98

348-8853   Hobo Clowns   *NEW*   6.98
348-423309   People at Leisure   3.98

ANIMALS

348-422301	Horses & Cattle	3.98

JUNE 17, 1832

❧ Today ❧
IN RAILROAD HISTORY

Annoyed with the noise of escaping steam from the pop valve, the fireman of the ''Best Friend of Charleston'' ties off the valve lever. Minutes later, the engine is destroyed by a boiler explosion.

HO SCALE (1/87) EASY-TO-BUILD

Manufactured by Wm. K. Walthers, Inc.

Classic American Cars Superdetail HO Scale Street Scenes!

Whether parked at the curb or on the roll, these detailed autos bring HO Scale streets to life! These American classics make the perfect superdetail for steam or diesel era scenes, and help set the time and place of your entire layout!

Each is a one-piece, resin casting, with all details molded in place. Cast metal wheels are included, and some models feature separate metal bumpers. Just assemble and paint, and these easy-to-build kits are ready for the road.

SERVICE/DELIVERY VEHICLES

Making local deliveries from the freight house to homes and industries, trucks like this were in service throughout the 1950's and early 60's. Decals, including the colorful REA logos, are provided.

Railway Express Agency Delivery Truck
439-923   each 7.98

Sedan deliveries were popular with department stores, laundry services and drug stores for making home deliveries. (Use Walthers decals to letter the finished vehicles for stores on your layout!)

'39 Sedan Delivery
439-911   pkg(2) 7.98

'59 CHECKER MARATHON TAXI

You can always find a taxi when you need one with this super kit! The prototype used this same body for years, so your model is right at home in various time periods. Decals for Checker, Yellow Cab and Veteran Taxi Service are included!

439-914 '59 Checker Marathon Taxi   pkg(2) 7.98

WALTHERS VEHICLES

Look under Walthers in the Freight Cars section for the complete selection of Walthers intermodal vehicles, including the Kalmar Container Crane, 20, 40 and 48′ Containers and 32, 40 and 48′ Semi Trailers.

SERVICE/DELIVERY VEHICLES (continued)

A must for busy city scenes, vans like this make local deliveries of all sorts of products. Based on a 1963 model, our kit has a one-piece body and colorful decals.

1964 Step Van
439-931   pkg(2) 7.98

AUTOMOBILES

This big sedan is the perfect family car or public service vehicle. Decals for police, fire, military and taxi cab versions are included.

'40 Traveler 4-Door Sedan
439-920   pkg(2) 7.98

The whole HO Scale family will enjoy a drive in this super postwar coupe! The model has individual front and rear bumpers.

'48 Coupe
439-910   pkg(2) 7.98

You'll wish you could slide behind the wheel of this sporty Chevy! The two-door hardtop has lots of chrome trim molded in place, which looks super when painted!

'53 Hardtop
439-912   pkg(2) 7.98

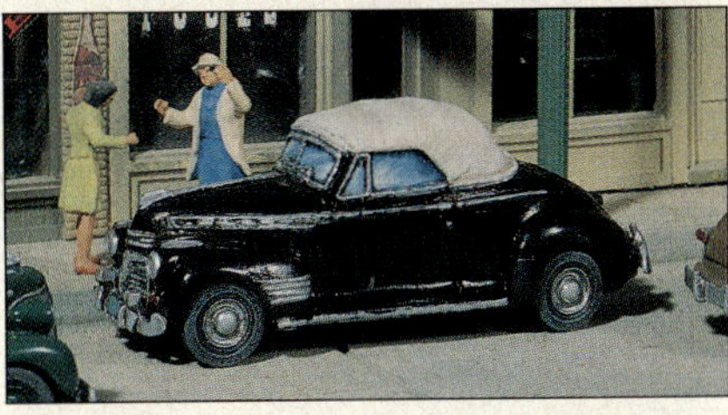

This handsome prewar "rag top" is ready for rough weather, with it's realistic canvas top molded in the up position.

'41 Convertible with top up
439-913   pkg(2) 7.98

Memories of sock hops and soda fountains come back every time you see this cool 50s cruiser! Perfect for steam-to-diesel layouts, or a restored collector car in a modern scene.

'56 Hardtop *NEW*
439-946   pkg(2) 7.98

prototype photo

(not illustrated)
439-303 Piggyback Ramp   each 4.98

HO SCALE
(1/87)
EASY-TO-BUILD

Manufactured by Wm. K. Walthers, Inc.

Classic American Cars Superdetail HO Scale Street Scenes!

Whether parked at the curb or on the roll, these detailed autos bring HO Scale streets to life! These American classics make the perfect superdetail for steam or diesel era scenes, and help set the time and place of your entire layout!

Each is a one-piece, resin casting, with all details molded in place. Cast metal wheels are included, and some models feature separate metal bumpers. Just assemble and paint, and these easy-to-build kits are ready for the road.

MILK TRUCK

preproduction model

The Divco was a common sight in every city when milk was delivered to your front door! The model is typical of Divcos built from the late 30's to the 60's. Full-color decals for three dairies are included.

Divco Milk Truck
439-917   pkg(2) 7.98

TRUCKS

This rugged workhorse is ready to do the job for any small business or farm. For extra detail, a load can be added to the open bed. A sheet of decals with various company names are included.

'41 Pickup Truck
439-919   pkg(2) 7.98

Local oil distributors will need several of these husky tankers for hauling fuel oil, gasoline or diesel fuel to their customers. Decals are included for several oil companies.

'53 Tank Truck
439-921   each 7.98

Here's a truck that can really deliver! The prototype was used for in-town deliveries of dry cleaning, newspapers, baked goods and much more. Decals for stores and other businesses are provided.

'54 Panel Truck
439-922   pkg(2) 7.98

Head down the highway in style at the wheel of this rugged semi tractor. It's a perfect accessory for modeling early piggyback service when used with Walthers 32' trailers and 75' flat cars. Decals for various truck lines are provided.

'56 Tractor
439-924   pkg(2) 7.98

Get heavy loads to customers safely with this big box van. Used for all types of local freight forwarding, the model features a one-piece body and a variety of decals.

'56 Delivery Truck
439-926   each 7.98

There's lots of room for tools and supplies in the back of this handsome panel truck, making it a favorite with plumbers, railroad maintenance crews and utility workers. The kit includes cast metal ladders, plus decals for a MOW truck, Public Utilities and more.

'40 Panel Truck
439-928   pkg(2) 7.98

Keep on truckin' down HO Scale highways with the Model R Introduced in 1967 as a replacement for the Model B, this popular semi tractor is still one of the most commonly seen trucks today.

Model "R"
Semi Tractor
439-929   pkg(2) 7.98

Bring your oil terminal or bulk oil distributor up-to-date with this Oil Truck. This rugged model is typical of the heavy trucks now in use for small deliveries of heating oil, gasoline, diesel fuel and other petroleum products.

Oil Truck
439-930   7.98

Keep HO Scale folks warm when you deliver their monthly fill-up of propane with this handsome hauler! This kit features the "C" cab, a one-piece tank body and full-color decals.

1957 LPG
Delivery Truck
439-934   each 7.98

HO SCALE (1/87) EASY-TO-BUILD

Manufactured by Wm. K. Walthers, Inc.

Classic American Cars Superdetail HO Scale Street Scenes!

TRUCKS (continued)

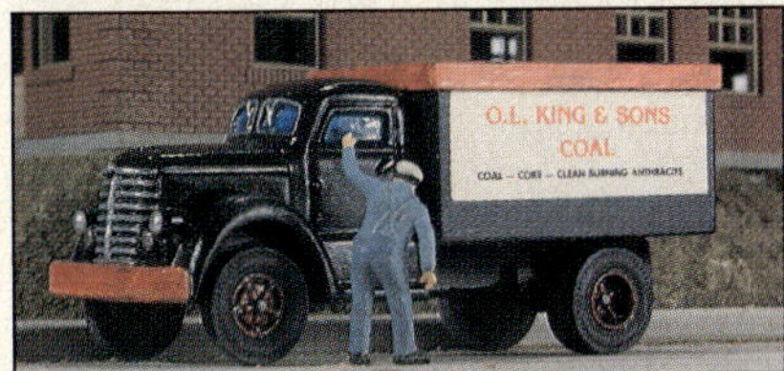

Keep your citizens warm all winter, with coal delivered in these vintage haulers.

1948 Diamond T Coal Truck
439-932   7.98

Got a bulky, heavy or oversize load? It's no problem for this rugged flatbed.

1953 Flatbed Truck
439-935   7.98

Send crews out to the job sight in this pick-up, a favorite with railroads, highway departments and industries. Includes cast metal hy-rail wheels.

Crew-Cab Pick-Up
439-933   7.98

This rough-and-ready truck is perfect for mine service or other types of off-road work.

Heavy-Duty Coal Truck
439-936   7.98

Carry big loads securely on the back of this truck, which is complete with a full set of cast-metal stakes.

Stake Truck
439-937   **NEW**   7.98

On or off the road, this big concrete carrier can deliver the goods to your job site. Features the famous "sidewinder" cab.

Model U Heavy Duty Concrete Truck
439-938   **NEW**   9.98

Great for cross-town trucking, or add your own customized body and build a unique model for your collection.

IH Tractor   **NEW**
439-939   7.98

TRUCKS (continued)

Your local Power & Light crews will be ready for any repair when they head out with this all-purpose repair truck.

'82 Line Truck   **NEW**
439-942   7.98

This sleek cab-over has become a favorite with large fleet operators. Looks great pulling Walthers 48' trailers too!

Semi Tractor   **NEW**
439-944   pkg(2) 7.98

Get the grain out of the fields and off to the elevator with this specially-equipped rig. Detailed grain box has dumper doors and canvas cover.

Grain Truck   **NEW**
439-947   7.98

(not illustrated)

439-943 Cab-over Reefer Truck   **NEW** 7.98
Rush fresh food to your local stores in a fleet of these trucks. Includes separate body and reefer unit.

YARD TRACTOR

Moving trailers or containers, these tractors look great at any modern freight terminal.

Ottawa Yard Tractor
439-941   pkg(2) 7.98

A must for the modern intermodal terminal!! Higher cab has more windows, making it easier for drivers to hitch to high-cube containers or tall trailers.

Ottawa HI-Cab Yard Tractor   **NEW**
439-945   pkg(2) 7.98

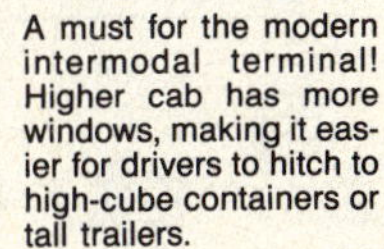

TRACKMOBILE

Equipped with railroad wheels and couplers for switching, and highway wheels for fast movement, these versatile vehicles are used by all types of industries. Powered version has a self-contained power truck.

Trackmobile®   **NEW**
439-953 Powered ea 39.98
439-952 Dummy   ea 19.98

prototype photo

ALLOY FORMS, INC.

HO SCALE (1/87) CRAFT TRAIN KITS

Kits consist of unpainted white metal detail parts. Truck kits include styrene, brass and rubber parts.

TRUCKS

PICKUP & PANEL

'56 Ford Pickup
119-2021   7.95

'56 Ford Pickup w/Camper
119-2042   9.95

'51 Ford Panel Delivery Truck
119-2041   7.95

(not illustrated)
119-2043 '56 Ford Pickup w/Rack   9.95

STAKE

'55 Chevy 2 Ton
119-2044   9.95

1954 B-42 Mack Flatbed
119-3001   17.95

(not illustrated)
119-3107 Mack BQ, 3-Axle   17.95
119-3105 Mack CJ COE, 3-Axle   17.95

BLOCK

B-42 Mack 3-Axle
119-3009   19.95

(not illustrated)
Autocar Block Truck
119-3202   19.95
Ford Lts Block Truck
119-7023   19.95

AUTOS

'48 Studebaker Starline
119-2040   6.95

'56 Ford Thunderbird
119-2022   6.95

'48 Ford Convertible
119-2030   7.95

'53 Chevy Bel-Air
119-2037   6.95

'49 Buick Roadmaster
119-2031   6.95

'49 Mercury, 2-Door
119-2028   6.95

'57 Chevy Bel-Air Sport Coupe
119-2008   7.95

'55 Chevy Bel-Air 2-Door
119-2020   6.95

'59 Cadillac Eldorado Convertible
119-2032   6.95

'53 Corvette
119-2025
6.95

'53 Buick Skylark Cv w/continental
119-2033
6.95

'59 Chevy Impala Convertible
119-2039   6.95

'55 Chevy Nomad Wagon
119-2029   6.95

'49 Hudson 4-Door
119-2023   6.95

'49 Ford Club Coupe w/Engine
119-2066   7.95

'55 Cadillac Fleetwood
119-2024   6.95

'59 Chevy El Camino
119-2045   6.95

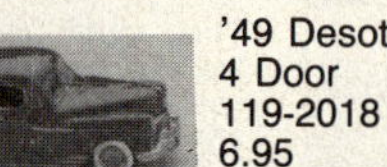

'49 Desoto, 4 Door
119-2018
6.95

'50 Chevy, 4-Door Fastback
119-2019
6.95

(not illustrated)
119-2026 Plymouth Coupe wo/engine   7.95
119-2027 Plymouth Coupe   7.95

TRACTORS

Mack B-70 w/Universal Chassis
119-3137   14.95

Ford LNT Cab w/Universal Chassis
119-3135   14.95

Astro, 3-Axle w/Rectangular Gas Tanks
119-3012   14.95

Astro Short Cab, 2-Axle
119-3025   14.95

Astro Short Cab, 3-Axle
119-3026   14.95

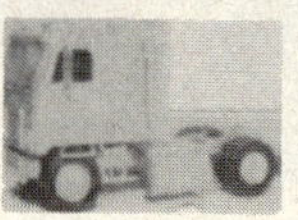

GMC Astro, 2-Axle
119-3036   14.95

Astro Sleeper
119-3013   14.95
w/Disc Wheels, Tandem Axle & Dual Exhausts

(not illustrated)

119-3010 Sleeper Box 2.95	119-3200 Autocar Chassis 14.95	119-7040 Mack CF/Pierce 29.95
119-3023 B-61 Mack Tank 2-Axle 19.95	119-3204 Diamond REO Universal Chassis 14.95	119-7041 Mack CF w/Univ Chassis 19.95
119-3146 33 Mack CJ 14.95		119-7043 Mack CF 4-Door 19.95
119-3138 B-61 Mack Universal Chassis 14.95	119-7020 Ford LTS w/Universal Chassis 14.95	119-7052 Mack DM-800 14.95 Offset Cab w/Universal Chassis

VAN

B-61 Mack, 2-Axle Refrigerated Type
119-3007   19.95

Mack BQ, 3-Axle
119-3106   19.95

(not illustrated)
119-3018 B-61 Mack w/16' Body   19.95
119-3022 GMC Astro Short Cab w/16' Body   19.95
119-3043 Ford LNT, 2-Axle w/Refrigerated Body   19.95
119-7049 Diamond REO BBC Refrigerated   19.95
119-3205 Diamond REO Delivery   19.95

ALLOY FORMS, INC.

HO SCALE (1/87) CRAFT TRAIN KITS

Kits consist of unpainted white metal detail parts. Truck kits include styrene, brass and rubber parts.

TRUCKS

DUMP

B-61 Mack Universal Chassis
119-3049   19.95
w/12' Theile Body, DW and Tandem Axle

B-61 Mack 2-Axle
119-3028   19.95

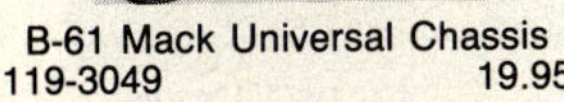

B-71 mack w/#3110 30' 3-Axle Trailer
119-3140   34.95

Ford LNT, 3-Axle
119-3044 w/3-Axle Trailer 34.95

B-61 Mack 3-Axle
119-3034   19.95

(not illustrated)

119-3041	Ford LNT 2-Axle w/7' Dump	19.95
119-3042	Ford LNT 3-Axle w/7' Heil Body	19.95
119-3143	Diamond Reo Dump Truck 11'b	19.95
119-3145	Diamond REO w/7' Bed	19.95
119-3201	Autocar Dump Truck 12' Box	19.95
119-7001	Autocar Dump Truck Large	24.95
119-7008	B-71 20' Coal/Gravel w/Tandem Axle	22.95
119-7009	Ford LNT Coal/Gravel w/20' Dump & Tandem Axle	22.95
119-7011	B-61 Mack	24.95
119-7014	Diamond Reo w/22' Dump Tr	24.95
119-7016	Autocar Special Dump Trucks	34.95
119-7021	Ford LTS w/12' Heil Dump	19.95
119-7022	Ford Lts w/Dump Body	22.95
119-7024	Ford Lts w/22' Dump Trailer	24.95

FLATBED TRAILER

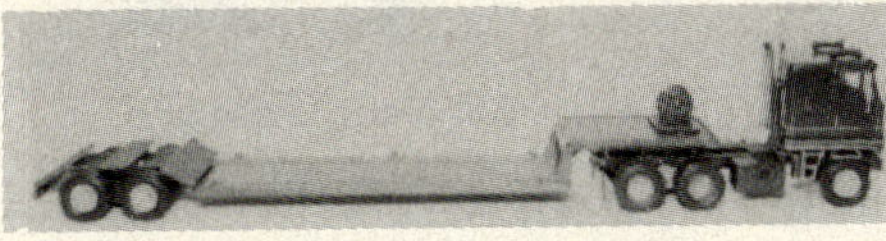

GMC Astro Tandem Axle w/40' ''Lowboy'' 16-Wheel
119-3016   29.95

(not illustrated)

119-2045	37' Depressed Center Trailer	19.95
119-3139	B-71 Mack w/Heavy Duty Flatbed	17.95
119-3047	Ford LNT, 3-Axle	17.95
119-3206	Diamond REO w/40' Flatbed	17.95
119-3142	Autocar w/45' Lowboy	29.95

TRAILER

30' 3-Axle Dump
119-3110   24.95

(not illustrated)

119-3017	45' 16 Wheel Lowboy	19.95
119-3029	30' Logging Trailer	19.95
119-3030	B-61 Mack w/Logging Trailer	29.95
119-3144	Autocar c w/log trailer	29.95
119-7010	22' Dump Trailer 2-Axle	17.95
119-7012	GMS Astro w/22' Dump Trailer	24.95
119-7013	Autocar w/22' Dump Trailer	24.95
119-7015	22' Dump Trailr w/Bogie	19.95

EMERGENCY EQUIPMENT

B-61 Mack 2-Axle Fire Pumper
119-3035   29.95

B-61 Mack Open Fire Truck
119-3136   26.95

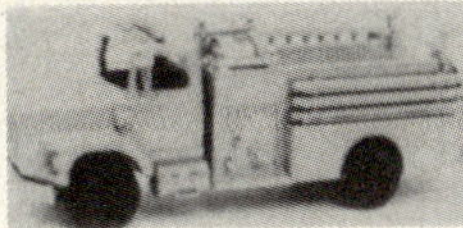

Ford LS Fire Pumper
119-7025   26.95

Ford LNT Fire Pumper
119-7007   26.95

(not illustrated)

119-3086	B-61 Mack Fire Pumper Body Kit	19.95
119-3141	B-61 Mack Fire Tanker	19.95
119-3203	B-71 Mack CF NYC Fire Pumper	29.95
119-7002	Mack Pumper Body Kit	19.95
119-7017	Mack CF Fire Pumper	29.95
119-7029	Pierce Ford Ln Pumper	26.95
119-7030	Pierce Ford Ls Pumper	26.95
119-7037	Pierce Lst Ford Fd Tanker	26.95
119-7038	Pierce Lnt Ford Fd Tanker	26.95
119-7039	Diamond REO Pierce Tanker	26.95
119-7042	Mack Pierce CRV-18	29.95
119-7044	Mack of Pierce 2500 Tanker	29.95
119-7046	Mack CF NYC Fire Pumper, Body Only	19.95
119-7031	Ford LNT Pierce Rescue	24.95
119-7032	Diamond REO Pierce Rescue	24.95
119-7036	Pierce REO Suburban Pumper	26.95
119-7035	Pierce Extended Pumper Body Only	19.95

ACCESSORIES

Wheel sets include wheels, axles and hubs.

119-2036	24' Roll Off Body		6.95
119-2047	Assorted Auto Parts		6.95
119-2051	Brass Airplane Hood Ornament		2.95
119-2053	CS Snowplow & Beam		6.95
119-2060	Budd/Alco Wheelset 3-Axle		2.50
119-3037	Bed Stakes		2.95
119-3038	Wheel Bogies		2.95
119-3039	Bud Disc Wheel Rims/Tires		2.95
119-3040	6 Spoke Wheel Rim/Tires		2.95
119-3045	Low Boy Wheel Rims/Tires		2.95
119-3046	Dual Exhaust Pipes/Mack H		1.95
119-3058	Cab Seats Standard		1.95
119-3061	Large Truck Tires		2.95
119-3062	Single Exhaust Pipe/Air Cleaner		1.95
119-3064	Tractor Detail Kit Athearn		2.95
119-3070	Fender for Dual Axles		2.95
119-3071	Truck Seat Bench Type		1.95
119-3072	Small Truck Tires		2.95
119-3073	Handle-Brass	pkg(4)	2.95
119-3075	Lumber Headache Rack		2.95
119-3077	Dolly Wheels for Trailers	pkg(2)	1.95
119-3078	5th Wheel Dolly Tandem Axles		7.95
119-3079	5th Wheel Dolly Single Axles		6.95
119-3083	Battery Box w/Air Tank	pkg(4)	2.95
119-3084	Battery Box w/Small Tank	pkg(4)	2.95
119-3088	Tri Axle Conversion Kit		6.95
119-3090	Gas Tank Autocar Rect		2.95
119-3091	Air Cleaner Horizontal	pkg(4)	2.95
119-3093	Torpedo Running Lites	pkg(2)	2.95
119-3094	Headlight Autocar Styl	pkg(4)	2.95
119-3095	Tail Lights/Tractors		2.95
119-3096	Tail Lights/Trailers		2.95
119-3097	Air Horns		1.95
119-3099	Update Detail Parts/Fire		2.95
119-7054	Trash Compactor Body		11.95
119-12040	6-Spoke Wheelset		2.50

MISCELLANEOUS

'47 Clark Forklift
119-2004   kit 4.95

(not illustrated)

119-3013	MAC BM Tractor	14.95
119-3032	MAC BQ Tractor	14.95
119-3148	Diamond REO Rack Truck	19.95

HO SCALE (1/87)
Pre-assembled in appropriately colored plastic. Painted details.

NON-OPERATING VEHICLES

160-42206
Automobile Set
pkg(6)   4.00

HO EASY-TO-BUILD KITS

These easy-to-build kits consist of pre-colored plastic parts and complete instructions.

SEMI TRUCK

Ford Tractor w/Van Trailer Kit
322-6023   5.50

METAL MINIATURES

HO SCALE (1/87) EASY-TO-BUILD KITS

Unpainted, one-piece cast metal vehicles.

CONSTRUCTION

Caterpillar Tractor
340-44
2.50

"It says, 'This end up.'"

Cartoon courtesy of *Model Railroader* Magazine.

DYNA-MODEL PRODUCTS COMPANY

HO SCALE (1/87) EASY-TO-BUILD

One-piece cast metal body. Tires & steering wheel need assembly. Available prepainted or unpainted.

AUTOS & TRUCKS

1914 Stutz Bearcat	1908 Buick	1911 Maxwell
Painted	Painted	Painted
260-20011 ea 7.50	260-20021 ea 7.50	260-20031 ea 7.50
Unpainted	Unpainted	Unpainted
260-2001 ea 3.95	260-2002 ea 3.95	260-2003 ea 3.95

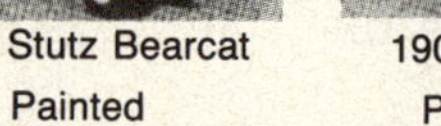

1916 Twin Six Packard	1909 Stanley Steamer	1947 Ford Pickup Truck
Painted	Painted	Painted
260-20041 ea 7.50	260-20051 ea 7.50	260-20061 ea 7.50
Unpainted	Unpainted	Unpainted
260-2004 ea 3.95	260-2005 ea 3.95	260-2006 ea 3.95

COAL CONVEYOR

Painted
260-20001   each 4.50

Unpainted
260-2000   each 3.95

CONSTRUCTION

Caterpillar Crawler	Caterpillar Bulldozer
Painted	Painted
260-20101 8.50	260-20111 10.50
Unpainted	Unpainted
260-2010 5.50	260-2011 6.50

Forklifts
Painted
260-20121 pkg(2) 9.95
Unpainted
260-2012 pkg(2) 5.95

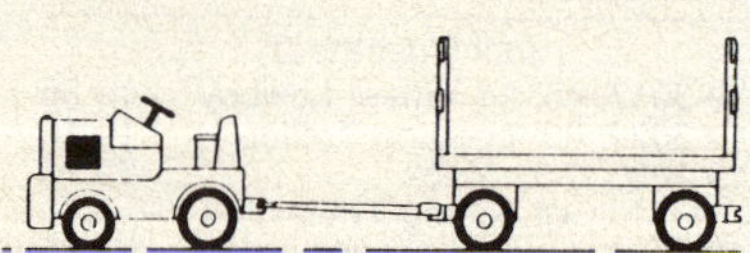

Platform Tractor & Two Baggage Wagons
Painted
260-20131   8.50
Unpainted
260-2013   5.95

CON-COR

HO SCALE (1/87) READY-TO-RUN

Vehicles are prepainted and feature full color lettering on sides and ends. All vehicles are assembled, unless noted.

SEMI w/TRAILER

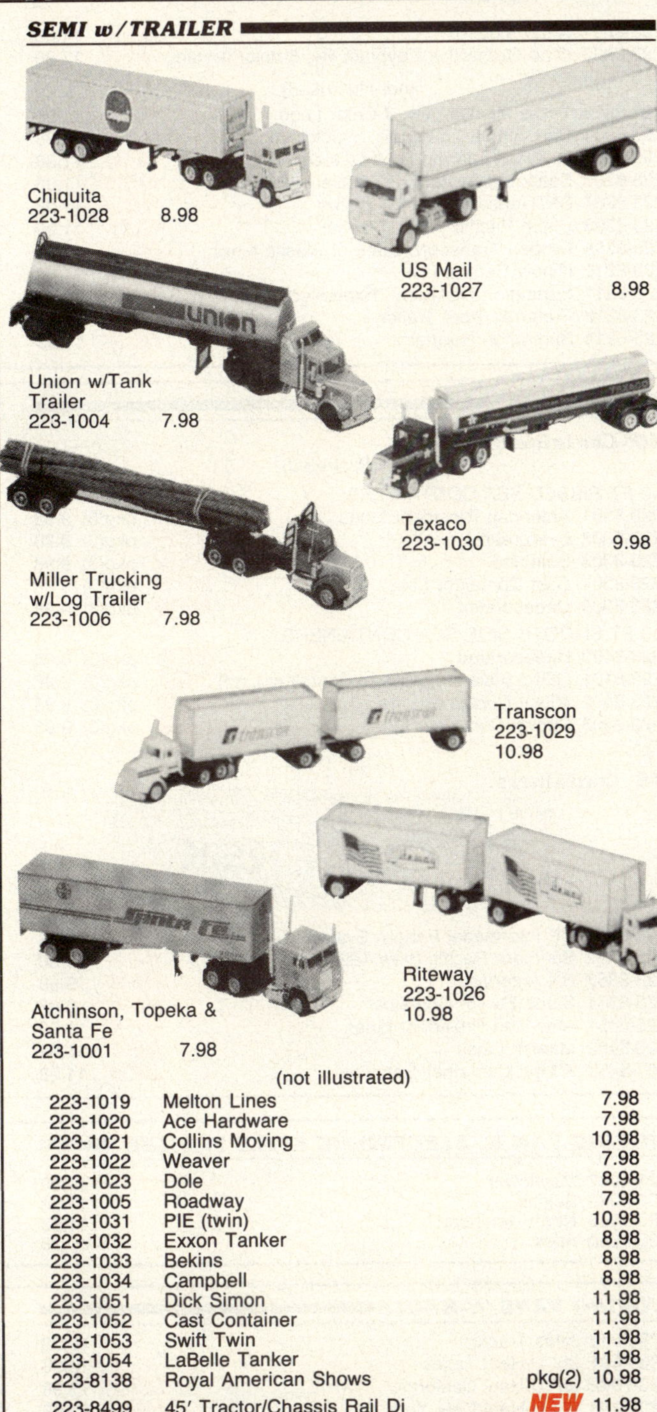

Chiquita
223-1028   8.98

US Mail
223-1027   8.98

Union w/Tank Trailer
223-1004   7.98

Texaco
223-1030   9.98

Miller Trucking w/Log Trailer
223-1006   7.98

Transcon
223-1029
10.98

Riteway
223-1026
10.98

Atchinson, Topeka & Santa Fe
223-1001   7.98

(not illustrated)

223-1019	Melton Lines		7.98
223-1020	Ace Hardware		7.98
223-1021	Collins Moving		10.98
223-1022	Weaver		7.98
223-1023	Dole		8.98
223-1005	Roadway		7.98
223-1031	PIE (twin)		10.98
223-1032	Exxon Tanker		8.98
223-1033	Bekins		8.98
223-1034	Campbell		8.98
223-1051	Dick Simon		11.98
223-1052	Cast Container		11.98
223-1053	Swift Twin		11.98
223-1054	LaBelle Tanker		11.98
223-8138	Royal American Shows	pkg(2)	10.98
223-8499	45' Tractor/Chassis Rail Di	**NEW**	11.98
223-408137	40' Tanker Royal American	**NEW** pkg(2)	11.98
223-408138	Tractor Royal American	**NEW** pkg(2)	10.98
223-511000	45' Mac Tractor	**NEW**	6.98

Pepsi
223-1003   7.98

Safety Kleen
223-1025   9.98

Brillion
223-1008   7.98

Texas Oil
223-1009   7.98

Palumbo
223-1010   7.98

Evergreen
223-1011   7.98

SP Fruit Express
223-1016   7.98

Hi-Way Dispatch
223-1014   7.98

Rollins
223-1017   7.98

Ka-Bob
223-1018
7.98

SEMI W/TRAILER SPECIAL EDITION   *NEW*

New York Skyline
223-199201
16.98

Wild West
223-199202
16.98

HO SCALE
(1/87)
READY-TO-RUN

SEMI W/TRAILER SPECIAL EDITION (cont)

Monuments
223-199203
16.98

US Capital
223-199205
16.98

(not illustrated)

223-199204	Space	16.98
223-199206	Columbus	16.98
223-401992	Route 66 ''500 Years America''	203.76

includes two each of #'s 199201, 199202, 199203, 199204, 199205, 199206

SEMI TRAILERS

Route 66 series.

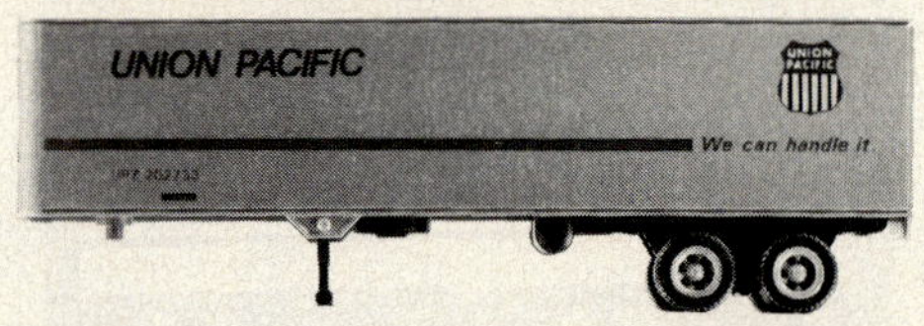

223-8107	Union Pacific	pkg(3)	9.98
223-8108	Budd of California	pkg(3)	10.98
223-8109	Illinois Central Gulf	pkg(3)	9.98
223-8110	Leaseway	pkg(3)	10.98
223-8111	Boston & Maine	pkg(3)	10.98
223-8112	Santa Fe #2	pkg(3)	9.98
223-8113	UPS	pkg(3)	9.98
223-8114	Norfolk & Western	pkg(3)	10.98
223-8115	D&RGW	pkg(3)	10.98
223-8127	Illinois Central-Modern	pkg(3)	9.98
223-8128	Royal American Shows +	pkg(3)	9.98
223-8129	New York Central ''Pacemaker'' +	pkg(3)	11.98
223-8130	Southern Pacific ''Daylight'' +	pkg(3)	11.98
223-8131	Seaboard Coast Line ''Old''	pkg(3)	11.98
223-8133	28' Ribbed Side		10.98
223-8134	28' Smooth Side		10.98
223-8135	''World's Largest''		10.98
223-8136	Royal American		10.98
223-8200	Smooth Side		9.98
223-8250	45' Rivet Side		9.98
223-8350	45' Smooth Side		9.98
223-8450	45' Ribbed Side		9.98

Van Trailer

Easy-to-build unprinted plastic kits with decals included.

Western Pacific
223-8117
9.98

(not illustrated)

223-8101	AT&SF	pkg(3)	9.98
223-8102	Burlington Northern	pkg(3)	9.98
223-8103	Consolidated Rail	pkg(3)	9.98
223-8104	Transamerica	pkg(3)	9.98
223-8105	Southern Pacific (PIG)	pkg(3)	9.98
223-8106	C&NW	pkg(3)	9.98
223-8116	Pennsylvania RR		9.98
223-8117	Western Pacific		9.98
223-8118	Union Pacific		9.98
223-8119	Pacific Fruit Express		9.98
223-8120	Wabash		9.98
223-8121	Great Northern		9.98
223-8122	Illinois Central		9.98
223-8123	Santa Fe		9.98
223-8100	Undecorated	pkg(3)	9.98

40' OLDIE TRAILER

223-8139	Northern Pacific	NEW	pkg(2) 11.98
223-8140	Norfolk & Western	NEW	pkg(2) 11.98
223-8141	Western Pacific	NEW	pkg(2) 11.98
223-8142	Baltimore & Ohio	NEW	pkg(2) 11.98

45' MODERN TRAILER

8202   8201

223-8201	Nitrol Modern	NEW	11.98
223-8202	Crab Orchard & Egyptian Ry, 6 color printing	NEW	11.98

(not illustrated)

223-8203	Texas-Mexican Ry, 4-Color Logo	NEW	11.98
223-8204	Cornucopia Transport, 5 Color Logo	NEW	11.98
223-8205	C P Rail Intermodal 45' Trailer	NEW	11.98
223-8206	Seaboard System 45' Trailer	NEW	11.98
223-8207	BN/Transamerica 45' Trailer	NEW	11.98
223-8208	Union Pacific ''Flag'' Trailer	NEW	11.98
223-8209	Lynden Transport (State of Alaska Map)	NEW	11.98
223-8210	Illinois Central Gulf	NEW	11.98
223-8211	Burlington Northern ''Expediter'' logo	NEW	11.98
223-8212	Preferred Pool Trailer	NEW	11.98
223-8214	Burlington Northern	NEW	11.98

CONTAINERS

40' Containers

(not illustrated)

40 FT RIBBED SEA CONTAINERS

223-8301	American President Lines	NEW	pkg(3) 9.98
223-8302	Evergreen Lines	NEW	pkg(3) 9.98
223-8303	SeaLand	NEW	pkg(3) 9.98
223-8304	Cast Container Line	NEW	pkg(3) 9.98
223-8300	Undecorated	NEW	pkg(3) 9.98

40 FT SMOOTH SIDE SEA CONTAINERS

223-8400	Undecorated	NEW	pkg(3) 8.98
223-8401	OOCL (Overseas Ocean Container Line)	NEW	pkg(3) 9.98
223-8402	Mitsui Container Line	NEW	pkg(3) 9.98
223-8403	Showa Container Line	NEW	pkg(3) 9.98

45' Containers

223-8351	CP Intermodal Freight Systems	NEW	9.98
223-8352	Southern Pacific (new 1992 logo)	NEW	9.98
223-8353	BN America	NEW	9.98
223-8354	Santa Fe 45' Container	NEW	9.98
223-8451	American President Lines	NEW	11.98
223-8452	Maersk Lines	NEW	11.98
223-8453	K Line Container Service	NEW	11.98

MOVING VAN W/ELECTRONIC STYLE TRAILER

223-1047	Mayflower	11.98
223-1048	Bekins	11.98
223-1049	North American	11.98
223-1050	Atlas	11.98

MOVING VANS/U-HAULS

223-1042	Atlas Tractor		10.98
223-7001	26' U-Haul Texas		13.98
223-7002	26' U-Haul California	NEW	13.98
223-7003	26' U-Haul New York	NEW	13.98
223-7004	26' U-Haul Ohio	NEW	13.98
223-7005	26' U-Haul New Mexico	NEW	13.98
223-7006	26' U-Haul Oregon	NEW	13.98
223-7000	26' U-Haul Undecorated	NEW	13.98

CON-COR

HO SCALE (1/87) READY-TO-RUN

Vehicles are prepainted and feature full color lettering on sides and ends. All vehicles are assembled, unless noted.

AUTOS

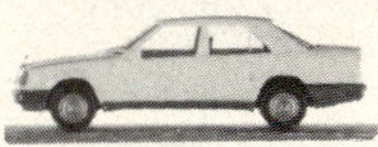

Mercedes 300E
223-225   2.89

(not illustrated)

223-250	Ford Mustang		7.98
223-4001	57 Chevy Mini Exact	**NEW**	7.98
223-4002	Lamborghini Mini Exact	**NEW**	7.98
223-4003	69 Mustang	**NEW**	7.98
223-4004	Ferrari Testerosa	**NEW**	7.98

EMERGENCY VEHICLE

Fire Chief 4 x 4
223-236   3.49

DUMP TRUCK

(not illustrated)

State Highway Dept
223-1012   5.98

Terra Short Dumper
223-1015   7.98

Terra Highway Dumper
223-1024   5.98

Stevens w/Dump Trailer
223-1002   7.98

SCHOOL BUS

Unified #2
223-1037
10.98

Helping Hand
223-1038
10.98

(not illustrated)

223-1036	County #4	10.98
223-1039	Maintenance-of-Way	10.98
223-1043	US Army	10.98
223-1044	Camp Woebegon	10.98
223-1045	Washington HS	10.98
223-1046	Good Shepard	10.98
223-1035	Undecorated	10.98

1993/'94 CATALOG   NEW

Full color, with complete line of route 66 trucks, trailers, busses, circus trailers, cars and containers. 24 pages.

223-9999   2.50

Many a local railfan is dreaming of the day this impressive house comes up for sale. Those large rooms would be perfect for a layout and it's next door to a busy right-of-way too. Known as ''John's Estates'' in honor of builder Terry Johns, the Pola Mansion is located on the ''Superior Short Line'' modular layout. This Minneapolis based group's layout measures 12 x 50' when all 25 modules are in use.   *Photo by Greg Smith*

When snow blows, the call goes out for the push plow. Bucking drifts along the Trout Creek Lumber Co. right-of-way is a Durango Press plow, pushed by a Westside brass import of an outside frame 2-8-0. The tank and trestle were scratch-built by Pete Moffett. Hydrocal® was sifted to create the snow.

Models and Photo by Pete Moffett

HO SCALE (1/87) READY-TO-RUN

Imported from Spain by *WALTHERS*

Vehicles are molded in appropriately colored plastic, with painted details. Marking may vary from what is shown in catalog.

AUTOMOBILES

CITROEN

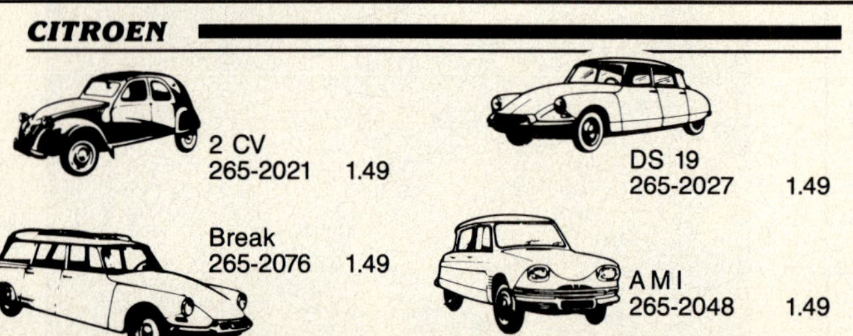

2 CV
265-2021   1.49

DS 19
265-2027   1.49

Break
265-2076   1.49

A M I
265-2048   1.49

FIAT

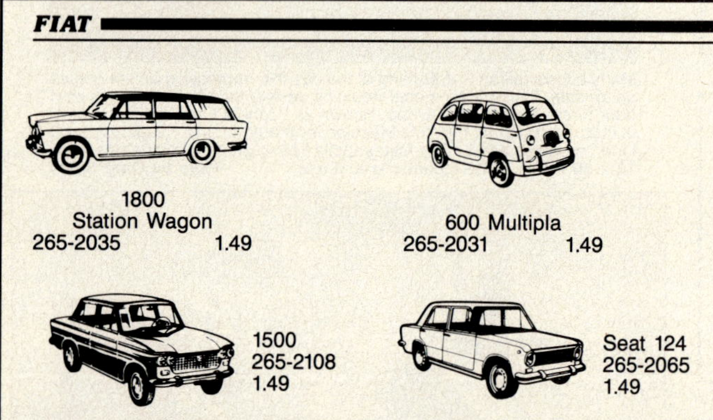

1800 Station Wagon
265-2035   1.49

600 Multipla
265-2031   1.49

1500
265-2108
1.49

Seat 124
265-2065
1.49

OPEL

Rekord
265-2039
1.49

RENAULT

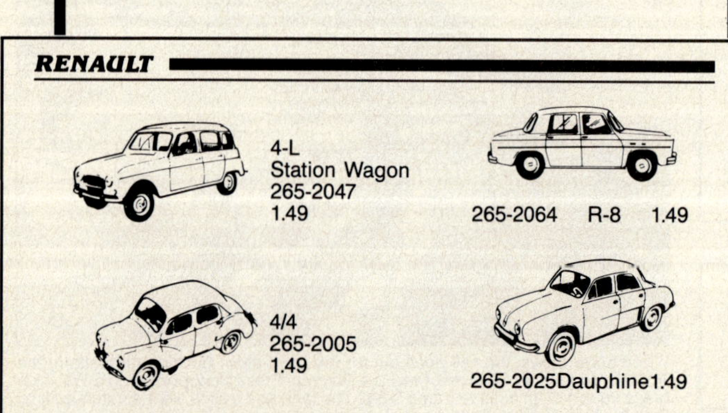

4-L Station Wagon
265-2047
1.49

265-2064   R-8   1.49

4/4
265-2005
1.49

265-2025 Dauphine 1.49

FORD

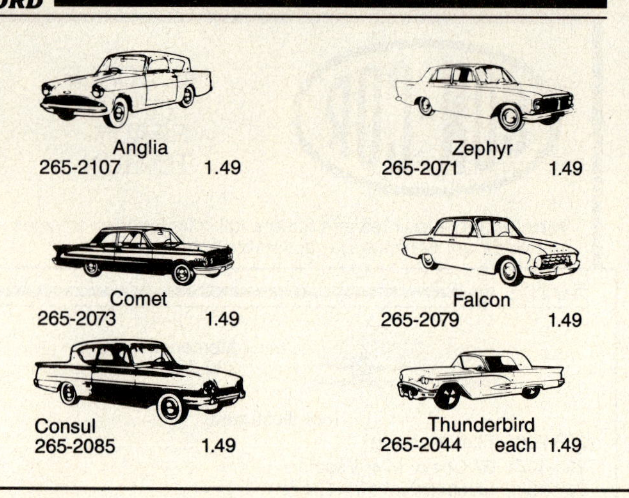

Anglia
265-2107   1.49

Zephyr
265-2071   1.49

Comet
265-2073   1.49

Falcon
265-2079   1.49

Consul
265-2085   1.49

Thunderbird
265-2044   each 1.49

MISCELLANEOUS

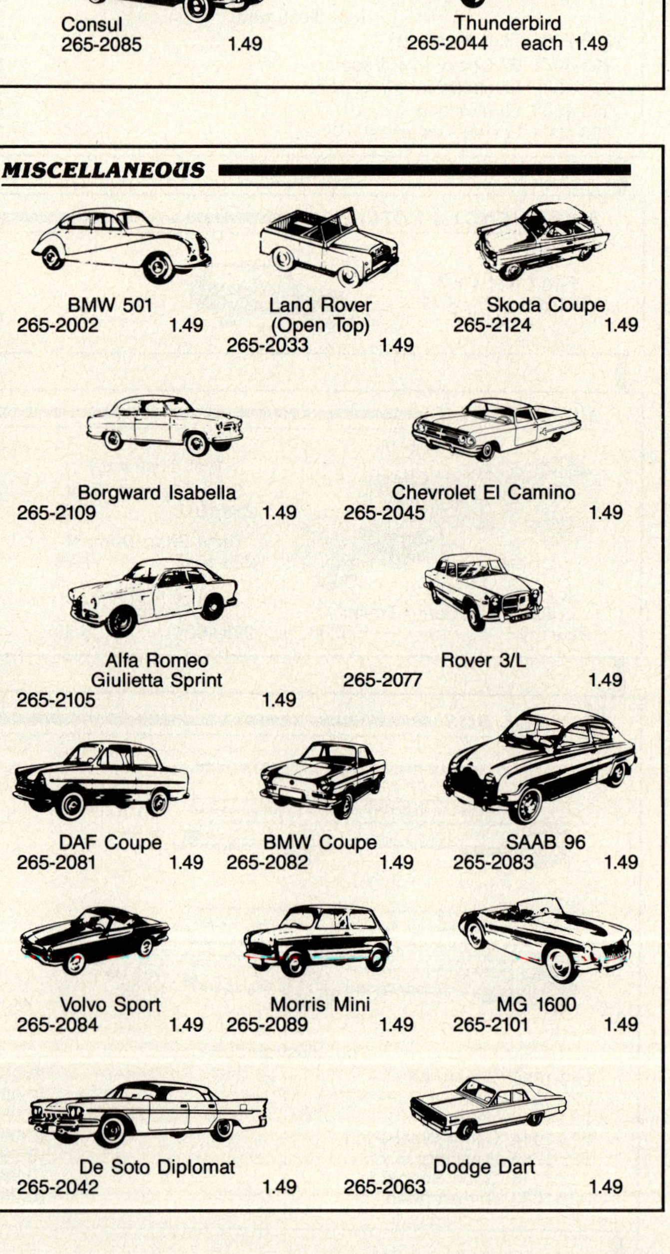

BMW 501
265-2002   1.49

Land Rover (Open Top)
265-2033   1.49

Skoda Coupe
265-2124   1.49

Borgward Isabella
265-2109   1.49

Chevrolet El Camino
265-2045   1.49

Alfa Romeo Giulietta Sprint
265-2105   1.49

Rover 3/L
265-2077   1.49

DAF Coupe
265-2081   1.49

BMW Coupe
265-2082   1.49

SAAB 96
265-2083   1.49

Volvo Sport
265-2084   1.49

Morris Mini
265-2089   1.49

MG 1600
265-2101   1.49

De Soto Diplomat
265-2042   1.49

Dodge Dart
265-2063   1.49

HO SCALE (1/87) READY-TO-RUN

Imported from Spain by *WALTHERS*

Vehicles are molded in appropriately colored plastic, with painted details. Marking may vary from what is shown in catalog.

AUTOMOBILES (continued)

Manufacturer	Country	Manufacturer	Country
Alfa-Romeo	Italy	MG	Britain
Barreiros	Spain	Magirus	Germany
BMC	Britain	Mercedes	Germany
BMW	Germany	Morris	Britain
Borgward	Germany	Opel	Germany
Caterpillar	USA	Pala	Spain
Chausson	France	Pegaso	Spain
Chevrolet	USA	Plymouth	USA
Citroen	France	Renault	France
DAF	Netherlands	Rover	Britain
DeSoto	USA	SAAB	Sweden
DKW	Germany	Sava	France
Dodge	USA	Seat	Spain
Fiat	Italy	Simca	France
Ford	USA/Europe	Studebaker	USA/Canada
GMC	USA	Thames	Britain
Hanomag	Germany	Thornycroft	Britain
Jaguar	Britain	Unic	France
Jeep	USA	Volkswagen	Germany
Lincoln	USA	Volvo	Sweden

JEEP

265-2026
1.49

JAGUAR

E Coupe	Racer	Mark Nine
265-2098 1.49	265-2100 1.49	265-2106 1.49

SEAT

 Sedan 1400
265-2006
1.49

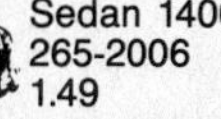 Seat 1400
Panel Truck
265-2037
1.49

 Sedan 1400C
265-2032
1.49

 Coupe 600
265-2036
1.49

STUDEBAKER

Hawk	Avanti
265-2070 1.49	265-2075 1.49

VOLKSWAGEN

 265-2001 1.49

 Convertible
Cabriolet
265-2009   1.49

 VW Karmann
Ghia
265-2099   1.49

MERCEDES BENZ

 265-2003   300   1.49

 190SL
265-2010   1.49

 265-2049   Racer   1.49

 190SL Coupe
265-2011   1.49

 220
265-2074 1.49

CARS & BOATS

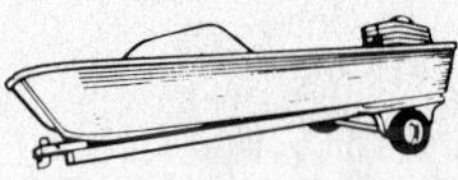 Boat & Motor
w/Trailer
265-2052   1.49

 De Soto w/Boat
265-2054   2.99

 Plymouth w/Motor Boat
265-2055   2.99

 Cabin Boat & Motor
w/Trailer
265-2053   1.49

HO SCALE (1/87) READY-TO-RUN

Imported from Spain by WALTHERS

Vehicles are molded in appropriately colored plastic, with painted details. Marking may vary from what is shown in catalog.

2-AXLE TRUCKS

Panel Truck Furgon
265-2090   1.99

Sava Garbage Truck
265-2123   2.49

Thames Beer Delivery Truck
265-2121   2.49

Thames Soda Delivery Truck
265-2120   2.49

Magirus Tank Truck
265-2024   2.49

Thames Flatbed Truck
265-2119   2.49

Pegaso Tank
265-2094   2.49

Sava Butano Delivery
265-2122   2.49

Gas Oil Tank Truck Ford
265-2020   2.49

Pegaso Cement Delivery Truck
265-2066   2.49

Ford Thames/Flat Bed
265-2091   1.99

Eko Cola Truck
265-2017   2.49

Piper Cola Truck
265-2018   2.49

Ford Flat Bed w/Canvas Top
265-2014   1.99

Pegaso Truck Delivery
265-2092   2.49

Magirus Flat Bed w/Canvas Top
265-2016   1.99

(not illustrated)

265-2013   Ford Flat Bed   1.99
265-2015   Magirus Flat Bed   1.99
265-2067   Body Truck Barreiros Van   2.49

VAN & SMALL PANEL TRUCKS

Ford Panel Truck
265-2028 1.49

Ford Microbus
265-2030 1.49

Mercedes Microbus
265-2088   1.99

SEMI TRUCKS

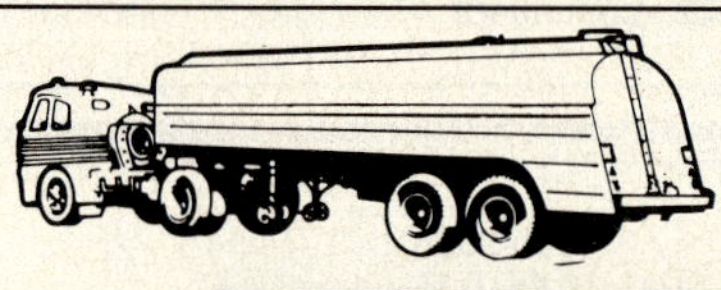

Pegaso Semi Tank Truck
265-2095   3.99

Titan Semi Lo-Boy w/Cargo
265-2118   4.99

Pegaso Transport w/5 Autos
265-21155   8.49

Semi w/Van Trailer Pegaso
265-2126   3.99

Tank Transport
265-2046   3.99

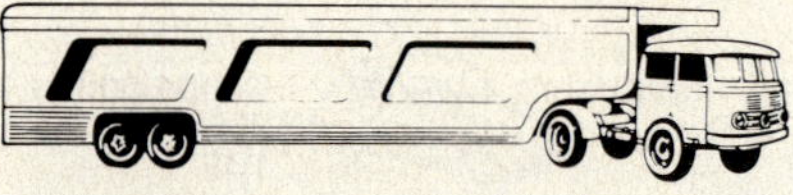

Mercedes Car Transport
265-2023   4.49

Antar Semi Lo-Boy w/Cargo
265-2111   3.49

Double Bottom Truck
265-2068   3.99

MISCELLANEOUS

Land Rover Safari
265-2116   1.99

Hanomag Farm Tractor
265-2114   1.99

EKO

HO SCALE (1/87) READY-TO-RUN

Imported from Spain by WALTHERS

Vehicles are molded in appropriately colored plastic, with painted details. Marking may vary from what is shown in catalog.

BUSES

Pegaso Motor Bus
265-2102   2.99

Double Decker Alco Bus
265-2110   2.99
Dealers: Must order dealer pack of 6.

Chausson Motor Bus
265-2117   2.99
Dealers: Must order dealer pack of 3.

EMERGENCY VEHICLES

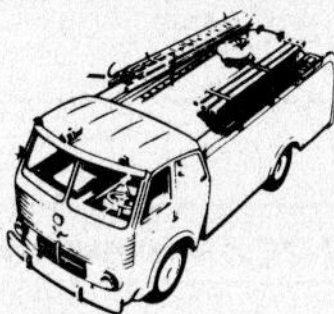

Fiat 1800 Ambulance
265-2041   1.49

Ford Ambulance
265-2029   1.49

Pegaso Fire Truck
265-2093   2.49

Fire Truck w/Ladder
265-2019   2.49

Pegaso Hook/ Ladder Truck
265-2097   2.49

CONSTRUCTION

Dump Truck
265-2087   2.49

HD Dump Truck Berliet
265-2125   2.49

Dump Truck Camion
265-2069   1.99

Caterpillar Earth Mover
265-2112   2.99

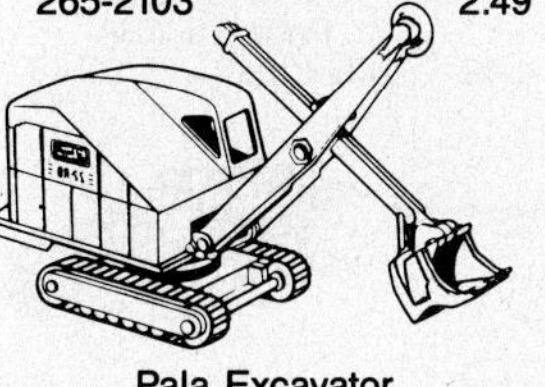

Unic Cement Mixer
265-2103   2.49

Pegaso Cement Mixer
265-2104   2.49

Pala Excavator
265-2113   2.99

4-Wheel Const Crane
265-2086   2.99

Pegaso Cement Truck-Semi
265-2096   3.99

3-AXLE TRUCKS

Flat Bed Army- GMC Truck w/Top
265-2057   2.49

GMC Truck Flat Bed
265-2056   2.49

GMC Tank Truck
265-2058   2.49

PICK UP TRUCKS

Jeep Truck
265-2008
1.49

DKW Pick-Up
265-2007
1.49

CARS & CAMPERS

Camping Trailer 2 Wheel
265-2022   1.49

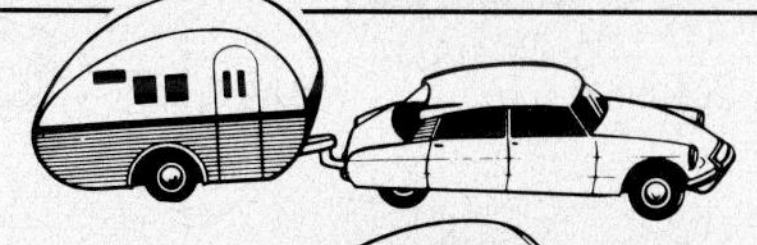

Citroen DS-19 w/Trailer
265-2059   2.99

Fiat 1800 w/Trailer
265-2060   2.99

Volkswagen w/Trailer
265-2061   2.99

HO SCALE (1/87) READY-TO-RUN

Imported from Spain by WALTHERS

Vehicles are molded in appropriately colored plastic, with painted details. Marking may vary from what is shown in catalog.

MILITARY VEHICLES

TANKS

T 34-Tipo USSR Standard
265-4001   2.49

M8 Coche Armored Car-USA
265-4002   1.99

M 48 General Patton II-USA
265-4003   2.49

Centurion-England
265-4004   2.49

M-47 General Patton-USA
265-4008   2.49

Wheeled Tank EBR-75 France
265-4017   1.99

German Tiger
265-4010   2.49

AMX 13-France
265-4011   1.99

M-4 Sherman USA
265-4012   2.49

T-54 USSR
265-4013   2.49

M-41 Bulldog USA
265-4014   2.49

German Panther
265-4009   2.49

Anti-Aircraft M-42
265-4018   2.49

M-40 USA
265-4019   2.49

PT-76 USSR
265-4020   2.49

BTR-50 USSR Personnel Carrier
265-4021   2.49

Stalin-USSR
265-4029   2.49

T-235 USA
265-4030   2.49

T-245 USA
265-4031   2.49

TANKS (continued)

Crane USA T-120
265-4032   2.49

T-98 USA
265-4033   2.49

T-113 Troop Transport USA
265-4034   2.49

Panzer P-111 German Assault
265-4040   2.49

Panzer III-Germany
265-4039   2.49

Matilda MK II-England
265-4043   2.49

AMX30-France
265-4038   2.49

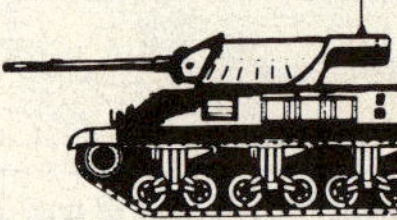

M-36 USA
265-4041   2.49

TRUCKS

Mercedes Unimog German
265-4005   1.99

Jeep Truck USA
265-4007   1.49

Military Truck w/Cargo
246-4016   2.49

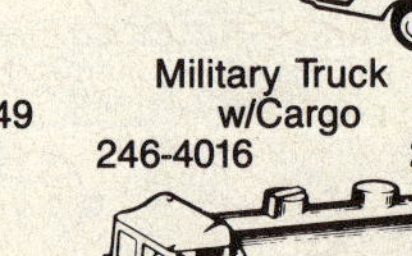

Military Jeep USA
265-4022   1.49

GMC 2.5T M-35
265-4024   2.49

GMC 2.5T Tank/ Truck M-35 USA
265-4025   2.49

GMC Lab Truck M-35 USA
265-4026   2.49

USA M-35 GMC Truck w/Rocket
265-4027   3.49

Thornycroft Mighty Antar Transport-Spain
265-4037   3.49

(not illustrated)
265-40051 Unimog w/Lt Cannon   2.49

HO SCALE (1/87) READY-TO-RUN

Imported from Spain by WALTHERS

Vehicles are molded in appropriately colored plastic, with painted details. Marking may vary from what is shown in catalog.

TRUCKS (continued)

Land Rover England	GMC M-35 Canvas Truck	TT 90.22 Truck
265-4023 1.49	265-4028 USA 2.49	SPANISH
		265-4035 1.99

(not illustrated)

265-4015	Military Truck	2.49
265-4045	Land Rover, Large	1.99

MISCELLANEOUS

German KM 8 Ton Anti-Aircraft 1/2 Track	Salva BMC Ambulance BRITAIN
265-4042 2.49	265-4044 1.99

USA Amphibious Duck	Light Cannon German
265-4036 3.49	265-4006 1.49

(not illustrated)

265-1	1992 EKO Catalog	TBA

BRAWA

HO SCALE (1/87) READY-TO-RUN

Imported from Germany by WALTHERS

Models ride on rubber tires, are powered and illuminated. Buses feature prepainted plastic bodies, in red, blue or yellow. Both standard or articulated types are available. Buses are available in sets with poles and wire or separately.

Buses require 12-16V AC or DC power supply. AC power supply needs a rectifier, but both require a 6150 speed controller. Minimum radius: 8″ with poles on inside of curve. Maximum Grade: 30%.

TROLLEYBUSES

Trolleybuses replaced streetcars in many cities and are still a familiar sight in some areas. These buses draw power from overhead electrical wires providing quiet, non-polluting transportation.

MINIMUM ROAD DIMENSIONS
Road width: Approx 2″, standard bus (one-way street) Width at corners: Artic. or Standard Bus pulling trailer: 2-1/2″ Width at Corners (two-way street) Approx 5″.

Power Car
186-6100 114.99
Approx. 5″. Poles measure approx. 3-1/2″ high.

Trailer
186-6106 24.99
Approx 5″

186-6102 Standard Trolley Bus Set 195.49
Includes standard power car and trailer, 8 polls, two power supply poles and 20 sections of wire, each about 10″. Less transformer.

Articulated Trolleybus
186-6104 134.49

186-6103 Articulated Trolleybus Set 190.99
Includes articulated trolleybus, 8 polls, two power supply poles and 20 sections of wire, each about 10″. Less transformer.

ACCESSORIES

186-6101	Replacement Pantograph	10.49

for use with buses 6100 or 6104

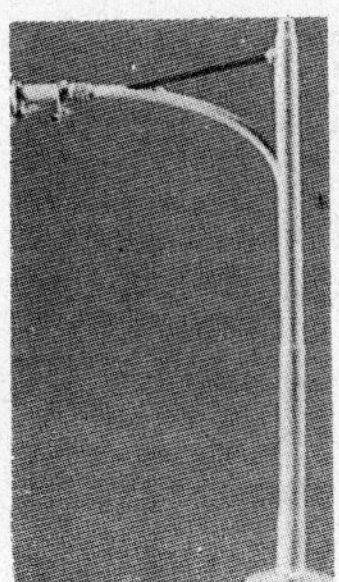

Overhead Mast 186-6111 5.99	Overhead Electric Switch 186-6120 37.99

186-6112	Overhead Power Mast	12.49
186-6127	Insulating Mast	6.99
186-6148	Overhead Reversing Loop	24.99

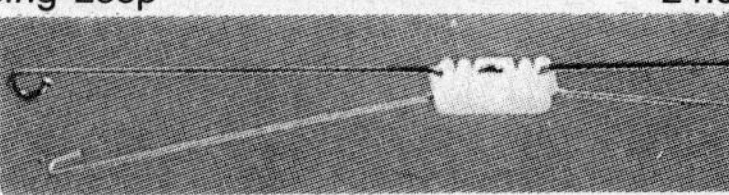

186-6117 Crossing 10.49	186-6140 Overhead Wire Crossing 8.49

between train and trolleybus wires

(not illustrated)

186-6115	Overhead Wires	pkg(20) 8.99
186-6143	Wire Connector Sleeves	pkg(10) 6.49
186-6144	Insulating Connector Sleeves	4.49
186-6126	Contact Switch Pole	7.99
186-6133	Rubber Tires	pkg(10) 5.99

to fit 6100 and 6104

186-60	Trolley Bus Catalog (English/German text)	17.49

Information on operations, maintenance and circuits for the Brawa Trolley Bus. Illustrations, color photos, 39 pages, 11 x 8-1/2″.

FALLER  

Imported from Germany and marketed by WALTHERS

Keep traffic moving on your layout with the exciting car system by Faller. Vehicles operate at a realistic speed without any unsightly slots in the roadway, power feeds or additional wiring. The FALLER car system is a fascinating technical innovation for modelers!

The integral motor drives the vehicle along, powered by re-chargeable batteries, while a steerable front axle guides the vehicles through the streets, using a specially strong magnet mounted on a triple steering link on the front axle, to actually steer the vehicles along the roads.

CAR SYSTEM VEHICLES

Assembled, precolored and lettered plastic vehicles feature long running, powerful, fully enclosed motor, rubber tires, two rechargeable batteries and built-in charging socket (no need to remove batteries to charge). Charging time for batteries approximately seven hours. Many hours of running following each charge. Colors of vehicles may vary.

VANS & RV'S

Mercedes G
w/Trailer
272-1641
106.49

MB T2 Express (blue, white)
272-1623   106.49

272-1635   VW Bus   103.49

VW Bus
w/Windows
272-1636
103.49

BUSES

MB O 5000
272-1607   *NEW* 106.49

MB O 303
"Touring"
272-1611   105.99

MB O 303
"Der O 303"
(Limited Edition)
272-1613   105.99

MB O 303
"En Vogue"
272-1614   106.49

We have worked closely with this manufacturer to provide accurate availability information at the time this catalog was published. Items listed in *blue ink* may not be available at all times. Please see your dealer for current delivery information.

TRUCKS

Scania Delivery
272-1602
106.49

DAF Delivery
272-1603
106.49

272-1605   Lorry w/Trailer   122.99

272-1606   MB w/Trailer "Dischinger"   121.49

272-1608   MB O 6600 Truck w/Trailer   *NEW* 121.49

MAN F90
Delivery Truck
272-1604 118.49
NEW

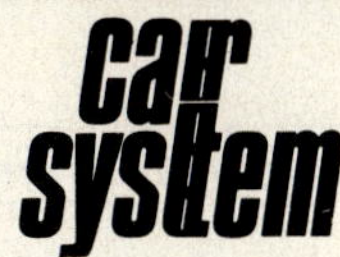

FALLER car system

Imported from Germany and marketed by WALTHERS

HO SCALE (1/87)   READY-TO-RUN

ROADWAY SECTIONS

The layout of your routes is entirely up to you, for the FALLER assortment of roadway sections is designed in such a way that buses and trucks can run through narrow and wide curves, and drive over and under bridges, on straight routes and gradients with no problems whatsoever.

You can build multi-plane routes and run your vehicles in one direction or in two directions. It's like road traffic in real life.

Each roadway package includes top road surface, die cut under boards and wire.

STRAIGHT & CURVED SECTIONS

272-1650 Straight 20.99
Includes six straight 2-lane roadway sections, each 30 cm long.

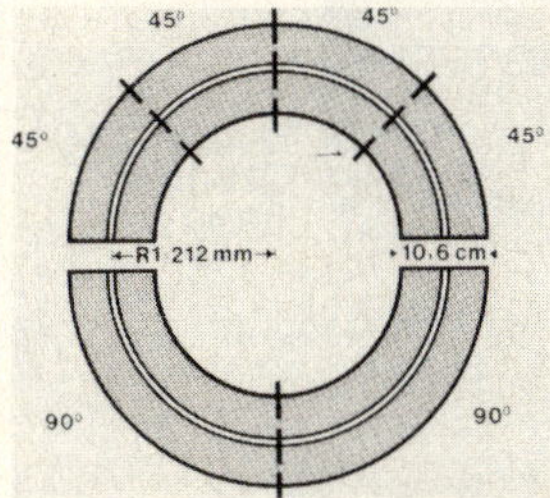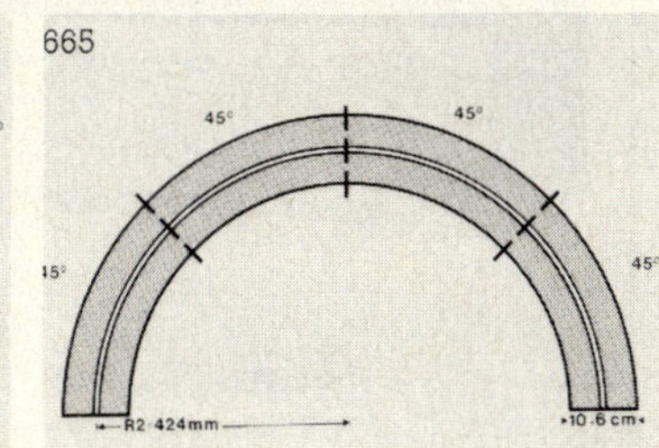

272-1660 Small 2-Lane Curve 20.99
Includes two 90° (212mm) curved sections and four 45° (212mm) curved sections.

272-1665 Large 2-Lane Curve 20.99
Includes four 45° (424mm) curved roadway sections.

PARTS

272-1670	Driving Wire 33′	7.99
272-1720	Traction Tires	pkg(10) 5.49
272-1730	Steering Wiper w/Magnet	pkg(5) 10.99

CAR SYSTEM LAYOUT **NEW**

272-1590 469.99

CAR SYSTEM CHARGER

Charge unit charges batteries in approximately seven hours. Input: 12VA 60 Hz 5W Output: 3V DC 200 mA.

272-16000 18.99

PLANNING TEMPLATE

272-1671 Car System Planning Template 4.49
Wiring planning for single and double-lane roads using the Faller Car System. Hard shoulders and central reserves can also be marked. Includes instructions.

The roadway system has been designed to be simple to lay.

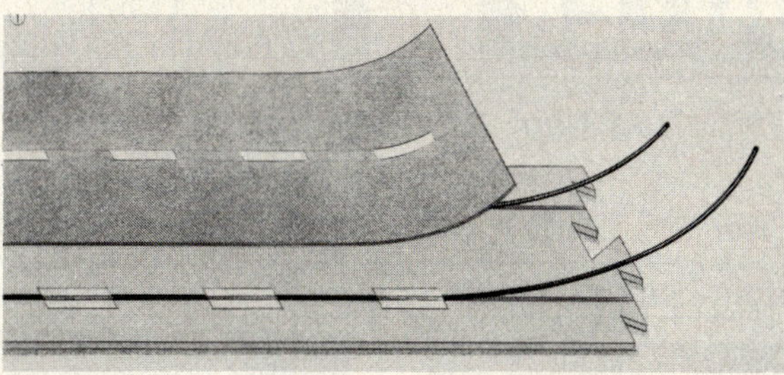

Those who wish for the simple life can make up the roads using the specially made 2-lane, die cut boards which already include guides for the wire.

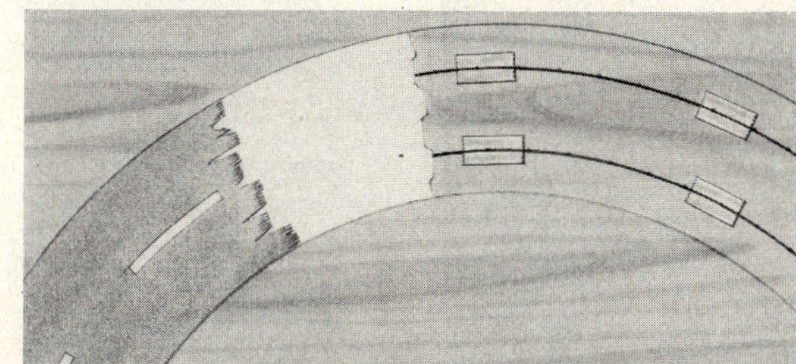

Those who enjoy a challenge can simply lay the special fine guide wire onto the road surface in either new or ready-made layouts or dioramas - with no problems whatsoever.

TURNOUTS & CROSSINGS

272-1661 Crossover Junction 20.99
Double lane with four roadway sections to make up a crossover junction with roadway sections 1650, 1660 & 1665. 5-7/8 x 5-7/8″ (15 x 15 cm).
272-1657 Level Crossing 7.99
To easily cross over model railway tracks. Suitable for the most track systems.
272-1675 Stop Section 14.49
Electro-mechanically operated with permanent magnet. The magnet cuts off the battery power with a special switchmounted inside the vehicle.
272-1676 Branch-Off Junction 20.99
Electro-mechanically operated with moving parts.
272-1662 Branch-Off 20.99
Includes one left & one right hand Branch-off road section.

CONTROL SWITCHES

272-1679 Control Switch 18.99
Four terminals with integrated rectifier for switching stop sections and branch-off sections.

AUTOS FOR CAR SYSTEM

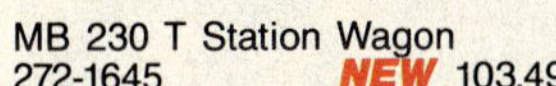

MB 230 T Station Wagon
272-1645 **NEW** 103.49

MB 230 T Taxi
272-1646 **NEW** 103.49

We have worked closely with this manufacturer to provide accurate availability information at the time this catalog was published. Items listed in *blue ink* may not be available at all times. Please see your dealer for current delivery information.

FALLER

HO SCALE (1/87) READY-TO-RUN

Imported from Germany and marketed by *WALTHERS*

Assembled precolored plastic vehicles.

EMERGENCY VEHICLES FOR CAR SYSTEM

LF16 Fire Truck
272-1620   121.49

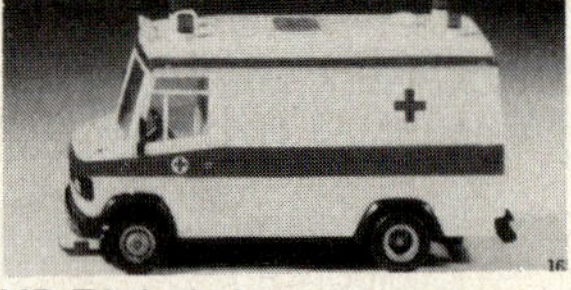

MB T2 Ambulance
272-1621   106.49

MB G Jeep (red)
272-1643   100.49

Mercedes G
272-1640   103.49

TRUCKS

MAN F90 w/Self-Loader
272-1020   15.49

MAN F90
272-1021   15.49

MAN F90 Shark Show
272-1024
20.49

MB Lorry "Dischinger" (Limited Run)
272-984
20.49

MB Van "Dischinger" (Limited Run)
272-985
21.99

MB Service Truck
272-1025   **NEW** 19.49

MB Service Truck "Break Dancer"
272-1026   **NEW** 22.99

(not illustrated)
272-1039   Fair Personnell Truck 2-axle   **NEW** 24.99

TRAILERS

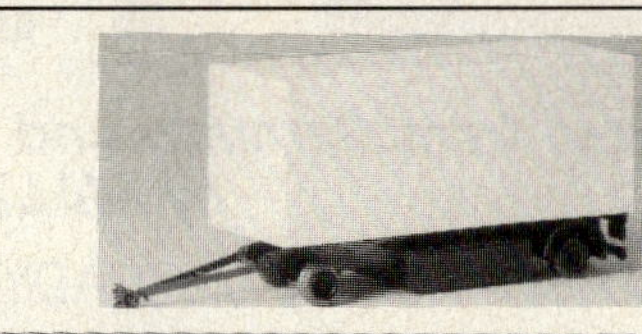

2-Axle
272-1035
15.49

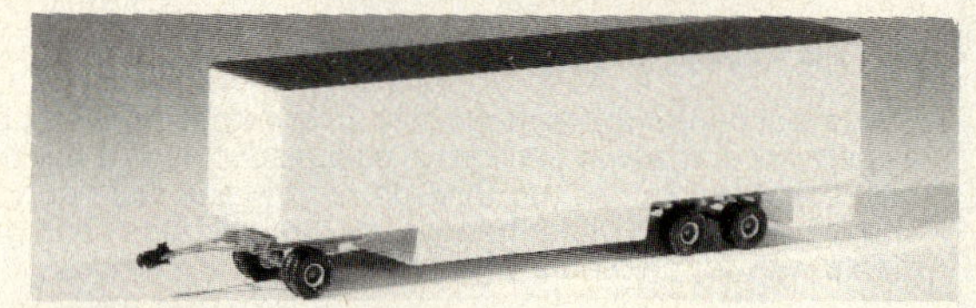

272-1036   3-Axle   16.49

2-Axle "Jupiter"
272-1034   15.49

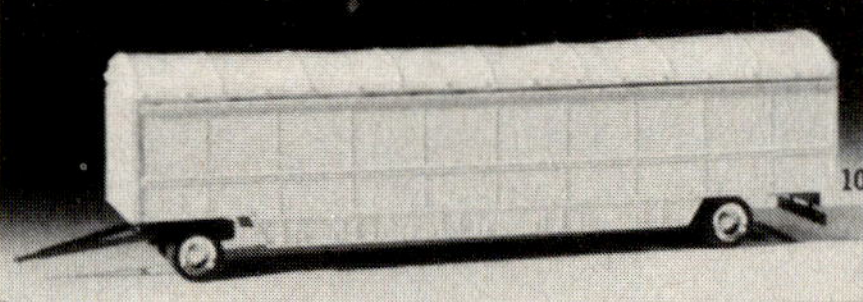

2-Axle, Long
272-1032
19.49

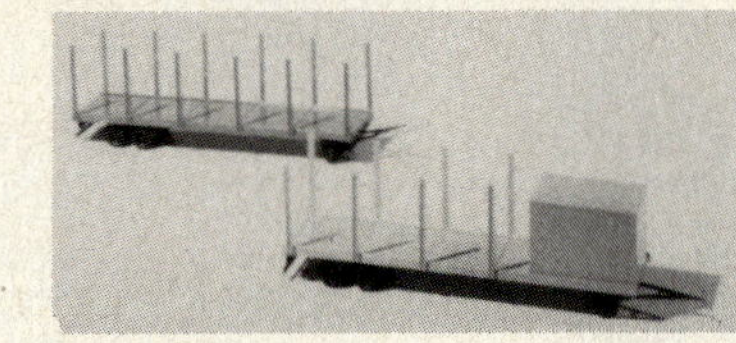

272-1037   3-Axle w/Stakes   15.49
272-1038   3-Axle w/Container   17.49

ACCESSORIES

591

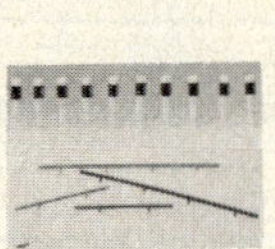
592

506

1655

272-591   Roadway Markings   8.49
Self-adhesive rub-on transfers.
272-592   Crash Barriers   8.49
Includes 32 marker posts and 80 cm length of crash barrers.
272-506   Roadway paint for car system   bottle(250ml)   6.49
272-1655   Traffic Lights w/Switch   pkg(2) 71.49
Micro-processor controlled traffic light electronics can operate four traffic lights. 12-16V AC/DC.
272-1656   Traffic Lights Less Switch   pkg(2) 37.49
For use with operating switch included in #272-1655.

MAY 1, 1888

Today
IN RAILROAD HISTORY

The Atchinson, Topeka & Santa Fe completes its route from Chicago to California.

herpa

HO SCALE (1/87)

Assembled vehicles are molded in appropriately colored plastic. Vehicles marked as "metallic paint" are painted plastic, simulating a shiny, metal finish.

AUTOS

Porsche 944
326-20398   5.00
326-30397   5.50
metallic paint

Porsche 928 S4
326-20718   6.50
326-30717   7.00
metallic paint

Porsche 928 S4
326-100144   20.00
metallic paint

Porsche 911 Turbo 87
326-20602   6.50
326-30601   7.00
metallic paint

Porsche 956 MG
(white)
326-25034   12.00

Porsche 911 Turbo
Private Collection
326-100106   20.00
metallic paint

BMW 325i Coupe
(metallic) **NEW**
326-30977   9.50

BMW 325i Cabriolet
326-20596   6.00
326-30595   6.50
metallic paint

BMW 325i Touring
Station Wagon
326-20633   6.50
326-30632   7.00
metallic paint

BMW 325i
326-20893   7.00
326-30892   7.50
metallic paint

BMW 535i
326-20657   6.60
326-30656   7.00
metallic paint

BMW 750i
326-25041   12.00
metallic paint

BMW 750il
326-25058   12.00

BMW 735i
326-20435   6.50
326-30434   7.00
metallic paint

BMW Z-1
326-20749   7.00
326-30748   7.00
metallic paint

326-20794 BMW 850i Coupe (metallic) 8.00
326-30793 BMW 850i Coupe (metallic) 8.50

BMW NEW
325i Coupe
326-21036   9.00

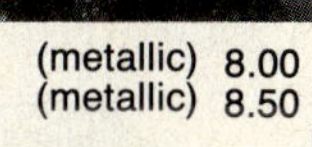

BMW M1
326-20183   5.00

BMW M3
326-20619   6.00
326-30618   6.50
metallic paint

BMW M3
Herpa-Motorsport
326-35309   22.00

BMW 525i
Touring
326-20961   7.50
326-30960   8.00
metallic paint

BMW Team
Linder
326-35330   22.00

BWM Team MM
326-35347   22.00

BMW 325i
Cabrio Carribean
326-45001   29.00

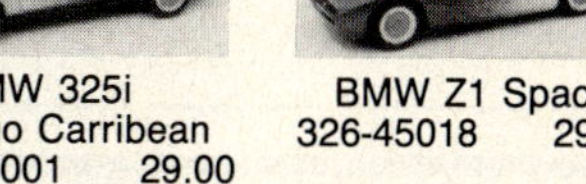

BMW Z1 Space
326-45018   29.00

BMW 735i B11
326-100090   20.00
metallic paint

BMW Alpina B10
326-100151   22.00

BMW M3 NEW
326-21173   9.00

BMW 74011 NEW
326-25430   12.00
(green/metallic)

BMW M3 NEW
326-31172   9.50
(metallic)

BMW M# NEW
Herpa DTT 92
326-35484   23.00

BMW M3 NEW
Schnitzer A Hager
326-35514   23.00

BMW NEW
525i Taxi
326-41102   8.50

Volkswagen Passat
326-20688   6.50
326-30687   7.00
metallic paint

VW Passant Caravan
326-20831   7.50
326-30830   8.00
metallic paint

VW Passat Taxi
326-41317   9.00

VW Golf 4-Door
326-20480   5.00

VW Golf GTi 2-Door
326-20510   5.50

VW Corrado
326-20671   6.50
326-30670   7.00
metallic paint

VW Golf NEW
GL 4-Door
326-21098   8.00

VW Golf NEW
GL 2-Door
326-21159   8.00

VW Golf NEW
BR6 4-Door
326-21166   8.00

VW Golf NEW
GL 4-Door
326-31097 met 8.50

VW Golf NEW
2-Door (metallic)
3267-31158   8.50

VW Golf NEW
VR6 4-Door (met)
326-31165   8.50

Opel Kadett GL
326-20459   5.50

Opel Kadett GSi
326-20466   5.50

Opel Kadett
Cabriolet
326-20589   6.50
326-30588   7.00
metallic paint

Opel Corsa
Hatchback
326-20367   5.00

Opel Vectra
Stufenheck
326-20725   6.50
326-30724   7.00
(metallic paint)

herpa

HO SCALE (1/87)

Assembled vehicles are molded in appropriately colored plastic. Vehicles marked as "metallic paint" are painted plastic, simulating a shiny, metal finish.

AUTOS (continued)

Opel Vectra
Fliebheck
326-20732 6.50
326-30731 7.00
metallic paint

Opel Omega
326-20572 5.50

Opel Omega
Caravan
326-20664 6.50

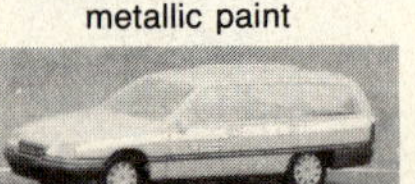

Opel Omega
Caravan
326-41294 8.00

Mercedes 190E
326-20404 5.00
326-30403 5.50
metallic paint

Mercedes 300 CE
326-20640 6.50

Mercedes 500Sl
326-25157 Blk 12.50
326-25164 Rd 12.50
metallic paint

MB 190E Evolution 1
326-30908 7.00
metallic paint

MB 300 CE Brabus
Private Collection
326-100021 20.00

MB 300 CE **NEW**
Convertible
326-21128 8.50

MB 600 **NEW**
SEC
326-21135 9.50

MB 560 SEC
Cabriolet
326-20879 6.00
326-30878 6.50
metallic paint

MB 230 GE
Cabriolet
326-30755 6.50
metallic paint

MB 560 SEC
Brabus
326-100014 20.00

MB 300 GE
326-20855 7.50
326-30854 8.00
metallic paint

MB 300 E
"Facelifting"
326-20916 7.50
326-30915 8.00
metallic paint

MB 300 TE
Standard
326-20930 7.50
326-30939 8.00
metallic paint

MB 600 SEL
326-20947 9.50
326-30946 9.90

MB 500 SL
Private Collection
326-25409 14.00

MB 190 E2.5
Evolution II
326-30953 9.50
metallic paint

MB 190
Evolution II
"Zakspeed"
326-35385 23.00

MB 300 E
Private Collection
326-100168 22.00

MB 300 CE **NEW**
326-30649 7.00
metallic paint

MBG 300 **NEW**
Conversion
326-30847 (met) 8.00

MB 300 CE
Convertible
326-31127 9.00
Metallic

MB600 SEC **NEW**
326-31134 9.90
metallic paint

MB 190 **NEW**
Evolution II Snobeck
326-35415 23.00

MB 300E **NEW**
Taxi
326-41591 9.00

MB 6.0 **NEW**
SL Brabus
326-100069 22.00

MB 600 SEL **NEW**
326-100113 22.00

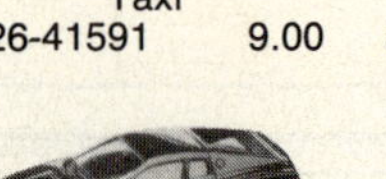

Ferrari **NEW**
Testarossa (blk)
326-25027 12.00

Ferrari Testarossa
326-25003 12.00

Ferrari Testarossa
(red)
326-100038 22.00

Ferrari Testarossa
(white)
326-100045 22.00

Ferrari 348 ts
(red)
326-25300 13.50

Ferrari 348 tb
326-25256 13.50

Ferrari F40 **NEW**
(red)
326-25102 12.50

Ferrari **NEW**
348tb
326-100267 25.00

Audi Conv **NEW**
326-21074 8.50

Audi **NEW**
Convertible (met)
326-31073 9.00

Audi **NEW**
Coupe (met)
326-31080 9.00

Audi V8 **NEW**
Evolution AZR #45
326-35392 23.00

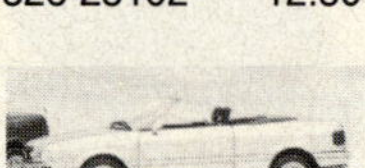

Audi V8 **NEW**
Evlution AZR #44
326-35408 23.00

Audi **NEW**
Convertible Fresh
326-45025 29.00

Audi V8 **NEW**
"SMS"
326-35354 23.00

Audi Quattro
326-20442 5.00

Audi 90 Quattro
Coupe
326-25201 13.00
metallic paint

Audi V8
326-30922 9.50
metallic paint

Audi V8 "SMS"
Evolution
326-35361 23.00

Citroen 2CV **NEW**
Charlston
326-20817 6.50

Citroen 2CV
326-20824 5.50
metallic paint

Mini Cooper **NEW**
326-21104 8.00

Mini Cooper **NEW**
German
326-21210 12.00

Mini Cooper **NEW**
(metallic)
326-31103 8.50

herpa
HO SCALE (1/87)

Assembled vehicles are molded in appropriately colored plastic. Vehicles marked as "metallic paint" are painted plastic, simulating a shiny, metal finish.

AUTOS (continued)

Peugeot 205
Turbo 16V
326-20695   6.00

Trabant *NEW*
601S Universal
326-20770   6.50

MBG 300 *NEW*
GE Conversion
326-20848   7.50

Trabant 601 S
326-20763   6.50

Trabant 601S
German
Postal Service
326-41324   8.00

Trabant 601
Private Collection
326-100076   15.00

Renault R4
326-20190   5.00

Jaguar XJ12
326-20206   5.00
326-30205   5.50
metallic paint

Jaguar XJ12
Private Collection
326-100083   20.00
metallic paint

Fiat *NEW*
Cinquecento
326-21142   6.00

Fiat *NEW*
Cinquecento (met)
326-31141   6.50

Lamborghini *NEW*
Diablo (red)
326-25423   14.00

(not illustrated)

326-21081	Audi Coupe	*NEW*	8.50
326-21357	Opel Corsa GLS 2-door	*NEW*	7.00
326-21364	Renault Clio 16V 2-Door	*NEW*	7.00
326-31356	Opel Corsa GLS 2-Door	*NEW* (met)	7.50
326-31363	Renault Clio 16V 2-door	*NEW* (met)	7.50
326-35422	MB 190 Evolution II AMG #78	*NEW*	23.00
326-35590	MB AMG Ommen	*NEW*	23.00
326-35606	BMW M3 Valier Engstler	*NEW*	23.00
326-35637	Audi V8 SMS Hanstuck	*NEW*	23.00
326-35644	Audi V8 AZR Frk Biola	*NEW*	23.00
326-35774	BMW M3 Auto Maass #18	*NEW*	23.00
326-35781	BMW M3 Kaucak #32	*NEW*	23.00
326-41096	BMW 535i Notarzt		8.50

EMERGENCY VEHICLES

Mercedes 300E
Fire
326-4103   5.29

MB 300 E
Police
326-41416   9.90

■ **LTD QTY** ■
MB 190 E Fire Car
326-4058 plastic 5.79

EMERGENCY VEHICLES (continued)

BMW *NEW*
325i Police
326-41584   11.50

MB 300TE *NEW*
Police
326-41638   9.90

Opel Vectra *NEW*
Lft-bk Police
326-41713   9.50

MB 207D Van *NEW*
Ambulance
326-41157   9.00

MB Gloria LVF *NEW*
112 Firetruck
326-41263   13.00

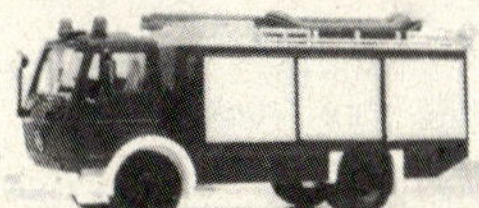
MB Pumper RW-2 *NEW*
326-41492   14.50

MAN M90 DKL *NEW*
Aerial Ladder
326-41515   19.50

Mercedes 711 Fire Truck
326-41065   13.50

MB 814/TLF Fire Truck
326-41508   12.98

MB T2 Fire Truck
326-41423   9.50

MB LP 813 Fire Truck
326-814302   5.98

MB T2 Truck Rotkrz
326-41218   13.50

MB T2 Rescue Truck
326-41256   8.00

VW Passat *NEW*
Police Station Wagon
326-41362   9.50

Renault R4 Fire Dept
326-41195   7.50

BMW 323i Police
326-41164   8.50

BMW 528i
Emergency Services
326-4061 plastic 4.79

BMW 525i Police
326-41126   8.50

VW Bus Bah Polizei *NEW*
326-41645   9.00

Opel Omega Fire Car
326-4084   plastic   5.29

Opel Vectra Police
326-41300   8.50

VW Passat Fire Dept
326-41331   9.00

VW Passat Police Car
326-41409   9.50

herpa

HO SCALE (1/87)

Assembled vehicles are molded in appropriately colored plastic. Vehicles marked as "metallic paint" are painted plastic, simulating a shiny, metal finish.

EMERGENCY VEHICLES (continued)

MAN M90 TLF16 Fire Truck
326-41430   22.50

MAN LKW 5TFire Truck
326-820034   12.98

Fire Truck Accessories
326-50135   5.00

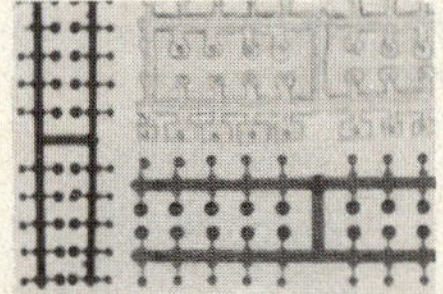

Warning Lights (blue)
326-50142   5.00
326-50494   5.50

(not illustrated)
326-41836 MB T2 Police Van   *NEW* 13.50
326-806057 MB Rescue Vehicle   11.49

TRUCKS

326-859126 MAN F90 Semi Truck Wandt   22.98

MB Truck w/Snowplow
326-140027   15.00

MB Semi Truck Truck Kieserling
326-811155   15.98

MB Dumpster
326-140041   13.50

MB Flatbed w/Tarp
326-41348   11.50

326-140058 MB Auto Transporter   18.00

MB Garbage Truck
326-140034   13.50

MB Garbage Truck
326-41201   13.50
(By Special Order Only.)

MB 207D Truck Post *NEW*
326-41232   8.50

Flatbed w/Hoist "Schenker"
326-140096   17.50

MB Tractor Private Collection
326-110013   28.00

MB Sweeper Set
326-140089   22.00

326-140188 MB Tanker "Willi Betz"   24.00

MB Sk Box Trailer "Veltins"
326-140522   29.00

MB SK 2A *NEW* w/Chassis Cov
326-110099   29.00

MB Ruthman - *NEW* Stieger Ch/Pkr
326-140102   18.50

MB Tractor 3-Axle w/Air Dam *NEW*
326-140423   13.50

MB Tractor w/Flatbed *NEW*
326-140461   17.50

herpa

HO SCALE (1/87)

Assembled vehicles are molded in appropriately colored plastic. Vehicles marked as "metallic paint" are painted plastic, simulating a shiny, metal finish.

TRUCKS (continued)

MB Sk w/Dump Trailer NEW
326-141215   16.50

MB 814 Car Transport NEW
326-141246   26.00

MB Sk Tranker Talke NEW
326-141581   28.00

MB Sk 1748 NEW
w/Trailer Canvas
326-141949   27.00

MB SK Car Transporter NEW
326-141567   18.50

MB SK Low Loader NEW
326-141963   w/Lights   18.50

MAN F90 2-Axle Prvt Coll NEW
326-110044   28.00

MAN F90 Chassis NEW
326-110105   29.00

MAN F90 w/Dump Trailer NEW
326-141222   16.50

MAN G90 Car Transport NEW
326-141239   26.00

MAN F90 Concrete
326-141574   16.50

MAN F90 NEW
Double Bottom RB
326-141956   26.00

MAN F90 Semi SMS
326-35439   29.00

Freightliner w/Cont Amer NEW
326-140324   22.00

MB SK Tractor
w/Dump Trailer
326-140591   16.50

MB SK
Cement Truck
326-140607   16.50

MB SK Truck
w/Rear Tailboard
"Schenker"
326-140638   18.50

MB SK Canvas
Tailer "SIXT"
326-140669
26.00

MB SK
4-Axle Dump Truck
326-140683   16.50

MB SK-DLK
23-12 w/Basket
326-41522
19.50

MAN
Double
Bottom
Edeka
326-140126
24.00

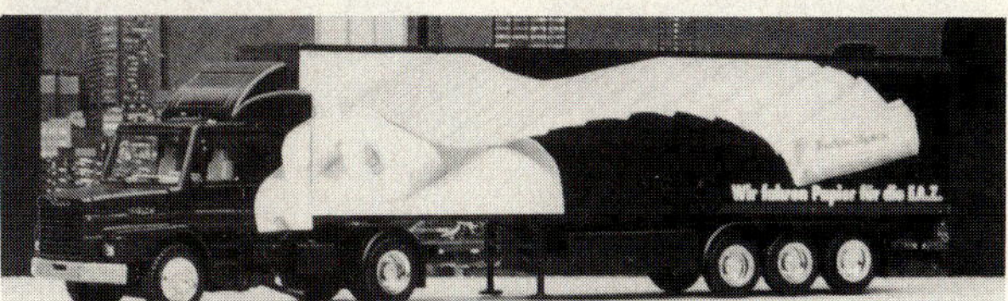

326-140263 Scania Semi-Truck F.A.Z.   30.00

Scania
Tank Trailer
326-140539
28.00

326-140652 Scania Canvas Truck/Trailer "ASG"   28.00

herpa

HO SCALE (1/87)

Assembled vehicles are molded in appropriately colored plastic. Vehicles marked as ''metallic paint'' are painted plastic, simulating a shiny, metal finish.

TRUCKS (continued)

Scania 2-axle Tractor
326-140294   12.50

Scania Semi (undec) **NEW**
326-140225   18.50

Scania w/Trailer Spoilers **NEW**
326-141451   13.50

Renault w/Trailer Escom **NEW**
326-141055   26.00

VW Platform Truck **NEW**
326-41676   7.50

Peterbuilt w/Cont Dole **NEW**
326-140546   22.50

Peterbilt w/Trailer Nitrol **NEW**
326-141352   24.00

Kenworth Semi Ple **NEW**
325-140300   22.00

Kenworth w/Trailer Sixt **NEW**
326-141604   24.00

Kenworth Tractor **NEW**
w/Moving Van ''Mayflower''
326-65054   20.00

Mack Slp w/Trailer UP **NEW**
326-141987   22.00

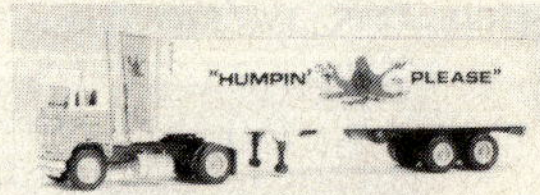

Tractor/Trailer **NEW**
''Humpin to Please''
326-140553   22.50

Tractor w/Double **NEW**
Trailer Preston
326-140690   22.50

Mack w/Trailer Feed Rite
326-141048   26.00

Iveco Truck/ **NEW**
Trailer Danzas
326-140287   22.00

Iveco Turbo Tractor **NEW**
2-Axle
326-141932   12.50

Iveco Turbo Trans Herpa **NEW**
326-35521   29.00

Mack w/Slp Mayflower
326-141406   23.00

Tanker Set
326-75855
pkg(3) 22.00

326-140270   Renault Semi-Truck ACL   24.00

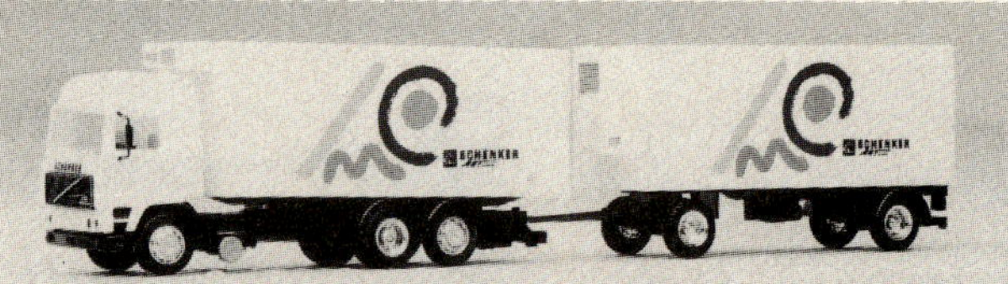

326-140119   Volvo Double-Bottom Van ''Schenker''   24.00

Mack CH603 Semi
Kuehne & Nagel
326-140737
24.00

Mack CH600 Solo Tractor Metallic
326-140614
14.50

Semi Dump Truck ''Gray''
326-140720
22.50

LIMITED QUANTITIES AVAILABLE

326-859185   MAN Double-Bottom Van ''Schenker''   22.98

herpa®

HO SCALE (1/87)

Assembled vehicles are molded in appropriately colored plastic. Vehicles marked as "metallic paint" are painted plastic, simulating a shiny, metal finish.

MAN M90 Three Side Dump Truck
326-140416   14.50

MAN F90 Double Bottom Van
326-140560   24.00

MAN 690 Canvas Truck "Blave Flotte"
326-140577   18.50

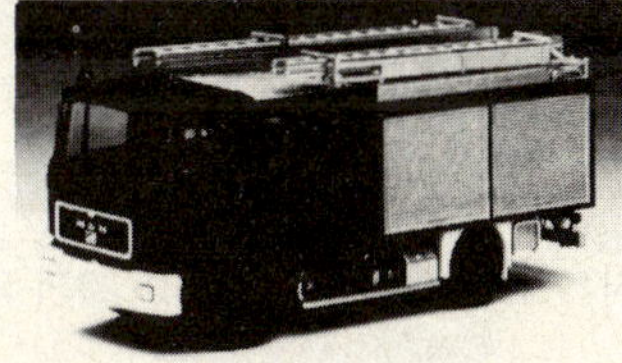

MAN M90 LF-16 Fire Truck
326-41447   22.00

MAN Tank Aral
326-864001   15.98

DAF 95 Truck w/Trailer "Blue Fleet"
326-140164   19.00

DAF 95 Tractor
326-140447   12.50

Iveco, Ferrymasters
326-813001   15.98

Iveco Semi-Truck "Private Collection"
326-110020   28.00

MAN F90 Tractor Truck
326-140579   12.50

(not illustrated)

326-4122	Opel Omega Caravan Maltes	8.49
326-120005	MB SK 2a w/Trailer Wemberger	49.00
326-140010	MB concrete	15.00
326-35613	MB Transport Diebels Alt	29.00
326-140010	MB Concrete +	15.00
326-140065	MB Double Bottom Van "Bavaria"	22.00
326-140454	Setra 215HDH Express Tour	26.00
326-141475	Iveco Concrete Mixer	16.50
326-811499	MB 2235	13.98
326-811557	MB Double Bottom Scholr Manhattan	22.98
326-825000	DAF Space Cab 3-Axle Tractor	10.49
326-843022	Scania Satlzg Wernberger	23.98
326-854004	Freightliner Tanker Safety Klen	18.98
326-855000	Freightliner Bottom Riteway	18.98
326-864004	MAN F90 Dump Truck	13.98

VANS & LIGHT TRUCKS

MB 207D Truck Schenker
326-41249   9.50

326-41041   MB100   7.50

MB100
326-40921   7.00

MB100w/Windows
326-40884   7.00

MB 100 Delivery Van
326-41393   7.00

MB 814 Delivery Van "Sixt"
326-140645   16.50

VW T Van
326-41614   7.50

Trailers Set-3
326-75800   29.50

Mack Moving Van N America
326-140706   26.00

(not illustrated)

326-75336	Semi **NEW** Trailer Set	19.50
326-822044	Scania Double Bottom Van	13.98
326-824000	DAF Double Van Spedition	19.98
326-826052	MB Double-Bottom Van Mltzr & Mnch	22.98
326-839041	Volvo Double Bottom Van	17.98
326-843014	Scania w/Van Nogger	19.98

herpa®

HO SCALE (1/87)

Assembled vehicles are molded in appropriately colored plastic. Vehicles marked as "metallic paint" are painted plastic, simulating a shiny, metal finish.

BUSES

VW "Zoll"
326-41379   8.00

MB 100 Metallic
326-41386   8.00

Setra 5215 "Wild"
326-140584
26.00

Setra S221 UL Art **NEW**
326-141598   But RVO   26.00

Setra S228DT **NEW**
326-141284   Nothegger   26.00

VW Postal Bus **NEW**
326-41270   8.00

VW Caravelle **NEW**
326-41652   Schoolbus   11.50

MB 100 Bus **NEW**
326-41621   7.50

MAN SU 240 Bus **NEW**
326-140485   15.00

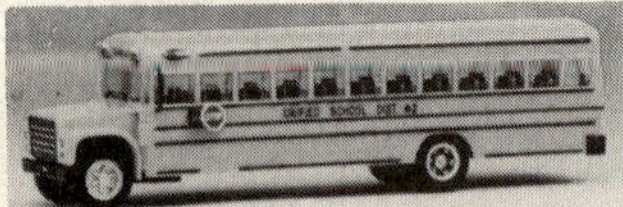

US School Bus **NEW**
326-140492   Harvestor   20.00

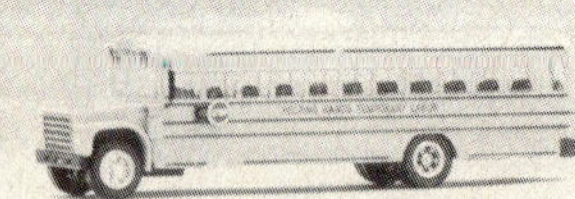

US School Bus Helping **NEW**
326-140508   Hands   20.00

MAN City Bus "Night & Day" **NEW**
326-141383   23.00

S215 HD Muler **NEW**
326-141369   26.00

(not illustrated)

326-35620	MB 100 Bus Diobels	**NEW**	23.00
326-35651	MAN w/Chas Cov & SMS	**NEW**	29.00
326-35798	MB 190E DTM Jr Team #20	**NEW**	23.00
326-35804	MB SK Trailer DTM Jr Team	**NEW**	29.00
326-868001	Setra HDH Bus Becker		22.98

ACCESSORIES

326-75374   40' Container   8.00

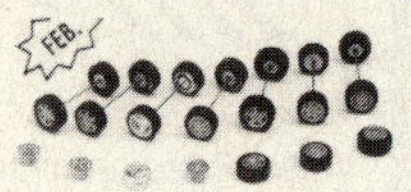
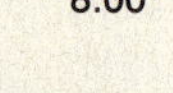

Sport Tire **NEW**
Accessories
326-50661   7 x 4   6.50

20' Container
326-75381   pkg(2) 8.00

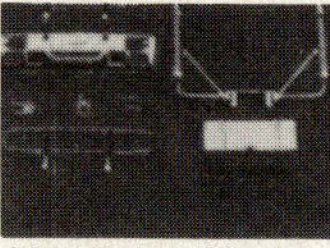

Mercedes Chrome
326-50579   5.50

Truck
326-50524   5.50

Tail Lights Assorted Colors
326-50425   5.00

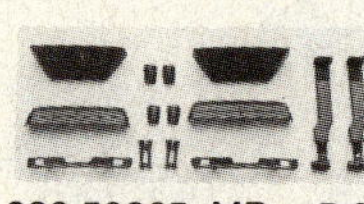

326-50265 MB   5.00
Includes horns, sun visors, wind deflectors and bug screens.

Wheelset
326-50548   5.50

Warning Lights
326-50159   5.00

Gas Cylinders on Pallets
326-50470   5.50

Wheelset
326-50531   5.50

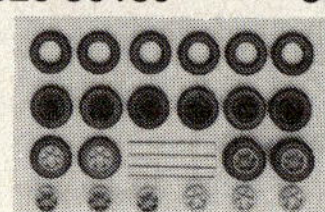

Wheels
326-50197   5.00

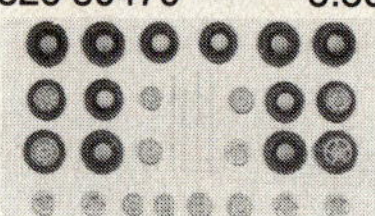

Auto Wheels
326-50401   5.00

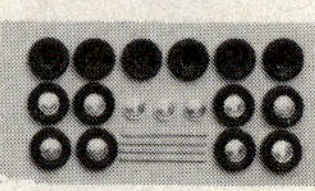

Bus Wheels
326-50357   5.00

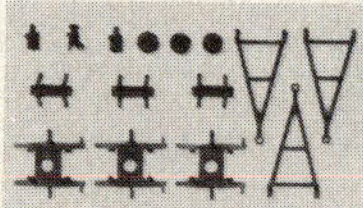

Tow Bar & 5th Wheel
326-50227pkg(3) 5.00

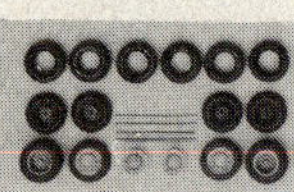

Truck Wheels
326-50326 +   5.00

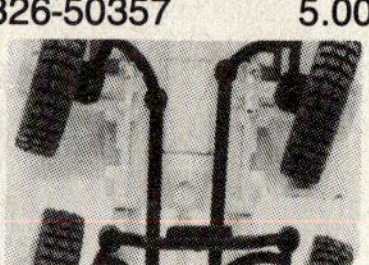

Road Vehicle Set
326-50517   5.50

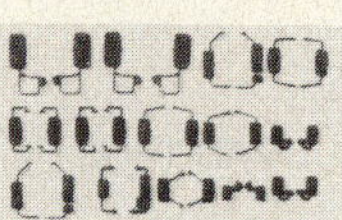

Rear View Mirrors
326-50203   5.00

Cable Reels
326-50487   5.50

Sport Car Tires
326-50500   5.50

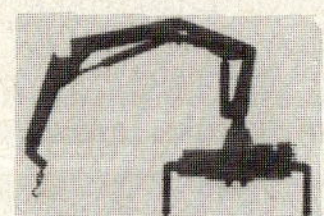

Truck Loading Crane
326-50449   5.00

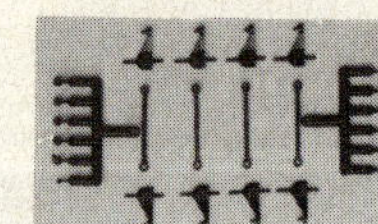

Truck
326-50333   5.00

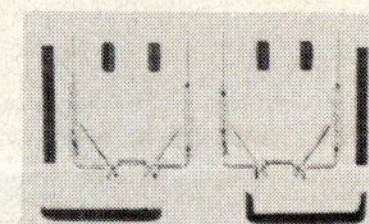

Exhaust/Spoiler
326-50364   5.00

Spoilers for MAN Trucks
326-50371   5.00

Extra Fuel Tanks & Windscreen
326-50234   5.00

Motorsport **NEW**
Sts/Crsh Cgs
326-50562   5.50

herpa®
HO SCALE (1/87)

Assembled vehicles are molded in appropriately colored plastic. Vehicles marked as "metallic paint" are painted plastic, simulating a shiny, metal finish.

ACCESSORIES (continued)

(not illustrated)

License Plate Set German **NEW**
326-50692   5.00

Herpa Catalog English **NEW**
326-199315   3.00

Cable Drums **NEW**
326-50555   5.50

DECAL

Presized, multi-colored decal.

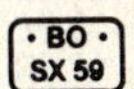

Enlarged to show details

MAN Truck Decal
326-5038   3.79

Fire Truck Decals **NEW**
326-50074   5.00

(not illustrated)

326-50395   Scania Truck Decal   5.00
326-50029   License Plates   5.00

DISPLAY CASE

Precolored (white or brown as noted) molded plastic. Inserts are vacuformed plastic with holes for wall mounting and a clear plastic dust cover. Each measures about 15 x 22." For more stylish display, individual insert boxes can be framed using the Display Case Frames. For added protection and appearance, a plexiglass cover that fits the frame is also available. Each item is sold separately.

Display Case Frame, Mixed
326-29520
70.00

Showcase Car/Van **NEW**
326-29209   (white)   19.95

Showcase Car **NEW**
326-29339   (white)   9.95

(not illustrated)

326-29308   Insert, Car & Truck   (brown)   19.95
326-29315   Insert, Truck   (brown)   19.95
326-29322   Insert, Car   (brown)   19.95
326-29216   Insert, Truck   (white)   19.95
326-29223   Insert, Car   (white)   19.95
326-29704   Plexiglass Cover   15.00

A-LINE
A division of **PROTO POWER WEST**
HO SCALE (1/87)
EASY-TO-BUILD KITS

FRUEHAUF "Z" VAN

Commonly seen on piggyback trains and highways, the prototype 40' Fruehauf "Z" van has been in production since 1960. Kits are molded in aluminum and black styrene with separate tires, spoked wheel hubs, mudflaps, doorbars and other details. Each kit includes two undecorated trailers with complete instructions and a list of correct decals.

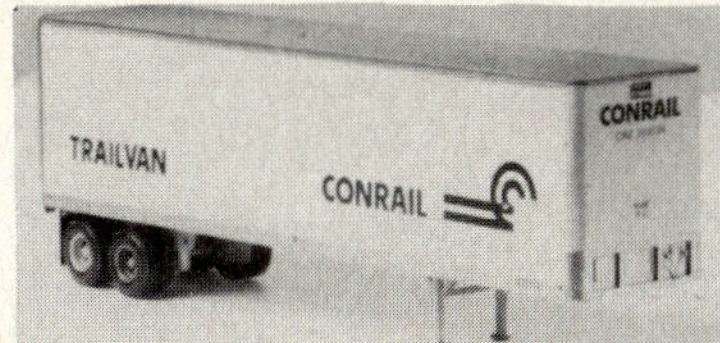

Van, Undecorated
116-50101
pkg(2) 10.95
Smooth-side van, manufactured from 1979-1986.

Original Van
116-50102
pkg(2) 10.95
Beaded-side van includes disc and spoked hubs. Manufactured from 1965-1978.

116-50115   Van, 5' Extension Kit   **NEW**   3.95
Replicates prototype practice of extending a 40' van to 45' length.

28' Parcel Van, Undecorated
116-50113   TBA

Parcel Van, Fifth Wheel Dolly
NEW   116-50114   TBA
Allows two 28' Parcel Vans to be operated as "doubles".

VAN ACCESSORIES

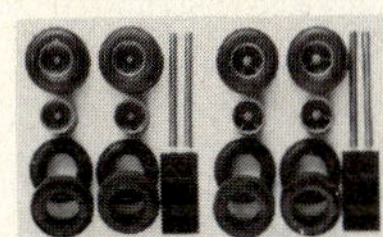

116-50103   Van Up-Grade Kit   pkg(2)   4.25
Contains tires, hubs, axles and mud flaps for two vans.

116-50104   Tire Pack (Vinyl)   each   4.25
Contains 24 tires and 12 mud flaps. Fits Con-Cor, Roco and Lindberg.

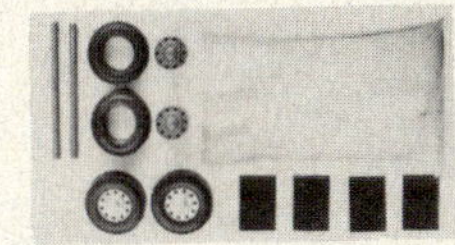

116-50105   Tractor Wheels   each   4.25
Contains Budd 2-hole disc hubs (two front, four driven), ten tires, axles and mud flaps for one tractor.

116-50106   Front Tractor Wheels   each   4.25
Contains four cast 10-hole hubs (Budd), four tires, axles and mud flaps for two tractors.

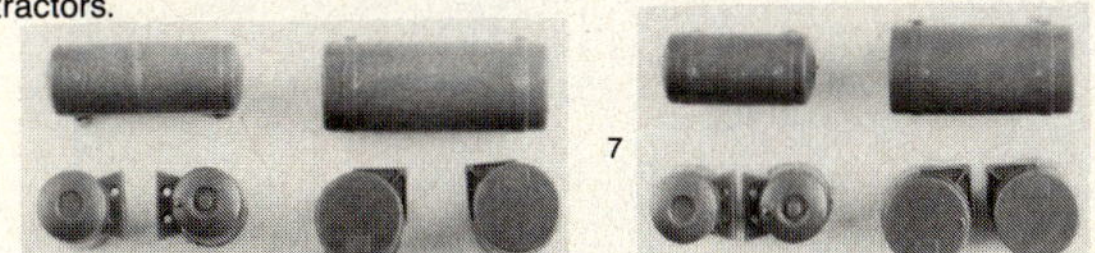

116-50107   Fuel Tanks, Long   pkg(4)   3.80
Contains two 150 gallon fuel tanks and two 60" refrigerator fuel tanks.

116-50108   Fuel Tanks, Short   pkg(4)   3.80
Contains two 120 gallon fuel tanks and two 47" refrigerator fuel tanks.

(not illustrated)

116-50110   Roll-Up Door (styrene)   pkg(2)   2.95
116-50111   Van Landing Gear (Up) (styrene)   pkg(2)   2.95
Two sets of trailmobile style landing gear.
116-50112   Van Landing Gear (Down)   2.95
Two sets of trailmobile style landing gear.

International Hobby Corp.
HO (1/87) READY-TO-RUN

Assembled, appropriately colored plastic vehicles, unless noted.

FIRE ENGINES

348-4200 Pumper (red) 5.49

348-4210 Ladder Truck (red) 5.98

CONSTRUCTION VEHICLE

348-4220 Road Grader (yellow) 3.98

MISCELLANEOUS

348-422306 Automobile Set 3.98

U-HAUL TRUCKS — NEW

348-1011	Alabama	12.98	348-1128	Nevada	12.98
348-1012	Alaska	12.98	348-1129	New Hampshire	12.98
348-1013	Arizona	12.98	348-1130	New Jersey	12.98
348-1014	Arkansas	12.98	348-1131	New Mexico	12.98
348-1015	California	12.98	348-1132	New York	12.98
348-1016	Colorado	12.98	348-1133	North Carolina	12.98
348-1017	Connecticut	12.98	348-1134	North Dakota	12.98
348-1018	Delaware	12.98	348-1135	Ohio	12.98
348-1019	Florida	12.98	348-1136	Oklahoma	12.98
348-1110	Georgia	12.98	348-1137	Oregon	12.98
348-1111	Hawaii	12.98	348-1138	Pennsylvania	12.98
348-1112	Idaho	12.98	348-1139	Rhode Island	12.98
348-1113	Iowa	12.98	348-1140	South Carolina	12.98
348-1114	Ilinois	12.98	348-1141	South Dakota	12.98
348-1115	Indiana	12.98	348-1142	Tennessee	12.98
348-1116	Kansas	12.98	348-1143	Texas	12.98
348-1117	Kentucky	12.98	348-1144	Utah	12.98
348-1118	Louisiana	12.98	348-1145	Vermont	12.98
348-1119	Maine	12.98	348-1146	Virginia	12.98
348-1120	Maryland	12.98	348-1147	Washington	12.98
348-1121	Massachusetts	12.98	348-1148	Washington DC	12.98
348-1122	Michigan	12.98	348-1149	West Virginia	12.98
348-1123	Minnesota	12.98	348-1150	Wisconsin	12.98
348-1124	Mississippi	12.98	348-1151	Wyoming	12.98
348-1125	Missouri	12.98	348-1152	British Columbia	12.98
348-1126	Montana	12.98	348-1156	Quebec	12.98
348-1127	Nebraska	12.98	348-4221	Undecorated	12.98

CLASSIC VEHICLES

Die cast metal body with plastic details and underframe.

Classic Car Assortment
348-1720   pkg(6) 9.98

348-1721 Classic Truck Assortment — NEW   pkg(6) 9.98

This mountain pass must be quite a place for a picnic, especially when heavy freight trains roll by overhead! The rugged beauty of the Rocky Mountains combines with the heavy motive power of western railroads in this dramatic scene, built by Klaus Schubert of Monchengladbach, Germany.

Models and Photo by Klaus Schubert

JORDAN
HIGHWAY MINIATURES

HO SCALE (1/87) CRAFT TRAIN KITS

"Highway Miniatures" models are molded of high impact polystyrene in appropriate colors and require only minimum painting.

FORD MODEL T's

1911 Delivery Truck
360-207   4.95

1913 Fire Truck
360-208   4.95

1925 Mail Truck
360-215   4.95

1925 Panel Truck
360-216   4.95

1920 Model T Sedan
360-226   4.95

Air Calliope Truck
360-233   6.95

FORD

REA Truck 1929 AA
Railway Express Agency   4.95
360-214

Station Wagon 1929 Model A
360-217   4.95

1940 Standard - V8 Sedan
360-225   4.95
Includes optional engine assembly for "hood-up" scenes.

AUTOS

360-222 1926 Essex 4.95
First popular priced closed car.

360-213 1925 Roadster or Pick Up   4.95
Can be built as a Roadster or Pick-Up w/top up or top down.

1904 Inspection Car and
1904 Curved Dash
Oldsmobiles
360-228   4.95

FORDSON TRACTORS

1920 Farm
360-218   3.95
1920 Industrial
360-219   3.95

218   219

1923 MACK TRUCKS

1923 Dump Truck
360-210   6.95

1923 Tank Truck
360-212   6.95

1923 Mack
Aerial Ladder
Fire Truck
360-220   7.95

1923 Stake Truck
360-209   6.95

1923 Mack Hi-Lift Truck
360-227   6.95

Mack Water Tank
360-232   6.95
Less driver.

WAGONS W/HORSES

Light Delivery
360-101   3.95

Standard Delivery
360-102   3.95

Buckboard
360-104   3.95

1913 Popcorn Wagon
with Horse
360-235   6.95

Brougham (Broo'am)
360-103   3.95

Beer Wagon w/8 Horses
360-105   7.95

Stage
Coach
360-234
7.95

JORDAN
HIGHWAY MINIATURES

HO SCALE (1/87) CRAFT TRAIN KITS

"Highway Miniatures" models are molded of high impact polystyrene in appropriate colors and require only minimum painting.

MISCELLANEOUS

1927 Ahrens Pump & Hose Car
360-221   5.95

1934 Ford 21 Passenger Bus
360-229   6.95

Depot Baggage Wagon w/Bags
360-301   3.95

1922 Packard Stake Truck
360-231   6.95

1928 Model A Sedan
360-236   5.95

Finishing Touches
SELLEY

HO SCALE (1/87) EASY-TO-BUILD KITS

Kits are easy-to-build and feature cast metal construction.

FARM EQUIPMENT

675-226 Farm Tractor #2   1.75

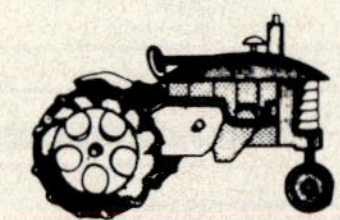

675-227 Farm Tractor #1   1.75

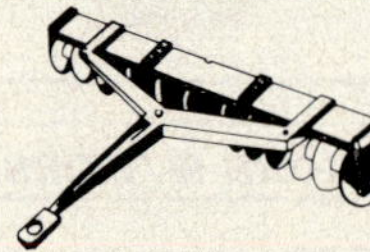

675-228 Harrow for Tractor   1.25

(not illustrated)
675-157 Farm Wagon   2.60

MISCELLANEOUS

675-642 Crazy Inspection Car   2.95

675-146 Forklift Truck   .95

675-147 Platform "Mule"   .95

(not illustrated)
675-288 Sherman Tank   2.95

Keil-Line Models
HO SCALE (1/87)

AUTOMOBILES

382-106 1932 Ford Roadster   3.95

Athearn
TRAINS IN MINIATURE

HO SCALE (1/87) EASY-TO-BUILD KITS

Prepainted and prelettered styrene kits. Can be assembled with plastic adhesive and a screwdriver.

TRACTOR   pkg(2) 5.50

140-5512 Union Pacific	140-5500 Undecorated

45' PIGGYBACK TRAILER   pkg(2) 7.00

140-5601 Burlington Northern	140-5605 Denver & Rio Grande Western
140-5602 Conrail	
140-5603 CSX	140-5606 Santa Fe
140-5604 Norfolk Southern	140-5600 Undecorated

40' CONTAINER   6.75

140-5741 Matson	140-5745 Itel-Maersk	140-5748 NYK
140-5742 Genstar	140-5746 Tiphook-Triton	140-5749 Zim
140-5743 Hanjin	140-5747 Evergreen	140-5740 Undec
140-5744 APC-APL		

48' CONTAINER   8.75

140-5701 American President Lines	140-5706 Santa Fe
140-5702 APC	140-5707 BN
140-5703 CSX-CSL	140-5708 TransAmerica
140-5704 NYK	140-5709 Itel
140-5705 Southern Pacific	140-5700 Undecorated

VAN/TRACTOR PARTS

140-14257 50' Flat Dual Trailer Mount	pkg(4) 1.60

VAN

140-14240 25' Body, Undecorated	pkg(2) 1.70
140-14251 25' Underframe	pkg(4) 1.00
140-14252 25' Stand	pkg(6) 1.20
140-14253 25' Wheel Assembly	pkg(4) 1.40
140-51511 40' Underframe	pkg(4) 1.40
140-51512 40' Bogey	pkg(4) 1.00
140-51513 40' Dual Wheel Assembly	pkg(2) 1.20
140-51515 40' Refrigeration Unit	pkg(4) 1.00
140-51516 40' Fuel Tank	pkg(4) 1.00

TRACTOR

140-55000 Cab, Undecorated	each 1.15
140-55001 2-Axle Frame	pkg(2) .70
140-55002 Frame, 3-Axle Tractor	pkg(2) .70
140-55008 Fuel Tank, Tractor	pkg(6) 1.50
140-55009 Battery Box	pkg(6) .90
140-55011 Fifth Wheel	pkg(6) 1.20
140-55012 Tires	pkg(8) .80
140-55013 Windshield	pkg(4) .80
140-55014 Axle	pkg(12) .90
140-55015 Accessory Set	pkg(2) 1.20

We have worked closely with this manufacturer to provide accurate availability information at the time this catalog was published. Items listed in *blue ink* may not be available at all times. Please see your dealer for current delivery information.

kibri

HO SCALE (1/87)

Imported from Germany by WALTHERS

Prepainted, easy-to-build kits and ready-to-run vehicles. Markings and colors may vary from illustrations in the catalog.

CONSTRUCTION VEHICLES

DUMP TRUCK

Meiller Heavy Duty
405-10004   kit 17.49

Heavy Duty Semi
405-10006   kit 17.49

Dump Trailer
405-10028   kit 15.99

Heavy Duty Semi
405-10012   kit 17.49

Pivoted Chassis
405-10124   assembled 20.99

Double-Bottom
405-10212   17.49

MB w/Flat Trailer
405-10124   assembled 20.49

MAN Double-Bottom
405-10212   20.49

DB 4-Axle
405-10352   19.99

Scania Heavy Duty
405-10274   16.49

MB, High Capacity
405-10416   21.49

MB, 3-Axle
405-10410   13.99

MB, 3-Axle w/Trailer & Load
405-10408   33.99

MB 3 Axle Dump Truck
405-10520
16.49

(not illustrated)
MAN 4-Axle
405-10014   13.49

CRANES

Telescopic Crane w/extended jib
405-10496
41.99
Get big jobs done at construction sights in a hurry with this heavy-duty crane. Model can be built with boom retracted for transport, or extended and ready to go to work.

Twin & Pivot Crane
405-10492   268.99

Liebherr LTM1800
405-10494   124.49

On Truck Chassis
405-10108   22.49

120T Mobile
405-10130   (yellow) 29.99

Kalmar Container Crane w/Three 20′ Containers
405-10432   27.99

MAN Tow Truck w/Large Crane
405-10376   22.99

Liebherr Mobile
405-10328   (yellow) 30.99
Liebherr Ltm 1050/3
405-10330   30.99

kibri

HO SCALE (1/87)

Imported from Germany by WALTHERS

Prepainted, easy-to-build kits and ready-to-run vehicles. Markings and colors may vary from illustrations in the catalog.

CRANES (continued)

Rising over the city skyline, this tall crane is an impressie model in any setting! The boom can be moved and includes steel colored thread to simulate cables.

Gottwald Construction
405-10326   90.49

Get your next construction project off the ground with this heavy duty crane! The telescoping boom can be positioned in lots of ways so the model can be displayed on the road (boom down and retracted), or on the job (boom extended and raised).

Gottwald Tele-Crane
405-10388   90.49

Liebherr
20K Crane
405-10390 39.99

405-10418 MB   24.99

Liebherr, Transport
405-10428   26.49

Liebherr 4 axle LTM 1050
405-10518   32.49

Gottwald, Maxilift
405-10426   106.49

■ **LTD QTY AVAILABLE** ■
Girder-Frame Crane
405-10438 w/Pivoted Jib 127.49

Mobile Crane w/High Level Cab
405-10490   14.49

Pivoted Jib
405-10440
39.99

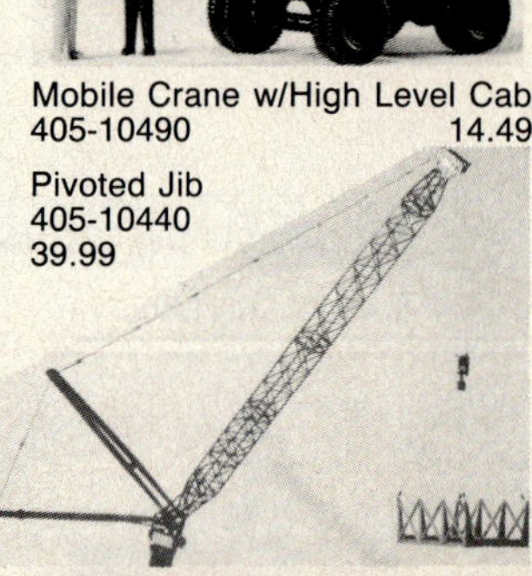

Mobile Crane w/Low Level Cab
405-10488   14.49

Crane Support
Transporter
405-10532
37.99
NEW

Liebherr
Telescopic
Crane w/Jib
405-10544
42.49
NEW

Liebherr LTM
1050/4 Fire
405-10554
33.99
NEW

Liebherr LTM 1025
405-10556
29.99
NEW

Telescopic Crane
& Transporter
405-10452   220.99

kibri

HO SCALE (1/87)

Imported from Germany by WALTHERS

Prepainted, easy-to-build kits and ready-to-run vehicles. Markings and colors may vary from illustrations in the catalog.

CRANES (continued)

Liebherr Railway Mounted Crane
405-10558
36.49
NEW

Liebherr LTM 1400 Crane w/JIB
405-10560
115.49
NEW

(not illustrated)
Liebherr 974
405-10550   **NEW** 50.99

Menck Excavator w/3 assorted grabs
405-10562
42.49
NEW

BACKHOE

405-10370 Large Transporter w/Excavator   45.99

Modern, Tracked
405-10142   kit 25.99

Modern on Wheels
405-10140   25.99

Transporter w/Atlas Excavator
405-10528   41.99
Move to the next job sight in style with this heavy transport rig. Includes kits for a DAF tractor, low-boy trailer and Atlas shovel.

LIMITED QUANTITIES AVAILABLE

Liebherr w/Acessories
405-10322   26.49

Tracked Excavator
405-10434   29.99

Road/Rail
405-10204   25.99

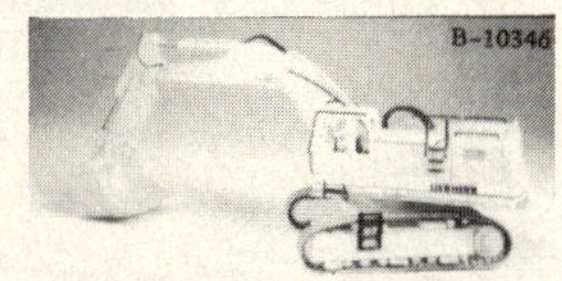

Manck Exctor w/Drag Bucket
405-10384   42.99

Liebherr Tractor Backhoe
NEW 405-10346   42.99

UTILITY TRUCK

Road/Land Grader
405-10430   26.49

Heavy Duty
405-10106   kit 16.49

Utility Truck
405-10100
kit 12.99
(By Special Order Only.)

MB Repair w/vehicle-Mounted Crane and Grab
405-10474   14.49

CEMENT TRUCKS

Readymix Concrete Truck
405-10042   kit 20.49

405-10254 MAN 4-axle   16.49

405-10044 MB   pkg(2) 20.49

Pumping
405-10200   (yellow) 32.49
Pumping
405-10250   (green) 29.49

kibri
HO SCALE (1/87)

Imported from Germany by WALTHERS

Prepainted, easy-to-build kits and ready-to-run vehicles. Markings and colors may vary from illustrations in the catalog.

FRONT END LOADER

405-10146   Tracked   kit 20.49

Faun
405-10208   (yellow) 20.49
Faun
405-10294   (red) 20.49

Kaelble SL30
Pivoted Shovel
405-10512   38.99

405-10340   Zettelmeyer w/Accessories   29.99

MISCELLANEOUS

Hamm Road Roller
405-10280   18.99

Hamm Soil Conpactor
405-10300   18.99

Liebherr Bulldozer
405-10324   29.99

Tractors w/2 Trailers
405-10350   29.99

DB Wrecking Crane
405-10292   pkg(2) 22.99

Portable Offices
405-10278   pkg(2) 13.99

Weight Spreading
Trailer & Load
405-10460   35.99

Excavator w/Ram
and Pulley Attachment
405-10462   50.49

FIRE VEHICLES

405-10354   DB TLF Pumper   27.99

DAF 95 Tractor Unit
405-10458   24.99

DB Snorkel Truck
405-10296   32.49

FORK LIFT

Kalmar LMV
405-10564
20.99
NEW

405-10002
6.19

MB, Road
& Rail
405-10422
24.99

SEMI-TRAILER TRUCKS

TANK TRUCK

British Petroleum
405-10076   kit 16.49

kibri

HO SCALE (1/87)

Imported from Germany by WALTHERS

Prepainted, easy-to-build kits and ready-to-run vehicles. Markings and colors may vary from illustrations in the catalog.

TANK TRUCKS (continued)

MAN 4-Axle, BP
405-10258   16.49

Artic Bulk Carrier
405-10030   kit 17.49

LOWBOY TRAILER

MAN w/Trailers & MB w/Trailers
405-10568   84.49
NEW

MAN W/Trailer & Boiler
405-10570   50.49
NEW

Scania w/Load
405-10094   19.99

MAN Tractor w/Trailer
405-10342   29.49

DB Tractor w/Trailer
405-10344   26.49

405-10122   w/Truss   kit 22.99

MAN Low Loader w/Container
405-10380   22.99

Tractor w/Lowboy Kit
405-10118   kit 19.99

LIMITED QUANTITIES AVAILABLE

MAN w/5-Axle Trailer
405-10366
26.49

Artic Low-Loader
405-10448   22.99

Triple-Axle Low-Loader
405-10466   19.99

DB w/5-axle Trailer Platform
405-10368   22.99

MB w/Road Surfacer
405-10404   44.99

MB w/Trailer & Crane
405-10406   27.99

Scania w/Boat Load
405-10414   53.99

MAN w/Excavator
405-10402   59.99

MAN, Scheurle
405-10360   20.49

Moving Trailers
405-10116   22.49

Triple Axle w/Bulldozer
405-10468   35.99

FLATBED TRAILER

405-10336   MAN DB Trailer 26.49

405-10216   MAN Semi   15.99

405-10312   Scania   22.19

Heavy Duty
405-10120   kit 22.99

kibri

HO SCALE (1/87)

Imported from Germany by WALTHERS

Prepainted, easy-to-build kits and ready-to-run vehicles.
Markings and colors may vary from illustrations in the catalog.

FLATBED TRAILER (continued)

MAN Stake Trailer
w/Girder Load
405-10378   21.49

405-10248 DAF Semi   12.99

Scania Well-Bed
405-10268   20.49

Flatbed w/Trailer
405-10446   35.49

Artic w/Rungs
405-10450   14.49

SEMI w/VAN TRAILER

DB, Stinnes
405-10246
12.99

Man, Kolb-Wellpappe
405-10244   11.99

DB, Kuhne & Nagel
405-10240   10.49
405-10242 MAN Sudzuker 10.49

DOUBLE-BOTTOM

Jagermeister
405-10170   kit 14.99

Gravel w/Trailer
405-10010   kit 16.49

DAF Stock Truck
405-10214   22.49

Covered-Paulaner
405-10180   14.99

MAN, DB ''Schenker''
405-10338   17.49

MAN, DB Container
405-10264   20.49
MAN, Dietrich
405-10262   14.99
MAN, Post-LKW
405-10260   16.49

HEAVY DUTY TRANSPORTERS

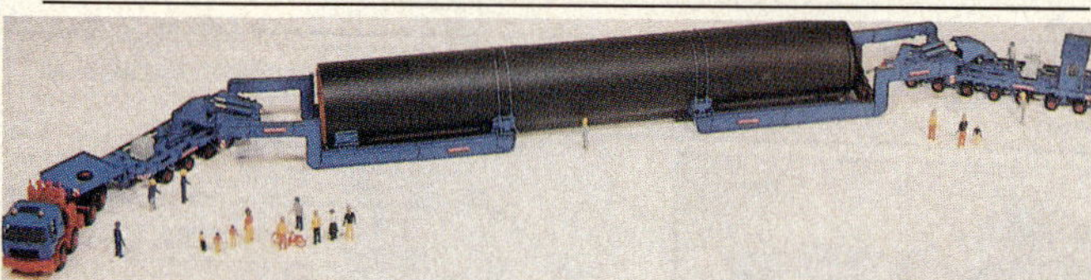

405-10498 150t VAT and Heavy Hauler
w/Rear Control Cabin   64.49

405-10386 Generator Transport   36.99

405-10128 Transformer Transport   54.99

405 10306 DB Transporter w/Transformer   45.99

405-10444 DB Transport w/6-axle Trailer   27.99

405-10442 Crane Mast Transporter   39.99

kibri

HO SCALE (1/87)

Imported from Germany by WALTHERS

Prepainted, easy-to-build kits and ready-to-run vehicles.
Markings and colors may vary from illustrations in the catalog.

HEAVY DUTY TRANSPORTER (continued)

405-10456 Triple Axle Artic   39.99

405-10464 4-Axle w/Vat and Support   50.49

405-10472 MB w/Crane   27.49

405-10476 w/Transformer Load   80.49

DAF Transport w/Truck Cabs
405-10534
29.99
NEW

405-10536 MB Transport w/Dumper   **NEW** 25.49

MB Transport w/Construction Trailer, Hut
405-10538
33.99
NEW

405-10412 MAN w/Girder Load   26.49

405-10420 MAN w/Transformer   42.99

405-10508 MB 4 Axle Tractor Unit   43.99

405-10502 Culemeyer LR40 Trailer
w/Cable Tractor Unit   22.99

405-10530 MB Transporter w/Grader   44.99

405-10540 MB Transport Trailer w/Crane   **NEW** 25.49

405-10542 Transport w/Construction Buildings   **NEW** 33.99

kibri
HO SCALE (1/87)

Imported from Germany by WALTHERS

Prepainted, easy-to-build kits and ready-to-run vehicles.
Markings and colors may vary from illustrations in the catalog.

ACCESSORIES

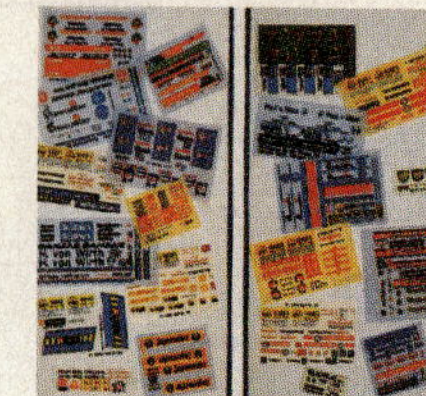
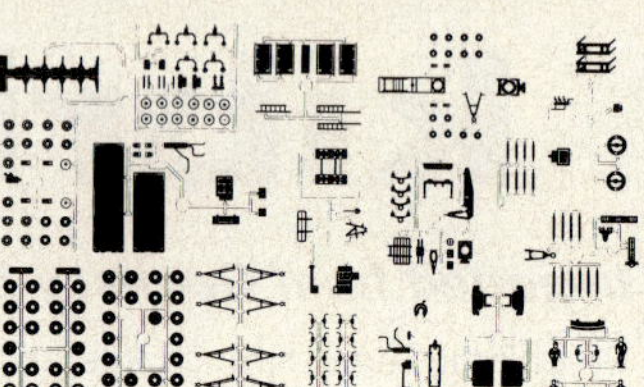

Lettering Set for Lorries
405-10500
18.99

Truck Accessory
405-11980
22.99

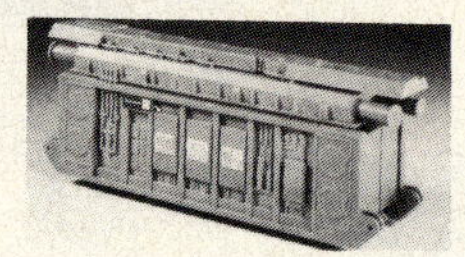

Metal Sheet Loads
405-11984
pkg(3) 11.49

Transformer 300 MVA
405-10286   each 16.49

TRANSPORTERS (continued)

Truck w/Trailer
405-10110
kit 16.99

405-10356   Gottwald Construction Set   152.99

405-10546   Kalmar Transporter w/Carrier   **NEW** 51.49

Transporter w/Pile Driver
405-10552   **NEW** 59.49

405-10548   MB Heavy Transporter   **NEW** 42.49

405-10524   MB Transport Lorry w/Lorry Cabs   25.99

405-10526   MB Transport Lorry w/Pipe Load   18.99

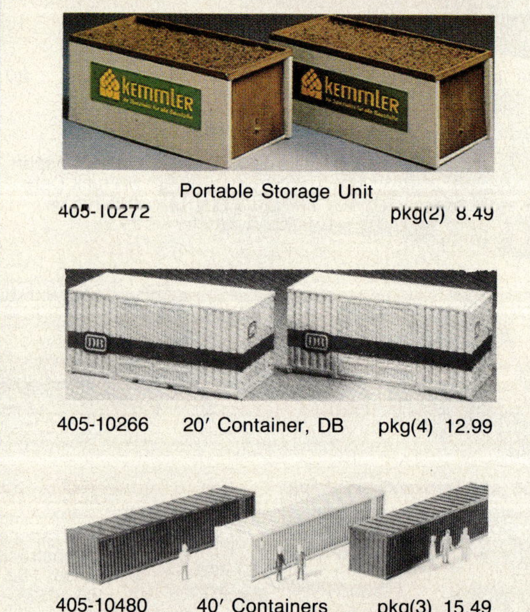

Portable Storage Unit
405-10272   pkg(2) 8.49

405-10266   20' Container, DB   pkg(4) 12.99

405-10480   40' Containers   pkg(3) 15.49

kibri

HO SCALE (1/87)

Imported from Germany by WALTHERS

Prepainted, easy-to-build kits and ready-to-run vehicles.
Markings and colors may vary from illustrations in the catalog.

MISCELLANEOUS

MB,3-Axle
405-10400   22.99

Scania Towing & Salvage
405-10436   22.49

Bulk Cement
405-10036   kit 17.49

MAN w/Loading Crane
405-10282   25.99

DB Container Truck w/Lift
405-10306   29.99

Glass Truck-Pilkington
405-10096 Langendorf 22.49

MAN Dumpster
405-10276
20.49

RAU MB 4 Axle Recovery Vehicle
405-10514
25.99

LKW Silo Tipper
405-10470   20.49

MB Container
405-10478   15.49

Container Stacker Truck w/40' Containers
405-10482   27.99

MB Tractor w/Silo Trailer
405-10486   27.49

MB Tractor w/Tank Trailer
405-10484
27.49

MISCELLANEOUS (continued)

Logging Truck & Crane
405-10334   20.49

Lumber Trailer
405-10020   kit 17.49

Scania Tractor
405-10218   16.49

DB 2-axle Tipper Lorry
405-10392
11.99

MB 3 Axle Tractor Unit
405-10510   25.99

MB 4 Axle Tractor Unit
405-10506   25.99

405-10504   Showmans Caravan w/MB Tractor Unit   32.49

405-10516   Short Log MB Transporter   25.99

405-10522   MB Tractor Unit and Trailor   17.99

MERTEN
HO SCALE (1/87)

Imported from Germany by WALTHERS

Wagons are appropriately colored plastic. All kits with figures are assembled (unless noted.)

PASSENGER WAGONS

Horse Drawn
Sleigh w/Figures
447-2419   15.49

Postal Stage
Coach w/Figures
447-2472   15.49

Western Stage
Coach w/Figures
447-2476   15.49

Cab-One Horse
w/Figures
447-2480   15.49

Cab Two-Horse
w/Figures
447-2478   15.49

Buggy w/Figures
447-2495
pkg(2)   15.49

Wedding Coach
w/Figures
447-2474   15.49

WORK WAGONS

Wagon w/Figures
and Horses
447-2424   15.49

Beer Wagon
w/Figures and Horses
447-2425   15.49

Farmers Box Wagon
w/Figures
447-2470   15.49

Butcher's Cart
w/Figures
447-2494   15.49

Lumber Wagon
w/Figures
447-2496   15.49

Box Cart w/Figure
447-2497   15.49

TEAM OF HORSES ONLY

Team Horses
447-2492   7.49

model power
HO SCALE (1/87)
READY-TO-RUN

Ready-to-run, precolored and lettered die cast metal vehicles and containers.

EMERGENCY VEHICLES

Aerial Ladder
Fire Truck
490-7767   7.98

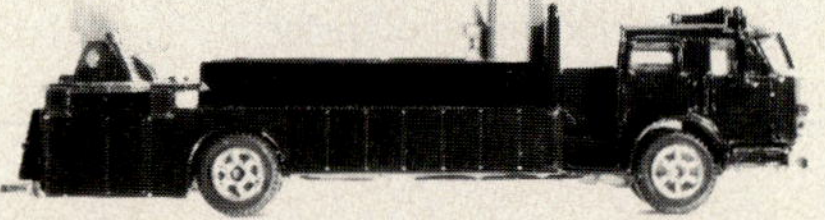

Aerial Bucket
Fire Truck
490-77671   7.98

GLOOR·CRAFT MODELS
HO SCALE (1/87)
CRAFT TRAIN KITS

STEP VAN

Kit features cast metal construction.

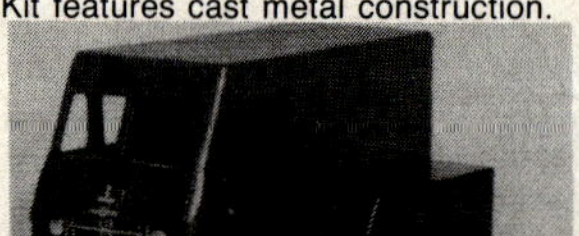

1960s Chevrolet
288-3800   7.95

TRAILERS

Wood construction with cast metal details.

45' Box Van
Undecorated
288-3803   15.95

45' Refrigerated
Undecorated
288-3804   16.95

N.J. International

HO SCALE (1/87) CAST METAL KITS

EMERGENCY EQUIPMENT

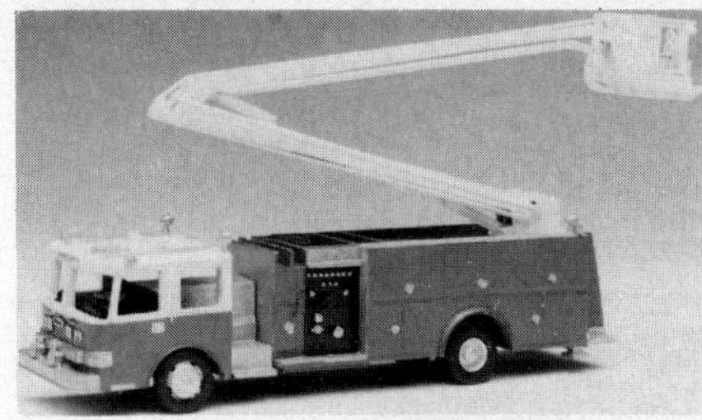

Snorkel
525-107   39.95

Aerial Ladder
525-106   39.95

Pierce
Mid-Ship Pumper
525-116   35.95

Pumper Kit w/4-Door
Closed Cab
525-117   37.95

Mack C
ladder Truck
525-130   69.95

(not illustrated)
525-139   Pierce Heavy Rescue   TBA

TRUCKS

1967 Jeep Pickup
525-112   6.95
Assembled & painted
525-115   9.95

UPS Delivery
525-104   19.95

AUTOMOBILES

1965, Shelby GT-350 Mustang
525-101   kit 6.95
Assembled & painted
1964 Corvette Sting Ray
525-102   6.95   525-113   9.95

(not illustrated)
525-114   1964 Corvette, assembled & painted   9.95
525-159   Assorted Windows, fits cars 101, 102, 112   pkg(3) 1.00

FIRE TRUCKS

Mack MB Tractor
Tilt Cab
525-138   25.95

Mack C, tractor only
525-1301   29.95

(not illustrated)
525-1302   Trailer w/85' Aerial Ladder   49.95
525-1303   Mac C Cab w/100' Ladder   69.95
525-1304   Mack Tillered Trailer w/100' Load   49.95
525-1385   Mack MB Tractor w/85' Ladder   66.95

MODEL TRACTION SUPPLY COMPANY

HO SCALE (1/87)

Kits consist of metal castings-sides, ends,
roof, floor and roof vents-wheels & axles.

BUSES

ACF H-17-S Bus Kit
505-3000   19.00
Produced from 1935 through
1938 the ACF H-17-S was used
by 30 different companies from
coast to coast.

Ford 19B "Crackerbox"
Bus Kit
505-3001   17.00

ACF Trackless Trolley Kit
505-3002   21.00
Includes dummy trolley poles

Praliné
HO SCALE (1/87) READY-TO-RUN

Imported from Germany by WALTHERS

Assembled, precolored plastic European autos, trucks and buses. Markings and colors may vary from what is shown in catalog.

We have worked closely with this manufacturer to provide accurate availability information at the time this catalog was published. Items listed in *blue ink* may not be available at all times. Please see your dealer for current delivery information.

AUTOMOBILES

PORSCHE 356
Coupe
583-1600   5.99
Coupe Metallic
583-1601   6.49

PORSCHE 356
Convert, Top Down
583-1602   5.99
TD Metallic
583-1603   5.49

PORSCHE 356
TU Metallic
583-1605   6.49
w/Sunroof
583-1611   5.99

PORSCHE 356
Gold Deluxe **NEW**
583-1677   13.49

PONTIAC
TRANS AM
583-1701   4.99

'50 BUICK
Military, US **NEW**
583-4714   7.49

'50 BUICK
Limousine
583-4701   5.49

'50 BUICK
Convert, Top Down
583-4702   5.49
Convert, Top Down
583-4707   7.49

'50 BUICK
Conversion Deluxe,
Metallic
583-4705   7.49

'50 BUICK
Conversion, Top Up
583-4706   7.49
Metallic

'50 BUICK
Conversion Deluxe,
Metallic
583-4708   7.49
Limo Deluxe
583-4709   7.49

CITROEN CX
583-3300 Break 6.49
Break, Metallic
583-3301   5.49

CITROEN CX
Metallic
583-3102   6.49
Undecorated
583-3100   5.99

CITROEN AX
583-5603   5.99
Limo
583-5600   5.49
Metallic
583-5601   5.49
w/Sunroof
583-5602   5.99

CITROEN AX
Telecom
583-5604   5.99

CITROEN AX
Pompiers
583-5605   6.49

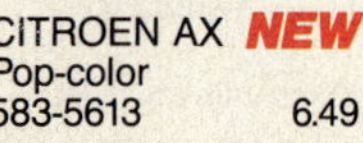

CITROEN AX **NEW**
Pop-color
583-5613   6.49

CITROEN AX **NEW**
Two-tone, Metallic
583-5614   6.49

FERRARI GTO
583-2605 1962   6.49

FERRARI GTO
Race Car
583-2607   7.49

VOLVO 544 SEDAN
Deluxe
583-3904   6.99
Sunroof, Metallic
583-3905   6.99

RENAULT R5 **NEW**
Adv Fr Canon
583-2515   6.49

RENAULT
R5GTL Turbo
583-2504   4.79

RENAULT 5TS
Pattex
583-2510   9.99

RENAULT R5
EDF/GDF
583-2511   5.99
Postal
583-2512   5.99

583-1306   1936 HORCH 853 w/Top Up   7.49

'38 HORCH 853
Convertible Deluxe
583-1305   7.49
Convertible
583-1302   5.49

'38 HORCH 853
Coupe
583-1301   5.49

'36 HORCH
Conversion LX
583-1316   8.99

'42 HORCH 853
w/Top Down
583-1307   7.99

'38 BMW 327
Convertible, Top Up
583-2001   4.99

'38 BMW 327
Deluxe Convertible
583-2005   6.99

'38 BMW 327
Convert, Top Down
583-2002   4.99
Convert, Top Down
583-2004   6.99

■ LTD QTY AVAIL
'38 BMW 327
Hard Top
583-2003   4.99

MB 170V
Hotel Car
w/Bag Deluxe **NEW**
583-1418   7.49

MORGAN PLUS 8
583-7100   7.49
Top Up
583-7101   7.49
Luxury
583-7102   8.49
Cabrio Plus Luxury
583-7103   8.49

MB 220 SE LIMO
w/Sunroof
583-418   7.49
MB 300S
DELUXE CONV
Top Up
583-4205   7.99
Top Down
583-4204   7.99

MB 1/05
Deluxe Convertible
w/Top Up
583-506   6.99

MB 170V Taxi
583-1412   7.49

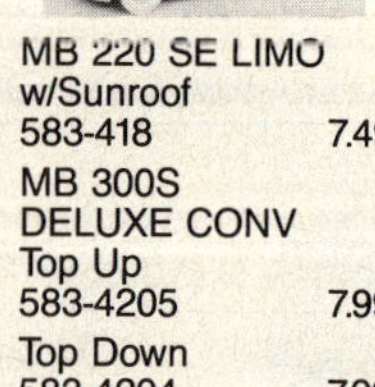

ROLLS
Silver Cloud, Metallic
583-4413   7.49
w/Trailer
583-4408   13.49

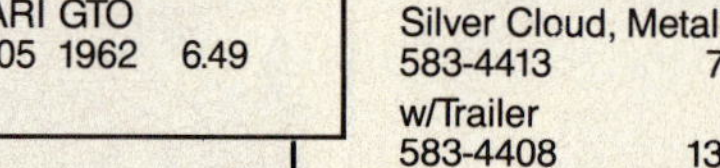

ROLLS ROYCE
Convertible SC,
Top Down
583-4409   6.99

ROLLS ROYCE
Convertible SC,
Top Up
583-4410   6.99

Praliné

HO SCALE (1/87) READY-TO-RUN

Imported from Germany by WALTHERS

Assembled, precolored plastic European autos, trucks and buses. Markings and colors may vary from what is shown in catalog.

AUTOMOBILES (continued)

ROLLS ROYCE
Silver Cloud, Gold
583-4477 **NEW** 7.49
Silver Cloud
Deluxe (2 Tone)
583-4404 6.99

BENTLEY
S2 Limo Deluxe
(2 Tone)
583-4406 6.99

BENTLEY
Convertible Top Down
583-4411 6.99

BENTLEY
Convert, Top Up
583-4412 6.99

BENTLEY
Series 2, Metallic
583-4414 7.49

'50 CADILLAC CAB
Convert, Top Up
583-3404 5.49

VW NEW
Make Love, Not War
583-2742 6.99

VW 1200
Gold Deluxe **NEW**
583-2777 13.49

■ **LTD QTY AVAIL** ■
MERCEDES 300S
Conv, Top Up
583-4201 5.99

'54 CADDY J NEW
Fox Furs Deluxe
583-3455 7.99

'54 CADDY NEW
Country Club Deluxe
583-3456 7.99

'54 CADDY NEW
Gold Deluxe
583-3477 13.49

300S
Convertible Deluxe
Top Up
583-4203 7.49

'50 COUPE DEVILLE
Convertible
583-3407 7.49
"Marilyn Monroe" (pink)
Convertible
583-3412 7.49

'59 CADILLAC
Hardtop
583-5100 7.49
Deluxe
583-5101 7.99
w/top up
583-5103 7.99

'50 COUPE DEVILLE
President Limo
583-3408 6.49
Luxury Limousine
583-3414 8.99

'50 COUPE DEVILLE
Convertible
583-3406 7.49

MB 300
Adenauer JFK
583-4801 23.99

'70 CADILLAC
Station Wagon
w/Trailer
583-2907 9.99

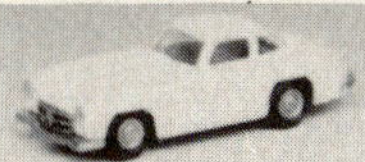
300 SL
Gullwig Coupe
583-800 4.49
583-804 Metallic 7.49
583-806 Deluxe 6.99
583-807 Ralley 7.99
Deluxe

170V
Limo w/Symbol
583-1416 7.49
Convertible Limo
Top Down
583-1403 4.99

170S
Convertible Deluxe
583-505 6.99
Convertible
583-501 4.99
Coupe
583-502 4.99
Convertible, Spoked
583-503 5.49
(By Special Order Only.)

60s MB 300
Pope w/Tiara **NEW**
583-4803 12.49

60s MB 300 NEW
Adenauer Deluxe
583-4802 12.49

170V
1948 Limo
583-1400 4.99
1948 Limo Deluxe
583-1409 6.99

'57 BELAIR
Deluxe (gold) **NEW**
583-5077 13.49

300S
Convertible, Top
Down
583-4200 5.99
Convertible Deluxe
Top Down
583-4202 7.49

VW HEBMULLER
Covertible CL
Metallic **NEW**
583-6704 8.49

220 SE
Diplomat
583-412 4.99
200/300
Diplomat
583-419 6.99
Luxury
583-420 7.49

'50 CADILLAC
STATION WAGON
583-3450 6.49
Metallic
583-3451 7.49
'54 CADILLAC
Texas Millionaire
583-3415 8.49

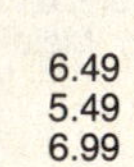
'50 COUPE DE VILLE
583-3402 Limousine 6.49
583-3401 Limousine 5.49
583-3405 Limousine 6.99

'38 OPEL OLYMPIA
Limo w/Top Down
583-1108 6.99

'38 OPEL OLYMPIA
Limo w/Top Up
583-1109 6.99

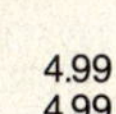
'38 OPEL OLYMPIA
583-1101 Limousine 4.99
583-1102 Convertible 4.99

'52 OPEL OLY
Limousine
583-6501 7.49

'52 OPEL OLY
Wagon
583-6551 7.49

'52 OPEL OLY
DRK Wagon
583-6552 8.49
Yellow Wagon
583-6553 8.49

'38 OPEL OLYMPIA
Taxi
583-1110 7.49

'52 VW w/Sunroof
583-2731 6.49

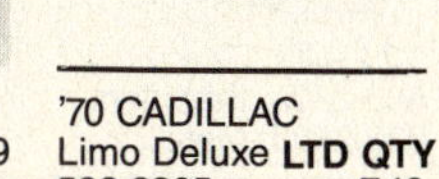
'70 CADILLAC
Limo Deluxe **LTD QTY**
583-2805 7.49

Praliné
HO SCALE (1/87) READY-TO-RUN

Imported from Germany by WALTHERS

Assembled, precolored plastic European autos, trucks and buses. Markings and colors may vary from what is shown in catalog.

We have worked closely with this manufacturer to provide accurate availability information at the time this catalog was published. Items listed in *blue ink* may not be available at all times. Please see your dealer for current delivery information.

AUTOMOBILES (continued)

'59 CADDY NEW
Convertible OP
Metallic Deluxe
583-5106   8.99

'59 CADDY NEW
Hardtop
Metallic Deluxe
583-5107   8.99

'59 CADDY NEW
Convertible
Metallic Deluxe
5108   8.99

'59 CADDY NEW
Convertible OP
Deluxe
583-5109   8.99

220SE
Convertible Top Down
583-3403   5.49

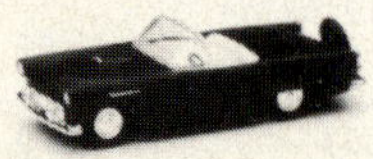

'56 T-BIRD NEW
Convertible OP
Deluxe
583-5209   7.99

'56 FORD T-BIRD
Cabrio, Metallic
583-5205   8.49

'56 FORD T-BIRD
Hardtop, Metallic
583-5206   8.49

'56 FORD T-BIRD
Marilyn Monroe Pink
583-5207   7.99

CHEVY CORVETTE
583-5400 Hdtop   6.49
583-5401 Deluxe   7.99
Convertible
583-5402   6.49
583-5403 Deluxe   7.99

CHEVY CORVETTE
Conversion, Metallic
583-5404   8.49
583-5406   9.49

'56 FORD T-BIRD
Conversion, Metallic
583-5204   8.49

■ **LTD QTY AVAIL** ■
Convertible Top Down
583-5202   6.49

'56 FORD THUNDERBIRD
Hardtop
583-5200   6.49
Hardtop Deluxe
583-5201   7.99
Deluxe
583-5203   7.99

'38 FORD EIFEL
w/Top Down
538-1211   6.99

'38 FORD EIFEL
Limo Conversion
583-1206   4.99

'52 VW
Undecorated
583-2701   5.99

'52 VW
ADAC Streetwatch
583-2707   4.99

'52 VW
Post Office
583-2708   4.99

'70 LIMO
583-2802 President   5.99
583-2803 Metallic   6.99

'70 LIMO
583-2804 Texas   6.49

VW POST PTT
583-2738   6.49
VW 1200 Military
583-2739   6.49
Cabrio Top Down
583-6701   7.49
Cabrio Top Up
583-6702   7.49

VW SEDAN
Metallic
583-2735   6.99
Deluxe
583-2736   6.99

'52 VW
Cabrio Limo
583-2732   6.49
Cabrio Limo Metallic
583-2733   6.99

'57 CHEVY BELAIR
583-5002 Limo   7.49
583-5004 Limo, Metallic 7.49
583-5005 Bel Air   7.49
583-5006 Bel Air, Deluxe 7.49

'57 CHEVY BELAIR
Highway Patrol
583-5008   8.49

'70 CADILLAC LIMO
Deluxe President
583-2806   7.49

DODGE MONACO
Limo
583-6603   7.99

'70 CADILLAC LIMO
Station Wagon
583-2902   5.49

'57 CHEVY BELAIR
Limo, Metallic
583-5007   7.99

CHEVY CORVETTE
Racing "3"
583-5405   9.49

'38 FORD EIFEL
Cabrio
583-1209   6.99

'38 FORD EIFEL
Cabrio Limo
538-1210   6.99

FORD ESCORT
Pop-color
583-5717 NEW TBA

FORD ESCORT
Telecom Green
583-5718 NEW 7.49

FORD ESCORT GHIA
Sunroof
583-5703   7.49

FORD ESCORT
583-5704   7.99

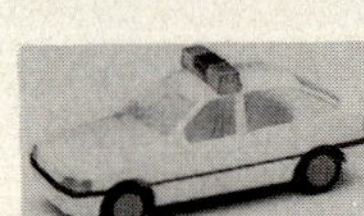

FORD ESCORT GHIA
Conversion
583-5705   7.49

FORD ESCORT GHIA
Conversion, Metallic
583-5706   7.49

FORD ESCORT GHIA
583-5708   7.99
Metallic
583-5715   7.99

FORD ESCORT GHIA
Kurier
583-5709   7.49

FORD ESCORT GHIA
Bild-Test
583-5713   7.49

KARMANN GHIA
1600 Limo
583-5811   6.99

KARMANN GHIA
Limo, Metallic
583-5812   7.49
w/Trailer
583-5813   14.99

MG MIDGET TC
OP Metallic Deluxe
583-5904 NEW 9.49

Praliné

HO SCALE (1/87) READY-TO-RUN

Imported from Germany by WALTHERS

Assembled, precolored plastic European autos, trucks and buses. Markings and colors may vary from what is shown in catalog.

AUTOMOBILES (continued)

MG MIDGET TC
Metallic Deluxe
583-5905 **NEW** 9.49

MG MIDGET TC
Racing Union **NEW**
583-5906   9.49

MG MIDGET TC
Conversion
583-5900   7.49

MG MIDGET TC
Cabrio
583-5901   7.49

MG MIDGET TC
Conversion, Deluxe
583-5902   8.49

MG MIDGET TC
Cabrio Deluxe
583-5903   8.49

PONTIAC TRANS AM
583-1711 w/T-Bar   7.49
583-1712 Deluxe   7.49

(not illustrated)
FORD ESCORT
583-5702 Post Ghia   7.49

CITROEN AX
Ralley
583-5607   7.99

CITROEN AX
RTT
583-5608   6.49

CITROEN AX
EDF/GDF
583-5609   6.49

CITROEN AX
Postal
583-5610   5.49

CITROEN AX
w/Design
583-5611   5.99

'36 HORCH 853
Gold Deluxe **NEW**
583-1377   13.49

DODGE MONACO
Kojack's Deluxe
583-6604 **NEW** 8.99

DODGE MONACO
Sedan **NEW**
Metallic Deluxe
583-6605   8.99

DODGE MONACO
Yellow Cab **NEW**
583-6606   8.99

PLYMOUTH FURY
Sedan Deluxe **NEW**
583-6651   7.99

PLYMOUTH FURY
Sedan Metallic
583-6652 **NEW** 8.99

(not illustrated)
PLYMOUTH FURY
Special Edition
583-6699 **NEW** 7.99

VANS & TRAILERS

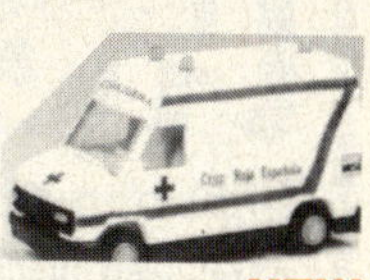

242 FIAT
Vigil Del Fuoco
583-348   5.49

FIAT DUCATO
Trans Caution **NEW**
583-3246   12.49

FIAT DUCATO **NEW**
Red Cross, French
583-3288   7.49

DKW SCHELL
Suchard
583-931   5.49

DKW
Sunlicht Seife
583-936   7.49

DKW
Persildame
583-937   7.49

DKW
Dienstmann
w/Luggage
583-938   7.49

■ **LTD QTY AVAIL** ■
FORD TRANSIT
Siemens
583-2422   2.99

'48 MB 170V
Panel Van Asbach
583-1521   5.49

MB 170V
Panel Van Kasten
583-1530   5.49

MB 170V
Panel Van Hiller
583-1531   6.49

'48 MB 170V
Pickup DB-WK
583-1523   5.49

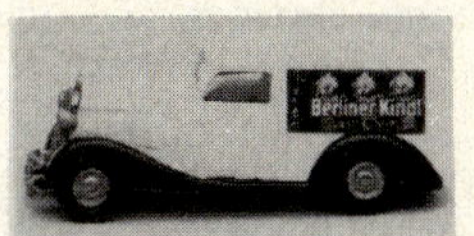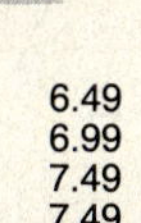

MB170V PANEL VAN
583-1532 Berliner   6.49
583-1533 4711   6.99
583-1535 ADAC   7.49
583-1536 Esso   7.49

MB 507D
583-4304 Undecorated   5.99

MB 507D
Jacky Maedr
583-4372   13.99
Reiterequippe
583-4373   14.49

FORD VAN **NEW**
Sinalco Frt Dnk
583-2430   7.49

FORD VAN **NEW**
Tech Serv, Green
583-2431   7.49

FORD VAN
Ice Cream **NEW**
583-2432   7.49

■ **LTD QTY AVAIL** ■
FORD TRANSIT
583-4311 ADAC 7.49

FORD TRANSIT
Essen Auf
583-3743   5.99

FORD TRANSIT
Gotano-Weinh
583-2428   6.49

Praline
HO SCALE (1/87) READY-TO-RUN

Imported from Germany by WALTHERS

Assembled, precolored plastic European autos, trucks and buses. Markings and colors may vary from what is shown in catalog.

We have worked closely with this manufacturer to provide accurate availability information at the time this catalog was published. Items listed in *blue ink* may not be available at all times. Please see your dealer for current delivery information.

VANS & TRAILERS (continued)

FORD **NEW** Kleindienst Car Wash 583-3763 7.49	FORD **NEW** Parcel Serv, Spain 583-3770 7.49	FORD **NEW** Bus-Serv, Austria 583-3771 7.49

CITROEN C25 Kommunal 583-3274 5.49	CITROEN Fish Delivery 483-1920 6.49	CITROEN C25 **NEW** Van Fret 583-3280 6.99

CITROEN H DLVRY Glass 583-1922 7.49 Suchard 583-1924 7.49	CITROEN C25 Europost 583-3276 6.99	CITROEN C25 Frankreich 583-3278 7.49

CITROEN C25 Van w/Ladder 583-3277 6.99	M5 507D w/Glass Transporter 583-4374 8.49	507D Schreib 583-4313 7.49

MB 507D Hor zo 583-4301 5.49	MB 507D Alligator 583-4302 4.99	MB 507D Inter Rent 583-4312 7.49

MB 507D **NEW** Eduscho-Kaffee 583-4319 7.99	MB 507D **NEW** Caute Trans Vehicle 583-4339 13.49	Peugot J5 **NEW** Military, French 583-3287 7.49

Peugot J5 DKW Schell
583-930 Werkstatt 4.49
583-932 DKW ADAC 4.99

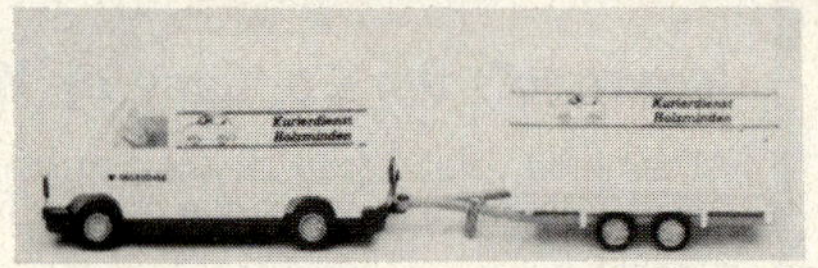

PEUGEOT J5 VAN 583-3244 5.99	583-3243 PEUGEOT J5 Kurierd w/Trailer 11.49

PEUGEOT J5 VAN 583-3299 6.49	PEUGEOT J5 583-3245 Hertz w/Trailer **NEW** 12.99

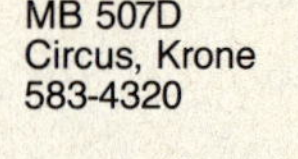

FIAT 242 Schenker 583-346 5.49	FORD TRANSIT Federal Express 583-3746 5.49	MB 507D Circus, Krone 583-4320 7.49

RENAULT TAXI 583-5503 7.49	RENAULT VAN 583-5500 6.49 Metallic 583-5501 7.49	RENAULT ESPACE Telecom 583-5508 7.49 Bild Test 583-5510 7.49

RENAULT ESPACE Pompiers 583-5512 8.49	RENAULT ESPACE MDK/JUB-FA 583-5511 6.99	RENAULT **NEW** Courtesy LeDome 583-5514 7.49

RENAULT **NEW** Air France 583-5515 7.49	RENAULT **NEW** French Video 583-5516 7.49	RENAULT **NEW** French Inter 583-5517 7.49

RENAULT **NEW** French LeParisien 583-5518 TBA		RENAULT **NEW** Red Cross, Austria 583-5519 TBA

(not illustrated)

583-343	FIAT 242 Kuhne Nagel		2.99
583-3228	FIAT DUCATO Courtesy U.N.	**NEW**	7.49
583-3708	FORD TRANSIT Funny Frisch		3.99

Praliné
HO SCALE (1/87) READY-TO-RUN

Imported from Germany by WALTHERS

Assembled, precolored plastic European autos, trucks and buses. Markings and colors may vary from what is shown in catalog.

VANS & TRAILERS (continued)

CITROEN C25
Dachser, w/Trailer
583-3223   12.49

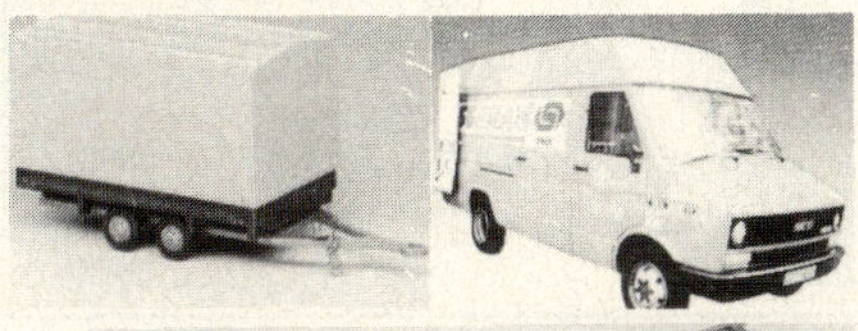

CITROEN C25
w/Trailer
583-3275   12.49

FORD TRANSIT
w/Glass Carrier
583-2427   11.99

ADAC
w/Trailers & Auto
583-4371   14.99

■ LTD QTY AVAIL ■
MB 1320
w/Trailer Karcher
583-4110   16.49

MB 1320
w/Trailer Lowensenf
583-4111   21.99
Pampers
583-4112   18.99

■ LTD QTY AVAIL ■
FIAT DUCATO
w/Trailer Ytong
583-3226   10.99

RENAULT ESPACE
w/Car & Trailer
583-5513   16.99

FORD TRANSIT
w/Trailer & Ralley Car
583-3760   16.49

(not illustrated)
583-3234   J5 Danzas   5.99
583-4902   Tandem Trailer for Vans   5.49

BUSES

RENAULT	R312
583-7200 Tour #1	29.49
583-7201 Tour #2	29.49
583-7202 Tour #3	29.49

■   LIMITED QUANTITY   ■
583-1029   500 Jahre Post   10.99
Deluxe Old Timer
583-1028   10.49

RENAULT RT1
583-5301   Undecorated   14.99
Air France
583-5302   19.49
Pan Am
583-5303   19.49

MB 03500 Sachsen
583-1030   12.49
(By Special Order Only.)
MB 03500 Sachsen-Anh
583-1031   12.49
MB 03500 Thuringen
583-1032   12.49

MB 03500 M. Brandenb
583-1033   12.49
MB 03500 Mecklenburg
583-1034   12.49
MB 03500 Schweizer
583-1035   12.49

MB 507
583-4322   Schoolbus   7.49

FORD TRANSIT
583-3704   Passenger   4.99

FORD TRANSIT
583-3749   Klenk   5.49

FIAT DUCATO
583-3218   Cinzano   6.49

FORD TRANSIT
583-3750   KHS   6.99
583-3758   Duisberger   6.49
583-3761   DB   7.49

MB 03500   *NEW*
583-1037   Meichsner   15.49

MB 03500   *NEW*
583-1038   Krone   13.99

Praline

HO SCALE (1/87) READY-TO-RUN

Imported from Germany by WALTHERS

Assembled, precolored plastic European autos, trucks and buses. Markings and colors may vary from what is shown in catalog.

We have worked closely with this manufacturer to provide accurate availability information at the time this catalog was published. Items listed in *blue ink* may not be available at all times. Please see your dealer for current delivery information.

BUSES (continued)

MB 507D
Kleber
583-4323   7.49
Gemballa
583-4309   7.49

MB 507D
Martika
583-4324   7.49
Duisberger
583-4333   7.49
Van Bus-Metallic U
583-4337   8.49

MB 507D
Cable-TV
583-4325   10.49
Telekommunik
583-4326   8.99

MACK
Privilege
583-5304   19.99

MACK
Travel Service
583-5305   24.99

MACK
Service Transport
583-5306   17.49

MACK
American Airline
583-5350   21.99

MACK
Gulf Coast
583-5351   21.99
NYC Circle Tour
583-5352   24.49

RENAULT BUS
FR1 RLE
583-5307   24.99

■ LTD QTY AVAIL ■
Ski Albertville
583-5308   23.49

RENAULT FR1
583-5311   Lilac   **NEW**   26.99

RENAULT FR1
Passenger Bus, Metallic   **NEW**
583-5312   31.99

RENAULT FR1
583-5313   Arnstadt   **NEW**   26.99

RENAULT FR1
583-5314   Charter   **NEW**   25.49

RENAULT FR1
583-5315   Savac Fr   **NEW**   21.99

RENAULT R312
583-7204   City Bus   **NEW**   29.49

(not illustrated)
583-5355   MACK US Deluxe Metallic   **NEW**   30.39

TRUCKS

DKW Flatbed Cargo
583-933   6.49

DKW Jacobs-Kaffee
583-934   6.49

FORD FIORINO
T-e-l-e-k-o-m
583-132   5.99

MB 170V
Pickup
583-1513   5.49

MB 507D
Truck w/Ladder & Trlr
583-4336   15.49

■ LTD QTY AVAIL ■
MB LP809
Herrenhauser
583-776   8.49

JULY 4, 1869

❖ Today ❖

IN RAILROAD HISTORY

The first railroad bridge to cross the Missouri River is opened for traffic, providing a through route from Kansas City to Chicago.

Praliné

HO SCALE (1/87) READY-TO-RUN

Imported from Germany by WALTHERS

Assembled, precolored plastic European autos, trucks and buses. Markings and colors may vary from what is shown in catalog.

TRUCKS (continued)

MB LP 809
w/Beer Barrel
583-775   12.99

LP 809
583-748 Clausthaler   9.99

LP 809
583-3804 Tow Truck   10.99

LP 809
Meyerhoff #7001
583-786   9.99

LP 809
Wernesgruner
583-787   9.99

LP 809
Der Alte Hoch
583-788   10.49

MB 1320
583-4002 Hellman   5.99

MB LP 809
Nordhauser
583-779   8.49

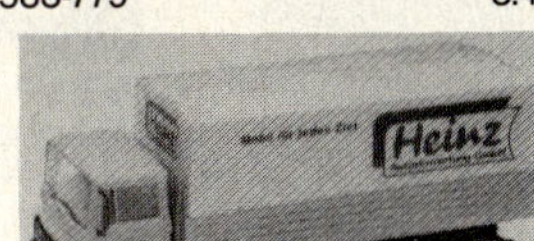
MB LP 809
Apolda-Bier
583-781   8.49

■ LIMITED QUANTITY AVAIL ■
583-782 MB LP 809 Heinz 8.49

MB LP 809
w/Accessories
583-774   12.99

MB LP 809
w/Glass Transporter
583-773   9.49

MB LP 809
Tech Service Truck
583-764   13.99

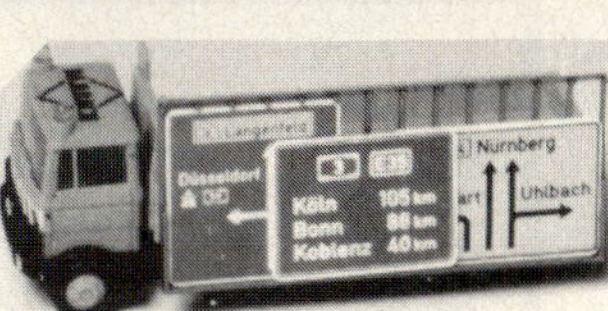
MB LP 809
Trans Truck w/Signs
583-791   15.49

VOLVO F10
583-4602 w/Trailer   25.49

VOLVO F10
583-4603 Jacky Maeder   13.99

VOLVO F10
Air France w/Trailer
583-4604   28.49

MAN F90
583-6102 Euro w/Trailer 32.99

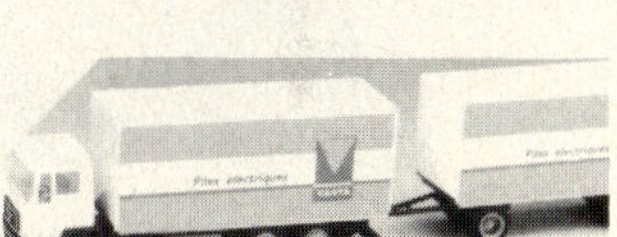
MAN F90
Clemens Muller
583-6103   13.49

MAN F90
Varta w/Trailer
583-6104   30.49

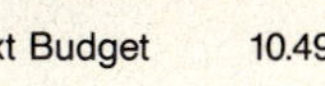
MB LP 814
583-7001 Meyerhoff   10.49

MP LP 814
583-7002 Sixt Budget   10.49

MB 1320
Tractor/Trailer Edeka
583-3507   17.99

583-2113 "BP"   9.99

(not illustrated)

583-7000 MB LP   10.99
814 German Railway

583-3003 Sinalco   6.49
583-3504 Pasin Papir   14.99

Praline

HO SCALE (1/87)
READY-TO-RUN

Imported from Germany by **WALTHERS**

Assembled, precolored plastic European autos, trucks and buses. Markings and colors may vary from what is shown in catalog.

We have worked closely with this manufacturer to provide accurate availability information at the time this catalog was published. Items listed in *blue ink* may not be available at all times. Please see your dealer for current delivery information.

TRUCKS (continued)

583-1816 Scania Navajo 17.49

583-1815 Scania Mayflower Moving Co. 17.49

MB 1320
Sped Emons
Double Tanker
583-4102 9.99

Marl w/Trailer
583-4101 9.99

MB 1320 w/Trailer
Bundepost Truck
583-4106 20.99

DELIVERY TRUCKS

TEMPO DREIRAD
583-631 Persil 6.99

(not illustrated)
583-131 Bad Ems 4.99

MB 170V
BW-Aral Tankstellen Service
583-1527 5.49

His Masters Voice
583-1526 5.49

Tempo Dreirad Zwieback
583-620 6.99

Tempo Dreirad Lindes
583-621 7.49

PEUGEOT 403
583-2308 5.49
583-2312 "BP" Tow 6.99

PEUGEOT 403
583-2309 7.49
583-2311 Glass Delivery 6.49

PEUGEOT 403
Delivery Truck & Trailer
583-2313 11.99

TD Rollmops
583-634 5.99

TD Lesezirkel
583-627 5.49

TD Briketts
583-632 6.99

TD Sinalco
583-635 6.99

FIAT FIORINO
Pizza Delivery
583-133 **NEW** 5.99

FIAT FIORINO **NEW**
Spanish Telephone
583-134 5.99

FIAT FIORINO
French Pizza
583-135 **NEW** 5.99

FIAT FIORINO
Martini
583-136 **NEW** 5.99

MB LP 809
Migro-Bakery **NEW**
583-723 13.99

MB LP 809 **NEW**
Schneider & Sohn
583-745 12.49

DKW **NEW**
Singer Sewing Mach
583-940 7.49

DKW **NEW**
Sinalco Fruit Drink
583-941 7.49

MB 170V **NEW**
Sinalco Fruit Drink
583-1537 7.49

MB 170V
Krone Circus **NEW**
583-1538 7.99

MB 179V **NEW**
German Police
583-1539 8.49

MB 170V
St. Raphael **NEW**
583-1540 6.99

CITROEN H **NEW**
French Cheese
583-1927 7.99

Praline

HO SCALE (1/87) READY-TO-RUN

Imported from Germany by WALTHERS

Assembled, precolored plastic European autos, trucks and buses. Markings and colors may vary from what is shown in catalog.

DELIVERY TRUCKS (continued)

CITROEN H NEW
French Waterman
583-1928   7.49

CITROEN H NEW
French Pinder
583-1929   7.49

CITROEN H NEW
French Banania
583-1930   7.49

CITROEN H NEW
Spanish Mail Correos
583-1931   7.49

PEUGEOT 403
French Pinder NEW
583-2315   6.49

PEUGEOT 403
French Nicolas
583-2316 NEW   6.49

EMERGENCY

MB 1320
583-4045   GW-Chemmie   13.49

MB LP 809
DRK-Red Cross Delivery
583-777   9.99

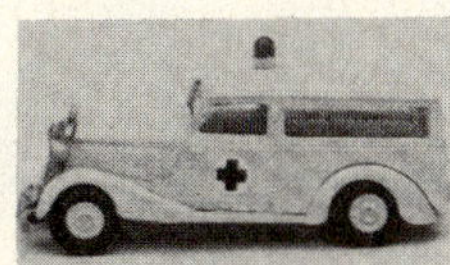
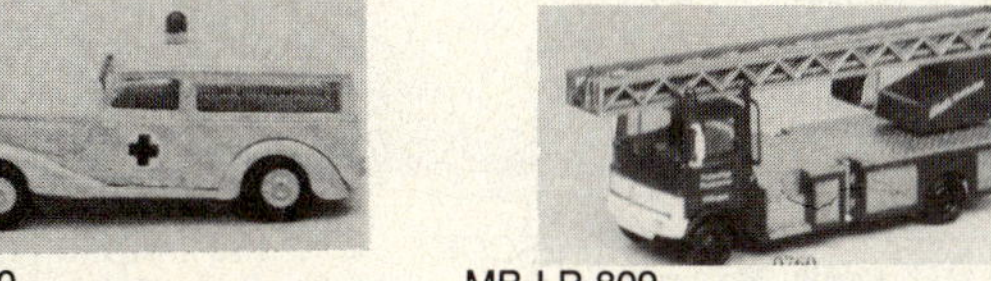

MB 170
Emergency Panel Van
583-1534   7.49

MB LP 809
Ladder Truck, Drehlit
583-760   14.49
583-765   Blemen UIT Holland   7.99

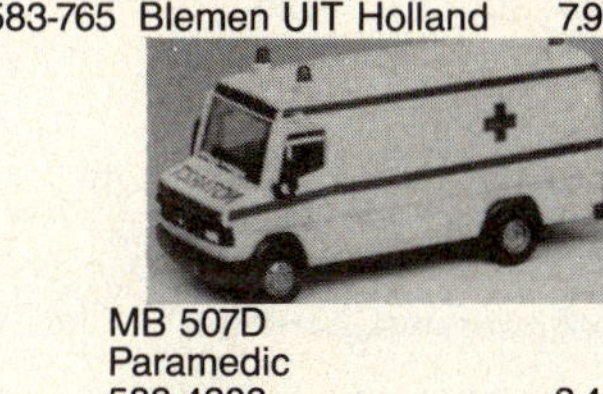

MB 507D
583-4307   Fire Dept   7.49
583-4308   Police   7.49

MB 507D
Paramedic
583-4303   8.49

PEUGEOT
French Fire NEW
583-2314   6.49

FIAT DUCATO
Ambulance NEW
583-3289   8.49

PORSCHE 356
583-1612 NEW   7.99

VW 1200
German Police NEW
583-2741   8.99

'54 CADILLAC WAGON NEW
Fire Chief, Deluxe
583-3454   8.99

MB 507D
Fire Dept
583-4318   7.49

583-4321   MB 507D   14.99
Fire Bus with ladder, trailer and boat
583-4317   MB 507D   8.49
with ladder only

MB 507D
Rescue MD "ASB" NEW
583-4338   9.99

FORD TRANSIT
Police Bus
583-3710   5.49

FORD
Rescue MD "ASB" NEW
583-3725   10.49

FORD TRANSIT
Fire Truck
583-3722   7.49

FORD TRANSIT
Fire Dept Van
583-3721   5.99

FORD TRANSIT
Ambulance
583-3713   5.99

FORD TRANSIT
Fire Dept Van
w/Ladder
583-3745   7.99

FORD TRANSIT
Fire Dept
583-3744   7.99

FORD TRANSIT
Police
583-3709   5.49

FORD TRANSIT
583-3707   Falck   5.99
583-2425   ASB   6.99
583-3724   Maredo   5.49
583-3723   Emergency Van   8.49

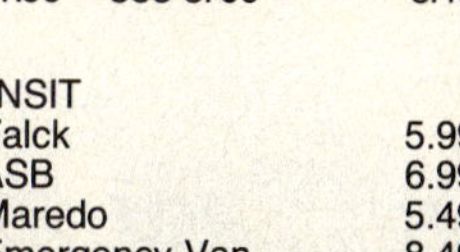

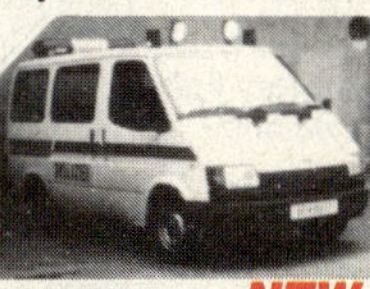

FORD NEW
British Ambulance
Wymas
583-3726   10.49

FORD NEW
Ambulance NL
583-3742   10.49

FORD NEW
Austrian Police
583-3772   8.49

FORD NEW
Austrian Rescue MD
583-3773   8.49

FORD ESCORT
Rescue MD NEW
583-5719   10.49

FIRE TRUCK NEW
USA, Wht w/Ladder
583-6006   35.99

(not illustrated)

583-421	MB 220 German Police Deluxe	NEW	7.99
583-2910	1970 Caddy Ambulance UD Deluxe	NEW	11.99
583-6007	Fire Engine, USA White Pumper	NEW	27.49

HO SCALE (1/87)
READY-TO-RUN

Imported from Germany by WALTHERS

Assembled, precolored plastic European autos, trucks and buses. Markings and colors may vary from what is shown in catalog.

We have worked closely with this manufacturer to provide accurate availability information at the time this catalog was published. Items listed in *blue ink* may not be available at all times. Please see your dealer for current delivery information.

EMERGENCY (continued)

MERCEDES 200 SE
Fire Dept
583-417 Deluxe   7.49

FIAT FIORNIO
Gratz Fire Dept
583-115   2.99

RENAULT
Ambulance
583-5502   8.49

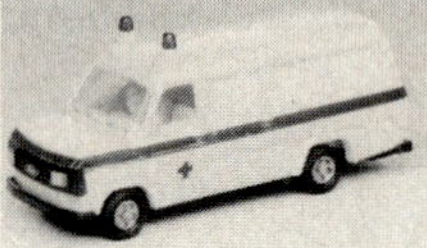
FORD TRANSIT
DRK-Krankenwagon
583-2402   6.49

FIAT DUCATO
Bus Ambulance
583-3227   7.49
Rescue Van
583-3229   7.49

1950 BUICK
Firecar Chicago
583-4712   7.99

FIAT DUCATO
Military Ambulance
583-3283   7.49

FIAT DUCATO
Van Ambulance
583-3281   7.49

CHEVY BELAIR
Military Police
583-5009   8.49

Military Police
583-4716   7.99

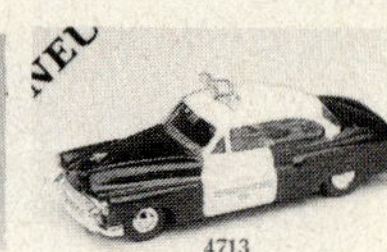
BUICK
Chicago Police Car
583-4713   7.99

'70 CADILLAC
Station Wagon
Fire Chief
583-2908   7.49

CITROEN AX
Police
583-5606   6.49

'54 CADILLAC
Ambulance Deluxe
583-3452   8.49
Fire Chief
583-3453   8.99

MERCEDES 170V
Police 1942 Top Up
583-1414   7.99

MERCEDES 170V
Police 1942 Top Down
583-1415   7.99

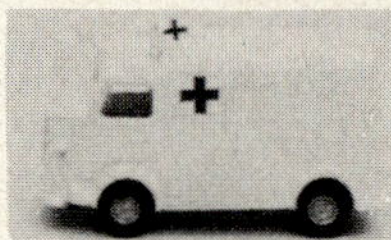
CITROEN H
Emergency Van
583-1925   7.49

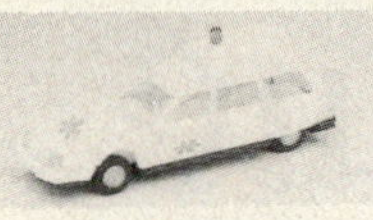
CITROEN CX
Break Ambulance
583-3308   7.99
Break Medicine
583-3309   7.99

CITROEN CX
Break Station Wagon
583-3310   6.99

CITROEN C25
Van Police
583-3279   8.49

CITROEN H VAN
Fire Van w/Ladder
583-1923   7.49

CITROEN
Police Van
583-1921   7.49

DODGE MONACO
Police
583-6601   9.99
583-6602   Fire   9.99

PORSCHE 356
Police Convertible
583-1606   7.49

Fire Dept
583-3903   5.49

■ **LTD QTY AVAIL** ■
VOLVO PV544
583-3901   Police   5.49

VW Police
583-2702   6.49
Fire Dept
583-2703   6.49

PONTIAC TRANS AM
Fire Chief
583-1705   5.49
Military Police
583-1708   5.49
583-1710   7.49

PONTIAC TRANS AM
Fire Chief
583-1713   7.49

■ **LTD QTY AVAIL** ■
PEUGEOT 403
Military Ambulance
583-2310   5.49

FORD ESCORT
Ghia Police
583-5714   8.49

KARMAN
Ghia 1600
583-5814   7.99

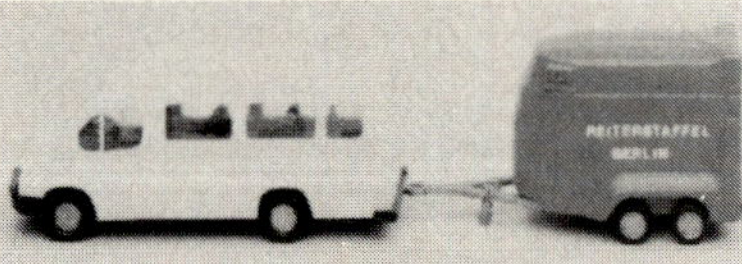
FORD TRANSIT
583-3759   Police Van & Trailer   13.49

ESPACE Van
583-5504   7.49

SCANIA H240
583-3609   Fire Truck   13.99
583-3610   Airport Rescue 13.99

ESPACE Van Police
583-5505   8.49

Praliné

HO SCALE (1/87) READY-TO-RUN

Imported from Germany by WALTHERS

Assembled, precolored plastic European autos, trucks and buses. Markings and colors may vary from what is shown in catalog.

EMERGENCY (continued)

Wht w/grn ladder
583-6003   35.99

	Fire Truck, New York City	
583-6000		27.49
	Fire Truck, San Francisco	
583-6001		27.49
583-6004	Wht w/red ladder	35.99
583-6002	Fire Truck, Chicago	27.49
583-6005	Wht w/ylw ladder	35.99

(not illustrated)

583-2513	Medicine SOS	5.99
583-3608	Airport Fire Truck	12.49
583-5507	ESPACE	8.49

ESPACE Police
583-5509   8.49

■ LIMITED QUANTITY AVAILABLE ■

| 583-2904 | '70 Cadillac w/Chrome | 7.99 |

RECREATIONAL VEHICLE

Fiat Ducato Camper
583-3285   8.49

ACCESSORIES

■ LTD QTY AVAIL
Freight Load
583-4500   5.49

Trailer w/Boat
583-4901   5.49

Tandem Trailer Ytong
583-4907   5.49

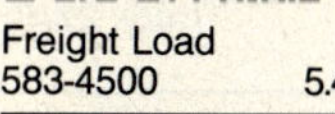

Enclosed
Tandem Trailer
583-4904   5.99

Trailer Glass Carrier
583-4906   5.49

Trailer
Fire & Emergency
583-4908   5.99

Tandem Trailer for
Auto Transport
583-4903   5.49

Small Trailer with
Air Equipment
583-4970   5.49

Glider w/Trailer
583-4951   7.99

VEHICLE SETS

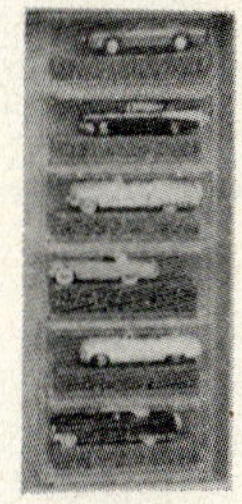

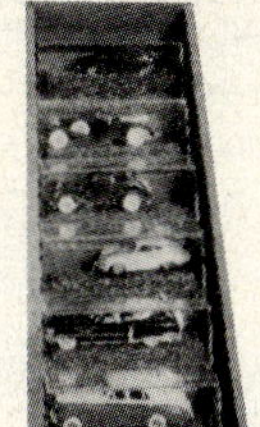

SET 1 (USA)
1954 Cadillac Limo
1954 Cadillac Limo
   Convertible
Buick Sedan
Buick Convertible,
   Top Down
Chevy Belair Sedan
1959 Cadillac Hard Top
583-10   35.99

SET 2 (GERMANY)
MB 170S Convertible
   Top Up
1938 Opel Olympia
1938 Ford Eifel
1936 Horch 853
   Convert, Top Down
MB 170V Sedan
1938 BMW 327
   Convert, Top Down
583-20   33.99

SET 3 (EUROPE)
Citroen H Metallic
Ferrari GTO
Volvo 544, Sedan
RR Sedan
Renault Espace Sedan
Citroen AX Sedan
583-30   29.99

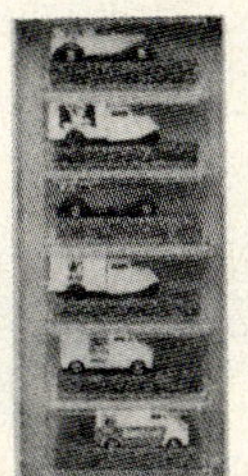
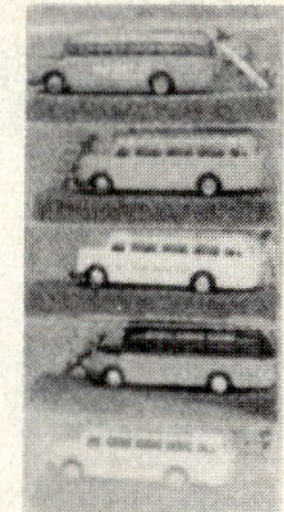

SET 4
Includes two each of the following models:

Tempo 3-Wheeler
DKW-Small Truck
Mercedes Benz 170V

583-40   29.99

**SET 5
(MERCEDES BENZ BUS)**
Includes one deluxe bus for each of the 5 new federal states of Germany (former socialistic German Republic) with their emblems.
583-50   49.99
(By Special Order Only.)

**SET 6
(10 Year Gift Set)**
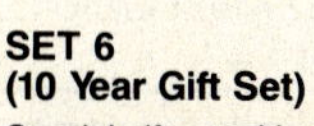
Special gift set with six different miniature model cars in a special paint, all parts are gold- and silver-vacuumplated. The models are printed in German "10 Years Praline " Le Must De Praline", 1981-1991.

Porsche 356 Limo	VW-1200 Limo
Cadillac 54	MB 300 SL
Horch 853	Chevy-Corvette

583-60   74.99

**SET 8
(Peacevillage Set)**
583-80   **NEW**   TBA

ORIGINAL Preiser

HO SCALE (1/87) EASY-TO-BUILD KITS

Imported from Germany by WALTHERS

Trucks are appropriately colored plastic.
All are kits (unless noted).

DUMP TRUCKS

590-1162 MB LA1924 14.99
3-Way Tipper

590-31226 MB LAK 1113 18.49
590-1228 MB LAK 1113 15.49

Magirus F150 w/Trailer
590-31262 21.49

Magirus 150D w/Trailer
3-Way Tipper
590-31215 21.49

590-1190 Magirus 120AK 13.99
Tipper assembled

590-37010 MB 3-Way 18.49

590-38000 MB LAK 2624 19.49
Heavy Duty asmb

590-1194 MB LA1924 w/Lift 15.99

There's lots of scrap to be hauled away during this building renovation project. Another dumpster is almost ready to haul away on the truck parked nearby. Preiser vehicles make it easy to add action to any scene. With their fine detail, realistic colors and add-on accessories, you'll be proud to display them on your layout.

TELESCOPING MOTORIZED CRANE

590-31100 Fire Company (red) 27.49

AUTOMOBILES

Audi 100
590-25104 NEW 21.49

Opel Astra
590-25105 NEW 21.49

Audi 200
590-25106 NEW 30.49

Suzuki w/Passengers
in Sports Clothing
590-33200 14.49

DUMPSTERS

590-31210 Meiller MB1632 21.49

590-1208 Meiller LAK911 15.99   590-31222 MB LA1519 21.49

ORIGINAL Preiser

HO SCALE (1/87) EASY-TO-BUILD KITS

Imported from Germany by WALTHERS

Trucks are appropriately colored plastic. All are kits (unless noted).

+ (Plus Sign) = Special Order Only Items

DUMPSTERS (continued)

Meiller MB 1419L Fire Brigade assembled
590-35004   21.49

Meiller MB L1513/42 assembled
590-38002   21.49

Meiller MB 1722L assembled
590-38003   21.49

MISCELLANEOUS TRUCKS

Road Maintenance Truck
590-37018   **NEW** 13.49

MB 1924 w/Cherry Picker
590-1196   22.99

(not illustrated)
590-21153   MB 508 Publicity Van   **NEW**   15.49

MISCELLANEOUS TRUCKS (continued)

MB LA911 Van
590-1232   15.99

MB LA911/42 Tank
590-31264 for Helicopters 21.49
590-37005 assembled   20.49

MB LA911/42 Driving School
590-31266   20.49
590-37006 assembled   21.49

Magirus M125A Covered
590-31282   Delivery 18.49

Magirus Generator Truck
590-31307   21.49

Armored Van assembled
590-38001   10.99

Federal Postal Service Van asmb
590-38007   12.99

MB L322/42 Cattle assembled
590-38004   21.49

MB1017 Cattle Carrier asmb
590-38010   21.49

MB L322/42 Brewery Truck asmb
590-38005   23.49

MB 1625 S/32 Refrigerator asmb
590-38006   Sturm   29.49

TRACTORS

MB Schmidbauer KG assembled
590-38008   29.49

MG Brabender assembled
590-38009   29.49

Semi-Trailer MB LAK 2624/36
590-1120   10.99

Titan Heavy Duty
590-31158 +   21.49

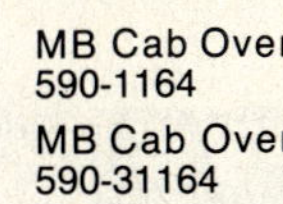

MB Cab Over
590-1164   (red) 15.49
MB Cab Over
590-31164   (beige) 13.99

Schnirle Flatbed Trailer
590-31154   19.49

Titan Open Cab
590-31156   19.49

Single Axle
590-17917 **NEW** 11.99

(not illustrated)
590-31176 Container Trailer   17.49

ORIGINAL Preiser

HO SCALE (1/87) EASY-TO-BUILD KITS

Imported from Germany by WALTHERS

Trucks are appropriately colored plastic.
All are kits (unless noted).

+ (Plus Sign) = Special Order Only Items

Smoke is pouring out of the windows, but this fire company will soon have things under control! Preiser kits build into authentic replicas of contemporary German fire and emergency vehicles. The unfinished models are perfect for use on layouts or dioramas, or for collecting.

VANS

Mitsubishi L300 w/Figures
590-33205 +   asmb 20.49

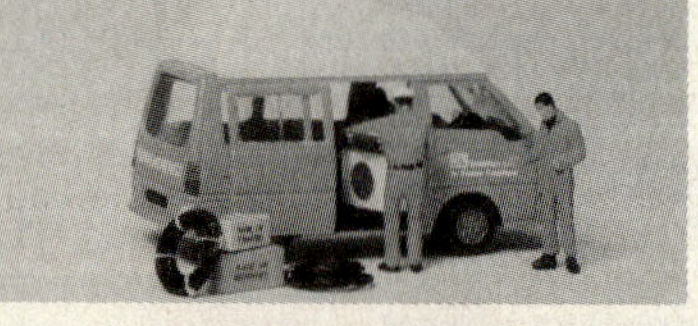

Mitsubishi L300 w/Figures
590-33206 assembled 19.49

MMC L300 w/Figures & Accessories assembled
590-33209   23.49

FARM EQUIPMENT

Deutz Farm Tractor assembled
590-17913   9.99

Deutz Farm Tractor w/Trailer
590-17914   assembled 13.49

Hanomag R55 Agriculture asmb
590-17915   10.99

Hanomag R55 Forestry asmb
590-17916   10.99

Hanomag R55 assembled
590-21000   11.99

Hanomag R55
590-24679   16.49

Hanomag R55 Tractor NATO assembled
590-37015 +
10.49

EMERGENCY EQUIPMENT

Magirus
MB LF1313
Turntable Ladder
DLK 23-12 St
590-31268   28.49

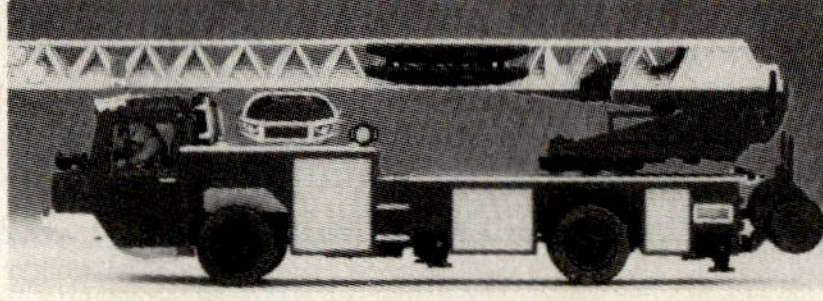

Magirus
MB LF1313
Turntable Ladder
DLK 23-12 Tr
590-31270   28.49

Magirus DLK23
Ladder (red)
590-31134 +   27.49

Mitsubishi L300
Belgian Police Van
Open Door w/Access
assembled
590-33212   23.49

Mitsubishi L300
Belgian Police Van
Closed Door w/Access
assembled
590-33213 +   21.99

Chevy Blazer w/Figures
Firebrigade Bregenz
assembled
590-33211   15.99

LF-16
Fire Truck
590-1129   15.49

Preiser

HO SCALE (1/87) EASY-TO-BUILD KITS

Imported from Germany by WALTHERS

Trucks are appropriately colored plastic.
All are kits (unless noted).

+ (Plus Sign) = Special Order Only Items

EMERGENCY EQUIPMENT (continued)

MB1019 TLF16 Pumper
590-35001 + asmb 20.49

MB1019 TLF16
Dry Powder assembled
590-35002   20.49

MB 1419 F/42
DLK23-12 Ladder asmb
590-35003   28.49

MAN 9.168 Tool and
Gear Carrier assembled
590-35007   21.49

MB L1519/48 DLK23-12
Ladder assembled
590-35009   28.49

TLF 15/53 Tank Pumper
590-31217   18.49

MB O 309 Command Van
assembled
590-35011   12.99

MB L 407D Emergency
Service assembled
590-37007   19.49

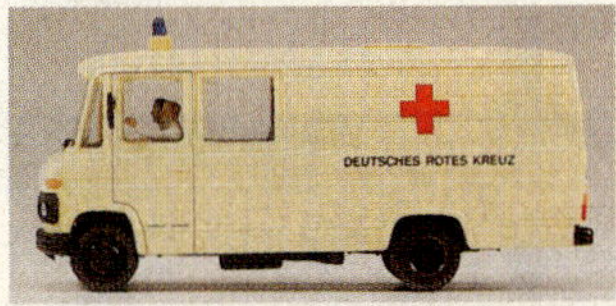

MB L 407D
Medical Van assembled
590-37008   12.99

MB L 508 Van assembled
590-37009 +   11.99

MB Covered Truck asmb
590-37011   20.49

FLF80/200 Airfield Fire Engine
590-35008 assembled   27.49

590-31167 Kit   17.49

MB LF322/36 Pumper TLF
TLF 16/28-5 Tr, METZ
590-31286   20.49

MAN 11.168 HA LF
Water/Dry Powder, Ziegler
590-31296   23.49

Rescue Tools & Gear Truck
590-31306   21.49

MAN 11.192 HA LF Pumper
590-31298 Ziegler   23.49
590-35005 assembled 20.49

Magirus M126D 10A Tanker
590-31278   21.49

LA 911A Emergency Service
590-1169   16.99
Same as 31168 less interior equipment

Magirus F200D Ambulance
590-31250   18.49

Fire Dept Tools & Gear Truck
590-31308   21.49

Magirus 200 D16
Articulated Elevating
Platform
590-31292   27.49

Rescue Equipment
590-31193   15.49

CO_2 & Pressure/ Suction
Container for #1116
590-31152   16.49

MB LA911A Fire Truck
590-31168 w/Interior kit 20.49
590-37000 assembled   21.49
            less Interior

Meiller Container Truck
w/4 Containers
590-31116   23.49

ORIGINAL Preiser

HO SCALE
(1/87)
EASY-TO-BUILD
KITS

Imported from Germany by WALTHERS

Trucks are appropriately colored plastic.
All are kits (unless noted).

+ (Plus Sign) =
Special Order Only Items

EMERGENCY EQUIPMENT (continued)

MB LA 1924 Snorkel
590-31180   26.99

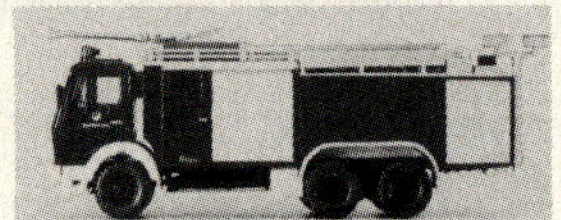

TLF 40/50-5 Ziegler MB 2632
590-31172 AK/38 Pumper 27.49

Rescue w/Crane MB1017
590-31182   23.49

MB TLF16 Pumper
590-31248   21.49

Magirus 1500 Salter
590-1206   15.99

Magirus F150D
590-31224+   19.49

MB 1113 Airport Pumper
590-31294   20.49

Magirus M125A
Hose SW2000
590-31276 21.49

GTLF18 Airport Fire Truck
590-31165   20.49

MB LAF1113 LF16TS, Lentner
590-31280   21.49

Magirus M125A LF 16TS
590-31272   21.49

Magirus M125A Pumper, TLF16
590-31274   21.49

F-16-2 Compartment Pumper
590-31128 Kit   18.49
590-35000 assem (red) 20.49

590-31144 LF1b Fire   16.49
Truck Kit

MAN 11.168 Tender HA LF
590-31302 Ziegler   23.49
590-35006 assembled   21.49

MAN 19.321 HAK Three-Way
590-31300   Tipper   21.49

F200D Water Tank
590-31202   20.49

TLF 24/50 Bachert MB
1922/AK Pumper
590-31178   19.49

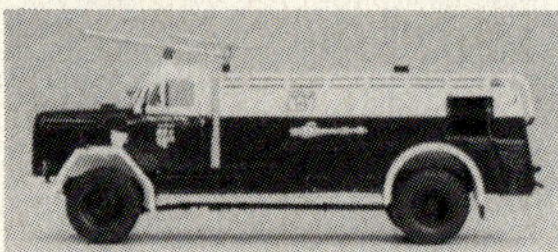

Magirus F200D 16A
Water Container ZB6
590-31260   21.49

Magirus F125A Pumper
590-1216   15.49

MB LAF1113 Squad Tender
590-31230   21.49

Magirus 150D 10FA Pumper
590-31218   18.49

MB LA911
590-1234   Red Cross   15.49
590-37003   assembled   20.49
590-1236   Police   15.99
590-37004   assembled   20.49
590-31238   Rescue   18.49
590-37002   assembled   20.49

Magirus FLF24 Pumper
590-31188   18.49

Magirus 125A Foam
590-31242   18.49

Magirus ZLF3000 Pumper
590-1198   15.99

MB LAF1113
590-31246   Hose   21.49
590-1250   Dry Powder   18.49

Magirus 150D/TLF16
590-1186   15.49

MB 1922AK Pumper
590-1258 Export   15.99

MB LA1113B (blue)
590-31192   20.49
590-37001 assembled   21.49

Magirus F125A Driving Training
590-31200   15.99

MB LAF911 Emergency
590-31252   21.99

590-31204 F200D Rescue 20.49

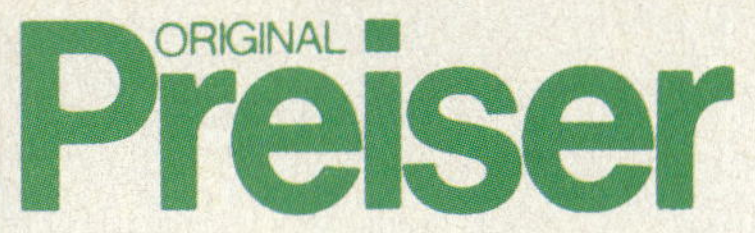

ORIGINAL **Preiser**

HO SCALE (1/87) EASY-TO-BUILD KITS

Imported from Germany by **WALTHERS**

Trucks and wagons are appropriately colored plastic. All are kits (unless noted).

+ (Plus Sign) = ■ Special Order Only Items

EMERGENCY EQUIPMENT (continued)

Hand-operated Fire Brigade
590-30405 **NEW** 27.49

Steam Fire Brigade
590-30406 **NEW** 17.49

Airport Fire Truck FTLF8000
590-31163 20.49

MB L508 BGS Police Van
590-37017 **NEW** 12.99

MB LF 710/32 Dry Powder
590-31284 20.49

■ **LTD QTY AVAILABLE** ■

Chevy Blazer FD
590-33210 13.99

EMERGENCY EQUIPMENT ACCESSORIES (cont)

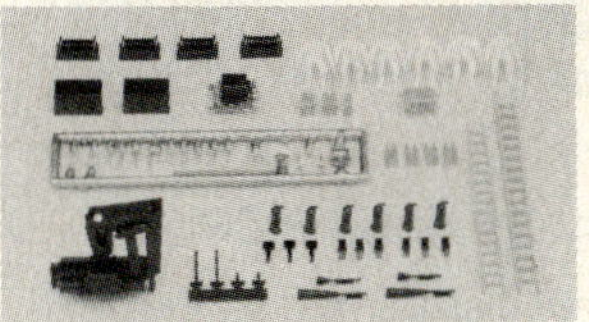

Firefighting Accessories
w/Loading Crane
590-31013 + 9.99

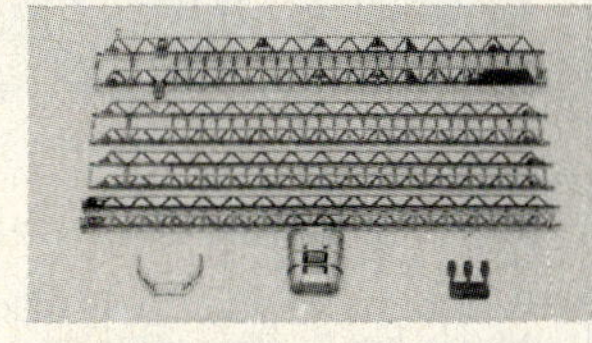

Magirus Ladder w/Rescue Basket
590-31015 7.49

Firefighting Trailer
590-31112 + 7.49

Ziegler Hose Trailer
590-31254 9.99

Fire Brigade
Accessories
590-31016 9.99

CRANE

35T w/Wheels
590-31138 21.49

EMERGENCY EQUIPMENT ACCESSORIES

Hose Reels
590-31012
pkg(6) 10.49

Water Container
590-31244 pkg(2) 10.99

Firefighting Accessories
590-31010 10.99

Water Cannon Set
590-31114 pkg(2) 7.49

590-31007 Ladders 9.99

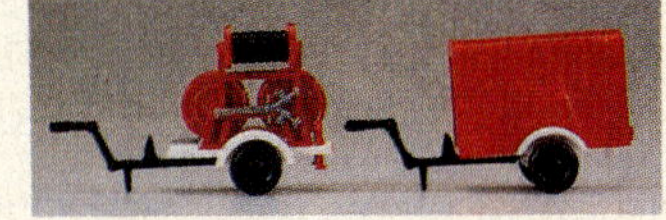

Ziegler 2B/2C w/Hose Trailer
590-35010 + 10.49

RECREATION

Mitsubishi Camping Bus
w/Figures assembled
590-33201 19.49

Fiat Tipo Escort
assembled
590-25103 + 20.49

TRAILERS

Flatbed
590-31174
15.49

Car Trailer
590-31150 pkg(2) 7.99

Bockmann TII Horse Trailer
590-31160 9.99

ORIGINAL Preiser

HO SCALE (1/87) EASY-TO-BUILD KITS

Imported from Germany by WALTHERS

Trucks are appropriately colored plastic.
All are kits (unless noted).

+ (Plus Sign) = Special Order Only Items

Traveling in style aboard an open carriage is a fine way to see the city sights. Whether at the turn-of-the-century or on modern highways, Preiser vehicles are the finishing touch to any scene. This detailed carriage comes complete with figures and horses, and is available assembled or as a kit.

HORSE DRAWN WAGON ■

Fire Wagon w/Pump assembled
590-30428   29.49

1890's Beer Wagon
590-30462   23.49

Furniture Wagon Hartleb asmb
590-30458   19.99

Royal Bavarian
590-30430   assembled   23.49

Fire Dept Hand Pumper asmb
590-30425   23.49

Log Wagon w/Driver & Load
590-30465   assembled   23.49

Fire Dept Water Wagon
590-30426   assembled   23.49

Furniture Wagon w/Two Horses
590-30457 +   assembled   23.49

Manure Wagon w/Driver asmb
590-30474 +   Load & Ox   21.49

Fire Coal Tender assembled
590-30429   23.49

Ore Wagon w/Driver & Horses
590-30468   assembled   17.49

Hay Wagon w/Driver & Load
590-30477 +   assembled   23.49

White Coach
590-30400   15.49

Furniture Wagon
590-30404   20.49

HORSE-DRAWN WAGON (continued) ■

Closed White Marriage Coach w/4
590-30450   Figures asmb   23.49

1900 German Coach w/Figures
590-30454   assembled   23.49

Open White Marriage Coach w/4
590-30451   Figures asmb   23.49

Closed Horse-Drawn Taxi w/3
590-30452   Figures asmb   23.49

Hay Wagon w/Driver & Load asmb
590-30472 +   21.49

Black Coaches
590-30401   15.49

Delivery & Parcel Post Carts
590-30403   15.49

Rack & Box Carts
590-30402   15.49

Fire Dept Wagon assembled
590-30427   23.49

Cargo Wagon w/Horses asmb
590-30470   21.49

Preiser

ORIGINAL Preiser

HO SCALE (1/87) EASY-TO-BUILD KITS

Imported from Germany by **WALTHERS**

Trucks are appropriately colored plastic.
All are kits (unless noted).

+ (Plus Sign) = Special Order Only Items

MISCELLANEOUS

Kuli Portable Lighting
590-31148   pkg(2) 10.99

Dumpster Container
590-31214   pkg(4) 10.99

Truck Accessories
590-31014   9.99

(not illustrated)
590-17202   Waste Container/Dustbin   **NEW** 10.49

PIRATE MODELS LTD. HO SCALE (1/87) CRAFT TRAIN KITS

Imported from Great Britain by **WALTHERS**

GMC

GMC PD4903/4905A Coach
559-353   43.99

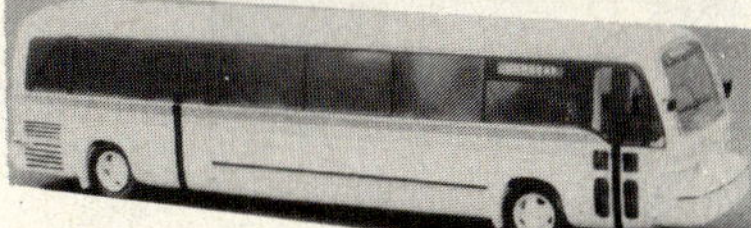

GMC RTS Mark 3 Coach
559-359   47.99
Less seats, interior detail and decal.

GMC RTS Mark 4
559-3510   47.99

GMC 4509/12 Transit
559-357   43.99

PIRATE MODELS LTD. HO SCALE (1/87) CRAFT TRAIN KITS

Imported from Great Britain by **WALTHERS**

TRANSIT

53SER 40'
559-351   43.99

4502/7
559-352   43.99

FLEXIBLE

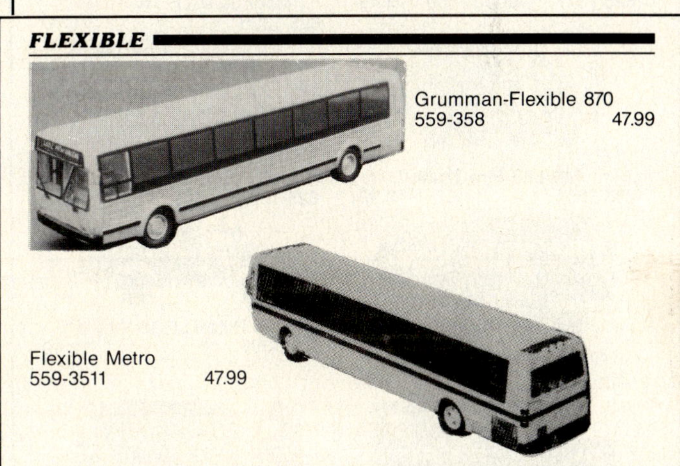

Grumman-Flexible 870
559-358   47.99

Flexible Metro
559-3511   47.99

MISCELLANEOUS

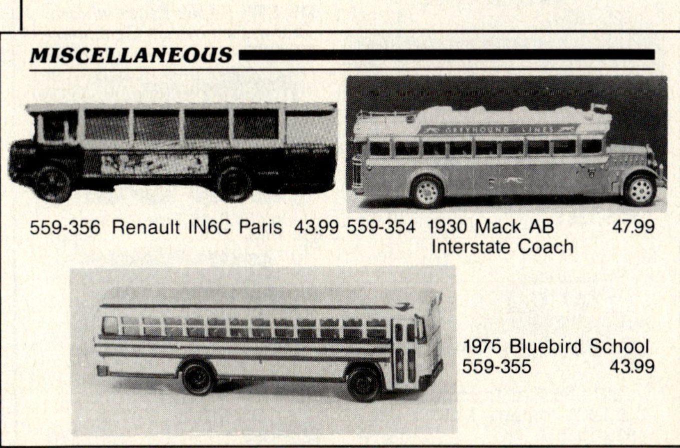

559-356   Renault IN6C Paris   43.99

559-354   1930 Mack AB Interstate Coach   47.99

1975 Bluebird School
559-355   43.99

Roco
Imported from Austria
by WALTHERS
HO SCALE (1/87)

Ready-to-run, pre-colored vehicles. Markings and colors may vary from what is shown in catalog.

EMERGENCY VEHICLES

DLK 23-12 w/Renault Cab
625-1371   19.99

Magirus 2312, Ladder
625-1349   19.99

625-1377   Ambulance   7.49

Magirus D LF 16 **NEW**
625-1396   15.99

MB LF8 Fire Truck
265-1351   10.99

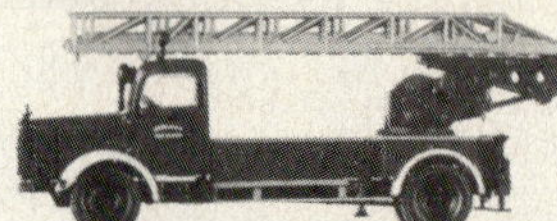

MB DL Ladder **NEW**
625-1397   19.99

Steyr 680 TLF Fire Truck
265-1342   13.99

Opel Blitz TLF 15 **NEW**
625-1398   12.49

Mercedes LF 25
625-1374   17.99

MB SRF Repair Truck w/Hiab
Crane, Removable Container
625-1369   18.99

Land Rover
625-1381   10.49

Mag TLF 16 Fire Pumper
625-1366   14.99

MB LF8 Fire Truck w/Trailer
& DKW Portable Motor Pump
625-1375   14.99

VW Typ 2
DB Railway Police
625-1382   7.49

Opel Blitz
w/Fire Extinguisher Trailer
625-1337   14.49

625-1376   VW-Bus and Truck
Field Kitchen Unit   18.49

MB L4500 D122 Ladder
625-1361   19.99

MAG DLK 23-12
w/Turn Ladder
625-1346   21.49

Unimog 1300L Fire
625-1364   Ambulance   8.99

VW Double Cab, Fire Fighting
625-1362   6.49

"Willys Jeep" Fire Dept.
625-1365   6.99

Pinzgauer 6x6 Command Car
625-1310   8.49

VW 2-Unit Mini Bus Set
625-1385   18.49

Magirus TLF Fire Truck
625-1386   14.99

Unimog 4-Wheel Drive
Fire Engine
625-1304   9.49

Red Cross Dodge
Jeep & Trailer
625-1388   10.49

Dodge, Swiss (yellow)
625-1348   9.99

Land Rover Red Cross
625-1380   10.49

Mercedes TLFA 4000
Rosenbauer
625-1379   16.49

Roco

Imported from Austria
by WALTHERS
HO SCALE (1/87)

Ready-to-run, pre-colored vehicles. Markings and colors may vary from what is shown in catalog.

EMERGENCY VEHICLES (continued)

Unimog S w/Canvas Hood
625-1338 Red Cross 7.99

KLFA Fire Land Rover
625-1359 10.49

Covered Trailer
625-1309
3.99

625-1323 THW VW 5.49

EMERGENCY VEHICLES (continued)

THW MAN 5 Ton
w/Canvas Hood
625-1302 8.49

THW MAN 5 Ton Equipment
Truck
625-1308 6.49

MAN 630 L2A
Technical Rescue Service
625-1378 9.99

VW Type 2 Command Car
625-1370 7.99

VW Type 2 Ambulance
625-1372 7.99

VW Ambulance
625-1355 7.49

LIMITED QUANTITY AVAILABLE

DKW Munga, Red Cross
625-1301 5.49

Munga Radio Car, Fire Dept
625-1300 5.49

Mercedes 1017 Police Truck
w/Canvas
625-1383 10.99

VW Mini bus w/horse trailer
625-1384 17.99

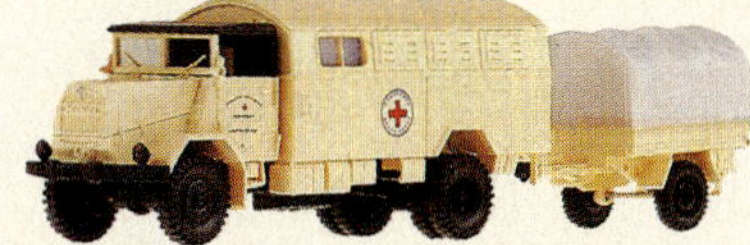

Munga Jeep, Red Cross
625-1329 4.49

MAN 630L 2 A Red Cross
Bus & Trailer
625-1387 11.49

MAN 5T w/Trailer, Red Cross
625-1339 8.49

THW Field Kitchen
625-1320 3.99

EMERGENCY HELICOPTERS

MBB BO 105 Rescue
625-1392 9.49

MBB BO 105 Rescue
625-1390 9.49

MBB BO 105 Police
625-1391 kit 9.49

CONSTRUCTION VEHICLES

625-1516 Tractor w/Load, Steyr 91 37.49

Dump Truck, Magirus
625-1527 15.49

625-1533 Construction Vehicle w/Accessories 24.99

Roco
Imported from Austria
by WALTHERS
HO SCALE (1/87)
Ready-to-run, pre-colored vehicles. Markings and colors may vary from what is shown in catalog.

CONSTRUCTION VEHICLES (continued)

Magirus D
Tipping
Semi Trailer
625-1546
19.99

Road Building
Vehicle Set
Add-On
625-1547
49.99

Mercedes 4500 Tanker
625-1588 TBA
NEW

Construction Site Set
Unimog 1300
& Sauer Komet
625-1526 19.49

Volvo FL10
w/Silo Moving
Equipment
625-1561   23.99

3-Axle Dump
w/Trailer, Magirus
625-1543 22.99

625-1545 Construction Set   25.99

SEMI TRUCKS

Mercedes 1838
625-1579
28.49
NEW

Mercedes 1838
625-1577
27.49
NEW

SEMI TRUCKS (continued)

Magirus M5
625-1569   12.49

Renault 3-Axle Tractor Trailer
625-1567   17.49

625-1589   Volvo FL10 ''Maxilaterale''   **NEW**   24.49

625-1430   Volvo FL10   **NEW**   10.99
(not illustrated)
625-1570 Volvo FL10 ''Kuhne & Nagel   24.99
625-1571 Mercedes 1838 ''Kieserling''   28.49

625-1581 ''Kuhlzug'' Refrigerator Truck & Trailer   28.49
625-1582 ''Bahlsen'' Truck & Trailer Vans   33.99

Tractor Trailer, Renault
625-1528   14.99

Tractor Trailer, Magirus
625-1538   15.49

Steyr 91
Gondrand 3-Axle
625-1557
16.99

Tractor & Trailer
Magirus
625-1524
16.99

Volvo FL10
625-1575
TBA
NEW

Mercedes 1838
Schenker
625-1576
TBA
NEW

Roco

Imported from Austria by WALTHERS

HO SCALE (1/87)

Ready-to-run, pre-colored vehicles. Markings and colors may vary from what is shown in catalog.

SEMI TRUCKS (continued)

Semi, Ischler Saltz (salt) Steyr 91
625-1520
15.99

Tractor Trailer Steyr 91
625-1514
14.99

Volvo "Laura Ashley" **NEW**
625-1583   11.99

Renault **NEW**
625-1584   TBA

Mercedes "Radeberger"
625-1573
21.49
NEW

(not illustrated)

625-1793	Volvo Advertisement Truck	4.49
625-1580	Volvo FL 10 Truck Trailer	19.99
625-1565	Ford Cargo w/large trailer	21.99

625-1406 Faun HD Transporter   16.99

SAURER BUSES

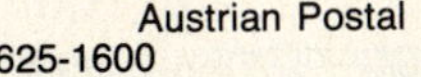

Austrian Postal
625-1600   15.49

Tour Bus "Komet"
625-1602   15.49

MAINTENANCE/UTILITY VEHICLES

Tow Truck, Dodge
625-1712   8.49

MAN 630 w/Repair Shop
625-1410   12.49

Service, Renault G
625-1656   15.49

Utility, Unimog 1300
625-1503   pkg(6) 29.99

Highway Maintenance Magirus
625-1655   17.49

6-WHEEL TRUCKS

Margirus M5t
625-1559   10.49

Steyr 680 w/flatbed
625-1562   8.49

Margirus D Dumptruck
625-1563   11.99

Steyr 680 w/Trailer
625-1564   13.49

625-1536 Delivery Van, GPR Magirus   9.99

LIMITED QUANTITIES AVAILABLE

625-1537   Van, Magirus   9.99

HO SCALE (1/87)

Ready-to-run, pre-colored vehicles. Markings and colors may vary from what is shown in catalog.

PIGGYBACK FLAT

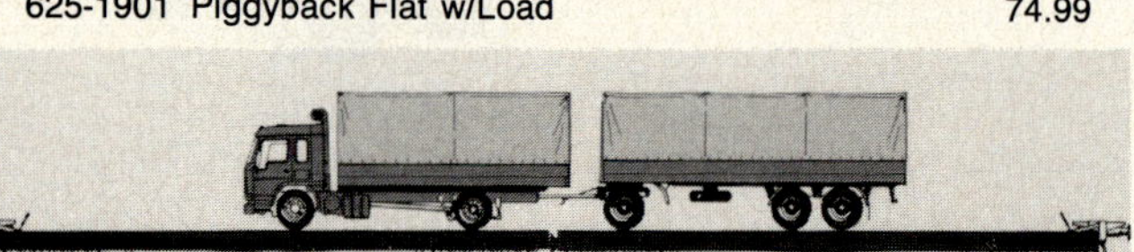

625-1901 Piggyback Flat w/Load   74.99

625-1902 Piggyback Flat w/Truck & Trailer   74.99

TRAILER TRAIN

"Road Railer"
DB Trailer Train
625-1903   TBA

RECREATIONAL VEHICLES

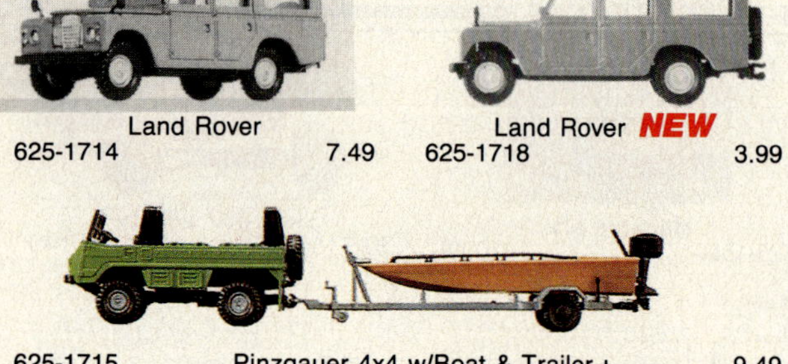

Land Rover
625-1714   7.49

Land Rover **NEW**
625-1718   3.99

625-1715   Pinzgauer 4x4 w/Boat & Trailer +   9.49

Jeep "Renegade"
w/Trailer
625-1719   9.49
NEW

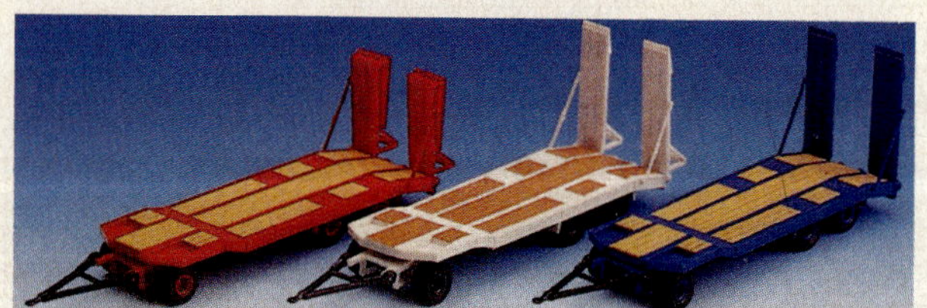

TRAILERS

625-1402 "Goldhofer" Trailers   pkg(3) 24.49

TRAILERS (continued)

625-1407   Goldhofer Low Boy Trailer, 12-Wheel Flat   8.49

625-1529   Trailer Set   pkg(3) 26.99

VANS

VW, Varta Flatbed
625-1412   9.49

VW Typ 2
625-1427   6.99

625-1550 VW MiniVan   7.49

VW Telekom **NEW**
625-1433   8.49

VW Type II
625-1428   7.49

VW Type II Syncro **NEW**
625-1432   6.99

Type II, Syncro, VW
625-1422   6.99

VW Type II "NDR" **NEW**
625-1429   8.49

VW Type II Transporter
625-1424   7.99

VW Type II "M.A.N."
625-1411   8.49

VW Type II Double Cab
625-1425   5.99

VW Type II w/covered
flatbed
625-1426   5.99

VW-German Federal
Mail Postal Carrier
625-1554   9.49

Roco
Imported from Austria
by *WALTHERS*
HO SCALE (1/87)

Ready-to-run, pre-colored vehicles. Markings and colors may vary from what is shown in catalog.

VANS (continued)

VW Type 2 Double Cab
625-1555   6.99

VW Type II Taxi
625-1423   7.49

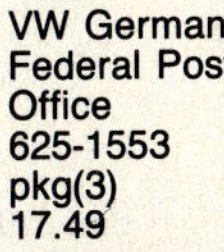

VW German Federal Post Office
625-1553
pkg(3)
17.49

625-1434   VW Type 2 Van w/Trailer   **NEW** TBA

625-1566   VW 3 Unit Set   21.99

ACCESSORIES

CONTAINERS

625-1797   20' Container Set   pkg(3) 12.49

DECALS & DRY TRANSFERS

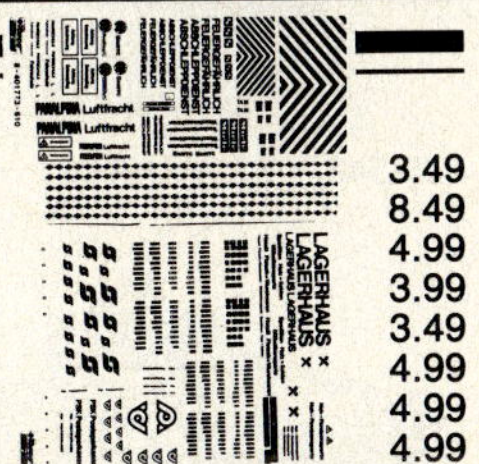

All sets are decals unless noted.

625-1764	for Fire Engines	3.49
625-1765	F.D. Lettering Dry Transfer	8.49
625-1768	Day Glow Red	4.99
625-1773	for Trucks/Trailers #1	3.99
625-1774	for Trucks/Trailers #2	3.49
625-1784	for Trucks (self-adhesive)	4.99
625-1785	Vehicle I.D. (self-adhesive)	4.99
625-1787	50's Vehicles Decals	4.99

MISCELLANEOUS

Crane Attatchments
625-1778   4.99

Coupling For Semi Trailers
625-1794   3.99

MISCELLANEOUS (continued)

Salt Spreader
625-1777
4.99

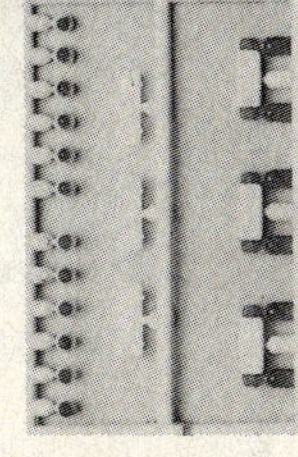

Headlight for Emergency Vehicles
625-1749
3.99

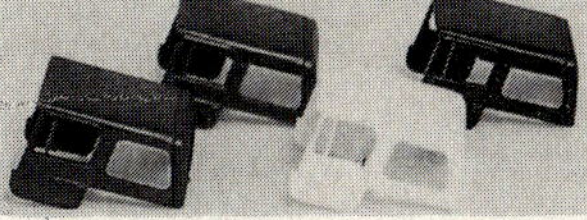

625-1756   Jeep Hard Top   3.49

Snowplow Kit
625-1775
pkg(2) 4.99
Type "Kahlbach", attachment plates for 2 trucks are supplied.

(not illustrated)
625-1745   Forklift Truck w/Pallets   **NEW** 3.99

ACCESSORY SETS

625-1748	Fire Fighting Set VI	3.99
625-1759	Fire Truck Parts	3.99
625-1788	Fire Truck Detail Set	3.99
625-1792	Steering Set Accessory for #625-1366	3.99
625-1772	Steering Set	3.99
	for truck models: Steyr 91 or Steyr 660, includes parts to change other vehicles.	
625-1751	Mirrors	3.99
	rear-view for passenger cars & trucks	
625-1752	Accessories	3.99
	for trucks, mainly US-chrome & colored	
625-1753	Head & Spot Light Accessories	3.99
625-1754	Accessories	3.99
	for hitches and trailers	
625-1755	Roof Spoilers	pkg(3) 3.99
625-1760	Accessories	3.99
	for fire engine models: 1300, 1303, 1304, 1311 & others	
625-1761	Accessories	3.99
	for fire engine models: 1304, 1311 & others	
625-1762	Accessories	3.99
	for fire engines—includes: fire hoses, portable foam generator, louvres, etc.	
625-1763	Fire Engine Ladders	3.99
625-1781	Michelin Figures +	pkg(10) 3.99
625-1783	Bottle Case Load	3.99
625-1758	Emergency Lights	(blue) 3.99
625-1795	Warning Device for Emergency Vehicles	3.99

RIETZE AUTOMODELLE

HO SCALE
READY-TO-RUN
Imported from Germany by *WALTHERS*
Assembled plastic vehicles are molded in appropiate colors.

VEHICLES

AUDI 80
633-10320   4.49

AUDI 80 Taxi
633-30320   5.29

(not illustrated)
AUDI 80 Metallic
633-20320   5.29
MITSUBISHI L300
Panel Van Metallic
633-20220   5.29

AUDI 80 Notarzt
633-50321   6.29

AUDI 80 Hessen Police
633-50322   5.49

633-60131   FORD Cargo Trailer   16.98

(not illustrated)

633-50230	Audi 200 Fire Department	5.29
633-50236	Audi 200 Fire Department Braunsc	6.29
633-50250	Audi Avant 200 Fire Dept	6.29
633-70023	Bumpers for Trucks	1.98

Roco MINITANKS

Imported from Austria

by WALTHERS

HO SCALE (1/87) READY TO RUN

Appropriately colored plastic vehicles.

MILITARY VEHICLES

UNITED STATES

625-202 MH A3 Sherman 5.50

Tank Destroyer, M10/M36
625-205 5.25

M41 Walker Bulldog
625-207 5.25

M47, General Patton
625-221 6.00

625-220 M48 A1 90mm 6.75

625-254 M551 Sheridan 5.75

625-182 M103 120mm 6.25

625-181 M60/M60A1 105mm 6.25

625-419 M1 E1 Abrams 10.25

625-435 Bradley M2 10.00

625-208 M42 AA 5.25

M40 155mm Gun Carriage
625-104 5.50

M53 203mm SPH
625-157 6.50

M107 SF Gun Carriage
625-388 7.00

M1A1 Abrams
625-519 9.75

M2 Bradley
625-520 10.50

M109 A2
625-521 11.25

M901 Tow or M981 Fist
625-527 10.75
Choice by accessory kit.

M4 Tractor
625-178 6.00

Armored Mortar
M113 A1G w/20mm
Mortar
625-351 8.50

Mine Launcher
on M548
625-376 11.50

Missile Carrier
M667
625-283 8.00

Anti-Aircraft Missile
Launcher M730
625-290 8.75

M 901/M981
625-406 11.25

M113 A3 ACAV
625-469 10.00

M88 Recovery Vehicle
625-232 7.75

625-346 M113 8.00

Command Post M577 A1
625-348 10.00

M3 Bradley CFV **NEW**
625-494 10.00

M977 Cargo Truck **NEW**
625-528 TBA

625-467 M109 A2 w/M548 and M10
Howitzer with add-on parts pkg(3) 22.00

ROCO MINITANKS

HO SCALE (1/87) READY TO RUN

Imported from Austria

by WALTHERS

Appropriately colored plastic vehicles.

MILITARY VEHICLES

UNITED STATES (continued)

625-806   M3, M16 and M21   pkg(3) 22.00

625-485   M934 Van 5 ton   TBA

M35 A2 2.5 ton w/flatbed
625-484   TBA

625-526   M923   17.00    625-522   M923 & M105   17.00

M923 Transport
625-518   13.25

Tow Missile Carrier
625-524   12.50

M1038 & M101
625-523   12.50

M923 5 ton w/Canvas & Wench
625-517   13.25

625-461   M54 A2   10.25

M62 Wrecker
625-432   10.25

M1038 Hummer
625-530 **NEW** TBA

625-477   M977 Cargo   16.49

Tow Missle Carrier
625-478   11.25

M923 Signal Truck
w/generator Trailer
625-460   16.25

Dodge 3/4 Ton
with M3A1 gun
625-480   7.25

Pontoon Semi-
Trailer
625-196   9.25

M26 Tank
Transporter
625-179   10.00

M1038 "Hummer"
625-479   8.75

625-525   Fuchs   10.75

Willy's Jeep
625-393   6.50

Willy's Jeep
625-444   9.75

AM General M151 A2
625-282   5.75

Ford Mutt w/Trailer
M151 A2
625-482   10.25

Cargo/Troop Carrier
625-428   8.75

M1038 Hummer
625-486 **NEW** 7.99

M1038 Hummer/Shelter
625-487   **NEW** TBA

M1038 Hummer
625-489   **NEW** 7.99

M561 Gama Goat
Radio
625-389   8.00

Dodge M880
w/Signal Cabin
625-359   8.00

4 x 4 Dodge, Closed
625-225   5.50

ROCO MINITANKS

Imported from Austria

by WALTHERS

HO SCALE (1/87) READY TO RUN

Appropriately colored plastic vehicles.

MILITARY VEHICLES

UNITED STATES (continued)

Long Tom Field Gun
M2/M59
625-120   155mm   7.75

Honest John,
Launcher w/Rocket
625-113   7.75

Heavy 8 inch Howitzer
M1/M115
625-119   7.75

Lacrosse, Launcher
w/Rocket
625-114   6.75

Medium Howitzer
M1/M114
625-187   155mm   5.99

Light Howitzer
M2A1 105mm
625-183   5.50

Fuel Supply
Equipment
625-488
TBA
NEW

GERMAN ARMY

Panzer III Short Gun
625-174   5.00

Panzer IV-F2 & H-K
625-107   5.50

625-102   Panther V   5.25

625-170   Panzer VI Tiger I   4.50

Panzer VI Hunting Tiger
625-171   5.75

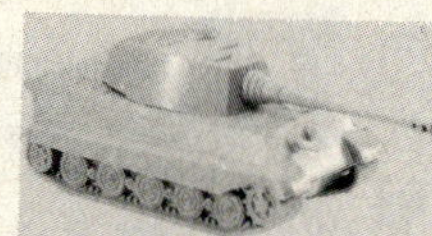

Panzer VI King Tiger
625-134   5.25

625-172   Leopard   5.75

625-256   Leopard   8.50

625-275   Leopard 1A4   8.50

625-391   Leopard 1A1A1   9.00

625-329   Leopard 2, Battle   8.25

HS30 Rocket Carrier
625-212   5.25

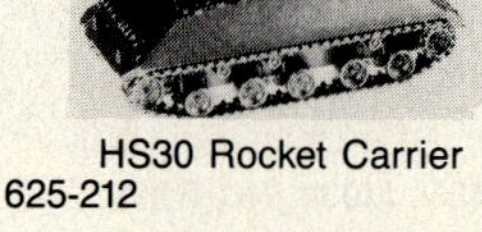

Luch Spatch Pz2
625-453   10.50

Transport & Loading
Vehicle
625-284   8.00

Marder 1 A2
625-475   6.00

Roland II w/Marder Chassis
625-476   10.99

625-257   Recovery   8.50

625-448   Hummel   11.25

625-347   M113 A1G   8.00

Command Control w/Tent
625-349   10.00

Roco
MINITANKS
Imported from Austria
by WALTHERS

HO SCALE (1/87) READY TO RUN

Appropriately colored plastic vehicles.

MILITARY VEHICLES

GERMAN ARMY (continued)

Grille, Anti-Aircraft
625-105   5.25

200mm Anti-Aircraft Twin Quad
625-111   5.50

625-176   Assault Gun III   5.50

Half Track
625-228   w/20 mm Gun   6.25

90mm
625-173   Assault Gun   5.75

625-270   AA Gepard   8.50

M109 A3 *NEW*
625-416   TBA

625-262   Marder   5.75

TPz1A Armour
Carrier Eloka
625-306   7.25

Recon Spz 22-2
625-216   5.00

M113A1G and M577A1G
625-804   71.25
with Railway Transport Stake Wagon

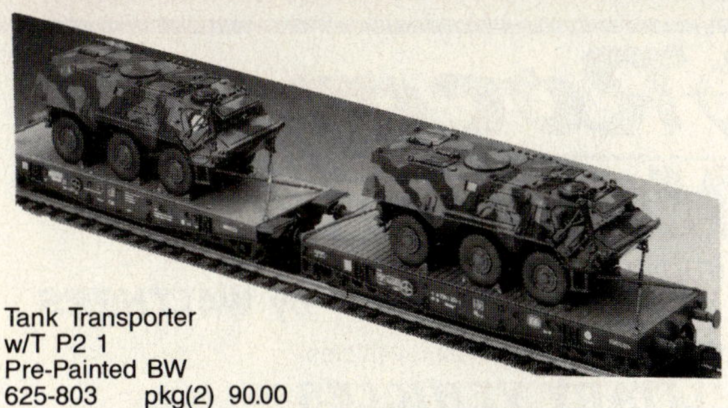

Tank Transporter
w/T P2 1
Pre-Painted BW
625-803   pkg(2) 90.00

Flat DB
w/Container
625-812
TBA
NEW

Flat DB
Leopard
625-813
TBA
NEW

Pioneer Set
625-409   32.25

Mag 320D
Tank Truck
625-436   18.25

Mercedes 1017A Fuel Truck
625-502   12.00

MAN 630 L2A Ambulance DB
625-503   11.75

Multiple Rocket Launcher
110 SF2
625-504   14.25

VW Transporter and VW
Flatbed Truck
625-807   pkg(2) 26.75

Open Truck FAWN L908
625-190   6.00

MAN N4520/4620 Closed
625-294   8.75

ROCO MINITANKS
Imported from Austria
by WALTHERS

HO SCALE (1/87)
READY TO RUN

Appropriately colored plastic vehicles.
MILITARY VEHICLES

GERMAN ARMY (continued)

MAN 630 L 2 AE
625-259　　6.25

MAN 630 L 2 A, Radio
625-260　　6.25

Dump Truck FAWN L912
625-189　　5.75

Jupiter MD 7 + 6 x 6, Closed
625-246　　6.75

MAN N4510
625-470　　9.50

MAN N4540, Closed
625-296　　11.25

Opel Blitze w/Canvas
625-370　　7.25

Daimler Benz 1017A
625-501　　12.25

Magirus/Iveco 16811FI
625-454　　10.50

MAN N 4530
625-449　　12.00

Unimog U 1300L w/Trailer
625-452　　11.00

Magirus 168M11FL
w/ Tanks
625-420　　14.25

L912 FAWN Ammo Truck
625-230　　6.75

Z912/21-155 Artillery Tractor
625-229　　6.75

MAN 630L2AE
625-411　w/water tanks　8.25

Magirus Jupiter
625-390　　10.75

Multiple Rocket Launcher
625-336　　7.50

Unimog U1300L
Communications Truck
625-472　　8.75

VW Transporter Set
625-807　　26.75

■ LTD QTY AVAILABLE ■

VW Ambulance 4x4
625-447　　10.00

Mercedes 0321H
625-808　　15.49

VW Typ2 Follow Me
625-811　　10.99

VW Fire Brigade
625-810　**NEW**　TBA

Unimog 1300L
Fire Brigade
625-344　　11.25

Opel Tank Fire
Extinguisher TLF 15
625-338　　13.75

VW, Cross Country
625-327　　6.25

VW Jeep Type 82
625-235　　5.50

Jeep, Munga
625-281　　5.50

VW Amphibian
625-236　　5.50

Unimog S404, Radio
625-242　　6.25

Audi 100 MS
625-481　　8.25

Roco MINITANKS

HO SCALE (1/87) READY TO RUN

Imported from Austria

by WALTHERS

Appropriately colored plastic vehicles.

MILITARY VEHICLES

625-809	Railway Transport Stake Wagon Kb(g)s 442 w/Lorry MAN 10t gl, mW, 8x8 — 43.49

GERMAN ARMY (continued)

MSN 4520/N
625-505 **NEW** 7.49

Fuchs ABC Armed Radiation Vehicle
625-507 **NEW** TBA

Unimog U 1300 L DB Ambulance
625-508 **NEW** TBA

Type 2 Syncro Mini Bus NEW
625-509 TBA

Daimler Benz 1017 A DB
625-510 **NEW** TBA

MB4500 DL Ladder Truck
625-418 19.50

Unimog 1300L KrKw Ambulance
625-325 9.00

Unimog S 404 Ambulance
625-241 6.25

M923
625-529
TBA
NEW

VW Typ2, Flatbed Truck
625-414 6.50

MAN 630 L2a w/Van
625-431 8.50

Daimier Benz 1017A
625-451 10.50

FEDERAL GERMAN FRONTIER GUARD

625-383   Border Patrol   set(5) 30.50

Dodge M886 1/1-4 ton 4 x 4
625-471 9.75

Unimog TLF 8/18 Truck
625-433 11.25

LKW Unimog S
625-240 6.25

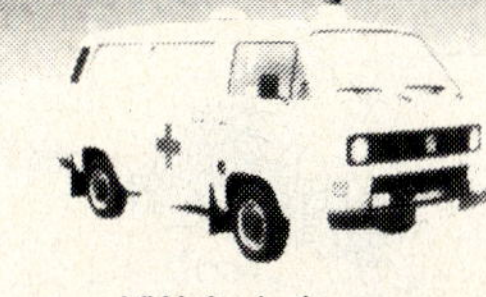

625-458   VW Bus Type 2   8.75

VW Ambulance
625-456 9.50

■ LTD QTY AVAILABLE ■

Amphibious Duck
625-455 21.50

Field Howitzer 199mm
625-186 5.75

AUSTRIAN MILITARY

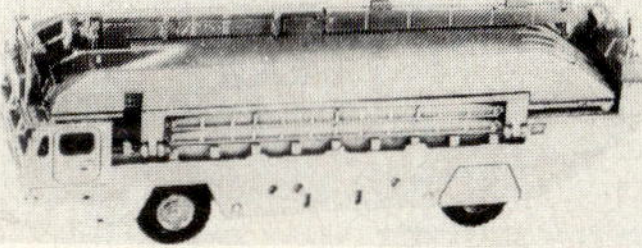

Steyer 586 TLF 2000
625-380 13.00

4 x 4 Troop Transport
625-330 8.50

6 x 6 Troop Transport
625-331 8.75

M2 Alligator Bridge
625-222 10.75

Armored Bridge Erector
625-427 18.25

Steyer, TLF2000 Tank Fire Extinguisher
625-337 11.75

4 x 4 Personnel Carrier
625-320 6.50

Steyer 680 M
625-372 9.25

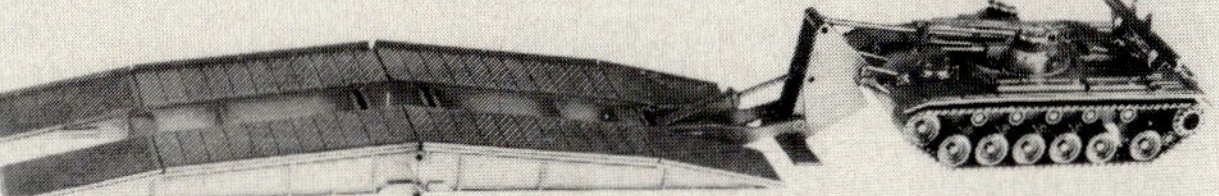

625-219   Armored Bridge Launcher   7.75

Roco MINITANKS — Imported from Austria
by WALTHERS

HO SCALE (1/87) READY TO RUN

Appropriately colored plastic vehicles.

MILITARY VEHICLES

BOATS

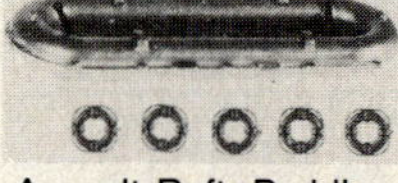
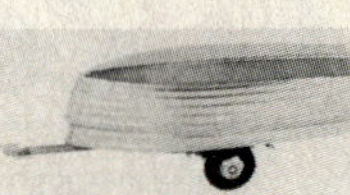

Assault Raft
625-239   3.50

Assault Raft, Paddles & Life Preservers
625-363   4.75

Trailer w/2 Assault Boats
625-151   5.25

BRITISH & SOVIET

SCUD-A Missle Carrier
625-250   8.50

625-237 Saladin Recon 6.25

Chieftan
625-200
6.00

UNITED NATIONS

VW Ambulance
625-430
8.50

AIRCRAFT

Bell Huey AH Cobra
625-247   8.75

Bell UH-1D
625-248   8.75

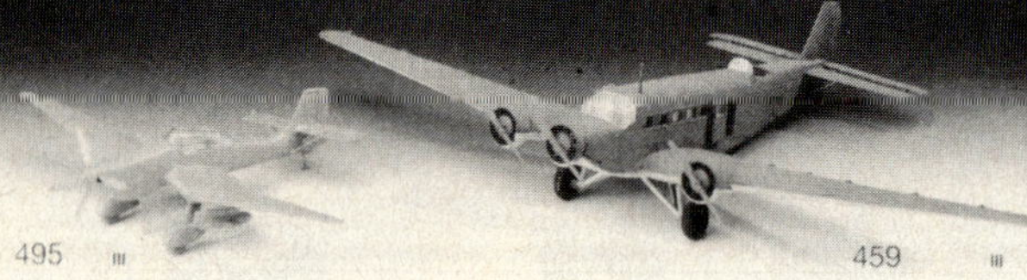

JU 87 G2 Luftwaffe **NEW**
625-495   TBA

JU 52 G2 Luftwaffe **NEW**
625-459   TBA

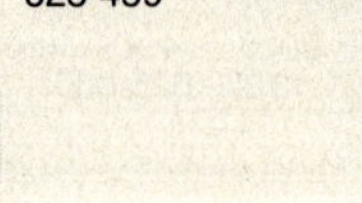

Lockheed P38J
625-439   12.25

(not illustrated)
Junkers JU52 Airplane
625-1800   12.49

FIGURES

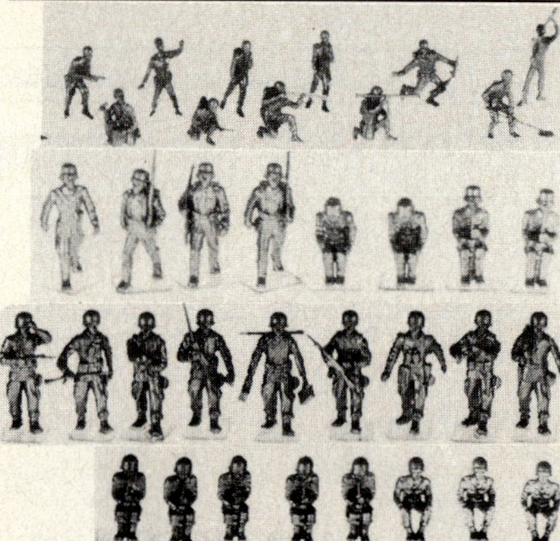

Combat Group
625-117   3.50
pkg(12)

WWII German Soldiers
625-263   3.50
pkg(15)

Infantry Assault Group
625-272   3.50
pkg(18)

Soldiers, Sitting
625-298   3.50
pkg(16)

Soldiers, Sitting
625-299   3.50
pkg(18)

Commander Group
625-300   3.50
pkg(8)

Infantry Soldiers
625-302   3.50
pkg(16)

Tank Commanders & Divers
625-309   3.50
pkg(14)

Russian Soldiers
625-265   3.50
pkg(10)

(not illustrated)
625-463 Tank Commanders   3.50

DECALS & PAINT

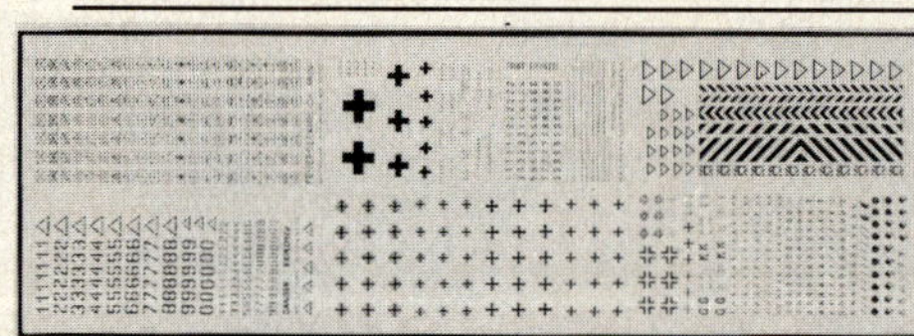

Assortment #2
625-269   4.75
USA/BW Military Police, Red Cross

(not illustrated)

625-386 Tactical Signs		4.75
625-371 Tactical Signs		4.75
625-373 Decal Set 6.		4.49
For tank lorries, danger & flammable contents		
625-465 Decals for Vehicles		6.25
625-499 Paint Set - green, Brown, Black		11.25
625-500 MT Plus Accessory Set		5.50

Assortment #4
625-335 A/UN 4.75

Roco MINITANKS — HO SCALE (1/87) READY TO RUN

DETAIL PARTS

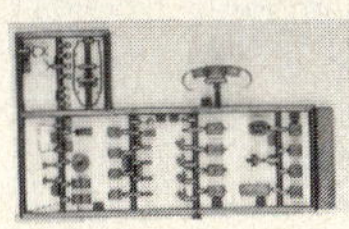

625-364	Accessories for M60 A1	3.50
	(not illustrated)	
625-365	Radio Boxes	pkg(2) 3.50
625-277	Accessory Set	3.50
	Includes rifles, shovels, axes, tripod and more.	
625-362	Machine Guns	4.75
625-377	Steering Accessory Set	4.75
625-400	Window Set	3.50
625-438	Accessory Bag for Tanks	4.75
625-441	Steering Set for #417	3.50
625-464	Flashing Lights	3.50
625-496	Rubber Tires for US Trucks	**NEW** 4.99
625-497	Antenna (aerial) wire, oxidized	3.50
625-500	MT Plus Accessory Set	5.50

LIMITED QUANTITIES AVAILABLE
625-425	Rearview Mirrors	(bronze,green) 4.75

MISCELLANEOUS

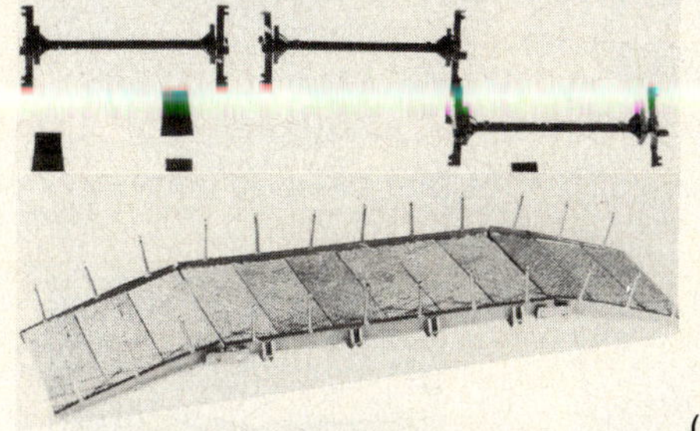

Anti-Tank Obstacles
625-192   8.50

Pontoon Bridge
625-197   3.50

(not illustrated)
Machine Gun Set
625-442   4.75

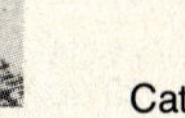

625-422	Gas Cans w/Pallets	4.75	
	Catalog of Vehicle Types	625-1001	21.99

TRAILERS

Jeep Trailers
625-443
pkg(2) 4.99

M101A/M105A2
Trailer Set
625-462   6.25

M10 Munitition
Trailer
625-287   3.50

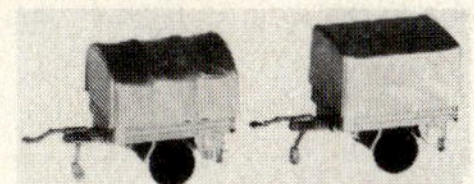
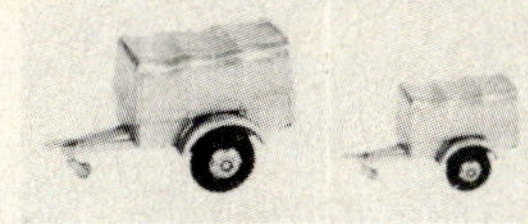

1-1/2 Ton 1 Axle Trailer
625-328   pkg(2) 5.25

3/4 x 1T Trailers
625-152   5.25

TENTS AND STRUCTURES

Gate & Guard House
625-258   3.50

Holding Tanks
625-421   4.75

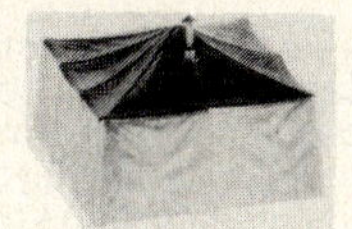

2-Stall Garage
625-292   13.25

10-Man Tent
625-255   3.50

Assorted Tents & Cargo
625-218   3.50

MOTORCYCLES

Motorcycles
625-233   pkg(2) 3.50

BMW Motorcycle
w/Side Car
625-238   3.50

ARMOR TRIVIA

In August of 1942, the first German Tiger tanks went into production. At the time of its introduction, and for some time afterwards, the Tiger was the most formidable tank in the world, retaining its reputation until the end of WWII. The 88mm main gun could put a hole into 100mm of armor at 1,000 meters and its frontal armor was impervious to any allied gun except at suicidally short ranges. Due to its weight, however, the engine had to be geared down and thus performance suffered. Another problem was that the turret had to be traversed by hand when the engine was not running. This put the Tiger at a disadvantage when caught from the rear.

Scale Scenics — Division of CIRCUITRON

HO SCALE (1/87) CRAFT TRAIN KITS

Unpainted white metal kits unless noted.

CONSTRUCTION VEHICLES

3- Wheel Road Roller
652-3516   each 7.95
Prototype of this model was found on road and construction sites from the 1940's to present. Yellow styrene and brass kit.

Fork Lift Truck
652-3515
each 6.95
Gasoline engine powered fork lift commonly used in industry. Non-operating kit includes several pallets.

trident

HO SCALE (1/87)
CRAFT TRAIN KITS

Imported from Austria by WALTHERS

Here's a line of modern military vehicles that are perfect for flat car loads, war games or collecting. Many of the U.S. prototypes can be converted as "military surplus" vehicles for civilian use on your layout. The HO Scale kits consist of detailed metal castings (unless noted).

SOVIET MAIN BATTLE TANKS & SELF-PROPELLED GUNS

T-72 w/125mm Gun
729-80020   26.99

T-64 w/125mm Gun
729-80025   28.99

T-72 w/125mm Gun
729-80043   28.99

T-72 M1 w/125mm Gun
729-80094   28.99
(By Special Order Only.)

T-62A w/115mm Gun
729-80032   26.99

2S3 "Akatsiya" 152mm Howitzer
729-80034   29.99

2S1 "Gvozdika" 122mm Howitzer
729-00038   26.00

T-62 w/115mm Gun
729-80063   26.99

T-80 ERA w/125mm Gun & Reactive Armor
729-80131   29.99

ENGINEERING VEHICLE

DOK-L Engineering Tractor/ End Loader
729-80136   38.99
(By Special Order Only.)

SOVIET AIRBORNE ASSAULT WEAPONS

BMD-2 Airborne Combat Vehicle
729-80133   24.99

ASU-57 w/57mm Gun
729-80021   18.49

ASU-85 w/85mm Gun
729-80033   24.99

SOVIET ARMORED PERSONNEL CARRIERS

MT-LBW Troop Transporter/ Artillery Tractor
729-80031   24.99

BTR 60PB Armored
729-80037   28.99

BRM-1 Reconnaissance Vehicle w/73mm Gun
729-80039   24.99

BMP-1 Armored w/73mm Gun
729-80040   24.99

BRDM2 Reconnaisance Vehicle
729-80041   25.99

BTR-60PA Armored
729-80064   28.99

BTR-70 Armored
729-80049   28.99

BMP-2 w/30mm Gun
729-80050   28.99

BTR-80 Armored
729-80121   30.49

PTS-M Amphibious Armored
729-80129   40.99

BRDM-26 Armored Command Vehicle
729-80132   25.99

trident

HO SCALE (1/87) CRAFT TRAIN KITS

Imported from Austria by WALTHERS

Here's a line of modern military vehicles that are perfect for flat car loads, war games or collecting. Many of the U.S. prototypes can be converted as "military surplus" vehicles for civilian use on your layout. The HO Scale kits consist of detailed metal castings (unless noted).

Missile System
729-80146   30.49
(By Special Order Only.)

M119 Light Gun
729-90025   plastic, assmb 7.99

(not illustrated)
729-90029   M105 Light Gun   **NEW**   7.99

SOVIET MISSILE WEAPONS

BRDM-2/AT5 "Spandrel"
Tank Destroyer
729-80042   26.99

BRDM-2/PUR-64
Tank Destroyer
729-80028   26.99

BM21 sf-pro Ural 122mm
Rocket Launcher
729-80075   29.99

M78 Launcher
729-80081   24.99
w/3 Surface-to-Air Missiles

SA-13 TELAR 1 "Strela 10"
Anti-Aircraft System
729-80093   29.99

HAWK MISSILE SYSTEM MIM-23B U.S.

AN/MPQ-55 Acquisition Radar
729-80085   24.99

AN/MPQ-46 Target
Illuminator Radar
729-80086   25.99

AN/MPQ-35 Target
Acquisition Radar
729-80087   29.99

AN/TSW-11 Battery Control Center
729-80090   18.49

HF45D Generator
729-80091   10.49

AUSTRIAN ARMY TRUCKS

Assembled plastic models.

OAF 16.192 FAK Service
729-90016   14.49

OAF 16.192 FAK, 5t
729-90019   11.99

OAF 19.240 FAK, 5t
w/Snowplow Adapter
729-90022   TBA
(By Special Order Only.)

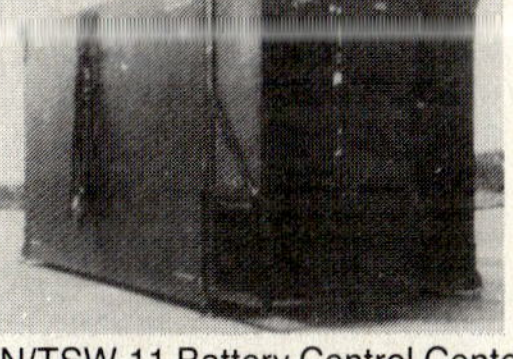
M501 Loader
729-80082   18.49

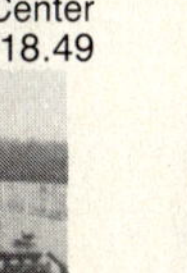

M390C Transporter
w/3 Surface-to-Air Missiles
729-80083   23.99

AN/MPQ-51 Range Only Radar
729-80084   24.99

AN/MSQ-110 Information
Coordination Center
729-80088   24.99

AN/MSM-43 Missile Test Shop
729-80089   12.49

ANTI-AIRCRAFT & ARTILLERY

BMP-SON
Soviet
Artillery
Radar Vehicle
729-80065   26.99

M247 "Sergeant York"
w/Twin 40mm Guns USA
729-80070   29.99

ZSU-23-4 Gun
w/Quad 23mm Guns CCCP
729-80052   28.99

trident

HO SCALE (1/87)
CRAFT TRAIN KITS

Imported from Austria by WALTHERS

Here's a line of modern military vehicles that are perfect for flat car loads, war games or collecting. Many of the U.S. prototypes can be converted as ''military surplus'' vehicles for civilian use on your layout. The HO Scale kits consist of detailed metal castings (unless noted).

US MILITARY TRUCKS

Assembled, plastic models based on prototypes.

M1009 Utility
Blazer Body
729-90003 plastic 8.99

M1008 Troop Carrier
Pickup w/Side Rails
729-90004 plastic 9.99

M1028 Radio Truck
Pickup Body
729-90006 plastic 10.49

M988 ''Hummer'' One Ton
Multi-Purpose (US)
729-80141 19.99

M715 Cargo
729-80144 20.99

M1008 Troop Carrier
w/Canvas Cover
729-90005 plastic 9.49

M1010 Ambulance
Pickup Cab
729-90007 plastic 10.49

MTV, 5t
729-90048 TBA

STEYR 12MIB, 5t
729-90045 TBA

M1031 CoE Maintenance
729-90020 plastic TBA

(not illustrated)

729-90030	M1008 Troop Carrier US DS	9.99
729-90031	M1008 Cargo w/Canvas US DS	9.49
729-90032	M1009 Utility US DS	8.99
729-90033	M1010 Ambulance US DS	10.49
729-90034	Shelter Carrier US DS	10.49

US 2-1/2 TON TRUCKS

CCKW 353 ''Le-Roi''
w/Air Compressor
729-80106 29.99

M35A2 Cargo w/Sidewalls
729-80142 28.99

M36A2 Flatbed
729-80143 TBA

CCKW 352 Utility w/Canvas Top
729-80111 25.99

CCKW 352 Wrecker
729-80112 25.99

ZIL-131, 3, 5t Cargo
Canvas Top
729-80137 TBA

OAF 16.240 FAK
Service Truck
729-90009 13.99

LMTV 2 Cargo 5t
729-90047 US Army TBA

LIGHT ASSAULT VEHICLES

Assembled plastic models.

LAV-AT Anti Tank
729-90011
12.49

LAV-M Mortar Carrier
729-90012 11.99

LAV-C2
Command Control Vehicle
729-90013 10.49

LAV-L USMC Logistics
729-90026 plastic 11.99

LAV-R Recovery
729-90027 plastic 10.99

(not illustrated)

729-90035	LAV 25 USMC Tank w/c Sand		11.99
729-90036	LAV Anti-Tank US DS	**NEW**	10.99
729-90037	LAV Mortar/carrier US DS	**NEW**	10.49
729-90038	LAV Com/con veh US DS	**NEW**	10.49
729-90039	LAV Logistics vehicle USMC DS	**NEW**	10.49
729-90040	LAV Recovery arm USMC DS	**NEW**	10.99

trident

HO SCALE (1/87)
CRAFT TRAIN KITS

Imported from Austria by WALTHERS

Here's a line of modern military vehicles that are perfect for flat car loads, war games or collecting. Many of the U.S. prototypes can be converted as "military surplus" vehicles for civilian use on your layout. The HO Scale kits consist of detailed metal castings (unless noted).

TRUCKS & VANS

These "civilian" trucks are assembled, plastic models; ready to use on your layout.

Blazer-Full Size
729-90001   8.99

Four-Wheel Drive Pickup
729-90002   8.99

"Fleetside" Long Box Pickup
729-90008   9.49

"Suburban" Nine Passenger
729-90014   TBA

GMC Fenderside Pickup
729-90015   8.99

USAF Firetruck Command
729-90018   TBA

M1031 USAF Maintenance
729-90017   TBA

"Fleetside Pickup"
729-90023   13.99

Ambulance
729-90021   10.99

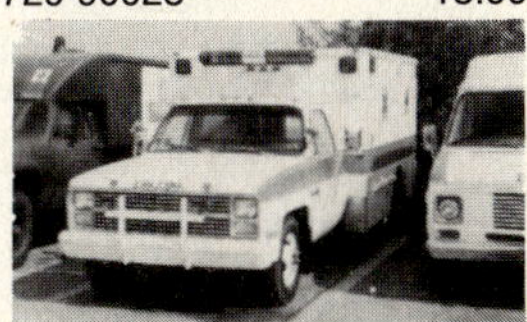

USAF Ambulance
729-90024   11.99

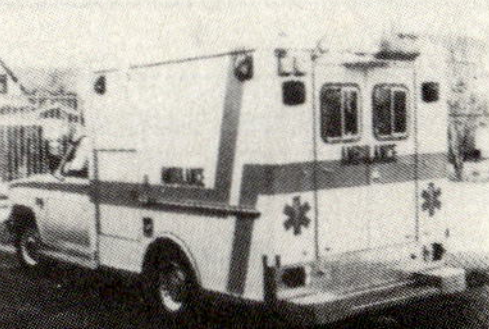

Ambulance *NEW*
729-90044   11.99

Sheriff *NEW*
729-90042   TBA

Sport *NEW*
729-90041   TBA

Rescue *NEW*
729-90049   TBA

Cargo *NEW*
729-90046   TBA

M915 & M872 US *NEW*
729-90028   TBA

729-90043   M915 & Semitrailer MILVAN Refrigerator   *NEW*   TBA

(not illustrated)

729-900011 Blazer 4 x 4	(red) *NEW*	8.99
729-900021 Pickup 4x4	(red) *NEW*	8.99
729-900151 GMC Step-Side 4x4	(red) *NEW*	8.99

ACCESSORIES   *NEW*

729-96001 Tires	3.49
729-96002 Tires f/Trucks Rubber	3.49
729-96003 Lights f/US Emergency Vehicle (blue)	TBA

VEHICLE CATALOG

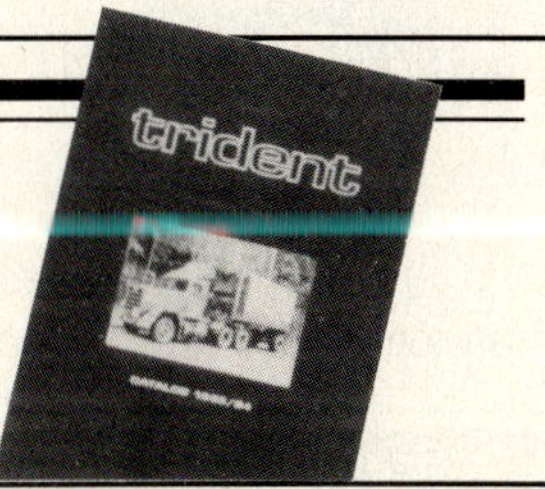

Trident 1993-94 Vehicle Catalog
729-91000   6.99
Complete listing of all Trident military and civilian vehicle kits, illustrated with black and white prototype photos.

Sequoia SCALE MODELS

HO SCALE (1/87) CRAFT TRAIN KITS

Kits feature cast metal construction.

VELOCIPEDES

HO	135-12	7.95
HOn3	135-13	7.95

WALKER Model service

HO SCALE (1/87) CRAFT TRAIN KITS

Kits feature unpainted cast white metal parts and styrene, wire and wood details. (Photos of Production models.)

INTERNATIONAL TRANSTAR 4200

786-5018	3-axle Tractor		14.95
786-7018	Semi Tractor	pkg(4)	44.95
786-5025	3-axle Tractor w/Sleeper		16.95
786-5024	Sleeper Only		4.95

w/Wrecker Body
786-5029   24.95

786-5028 w/Flatbed Trailer   23.95
786-5027 w/Flatbed Trailer & Sleeper 25.95

INTERNATIONAL TRANSTAR II

Cabover w/Sleeper
786-5020   14.95

786-5031 w/5020 & Flatbed Trailer 22.95

Suicide Cab
(less Sleeper)
786-5021   14.95
Suicide Cab
786-7021   41.95

786-5034 w/5021 & Flatbed Trailer 21.95

(not illustrated)
786-7020 Cab Over   pkg(4) 44.95

TRAILERS

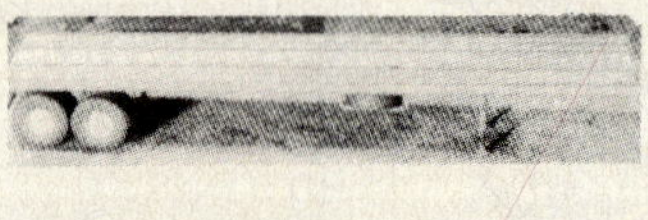

40′ Flatbed
786-5022   10.95
786-7022 pkg(4) 35.95

32′ 1-axle Flatbed
786-5043   11.95

(not illustrated)
28′ Fruehauf Piggyback
786-6000   10.95
786-7000 pkg(4) 39.95

1947 INTERNATIONAL KB11

Flatbed Truck
786-5040   15.95

Dump Truck
786-5042   15.95
786-7042 pkg(3) 41.95

2-Axle Semi Tractor
786-5041   14.95
786-7041 pkg(4) 49.95

Stakebed Truck
786-5045   15.95
786-7045 pkg(3) 41.95

786-5080 Produce   17.95

Flatbed with Details
786-5049   17.95
786-7049 pkg(4) 49.95

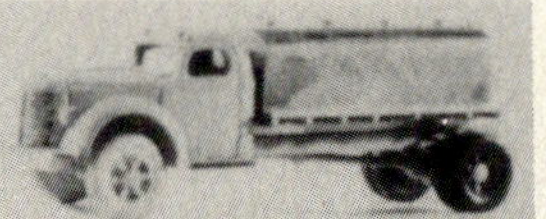

Basic Body
786-5048   14.95
486-7048 pkg(4) 49.95

786-5081 Tank   16.95

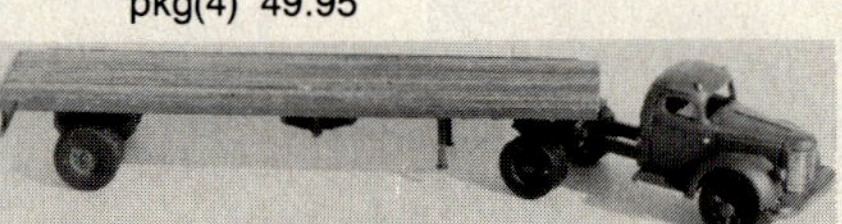

786-5046 Log Truck   17.95
786-7046 Log Truck pkg(3) 47.95

786-5044 Semi Tractor w/5043   19.95
786-7044 Semi Tractor w/5043 pkg(2) 35.95

(not illustrated)

786-5047	28′ Van Trailer		20.95
786-5082	Crane Truck		18.95
786-5083	Canopy Truck		17.95
786-5084	Tank Truck		18.95
786-7047	28′ Van Trailer	pkg(2)	38.95

MISCELLANEOUS

JI Case Steam Tractor
786-5201   69.95
Intricately detailed model of 1900's era steam powered tractor.

Lumber Carrier
786-5109   20.95

(not illustrated)
786-5023 Wrecker Body Only   11.95
786-5157 1920's Wrecker Body   10.95

WALKER Model service

HO SCALE (1/87) CRAFT TRAIN KITS

Kits feature unpainted cast white metal parts and styrene, wire and wood details. (Photos of Production models.)

1947 INTERNATIONAL KBII RAIL TRUCK

Highway truck fitted with flanged railroad wheels.

786-5072 Stakebed   15.95

Basic Chassis
786-5070   14.95

786-5073 Flatbed w/Load 17.95

(not illustrated)
Set of Four Trucks
786-5074   55.95
Includes one each of #5070, 5071, 5072 and 5073.

1926 WHITE TRUCK

Basic
786-5050   13.95
786-7050   pkg(4) 49.95

Flatbed
786-7051   pkg(3) 41.95

Stakebed
786-5052   15.95
786-7052   pkg(3) 43.95

Tank
786-5053   15.95
786-7053   pkg(3) 43.95

Log
786-5055   17.95
786-7055   pkg(3) 49.95

Produce
786-5056   15.95
786-7056   pkg(3) 43.95

Flatbed with Details
786-5057   17.95
786-7057   pkg(3) 49.95

Sand
786-5058   15.95
786-7058   pkg(3) 41.95
(not illustrated)

786-5156 Cement   18.95

1926 WHITE RAIL TRUCK

786-5060 Basic Chassis 13.95

786-5061 Flatbed   14.95

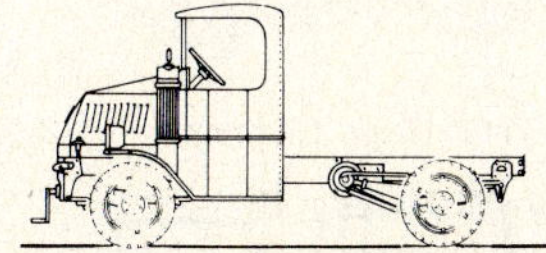

Flatbed with Load
786-5063   17.95

(not illustrated)
786-5062 Stakebed   15.95
786-5064 Set of 4 Trucks   50.95
Includes each of #'s
5060, 5061, 5062, 5063.

1924 MACK TRUCK

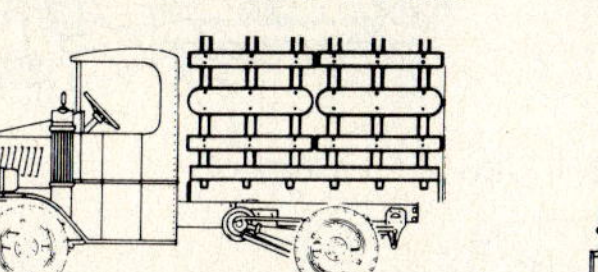

786-5128 Short Chassis + 14.95   786-5131 Flatbed w/Load 17.95

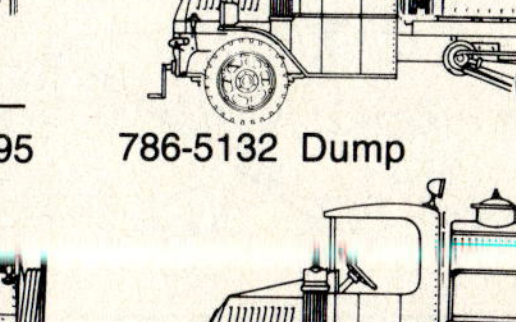

786-5130 Stakebed   17.95   786-5132 Dump   16.95

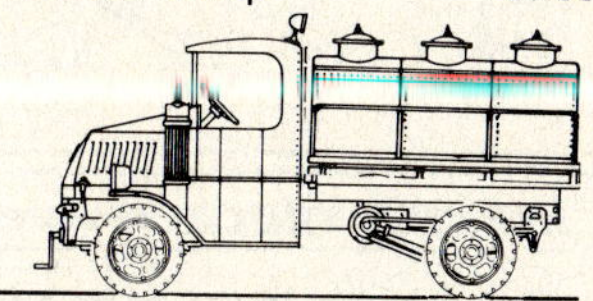

786-5134 Round Tank   16.95   786-5135 Kerosene Tank   17.95

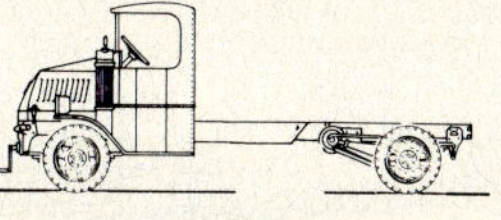

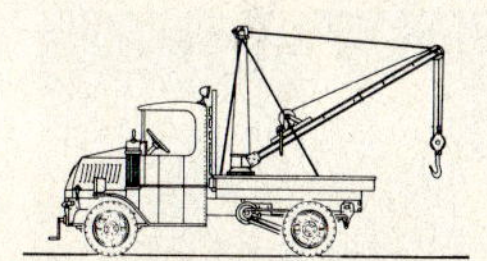

786-5136 Long Chassis 14.95   786-5137 Wrecker   17.95

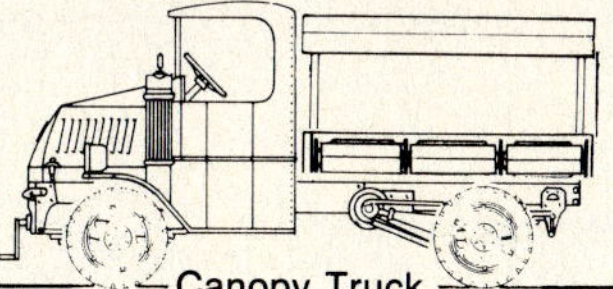

Canopy Truck
786-5138   16.95

Lite Delivery
786-5139   16.95

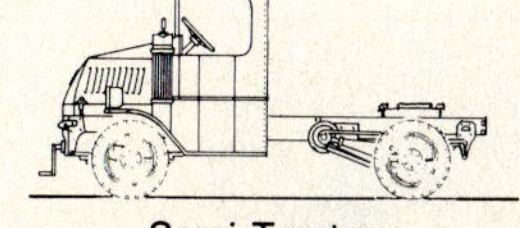

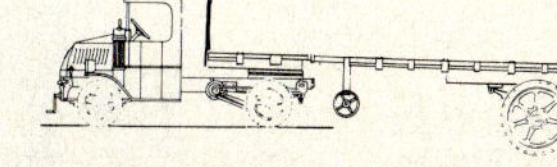

Semi Tractor
786-5144   15.95

Semi Tractor with Trailer
786-5145   21.95

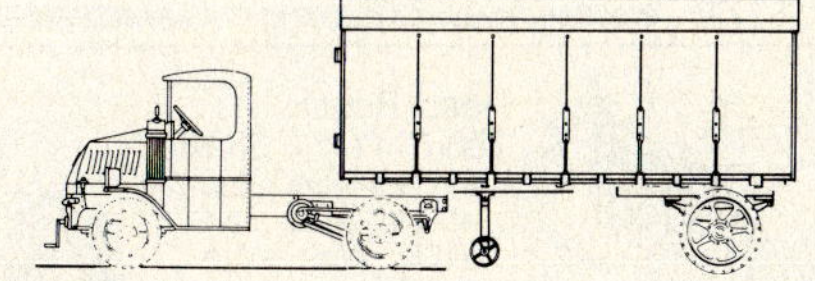

786-5146 Semi with Tractor   23.95

(not illustrated)
Square Tank
786-5133
16.95

WALKER Model service

HO SCALE (1/87) CRAFT TRAIN KITS

Kits feature unpainted cast white metal parts and styrene, wire and wood details. (Photos of Production models.)

AUTOCAR TRUCK

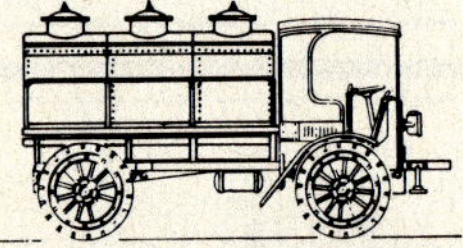

786-5116 Light Delivery 15.95

Canopy Truck
786-5140 15.95

786-5126 Kerosene Tank 17.95

786-5117 Basic Chassis 13.95

786-5154 Tank 17.95

786-5155 Cement 17.95

Wrecker
786-5147
16.95

(not illustrated)
786-5118 Flatbed 14.95
786-5119 Flatbed 16.95
with Load

KLEIBER TRUCK

Built from 1914 to 1937 by the Kleiber Motor Company of San Francisco, California.

Semi/Tractor
786-5100 15.95

Semi/Tractor/Trailer
786-5101 19.95

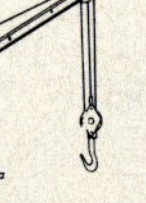

Semi Tractor
786-5141 14.95

27' Semi Tractor
w/Flatbed Trailer
786-5142 20.95

27' Semi Tractor
w/Van Trailer
786-5143
22.95

KLEIBER TRUCK (continued)

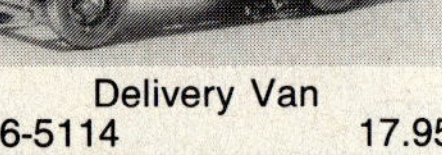

Rail Speeder
786-5102 15.95

786-5103 Dump 15.95

786-5104 Tank 15.95

786-5113 Stakebed Semi 22.95

Delivery Van
786-5114 17.95

Stakebed (Closed Cab)
786-5115 15.95

Moving Van
786-5121 22.95

786-5122 Flatbed 15.95
786-5123 Flatbed w/Load 17.95

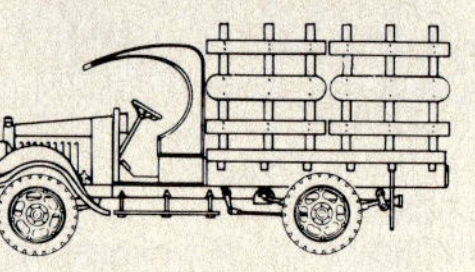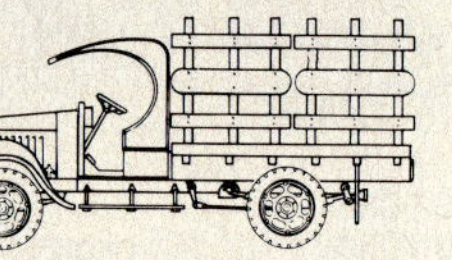

786-5124 Cement 18.95

786-5125 Station Jitney 18.95

786-5149 Tank 17.95

786-5150 Light Delivery 15.95

786-5151 Stakebed 16.95

786-5152 Dump 17.95

Kerosene Tank
786-5127 18.95

Canopy
786-5153 15.95

(not illustrated)
786-5148 Basic Chassis 14.95
786-5106 Set of Four Trucks 50.95
Includes one each of #'s 5100, 5102, 5103 and 5104.

ROAD REPAIR

Road Repair
786-5111 35.95
Includes one each
of #'s 5107 and
5108, plus extra
details.

Steam
Road Roller
786-5108
18.95

Concrete Mixer
786-5107 19.95

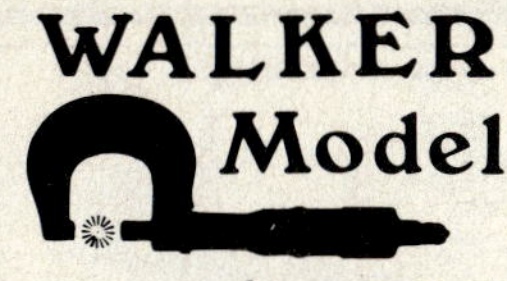

WALKER Model Service

HO SCALE (1/87) CRAFT TRAIN KITS

Kits feature unpainted cast white metal parts and styrene, wire and wood details.

BY SPECIAL ORDER ONLY

786-5054	1926 White Truck Assortment		50.95
786-7025	Transtar 4200 w/Sleeper	pkg(4)	49.95

NOW AVAILABLE

786-5022	40' Flatbed Trailer		10.95
786-5051	1926 White Flatbed Truck		14.95
786-5071	1947 KB-11 Railtk Flatbed		15.95
786-5081	1947 KB-11 Tank Truck		16.95
786-5085	26' White Crane Truck		17.95
786-5086	26' White Tank—RND		17.95
786-5087	26' White Lite Delivery		17.95
786-5088	26' White Canopy Truck		17.95
786-5105	Auto Car Stake Bed Truck		14.95
786-5110	1920 Fruehauf Semi Van		13.95
786-5112	Basic Kleber Chassis		14.95
786-5120	Moving Van Body		10.95
786-5125	Station Jitney		18.95
786-5129	24 Mack Flatbed		15.95
786-7029	Transtar 4200 w/Wrecker	pkg(2)	39.95
786-7040	IH KB-11 Flatbed	pkg(3)	41.95
786-7041	1947 IH KB-11 Flatbed Tractor	pkg(4)	49.95
786-7043	32' Flatbed Semi-Trailers	pkg(4)	35.95

LIFE-LIKE

HO SCALE (1/87) EASY-TO-BUILD KITS

Appropriately colored, molded plastic.

VEHICLE SETS

American Cars	American Pick-up Trucks
433-1117 pkg(4) 5.00	433-1120 pkg(3) 5.00

McKean

HO SCALE (1/87) EASY-TO-BUILD KITS

Kits feature prepainted and lettered, molded styrene body.

45' TRAILER 2-PACK

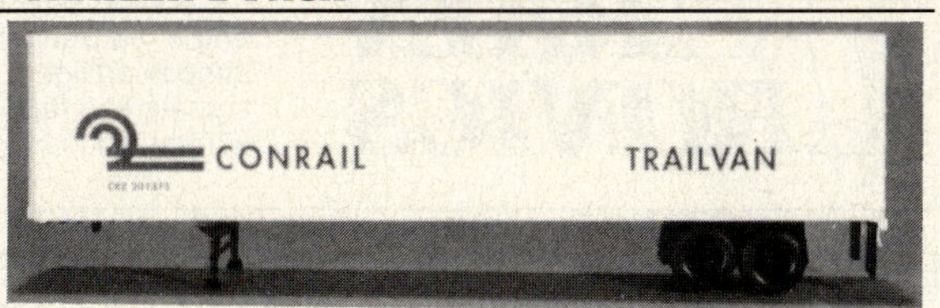

457-502	Burlington Northern	8.95
457-506	Boston & Maine	8.95
457-508	Trans America	8.95
457-510	Preferred 102	8.95
457-511	Santa Fe #2	8.95
457-512	Preferred 45	8.95
457-515	Southern	8.95
457-517	Union Pacific	8.95
457-522	Canadian Pacific	8.95
457-523	Canadian National	8.95
457-500	Undecorated	8.95

TRAILER FLATS   NEW

457-550	45' Trailer Flats TOFC	pkg(4)	18.95

WILLIAMS BROS. INC.

HO SCALE (1/87) PLASTIC KITS

AUTOMOBILES AND TRUCKS

'40 Ford Coupe			'32 Chevy Pickup		
782-535		5.45	782-546		5.45
782-5353	3-Pack	11.95	782-5463	3-Pack	11.95

'32 Chevy Cabriolet
782-545   5.45
Build as a Convertible or Hardtop.
782-5453   3-Pack   11.95

(not illustrated)

782-536	1935 Ford 4-Door	NEW	5.45
782-5363	1935 Ford 4-Door 3-Pack	NEW	11.95
782-538	Ford Taurus 4-Door	NEW	5.45
782-5383	Ford Taurus 4-Door 3-Pack	NEW	11.95

AIRCRAFT

Pitcairn Autogiro Helicopter		Corben Super-Ace	
782-526	less Decals 5.95	782-525	5.95
782-5264	w/Decals 6.95		

(not illustrated)

782-527   P2-17 Stearman   NEW   5.95

The Wheel Works

HO SCALE (1/87) CRAFT TRAIN KITS

Kits feature white metal parts.

AUTOS

1932 Ford Roadster (Top Down)
778-96105   8.95

1932 Ford Roadster (Top Up)
778-96106   8.95

1932 Ford Coupe
778-96122   8.95

1932 Ford Victoria Sedan
778-96121   8.95

34' Ford Station Wagon
778-96130   8.95

MISCELLANEOUS

Fordson Tractor
778-96115   6.50

HOn3 Rail Truck
778-96111   10.95
HO Rail Truck
778-96113   10.95

TRUCKS

1934 Ford Cab & Chassis
778-96108   8.95

1934 Ford REA Panel Truck
778-96114   12.95

1934 Ford Log Truck (includes logs)
778-96112   14.95

1934 Ford Stake Body Truck (decals included)
778-96103   11.95

1934 Ford Dump Truck
778-96129   9.95

1934 Small Stake Truck
778-96109   8.95
(features plastic stake bed)

1934 Ford Flatbed w/tractor
778-96128   14.95

1934 Panel Truck (decals included)
778-96102   9.50

1934 Ford Pick-Up
778-96101   8.95

Terminal Tractor
778-96157   10.95

34' Ford Service Truck
778-96117   10.95

34' Ford Flatbed Truck
778-96127   9.50

Ye Olde Huff-N-Puff

HO SCALE (1/87) CRAFT TRAIN KITS

Detailed, Cast Metal Kits.

COUNTRY VEHICLES

792-1025 Farm Tractor & Disc   7.00

792-1026 Amish Buggy w/Horse and Ma & Pa Figures   11.50

See also: FREIGHT & STRUCTURES for additional YE OLDE HUFF-N-PUFF

Train Tronics

Kit contains two HO autos featuring operating head lights, turn signals and tail lights w/fiber optics.

AUTOS

723-901 VW & Jeep Wagon   7.95
723-902 Continental & El Camino   7.95
723-903 Plymouth Suburban & DeSoto Diplomat   7.95

JANUARY 12, 1929

❧ Today ❧
IN RAILROAD HISTORY

The Cascade Tunnel opens on Great Northern's main line from Spokane to Seattle. This is the longest railroad tunnel in the United States, measuring over seven miles in length.

 **HO SCALE (1/87)**

Imported from Germany by WALTHERS

Gentlemen, start your engines! There's something for everyone from this large selection of vehicles. Autos from VW to Mercedes, classic autos and trucks, vans, emergency, construction and recreation vehicles. Each item is preassembled in appropriately colored plastic. (Markings and colors may vary from what is shown in catalog.)

We have worked closely with this manufacturer to provide accurate availability information at the time this catalog was published. Items listed in *blue ink* may not be available at all times. Please see your dealer for current delivery information.

Bring your layout up to speed with Wiking vehicles! Great for detailing your HO Scale streets and highways, these contemporary vehicles will be right at home on your layout or in your collection.

AUTOS

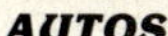

VW Golf GTI
781-5201 white 8.49
781-5202 blk 7.99

VW Golf (Postal)
781-4901 9.49

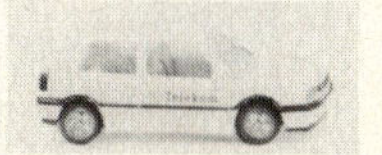

VW Golf (Telekom)
781-4902 10.49

Audi 80
781-121 5.49

MB 500 SL
781-141 6.49

MB 260E
781-153 6.49

MB 230TE Station Wagon
781-154 5.49

Porsche 911 Convertible
781-162 5.49

VW Cabriolet
781-33 5.49

Saab 900 Turbo
781-215 5.49

BMW 750i
781-192 6.49

Mercedes 190E
781-145 5.49

Trabant 601S
781-129 6.49

Porsche Carrera 4
781-164 6.99

MB 260E Taxi
781-149 6.49

Jaguar Type E
781-22 4.99

Jaguar Sport
781-20 4.99

BMW 520i
781-193 5.49

Mercedes 300CE
781-143 5.49

Opel Senator
781-82 6.99

Ford Sierra XR4
781-204 7.99

Porsche Carrera 4 Convertible
781-165 8.49

RR Silver Shadow
781-837 8.49

VW Passat Variant
781-42 8.49

VW Post 1200
781-831 5.49

BMW 325i Convertible
781-191 6.49

Audi Front
781-826 8.49

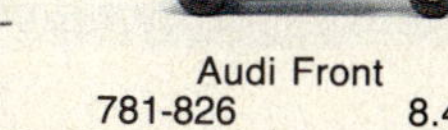

VW Golf Cabriolet
781-46 8.49

AUTOS (continued)

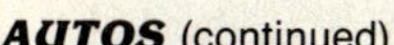

Ford Taunus
781-820 4.99

Mercedes 300 SL Roadster
781-834 9.49

Borgward Isabella
781-823 4.99

VW 1200
781-830 4.99

Citroen 15 Six
781-822 5.49

Rolls Royce 51
781-838 8.49

1936 Mercedes 540K
781-835 5.49

1937 Mercedes 260D
781-832 5.49

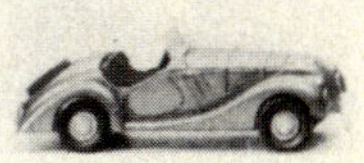

1938 BMW 328
781-828 4.99

1937 Horch 850
781-825 5.49

(not illustrated)

781-14201 MB 500 SL Cabrio Conv 9.49
781-16502 Porsche Carerra Conv **NEW** 8.49
781-18901 Ferrari 348ts (red) 9.49
781-18902 Ferrari 248ts (yellow) 9.49

RECREATIONAL

MB230G w/Horse Trailer
781-66 10.99

TRAILERS **NEW**

781-382 Vacuum Trailer 7.99

WIKING

HO SCALE (1/87)

Imported from Germany by *WALTHERS*

Gentlemen, start your engines! There's something for everyone from this large selection of vehicles. Autos from VW to Mercedes, classic autos and trucks, vans, emergency, construction and recreation vehicles. Each item is preassembled in appropriately colored plastic. (Markings and colors may vary from what is shown in catalog.)

We have worked closely with this manufacturer to provide accurate availability information at the time this catalog was published. Items listed in blue ink may not be available at all times. Please see your dealer for current delivery information.

TRUCKS

THW-MBL 408 Covered Van
781-695   8.49

THW-MB Covered Van
781-696   9.49

MB Street Cleaning Truck
781-642   12.49

MB Recycling Container
781-643   9.49

Mercedes 814 Van
781-431   8.49

Unimog 1700L
781-375   9.49

Peterbilt Wrecker
781-631   14.49

MB L2500 Truck Maggi's
781-842   10.99

■ LTD QUANTITY AVAIL ■

MB Garbage Truck
781-641   12.49

MB 507D Delivery
781-272   8.49

Dump Truck
781-676
13.49

(not illustrated)

781-689	Man F90 Asphalt	**NEW**	12.49
781-770	MB 1850 Truck Cab	**NEW**	TBA
781-846	LKW Delivery	**NEW**	10.99
781-859	MB L 6600 Delivery	**NEW**	12.49

ACCESSORIES

781-10 Truck Accessories   6.49
Assorted details include windshields, bumpers, mirrors and more.

TRUCKS (continued)

1939 Opel
Blitz Military
781-840
10.99

MAN Post Lorry
781-552
12.49

BUSES

Berlin Double
Decker D89
781-731
18.99

781-705 Mercedes 0305G Articulated City Bus   22.99

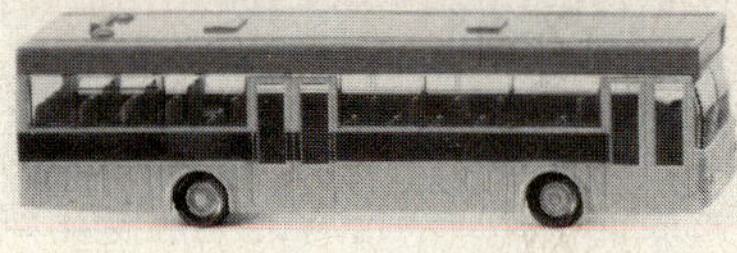

MAN SL202 City Bus
781-703   12.49

MAN SD200
Double-Deck Bus
781-730   16.49

1939 Mercedes
Double Deck Bus
781-873   14.49

MB 0405 Transit
781-702   22.99

MB 0305 City
Bus-Alliz-wb
781-700   12.49

MB 0303 RHD
Hi-Level
781-712   21.49

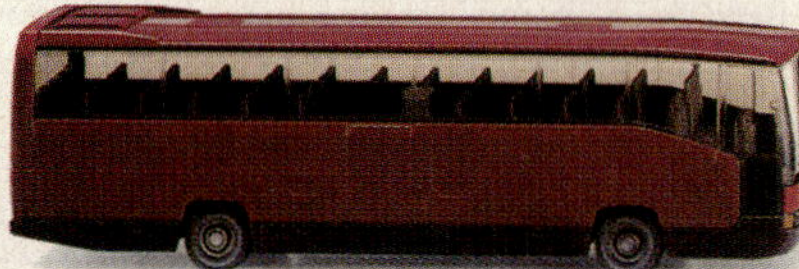

Reisebus
MB 0404 RHD
781-714   26.99

(not illustrated)
MB 404 RH Bus
781-713   **NEW** 26.99

WIKING

HO SCALE (1/87)

Imported from Germany by WALTHERS

Gentlemen, start your engines!
There's something for everyone from this large selection of vehicles. Autos from VW to Mercedes, classic autos and trucks, vans, emergency, construction and recreation vehicles. Each item is preassembled in appropriately colored plastic. (Markings and colors may vary from what is shown in catalog.)

SEMI TRUCKS

781-882 Benzin Diesel Tank Truck   14.49

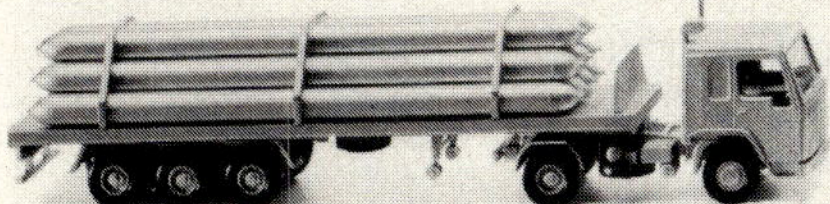

Volvo FL10 w/Gas Cylinders
781-787   14.49

Tractor Truck w/Tar Kettle Trailer
781-405   12.49

Double-Bottom DAF Van
781-467   18.99

MB Covered Flatbed
781-511   16.99

Covered Flatbed
781-541   16.99

Double-Bottom Live Stock Truck
781-565   16.99

MB Double-Bottom Trailer Truck
781-571   22.99

Liquid Gas Transporter
781-786   22.99

MB 2632 Double-Bottom Covered Flatbed
781-456   13.49

Bussing 8000 Lorry
781-478   17.49

MB Tractor (Service 24th)
781-441   31.49

781-518   MB Covered Flatbed (Scania)   27.99

STORAGE

781-12000 Clear storage box 8″ x 6″ x 2″   4.49

Keep freight rolling on your layout with Wiking's wide assortment of detailed trucks! Based on authentic European prototypes, each model comes fully assembled and ready for the road.

WIKING

HO SCALE (1/87)

Imported from Germany by WALTHERS

Gentlemen, start your engines!
There's something for everyone from this large selection of vehicles. Autos from VW to Mercedes, classic autos and trucks, vans, emergency, construction and recreation vehicles. Each item is preassembled in appropriately colored plastic. (Markings and colors may vary from what is shown in catalog.)

SEMI TRUCKS (continued)

BP Stromeyer Tanker
781-780
26.99

Transport Truck w/Cable
781-852
16.99

Iveco w/40' Container
781-523
18.99

Iveco 190.36 Double-Bottom Turbo Star
781-475
18.99

MAN Bussing Double-Bottom Flatbed
781-473
14.49

DAF 330 w/Trailer
781-468
16.99

MB Tractor w/Lowboy Trailer
781-504
18.99

Unimog U1500 w/2 Coal Trailers
781-404
16.99

Unimog U1500 w/Trailer & Building Scaffold
781-392
14.49

781-474 Iveco Double-Bottom Van   16.99

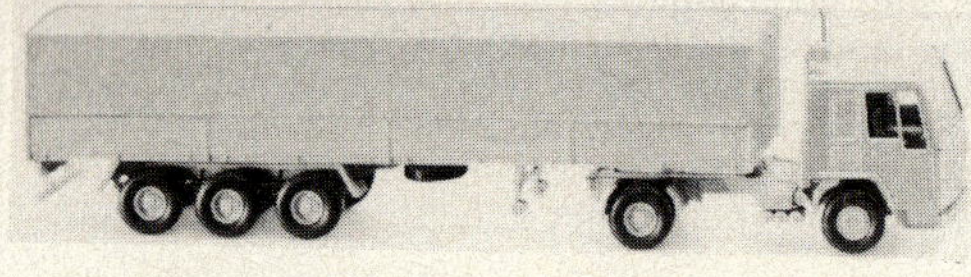

Volvo FL10 Semi-Van
781-519
16.99

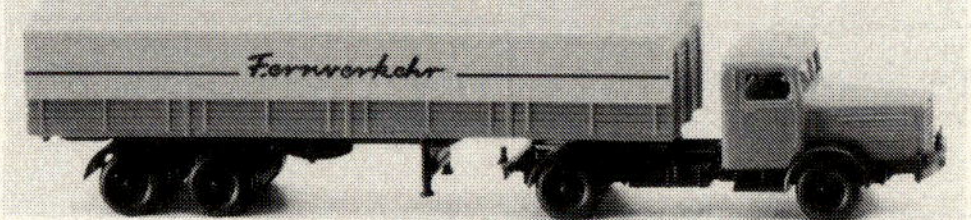

Bussing 8000 Old Time
781-890
12.49

781-570 MAN F90 Truck w/Trailer   19.99

781-850 Hanomag ST100 w/Two Trailers   18.99

Bussing 8000 Tank Truck
781-883
10.99

781-573 MB Double-Bottom Deutsche   26.99

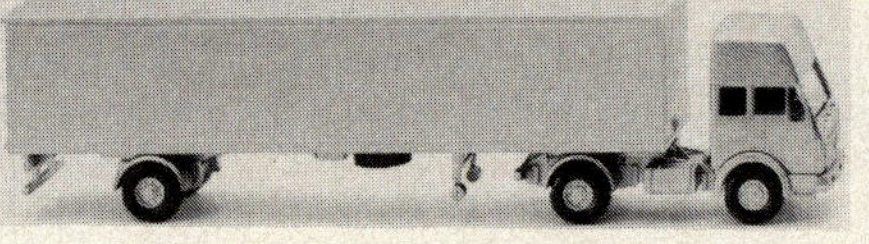

MB Tractor w/Van
781-544   14.49

MB Double-Bottom Van
781-459
16.99

781-580 MB 1622 Auto Transport   16.99

781-458 MB Semi w/Trailer   21.49

WIKING

HO SCALE (1/87)

Imported from Germany by WALTHERS

Gentlemen, start your engines!
There's something for everyone from this large selection of vehicles. Autos from VW to Mercedes, classic autos and trucks, vans, emergency, construction and recreation vehicles. Each item is preassembled in appropriately colored plastic. (Markings and colors may vary from what is shown in catalog.)

SEMI TRUCKS (continued)

MB 2244 Silo Transporter
781-575
21.49

Mercedes 1626 Semi-Van
781-542
18.99

Mercedes 1616 Semi Reefer Van
781-543
18.99

781-845 Mercedes LS2500 Double-Bottom Moving Van   16.49

Honomag Double-Bottom Covered Flatbed
781-857   16.99

Bussing 8000 Double-Bottom Truck
781-886   18.99

MB 2632 Double-Bottom
781-457
18.99

Truck w/40' Container
781-527
19.99

MAN Double-Bottom Post Office
781-551
18.99

781-853 HM ST 100 w/2 circus wagons   19.99

CONSTRUCTION VEHICLES

MAN Dump Truck
781-673   8.49

Haywagon
781-381   5.49

Open Trailer
781-879   4.49

Mercedes Cement Truck
781-682   8.49

Unimog Highway Dept Truck
781-646   8.49

MAN HD Dump Truck
781-671   8.49

Grove Hydraulic Crane 6-Axle
781-632
42.99

781-650 Road Roller   9.49

Liebherr 531 Front Loader
781-651   10.99

781-656 Trailer   8.49

781-660 O&K Caterpillar   12.49

4-Axle Dump Truck
781-674   10.99

4-Axle Cement Truck
781-681   12.49

Still R70 Forklift
781-659   5.49

1938 Lanz Bulldog Tractor
781-880   4.49

Mercedes 700 Farm Tractor
781-385
6.99

Bulldozer w/Cover
781-655   6.49

Deutz Farm Tractor
781-386   6.99

(not illustrated)
781-663 Forklift SPO   NEW 8.49

HO SCALE (1/87)

Imported from Germany by WALTHERS

Gentlemen, start your engines!
There's something for everyone from this large selection of vehicles. Autos from VW to Mercedes, classic autos and trucks, vans, emergency, construction and recreation vehicles. Each item is preassembled in appropriately colored plastic. (Markings and colors may vary from what is shown in catalog.)

EMERGENCY VEHICLES

VW Ambulance (ADAC)
781-78   10.99

ADAC-VW Golf Police Car
781-48   6.99

VW Caravelle Fire Dept
781-601   8.49

MB VRW Land Rover Command Car
781-609   7.99

MB 230G Land Rover Police Car
781-106   6.99

Golf Police Car
781-104   12.49

Mercedes Fire Chief
781-600   7.99

MB 230TE Autobahnpolizei
781-103   10.99

39 Opel Ladder Fire Truck
781-862   8.49

Magirus DLK 23-12 Aerial
781-620   Ladder   12.49

MB-1617 Fire Truck
781-628   9.49

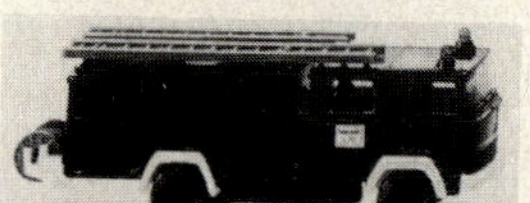
Mercedes Pumper
781-616   12.49

MB Police-Station Wagon
781-71   12.49

Unimog TLF 8/18 Fire Water Truck
781-622   10.99

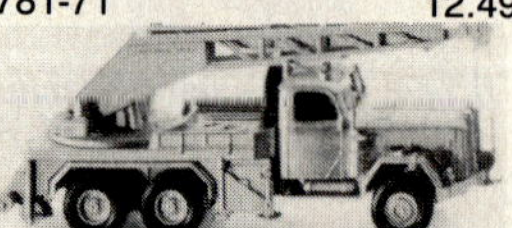
Magirus KW15 Fire Wrecker
781-694   (blue) 12.49

Magirus KW15 Fire Wrecker
781-630   (red) 10.99

VW Fire LF16 FD Hose Truck
781-610   16.49

Magirus Fire Water Truck
781-693   12.49

ACCESSORIES

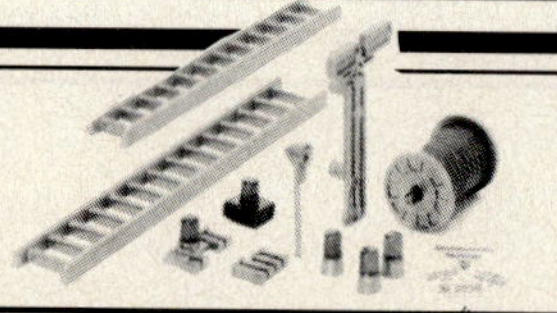
Firefighting Accessories
781-12
6.49

Opel LF8 Blitz 39 Fire Truck
781-863   9.49

MB 230 TE Ambulance
781-70   9.49

VW Fire Dept Van
781-692   8.49

VW Police Van
781-109   8.49

Fire Dept Van
781-605   9.49

Fire Dept Ambulance
781-607   9.49

Opel 39 Fire Truck
781-861   7.99

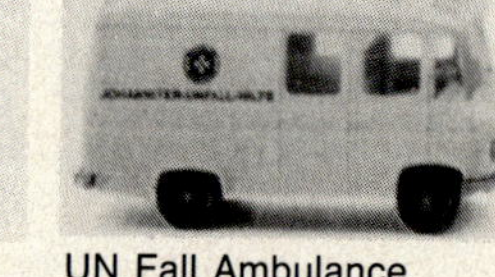
MB Ladder Truck
781-618   16.49

UN Fall Ambulance
781-278   9.49

TLF Water Cannon
781-621   12.49

VW Fire Command Car
781-603   6.99

VANS

VW Electronic Van
781-303   6.99

Camper
781-267   6.49

MB 207D Passenger Mini Bus
781-282 (blue)   4.99

VW Camper
781-294   8.49

VW Caddy w/top
781-47   6.49

MB L406 (Postal)
781-277   8.49

VW Panel Van
781-304   5.49

Van Caravelle
781-320   9.49

VW Transporter
781-290   4.99

781-548   Volvo FL 10 Moving Van   16.49

(not illustrated)

781-434   MB 814   **LIMITED QUANTITIES AVAILABLE**   10.99

kibri

HO SCALE (1/87) EASY-TO-BUILD KITS

Imported from Germany by WALTHERS

Keep your waterways busy with these boat kits from Kibri! The models are easy-to-build and molded in realistic colors, so no painting is required. Complete instructions are also included.

AMPHIBIOUS BOAT ■■■■■ ■ FIRE BOAT ■

■ LIMITED QUANTITIES ■
AVAILABLE

405-8269 THW   15.49

405-8257   29.49

BARGE

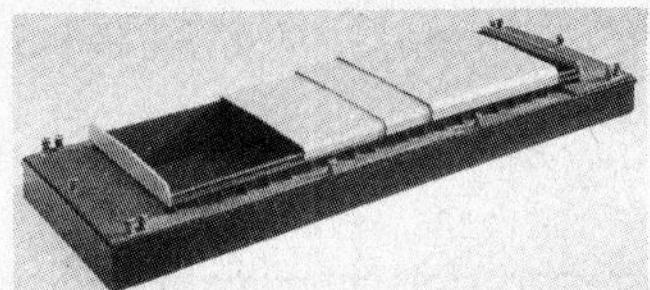

405-8514 w/Sliding Cover   20.49

PONTOON BOATS

w/Working Cranes
405-8518   29 x 9 cm   63.99

w/Bridge
405-8272   20 x 15 cm   16.49

MISCELLANEOUS

Push-Pull Tug Boat
405-8512   29.99

Small Boat Assortment
405-8270   pkg(8) 11.49

WOODLAND SCENICS

HO SCALE (1/87) CRAFT TRAIN KITS

Easy-to-assemble kits are unpainted, soft-metal castings and include complete instructions.

TRUCKS

1914 Diamond T
Service Truck
785-217   6.98
Dry transfers included

1914 Diamond T
Tank Truck
785-242   7.98
Dry transfers included

Diamond T
Grain Truck
785-218   6.98

Federal Dump Truck
785-247   7.98

Diamond T Tractor & Trailer
785-244   7.98

MOTORCYCLES

Motorcycle Set
785-228   3.98
Set includes two motorcycles, one side car and one motorcycle rider.

HEAVY EQUIPMENT

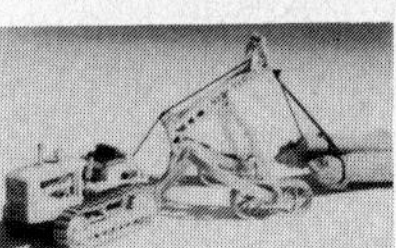

Hyster Logging Cruiser
785-246   9.98

Track Type Loader
Traxcavator
785-235   6.98

Bulldozer-Tractor
w/Blade
785-233   6.98

Back Hoe-
Insley
Model "K"
785-237   9.98

Motor Grader
785-234   6.98

JOHN DEER TRACTOR

w/Disc (1938 & 1946)
785-207   5.98

w/Seeder (1938-1946)
785-208   5.98

(1929-1938)
785-211   pkg(2) 5.98

NOCH
HO SCALE (1/87)

Imported from Germany by **WALTHERS**

Add to waterways with this assortment of boats and aircraft. Assembled (unless noted), appropriately colored plastic.

INCREASE OPERATIONS WITH A WHARF SCENE

Wherever ships make port, you'll find railroad facilities nearby. Many of the nation's railroads serve major ports on the east and west coasts as well as the Great Lakes states. Modeling a small wharf scene on your layout is a great way to add realistic scenery and new operating possibilites.

AIRCRAFT

Light Aircraft Mid-Wing
528-1145   9.99

High Performance Glider
528-1147   9.99

BARGE & TANK

These N Scale items are excellent background models.

Coal Barge
528-3572
kit 22.99

Motor Tank
528-3574
kit 26.99

CATAMARAN BOAT

528-1077
6.49

w/Figure
528-1124
9.99

ROW BOAT

528-1078   5.49

528-1126 w/Two People 9.99

MISCELLANEOUS

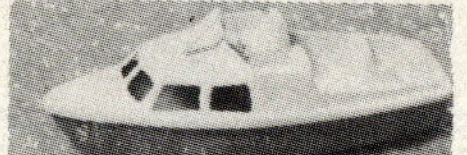

Motor Boat
528-1073   5.49

Kayak
528-1075   pkg(2) 3.99

TUG BOAT

These N Scale items are excellent background models.

528-3571 Tug Boat   kit 29.99

528-3575 Pilot Boat   kit 30.99

SAILBOATS

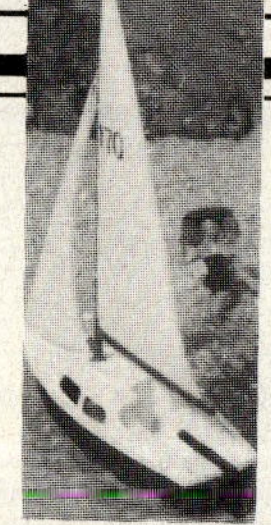

w/Fisherman
528-1121   8.49

528-1079   6.49

528-1071   6.49

w/Figure
528-1125   9.99

w/Spinnaker
528-1130   8.49

POLA
HO SCALE (1/87)

Imported from Germany by **WALTHERS**

FREIGHT BARGE

578-470 ''Marijke'' Barge   17.49
Authentic model of small barges found in Europe. Movable rudder, detailed deck construction. (6-1/3 x 1-3/4"   16 x 4.8 cm)

WALTHERS

Decals are a great way to expand your railroad with dozens of unusual paint and lettering schemes that aren't available on factory decorated cars. Decals also add more realism to ready-to-run equipment. Applying decals is easy, and doesn't require special skills or tools. First, try decaling a smooth sided car, then one with rivets and finally a scribed sided car. These four steps provide a basic guide to applying decals.

DECALING IS EASY!

Solvaset
904-470 (2oz btl) 2.98

Decals:
HO Scale 3.98

HERE ARE FOUR EASY STEPS TO A PROFESSIONAL LOOKING DECAL JOB.

1 **APPLY DECALS ON A GLOSSY SURFACE.** A gloss finish is needed for a good decal job. Glaze or gloss can be added to paint that dries dead flat, or sprayed on the model after the paint has dried. When spraying gloss, window "glass" and other areas can be protected by using Magic Masker. The gloss is NOT the final finish, it is only the surface to which the decal will be applied.

2 **TRIM THE DECAL PROPERLY.** Patches of excess decal film will show on the model, so trim as close to the lettering as possible and make all cuts parallel to the edges of the design. Use a sharp razor blade or modeling knife and cut on a piece of glass. Soak the individual decal pieces in clean water until they release from the backing sheet.

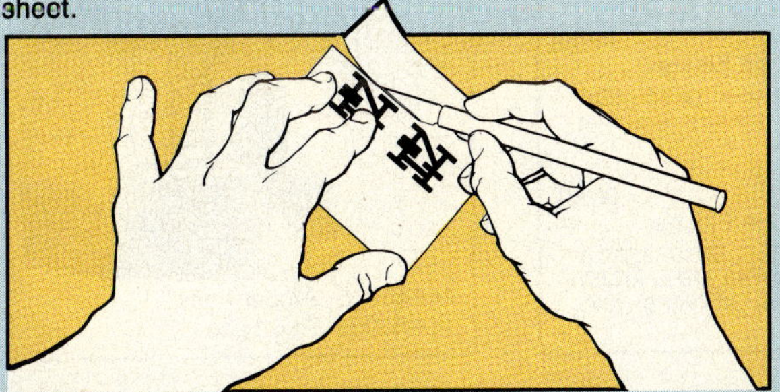

3 **USE SOLVASET™ TO MAKE THE DECAL STICK.** Position the decal on your model, and then apply a drop of SOLVASET™ on top. This will drive out air bubbles and soften the decal film so it can snuggle down around rivets, irregular surfaces and into crevices. NEVER touch the decal while the SOLVASET™ is working — and don't be alarmed if the decal appears to wrinkle. These small wrinkles will come out as the decal dries.

When the decal is throughly dry, check for any trapped air bubbles. Prick them with the point of a small pin or modeling knife blade and apply more SOLVASET.™ (On scribed siding some modelers prefer slitting the decal with a razor blade, then applying more SOLVASET.™)

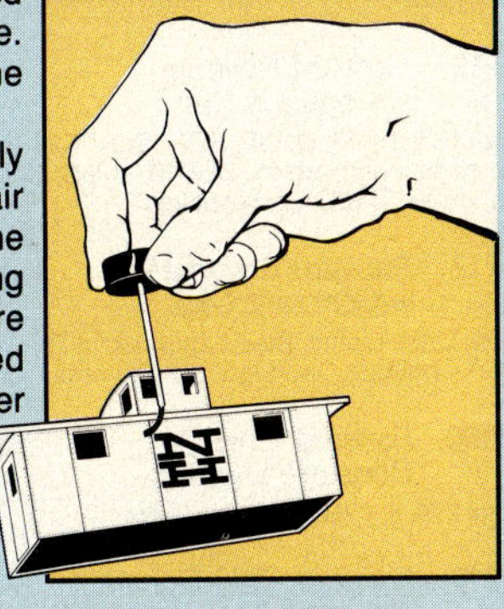

4 **USE DDV™ FOR A FINAL DULL FINISH.** When the decal is throughly dry, (24 hours) brush or spray DDV™ on model. This provides a uniform dull finish to the entire model.

If followed carefully, these four easy steps will give you excellent results every time you apply decals.

The Walthers Decal Catalog and Reference Manual lists hundreds of decal sets and lettering diagrams, so it's easy to choose the exact set in what you want. Capsule histories of prototype railroads provide information on color schemes, equipment, mergers and much more!

ACCURATE LIGHTING

LIGHTING KITS

NEW

CONSTANT LIGHTING KITS

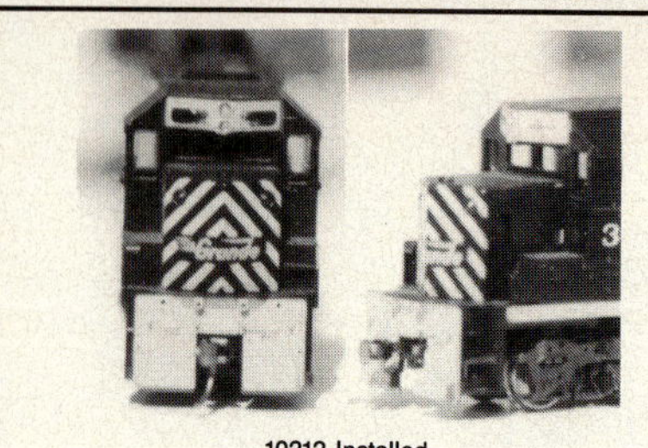

10212 Installed

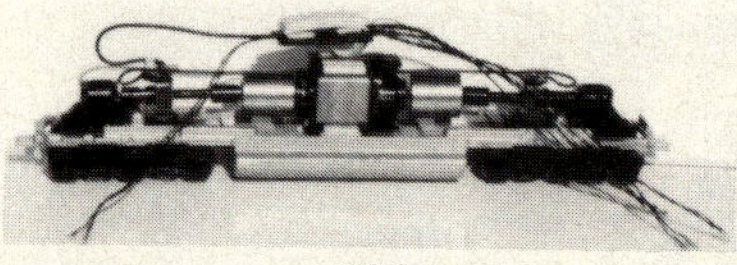

10212

10101

144-10101 Forward/Reverse 25.50
Athearn SW7 Cow, SW7 Calf & S-12 Switchers

144-10202 Forward/Reverse 25.50
Athearn SW1000, SW15 Switchers (except SP Version)

144-10404 Forward/Reverse 26.50
Athearn, SP Version of the SW1500 Switcher

**144-10212 Forward/Reverse 27.50
w/Constant Cab**
Athearn GP9, GP38-2, GP40-2, GP50, SD9, SD40-2, SD40T-2 (except SP & CB versions) Locomotives

**144-12212 Forward/Reverse 29.50
w/Constant Cab**
Athearn F45, FP45, GP35, RDC, SD40T-2 (SP & CB versions only), SD45, SDP40, U28B, U28C, U30C, U33B, U33C Locomotives

**144-14212 Forward/Reverse 29.50
w/Constant Cab**
Athearn, Ditch Lights, Step Lights, etc. 6 Forward Lights, 1 Constant Cab Light & 2 Reverse Lights

**144-22000 Forward Only 27.50
Constant Lighting**
Athearn F7A & F7B Powered Units

**144-20210 Forward Only Constant 25.50
Lighting w/Directional Cab Light
for Locomotives in Multi Units**
Athearn GP9, GP38-2, GP40-2, GP50, SD9, SD40T-2 (except SP & CB versions)

**144-22210 Forward Only Constant 27.50
Lighting w/Directional for
Locomotives in Multi Units**
Athearn F45, FP45, GP35, RDC, SD40T-2 (SP & CB versions only), SD45, SDP40, U28B, U28C, U30B, U30C, U33B, U33C

**144-24210 Forward Only Constant 27.50
Lighting w/Directional Cab for
Locomotives in Multi Units**
Athearn Locomotives needing extra lights for Ditch Lights, Step Lights, Truck Lights, etc. 6 Forward Lights, 1 Directional Cab Light

CONSTANT LIGHTING KITS
(continued)

144-30010 Constant Light Module 23.50
Athearn, all powered locomotives run in Multi Units which do not require lighting; one constant bulb which may be used to light number boards

144-11101 Forward/Reverse 25.50
Walthers Fairbanks Morse H10-44 and EMD SW1 Switchers

144-50212 Forward/Reverse 29.50
Kato GP35

144-101016 Forward/Reverse 25.50
Overland Model Drives, SW7, SW12 Switchers

144-102026 Forward/Reverse 25.50
Overland Model Drives, SW1000, SW1500 Switchers

144-102126 Forward/Reverse 28.50
Overland Model Drives, for Locomotives requiring 2 Roof Lights, 1 Constant Cab Light, 2 Back-up Lights

144-122126 Forward/Reverse 30.50
Overland Model Drives, for Locomotives requiring 2 Roof Lights, 2 Nose Lights, 1 Constant Cab Light, 2 Back-up Lights

144-142126 Forward/Reverse 32.50
Overland Model Drives, for Locomotives requiring 2 Roof Lights, 1 Constant Cab Light, 2 Back-up Lights

144-220006 Forward Only 29.50
Overland Model Drives, F Series Locomotives

**144-102125 Forward/Reverse 39.50
w/Amber Strobe Flasher**
Athearn GP9, GP38-2, GP40-2, GP50, SD9, SD40-2, SD40T-2 (except SP & CB versions), including roof-mounted beacon detail

**144-122125 Forward/Reverse 39.50
w/Amber Strobe Flasher**
Athearn F45, FP45, GP35, RDC, SD40T-2 (SP & DC versions only), SD45, SDP40, U28B, U28C, U30B, U30C, U33B, U33C, including roof-mounted beacon detail

**144-220005 Forward Only 39.50
w/Amber Strobe Flasher**
Athearn F7A, including Western Cullen style beacon detail

**144-202105 Forward Only 39.50
w/Amber Strobe Flasher**
Athearn GP9, GP38-2, GP40-2, GP50, SD9, SD40T-2 (except SP & CB versions), including roof-mounted beacon detail

**144-222105 Forward Only 39.50
w/Amber Strobe Flasher**
Athearn F45, FP45, GP35, RDC, SD40T-2 (SP & CB versions only), SD45, SDP40, U28B, U28C, U30B, U30C, U33B, U33C, including roof-mounted beacon detail

STROBE FLASHERS

.90L x .55W x .32H Battery Pack & Flasher Unit, On/Off Switch—suited for Diesel Roof Flashers and Emergency Vehicle Warning Lights

144-62001 Red 9.50
144-62002 Amber 9.50
144-62003 Yellow 9.50
**144-62009 Replacement Batteries 1.79
for 62001, 62002, 62003**

2.25L x .62W x .60H Single AA Battery Holder w/Surface-Mounted Flasher, Flasher 1.5V Bulb—suited for simulated Diesel Roof Beacon when combined with Roof-Mounted Beacon Details.

144-62010 Basic Unit 12.95
**144-62011 Same as 62010 w/Single 16.95
Bulb & Reed Switch**
**144-62012 Same as 62010 14.95
w/Dual Bulb**
**144-62013 Same as 62010 w/Dual 18.95
Buld & Reed Switch**

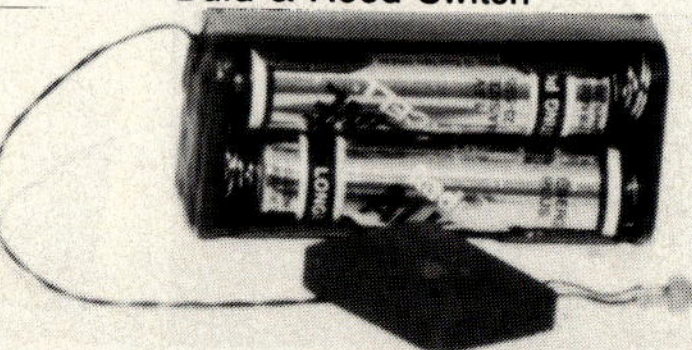

2.18L x .97W x .58H Double AAA Battery Holder w/Surface-Mounted Flasher, On/Off Reed Switch, Magnet, Flashing LED—suited to simulate Roof Beacon when combined with roof-mounted details.

144-62020 Red 19.95
144-62021 Amber 19.95
144-62022 Yellow 19.95

END OF TRAIN DEVICE

Mounted on Kadee #5 Coupler, Flashing Bulb (1.5V) installed in casting—unit surface-mounted on AA Battery Holder, wiring complete.

144-61001 Amber Lens 19.95
144-61002 Red Lens 10.05

CABOOSE FLASHER

Caboose Flasher with plastic details to make a round or square light receptacle

144-61005 Amber Lens 15.95
144-61006 Red Lens 15.95

ARNOLD

ELECTRICAL SYSTEMS AND PARTS

Imported from Germany and marketed by **WALTHERS**

BULBS

125-7960 Controller Bulb each 2.99
16v, yellow for use w/#'s 7220, 7230 & 7240.
Dealers: MUST Order Dealer Pack of 10.
Mini-Bayonet
125-791 (red) 3.49
Mini-Bayonet
125-792 (green) 3.49
125-793 Screw Base (clear) 3.49
125-794 Bayonet (clear) 3.49
125-797 Bayonet 12V (clear) 3.49
125-798 Bayonet 12V (red) 3.49

GOW 12V
125-736154 (clear) 3.49
GOW 16V
125-760305 (green) 3.49
125-760306 GOW16V (red) 3.49
125-760307 GOW 16V (yellow) 3.49

ELECTRICAL CONTROLS

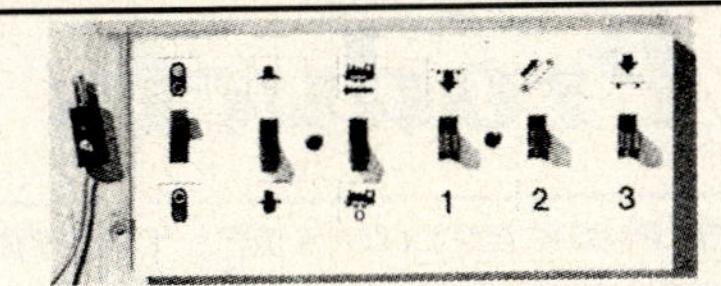

125-7260 Universal Control Panel 22.49
For all model railroad systems. Six functions. Suitable for operating turnouts as well as single-pole and momentary operation. Connections accept plug-in type wires.

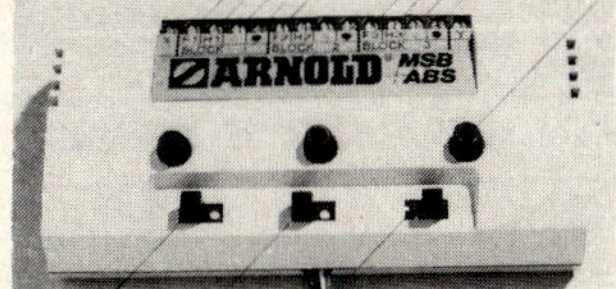

125-7695 Multi-Train Control Block 245.49
w/starting and braking system
A compact panel for safe multi-train operation. Three block sections w/integrated automatic signals and starting -- braking system. The length of the starting and braking distance can be adjusted individually. This system may be used for all direct current trains up to 16v, 1 amp with the exception of LGB™ and miniclub.

Automatic Braking System Auto Train Control
125-7696 70.99
for use of automatic and block service.

Use w/#7693 Control Block or may be used alone or for all direct current trains up to 16v, 1 amp with the exception of LGB™ and miniclub.

LIMITED QUANTITIES AVAILABLE

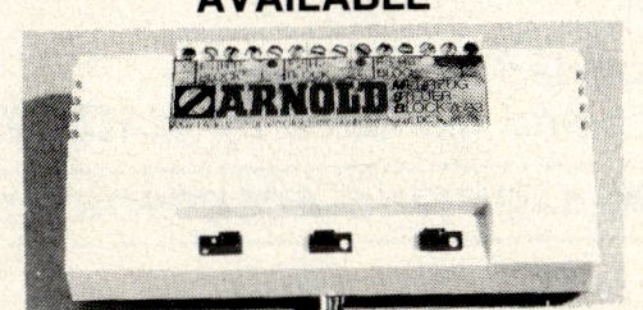

125-7693 Multi-Train Control Panel 138.99
Compact panel for safe multi-train operation with automatic signals. Can be used with any DC transformer up to 16 volts, 1 amp. Three track blocks and signals may be connected to one MSB. The three slide switches control direction of travel in the block. 4-3/16 x 2-1/4", 115 x 57 mm.

ACCESSORIES

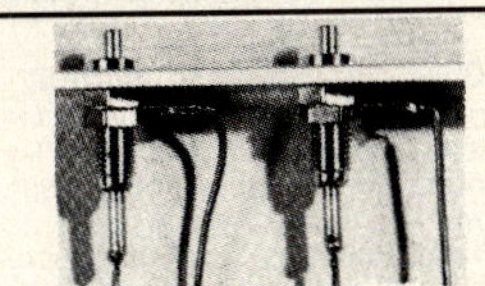

125-7200 Push Button SPST Switch pkg(2) 12.49

125-7230 Double Slip Controller 18.99

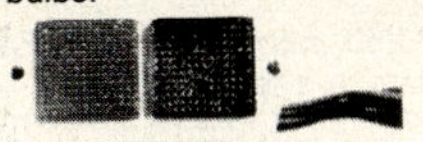

125-7220 Turnout Controller pkg(2) 23.99
Illuminated push buttons, wire length, 11-13/16" (30 cm). Less bulbs.

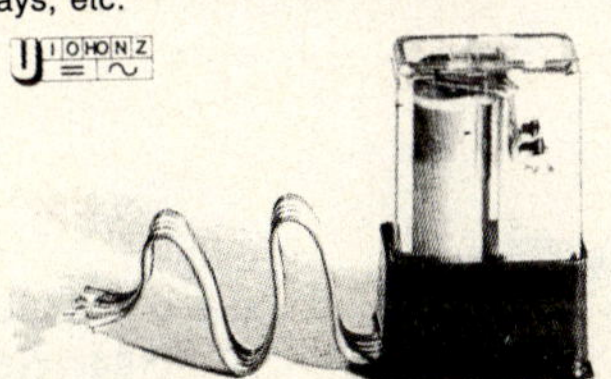

125-7240 Twin Push Button Control 16.49
with red and green keys for activating signals, relays, etc.

125-7452 Latching Relay 54.99
Used for operating crossing gate lamps, bells, flashers, automatic operation of reverse loops, signals and more. Relay can be connected to either DC or AC for continuous operation up to 18 volts. Features: switching capacity, 2.5 Amp. 9 lead connections 3-15/16" (10 cm), silver plated contacts, dust-proof enclosed case. Operates in any position. Base, 1 x 1-3/8" (24 x 34mm). Height, 2-1/8" (53mm).

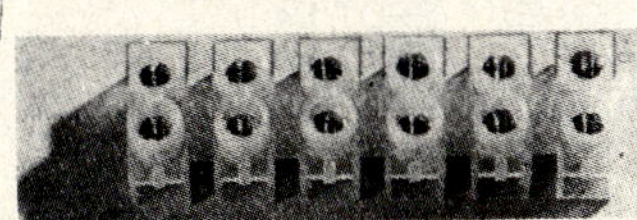

Universal Controller DPDT
125-7250 16.49
Easy access screw connections will accommodate up to 6 wires when used with a momentary switch. This universal switch can be used to operate the turntable.

Indicator tabs are included.

125-7150 Terminal Connecting Strip 1.99
6 poles with 12 terminals and screw type contacts. Requires an area of 1-3/4 x 5/8" (45 x 16 mm).

125-7160 Wire Hold Down Clip pkg(10) 9.49
for 10 and 30 strands

ACCESSORIES (cont.)

(not illustrated)
125-7235 3-Way Switch Control Box 28.99

TWO-STRAND CONDUCTOR WIRE

125-7120 Red, Black 1.99
19" (50 cm) w/2 plug-in connectors

PANEL LIGHTS

125-7316 Red ea 6.99
125-7317 Green ea 6.99
125-7318 Yellow ea 6.99
125-7319 White ea 6.99
Multi-purpose panel lights, 12-16 V, 30mA. Includes 3-9/16" (90 cm) wire. For interior illumination of buildings, tunnels or as control panel switch indicator lights.

MISCELLANEOUS **NEW**

Simplex Control Switch
125-7252 27.49
125-7310 Lighting Strip for #3850 21.99

LIGHTING GENERATOR

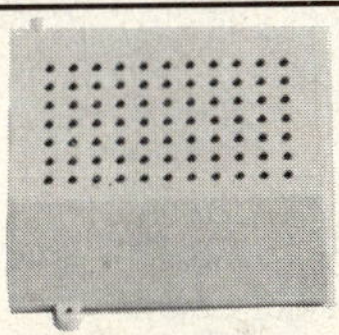

125-7097 Lighting Generator 155.99

Constant intensity lighting generator. Operates independently of track voltage. AC voltage, output of 14 to 16 volts. Unit can handle up to 25 bulbs of 12v, 50 mA each. Short circuit protection, and radio interference suppressor are built in. Suitable for all gauges except G scale equipment.

BACHMANN
QUALITY SINCE 1833

STRUCTURAL ELECTRICAL ACCESSORIES

Water Pump Electric, Mini
160-42219 8.00

Interior Lighting Kit w/Wire
160-42240 pkg(2) 4.00

MISCELLANEOUS

160-44207 Power Pack 22.00

B L HOBBY PRODUCTS

DIODES

183-261	Diodes	pkg(5) 2.50

LED LENSES

183-250	Small (red), 3/32" lens	pkg(4) 3.50
183-251	Small (green), 3/32" lens	pkg(4) 3.50
183-252	Small (yellow), 3/32" lens	pkg(4) 3.50

183-253	Regular T-1 (red)	pkg(4) 3.50
183-254	Regular T-1 (grn)	pkg(4) 3.50
183-255	Regular T-1 (ylw)	pkg(4) 3.50

RESISTOR

183-260	Drop 560 ohms	2.00
183-262	Sensing	pkg(10) 4.00

4700 ohm surface mount resistors are used across wheels of cars to sensitize the cars for operating the auto block control. Instructions included.

FIBER OPTICS

183-700	Fiber Optic Assortment	4.00
	5' each, 10, 20 and 30mm fiber	
183-701	100', 10mm fiber	6.00
183-702	30', 20mm fiber	5.50
183-703	15', 30mm fiber	5.00
183-704	15', 40mm fiber	6.25
183-711	*Clear Fiber w/Light Source	4.75
183-712	*Green Fiber w/Light Source	4.75
183-713	*Red Fiber w/Light Source	4.75
183-714	*Yellow Fiber w/Light Source	4.75

* w/2' each of 20 and 30mm optic fiber.

FIBER OPTIC LIGHT KIT

183-532	Stars In Your Sky **NEW**	42.00

Places lighted stars in your backdrop sky. Includes various sizes of fiber optic, light source and full instructions.

183-535	Moon In Your Sky **NEW**	12.00

Places a moon in your sky backdrop. Light source, materials and instructions included.

183-720	Automatic	6.25

with 1 red and 1 clear bulb, 3 feet each of 20 and 30mm fiber optic material.

183-721	Flasher	6.25

with 2 red bulbs.

Master Creations

LIGHT SENSITIVE CIRCUIT **NEW**

464-1200 Light Sensitive Circuit 19.95
Unit controls 3 1.5mv bulbs. Circuit includes a photo-cell which activates the 3 lights at 3 different times when room lights are dimmed. The 3 lights also turn off at 3 different times when light in room is increased. The unit's light sensitivity is adjustable. The unit accepts 7.5 to 12 volts in either AC or DC for power input.

LIGHT SENSITIVE CIRCUIT II **NEW**

464-1210 Light Sensitive Circuit II 21.95
Unit controls 6 1.5mv bulbs. Circuit includes a photo-cell which activates the 6 lights at 3 different times when room lights are dimmed. The 6 lights also turn off at 3 different times when light in room is increased. The unit's light sensitivity is adjustable. The unit accepts 7.5 to 12 volts in either AC or DC for power input.

MINIATURE LIGHT BULB **NEW**

464-1250 Miniature Light Bulb 1.25
1.5mm in size, designed for long life. Accepts only 1.5 volts for power (more volts will destroy bulb).

MODEL RECTIFIER CORPORATION

POWER SUPPLY ACCESSORIES

SWITCHES

500-2001	SPST Slide	ea	.60
500-2003	DPDT Slide	ea	.80
500-2011	SPST Toggle	ea	2.25
500-2012	DPST E2 Toggle	ea	2.25
500-2013	DPDT E3 C-Off Toggle	ea	3.50
500-2014	SPDT E4 C-Off Toggle	ea	2.95
500-2015	DPDT E5	ea	2.75
500-2016	DPDT 3W C-Off-Wired	ea	4.50
500-2017	SPDT E7 C-Off Momentary	ea	4.95

ACCESSORIES

500-40	Rheostat HO Scale (40 ohms; 1.5 amps)	ea	12.98
500-2040	Terminal Strip-Plain	ea	3.95
	Dealer: MUST order Dealer pack of 10.		
500-2041	Terminal Strip-Wired	ea	4.95
	Dealer: MUST order Dealer pack of 10.		

kibri

Imported from Germany by WALTHERS

BULB

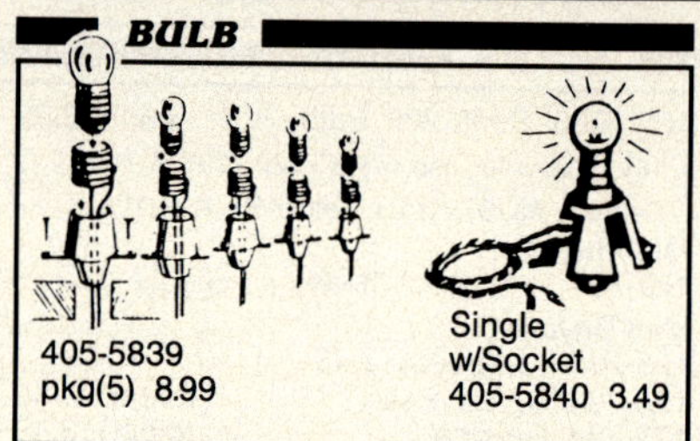

405-5839	pkg(5)	8.99
405-5840	Single w/Socket	3.49

Rix Products

PUSH BUTTONS

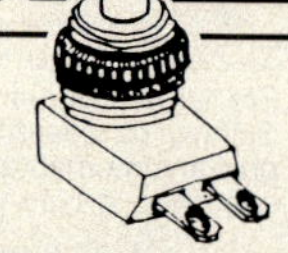

Buttons are complete with mounting nut and soldering terminals. 125v, 3 amps.

628-16	Momentary Contact	pkg(4) 3.49

DIODE MATRIX **NEW**

Diode Matrix board makes it possible to control several switch machines at once so that an entire route can be aligned with the push of one button. Will work with most twin coil switch machines and motor drives, including Hankscraft and Tortoise. Use 1 amp diodes with motor drives and 3 amp diodes with twin coil switch machines.

628-50	RIX Diode Matrix Board	9.95
628-52	RIX 1K Resistors	pkg(12) 1.20
628-51	One Amp Diode	pkg(14) 2.99
628-53	Three Amp Diode	pkg(14) 3.99

VOLLMER

Imported from Germany and marketed by WALTHERS

LIGHTING ACCESSORIES

770-6550	Lighting Strip 2-Socket	6.49

BRAWA

Brawa offers a comprehensive line of electrical accessories, suitable for use with all model railroad systems.

Imported from Germany by **WALTHERS**

SUPER HIGH-PERFORMANCE RELAY

Electronic Reversing Relay
186-6421 73.99

The Brawa polarity reversing switch will automatically change direction of DC motors. The unit features a built-in speed control and can be used with Brawa cableways, rope hoists and funiculars, or where automatic reversal of trains is desirable.

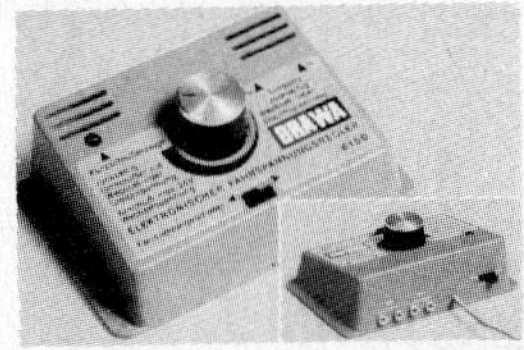

186-6150 Electronic Speed Controller 71.49
Variable speed throttle for Brawa cableways, trolleybuses and DC railroad systems. Unit operates from AC contacts on transformer (24V maximum). Can power AC or DC accessories. Built-in short circuit protection w/red LED indicator.

SUPER SIGNAL RELAY

Relays 2760 or 2761 feature matching color-coded wiring for Brawa signals and accessories. Units may be operated manually, or automatically with reed switches.

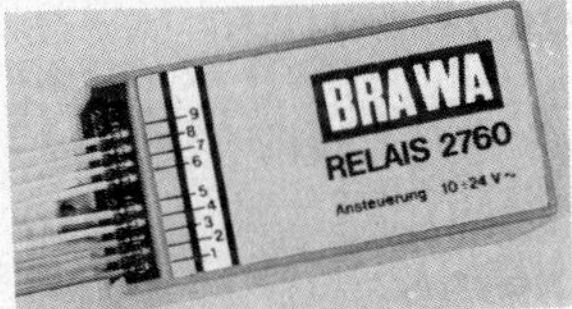

186-2760 Double 42.99
10-24V AC

186-2761 Triple 57.49
10-24V AC

MODEL RAILROAD ACCESSORIES

6154
3529

186-6154 Adjustable Resistor 16.99
Adjustable output clip. Reduces train speed for slow-running track blocks. 0-100ohms; 1/4 x 2".

186-3529 Time Delay Switch 10.49
Regulates time loco or other powered vehicles will stop at stations etc. Adjustable for long or short stops. 2-1/4 x 1/2 x 1/2".

MODEL RAILROAD ACCESSORIES (continued)

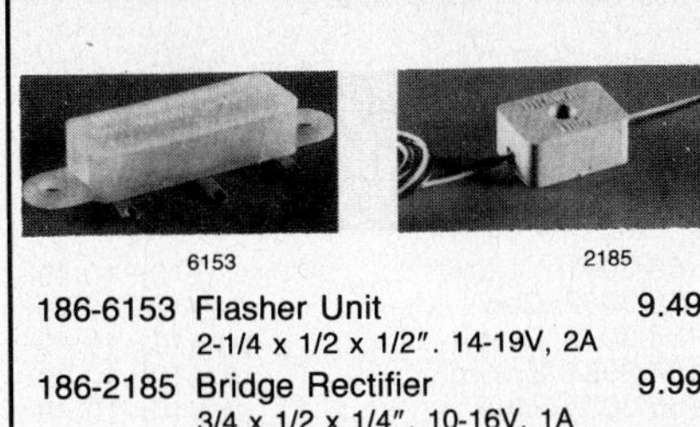
6153
2185

186-6153 Flasher Unit 9.49
2-1/4 x 1/2 x 1/2". 14-19V, 2A

186-2185 Bridge Rectifier 9.99
3/4 x 1/2 x 1/4". 10-16V, 1A

DISTRIBUTOR

Several distributors can be connected to supply more accessories.

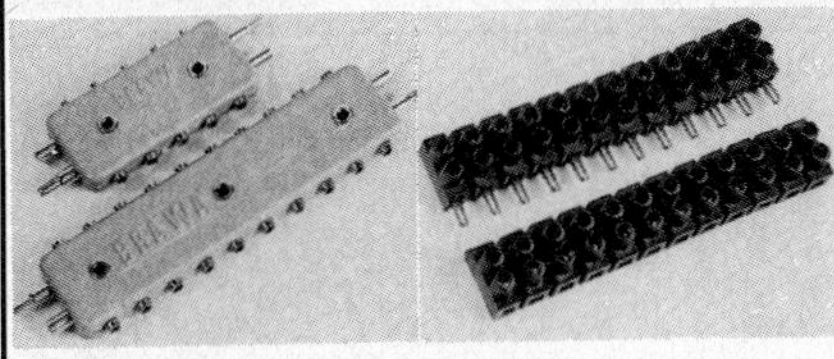
2591   2592   3093

186-2591 5-Way, 2-Pole 4.49
186-2592 10-Way, 2-Pole 6.49
186-3093 Plug & Socket Strip 8.99
12 way; 4" long.

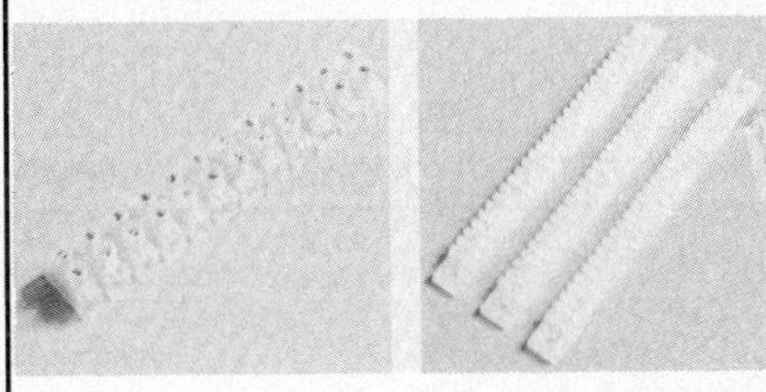
3094   3910

186-3094 Screw Terminal Strip 2.49
12 way; 4" long.
186-3910 Wire Holder pkg(10) 4.49
Holds up to 25 wires or leads securely.

PUSHBUTTON

186-3500 Panel, Nickel-Plated 4.49
Multi-purpose on/off switch, with retaining clip. 1/4 x 1-1/2".

186-3573 Pushbutton pkg(4) 5.49
3/4"

MOMENTARY CONTACT PUSHBUTTON

1/4 x 1-1/2"

186-3501 Yellow pkg(2) 5.99
186-3502 Red each 2.99
186-3503 Green each 2.99
186-3505 Blue pkg(2) 5.99
186-3508 Black pkg(2) 5.99
186-3509 White pkg(2) 5.99

ILLUMINATED PUSHBUTTON

1/4" diameter

186-3511 Yellow 7.99
186-3512 Red 7.99
186-3513 Green 7.99
186-3519 White 7.99

NON-ILLUMINATED PUSHBUTTON

1/4" diameter
186-3471 Yellow 3.49
186-3472 Red 3.49
186-3473 Green 3.49
186-3475 Blue 3.49
186-3478 Black 3.49
186-3479 White 3.49

PANEL PUSHBUTTON SWITCH W/NUT

SPST Pushbutton Switch w/nut
186-3524 pkg(2) 4.99
Base approx 1 x 1/2"; threaded neck length is approx 1/2".

SIGNAL SWITCH

For manual operation of signals. 1A/25V

Two-Way
186-2755
17.49
Red-green; 1-1/2"

Three-Way
186-2756
20.49
Red-green-yellow; 2"

2755   2756

Four-Way
186-2757
26.49
Red-green-yellow-white; 2-1/2"

2757

TOGGLE SWITCH—ON/OFF

220 V/2A

Single-Pole
186-3520 5.99

186-3574 Tumbler Toggle pkg(4) 5.49
Switch 3/4"

BRAWA

Brawa offers a comprehensive line of electrical accessories, suitable for use with all model railroad systems.

Imported from Germany by **WALTHERS**

TOGGLE SWITCH— POLARITY REVERSING

186-3521	Single-Pole	5.49

MAGNETIC REED SWITCH

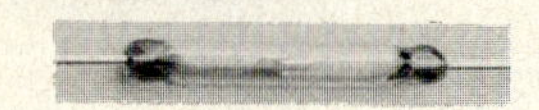

186-3530	Inert Gas-Filled Tube Contact	3.99

Contact load is 0.5A capacity, 3/4 x .1″

MAGNET

3543

186-3541	Rod Magnet	6.99

for use with 3531; 1/3 x 1″ (8 x 26mm)

186-3543	Bar Magnet	1.99

for use with 3530; 1/4 x 1/2″ (6 x 12 x 4mm)

PLUG & SOCKET

186-3070	for Marklin	set 4.49

8 crosshole plugs, 8 sleeves

186-3071	30 pieces	set 7.99

15 plugs, 15 sockets in 5 colors

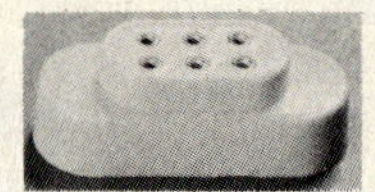

3570 3571 3572

186-3570	Socket 2-Pole	pkg(5) 4.49

1/3″ centers

186-3571	Plug 2-Pole	pkg(5) 4.49

1/3″ centers

186-3572	Battery Cap Socket 6-Pole	1.49

ROUND PLUGS

with crossover hole

186-3051	Yellow	pkg(10) 2.99
186-3052	Red	pkg(10) 2.99
186-3053	Green	pkg(10) 2.99
186-3054	Brown	pkg(10) 2.99
186-3055	Blue	pkg(10) 2.99
186-3056	Orange	pkg(10) 2.99
186-3057	Gray	pkg(10) 2.99
186-3058	Black	pkg(10) 2.99
186-3059	White	pkg(10) 2.99

PANEL SOCKETS

For use on control panels.

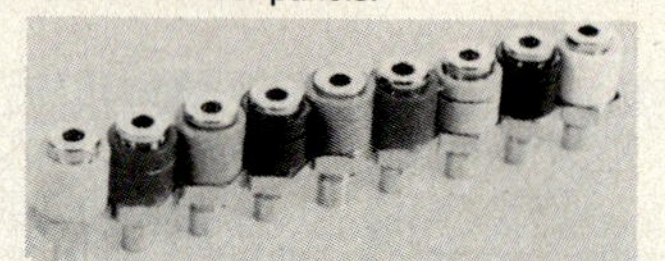

186-3081	Yellow	pkg(10) 10.49
186-3082	Red	pkg(10) 10.49
186-3083	Green	pkg(10) 10.49
186-3084	Brown	pkg(10) 10.49
186-3085	Blue	pkg(10) 10.49
186-3086	Orange	pkg(10) 10.49
186-3087	Gray	pkg(10) 10.49
186-3088	Black	pkg(10) 10.49
186-3089	White	pkg(10) 10.49

ROUND SOCKET

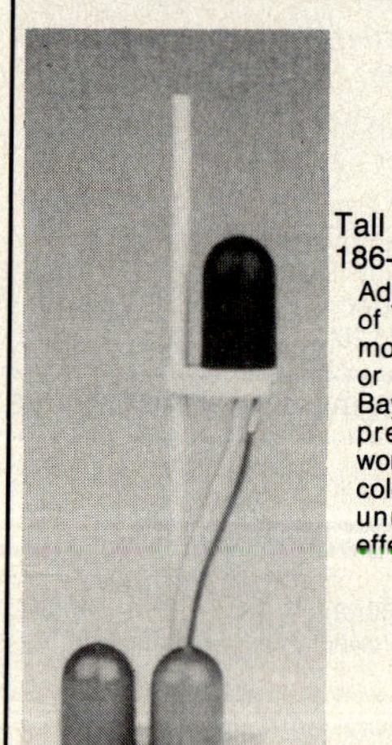

Yellow
186-3041
pkg(10)
2.99

186-3042	Red	pkg(10) 2.99
186-3043	Green	pkg(10) 2.99
186-3044	Brown	pkg(10) 2.99
186-3045	Blue	pkg(10) 2.99
186-3046	Orange	pkg(10) 2.99
186-3047	Gray	pkg(10) 2.99
186-3048	Black	pkg(10) 2.99
186-3049	White	pkg(10) 2.99

LIGHTING

Tall Structure Lights
186-3405   4.49
Adjustable for all sizes of structures. Can be mounted in buildings, or under benchwork. Bayonet fitting helps prevent bulb from working loose. Includes colored bulb cover for unusual lighting effects. 16V.

LED PANEL LIGHT

Each LED features a built-in ballast resistor. Each measures 1/4″ diameter, installed depth 1″. 14-16V

186-3481	Yellow	6.49
186-3482	Red	6.49
186-3483	Green	6.49

SCREW PANEL LIGHT

Size E5.5 for use on control panel. Current draw 50mA at 14-16V

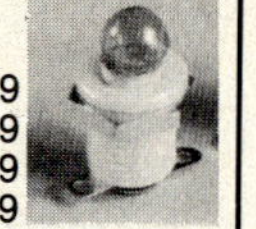

186-3441	Yellow	pkg(2) 8.49
186-3442	Red	pkg(2) 8.49
186-3443	Green	pkg(2) 8.49
186-3449	White	pkg(2) 8.49

PUSH IN PANEL LIGHTS

For control panels and other installations where small diameter indicator lamps are needed. Units feature heat-resistant black plastic body with colored cap, nickel-plated mounting ring, long-life bulb and 6″ leads. Fits mounting hole of 3/16″. 12-14V, 60mA

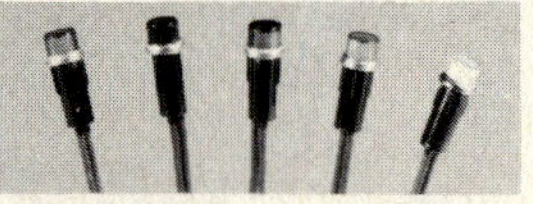

186-3461	Amber	8.49
186-3462	Red	8.49
186-3463	Green	8.49
186-3465	Blue	8.49
186-3469	White	8.49

INDICATOR BULB COVER

For use only with 3304 spherical bulbs.

186-3451	Yellow pkg(2)	6.49
186-3453	Green pkg(2)	6.49
186-3455	Blue pkg(2)	6.49
186-3459	White pkg(2)	6.49

LIGHT-EMITTING DIODE—LEDs

Connect only through 1000 Ohm resistor.

186-3295	Yellow, 2mm	pkg(2) 4.49
186-3296	Red, 2mm	pkg(2) 4.49
186-3297	Red, 1mm	pkg(2) 7.49
186-3298	Red, 3mm	pkg(2) 5.49

Miniature Type for #4806. Approximate size 1/4″ x 5/32″

186-3360	Yellow	pkg(2) 5.49
186-3361	Red	pkg(2) 5.49
186-3362	Green	pkg(2) 5.49
186-3339	for Marklin Loco	pkg(4) 4.99

(not illustrated)

186-3913	1000 OHM Resistor	pkg(10) 2.49

MINIATURE BULB

14V, 30 mA; for Brawa metal signals.

186-3259	Clear	pkg(2) 6.99
186-3260	Yellow	pkg(2) 6.99
186-3261	Red	pkg(2) 6.99
186-3262	Green	pkg(2) 6.99

SPECIAL BULB

With 2 electrodes. Replacement bulb for Brawa HO and N plastic signals made before 1981. 16V, 30 mA

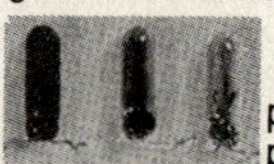

186-3257	Green	pkg(2) 4.99
186-3258	Yellow	pkg(2) 4.99

BRAWA

Brawa offers a comprehensive line of electrical accessories, suitable for use with all model railroad systems.

Imported from Germany by **WALTHERS**

LILIPUT BULB

16V, 35 mA
186-3263	24V, Clear	pkg(2)	8.49
186-3271	Clear	pkg(2)	4.49
186-3272	Red	pkg(2)	4.99
186-3273	Green	pkg(2)	4.99
186-3274	Yellow	pkg(2)	4.99

GRAIN-O-WHEAT BULB

16V, 30 mA, unless otherwise noted.
186-3269	Short, Clear	pkg(2)	6.99
186-3270	Long, Clear	pkg(2)	6.99
186-3284	60 mA, 16V	pkg(2)	5.49
	for #4538 to '81		

LIMITED QUANTITIES AVAIL

186-3285	Short, Yellow	pkg(2)	5.99
186-3286	Short, Green	pkg(2)	6.99
186-3287	2-Wire, Clear	pkg(2)	7.99
186-3288	Clear for 5760, 14V, 40mA	pkg(2)	7.99
186-3291	Clear for Z Lights, 10V, 30mA	pkg(2)	7.49
186-3293	Clear, 1 Blk Wire	pkg(2)	6.99
186-3254	Clear 2 exposed electrodes, 16V, 35mA	pkg(2)	5.49
186-3290	Spare Bulb for Z Lights 2 exposed electrodes, clear, 10V, 30 mA	pkg(2)	6.49
186-3292	Miniature Bulb 2 electrodes for 7942; 1.5V 15 mA; connect only through resistor.	pkg(2)	7.49
186-3267	Micro Bulb, Clear, 3V	pkg(2)	7.49
186-3268	Mini Bulb, Clear, 3V	pkg(2)	7.99

MISCELLANEOUS BULBS

3252
186-3252	M 3.5 x 0.35 Micro-Thread short/clear, 16V, 30 mA	pkg(2)	6.99
186-3264	Screw-In Bulb for #4621 & 4591	pkg(2)	6.99
186-3265	for Spotlight 6V, (HO, N)	pkg(2)	6.49
186-3289	for Z Spotlight, 6V	pkg(2)	5.99
186-3279	Valve Base 16V Clear	pkg(2)	5.99
186-3337	Flat Top 19V Red	pkg(4)	6.99
186-3338	Replacement Bulb for Marklin #60008	pkg(4)	6.49
186-3344	14V Fleischmann Bulb	pkg(4)	5.49
186-3345	14V Trix Bulb	pkg(4)	5.49
186-3348	Mini Bayonet Bulb, 14V	each	1.99

FESTOON BULB

Candle Bulb, Amber
186-3276 pkg(4) 6.49
fits socket size E5.5, 19v 65 mA
186-3250	Frosted 16V, 30 mA	pkg(2)	6.49
186-3277	Candle Bulb, Clear fits socket size E5.5., 19V, 65mA	pkg(4)	5.99

Reflector Bulb, Clear
186-3278 pkg(2) 8.49
80 mA, 1 watt, approx total length 3/4", 16V

19v TUBULAR BULB

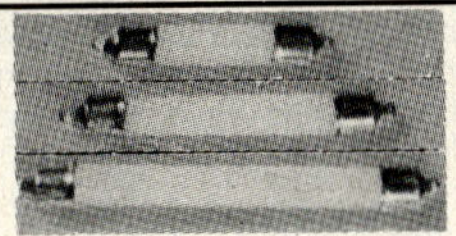
186-3281	22mm	pkg(2)	4.99
186-3282	32mm	pkg(2)	4.99
186-3283	42mm	pkg(2)	6.49

PUSH-IN BULB

186-3344	Clear for Fleischmann, 14V 50 mA	pkg(4)	5.49
186-3345	Clear for Trix, 14V, 50 mA	pkg(4)	5.49
186-3340	Clear for Marklin, 19V, 50mA	pkg(4)	4.49
186-3341	Red for Marklin, 19V, 50mA	pkg(4)	4.99
186-3342	Green for Marklin, 19V, 50mA	pkg(4)	4.99

3343   3251
186-3343	Clear Marklin, new pattern w/locating lugs; 19V, 50mA	pkg(4)	5.49
186-3251	Clear 3 x 2.55, 16V, 30 mA	pkg(2)	6.49

THREAD SPHERICAL BULB

FITS E5.5 SIZE SOCKETS

186-3275	19V, 50mA Clear	pkg(4)	4.49
186-3315	1.5V Clear, 100 mA, 8mm	pkg(4)	4.99
186-3316	3.5V Clear, 200 mA, 8mm	pkg(4)	4.99
186-3318	14V Clear, 50 mA, 8mm	pkg(4)	4.49
186-3319	19V Clear, 50 mA, 8mm	pkg(4)	3.99
186-3322	19V Green, 50 mA, 8mm	pkg(4)	4.99
186-3325	19V Red, 50 mA, 8mm	pkg(4)	4.99
186-3300	1.5V Clear, 100 mA, 5mm	pkg(4)	4.99
186-3301	3.5V Clear, 200 mA, 5mm	pkg(4)	4.99
186-3302	6V Clear, 100 mA, 5mm	pkg(4)	4.99

S-O-B   NEW

186-48401	KOF II DB Orange DC	264.99
186-48501	KOF II DB Orange AC	376.99

THREAD SPHERICAL BULB

(continued)
186-3303	14V Clear, 50 mA, 5mm	pkg(4)	4.49
186-3304	19V Clear, 60 mA, 5mm	pkg(4)	4.49
186-3307	19V Green, 50 mA, 5mm	pkg(4)	4.49
186-3310	19V Red, 50 mA, 5mm	pkg(4)	4.99
186-3311	19V Yellow, 60 mA, 5mm	pkg(4)	4.99

FITS E10 SIZE SOCKETS

186-3330	3.5V Clear, 200 mA	pkg(4)	4.49
186-3331	19V Clear, 100 mA	pkg(4)	5.99
186-3332	3.5V Red, 200 mA	pkg(4)	5.49
186-3333	19V Red, 100 mA	pkg(4)	6.99
186-3334	3.5V Green, 200 mA	pkg(4)	5.49
186-3335	19V Green, 100 mA	pkg(4)	6.99

BULB ACCESSORIES

3400   3404
186-3400	Building Light Plastic, w/brass socket (male) and 16" brown and yellow leads 16V; 2 (female) plastic plugs for simple hook up.	pkg(4)	5.99
186-3404	Plug-In Light For building illumination. E5.5 socket with bulb and wire. 14-19v.	pkg(2)	5.49

3420   3421   3422   3423
186-3420	Metal Plain Screw Base Size E5.5, insulated socket.	pkg(20)	6.49
186-3421	Screw Base w/1 connector Size E5.5	pkg(10)	6.49
186-3422	Screw Metal Base w/2 connectors Size E5.5	pkg(10)	7.49
186-3423	Recessed Base w/Bracket Size E5.5	pkg(10)	11.99

(not illustrated)
186-3424	E5 Screw Base, Raised	pkg(10)	10.49
186-3433	E10 Screw Base, Raised	pkg(10)	9.49

BRAWA

Imported from Germany by WALTHERS

Brawa offers a comprehensive line of electrical accessories, suitable for use with all model railroad systems.

WIRE

Solid strand copper wire with PVC insulation. Max load 6A; length, 11 yards per coil, approx diameter, .048

33' Roll
1.49 each

Dealers: MUST order Dealer Pack of 10.

186-3100	Purple	pkg(33')	1.49
186-3101	Yellow	pkg(33')	1.49
186-3102	Red	pkg(33')	1.49
186-3103	Green	pkg(33')	1.49
186-3104	Brown	pkg(33')	1.49
186-3105	Blue	pkg(33')	1.49
186-3107	Gray	pkg(33')	1.49
186-3108	Black	pkg(33')	1.49
186-3109	White	pkg(33')	1.49
186-3201	Yellow	pkg(80')	4.49
186-3202	Red	pkg(80')	4.49
186-3203	Green	pkg(80')	4.49
186-3204	Brown	pkg(80')	4.49
186-3205	Blue	pkg(80')	4.49
186-3207	Gray	pkg(80')	4.49
186-3208	Black	pkg(33')	4.49
186-3209	White	pkg(33')	4.49
186-3110	Purple	pkg(328')	14.49
186-3111	Yellow	pkg(328')	14.49
186-3112	Red	pkg(328')	14.49
186-3113	Green	pkg(328')	14.49
186-3114	Brown	pkg(328')	14.49
186-3115	Blue	pkg(328')	14.49
186-3117	Gray	pkg(328')	14.49
186-3118	Black	pkg(328')	14.49
186-3119	White	pkg(328')	14.49
186-3197	Brown	pkg(33')	6.99
186-3198	Brown	pkg(130')	61.99

Fine stranded copper wire, approx .036 diameter. Maximum load 2.5A.

186-3160	Purple	pkg(33')	1.49
186-3161	Yellow	pkg(33')	1.49
186-3162	Red	pkg(33')	1.49
186-3163	Green	pkg(33')	1.49
186-3164	Brown	pkg(33')	1.49
186-3165	Blue	pkg(33')	1.49
186-3168	Black	pkg(33')	1.49
186-3222	Red	pkg(131')	15.99
186-3228	Black	pkg(131')	15.99

#16 stranded wire in assorted colors.

186-3236	Yellow	pkg(33')	6.99
186-3237	Red	pkg(33')	6.99
186-3238	Black	pkg(33')	6.99

Teflon insulated #30 solid core wire.

186-3191	Black	pkg(33')	5.99

SINGLE CONDUCTOR EXTRA-FLEXIBLE WIRE

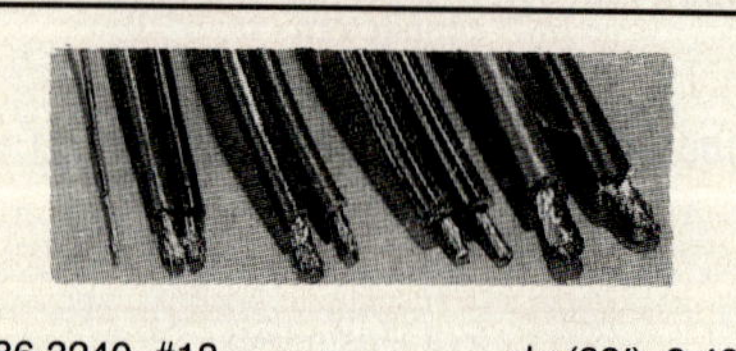

186-3240	#18	pkg(33')	3.49
186-3242	#17	pkg(10')	4.49
186-3244	#16	pkg(10')	5.49
186-3246	#15	pkg(10')	5.99
186-3248	#12	pkg(10')	8.49

MULTI—CONDUCTOR FLAT CABLE HOOK-UP WIRE

#24 solid copper wires in assorted colors, maximum load, 6A per wire.

186-3170	Brown/Yellow	pkg(16')	1.99
186-3171	Brown/Yellow	pkg(164')	17.49
186-3172	Blue/Ylw/Blue for use with Marklin	pkg(16')	2.99
186-3173	Blue/Ylw/Blue for use with Marklin	pkg(164')	28.49
186-3174	Ylw/Red/Blue for use with Marklin	pkg(16')	2.99
286-3175	Yellow/Red/Blue for use with Marklin	pkg(164')	28.49
186-3176	Gray/Violet/Blue for use with Arnold	pkg(16')	2.99
186-3177	Gray/Violet/Blue for use with Arnold	pkg(164')	28.49
186-3182	Blue/Ylw/Red/Grn	pkg(16')	3.99
186-3184	Five Conductor	pkg(16')	4.99
186-3186	Blue/Brown/Ylw/ Red/Green/Black	pkg(16')	8.99
186-3188	Ylw/Brown/Red/ Green/Blue/Gray/Black/White	pkg(16')	8.99
186-3189	Same as 3188	pkg(164')	87.99
186-3192	Coil Control Cable	pkg(16')	11.99

Round sheath contains 10 wires in various colors

186-3139	#24 2 Conductor, white	pkg(164')	13.49
186-3193	#24 10 Cond, white	pkg(164')	117.49
186-3230	#18 2 Conductor, orange/white	pkg(65')	19.49
186-3235	#18 3 Conductor, yellow/white/green	pkg(65')	28.49

Dealers: MUST order Dealer Pack of 10 (3122, 3123, 3128, 3129).

186-3122	#24 2 Cond, red	pkg(16')	1.49
186-3123	#24 2 Conductor, green	pkg(16')	1.49
186-3128	#24 2 Conductor, black	pkg(16')	1.49
186-3129	#24 2 Conductor, white	pkg(16')	1.49

WIRE ACCESSORIES

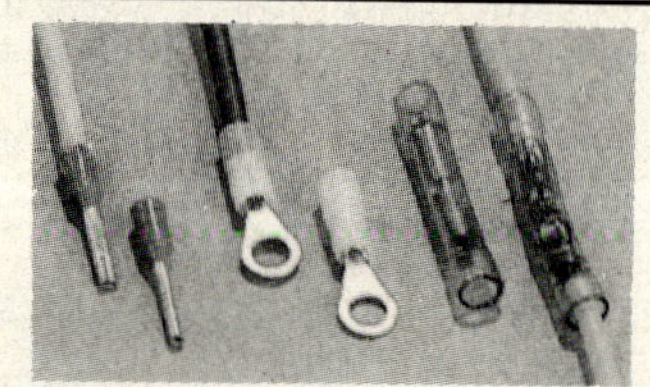

186-3095	Terminal Plugs	pkg(50)	9.99
186-3096	Terminal Eyes	pkg(10)	5.49
186-3097	Quick Connectors	pkg(10)	5.49

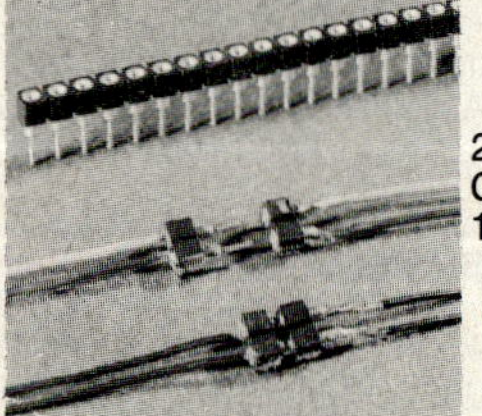

20 Pin Miniature Connector
186-3091   10.49

186-3914   Terminal Strip, 30 Position   7.99

WIRE ACCESSORIES

(continued)

(not illustrated)

186-3913	Resistor 1000 ohm	pkg(10)	2.49
186-3211	Stand for Spooled Wire		28.99
186-3212	Wire Assortment w/Stand		68.99

Soldering Plates 10 Terminal 186-3915		7.49
Soldering Plates 20 Terminal 186-3916		12.99

MODELTRONICS

LIGHTING ACCESSORIES FOR MODEL LOCOS

CONSTANT BRIGHTNESS KITS

510-6001	Light/Speed Reducer	11.95

Will slow locos not equipped with Modeltronics sound system and provide constant lighting.

SUB-MINI CONNECTOR GOLD PLATED

510-1339	One Pin	5.95
510-1340	Two Pin	6.95
510-1341	Three Pin	7.95
510-1342	Four Pin	8.95
510-1343	Six Pin	9.95

BATTERY HOLDER

510-1350	Small	2.95
510-1351	Large	2.95

FLEXIBLE WIRE- 10' LENGTH

510-3020	28 Gauge	**NEW** (black)	1.75
510-3022	30 Gauge	(black)	1.75
510-3024	30 Gauge	(red)	1.75
510-3002	Reversing, (HO/N) motor current MAX 1.0 amp		9.95
510-3003	Reversing, (HO/O) motor current MAX 3.0 amp		15.98
510-3004	Non-Reversing, (HO/N) motor current MAX 1.0 amp		7.95
510-3005	Non Reversing, (HO/O) motor current MAX 3.0 amp		13.98
510-3006	Non-Reversing, (HO/O) motor current MAX 2.0 amp		11.95

MISCELLANEOUS   **NEW**

510-3015	Solder kit	4.95

Circuitron
Electronics for Model Railroads

CIRCUITRON products constructed on printed circuit boards are designed to mount by snapping them into a section of CIRCUITRON's PCMT (Printed Circuit Mounting Track). Solid State integrated circuit technology. Connections to any CIRCUITRON printed circuit board can be made using .110″ female solderless connectors or by soldering the leads directly to the terminals on the board. Complete instructions are included. One year limited warranty.

STROBE FLASHERS

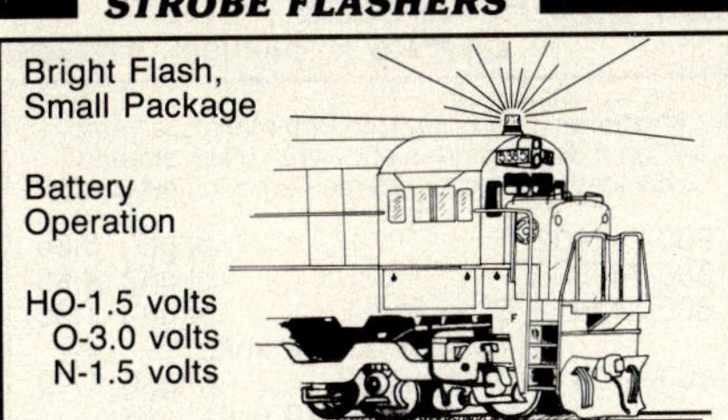

Bright Flash, Small Package

Battery Operation

HO-1.5 volts
O-3.0 volts
N-1.5 volts

Long battery life, 6 months continuous from one AA Alkaline Cell. Will operate off hearing aid or watch cell. 1/2″ x 1/2″ x 3/4″ high

800-1001	HO Scale, Orange LED	12.95
800-1002	HO Scale, Red LED	12.95
800-1003	HO Scale, Yellow LED	12.95
800-1011	O Scale, Orange LED	12.95
800-1012	O Scale, Red LED	12.95
800-1013	O Scale, Yellow LED	12.95
800-1021	N Scale Orange LED	12.95
800-1022	N Scale, Red LED	12.95
800-1023	N Scale, Yellow LED	12.95

FLA AMTRAK STYLE STROBE FLASHER

The FLA White Strobe Flasher duplicates the action of twin Xenon strobes found on many of the current Amtrak locos. The FLA is designed for mounting inside HO Scale dummy locos and uses 9v transistor type battery to provide approximately 100 hours of flashing. Twin lamps flash brightly about once a second.

800-1100	FLA Amtrak Style White Strobe Flasher, Twin Lamp	18.95
800-9341	Amtrak Strobe Lampset Replacement, 0.1″ dia, lamp	pkg(2) 5.95

ML-1 MARS LIGHT

The ML-1 Mars Light provides realistic simulation of the gyrating beacon seen on many locos. Utilizing a special design, high intensity, lens end, dual-filament lamp, the ML-1 can be used in most HO locos. Uses 2.4-3.0 volt DC input obtained from batteries 800-2002 TP-2 or the 800-2003 TP-3 Track Power Adapter.

800-1500	ML-1 Mars Light	16.95
800-9340	Replacement Dual Filament Lamp, 3v	ea 2.95

ML-2 MARS LIGHT

The ML-2 alternately flashes two 1.7mm diameter, high intensity, lens-end lamps (included) at a prototypical speed. The lamps may be mounted in dual headlight housings, or side by side in larger headlight openings. The ML-2 requires a 2.4 - 3.0 volt DC input which can be provided by batteries, 800-2002 TP-2 or 800-2003 TP-3 Track Power Adapters.

800-1502		14.95

DITCH LIGHTS

The DL-1 alternately flashes two 1.7mm diameter, high intensity, lens-end lamps (included) at a slow rate to simulate the pilot mounted safety lamps currently in use on most railroads. With the addition of an optional DPST or DPDT switch, the DL-1 circuit can be easily bypassed to turn the ditch lights continuously on. The DL-1 requires a 2.4 - 3.0 volt DC input which can be supplied by batteries, 800-2002 TP-2 or 800-2003 Track Power Adapters.

800-1400	DL-1 Oscillating Ditch Lights	14.95
800-9123	Submini Slide Switch, DPDT	(2) 2.95

BATTERY HOLDERS

For use with HO and O Scale Strobe Flashers.

800-9611	AA Battery Holder	2.00
	1 cell, 1.5 volts	
800-9612	AA Battery Holder	2.00
	2 cell, 3.0 volts	

HIDDEN ACCESSORY SWITCH

To provide a completely hidden switch for controlling Strobe Flashers, marker lights or other rolling stock electrical accessories. Reed Switch Kits are turned on and off simply by bringing an external magnet up to the outside of the locomotive or car body. No external projections to detract from the appearance of the model. Kits contain a subminiature reed switch and a tiny bias magnet.

800-9101	RS-1 Reed Switch Kit	4.95
	requires adjustment before mounting	
800-9102	RS-2 Reed Switch Kit	6.95
	requires no adjustment	
800-9100	External Magnet for actuating Reed Switches	1.50
800-9103	Sub-miniature Slide switches SPDT	pkg(2) 2.95

CF-1 CABOOSE FLASHER

Single rear facing bulb slowly flashes on and off to comply with current regulations requiring a red lamp at rear of train. Includes CF-1 circuit board, subminiature LED and battery clip. A single 9 volt battery will provide about 100 hours of flashing.

800-1200	CF-1	(red) 12.95
800-1201	CF-1	(yellow) 12.95

EOT / FRED FLASHERS ■ NEW

The EOT flasher includes a scale size flasher housing which is easily mounted above the coupler on any freight car. The high-intensity LED chip contained in the housing projects a bright, slowly flashing light rearward to protect the end of the train. The EOT requires a 3 volt input which is most easily obtained from a pair of small batteries, although the TP-1 Track Power Adapter, 800-2001, could be used if the car was equipped with track power pickups.

800-1302	EOT Flasher with Red Light	12.95
800-1303	EOT Flasher w/Yellow Lights	12.95

EMERGENCY FLASHER & POWER SUPPLY

The EF-1 Emergency Flasher is a low-cost circuit designed to alternately flash two Light Emitting Diodes at a constant rate. Available with either .080″ LEDs or .120″ LEDs in either red or yellow. Add action to emergency vehicles, barricades, signs, towers, etc. Simple to install. Powered by a 9 volt battery, or by using a PS-3.

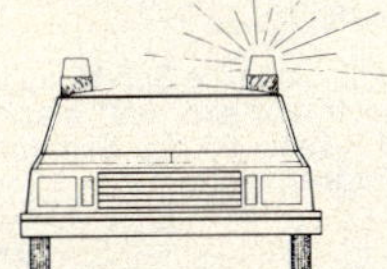

800-3002	EF-1 Emergency Flasher, .120 Red LEDs	14.95
800-3003	EF-1 Emergency Flasher .120 Yellow LEDs	14.95

EMERGENCY FLASHERS & POWER SUPPLY (continued)

800-3022	EF-1 Emergency Flasher, .080 Red LEDs	14.95
800-3023	EF-1 Emergency Flasher, .080 Yellow LEDs	14.95

The PS-3 Power Supply designed to power the EF-1 Emergency Flasher in situations where battery operation is undesirable. Accepts AC or DC input of 10 to 18 volts and converts it to 9 volts DC.

800-5304	PS-3 Emergency Flasher— Power Supply	10.95

TL-1 TRAFFIC LIGHT CONTROLLER

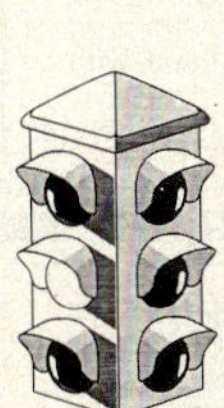

The TL-1 provides the timing circuitry to accurately reproduce the standard four step traffic light sequence. The outputs will drive LED or incandescent lamp signals (not included). If LED signals are used, they must be common anode design. All four time periods are individually adjustable. The TL-1 requires a 10-18 volt AC or DC input. Standard red, yellow and green outputs are provided for each direction (6 total) and each can drive a 250 ma. maximum load. Adaptable for all scales.

800-5820	TL-1 Traffic Light Controller	24.95

PL-8, PL-12 PROGRESSIVE LAMP CIRCUITS

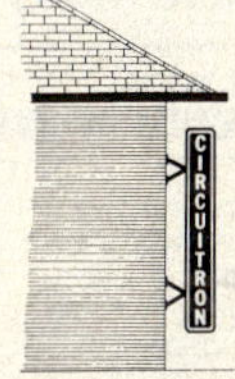

The PL-8 and PL-12 circuits are used for moving signboard applications. The sequence for both circuits is the same, only the maximum number of letters (and thus lamps) is different. Either circuit will light signs with fewer than the maximum letters without modification. The Progressive Lamp sequence lights each lamp in succession with all previous lamps remaining on until all lamps are lit. The step speed of the succession is adjustable. All lamps then remain on for a time period (adjustable). Then all the lamps go out for a time period (adjustable). Finally, all the lamps come on together for a short time (adjustable) and then all go out. The sequence then repeats. The PL-8 and PL-12 include 8 and 12 lamps respectively (12-18 volts, 3 mm dia.) but other size and voltage lamps m ay be substituted for specific application. Construction of the actual sign will depend upon application and is left to the modeler. The PL-8 and PL-12 require a 12 volt AC or DC supply for proper operation. Adaptable for HO and larger scales.

800-5808	PL-8 Progressive Lamp Circuit	44.95
800-5812	PL-12 Progressive Lamp Circuit	54.95

TRACK POWER ADAPTERS

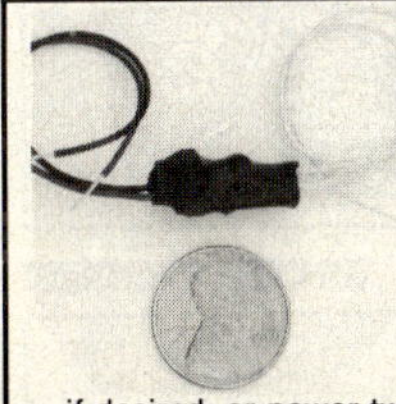

This miniature voltage regulator can power any CIRCUITRON Strobe Flasher from track power. Can be used as a constant lighting kit in unpowered rolling stock. Sufficient to power any number of CIRCUITRON Strobe Flashers if desired, or power two 1.5 volt grain of wheat or rice lamps connected in series. Bi-directional, output will be present if train is moving forward or backward. May be used with AC track power, although slightly irregular flashing may occur. The TP-1 measures 0.3″ x 0.3″ x 0.8″.

800-2001	TP-1 Track Power Adapter	8.95

CIRCUITRON
Electronics for Model Railroads

CIRCUITRON products constructed on printed circuit boards are designed to mount by snapping them into a section of CIRCUITRON's PCMT (Printed Circuit Mounting Track). Solid State integrated circuit technology. Connections to any CIRCUITRON printed circuit board can be made using .110" female solderless connectors or by soldering the leads directly to the terminals on the board. Complete instructions are included. One year limited warranty.

TRACK POWER ADAPTERS (continued)

TP-3 Track Power Adapter has adjustable output (1.5 or 3.0v DC). Ideal for constant lighting source In unpowered rolling stock. No ballast lamps or motors required. Will power Mars Flasher in models driven by low current can motors. Works with all forms of track power. Max current output is 1/2 amp.

800-2003 TP-3 Track Power Adapter 14.95

The TP-2 will power the ML-1 Mars Light and Strobe Flashers and also has outputs that will provide directional constant lighting. Able to fit most HO locos, the TP-2 can be used with motors drawing up to 1 amp.

800-2002 TP-2 Track Power Adapter 9.95

SQ-8 SEQUENCING STROBE

The SQ-8 provides a rapid sequencing of 8 high intensity white strobe lamps (included). When the lamps are arranged in a linear fashion, the effect is one of a light sweep from one end to the other. This type of lighting effect is commonly used near airports on the approach towers but can also be very effective on signs and other applications. Both the sweep speed and the delay between sweeps are independently adjustable. The SQ-8 requires a 10-18 volt AC or DC input. For use with HO and larger scales.

800-5838 SQ-8 Sequencing Strobe 39.95

AW-1, AW-2 ARC WELDER CIRCUITS

The CIRCUITRON Arc Welder Circuits utilize 2 lamps, one yellow and one blue, along with a circuit that provides a random flickering effect of the lamps. The result is a very convincing representation of an arc welder in operation.

The AW-1 includes micro-bulbs and is designed for direct viewing in all scales. A small wisp of cotton placed over the lamps will serve to diffuse the light and produce a very realistic smoke effect.

The AW-2 includes larger lamps and is designed to illuminate a window in from a structure. If the window is frosted to represent years of grime, the flickering effect is very realistic. The AW-1 and AW-2 require a 10-18 volt AC or DC input for proper operation. Adaptable for all scales.

800-5841 AW-1 Arc Welder Circuit 16.95
800-5842 AW-2 Arc Welder Circuit 16.95

CATALOG

Catalog & Application Book
800-9999
4.00

ACCESSORIES

800-9350	3 amp Diode	pkg(2)	1.50
800-9351	1 amp Diode	pkg(6)	1.50

Opto-Sensors (.185" diameter). For use with all CIRCUITRON Detection Circuits.

800-9201	1 Opto-Sensor	each	3.95
800-9202	2 Opto-Sensors	pkg(2)	7.50
800-9206	6 Opto-Sensors	pkg(6)	19.95

SUB-MINIATURE LAMPS

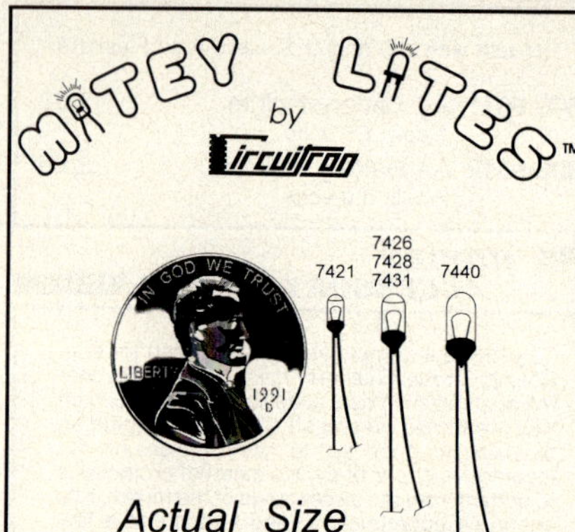

Sub-Micro, 0.75mm diameter axial lead. 1.5 volts, 18 ma.w/1" bare wire leads. Use for marker lights, number boards, step lights, etc.

800-740002	pkg(2)	3.95
800-740006	pkg(6)	9.95
800-740012	pkg(12)	16.95
800-940012	Dropping resistor pkg(10) for 12 volts	1.95
800-940016	Dropping resistor pkg(10) for 16 volts	1.95

Standard output, Long life Micro-lamp. 1.40mm diameter lens end, w/ 8" black stranded wires. 1.5 volts, 13 ma.

800-741102	pkg(2)	3.50
800-741106	pkg(6)	7.75
800-741112	pkg(12)	12.95
800-741125	pkg(25)	24.95
800-941112	Dropping pkg(10) Resistor for 12 volts	1.95
800-941116	Dropping pkg(10) Resistor for 16 volts	1.95

High output, long life Micro-Lamp. 1.40mm diameter lens end, w/8" black stranded wire leads. 1.5 volts, 60 ma. Very bright! Use for headlights, etc.

800-741602	pkg(2)	4.95
800-741606	pkg(6)	11.95
800-741612	pkg(12)	16.95
800-941612	Dropping pkg(6) Resistor for 12 volts	1.95
800-941616	Dropping pkg(6) Resistor for 16 volts	1.95

Very high output, long life Micro-Lamp. 1.70mm diameter lens end, w/8" black stranded wire leads. 1.5 volts, 75 ma. Extremely bright! Ideal for headlights, mars lights, or ditch lights.

800-742102	pkg(2)	4.95
800-742106	pkg(6)	11.95
800-942112	Dropping pkg(4) Resistor for 12 volts	1.95
800-942116	Dropping pkg(4) Resistor for 16 volts	1.95

Very high output, long life Sub-Miniature Lamp. 2.4mm diameter lens end, w/8" black stranded wire leads. 1.5 volts, 90 ma. Extremely bright! Use for headlights, etc.

800-742602	pkg(2)	3.95
800-742606	pkg(6)	9.95
800-942612	Dropping pkg(4) Resistor for 12 volts	1.95
800-942616	Dropping pkg(4) Resistor for 16 volts	1.95

SUB-MINIATURE LAMPS (continued)

Maximum output, long life Sub-Miniature Lamp. 2.4mm diameter lens end, w/8" black stranded wire leads. 3.0 volts, 120 ma. Our brightest lamp!

800-742802	pkg(2)	3.95
800-742806	pkg(6)	9.95
800-942812	Dropping pkg(4) Resistor for 12 volts	1.95
800-942816	Dropping pkg(4) Resistor for 16 volts	1.95

Very high output, long life Sub-Miniature Lamp. 2.4mm diameter lens end, w/8" black stranded wire leads. 12 - 14 volts, 50 ma. Ideal for headlights in locomotives not equipped with constant lighting and for structure lighting.

800-743102	pkg(2)	3.95
800-743106	pkg(6)	9.95

General purpose, long life Miniature Lamp. 3.0mm diameter lens end, w/8" stranded wire leads. 14 - 16 volts, 30 ma. Use for equipment and structure lighting.

800-744006	pkg(6)	3.95
800-744012	pkg(12)	5.95
800-744025	pkg(25)	10.95

LIGHT EMITTING DIODES

(Super Bright)

800-9301	Orange	.125" dia	pkg(2)	2.95
800-9302	Red	.125" dia	pkg(2)	2.95
800-9303	Yellow	.125" dia	pkg(2)	2.95
800-9304	Green	.125" dia	pkg(2)	2.95
800-9306	Red/ Green, Bi-Color	.125" dia	ea	2.95
800-9311	Orange	.200" dia	pkg(2)	2.95
800-9312	Red	.200" dia	pkg(2)	2.95
800-9313	Yellow	.200" dia	pkg(2)	2.95
800-9314	Green	.200" dia	pkg(2)	2.95
800-9316	Red/ Green, Bi-Color	.200" dia	ea	2.95
800-9321	Orn	.075" dia	pkg(2)	2.95
800-9322	Red	.075" dia	pkg(2)	2.95
800-9323	Yellow	.075" dia	pkg(2)	2.95
800-9324	Grn	.075" dia	pkg(2)	2.95

ADJUSTABLE CONVERTER AND REGULATOR

A self-contained AC to DC converter with an adjustable voltage regulated output. The output voltage can be adjusted anywhere between 1.25 and 12.00 volts DC. Maximum continuous current output of the PS-2A is in excess of one amp. The PS-2A is ideal for powering any low current DC accessories including 1.5 volt micro-lamps. The AC or unfiltered DC input to the PS-2A should be about 5-6 volts higher than the desired regulated output voltage to allow maximum current output. The input voltage may be as high as 22 volts, but this may result in reduced current available at the output, particularly at lower voltage settings.

800-5305 PS-2A 24.95

SOLDERLESS CONNECTORS

Female .110" Solderless Connectors for all Circuitron printed circuit boards.

800-9602	Non-Insulated	pkg(6)	2.50
800-9603	Insulated	pkg(6)	2.50

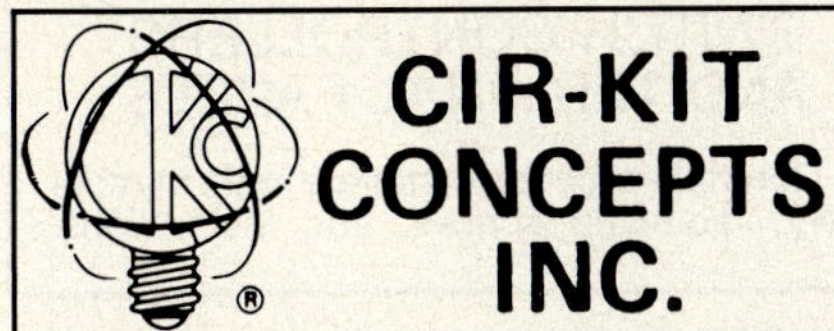

CIR-KIT CONCEPTS INC.

The Cir-Kit "concept" of electrical interconnection provides one of the most flexible means of circuit wiring to be found anywhere in model railroading. The Cir-Kit wiring system uses flat, pressure-sensitive adhesive backed Mylar tapewire for low voltage wiring. The tape is only .005" thick, and can be painted. The tape can be used throughout the layout, but is most useful where "invisible" wiring is desired.

Connections are pinned together (with brads) and do not require soldering.

The system includes sockets and adapters for joining the tapewire to conventional wiring systems, tools and complete instructions for installation.

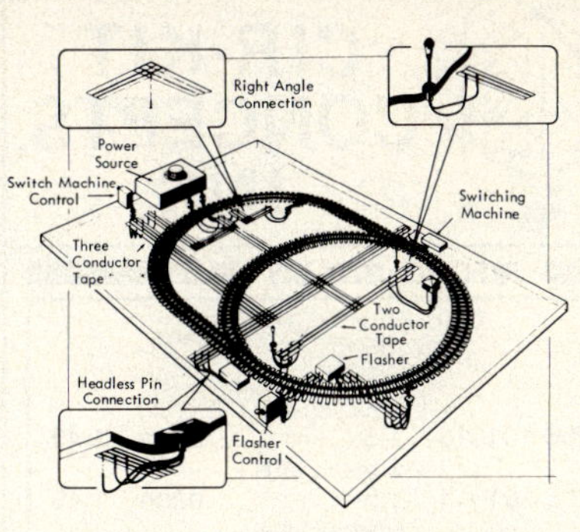

BASIC WIRING KIT

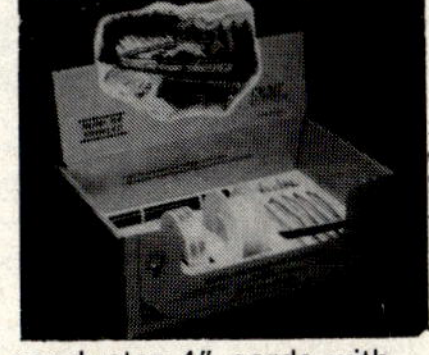

Contains everything required to get started. A 15' roll of two-conductor tape, a 10' roll of three-conductor tape, (60) 1/8" brass brads, (36) headless pins, (22) wire sockets, (5) two-conductor 4" cords with sockets, map tack, pilot hole punch, instruction book, GOW bulb and test probe for trouble shooting.

206-1040 Basic Wiring Kit   31.95

TAPEWIRE

Tapewire is an adhesive-backed Mylar tape containing electrical conductors. The tape is .005" thick by 5/8" wide and can be painted. It can be run under grass mats or behind wallpaper. Tapewire can be used throughout the layout, but is most useful where "invisible" wiring is desired. Connections are pinned together (with brads) and do not require soldering.

206-1001   2 Conductor pkg(15' roll)   7.95
206-1017   2 Conductor pkg(50' roll) 23.95
206-10291 3 Conductor pkg(50' roll) 27.95
206-10292 3 Conductor pkg(10' roll)   6.98

BRASS BRADS AND HEADLESS PINS

Brass brads and headless pins are used for connecting tapewire and conventional wiring systems. No soldering is required.

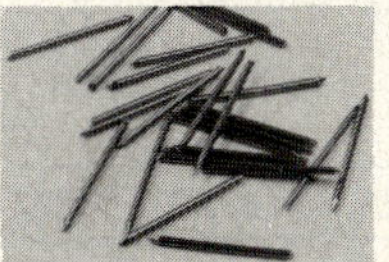
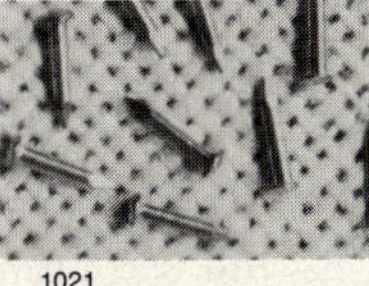

206-1021   1/8" Brass Brads pkg(300) 4.98
206-10211 1/8" Brass Brads pkg(60)   1.49
206-1031   Headless Pins   pkg(36)   .69

CORD W/WIRE SOCKET

A four inch length of conductor cord with pin sockets on one end. For connecting tape to conventional wiring systems.

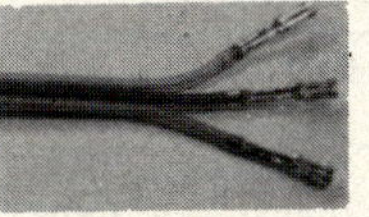

206-10282 Two Conductor Cord   ea   .99
206-10283 Three Conductor Cord ea 1.19

PILOT HOLE PUNCH

For making small holes for brass brads. Eliminates the risk of making holes that are too large.

206-10141 Pilot Hole Punch   each 2.29
206-10143 Pilot Hole Punch   pkg(3) .98
           Needles

SOCKETS

One end is crimped onto conventional wire. The other end may be plugged into headless pins and pinned to tapewire systems.

206-1032   Wire Sockets   pkg(22) 3.98
206-10321 Wire Sockets   pkg(60) 8.98

12V PLUG IN TRANSFORMER

Provides AC power for lights. Not for running trains. Will handle up to 23 16v bulbs. 10 watt rating. Built-in circuit breaker.

12-Volt Plug In
Lighting Transformer
206-10090
18.95

TRANSFORMER LEAD-IN

For connecting transformer to tapewire system. Plug on one end mates with Junction Splice (206-1007). Opposite (spade lug) ends of 6' lead connect to transformer terminals.

Transformer Lead-In Wire
206-1008   4.75

JUNCTION SPLICE

For connecting tapewire system to transformer lead-in. Use with 206-1008.

Junction Splice
206-1007   each 2.98

ADAPTER CORD

Plug on one end accepts tape conductors. Opposite (stripped) ends may be connected to screw terminals, track, or conventional wiring.

206-10281 18" Long Adapter Cord   1.98

MINIATURE WIRE

For connections where flat tape is not practical.

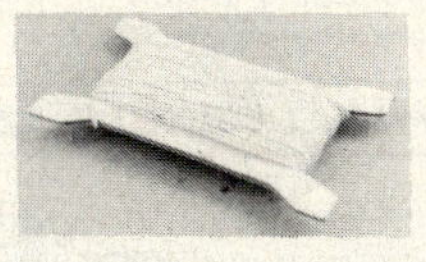

206-203   2 Conductor Hookup pkg(25') 2.98
           Very fine, stranded, #34 gauge

206-2032   1 Conductor   1.98
           #32 gauge w/50' shank, white

SWITCH

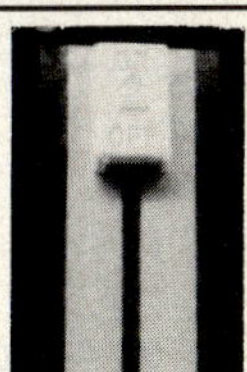

SPDT, for turning lights and accessories on and off. Only 1/4" x 7/16" in size. For tape or conventional wiring systems. Instructions included. Pound in construction.

206-1011   Miniature Slide   each 3.69
           Switch
206-10481 Small Slide Switch   1.98
206-1048   In-Line Switch   2.29

IN-LINE FUSE HOLDER

Fuse holder and wire sockets for in-line connection. Fuse not included.

206-1026   In-Line Fuse Holder   each 1.75

GRAIN-OF-WHEAT BULBS

Bulb consumes between 50 and 60 milliamps at 12 volts. Outside diameter approximately 1/8".

12v Clear
w/8" black wire
206-10101   each 1.15

206-10102   16v Clear   ea 1.15
            w/8" black wire
206-101018 3v w/8" white wire   1.15
206-101021 12v w/12" brown wire   1.20
206-101022 12v w/18" brown wire   1.25

GRAIN-OF-RICE BULBS

206-10106   12v Clear w/black wire ea 1.39
206-10107   12v Clear w/white wire ea 1.39
206-10108   16v Clear w/black wire ea 1.39
206-10109   16v Clear w/white wire ea 1.39
206-101020 12v w/12" brown wire   1.25
206-101023 12v w/8" brown wire   1.20
            (By Special Order Only.)

SWIVEL SPOTLIGHT

Miniature swivel spotlight features top mounted 360 degree rotation and 180 degree side-to-side movement. Large size bulb is a highly focused lens for light concentration and will burn for 5000 plus hours. Bulb snaps in and works on a 12-volt system. 7/8" long, 3/8" diameter.

206-101010 Swivel Spotlight Bulb   2.98

CIR-KIT CONCEPTS, INC.

MICRO BULBS

206-101013	1.5v, w/black wire	each	1.49
206-101014	1.5v, w/white wire	each	1.49
206-101015	1.5v, w/wire terminals	each	1.49
206-1010130	1.5v w/black wire	pkg(100)	126.65

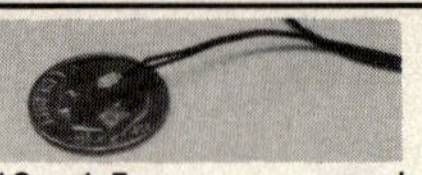

206-1100 Dropping Resistor pkg(3) .98
for Micro Bulbs

Used to directly connect 1.5v micro bulbs to a 12v source. A resistor must be connected to each bulb.

MISCELLANEOUS

206-10223	Brass Pins, #18	pkg(50)	1.59
206-1023	Hollow Eyelets, small	pkg(20)	.98
206-10231	Hollow Eyelets, small	pkg(110)	4.98
206-1049	2-Pole Terminal Block		1.98
206-10491	4-Pole Terminal Block		2.49
	(By Special Order Only.)		
206-10492	6-Pole Terminal Block		2.98
206-1045	#0 Wood Screws	pkg(20)	1.79
206-865	Glowing Embers **NEW**		9.95

Works with any 12-volt system and requires no separate transormer. The orange-colored bulb is a replaceable screw-base type with a MH658 plug attached to the small gauge along with a 24" long power cord.

Installation Instruction Booklet
206-1039 1.95

Illustrated 22 page instruction booklet outlining all steps necessary for installing Cir-Kit Concepts electrical components. Explains how to use brads, make solderless connections, interconnect conventional and tape wiring systems, and how to test circuits. Included with Basic Wiring Kit 206-1040.

BASIC WIRING KIT **NEW**

Includes:
Transformer lead-in wire, junction splice, pilot hole punch and needles, 15" tapewire, test probe and 1/8" brass brads.

Basic Wiring Kit
206-105 23.95

DIMMER **NEW**

With this all-electric, variable controller any lamp up to 300 watts may be dimmed or the speed regulated for a small power tool up to 2.5 amps.

206-802 Dimmer Extension Cord 24.95

LIGHTED CONTROLLERS

Will operate all switches and switch motors including Lionel and Atlas. Can be wired so light remains on after button is pressed. Each controller includes red and green bulbs, contact plate, pressure sensitive number sheet, mounting screws, and instructions.

105-444	Switch Control Panel w/mounting frame (surface mount)	ea	7.15
105-498	Switch Control panel (flush mounting)	ea	6.20
105-4995	GE Bulb 12-18V (blue)	ea	.70

FRAME - MOUNTED PANELS

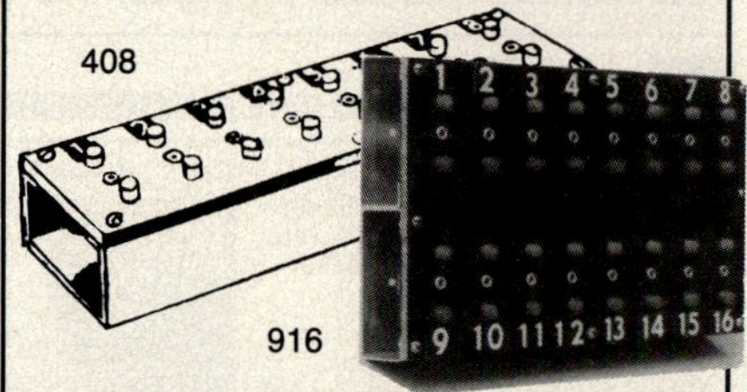

With polished aluminum mounting frame.

105-401	Operates 1 switch	4.20
105-402	Operates 2 switch	5.65
105-403	Operates 3 switch	7.15
105-404	Operates 4 switch	8.60
105-405	Operates 5 switch	9.50
105-406	Operates 6 switch	11.10
105-407	Operates 7 switch	12.55
105-408	Operates 8 switch	14.35
105-916	Operates 16 switch	27.20

FLUSH - MOUNTED PANELS

EXCLUSIVE FEATURE

All Acme switch controllers are equipped with crimp or solder terminals.

105-301	Operates 1 switch	3.50
105-302	Operates 2 switch	4.65
105-303	Operates 3 switch	6.05
105-304	Operates 4 switch	7.50
105-305	Operates 5 switch	8.60
105-306	Operates 6 switch	10.05
105-307	Operates 7 switch	11.45
105-308	Operates 8 switch	12.90
105-816	Operates 16 switch	23.70

TERMINAL PANELS

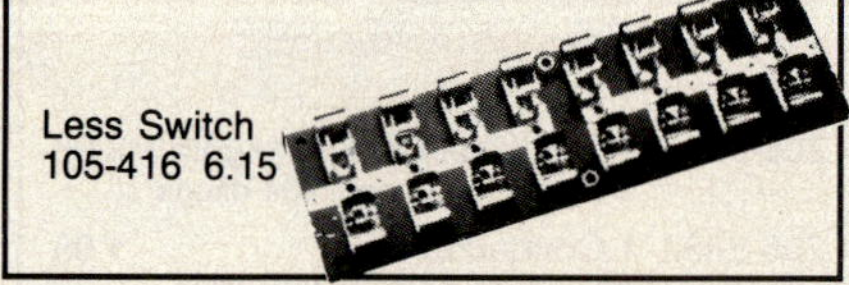

Less Switch
105-416 6.15

SWITCH CONTROLLERS AND TERMINAL PANELS

All Controllers come complete with number sheet, mounting screws, and instructions.

TERMINAL PANELS

With Switch
105-516 7.65

PUSH BUTTON UNITS

Can be installed in any position

Double Push Button Unit
105-439 1.39

DEALERS: MUST order dealer pack of 12.

Pacific Rail Products

MINIATURE ELECTRICAL CONNECTORS

544-401	One Pin	1.50
544-402	Two Pin	2.50
544-403	Three Pin	3.50
544-404	Four Pin	4.50

BULK PACKS

544-4016	One Pin	pkg(7)	9.00
544-4026	Two Pin	pkg(7)	15.00
544-4036	Three Pin	pkg(7)	21.00
544-4046	Four Pin	pkg(7)	27.00

MINIATURE WIRE

544-501	34 Gauge	1.95
544-502	32 Gauge	1.95
544-503	30 Gauge	1.95

HEAT SHRINK TUBING

544-510	3/32 Diameter	1.75
544-511	1/16 Diameter	1.50

MINIATURE SWITCHES

544-525	Subminiature SPDT	1.75
544-526	Miniature DPDT	1.75

BATTERY HOLDERS

544-528	1 Cell 1.5V AA Penlight	1.95
544-529	2 Cl 3V AA w/Wire Leads	1.95

9V "RADIO BATTERY" HOLDER

Formed Metal.

544-530	Horizontal Mount	1.50
544-531	Vertical Mount	1.50

MINI PANEL LAMPS & ACCESSORIES

544-541	10V w/Rd, Wht, Grn Lenses	2.50
544-545	Panel Lamp Set pkg(10)	11.95

Lamps only, use w/Lenses #546-548

LENSES

544-546	Red	pkg(5)	2.50
544-547	White	pkg(5)	2.50
544-548	Green	pkg(5)	2.50

FALLER

Imported from Germany and marketed by WALTHERS

- MOTORS
- FIRE SIRENS
- TRANSFORMERS
- BLINKERS
- LIGHTS
- CLIPS
- SWITCHES
- GEARS

ELECTRICAL ACCESSORIES

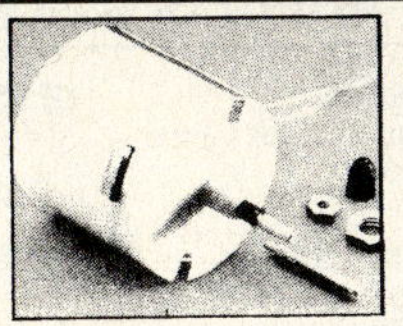

Synchronous Motor
272-629
ea 20.99
18 RPM, 16v AC, revolves clockwise or counter-clockwise.

Drive Gear
272-635 11.99
Momentary contact, turns 90°
For #147.

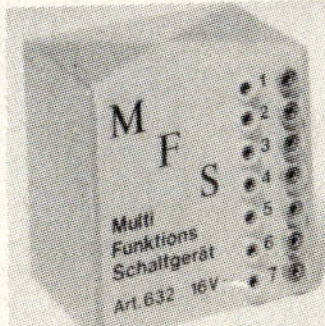

Multi-Function Switch Unit
272-632 35.99
NEW
Electro-mechanical for switching functions, one connection for permanent contact. Ready for operation with 12-16V AC.

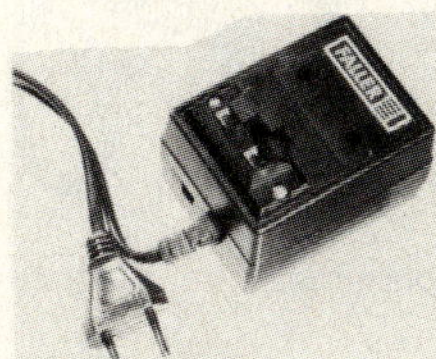

AC Transformer 16V 2A
272-641 67.99
NEW
For high output. Specially for operating fairground equipment, electrical articles and lighting.

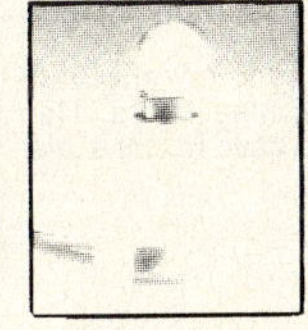

Motorized Blinker
272-631 ea 35.99
Pulses are used for rhythmic switching, blinkers or church bells.

Structure Light
272-670 ea 1.49
Set comes with lighting socket, bulb cable & plugs.

272-640 Welding Flash Module 34.49
16v AC, generates a bluish-white flickering light.

Plug Strip
272-686
3.49
Features 10 pairs of sockets.

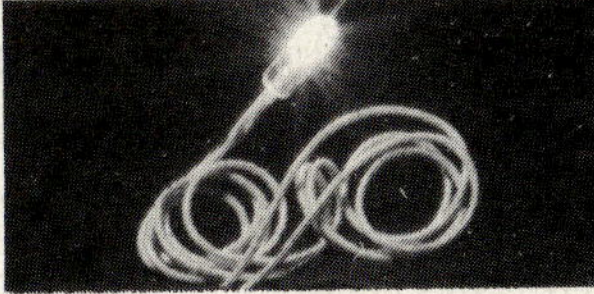

272-671 12-16V Grain of Wheat Bulb ea 2.99

ELECTRICAL ACCESSORIES (cont.)

272-687 Cable Clips pkg(10) 3.99

(not illustrated)

272-633 Vario-Light **NEW** 42.99
For illuminating .10m of flexible light fibres enclosed. Ready to plug-in for 12-16V AC.

272-634 Light Conductor Filament **NEW** 15.49
For #633. 10m of flexible light filament.

272-637 Electronic Fire Siren **NEW** 36.99
Ready for use for 12-16V DC or AC. Loudspeaker included.

CONSTANT LIGHTING KIT

Reversing headlight and back-up light. Constant light for number boards, cab lights, etc. Kit includes diodes and polarity board. Less light bulbs.

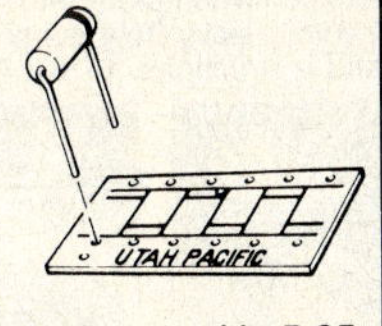

755-96 Loco kit 5.95

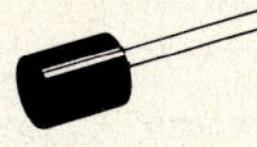

755-66 Non-Directional kit 4.00

TRAIN TRONICS

- FIBER OPTICS
- AUTOMOTIVES

SWITCHES

723-406 Reed Switch & Magnet 5.95
Provides momentary switch that is activated by magnets placed on bottom of train. Use to operate various track detection systems, controls and signals.

723-407 Pushbutton each 5.95
SPST - normally open, momentary, mounts in 5/16" hole. Kit contains 4 switches.

TRAIN TRONICS

CONSTANT LIGHT KITS

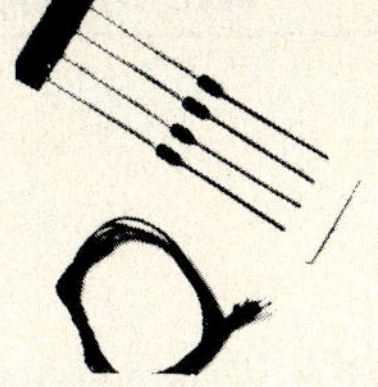

Installed in any HO or N Scale engine the headlight remains "on" even when engine is stopped. 102 contains 2 bulbs; may be used for cab light & 1 headlight or dual headlight engines.
102

723-101 Bulb Constant Light Kit 3.65
723-102 Bulb Constant Light Kit 3.95
723-103 2 Bulb Reversing Constant Light Kit 4.65
(Rear light operates when reversing. Front headlight stays on without dimming as on the real railroads. Rear light will go out when loco again moves forward.)

723-105 Constant Lighting 1 Bulb Kit 5.95
O, S Scale

723-106 Constant Lighting 2 Bulb Kit 6.95
O, S Scale
(For double headlights on engine or as an artificial glow in fire box, light in cab, or boiler.)

REPLACEMENT BULBS

1.5 volt Replacement Bulb (For #101/102/103)
723-104 3.65

12v-.080 Amps Replacement Bulbs .2 Diameter 6" Leads
723-108 pkg(3) 2.99

723-107 12v Replacement Bulbs, GOW, Red pkg(3) 3.65

723-109 12v-.27 Amps Bulbs pkg(3) 3.95
Flasher Type, Min. Bayonet Base

723-110 12v-.2 Amps Bulbs pkg(3) 2.99
Min. Bayonet Base, Clear

LIGHT EMITTING DIODES LED's

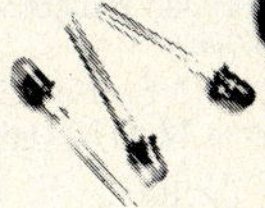

No heat, low current drain, low voltage. .120 diameters.

723-402 Red pkg(4) 2.99
723-403 Green pkg(4) 2.99
723-404 Yellow pkg(4) 2.99

FIBER OPTICS

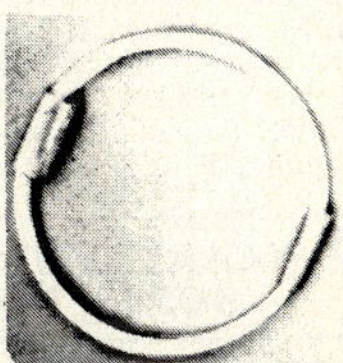

Fiber optics can be used in dwarfs, street lights, airplane marker lights and railroad block signals to name but a few applications. 401 optics can be used with Train Tronics Chase Light Kit #201 to make larger illuminated or animated signs.

723-401 Fiber Optics .020" diameter pkg(25') 7.95

723-413 Fiber Optics .030" diameter pkg(25') 7.95

723-414 Fiber Optics .040" diameter pkg(25') 11.95

LIGHTING KITS

ULTIMATE MICROLAMPS

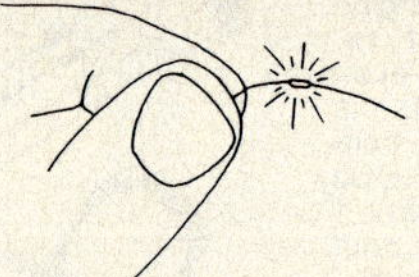

296-500 Ultimate MicroLamp™ 2.98
Can be used with the CLM series Loco Liting modules for working head, ditch, marker or numberboard lights on locos, plus marker lights for cabooses and passenger equipment. Also used for military, aircraft and vehicle models. Requires 1.5V power source, draws a low 15mA of current. Using the CIL-125 LitePac™, (#269-125) 50 to 75 of these bulbs can be used on a layout. Includes one assembled axial design bulb with one 1″ wire leads, (bulbs are pretested before packaging) insulation material and instructions.

SUPER MICROLAMPS

These tiny light bulbs are perfect for use with signals, headlights or wherever space is limited. Bulbs are designed for use with 1.5 volts DC (15mA) and measure 1.4mm. Long life design.

296-100	Clear	1.98
296-101	Red	2.19
296-102	Green	2.19
296-103	Amber	2.19
296-104	Flame	2.19
296-10001	Clear pkg(25)	34.95

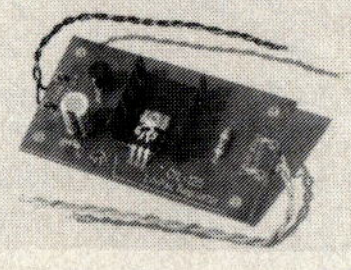

Litepac™ 1.5V
296-125 29.95
Powers up 50 or more micro15mA bulbs on a layout, diorama or module using any 4-20 volt AC or DC power source. Unlike AC transformer devices, the Litepac™ provides fully regulated and filtered DC voltage which can extend lamp life up to 30%. The "Lamp Saver" circuit helps prevent harmful AC over-volt conditions from destroying delicate 1.5 volt microlamps. Litepac™ comes fully assembled, with built in overload protection, instructions & mounting hardware.

296-135 Litepac™ Starter Set 42.95
Includes 12 #100 Light bulbs.

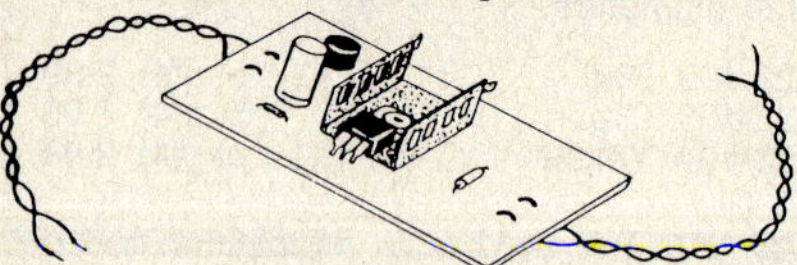

296-140 LED Power Converter 29.95
Converter can power up to 50 20mA 2.1 to 3.0V LED's. Automatic safety feature shuts down the unit in event of overload, overheating or short. Ballast resistors are not required. Input: 6-20V AC/DC (variable or steady); output: 2.4V DC (regulated) 1.0 amp. max.

HEAVY DUTY SUPER MICROLAMPS

Bulbs are designed for use with 1.8 volt DC (60mA) and measure 1.3mm in diameter.

296-200	Clear	3.29
296-201	Red	3.29
296-202	Green	3.29
296-203	Strobe Blue	3.29
296-204	Clear w/Brass Painted Shade	3.98
296-205	Flamemaker™ Lamp Kit	3.49
296-301	Frosted Globe	4.49
	6.0 mm diameter	

HEAVY DUTY FLUORETTE LAMPS

Can be used to light building interiors or passenger car interiors. 12-16 volt AC/DC.

296-400	Frosted	each	1.89
296-401	Frosted	pkg(6)	9.95
296-402	Lamp Holder	each	1.89
296-403	Lamp Holder	pkg(6)	9.95

STREET LAMPS

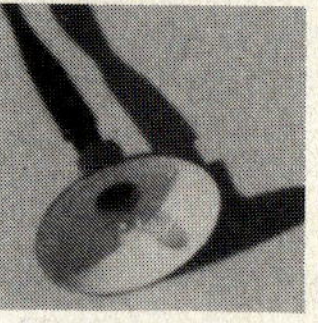

Lamp w/Painted Shade
296-105 3.29
Typical outdoor/security lamp, found on all types of buildings. Includes 1.5V bulb and painted, metal shade with instructions. HO & up.

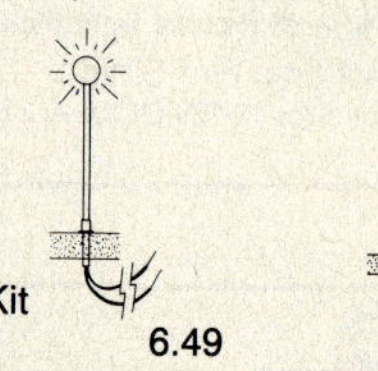

Street Light Kit
296-302 6.49
Typical street light includes 4″ diameter post adjustable to 12′ high (HO Scale feet), 1.8 volt DC Frosted Globe lamp (6mm), and instructions. Can also be used on N & S Scales.

Old Time Gas Street Light HO & up.
296-303 6.49

VEHICLE LIGHTING KITS

Kits come complete with assembled electronics, 1.8 volt Heavy Duty Super Microlamps, hardware and instructions. 6-18V AC/DC.

1005, 1011	1007,10111		1008

296-1005	Rotating Beacon	(red)	23.95
296-1008	Dual Litebar	(red/blue)	34.95
296-1011	Rotating Beacon	(yellow)	23.95

LIMITED QUANTITIES AVAILABLE

296-1007	Rotating Beacons	(red/blue)	29.95
296-10111	Rotating Beacon	(dual ylw)	29.95

Basic Vehicle Lighting Kit
296-1012 14.45

LOCOMOTIVE CONSTANT LIGHTING MODULES

CLM LOCOLITE™
Fully assembled, ready for installation. HO and larger.
Single Headlamp
296-900 9.95
w/one Microlamp

Two Headlamps
296-901 12.95
w/auto reverse on one lamp w/two micro lamps.

LOCOMOTIVE CONSTANT LIGHTING MODULES (cont)

296-902 Two Headlamps 12.95
w/auto-reverse on both lamps w/two micro lamps.

296-908 Replacement Lamp 1.98
for #s 900, 901 and 902. 1.4V DC 1.3mm dia 10mA.

FLAMEMAKER™

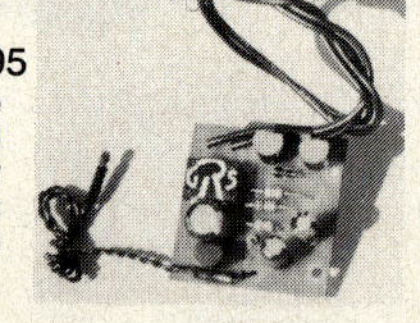

Micro Flamemaker™
296-1000 23.95
Unit simulates the flickering light produced by a small bonfire or campfire. 6-20 volts AC/DC. Used with all scales. 1 × 1 × 3/8″.

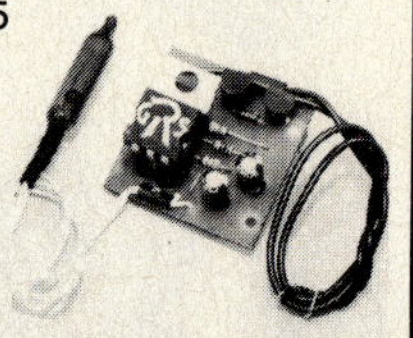

Super Flamemaker™
296-1004 23.95
Unit simulates larger fires such as a working blast furnace or a burning structure. Can be used in any scale. 16-20 volts AC. Circuit board 1 × 1 × 5/8″ high. Lamp assembly 3/16″ diameter, 7/8″ long.

296-300 Lamp Replacement 3.49
For #1004

MICROFLASHER™

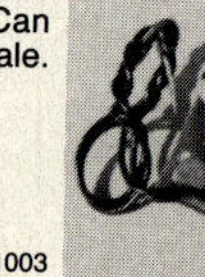

Used to simulate flashing lights. Can be used in any scale.

296-1003

296-1001 Slow 23.95
For model signs, billboards, beacons, etc. Includes two clear heavy duty microbulbs. 12-20 volts.

296-1002 Fast 23.95
For model signs, billboards, emergency vehicles, planes, boats, etc. Flashes two clear heavy duty microlamps which are included. 12-20 volts.

296-1003 MicroStrobe™ 23.95
Pure white strobe effect achieved thru two strobe blue microlamps, included. For use on model signs, trains, planes, boats, etc. 6-20 volts.

2-PIN MICRO CONNECTOR™

Gold plated, assembled.

296-906 With 5″ 30ga 3.95
color-coded leads (1 set)

296-907 Less leads pkg(2 sets) 4.95

296-5006 Sub-Miniature MicroWire™ 3.49
2-Conductor Stranded, 25′
32 gauge, flexible & paintable. Ideal for loco lighting & sound system.

See also: SCENERY for additional GRS Micro-Liting™ items.

Labelle industries

ASSORTED BULBS & LIGHTING KITS

We have worked closely with this manufacturer to provide accurate availability information at the time this catalog was published. Items listed in *blue ink* may not be available at all times. Please see your dealer for current delivery information.

14V ATHEARN LOCO

430-6630 Clear   pkg(3) 1.69

0.2A "BLINKER" BULBS

430-6461 Clear 16v   pkg(2) 1.69
430-6462 Red 16v   pkg(2) 1.69

16V, 0.06A FLORESCENT

430-6685 Fluorette Type   pkg(2) 1.69

14V GRAIN-O-SAND

430-6664 Yellow   pkg(2) 1.98

12V GRAIN-O-WHEAT

430-6641 Clear   pkg(3) 1.69
430-6642 Red   pkg(3) 1.69
430-6643 Green   pkg(3) 1.69
430-6644 Yellow   pkg(3) 1.69
430-6645 Frosted   pkg(3) 1.69

16V GRAIN-O-WHEAT

430-6651 Clear   pkg(3) 1.69
430-6653 Green   pkg(3) 1.69
430-6654 Yellow   pkg(3) 1.69
430-6655 Frosted   pkg(3) 1.69

1.2V ANGEL HAIR

430-6663 Clear   pkg(2) 1.98

14V SUB-GOW

430-6551 Clear   pkg(2) 1.89

16V "ROUND"

430-6441 Clear   pkg(2) 1.69
430-6442 Red   pkg(2) 1.69
  (track bumpers)
430-6443 Green   pkg(2) 1.69
430-6444 Yellow   pkg(2) 1.69
430-6445 Frosted   pkg(2) 1.69
  (street lamps)

HOOK-UP WIRE, MULTI-STRAND - 33'

430-6001 23 Ga. Single Conductor   1.79
  Black, Red, Green
430-6002 23 Ga. Two Conductor   3.19
  Brown, Yellow
430-6003 23 Ga. Three Conductor   3.99
  Red, Green, Yellow
430-6004 23 Ga. Four Conductor   4.99

LOCOMOTIVE HEADLIGHT

430-2430 12V   each 1.75
430-2431 Small   each 1.99

"PEPPER BULBS"

430-6401 Clear 1.5v   pkg(3) 1.69
430-6411 Clear 3v   pkg(3) 1.69

LIGHTING KITS

430-6675 Loco Direction Light Kit   2.98
430-6676 Interior Lighting Kit   1.89
430-6677 Bulb for #6676   1.69

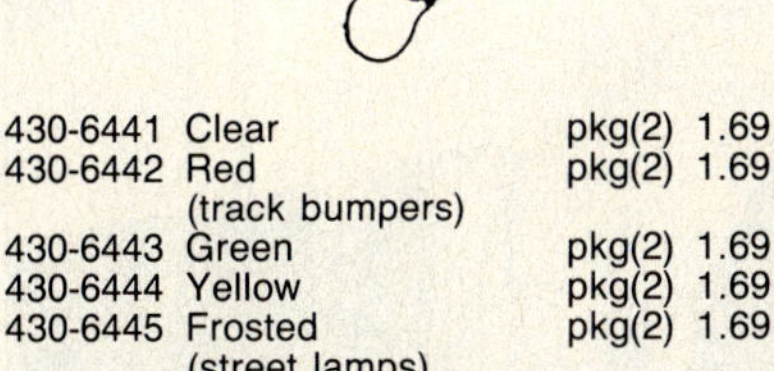
LIFE-LIKE®

BULBS

Grain of Wheat
(for 1206,1505,1507)
433-1210
pkg(2) 3.00

w/Wired Socket
433-1204
pkg(2) 3.00

Blinking
(for 1212)
433-1223
pkg(2) 3.00

Lamp Bulb
(for 1201)
433-1203
pkg(3) 3.00

HOOK-UP WIRE

2-Strand, Brown
433-1431
pkg(10') 3.00

MISCELLANEOUS

House Lighting Kit
433-1200   ea 3.00

Light-Up Assortment Pack
433-1240   168.00
(By Special Order Only.)

HO SCALE (1/87) EASY-TO-BUILD KIT

LIGHTING KIT

236-8000 Passenger Car, Athearn   6.95

PRECISION SCALE Co.

BULBS

12V SMALL SCREW

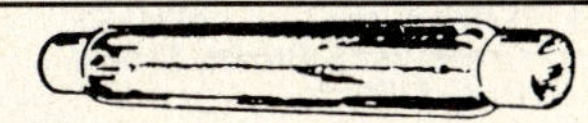

585-48300 Amber   pkg(2) 2.25
585-48301 Green   pkg(2) 2.25
585-48302 Red   pkg(2) 2.25

12V TUBULAR

585-48308 Amber Clip-in   each 2.25
585-48309 Green Clip-in   each 2.25
585-48310 Blue Clip-in   each 2.25
585-48311 Red Clip-in   each 2.25

12V BRASS BASE

585-48303 Clear   pkg(2) 2.25
585-48304 Amber   pkg(2) 2.25
585-48305 Green   pkg(2) 2.25
585-48306 Red   pkg(2) 2.25

12V GRAIN-OF-WHEAT

585-48294 Clear 18v   pkg(2) 2.25
585-48295 Amber 18v   pkg(2) 2.25
585-48296 Red 6v   pkg(2) 2.25
585-48298 Green 6v   pkg(2) 2.25

ELONGATED 12V GRAIN-OF-WHEAT

Designed for trackside signals of all types.
585-400 Clear   pkg(4) 3.75
585-401 Red   pkg(4) 3.75
585-402 Green   pkg(4) 3.75
585-403 Amber   pkg(4) 3.75

2.5 V GRAIN-OF-WHEAT

585-48297 Red   pkg(2) 2.25

4.5V GRAIN-OF-WHEAT

585-48313 Clear   pkg(2) 2.25
585-48314 Red   pkg(2) 2.25

DUAL FILAMENT

585-48315 1.5v, clear   pkg(2) 3.25
585-48316 2.5v, clear   pkg(2) 3.25
585-48317 3.0v, clear   pkg(2) 3.25

MISCELLANEOUS

585-405 12v, Clear   pkg(2) 2.75
Bulb has diffused lens, use for diesel headlight.

585-410 Micro-Mini Bulbs   pkg(8) 9.50
1.5v

Bulb for Caboose 12 v
585-48307   ea 3.00
In special case, red & green light.

HOOK-UP WIRE & BULBS

HOOK-UP WIRE

All purpose, color coded, flexible pre-tinned wire.

490-5201	1 Conductor Red pkg(500')		22.00
490-5202	2 Conductor Red, pkg(200') Black		24.00
490-5203	3 Conductor pkg(100') Red, White, Black		22.00
490-5204	4 Conductor pkg(100') Red, White, Yellow, Black		24.00
490-2401	1 Conductor pkg(35') Green, Red, Brown, Blue, Gray & Black		1.89
490-2402	2 Conductor pkg(17.5') Red, Black		1.89
490-2403	3 Conductor pkg(11.5') Blue, White, Black		1.89
490-2404	4 Conductor pkg(8.5') Green, Red, White, Black		1.89
490-2300	72 Cds assort	**NEW**	143.28
490-2301	1 Conductor cd	**NEW**	1.99
490-2302	2 Conductor cd	**NEW**	1.99
490-2303	3 Conductor cd	**NEW**	1.99
490-2304	4 Conductor cd	**NEW**	1.99
490-2310	18 gauge wire	**NEW**	2.98
	1 Conductor 25'		
490-2311	18 gauge wire	**NEW**	2.98
	2 Conductor 12.5'		

14v GRAIN-O-SAND

490-146	Clear, 1.2mm	pkg(3)	3.98
490-147	Red, 1.2mm	pkg(3)	3.98
490-148	Green, 1.2mm	pkg(3)	3.98
490-149	Amber, 1.2mm	pkg(3)	3.98

1.5v GRAIN-O-RICE

490-152	Clear, 2.2mm	pkg(3)	3.98
490-153	Red, 2.2mm	pkg(3)	3.98
490-154	Green, 2.2mm	pkg(3)	3.98
490-155	Amber, 2.2mm	pkg(3)	3.98

3v GRAIN-O-RICE

490-345	Clear, 150MA	pkg(3)	2.98

14v GRAIN-O-RICE

490-252	Clear, 2.2mm	pkg(3)	3.98
490-253	Red, 2.2mm	pkg(3)	3.98
490-254	Green, 2.2mm	pkg(3)	3.98
490-255	Amber, 2.2mm	pkg(3)	3.98

1.5v GRAIN-O-WHEAT

490-344	Pointed, 150MA	pkg(3)	2.98

3v GRAIN-O-WHEAT

490-391	Clear, 3.2mm	pkg(3)	1.98
490-392	Red, 3.2mm	pkg(3)	1.98
490-393	Green, 3.2mm	pkg(3)	1.98
490-394	Amber, 3.2mm	pkg(3)	1.98

14v GRAIN-O-WHEAT

490-381	Clear, 3.2mm	pkg(3)	1.98
490-382	Red, 3.2mm	pkg(3)	1.98
490-383	Green, 3.2mm	pkg(3)	1.98
490-384	Amber, 3.2mm	pkg(3)	1.98

HEADLIGHTS

490-340	16v 70MA Wired Flat Head	pkg(3)	2.98
490-341	14v 70MA Flat Head Screw	pkg(3)	2.98
490-342	14v Oval Screw	pkg(3)	2.98
490-343	14v Oval Bayonet	pkg(3)	2.98

14v GAS PEA LAMPS

490-395	Clear, 6mm	pkg(2)	2.98
490-396	White, 6mm	pkg(2)	2.98

BAYONET BASE 6v

490-51961	#51 Clear	pkg(2)	2.29

BAYONET BASE 14v

490-398	Pointed, N Scale pkg(3) w/14v G-O-W bulbs		2.98
490-53961	#53 Clear	pkg(2)	1.98
490-53962	#53 Red	pkg(2)	1.98
490-257962	#257 Red	pkg(2)	1.98
490-257961	BB	pkg(2)	1.98
490-363961	#363 Clear	pkg(2)	1.98

BAYONET BASE 18v

490-144596	#1445 Clear	pkg(2)	1.98

BUILDING LIGHTS

490-491	Socket Stand & Bulb	pkg(2)	2.98
490-492	12v w/Screw Base	pkg(6)	3.98
490-10096	w/Screw Base	pkg(2)	2.98

LAMP POST BULBS **NEW**

490-10095		pkg(2)	2.98

SCREW BASE 14v

490-144996	#1449 Clear	pkg(2)	1.98
490-144997	#1449 Red	pkg(2)	1.98
490-144998	#1449 Green	pkg(2)	1.98
490-258961	#258 Clear	pkg(2)	1.98
490-430961	#430 Clear	pkg(2)	1.98
490-432961	#432 Clear	pkg(2)	1.98
490-432962	#432 Red	pkg(2)	1.98
490-432963	#432 Green	pkg(2)	1.98
490-461961	#461 Clear	pkg(2)	1.98

SCREW BASE 18v

490-144796	#1447 Clear	pkg(2)	1.98

1.5v SUB-MINI

Angels Hair 1.2mm

490-145	Clear, 12.5MA	pkg(3)	3.98

3v BRITE

490-397	Clear, GOW	pkg(3)	2.98

14v BLINKER

Blinks after 20 second warm-up

490-10097	Clear, 250MA	pkg(2)	2.50
490-10098	Red, 250MA	pkg(2)	2.50
490-10099	Amber, 250MA	pkg(2)	2.50

Wonder if anybody's New Year's resolutions included finding work in the deep south? The new year brought several inches of fresh snow to the Canadian forests and several hours of work for the section gang. Such events are an everyday part of the job on the Maritime Lumber line. This 2 x 4' module was built by Gerry Gilliland and features a scratch-built engine house constructed with Northeastern Lumber and Campbell shingles. Parked nearby are Jordan and Wheelworks vehicles, while the crew members are from Campbell. *Models and Photo by Gerry Gilliland*

N.J. International

Bulbs, wire, meters, miniature switches and plugs.
Bulbs shown approximately actual size.

BRASS ENCASED 12V

525-9006	Clear	pkg(2)	2.99
525-9007	Red	pkg(2)	2.99
525-9008	Green	pkg(2)	2.99
525-9009	Amber	pkg(2)	2.99

PANEL INDICATOR 12V

525-9026	White	each	3.59
525-9027	Red	each	3.59
525-9028	Green	each	3.59
525-9029	Yellow	each	3.59

SMALL CLEAR BULBS

9185 9255 9145

525-9185	Micro 1.8mm, 1.5v	ea	2.99
525-9255	Submin 2.5mm, 1.5V	ea	2.59
525-9145	Super Micro 1.4mm, 1.5V	pkg(3)	13.99
525-9182	Micro 1.8mm, 12V	each	2.99
525-9252	Submin 2.5mm, 12V	each	2.59

GRAIN OF RICE 2.5mm, 12V

525-9256	Clear	pkg(2)	3.29
525-9257	Red	pkg(2)	3.29
525-9258	Green	pkg(2)	3.29
525-9259	Amber	pkg(2)	3.29

GRAIN OF WHEAT 1.5V

525-9306	Clear	pkg(2)	2.99
525-9307	Red	pkg(2)	2.99
525-9308	Green	pkg(2)	2.99
525-9309	Amber	pkg(2)	2.99

GRAIN OF WHEAT 3V

525-9316	Clear	pkg(2)	2.99
525-9317	Red	pkg(2)	2.99
525-9318	Green	pkg(2)	2.99
525-9319	Amber	pkg(2)	2.99

GRAIN OF WHEAT 3.2mm, 12V

525-9326	Clear	pkg(2)	2.99
525-9327	Red	pkg(2)	2.99
525-9328	Green	pkg(2)	2.99
525-9329	Amber	pkg(2)	2.99

RUNNING LITE FITTINGS 3V

525-9750	Small	(red)	ea	2.79
525-9751	Small	(green)	ea	2.79
525-9752	Medium	(red)	ea	2.99
525-9753	Medium	(green)	ea	2.99
525-9754	Large	(red)	ea	2.99
525-9755	Large	(green)	ea	2.99

SEARCH LITE FITTINGS 3V

525-9761	Small	ea	2.49
525-9762	Medium	ea	2.99
525-9763	Large	ea	2.79

DOME LITE

525-9771		ea 2.39

MISCELLANEOUS BULBS, 12V UNLESS NOTED

9612 9615 8804

525-9612	White Globe	pkg(2)	2.99
525-9615	Pea Lamp, 12V Clear	pkg(2)	2.79
525-8804	Socket Base for Bulb #9615	pkg(2)	1.09
525-9617	Flat Face		2.99
525-9618	Red (MS 2/8)	pkg(2)	3.29
525-9620	White (4x20)	pkg(2)	3.99
525-9622	Clear (2.2S)	pkg(2)	2.99
525-9624	Clear (E-4)	pkg(2)	2.99
525-9625	Blinker w/3" Lead	pkg(2)	3.29
525-9626	Blinker w/E-5 Base	pkg(2)	4.29
525-9628	Clear (28x5)	pkg(2)	2.99
525-9629	Clear (2.8x9)	pkg(2)	2.99
525-9638	Blue (38x6)	pkg(2)	2.99
525-9644	Clear (MS-4)	pkg(2)	2.99
525-9645	Clear (3.17x4) 3V	pkg(2)	2.99
525-9646	Clear (4x45) 3V	pkg(2)	2.99
525-9648	Clear (48x6)	pkg(2)	2.99
525-9649	Clear (48x7)	pkg(2)	2.99
525-9666	6MM Flat Face	pkg(2)	2.99

LIGHTING KIT

Use for lighting structures. Kit includes bulb socket, mounting base, bulb, wire and screws.

525-8801	Lighting Kit	1.99

LED PANEL LITES 12V

525-9057	Red	3.59
525-9058	Green	3.59

MINIATURE BULB CAP

525-8901	Red	pkg(12)	.99
525-8903	Amber	pkg(12)	.99

MINIATURE SCREW BASE 4 MM 12V

525-9603	Clear w/Base	2.49
525-9604	Clear	2.49
525-9605	Red	2.49
525-9606	Green	2.49
525-9607	Yellow	2.49
525-9608	Blue	2.49

CONDUCTOR WIRE

525-8421	1-strand Green,	pkg(50')	2.49
525-8420	1-strand Red,	pkg(50')	2.49
525-8425	1-strand Blue,	pkg(50')	2.49
525-8426	1-strand Gray,	pkg(50')	2.49
525-8422	2-strand Red, Black	pkg(35')	4.75
525-8423	3-strand Red, Black, Yellow	pkg(30')	4.79
525-8424	4-strand Red, Black, Yellow, Green	pkg(20')	4.99

METERS

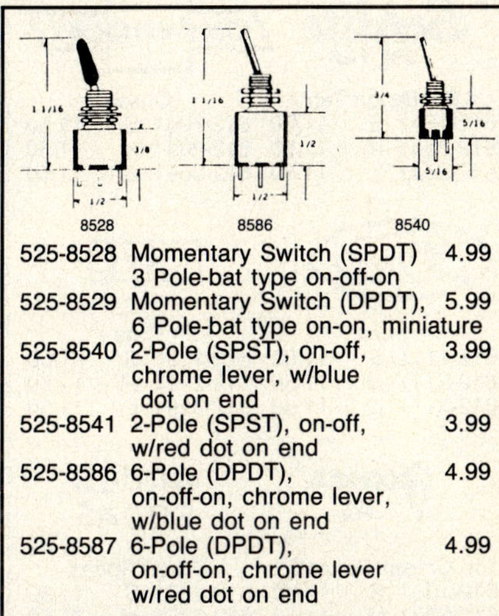

- Center Zero Scale
- Easy Installation
- HO-N-O Scale Use
- 2-3/8" x 2-3/8" Square Face
- Metal Bezel-Black Finish

DC Volt Meter 20-0-20
525-8360   13.99

DC Amp Meter, 5-0-5
525-8361   12.99

DC Amp Meter, 0-2
525-8362   12.99

525-8363 DC Volt Meter 0-16   12.99

MINIATURE SWITCHES

8528 8586 8540

525-8528	Momentary Switch (SPDT) 3 Pole-bat type on-off-on	4.99
525-8529	Momentary Switch (DPDT), 6 Pole-bat type on-on, miniature	5.99
525-8540	2-Pole (SPST), on-off, chrome lever, w/blue dot on end	3.99
525-8541	2-Pole (SPST), on-off, w/red dot on end	3.99
525-8586	6-Pole (DPDT), on-off-on, chrome lever, w/blue dot on end	4.99
525-8587	6-Pole (DPDT), on-off-on, chrome lever w/red dot on end	4.99

PLUGS

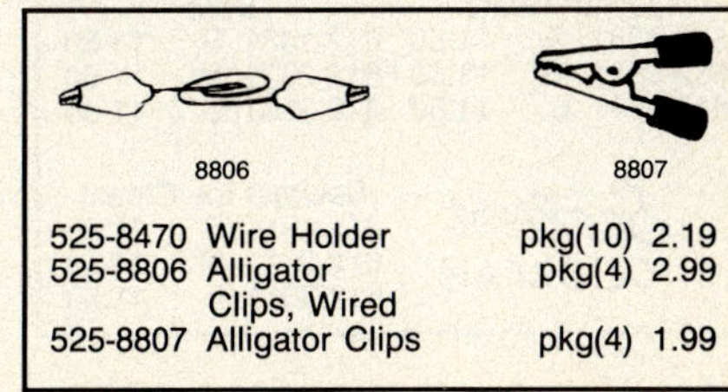

525-8450	Male Red	pkg(10)	2.99
525-8451	Male Green	pkg(10)	2.99
525-8452	Male Orange	pkg(10)	2.99
525-8453	Male White	pkg(10)	2.99
525-8454	Male Black	pkg(10)	2.99
525-8455	Male Blue	pkg(10)	2.99
525-8456	Male Gray	pkg(10)	2.99
525-8457	Male Brown	pkg(10)	2.99
525-8458	Male Yellow	pkg(10)	2.99
525-8460	Female Red	pkg(10)	2.99
525-8461	Female Green	pkg(10)	2.99
525-8462	Female Orange	pkg(10)	2.99
525-8463	Female White	pkg(10)	2.99
525-8464	Female Black	pkg(10)	2.99
525-8465	Female Blue	pkg(10)	2.99
525-8466	Female Gray	pkg(10)	2.99
525-8467	Female Brown	pkg(10)	2.99
525-8468	Female Yellow	pkg(10)	2.99

WIRE HOLDER

8806 8807

525-8470	Wire Holder	pkg(10)	2.19
525-8806	Alligator Clips, Wired	pkg(4)	2.99
525-8807	Alligator Clips	pkg(4)	1.99

Quality Products Co.

NEON SIGN KITS

Signs are clear plastic, dyed various colors to give the effect of a neon-like sign. Material size (2 x 2″) serves as the window in your building. Signs can be made to flash on and off or have various parts flash alternately. Includes mounting channels, bulb(s), instructions. Flasher unit not included.

S = Small, **M** = Medium, **L** = Large

■ SINGLE-FLASH SIGNS ■

Entire sign lights up at one time constantly or may be made to flash on and off with either #1220 or #1230 flasher unit (not included).

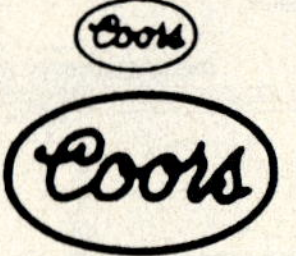

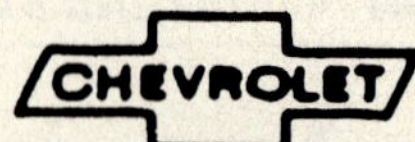

Coors			Tony's Barber Shop		
612-1041	S	11.50	612-1021	S	11.50
612-2041	M	11.50	612-2021	M	11.50
612-3041	L	11.50	612-3021	L	11.50

Schlitz on Tap			Chevy		
612-1541	S	11.50	612-1091	S	11.50
612-2541	M	11.50	612-2091	M	11.50
612-3541	L	11.50	612-3091	L	11.50

Ford			Cafe		
612-1111	S	11.50	612-1191	S	11.50
612-2111	M	11.50	612-2191	M	11.50
612-3111	L	11.50	612-3191	L	11.50

DRUGS SODAS

Ice Cream Cones/5¢			Drugs/Sodas		
612-1301	S	11.50	612-1321	S	11.50
612-2301	M	11.50	612-2321	M	11.50
612-3301	L	11.50	612-3321	L	11.50

HIRES OPEN

Hires Root Beer			Open		
612-1361	S	11.50	612-1431	S	11.50
612-2361	M	11.50	612-2431	M	11.50
612-3361	L	11.50	612-3431	L	11.50

Fish-Sea Food			John Deere		
612-1391	S	11.50	612-1681	S	11.50
612-2391	M	11.50	612-2681	M	11.50
612-3391	L	11.50	612-3681	L	21.75

QUALITY MEATS   BEER

Quality Meats			Beer		
612-1381	S	11.50	612-1031	S	11.50
612-2381	M	11.50	612-2031	M	11.50
612-3381	L	11.50	612-3031	L	11.50

ICE CREAM

Sealtest Ice Cream		
612-1311	S	11.50
612-2311	M	11.50
612-3311	L	11.50

■ SINGLE-FLASH SIGNS (cont) ■

PAWN SHOP

Robert's Florist			Pawn Shop		
612-1151	S	11.50	612-1421	S	11.50
612-2151	M	11.50	612-2421	M	11.50
612-3151	L	11.50	612-3421	L	11.50

Oly			White Castle		
612-1531	S	11.50	612-1561	S	11.50
612-2531	M	11.50	612-2561	M	11.50
612-3531	L	11.50	612-3561	L	11.50

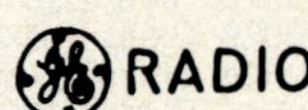

RADIO

Schlitz			GE Radio		
612-1591	S	11.50	612-1441	S	11.50
612-3591	L	11.50	612-2441	M	11.50
			612-3441	L	11.50

Budweiser			Stroh's		
612-1611	S	11.50	612-1621	S	11.50
612-2611	M	11.50	612-2621	M	11.50
612-3611	L	21.75	612-3621	L	11.50

Coca-Cola			Good Year		
612-1631	S	21.75	612-1661	S	11.50
612-2631	M	11.50	612-2661	M	11.50
612-3631	L	11.50	612-3661	L	11.50

DR HELMS

7-Up			Dr. Helms		
612-1641	S	11.50	612-1521	S	11.50
612-2641	M	11.50	612-2521	M	11.50
612-3641	L	11.50	612-3521	L	11.50

MIKE S GARAGE

Marlboro			Mike's Garage		
612-1551	S	11.50	612-1131	S	11.50
612-2551	M	11.50	612-2131	M	11.50
612-3551	L	11.50	612-3131	L	11.50

AVENUE BARBER SHOP

NEW

Avenue Barber Shop		
612-1011	S	11.50
612-2011	M	11.50
612-3011	L	11.50

■ SINGLE-FLASH SIGNS (cont) ■

Lunch 45¢			Ritz Hotel		
612-1231	S	11.50	612-1401	S	11.50
612-2231	M	11.50	612-2401	M	11.50
612-3231	L	11.50	612-3401	L	11.50

Winchell's			Zenith		
612-1271	S	11.50	612-1451	S	11.50
612-2271	M	11.50	612-2451	M	11.50
612-3271	L	21.75	612-3451	L	11.50

Hires			Shoe Repair		
612-1351	S	11.50	612-1501	S	11.50
612-2351	M	11.50	612-2501	M	11.50
612-3351	L	11.50	612-3501	L	11.50

NEW

Duffy's Tavern			Pabst		
612-1051	S	11.50	612-1061	S	11.50
612-2051	M	11.50	612-2061	M	11.50
612-3051	L	11.50	612-3061	L	21.75

Pool			Wines/Liquors		
612-1071	S	11.50	612-1081	S	11.50
612-2071	M	11.50	612-2081	M	11.50
612-3071	L	11.50	612-3081	L	11.50

Gateway Chevy			Hughson Ford		
612-1101	S	11.50	612-1121	S	11.50
612-2101	M	11.50	612-2121	M	11.50
612-3101	L	11.50	612-3121	L	11.50

Used Cars			Bevin Furs		
612-1141	S	11.50	612-1161	S	11.50
612-2141	M	11.50	612-2161	M	11.50
612-3141	L	11.50	612-3161	L	11.50

Food			Bar & Grill		
612-1171	S	11.50	612-1181	S	11.50
612-2171	M	11.50	612-2181	M	11.50
612-3171	L	11.50	612-3181	L	21.78

Chop Suey			Dell's Cafe		
612-1201	S	11.50	612-1211	S	11.50
612-2201	M	11.50	612-2211	M	11.50
612-3201	L	11.50	612-3211	L	11.50

Kasper's Hot Dogs			Steaks & Chops		
612-1221	S	11.50	612-1241	S	11.50
612-2221	M	11.50	612-2241	M	11.50
612-3221	L	11.50	612-3241	L	11.50

Bake Shop			Maler's Bakery		
612-1251	S	11.50	612-1261	S	11.50
612-2251	M	11.50	612-2261	M	11.50
612-3251	L	11.50	612-3261	L	11.50

See's Candy			Karmel Korn		
612-1281	S	11.50	612-1291	S	21.75
612-2281	M	21.75	612-2291	M	21.75
612-3281	L	21.75	612-3291	L	21.75

Prescriptions			Rx		
612-1331	S	11.50	612-1341	S	11.50
612-2331	M	11.50	612-2341	M	11.50
612-3331	L	11.50	612-3341	L	11.50

Meat			Loans		
612-1371	S	11.50	612-1411	S	11.50
612-2371	M	11.50	612-2411	M	11.50
612-3371	L	11.50	612-3411	L	11.50

Real Estate			Radio Repair		
612-1471	S	11.50	612-1461	S	11.50
612-2471	M	11.50	612-3461	L	11.50
612-3471	L	11.50			

Ben's Records			Sheet Music		
612-1481	S	11.50	612-1491	S	11.50
612-2481	M	11.50	612-2491	M	21.75
612-3481	L	11.50	612-3491	L	11.50

Checker's Cleaners			Freeman-Spicer Studebaker		
612-1511	S	11.50	612-1571	S	11.50
612-2511	M	11.50	612-2571	M	11.50
612-3511	L	11.50	612-3571	L	11.50

IGA			Firestone		
612-1651	S	11.50	612-1671	S	11.50
612-2651	M	11.50	612-2671	M	11.50
612-3651	L	11.50	612-3671	L	21.75

Quality Products Co.

NEON SIGN KITS

Signs are clear plastic, dyed various colors to give the effect of a neon-like sign. Material size (2 x 2″) serves as the window in your building. Signs can be made to flash on and off or have various parts flash alternately. Includes mounting channels, bulb(s), instructions. Flasher unit not included.

S = Small, **M** = Medium, **L** = Large

■ ALTERNATE FLASHING SIGNS ■

Two parts of each sign can flash alternately on and off when used with #1220 flasher unit (not included).

Zenith Radio-TV	Shoe Repair	Marlboro	Mike's Garage	Kaaren's Bake Shop
612-1452 S 21.75	612-1502 S 21.75	612-1552 S 21.75	612-1132 S 21.75	612-1252 S 21.75
612-2452 M 21.75	612-2502 M 21.75	612-2552 M 21.75	612-2132 M 21.75	612-2252 M 21.75
612-3452 L 21.75	612-3502 L 21.75	612-3552 L 21.75	612-3132 L 21.75	612-3252 L 21.75

White Castle	Sealtest Ice Cream	The Ritz Hotel	Winchell's Donuts	Lunch 45¢
612-1562 S 21.75	612-1312 S 21.75	612-1402 S 21.75	612-1272 S 21.75	612-1232 S 21.75
612-2562 M 21.75	612-2312 M 21.75	612-2402 M 21.75	612-2272 M 21.75	612-2232 M 21.75
612-3562 L 21.75	612-3312 L 21.75	612-3402 L 21.75	612-3272 L 21.75	612-3232 L 21.75

Coca-Cola	Tony's Barber Shop	Robert's Florist	Drugs/Soda	Hires
612-1632 S 21.75	612-1022 S 21.75	612-1152 S 21.75	612-1322 S 21.75	612-1352 S 21.75
612-2632 M 21.75	612-2022 M 21.75	612-2152 M 21.75	612-2322 M 21.75	612-2352 M 21.75
612-3632 L 21.75	612-3022 L 21.75	612-3152 L 21.75	612-3322 L 21.75	612-3352 L 21.75

Hires	Quality Meats	Pawn Shop	GE Radio	Dr Helms
612-1362 S 21.75	612-1382 S 21.75	612-1422 S 21.75	612-1442 S 21.75	612-1522 S 21.75
612-2362 M 21.75	612-2382 M 21.75	612-2422 M 21.75	612-2442 M 21.75	612-2522 M 21.75
612-3362 L 21.75	612-3382 L 21.75	612-3422 L 21.75	612-3442 L 21.75	612-3522 L 21.75

Oly	Schlitz	Budweiser	Stroh's	Good Year
612-1532 S 21.75	612-1542 S 21.75	612-1612 S 21.75	612-1622 S 21.75	612-1662 S 21.75
612-2532 M 21.75	612-2542 M 21.75	612-2612 M 21.75	612-2622 M 21.75	612-2662 M 21.75
612-3532 L 21.75	612-3542 L 21.75	612-3612 L 21.75	612-3622 L 21.75	612-3662 L 21.75

— NEW —

Avenue Barber Shop	Duffy's Tavern	Pabst	Wines/Liquors	Freeman-Spicer Studebaker
612-1012 S 21.75	612-1052 S 21.75	612-1062 S 21.75	612-1082 S 21.75	612-1572 S 21.75
612-2012 M 21.75	612-2052 M 21.75	612-2062 M 21.75	612-2082 M 21.75	612-2572 M 21.75
612-3012 L 21.75	612-3052 L 21.75	612-3062 L 21.75	612-3082 L 21.75	612-3572 L 21.75

Gateway Chevy	Hughson Ford	Used Cars	Bevin Furs	Bar & Grill
612-1102 S 21.75	612-1122 S 21.75	612-1142 S 21.75	612-1162 S 21.75	612-1182 S 21.75
612-2102 M 21.75	612-2122 M 21.75	612-2142 M 21.75	612-2162 M 21.75	612-2182 M 21.75
612-3102 L 21.75	612-3122 L 21.75	612-3142 L 21.75	612-3162 L 21.75	612-3182 L 21.75

Chop Suey	Dell's Cafe	Kasper's Hot Dogs	Steaks & Chops	Maler's Bakery
612-1202 S 21.75	612-1212 S 21.75	612-1222 S 21.75	612-1242 S 21.75	612-1262 S 21.75
612-2202 M 21.75	612-2212 M 21.75	612-2222 M 21.75	612-2242 M 21.75	612-2262 M 21.75
612-3202 L 21.75	612-3212 L 21.75	612-3222 L 21.75	612-3242 L 21.75	612-3262 L 21.75

See's Candy	Real Estate	Ben's Records	Sheet Music	Firestone
612-1282 S 21.75	612-1472 S 21.75	612-1482 S 21.75	612-1492 S 21.75	612-1672 S 21.75
612-2282 M 21.75	612-2472 M 21.75	612-2482 M 21.75	612-2492 M 21.75	612-2672 M 21.75
612-3282 L 21.75	612-3472 L 21.75	612-3482 L 21.75	612-3492 L 21.75	612-3672 L 21.75

■ NEON CLOCK KITS ■

Clocks are based on the Glo-dial, popular from the 30s to the 50s, which were illuminated with a ring of Neon. Require some basic skills to complete electrical hook up. Use in windows or mount on buildings & towers.

Clock and sign kit include Neon message and is designed for window mounting. Size is approximate outside diameter.

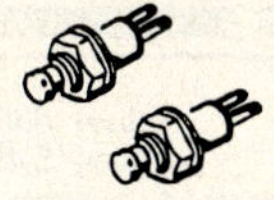

Clock
612-5011	1/8″	11.25
612-5012	1/4″	10.00
612-5013	3/8″	10.50
612-5014	1/2″	11.00
612-6011 same as 5011 asmb **NEW**		15.50
612-6012 same as 5012 asmb **NEW**		14.25
612-6013 same as 5013 asmb **NEW**		14.75
612-6014 same as 5014 asmb **NEW**		15.25

Clock w/Sign
612-1581	3/8″	21.00
612-2581	1/2″	18.00
612-3581	3/4″	20.25
612-4581	1″	20.75

Ford
612-1691	Small	21.00
612-2691	Medium	19.75
612-3691	Large	20.25
612-4691	X-large	20.75

Chevy
612-1701	Small	21.00
612-2701	Medium	19.75
612-3701	Large	20.25
612-4701	X-large	20.75

■ FLASHER UNITS ■

612-1220 Flasher Unit — 14.25
Solid-state, self-contained flasher unit operates on 9-18 volts AC or DC. Unit lights LEDs or grain-of-wheat bulbs in the following manner: A single lamp flashing at a rate of 60 flashes per minute, or two lamps flashing alternately 60 flashes per minute (for a total of 120 flashes per minute).

612-1230 Adjustable Flasher Unit — 20.25
Flash rate can be adjusted from 28 flashes per minute per lamp (a total of 2 lamps, 56 flashes per minute) to almost constant for each lamp-creating a rapid flickering effect.

WESTERN RAIL PRODUCTS NEW

■ LIGHTING KITS ■

757-101 End of Train 10.95 Flasher w/Batteries
EOT device w/Flashing red LED, electronic circuit, on/off switch & batteries included.

757-103 Diesel Engine 9.95 Strobe Flasher w/Batteries
Kit includes flashing yellow strobe LED, electronic control circuit, switch & batteries.

757-105 Caboose 9.95 Flashing, Warning Lights
Kit comes completely wired and ready for installation.

■ LED's ■

With resistors
757-301	5mm Red	pkg(3)	1.95
757-302	5mm Green	pkg(3)	1.95
757-303	5mm Yellow	pkg(3)	1.95
757-310	5mm Red/Green	pkg(2)	1.95
757-304	3mm Red	pkg(3)	1.95
757-305	3mm Green	pkg(3)	1.95
757-306	3mm Yellow	pkg(3)	1.95
757-311	3mm Red/Green	pkg(2)	1.95
757-307	1.8mm Red	pkg(3)	1.95
757-308	1.8mm Green	pkg(3)	1.95
757-309	1.8mm Yellow	pkg(3)	1.95

■ SWITCHES ■

757-401 SPDT pkg(2) 4.95
Single pole double throw miniature toggle switch. On-Off-On positions. Rated 6 amps of 125 volts.

757-402 DPDT pkg(2) 5.95
Double Pole Double Throw miniature toggle switch. On-off-on positions. Rated 6 amps at 125 volts.

■ SWITCHES (continued) ■

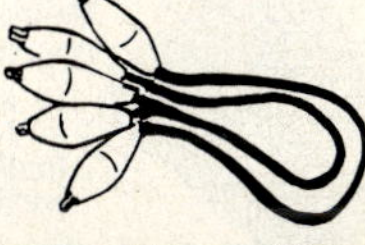

Switch Push Button
757-403 pkg(2) 1.95
Miniature push button switches. Momentary-on pushbuttons.

■ TEST LEADS ■

Insulated Alligator Clip Test Leads
757-901 pkg(5) 4.95
15″ in length, each lead is a different color.

■ BATTERIES ■

Batteries
757-902 pkg(2) 1.95
Small "watch type" batteries are replacements for original batteries sold with EOT flasher (#101) Diesel Engine Strobe Light (#103 and the Caboose Flasher (#105).

Roco

SWITCHES, CONNECTORS BULBS & WIRE

Imported from Austria by WALTHERS

SWITCHES

Each switch unit contains 4 single pushbuttons or switches. The switch unit intended for turnout control has an additional position indication return, which is a true return indication and does not require additional cabling. Manual operation at the turnout will produce a correct red or green indication.

625-10520	w/Return Indication	25.49
625-10521	2-Position	18.49
	w/o return indication	
625-10522	Pushbutton	14.99
625-10524	2-Position	18.49
	w/center Off switch	

Circuit Control Unit
625-10700 75.99
to be used with universal transformers —continuous voltage regulation & polarity reverse with "O" position.

Switch Control 2/3-Way
625-10526 25.49
Two-position switch with return indication for single slips and symmetrical 3-way turnouts. These two turnout designs require—if properly controlled—the exclusion of one of the four possible turnout positions. The switch 10526 offers a definite control of the three permissible turnout settings.

LEVER SWITCHES

625-10503	On-Off Switch	(blue)	5.49
625-10504	2-Way	(yellow)	5.49

for signals, alternating power feed to track sections

Multi-Function
625-10505 9.99
for signals—corresponding to the signals indication (red/green), power to track section is cut off or supplied.

CONNECTORS

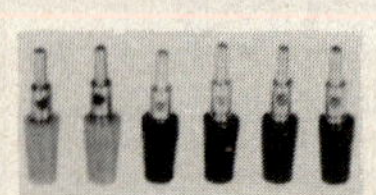

Plug Connectors
625-10601
pkg(6) 3.49

BULBS

625-85500	Bulb w/wire leads	each	2.49
625-10024	12v Bayonet, Clear E5-5	each	2.49
625-10026	12v Bayonet, Short	each	2.49

1-CONDUCTOR WIRE

10 meter length per roll. 6 rolls per pkg. 18.49 each.

625-10630	Black	625-10635	Green
625-10631	Brown	625-10636	Blue
625-10632	Red	625-10637	Violet
625-10633	Orange	625-10638	Green
625-10634	Yellow		

RELAYS

625-10019	Universal Relay	16.99

TAURUS PRODUCTS

HO SCALE CRAFT TRAIN KITS

POWER PICK—UP

Track Slider Power Pick-Up System
707-100 pkg(4) 2.50

POLA

HO SCALE (1/87)

Imported from Germany by WALTHERS

LAMP STAND

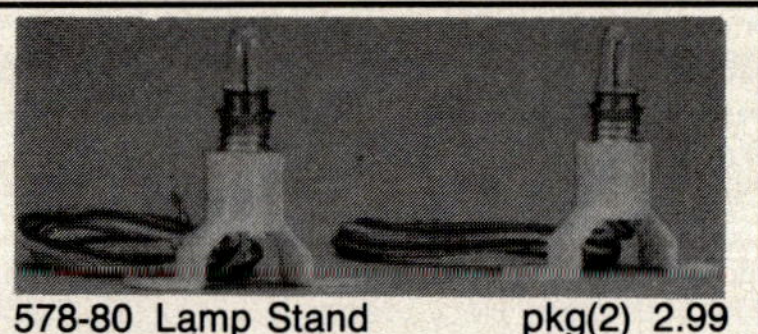

578-80 Lamp Stand pkg(2) 2.99
w/bulb and flex wire, 14-19V

International Hobby Corp.

25' WIRE

348-4411	Multi-Strand	1.49

LIGHTING KITS *NEW*

For passenger cars

348-4245	4-wheel	pkg(12)	12.98
348-4246	6-wheel	pkg(12)	14.98

RIBBONRAIL
by Earl Eshleman

Pilot lights for compact panel mounting. Features all brass housing, colored lens and simple wiring. 5/16" mounting hole, fits up to 3/8" thick panel.

14V PILOT LIGHT W/GOW BULB

Includes rubber retainer and clear grain-o-wheat bulb (12-16 volts).

enlarged to show detail

170-141	Red lens	each	2.00
170-142	Amber lens	each	2.00
170-143	Green lens	each	2.00
170-144	Blue lens	each	2.00
170-145	White lens	each	2.00

14V PILOT LIGHT W/AUTOMOTIVE BULB

Includes spring retainer and clear automotive bulb (grounded one wire, brass 12-16 volts).

enlarged to show detail

170-151	Red lens	each	2.15
170-152	Amber lens	each	2.15
170-153	Green lens	each	2.15
170-154	Blue lens	each	2.15
170-155	White lens	each	2.15

PILOT LIGHT HOUSING

Includes rubber retainer, less bulb.

170-161	Red lens	each	1.50
170-162	Amber lens	each	1.50
170-163	Green lens	each	1.50
170-164	Blue lens	each	1.50
170-165	White lens	each	1.50

MINIATURE SWITCHES

Functions as a single pole switch or as a momentary push-button contact in one unit, with one hole mounting. Both the Midget Switch (7/16" dia) and the Mini Switch (1/4" dia) come in two mounting styles: the "press mount" (drill hole & tap into it, for thicker panels 3/16" & up) and the "ring & nut mount" (for thinner panels under 3/16").

170-1	Midget, press mount	ea	1.25
170-2	Midget, screw mount	ea	2.75
170-3	Mini, press mount	ea	1.00
170-4	Mini, screw mount	ea	2.50

TARGET FACES *NEW*

348-4425	Pennsylvania Position Lights	pkg(12)	2.98
348-4426	Baltimore & Ohio Position Lights	pkg(12)	2.98
348-4427	Norfolk & Western Position Lights	pkg(12)	2.98

MISCELLANEOUS *NEW*

348-4415	High Tension Tower		9.98
348-4420	Marker Light	pkg(12)	2.98

SCALE SHOPS

HO SCALE (1/87)

Make your models more realistic with this assortment of miniature electronic supplies!

We have worked closely with this manufacturer to provide accurate availability information at the time this catalog was published. Items listed in *blue ink* may not be available at all times. Please see your dealer for current delivery information.

SUPER CONSTANT LIGHTING UNITS

Add battery powered lights to cars or locos with these lighting units. These units charge a battery which provides power for the bulb.

649-7065	Less Battery	kit	6.98
649-7066	#7065, less Battery	assembled	25.95
649-7075	Less Battery	kit	5.98
649-7076	#7075, less Battery	assembled	23.95
649-7080	AA Battery 12V 500MH with solder tabs		4.98

LIGHTING CONTROLLERS

Provides enough power to illuminate over 50 1.5 volt micro-bulbs. The unit can be used with any 6 or 12 volt CT power source and puts out a steady 1.5 volts up to 750MA.

649-7090	Kit	7.98
649-7091	Assembled	19.95

CROSSING FLASHER

Control Unit

649-7010	Kit	3.98
649-7011	Assembled	12.98

CONNECTORS

Small size, multi-pin connectors feature gold-plated contacts for reliable operation.

649-3020	2-Pin Connector	1.49
649-3030	3-Pin Connector	1.98
649-3040	4-Pin Connector	2.98
649-3200	20-Pin Connector, separable	13.98
649-3021	2-Pin, Indexed	1.98
649-3041	4-Pin, Indexed	3.98
649-3061	6-Pin, Indexed	5.98
649-3420	2-Pin, Sub-miniature	1.98
649-3430	3-Pin, Sub-miniature	2.98
649-3440	4-Pin, Sub-miniature	3.98
649-3442	20-Pin, Sub-miniature	18.98

DIODE

649-4009	3 amp, 50 PIV	pkg(3)	.98
649-4010	1 amp, 50 PIV	pkg(10)	.98

LIGHT-EMITTING DIODE (LEDs)

649-5030	.085" dia x .115" high	NEW	(red)	.98
649-5031	.085" dia x .115" high	NEW	(green)	.98
649-5040	T1, 3 mm	NEW	(blue)	3.49
649-5049	R-Y-G, 5 mm dia		each	.98
649-5050	Red, 4 mm dia		pkg(2)	.98
649-5070	Yellow, 4 mm dia		pkg(2)	.98
649-5080	Red, 3 mm dia		pkg(2)	.98
649-5090	Green, 3 mm dia		pkg(2)	.98
649-5100	Yellow, 3 mm dia		pkg(2)	.98
649-5110	R-Y-G, Right Angle		each	.98
649-5130	Mounting Clip T1 in Panels		pkg(10)	1.98
649-5131	Mounting Clip T1-1/2 LED's		pkg(10)	1.98
649-5132	Mounting Clip T1-3/4 LED's		pkg(10)	1.98

BULBS

649-5001	Grain-O-Wheat, 6v Clear	pkg(4)	.98
649-5020	Micro, 1.4V Clear .052" diameter	pkg(2)	2.98

SWITCHES

649-4049	Toggle Switch, SPST Miniature		2.59
649-4050	Toggle Switch, SPDT Miniature		2.79
649-4052	Slide Switch, DPDT Miniature	NEW	.98
649-4053	Slide Switch, SPDT Sub-Miniature		.98
649-4060	Toggle Switch, DPDT/CO Sub-Miniature		2.98
649-4070	Toggle Switch, DPDT Sub-Miniature		2.89

HEAT SHRINKING TUBING

649-4501	3/64" dia	(black)	pkg(12")	1.29
649-4502	1/16" dia	(black)	pkg(12")	1.39
649-4503	1/8" dia	(black)	pkg(12")	1.59
649-4504	3/16" dia	(black)	pkg(12")	1.79
649-4505	3/32" dia	(black)	pkg(12")	1.49
649-4600	Assortment	(black)	pkg(20")	2.98
	4" of each listed above			
649-4601	3/64" dia	(red)	pkg(12")	1.29
649-4602	1/16" dia	(red)	pkg(12")	1.39
649-4603	1/8" dia	(red)	pkg(12")	1.59
649-4604	3/16" dia	(red)	pkg(12")	1.79
649-4605	3/32" dia	(red)	pkg(12")	1.49
649-4700	Assortment	(red)	pkg(20")	2.98
	4" of each listed above			

MISCELLANEOUS

649-7028	Power Regulator	assembled	12.98
649-7029	Power Regulator	kit	2.98
649-7030	Mars Light Control Unit requires #7029 or #7028	kit	6.98
649-7031	Mars Light Control Unit assembled requires #7028 or #7029		15.98
649-7040	Strobe/F.R.E.D. Control Unit	kit	4.98
649-7041	Strobe/ F.R.E.D. Unit	assembled	14.98
649-7042	Strobe F.R.E.D. Unit 1.5v bulb requires #7028 or #7029	assembled	14.98
649-7051	Constant/Directional Lighting Diodes	kit	1.98
649-8003	Phosphor Bronze Sheet 1-5/8 x 6 x .003"		1.39
649-8008	Phosphor Bronze Sheet 1-5/8 x 6 x .088"		1.29
649-4106	Transformer, 6.3v AC 1.2 amp use with #7090 & 7091		4.98
649-4242	24 AWG Wire		6.98
649-4245	6' Five Conductor Flexible Cable		4.98
649-6015	Connector Clip Replacement Kit for Athearn engines, 1 set	pkg(6)	1.98

MISCELLANEOUS

649-6025	Reverse Loop Control Kit		7.98
649-6030	Snap Wipers, phosphor bronze for Athearn SW1500, S12	pkg(4)	1.98
649-4048	Latching Reed Switch, 3/32" x 1-3/16" Magnet actuated	NEW pkg(2)	2.39
649-4243	Flexible (red) Wire 24AWE	NEW pkg(10')	6.98
649-5021	Micro Mini Bulb 1.5v, .052" dia	NEW	1.39
649-7012	Crossing Flasher Control, actuates #7010	NEW kit	2.98
649-7013	Magnets for engines #7012, 4048	NEW	3.98
649-7014	Magnets for caboose, rolling stock	NEW pkg(4)	2.39

Scale Scenics
Division of CIRCUITRON

CONSTRUCTION SIGNS

Multiple Flashing Barricade Kit
652-1505 19.95
Includes circuit and materials to construct 5 operational Flashing Barricades. Each barricade will flash independently, but in a specific sequence. Use of two or more FBK-5 kits to construct a complete construction scene will result in a seemingly random flash sequence among all the barricades.

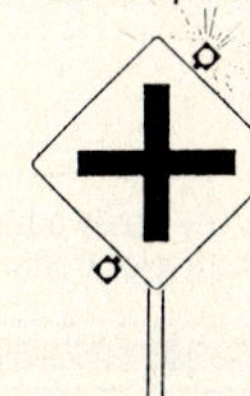

Flashing Highway Sign Kit
652-1520 14.95
Includes materials and circuit to construct one operational diamond shaped highway warning sign with dual alternating yellow flashing lamps. The sign can be assembled in a number of ways to duplicate most prototype situations. Pre-printed yellow and black signboards in a large variety of styles are included. The FS-1 requires a 9 volt DC power source or the CIRCUITRON PS-3 may be used to power the FS-1 directly from a power pack.

STOP SIGNS   NEW

Post mounted, scale sized sign kit includes preassembled electronic flasher circuit. 9 volt DC operation. May be battery powered, or Circuitron PS-3 to power from powerpack. Circuit can flash up to 3 additional signs.

652-1525	w/Red Flashing Light	kit	14.95
652-1526	w/Red Flashing Light	preassembled	22.95
652-1528	Stop Sign	kit	6.95
652-1529	Stop Sign	preassembled	12.95

Vintage Reproductions

We have worked closely with this manufacturer to provide accurate availability information at the time this catalog was published. Items listed in *blue ink* may not be available at all times. Please see your dealer for current delivery information.

MODEL RAILROAD ELECTRONICS LETTERING

Black dry transfers will letter any model railroad electronic control or sound system. If a special word isn't included, there is an extra mini-alphabet and numeral set to create omissions. Sets have two high-tech lettering styles in three sizes, including vertical. Sized especially to fit hand-held or walk around controls. Slash marks to index controls and border and corner lines are included.

CONTROL SYSTEM POWER
THROTTLE CLOCK LIGHTS
BRAKES MOMENTUM INERTIA

766-562 Control Systems Lettering 5.50

SOUND SYSTEM STEAM
DIESEL VOLUME BELL
REVERBERATION HORN
EXHAUST HISS AIR PUMP
WHISTLE GENERATOR

766-563 Sound Systems Lettering 5.50
766-564 Economy Pack 10.00
   Includes one each of #562 and #563.
766-565 Economy Pack & 13.00
   Glo-Sheet Panel Lighting
Includes one each of #'s 562, 563 and 326. Glo-sheet is used to back light lettering for night operation.

WIRE WORKS
NEW

A wide range of electrical wire easily adaptable to any sort of miniature electronics.

WIRE

One Conductor - 7/30-50'		
851-122070500	Black	2.50
851-122070501	Brown	2.50
851-122070502	Red	2.50
851-122070503	Orange	2.50
851-122070504	Yellow	2.50
851-122070505	Green	2.50
851-122070506	Blue	2.50
851-122070509	White	2.50

One Conductor - 7/30-90'		
851-122070900	Black	4.00
851-122070902	Red	4.00
851-122070905	Green	4.00
851-122070909	White	4.00

Two Conductor - 30'		
851-222070300	Black/Red	4.00
851-222070304	Yellow/Blue	4.00
851-222070305	Green/Brown	4.00

Three Conductor - 23'		
851-322070230	Black/Red/Green	4.00
851-322070234	Yellow/Blue/White	4.00

WALTHERS

1.5v MICRO BULB

942-433	Clear	each 4.98

1.5v GRAIN-O-RICE

942-435	Clear	pkg(3) 3.98
942-464	Amber w/10" leads	pkg(3) 1.98

12v GRAIN-O-RICE

942-436	Clear	pkg(3) 3.98

6v GRAIN-O-WHEAT

942-441	Clear	pkg(2) 2.98

16v GRAIN-O-WHEAT

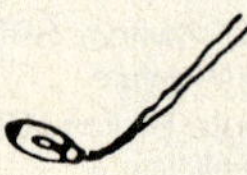

942-3451	Amber	pkg(3)	3.98
942-3453	Clear	pkg(3)	3.98
942-3455	Green	pkg(3)	3.98
942-3456	Red	pkg(3)	3.98
942-13453	Clear	pkg(50)	49.98

16v SUB-MINIATURE BULB

942-365	Clear	pkg(3) 5.98

FLUORETTES - 3 PACK

942-352	16v White	5.98

FLUORETTE SOCKETS

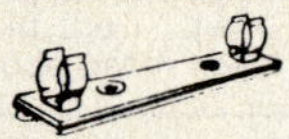

942-362	Panel w/clips	pkg(3) 3.98

16v MINI-BULB

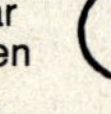

942-3491	Amber	pkg(3) 3.98
942-3493	Clear	pkg(3) 3.98
942-3495	Green	pkg(3) 3.98
942-3496	Red	pkg(3) 3.98

SOCKETS

942-350		pkg(6) 2.98

LIGHTING KITS

EASILY INSTALLED, these insulated sockets can be connected directly to a metal, plastic or wood roof. Frosted tubular bulbs fit snugly out of the way of interior details, give uniform, diffuse lighting over a large area. Wired as directed, bulbs give realistic illumination, last for hundreds and hundreds of hours. Kit contains bulbs, sockets and wiring diagrams.

933-963	Lighting Kit 1-Bulb	3.98
933-717	Standard 2-Bulb Kit	5.98
	(Two 942-352 16v bulbs included)	

LIGHT BULBS, SOCKETS, LIGHTING KITS

Our 16 volt bulbs, when operated from a 12 volt power source, result in a much longer bulb life.

CONSTANT LIGHTING KITS

933-961	Constant Light Unit 1 amp	5.98
933-964	Reversing Headlight Kit	3.98
933-965	Reversing 1 amp	10.98
933-968	Constant Car Light Kit	7.98

DIODES

942-455	Silicon Diode 1 amp	pkg(6) 3.29

18v PANEL BULBS

(mount in 3/8" hole)
"Bulb Only"

942-4000	Extra Bulb	pkg(3) 3.29

HOOK-UP WIRE

942-414	6', 4 Colors	1.98

"N"-WAY PRODUCTS

FLASHING DIESEL BEACON

535-551	Orange, track operated	7.95
535-552	Red, track operated	7.95
535-555	Orange, battery powered	7.95
535-556	Red, battery powered	7.95

Prototype Flashing Warning Beacon lights sit atop modern diesels and emit a colored flash from a LED. Require drilling and soldering.

FLASHING STROBES

535-553	White, track operated	12.95
535-557	White, 9 volt	12.95
	battery powered	

Flashing Strobe unit produces a pure white flash from small light bulb, and instructions included.

EMERGENCY FLASHING LIGHT KIT

535-651	Orange Lights w/Flasher	9.95
535-652	Red Lights w/Flasher	9.95
535-655	Orange Lights only	4.95
535-656	Red Lights only	4.95

Can be attached to all plastic HO cars, fire engines and trucks to transform them into police, fire and highway emergency vehicles. The Flasher will operate 3 sets of emergency lights. Requires two 9 volt batteries or the "N"-Way Power Supply Kit. Vehicle not included.

A-LINE
A division of PROTO POWER WEST

HO SCALE (1/87)

CAN MOTOR

Five-pole with skewed armature and 2.0 mm shaft.

116-40321	Flat, 18 x 33 mm, DS	24.00
116-40322	Flat, 18 x 24 mm, DS	24.00
116-30321	Holland	21.50

MOTOR MOUNT TAPE

Two-sided foam tape motor mount.

116-12020 Motor Mount Tape   pkg(8) 1.35

ELECTRICAL HOOK-UP

116-12040 Hook-up Kit   2.85
For upgrading electrical connections on stock Athearn locos. Also for installing can motors in Athearn and other locos. Will complete two locos.

116-12041 Hook-up Wire   pkg(2') 1.45
Very fine, white flexible multi-stranded wire for all repowering jobs.

LOCOMOTIVE REPOWERING KITS

For use with Athearn diesels, kits include can motor, brass flywheels, wiring hardware and instructions.

116-70321	Basic 4 and 6 axle diesels (18 x 33 mm motor)	30.50
116-80321	Diesel Switchers (18 x 33 mm motor, tapered #20021 flywheels)	32.00
116-90321	Short Wheel Base Diesel/ Steam Loco (18 x 24 mm motor, fits Athearn GP38, GP40 & GP50; also can be used for steam locomotive repowering)	30.50

FLYWHEELS

Precision machined from brass stock, flywheels are drilled and reamed for slip fit on drive shaft. Each pack includes two flywheels, with Athearn couplings installed and complete instructions. Dimensions shown are outside diameter, length and shaft size. Possible applications are listed with each item.

116-20011 3/4 x 11/16" x 2.4   6.50
Can motor fits most Athearn units, except GP35, GP9, S12 amd SW1500. Also fits wide hood brass imports and plastic diesels.

116-20013 3/4 x 3/8" x 2.4   6.50
Can motor fits Athearn S12, SW1500 and most short wheel base locomotives.

116-20004 1 x 1/2" x 3.0   6.50
Micro or Holland can motor fits Athearn F7, PA F&FP45, Cary F&E, Train Miniature, Bachmann F9, Model Power/AHM E and most wide hooded units.

116-20015 3/4 x 11/16" x 2.0   6.50
Can motor fits most Athearn units, except S12, SW1500, GP9 and GP35. Also fits many wide hood brass imports and plastic diesels.

116-20006 21/32 x 11-16" x 2.0   6.50
Flat can motor fits narrow hood units; Atlas, Athearn/GSB SD40-2, SD40T-2, Mantua GP20, Bachmann GP30, DD40X, BQ23-7, AHM RS2, SD40. Fits on stock motored Atlas units. Also fits narrow hood brass imports and plastic diesels.

FLYWHEELS (continued)

116-20021 3/4 x 3/8" x 2.0   7.50
Flat can motor fits Athearn S12, SW1500 and most narrow hood units with short wheelbase, AHM, ALCO 1000. Can also be used for steam locomotive repowering.

116-20020 21/32 x 11/16 x 1/8"   6.50
All Athearn units except SW and SW12.

LIMITED QUANTITIES AVAIL

116-20017 3/4 x 11/16 x 1/8"   6.50
Athearn 4 and 6-axle, wide body units; F7, FP45 and PA.

FLYWHEEL CEMENT

116-20010 Flywheel Cement   2.50

COUPLINGS   NEW

116-12030 Universal Coupling Assortment   6.00
21-piece kit includes assorted male and female universal joints and varous length splines, all cast in Delrin®.

116-12031 Universal Coupling Kit   6.00
8-piece kit includes two 105 mm steel shafts with plastic splines and universal joint components (enough parts to retrofit one brass or plastic locomotive.

Athearn
TRAINS IN MINIATURE

HO SCALE (1/87)

NARROW CAN MOTORS

140-84030	Small	each 7.50
140-84040	Large	each 7.50

ARMATURES

140-86011 1/2", Jet 600   each 3.50

END BELL ASSEMBLIES

140-84013 Jet 400/600   each .80

ASSEMBLY CLIP

140-84017	Jet 400	pkg(6)	.90
140-84025	Bottom, Jet 400	pkg(6)	.90
140-86017	Jet 600	pkg(6)	1.20
140-86025	Bottom, Jet 600	pkg(6)	1.20

MOTOR MOUNT PADS

140-84020	Jet 400	pkg(6)	.90
140-84021	Jet 600	pkg(6)	.90

MISCELLANEOUS

140-84014	Brush Spring Jet 400	pkg(12)	.75
140-84019	Thrust Washer 1/8" (24)		1.00
140-90036	Motor Brush for Jet 400/600	pkg(6)	1.05
140-90043	Motor Bearing Oilite	pkg(4)	1.40
140-90107	Spline Hollow 7/16" (6)		1.20
140-90108	Ball Coupling Jet 400/600	pkg(6)	.90
140-90586	Connector Clip GP35	pkg(4)	1.40

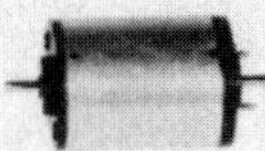

RO CO Roco
Imported from Austria by WALTHERS

HO SCALE (1/87)

CAN

Five-pole, 14V DC, open and can motors.

17,000 RPM
120mA(23x17mm)
Single-End Shaft Flat
625-85025   18.99

625-85029	Single-End Shaft Flat	18.99
625-85030	Single-End Shaft Flat	18.99

OPEN FRAME

17,000 RPM, 85mA (21x14mm)
Double-End Shaft
625-85020   18.99

625-85033	Double Shaft 33x20mm	18.99
625-85035	Single Shaft 33x20mm	18.99
625-85018	17,000 RPM, 100mA Double-End Shaft 17x14mm	18.99
625-85016	Single End Shaft-B	18.99
625-85017	Single End 16,000 RPM, 90mA	18.99

RIBBONRAIL
by Earl Eshleman

+ (PLUS SIGN) =
SPECIAL ORDER ONLY ITEMS
Supplied with 4-40 set screws & allen wrench to fit.

DUAL FLYWHEEL

Item No	O D	Length	Hole & Shaft	Price
170-52 +	11/16"	5/8"	3/32"	6.00
170-53	11/16"	5/8"	1/8"	6.00
170-54	3/4"	19/32"	1/8"	6.00
170-56	15/16"	3/8"	1/8"	7.00
170-57	1"	3/8"	1/8"	7.00
170-58	1"	5/8"	2mm	8.00
170-59 +	1"	5/8"	3/32"	8.00
170-60	1"	5/8"	1/8"	8.00

SINGLE FLYWHEEL

Item No	O D	Length	Hole & Shaft	Price
170-61	11/16"	5/8"	3/32"	3.25
170-62 +	11/16"	5/8"	1/8"	3.25
170-63 +	3/4"	.600"	1/8"	3.25
170-64 +	15/16"	3/8"	1/8"	3.75
170-65	1"	3/8"	1/8"	3.75
170-66	1"	5/8"	2mm	4.25
170-67	1"	5/8"	3/32"	4.25
170-68	1"	5/8"	1/8"	4.25

Grandt Line

HO SCALE (1/87)

- MABUCHI MOTORS
- GEARS
- UNIVERSAL JOINTS
- PICK-UP SHOES
- DELRIN SPROCKETS

MABUCHI MOTORS

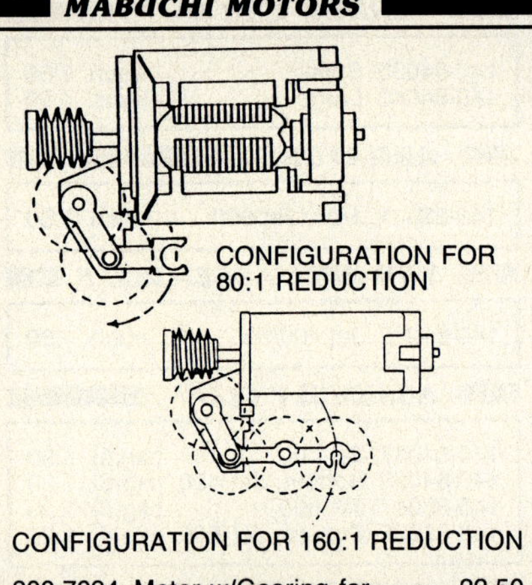

300-7094 Motor w/Gearing for 80:1 or 160:1 Reduction   22.50

GEARS

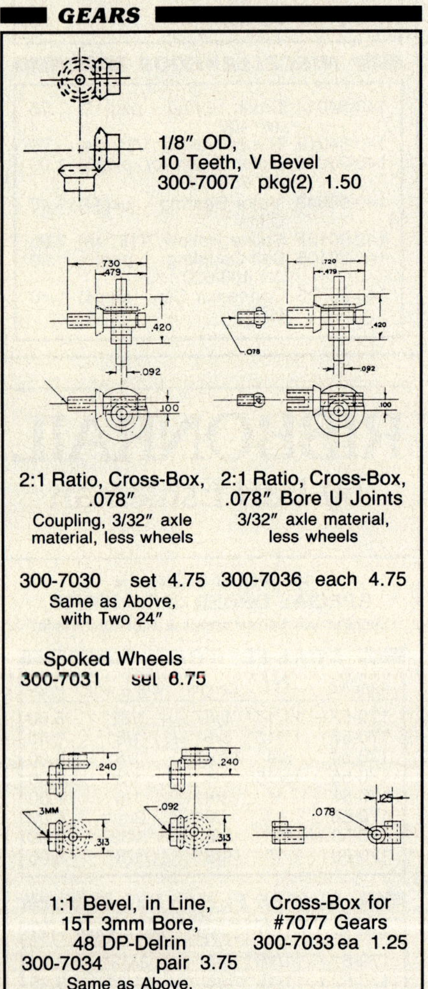

1/8" OD, 10 Teeth, V Bevel
300-7007   pkg(2) 1.50

2:1 Ratio, Cross-Box, .078"
Coupling, 3/32" axle material, less wheels
300-7030   set 4.75

2:1 Ratio, Cross-Box, .078" Bore U Joints
3/32" axle material, less wheels
300-7036   each 4.75

Same as Above, with Two 24"
Spoked Wheels
300-7031   set 6.75

1:1 Bevel, in Line, 15T 3mm Bore, 48 DP-Delrin
300-7034   pair 3.75

Cross-Box for #7077 Gears
300-7033 ea 1.25

Same as Above, w 3/32" Bore
300-7035   pair 3.75

GEARS (continued)

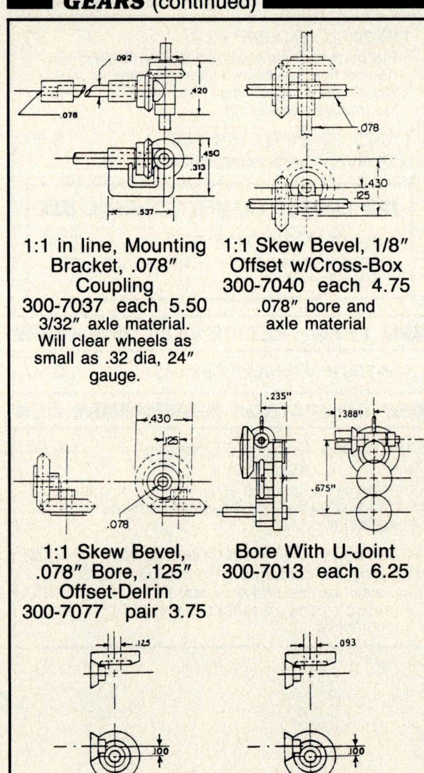

1:1 in line, Mounting Bracket, .078" Coupling
300-7037 each 5.50
3/32" axle material. Will clear wheels as small as .32 dia, 24" gauge.

1:1 Skew Bevel, 1/8" Offset w/Cross-Box
300-7040 each 4.75
.078" bore and axle material

1:1 Skew Bevel, .078" Bore, .125" Offset-Delrin
300-7077   pair 3.75

Bore With U-Joint
300-7013 each 6.25

2:1 Skew Bevel, .062" & .125" Bore
300-7078   pair 3.75
.100" offset, Delrin

Bore with Cross-Box
300-7012 each 3.95
(By Special Order Only.)

UNIVERSAL JOINTS

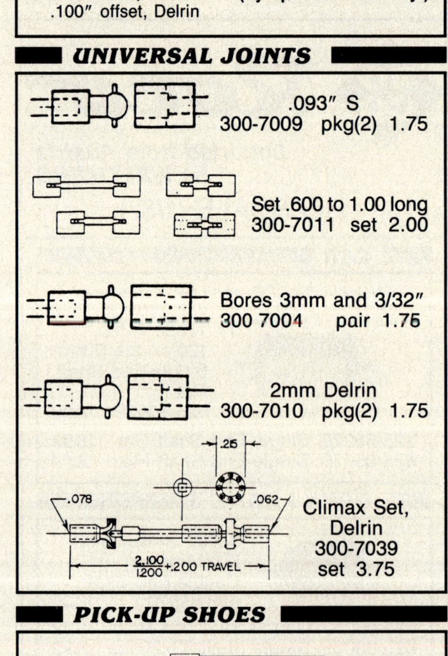

.093" S
300-7009   pkg(2) 1.75

Set .600 to 1.00 long
300-7011   set 2.00

Bores 3mm and 3/32"
300-7004   pair 1.75

2mm Delrin
300-7010   pkg(2) 1.75

Climax Set, Delrin
300-7039   set 3.75

PICK-UP SHOES

Electric (Loco Drivers)
300-7005   ea 4.50

MISCELLANEOUS

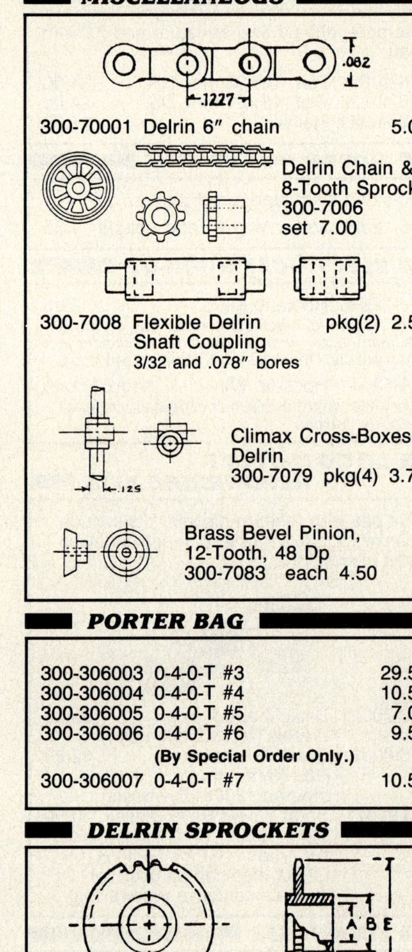

300-70001 Delrin 6" chain   5.00

Delrin Chain & 8-Tooth Sprocket
300-7006   set 7.00

300-7008 Flexible Delrin Shaft Coupling   pkg(2) 2.50
3/32 and .078" bores

Climax Cross-Boxes, Delrin
300-7079 pkg(4) 3.75

Brass Bevel Pinion, 12-Tooth, 48 Dp
300-7083   each 4.50

PORTER BAG

300-306003	0-4-0-T #3	29.50
300-306004	0-4-0-T #4	10.50
300-306005	0-4-0-T #5	7.00
300-306006	0-4-0-T #6	9.50
	(By Special Order Only.)	
300-306007	0-4-0-T #7	10.50

DELRIN SPROCKETS

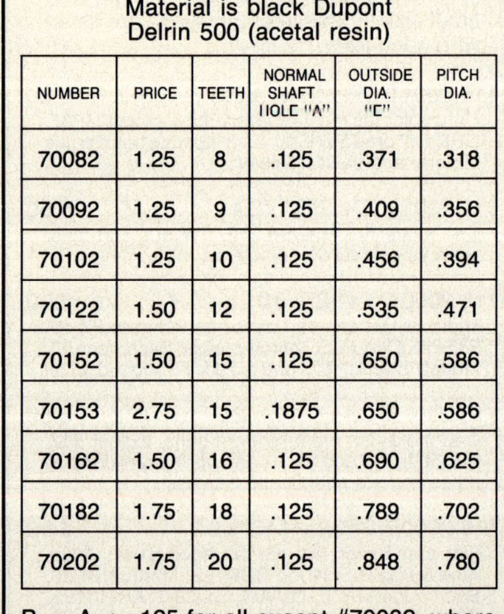

Material is black Dupont Delrin 500 (acetal resin)

NUMBER	PRICE	TEETH	NORMAL SHAFT HOLE "A"	OUTSIDE DIA. "C"	PITCH DIA.
70082	1.25	8	.125	.371	.318
70092	1.25	9	.125	.409	.356
70102	1.25	10	.125	.456	.394
70122	1.50	12	.125	.535	.471
70152	1.50	15	.125	.650	.586
70153	2.75	15	.1875	.650	.586
70162	1.50	16	.125	.690	.625
70182	1.75	18	.125	.789	.702
70202	1.75	20	.125	.848	.780

B = A + .125 for all except #70082, where B = .236   L = .312 for all

MIL-SCALE Products

COMPUTER PROGRAMS

These products are special order items. When ordering, please request that your Dealer "Back Order" the item, or the order cannot be processed. Please allow 2-3 weeks for delivery.

CARTRACKER

Realistic operation is easy with a copy of Car-Tracker for your computer. This IBM/compatibles program simplifies and defines car forwarding and routing on your layout. Cars can be moved between yards, routed to points on the layout or moved to and from staging areas. Way freight routings to on-line industries can also be generated and the program can match car contents to industry requirements, including special lading or restricted loads. The computer will also keep track of loaded and empty cars and can provide train lists and car location lists for crews. Many other exciting features are included. Program requires 512K RAM and hard disk. Complete unit includes CarTracker master disks, a user manual and a vinyl binder.

477-1117 CarTracker 119.95

T/D CALC

Program computes scale time and distance. Can be used to calculate running times between stations or terminals.

477-1101 Commodore 64, 128 Disk 14.95

INVENRAIL **NEW**

Complete program keeps track of your entire model railroad inventory. IBM and Compatible. Requires 512K, hard disk. Color Monitor suggested. Ready to use.

477-1118 InvenRail Software 59.95

MANIFEST

Based on your roster, this program automatically determines train length and consist. Will accomodate 100 cars. List is printed automatically when computer is used with a printer.

477-1102 Commodore 64, 128 Disk 20.95
477-1113 IBM & Compatible 26.95

SWITCH

This program classifies and consigns freight cars to industrial sidings on your layout. Program accomodates 100 cars and 25 shippers. Requires input of car roster, shipper list and siding capacities. List is printed automatically when computer is used with a printer.

477-1103 Commodore 64, 128 Disk 20.95
477-1114 IBM & Compatible 39.95

CLOCK

An adjustable fast clock, with large digital readout, suitable for model railroad use. Can be adjusted from normal time to 15:1 fast time. Unit can also display scale time and distance.

477-1104 Commodore 64, 128 Disk 19.95

LOCO

Based on your locomotive roster, this program assigns engines based on train length and type. List is printed automatically when computer is used with a printer.

477-1105 Commodore 64, 12 Disk 24.95

MAINTENANCE MANAGER

Maintains a repair history of all cars or locos and indentifies equipment due for service. Compatible with Commodore 64/128.

477-1106 Cars 36.95
477-1107 Locomotives 36.95
477-1108 Cars & Locomotives 57.95

RAILSTARR II COMPUTER PROGRAMS

Generates consists, switch lists and assigns locomotives to trains.

477-1116 IBM & Compatible 73.95

DILOCRON

Provides complete historical information and profiles of over 50 types of diesels. Includes number built, average number in service for a given year and more, which can be used to create an accurate roster for your layout. The file can be revised and calculations are automatically updated.

477-1112 IBM & Compatible 31.95

ARNOLD

HO SCALE (1/87) **NEW**

MOTORS

125-776	for #2220's-2250-60's	31.99
125-778	for #2402	31.99
125-205006	for 2051-52-53-54	23.99
125-231080	for #2310-11-30	23.99
125-245001	for #2450-57	23.99
125-246003	for #2460-61	33.99
125-253020	for #2350-35-40-2210	33.99
125-254503	for #2545-46	23.99
125-293000	for #2930-35	23.99
125-296000	for #2960-63	23.99

MOTOR BRUSH

125-224016 Motor Brushes pkg(2) 3.49

N.J. International

HO SCALE (1/87)

OPEN FRAME

525-8805 8.95

TIMEWELL PRECISION FLYWHEELS

HO SCALE (1/87)

FLYWHEELS

These Precision Flywheels may be used as Athearn replacement parts or on other motors.

712-101 for: Alco, Balboa, Trains, Hallmark, Westside Imports, Athearn Hi-F (old) 2.00

for: Suydam, Custom Brass Electrics
712-102 2.00

712-1032 for: Athearn F7, GP9, SD9, RDC, GP30, FP35 and BART 2.50

712-1034 for: Athearn F45, FP45, SDP40, SD45 2.50
712-1031 for: Athearn U28, U30, U33, PA1 2.50
712-1033 for: Athearn S12, SW1500 2.00
712-115 for: NWSL Can Motors, w/1.5 mm shaft diameter 2.00
712-120 for: NWSL Can Motors w/2.0mm shaft diameter 2.00
712-124 for:NWSL Can Motors w/2.4mm shaft diameter 2.00
712-130 for: NWSL Can Motors w/2.4mm shaft diameter 3.00
712-135 for: NWSL Can Motors w/2.4mm shaft diameter 3.50

SPECIFICATIONS

Number	Outside Diameter	Length	Shaft Diameter
712-101	3/4"	3/8"	3/32"
712-102	11/16"	3/8"	3/32"
712-1031	5/8"	5/8"	1/8"
712-1032	3/4"	1/2"	1/8"
712-1033	3/4"	5/16"	1/8"
712-1034	3/4"	3/4"	1/8"
712-115	1/2"	3/16"	1.5 mm
712-120	5/8"	5/16"	2.0 mm
712-124	3/4"	5/16"	2.4 mm
712-130	7/8"	3/8"	2.4 mm
712-135	1"	3/8"	2.4 mm

NorthWest Short Line

Specify Mfr #053 When Ordering

NOTE: We can NOT set up gearing arrangements. See November, 1976 NMRA Bulletin for gear information.

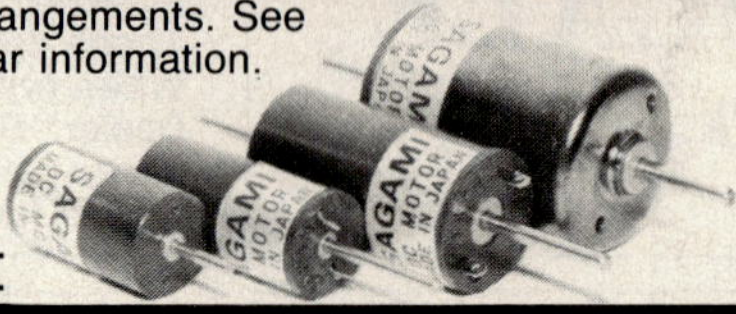

12 VOLT CAN TYPE MOTORS

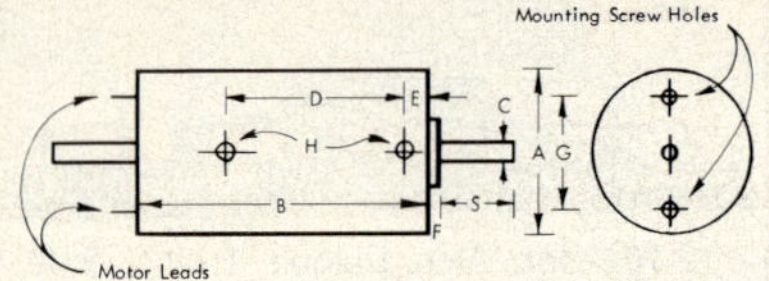

These high precision heavy duty motors, with skewed 5 pole armatures, diameters ranging from less than 1/2″ to 1-1/4″, are suitable for all scales from O to N. They have a high efficiency (low battery drain) with high torque/ speed characteristics, plus silent and maintenance free operation. Fully enclosed cylindrical type. Mounting screws (packed with motor) must not be inserted more than 2mm into motor case. Uses long life ceramic & ferrite magnets.

The first two digits in the number indicate the diameter in millimeters. The second two digits indicate the length. Fifth digit even (0,2) = single shaft, odd = double shaft. When single or shorter double shaft is desired use cut-off disk to remove excess. Specifications and prices subject to change without notice.

NOTE: All dimensions on the chart are in millimeters. →

number	price	A	B	C	D	E	F	G	H	S	stall# torque	12 volt no load rpm	amp	ef%	HP
101319*	26.95	10.5	13	1.5			1.1	8		15	.05	27500	.17		
101519*	26.95	10.5	15	1.5			1.1	8		15	.10	27500	.09		
102019*	27.95	10.5	20	1.5			1.1	8		15	.15	27500	.05		
122029	24.95	12	20.0	1.5	11.5	2	1.0	8	1.4	6	0.135	24500	0.18	20.5	.0008
122039	24.95	12	20.0	1.5	11.5	2	1.0	8	1.4	15	0.135	24500	0.18	20.5	.0008
122539	26.95	12	25.0	1.5	16.5	2	1.0	8	1.4	15	0.187	17800	0.04	43.5	.0010
123039	29.95	12	30	1.5	16.5	2	1.0	8	1.4	15	.35	15000	.04		
142039	27.45	14	20.0	1.5	11.5	2	1.0	10	1.4	15	0.225	28000	0.24	23.4	.0012
142539	27.95	14	25.0	1.5	16.5	2	1.0	10	1.4	15	0.43	17000	0.05	50.0	.0014
162039	21.95	16	20.0	2.0	13.0	1.5	1.9	12	2.0	15	0.31	16800	0.14	39.3	.0015
163029	22.95	16	29.5	2.0	19.0	3	0.5	12	2.0	25	0.68	14900	0.10	48.4	.002
163039	22.95	16	29.5	2.0	19.0	3	0.5	12	2.0	15	0.68	14900	0.10	48.4	.002
202739	21.95	20	26.5	2.4	13.0	4	1.0	13	2.0	15	1.10	9100	0.10	47.9	.003
203229	22.95	20	31.5	2.4	19.0	4	1.0	13	2.0	25	1.20	9800	0.10	50.0	.0040
203239	22.95	20	31.5	2.4	19.0	4	1.0	13	2.0	15	1.20	9800	0.10	50.0	.0040
203279*	22.95	20	31.5	2.4	19.0	4	1.0	13	2.0	15	2.0	16500			
222419	19.50	22	24.0	2.4	15.0	2	1.5	15	2.0	15	0.63	17000	0.16	44.25	.0031
223119	20.95	22	31.0	2.4	20.0	2	1.5	15	2.0	15	1.10	11000	0.11	53.1	.0037
223619	22.95	22	36.0	2.4	26.0	2	1.5	15	2.0	15	1.42	9800	0.075	60.9	.0042
224019	23.95	22	40.0	2.4	27.0	2	2.0	15	2.0	15	1.60	9500	0.075	57.6	.0043
282419	20.95	28	24.0	2.4	11.0	5	2.0	15	2.0	15	1.45	9800	0.13	49.3	.0043
283019	22.95	28	30.0	2.4	16.0	5	2.0	15	2.0	15	2.50	8200	0.09	61.8	.0058
283519	23.95	28	35.0	2.4	21.0	5	2.0	15	2.0	15	3.40	7000	0.10	70.2	.0065
284019	24.95	28	40.0	2.4					2.0	15	4.0	8300	.010	77.0	.0087

*Can Motor has double shafts to serve as a replacement in Tenshado or AHM regeared locos. This motor is designed to perform 70% faster than a standard 20 x 32 motor.

12 VOLT DC FLAT CAN MOTORS

Flat sides permit more power in narrow spaces.

053-183349 Single Shaft **NEW** 26.95
18 x 23 x 33mm
053-183359 Double Shaft **NEW** 26.95
18 x 23 x 33mm
053-183659 15 x 2.4mm **NEW** 26.95
Double Shaft
18 x 23 x 36mm

BRUSH CAP

For can motors only.
053-100169 16mm diameter 5.50
053-100209 20mm diameter 5.50
(By Special Order Only.)

OPEN FRAME MOTORS

All dimensions on the chart are in millimeters. #101539 has a double shaft.

Open Frame Motor
053-101539 18.95

A1	A2	B	C	F	S
10	15	23	1.5	1.5	15

MOTOR MOUNT

053-1996 Sticky Plastic 1.00
for temporary or permanent attachment

MOTOR SHAFT BUSHING

Bushings increase small shafts to normal 3/32″ or 1/8″ press fit.

Number	Bore	O.D.	Qty.	Price
053-1524	1.5mm	3/32″	pkg(2)	1.00
053-1544	1/16″	3/32″	pkg(2)	1.00
053-11524	1.5mm	3/32″	pkg(24)	9.50
053-11544	1/16″	3/32″	pkg(24)	9.50
053-11574	1.2mm	3/32″	pkg(12)	9.50

NorthWest Short Line

Specify Mfr #053 When Ordering

NOTE: We can NOT set up gearing arrangements.
See November, 1976 NMRA Bulletin for gear information.

■ 72' DP GEARS pkg(6) 18.00 ■

All bores are light press fit. All gears are machine cut, not injection molded.

72' DP GEAR TYPES & BORES

3.0mm Bore (.118")				
# of teeth	spur gear	worm gear	reverse worm gear	type	O.D.
15	177156	117156	147156	Brass	.240
15	187156	127156	157156	Delrin	.240
20	177206	117206	147206	Brass	.306
20	187206	127206	157206	Delrin	.306
24	177246	117246	147246	Brass	.361
24	187246	127246	157246	Delrin	.361
30	177306	117306	147306	Brass	.444
30	187306	127306	157306	Delrin	.444
36	177366	117366	147366	Brass	.527
36	187366	127366	157366	Delrin	.527
40	177406	117406	147406	Brass	.583
40	187406	127406	157406	Delrin	.583

3/32" Bore (.0937")				
# of teeth	spur gear	worm gear	reverse worm gear	type	O.D.
10	170106	110106	140106	Brass	.178
15	170156	110156	140156	Brass	.240
15	180156	120156	150156	Delrin	.240
20	170206	110206	140206	Brass	.306
20	180206	120206	150206	Delrin	.306
24	170246	110246	140246	Brass	.361
24	180246	120246	150246	Delrin	.361
30	170306	110306	140306	Brass	.444
30	180306	120306	150306	Delrin	.444
36	170366	110366	140366	Brass	.527
36	180366	120366	150366	Delrin	.527
40	170406	110406	140406	Brass	.583
40	180406	120406	150406	Delrin	.583

■ SHAFT/AXLE STOCK ■

Precision ground steel drill rod for shafts, axles and worm shafts. Each package includes one 6" length.

053-20154 O.D. 1.5mm 1.00
053-20204 O.D. 2.0mm 1.00
053-20244 O.D. 2.4mm 1.00
often used in place of 3/32 in import models

053-20254 O.D. 2.5mm 1.00
053-20304 O.D. 3.0mm 1.00
used in place of 1/8 in import models and axles

053-20404 O.D. 4.0mm 1.50
053-20504 O.D. 5.0mm 1.50
053-20584 O.D. 5.8mm 1.50
053-20604 O.D. 6.0mm 1.50
053-20624 O.D. 1/16" 1.00
053-20934 O.D. 3/32" 1.00
common as motor shaft size

053-21254 O.D. 1/8" 1.00
loco axles, some motor shafts in US models

053-21564 O.D. 5/32" 1.50
053-21874 O.D. 3/16" 1.50
053-22504 O.D. 1/4" 1.50

■ KMT BRASS TOWER GEARS ■

Will also fit Tenshoda diesels and some others.

053-776096 9T pkg(6) 16.20
053-776106 10T pkg(6) 16.20
053-776116 11T pkg(6) 16.20
053-776126 12T pkg(6) 16.20
053-776136 13T pkg(6) 16.20
053-776146 14T pkg(6) 16.20
053-776156 15T pkg(6) 16.20
053-776166 16T pkg(6) 16.20
053-776176 17T pkg(6) 16.20
053-776186 18T pkg(6) 16.20
053-776196 19T pkg(6) 16.20
053-776206 20T pkg(6) 16.20
053-776216 21T pkg(6) 16.20
053-776226 22T pkg(6) 16.20
053-776236 23T pkg(6) 16.20
053-776246 24T pkg(6) 16.20
053-776266 26T pkg(6) 16.20
053-1056 KMT Tower Gear Service 49.95

■ 72' DP STEEL WORMS ■

.1875 O.D. Worms match gears listed above.
053-100006 3/32" Bore pkg(6) 16.20
053-104006 1.5mm Bore pkg(6) 17.55
053-105006 2mm Bore pkg(6) 17.55

■ FLANGED BEARINGS ■

053-3546 Brass, 3/32 x 1/8" pkg(8) 1.95
053-3556 Brass, 9/64 x 5/32" for WSM K-37 pkg(8) 1.95
053-3566 Bronze, 2.0mm x 1/8" pkg(2) 1.50
053-3576 Bronze, 1.5mm x 4.0mm pkg(2) 1.50
053-3586 Bronze, 2.4mm x 3.9mm pkg(2) 1.50
053-3596 Bronze, 2.0mm x 3.9mm pkg(2) 1.50
053-3606 Bronze, 1.5mm x 3.9mm pkg(2) 1.50
053-3616 Bronze, 1/8 x 3/16" pkg(2) 1.50
053-3636 Bronze, 1.5mm x 2.5mm pkg(2) 1.50
053-3706 Pillow Block 2.4 hole each 2.50

■ THRUST WASHER ■

For miscellaneous fine tuning application. All slip fit dimensions listed.

053-1004 3/32" I.D., 3/16" pkg(10) .90
  O.D. .005" thick, bronze
053-1014 3/32" I.D., 3/16" pkg(100) 4.50
  O.D. .005" thick, bronze
053-1024 3/32" I.D., 3/16" pkg(100) 4.50
  O.D. .010" thick, bronze
053-1034 3/32" I.D., 3/16" pkg(10) .90
  O.D. .010" thick, bronze
053-1064 1/8" I.D., 3/16" pkg(10) .90
  O.D. .010" thick, bronze
053-1074 1/8" I.D., 3/16" pkg(100) 4.50
  O.D. .010" thick, bronze
053-1084 2.0mm I.D., 3.0mm pkg(10) .90
  O.D. .010" thick, bronze
053-1094 2.0mm I.D., 3.0mm pkg(100) 4.50
  O.D. .010" thick, bronze
053-1104 1/16" I.D., 3.0mm pkg(10) .90
  O.D. .010" thick, bronze
053-1114 1/16" I.D., 3.0mm pkg(100) 4.50
  O.D. .010" thick, bronze

■ THRUST WASHER (continued) ■

053-1124 .064" I.D., pkg(10) .90
  .120" O.D. .020" thick, nylon
053-1134 .060" I.D., pkg(100) 5.50
  .120" O.D. .020" thick, nylon
053-1144 3/32" I.D., pkg(10) .90
  1/4" O.D. .016" thick, bronze
053-1154 3/32" I.D., pkg(100) 4.50
  1/4" O.D. .016" thick, bronze

■ GEARBOXES ■

Idler and standard gearboxes and a "high-rise" double idler to allow horizontal motor installation in the boiler. Power is transferred to driven axle via quiet, slow speed worm gears.

053-1366 28:1 Double Idler, 3.0mm axle 15.95
053-1396 28:1 Idler, 3.0mm axle 12.95
053-1406 28:1, 3.0mm axle 10.95
053-1416 28:1 Double Idler, 1/8" axle 15.95
053-1426 28:1 Idler, 1/8" axle 12.95
053-1436 28:1, 1/8" axle 10.95
053-1466 28:1 Idler, 2.4mm axle 12.95
053-1476 28:1, 2.4mm axle 10.95
053-1506 36:1 Idler, 3.0mm axle 12.95
053-1516 36:1, 3.0mm axle 10.95
053-1536 36:1 Idler, 1/8" axle 12.95
053-1546 36:1, 1/8" axle 10.95
053-2116 14:1, 2.4/3.0 mm axle 10.95
053-2216 Transfer Gearbox 13.95
053-2236 Transfer Gearbox, 1:89, 2.4 mm axle 14.95
053-2246 Transfer Case, 1:1 2.4 mm axle 18.95
053-2406 28:1 Idler, 3.0mm axle 13.95
053-2416 28:1, 3.0mm axle 11.95
053-2426 28:1 Idler, 1/8" axle 13.95
053-2436 28:1, 1/8" axle 11.95
053-2446 28:1 Idler, 4.0mm axle (5/32") 13.95
053-2456 28:1, 4.0mm axle (5/32") 11.95
053-2606 12.5:1 Idler, 3/16" axle 21.95
053-2616 12.5:1, 3/16" axle 16.95
053-2626 12.5:1 Idler, 1/4" axle 21.95
053-2636 12.5:1, 1/4" axle 16.95
053-2646 12.5:1 Idler, 5.0mm axle 21.95
053-2656 12.5:1, 5.0mm axle 16.95
053-2666 12.5:1 Idler, 5.8mm axle 21.95
053-2676 12.5:1, 5.8mm axle 16.95
053-2686 12.5:1 Idler, 6.0mm axle 21.95

■ GEAR ALIGNER ■

A gear trueing tool designed to check and minimize gear wobbling which can occur when installing gears on axles and shafts.

053-324 for 2.4mm (3/32") axles & shafts 5.95
053-334 for 3.0mm axles & shafts 5.95
053-384 for 1/8" axles & shafts 5.95

■ GEARBOX INPUT SHAFT CONVERSION ■

053-1446 2.0mm Right Hand 4.00
053-1456 1.5mm Right Hand 4.00
Converts wormshaft (double idler and non-idler types only).

053-1646 2.0mm Left Hand 4.00
053-1656 1.5mm Left Hand 4.00
Converts worm shaft for idler styles 1396, 1426, 1506, 1536 and 1466 (idler style only).

NorthWest Short Line

NOTE: We can NOT set up gearing arrangements.
See November, 1976 NMRA Bulletin for gear information.

HI-LOW GEARBOXES

For quiet HO mallets and articulated locos. Features a quiet direct line drive system, molded of celcon acetal plastic with bronze worm shaft bearings, steel worm and machined brass gears.

053-1486	28:1, 3mm axle	29.00
053-1496	28:1, 1/8″ axle	29.00
053-1586	36:1, 3mm axle	29.00
053-1596	36:1, 1/8″ axle	29.00
053-2486	28:1, .04 module	29.00

GEAR AND RE-GEAR SETS

053-1006	4-axle KMT Diesel Re-gear Kit	14.95
053-1016	6-axle KMT Diesel Re-gear Kit	19.95
053-1206	Speed Reduction Gear Set for Benson Shay	10.95
053-1216	Speed Reduction Gear Set for PC Shay **(By Special Order Only.)**	10.95
053-1236	Re-gear for PFM Shay (7T) 2mm Bore	14.50
053-1246	Re-gear for PFM Shay (12T) 2.6mm Bore	13.00
053-1266	Re-gear for PFM Shay (7T) 2.4mm Bore	14.00
053-1276	Re-gear for PFM Shay (7T) 2.4mm Bore	13.00
053-1806	72:1 for Small Motor, 2.0mm shaft on MDC Locos	12.95
053-1816	45:1 for Small Motor, 2.0mm shaft on MDC Locos	12.95
053-1826	72:1 for Large Motor, 3/32″ shaft on MDC Locos	12.95
053-1836	45:1 for Large Motor, 3/32″ shaft on MDC Locos	12.95
053-1846	Loco Re-gear Set for HOn3 on MDC Locos uses existing motor	10.95
053-1856	Loco Re-gear Set for HOn3 on MDC Locos includes 1225 can motor	34.95
053-1866	Partial Re-gear Kit for MDC 2-truck Shay	18.50
053-1876	Partial Re-gear Kit for MDC 3-truck Shay	22.50
053-1886	Gear Upgrade Kit for MDC Shay Bull Gear	9.50
053-3016	Re-gear Kit for AHM Locos 2-8-4 and larger, except 4-8-4	7.95
053-3056	HOn3, 26 tooth Idler Gear Westside Models	4.50
053-3066	for Life-Like GP-38, etc.	8.95
053-3076	Speed Reduction Gear Set for AHM, HUD & PAC	9.95
053-3086	for AHM MIKADO	8.95
053-3096	for AHM 0-4-0 & 0-6-0T	8.95
053-3106	for AHM USRA 0-6-0	9.95
053-3126	42% Speed Reduction, for AHM 0-8-0 vertical motor shaft type only	8.95
053-3136	Speed Reduction Gear Set for AHM 4-8-4	8.95
053-3166	Main Gear for Life-Like GP-38	4.50
053-3206	Replacement Gear for Mantua	8.95
053-3226	Gear for Sambongsa E-B (22T) pkg(2)	8.95
053-3296	Spur Gear for Suydam (10T) pkg(4)	11.95
053-3336	Replacement Gear pkg(2) (21T) for Alco, SHS, etc.	8.95
053-3346	Kit for WSM E Unit **(By Special Order Only.)**	16.95

GEAR AND RE-GEAR SETS (continued)

053-3356	Replacement Gear pkg(2) (15T) for Alco, SHS, etc.	8.95
053-3366	Idler Worm Gear pkg(2) for Keystone/Samhongsa GP-7 (28T)	8.95
053-3376	Idler Worm Gear pkg(2) for Samhongsa H15-44/GP-7 (23T)	8.95
053-3386	Re-gear Kit for pkg(2) Keystone/Samhongsa Shay	8.95
053-3396	Replacement Gear for pkg(2) Keystone/Samhongsa Shay (27T)	8.95
053-3416	Spur Gear for pkg(2) Samhongsa SD38-2 (14T)	9.95
053-3426	Spur Gear for pkg(2) Samhongsa SD38-2 (15T)	9.95
053-3436	Spur Gear for pkg(2) Samhongsa RSD-15/DL600B (15T)	9.95
053-3446	Spur Gear for pkg(2) Samhongsa (20T)	9.95
053-3456	Spur Gear for pkg(2) Samhongsa RSD-15/DL600B (21T)	9.95
053-3466	Spur Gear for pkg(2) Oriental F-3 (20T)	9.95
053-3476	Spur Gear for pkg(2) Samhongsa RS-3/RS-32 (21T)	9.95
053-3486	Reverse Worm Gear pkg(2) for Hallmark Whitcomb (25T) **(By Special Order Only.)**	8.95
053-3496	Reverse Worm Gear pkg(2) (hi-angle) for Samhongsa Diesels (15T)	8.95
053-3516	WS-K-36 Worm & Idler Replacement **(By Special Order Only.)**	8.95

ARMATURE

Double shaft Sagami 5 pole armature upgrades the Rivarossi 14 x 20mm 3 pole motor used in N Scale articulated locos and Atlas 4-6-2.

053-100529	Rivarossi Armature	8.95
053-100869	for #101539 Motor	8.95
053-100879	for #101319 Motor	8.95
053-100889	for #101519 Motor	8.95
053-100899	for #102019 Motor	8.95

ATHEARN RE-POWER KITS

Athearn diesel re-motor kit with Sagami motor and NWSL flywheel allows slower, smoother speed, more power with lower amp draw (run more locos at a time) and no need to re-gear. Plugs directly to Athearn Universals.

053-1614	All but Narrow Hood	29.95
053-1624	Large	26.95
053-1634	SD40-2	32.95

Includes two precision turned brass flywheels and shafts bushed to fit the existing Athearn couplings.

053-1654	Switcher	29.95

Includes #1833 motor, NWSL flywheel & universal couplings.

ATLAS RE-POWER KITS

053-1664	FP7	29.95

FLYWHEELS

053-4006	10mm diameter, F/1.5mm	2.50
053-4016	12mm diameter, F/1.5mm	2.50
053-4026	16mm diameter, F/2.0mm	2.50
053-4036	18mm diameter, F/2.4mm	3.00
053-4046	1″ diameter, F/2.4mm	3.00

POWER SYSTEM PLANNING KIT

Consists of translucent sheets of motor, gearbox and drive unit outlines printed actual size. Sheets can be overlaid on scale drawings of the model to determine fit, position and location of components.

053-26	Power System Planning Kit	2.00

KEYSTONE DRIVE KITS

Kit will convert the dummy Keystone Shay to a powered version; all four axles.

053-2086	HO (fits KLW 105)	60.00
053-2096	HOn3 (fits KLW 1053)	60.00
053-2106	HOn2-1/2 (fits KLW 1053)	64.95

SPECIFICATION & USAGE INFORMATION BOOKLET

053-9	Sagami Motor Specifications Usage Information Booklet	ea .50

UNIVERSAL DRIVELINE COUPLER SETS

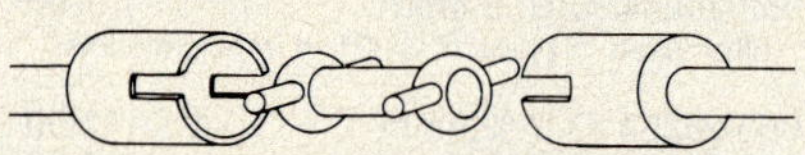

Ball type universal driveline coupling for use as double universal or as two single joints. Sets with the same ball sizes may be combined to couple different shaft sizes. Easy to install press-fit or cup can be drilled and tapped for set screw.

Made of Celcon Acetal engineering plastic and will fit 1.2, 1.5, 2.0, 2.4, 3.0mm and 3/32 and 1/8mm motor/gearbox shafts.

No.	Primary Cups Shaft Size	Add'l Cups	Horned Shaft Shaft Size	Ball Dia″	Price
4806	1/8″	None	2.4mm	3/16	1.95
4816	2.4mm	None	2.4mm	3/16	1.95
4826	2.0mm	1.5 & 2.4mm	2.0mm	1/8	2.95
4836	1.5mm	2.0 & 2.4mm	1.5mm	3/32	2.95
4846	2.4mm	2.4mm	2.0mm	1/8	2.95
4856	1.2mm	1.5 & 2.0mm	1.5mm	3/32	2.95
4866	3.0mm	None	2.4mm	3/16	1.95
4876	1.5mm	1.5mm	1.5mm	3/32	2.95
4886	2.4mm	2.0mm			2.95
4896	2.0mm	2.0mm			2.95
4906	2.4mm				2.95
4956	5/32-1/8″ Shaft Universal Connection				2.95

Circuitron
Electronics for Model Railroads

CIRCUITRON products constructed on printed circuit boards are designed to mount by snapping them into a section of CIRCUITRON'S PCMT (Printed Circuit Mounting Track). Solid state integrated circuit technology. Complete instructions are included. One year limited warranty.

SNAPPER POWER MACHINE

Designed to provide positive power to all dual-coil switch machines. Provides protection from burnout due to stuck pushbuttons, short circuits, etc. Operates off accessory terminals of power pack, or any 25 volt input, it will activate between 5 and 10 switch machine coils simultaneously if they are connected to the same control. Recycle time is instantaneous. A section of Printed Circuit Mounting Track (PCMT) is included.

800-5303 SNAPPER		24.95
800-9350 3 Amp Diode for Matrix Control	pkg(2)	1.50

ADJUSTABLE CONVERTER & REGULATOR

A self-contained AC to DC converter with an adjustable voltage regulated output. The output voltage can be adjusted anywhere between 1.25 and 12.00 volts DC. Maximum continuous current output of the PS-2A is in excess of one amp. The PS-2A is ideal for powering any low current DC accessories including 1.5 volt micro-lamps. The AC or unfiltered DC input to the PS-2A should be about 5-6 volts higher than the desired regulated output voltage to allow maximum current output. The input voltage may be as high as 22 volts, but this may result in reduced current available at the output, particularly at lower voltage settings.

800-5305 PS-2A   24.95

POWER SUPPLIES

Most CIRCUITRON accessories are designed to operate off AC or DC supplies, but best performance is achieved when a DC supply is used. A section of PCMT is supplied with both the PS-1 and PS-2.

800-5301 PS-1 Filtered AC to DC Converter   13.95

PS-1: A highly filtered AC to DC converter. Maximum load capacity of 1 amp, and maximum input voltage of 22 volts AC. Output is not regulated; thus output voltage will vary depending upon input voltage and output load. (Requires transformer or power pack of AC input.)

800-5302 PS-2 Filtered & Regulated AC to DC Converter   22.95

PS-2: Filtered and fully regulated AC to DC converter which will provide a 1 amp output at a constant 12 volts. DC independent of input voltage and output load. The PS-2 has a maximum input of 18 volts AC. (Requires a transformer or power pack for AC input).

POWER SUPPLIES (cont)

800-9601	Inline Fuse Holder	2.00
800-5304	PS-3 Emergency Flasher Power Supply	10.95

The PS-3 Power Supply is designed to power the EF-1 Emergency Flasher in situations where battery operation is undesirable. Accepts AC or DC input of 10 to 18 volts and converts it to 8 volts DC. Maximum current output of 50 ma. is sufficient to power up to 5 EF-1's.

A.J. FRICKO COMPANY

"making toy trains run like real trains"

Electrical accessories for HO & Larger Scales.

CONVERTO

Solid state electronic device converts AC universal motor. Direction is then controlled by polarity in rail, not by the traditional E unit. (For Marklin, Lionel, American Flyer or any AC transformer.)

274-805 Converto   9.95

TRANSVERTO

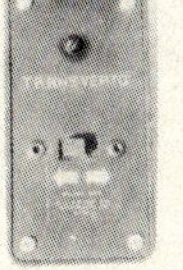

Control box changes the output of a toy train transformer from 18 volt AC to 18 volt DC, and can also reverse polarity. (For Marklin, Lionel, American Flyer or other AC transformers.)

274-804 Transverto   49.95

Rix Products

HANDHELD TRANSISTOR THROTTLE

628-8 Handheld Transistor Throttle 79.95

Offers easy one hand operation, Rix throttle includes automatic circuit breaker, track voltage lamp, overload lamp, PC board mounting rack and 12' cord. 4 amps, 6-24 volts.

DIAMOND SCALE CONST.

TURNTABLE INDEXING KIT

Index kit is designed to control the operation of the motor, to stop turntable in correct rail alignment at track selected. Operator selects track, determines direction of bridge rotation and starts unit with the push of a button. Turntable turns until it comes within 3/4" of selected track, then automatically slows until final alignment is made.

Kit consists of prewired electronic board, six track senors, twelve-position rotary selector switch, switch knob, two push buttons and control rotor.

239-110	for 105 ft and under Turntables N and Sn3 Scales	90.25
239-114	for 115 ft and over Turntables HO and O Scales	90.25

TURNTABLE MOTOR & GEAR BOX

Designed to operate all Diamond Scale turntables through the 3/16" steel worm shaft supplied in each turntable kit. Attaches to underside of pit and requires indexing kit to achieve total automatic operation. Reversing switch included.

239-111 Turntable Motor & Gear Box Kit   49.50

INDEX KIT ACCESSORIES

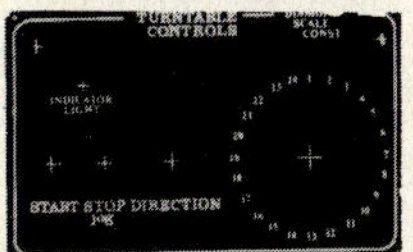

Control Panel Plate 239-74   7.95

Silk-screened control panel plate for the Turntable Indexing Kits. Aluminum plate is punched to receive push buttons, direction switch, rotary switch and indicator light.

(not illustrated)

239-1151 Indexing Sensor   2.25
Track sensors for use with Turntable Indexing Kit.

JANUARY 22, 1912

❀ Today ❀
IN RAILROAD HISTORY

Florida East Coast opens its 41 mile extension from Miami to Key West, Florida.

MODEL RECTIFIER CORPORATION

TECH II SERIES

The TECH II Series introduces PTC (proportional tracking control.) Instant response from locos throughout the entire speed range. Automatically adjusts pulse characteristics to match locos motor.

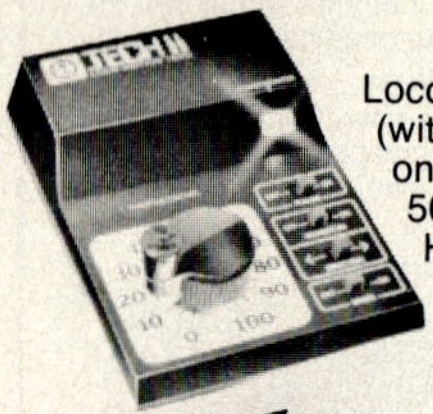

SPECIFICATIONS

All MRC power packs are guaranteed against defects in material and workmanship for five years when properly used, and include the following basic features: UL listed (except 550, 55 & 135 and cab controls: which cannot be UL listed). On-off switch (except as noted). Overload indicator light (except as noted). Circuit breaker protected. Directional control (reverse switch). 16v AC for accessories. Taper-wound rheostat speed control (except as noted). All power packs have AC Terminal for accessories.

MANUFACTURERS RATING

1 amp will handle one average HO or two average N Scale trains.

FIXED 12v DC expansion terminals, (where noted) allow you to add another speed & direction control as long as capacity of the pack is not exceeded. MRC Power Packs meet governmental regulations.

Locomotion 1500
(with momentum ontrol)
500-1500   49.98
HO, HOn3, N, TT, Z

Railpower 1400
500-1400
40.98
HO, HOn3, TT,N

Dualpower 2800
500-2800   64.98
HO, HOn3, N

Railmaster 2400
500-2400 51.98
HO, HOn3, O, On3, N, Z, S, TT,G

TECH II SERIES (cont)

Locomotion 2500
(with momentum control)
500-2500 65.98
HO, HOn3, O, On3, N,Z, S, TT, G

Railpower 1300
500-1300   29.98
For use with HO and NZ. Total output - 7VA on this solid state circuitry designed to deliver superior slow speed acceleration for increased realism. Features a main line direction switch, 300° speed control, circuit protection guards against overload and more.

Cab Control
500-135   54.98
An advanced, transistorized, walk-around unit with Proportional Tracking Control, can be connected to AC power supply. For HO, HOn3, TT, N.

TECH III SERIES

Extra power for various scales of operation. Available either 30VA or 19VA of power. Both packs are covered by a five year warranty, and come with Throttle Master control knob, 300° of control, thermostat protection, momentum switch and more.

500-9500 Power Command (30VA)   99.98
(not illustrated)
500-9000 Power Command (19VA)   79.98

ADVANCED PERFORMANCE

500-1100 N Scale   35.98

CONTROL MASTER 20

LTD QUANTITIES AVAILABLE

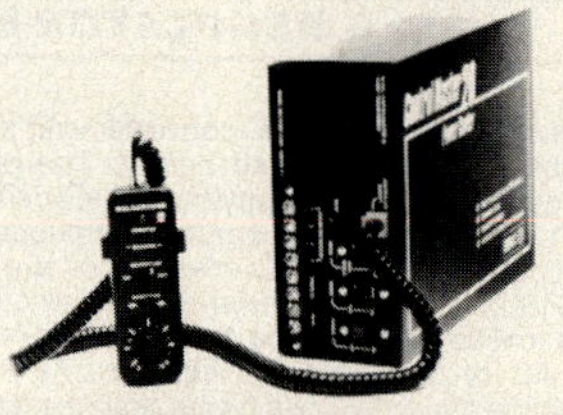

500-444   Control Master 20   169.98
Has Walkaround hand held control with memory function, for right or left hand. Can be unplugged and moved. Delivers 85VA for G Scale, 57VA for HO/N Scale. Terminals for ammeter and voltmeter hookup, filtered and regulated DC output, momentum circuitry, nudge switch control and a mode switch. 5.0 amps plus reserve power.

MRC POWER PACK SELECTION CHART

Part Number	Description	Transistorized Control	Taper-Wound Rheostat Speed Control	Extended Range Speed Control	Automatic Circuit Protector	Overload Indicator Light	Direction Control	Reverse Loop Switch	On-Off Switch	Automatic Pulse or Pulse Power Switch	Throttle-Master Control Knob	Ammeter And Voltmeter	Total Amperage	Power for Average Trains	Fixed 12 volt DC for Expansion	U.L. Inc. Listed
500-27	Trainpower 027				X	X	X		X		X		2.5	4		
500-55	Cab Control	X		X	X		X						N/A	N/A	N/A	N/A
500-100	Trainpack 100		X		X		X						.65	2		X
500-160	Dual Loco Pack V	2X		X	2X	2X	X		X	2X	X		2.20	6-8	X	X
500-501	Throttlepack 501		X	X	X	X	X		X	X	X		1.90	5	X	X
500-770	Dualpack 770		2X		2X	2X	2X		X				1.60	4	X	X
500-1100	Trainpack 100N		X		X		X						.65	3		X
500-1300	Railpower 1300	X		X	X		X		X		X		.6	3		X
500-1400	Railpower 1400	X		X	X	X*	X		X	X	X		1.20	2-3		X
500-1500	Locomotion 1500	X		X	X	X*	X		X	X	X		.90	2-4	X	X
500-1501	Throttlepack 501N		X	X	X	X	X		X	X	X		1.90	6	X	X
500-1770	Dualpack 770N		2X		2X	2X	2X		X				1.60	5	X	X
500-2400	Railmaster 2400	X		X	X	X	X		X	X	X		1.65	4-5	X	X
500-2500	Locomotion 2500	X		X	X	X	X		X	X	X		2.00	4-6	X	X
500-2800	Dualpower 2800	2X		2X	2X	X	2X		X	X	X		1.2	2-3		X
500-7000	Sound 'n Power	X			X	X	X		X		X		2.5	4-6		X
500-9000	Power Command (19VA)	X			X	X	X		X		X	X	1.5	4		X
500-9500	Power Command (30VA)	X			X	X	X		X		X	X	2.5	4-6		X

MODEL RECTIFIER CORPORATION

The difference between HO and N gauge packs is usually the resistance of the speed control. An HO pack does not have enough resistance to stop an N gauge loco, but any N gauge can be used with HO locomotives.

SOUND 'N POWER

Delivers 60VA output power for G Scale, 57VA for NO/N Scale. Momentum switch, pump action brake switch, mode switch, On-Off power switch and 300 degree throttle control. 4 sounds: Steam Chuff, Steam Whistle, Diesel Generator and Diesel horn. Chuff or Generator sound can be synchronized to the motion of your locos plus a volume control. 8 ohm 4 inch round speaker and 12 foot 2 conductor cable included. Delivers 2.5 Amps of power.

Sound 'N Power 7000 System
500-7000   159.98

DUAL POWER

Dual Loco Pack V
HO, HOn3, O.On3, N,Z, TT, SS, G
500-160   114.98

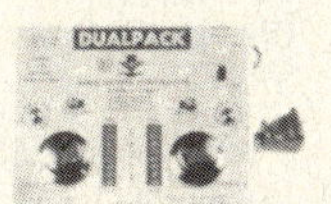

Dualpack 770
HO, HOn3
500-770   66.98
500-1770   N
66.98

MORE POWER & CONTROL

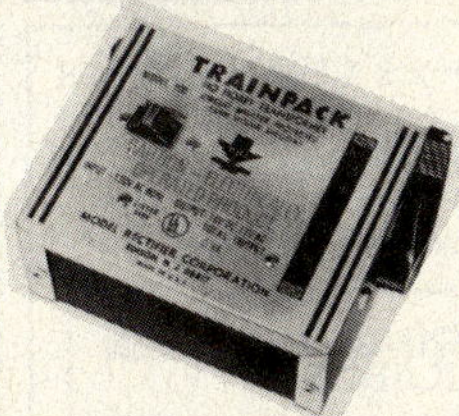

Trainpack 100
HO, HOn3
500-100   35.98
500-1100   N
35.98

Throttlepack 501
500-501 60.98
HO, HOn3
500-1501 N
60.98

Trainmaster 6200
500-6200   89.98
Unit delivers a total of 60VA output power, plus 0-18.5 volts DC track voltage. Includes AC output for accessories, a mode switch to select use for HO & N Scale or Large Scale layouts and a power monitor lamp. Delivers 2.2 Amps of power.

ADD-ONS

Cab Control
500-55   22.98
HO, HOn3, N, TT, Z

SWITCHES

500-2001	SPST Slide	ea	.60
500-2003	DPDT Slide	ea	.80
500-2011	SPST Toggle Switch	ea	2.25
500-2012	DPST Toggle Switch	ea	2.25
500-2013	DPDT C-Off Toggle Switch	ea	3.50
500-2014	SPDT C-Off Toggle Switch	ea	2.95
500-2015	DPDT E5 Switch	ea	2.75
500-2016	DPDT 3W C-Off SW Wired Switch	ea	4.50
500-2017	SPDT E7 C-Off Momentary Switch	ea	4.95

ACCESSORIES

500-2025	Circuit Breaker Loco GD 1	2.75
500-2026	Circuit Breaker Pike GD2	1.00
500-2030	Throttlemaster Knob	1.50
500-2040	Terminal Strip-Plain ea	3.95
500-2041	Terminal Strip-Wired ea	4.95

TRAIN TRONICS

SWITCH MACHINE POWER UNIT

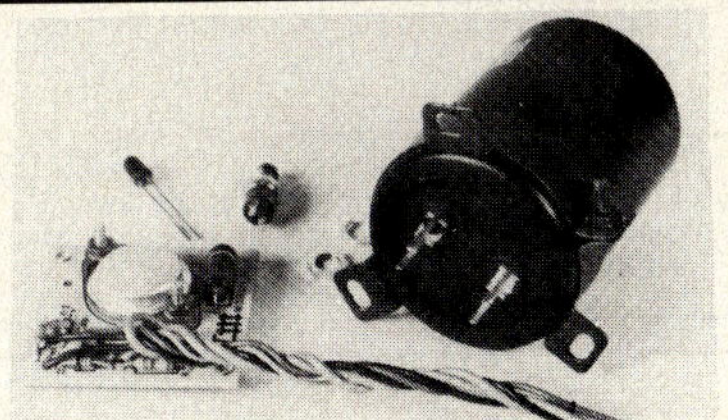

723-603 Switchman Capacitive   38.95
Discharge Unit

Capable of operating up to twenty turnouts simultaneously, with "positive snap-action". Features instantaneous recycling with LED ready indicator, current limiting to prevent coil burnout and operates any type of dual coil switch machine.

723-1801 AC Converter for   7.95
Zero-1
(By Special Order Only)

723-1804 Conductive Paint for   2.00
Zero-1
(By Special Order Only)

723-1805 Power Booster for   99.95
Zero-1
(By Special Order Only)

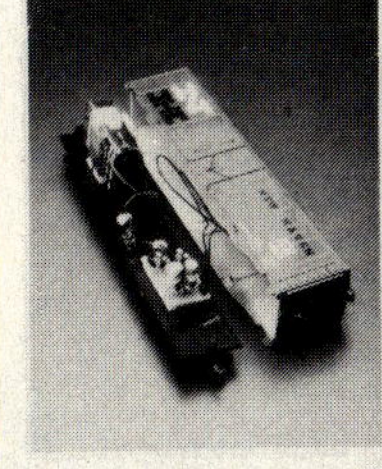

A-B TECH INC.

Animate your models with these working electrical accessories. Designed for easy construction, they can be used in all types of applications to simulate warning lights.

FLASHER KITS

Simulate strobe and warning lights on locos, cabooses, End-Of-Train Devices and vehicles with these flasher kits. Each is complete with assembled circuit board, LED, on/off switch, and battery terminals for a 9V battery (sold separately).

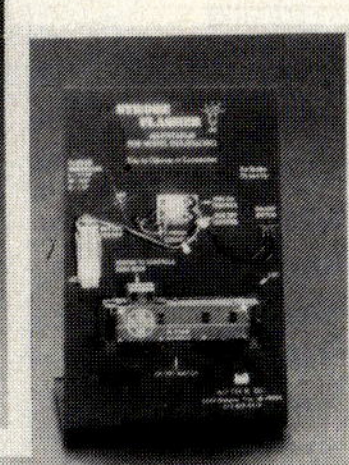

STANDARD FLASHER
106-101 Red LED   15.95
106-102 Yellow LED   15.95

LARGE FLASHER
106-201 Red LED   15.95
106-202 Yellow LED   15.95

SUBMINIATURE FLASHER W/2 LEDs
106-301 Red LED   15.95
106-302 Yellow LED   15.95
106-402 Green LED   15.95

CROSSING FLASHER KIT

Protect highway crossings on your railroad with this working accessory. The kit powers up to eight LEDs, enough for two sets of crossing signals. A pair of controllers regulate the "on" and "off" time of the LEDs. Each unit includes an assembled control module which measures 1-1/4 x 7/8 x 1/2". Also included are three feet of color coded hook-up wire, wire leads for the LEDs, an on/off switch and four red LEDs which can be adapted to various crossing flashers (sold separately).

106-501 For N&Z   17.95
106-502 For HO   17.95

WALTHERS

HO SCALE (1/87)

TURNTABLE DRIVE

1 rpm Motor, Bracket and mounting hardware. For use with Heljan #322-804 HO Scale and Cornerstone #933-3203 N Scale Turntables.

942-472 Turntable Drive   24.98

NEW

P.H. Hobbies, Inc.

POWER PACKS

The PS3 has a 16 gauge aluminum case with a flat black finish. Fully filtered 3 amp pure DC power supply, with power indicator light.

PS3 3-Amp Throttle	567-3	89.45

PS6&10 Series Power Supplies have a 16 gauge aluminum case with a baked gunmetal gray metallic finish upper case, and a black lower case. All 6&10 amp models are fan cooled and for use with all DC trains in all gauges and scales.

 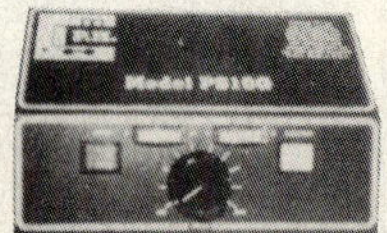

6&10   67&107

567-6	PS6—6 Amp	228.08
567-10	PS10—10 Amp	295.55
567-67	PS6G—6 Amp w/Volt & Ammeter	279.78
567-107	PS10G—10 Amp w/Volt & Ammeter	344.25

	PS6DG—6 Amp Dual Throttle w/Gauges	
	567-647	348.68

567-1047	PS10DG—10 Amp Dual Throttle w/Gauges	413.13

SOUND

Railbus sound system, digitally recorded sounds w/Oogah horn, bell and motor sounds. On-board system can be used with all scales from HO to G.

567-300318		163.47

Spectrum

(Division of Bachmann)

POWER PACKS

Powerpacks feature: Precision throttle control, master on-off switch, direction control, AC output for accessories, shockproof casing, and a lifetime warranty.

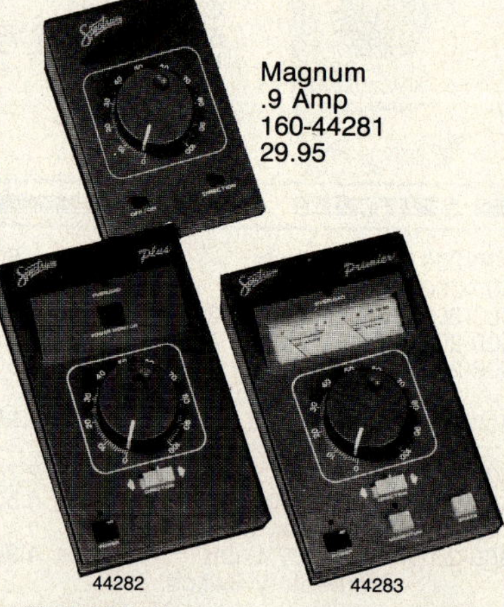

Magnum
.9 Amp
160-44281
29.95

44282   44283

160-44282	Plus	49.95

1.5 amp, power monitor LED overload indicator, fixed DC output for expansion.

160-44283	Premier	79.95

1.5 amp, momentum switch, brake switch, lighted DC amp and volt meter, LED overload indicator, fixed DC output for expansion.

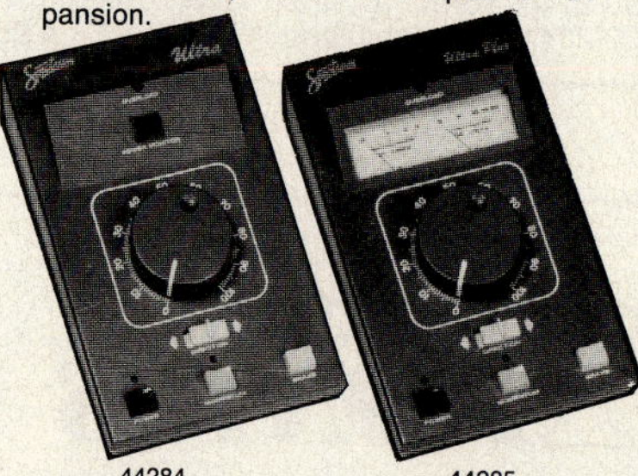

44284   44285

160-44285	Ultra Plus	99.95

2.5 amp, momentum switch, brake switch, lighted DC amp and volt meters, LED overload indicator, fixed DC output for expansion.

160-44284	Ultra	69.95

2 amp, momentum switch, brake switch, powre monitor, LED overload indicator, fixed DC output for expansion.

SCALE SHOPS

VOLTROLLER

Voltrollers are offered in two different versions. The hand-held throttle is primarily designed for CAN motors, while the cabinet/panel models are intended for all motors. Most units available assembled or in kit form. All units are DC less momentum, pulse or brake. Power is controlled by a rotational knob for speed, and a slide switch for direction.

HANDHELD

	3 amp, 6′ cable		
	649-1203	kit	39.98
	3 amp, assembled		
	649-12031		59.98
	(By Special Order Only)		
649-1215	1.5 amp, 6′ cable	kit	29.98
649-12151	1.5 amp, assembled		52.95
	(By Special Order Only)		

CABINET & PANEL

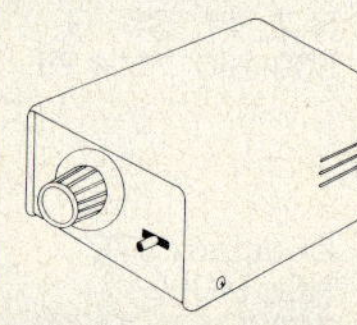

	Cabinet, 3 amp assembled		
	649-12033		62.50
	Cabinet, 3 amp		
	649-12034	kit	42.95
	(By Special Order Only)		
649-12153	Cabinet, 1.5 amp, asmb		41.98
649-12154	Cabinet, 1.5 amp	kit	32.50
	(By Special Order Only.)		
649-12032	Panel, 3 amp	kit	29.98
649-12152	Panel, 1.5 amp	kit	19.98
	(By Special Order Only.)		

ACCESSORIES

649-3500	Velcro Hook & Loop, 1 x 2″	.98

adhesive back for throttle mount

649-3501	Velcro Hook, 1 x 4″	.98

adhesive back, for extra throttle mounts

LIMITED QUANTITIES AVAILABLE

649-4092	RCA Dual Jack	.79
649-4093	DIN Plug and Socket	4.98

"N"-WAY PRODUCTS

POWER SUPPLY KIT

535-425	Power Supply Kit	12.95

This kit will eliminate the two 9 volt batteries necessary to power the N-Way Flashing Crossing Signals & Boulevard Crossing Signals. One power supply kit will power 4 sets of signals. This kit will also power the N-Way Train Detection Kit. Requires 110 volts input for operation.

JANUARY 2, 1935

❧ Today ❧

IN RAILROAD HISTORY

Chicago & North Western operated first "400" passenger trains between Chicago, Illinois and Minneapolis, Minnesota.

LIFE-LIKE®

SMOKE FLUID

Can be used in any smoke generator designed for petroleum based smoke fluid.

1 fl oz		
433-1417		4.50

MODELTRONICS

Sound For Model Locos

SIMPLE 3 STEP ORDERING PROCEDURE

For a complete system order a sound system kit, plus a speaker kit. For additional effect you can order air pump kits.

1) Select either #1000 or #2000 depending on engine size.
2) Select speaker size to fit engine - tender - car.
3) Select air pump - see picture in air pump listing and match to type that is on your engine. If engines require two - then order two air pumps.

■ SYSTEM FEATURES ■

• **TOTALLY SELF CONTAINED**
Designed for use in steam or diesel locos. Modular units for limited space requirments may be fitted in a space as small as a 50' N Scale box Car of loco tender. Totally portable.

• **OPERATES WITH ANY THROTTLE**
Self containment allowing for locos with independent sound systems to operate at the same time.

• **OPERATES ON ANY LAYOUT**
With no external attachments, system will operate on "common rail" layouts and those with "signal detection systems".

• **FULLY SYNCHRONIZING SOUND WITH DRIVE WHEELS**
The method of synchronizing sound with the driving wheels consists of a formed wire for the pickup switch, acetate material for partial driver insulation, and the copper clad epoxy board for mounting the switch. The method avoids cutting the Loco frame or cover plate. The superstructure, cover plate, and drive wheelset must be removed but are easily reassembled.

• **Complete special sound effects possible;** ARTICULATED, COMPOUND, #CYLINDER

• **BLOWER SOUNDS (constant hiss)**

• **EXHAUST CUTOFF & DRIFT CONTROL**
As the load levels off so does the exhaust. Self-adjusting exhaust control regulated by engine power. The harder the loco works the louder it snorts.

• **SINGLE & COMPOUND AIRPUMP SOUNDS**
Micro modules make possible the installation of a number of arrangements of airpump sounds. Single compound and dual compound pump sounds are available as accessory units & can be added at anytime.

• **SIZED FOR ALL GAUGES**
Can be installed in a 50' N Scale box car or loco tender, most HOn3 tenders and all other larger gauge locomotives.

• **EASY TO INSTALL**
Easy to follow instructions plus a screwdriver, soldering iron and a few small hand tools are all that is needed to assemble the basic kit; consisting of inter-connected sound modules with pre-stripped and tinned wiring for instant soldering (solder included) along with heat shrinkable plastic sleeve.

■ SOUND SYSTEM KITS - DIESEL ■

510-6200 Diesel, Sound System MKII 69.95
Will fit Athearn dummy, SW's Athearn SD45 and SDP40 if the rear flywheel is removed. Will also fit into a N Scale boxcar. 3/4x2/3/16x5/8".

■ SOUND SYSTEM KITS - STEAM ■

Kits do not include speakers or airpumps.
510-1000 Micro-Sound I, steam 69.95
(For N-HOn3, this is the smallest system)
510-2000 Micro-Sound II, steam 69.95
(For small HO to 1-1/2" Scale)

■ SOUND CAR KITS ■

Good for Short Line, Logging, N Scale or...Low Cost Per Engine.
510-2200 System-B Sound Car Kit 12.95
510-2201 System-B Engine Kit 8.95
510-2202 System-C Sound Car Kit 7.95
510-2203 System-C Engine Kit 5.95

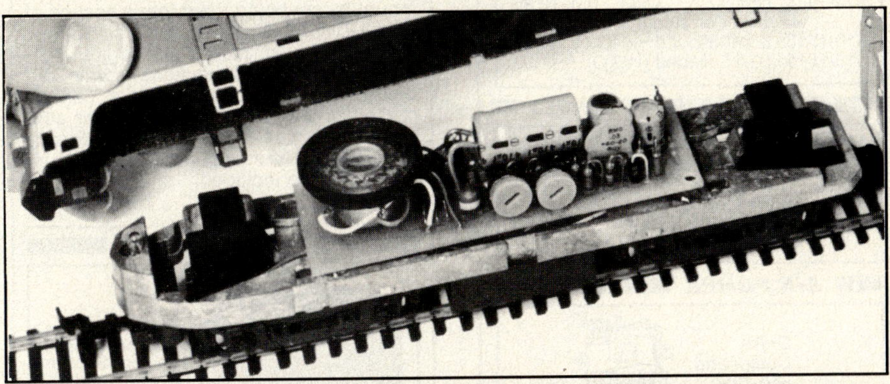

■ SYSTEM EXPLANATION ■

"Head End Car" method. The electronic equipment is installed in a head end car, (such as a RPO car or express reefer). System B (510-2200) or System C (510-2202) sets up one car and engine. Additional locos can be plugged into the head end car (thereby making the additional Loco a sound producer), by using engine kit 510-2201 for System B or engine kit 510-2203 for System C. (System B also requires an additional loco.) System C differs from B in that the speaker is mounted in the head-end car instead of tender like B.

Initial Sound System & System C Sound Car Kit		
510-2000 Micro Sound II		69.95
510-1930 Air Pump		34.95
510-1511 Speaker		11.95
510-2202 Sound Car kit	C	7.95
total:		124.80
1st Additional Engine		
510-2203 Engine Kit		5.95
Example of the total costs:		
Each Additional Engine Costs		5.95
A modeler using System C to equip a motive power roster of five locos total cost:		154.55
Average cost per engine:		30.91

Initial Sound System & System B Sound Car Kit		
510-2000 Micro Sound II		69.95
510-1930 Air Pump		34.95
510-1511 Speaker		11.95
510-2200 Sound Car Kit	B	12.95
total:		129.80
1st Additional Engine		
510-2201 Engine Kit		8.95
510-1511 Speaker		11.95
total:		20.90
Example of the total cost:		
Each Additional engine Costs;		
A modeler using System B to equip a motive power roster of five locos total cost:		104.50
Average cost per engine:		46.86

■ LOCOMOTIVES w/SOUND ■   NEW

(All Locomotives By Special Order Only.)

510-8321	GP35 ACL	pkg(2)	137.95
510-8322	GP35 B&O	pkg(2)	137.95
510-8323	GP35 CB&Q	pkg(2)	137.95
510-8324	GP35 IC	pkg(2)	137.95
510-8325	GP35 SF Freight	pkg(2)	137.95
510-8326	GP35 SP	pkg(2)	137.95
510-8327	GP35 EL	pkg(2)	137.95
510-8328	GP35 CHSY	pkg(2)	137.95
510-8331	GP9 B&O	pkg(2)	137.95
510-8332	GP9 CB&Q	pkg(2)	137.95
510-8333	GP9 SF Freight	pkg(2)	137.95
510-8334	GP9 SP	pkg(2)	137.95
510-8335	GP9 UP	pkg(2)	137.95
510-8336	GP9 GN	pkg(2)	137.95
510-8337	GP9 MILW	pkg(2)	137.95
510-8341	EMD F7A&B powered SF Passenger	pkg(2)	137.95
510-8342	EMD F7A&B powered SF Freight	pkg(2)	137.95
510-8343	EMD F7A&B powered SP	pkg(2)	137.95
510-8344	EMD F7A&B powered BN	pkg(2)	137.95
510-8345	EMD F7A&B powered UP	pkg(2)	137.95
510-8346	EMD F7A&B powered B&O	pkg(2)	137.95

■ LOCOMOTIVES w/SOUND ■ (continued)

510-8347	EMD F7A&B powered AMT	pkg(2)	137.95
510-8421	GP35 Dummy ACL		117.95
510-8422	GP35 Dummy B&O		117.95
510-8423	GP35 Dummy CB&Q		117.95
510-8424	GP35 Dummy IC		117.95
510-8425	GP35 Dummy SF Freight		117.95
510-8426	GP35 Dummy SP		117.95
510-8427	GP35 Dummy EL		117.95
510-8428	GP35 Dummy CHSY		117.95
510-8431	GP9 Dummy B&O		117.95
510-8432	GP9 Dummy CB&Q		117.95
510-8433	GP9 Dummy SF Freight		117.95
510-8434	GP9 Dummy SP		117.95
510-8435	GP9 Dummy UP		117.95
510-8436	GP9 Dummy GN		117.95
510-8437	GP9 Dummy MILW		117.95
510-8441	EMD F7B dummy SF Passenger		117.95
510-8442	EMD F7B dummy SF Freight		117.95
510-8443	EMD F7B dummy SP		117.95
510-8444	EMD F7B dummy BN		117.95
510-8445	EMD F7B dummy UP		117.95
510-8446	EMD F7B dummy B&O		117.95
510-8447	EMD F7B dummy Amtrak		117.95

MODELTRONICS

Sound For Model Locos

SPEAKERS

510-1511	1" Round	(N, HO)	11.95
510-1523	1.85"x2.85" Oval (O) diesel or steam		12.95
510-1513	1-1/4" Round (HO,O)		11.95
510-1515	1-1/2" Round (HO,O)		11.95

FLEXIBLE WIRE-10' LENGTH

510-3022	30 Gauge (black)	1.75
510-3024	30 Gauge (red)	1.75
510-3026	30 Gauge (blue)	1.75
	(By Special Order Only.)	
510-3028	30 Gauge (yellow)	1.75
	(By Special Order Only.)	

AIR PUMPS

Cross Compound
510-1930
34.95

Single Phase
510-1940
34.95

When ordering, choose the airpump that looks like the one on your loco, for a proto-typical sound.

CONSTANT BRIGHTNESS KITS

510-3002	Reversing, (HO & N) motor current MAX 1.0 amp	9.95
510-3003	Reversing, (HO & O) motor current MAX 3.0 amp	15.95
510-3004	Non-Reversing, (HO & N) motor current MAX 1.0 amp	7.95
510-3005	Non-Reversing, (HO & O) motor current MAX 3.0 amp	13.95
510-3006	Non-Reversing, HO & O motor current MAX 2.0 amp	11.95
510-6001	Light/Speed Reducer	11.95

Will slow locos not equipped with Modeltronics sound system and provide constant lighting.

SUB-MINI CONNECTOR-GOLD PLATED

510-1339	One Pin	5.95
510-1340	Two Pin 1/16x1/8"	6.95
510-1341	Three Pin	7.95
510-1342	Four Pin	8.95
510-1343	Six Pin	9.95

BATTERY HOLDER

510-1350	Small	2.95	510-1351 Large	2.95

MISCELLANEOUS

510-1300	Articulated Synchro Kit	2.95
510-1330	Power Filter (adds echo)	2.95
510-1370	Small ON/OFF Switch	2.95
510-3010	Shrink Sleeve Asst.	2.95
	3/64", 3/82", 1/16" 2-4" lengths.	

CIRCUITRON

Electronics for Model Railroads

CIRCUITRON products constructed on printed circuit boards are designed to mount by snapping them into a section of CIRCUITRON'S PCMT (Printed Circuit Mounting Track). Solid state integrated circuit technology. Connections to any CIRCUITRON printed circuit board can be made using .110" female solderless connectors or by soldering the leads directly to the terminals on the board. Complete instructions are included.

DH-1 DIESEL HORN

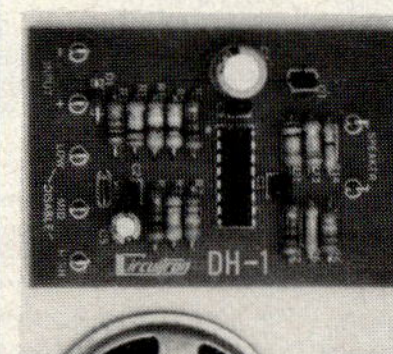
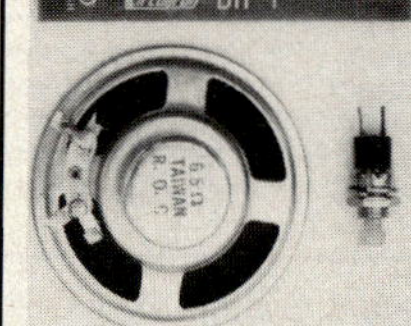

Electronic multi-chime diesel horn with speaker and push button. With external switches, the DH-1 can produce three different single frequency tones, three different dual chime tones and a three chime tone. Requires a 10-18 volt AC or DC input.

800-5701	DH-1 Diesel Horn	26.95
800-9150	Speaker 2-1/4" (8 ohm)	4.95
800-9610	Push Button	1.50

SS-1 STEAM SOUND KIT

Realistic steam sound generator is easily installed in HO Scale or larger models. Circuitry has individually controlled accurate "chuff" sound with constant background hiss. Self-contained SS-1 is powered by 9 volt transistor-type battery and may be used with any form of track power. Includes 1 x 1 x 0.5" (1/2") circuit board, 9V battery holder, subminiature slide switch, 1" diameter speaker, volume control resistors, chuff contact wire, insulating material and complete instructions.

800-4000	SS-1 Steam Sound Kit	39.95
800-9104	Spring Pickup Wirepkg(4)	1.00

Four 3" lengths, 28 gauge (.0126") Beryllium Copper spring wire.

800-9105	Sound System Synchronizing Insulation	each 2.00
800-9151	Speaker	each 9.95

23mm (7/8") diameter, 3/8" thick high-output transducer.

BELL RINGER CIRCUITS

Bell Ringer circuitry allows for adjustment of ring rate and strike force (volume). Use with 10-18V AC or DC.

800-5700	BR-1 with Bell	39.95
800-5702	BR-2 less Bell	24.95

FALLER

Imported from Germany and marketed by WALTHERS

SOUND ACCESSORIES

Electrical Bell-Set
272-638   ea 30.49
Church bell sound.

Motorized Blinker
272-631   ea 35.99
Pulses are used for rhythmic switching; blinkers or church bells.

STEREO BOOSTER

LIMITED QUANTITIES AVAILABLE

522-7024	Micro Personal Stereo Booster	20.50

DC Adapter Input: 6V-9V. Uses 9V battery or equivalent, power output of 100mW at 30ohm 9V VCC.

"N"-WAY PRODUCTS

RAILROAD CROSSING BELL

535-191	Railroad Crossing Bell Kit	19.95

Requires 110 volt, AC and 12 volts DC to operate. Kit includes bell, sheet metal timing box, 4ft cord and instructions.

VOLLMER

Imported from Germany and marketed by WALTHERS

SMOKE UNIT

With large tank for smoke making. Includes fluid to last for 70 minutes.

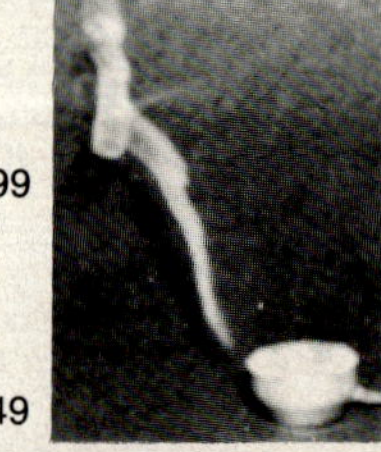

Smoke Generator
770-4114   26.99

Smoke Fluid Refill bottle (50ml)
770-4115   6.49

SEUTHE ®
Imported from Germany by WALTHERS

HO SCALE (1/87)
Smoke/Steam generators for various foreign and domestic locomotives. Generators for structures and ships are also available.

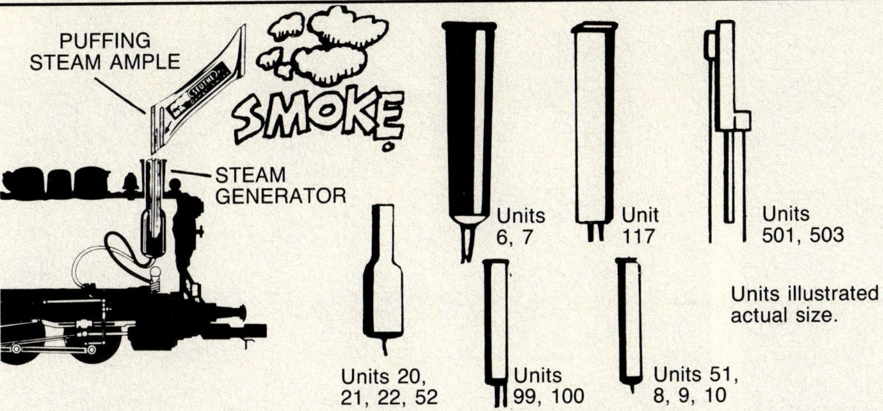

STEAM GENERATORS

667-9 Operating voltage: 14v — 17.99
For Fleischmann 4170, 4175, 4177 & 4178 also, Marklin-Hamo DC (8335).

667-10 Maximum: 16v AC/DC — 17.99
For Marklin 3046, 3047, 3048, 3084, 3085, and 3102 locomotives as well as Fleischmann and Liliput locomotives.

667-11 Maximum: 16v AC/DC — 17.99
Same as #10 except for Marklin digital

667-12 Maximum: 16v — 17.99
Same as #100 except for Marklin digital

667-20 Maximum: 16v AC/DC — 17.99
For Markling 3083, 3091, 3093, Hamo 8391, 8392, 8393.

667-21 Maximum: 16v AC/DC — 17.99
Universal type for all types of locomotives with metal bodies and extremely slim chimneys.

667-22 Maximum: 16v AC/DC — 17.99
Universal type for all types of locomotives with plastic bodies and extremely slim chimneys.

667-23 Maximum: 16v AC/DC — 17.99
Same as #22 except for Marklin digital

667-24 Maximum: 16v AC/DC — 17.99
Same as #20 except for Marklin digital

667-99 Operating voltage: 14v — 17.99
For all types of locomotives with plastic bodies.

667-100 Operating voltage: 16v — 17.99
For all types of locomotives with plastic bodies.

CONSTANT GENERATOR

Generator creates realistic puffing smoke while loco is stationary or in motion. #50 Electronic Smoke Unit is to be used with #51 and 52 smoke generators. #50 regulates the current flow for the proper amount to operate #51 or 52.

667-117 Smoke Chimney 12-16v — 9.49
For house or building.

667-50 Electronic Control (SDE #50) — 22.99
HO Steam Generators for connection with Seuthe steam Electronic Control (SDE #50). Working voltage of 3 to 5.5v.

667-51 Smoke Generator – small stack — 17.99
For locomotives of all makes.

667-52 Smoke Generator – large stack — 17.99
For locomotives with especially narrow chimneys.

667-5 Smoke Generator for ships — 17.99
and similar models, 4-6v.

667-501 Super Smoke Unit 12v w/Smoke fluid — 22.99

667-503 Super Smoke Unit 16v w/Smoke fluid — 22.99

PUFFING STEAM AMPULE

667-101 Loco Smoke 4cc pkg(3) — 3.49
for Arnold and Marklin

667-103 Steam Distillate 4cc pkg(3) — 2.99
3 tubes (neutral, pine, loco scent)

667-400 Neutral Scent 4cc pkg(3) — 2.99
667-401 Loco Smoke 4cc pkg(3) — 2.99
667-402 Pine Scent 4cc pkg(3) — 2.99
667-404 Continuous Smoke pkg)3) — 2.99
For use w/Chimney.

ACCESSORIES

667-105 Steam Distillate Neutral, 55c bottle — 6.99

667-200 Steam Pipes pkg(3) — 5.99
For use w/#8,9,10 & 99.

667-106 Smoke distillate, neutral, 250m — 14.49

SCALE SHOPS

"CHEAP CHUG" SOUND UNITS

Operated from a cam or opto-sensors, can be used with #4090 speaker. Power for the units can be supplied by batteries or the track and 4091 speaker.

649-6046 Kit — 12.98
649-6047 Assembled — 25.95

SPEAKER

8 ohm, .2 watts; for on-board sound systems.
649-4090 1" Round — 8.98
649-4091 3/4" Round — 4.98

See also: POWER SUPPLIES, LIGHTING & ELECTRICAL, TRACK and SIGNALS & DETECTION for additional SCALE SHOPS items.

DIESEL HORN SOUND

3-Toned Diesel Horn
723-301 kit 23.95

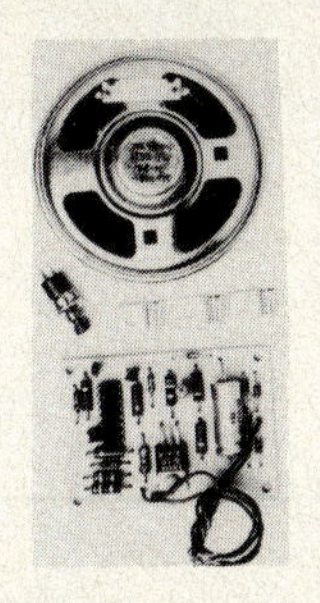

Tones of 311, 370, and 420 cycles are duplicated simultaneously. Solid state circuitry throughout can be connected to 6 to 16 volt AC/DC (not included). Kit includes pushbutton speaker mounting clips and 3" speaker. To expand system add 723-415 speakers at various points around layout.

STEAM WHISTLE w/DIESEL HORN

723-305 Steam Whistle — 89.95
Provides both 3-toned steam whistle and 3-chimed diesel horn. For authenticity steam whistle provides background steam hiss; use slide control on steam for varying pitch and volume of whistle. Kit contains solid state prebuilt and tested circuit, pushbutton, slide control, speaker and mounting clips.

723-415 Accessory Speaker each 4.95
Can be used in conjunction with Train Tronics #301 3-Toned Diesel Horn or #305 Steam Whistle to add diesel horn or steam whistle sound to other areas of layout. 8 OHM, 3" in diameter.

CROSSING CONTROL WITH BELL

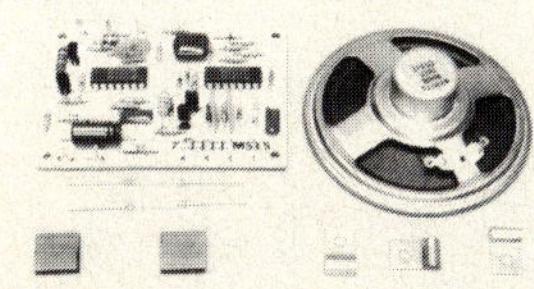

723-515 Crossing Control with Bell 29.95
Realistic crossing control complete in one piece allows for crossing signals and electronic bell to be turned off & on automatically as train enters & leaves crossing area. This unit is bi-directional, and comes complete with track detector, crossing flasher, and electronic bell & speaker. This unit for LED crossing signals only. (723-510 suggested crossing signals.)

JANUARY 21, 1963
❦ Today ❦
IN RAILROAD HISTORY
At 2:55 a.m., the last northbound train of the Chicago, North Shore & Milwaukee arrives in Milwaukee, ending operations of the railroad.

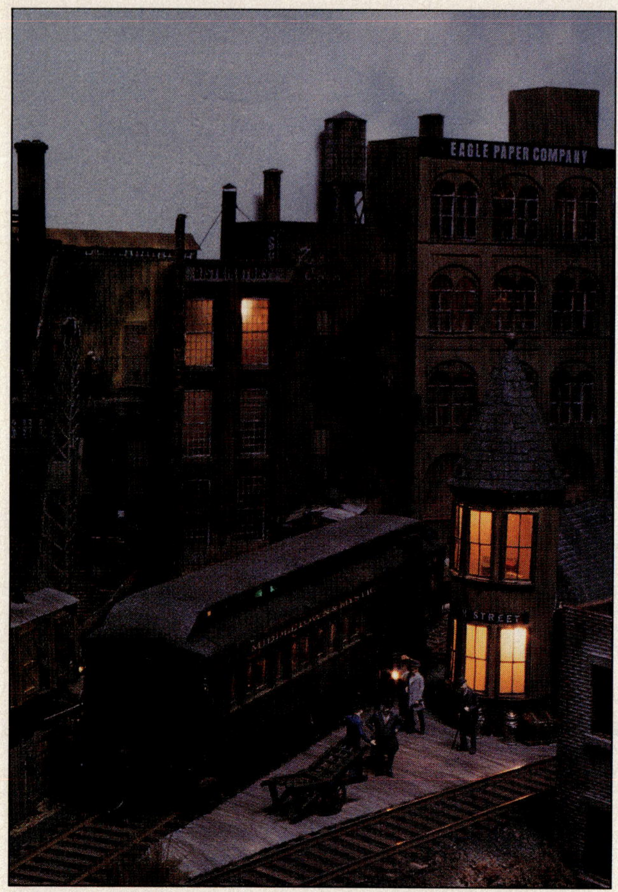

Darkness is descending rapidly as a few late evening passengers depart from Middletown. Boarding at the High Street Station are a few Preiser figures, who have been waiting patiently under Brawa street lamps. This is one of many detailed scenes along the Middletown & Mystic Mines, built by Earl Smallshaw of Middletown, Connecticut. *Models and Photo by Earl Smallshaw*

Many a fortune has been made and lost here in the Colorado Rockies and these ornate homes are status symbols for the wealthy and powerful. Chris Comport of Arlington, Texas, built the Classic Miniatures Leadville House right from the box, but added a driveway made from Holgate & Reynolds brick and a stone foundation of self-hardening clay. This is one of several small, HO Scale dioramas Chris has built after many years of working in On3. *Models and Photo by Chris Comport.*

ADHESIVES AND THEIR PROPERTIES

ADHESIVE	BASE	SETTING TIME	CURING TIME	STRENGTH	COLOR WHEN DRY	BEST APPLICATIONS
White Glue	Polyvinyl	30 to 60 minutes	24 hours	high	clear	wood, ground cover
Yellow Glue	Aliphatic resin	20 to 40 minutes	24 hours	high	clear	wood, paper, cardboard
Contact Cement	Synthetic rubber	on contact	24 hours	medium	light brown	plastic, wood, cardboard
Plastic Cement	Allyl Isothiocyanate	30 seconds to 1 minute	8 hours	medium	clear	wood, plastic, styrene
Cyanoacrylate	Cyanoacrylate	5 to 30 seconds	2 hours	high	clear	wood, metal, plastics
Epoxy (quick set)	Epoxy and polyamine resin	5 to 10 minutes	12 hours	high	clear, amber	metal, cardboard, wood, plastic
Epoxy (slow set)	Epoxy and polyamine resin	2 to 4 hours	24 hours	high	clear, amber	metal, cardboard, wood, plastic

AMBROID®

LIQUID CEMENT

For use on wood, leather, canvas, metal, most fabrics and glass. Waterproof.

130-102 3.2 oz Tube   3.33
Dealers: MUST order Dealer Pack of 12
130-101 1.8 oz Tube   2.13
130-151 Regular Cement   1-3/4oz 2.43

STYRENE PLASTIC CEMENT

Resistant to running.

130-152 1-3/4 oz Tube   2.13

PLASTIC WELDER   **NEW**

A water clear plastic fusing adhesive. Dissolves a thin layer of each surface to form a welded joint. Bonds styrene, butyrate, ABS and acrylic. Nonflammable, leaves no residue. SUPER FAST formula. Applicator brush included.
Proweld
130-110   2oz 2.69

RESIN GLUE   **NEW**

Sandable resin glue will not stain and is non-flammable. For all arts and crafts as well as home repairs, hardwoods, balsa, plywood, styrofoam, cloth paper, ceramics and other porous materials.
Se·Cur·It
130-126   4oz 2.29

N.J. International

SOLDER

Extra fine solder for electrical use.
525-6603 Solder   1/2oz 2.99

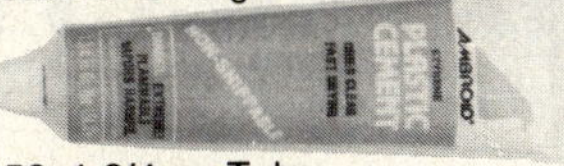
Imported from Germany and marketed by WALTHERS

PLASTIC CEMENT

Expert Liquid
272-492   25ml 3.77
Liquid cement in a plastic bottle with needle applicator for very fine work. Nontoxic, Nonflamable.
Dealers MUST order Dealer pack of 24.

272-494 Liquid   75ml 4.49
for polystyrene

LUBRICANT

Special Oiler
272-489   25g 5.49
All-around oiler for small motors and gears. Resin and acid free.

FLOQUIL~POLLY S COLOR CORP.

An RPM Company

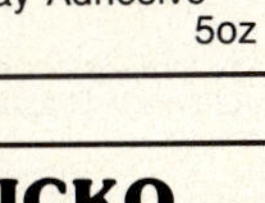

ALL PURPOSE SCENERY SPRAY ADHESIVE

Railroad Spray Adhesive
270-130602   5oz 5.19

A.J. FRICKO COMPANY

"making toy trains run like real trains"

TRACK & MOTOR CLEANER

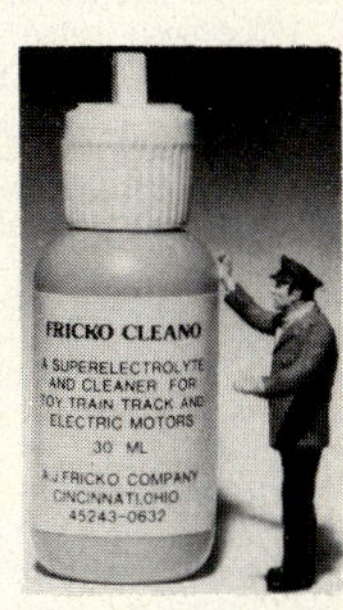
A superelectrolyte and anti-toxidant. A universal track and motor cleaner for scale and tinplate layouts & locos.

Use one drop per rail per 4 x 8' area. One drop will remain effective for 1 year. Cleano will protect against oxidation (rust) even in damp basements.

274-8 Cleano   30ml 19.95

⊘ARNOLD

Imported from Germany and marketed by WALTHERS

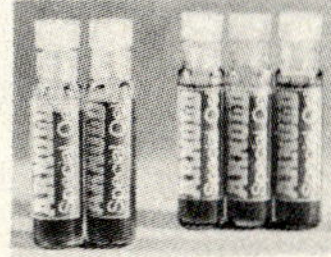

LUBRICANT

For motor bearings, wheel bearings and gears. Use sparingly.

125-7998 Lubricating Oil   pkg(5) 10.49

CARL GOLDBERG MODELS, Inc.

INSTANT ADHESIVES (CYANOACRYLATES)

Normal shelf life is approximately 12 months, which can be extended by refrigeration.

289-767 Super Jet 1/2oz 3.49
289-768 Super Jet 1oz 5.99
Super Jet may be used to bond balsa, hardwood, celluloid, polyester and epoxy fiberglass, epoxy castings, metals, rubber, ceramics, leather, naugahyde, most plastics and some fabrics. It has gap filling qualities and sets up in 15-20 seconds.

289-762 Instant Jet 1/2oz 3.49
289-763 Instant Jet 1oz 5.99
Jet instant glue flows like water through 1/4 to 1/2" of a tightly fitted joint. May be used to bond balsa, hardwood, plywood, many plastics, rubber, glass, ceramics, metal, leather and some fabrics. Apply sparingly and hold parts firmly together for about 15 seconds. Nontoxic.

289-776 Jet Set Aerosol 3oz 5.79
289-777 Jet Set Pump **NEW** 2oz 5.99
289-778 Pump Refill **NEW** 8oz 9.99
Works with all brands of cyanoacrylate adhesives for fast setting and strong glue joints. Can also be used to make instant bonds and fillets for large and small gaps. Pump is freon-free with a very mild odor.

289-772 Slow Jet 1/2oz 3.49
289-773 Slow Jet 1oz 5.99
289-774 Slow Jet 2oz 10.99
Slow drying, thick formula is excellent for gap filling and delicate critical fit applications. Dries in one to two minutes.

289-781 Jet DeSolv 1oz 3.79
Will desolve Instant Jet, Super Jet, Slow Jet and other brands of CA glue. Excellent for clean up.

289-789 Jet Pac Cap & Tips 3.99
Includes cap, five sizes of tips and 12" of pipette tubing. Fits Goldberg adhesive bottles.

289-790 Epoxy Plus 2oz 9.99
Eight minute set-up epoxy is non-sagging, sandable, carvable and paintable. Is 25% lighter than other epoxies.

Model Magic Filler
289-795 5.99
Filler material for wood, fiberglass or styrofoam. Putty is nonshrinking, odorless and nontoxic. Easily sanded. Compatible with all types of paints and finishes, can be colored using water colors or latex pigments.

289-782 Jet Free Penetrate 1/2oz 6.99
289-783 Jet Free 1oz 10.99
289-784 Jet Free Penetrate 2oz 19.99
289-791 Jet Epoxy 6 min 11.99
289-792 Jet Epoxy 20 min 9.99

Hob-E-Lube
by Woodland Scenics

HOB-E-LUBE OILS & GREASE

Complete line of oils, greases and dry lubricants for model railroad equipment in various scales. **All seven are paint and plastic compatible.**

785-650 Workbench Assortment 14.98
Includes one of each listed below and complete instructions.

785-651 Dry Graphite 2.98
With molybdenum. Does not attract dust and dirt.

785-652 Dry White Lube w/Teflon 2.98
White, nonstaining lube doesn't conduct electricity. Use on electrical switches, N&Z worm and gears.

785-653 Ultra Lite Oil 2.98
Use with close tolerance precision parts.

785-654 Lite Oil 2.98
General purpose hobby lube, rust preventing.

785-655 Gear Lube 2.98
Tough, long-lasting lube with high adhesion to prevent dripping.

785-656 Moly Grease 2.98
With molybdenum, covers entire surface and maintains high viscosity. Ideal for parts exposed to water.

785-657 White Grease w/Teflon 2.98
Non-staining lube with corrosion protection and water proof lubrication. Good for outside.

LUBRICANT

Lubricating oil packaged in easy to use tube. Safe for plastics.

490-5300 General Purpose Oiler 1/4oz 2.98
490-5305 Gear Oiler 1/4oz 2.98

Kadee

SPEEDI-DRIVER CLEANER

No special wiring needed to operate. Cleans corrosion from loco driver threads to improve electrical conductivity.

Speedi Driver Cleaner Brush
380-236 each 7.95

LUBRICANT

380-231 Greas-Em tube 1.95
A dry lubricant for couplers.

kibri
Imported from Germany
by WALTHERS

PLASTIC CEMENT
Liquid cement with brush.

405-9996 3.4oz, 100ccm 6.49
405-9995 .45oz, 15ccm 2.99

LIFE-LIKE®

TRACK CLEANER

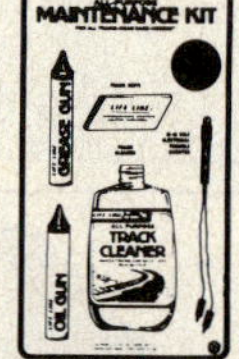

433-1440 Track Brite 3.00
433-1415 Track Cleaner 8oz 3.75

MAINTENANCE KIT

All-Purpose Maintenance Kit
433-8629 11.00
Includes one each: Grease Gun, Oil Gun, Track Cleaner, Track Brite & Trouble Shooter, (an electric circuit tester).

LANDSCAPING CEMENT

Landscaping Cement
433-1403 1pt 5.00
Clean, non-toxic, non-flammable adhesive. Dries hard and clean on almost any surface.

MASCOT™
PRECISION TOOLS

NEW

GEL ADHESIVE

230-751 Adhesive 1.99
230-752 Instant Gel Adhesive Tube 2.99

POLISH

230-975 Flitz Metal Polish 3.30

Satellite City "HOT STUFF"

- HOT STUFF
- SUPER T
- SPECIAL T
- HOT SHOT
- KICK-IT
- SOLVENT

HOT STUFF

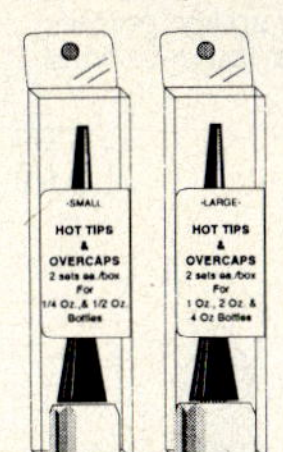

Cyanoacrylate, colorless liquid instant adhesive that bonds wood, glass, metal, leather, fabric, rubber and most plastics in 5-10 seconds. Non-toxic.

639-501 14.2gm (1/2oz) **3.60**
Includes Teflon® Tube.

639-504 28.4gm (1oz) **5.75**

SUPER T

GAP-FILLING cyanoacrylate glue with a cure rate of 10-25 seconds, allowing time to position parts after glue is applied. Besides having the speed and strength of "HOT STUFF", SUPER T's thick density makes it especially suitable for joining parts that don't fit perfectly.

639-506 14.2gm (1/2oz) **3.60**
639-505 28.4gm (1oz) **5.75**

SPECIAL T

Thick cyanoacrylate glue with a consistency five times that of Super T. Thick consistency allows for up to 50 seconds positioning time (most materials bond 30 to 50 seconds).

639-515 56.7gm (2oz) **10.95**
639-516 28.4gm (1oz) **6.50**

UFO™ INSTANT GLUE — THIN

Penetrating, odorless and no curing fumes. Instant glue for the cyano-sensitive modeler. Will not attack white foam, allows full joint coverage of all bonds.

639-519 20 gram **7.95**

UFO™ INSTANT GLUE — THICK

Odorless and no curing fumes. Ultra Gap Filling instant glue. Set time of 50-60 seconds. Use for assembly work.

639-521 20 gram **7.95**

HOT SHOT

Instant cure can be used before or after glue is applied. Gap filling is greatly increased and strong fillets can be made in seconds. "HOT SHOT" and "SUPER T" are excellent for laying track & cork roadbed.

639-503 3oz Pump **5.95**
639-513 6oz Refill for #503 **9.95**

KICK-IT

Power cure accelerator.
639-517 3oz Pump **6.95**
639-518 6oz Refill **11.95**

SPRAY 'N CURE

Pump spray accelerator.

639-510 2oz **5.25**

REPLACEMENT ACCESSORIES

639-500 18" Tube Teflon pkg(10) **5.00**
for #'s 501 and 504

639-509 12" Tube Super T pkg(10) **5.00**
for #'s 506, 505 and 508
(Dealers: MUST order pack of 10)

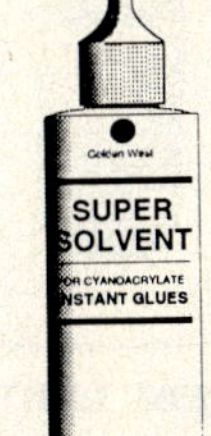

Small Hot Tips
639-511 pkg(2) **1.95**
no clog, for 501 & 506

Large Hot Tips
639-600 pkg(2) **1.95**

511   600

SOLVENT

Nitroparaffin based for cyanoacrylate/super glues

Ultra Super Solvent
639-512 2oz **5.98**

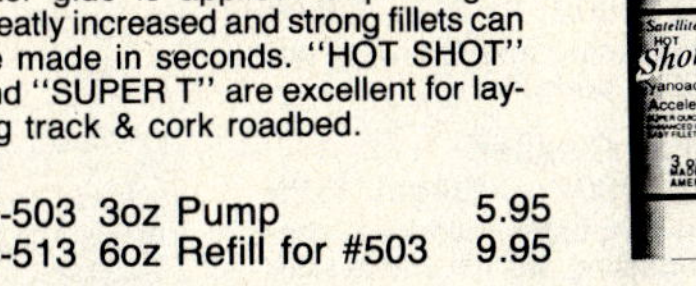

International Hobby Corp.

TRACK CLEANERS

348-4398 Car Pads pkg(6) **2.98**
Replacement Pads for IHC Track Cleaning Car.

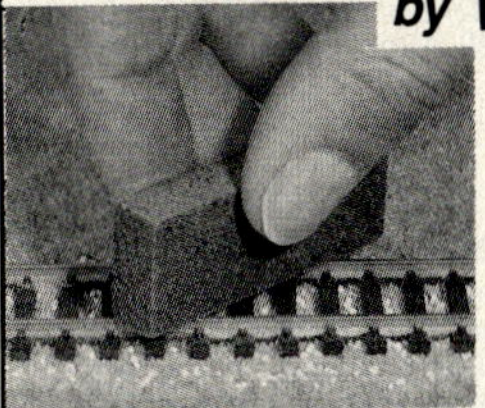

NOCH

Imported from Germany by WALTHERS

Track Cleaning Block
528-5014 **6.99**

AC/CA/ACC = SUPER GLUE

AC, C and ACC are all common abbreviations used in hobby magazines for cyanoacrylate cement, or instant bonding "super" glues. Be sure to read and follow ALL safety precautions when working with these adhesives.

labelle industries

Lubricants contain rust inhibitors. Wipe the lubricants on metal parts to prevent rust.

LUBRICANTS

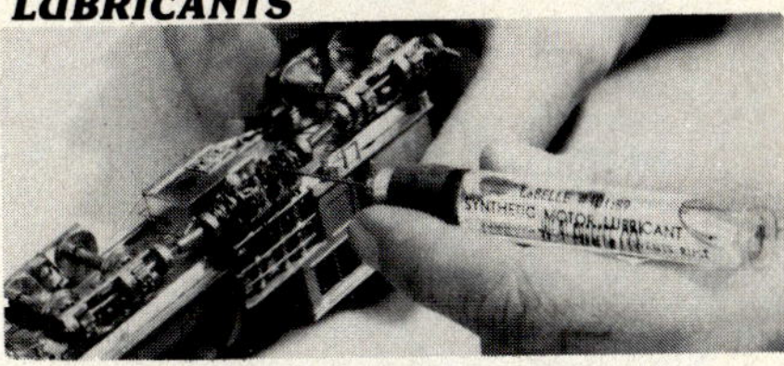

430-101 Synthetic Multi-Purpose Oil 1/2oz **3.79**
Very light oil for motors, bearings, etc. Natural penetrating action will usually free a "frozen" motor. Will damage paints and some plastics.

430-102 Plastic Compatible Gear Lubricant 1/2oz **3.59**
A true gear oil. Should NOT be used on bushing, bearings, etc. Can be used on plastic.

430-104 Synthetic Multi-Purpose Oil 1/2oz **3.59**
Medium weight, non-gumming, long lasting. For small power tools, major appliances, etc. Will damage paints and some plastics.

430-106 Plastic Compatible Grease with Teflon™ 1/2oz **3.59**
Compatible with other lubricants and can be applied over them if necessary. Non-staining, non-toxic.

430-107 Plastic Compatible Motor Oil 1/2oz **3.59**
Medium weight lubricant for large scale models with high torque motors.

430-108 Plastic Compatible Motor Oil 1/2oz **3.59**
Light weight lubricant for small locomotives with low and medium torque motors, precision instruments, sewing machines, etc. Will not harm plastics, painted surfaces. Non-staining.

430-134 Micro-Fine Powdered Teflon™ **3.79**

430-111 Racing Oil 1/2oz **3.59**
For road race cars. A clean, white, dry, non-staining powdered lubricant. Will not harm plastics or paints. Use dry or add to oils or greases to make them "slipperier".

SAFETY WARNING

Pacer Zap, Hot Stuff and Goldberg Super Jet all contain Cyanacrylates (bonds skin instantly).

Apply only to surface to be bonded. In case of body contact, flush with water. Get immediate medical attention for any eye or internal contact. Keep away from children. As with all adhesives—use with adequate ventilation!

MICROSCALE®

LIQUID CEMENT

Micro Weld—Plastic
460-109
1 oz bottle **2.00**
Colorless liquid plastic-fusing adhesive. (Dissolves a thin layer of each surface to be joined and forms a welded joint.)

460-116 Metal Foil Adhesive 1oz **2.00**
Bonds aluminum foil to models.

MICRO MASK

460-110 Micro Mask bottle 1oz **2.00**
Liquid masking, which can be brushed on plastic, wood, metal and over paints, etc. Then after spraying on paint, the mask can be peeled off, leaving a good delineation.

- ADHESIVES
- GLUES
- PRIMERS
- DEBONDING AGENTS

452 431 430

RAIL ZIP

Track cleaner & corrosion inhibitor. Penetrates existing corrosion layers and restores electrical conductivity to the track. Also retards future corrosion by a molecular reaction with the base metal. Non-toxic, contains no solvents, acids, alkalis or alcohols — safe for all metals and plastics.

547-452 1oz 4.49

ZAP/CA+
SUPER THIN INSTANT ADHESIVE

Bonds woods, veneers, cork, vinyl, fabrics, rubber, leather, plastics, metals, stone and porcelain. Also works on oily, fuel-soaked surfaces or prestained miniature pieces.

547-425 4oz 20.99
547-429 2oz 11.99
547-431 1oz 6.59
547-433 1/2oz 3.99
547-435 1/4oz 2.99

ZAP-A-GAP
FILLING ADHESIVE

Very thin, penetrating, instant curing cyanoacrylate adhesive. Parts are held tightly together and a drop of ZAP/CA is applied to the joint and cures in 1-5 seconds. Bonds close fitting balsa, cloth, all woods, veneers, plastics, metals, rubber, oily surfaces, etc.

547-426 4oz 20.99
547-428 2oz 11.99
547-430 1oz 6.59
547-432 1/2oz 3.99
547-434 1/4oz 2.99

ZAP-O-CA + ODORLESS

Bonds balsawood, plywood and fiberglass to Styrofoam without any primers. Bonds Styrofoam to Styrofoam without melting the foam pieces.

547-458 20 grams 9.99

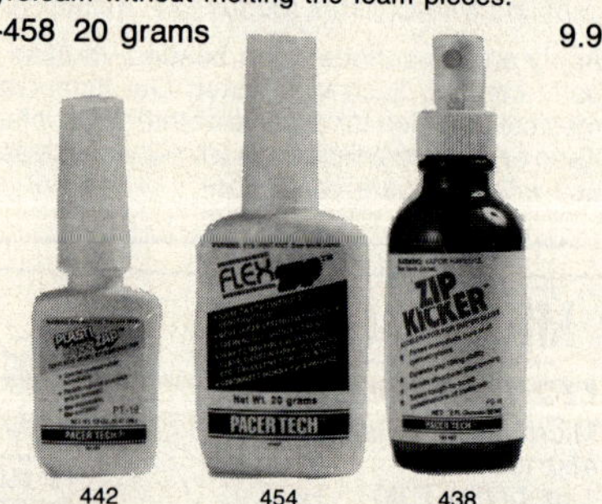

442 454 438

FLEX ZAP

For use on fiberglass, carbon fiber and plywood. 10-15 second set time.

547-454 20 grams 7.99

PLASTI-ZAP CA + +
INSTANT PLASTIC GLUE

For assembly of plastic parts or kits. Will not attack painted surfaces, tacking cures in 10-20 seconds, full cure in 1-3 minutes. Can be removed with debonder or accelerated with ZIP-KICKER. Non-flammable, non-sniffable.

547-442 1/3oz 3.49

ZIP-KICKER GLUE ACCELERATOR

"ZIP-KICKER" accelerator for super glues forces immediate cure for all cyanoacrylates. Use of this accelerator also expands gap filling ability, permits structural fillet forming and solves tough-to-bond combinations of materials.

547-438 2oz 5.99
547-453 8oz Refill 9.99

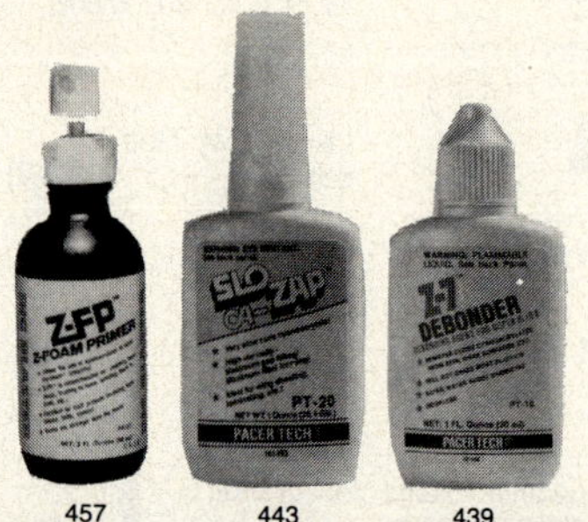

457 443 439

<hr>

LIMITED QUANTITIES AVAILABLE

Z-FOAM PRIMER (Z-FP)

Bonds foam boards instantly and prevents melting. Slow cure time.

547-457 2oz 5.79

SLO-ZAP CA –
SLOW CURE ADHESIVE

High viscosity, slow cure adhesive has a 30-40 second positioning time and cures in 1-2 minutes. The high viscosity formula permits use on poorly fitting surfaces, large bond areas and is a surface sealing agent for cloth and porous surfaces. Bonds oily surfaces.

547-443 1oz 6.89

Z-7 DEBONDER
DEBONDING AGENT

Waterbased material softens and removes cured cyanoacrylates, paint and hobby decals. Also removes ball point pen inks, permanent marker inks, typist correction fluid, nail polish and scuff marks from painted surfaces. Safe for most plastics.

547-439 1oz 3.99

Z-ENDS
DISPENSING TIPS & TUBES

Extra nozzle extension reaches into tight fitting spots and has a molded ring for storage on bottle neck. 10 Z-Ends tips plus 10 teflon micro dropper tubes included.

547-441 Z-Ends pkg(10) 3.59

ZAP-LOCK
THREAD LOCKING COMPOUND

Medium strength adhesive for locking fasteners, bearing bushings, sleeves, etc. "ZAP-LOCK" provides locking under heavy vibration but is easily disassembled with ordinary hand tools. Sets in 1-5 minutes, full cure after 5 minutes.

547-444 1/4oz 2.99

POLY-ZAP

Glues and repairs Lexan®. Glues space age plastics and nylons. Doesn't fog parts if glue is applied to film. Repairs EZ kits, too.

547-422 1/2oz 5.49

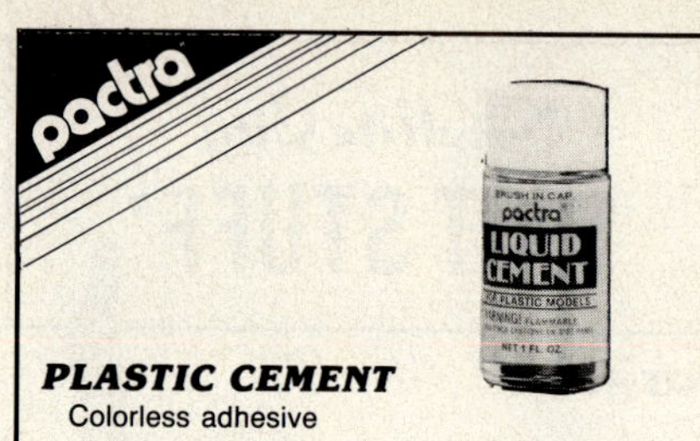

PLASTIC CEMENT

Colorless adhesive

545-230 Liquid 1 oz 1.25
Dealers: MUST order Dealer Pack of 12.

Plastruct

PLASTIC SOLVENT CEMENT

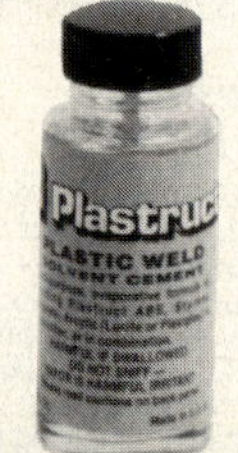

A colorless liquid plastic-fusing type adhesive. Dissolves a thin layer of each surface to join and form a welded joint as strong as the surrounding area. Bonds Styrene, ABS, Butyrate, and Acrylics.

Plastic Weld
570-2 2oz bottle 2.75

PECO

Imported from Great Britain by WALTHERS

LUBRICANT

552-640 Electro Lube Cleaner and Oil 5.99
Safe for most plastics, use to lube motors, gears, commutators and bearings. Pen type applicator for reaching small parts.

Roco

Imported from Austria by WALTHERS

CLEANERS

Rubber Track Cleaner
625-10002 8.49
for cleaning and removing dirt and oil deposits

Spray Cleaner
625-10904 194gm 13.99
non-flammable, odorless, non-conducting, will not irritate skin. Does not attack insulating materials, plastics, rubber, etc.

625-10902 Oiler NEW 9.49
625-10905 Grease for Loco NEW 6.49
Gears

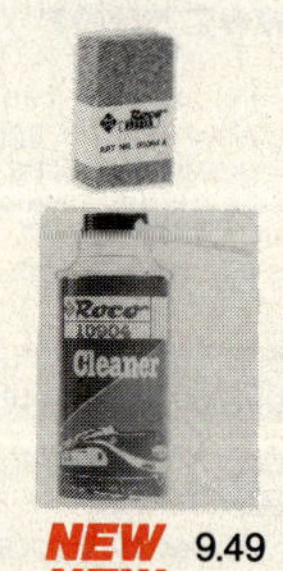

RIBBONRAIL
by Earl Eshleman

TRACK CLEANING BLOCK

Manual cleaning block for rail and wheels consists of an abrasive stone block (1 x 3 x 1/4").

170-11 Less Handle each 3.75
170-12 With Handle each 4.75

TIX

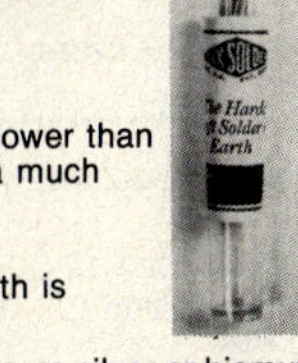

SOLDER
- Indium-based solder
- Melts at 275° F (150° lower than lead-tin solders—with a much higher wetting ability)
- Specific Gravity is 8.6
- Bonding holding strength is 4,000 lbs. PSI

Will never tarnish; contains no silver or bismuth and will solder to Platinum, Gold, Silver, and numerous alloys. Solid state components can be soldered without using a heat sink. Repairs to printed circuit boards are simple as the low melting point will not damage the board. Use with any Flux, rosin, chloride or acid.

| 118-1 Solder | pkg(20) 10.45 |

ANTI-FLUX
Fast drying liquid inhibitor. Apply over area where solder is not wanted. Solder immediately after applying. Water soluble, may be washed or brushed off and used with any soft solder.

| 118-7 Anti-Flux | 1/2oz 2.75 |

FLUX
Works on most metals and alloys and may be used with any soft solder. Water soluble and will wash off after drying. If a possibility of corrosion exists, may be neutralized by a solution of bicarbonate of soda.

| 118-3 Flux | 1/2oz 2.75 |

Scale Scenics
Division of CIRCUITRON

SOLDER
| 652-1502 Solder | pkg(10') 2.95 |

Ultra-fine rosin core solder (.014" diameter), is electronics grade (60% tin, 40% lead). Ideal for soldering miniature circuits, detailing for brass models or to simulate scale size hose or piping.

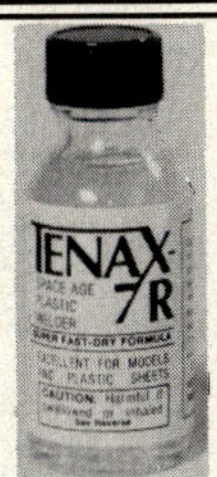

TENAX-7R
The Space Age Plastic Welder

PLASTIC WELDER
Tenax-7R causes plastic to become its own bonding agent. Works on styrene, butyrate, ABS and acrylic plastics. Apply Tenax-7R with a fine hair or nylon bristled brush. Non-flammable, non-sniffable, non-sticky and leaves no residue. Tenax-7R bonds in seconds and drys in minutes.

| 731-7 Tenax-7R | 1.35 |

Dealers: Must Order Dealer Pack of 12

STEWART PRODUCTS
HO SCALE (1/87)

TRACK CLEANER
| 683-501 Track Cleaner | 9.95 |

The track cleaner slips over the fuel tank of the Athearn SW-1500 and rubs rails by gravity. Each cleaner includes 15 self-abrasive sanding pads for easy replacement.

| 683-502 Replacement Pads | pkg(30) 6.95 |
| for 501 | |

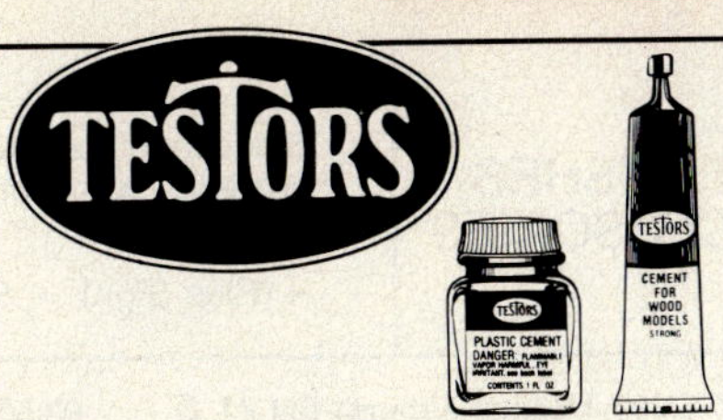

TESTORS

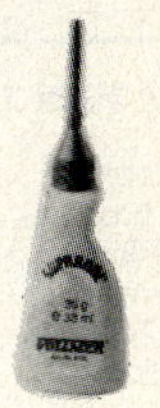

Fast drying non-yellowing cements.

PLASTIC CEMENT
| 704-3501 Tube | 5/8oz .98 |

Dealers: MUST order Dealer Pack of 48

| 704-3502 Liquid | bottle 1oz 1.55 |

for clean, transparent plastic-to-plastic joints.
Dealers: MUST order Dealer Pack of 12

| 704-3507 Liquid Cement | **NEW** 3.25 |
| w/Precision Applicator | |

Dealers: MUST order Dealer Pack of 6.

NON-TOXIC PLASTIC CEMENT
for use by children.
Dealers: MUST order Dealer Pack of 48.

| 704-3521 Tube | 5/8oz .98 |

CEMENT PEN
Fast drying high strength cement for plastic.

| 704-3532 Cement Pen | 1/3oz 2.59 |

WOOD CEMENT
| 704-3503 Extra-Fast Drying tube 5/8oz .98 |
| hot fuel proof |

Dealers: MUST order Dealer Pack of 24

| 704-3504 Extra-Fast Drying 1-3/4oz 1.55 |
| hot fuel proof |

Dealers: MUST order Dealer Pack of 12

| 704-3505 Fast Drying tube 5/8oz .98 |

Dealers: MUST order Dealer Pack of 24

| 704-3506 Fast Drying tube 1-3/4oz 1.55 |

Dealers: MUST order Dealer Pack of 12

GLUING TIPS
Fits most tubes of glue—for precise glue application.
Dealers: MUST order Dealer Pack of 12

| 704-8805 Gluing Tips | pkg(5) 1.39 |

DECAL SETTING SOLUTION
Dealers: MUST order Dealer Pack of 12

| 704-8804 Bottle | 1/4oz .98 |
| 704-1737 Bottle | 1/2oz 1.75 |

PLASTIC PUTTY
Can be used to fill, sculpture or redesign a surface.
Dealers: MUST order Dealer Pack of 24

| 704-3511 Plastic Putty | tube 5/8oz .98 |

TWINN - K

TRACK CLEANING FLUID
Cleans parts, wheels & track
TNT Track Cleaner
| 743-8501 | 1-1/4oz 1.60 |

GREASE
Lubricant with teflon, for all moving parts. Safe on plastics. Tube.

| 743-197 Magic Grease | 3/4oz 3.25 |

Ye Olde Huff-N-Puff

FLUX
Non-corrosive soft solder liquid flux.

Super Safe Solder Flux
| 792-2015 btl 1oz 2.00 |

VOLLMER
Imported from Germany and marketed by WALTHERS

CLEAR PLASTIC CEMENT
A clear plastic cement, for use on plastic kits. Delayed drying time allows gluing of larger surface areas. Nontoxic, nonflamable.

| 770-6115 Supranol 33 ml 4.49 |

Supercement
| 770-6016 | 25 ml 3.49 |
| 770-6116 | 100 ml 5.99 |

WALTHERS

BRIGHT BOY ABRASIVE TRACK CLEANER

For better conductivity. Clean track conducts better. Easy-to-Use Bright Boy will make your rails shine.

| 949-521 | 3.98 |

WELDBOND
All around wood glue, ballast cement, sealer, hardener, weather-proofer and more.

For ballast cement; mix one part Weldbond with two parts water.

797-125	4oz	2.98
797-185	8oz	4.35
797-795	1/2 gallon	19.45
797-1395	1 gallon	32.50

A Weldbond application book is available at no charge. Please send a stamped self-addressed envelope to Walthers.

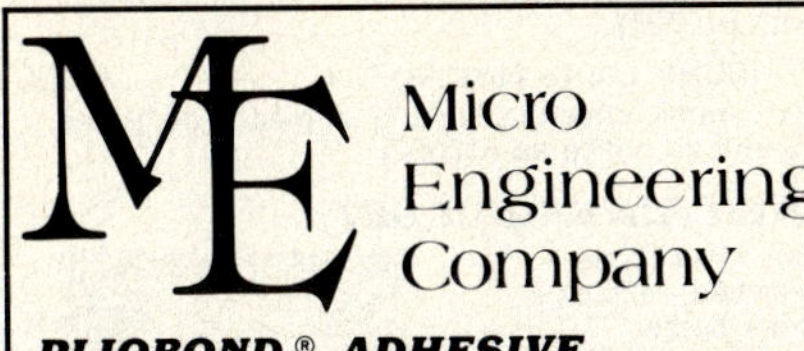

ME Micro Engineering Company

PLIOBOND ® ADHESIVE
For gluing Delrin track or hand-laid rail to ties.

| 255-49101 | w/Brush Top | 3oz 5.50 |
| 255-49102 | w/Fine Tip Tube | 1oz 3.50 |

MODELING SUPPLIES
255-49103	Rail Weather Solution 3oz 5.95
255-49104	Aluminum **NEW** 7 grams 4.95
	Solder Paste
255-49106	Zinc Solder **NEW** 7 grams 6.25
	Paste

AIRBRUSHES & ACCESSORIES

Binks manufactures airbrushes, airbrush sets and outfits, compressors, propellent, air hoses, accessories and parts for specific airbrushes.

+ (Plus Sign) = Special Order Only Items

RAVEN II AIRBRUSH

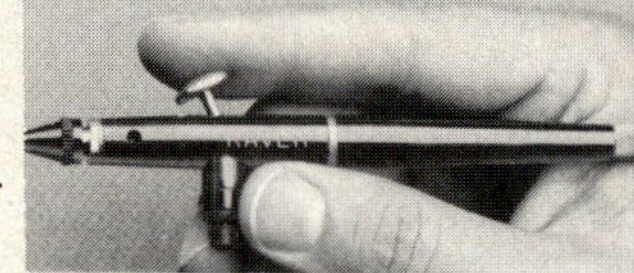

Raven II Airbrush w/Plastic Handle
177-59220 + 205.00

Set includes 59225 airbrush, spare needle, airbrush hanger & screws, wrench, needle seal tool, instruction manual & wooden box.
- Reversible color cup converts to right or left hand user
- Air and fluid seals made of self-lubricating Teflon
- Delrin needle chuck for alignment and cleaning device
- Double acting, internal mix, siphon type, adjustable feed. Both air and paint are controlled by the valve (double action) and they are mixed inside the body (internal mix). Either siphon or gravity paint feed is used and this is controlled by the trigger (adjustable feed).
- Raven II Airbrush will apply inks, dyes, watercolors, acrylics, oils, enamels and lacquers from 1/2" to a pencil line spray.

RAVEN II AIRBRUSH SET

Raven II Airbrush Set
177-59221 + 180.00

Set includes Raven II Airbrush, spare needle, airbrush hanger and screws, wrench, needle seal tool and instruction manual; packaged in a durable cardboard box.

WREN AIRBRUSH

Single acting, external mix, siphon type, adjustable feed.
The valve or trigger regulates only the air (single action). The paint and air are mixed outside the body (external mix). Siphon paint feed is used. Paint flow can vary from 1/16 to 1-1/2" wide depending on the adjustment of the cone (adjustable feed).

177-10001   Small Nozzle, A +   67.00
for inks, stains, dyes, etc., sprays a fine line

177-10002   Medium Nozzle, B   67.00
for thinned lacquers, enamels, etc. (Interchanges with #10021)

177-10021   Large Nozzle, C +   67.00
for ceramic underglazing and thinned underglazes. (Same air orifice as #10002)

WREN AIRBRUSH SET

Set #1 includes airbrush, 1/2fl oz color bottle assembly.

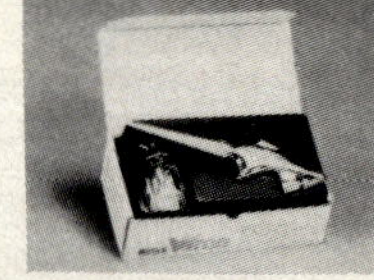

177-10003   Small Airbrush Set #1, A +   74.50
177-10004   Medium Airbrush Set #1, B   74.50
177-10022   Large Airbrush Set #1, C +   74.50

Set #2 includes 1/4, 1/2 & 2-1/2 fl oz color bottle assemblies and #60 hose with connections.

177-10005   Small Airbrush Set #2, A +   93.50
177-10006   Medium Airbrush Set #2, B   93.50
177-10023   Large Airbrush Set #2, C +   93.50

WREN AIRBRUSH OUTFIT

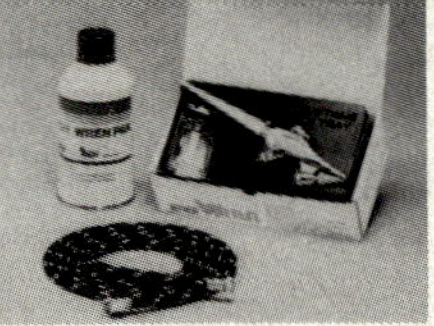

Includes one airbrush set #1 plus one #65 Wren-Pak Valve, one #70 Wren-Pak and one #61 hose with connections.

177-10007   Small Airbrush Outfit #3, A   102.50
177-10008   Medium Airbrush Outfit #3, B   102.50

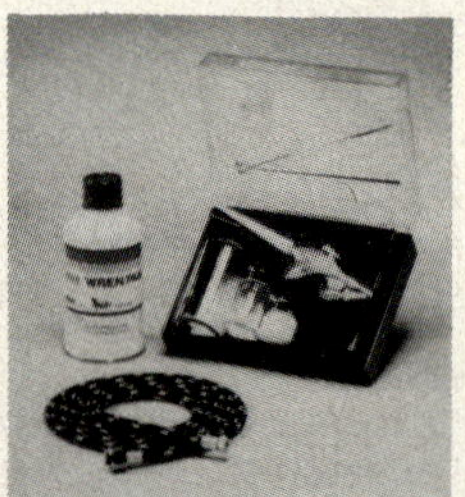

Includes one airbrush set #2, one #65 Wren-Pak Valve, one #70 Wren-Pak and one #61 hose with connections. #10011 and #10012 include two #70 Wren-Paks.

177-10009   Small Airbrush Outfit #4, A +   117.00
177-10010   Medium Airbrush Outfit #4, B +   117.00
177-10011   Small Airbrush Outfit #5, A +   124.00
177-10012   Medium Airbrush Outfit #5, B +   124.00

WREN AIRBRUSH w/COMPRESSOR

Consists of one airbrush set #1, one #61 hose with connections and one #342025 air compressor.

177-10015   Small w/Compressor, A +   282.00
177-10016   Medium w/Compressor, B +   282.00
177-10025   Large w/Compressor, C +   282.00
177-342025 Air Compressor Only +   200.00
Electric motor delivers 1/15 HP; 30 PSI w/10001, 28 PSI w/10002 and 10021 airbrushes. Permits continuous running without overheating. Weight 9 lbs.

177-5984   Foot Switch with Cord   36.75
Turns compressor on/off without having to plug and unplug. Capacity to 7 amp, 125/250 VAC. Comes with 6 foot cord.

WREN-PAK PROPELLENT

177-5970   Pea Can   each   7.00
177-5975   Pea Can   pkg(12) 75.00
Harmless Freon propellent for use with Wren Airbrush. Supplies power for spraying liquid material. Sufficient to airbrush the contents of a 2-1/2oz color bottle. (PAK life dependent upon material viscosity.)

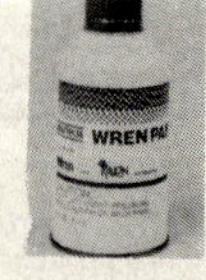

177-5962   Valve Body   5.00
177-5963   Needle Stem +   2.40

177-5964   Propellent Valve Seat +   pkg(2) 1.60

177-5965   Valve 12.50
connects hose to Wren Pak

AIR HOSE

177-715003   5'   9.55
for hook-up of #152 blow gun to #86836 extractor or compressor; comes w/#72312 connections

177-72312   Connector, 1/4" ID hose   3.15
For use with #715003.

Light Weight Vinyl
177-5960   6'   4.50
177-5994   10'   5.15
177-5995   12' + 5.50
177-5996   15' + 6.00

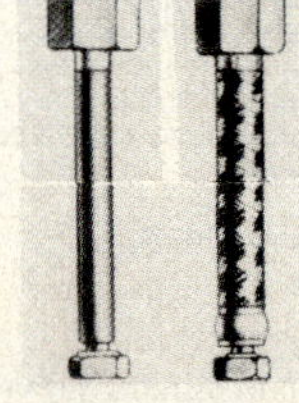

Heavy Duty Braided
177-5961   6'   8.00
177-5997   10'   10.00
177-5998   12'   11.00
177-5999   15'   12.50

CAP ASSEMBLY

177-5927   Cap Assembly for 1/4oz   5.40
177-5928   Cap Assembly for 1/2oz   6.00
177-5929   Cap Assembly for 2.5oz   6.30

SIPHON BOTTLE ASSEMBLY

with friction connection
177-5930   Glass 1/4oz 6.90
177-5931   Glass 1/2oz 7.50
177-5932   Glass 2.5oz 7.80
177-5981   Plastic 2oz 11.50

BOTTLE & CAP ASSEMBLY

with seal tight cover
177-5933   Glass   1/4oz 2.25
177-5934   Glass   1/2oz 2.25
177-5935   Glass   2.5oz 2.25
177-5978   Plastic   2oz   3.55

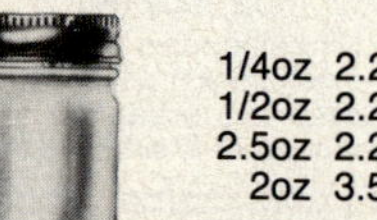

ACCESSORIES

177-5940   Siphon Tube   2.55
177-5941   Bottle less Cap +   1/4oz   1.50
177-5942   Bottle less Cap   1/2oz   1.50
177-5943   Bottle less Cap +   2.5oz   1.50
177-5950   Nut for Hose-Airbrush + pkg(3)   1.35
177-5951   Tailpiece for Hose- +   pkg(2)   1.50
           Airbrush
177-5952   Tailpiece for Hose-Compressor +   1.50
177-5953   Ferrule for Hose-Tailpiece +   .75
177-5957   Cap for 1/4oz Jar +   pkg(2)   1.50
177-5958   Cap for 1/2oz Jar +   pkg(2)   1.50
177-5959   Cap for 2.5oz Jar +   pkg(2)   1.50

Airbrush Repair Kit
177-59102
9.20

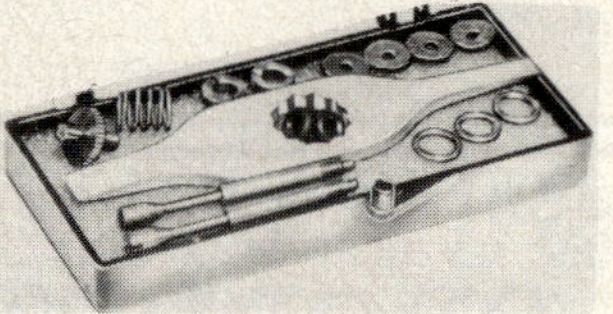

Contains special tool for disassembly of airbrush and extra spare parts.
177-5983   Airbrush Wrench +   1.00
177-83576 DM Nipple for Blow Gun +   1.70
to connect #715003 Hose to #152 Blow Gun

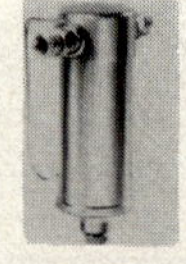

Extractor, Belt Type +
177-86836   80.00
Removes moisture and foreign matter from air delivered to airbrush. Hook up to compressor using #715003 Hose Assembly. Order hose separately.

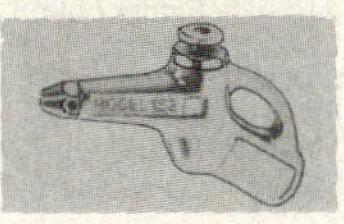

W. R. BROWN INCORPORATED

AIRBRUSH & ACCESSORIES
CAUTION: We strongly recommend the use of a respirator for your safety, when doing any airbrush painting!

ACCESSORIES (continued)
177-40145 Respirator pkg(10) 24.00
MSHA and NIOSH approved. Filters out silica, fiberglass, saw dust and crop grains. Soft, noncollapsible piece conforms comfortably to face.

Blow Gun
177-152 15.00
(By Special Order Only.)
for cleaning, dusting or releasing casting from mold

177-202673 Hanger Screw pkg(20) 2.00
177-59100 Airbrush Repair Kit 108.00

RAVEN PARTS
177-59206 Repair Kit #1 13.00
(By Special Order Only.)
Includes two each of 59146, 59144, 59134, 59140 and one of 59175.

177-59207 Repair Kit #2 42.00
(By Special Order Only.)
Includes 1 ea 59143, 59136, 59138, 59135, 59171, 59147, 59139 & 59141. 2 ea 59162, 59146, 59144, 59134, 59170, & 59175. 6 ea 59171 & 59135.

177-59131 Handle Only, Plastic 2.50
177-59135 Fine Point Needle pkg(2) 15.20
177-59137 Needle Chuck Nut 2.50
177-59141 Air Valve Spring pkg(10) 5.00
177-59143 Fluid Nozzle 19.25
(By Special Order Only.)
177-59145 Air Cap 2.60
177-59151 Cup Assembly 1/16oz 20.00
177-59152 Cup Base 1/16 & 1/8oz 4.55
(By Special Order Only.)
177-59153 Cup Sub-Assembly 1/16oz 15.25
177-59164 Color Cup Assembly 1/8oz 29.00
177-59165 Cup Sub-Assembly 1/8oz 24.25
177-59156 Protective Cap 4.45
177-59157 Airbrush Wrench pkg(2) 1.30
177-59160 Hanger 2.15
177-59169 Lower Case Insert 1.50
177-59170 Spring Retainer 2.40
177-59172 Gasket pkg(2) .50
for #142 Hose
177-59176 Fluid Nozzle Insert 6.00
(By Special Order Only.)
177-59181 Spare Parts Kit 8.65
177-59184 Adapter 4.30
177-59209 Fine Needle pkg(6) 36.00
177-59226 Body Assembly for Raven II 55.00
shell only
177-59229 Air Valve 2.20
177-59233 Needle Adjustment 1.35
177-59234 Adjustment Knob 3.90
177-59235 Lock Knob .85
177-59236 Needle Adjustment Assembly 15.50
177-59238 Trigger Assembly 17.50
177-59242 Needle Chuck 4.00
177-59244 Trigger Cam .80

WREN PARTS
177-591 10001 A Body Only 45.00
(By Special Order Only.)
177-592 10002 B Body Only 45.00
177-595 10021 C Body Only 45.00
177-593 Trigger Button 2.50
177-599 10001 Fluid Control 24.75
177-5910 10002 Fluid Control Assmb. 24.75
177-59101 10021 Fluid Control 24.75
177-5920 Air Valve Housing 4.35
177-5137 Handle Only 1.85

AIRBRUSH / COMPRESSOR SETS

787-211 Hobby Spray Set 139.95
Includes: #201 Compressor, Hobby Gun, 8ft air hose and extra 1oz and 2oz jars w/covers.

787-430 Complete Airbrush Kit 209.95
Set includes: 1/10 HP compressor with bleeder valve and on/off switch, external mix airbrush with adjustable air flow and 8ft hose.

COMPACT SPRAY GUN
External mix siphon feed w/adjustable nozzles, convertible bleeder and non-bleeder operation. Includes 1oz jar & 8ft air hose.

Hobby Gun
787-812 19.95

LIMITED QUANTITY
787-834 Air Brush 64.95
with fine-med heavy nozzles.

AIR COMPRESSORS

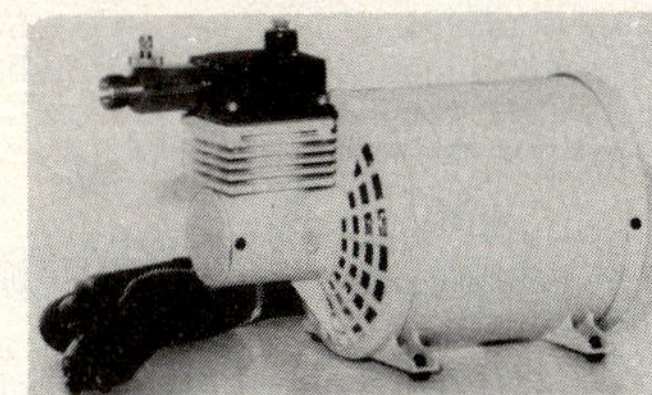

787-201 Piston Air Compressor 119.95
1/12 horsepower oil-less piston compressor, delivers up to 40 PSI. Operates on 115 volt, 60 cycle. Includes bleeder valve. Weight 6-1/2 lbs.

787-410 Diaphragm Air Compressor 175.95
1/10 horsepower oil-less diaphragm air compressor, delivers up to 45 PSI. Operates on 115 volts, 60 cycle. Includes bleeder valve.

AIRBRUSH SET *NEW*

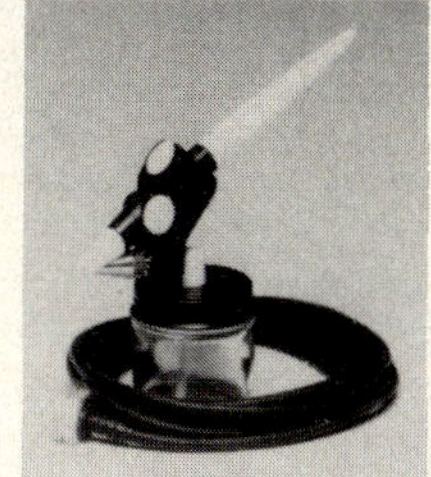

Air Brush
787-1832
41.95
Unique, quick change jar and nozzle assembly allows easy clean up and facilitates color changes. Wide base allows unit to stand on any horizontal surface. Comes with medium top.

JAR & NOZZLE ASSEMBLIES *NEW*

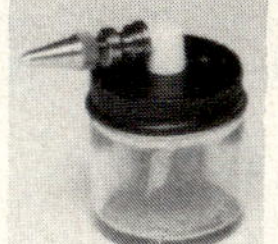

787-31 Light 18.50
787-32 Medium 18.50
787-33 Heavy 18.50

AIRBRUSH ACCESSORIES

787-822 Regulator w/Gauge 29.95
Provides constant, uniform pressure up to 0-50 PSI.
787-1520 Paint Jars 1oz pkg(3) 5.95
787-1521 Paint Jars 2oz pkg(3) 6.50
787-1522 Paint Jars 4.5oz pkg(3) 7.25
(By Special Order Only.)
787-803 Foot Control Switch 49.95

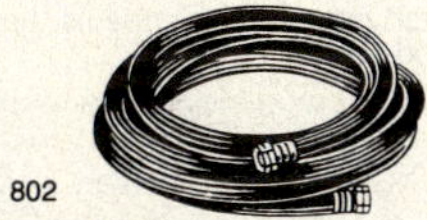

787-802 1/4" Bleeder Valve 9.95
787-415 15 Foot Hose 11.95
1/4" thread, 1/4" fittings
(not illustrated)
787-833 Nozzle, Heavy 18.50

LIMITED QUANTITY
787-818 8 Foot Hose 9.95

MINI-SANDBLAST GUN

Mini-Sandblast gun for cleaning curved surfaces or hard to reach areas or etching designs on glass or wood.

Unit includes: 4oz jar, 8' air hose, 12oz of 220 grit aluminum oxide and a face mask. Use with a 1/10th horsepower or higher compressor (not included).
787-342 Mini-Sandblast Gun 41.95
787-452 Complete Mini-Sandblaster 205.95
(By Special Order Only.)
Includes #410 compressor, #342 mini blaster, 8ft of air hose, 12oz package of aluminum oxide & face mask shield.
787-805 Mini-Sandblast Booth 39.95
(By Special Order Only.)
for use with Mini-Sandblast guns.

ALUMINUM OXIDE
787-35100 100 Grit pkg(12oz) 5.95
(By Special Order Only.)
787-35180 180 Grit pkg(12oz) 5.95
(By Special Order Only.)
787-35220 220 Grit pkg(12oz) 5.95

BADGER AIR-BRUSH CO.

Airbrushes, Airbrush Parts & Accessories, Compressor, Compressor Parts & Accessories.

CAUTION: We strongly recommend the use of a respirator for your safety, when doing any airbrush painting!

MODEL 100 AIRBRUSH KIT

For extra fine lines and fine detail work. Spray ranges from fine lines to soft continuous tones. This is a double action airbrush (finger controls both the amount of paint and air pressure with the same button).

Kits include Model 100 series airbrush, 1/16oz self-standing color cup, protective cap, extra needle, case, holder and a wrench.

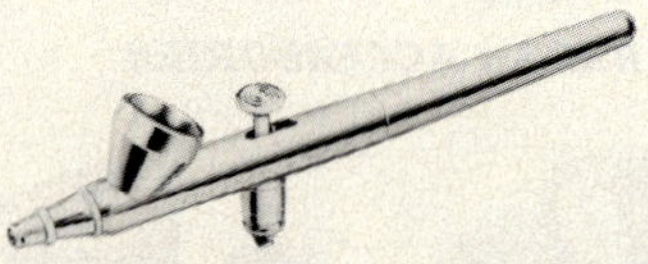

165-100	Extra Fine Line	83.00
165-101	Medium Standard Illustration	83.00

MODEL 100 GRAVITY FEED AIRBRUSH KIT

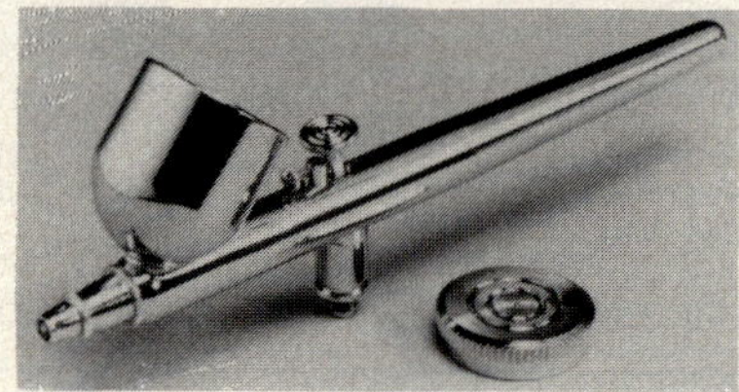

165-102 Gravity Feed Extra Fine Line 89.00
Includes: Model 100 airbrush with extra fine line gravity feed permanently mounted top color cup, protective cap, extra needle, case, holder and a wrench.

MODEL 100 (LARGE) GRAVITY FEED, DUAL ACTION AIRBRUSH KIT

Allows you to convert any model to another by simply changing two parts: complete head assembly and needle.

Each kit includes: model LG series airbrush, 1oz permanently mounted top color cup (with fitted cover), counter balanced handle (to prevent forward tipping), airbrush hanger, extra needle, tip cap, wrench and padded case.

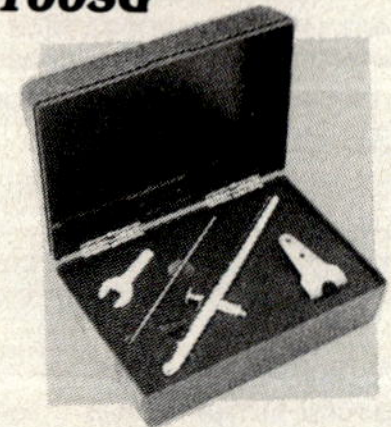

165-1005	Extra Fine	94.00

for extra fine lines and fine detail work
(By Special Order Only.)

165-1006	Illustration	94.00

for fine lines and detail work, has slightly wider spray than #1005

165-1007	Heavy Duty	94.00

for medium lines and an extra wide range of spray

MODEL 100SG

165-1008	Extra Fine	83.00
	(By Special Order Only.)	

Fine detailed work, has a small built in fluid cavity. Will spray inks, dyes and water colors.

MODEL 150 AIRBRUSH KIT

165-1507	150 Airbrush Kit	110.00
	(By Special Order Only.)	

MODEL 250 AIRBRUSH KIT

Single action external mix airbrush. Finger button controls the amount of air pressure. Turning the paint tip can adjust spray from 3/4" to 2" pattern.

All kits include Model 250 series airbrush, 6' hose, propel regulator and two 3/4oz jars; unless otherwise noted.

165-2501	Basic	19.00
165-2502	Basic	15.95
	w/one attached 3/4oz jar	
165-2503	Basic w/Propel Can	25.95
165-2504	Mini	25.95

Includes 8' hose, propel regulator, propel can and one attached 4oz jar.

MODEL 200 AIRBRUSH KIT

Single action internal mix airbrush. Finger button controls the amount of air pressure. Turning needle valve screw adjusts pattern of spray from lines less than 1/16" up to 1-1/2".

Kits include: Model 200 airbrush protective cap & case unless otherwise noted.

165-2001	Fine Line	57.00
	w/two 3/4oz jars with 1 cover	
165-2002	HD Airbrush Kit	57.00
165-2005	Ex Airbrush Kit Fine	64.00
	(By Special Order Only.)	
165-2003	Fine Deluxe	71.00

w/attached 3/4oz jar, 6' hose, propel regulator, three 3/4oz jars with covers, propel can, less case.

165-2004	Fine Hobby & Touch Up	245.00
	(By Special Order Only.)	

w/Model 180 Portable Diaphragm Compressor, two 3/4oz jars w/1 cover, 10' hose, 1/4" pipe thread fitting (adapts brush to compressor or CO2 tank), less protective cap.

165-2009	Extra Fine	57.00

Model 200-9-XF with a top mounted 1/16 oz color cup.

165-20010	Medium	57.00
165-20011	Extra Fine less Cup	52.00

MODEL 150 AIRBRUSH KIT

For fine lines & fine detail work where larger coverage is needed. (Paint jar instead of color cup is the only difference between this brush & Model 100).

All kits include: Model 150 series airbrush, attached 3/4oz jar, protective cap, 2oz jar with cover, case, holder and wrench.

165-150	Fine Line	89.00
	w/extra needle	
165-151	Extra Fine Line	89.00

w/extra needle & 1/4oz color cup (for light material and very fine details)

165-152	Professional	120.00

with 1/4oz color cup, additional 3/4oz jar with cover, braided air hose, 1/4" pipe thread fitting, heavy duty head assembly & needle (for light to medium material & faster feed) and wood case.

165-153	Heavy Duty	89.00

MODEL 350 AIRBRUSH KIT

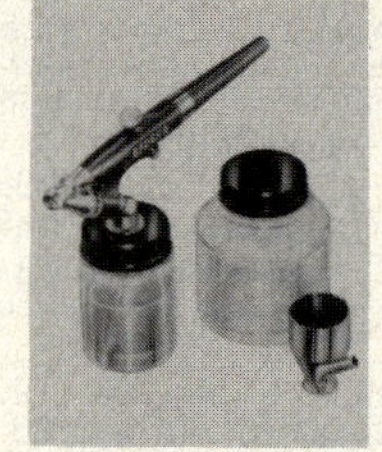

Single action external mix airbrush. Finger button controls the amount of air pressure. Turning the paint tip can adjust spray from 1/8 to 1-1/2" depending on tip.

All kits include: Model 350 series airbrush, 2oz jar w/cover, 3/4oz jar.

165-3501	Fine Line	40.00
165-3502	Medium Line	46.00
	w/6' vinyl air hose & propel regulator	
165-3503	Medium Line	54.00

w/6' vinyl air hose, 1/4oz color cup, propel regulator and propel can

165-3504	Medium Line	40.00
	sprays from 1/4" to 1-1/2"	
165-3505	Heavy Duty	40.00
	sprays from 1/2 to 2"	
	(By Special Order Only.)	
165-35004	350 Airbrush Kit	72.00
	(By Special Order Only.)	

MODEL 400 TOUCH-UP GUN

Detail/touch-up gun is ideal for larger scale models. Provides intricate spraying where delicate control is necessary.

Easily adjusted for use by a right or left hand modeler. "Trigger control" enables a wide spray for larger areas, as well as a narrow spray for precise detail.

165-4001	Fine w/cup	114.00
	(By Special Order Only.)	
165-4002	Medium w/cup	114.00
	(By Special Order Only.)	
165-4003	Heavy w/cup	114.00
	(By Special Order Only.)	

CRESCENDO MODEL 175 AIRBRUSH KIT   *NEW*

Bottom feed dual action, internal mix airbrush that adapts to either color cups or jars.

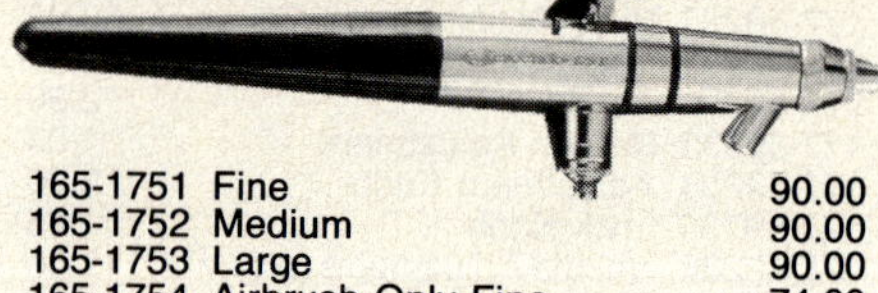

165-1751	Fine	90.00
165-1752	Medium	90.00
165-1753	Large	90.00
165-1754	Airbrush Only Fine	74.00
165-1755	Airbrush Only Medium	74.00
165-1756	Airbrush Only Large	74.00
165-1757	Crescendo Kit	105.00

SPRAY BOOTH

Booth has a lightweight, translucent polypropolene case. Contains 3100 rpm blower, filter, 8 x 5" plexiglass window. Blower measures 20 x 12 x 12". 110V.
(NOTE: Hobby Spray Booth **MUST** be vented! Instructions are included, less venting hardware.)

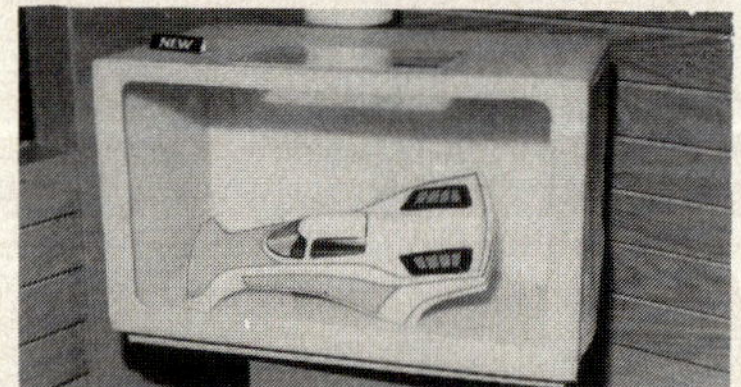

165-135	Hobby Spray Booth	235.00
165-136	Replacement Filter for Spray Booth	3.50

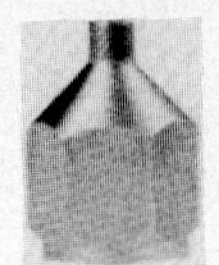

BADGER AIR-BRUSH CO.

Airbrushes, Airbrush Parts & Accessories, Compressor, Compressor Parts & Accessories.

CAUTION: We strongly recommend the use of a respirator for your safety, when doing any airbrush painting!

COMPRESSOR

Silent I Compressor 1/3 HP
165-38011   685.00
(By Special Order Only.)
Quiet portable air compressor. Features: automatic on/off pressure switch, intake air filter, 1 gal (4 ltr) tank, thermal overload protection, pressure relief safety valve, operates 3 artist air-brushes (any make), 6 ft. Electric cord with 3 prong plug, in-line oil filter 99.9% effective, pressure gauges for air, tank, oil level & line.

Silent II Compressor 1/2 HP
165-3802   815.00
(By Special Order Only.)
Quiet portable air compressor. Allows 4-5 airbrushes to operate at a time. No pulsation. Features: on/off switch, automatic on/off pressure switch, intake air filter, safety relief and pressure relief safety valve, 1.3 gal (5 ltr) storage tank, adjustable air pressure regulator, thermal overload protection, will operate up to 5 air-brushes, 6 ft. electric cord 3 prong plug, gauges for oil level, line & tank pressure.

Silent 1/6 HP Compressor
165-3806   580.00
(By Special Order Only.)
Piston motor. Allows 1 air brush without pulsation; portable with no noise. Features: on/off switch & automatic on/off pressure switch, intake air filter, 1 gallon (4 ltr) tank, thermal overload protection, adjustable air pressure regulator, gauges for tank pressure, oil level & line pressure, 6 ft. Electric cord with 3 prong plug. **(By Special Order Only.)**

Air Compressor 1/12 hp
165-1801   185.00
This portable oil-less diaphragm type compressor is a "bleeder" type that develops 25PSI at 1.0 CFM. Compact, lightweight & quiet.

165-18011 Air Compressor   235.00
Same as 1801 but, with automatic shutoff.
(By Special Order Only.)

165-802 Whirlwind II Air Compressor 135.00
1/20 horsepower, maximum pressure: 35PSI. Approximately .40 CFM at 20PSI when airbrushing.
FEATURES:
• Lightweight/Portable   • Oil-less diaghragm
• Use with most Artist or Hobby Airbrushes
• 6' Electric Cord

COMPRESSOR ACCESSORIES

165-50023 1/4" Pipe Thread Fitting   3.00
Adaptor
Adapts airhose to compressor or CO_2 tank.

165-50057 CO_2 Regulator & Gauge   70.00

165-50051 Moisture Trap   35.00
Air filter and water trap for air compressors.

165-50054 Air Regulator, Filter &   52.50
Gauge Set

AIRBRUSH ACCESSORIES

165-1	Cork Gasket (for Mini Gun)	1.10
165-2	Paint Jar, 4oz (Mini Gun)	1.35
165-3	Paint Hose, 4" (Mini Gun)	1.10
165-4	Air Hose, 8' (Mini Gun)	5.25
165-50021	Airbrush Holder	2.50

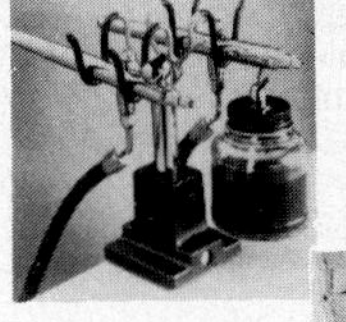

Airbrush Holder
165-125   24.95
Holds two airbrushes; rotates, swivels and clamps on to surface up to 2" thick.

165-50048	1/8oz Color Cup	5.80
165-500482	1/4oz Color Cup	5.80
165-500483	1/4oz Color Cup for Model 350	5.80
165-50029	Tire Adapter	3.25
165-50047	1/16oz Color Cup	5.25

165-502016 Paint Filter   5.25
Stainless steel mesh fits in airbrush bottle and filters out large particles. Easy removal for cleaning.

165-50050	Prepared Beeswax		3.15
165-50056	Polishing Paper	pkg(3)	3.15
	(By Special Order Only.)		
165-50060	Cleaning Reamer for Head 100-200		3.75
165-50061	3-Cornered Reamer Models 100 & 200		4.75
165-500052	Jar & Cover Models 200, 250, 350 & 150	3/4oz	1.05
165-500053	Jar & Cover Models 200, 250, 350, & 150	2oz	1.35
165-50200	Propel Regulator		5.25
165-50117	Propel Regulator Stem with O-Ring		2.50
165-50118	Propel Regulator O-Ring		.80
165-50119	Propel Regulator Washer		.80

Badger Propel, Can
165-50002   11oz 7.00

Badger Propel, Can
165-50202   17oz 9.00
*environmentally safe

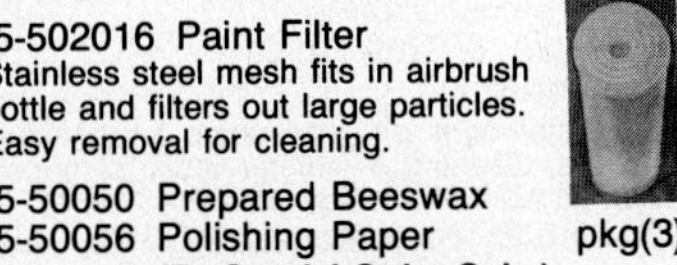

165-50001 6' Vinyl Air Hose   4.25

165-500011	10' Vinyl Air Hose w/1/4" pipe thread fitting	7.00
165-504011	10' Recoil Hose for Badger	14.00
165-504012	10' Recoil Hose for Binks	14.00
165-502011	10' Braided Air Hose w/1/4" pipe thread fitting	11.50
165-502012	Moisture Filter w/Hoses	26.50
165-502015	Moisture Filter Only	16.00
165-502016	Inside Jar Paint Filter	4.75
165-600	Foto-Frisket Film pkg(10)	11.00

Low tack, easy lift-off masking film. Leaves no residue after removal and will not lift the surface or strip gloss finish off work already completed. Use for making hard edges and controlling color, stencils and mask-making and temporary overlays. Reusable. 8-1/2 x 11".

DOUBLE CARTRIDGE RESPIRATOR

Double Cartridge Respirator
165-1901   63.00

Provides protection against paint mists & vapors. May be worn on or under the chin, adjustable straps ensure a comfortable fit. Double cartridge design provides protection & low breathing resistance where single cartridge designs may clog or load up. Built in anti-bacterial agent may be taken apart for easy cleaning.

165-1902 Replacement Cartridge   13.75
for #1901
165-1903 Replacement Pre-Filter   6.50
for #1901

AIR ABRASIVE GUN

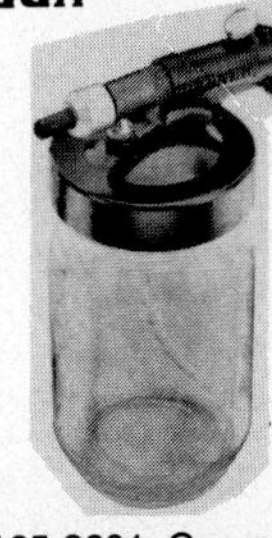

Removes paint, rust and corrosion; leaves surface ready for refinishing. Set includes: gun w/attached 4oz jar, 8' hose and 12oz net weight jar of aluminum oxide plus face mask. Use of wrap-around safety goggles is recommended.

165-2601 Gun only   25.95
165-2603 Gun   37.95
Also includes propel can and propel regulator.

AIR ABRASIVE GUN ACCESSORIES

165-50260	Abrasive	12oz	4.75
165-50261	Gun Body **(By Special Order Only.)**		8.50
165-50262	Gun Main Shaft		4.75
165-50263	Gun Tip		3.75
165-50264	Gun Pick-up Tube **(By Special Order Only.)**		1.50
165-50265	Gun Adjustable Screw		2.00
165-50266	Air Hose		6.50
165-50268	Gun Collar		2.00

AIRBRUSH PARTS
MODELS 100 & 150

165-50033	Aluminum Handle **(By Special Order Only.)**	3.70
165-50034	Shell (Model 100) **(By Special Order Only.)**	25.50
165-50035	Shell (Model 150) **(By Special Order Only.)**	27.50
165-500332	Counter Balanced Handle	8.95

Made of solid brass and chrome plated, this handle prevents forward tipping.

165-500341 Shell   25.50
Model 100, extra fine line, w/gravity feed.

Airbrushes, Airbrush Parts & Accessories, Compressor, Compressor Parts & Accessories.

CAUTION: We strongly recommend the use of a respirator for your safety, when doing any airbrush painting!

+ = Special Order Only

MODEL 200

165-50011	Handle +	4.25
165-50012	Shell +	22.00
165-500162	Head Assembly, Complete	11.50
165-50017	Needle, Nickel Silver	4.25
165-50208	Jar Adapter	2.85

Model 150 & 200, use for newer guns.

165-500171	Needle, Nickel Silver heavy duty	4.25
165-500172	XF Needle	4.25

MODEL 250

165-50028	Paint Tip & Spring	3.15

MODEL 350

165-50070	Plunger	2.90
165-50071	Air Hose Fitting	1.85
165-50072	Plunger Head	1.85
165-50073	Air Tip Busing	3.15
165-50074	Air Tip Seal	1.35
165-50075	Air Tip Fine	3.45
165-50076	Fluid Cap Fine	4.75
165-50077	Paint Seal	.85
165-50078	Paint Seal Nut	1.35
165-50079	Lock Nut	1.35
165-50080	Body Fine	8.40
165-50081	Fluid Needle Fine	7.35
165-50082	Fluid Needle Assy Fine	11.60
165-50083	Fluid Needle Assy Medium	11.60
165-50084	Fluid Needle Assy Heavy	11.60
165-50085	Spacer	1.35
165-50308	Jar Adapter	2.85
165-500751	Air Tip Medium	3.45
165-500752	Air Tip Heavy	3.45
165-500761	Fluid Cap Medium	4.75
165-500762	Fluid Cap Heavy	4.75
165-500811	Fluid Needle Medium	7.35
165-500812	Fluid Needle Heavy	7.35

MISCELLANEOUS PARTS

165-50007	Jar Cover 3/4 & 2oz	2.50

use for old style guns only—pre-1982

165-50010	Needle Chuck	2.10
165-50013	Valve Casing	6.50
165-50014	Plunger & "O" Ring	2.65
165-50015	Valve Screw	1.85
165-50019	Trigger	4.50
165-50020	Plunger Spring	1.35
165-50022	Protective Cap for Airbrush	2.50
165-50025	Paint Hose Siphone Tube	.90
165-50027	Needle Adjusting Screw	1.85
165-50030	Tube Shank +	4.20
165-50031	Spring Screw	2.35
165-50032	Needle Tube	3.70
165-50036	Complete Assembled Valve	9.75
165-50038	Head Only	7.10
165-50042	Back Lever	2.50
165-50043	Adjusting Screw +	1.85
165-50044	Spring for Needle Tube	1.35
165-50046	Needle bearing, Teflon	3.15
165-50055	Head Washer/Seal, Teflon	1.35
165-50086	Wrench	1.35
165-50090	Badger/Paasche Airline Adaptor	2.50
165-50111	Coupling Nut +	1.50
165-50112	Coupling Nipple	1.10
165-500141	"O" Ring	1.05
165-500142	"O" Ring	1.05

for models 250 and 350

165-500161	Head Assembly, Complete	11.50

extra fine line models

165-500163	Head Assembly, Complete	11.50

heavy duty models

165-500241	Gasket pkg(3)	1.50

Models 150, 200, 250 & 350

165-500371	Spray Regulator, Extra Fine	4.75
165-500372	Spray Regulator, IL Models	4.75
165-500373	Spray Regulator, Heavy Duty	4.75
165-500381	Head & Tip, Extra Fine	10.50
165-500382	Head & Tip, IL Models	10.50
165-500383	Head & Tip, Heavy Duty	10.50

165-500391	Tip, Extra Fine	4.75
165-500392	Tip, Illustration Models	4.75
165-500393	Tip, Heavy Duty	4.75
165-500401	Needle, Extra Fine	3.75
165-500402	Needle, Illustration Models	3.75
165-500403	Needle, Heavy Duty	3.75
165-500841	Badger/Paasche Needle Adaptor	2.10

(By Special Order Only.)

CRESCENDO (MODEL 175) REPLACEMENT PARTS *NEW*

165-41003	Tip Fine SS	3.25
165-41004	Tip Medium SS	3.25
165-41005	Tip Large SS	3.25
165-41006	Needle SS Fine	3.75
165-41007	Needle SS Medium	3.75
165-41008	Needle SS Large	3.75
165-41009	Case & Insert	8.50
165-41013	Back Lever	3.00
165-41014	Tube Shank	5.50
165-41015	Shell w/Needle Bearings	30.00
165-41016	Needle Tube	5.50
165-41017	Needle Chuck	3.00
165-41018	Trigger Straight	5.50
165-41019	Trigger Angled	5.50
165-41021	handle pkg(2pcs)	3.75
165-41023	Head	7.75
165-41025	Protective Cap	3.00
165-41026	Spring Needle Tube	2.00
165-41027	Body "O" Rings pkg(2)	1.75
165-41028	Trigger Pad pkg(3)	1.00
165-41033	Spray Regulator Fine	4.00
165-41034	Spray Regulator Medium	3.00
165-41035	Spray Regulator Large	4.00

INSTRUCTION BOOKLET

165-314	for Model 200 +	1.25
165-316	for Kit 2504	1.00

(By Special Order Only.)

165-318	for Kits 2501 & 2503	1.00

(By Special Order Only.)

165-319	for Models 100 & 150	2.25

(By Special Order Only.)

165-324	for Model 350 +	2.25
165-500	Hobby & Craft Guide to Airbrushing	5.95

Includes instructions on preparation for painting, mixing paint, cleaning & maintenance. 32 pages, over 130 full color illustrations, 8-1/2 x 11".

165-505	Step By Step Modelers Guide to Airbrushing	8.95

Covers painting models, figures and dioramas. Includes techniques from shadowing to mixing paint. Over 180 color photos, 32 pages, 8-1/2 x 11".

AIR BRUSH COLORS

AIR-OPAQUE COLOR SET

165-7010	Primary Color Set	18.00

Set includes one of each: Magenta, yellow, blue, green, brown, white and black.

165-7020	Secondary Color Set	18.00

Set includes one of each: Scarlet, crimson, orange, violet, indigo, aqua and turquoise.

165-7030	Supplementary Color Set	18.00

Includes 1 of each: Lime green, chrome oxide green, sepia, amber, flesh, warm yellow & powder blue.

165-7050	Loco Weathering Set	18.00

Set includes one each: Sepia — dark rust, Amber — light rust, gray 2 — light dust, gray 4 — dark dust, brown, white and black.

165-7060	Scenery Weathering Set	18.00

Set includes one each: gray 3 — dust, green, warm yellow, brown, chrome oxide green, white and black.

165-7070	Neutral Grays Color Set +	18.00

Set includes one of each: Gray #1/2, 1, 2, 3, 4, 5 & 6.

AIR-OPAQUE COLORS

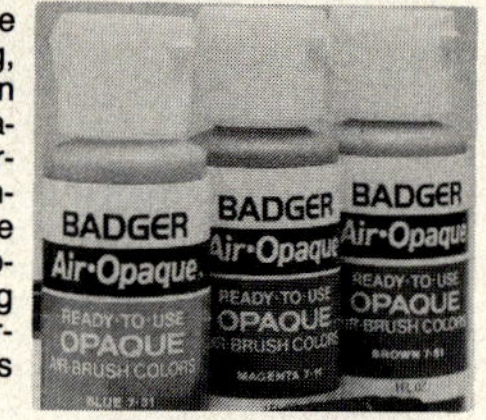

Ready-to-use paints are waterproof, quick-drying, easy-to-clean up and can be used without a ventilation system (since Air-Opaque colors are non-toxic). The unbreakable plastic bottles have a no-clog, easy dispensing closure. Use with air-brushes, artist's brushes and technical pens.

165-701	Black	1oz	3.00
165-702	White	1oz	3.00
165-703	Gray #1/2	1oz	3.00
165-704	Gray #1	1oz	3.00
165-705	Gray #2	1oz	3.00
165-706	Gray #3	1oz	3.00
165-707	Gray #4	1oz	3.00
165-708	Gray #5	1oz	3.00
165-709	Gray #6	1oz	3.00
165-710	Flesh	1oz	3.00
165-711	Magenta	1oz	3.00
165-712	Scarlet	1oz	3.00
165-713	Crimson	1oz	3.00
165-719	Orange	1oz	3.00
165-720	Warm Yellow	1oz	3.00
165-721	Yellow	1oz	3.00
165-722	Amber	1oz	3.00
165-728	Powder Blue	1oz	3.00
165-731	Blue	1oz	3.00
165-732	Violet	1oz	3.00
165-733	Indigo	1oz	3.00
165-734	Aqua	1oz	3.00
165-738	Lime Green	1oz	3.00
165-740	Oxide Green	1oz	3.00
165-741	Green	1oz	3.00
165-742	Turquoise	1oz	3.00
165-751	Brown	1oz	3.00
165-754	Sepia	1oz	3.00

ACCU-FLEX PAINT SETS *NEW*

165-1701	Railroad Rolling Stock Colors	21.00

Set includes one of each: Engine black, reefer white, reefer gray, reefer yellow, reefer orange, dark tuscan red, light tuscan red.

165-1702	Weathering & Railroad Off Line Colors Set	21.00

Set includes: Weathered black, antique white, primer gray, concrete gray, sand, signal red, light green.

165-1703	Railroad Private Colors Set	21.00

Set includes one of each: Caboose red, rail box yellow, mo pac blue, pullman green, super gloss black, maroon tuscan red, Santa Fe silver.

165-1704	Military Colors Set	21.00

Set includes one of each: Forest green, olive drab, European dark green, armor sand, field drab, medium green, camouflage gray.

165-1705	Auto Colors Set	21.00

Set includes one of each: Gloss black, gloss white, gloss red, gloss blue, gloss brown, gloss yellow, gloss green.

ACCU-FLEX PAINTS *NEW*

165-1601	Engine Black	1oz	3.40
165-1602	Reefer White	1oz	3.40
165-1603	Grimy Black	1oz	3.40
165-1604	Reefer Gray	1oz	3.40
165-1605	Weathered Black	1oz	3.40
165-1606	Antique White	1oz	3.40
165-1607	Signal Red	1oz	3.40
165-1608	Caboose Red	1oz	3.40
165-1609	Reefer Orange	1oz	3.40
165-1610	Reefer Yellow	1oz	3.40
165-1611	Concrete Gray	1oz	3.40
165-1612	Primer Gray	1oz	3.40
165-1613	Dark Tuscan Oxide Red	1oz	3.40
165-1614	Light Tuscan Oxide Red	1oz	3.40
165-1615	Maroon Tuscan Oxide Red	1oz	3.40
165-1616	Brunswick Green	1oz	3.40
165-1617	Pullman Green	1oz	3.40
165-1618	Soo Line Maroon	1oz	3.40

BADGER AIR-BRUSH CO.

Airbrushes, Airbrush Parts & Accessories, Compressor, Compressor Parts & Accessories.

CAUTION: We strongly recommend the use of a respirator for your safety, when doing any airbrush painting!

ACCU-FLEX PAINTS (continued)

165-1619	Soo Line Delux Gold	1oz	3.40
165-1620	Super Gloss Black	1oz	3.40
165-1621	Pennsy Green	1oz	3.40
165-1622	Pennsy Maroon	1oz	3.40
165-1623	C&NW Dark Green	1oz	3.40
165-1624	UP Armor Yellow	1oz	3.40
165-1625	UP Harbor Mist Gray	1oz	3.40
165-1626	Burlington Northern Green	1oz	3.40
165-1627	NYC Gray Dark 1	1oz	3.40
165-1628	NYC Gray Light 1	1oz	3.40
165-1629	Conrail Blue	1oz	3.40
165-1630	Sand	1oz	3.40
165-1631	Santa Fe Red	1oz	3.40
165-1632	Santa Fe Silver	1oz	3.40
165-1633	Santa Fe Yellow	1oz	3.40
165-1634	Santa Fe Blue	1oz	3.40
165-1635	SP Lark Light Gray	1oz	3.40
165-1636	SP Daylight Red	1oz	3.40
165-1637	SP Scarlet Red	1oz	3.40
165-1638	SP Daylight Orange	1oz	3.40
165-1639	SP Letter Gray	1oz	3.40
165-1640	SP Lark Dark Gray	1oz	3.40
165-1641	SP Armor Yellow	1oz	3.40
165-1642	Milwaukee Orange	1oz	3.40
165-1643	Milwaukee Maroon	1oz	3.40
165-1644	Milwaukee Gray	1oz	3.40
165-1645	Milwaukee Brown	1oz	3.40
165-1646	Southern Sylvan Green	1oz	3.40
165-1647	Light Green	1oz	3.40
165-1648	Weyerhauser Yellow Green	1oz	3.40
165-1649	CSX Blue	1oz	3.40
165-1650	Insignia Yellow	1oz	3.40
165-1651	Erie Lackawanna Gray	1oz	3.40
165-1652	Erie Lackawanna Yellow	1oz	3.40
165-1653	Erie Lackawanna Maroon	1oz	3.40
165-1654	Rail Box Yellow	1oz	3.40
165-1655	C&NW Old Yellow	1oz	3.40
165-1656	C&NW New Zeto Yellow	1oz	3.40
165-1657	Soo Line Red	1oz	3.40
165-1658	Amtrak Red	1oz	3.40
165-1659	Amtrak Blue	1oz	3.40
165-1660	B&M Blue	1oz	3.40
165-1661	D&RGW Orange	1oz	3.40
165-1662	D&RGW Gold	1oz	3.40
165-1663	GN Big Sky Blue	1oz	3.40
165-1664	GN Orange	1oz	3.40
165-1665	GN Green	1oz	3.40
165-1666	Grand Trunk Western Blue	1oz	3.40
165-1667	C&O Royal Blue	1oz	3.40
165-1668	C&O Yellow	1oz	3.40
165-1669	B&O Enchantment Blue	1oz	3.40
165-1670	CSX Gray	1oz	3.40
165-1671	Wisconsin Central Maroon	1oz	3.40
165-1672	Wisconsin Central Cream	1oz	3.40
165-1673	Illinois Central Orange	1oz	3.40
165-1674	Illinois Central Brown	1oz	3.40
165-1675	GMO Red	1oz	3.40
165-1676	Delaware & Hudson Blue	1oz	3.40
165-1677	Northern Pacific Lt Green	1oz	3.40
165-1678	GN Pacific Yellow	1oz	3.40
165-1679	Rock Island Blue	1oz	3.40
165-1680	Katy Green	1oz	3.40
165-1681	Katy Yellow	1oz	3.40
165-1682	Louisville & Nashville Blue	1oz	3.40
165-1683	Louisville & Nashville Gray	1oz	3.40
165-1684	Louisville & Nashville Yellow	1oz	3.40
165-1685	Reading Green	1oz	3.40
165-1686	Mo Pac Blue	1oz	3.40
165-1687	DM&IR Maroon	1oz	3.40
165-1688	DM&IR Yellow	1oz	3.40
165-1689	Western Pacific Orange	1oz	3.40
165-1690	Penn Central Green	1oz	3.40
165-1691	Bomber Green	1oz	3.40
165-1692	SAC Bomber Green	1oz	3.40
165-1693	Bomber Blue	1oz	3.40
165-1694	Field Drab	1oz	3.40
165-1695	Green Drab	1oz	3.40
165-1696	Olive Drab	1oz	3.40
165-1697	Camouflage Gray	1oz	3.40
165-1698	Camouflage Brown	1oz	3.40
165-1699	Flat Gull Gray	1oz	3.40

165-16100	Euro Dark Green	1oz	3.40
165-16101	Medium Field Green	1oz	3.40
165-16102	Forest Green	1oz	3.40
165-16103	Armor Sand	1oz	3.40
165-16104	Dark Green	1oz	3.40
165-16105	Medium Green	1oz	3.40
165-16106	Gloss Black	1oz	3.40
165-16107	Gloss White	1oz	3.40
165-16108	Gloss Red	1oz	3.40
165-16109	Gloss Orange	1oz	3.40
165-16110	Gloss Blue	1oz	3.40
165-16111	Gloss Green	1oz	3.40
165-16112	Gloss Yellow	1oz	3.40
165-16113	Gloss Brown	1oz	3.40
165-16114	Gloss Silver	1oz	3.40
165-16115	Midnight Blue	1oz	3.40
165-16116	Deep Red	1oz	3.40
165-16117	Bright Orange	1oz	3.40
165-16118	Sunset Yellow	1oz	3.40
165-16119	Flat Black	1oz	3.40
165-16120	Flat White	1oz	3.40
165-16600	Extender	1oz	3.40
165-16601	Clear Flat	1oz	3.40
165-16602	Clear Satin	1oz	3.40
165-16603	Clear Gloss	1oz	3.40

CLEANER & COATINGS

165-7100	Air-Opaque Cleaner	1oz	1.50

NORTON SAFETY PRODUCTS

RESPIRATOR

Approved for respiratory protection against mists of paints, lacquers, and enamels, not more than 1,000 parts per million organic vapors by volume, or any combination thereof and pesticides. (*NIOSH approval #TC-23C-354).

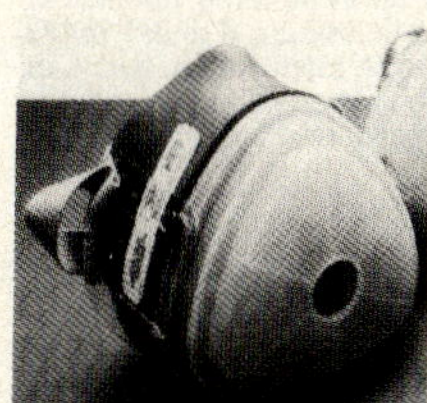

Disposable Spray Respirator
774-10041   38.95

* Disposable—eliminates time spent on cleaning and maintenance.
* Cradle Suspension System with Continuous Headband strap for more comfort provides a secure, even seal to the face.

* Elastomeric Facepiece to prevent slippings or sticking to the face.
* Low Inhalation/Exhalation resistance to make respirator easy to breathe through and more comfortable to use.
* Low Profile on nose provides good field of vision and does not interfere with glasses.
* Replaceable Pre-filters available to extend respirator service life, reducing cost of respiratory protection program.

774-10056   Pre-filter for 10041   pkg(10) 48.75
Keep respirator costs down by extending the usable life of the respirator in paint spraying or other environments containing dust or mist.

EYE PROTECTORS

■ **LIMITED QUANTITIES AVAILABLE** ■

774-1010   Clear Lens Soft Goggles   3.75
Features air vents around lenses to help prevent fogging. Impact-resistant lenses meet American Standards Institute Z87.1 standard for eye protection. Molded-in temple groove for use with prescription glasses. Can be worn with Norton Dust Mask.

GRUMBACHER

+ = Special Order Only

Rustproof, nickel plated, seamless ferrules. Polished hardwood handles. Natural tips, hand cupped. Rubens and Beaux Arts Series brushes also have split-proof tips, and are the top of the Grumbacher Red Sable brush line.

BEAUX ARTS SERIES

ROUND: FINEST PURE RED SABLE

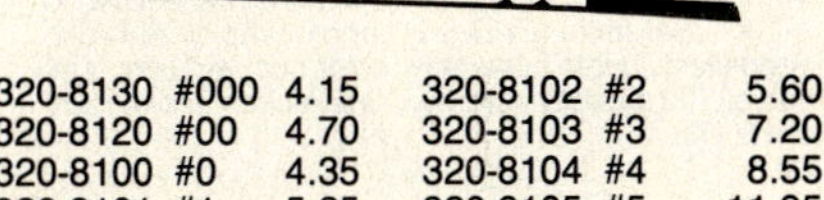

320-1930	#000	5.15		320-1901	#1	7.15
320-1920	#00	5.45		320-1902	#2	8.35
320-1910	#0	5.85	+	320-1903	#3	11.65
			+	320-1904	#4	13.65

GRUMBACHER SERIES

ROUND: FINE PURE RED SABLE

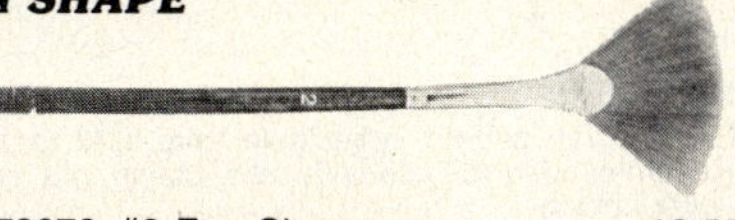

320-8130	#000	4.15	320-8102	#2	5.60
320-8120	#00	4.70	320-8103	#3	7.20
320-8100	#0	4.35	320-8104	#4	8.55
320-8101	#1	5.25	320-8105	#5	11.95

FLAT: RED SABLE

320-7700	#0		6.05
320-7701	#1	NEW	6.20
320-7702	#2	NEW	6.70
320-7704	#3	NEW	8.85
320-7720	#0	NEW	5.55

ROUND: RED SABLE   NEW

320-7740	#0000	4.70	320-7750	#00000	4.70

CONTROL PLUS SERIES

Synthetic hair brushes with the look and feel of red sable.

FAN SHAPE

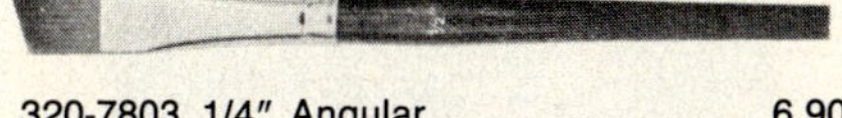

320-78072	#2 Fan Shape		10.55

SHORT LINER

320-78082	#2 Short Liner		4.25

ANGULAR SHADER

320-7803	1/4" Angular		6.90

MATTE FIXITIVE SPRAY

Crystal clear, non-yellowing, flexible, acrylic dull coat final varnish for models. An aerosol acrylic solution resin.

320-549	12oz		6.95
320-649	5oz		5.45
320-5288	8oz		7.35

BRUSH SOAP   NEW

320-589		7.90

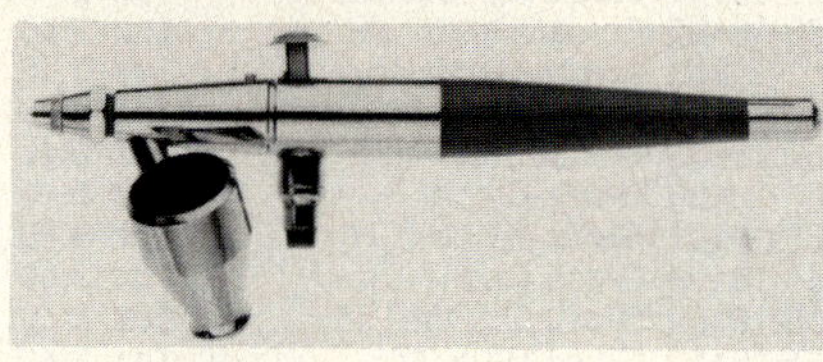

Single and double action airbrushes, parts and accessories, compressors and accessories.

CAUTION: We strongly recommend using an approved respirator for your safety when doing any airbrush painting!

AIRBRUSHES

SETS

542-3 H #3 Travel Set   66.00
Includes H3 single action airbrush, with separate air and paint controls. Medium spray pattern adjusts from 1/32 to 1-1/4". Set includes two 8 ounce cans of Airbrush Propellent, bottle assembly, color cup, airhose, tank valve, "22 airbrush lessons", instruction booklet and parts list.

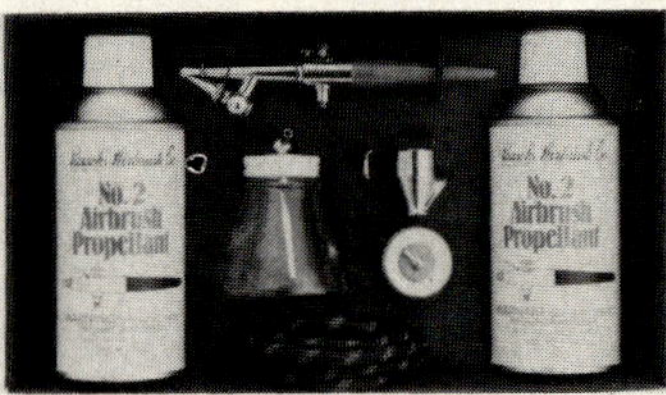

542-11 VL#3 Travel Set   96.00
The VL3 double action airbrush provides control of air pressure and paint flow with a single lever. Medium spray pattern is adjustable from 1/32 to 1-1/4". Set includes two 8 ounce cans of Airbrush Propellent, bottle assembly, color cup, airhose, tank valve, "22 airbrush lessons", instruction booklet and parts list.

542-19 Air Eraser Set   76.00
This miniature sand blasting gun is designed for delicate work and can be used for etching glass, or removal of paint and rust. Set includes air eraser, fast cutting compound, airhose with moisture trap, wrench, hanger and pack of five disposable respirators (NIOSH and MSHA approved for dust and mists.)

SINGLE ACTION

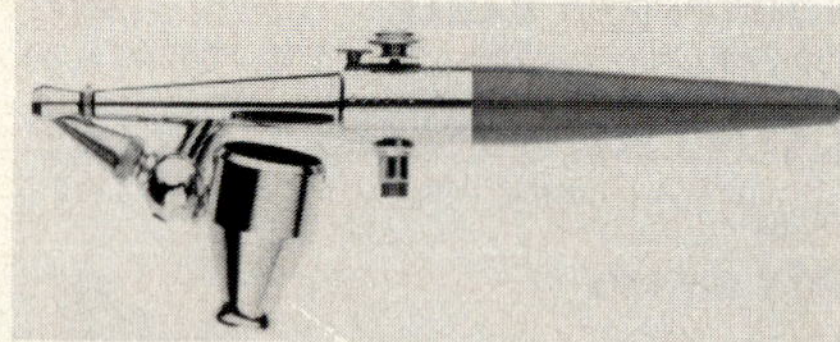

542-25 H#1   38.00
Small spray pattern, adjustable from 1/32 to 1". Recommended for use with inks, stains, oils and water colors.

542-26 H#3   38.00
Medium spray pattern, adjustable from 1/32 to 1-1/4". Recommended for use with thinned lacquers, enamels, varnishes and glazes.

542-27 H#5   38.00
Large spray pattern, adjustable from 1/32 to 1-1/2". Recommended for free-flowing lacquers, enamels and acrylics.

542-31 H Series — Complete Set   68.00
Includes H1 single action airbrush (spray pattern from 1/32 to 1"), 1/4 ounce color cup, 3 and 1 ounce bottle assemblies, 1 ounce bottle and cap, color adjusting parts, hanger, wrenches, air hose with couplings, aircaps, "22 airbrush lessons" instruction booklet and parts list.

DOUBLE ACTION

542-46 Model VL#1   85.00
Small spray pattern, adjustable from 1/32 to 1". Recommended for use with inks, stains, oils and water colors.

542-47 Model VL#3   85.00
Medium spray pattern, adjustable from 1/32 to 1-1/4". Recommended for use with thinned lacquers, enamels, varnishes and glazes.
(By Special Order Only.)

542-48 Model VL#5   85.00
Large spray pattern, adjustable from 1/32 to 1-1/2". Recommended for free-flowing lacquers, enamels and acrylics.
(By Special Order Only.)

542-52 VL Series — Complete Set   97.00
Includes VL#1 double action airbrush, (spray pattern can be adjusted from 1/32 to 1"). Multi-heads for VL3 (medium) and VL5 (large) spray patterns, needles for VL3 and VL5, 1/4 ounce color cup, 3 and 1 ounce bottle assemblies, 1 ounce plain bottle and cap, hanger, wrench, air hose with couplings, head protector cap, "22 airbrush lessons", instruction booklet and parts list.

542-53 Airbrush VLS-Complete Set   103.00
Features hand-crafted construction using machined brass, polished and chrome plated. Includes air brush, 1/4 oz color cup, 3 oz color bottle assembly, 1 oz bottle with plain cap, 2 multiple heads, 2 needles, hanger, wrench and air hose with couplings.

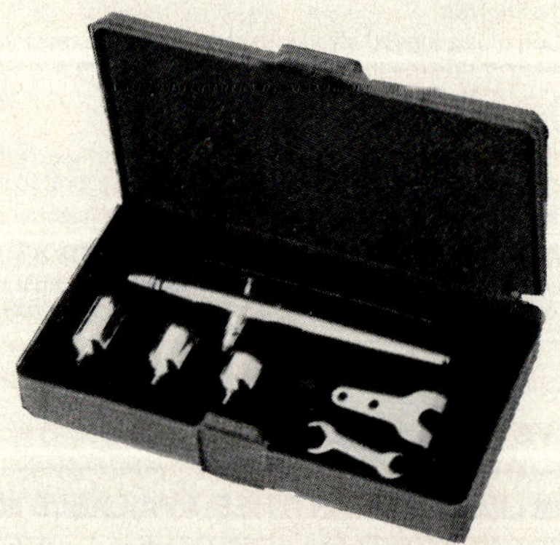

542-55 VSR90#1 — Complete Set   87.00
Includes VSR90#1 double action airbrush. 1/8oz, 3/16oz, and 1/4oz color cups, spare needle, head protector cap, wrench, airbrush hanger, vinyl case, parts list and instruction booklet.
(By Special Order Only.)

AIR HOSE AND ACCESSORIES

542-2118 Air Hose w/Couplings   8.40
1/8" diameter hose, for use with all Paasche airbrushes, measures 8' in length.

542-6171 Moisture trap   12.10
Unit inserts into 1/8" airhose to remove water from air line.

COMPRESSORS

62

63

542-62 Compressor 1/4 HP   225.00
This small, quiet compressor with oil-less diaphragm, is designed for home, office or studio use. Delivers up to 30 pounds of pressure and can be used with any airbrush. Equipped with three-wire cord and on/off switch. Weighs approximately 24 pounds.
(By Special Order Only.)

542-63 Compressor 1/10 HP   150.00
An economical compressor with oil-less diaphragm, suitable for use with properly thinned fluids. Delivers up to 30 pounds of pressure and can be used with any airbrush. Equipped with three-wire cord. Weighs approximately 12 pounds.

AIRBRUSH PROPELLENT

Replaceable cans of airbrush propellent, for use when a compressor or electricity is not available. Provides air pressure for varying amount of time, depending on airbrush and type of work. Propellant blend: DuPont-DYMEL® 22/DYMEL® A, which is considered less hazardous to the ozone in the upper atmosphere.

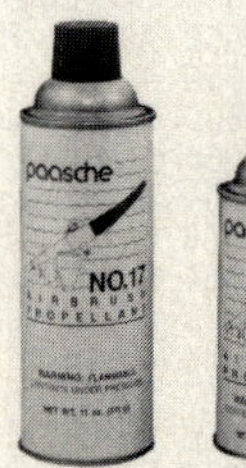
6236   6238

542-6236 Pressure Tank   17oz   9.00
542-6238 Pressure Tank   8.5oz   7.00
542-1456 Pressure Tank Valve   5.80
For use with 8 or 11 ounce pressure tanks, controls air volume from tank to airbrush. All brass construction.

REPLACEMENT PARTS

542-190	3oz Plain Cover	**NEW**	.35
542-191	1oz Plain Cover	**NEW**	.35
542-1455	"O" Ring		.50
542-5381	Color Adjusting Parts for #H1		9.50
542-5429	Color Adjusting Parts for #H3		9.50
542-5433	Color Adjusting Parts for #H5		9.50
542-5516	Aircap for #H1		2.90
542-5518	Aircap for #H3		2.90
542-5519	Aircap for #H5		2.90
542-5621	Tip #H1	**NEW**	4.25
542-5623	Tip #H3	**NEW**	4.25
542-5625	Tip #H5	**NEW**	4.25
542-9552	Reamer for VL		3.30

VL SERIES MULTIHEAD ASSEMBLIES

542-9575	Small #VL1		15.50
542-9576	Medium #VL3		15.50
542-9577	Large #VL5		15.50
542-9675	#VM-1	**NEW**	14.50

Paasche Airbrush Co.

Single and double action airbrushes, parts and accessories, compressors and accessories.

CAUTION: We strongly recommend using an approved respirator for your safety when doing any airbrush painting!

VL SERIES REPLACEMENT NEEDLES

542-9578	#1 (small)	2.90
542-9581	#3 (medium)	2.90
542-9583	#5 (large)	2.90
542-9681	#VN1	**NEW** 2.90
542-9683	#VN2	**NEW** 2.90

ACCESSORIES

VL SERIES AIRBRUSHES

542-9511	1 oz Bottle Assembly	3.90
542-9515	Metal Color Cup	4.75
542-9549	3 oz Bottle Assembly	4.05
542-5430	3 oz Bottle Assembly	4.05
542-5435	1 oz Bottle	.70
542-5383	1 oz Bottle Assembly	3.90
542-5387	Metal Color Cup	4.75
542-5388	3 oz Bottle	.85

WALTHERS

PROFESSIONAL DECAL FINISH

904-470 Solvaset 2oz 2.98
Makes decals snuggle down over irregular surfaces. Eliminates air bubbles, white spots and draping, without hiding surface detail.

904-537 DDV 2oz 2.98
Dull, flat finish hides decal film, protects model finishes. Brush or spray it on, safe for plastics.

MAGIC MASKER™

Brush it on the area to be masked off. Then spray your color, let dry and peel off Magic Masker.™ Works on plastic, wood, metal, paint, dope, chrome and silver.

904-106 Magic Masker™ btl(20cc) 2.98
Dealers: MUST Order Dealer Pack of 12

MAY 13, 1829

❧ Today ❧
IN RAILROAD HISTORY

The English-built steam locomotive "Stourbridge Lion" arrives in New York, for service on the Delaware & Hudson.

FLOQUIL~POLLY S COLOR CORP.

An **RPM** Company

All brushes set in seamless nickel furrules. Illustrations show style - not actual size.

Dealers: MUST Order Six of One Part Number.

PAINT BRUSHES

RND RED SABLE
270-677000	#0	2.90
270-677001	#1	3.15
270-677002	#2	3.40
270-677003	#3	4.15
270-677004	#4	5.20
270-677010	10/0	4.40
270-677030	3/0	2.70
270-677050	5/0	3.15

FLAT RED SABLE
270-622001	#1	3.20
270-622002	#2	3.95
270-622003	#3	4.15
270-622004	#4	5.15

THE FLOQUIL ULTIMATE

Red Sable brush features re-useable screw top case.
270-655001	#1 round	7.99
270-655002	#2 Scroller	7.99
270-655003	#3 Flat	7.99

WHITE BRISTLE
270-768212	1/2"	1.75

FLAT WHITE BRISTLE
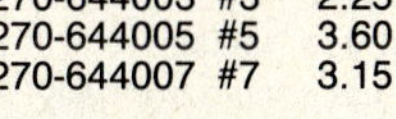
270-633001	#1	2.70
270-633002	#2	2.90
270-633003	#3	3.40
270-633004	#4	3.65

FLAT OX HAIR SINGLE STROKE
270-666012	1/2"	5.15
270-666014	1/4"	3.15
270-666018	1/8"	2.70
270-666038	3/8"	4.25

CAMEL HAIR: WATER COLOR ROUND
Dealer Must Order Pack of 12
270-644003	#3	2.25
270-644005	#5	3.60
270-644007	#7	3.15

CAMEL HAIR
Dealer pack of 12
270-651101	#1	.55
270-651102	#2	.60
270-651103	#3	.65
270-651104	#4	.70
270-651105	#5	.75
270-651106	#6	.85

CAMEL HAIR: LACQUER FLAT
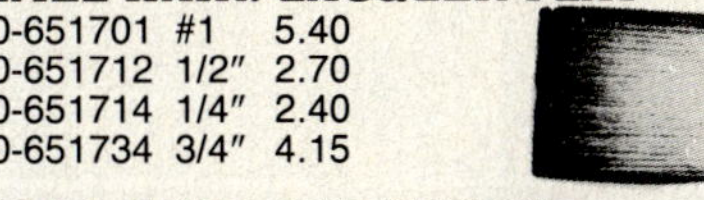
270-651701	#1	5.40
270-651712	1/2"	2.70
270-651714	1/4"	2.40
270-651734	3/4"	4.15

CAMEL HAIR ONE STROKE
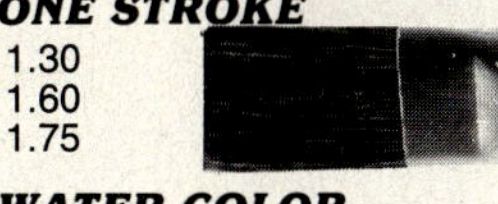
270-768314	1/4"	1.30
270-768338	3/8"	1.60
270-768312	1/2"	1.75

CAMEL HAIR WATER COLOR
270-768401	#1	.40
270-768402	#2	.45
270-768403	#3	.50
270-768404	#4	.55
270-768405	#5	.60
270-768406	#6	.60

ROUND SILVER FOX
270-688200	#0	3.15		
270-688201	#1	3.75	270-688203 #3	5.15
270-688202	#2	4.40	270-688230 #3/0	2.95

FLAT SILVER FOX
270-688001	#1	3.15	270-688003 #3	3.70
270-688002	#2	3.40	270-688004 #4	3.95

FLAT: SILVER FOX SINGLE STROKE
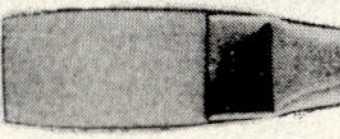
270-688112	1/2"	6.75
270-688114	1/4"	4.15
270-688138	3/8"	5.60

GOLDEN FOX DETAIL ROUNDS
270-768000	#0	2.25

(By Special Order Only.)
270-768001	#1	2.50
270-768010	10/0	3.45
270-768020	20/0	3.75
270-768030	3/0	1.99
270-768050	5/0	2.60

GOLDEN FOX FLATS
270-768102	#2	2.55
270-768104	#4	2.90

FLOQUIL SUPREMES
270-699000	#0	4.70

(By Special Order Only.)
270-699001	#1	5.15
270-699002	#2	5.90
270-699003	#3	7.10
270-699030	3/0	3.40
270-699050	5/0	3.15

PRECISION LINERS
270-688300	#0	3.40
270-688302	#2	4.50
270-688350	5/0	3.20

SETS
270-606000	Starter Set	10.99

Includes 5 assorted brushes.

270-606025 Silver Edition Brush **NEW** 45.00
Gift Set
Includes: 1 each Floquil supremes, pure Kolinsky Sable Rounds (990 series), 1 each Floquil duster brushes (669006) and a diecast figurine of an American Indian Chief.

robart

HOBBY PAINT SHAKER

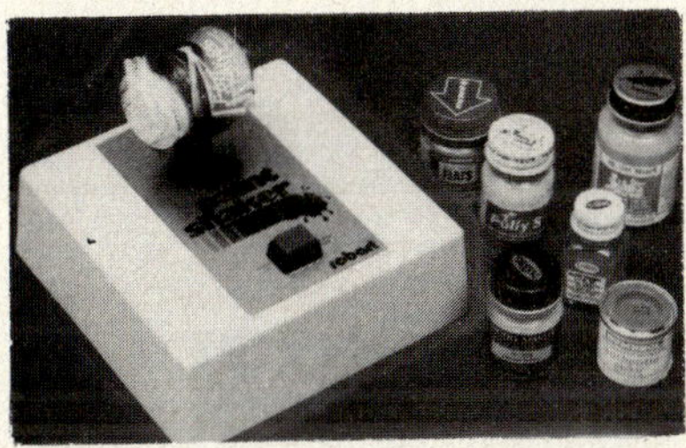

Electric or battery operated paint shaker mixes hobby paint by shaking at 5,000 cycles per minute. Accommodates 1/4, 1/3, 1/2, 5/8 and 1oz size bottles.

547-410	Paint Shaker (battery operated)	19.95
547-411	Paint Shaker (electric) 110 volt AC powered	29.95
547-415	Paint Shaker Straps pkg(5)	5.95

MICROSCALE®

DECAL FINISHING PRODUCTS

DECAL COATINGS

Micro Set   1 fl oz
460-104   2.00
A fast decal softener & surface cleaner combined.

460-103   Micro Coat Flat   2.00
Decal overcoat evens & protects finish.

460-105   Micro Sol   1 fl oz 2.00
A deep drawing decal softener with a solvent base for difficult problem areas.

460-106   Micro Coat Satin   2.00
Decal overcoat evens & protects finish.

460-108   Micro Coat Gloss   2.00
Decal under & overcoat for even high gloss finish.

460-117   Micro Liquid Decal Film   1 fl oz   2.00
Ultra thin decal film allows you to create your own decals or save old decals. To make your own decals, brush super film on a flat clean surface, allow to dry and draw or paint on your image. When brushed over an old decal, superfilm seals and provides a new surface.

MISCELLANEOUS

460-109   Micro Weld Plastic Cement   1 fl oz 2.00
460-110   Micro Mask   1 fl oz 2.00
460-114   Micro Krystal Kleer   1 fl oz 2.00
460-115   Micro Liquitape   1 fl oz 2.00
460-116   Micro Metal Foil Adhesive   1 fl oz 2.00

RIBBONRAIL
by Earl Eshleman
formerly Wallace Metal Products

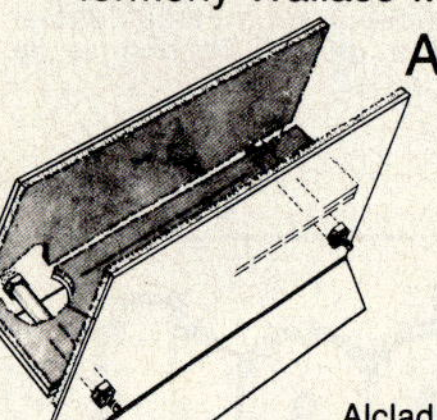

ADJUSTABLE METAL CRADLE

Engine & Car Service Cradle
170-55   9.95

Alclad aluminum HO engine and car cradle is self adjustable and fully felt padded. Easy-to-Assemble.

gb Engineering

Painting Handle
298-600   4.98

The painting handle eliminates the problem of cleaning paint off your hands after painting. Its secure grip gives you the freedom to turn a model to any position while painting and keeps your hand free of paint. The ''V'' shaped aluminum handle has closed cell foam pads at the ends and a spring between the ''V'' legs to provide a constant holding force by adjusting the screw and nut that holds the spring in its place.

GYROS

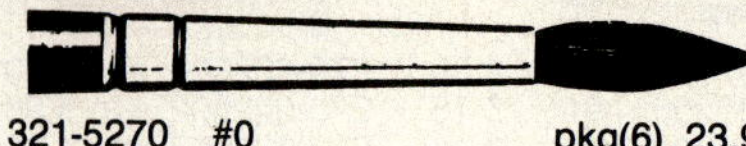

BRUSH SETS
Red sable brush sets can be used with all kinds of color or paint, water, oil, enamels, varnish, lacquer, etc.

321-1900	3/0-00-0	4.99
321-1910	1/3/5	5.85
321-1920	10/0-5/0-4/0	5.85

PURE RED SABLE WATER COLOR BRUSHES   TBA
Short Handle

321-5270	#0	pkg(6)	23.95
321-5271	#1	pkg(6)	25.95
321-5272	#2	pkg(6)	29.20
321-5273	#3	pkg(6)	34.40
321-52720	#00	pkg(6)	23.35
321-52730	#000	pkg(6)	23.35
321-52740	#0000	pkg(6)	23.35

K-Tool Products

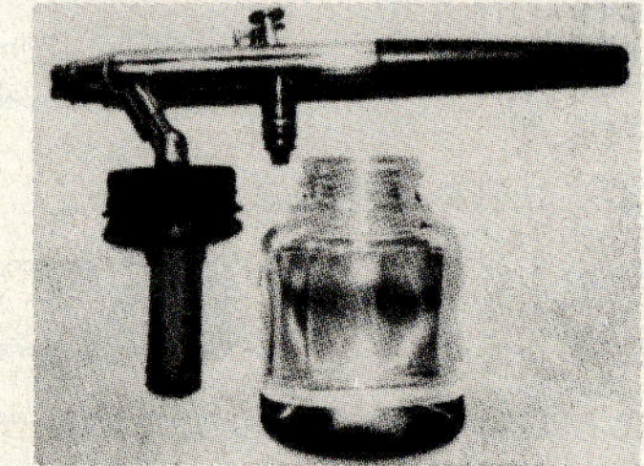

AIRBRUSH PAINT STRAINER

- Stainless steel mesh screen
- Fits all airbrushes that use bottles
- Passes only particles that should normally flow through airbrush
- Slides on & off siphon tube for easy cleaning

211-1   Airbrush Paint Filter   each 3.98
(not illustrated)
211-200   Ultimate paint booth   **NEW**   TBA

C-THRU®
GRAPHICS/TAPES
Please Specify Mfr #470 When Ordering

MATTE COLOR TAPES

	Size & Price (per roll)				
	1/64″ x648″	1/32″ x648″	1/16″ x648″	3/32″ x324″	1/8″ x324″
Color	2.35	2.35	2.35	2.35	2.60
Black	1641	1321	1161	3321	4321
Red	1642	1322	1162	3322	4322
Yellow	1643	1323	1163	3323	4323
White	1644	1324	1164	3324	4324

METALLIC TAPES

	Size & Price (per roll)			
	1/64″ x648″	1/32″ x648″	1/16″ x648″	1/8″ x324″
Color	3.00	3.00	3.00	3.50
Silver	1649	1329	1169	4329
Gold	1640	1320	1160	4320

VOLLMER
Imported from Germany and marketed by WALTHERS

WEATHERING PAINTS
Vollmer weathering paints are water soluble.

770-6050	Red	(15ml) btl	2.99
770-6051	Black	(15ml) btl	2.99
770-6052	White	(15ml) btl	2.99
770-6053	Yellow	(15ml) btl	2.99

We've found a parking spot and it looks like there's an open gate where we can get some better shots of this RS-18! Alcos are getting rarer every day, so any chance to shoot the big units is a welcome opportunity! It's a sunny afternoon in the metropolitan Toronto area, ideal for railfanning on this diorama built by Brian Rudko. We've parked our Herpa vehicle next to some Pikestuff buildings, which are protected by Builders-in Scale chainlink fence. The diesel was rebuilt from an Atlas RS-11 by Jay Rotsch. The diorama was photographed out-of-doors for realistic lighting and shadows.
Photo by Brian Rudko

SMP INDUSTRIES Accu-paint

Non-lead, low odor pigments. Brush or spray directly on wood, metals or plastics. Dries to a hard, glossy finish in minutes.

RAILROAD COLORS

102-1	Stencil White	1oz	3.15
102-2	Stencil Black	1oz	3.15
102-3	Boston & Maine Blue	1oz	3.15
102-4	Bangor & Aroostook Blue	1oz	3.15
102-5	Delaware & Hudson Blue	1oz	3.15
102-6	GTW Blue	1oz	3.15
102-7	Conrail Blue	1oz	3.15
102-8	Vermillion	1oz	3.15
102-9	Cornell Red	1oz	3.15
102-10	Chinese Red	1oz	3.15
102-11	CP Rail Action Red	1oz	3.15
102-12	Oxide Brown	1oz	3.15
102-14	Socony Red	1oz	3.15
102-15	Warm Orange	1oz	3.15
102-16	NH Red-Orange	1oz	3.15
102-17	CN Orange	1oz	3.15
102-18	CN Red-Orange	1oz	3.15
102-19	CN Yellow	1oz	3.15
102-20	Medium Yellow	1oz	3.15
102-21	MEC Harvest Yellow	1oz	3.15
102-22	Imitation Gold	1oz	3.15
102-23	Delaware & Hudson Yellow	1oz	3.15
102-24	E-L Yellow	1oz	3.15
102-25	Hunters Green	1oz	3.15
102-26	MEC Pine Green	1oz	3.15
102-27	#401 Green	1oz	3.15
102-30	CN Green	1oz	3.15
102-31	Brunswick Green	1oz	3.15
102-32	Jade Green	1oz	3.15
102-33	Reading Green	1oz	3.15
102-34	E-L Maroon	1oz	3.15
102-35	Passenger Maroon	1oz	3.15
102-36	Engine Maroon	1oz	3.15
102-37	PRR Maroon	1oz	3.15
102-38	CP Tuscan Red	1oz	3.15
102-39	Alkyd Brown	1oz	3.15
102-40	Aluminum	1oz	3.15
102-41	Rich Gold	1oz	3.15
102-42	CN Lettering Gray	1oz	3.15
102-43	CP Gray	1oz	3.15
102-45	NYC Light Gray	1oz	3.15
102-46	NYC Dark Gray	1oz	3.15
102-47	Delaware & Hudson Gray	1oz	3.15
102-48	E-L Gray	1oz	3.15
102-51	CP Rail Action Green	1oz	3.15
102-52	CP Rail Action Yellow	1oz	3.15
102-53	Deep Red	1oz	3.15
102-54	Rich Oxide Brown	1oz	3.15
102-55	Erie Green	1oz	3.15
102-56	Gray-Green	1oz	3.15
102-57	Imitation Aluminum	1oz	3.15
102-58	Vermont Green	1oz	3.15
102-59	Iron Oxide	1oz	3.15
102-60	Light Imitation Gold	1oz	3.15
102-61	VIA Blue	1oz	3.15
102-62	Weathered Black	1oz	3.15
102-63	ATSF War Bonnet Blue	1oz	3.15
102-64	ATSF War Bonnet Yellow	1oz	3.15
102-65	SP Lark Dark Gray	1oz	3.15
102-66	SP Scarlet	1oz	3.15
102-67	UP/Milw Armour Yellow	1oz	3.15
102-68	UP/Milw Harbor Mist Gray	1oz	3.15
102-69	ATSF War Bonnet Red	1oz	3.15
102-70	BN Green	1oz	3.15
102-71	ICG Orange	1oz	3.15
102-72	D&RGW Yellow	1oz	3.15
102-73	Chessie Yellow	1oz	3.15
102-74	Chessie Blue	1oz	3.15
102-75	Southern Green	1oz	3.15
102-76	Gilford Gray	1oz	3.15
102-77	Gilford Orange	1oz	3.15
102-78	NP Dark Green	1oz	3.15
102-79	NP Light Green	1oz	3.15
102-80	CSX Blue	1oz	3.15
102-81	CSX Gray	1oz	3.15

THINNERS & COATINGS

102-98	Metal-Plastic Primer	1oz	3.15
102-100	Thinner-Solvent	1oz	3.15
102-10016	Accu-Paint Thinner	16oz	14.50
102-101	Satin Finish-Plastics	1oz	3.15

102-102	Semi-Gloss Finish	1oz	3.15
102-103	Gloss Finish	1oz	3.15
102-104	Weathering Finish	1oz	3.15

DECAL SETTING SOLUTION

102-500	Accu-Set	1oz	3.39

SCALECOAT

MODEL RAILROAD PAINT

Non-Toxic when wet. Can be further diluted for spraying: 3 parts paint/1 part thinner. 640-1, 2 & 3 have a very low gloss finish. When ordering Scalecoat Paint ask for the free technical sheet.

Scalecoat II is plastic compatible - to be used primarily on plastic.

SCALECOAT PAINT

For brass, wood and most plastics. No primer needed, one coat covers with a semi-gloss finish.

LOCOMOTIVE COLORS

640-1	Locomotive Black	2oz	2.95
640-2	Oxide Red	2oz	2.95
640-3	Graphite & Oil	2oz	2.95
640-4	Keystone Black	2oz	2.95
640-5	Smoke Box Gray	2oz	2.95
640-6	PRR Brunswick Green	2oz	2.95
640-7	EMD Demo Blue	2oz	2.95

STANDARD COLORS

640-8	D&H Yellow	2oz	2.95
640-9	D&H Blue	2oz	2.95
640-10	Black	2oz	2.95
640-11	White	2oz	2.95
640-12	Tuscan Red	2oz	2.95
640-13	Box Car Red	2oz	2.95
640-14	Caboose Red	2oz	2.95
640-15	Reefer Yellow	2oz	2.95
640-16	Reefer Orange	2oz	2.95
640-17	Pullman Green	2oz	2.95
640-18	Coach Olive	2oz	2.95
640-19	Southern Green	2oz	2.95
640-20	Maintenance of Way Gray	2oz	2.95
640-21	Roof Brown	2oz	2.95
640-22	UP Armour Yellow	2oz	2.95
640-23	Silver (or Aluminum)	2oz	2.95
640-24	Santa Fe Blue	2oz	2.95
640-25	GN Green	2oz	2.95
640-26	Santa Fe Red	2oz	2.95
640-27	IC Orange	2oz	2.95
640-28	SP Dark Gray	2oz	2.95
640-29	SP Scarlet	2oz	2.95
640-30	SP Daylight Orange	2oz	2.95
640-31	SP Daylight Red	2oz	2.95
640-32	UP Harbor Mist Gray	2oz	2.95
640-33	UP Dark Gray	2oz	2.95
640-34	Penn Central Green	2oz	2.95
640-35	C&NW Canary Yellow	2oz	2.95
640-36	C&NW Green	2oz	2.95
640-37	B&O Royal Blue	2oz	2.95
640-38	BN Cascade Green	2oz	2.95
640-39	D&RGW Old Frt Car Yellow	2oz	2.95
640-40	D&RGW New Orange	2oz	2.95
640-41	Erie-Lackawanna Gray	2oz	2.95
640-42	Erie-Lackawanna Maroon	2oz	2.95
640-43	Erie-Lackawanna Yellow	2oz	2.95

640-44	Trailer Train Yellow	2oz	2.95
640-45	GN Empire Builder Green	2oz	2.95
640-46	GN Empire Builder Orange	2oz	2.95
640-47	Aluminum	2oz	2.95
640-48	NYC Pacemaker Red	2oz	2.95
640-60	NP Light Green	2oz	2.95
640-61	NP Dark Green	2oz	2.95
640-62	LV Cornel Red	2oz	2.95
640-63	D&H Gray	2oz	2.95
640-64	Weyerhaeuser Green	2oz	2.95
640-65	NYC Light Gray	2oz	2.95
640-66	NYC Dark Gray	2oz	2.95
640-67	CP Yellow	2oz	2.95
640-68	CP Gray	2oz	2.95
640-69	CP Tuscan Red	2oz	2.95
640-70	CP Action Red	2oz	2.95
640-71	CN Yellow	2oz	2.95
640-72	CN Green	2oz	2.95
640-73	Bright Caboose Red	2oz	2.95
640-74	Loco Grime	2oz	2.95
640-75	Conrail Blue	2oz	2.95

QUICK DRY

640-54	Quick-Dry	2oz	2.95

Used to shorten the drying time of Scalecoat Paints.

PAINT REMOVER

640-56	Paint Remover	pint	8.95

Apply to car or engine, then rinse. Will not harm plastic. Can be re-used.

640-59	Metal Stripper	32oz can	10.95

Immerse model in Metal Stripper then use paint brush or tooth brush for abrasive action to remove paint. Re-usable.

SPECIAL COATINGS

640-55	Shieldcoat	2oz	2.95

With the possibility of plastic not being of the best quality in the future, Shieldcoat has been developed to be used as a barrier . . . to prevent Scalecoat from crazing.

640-51	Flat Glaze	2oz	2.95
640-52	Gloss Glaze	2oz	2.95
640-53	Sanding Sealer	2oz	2.95
640-57	Sanding Sealer Thinner	2oz	2.50

(Use only with #53 Sanding Sealer)

THINNER

640-48	Thinner	8oz	3.95
640-49	Thinner	1 qt	7.50
640-50	Thinner	2oz	2.50

SCALECOAT II PAINTS

Scalecoat II is plastic compatible— to be used primarily on plastic.

PLASTIC PAINTS

Fast drying and adheres to semi-gloss finishes.

640-2001	Locomotive Black	2oz	2.95
640-2002	Oxide Red	2oz	2.95
640-2003	Graphite & Oil	2oz	2.95
640-2006	PRR Brunswick Green	2oz	2.95
640-2010	Black	2oz	2.95
640-2011	White	2oz	2.95
640-2012	Tuscan Red	2oz	2.95
640-2013	Box Car Red	2oz	2.95
640-2014	Caboose Red	2oz	2.95
640-2015	Reefer Yellow	2oz	2.95
640-2016	Reefer Orange	2oz	2.95
640-2017	Pullman Green	2oz	2.95
640-2019	Southern Green	2oz	2.95
640-2020	Maintenance of Way Gray	2oz	2.95
640-2021	Roof Brown	2oz	2.95
640-2022	UP Armour Yellow	2oz	2.95
640-2023	Silver (or Aluminum)	2oz	2.95
640-2024	Santa Fe Blue	2oz	2.95
640-2025	Great Northern Green	2oz	2.95
640-2026	Santa Fe Red	2oz	2.95
640-2032	UP Habor Mist Gray	2oz	2.95
640-2037	B&O Royal Blue	2oz	2.95
640-2038	BN Cascade Green	2oz	2.95
640-2047	Aluminum	2oz	2.95
640-2073	Bright Caboose Red	2oz	2.95
640-2074	Loco Grime	2oz	2.95
640-2075	Conrail Blue	2oz	2.95

SCALECOAT II THINNER

640-2048	Thinner	8oz	3.95
640-2049	Thinner	1qt	7.50
640-2050	Thinner	2oz	2.95

FLOQUIL~POLLY S COLOR CORP.

An **RPM** Company

Floquil paints are designed for miniatures. Floquil colors are solvent base enamels. Polly S are water soluble acrylics.

Dealers: Ask about merchandising (display) racks.

RAILROAD COLORS

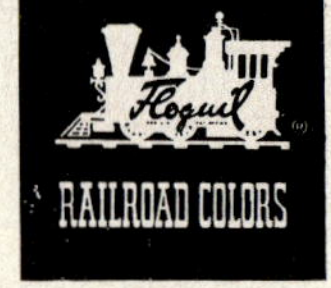

Made for miniatures; designed to cover without hiding detail. Permanent on all surfaces including plastic and plaster. Dries "dust free" in 2-5 minutes. Will not crack, peel, or chip. For best results use only Dio-Sol for thinning.

270-110009	Primer	1oz	2.19
270-110010	Engine Black	1oz	2.19
270-110011	Reefer White	1oz	2.19
270-110012	Reefer Gray	1oz	2.19
270-110020	Caboose Red	1oz	2.19
270-110023	Flesh	1oz	2.19
270-110025	Tuscan Red	1oz	2.19
270-110030	Reefer Orange	1oz	2.19
270-110031	Reefer Yellow	1oz	2.19
270-110033	Railbox Yellow	1oz	2.19
270-110034	Brunswick Green	1oz	2.19
270-110035	BN Cascade Green	1oz	2.19
270-110040	Dark Green	1oz	2.19
270-110041	Light Green	1oz	2.19
270-110044	Depot Olive	1oz	2.19
270-110045	Pullman Green	1oz	2.19
270-110048	Coach Green	1oz	2.19
270-110050	Dark Blue	1oz	2.19
270-110051	Light Blue	1oz	2.19
270-110056	GN Big Sky Blue	1oz	2.19
270-110065	Signal Red	1oz	2.19
270-110070	Roof Brown	1oz	2.19
270-110074	Box Car Red	1oz	2.19
270-110081	Earth	1oz	2.19
270-110082	Concrete	1oz	2.19
270-110084	Foundation	1oz	2.19
270-110085	Antique White	1oz	2.19
270-110087	Depot Buff	1oz	2.19
270-110088	D&H Caboose Red	1oz	2.19
270-110166	UP Armour Yellow	1oz	2.19
270-110167	UP Harbor Mist Gray	1oz	2.19
270-110168	UP Light Orange	1oz	2.19
270-110174	SR Green	1oz	2.19
270-110175	SR Freight Car Brown	1oz	2.10
270-110176	AT&SF Red	1oz	2.19
270-110177	AT&SF Blue	1oz	2.19
270-110178	AT&SF Yellow	1oz	2.19
270-110179	AT&SF Mineral Brown	1oz	2.19
270-110183	Reading Green	1oz	2.19
270-110184	Tuscan Red #2	1oz	2.19
270-110186	RR Oxide Red	1oz	2.19
270-110250	CN Orange #11	1oz	2.19
270-110252	CN Grey #17	1oz	2.19
270-110254	CN Yellow #12	1oz	2.19
270-110256	CN Green #12	1oz	2.19
270-110260	CNW Yellow	1oz	2.19
270-110262	CNW Green	1oz	2.19
270-110280	Wisc Central Gold	1oz	2.19
270-110282	Wisc Central Maroon	1oz	2.19
270-110310	TTX Yellow	1oz	2.19
270-110320	M.K.T. Green	1oz	2.19
270-110330	NYC Jade Green	1oz	2.19
270-110350	CSX Grey	1oz	2.19
270-110352	CSX Blue	1oz	2.19
270-110356	CSX Yellow	1oz	2.19
270-110450	Soo Line Red	1oz	2.19

270-120009	Primer	2oz	3.50
270-120010	Engine Black	2oz	3.50
270-120011	Reefer White	2oz	3.50
270-120020	Caboose Red	2oz	3.50
270-120025	Tuscan	2oz	3.50
270-120030	Reefer Orange	2oz	3.50
270-120031	Reefer Yellow	2oz	3.50
270-120070	Roof Brown	2oz	3.50
270-120074	Box Car Red	2oz	3.50
270-120082	Concrete White	2oz	3.50
270-120085	Antique White	2oz	3.50

270-130007	Rail Brown Spray	5oz	5.19
270-130009	Primer Spray	5oz	5.19
270-130010	Engine Black Spray	5oz	5.19
270-130011	Reefer White Spray	5oz	5.19
270-130012	Reefer Gray Spray	5oz	5.19
270-130020	Caboose Red Spray	5oz	5.19
270-130025	Tuscan Red Spray	5oz	5.19
270-130030	Reefer Orange Spray	5oz	5.19
270-130031	Reefer Yellow Spray	5oz	5.19
270-130040	Dark Green Spray	5oz	5.19
270-130045	Pullman Green Spray	5oz	5.19
270-130048	Coach Green Spray	5oz	5.19
270-130050	Dark Blue Spray	5oz	5.19
270-130070	Roof Brown Spray	5oz	5.19
270-130074	Box Car Red Spray	5oz	5.19
270-130081	Earth Spray	5oz	5.19
270-130082	Concrete Spray	5oz	5.19

■ LIMITED QUANTITIES ■ AVAILABLE			
270-110058	Conrail Blue	1oz	2.19
270-120081	Earth	2oz	3.50
270-120184	Tuscan Red #2	2oz	3.50

SOUTHERN PACIFIC COLORS

270-110130	SP Lettering Gray	1oz	2.19
270-110131	SP Lark Light Gray	1oz	2.19
270-110132	SP Lark Dark Gray	1oz	2.19
270-110133	SP Armour Yellow	1oz	2.19
270-110134	SP Daylight Orange	1oz	2.19
270-110135	SP Daylight Red	1oz	2.19
270-110136	SP Scarlet	1oz	2.19

METALLIC COLORS

270-110100	Old Silver	1oz	2.19
270-110101	Bright Silver	1oz	2.19
270-110103	Bright Gold	1oz	2.19
270-110104	Brass	1oz	2.19
270-110105	Copper	1oz	2.19
270-110108	Gun Motal	1oz	2.10
270-110119	Graphite	1oz	2.19
270-110144	Platinum Mist	1oz	2.19
270-130101	Bright Silver	5oz	5.19

THINNERS & COATINGS

RETARDER

Used to slow drying time of paint (helpful with air-brushes and on large surfaces).

270-110002	Retarder	1oz	1.79

CRYSTAL COTE

Clear gloss protective coating and fixative. Quick drying, non-yellowing, durable. Resists abrasion and most common chemicals (except alcohol).

270-110004	Crystal Cote	1oz	1.99
270-130004	Crystal Cote Spray	5oz	5.19
270-140004	Crystal Cote	8oz	7.25

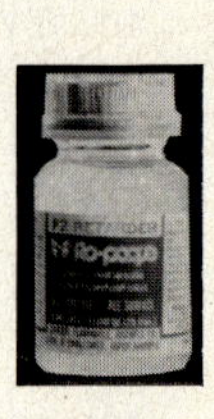

DIO-SOL

Only chemically compatible solvent for Floquil colors. Use for thinning, mixing, correcting, cleaning brushes, air brushes, and surfaces to be painted.

270-110001	Dio-Sol	1oz	1.79
270-120001	Dio-Sol	2oz	2.29
270-140001	Dio-Sol	8oz	5.25
270-150001	Dio-Sol	pint can	6.25
270-160001	Dio-Sol	quart can	8.75
270-170001	Dio-Sol	1gal	19.99
270-151611	Airbrush Thinner	16oz	6.50

HIGH-GLOSS

For a high gloss finish apply over colors. Water and alcohol resistant. Drying time is four hours.

270-110003	Hi-Gloss	1oz	1.99

FLAT FINISH

270-110015	Flat Finish	1oz	2.19
270-120015	Flat Finish	2oz	3.50
270-130015	Flat Finish Spray	5oz	5.19

GLAZE

For medium gloss coating or, when mixed with colors, to provide an egg-shell or semi-gloss finish. Resistant to water and most common chemicals.

270-110005	Glaze	1oz	1.99
270-120005	Glaze	2oz	3.50
270-140005	Glaze	8oz	9.75
270-300005	Glaze	1/2 oz	1.49

BARRIER

Crystal-clear, primer sealer for polystyrene plastics. Simply brush or spray on model, let dry, then apply regular colors.

270-110019	Barrier	1oz	1.99
270-110008	Barrier Thinner	1oz	1.79
270-120008	Barrier Thinner	2oz	2.29
270-120019	Barrier	2oz	3.50
270-131711	Barrier Spray Glossing Shield	12oz	6.50

ZINC CHROMATE PRIMER

270-110601	Zinc Chromate Primer	1oz	2.19
270-120601	Zinc Chromate Primer	2oz	3.50
270-130601	Zinc Chromate Spray	5oz	5.19

AEROSOL FIGURE PRIMER

Permanent, high-adherence prime coat for metal figures and miniatures. Use under water based or solvent based paints.

270-330009	Light Gray	5oz	5.19
270-330010	Base Black	5oz	5.19
(By Special Order Only.)			
270-330021	Base White	5oz	5.19
270-330022	Figure Flat	5oz	5.19

WEATHERING COLORS

Weathering colors are a special consistency (thinner than standard railroad colors).

270-110006	Dust	1oz	2.19
270-110007	Rail Brown	1oz	2.19
270-110013	Grimy Black	1oz	2.19
270-110017	Weathered Black	1oz	2.19
270-110073	Rust	1oz	2.19
270-110083	Mud	1oz	2.19
270-110086	Grime	1oz	2.19

FLOQUIL~POLLY S COLOR CORP.

An **RPM** Company

Floquil paints are designed for miniatures. Floquil colors are solvent base enamels. Polly S are water soluble acrylics.

Dealers: Ask about merchandising (display) racks.

WEATHERING COLORS (continued)

Weathering colors are a special consistency (thinner than standard railroad colors).

270-120007	Rail Brown	2oz	3.50
270-120013	Grimy Black	2oz	3.50
270-120017	Weathered Black	2oz	3.50
270-120073	Rust	2oz	3.50
270-130013	Grimy Black Spray	5oz	5.19
270-130016	Instant Weathering Spray	5oz	5.19

FLOQUIL PAINT KITS

270-190210 Railroad Color Kit 7.49
(Contains one each: Engine Black, Reefer White, Caboose Red, Tuscan Red, Box Car Red & Dio-Sol)

270-190211 Railroad Weathering Kit 7.49
(Contains one each: Dust, Grimy Black, Rust, Mud, Grime and Dio-Sol)

MILITARY COLOR SERIES

■ LIMITED QUANTITIES AVAILABLE ■

270-300030	Bright Orange	1/2oz	1.49
270-300031	Yellow	1/2oz	1.49
270-300103	Bright Gold	1/2oz	1.49
270-300120	Platinum Mist	1/2oz	1.49
270-300185	Sand (AN616)	1/2oz	1.49

MILITARY PAINT ACCESSORIES

270-300001	Dio-Sol	1/2oz	1.49
270-300002	Retarder	1/2oz	1.49
270-300008	Barrier/Thinner	1/2oz	1.49
270-300015	Flat Finish	1/2oz	1.49

MARINE COLORS

For ship and boat builders, compatible with plastic, as well as fiberglass, woods, metals and Lexan.

MODERN VESSELS

270-818610	Black Boottopping A/N514	2.19
270-818612	Red Boottopping FS1705	2.19
270-818614	Anti-Fouling Red FS1020	2.19
270-818616	Deck Green A/N503	2.19
270-818618	Deck Tan FS1735	2.19
270-818620	Quartermaster Brown FS1005	2.19
270-818622	Navy Brown #41 A/N510	2.19
270-818624	Navy Buff #22 FS1750	2.19
270-818626	Panama Buff A/N507	2.19
270-818628	Navy Red #40 FS1110	2.19

270-818630	Navy White #30 A/N511	2.19
270-818632	Coast Guard Red A/N508	2.19
270-818634	Coast Guard Orange A/N508	2.19
270-818636	Marine Corps Green FS1415	2.19
270-818638	Sea Blue A/N623	2.19
270-818640	Navy Blue A/N502	2.19
270-818642	Maritime Blue A/N501	2.19
270-818644	Navy Light Blue #43 FS1525	2.19
270-818646	Navy Dark Gray #21 A/N513	2.19
270-818648	Navy Medium Gray FS1615	2.19
270-818650	Navy Light Gray FS1650	2.19
270-818652	Battleship Gray FS1640	2.19

CLASSIC VESSELS

270-818654	Bright Silver	2.19
270-818656	Iron Black	2.19
270-818658	New Manila Stain	2.19
270-818660	Weathered Manila Stain	2.19
270-818662	Light Stockholm Tar	2.19
270-818664	Dark Stockholm Tar	2.19
270-818666	Teak	2.19
270-818668	Mahogany	2.19
270-818670	Bright Oil	2.19
270-818672	Tallow Coat	2.19
270-818674	Pine Tar Oil	2.19
270-818676	Tar	2.19
270-818678	Salmon Buff	2.19
270-818680	Yellow Ochre	2.19
270-818682	Orange Ochre	2.19
270-818684	Umber	2.19
270-818686	Slate Gray	2.19
270-818688	Midship Blue	2.19
270-818690	Caprail Green	2.19
270-818692	Bulwarks Red	2.19
270-818694	Hull Cream	2.19
270-818696	Verdigris	2.19
270-898500	Marine Colors Set	18.99

THINNERS

270-818603	Thinner & Brush Cleaner	1oz	1.79
270-848601	Airbrush Thinner	8oz	5.30

REFLECTANCE REDUCER

270-818604	1oz	2.19
270-848602	8oz	8.25

FLO STAINS

Pigmented, penetrating stains for wood or most light colored surfaces. Easy to apply (wipe or brush on), fast drying, permanent, non-fading, require no waxing.

270-110701	Dio-Sol	1oz	1.79
270-110703	Al-pro Cote	1oz	1.99
270-110704	Crystal Cote	1oz	1.99
270-110705	Glaze	1oz	1.99
270-110720	Driftwood	1oz	1.79
270-110721	Rosewood	1oz	1.79
270-110722	Natural Pine	1oz	1.79
270-110723	Oak	1oz	1.79
270-110724	Maple	1oz	1.79
270-110725	Cherry	1oz	1.79
270-110726	Walnut	1oz	1.79
270-110727	Mahogany	1oz	1.79
270-110728	Teak	1oz	1.79
270-110784	Foundation	1oz	2.19
270-190700	Flo Stain Master Set		6.79

Contains six 1/2 fluid ounce jars: Dio-Sol, Glaze, Wood Oil, Teak, Oak and Mahogany.

WOOD OILS

270-110730	Swedish Wood Oil	1oz	1.79
270-190730	Swedish Wood Oil	4oz	4.50

POLLY S RR COLORS

Water soluble paint for styrene, wood, plaster, cardboard. Thins with water. Easy cleanup for brushes, mixing bottles and spray equipment.

NOTE: Because Polly S handles differently than solvent base paints, be sure to ask for and read the Polly S instruction sheet.

270-400400	Monon Gold	1/2oz	1.69
270-400402	B&M Red	1/2oz	1.69
270-400404	B&M Yellow	1/2oz	1.69
270-400406	MEC Pine Green	1/2oz	1.69
270-400408	WP Orange	1/2oz	1.69
270-400410	PRR Buff	1/2oz	1.69
270-400412	Oxide Red	1/2oz	1.69
270-400414	Roof Red	1/2oz	1.69
270-400416	Signal Yellow	1/2oz	1.69
270-400418	Signal Green	1/2oz	1.69
270-400420	Signal Red	1/2oz	1.69
270-400422	Utility Orange	1/2oz	1.69
270-400424	Prussian Blue	1/2oz	1.69
270-400426	Vermillion	1/2oz	1.69
270-400428	TH&B Cream	1/2oz	1.69
270-400430	VIA Blue (Gloss)	1/2oz	1.69
270-400432	CP Yellow	1/2oz	1.69
270-400434	CP Red	1/2oz	1.69
270-410003	Dust	1oz	2.19
270-410005	Flat Finish	1oz	2.19
270-410006	Metal Primer	1oz	2.19
270-410010	Black	1oz	2.19
270-410011	Reefer White	1oz	2.19
270-410012	Reefer Gray	1oz	2.19
270-410013	Grimy Black	1oz	2.19
270-410015	Oily Black	1oz	2.19
270-410020	Caboose Red	1oz	2.19
270-410025	Tuscan Red	1oz	2.19
270-410030	Reefer Orange	1oz	2.19
270-410031	Reefer Yellow	1oz	2.19
270-410040	Dark Green	1oz	2.19
270-410044	Depot Olive	1oz	2.19
270-410045	Pullman Green	1oz	2.19
270-410048	Coach Green	1oz	2.19
270-410058	Conrail Blue	1oz	2.19
270-410069	Dirt	1oz	2.19
270-410070	Roof Brown	1oz	2.19
270-410073	Rust	1oz	2.19
270-410074	Box Car Red	1oz	2.19
270-410081	Earth	1oz	2.19
270-410082	Concrete	1oz	2.19
270-410083	Mud	1oz	2.19
270-410087	Depot Buff	1oz	2.19
270-410170	Gloss Finish	1oz	2.19
270-410436	Atlantic Coast Purple	1oz	2.19
270-410438	Atlantic Coast Yellow	1oz	2.19
270-410440	B&M Blue	1oz	2.19
270-410442	Montana Rail Link Blue (Gloss)	1oz	2.19
270-410444	MEC Harvest Gold	1oz	2.19
270-410446	Monon Blk (Gloss)	1oz	2.19
270-410448	PRR Freight Car Red	1oz	2.19
270-410450	PRR Camp Car Yellow	1oz	2.19
270-410452	PRR Dark Green	1oz	2.19
270-410454	Bar Blue	1oz	2.19
270-410456	Bar Gray	1oz	2.19
270-410458	TH&B Maroon	1oz	2.19
270-410460	Via Yellow (Gloss)	1oz	2.19
270-410462	CP Gray	1oz	2.19
270-410464	CP Tuscan	1oz	2.19
270-410466	Amtrak Red	1oz	2.19
270-410468	Amtrak Blue	1oz	2.19
270-411995	Flat Aluminum	1oz	2.19
270-411990	Bright Aluminum	1oz	2.19
270-412000	Brass	1oz	2.19
270-411997	Stainless Steel	1oz	2.19

FLOQUIL~POLLY S COLOR CORP.

An **RPM** Company

Floquil paints are designed for miniatures. Floquil colors are solvent base enamels. Polly S are water soluble acrylics.

Dealers: Ask about merchandising (display) racks.

METALLINE COLORS

270-501990	Bright Silver	1/2oz	1.69
270-501991	Burnt Aluminum	1/2oz	1.69
270-501992	Oxided Aluminum	1/2oz	1.69
270-501993	Metallic Green	1/2oz	1.69
270-501994	Anodized Blue Metal	1/2oz	1.69
270-501997	Stainless Steel	1/2oz	1.69
270-501998	Copper	1/2oz	1.69
270-501999	Graphite	1/2oz	1.69
270-502000	Brass	1/2oz	1.69
270-502001	Pewter	1/2oz	1.69

POLLY S "FLATS"

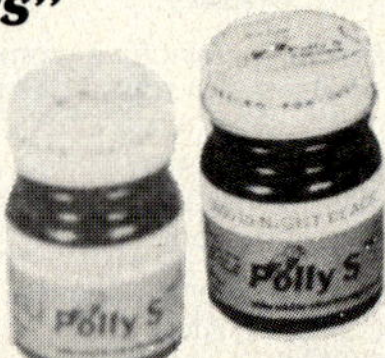

270-500003	Dust	1/2oz	1.69
270-500005	Flat Finish	1/2oz	1.69
270-500006	Metal Primer	1/2oz	1.69
270-500010	Night Black	1/2oz	1.69
270-500011	White	1/2oz	1.69
270-500012	Equipment Lt Gray	1/2oz	1.69
270-500013	Battle Dark Gray	1/2oz	1.69
270-500014	Grimy Black	1/2oz	1.69
270-500015	Oily Black	1/2oz	1.69
270-500020	Fire Red	1/2oz	1.69
270-500021	Venetian Dull Red	1/2oz	1.69
270-500023	Flesh	1/2oz	1.69
270-500024	International Orange	1/2oz	1.69
270-500030	Blue	1/2oz	1.69
270-500031	Sea Blue	1/2oz	1.69
270-500032	Sky Blue	1/2oz	1.69
270-500040	Yellow	1/2oz	1.69
270-500050	Jungle Green	1/2oz	1.69
270-500051	Grass Green	1/2oz	1.69
270-500052	Olive Drab	1/2oz	1.69
270-500060	Khaki	1/2oz	1.69
270-500061	Wood Tan	1/2oz	1.69
270-500062	Sahara Sand	1/2oz	1.69
270-500063	Desert Light Brown	1/2oz	1.69
270-500064	Dark Earth Brown	1/2oz	1.69
270-500065	Military Medium Brown	1/2oz	1.69
270-500067	Mud	1/2oz	1.69
270-500068	Rust	1/2oz	1.69
270-500069	Dirt	1/2oz	1.69
270-500070	Gloss Finish (clear)	1/2oz	1.69
270-500075	Dark Green	1/2oz	1.69
270-500076	Dark Earth	1/2oz	1.69
270-500077	Light Green	1/2oz	1.69
270-500084	Dark Gray (74)	1/2oz	1.69
270-500085	Medium Blue	1/2oz	1.69
270-500086	Black/Green (70)	1/2oz	1.69
270-500087	Dark Green (71)	1/2oz	1.69
270-500000	Light Gray (76)	1/2oz	1.60
270-500101	Black (37038)	1/2oz	1.69
270-500102	White (37875)	1/2oz	1.69
270-500103	Brown (30117)	1/2oz	1.69
270-500104	Red (31136)	1/2oz	1.69
270-500105	Light Red (31158)	1/2oz	1.69
270-500106	Yellow (33538)	1/2oz	1.69
270-500107	Dark Green (34108)	1/2oz	1.69
270-500108	Light Green (34558)	1/2oz	1.69
270-500109	Light Blue (35109)	1/2oz	1.69
270-500110	Gray (36231)	1/2oz	1.69
270-500201	Marker Red	1/2oz	1.69
270-500202	Marker Yellow	1/2oz	1.69
270-500203	Earth Brown	1/2oz	1.69
270-500204	Earth Gray	1/2oz	1.69
270-500205	Topside Blue	1/2oz	1.69
270-500206	Topside Green	1/2oz	1.69
270-500207	Underside Blue	1/2oz	1.69
270-500209	Underside Gray	1/2oz	1.69
270-500218	Topside Gray	1/2oz	1.69
270-500301	Light Yellow (4B4)	1/2oz	1.69
270-500302	Cl Doped Linen	1/2oz	1.69
270-500303	Roundel Blue	1/2oz	1.69

270-500304	Roundel Red	1/2oz	1.69
270-500305	Battleship Gray	1/2oz	1.69
270-500306	Pale Green (29E5)	1/2oz	1.69
270-500307	Blue (UB2-2007)	1/2oz	1.69
270-500308	Brown (8E8)	1/2oz	1.69
270-500309	Lilac (18D6)	1/2oz	1.69
270-500702	Armor Panzer Gray	1/2oz	1.69
270-500703	Armor Dark Yellow	1/2oz	1.69
270-500704	Armor Dark Green	1/2oz	1.69
270-500705	Armor Red-Brown	1/2oz	1.69
270-500706	Green	1/2oz	1.69
270-500707	Medium Gray	1/2oz	1.69
270-500708	Sand Yellow	1/2oz	1.69
270-500709	Olive Green	1/2oz	1.69
270-500710	Field Gray	1/2oz	1.69
270-500711	Light Gray	1/2oz	1.69
270-500802	Interior Green	1/2oz	1.69
270-500803	Sea Blue NS	1/2oz	1.69
270-500804	Inspection Blue NS	1/2oz	1.69
270-500805	Dirty White	1/2oz	1.69
270-500809	Neutral Gray	1/2oz	1.69
270-500810	Desert Pink	1/2oz	1.69
270-500811	Sea Green	1/2oz	1.69
270-500812	Sand	1/2oz	1.69
270-500813	Azure Blue	1/2oz	1.69
270-500814	Dark Green (34079)	1/2oz	1.69
270-500815	Med Army Grn (34102)	1/2oz	1.69
270-500816	Tan (30219)	1/2oz	1.69
270-500817	Gray (36622)	1/2oz	1.69
270-500822	Sea Gray (36118)	1/2oz	1.69
270-500823	Ocean Gray (36176)	1/2oz	1.69
270-500824	Dark Gull (36231)	1/2oz	1.69
270-500825	Light Gull (36440)	1/2oz	1.69
270-500826	Desert Sand	1/2oz	1.69
270-500827	Sand (30277)	1/2oz	1.69
270-500828	Earth Yellow	1/2oz	1.69
270-500829	Earth Red	1/2oz	1.69
270-500830	Field Drab	1/2oz	1.69
270-500831	Earth Brown	1/2oz	1.69
270-500836	Ghost Gray-Light	1/2oz	1.69
270-500837	Ghost Gray-Dark	1/2oz	1.69
270-500838	Light Gray FS 36440	1/2oz	1.69
270-500839	Medium Gray FS 36375	1/2oz	1.69
270-500840	Dark Gray FS36320	1/2oz	1.69
270-500841	Deep Gray FS 36081	1/2oz	1.69
270-500842	Aircraft Untinted White FS 17925	1/2oz	1.69
270-500843	Sand FS 33303	1/2oz	1.69
270-500844	Tan 686 FS 33446	1/2oz	1.69
270-500845	Brown 383 FS 30051	1/2oz	1.69
270-500846	Dark Sandstone FS 33510	1/2oz	1.69
270-500847	Aircraft Gray FS36300	1/2oz	1.69
270-500848	Aircraft Green FS34031	1/2oz	1.69
270-500849	Int. Air. Black FS37031	1/2oz	1.69
270-500850	Olive Drab FS33070	1/2oz	1.69
270-500851	Field Drab FS 33105	1/2oz	1.69
270-500852	Earth Red FS31090	1/2oz	1.69
270-500853	Earth Brown FS 30097	1/2oz	1.69
270-500854	Red FS 11136	1/2oz	1.69
270-500855	Orange-Yellow FS13538	1/2oz	1.69
270-500874	Brown (30219)	1/2oz	1.69
270-500875	Yellow (33531)	1/2oz	1.69
270-500876	Green (34277)	1/2oz	1.69
270-500877	Blue (35622)	1/2oz	1.69
270-500878	Blue (35045)	1/2oz	1.69
270-500879	Gray (30372)	1/2oz	1.69

"GLOSS" COLORS

270-500910	Ebony Black	1/2oz	1.69
270-500911	Polar White	1/2oz	1.69

POLLY S PAINT SETS

Hobbycraft Paint Set
270-591481
6.29

Includes eight 1/3 fluid ounce jars: primary colors for model, hobby, art or craft projects.

270-591407 Creature Color Set 6.95
Eight 1/3 fluid oz jars included: yellow, yellow-green, yellow-brown, dull green, light green, orange, ivory, and red; plus a detailing brush.

270-591480 Deluxe Hobbycraft Paint Set 11.95
Sixteen 1/3 fluid oz jars: primary colors and priming brush.

POLLY S PAINT KITS

Each kit contains 1/2 ounce bottles

270-290212 Boat Color Kit 7.49
Permanent, water proof color can be applied to any surface. Includes one each: black, white, red, copper, glaze and Dio-Sol.

270-590208 Weathering Kit 7.49
Contains one each: Dust, Grimy Black, Mud, Oily Black, Rust and Dirt

270-490213 Polly S RR Color Kit 10.14
Contains one each: Grimy Black, Boxcar Red, Tuscan Red, Reefer White, Caboose Red and Reefer Yellow

270-590229 Polly S Paint Factory Kit 8.95
270-591989 "Silver" Metalline Kit 19.99
Set includes one bottle each of the six water-based Metalline colors (Bright Silver, Oxidized Aluminum, Burnt Aluminum, Green Metallic, Anodized Blue Metallic and Flat Aluminum), a jar of Base White, Base Black, Airbrush Thinner and Plastic Prep, two #3 flat sable brushes and a handy storage tray.

270-591415 Figure Painting Kit 19.99
Includes 15 assorted jars of water reducible paint (including 3 metalline colors), a priming brush and a reusable 10/0 brush.

270-592020 "Gold" Metalline Kit 19.99
Set is complete with bright gold, stainless steel, brass, pewter, graphite, copper, and base white & black. Also includes brushes, airbrush thinner and plastic prep.

270-190300 CSX Color Set w/Decal 15.99
270-190400 Soo Line Color w/Decal 15.99

DESERT STORM PAINT KITS

Each kit contains 8 different colors, plastic prep, airbrush thinner, and brushes.

270-590600 Air Colors 19.99
270-590700 Armor Colors 19.99

FLOQUIL~POLLY S COLOR CORP.

An **RPM** Company

DESCRIPTIONS OF ACCESSORY PREPARATIONS & COATINGS

FRR AIRBRUSH THINNER
Used for thinning Polly S colors for airbrushing.

DIO-SOL
The only chemically compatible solvent for FMC. Used for thinning, mixing, making corrections and cleaning surfaces, brushes, air brushes, etc. Use Dio-Sol generously. It is inexpensive and makes your paint go further.

RETARDER
Used to slow drying time of FMC for use with air brush application, large surfaces, etc.

HI-GLOSS
Light amber colored coating. For indoor use. Heat, water and alcohol resistant. Drying time approximately 4 hours. Produces an extremely high gloss finish.

CRYSTAL-COTE
Water-clear, glossy, quick-drying coating and fixative. For indoor and outdoor use. Does not yellow. Durable. Resists abrasion and most common chemicals (except alcohol).

GLAZE
Amber colored, medium gloss coating. For indoor and outdoor use. Quick drying (15-20 minutes). Resistant to water, alcohol, and most common chemicals. Dielectric. Also used for priming and to produce an eggshell finish when mixed with the colors.

ACCESSORIES

AIRBRUSH THINNER FOR ACRYLICS
Made for airbrush application of Polly S model and hobby colors. For smoother mixing, better flow and faster drying.

270-546008	Airbrush Thinner	8oz 4.69
270-556008	Airbrush Thinner	16oz 6.79

PLASTIC PREP
Removes mold release silicones, grease, etc. Makes plastic clean, static-free, dust-free.

270-546007	Plastic Prep	8oz 4.69
270-556007	Plastic Prep	16oz 6.79

PAINT & DECAL REMOVER
Slow acting, safe for plastics. Removes both paint and decals.

Polly S Elo Remover
270-542143   8oz 6.79

DUST FLOGGER BRUSH SET

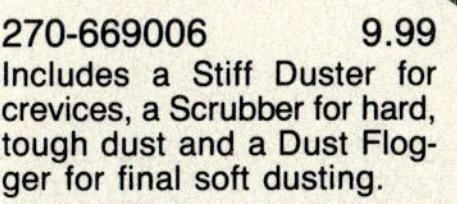

270-669006   9.99
Includes a Stiff Duster for crevices, a Scrubber for hard, tough dust and a Dust Flogger for final soft dusting.

COLOR CARDS & COLOR CHARTS

270-190240	Floquil RR Chart (small)	2.00
270-490251	Polly RR Chart	2.00

BRUSHES

See Painting Supplies Section for FLOQUIL Brushes. Types of brushes included in this series are Red Sable, White Bristle, Ox Hair, Camel Hair, Silver Fox and FLOQUIL Supremes.

270-890689	Floquil Marine Card	2.00
270-890789	Floquil Classic Ship Card	2.00
270-590246	Polly S Camouflage Color Card	2.00
270-590244	Polly S Model & Hobby Color Card	2.00

MISCELLANEOUS

270-190231	1/2oz Bottles w/Cap	pkg(6)	3.49
270-190232	1oz Mixing Bottles w/Cap	pkg(6)	3.69
270-190243	Painting Miniatures Manual		4.25

AIR BRUSH INFORMATION

RECOMMENDED AIR PRESSURES AND THINNING RATIOS FOR AIRBRUSHING

Model Railroad Colors
Thinning Ratio:
   75% color, 5% glaze, 20% Dio-Sol
Approximate Pressure: 12-20 lbs.

Military Miniature Colors
Thinning Ratio:
   75% color, 5% glaze, 20% Dio-Sol
Approximate Pressure: 12-20 lbs.

Clear Coatings
Al-Pro-Cote Thinning Ratio:
   Usually none required, if needed use Dio-Sol

Crystal-Cote Thinning Ratio:
   Usually none required, if needed use Dio-Sol as a thinner

Barrier Coat
   If thinning required, use only the special #8 Barrier-Thinner.
   75% Barrier, 25% Barrier-Thinner.
Approximate Pressure: 12-20 lbs.

Scale Marine Colors
Thinning Ratio:
   75% color, 25% Dio-Sol
Approximate Pressure: 15-20 lbs.

Polly S Colors
Thinning Ratio:
   60-65% color, 35-40% thinner
Approximate Pressure: 15-20 lbs.

Metalline Series
Thinning Ratio:
   50% color, 50% thinner
Approximate Pressure 15-20 lbs.

IMPORTANT NOTES

It is imperative that your air brush is cleaned thoroughly, immediately after use with Polly S Colors. Acrylics set up fast and can clog air brush if not cleaned immediately.

All measurements are approximate. Thinning ratio and pressure needed may vary, depending upon the type of finish required or brand of compressor.

ALWAYS TEST FIRST!

hobby helpers

CHALK-EZ   pkg(1oz) 1.08
"CAKE FORM" chalk is easily applied with fingertip or a cotton swab. For best results, apply desired color or blended shade and dust lightly with a flat artist's brush. If project is to be handled heavily, we suggest you seal it with a flattener such as Testors Dullcote.

Many desirable shades may be achieved by blending colors. If desired effect is not achieved with first application, Chalk-EZ is easily removed with water.

099-103 Lt Brown	099-113 Orange
099-104 Grey	099-114 Light Blue
099-106 White	099-115 Red-Orange
099-107 Black	099-116 Yellow-Green
099-108 Rust	099-117 Turquoise
099-109 Yellow	099-118 Amber/Lt Rust
099-110 Blue	099-119 Yellow-Orange
099-111 Red	099-120 Dark-Green
099-112 Green	

WEATHERING SETS
099-101 For Railroad Equipment   10oz 6.99
Set of ten cake form chalks: tan, light brown, black, white, grey, red, yellow, rust, blue and green.

099-102 For Buildings and Scenery 10oz 6.99
Set of ten chalks include: orange, red orange, light rust, yellow orange, yellow green, turquoise, light blue, dark green, white and black.

099-301 Master Set   ea 16.68
Set includes both #101 and 102 cake form sets and #516 white bristle brush set.

BRUSHES
For Chalk-Ez weathering colors and general painting.

PAINTS & PEWTER FINISH

Paint Set
785-125   3.49
Set includes one 1-1/2 fl oz bottle of the following colors: red, yellow, blue, white, grey, black, earth, clay, terra cotta, sand, beige, and goldenrod.

Pewter Patina Finish
785-126   1/2oz .98
Dealers: MUST order Dealer pack of 5.

VOLLMER

Imported from Germany and marketed by WALTHERS

WEATHERING PAINTS
Vollmer weathering paints are water soluble.

770-6050	Red	(15ml) btl 2.99
770-6051	Black	(15ml) btl 2.99
770-6052	White	(15ml) btl 2.99
770-6053	Yellow	(15ml) btl 2.99

ENAMEL PAINTS

Testors Pla Enamel paints are available in 1/4 oz bottles and 3oz spray cans. (Enamels are gloss finish unless noted.)

Also available are Thinners and Coatings.

+ (PLUS SIGN) = SPECIAL ORDER ONLY ITEMS

PLA ENAMELS

Pla Brush-On Enamels in 1/4 ounce bottles. Colors dry fast to a hard finish. (Enamels are gloss finish unless noted).

Dealers: MUST Order Dealer Pack of 12.

704-1103	Red	1/4oz	.98
704-1104	Dark Red	1/4oz	.98
704-1108	Light Blue	1/4oz	.98
704-1110	Medium Blue	1/4oz	.98
704-1111	Dark Blue	1/4oz	.98
704-1112	Pale Yellow	1/4oz	.98
704-1114	Yellow	1/4oz	.98
704-1116	Cream	1/4oz	.98
704-1124	Green	1/4oz	.98
704-1127	Orange	1/4oz	.98
704-1133	Light Brown	1/4oz	.98
704-1134	Purple	1/4oz	.98
704-1138	Gray	1/4oz	.98
704-1140	Brown	1/4oz	.98
704-1141	Wood	1/4oz	.98
704-1144	Gold	1/4oz	.98
704-1145	White	1/4oz	.98
704-1146	Silver	1/4oz	.98
704-1147	Black	1/4oz	.98
704-1149	Flat Black	1/4oz	.98
704-1150	Flat Red	1/4oz	.98
704-1151	Copper	1/4oz	.98
704-1152	Metallic Red	1/4oz	.98

BRUSH-ON METAL FLAKE

704-1529	Ruby Red	1/4oz	.98
704-1530	Jade Green	1/4oz	.98
704-1531	Burgundy Purple	1/4oz	.98
704-1539	Sapphire Blue	1/4oz	.98
704-1542	Lime Gold	1/4oz	.98

MILITARY FLAT COLORS

704-1162	Sky Blue	1/4oz	.98
704-1163	Battle Gray	1/4oz	.98
704-1164	Olive Drab Green	1/4oz	.98
704-1165	Army Olive	1/4oz	.98
704-1166	Military Brown	1/4oz	.98
704-1167	Desert Tan	1/4oz	.98
704-1168	White	1/4oz	.98
704-1169	Yellow	1/4oz	.98
704-1170	Light Tan	1/4oz	.98
704-1171	Beret Green	1/4oz	.98
704-1172	Sea Blue	1/4oz	.98
704-1180	Steel	1/4oz	.98
704-1181	Aluminum	1/4oz	.98
704-1182	Brass	1/4oz	.98
704-1183	Rubber	1/4oz	.98
704-1184	Zinc Chromate	1/4oz	.98
704-1185	Rust	1/4oz	.98

PLA SPRAY ENAMELS

Pla Spray Enamels come in cans with color coded, tamper-proof caps. Colors match Pla Brush-On Enamels. (Enamels are gloss finish unless noted).

Dealers: MUST Order Dealer Pack of 3.

704-1203	Red		3oz	2.75
704-1204	Dark Red		3oz	2.75
704-1208	Light Blue		3oz	2.75
704-1210	Brown	NEW	3oz	2.75
704-1211	Dark Blue		3oz	2.75
704-1214	Yellow		3oz	2.75
704-1224	Green		3oz	2.75
704-1226	Aircraft Green	NEW	3oz	2.75
704-1231	Bright Red	NEW	3oz	2.75
704-1233	Flat Light Green	NEW	3oz	2.75
704-1234	Purple		3oz	2.75
704-1237	Primer	NEW	3oz	2.75
704-1238	Gray		3oz	2.75
704-1240	Brown		3oz	2.75
704-1241	Wood		3oz	2.75
704-1244	Gold		3oz	2.75

704-1245	White	3oz	2.75
704-1246	Silver	3oz	2.75
704-1247	Black	3oz	2.75
704-1249	Flat Black	3oz	2.75
704-1250	Flat Red	3oz	2.75
704-1251	Copper	3oz	2.75
704-1255	Transparent Red	3oz	2.75
704-1256	Transparent Green	3oz	2.75
704-1257	Transparent Blue	3oz	2.75
704-1258	Flat White	3oz	2.75
704-1265	Flat Olive NEW	3oz	2.75

CUSTOM COLORS

704-1601	Candy Emerald Green	3oz	2.75
704-1605	Candy Apple Red	3oz	2.75
704-1607	Candy Hot Rod Red	3oz	2.75
704-1617	Candy Grape	3oz	2.75
704-1628	Competition Orange	3oz	2.75

SPRAY METAL FLAKE

704-1629	Ruby Red	3oz	2.75
704-1630	Jade Green	3oz	2.75
704-1631	Burgundy Purple	3oz	2.75
704-1639	Sapphire Blue	3oz	2.75
704-1642	Lime Gold	3oz	2.75

CHROME SPRAY

704-1290	Chrome	3oz	2.75

MODEL MASTER

FS ENAMELS BOTTLES

The FS Series of Model Master colors will match the Federal Standard number indicated. 1/2 ounce bottles.

Dealers: MUST order Dealer Pack of 9.

704-1701	Military Brown (30117)	1.75
704-1702	Field Drab (30118)	1.75
704-1704	Armor Sand (30277)	1.75
704-1705	Insignia Red (31136)	1.75
704-1706	Sand (33531)	1.75
704-1707	Chrome Yellow (13538)	1.75
704-1708	Insignia Red (33538)	1.75
704-1709	Radome Tan (33613)	1.75
704-1710	Dark Green (34079)	1.75
704-1711	Olive Drab (34087)	1.75
704-1712	Field Green (34097)	1.75
704-1713	Medium Green (34102)	1.75
704-1714	Forest Green (34127)	1.75
704-1715	Interior Green (34151)	1.75
704-1716	Pale Green (34227)	1.75
704-1717	Sea Blue (15042) Dark	1.75
704-1718	Sea Blue (35042) Flat	1.75
704-1719	Insignia Blue (35044)	1.75
704-1720	Intermediate Blue (35164)	1.75
704-1721	Medium Gray (35237)	1.75
704-1722	Duck Egg Blue (35622)	1.75
704-1723	Gunship Gray (36118)	1.75
704-1725	Neutral Gray (36270)	1.75
704-1726	Light Sea Gray (36307)	1.75
704-1728	Light Ghost Gray (36375)	1.75
704-1729	Gloss Gull Gray (16440)	1.75
704-1730	Gull Gray (36440) Flat	1.75
704-1731	Aircraft Gray (16473)	1.75
704-1732	Light Gray (36495)	1.75
704-1733	Camouflage Gray (36622)	1.75
704-1734	Zinc Chromate Green	1.75
704-1735	Wood	1.75
704-1736	Leather	1.75
704-1740	Dark Gull Gray (36231)	1.75
704-1741	Dark Ghost Gray (36320)	1.75
704-1742	Dark Tan (30219)	1.75
704-1744	Gold	1.75
704-1745	White (17875) Insignia	1.75
704-1747	Gloss Black (17038)	1.75
704-1749	Flat Black (37038)	1.75
704-1764	Dark Green (34092) Euro	1.75
704-1768	Flat White (37875)	1.75

704-1772	Blue Angel Blue (15050)	1.75
704-1775	Fluorescent Red (28915)	1.75
704-1780	Steel	1.75
704-1781	Aluminum	1.75
704-1782	Brass	1.75
704-1785	Rust	1.75
704-1786	Medium Field Green (34095)	1.75
704-1787	Green Drab (34086)	1.75
704-1788	Euro 1 Gray (36081)	1.75
704-1790	Chrome Silver (17178)	1.75
704-1791	Navy Gloss Gray (16081)	1.75
704-1792	SAC-Tan (34201) Bomber	1.75
704-1793	SAC-Green (34159) Bomber	1.75
704-1794	Aggressor Gray (36251) Navy	1.75
704-1795	Gunmetal	1.75
704-1796	Jet Exhaust	1.75

ACRYLIC

1/2 ounce bottles. Dealers: MUST order Dealer pack of 9.

704-50101	Military Brown (30117)	NEW	1.80
704-50102	Field Drab (30118)	NEW	1.80
704-50104	Armor Sand (30277)	NEW	1.80
704-50105	Insignia Red (31136)	NEW	1.80
704-50106	Sand (33531)	NEW	1.80
704-50108	Insignia Yellow (33538)	NEW	1.80
704-50109	Radome Tan (33613)	NEW	1.80
704-50110	Dark Green (34079)	NEW	1.80
704-50111	Olive Drab (34087)	NEW	1.80
704-50113	Medium Green (34102)	NEW	1.80
704-50117	Dark Sea Blue (15042)	NEW	1.80
704-50118	Flat Sea Blue (35042)	NEW	1.80
704-50120	Intermediate Blue (35164)	NEW	1.80
704-50121	Medium Gray (35237)	NEW	1.80
704-50123	Gunship Gray (36118)	NEW	1.80
704-50125	Neutral Gray (36270)	NEW	1.80
704-50128	Lt Ghost Gray (36375)	NEW	1.80
704-50129	Gloss Gull Gray (16440)	NEW	1.80
704-50130	Flat Gull Gray (36440)	NEW	1.80
704-50131	Aircraft Gray (16473)	NEW	1.80
704-50132	Light Gray (36495)	NEW	1.80
704-50133	Camouflage Gray (36622)	NEW	1.80
704-50134	Green Zinc Chromate (36622)	NEW	1.80
704-50135	Wood	NEW	1.80
704-50136	Leather	NEW	1.80
704-50137	Primer	NEW	1.80
704-50140	Dark Gull Gray (36231)	NEW	1.80
704-50141	Dark Ghost Gray (36320)	NEW	1.80
704-50142	Dark Tan (30219)	NEW	1.80
704-50145	Insignia White (17875)	NEW	1.80
704-50147	Gloss Black (17038)	NEW	1.80
704-50149	Flat Black (37038)	NEW	1.80
704-50150	Panzer Gray (36076)	NEW	1.80
704-50153	Desert Sand (33637)	NEW	1.80
704-50154	Light Earth (30140)	NEW	1.80
704-50155	Afrika Mustard (30266)	NEW	1.80
704-50159	Clear Satin (20000)	NEW	1.80
704-50160	Clear Flat (30000)	NEW	1.80
704-50161	Clear Gloss (10000)	NEW	1.80
704-50164	European Green (34092)	NEW	1.80
704-50168	Flat White (37875)	NEW	1.80
704-50172	Blue Angel Blue (15050)	NEW	1.80
704-50175	Flourescent Red (28915)	NEW	1.80
704-50180	Steel	NEW	1.80
704-50181	Aluminum	NEW	1.80
704-50185	Rust	NEW	1.80
704-50188	Euro I Gray (36081)	NEW	1.80
704-50191	Navy Gray (16081)	NEW	1.80
704-50192	SAC Tan (34201)	NEW	1.80
704-50193	SAC Green (34159)	NEW	1.80
704-50194	Aggressor Gray (36252)	NEW	1.80
704-50195	Gun Metal	NEW	1.80
704-50196	Jet Exhaust	NEW	1.80

SPRAY ENAMEL

Dealers: MUST order Dealer Pack of 3.

704-1910	Dark Green (34079)	3 oz	3.00
704-1911	Olive Drab (34087)	3 oz	3.00
704-1913	Medium Green (34102)	3 oz	3.00
704-1917	Dark Sea Blue (15042)	3 oz	3.00
704-1920	Intermediate Blue (35164)	3 oz	3.00
704-1923	Gunship Gray (36118)	3 oz	3.00
704-1926	Light Sea Gray (36307)	3 oz	3.00

TESTORS

ENAMEL PAINTS

Testors Pla Enamel paints are available in 1/4 oz bottles and 3oz spray cans. (Enamels are gloss finish unless noted.)

Also available are Thinners and Coatings.

MODEL MASTER

FS ENAMELS SPRAY (continued)

704-1929	Gloss Gull Gray (16440)	3oz	3.00
704-1930	Flat Gull Gray (36440)	3oz	3.00
704-1933	Camouflage Gray (36622)	3oz	3.00
704-1942	Dark Tan (30219)	3oz	3.00
704-1947	Gloss Black (17038)	3oz	3.00
704-1949	Flat Black (37038)	3oz	3.00
704-1950	Panzer Gray (36076)	3oz	3.00
704-1953	Desert Sand (33637)	3oz	3.00
704-1954	Light Earth (30140)	3oz	3.00
704-1955	Afrika Mustard (30266)	3oz	3.00
704-1959	Clear Satin Finish	3oz	3.00
704-1960	Clear Flat Finish	3oz	3.00
704-1961	Clear Gloss Finish	3oz	3.00
704-1972	Blue Angel Blue (15050)	3oz	3.00
704-1988	Euro I Gray (36081)	3oz	3.00
704-1992	SAC Bomber Tan (34201)	3oz	3.00
704-1993	SAC Bomber Green (34159)	3oz	3.00
704-1994	Navy Aggressor (36251) Gray	3oz	3.00

ACRYLIC

704-50401	Military Brown (30117)	NEW	1oz	2.50
704-50405	Insignia Red (31136)	NEW	1oz	2.50
704-50408	Insignia Ylw (33538)	NEW	1oz	2.50
704-50410	Dark Green (34079)	NEW	1oz	2.50
704-50411	Olive Drab (34087)	NEW	1oz	2.50
704-50423	Gunship Gray (36118)	NEW	1oz	2.50
704-50428	Lt Ghost Gray (36375)	NEW	1oz	2.50
704-50429	Gloss Gull Gray (16440)	NEW	1oz	2.50
704-50436	Leather	NEW	1oz	2.50
704-50437	Primer	NEW	1oz	2.50
704-50440	Dark Gull Gray (36231)	NEW	1oz	2.50
704-50442	Dark Tan (30219)	NEW	1oz	2.50
704-50445	Insignia White (17875)	NEW	1oz	2.50
704-50447	Gloss Black (17038)	NEW	1oz	2.50
704-50449	Flat Black (37038)	NEW	1oz	2.50
704-50468	Flat White (37875)	NEW	1oz	2.50
704-50475	Flourescent Red (28915)	NEW	1oz	2.50
704-50480	Steel	NEW	1oz	2.50
704-50481	Aluminum	NEW	1oz	2.50
704-50495	Gun Metal	NEW	1oz	2.50

MODEL MASTER METALIZER

Designed for airbrushing only, these pre-mixed colors are offered in buffing (which can be polished to various degrees of sheen) or nonbuffing colors.

BUFFING

Dealers: MUST order Dealer Pack of 9 Bottles.

704-1401	Aluminum Plate	1/2oz	1.98
704-1402	Stainless Steel	1/2oz	1.98
704-1403	Magnesium	1/2oz	1.98
704-1404	Titanium	1/2oz	1.98
704-1405	Gunmetal	1/2oz	1.98
704-1406	Exhaust	1/2oz	1.98
704-1412	Dark Anodonic Gray	1/2oz	1.98
704-1415	Burnt Metal	1/2oz	1.98

Dealers: MUST order Dealer Pack of 3.

704-1451	Aluminum Plate	3oz	3.00
704-1452	Stainless Steel	3oz	3.00
704-1453	Magnesium	3oz	3.00
704-1454	Titanium	3oz	3.00
704-1455	Gunmetal	3oz	3.00
704-1459	Metalizer Sealer	3oz	3.00

NONBUFFING

Dealers: MUST order Dealer Pack of 9 Bottles.

704-1417	Brass	1/2oz	1.98

704-1418	Aluminum	1/2oz	1.98
704-1420	Steel	1/2oz	1.98
704-1423	Gunmetal	1/2oz	1.98
704-1424	Burnt Iron		1.98

SEALER

1/2ounce bottles.
Dealers: MUST order Dealer Pack of 12.

704-1409	Sealer		1.55

THINNER

1-3/4 ounce bottles.
Dealers: MUST order Dealer Pack of 12.

704-1419	Thinner		1.55

PAINT MARKERS

Fast-drying, enamel with double chisel tip for fine lines or bold strokes. 10cc oz.

Dealers: MUST order Dealer Pack of 6.

704-2503	Gloss Red		2.59
704-2508	Gloss Light Blue		2.59
704-2511	Gloss Dark Blue		2.59
704-2514	Gloss Yellow		2.59
704-2524	Gloss Green		2.59
704-2527	Gloss Orange		2.59
704-2538	Gloss Gray		2.59
704-2540	Gloss Brown		2.59
704-2545	Gloss White		2.59
704-2547	Gloss Black		2.59
704-2544	Metallic Gold		2.59
704-2546	Metallic Silver		2.59
704-2549	Flat Black		2.59
704-2575	Fluorescent Red		2.59

MODELER'S KITS

704-9115	Enamel Kit	set	5.69

Six Pla Enamel and a bottle of thinner. Contains 1/4 ounce bottles of: Red, Yellow, Ultramarine, Silver, White and Black includes brush.

704-9117	Enamel Kit	set	7.99

Nine Pla Enamels and a bottle of thinner. Contains 1/4 ounce bottles of: Red, Yellow, Ultramarine, Emerald Green, Dark Brown, Gold, Silver, White and Black includes brush.

704-9131	Military Flats Kit	7.49

Eight Pla Enamels and a bottle of thinner. Includes brush and tray. Contains 1/4 ounce bottles of: Black, Blue, Gray, Green, Brown, Tan, White and Blue.

704-9146	Promotional Paint Set	6.29
704-9111	Model Building Supplies Kit	6.99

Contains drop cloth, three brushes, hobby knife, five gluing tips and five sanding films.

ACRYLIC PAINT KITS

704-50501	US Aircraft Detailing	6.30
704-50502	Modern US Air Force	6.30
704-50503	Modern US Navy	6.30
704-50504	US Vietnam	6.30
704-50505	US WWII Aircraft	6.30
704-50506	US Armor & Military	6.30

PLASTIC MODEL FINISHING KITS

704-9160	Flat	15.49
704-9161	Gloss	15.49

THINNERS & COATINGS

DECAL SETTING SOLUTION

704-8804	Decal Set	bottle 1/4floz	.98

Dealers: MUST order Dealer pack of 12.

704-1737	Decal Set	bottle 1/2floz	1.75

Dealers: MUST order Dealer pack of 9.

DULLCOTE

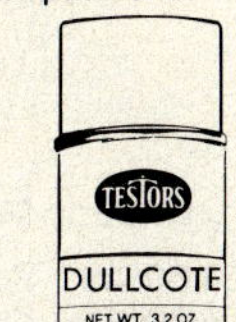

Dullcote is a protective, transparent satin finish that does not alter the color.

Lacquer Bottle

704-1160	1-3/4oz	1.59

Dealers: MUST order Dealer Pack of 12.

704-1260	Spray	3oz	2.75

Dealers: MUST Order Dealer Pack of 3.

GLOSSCOTE

Glosscote is a transparent, high gloss protective finish, that does not alter the color. (Lacquer)

704-1161	Bottle	1-3/4oz	1.59

Dealers: MUST order Dealer Pack of 12.

704-1261	Spray	3oz	2.75

Dealers: MUST Order Dealer Pack of 3.

THINNER & BRUSH CLEANER

704-1148	Thinner	bottle 1/4oz	.98

Dealers: MUST order Dealer Pack of 12.

704-1156	Thinner	bottle 1-3/4oz	1.59

Dealers: MUST order Dealer Pack of 12.

704-1159	Lacquer Brush Cleaner	1oz	1.49

Dealers: MUST order Dealer Pack of 12.

704-1799	Air Brush Thinner	8oz	4.25
704-1789	Air Brush Thinner	1-3/4oz	1.59

Dealers: MUST order Dealer Pack of 12.

704-8824	Air Brush Thinner	1/2pt	4.25
704-8825	Air Brush Thinner	1-3/4oz	4.58

Dealers: MUST order dealer pack of 3.

704-50498	Acrylic Enamel Cleaner		3.95
704-50499	Acrylic Enamel Thinner		3.95

FINISHING CENTER

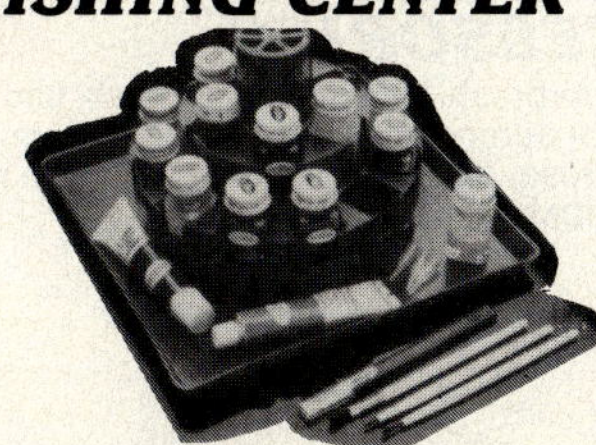

704-9172	Lazy Susan Finishing Center	19.98

Revolving carousel contains 9 gloss & flat enamels, thinner, plastic cement, putty, 3 brushes, knife, gluing tips and drop cloth.

PAINT BRUSHES

SYNTHETIC

Dealers: MUST Order Dealer Pack of 12.

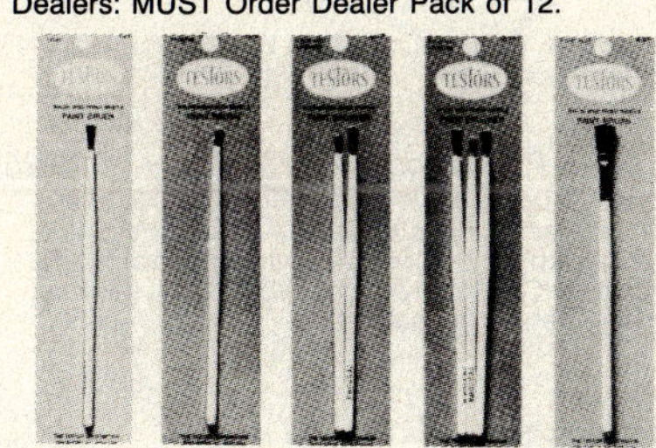

704-8701	Broad Tip	each	.75
704-8702	Fine Tip	each	.75
704-8703	Flat Tip	pkg(2)	.99
704-8704	2 Flat & 1 Pointed	set	1.29
704-8705	1/4" Tip	each	.1.19
704-8706	1 Flat, 1 Pointed, NEW pkg(3)	1.49
	1 — 1/4" Tip		

MODEL MASTER

Dealers: MUST Order Dealer Pack of 12.

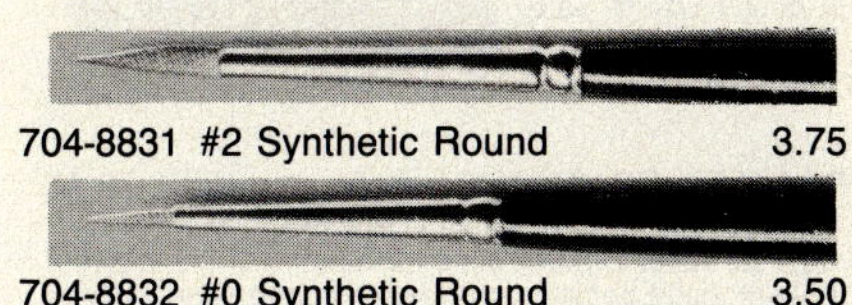

704-8831	#2 Synthetic Round	3.75
704-8832	#0 Synthetic Round	3.50

- PAINT BRUSHES
- AIRBRUSHES
- AIRBRUSH ACCESSORIES

TAMIYA
MODEL RECTIFIER CORP.

PAINT BRUSHES (continued)
MODEL MASTER (continued)

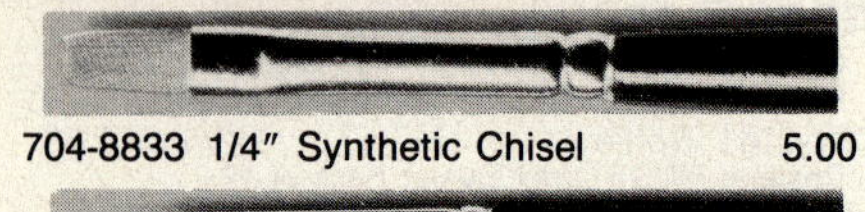

704-8833	1/4" Synthetic Chisel	5.00

704-8842	#3/0 Red Sable Round	3.50

704-8841	#2 Red Sable Round	4.00

704-8851	3/8" Camel Hair Flat	2.75

704-8861	1/2" Black Sable Flat	4.00

AIRBRUSH & ACCESSORIES **NEW**

Each airbrush includes 1 airbrush body, 1 general purpose nozzle, a 2.5cc paint cup, a 6' air hose, an instruction manual and a hard shell case.

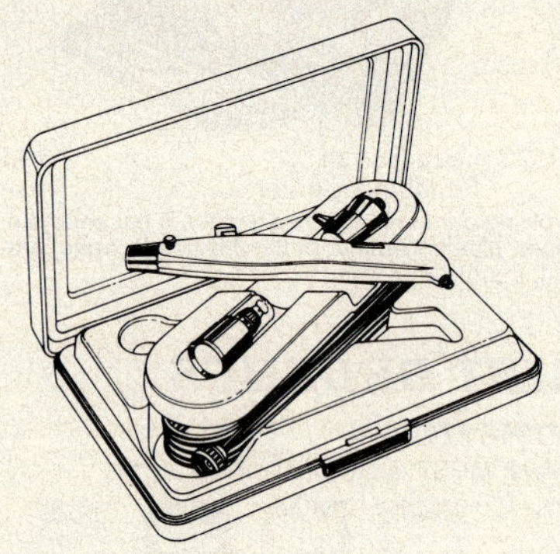

704-50601	Professional Air Kit	79.95

Airbrush is a suction/side feed internal mix instrument that works as both a single-action and double action airbrush. It works with all compressors and with the Air Can Hose Adapter (#50619). It will work with any aerosol propellant.

AIR BRUSH
Airbrush Set
704-8821   29.95

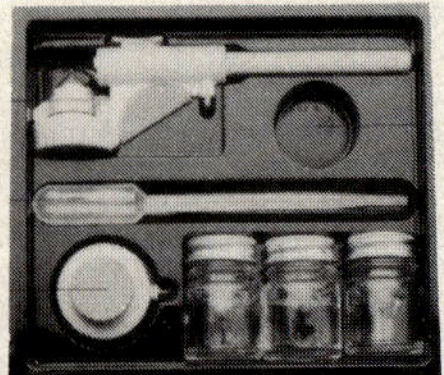

Set includes organizing tray, single-action external mix Airbrush, color mixing pipette, propellant control assembly, three 1/2 oz jars, 6 foot flexible hose, and instruction manual. Also includes 9 ounce Ozone Safe Propellant.

704-50652 GP100 Airbrush Starter Kit   79.95
Includes a GP100 airbrush with storage case, paint cup, air hose, airbrush cleaning station, airbrush propellant, paint bottles, compressor adaptor and more.

PROPELLENT

Ozone Safe
704-8822 15oz   9.00

Ozone Safe
704-8823 9oz   6.50

Nozzles
704-50610	General Purpose	9.95
704-50611	Fine Line	9.95
704-50612	High Flow	9.95
704-50613	Spatter	9.95

PAINT CUPS

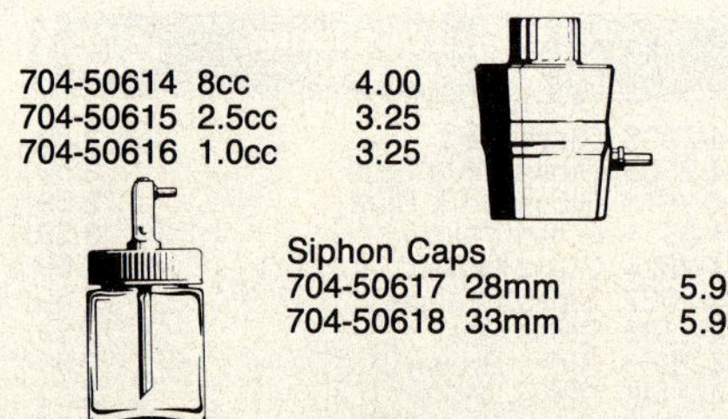

704-50614	8cc	4.00
704-50615	2.5cc	3.25
704-50616	1.0cc	3.25

Siphon Caps
704-50617	28mm	5.95
704-50618	33mm	5.95

Air Can
Hose Adaptor
704-50619
8.95

704-50620 10' Coiled Air Hose   18.95

Airbrush Cleaning
Station
704-50624   29.95

Cleaning Station Filters
704-50621
5.95

Masking Tape
704-50622
3.98

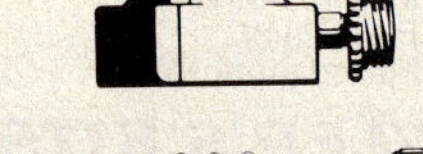

Paint Sprayer
704-50623 23.95

704-50625 Mixing Bottle & Pipette Set   2.98

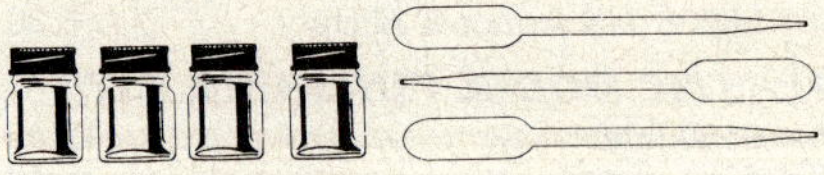

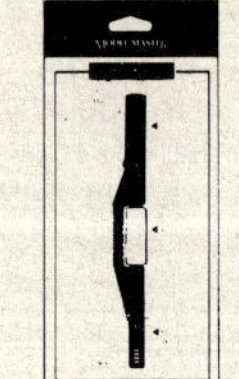

Hobby Knife
704-50626
5.95

Dealers: MUST order dealer pack of 6.

(not illustrated)
Dealers: MUST order dealer pack of 6.

704-50628	Sprue Cutters	12.50
704-50641	Parafilm M Masking Film	7.95
704-50642	Pipettes	2.50

Water soluble acrylic paints & Enamel Paint Markers.

GLOSS ACRYLIC

Tamiya Paints are made from water-soluble acrylic resins and are safe, non-toxic and easy-to-use. Good for use on wood, metal, styrol resins and styro-foam. Apply with brush or spray. 3/4 oz. bottles.

865-101	Black	3/4oz	2.49
865-102	White	3/4oz	2.49
865-103	Royal Blue	3/4oz	2.49
865-104	Blue	3/4oz	2.49
865-105	Green	3/4oz	2.49
865-106	Orange	3/4oz	2.49
865-107	Red	3/4oz	2.49
865-108	Lemon Yellow	3/4oz	2.49
865-109	Brown	3/4oz	2.49
865-110	Gun Metal	3/4oz	2.49
865-111	Chrome Silver	3/4oz	2.49
865-112	Gold Leaf	3/4oz	2.49
865-113	Metallic Blue	3/4oz	2.49
865-114	Sky Blue	3/4oz	2.49
865-115	Light Green	3/4oz	2.49
865-116	Purple	3/4oz	2.49
865-117	Pink	3/4oz	2.49
865-119	Smoke	3/4oz	2.49
865-123	Clear Blue	3/4oz	2.49
865-124	Clear Yellow	3/4oz	2.49
865-125	Clear Green	3/4oz	2.49
865-126	Clear Orange	3/4oz	2.49
865-127	Clear Red	3/4oz	2.49
865-128	Park Green	3/4oz	2.49
865-122	Clear	3/4oz	2.49
865-121	Flat Base	3/4oz	2.49

An agent for making glossy paints any degree of dullness desired. For semigloss add about 15% flat base; for full matt dullness add about 30% flat base.

SEMI-GLOSS ACRYLIC
865-118	Black	3/4oz	2.49

MATT ACRYLIC
865-201	Black	3/4oz	2.49
865-202	White	3/4oz	2.49
865-203	Yellow	3/4oz	2.49
865-204	Yellow Green	3/4oz	2.49
865-205	Green	3/4oz	2.49
865-206	Copper	3/4oz	2.49
865-207	Red	3/4oz	2.49
865-208	Blue	3/4oz	2.49
865-209	Hull Red	3/4oz	2.49
865-210	Brown	3/4oz	2.49
865-211	JN Green	3/4oz	2.49
865-212	JN Gray	3/4oz	2.49
865-213	JA Green	3/4oz	2.49
865-214	JA Gray	3/4oz	2.49
865-215	Flesh	3/4oz	2.49
865-216	Aluminum	3/4oz	2.49
865-217	Sea Blue	3/4oz	2.49
865-218	Medium Blue	3/4oz	2.49
865-219	Sky Gray	3/4oz	2.49
865-220	Medium Gray	3/4oz	2.49
865-221	Sky	3/4oz	2.49
865-222	RLM Gray	3/4oz	2.49
865-223	Light Blue	3/4oz	2.49
865-224	Dark Gray	3/4oz	2.49
865-225	Light Sea Gray	3/4oz	2.49
865-226	Deep Green	3/4oz	2.49
865-227	Black Green	3/4oz	2.49
865-249	Khaki	3/4oz	2.49
865-250	Field Blue	3/4oz	2.49
865-251	Khaki Drab	3/4oz	2.49

(continued on next page)

TAMIYA
MODEL RECTIFIER CORP.

(continued)

Water soluble acrylic paints & Enamel Paint Markers.

865-252	Earth	3/4oz	2.49
865-253	Neutral Gray	3/4oz	2.49
865-254	Dark Sea Gray	3/4oz	2.49
865-255	Deck Tan	3/4oz	2.49
865-256	Metallic Gray	3/4oz	2.49
865-257	Buff	3/4oz	2.49
865-258	Olive Green	3/4oz	2.49
865-259	Desert Yellow	3/4oz	2.49
865-260	Dark Yellow	3/4oz	2.49
865-261	Dark Green	3/4oz	2.49
865-262	Olive Drab	3/4oz	2.49
865-263	German Gray	3/4oz	2.49
865-264	Red Brown	3/4oz	2.49
865-265	Field Gray	3/4oz	2.49
865-266	Light Gray	3/4oz	2.49

ACRYLIC THINNER

Use for adjusting the thickness of the paints for brushing & spraying. For spray painting, about 15% of thinner to paint is recommended.

865-301	Thinner	3/4oz	2.49

ENAMEL GLOSS MARKERS

Enamel Paint Markers are used as you would use a marking pen. Good for use on plastic, wood, metal and glass, and can be applied over acrylics and lacquers. Tip is 4mm x 1mm. 8 grams.

865-505	Green	8 grams	3.31
865-506	Orange	8 grams	3.31
865-507	Red	8 grams	3.31
865-512	Gold Leaf	8 grams	3.31

ENAMEL MATT MARKER

865-531	Black	8 grams	3.31
865-532	Flesh	8 grams	3.31

BRUSHES

HORSE HAIR

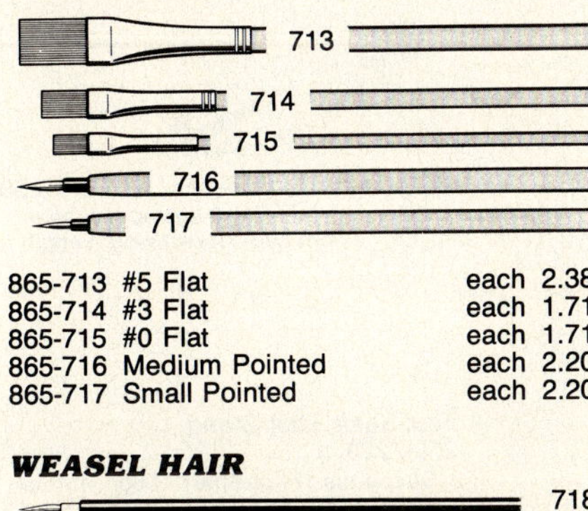

865-713	#5 Flat	each	2.38
865-714	#3 Flat	each	1.71
865-715	#0 Flat	each	1.71
865-716	Medium Pointed	each	2.20
865-717	Small Pointed	each	2.20

WEASEL HAIR

865-718	Medium Pointed	each	6.80
865-719	Small Pointed	each	5.56

AIR BRUSH

865-74501	Spray Works Airbrush System	**NEW**	177.76

pactra

ACRYLIC ENAMELS

Fast drying, non-toxic paint. Most flat colors match popular Federal Standard (FS) colors. Acrylic Enamels are water-based and non-flammable. Can be used on plastics, wood, metal, paper, plaster and other paintable surfaces. Can be brushed or sprayed without thinning (or mixed with water for thinner consistency). 2/3oz bottles fit most Badger airbrushes. Equipment can be cleaned with soap and water. Dries to a hard gloss or flat finish. Military colors match Federal Standard number shown on cap.

Dealer MUST order Dealer Pack of 6.

GLOSS

545-1101	Black	2/3oz	2.25
545-1102	White	2/3oz	2.25
545-1103	Royal Blue	2/3oz	2.25
545-1104	Medium Blue	2/3oz	2.25
545-1105	Sea Blue	2/3oz	2.25
545-1106	Dark Red	2/3oz	2.25
545-1107	Insignia Red	2/3oz	2.25
545-1108	Lemon Yellow	2/3oz	2.25
545-1109	Aircraft Gray	2/3oz	2.25
545-1110	Military Green	2/3oz	2.25
545-1111	Green	2/3oz	2.25
545-1112	Light Green	2/3oz	2.25
545-1113	Orange	2/3oz	2.25
545-1114	Brown	2/3oz	2.25
545-1115	Pink	2/3oz	2.25
545-1116	Purple	2/3oz	2.25
545-1117	Wood Tan	2/3oz	2.25
545-1118	Clear	2/3oz	2.25
545-1155	Pearl White	2/3oz	2.25

FLUORESCENT GLOSS

545-1156	Red	2/3oz	2.25
545-1157	Orange	2/3oz	2.25
545-1158	Yellow +	2/3oz	2.25
545-1159	Blue	2/3oz	2.25
545-1160	Magenta	2/3oz	2.25

FLAT

545-1119	Skin Tone Base	2/3oz	2.25
545-1120	Africa Yellow	2/3oz	2.25
545-1121	Hull Red	2/3oz	2.25
545-1122	Dark Earth	2/3oz	2.25
545-1123	Light Earth	2/3oz	2.25
545-1124	Drab Brown	2/3oz	2.25
545-1125	Dark Tan	2/3oz	2.25
545-1126	Insignia Red +	2/3oz	2.25
545-1127	Insignia Yellow	2/3oz	2.25
545-1128	Light Tan +	2/3oz	2.25
545-1129	Jungle Green	2/3oz	2.25
545-1130	Olive	2/3oz	2.25
545-1131	Dark Green	2/3oz	2.25
545-1132	Marine Green	2/3oz	2.25
545-1133	Medium Green	2/3oz	2.25
545-1134	Artillery Olive +	2/3oz	2.25
545-1135	Interior Green +	2/3oz	2.25
545-1136	Military Blue	2/3oz	2.25
545-1137	Medium Gray	2/3oz	2.25
545-1138	Dark Gull Gray	2/3oz	2.25
545-1139	Neutral Gray	2/3oz	2.25
545-1140	Light Gray	2/3oz	2.25
545-1141	Dark Flyer Gray	2/3oz	2.25
545-1142	Light Flyer Gray	2/3oz	2.25
545-1143	Gull Gray	2/3oz	2.25
545-1144	Light Gray	2/3oz	2.25
545-1145	Camouflage Gray	2/3oz	2.25
545-1146	Black	2/3oz	2.25
545-1147	White	2/3oz	2.25
545-1148	Clear	2/3oz	2.25
545-1149	Navy Blue +	2/3oz	2.25
545-1150	Zinc Chromate Green	2/3oz	2.25
545-1151	Rust	2/3oz	2.25
545-1152	Mud	2/3oz	2.25
545-1153	Weathering	2/3oz	2.25
545-1154	Gun Metal	2/3oz	2.25

ACRYLIC PAINT KITS

Includes an assortment of nine 1/4oz bottles of paints, 3 brushes (flat, pointed and 1/4" flat) and an organizing tray.

545-500	Hobby & Craft +	pkg(9 — 1/4oz)	7.49

545-501 +	Car Model Set	pkg(9—1/4oz)	7.49
545-505 +	Aircraft Model Set	pkg(9—1/4oz)	7.49

SPRAY ENAMEL SETS

Neon flourescent, fast drying durable paints.
Dealer MUST order Dealer Pack of 3.

LARGE

545-151	Orange	3oz	2.75
545-152	Green	3oz	2.75
545-153	Red	3oz	2.75
545-154	Yellow	3oz	2.75
545-155	Pink	3oz	2.75

FLECK STONE

Three-dimensional textured spray paint for scenery and landscaping. Contains one 12 ounce multi-hue textured base coat and one 6 oz clear, flat acrylic topcoat. Easy to follow instructions.

545-34	Ironstone		14.98
545-35	Serpentine Marble		14.98
545-36	Soap Stone		14.98
545-37	Rose Quartz		14.98
545-38	Canyon Rock		14.98
545-39	Alabaster		14.98
545-40	Sand		14.98
545-41	Turquoise Dust +		14.98
545-42	Pueblo Sunset		14.98
545-43	City Lights		14.98
545-44	Manhattan Mist		14.98
545-45	Gotham Gray		14.98
545-46	Earth Brown		14.98
545-47	Dark Meadow Green		14.98
545-48	Light Turf Green		14.98

THINNERS & COATINGS

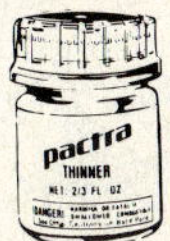

Enamel Thinner

545-204	3-1/2oz	2.89

Dealer must buy dealer-pack of 6.

Pactra Primer/Surfacer

545-4116+		16oz	7.49

Dual purpose primer and surfacer for filling nicks, dents and scratches. Can be used on plastics, wood, metal, fiberglass, silk or previously painted surfaces. May be brushed or sprayed.

545-4216	Pactra Prep Thinner+	16oz	5.29

Use to thin Pactra Prep for spraying.

DREMEL®
CREATIVE POWER TOOLS

WARNING: Wear safety glasses when using MOTO-TOOLS!

MOTO-TOOL®
- HOUSING — Sturdy, shockproof, double insulated housing of fiber reinforced nylon
- MOTOR SPECIFICATION — 115v, 50-60 Hz, AC, 1.15 amp
- CORD — 6 ft, 2-wire, cord does not require adapter plug
- COLLET SIZES — from 1/32 to 1/8"

MOTO-TOOL®
MINIMITE

250-750 Moto-Tool 50.50
Model 750 Cordless Rotary Tool with 5 accessories.

250-755 Removable Battery Pack 21.00
Model 750

250-756 Battery Charger 10.70
Model 750

VARIABLE SPEED

250-395 Variable Speed Moto-Tool only 115.50
Features 5,000 to 30,000 rpm, 6'2" wire flexible coil cord, 1/8" collet and finger tip control.

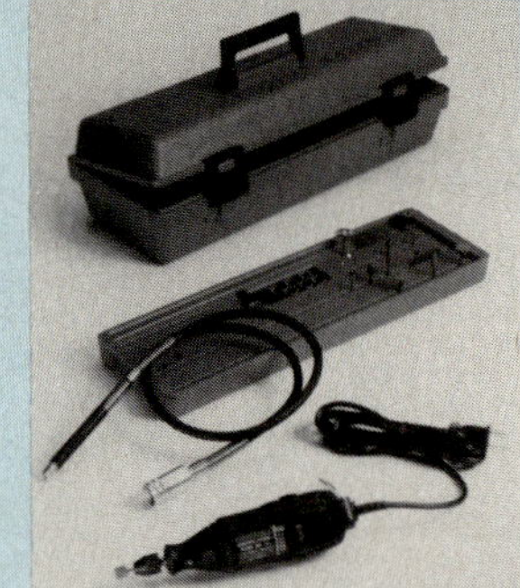

250-3952 Moto-Tool Super Kit NEW 149.00
(not illustrated)
250-5950 Variable Speed Moto-Tool 108.39

SINGLE-SPEED

250-275 1-Speed Moto-Tool only 60.00
28,000 rpm, high speed tool

CORDLESS

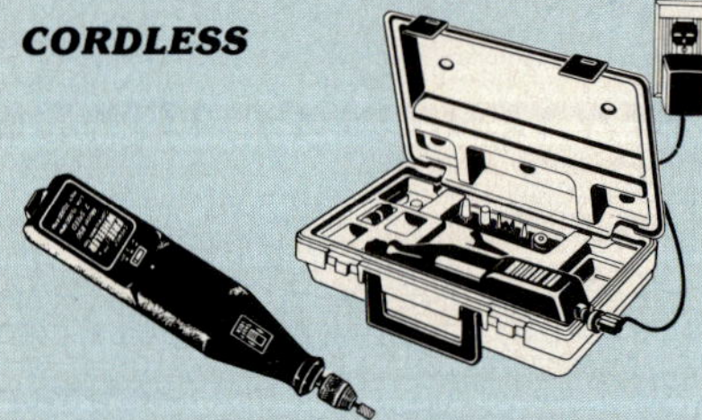

250-8508 FREEWHEELER™ 106.50
Includes cordless Moto-Tool and 30 bits and accessories for cutting, cleaning, engraving, grinding, sharpening, polishing, sanding and drilling. Keyless chuck for easy replacement of bits and accessories, plug-in charging; carrying case and book, *175+ USES.*

250-15008 Freewheeler Plug-In Case 9.45

KITS

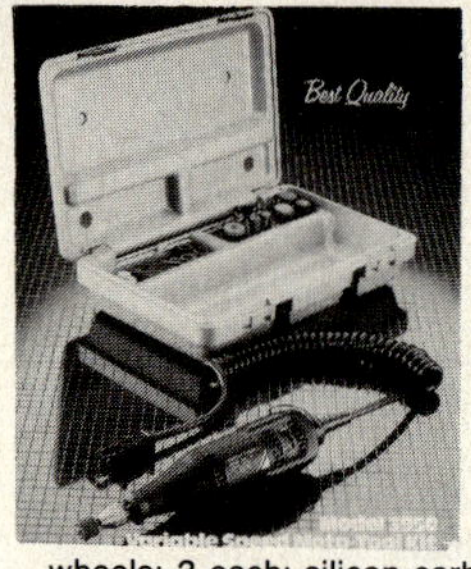

Variable Speed Moto-Tool w/Accessories
250-3950 131.50

Kit includes: #395 Moto-Tool, carrying case, 6 cutoff wheels, 7 sanding discs, 2 each: mandrels, engraving cutters, felt polishing wheels; 3 each: silicon carbide grinding stones, aluminum oxide grinding stones, sanding bands, cutters; 1 each: 3/32" collet, 1/8" drill, cup brush, paste brush, wrench, dressing stone, keyless chuck, polishing wheel and drum sander.

2-Speed Moto-Tool w/Accessories
250-2850 105.00

Kit includes: #285 Moto-Tool, carrying case, 6 cutoff wheels, 3 sanding discs, 2 each: mandrels, felt polishing wheels, silicon carbide grinding stones, aluminum oxide grinding stones, sander bands; 1 each: 3/32" collet, 1/8" drill, cup brush, paste brush, wrench, dressing stone, keyless chuck, polishing wheel, drumsander, cutter and engraving cutter.

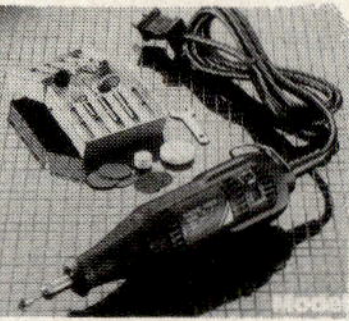

1-Speed Moto-Tool w/Accessories
250-2750 72.50
Kit includes: #275 Moto-Tool, accessory holder, 3 each: cutoff wheels & sanding discs; 2 each: mandrels & felt polishing wheels; 1 each: aluminum oxide grinding stone, silicon carbide grinding stone, wrench, cup brush and 1/8" drill.

ACCESSORY SETS
250-605 Cutting and Carving Bit Set 14.67
20 piece set to be used only with Moto-Tool and Flex-Shaft tools.

250-624 Cleaning and Polishing Bit Set 21.55
16 piece set to be used only with Moto-Tool and Flex-Shaft tools.

HOLDER
Holds Moto-Tool firmly in any desired position so you can use both hands to control work piece. Includes Moto-Tool holder, post and adjustable base.

MOTO-TOOL Holder & Base
250-2217 41.00

MOTO-FLEX®

250-232 MOTO-FLEX Tool 142.00
Motor: 1.0 amps, 115v, AC only, universal type, sleeve bearing. Speed: 25,000 rpm. Chuck Capacity: Max collet size 1/8". Furnished complete with motor, flexible shaft with 1/8" collet and base.

250-332 Variable Speed MOTO-FLEX Tool 150.50
(By Special Order Only.)

- Solid State Variable Speed Control-7,500-25,000 RPM
- 3-Position Selector Switch
- Lightweight Aluminum, Ball-Bearing Handpiece
- 34" Neoprene Covered Flex-Shaft with Spring Type Strain Reliefs
- Impact Resistant Motor Housing
- 360% Detachable Swivel Base
- Built-In Hanger
- .09 amp Motor

Includes 1 open end wrench, 1 right angle wrench.

MOTO-FLEX® ACCESSORIES

Right Angle Wrench
250-70126 1.10

For easy insertion and removal of accessories. To be used with #232 or #332.

250-90952 Shaft Lubrication 1oz 2.75
Helps increase shaft life for smooth, consistent, trouble free use. To be used with Moto-Flex Tool or variable speed Moto-Flex Tool. This lubricant is also helpful with the flexible shaft found in the Moto-Shop kits.

HEAVY DUTY FLEX-SHAFT TOOL

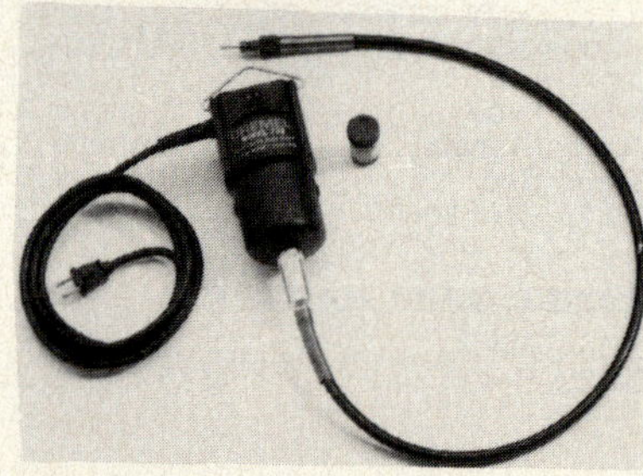

250-732 (By Special Order Only.) 153.00
High torque, ball bearing, smooth running motor with 1/5 horsepower for grinding & shaping. Base model includes H.D. Flex-Shaft tool, 39" Flex-Shaft with quick disconnect feature that will accept most standard handpieces.

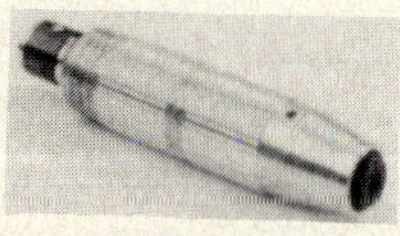

250-236 Heavy Duty Handpiece 75.50
1# diameter aluminum housing & sealed ball bearings for long life, smooth and cool running. Length 5-1/4".

Flex-Shaft Tool Stand
250-2222 35.50
Suspends Flex-Shaft Tool above workbench. Adjustable height from 12-42". Clamps to table or work bench 2" thick. Holds 12 bits & stores handpiece.

DREMEL®
CREATIVE POWER TOOLS

WARNING: Wear safety glasses when using MOTO-TOOLS!

PRO-BONDER GLUE GUN KIT
TABLE SAW
DISC AND BELT SANDER
MOTO-LATHE ®

SOLDERING IRONS
ELECTRIC ENGRAVER
SPEED CONTROLS
D-VISE

MOTO-SHOP ® ACCESSORIES

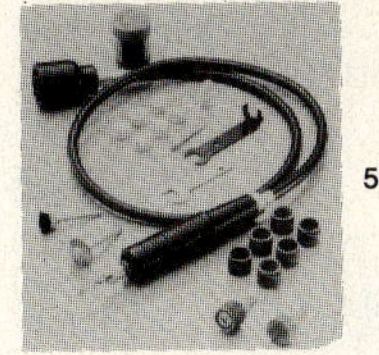
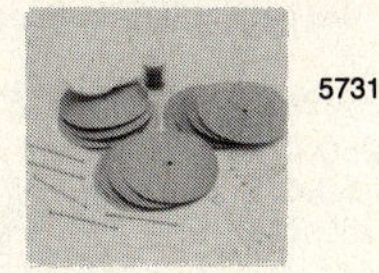

250-5730 Flexible Shaft Accessory Set 44.00
23 pieces **(By Special Order Only.)**

250-90199 Flexible Shaft 31.65
(By Special Order Only.)

ARBOR ADAPTORS
250-4211 for Pad & Cloth Wheel 3.35
250-4214 Rubber Backing Pad 2.75
4" dia for adapter 250-4211

SANDING DISCS
250-4227 1/2 Grit coarse pkg(6) 3.00
(By Special Order Only.)
250-4228 2/0 Grit medium pkg(6) 3.00
(By Special Order Only.)
250-4229 4/0 Grit fine pkg(6) 3.00
(By Special Order Only.)
250-4235 Buffing Wheel 3.00
3" dia, cloth, for adapter 250-4211
(By Special Order Only.)

SAW BLADES
for use with #1571 & 572
250-8029 Fine Blades pkg(5) 2.75
250-8030 Coarse Blades pkg(5) 3.00

SCROLL SAW

250-1571 Scroll Saw 15" 141.00
250-1671 Scroll Saw 16" 293.50
2 speed, 2" cutting capacity
(By Special Order Only.)

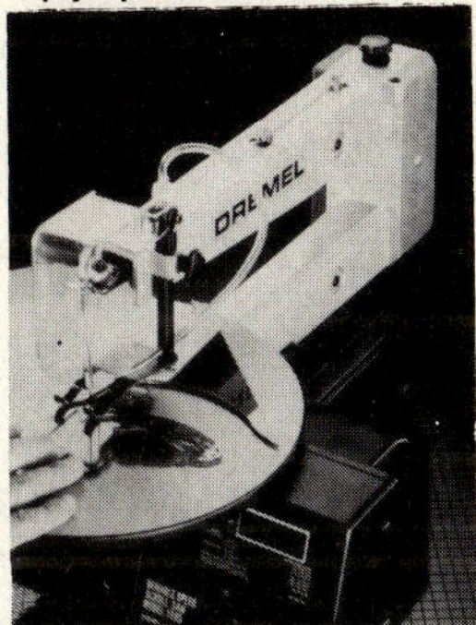

250-1695 Scroll Saw 16" 398.00
(By Special Order Only.)
Variable Speed, LED Blade Strokes per minute indicator, 120VAC Motor, 45° Tilt Table, Saw dust blower & Blade tension control. **(By Special Order Only.)**

250-16412 5" Blade Pin Type 10 pkg(5) 4.45
250-16413 5" Blade Pin Type 18.5 pkg(5) 4.20

TABLE SAW ACCESSORIES
250-8003 4" Combination Blade 10.65
1/2" Arbor, 30 teeth per inch
250-8004 4" Fine Tooth Blade 10.65
1/2" Arbor, 100 teeth per inch
250-8015 Drive Belt for #580 Table Saw 6.90

■ LIMITED QUANTITIES AVAILABLE ■
250-8013 Vacuum Cleaner Attachment 2.90

DISC AND BELT SANDER

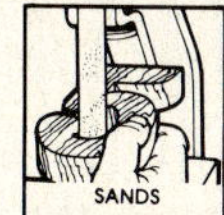

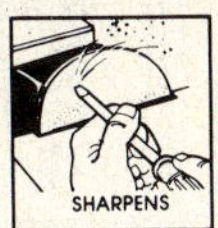

250-1731 Disc & Belt Sander 185.00
Portable lightweight, 15 lbs, 11-3/4 x 13-1/2 x 16", 45° up & down table adjustment with miter gauge. Sharpens, sands, deburrs, polishes and finishes woods, plastics, metals and ceramics.

BELTS
For Sander #'s 730, 1630, 1631 & 1731
Cloth belts 1" x 30"   pkg(2) 6.90
250-8040 50 grit   250-8043 180 grit
250-8041 80 grit   250-8044 240 grit
250-8042 120 grit 250-8045 320 grit

For Sander #'s 730 & 731
Cloth disc 5"   pkg(5) 6.90
250-8050 50 grit
250-8051 80 grit
250-8052 120 grit

D-VISE & ACCESSORIES

The D-Vise can accommodate objects up to 2-1/2" thick and has removable v-grooved jaws and soft jaw pads.

The 3-point, non-rocking base which can be mounted at edge of a workbench has a ball swivel with a twist-lock ring that can lock vise in any position.

Also the Moto-Tool Holder can be used with this base.

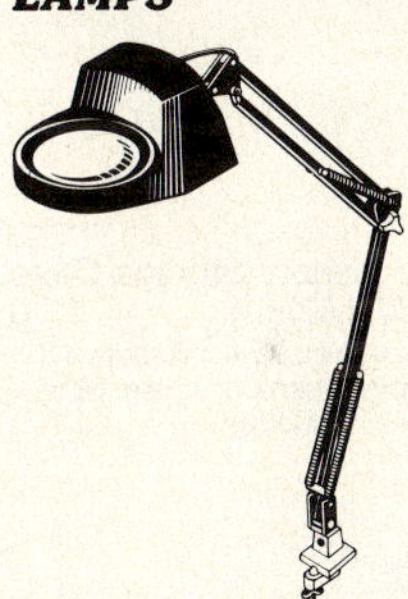

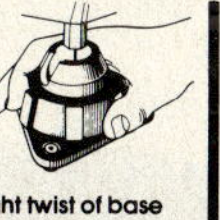

250-2214 D-Vise and Base 40.00
250-2213 Moto-Tool Holder & Clamp 20.50
(By Special Order Only.)

MISCELLANEOUS
ELECTRIC ENGRAVER

Electric Engraver
250-290
24.00

Writes like a pencil on metals, plastics or glass. With carbide point. Features adjustable dial to regulate engraving depth.

250-9924 Carbide Engraving Point 6.55
(By Special Order Only.)
250-9929 Diamond Engraving Point 20.55

SPEED CONTROLS
Motor Speed Controller
250-219   63.00

Solid state speed Controller is a perfect partner for the Moto-Tool kits. Dials any speed from 0 to full rpm.

SAFETY GLASSES
Safety Glasses
250-1228
6.90

LAMPS

3 Diopter Magnifier Lamp
250-1304   33.00
4" diameter lens & 40 watt incandescent bulb (included with lamp). 3 diopter lens enlarges the viewed area clearly and allows hands free to work. Constructed of metal and nylon; black enamel finish. 39" long flexible arm rotates 360%. Includes mounting bracket. (Black only)

WRENCH

250-90962 Open End Wrench 1.35

MOTO-TOOL ® ACCESSORIES
DRILL PRESS STAND

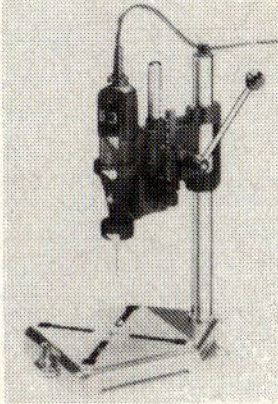

Drill Press Stand for models #275, 285 & 395
250-212   56.50
(Less Moto-Tool)

ROUTER/SHAPER TABLE
250-231 Router/Shaper Table 41.50
(By Special Order Only.)
Converts Moto-Tool into bench mounted wood shaper. Clamps on workbench for slotting, edge trimming, pilot bit routing and sanding. Use with #245, 250, 270, 275, 280, 285, 2750 and Freewheeler Model 850.

ROUTER ATTACHMENTS
250-616 Moto-Tool Finger Grip 2.75
Attaches to Moto-Tools #245, 260, 270, 280, 370 & 380 for easier handling and better control.

DREMEL®
CREATIVE POWER TOOLS

WARNING: Wear safety glasses when using MOTO-TOOLS!

LAMPS
MOTO-TOOL® ACCESSORIES
ROUTER BITS
MANDRELS

CUTTERS AND COLLETS
MOTOR BRUSHES
SANDERS

+ (PLUS SIGN) = SPECIAL ORDER ONLY ITEMS.

ROUTER ATTACHMENTS (continued)

250-55090 Adaptor Sleeve +   3.50
Required for #260 Moto-Tool when it is used with the #2215 or #2217 Moto-Tool Holder, #228 Deluxe Router Kit, #229 Router Attachment, and the #210 Drill Press.

Router Attachment
250-230   33.00
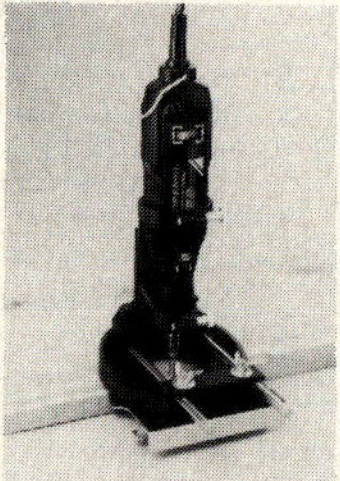
Attachment will shape edges, cut rabbets, dadoes, mortise, tongue and groove, slot and chamfer. Also rout circles from 2-1/2 to 4" radius. Features screw adjustment and lock for accurate depth settings as fine as .010 of an inch, large round base and reversible edge guide adjustable from 0 to 4-1/2".

250-221 Foot Operated   64.00
       Speed Control
Variable speed control to power HD Flex tool. Speed from 0-20,000 RPM.

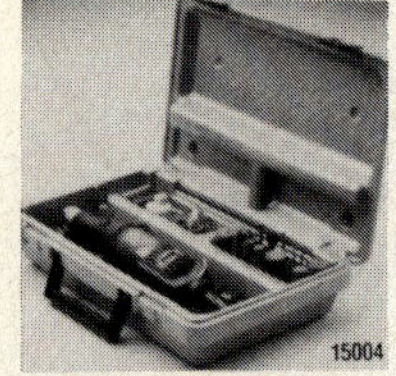
Moto-Tool Storage Case
250-15004   8.65
Holds Moto-Tool and wide assortment of bits. (Tool & bits not included)

15004

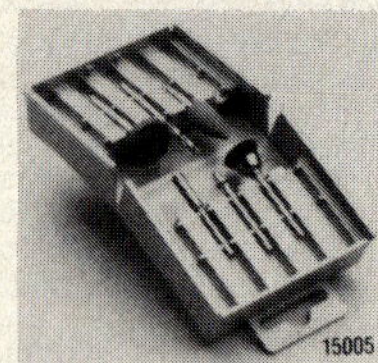
Accessory Storage Case
250-15005 +   1.90
Organizes & protects 10 bits when not in use. (Bits not included)

15005

HIGH SPEED STEEL CARVING CUTTERS   each 5.65
1/8" steel shanks

250-124   250-115
250-131 +   250-116
250-134   250-117
250-141 +   250-178
250-144   250-118
250-189   250-125

each 5.45

250-190   250-197
250-191   250-198
250-192   250-199
250-100 +   250-193
5.65

250-114   250-194
5.65
250-121   250-196
5.65

HIGH SPEED CUTTER SETS
250-326 6 pieces   25.00
Includes #'s 115, 125, 134, 144, 192 and 196.

SMALL ENGRAVING CUTTERS   ea 2.75
3/32" shanks only

ENLARGED VIEW   ENLARGED VIEW   ENLARGED VIEW

105   106   107   108   109   110   111   112   113

TUNGSTEN CARBIDE CUTTERS   each 10.45
1/8" shanks w/maximum cutting head of 1/8"

250-9901   250-9902
250-9903   250-9909
250-9904   250-9910
250-9905   250-9911
250-9906   250-9912

250-9923 3 Piece Set +   35.90
Includes #'s 9931, 9933 and 9935.
250-9925 5 Piece Set +   44.55
Includes #'s 9901, 9903, 9905, 9908 and 9912.
250-9931   Slim Taper   14.65
250-9932   Ball Nose   14.65
250-9933   Cylindrical   14.65
250-9936   Wheel Shape (rotor saw)   14.65
250-9934   Wide Taper   14.65
250-9935   Round   14.65

CHUCK COLLETS
for Moto-Tools 260, 270 & 280
250-434   1/8"   3.75
250-435   3/32"   7.20
250-436   1/16"   7.20
250-437   1/32"   7.20
for Moto-Tools Series 2 or later
250-480   1/8"   2.75
250-481   3/32"   2.75
250-482   1/16"   3.00
250-483   1/32"   3.00

MOTOR BRUSHES
250-90828   Carbon Brush   pkg(2) 3.90
250-90826   For #260 Moto-Tool   pkg(2) 3.90
250-90827   270, 280, 370, 380, 395   pkg(2) 3.90
250-90825   For #245, 250, 246, 275, 2750   pkg(2) 3.90
250-90929   For #275, 285, 395   pkg(2) 3.90

ALUMINUM OXIDE ABRASIVE WHEEL
250-500   1" Diameter Medium Grit   6.10
250-501   1" Diameter Fine Grit   6.10

CUT-OFF WHEELS
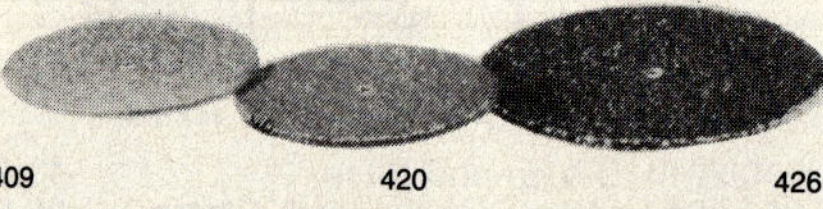
409   420   426
250-409   Cut-off Wheel   pkg(36) 5.65
.025" thick, 15/16" dia.

250-420 Heavy Duty   pkg(20) 6.10
.40" thick 15/16" dia.
250-426 Super Duty   pkg(5) 8.20
Fiberglass (1-1/4" dia.) long lasting. Larger diameter for cutting thicker materials.

SANDING DISCS   each 3.10
250-411   Coarse   pkg(36)
250-412   Medium   pkg(36)
250-413   Fine   pkg(36)

1/2" DIAMETER DRUM SANDER & BANDS
250-407   Drum Sander   ea 3.75
250-408   Coarse Grit   pkg(6) 2.75
250-432   Fine Grit   pkg(6) 2.75

BRUSHES
Not to be used over 15,000 rpm.

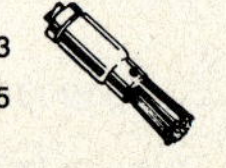
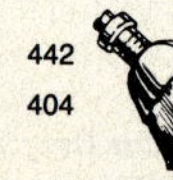

443   442   428
405   404   403

250-428   Wire   2.75   250-403   Bristle   2.75
250-442   Wire   2.75   250-404   Bristle   2.75
250-443   Wire   2.75   250-405   Bristle   2.75

MANDRELS
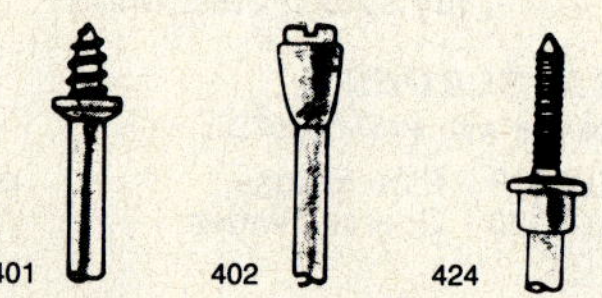
401   402   424

250-401   Screw Mandrel   2.75
used w/polishing accessories, 1/8" shank
250-402   Mandrel   2.75
used w/wheels, sanding discs, polishing wheels, 1/8" shank
250-424   Screw Mandrel used w/427   2.75
used w/427 polishing wheel, 1/8" shank
250-460   Polishing Point & Mandrel   5.00

STEEL ROUTER BITS

250-610   1/4" dia   8.75
250-632   1/4" dia   8.20
250-640   1/4" dia +   8.20
250-650   1/8" dia   8.20
250-652   3/16" dia   8.20
250-654   1/4" dia   8.20
250-612   3/32"   9.65
250-613   3/16"   9.65
250-614   1/8"   9.65

250-602   High Speed Router Bit Set +   45.35
Use with router attachment #229. Includes router bits #610, 613, 614, 615, 650 and 654.

DREMEL®
CREATIVE POWER TOOLS

WARNING: Wear safety glasses when using MOTO-TOOLS!

ROUTER BITS
GRINDING POINTS
TOOL KIT
WHEEL POINTS
DRILLS
BOOKS

MOUNTED EMERY WHEEL POINTS
each 2.75

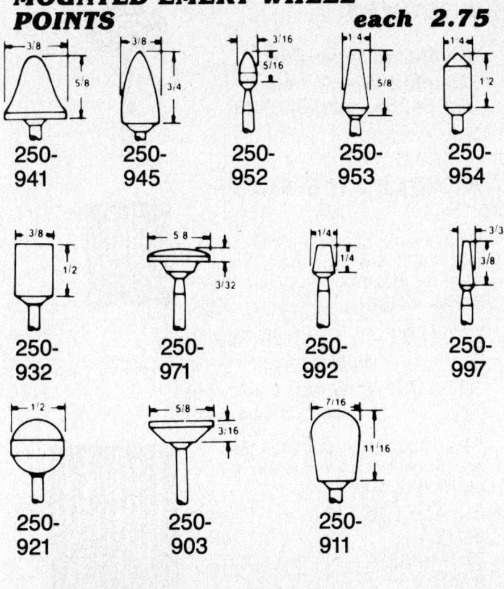

250-941	250-945	250-952	250-953	250-954
250-932	250-971	250-992	250-997	
250-921	250-903	250-911		

PLAIN SHAPED WHEEL POINTS
each 2.75

1/8" shanks
Dimensions in inches

Number	D	T	Number	D	T
250-8153	3/16x3/8		250-8173	3/8x1/8	
250-8215	1x1/8		250-8175	3/16x3/8	
250-8160	1/4x1/4		250-8181	5/8 x 1/8	
			250-8193	5/8x3/8	

DIAMOND WHEEL POINTS

250-7103	11.55	250-7117	11.55
250-7105	11.55		
250-7122	11.55	250-7120	11.55
250-7134	11.55		
250-7144	11.55	250-7123	11.55

250-9927 4 Piece Set 31.10

POLISHING WHEELS

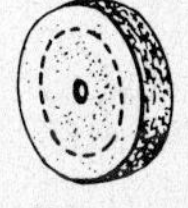

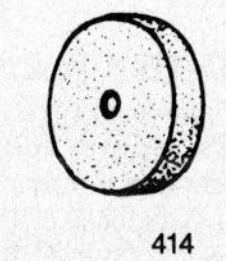

250-423 Cloth Polishing Wheel 1" dia 2.75
use 402 mandrel

250-422 Felt Polishing Tip 3/8" diameter 2.75
use 401 mandrel

250-414 1/2" dia Felt Polishing Wheel 2.75
use 402 mandrel

250-429 1" dia Felt Polishing Wheel 2.75
use mandrel 402, 1/2" diameter

250-425 Emery Impregnated 2.75
used with #402 mandrel, 7/8" dia

250-421 Polishing Compound 2.75

POLISHING POINTS

250-427 Emery Impregnated 2.75
use with #424 mandrel

250-303 6 Piece Rubber Set 12.65
250-461 Polishing Rubber Cylinder 2.75

SILICON GRINDING POINTS ea 2.75

250-83142		
250-83322		250-85422
250-83702		250-85562
250-84382		250-85602
250-84642		250-85622
250-84922		

250-306 6 Piece Silicon Carbide Grinding Stone Set 12.65

DRILLS

250-150 1/8" Drill, HS Steel 2.75

CHAIN SAW SHARPENING TOOL KIT

250-452 Attachment Kit 17.50
Fastens to Moto-Tools 245, 250, 260, 275, 2170, 280, 370, 380, 295 & 2401. Includes sharpening attachment, 3 grinding wheels, gauge, spacers and instructions.

GRINDING WHEELS FOR CHAINSAW SHARPENING KIT

250-453 5/32" grinding wheel pkg(2) 5.00
250-454 3/16" grinding wheel pkg(2) 5.00
250-455 7/32" grinding wheel pkg(2) 5.00

ACCESSORY SETS

250-90349 Accessory Set (34pc) 52.45
Includes the following:

1 mandrel (402)	1 collet (481)
1 bristle brush (403)	3 cutoff wheels (409)
1 bristle brush (404)	7 sanding discs (412)
1 bristle brush (405)	3 sanding discs (408)
1 drum sander (407)	1 polishing wheel (414)
1 dressing stone (415)	1 polishing wheel (425)
1 emery wheel point (921)	1 polishing wheel (429)
1 emery wheel point (932)	1 twist drill (150)
1 emery wheel point (952)	1 HS steel cutter (192)
1 emery wheel point (973)	1 mandrel (401)
1 plain shaped whl pt (8208)	1 wrench
1 silicon grinding point (85422)	
1 silicon grinding point (85602)	

250-300 6 Piece Engraving Cutter Set 12.65
250-316 6 Piece Aluminum Grinding Stone Set 12.65

MISCELLANEOUS

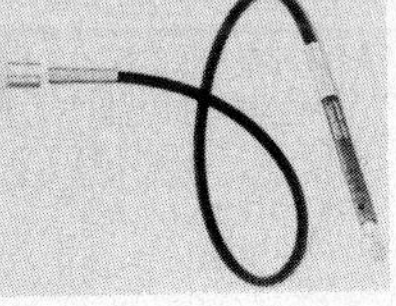

MOTO-TOOL Flex-Shaft
250-225 36.50

250-415 Dressing Stone 2.75
250-90800 Repair Kit for Moto-Tools 8.20

Keyless Finger Chuck
250-4480 6.55
for #s 275, 285 & 395

Adapter Sleeve
250-55091 3.65
for #'s 275, 285 & 395

250-851 Freewheeler Charger Unit 10.70
For model #850, three hour re-charge time.

250-852 Freewheeler Charger Stand 6.10

CORDLESS TOOLS

348-11001 Soldering Iron 14.98
Operates on 4(C-size) batteries. Heats in ten seconds. After use, tip can be retracted. An inlet is provided for battery recharging from any AC/DC adapters with output between 4.5 to 6 volts. Spare soldering tip and flux wire included.

348-11002 Power Scissors 13.98
Operates on 2 (C-size) batteries. Rapid cutting movements provides fast, precise cuts. Blades are stainless tool steel, heat treated to 58 degree of hardness.

The unit stands upright and is covered with a clear lid which is a magnifying glass by itself.

RIGHT ANGLE DRIVE

Drill, grind, polish and more in places that are tight or around corners. Easy to attach and uses the same collet system as the Moto-Tool.

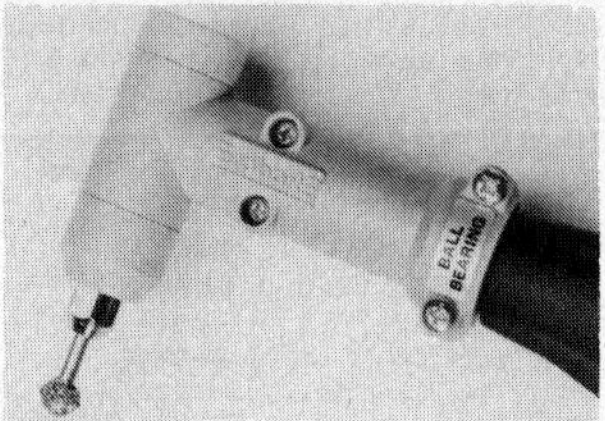

547-421 Ball Bearing 34.95
for use with Moto-Tool #s 395, 285, 275 series and #800 freewheel.

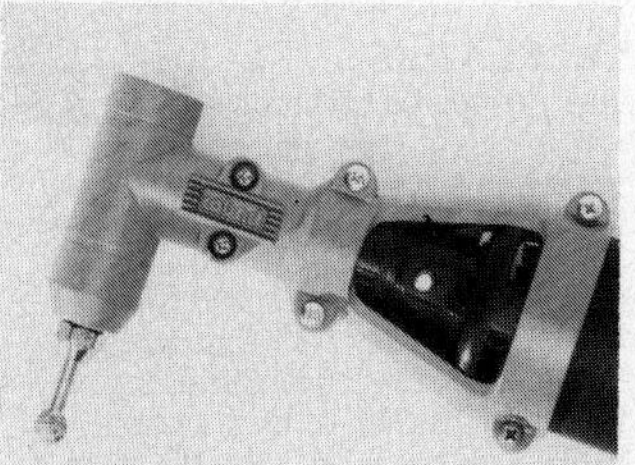

547-4200 Ball Bearing 34.95
for use with older model Moto-Tools

- Tungsten Steel Taps
- Tap Wrench
- Adjustable Split Dies
- Die Holder
- Swivel Head Pinvise
- Saw Blades
- Fiber-Disk
- Mandrels
- Needle File Sets
- Needle Rasp Assortment
- Tap & Die Set
- Ratchet Drill Vise
- Adaptor Chuck
- Dressing Stone
- Mini Vise

TUNGSTEN STEEL TAPS

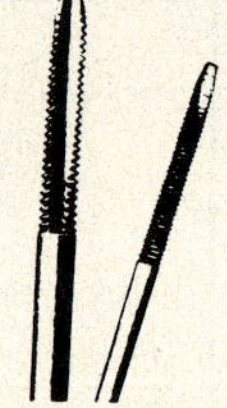

321-1700	#00-90	5.55
321-1701	# 0-80	4.15
321-1702	# 1-72	3.98
321-1703	# 2-56	3.25
321-1704	# 3-48	3.25
321-1705	# 4-40	3.05
321-1706	# 5-40	3.05
321-1707	# 6-32	3.05
321-1708	# 8-32	2.69

321-1714 Tap Set   16.99
Consist of one each: #00-90, 0-80, 1-72 & 2-56.

321-1712 Tap Set   16.99
Consist of one each: #2-56, 3-48, 4-40, 6-32 & 8-32.

TAP WRENCH

321-1710 Tap Wrench #0-1/4"   10.55

ADJUSTABLE SPLIT DIES 13/16" dia

321-1720	#00-90	11.10
321-1721	# 0-80	10.59
321-1722	# 1-72	10.59
321-1723	# 2-56	7.40
321-1724	# 3-48	8.11
321-1725	# 4-40	7.40
321-1726	# 5-40	7.40
321-1727	# 6-32 (By Special Order Only.)	7.40

13/16" DIAMETER DIE HOLDER

321-1728 13/16" diameter Die Holder   7.25

TAP & DIE SET

Tap & Die Set
321-1716
100.85

Sixteen piece set in-
cludes die holder, tap
wrench, seven taps &
seven dies, numbers:
00-90, 0-80, 1-72, 2-56,
3-48, 4-40 & 6-32, and
a 10 x 6-3/4" molded
storage case.

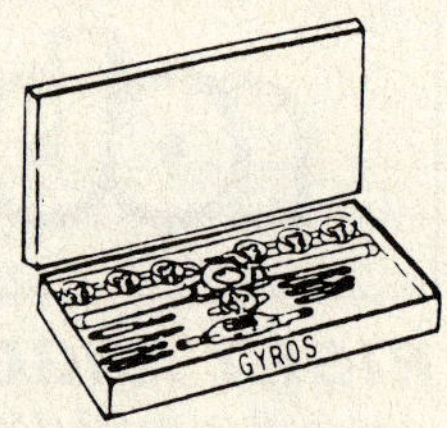

RATCHET DRILL/VISE

Tool can be used as pin vise or as hand drill by
pushing the quick return center piece along the
twisted bar.

321-1837 Ratchet Drill/Vise   14.69
Uses drills 61 thru 80.

SWIVEL HEAD PIN VISE

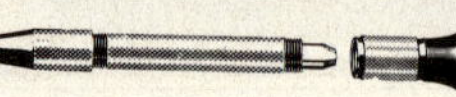

Swivel Head
Pin Vise
321-1818   7.65

Holds drills, taps, reamers, etc from 0 to 1/8"
diameter. Steel 4" long.

SAW BLADES

Circular, tempered carbon steel
blades with 1/8" hole. Use with
mandrel #2, 321-83985.

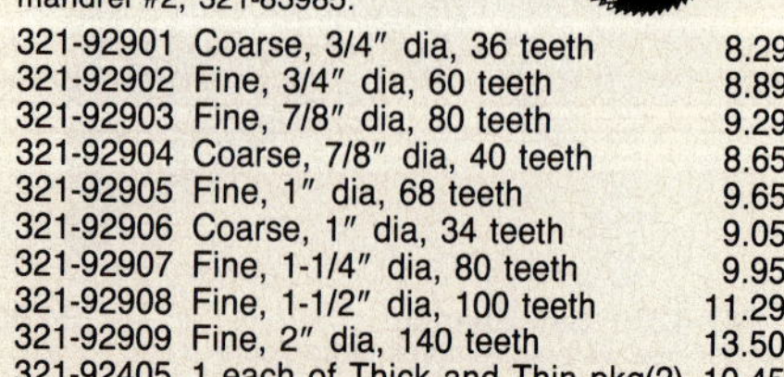

321-92901	Coarse, 3/4" dia, 36 teeth	8.29
321-92902	Fine, 3/4" dia, 60 teeth	8.89
321-92903	Fine, 7/8" dia, 80 teeth	9.29
321-92904	Coarse, 7/8" dia, 40 teeth	8.65
321-92905	Fine, 1" dia, 68 teeth	9.65
321-92906	Fine, 1" dia, 34 teeth	9.05
321-92907	Fine, 1-1/4" dia, 80 teeth	9.95
321-92908	Fine, 1-1/2" dia, 100 teeth	11.29
321-92909	Fine, 2" dia, 140 teeth	13.50
321-92405	1 each of Thick and Thin pkg(2)	10.45

321-92406	Coarse 7/8" dia		5.75
321-92407	1-1/4" dia		5.75
321-92408	7/8" dia & Mandrel	pkg(2)	11.50
321-92409	1-1/4" dia & Mandrel	pkg(2)	8.82
321-92410	Coarse 1-1/4"		8.82
321-92412	Coarse 1-1/4" w/mandrel		10.33
321-92800	Saw Mounted Med 1/2" dia		8.05
321-92801	Coarse 3/4" w/mandrel (By Special Order Only.)	pkg(3)	31.15
321-92802	Fine 3/4" w/mandrel (By Special Order Only.)	pkg(3)	31.15
321-92803	Fine 7/8" w/mandrel (By Special Order Only.)	pkg(3)	37.60
321-92804	Coarse 7/8" mandrel (By Special Order Only.)	pkg(3)	32.19
321-92805	Fine 1" w/mandrel (By Special Order Only.)	pkg(3)	33.29
321-92806	Coarse 1" w/mandrel	pkg(3)	33.29
321-92807	Fine 11/4" w/mandrel (By Special Order Only.)	pkg(3)	42.00
321-92808	Fine 11/2 w/mandrel	pkg(3)	46.75
321-92809	Fine 2" w/mandrel	pkg(3)	43.29
321-92900	Medium 1/2" dia		5.98

CIRCULAR STEEL SAWS

For wood, plastic and soft metal. Includes two
washers.

321-92400	.005"	4.39
321-92404	.005" with Mandrel	5.59

FIBER-DISK

Cuts & grinds many
materials, and resists
breakage.

93102 & 93104 can be used on glass, plastic, stone,
ceramic, wood, aluminum, copper, brass and other
low tensile strength materials. 1/16" hole use mandrel #4, 321-84025.

321-93102	1" dia x 1/32", soft	pkg(2)	2.69
321-93104	1-1/2" dia x 1/32", soft	pkg(2)	3.29

Heavy duty—93106 & 93108 are ideal on steel, steel
alloys, hard bronze and other high tensile strength
materials.

321-93106	1-1/2" dia x 1/32", hard	pkg(2)	3.29

1/16" hole, use with mandrel #4, 321-8025.

321-93108	2" dia x 1/32", hard	pkg(2)	4.29

1/8" hole, use w/mandrel #2, 321-83985.

321-93109	2-1/2" hard	2.80

1/8" MINI-CHUCK

321-1801 1/8" to #61-80   5.35

MANDRELS

Mandrels for saws & fiber cut-off discs.

Mandrel #2
1/8" shank
321-83985
2.79

Mandrel #4
1/8" shank
321-84025
2.10

Mandrel
1/4" screw, 1/8" shank
321-840252   2.45

Saw Mandrel
Small dia
321-839851
2.10

FLAP WHEEL

For use on metal and wood. Polishes, sands, deburs,
blends seams, removes old finished, rust and scale.
1/2 x 3/8" with 1/8" shank.

321-94207	80 Grit, medium	6.85
321-94208	180 Grit, fine	6.85
321-94209	360 Grit, very fine	6.85

BRUSHES

(By Special Order Only)
Mounted Wire Wheel
321-84285   pkg(3) 7.20

NEEDLE FILE SETS

With round handles. Sets 1403
and 1402 are four inch ''mini''
files for delicate filing and tiny
areas. #2 cut.

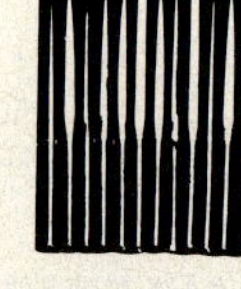

321-1403 4" 12 piece File Set   19.35
w/plastic folding wallet

321-1402 4" 6 piece File Set   8.85
w/plastic folding wallet

Sets 1400, 1401 and 1404 files
are for all metals and wood. #2
cut unless noted.

6 piece File Set
5-1/2"
321-1400
9.90
w/plastic folding wallet

321-1401 12 piece File Set, 5-1/2"   17.59
w/plastic folding wallet

321-1404 4 piece File Set, 4"   7.10
4 extra fine cut files
(equal, round, 1/2 round, 3 square)

321-1406 Economy 6 piece   6.15
Contains six #3 cut 5-1/2" files w/plastic pouch. One
each: Flat pointed, rat tail, equalizing, square, half-
round and triangular.

321-1407 7" 5 piece File Set   12.29
(By Special Order Only.)
Contains five #0 cut 7" files with plastic pouch. One
each: triangular, square, 1/2 round, round and flat.

5-1/2" FILES

Dealers: MUST order Dealer Packs of 12.

321-1460	1/2" Round (By Special Order Only.)	1.13
321-1461	Knife	1.00
321-1462	Round (By Special Order Only.)	1.13
321-1463	Square (By Special Order Only.)	1.00
321-1464	Triangle	1.13
321-1465	Equaling	1.00
321-1466	Flat	1.13

RASP ASSORTMENTS

321-1405 Needle Rasp Set   13.65
w/plastic wallet
Coarse cut for plaster, wood plastic & stone. Includes
square, equal, 1/2 round, 3 square, round & flat.
5-1/2"

321-1485 6-piece Curved Rasp Set   26.95

HOBBY HAND BRUSH

Fine wire brush cleans files, saws, drill bits. Removes
rust, tarnish, dirt. 3/8" wire bristles, .005"; 8" overall.
Smooth wood handles.

321-1822	Stainless	3.29
321-1824	Brass	3.29

MINI-VISE

Mini-Vise
321-1827
7.53
Clamp-on, tiny die cast
steel vise fits 3/4" table
top. 7/8" opening.

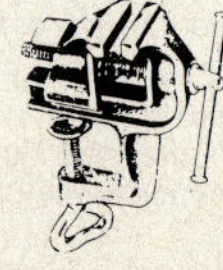

- Pliers
- Tweezers
- Clamps
- Drills & Accessories

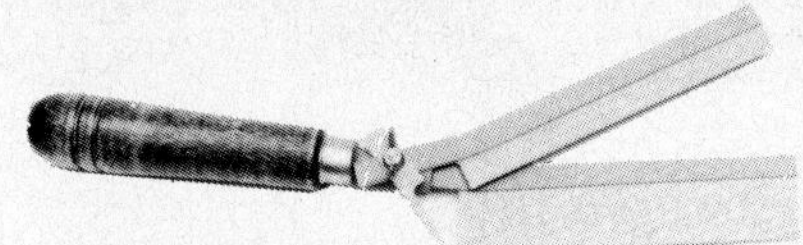

RIFFLER SETS

Double ended riffler files for wood, metal, plastic & stone. 6″ long. Each tool has two shaped ends.

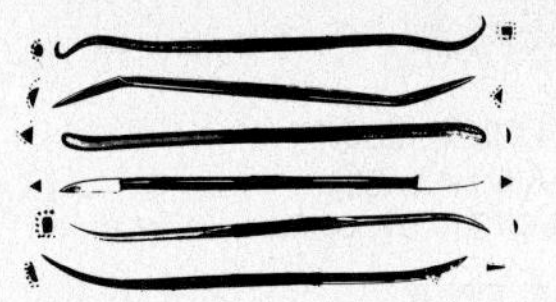

321-1486 12 Piece Set, medium cut 37.15

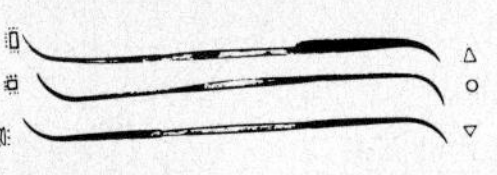

321-1488 6 Piece Set 23.35

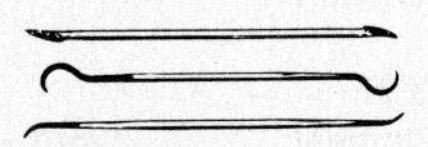

321-1489 Mini Riffler File Set 3 pc 11.95
321-1490 Mini Riffler File Set 4 pc 17.53
All shapes different

MINI-PICK ASSORTMENT

Stainless, tiny picks, probes, scrapers, hooks. 6″ long.

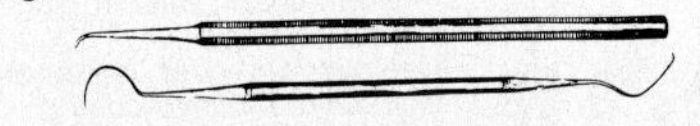

321-1840 5 Piece Assortment 21.67

MINI WATCHMAKERS PLIERS

Smooth jaw, box joint, 4-1/2″ set includes flat, round and chain.

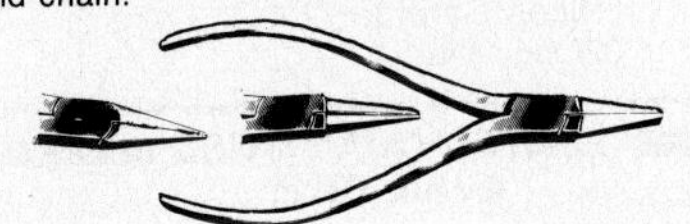

321-1333 Pliers Set 19.42

END CUTTER PLIERS

End Cutter Pliers
321-1307 6.25

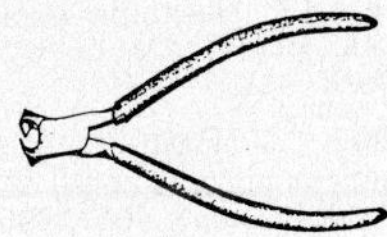

TWEEZERS

Non-Magnetic, stainless steel, fine point. 4-5/8″ long, Swiss style watchmakers tweezers.

321-1741 Straight 5.35

321-1742 Curved 5.35

HEMOSTAT

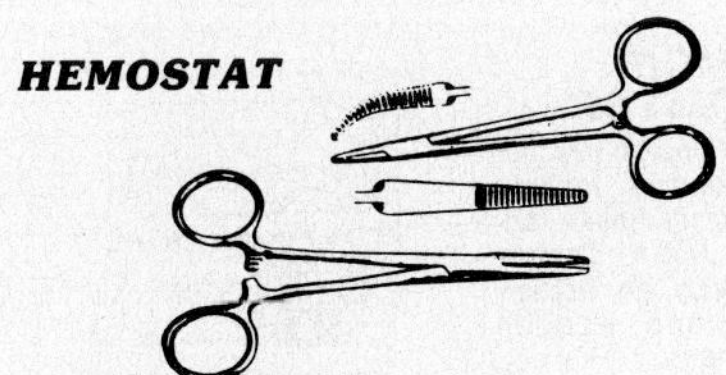

321-1820 Curved, 5-1/2″ long 7.35
321-1821 Straight, 5-1/2″ long 7.35

TINY TINSNIP

Tiny Tinsnip
321-1830
5.75
4-1/4″ one
serrated jaw

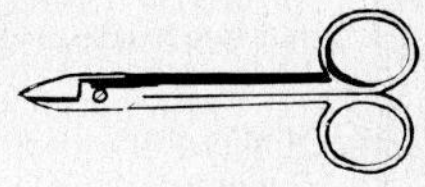

■ LIMITED QUANTITIES ■
AVAILABLE

C-CLAMPS

Steel screws w/sliding cross bar handle.

321-1868 1″ Opening 3.98

CORDLESS ELECTRO POWER DRILL

For drilling, grinding, engraving, sanding, sawing, polishing and deburing. Holds drills 55 thru 80, plus 3/32″ and 1/8″ shank accessories. Powered by three standard C batteries, runs at 12,000 RPM and features button control with locking on/off switch. Comes with carving cutter assortment and grinding point.

321-15000 Electric Power Drill 37.89
            with accessories
321-15001 Electric Power Drill Only 32.15
321-15010 Collet Set for 15000 5.59

DRILL ACCESSORIES

20 high speed drills sizes 61-80. Includes storage box w/plastic dome.

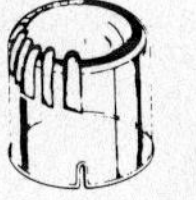

321-1285 Drill set #61-80 33.75

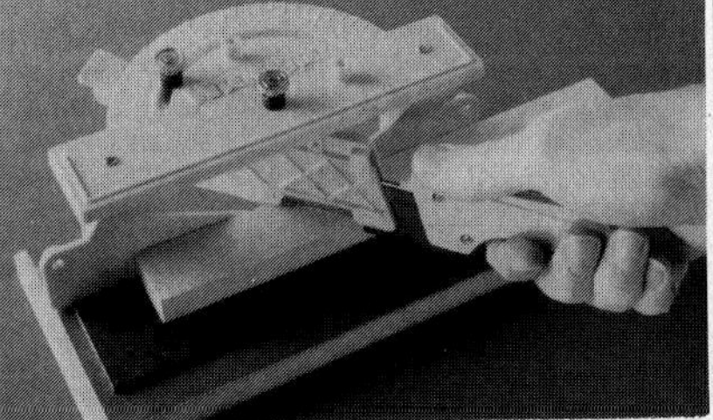

MITER SAW

This ready to use, plastic miter saw allows you to adjust the angle of your cut from 25 to 90° left or right. Saw includes cutting board and X-acto sawblade. Cuts wood, plastic and soft metal.

658-1001 Miter Saw 27.95
658-1002 Miter-Rite 3.25
            Replacement Blade

SAWS AND SAW SETS

Cut thin wall tubing, wire, sheet metal fittings, screws, etc.

795-100 Saw Set, Complete 5.50
(1 each: razor saw, sabre saw, homecraft saw blades, interchangeable handle)

795-400 Sabre Saw w/extra blade 3.50

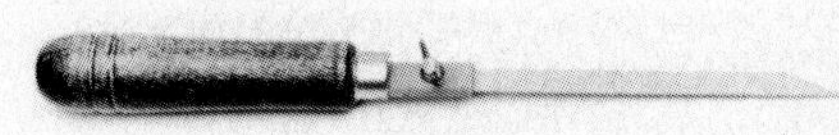

795-150 Razor "42" Saw 3.49
Like the #200 Razor Saw except has 42 teeth per inch for even finer work. Improved cutting for wood & plastic. Shorter blade life if used with metals.

795-200 Razor Saw 3.49
32 teeth per square inch.

795-450 Super Sabre Saw 3.65
4-1/2″ blade has no backing or stiffener. Flexible enough that it can be bent to any shape.

795-300 Homecraft Saw 3.75
24 teeth per square inch.

795-500 Universal Saw 3.80
Same length as Homecraft Saw but has deeper cut (1-3/16″) and much thinner blade (.010), almost as thin as Razor Saw. 32 teeth per square inch.

REPLACEMENT BLADES

795-112 4-1/2″ Homecraft pkg(3) 3.00
            for Sawset #100 only
795-308 6-1/2″ Homecraft pkg(3) 3.60
            for #300
795-158 Razor "42" pkg(3) 2.85
795-208 Razor Saw pkg(3) 2.85
795-408 Sabre (push) pkg(3) 1.80
795-409 Sabre (pull) pkg(3) 1.80
795-458 Super Sabre pkg(3) 3.00
795-508 Universal Blade pkg(3) 3.90
795-608 6″ Hacksaw pkg(3) 2.25

MINI MITER BOX

795-250 Mini-Miter Box 3.55
Designed to fit all razor-type saws. Adjustable stop & beveled channel.

795-251 Mini-Miter Box w/Saw 6.55
Razor Saw Combination (w/#200 saw)

K&S ENGINEERING

Soldering tools, various tool sets and accessory items for model builders.

SOLDERING GUN

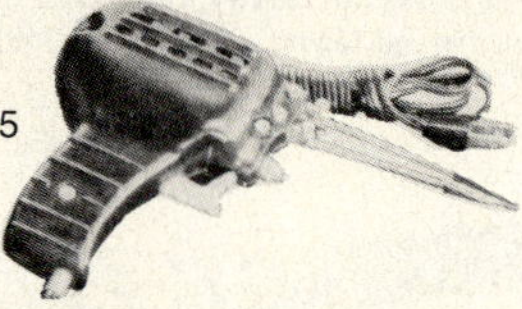

Electric
Soldering Gun
370-1210   15.95
with tip, 110V,
100 watts

SOLDERING IRON

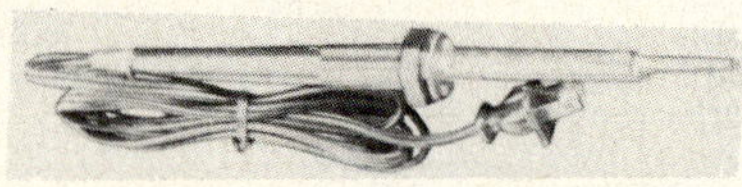

370-300   Soldering Iron w/tip, 30 watts   6.95

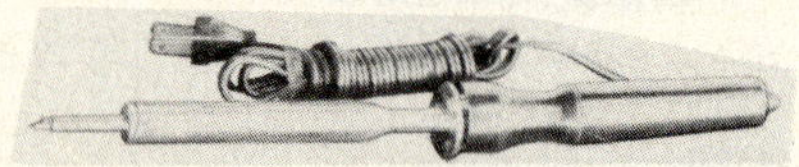

370-910   Heavy Duty Soldering   7.95
Iron w/tip, 60 watts

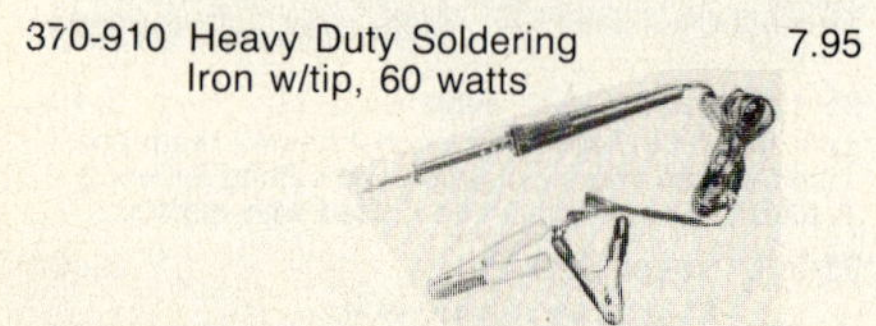

370-212   Soldering Iron Pencil   5.95
12v, 30 watt capacity. Features 6' cord, lightweight
construction, clips onto car battery for outdoor use.

ELECTRICAL TESTERS

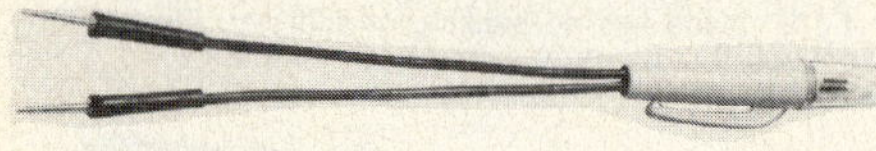

370-290   Electrical Tester, 90-500V   1.50
Tests electrical appliances, fuses, wall plugs, spark
plugs and switches.

370-293   Low Voltage Tester   4.95

WIRE BENDERS

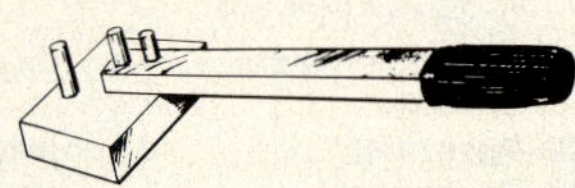

370-322   Mighty   19.95
Bends 1/4" music wire and square or rectangular
shaped metal. You can produce your own clamps,
brackets, landing gear, hangers and more.

370-323   Mini   8.95
Bends music wire or brass wire diameters of 1/8" and
smaller as well as square and rectangular shaped
metal.

COIL WINDER

370-324   Coil Winder   19.95
For winding wire up to 1/4" in diameter.

TUBING BENDER

Bend tubing in the
following sizes:
1/16", 3/32", 1/8",
5/32", 3/16" OD

Tubing Bender Kit
370-321   set 1.75

SCREWDRIVER SET

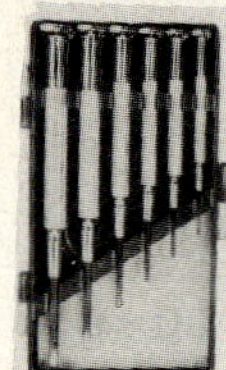

"Quality" sets: each tip comes with its
own handle. "Quick Change" precision
sets: one handle, with interchangeable
tips.

Quality Set
(6 assorted in plastic box)
370-426   9.95

Precision Set
(5 interchangeable
tips, handle & case)
370-425   7.95

NUT DRIVER SET

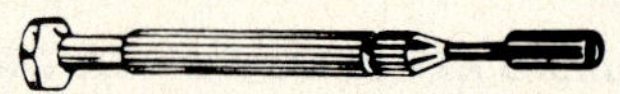

370-422   Quality Nut Driver Set   9.95

OPEN END WRENCH SET

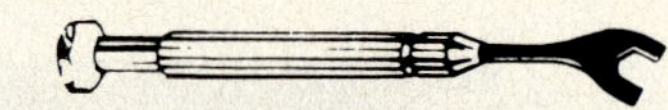

370-423   Open End Wrench Set   9.95
Includes #0 and #1 crosspoint screwdrivers and
.050", 1/16" and 5/64" hex keys with handles and
case.

PHILLIPS-ALLEN SET

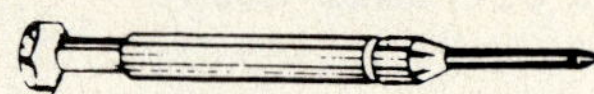

370-424   Quality Driver Set   9.95
Includes #1 and #2 crosspoint screwdrivers and
.050", 1/16" and 5/64" hex keys and case.

TAPS

370-436	#1-72	each 2.95
370-437	#2-56	each 2.95
370-438	#3-48	each 2.95
370-439	#4-40	each 2.95
370-434	Tap Handle	4.95

ADJUSTABLE THREADING DIES

High speed, steel, 13/16" diameter dies, with unified
threads.

370-415	#0-80	each 5.95
370-416	#1-72	each 5.95
370-417	#2-56	each 5.95
370-418	#3-48	each 5.95
370-419	#4-40	each 5.95

Carbon Steel, positive lock die stock handle.

370-420   Die Handle   9.95

DRILL BITS, 6"

For drilling light metals & woods, plus composite
materials (araphite, carbon fiber kevlar, etc.) Useful
for drilling fusalages, firewalls, stuffing boxes, etc.

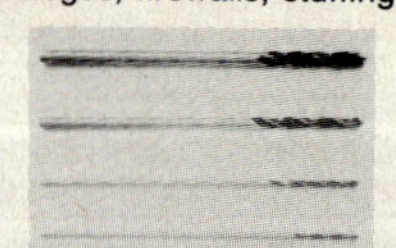

370-482	3/32	2.50	370-488	1/8	**NEW** 1.10
370-483	1/8	2.50	370-489	5/32	**NEW** 1.10
370-484	3/16	2.50	370-490	3/16	**NEW** 1.10
370-485	1/4	2.50	370-491	7/32	**NEW** 1.25
370-486	1/16	**NEW** 1.00	370-492	1/4	**NEW** 1.50
370-487	3/32	**NEW** 1.00			

TUBING CUTTER

Tubing Cutter
370-296   3.95

ALLIGATOR CLIP

370-305   Alligator Clip   pkg(2) .59
Dealer: MUST order dealer pack of 6.

NEEDLE FILE SET

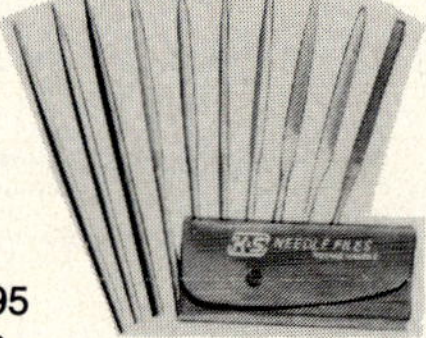

6" Needle File Set
370-430   pkg(10) 8.95
packed in plastic pouch

SANDPAPER

370-475   Assortment   pkg(9 sheets) .59
Dealers: MUST order 24 packs.

FLEX-I-GRIT SANDING SHEET

- Sand any surface
  wood, plastic, metal, paint
- Fit to any shape,
  won't crack, peel or clog
- Flex to clean

Use over and over, wet or dry.
Reusable abrasive coated
polyester.
Dealers: MUST order dealer
pack of 36.

370-4011   Silicon Carbide   pkg(5) 1.19
150 grit, coarse
370-4031   Silicon Carbide   pkg(5) 1.19
320 grit, fine

LIMITED QUANTITIES AVAILABLE

370-4021   Garnet   pkg(5) 1.19
280 grit, medium

FLEX-I-GRIT PACK

Five 4 x 5.5" sheets per pack.
Dealers: MUST order dealer pack of 36 (all one
number).

370-4001   "A" Regular, Assorted Grits   1.09
For general purpose hobby sanding, 1 sheet each,
#4011, 4021, 4031, 4041, 4051.

370-4002   "B" Micro-Fine, Assorted   1.09
For exceedingly high finishes.
1 sheet each: 23 micron silicon carbon, light gray,
23 micron aluminum oxide, tan, 8 micron silicon carbide, dark gray, 0.5 micron chromium oxide, green,
1.5 micron cerium oxide, burnt orange (Micron = 1
millionth of a meter).

TACK CLOTH

370-480   Tack Cloth   .89
Removes dust, lint and other particles from the sur-
face to be finished.
Dealers: MUST order dealer pack of 36.

PRECISION MICROMETER

High quality design, ratchet
thimble, positive locking
clamp, enamel finish, ac-
curacy to .0001. Comes
complete with an adjust-
ment tool and wooden
storage case.

370-800   Precision Micrometer   29.95

K-Tool Products

MITER BOX

- Cuts any angle from 0° to 60°, in 5° increments, right or left (plus 22-1/2°, half of 45°).
- Cutting depth 1/4" w/razor blade (more w/saw blade)
- Cuts all woods, plastics and thin wall metal tubings.
- Handle accepts "Zona" saw or single edged razor blades. (One of each included).
- Adjustable slide-stop for cutting many same length pieces.
- 7-1/2 x 7-1/2" cutting surface.
- Lexan base with non-skid rubber feet.
- Designed for either right or left hand operation.

211-2	Miter Box	27.95
211-21	Model Miter Handle	8.50

Roco

Imported from Austria
WALTHERS

625-10903 Crankpin Wrench 6.99
Box spanner socket wrench for removal of crankpins on locomotives with coupling rods.

FALLER

Imported from Germany and marketed by WALTHERS

Cutter for Styrene
272-688   23.99
Special side cutter for cutting off ultra-fine molded parts without burrs. Tip angle 48°. Only suitable for polystyrene and copper wires.

A.J. FRICKO COMPANY

"making toy trains run like real trains"

PINHOLE BOX CAMERA

The box camera is perfect for photographing models, as it allows for a trackside perspective (as would be seen by a scale figure) and a wide depth of field. The Fricko box camera uses 4" x 5" cut sheet film and is equipped with a pinhole aperture (0.016 dia.) with an f/stop of f 256. **(By Special Order Only.)**

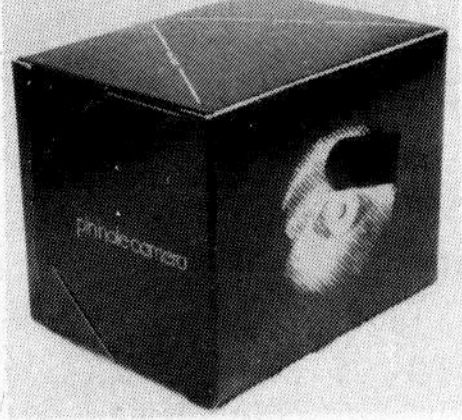

Fricko Peekaboo Pinhole Box Camera
274-831   74.95

PINHOLE LENS
for 35mm SLR CAMERA*

Focusing pinhole lens w/colens to overcome fuzziness.

*Must have a camera with removable lens. Pinhole lens fits onto a camera body.

Lens features:
- 0.018 diameter aperture
- 105 f stop
- etched in stainless steel
- a much sharper image
- a brighter viewing screen
- a shorter exposure time
- depth of field from 1" to infinity

274-842	for Canon (manual focus camera body)	89.95
274-843	for Konika	89.95
274-844	for Minolta (manual focus camera body)	89.95
274-845	for Nikon (either manual or auto focus camera body)	89.95
274-846	for Olympus	89.95
274-847	for Pentax K (bayonet mount, also works for Ricoh)	89.95
274-848	for Pentax S (universal screw mount for all screw mount body types)	89.95
274-849	for Yashica/Contax	89.95
274-851	for Maxxum (Minolta auto focus camera body)	89.95
274-852	for EOS (Canon auto focus camera body)	89.95

model power

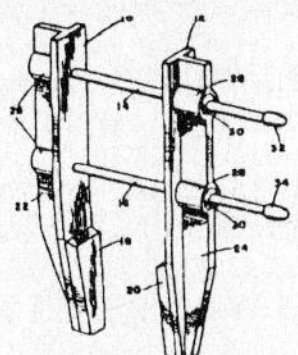

490-5366 Pocket Screwdriver pkg(2) 2.98
all metal with storage area

(not illustrated)
490-5350	Track Hammer	6.98
490-5386	Track Saw Set	6.98
490-5484	Spike Pliers 6-1/2"	6.98

Evergreen Workbench

Get a grip on your next project with these quick-release clamps, that allow you to tighten or release the jaws in seconds. Ideal for any project, two sizes are available and self-sticking replacement pads allow for quick repair, or conversion for use with solvents, chemicals or heat.

STANDARD CLAMP

256-001	Small, Opens to 5-1/4"	4.95
256-002	Large, Opens to 9-1/2"	5.45

REPLACEMENT JAW PADS

256-201	Cork	pkg(4) 1.95
256-202	Rubber	pkg(4) 1.95
	Fuel and Solvent Resistant	
256-203	Teflon (Gore-Tex)	pkg(2) 2.95
	Heat and Chemical Resistant	

CIR-KIT CONCEPTS, INC.

DRILL

206-201 Mini Drill 5.95
High speed and hand operated; will drill small accurate holes in all types of material. 4-1/2" long, 3 to 1 ratio and accepts number size bits 61 thru 80. Hollow handle stores your extra bits.

HAMMER

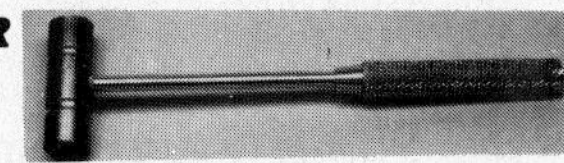

206-1041 Brass Head Hammer 9.95
Designed to pound brass brads. Hammer is 5-1/2" long with a solid brass head and serrated steel handle.

MASCOT™
PRECISION TOOLS

Mascot tools are quality engineered to give top performance and satisfaction.

KNIVES

230-110   Mini Utility Knife   3.79

230-1   #1 Lightweight Knife w/ blade   2.40
230-111   #1 Lightweight Knife w/3 blades 4.80

230-2   #2 Med Weight Knife w/blade   3.60

230-5   #5 Heavy Duty Knife w/blade   4.15

KNIFE SETS

Precision Knives
230-182 (3pc) 15.00

Includes a lightweight, medium weight and heavy duty knife plus a plastic storage tray.

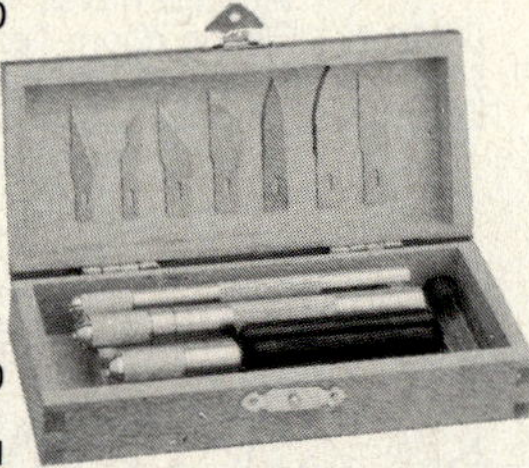

Precision Knives
230-865 (3pc) 17.50
Sames knives as #182 plus assorted blades and wooden storage box.

KNIFE BLADES w/SAFE VIAL

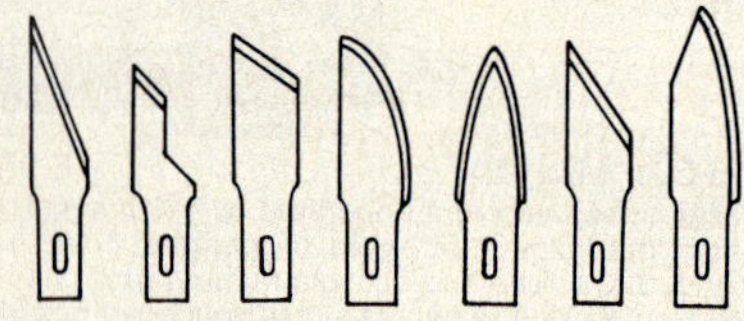

#11   #16   #19   #22   #23   #24   #25

Blades for 230-1 knife handles:
230-11   #11   pkg(5) 1.99
230-16   #16   pkg(5) 1.85

Blades for 230-2, 230-5, 230-9 knife handles:
230-19   #19   pkg(5) 2.29
230-22   #22   pkg(5) 3.29
230-23   #23   pkg(5) 5.29
230-24   #24   pkg(5) 2.19
230-25   #25   pkg(5) 5.49

Blades for 230-110 knife handles:
230-1101 Mini Knife Blades   pkg(5) 2.60
   (By Special Order Only.)

SAWS

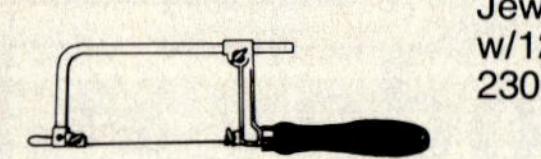

Jewelers Saw
w/12 blades
230-100   14.50

Frame adjusts from 2-1/2" to 6-1/2" to fit the twelve assorted blades included in this set. 2-1/2" deep frame.

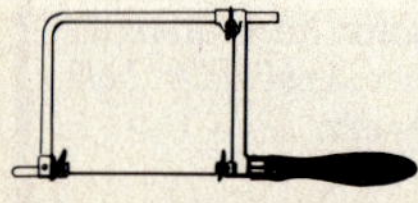

5" Deep Jewelers
Saw Frame
w/12 #4 Saw Blades
230-103   19.80

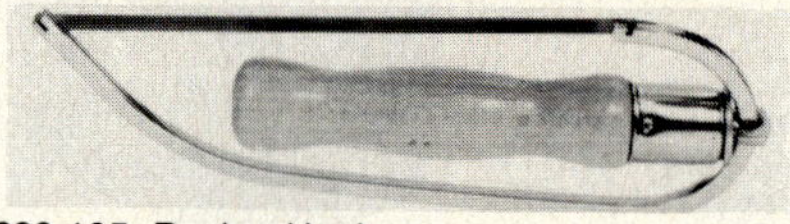

230-101   Brass Back Razor Saw   8.50
          with 1-1/4" replaceable blade

230-104   Brass Back Razor Saw   9.00
          w/3/4" replaceable blade

230-106   Brass Back Razor Saw   11.99
          w/ 3/4", 1", 1-1/4" replaceable blades

230-105   Pocket Hacksaw   10.50
          7-1/2" folded

SAW BLADES

230-1001 Jewelers   pkg(24) 6.50
          12 coarse #8, 12 medium #4
230-1004 Jewelers   pkg(24) 5.50
          12 fine #1, 12 extra fine #2/0
230-1005 Jewelers   pkg(24) 5.70
          12 super fine #4/0, 12 ultra fine #8/0
230-107   3/4" Saw Blade   each 2.60
          w/34 teeth per inch
230-108   1" Saw Blade   each 2.60
          w/42 teeth per inch
230-109   1-1/4" Saw Blade each 2.60
          w/34 teeth per inch

230-120   Blade #3   pkg(144) 25.92
230-121   Blade #2   pkg(144) 25.92
230-122   Blade #1   pkg(144) 25.92
230-123   Blade #0   pkg(144) 25.92
230-124   Blade #2/0   pkg(144) 25.92
230-125   Blade #4/0   pkg(144) 25.92
230-1051 Blades for pocket pkg(3) 2.40
          hacksaw
230-492041 Blades #4 Flat   4.08
          (By Special Order Only.)

230-1003 Spiral Saw Blades   pkg(24) 6.60
Contains 12 each, medium and coarse blades, fitting all jeweler's saw frames.

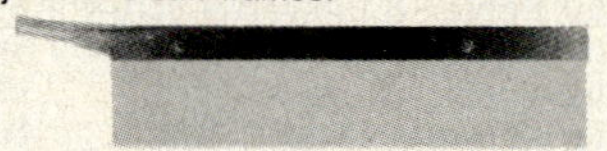

230-102   1-1/4" Razor Saw Blade   4.10
          fits #2 and #5 handles

MITRE BOX

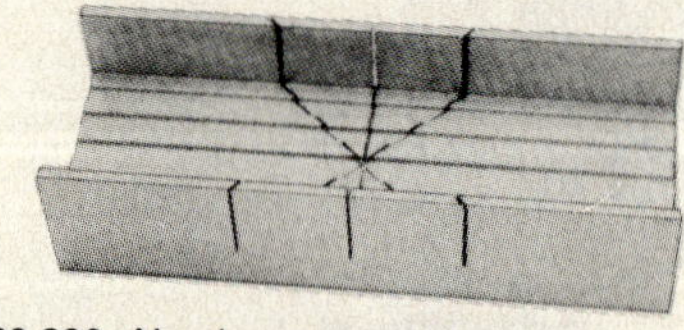

230-206   Aluminum   7.29
          uses 1-1/4" blade, has two 45° slots & one 90° slot
230-207   Mitre Box & Razor Saw Set   15.50

FILES

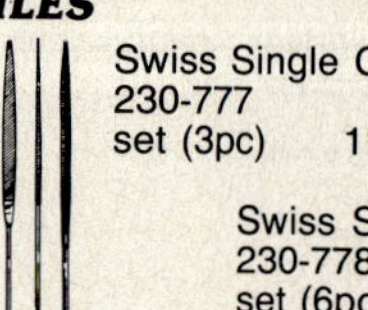

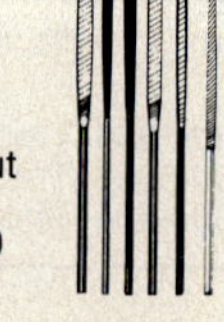

Swiss Single Cut
230-777
set (3pc)   11.00

Swiss Single Cut
230-778
set (6pc)   21.50

5-1/2" SWISS NEEDLE FILES IN POUCHES

Single cut needle files w/vinyl pouch

230-770   Flat   3.90
230-771   1/2 Round   3.90
230-772   Round   3.90
230-773   Square   3.90
230-774   Equalling   3.90
230-775   3 Square   3.90

HOBBY TOOL SET

230-860   Woodcarving Knife Set (4pc) 43.50
Finely balanced knives with alloy blades and wooden handles; designed for carving, incising, shaving, splicing and notching.

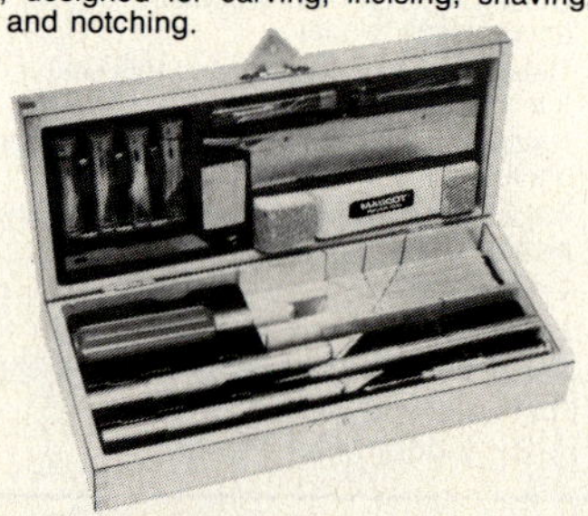

230-866   Deluxe Hobby   39.90
Contains 1 each lightweight, medium weight, heavy-duty knife, hobby awl, mitre box, razor saw, sander, screwdriver and 20 assorted blades.

230-861   Woodworking w/Ball Handles   37.50
Includes one each of the following: a bent square chisel (5/16"), straight skew chisel (5/16"), straight small gouge (5/32"), bent large gouge (5/16") and a bent "V" parting tool (5/32").

230-862   Woodworking   37.50
Set #2 includes one each of the following: a bent square chisel (5/16"), straight skew chisel (5/16"), straight small gouge (5/32"), bent large gouge (5/16") and a bent "V" parting tool (5/32").

WOOD WORKING TOOL SET

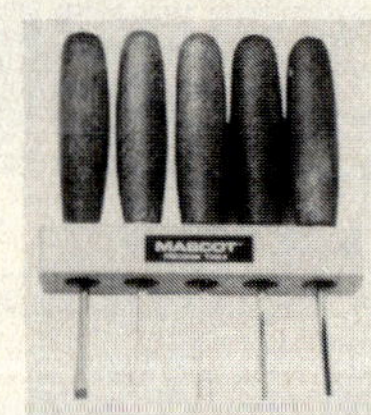

Conventional
Straight Handles
230-864   42.00

Palm Grip
Mushroom Shaped
Handles
230-863   42.00

DRILLS

230-840   Mini Hand Drill   9.25

230-841   Spiral Drill   14.99

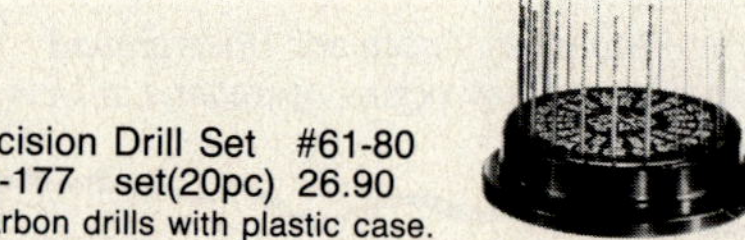

Precision Drill Set #61-80
230-177   set(20pc) 26.90
carbon drills with plastic case.

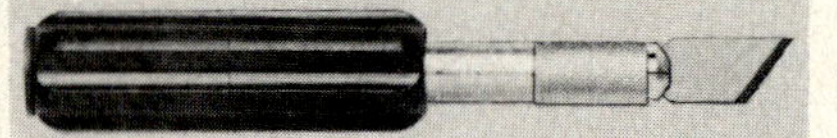

MASCOT™
PRECISION TOOLS

Mascot tools are quality engineered to give top performance and satisfaction.

DRILLS (continued)

To order individual drills specify manufacturer's number and drill size number. (i.e. 230-70)

Drills 50-60   each .75
Drills 61-67   each .92
Drills 68-80   each 1.00
Dealers: MUST order pack of 12 (one size to a pack).

HSS TWIST DRILLS
Dealers: MUST order Dealer pack of 12 (one size per Dealer pack).

230-643	#43	1.09	230-670	#70	1.15
230-648	#48	1.09	230-672	#72	1.15
230-650	#50	1.09	230-674	#74	1.38
230-656	#56	1.09	230-675	#75	1.38
230-660	#60	1.15	230-676	#76	1.38
230-665	#65	1.15	230-678	#78	1.38
230-667	#67	1.15	230-679	#79	1.38
230-668	#68	1.15	230-680	#80	1.88

CARBON TWIST DRILLS

230-86   6 Carbon Twist Drills   5.99
Assortments of the top six drill sizes preferred by hobbyists and craftsmen.

230-178   12 Carbon Twists Drills   10.50
Includes two of each size.

DRILL, TAP & DRIVER SET

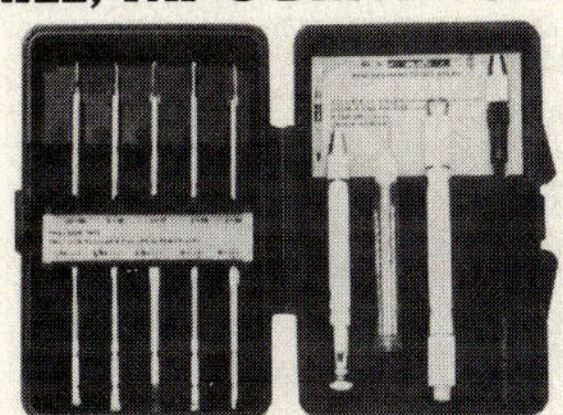

230-833   Drill, Tap & Driver Set   37.50
Includes chuck handle, double end pin vise, flexible extender, 9 tap drills, taps 00-90, 0-80, 1-72, 2-56, 2-64, regular & Phillips screwdrivers.

ADAPTER CHUCK

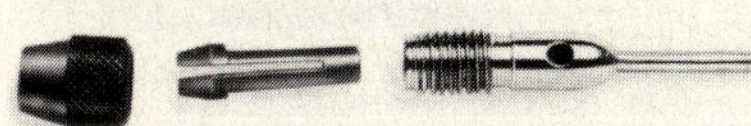

230-982   w/2 Collets #80-43   6.30
The 3/32″ shaft fits all portable electric rotary tools. Holds miniature drills .014 to .089″.

PIN VISES

230-811   Swivel Head Pin Vise   6.30
230-822   Pin Vise & Drill Set   11.90

230-815   Slide Lock Pin Vise   **NEW** 6.90

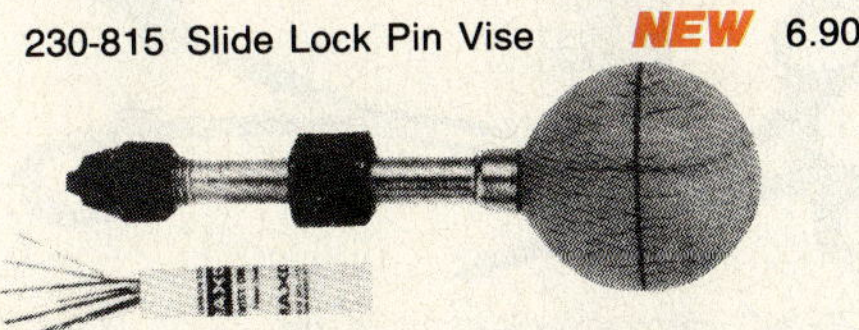

230-812   Wood Head Pin Vise, Drill Set   13.99

SANDERS

Rotary Tool Accessory Kit
230-980   27.50
(18 pieces) 1/8″ & 1/32″ shanks. Fits all electric portable rotary tools.

CLAMPS

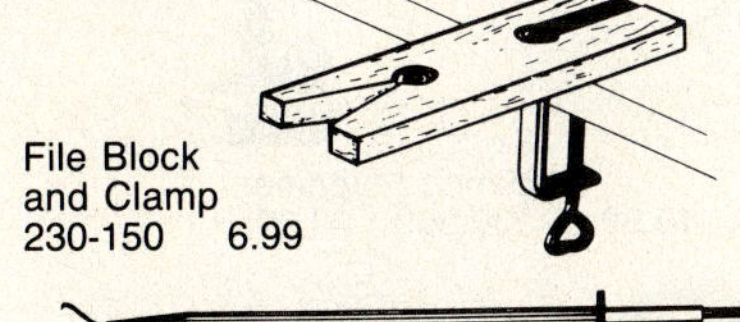

File Block and Clamp
230-150   6.99

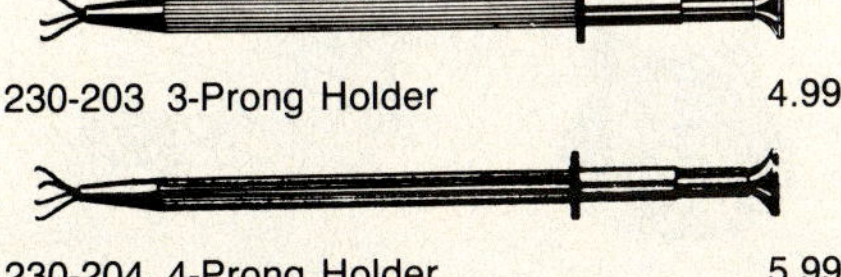

230-203   3-Prong Holder   4.99

230-204   4-Prong Holder   5.99

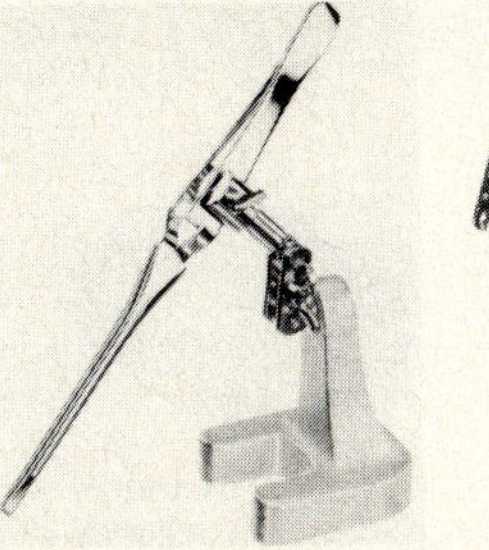

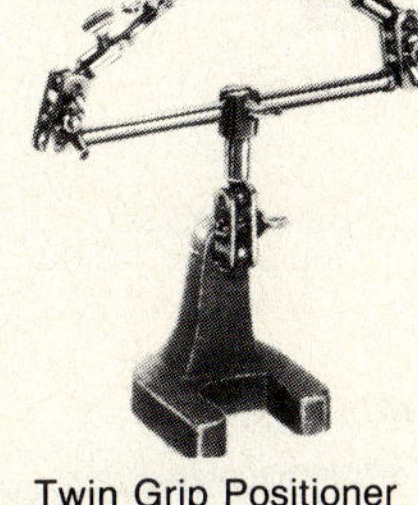

The Third Hand
230-200   13.95
(tweezer-mounted work positioner)

Twin Grip Positioner
230-201   18.49

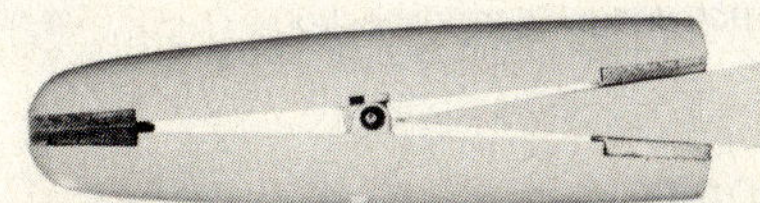

230-202   Non-Mar Wedge Clamp   9.90
Leather-lined jaws grip securely without marring. Resin body.

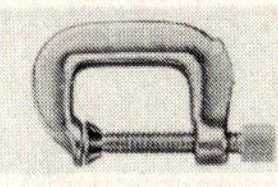

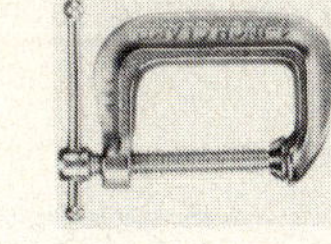

230-210   Mini-Clamps   pkg(2) 4.60
1″ and 3/4″

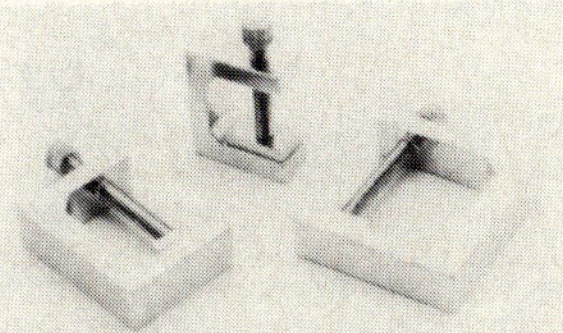

C-Clamp Set
230-212
6.50
NEW

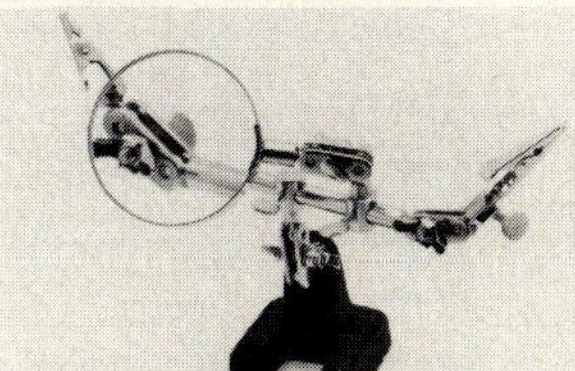

Twin Grip w/Magnifier
230-205
19.75

SLIMLINE PLIERS

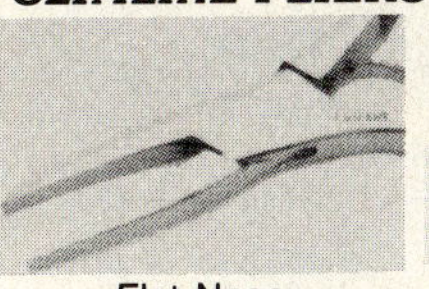

Flat Nose
230-400   21.50

Needle
230-401   21.50

Wire Cut
230-403   28.90

HOBBY PLIERS

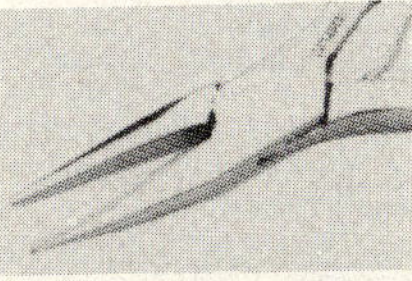

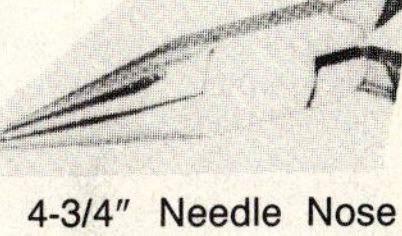

5″ Flat Nose
230-350   11.99

4-3/4″ Needle Nose
230-351   11.99

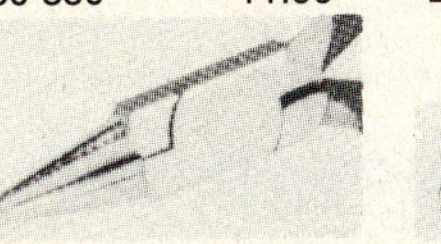

4-3/4″ Round Nose
230-352   11.99

4-3/4″ Diagonal Cutter
230-353   12.50

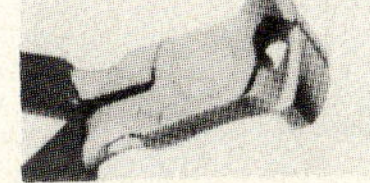

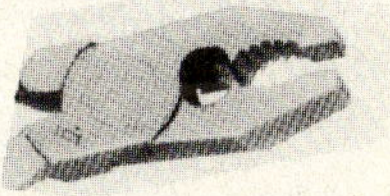

4-1/4″ End Nipper
230-354   12.50

4-1/2″ Midget Lineman
230-355   12.50

5-1/2″ Long Bent Nose
230-356   12.99

ELECTRONIC PLIERS

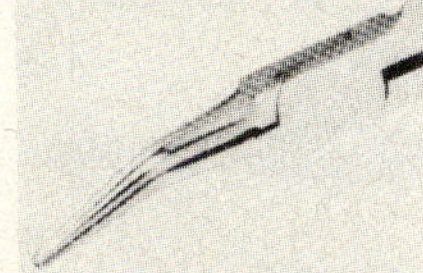

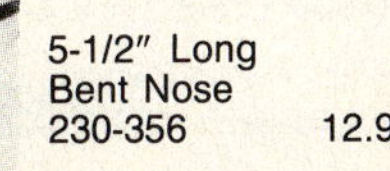

4-1/2″ Needle Nose
230-361   12.99

4-1/2″ Diagonal Cut
230-363   12.99

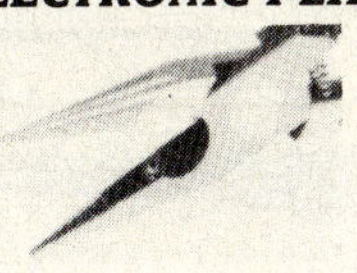

4-3/4″ Tapered Wire Cutter
230-364   12.99

5-1/2″ Bent Long Needle Nose
230-365   13.75

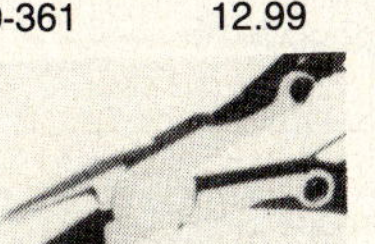

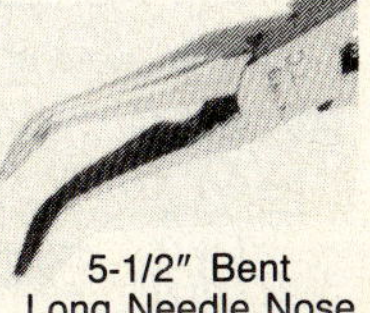

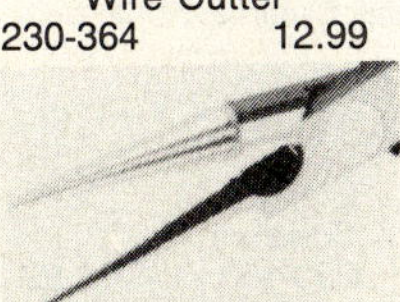

5-1/2″ Long Needle Nose
230-366   13.75

4-1/2″ Mini Lineman
230-367   13.75

MASCOT™
PRECISION TOOLS

Mascot tools are quality engineered to give top performance and satisfaction.

TWEEZERS

230-500 Cross-Locking 6-3/8″ 4.40
Tips serrated for sure grip. 1-12lb tension. Fits #200

230-501 Fine Pointed 5″ 9.98
Sharp tips and light tension for fine work. Nickel-plated steel. Magnetic.

230-503 Stamp 4-1/2″ 2.79
Smooth, wafer thin points. Nickel-plated steel.

230-504 Slide Lock 5-7/8″ 7.75
Thin serrated tips for firm grip, thin flat back permits holding tweezer in vise. Chrome plated.

230-505 Curved 6″ 4.99
Nickel plated steel with slender tips, serrated for positive grip.

230-506 Sharp Pointed 4-3/4″ 3.99

230-507 Slide Lock 4-3/4″ 4.29

230-508 Curved 4-1/2″ 4.39

230-509 Cross Lock 4-1/2″ 4.29

230-510 Curved 6-7/8″ 4.39

230-511 Straight 7″ 4.29

230-512 Round Point 6″ 4.29

230-520 Retrieving 8″ 7.95

**All Purpose Set
230-521** 17.99
Contains 1 each:
4-3/4″ stamp, 4-1/2″ sharp pointed, 6″ retrieving, 6″ curved, 6-1/2″ self-closing

**Electrician Scissors
230-163** 12.50
Double plated, chrome over nickel with notches for stripping wire, 5″ long.

CUTTERS

**6″ Flush Cut Rail Nipper
230-413** 24.99

MAGNIFIERS

**4x & 5x w/case
230-903** 10.50

**3x Bench Magnifier
230-909** 22.99

900 901

230-900 Eyepiece (2.5x) 4.50
230-901 Pocket (10x) 10.50

**Binocular (3x)
230-910** 18.00

MIRRORS

230-905 Inspection, plain 5.99
3/4″ with 8″ handle
230-906 Magnifying Inspection 5.99
1″ with long handle

PROBES

230-303 Probes set(3) 7.20

MALLETS

230-602 Brass Head 1/2 x 2 8.99

230-603 Brass & Fibre Head 15.99
2-1/2 x 1/2

WRENCHES

**Miniature Open End Wrench Set
230-856** 14.75

SCREWDRIVERS

**230-604 Hammer
w/4 Screwdrivers** pkg(5) 13.99

230-853 Metric Screwdriver Set pkg(6) 4.99
w/2 Phillips

230-800 Reversible Blade, Swivel Head 5.95
(blade width 3/32″ & 1/16″)
230-806 Reversible Blade, Phillips 6.90

230-804 Pocket Eyeglass 1.70

230-801 Mini Pocket w/Keychain 3.00

230-855 Precision set(5pc) 9.49
Nickel plated, w/swivel heads. 3″ to 3-5/8″ length, sizes .048″ to .085″. Blades permanently fixed in handles.

MISCELLANEOUS

**Wood Rasp Set
230-779** 21.90

**Pocket Level
230-805** 2.08

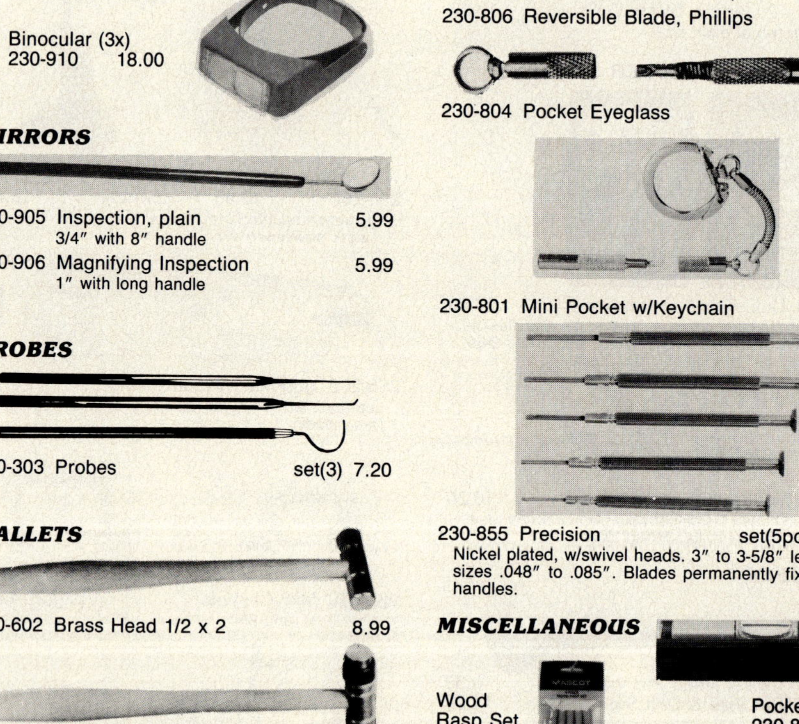

230-340 Hemostat-Straight Blade 7.90
230-341 Hemostat-Curved Blade 7.90

MASCOT™
PRECISION TOOLS
Mascot tools are quality engineered to give top performance and satisfaction.
•Punches •Burnishers •Reamers •Vises

MISCELLANEOUS (continued)

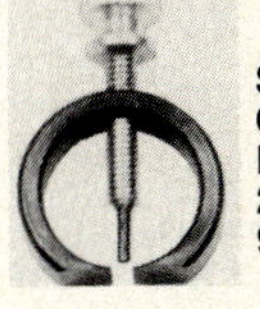

Solder Bulb/Blower
230-915
6.99

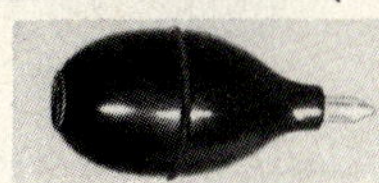

230-301 Mini-Automatic Punch   19.90

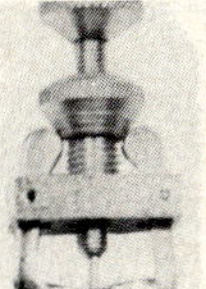

Stationary Gear Puller
230-220
9.00

Adjustable Gear Puller
230-221
17.50

230-300 Double End Scriber-7"   7.20

230-710 6" Metric/English Ruler   2.69

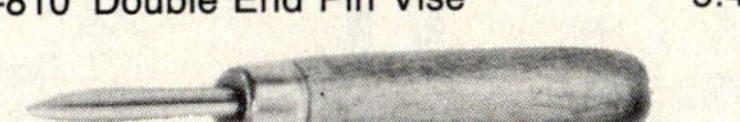

230-711 12" Model RR Scale   8.99
Scale conversions for HO, O and S Gauges

230-810 Double End Pin Vise   5.49

230-295 Straight Blade Burnisher   5.50

230-296 Curved Blade Burnisher   5.50

230-297 Scraper   7.50
(By Special Order Only.)

Metric Nut Driver Set
230-858
pkg(5)
5.80

Track & Tool Cleaning Tablet
230-970   3.69
NEW

Wood Handle Handvise
230-199   10.70
NEW

(not illustrated)
230-311 Reamers   set(6)   14.50
230-986 Denim Apron Bib   8.99

microflame

MINIATURE TORCH SETS

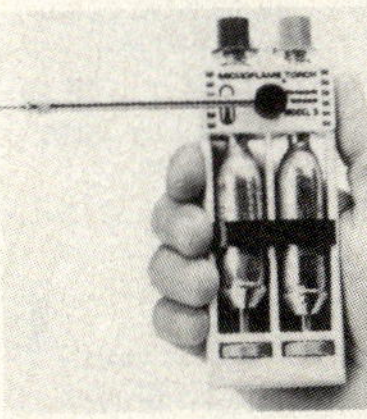

Hobby
450-1000
34.95

Torch set solders & brazes and has a 5000°F pin-point flame. Contains: torch, flame tips, gaskets, 1 butane & 2 Micronox cylinders, brazing rod and flux. Also included is a 1/2" thick fireproof board — a working surface on which the Microflame torch can be used safely.

Economy
450-1201   19.95
Contains torch, flame tip, one Micronox, butane cylinder and instructions.

450-4200 Standard   29.95
Contains torch, two flame tips, gaskets, one butane and two Micronox cylinders, three brazing rods and flux tube.

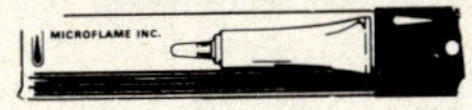

450-4400 Deluxe Hardware-Gas Set   49.95
Injection molded carrying case with form-fitted recessed compartments. Contains torch, 2 flame tips, 1 butane tip, 6 Micronox and 3 butane cylinders, spark lighter, 6 brazing rods, tube of flux.

BRAZING RODS & FLUX
450-3000 Brazing Rods   pkg(4) 15.75
gold colored/silver alloy w/flux core
450-3102 Alum Brazing Rods   pkg(6) 2.00
450-3104 Flux Aluminum   jar(1.5oz) 2.25

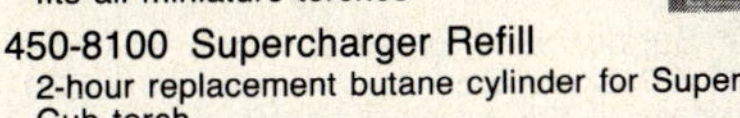

450-3111 Silver Alloy Rod   pkg(6) 6.04
1/32" dia, contains self-dispensing tube of brazing rod flux.

BUTANE TORCH SETS
450-9510 Dragon Torch Head Only   13.80

Super Cub
450-8000   12.95
Delivers more than 2 hours of burning time, controlled high temperature flame (2000°F, 1080°C).

Contains threaded torch head and 25 gram butane cylinder.

REPLACEMENT CYLINDERS
Micronox
450-1001 pkg(2) 2.99
fits all miniature torches
450-8100 Supercharger Refill   3.99
2-hour replacement butane cylinder for Super Cub torch.

TORCHES & ACCESSORIES
Note: Microflame features "Micronox" a laboratory tested and proven gas used as a fuel oxidizer. It has a longer operating and shelf life than oxygen, extends operating life of butane and produces a neutralizing flame.

Butane
450-1002   pkg(2) 4.49   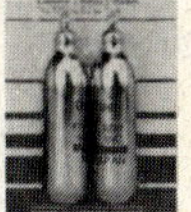
fits all miniature torches   1002
450-4300 Cylinder Kit   9.99
Contains 4 Micronox and 2 butane cylinders.

ACCESSORIES
450-7400   Orifice Cup   pkg(3) 2.46
450-10031 Flame Tip, Threaded pkg(2) 2.46

450-1003   Flame Tips, Slotted pkg(2) 2.46
16-gauge tips to fit all torches
450-10040 Cylinder Gaskets   pkg(4) .99
fits all torches mfg'd before 4/77
450-1004   Cylinder Gaskets   pkg(4) .99
fits all Model B Dual Cylinder Miniature Torches
450-10060 Micronox Piercing Knob   2.99
fits all Dual Cylinder torches mfg'd prior to 4/77

450-1006   Micronox Piercing Knob   2.99
fits all Model B Dual Cylinder Miniature Torches mfg'd after 1977
450-10070 Butane Piercing Knob   2.99
fits Dual Cylinder torches mfg'd prior to 4/77

450-1007   Butane Piercing Knob   2.99
fits all Model B Dual Cylinder Miniature Torches mfg'd after 1977
450-1008   Spark Lighter   1.95

450-1009   Butane Tip, Slotted   6.25
Attaches to any torch to permit use of butane gas only
450-10091 Butane Tip, Threaded   6.25

450-1005   Rotary Assembly, Threaded   4.12

---

kibri
Imported from Germany
by WALTHERS

HOBBY BOARD

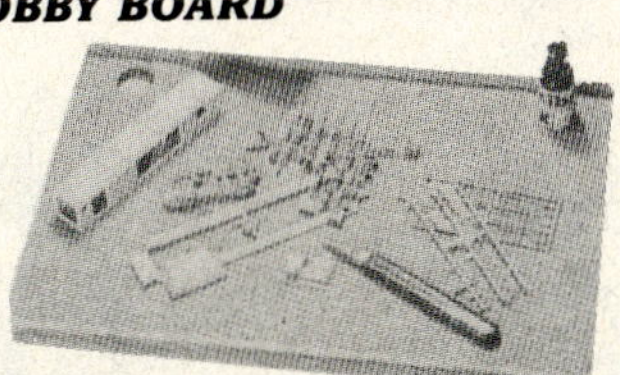

405-5092 Cutting & Work Board   14.49
15-3/4" x 10-1/2"   40 x 26.5 cm
Fiberboard surface with built-up wood edges and a 2" wood slant. Screws for permanent mounting included.

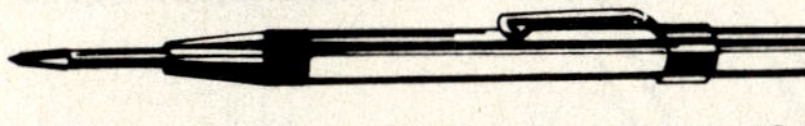
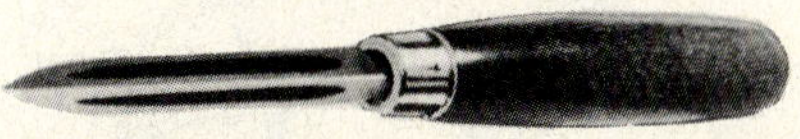

PanaVise®
WORK POSITIONERS

WORK HOLDER TOOL SYSTEMS

PanaVise work holder tool systems are very versatile. All movements are controlled by one variable-pressure knob, making it possible to move the work to any desired position.

SETS

550-302 Starter Kit   65.49
This combination features the #303 Standard Head with #343 Nylon Jaws, and the #366 Wide Opening Head with deep-ribbed Neoprene jaw pads. Both heads are interchangeable with the #300 Standard Base also included.

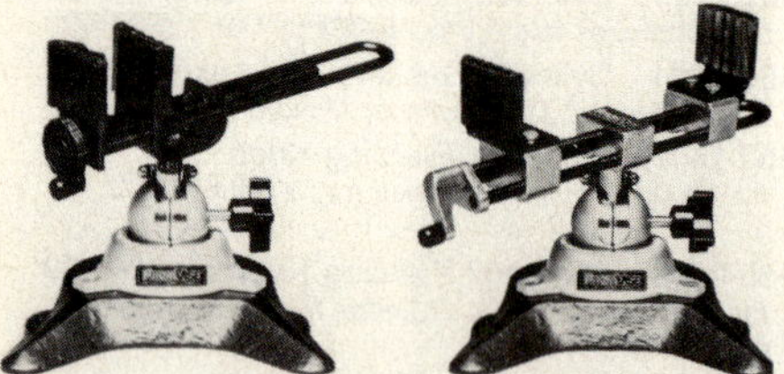
309   334

550-309 Wide Opening Head Portable PanaVise   64.49
Standard Base #300 with Weighted Base Mount #308. Wide Opening Head #366 with Neoprene jaw pads.

550-334 Extra-Wide Opening Head Portable PanaVise   73.99
Standard Base #300 with Weighted Base Mount #308. Extra-Wide Opening Head #376. Reversible jaw pads are ribbed on one side and "V" grooved on the other side.

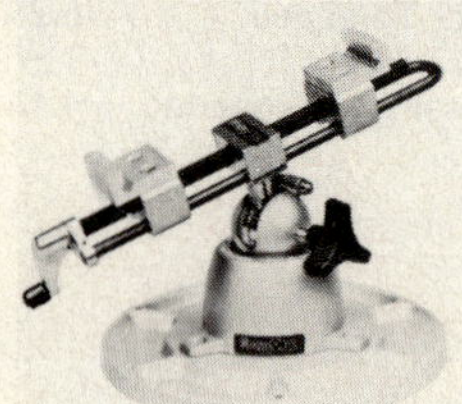

RC Car Chassis PanaVise
550-375   79.95
Standard Base #300 with Tray Base Mount #312. Extra-Wide Opening Jaws with reversible Neoprene jaw pads.

301   324

550-324 Work Center   70.99
(By Special Order Only.)
Standard base, tray base mount, circuit board holder & solder station. (Solder & soldering iron not included.)

550-301 Standard PanaVise   39.99
Standard height base and vertical jaw vise head with nylon jaws.

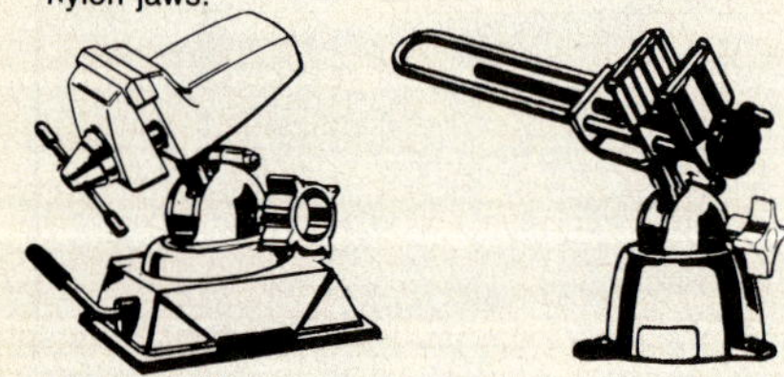
381   396

550-381 Vacuum Base PanaVise   51.99
Vacuum base and vertical jaw vise head with nylon jaws included.

550-396 Wide-Opening Head PanaVise 44.49
Standard height base and wide opening jaw vise head #366 with Neoprene jaw pads.

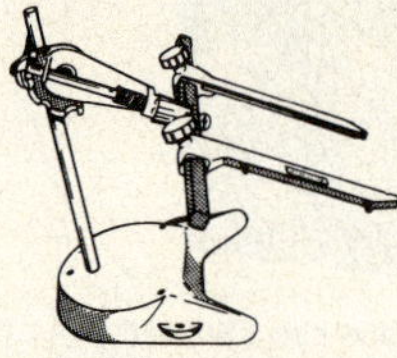
333   350

550-333 Circuit Board Holder   60.99
Spring loaded circuit board holder features 8-position rotating adjustment, indexing at 45% increments & 6 lock positions. Extra arms can be added for multiple board holding. Includes two pre-drilled & tapped flanges.

550-350 Multi-Purpose Work Center   72.99
Wide opening head, standard base and tray base mount with 6 trays for small parts and tools.

UP-DOWN BASES

Bench Mount Positioner
550-325   33.99
(By Special Order Only.)

HEADS

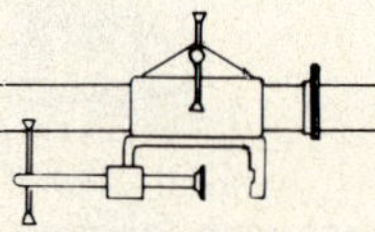
376

550-376 Extra Wide Opening   35.99
Self-centering, double action jaws (opens to 9") & reversible jaw pads. Fits #300 Series bases. (Base not included).

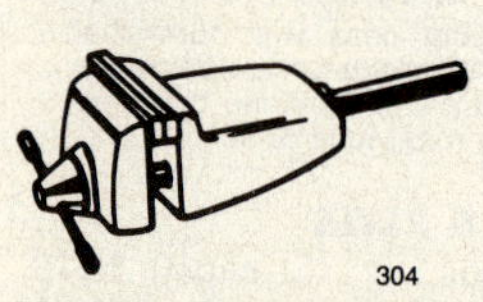
304   303

550-303 Original Vise Head   21.99
Nylon jaws. Fits #300 Series bases.

550-304 Low Profile Vise Head   26.99
Steel jaws. Fits #300 Series bases.

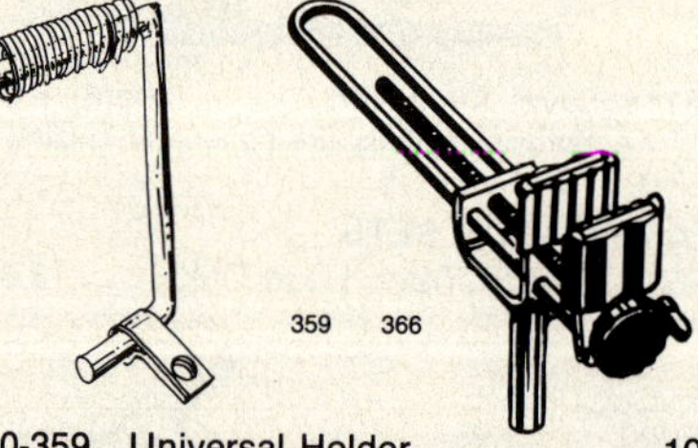
359   366

550-359 Universal Holder   10.99
550-366 Wide Opening Head   26.49
Wide opening head features Neoprene jaw pads. Fits all #300 Series bases.

317   318

550-317 Support Unit for #315   10.49
550-318 12" Cross Bar   4.29
for #315 circuit board holder (lengths to 30" on special order)

---

315   316

550-315 Circuit Board Holder   25.99
Complete w/14" cross-bar. Fits all #300 Series bases. Ideal for holding boxcars for lettering.

550-316 Extra Arms   pair 13.99
(By Special Order Only.)
for #315 circuit board holder

(not illustrated)
550-42000 Tension Arm   9.12
(By Special Order Only.)
Left side, for #315 circuit board holder.

550-44000 Solid Arm   4.60
Grooved, for #315 circuit board holder.

Solder Station
550-371   7.99
Solder and iron holder attach to #312 & all bases (except #380), to bench, wall, or free standing. Includes two sponges & mounting screws.

371

BASES

305   300   336

550-300 Standard Height (Original)   18.99
550-305 Low Profile   18.99
550-336 Up/Down Converter   25.99
attachment for #325 and #331

380   400

550-380 Vacuum PanaVise Base   30.99
550-400 Heavy Duty PanaVise Base   36.99
(By Special Order Only.)

PANAPRESS

501   502

Although it weighs less than 6 pounds and stands only 7 inches high, this hand arbor press exerts pressure up to a quarter-ton. Ideal for pressing bearings, sleeves or collars, forming and assembling small parts, punching, riveting, broaching, staking and dozens of other operations.

CONSTRUCTION: Arbor and table-plate diecast of high strength Zamak III. Operating mechanism of hardened and ground steel. Ram is reversible.

550-501 Panapress—500 psi   89.99
(By Special Order Only.)
Hand operated arbor press, 1/4 ton capacity, pressure die-cast.

550-502 Precision Panapress   99.99
Same as #501, but with adjustments for close tolerance work.

PANAVISE®
WORK POSITIONERS

REPLACEMENT JAWS

343		344

550-343   Nylon Jaws   pair   2.49
for #303 and #304 heads with screws

550-344   Grooved Nylon Jaws   pair   3.49
w/horizontal groove, for #303 and #304 heads
with screws

(not illustrated)
550-346   Deluxe Neoprene Jaw Pads   pr   2.99
grooved, for #366 head

550-352   Teflon Jaws   each   8.49
for #'s 303 and 304 with screws

550-353   Plated Steel Jaws   pair   5.49
for #303 and #304 heads with screws

550-354   Brass Jaws   pair   6.99
for #'s 303 and 304 with screws

CROSSBARS
for 315, 324, 333 & 372
20"
550-31820   5.89
30"
550-31830   7.89

FIXTURING HEADS

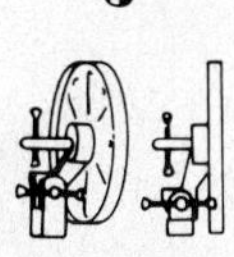

Fixturing Head Face Plate
550-337   15.99
fits all #300 Series bases

340

437

550-340   Deluxe Tilt & Turn Plate   18.99
(By Special Order Only.)
for #325, #330 & #331 assemblies

550-437   Heavy Duty Face Plate   19.99
(By Special Order Only.)
for #400 Series heavy duty base

MOUNTINGS

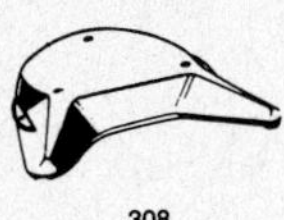

308   310

550-308   Mounting Plate, Weighted   20.99
complete w/mounting holes and mounting screws,
for #300 and #305 bases

550-310   Surface Plate   65.99
blanchard ground, w/mounting holes for #300 and
#305 bases with mounting screws

312   311

550-311   Bench Clamp   34.99
complete w/mounting screws, for #300 and #305
bases

550-312   Tray Base Mount   19.99
includes mounting screws, for #300 and #305 bases

ACCESSORIES
550-319   Circuit Board   pkg(4)   3.99
       Replacement Knobs

GENERAL®

Measuring, marking and assembly tools
for hobbyists, industry or specialty trades.

PUNCH

285-79   Automatic Center Punch   18.89
(not illustrated)
285-7924   Solid Point   **NEW**   2.96

CALIPER

285-142   6" Dial Caliper   31.44
Fiberglass reinforced plastic

LEVELS

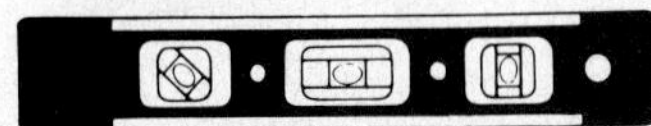

Bull's Eye Level
285-847   3.91
plastic, 1-3/8" dia

285-839   9" Magnetic Torpedo Level   18.62

MECHANICS STEEL SQUARE

285-2702	2"	13.96
285-2703	3"	15.67
285-2704	4"	16.78

MINI MECHANICAL PICKUP
Three prong steel jaws retrieve small objects up to
1/2" (14mm). Tapered point for hard-to-reach work
areas.

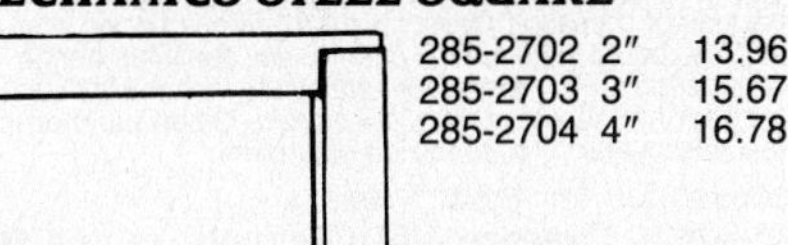

285-388   Pickup   4.51

NEEDLE FILE SET

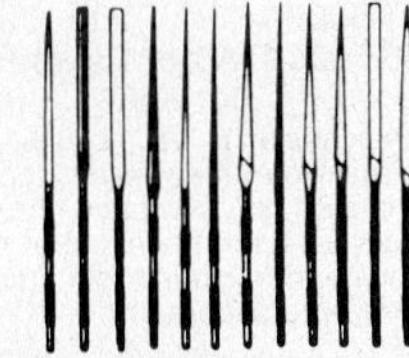

Swiss Pattern
Needle File Set
285-475
(12 pcs)   21.44

POCKET SCRIBER

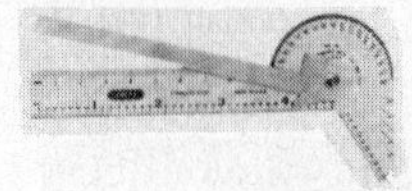

285-81   Pocket Scriber 3/8" Body   4.13

RULES

285-16   Multi Use Rule & Gauge   each   9.02
Stainless steel, can be used as a square, 4" rule has
etched graduations in 64th & millimeters, plus performs these five functions:
• drill point gauge checks 59° angle drill points
• bevel protractor for measuring angles
• center finder locates center of shafts & circles
• circle divider for dividing circles into sectors
• tap & drill table for National form of thread

285-1203   12" Flexible Rule   5.58
Stainless steel, inches & metric, 15/32" wide.

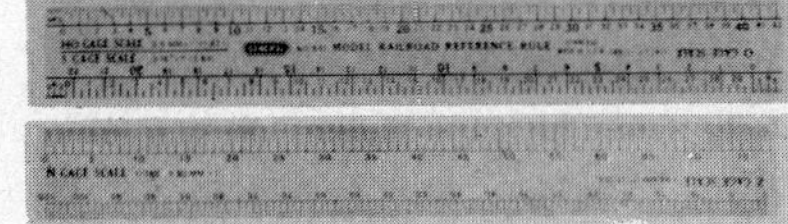

285-651   6" Railroad Scale Rule   3.56
Stainless steel, includes HO, N, Z, O and S Scales.

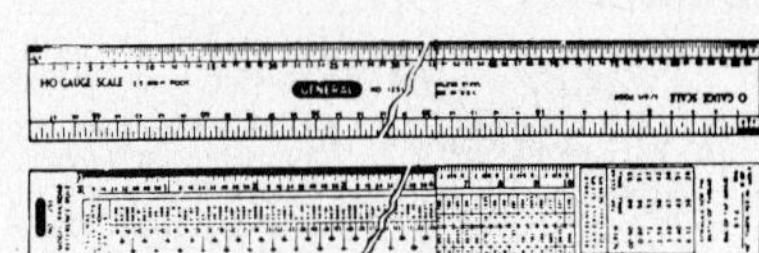

285-1251   12" Railroad Scale Rule   6.11
Stainless steel, includes HO, N, O and S Scales.

SCREW DRILL SET

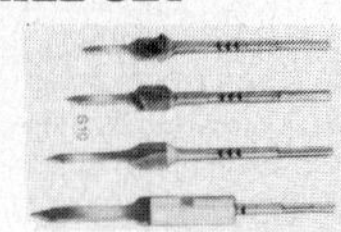

285-10   Countersink & Screw Drill Set   17.82
Drills & countersinks screw holes in one operation.
Includes 4 popular size bits, adjustable depth stop
for making flush, countersunk or plug depth holes,
snap button plastic case & instructions. Screw sizes:
6 thru 10 & 12.

TRAMMEL
Precision Adjustable
Trammel
285-520   26.84

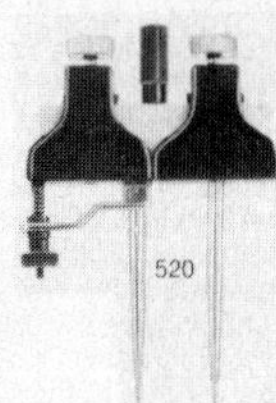

Die-cast body with hardened and
ground 3" needlepoint legs will
draw circles & measure sizable
distances with the accuracy of a
divider. Points are removable &
accurately set with fine adjusting
screws, clamp opening for beam
is 3/8 x 3/4".

520

TWEEZERS

285-411   Cross-lock Tweezers   each   3.62
nickel plated, self-closing points

Tweezer Set
285-422
set(5)   14.51

VISES

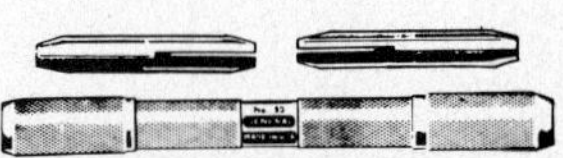

285-90   Pin Vise, double end   each   10.31
w/2 double end collets, .00 — .125

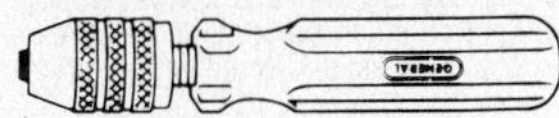

285-93   Heavy Duty Adjustable Pin Vise   9.56
Pin Vise (.00 — 125)

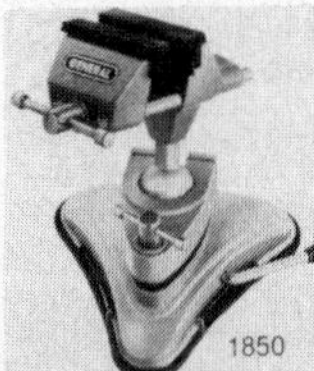

Vacuum Vise
285-1850
60.39
Multi-angle swivel
Vacuum Vise
holds firmly in any
position. This port-
able vise attaches
instantly with quick
lever action and

1850

features a universal ball joint with positive lock, "V"
grooved steel jaws (3" wide, 2-5/8" capacity) as well
as slide-on soft jaws for fragile work.

POWER MAGNET

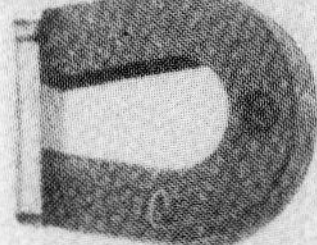

4 oz
285-3704   15.47

NorthWest Short Line

DRILL
CUTTERS
RIVET TABLE
PUNCH PRESS

PUNCH & DIES
METAL BENDER
ACCESSORIES
DRILL & TAP SETS

QUARTER CHECKER
REMOVING TOOL
(wheels, drivers &
gears from axles &
shafts)

THE PULLER

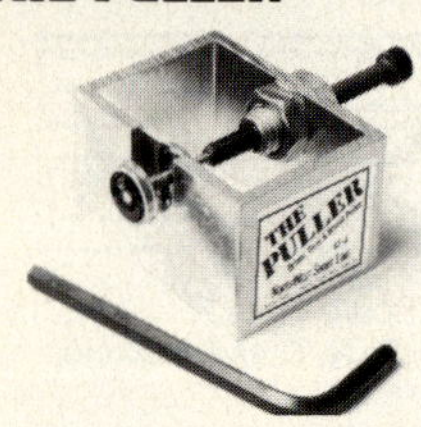

The Puller
053-454   6.95
A rigid, precision tool for removing wheels, drivers and gears from axles and shafts. Made for HO Scale modeling, but handles larger and smaller scales. Capacity: axles 1/16″ to 1/8″; drivers, wheels and gears up to 1-5/8″ O.D.; maximum press depth 1″. Puller comes complete with 2 press screws, V-plate, Allen wrench and operation suggestions. Allen wrench not usually needed, finger pressure being adequate in most cases.

Optional press screws for #454 with thumb screw head (will not accept Allen wrench).

053-45314	1/16″ Tip	each 1.75
053-45324	3/32″ Tip	each 1.75
053-45334	Cone Tip	each 1.50
053-45344	Flat Tip	each 1.50

THE QUARTERER

HO Scale
053-444   26.95

For quartering or quarter checking of drivers up to 1″ O.D. on 1/8″ or 3.0mm axles. Permits quartering either right or left lead. Wheel is pressed onto axle while wheelset is still securely held in tool to avoid possibility of slippage. Can be used to compare quartering of existing drivers. Includes operating instructions and 2 index pins (crankpin substitutes). Requires .100″ space on each side of gear to fit driver into tool.

THE BENDER

The Bender
053-484
32.95

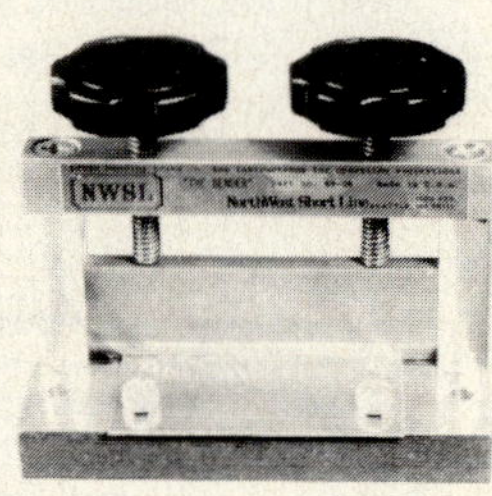

Press bending brake to bend brass or other light sheet metals up to 90°, (depends on how far you tighten press screws) up to 3″ bend length, up to .020″ half hard brass capacity. Depth guide permits duplication of bend placement on stock being bent. Includes reversible die operation suggestions and alternate urethane die material.

053-48154   Urethane Die Material   pkg(3) 2.00
permits bends without marking material, for #484

053-48164   Replacement Press   pkg(2) 2.00
Screw **(By Special Order Only.)**
w/1-1/2″ head, 1/4″ diameter & 20 threads per inch for #484

SANDING STICKS

		NEW
053-25019	120 grit (red)	2.95
053-25029	240 grit (blue)	2.95
053-25039	320 grit (green)	2.95
053-25049	400 grit (yellow)	2.95
053-25059	600 grit (black)	2.95

REPLACEMENT BELTS FOR SANDING STICKS

		NEW
053-28069	for #25019	.79
053-28079	for #25029	.79
053-28089	for #25039	.79
053-28099	for #25049	.79
053-28109	for #25059	.79

THE DUPLICUTTER

The Duplicutter
053-524   19.95
Designed for working with sheet styrene (scribing, squaring and cutting to size), but can also be used with wood modeling and cutting locomotive window glass to size. Accepts standard size styrene sheets 6-1/2″. Comes complete with a set of 4 scales O, HO, S, N.

THE SENSIPRESS +

Arbor
Punch Press

The Sensipress +
053-504   74.95
Use the press for assembling parts, wheels, etc. and as a gear puller to disassemble. Small enough to give a sensitive touch and also sturdy enough to supply up to 250 pounds of pressure. Reversible 3/8″ ram is flat on one end and bored 3/16″ on the other so you can interchange various tools. Ram set screw retains the tool. A 3/32″ tip for gear and wheel pulling is included. Gibbed and adjustable overarm for precision alignment.

Accessories for Arbor Press:

053-50504	Oversize 1/2″ OD Tool	1.50
053-50514	Blank Flat End Tool	.75
053-50524	1/16″ Diameter Tip	1.50
053-50534	3/32″ Diameter Tip	1.50
053-50544	Cone End, Concave	1.00
053-50564	Bored 2.0mm Tool	1.00
053-50574	Bored 3/32″ Tool	1.00
053-50584	Bored 1/8″ Tool	1.00
053-50594	Interchange Tool Set	7.75
	(Set of all the above except 50534)	
053-50604	''V'' Plate	3.00
053-50014	Arbor Press Punch Adapter	3.95
	for #504	

Punches up to 1/8″ holes easily in brass and styrene, larger holes may exceed tool capacity depending on material and thickness. You can "nibble" your way with adjacent punching to make car window openings, etc. Includes ram adapter. Punches and dies available separately.

Round Hole Punches & Dies for #504   ea 4.05

SIZE	PUNCH	DIE
1/16″	053-50104	053-50114
5/64″	053-50124	053-50134
3/32″	053-50144	053-50154
1/8″	053-50164	053-50174

THE RIVETER +

Rivet Embossing Table
053-514   44.95

Rivet table can be easily attached to Sensipress + (not included). Comes with .015 (1-1/2 HO) rivet embossing punch and die. Tool enables "accurate rivet spacing". Advancing knob is calibrated in .001″ increments.

Optional Embossing Punches & Dies for #514:

SIZE	PUNCH	each	DIE	each
universal	053-51004	3.00		
.010″	053-51104	4.00	053-51114	4.00
.015″	053-51154	4.00	053-51164	4.00
.020″	053-51204	3.00	053-51214	3.00
.030″	053-51304	3.00	053-51314	3.00
.040″	053-51404	3.00	053-51414	3.00
.050″	053-51504	3.00	053-51514	3.00

053-51014   Rivet Embossing   27.95
Punch/Die Set for Riveter +
Includes one each of the following sizes of punches and dies: .010″, .020″, .030″, .040″, .050″ and a universal punch.

THE CHOPPER

The Chopper
053-494   19.95
Heavy duty strip wood length cutter. Also can do mitre cuts (guides for 30, 45 & 60 included). Adjustable stop piece permits setting any cut length up to 3-1/4″, for exactly duplicate cut pieces — for car decking, ties, trestle building, etc. Four blades and operating suggestions included. No special blades needed, uses single edge razor blades. Also cuts styene and other model making plastics. Safety top keeps handle from slipping or raising dangerously high.

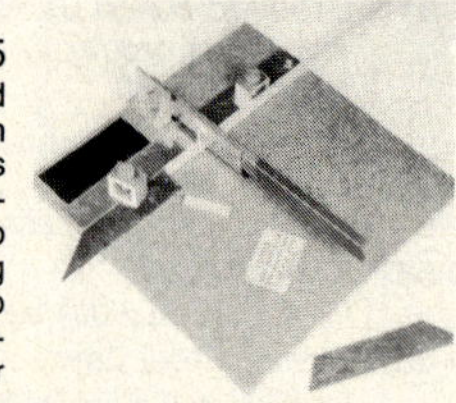

053-49154   Extra Blades for #494   pkg(8) 1.00

053-594   Chopper III   27.95
Heavy duty wide base version of the Chopper allows easier handling of long pieces of material. Chopper III provides for installation of up to 3 handles, permitting multiple set-ups. Includes one handle only, additional handles are available (see #49144 below). The 18″ wide base is a sturdier work area and the safety top keeps handle from slipping or raising dangerously high.

053-49144   Extra Handle   8.95
Complete handle assembly for The Chopper and Chopper III.

THE TRUE-SANDER

True-Sander
053-574   26.95
Combination holding jig and sanding block for finishing and squaring off stripwood and strip styrene. Jig can be adjusted to hold anything from thinnest stripwood up to an HO body shell (angle adjustment to 90 degrees). Makes perfect fits easier.

EXTRA FLEXIBLE STRAND WIRE

053-100019	30 Gauge, black, 4′	.95
053-100029	30 Gauge, red, 4′	.95
053-100039	28 Gauge, black, 4′	.95
053-100059	30 Gauge, brown, 4′	.95
053-100069	28 Gauge, brown, 4′	.95
053-100079	29 Gauge (super flexible), black, 2′	.95

DRILL AND TAP SETS

053-30505	1/6-60W	each 15.75
	(By Special Order Only.)	
053-30605	1.0mm x 0.25	each 10.75
053-30625	1.2mm x 0.25	each 10.50
053-30645	1.4mm x 0.3	each 9.75
053-30675	1.7mm x 0.35	each 9.25
053-30705	2.0mm x 0.4	each 9.00
053-30765	2.6mm x 0.45	each 8.25
053-30805	3.0mm x 0.5	each 8.25

HAND TAP

053-30005	1/16-60W	each 9.75
	(By Special Order Only.)	
053-30145	1.4mm x 0.3	each 3.25

THE ALIGNER GEAR ALIGNMENT TOOL

Installing a gear squarely (without wobble) on a shaft or axle is tedious and sometimes unsuccessful. This tool will "square-up" and salvage most such problemsome gears in place.

053-324	for 2.4mm or 3/32″ axle	5.95
053-334	for 3mm axle	5.95
053-384	for 1/8″ axle	5.95

SHERLINE

Milling Machine can be used for milling, drilling, fly-cutting and boring. Use lathe for turning wood, plastic or metal. Sherline machines have inch-feed threads.

VERTICAL MILL

Features precision spindle adjustable pre-load bearings, anti-backlash feed screws, table locks and variable speed control. Complete instructions.

677-5000 Vertical Milling Machine 470.00
with 1/2 HP DC motor.

677-5100 Vertical Milling Machine 480.00
Metric version of #5000.
(By Special Order Only.)

677-5201 XYZ BASE 300.00
The Vertical Mill can be purchased without the Headstock and Motor/speed control. This allows Lathe owners to swap their headstock and motor/speed control from the lathe to the mill in approximately 30 seconds.

SPECIFICATIONS

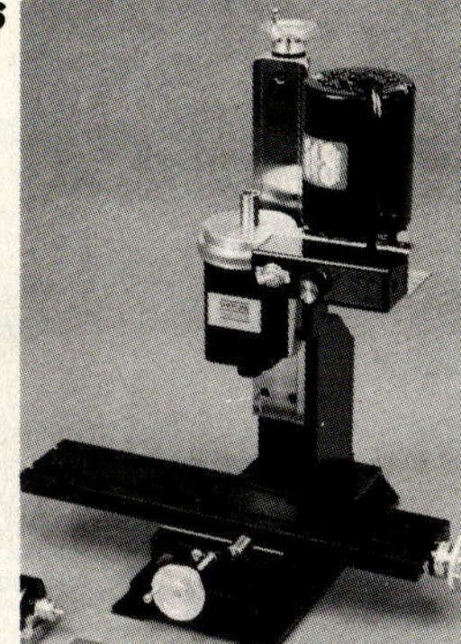

SPEEDS: 70-3000 RPM

CAPACITY: 13" x 2-3/4" tee slotted work table with 9" of movement on the 'X' axis and '3' on the 'Y' axis. In its uppermost position the spindle nose is 8" from the table and has 6-1/2" movement on the 'Z' (vertical) axis. (Head may be rotated for machining angles.)

CONTROLS: Movements on all axes are controlled by handwheels calibrated in 1/1000" divisions.

CONSTRUCTION: Fully dovetailed machined slides with adjustable gibs, solid base with mounting holes. Permanently lubricated ball bearing used with spindle, which has a morse no. 1 inside taper and 3/4"-16 TPI male thread. (Design permits conversion to metric callibration.)

OVERALL DIMENSIONS:
12" x 14-1/2" x 17" high.

TABLES

677-1185 Vertical Milling Table 75.98
Table mounts on the cross-slide allowing stock to be moved in three axes. Cutters held in headstock for milling. Not as sturdy as #3050 but performs same basic functions.
(By Special Order Only.)

677-1184 Vertical Milling Table 75.98
Metric version of #1185.
(By Special Order Only.)

COVER

677-5150 Vinyl Mill Cover 10.98

4" ROTARY TABLE   *NEW*

677-3700 Rotary Table 250.00
Designed to work with their Model 5000 and 5100 milling Machines. Can be used on any mill whenever the 4-inch size would be an advantage. 2" high and 4" (100mm) in diameter. Features solid bar stock steel and weighs 7 pounds. Hardened worm gear case. Engraved with a laser, giving sharp and precise lines every 5°, numbered every 15°. These lines are calibrated with the 72-tooth worm gear which is driven by the handwheel. The handwheel is divided into 50 parts, making each line on the handwheel 1/10 degree. This allows a circle to be divided into 3600 increments without interpolation. It takes 72 revolutions of the handwheel to rotate the table one revolution. Includes two holddown clamps and "T" nut fasteners. Plus an adapter that allows the Sherline 3- and 4-jaw chucks to be mounted directly to the Rotary Table & 6 page instruction manual.

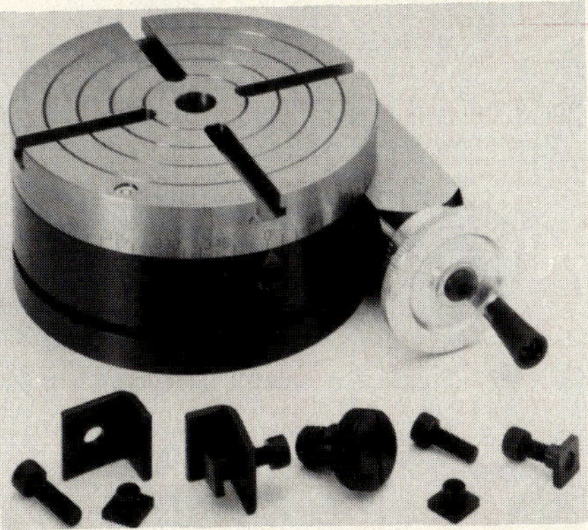

677-3701 Right Angle Attachment *NEW* 50.00
For use with #3700. Mounts the table in the vertical position. Has a locking mechanism that is positive and does not move the table as it is locked. Black oxide base.

3" LATHE

Features fully dovetailed slides, adjustable gibs on cross-slide and saddle, protected lead and feed screws, adjustable headstock bearings that are prelubricated for life, hollow headstock spindle and a variable speed 115v motor. (220v 50Hz motors are also available.) Complete instructions.

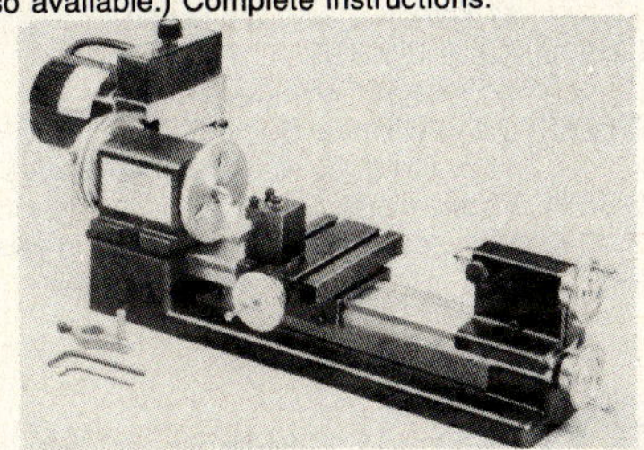

677-4000 Lathe Machine Base 390.00
with 1/2 HP DC motor.

677-4100 Lathe Machine Base 400.00
Metric version of #4000.
(By Special Order Only.)

677-4150 Lathe Cover 8.00
677-40001 Lathe Starter Package 460.00
Includes 4000, 1041, 1072

LATHE ACCESSORY

677-3050 Vertical Milling Column 110.00
Attachment features solid aluminum base, dovetailed vertical column and adjustable saddle. Various functions possible include grooving, keyway cutting and flycutting.
(By Special Order Only.)

677-3053 Vertical Milling Column 110.00
Metric version of #3050.
(By Special Order Only.)

MODEL 4000 SPECIFICATIONS

Swing Over Bed	3.5"
Swing Over Carriage	1.75"
Distance Between Centers	8.00"
Hole Through Spindle	0.405"
Spindle Nose Thread	3/4" x 16 T.P.I.
Spindle Nose Taper	No. 1 Morse
Travel of Cross Slide	2.25"
Travel of Tailstock Spindle	1.5"
Taper of Tailstock Spindle	No. 0 Morse
Headstock Swivel	360°
Protractor Graduations	0° to 45° by 5°
Handwheel Dial Graduations	0.001"
Electronic Speed Range	70-3000 RPM
Length Overall	18"
Width Overall	7-1/2"
Height Overall	6"
Shipping Weight	24lbs.

ACCESSORIES

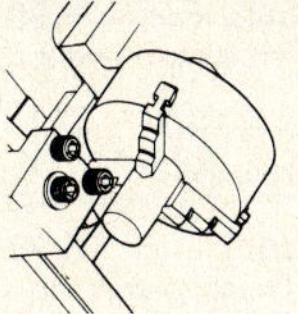

3-Jaw Self Centering Chuck
677-1041 75.00

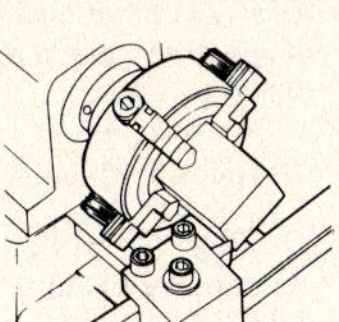

4-Jaw Chuck
677-1044 75.49

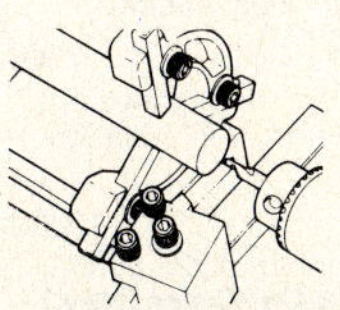

Steady Rest
677-1074 30.00

Tailstock Chuck & Key
677-1072 35.00

677-1160 Collet Set (1-5/16) set of 5 70.00
(By Special Order Only.)
677-1161 WW Collet Adapter & Draw Bar 32.49
677-1178 Collet Set, Metric set of 5 70.00

677-1187 Chuck to Tee Slot Adapter 4.00
677-1191 Live Center 30.00
677-1291 Spacer Block Kit 40.00
(By Special Order Only.)

677-3001 Power Feed for Lathe 60.00
677-3002 Cut-Off Tool & Holder 35.00
677-3003 Two Position Tool Post 15.00
677-3005 1/4" sq. High Spd Tool Blank 3.29
677-3006 Carbide Tool Set 19.49
677-3007 High Speed Tool Set 15.00
677-3012 Hold Down Set 21.98
677-3020 Allen "T" Driver 5.49
(For cap screws used on machines)
677-3021 Center Drill Set 16.29
677-3551 Milling Vise 60.00
677-3052 Fly Cutter 30.00
677-3054 Boring Head 50.00
677-3055 Morse No.1 Tool Blank 15.00
677-3056 T Nut 10/32 pkg(4) 2.20
677-3057 Rocker Tool Post 20.00
677-3058 4-Jaw Hold Down Set 5.45
677-3059 Slow Speed Attachment 30.00
not required w/DC models
677-3060 Milling Collets 35.00
677-3062 High Speed Attachment 12.00
not required w/DC models
677-3063 Boring Tool (1-5/16) 9.00
(By Special Order Only.)

677-3072 Drill Chuck and Draw Bar 32.50
677-3079 End Mill Holder 3/8" 27.10
677-3061 Boring Tool for #3054 8.98
677-3080 End Mill Set 25.98
677-3100 Screw Cutting Attachment 107.98
677-4004 Drive Belt 5.00
677-5300 Home Machinist's Handbook 19.00
677-5325 Mill Instruction Manual 2.00
677-5327 Complete Instruction *NEW* 10.00
Manual
Instructions for boring, screw cutting, knurling, indexing attachments, rotary table use and more. Includes a 24-page color catalog of tools and accessories plus the 24-page color instruction guide in a black 1" ring binder.

677-3200 Indexing Attachment 150.00
677-7505 Cutting Oil 1qt 12.35
(By Special Order Only.)

X-ACTO®

Designed for artist, craftsmen/women and hobbyists. X-Acto began producing precision knives and tools in 1935. Included are cutting tools and accessories, drills, tweezers, pliers, files, woodcarving sets and other craft tools that are ideal for miniature work.

HOBBY KNIVES

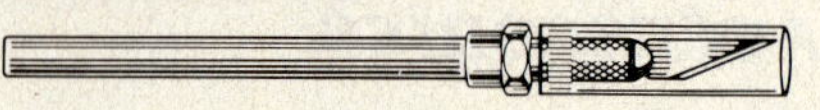

790-3021 #1 Knife w/Safety Guard Box 4.99
Includes #11 blade and hexagonal chuck to prevent rolling.

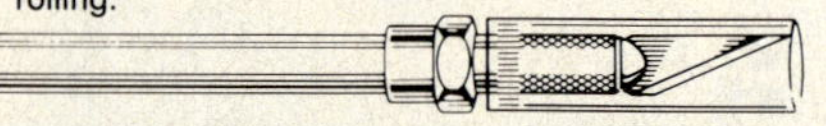

790-3022 #2 Knife w/Safety Guard 6.99
Includes #2 blade and hexagonal chuck to prevent rolling.

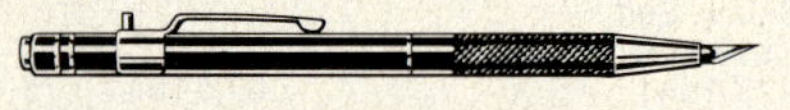

790-3295 X-Calibre Retractable Knife 10.99
Executive design with metal pocket clip. Balanced lightweight; perfect for most light duty cutting.

790-5090 X-Calibre Set 7.49
For delicate, precision cutting of lightweight materials. Includes safety cap and five #11 blades.
(By Special Order Only.)

790-5095 X-Calibre RT Set 13.50
Stainless steel blade retracts with push button. Pocket clip. **(By Special Order Only.)**

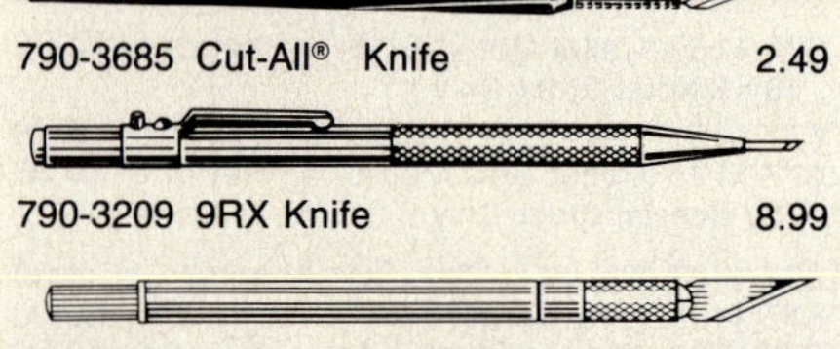

790-3685 Cut-All® Knife 2.49

790-3209 9RX Knife 8.99

790-3299 X-Press™ Rear Release Knife 4.69

#1 Knife w/#11 Blade

790-3201 #1 Light Duty Knife 2.39
790-3601 #1 Knife w/Safety Cap 2.79

#1 Knife w/#11 Blade

790-3211 #1 Super Knife w/Rear Blade Release 7.69

#2 Knife w/#22 Blade

790-3202 #2 Medium Duty Knife 3.39
790-3602 #2 Knife w/Safety Cap 3.99

Gold finish w/#10 Blade

790-3203 #3 Pen-Knife 4.69

w/#204 Blades

790-5204 #4 Stencil Knife w/5 #204 Blades 4.99

Plastic handle w/#19 Blade

790-3205 #5 Heavy Duty Knife 4.49

Aluminum Hexagonal handle w/#24 Blade

790-3206 #6 Heavy Duty Knife 6.99

The perfect precision tool for all light-duty cutting.
790-3241 Craft Swivel Knife 6.69

UTILITY KNIVES

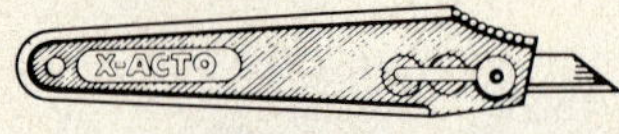

w/#8 Blade

790-3208 #8R Utility Knife (retractable) 1.69
Cycolac handle w/2 Blades

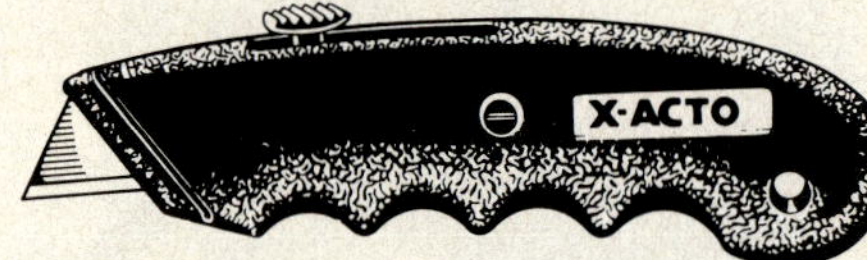

790-3272 Plastic Retractable Utility Knife 4.99

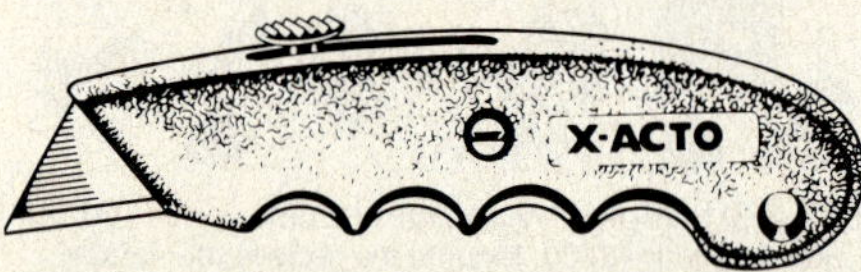

790-3274 Metal Retractable Utility Knife 6.79

KNIFE SETS

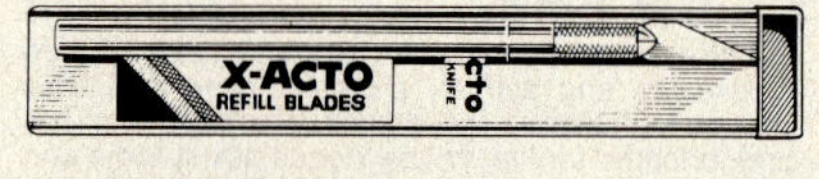

790-5211 Knife Set #51 3.99
#1 knife w/5 assorted blades
790-5212 Knife Set #52 5.69
#2 knife w/5 assorted blades
790-5262 Double Knife Set #62 9.99
#1 & #2 knives w/10 assorted blades
790-5281 Triple Knife Set 13.95
#1, #2 & #5 knives plus 10 assorted blades in plastic case.

Knife Chest #82
790-5282 19.95
#1, #2 & #5 knives plus 10 assorted blades.

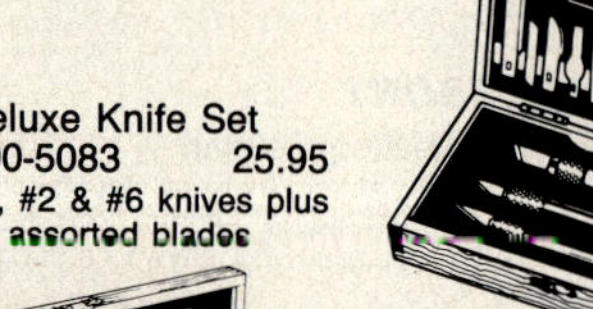

Deluxe Knife Set
790-5083 25.95
#1, #2 & #6 knives plus 14 assorted blades

Deluxe Knife Set
790-5021 34.95
#1, #2, #6 and woodcarving knives, plus 5 woodcarving blades and 12 assorted blades.

Do-It-Yourself Set
790-5028 19.95
#2 and woodcarving knives, plus 8 assorted blades.

MODEL RR TOOL SETS

Deluxe Model RR Set
790-5025 49.95
Contains: #5 knife w/#19 blade, #234 razor saw blade, hammer w/brass head, tweezer, jewelers screwdriver, long nose pliers and needle file.

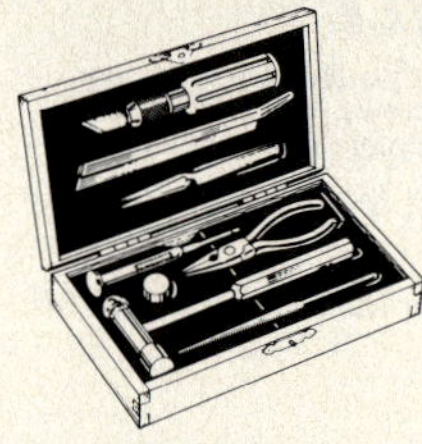

Model Builders Set
790-5026 42.95
Contains: #1 knife w/#11 blade, #8R knife, tweezer, jewelers screwdriver, long nose pliers, needle file, large and small plastic clamps and cross action clamp.

CARVING TOOL SETS

Carving Chest "The Leader"
790-5175 28.95

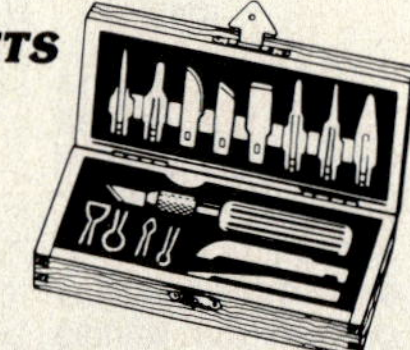

#5 handle with 5 assorted blades: two 3″ blades, 6 gouges and 4 routers. Wood chest.

790-5177 Woodcarving Set 14.95
#5 handle w/6 gouge-blades, 4 regular blades, 2 3-inch blades, in Vizi-dome plastic case.

Basic Whittlers Set
790-5023 28.95
Contains: #1 knife w/#11 blade, woodcarving knife w/#104 blade, #1 blade assortment, #'s 101 and 106 woodcarving blades, instruction booklet, whittlers pattern and abrasive and leather strop.

Standard Woodcarving Set
790-5024 22.95
Contains: #5 knife w/#19 blade, #'s 15, 18, 22, 24 and 26 blades, and A, B, C, D, E and F gouges.

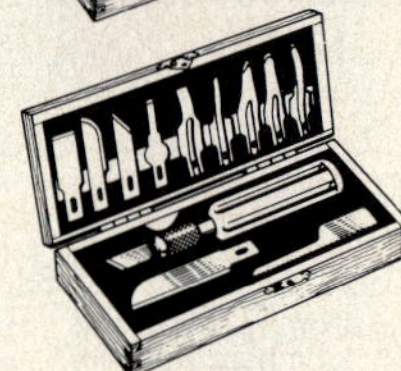

Carving Tool Set
790-5179 29.97
6 hardwood handled chisels

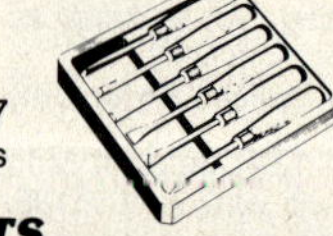

KNIFE & TOOL SETS

"The Crafter" Tool Set
790-5086 43.95
#1, #2 and #5 knives and assortment of blades, gouger, routers, plus plane, sander, spokeshave, balsa stripper in a wood chest.

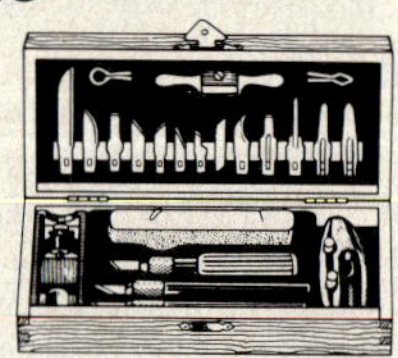

Deluxe Hobby Tool and Knife Set
790-5089 159.95
#1, #2 and #5 knives, stencil knife, craft swivel knife, burnisher and assortment of blades all in a wood chest.
(By Special Order Only.)

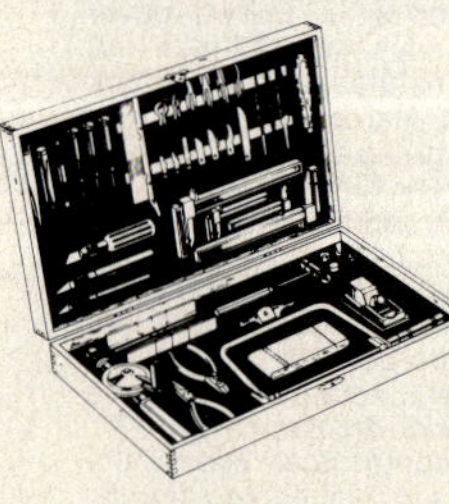

X-ACTO

Designed for artist, craftsmen/women and hobbyists. X-Acto began producing precision knives and tools in 1935. Included are cutting tools and accessories, drills, tweezers, pliers, files, wood-carving sets and other craft tools that are ideal for miniature work.

KNIFE BLADES

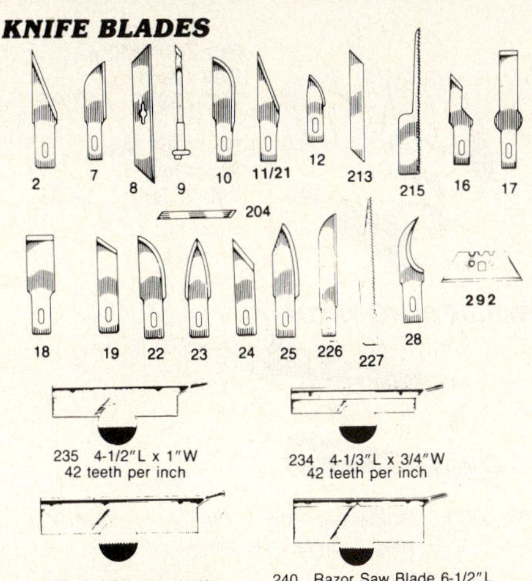

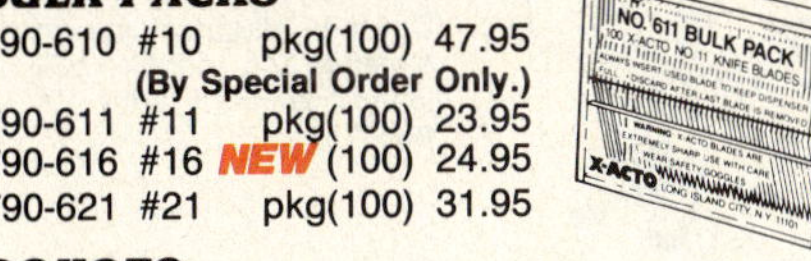

235 4-1/2" L x 1" W
42 teeth per inch

234 4-1/3" L x 3/4" W
42 teeth per inch

236 5-1/2" L x 1-1/4" W
24 teeth per inch

240 Razor Saw Blade 6-1/2" L
25 teeth per inch

239 54 teeth per inch

790-8	for #8R Utility Knife	pkg(5)	1.99
790-9	for #9 Retractable	pkg(5)	5.99
790-31	Blade Assortment #1	each	1.99

Includes two #11 and one each of #'s 10, 16 and 17.

790-32	Blade Assortment #2	each	2.79

Includes two #24 and one each of #'s 18, 19 and 22.

790-204	for #4 Stencil Knife	each	1.99
790-245	for Craft Swivel	pkg(2)	2.49
790-292	Heavy Duty Utility for #3272 & 3274	pkg(5)	2.39
790-295	for #5095	pkg(5)	5.99
790-411	#11 Fine Point in Safety Dispenser	pkg(15)	4.69
790-402	#2 in Safety Dispenser	pkg(12)	5.29
790-202	#2 Blade	pkg(5)	1.99
790-211	#11 Blade	pkg(5)	1.99

STAINLESS STEEL BLADES

790-221	#11 Blade	pkg(5)	1.99
790-421	#11 Blade in Safety Dispenser	pkg(15)	5.99

(By Special Order Only.)

RAZOR BLADES

790-270	Single Edge Blades	pkg(5)	1.69
790-271	Single Edge Blades	pkg(12)	2.99
790-670	Single Edge Blades	pkg(100)	12.79

BULK PACKS

790-610	#10	pkg(100)	47.95

(By Special Order Only.)

790-611	#11	pkg(100)	23.95
790-616	#16 **NEW**	(100)	24.95
790-621	#21	pkg(100)	31.95

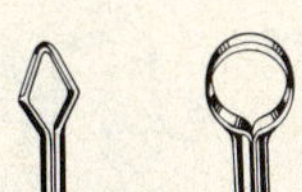

GOUGES

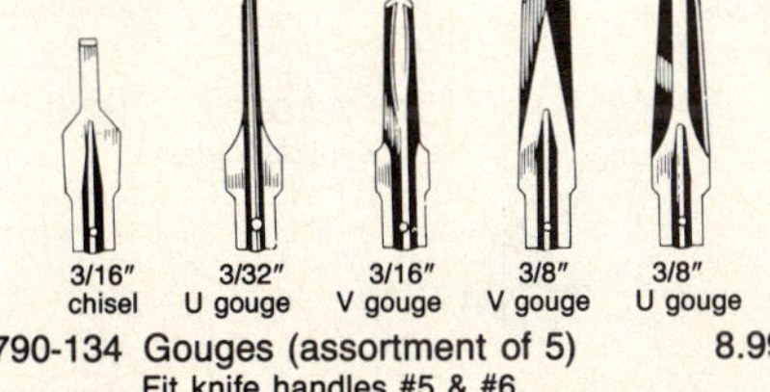

3/16" chisel	3/32" U gouge	3/16" V gouge	3/8" V gouge	3/8" U gouge

790-134 Gouges (assortment of 5) 8.99
Fit knife handles #5 & #6.

ROUTERS

.300 round	V shape	.550 round	.500 straight

790-135 Routers (assortment of 4) 8.99
Fit knife handle #5 & #6. For carving out grooves, hollows and recesses.

Blade No	Qty	Price/ Pkg	fit knife handle:				
			1	2	3	5	6
790-2	5	1.99		x		x	x
790-10	5	2.99	x		x		
790-11	5	1.89	x		x		
790-12	5	6.99	x		x		
790-213	5	2.99	x				
790-215	5	5.99		x		x	x
790-16	5	1.89	x		x		
790-17	5	1.89	x		x		
790-18	5	1.99		x		x	x
790-19	5	1.99		x		x	x
790-21	5	1.99	x		x		
790-22	5	3.49		x		x	x
790-23	5	7.29		x		x	x
790-24	5	1.89		x		x	x
790-25	5	6.49		x		x	x
790-226	5	3.99		x		x	x
790-227	5	4.99		x		x	x
790-28	5	9.79		x		x	x
790-234	1	2.79				x	x
790-235	1	2.99				x	x
790-236	1	3.69				x	x
790-239	1	4.49				x	x
790-240	1	6.99				x	x

x—Compatible Knife/Blade Combination

FILE SETS

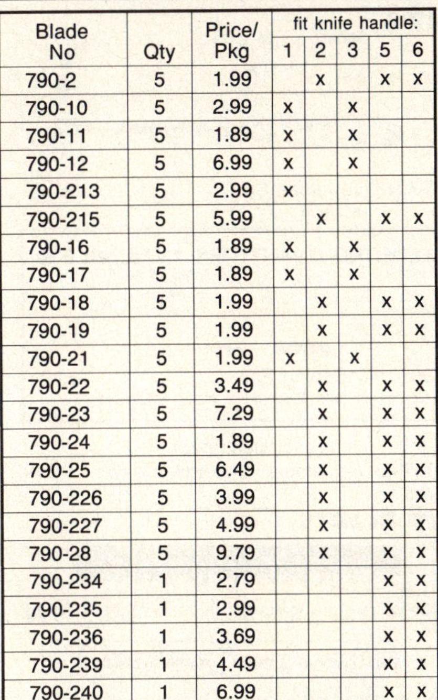

File Set
(3 files & handle)
790-73580   9.49

790-73560	Swiss Needle File Set, Assorted (12)	27.95
790-73600	Univ Needle File Handle	3.59

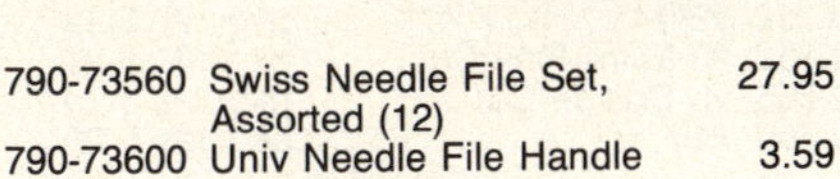

Swiss Needle File Set
(6 files and handle)
790-73610
17.95

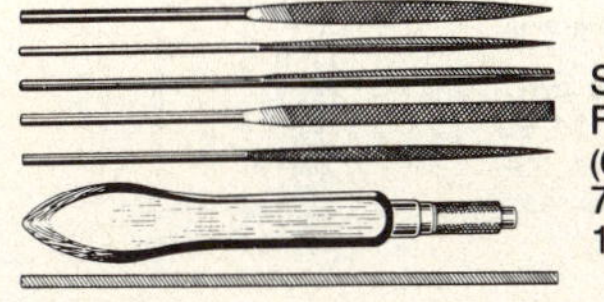

790-73650	Miniature File Set	each 14.95

3-1/8" long-storage pouch included.

790-73660	Needle Rasps Set	each 14.95

Storage pouch included.

NEEDLE FILES

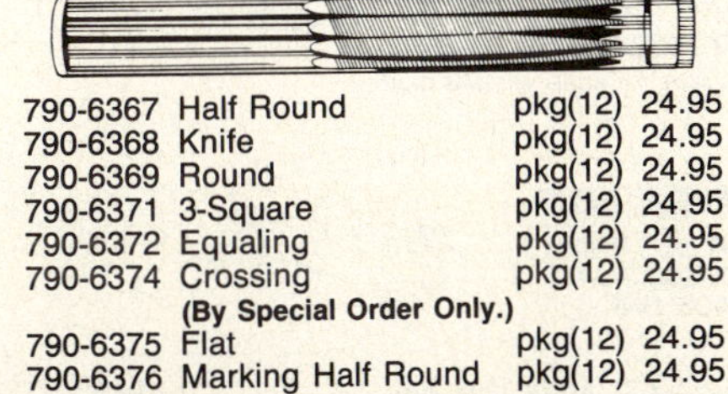

790-6367	Half Round	pkg(12) 24.95
790-6368	Knife	pkg(12) 24.95
790-6369	Round	pkg(12) 24.95
790-6371	3-Square	pkg(12) 24.95
790-6372	Equaling	pkg(12) 24.95
790-6374	Crossing	pkg(12) 24.95

(By Special Order Only.)

790-6375	Flat	pkg(12) 24.95
790-6376	Marking Half Round	pkg(12) 24.95

BURNISHERS

790-7701	Ball Burnisher, 1/16"	ea 3.99
790-7702	Ball Burnisher, 1/8"	ea 3.99

PINPOINT STYLUS & LIFTER

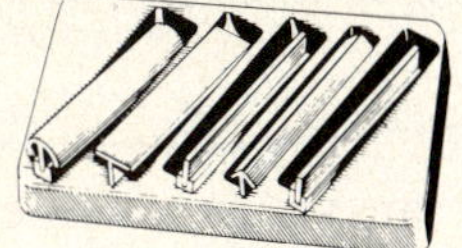

790-7705 Pinpoint Stylus & Lifter   3.99

SANDERS

Contour Sander w/5 heads
790-73510   13.95

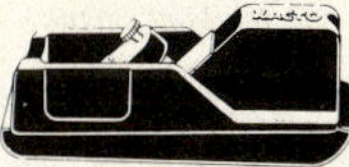

Block Sander 2 x 5"
790-7042   3.99

SANDING ACCESSORIES

790-7035	Sanding Stick w/Belt	each 4.29
790-7038	Sanding Stick	each 2.99

BLOCK PLANE

3-3/4" long single bevel steel blade steel bottom plate. Molded body for delicate and accurate planing.

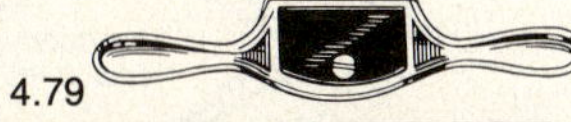

Block Plane
790-7040   6.49

SPOKE SHAVE

Solid, one-piece metal handle 3-5/8" long. Single bevel steel blade 7/8" wide. For fine shaving, rounding and shaping.

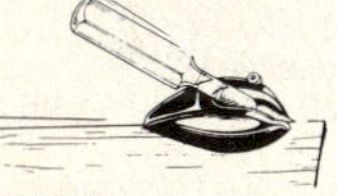

Spoke Shave
790-7045   4.79

LIMITED QUANTITIES AVAILABLE

790-30 Blade for Spoke Shave pkg(2) 1.79

BALSA STRIPPER

Precision cutter 3-3/4" long. Cuts sheets to 1/16" thick, in strips 1/16" thick, in strips 1/16" to 5/16" wide. Adjustable width. Use with #5 or #6 knife.

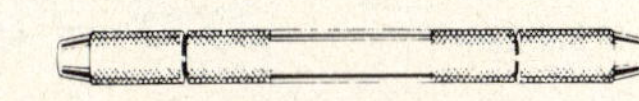

Balsa Stripper
790-7048   5.69

HAND DRILL PIN VISE

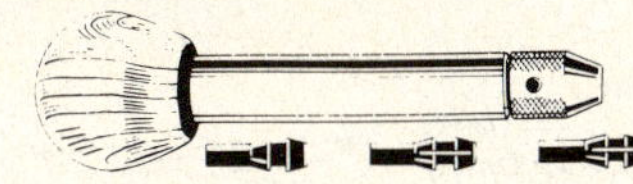

790-73220 Double-ended Hand Drill Pin Vise   4.99
Contains chucks that will accept #49-#80 bits.

DRILL CHUCK ADAPTER

790-73210 Precision Chuck Set   8.99
3 collets with interchangeable standard handle for sizes 45-80 drills.

TWIST DRILLS

790-6409	Drills 55-80	assorted (12)	12.95
790-6410	Drills 45-60	assorted (12)	12.95
790-6411	Drills 1/16-3/16"	assorted (9)	12.95

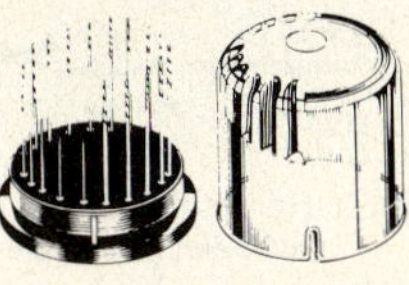

Drill Stand Set
790-6412   29.95
w/20 drills 61-80, stand & cover

X-ACTO

Designed for artist, craftsmen/women and hobbyists. X-Acto began producing precision knives and tools in 1935. Included are cutting tools and accessories, drills, tweezers, pliers, files, wood-carving sets and other craft tools that are ideal for miniature work.

TWEEZERS

790-73360 Soldering Tweezer 4-1/2″   3.99
medium sharp points

790-73370 Pointed Tweezer 6-1/2″   3.99
self-closing

790-73380 Soldering Tweezer 6-1/2″   4.49
self-closing blunt serrated points

790-73430 Angular Tweezer 6″   4.49
fine serrated points

(not illustrated)
790-73350 5″ Fine Point   10.99
(By Special Order Only.)

PLIERS

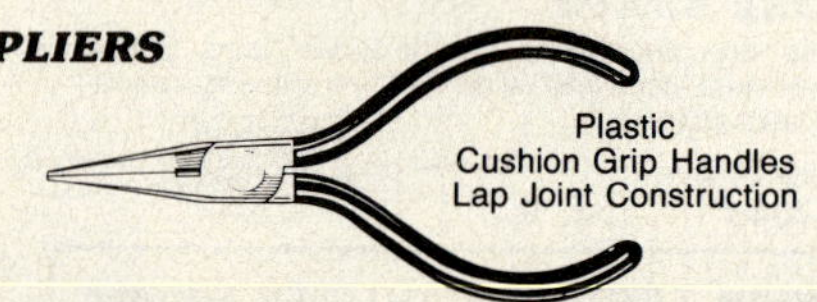

Plastic
Cushion Grip Handles
Lap Joint Construction

790-75040 Long Nose, Side Cutting   11.95

Diagonal Cutting
790-75050   11.95

Flat Nose, 4-1/2″
790-75060   11.95

Snipe Nose, 4-1/2″
790-75070   11.95

Bent Nose
790-75110   12.95
(By Special Order Only.)

Extra Long Nose
790-75100   15.95

VISE-GRIP® LOCKING PLIERS

Curved Jaws
790-7471   14.95
(By Special Order Only.)

Long Nose
790-7472   16.95
(By Special Order Only.)

SCREWDRIVERS

790-7068 Jewelers   pkg(5) 8.49
790-7069 Jewelers   8.49
w/Interchangeable Blades

HAMMER SET

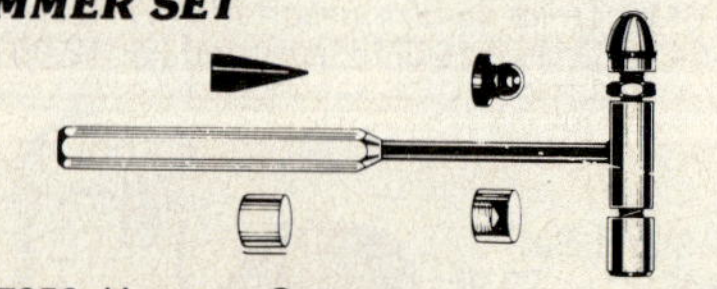

790-7050 Hammer Set   14.95
w/6 interchangeable heads

SAWS

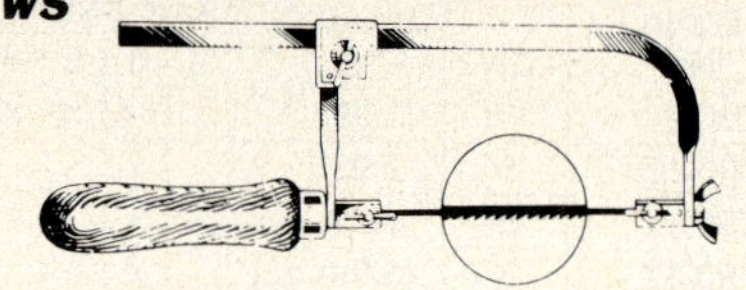

790-7043 Jeweler's Saw   21.95
w/blade

■ **LIMITED QUANTITIES AVAILABLE** ■

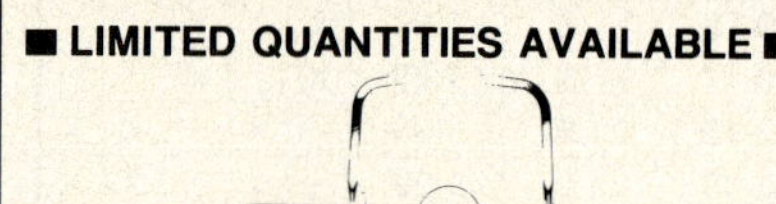

790-7044 Coping Saw   8.49
Comes with one standard saw blade. Adjustable grips.

(not illustrated)
790-7046 Adjustable Pocket Hacksaw   11.99

SAW BLADES

790-734 Coping Saw Blade   pkg(5) 5.29

790-735 Spiral Saw Blade   pkg(3) 5.29

(not illustrated)
790-246 Hacksaw   pkg(3) 1.99
Adjustable Blades

JEWELER'S SAW BLADES

for #7043 saw
790-746 #6/0   pkg(12) 5.29
790-752 #2/0   pkg(12) 5.29
790-753 #3 Extra Fine Cut   pkg(12) 5.29
790-755 #5 Coarse Cut   pkg(12) 5.29
790-759 #14   pkg(12) 5.29

RAZOR SAW SETS

Razor Saw & Knife Set
790-75310   14.95
#5 handle, 234, 235 & 236 blades, #15 keyhole saw blade, 5 knife blades

#5 Handle Set
790-75300   7.99
with #234 & #235 blades

Extra-Fine Set
790-75350   6.99

6-1/2″ Set
790-75380   7.99
Includes #5 knife w/#240 blade.

MITRE BOX

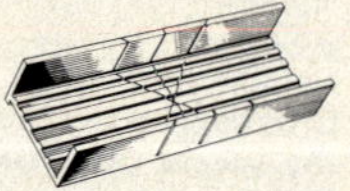

FOR USE WITH #790-236 SAW BLADE ONLY!

790-75320 Mitre Box Set   14.95
Contains aluminum mitre box #7533, #236 razor saw blade and #5 handle.

790-75330 Mitre Box Only   each 7.99
Extruded aluminum, 6″ long, 3/4 x 1-3/4″ capacity. Grooves on base to hold wood, etc., in from 1/16″ to 1/4″.

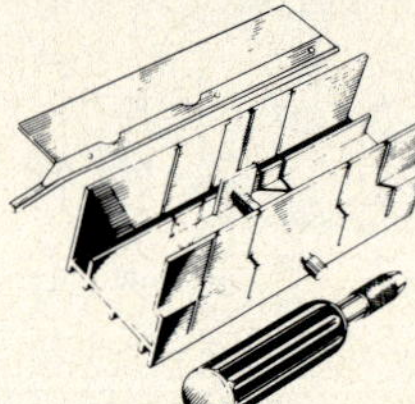

SurGrip® Mitre Box Set
790-75370   27.95

SurGrip® Mitre Box Only
790-75360   19.95

SOLDERING IRON

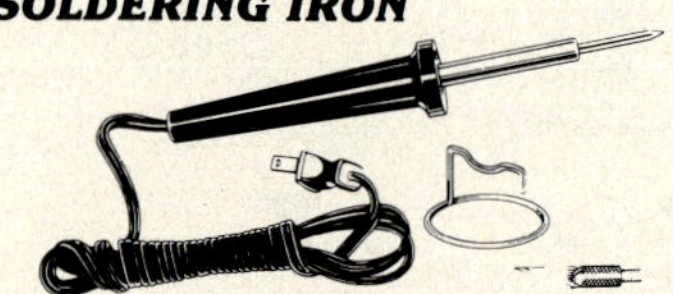

790-73780 Soldering Iron 110V   14.95
w/tip and hot knife blade

SOLDERING AIDS

790-7456 Cross-Action Clamp   pkg(3) 2.99
Heat Sink
790-73480 Soldering Aid Kit   14.95
6 tools with carrying case
(By Special Order Only.)

X-TRA HANDS

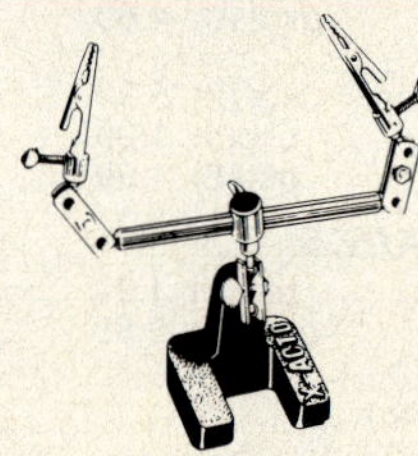

X-tra Hand (single)
790-75130   14.95

X-tra Hands (double)
790-75140   19.95

X-tra Hands w/Magnifier
790-75170   23.95
Double alligator spring clamps and double ball joints hold work firmly. 2X magnifier.

Magnifier
790-75160   15.95
2X magnification.

VISE & CLAMPS

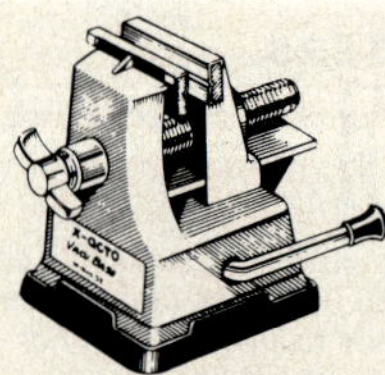

Mini Vacu-Vise
790-73700
8.99

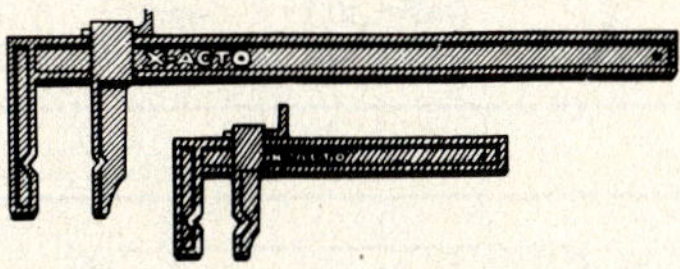

Designed for artist, craftsmen/women and hobbyists. X-Acto began producing precision knives and tools in 1935. Included are cutting tools and accessories, drills, tweezers, pliers, files, woodcarving sets and other craft tools that are ideal for miniature work.

THE NATIONAL MODEL RAILROAD ASSOCIATION, INC.

See also: BOOKS Section to join NMRA

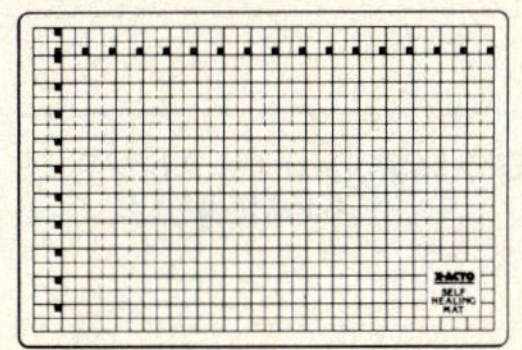

790-7446 ''C'' Clamp Set (4 clamps)   9.69

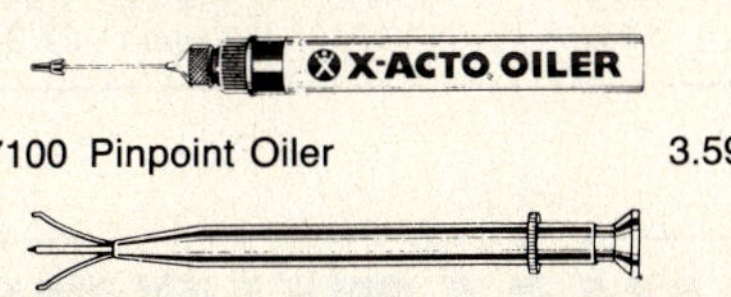

790-7003 Small Clamp (plastic)   pkg(2) 3.59
3-1/4'' long w/1'' throat depth.
790-7004 Large Clamp (plastic)   pkg(2) 6.79
7-1/4'' long w/2-1/16'' throat depth
790-7450 Mini ''C'' Clamp   pkg(3) 6.99
          Assortment

SELF-HEALING MAT
One-inch grid pattern, 3mm thickness, non-slip bottom.

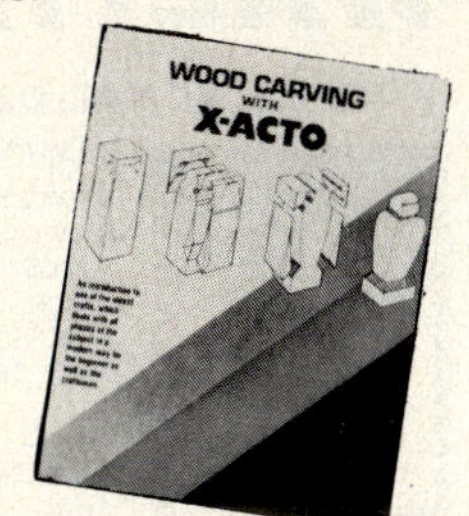

790-7760 8-1/2 x 12''   (gray) 10.95
790-7761 12 x 18''   (gray) 18.45

MISCELLANEOUS

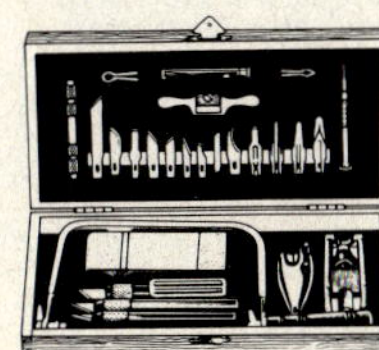

790-7100 Pinpoint Oiler   3.59

790-73800 Part Picker   6.99

Woodcarving Book
790-90001 10.95

NEW ITEMS

KNIFE & TOOL SETS

Deluxe Craft Tool Set
790-5087   59.95
Contains: Complete assortment of knives, blades and tools including coping saw, block plane, sander, jewelers screwdriver, spokeshave, balsa stripper, pin vise, 3 drill bits. 4 gouges, 2 routers and 9 assorted blades.

HOBBY RULERS
790-7720 18' Metric   8.99
790-7721 HO/O Inch Metric   7.99
790-7722 12'' 1/24, 1/32, 1/72   7.99
790-7723 6'' HO/O Inch Metric   3.99
790-7724 6'' 1/24, 1/32, 1/72   3.99
790-7725 3'' Triangle, Inches Only   6.99
790-7726 3 x 4 Square, Inches Only   6.99

HOBBY KNIVES

790-3628 Gripster Knife   3.99

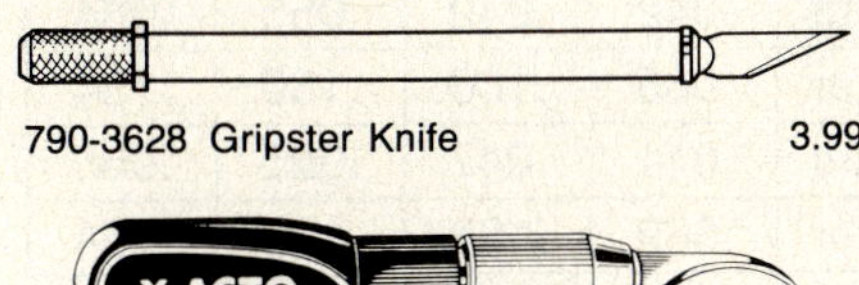

790-3261 Woodcarving Knife   7.49

TESTORS

HOBBY KNIVES

Specially designed for building plastic kits. Blade can be resharpened.
Hobby Knife
704-8801   1.29

Dealers: MUST order Dealer Packs of 12.

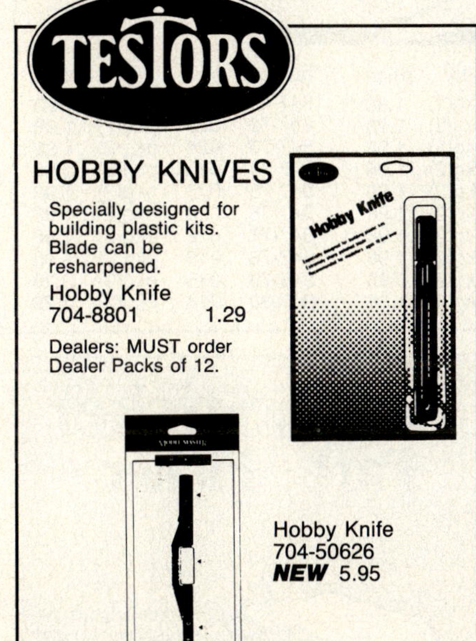

Hobby Knife
704-50626
NEW 5.95

? ? ? ? ? ? ? ? ?

__________ is a building where coal for steam locomotives is stored and shoveled or dumped through chutes into the locomotives' tenders. When the storage is usually called a __________. When the elevated storage bins are reached by a trestle so the coal can be dumped from the cars or shoveled right into the storage bins, the structure is usually called a __________.

(Answers: Coaling Station, Coaling Tower, Coaling Trestle)

STANDARDS GAUGE
Designed and developed by the NMRA (National Model Railroad Association) Engineering Committee; this pocket-sized gauge enables you to check all important dimensions on your track and rolling stock as follows:

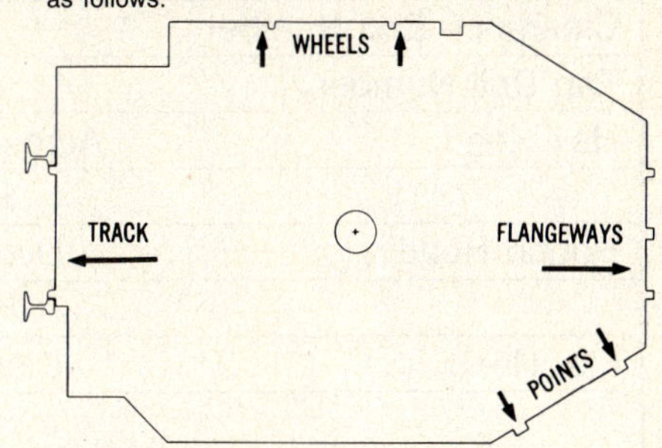

- Gauge of track and turnouts
- Flangeway depth and ''check gauge''
- Clearance
- Height of loading platform and coupler

If cars do not run correctly, this gauge will pinpoint the trouble for you. Complete instructions come with each gauge.

098-1 HO Standard Gauge   6.69
098-2 HOn3 Standard Gauge   6.69

donegan optical company

OPTIVISOR
The precision-made binocular magnifier that is worn on the head leaving both hands free. Can be instantly tilted downward when needed and upward when not is use. Can be worn over regular prescription or safety glasses.

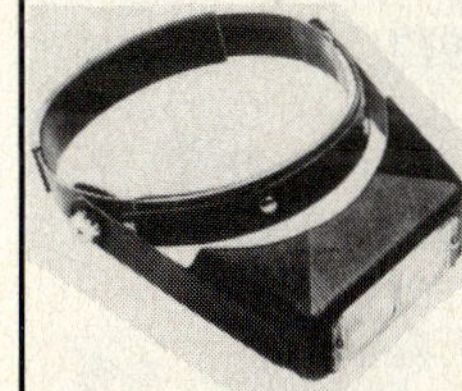

Comes with dial adjustable, conforming headband, ABS high impact visor, genuine feather padded comfort band, optical glass lenses mounted in an interchangeable frame. Six lens powers available, plus an attachable auxiliary OptiLOUPE lens for additional magnification.

240-402 1-1/2X, 20'' focal length   28.95
240-403 1-3/4X, 14'' focal length   28.95
for close work and will be most comfortable when worn for a long period of time
240-404 2X, 10'' focal length   28.95
ideal for model railroad work
240-405 2-1/2X, 8'' focal length   28.95
ideal for model railroad work
240-407 2-3/4X, 6'' focal length   28.95
240-410 3-1/2X, 4'' focal length   29.95
for extremely fine work

ACCESSORIES
240-300 OptiLOUPE   5.95
240-303 Replacement Leather   5.25
         Comfort Band
240-70   Headband w/Dial Adjustment   5.50

LENS PLATE ONLY
240-#2,3,4,5,7   each 16.95
240-10   17.85

WALTHERS

Walthers miniature hardware and accessories are perfect for your modeling projects. The complete selection includes wood, metal and machine screws from 00-99 to 2-56 with matching nuts and washers.

Fine detail work is easier with the right tools. Walthers offers miniature drill bits from size 43 to 80, pin vises, the Screw Sticker and more.

SIZE INFORMATION

Size		00-90	0-80	1-72	2-56
Screw Body Diameter		.047	.060	.073	.086
Clearance Drill Number		55	52	48	43
Tap Drill Number		61	55	53	50
Hex Head	Across Flat	5/64	3/32	7/64	1/8
	Height	.042	.042	.055	.064
Round Head	Diameter	.085	.106	.130	.154
	Height	.041	.047	.055	.065
Flat Head	Diameter	.089	.108	.136	.164
	Height	.024	.035	.043	.051

DRILLS

number	size	qty	price	number	size	qty	price	number	size	qty	price
947-43	.089	pkg(2)	1.79	947-61	.039	pkg(2)	1.98	947-71	.026	pkg(2)	1.98
947-48	.076	pkg(2)	1.79	947-62	.038	pkg(2)	1.98	947-72	.025	pkg(2)	1.98
947-50	.070	pkg(2)	1.79	947-63	.037	pkg(2)	1.98	947-73	.024	pkg(2)	1.98
947-52	.064	pkg(2)	1.79	947-64	.036	pkg(2)	1.98	947-74	.023	pkg(2)	1.98
947-53	.060	pkg(2)	1.79	947-65	.035	pkg(2)	1.98	947-75	.021	pkg(2)	1.98
947-55	.052	pkg(2)	1.79	947-66	.033	pkg(2)	1.98	947-76	.020	pkg(2)	1.98
947-56	.047	pkg(2)	1.79	947-67	.032	pkg(2)	1.98	947-77	.018	pkg(2)	1.98
947-57	.043	pkg(2)	1.79	947-68	.031	pkg(2)	1.98	947-78	.016	pkg(2)	1.98
947-58	.042	pkg(2)	1.79	947-69	.029	pkg(2)	1.98	947-79	.015	pkg(2)	2.29
947-60	.040	pkg(2)	1.79	947-70	.028	pkg(2)	1.98	947-80	.014	pkg(2)	2.29

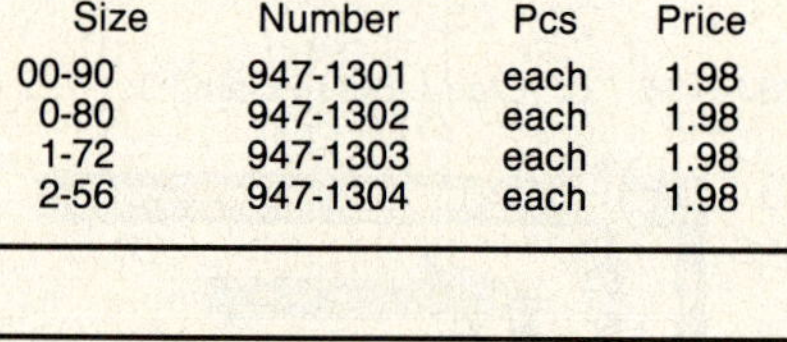

TAPS

Size	Number	Pcs	Price
00-90	947-1301	each	1.98
0-80	947-1302	each	1.98
1-72	947-1303	each	1.98
2-56	947-1304	each	1.98

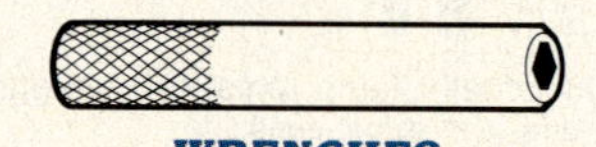

WRENCHES

Will fit Brass Hex Nuts & Hex Head screws.

Size	Number	Pcs	Price
#00	947-1321	each	3.98
#0	947-1322	each	3.98
#1	947-1323	each	3.98
#2	947-1324	each	3.98
#00—#2	949-662	set of 4	14.98

LIMITED QUANTITIES AVAILABLE

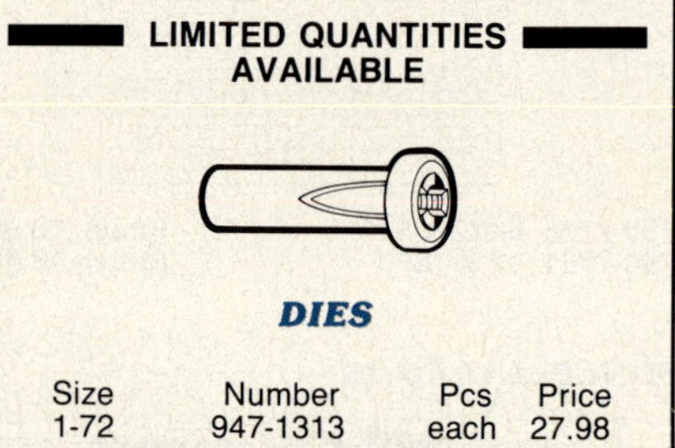

DIES

Size	Number	Pcs	Price
1-72	947-1313	each	27.98

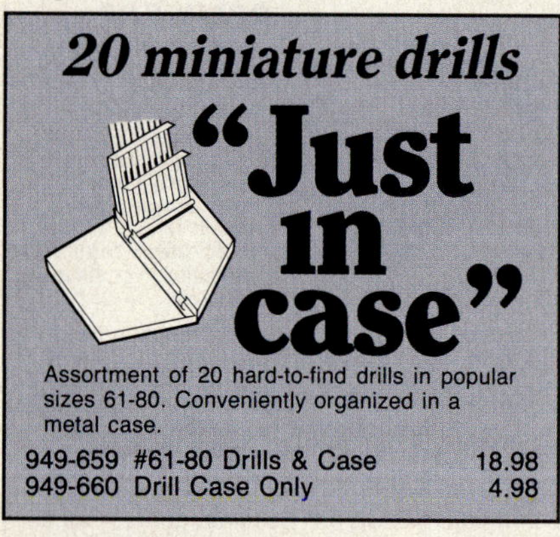

Assortment of 20 hard-to-find drills in popular sizes 61-80. Conveniently organized in a metal case.

949-659 #61-80 Drills & Case — 18.98
949-660 Drill Case Only — 4.98

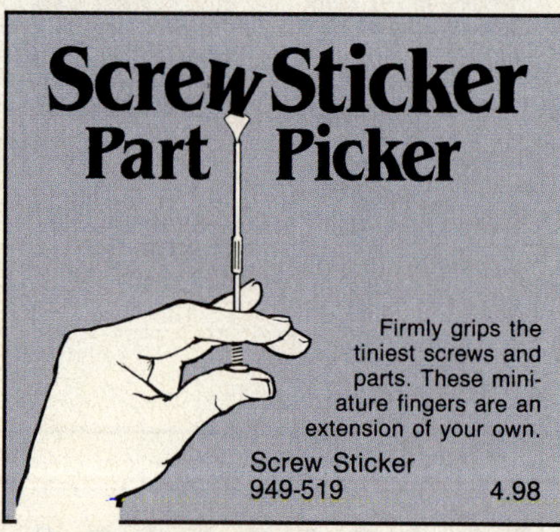

WALTHERS
PROFESSIONAL DECAL FINISH

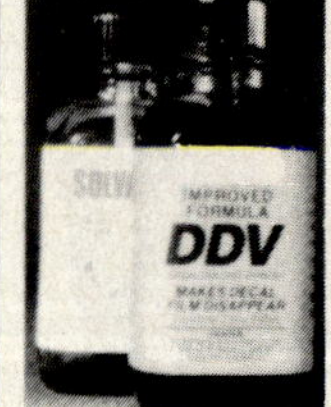

904-470 Solvaset 2oz 2.98
Makes decals snuggle down over irregular surfaces. Eliminates air bubbles, white spots and draping, without hiding surface detail.

904-537 DDV 2oz 2.98
Dull, flat finish hides decal film, protects model finishes. Brush or spray it on, safe for plastics.

MAGIC MASKER™

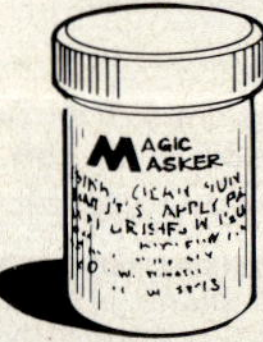

Brush it on the area to be masked off. Then spray your color, let dry and peel off Magic Masker.™ Works on plastic, wood, metal, paint, dope, chrome and silver.

904-106 Magic Masker™ btl(20cc) 2.98
Dealers: MUST Order Dealer Pack of 12

PIN-VISE

949-664 Double End Pin-Vise — 7.98
Includes two single end collets. Holds bits from #42 to #70.

CARBON STEEL MODELING BLADES

Stiffer and more satisfactory for cutting than stainless steel.

Modeling Blades
949-560
pkg(10) 2.29

TAP & DIE HOLDER

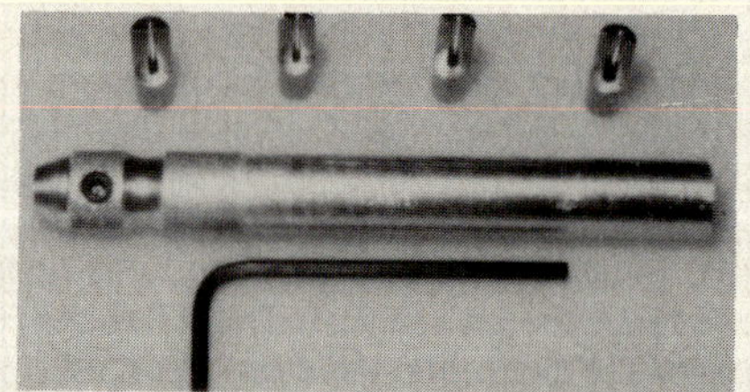

949-663 Tap and Die Holder — 14.98
Holds taps securely while cutting threads. Includes storage case, holder, Allen wrench and collets for 00-90, 0-80, 1-72 and 2-56 taps.

WAHL NEW

Originators of practical cordless soldering.

Butane not included with butane-powered soldering iron or kit pack. Butane is not available from Walthers, but can be purchased at your local hardware or convenience store.

SOLDERING IRON & TORCH

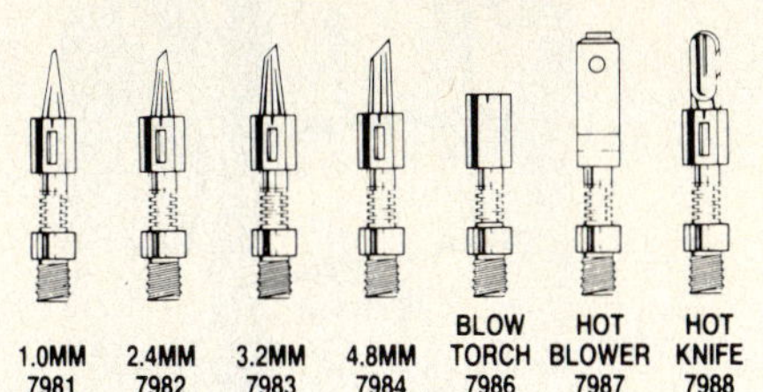

Cordless Wallmount
Soldering Iron
758-7775   39.95
Cordless soldering iron includes iron, wall plug recharger, mounting bracket, 7545 tip and instructions.

BUTANE TIPS

758-7981	Fine 1.0mm	each 8.95
758-7982	Medium 2.4mm	each 8.95
758-7983	Regular 3.2mm	each 8.95
758-7984	Heavy Duty 4.8mm	each 8.95
758-7986	Blow Torch	each 8.95
758-7987	Hot Blower	each 8.95
758-7988	Hot Knife	each 8.95

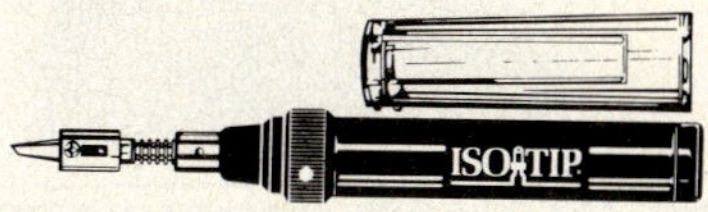

758-7980 Butane-Powered   29.95
Soldering Iron and Torch

758-7985 Butane-Powered Kit Pack   54.95
Kit pack includes soldering iron with protective igniter cap, torch attachment, medium (2.4mm), fine (1.0mm), & hot blower tip, wiping sponge/well and in-use stand/rest in reusable carrying case.

MINIDRILLS

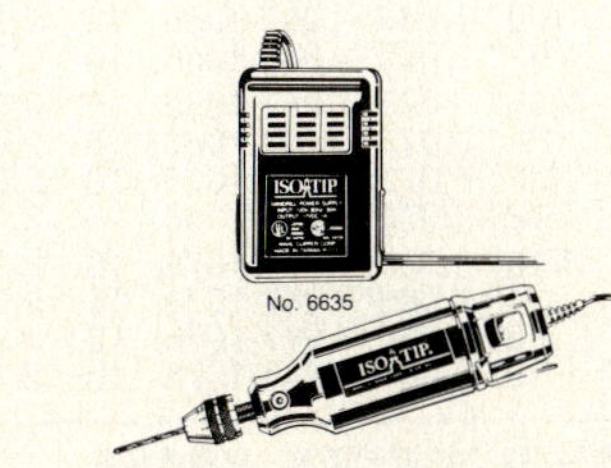

758-6635 Constant Speed   78.95
21,000 RPM
Low voltage/high power, fan-cooled, permanently lubricated ball bearing, three-jaw universal chuck up to .140″ shank & 6 ft cord.
758-6636 Variable Speed   61.95
10,000-21,000 RPM

N.J. International

TOOL SET

525-6606	5-pc Nut Driver Set	**NEW**	6.99
525-6607	5-pc Open End Wrench Set		6.99
525-6601	Screwdriver Set	pkg(6)	6.99
525-6608	Phillips/Allen Driver Set		6.99

PARTS PICKER

525-6604   Parts Picker   3.99
Three-prong end allows you to grasp onto hard to hold parts.

WOODLAND SCENICS

DIES

785-877	00-90	each	29.98
785-878	0-80	each	29.98
785-879	1-72	each	29.98
785-880	2-56	each	29.98

WRENCHES

785-885	00-90	each	3.98
785-886	0-80	each	3.98
785-887	1-72	each	3.98
785-888	2-56	each	3.98

TAPS

785-895	00-90	each	1.98
785-896	0-80	each	1.98
785-897	1-72	each	1.98
785-898	2-56	each	1.98

Judging from her polished appearance, engine #3 has had a recent date with the paint shop. Bob Blake built the Loco from a Bowser 0-6-0 kit, which was photographed on the Great South Bay Model Railroad club layout, in Freeport, Long Island, New York.
Model and Photo by Bob Blake

WALTHERS

Walthers provides a complete range of miniature hardware for hobby projects. Wood, machine and nylon screws, plus hex nuts and insulating washers in assorted sizes are available for your special needs. Look for the Walthers Miniature Screw display at your Dealer. (Machine and wood screws may be brass or brass plated.)

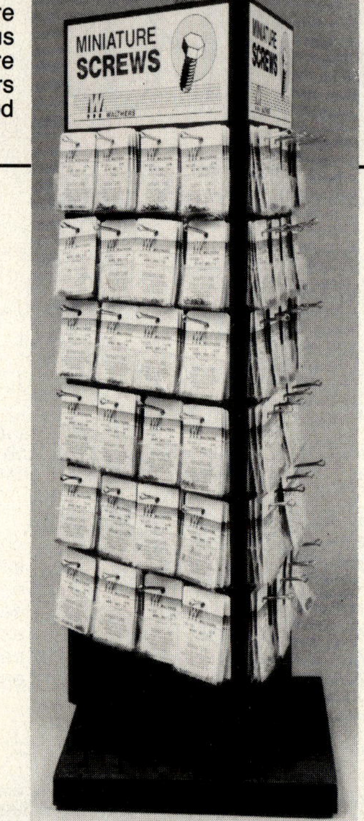

HEX HEAD BRASS MACHINE SCREWS

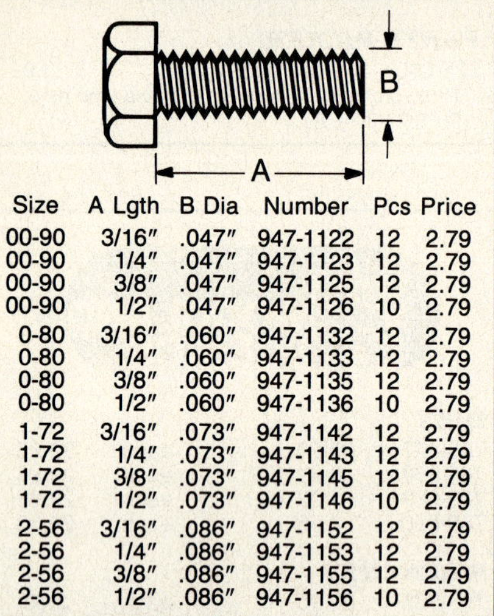

Size	A Lgth	B Dia	Number	Pcs	Price
00-90	3/16″	.047″	947-1122	12	2.79
00-90	1/4″	.047″	947-1123	12	2.79
00-90	3/8″	.047″	947-1125	12	2.79
00-90	1/2″	.047″	947-1126	10	2.79
0-80	3/16″	.060″	947-1132	12	2.79
0-80	1/4″	.060″	947-1133	12	2.79
0-80	3/8″	.060″	947-1135	12	2.79
0-80	1/2″	.060″	947-1136	10	2.79
1-72	3/16″	.073″	947-1142	12	2.79
1-72	1/4″	.073″	947-1143	12	2.79
1-72	3/8″	.073″	947-1145	12	2.79
1-72	1/2″	.073″	947-1146	10	2.79
2-56	3/16″	.086″	947-1152	12	2.79
2-56	1/4″	.086″	947-1153	12	2.79
2-56	3/8″	.086″	947-1155	12	2.79
2-56	1/2″	.086″	947-1156	10	2.79

FLAT HEAD BRASS MACHINE SCREWS

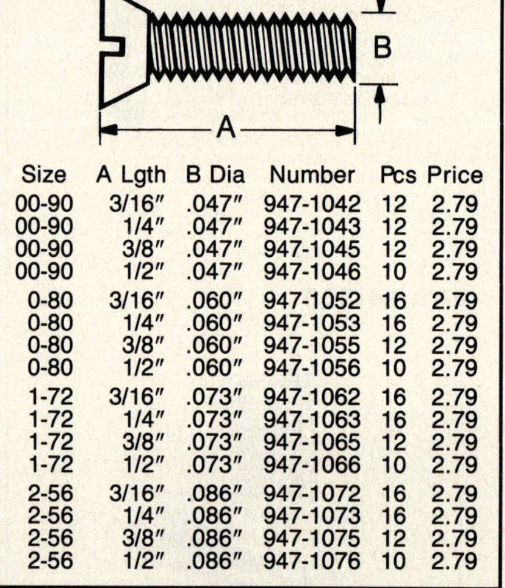

Size	A Lgth	B Dia	Number	Pcs	Price
00-90	3/16″	.047″	947-1042	12	2.79
00-90	1/4″	.047″	947-1043	12	2.79
00-90	3/8″	.047″	947-1045	12	2.79
00-90	1/2″	.047″	947-1046	10	2.79
0-80	3/16″	.060″	947-1052	16	2.79
0-80	1/4″	.060″	947-1053	16	2.79
0-80	3/8″	.060″	947-1055	12	2.79
0-80	1/2″	.060″	947-1056	10	2.79
1-72	3/16″	.073″	947-1062	16	2.79
1-72	1/4″	.073″	947-1063	16	2.79
1-72	3/8″	.073″	947-1065	12	2.79
1-72	1/2″	.073″	947-1066	10	2.79
2-56	3/16″	.086″	947-1072	16	2.79
2-56	1/4″	.086″	947-1073	16	2.79
2-56	3/8″	.086″	947-1075	12	2.79
2-56	1/2″	.086″	947-1076	10	2.79

ROUND HEAD BRASS MACHINE SCREWS

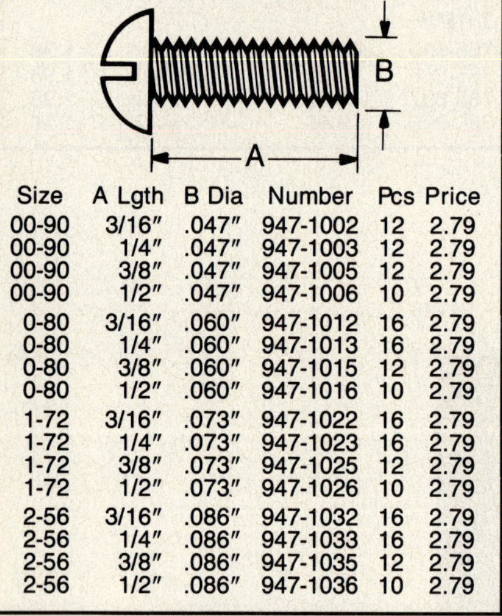

Size	A Lgth	B Dia	Number	Pcs	Price
00-90	3/16″	.047″	947-1002	12	2.79
00-90	1/4″	.047″	947-1003	12	2.79
00-90	3/8″	.047″	947-1005	12	2.79
00-90	1/2″	.047″	947-1006	10	2.79
0-80	3/16″	.060″	947-1012	16	2.79
0-80	1/4″	.060″	947-1013	16	2.79
0-80	3/8″	.060″	947-1015	16	2.79
0-80	1/2″	.060″	947-1016	10	2.79
1-72	3/16″	.073″	947-1022	16	2.79
1-72	1/4″	.073″	947-1023	16	2.79
1-72	3/8″	.073″	947-1025	12	2.79
1-72	1/2″	.073″	947-1026	10	2.79
2-56	3/16″	.086″	947-1032	16	2.79
2-56	1/4″	.086″	947-1033	16	2.79
2-56	3/8″	.086″	947-1035	12	2.79
2-56	1/2″	.086″	947-1036	10	2.79

WOOD SCREWS, BRASS OR BRASS PLATED

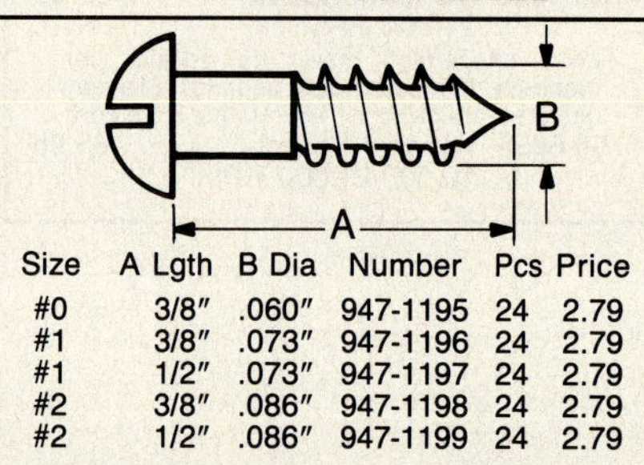

Size	A Lgth	B Dia	Number	Pcs	Price
#0	3/8″	.060″	947-1195	24	2.79
#1	3/8″	.073″	947-1196	24	2.79
#1	1/2″	.073″	947-1197	24	2.79
#2	3/8″	.086″	947-1198	24	2.79
#2	1/2″	.086″	947-1199	24	2.79

BRASS HEX NUTS

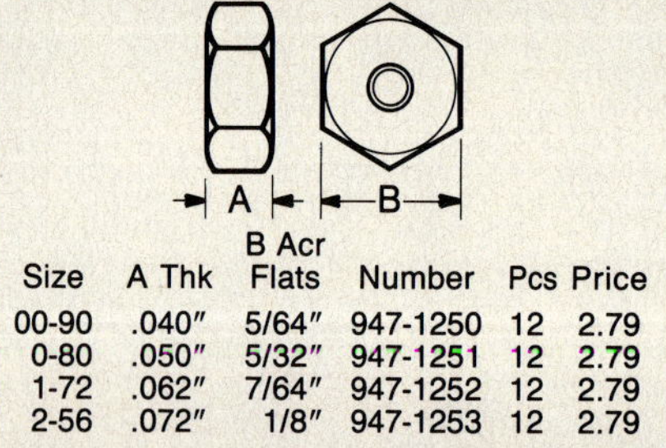

Size	A Thk	B Acr Flats	Number	Pcs	Price
00-90	.040″	5/64″	947-1250	12	2.79
0-80	.050″	5/32″	947-1251	12	2.79
1-72	.062″	7/64″	947-1252	12	2.79
2-56	.072″	1/8″	947-1253	12	2.79

NYLON HEX NUTS

Size	A Thk	B Acr Flats	Number	Pcs	Price
2-56	.075″	3/16″	947-1255	12	2.79
4-40	.100″	1/4″	947-1256	12	2.79

ROUND HEAD NYLON MACHINE SCREWS

Size	A Lgth	B Dia	Number	Pcs	Price
1-72	1/4″	.073″	947-1163	12	2.79
2-56	5/8″	.086″	947-1177	12	2.79
4-40	3/4″	.112″	947-1188	12	2.79

SELF TAPPING STEEL SHEET METAL SCREWS

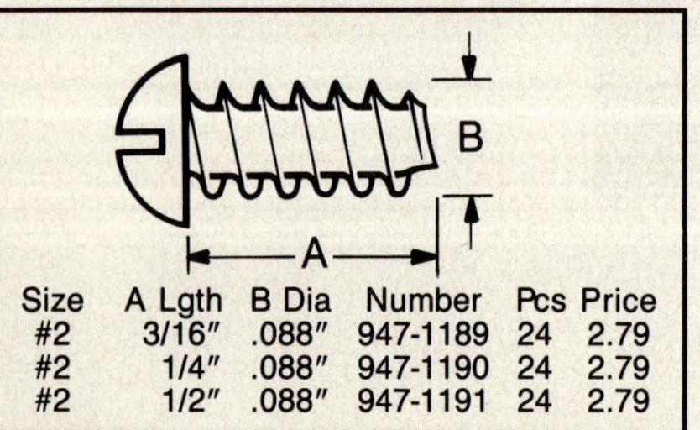

Size	A Lgth	B Dia	Number	Pcs	Price
#2	3/16″	.088″	947-1189	24	2.79
#2	1/4″	.088″	947-1190	24	2.79
#2	1/2″	.088″	947-1191	24	2.79

BRASS WASHERS

Package 2.79

Size	O.D.	I.D.	Thick	Number	Pcs
#00	.105″	.060″	.020″	947-1270	16
#0	.125″	.068″	.020″	947-1271	16
#1	.156″	.084″	.025″	947-1272	16
#2	.188″	.094″	.025″	947-1273	16

INSULATED BUSHINGS

ID takes #2 screw. OD as indicated

941-2046 3/16″ Diameter   pkg(24) 2.79

- **ALL PURPOSE ADHESIVE**
  GOO is the permanent rubber base adhesive that grips most anything. It never lets go.

- **FAST SETTING JOINTS**
  Easy contact action opens new possibilities for fast-setting joints with any material.

GOO is the perfect adhesive for building or repairing jobs on your layout and around the house!

The easy contact action of GOO produces fast-setting joints with any material. GOO works with all types of metals (including steel, brass, aluminum, copper and others) plus items like wood, plastic, cardboard, china, leather, vinyl, ceramics, paper, concrete and many more, on any smooth or porous surface.

GOO is a permanent rubber base adhesive that's shockproof, waterproof and crack proof — it's as flexible as rubber. Joints won't crack when flexed back and forth, won't break loose when the temperature changes and won't weaken when wet or damp. It sticks forever! (A technical data sheet is available on request with detailed instructions for use).

GOO Adhesive, Large Tube
904-299   (1-1/8 oz) 2.98

Hob-Bits
by Woodland Scenics

- Washers
- Screws
- Washers
- Nuts

Hob-Bits® screws are made of brass and are available in four types.

FILLISTER HEAD SCREWS

Size	Length	Dia	Number	Pkg	Price
00-90	1/8″	.046″	785-821	5	1.19
00-90	1/4″	.046″	785-822	5	1.19
00-90	3/8″	.046″	785-823	5	1.19
00-90	1/2″	.046″	785-824	5	1.19
0-80	1/8″	.058″	785-825	5	1.19
0-80	1/4″	.058″	785-826	5	1.19
0-80	3/8″	.058″	785-827	5	1.19
0-80	1/2″	.058″	785-828	5	1.19
1-72	1/8″	.072″	785-829	5	1.19
1-72	1/4″	.072″	785-830	5	1.19
1-72	3/8″	.072″	785-831	5	1.19
1-72	1/2″	.072″	785-832	5	1.19
2-56	1/8″	.085″	785-833	5	1.19
2-56	1/4″	.085″	785-834	5	1.19
2-56	3/8″	.085″	785-835	5	1.19
2-56	1/2″	.085″	785-836	5	1.19

FLAT HEAD SCREWS

Size	Length	Dia	Number	Pkg	Price
00-90	1/8″	.046″	785-841	5	1.19
00-90	1/4″	.046″	785-842	5	1.19
00-90	3/8″	.046″	785-843	5	1.19
00-90	1/2″	.046″	785-844	5	1.19
0-80	1/8″	.058″	785-845	5	1.19
0-80	1/4″	.058″	785-846	5	1.19
0-80	3/8″	.058″	785-847	5	1.19
0-80	1/2″	.058″	785-848	5	1.19
1-72	1/8″	.072″	785-849	5	1.19
1-72	1/4″	.072″	785-850	5	1.19
1-72	3/8″	.072″	785-851	5	1.19
1-72	1/2″	.072″	785-852	5	1.19
2-56	1/8″	.085″	785-853	5	1.19
2-56	1/4″	.085″	785-854	5	1.19
2-56	3/8″	.085″	785-855	5	1.19
2-56	1/2″	.085″	785-856	5	1.19

HEX HEAD SCREWS

Size	Length	Dia	Number	Pkg	Price
00-90	1/8″	.046″	785-861	5	1.19
00-90	1/4″	.046″	785-862	5	1.19
00-90	3/8″	.046″	785-863	5	1.19
00-90	1/2″	.046″	785-864	5	1.19
0-80	1/8″	.058″	785-865	5	1.19
0-80	1/4″	.058″	785-866	5	1.19
0-80	3/8″	.058″	785-867	5	1.19
0-80	1/2″	.058″	785-868	5	1.19
1-72	1/8″	.072″	785-869	5	1.19
1-72	1/4″	.072″	785-870	5	1.19
1-72	3/8″	.072″	785-871	5	1.19
1-72	1/2″	.072″	785-872	5	1.19
2-56	1/8″	.085″	785-873	5	1.19
2-56	1/4″	.085″	785-874	5	1.19
2-56	3/8″	.085″	785-875	5	1.19
2-56	1/2″	.085″	785-876	5	1.19

See also: SCENERY, STRUCTURES, FIGURES, VEHICLES and TOOLS for additional WOODLAND SCENICS products.

HEX NUTS

Size	Number	Package	Price
00-90	785-881	5	1.19
0-80	785-882	5	1.19
1-72	785-883	5	1.19
2-56	785-884	5	1.19

ROUND HEAD SCREWS

Size	Length	Dia	Number	Pkg	Price
00-90	1/8″	.046″	785-801	5	1.19
00-90	1/4″	.046″	785-802	5	1.19
00-90	3/8″	.046″	785-803	5	1.19
00-90	1/2″	.046″	785-804	5	1.19
0-80	1/8″	.058″	785-805	5	1.19
0-80	1/4″	.058″	785-806	5	1.19
0-80	3/8″	.058″	785-807	5	1.19
0-80	1/2″	.058″	785-808	5	1.19
1-72	1/8″	.072″	785-809	5	1.19
1-72	1/4″	.072″	785-810	5	1.19
1-72	3/8″	.072″	785-811	5	1.19
1-72	1/2″	.072″	785-812	5	1.19
2-56	1/8″	.085″	785-813	5	1.19
2-56	1/4″	.085″	785-814	5	1.19
2-56	3/8″	.085″	785-815	5	1.19
2-56	1/2″	.085″	785-816	5	1.19

WASHERS

Size	Number	Package	Price
00-90	785-891	5	1.19
0-80	785-892	5	1.19
1-72	785-893	5	1.19
2-56	785-894	5	1.19

NorthWest Short Line

NICKEL-PLATED METRIC SCREWS

FLAT HEAD

053-11535	1.4 x .3 x 3.0 mm	pkg(8)	.95
053-11565	1.4 x .3 x 6.0 mm	pkg(8)	.95
053-12255	2.0 x 4 x 5.0 mm	pkg(10)	.95
053-12755	2.6 x .45 x 5.0 mm	pkg(10)	.95
053-11995	1.7 x 16 x .35 mm	pkg(8)	.95
053-12295	2.0 x 18 x .4 mm	pkg(6)	.95

NorthWest Short Line

HEX NUTS

053-10105	1.0 x .25 mm	pkg(6)	.95
053-10125	1.2 x .25 mm	pkg(6)	.95
053-10145	1.4 x .3 mm	pkg(8)	.95
053-10175	1.7 x .35 mm	pkg(8)	.95
053-10205	2.0 x .4 mm	pkg(10)	.95
053-10265	2.6 x .45 mm	pkg(10)	.95
053-10305	3.0 x .5 mm	pkg(10)	.95

PAN HEAD

053-11035	1.0 x .25 x 3.0 mm	pkg(6)	.95
053-11255	1.2 x .25 x 5.0 mm	pkg(6)	.95
053-11435	1.4 x .3 x 3.0 mm	pkg(8)	.95
053-11465	1.4 x .3 x 6.0 mm	pkg(8)	.95
053-11755	1.7 x .35 x 5.0 mm	pkg(8)	.95
053-12035	2.0 x .4 x 3.0 mm	pkg(10)	.95
053-12045	2.0 x .4 x 4.0 mm	pkg(10)	.95
053-12055	2.0 x .4 x 5.0 mm	pkg(10)	.95
053-12065	2.0 x .4 x 6.0 mm	pkg(10)	.95
053-12085	2.0 x .4 x 8.0 mm	pkg(10)	.95
053-12635	2.6 x .45 x 3.0 mm	pkg(10)	.95
053-12655	2.6 x .45 x 5.0 mm	pkg(10)	.95
053-13055	3.0 x .5 x 5.0 mm	pkg(10)	.95
053-11235	1.2 x .25 x 3.0 mm	pkg(6)	.95
053-11885	1.7 x 18 x .35 mm	pkg(8)	.95
053-13105	3.0 x 10 x .5 mm	pkg(10)	.95

SET SCREW

053-16835	2.0 x 4 mm	pkg(6)	.95

PLASTIC INSULATING SCREWS

PAN HEAD — NEW

053-51435	1.4 x 3 mm	pkg(4)	.95
053-52055	2.0 x 5 mm	pkg(4)	.95
053-51745	1.7 x 4 mm x .35	pkg(4)	.95

NYLON SCREWS

FILLISTER HEAD

053-41745	0-80 x 1/8″	pkg(10)	1.25
053-41765	0-80 x 1/2″	pkg(10)	1.25

FLAT HEAD

053-42245	0-80 x 9/32″	pkg(10)	1.25
053-42365	1-72 x 7/16″	pkg(10)	1.00
053-42455	2-56 x 3/8″	pkg(10)	1.00

PAN HEAD

053-41135	00-90 x 1/8″	pkg(8)	1.25
053-41255	0-80 x 3/8″	pkg(8)	1.25
053-41365	1-72 x 1/2″	pkg(10)	1.00
053-41475	2-56 x 1/2″	pkg(10)	1.00

BLACK-PLATED SCREWS

PAN HEAD

053-211425	1.4 x 2 x .3 mm	pkg(8)	.95
053-211435	1.4 x 3 x .3 mm	pkg(8)	.95
053-211455	1.4 x 5 x .3 mm	pkg(8)	.95
053-211465	1.4 x 6 x .3 mm	pkg(8)	.95
053-211485	1.4 x 8 x .3 mm	pkg(8)	.95
053-212065	2.0 x 6 x .4 mm	pkg(8)	.95
053-212085	2.0 x 8 x .4 mm	pkg(8)	.95
053-216415	1.4 x 1.5 mm	pkg(6)	.95

STEEL SCREWS — NEW

053-18065	2.0 x 6mm	pkg(8)	.95

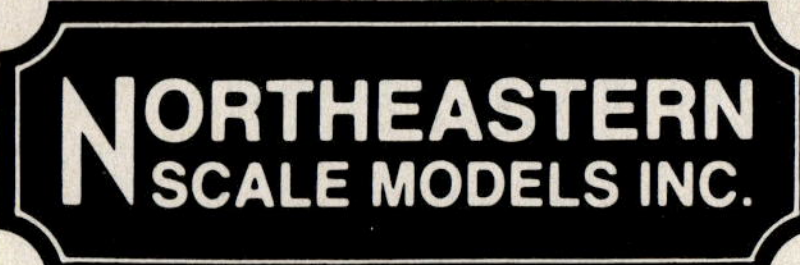

NORTHEASTERN SCALE MODELS INC.

HO SCALE (1/87)

[WOOD]

STRIPS, SHAPES AND PARTS ARE 24″ IN LENGTH (unless noted).

MINIMUM ORDER: Because the 24″ Length of these strips, shapes and parts requires special shipping containers and, in many cases, a separate package for mailing, we ask that you order at least $3.00 worth of wood or allow 50¢ for packaging on orders less than $3.00.

SCALE LUMBER

11″ Length PACKS 2.00 EACH
Decimal number represents the actual size in inches.

1 SCALE INCH

(actual size .012)

521-3001	x 2	(x .024)	pkg(17)
521-3002	x 3	(x .036)	pkg(17)
521-3003	x 4	(x .048)	pkg(17)
521-3004	x 6	(x .072)	pkg(15)
521-3005	x 8	(x .096)	pkg(15)
521-3006	x 10	(x .120)	pkg(15)

2 SCALE INCH

(actual size .024)

521-3010	x 2	(x .024)	pkg(17)
521-3011	x 3	(x .036)	pkg(17)
521-3012	x 4	(x .048)	pkg(17)
521-3013	x 6	(x .072)	pkg(15)
521-3014	x 8	(x .096)	pkg(15)
521-3015	x 10	(x .120)	pkg(15)
521-3016	x 12	(x .144)	pkg(13)

3 SCALE INCH

(actual size .036)

521-3020	x 3	(x .036)	pkg(17)
521-3021	x 4	(x .048)	pkg(17)
521-3022	x 6	(x .072)	pkg(15)
521-3023	x 8	(x .096)	pkg(15)
521-3024	x 10	(x .120)	pkg(15)
521-3025	x 12	(x .144)	pkg(13)

4 SCALE INCH

(actual size .048)

521-3030	x 4	(x .048)	pkg(15)
521-3031	x 6	(x .072)	pkg(15)
521-3032	x 8	(x .096)	pkg(15)
521-3033	x 10	(x .120)	pkg(15)
521-3034	x 12	(x .144)	pkg(15)

6 SCALE INCH

(actual size .072)

521-3040	x 6	(x .072)	pkg(15)
521-3041	x 8	(x .096)	pkg(13)
521-3042	x 10	(x .120)	pkg(13)
521-3043	x 12	(x .144)	pkg(13)

8 SCALE INCH

(actual size .096)

521-3050	x 8	(x .096)	pkg(13)
521-3051	x 10	(x .120)	pkg(13)
521-3052	x 12	(x .144)	pkg(13)

10 SCALE INCH

(actual size .120)

521-3060	x 10	(x .120)	pkg(13)
521-3061	x 12	(x .144)	pkg(10)

12 SCALE INCH

(actual size .144)

521-3070	x 12	(x .144)	pkg(10)

22″ LENGTH

Dealers must order Dealer Pack of 50. Refer to chart under Stripwood for Dealer prices. Price indicated is per piece. Dimensions are in HO Scale inches.

521-2001	1 x 2″	each .16
521-2002	1 x 3″	each .16

22″ LENGTH (continued)

521-2003	1 x 4″	each .16
521-2004	1 x 6″	each .18
521-2005	1 x 8″	each .18
521-2006	1 x 10″	each .18
521-2010	2 x 2″	each .16
521-2011	2 x 3″	each .16
521-2012	2 x 4″	each .16
521-2013	2 x 6″	each .18
521-2014	2 x 8″	each .18
521-2015	2 x 10″	each .18
521-2016	2 x 12″	each .23
521-2020	3 x 3″	each .16
521-2021	3 x 4″	each .16
521-2022	3 x 6″	each .18
521-2023	3 x 8″	each .18
521-2024	3 x 10″	each .18
521-2025	3 x 12″	each .23
521-2030	4 x 4″	each .18
521-2031	4 x 6″	each .18
521-2032	4 x 8″	each .18
521-2033	4 x 10″	each .18
521-2034	4 x 12″	each .18
521-2040	6 x 6″	each .18
521-2041	6 x 8″	each .23
521-2042	6 x 10″	each .23
521-2043	6 x 12″	each .23
521-2050	8 x 8″	each .23
521-2051	8 x 10″	each .23
521-2052	8 x 12″	each .23
521-2060	10 x 10″	each .23
521-2061	10 x 12″	each .28
521-2070	12 x 12″	each .28

STRIPWOOD

*Minimum Dealer Stripwood Order on these items is a tube of 50 pieces (all one item). Price indicated is per piece.

50 @ .16 = 8.00/tube	50 @ .25 = 12.50/tube
50 @ .18 = 9.00/tube	50 @ .28 = 14.00/tube
50 @ .20 = 10.00/tube	50 @ .30 = 15.00/tube
50 @ .22 = 11.00/tube	50 @ .32 = 16.00/tube
50 @ .24 = 12.00/tube	

SAMPLE PACKAGE

521-1001		2.00

Package of over 30 samples showing the different shapes, strips and car parts.

24″ COLOR CODED STRIPWOOD (pkg 50)

521-10	1/16 x 1/16″	(red)	11.50
521-13	1/16 x 1/8″	(yellow)	14.00
521-17	1/16 x 1/4″	(blue)	20.00
521-25	3/32 x 3/32″	(yellow)	14.00
521-30	1/8 x 1/8″	(yellow)	14.00
521-34	1/8 x 1/4″	(black)	22.50
521-40	5/32 x 5/32″	(orange)	18.00
521-45	3/16 x 3/16″	(green)	22.50
521-50	1/4 x 1/4″	(white)	29.00

22″ LENGTH

521-100	.012 x 1/32″	* each .16
521-101	.012 x .040″	* each .16
521-102	.012 x 3/64″	* each .16
521-103	.012 x 1/16″	* each .16
521-104	.012 x 5/64″	* each .20
521-105	.012 x 3/32″	* each .20
521-106	.012 x 1/8″	* each .20
521-110	.020 x 1/32″	* each .16
521-111	.020 x .040″	* each .16
521-112	.020 x 3/64″	* each .16
521-113	.020 x 1/16″	* each .16
521-114	.020 x 5/64″	* each .20
521-115	.020 x 3/32″	* each .20
521-116	.020 x 1/8″	* each .20

22″ LENGTH

521-117	.020 x 5/32″	* each .22
521-120	1/32 x 1/32″	* each .16
521-121	1/32 x .040″	* each .16
521-122	1/32 x 3/64″	* each .16
521-123	1/32 x 1/16″	* each .16
521-124	1/32 x 5/64″	* each .20
521-125	1/32 x 3/32″	* each .20
521-126	1/32 x 1/8″	* each .20
521-127	1/32 x 5/32″	* each .23
521-128	1/32 x 3/16″	* each .23
521-130	1/32 x 1/4″	* each .28
521-131	1/32 x 5/16″	each .31
521-132	1/32 x 3/8″	each .45
521-134	1/32 x 1/2″	each .51
521-135	1/32 x 3/4″	each .51
521-136	1/32 x 1″	each .58
521-137	1/32 x 2″	each 1.08
521-138	1/32 x 3″	each 1.45
521-139	1/32 x 4″	each 1.90
521-141	.040 x .040″	* each .21
521-142	.040 x 3/64″	* each .21
521-143	.040 x 1/16″	* each .21
521-144	.040 x 5/64″	* each .21
521-145	.040 x 3/32″	* each .21
521-146	.040 x 1/8″	* each .21
521-147	.040 x 5/32″	* each .25
521-148	.040 x 3/16″	* each .25
521-150	.040 x 1/4″	* each .30
521-151	.040 x 5/16″	each .35
521-152	.040 x 3/8″	each .45
521-154	.040 x 1/2″	each .51
521-155	.040 x 3/4″	each .51
521-156	.040 x 1″	each .58
521-157	.040 x 2″	each 1.14
521-158	.040 x 3″	each 1.45
521-159	.040 x 4″	each 1.90
521-161	3/64 x 3/64″	* each .23
521-162	3/64 x 1/16″	* each .23
521-163	3/64 x 5/64″	* each .23
521-164	3/64 x 3/32″	* each .23
521-165	3/64 x 1/8″	* each .23
521-166	3/64 x 5/32″	* each .28
521-167	3/64 x 3/16″	* each .28
521-169	3/64 x 1/4″	* each .36
521-170	3/64 x 5/16″	each .40
521-171	3/64 x 3/8″	each .45
521-173	3/64 x 1/2″	each .51
521-174	3/64 x 3/4″	each .51
521-175	3/64 x 1″	each .63
521-176	3/64 x 2″	each 1.39
521-177	3/64 x 3″	each 1.70
521-178	3/64 x 4″	each 2.21
521-180	1/16 x 1/16″	* each .23
521-181	1/16 x 5/64″	* each .23
521-182	1/16 x 3/32″	* each .23
521-183	1/16 x 1/8″	* each .28
521-184	1/16 x 5/32″	* each .28
521-185	1/16 x 3/16″	* each .31
521-187	1/16 x 1/4″	each .40
521-188	1/16 x 5/16″	each .40
521-189	1/16 x 3/8″	each .51
521-191	1/16 x 1/2″	each .58
521-192	1/16 x 3/4″	each .69
521-193	1/16 x 1″	each .83
521-194	1/16 x 2″	each 1.39
521-195	1/16 x 3″	each 1.70
521-196	1/16 x 4″	each 2.21
521-198	5/64 x 5/64″	* each .23
521-199	5/64 x 3/32″	* each .28
521-200	5/64 x 1/8″	* each .28
521-201	5/64 x 5/32″	* each .28
521-202	5/64 x 3/16″	* each .31
521-204	5/64 x 1/4″	* each .40
521-205	5/64 x 5/16″	each .40
521-206	5/64 x 3/8″	each .51
521-208	5/64 x 1/2″	each .58
521-209	5/64 x 3/4″	each .69

NORTHEASTERN SCALE MODELS INC.

HO SCALE (1/87)

WOOD

STRIPS, SHAPES AND PARTS ARE 24″ IN LENGTH (unless noted).

MINIMUM ORDER: Because the 24″ Length of these strips, shapes and parts requires special shipping containers and, in many cases, a separate package for mailing, we ask that you order at least $3.00 worth of wood or allow 50¢ for packaging on orders less than $3.00.

22″ LENGTH (continued)

521-210	5/64 x 1″	each	.83
521-211	5/64 x 2″	each	1.45
521-212	5/64 x 3″	each	1.84
521-213	5/64 x 4″	each	2.59
521-215	3/32 x 3/32″	* each	.28
521-216	3/32 x 1/8″	* each	.28
521-217	3/32 x 5/32″	* each	.28
521-218	3/32 x 3/16″	* each	.31
521-220	3/32 x 1/4″	* each	.40
521-221	3/32 x 5/16″	each	.45
521-222	3/32 x 3/8″	each	.58
521-224	3/32 x 1/2″	each	.63
521-225	3/32 x 3/4″	each	.69
521-226	3/32 x 1″	each	.83
521-227	3/32 x 2″	each	1.45
521-228	3/32 x 3″	each	1.84
521-229	3/32 x 4″	each	2.59
521-231	1/8 x 1/8″	* each	.28
521-232	1/8 x 5/32″	* each	.36
521-233	1/8 x 3/16″	* each	.38
521-235	1/8 x 1/4″	each	.45
521-236	1/8 x 5/16″	each	.45
521-237	1/8 x 3/8″	each	.58
521-239	1/8 x 1/2″	each	.76
521-240	1/8 x 3/4″	each	.89
521-241	1/8 x 1″	each	.94
521-242	1/8 x 2″	each	1.59
521-243	1/8 x 3″	each	2.02
521-244	1/8 x 4″	each	2.91
521-246	5/32 x 5/32″	* each	.36
521-247	5/32 x 3/16″	* each	.38
521-249	5/32 x 1/4″	each	.45
521-250	5/32 x 5/16″	each	.51
521-251	5/32 x 3/8″	each	.58
521-253	5/32 x 1/2″	each	.76
521-254	5/32 x 3/4″	each	.89
521-255	5/32 x 1″	each	.94
521-256	5/32 x 2″	each	1.77
521-257	5/32 x 3″	each	2.09
521-258	5/32 x 4″	each	2.91
521-260	3/16 x 3/16″	each	.45
521-262	3/16 x 1/4″	each	.51
521-263	3/16 x 5/16″	each	.58
521-264	3/16 x 3/8″	each	.74
521-266	3/16 x 1/2″	each	.83
521-267	3/16 x 3/4″	each	.93
521-268	3/16 x 1″	each	1.01
521-269	3/16 x 2″	each	1.77
521-270	3/16 x 3″	each	2.28
521-271	3/16 x 4″	each	3.22
521-285	1/4 x 1/4″	each	.58
521-286	1/4 x 5/16″	each	.58
521-287	1/4 x 3/8″	each	.81
521-289	1/4 x 1/2″	each	.94
521-290	1/4 x 3/4″	each	1.01
521-291	1/4 x 1″	each	1.27
521-292	1/4 x 2″	each	2.02
521-293	1/4 x 3″	each	2.59
521-294	1/4 x 4″	each	3.80
521-296	5/16 x 5/16″	each	.83
521-297	5/16 x 3/8″	each	.94
521-299	5/16 x 1/2″	each	1.01
521-300	5/16 x 3/4″	each	1.10
521-301	5/16 x 1″	each	1.27
521-302	5/16 x 2″	each	2.21
521-303	5/16 x 3″	each	3.04
521-304	5/16 x 4″	each	4.23
521-306	3/8 x 3/8″	each	.94
521-308	3/8 x 1/2″	each	1.01
521-309	3/8 x 3/4″	each	1.10
521-310	3/8 x 1″	each	1.27
521-311	3/8 x 2″	each	2.21
521-312	3/8 x 3″	each	3.04
521-313	3/8 x 4″	each	4.23
521-323	1/2 x 1/2″	each	1.01
521-324	1/2 x 3/4″	each	1.10
521-325	1/2 x 1″	each	1.32
521-326	1/2 x 2″	each	2.53
521-327	1/2 x 3″	each	3.47

22″ LENGTH (continued)

521-328	1/2 x 4″	each	4.88
521-330	3/4 x 3/4″	each	1.27
521-331	3/4 x 1″	each	1.38
521-332	3/4 x 2″	each	2.53
521-333	3/4 x 3″	each	3.85
521-334	3/4 x 4″	each	5.06
521-336	1 x 1″	each	1.59
521-337	1 x 2″	each	3.16
521-338	1 x 3″	each	4.37
	(By Special Order Only.)		
521-339	1 x 4″	each	5.50
521-341	2 x 2″	each	6.33
521-342	2 x 3″	each	8.60
521-343	2 x 4″	each	10.63

SIDING Milled Basswood. 3.50 x 24″ Sheets

BEAD AND BOARD SIDING

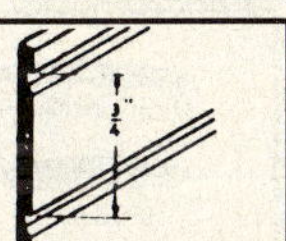

521-385	1/4 x 3-1/2″	each	2.65
521-386	1/8 x 3-1/2″	each	2.65

CAPPED SIDING

First dimension indicates cap spacing.

521-402	1/16 x 1/16″	each	2.65
521-403	3/32 x 1/16″	each	2.65
521-404	1/8 x 1/16″	each	2.65
521-405	3/16 x 1/16″	each	2.65
521-406	1/4 x 1/16″	each	2.65
521-407	3/8 x 1/16″	each	2.65
521-408	1/2 x 1/16″	each	2.65
521-409	3/4 x 1/16″	each	2.65

CLAPBOARD SIDING

First dimension indicates lap spacing.

521-375	1/32 x 1/16″	each	2.65
521-377	3/64 x 1/16″	each	2.65
521-378	1/16 x 1/16″	each	2.65
521-379	3/32 x 1/16″	each	2.65
521-380	1/8 x 1/16″	each	2.65
521-381	3/16 x 1/16″	each	2.65
521-382	1/4 x 1/16″	each	2.65
521-383	3/8 x 1/16″	each	2.65
521-384	1/2 x 1/16″	each	2.65

CORRUGATED SIDING

First dimension indicates corrugation spacing.

521-424	.040 x .040″	each	2.65
521-426	1/16 x .040″	each	2.65
521-436	3/32 x 3/64″	each	2.65
521-437	1/8 x 3/64″	each	2.65

IMPRINTED CONCRETE

521-415	1/16 x .040″	each	2.65
521-417	1/8 x .040″	each	2.65
521-418	3/16 x .040″	each	2.65

NOVELTY SIDING

1/16 x 3.5″
521-390
per sheet 2.65

OVERLAP CLAPBOARD SIDING

Milled Basswood sheets, .080 x 3.50 x 12″.

521-394	1/4″ lap spacing	each	1.20
521-395	3/8″ lap spacing	each	1.20
521-396	1/2″ lap spacing	each	1.20

OVERLAP CLAPBOARD SIDING (continued)

Milled Basswood Sheets, .080 x 3.50 x 36″.

521-391	1/4″ lap spacing	each	4.55
521-392	3/8″ lap spacing	each	4.55
521-393	1/2″ lap spacing	each	4.55

SCRIBED SHEATHING

First dimension indicates scribe spacing.

521-350	.025 x 1/32″	each	2.65
521-351	1/32 x 1/32″	each	2.65
521-352	.040 x 1/32″	each	2.65
521-353	3/64 x 1/32″	each	2.65
521-354	1/16 x 1/32″	each	2.65
521-355	3/32 x 1/32″	each	2.65
521-356	1/8 x 1/32″	each	2.65
521-357	3/16 x 1/32″	each	2.65
521-358	1/4 x 1/32″	each	2.65
521-359	3/8 x 1/32″	each	2.65
521-360	1/2 x 1/32″	each	2.65
521-361	Random 1/32″	each	2.65
521-362	.025 x 1/16″	each	2.65
521-363	1/32 x 1/16″	each	2.65
521-364	.040 x 1/16″	each	2.65
521-365	3/64 x 1/16″	each	2.65
521-366	1/16 x 1/16″	each	2.65
521-367	3/32 x 1/16″	each	2.65
521-368	1/8 x 1/16″	each	2.65
521-369	3/16 x 1/16″	each	2.65
521-370	1/4 x 1/16″	each	2.65
521-371	3/8 x 1/16″	each	2.65
521-372	1/2 x 1/16″	each	2.65
521-373	Random 1/16″	each	2.65

STEEL SIDING

521-347	1/8″		2.65
521-349	3/16″ space		2.65

HO SCALE STRUCTURAL SHAPES

ANGLES

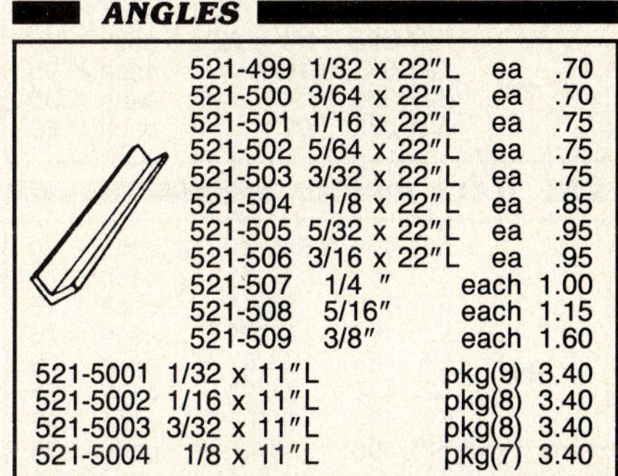

521-499	1/32 x 22″L	ea	.70
521-500	3/64 x 22″L	ea	.70
521-501	1/16 x 22″L	ea	.75
521-502	5/64 x 22″L	ea	.75
521-503	3/32 x 22″L	ea	.75
521-504	1/8 x 22″L	ea	.85
521-505	5/32 x 22″L	ea	.95
521-506	3/16 x 22″L	ea	.95
521-507	1/4 ″	each	1.00
521-508	5/16″	each	1.15
521-509	3/8″	each	1.60
521-5001	1/32 x 11″L	pkg(9)	3.40
521-5002	1/16 x 11″L	pkg(8)	3.40
521-5003	3/32 x 11″L	pkg(8)	3.40
521-5004	1/8 x 11″L	pkg(7)	3.40

CHANNELS

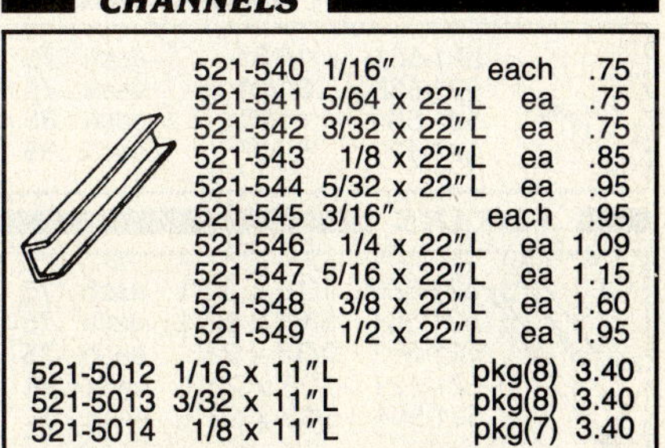

521-540	1/16″	each	.75
521-541	5/64 x 22″L	ea	.75
521-542	3/32 x 22″L	ea	.75
521-543	1/8 x 22″L	ea	.85
521-544	5/32 x 22″L	ea	.95
521-545	3/16″	each	.95
521-546	1/4 x 22″L	ea	1.09
521-547	5/16 x 22″L	ea	1.15
521-548	3/8 x 22″L	ea	1.60
521-549	1/2 x 22″L	ea	1.95
521-5012	1/16 x 11″L	pkg(8)	3.40
521-5013	3/32 x 11″L	pkg(8)	3.40
521-5014	1/8 x 11″L	pkg(7)	3.40

NORTHEASTERN SCALE MODELS INC.

HO SCALE (1/87)

WOOD

STRIPS, SHAPES AND PARTS ARE 24″ IN LENGTH (unless noted).

MINIMUM ORDER: Because the 24″ Length of these strips, shapes and parts requires special shipping containers and, in many cases, a separate package for mailing, we ask that you order at least $3.00 worth of wood or allow 50¢ for packaging on orders less than $3.00.

COLUMN

521-550	1/16 x 22″L	each	.75
521-551	5/64 x 22″L	each	.75
521-552	3/32 x 22″L	each	.75
521-553	1/8″	each	.85
521-554	5/32 x 22″L	each	.95
521-555	3/16 x 22″L	each	.95
521-556	1/4″	each	1.00
521-557	5/16 x 22″L	each	1.15
521-558	3/8″	each	1.60
521-559	1/2″	each	1.95
521-5018	1/16 x 11″L	pkg(8)	3.40
521-5019	3/32 x 11″L	pkg(8)	3.40
521-5020	1/8 x 11″L	pkg(7)	3.40

CORNER POSTS

521-593	1/8″	each	.85
521-595	3/16″	each	.95

COVE

521-91	1/16″	each	.75
521-92	5/64″	each	.75
521-93	3/12″	each	.75
521-94	1/8″	each	.90
521-95	5/32″	each	.95
521-96	3/16″	each	.95
521-98	1/4″	each	1.05

DOOR TRACK

521-576	3/32 x 22″L	each	.75
521-577	1/8″	each	.85
521-579	3/16″	each	.95

DOUBLE BEAD

521-871	1/8″	each	.90
521-872	3/32″	each	.75
521-873	5/64″	each	.75
521-874	1/16″	each	.75
521-875	3/64″	each	.70

FLANGES

521-582	3/32 x 22″L	each	.75
521-583	1/8 x 22″L	each	.85
521-585	3/16″	each	.95
521-586	1/4″	each	1.00
521-588	3/8″	each	1.60

HALF ROUND

521-490	3/64″ x 22″L	each	.70
521-491	1/16″	each	.75
521-492	5/64″	each	.75
521-493	3/32″	each	.75
521-494	1/8″	each	.90
521-495	5/32″	each	.95
521-496	3/16″	each	.95
521-498	1/4″	each	1.05

HAT SECTION

521-531	1/16″	each	.75
521-533	3/32″	each	.75
521-534	1/8″	each	.85
521-535	5/32″	each	.95

I BEAMS

521-560	1/16 x 22″L	each	.75
521-561	5/64 x 22″L	each	.75
521-562	3/32 x 22″L	each	.75
521-563	1/8 x 22″L	each	.85
521-564	5/32 x 22″L	each	.95

I-BEAMS (continued)

521-565	3/16 x 22″L	each	.95
521-566	1/4 x 22″L	each	1.00
521-567	5/16 x 22″L	each	1.15
521-568	3/8 x 22″L	each	1.60
521-569	1/2 x 22″L	each	1.95
521-5015	1/16 x 11″L	pkg(8)	3.40
521-5016	3/32 x 11″L	pkg(8)	3.40
521-5017	1/8 x 11″L	pkg(7)	3.40

QUARTER ROUND

521-570	3/64″	each	.70
521-571	1/16″	each	.75
521-572	5/64″	each	.75
521-573	3/32″	each	.75
521-574	1/8″	each	.90

ROUND

521-485	3/64″	each	.70
521-486	1/16″	each	.75
521-487	5/64″	each	.75
521-488	3/32″	each	.75
521-489	1/8″	each	.90

TEES

521-510	3/64 x 22″L	ea	.70
521-511	1/16 x 22″L	ea	.75
521-512	5/64 x 22″L	ea	.75
521-513	3/32 x 22″L	ea	.75
521-514	1/8 x 22″L	ea	.85
521-515	5/32″	each	.95
521-516	3/16″	each	.95
521-517	1/4″	each	1.00
521-518	5/16″	each	1.15
521-519	3/8″	each	1.60
521-525	1/32″	each	.70
521-5005	1/32 x 11″L	pkg(9)	3.40
521-5006	1/16 x 11″L	pkg(8)	3.40
521-5007	3/32 x 11″L	pkg(8)	3.40
521-5008	1/8 x 11″L	pkg(7)	3.40

WINDOW SASH

521-880	3/16″	each	.95
521-881	5/32″	each	.95
521-882	1/8″	each	.90
521-883	1/4″	each	1.05

ZEES

521-520	3/64″	each	.70
521-523	3/32″	each	.75
521-5009	3/64 x 11″L	pkg(9)	3.40
521-5010	1/16 x 11″L	pkg(8)	3.40
521-5011	3/32 x 11″L	pkg(8)	3.40

CAR PARTS

HO SCALE

OVERHANGING	521-602	2.50
RECESSED	521-612	2.50
CABOOSE	521-622	2.50
REFRIGERATOR	521-632	2.50
HOLLOW CABOOSE	521-642	1.55

HO SCALE (continued)

INNER ROOF	521-652	1.55
FREIGHT FLOOR	521-662	1.45
END BLOCKS	521-672	1.55
CLERESTORY	521-682	3.15
PASS. FLOOR	521-692	1.30
STREAMLINE	521-702	2.50
S-LINE FLOOR	521-712	2.50
COACH SIDE w/BELT RAIL	521-722	1.40
CENTERSILL (SOLID)	521-732	.70
CENTERSILL (GROOVED)	521-742	.85
CENTERSILL (DEEP)	521-752	.75
CENTERSILL (PASS)	521-762	1.20
ROOF WALK	521-772	.40
LATERAL WALKS (Dz)	521-782	.50
FRT BOLSTERS (Pair)	521-792	.45
PASS BOLSTERS (Pair)	521-802	.45
WINDOW MOULDING	521-812	.60
CORNER POST	521-822	.45
BELT RAIL	521-832	.40
THRESHOLD	521-842	.45
EYE PINS .018 x .750 gross	521-860	5.05

FOR MINIATURES (1/12)

BASEBOARD

521-939	1/4″	each	.95
521-945	1/2″	each	1.40
521-946	1/2″	each	1.40
521-947	1/2″	each	1.40
521-949	1/2″	each	1.40

CHAIR RAIL

521-951	3/16″	each	.90
521-952	1/4″	each	.95
521-957	1/4″	each	.95

NORTHEASTERN SCALE MODELS INC.

SCALE
1 inch = 1 foot

WOOD

STRIPS, SHAPES AND PARTS ARE 24″ IN LENGTH (unless noted.)

MINIMUM ORDER: Because the 24″ Length of these strips, shapes and parts requires special shipping containers and, in many cases, a separate package for mailing, we ask that you order at least $3.00 worth of wood or allow 50¢ for packaging on orders less than $3.00.

MINIATURES (1/12) (cont)

CHANNEL, DOLLHOUSE

521-1066	1/4 x 22″	each 1.00
521-1067	3/8 x 22″	each 1.30

CLAPBOARD

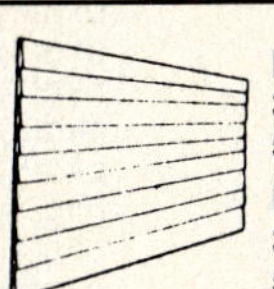

Beaded Clap Board 3-7/16″, 3/8″ spacing 521-387		ea 2.65
Beaded Clap Board 3-7/16″, 1/2″ spacing 521-389		ea 2.65

CORNER BLOCK

521-954	5/64 x 9/16 x 22″L	each 2.45
521-955	5/64 x 9/16 x 22″L	each 2.45

CORNER TRIM

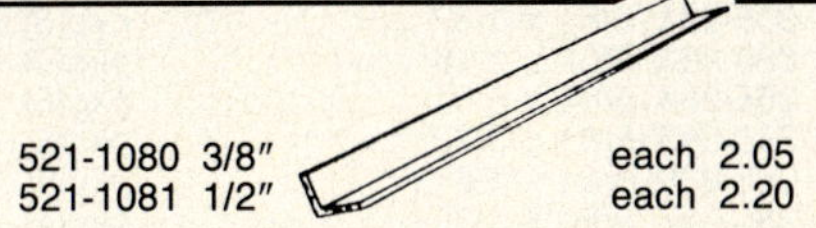

521-1080	3/8″	each 2.05
521-1081	1/2″	each 2.20

CORNICE

521-948	5/16″	each 1.05
521-950	1/2″	each 1.40
521-967	3/8″	each .90

DOOR CASING

1/2″	521-941	1.40
1/2″	521-942	1.40
3/8″	521-943	1.25
3/8″	521-944	1.25

DOOR/WINDOW CASING

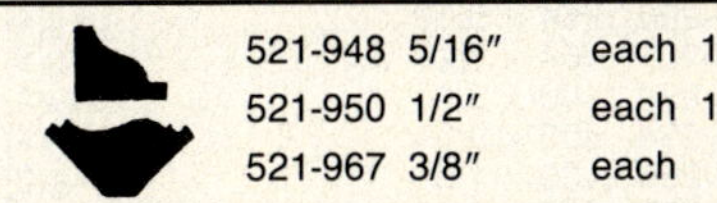

1/4″	521-929	.95
1/2″	521-930	1.40
1/4″	521-931	.95
3/8″	521-933	1.25
1/2″	521-940	1.40

DOOR FRAMES

521-1030	7/16″	each 1.60
521-1032	5/8″	each 1.75
521-1034	3/4″	each 1.90
521-1031	7/16″	each 1.60
521-1033	5/8″	each 1.75
521-1035	3/4″	each 1.90

DOOR JAMB

521-961	1/2″	1.40
521-966	1/2″	1.40

DOOR KNOBS

521-867	Dummy (Brass)	each 3.65
521-868	Working w/Latch	each 9.75
521-869	Template	each 2.90

DOOR PANEL TRIM

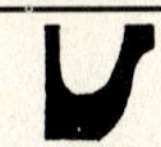

1075   1076   1077

521-1075	Back Band	each 1.05
521-1076	Cap	each 1.05
521-1077	Cap	each 1.05

GUTTER

521-956	3/8″ 1.60

HANDRAIL

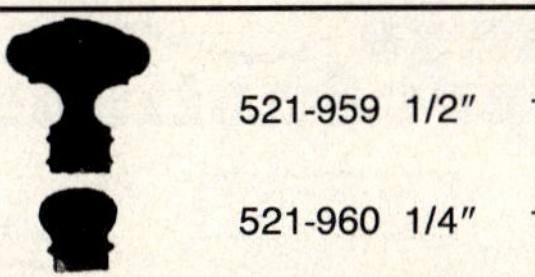

521-959	1/2″ 1.75
521-960	1/4″ 1.10

HINGES

521-1010 Butt Hinges (Brass) pkg(12) 5.75
Scale 4″ high. Removable pins make door hanging easy.
521-863 Piano Hinge   each 9.15

MISCELLANEOUS

521-1003 Dollhouse of a Dollhouse   13.75

PANEL, WAINSCOT

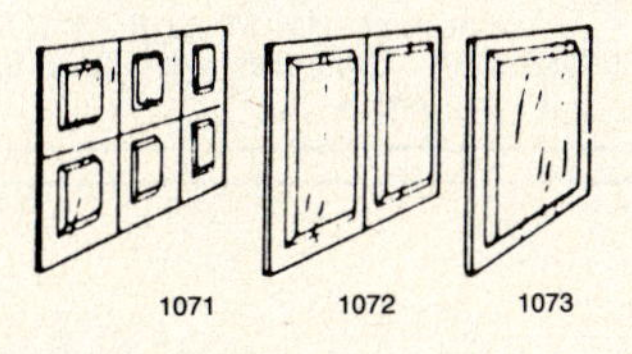

1071   1072   1073

521-1071	6 Panel x 3″	1.25
521-1073	1 Panel x 2-3/16″	1.00

PICTURE FRAME

521-901	3/32″	each	.75
521-902	1/8″	each	.90
521-904	3/16″	each	.95
521-905	1/4″	each	1.05
521-907	1/8″	each	.90
521-909	3/16″	each	.95
521-910	1/4″	each	1.05
521-914	3/16″	each	.95
521-915	1/4″	each	1.05
521-917	1/8″	each	.90
521-919	3/16″	each	.95
521-922	5/32″	each	.95
521-923	3/16″	each	.95

RAILING

521-1140	Fancy Hand Rail	each 1.50
521-1150	Top Porch Rail	each 1.40
521-1151	Bottom Porch Rail	each .95

RANDOM FLOORING

1/16 x 3-1/2″
2.65 per sheet
521-440

SHUTTER

521-1060	3-1/2″ each 4.25

SHUTTER FRAME

521-1025	5/32″	each .95
521-1026	3/16″	each .95

STAIR PARTS

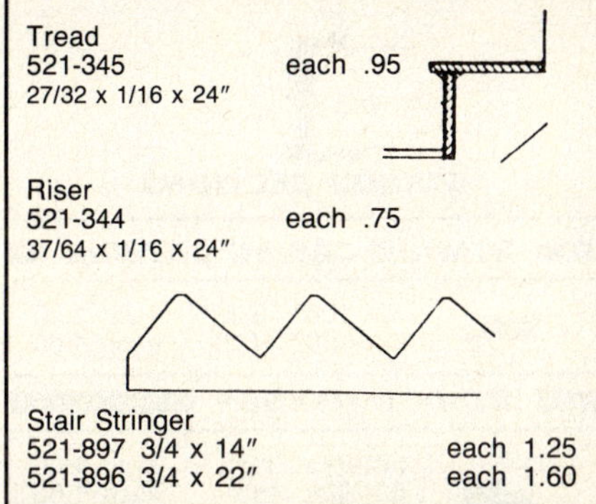

Tread
521-345   each .95
27/32 x 1/16 x 24″

Riser
521-344   each .75
37/64 x 1/16 x 24″

Stair Stringer
521-897 3/4 x 14″   each 1.25
521-896 3/4 x 22″   each 1.60

THRESHOLD

521-973	3/4 x 22″L 2.00

SIDING PACKS

Each pack includes two pieces of scale lumber 3 x 11″

BOARD AND BATTEN

521-6006	3/32″	each 3.25
521-6007	1/8″	each 3.25
521-6008	3/16″	each 3.25

CLAPBOARD

521-6001	1/16″	pkg(2) 3.25
521-6002	3/32″	pkg(2) 3.25
521-6003	1/8″	pkg(2) 3.25

CORRUGATED

521-6020	1/16″	pkg(2) 3.25
521-6021	3/32″	pkg(2) 3.25
521-6022	1/8″	pkg(2) 3.25

SCRIBED

521-6010	1/32″, 1/32″ thick	pkg(2) 3.25
521-6011	1/16″, 1/32″ thick	pkg(2) 3.25
521-6012	3/32″, 1/32″ thick	pkg(2) 3.25
521-6013	1/8″, 1/32″ thick	pkg(2) 3.25
521-6015	1/16″, 1/16″ thick	pkg(2) 3.25
521-6016	3/32″, 1/16″ thick	pkg(2) 3.25
521-6017	1/8″, 1/16″ thick	pkg(2) 3.25

NORTHEASTERN SCALE MODELS INC.
WOOD

MINIMUM ORDER: Because of the 24″ Length of these strips, shapes and parts requires special shipping containers and, in many cases, a separate package for mailing, we ask that you order at least $3.00 worth of wood or allow 50¢ for packaging on orders less than $3.00.

SIDING PACKS (continued)

WINDOW SASH RECESS

521-885 5/32″	each .95

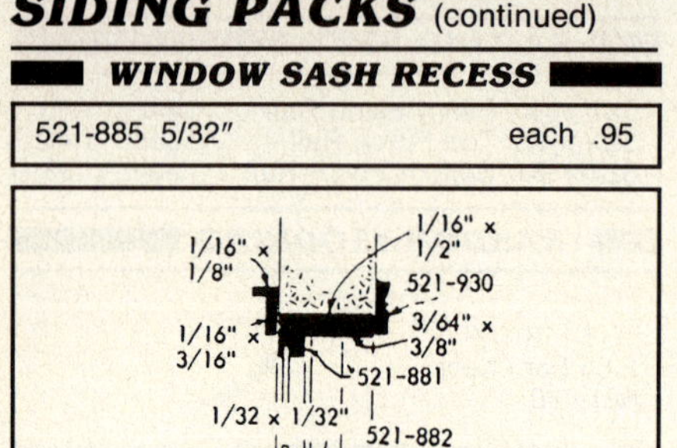
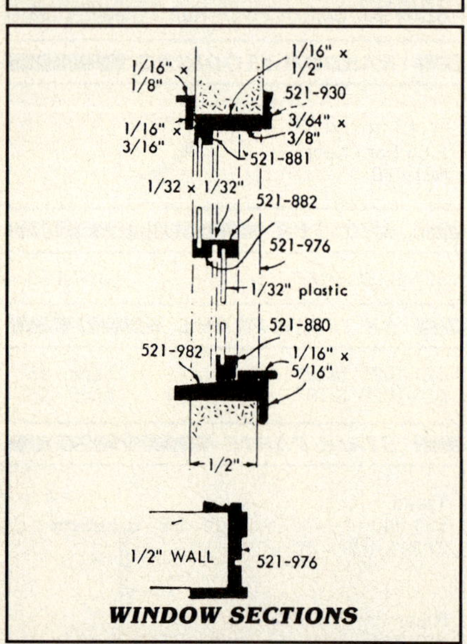
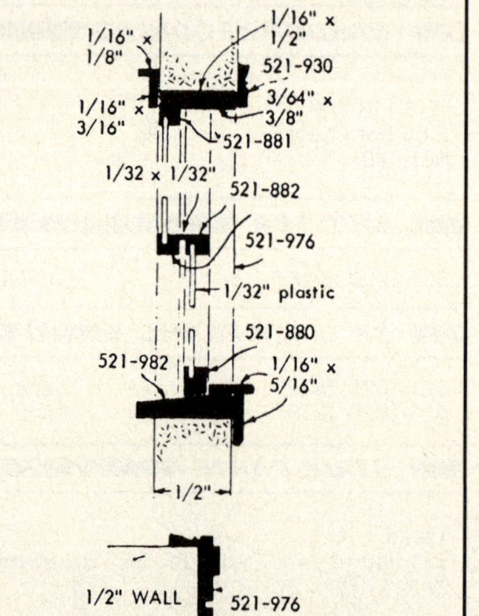

WINDOW SECTIONS

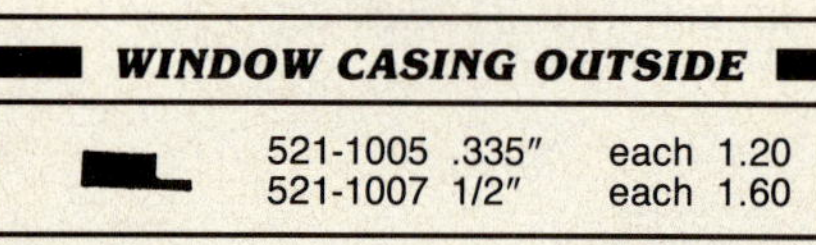

WINDOW CASING OUTSIDE

521-1005	.335″	each 1.20
521-1007	1/2″	each 1.60

WINDOW HEADER

521-995	.335″	each 1.20
521-996	.460″	each 1.60
521-997	1/2″	each 1.60

WINDOW JAMB

521-974	.335″	each 1.15
521-975	.460″	each 1.45
521-976	1/2″	each 1.45

WINDOW SILL

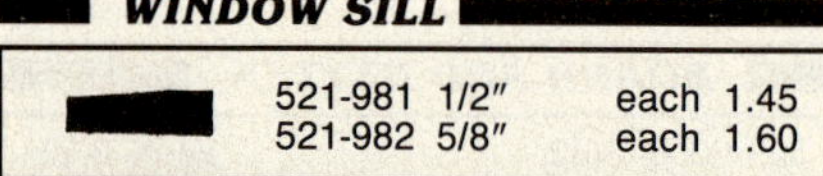

521-981	1/2″	each 1.45
521-982	5/8″	each 1.60

MOULDING PACKS

Each package decorates two or more dollhouse rooms.

BASEBOARD

4010   4011

521-4010	1/2″	pkg(3) 4.35
521-4011	1/2″	pkg(3) 4.35

CHAIR RAIL

521-4014	1/4″	pkg(5) 4.35

CASING DOOR/WINDOW

4015   4016   4017

521-4015	1/2″	pkg(3) 4.35
521-4016	1/4″	pkg(5) 4.35
521-4017	3/8″	pkg(4) 4.35

CORNER BLOCK

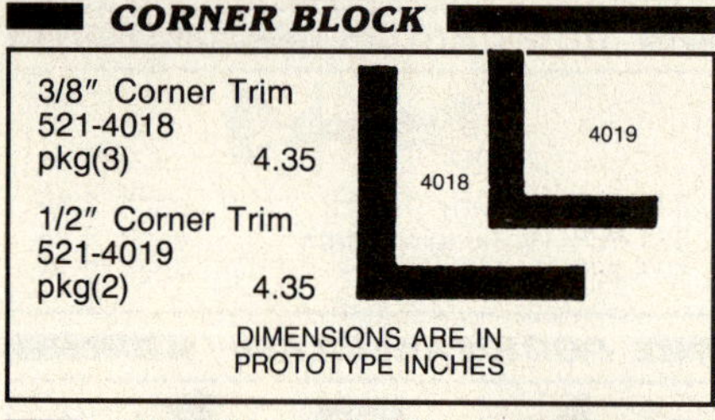

3/8″ Corner Trim
521-4018
pkg(3)   4.35
4018

4019

1/2″ Corner Trim
521-4019
pkg(2)   4.35

DIMENSIONS ARE IN PROTOTYPE INCHES

CROWN CORNICE

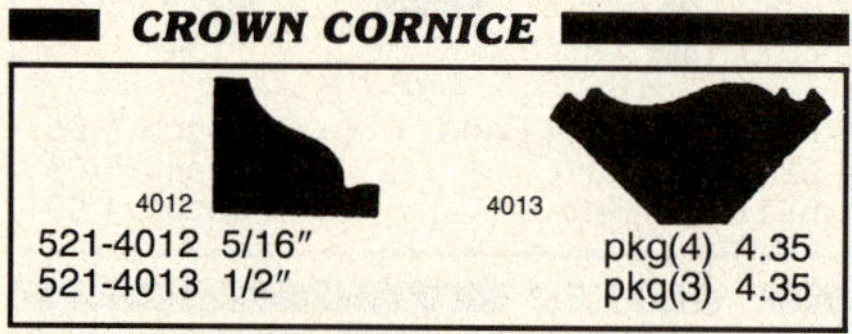

4012   4013

521-4012	5/16″	pkg(4) 4.35
521-4013	1/2″	pkg(3) 4.35

Vintage Reproductions
WOOD

MISCELLANEOUS

WOODEN DOWELS

Dowels are 12″ long unless noted.

766-303	1/12″ diameter	pkg(22)	1.75
766-314	1/8″ diameter	pkg(18)	1.75
766-316	3/16″ diameter	pkg(14)	1.75
766-317	1/4″ diameter	pkg(10)	1.75
766-318	5/16″ diameter	pkg(10)	1.75
766-319	Dowel Sampler	pkg(15)	2.50
	3 each of 1/12, 1/8, 3/16, 1/4 & 5/16		
766-362	3/16″ diameter	pkg(22)	5.00
	24″ length		

Cartoon courtesy of *Model Railroader* Magazine.

KAPPLER MILL & LUMBER CO.

STRIPWOOD   Packs **2.10** ea

24″ LENGTH

385-931	.020 x 1/4	pkg(4)
385-941	.040 x 1/32	pkg(8)
385-942	.040 x .040	pkg(8)
385-943	.040 x 3/64	pkg(8)
385-944	.040 x 1/16	pkg(6)
385-945	.040 x 5/64	pkg(6)
385-946	.040 x 3/32	pkg(6)
385-947	.040 x 1/8	pkg(5)
385-948	.040 x 5/32	pkg(5)
385-949	.040 x 3/16	pkg(5)
385-950	.040 x 7/32	pkg(5)
385-951	.040 x 1/4	pkg(4)
385-971	3/64 x 1/32	pkg(6)
385-972	3/64 x 3/64	pkg(6)
385-973	3/64 x 1/16	pkg(6)
385-974	3/64 x 5/64	pkg(6)
385-975	3/64 x 3/32	pkg(6)
385-976	3/64 x 1/8	pkg(5)
385-977	3/64 x 5/32	pkg(5)
385-978	3/64 x 3/16	pkg(5)
385-979	3/64 x 1/4	pkg(4)
385-981	5/64 x 1/32	pkg(6)
385-983	5/64 x 1/16	pkg(6)
385-984	5/64 x 5/64	pkg(6)
385-985	5/64 x 3/32	pkg(6)
385-986	5/64 x 1/8	pkg(5)
385-987	5/64 x 5/32	pkg(4)
385-988	5/64 x 3/16	pkg(4)
385-989	5/64 x 1/4	pkg(4)
385-990	5/64 x 5/16	pkg(4)
385-991	5/64 x 1/2	pkg(4)
385-992	.400 x 3/64	pkg(4)
385-994	.400 x 5/64	pkg(4)
385-996	.400 x 1/8	pkg(3)
385-997	.400 x 5/32	pkg(3)
385-998	.400 x 3/16	pkg(3)
385-999	.400 x 1/4	pkg(1)

STRUCTURAL ACCESSORIES

40′ FENCE

385-608	3 Rail	pkg(2) 2.75
385-610	4 Rail	pkg(2) 2.75

10′ GATE

385-609	3 Rail	2.25
385-611	4 Rail	2.25

MISCELLANEOUS

WOODEN LADDERS

26′ Length

385-600	HO Scale	pkg(2) 2.50

FUZZ

Fuzz is a prepackaged multi-scale wood material for use in scratch building and railroad scenery.

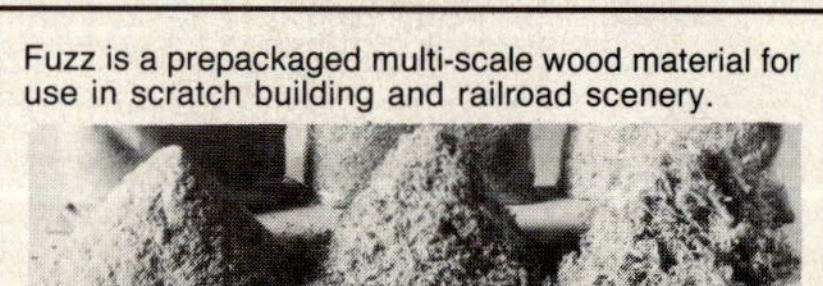

385-620	Extra Fine	pkg(7.5oz)	1.95
385-621	Fine	pkg(6.5oz)	1.95
385-622	Medium	pkg(4oz)	1.95
385-623	Coarse	pkg(1.5oz)	1.95
385-624	Extra Coarse	pkg(4.5oz)	1.95

Specify mfr #385 when ordering

WOOD

- STRIPWOOD
- HO SCALE LUMBER
- SIDING
- WOODEN LADDER
- SCALE TIES
- ALL ITEMS BASSWOOD EXCEPT WHERE NOTED

Items listed in *blue ink* may not be available at all times. Please see your dealer for current delivery information.

SCALE LUMBER

Packs **2.10** each
Dimensions are in prototype inches.

1" HO SCALE

	12" Length			24" Length	
200	x 2	pkg(11)	300	x 2	pkg(6)
201	x 3	pkg(11)	301	x 3	pkg(6)
202	x 4	pkg(10)	302	x 4	pkg(5)
203	x 6	pkg(10)	303	x 6	pkg(5)
204	x 8	pkg(9)	304	x 8	pkg(5)
205	x 10	pkg(8)	305	x 10	pkg(4)
206	x 12	pkg(7)	306	x 12	pkg(4)
207	x 14	pkg(7)	307	x 14	pkg(4)
208	x 16	pkg(6)	308	x 16	pkg(3)
209	x 18	pkg(6)	309	x 18	pkg(3)
210	x 20	pkg(6)	310	x 20	pkg(3)
212	x 24	pkg(6)	311	x 22	pkg(3)
			312	x 24	pkg(3)

2" HO SCALE

	12" Length			24" Length	
213	x 2	pkg(14)	313	x 2	pkg(7)
214	x 3	pkg(14)	314	x 3	pkg(7)
215	x 4	pkg(14)	315	x 4	pkg(7)
216	x 6	pkg(14)	316	x 6	pkg(7)
217	x 8	pkg(11)	317	x 8	pkg(6)
218	x 10	pkg(11)	318	x 10	pkg(6)
219	x 12	pkg(10)	319	x 12	pkg(6)
220	x 14	pkg(10)	320	x 14	pkg(5)
221	x 16	pkg(10)	321	x 16	pkg(5)
222	x 18	pkg(10)	322	x 18	pkg(5)
223	x 20	pkg(10)	323	x 20	pkg(5)
224	x 22	pkg(8)	324	x 22	pkg(5)
225	x 24	pkg(8)	325	x 24	pkg(5)

3" HO SCALE

	12" Length			24" Length	
226	x 3	pkg(14)	326	x 3	pkg(7)
227	x 4	pkg(14)	328	x 6	pkg(6)
228	x 6	pkg(12)	329	x 8	pkg(6)
229	x 8	pkg(12)	330	x 9	pkg(6)
230	x 9	pkg(11)	331	x 12	pkg(5)
231	x 12	pkg(10)	333	x 10	pkg(6)
233	x 10	pkg(11)	334	x 14	pkg(6)
234	x 14	pkg(12)	335	x 16	pkg(6)
235	x 16	pkg(12)	336	x 18	pkg(6)
236	x 18	pkg(12)	337	x 20	pkg(6)
237	x 20	pkg(12)			

4" HO SCALE

	12" Length			24" Length	
238	x 4	pkg(14)	338	x 4	pkg(7)
239	x 6	pkg(12)	339	x 6	pkg(6)
240	x 8	pkg(11)	340	x 8	pkg(6)
241	x 10	pkg(11)	341	x 10	pkg(6)
242	x 12	pkg(10)	342	x 12	pkg(5)
243	x 14	pkg(10)	343	x 14	pkg(5)
244	x 16	pkg(8)	344	x 16	pkg(4)
245	x 18	pkg(8)	345	x 18	pkg(4)
246	x 20	pkg(8)	346	x 20	pkg(4)
247	x 22	pkg(8)	347	x 22	pkg(4)
248	x 24	pkg(6)	348	x 24	pkg(3)

6" HO SCALE

	12" Length			24" Length	
249	x 6	pkg(12)	349	x 6	pkg(6)
250	x 8	pkg(11)	350	x 8	pkg(6)
251	x 10	pkg(10)	351	x 10	pkg(5)
252	x 12	pkg(9)	352	x 12	pkg(5)
253	x 14	pkg(9)	353	x 14	pkg(5)
254	x 16	pkg(9)	354	x 16	pkg(5)

6" HO SCALE (continued)

255	x 18	pkg(8)	355	x 18	pkg(4)
256	x 20	pkg(8)	356	x 20	pkg(4)
257	x 22	pkg(6)	357	x 22	pkg(3)
258	x 24	pkg(6)	358	x 24	pkg(3)

8" HO SCALE

	12" Length			24" Length	
259	x 8	pkg(10)	359	x 8	pkg(5)
260	x 10	pkg(10)	360	x 10	pkg(5)
261	x 12	pkg(9)	361	x 12	pkg(5)
262	x 14	pkg(8)	362	x 14	pkg(4)
263	x 16	pkg(8)	363	x 16	pkg(4)
264	x 18	pkg(6)	364	x 18	pkg(3)
265	x 20	pkg(6)	365	x 20	pkg(3)
266	x 22	pkg(6)	366	x 22	pkg(3)
267	x 24	pkg(6)	367	x 24	pkg(3)

10" HO SCALE

	12" Length			24" Length	
268	x 10	pkg(10)	368	x 10	pkg(5)
269	x 12	pkg(8)	369	x 12	pkg(4)
270	x 14	pkg(8)	370	x 14	pkg(4)
271	x 16	pkg(6)	371	x 16	pkg(4)
272	x 18	pkg(6)	372	x 18	pkg(3)
273	x 20	pkg(6)	373	x 20	pkg(3)
274	x 22	pkg(6)	374	x 22	pkg(3)
275	x 24	pkg(6)	375	x 24	pkg(3)

12" HO SCALE

	12" Length			24" Length	
276	x 12	pkg(8)	376	x 12	pkg(4)
277	x 14	pkg(6)	377	x 14	pkg(4)
278	x 16	pkg(6)	378	x 16	pkg(3)
279	x 18	pkg(6)	379	x 18	pkg(3)
280	x 20	pkg(6)	380	x 20	pkg(3)
281	x 22	pkg(6)	381	x 22	pkg(3)
282	x 24	pkg(6)			

STRIPWOOD Packs **1.95** ea

12" LENGTH

385-101	1/32 x 1/32	pkg(14)
385-102	1/32 x 1/16	pkg(14)
385-103	1/32 x 3/32	pkg(12)
385-104	1/32 x 1/8	pkg(12)
385-105	1/32 x 5/32	pkg(10)
385-106	1/32 x 3/16	pkg(10)
385-107	1/32 x 1/4	pkg(10)
385-108	1/32 x 5/16	pkg(8)
385-109	1/32 x 3/8	pkg(8)
385-110	1/32 x 7/16	pkg(6)
385-111	1/32 x 1/2	pkg(6)
385-112	1/32 x 3/4	pkg(6)
385-113	1/32 x 1"	pkg(4)
385-115	1/16 x 1/16	pkg(12)
385-116	1/16 x 3/32	pkg(12)
385-117	1/16 x 1/8	pkg(10)
385-118	1/16 x 5/32	pkg(10)
385-119	1/16 x 3/16	pkg(10)
385-120	1/16 x 1/4	pkg(8)
385-121	1/16 x 5/16	pkg(8)
385-122	1/16 x 3/8	pkg(6)
385-123	1/16 x 7/16	pkg(6)
385-124	1/16 x 1/2	pkg(6)
385-125	1/16 x 3/4	pkg(4)
385-126	1/16 x 1"	pkg(4)
385-128	3/32 x 3/32	pkg(10)
385-129	3/32 x 1/8	pkg(10)
385-130	3/32 x 5/32	pkg(10)
385-131	3/32 x 3/16	pkg(8)
385-132	3/32 x 1/4	pkg(8)
385-133	3/32 x 5/16	pkg(6)

12" LENGTH (continued)

385-134	3/32 x 3/8	pkg(6)
385-135	3/32 x 7/16	pkg(6)
385-136	3/32 x 1/2	pkg(4)
385-137	3/32 x 3/4	pkg(4)
385-138	3/32 x 1"	pkg(2)
385-140	1/8 x 1/8	pkg(10)
385-141	1/8 x 5/32	pkg(8)
385-142	1/8 x 3/16	pkg(8)
385-143	1/8 x 1/4	pkg(6)
385-144	1/8 x 5/16	pkg(6)
385-145	1/8 x 3/8	pkg(6)
385-146	1/8 x 7/16	pkg(4)
385-147	1/8 x 1/2	pkg(4)
385-148	1/8 x 3/4	pkg(4)
385-149	1/8 x 1"	pkg(2)
385-151	5/32 x 5/32	pkg(8)
385-152	5/32 x 3/16	pkg(8)
385-153	5/32 x 1/4	pkg(6)
385-154	5/32 x 5/16	pkg(6)
385-155	5/32 x 3/8	pkg(4)
385-156	5/32 x 7/16	pkg(4)
385-157	5/32 x 1/2	pkg(4)
385-158	5/32 x 3/4	pkg(4)
385-159	5/32 x 1"	pkg(2)
385-161	3/16 x 3/16	pkg(6)
385-162	3/16 x 1/4	pkg(6)
385-163	3/16 x 5/16	pkg(4)
385-164	3/16 x 3/8	pkg(4)
385-165	3/16 x 7/16	pkg(4)
385-166	3/16 x 1/2	pkg(4)
385-167	3/16 x 3/4	pkg(2)
385-168	3/16 x 1"	pkg(2)
385-170	1/4 x 1/4	pkg(6)
385-171	1/4 x 5/16	pkg(4)
385-172	1/4 x 3/8	pkg(4)
385-173	1/4 x 7/16	pkg(4)
385-174	1/4 x 1/2	pkg(2)
385-175	1/4 x 3/4	pkg(2)
385-176	1/4 x 1"	pkg(2)
385-178	5/16 x x 5/16	pkg(4)
385-179	5/16 x 3/8	pkg(4)
385-180	5/16 x 7/16	pkg(2)
385-181	5/16 x 1/2	pkg(2)
385-182	5/16 x 3/4	pkg(2)
385-183	5/16 x 1"	pkg(2)
385-185	3/8 x 3/8	pkg(4)
385-186	3/8 x 7/16	pkg(2)
385-187	3/8 x 1/2	pkg(3)
385-188	3/8 x 3/4	pkg(2)
385-189	3/8 x 1"	pkg(2)
385-191	7/16 x 7/16	pkg(2)
385-192	7/16 x 1/2	pkg(2)
385-193	7/16 x 3/4	pkg(2)
385-194	7/16 x 1"	pkg(2)
385-196	1/2 x 1/2	pkg(2)
385-197	1/2 x 3/4	pkg(2)
385-198	1/2 x 1"	pkg(2)
385-901	.012 x 1/32	pkg(5)
385-902	.012 x .040	pkg(6)
385-903	.012 x 3/64	pkg(6)
385-904	.012 x 1/16	pkg(6)
385-905	.012 x .12 x 3/32	pkg(5)
385-906	.012 x 3/32	pkg(5)
385-907	.012 x 1/8	pkg(5)
385-908	.012 x 5/32	pkg(5)
385-909	.012 x 3 /16	pkg(5)
385-910	.012 x 7/32	pkg(5)
385-911	.012 x 1/4	pkg(4)
385-921	.020 x 1/32	pkg(7)
385-922	.020 x .040	pkg(7)
385-923	.020 x 3/64	pkg(7)
385-924	.020 x 1/16	pkg(7)
385-925	.020 x 5/64	pkg(6)
385-926	.020 x 3/32	pkg(6)
385-927	.020 x 1/8	pkg(6)
385-928	.020 x 5/32	pkg(5)
385-929	.020 x 3/16	pkg(5)
385-930	.020 x 7/32	pkg(5)

SUPERIOR HOBBY PRODUCTS

WOOD

HO SCALE (1/87)
Rough sawn basswood lumber.

SCALE LUMBER PACKS
12" 1.79   24" 1.98

Dimensions are in prototype inches.

+ (PLUS SIGN) = SPECIAL ORDER ONLY ITEMS

2" HO SCALE

12" Length	24" Length
697-710 x 2 pkg(14)	697-744 x 2 pkg(7)
697-711 x 4 pkg(14)	697-745 x 4 pkg(7)
697-712 x 6 pkg(14)	697-746 x 6 pkg(7)
697-713 x 8 pkg(12)	697-747 x 8 pkg(6)
697-714 x 10 pkg(12)	697-748 x 10 pkg(6)
697-715 x 12 pkg(10)	697-749 x 12 pkg(6)

4" HO SCALE

12" Length	24" Length
697-716 x 4 pkg(14)	697-750 x 4 pkg(7)
697-717 x 6 pkg(12)	697-751 x 6 pkg(6)
697-718 x 8 pkg(12)	697-752 x 8 pkg(6)
697-719 x 10 pkg(10)	697-753 x 10 pkg(6)
697-720 x 12 pkg(10)	697-754 x 12 pkg(6)
697-721 x 14 pkg(8)	697-755 x 14 pkg(4)
697-722 x 16 pkg(6)	697-756 x16 pkg(3)

6" HO SCALE

12" Length	24" Length
697-724 x 8 pkg(12)	
697-725 x 10 pkg(10)	697-759 x 10 pkg(5)
697-727 x 14 pkg(6)	697-761 x 14 pkg(4)

8" HO SCALE

12" Length	24" Length
697-729 x 8 pkg(10)	697-763 x 8 pkg(5)
697-730 x 10 pkg(10)	697-764 x 10 pkg(5)
697-731 x 12 pkg(8)	697-765 x 12 pkg(4)
697-732 x 14 pkg(6)	697-766 x 14 pkg(3)
697-733 x 16 pkg(6)	697-767 x 16 pkg(3)

10" HO SCALE

12" Length	24" Length
+ 697-734 x 10 pkg(10)	697-768 x 10 pkg(5)
697-735 x 12 pkg(8)	697-769 x 12 pkg(4)
697-736 x 14 pkg(6)	697-770 x 14 pkg(3)
+ 697-737 x 16 pkg(5)	697-771 x 16 pkg(2)

12" HO SCALE

12" Length	24" Length
697-738 x 12 pkg(8)	697-772 x 12 pkg(4)
697-739 x 14 pkg(6)	697-773 x 14 pkg(3)
697-740 x 16 pkg(4)	697-774 x 16 pkg(2)

14" HO SCALE

12" Length	24" Length
697-741 x 14 pkg(6)	697-775 x 14 pkg(3)
697-742 x 16 pkg(4)	697-776 x 16 pkg(2)

16" HO SCALE

12" Length	24" Length
+ 697-743 x 16 pkg(3)	697-777 x 16 pkg(2)

JIG MATERIAL

697-700 5x10" 1.98   697-701 10x16" 2.98

HOLGATE REYNOLDS
1/8" SCALE

PLASTIC
BUILDING MATERIAL

Embossed surfaces are made of Vinylite plastic. They may be bent, scored and cut. The material is rigid enough to stand alone, but develops greater strength when glued to wood or cardstock backing. Illustration approximately 3/4 full size.

DEALERS: MUST order Dealer Packs (Dealer Pack: 6 sheets — all one number)

BRICK

White
340-1011   2.50
(3-1/2 x 20")

White
340-1013   5.00
(8-1/4 x 20")

340-1012 Red (3-1/2 x 20")   2.50
340-1014 Red (8-1/4 x 20")   5.00

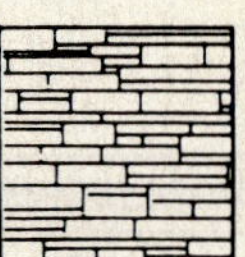
Stone
340-1020
2.50
3-1/2 x 18"

Asphalt
Roofing
340-1030
2.50
3-1/2 x 18"

Shake
Roofing
340-1040
2.50
3-1/2 x 18"

Cement
Block
340-1050
2.50
3-1/2 x 18"

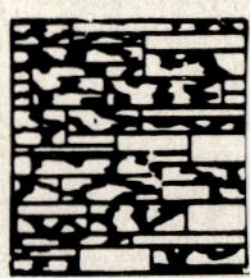
Lannon
Stone
340-1070
2.50
3-1/2 x 18"

Field
Stone
340-1220
2.50
3-1/2 x 18"

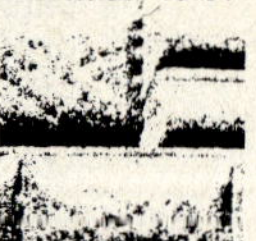
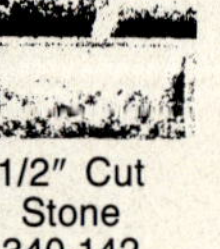
1/2" Cut
Stone
340-142
5.00
8-1/2 x 20"

Pebblestone
340-2127
3.50
5-1/8 x 14"

(not illustrated)

340-2121 1/2" Scale Brick   5.00
8 x 20"
340-2123 1/2" Scale Roof   5.00
8 x 18"
340-1411 1" Scale Brick   3.50
5-1/2 x 20"
340-1413 1" Scale Brick   5.00
8-1/4 x 20"

Grandt Line

PLASTIC

RODS
8" Long Flexible Plastic Rod

PLASTIC RODS

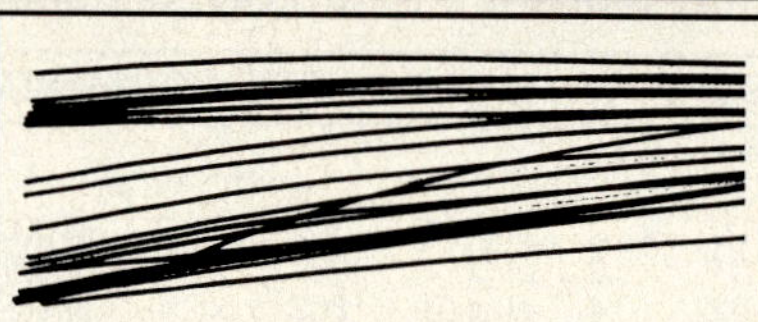

300-3901 .010" Diameter	pkg(12)	3.50
300-3902 .020" Diameter	pkg(12)	3.50
300-3903 .030" Diameter	pkg(12)	3.50
300-3904 .040" Diameter	pkg(12)	3.50
300-3905 .050" Diameter	pkg(12)	3.50

K&S ENGINEERING

PLASTIC

SHEETS

CLEAR PLASTIC

8 x 10" flexible sheets. Clear as glass, vacuum formable.

Part #	Size	Price Each	Pkg	Price Pkg
370-301	.010	.40	10	4.00
370-302	.0075	.30	15	4.50
370-304	.015	.60	10	6.00
370-306	.030	1.00	5	5.00

Vintage Reproductions

PLASTIC

MISCELLANEOUS

CLERESTORY WINDOWS

Colored polyester photographic film with clear design to simulate stained glass windows.

766-401	.23" Long	(red)	pkg(24)	2.25
766-402	.23" Long	(grn)	pkg(24)	2.25
766-403	.31" Long	(red)	pkg(24)	2.75
766-404	.31" Long	(grn)	pkg(24)	2.75
766-405	.42" Long	(red)	pkg(24)	3.25
766-406	.42" Long	(grn)	pkg(24)	3.25

evergreen scale models

STYRENE BUILDING MATERIALS

[PLASTIC]

May be scored with a sharp knife, and broken on the scored line. Joined by using plastic solvent adhesive. Before brush painting with Floquil, Scalecoat or lacquers, a primer coat of Floquil Barrier or Scalecoat Shieldcoat should be applied.

SIDING

◼ V-GROOVE SCRIBED (6 x 12")

Opaque white sheets. Used on freight and passenger cars as well as railroad, commercial and residential buildings. It was also used in combination with clapboard and novelty siding for decorative effects. Many turn-of-the-century structures used decorative panels of v-groove siding applied in horizontal, vertical and diagonal patterns.

Part	Thickness	Spacing	Qty	Price
269-2025	.020"	.025"	each	2.69
269-2030	.020"	.030"	each	2.69
269-2040	.020"	.040"	each	2.69
269-2050	.020"	.050"	each	2.69
269-2060	.020"	.060"	each	2.69
269-2080	.020"	.080"	each	2.69
269-2100	.020"	.100"	each	2.69
269-2125	.020"	.125"	each	2.69
269-4030	.040"	.030"	each	2.89
269-4040	.040"	.040"	each	2.89
269-4050	.040"	.050"	each	2.89
269-4060	.040"	.060"	each	2.89
269-4080	.040"	.080"	each	2.89
269-4100	.040"	.100"	each	2.89
269-4188	.040"	.188"	each	2.89
269-4250	.040"	.250"	each	2.89

◼ V-GROOVE SCRIBED (12 x 24")

Part	Thickness	Spacing	Qty	Price
269-12025	.020"	.025"	each	9.25
269-12030	.020"	.030"	each	9.25
269-12040	.020"	.040"	each	9.25
269-12050	.020"	.050"	each	9.25
269-12060	.020"	.060"	each	9.25
269-12080	.020"	.080"	each	9.25
269-12100	.020"	.100"	each	9.25
269-12125	.020"	.125"	each	9.25
269-14030	.040"	.030"	each	10.00
269-14040	.040"	.040"	each	10.00
269-14050	.040"	.050"	each	10.00
269-14060	.040"	.060"	each	10.00
269-14080	.040"	.080"	each	10.00
269-14100	.040"	.100"	each	10.00
269-14125	.040"	.125"	each	10.00
269-14188	.040"	.188"	each	10.00
269-14250	.040"	.250"	each	10.00

◼ NOVELTY (6 x 12")

Opaque white sheets. Many of the buildings of the mid 19th to early 20th century used novelty siding. Also known as shiplap or drop siding, it consisted of overlapping boards with a rabbet in the bottom of each board overlapping in the round cove on the top of the board below.

Part	Thickness	Spacing	Qty	Price
269-4062	.040"	.060"	each	2.89
(5-1/4 HO Scale inches, 9-1/2 N Scale inches)				
269-4083	.040"	.083"	each	2.89
(7-1/4 HO Scale inches)				
269-4109	.040"	.109"	each	2.89
(9-1/4 HO Scale inches)				
269-4150	.040"	.150"	each	2.89

◼ BOARD & BATTEN (6 x 12")

Part	Thickness	Spacing	Qty	Price
269-4542	.040"	.075	each	2.89
269-4543	.040"	.100	each	2.89
269-4544	.040"	.125	each	2.89

◼ BOARD & BATTEN (12 x 24") ◼

Part	Thickness	Spacing	Qty	Price
269-14542	.040"	.075	each	10.00
269-14543	.040"	.100	each	10.00
269-14544	.040"	.125	each	10.00

◼ CLAPBOARD (6 x 12") ◼

One of the most common types of sidings used on wood structures. Clapboard siding (often called lap siding) is a prominent feature of many railroad buildings as well as city, town and farm structures of all kinds.

Part	Thickness	Spacing	Qty	Price
269-4031	.040"	.030"	each	2.89
269-4041	.040"	.040"	each	2.89
269-4051	.040"	.050"	each	2.89
269-4061	.040"	.060"	each	2.89
269-4081	.040"	.080"	each	2.89
269-4101	.040"	.100"	each	2.89

◼ CLAPBOARD (12 x 24") ◼

Part	Thickness	Spacing	Qty	Price
269-14031	.040"	.030"	each	10.00
269-14041	.040"	.040"	each	10.00
269-14051	.040"	.050"	each	10.00
269-14061	.040"	.060"	each	10.00
269-14081	.040"	.080"	each	10.00
269-14101	.040"	.100"	each	10.00

◼ CORRUGATED METAL (6 x 12") ◼

Opaque white plastic sheets.

Part	Thickness	Spacing	Qty	Price
269-4525	.040"	.030"	each	2.89
269-4526	.040"	.040"	each	2.89
269-4527	.040"	.060"	each	2.89
269-4528	.040"	.080"	each	2.89
269-4529	.040"	.100"	each	2.89
269-4530	.040"	.125"	each	2.89

◼ CORRUGATED METAL (12 x 24") ◼

Opaque white plastic sheets

Part	Thickness	Spacing	Qty	Price
269-14525	.040"	.030"	each	10.00
269-14526	.040"	.040"	each	10.00
269-14527	.040"	.060"	each	10.00
269-14528	.040"	.080"	each	10.00
269-14529	.040"	.100"	each	10.00
269-14530	.040"	.125"	each	10.00

◼ PASSENGER CAR (6 x 12") ◼

Passenger car siding has grooves across the sheet to eliminate splicing. Thickness matches Grandt Line molded windows and doors 2-1/4" scale spacing.

Part	Thickness	Scale	Qty	Price
269-3025	.030"	HO	each	2.89

◼ CAR (6 x 12") ◼

Car siding has grooves across the sheet to eliminate splicing.

Part	Thickness	Scale	Qty	Price
269-2020	.020"	N	each	2.69
269-2037	.020"	HO	each	2.69
269-4037	.040"	HO	each	2.89

STRIPS

◼ DIMENSIONAL ◼

14" long opaque white strips

Part	Thickness	Spacing	Qty	Price
269-100	.010"	.020"	pkg(10)	1.59
269-101	.010"	.030"	pkg(10)	1.59
269-102	.010"	.040"	pkg(10)	1.59
269-103	.010"	.060"	pkg(10)	1.59
269-104	.010"	.080"	pkg(10)	1.59
269-105	.010"	.100"	pkg(10)	1.59
269-106	.010"	.125"	pkg(10)	1.59
269-107	.010"	.156"	pkg(10)	1.59
269-108	.010"	.188"	pkg(10)	1.59
269-109	.010"	.250"	pkg(10)	1.59
269-110	.015"	.090"	pkg(10)	1.59

GROOVE SPACING			PROTOTYPE INCHES				
Inches	Nearest Fraction	mm	N 1:160	TT 1:120:	HO 1:87	S 1:64	O 1:48
.010	—	.25	1-1/2	1-1/4	7/8	7/8	1/2
.015	1/64	.38	2-3/8	1-3/4	1-1/4	1	3/4
.020	—	.50	3-1/4	2-3/8	1-3/4	1-1/4	1
.025	—	.64	4	3	2-1/8	1-5/8	1-1/4
.030	1/32	.75	4-3/4	3-5/8	2-5/8	1-7/8	1-1/2
.040	—	1.0	6-3/8	4-3/4	3-1/2	2-1/2	1-7/8
.050	3/64	1.25	8	6	4-3/8	3-1/4	2-3/8
.060	1/16	1.5	9-5/8	7-1/4	5-1/4	3-7/8	2-7/8
.080	5/64	2.0	12-3/4	9-5/8	7	5-1/8	3-7/8
.100	3/32	2.5	16	12	8-3/4	6-3/8	4-3/4
.125	1/8	3.1	20	15	10-7/8	8	6
.188	3/16	4.8	30	22-1/2	16-3/8	12	9
.250	1/4	6.3	40	30	21-3/4	16	12

evergreen scale models

STYRENE BUILDING MATERIALS
PLASTIC

May be scored with a sharp knife, and broken on the scored line. Joined by using plastic solvent adhesive. Before brush painting with Floquil, Scalecoat or lacquers, a primer coat of Floquil Barrier or Scalecoat Shieldcoat should be applied.

DIMENSIONAL (continued)

Part	Thickness	Spacing	Qty	Price
269-111	.015″	.030″	pkg(10)	1.59
269-112	.015″	.040″	pkg(10)	1.59
269-113	.015″	.060″	pkg(10)	1.59
269-114	.015″	.080″	pkg(10)	1.59
269-115	.015″	.100″	pkg(10)	1.59
269-116	.015″	.125″	pkg(10)	1.59
269-117	.015″	.156″	pkg(10)	1.59
269-118	.015″	.188″	pkg(10)	1.59
269-119	.015″	.250″	pkg(10)	1.59
269-120	.020″	.020″	pkg(10)	1.59
269-121	.020″	.030″	pkg(10)	1.59
269-122	.020″	.040″	pkg(10)	1.59
269-123	.020″	.060″	pkg(10)	1.59
269-124	.020″	.080″	pkg(10)	1.59
269-125	.020″	.100″	pkg(10)	1.59
269-126	.020″	.125″	pkg(10)	1.59
269-127	.020″	.156″	pkg(10)	1.59
269-128	.020″	.188″	pkg(10)	1.59
269-129	.020″	.250″	pkg(10)	1.59
269-131	.030″	.030″	pkg(10)	1.59
269-132	.030″	.040″	pkg(10)	1.59
269-133	.030″	.060″	pkg(10)	1.59
269-134	.030″	.080″	pkg(10)	1.59
269-135	.030″	.100″	pkg(10)	1.59
269-136	.030″	.125″	pkg(10)	1.59
269-137	.030″	.156″	pkg(10)	1.59
269-138	.030″	.188″	pkg(10)	1.59
269-139	.030″	.250″	pkg(10)	1.59
269-142	.040″	.040″	pkg(10)	1.59
269-143	.040″	.060″	pkg(10)	1.59
269-144	.040″	.080″	pkg(10)	1.59
269-145	.040″	.100″	pkg(10)	1.59
269-146	.040″	.125″	pkg(10)	1.59
269-147	.040″	.156″	pkg(10)	1.59
269-148	.040″	.188″	pkg(10)	1.59
269-149	.040″	.250″	pkg(10)	1.59
269-153	.060″	.060″	pkg(10)	1.59
269-154	.060″	.080″	pkg(10)	1.59
269-155	.060″	.100″	pkg(10)	1.59
269-156	.060″	.125″	pkg(10)	1.59
269-157	.060″	.156″	pkg(9)	1.59
269-158	.060″	.188″	pkg(9)	1.59
269-159	.060″	.250″	pkg(8)	1.59
269-164	.080″	.080″	pkg(9)	1.59
269-165	.080″	.100″	pkg(8)	1.59
269-166	.080″	.125″	pkg(8)	1.59
269-167	.080″	.156″	pkg(8)	1.59
269-168	.080″	.188″	pkg(8)	1.59
269-169	.080″	.250″	pkg(7)	1.59
269-175	.100″	.100″	pkg(8)	1.59
269-176	.100″	.125″	pkg(7)	1.59
269-177	.100″	.156″	pkg(7)	1.59
269-178	.100″	.188″	pkg(7)	1.59
269-179	.100″	.250″	pkg(6)	1.59
269-186	.125″	.125″	pkg(6)	1.59
269-187	.125″	.156″	pkg(6)	1.59
269-188	.125″	.188″	pkg(6)	1.59
269-189	.125″	.250″	pkg(5)	1.59

SQUARE STRIPS

Part	Size	Qty	Price
269-196	3/16 x 3/16″	pkg(4)	1.59
269-199	1/4 x 1/4″	pkg(3)	1.59

HO SCALE

Dimensions are in HO Scale inches. Strips are 14″ long, opaque white and packed in resealable polyethylene bags.

Part	Size	Qty	Price
269-8102	1 x 2	pkg(10)	1.59
269-8103	1 x 3	pkg(10)	1.59
269-8104	1 x 4	pkg(10)	1.59
269-8106	1 x 6	pkg(10)	1.59

HO SCALE (continued)

Part	Size	Qty	Price
269-8108	1 x 8	pkg(10)	1.59
269-8110	1 x 10	pkg(10)	1.59
269-8112	1 x 12	pkg(10)	1.59
269-8202	2 x 2	pkg(10)	1.59
269-8203	2 x 3	pkg(10)	1.59
269-8204	2 x 4	pkg(10)	1.59
269-8206	2 x 6	pkg(10)	1.59
269-8208	2 x 8	pkg(10)	1.59
269-8210	2 x 10	pkg(10)	1.59
269-8212	2 x 12	pkg(10)	1.59
269-8404	4 x 4	pkg(10)	1.59
269-8406	4 x 6	pkg(10)	1.59
269-8408	4 x 8	pkg(10)	1.59
269-8410	4 x 10	pkg(10)	1.59
269-8412	4 x 12	pkg(10)	1.59
269-8606	6 x 6	pkg(10)	1.59
269-8608	6 x 8	pkg(10)	1.59
269-8610	6 x 10	pkg(10)	1.59
269-8612	6 x 12	pkg(10)	1.59

STRUCTURAL SHAPES

CHANNELS — NEW

14″ Length — Opaque white styrene

Part	Size	Qty	Price
269-262	.080″	pkg(4)	1.99
269-263	.100″	pkg(4)	1.99
269-264	.125″	pkg(4)	1.99
269-265	.156″	pkg(4)	1.99
269-266	.188″	pkg(3)	1.99
269-267	.250″	pkg(3)	1.99
269-268	.312″	pkg(2)	1.99

I-BEAMS — NEW

14″ Lengths — Opaque white styrene

Part	Size	Qty	Price
269-272	.080″	pkg(4)	1.99
269-273	.100″	pkg(4)	1.99
269-274	.125″	pkg(4)	1.99
269-275	.156″	pkg(3)	1.99
269-276	.188″	pkg(3)	1.99
269-277	.250″	pkg(2)	1.99
269-278	.312″	pkg(2)	1.99

TUBING

ROD & TUBING

14″ long white styrene

Part	Thickness	Qty	Price
269-216	Rod & Tube Assortment		3.99
269-219	.025 Rod	pkg(10)	1.89
269-220	.035 Rod	pkg(10)	1.89
269-221	.047 Rod	pkg(10)	1.89
269-222	.062 Rod	pkg(8)	1.89
269-223	.093 Tubing	pkg(6)	1.89

TELESCOPING

Part	Thickness	Qty	Price
269-224	1/8″	pkg(5)	1.89
269-226	3/16″	pkg(4)	1.89
269-228	1/4″	pkg(3)	1.89
269-230	5/16″	pkg(3)	1.89
269-232	3/8″	pkg(2)	1.89
269-234	7/16″	pkg(2)	1.89
269-236	1/2″	pkg(2)	1.89

STYRENE SHEETS

WHITE (6 x 12″)

Part	Thickness	Qty	Price
269-9001	Assortment		2.99
269-9002	Odds & Ends		3.99
269-9009	.005″	pkg(4)	1.99
269-9010	.010″	pkg(4)	1.99
269-9015	.015″	pkg(3)	1.99
269-9020	.020″	pkg(3)	1.99
269-9030	.030″	pkg(2)	1.99
269-9040	.040″	pkg(2)	2.49
269-9060	.060″	pkg(1)	1.99
269-9080	.080″	pkg(1)	2.49

WHITE (11 x 14″)

Part	Thickness	Qty	Price/Pack
269-9210	.010″	pkg(15)	14.40
269-9215	.015″	pkg(12)	14.40
269-9220	.020″	pkg(12)	14.40
269-9230	.030″	pkg(8)	14.40
269-9240	.040″	pkg(6)	14.40
269-9260	.060″	pkg(4)	14.40
269-9280	.080″	pkg(3)	14.40

WHITE (12 x 24″)

Part	Thickness	Price Each	Pack	Price/Pack
269-19009	.005″	1.44	15	21.60
269-19010	.010″	1.44	15	21.60
269-19015	.015″	1.80	12	21.60
269-19020	.020″	1.80	12	21.60
269-19030	.030″	2.70	8	21.60
269-19040	.040″	3.60	6	21.60
269-19060	.060″	5.40	4	21.60
269-19080	.080″	7.20	3	21.60
269-19100	.100″	9.00	2	18.00
269-19125	.125″	10.00	2	20.00

CLEAR (6 x 12″)

Part	Size	Qty	Price
269-9005	.005″	pkg(4)	1.99
269-9006	.010″	pkg(3)	1.99
269-9007	.015″	pkg(2)	1.99

TILES
Opaque white sheets.

SQUARE (6 x 12″)

Part	Thickness	Size	Qty	Price
269-4501	.040″	1/16″ sq	each	2.89
269-4502	.040″	1/12″ sq	each	2.89
269-4503	.040″	1/8″ sq	each	2.89
269-4504	.040″	1/6″ sq	each	2.89
269-4505	.040″	1/4″ sq	each	2.89
269-4506	.040″	1/3″ sq	each	2.89
269-4507	.040″	1/2″ sq	each	2.89

SQUARE (12 x 24″)

Part	Thickness	Size	Qty	Price
269-14501	.040″	1/16″ sq	each	10.00
269-14502	.040″	1/12″ sq	each	10.00
269-14503	.040″	1/8″ sq	each	10.00
269-14504	.040″	1/4″ sq	each	10.00
269-14505	.040″	1/6″ sq	each	10.00
269-14506	.040″	1/3″ sq	each	10.00
269-14507	.040″	1/2″ sq	each	10.00

evergreen scale models — STYRENE BUILDING MATERIALS

PLASTIC

May be scored with a sharp knife, and broken on the scored line. Joined by using plastic solvent adhesive. Before brush painting with Floquil, Scalecoat or lacquers, a primer coat of Floquil Barrier or Scalecoat Shieldcoat should be applied.

MISCELLANEOUS

SIDEWALKS

Opaque white sheets (6 x 12")

Part	Thickness	Size	Qty	Price
269-4514	.040"	1/8" sq	each	2.89
269-4515	.040"	3/16" sq	each	2.89
269-4516	.040"	1/4" sq	each	2.89
269-4517	.040"	3/8" sq	each	2.89
269-4518	.040"	1/2" sq	each	2.89

Opaque white sheets (12 x 23")

Part	Thickness	Size	Qty	Price
269-14514	.040"	1/8" sq	each	10.00
269-14515	.040"	3/16" sq	each	10.00
269-14516	.040"	1/4" sq	each	10.00
269-14517	.040"	3/8" sq	each	10.00
269-14518	.040"	1/2" sq	each	10.00

LADDER KITS

Slotted stringers — makes 24" of ladder

Part	Scale	Price
269-201	HO Scale (1/810)	1.59

STAIRWAY KITS

Slotted stringers — makes 22" of ladder

Part	Scale	Price
269-204	HO Scale (1/810)	2.99

STANDING SEAM ROOFING

6 x 12" with seam strips

Part	Thickness	Size	Qty	Price
269-4521	.040"	3/16"	each	3.99
269-4522	.040"	1/4"	each	3.99
269-4523	.040"	3/8"	each	3.99
269-4524	.040"	1/2"	each	3.99

STYRENE HANDBOOK

269-12	Styrene Handbook	1.00

OCTOBER 10, 1848

❧ Today ❧

IN RAILROAD HISTORY

The steam locomotive "Pioneer," the first locomotive in Chicago, arrives aboard a sailing ship. Built by Mathias Baldwin, the loco will pull its first train two days later.

BRAWA

Plastic sheet building material. Includes two sheets, 4 x 6". Thickness varies from 1/32 to .039.

PLASTIC

Imported from Germany by WALTHERS

BUILDING MATERIAL — SHEETS

Cobblestones
186-2805   3.99

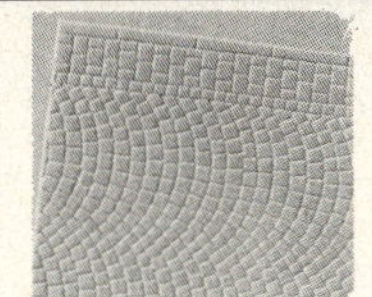

Curved Cobblestones
186-2810   3.99

Ribbed Metal Sheet
186-2835   (silver) 3.99
Ribbed Metal Sheet
186-2836   (black) 3.99

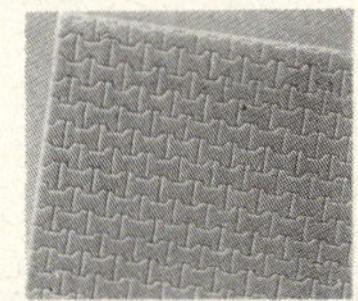

Sidewalk Paving
186-2830   3.99

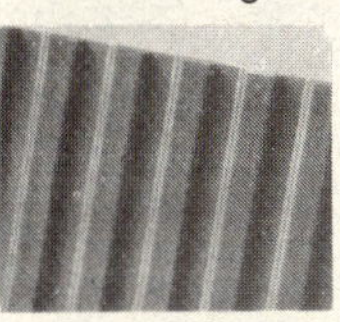

Artificial Stone
186-2845 Paving 3.99

Brick Wall (bk red)
186-2827   3.99

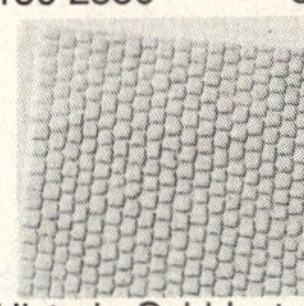

Sheet Piling
186-2850   3.99

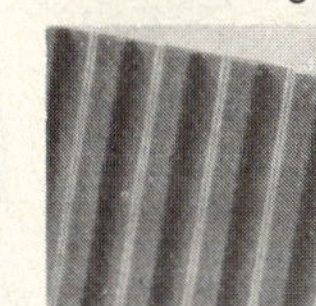

Masonry Slabs
(sandstone)
186-2825   3.99

Historic Cobblestones
(gray)
186-2806   3.99

Wood Flooring
(dark brown)
186-2800   3.99

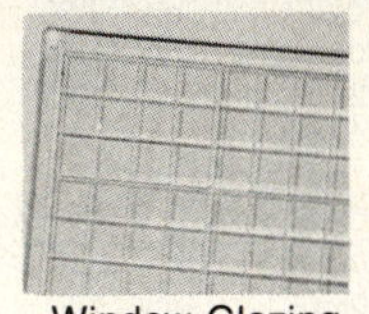

Window Glazing
186-2840   3.99

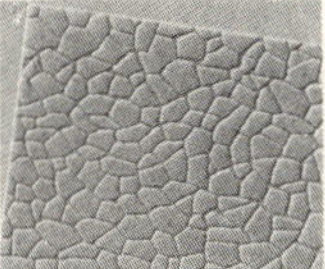

Random Stone Paving
186-2815   3.99

Masonry Slabs
(brick red)
186-2826   3.99

Wall Tiles, HO Scale
(brick red)
186-2867   3.99

Wood Flooring
(natural finish)
186-2801   3.99

Corrugated Metal Sheet (gray)
186-2855   3.99

Corrugated Sheet
(translucent)
186-2856   3.99

WALTHERS — BUILDING MATERIAL

PLASTIC

LIMITED QUANTITIES AVAILABLE

STYRENE SHEETS (6-1/2 x 12" white opaque sheets unless noted).

Part	Thickness	Qty	Price		Part	Thickness	Qty	Price
949-592	.010	(4 sheets)	2.98		949-603	.100	(1 sheet)	2.98
949-593	.015	(3 sheets)	2.98		949-598	.075" Clear 6-1/4 x 12"	(4 sheets)	2.98
949-594	.020	(3 sheets)	2.98					
949-595	.040	(2 sheets)	2.98		949-599	.015 Clear	(3 sheets)	2.98
949-596	.030	(2 sheets)	2.98		949-600	Assortment	(5 sheets)	3.98
949-601	.060	(1 sheet)	1.98			Includes one each .010, .015, .020, .030, and .040.		
949-602	.080	(1 sheet)	1.98					

TRANSPARENT WINDOWS

These sash designs are silk-screened in .0075" clear transparent styrene ("cellutate"). They will not warp when cemented in place. Residential windows are printed with white sash lines, for use in homes, stores, offices, farm houses, etc. The industrial sheet is printed with black sash lines and should be used for factories, warehouses, roundhouses and other yard buildings.

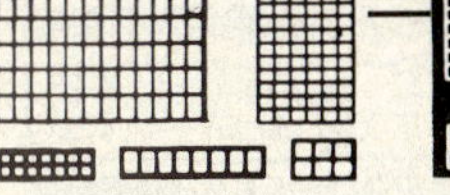

Industrial
949-340 (2 sheets) 1.98

Residential
949-506 (2 sheets) 1.98

Plastruct

PLASTIC

SCALE PLASTIC STRUCTURAL SHAPES AND COMPONENTS

Material ABS plastic, precision injection molded or extruded. Can be sawed, blade-cut, drilled or sanded. Use liquid or solvent cement to join. ANY type of paint, even lacquer can be used. Brush or spray on.

Dealers MUST order Dealer Packs on Structural Shapes, Tubing, Pipe Fittings, Strips & Sheets and Plastic Weld.

STRIPS & SHEET

STRIPS - 1-1/4" x 24"

570-901	Conc. .020	pkg(10)	8.50
570-902	Conc. .030	pkg(10)	10.00
570-951	Steel .020	pkg(10)	8.50
570-952	Steel .030	pkg(10)	10.00

PLAIN SHEET - 12" Long

570-7000	Clear .040 x 4"	pkg(10)	15.00
570-7001	Gray .025 x 4"	pkg(20)	13.00
570-7003	Gray .031 x 4"	pkg(15)	12.00
570-7006	Gray .062 x 4"	pkg(10)	10.50
570-7009	Gray .093 x 4"	pkg(7)	9.45
570-10000	Clear .010 x 7"	pkg(3)	9.75
570-10001	Red .030 x 7"	pkg(3)	6.75
570-10002	Beige .030 x 7"	pkg(3)	6.75
570-10003	Gray .030 x 7"	pkg(3)	6.75

TUBING & ROD

ROUND TUBING

570-601	1/32" x 15" Wire	pkg(40)	10.00
570-602	1/16" x 15" Wire	pkg(40)	12.00
570-603	3/32" x 15"	pkg(35)	12.25
570-604	1/8" x 15"	pkg(30)	12.00
570-606	3/16" x 15"	pkg(20)	9.00
570-608	1/4" x 15"	pkg(15)	9.00
570-610	5/16" x 15"	pkg(10)	7.50
570-612	3/8" x 15"	pkg(8)	7.20

SQUARE TUBING

570-704	1/8" x 15"	pkg(15)	9.00
570-706	3/16" x 15"	pkg(15)	10.50
570-708	1/4" x 15"	pkg(10)	8.00
570-710	5/16" x 15"	pkg(10)	9.00
570-712	3/8" x 15"	pkg(7)	7.35

RECTANGULAR TUBING

570-808	1/4" x 15"	pkg(10)	7.00
570-810	5/16" x 15"	pkg(10)	7.50
570-812	3/8" x 15"	pkg(10)	8.50
570-814	7/16" x 15"	pkg(5)	4.50

STYRENE MICRO ROD

570-1310	.010 x 10"	pkg(10)	3.00
570-1320	.020 x 10"	pkg(10)	3.00
570-1000	.000 x 10"	pkg(10)	3.50
570-1340	.040 x 10"	pkg(10)	4.00
570-1350	.050 x 10"	pkg(10)	4.00

ACRYLIC CLEAR ROD

570-7162	1/16" x 8-1/2"	pkg(40)	5.20
570-7164	1/8" x 8-1/2"	pkg(30)	5.40

FLUORESCENT ROD

570-17365	5/32" x 9" Blue	pkg(6)	5.10
570-17465	5/32" x 9" Green	pkg(6)	5.10
570-17565	5/32" x 9" Red	pkg(6)	5.10
570-17665	5/32" x 9" Yellow	pkg(6)	5.10

ABS ROD

570-854	1/8" x 1/8" x 15"	pkg(5)	4.25
570-858	1/8" x 1/4" x 15"	pkg(5)	4.50

HALF ROUND PROFILES

570-1203	3/32" x 15"	pkg(5)	4.75
570-1204	1/8" x 15"	pkg(5)	5.00
570-1206	3/16" x 15"	pkg(5)	5.25

STRUCTURAL SHAPES

ANGLES

570-101	3/64" x 10"	pkg(20)	7.00
570-102	1/16" x 10"	pkg(20)	8.00
570-103	3/32" x 15"	pkg(15)	6.75
570-104	1/8" x 15"	pkg(15)	8.25
570-106	3/16" x 24"	pkg(10)	8.00
570-108	1/4" x 24"	pkg(10)	9.50
570-110	5/16" x 24"	pkg(5)	5.50
570-112	3/8" x 24"	pkg(5)	6.50

I BEAMS

570-202	1/16" x 10"	pkg(15)	6.00
570-203	3/32" x 10"	pkg(15)	6.75
570-204	1/8" x 15"	pkg(15)	9.00
570-206	3/16" x 24"	pkg(10)	8.00
570-208	1/4" x 24"	pkg(10)	9.00
570-210	5/16" x 24"	pkg(10)	10.50
570-212	3/8" x 15"	pkg(10)	8.00
570-214	7/16" x 15"	pkg(10)	9.00
570-216	1/2" x 15"	pkg(8)	8.00
570-218	9/16" x 15"	pkg(7)	7.70
570-220	5/8" x 15"	pkg(5)	6.25

CHANNELS

570-302	1/16" x 10"	pkg(20)	8.00
570-303	3/32" x 10"	pkg(15)	7.50
570-304	1/8" x 15"	pkg(15)	9.00
570-306	3/16" x 15"	pkg(15)	11.25
570-308	1/4" x 24"	pkg(10)	9.00
570-310	5/16" x 15"	pkg(10)	10.50
570-312	3/8" x 15"	pkg(5)	3.50

H COLUMNS

570-402	1/16" x 10"	pkg(20)	11.00
570-403	3/32" x 15"	pkg(15)	9.75
570-404	1/8" x 15"	pkg(15)	11.25
570-406	3/16" x 24"	pkg(10)	10.00
570-408	1/4" x 15"	pkg(10)	7.50
570-410	5/16" x 15"	pkg(10)	8.00
570-412	3/8" x 15"	pkg(7)	6.30

TEES

570-501	3/64" x 10"	pkg(20)	8.00
570-502	1/16" x 10"	pkg(20)	9.00
570-503	3/32" x 15"	pkg(15)	7.50
570-504	1/8" x 15"	pkg(15)	9.00
570-506	3/16" x 24"	pkg(10)	8.50
570-508	1/4" x 15"	pkg(10)	10.00

STAIRS

570-1500 N Scale 3" Long	pkg(2)	3.00
570-1504 HO Scale 5" Long	pkg(2)	2.60

LADDERS

570-1600 N Scale 3" Long	pkg(2)	1.90
570-1601 HO Scale 5" Long	pkg(2)	1.50

LADDER W / SAFETY CAGE

570-1704 HO Scale 5" Long	each	2.95
570-1708 O Scale 12" Long	each	4.95

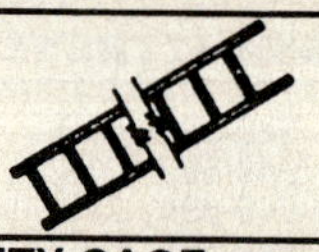

BALCONY RAILINGS

570-1931 HO Scale 6-1/2" Long	pkg(2)	4.50
570-1932 N Scale 6-1/2" Long	pkg(2)	4.50

STRUCTURAL SHAPES

HANDRAILS

570-1900 N Scale 3-5/8" Long	pkg(2)	2.00
570-1904 HO Scale 6" Long	pkg(2)	1.60

STAIR RAILS

570-1800 N Scale 3-5/8" Long	pkg(2)	2.00
570-1804 HO Scale 6" Long	pkg(2)	1.60

STEPS

570-1552 N Scale 2" x 1"	pkg(2)	6.50
570-1554 HO Scale 2-7/8" x 1-3/8"	pkg(2)	7.50

OPEN WEB TRUSSES

570-1950	1/8"	pkg(2)	4.50
570-1951	13/64"	pkg(2)	5.50
570-1952	9/32"	pkg(2)	5.90
570-1953	13/32"	pkg(2)	6.50
570-1954	33/64"	pkg(2)	7.00
570-1955	5/8"	pkg(2)	7.50
570-1956	3/4"	pkg(2)	7.90
570-1957	1"	pkg(2)	9.00

TUBING FITTINGS

90° ELBOWS

570-2303	To Fit 570-603	pkg(5)	1.25
570-2304	To Fit 570-604	pkg(5)	1.50
570-2306	To Fit 570-606	pkg(5)	1.50
570-2308	To Fit 570-608	pkg(5)	1.75
570-2310	To Fit 570-610	pkg(5)	1.75
570-2312	To Fit 570-612	pkg(5)	2.00

45° ELBOWS

570-2103	To Fit 570-603	pkg(5)	1.25
570-2104	To Fit 570-604	pkg(5)	1.50
570-2106	To Fit 570-606	pkg(5)	1.50
570-2108	To Fit 570-608	pkg(5)	1.75
570-2110	To Fit 570-610	pkg(5)	1.75
570-2112	To Fit 570-612	pkg(5)	2.00

TEES

570-2203	To Fit 570-603	pkg(5)	1.25
570-2204	To Fit 570-604	pkg(5)	1.50
570-2206	To Fit 570-606	pkg(5)	1.50
570-2208	To Fit 570-608	pkg(5)	1.75
570-2210	To Fit 570-610	pkg(5)	1.75
570-2212	To Fit 570-612	pkg(5)	2.00

SNAP-ON TEES

570-2501	To Fit 570-601	pkg(5)	1.25
570-2502	To Fit 570-602	pkg(5)	1.25
570-2503	To Fit 570-603	pkg(5)	1.50
570-2504	To Fit 570-604	pkg(5)	1.50
570-2506	To Fit 570-606	pkg(5)	1.75
570-2508	To Fit 570-608	pkg(5)	1.75
570-2510	To Fit 570-610	pkg(5)	2.00
570-2512	To Fit 570-612	pkg(5)	2.00

Plastruct
PLASTIC

SCALE PLASTIC STRUCTURAL SHAPES AND COMPONENTS

Material ABS plastic, precision injection molded or extruded. Can be sawed, blade-cut, drilled or sanded. Use liquid or solvent cement to join. ANY type of paint, even lacquer can be used. Brush or spray on.

Dealers MUST order Dealer Packs on Structural Shapes, Tubing, Pipe Fittings, Strips & Sheets and Plastic Weld.

TUBING FITTINGS

GATE VALVES

570-4001	To Fit 570-601	pkg(5)	1.50
570-4002	To Fit 570-602	pkg(5)	1.50
570-4003	To Fit 570-603	pkg(5)	1.75
570-4004	To Fit 570-604	pkg(5)	1.75
570-4006	To Fit 570-606	pkg(5)	2.00
570-4008	To Fit 570-608	pkg(5)	2.00
570-4010	To Fit 570-610	pkg(5)	2.25
570-4012	To Fit 570-612	pkg(5)	2.50

CONTROL VALVES

570-4101	To Fit 570-601	pkg(5)	1.50
570-4102	To Fit 570-602	pkg(5)	1.50
570-4103	To Fit 570-603	pkg(5)	1.75
570-4104	To Fit 570-604	pkg(5)	2.00
570-4106	To Fit 570-606	pkg(5)	2.25
570-4108	To Fit 570-608	pkg(5)	2.25

ANGLE VALVES

570-4302	To Fit 570-602	pkg(5)	1.50
570-4303	To Fit 570-603	pkg(5)	1.75
570-4304	To Fit 570-604	pkg(5)	2.00
570-4306	To Fit 570-606	pkg(5)	2.25
570-4308	To Fit 570-608	pkg(5)	2.75

NOZZLES

570-2901	To Fit 570-601	pkg(5)	1.25
570-2902	To Fit 570-602	pkg(5)	1.25
570-2903	To Fit 570-603	pkg(5)	1.50
570-2904	To Fit 570-604	pkg(5)	1.50
570-2906	To Fit 570-606	pkg(5)	1.75
570-2908	To Fit 570-608	pkg(5)	1.75
570-2910	To Fit 570-610	pkg(5)	2.00
570-2912	To Fit 570-612	pkg(5)	2.00

COUPLINGS

570-3401	To Fit 570-601	pkg(5)	1.00
570-3402	To Fit 570-602	pkg(5)	1.00
570-3303	To Fit 570-603	pkg(5)	1.00
570-3304	To Fit 570-604	pkg(5)	1.00
570-3306	To Fit 570-606	pkg(5)	1.25
570-3308	To Fit 570-608	pkg(5)	1.25
570-3310	To Fit 570-610	pkg(5)	1.25
570-3312	To Fit 570-612	pkg(5)	1.50

CONCENTRIC REDUCER

570-2603	To Fit 570-604	pkg(5)	1.50

MISCELLANEOUS

DOMES

570-5212	3/8" Ellipse	pkg(5)	1.25
570-5214	7/16" Ellipse	pkg(5)	1.25
570-5216	1/2" Ellipse	pkg(5)	1.50
570-5218	9/16" Ellipse	pkg(5)	1.50
570-5220	5/8" Ellipse	pkg(5)	1.75
570-5224	3/4" Ellipse	pkg(5)	1.75
570-5228	7/8" Ellipse	pkg(5)	2.00
570-5232	1" Ellipse	pkg(5)	2.25
570-5248	1-1/2" Ellipse	pkg(5)	4.00
570-5412	3/8" Hemi	pkg(5)	1.25
570-5414	7/16" Hemi	pkg(5)	1.25
570-5416	1/2" Hemi	pkg(5)	1.50
570-5418	9/16" Hemi	pkg(5)	1.75
570-5420	5/8" Hemi	pkg(5)	1.75
570-5424	3/4" Hemi	pkg(5)	2.00
570-5428	7/8" Hemi	pkg(5)	2.25
570-5432	1" Hemi	pkg(5)	2.50
570-5448	1-1/2" Hemi	pkg(5)	5.50

LIGHT SHADES

570-6303	5/16" O.D.	pkg(5)	1.50
570-6306	7/16" O.D.	pkg(5)	1.75

MISCELLANEOUS

ACRYLIC BALLS

570-7304	1/8" O.D.	pkg(10)	2.00
570-7308	1/4" O.D.	pkg(10)	2.50
570-7312	3/8" O.D.	pkg(10)	3.00
570-7316	1/2" O.D.	pkg(10)	3.50
570-7320	5/8" O.D.	pkg(10)	4.50
570-7324	3/4" O.D.	pkg(5)	4.25

SKYLIGHTS

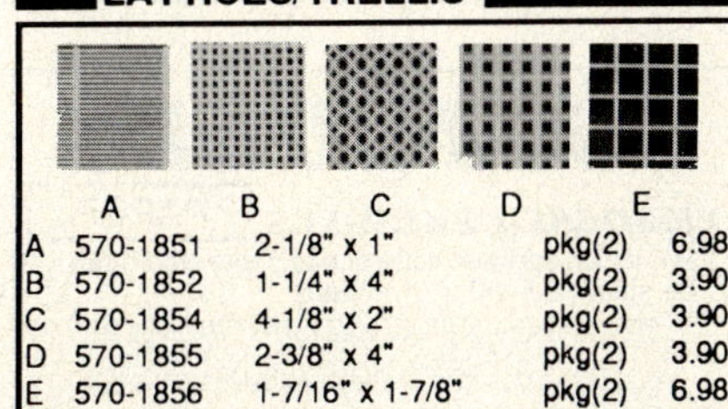

570-11008	1/4" Pyramid	pkg(2)	3.50
570-11012	3/8" Pyramid	pkg(2)	3.60
570-11108	1/4" Dome	pkg(2)	3.50
570-11112	3/8" Dome	pkg(2)	3.60

LATTICES/TRELLIS

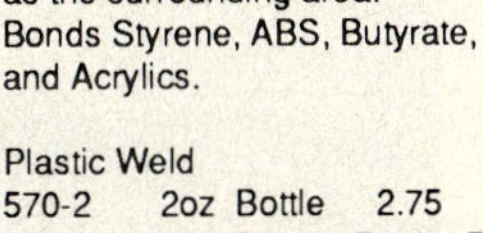

A	570-1851	2-1/8" x 1"	pkg(2)	6.98
B	570-1852	1-1/4" x 4"	pkg(2)	3.90
C	570-1854	4-1/8" x 2"	pkg(2)	3.90
D	570-1855	2-3/8" x 4"	pkg(2)	3.90
E	570-1856	1-7/16" x 1-7/8"	pkg(2)	6.98

PLASTIC WELD CEMENT

PLASTRUCT Plastic Weld Solvent Cement, a colorless, liquid, plastic-fusing type adhesive. Dissolves a thin layer of each surface to be bonded to form a welded joint as strong as the surrounding area. Bonds Styrene, ABS, Butyrate, and Acrylics.

Plastic Weld
570-2   2oz Bottle   2.75
Dealers MUST order Dealer Pack of 12 Bottles.

PATTERNED SHEETS

FLOORING, ROOFING & SIDING

7" x 12" Patterned Sheets Vacuum Formed from .030 Styrene Plastic   All HO Scale or Equivalent.

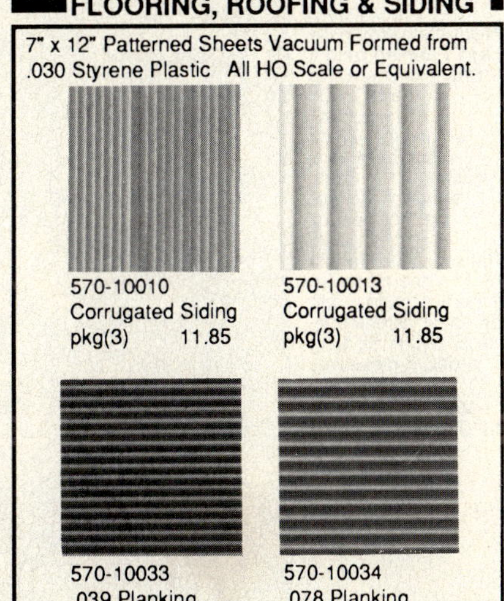

570-10010
Corrugated Siding
pkg(3)   11.85

570-10013
Corrugated Siding
pkg(3)   11.85

570-10033
.039 Planking
pkg(3)   11.85

570-10034
.078 Planking
pkg(3)   11.85

PATTERNED SHEETS

FLOORING, ROOFING & SIDING

7" x 12" Patterned Sheets Vacuum Formed from .030 Styrene Plastic   All HO Scale or Equivalent.

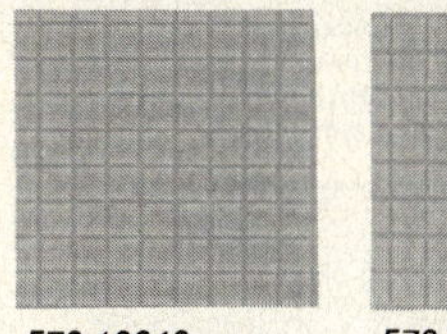
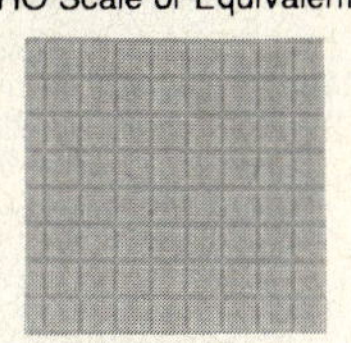

570-10040
1/16" Squares
pkg(3)   11.85

570-10041
1/13" Squares
pkg(3)   11.85

570-10043
1/10" Squares
pkg(3)   11.85

570-10047
1/16" Clapboard
pkg(3)   11.85

570-10049
1/8" Clapboard
pkg(3)   11.85

570-10091
Rough Brick
pkg(3)   11.85

570-10097
Brick
pkg(3)   11.85

570-10103
Concrete Block
pkg(3)   11.85

570-10112
Asphalt Shingles
pkg(3)   11.85

570-10122
Spanish Tile Roof
pkg(3)   11.85

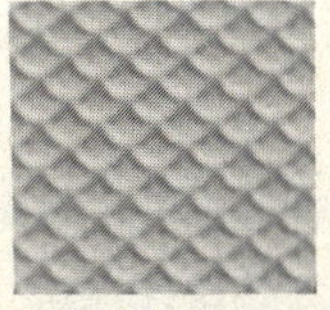
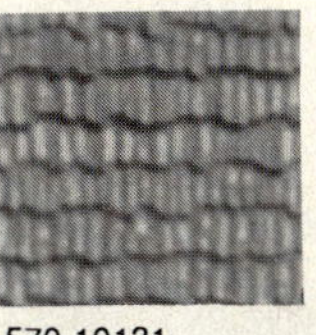

570-10124
Scalloped Tile Roof
pkg(3)   11.85

570-10131
Wood Shake Roof
pkg(3)   11.85

PLASTIC
Pikestuff
HO SCALE (1/87)

BUILDING MATERIAL

CONCRETE
BLOCK SHEETS

Concrete block sections are molded in gray plastic and can be used to create warehouses, gas stations, garages and other concrete structures. Measurement in scale HO feet.

541-1004	14-1/2 x 28'	pkg(4)	1.75
541-1005	14-1/2 x 18-1/2'	pkg(4)	1.75
541-1006	14-1/2 x 9-1/4'	pkg(8)	1.65
	& 14-1/2 x 4'		
	(4 of each size)		

CAP TILES

541-1008	For Concrete Sheets	1.15

ROOFING MATERIAL

541-1007	Shingle Panels	pkg(2)	2.25
	(7-3/16 x 2-1/32")		
541-1015	Shingle Roof (5 x 8")		2.95

PREFAB STEEL
WAREHOUSE WALLS

541-1011	2 Wall Panels & Downspouts (18 x 80' scale feet)		3.50
541-1012	Peaked End Panels	pkg(2)	3.00
541-1013	2 Roof Panels & Supports (15 x 80' scale feet)		3.50

SIDING

541-1014	Board & Batten (5 x 8')	2.95

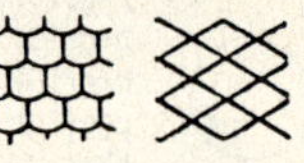
Builders In Scale
Fine Craft Models
HO SCALE (1/87)

VICTORIAN SHINGLES

Lasercut, Gummed | **PAPER**

504	505	506	507

169-504	Curved, "Fishscale"	each	3.49
	(approx 6 square inches)		
169-505	Diamond	each	3.49
	(approx 5 square inches)		
169-506	Octagonal	each	3.49
	(approx 6 square inches)		
169-507	Hexagonal	each	3.49
	(approx 6 square inches)		

CS MODELS

EMBOSSED SHINGLES | **PAPER**

Printed on appropriately colored paper stock, can be stained. 5-1/2 x 4" sheets.

546-9011	N Scale	**NEW** pkg(5)	2.95
546-9021	HO Scale	pkg(5)	2.95

NOCH
Imported from Germany
PAPER | by WALTHERS

CARDBOARD | NEW

528-6162	Corrugated	7.99

TAURUS PRODUCTS
NEW
PAPER

BUILDING MATERIAL

EMBOSSED PAPERS

707-1000	Wallpaper Assort	pkg(8)	2.95
707-1001	Small Brick/ Block Pattern	pkg(3)	2.95
707-1002	Large Brick/ Block Pattern	pkg(3)	2.95
707-1003	Fieldstone Pattern	pkg(3)	2.95

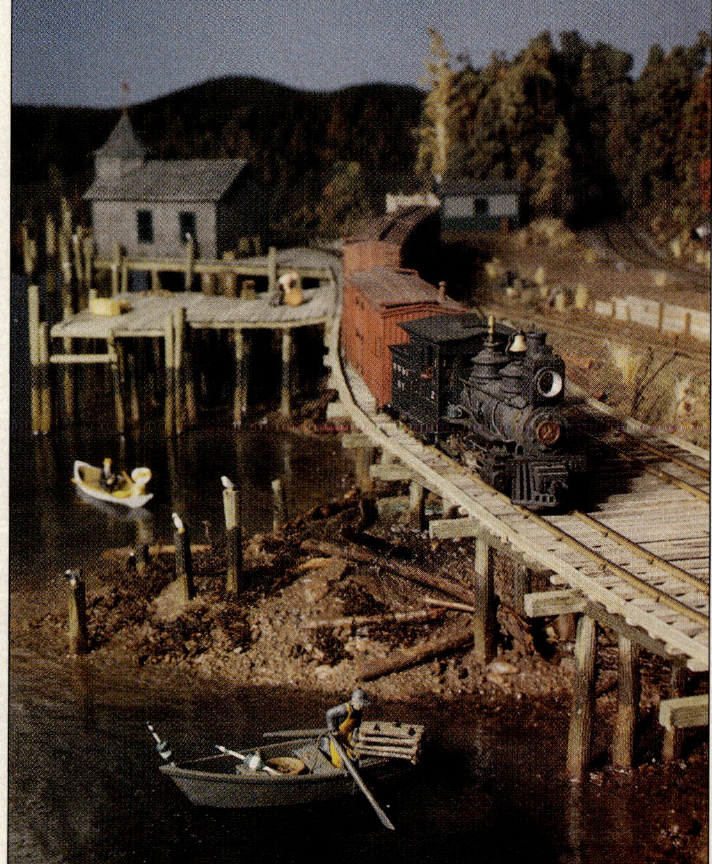

Suppose the passing train scares the lobsters out from under the pier? Ed Jones has fished this part of Maine for years and shows up every time a Wiscasset, Waterville and Farming freight arrives. Rollling along on the HOn30" narrow gauge is engine #2, which started out as a Bachmann N Scale switcher. Builder Chris McChesney of Carlisle, Pennsylvania, rebuilt the loco with numerous hand-made and some commercial parts, and in working order, it measures just 3-1/2" long! *Models and Photo by Chris mcChesney*

Builders In Scale
Fine Craft Models

SIDING | METAL

ALUMINUM SHEETS

Ribbed Seam, 7-1/2″ long.

169-500	4 scale feet wide	pkg(6)	3.29
169-501	8 scale feet wide	pkg(6)	3.29
169-502	12 scale feet wide	pkg(6)	3.29

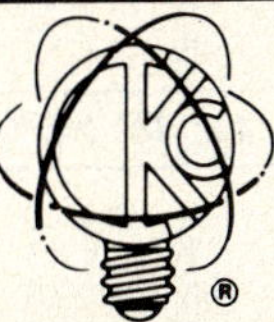

CIR-KIT CONCEPTS, INC.

METAL

MISCELLANEOUS

BRASS BRADS

Installation may be made with either small hammer and/or pliers. Measure approximately 1/8″ by .024″.

206-1021	1/8″	pkg(300)	4.98
206-10211	1/8″	pkg(60)	1.49

HEADLESS PINS

206-1031	Headless Pins	pkg(36)	.69

For connecting larger gauge wires into conductive tape runs. Approximately 1/2″ in length.

WILLIAMS BROS.

SIDING | METAL

ALUMINUM SHEETS

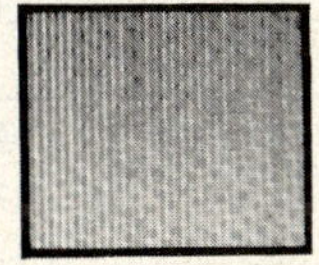 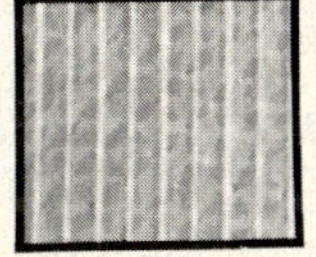

782-600	Corrugated Aluminum	pkg(2)	3.25
	(Total 69 square inches)		
782-601	Crimped Aluminum	pkg(2)	3.25
	(Total 69 square inches)		

TILE

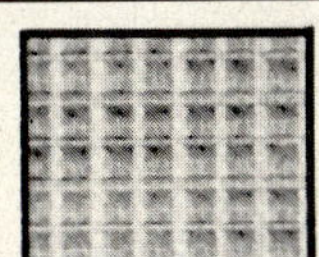

Tile Sheets
782-602
pkg(2) 3.25

PRECISION SCALE Co

METAL

HO SCALE (1/87)

All planking and tread is .020″ thick and 5x7″ unless noted. Screen is 4x6″.

+ (PLUS SIGN) = SPECIAL ORDER ONLY ITEMS

MISCELLANEOUS

ETCHED PLANKING

Wood sheathing for use on brass models. Suitable for car sides and floors, building siding and flooring, and such things as fences, packing crates, etc.

POSITIVE

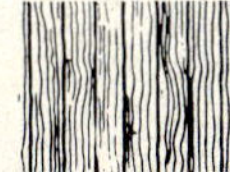 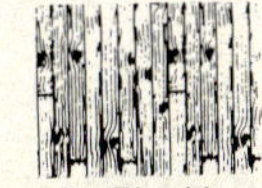

12″ Planking grained
585-48249
14.75

6″ Planking grained
585-48248
14.75

NEGATIVE

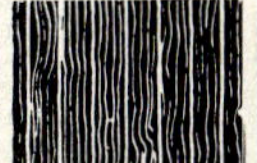 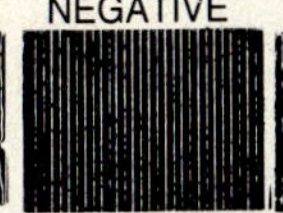

12″ Planking grained
585-48250
14.75

3″ Planking scribed
585-48247 +
14.75

6″ Planking grained
585-48245 +
14.75

SAFETY TREAD

Safety tread is used on locomotives, cars and all sorts of buildings and structures, for stairs, walk-ways, and platforms.

.012″ Thick

Raised Diamond
585-48260
14.75

BRASS WIRE SCREEN

  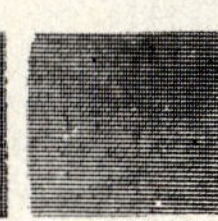

60 Mesh
585-48117
5.15

70 Mesh
585-48262
5.15

80 Mesh
585-48118
5.15

(not illustrated)
585-48119 #100 Mesh 5.15

BRAWA

Imported from Germany by WALTHERS

METAL

TUBING/RODS

Brass tube and angles are 12″ long, unless noted; dimensions shown are external diameter x wall thickness in millimeters.

Dealers: MUST order dealer pack of 10.

ROUND TUBE

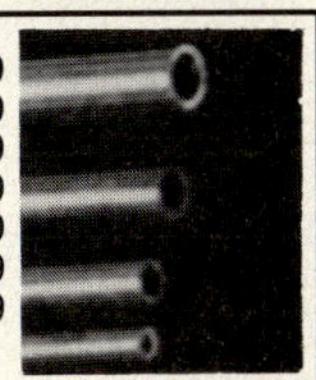

186-3700	0.8 x 0.30	1.49
186-3702	1.2 x 0.30	1.49
186-3704	1.5 x 0.30	1.49
186-3706	2.0 x 0.30	1.49
186-3708	2.5 x 0.30	1.49
186-3710	3.0 x 0.30	1.99
186-3712	4.0 x 0.30	1.99
(By Special Order Only.)		

RECTANGULAR TUBE

186-3726	1.0 x 1.5 x 0.30	2.49
186-3728	1.5 x 2.0 x 0.30	2.49
(By Special Order Only.)		
186-3730	1.5 x 3.0 x 0.30	2.49
186-3732	2.0 x 4.0 x 0.30	2.99

U-SECTION

186-3736	1.5 x 1.5 x 1.5 x 0.30	1.99
186-3738	2.0 x 2.0 x 2.0 x 0.30	1.99
186-3740	3.0 x 3.0 x 3.0 x 0.30	2.49
186-3742	4.0 x 4.0 x 4.0 x 0.30	2.49

T-SECTION

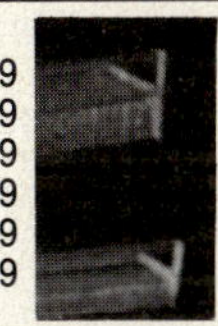

186-3771	1.0 x 1.0 x 0.35	2.99
186-3772	2.0 x 2.0 x 0.40	2.99
186-3773	3.0 x 3.0 x 0.50	3.49
186-3774	4.0 x 4.0 x 0.50	5.49
186-3775	1.5 x 1.5 x 0.30	2.99
186-3776	2.5 x 2.5 x 0.40	3.49

SQUARE TUBE

186-3716	1.5 x 1.5 x 0.30	2.49
186-3718	2.0 x 2.0 x 0.30	2.49
186-3720	3.0 x 3.0 x 0.30	2.99
186-3722	4.0 x 4.0 x 0.30	2.99

HEXAGON TUBE

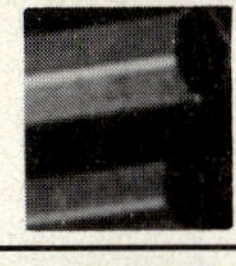

186-3746	1.5 x 0.30	2.49
186-3748	2.0 x 0.30	2.49
186-3750	3.0 x 0.30	2.49
186-3752	4.0 x 0.30	2.49

ANGLE

186-3761	1.0 x 1.0 x 0.35	2.49
186-3762	2.0 x 2.0 x 0.40	2.49
186-3763	3.0 x 3.0 x 0.50	3.49
186-3764	4.0 x 4.0 x 0.50	4.99
186-3765	1.5 x 1.5 x 0.30	2.99
186-3766	2.5 x 2.5 x 0.40	2.99
186-3767	3.5 x 3.5 x 0.30	3.99

H-SECTION

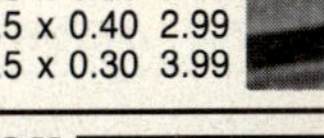

186-3781	2.5 x 1.5 x 0.50	3.49
186-3782	3.0 x 2.0 x 0.50	3.49
186-3783	4.0 x 3.0 x 0.50	3.99

K&S ENGINEERING [METAL]

TUBING: Brass (rectangular, soft, streamline), Aluminum, Copper and Square.
Brass Rods, Strips, Channels, Angles, Music Wire, Clear Plastic Sheets and assorted Strip & Sheet.
NOTE: Tubing size indicates outside diameter.

Dealer Displays available, write for information.
DEALERS MUST ORDER DEALER PACKS

STRIPS

BRASS STRIP 12"

PART#	SIZE	PRICE EACH	PACK	PRICE PACK
370-230	.016 x 1/4	.25	20	5.00
370-231	.016 x 1/2	.35	15	5.25
370-232	.016 x 1	.50	10	5.00
370-233	.016 x 3/4	.45	10	4.50
370-234	.016 x 2	.95	5	4.75
370-235	.025 x 1/4	.30	15	4.50
370-236	.025 x 1/2	.50	10	5.00
370-237	.025 x 1	.90	6	5.40
370-238	.025 x 3/4	.65	6	3.90
370-239	.025 x 2	1.70	3	5.10
370-240	.032 x 1/4	.35	15	5.25
370-241	.032 x 1/2	.55	10	5.50
370-242	.032 x 1	.95	5	4.75
370-243	.032 x 3/4	.75	6	4.50
370-244	.032 x 2	1.90	3	5.70
370-245	.064 x 1/4	.70	8	5.60
370-246	.064 x 1/2	1.15	4	4.60
370-247	.064 x 3/4	1.40	3	4.20
370-248	.064 x 1	1.90	2	3.80
370-249	.064 x 2	3.40	3	10.20

STRIP & SHEET ASSORTMENT

370-727	Strip & Sheet Assortment	3.95

Package contains brass, copper and aluminum strips and sheets in a variety of thicknesses, widths and lengths.

SHEETS

SHEET METAL 4x10"

370-250	.005 Brass	1.20	6	7.20
370-251	.010 Brass	1.40	6	8.40
370-252	.015 Brass	1.90	6	11.40
370-253	.032 Brass	3.50	3	10.50
370-254	.008 Tin	.90	6	5.40
370-255	.016 Aluminum	1.00	6	6.00
370-256	.032 Aluminum	1.40	6	8.40
370-257	.064 Aluminum	2.20	6	13.20
370-258	Assorted Brass	2.75	6	16.50
370-259	.025 Copper	3.50	3	10.50

TUBING / RODS

MUSIC WIRE 36"

370-497	.039	.20	25	5.00
370-498	.015	.20	50	10.00
370-499	.020	.12	42	5.00
370-500	.025	.15	04	5.00
370-501	.032 (1/32)	.15	34	5.00
370-502	.047	.20	34	6.80
370-503	.055	.20	32	6.40
370-504	.062 (1/16)	.25	25	6.25
370-505	.078	.35	20	7.00
370-506	3/32	.50	13	6.50
370-507	1/8	.65	9	5.85
370-508	5/32	.90	7	6.30
370-509	3/16	1.25	4	5.00
370-510	7/32	1.75	4	7.00
370-511	1/4	2.25	3	6.75

ROUND, BRASS 12"

PART#	SIZE	PRICE EACH	PACK	PRICE PACK
370-125	1/16	.35	20	7.00
370-126	3/32	.40	15	6.00
370-127	1/8	.40	15	6.00
370-128	5/32	.50	12	6.00

ROUND, BRASS (continued)

PART#	SIZE	PRICE EACH	PACK	PRICE PACK
370-129	3/16	.55	12	6.60
370-130	7/32	.60	10	6.00
370-131	1/4	.65	8	5.20
370-132	9/32	.70	8	5.60
370-133	5/16	.80	6	4.80
370-134	11/32	.90	6	5.40
370-135	3/8	1.00	6	6.00
370-136	13/32	1.10	4	4.40
370-137	7/16	1.20	4	4.80
370-138	15/32	1.30	4	5.20
370-139	1/2	1.40	4	5.60
370-140	17/32	1.50	3	4.50
370-141	9/16	1.60	3	4.80
370-142	19/32	1.75	2	3.50
370-143	5/8	1.85	2	3.70
370-144	21/32	1.95	2	3.90

ROUND, BRASS 36"

370-1143	1/16	1.05	10	10.50
370-1144	3/32	1.20	8	9.60
370-1145	1/8	1.20	8	9.60
370-1146	5/32	1.50	6	9.00
370-1147	3/16	1.65	6	9.90
370-1148	7/32	1.80	6	10.80
370-1149	1/4	1.95	5	9.75
370-1150	9/32	2.10	5	10.50
370-1151	5/16	2.40	4	9.60
370-1152	11/32	2.70	4	10.80
370-1153	3/8	3.00	3	9.00

ROUND, ALUMINUM 12"

370-100	1/16	.25	15	3.75
370-101	3/32	.30	12	3.60
370-102	1/8	.30	12	3.60
370-103	5/32	.35	12	4.20
370-104	3/16	.40	12	4.80
370-105	7/32	.45	10	4.50
370-106	1/4	.50	10	5.00
370-107	9/32	.55	8	4.40

ROUND, ALUMINUM 36"

370-1108	3/32	.90	8	7.20
370-1109	1/8	.90	8	7.20
370-1110	5/32	1.05	6	6.30
370-1111	3/16	1.20	6	7.20
370-1112	7/32	1.35	6	8.10
370-1113	1/4	1.50	5	7.50
370-1114	9/32	1.65	5	8.25
370-1115	5/16	1.80	4	7.20

STREAMLINE, ALUMINUM 36"

370-1100	1/4	1.85	5	9.25
370-1101	5/16	2.10	5	10.50
370-1102	3/8	2.35	4	9.40
370-1103	1/2	2.60	4	10.40
370-1104	5/8	3.10	3	9.30
370-1105	3/4	4.20	2	8.40

SQUARE, BRASS 12"

370-149	1/16	.65	12	7.80
370-150	3/32	.80	12	9.60
370-151	1/8	.90	12	10.80
370-152	5/32	1.00	10	10.00
370-153	3/16	1.10	6	6.60
370-154	7/32	1.20	6	7.20
370-155	1/4	1.40	6	8.40

ROUND, COPPER 12"

PART#	SIZE	PRICE EACH	PACK	PRICE PACK
370-117	1/16	.25	20	5.00
370-118	3/32	.30	15	4.50
370-119	5/32	.40	12	4.80
370-120	1/8	.35	12	4.20

RECTANGULAR, BRASS 12"

370-262	3/32 x 3/16	1.30	4	5.20
370-264	1/8 x 1/4	1.40	4	5.60
370-266	5/32 x 5/16	1.60	4	6.40
370-268	3/16 x 3/8	1.85	4	7.40

HEXAGON, BRASS 12" NEW

370-271	3/32	.55	8	4.40
370-272	1/8	.65	7	4.45
370-273	5/32	.75	6	4.50
370-274	3/16	.85	5	4.25

SOFT BRASS FUEL 12"

370-121	1/8	.50	10	5.00

BRASS STREAMLINE 12"

370-122	Small	.90	4	3.60

BRASS ROD 12"

370-159	.020	.10	50	5.00
370-160	1/32	.12	50	6.00
370-161	3/64	.15	34	5.10
370-162	1/16	.20	20	4.00
370-163	3/32	.25	16	4.00
370-164	1/8	.40	10	4.00
370-165	5/32	.60	8	4.80
370-166	3/16"	.80	5	4.00
370-167	.114"	.40	10	4.00
370-168	.081"	.40	10	4.00
370-169	.072"	.25	16	4.00

BRASS CHANNEL 12"

370-181	1/8	.70	10	7.00
370-182	5/32	.80	8	6.40
370-183	3/16	.65	7	4.55
370-184	7/32	.70	6	4.20
370-185	1/4	.75	5	3.75

BRASS ANGLE 12"

370-171	1/8 x 1/8	.55	10	5.50
370-172	5/32 x 5/32	.65	10	6.50
370-173	3/16 x 3/16	.55	8	4.40
370-174	7/32 x 7/32	.60	7	4.20
370-175	1/4 x 1/4	.65	6	3.90

ASSORTED TUBING

370-707	Sizes-Shapes	5.95

A large assortment of brass, copper and aluminum tubing and shapes.

370-320 Tube Assortment (small pcs) 2.95

Vintage Reproductions

METAL

SCALE CABLE
RUSTY CABLE
EMBOSSING KITS
ROOFING MATERIAL
RIVETING FOIL

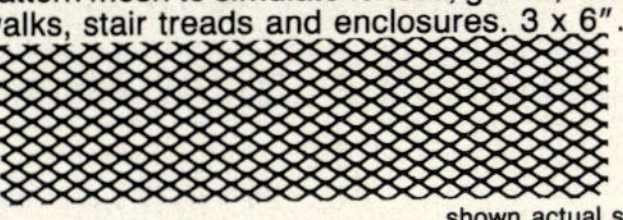

BUILDING MATERIAL

RIVET EMBOSSING KITS

Kits contain 6 sheets of silver foil/paper laminate. Each sheet is .004″ thick and 4-1/3 x 5″. Rivet embossing tools are also included in each kit.

766-320	14 rivets per inch tool	kit	8.00
766-321	24 rivets per inch tool	kit	8.00
766-322	Tool Set	kit	14.00

Includes foil/paper laminate sheets and both #320 & #321 embossing tools.

ROOFING FOIL

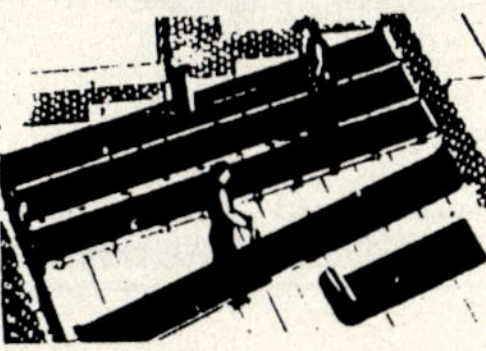

Metal roofing foil is very thin (.0005″) and coated with color lacquers that represent common roofing materials. Tissue-like thinness allows for seamed roofs to be modeled and includes tissue paper that can be painted and used for other roofing and wall covers. 4 x 8″ sheets, use burnishing tool #313 to smooth foil on.

766-332	Old copper (green)	3.25
766-333	New copper (copper)	3.25
766-334	Assorted colors	3.75

Includes 3 each of the following: old copper (green), new copper, gold, and faded red tin (red).

766-338	Assorted colors with Burnishing tool.	9.50

RIVETING FOIL

Foil/paper laminated is coated on one side with a metal look (lacquered aluminum foil), the other side is paper (for pattern drawing & gluing). Foils are 4-3/8 x 10″, .004″ thick. Use riveting tools #320 & #321 to emboss foil.

766-324	Dull Silver	3.25
766-329	Silver	3.50
766-330	Gold	3.50
766-331	Assorted	3.75

MISCELLANEOUS

"RUSTY" SCALE CABLE

766-325	49 strands (.036″ dia) Stainless Steel	2.75
766-335	7 strands (.012″ dia) Stainless Steel	1.75
766-336	7 strands (.018″ dia) Stainless Steel	1.75
766-337	7 strands (.024″ dia) Stainless Steel	2.25
766-340	21 strands (.031″ dia) Stainless Steel	2.25

STEVEDORE ROPE

Nylon rope with real tar coating.

766-349	017″	pkg(25′)	1.75
766-350	042″	pkg(25′)	1.75
766-351	046″	pkg(25′)	1.75
766-352	051″	pkg(25′)	1.75
766-353	058″	pkg(25′)	1.75
766-354	065″	pkg(25′)	1.75

SCALE CABLE

Industrial grade, tight wound, multi-strand steel wire. Galvanized cable can be chemically blackened and soldered.

766-301	7 strands (.016″ dia) Galvanized	10 ft	1.75

SCALE CABLE (continued)

766-304	19 strands (.032″ dia) Galvanized	8 ft	1.75
766-310	7 strands (.012″ dia) Stainless Steel	8 ft	1.75
766-311	21 strands (.009″ dia) Stainless Steel	2 ft	1.75
766-312	7 strands (.006″ dia) Stainless Steel	4 ft	1.75
766-315	Wire Assortment six sizes	(brown)	3.00

END LOOP SLEEVES SCALE CABLE FITTINGS

Black oxidized brass tubes for forming end loops or splicing scale cables.

766-341	.187″ L (.033″ dia) for cable to .016″	pkg(10)	1.75
766-342	.250″ L (.046″ dia) for cable to .021″	pkg(10)	1.75
766-343	.250″ L (.055″ dia) for cable to .027″	pkg(10)	1.75
766-344	.250″ L (.070″ dia) for cable to .035″	pkg(10)	1.75
766-345	Assortment, 4 each 4 sizes		2.75
766-358	Cable clamp crimp bead	NEW	2.00
766-359	Cast eyeblt/padeye .055	NEW	2.50
766-360	Mach eyeblts/padeye .055	NEW	2.50
766-361	Eyepin .07 hl .029 wire	NEW	2.00

SCALE CHAIN

766-323	Chain, 32 LPI	2.75
766-348	Brass Long Links, 12 LPI	2.50
766-355	Twisted Curb, 16-1/2 LPI	2.50
766-356	Oval, 17 LPI	2.50
766-357	Long Links, 11-1/2 LPI steel-colored	2.50

NYLON

For highly visible scale size trust rods and piping. Replacement for clear nylon truss rods. Needs no painting.

BLACK NYLON (opaque)

766-305	.008″ diameter	25 ft	1.75
766-306	.014″ diameter	25 ft	1.75
766-307	.023″ diameter	20 ft	1.75
766-309	.019″ diameter	20 ft	1.75

California Model Company

SIDING SHEETS

METAL

700-100	.010 Corrugated Tin, 4x12″		1.10
700-101	.010 Corrugated Tin, 2x12″		.75
700-102	.010 Plain Tin, 4x12″		.85
700-104	90° Tin Angle, 1/8x1/8x12″	each	.50
700-1001	Corrugated Aluminum Paper, 4x11-1/2″	pkg(6)	3.25

Scale Scenics

METAL

Division of CIRCUITRON

MICRO-MESH

Lightweight, non-woven, raised diamond pattern mesh to simulate fences, grilles, catwalks, stair treads and enclosures. 3 x 6″.

shown actual size

652-3500	Aluminum	3.95
652-3501	Brass may be soldered	4.50

GEAR ASSORTMENT

652-2001	3.95

Generous quantity of various size gears that may be used for scratchbuilding machinery or as junk on your layout. May include other heavy machinery parts.

FLAT WIRE

652-1504	Flat Wire, Nickel Silver	5ft	2.50

Measures .010 x .030″: may be used for strapping.

METAL

N.J. International

SHEETS

ETCHED BRASS SHEETS 3×8″

525-317	Alphabet, Future	9.95
525-318	Alphabet, Claren	9.95
525-319	Numbers	9.95

MAY 18, 1893

Today IN RAILROAD HISTORY

The Empire State Express of the New York Central and Hudson River Railroad, pulled by engine #999, hits a record speed of 112.5 mph.

Alexander scale models

HO SCALE (1/87)

Parts are metal castings unless noted. Illustrations are approximately full size unless noted.

CABOOSE AWNING

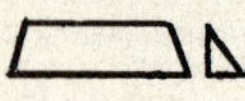

24" Scale Width
120-2201
pkg(4) .59

30" Scale Width
120-2202
pkg(4) .59

CHIMNEYS & VENTS

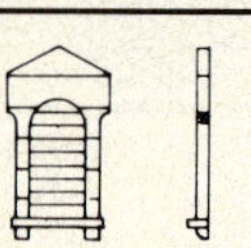 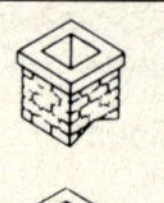 

Brick
120-2705
pkg(2) .59

Exhaust Fans
120-701
pkg(4) .59

Louvered Vent
120-1901
pkg(4) .59

Stone
120-2706
pkg(2) .59

Fancy
120-2701
pkg(2) .59

Passenger Car Vent
120-1701
pkg(4) .59

COACH SEATS

120-3401 Two Seater pkg(6) .95
120-3402 Three Seater pkg(4) .95
120-3403 Four Seater pkg(4) .95

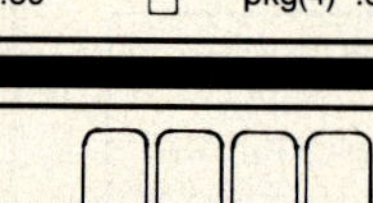

CORBELS

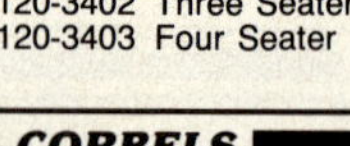 

120-1401
pkg(12) .95

120-1404 pkg(4) .95

120-1403 pkg(4) .95

DOORS

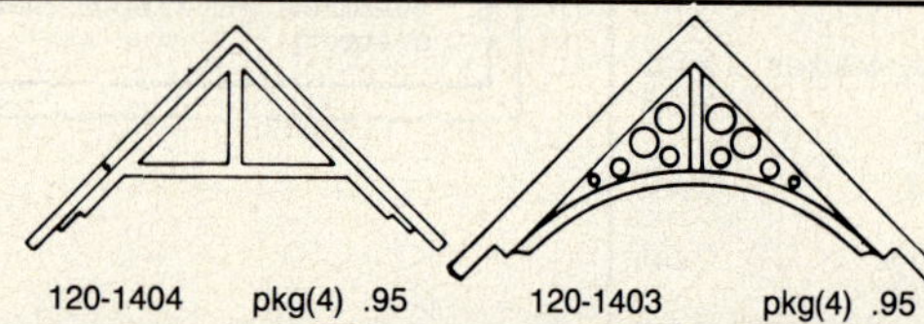

Freight
120-2401 each .59

Freight
120-2402 each .59

w/Transom
120-2404
pkg(4) 1.25

Ghost Town Freight
120-1602 each .49

120-2406 Double Entry pkg(2) 1.75

Entry Door & 4 Pane Windows
120-2403
pkg(4) 1.75

4-Panel
120-2410
pkg(4) 1.25

120-2405

4-Panel Entry
pkg(4) 1.25

DOORS (continued)

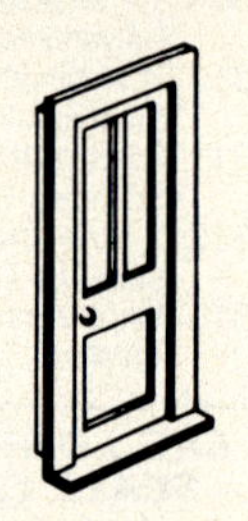 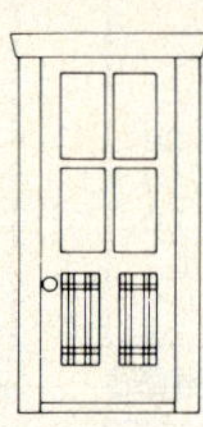  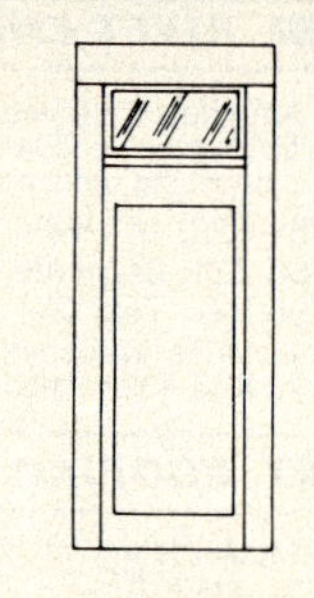

3-Panel
120-2408
pkg(4) 1.25

w/4 Windows
120-2411
pkg(4) 1.25

w/2 Windows
120-2409
pkg(4) 1.25

Solid Panel
120-2407
pkg(4) 1.25

GEARS

 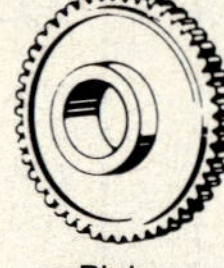 

Large
(9/16" dia)
120-414
pkg(2) .59

Pinion
(9/16" dia)
120-416
pkg(2) .59

Small
(7/32" dia)
120-422
pkg(2) .65

Large
(5/16" dia)
120-423
pkg(2) .59

Small
(7/16" dia)
120-415
pkg(2) .59

GINGERBREAD

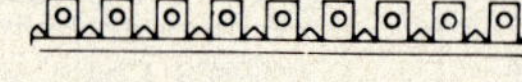

120-1102 pkg(10) 1.25

120-1105 pkg(10) 1.25

120-1104 pkg(10) 1.49

120-1106 Ridge Trim pkg(10) 1.25

120-1101 pkg(10) 1.49

120-1103 pkg(10) 1.25

120-2900
Lattice Trim
pkg(6)
1.25

HATCH

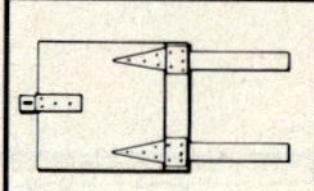 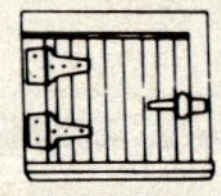

Ice, Narrow Gauge
120-4000
pkg(4) .59

Small
120-4002
pkg(4) 1.25

LAMPS

Outside Kerosene Lamp
120-1800 pkg(6) 1.25

LOCOMOTIVE DETAILS

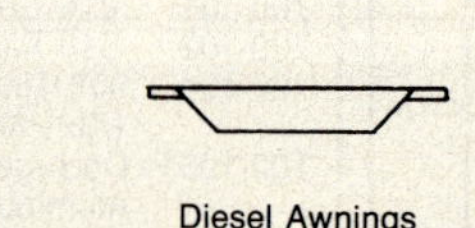 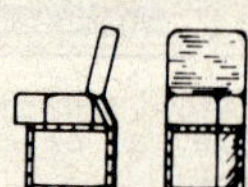

Diesel Awnings
120-2203 pkg(2) .59

Engineer's & Fireman's Seats
120-1301 (1 each) 1.25

Alexander scale models

HO SCALE (1/87)

Parts are metal castings unless noted. Illustrations are approximately full size unless noted.

MINE EQUIPMENT

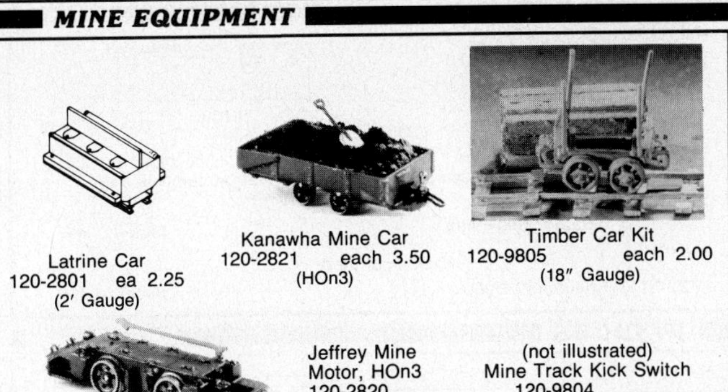

Latrine Car
120-2801 ea 2.25
(2' Gauge)

Kanawha Mine Car
120-2821 each 3.50
(HOn3)

Timber Car Kit
120-9805 each 2.00
(18" Gauge)

Jeffrey Mine Motor, HOn3
120-2820 each 4.50

(not illustrated)
Mine Track Kick Switch
120-9804 pkg(2) 1.25

MISCELLANEOUS

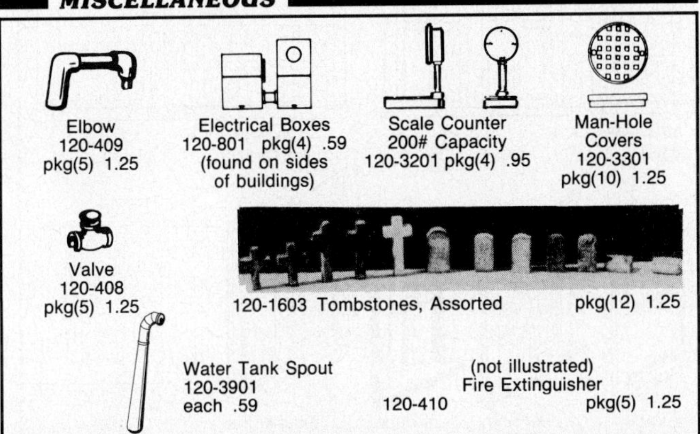

Elbow
120-409
pkg(5) 1.25

Electrical Boxes
120-801 pkg(4) .59
(found on sides of buildings)

Scale Counter 200# Capacity
120-3201 pkg(4) .95

Man-Hole Covers
120-3301
pkg(10) 1.25

Valve
120-408
pkg(5) 1.25

120-1603 Tombstones, Assorted pkg(12) 1.25

Water Tank Spout
120-3901
each .59

(not illustrated)
Fire Extinguisher
120-410 pkg(5) 1.25

PLUG DOORS

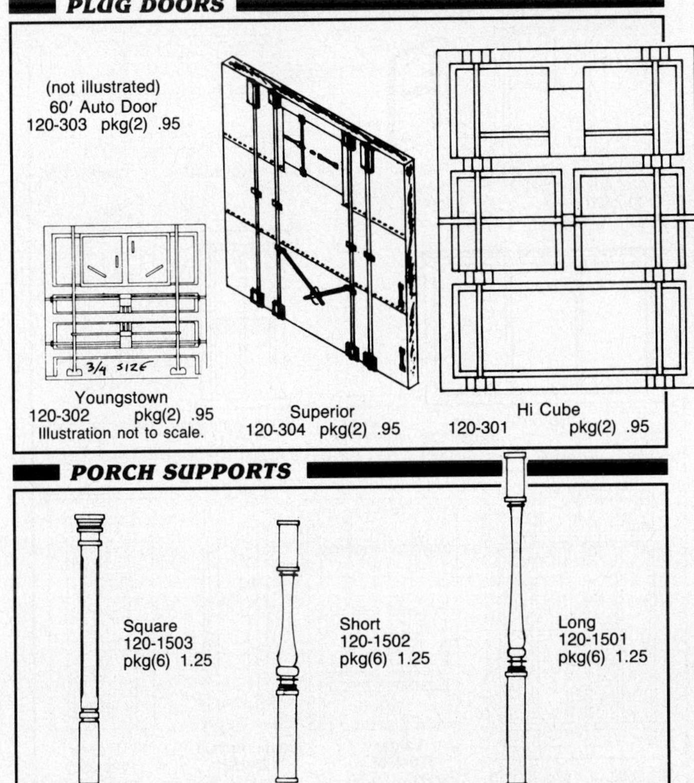

(not illustrated)
60' Auto Door
120-303 pkg(2) .95

Youngstown
120-302 pkg(2) .95
Illustration not to scale.

Superior
120-304 pkg(2) .95

Hi Cube
120-301 pkg(2) .95

PORCH SUPPORTS

Square
120-1503
pkg(6) 1.25

Short
120-1502
pkg(6) 1.25

Long
120-1501
pkg(6) 1.25

PULLEYS

Large 1/4" Diameter
120-424 pkg(4) .59

Small 3/16" Diameter
120-425 pkg(4) .59

RAILINGS & GATES

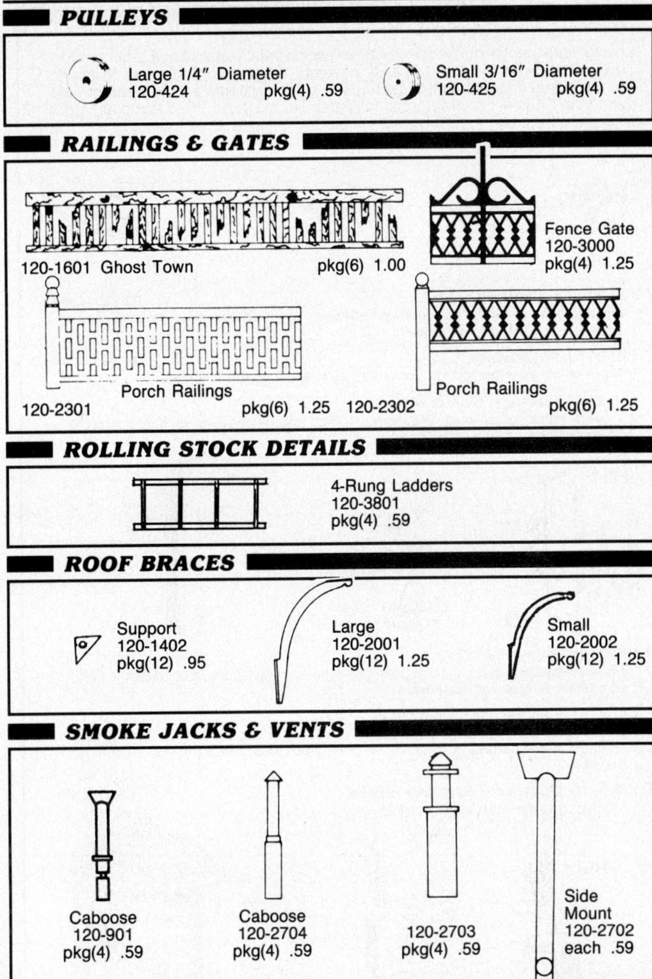

120-1601 Ghost Town pkg(6) 1.00

Fence Gate
120-3000
pkg(4) 1.25

Porch Railings
120-2301 pkg(6) 1.25

Porch Railings
120-2302 pkg(6) 1.25

ROLLING STOCK DETAILS

4-Rung Ladders
120-3801
pkg(4) .59

ROOF BRACES

Support
120-1402
pkg(12) .95

Large
120-2001
pkg(12) 1.25

Small
120-2002
pkg(12) 1.25

SMOKE JACKS & VENTS

Caboose
120-901
pkg(4) .59

Caboose
120-2704
pkg(4) .59

120-2703
pkg(4) .59

Side Mount
120-2702
each .59

STAIRS & STEPS

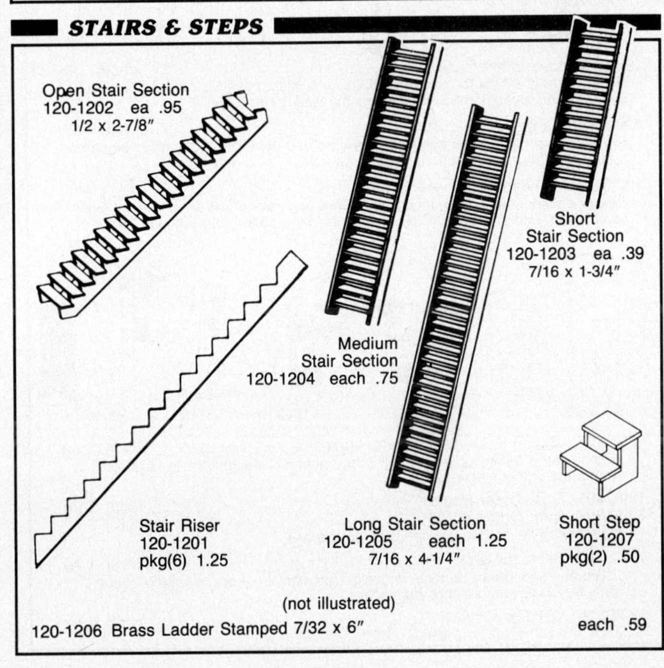

Open Stair Section
120-1202 ea .95
1/2 x 2-7/8"

Short Stair Section
120-1203 ea .39
7/16 x 1-3/4"

Medium Stair Section
120-1204 each .75

Stair Riser
120-1201
pkg(6) 1.25

Long Stair Section
120-1205 each 1.25
7/16 x 4-1/4"

Short Step
120-1207
pkg(2) .50

(not illustrated)
120-1206 Brass Ladder Stamped 7/32 x 6" each .59

Alexander scale models

HO SCALE (1/87)

Parts are metal castings unless noted. Illustrations are approximately full size unless noted.

◼ WAYSIDE DETAILS

Smaller items are single pieces, ready for painting and installation. Larger models have a minimum of parts for easy assembly. Illustrations are not to scale. For additional information and pictures of signal systems and equipment, see the article "Add Right-of-Way Signal Detail" in the June, 1975 issue of *Model Railroader*"

3105

3110

3107

120-3105 Battery Box, Double   pkg(2) .95
Used to enclose primary or back-up batteries. Also used as a relay housing where batteries are the primary power.

120-3110 Vault Cover   pkg(4) .95
Used to cover underground concrete vaults at all signal locations.

120-3107 Electrical Switch Motor   pkg(6) 1.25
Powers mainline turnouts at passing sidings and crossovers, enabling them to be thrown remotely by towerman or dispatchers.

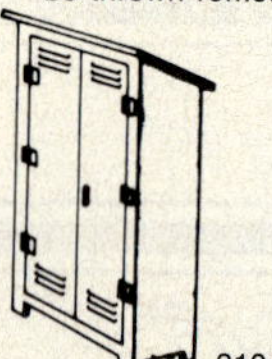
3104

3111

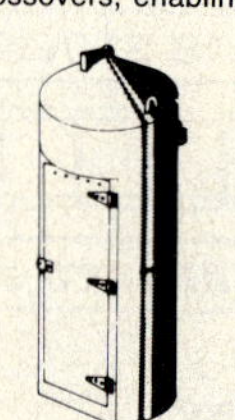
3115

120-3104 Relay Enclosure   each .95
House relays and electrical equipment for smaller installations such as single pairs of signals or crossing flashers.

120-3111 Remote Signal Indicator   pkg(3) 1.25
A low-level, dual block signal indicator used to guide track crews and switchmen. Repeats distant signal aspect. Sometimes used to indicate position of remote turnout.

120-3115 Concrete Telephone Shelter   each 1.25
Modern, smaller unit used like #3114.

3102

3109

3114

120-3102 Instrument Case   each .95
Houses circuit relays for smaller installations. Mast provides connections from underground signal cables to line wire paralleling the track.

120-3109 Cable Junction Box   pkg(3) 1.25
Provides a terminal point between overhead and underground lines to signals. It may also house a telephone or a signal relay.

120-3114 Wooden Telephone Shelter   each 1.50
Provides shelter and communications for road and track crews at unmanned junctions, spurs and crossings. Cast interior includes phone and junction box.

3103   1001   1002   3112   9515

120-3103 Signal Relay Equipment House   each 1.50
For housing banks of relays and other electrical equipment at large and important signal installations.

120-1001 Train Order Board   each 1.25
120-1002 Train Order Board   pkg(2) 1.25
Non-operating boards are mounted on stations.

120-3112 Electrical Lock   pkg(3) 1.25
Secures hand-thrown turnouts on a signaled mainline. Lock may be released only by tower personnel or dispatcher.

120-9515 AC1 Car Counter   each 4.49

◼ WAYSIDE DETAILS (continued)

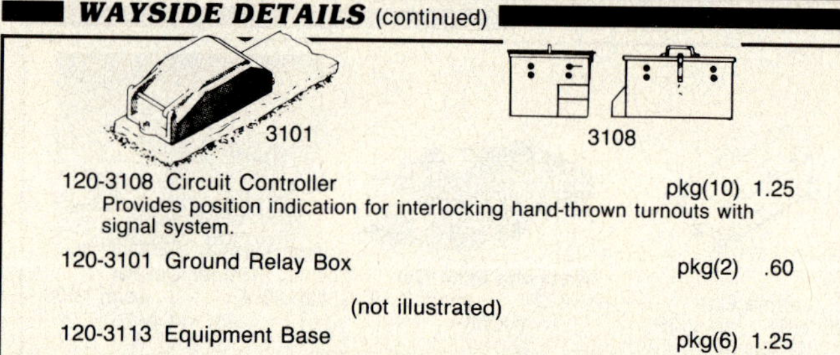
3101   3108

120-3108 Circuit Controller   pkg(10) 1.25
Provides position indication for interlocking hand-thrown turnouts with signal system.

120-3101 Ground Relay Box   pkg(2) .60

(not illustrated)

120-3113 Equipment Base   pkg(6) 1.25

◼ WINDOWS

120-2506
pkg(4) 1.25

120-2505
pkg(4) 1.25

120-2511
pkg(4) 1.50

120-2504
pkg(4) 1.25

2-Pane
120-2522
pkg(4) 1.25

12-Pane
120-2512
pkg(4) 1.50

4-Pane
120-2514
pkg(4) 1.25

Double For
Interlock Tower
120-2517
pkg(4) 1.25

Ticket
120-2101 ea 1.25

Small
Arched
120-2520
pkg(4) 1.25

120-2501
pkg(4) 1.25

Transom
120-2513
pkg(4) 1.25

120-2503
pkg(4) 1.25

120-2510   pkg(4) 1.50

Curio Shop
120-2518   pkg(2) 1.75

120-2502
pkg(4) 1.25

Single Window
120-2515
pkg(4) 1.25

Single Interlock
120-2516
pkg(4) 1.25

Large
120-2509   120-2508
pkg(2) 1.75   pkg(2) 1.00

Large, Arched
120-2521
pkg(4) 1.25

French
120-2507
pkg(4) 1.75

A M Models

HO SCALE (1/87)

Parts are molded in brown plastic (unless noted).

DOORS & WINDOWS

Doors and Windows
129-201   1.50
Includes four doors and twelve windows.

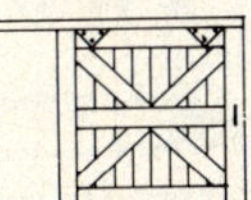

Freight Set, (white plastic)
129-203   pkg(4) 1.50

PALLETS

129-50112 Skids and Pallets pkg(12) 1.50
129-50136 Skids and Pallets pkg(36) 3.50

Columbia Valley Model

HO SCALE (1/87)

Cast white metal detail parts.

STRUCTURE DETAILS

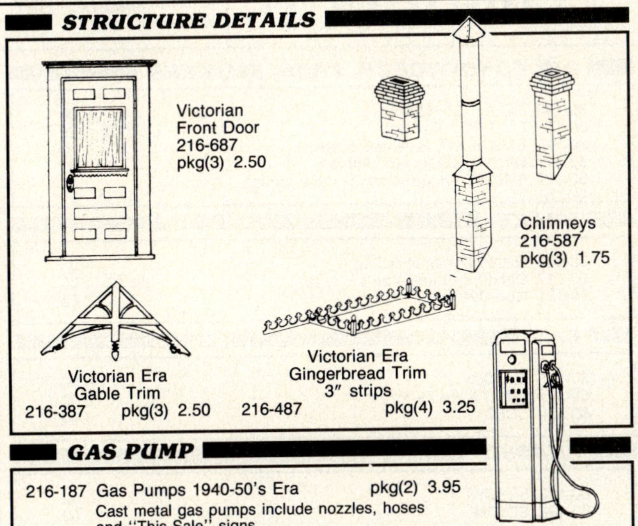

Victorian Front Door
216-687
pkg(3) 2.50

Chimneys
216-587
pkg(3) 1.75

Victorian Era Gable Trim
216-387   pkg(3) 2.50

Victorian Era Gingerbread Trim 3" strips
216-487   pkg(4) 3.25

GAS PUMP

216-187 Gas Pumps 1940-50's Era   pkg(2) 3.95
Cast metal gas pumps include nozzles, hoses and "This Sale" signs.

EASTERN CAR WORKS

PASSENGER / FREIGHT CAR   **NEW**

117-9100	M&K Ballast Doors	3.00
117-9101	P/R/R Ice Air Conditioner	3.00
117-9102	Car Roof Vents	3.00
117-9103	PRR/Pullman Undercar Details	5.00
117-9104	NH Undercar Details	5.00
117-9105	Covered Hopper Details	4.00
117-9106	Caboose Grab Irons	4.00
117-9107	Caboose Details Parts	TBA
117-9108	Windoe's Bowser N5cCaboose	3.00

CENTURY FOUNDRY METAL WORKS

HO SCALE (1/87)

Metal castings unless noted. Illustrations are not to scale.

BATTERY BOX & COVER

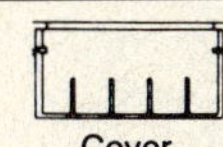

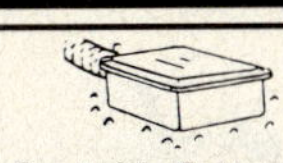

Cover
215-213   pkg(4) 1.75

Pullman Cover
215-211   pkg(4) 1.50

Trackside Battery Box
215-113   pkg(6) 1.75

FINIAL

For side mounted signals.

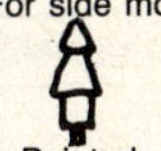

Pointed
215-1361
pkg(6) 1.50

Round
215-1362
pkg(6) 1.50

Teardrop
215-1363
pkg(6) 1.50

Dome
215-1364
pkg(6) 1.50

MISCELLANEOUS

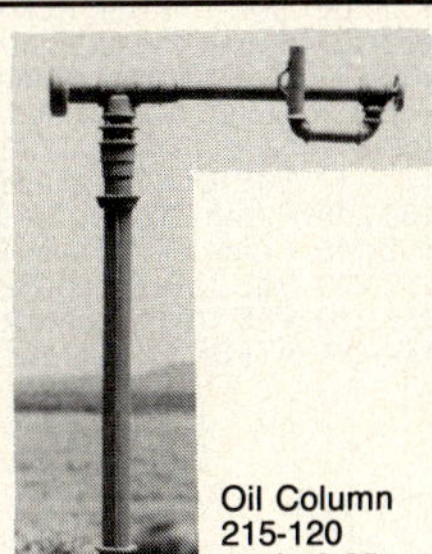

Gas Pump
215-100
pkg(2) 1.75

Moonshine Still
215-180
kit 3.25

Oil Column
215-120
each 2.25

Ice Engine   Sub Cooler   Bottled Gas Box   Engine Generator
215-200 Waukesha Air Conditioners   kits 2.00   215-205   kit 1.75

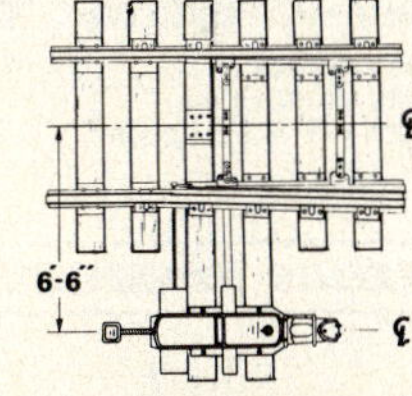
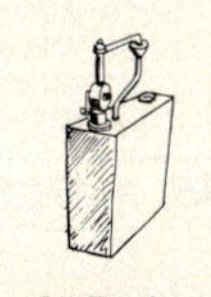

Electric Car Puller
215-125   each 2.25

Switch Motor
215-135   pkg(2) 2.75

Oil Bunker
215-101
pkg(4) 1.75

6-6"

PASSENGER CAR DETAILS

Water Fill Hatch
215-220 (2 pair) 1.50

(not illustrated)
Waste Drain Pipe
215-221 pkg(6) 1.50

STAIRS

45 Degree Stairway
215-155   pkg(2) 1.50

VENTS

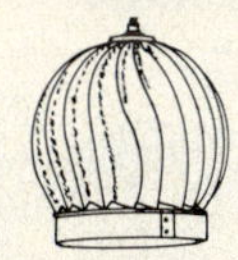
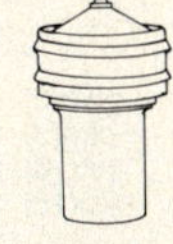

Streamlined Car Roof Vent
215-255
pkg(8) 1.75

Large Cyclone
215-151
pkg(3) 1.50

Roof
215-150
pkg(3) 1.50

Utility, Round Roof
215-250
pkg(12) 2.25
heavyweight passenger car

AMERICAN MODEL BUILDERS, INC.

NEW

Add the finishing touch of realism to your Models with this selection of white metal, wood, plastic and brass (as noted) parts.

FREIGHT CAR DETAILS

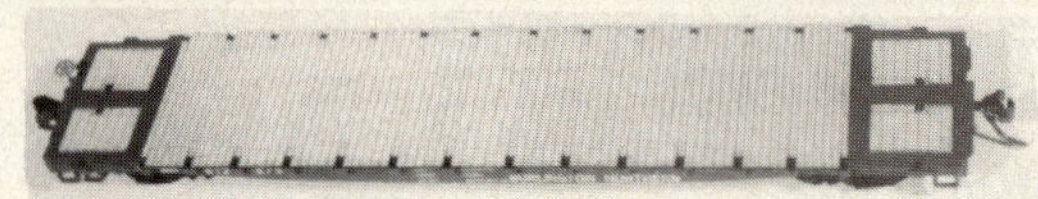

152-233	Wood Deck w/Bolt Holes for Walthers 54' GSC Flat Car	7.95
152-234	Wood Deck for Walthers 54' GSC Flat Car	3.25

LOCOMOTIVE DETAILS

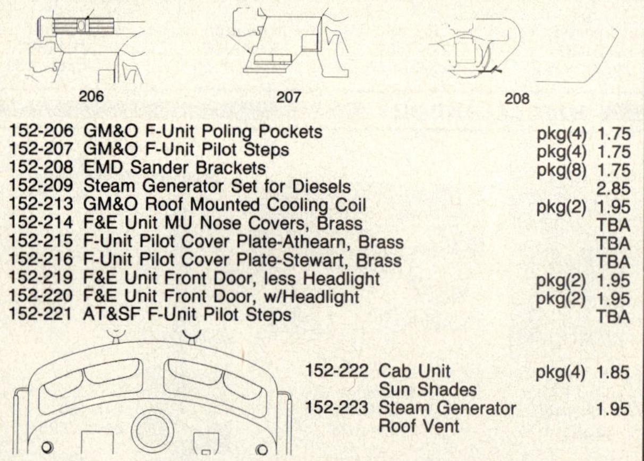

206   207   208

152-206	GM&O F-Unit Poling Pockets	pkg(4)	1.75
152-207	GM&O F-Unit Pilot Steps	pkg(4)	1.75
152-208	EMD Sander Brackets	pkg(8)	1.75
152-209	Steam Generator Set for Diesels		2.85
152-213	GM&O Roof Mounted Cooling Coil	pkg(2)	1.95
152-214	F&E Unit MU Nose Covers, Brass		TBA
152-215	F-Unit Pilot Cover Plate-Athearn, Brass		TBA
152-216	F-Unit Pilot Cover Plate-Stewart, Brass		TBA
152-219	F&E Unit Front Door, less Headlight	pkg(2)	1.95
152-220	F&E Unit Front Door, w/Headlight	pkg(2)	1.95
152-221	AT&SF F-Unit Pilot Steps		TBA
152-222	Cab Unit Sun Shades	pkg(4)	1.85
152-223	Steam Generator Roof Vent		1.95

222

WINDOW SETS

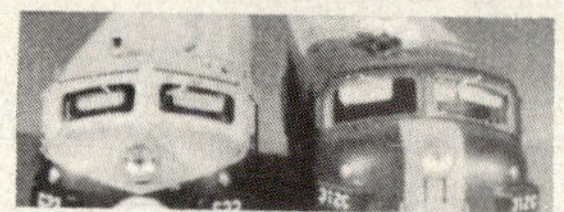

152-228	Athearn F-Units (Scale)	5.95
152-229	Athearn F-Units (Semi-Scale)	4.95
152-230	Athearn Modern GP & SD Locos	3.95
152-231	Athearn SW-7	3.95
152-232	Athearn SW-1000/1500	3.95

MISCELLANEOUS

101   102   103

152-101	Jaw Crusher Kit		14.50
152-102	Ten Stamp Kit		44.95
152-103	Ore Feeders Kit	pkg(2)	9.95
152-105	Grizzley	pkg(2)	4.95
152-106	Stationary Boiler Kit		28.95
152-107	Stationary Steam Engine Kit		32.95
152-109	Steam Piping Kit		TBA
	for use with kits 106 & 107		
152-203	Hose Reel		2.00
152-205	Wheelstops	pkg(2)	1.95
152-217	Checker Plate, Brass		TBA
152-218	Diamond Plate, Brass		TBA
152-224	Steam Driven Water Pump	pkg(2)	3.00
152-225	Piping Flanges & Valves		TBA
152-226	Caboose Axle Generator	pkg(2)	5.95
152-227	Modernization Kit Athearn AT&SF Caboose		11.95

152-401	Winches	pkg(2)	6.60
152-402	Hooks	pkg(5)	2.75
152-404	Hydrants	pkg(8)	2.75
152-411	Pillow Blocks	pkg(16)	2.75
152-413	Gas Engine		5.95
152-10401	Wifley Table-Left		9.95
152-10402	Wifley Table-Right		9.95

10401   10402

American Limited Models

NEW
HO SCALE (1/87)

DIAPHRAGM

Operating passenger car diaphragms are injection molded plastic kits and are accurate models of the specific prototype. Sprung to hold together in turns down to 24" radius—no minimum radius limitation. They do not interfere with operation of most couplers. All kits are in pairs, enough for one car.

147-9000	Streamline Cars	pair 3.95
	ACF style can be modified to look like Pullman or Budd disphragm. Fit directly on Athearn Streamliners.	
147-9100	Athearn Standard Heavyweight Cars	pair 3.95
147-9200	Rivarossi & other Heavyweight Cars	pair 3.95
147-9900	Stewart F-Units Diesel	pair 4.49
	Includes alignment spacers and works with the close coupling adapter.	

RAIL POWER PRODUCTS

NEW
HO SCALE (1/87)

Parts are injection molded gray plastic. Chassis are die cast metal.

AIR CONDITIONER, FANS, BLOWERS

60-103	GE Air Conditioner		1.00
60-104	EMD "Q" Fan set	pkg(3)	1.25
60-108	EMD SD-60 Blower Housing		1.00
60-111	Dash 8 GE Air Conditioner		1.00
60-127	8-40CW Air Conditioner deck mount		1.50

BRAKE

60-120	GP-35 Dynamic w/Fan		1.25
60-117	Dynamic Brake Vents	pkg(8)	1.00
60-121	Non-Dynamic GP-35		1.25

CAB

60-122	8-40CW	6.00
60-129	8-40CW Santa Fe	6.00
60-130	SD60	6.00

CHASSIS

60-123	8-40CW	10.00
60-128	SD60M	10.00

EXHAUST

60-101	Dash 8 Early Exhaust Stack		.50
60-102	Dash 7/8 Large Exhaust Stack		.50
60-105	EMD Exhaust Silencer	each	.75
60-112	GE Bathtub Silencer Exhaust		.50
60-125	8-40C W&B Exhaust Stack		.50

MISCELLANEOUS

60-106	EMD 116" Snoot Nose Kit		3.00
60-107	Loco Brake Wheel	pkg(6)	1.00
60-110	EMD Hood Unit Cab Doors		1.00
60-114	FB-2 Sideframes	pkg(4)	4.00
60-115	8-40B Frame		10.00
60-118	8-40B Air Tanks	set	1.00
60-119	CF-7 Frame		10.00
60-124	Container Braces for Athearn Impac	pkg(4)	2.50
60-126	8-40CW Air Tanks	pkg(2)	1.00

NUMBER BOARDS

60-109	C32-8	2pr	.50
60-116	CF-7 Light/Number		1.00

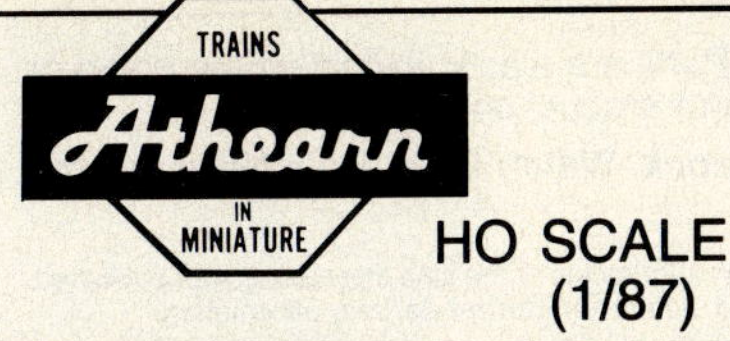

TRAINS IN MINIATURE — Athearn

HO SCALE (1/87)

Plastic bodies and parts for kitbashing & scratchbuilding. Parts are plastic except where noted or obvious (light bulbs etc.). Parts are available only for current production models.

Items not listed in this catalog are temporarily out of stock. **Watch Craft Train News for the latest delivery information on these products.**

We have worked closely with this manufacturer to provide accurate availability information at the time this catalog was published. Items listed in *blue ink* may not be available at all times. Please see your dealer for current delivery information.

CAR PARTS

CAR PARTS

140-12000	40' Body, Undecorated	each	1.50
140-12022	Steeel Door	pkg(12)	1.20
140-12023	Door Guide	pkg(12)	1.20
140-12024	40' Box, Floor Simulated Wood Floor	pkg(4)	1.60
140-12025	40' Modern Roofwalk	pkg(4)	1.00
140-12026	40' Underframe	pkg(4)	1.20
140-12027	40' Hi-Cube, Floor	pkg(4)	1.40
140-12028	40' Hi-Cube, Door	pkg(6)	.90
140-12029	40' Hi-Cube, Door Guide	pkg(8)	1.20
140-13090	50' Double Door Body Shell	each	1.60
140-13102	50' Double Door Box Door	pkg(12)	.90
140-13103	50' Door Guide Double Door Box	pkg(24)	1.20
140-13104	50' Double Door Box Flooe	pkg(4)	1.60
140-13105	50' Double Door Roofwalk	pkg(4)	1.00
140-13106	50' Double Door Underframe	pkg(4)	1.20
140-13108	50' Plug Door Box/57' Reefer Fuel Tank	pkg(12)	1.20
140-13113	50' Door Guide Sliding Box	pkg(12)	1.20
140-13098	50' Sliding Door Box Door	pkg(6)	.90
140-13109	50' Sliding Door Box Floor	pkg(4)	1.60
140-13107	50' Plug Door Box Floor	pkg(4)	1.60
140-20900	40' Grain Box, Undecorated	each	1.50
140-52300	40' Wood Box, Shell, Undec	each	1.75

HIGH-CUBE BOX CAR

140-19740	86' Body, 4-Door, Undecorated	each	3.60
140-19741	86' Floor	pkg(2)	1.60
140-19743	86' Drawbar	pkg(4)	1.20
140-90717	86' Steel Weight	pkg(2)	1.20

STOCK CAR

140-17740	Shell, Undecorated	each	1.50
140-17752	Door	pkg(8)	1.20
140-17753	Floor	pkg(4)	1.60
140-17754	Roofwalk	pkg(4)	1.00
140-17755	Underframe	pkg(4)	1.20

FLAT CAR

140-13002	HD Floor	pkg(4)	1.60
140-13005	HD Span Bolster	pkg(6)	1.20
140-13009	HD Underframe, Undecorated	pkg(2)	1.20
140-13040	HD Body Shell	each	1.25
140-13502	40' Upper Underframe	pkg(4)	1.00
140-13503	40' Lower Underframe	pkg(4)	1.00
140-13504	40' Stake	pkg(36)	1.80
140-13990	50' Body Shell, Undecorated	each	1.25
140-14002	50' Upper Underframe	pkg(4)	1.50
140-14003	50' Lower Underframe	pkg(4)	1.00
140-20000	85' PB Floor, Undecorated	each	1.50
140-20013	85' PB, Body Bolster	pkg(4)	1.40
140-20025	85' PB Trailer Hitch Set	pkg(2)	1.60
140-20021	85' PB Steel Weight	pkg(2)	1.30
140-20022	85' PB Coupler Draw Bar	pkg(4)	1.20
140-20026	85' PB Container Shoe Set	pkg(4)	1.20
140-20150	85' AP Floor, Undecorated	each	1.50
140-90706	HD Large Weight	pkg(6)	1.40
140-90707	HD Small Weight	pkg(6)	1.20

CONTAINERS

140-20601	20' Floor	pkg(4)	1.40

TANK CAR

140-14990	3-Dome Shell, Undecorated		1.25
140-15200	62' Shell, Undecorated		1.35
140-15231	62' Bottom Sheet	pkg(4)	2.00
140-15232	62' Underframe	pkg(4)	1.40
140-15233	62' Center Sill	pkg(4)	1.00
140-15234	62' Ladder	pkg(12)	.75
140-15235	62' Rail Platform	pkg(4)	1.20
140-15236	62' Handrail	pkg(6)	1.20
140-15239	62' Manway Cover	pkg(12)	1.80
140-15241	62' Safety Valve	pkg(12)	1.80
140-15243	Outlet Valve Wrench	pkg(12)	1.80
140-15502	40' Bottom Sheet	pkg(4)	1.20
140-15503	40' Tank Underframe	pkg(4)	1.20
140-15504	40' Center Sill	pkg(4)	1.00
140-15505	40' Brake Gear Box	pkg(6)	1.20
140-15506	40' Placard Holder	pkg(12)	.75
140-15507	40' Ladder	pkg(12)	.75
140-15508	40' Handrail	pkg(6)	1.20
140-15511	40' Manway Cover	pkg(12)	1.80
140-15512	40' Chemical, Platform	pkg(4)	1.20
140-15513	40' Chemical, Platform Rail	pkg(6)	1.20
140-15700	1-Dome Body, Undecorated	each	1.25
140-90705	40' Steel Weight	pkg(4)	1.20
140-90716	50' Steel Weight	pkg(4)	1.40

PICKLE CARS

140-14752	Floor	pkg(4)	1.40
140-14753	Underframe	pkg(4)	1.20

PICKLE CARS (continued)

140-14754	Center Support	pkg(4)	1.00
140-14755	Roofwalk	pkg(4)	1.00
140-14756	Hatch Cover	pkg(12)	1.20
140-14757	Tank	pkg(4)	1.20
140-14758	Truss Rod	pkg(48)	2.40
140-14759	Side, Undecorated		.85

REEFER

140-16002	Ice Hatch/Latch Set	pkg(2)	1.10
140-16005	40' Roofwalk	pkg(6)	1.50
140-16006	40' Underframe	pkg(4)	1.20
140-16240	50' Shell SS, Undecorated	each	1.50
140-52000	40' Wood, Shell, Undecorated	each	1.75
140-53301	50' Express, Floor	pkg(4)	1.60
140-53302	50' Express Underframe	pkg(4)	1.40
140-53308	Express Truck	each	1.00
140-54600	57' Shell, Undecorated	each	2.00
140-54601	57' Floor	pkg(2)	.90
140-54602	57' Underframe	pkg(2)	.90
140-54603	57' Steel Weight	pkg(2)	.90
140-16310	50' Body OB, Undecorated	each	1.50

GONDOLA

140-16523	50' Cannister, Undec	pkg(4)	1.40
140-16755	Frozen Food Locker	pkg(4)	1.40
140-16756	50' Roof	pkg(4)	1.60

HOPPER

140-17503	Quad Door	pkg(12)	1.80
140-17504	Quad Underframe	pkg(4)	1.60
140-19000	Center Flow Body, Undec	each	1.75
140-19057	54' Center Flow, Steel	pkg(4)	1.60
140-53000	54' Covered, Body, Undecorated	each	1.75
140-53002	54' Covered, End A	pkg(4)	1.20
140-53003	54' Covered, End B	pkg(4)	1.20
140-53004	54' Covered, Roofwalk	pkg(2)	.90
140-53006	54' Covered, Outlet	pkg(12)	1.80
140-53007	54' Covered, Brakewheel	pkg(12)	1.80
140-53008	54' Covered, Brake Set	each	.35
140-53009	54' Covered, Round Signboard	pkg(6)	1.20
140-53011	54' Covered, Square Signboard	pkg(6)	1.20
140-53012	54' Covered, Rect Signboard	pkg(6)	1.20
140-53001	54' Covered Hopper Underframe	pkg(2)	1.00
140-53005	54' Covered Hopper Hatch	pkg(4)	1.20
140-54001	34' Underframe	pkg(2)	.80
140-54200	34' Composite Body, Undec	each	1.50
140-54400	34' Body, Rib/Pk, Undecorated	each	1.50
140-90701	34-40' Steel Weight	pkg(2)	1.40

DERRICK CAR

140-17254	Right & Left Hand Tool Box	pkg(4)	.80
140-17256	Mast Base	pkg(4)	1.60

200 TON CRANE

140-16990	Cab, Undecorated	each	2.00
140-17002	Chassis, Undecorated	each	2.00
140-17003	Spt-Right and Left	pkg(4pr)	.40
140-17007	Boom	pkg(2)	1.50
140-17015	Large Sheave	pkg(12)	1.80
140-17016	Small Sheave	pkg(12)	1.80
140-17017	Large Hook	pkg(4)	1.20
140-17018	Small Hook	pkg(6)	1.20
140-17019	Snatch Block	pkg(4)	1.20
140-90704	Steel Weight	pkg(4)	.80
140-99205	Crane Pins Assorted	pkg(36)	1.05

SNOW PLOW

140-11961	Long Roofwalk	pkg(4)	1.00
140-11962	Short Roofwalk	pkg(6)	1.20
140-11963	Smokebox Door	pkg(4)	1.00
140-11940	Body Shell, Undecorated	each	2.25
140-11964	Deflector	pkg(4)	.80
140-11965	Rotor with Shaft	pkg(2)	1.20
140-11966	Rotor Housing Subframe	each	1.50
140-11969	Thrust Washer	pkg(12)	.60
140-11971	Retainer	pkg(12)	.60
140-11972	Underframe	pkg(2)	1.40
140-11973	Flanger	pkg(4)	1.40
140-11975	Coupler Box	pkg(6)	.90

CABOOSE

140-12490	Shell, Undecorated	each	1.50
140-12503	Regular Floor	pkg(2)	.80
140-12504	Regular Ladder	pkg(6)	1.20
140-12506	Regular Short Roofwalk	pkg(6)	1.50
140-12507	Railing	pkg(12)	1.20
140-12508	Smoke Jack	pkg(6)	.90
140-12509	Regular Underframe	pkg(2)	.70
140-12512	Cupola	pkg(4)	1.40
140-12513	Brake Gear Box	pkg(12)	1.80
140-12740	Work, Shell, Undecorated	each	1.50
140-12756	Work Long Roofwalk	pkg(6)	1.20
140-12757	Work Short Roofwalk	pkg(6)	1.20
140-12758	Boom Support	pkg(8)	1.60
140-12759	Work Smoke Jack	pkg(6)	.90

CABOOSE (continued)

140-12850	Brake Wheel, Shell, Undecorated		1.50
140-12851	Brake Wheel, Floor	pkg(4)	1.60
140-12852	Brake Wheel, Underframe	pkg(4)	1.40
140-12853	Brake Wheel, Steel Weight	pkg(4)	1.20
140-12854	Brake Wheel, Roofwalk	pkg(4)	1.20
140-12855	Brake Wheel, Smoke Jack	pkg(6)	.90
140-12911	Work, Floor	each	1.00
140-12912	Work, Cab	pkg(2)	1.00
140-12913	Work, Cupola	pkg(4)	1.40
140-12914	Work, Tool Box R&L	pkg(4)	1.60
140-53600	WV Shell, Undecorated	each	2.25
140-53601	WV Cupola, Undecorated	pkg(4)	1.40
140-53602	WV Roofwalk (Short)	pkg(4)	1.00
140-53604	WV Floor	pkg(2)	.80
140-53606	WV Air Brake Set	pkg(4)	1.40
140-53607	WV Steel Weight	pkg(4)	1.20
140-53608	WV Smoke Jack	pkg(6)	.90
140-90600	Brake Wheel, Freight	pkg(12)	1.20

MISCELLANEOUS

140-14072	Side Auto Loader	pkg(4)	1.40
140-14073	Upper Deck Auto Loader	pkg(2)	1.00
140-14074	Lower Deck Auto Loader	pkg(4)	1.20
140-14075	Shell, Undecorated, Auto Loader	each	1.25
140-90700	40' Freight Car Steel Weight	pkg(4)	1.20
140-90702	Regular Steel Weight	pkg(4)	1.80
140-90703	50' Freight Car Steel Weight	pkg(4)	1.40

DIESEL POWER UNIT

WORM ASSEMBLY

140-40054	GP9 and GP35	pkg(2)	1.70
140-41032	S12 and SW1500	pkg(2)	1.70
140-41037	F7	pkg(2)	1.70
140-41031	Worm Housing, SW/S12	pkg(2)	1.70
140-41034	Worm Coupling, SW1500/S12	pkg(6)	1.20
140-42000	DD40 and PA	pkg(2)	1.70

LOCO DETAILS / ACCESS

HUSTLER

140-29900	Shell, Undecorated	each	2.25
140-29912	Master Shaft Pulley	pkg(6)	.90
140-29915	Insulated Plate	pkg(6)	.90
140-29916	Insulated Washer	pkg(24)	1.00

GP-9

140-10511	Undecorated Cab	pkg(4)	1.00
140-10522	Radiator	pkg(8)	1.20
140-10523	Right Hand Step Guard	pkg(12)	1.50
140-10524	Left Hand Step Guard	pkg(12)	1.50
140-11529	Handrail Set	each	1.75
140-10536	Air Tank	pkg(8)	1.40
140-42004	Underframe	each	2.75
140-90604	Horns	pkg(12)	1.80

GP50/38-2

140-46026	Connector Clip	each	1.60
140-46027	Handrail Set	each	2.00
140-46029	Underframe GP38-2	each	5.00
140-46031	Window & Lens Set	each	.85
140-46037	Truck Accessory Set	each	1.20
140-46038	Hatch, Dynamic	pkg(2)	1.00
140-46039	Hatch, Non-dynamic GP38-2	each	1.00
140-46040	Weights, GP38-2	pkg(12)	1.20
140-46638	Dynamic Housing, GP50		1.00
140-46729	Underframe GP50	each	5.00
140-46740	Weights, GP50		1.20

F7

140-42005	Underframe, Black	each	2.75
140-90609	Horns	pkg(12)	1.80
140-90709	Weight	each	.65
140-90710	Super Gear Weights	each	2.75

RDC

140-11713	Underframe	each	3.00
140-11714	Coupler Box	pkg(6)	.90
140-11715	Coupler Box Cover	pkg(12)	.90
140-11716	Centering Spring	pkg(12)	.75
140-11717	Drive Shaft	pkg(6)	.90
140-11720	Motor Connector Clip	pkg(4)	1.00
140-11726	Window Set, RDC1	pkg(2)	1.50
140-11727	Window Set, RDC3	pkg(2)	1.50

HO SCALE (1/87)

Plastic bodies and parts for kitbashing & scratchbuilding. Parts are plastic except where noted or obvious (light bulbs etc.). Parts are available only for current production models.

Items not listed in this catalog are temporarily out of stock. Watch Craft Train News for the latest delivery information on these products.

We have worked closely with this manufacturer to provide accurate availability information at the time this catalog was published. Items listed in *blue ink* may not be available at all times. Please see your dealer for current delivery information.

PA1, PA & PB

140-33214	Lens Headlight PA1	pkg(6)	1.20
140-33218	Window Set PA1/PB1	pkg(2)	1.20
140-33221	Underframe, PA & PB	each	3.25
140-33226	Trunk Front Power PA1	each	4.50
140-33227	Trunk Rear Power PA/PB1	each	4.50
140-33228	Cover Gear Box Front PA1	pkg(2)	.80
140-33229	Cover Rear Gear Box PA & PB	pkg(2)	.80
140-33232	Motor Connection Clip PA/PB	pkg(2)	.90
140-33237	Truck Front Dummy PBI	each	3.00
140-33235	Numberboard Set PA1	each	1.60
140-33238	Porthole Window Set, PA/PB	pkg(4)	1.80
140-33215	Cab Window PA1	pkg(4)	1.20

U-BOAT (U28B, U28C, U33B & U33C)

140-34003	Numberboard Set	pkg(6)	1.20
140-34005	Brake Wheel	pkg(12)	1.80
140-34006	3 Horn Cluster, U33B/C	pkg(6)	.90
140-34007	Bell	pkg(6)	.90
140-34212	Truck Front Power U28, 30, 33C	each	4.50
140-34019	Handrail Set, U28B/U30B	each	1.90
140-34214	Truck Front Dummy U28, 30, 33C	each	2.55
140-34229	Handrail Set, U28C/U30C	each	2.15

GE

140-34015	Air Tank	pkg(4)	1.20
140-34027	Motor Drive Assembly	pkg(2)	1.70
140-34028	Sideframe GE-B	each	1.50
140-34206	Underframe, GE-C	each	3.25
140-34217	C Spline 1"	pkg(6)	1.20
140-34218	Sideframe, GE-C	pkg(4)	1.50
140-34228	Window Lens	pkg(4)	1.40
140-34001	Loco Cab, Undecorated	pkg(2)	2.20
140-34010	Underframe, GE-B	each	2.75
140-40002	Windshield	pkg(4)	1.20

F45 & FP45

140-36071	Underframe FP45	each	3.25
140-36101	Numberboard F45/FP45	pkg(4)	1.60
140-36105	Cab Window	pkg(4)	.60
140-36106	Window Seat F45/FP45	each	.85
140-36111	Handrail Set	each	1.25
140-40067	Brake Cylinder	pkg(8)	1.00

S12 & SD9

140-37211	Handrail Set, S12	each	1.60
140-38005	Window/Numberboard SD-9	pkg(2)	1.40
140-38018	Underframe SD9	each	2.75
140-38017	Handrail Set, SD9	each	1.60
140-38025	Sideframe SD9, Plastic	pkg(4)	1.50

DD40

140-40049	Spline 7/8" Long	pkg(6)	1.20
140-42033	Underframe	each	5.50

SW1000, SW1500, SW1500 SP

140-39001	Cab, SW1500		TBA
140-39002	Cab, SP/SW1500		TBA
140-39003	Numberboard SP/SW1500		TBA
140-39008	Window Lens Board	each	1.50
140-39015	Handrail Set	each	1.75
140-39020	Sideframe Set	each	2.00
140-41001	Hood Shell, SW/Calf Undecorated	pkg(4)	1.80
140-41002	Cab SW, Undecorated	pkg(4)	1.80
140-41003	Headlight Lens, SW	pkg(6)	1.20
140-41004	Front Window, Cow SW1500	pkg(4)	1.00
140-41005	Side Window, Cow SW1500	pkg(6)	1.20
140-41006	Rear Window, Cow SW1500	pkg(4)	1.20
140-41007	Bell, SW1500	pkg(6)	.90
140-41015	Horn SW	pkg(12)	1.80
140-14018	Underframe SW1500 & S12	each	2.75
140-14021	Sideframe SW7/1000 Plastic	pkg(4)	1.50
140-41023	Truck Rear Power SW7, 1000	each	3.00
140-41024	Truck Front Power SW7, 1000	each	3.00
140-41029	Handrail Set, Cow & Calf	each	1.50

H24-66

140-43210	Shell, Southern Pacific Type, Undec	each	4.50

GP35, SD40, SD45

140-40002	Lens Numberboard	pkg(6)	1.20
140-40003	Cab Window	pkg(6)	1.00
140-40004	Lens Headlight	pkg(6)	1.20
140-40006	Radiator SD45	pkg(8)	1.60
140-40007	Cab Roof	pkg(6)	1.60
140-40066	Sideframe Set, All 45s	pkg(12)	2.00

SD40-2

140-44042	Pwrd Mechanism	ea	25.00
140-44106	Window Lens Brd	ea	1.00
140-45019	Underframe Casting	ea	5.00
140-45036	Sideframe Set	each	2.00
140-45038	Dynamic Hatch	each	1.00
140-45039	Non-dynamic hatch	pkg(2)	1.00
140-45042	Power Mechanism, SD40T2	each	25.00
140-45106	Window Set Long	each	1.00
140-45529	Underframe, SD40T2	each	5.00

HANDRAIL SET

140-42019	GP35	each	1.75
140-43101	H24-66	each	1.90
140-44029	SD40-2	each	2.00
140-45580	SD40T2, Long	each	2.15
140-45590	SD40T2, Short	each	2.15
140-40035	SDP40 & SD45	each	2.25

HEADLIGHTS & LIGHTING

140-10533	Lens, GP9	pkg(6)	1.20
140-11015	Lens, F7A	pkg(6)	1.20
140-43107	Lens & Marker Boards	pkg(2)	.70
140-90200	4-Wheel Truck Light Kit	each	1.00
140-90201	6-Wheel Truck Light Kit	each	1.00
140-90360	Headlight Bulb	pkg(2)	1.00
140-90378	Lit Kit Conductor Strip	pkg(6)	1.20
140-90587	Light Bracket, F7 & GP	pkg(6)	1.20
140-95010	Bracket Recept Loco	pkg(6)	1.20
140-95011	Bulb Retainer Clip Loco	pkg(6)	1.20

MISCELLANEOUS

140-42012	Blomberg B Truck Details	pkg(12)	1.20
140-43015	Underframe H24-66	each	3.00
140-40001	Horn GP35,38,50 & SD40,45	each	1.80
140-42003	Underframe, GP35	each	2.75
140-44501	Cab, SD40-2, GP50 & GP38-2	each	1.00

STANCHIONS

140-10424	Short	pkg(24)	1.50
140-10425	Long	pkg(24)	1.50
140-10426	TM Long	pkg(24)	1.50

STEP GUARD

140-46017	Right, GP38-2 & GP50	each	1.80

LOCO POWER TRAIN PARTS/UNIVERSALS

FLYWHEELS w/BUSHINGS

140-95003	5/16" Long, 3/4" Diameter	pkg(2)	2.00
140-95007	GP 50/38-2	each	1.50
140-95001	5/8" Long	pkg(6)	1.20
140-95004	5/16" Long	pkg(6)	1.20
140-95008	Brass, 3/4" long, .670 Dia	each	1.50

COUPLINGS

140-40020	Worm & Shaft Assembly	pkg(3)	1.35
140-40022	1/4" Worm	pkg(6)	1.20
140-41017	Univ Slotted, S12	pkg(6)	1.20
140-90105	Female w/Keyway	pkg(6)	1.20
140-40051	1/4" Worm, DD40	pkg(6)	1.20
140-90103	5/16" Female	pkg(6)	1.20

GEARS, GEAR PLATE & BOX COVER

140-36115	Top Box, Clip 6-Axle	pkg(6)	1.20
140-36116	Bottom Box, Clip 6-Axle	pkg(4)	1.60
140-40055	Bottom Box, Clip F7/GP	pkg(4)	1.20
140-40056	Top Box, Clip F7/GP	pkg(6)	1.20
140-40030	23-Tooth	pkg(4)	1.00
140-40058	30-Tooth, DD40	pkg(4)	1.00
140-40031	45-Tooth	pkg(4)	1.20
140-41020	16-Tooth, SW & S12	pkg(6)	1.20

MISCELLANEOUS

140-40019	40" Drive Wheel	pkg(2)	1.50
140-90101	HI-F Drive Belt "Rubber Band"	pkg(12)	.25
140-40057	Oilite Sideframe Bearing	pkg(6)	1.20
140-95012	Loco Wiper Clip	pkg(6)	1.20

SPLINES

140-34025	3/4" Long, GE-B	pkg(6)	1.20
140-40015	1-1/4" Long, FP45	pkg(6)	1.20
140-90099	5/8" Long, Coupling	pkg(6)	1.20
140-90106	1/2" Long, Coupling	pkg(6)	1.20

THRUST WASHERS

140-99201	3/32"	pkg(36)	1.05

WORM BEARINGS & HOUSING

140-40021	Rnd, PA/DD	pkg(6)	1.20
140-40052	Square, DD40	pkg(6)	1.20
140-40053	Housing, DD40	pkg(4)	1.00
140-42007	Housing, Half L PA/DD	pkg(4)	1.00
140-42008	Housing, Half S PA/DD	pkg(4)	1.00
140-46639	Housing, Nondynamic GP50	pkg(2)	1.00

LOCO PARTS

SHELLS

140-15490	40' Chemical Tank, Undecorated	each	1.25
140-30230	F-7A, Undecorated	each	2.75
140-30240	F-7B, Undecorated	each	2.75
140-34100	U28B, Undecorated	each	4.00
140-38200	SD9, Undecorated	each	4.50
140-39200	SW-1000, Undecorated	each	TBA
140-39210	SW-1500 SP, Undecorated	each	TBA
140-39500	SW-1000, Undecorated	each	TBA
140-40760	SW-1500 Calf, Undecorated	each	3.00
140-30510	GP9, Undecorated	each	3.00
140-42200	GP35, Undecorated	each	3.00
140-41800	SD45, Undecorated	each	3.00
140-42600	DD40, Undecorated	each	5.00
140-34700	U30C, Undecorated	each	4.25
140-44590	SD40-2, Nondynamic, Undecorated	each	6.00
140-37200	S12, Undecorated	each	3.00
140-44500	SD40-2, Undecorated Dynamic	each	6.00
140-33210	PA-1, Undecorated	each	3.75
140-33610	PB-1, Undecorated	each	3.75
140-20700	RDC-1, Undecorated	each	2.75
140-20750	RDC-3, Undecorated	each	2.75
140-43200	H24-66, Undecorated	each	4.50
140-40510	SW-1500 Cow, Undecorated	each	3.00
140-46620	GP38-2, Undec, Non-Dynamic	each	4.00
140-46500	GP38-2, Undecorated, Dynamic	each	4.00
140-41200	SDP40, Undecorated	each	3.00
140-34300	U28C, Undecorated	each	4.25
140-34500	U30B, Undecorated	each	4.00
140-34900	U33B, Undecorated	each	4.00
140-35100	U33C, Undecorated	each	4.25
140-36100	F45, Undecorated	each	4.00
140-36300	FP45, Undecorated	each	4.25
140-45500	SD40T-2, Undec (LONG NOSE)	each	7.00
140-45540	SD40T-2, Undecorated	each	7.00

PASSENGER CAR PARTS

140-17800	Baggage, Sline Body, Undecorated	each	2.25
140-17803	Baggage, Sline Window	pkg(2)	1.60
140-17900	Diner, Sline Body, Undecorated	each	2.25
140-17903	Diner, Sline Window	pkg(2)	1.80
140-18000	RPO, Sline Body, Undecorated	each	2.25
140-18102	Coach Floor, Streamline	pkg(2)	1.60
140-18103	Coach Window Set	pkg(2)	1.70
140-18203	Vista-Dome Window Set	pkg(2)	1.70
140-18204	Vista-Dome Window	pkg(4)	1.20
140-18303	Observation, Sline Window Set	pkg(2)	1.70
140-18402	RPO, Floor, Standard	pkg(2)	1.60
140-18500	Coach Std Mon Shell, Undec	each	2.25
140-18502	Coach Std Floor Coach/Pullman	pkg(2)	1.60
140-18503	Coach Std Window Set	pkg(2)	1.70
140-18540	Coach Std Clerestory Shell, Undec	each	2.25
140-18103	Coach Window Set	pk(2)	1.70
140-18603	Pullman Window	pkg(2)	1.70
140-18703	Observation, Standard Window-Set	pkg(2)	1.70
140-18709	Vista-Dome Railing	pkg(4)	1.60
140-18800	Baggage, Std Shell, Undecorated	each	2.25
140-18900	Diner, Std Shell, Undecorated	each	2.25
140-90376	Offset Steel Weight	pkg(4)	1.60
140-90377	Steel Weight, Flat	pkg(4)	1.40
140-90598	Streamline Brakewheel	pkg(12)	1.80
140-90599	Standard, Brakewheel	pkg(12)	1.80

SCREWS

MISCELLANEOUS

2-56 machine screws available in the following lengths:

140-99000	1/8"	pkg(12)	.30
140-99001	3/16"	pkg(12)	.30
140-99002	1/4"	pkg(12)	.30
140-99003	5/16"	pkg(12)	.30
140-99004	3/8"	pkg(12)	.30
140-99005	7/16"	pkg(12)	.30
140-99006	1/2"	pkg(12)	.30

BH MODELS

HO SCALE (1/87)

TOPS FOR WATER/OIL TANKS

Molded plastic, use with other tank kits or for scratchbuilding.

FLAT TOPS

159-1	24' Diameter — Black	2.50
159-5	24' Diameter — Silver	2.50

15 DEGREE, PEAKED TOPS

159-2	24' Diameter — Black	3.00
159-6	24' Diameter — Silver	3.00

30 DEGREE, PEAKED TOPS

159-3	24' Diameter — Black	3.00
159-7	24' Diameter — Silver	3.00

DOORS/WINDOWS/BRACKETS — NEW

Various doors, windows and other trim parts, typical of items used on stations and other buildings from the period. Windows and doors separate from frames for easy painting and are molded in white styrene.

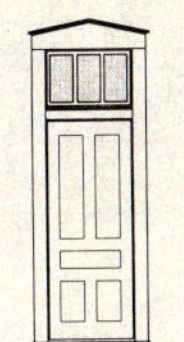
Standard Depot Door With Transom

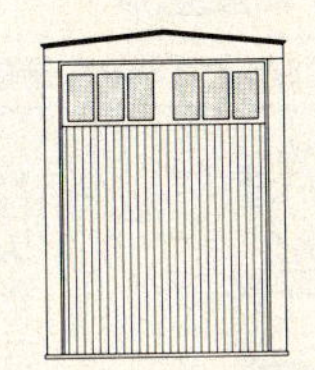
Standard Freight Door With Stationary Transom

Standard Freight Door With Sliding Door and Transom

Standard Utility Window

Pedimented Lintel For 8-Light Windows

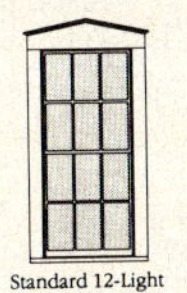
Standard 12-Light Depot Window

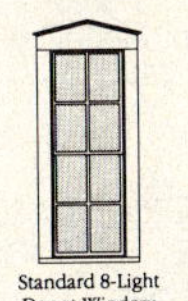
Standard 8-Light Depot Window

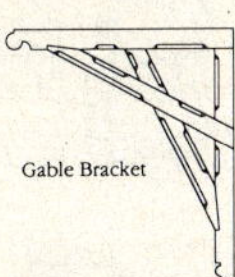
Gable Bracket

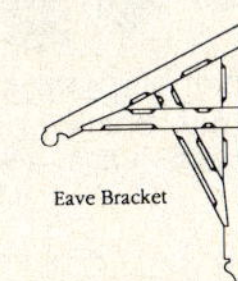
Eave Bracket

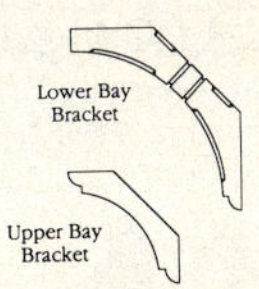
Lower Bay Bracket

Upper Bay Bracket

Bracket Set

159-404 Depot Doors & Windows w/Brackets — 19.95
Includes 18 12-Light Windows, 12 8-Light Windows, 3 each Utility Door, Entrance Door w/Transom, Freight Door w/Stationary Transom and Freight Door w/Sliding Transom, 10 Gable Brackets, 20 Eave Brackets, 4 Lower Bay Brackets, Two Upper Bay Brackets.

159-405 Depot Doors & Windows — 13.95
Includes twelve 12-Light Windows, eight 8-Light Windows, and two each Utility Windows, Entrance Door w/Transom, Freight Door w/Stationary Transom, Freight Door w/sliding Transom.

159-406 Depot Brackets — 5.95
Includes 10 Gable Brackets, 20 Eave Brackets, 4 Lower Bay Brackets, Two Upper Bay Brackets.

HO SCALE (1/87)

Detail parts are metal castings unless otherwise noted.

BARGES, BOXES, BUCKETS & PALLETS

Wood Style

HO	HO/N	Coal Buckets w/Handle
254-15	254-23	HO/O
		254-76
pkg(4) 2.25	pkg(10) 2.25	pkg(2) 2.95

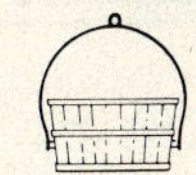

(not illustrated)

254-107 Large Tool Boxes — pkg(2) 1.95

DOORS

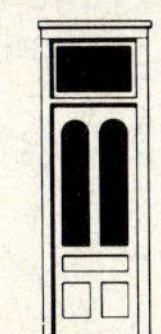
with Transom
254-62
pkg(4) 1.95
plastic

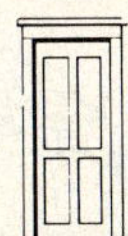
Four Panel
254-63
pkg(4) 1.95
plastic

MISCELLANEOUS

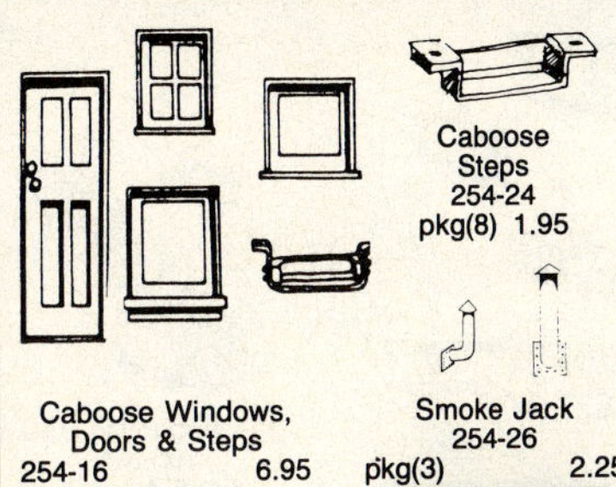

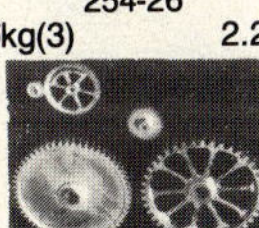
Caboose Steps
254-24
pkg(8) 1.95

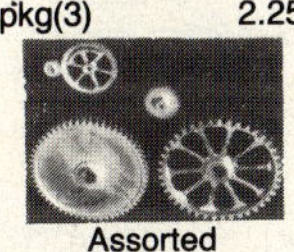

Caboose Windows, Doors & Steps
254-16 — 6.95

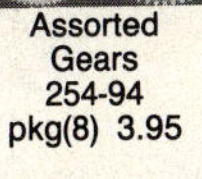
Smoke Jack
254-26
pkg(3) 2.25

Victorian Chimney
254-18
1.95

Headlight, D&RGW, Early Box
254-45
pkg(2) 2.25

Assorted Gears
254-94
pkg(8) 3.95

Stove
254-108
1.95

Auto Tires
254-93 pkg(12) 3.95

(not illustrated)

254-25	Mailbox	pkg(5)	1.95
254-34	Bridge Shoe	pkg(4)	1.95
254-104	Ladder, Plastic	pkg(2)	2.25
254-106	Rerailer Shoes	pkg(4)	1.95
254-109	Lanterns	pkg(4)	1.95
254-110	Shovels	pkg(4)	1.95
254-111	Brooms	pkg(4)	1.95
254-121	Brass Chain (12")		2.50
254-122	Box of Bottles	pkg(4)	1.95
254-123	Cafe Chairs (used in Columbine Cafe #118)	pkg(8)	1.95
254-124	Round Water Tank Roof		5.95

WINDOWS

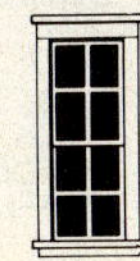
Tall Double-Hung
254-60
pkg(4) 1.95
plastic

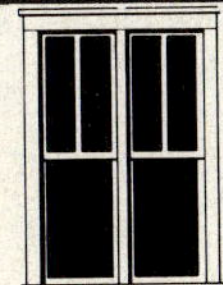
Double Double-Hung
254-61
pkg(2) 1.95
plastic

HO SCALE (1/87)

Parts are lost wax brass castings unless noted. Black silhouette illustrations are approximately full size.

AIR BRAKES

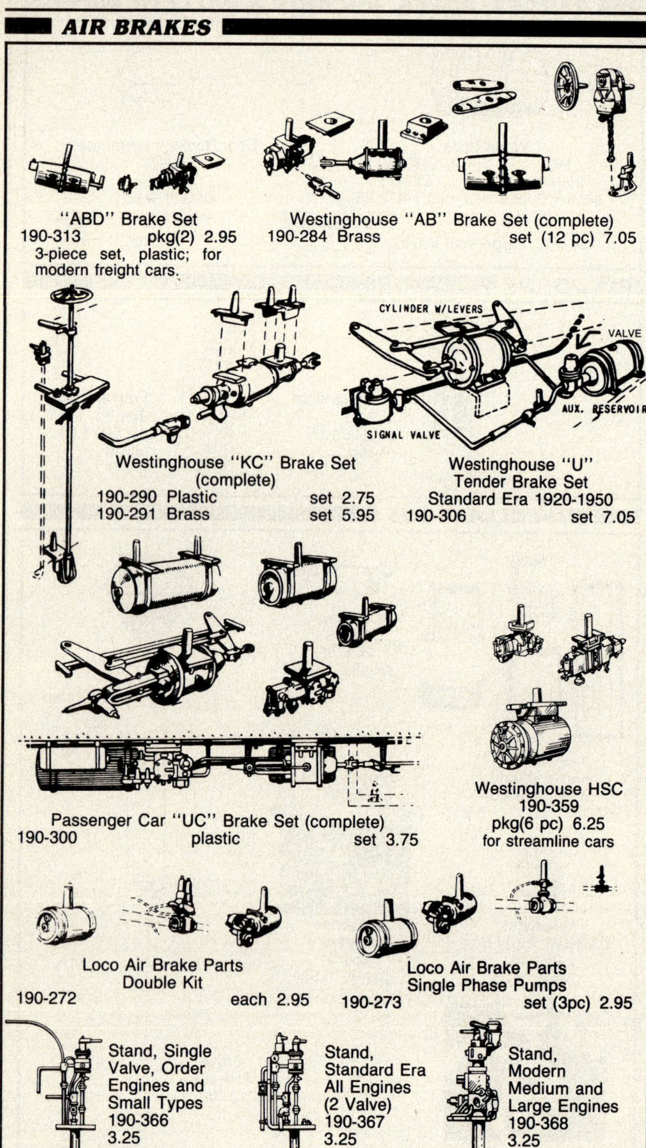

"ABD" Brake Set
190-313   pkg(2) 2.95
3-piece set, plastic; for modern freight cars.

Westinghouse "AB" Brake Set (complete)
190-284 Brass   set (12 pc) 7.05

Westinghouse "KC" Brake Set (complete)
190-290 Plastic   set 2.75
190-291 Brass   set 5.95

Westinghouse "U" Tender Brake Set
Standard Era 1920-1950
190-306   set 7.05

Westinghouse HSC
190-359
pkg(6 pc) 6.25
for streamline cars

Passenger Car "UC" Brake Set (complete)
190-300   plastic   set 3.75

Loco Air Brake Parts
Double Kit
190-272   each 2.95

Loco Air Brake Parts
Single Phase Pumps
190-273   set (3pc) 2.95

Stand, Single Valve, Order Engines and Small Types
190-366
3.25

Stand, Standard Era All Engines (2 Valve)
190-367
3.25

Stand, Modern Medium and Large Engines
190-368
3.25

AIR CONDITIONING RECEPTACLE

190-355 Air Conditioning Receptacle   pkg(2) 2.75

AIR HORNS—NATHAN   SEE DIESEL DETAILS

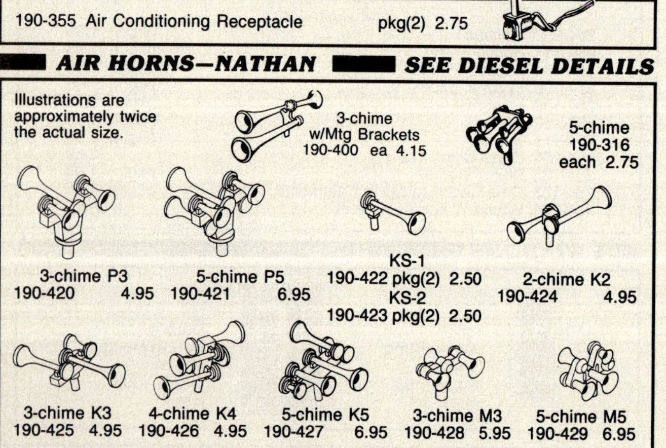

Illustrations are approximately twice the actual size.

3-chime w/Mtg Brackets
190-400 ea 4.15

5-chime
190-316
each 2.75

KS-1
190-422 pkg(2) 2.50
KS-2
190-423 pkg(2) 2.50

3-chime P3
190-420   4.95

5-chime P5
190-421   6.95

2-chime K2
190-424   4.95

3-chime K3
190-425   4.95

4-chime K4
190-426   4.95

5-chime K5
190-427   6.95

3-chime M3
190-428   5.95

5-chime M5
190-429   6.95

AIR HOSES

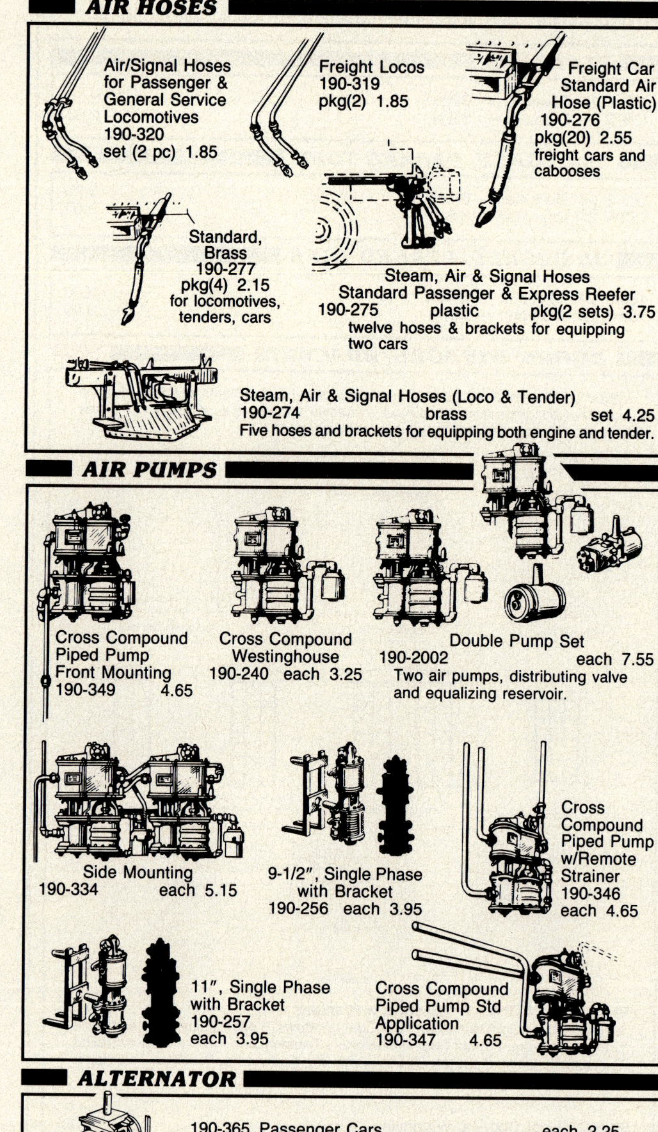

Air/Signal Hoses for Passenger & General Service Locomotives
190-320
set (2 pc) 1.85

Freight Locos
190-319
pkg(2) 1.85

Freight Car Standard Air Hose (Plastic)
190-276
pkg(20) 2.55
freight cars and cabooses

Standard, Brass
190-277
pkg(4) 2.15
for locomotives, tenders, cars

Steam, Air & Signal Hoses
Standard Passenger & Express Reefer
190-275   plastic   pkg(2 sets) 3.75
twelve hoses & brackets for equipping two cars

Steam, Air & Signal Hoses (Loco & Tender)
190-274   brass   set 4.25
Five hoses and brackets for equipping both engine and tender.

AIR PUMPS

Cross Compound Piped Pump Front Mounting
190-349   4.65

Cross Compound Westinghouse
190-240 each 3.25

Double Pump Set
190-2002   each 7.55
Two air pumps, distributing valve and equalizing reservoir.

Side Mounting
190-334   each 5.15

9-1/2", Single Phase with Bracket
190-256   each 3.95

Cross Compound Piped Pump w/Remote Strainer
190-346
each 4.65

11", Single Phase with Bracket
190-257
each 3.95

Cross Compound Piped Pump Std Application
190-347   4.65

ALTERNATOR

190-365 Passenger Cars   each 2.25
Converts DC to AC for the lighting systems on cars

ANTENNA SUPPORT

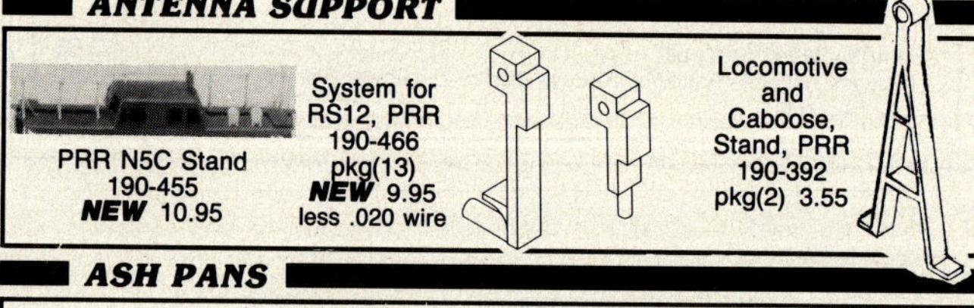

PRR N5C Stand
190-455
NEW 10.95

System for RS12, PRR
190-466
pkg(13)
NEW 9.95
less .020 wire

Locomotive and Caboose, Stand, PRR
190-392
pkg(2) 3.55

ASH PANS

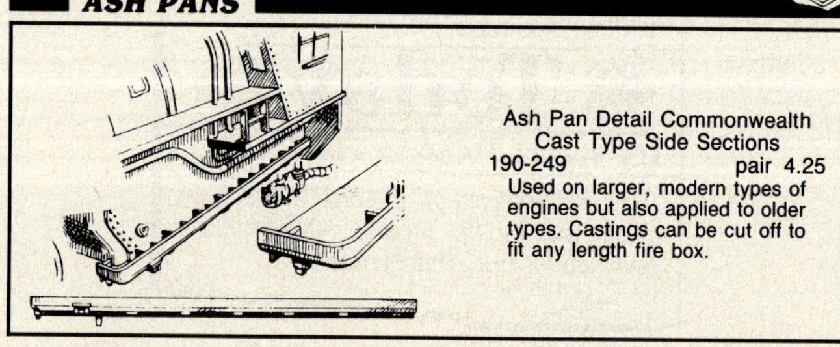

Ash Pan Detail Commonwealth Cast Type Side Sections
190-249   pair 4.25
Used on larger, modern types of engines but also applied to older types. Castings can be cut off to fit any length fire box.

Scale
CAL-SCALE

HO SCALE (1/87)

Parts are lost wax brass castings unless noted. Black silhouette illustrations are approximately full size.

ASH PANS (continued)

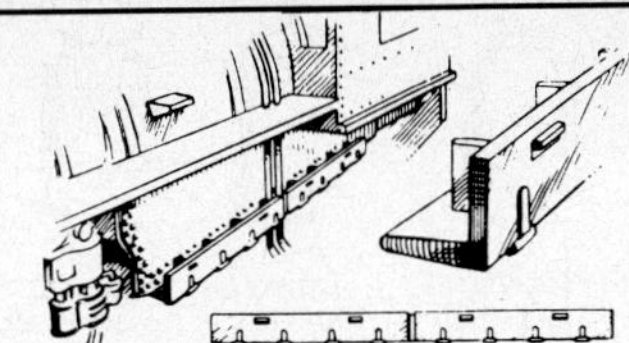

Ash Pan Detail Drop-Door Type Side Sections
190-248   pair 3.25
Used on engines with small fire boxes. Usually engines built between 1900 and late 1930's.

BACKHEAD DETAILS

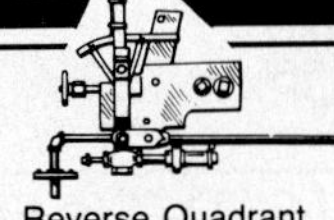

Gages, Engineer and Fireman Set
190-372   2.95

Small Quadrant
190-374   pkg(2) 2.95
Can be used for injectors, small power reverses, etc.

Reverse Quadrant for Power Reverse
190-373   3.65

BATTERY RECEPTACLES

190-354 Battery Receptacles   pkg(2) 2.75

BELLS

Standard Rope Pull
190-281   each 2.95

Bell w/Top Bar
190-328   each 2.95

Modern Steam Loco
190-317   each 2.95

Air Ringer
190-285   each 2.95

Rigid Old Ball Top
190-329   each 2.25

Angle Bracket Boiler Front Mounting
190-299   each 3.45

BRAKE CYLINDER

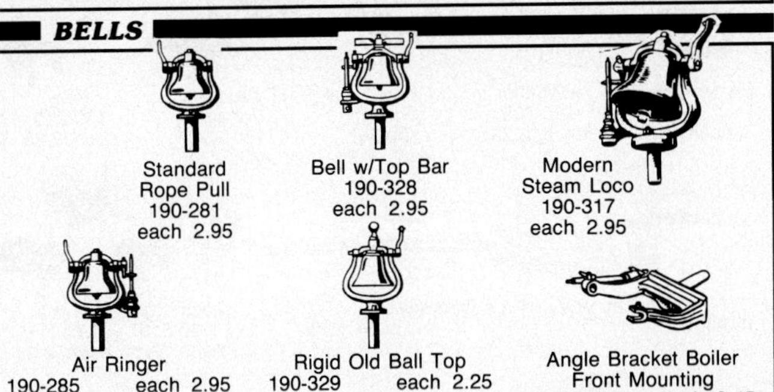

Loco Blow-Off Cocks (2) & Inspection Plugs (6)
190-308   pkg(8) 3.25

Engine Brake Cylinder
190-219   pair 3.25

Tender Brake Cylinder
190-221   2.45

Cylinder w/levers and Triple Valve

Auxiliary Reservoir

Reducing Valve

Westinghouse "PC" High Speed Old Tender & Passenger System
190-220   set(3 pc) 5.75
This same system was used on both tenders and passenger cars and in many cases is in use to this day.

BRAKE SHOES

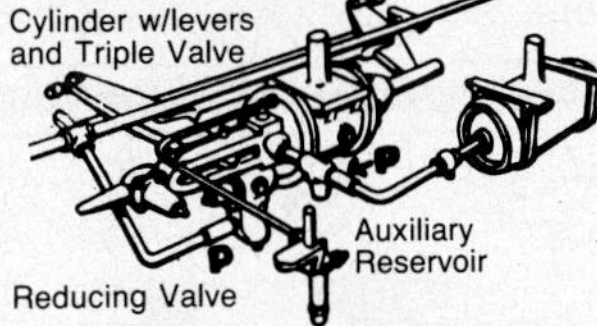

All brake shoes have insulated bushing.
190-444 Fits 57 to 64"   9.95
190-445 Fits 64 to 80"   9.95
190-446 Fits Bowser M1, M1A   9.95
          Northern & USRA Mountain
190-447 Bowser G-5   9.95

BRAKE WHEELS

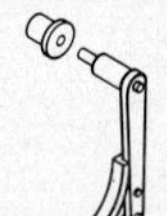

Brass, 6-Spoke
190-289   pkg(6) 3.25
Three of each type

Plastic
190-351   set(6) 3.65

CAB DETAILS

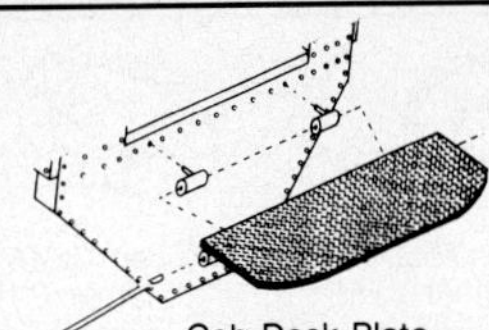
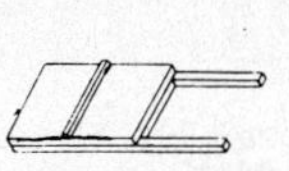

Cab Walk
190-379   pair 2.45
25/32" long

Cab Deck Plate w/Hinges
190-385   4.25

Cab Roof Hatch
190-381   2.15

Cab Walk
190-380   pair 2.45
1-1/16" long

COAL PUSHER

190-255 Standard   each 3.95

DETAILING KITS

Dual Service Express Reefer Detailing Kit (Plastic)
190-324   set 3.95

Modernize your BOWSER engines with this detailing kit in HO Scale. Used in combination with #236 Smoke Box front:

Front End for Modern PRR Freight Engines
190-2001   set 9.05

Set includes: modern headlight, Pyle dual generator, bracket for generator, PRR marker lights, keystone number plate and chin platform.

DIESEL DETAILS

See AIR HORNS for more DIESEL DETAILS

Windshield Wiper
190-419
2 pair 3.50

Ladder Shark Nose
190-418 ea 2.75

MU Stand with Battery Connection
190-393 pair 2.45

Nose Lift Rings EMD F&E
190-415
pair 1.95

Step
190-399
pair 2.15

Diesel, Bracketed
190-322
each 2.45
for hood units

MU Stand w/Battery Connection
190-394
pair 2.45

Mars Light F3A
190-417
each 1.75

Fuel Fills
190-431   2.50

Fuel Filters
190-432   pkg(2) 3.75

Diesel Bell Underfloor
190-430
pkg(2) 2.95

RS w/Bracket
190-435 3.50

RS Marker Lights EL
190-433
pkg(4) 3.95

Water Tank FP-7
190-451
each 5.95

Scale
CAL-SCALE

HO SCALE (1/87)

Parts are lost wax brass castings unless noted. Black silhouette illustrations are approximately full size.

DIESEL DETAILS (continued)

Pyle Nat'l Dual Sealed Beam
190-395
pair 2.45

Pyle Nat'l Single Beam
190-396
pair 2.45

Modern GE44 Tonner
190-413
pair 2.25

w/Visor, GE44 Tonner
190-414
pair 2.50

Brake Access Panel, Dynamic
190-436   1.95

Sunshade w/Mounting Lugs
190-437   3.95

Spark Arrestor pkg(2)
190-439   2.75

Spark Arrestor pkg(2)
190-440   2.75

F-Unit
190-416 pr 2.50

5-Character
190-398 pr 3.05

3-Character
190-397 pr 2.75

PRR E&F Unit
190-443 pkg(2) 2.50

F-Unit Pilot Doors
190-441   2.50

Passenger Pilot w/Coupler Cover for Athearn "F" & Cary "E" Units
190-442   10.95

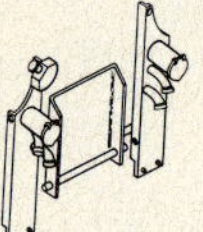

Stanchion Step End Platform EL
190-434   5.95

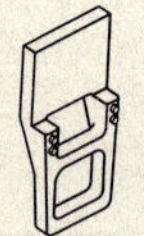

E, F & BL2 Step
190-448   pkg(6) 3.50

Modern Pilot Plow
190-456   5.95

GP7 & GP9 PRR Receiver
190-457   1.75

PRR Trainmaster Receiver
190-458   1.75

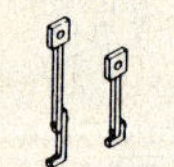  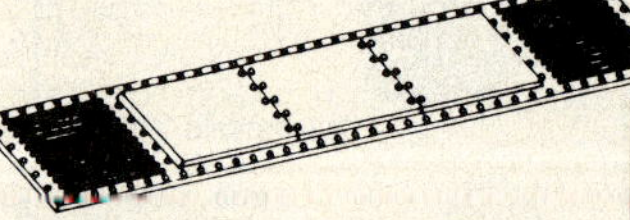

FA PRR Antenna Support Set
190-459   8.95

FA Water Cooled Turbo Exhaust Stack
190-460   1.75

FA Dynamic Brake Plastic
190-461   1.95

FA Dynamic Brake Brass
190-462   5.15

ANTENNA SUPPORT SETS

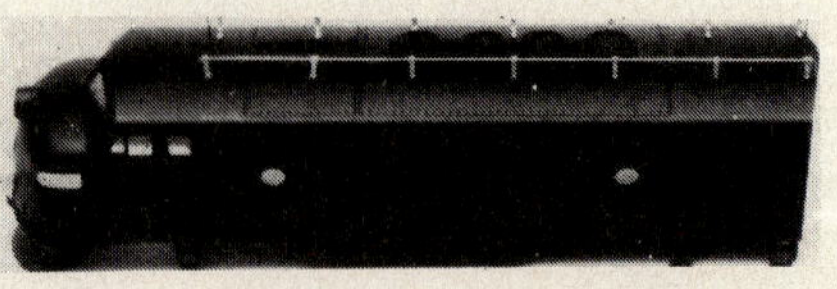

190-401	RS-3	each 8.95	190-407	RS-1	each 8.95
190-402	F-Unit	each 8.95	190-408	GP-7/GP-9	each 8.95
190-403	Alco PA	each 8.95	190-409	Shark	each 8.95
190-404	FM Trainmaster	each 8.95	190-410	U-25B	each 8.95
190-405	Baldwin S-12	each 8.95	190-411	RS-11	each 8.95
190-406	GP-30	each 9.95	190-412	E-Unit	each 9.95
			190-438	FP-7	each 9.95

DOMES

 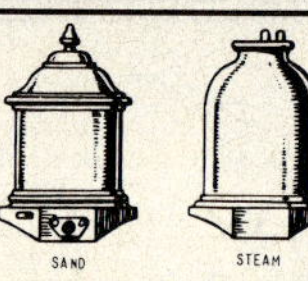 

Damper Control
190-269   each 1.85

Dome Set (1860-70)
190-338   set 7.25
One each sand & steam

Dome Set (1860-70)
190-342   set 7.25
One each sand & steam

 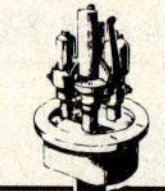

Auxiliary Exposed
190-227
set(4 pc) 3.85

Auxiliary w/Fittings
190-228
set (4 pc) 3.25

ECCENTRIC CRANK

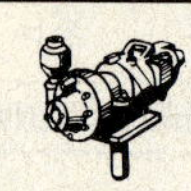

Eccentric Crank
190-384   pkg(2) 4.25

GENERATORS

Passenger Car
190-348
each 2.25

w/Muffler
190-335
each 2.25

Large, Dual Voltage
190-362
each 2.25

Pyle, Dual Voltage
190-234
each 2.25

Pyle
190-215
each 2.25

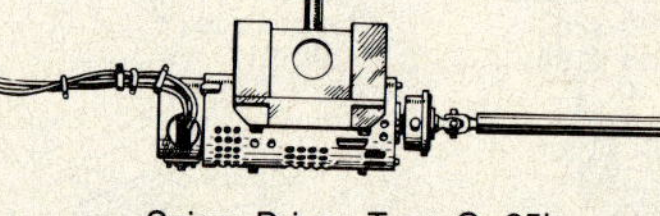

Spicer Driven Type G, 35kw
190-357   each 5.75

Loco Light
190-213
each 2.25

Turbo
190-211
each 2.25

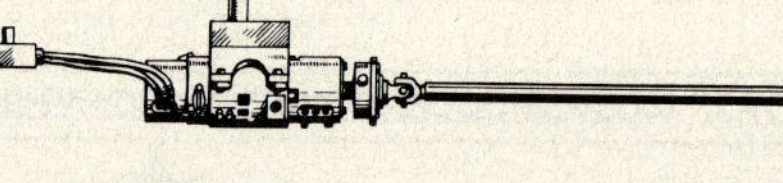

Spicer Driven Type GL, 25kw
190-353   each 5.25

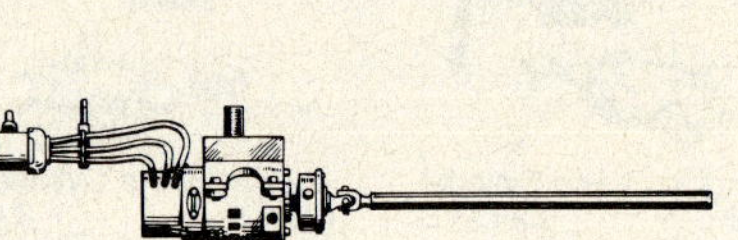

Spicer Driven Type GK, 20kw
190-352   each 5.25

Sunbeam
190-212
each 2.25

Buda Ross
190-214
each 2.25

HEADLIGHTS

F&R Style Switcher
190-304
each 2.95
also used as back-up light

Large Santa Fe Type, Old
190-203
each 2.25

Pyle Wing Board
190-205
each 2.25

Std Wing Board w/Visor
190-206
each 2.25

Mars Light Twin Type
190-263
each 2.45

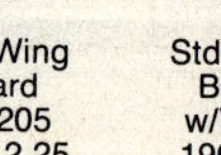

Baldwin Oil (1890)
190-305
each 3.45

Great Northern
190-282
each 2.25

Santa Fe Standard
190-210
each 2.25

Pyle Twin Sealed Beam
190-230
each 2.25

Sunbeam w/Visor
190-229
each 2.25

Scale
CAL-SCALE

HO SCALE (1/87)

HEADLIGHTS (continued)

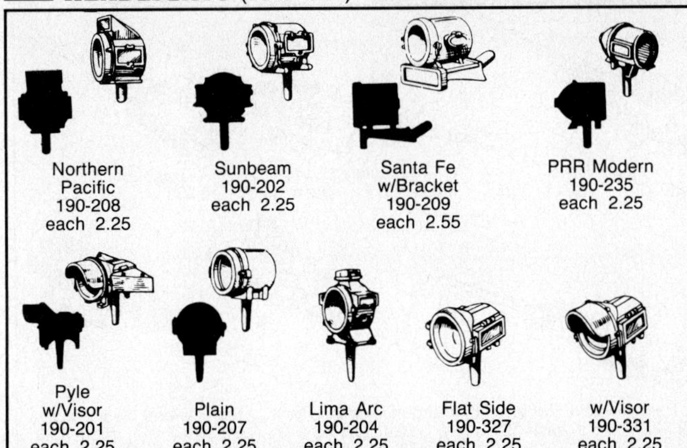

Northern Pacific
190-208
each 2.25

Sunbeam
190-202
each 2.25

Santa Fe w/Bracket
190-209
each 2.55

PRR Modern
190-235
each 2.25

Pyle w/Visor
190-201
each 2.25

Plain
190-207
each 2.25

Lima Arc
190-204
each 2.25

Flat Side
190-327
each 2.25

w/Visor
190-331
each 2.25

HEADLIGHT BRACKETS

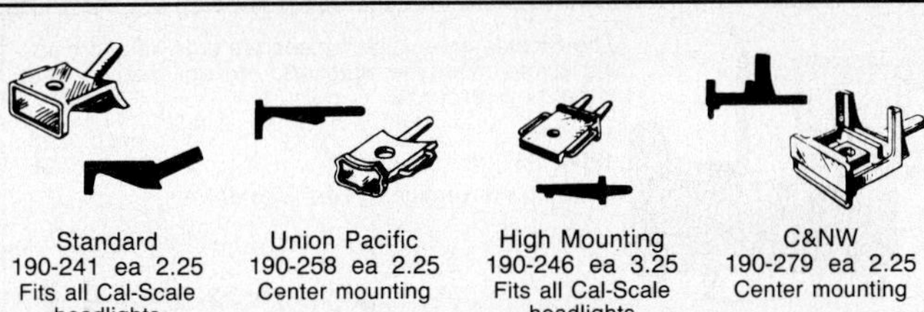

Standard
190-241 ea 2.25
Fits all Cal-Scale headlights

Union Pacific
190-258 ea 2.25
Center mounting

High Mounting
190-246 ea 3.25
Fits all Cal-Scale headlights

C&NW
190-279 ea 2.25
Center mounting

HEATERS

ELESCO Pipe Set
190-343   set 4.65
(1 each hot & cold water)

The plain pipe carries cold water from pump to heater. The wrapped pipe carries the heated water to the left side injector. Bend pipes with care to fit your application.

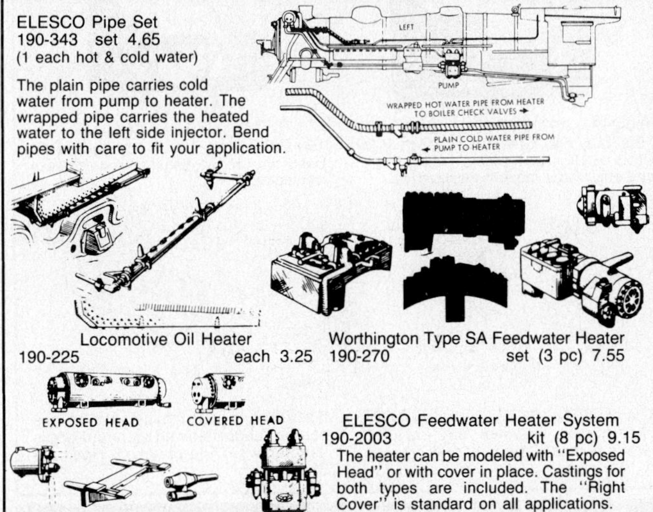

Locomotive Oil Heater
190-225   each 3.25

Worthington Type SA Feedwater Heater
190-270   set (3 pc) 7.55

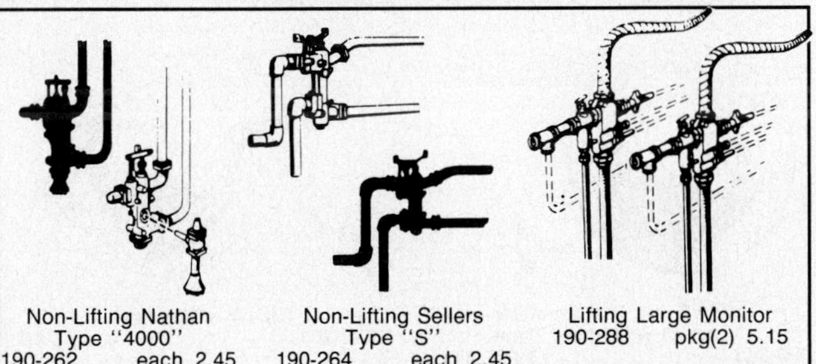

ELESCO Feedwater Heater System
190-2003   kit (8 pc) 9.15
The heater can be modeled with "Exposed Head" or with cover in place. Castings for both types are included. The "Right Cover" is standard on all applications.

INJECTORS

Non-Lifting Nathan Type "4000"
190-262   each 2.45

Non-Lifting Sellers Type "S"
190-264   each 2.45

Lifting Large Monitor
190-288   pkg(2) 5.15

INJECTORS (continued)

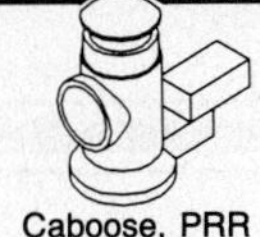

Check Valve & Injector
190-337
set 5.05

Check valves and pumps mount on each side of boiler, injector on the left side only.

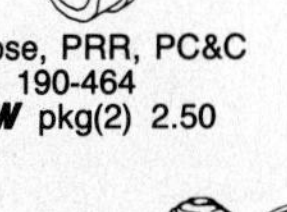

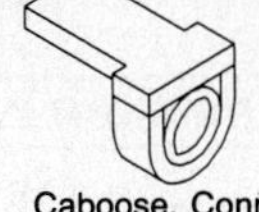

Check Valve & Injector
190-341   pkg(3 pc) 5.75

MARKERS

Caboose, PRR
190-463
NEW pkg(2) 2.50

Caboose, PRR, PC&C
190-464
NEW pkg(2) 2.50

Caboose, Conrail
190-465
NEW pkg(2) 2.50

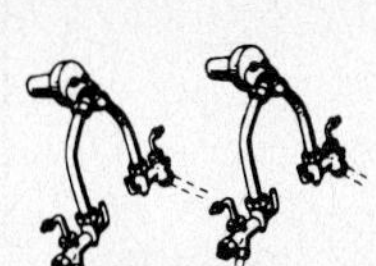
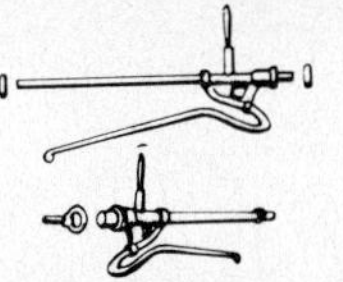
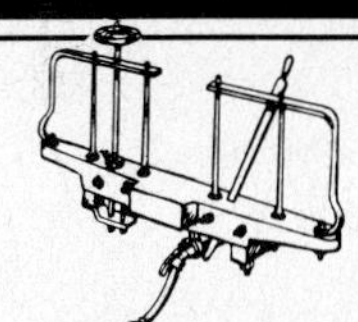

Loco, Modern
190-280
pkg(2) 2.15

Caboose
190-325
pkg(2) 2.15
Less jewels

Loco "Standard Era" including USRA
190-312
pkg(2) 2.15

Standard A&W
190-375 pair 2.15
Passenger, standard cabooses, and some early engines.

MISCELLANEOUS

Sanders
190-286   pkg(2) 2.95

Mail Catcher for RPO Cars
190-345   pkg(2) 4.05

End Railing Set Wood Passenger Car
190-321   set 8.25

3-Way Junction Box
190-383   pkg(2) 2.15

Mechanical Lubricators w/Brackets
190-271   pkg(4) 4.95

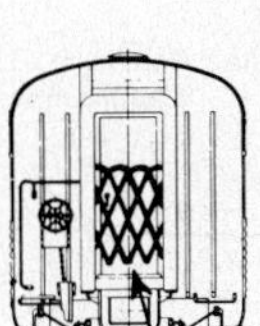

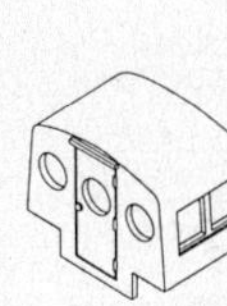
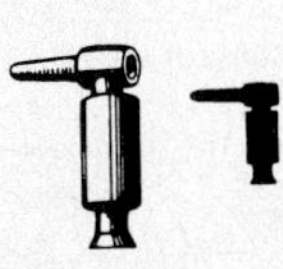

Tailgate (Brass) Passenger Standard
190-309
pkg(2) 3.25
(Illustration is half of actual size)

Wood Burning Style Stack with Spark Arresting Screen (circa 1860)
190-326
each 7.55

PRR Modern Dog House
190-452
7.95

Used on the prototype to create better combustion in the fire box, these jets add much detail to a modern locomotive.

Over-Fire Jets
190-239
set (16 pc) 6.45

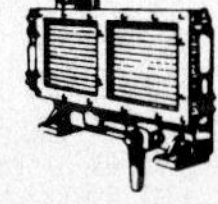
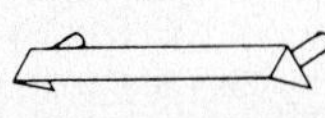

Water Scoop Set
190-2004   kit 7.55

Locomotive Radiator
190-226   each 2.55

Window Shade
190-382   pkg(2) 2.45

MUFFLERS

Exhaust w/Valve
190-222
each 2.45

Exhaust, Wilson
190-223
each 2.25

Scale
CAL-SCALE

HO SCALE (1/87)

Parts are lost wax brass castings unless noted. Black silhouette illustrations are approximately full size.

NUMBER BOARDS

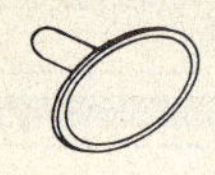

Oval
190-389
pkg(2) 2.15

Right & Left Set
190-260
set 2.95

NUMBER PLATES

Pennsylvania
190-238   pkg(3) 1.85

Baltimore & Ohio
190-244   pkg(2) 1.85

Plain
190-245   pkg(3) 1.85

PILOTS

Commonwealth Drop Coupler
190-261   each 6.55
Used on 4-8-4's Big Boy & Challenger

Pennsylvania
190-387
each 5.95

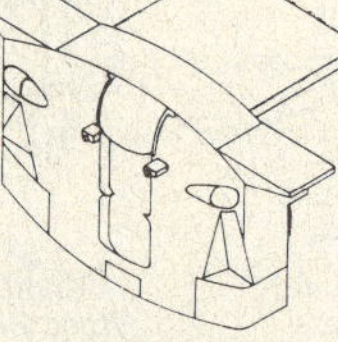

General Steel Castings, w/Coupler
190-298   each 6.55

Pennsylvania Slatted w/Stops
190-388   each 5.95

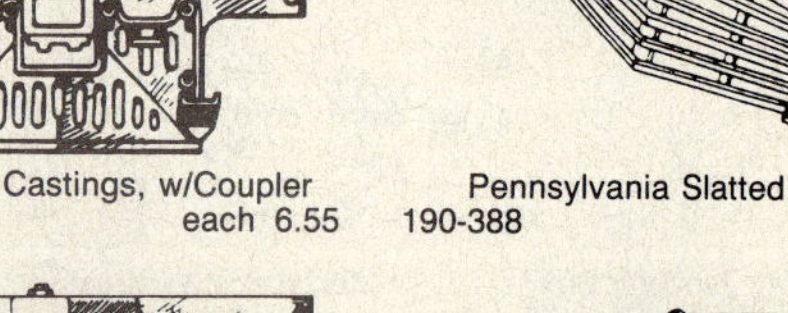

Commonwealth Swing Coupler
190-296   pkg(5 pc) 6.55

Wood, 5'6", Canadian Pacific
190-336   each 6.55

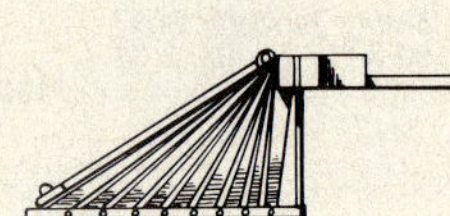

Commonwealth Cast Late Version
190-344   w/couplers   each 6.55

Wood, 4'6", Union Pacific
190-340   each 6.55

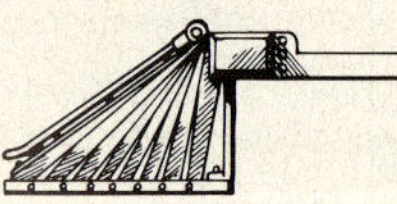

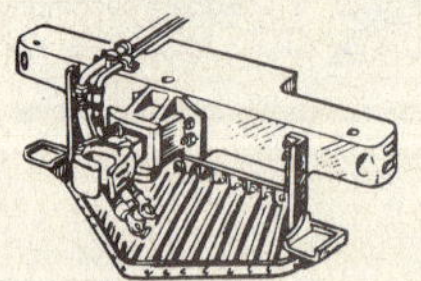

Standard Boiler Tube
190-315   each 6.55

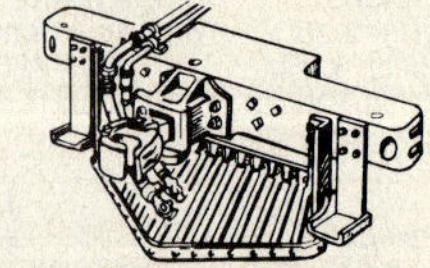

Boiler Tube w/Coupler & Hoses
Sheet Metal Setup Guard
190-318   each 6.55

POWER REVERSE

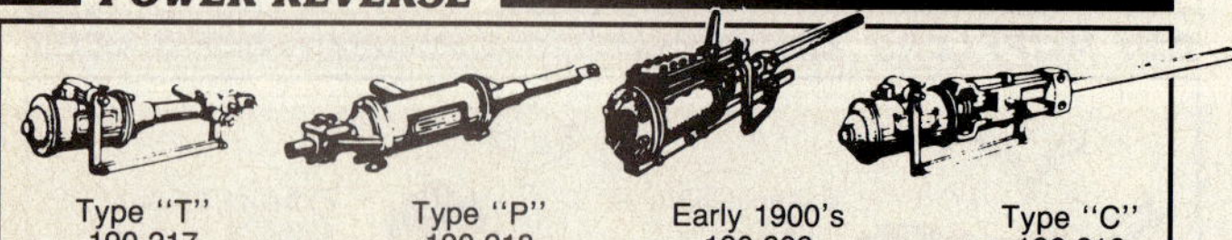

Type "T"
190-217
each 3.25

Type "P"
190-218
each 2.75

Early 1900's
190-303
each 3.25

Type "C"
190-216
each 3.25

POWER REVERSE (continued)

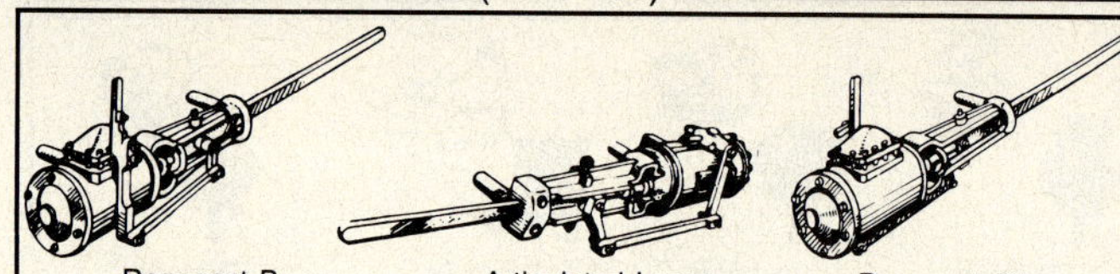

Ragonnet B
190-330   each 3.25

Articulated Locos
190-297   each 3.25

Ragonnet B1
190-332   each 3.25

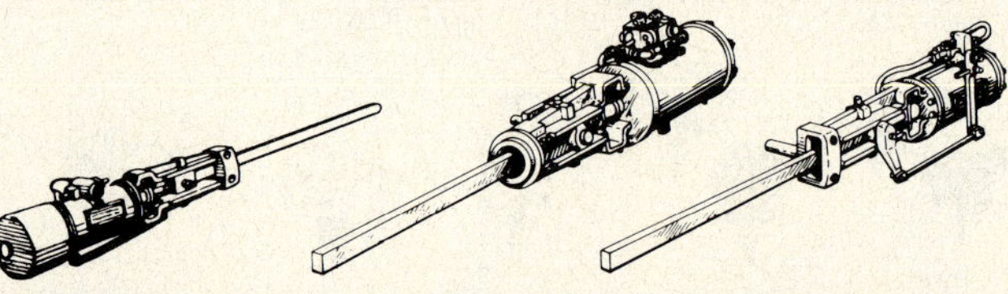

Pennsylvania Modern
190-237   each 3.25

Large Reverse Gear
Rear Facing
190-363   each 3.25

Std Reverse Gear (Rear)
190-360   each 3.25
Typical use small engines

SHIELDS

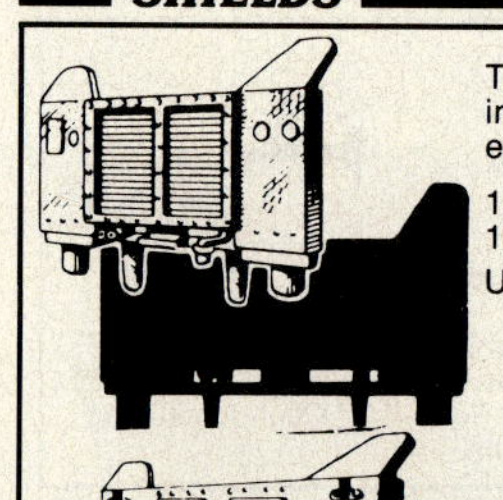

The Shields are available separate or in kits containing pump mounting brackets, radiator casting and equalizing reservoir.

190-267   7'3" Shield   each 4.25
190-2006 7'3" Shield Kit   each 7.35
Used on conventional sized locomotives.

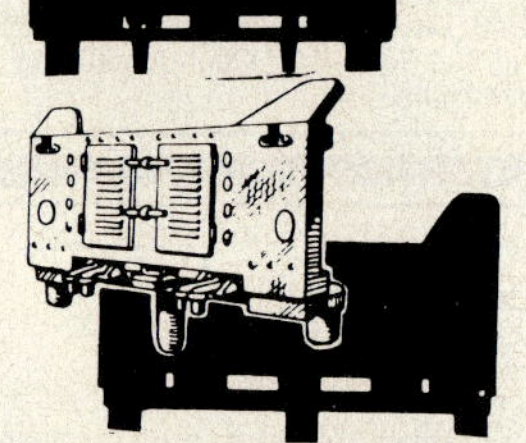

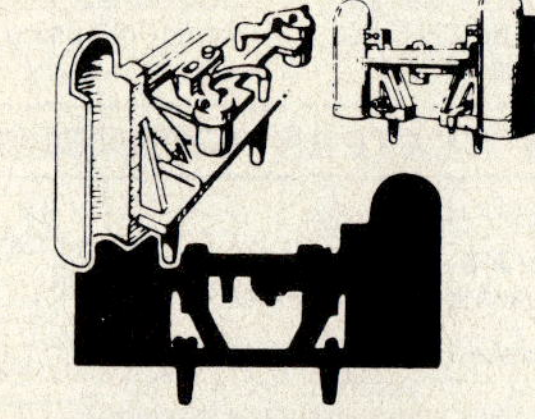

190-266   7'9" Shield   each 4.25
190-2005 7'9" Shield Kit   each 7.35
Used on UP "Challengers", "Big Boys" and other large modern locomotives.

7'3" Air Pump Shield
190-259   each 5.15
Used on conventional sized modern locomotives.

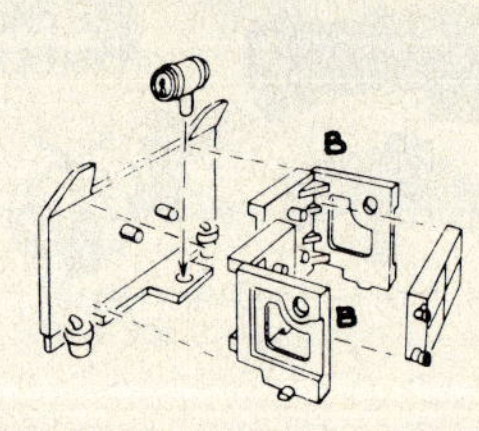

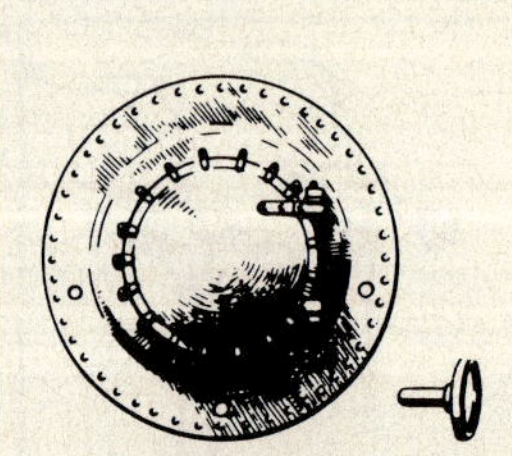

The brackets "B" are designed for the #240 pumps. However, any manufacturer's pumps of this type may be used.

If you wish to go to this detail, the pipes can be fabricated with standard brass handrail wire. The prototype pipes are 2" OD.

SMOKE BOX FRONTS

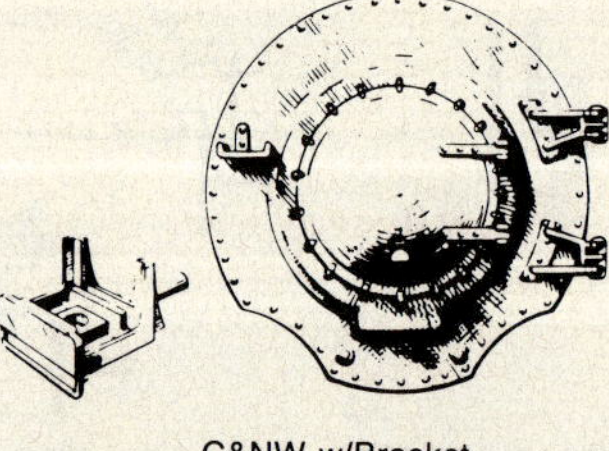

USRA Type, 81" Diameter
Complete w/Number Plate
190-243   each 4.05

C&NW w/Bracket
190-278   each 3.95

HO Scale (CAL-SCALE)

HO SCALE (1/87)

Parts are lost wax brass castings unless noted. Black silhouette illustrations are approximately full size.

SMOKE BOX FRONTS

PRR Modern 7'6"
190-236 each 3.95
As used on K-5's and M-1's complete with number plate.

Harriman Type 86" Dia
190-242 each 4.05
Complete with number plate.

STEPS

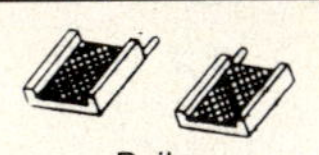

Boiler
190-377 pkg(2) 1.85

Passenger/Baggage Car
190-386 pkg(4) 5.75

Passenger Car Standard Era
190-356 pkg(4) 6.45

For FP-45 & F45
4 large & 1 small
190-449 pkg(5) 3.50

For PA, PB's & FA's
190-450 pkg(4) 3.50

STOKER ENGINES

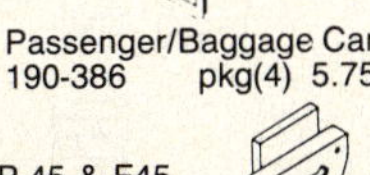

Standard Two Cylinder
190-224 set 4.25

Single Cylinder Duplex Type
190-254 each 2.95

TENDER HATCHES

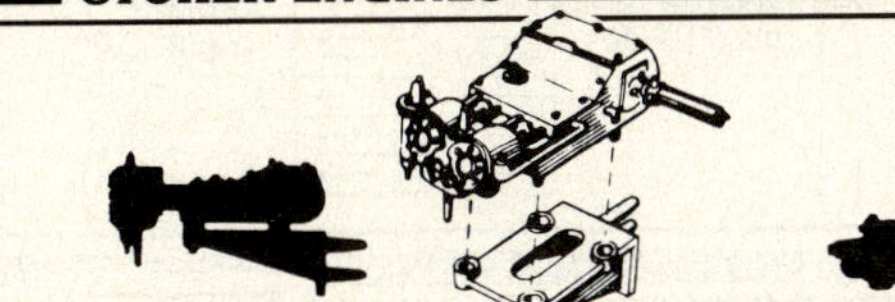

Tool Box, Tender
190-364 each 3.65
Under slung between trucks

Rounded Base
190-233 each 2.95

Large
190-231 each 3.85

Loco Tool Box
190-295 each 2.75

Rectangular Base
190-232 each 2.95

THROTTLES

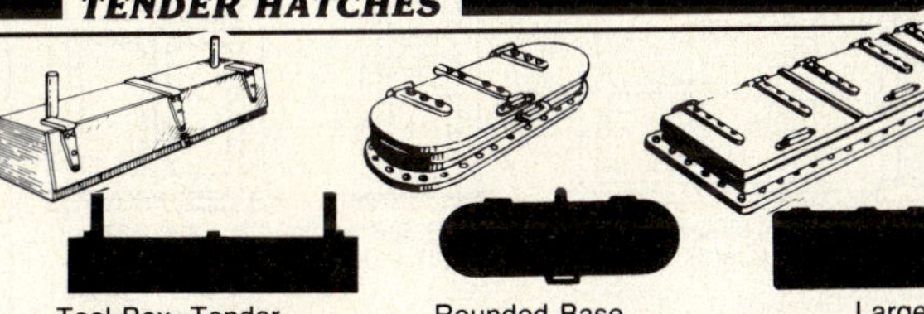

Front End w/Rods & Guides
190-268 set 2.95

Horizontal Early Engines
190-369 each 2.75

Dome, Mounts on Side of Steam Dome
190-376 each 2.25

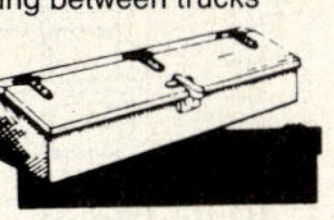

Front End, Medium & Large #2
190-371 each 3.25

Front End, Medium & Large #1
190-370 each 3.25

TRAIN CONTROL

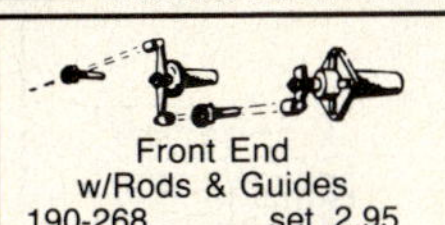

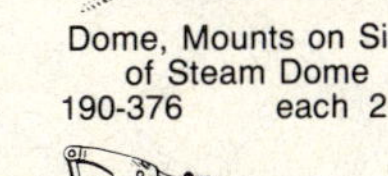

Trailing Truck Bearing Plates
190-390 pair 2.45

Transmitter Loco & Caboose
190-391 each 3.25

Steam Turret Medium & Large Locos
190-323 each 5.15

TRAIN CONTROL (continued)

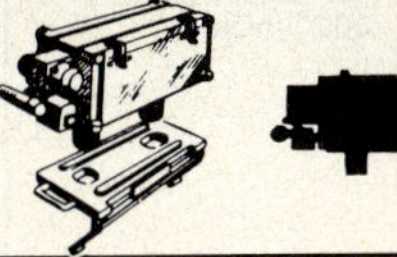

Train Control Box w/Bracket, Union 3-Speed
190-252 each 4.95

The Union 3-Way Train Control Box is the "brain" of automatic train control. It may be mounted on the boiler, under or on the walks, either side, or on the pilot deck.

UNDERBODY

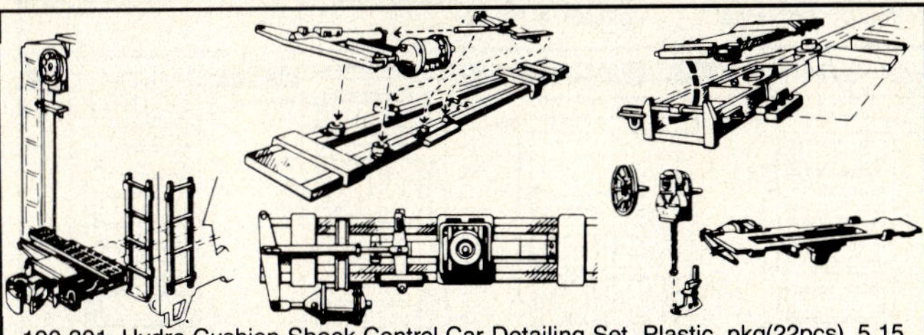

190-301 Hydra-Cushion Shock Control Car Detailing Set, Plastic pkg(22pcs) 5.15
This kit is designed to complement Athearn, MDC and Silver Streak Golden Spike Series cars. Set includes:

Coupler pockets	Coupler Pocket Lids	Air Line Pipe
Air Cylinder/Slack Adjuster	Small Lever & Piston	Central Frame Cover
End Frame Covers	Hydra Cylinder	3-Piece Brake Wheel Set
Lift Bar Brackets	Special End Walks	End Ladders
Side Ladders		

VALVES

Check Valve Nathan Double Top Feed
190-251 ea 2.25

Pop-Valves, Large
190-247 set(6 pc) 1.85
modern steam engine

Check Valve, Vertical
190-265 pair 2.45

Boiler Check Valve w/Stop Valve
190-253 pair 2.45

Globe Valve & Drain Cocks (Assorted)
190-314 pkg(13) 4.25

Globe Valve 2 & 3"
190-361 pkg(4) 3.25

Large (Left Hand) Starter Valve
190-293 each 2.95

Small (Right & Left Hand) Starter Valves
190-294 pair 3.25

VAPOR TRAPS

Steam Vapor Traps Passenger Cars
190-350 pkg(2) 2.75

Vapor Traps Streamline Cars
190-358 pkg(2) 3.25

WATER PUMP

Low Water Alarm
190-333 each 2.95

Fairbanks, Morse Steam Driven, w/Bracket, Valve & Hose Reel
190-287 set 5.15

WHEELSETS

Nickel plated, insulated on one side only for electrical pick-up. 3/32" axle w/1/16" diameter shoulder.

36" Nonmagnetic
190-453 pkg(4) 3.95

33" Nonmagnetic
190-454 pkg(4) 3.95

WHISTLES

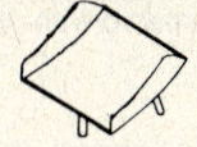

Large, Modern Type
190-250 ea 1.85
Mounted on boiler proper or on smoke box by stack.

Whistle Shield
190-378 ea 2.15

Whistles, Asstd
190-339 pkg(3) 3.55

Saturated Steam w/Steam Pipe
190-307 ea 3.25

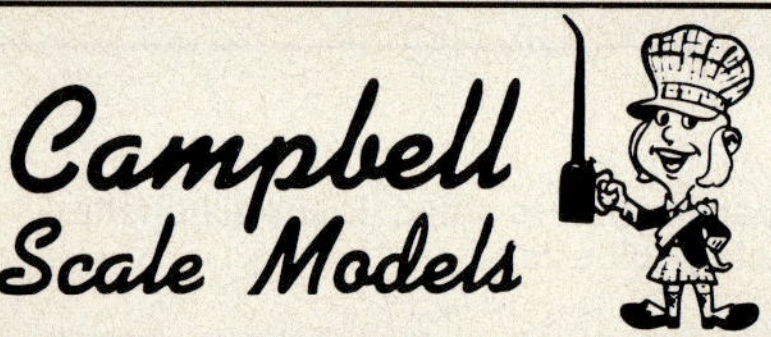

Campbell Scale Models

HO SCALE (1/87)

Most of these products are non-period and can be used on modern, Old West or Victorian era buildings. Windows, doors and trim are molded in white plastic unless noted. Illustrations are approximately full size, except where enlarged to show detail.

CORRUGATED ALUMINUM

HO Scale Feet
.002" thick

200-801 7.5" x 8'	pkg(9) 4.15	200-804 7.5" x 4'	pkg(10) 4.15
200-802 7.5" x 10'	pkg(7) 4.15	200-805 7.5" x 6'	pkg(9) 4.15
200-803 7.5" x 12'	pkg(6) 4.15		

DOORS

200-916 pkg(3) 2.00
200-919 pkg(2) 2.00
200-917 pkg(2) 2.00
200-918 pkg(2) 2.00

200-912 pkg(3) 2.00
200-913 pkg(3) 2.00
200-914 pkg(2) 2.00
200-915 pkg(3) 2.00

200-941 Victorian Vent (not illustrated) pkg(2) 2.00

MISCELLANEOUS

Brass Light Shades
200-255 pkg(6) 3.00
Dealers: Must order dealer pack of 6.

Nuts & Bolts
200-925 pkg(60) 2.00
Gunmetal gray

Black Chain 12" Length
200-256 3.50
36 links per inch
Dealers: Must order dealer pack of 6.

Air Cooler Evaporator
200-938 pkg(2) 2.00

Hinges, Large
200-935 pkg(8) 2.00
Black plastic

Smoke Stack
200-934 pkg(2) 2.00
Black plastic

OIL DRUMS

200-251 Plain	pkg(12) 3.00	200-253 Black	pkg(12) 3.50
200-252 Silver	pkg(12) 3.50	200-254 Red	pkg(12) 3.50

SHINGLES

Profile shingles come in a long roll and are back coated with glue for easy application.

200-800 Profile Shingles (100 foot roll) 5.95
Matte-surfaced, natural wood color, edge notched. Enough shingle material to cover approximately 9 x 12" roof area.

STRUCTURAL DETAILS

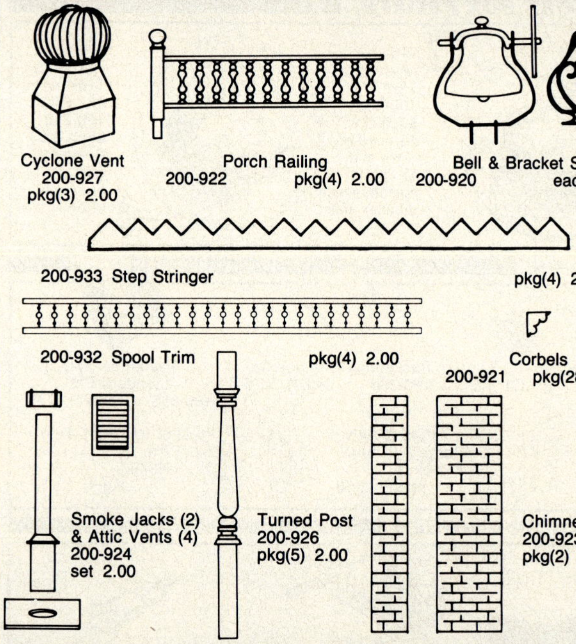

Cyclone Vent
200-927 pkg(3) 2.00

Porch Railing
200-922 pkg(4) 2.00

Bell & Bracket Set
200-920 each 2.00

200-933 Step Stringer pkg(4) 2.00

200-932 Spool Trim pkg(4) 2.00

Corbels
200-921 pkg(28) 2.00

Smoke Jacks (2) & Attic Vents (4)
200-924 set 2.00

Turned Post
200-926 pkg(5) 2.00

Chimneys
200-923 pkg(2) 2.00

WINDOWS

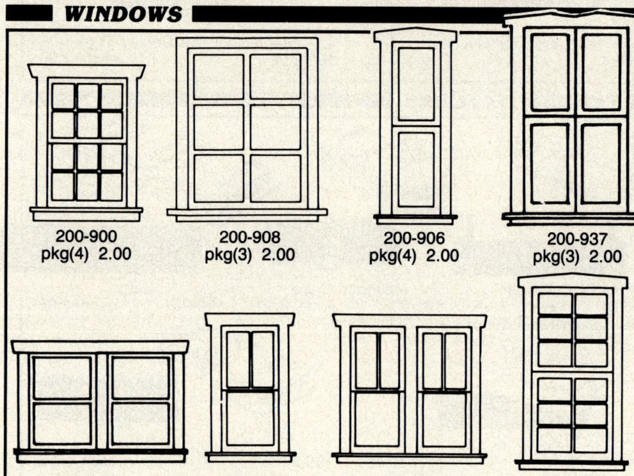

200-900 pkg(4) 2.00
200-908 pkg(3) 2.00
200-906 pkg(4) 2.00
200-937 pkg(3) 2.00

200-911 pkg(3) 2.00
200-905 pkg(4) 2.00
200-904 pkg(3) 2.00
200-907 pkg(4) 2.00

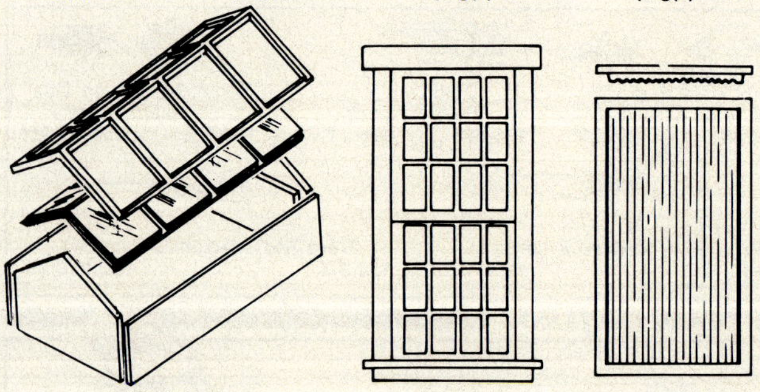

Skylight
200-909 pkg(2) 2.00

200-929 pkg(2) 2.00

Skylight, Corrugated
200-910 pkg(4) 2.00

(not illustrated)
200-939 Large Victorian pkg(3) 2.00
200-940 Small Victorian pkg(3) 2.00

 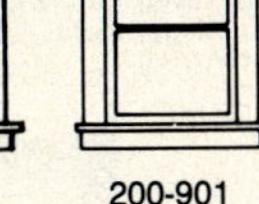 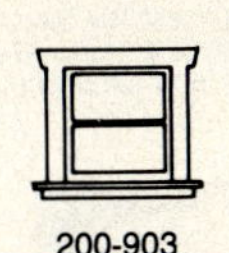 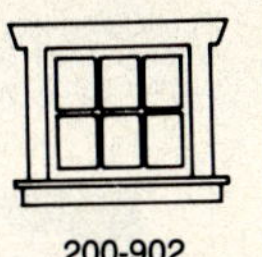

Campbell Scale Models

HO SCALE
Illustrations are approximate size except where enlarged to show detail.

WINDOWS (continued)

200-936	200-901	200-903	200-902
pkg(3) 2.00	pkg(5) 2.00	pkg(6) 2.00	pkg(5) 2.00

WOODEN BARRELS

Made from turned hardwood, with raised trim and bands.

| 200-249 Red | pkg(12) 3.50 |
| 200-250 Plain | pkg(12) 3.00 |

Builders In Scale
Fine Craft Models

HO SCALE (1/87)

CHAIN

| 169-250 | Black, 40 links per inch | pkg(18") 2.98 |
| 169-251 | Natural Brass, 40 links per inch | pkg(18") 2.59 |

VENETIAN BLINDS

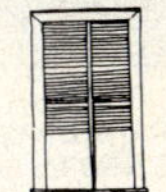 

Venetian Blinds
169-503
set(6)   3.29
Angle of slats can be adjusted.
Set of six different size blinds.

ORE SKIPS

Mine Hoist
w/Ore Skip
169-609
14.49

ROUNDHOUSE Products

HO SCALE (1/87)

Detail parts are plastic unless noted.

HANDRAIL

| 480-2977 Locomotive Post | pkg(12) 1.75 |
| 480-2978 Caboose (curved, angled & platform) | pkg(12) 1.50 |

LOCO DETAILING SET

Set includes molded plastic detail parts illustrated here. (Less cab and boiler).

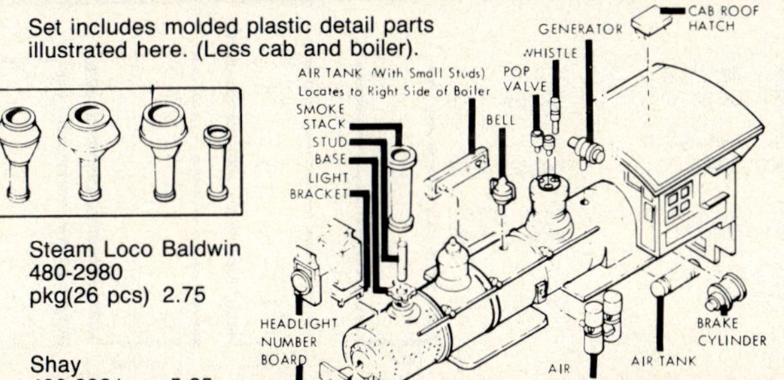

Steam Loco Baldwin
480-2980
pkg(26 pcs) 2.75

Shay
480-2981   5.25

MARKER / HEADLIGHT JEWELS

480-2961	Red	pkg(12) 1.25
480-2962	Green	pkg(12) 1.25
480-2963	Amber	pkg(12) 1.25
480-2964	White	pkg(12) 1.25
480-2970	Headlight, 3/16" diameter	pkg(2) 1.50
480-2971	Headlight, 5/32" diameter	pkg(2) .75

MARKERS

| 480-2956 | Classification Lamp | 1.75 |

Includes 2 marker lamps and assorted jewels.

MISCELLANEOUS

480-2959	Screw Assortment	pkg(36) 1.50
480-2990	AB Brake Set	pkg(3) 1.50
480-2991	Oval Hopper Ends	pkg(6) 1.00
480-2992	Box Car Doors 6'	pkg(4) 1.50
480-2993	Peak Ends	6 each 1.50
480-2999	50' Clerestory Passenger Car Roof	each 2.25

VALVE GEAR KITS

Brass and plastic detail parts.

| 480-2841 | 2-6-2 Prairie | 7.50 |
| 480-2840 | 4-4-2 Atlantic | 7.50 |

WALTHERS

HO SCALE (1/87)

COIL SPRING

■ **LTD QTY AVAILABLE** ■
945-3005 Metal   pkg(20) 1.98

JEWELS

■ **LIMITED QUANTITY AVAILABLE** ■

MARKER JEWELS (.062" diameter)

949-5291	Amber	pkg(12) 1.98
949-5293	Clear	pkg(12) 1.98
949-5295	Green	pkg(12) 1.98
949-5296	Red	pkg(12) 1.98

TEMP-LOW™

THE "LOW TEMP" METAL THAT MELTS IN HOT WATER (158° to 190° F)

- Weighting Locomotives. Just melt and pour in. Won't disturb soldered detail.
- Casting-Make your own castings in cardboard, rubber or plaster molds.
- Use as a filler to support tubing while bending.

949-525 Temp-Low™   pkg(approx 3 oz) 4.98

CANNON & COMPANY
DIESEL COMPONENTS

HO SCALE (1/87)

Injection molded kits and parts for major structural components of EMD locomotives.

Southern Pacific SD45T-2 #9231 displays the potential of Cannon & Company diesel components; kit bashed on a modified Athearn SD40T-2. The following components are correct for any SD45T-2 model:

191-1001, 1002, 1005, 1006, and 1009 EMD Hood Doors
191-1103 81″ Low Short Hood Kit
191-1304 Inertial Filter Screens
191-1202 Cab Sub Base Kit
191-1203 EMD Optional Doors SP "Split" Equipment Doors
191-1501 Thinwall Dash 2 Cab Kit

BLOWER HOUSING

EMD 50/60 Angled
191-1601
pkg(2) 3.50

EMD DIESEL CAB KITS

Designed to fit various EMD locomotives. Kits include two styles of fronts, separate doors, handles, side windows and sunshade brackets. The cabs feature prototypically correct roof contour, reversed louvers and separate numberboard assembly.

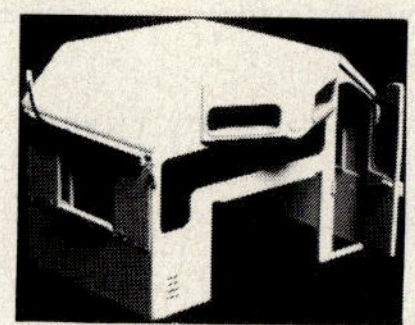

191-1501   Dash-2   5.95
Modern cab with "L" window front, used on EMD Dash-2 models since 1972 & current 50/60 series engines. Fits Athearn SD40-2, SD40T-2, GP38-2, GP40-2 and GP50.

191-1502   "35" line   5.95
Used on EMD locos built from 1964 to 1971. Fits Athearn GP35, SDP40, SD45, Atlas GP38 and 40, and Kato SD-40 (locos require some modification).

EMD Switcher Cab Kit Early
191-1503   8.50
Kit #1503 features the arched front windows and large air intake used on the early SW1/NW2 and Phase I SW7, as produced by EMD from 1939 to 1950.

EMD Switcher Cab Kit Late
191-1504   8.50
Kit #1504 has the squared windows and battery box details as seen on Phase II SW7's through the last of the SW1200's, produced from 1950 - 1966.

EMD HIGH SHORT HOOD

191-1101   Conversion   6.95
Shortnose version for EMD GP and SD35 thru 50 Series units. Includes clear numberboard.

EMD LONG HOOD END

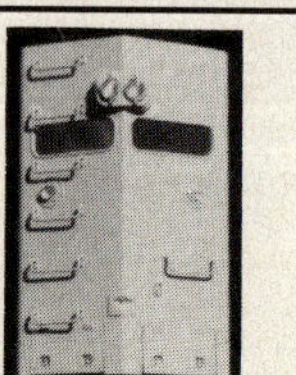

191-1151   Conversion   pkg(2) 3.50
EMD Long Hood End for scale hood width 35 Line units. Fits GP28, GP35, SD28 and SD35

LOW SHORT HOOD KITS

Conversion kits duplicate the low short hoods found on EMD locos from 1963 to the present. Each includes at least 40 parts to cover the many variations of brake gear, marker lights, vents and other appliances. All parts are molded in light gray styrene.

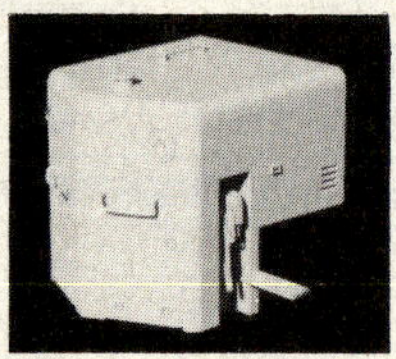

191-1103   81″   6.95
Introduced in 1963, used on all hood units through early Dash-2's.

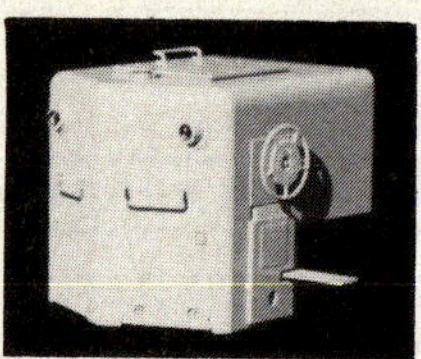

191-1104   88″   6.95
Introduced in 1977, this is the standard nose for all current EMD units.

191-1105   116″   6.95
The first of the longer "snoots," used on SP tunnel motors and early UP SD40-2's.

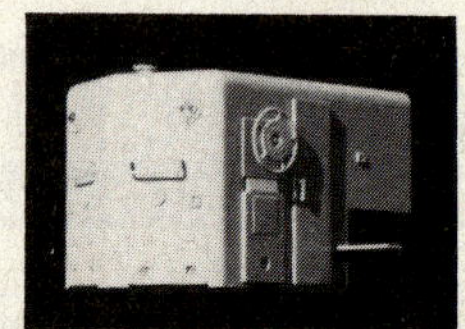

191-1106   123″   6.95
The latest version of the "snoot," used on ATSF and UP SD40-2's, plus SP and SSW SD 40T-2's.

EMD HOOD UNIT DOORS

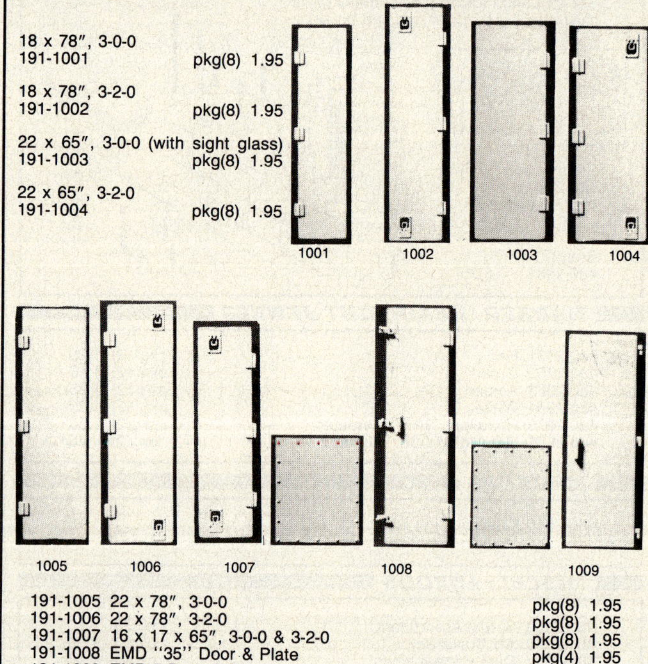

18 x 78″, 3-0-0
191-1001   pkg(8) 1.95

18 x 78″, 3-2-0
191-1002   pkg(8) 1.95

22 x 65″, 3-0-0 (with sight glass)
191-1003   pkg(8) 1.95

22 x 65″, 3-2-0
191-1004   pkg(8) 1.95

1001   1002   1003   1004

1005   1006   1007   1008   1009

191-1005   22 x 78″, 3-0-0   pkg(8) 1.95
191-1006   22 x 78″, 3-2-0   pkg(8) 1.95
191-1007   16 x 17 x 65″, 3-0-0 & 3-2-0   pkg(8) 1.95
191-1008   EMD "35" Door & Plate   pkg(4) 1.95
191-1009   EMD-2 Door & Plate   pkg(4) 1.95

HATCHES

GP/SD38-2 Angled Filter
191-1901
each 2.95

EMD Low Nose Toilet Hatch
191-1102
pkg(4) 1.95

CANNON & COMPANY
DIESEL COMPONENTS

HO SCALE (1/87)

■ EMD CAB SUB BASE & OPTIONAL DOORS ■ NEW

These kits replace the entire structure under the cab and nose with enough parts to build two different sub bases including all prototype variations for the period covered. Photos show only some of the possible door arrangements. Optional doors are shown installed on appropriate sub bases.

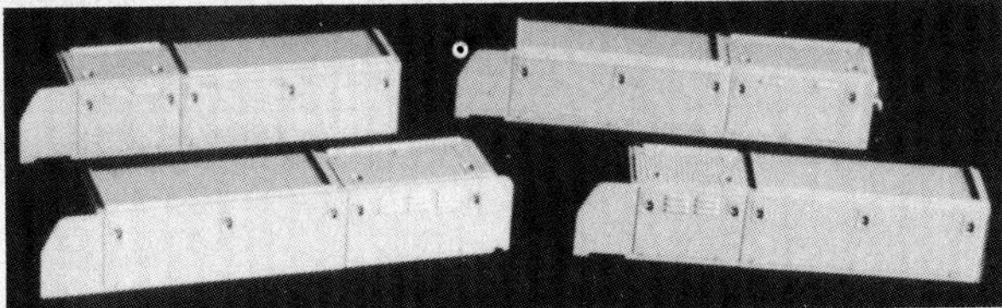

191-1201 All 35 Line and 40 Series Units   pkg(2pr) 6.95

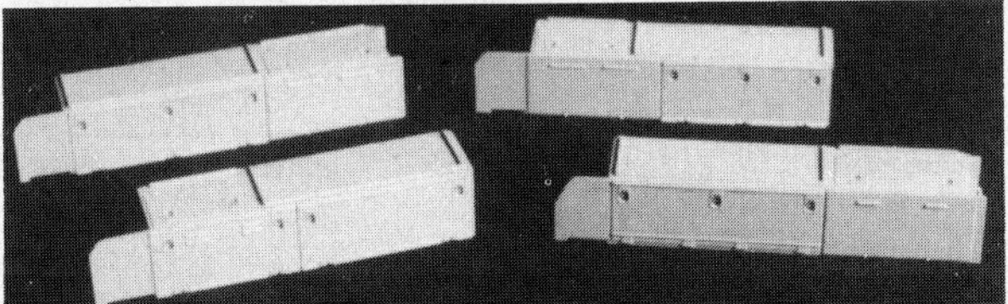

191-1202 All Dash 2 and 50/60 Series Units   pkg(2pr) 6.95

191-1203 SP "Split" Equipment Doors   pkg(6) 2.95

Conrail "Split" Battery Box Doors, Chessie "Mailslot" Battery Box Doors
191-1204   pkg(8) 2.95

■ SCREENS — INERTIAL FILTER ■

Late Dash-2 GP's
191-1301 pkg(4) 1.95

35 Line
191-1302 pkg(4) 2.95

For the post 1984 EMD SD40-2.
191-1305 pkg(4) 2.50

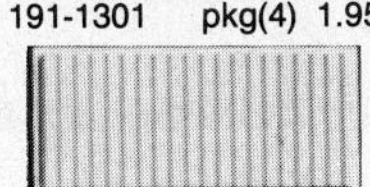

GP38, GP39, GP40 to early Dash-2, some SD39's, GP15-1, GP38-2, GP39-2, GP40-2 & SD38-2
191-1303 pkg(4) 2.50

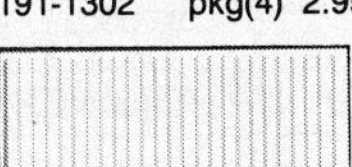

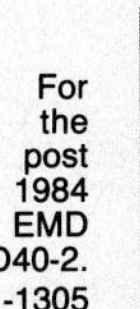

For the SD38, SD40, SD45 to early Dash 2, SD40-2, and SD45-2.
191-1304 pkg(4) 2.50

■ SCREENS — RADIATOR ■

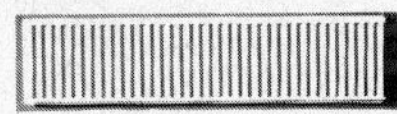

GP38-2, GP 39-2
191-1401   pkg(4) 2.50

Grill & Shutter Assembly, 35 Line
191-1402   pkg(4) 3.50

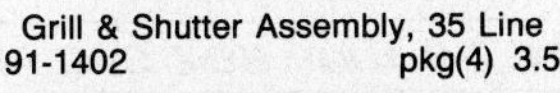

For the post 1976 EMD GP40-2 and SD40-2.
191-1403   pkg(4) 3.50

Grilles & Shutters for the EMD GP/SD40 to Early GP/SD40-2.
191-1404   pkg(4) 3.95

California Model Company

HO SCALE (1/87)
Illustrations are approximately 3/4 actual size.

■ CAR SEATS ■

700-160 Cast Metal	pkg(24)	3.25
700-161 Cast Metal	pkg(100)	10.95

■ CRATES & BARRELS ■

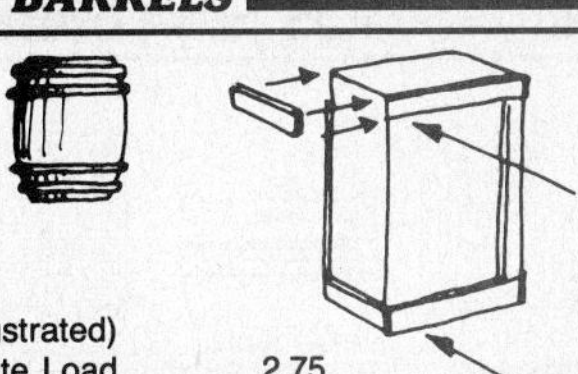

Barrels
700-513
pkg(6) 1.10

Wood Platform Crates
700-512
kit 2.25

(not illustrated)
700-431 Flat Car Crate Load   2.75
2 large and 1 small machinery crates.

■ DOORS ■

Sheet Metal
700-109
pkg(6) 1.75

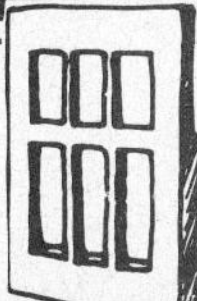

Baggage
3 panel type (brass)
700-188 pkg(2) 2.10

■ ICE ■

700-569 Ice 300lb Cakes   pkg(12) 2.25

■ MISCELLANEOUS ■

Dynamotor/Compressor (brass)
700-177   each 1.35

(not illustrated)
700-173 Motor Pulley Twin Groove   pkg(3) 3.95
700-146 Spring Drive Belt   pkg(6) 2.75

■ PILOTS ■

700-185 PE Standard Wood   2.75
700-184 PE Steel   2.75

■ STRUCTURAL DETAILS ■

5 Tread Steps (Wood)
700-106 pkg(6) 2.50

■ TRACTION DETAILS ■

Roof Traction Details (Brass)
700-183   set 1.35
(Roof mat, 2 small gongs & 2 retrievers)

■ WINDOWS ■

Windows printed on acetate sheets.

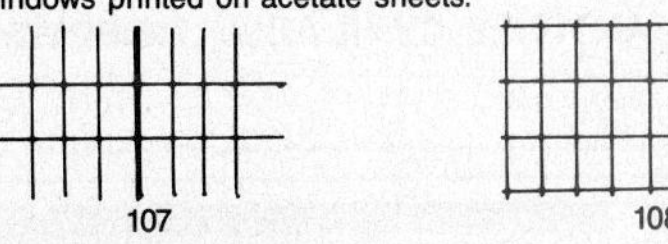

700-107 Industrial   each 1.10
700-108 Skylights   each 1.10
700-118 House   each 1.10

■ VENTS ■

Cast Roof
700-114 pkg(6) 3.10

Cast "A"
700-113 pkg(12) 3.10

HO SCALE (1/87)

Styrene parts with details cast in. Illustrations are not to scale.

BOILER FRONTS

197-31353	84" diameter	each 1.25
197-31359	72" diameter	each 1.25

CAR ENDS pair 1.25

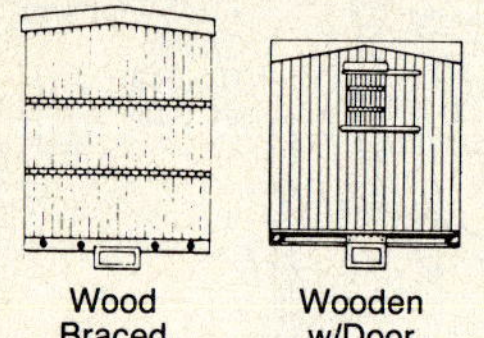
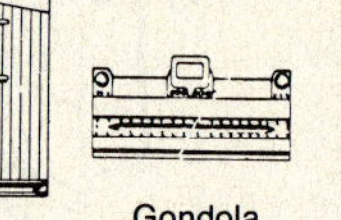
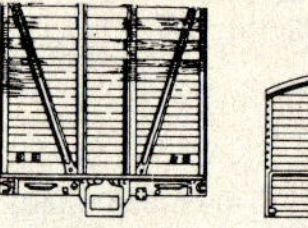
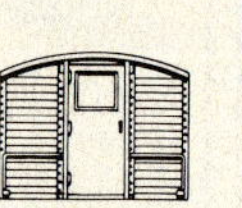

Wood Braced 197-31516
Wooden w/Door 197-31520
Gondola Pressed Steel 197-31166 pkg(4)
Stock Car Wooden 197-31271
Caboose Wooden 197-31206

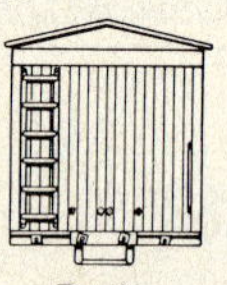

Reefer Wooden 197-31510
Low Peaked 197-31512
Medium Wooden 197-31521
Express Reefer 197-31540
Early Merchandise Steel 197-31558

Container Car, Wooden 197-31548
X-28 Auto Car, Steel 197-31552

(not illustrated)
197-31124 Tall Braced, Wooden
197-31223 Youngstown, Tall
197-31342 Union Pacific Photo Car
197-31504 Box Car, Flat Top

LIMITED QUANTITIES AVAILABLE

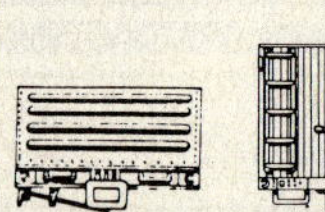
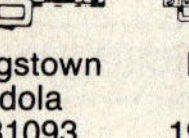
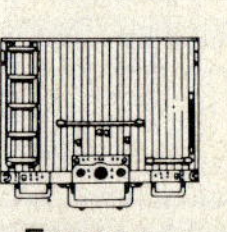
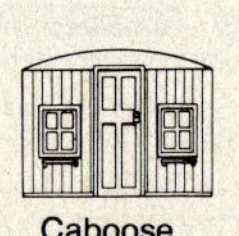
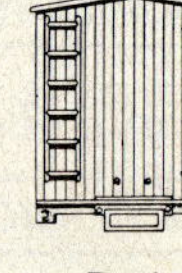

Youngstown Gondola 197-31093
Express Reefer 197-31549
Caboose Wooden 197-31066
Caboose Wooden 197-31250
Reefer Wooden 197-31509

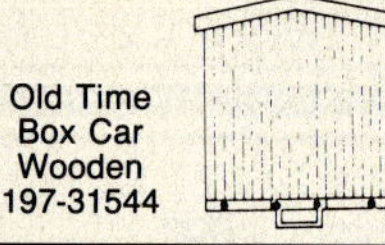

Old Time Box Car Wooden 197-31544

(not illustrated)
197-30006 Dreadnaught Reefer

CAR SIDES

197-30013	40' Steel Reefer Sides	pair 2.00
197-30204	40' Gondola Sides, Med Undec	pair 5.00

LIMITED QUANTITIES AVAILABLE

197-30204	40' Gondola Sides, Med Undec	pair 4.00

CONVERSION KITS

Parts are molded styrene.

197-32009 Passenger Vestibule — 9.00
Includes door and ends to modify MDC Overland combine into 50' RPO.

LIMITED QUANTITIES AVAILABLE

197-32310 33' Panel Hopper Side — 5.00
Fits Life-Like or Varney two-bay hoppers.

197-32527 50' Coach Sides — 5.00
Fits MDC Overland cars, allowing conversion to several styles of daycoach, Jim Crow, etc.

CUPOLAS

LIMITED QUANTITIES AVAILABLE

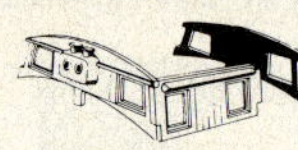

PRR, Old Time w/Signal Lamp 197-31078 2.00
Standard Slope Side 197-31126 2.00

DOORS pkg(2) 1.25 (unless noted)

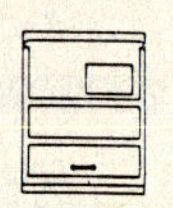

6' Low Steel 197-31302

(not illustrated)
197-31222 Corrugated Mtl pkg(2) 1.25
197-31600 Semi-Trailer Rear 1.25

LIMITED QUANTITIES AVAILABLE

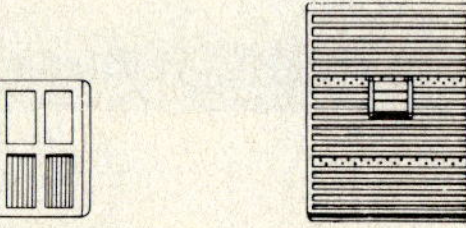

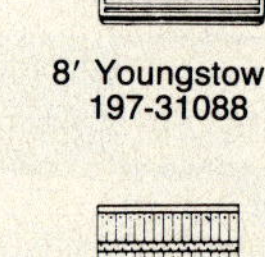

4' Wooden 197-31149
8' Youngstown 197-31088
Caboose/ Baggage 197-31233
Caboose End Door 197-31144

5'4" Wooden 197-31148
6 x 9' Wooden 197-31191
Creco Steel 197-31216
6' Youngstown 197-31217

Box Car Wooden 197-31364
3' Wooden 197-31309

(not illustrated)
31023 Reefer Wood pkg(2) 1.25

HATCHES

LIMITED QUANTITIES AVAILABLE

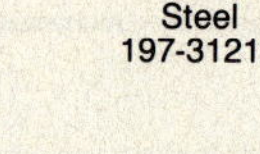

Old Time Reefer 197-31019 pkg(4) 1.25
Ice, Wooden 197-31038 pkg(4) 1.25

LATERAL ROOFWALK

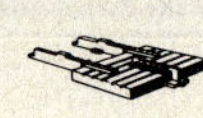

Wooden 197-31082 pkg(4) 1.25

MISCELLANEOUS

197-32010	Smoke Deflector	each 2.00
197-32020	Box Car Details	each 2.00

LIMITED QUANTITIES AVAILABLE

197-30009	Dummy Coupler AAR	pkg(6) 1.25
197-31073	Turnbuckle	pkg(18) 1.25
197-32021	B&O Wagon Top Car Body	each 7.00

PS-1 40' BOX CAR ASSEMBLY

LIMITED QUANTITIES AVAILABLE

197-30001	Steel Car Roof w/Walk	each 1.25
197-30008	Box Car End	pair 1.25
197-30011	40' Box Car Sides	pair 2.00

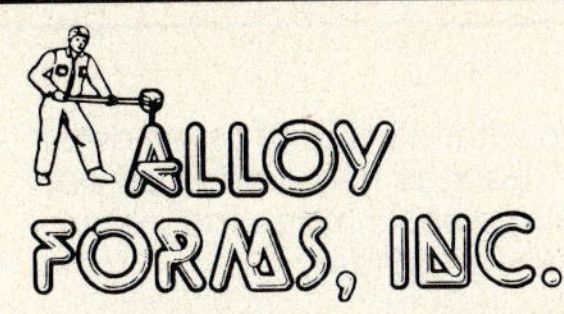

ALLOY FORMS, INC.

HO SCALE (1/87)

Kits feature unpainted metal castings. Illustrations are not to scale.

AIR CONDITIONERS

(not illustrated)
Roof A/C
119-2016   3.95

Window
119-2007
pkg(7) 2.95

3004

DRUMS & BARRELS

55 Gallon—Used Looking
119-2002   pkg(7) 2.95

55 Gallon—New Condition
119-2003   pkg(7) 2.95

(not illustrated)
119-2011 Barrel Rack Set   each 5.95

JUNK YARD DETAILS

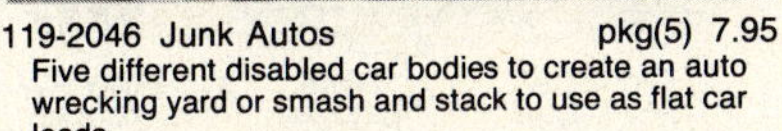

119-2046 Junk Autos   pkg(5) 7.95
Five different disabled car bodies to create an auto wrecking yard or smash and stack to use as flat car loads.

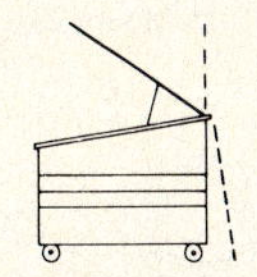

Rubbish Bin
119-2001   2.95
Includes brass dumpster top.

119-2010 A-Frame w/Chain Hoist   4.95
Includes brass parts and copper chain.

24″ Roll-Off Body
119-2036   kit 5.95

MISCELLANEOUS

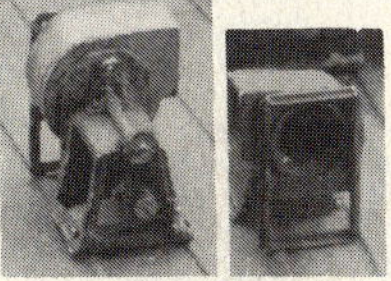

Squirrel Cage
Exhaust Blower
119-2015   3.95

Hydraulic Pallet Jack
119-2006   2.95

Wooden Step Ladder
119-2014   2.95

Work Table Set
119-2012
(3 pieces)   5.95

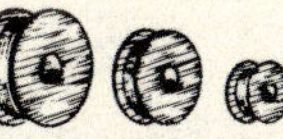

Wooden Reels
w/Cable
119-2017
pkg(3) 2.95

Diamond
Plate Sheet
119-2005
pkg(7) 2.95

(not illustrated)
119-1000 24″ Copper Chain (36 links per inch)   each 2.95
119-2013 Corrugated Iron Fence   kit 9.95
119-2034 Roof Top Water Tower   each 4.95
119-2048 Dog Fence   pkg(2) 2.95
119-3085 Air Tank with Mounting Bracket   each 2.95

VEHICLE DETAILS

CAB DETAILS

Air Deflector, Conventional
119-3004   each 2.95

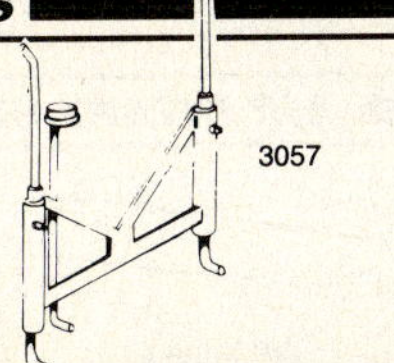

(not illustrated)
119-3060 Mirrors, GMC (plastic)   pkg(2) 1.95
119-3065 Mack Bulldog Radiator Caps (brass)   pkg(3) 2.95
119-3066 Mirrors (etched brass for B-61)   pair 1.95
119-3069 1/4 Fenders for Truck Tractors   each 1.95
119-3081 Sun Visors for B-42/61 Macks   pkg(3) 1.95

EXHAUST PIPE & ACCESSORIES

Dual w/Air Cleaner for Athearn Freightliner
119-3057   each 1.95

3057

(not illustrated)
119-3054 Dual   each 2.95
119-3063 Dual w/"Snorkel" Air Cleaner   each 1.95

GAS TANKS

119-3050 Rectangular with Steps R&L   each 2.95
119-3051 Cylindrical   pair 1.95
119-3067 Gas Tank for B-42/61   pair 1.95
119-3082 Round with Step   pkg(2) 1.95

MISCELLANEOUS

119-3059 Modern Cab Seat   pair 1.95
119-3068 Mud Flaps   2 pair 1.95
119-3076 Radiator Guards   pkg(2) 1.95
119-3087 Hose Reel & Fire Extinguisher   pkg(2) 6.95
119-3089 Truck Loading Boom   each 4.95
119-3092 Oil Cooler & Oil Filter   pkg(4) 2.95
119-3098 Mirrors, Autocar Set (brass)   each 1.95

CENTRAL VALLEY

HO SCALE

Parts are injection molded, black plastic styrene. Illustrations are not to scale.

BRAKE SHOE END BEAM

210-1124 Brake Shoe End Beam   each 2.49
Includes parts for one pair each of 6-wheel and 4-wheel CV passenger trucks featuring the 4-wheel style. The parts can also be adapted to fit 6-wheel trucks and other truck brands.

UNDERFRAME KIT

210-1000 Steel   pkg(3) 4.95

DEPOTS BY JOHN

CUSTOM BUILT STRUCTURES IN SCALE

NEW
HO SCALE (1/87)

AIR CONDITIONER

87-109 Window Air Conditioner Kit   pkg(2) 3.50
Wood, metal grill & foil

Custom Finishing

HO SCALE (1/87)

Add a new dimension to your models with this line of brass detail parts for locos and passenger cars. Each is finely detailed and ready for installation. Most items include basic mounting instructions and can be attached using ACC or solder.

AIRHORNS, LESLIE

  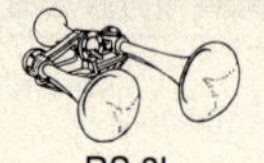

RS-25 Single Chime
247-219   2.29

RSM-25-2R Double Chime
247-220   2.79

RSL-3L Three Chime
247-221   3.69

RS-3L Three Chime
247-222   3.69

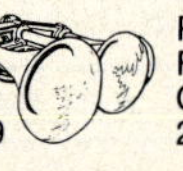 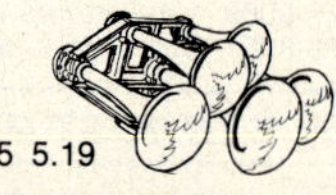

RSU-3L Three Chime
247-223   3.69

RSU-3C Three Chime
247-224   3.69

RS-5T Five Chime
247-225   5.19

AIR INTAKE SNOW SHIELD

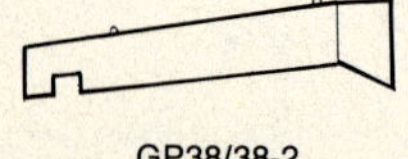

GP38/38-2 Short notch (2 piece set)
247-265   8.95

GP38/38-2 Long notch (2 piece set)
247-266   8.95

GP38-2 (2 piece set)
247-270   8.95

SD40/SD40-2 Short notch (2 piece set)
247-271   8.95

SD40/SD40-2 Long notch, (2 piece set)
247-272   8.95

AIR PUMP GOVERNORS

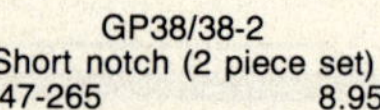

Cored for use with .018″ wire

Westinghouse AD
247-156   pair 2.59

Westinghouse SD
247-157   pair 2.59

AIR RESERVOIRS

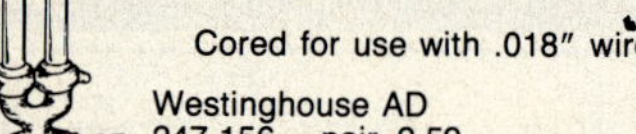

12′ Roof Top
247-235
pkg(2) 4.95

Extended Range Fuel Tank and Air Reservoir (Fits Athearn SW-7)
247-290   pkg(4) 3.29

ALCO RS SERIES LOCO PARTS

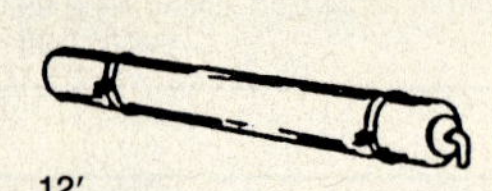 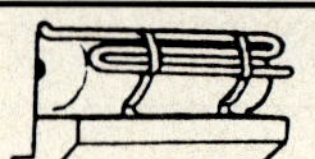

Turbo Stack
247-122   3.09
Use to simulate engines with the original aircooler or rebuilt with turbochargers.

Steam Generator Stack
247-151   2.69

Cooling Coils
247-152
pair 4.19
Commonly used on passenger service engines.

Hand Brake Chain Guide
247-147
pkg(6) 5.19

 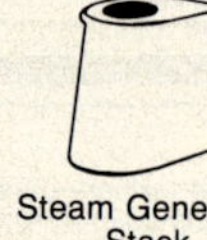

Horn
247-120
each 2.39

RS-2/3 Curved Grab Irons
247-205
pkg(10) 2.69

Steam Generator Intake
247-206
pkg(2) 1.59

RS1/RS3 Steam Generator Stack
247-207
pkg(2) 1.59

RS11 Steam Generator Stack Set
247-211   2.39

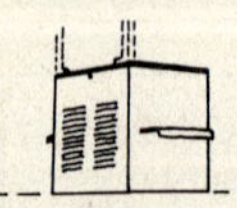 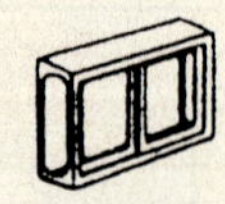 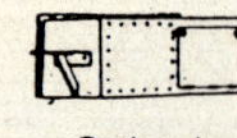 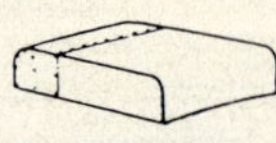

RS3 Lighting Box
247-212   3.09

Extended Vision Side Windows
247-239
(pr) 5.69

Optional Equipment Box
247-245
3.59

Winterization Hatch RS2/3's CP Recirculating Type
247-261
4.98

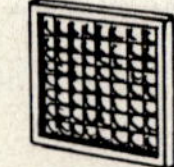 

Car Body Filters (12 pieces)
247-268
9.98

Extended Height Turbo Cooled Exhaust Stack
247-269
each   2.59

ALCO FA SERIES LOCO PARTS

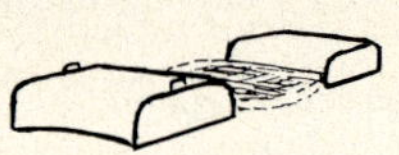 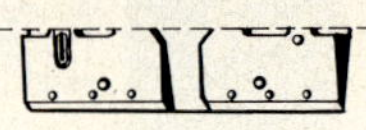 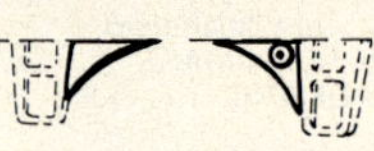

Split Winterization Hatches, CP Style (fits Life-Like FA-2)
247-259   set 9.95

Fuel Tank Skirts (FA-2) Left & Right Pair
247-262   set 9.98

EMD/MLW F-B Unit End Step Skirts (Passenger Units)
247-263   pkg(4) 5.29

BELLS

  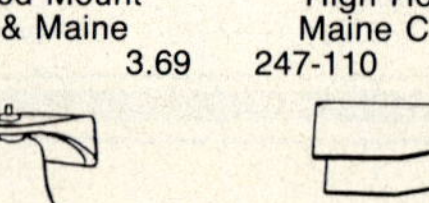  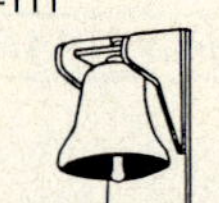

High Hood Mount Boston & Maine
247-109   3.69

High Hood Mount Maine Cntl Type 1
247-110   3.69

High Hood Mount Maine Cntl Type 2
247-111   3.69

Side Mount Bell
247-137   2.69

Bell Hood Mounted
247-230   3.09

Bell Cab Mounted
247-231   3.09

Dual Lever
247-138
2.69

Boiler Side Mount
247-139   2.79

Old Time New Haven
247-140   3.09

Hood
247-246
3.09

EMD SW
247-250
2.79

CONVERSION KIT

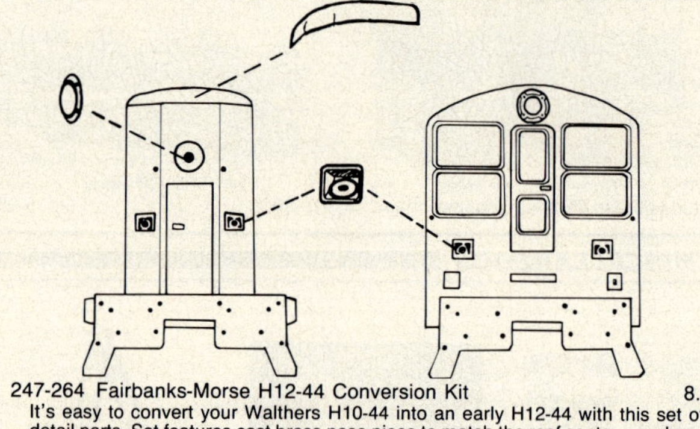

247-264 Fairbanks-Morse H12-44 Conversion Kit   8.79

It's easy to convert your Walthers H10-44 into an early H12-44 with this set of detail parts. Set features cast brass nose piece to match the roof contour, replacement front headlight (accepts 1.5V mini-bulb and MV lens #159, both sold separately) and sloped sand filler hatches for nose and rear of cab. Illustrated instruction sheet covers basic body modifications and installation of new parts.

DIESEL PARTS

 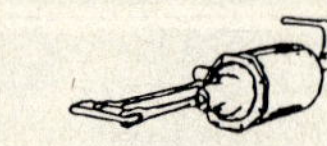  

Shrouded Horn CB&Q
247-197   2.09

12x10 Brake Cylinder w/Lever
247-198 pkg(4) 7.29

Slack Adjustor
247-199 pkg(4) 4.39

Bolster Anchor
247-200
pkg(4) 4.39

 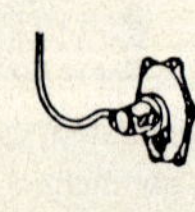 

Ground Light w/Bracket
247-112
pair 3.09

Wheel Slip Modulator
247-195
pkg(4) 4.39

Speed Recorder
247-196
pkg(4) 4.39

Firecracker Radio Antenna
247-113
pkg(2) 3.09

Spark Arrestor
247-131
pkg(2) 2.59
Used on Boston & Maine and Springfield Terminal GP7 and GP9 locos.

Custom Finishing

HO SCALE (1/87)

Add a new dimension to your models with this line of brass detail parts for locos and passenger cars. Each is finely detailed and ready for installation. Most items include basic mounting instructions and can be attached using ACC or solder.

DIESEL PARTS (continued)

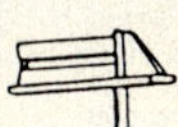
Sinclair Antenna
247-201 pkg(4) 3.79

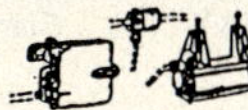
ATS Pick-Up & Connector
247-202 pkg(3) 3.79

Number Boards
CV, GT, CP
247-203
pkg(2) 2.39

EMD Steam
Generator
247-214
pkg(2) 2.09

Flag Stanchion
w/Saddle
247-204
pkg(4) 2.39

BL2 Single
Headlight for
Proto 2000
247-210 2.39

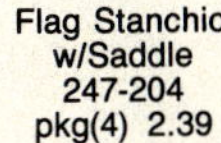
EMD Single
Chime Horn
247-215
pkg(2) 2.69

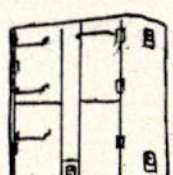
GP-7 Light
Equipment Box
247-213
pkg(2) 9.39

Automatic Train Stop
247-229   2.29
Pickup shoe for mounting on truck side frames.

Pilot Plow
w/Hoses
247-243
3.69

Extended
Height Exhaust
Stack GP, SD
247-247
pair 2.39

Diesel End
Platform Lift
Rings (4 pieces)
247-248
3.49

Diesel MU's
247-257 4.95
3 hose w/bracket
2 lefts & 2 rights

Diesel MU's
247-258   4.95
4 hose w/bracket,
2 lefts and 2 rights

Air Infiltration
Unit/HORST
247-260   6.98
Fits Atlas GP-7 locos

Spark Arrestor
247-234   2.39

ELECTRICAL BOXES

Round
Junction
247-145
pkg(8) 2.39

Rectangular
Electrical
247-148
pkg(6) 2.69

Small
Junction
247-154
pkg(6) 2.39

ELECTRICAL INSULATORS

New Haven
247-105
pkg(2) 3.09

Short
247-119
pkg(6) 3.69

EMD F&E SERIES LOCO PARTS

Winterization
Hatch, High Type
F-Units
247-240   each 2.59

(not illustrated)
Icicle Breakers
E&F Units
(3 piece set)
247-249   9.59

EMD SWITCHER STANCHIONS

EMD Switcher End
Platform Stanchions
(6 piece set)
247-241   8.99

EMD Switcher
Side Handrail
Stanchion
(14 piece set)
247-242   8.99

END PLATFORM STEPS

Loco Steps
Three Straight Up
GP38-2
247-276   9.95

Loco Steps
Three Up
SD40
247-277   9.95

HEADLIGHTS

12" Pyle Nat'l
247-102 3.69
Steel wrapped
headlight, used
by NYC and
B&A. Can be il-
luminated with
modification.
Accepts MV
Products lens
#136.

EMD
Back-Up Light
247-106 3.69
Applied to many
E units, cored
for 1.5 volt bulb
(.055 diameter).
Accepts MV Pro-
ducts lens #29.

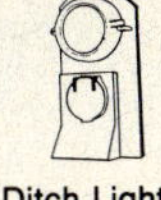
Ditch Lights
Deck Mounted
247-126
pkg(2) 3.79
Applied to mod-
ern diesels, in-
cludes left and
right lights with
MU stand.

Golden Glow
New Haven
247-123 3.49
Can be illum-
inated with mod-
ification. Accepts
MV Products
lens #166. Used
on many types
of New Haven
steam locos.

Bracket for #123
247-124   3.09
Use for mounting
Golden Glow head-
light on smokebox
door.

Pyle Dual Sealed
Beam Headlight
247-253
1.95
Visors, VERT, cored
for lighting.

Pyle Dual Sealed
Beam Headlight
247-254
1.95
Visors, HORIZ
cored for lighting

Pyle Dual Sealed
Beam Headlight
247-255
1.95
Cored for lighting

Pyle Twin
MARS Light
(CB&Q Style)
247-256
2.89

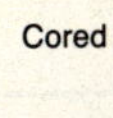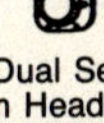
Ditch Lights
Bracket
Mounted
247-236
pkg(2) 1.89

Ditch Lights
(Built-on Type)
247-237
pkg(2) 1.79

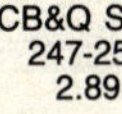
Ditch Lights
(Built-on Type)
247-238
pkg(2) 1.69
Left & Right,
E&F Units

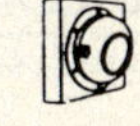
Ditch Lights
Platform End
Mount
247-251
pkg(2) 2.69
Cored for lighting

LATCHES

"Wine" Twin
Hopper
247-273   pkg(2) 2.98

"Wine" Triple
Hopper
247-274   pkg(2) 5.49

"Wine" Quad
Hopper
247-275   pkg(2) 5.49

MARKER LIGHTS

Early
247-114
pkg(2) 3.59
Single lens, accepts
jewels .042" in dia.

Bracket
247-179
pkg(8) 2.69

MARKER LIGHT JEWELS

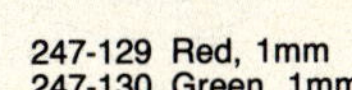
Sized to fit most steam and diesel marker lights, 1mm size is just under four HO Scale inches.

247-127 Clear, 1mm   pkg(12) 2.69
247-129 Red, 1mm   pkg(12) 2.69
247-130 Green, 1mm   pkg(12) 2.69

MISCELLANEOUS

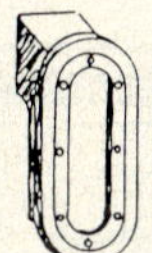
Fuel Tank
Sight Glass
247-226
pkg(2) 2.09

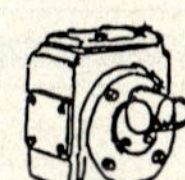
EMD Speed
Recorder
Drive Unit
247-228
1.59

EMD Early
Switcher
Exhaust
Stack/Short
247-284
pkg(2) 2.59

EMD Cast Iron
Brake Wheel
247-278   1.98

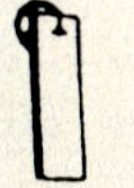
EMD Loco
Brake Stand
w/Wheel
247-279   3.59

Peacock
Brake Stand
247-280   TBA

Side Mount Bell
247-281   2.59

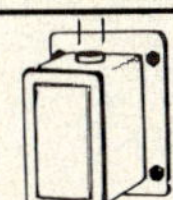
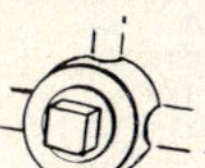

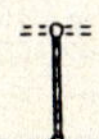

Custom Finishing

HO SCALE (1/87)

Add a new dimension to your models with this line of brass detail parts for locos and passenger cars. Each is finely detailed and ready for installation. Most items include basic mounting instructions and can be attached using ACC or solder.

PASSENGER CAR PARTS

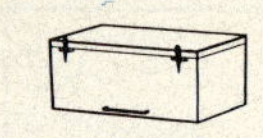
Tool Box
247-162   2.39
Can also be used on cabooses, tenders or maintenance equipment.

Diaphragm Buffer Springs
247-161
pkg(2) 3.69

Amplidyne Invertor
247-164   4.59

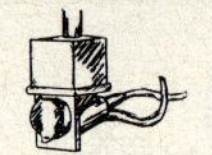
Air Conditioning Receptacle
247-163
pkg(2) 2.49

PIPE HANGERS

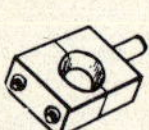
247-136 Pipe Hangers   pkg(2) 2.19
Cored .040″, generally used on the injector pipe to check valves.

PROTO 2000 by LIFE-LIKE BLT

ATS Motor Generator
247-208
2.09

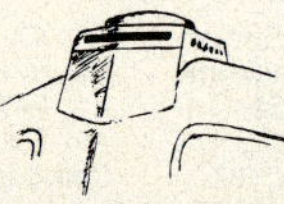
BL2 Steam Generator Stack
247-209
2.19

QUEEN POSTS

Ideal for use with turnbuckles #165 and 166.

247-168 6″   pkg(8) 2.59
247-169 8″   pkg(8) 2.59

Flush Type
247-184   pkg(8) 2.59

RETURN SPRING

Return Spring .062″ Diameter .050″ Eye Diameter, .655″ Eye Centers
247-252   pair 2.69

REFRIGERATION UNITS

Freight Car Retrofit Unit (white metal)
247-286
2.59

Modern Trailer Diesel Unit
247-287
2.98

Medium Duty Truck Unit
247-288
pkg(2) 2.59

Older Style Gas Powered Unit
247-289
pkg(2) 2.49

SAND DOME/SANDER PARTS

Dome Fittings
247-142
pkg(8) 2.69
Accepts up to .028″ wire for discharge pipes.

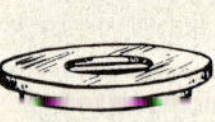
Oval Dome Covers
247-178
pkg(4) 3.79

Sander Valves
247-143
pkg(16) 3.69
Accepts up to .028″ wire for discharge pipes.

Sander Valves
247-144
pkg(2) 3.09
Can be used with #142.

SIGNAL BOXES

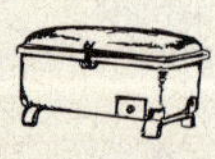
CTC for NYC/B&O
247-101 3.79

Cab Type for NYC
247-116 3.79
Commonly used on passenger service RS-3's.

Cab Type Box w/Exiter
247-125 5.19
Used on New Haven RS-3's, can be adapted to other New Haven engines.

Modern Cab Type
247-149 2.69

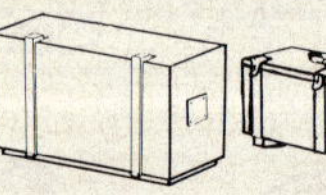
PRR
247-153 2.79

STEAM ENGINE PARTS

Boiler Strap Stays
247-141
pkg(9) 2.69

Air Strainer
247-135
each 2.09

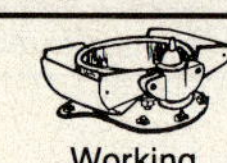
Working Clamshell Stack
247-150
each 5.19

Cab Seats- Left & Right
247-170
pkg(2) 3.69

STEPS

Walkway Step for Steam Loco
247-108
pkg(2) 3.79

Steam Loco Pilot Steps
247-115
pkg(2) 4.19

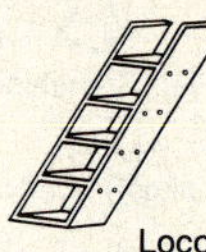
Loco Ladder
247-155
pkg(2) 4.19

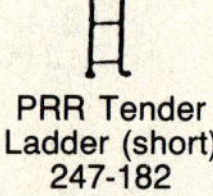
PRR Tender Ladder (short)
247-182
each 7.09

PRR Tender Ladder (long)
247-183
each 7.09

(not illustrated)
247-267 GP/SD End Platform Steps (Four Straight Up)   9.95

TENDER PARTS

Stoker Feed (Alco)
247-133 2.69
Mounts under front main deck of tender, simulates connection for automatic stoker.

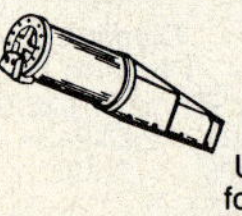
Coal Pusher (Alco)
247-134 3.79
Used to move forward in tenders.

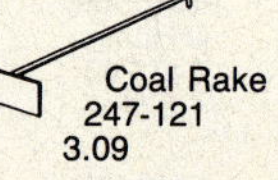
Coal Rake
247-121
3.09

TRACKSIDE DETAILS

Trackside Battery Box
247-172
pkg(2) 3.09

Buda Wheel Stops
247-171
pkg(2) 3.69

Remote Block Signal Indicator
247-175
3.79

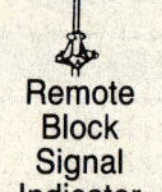
Switch Lock Box
247-176
3.09

Pole Mounted Relay
247-173
4.19

Large Relay Box
247-174
4.79

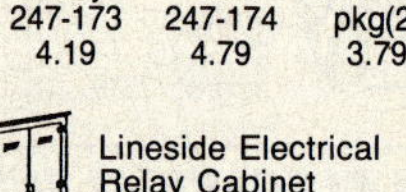
Flanger Sign
247-192
pkg(2)
3.79

Durable Bumper Model D
247-194   5.19

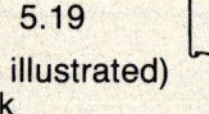
Lineside Electrical Relay Cabinet
247-193   6.95

(not illustrated)
247-283 Switch Heater w/Tank   2.95

TURNBUCKLES

Cored for use with .015″ wire, ideal for use with Queenposts #168 and 169.

Short for Freight Cars
247-165
pkg(4) 3.79

Long for Passenger Cars
247-166
pkg(4) 3.79

VALVES

Check Valves Left & Right
247-158
pkg(2) 2.98

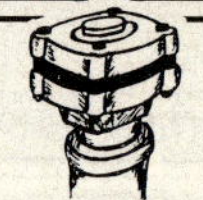
Relief Valves
247-159
pkg(2) 2.49

Drain Cock
247-160
pkg(6) 2.49

Globe Valve Long Stem
247-167
pkg(4) 4.49

VENTS

Globe
247-117   pkg(2) 3.09
Used for passenger car washrooms; angled base

Pintsch Roof
247-118
pkg(10) 3.69
Includes 8 short vents with flat bases for roof mounting and two long vents with angled bases for mounting over vestibules. Used on early cars equipped with gas lights and frequently left in place after electric lighting was installed.

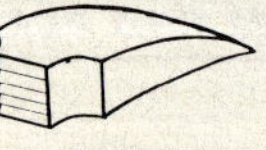
Garland
247-146 pkg(8) 5.98

Custom Finishing

HO SCALE (1/87)

WHISTLES

Electric
New Haven
247-103
pkg(2) 3.09

New York Central
Boston & Albany
247-104
pkg(2) 3.09

Electric
New York Central
Great Northern
247-107
pkg(2) 3.09

WINTERIZATION HATCHES

High Type
F-Units
247-240
2.59

Split, CP
Style (Fits
Life-Like FA-2)
247-259 9.95

RS2/3's CP
Recirculating
Type
247-261 4.98

DYNA-MODEL COMPANY PRODUCTS

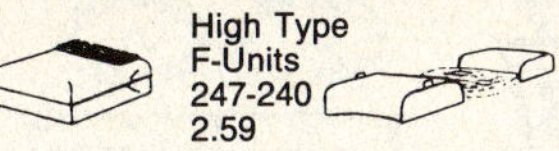

HO SCALE (1/87)
Cast metal, unpainted doors and windows. Illustrations are 3/4 size.

DOORS

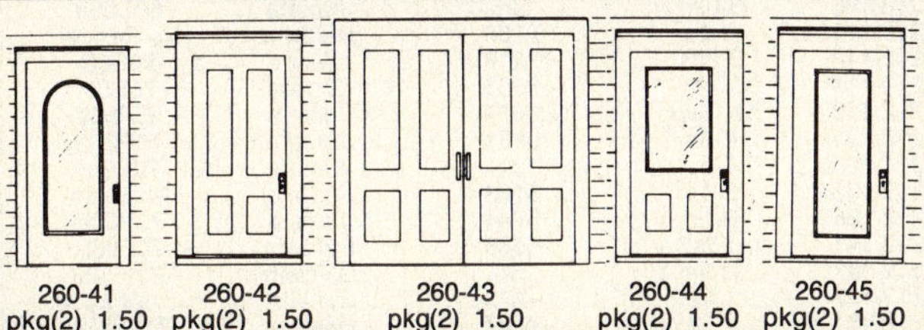

260-41
pkg(2) 1.50

260-42
pkg(2) 1.50

260-43
pkg(2) 1.50

260-44
pkg(2) 1.50

260-45
pkg(2) 1.50

ROOF SHINGLES & BRACKET

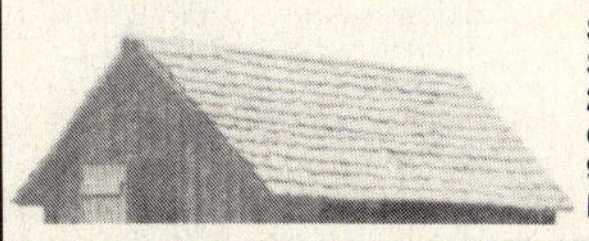

Shake
Shingle
260-61
each 2.00
9 x 9″ formed
plastic sheet

Bracket
260-71
pkg(6) 1.50

UTILITY POLE ACCESSORIES

260-2025   each 4.95
Includes 10 cast metal six insulator crossarms, crossarm braces, 10 side mount telephone line insulators and a transformer.

WINDOWS

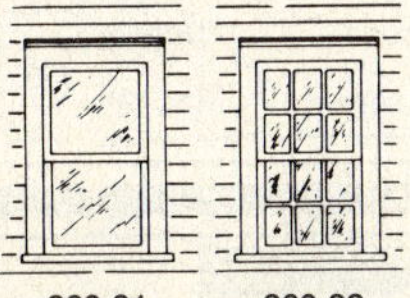
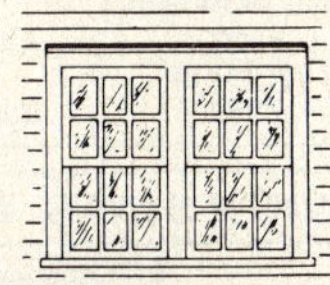
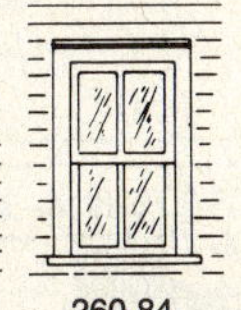

260-81
pkg(6) 1.95

260-82
pkg(6) 1.95

260-83
pkg(2) 1.50

260-84
pkg(6) 1.95

260-85
Attic/Tower
pkg(6) 1.50

A-LINE

A division of PROTO POWER WEST

HO SCALE (1/87)

DETAIL PARTS

Style "A"
Stirrup Step
116-29000 pkg(25) 2.80

Style "B"
Stirrup Step
116-29001 pkg(25) 2.80

Style "C"
Stirrup Step
116-29002 pkg(25) 2.80

(not illustrated)

116-29100	Grab Irons		pkg(50) 2.75
116-29200	Windshield Wipers, Long & Short		pkg(8) 1.85
116-29201	Windhsield Wipers, Short	NEW	pkg(8) 1.85
116-29210	Diesel Sun Shades (Adjustable, durable etched blass)		pkg(6) 1.95
116-29211	E&F Unit Sunshades	NEW	pkg(6) 1.95
116-29212	Comfort Cab Sunshades	NEW	pkg(4) 1.95
116-29230	Diesel Steps RPP SD45	NEW	2.95
116-29231	Diesel Steps RPP SD60	NEW	2.95
116-29232	Diesel Steps RPP 8-40CW	NEW	2.95
116-29233	Diesel Steps RPP B23-7	NEW	2.95
116-29234	Diesel Steps RPP SD60M	NEW	2.95
116-29235	Diesel Steps RPP GP35	NEW	2.95
116-29236	Diesel Steps Athearn SD40-2	NEW	2.95
116-29237	Diesel Steps Athearn GP50	NEW	2.95
116-29238	Diesel Steps Kato SD40	NEW	2.95
116-29239	Diesel Steps Front Range GP7/9	NEW	2.95
116-29240	Diesel Steps Spectrum 8-40C	NEW	2.95
116-29241	Diesel Steps Atlas/Con-Cor GP40	NEW	2.95
116-29242	Diesel Steps Stewart U25-B	NEW	2.95
116-29243	Diesel Steps Mantua/A-Line GP20 (Steps are see-through photo-etched brass)	NEW	2.95
116-29300	E-Unit Sideframe Set (fits Athearn SD45, UC, F45 & FP45 3-axle truck)		7.85
116-29301	E-Unit Fuel Tank Skirt/Air Tank Set		3.00
116-29400	Tank Car Ends (GATX, ACF & Recessed, fits MDC cars)		3.50

FLAT CAR WEIGHTS

White metal weights custom cast to fit the ends and center sill of Athearn 85′ flat cars. The end weights have the option of cushion or non-cushion coupler box, will lower the car to a prototypical scale height, and will give the car end a more realistic appearance. The center sill weights improve the tracking ability of the car by lowering the center of gravity with additional weight and enabling the modeler to operate the flat car without a load.

116-13200	85′ Flat Car End Weight Kit	5.20
	(fits Athearn 85′ Custom Rail 89′ flat cars, Walthers' Auto Rack)	
116-13201	85′ Flat Car Center Sill Weight Kit	5.20
116-13202	85′ Flat Car w/End Weight Kit	10.95
116-13203	89′ Flat Car Center Sill Weight Kit	TBA

LEAD WEIGHTS

For adding extra weight to locos and cars. Lead is precut, with double sided backing tape for easy installation. Thickness dimension includes tape.

116-13000	1/2 x 1/2 x 3/16″ (3 ounce strips)	pkg(2) 3.50
116-13001	1/2 x 3/4 x 5/32″ (3 ounce strips)	pkg(2) 3.50
116-13002	1/2 x 3/4 x 1/4″ (6 ounce strips)	3.50

MOLDABLE LEAD

Lead putty contains over 90% lead, yet is easily shaped with fingers. Nonhardening, can be glued with most adhesives.

116-13010 Moldable Lead   1oz 2.25

SCALE LABEL SET

Labels shown on scale
(scale not included)

Converts a 16 ounce postal scale to a E-Z read modelers weighing scale. Used for weighing rolling stock to NMRA standards. Use with A-Line "weigh-it yourself" lead weights.

116-13111   2.50

CUSTOM RAILWAY SUPPLY

HO SCALE (1/87)

Photo-etched, brass sign castings. The castings are soft enough to be trimmed with a modeler's knife for proper shape and fit and can be painted for added detail. Illustrations are not to scale.

BRASS LOCO FRAMES

212-1055 7" Frame — pair 23.50
Loco frames can be used to make a PRR Q-1 or a customized 2-10-4 by using Bowser T-1 80" wheels.

(The locomotive frame is a kitbashing item intended for the experienced modeler.)

LOCO INTERIOR KITS

Kits are cast metal construction.

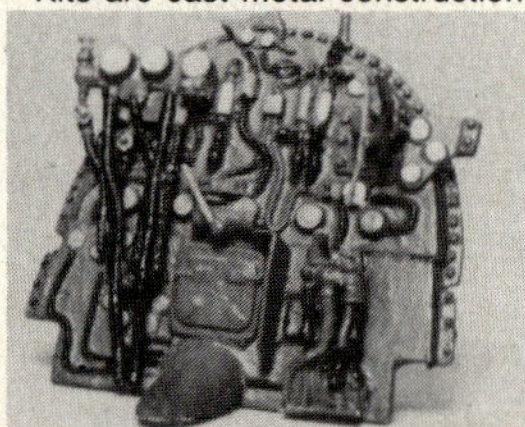

Complete Backhead
for Radial Stay Firebox Steam Locos
212-1052 — each 6.85

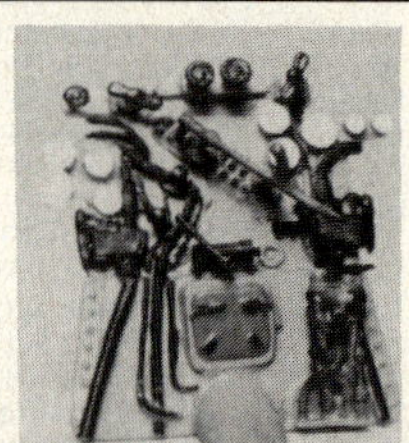

Complete Backhead
for Belpaire Firebox Steam Locos
212-1053 — each 6.85

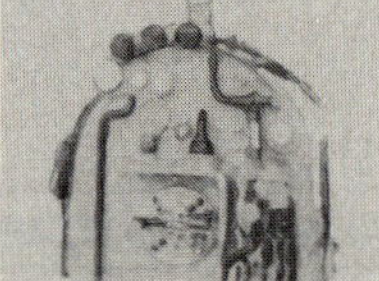

1895 Era Boiler Backhead
for use with MDC
212-1057 — each 6.85
backhead approximately 3/4" wide

1905 Era Boiler Backhead
for use with MDC
212-1058 — each 6.85
backhead approximately 15/16" wide

"Roundhouse" Brand Kit Loco

Example of application of engine backhead #1057 used in Model Die Casting's loco #480-480. #'s 1057 & 1058 backheads are for use with MDC kits, and are sized the same as those used in many MDC kits.

Diesel Cab Interior for Hood Type Road Locos, Less Crew Figures
212-1054 — each 6.85

POSTAGE STAMP SERIES

Chemically milled free brass kits require a minimum of cutting, filing, bending and painting.

1060

1061

1062

212-1060 Bicycle and Park Bench — set 1.75
212-1061 Two Bicycles and One Bike Rack — set 1.75
212-1062 Tools — set 1.75

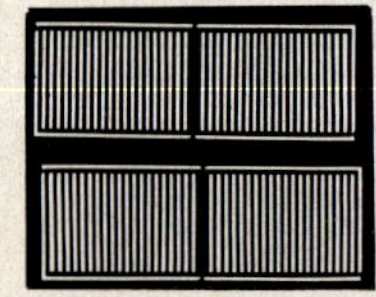

SD40T-2 Intake Grill
212-1064
pkg(4) 3.95

Locomotive Weather Vane
212-1063
each 1.75

PRR LOCOMOTIVE PLATES (set 6.45)

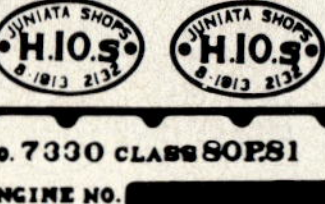

151

167

Part #	Class	Locomotive #	Builder	Tender Type
212-151	H-10s	7669	Juniata	80F81
212-167	J-1	6455	Altoona	210F84
212-190	K-4s	3875 "Broadway Ltd"	Juniata	110P57a
212-101	A-55	730	Juniata	55S66a
212-105	B-6sb	525	Juniata	60S66a
212-111	B-8a	2788	Baldwin	No Tender
212-112	B-28s	7216	Alco	80S65
212-114	C-1	6551	Juniata	70S66
212-118	D-16sb	5079	Juniata	55P55a
212-123	E-5s	9831	Juniata	70P85a
212-129	E-6s	1211	Juniata	70P66f
212-133	F-3c	5163	Juniata	No Plate
212-138	G-5s	5744	Juniata	70P82a
212-141	H-6sb	8568	Baldwin	70F66b
212-147	H-9s	54	Baldwin	70F70a
212-157	I-1s	4273	Juniata	90F82
212-161	I-1s	4587	Baldwin	210F82a
212-162	I-1sa	4485	Baldwin	90F82
212-169	J-1a	6464	Altoona	210F84
212-175	K-2s	150	Juniata	70P66
212-178	K-3s	7161	Baldwin	70P78
212-184	K-4s	1330	Juniata	90P75
212-187	K-4s	3867 "Jeffersonian"	Juniata	90P75
212-188	K-4s	3872 "Red Arrow"	Baldwin	90P75
212-198	K-5	5698 "Liberty Limited"	Altoona	130P75
212-201	L-1s	1696	Juniata	90F75
212-209	M-1	6845	Baldwin	110P75a
212-211	M-1a	6752 "The Union"	Altoona	110P75a
212-213	M-1a	6781	Lima	210F75a
212-214	M-1b	6761	Baldwin	210F75
212-219	N-1s	7243	Alco	100F85
212-221	N-2s	7126	Baldwin	120F78
212-222	N-2sa	7343	Baldwin	120F78
212-226	Q-2	6131	Altoona	180F84
212-233	S-2	6200	Altoona	180P85
212-236	T-1	5513 "Spirit of St Louis"	Altoona	180P84
212-237	T-1	5523 "Trail Blazer"	Altoona	180P84
212-245	CC-2s	7332	Baldwin	100F85

PRR STATION & TOWN SIGNS

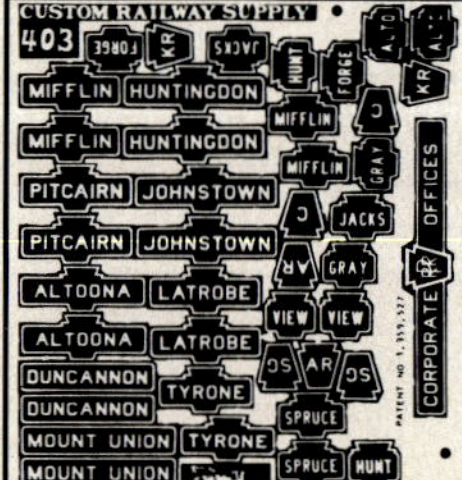

Mountain Main Line Cut
212-4031
pkg(43)
9.65

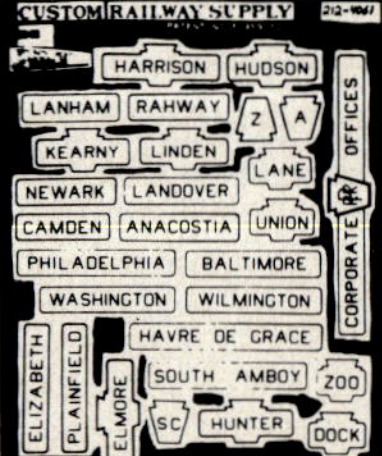

NE Corridor
212-4061
pkg(28)
9.65

CUSTOM RAILWAY SUPPLY

HO SCALE (1/87)

Photo-etched, brass sign castings. The castings are soft enough to be trimmed with a modeler's knife for proper shape and fit and can be painted for added detail. Illustrations are not to scale.

PRR STATION & TOWN SIGNS (continued)

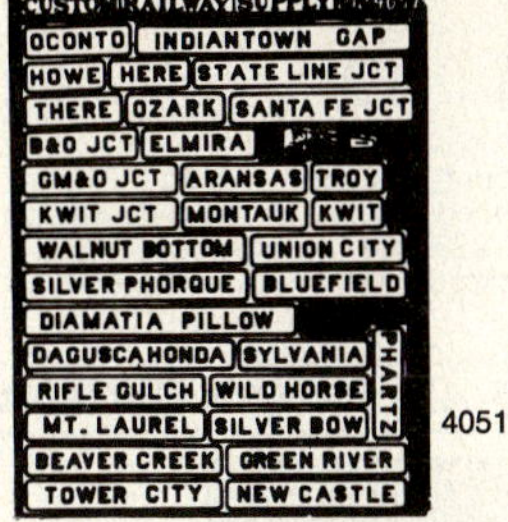

212-4021	Mountain Branch Line, Cut	pkg(35) 9.65
212-4051	Station & Tower	pkg(32) 9.95

PRR TRUST PLATES (pair 1.95)

PENNSYLVANIA RAILROAD
EQUIPMENT TRUST SERIES X
FIDELITY-PHILADELPHIA TRUST CO.,
TRUSTEE, OWNER AND LESSOR.

212-282	N-8 Cabin Car (enlarged to show detail)
212-276	GG-1, VO-660, SW-1, VO-1000
212-277	NW-2
212-278	Baldwin Centipede
212-279	E-7, Alco PA
212-280	F-3, Erie Built
212-281	F-3, BF-15, H-10-44
212-283	FM "C Liner", Alco S-1
212-284	SW-1, SW-7, SW-9, RS-1
212-285	VO-660, P-85
212-275	Passenger & Freight Cars pkg(20) 6.45

RIGHT-OF-WAY SIGNS

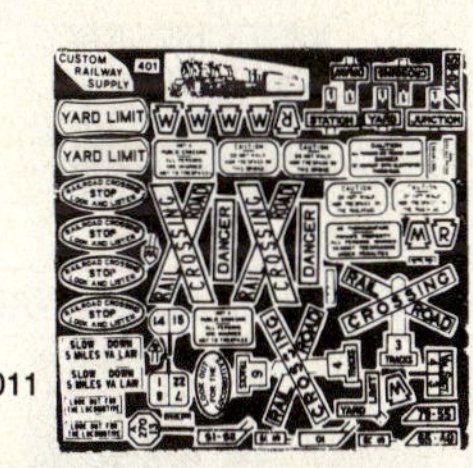

212-4011	Circa 1945, Cut	pkg(55) 9.65
212-4041	Circa 1920, Cut	pkg(52) 9.65

TUBING

212-1068	Drive Coupling Tubing	pkg(3) 2.59
	1" long, 1/16" round hole, oil resistant	

WINDSHIELD GRILL BARS

Windshield Grill Bars
212-1067   pair 2.95
Locomotive windshield crew protection grill bars. Trim to size to fill all windshields.

BALCONY **NEW**

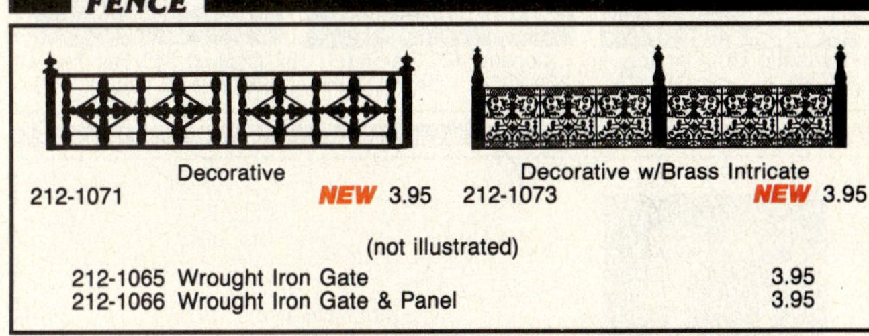

Iron w/Brass Banister
212-1070   4.95

Elevated Walkway Banister
212-1074   3.95

Walkway Banister
212-1076   3.95

FENCE

Decorative
212-1071   **NEW** 3.95

Decorative w/Brass Intricate
212-1073   **NEW** 3.95

(not illustrated)

212-1065	Wrought Iron Gate	3.95
212-1066	Wrought Iron Gate & Panel	3.95

STAIRWAY **NEW**

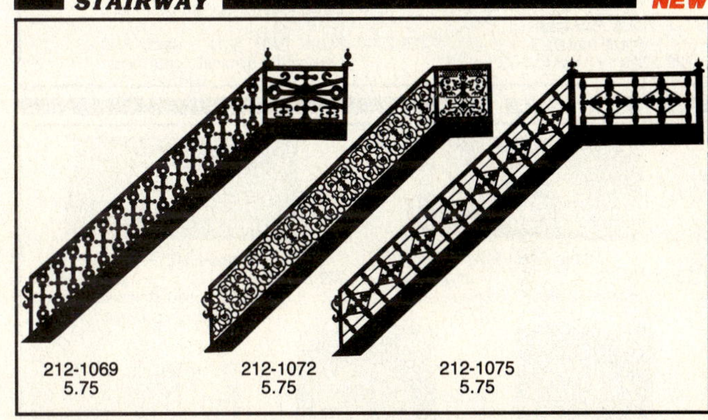

212-1069	212-1072	212-1075
5.75	5.75	5.75

THE CAR SHOP

HO SCALE (1/87)
NEW

HOPPER CONVERSION KIT

227-1607	Model Power Cylindrical Hopper Conversion	kit 13.50
	(Hopper not included in kit)	

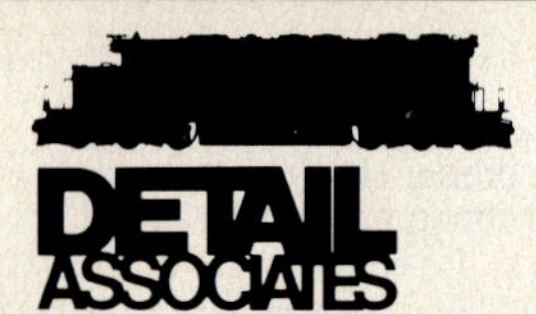
DETAIL ASSOCIATES

HO SCALE (1/87)

All parts are black injection molded styrene plastic unless noted. Illustrations are approximately 1-1/2 times HO Scale unless noted.

AIR HORNS

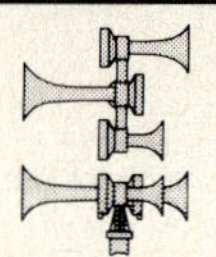 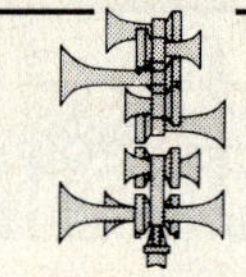 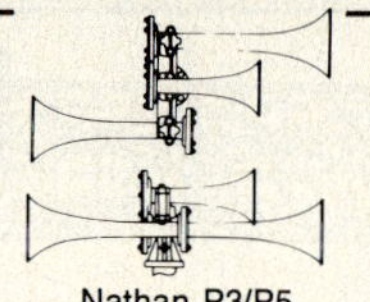

3-Chime Nathan M3	5-Chime Nathan M5	Nathan P3/P5
229-1601 pkg(2) 1.75	229-1602 pkg(2) 1.75	229-1603 pkg(2) 1.75

(not illustrated)

229-1608 Leslie Tyfon A200   pkg(4) 2.00

AIR FANS

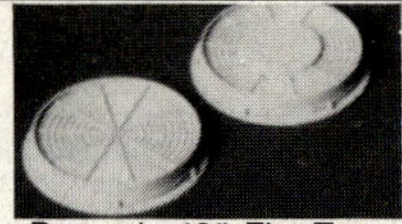 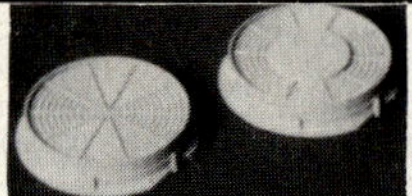 

Dynamic 48" Flat Top	Cooling 48" Flat Top	Cooling 34" Flat Top
229-2003 pkg(4) 2.75	229-2004 pkg(4) 2.75	229-2001 pkg(4) 2.75

AIR FILTERS

(not illustrated)

229-2707 Horst Paper   each 3.50
Large weather hoods, cast metal

229-2708 Paper, AMT Type   each 3.00
Low profile dynacell, cast metal

Horst Paducah (cast metal)
229-2706   each 2.75

AIR GRILLS

Intake EMD F7A	Intake EMD F7B
229-2704 pkg(2) 4.50	229-2705 pkg(2) 4.50
Unit boosters, etched stainless steel	Unit boosters, etched stainless steel

Cooling Fan	Cooling Fan	Exhaust, Vent & Intake
229-2702 pkg(2) 3.00	229-2703 pkg(2) 3.00	229-2712 pkg(4) 2.50
Alco 64" diameter	Alco 57" diameter	GM, etched metal

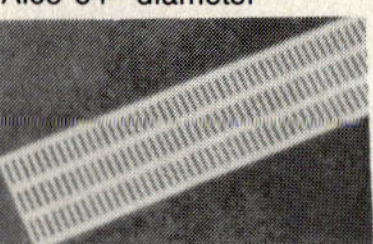 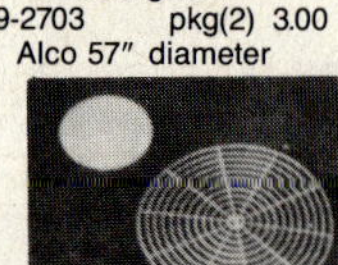 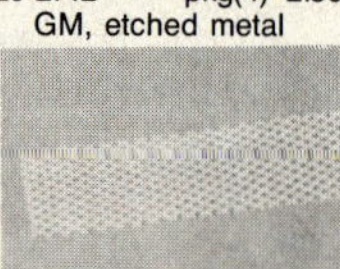

Intake "Farr" F&E Units	Fan, 48" Flat Top	Air EMD F Unit
229-2701 pkg(2) 8.00	229-2012 pkg(2) 3.00	229-2711 pkg(2) 8.00
Photo etched stainless steel		Chicken wire type etched metal

(not illustrated)

229-2717 Grill Set GE8-40C   **NEW** 5.00
229-2718 Grill Set GE8-40B   **NEW** 5.00

AIR RESERVOIRS

 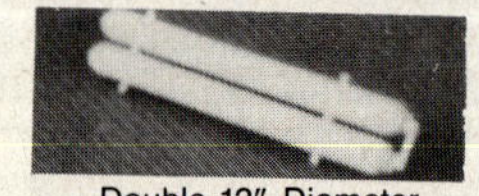

Single 15" Diameter	Double 12" Diameter
229-3201 pkg(2) 2.25	229-3202 pkg(2) 2.25
Top or side mount	Top mount

(not illustrated)

229-3203 15" GP 35-40 side mount   pkg(4) 2.25

AIR VENTS

 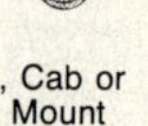 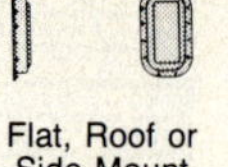  

Round, Cab or Hood Mount	Flat, Roof or Side Mount	Flat, Roof Mount	Dynamic Brake Hood Roof Mount
229-1901 pkg(12) 1.00	229-1902 pkg(8) 1.00	229-1903 pkg(4) 1.00	229-1904 pkg(4) 1.00
		2 times actual size	2 times actual size

AIR HOSES

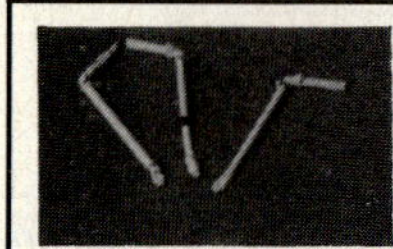 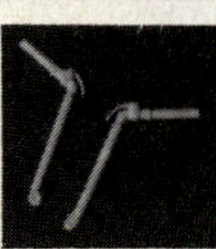

MU	Freight Car
229-1508 pkg(16) 2.50	229-6206 pkg(6) 1.25

BELLS

EMD Cab Mount	Underframe Mount	Western
229-1201 pkg(2) 1.50	229-1202 pkg(2) 1.25	229-1204 pkg(2) 1.25

BRAKE CYLINDERS

Diesel Trucks
229-2801   pkg(8) 2.00

BRAKE WHEELS

229-6402 Gear Miner   pkg(2) 1.25

(not illustrated)

229-6238 Hand Brake & Valve   pkg(2) 1.50
229-6401 Gear Equipco   pkg(2) 1.25
229-6403 Gear Ukeco   pkg(2) 1.25

CAB DETAILS

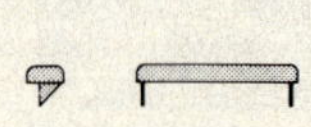 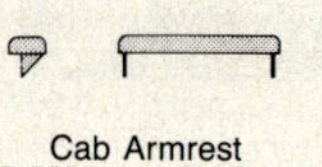 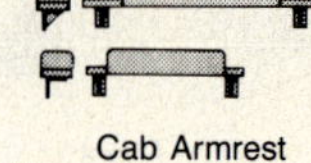 

Cab Armrest	Cab Armrest	All Weather Window Double Type for GP, SD
229-2302 pkg(8) 1.25	229-2303 pkg(4) 1.25	229-2301 pkg(2) 1.75
24" plain type	24 & 36" stepped	

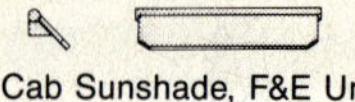

Cab Sunshade, F&E Unit Type		Cab Sunshade
229-1302 pkg(8) 1.25	229-1301	pkg(6) 1.50

(not illustrated)

229-1303 EMD Wide Cab	**NEW**	pkg(4) 1.50
229-2308 Cab AC "Prime"		1.50
229-2309 Cab AC "Vapor"		1.50
229-2310 Cab Deflector/Mirror	**NEW**	pkg(4) 1.25
229-2311 Cab Deflector "Prime"	**NEW**	pkg(4) 1.25
229-2312 Cab Deflector "Prime" Str	**NEW**	1.25
229-2551 Clear Plastic Window Material (.010 x 1 x 8")		pkg(5) 1.00
229-3306 Extra Cab Windows EMD		pkg(4) 1.25
229-3307 Window plugs, Athearn "GE"		pkg(4) 1.25

CLASSIFICATION LIGHTS

Shown 2 times actual size.

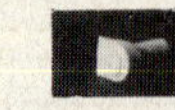    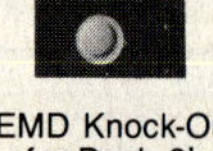

Early EMD, GP7 GP9, 18/20, SD24	Access Door SD7	Late EMD GP-30	EMD Knock-Out for Dash 2's
229-1017	229-1018	229-1019	229-1020
pkg(6) 1.25	pkg(4) 1.50	pkg(8) 1.25	pkg(8) 1.25
	Converts Athearn SD-9 to SD-7	Designed to be illuminated inside	

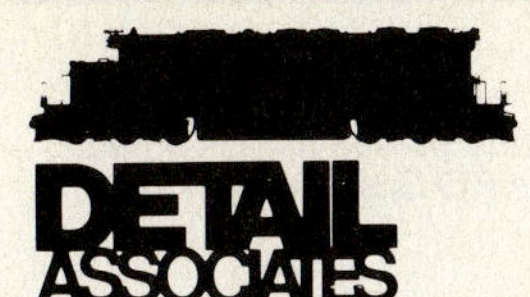

DETAIL ASSOCIATES

HO SCALE (1/87)	All parts are black injection molded styrene plastic unless noted. Illustrations are approximately 1-1/2 times HO Scale unless noted.

COUPLER LIFT BARS

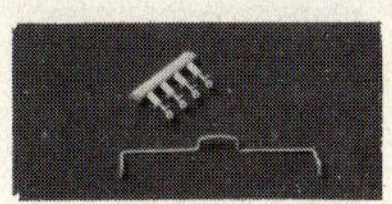
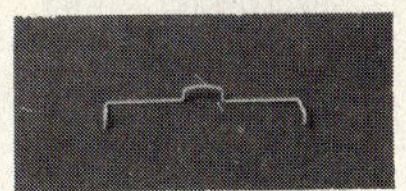

w/Bracket
229-2204   pkg(2) 2.00
Formed wire and plastic

Formed Wire
229-2205   pkg(10) 2.75
Formed wire

w/Bracket, AAR Type 1
229-2211   pkg(2) 2.25
Formed wire and plastic

(not illustrated)
229-2212   w/Bracket, AAR Type 2 (formed wire/plastic)   pkg(10) 3.50
229-2213   Bracket   pkg(4) 2.50
229-102213   Bracket (brass)   pkg(8) 1.75

DETAIL KITS

229-501   CB&T Shops — 40' Steel Box Car, SD & DD   10.50
229-701   Stewart F-3A, F-7A, F-9A Units   7.50
229-702   Stewart F-3B, F-7B, F-9B Units   7.00
229-704   Highliner EMD F-B Units   7.00

DIESEL PARTS

229-2716   Brake Grid Alco/Century (brass)   pkg(2) 1.25
229-101507   MV Receptacles (brass)   pkg(30) 2.25

DIESEL TRUCK JOURNAL

Hyatt Roller Bearing
229-2804   pkg(8) 2.25

EMD Blomberg Square Type
229-2805   pkg(8) 2.25

EMD Blomberg Slope Style
229-2806   pkg(8) 2.25

DOORS

Illustrations are actual size.

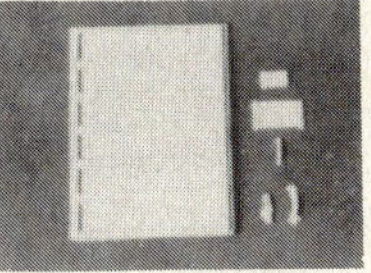

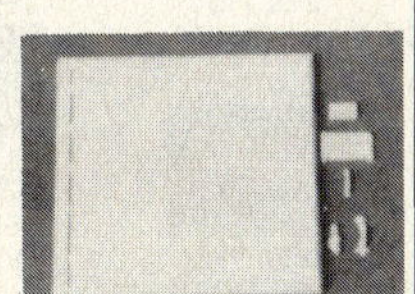

Superior Panel
6 x 8'3", 6-Panel
229-6302   pkg(2) 2.85

Superior Panel
6 x 8'3", 5-Panel
229-6301   pkg(2) 2.85

Superior Panel
10' x 9'3", 6-Panel
229-6311   pkg(2) 2.85

Superior Panel
8 x 9', 7-Panel
229-6306
pkg(2) 2.85

(not illustrated)
229-6216   Hennessy Door Opener   pkg(2) 1.75

EXHAUST STACKS

EMD F3, F7, F9, BL2
229-2401   pkg(2) 1.25

EMD Non-Turbo
229-2402   pkg(2) 1.25

EMD GP20/SD24
229-2403   pkg(2) 1.50

FOOTBOARD PILOTS

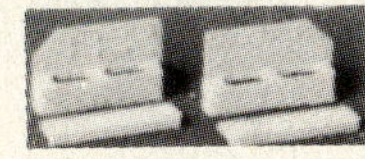
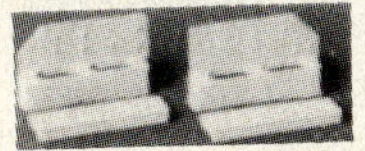

Metal Type
229-2208
pair 3.25

Wood Type
229-2209
pair 3.25

FREIGHT CAR STIRRUP STEPS

Measured in scale inches.

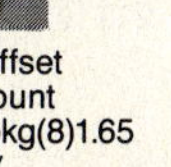

Angled Offset Bottom Mount
229-6411   pkg(8) 1.65
18 x 12-1/2"

Stepped Offset Bottom Mount
229-6412   pkg(8)1.65
17 x 14"

Double Offset Bottom Mount
229-6413   pkg(8)1.65
18-1/2 x 12"

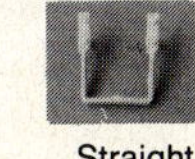

Straight Bottom Mount
229-6414
pkg(8) 1.65
16 x 11-1/2"

Slant, Side Mount
229-6415
pkg(8) 1.65
13-1/2 x 13"

Straight Side Mount
229-6416
pkg(8) 1.65
9 x 12"

Straight Bottom Mount
229-6417
pkg(8) 1.65
8-1/2 x 13"

(not illustrated)
229-6237   Tank Car Placards   pkg(8) 1.25
229-6418   Mech Reefer   pkg(7) 1.75
229-6419   Gunderson   pkg(8) 1.75
229-6420   Thrall   pkg(8) 1.75
229-6606   Superliner   pkg(8) 1.75

GONDOLA CAR ENDS

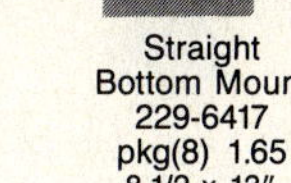

Drop Doors
229-6223   pkg(8) 2.50

Dreadnaught
229-6221   pkg(2) 1.75

Riveted
229-6222   pkg(2) 1.75

(not illustrated)
229-6225   GS Steel Plate   pkg(8) 2.50

GRAB IRONS

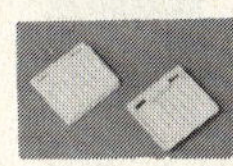
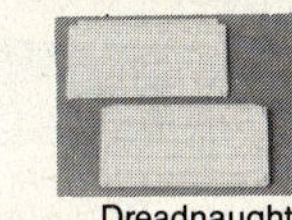
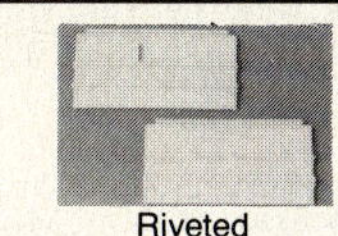

Scale
229-2201   pkg(18) 2.00
Includes plastic nut castings

Scale, Formed Wire
229-2202   pkg(48) 2.50

Vestibule Passenger Car
229-6601   pkg(12) 1.75

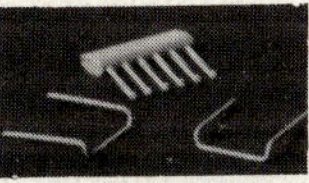

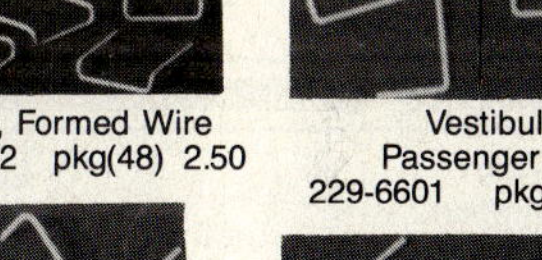

Caboose End
229-6503   pkg(12) 2.25

Caboose End
229-6504   pkg(12) 2.25

Roof Passenger Car
229-6602   pkg(12) 1.75

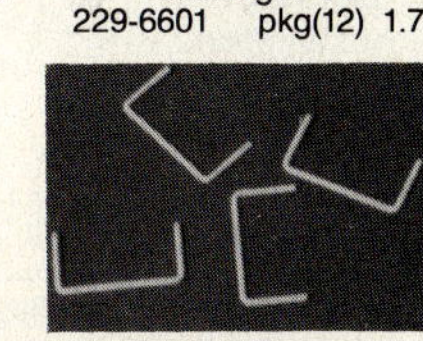

Straight Type
229-6210   pkg(12) 1.75

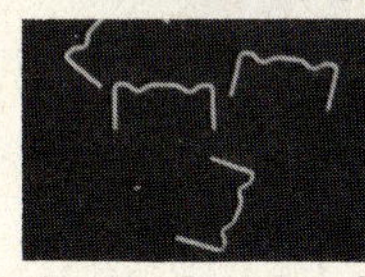

Running Board Corner Freight Car
229-6205   pkg(12) 2.00

Roof Ladder Passenger Car
229-6603   pkg(12) 1.75

(not illustrated)
Bracket Type
229-6209   pkg(8) 1.50

Ladder-Cab Unit
229-2215   pkg(12) 2.00

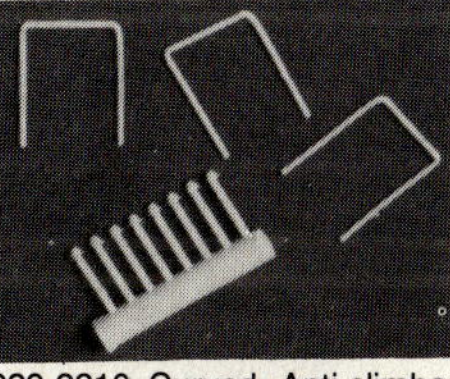

229-2216   Curved, Anti-climber   pkg(12) 2.00
229-2217   Circular Fan, GP30-GP/SD60   pkg(3) 1.50
229-2218   Angular Fan, Dash 2   pkg(3) 1.50
229-2219   Walkway Guard EMD 60 ser   **NEW** 1.00
229-2220   Pilot Grab Bar   **NEW** pkg(6) 1.25
229-2221   Cab Roof Grab Bar   **NEW** pkg(6) 1.25
229-6217   Curved,Tank Car   pkg(12) 1.25
229-6602   24" Passenger Roof   pkg(12) 1.75
229-6605   36" Straight   pkg(12) 2.00

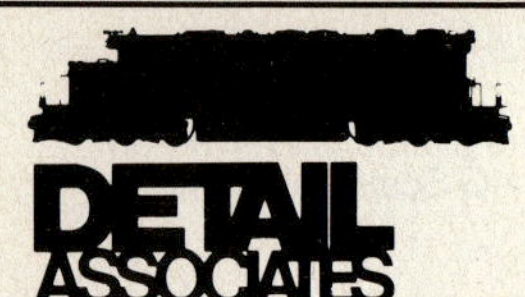

DETAIL ASSOCIATES

HO SCALE (1/87)

All parts are black injection molded styrene plastic unless noted. Illustrations are approximately 1-1/2 times HO Scale unless noted.

HEADLIGHTS

Oscillating Pyle Gyralite
229-1001 pkg(2) 1.00
229-101001 Brass 1.35

Oscillating Mars
229-1005 pkg(2) 1.00
229-101005 Brass 1.35

Oscillating Dual Pyle Gyralite
229-1002 pkg(2) 1.00
229-101002 Brass 1.35

Dual, Pyle or EMD Late
229-1003 pkg(2) 1.00
229-101003 Brass 1.35

Dual, Pyle Early Type
229-1004 pkg(2) 1.00
229-101004 Brass 1.35

Oscillating Dual, Mars
229-1008 pkg(2) 1.00
229-101008 Brass 1.50

Pyle, Large Type for WP, CN, CP
229-1010 pkg(2) 1.25
229-101010 Brass 1.50

Dual, Pyle **NEW**
Horizontal w/Shield
229-1023 pkg(2) 1.00

Dual, Pyle **NEW**
Vertical w/Shield
229-1024 pkg(2) 1.00

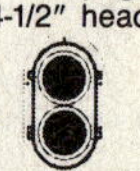

Dual, Pyle Conversion Plate
229-1012 pkg(2) 1.00
for 14-1/2" headlight

Dual, Pyle EMD SW Series Type
229-1011 pkg(2) 1.50

Dual, Mars
229-1006 pkg(2) 1.00

Oscillating Dual Recessed Mars
229-1007 pkg(2) 1.00

Oscillating Dual Recessed Pyle Gyralite
229-1009 pkg(2) 1.00

Housing SP Baldwin NW/SW
229-1016 set 3.50
50% HO size

Large "EMD" NW/SW
229-1015 pkg(2) 1.50
2 times HO size

(not illustrated)

Rear Light Bracket SP Late GP/SD's
229-1021 pkg(2) 1.25

229-1022 Ditch Light and Stand **NEW** pkg(4) 1.25
229-1013 Ditch Light Canadian pkg(2) 1.00
229-1014 Backup Light Canadian pkg(2) 1.00

LADDERS

(not illustrated)
Freight Car, Short
229-6208 1.75
Ladder Set, 8-rung
229-6241 set 2.25
Ladder Set, 7-rung
229-6242 set 2.25

SD 7/9
229-2207 kit 3.50

Freight Car, Short
229-6208 pkg(8) 1.75

Freight Car, Long
229-6207 pkg(10) 2.50

LENS

229-1708 Classification Light Lens pkg(12) 1.25
4-1/2" (.052") diameter, clear

229-1709 Classification Light Lens pkg(12) 1.25
7" (.080") diameter, clear

229-1710 Headlight Lens pkg(12) 1.25
12" (.138") diameter, clear

229-1711 Headlight Lens pkg(12) 1.25
14-1/2" (.167") diameter, clear

LIFT RINGS

EMD 3.5" Eye Bolt
229-1101 pkg(36) 1.25

Tabs, Roof and Side Hood Mount
229-1104 pkg(16) 1.00

EMD F&E Unit Nose
229-1102 pkg(6) 1.00

Flat Mounts on Pilot Beam
229-1103 pkg(8) 1.00

Switcher Side Mount
229-1105 pkg(4) 1.25

Alco FA/PA Century Type
229-1106 pkg(12) 1.25

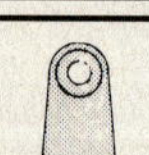

Alco S/RS Type
229-1107 pkg(12) 1.25

(not illustrated)

229-1108 GE w/Hinges **NEW** pkg(12) 1.50
229-101101 3-1/2" Eye Bolt (scale inches), Brass pkg(24) 1.75

MISCELLANEOUS

Covered Hopper Square Hatch
229-6212 pkg(8) 2.75

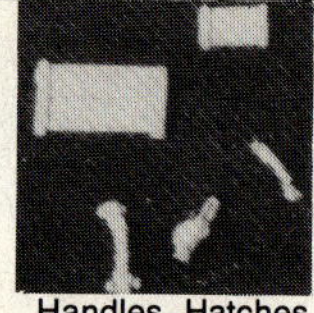

Handles, Hatches & Tac Boards
229-6213 (14 pcs) 2.25

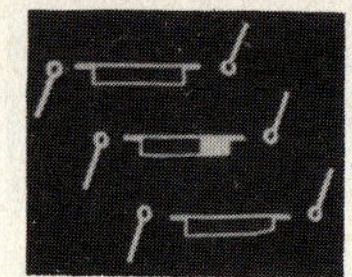

Wind Deflector Set
229-2304 pkg(3) 2.50

Tool Set, Photo Etched
229-7101 set(35 pieces) 3.25

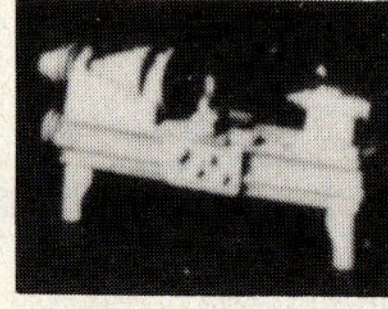

Lathe, 24" Belt Driven
229-7106 each 3.00

Drill Press, Belt Driven
229-7107 each 2.00

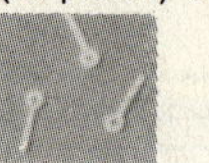

Eye Bolt, Formed Wire
229-2206 pkg(36) 3.25

Passenger Car Roof Vent-Harriman Type
229-6604 pkg(12) 1.75

Footing Piers, Concrete
229-7202 pkg(12) 1.50

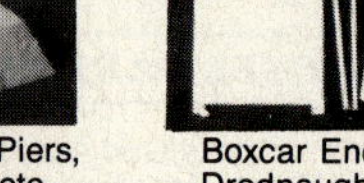

Boxcar End Drednaught
229-6235 pkg(4) 1.75

Coupler Cut Bar Standard
229-6215 pkg(10) 2.50

Passenger Pilots for Cab Units
229-2214 ea 5.50

Oil Can
229-7104 pkg(2) 1.00

Box Car Roof Plug
229-6224 pkg(8) 1.50

Water Bag
229-7105 pkg(2) 1.00

Screw Jack
229-7102 pkg(2) 1.00

Rerail Frog
229-7103 pkg(2) 1.00

Brake Platform
229-6211 pkg(4) 2.75

Fuel Gauge EMD
229-3101 pkg(6) 1.00

SD7-35 Circular Access Cover
229-2307 pkg(6) 1.00

(not illustrated)

229-100 Detail Associates Catalog 3.50
Complete item listing with pictures. 28 pages, 8-1/2 x 11".
229-102203 Hex Nut, Brass 3/4" diameter pkg(18) 1.50
229-2203 Hex Nut-Bolt-Washer pkg(48) 1.75
3/4" diameter bolt with 2" diameter washer
229-2901 Flasher, wch (2) **NEW** 1.50
229-2902 Flasher, Stratolite (2) **NEW** 1.50
229-2903 Flasher, Xenon Strobe (2) **NEW** 1.50
229-3102 Fuel Tank Fittings **NEW** (set) 1.00
229-6218 Covered Hopper Hatch Round pkg(8) 2.00
229-6226 GS-Drop Chain, Open/Closed "Enterprise" pkg(32) 4.50
229-6227 AB Brake Set, Freight Car each 3.00
229-6229 Covered Hopper Discharge gate pkg(4) 2.00
229-6236 Boxcar End, Dreadnaught pkg(5) 1.75

MU STANDS

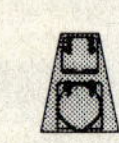

EMD Late GP SD Type Sgle
229-1505 pkg(2) 1.25

EMD Early GP Types
229-1501 pkg(2) 1.25

EMD Intermed GP, SD Double
229-1504 pkg(2) 1.25

EMD Intermed GP, SD Single
229-1503 pkg(2) 1.25

EMD Late GP SD Type Double
229-1506 pkg(2) 1.25

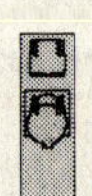

MU Receptacles 3 Types and 2 Blank Covers
229-1507 pkg(30) 1.25

EMD Early GP Type, High
229-1502 pkg(2) 1.25

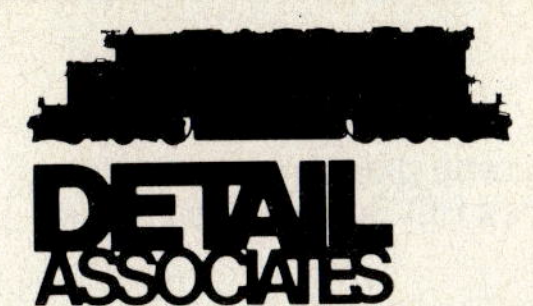

DETAIL ASSOCIATES

HO SCALE
(1/87)

All parts are black injection molded styrene plastic unless noted.
Illustrations are approximately 1-1/2 times HO Scale unless noted.

NUMBER BOARDS

NEW
Number Board & Headlight
WP/UP GP35/40
229-2604   each 3.50

Stencils (photo etched brass)
229-2601   pkg(2) 2.50

Alco Curved Back
229-2602
pkg(4) 3.00

Alco Angled Back
229-2603
pkg(4) 3.00

RADIATOR FRAME & SCREEN

Illustrations are shown 2 times actual HO size.

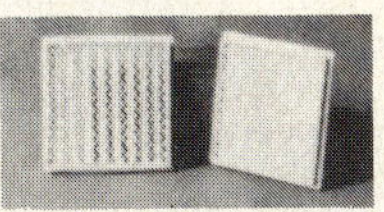

EMD SW Switchers
(Plastic & Etched Metal)
229-2709 pkg(2) 3.50

EMD NW Switchers
(Plastic & Etched Metal)
229-2710 pkg(2) 3.50

Radiator Fan Screen
F, Etched Metal
229-2713 each 2.75

RADIATOR GRILLS

EMD SD45
Late Type
229-2714
pkg(2) 1.25

EMD SD45
Early Type
229-2715
pkg(2) 1.25

RADIO ANTENNAS

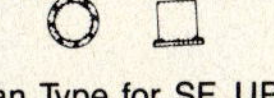

Can Type for SF, UP
229-1801 pkg(6) 1.00
Brass
229-101801 pkg(3) 1.35

Whip Type for SF, UP
229-1802 pkg(6) 1.00
Brass
229-101802 pkg(3) 1.35

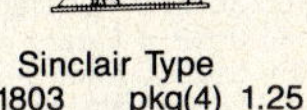

Sinclair Type
229-1803 pkg(4) 1.25
Brass
229-101803 pkg(4) 2.00

Wagon
Wheel Type
229-1804
pkg(3) 3.25
Photo etched brass with plastic
antenna casting.

Caboose
Dish Type
229-6501
pkg(3) 2.50

(not illustrated)
NEW
Motorola
Firecracker
229-1805
pkg(6) 1.25

RUNNING BOARDS (FREIGHT CARS)

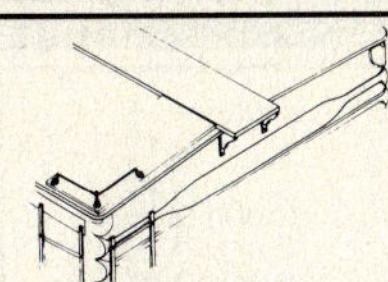

229-6201 40' Wood   each 2.50
229-6202 50' Wood   each 3.50
229-6203 40' Metal   each 6.00
229-6204 50' Metal   each 6.00

SAND HATCHES

Illustrations are shown 2 times actual HO Scale size.

Sandfiller Cover
EMD Late, GP35
229-3001
pkg(6) 1.25

EMD GP-7
& GP-9 Early
229-3002
pkg(4) 1.00

EMD Cab
Unit Early
229-3003
pkg(4) 1.00

EMD Cab
Unit Late
229-3004
pkg(4) 1.00

SHOCK ABSORBER/SNUBBER

EMD
229-2802
pkg(4) 1.75

GE
229-2803
pkg(4) 1.75

SIGNAL BOXES

3 Strap Early
229-2305
pkg(2)   1.50

2 Strap Late
229-2306
pkg(2)   1.50

SCALE WIRE & PIPE

Pipe Dimensions are HO Scale. Piping is Brass Wire.

Number	Size		Outside Dia	Brass Wire Size	Pkg	Price
229-2501	1/4"	Iron Pipe	.540"	.006"	5	2.50
229-2502	3/8"	Iron Pipe	.675"	.008"	5	2.50
229-2503	1/2"	Iron Pipe	.840"	.010"	10	2.50
229-2504	3/4"	Iron Pipe	1.050"	.012"	10	2.50
229-2505	1"	Iron Pipe	1.215"	.015"	10	2.50
229-2506	1-1/4"	Iron Pipe	1.660"	.019"	10	2.50
229-2507	1-1/2"	Iron Pipe	1.990"	.022"	10	2.50
229-2508	2"	Iron Pipe	2.375"	.028"	10	2.50
229-2509	2-1/2"	Iron Pipe	2.875"	.033"	10	2.50
229-2510	3"	Iron Pipe	3.5"	.040"	10	2.50
229-2511	3-1/2"	Iron Pipe	4.0"	.046"	10	2.50
229-2512	4"	Iron Pipe	4.5"	.052"	10	2.50
229-2513	Brass Wire, Round (.0625" dia)			*NEW*		2.50
229-2530	Brass Wire, Flat (.015 x 060)			*NEW*		2.50
229-2522	Brass Wire, Flat (.010 x .018)			pkg(6)		2.50
229-2524	Brass Wire, Flat (.010 x .030)			pkg(6)		2.50
229-2526	Brass Wire, Flat (.015 x .024)			pkg(6)		2.50
229-2528	Brass Wire, Flat (.015 x .042)			pkg(6)		2.50
229-2550	Silver Plating Powder			(5 grams)		4.50

SCREWS

229-2552	2-56 x 1/8"	Pan Head	pkg(12) .85
229-2553	2-56 x 3/16"	Pan Head	pkg(12) .85
229-2554	2-56 x 1/4"	Pan Head	pkg(12) .85
229-2555	2-56 x 1/2"	Pan Head	pkg(12) .85

SPARK ARRESTORS

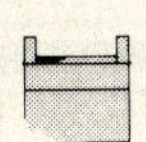

Super Flared
Switcher Type
229-2101
pkg(2) 1.25

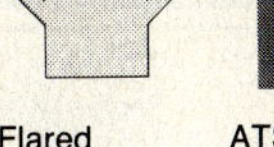

ATSF Type
Cast Metal
229-2104
pkg(2) 1.50

Round Type
229-2102
pkg(2) 1.25

Round Wire
Screen Type
229-2103
pkg(2) 1.50
EMD switcher
cast metal type

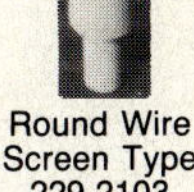

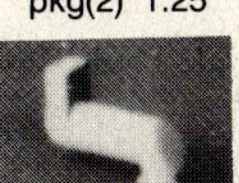

Milwaukee
SW Type
229-2105
pkg(2) 2.00
cast metal

Milwaukee
F Type
229-2106
pkg(2) 2.00
cast metal

(not illustrated)
229-4001   Steam Locos   ea 2.00
229-102102   Round, Brass   pr 2.35

SPEED RECORDERS

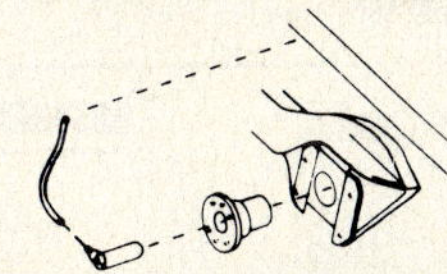

Flange Type
229-2807   pkg(4) 1.50

GE Type
229-2808   pkg(4) 1.75

STEPS

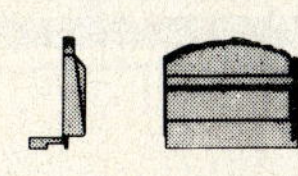

Drop, EMD
Late GP, SD Type
229-1402   pkg(2) 1.50

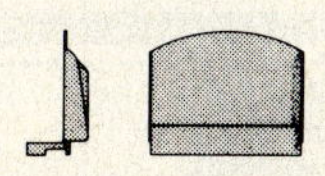

Drop EMD-2 Series Type
229-1404   pkg(2) 1.50

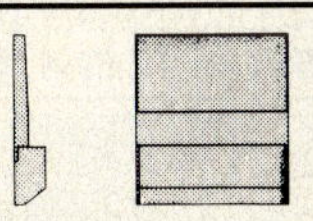

Drop GE U Series Type
229-1403   pkg(2) 1.50

Caboose with
End Platform
229-6502   pkg(2) 2.50

DETAIL ASSOCIATES

HO SCALE (1/87)

All parts are black injection molded styrene plastic unless noted. Illustrations are approximately 1-1/2 times HO Scale unless noted.

STEPS (continued)

Drop, EMD Early GP, SD, SW Type
229-1401 pkg(2) 1.50

Drop, Alco Short RS/RSD's
229-1405 pkg(2) 3.00

Drop, Alco Long Century
229-1406 pkg(2) 3.00

(not illustrated)

229-1407	Drop FM Trainmaster Type	each 3.00
229-1408	Drop Alco Long, RSD Type	each 3.00

SUNSHADES

229-101301	Sunshade (brass)	pkg(2) 1.75
229-101302	Sunshade F&E (brass)	pkg(4) 1.75

WINDOWS

229-3301	Athearn SW	each 1.75	229-3304	Athearn F7B	each 1.00
229-3302	Athearn S-12	each 1.75	229-3305	Atlas FP7	each 1.75
229-3303	Athearn F7A	each 1.75			

WINTERIZATION HATCHES

229-2013	GP9 & GP18	*NEW*	each 2.00
229-2014	GP/SD 60	*NEW*	each 2.00

BRAWA

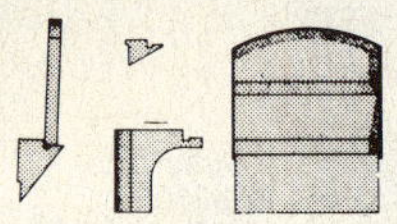
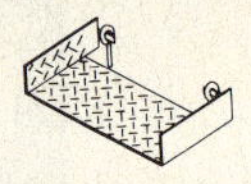

HO SCALE (1/87)

Imported from Germany by WALTHERS

Metal details, unless noted. Illustrations are not to scale.

+ (PLUS SIGN) = SPECIAL ORDER ONLY ITEMS

BUMPERS

186-672	Open Frame (resin cast)	each 6.49
186-674	Closed Frame (resin cast)	each 6.49

186-673	Brass Post	pkg(2) 33.99

COUPLINGS

DRG "Hook"
186-560 pkg(2) 10.99
Hook type coupling used on DRG and early DB equipment.

Rangier Automatic, Brass
186-561 pkg(2) 15.99
Prototype used on Rangier industrial locos, will fit most small switch engines.

Automatic Couplings
186-564 11.49
Brass, for KOFII switcher

DETAIL SET

KOF2 Detail Set
186-562 each 114.99
Brass details, less loco

FUEL PUMP

Diesel Fuel Pump
186-675 each 19.99
Two piece metal casting, approximately 3/4" high, painted.

WHEELS

KOF Diesel Spokewheels
186-563 pkg(2) 42.99

ORNAMENTAL SHEETS

Detail items are etched from 0.20 and 0.30 brass sheets.

186-3601	Grids and Gates, Large (3-3/4 x 6")+	20.49
186-3621	Grids and Gates, Small (2-1/2 x 4")	12.49
186-3603	6 Guard Rails, Large (3-3/4 x 5-1/2")	20.49
186-3623	6 Guard Rails, Small (2-1/2 x 4")	12.49
186-3606	6 Handrails, Large (to match #3602, 4 x 5-1/2")	20.49
186-3626	6 Handrails, Small (to match #3622, 2-1/2 x 4")	12.49
186-3602	6 Guard Rails, Large (4 x 6")	20.49
186-3622	6 Guard Rails, Small (2-1/2 x 4")	12.49
186-3607	6 Handrails, Large (to match #3603, 4 x 5-1/2")	20.49
186-3627	6 Handrails, Small (to match #3623, 2-1/2 x 3-3/4")	12.49

McKean

HO SCALE (1/87)

FREIGHT CAR DETAIL

457-10	Modern Brake Set (fits any car)	pkg(3)	1.25
457-11	Box Ladders & Appliances		1.95
457-12	40' Frame Kit		2.95
457-13	PS-1 Ladder	pkg(4)	2.95
457-14	Door-8' Pullman Standard	2 pair	1.00
457-15	Door-6' Pullman Standard	2 pair	1.00
457-16	Roofwalks-PSL	pkg(3)	1.50
457-20	Modern Box Car Detail Set		2.95
457-21	50' Overhang Roof		1.95
457-22	50' Underframe/Ladder Sets/Details		2.95
457-26	Door 8' Corrugated Pullman Standard	pkg(4)	1.00
457-27	Door 6' Corrugated Pullman Standard	pkg(4)	1.00
457-28	6' 7-Panel Doors	pkg(4)	1.00
457-29	6' 5-Panel Doors	pkg(4)	1.00
457-30	7' Plug Doors	pkg(4)	1.00
457-31	8' Plug Doors	pkg(4)	1.00
457-32	40'/50' Boxcar Details	pkg(4)	1.95
457-33	50' Diagonal Panel Roof w/walk	each	1.95
457-36	10' Plug Doors	pkg(4)	1.00
457-37	ACF Hopper 20" hatch details	each	1.50
457-38	ACF Hopper Lower Hatches and Tubes	each	1.75
457-39	ACF Hopper 30" hatch details	each	1.50
457-40	ACF Hopper Ladders 1-pc	each	1.95
457-47	40' Straight-Panel Roof	*NEW*	1.75
457-48	40' Diagonal-Panel Roof	*NEW*	1.75
457-50	Hopper Toppers—White	*NEW*	3.95
457-51	Hopper Toppers—Yellow	*NEW*	3.95

DETAILS WEST

HO SCALE (1/87) SUPER DETAIL PARTS

These diesel detail parts are white metal castings unless noted. Illustrations are not to scale.

This custom painted Bachmann GP-30 is equipped with the following Details West parts.

- #120 Plow
- #186 M3 Horn
- #157 "Firecracker Antenna"
- #117 Twin Beam Headlight
- #137 Nose Light
- #119 Rerail Frog
- #172 Step Light
- #154 Air Filter
- #195 Pilot Buffer Plate
- #193 Pilot Beam
- #166 Fuel Filters
- #203 GE Sand Fillers
- #127 Underframe Bell
- #132 Hand Brake

AIR CONDITIONERS

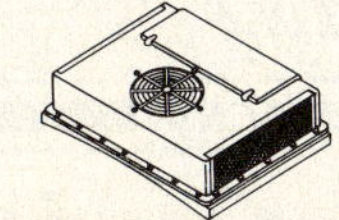

235-158 Vapor Type   each 1.00
Mounted atop cab of 2nd generation hood units. Styrene.

235-159 Prime Type   each 1.25
Roof mount with adaptor for GE hood units. Styrene.

AIR FILTERS

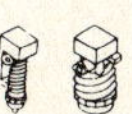

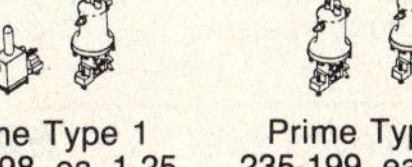

235-139 pr 1.00
For most 2nd generation GE and EMD hood units.

235-154 ea .70
Common in 1st and early 2nd generation hood units.

Prime Type 1
235-198 ea 1.25
2nd generation EMD hood units.

Prime Type 2
235-199 ea 1.25
2nd generation EMD hood units.

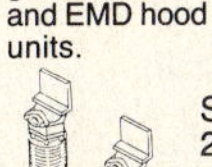
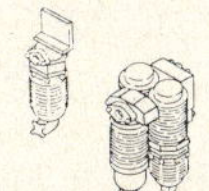

Salem Small
235-225
pkg(2) 1.50

Salem Set
235-226
pkg(2) 1.75

AIR HORNS

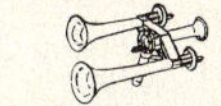

Nathan M3
235-186   ea 2.50

Nathan M5
235-187   ea 2.50

Leslie RSL-3L-R
235-190   ea 2.50

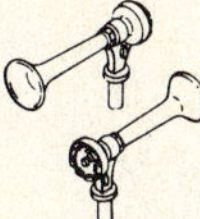
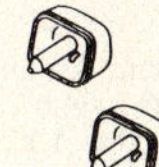

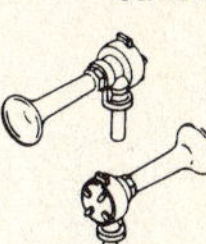

Wabco Type E, Single Chime
235-174
pkg(2) 2.00
For 1st generation cab and hodd units and switchers

Hancock Type 4700
235-131
pkg(2) 1.00
For a variety of of units of PC, MILW, L&N, SCL & others.

Nathan P3, Three Chime
235-175
each 2.50
For all types of 1st and 2nd gneration units, brass.

Blat Type Single Chime
235-173
pkg(2) 2.00
For 1st generation cab and hood units and switchers, brass.

AIR TANKS

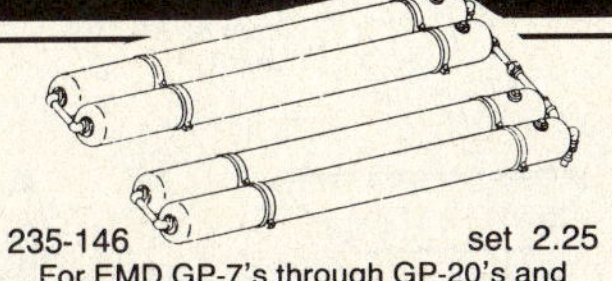

235-204 Underframe   pair 1.95
For EMD Hood Units

235-146   set 2.25
For EMD GP-7's through GP-20's and C&NW GP-35's.

ANTENNA STANDS

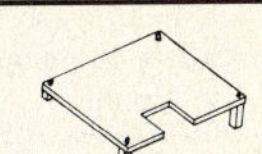
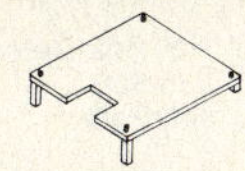

Style 1
235-222
pkg(2)   1.75

Style 2
235-223
pkg(2)   1.75

BELLS

Frame Mount
235-127   pkg(2) 1.25
For all types of units.

Fabricated Type
235-128   pkg(2) 1.25
Standard equipment for EMD switchers, post 1952.

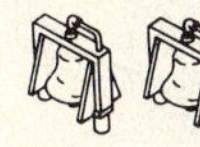

Hood Side Mount
235-129   pkg(2) 1.25
For GE & other hood units.

Roof Mount
235-134   pkg(2) 1.25
For GE hood units.

Front Mount
235-135   pkg(2) 1.50
For hood units of N&W and Southern.

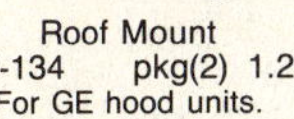
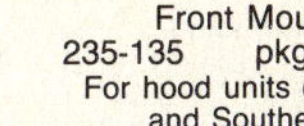

Curved Base Fabricated Type
235-151   pkg(2) 1.25
For Alco-built switchers.

Gong Type
235-152   pkg(2) 1.00
For noses of C&NW and DT&I units and to locos of BAR, BN and MP.

Hood Side Mount
235-176   pkg(2) 1.25

BRAKE WHEELS & HANDBRAKE

EMD/GE Loco
235-179
pkg(2) 1.00

Handbrake
235-132 ea 1.00
Standard on most EMD and other hood units.

with Gear Box
235-177 1.50

CAB & BODY VENTS

235-121 Styrene   pkg(12) .75
For hood units and cabooses.

235-122 Styrene   pkg(12) .75
For 2nd generation EMD and GE units.

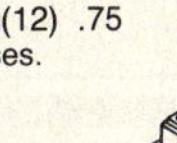

w/Electrical Cabinet Filter
235-107   set (2 pieces) .75
Late 2nd generation hood units.

w/Electrical Cabinet Filter
235-161   set (2 pieces) .75
Standard equipment on EMD Dash-2 hood units.

COOLING FANS

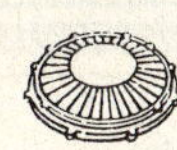
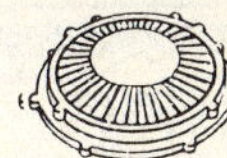

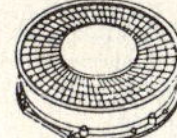

36" Cap-Top Type for Radiator and/ or Dynamic Brake
235-142
pkg(4) 1.25
For F-7's, F-9's, GP-20's, GP-30's, GP-35's, SD-7's, SD-9's, SD-18's, SD-24's, SD-35's, F-8's, F-9's.

48" Cap-Top Type for Dynamic Brake
235-143
pkg(2) .70
For F-7's, F-9's, GP-7's, GP-9's, E-8's, E-9's.

48" Pan-Top Type for Radiator and/ or Dynamic Brake
235-144
pkg(3) 1.25
For late GP-9's, GP-18's, GP-20's, GP30's, GP-35's, late SD-9's, SD-18's SD-24's.

48" Flared-Top Type for Radiator
235-145
pkg(4) 1.25
For EMD GP-20's.

4-4 DREADNAUGHT ENDS

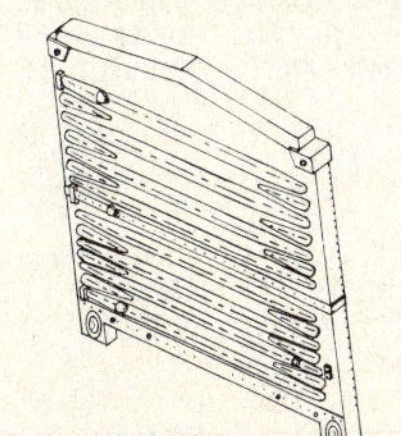
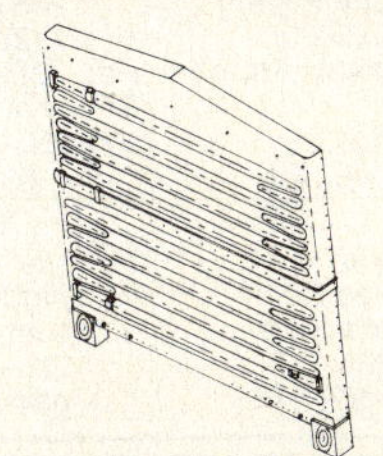

235-1000 Square Corner   pkg(2) 2.00
1930-1940

235-1001 Round Corner pkg(2) 2.00
1940-1950

ELECTRIC RELAY

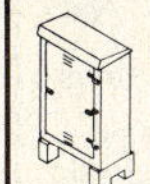
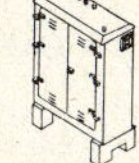
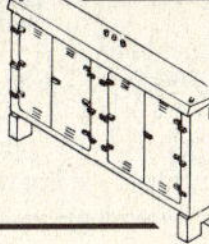

Cabinet, 1 Door
235-901
each 1.75

Cabinet, 2 Door
235-902
each 1.85

Cabinet, 4 Door
235-904
each 1.95

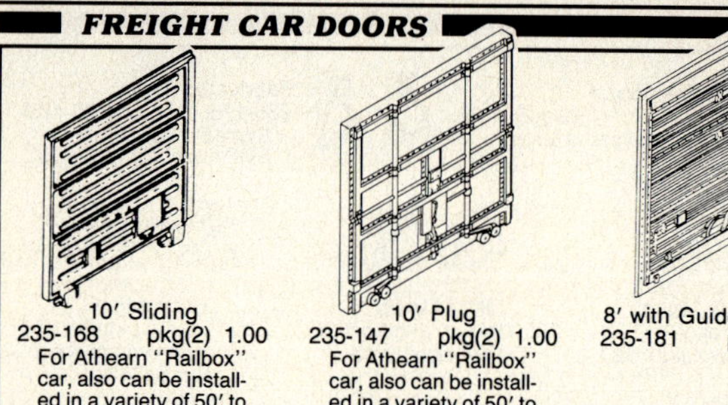

DETAILS WEST

HO SCALE (1/87)
SUPER DETAIL PARTS

These diesel parts are white metal castings unless noted. Illustrations are not to scale.

FREIGHT CAR DOORS

10' Sliding
235-168   pkg(2) 1.00
For Athearn ''Railbox'' car, also can be installed in a variety of 50' to 60' cars.

10' Plug
235-147   pkg(2) 1.00
For Athearn ''Railbox'' car, also can be installed in a variety of 50' to 60' cars.

8' with Guides & Board
235-181   pkg(2) 1.75

FUEL FILLERS

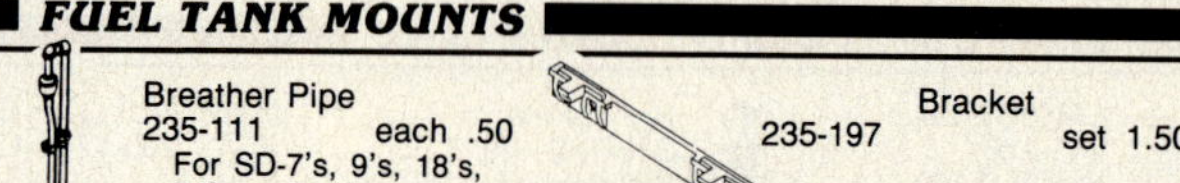

GE Hood Units
235-149   pkg(4) 1.00

EMD Road Units
235-166   pkg(4) 1.00

EMD Switcher Type
235-167   pkg(4) 1.00

FUEL TANK MOUNTS

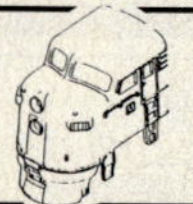

Breather Pipe
235-111   each .50
For SD-7's, 9's, 18's, 24's and 26's.

Bracket
235-197   set 1.50

F-UNIT PARTS

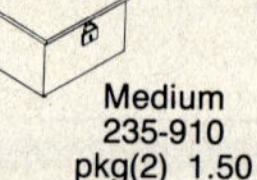

A-Units
235-208   set 5.50

B-Units
235-209   set 5.50

GROUND BOXES

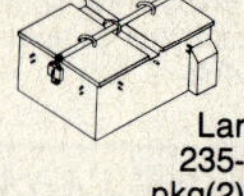

Small
235-909
pkg(2) 1.25

Medium
235-910
pkg(2) 1.50

Large
235-911
pkg(2) 1.75

HEADLIGHTS

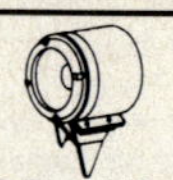

SP Barrel Type, Bolted Face
235-108   ea 1.25
For first generation GP's and SD's

SP Barrel Type, Hinged Face
235-109   ea 1.25
For first generation GP's and SD's

''Pyle'' Twin Gyralight Flush Mount Type
235-138   ea .70
For low hood of EMD 2nd generation hood units.

''Pyle'' Gyralight
235-115   pkg(2) .70

''Pyle'' Twin Sealed Beam, Early Style
235-114   pkg(2) .70

''Pyle'' Barrel Type
235-133   pkg(2) 2.00
For GP-7's an GP-9's of EWP and CN.

''Pyle'' Type Back-up Light, Sgl Sealed Beam
235-162   pr .70
For E and F-units.

Oscitrol Type
235-153   pr .75
For Amtrak E-units and ICG rebuilt hood units.

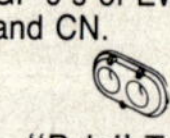

''Pyle'' Twin Sealed Beam, Late Style
235-117   pkg(2) .70

''Pyle'' Twin Graylight, Flush Mount Type
235-148   pair .70

''Pyle'' Twin Gyralight
235-116   pkg(2) .70

Nose Headlight Southern Pacific
235-200   ea 1.25

HEADLIGHT SETS — SP

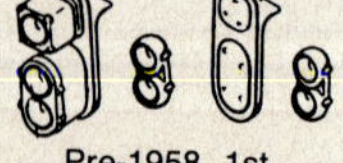
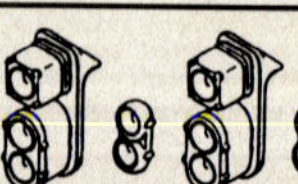
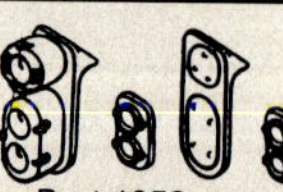

Pre-1958, 1st Generation Hood Units
235-100
set (6 pieces) 2.25
For single end Mars group.

Pre-1958, 1st Generation Hood Units
235-101
set (8 pieces) 2.75
For double end Mars group.

Post-1958, 1st Generation Hood Units
235-102
set (6 pieces) 2.25
For single end Pyle group.

HEADLIGHT SETS — SP (cont)

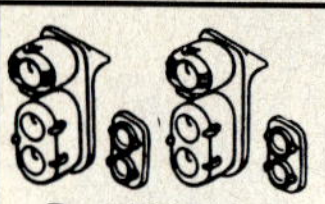

Post-1958, 1st Generation Hood Units
235-103
set (8 pcs) 2.75
For double end ''Pyle'' group.

SD-7, SD-9
235-104
set (6 pcs) 2.25
For single end ''Mars'' group.

SD-7, SD-9
235-105
set (8 pcs) 2.75
For double end ''Mars'' group.

SP Rebuilt Rear
235-178
set 1.50

INSTRUMENT SHEDS

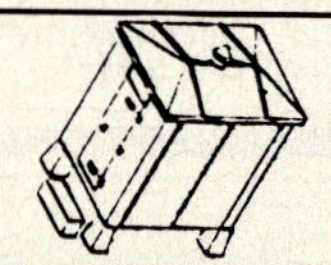
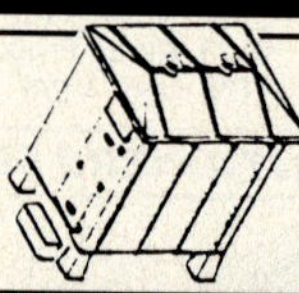

6x8
235-907
3.95

5x7
235-908
2.95

LADDERS

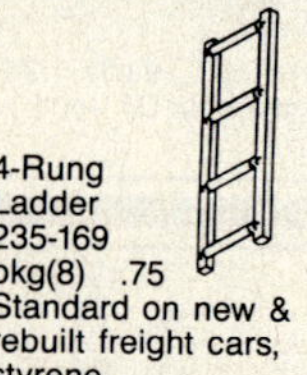

4-Rung Ladder
235-169
pkg(8) .75
Standard on new & rebuilt freight cars, styrene.

7-Rung Ladder w/brackets
235-1006
pkg(4) 1.25

8-Rung Ladder
235-1005
pkg(4) 1.25

MARS LIGHTS

Signal
235-112   pkg(2) .70

Twin Signal
235-113   pkg(2) .70

Twin Signal Light, Flush Mount Type
235-137   each .70
For low hood of EMD 2nd generation hood units.

MISCELLANEOUS

Steam Generator Set
235-118
3 pieces 1.50

Re-Rail Frog Set
235-119
4 pieces 1.50
with right and left hangers

Loco and Cab Step Lights
235-172
pkg(8) 1.25
For virtually all diesels and many road's cabooses.

Automatic Train Control Box
235-170   ea 1.50
For hood units of PRR (PC, CR) AT&SF, UP and others.

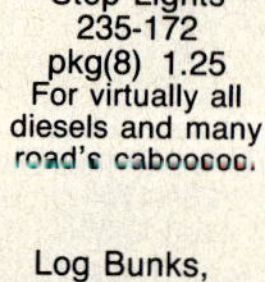

Log Bunks, Pacific Car & Foundry Type
235-171
pkg(4) 2.25
For 40' and 50' flat cars of BN, MILW, and UP.

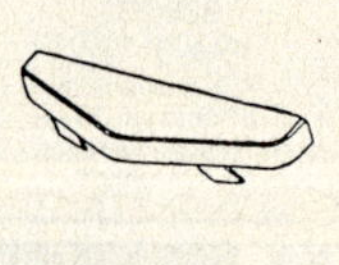

Anti-Climber
235-189   ea 1.25
For EMD SD locos, styrene.

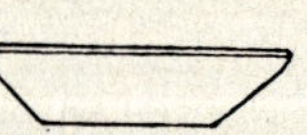

Diesel Sun Visor, Styrene
235-188   pkg(4) .80

Spare Knuckle/Bracket
235-196   pkg(2) 1.00

Awning/Smoke Deflector
235-194   each 1.50

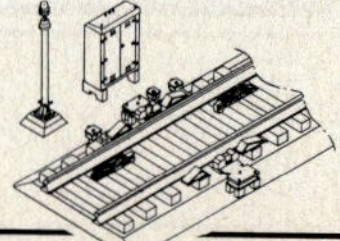
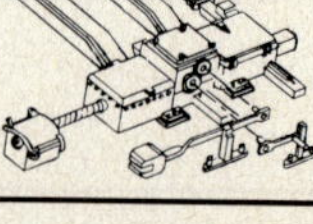

Hot Box Detector
235-900
set 7.95

Switch Motor & Tie Mount
235-903   ea 1.50

DETAILS WEST

HO SCALE (1/87) SUPER DETAIL PARTS

These diesel parts are white metal castings unless noted. Illustrations are not to scale.

■ MISCELLANEOUS (continued)

Automatic Train Stop Santa Fe, Amtrak
235-184   1.25

Sinclair Radio Antenna: SP, Santa Fe And Others
235-214   1.50

Drag Detector Set
235-905   4.95

Flange Lubricator Set
235-906   2.95

Refrigerator Car Details
235-215   1.75

Radio Antenna
235-157
pkg(5) 1.50
Brass "Firecracker" type

Traction Motor Cable Set
235-224 1.95

End of Train Device
235-227
pkg(2) 1.95

Air Jack and Car Stands
235-450
pkg(2) 2.25

Men at Work Sign
235-451 1.95

Telephone Box w/Wood Post
235-912 1.50

Reefer Hatch Equipco Set
235-1003 2.00

Crossing Signal w/LED's
235-913 19.95

Trailer Hitch Piggyback
235-1004 6.95

8 Ft Panel Door
235-1002
pkg(2) 2.00

Knuckle Holder GP50/60
235-210   each 1.75

(not illustrated)

235-916	Ground Throw Switch	2/sets 2.75	
235-228	EMD Ditch Lights w/bulb	**NEW**	TBA
235-1007	Flat Car Trailer Hitch #1	**NEW**	TBA
235-1008	Flat Car Trailer Hitch #2	**NEW**	TBA

■ MU CABLES

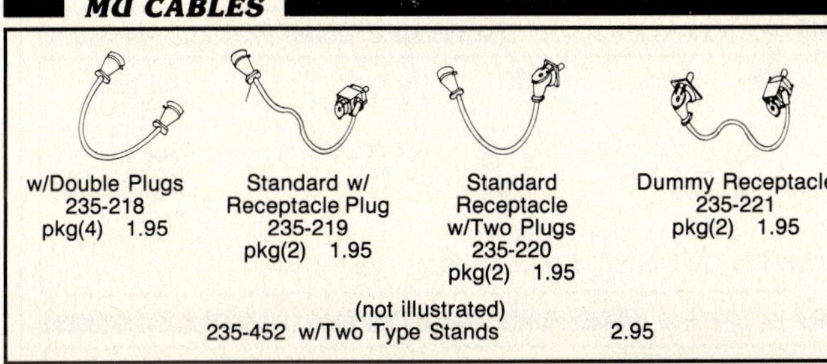

w/Double Plugs
235-218
pkg(4) 1.95

Standard w/ Receptacle Plug
235-219
pkg(2) 1.95

Standard Receptacle w/Two Plugs
235-220
pkg(2) 1.95

Dummy Receptacle
235-221
pkg(2) 1.95

(not illustrated)
235-452 w/Two Type Stands   2.95

■ NUMBER BOARDS

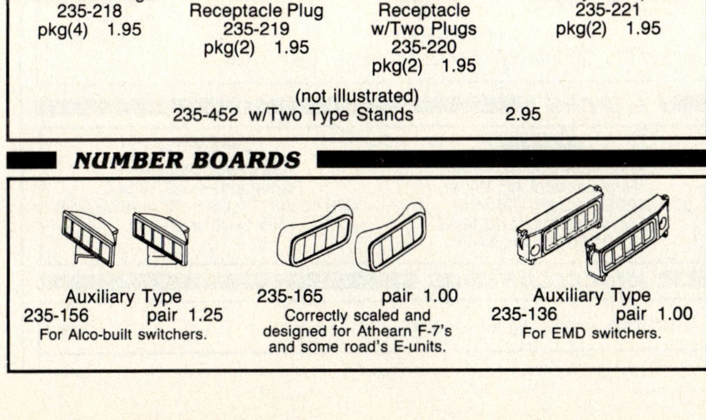

Auxiliary Type
235-156   pair 1.25
For Alco-built switchers.

235-165   pair 1.00
Correctly scaled and designed for Athearn F-7's and some road's E-units.

Auxiliary Type
235-136   pair 1.00
For EMD switchers.

■ PILOTS

Snow Plow
235-130   each 1.50
Replaces footboards on 2nd generation EMD and GE hood units.

235-141   pair 2.50
For SP passenger service GP-9's.

Beam with Footboards
235-192   pkg(2) 1.50

Beam
235-193
pkg(2) 1.25

Buffer Plate
235-195
pkg(2) 1.50

■ ROTARY BEACON

White metal castings with styrene lens.

Roof Mount
235-106   each 1.00

"Western-Cullen" Type D-312
235-126   each 1.00
For UP, BN, AT&SF and others.

■ SAND FILLER HATCHES

EMD GP-7's to GP-20's
235-201
pkg(4) 1.25

Alco
235-202
pkg(4)
1.25

GE
235-203
pkg(4) 1.25

■ SNOW PLOWS

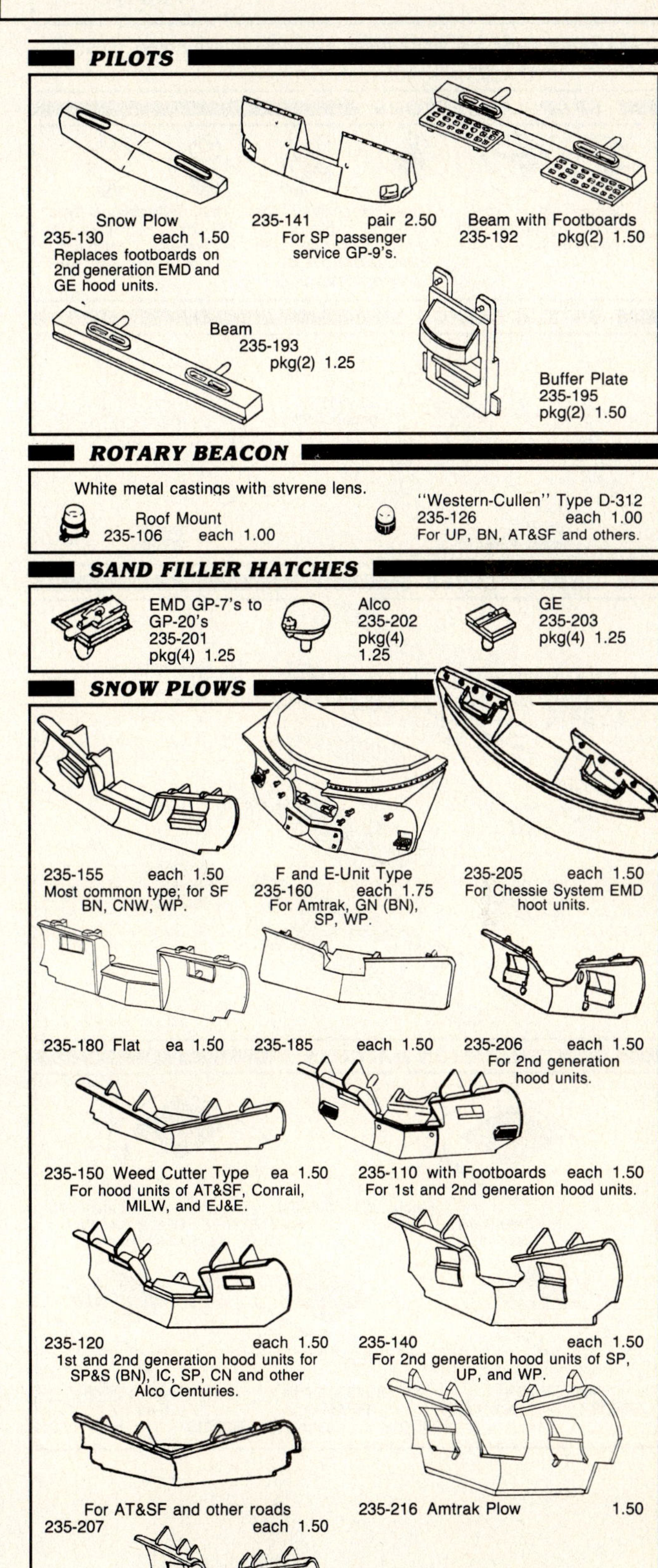

235-155   each 1.50
Most common type; for SF BN, CNW, WP.

F and E-Unit Type
235-160   each 1.75
For Amtrak, GN (BN), SP, WP.

235-205   each 1.50
For Chessie System EMD hoot units.

235-180 Flat   ea 1.50

235-185   each 1.50

235-206   each 1.50
For 2nd generation hood units.

235-150 Weed Cutter Type ea 1.50
For hood units of AT&SF, Conrail, MILW, and EJ&E.

235-110 with Footboards   each 1.50
For 1st and 2nd generation hood units.

235-120   each 1.50
1st and 2nd generation hood units for SP&S (BN), IC, SP, CN and other Alco Centuries.

235-140   each 1.50
For 2nd generation hood units of SP, UP, and WP.

For AT&SF and other roads
235-207   each 1.50

235-216 Amtrak Plow   1.50

"Hood Unit" EMD Passenger Plow
235-217   each 1.50

DETAILS WEST

HO SCALE (1/87)
SUPER DETAIL PARTS

These diesel parts are white metal castings unless noted. Illustrations are not to scale.

SPARK ARRESTORS

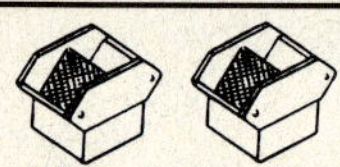
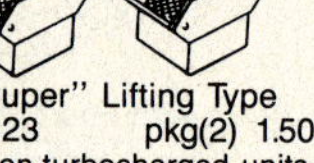

"Super" Lifting Type
235-123   pkg(2) 1.50
For non-turbocharged units.

"Super" Non-Lifting Type
235-124   pkg(2) 1.50
For non-turbocharged EMD units of D&RGW, MP, G&NW, GM&O, SOO

"Harco" Centrifugal Type
235-125   pkg(2) 1.50
For non-turbocharged EMD units of UP, BN, BAR, ARR

SWITCH STANDS

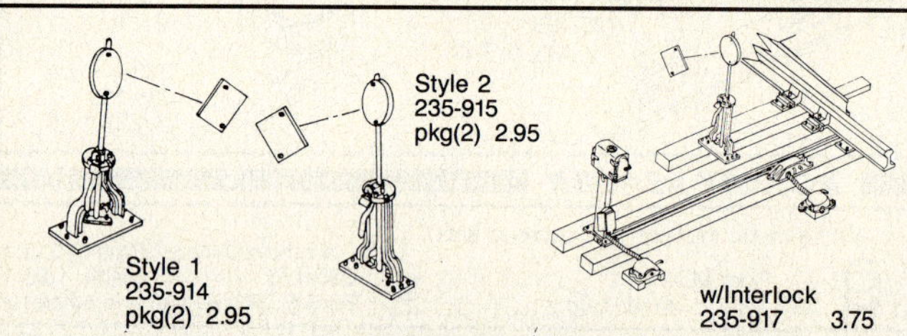

Style 2
235-915
pkg(2) 2.95

Style 1
235-914
pkg(2) 2.95

w/Interlock
235-917   3.75

UNDERFRAMES

50' Hydra-Cushion
235-182   1.75
Styrene

50' Evans
235-183   1.75
Styrene

WINTERIZATION HATCHES

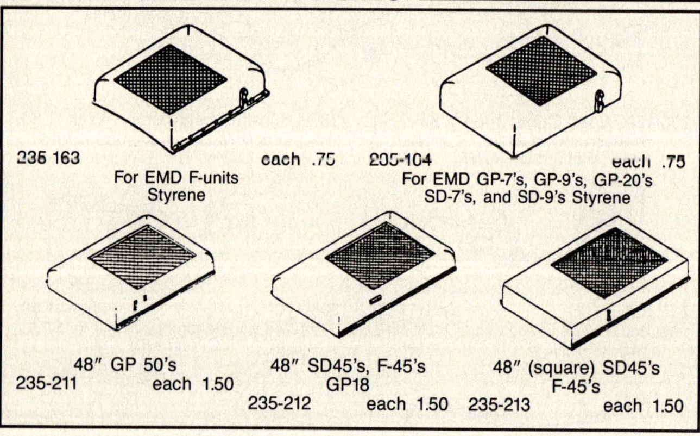

235-163   each .75
For EMD F-units
Styrene

235-164   each .75
For EMD GP-7's, GP-9's, GP-20's SD-7's, and SD-9's Styrene

48" GP 50's
235-211   each 1.50

48" SD45's, F-45's
GP18
235-212   each 1.50

48" (square) SD45's
F-45's
235-213   each 1.50

kibri

Imported from Germany
by **WALTHERS**

HO SCALE (1/87)

CARGO

Shipping Container Pallets, Oil Drums
405-9458   18.49

2 Wire Cable Drums
405-9921   pkg(2) 9.99

High Voltage Transformer
405-9922   11.99

Assorted Oil Drum
405-9386   pkg(24) 8.99

INTERIORS

General Office
405-8120   12.99

Design Office
405-8122   12.99

Keil-Line Models

HO SCALE (1/87)

WEIGHTS

Designed for hidden installations, hopper car weights add necessary weight to ensure good tracking qualities.

382-8706	Athearn Quad Hopper	pkg(2) 2.95
382-8707	TMI Twin Hopper	pkg(2) 2.95
382-8708	Athearn 2-Bay Hopper	pkg(2) 2.95
382-8709	MDC 3-Bay Hopper	pkg(2) 2.25
382-8710	McKean 100T Hopper	each 2.95
382-8711	MDC 5-Bay Rapid Discharge Hopper	pkg(2) 1.85

Roco

Imported from Austria
by **WALTHERS**

HO SCALE (1/87)
Metal working pantographs.

DESTINATION BOARDS

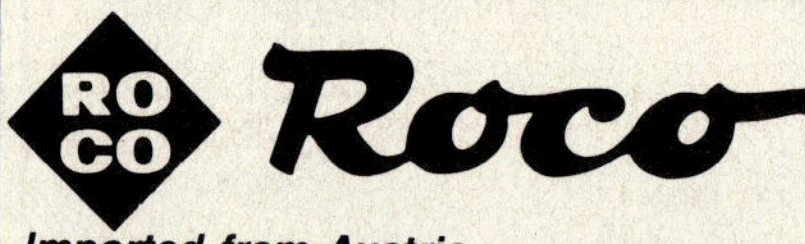

Destination Boards Assortment
625-40012   3.49

PANTOGRAPHS

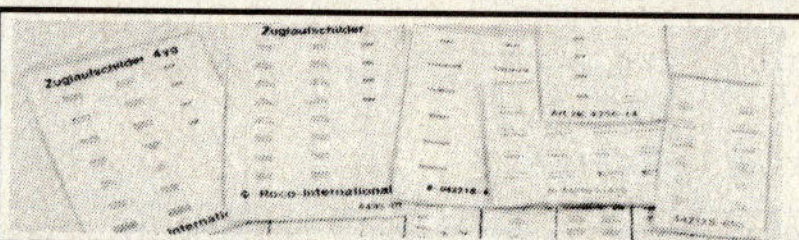

Austrian Type II
625-85225
pkg(2) 10.99
w/"Wanisch" mount

DB Type SBS (black)
#67
625-85216   10.99

#67 (red)
625-85234   10.99
Same as #85216, but with wider wiper to fit 3-rail AC systems.

(not illustrated)
625-85233 DB Type SBS #54 for AC, Black   each 10.99

WIPERS

Replacement AC Wiper
625-40002   (2.2" 56 mm)   2.99
Fits 14111,14120,14126,14138, 14145,14148 and 14191

Replacement AC Wiper
625-40003   (1.6" 42 mm)   2.99
Fits 14178 and 14183.

MISCELLANEOUS

625-10006 Drilling Jig for #10004   2.99

EVERGREEN HILL designs

HO SCALE (1/87)

Detail parts are metal castings. Illustrations are not to scale.

AUTO PARTS

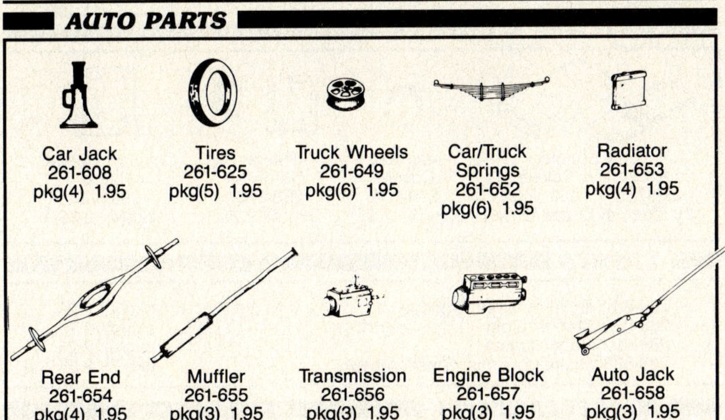

Car Jack
261-608
pkg(4) 1.95

Tires
261-625
pkg(5) 1.95

Truck Wheels
261-649
pkg(6) 1.95

Car/Truck Springs
261-652
pkg(6) 1.95

Radiator
261-653
pkg(4) 1.95

Rear End
261-654
pkg(4) 1.95

Muffler
261-655
pkg(3) 1.95

Transmission
261-656
pkg(3) 1.95

Engine Block
261-657
pkg(3) 1.95

Auto Jack
261-658
pkg(3) 1.95

BOXES & CRATES

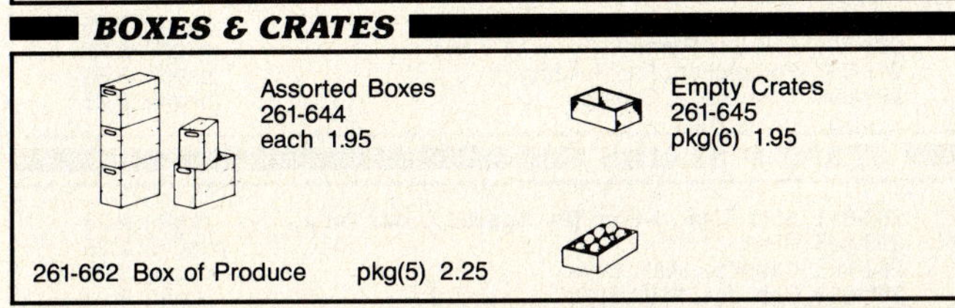

Assorted Boxes
261-644
each 1.95

Empty Crates
261-645
pkg(6) 1.95

261-662 Box of Produce   pkg(5) 2.25

CANS & DRUMS

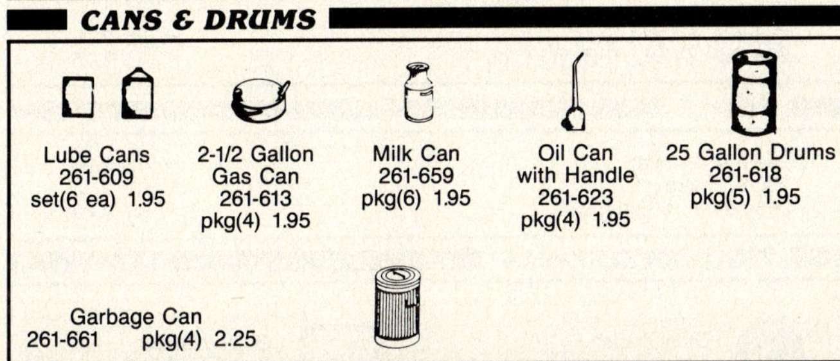

Lube Cans
261-609
set(6 ea) 1.95

2-1/2 Gallon Gas Can
261-613
pkg(4) 1.95

Milk Can
261-659
pkg(6) 1.95

Oil Can with Handle
261-623
pkg(4) 1.95

25 Gallon Drums
261-618
pkg(5) 1.95

Garbage Can
261-661   pkg(4) 2.25

BOILERS

261-505 AH&D Boiler Only   kit 5.95

FURNISHINGS

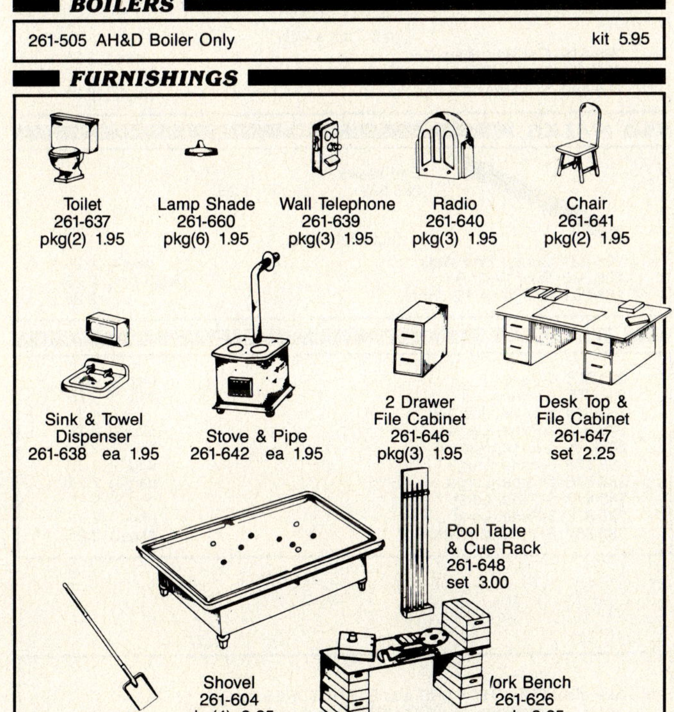

Toilet
261-637
pkg(2) 1.95

Lamp Shade
261-660
pkg(6) 1.95

Wall Telephone
261-639
pkg(3) 1.95

Radio
261-640
pkg(3) 1.95

Chair
261-641
pkg(2) 1.95

Sink & Towel Dispenser
261-638   ea 1.95

Stove & Pipe
261-642   ea 1.95

2 Drawer File Cabinet
261-646
pkg(3) 1.95

Desk Top & File Cabinet
261-647
set 2.25

Pool Table & Cue Rack
261-648
set 3.00

Shovel
261-604
pkg(4) 2.25

Work Bench
261-626
each 2.25

MISCELLANEOUS

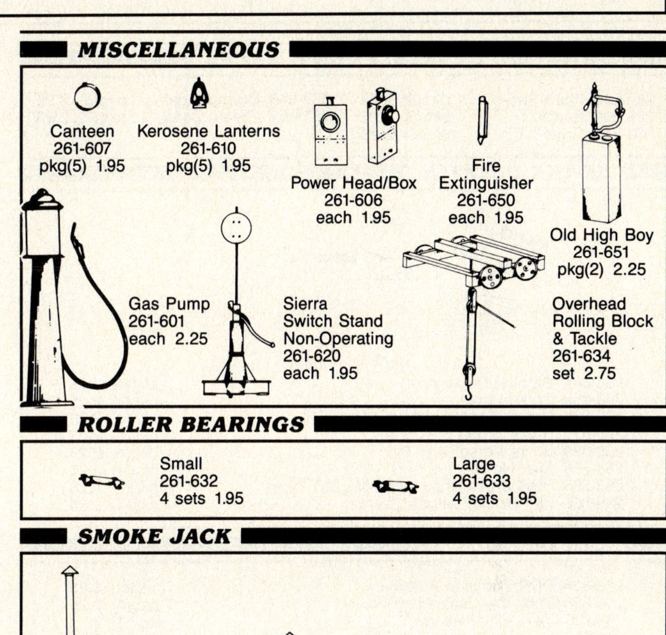

Canteen
261-607
pkg(5) 1.95

Kerosene Lanterns
261-610
pkg(5) 1.95

Power Head/Box
261-606
each 1.95

Fire Extinguisher
261-650
each 1.95

Old High Boy
261-651
pkg(2) 2.25

Gas Pump
261-601
each 2.25

Sierra Switch Stand Non-Operating
261-620
each 1.95

Overhead Rolling Block & Tackle
261-634
set 2.75

ROLLER BEARINGS

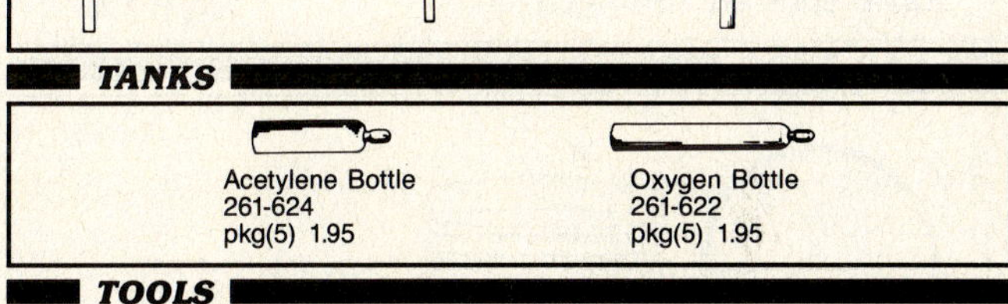

Small
261-632
4 sets 1.95

Large
261-633
4 sets 1.95

SMOKE JACK

Smoke Jack Tall
261-617
pkg(2) 1.95

Smoke Jack Short
261-619
pkg(2) 1.95

Smoke Jack
261-643
pkg(3) 1.95

TANKS

Acetylene Bottle
261-624
pkg(5) 1.95

Oxygen Bottle
261-622
pkg(5) 1.95

TOOLS

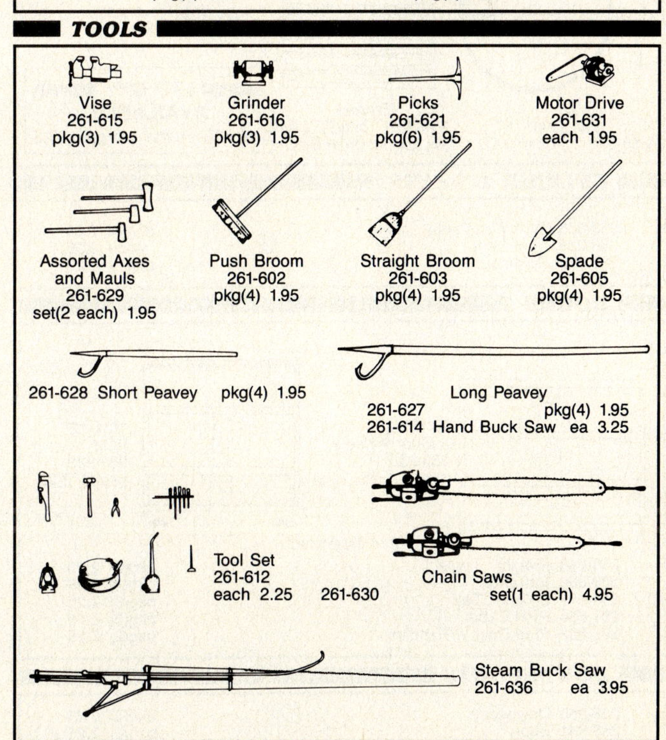

Vise
261-615
pkg(3) 1.95

Grinder
261-616
pkg(3) 1.95

Picks
261-621
pkg(6) 1.95

Motor Drive
261-631
each 1.95

Assorted Axes and Mauls
261-629
set(2 each) 1.95

Push Broom
261-602
pkg(4) 1.95

Straight Broom
261-603
pkg(4) 1.95

Spade
261-605
pkg(4) 1.95

261-628 Short Peavey   pkg(4) 1.95

Long Peavey
261-627   pkg(4) 1.95
261-614 Hand Buck Saw ea 3.25

Tool Set
261-612
each 2.25

Chain Saws
261-630   set(1 each) 4.95

Steam Buck Saw
261-636   ea 3.95

GLOOR·CRAFT MODELS

HO SCALE (1/87)

Parts cast in white metal.

Illustrations not to scale.

BARRELS, CRATES, CANS & SACKS

288-845	Flour Sacks	pkg(6)	2.25
288-846	Barrel	pkg(3)	2.25
288-847	Crate	pkg(3)	2.25
288-848	Drum 55 gal	pkg(3)	2.25
288-851	Cream Cans	pkg(3)	2.25

BRAKE DETAILS

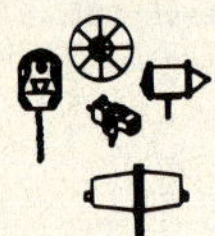

5 Piece Brake Set
288-826   2.25

(not illustrated)

288-844	Ratchet Brake Arm	pkg(4)	2.25
288-862	Brake Wheel	pkg(4)	2.25
288-822	Brake Wheel Platform	pkg(6)	2.25
288-813	Brake Wheel Platform	pkg(6)	2.25
288-888	Brake Wheel with Pin	pkg(4)	2.25
288-890	Ajax Holder	pkg(4)	2.25
288-895	PRR Brake Shoe with Arm, ND Type	pkg(8)	2.25
288-896	"K" Brake Cylinder, Large	pkg(4)	2.25

CAR DETAILS

288-824	PRR Caboose Antenna	each	3.25
288-836	Tank Car, Unloading Valves	pkg(4)	2.25
288-837	Tank Car Placard	pkg(12)	2.25
288-859	Coupler Pocket, Flared	2 pair	2.25
288-861	Grab Irons	pkg(12)	3.25
288-870	Smoke Jack, PRR Style	pkg(2)	2.25
288-885	Flatcar Stake Pocket	pkg(12)	2.25
288-889	End Sill, Flatcar	pkg(2)	2.25
288-894	PRR Wheel Housing ND Type	pkg(4)	2.25
288-897	Poling Pocket	pkg(12)	2.25
288-898	"Z" Braces	pkg(8)	2.25
288-899	Bolster End Plate-Hopper	pkg(2)	2.25

CAR ENDS

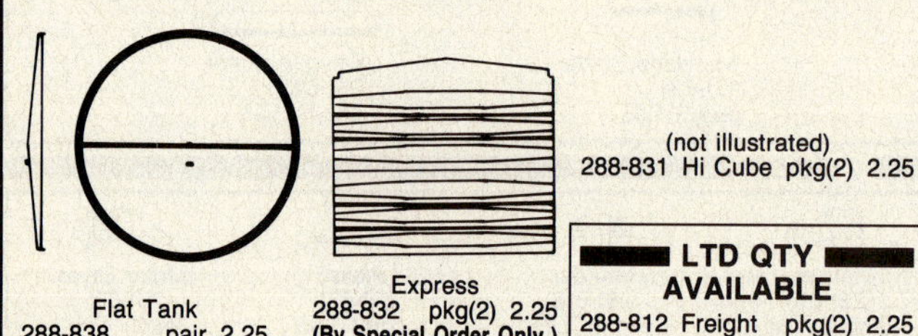

(not illustrated)
288-831 Hi Cube pkg(2) 2.25

LTD QTY AVAILABLE
288-812 Freight   pkg(2) 2.25

Flat Tank
288-838   pair 2.25

Express
288-832   pkg(2) 2.25
(By Special Order Only.)

CHIMNEY & VENTS

288-835	Tank Car Vents	pkg(4)	2.25
288-865	Roof Vent	each	2.25
288-872	Chimney, Short	pkg(2)	2.25

DOORS

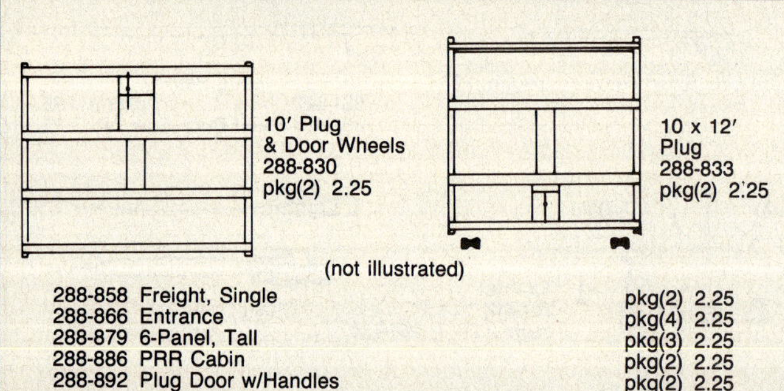

10' Plug & Door Wheels
288-830
pkg(2) 2.25

10 x 12'
Plug
288-833
pkg(2) 2.25

(not illustrated)

288-858	Freight, Single	pkg(2)	2.25
288-866	Entrance	pkg(4)	2.25
288-879	6-Panel, Tall	pkg(3)	2.25
288-886	PRR Cabin	pkg(2)	2.25
288-892	Plug Door w/Handles	pkg(2)	2.25

DOWNSPOUTS

288-868	Downspout	pkg(4)	2.25
288-881	Short	pkg(6)	2.25

HATCHES & COVERS

Long Coupler Pockets & Covers
288-825   pair 2.25
(By Special Order Only.)

Mainway Covers
288-834
pkg(3) 2.25

Reefer Hatches
288-839
pkg(4) 2.25

Covered Hopper Hatch
288-840
pkg(4) 2.25

LIGHTS

288-849	Building Light, Antique	pkg(4)	2.25
288-871	Marker Light	pkg(4)	2.25
288-882	Vapor Lights	pkg(4)	2.25
288-883	Building Lights, Small, Modern	pkg(3)	2.25

MISCELLANEOUS

288-823	Wire Coil	pkg(6)	2.25
288-841	Flat Car Ramp	pkg(6)	2.25
288-867	Foundation, For Building	pkg(2)	2.25
288-880	Trim Brace, Ornate	pkg(6)	2.25

STEPS & STAIRS

288-811	Stair Riser, 9-Step **(By Special Order Only.)**	pkg(6)	2.25
288-855	Riser	pkg(15)	2.25
288-863	Caboose, AAR Style	pkg(3)	3.25
288-869	Caboose, PRR Style	pkg(4)	3.25
288-820	Freight Car	pkg(2)	2.25
288-884	Freight Car	pkg(8)	2.25
288-893	STEP, PRR ND Type		3.25

TOOLS

288-852	Shovel	pkg(3)	2.25
288-853	Broom	pkg(3)	2.25
288-854	Fire Extinguisher	pkg(6)	2.25

TRAILER DETAILS

Dual Trailer and Axle Set
288-827   pkg(4) 4.35

Dolly Wheels (Landing Gear)
288-828   pkg(2) 2.25

(not illustrated)

288-819	Flat Bed Hitch Set	each	2.25
288-842	Trailer Bumper	pkg(4)	2.25
288-843	Suspension	pkg(2)	2.25

WALKS

End Walks
288-829   pkg(6) 2.25

(not illustrated)

288-821	Corner End Walk	pkg(4)	2.25
288-860	Roof Walk Set	pkg(3 pcs)	2.25
288-891	End Walk Platform		2.25

WINDOWS

288-856	4-Pane	pkg(4)	2.25
288-857	12-Pane	pkg(4)	2.25
288-864	Bay Window Set	each	4.35
288-873	2-Pane, Large	pkg(3)	2.25
288-874	5-Pane, Narrow	pkg(4)	2.25
288-875	6-Pane, Large	pkg(3)	2.25
288-876	1-Pane, Large	pkg(4)	2.25
288-877	6-Pane, Long	pkg(3)	2.25
288-878	5-Pane, Long	pkg(3)	2.25
288-887	PRR Cabin Window	pkg(4)	2.25

See also: FREIGHT CARS and STRUCTURES for additional GLOOR CRAFT products.

Grandt Line

HO, HOn3 (1/87)

Detailed castings are injection molded black styrene plastic unless noted.

BAGGAGE WAGON

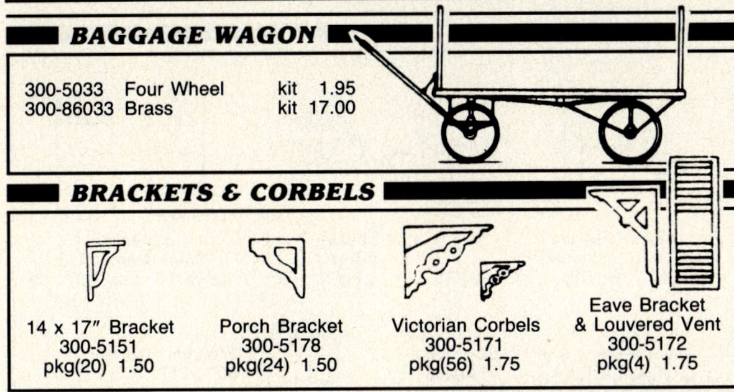

300-5033	Four Wheel	kit 1.95
300-86033	Brass	kit 17.00

BRACKETS & CORBELS

14 x 17″ Bracket
300-5151
pkg(20) 1.50

Porch Bracket
300-5178
pkg(24) 1.50

Victorian Corbels
300-5171
pkg(56) 1.75

Eave Bracket & Louvered Vent
300-5172
pkg(4) 1.75

BRAKE CYLINDER SETS

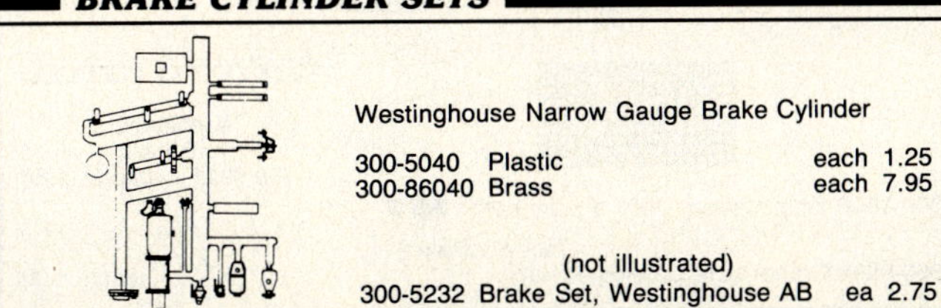

Westinghouse Narrow Gauge Brake Cylinder

300-5040	Plastic	each 1.25
300-86040	Brass	each 7.95

(not illustrated)
300-5232 Brake Set, Westinghouse AB   ea 2.75

BRAKE WHEELS

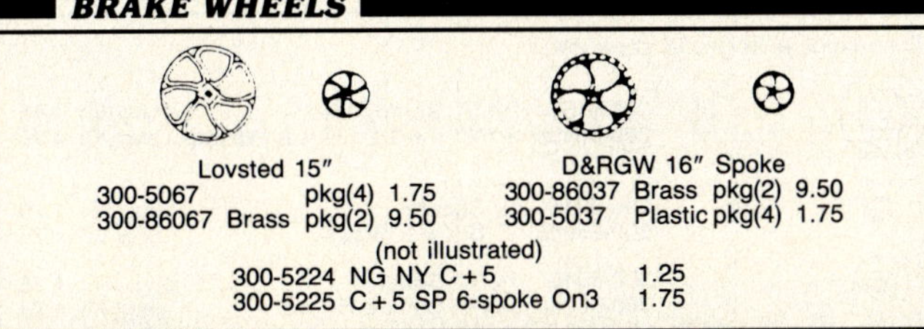

Lovsted 15″
300-5067   pkg(4) 1.75
300-86067 Brass pkg(2) 9.50

D&RGW 16″ Spoke
300-86037 Brass pkg(2) 9.50
300-5037   Plastic pkg(4) 1.75

(not illustrated)
300-5224 NG NY C+5   1.25
300-5225 C+5 SP 6-spoke On3   1.75

CHIMNEY & VENTS

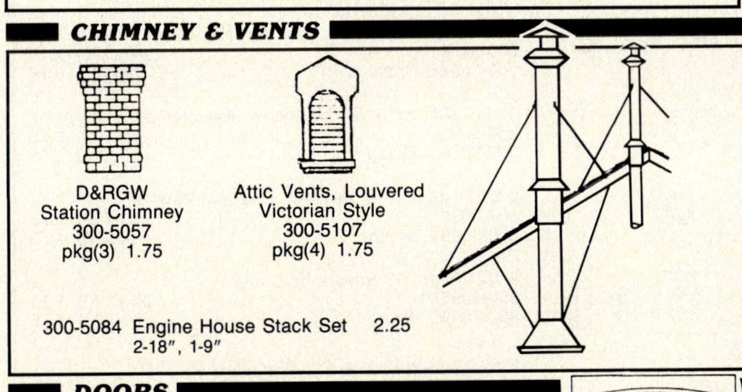

D&RGW Station Chimney
300-5057
pkg(3) 1.75

Attic Vents, Louvered Victorian Style
300-5107
pkg(4) 1.75

300-5084 Engine House Stack Set   2.25
2-18″, 1-9″

DOORS

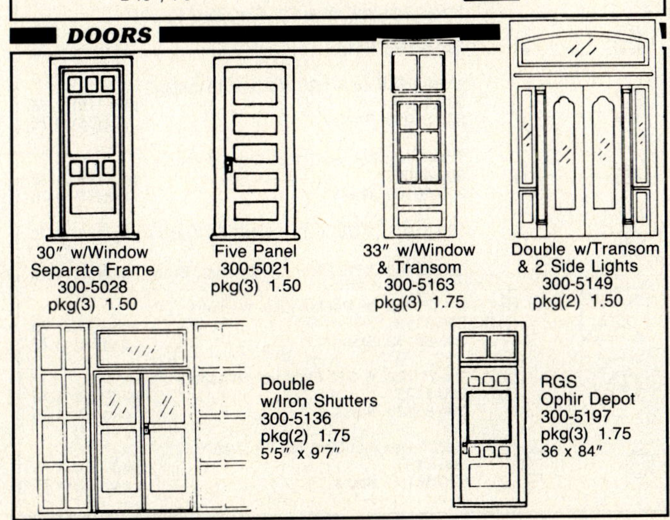

30″ w/Window Separate Frame
300-5028
pkg(3) 1.50

Five Panel
300-5021
pkg(3) 1.50

33″ w/Window & Transom
300-5163
pkg(3) 1.75

Double w/Transom & 2 Side Lights
300-5149
pkg(2) 1.50

Double w/Iron Shutters
300-5136
pkg(2) 1.75
5′5″ x 9′7″

RGS Ophir Depot
300-5197
pkg(3) 1.75
36 x 84″

DOORS (continued)

"Assay Office" Double, 5′ x 9″
300-5022   pkg(2) 1.50

Durango Station w/Oval Window
300-5042   pkg(2) 1.50

Roundhouse for 14′6″ x 19″ opening w/Windows & Doors
300-5133   2.25

2-Panel w/Frame (Tongue & Groove)
300-5131   pkg(3) 1.50

RGS Ophir Depot, Freight
300-5198   pkg(3) 2.25

Single w/Iron Shutters
300-5137   pkg(2) 1.75
4′2″ x 9′7″

36″ w/Window and Transom
300-5134
pkg(3) 1.50

D&RGW Station Frame & Transom
300-5058
pkg(3) 1.75

Factory Front w/Transom
300-5139
pkg(4) 1.50
masonry buildings, 39x92″

Station 4-Panel
300-5088
pkg(3) 1.75
2′6″ x 7′6″

Warehouse, Roll-Up & 36″ Personnel
300-5158   (2 sets) 1.75

Durango Station
300-5013
pkg(2) 1.50

4-Light
300-5072
pkg(4) 1.75

Double
300-5073
pkg(2) 1.50

Double w/Transom Round & Rectangular Panes
300-5109
pkg(2) 1.75

Grandt Line

HO, HOn3 (1/87)

Detailed castings are injection molded black styrene plastic unless noted.

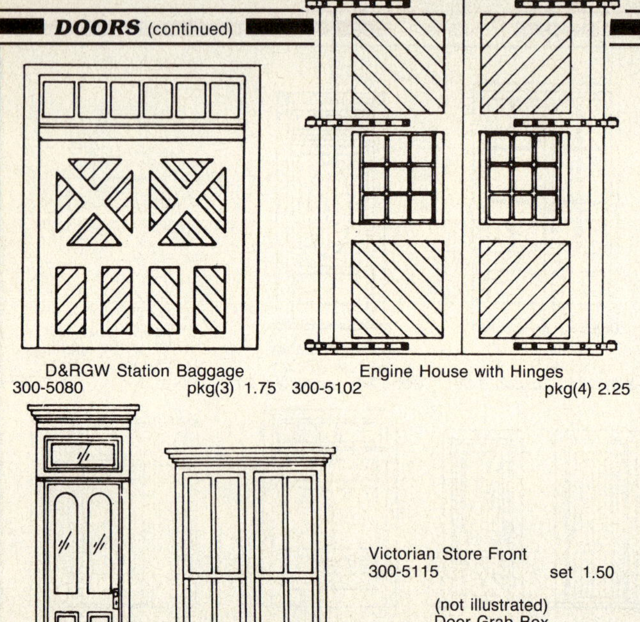

DOORS (continued)

D&RGW Station Baggage
300-5080   pkg(3) 1.75

Engine House with Hinges
300-5102   pkg(4) 2.25

Victorian Store Front
300-5115   set 1.50

(not illustrated)
Door Grab Box
300-5243   13.00

DRIVE CENTERS

Unmachined brass
300-86101   BLW 36" D&RGW C-16   pkg(8) 23.99
300-86102   BLW 46" D&RGW T-12   pkg(6) 21.75

FAIRMONT PUSH CAR

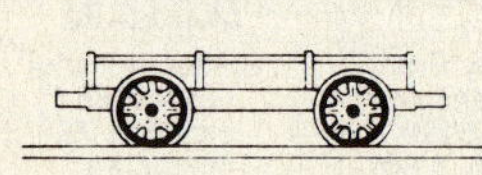

300-5164   HO   kit 1.50
300-5024   HOn3   kit 1.75
300-86024   HOn3, Brass   kit 10.50
300-86104   16" Pressed Steel   pkg(4) 9.50
Wheels for Push Car, Brass

HINGES

Reefer
300-5168   pkg(48) 1.75
300-5095   Assortment   1.50
300-86095   Assortment (Brass)   4.75

LOUVERED SHUTTERS

300-5173   18 x 56"   pkg(16) 1.75
300-5174   18 x 68"   pkg(16) 1.75
300-5175   18 x 87"   pkg(16) 1.75

MISCELLANEOUS

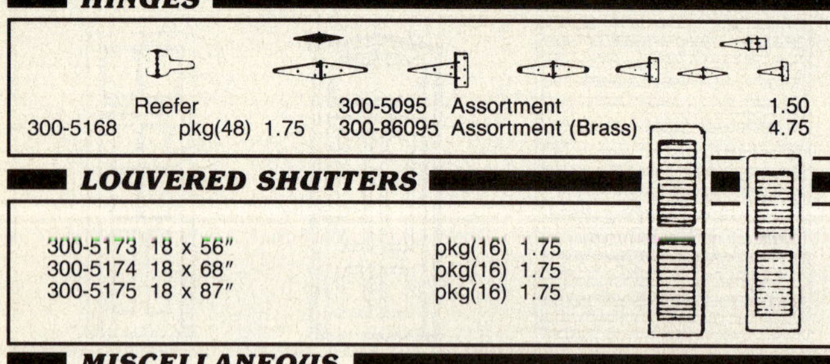

Water Tank Hoop Fasterners
300-5038   pkg(99) 2.75

Lift Ring Assortment
300-5085   Plastic   pkg(108) 1.75
300-86085   Brass   pkg(35) 4.75

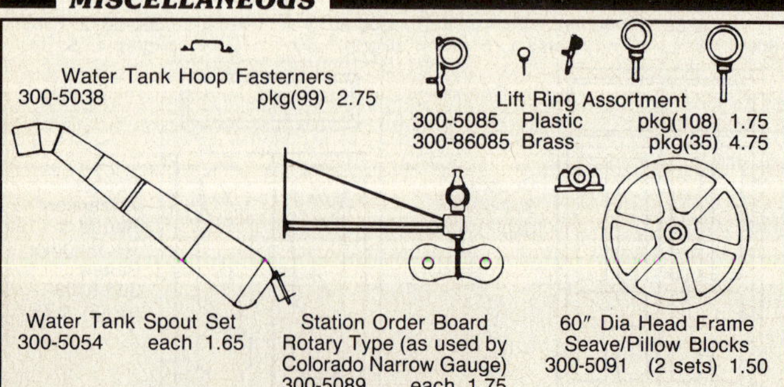

Water Tank Spout Set
300-5054   each 1.65

Station Order Board
Rotary Type (as used by
Colorado Narrow Gauge)
300-5089   each 1.75

60" Dia Head Frame
Seave/Pillow Blocks
300-5091   (2 sets) 1.50

MISCELLANEOUS (continued)

Lamp Reflectors
Bulbs (translucent)
300-5062   pkg(18) 1.75

Cable Sheave
43" w/Brgs
300-5122   pkg(2) 1.50

55 Gallon
Steel Drum w/Lid
300-5041   pkg(12) 1.75

Scalloped
Shingles
300-5216
pkg(2) 1.75

Wooden Barrels
300-5217
pkg(12) 1.95

Architectural
Details
300-5211   pkg(3) 1.50

300-3906   Ship Grating, 100" square hole   **NEW** 1.75
(not illustrated)

300-9991 Grandt Line Catalog 1   each 4.00

NUT-BOLT-WASHER

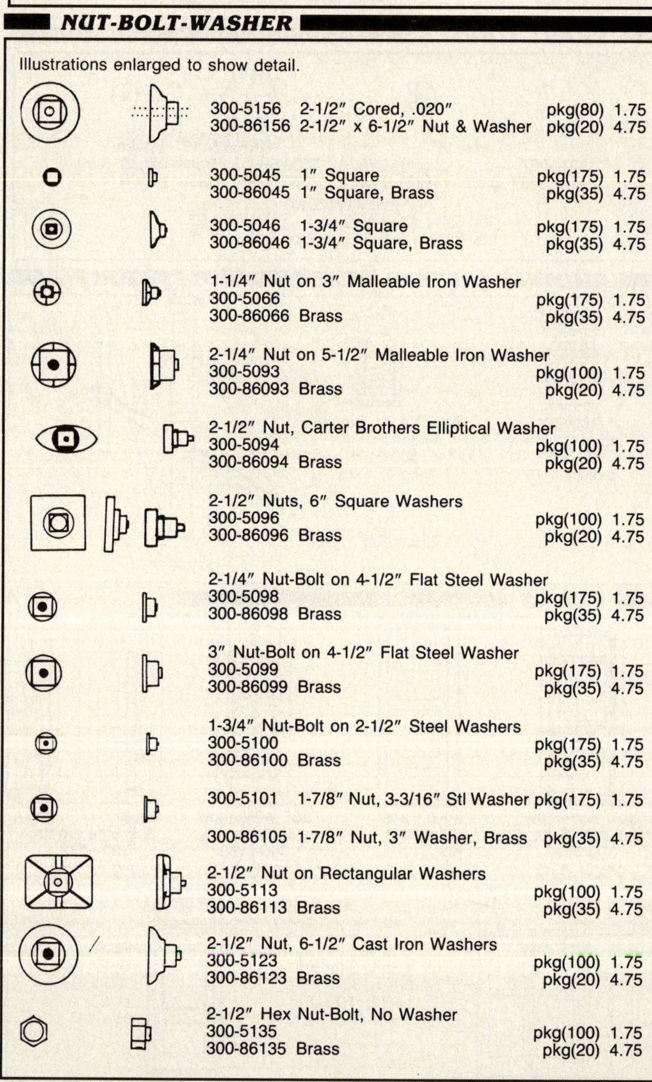

Illustrations enlarged to show detail.

300-5156 2-1/2" Cored, .020" pkg(80) 1.75	
300-86156 2-1/2" x 6-1/2" Nut & Washer pkg(20) 4.75	
300-5045 1" Square pkg(175) 1.75	
300-86045 1" Square, Brass pkg(35) 4.75	
300-5046 1-3/4" Square pkg(175) 1.75	
300-86046 1-3/4" Square, Brass pkg(35) 4.75	
1-1/4" Nut on 3" Malleable Iron Washer	
300-5066 pkg(175) 1.75	
300-86066 Brass pkg(35) 4.75	
2-1/4" Nut on 5-1/2" Malleable Iron Washer	
300-5093 pkg(100) 1.75	
300-86093 Brass pkg(20) 4.75	
2-1/2" Nut, Carter Brothers Elliptical Washer	
300-5094 pkg(100) 1.75	
300-86094 Brass pkg(20) 4.75	
2-1/2" Nuts, 6" Square Washers	
300-5096 pkg(100) 1.75	
300-86096 Brass pkg(20) 4.75	
2-1/4" Nut-Bolt on 4-1/2" Flat Steel Washer	
300-5098 pkg(175) 1.75	
300-86098 Brass pkg(35) 4.75	
3" Nut-Bolt on 4-1/2" Flat Steel Washer	
300-5099 pkg(175) 1.75	
300-86099 Brass pkg(35) 4.75	
1-3/4" Nut-Bolt on 2-1/2" Steel Washers	
300-5100 pkg(175) 1.75	
300-86100 Brass pkg(35) 4.75	
300-5101 1-7/8" Nut, 3-3/16" Stl Washer pkg(175) 1.75	
300-86105 1-7/8" Nut, 3" Washer, Brass pkg(35) 4.75	
2-1/2" Nut on Rectangular Washers	
300-5113 pkg(100) 1.75	
300-86113 Brass pkg(35) 4.75	
2-1/2" Nut, 6-1/2" Cast Iron Washers	
300-5123 pkg(100) 1.75	
300-86123 Brass pkg(20) 4.75	
2-1/2" Hex Nut-Bolt, No Washer	
300-5135 pkg(100) 1.75	
300-86135 Brass pkg(20) 4.75	

Grandt Line

HO SCALE (1/87)

Detailed castings are injection molded black styrene plastic unless noted.

PORCH RAILING

Porch Pillar Turned Wood Type
300-5079
pkg(8) 1.75

300-5035 Turned Spindle   pkg(3) 1.75
(Enlarged to show detail)

"Wells Fargo" Balcony
300-5017   pkg(3) 1.75

"Masonic Hall" Balcony, Brackets
300-5065   set(3) 1.85

Ornamental Wood w/Roof Bracket
300-5034   pkg(5) 1.75

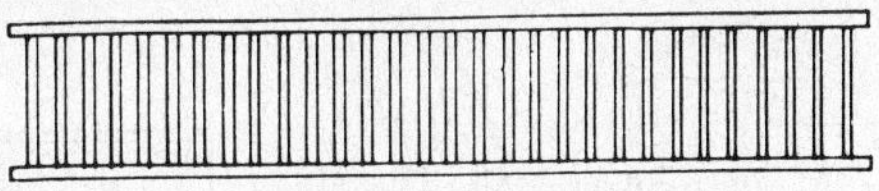

35" High, 1" Bars on 6" Centers
(approximately 100 scale feet)
300-5083   pkg(6) 2.25

Band Stand Lattice Work
300-5064   pkg(8) 2.25

"Gay Nineties"
300-5019   pkg(4) 1.75

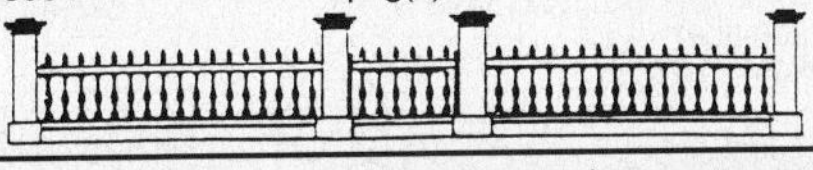

Victorian Picket Fence Set
300-5119   1.75

STAIRCASES

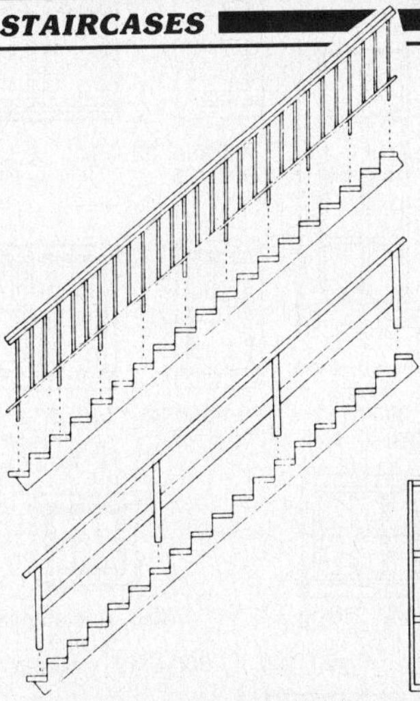

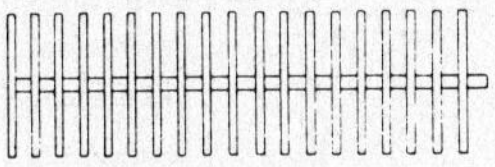

Modern Cast
300-5176   each 1.75

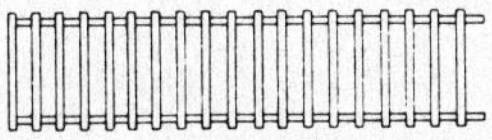

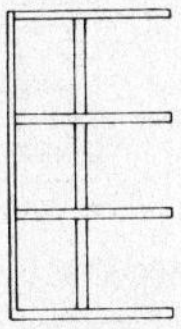

Open Wood
300-5177   each 1.95

STOVES

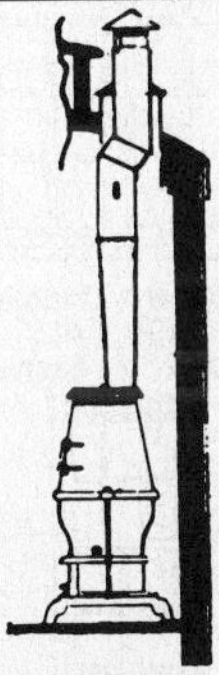

D&RGW Passenger Car with Stack
300-5008   each 1.50

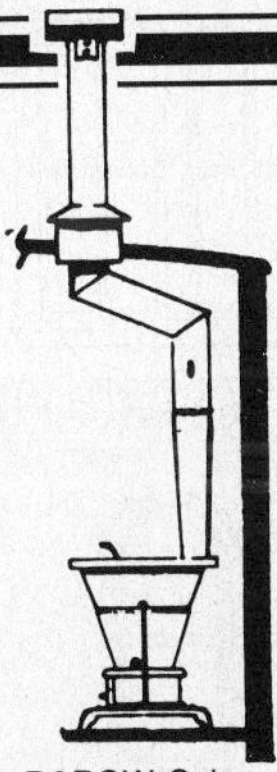

D&RGW Caboose with Stack
300-5007   each 1.50

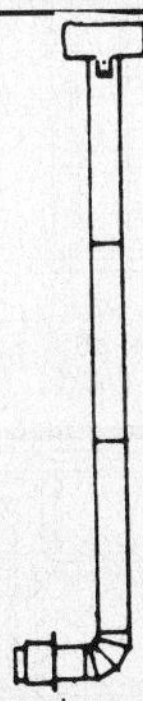

Stovepipe w/Elbow Bonnet, Thimble
300-5023   set(2) 1.50

TRIM

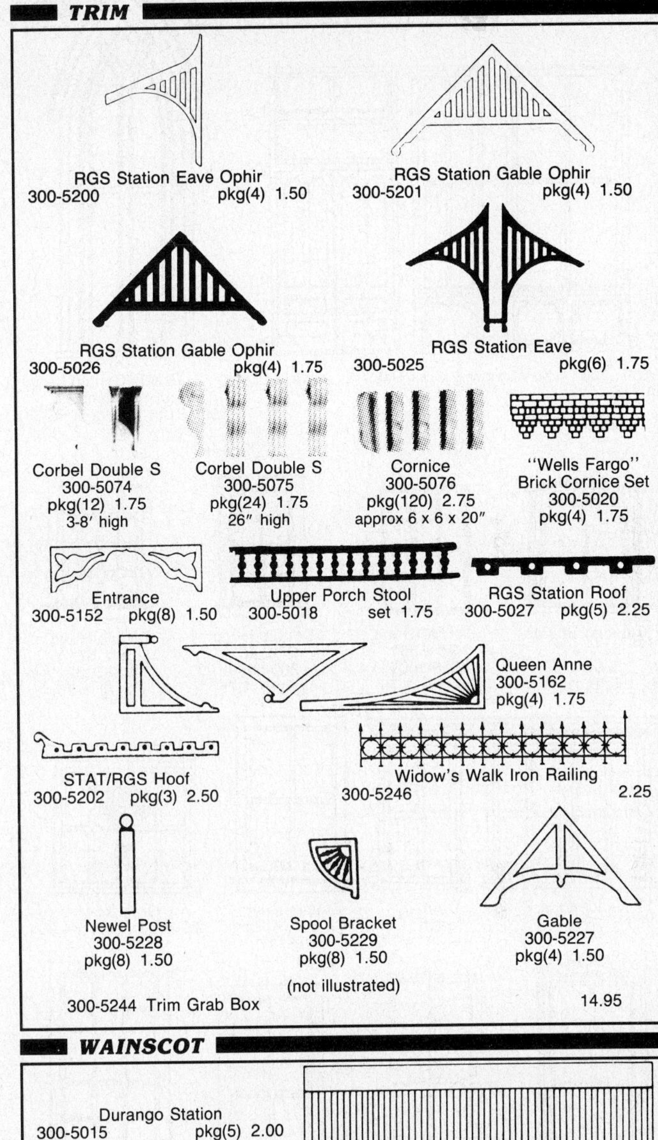

RGS Station Eave Ophir
300-5200   pkg(4) 1.50

RGS Station Gable Ophir
300-5201   pkg(4) 1.50

RGS Station Gable Ophir
300-5026   pkg(4) 1.75

RGS Station Eave
300-5025   pkg(6) 1.75

Corbel Double S
300-5074
pkg(12) 1.75
3-8' high

Corbel Double S
300-5075
pkg(24) 1.75
26" high

Cornice
300-5076
pkg(120) 2.75
approx 6 x 6 x 20"

"Wells Fargo" Brick Cornice Set
300-5020
pkg(4) 1.75

Entrance
300-5152   pkg(8) 1.50

Upper Porch Stool
300-5018   set 1.75

RGS Station Roof
300-5027   pkg(5) 2.25

Queen Anne
300-5162
pkg(4) 1.75

STAT/RGS Hoof
300-5202   pkg(3) 2.50

Widow's Walk Iron Railing
300-5246   2.25

Newel Post
300-5228
pkg(8) 1.50

Spool Bracket
300-5229
pkg(8) 1.50

(not illustrated)

Gable
300-5227
pkg(4) 1.50

300-5244 Trim Grab Box   14.95

WAINSCOT

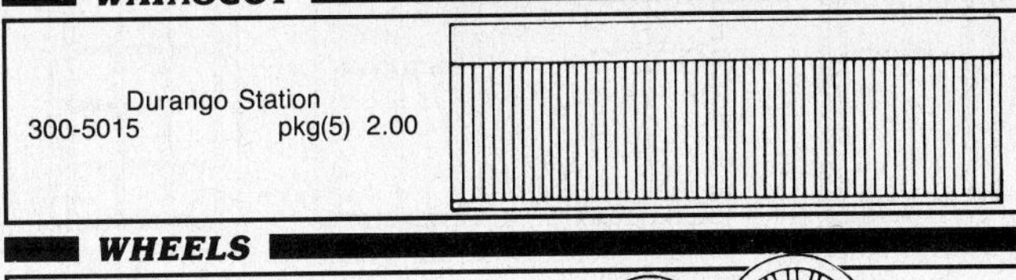

Durango Station
300-5015   pkg(5) 2.00

WHEELS

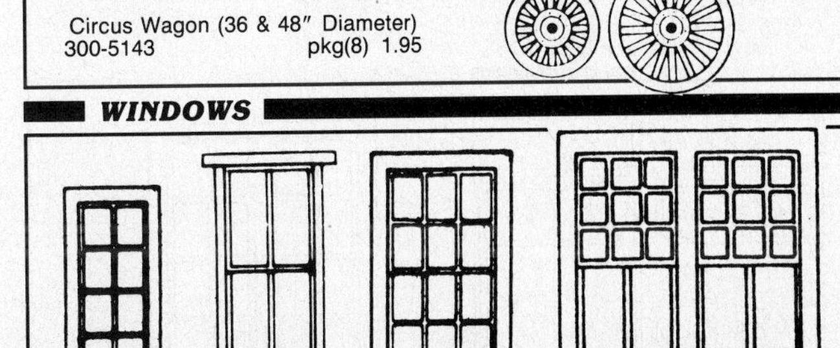

Circus Wagon (36 & 48" Diameter)
300-5143   pkg(8) 1.95

WINDOWS

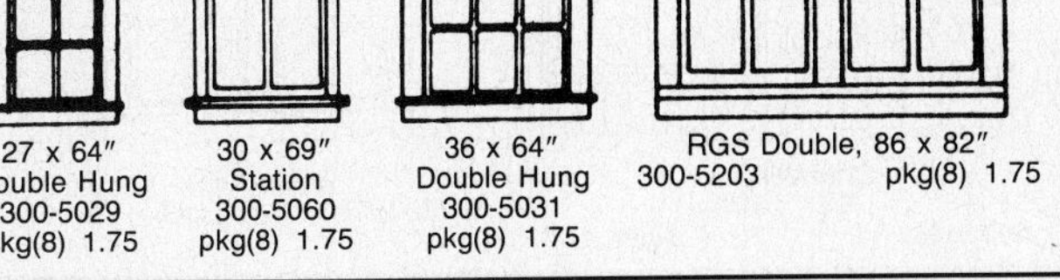

27 x 64" Double Hung
300-5029
pkg(8) 1.75

30 x 69" Station
300-5060
pkg(8) 1.75

36 x 64" Double Hung
300-5031
pkg(8) 1.75

RGS Double, 86 x 82"
300-5203   pkg(8) 1.75

Grandt Line

HO SCALE (1/87)

Detailed castings are injection molded black styrene plastic unless noted.

WINDOWS (continued)

300-5165   Window & Door Set   each 2.25

Gothic Church and Residence
300-5126   pkg(4) 1.75

Durango Station
36 x 44"
300-5016
pkg(8) 1.75

Double Hung
36 x 56"
300-5009
pkg(8) 1.75

Double Hung
27 x 48"
300-5030
pkg(8) 1.75

Double Hung
36 x 52"
300-5032
pkg(8) 1.75

Victorian, 4 Single, 2 Double
300-5116   each 1.75

Double Hung
36 x 64", 4-Pane
300-5117
pkg(8) 1.75

Grab Box
300-5192 each 14.95

Durango Station
36 x 87"
300-5014
pkg(8) 2.25

Double Hung
4-Pane Factory
42 x 91"
300-5140
pkg(4) 1.75
masonry buildings

RGS, 4-Pane
48 x 90"
300-5195
pkg(4) 1.75

Engine House
18-Pane, 42 x 91"
300-5097
pkg(6) 1.75

Store Windows
5'5" x 9'7"
300-5138   pkg(4) 1.75

Queen Anne
300-5160   pkg(3) 1.75

WINDOWS (continued)

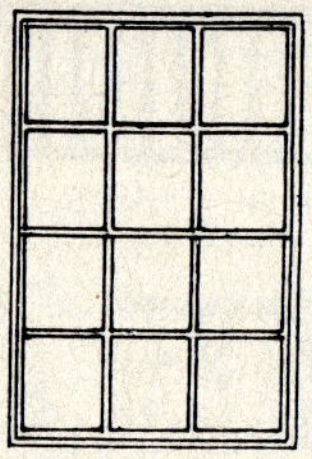

Store Front, 72 x 103"
300-5077   pkg(4) 1.75

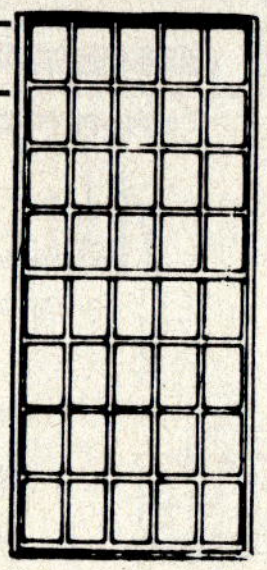

Roundhouse, 60 x 120"
300-5010   pkg(6) 1.75

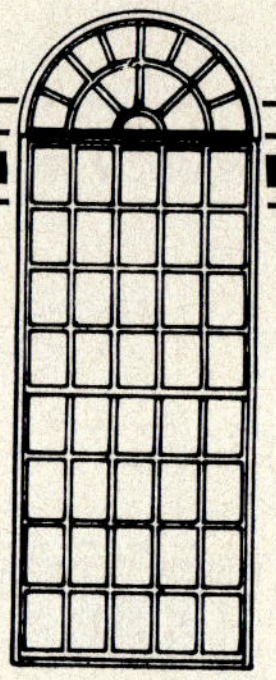

Round Top, 60 x 150"
300-5092   pkg(4) 1.75

Peak Cap
41 x 90"
300-5150
pkg(8) 1.75

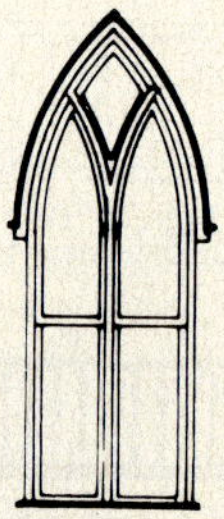

Gothic Church
48 x 90"
300-5087
pkg(4) 1.75

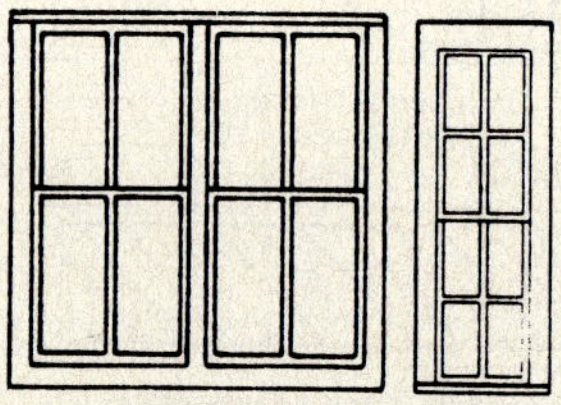

RGS Single/Double
300-5196   pkg(4) 1.75

10-Pane, 32 x 54", 58 x 60"
300-5199   each 1.75

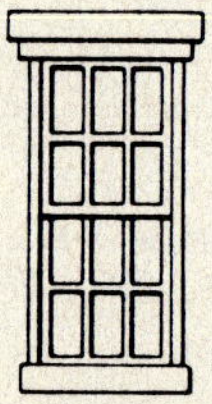

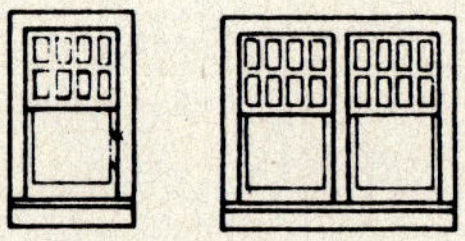

9-Pane 32 x 53", 58 x 53"
300-5194   each 1.75

Mason, 30 x 65"
300-5154
pkg(8) 1.75

RGS, 36 x 76"
300-5193
pkg(8) 1.75

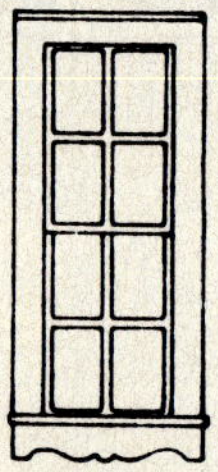

Queen Anne
Single
300-5161
pkg(6) 1.75

30" Silverton
Station Attic
300-5011 pkg(4) 1.75

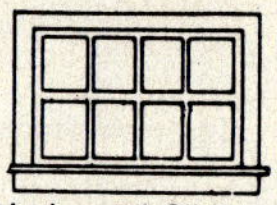

Horizontal Sliding
52 x 33"
300-5081   pkg(8) 1.75

Attic, Rectangular
6-Light
300-5112   pkg(8) 1.75

Double Pointed,
33 x 88"
300-5220 pkg(8) 1.75

8-Pane Double,
63 x 69"
300-5221   each 1.75

16-Pane Double,
59 x 64"
300-5222   each 1.75

Dormer/Gable
300-5223   each 1.75

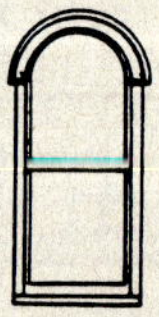

Round Top, 2'3" x 6'3"
300-5230   each 1.75

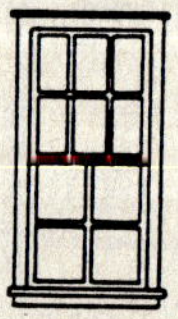

Double Hung, 32 x 70"
300-5233   each 1.75

Grandt Line

HO SCALE (1/87)

Detailed castings are injection molded black styrene plastic unless noted.

■ WINDOWS (continued)

Double Hung, 42 x 72"
300-5179
pkg(6) 1.75

6-Pane Double Hung, Triple 100 x 92"
300-5204   each 1.75

Diamond Patterned
300-5206   ea 1.50

Pointed Top 30 x 86"
300-5234
pkg(8) 1.75

4-Pane Double Hung, Double 65 x 92"
300-5205
each 1.75

300-5210 48-Pane Double Hung 186 x 70", Bagby Station   pkg(2) 1.75

Double Hung 85 x 48"
300-5208   pkg(4) 1.75

16-Pane Double Hung Single 34 x 67", Bagby Station
300-5209
pkg(6) 1.75

Paired, Round Top Double Hung, 4'6" x 6'3"
300-5212
pkg(4) 1.75

4-Pane Double Hung, 30 x 62"
300-5215
pkg(8) 1.75

Shed or Attic
300-5241
pkg(8) 1.75

Horizontal
300-5242
each 1.75

Single Sash 28 x 26"
300-5239
pkg(4) 1.75

Round, Masonry 65" diameter
300-5240
pkg(2) 1.50

(not illustrated)

300-5157	Window & Door Set, 96 x 108"		each 1.75
300-5245	Window/Transom Set		each 1.75
300-5138	Store Window, 65 x 115"		pkg(4) 1.75
300-5160	Queen Anne, Double Hung		pkg(3) 1.75
300-5199	10-Pane, 32 x 54", 58 x 60"		1.75
300-5247	Double Hung 11-Pane	NEW	pkg(8) 1.75
300-4248	Attic Peaked Single Pane	NEW	pkg(8) 1.75
300-5249	Victorian Attic	NEW	pkg(8) 1.75
300-5250	Gothic church	NEW	pkg(8) 1.75

FREIGHT CAR DETAILS

■ BRAKE RODS

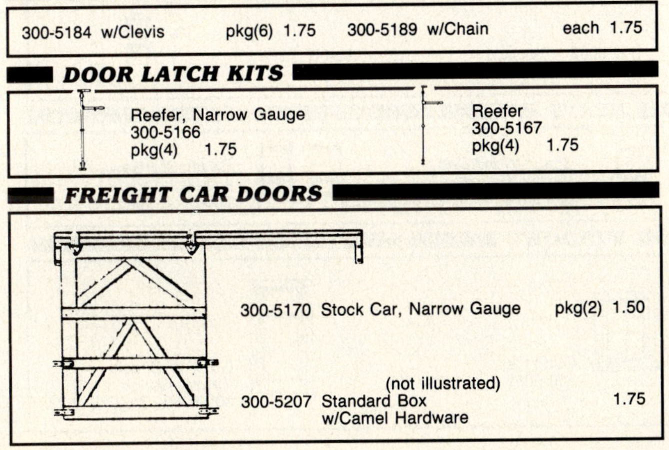

300-5184 w/Clevis   pkg(6) 1.75   300-5189 w/Chain   each 1.75

■ DOOR LATCH KITS

Reefer, Narrow Gauge
300-5166
pkg(4)   1.75

Reefer
300-5167
pkg(4)   1.75

■ FREIGHT CAR DOORS

300-5170 Stock Car, Narrow Gauge   pkg(2) 1.50

(not illustrated)

300-5207 Standard Box w/Camel Hardware   1.75

■ HARDWARE KITS

(illustrations not to scale)

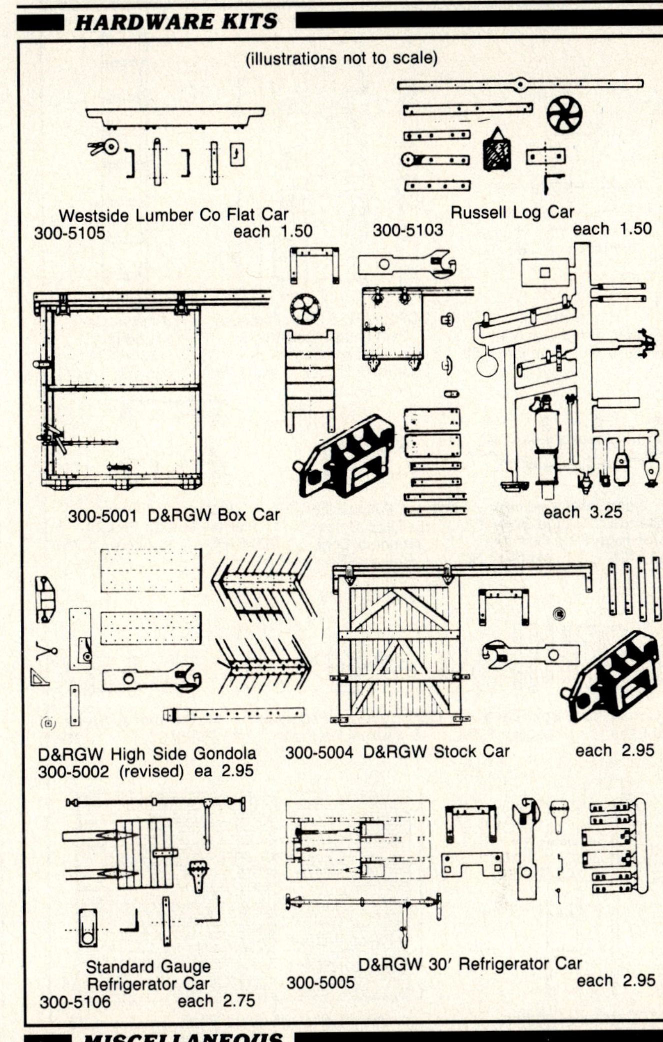

Westside Lumber Co Flat Car
300-5105   each 1.50

Russell Log Car
300-5103   each 1.50

300-5001 D&RGW Box Car   each 3.25

D&RGW High Side Gondola
300-5002 (revised) ea 2.95

300-5004 D&RGW Stock Car   each 2.95

Standard Gauge Refrigerator Car
300-5106   each 2.75

D&RGW 30' Refrigerator Car
300-5005   each 2.95

■ MISCELLANEOUS

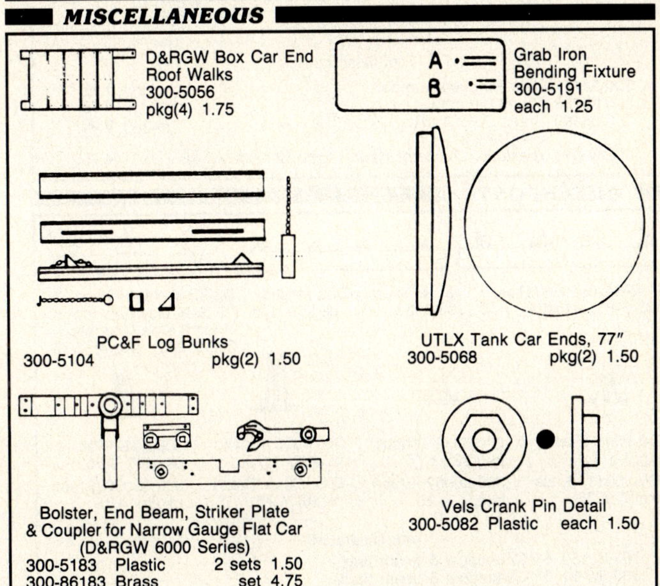

D&RGW Box Car End Roof Walks
300-5056
pkg(4) 1.75

Grab Iron Bending Fixture
300-5191
each 1.25

PC&F Log Bunks
300-5104   pkg(2) 1.50

UTLX Tank Car Ends, 77"
300-5068   pkg(2) 1.50

Bolster, End Beam, Striker Plate & Coupler for Narrow Gauge Flat Car (D&RGW 6000 Series)
300-5183 Plastic   2 sets 1.50
300-86183 Brass   set 4.75

Vels Crank Pin Detail
300-5082 Plastic   each 1.50

Grandt Line

HO, HOn3 (1/87)

Detailed castings are injection molded black styrene plastic unless noted.

◼ MISCELLANEOUS (continued)

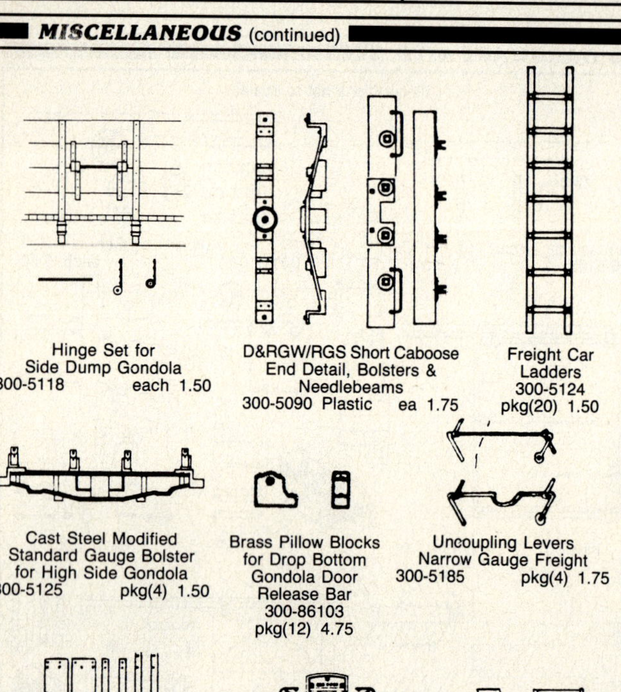

Hinge Set for Side Dump Gondola
300-5118   each 1.50

D&RGW/RGS Short Caboose End Detail, Bolsters & Needlebeams
300-5090 Plastic   ea 1.75

Freight Car Ladders
300-5124   pkg(20) 1.50

Cast Steel Modified Standard Gauge Bolster for High Side Gondola
300-5125   pkg(4) 1.50

Brass Pillow Blocks for Drop Bottom Gondola Door Release Bar
300-86103   pkg(12) 4.75

Uncoupling Levers Narrow Gauge Freight
300-5185   pkg(4) 1.75

Corner Iron, Box/Stake
300-5169   pkg(4) 1.75

C&S Caboose Pedestals & Journal Box Lids
300-5236   2.00

C&S Caboose Steps
300-5237   1.25

C&S Caboose Ladders
300-5238   pkg(2) 2.00

300-5218 Corrugated Roof   1.75
(1.85 x 4.4")

(not illustrated)

300-5219	Date Plaques/Number	set 1.75
300-86082	Crank pin detail	4.75
300-86090	Brass D&RGW/RGS Short Caboose End Details	pkg(2) 9.00
300-86091	Brass 60' Diameter Head-Frame Sheave w/brgs	4.75

◼ QUEENPOSTS

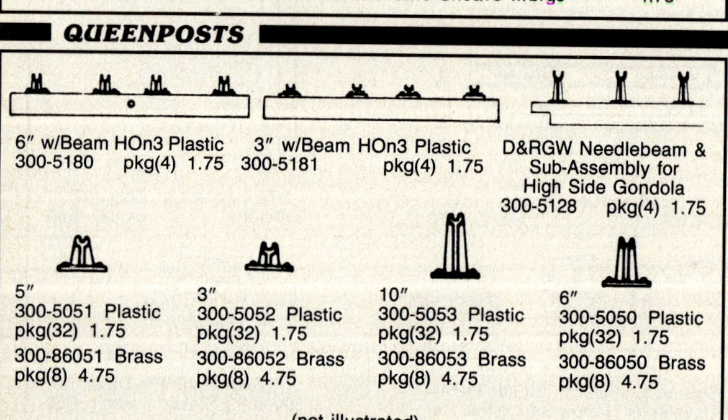

6" w/Beam HOn3 Plastic
300-5180   pkg(4) 1.75

3" w/Beam HOn3 Plastic
300-5181   pkg(4) 1.75

D&RGW Needlebeam & Sub-Assembly for High Side Gondola
300-5128   pkg(4) 1.75

5"
300-5051 Plastic pkg(32) 1.75
300-86051 Brass pkg(8) 4.75

3"
300-5052 Plastic pkg(32) 1.75
300-86052 Brass pkg(8) 4.75

10"
300-5053 Plastic pkg(32) 1.75
300-86053 Brass pkg(8) 4.75

6"
300-5050 Plastic pkg(32) 1.75
300-86050 Brass pkg(8) 4.75

(not illustrated)

300-86180	6" Queenpost & beam brass	4.75
300-86181	3" Queenpost & beam brass	4.75

◼ STAKE POCKETS

One U-Bolt, Plastic
300-5012   pkg(24) 1.75

One U-Bolt, Brass
300-86012   pkg(12) 9.00

2 U-Bolt, Plastic D&RGW
300-5036   pkg(24) 1.75

2 U-Bolt, Brass D&RGW
300-86036   pkg(12) 9.00

Gondola for 12" Wide Boards with Pocket
300-5108   pkg(40) 2.25

◼ STIRRUP STEPS

300-5190   Drop Bottom for D&RGW Gondola   pkg(20) 1.75
D&RGW for box, flat, stock cars, high side gondolas

300-5129   Brown Delrin   pkg(24) 1.75
300-5130   Black Delrin   pkg(24) 1.75

(not illustrated)

300-86129   Freight Car Stirrup Sets   pkg(5) 5.25

◼ TURNBUCKLES

Holes are cored for .015 wire

300-5039   D&RGW Scale, Plastic   pkg(24) 1.75
300-86039   Brass   pkg(18) 9.00

PASSENGER CAR PARTS

◼ DOORS

D&RGW Combine Baggage
300-5071   pkg(4) 1.75

D&RGW Caboose
300-5063   pkg(4) 1.75

D&RGW Coach/Combine End
300-5070   pkg(4) 1.75

D&RGW Coach Arch Top
300-5078   pkg(4) 1.75

◼ ROOF DETAIL

300-5043   Plastic   set(4) 1.75
300-86043   Brass   set(4) 4.75

◼ SEATS

Coach-Wood End Narrow Gauge
300-5048   pkg(12) 2.50

Coach-Std Gauge w/2 Wood Ends
300-5049   pkg(12) 2.75

◼ WINDOWS

Outfit Car
300-5059   pkg(8) 1.75

D&RGW Coach Narrow Gauge
300-5069   pkg(30) 2.25

Keystone Locomotive Works

HO SCALE (1/87)

SUPER DETAIL PARTS

Metal pressure castings, brass rod, wire as required.
Illustrations NOT to scale.

BOILERS

395-101 Horizontal Portable   kit 13.95
Used wherever a supply of steam or compressed air was needed.

395-20 Small Vertical   1.75

CAST RAFTERS

395-43	13-1/2′	pkg(6) 1.95
395-44	25′	pkg(6) 2.25
395-45	48-1/2′	pkg(6) 2.75

DOMES

395-26	Shay Steam .75
395-27	Shay Sand .75

JUNK

Set of 8 Drivers and Axles
395-12   4.50
(64″ spoked)
Engine House Scenery

395-14 Logging   2.95
Includes 70 and 90-Ton Shay sideframes, Shay sandbox, domes and cab front, headlight, backhead and tender filler hatch, geared Shay drivers and tires, log bunks, compressors and cylinders.

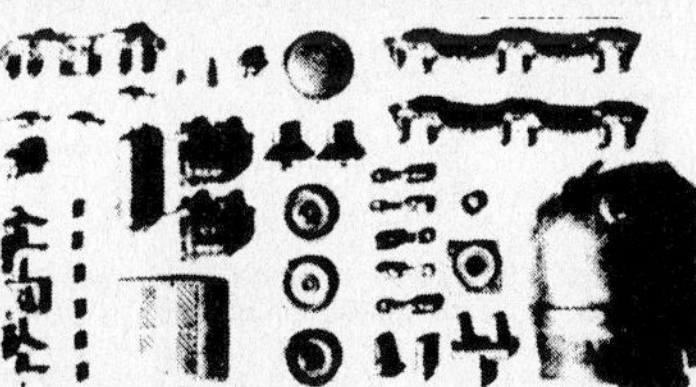

395-15 Diesel Engine House   4.75
Approximately 35 pieces of assorted "scrapped" diesel parts — EMD, Alco, GE, etc., sideframes, roof fans, spark arresters, stacks, traction motors, loco brake cylinders, wheels, brake shoes, nose assembly. . . scrap from the 1950's to the present.

(not illustrated)

395-2 Engine House   2.95
Includes stacks, domes, sideframes, drivers, rods, loco fittings and lots of etcetera.

LOCO & FREIGHT DETAILS

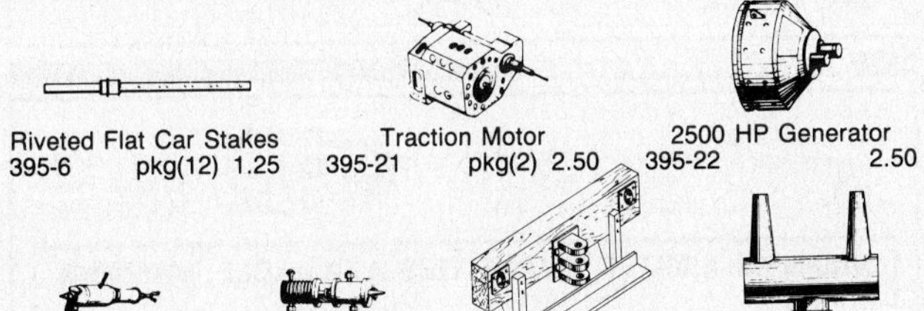

Riveted Flat Car Stakes
395-6   pkg(12) 1.25

Traction Motor
395-21   pkg(2) 2.50

2500 HP Generator
395-22   2.50

Small Brake Cylinder w/Clevis
395-4   .75

Single Stage Air Compressor
395-8   each .75

Pilot
395-10   .95
(Provision for Kadee coupler)

CN & Grand Truck Diesel Spark Arrestor
395-11   each .95

LOCO & FREIGHT DETAILS (continued)

(not illustrated)

395-23	Old Time Headlight	.65
395-49	GE44-Tonner Delrin U-Joint Retrofit	3.00
	To replace early model's rubber tubing, later models come with Delrin U-joints.	
395-51	Air Tank (approx 2 x 6′)	.95
395-5	Log Buggy Shoo-fly	pkg(2) .50
395-52	Rack Flat Bulkhead End (Converts flat car to pulpwood car)	2.95
395-53	Gondola, Low End, Solid Bulkhead Kit (Converts Gon. for pulp)	2.95
395-54	Gondola, Tall, Open End Bulkhead Kit (Converts for pulpwood)	2.95
395-58	Pilot Filler Piece for Athearn SD-9 (Fits under coupler)	pkg(2) 1.95
395-59	DM&IR Taconite Extension to Convert Ore Car for Taconite use	TBA

LOGGING TOOLS

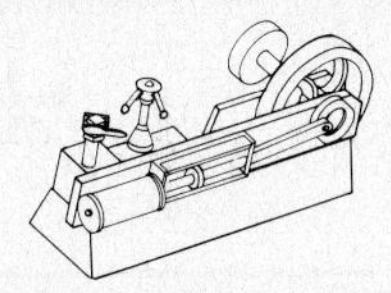

395-1 Logging Tools   set 2.95
Set includes two peaveys, two pikes, one saw and two axes.

MILL ENGINE

395-1106 Horizontal   11.95
Usable in HO Scale as a large engine.

(not illustrated)
395-32 Boiler w/mill engine (small)   9.95

MISCELLANEOUS

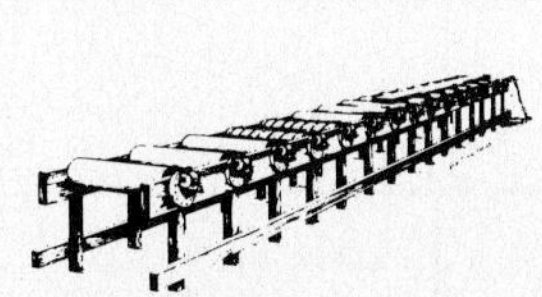

395-31 Donkey Engine   10.95

(not illustrated)

395-17	Corrugated Metal Roll, 5′ x 1-1/4″		1.95
395-18	Switch Stand	pkg(2)	2.95
395-19	Cheese Blocks	pkg(4)	.75
395-29	Shay Steam Engine with U-joints		8.95
395-33	Blacksmith Forge & Anvil		2.75
395-42	Outhouse		1.95
395-46	Concrete Pier, 1/8 x 1/8″	pkg(15)	1.95
395-47	Angle Brace	pkg(24)	1.95
395-50	Passenger Shelter Columns	pkg(6)	4.95
	Includes uprights, cross arms, and scroll work.		

SAWMILL DETAILS

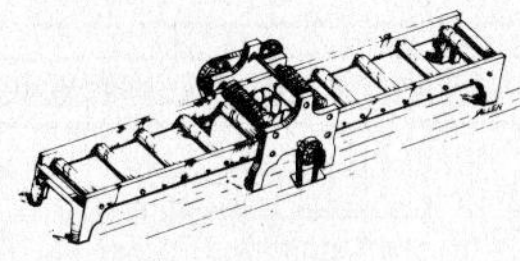

395-37 Live Rolls   8.95
Used to carry boards to the edger or sorting table.

Lumber Carts 2′ Gauge
395-48   pkg(2) 1.75

395-36 Edger   kit 8.95
Used to cut boards to width.

Shotgun Carriage with Ways & Track
395-35   8.95

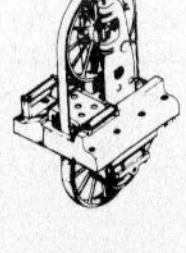

Log Deck & Jack Slip
395-40   10.95
Used to carry logs from mill pond into mill and transfer them to the carriage for cutting into boards.

Sumner 6′ Band Saw
395-34   10.95

Working Jill Poke Unloader
395-102   kit 7.95
Used to unload logs into log ponds.

(not illustrated)
395-41 Grinder   pkg(2) 1.50

Keystone Locomotive Works

HO SCALE (1/87)

■ SAWMILL DETAILS (continued)

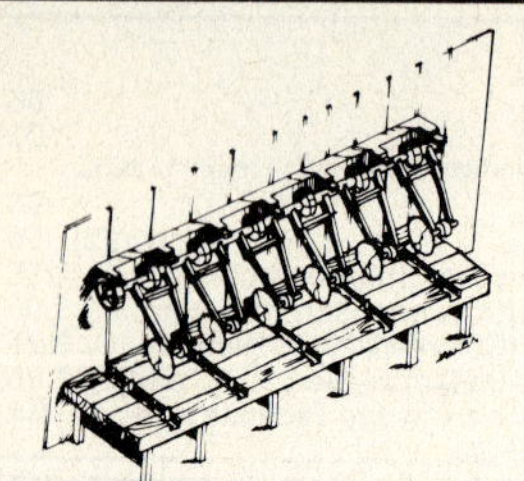

395-38 Cut-off Saw   8.95
Used to cut sawn lumber to length.

Logging Mill Transfer Table
395-39   7.95
Used to move cut boards to sorting area and cut off saws from live roll systems.

■ STACKS

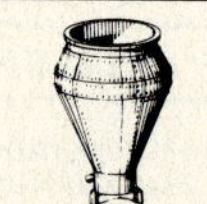

Shotgun	Small Diamond	Lima Diamond	Congdon Type
395-25 .75	395-24 .75	395-3 2.25	395-7 1.25
		replaces PFM B-2 & B-3 stack	

■ WINDSHIELD WIPERS

395-3401	Cast Metal for any HO diesel	pkg(4) 1.98
395-3405	Plastic for 2nd generation hood diesels	1.98

■ WINTERIZATION HATCHES

395-55	48" to fit SD18 & others	1.45
395-56	48" long for 2nd Generation Diesels	1.45
395-57	48" short for GP38-2 & others	1.45

Kadee ®

HO SCALE (1/87)

■ MISCELLANEOUS

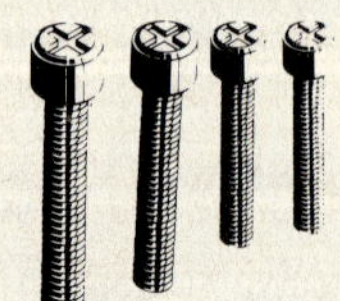

Delrin Insulating Roundhead Screws
380-256 pkg(12) 1.65

(not illustrated)
Air Hose & Angle Cock w/Mounting Bracket
380-438 pkg(20) 1.35
Nut-Bolt-Washer Detail
380-439 pkg(36) 1.35
18" Brake Wheel, Metal
380-440 pkg(6) 1.35

M**ETAL** M**INIATURES**

HO SCALE (1/87)
Parts are lead alloy castings. Illustrations are not to scale.

■ CAR WEIGHTS

340-175	Metal	pkg(8) 2.50
340-176	Athearn PA-1	each 2.50
340-177	Athearn SW1500 Switcher	each 2.50
340-178	Athearn GE U28B & U28C	each 2.50

■ DIESEL SNOW PLOWS

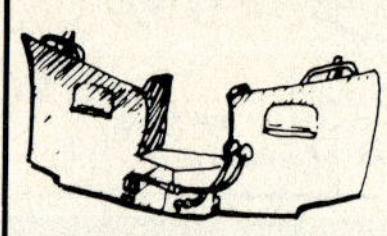
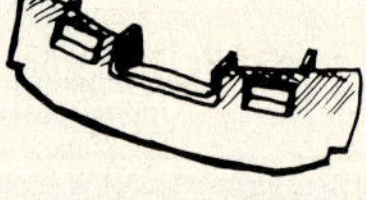
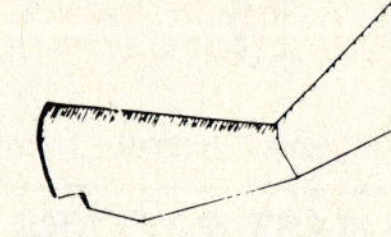

340-50   each 2.50
340-52   each 2.50
For GP, SD series locos. The 52 is slightly different than the 50 and is used by the SP and other major systems. Fits Athearn locos, adaptable to Tyco and Tenshodo (PFM) locos.

340-56   each 2.50
Latest type plows being used on GP, SD type diesels. Fits Athearn, Life-Like and Bachmann locos as well as Alco imported brass loco. Can also be used on Athearn GE U28-33 series locos.

340-61   each 2.50
New type, below the coupler. Use on GP, SD's by EJ&E, Long Island and others. Fits Athearn, Life-Like, Bachmann, Alco brass locos. Also used on GE U28-33.

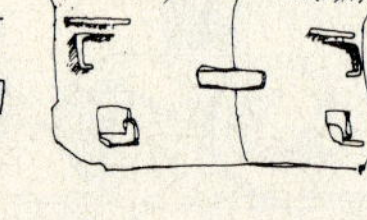
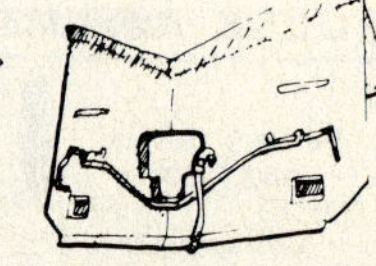
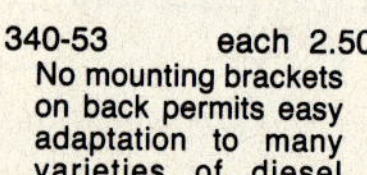

340-53   each 2.50
No mounting brackets on back permits easy adaptation to many varieties of diesel models.

340-55   each 2.50
Suitable for mounting on Athearn PA and Train-Mini FA square nose models.

340-51   each 2.50
Fits Athearn F-9A unit diesels, adaptable to Tyco and Tenshodo models also.

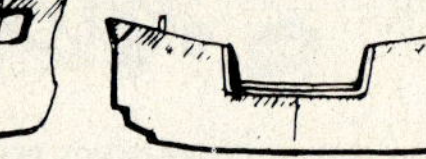

340-57   each 2.50
same description as #56

340-58   each 2.50
same description as #56

340-59   each 2.50
same description as #56

340-60   each 2.50
Used by C&NW and others on GP, SD types, fits Athearn, Bachmann and imported brass, also Athearn GE U28-33.

340-63   each 2.50
same description as #56

340-62   each 2.50
Used on GP, SD's by the Chessie System. Fits Athearn, Life-Like, Bachmann, Alco brass and GE U28-33's.

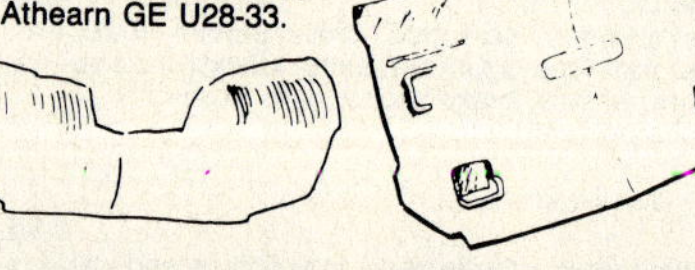
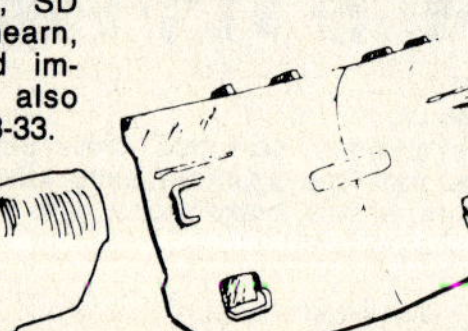
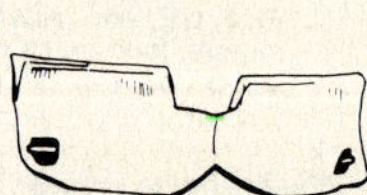

340-64   each 2.50
Typical of new plow fitted on new U28-33 GE diesels. Will fit most HO engine models currently on market.

340-54   each 2.50
Medium sized, used for clearing yards and sidings. Fits Athearn SW, SP & SD models, also AHM S-1's.

340-65   each 2.50
Type of snow plow pilot the SP used on F units for many years.

■ MISCELLANEOUS

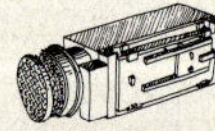
Air Conditioning Unit
340-75   each 2.50
Pullman type, 1931

Track Siding Bumper Post
340-100   2.50

■ LIMITED QUANTITIES AVAILABLE

Portable Generator
340-33   2.50

Micro Engineering Company

HO SCALE (1/87)

Detailed, injection molded styrene plastic, unless noted.

BARRELS

White Metal.

Large
255-80015
pkg(4) 2.25

Small
255-80023
pkg(10) 2.25

Platform
w/Barrel
255-80174
2.25

BOXES

Box of Bottles
White Metal
255-80112
pkg(4) 1.95

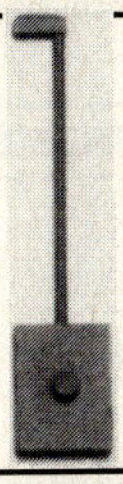

Electric Meter
Boxes
255-80164
pkg(2) 1.75

Mail Boxes
White Metal
255-80025
pkg(5) 1.95

BRIDGE SHOES

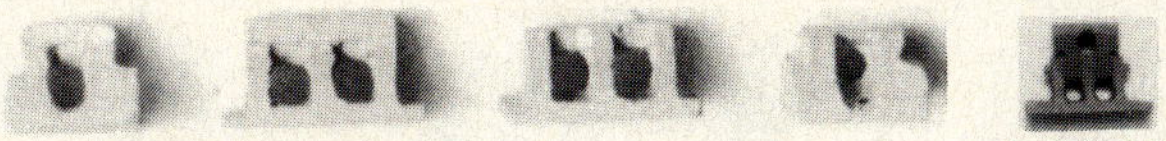

255-80035 Assorted   pkg(16) 5.95
255-80034 Bridge Shoes   pkg(4) 1.95

DOORS

Warehouse Overhead
255-80160
pkg(3) 1.75

Office Windows &
Doors
255-80161
pkg(8) 1.75

Warehouse Personnel
255-80162
pkg(4) 1.75

(not illustrated)

255-80062 Transom   pkg(4) 1.75
255-80063 Four Panel   pkg(4) 1.75
255-80065 Baggage   pkg(3) 1.75
255-80165 False Front   pkg(4) 1.75

MISCELLANEOUS

255-80166 50' Plate Girder   pkg(4) 2.25
255-80167 30' Plate Girder   pkg(4) 2.25
255-80043 Mine Car, white metal   3.25
255-80108 Pot Belly Stove, white metal   1.95
255-80026 Smoke Jacks, white metal   pkg(3) 2.25
255-80066 Board Walks   pkg(2) 1.75
255-80173 Ore Gate Mechanism   1.95
255-80093 Auto Tires, white metal   pkg(12) 2.95

STRUCTURAL DETAILS

Gutters &
Downspouts
255-80163
pkg(6) 1.75

Victorian Chimney,
white metal
255-80018 2.25

TOOLS

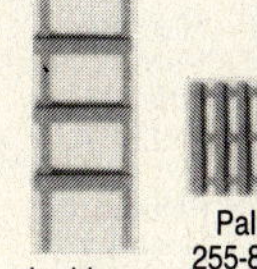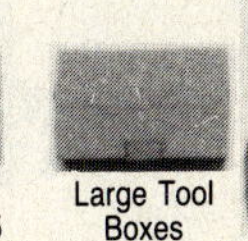

Ladders
255-80104
pkg(4) 2.25

Pallets
255-80105
pkg(12) 1.75

Large Tool
Boxes
white metal
255-80107
pkg(2) 1.95

Shovels,
white
metal
255-80110
pkg(4)
1.95

Lanterns,
white
metal
255-80109
pkg(4)
1.95

Brooms,
white
metal
255-80111
pkg(4)
1.95

WINDOWS

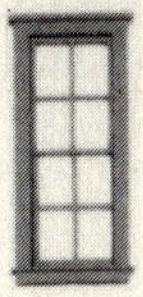

30 x 81"
255-80060
pkg(8)
1.75

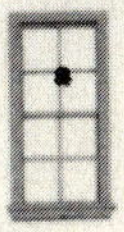

28 x 64"
255-80064
pkg(8)
1.75

Double
66 x 104"
255-80061
pkg(2) 1.75

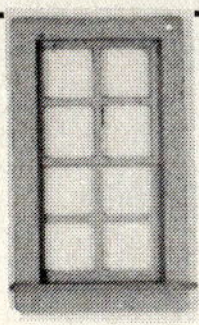

25 x 50"
8 pane
255-80067
pkg(8) 1.75

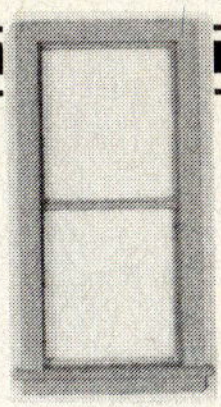

28 x 64"
2 pane
255-80068
pkg(8) 1.75

N.J. International

HO SCALE (1/87)

Accessories are all brass castings unless noted.

ALDON CAR ACCESSORIES

White Metal Cast Kits.

pkg(4) 4.29

We have worked closely with this manufacturer to provide accurate availability information at the time this catalog was published. Items listed in *blue ink* may not be available at all times. Please see your dealer for current delivery information.

525-331 Retarder

MISCELLANEOUS

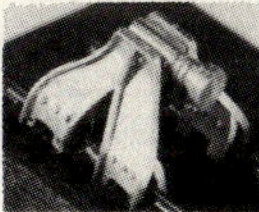

327   332   311

525-326   Switch Indicator - Union   1.59
525-327   Bumping Post - Halie   2.69
525-332   Nolan Car Stops CCS-1   pkg(2)   1.99
525-407   Brass Chain, 18" long (24 links per inch)   pkg(2)   1.99
525-411   Steam Snow Pilot   3.50
525-4023 Handrail Detail Kit, 68'   **NEW** 3.99
525-311   Containers, ACF LCL Cement (cast metal)   each   2.49
525-410   Air Horn   pkg(2)   .99

NorthWest Short Line

HO SCALE (1/87)

BALDWIN DETAILS

053-4625 Cylinder Saddle, HOn3   each .50
Baldwin slide valve style saddle as used on 4-4-0 and 2-6-0 locos circa 1880-1910. Brass plated die casting.

LOCO DRIVER SPRINGS

4mm long springs w/2mm diameters

053-14004 Wimpy   pkg(8)   1.95
053-14014 Light   pkg(8)   1.95
053-14104 Wimpy   pkg(100) 9.95
053-14114 Light   pkg(100) 9.95

MODEL MASTERPIECES LTD

HO SCALE
(1/87)

Parts are unpainted metal castings. Illustrations are actual size unless noted.

We have worked closely with this manufacturer to provide accurate availability information at the time this catalog was published. Items listed in *blue ink* may not be available at all times. Please see your dealer for current delivery information.

BOILERS

Cripple Creek
Horizontal Boiler
485-303   8.00

American Hoist
and Derrick
Vertical Boiler
485-301   9.00

Can be used to power the Steam Mill Engine #501 and shop equipment. Measures 14 × 6'6".

CHIMNEYS

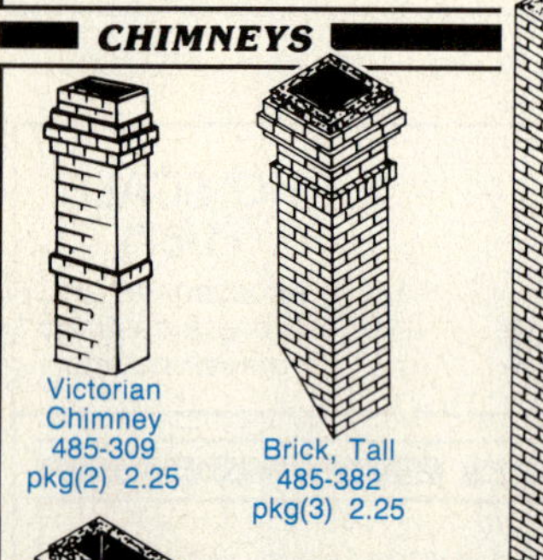

Victorian
Chimney
485-309
pkg(2) 2.25

Brick, Tall
485-382
pkg(3) 2.25

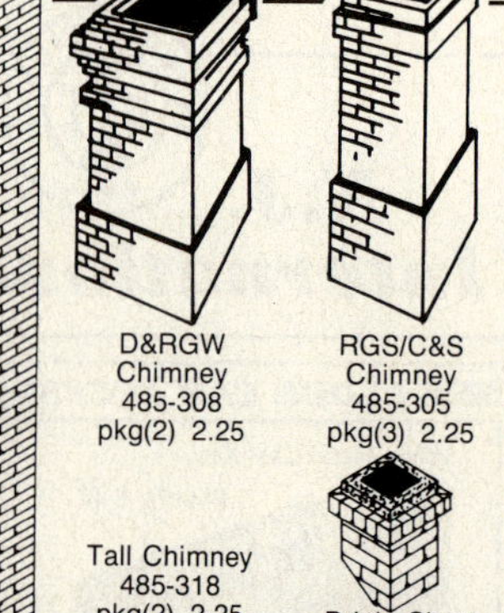

D&RGW
Chimney
485-308
pkg(2) 2.25

RGS/C&S
Chimney
485-305
pkg(3) 2.25

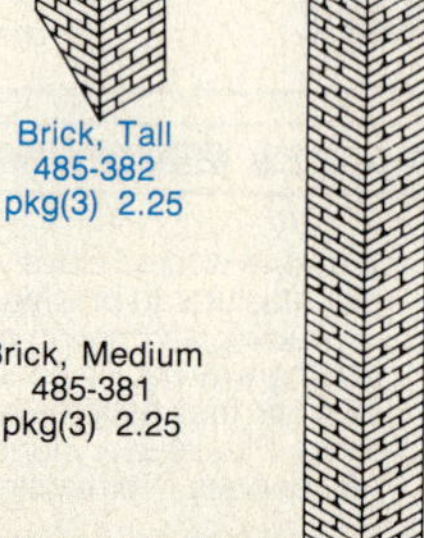

Brick, Medium
485-381
pkg(3) 2.25

Tall Chimney
485-318
pkg(2) 2.25
Solid, use with
#379 or #319

Brick, Short
485-380
pkg(4) 2.25

CONVEYORS

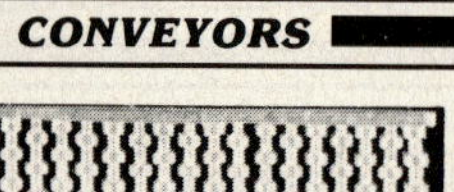

Skate
Wheel
485-3117
pkg(4) 2.25

(not illustrated)
485-3118 Roller   pkg(4) 2.25

DOORS

Double Arch Top
485-314   pkg(3) 3.50
styrene

Tall Double
485-364   pkg(2) 2.00
with transom, fits inside
masonry wall

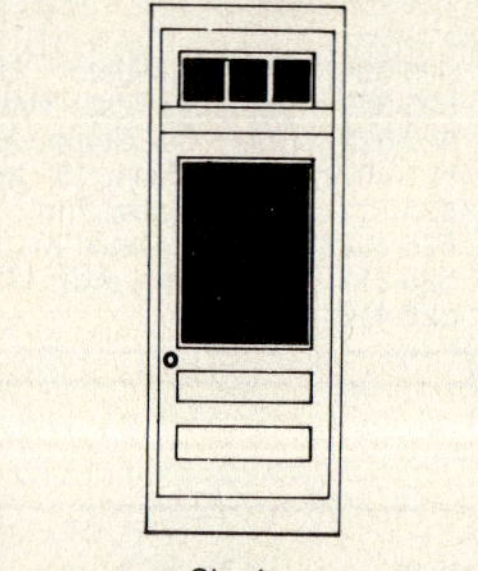

Single
485-366   pkg(2) 2.00
with transom, fits inside
masonry wall, use with
3/32" step

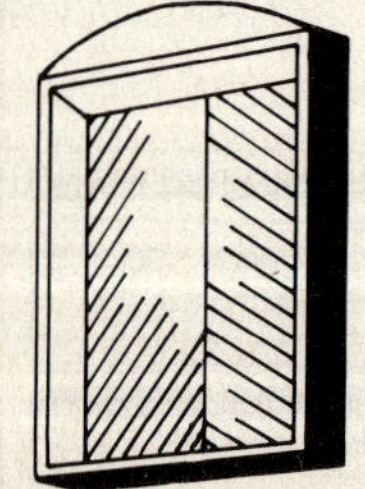

Arch Top Baggage
of Loft
485-369 pkg(3) 2.25

Double 4-Lite Industrial
485-365   pkg(2) 2.25
detailed both sides

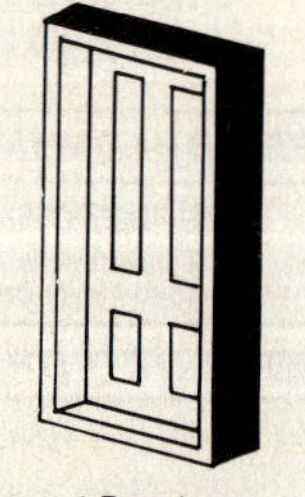

4-Panel
485-388   pkg(3) 2.25
for masonry walls

DOORS (continued)

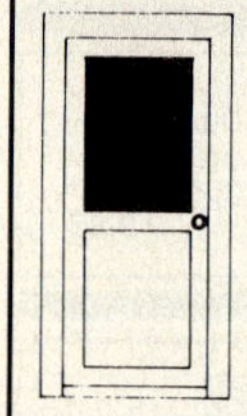

Single w/Sill
485-368
pkg(4) 2.00
detailed
both sides

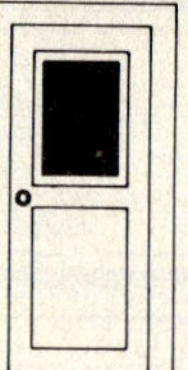

Single
485-367
pkg(4) 2.00

(not illustrated)
Gothic Double
485-391 pkg(2) 2.00
detailed frame

EXTERIOR DETAILS

Wooden Box
485-333
pkg(6) 1.75

Wood Keg
485-331
pkg(6) 2.00

Oak Bucket
485-334
pkg(6) 2.00

Mail Box
on Post
485-337
pkg(4) 2.00

Bumper Post
485-383
pkg(2) 2.25

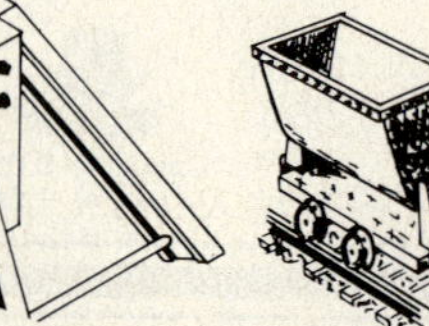

18" Gauge Side
Dump Mine Car
485-335
pkg(2) 2.25

Wood Pallet
485-338
pkg(4) 2.25

Street Lamp
485-356
pkg(3) 2.00
non-illuminating

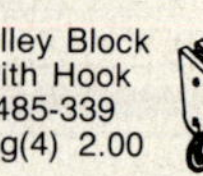

Wooden
Shipping Crate
485-332
pkg(4) 1.75

Fire Hydrant
485-336
pkg(6) 1.75

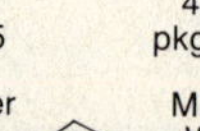

5 Gallon Can
485-362
pkg(6) 1.75

Old Wooden
Barrel/Keg
485-363
pkg(6) 2.25

Pulley Block
with Hook
485-339
pkg(4) 2.00

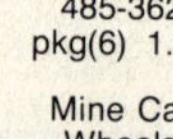

Bolt Retainer
Plate
485-350
pkg(6) 1.50

Mine Car
Wheels
485-359
pkg(8) 1.75

Industrial Lamp
Shade & Bulb
485-357
pkg(4) 2.00
non-operating

(not illustrated)

485-330 Platform Detail Set   pkg(6) 2.00
Set includes two wooden kegs, two wooden shipping crates and two wooden boxes.

485-360 Drum & Barrel Set   pkg(6) 2.00
Set includes two 55-gallon oil drums, two 5-gallon drums and two wooden barrels.

485-361 55-Gallon Oil Drum   pkg(5) 2.00

INTERIOR FURNISHINGS

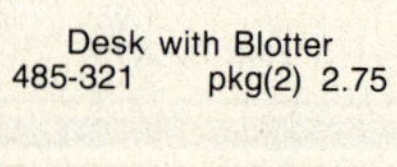

Desk with Blotter
485-321   pkg(2) 2.75

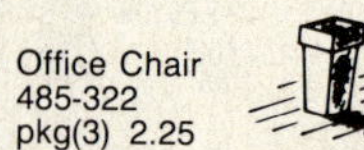

5' Round Dining Table
485-349   pkg(2) 2.25

42" Saloon Table
485-329   pkg(2) 2.25

1870 Chord Pump Organ
with Bench
485-345   set 2.50

High Back
Velvet Chair
485-346
pkg(2) 2.00

Office Chair
485-322
pkg(3) 2.25

Square
Waste Basket
485-326
pkg(6) 2.00

Flourescent
Desk Lamp
485-328
pkg(4) 2.00

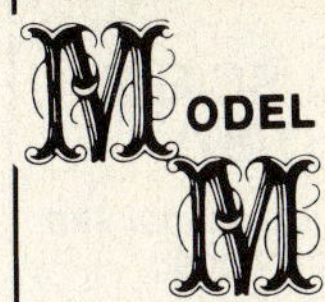

MODEL MASTERPIECES LTD

HO SCALE (1/87)

Parts are unpainted metal castings. Illustrations are actual size unless noted.

We have worked closely with this manufacturer to provide accurate availability information at the time this catalog was published. Items listed in *blue ink* may not be available at all times. Please see your dealer for current delivery information.

INTERIOR FURNISHINGS (continued)

Oil Stove w/Pipe
485-348
pkg(2) 2.00

2-Drawer Filing Cabinet
485-323
pkg(4) 2.00

3-Drawer Filing Cabinet
485-324
pkg(3) 2.00

Roundhouse Stove Set
485-311
each 2.50

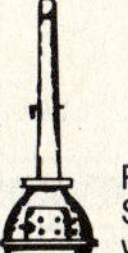

Pot Belly Stove with Pipe
485-347
pkg(2 sets) 2.00

Small Hook
485-392
pkg(8) 2.00

Filing Tray
485-327
pkg(6) 2.00

Books
485-325
pkg(6) 2.00 clustered & single

(not illustrated)

485-320 Office Furniture Set — pkg(8) 5.00
Set includes desk with blotter, office chair, 2-drawer filing cabinet, display of books (both single and clustered), square waste basket, filing tray and fluorescent desk lamp.

485-3128 Conference Table	pkg(3) 2.25
485-3129 CRT Terminal with Table	each 2.50
485-3130 Portable Shop Steps	pkg(3) 2.25
485-3131 Shelving Unit (87 × 36")	pkg(3) 2.25
485-3132 Workbench with Drawers 60"	pkg(2) 2.25
485-3133 Workbench with Drawers 72"	pkg(2) 2.25

MINIATURE MACHINE WORKS

A Craft Train Kit series of shop machinery cast in jewelers metal. Illustrations are not actual size.

506   505   504

485-504 Drill Press — 8.00
Six detail castings with belt drive wheel and adjustment handles.

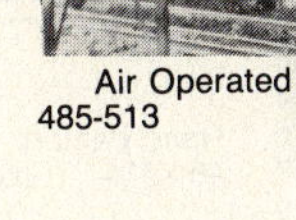

Air Operated Hoist
485-513   14.50

485-501 Steam Mill Engine   22.50

(not illustrated)

485-505 Shop Lathe — 8.00
Includes nine castings with belt drive wheel and positionable tool post.

485-506 Band Saw — 8.00

485-502 Steam Piping Set — 8.00
Supply of straight and right angle piping (4" diameter) for connecting boiler to mill engine. Valves can be used in many ways for the piping required by modeler. 11 pieces.

485-503 Overhead Belt Drive System — 9.95

MISCELLANEOUS

485-3125 Bridge Plate	pkg(2) 2.25
485-3126 Crane Electro-Magnet	each 2.25
485-3119 Storage Locker, 3 x 6'	pkg(4) 2.25
485-3134 Rotary Parts Bin	pkg(2) 2.25
485-3135 Pallet Jack, Hand Truck	each 2.25
485-117 Ashpit HO/HOn³/ON²ON³/Sn³	9.25

MISCELLANEOUS (continued)

485-3136 Roof Ventilator, Round	pkg(2) 2.25
485-3138 Building Name Plate Set	each 3.15
485-3143 Platform Scale with Desk	each 3.00
485-304 Strap Iron Hinges	pkg(36) 1.50

120T WRECKING DERRICK DETAILS

485-3121 Double Crane Hook	pkg(3) 2.25
485-3122 4-Pulley Sheave	each 2.25
485-3123 Cable Shackle/Clevis	pkg(6) 2.25
485-3124 Crane Equalizer Bar	pkg(2) 2.25

ORE HATCHES

485-397 Rectangular	pkg(3) 2.25
485-398 Square	pkg(3) 2.25
485-3127 Coal/Ore Chute	3.00

SMOKE JACKS

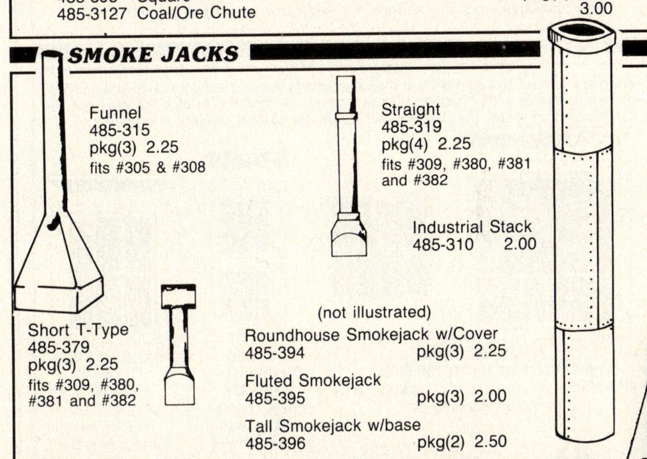

Funnel
485-315
pkg(3) 2.25
fits #305 & #308

Straight
485-319
pkg(4) 2.25
fits #309, #380, #381 and #382

Industrial Stack
485-310   2.00

Short T-Type
485-379
pkg(3) 2.25
fits #309, #380, #381 and #382

(not illustrated)

Roundhouse Smokejack w/Cover
485-394   pkg(3) 2.25

Fluted Smokejack
485-395   pkg(3) 2.00

Tall Smokejack w/base
485-396   pkg(2) 2.50

STRUCTURAL DETAILS

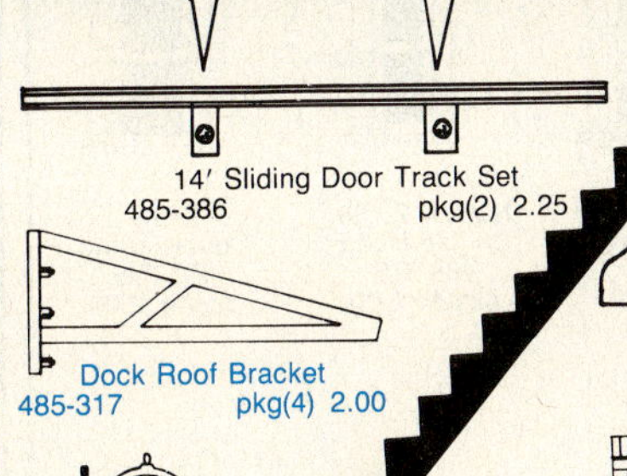

14' Sliding Door Track Set
485-386   pkg(2) 2.25

Dock Roof Bracket
485-317   pkg(4) 2.00

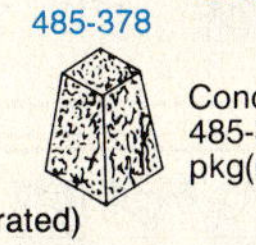

Bell with Supports and Wheel
485-344
pkg(2 sets) 2.00

Stair Stringer
485-306
pkg(4) 2.25

Sand Spout with Hanging Plate
485-387   2.25

Brick Cornice
485-378   pkg(4) 2.00

Concrete Pier
485-316
pkg(6) 2.25

(not illustrated)

485-389 Downspout Scupper	pkg(8) 1.75
485-393 Steel Bridge Shoes	pkg(4) 2.00
485-3115 Porch Post	pkg(12) 2.10
485-3120 Large Electric Motor	pkg(3) 2.25

TOOLS

Motor Driven Centrifugal Pump
485-510
pkg(2) 2.50

Mop-Leaning
485-353
pkg(4) 2.00

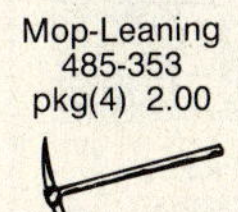

Pick
485-342
pkg(6) 1.75

Ladder
485-354
pkg(4) 2.00

Scoop Shovel
485-351
pkg(4) 2.00

MODEL MASTERPIECES LTD

HO SCALE (1/87)
Parts are unpainted metal castings. Illustrations are actual size unless noted.

■ TOOLS (continued)

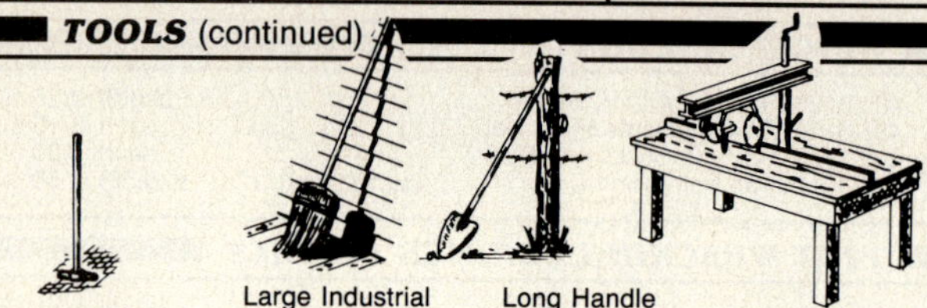

Maul
485-341
pkg(6) 1.75

Large Industrial Broom
485-352
pkg(5) 2.00

Long Handle Spade
485-343
pkg(6) 1.75

Radial Arm Saw with Bench
485-355   2.75

(not illustrated)

485-340 Tool Set #1   pkg(6) 2.00
Set includes two mauls, two picks and two long handled spades.

485-390 Tool Set #2   pkg(6) 2.00
Set includes two scoop shovels, two large brooms and two leaning mops.

■ WINDOWS

We have worked closely with this manufacturer to provide accurate availability information at the time this catalog was published. Items listed in *blue ink* may not be available at all times. Please see your dealer for current delivery information.

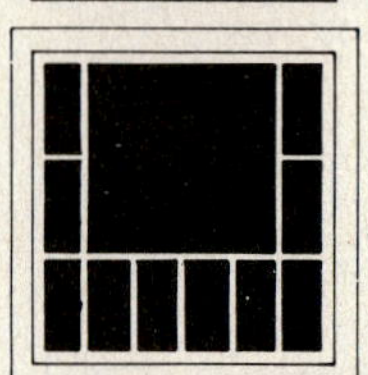
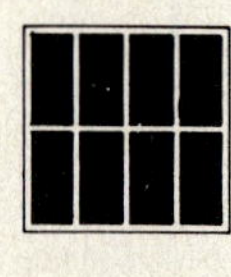

18-Lite Industrial with Working Insert Sill Detail
485-370   pkg(2) 2.00
fits inside masonry wall

12-Lite Double Hung
485-374
pkg(4) 2.00
fits inside masonry wall

6-Lite Interior Sill Detail
485-372
pkg(2) 2.00
fits inside masonry wall

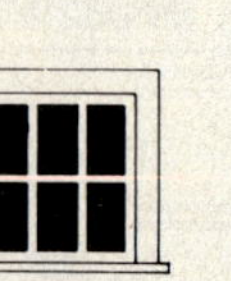
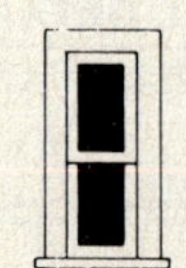
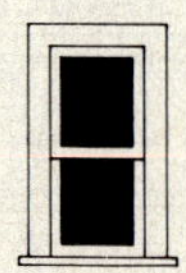

8-Lite Gothic Double Hung
485-377
pkg(3) 2.00

6-Lite Single Hung
485-373
pkg(4) 2.00

Narrow 2-Lite Double Hung
485-376
pkg(4) 2.00

2-Lite Double Hung
485-375
pkg(4) 2.00

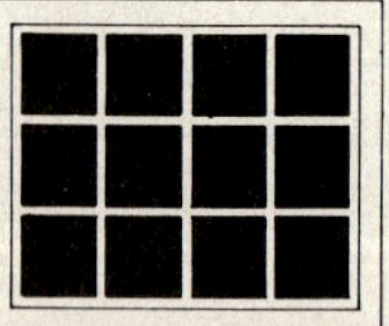

12-Lite Industrial
485-371
pkg(2) 2.00

(not illustrated)
Dormer Front with Window
485-399 pkg(2) 2.25

MERTEN

HO SCALE (1/87)

Imported from Germany by WALTHERS

Accessories are hand-painted plastic.

■ BARRELS & BOXES

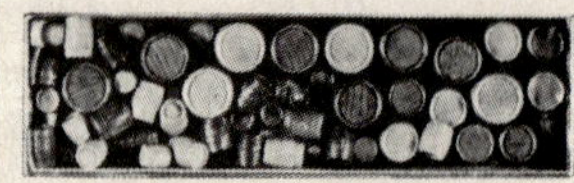
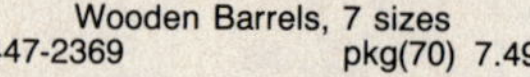

Wooden Barrels, 7 sizes
447-2369   pkg(70) 7.49

Wooden Boxes, 6 sizes
447-2370   pkg(90) 7.49

Master Creations

HO SCALE (1/87)

Parts are unpainted metal castings.

■ AUTO PARTS

464-716	Pierce Arrow Truck's Front Wheel/Tire	pkg(2) 1.00
464-718	Pierce Arrow Truck's Rear Wheel/Tire	1.00
464-755	Pierce Arrow Radiator	*NEW* 1.00
464-756	Pierce Arrow Engine	1.50
464-758	Automobile Transmission	1.50

■ CANS & DRUMS

Five Gallon Can
464-730   pkg(6) 1.00

55 Gallon Drum
464-760   pkg(4) 1.25

Jug
464-720   pkg(6) 1.00

■ DOORS & WINDOWS

464-710 Station Window   pkg(4) 1.00

Station Door with Transom
464-770   each 1.00

Freight Door Single
464-780   each 1.50

710   770   780

(not illustrated)

464-706	Freight Door, Plastic	1.00
464-708	Weathered Door, Plastic	1.00
464-766	Double-Hung Window, Plastic	pkg(3) 1.00
464-784	Skylight Window, Acetate	1.00

■ GAS STATION DETAILS

Gas Pump-Filter Style
464-762   each 2.50

Gas Pump-Glass Style
464-764   each 3.00

762   764

464-772 Gas Pump Island Set   7.95
Includes urethane island, two pumps, oil bottles, water can and decals.

464-774 Gas Station Detail Set   19.95
Contains a complete set of three color decals, two oil bunkers with crank arms, filler pipe stand and vapor vents for two large underground storage tanks, air compressor, innertube tesk tank, concrete lube pad, pump island, vehicle lift, two pumps and other details.

■ MISCELLANEOUS

Hand Lantern
464-714   pkg(2) 1.00

Lightning Rod
464-740   pkg(6) 1.00

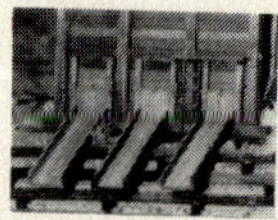

Mine Chute Assembly
464-792   2.25

(not illustrated)

464-712	Franz Falk Finial	pkg(2) 1.00
464-722	Metal Lunch Box	pkg(2) 1.00
464-724	Hi-Boy Oil Container	ea 1.00
464-726	Air Compressor Set	ea 2.00
464-728	Tube Test Tank w/Tire	pkg(2) 1.00

464-701	Water Melons	*NEW*	pkg(6) 1.00
464-702	Pumpkins	*NEW*	pkg(6) 1.00
464-704	Gourds	*NEW*	pkg(6) 1.00
464-731	Roof Brackets	*NEW*	pkg(4) 1.00
464-734	Tiffany Reefer Hinges		1.25
464-738	Clear Creek Freight Car Hardware		1.75
464-742	Junk Barrel	*NEW*	1.00
464-759	Bent Smokejack	*NEW*	pkg(2) 1.00
464-761	T Top Smokejack	*NEW*	pkg(2) 1.00
464-781	Cone Top Smokejack	*NEW*	pkg(2) 1.00
464-782	Corbel #1, Laser Cut Wood		pkg(6) 1.25
464-783	Corbel #2, Laser Cut Wood		pkg(6) 1.25
464-785	Corbel #3, Laser Cut, Wood		pkg(6) 1.25
464-794	1893 D&RG Reefer Vents		pkg(2) 1.00
464-796	Mine Head Gear		1.00
464-797	Water Bottle	*NEW*	pkg(6) 1.00
464-798	Smokejack		pkg(2) 1.00
464-799	Leaning Sacks		pkg(4) 1.00

M.V. PRODUCTS

HO SCALE HEADLIGHT & MARKER LENSES

CLASS/MARKER LIGHT LENS SETS FOR STEAM & DIESEL

516-22 4 Clear — 1.15
Class lights for Athearn, Atlas, AHM & Brass EMD Units & U-Boats. Class (Marker) lights for CAL Scale 280, 312, 325 and Kemtron 1408, 5353, 5359, 6101, 6102, 6103, 6106, & 6110 Castings & Marker Castings on most brass steam engines. Headlights for Alco models S5 & S6, RS3, RS4 & RS5, U33C, C628 LH & HH, DL600b LH & HH, DL702 LH & HH, PRR E44, PRR DL440, SD40 HH, C855A, RSD12, DL440 T6 N&W, SW1, SW1500. Custom brass GMD1, GP30, FP45, RDC1, RDC2 & RDC3. Athearn RDC cars. Hallmark GP7 & GP9. Scale 5-1/2″, actual .063″, drill #52

516-220 4 Red, same as #22 — 1.15
516-221 4 Green, same as #22 — 1.15
516-222 4 Amber, same as #22 — 1.15
516-501 1 Red, 1 Green & 1 Amber, same as #22 — 1.00

516-300 4 Clear — 2.00
Marker castings for CAL Scale 280, 312, 325 and Kemtron 1408, 5353, 5359, 6101, 6102, 6103, 6106 & 6110. All Precision Scale castings. Also fits most HO brass steam engines. Exact drop in—no drilling required. actual .052″

516-301 4 Red, same as #300 — 2.00
516-302 4 Green, same as #300 — 2.00
516-303 4 Amber, same as #300 — 2.00
516-500 1 Red, 1 Green & 1 Amber, same as #300 — 1.50

516-20 4 Clear — 1.50
Athearn EMD GP9, Atlas GP38, SD24, SD35, American GK GE E60 CP & CF. Class Lights for Athearn F7's & all other plastic & brass cab units. Scale 7-1/2″, actual .086″, drill #44

516-200 4 Red, same size as #20 — 1.30
516-201 4 Green, same as #20 — 1.30
516-202 4 Amber Lenses, same as #20 — 1.30
516-502 1 Red, 1 Green & 1 Amber, same as #20 — 1.00

DIESEL/ELECTRIC REFLECTIVE LENS SET

516-11 2 Clear, Athearn F7 — 1.50
516-111 1 Clear & 1 Red, Athearn F7 — 1.50
516-12 2 Clear, Athearn PA — 1.30
516-17 2 Clear — 1.30
Athearn SW 1500 Cow, Alco/Westside, GE 44 ton Diesel

516-18 6 Clear & 1 Red — 2.25
Athearn U-Boats, Details West HS102. Scale 6-1/2″, actual .073″, drill #49

516-19 6 Clear & 1 Red — 2.25
Athearn EMD Units, Atlas GP 40, AHM GE & U25C, Gem SDP 40F. AHM/Model Power Trains Inc PMI EMD FP45. Details West HS100 & 104. Scale 6-3/4″, actual .078″, drill #47

516-21 2 Clear, Athearn Baldwin S12 — 1.40
516-23 4 Clear & 1 Red — 1.65
Athearn F45, FP45, SD9. Alco Models C420 LH, C430, C630 HH, SD40 LH, GP40 LH & HH, C643 DH. Details West HS101 & HS105. (Use two sets) scale 6-3/4″, actual .078″, drill #47

516-24 2 Red — .75
Details West HL112, HL113, HL115 & HL116. Detail Associates LT1001, LT1002, LT1005, LT1007, LT1008 & LT1009. Utah Pacific SG70, GB71 & GB84. Scale 6-3/4″, actual .078″, drill#47.

516-25 4 Clear — 1.30
Athearn SD9. Details West HL113, HL114, HL116 & HL137. Detail Associates LT1002, LT1003, LT1004, LT1006, LT1007, LT1008, LT1009 & LT1011. Scale 6-3/4″, actual .078″, drill #47

516-26 4 Clear — 1.30
Details West HL117 & HL138. Detail Associates LT1003. Scale 6-1/2″, actual .073″, drill #49

516-103 8 Clear & 2 Red, Details West HS103 — 3.25

516-280 4 Clear — NEW 1.50
Scale 7″ Sealed Beam Headlights for EMD Hood Units, GE U-Boat & Electrics - all manufacturers, actual .082″, drill #45.

516-281 4 Red, Same as #280 — NEW 1.50

MISCELLANEOUS LENS SET

516-27 2 Clear — .75
Tenshodo N3, R2, P2, S1, S2 & M2 Tenders. WSM #50 D&RGW Diesel. Kemtron Alco Tender & Casting 1447 & 7502. Scale 7-1/2″, actual .086″, drill #44

516-28 1 Clear & 1 Red — .75
CAL Scale HL263 Mars Light Twin, scale 7″, actual .082″, drill #45

516-29 2 Clear — 1.00
Marklin engines 3096, 8396, 8322, 3034, 3037, 3038, 3035, 3041, 3050, 3043, 3075, 3066, 3067, 3068, 3076 & 3071. SS Ltd Old Time Trucks 7104, 7105, etc. Scale 9″, actual .101″, drill #38. 1/43 Scale 4.46″ Auto, Trucks, Emergency Vehicle lights.

516-30 2 Red, Same as #29 — 1.00
516-31 2 Amber, Same as #29 — NEW 1.00
516-32 2 Blue, Same as #29 — NEW 1.00

NON-OPERATING LENSES

Lenses provide the ultimate in realism with a lens system consisting of a 0.0012″ parabolic metal mirror and a solid lens made of a hybrid polymer. The lenses are available clear, or tinted in red, green, amber or blue. The lens system is designed to pick up and reflect all available light providing a prototype appearance to the model. Lens may be used with a lighting system due to the heat resistant properties of the hybrid polymer.

Lighting the lens — Locate a starter hole (using a sharp tool such as an awl) in the center of metal backing. Drill a small hole approximately 1/2 way through the solid lens (select a drill size that looks good for the size of the lens to be lighted). During **power on** operation the light will shine through the hole resulting in the whole lens glowing with its bright center giving the appearance of a scale bulb.

Lens sizes are given for each part number. First in scale inches for HO gauge and then actual diameter in inches and drill number.

For a complete usage listing and catalog send a large (#10) stamped, self-addressed envelope with two 1st Class stamps to Walthers. (516-1001   .50)

MISCELLANEOUS LENS SETS (continued)

516-203 4 Blue, Same as #20 — NEW 1.50
Railroad Signal Lights, 1/32 & 1/24 Scale Aircraft Formation Lights

516-223 4 Blue, Same as #22 — NEW 1.50
Railroad Signal Lights, 1/48 & 1/32 Scale Aircraft Formation Lights

516-304 4 Blue, Same as #300 — NEW 2.00
Railroad Signal Lights, 1/72 & 1/48 Scale Aircraft Formation Lights

516-600 .070″ diameter, clear — NEW pkg(4) 1.50
516-601 .070″ diameter, red — NEW pkg(4) 1.50
516-602 .070″ diameter, green — NEW pkg(4) 1.50
516-603 .070″ diameter, amber — NEW pkg(4) 1.50
516-800 1 Red, 1 Green & 1 Amber — NEW 2.25
Scale 11″ actual .125″, drill #1/8, 1/32 Scale Aircraft Recognition Lights, (Use #500 for 1/72 & #502 for 1/48 Scale Aircraft Formation Lights)

STEAM ENGINE & TENDER REFLECTIVE LENS SET

516-1 1 Clear & 1 Red, PFM SF 4-6-4, 4-8-4, 2-10-4 — 1.50
516-2 2 Clear — 1.65
PFM SF 1/137′ 4-6-2, B2 & B3 Shays with balloon stacks, Mich 3 Cylinder Shay. CB A & A1 4-8-4

516-3 2 Clear, Balboa/Hallmark SF 9000 0-6-0 — 1.50
516-4 2 Clear & 1 Red — 2.00
Sunset Models SF 0-6-0 & 2-8-0, Custom Brass/Balboa SF 2-6-2

516-5 2 Clear, Hallmark SF 2-8-0 '2507' — 1.65
516-6 2 Clear — 1.30
Tenshodo GN M2, N3, R2, P2 & Q1. WSM NYC J1e 4-6-4

516-7 2 Clear — 1.30
Tenshodo GN S1, S2 and O8. Van Hobbies CN N5d & S2, CP T-la

516-8 3 Clear, Westside/Balboa/Max Gray SP GS4 — 2.25
516-9 2 Clear & 1 Red — 2.25
PFM C&NW 4-6-2 E2a. Westside/Max Gray UP FEF2 & FEF3

516-10 2 Clear, PFM SOU F1 & PS4, WP 4-8-2 — 1.55

516-13 2 Clear Lenses — 1.65
PFM Pacific Coast Shay & NP S4 4-6-0. NWSL N&W E2a circa 1910 4-6-2

516-14 2 Clear — 1.65
PFM Frisco 2-10-0, WSM SP B1. Alco Models SP C15

516-15 2 Clear — 1.55
PFM WP 2-8-2, D&RGW L131, C&O K4, UP FEF1, Milwaukee Road F6a

516-16 2 Clear — 1.30
PFM D&RGW & WP 4-6-0, MoPac 4-6-2 & 4-8-4. WSM NYC J3a, J3b & J1e 4-6-4's. Van Hobbies CN #6060 4-8-2

INDIVIDUAL HEADLIGHT LENSES

516-116 Clear, scale 10″, actual .116″, drill #32 — .75
516-117 Red, scale 10″, actual .116″, drill #32 — .75
516-128 Clear, scale 11″, actual .128″, drill #30 — .85
516-129 Red, scale 11″, actual .128″, drill #30 — .85
516-130 Amber, Same as #128 clear & #129 red — NEW .85
516-131 Blue, 1/35 Scale 4.46″ & 1/43 Scale 5.57″ — NEW .85
516-136 Clear, scale 12″, actual .136″, drill #29 — .75
516-137 Red, scale 12″, actual .136″, drill #29 — .85
516-138 Amber (Same as #136 clear & #137 red) 1/32 Scale — NEW .85
516-139 Blue, 4.46″ Auto/Truck/Emergency/Military Vehicles — NEW .85
516-149 Clear, scale 13″, actual .149″, drill #25 — .75
516-150 Red, scale 13″, actual .149, drill #25 — .85

M.V. PRODUCTS

HO SCALE HEADLIGHT & MARKER LENSES

HO SCALE HEADLIGHT & MARKER LENSES

■ INDIVIDUAL HEADLIGHT LENSES (continued) ■

516-159	Clear, scale 14″, actual .159″, drill #21	.75
516-160	Red, scale 14″, actual .159″, drill #21	.85
516-166	Clear, scale 14-1/2″, actual .166″, drill #19	.85
516-167	Red, scale 14-1/2″, actual .166″, drill #19	.85
516-168	Amber (Same as #166 clear & #167 red) 1/35 Scale **NEW**	.85
516-169	Blue, 5.7″ & 1/43 Scale″ 7″ Auto/Truck/ Emergency Vehicles **NEW**	.85
516-173	Clear, scale 15″, actual .173″, drill #17	.85
516-174	Red, scale 15″, actual .173″, drill #17	.85
516-180	Clear, scale 15-1/2″, actual .180″, drill #15	.85
516-181	Red, scale 15-1/2″, actual .180″, drill #15	.85
516-182	Amber (Same as #180 clear & #181 red) 1/32 Scale 5.7″ **NEW**	.85
516-183	Blue, & 1/24 Scale 4.46″ Auto/Truck/Emer. Vehicle Signal Fog Lamps	.85
516-185	Clear, scale 16″, actual .185″, drill #13	.85
516-193	Clear, scale 17″, actual .193″, drill #10	.85
516-197	Amber(Same as #199 clear & #197 red) 1/35 Scale 7″ Auto/Truck/Emergency Vehicles Fog/Signal **NEW**	.85
516-198	Red, scale 17-1/2″, actual .199″, drill #8	.85
516-199	Clear, scale 17-1/2″, actual .199″, drill #8	.85
516-204	Clear, scale 18″, actual .204″, drill #6	.85
516-209	Clear, scale 18-1/2″, actual .209″, drill #4	.85
516-210	Red (Same as #209 clear) 1/2 gauge Railroad 4-1/2″ **NEW**	.85
516-211	Green, Steam Engine, Caboose, Switch Stand Marker **NEW**	.85
516-212	Amber, Lenses, Diesel/Electric Class Lights **NEW**	.85
516-216	Red (Same as #218 clear) 1/32 Scale 7″ Signal/Fog **NEW**	.85
516-217	Amber, Lamps for Autos/Trucks/Emergency Vehicle **NEW**	.85
516-218	Clear, scale 19″, actual .221″, drill #2	.85
516-228	Clear, Scale 20″, actual .228″, drill #1 **NEW**	.85
516-229	Red, 1/24 - 1/25 Scale 5.7″ Auto/Truck/ Emergency Vehicle **NEW**	.85
516-230	Amber, Headlamps, Red, Amber & Blue Signal Lamps **NEW**	.85
516-231	Blue, and AMber Fog Lamps **NEW**	.85
516-248	Clear, scale 22″, actual .248″, drill 1/4″	1.00
516-401	Clear, scale 20-1/2″, actual 15/64″, drill 15/64″	1.75
516-402	Clear, scale 23″, actual 17/64″, drill 17/64″	1.75
516-403	Clear, scale 24-1/2″, actual 9/32″, drill 9/32″	1.75
516-404	Clear, scale 26″, actual 19/64″, drill 19/64″	1.75
516-414	Red, (Same as #403 clear) 1/24 Scale 7″ Signal/Fog **NEW**	1.75
516-415	Amber, Lamps for Autos/Trucks/Emergency Vehicles **NEW**	1.75

MODEL TRACTION SUPPLY COMPANY

HO SCALE (1/87)

Detail parts are metal castings, unless noted. Illustrations are approximately full size.

■ MISCELLANEOUS ■

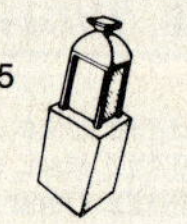

Troley Pole w/Wheel
505-501
pkg(2) 16.00

Fare Box
505-600 pkg(2) 2.95
(brass)

(not illustrated)

505-2000	Road Safety Cone	pkg(18) 1.00
505-2002	Rural Mailbox **(By Special Order Only.)**	pkg(5) 1.00

■ 'EL CAR' FLOORS ■

Floors are designed for the Q-Car epoxy body shells.

505-4000	R9 IND Power Floor	6.00
505-4004	CTA 4000 Power Floor	6.00
505-4005	CTA 4000 Trailer Floor	6.00

New England Rail Service, Inc.

HO SCALE (1/87)

Pullman Detail Parts Plastic unless noted.

■ AIR CONDITIONING DUCT ■

529-250	Air Conditioning Duct	pkg(2) 5.95

■ ICE BUNKERS ■

529-151	6 foot, brass	each 12.95
529-251	6 foot	pkg(2) 3.95
529-152	Double, brass	each 12.95
529-252	Double	pkg(2) 3.95

■ PULLMAN CAR PARTS ■

The addition of new parts transforms a stock model into a one-of-kind replica! This rebuilt Rivarossi 12-1 Sleeper now matches Pullman Plan #3410 and is fitted with Pullman Air Conditioning Ducts, Ice Bunkers, Water Tank, and different styles of Paired Windows.

529-230 Pullman Pressurized Water Tanks pkg(2) 3.95
Correct 145 gal. water tanks with five way valves.

529-350 Pullman Ice Activated Air Conditioning Kit 23.95
Four duct pieces, two #251 and four #252 ice bunkers plus two #230 water tanks. Enough parts to equip two Pullmans with ice activated air conditioning.

529-202	Miscellaneous Single Windows	3.95
529-203	Single Coach Windows	1.95
529-204	Coach Toilet Windows	TBA
529-210	Interior Vestibule Wall & Door Section	TBA
529-211	Baggage Doors	1.95
529-254	Air Conditioner Compressor Box	3.95
529-255	Holdover Coil Box for Mechanical Brine A/C	TBA
529-270	242-A Top Equalized Trucks	TBA
529-300	Coach Conversion Kit	4.95
529-301	Combination Car Conversion Kit	3.95

■ WINDOWS ■

These styrene windows make it easy to convert or rebuild AHM/Rivarossi/ IHC 12-1 Pullmans to other sleeper types. Each set of windows is molded in gray styrene with rivet details. Set 200 provides six windows and two filler panels, with basic instructions.

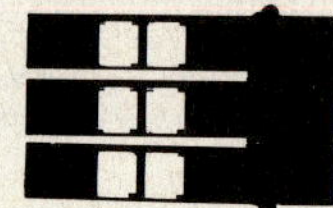

Paired
529-200
pkg(6) 3.95

24″ Single
529-201
pkg(12) 3.95

(not illustrated)

529-205 Pullman Sun Room pkg(4) 3.95
Lounge Observation
Includes four windows and four filler pieces

529-212 Pullman Diner Window/Food Doors pkg(10) 3.95
Includes four food service doors, four paired kitchen windows and two diner windows

EKO

HO SCALE (1/87)

Molded in appropriately colored plastic.

■ BARRELS, BOXES & SACKS ■

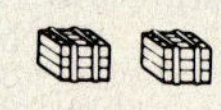

Assortment
265-2204 pkg(8) 1.49

PRECISION INVESTMENT ASSOCIATES

HO SCALE (1/87)

All PIA parts are brass castings unless noted.
Illustrations are not to scale.

AIR FILTER

Piping for Cross Compound Pump
063-56   each 1.98

(not illustrated)
063-108 Westinghouse Type G ea 1.95
063-103 Northern Pacific Style 1.98

AIR HORN

Boiler Mounting
063-33   each 2.25

Leslie S, 3-Chime (Standard Diesel)
063-155   each 3.25

AIR PUMPS

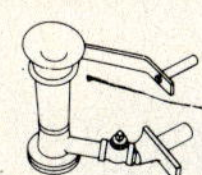

Intake Piping
063-105
pkg(2) 1.98

Hinged Bracket Smokebox Mounted
063-23 pair 2.98

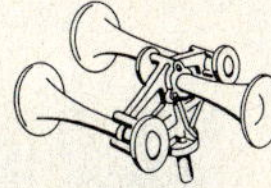

Westinghouse 8-1/2" Cross Compound
063-22 ea 3.25

Drip Pans (cross compound)
063-24 pair 2.50

AIR TANK HANGERS

Air Tank Hangers
063-104   pair 2.25

BELLS

NP Style
063-107
each 2.50

Air Ringer Boiler Top Mount
063-53   each 2.50

(not illustrated)
063-114 Smoke Box Front Angle Mount   each 2.98
063-115 Bell Only   each 1.79
063-116 Bracket, Hand Ringer (use #115 bell)   each 1.95
063-117 Bracket Air Ringer (use #115 bell)   each 1.95

BLOW OFF COCK

Okadee Type
063-76   pkg(2) 2.25

BRAKE CYLINDERS

Tenders
063-54   each 2.25

Trailing Truck
063-106   pkg(2) 2.50

Trailing Truck
063-55   pkg(2) 2.98

BRAKE STANDS

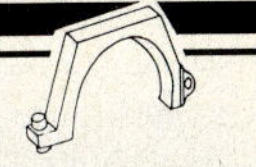

Westinghouse E-6 Type (cab interior)
063-1   each 2.50

CAB SEATS

Wood Box
063-3
pair 2.25

Box Type
063-5
pair 2.25

Modern Pedestal
063-4
pair 2.50

CROSSHEADS

Alligator (Small Loco)
063-110   pkg(2) 3.25

Alligator MoPac Style
063-112   pkg(2) 3.25

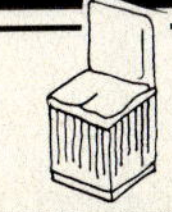

w/Guide, Laird Type
063-113   pkg(2) 5.98

Alligator (Large Loco)
063-111   pkg(2) 3.25

FIREDOORS

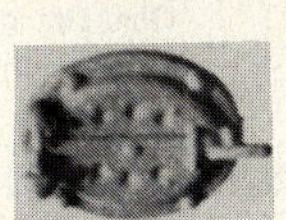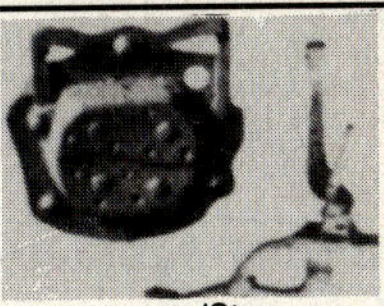

Small, Oil Type
063-90   ea 2.25

Small, Old Style Baldwin
063-91   ea 2.25

w/Step "Butterfly" Type (cab interior)
063-6   ea 2.50

w/Step "Economy" Type (cab interior)
063-7   ea 2.50

FLAG STANCHIONS

Tall
063-67 pkg(4) 2.50

Short
063-68 pkg(4) 2.50

GAUGE CLUSTERS

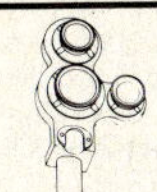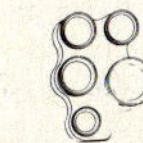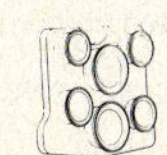

3 Older Style (cab interior)
063-11 ea 1.98

4 Modern Style (cab interior)
063-12 ea 1.95

5 Modern Gauges for Engines or (cab interior)
063-13 ea 2.25

6 Modern Gauges for Engines or (cab interior)
063-14 ea 2.25

GAUGES

Steam, 6" Backhead Mounted (cab interior)
063-9   each 1.75

Duplex Air for Brake System (cab interior)
063-10   each 1.75

GENERATORS

Pyle National Type (M-06)
063-64   each 2.25

Pyle National Type K-2
063-62   each 2.25

Sunbeam Turbo
063-63   each 2.25

GOVERNOR

Pump, Westinghouse Type SD
063-77   pkg(2) 2.25

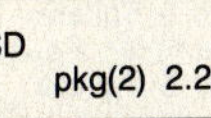

HATCH

063-31 Oil Tender   each 2.25

HEADLIGHTS

Mars Type
063-120
each 2.25

Pyle National without Visor
063-71
each 2.25

NP Style
063-72
each 2.25

Direct Mounting B&M Type
063-73 each 2.25

Bracket Boiler Front
063-69   each 2.25

Pyle National w/Visor
063-70   each 2.25

(not illustrated)
063-119 Pennsylvannia RR Style   2.25

HINGE

Okadee Boiler Front
063-32   pair 2.98

PRECISION INVESTMENT ASSOCIATES

HO SCALE (1/87)

All PIA parts are brass castings unless noted. Illustrations are not to scale.

INJECTORS

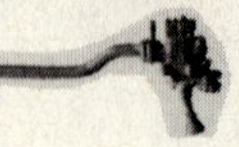

Hancock Non-Lifting Type
063-37   pair 3.24

Ohio Lifting Type
063-36   pair 3.25

MISCELLANEOUS

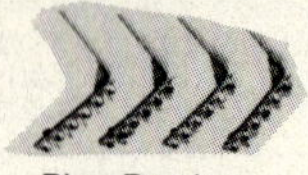

Pipe Brackets for Cooling Coils
063-123
pkg(4) 2.50

Lagging Clamps for Boiler Jacketing
063-34
pkg(25) 2.98

Stoker, Elevator Type
063-18
pkg(2) 3.95

Backhead Shelf w/Oil Cans
063-2
each 2.25

Drive Head Speed Recorder
063-154
pkg(2) 2.98

Bearing Cap EMD Hyatt
063-153
pkg(8) 3.98

Back-Up Light (Modern Locos)
063-25
each 1.95

Junction Boxes Elec, Loco Wiring
063-87
pkg(25) 3.95

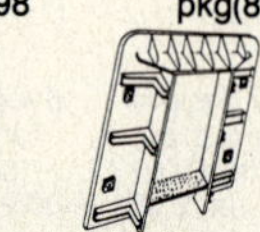
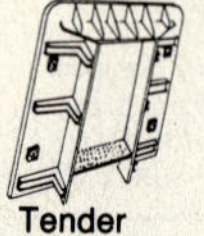

Soot Blowers L&R
063-137
pair 2.75

Tender Vestibule
063-150
each 6.95

6 Cylinder Steam Turrent
063-88
each 3.25

Tool Box Tender Mounting
063-61
each 2.79

Pedestals, for Vanderbilt Tender Tanks
063-125
pkg(18) 7.95

(not illustrated)

063-89	Steam Turret 6-Round	each 3.25
063-109	Exhaust Muffler Centrifugal Blow-Off	each 2.25
063-124	Sand Box Geared Loco's	each 3.50
063-15	Lubricator, 3 feed Detroit "Bullseye"	each 2.75
063-49	Drain Cook for Air Tanks	each 1.95

NUMBER BOARDS

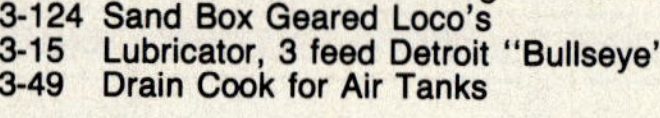

C&O Extended Type
063-74 pkg(2) 2.75

General Design
063-75   each 2.75

PIPE FLANGES

063-40	0.8" Diameter, Round & Square	(20 pieces) 3.95
063-41	Pipe Flange, 1.2" Diameter, Round & Square	(20 pieces) 3.95
063-42	1.8" Diameter, Round & Square	(20 pieces) 4.00

PILOTS

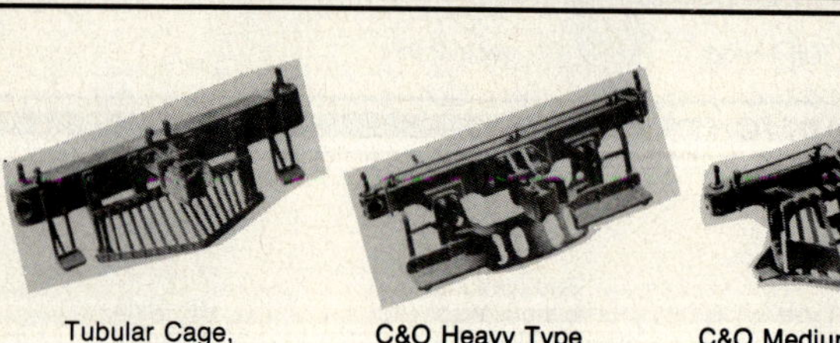

Tubular Cage, General Design
063-79   kit (7 pcs) 9.98

C&O Heavy Type
063-78   kit (7 pcs) 10.98

C&O Medium Type
063-80   kit (7pcs) 11.00

SP/TN&O
063-165   each 9.98

Drop Coupler, Commonwealth
063-39 kit (7 pieces) 9.95

Northern Pacific Wood Pilot Kit
(contains 4 coupler lift stanchions, 2 flag stanchions, coupler & coupler pocket, pilot beam, cage and footboard)
063-38   Kit (10pcs) 9.98

PILOTS (continued)

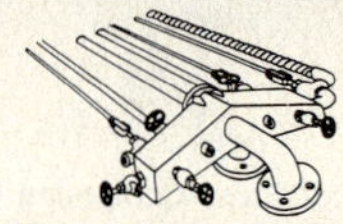

Pilot Kit L&A
063-171   7 pc   9.98

Turret, Front of Cab w/Control Rods
063-149   each 4.98

Pilot Kit NP
063-172   7 pc   9.98

Pilot Kit Soo Line
063-179   9 pc   9.98

Pilot Kit WP
063-173   9 pc   9.95

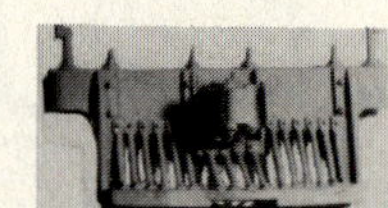

UP FEF-1
063-166 8 pc ea 9.95

SP Tube
063-167 5 pc ea 9.95

CPR Silkerk
063-168 9 pc ea 9.98

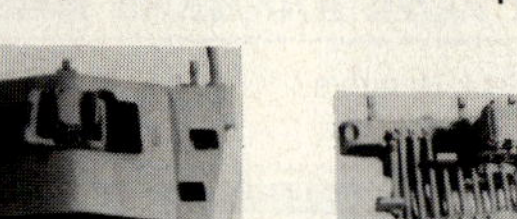

SR Tube Style
063-174 9 pc ea 9.95

C&O S3-A
063-175 9 pc ea 9.95

GN Tube Style
063-176 8 pc ea 9.98

SP Switcher
063-178 7 pc ea 8.98

C&O K-3
063-177 10 pc ea 9.95

Beams, Shay Type w/Coupler Pocket
063-128 4 pc ea 14.98

(not illustrated)
Pilot Kit CNR
063-164
each 8.95

Deck Step
063-122
each 2.95

w/Drop Coupler, PRR
063-127 4 pc ea 5.95

B&M
063-169 7 pc ea 8.98

POWER REVERSE

Alco Type E
063-81   each 2.98

(not illustrated)
Reverse Power Quadrant (cab interior)
063-17   each 1.95

REVERSE QUADRANTS

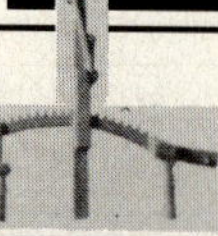

Screw
063-102
each 2.50

Manual Floor Mount, Cab Interior
063-16
each 2.50

RERAIL FROGS

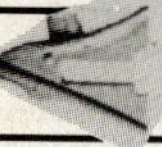

Standard Cast Iron Type
063-82   pkg(2) 2.79

Butterfly Type
063-131   pkg(2) 2.50

SANDERS

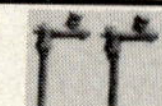

Viloco Type, Single
063-136   pair 2.25

Valves, Graham-White Co
063-50   pair 2.25

063-126 Valve

(not illustrated)
each 2.79

PRECISION INVESTMENT ASSOCIATES

HO SCALE (1/87)

All PIA parts are brass castings unless noted.
Illustrations are not to scale.

STACK DETAILS

Double Exhaust
063-21   each 2.50

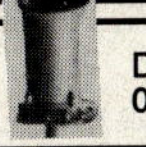
D&RGW, K-36, 37
063-85   each 2.79

STEPS

35 Degree Running Board Loco
063-121   pkg(2) 5.98

SUPER DETAILING KIT, SD40-2

For Athearn and GSB SD40-2 plastic models.

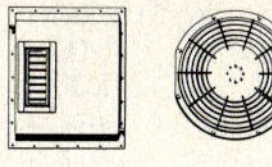
063-156 Quiet Kit   17.50
For post 1980 EMD units. Kit includes 3 Q fans (brass open and grid & visible blades) and one plastic exhaust silencer hatch.

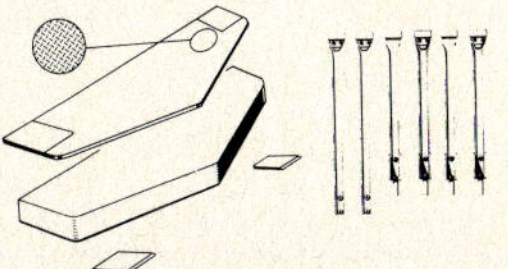
063-157 Jumbo Anti-Climber Kit 7.98
For EMD hood units, includes 3 styles of posts, handrail, wire & bending template, tread and plastic anti-climber.

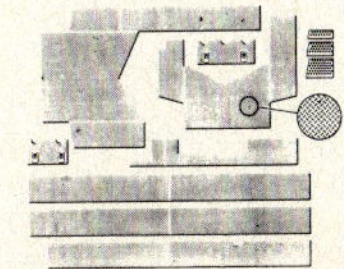
063-159 Walkway Tread Kit   11.95
Walkway tread pieces for SD40-2 and other EMD units.

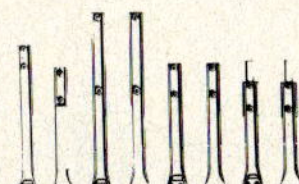
063-158 Handrail Kit   14.95
40 handrail posts of eight styles and .015″ brass handrail with bending template.

(not illustrated)
063-160 SD40-2 Super Detailing Package   24.95
#'s 154, 155, 158 and 159 and includes: walkway tread (sized to fit all), etched brass Leslie S 3-chime horn, handrail posts (8 different styles), speed recorder head, handrail wire & bending templates and cab & end steps (etched brass, sized to fit).

TENDER STEP

TS-7
063-146   pair 2.50

TS-2
063-143   pair 2.98

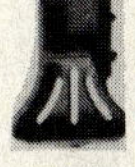
TS-8
063-147   pair 2.98

TS-5
063-145   pair 2.98

(not illustrated)
063-144 D&RGW Rear TS-3   pair 2.50

TRUCK DETAILS

For super-detailing the basic Athearn and Atlas trucks, lost wax brass parts.

EMD Type B-2 Truck Kit
063-152   each 14.95

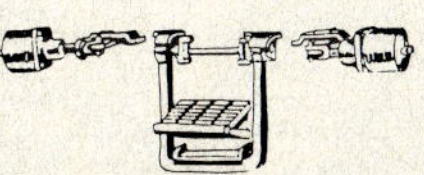
EMD Type B Truck Kit
063-151   each 14.95

THROTTLES

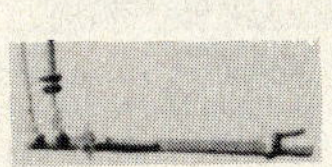
Backhead Mounting, Long
063-95   each 2.50

Side Mount Chambers
063-94   each 2.79

THROTTLES (continued)

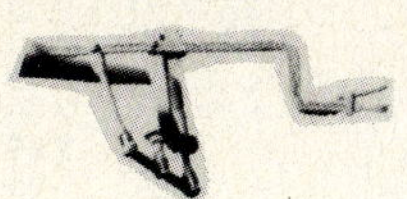
D&RGW, Long Reach Backhead Mount
063-20   each 2.95

Backhead Mounting, Short
063-93   each 2.50

(not illustrated)
063-96 Back Mounting Chamber   each 2.75
063-140 Large Front End   each 4.95

VALVES

Globe Short Stem
(cored .012″ wire)
063-29   pkg(3) 2.25

Globe Long Stem
(cored .012″ for wire)
063-30   pkg(3) 2.25

Hanger, Baker Modern
063-47   pair 5.95

Cylinder Relief
Recessed, Small
063-84   pkg(2) 2.75

Check Nathan Type T
063-118   each 2.50

Check Edna
High-Pressure Type
063-28   pair 2.25

Tri-Cock and Funnel
063-92   pkg(4) 2.79

Globe, Small on Pipe
063-65   pkg(3) 2.25

(not illustrated)
063-19   Turrent Control   each 2.25
063-83   Large Cylinder Relief   pkg(2) 2.25
063-139   Starter, Seller VC   each 2.25
063-141   Pop Open   each 2.25
063-142   Pop Housing   each 2.50

WATER DETAILS

Water Glass, Sargent
063-98   pkg(2) 2.50

Tender Water Hatch
063-66   each 2.50

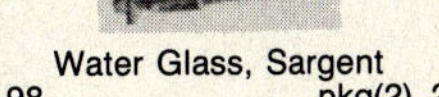

Water Column Nathan Type w/Funnel
063-97   pkg(2) 2.50

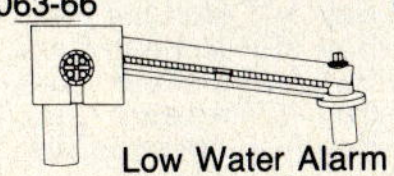
Low Water Alarm
Nathan Boiler, Top Mounting
063-35   each 2.25

WATER LEG VALVES

Modern
Quick Acting Type
063-99   pair 2.50

Old Time
063-100   pair 2.50

WHISTLES

5-Chime
063-48   each 2.25

Single Chime Arm Down
063-133   each 1.95

(not illustrated)
063-132   Single Chime, Arm Up   each 1.95
063-138   Single Chime, Elbow Up   each 2.25
063-134   Six Chime, Arm Up   each 1.95
063-135   Six Chime, Arm Down   each 1.95

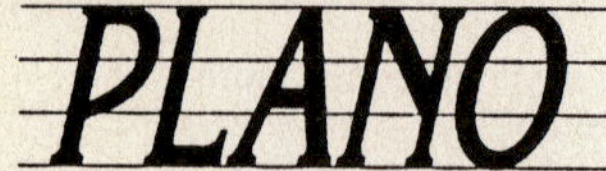

HO SCALE (1/87)

HO Scale Freight car details. Features see-through walkways of etched stainless steel and brass to replace plastic parts in kits.

DETAIL PARTS

565-116	ACF Risers, McKean - Same Size		2.00
565-117	ACF Risers, McKean - Two Sizes		2.00
565-118	ACF Risers, Athearn - Same Size		2.00
565-119	ACF Risers, Athearn - Two Sizes		2.00
565-127	Coupler Platform, Round	pkg(2)	1.95
565-128	Coupler Platform, Slotted	pkg(2)	1.95
565-129	Coupler Platform, Open Diamond	pkg(2)	1.95
565-130	Box Car Brake Platform, Open Round	pkg(2)	1.25
565-131	Box Car Brake Platform, Slotted	pkg(2)	1.25
565-132	Box Car Brake Platform, Diamond	pkg(2)	1.25
565-133	Coupler Platform, Round		2.75
565-134	Coupler Platform, Slotted Pattern		2.75
565-136	Brake Rod Support, Gunderson Cont.		1.00
565-137	End Load Guides, Thrall Container		1.75
565-138	Locator Boxes, Thrall Container		2.75
565-139	Lift Rings w/Gussets, Thrall Container		2.00
565-140	Freight Car Lift Rings		1.00
565-171	Husky Stack Replacement Detail Parts		3.00
565-181	Farr Grille, Rock Island U25B	pkg(2)	2.75
565-189	EMD Blower Housing Step Guards	pkg(4)	1.00
	Angled Slots, Brass		
565-201	Slotted Pattern Builders Material 1.8" x 8.5" Stainless		10.50
565-202	Slotted Pattern Builders Material 1.8" x 8.5" Brass		10.50

DRILL TEMPLATES

565-175	Husky Stack	4.50
565-176	Thrall Long & Short Ends, Standard 40' & 45' APL	6.50
565-177	Thrall 45' TTX Short End	2.75
565-178	Thrall Electric Long & Short Ends	6.50
565-179	40' Gunderson Car	2.50

THRALL FRAME KITS

40' DOUBLE STACK CARS

565-161	End Units	pkg(2)	8.75
565-162	Mid Units	pkg(2)	8.25
565-163	Five Unit Set	pgk(5)	17.95

45'

565-164	APL Style Mid Units	pkg(2)	8.95
565-165	APL Style Five Unit Set	pkg(5)	18.95
565-166	APL Style Mid Units	pkg(2)	8.95
565-167	TTX Style Five Unit Set	pkg(5)	18.95
565-168	40' Gunderson, Five Unit	pkg(5)	4.50
565-169	Electric Version, End Units	pkg(2)	TBA
565-170	Electric Version, Five Units	pkg(5)	TBA

WALKWAYS

COVERED HOPPERS

565-80	MDC FMC-Round Pattern	9.25
565-86	2-Bay Cement Hopper, WKW car	5.75
565-89	MDC PS2 2-Bay	3.50
565-92	Con-Cor PS2 3-Bay	4.50
565-101	2-Bay ACF-McKean Cars, Round	7.50
565-102	2-Bay ACF-McKean Cars, Slotted	7.50
565-104	3-Bay ACF-McKean Cars, Round	8.25
565-105	3-Bay ACF-McKean Cars, Slotted	8.25
565-107	4-Bay ACF-McKean Cars, Round	9.50
565-108	4-Bay ACF-McKean Cars, Slotted	9.50
565-110	4-Bay ACF-Athearn Cars, Round	9.25
565-111	4-Bay ACF-Athearn Cars, Slotted	9.25

CYLINDRICAL HOPPERS

565-100	Canadian Grain Car - Intermountain	8.25

WALTHERS AIRSLIDE HOPPERS

565-95	Single Bay	3.75
565-92	Double Bay	4.50

WALTHERS COIL CARS

565-121	Full Length-Round	5.50
565-122	Car Ends Only, Round	3.75
565-123	Full Length-Slotted	5.50
565-124	Car Ends Only, Slotted	3.75

THRALL DOUBLE STACK

565-141	40' End Units Only	2.75
565-142	40' Mid Units Only	2.75
565-143	40' Five Unit Set	5.75
565-144	45' APL Style Mid Unit	3.00
565-145	APL Style Five Unit Set	5.95
565-146	45' TTX Style Mid Unit	3.00
565-147	45' TTX Style Five Unit Set	5.95
565-148	40' Gunderson Five Unit Set	1.75
565-149	Electric Version-End Unit	2.75
565-150	Electric Version-Five Unit	5.75

WALKWAYS (continued)

HUSKY STACK

565-151	Walkway & Detail Parts	7.75

ATHEARN IMPAC CARS

565-152	Walkway Set-Round	2.00

WALTHERS STAND ALONE CARS

565-153	Thrall 48', Round	4.25

FRONT RUNNER

565-159	Walkway Platform, Round	2 Sets	2.25
565-160	Walkway Platform, Diamond	2 sets	2.25

40' BOX CAR

565-190	Round	pkg(2)	4.00
565-191	Slotted		4.00
565-192	Diamond		4.00

Now you know why they call it the "Great White North!" Last night's snowfall deposited several scale inches of Hydrocal® on Pete Moffet's Trout Creek Lumber Co. narrow gauge, creating extra work for the South River section gang. The hy-rail truck combines a scratchbuilt body with a Wheel Works chassis, while the driver is a Campbell figure.

Models and Photo by Pete Moffett

Pikestuff

HO SCALE (1/87)

Parts are molded in plastic.
Illustrations are 2/3 size.

DOORS

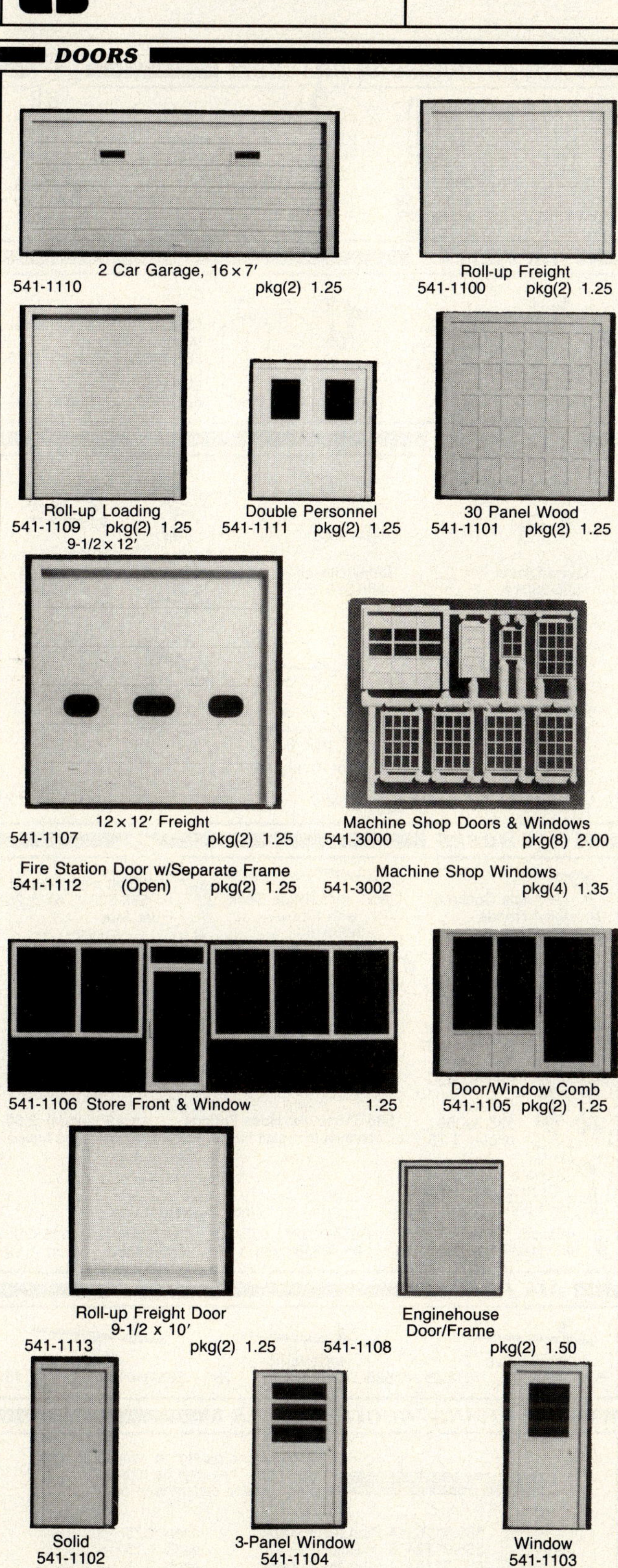

2 Car Garage, 16 × 7′
541-1110   pkg(2) 1.25

Roll-up Freight
541-1100   pkg(2) 1.25

Roll-up Loading
541-1109   pkg(2) 1.25
9-1/2 × 12′

Double Personnel
541-1111   pkg(2) 1.25

30 Panel Wood
541-1101   pkg(2) 1.25

12 × 12′ Freight
541-1107   pkg(2) 1.25

Machine Shop Doors & Windows
541-3000   pkg(8) 2.00

Fire Station Door w/Separate Frame
541-1112   (Open)   pkg(2) 1.25

Machine Shop Windows
541-3002   pkg(4) 1.35

541-1106 Store Front & Window   1.25

Door/Window Comb
541-1105 pkg(2) 1.25

Roll-up Freight Door
9-1/2 × 10′
541-1113   pkg(2) 1.25

Enginehouse Door/Frame
541-1108   pkg(2) 1.50

Solid
541-1102
pkg(3) 1.25

3-Panel Window
541-1104
pkg(3) 1.25

Window
541-1103
pkg(3) 1.25

DOORS (continued)

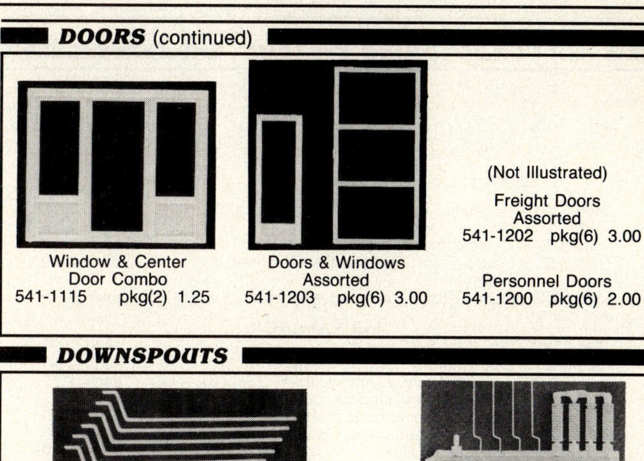

Window & Center Door Combo
541-1115   pkg(2) 1.25

Doors & Windows Assorted
541-1203   pkg(6) 3.00

(Not Illustrated)

Freight Doors Assorted
541-1202   pkg(6) 3.00

Personnel Doors
541-1200   pkg(6) 2.00

DOWNSPOUTS

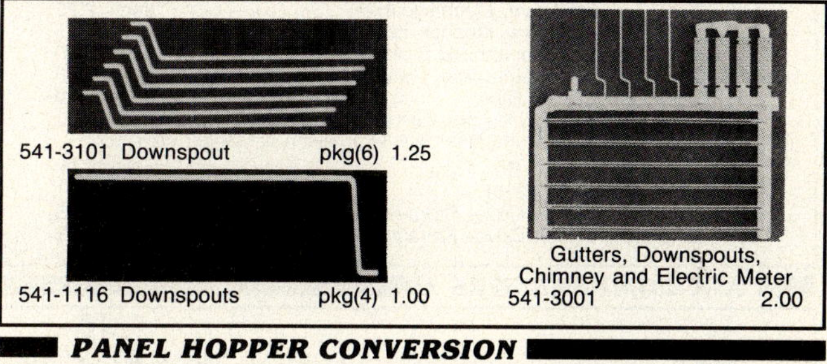

541-3101 Downspout   pkg(6) 1.25

541-1116 Downspouts   pkg(4) 1.00

Gutters, Downspouts, Chimney and Electric Meter
541-3001   2.00

PANEL HOPPER CONVERSION

541-4000 Panel Hopper Conversion   1.50
Panels are designed to be applied to the Athearn 34′ ribbed side hoppers.

PASSENGER CAR SEATS

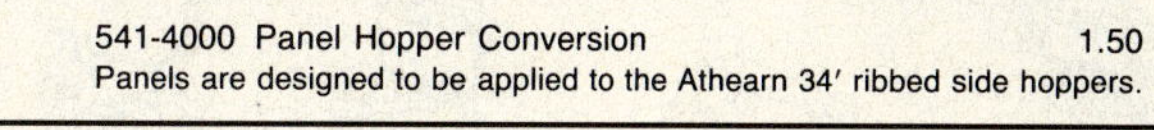

541-4101 Lightweight Gray   pkg(36) 3.25
541-4100 Lightweight Brown   pkg(36) 3.25
541-4102 Lightweight Red   pkg(36) 3.25
541-4103 Lightweight Blue   pkg(36) 3.25

STAIRCASE

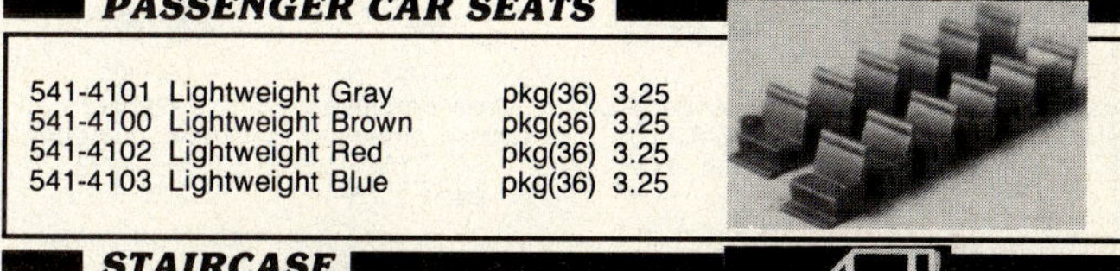

Concrete Staircase
541-1010   pkg(3) 1.25

Staircase Handrails
541-1114   pkg(2) 1.25

VENTILATORS

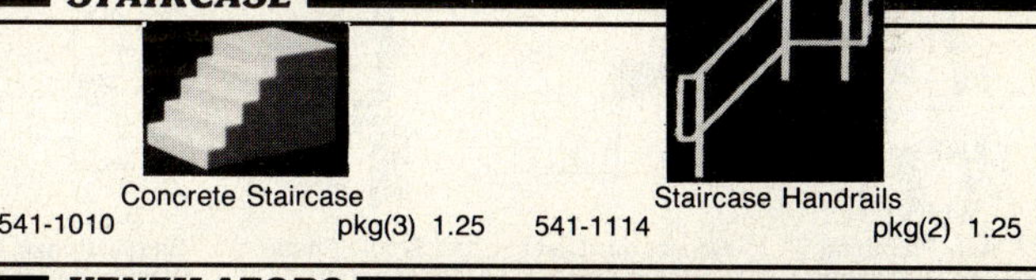

Louvered
541-1009
pkg(3) 1.25

Roof Ridge
541-3102
pkg(4) 1.50

WINDOWS

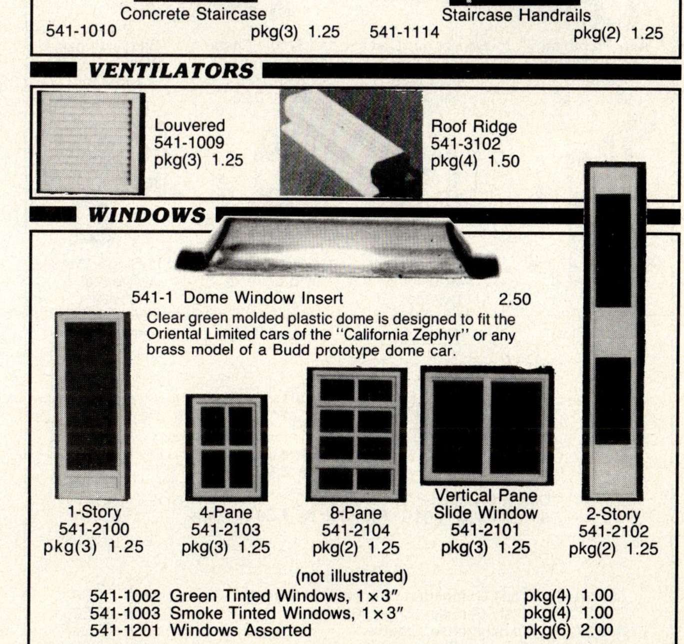

541-1 Dome Window Insert   2.50
Clear green molded plastic dome is designed to fit the Oriental Limited cars of the "California Zephyr" or any brass model of a Budd prototype dome car.

1-Story
541-2100
pkg(3) 1.25

4-Pane
541-2103
pkg(3) 1.25

8-Pane
541-2104
pkg(2) 1.25

Vertical Pane Slide Window
541-2101
pkg(3) 1.25

2-Story
541-2102
pkg(2) 1.25

(not illustrated)

541-1002 Green Tinted Windows, 1 × 3″   pkg(4) 1.00
541-1003 Smoke Tinted Windows, 1 × 3″   pkg(4) 1.00
541-1201 Windows Assorted   pkg(6) 2.00

HO SCALE (1/87)

All Precision Scale Company parts are brass castings, unless noted. Illustrations are not to scale.

+ (PLUS SIGN) = SPECIAL ORDER ONLY ITEMS

AIR CONDITIONING SYSTEMS

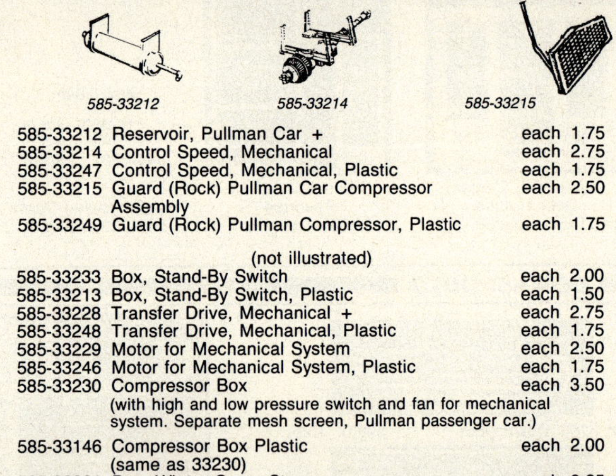

585-33212   585-33214   585-33215

585-33212	Reservoir, Pullman Car +	each 1.75
585-33214	Control Speed, Mechanical	each 2.75
585-33247	Control Speed, Mechanical, Plastic	each 1.75
585-33215	Guard (Rock) Pullman Car Compressor Assembly	each 2.50
585-33249	Guard (Rock) Pullman Compressor, Plastic	each 1.75

(not illustrated)

585-33233	Box, Stand-By Switch	each 2.00
585-33213	Box, Stand-By Switch, Plastic	each 1.50
585-33228	Transfer Drive, Mechanical +	each 2.75
585-33248	Transfer Drive, Mechanical, Plastic	each 1.75
585-33229	Motor for Mechanical System	each 2.50
585-33246	Motor for Mechanical System, Plastic	each 1.75
585-33230	Compressor Box	each 3.50

(with high and low pressure switch and fan for mechanical system. Separate mesh screen, Pullman passenger car.)

585-33146	Compressor Box Plastic (same as 33230)	each 2.00
585-33231	Box, Winter Cover Storage	each 3.25
585-33245	Box, Winter Cover Storage, Plastic	each 1.75

AIR COMPRESSORS

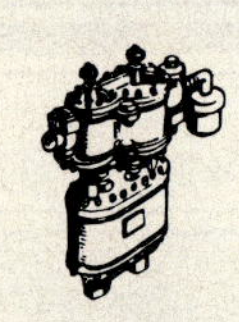   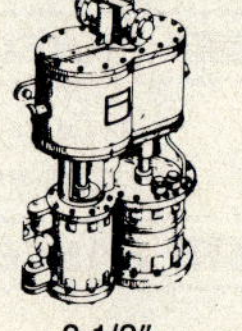

8-1/2" New York Cross Compound
585-31022
each 3.50

Passenger AC
585-31003
each 4.00

8-1/2" Westinghouse Cross Compound
585-31581
each 2.75

8-1/2" Wabco Cross Compound
585-3092
each 3.25

 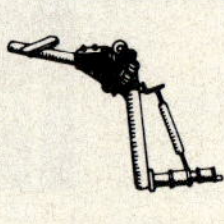 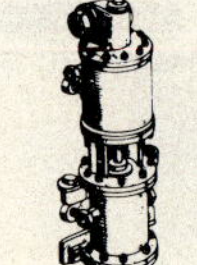 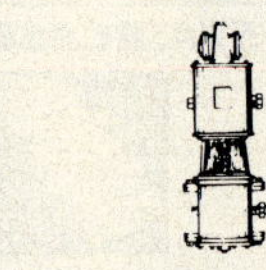

with Plumbing, Small Strainer
585-30921
each 3.50

Passenger Car Steam Line
585-33125
pair 2.50

11" Single Phase Westinghouse
585-3333
each 2.25

9-1/2" Single Phase Westinghouse
585-3188
each 2.50

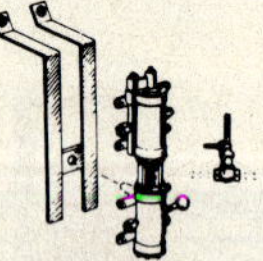 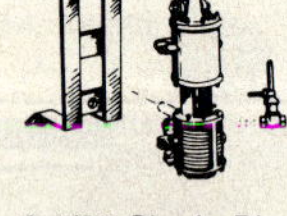  

6" Single Phase w/braket & govenor
585-31024
each 3.50

9-1/2" Single Ph. w/bracket & govenor
585-31025
each 3.50

11" Single Phase w/bracket & govenor
585-31026
each 3.50

11" Single Phase w/bracket & govenor
585-31027
each 3.50

8-1/2" Westinghouse Dual X Compound
585-3449 ea 4.00

Vapor Type
585-3987 ea 3.00
(plastic)
585-3988 ea 1.50

EMD 2nd Generation hood unit top mount air conditioner with fan and open screens.

(not illustrated)

585-3416	Cross Compound Lubricator w/Bracket	each 1.75
585-3723	Westinghouse, Single Kit +	each 22.50
585-3724	Westinghouse, Double Kit +	each 25.00
585-31023	6" Single Phase	each 2.25

AIR COMPRESSOR BRACKETS

  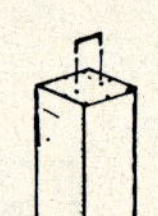

Air inlet manifold, Type B

585-31029 each 1.50 for #31026	585-31030 each 1.50 for #31027 & 31025	585-30923 each 1.50 for #3092	585-31028 each 1.50 for #31024

AIR FILTERS

Early EMD
585-39051
pkg(2) 2.00

Late EMD
585-39052
pkg(2) 2.00

Electric Air Filter Outside Mount, EMD cat
585-3956   each 2.25
(plastic)
585-3957   each 1.50

AIR HORNS

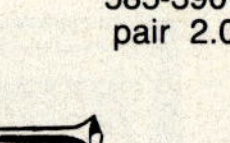 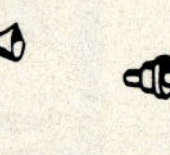

Large Diesel
585-39014
pair 2.00

Small Diesel
585-39015
pair 2.00

3-Chime w/Bracket
585-39085
each 2.75

3-Chime w/Ring Mount
585-39084
each 2.75

Short
585-39093
pair 2.00

585-39016
pair 2.00

Alco
585-39044
pair 2.00

Alco
585-39083
pair 2.00

2-Post Diesel
585-39043
pair 2.00

(not illustrated)

585-39140	3-Chime, Leslie	each 2.00
585-39141	3-Chime, Leslie, Plastic	pair 1.50

AIR HOSES

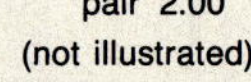

w/Angle Cocks & Glad Hands
585-3150
pkg(6) 2.00
(plastic)
585-3151   pkg(10) 1.75

less Angle Cock, with Elbow
585-3152
pkg(6) 1.75
(plastic)
585-3153   pkg(10) 1.50

Dual with Bracket
585-3281 ea 1.75
for Pilot
Plastic
585-32811 pkg(2) 1.50

Air Hose Material
585-31015   ea 2.25
Armored, .045 × 8"

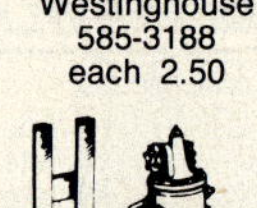

EMD MU w/ Bracket, L&R
585-39058
pkg(4) 2.50
(plastic)
585-39059
pkg(4) 1.75

Angle Cocks
585-31017   pkg(6) 2.50

Glad Hands
585-31018   pkg(4) 1.75

585-31016   Air Hose Fittings   pkg(9 pieces) 2.50
contains four glad hands, four angle cocks and hose

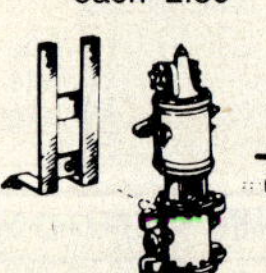

Short, w/Angle HOn3 Cock & Glad Hand
585-3307   pkg(8) 2.00
(plastic)
585-31638   pkg(8) 1.75

(not illustrated)
Rubber, 12", .055 OD
585-48388 each 1.50

Rubber, 12", .045 OD
585-48387   each 1.50

AIR PIPE

w/Valve	w/Governor	w/Valve
585-48203 2.25	585-31020 1.75	585-31019 1.75

AIR PIPING/COOLING COILS

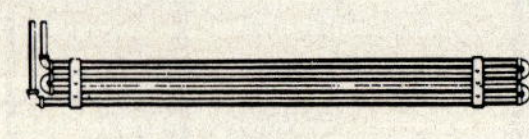

Replace the piping on your locos with castings. They can be altered to 2 or 3 pipe units to satisfy your need.

585-31163	4 Pipe for 8' Tank	each 2.75
585-31724	8' Plastic	each 1.75
585-31164	4 Pipe for 7' Tank	each 2.75
585-31723	7' Plastic	each 1.75
585-31165	4 Pipe for 6' Tank	each 2.75
585-31722	6' Plastic	each 1.75

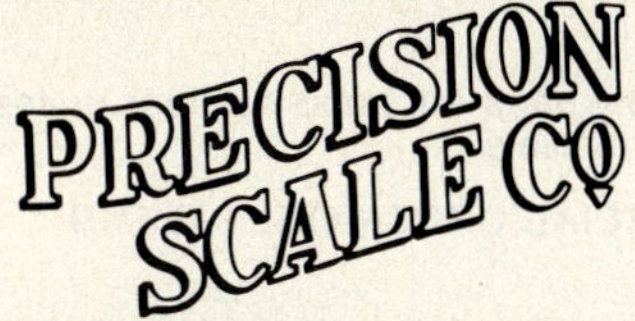

PRECISION SCALE Co

HO SCALE (1/87)

All Precision Scale Company parts are brass castings, unless noted. Illustrations are not to scale.

+ (PLUS SIGN) = SPECIAL ORDER ONLY ITEMS

AIR PIPING / COOLING COILS (continued)

585-31160 4 Pipe for 10' Tank	each 3.00
585-31898 4 Pipe for 10' Tank, Plastic	1.75
585-31161 For 9'3" Tank, Wabash	each 2.75
585-31726 Wabash, Plastic +	1.75

Ends, .028" Core
585-48104
pkg(6) 2.50

Ends, .020" Core
585-48105
pkg(6) 2.50

(not illustrated)

585-31162 4 Pipe for 9' Tank	each 2.75
585-31725 4 Pipe for 9' Tank, Plastic	1.75

AIR PUMP GOVERNORS

Governors have hole cast through for piping

Westinghouse AD Bored .015" Core
585-3212 2.50

Westinghouse AD w/Piping
585-3093 2.00

Air Pump Governor cored
585-31031 pkg(8) 2.75

Single Bored w/.012" Core
585-3195 1.75

(not illustrated)
585-3456 Westinghouse, Duplex .012 Core   each 1.75

AIR PUMP PIPING

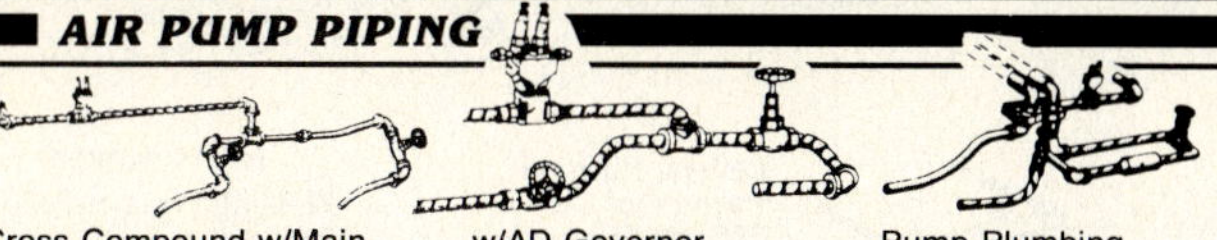

Cross Compound w/Main Stream Supply w/Governor
585-3389   each 2.75

w/AD Governor SP AC-10/11/12
585-3423   each 2.75

Pump Plumbing w/Governor SP AC-9
585-3554 +   each 2.75

AIR STRAINERS

Small
585-30925
ea 1.75

Large
585-30924
ea 1.75

Large w/ Plumbing
585-30927
ea 1.75

Old Style D&RGW
585-30926
pair 1.75

Westinghouse Short, Modern
585-3445
pair 1.75

Westinghouse Large
585-3537 + ea 2.25

Westinghouse Air System Vent Valve
585-3420   ea 2.25

Westinghouse Small, Modern
585-3543
each 2.75

AIR TANKS

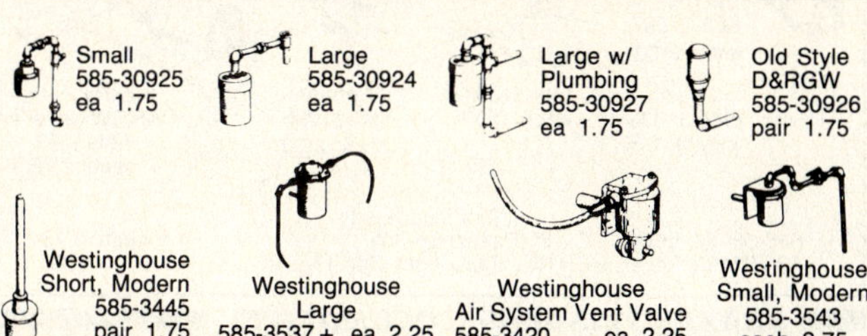

27" C-16 Tender
585-31034
each 2.50
9'3" length

14" Long
585-31038
each 2.00

24" C-16 Tender
585-31035   each 2.50
6'7" length

Equalizing Small
585-3404 each 1.75

Westinghouse AB
585-3373
pair 2.00

(not illustrated)
Plastic
585-3374   pkg(4) 1.75
Wabash Air Tank Kit
585-31033   each 5.00
Includes six cast ends and three brass tubes.

TANKS   4.50 each (Unless otherwise noted).
Kits include detailed cast ends and drain valve, plus 2-1/2" of tubing which you can cut to desired length for a specific tank.

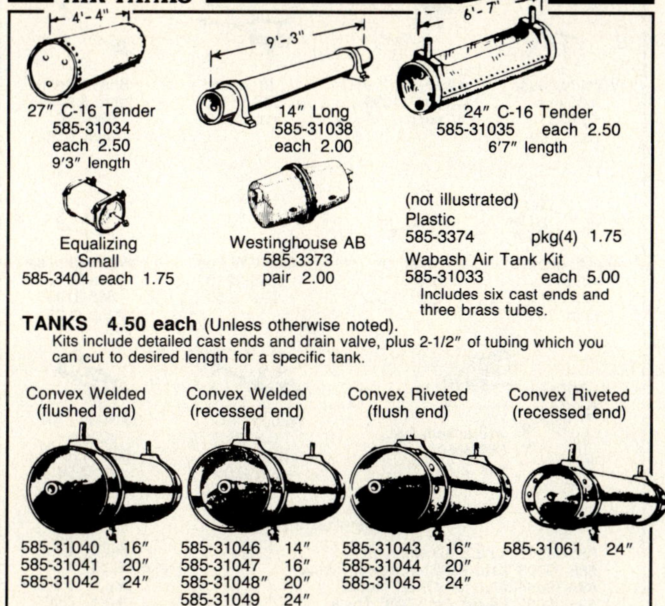

Convex Welded (flushed end)

Convex Welded (recessed end)

Convex Riveted (flush end)

Convex Riveted (recessed end)

585-31040	16"	585-31046	14"	585-31043	16"	585-31061 24"
585-31041	20"	585-31047	16"	585-31044	20"	
585-31042	24"	585-31048	20"	585-31045	24"	
		585-31049	24"			

AIR TANKS (continued)

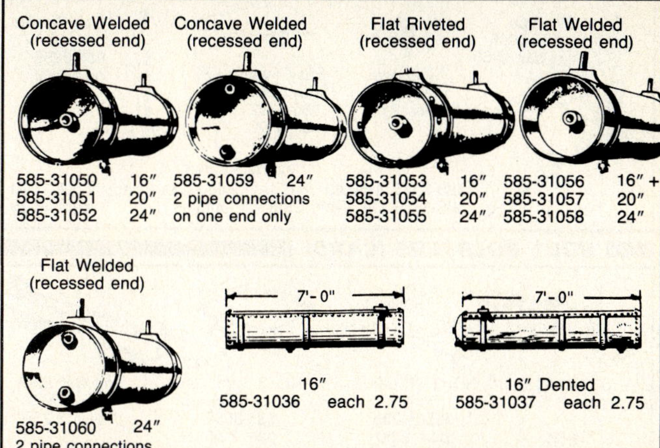

Concave Welded (recessed end)

Concave Welded (recessed end)

Flat Riveted (recessed end)

Flat Welded (recessed end)

585-31050	16"	585-31059	24"	585-31053	16"	585-31056	16" +
585-31051	20"	2 pipe connections		585-31054	20"	585-31057	20"
585-31052	24"	on one end only		585-31055	24"	585-31058	24"

Flat Welded (recessed end)

585-31060   24"
2 pipe connections on one end only

16"
585-31036   each 2.75

16" Dented
585-31037   each 2.75

BELLS & BRACKETS

Working Side Mounting
585-31069
each 3.00

Rigid Top, Mounting Modern
585-31068
each 2.25

AM-2 SP Cab Forward, w/Platform
585-3209
each 2.75

5.0 mm Working
585-31064
each 2.50

4.7 mm Angle Smokebox Mounting
585-31601
each 2.25

22" Working
585-3004
each 2.75

5.0 mm Bell & Ornate Bracket
585-31063
set 3.50

4.6 mm D&RGW Air Ringer
585-3089
each 2.50

Old Style 5.0 mm, platform
585-31071
each 4.00

(plastic)
585-31416
2.00

(plastic)
585-31415
2.00

(not illustrated)
Air Ringing
585-3588 +
each 2.50

Wm Shaw w/brkt
585-31836
each 2.75

4.6 mm PRR w/Bracket
585-3155
each 2.50

w/Bracket Side Mount
585-31070 +
each 2.25

5.5 mm Working w/Brass Brkt
585-31067   3.50

3.5 mm Rigid
585-31065
each 2.00

5.5 mm D&RGW Class 45, HOn3
585-31072
each 2.75

585-39152 EMD Roof Mounted, Diesel   pair 2.50
585-39153 EMD Roof Mounted, Plastic   pair 1.75

BLOWER CONTROL VALVES

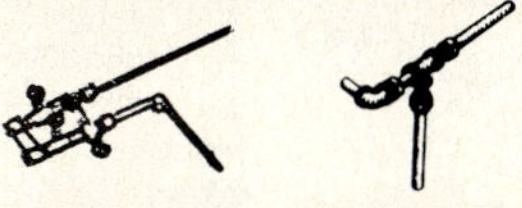

w/4 Valves Style #3
585-3438 ea 3.00

Wm Shay, Pipe
585-31835
each 2.50

Style #1
585-3436
each 3.00

w/3 Valves Style #2
585-3437 ea 3.00

BLOW DOWN MUFFLERS

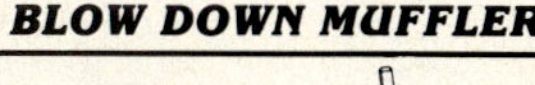

585-31077
pair 1.75

Common Standard
585-3147
pair 1.75

w/Mounting Bracket, Long Pipe & Union
585-3435
each 2.25

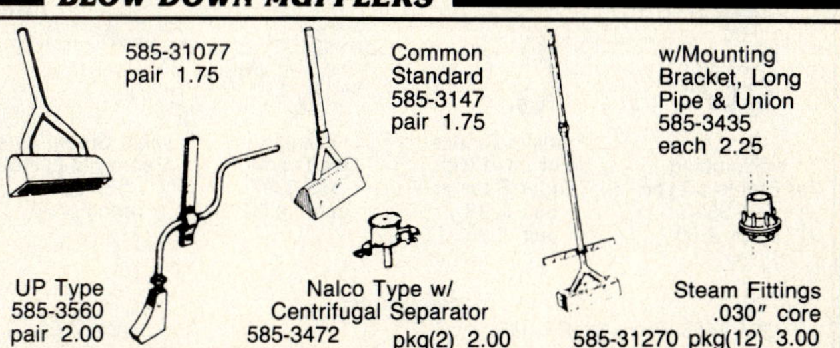

UP Type
585-3560
pair 2.00

Nalco Type w/ Centrifugal Separator
585-3472   pkg(2) 2.00

Steam Fittings .030" core
585-31270 pkg(12) 3.00

PRECISION SCALE CO.

HO SCALE (1/87)

All Precision Scale Company parts are brass castings, unless noted. Illustrations are not to scale.

+ (PLUS SIGN) = SPECIAL ORDER ONLY ITEMS

BLOW-OFF COCKS

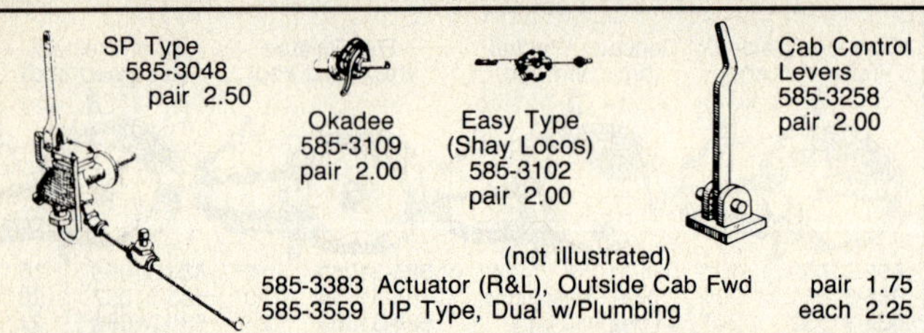

SP Type
585-3048
pair 2.50

Okadee
585-3109
pair 2.00

Easy Type
(Shay Locos)
585-3102
pair 2.00

Cab Control
Levers
585-3258
pair 2.00

(not illustrated)
585-3383 Actuator (R&L), Outside Cab Fwd — pair 1.75
585-3559 UP Type, Dual w/Plumbing — each 2.25

BODY BOLSTERS (CARS)

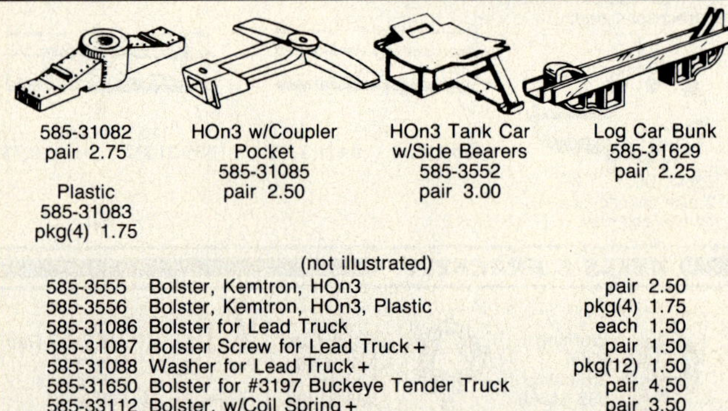

585-31082
pair 2.75

HOn3 w/Coupler
Pocket
585-31085
pair 2.50

HOn3 Tank Car
w/Side Bearers
585-3552
pair 3.00

Log Car Bunk
585-31629
pair 2.25

Plastic
585-31083
pkg(4) 1.75

(not illustrated)
585-3555 Bolster, Kemtron, HOn3 — pair 2.50
585-3556 Bolster, Kemtron, HOn3, Plastic — pkg(4) 1.75
585-31086 Bolster for Lead Truck — each 1.50
585-31087 Bolster Screw for Lead Truck + — pair 1.50
585-31088 Washer for Lead Truck + — pkg(12) 1.50
585-31650 Bolster for #3197 Buckeye Tender Truck — pair 4.50
585-33112 Bolster, w/Coil Spring + — pair 3.50
585-33113 Bolster, w/Coil Spring, Plastic + — pair 1.75

BOILERS

C-16 Original, Drilled, HOn3
585-31073 — each 16.50

C-16 Modern, Drilled
585-31075 — each 16.50

Backhead
Fits C-16 Boilers
585-31062
each 2.75

Plastic
585-31675
each 2.00

(not illustrated)
C&NW E/4-2-0 Left & Right
585-31867 — 2 pcs 9.00

Intermediate C-16, HOn3
585-31074 — each 16.50
(formed & drilled)

BOOSTER ENGINES

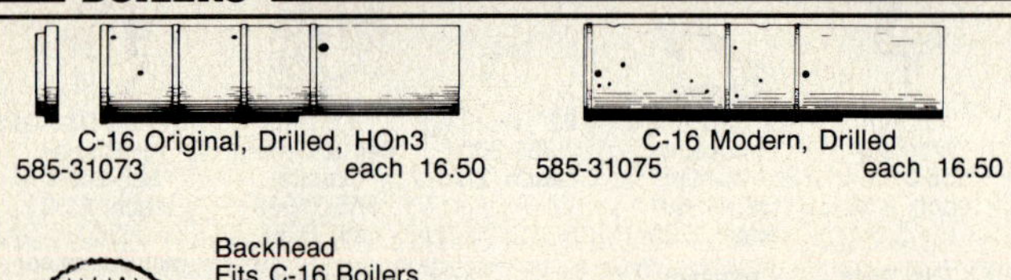

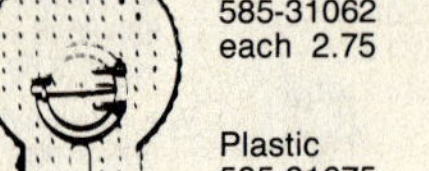

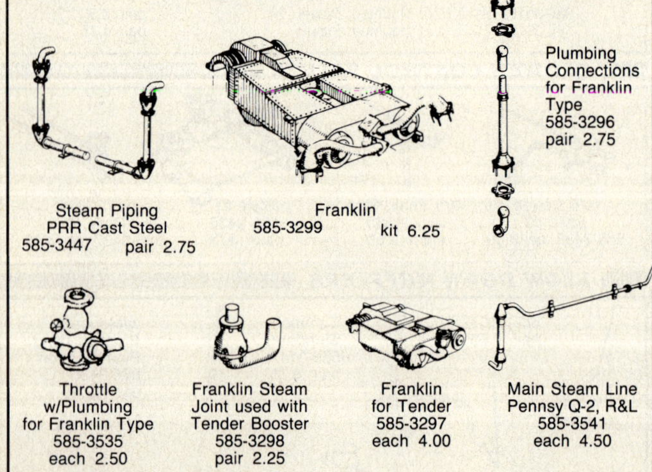

Plumbing
Connections
for Franklin
Type
585-3296
pair 2.75

Steam Piping
PRR Cast Steel
585-3447
pair 2.75

Franklin
585-3299
kit 6.25

Throttle
w/Plumbing
for Franklin Type
585-3535
each 2.50

Franklin Steam
Joint used with
Tender Booster
585-3298
pair 2.25

Franklin
for Tender
585-3297
each 4.00

Main Steam Line
Pennsy Q-2, R&L
585-3541
each 4.50

(not illustrated)
585-3453 Franklin, SP, GS — each 4.00

BRAKE CONTROLS

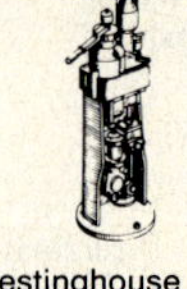

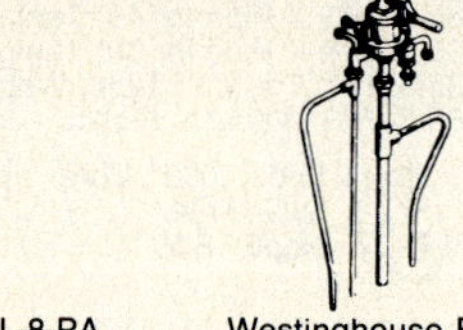

Westinghouse H-6 & S-6
585-3044 — each 3.50

Westinghouse L-8-PA
585-3179 — each 3.50

Westinghouse E-6
with Plumbing
585-3063 — each 3.50

3-Way
Westinghouse
Straight Air
585-3266
each 3.00

Independent
Westinghouse
S-6
585-3325
each 3.00

Steam or Air
for Shays
585-3094
each 3.00

Brake Levers for
Freight Cars &
Tenders, Universal
585-3358 pair 1.75

Plastic
585-3357 pair 1.50

Ashton, Brake Stand
w/Gauges, DP Recorder
for Cab Forward
& Larger Locos
585-3245 each 3.25

Levers, Pullman
Passenger Car
585-33126
pkg(2) 2.75

(not illustrated)
Westinghouse H-6
Automatic
585-3324 — each 3.25

BRAKE CYLINDERS (TENDERS)

Tender
585-31097
each 2.50

Plastic
585-31098
pkg(4) 1.50

585-31091
each 2.00

Wabash
585-31095
each 2.50

Westinghouse
D&RGW w/Levers
585-3169
each 2.75

(not illustrated)
585-33167 Lever, UC 16" Passenger Car — each 2.75
585-33168 Lever, UC, 16", Passenger Car, Plastic — each 2.00

BRAKE CYLINDERS (LOCOMOTIVE)

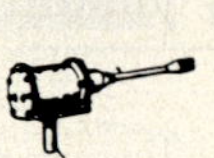

Westinghouse
w/Clevis
585-3515
pair 2.00

w/Levers (2 each)
585-31099
each 2.75

Wabash
585-31100
pair 2.00

Shay, Steam
Jamb & Clevis
585-3101
each 4.00

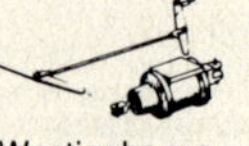

Westinghouse
w/Levers
585-3211
each 2.75

Wabash
585-31102
pair 1.50

D&RGW Loco
585-3210
pair 2.50

Westinghouse
Type D "6"
585-3193
each 2.25

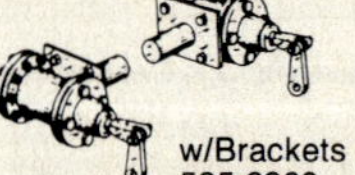

w/Brackets R&L
585-3360
pair 2.75

Wabco "KC"
6 x 8"
585-3123 +
each 2.00

D&RGW L&R
(C-16)
585-31101
pair 2.50

(not illustrated)
585-39002 Late EMD w/Levers — pkg(8) 4.50
585-39003 Late EMD w/Levers, Plastic — pkg(16pcs) 3.00
585-39034 Alco for #7468 Trucks — pkg(4) 3.00
585-39035 Levers for #7468 Truck — pkg(4) 2.00

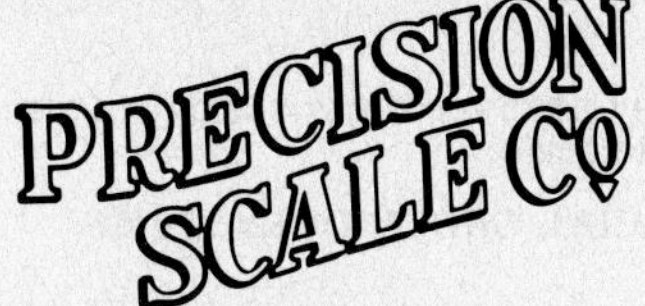

PRECISION SCALE Co.

HO SCALE (1/87)

All Precision Scale Company parts are brass castings, unless noted. Illustrations are not to scale.

+ (PLUS SIGN) = SPECIAL ORDER ONLY ITEMS

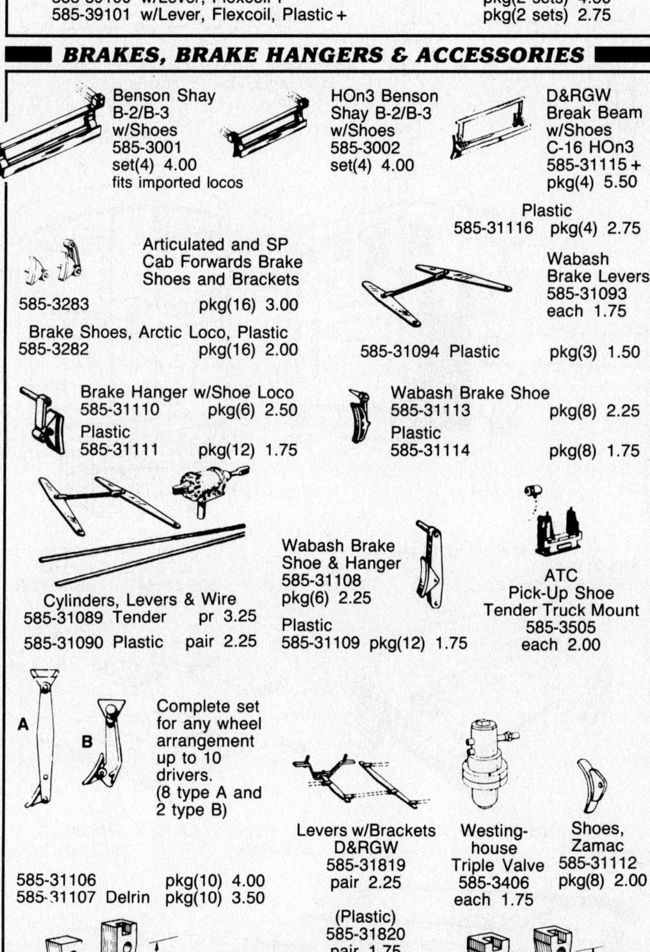

■ BRAKE CYLINDERS (CAR) ■

Westinghouse Type "C"
585-31104
each 2.25

HOn3
585-31103
pair 1.50

Westinghouse Type KC Freight
585-3461
pair 2.50

Zamac
585-31603
3 pair 1.75

Plastic
585-31105
pkg(3) 2.00

Modern 10″ OD Westinghouse w/Clevis
585-3481   pair 2.25

D&RGW C-Class w/Brkt & Levers
585-3194   pair 2.50

(not illustrated)

585-3233	Westside Shay	pair 2.00
585-31096	Delrin	pkg(4) 2.00
585-33110	for UP, SP and C&NW +	pkg(4) 2.50
585-33111	for UP, SP and C&NW, Plastic +	pkg(4) 1.75
585-39100	w/Lever, Flexcoil +	pkg(2 sets) 4.50
585-39101	w/Lever, Flexcoil, Plastic +	pkg(2 sets) 2.75

■ BRAKES, BRAKE HANGERS & ACCESSORIES ■

Benson Shay B-2/B-3 w/Shoes
585-3001
set(4) 4.00
fits imported locos

HOn3 Benson Shay B-2/B-3 w/Shoes
585-3002
set(4) 4.00

D&RGW Break Beam C-16 HOn3
585-31115 +
pkg(4) 5.50

Plastic
585-31116   pkg(4) 2.75

Articulated and SP Cab Forwards Brake Shoes and Brackets
585-3283   pkg(16) 3.00

Brake Shoes, Arctic Loco, Plastic
585-3282   pkg(16) 2.00

Wabash Brake Levers
585-31093
each 1.75

585-31094 Plastic   pkg(3) 1.50

Brake Hanger w/Shoe Loco
585-31110   pkg(6) 2.50
Plastic
585-31111   pkg(12) 1.75

Wabash Brake Shoe
585-31113   pkg(8) 2.25
Plastic
585-31114   pkg(8) 1.75

Cylinders, Levers & Wire
585-31089 Tender   pr 3.25
585-31090 Plastic   pair 2.25

Wabash Brake Shoe & Hanger
585-31108
pkg(6) 2.25
Plastic
585-31109 pkg(12) 1.75

ATC Pick-Up Shoe Tender Truck Mount
585-3505
each 2.00

A   B   Complete set for any wheel arrangement up to 10 drivers. (8 type A and 2 type B)

585-31106   pkg(10) 4.00
585-31107 Delrin pkg(10) 3.50

Levers w/Brackets D&RGW
585-31819
pair 2.25
(Plastic)
585-31820
pair 1.75

Westinghouse Triple Valve
585-3406
each 1.75

Shoes, Zamac
585-31112
pkg(8) 2.00

.570   .400

.500   .350

.580   .345

Long Loco Brakes (Plastic)
585-3322   pkg(8) 2.00

Short Loco Brakes (Plastic)
585-3323   pkg(8) 2.00

Loco Brakes, Standard Gauge
585-3091 pkg(12) 3.50
(Plastic)
585-31643 pkg(12) 2.25

■ BRAKES, BRAKE HANGERS & ACCESS (cont) ■

(not illustrated)

Dynamic Brake Housing w/Ventilators, 48″ Diameter Open Fan & Blower, EMD DP-7, GP-9

585-3939		pkg(3pcs) 7.00
585-3940	Plastic	pkg(3pcs) 2.50

Dynamic Brake Fan Housing, 48″ Diameter w/Open Ribs F-7/9, GP7/9, E8/9 and some modified SD-9's.

585-3991		pkg(4) 4.75
585-3992	Plastic	pkg(4) 2.25
585-3342	Freight Car Brake Detail Set	each 2.50
585-3350	Brake Staff Bracket	pkg(2) 1.50
585-3351	Roller Chain, Lower Brake Staff +	pkg(4) 2.00
585-3521	Slack Adjustor for Brakes	each 2.00
585-3727	Westinghouse Air Brake Detail	each 9.75
585-3728	Westinghouse Air Brake Detail, Freight	each 4.75
585-3738	Westinghouse Brake Detail Kit +	each 6.75
585-3740	Westinghouse Air Brake Detail, Hopper	each 6.75
585-3767	Westinghouse Brake Gear, HOn3	each 4.75
585-31129	Brake Wheel 5-Spoke HOn3 +	pkg(6) 5.00
585-33104	Shock Absorbers, Standard +	pkg(4) 2.25
585-33105	Shock Absorbers, Standard, Plastic +	pkg(4) 1.50
585-33106	Slack Adjustors for UP/SP +	pkg(4) 2.00
585-33107	Slack Adjustors for UP/SP, Plastic +	pkg(4) 1.50
585-33196	Westinghouse D-22 Brake System	pkg(2) 2.75
585-33197	Westinghouse D-22 Brake System, Plastic	pkg(2) 2.00
585-33232	Pulley/Cam Underbody Mount	each 2.25
585-37281	Westinghouse Air Brake, Plastic	each 3.50
585-37381	Westinghouse Brake, Standard, Plastic	each 3.75
585-37401	Westinghouse AB for Hopper, Plastic	each 3.75
585-37671	Westinghouse Gear, HOn3, Plastic +	each 3.50
585-39049	Brake Stand EMD +	each 2.50
585-39050	EMD Brake Stand, Plastic	each 2.00
585-39105	Dynamic Brake Housing R&L	pkg(2) 6.00

■ BRAKE STAFFS & BRACKETS ■

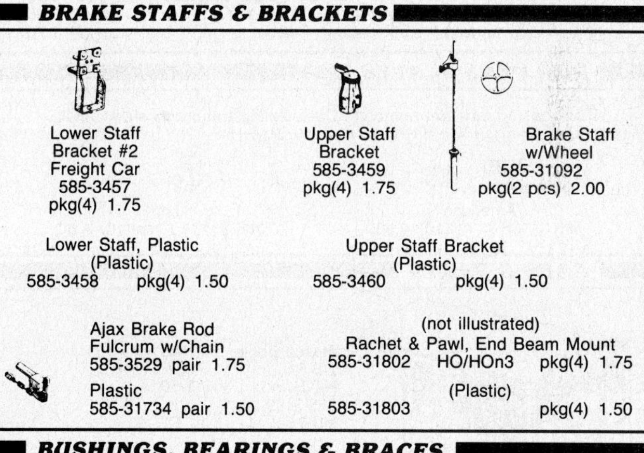

Lower Staff Bracket #2 Freight Car
585-3457
pkg(4) 1.75

Upper Staff Bracket
585-3459
pkg(4) 1.75

Brake Staff w/Wheel
585-31092
pkg(2 pcs) 2.00

Lower Staff, Plastic (Plastic)
585-3458   pkg(4) 1.50

Upper Staff Bracket (Plastic)
585-3460   pkg(4) 1.50

Ajax Brake Rod Fulcrum w/Chain
585-3529 pair 1.75
Plastic
585-31734 pair 1.50

(not illustrated)
Rachet & Pawl, End Beam Mount
585-31802   HO/HOn3   pkg(4) 1.75
(Plastic)
585-31803   pkg(4) 1.50

■ BUSHINGS, BEARINGS & BRACES ■

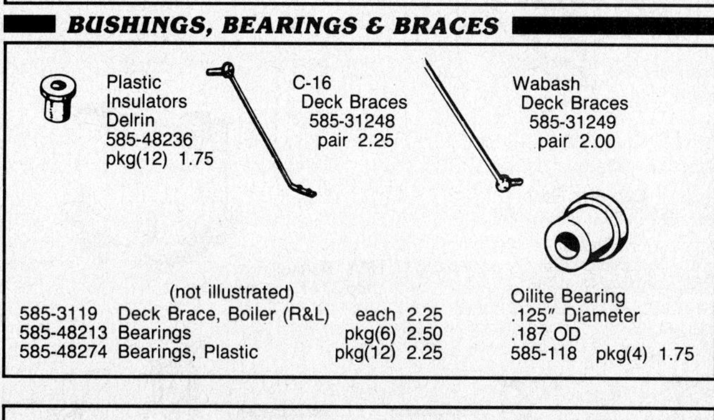

Plastic Insulators Delrin
585-48236
pkg(12) 1.75

C-16 Deck Braces
585-31248
pair 2.25

Wabash Deck Braces
585-31249
pair 2.00

(not illustrated)
585-3119 Deck Brace, Boiler (R&L)   each 2.25
585-48213 Bearings   pkg(6) 2.50
585-48274 Bearings, Plastic   pkg(12) 2.25

Oilite Bearing .125″ Diameter .187 OD
585-118   pkg(4) 1.75

See also: FREIGHT CARS, TRUCKS, COUPLERS and SCRATCH-BUILDING SUPPLIES for additional PRECISION SCALE items.

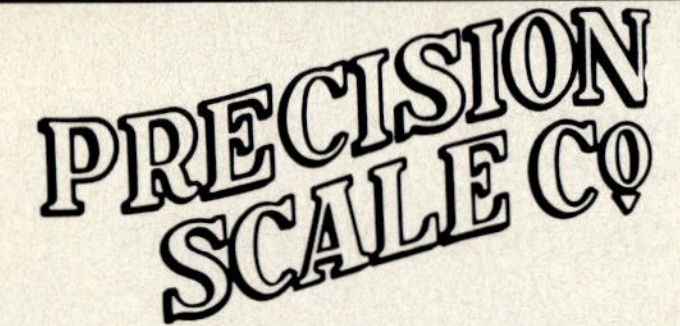

PRECISION SCALE CO.

HO SCALE (1/87)

All Precision Scale Company parts are brass castings, unless noted. Illustrations are not to scale.

+ (PLUS SIGN) = SPECIAL ORDER ONLY ITEMS

BRAKE WHEELS

Use Mfr #585 to order	22"	21"	22"	12"	13"	12"	12"

Brass pkg(6)	31121 2.25	31119 3.00	31117 3.00	31636 2.25	31123 2.25	31125 2.50	31127 2.50
Plastic pkg(8)	31122 1.75	31120 1.75	31118 1.75	31637 1.75	31124 1.75	31126 1.75	31128 1.75

Ajax
585-3246
pkg(4) 2.50

Plastic
585-3247
pkg(2) 1.50

D&RGW 16"
Five Spoke
585-3181
pkg(6) 3.00

Plastic
585-3182
pkg(8) 1.75

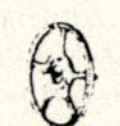

Peacock Brake
Wheels, 3rd
Generation EMD
585-3959
pkg(4) 2.25

Plastic
585-3960   pkg(4) 1.75

Ajax Housing
585-3251
pkg(4) 2.75

(Plastic)
585-3252
pkg(4) 2.00

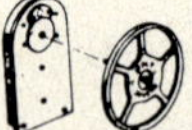

Brake Wheel
Housing, 3rd
Generation EMD
585-3961 pair 2.25

Plastic
585-3962
pkg(4) 1.75

Ajax Housing
585-3248
pkg(4) 2.75

Plastic
585-3249
pkg(4) 2.00

Miner Hand Brake
585-39081
pkg(2) 2.00

Plastic
585-39082
pkg(2) 1.50

(not illustrated)

585-3567	Miner Ideal Brake Handle, Tender/Caboose	each 1.75
585-39148	Housing for EMD/Miner	pkg(2) 2.25
585-39149	Housing for EMD/Miner, Plastic	pkg(2) 1.75

BUILDERS PLATES

Packages 10 different numbers. Oversize illustrations to show detail.

American
585-31136   set(10) 4.50

Lima
585-31138   set(10) 4.50

CABS & PARTS

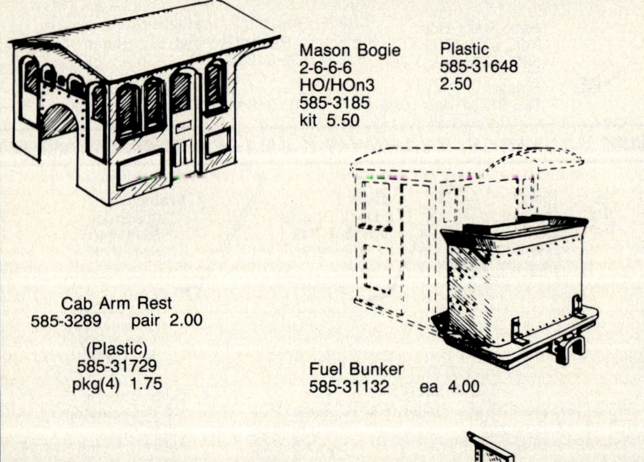

Mason Bogie
2-6-6-6
HO/HOn3
585-3185
kit 5.50

Plastic
585-31648
2.50

Cab Arm Rest
585-3289   pair 2.00

(Plastic)
585-31729
pkg(4) 1.75

Fuel Bunker
585-31132   ea 4.00

HOn3 Cab Support, C-16
585-31146   each 2.00

(Plastic)
585-31694   each 1.50

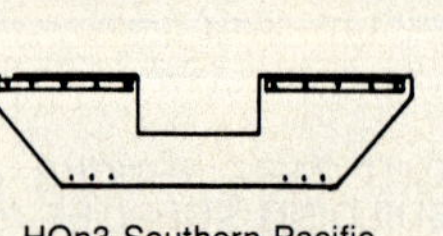

HOn3 Southern Pacific
Cab Support
585-31157   each 1.50

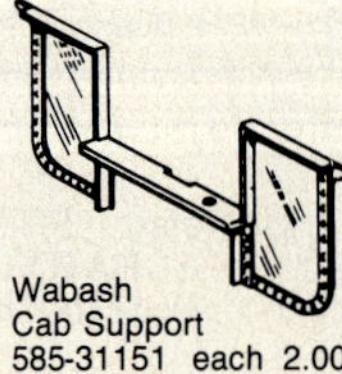

Wabash
Cab Support
585-31151   each 2.00

CABS & PARTS (continued)

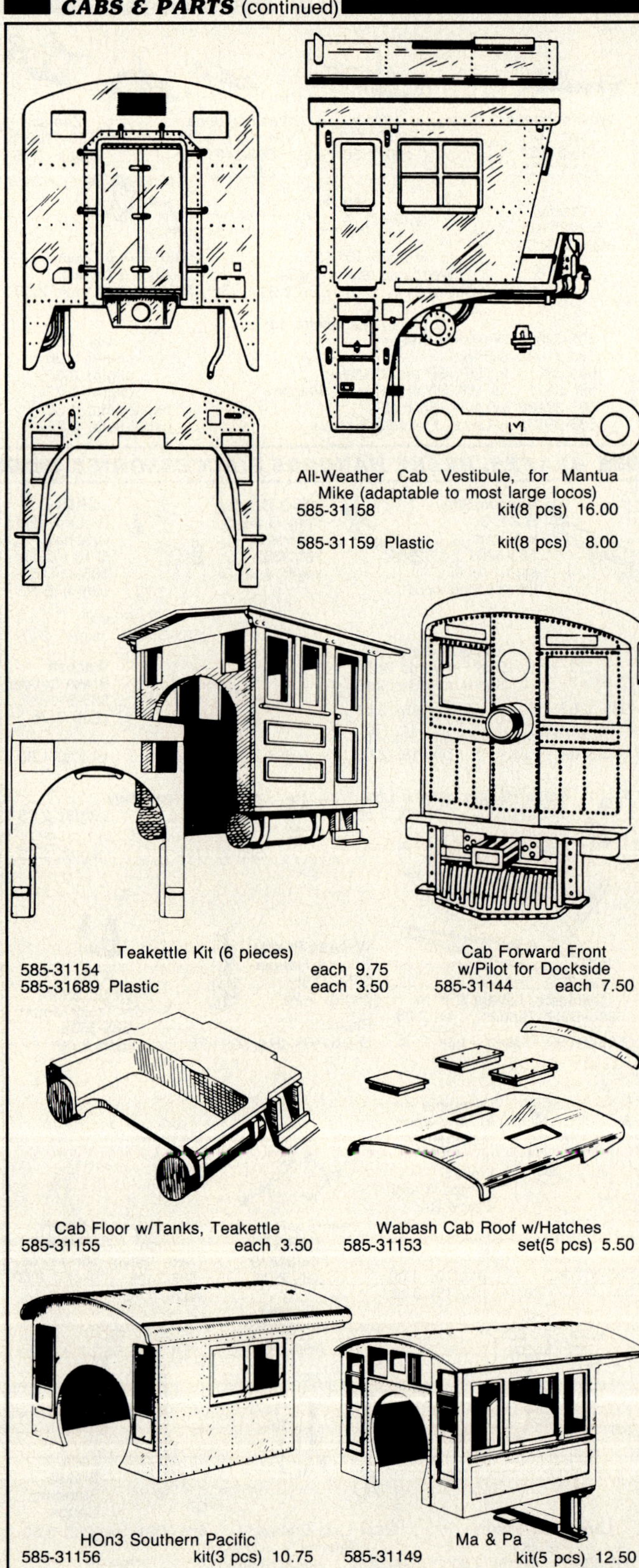

All-Weather Cab Vestibule, for Mantua
Mike (adaptable to most large locos)
585-31158   kit(8 pcs) 16.00

585-31159 Plastic   kit(8 pcs) 8.00

Teakettle Kit (6 pieces)
585-31154   each 9.75
585-31689 Plastic   each 3.50

Cab Forward Front
w/Pilot for Dockside
585-31144   each 7.50

Cab Floor w/Tanks, Teakettle
585-31155   each 3.50

Wabash Cab Roof w/Hatches
585-31153   set(5 pcs) 5.50

HOn3 Southern Pacific
585-31156   kit(3 pcs) 10.75

Ma & Pa
585-31149   kit(5 pcs) 12.50
585-31691 Plastic   kit(5 pcs) 5.50

PRECISION SCALE Co.

HO SCALE (1/87)

All Precision Scale Company parts are brass castings, unless noted. Illustrations are not to scale.

+ (PLUS SIGN) = SPECIAL ORDER ONLY ITEMS

CABS & PARTS (continued)

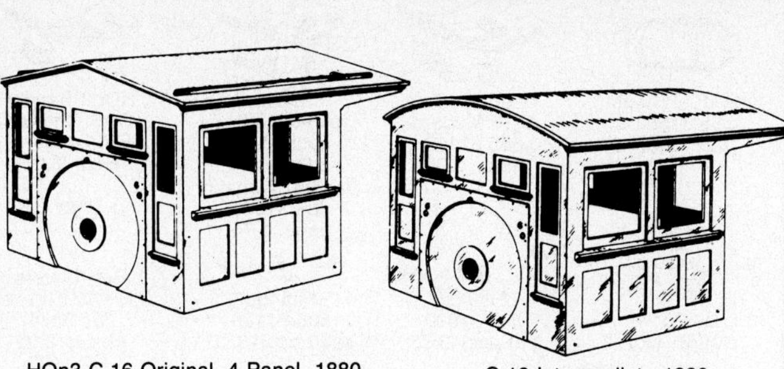

HOn3 C-16 Original, 4 Panel, 1880
585-31140　　kit(6 pcs) 12.50
585-31685 Plastic　　4.50

C-16 Intermediate 1880 4 Panel, Arched Roof
585-31141　　kit(6 pcs) 12.50
585-31687 Plastic　　4.50

C-16 Intermediate, 1 Panel 1905
585-31142　　kit(5 pcs) 12.25
585-31688 Plastic　　5.50

C-16 Modern 1920
585-31143　　kit(5 pcs) 12.25
585-31686 Plastic　　4.50

585-31692 Plastic, No Roof　ea 5.50
585-31148 PRR　　kit (5 pcs) 12.50
585-31150 Wabash　　(10 pcs) 12.50
585-31690 Wabash, Plastic　　6.50

(not illustrated)

585-3720　Interior Detail Kit for AC-6 Cab Forward　each 26.00
Includes one each:　simplex injectors, D&RGW tricox, H-6, S-6 control, blower reverse, throttle, signal indicator with control box, water glass, oil fire door, lubricator, cab stand gauges, oil can shelf, turret controls, main steam engine, plumbing cluster, fireman's side, seat boxes, five gauge cluster w/oil firing valve and tool box.

585-3721　Detail Kit Cab Forward AM-2 Cab +　　25.00
585-3508　SP Main Steam Lines, Cab Floor　pair 4.00
585-4863　Pipe Cluster #1 +　each 3.00
585-4864　Pipe Cluster #2 +　each 2.75
585-4865　Style #1 +　each 2.75
585-4866　Fireman Side Cluster Pipe #2 +　each 2.75
585-36751　EMD Cab Interior Detail, Plastic +　13.75
585-37651　EMD Cab Interior, Plastic　each 13.75
585-39045　EMD Cab Arm Rest, Brass　pkg(4) 2.25
585-39046　EMD Cab Arm Rest, Plastic　pkg(4) 1.75
585-39047　EMD Shade, Brass　pkg(4) 2.25
585-39048　EMD Shade, Plastic　pkg(4) 1.50
585-39121　24" Arm Rest, MT　pkg(6) 2.50
585-39122　24" Arm Rest, MT, Plastic　pkg(6) 1.25
585-39123　36" Arm Rest, MT　pkg(6) 2.50
585-39124　36" Arm Rest, MT, Plastic　pkg(6) 1.25
585-39127　RE16 Roof Detail +　pkg(3) 3.00
585-39150　EMD Cab Deflectors +　pkg(3) 2.25

CHAIN & CHAIN HOOKS

10" brass chain. Chain actual size.

18 link
20 link
26 link

585-48194　10 links per inch　2.75
585-48348　18 links per inch　2.75
585-48349　20 links per inch　2.75
585-48237　26 links per inch　2.75

Tender Chain Inboard Hung
585-3304　pkg(5) 2.00
Plastic
585-32042　pkg(10) 1.75

Tender Chain Outboard Hung
585-3305　pkg(5) 2.00
Plastic
585-32043　pkg(10) 1.75

Large
585-48208　pkg(4) 2.50

Small
585-48209　pkg(4) 2.25

4" Chain w/3 Large Hooks
585-48207　each 3.50

4" Chain w/3 Small Hooks
585-48206　each 3.50

CHECK VALVES

Boiler Shay with Flanged Gland
585-3130　pair 2.75

Early Baldwin
585-3099　pair 2.00

Top Mount Hancock
585-3080　each 2.25

Nathan Boiler Left & Right
585-3142　pair 2.00

Westside Shay
585-3412 +　each 1.75

Exhaust, Worthington
585-3410　pair 2.25

Hancock Vertical Valve w/o Elbow
585-3343　pair 1.75

Elesco Siphon on Suction
585-3484 pr 2.00
.025 and .045" core

Boiler
585-31079　pair 1.75

w/Plumbing PRR, M-1, M-1a
585-3471　each 1.75

Nathan Boiler
585-3376　pair 2.25

Boiler, Left & Right Rutland Locos
585-3429 pair 2.00

(not illustrated)
585-3483　Worthington SA Inline Type, .020" core +　each 1.75

CLEANOUT PLUGS

Cleaning Hole Lids
585-31133　pkg(4) 2.00

Common Standard
585-3329　pair 1.75

Baldwin or Santa Fe
585-3306　pair 1.75

CLEVISES

.120L x .040T"
585-48133　pkg(4) 2.25

.100L x .045T"
585-48134　pkg(4) 2.25

.100L x .065T"
585-48135　pkg(4) 2.25

Double End .060" Overall
585-48136　pkg(4) 2.50

Rod, .200" .400" Overall
585-48139　pkg(4) 2.25

Rod, .090" .275" Overall
585-48143　pkg(4) 2.25

for Brake Linkage
585-48151　pkg(4) 2.25

Double End .062" Overall
585-48137　pkg(4) 2.25

(not illustrated)
585-48138　Strap .200" +　pkg(4) 2.25

CONNECTORS-ELECTRICAL

Conduit Junction Box, Right Angle
585-3317　pkg(6) 2.25
Plastic
585-31751　pkg(18) 2.00

"Tee" Type Round
585-3318　pkg(6) 2.25
Plastic
585-31752　pkg(18) 2.00

"Tee" Type Square
585-3319　pkg(6) 2.25
Plastic
585-31747　pkg(18) 2.00

Terminal
585-3320　pkg(6) 2.25
Plastic
585-31748　pkg(18) 2.00

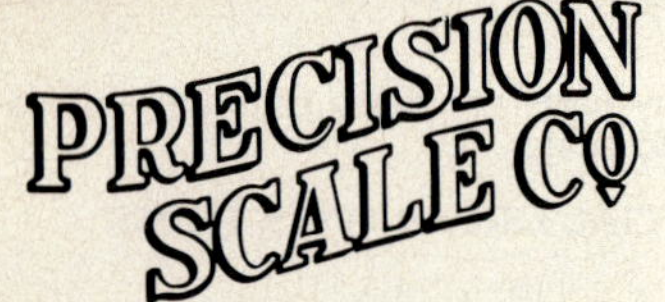

PRECISION SCALE Cº

HO SCALE (1/87)

All Precision Scale Company parts are brass castings, unless noted. Illustrations are not to scale.

We have worked closely with this manufacturer to provide accurate availability information at the time this catalog was published. Items listed in *blue ink* may not be available at all times. Please see your dealer for current delivery information   + (PLUS SIGN) = SPECIAL ORDER ONLY ITEMS.

CONNECTORS-ELECTRICAL (continued)

For Battery Charger, Alco Diesel +
585-3912   pkg(2) 2.25
585-3913 Plastic   pkg(2) 1.50

Cab Front Fuse Box
585-3355
each 2.00

CRANK PIN SCREWS

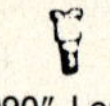

.090" Long
585-335
pkg(8) 3.50

.070" Long
585-336
pkg(8) 3.00

.260" Long
585-333
pair 1.50

.230" Long
585-334
pair 1.50

0-80 x 085L (shown enlarged)
585-505 pkg(2) 1.75

CROSSHEADS

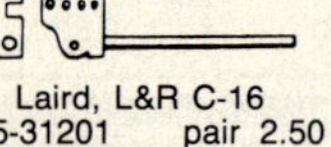

Laird, L&R C-16
585-31201   pair 2.50
fits #31184 Cyl

Alligator Type, L&R
585-31200   pair 2.50
fits #31191 Cyl

N/S SP AM-2, Std Gauge
585-3409   pair 2.75

Alligator Type
585-31206
pair 2.25
fits #31193 Cyl

Alligator Type
585-31204 pr 2.50
fits #31185, 31186 & 31187 Cyl

Alligator Type
585-31205 pr 2.50
fits #31185, 31186 & 31187 Cyl

Alligator Type
Left & Right
585-31202
pair 3.00

Alligator Type, Wabash
585-31203 pair 2.75
fits #31189 Cyl

HOn3 Laird Type
less Piston Rods
585-31207 pair 2.00

CYLINDERS

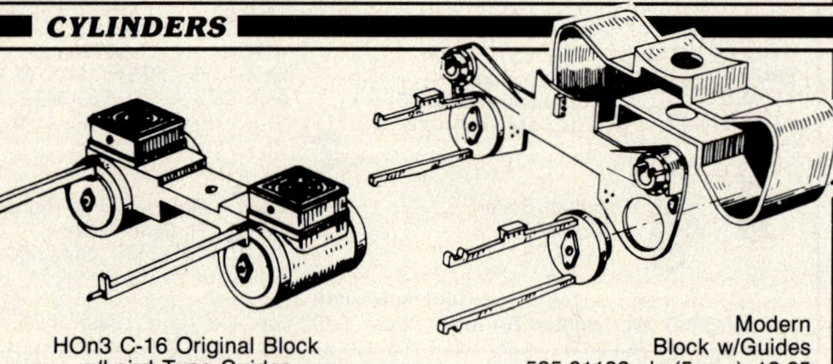

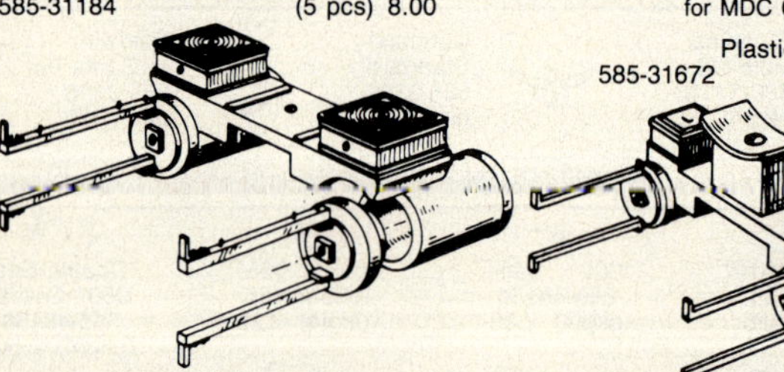

HOn3 C-16 Original Block w/Laird Type Guides
585-31184   (5 pcs) 8.00

Modern Block w/Guides
585-31193 pkg(5 pcs) 12.25
for MDC 0-6-0

Plastic
585-31672   pkg(5) 4.00

Wabash Block, Slide Valve Type
585-31189   w/Guides   (5 pcs) 8.25

Plastic
585-31671   (5 pcs) 4.00

HO Block
585-31187   (5 pcs) 8.00

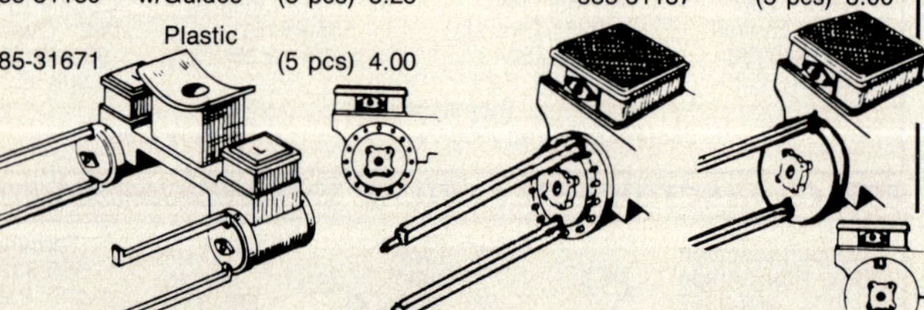

HOn3 Block Kit
585-31186
set(5 pcs) 8.00

HOn3 Southern Pacific
585-31192
pkg(5 pcs) 8.00

HOn3 Southern Pacific
585-31191
pkg(6) 8.00

CYLINDERS (continued)

Individual Steam
585-31632
pair 2.25

Saddle HOn3 C-16 Modern
585-31182
each 3.00

Saddle
585-31188 +
each 3.00
Plastic Saddle, Wabash
585-31670
each 1.75

HOn3 Saddle C-16 Original
585-31183 +
each 3.00

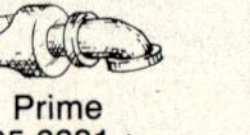   

Prime
585-3381 +
pkg(8) 2.25

Fittings
585-31630
(10 pcs) 3.75

Fittings
585-31190
set(6 pcs) 3.00

Port Covers D&RGW K-Series
585-3174
pkg(4) 2.00

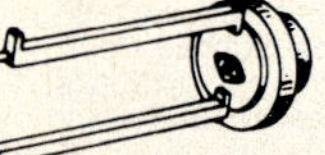 

HOn3 C-16 Original & Intermediate Blk
585-31185
(5 pieces) 8.00
w/alligator guides

Valve Spindle Guides, D&RGW K's
585-3214   pair 3.00

(not illustrated)
585-3213   Denver & Rio Grande Western K-27 #455   each 5.50
585-3250   12 x 15 3-Cylinder Shay   each 4.00
585-3523   Cylinder Block, 4-6-0 RGS +   each 5.50
585-31758   Chicago & North Western Pioneer   each 3.00

DIRT COLLECTORS

Westinghouse Centrifugal
585-3433
pair 2.25

Westinghouse Early Type Centrifugal .010" core
585-31755 pkg(3) 2.50
Plastic
585-31756   pkg(3) 2.00

Westinghouse Modern
585-3391
pkg(3) 2.50

Plastic
585-31754 + pkg(3) 2.25

DISTRIBUTING VALVES

Westinghouse #6 w/Reservoir
585-3175 +
each 2.75

Westinghouse AB w/Dirt Collector & Cut-Off Cock
585-3520 ea 2.00
Plastic
585-31934 pkg(2) 1.50

Westinghouse #8-A
585-31021
each 2.00

Westinghouse #8-ET
585-3415
each 2.00

Westinghouse #6 less reservoir
585-3162
each 1.50

DOMES

Steam Small Modern
585-31237
each 2.75

Sand Medium Modern
585-31238
each 3.25

Sand, SP & Wabash
585-31224
each 2.75

Steam, SP
585-31223
each 3.00

Steam HOn3 & TT
585-31227
each 3.00

Steam Saddle Tanker
585-31229
each 2.75

Steam
585-31221
each 3.00

Sand, HOn3 C-16 Modern
585-31218
each 2.50

Sand, Saddle Tanker
585-31230
each 3.00

Sand HOn3 & TT
585-31228
each 3.00

Steam, Large
585-31239
each 3.00

Sand, HOn3 DSP&P
585-31236
each 3.50

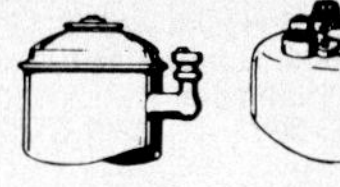

PRECISION SCALE CO.

HO SCALE (1/87)

All Precision Scale Company parts are brass castings, unless noted. Illustrations are not to scale.

We have worked closely with this manufacturer to provide accurate availability information at the time this catalog was published. Items listed in *blue ink* may not be available at all times. Please see your dealer for current delivery information   + (PLUS SIGN) = SPECIAL ORDER ONLY ITEMS.

◼ DOMES (continued) ◼

for Tank Cars
585-31246
each 2.25

for Tank Cars
585-31247
each 2.25

Sand, Old
Style, Rect
585-31243
each 2.00

Steam
C-16 Modern
585-31219
each 3.00

Sand
C-16 Modern
585-31220
each 2.75

Steam
Wabash
585-31231
each 3.00

Steam, PRR
Old Time
585-31233
each 4.50

Sand, PRR
Old Time
585-31234
each 4.50

Steam, C-16
(Early)
585-31225
each 3.00

Sand, C-16
(Early)
585-31226
each 2.75

HOn3
D&RGW
Sand, K-37
585-3014
each 2.75

HOn3
D&RGW
Steam, K-37
585-3016
each 2.75

Sand, Wabash
585-31232
each 2.75

HOn3, C-16
Steam
Modern Style
585-31217
each 3.00

Sand
585-31222
each 2.50

HOn3
D&RGW
Sand, K-36
585-3030
each 2.75

HOn3
D&RGW
Sand, K-28
585-3032
each 2.75

HOn3
D&RGW
Steam, K-36
585-3031
each 3.00

HOn3
D&RGW
Steam, K-28
585-3033
each 3.00

SP Sand
Pacifics
585-3034
each 3.25

Steam, HOn3
DSP&P
585-31235
each 4.50

Pop Valve
Cluster
585-31245
each 2.50

Steam
585-31244
each 2.25

Sand, Large w/Removable
Hatches for NYC Niagara
585-31240   each 6.00

Sand w/Operating Hatches
585-31242   set 6.00

Sand w/Operating Hatches
585-31241   each 6.00

(not illustrated)

585-3575   Platform, 10,000-gallon Tank   each 2.75
585-3576   Platform, 8,000-gallon Tank   each 2.75
585-31005 Modern Tank Car   pair 2.25

◼ DOORS & ACCESSORIES ◼

Working Stock Car
D&RGW
585-3494   pr 3.00

Plastic
585-3495   pr 2.00

Coal Bunker
Wabash Tender
585-31252   ea 2.50

Stock Car
585-31250   pair 2.50

Plastic
585-31251   pair 1.75

◼ DOORS & ACCESSORIES (continued) ◼

EMD Hood Unit Cab
w/Window Glass
& Door Handles
585-3995   pair 3.00

Plastic
585-3996   pair 2.00

Handles,
Cab, EMD
585-3997
pkg(6) 2.00
Plastic
585-3998
pkg(6) 1.50

(not illustrated)

585-3096   Butterfly Door, Open   each 2.75
585-3242   BH Fire Door Shield w/Guard +   each 2.00
585-3920   EMD Latches, Plastic   pkg(20) 2.25
585-3921   EMD Latches, Brass   pkg(20) 3.00
585-3999   Glass for EMD Cab Door   pair 1.50

◼ DRAIN VALVES ◼

Air Tank
Small
585-4854
pkg(4) 2.50

Air Tank
Large
585-4853
pkg(4) 2.50

Peacock
Type
585-4830
pkg(3) 2.50

Drain Cock
585-48267
pkg(12) 3.50

Plastic
585-48121
pkg(6) 2.00

Plastic
585-48120
pkg(6) 2.00

(not illustrated)
Elesco Steam Drain
585-3485   pair 1.75

◼ DRAW BARS ◼

Illustrations shown actual size.

585-48188   Delrin, Short   pkg(3) 2.25
585-48187   Delrin, Medium   pkg(3) 2.25
585-48186   Delrin, Long   pkg(3) 2.25
585-48271   Delrin w/Screws   pkg(3 pcs) 2.25
Includes one each of #48188, 48187 & 48186.

Set (S/M/L)
585-48380
pkg(3) 1.75

Small, Delrin
585-48189   pkg(3) 2.25

Front Delrin
585-31253
each 1.50

Automatic Spring Loaded
Insulated
585-3117   each 4.50

◼ DRIVER CENTERS ◼

63″ Spoked, Light
Counter Weight,
Unmachined
585-3159   pkg(4) 5.75
Plastic
585-31892   pkg(4) 2.25

63″ Spoked, Medium
Counter Weight
Unmachined
585-3160   pkg(4) 5.75
Plastic
585-31893   pkg(4) 2.25

63″ Spoked, Heavy
Counter Weight
Unmachined
585-3161   pkg(4) 5.75
Plastic
585-31894   pkg(4) 2.25

79″ Box Pok, Light Counter
Weight, Unmachined
585-3134   pkg(4) 6.75
Plastic
585-31890 +   pkg(4) 3.50

79″ Box Pok, Med
Counter Weight
Unmachined
585-3135
pkg(4) 6.75
Plastic
585-31891   pkg(4) 3.50

◼ ELECTRICAL PARTS ◼

MU Connector
Plug Head
585-39038
pkg(6) 2.25

Plastic
585-39039
pkg(6) 1.50

(not illustrated)

Electrical
Pick-Up Rod,
Locomotive
585-4898
each 4.55

Late GP & SD Dual MU
End Receptacle Stand
585-39053   pkg(2) 2.25

Plastic EMD
585-39054
pkg(2) 1.50

PRECISION SCALE Co.

HO SCALE (1/87)

All Precision Scale Company parts are brass castings, unless noted. Illustrations are not to scale.

We have worked closely with this manufacturer to provide accurate availability information at the time this catalog was published. Items listed in *blue ink* may not be available at all times. Please see your dealer for current delivery information   + (PLUS SIGN) = SPECIAL ORDER ONLY ITEMS.

ENDS

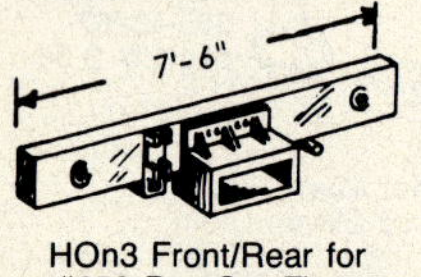
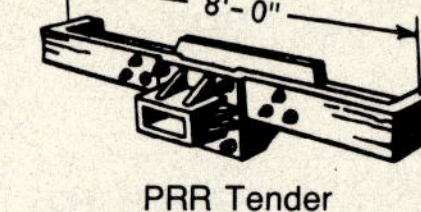
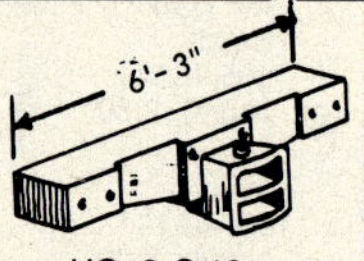

UP Streamlined
585-3561   pair 3.50

HOn3 Combine
585-31208   pair 3.50

HOn3 Coach
585-31209   pair 3.50

Plastic
585-3562   pair 2.00

END SILLS & PLATFORMS

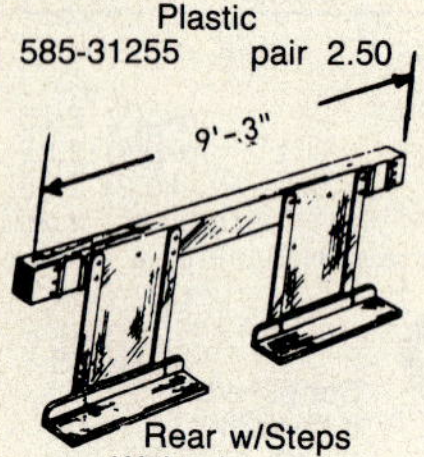

HOn3 Front/Rear for
#653 Box Car Floor
585-31254   pair 4.50

Plastic
585-31255   pair 2.50

PRR Tender
for #307 Floor
585-31258 +   each 2.75

HOn3 C-16
Tender Frame
585-31256   each 2.75

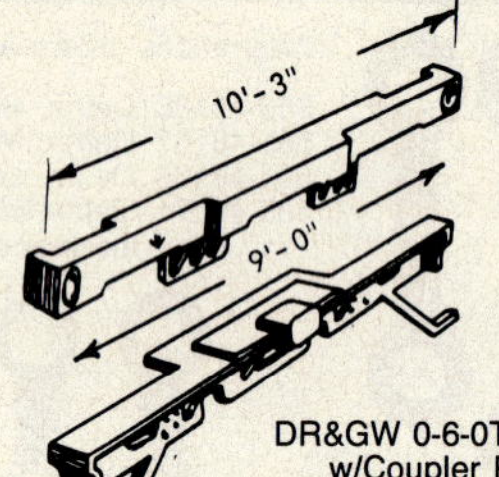

Front/Rear
Vanderbilt
585-31257 +
pair 3.50

Rear w/Steps
Wabash
585-31262   each 3.50

DR&GW 0-6-0T Switcher
w/Coupler Pocket
585-3066 Front Pilot +   ea 3.50
585-3067 Rear Pilot +   ea 3.50

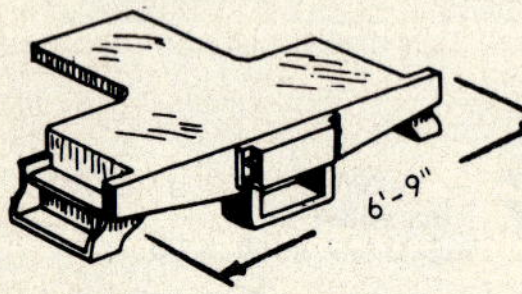

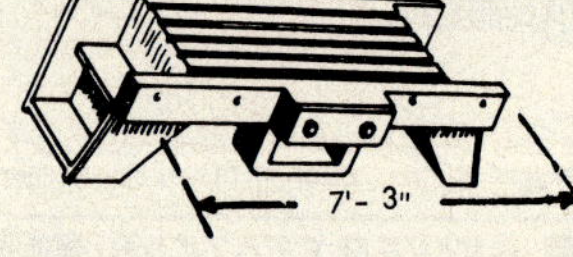

HOn3 End Platform D&RGW Coach
585-31259   pair 4.50

EMD Platform, 4-Wheel Caboose C&S
585-31261   pair 5.50

HOn3 Rear End Platform D&RG Caboose
585-31260   pair 5.50

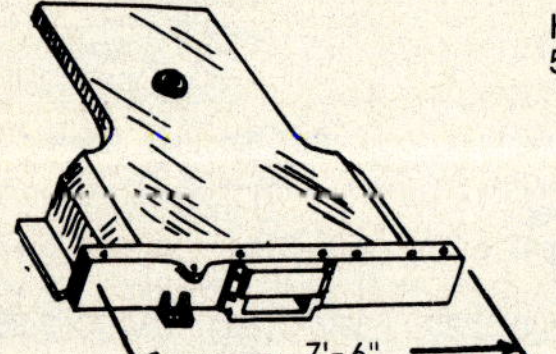

(not illustrated)
Rear for #1700 Tender
585-31406 +   each 2.25
Front for #1700 Tender
585-31495 +   each 2.50
Carrier Bar Pullman Passenger
585-33234   pkg(2) 4.25

ETCHED PARTS

Sheets are 102 x 57 HO Scale feet.

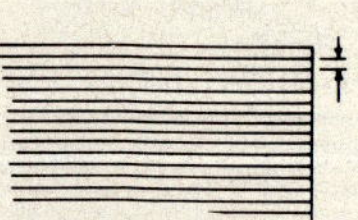
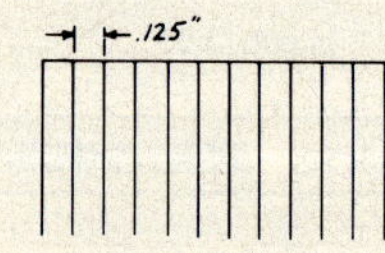
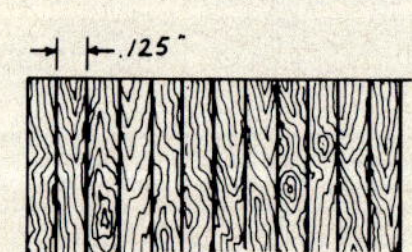

Planks without Grain
Depressed Lines
585-3660   4.00
.016" thick, .038"
between lines, HO-4"

Planks without Grain
Depressed Lines
585-3661   3.25
.014" thick, .123"
between lines, HO-10"

Planked Wood Grain
Single Side, Lines Raised
585-3662   3.25
.025" thick, .123"
plank width, HO-10"

(not illustrated)
585-3663 Planked Wood Grain, Double Sided, Lines Raised   4.00
.123" plank width, .025" thick, HO-10"

FANS & ACCESSORIES

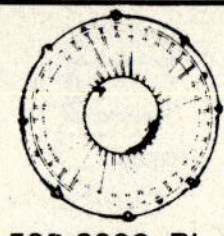

48" Dynamic Brake
Housing w/Open Ribs
(F-7/9, GP7/9, E-8/9 &
some modified SD-9's)
585-3991   pkg(4) 4.75

585-3992 Plastic   pkg(4) 2.25

Intake House w/Grill
& Grill Guard, EMD
48" diameter
585-3963   pair 2.75

585-3964 Plastic   pair 2.25

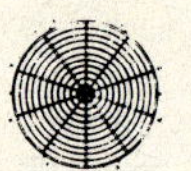

Intake
Housing
w/Grill less
Guard 48"
dia EMD
585-3965   pair 2.75

Plastic
585-3966   pair 2.00

Dynamic
Brake
Housing
48" dia
EMD
585-3931   pkg(4) 3.00

Plastic
585-3932   pkg(4) 2.25

Old
Cooling
Housing
or Dynamic
Brake
Housing w/Open Ribs
36" diameter
585-3989   pkg(4) 4.75
F-7/9, GP7/9/20/30/35,
E8/9, SD7/9/19/24/35

Plastic
585-3990   pkg(4) 2.25

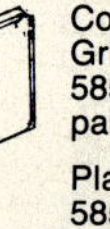

EMD SD40T-2
Cooling Intake
Grilles
585-39075
pair 4.00

Plastic
585-39076
pair 2.75

Housing, Early Style
36" dia, EMD GP-7
585-3946   pkg(2) 3.50

Alco
Exhaust
w/Screen
585-39086 +   1.75

(not illustrated)

585-3930   Fan Enclosure   each 3.00
585-39301   Fan Enclosure, Plastic   each 2.25
585-39087   Headlight Grille, Alco FA   each 2.25

FEEDWATER HEATERS

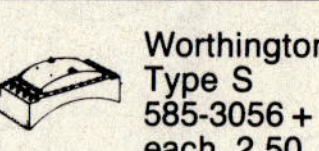

Worthington
Type S
585-3056 +
each 2.50

Worthington
Type SA
585-3164
each 2.75

Elesco Coil Type
585-3154
each 2.50

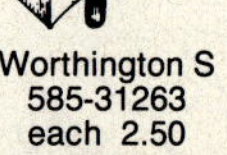

Worthington S
585-31263
each 2.50

Plastic
585-31662
each 1.50

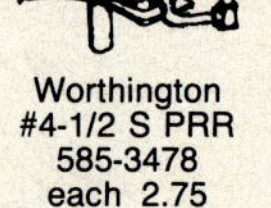

Worthington
#4-1/2 S PRR
585-3478
each 2.75

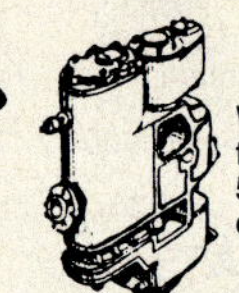

Worthing-
ton, BL-2
585-31265
ea 3.00

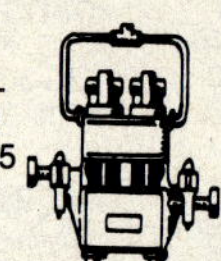

Elesco
Pump
Type CF-1
585-31080
ea 2.50

Worthington Type SA Kit w/Plumbing
585-3166   kit 6.50

Worthington BL-4
585-3337   each 3.00

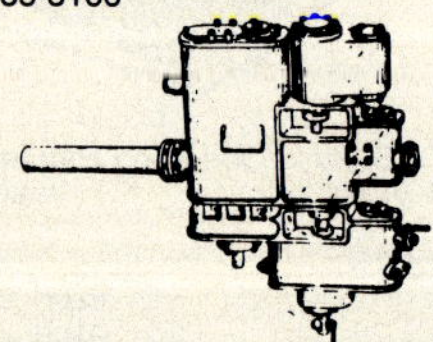

Worthington BL-4B
585-3338   each 3.00

FIREBOXES

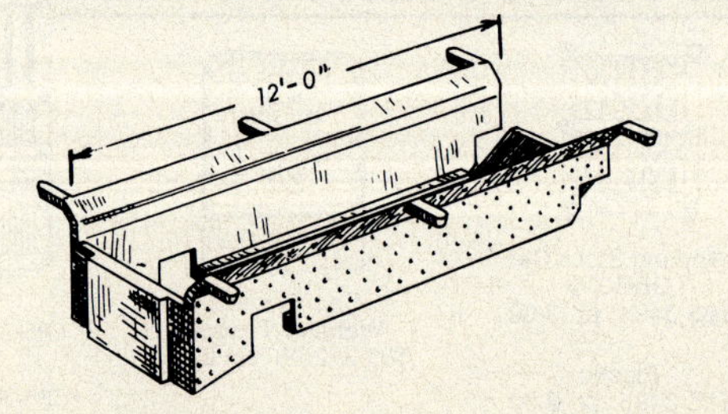

Wabash, Brass
585-31728
each 6.75

Plastic
585-31266
each 3.75

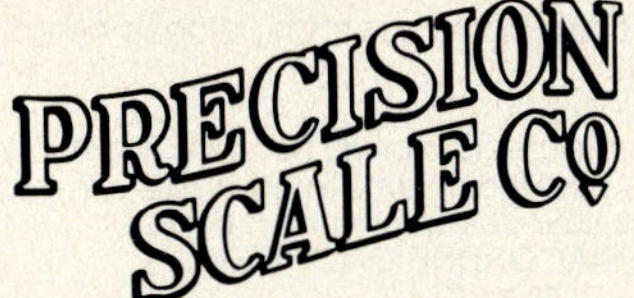

PRECISION SCALE Co

HO SCALE (1/87)

All Precision Scale Company parts are brass castings, unless noted. Illustrations are not to scale.

We have worked closely with this manufacturer to provide accurate availability information at the time this catalog was published. Items listed in *blue ink* may not be available at all times. Please see your dealer for current delivery information   + (PLUS SIGN) = SPECIAL ORDER ONLY ITEMS.

FIRE DOORS

Oil Early Type
585-3045   each 2.50

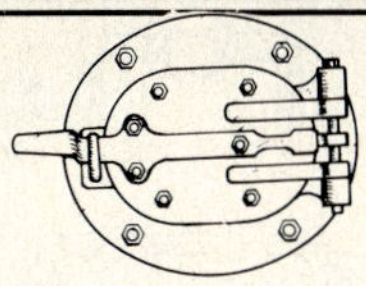

Oil Type w/Oval Frame
585-3327   each 2.25

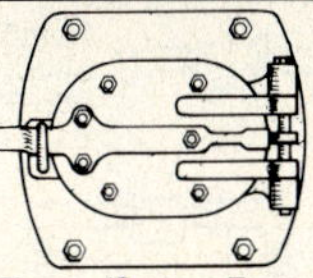

Oil Type w/Square Frame
585-3328   each 2.25

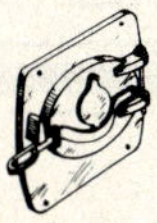

SP Oil Type Large Modern
585-3042   each 2.25

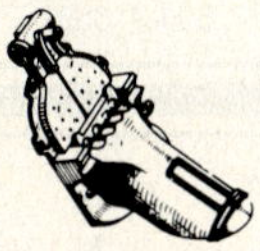

Hanna HT w/Butterfly Door
585-3144   each 3.00

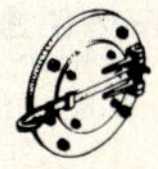

Round Early Type
585-3069   each 2.00

Santa Fe w/Draft Housing
585-3183   each 2.25

Shield w/Tray D&RGW K Series, SP & Common Std
585-3229   2.00

Butterfly, non-working
585-3055   each 2.75

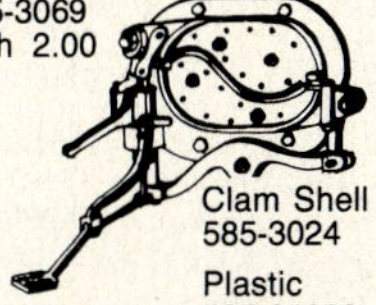

Clam Shell
585-3024   each 3.00

Plastic
585-31639   each 2.25

(not illustrated)
585-3259 Baldwin Oval Oil Fire Door +   each 2.00
585-3273 Large Loco (RI) Oil Fire Door +   each 2.75

FLAG HOLDERS

Flat, for Pilot Beam
585-3206
pair 1.75

2 Holders & Lead Truck Kingpin Kit
585-31268
(3 pcs) 1.75

Flag Holders
585-31267 pair 1.75

FLAT CAR PARTS

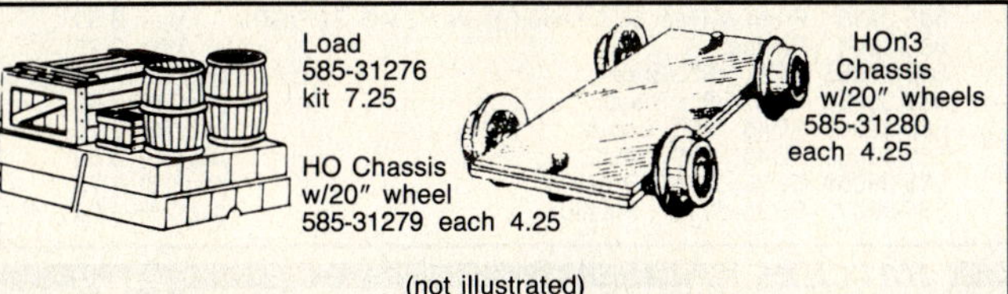

Load
585-31276
kit 7.25

HOn3 Chassis w/20" wheels
585-31280
each 4.25

HO Chassis w/20" wheel
585-31279 each 4.25

(not illustrated)
585-3700   Bulkhead Kit   7.50   585-37003 Bulkhead Kit   7.50
585-37002 Bulkhead Kit, HOn3   3.75   585-37004 Bulkhead Kit, Plastic + 3.75

FLOORS

HOn3

Combine, Wood
585-31212   each 2.00

Coach, Wood
585-31213   each 2.00

(not illustrated)
585-31032 Box Car Floor   each 9.75

FRAMES, LOCO

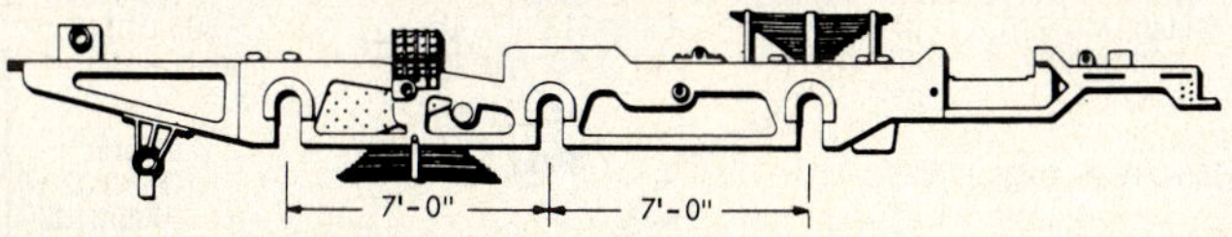

585-31271 Wabash, Unmachined   each 20.00

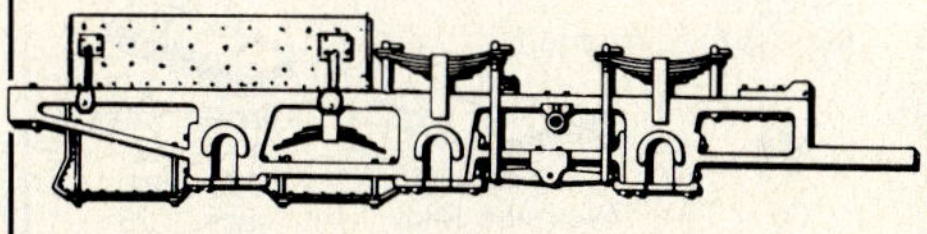

Frame, Machined 0-6-0T & Plastic Cover Plate
585-31275 ea 15.75

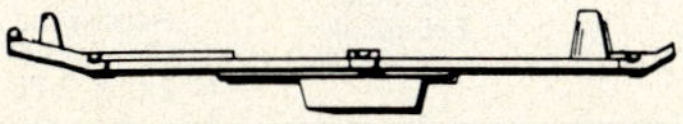

Cover Plate, Wabash
585-31272 + each 2.75

FRAMES, LOCO (continued)

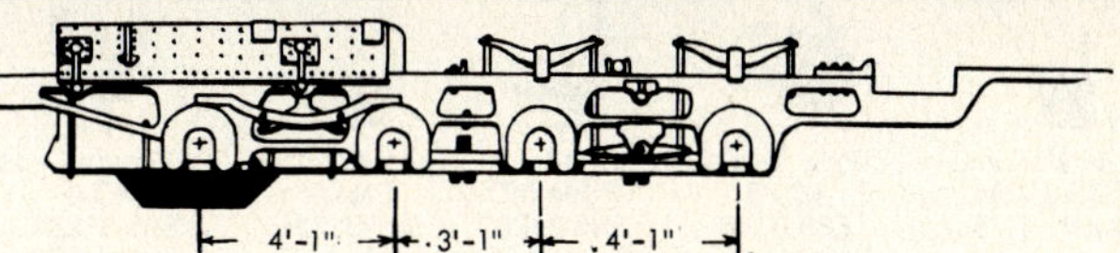

Frame & Cover Plate, C-16 Unmachined
585-31273   15.75

Frame & Cover Plate, Modern C-16 w/Brackets to Mount Brake Rigging, Unmachined
585-31274   15.75

(not illustrated)
585-3592 Front Reinforcing Plates UP 7000 Class 4-8-2   pair 2.25
(Right & Left)

GAUGES

Steam w/Lamp for Top Mount Throttle
585-3070   each 2.00

6-Valve Fireman's Control Box
585-3394   each 2.00   Use w/#3393

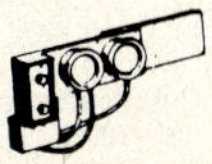

Ashton Signal Indicator w/Dual Pressure Gauge
585-3393   2.75

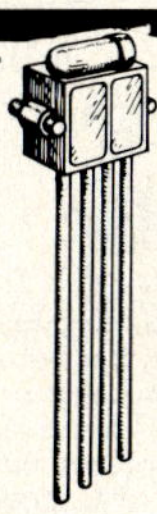

Ashton Quadruplex for Modern Steam Locos
585-3230   2.25

Large, Modern Steam Locos
585-3071   each 2.25

Ashton Double Sided
585-3256   each 1.75

Pressure w/ Bracket Common Std
585-3257   each 1.75

3-Gauge Top Mount D&RGW
585-3287   each 2.25

3-Gauge Side Mount Common Std
585-3288   each 2.25

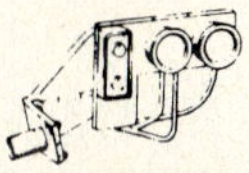

Main Stream w/Control Box
585-3362 ea 3.00

Dual General Purpose
585-3226 ea 1.75

w/Bracket
585-3227
each 1.50

Lamp Early Style
585-3312 + pr 1.50

(not illustrated)
585-31582 Steam   each 1.75
585-31583 Steam, Plastic +   each 1.50
585-32115 Handrail   each 1.25
585-39036 Fuel Pressure, Brass   pkg(6) 2.25
585-39037 Fuel Pressure, Plastic   pkg(6) 1.50

GEARBOXES

Worm, Short 13:1 Steel
585-48283
each 1.75

Worm, Long 13:1 Steel
585-48284
each 1.75

Worm Gear 13:1 Bronze
585-48285
each 2.00
for WA wheel sets

ACCESSORIES

585-108	Washer (.300 OD)	pkg(12) 2.25
585-119	Washer (.190 OD)	pkg(12) 2.00
585-123	Washer (.317 OD) +	pkg(12) 2.25
585-124	Washer (.299 OD)	pkg(12) 2.00
585-125	Washer, Plastic (.237 OD)	pkg(12) 2.00
585-127	Washer (.278 OD) +	pkg(12) 2.00
585-128	Washer (.275 OD) +	pkg(12) 2.00
585-129	Washer (.237 OD)	pkg(12) 2.00
585-130	Washer (.241 OD) +	pkg(12) 2.00
585-131	Crankpin Screw, Small	pkg(4) 2.50
585-132	Crankpin Screw, Large	pkg(4) 2.50
585-105	Worm Gear	each 4.00
585-8338	Pinion Gear	each 3.50
585-31214	HOn3 C-16 Gear Cover	each 1.50
585-31215	Universal Draft Gear	pkg(4) 2.75
585-31216	Universal Draft Gear, Plastic	pkg(2) 2.25
585-40184	Skewed Bevel Gear Box 1:1 +	5.50
585-48319	4" Shaft	each 1.50
585-48320	30:1 Steel Worm	each 1.75
585-48321	30:1 Brass Gear	each 1.75
585-48322	40:1 Steel Worm	each 1.50
585-48323	40:1 Brass Gear +	each 1.75
585-48324	13:1 Nylon Gear	each 1.50

PRECISION SCALE CO

HO SCALE (1/87)

All Precision Scale Company parts are brass castings, unless noted. Illustrations are not to scale.

We have worked closely with this manufacturer to provide accurate availability information at the time this catalog was published. Items listed in *blue ink* may not be available at all times. Please see your dealer for current delivery information   + (PLUS SIGN) = SPECIAL ORDER ONLY ITEMS.

GENERATORS

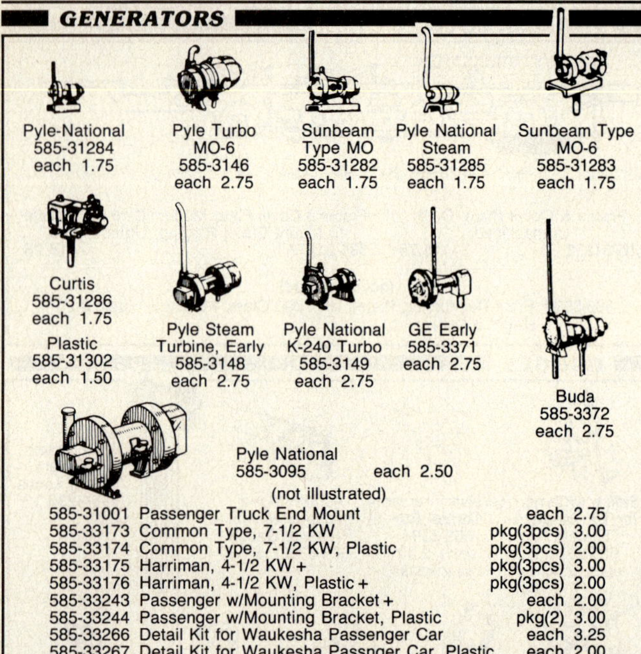

(not illustrated)

585-31001	Passenger Truck End Mount		each 2.75
585-33173	Common Type, 7-1/2 KW		pkg(3pcs) 3.00
585-33174	Common Type, 7-1/2 KW, Plastic		pkg(3pcs) 2.00
585-33175	Harriman, 4-1/2 KW +		pkg(3pcs) 3.00
585-33176	Harriman, 4-1/2 KW, Plastic +		pkg(3pcs) 2.00
585-33243	Passenger w/Mounting Bracket +		each 2.00
585-33244	Passenger w/Mounting Bracket, Plastic		pkg(2) 3.00
585-33266	Detail Kit for Waukesha Passenger Car		each 3.25
585-33267	Detail Kit for Waukesha Passnger Car, Plastic		each 2.00

GLOBE VALVES

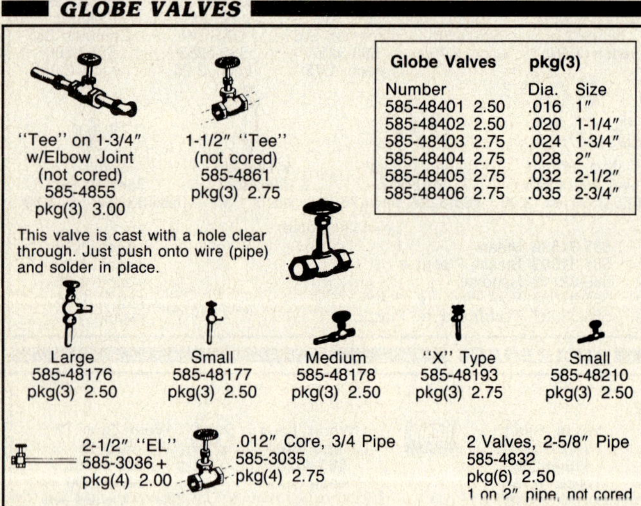

Globe Valves	pkg(3)		
Number		Dia.	Size
585-48401	2.50	.016	1"
585-48402	2.50	.020	1-1/4"
585-48403	2.75	.024	1-3/4"
585-48404	2.75	.028	2"
585-48405	2.75	.032	2-1/2"
585-48406	2.75	.035	2-3/4"

This valve is cast with a hole clear through. Just push onto wire (pipe) and solder in place.

(not illustrated)

585-4862	4-1/2" Tee, Less Core (2" valve cored .40)		pkg(3) 2.75
585-4841	3/4" EL with 1-1/4" Handle, No Core +		pkg(4) 2.50

GRAB IRONS

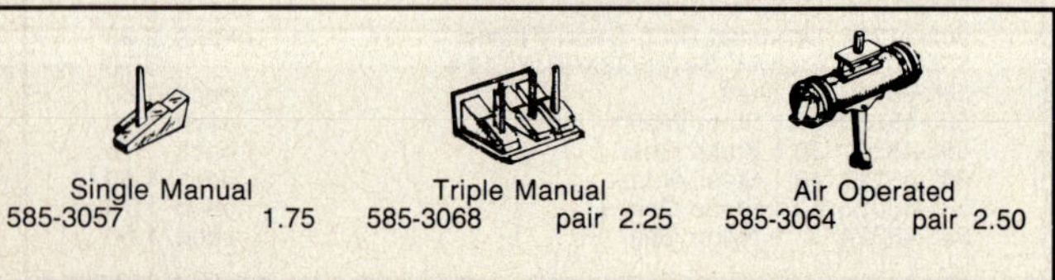

(not illustrated)

585-3582	Wide, HOn3		pkg(28) 2.25
585-3583	Plastic		pkg(28) 1.50
585-3584	Narrow, Gondola, HOn3		pkg(24) 2.25
585-3585	Plastic		pkg(24) 1.50
585-31659	Plastic		pkg(4) 1.50

GRATE SHAKERS

GUIDE YOKES

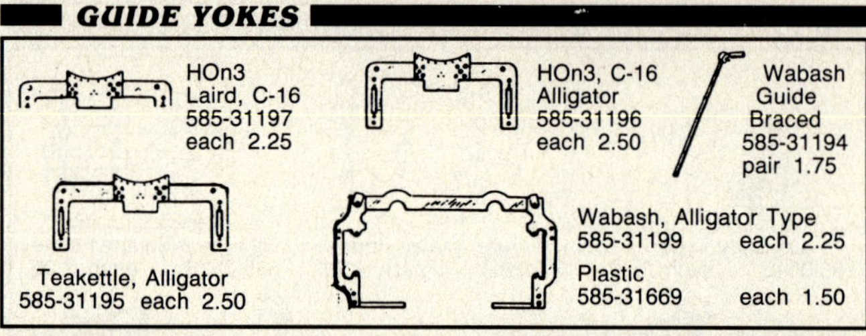

HANDRAIL STANCHIONS

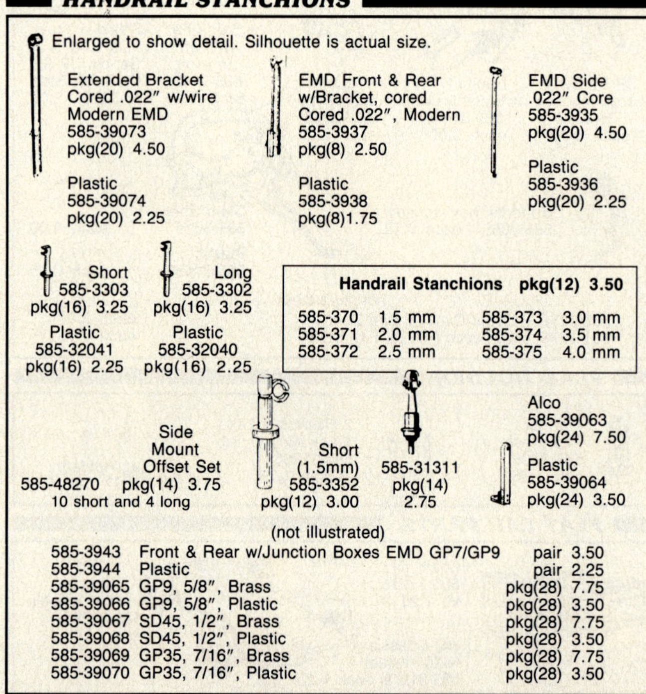

Handrail Stanchions	pkg(12) 3.50		
585-370	1.5 mm	585-373	3.0 mm
585-371	2.0 mm	585-374	3.5 mm
585-372	2.5 mm	585-375	4.0 mm

(not illustrated)

585-3943	Front & Rear w/Junction Boxes EMD GP7/GP9		pair 3.50
585-3944	Plastic		pair 2.25
585-39065	GP9, 5/8", Brass		pkg(28) 7.75
585-39066	GP9, 5/8", Plastic		pkg(28) 3.50
585-39067	SD45, 1/2", Brass		pkg(28) 7.75
585-39068	SD45, 1/2", Plastic		pkg(28) 3.50
585-39069	GP35, 7/16", Brass		pkg(28) 7.75
585-39070	GP35, 7/16", Plastic		pkg(28) 3.50

HATCHES

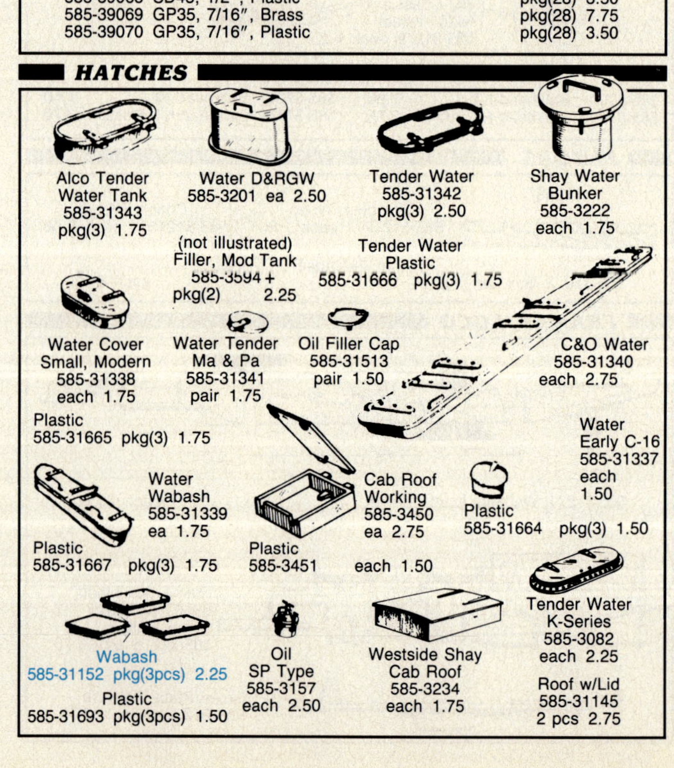

PRECISION SCALE Co

HO SCALE (1/87)

All Precision Scale Company parts are brass castings, unless noted. Illustrations are not to scale.

We have worked closely with this manufacturer to provide accurate availability information at the time this catalog was published. Items listed in *blue ink* may not be available at all times. Please see your dealer for current delivery information   + (PLUS SIGN) = SPECIAL ORDER ONLY ITEMS.

HARDWARE — HALF ROUND

HALF ROUND WIRE pkg(6-12" pieces) 2.25

Part #	Outside Dia in MM	Outside Diameter in Thousandths
585-4877	1.35 x .75	.056 x .031
585-4878	.70 x .25	.028 x .014

HARDWARE - STRAIGHT BRASS WIRE

STRAIGHT BRASS WIRE 12" pcs

Part #	Outside Diam in MM	Outside Diam Thousandths	Outside Diam HO Scale
585-4867 pkg(6) 1.75	.2	.008	3/4"
585-4868 pkg(6) 1.75	.3	.012	1"
585-4869 pkg(10) 2.50	.4	.016	1-3/8"
585-4870 pkg(10) 2.50	.5	.020	1-3/4"
585-4871 pkg(10) 2.50	.6	.024	2"
585-4872 pkg(10) 2.50	.7	.028	2-1/2"
585-4873 pkg(10) 3.00	.8	.032	2-3/4"
585-4874 pkg(10) 2.50	.9	.035	3"
585-4875 pkg(10) 2.50	1.0	.040	3-1/2"
585-4876 pkg(10) 2.50	1.2	.045	4"

HARDWARE - NUTS & BOLTS

Small, Medium and Large Square Assortment
585-48346   pkg(24) 2.75
.045"/.035" sq & .030" hex

Plastic
585-48263   pkg(48) 2.00

HEADLIGHTS

Alco Front & Rear
585-3914 pr 1.75

Pyle w/Visor
585-3085   2.25
Includes lens & number board

D&RGW Box
585-3076   2.75

Plastic
585-3915 pr 1.50

Great Northern
585-3000   2.50

NYC Type
585-3189
ea 2.25

Pyle Streamline
585-3380 1.50

Pyle w/o Visor
585-3428
ea 2.00

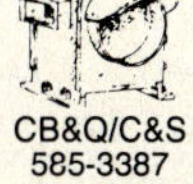
CB&Q/C&S
585-3387
ea 2.75

Early Great Northern
585-3503 2.25

Back-up Light Wabash Tender
585-31298
each 1.75

Back-up Light #1747 Tender
585-31297
each 1.50

Arc Type
585-31289
ea 2.50
Plastic
585-31301
each 1.50

Stubby
585-31288
ea 2.25

Hollow C-16 Modern
585-31292
each 2.50

Hollow with Number Boxes
585-31293
each 2.25

D&RGW Pagosa Junction Cupolas or Caboose
585-3432   2.00

Modern w/Visor
585-31290
ea 1.50

PRR with Bracket
585-31291
ea 2.50

Pyle National Hollow w/Visor
585-31295
each 2.25

Plastic
585-31299
each 1.50

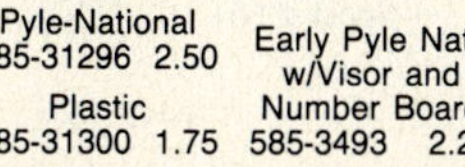
Pyle-National
585-31296 2.50
Plastic
585-31300 1.75

Early Pyle Nat'l w/Visor and Number Board
585-3493   2.25

Common Standard Visor
585-3388
pair 1.50

Incandescent Interurban Cars
585-31004
ea 2.00

HEADLIGHTS (continued)

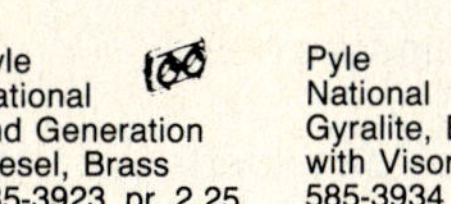

Pyle National Gyralite Red Warning
585-3971 Brass +   pr 1.75
585-3972 Plastic +   pr 1.50

Pyle National Twin Sealed Beam
585-3973 Brass   pr 2.25
585-3974 Plastic   pr 1.50

Pyle National 2nd Generation Diesel, Brass
585-3923 pr 2.25
Plastic
585-3922 pr 1.50

Pyle National Gyralite, EMD with Visor, Brass
585-3934 pr 2.50
Plastic
585-3933 pr 2.25

Mars Dual Signal Oscillating, Brass
585-3969 pr 2.50
Plastic
585-3970 pr 1.50

Early EMD w/Number Board
585-3948
ea 2.00

(not illustrated)

585-31596	Pyle National, Hollow w/Visor & Bulb	each 2.50
585-31597	Pyle National, Hollow w/Visor, Bulb & Bracket +	each 4.00
585-31598	Pyle National, Hollow less Visor w/Bulb	each 2.25
585-31599	Pyle National, Hollow w/Bracket & Bulb	each 3.50
585-31633	Old Style Oil Bulb-Hollow	each 3.50
585-31634	Marker Lamp, Round Lens, less Jewels	pair 2.50
585-31822	Early Pyle +	each 2.00
585-39019	EMD Class, Modern	pkg(2) 1.75
585-3367	CS/CB&Q Without Visor +	each 2.50
585-39125	Mars Dual Oscillating +	pkg(2) 1.75
585-39126	Mars Dual Oscillating Plastic	pkg(4) 1.75
585-39136	Saturn Safety Light	pkg(3) 1.50
585-39137	Saturn Safety Light Plastic +	pkg(3) 1.25
585-39138	Rotary Beacon w/Lens	pkg(3) 1.50
585-39139	Rotary Beacon w/Lens Plastic	pkg(3) 1.25
585-39142	Gyrolite Cover Plate, SP	pkg(3) 2.00
585-39143	Gyrolite Cover Plate, SP Plastic	pkg(3) 1.50
585-39144	Hood Cover Plate, SP, Rect	pkg(3) 2.00
585-39145	Hood Cover Plate, SP, Rect Plastic	pkg(3) 1.50
585-39146	Hood Cover Plate, Oval	pkg(3) 2.00
585-39147	Hood Cover Plate, SP, Oval Plastic	pkg(3) 1.50

HEADLIGHT BRACKETS

These brackets are for center mounting on Smoke Box Door.

585-31605   2.00
585-31606 Plastic +   1.75

for "Frisco"
585-31607   2.00
585-31608 Plastic   1.50

for "UP"
585-31609   2.00
585-31610 Plastic +   1.50

for 4 Digit Numbers
585-31613   2.25
585-31614 Plastic   1.50

for 1, 2 or 3 Digit Numbers
585-31611   2.00
585-31612 Plastic   1.50

with Hand Grab
585-31310 +   1.75

585-31309
each 1.50

SP Type for #31798 Headlight
585-31799
each 2.50

SP Common Standard
585-3232   2.00

Pennsy
585-3536 +
2.00

Rear Bracket Westside
585-3122   1.75

These brackets are for mounting above Smoke Box Door. Grab Iron is on one side only.

High Mount
585-31615   2.00
585-31616 Plastic   1.50

for 3 Digit Numbers
585-31617   2.25
585-31618 Plastic +   1.50

w/Number Board & 1 Grab Iron
585-31619   2.25
585-31620 Plastic   1.50

Platform, RGS 20, 22 and 25, HOn3
585-3359   1.75

Old Style for #6007
585-31306   2.00
Plastic
585-31304   1.50

Ornate for #31633
585-31307
each 2.25

C-16, Modern HOn3
585-31308
each 1.75

PRECISION SCALE Co.

HO SCALE (1/87)

All Precision Scale Company parts are brass castings, unless noted. Illustrations are not to scale.

+ (PLUS SIGN) = SPECIAL ORDER ONLY ITEMS

HEADLIGHT BRACKETS (continued)

Mason Bogie
585-3558
each 2.25

Front, Shay
585-3120
each 1.75

This bracket is for mounting on top of Smoke Box, or Deck of Tender.

585-31305   1.75   585-31303 Plastic   1.50
(not illustrated)
585-3106 Number Board & Headlight Bracket K-28 +   each 1.75
585-3107 Number Board & Headlight Bracket 0-6-0 HOn3 +   each 1.75

HEATERS

Oil
585-3293
each 3.00

SP, Oil
585-3532
each 2.50

HINGES

Large Working
585-320 pkg(12) 4.50

Small Working
585-319 pkg(12) 4.25

Etching Non-working
585-4899 pkg(36) 2.25

INJECTORS

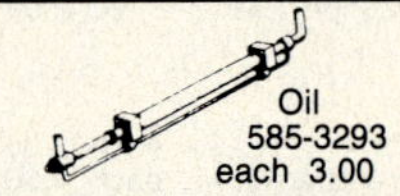
Elesco Type SF
585-3335
each 3.50

Edna Type
585-3203
pair 2.00

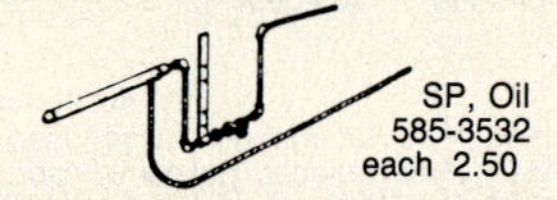
Nathan Non-Lifting
Left & Right
585-31313 pr 2.75

Old Style
Lifting Type
585-31312 pr 2.25

Non-Lift Hancock w/Starter Valve Assembly
585-3077
pkg(2 pcs)
3.00

Nathan-Simplex
585-3143
pair 3.00

Overflow Pipe with Bracket
585-3313
pair 2.25

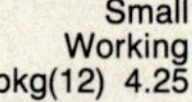

Valve Handles 1-EL, 1-Tee, & 1-Crank
585-4831
pkg(3) 2.25

Drain Line, SP
585-3465
each 2.25

Elesco Starter Valve
585-3336
each 1.75

Long Stem 7-5/8" Dia
585-4884
pkg(3) 2.50

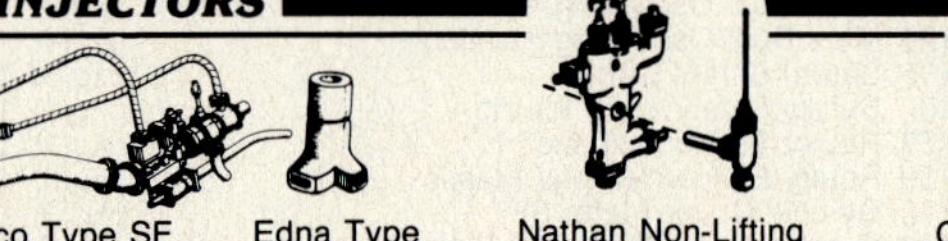
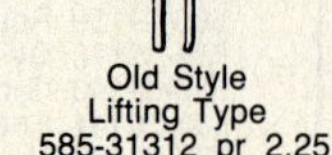

Non-Lifting, Sellers Type K
585-3504   each 2.75

Lifting, Sellers Improved Class N
585-3507   each 2.75

Hancock Non-Lifing Right & Left
585-31314
pair 2.75

Simplex w/Extra Long Plumbing
585-3349
pair 3.00

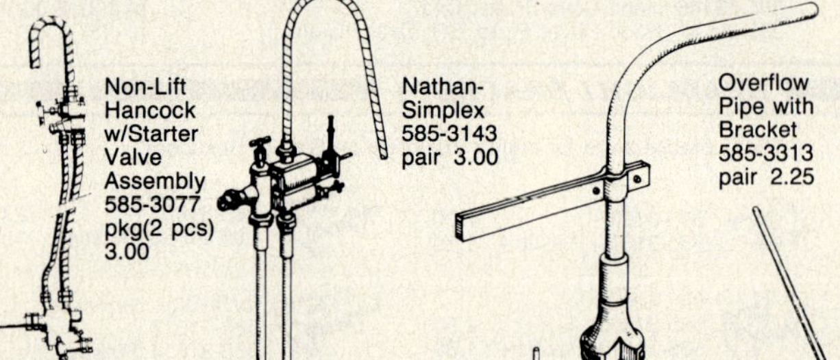
Nathan #4000
585-3375   each 2.50

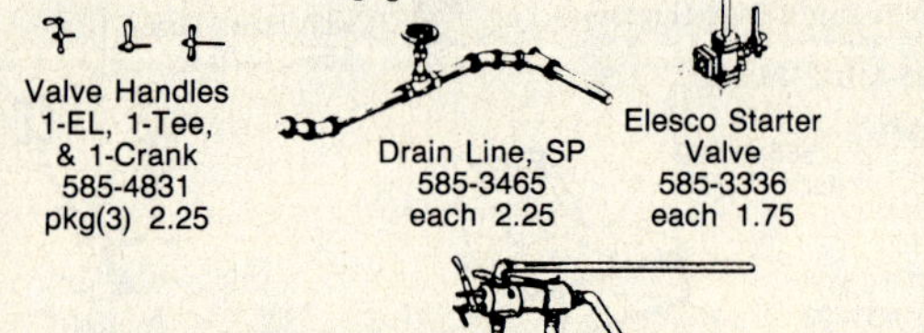

Overflow, SP
585-3023
pkg(2) 3.00

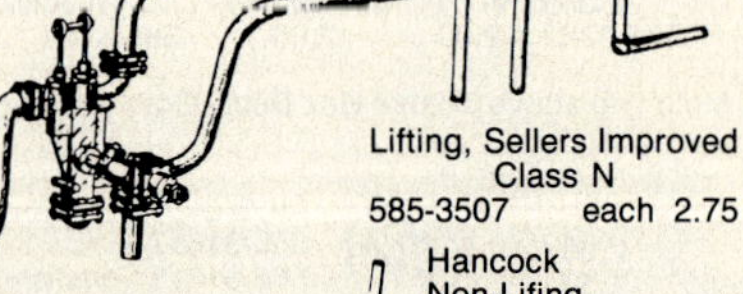
(not illustrated)
SP Auxiliary Water Line Connector
585-31823   each 1.75

JEWELS

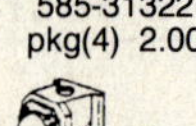

Number	MM	Thousands	Color	Quantity	Price
585-48289	1.3	.053	Red	pkg(12)	2.50
585-48290	1.3	.053	Green	pkg(12)	2.50
585-48291	1.3	.053	Clear	pkg(12)	2.50
585-48292	1.9	.075	Amber	pkg(12)	2.50
585-48293	1.9	.075	Blue	pkg(12)	2.50
585-48373	3.4	.136	Clear	pkg(12)	2.50
585-48374	3.8	.155	Clear	pkg(12)	2.50
585-48375	1.9	.081	Clear	pkg(12)	2.50
585-48376	1.9	.081	Red	pkg(12)	2.50
585-48377	1.7	.079	Clear	pkg(12)	2.50
585-48378	3.0	.118	Amber	pkg(12)	2.50

(not illustrated)
585-48327 Red, Large .112   pkg(12) 2.75
585-48328 Green, Large .112   pkg(12) 2.75
585-48329 Clear, Large .112   pkg(12) 2.75
585-48331 Clear, Small .042   pkg(12) 2.50

JOURNAL BOXES

Roller Bearing
585-31318 +
pkg(4) 3.00

Plain Bearing
585-31317
pkg(4) 3.00

Pedestal with Journal, Old
585-31322
pkg(4) 2.00

Lid
585-31321
pkg(4) 1.50

Plain Bearing
585-31319 +
pkg(4) 2.25

Roller Bearing
585-31320
pkg(4) 2.25

Roller Bearing Delta Trailing Trucks
585-31316
pkg(4) 2.25

Plain Delta
585-31315
pkg(4) 2.25

(not illustrated)
585-3403   Roller Bearing Cap, Timken   pkg(4) 3.00
585-33180   Equalizing Bar PRR +   pkg(4) 2.75
585-33181   Equalizing Bar PRR Plastic +   pkg(4) 1.75

JUNCTION BOXES

EMD, MU Extension
585-39060   pkg(2) 2.25

Plastic
585-39061   pkg(2) 1.75

3-Kinds, 2 Sizes Each
"T" Connector End Type
585-3427   pkg(16) 3.50

Plastic
585-31753   pkg(32) 2.25

EMD Deck Mount
585-39040   pkg(2) 2.75

Plastic
585-39041   pkg(6) 1.75

Modified MU
585-39056 +   pkg(2) 2.25

Plastic
585-39057   pkg(3) 1.75

(not illustrated)
585-31751 Round, Right Angle   pkg(18) 2.00
585-31752 Round, Right Angle Plastic   pkg(18) 2.00

LADDERS

HOn3 & TT
585-31602
pkg(3)
3.50
4" long

Wabash, Loco
585-31328
each 2.00

SP AC-4, Cab
585-3519
pair 2.50

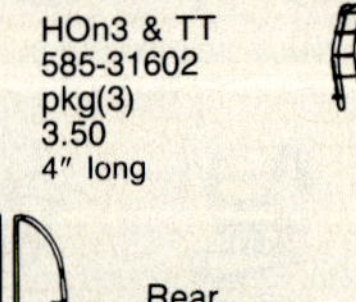
Rear, Right & Left for #1700 tender
585-31323
pair 4.50

Plastic
585-31719
pair 2.75

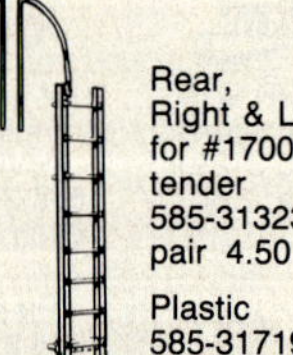
Front Right & left for #1700 tender
585-31324
pair 4.00

Plastic
585-31720
pair 2.50

Tender Rear & 2 Front Steps
585-31325
set(4pcs) 4.00

Ladder & Steps Vandy, Plastic
585-31721 +
4(pcs) 2.50

Strip
585-31327
pkg(12") 2.75

D&RGW Cab w/Extended 4 Steps
585-31971
pair 3.00

(not illustrated)
585-39151 For SD7&9 Locos   each 3.25

PRECISION SCALE CO

HO SCALE (1/87)

LIFT RINGS

Small	Large	Small	Large
585-48276	585-48277	585-48278	585-48279
pkg(12) 2.25	pkg(12) 2.25	pkg(12) 2.25	pkg(12) 2.25
Plastic	Plastic	Plastic	Plastic
585-482761	585-482771	585-482781	585-482791
pkg(12) 1.75	pkg(12) 1.75	pkg(12) 1.75	pkg(12) 1.75

585-39110 Plastic   pkg(16) 1.75   585-39109 Steel   pkg(16) 2.50

Number		Core Dia	Quantity	Price
585-4856	Brass	.080	pkg(6)	2.25
585-4857	Brass	.062	pkg(6)	2.50
585-4858	Brass	.040	pkg(6)	2.50
585-48582	Brass	.036	pkg(6)	2.50
585-48583	Brass	.032	pkg(6)	2.50
585-48584	Brass	.024	pkg(6)	2.50
585-48585	Brass	.020	pkg(6)	2.50
585-48586	Brass	.016	pkg(6)	2.50
585-48587	Brass	.012	pkg(6)	2.50
585-48588	Brass	.008	pkg(6)	2.50
585-485811	Plastic	.040	pkg(12)	2.00
585-485822	Plastic	.036	pkg(12)	2.00
585-485833	Plastic	.032	pkg(12)	2.00
585-485844	Plastic	.024	pkg(12)	2.00
585-485855	Plastic	.020	pkg(12)	2.00
585-485866	Plastic	.016	pkg(12)	2.00
585-485877	Plastic	.012	pkg(12)	2.00
585-485888	Plastic	.008	pkg(12)	2.00

LUBRICATORS

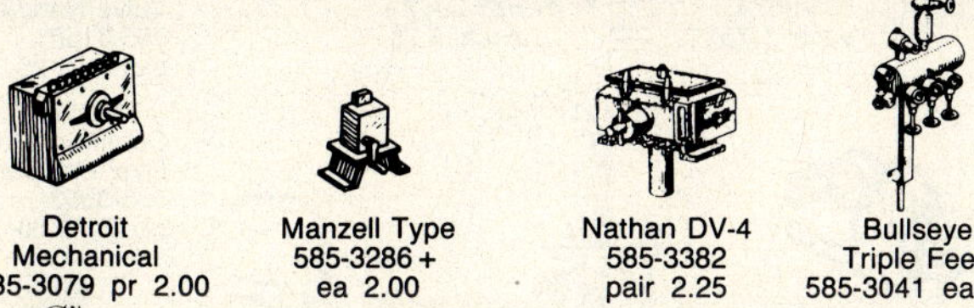

Detroit Mechanical
585-3079 pr 2.00

Manzell Type
585-3286 +
ea 2.00

Nathan DV-4
585-3382
pair 2.25

Bullseye Triple Feed
585-3041 ea 2.25

Detroit 3-Feed
585-3145
ea 2.25

Steam Chest
585-31329
pair 1.50

Pump F-1A Westinghouse
585-3139
ea 2.00

Brass
585-31330
pair 1.75

Plastic
585-31656 +
pkg(4) 1.75

MARKER LAMPS

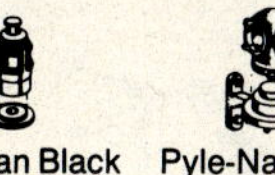
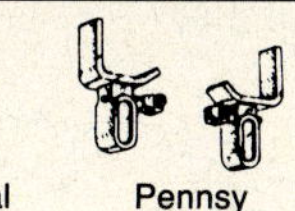

Light Box, SP
585-3049
each 1.50

Handlan Black
585-3124
pair 2.25

Pyle-National
585-3314
pair 2.25

Pennsy Modern
585-3501
pair 2.25

Pennsy Type on Stand
585-3331
pair 2.75

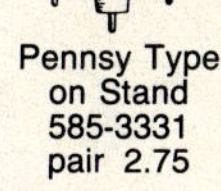
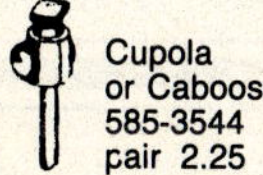

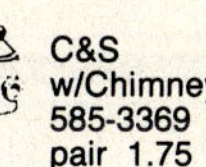
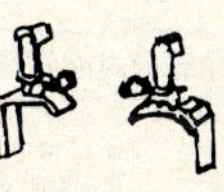

Cupola or Caboose
585-3544
pair 2.25

C&S w/Chimney
585-3369
pair 1.75

Pennsy Modern w/Bracket
585-3502
pair 2.25

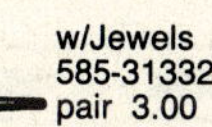
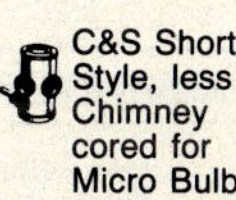

w/Jewels
585-31334
pair 3.00

w/Jewels
585-31332
pair 3.00

C&S Short Style, less Chimney
cored for Micro Bulb
585-3370 pr 2.00

w/Jewels Left & Right
585-31335
pair 3.00

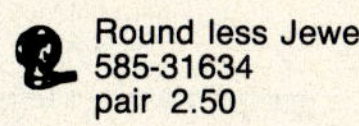

w/Jewels
585-31333
pair 3.00

Drum Style less Jewels
585-31336
pair 1.50

Round less Jewels
585-31634
pair 2.50

(not illustrated)

585-31331 Early Style w/Jewels   pair 3.00

MISCELLANEOUS

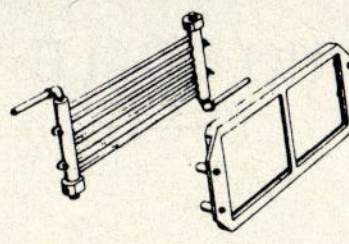

Westinghouse Air System After-Cooler w/Radiator Mounting Frame and Screen
585-3514   set 3.75

Low Water Alarm
585-31997
ea 2.50

Sinclair Radio Antenna
585-39115
pkg(2) 1.75

Plastic
585-39116
pkg(2) 1.25

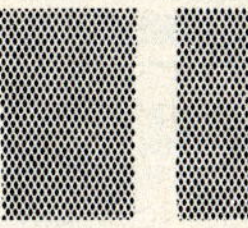

Blower Housing, EMD
585-3975   each 2.75
585-3976 Plastic each 2.50

HO Diesel Catalog #2 Complete Listing of PSC Parts
585-9741   5.00

EMD SD 2nd Gen HT-C, 6-Wheel Truck Side Frame-to-Bolster Cushion Unit, Right & Left
585-39006 pkg(8) 2.00

Plastic +
585-39007 pkg(8) 1.50

Anti-Skid Apron Etched, 3/8″ x 7/16″
585-31397   pair 1.50

EMD Rear Runlight
585-39112   each 2.00

Fuel Sight Glass
585-39010 Brass   pkg(2) 1.75
585-39011 Plastic   pkg(2) 1.50

Jacking Pads
585-3910 Alco   pkg(4) 1.75
585-3911 Plastic   pkg(4) 1.50

Lagging Clamps
585-3038   pkg(6) 2.00

Plastic
585-31744   pkg(6) 1.50

Small
585-3332   pkg(6) 1.75

Shay, Sandbox Left & Right
585-3221   pair 2.75

Western Maryland Shay Sandbox
585-31834 each 2.50

Gerlinger Stack
585-31998 +   ea 2.75

Old Style Stake Pockets
585-31470
pkg(12) 4.00

Plastic
585-32019
pkg(24) 1.25

Temperature Control Panel Late Version, EMD Hallowed for Bulb
585-3928   ea 2.00
585-3929 Plastic   ea 1.50

Truck Shock Absorber or Hydraulic Stabilizer Bars
585-39004 pkg(4) 2.00

Plastic
585-39005   pkg(4) 1.50

EMD SD 2nd Gen, HT-C, 6-Wheel Truck Slack Adjustors
585-39008 pkg(8) 1.75

Plastic
585-39009 pkg(8) 1.50

Drain Funnel Try-Cock with Drain Pipe Backhead
585-3255
each 2.00

Backhead Tricox & Funnel, Nathan
585-3008
each 2.25

585-48234 Brass Turnbuckles   pkg(8) 2.25
585-48235 Plastic Turnbuckles   pkg(16) 1.75
585-48323 Brass Gear, 40:1 Ratio   pkg(12) 1.75

Barko Low Water Alarm
585-3490
each 2.50

Westinghouse Early Type Water Trap
585-3205 1.50

Windshield Wipers
585-3967 pkg(4) 2.25

Plastic
585-3968 pkg(4) 1.50

Wrenches
585-48191 Hex Wrench 5/64″ +   each 2.00
585-48190 Hex Wrench 3/32″   each 2.00

(not illustrated)

585-3264	Foot Grate, D&RGW	pair	2.50
585-3431	Footrail w/Full Step +	each	2.25
585-3467	Flag Holder/Pilot BM	pkg(4)	1.75
585-3506	Condensation Trap, Elesco +	each	2.00
585-3654	Engraving Porter 0-4-0T +	each	6.50
585-3655	Engraving Porter NCNG #8	each	14.00
585-3726	Woth Feedwater Steam SA +	each	10.00
585-3837	Rear Sideframe Mack ACK	pkg(2)	4.50
585-31013	Caboose End Grate Railing +	each	2.25
585-31081	Bridge Shoes	pkg(4 sets)	2.75
585-31442	West Side Lumber Shay-14 Boiler Check +	pair	2.75
585-31491	Coal Bunker Slope Sheet	each	2.00
585-32024	Bridge Shoes, Plastic	pkg(4 sets)	2.00
585-33108	Anti-Sway Bar UP/SP/C&NW	pkg(4)	2.00
585-33109	Anti-Sway Bar UP/SP/C&NW, Plastic +	pkg(4)	1.50
585-33120	Support Center Torque, UP +	pkg(4)	2.00
585-33121	Support Center Torque, UP, Plastic +	pkg(4)	1.50
585-33123	Vapor Trap (R&L) +	pkg(2pr)	3.25
585-33124	Passenger Car Diaphragm	each	2.65
585-33127	Reservoir, Passenger Car +	each	2.25
585-33184	Diaphragm, Spring Loaded, Working +	pkg(6pr)	7.90
585-33193	Catcher Mail Sack, RPO	pkg(2)	2.50
585-33194	Conduit Lighting, Roof Mount +	pkg(3)	3.00
585-33216	Water Tank End Pullman Passenger Car +	each	1.75
585-33240	Battery Box Standard HW +	each	3.00
585-33195	Box Conduit, Junction, RPO +	pkg(8)	3.00
585-33260	Recepticle, Pullman (220V)	pkg(4)	2.50
585-33261	Recepticle, Pullman (220V), Plastic	pkg(8)	2.00

PRECISION SCALE Co

HO SCALE (1/87)

All Precision Scale Company parts are brass castings, unless noted. Illustrations are not to scale.

We have worked closely with this manufacturer to provide accurate availability information at the time this catalog was published. Items listed in *blue ink* may not be available at all times. Please see your dealer for current delivery information   + (PLUS SIGN) = SPECIAL ORDER ONLY ITEMS.

MISCELLANEOUS (continued)

585-33265	Window Trim, Budd	pkg(12)	2.25
585-33268	Engine Waukesha Interior Detail	each	3.50
585-33269	Engine Waukesha Interior Detail, Plastic +	each	2.25
585-33272	Lid, Fuel Box, Waukesha +	pkg(4)	2.25
585-33273	Lid, Fuel Box, Waukesha, Plastic +	pkg(4)	2.00
585-39102	Air Intake Grill w/Screen	pkg(2)	3.75
585-39103	Air Intake Grill w/Screen, Plastic	pkg(2)	2.25
585-39106	Air Intake Frame	pkg(2)	3.50
585-39114	EMD Housing Exhaust Sheet	each	5.75
585-39117	Hoses, Diesel, MU	pkg(6)	1.75
585-39118	Hoses, Diesel MU, Plastic	pkg(10)	1.50
585-39128	EMD Interior Window Visor	pkg(4)	3.75
585-39129	EMD Interior Window Visor, Plastic	pkg(4)	2.00
585-39130	Auxiliary Engineer Cabinet +	pkg(4)	3.50
585-39131	Auxiliary Engineer Cabinet, Plastic	pkg(2)	2.00
585-39132	EMD Firecracker Antenna, Plastic	pkg(4)	1.50
585-39133	EMD Firecracker Antenna	pkg(4)	1.30
585-39134	GE Firecracker Antenna, Plastic	pkg(4)	1.50
585-39135	GE Antenna Firecracker, Plastic	pkg(4)	1.25

MOTORS & ACCESSORIES

Manzell Lubricator
585-31883   each 1.75

NUMBER BOARDS

EMD Hood Unit Front Housing w/Lenses & Headlight, GP-15/18/35/38/39 and SD-Series

585-3985 Modern, Brass   set 4.50
585-3986 Modern, Plastic   set 2.75

Common Standard
SP Cab Forward
585-3202 pr 2.50

HOn3 Tank Car, Destination
585-31364 pkg(4) 1.50

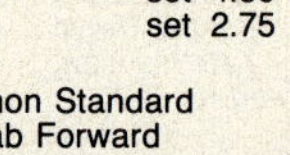

Common Standard, R&L
585-3176 D&RGW pr 2.50

5-Digit Standard
585-31359   pair 2.25

Plastic
585-31661   pair 1.50

Alco, Brass
585-3958
pkg(4) 2.50

NUMBER PLATES

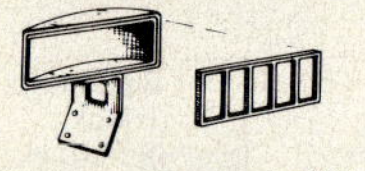

585-31355	Various	set(6)	2.50
585-31715	Plastic +	set(6)	2.00

(#497, 41, 483, 22, 478 & 15)

585-31357	Various	set(6)	2.50
585-31717	Plastic	set(6)	2.00

(#74, 40, 36, 21, 14 & 1)

585-31356	Various	set(6)	2.50
585-31716	Plastic	set(6)	2.00

(#416, 13, 455, 3, 361 & 268)

585-31358	Various	set(6)	2.75
585-31718	Plastic	set(6)	2.00

(#341, 267, 107, 168, 153, 100)

585-31347	1 to 5	pkg(5)	2.00	585-31351	21 to 25	pkg(5)	2.00
585-31695	Plastic +	pkg(5)	1.75	585-31699	Plastic	pkg(5)	1.75
585-31348	6 to 10 plus Star	pkg(6)	2.00	585-31352	26 to 30 plus Bank	pkg(6)	2.00
585-31696	Plastic	pkg(6)	1.75	585-31700	Plastic +	pkg(6)	1.75
585-31349	11 to 15	pkg(5)	2.00	585-31353	31 to 35	pkg(5)	2.00
585-31697	Plastic	pkg(5)	1.75	585-31701	Plastic	pkg(5)	1.75
585-31350	16 to 20 plus Blank	pkg(6)	2.00	585-31354	36 to 40 plus Blank	pkg(6)	2.00
585-31698	Plastic +	pkg(6)	1.75	585-31702	Plastic	pkg(6)	1.75

585-31360	Pennsy, Keystone	pkg(2)	1.75
585-31711	Plastic	pkg(4)	1.75
585-31361	Union Pacific	pkg(2)	1.75
585-31712	Plastic	pkg(4)	1.75
585-31362	D&RGW	pkg(2)	1.75
585-31713	Plastic	pkg(4)	1.75
585-31363	Wabash	pkg(2)	1.75
585-31714	Plastic	pkg(4)	1.75

(not illustrated)
Rear Inspection Plate
for SP Vanderbilt Tender
585-31837   pair 1.50

NUT-BOLT-WASHER SETS

585-48216	Square	Medium	.040″	pkg(18)	2.50
585-48222	Hex	Medium	.040″	pkg(18)	2.50
585-48218	Square	Small	.030″	pkg(18)	2.50

NUT-BOLT-WASHER SETS (continued)

585-48224	Hex		Small	.030″	pkg(18)	2.50
585-48220	Square		Very Small	.025″	pkg(18)	2.50
585-48217	Square	Plastic	Medium	.040″	pkg(48)	2.50
585-48223	Hex	Plastic	Medium	.040″	pkg(48)	2.50
585-48219	Square	Plastic	Small	.030″	pkg(48)	2.50
585-48225	Hex	Plastic	Small	.030″	pkg(48)	2.50
585-48226	Hex		Very Small	.025″	pkg(18)	2.50
585-48221	Square	Plastic	Very Small	.025″	pkg(48)	2.50
585-48227	Hex	Plastic	Very Small	.025″	pkg(48)	2.50
585-48228	Square		Large	.045″	pkg(12)	2.75
585-48230	Square		Medium	.035-.040″	pkg(12)	2.75
585-48232	Square		Small	.030-.030″ hex	pkg(12)	2.75
585-48229	Square	Plastic	Large	.045″	pkg(36)	2.50
585-48231	Square	Plastic	Medium	.035-.040″ hex	pkg(48)	2.50

585-48263	Plastic (#48346)	pkg(48)	2.00
585-48233	Assortment Set (.030″ square, .030″ hex)	pkg(48)	2.50
585-48346	Assortment Set (.045″/.035″ square, .030″ hex)	pkg(24)	2.75

OILERS

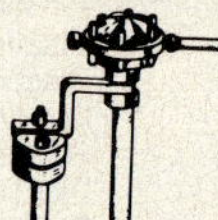

Detroit High Pressure Cylinder, Dual
585-3171
pkg(2) 2.50

Oil Dip Stick SP
585-31833
each 1.50

Detroit High Pressure Cylinder, Single
585-3170 +
pkg(2) 2.00

OIL-FIRING CONTROLS

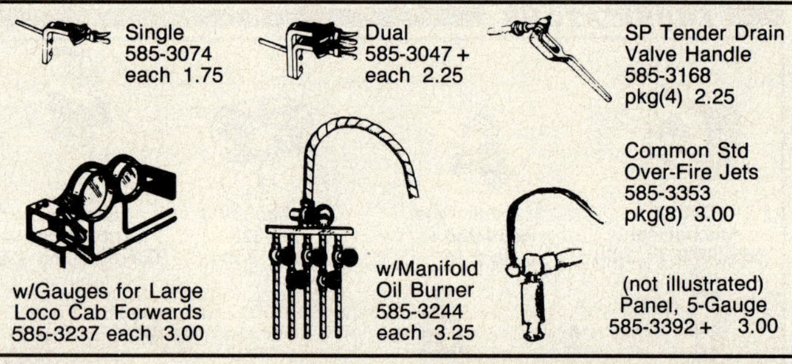

Single
585-3074
each 1.75

Dual
585-3047 +
each 2.25

SP Tender Drain Valve Handle
585-3168
pkg(4) 2.25

w/Gauges for Large Loco Cab Forwards
585-3237 each 3.00

w/Manifold Oil Burner
585-3244
each 3.25

Common Std Over-Fire Jets
585-3353
pkg(8) 3.00

(not illustrated)
Panel, 5-Gauge
585-3392 +   3.00

ORE CAR SIDE DUMPS

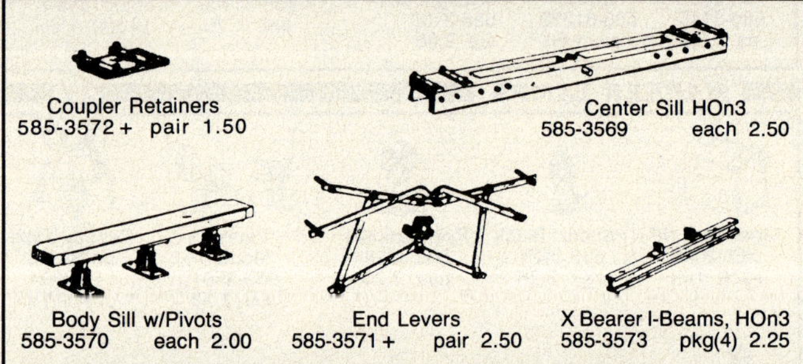

Coupler Retainers
585-3572 + pair 1.50

Center Sill HOn3
585-3569   each 2.50

Body Sill w/Pivots
585-3570   each 2.00

End Levers
585-3571 +   pair 2.50

X Bearer I-Beams, HOn3
585-3573   pkg(4) 2.25

PANTOGRAPHS

AC Insulators Large, Plastic
585-3261
pkg(8) 2.25

DC Insulators Small, Plastic
585-3262
pkg(8) 2.25

PILOTS

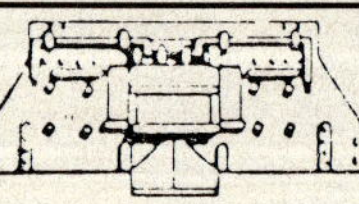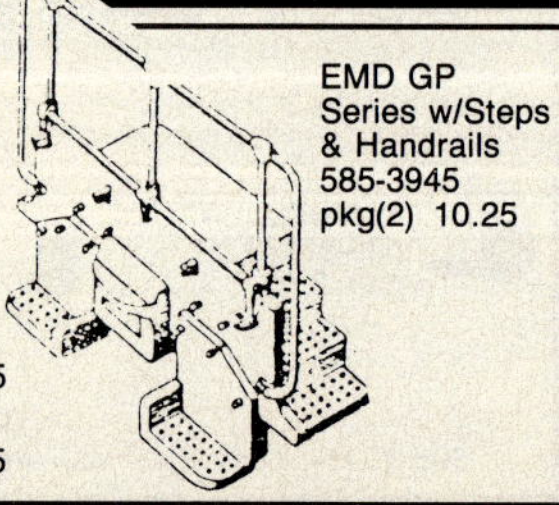

Alco w/Side Steps, Brass
585-3947
pair 7.00

EMD GP Series w/Steps & Handrails
585-3945
pkg(2) 10.25

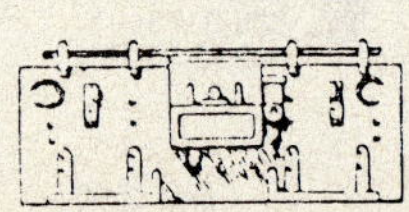

Front & Rear Industrial Switcher
585-3952 pair 4.75

Plastic
585-3953 pair 2.25

PRECISION SCALE Co

HO SCALE (1/87)

All Precision Scale Company parts are brass castings, unless noted. Illustrations are not to scale.

We have worked closely with this manufacturer to provide accurate availability information at the time this catalog was published. Items listed in *blue ink* may not be available at all times. Please see your dealer for current delivery information   + (PLUS SIGN) = SPECIAL ORDER ONLY ITEMS.

■ PILOTS (continued)

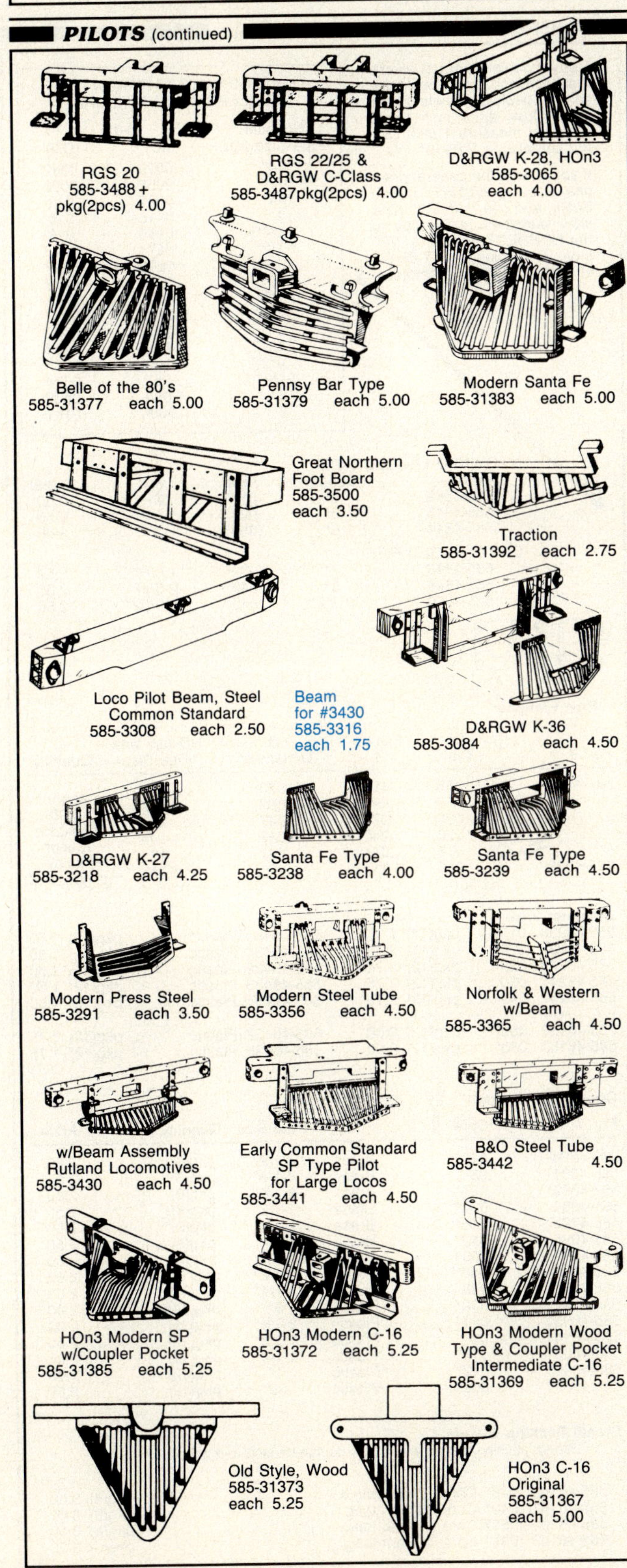

RGS 20
585-3488 +
pkg(2pcs) 4.00

RGS 22/25 &
D&RGW C-Class
585-3487pkg(2pcs) 4.00

D&RGW K-28, HOn3
585-3065
each 4.00

Belle of the 80's
585-31377   each 5.00

Pennsy Bar Type
585-31379   each 5.00

Modern Santa Fe
585-31383   each 5.00

Great Northern
Foot Board
585-3500
each 3.50

Traction
585-31392   each 2.75

Loco Pilot Beam, Steel
Common Standard
585-3308   each 2.50

Beam
for #3430
585-3316
each 1.75

D&RGW K-36
585-3084   each 4.50

D&RGW K-27
585-3218   each 4.25

Santa Fe Type
585-3238   each 4.00

Santa Fe Type
585-3239   each 4.50

Modern Press Steel
585-3291   each 3.50

Modern Steel Tube
585-3356   each 4.50

Norfolk & Western
w/Beam
585-3365   each 4.50

w/Beam Assembly
Rutland Locomotives
585-3430   each 4.50

Early Common Standard
SP Type Pilot
for Large Locos
585-3441   each 4.50

B&O Steel Tube
585-3442   4.50

HOn3 Modern SP
w/Coupler Pocket
585-31385   each 5.25

HOn3 Modern C-16
585-31372   each 5.25

HOn3 Modern Wood
Type & Coupler Pocket
Intermediate C-16
585-31369   each 5.25

Old Style, Wood
585-31373
each 5.25

HOn3 C-16
Original
585-31367
each 5.00

■ PILOTS (continued)

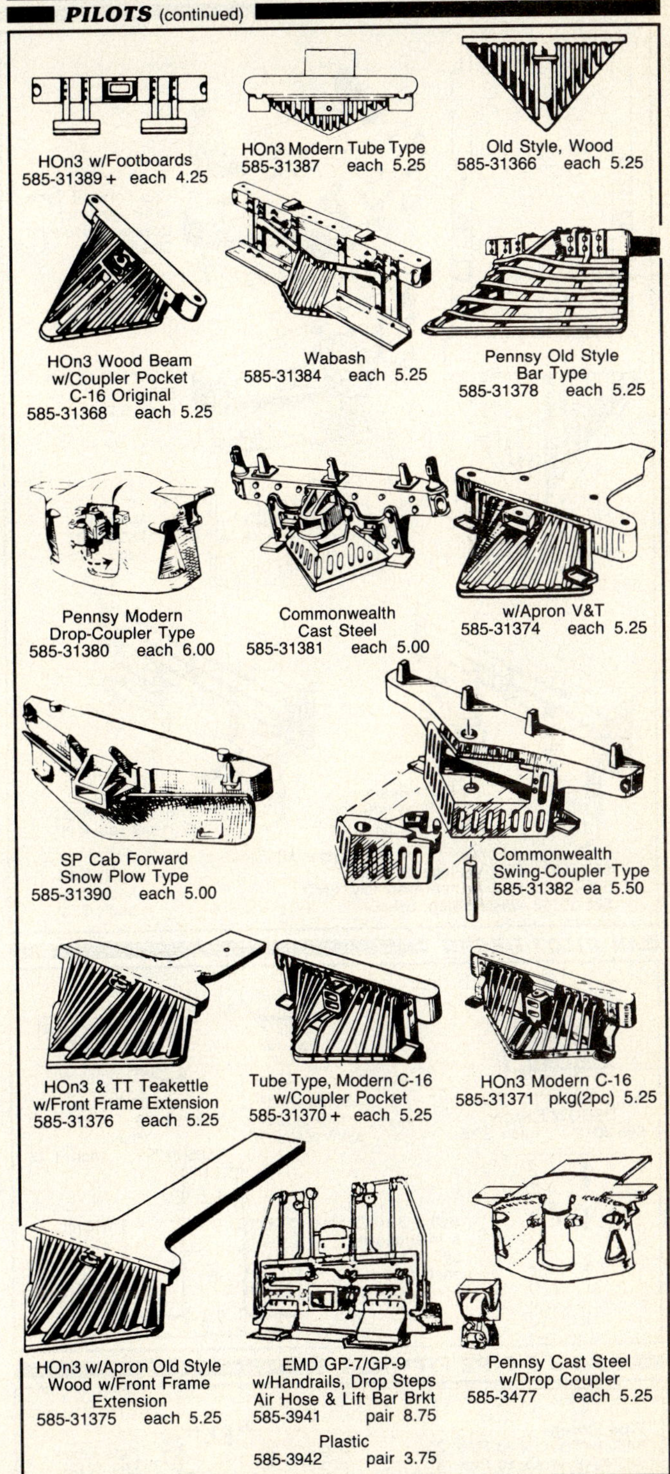

HOn3 w/Footboards
585-31389 +   each 4.25

HOn3 Modern Tube Type
585-31387   each 5.25

Old Style, Wood
585-31366   each 5.25

HOn3 Wood Beam
w/Coupler Pocket
C-16 Original
585-31368   each 5.25

Wabash
585-31384   each 5.25

Pennsy Old Style
Bar Type
585-31378   each 5.25

Pennsy Modern
Drop-Coupler Type
585-31380   each 6.00

Commonwealth
Cast Steel
585-31381   each 5.00

w/Apron V&T
585-31374   each 5.25

SP Cab Forward
Snow Plow Type
585-31390   each 5.00

Commonwealth
Swing-Coupler Type
585-31382 ea 5.50

HOn3 & TT Teakettle
w/Front Frame Extension
585-31376   each 5.25

Tube Type, Modern C-16
w/Coupler Pocket
585-31370 +   each 5.25

HOn3 Modern C-16
585-31371   pkg(2pc) 5.25

HOn3 w/Apron Old Style
Wood w/Front Frame
Extension
585-31375   each 5.25

EMD GP-7/GP-9
w/Handrails, Drop Steps
Air Hose & Lift Bar Brkt
585-3941   pair 8.75

Plastic
585-3942   pair 3.75

Pennsy Cast Steel
w/Drop Coupler
585-3477   each 5.25

See also: TRUCKS, COUPLERS, SCRATCH-BUILDING SUPPLIES and BOOKS for additional PRECISION SCALE CO products.

PRECISION SCALE Co

HO SCALE (1/87)

All Precision Scale Company parts are brass castings, unless noted. Illustrations are not to scale.

We have worked closely with this manufacturer to provide accurate availability information at the time this catalog was published. Items listed in *blue ink* may not be available at all times. Please see your dealer for current delivery information   + (PLUS SIGN) = SPECIAL ORDER ONLY ITEMS.

■ PILOTS (continued)

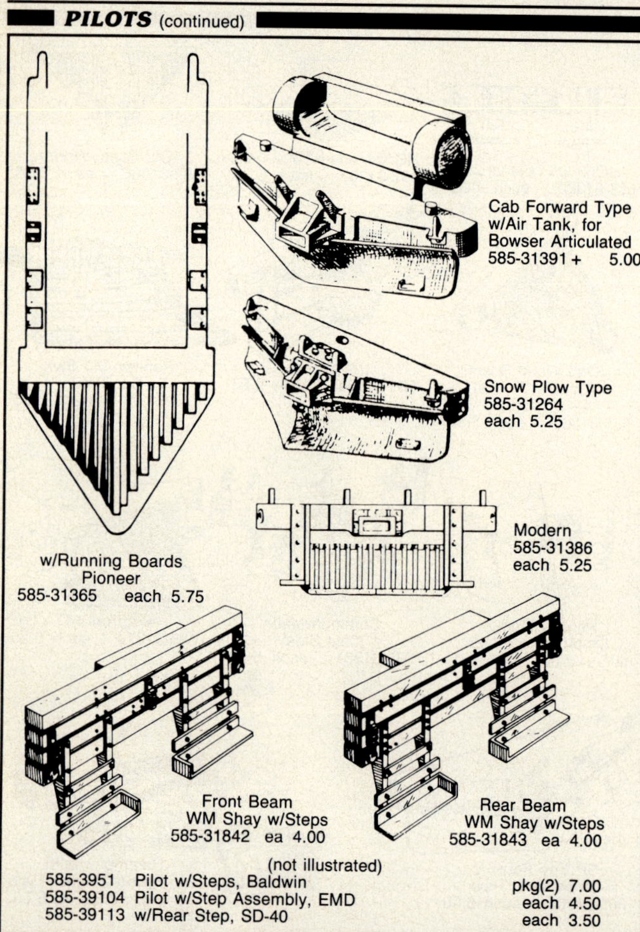

Cab Forward Type w/Air Tank, for Bowser Articulated
585-31391 +   5.00

Snow Plow Type
585-31264
each 5.25

Modern
585-31386
each 5.25

w/Running Boards Pioneer
585-31365   each 5.75

Front Beam WM Shay w/Steps
585-31842   ea 4.00

Rear Beam WM Shay w/Steps
585-31843   ea 4.00

(not illustrated)

585-3951   Pilot w/Steps, Baldwin   pkg(2) 7.00
585-39104 Pilot w/Step Assembly, EMD   each 4.50
585-39113 w/Rear Step, SD-40   each 3.50

■ PILOT DECKS

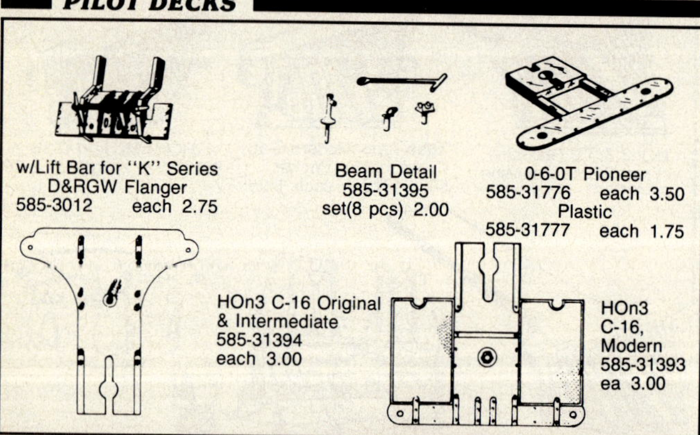

w/Lift Bar for "K" Series D&RGW Flanger
585-3012   each 2.75

Beam Detail
585-31395
set(8 pcs) 2.00

0-6-0T Pioneer
585-31776   each 3.50
Plastic
585-31777   each 1.75

HOn3 C-16 Original & Intermediate
585-31394
each 3.00

HOn3 C-16, Modern
585-31393
ea 3.00

■ PIPE & PIPE FITTINGS

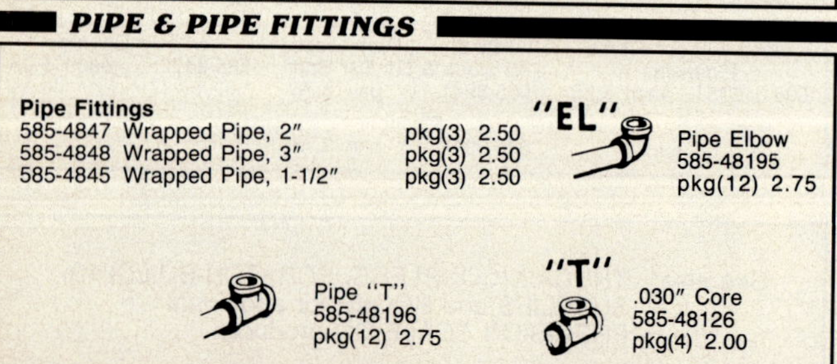

Pipe Fittings
585-4847 Wrapped Pipe, 2"   pkg(3) 2.50
585-4848 Wrapped Pipe, 3"   pkg(3) 2.50
585-4845 Wrapped Pipe, 1-1/2" pkg(3) 2.50

"EL"   Pipe Elbow
585-48195
pkg(12) 2.75

Pipe "T"
585-48196
pkg(12) 2.75

"T"   .030" Core
585-48126
pkg(4) 2.00

■ PIPE & PIPE FITTINGS (continued)

Many modelers are not aware that "nominal" pipe sizes represent the INSIDE diameter of the pipe. Thus, a "1 inch pipe" does not measure 1 inch OD, but actually, is 1-15/16" OD.

If you accept the general practice of using .010 = 1" in HO Scale, and use it as a 1" pipe size, your pipe is really closer to the CORRECT size for a 1/2" pipe. A 1" pipe in HO Scale, should be .015" in diameter.

TABLE OF WROUGHT IRON PIPE SIZES (BRIGGS STANDARD)

Nominal Pipe Size (ID)	HO (ID)	(OD)
1/4"	.0029	.0062
1/2"	.0058	.0096
3/4"	.0087	.012
1"	.0116	.015
1-1/4"	.0145	.019
1-1/2"	.0174	.0218
1-3/4	.0203	.0247
2"	.0236	.0272
2-1/2"	.029	.033
2-3/4"	.0319	.0377
3"	.0348	.0402
3-1/2"	.0406	.0459
4"	.0464	.0517
4-1/2"	.052	.0574
5"	.058	.0639
6"	.0696	.0761

MACHINED LAGGED PIPE

Part #	Length	Pipe	HO	pkg(3)
585-4842	6"	.019"	3/4"	2.50
585-4843	6"	.028"	1-1/2"	2.50
585-4844	6"	.052"	3"	3.00

CAST LAGGED PIPE

Part #	Length	Pipe	HO	
585-4846	2"	.032"	1-3/4"	2.50
585-4848	3"	.042"	2-3/4"	2.50
585-4850	2-1/2"	.045"	3-15/62"	2.50

Pipe Flanges

Part #	Core Dia C	Flange A	B Dimension	HO use with Pipe Size	Quantity
585-4827	.055	.123	.083	4-1/4"	pkg(8) 3.00 (includes 2 each size)
	.040	.097	.068	2-3/4"	
	.030	.070	.048	2"	
	.020	.060	.037	1-1/4"	
	.018	.044	.027	1"	
585-4828	.050	.117	.075	3-3/4"	pkg(2) 2.50

Diameter Wire

Part #			Part #		
585-48238	.015	pkg(12) 2.75	585-48430	Plastic	pkg(12) 1.50
585-48239	.020	pkg(12) 2.75	585-48431	Plastic	pkg(12) 1.50
585-48240	.025	pkg(12) 2.75	585-48432	Plastic	pkg(12) 1.50
585-48241	.030	pkg(12) 2.75	585-48433	Plastic	pkg(12) 1.50
585-48242	.040	pkg(12) 2.75	585-48434	Plastic	pkg(12) 1.50
585-48180	.050"	pkg(12) 3.00	585-48437	Plastic	pkg(12) 1.75
585-48181	.040"	pkg(12) 3.00	585-48438	Plastic	pkg(12) 1.75

Cored Pipe Bracket

Part #	Core		Pipe Size	Quantity	Price
585-4890	.040"	Brass	3-1/2"	pkg(6)	2.50
585-4891	.036"	Brass	3-1/4"	pkg(6)	2.50
585-4893	.024"	Brass	2-1/4"	pkg(6)	2.50
585-4894	.020"	Brass	1-1/2"	pkg(6)	2.50
585-4895	.016"	Brass	1-1/4"	pkg(6)	2.50
585-4896	.012"	Brass	1"	pkg(6)	2.50
585-4897	.008"	Brass	1/2"	pkg(6)	2.50
585-48901	.040"	Plastic	3-1/2"	pkg(12)	2.00
585-48911 +	.036"	Plastic	3-1/4"	pkg(12)	2.00
585-48921	.032"	Plastic	3"	pkg(12)	2.00
585-48931	.024"	Plastic	2-1/4"	pkg(12)	2.00
585-48941	.020"	Plastic	1-1/2"	pkg(12)	2.00
585-48951	.016"	Plastic	1-1/4"	pkg(12)	2.00
585-48961	.012"	Plastic	1"	pkg(12)	2.00
585-48971	.008"	Plastic	1/2"	pkg(12)	2.00

Steam Packing Glands

Steam packing glands are round, double-flanged and bolted.

585-48100	.028" Core, .7mm long +	pkg(6) 3.00
585-48101	.040" Core, 1.0mm long	pkg(6) 3.00
585-48102	.060" Core, 1.5mm long	pkg(6) 3.00
585-48103	.085" Core, 2.1mm long	pkg(6) 3.25

PRECISION SCALE Co

HO SCALE (1/87)

All Precision Scale Company parts are brass castings, unless noted. Illustrations are not to scale.

We have worked closely with this manufacturer to provide accurate availability information at the time this catalog was published. Items listed in *blue ink* may not be available at all times. Please see your dealer for current delivery information   + (PLUS SIGN) = SPECIAL ORDER ONLY ITEMS.

PIPE & PIPE FITTING (continued)

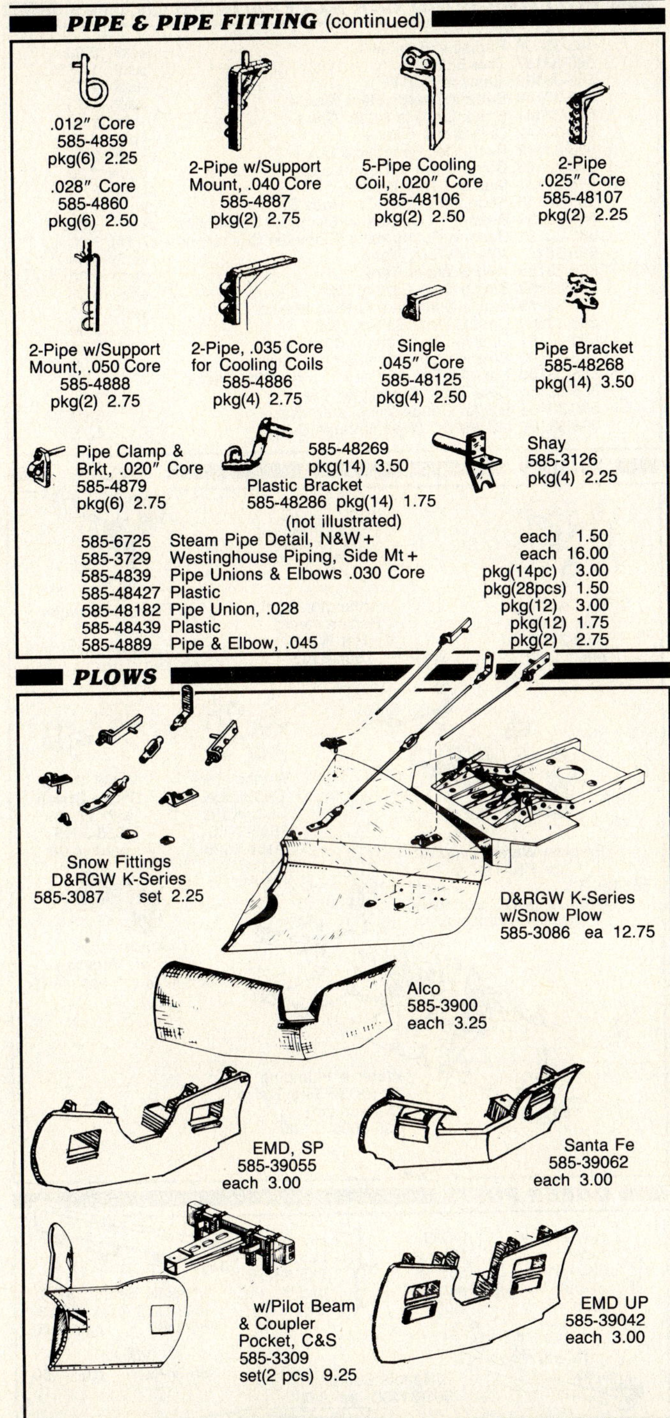

.012" Core
585-4859
pkg(6) 2.25

.028" Core
585-4860
pkg(6) 2.50

2-Pipe w/Support Mount, .040 Core
585-4887
pkg(2) 2.75

5-Pipe Cooling Coil, .020" Core
585-48106
pkg(2) 2.50

2-Pipe .025" Core
585-48107
pkg(2) 2.25

2-Pipe w/Support Mount, .050 Core
585-4888
pkg(2) 2.75

2-Pipe, .035 Core for Cooling Coils
585-4886
pkg(4) 2.75

Single .045" Core
585-48125
pkg(4) 2.50

Pipe Bracket
585-48268
pkg(14) 3.50

Pipe Clamp & Brkt, .020" Core
585-4879
pkg(6) 2.75

585-48269
pkg(14) 3.50

Plastic Bracket
585-48286 pkg(14) 1.75
(not illustrated)

Shay
585-3126
pkg(4) 2.25

585-6725	Steam Pipe Detail, N&W +	each 1.50
585-3729	Westinghouse Piping, Side Mt +	each 16.00
585-4839	Pipe Unions & Elbows .030 Core	pkg(14pc) 3.00
585-48427	Plastic	pkg(28pcs) 1.50
585-48182	Pipe Union, .028	pkg(12) 3.00
585-48439	Plastic	pkg(12) 1.75
585-4889	Pipe & Elbow, .045	pkg(2) 2.75

PLOWS

Snow Fittings D&RGW K-Series
585-3087   set 2.25

D&RGW K-Series w/Snow Plow
585-3086   ea 12.75

Alco
585-3900
each 3.25

EMD, SP
585-39055
each 3.00

Santa Fe
585-39062
each 3.00

w/Pilot Beam & Coupler Pocket, C&S
585-3309
set(2 pcs) 9.25

EMD UP
585-39042
each 3.00

PLUMBING

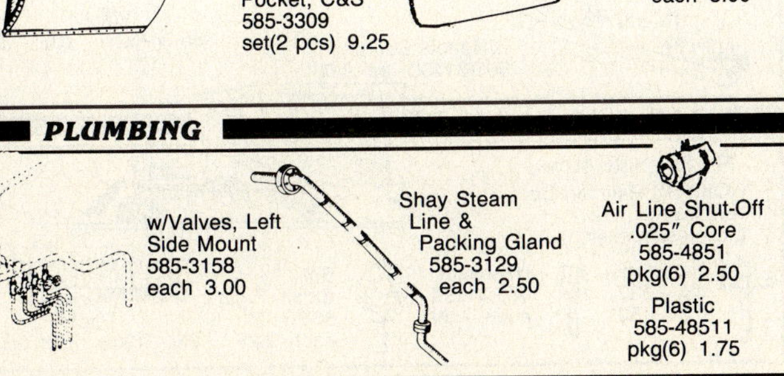

w/Valves, Left Side Mount
585-3158
each 3.00

Shay Steam Line & Packing Gland
585-3129
each 2.50

Air Line Shut-Off .025" Core
585-4851
pkg(6) 2.50

Plastic
585-48511
pkg(6) 1.75

PLUMBING (continued)

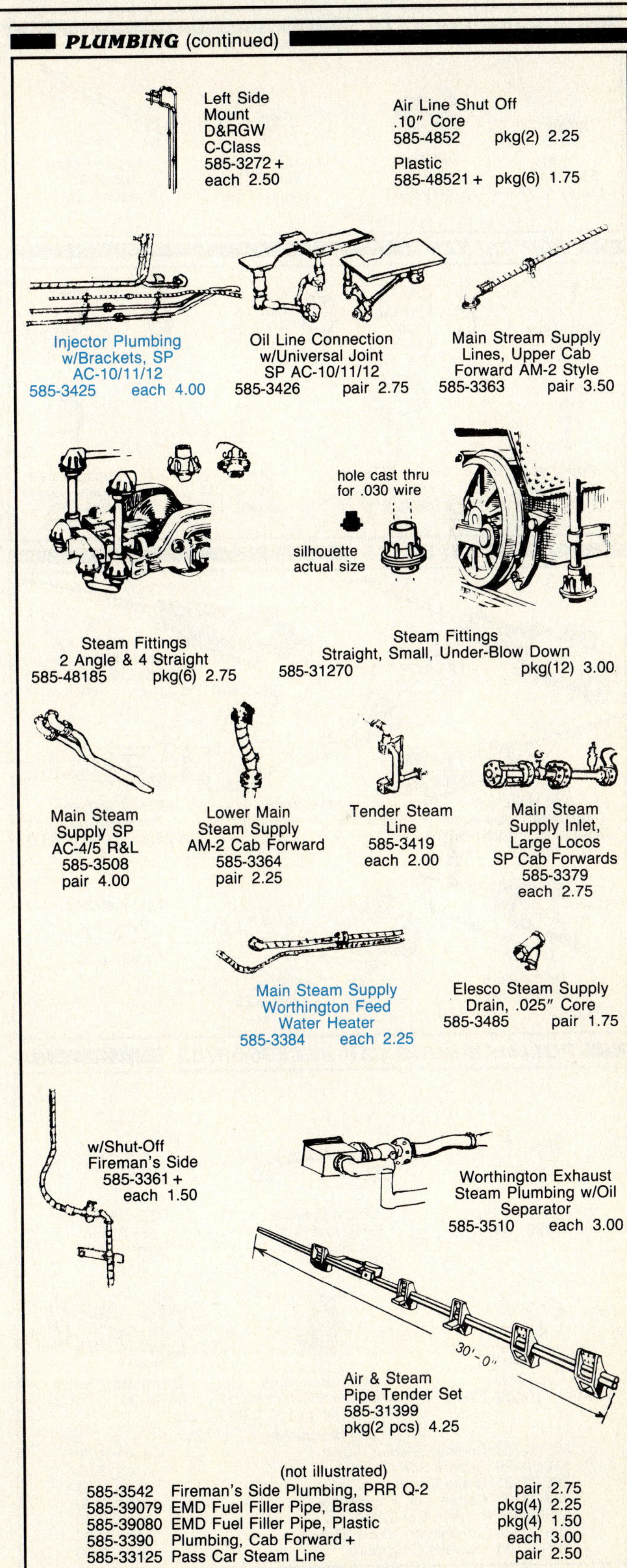

Left Side Mount D&RGW C-Class
585-3272 +
each 2.50

Air Line Shut Off .10" Core
585-4852   pkg(2) 2.25

Plastic
585-48521 + pkg(6) 1.75

Injector Plumbing w/Brackets, SP AC-10/11/12
585-3425   each 4.00

Oil Line Connection w/Universal Joint SP AC-10/11/12
585-3426   pair 2.75

Main Stream Supply Lines, Upper Cab Forward AM-2 Style
585-3363   pair 3.50

hole cast thru for .030 wire

silhouette actual size

Steam Fittings 2 Angle & 4 Straight
585-48185   pkg(6) 2.75

Steam Fittings Straight, Small, Under-Blow Down
585-31270   pkg(12) 3.00

Main Steam Supply SP AC-4/5 R&L
585-3508
pair 4.00

Lower Main Steam Supply AM-2 Cab Forward
585-3364
pair 2.25

Tender Steam Line
585-3419
each 2.00

Main Steam Supply Inlet, Large Locos SP Cab Forwards
585-3379
each 2.75

Main Steam Supply Worthington Feed Water Heater
585-3384   each 2.25

Elesco Steam Supply Drain, .025" Core
585-3485   pair 1.75

w/Shut-Off Fireman's Side
585-3361 +
each 1.50

Worthington Exhaust Steam Plumbing w/Oil Separator
585-3510   each 3.00

30'-0"

Air & Steam Pipe Tender Set
585-31399
pkg(2 pcs) 4.25

	(not illustrated)	
585-3542	Fireman's Side Plumbing, PRR Q-2	pair 2.75
585-39079	EMD Fuel Filler Pipe, Brass	pkg(4) 2.25
585-39080	EMD Fuel Filler Pipe, Plastic	pkg(4) 1.50
585-3390	Plumbing, Cab Forward +	each 3.00
585-33125	Pass Car Steam Line	pair 2.50

 **PRECISION SCALE Co.**

HO SCALE (1/87)

★ Note: Rail bus parts are for a Silverton Northern Rail Bus, a Cadillac powered rail car that operated between Silverton & Eureka, Colorado, during the 1930's. Many of these Rail Bus parts can be used to scratchbuild a "Galloping Goose" — the Rail Bus used by the Rio Grande Southern.

+ (PLUS SIGN) = SPECIAL ORDER ONLY ITEMS

POLING POCKETS

   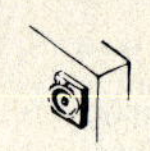 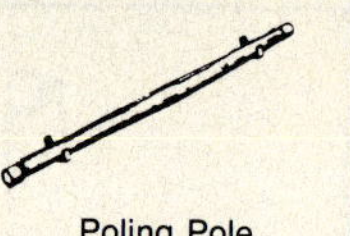

Large 585-3443 pkg(4) 1.50	D&RGW 585-3061 pkg(4) 1.50	Loco End Beams 585-3215 pkg(4) 1.50	Poling Pole 585-31571 each 1.50

POP VALVES

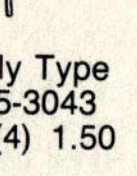 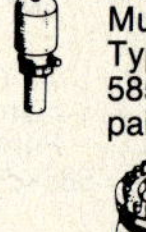  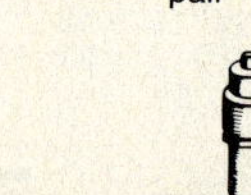

Early Type 585-3043 pkg(4) 1.50	Coal Muffled Type 585-3199 pair 1.75	Coal Muffled 4" Type 585-3294 pair 1.75	Ashton Type, 4" Unmuffled 585-3295 pair 1.75
Pop Valve 585-31396 pkg(4) 1.75	Cluster w/Dome 585-31245 each 2.50	Unmuffled 585-31134 pkg(4) 1.75	Consolidated Modern Steam 585-3200 pair 1.75

POWER REVERSES

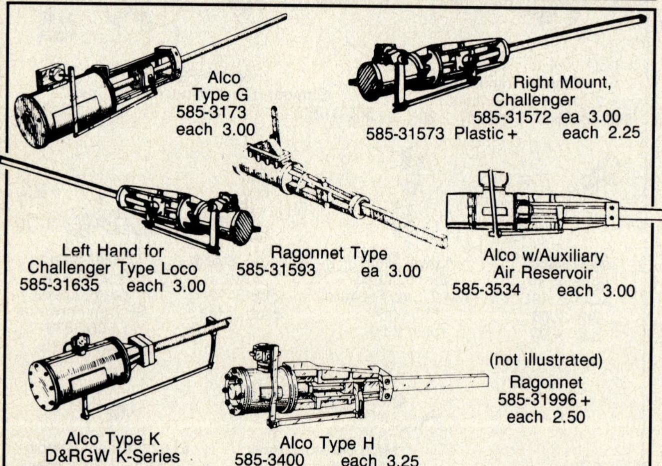

Alco Type G
585-3173
each 3.00

Right Mount, Challenger
585-31572 ea 3.00
585-31573 Plastic +   each 2.25

Left Hand for Challenger Type Loco
585-31635   each 3.00

Ragonnet Type
585-31593   ea 3.00

Alco w/Auxiliary Air Reservoir
585-3534   each 3.00

(not illustrated)
Ragonnet
585-31996 +
each 2.50

Alco Type K
D&RGW K-Series
585-3172 +   each 3.00

Alco Type H
585-3400   each 3.25

PULLMAN-BUDD CAR ACCESSORIES

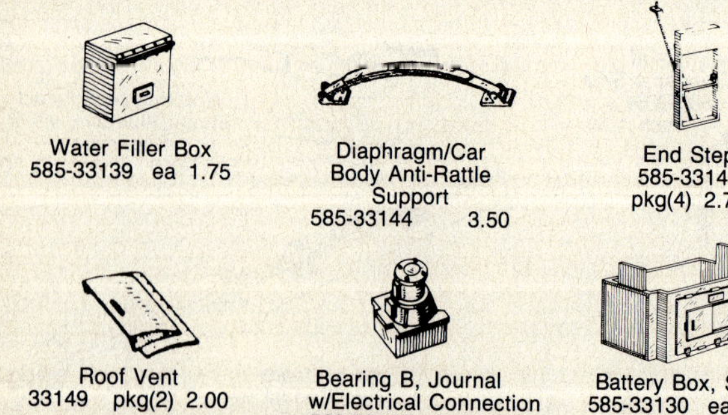

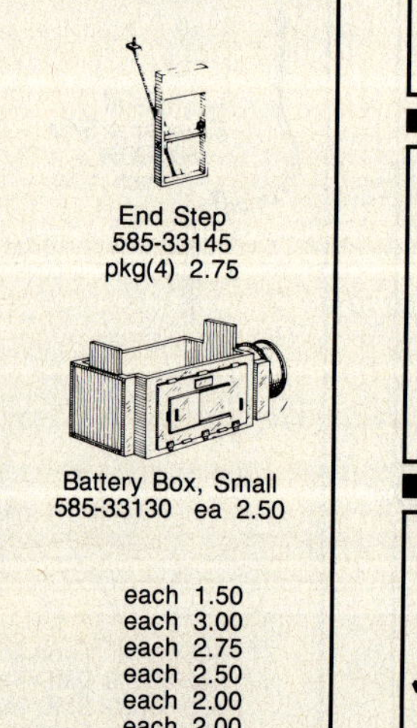

Water Filler Box
585-33139 ea 1.75

Diaphragm/Car Body Anti-Rattle Support
585-33144   3.50

End Step
585-33145
pkg(4) 2.75

Roof Vent
33149   pkg(2) 2.00

Bearing B, Journal w/Electrical Connection
585-33150 pkg(4) 3.00

Battery Box, Small
585-33130 ea 2.50

(not illustrated)

585-33128	Engine Exhaust Piping +	each 1.50
585-33129	Battery Box, Large	each 3.00
585-33131	Brake System	each 2.75
585-33132	Condensor, Frigidaire +	each 2.50
58533133	Pullman Condensor +	each 2.00
585-33134	Condensor w/Fan, Frigidaire	each 2.00
585-33135	Radiator, Frigidaire	each 2.00

PULLMAN-BUDD CAR ACCESSORIES (continued)

585-33136	Radiator, Frigidaire	each 2.00
585-33137	Tool Box +	each 1.75
585-33138	Junction Box +	each 1.75
585-33140	Battery Charge Recepticle +	each 1.75
585-33141	Break Light Indicator Box +	pair 2.00
585-33142	Dehydrator Filter +	pair 2.00
585-33143	Fuel Filler Recepticle Box +	pkg(2) 2.00
585-33146	Compressor w/High & Low	each 2.00
585-33147	Marker Lamp Bracket	pkg(4) 2.00
585-33148	Recepticle, MU, Car Body End	pkg(2) 1.50
585-33150	Bearing A, Journal w/Electrical Connection	pkg(4) 3.00
585-33151	Bearing B, Journal w/Electrical Connection +	pkg(4) 3.00
585-33156	AWPS Water Tank	each 3.00
585-33157	AWPS Water Tank	each 2.00
585-33158	Single-Door Battery Box	each 3.00
585-33159	Single-Door Battery Box, Plastic	each 2.00
585-33160	Double-Door Battery Box	3.50
585-33161	Double-Door Battery Box, Plastic	each 2.25
585-33162	Box, Air Conditioning Compressor	3.00
585-33163	Box, Air Conditioning Compressor, Plastic	3.00
585-33164	Co-2 Tank, Commuter Car	2.00
585-33165	GE Air Conditioning Unit, Diesel	3.00
585-33166	UC Valve, Westinghouse U-12 +	1.75

PUMPS

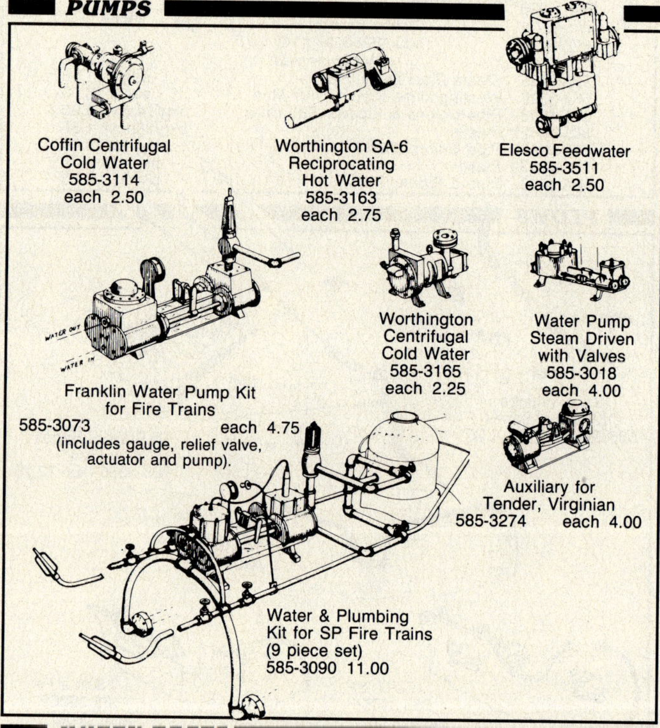

Coffin Centrifugal Cold Water
585-3114
each 2.50

Worthington SA-6 Reciprocating Hot Water
585-3163
each 2.75

Elesco Feedwater
585-3511
each 2.50

Franklin Water Pump Kit for Fire Trains
585-3073   each 4.75
(includes gauge, relief valve, actuator and pump).

Worthington Centrifugal Cold Water
585-3165
each 2.25

Water Pump Steam Driven with Valves
585-3018
each 4.00

Auxiliary for Tender, Virginian
585-3274   each 4.00

Water & Plumbing Kit for SP Fire Trains (9 piece set)
585-3090 11.00

QUEEN POSTS

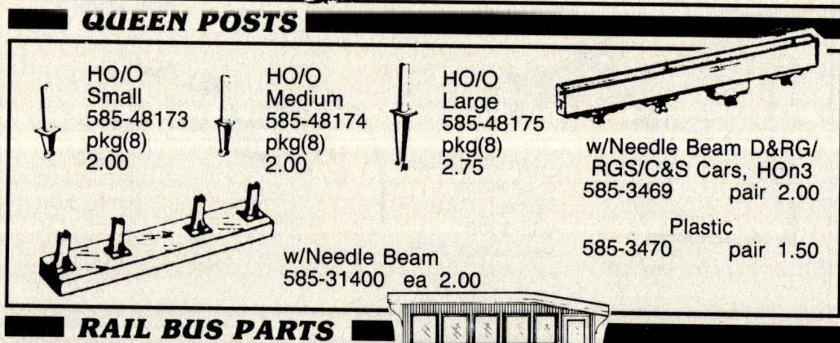

HO/O Small 585-48173 pkg(8) 2.00	HO/O Medium 585-48174 pkg(8) 2.00	HO/O Large 585-48175 pkg(8) 2.75

w/Needle Beam D&RG/RGS/C&S Cars, HOn3
585-3469   pair 2.00

Plastic
585-3470   pair 1.50

w/Needle Beam
585-31400 ea 2.00

RAIL BUS PARTS

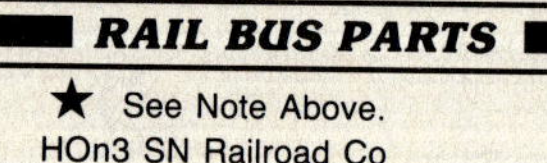

★ See Note Above.
HOn3 SN Railroad Co Rail Bus
(pre-design sketch)

Headlight
585-3832
pair 1.50

Headlight
585-31294
each 1.50

Bell, Small, Rigid
585-31066
each 2.25

Pilot
585-31388 each 3.50

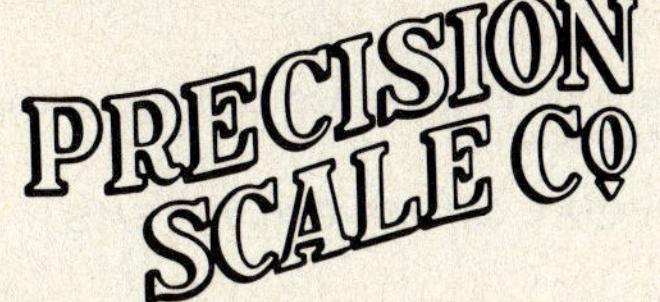

PRECISION SCALE CO

HO SCALE (1/87)

All Precision Scale Company parts are brass castings, unless noted. Illustrations are not to scale.

We have worked closely with this manufacturer to provide accurate availability information at the time this catalog was published. Items listed in *blue ink* may not be available at all times. Please see your dealer for current delivery information   + (PLUS SIGN) = SPECIAL ORDER ONLY ITEMS.

RAILBUS PARTS (continued)

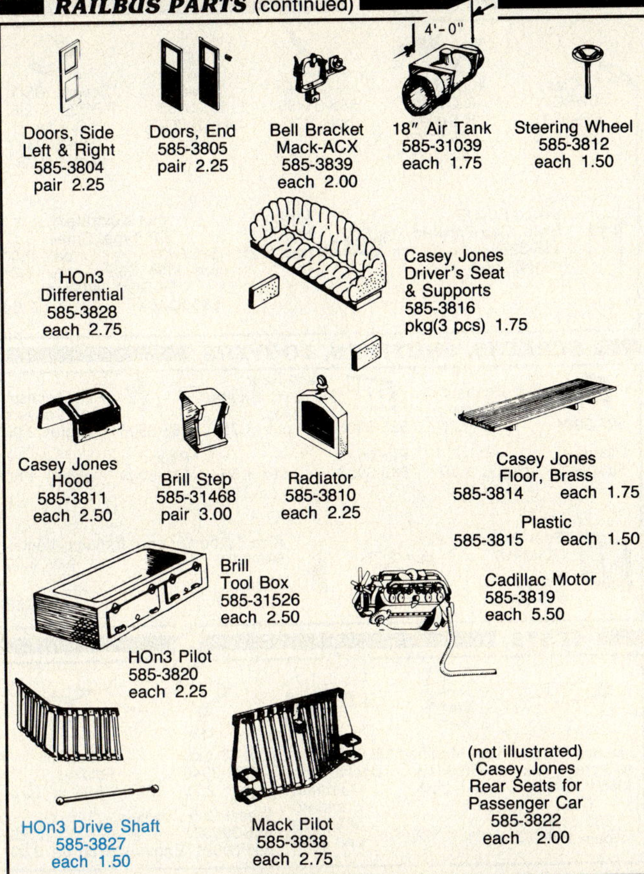

Doors, Side Left & Right
585-3804
pair 2.25

Doors, End
585-3805
pair 2.25

Bell Bracket Mack-ACX
585-3839
each 2.00

18" Air Tank
585-31039
each 1.75

Steering Wheel
585-3812
each 1.50

HOn3 Differential
585-3828
each 2.75

Casey Jones Driver's Seat & Supports
585-3816
pkg(3 pcs) 1.75

Casey Jones Hood
585-3811
each 2.50

Brill Step
585-31468
pair 3.00

Radiator
585-3810
each 2.25

Casey Jones Floor, Brass
585-3814   each 1.75

Plastic
585-3815   each 1.50

Brill Tool Box
585-31526
each 2.50

Cadillac Motor
585-3819
each 5.50

HOn3 Pilot
585-3820
each 2.25

(not illustrated)
Casey Jones Rear Seats for Passenger Car
585-3822
each 2.00

HOn3 Drive Shaft
585-3827
each 1.50

Mack Pilot
585-3838
each 2.75

REGULATORS

585-33169 Type 1, Passenger Car — pkg(4) 2.25
585-33170 Type 1, Passenger Car, Plastic — pkg(4) 1.75
585-33171 Duel Vapor, Type 2 + — pkg(2) 2.50
585-33172 Duel Vapor, Type 2, Plastic — pkg(4) 3.00

RELIEF VALVES

Cylinder, Baldwin Early, 0-6-0
585-3103   pair 2.00

Prime Cylinder Top Mount
585-3418   pkg(4) 2.50

585-32103 Plastic **NEW** pkg(4) 1.75

RERAIL FROGS

2.5mm & 9mm
585-3110
pair 2.25

Plastic
585-31644
pair 1.50

585-31269
pair 2.25

3.5mm x 10.5mm
585-3115
pair 2.25

Plastic
585-32102
NEW pair 1.50

Wedge & Bracket D&RGW Noland Type, Left/Right
585-3204
pkg(8pcs) 3.50

RETAINER VALVES

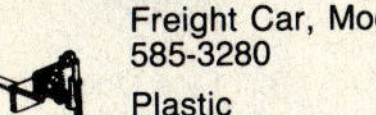

D&RGW Tender
585-3263   pair 1.75

Plastic
585-31796   pkg(4) 1.50

Freight Car, Modern
585-3280   pkg(2) 1.75

Plastic
585-31797   pkg(4) 1.50

(not illustrated)
585-3448 Shay Line Shaft +   pkg(4) 1.50

REVERSE LEVERS

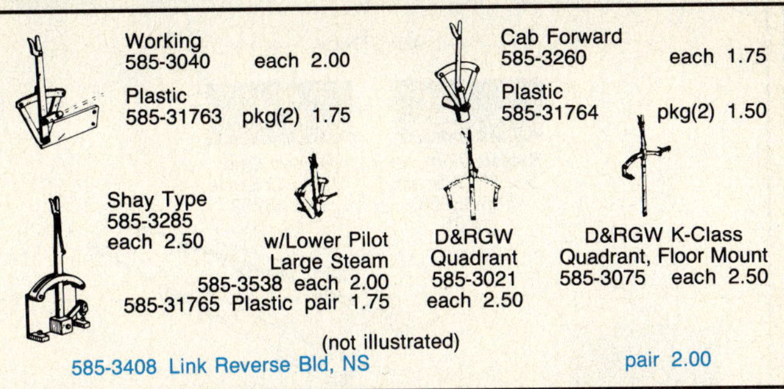

Working
585-3040   each 2.00

Plastic
585-31763   pkg(2) 1.75

Shay Type
585-3285
each 2.50

w/Lower Pilot Large Steam
585-3538 each 2.00
585-31765 Plastic pair 1.75

Cab Forward
585-3260   each 1.75

Plastic
585-31764   pkg(2) 1.50

D&RGW Quadrant
585-3021
each 2.50

D&RGW K-Class Quadrant, Floor Mount
585-3075   each 2.50

(not illustrated)
585-3408 Link Reverse Bld, NS   pair 2.00

RODS

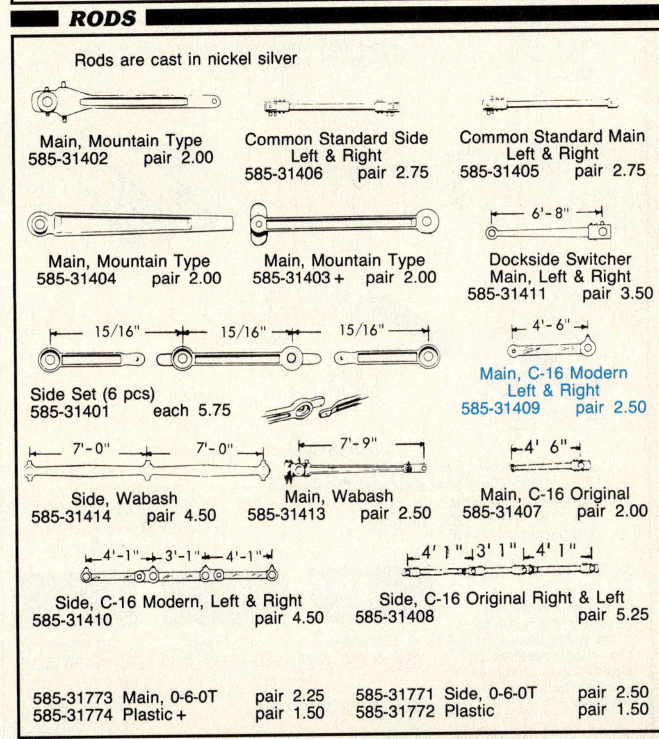

Rods are cast in nickel silver

Main, Mountain Type
585-31402   pair 2.00

Common Standard Side Left & Right
585-31406   pair 2.75

Common Standard Main Left & Right
585-31405   pair 2.75

Main, Mountain Type
585-31404   pair 2.00

Main, Mountain Type
585-31403 + pair 2.00

Dockside Switcher Main, Left & Right
585-31411   pair 3.50

Side Set (6 pcs)
585-31401   each 5.75

Main, C-16 Modern Left & Right
585-31409   pair 2.50

Side, Wabash
585-31414   pair 4.50

Main, Wabash
585-31413   pair 2.50

Main, C-16 Original
585-31407   pair 2.00

Side, C-16 Modern, Left & Right
585-31410   pair 4.50

Side, C-16 Original Right & Left
585-31408   pair 5.25

585-31773 Main, 0-6-0T   pair 2.25
585-31774 Plastic +   pair 1.50

585-31771 Side, 0-6-0T   pair 2.50
585-31772 Plastic   pair 1.50

ROOFS

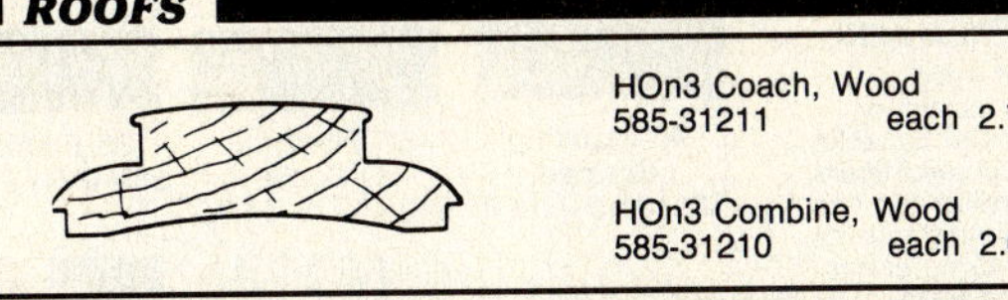

HOn3 Coach, Wood
585-31211   each 2.75

HOn3 Combine, Wood
585-31210   each 2.00

RUNNING BOARDS

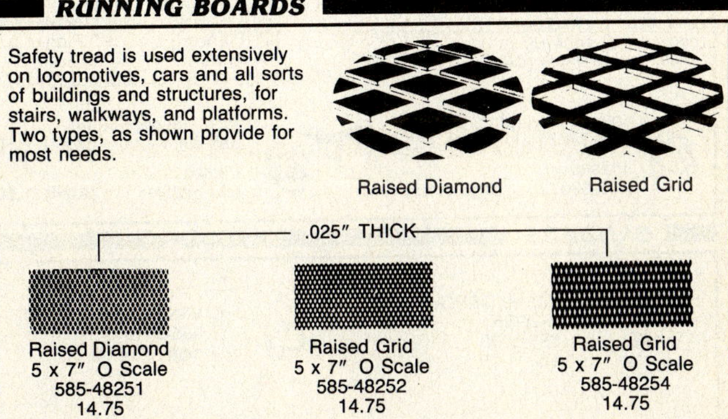

Safety tread is used extensively on locomotives, cars and all sorts of buildings and structures, for stairs, walkways, and platforms. Two types, as shown provide for most needs.

Raised Diamond

Raised Grid

.025" THICK

Raised Diamond 5 x 7" O Scale
585-48251
14.75

Raised Grid 5 x 7" O Scale
585-48252
14.75

Raised Grid 5 x 7" O Scale
585-48254
14.75

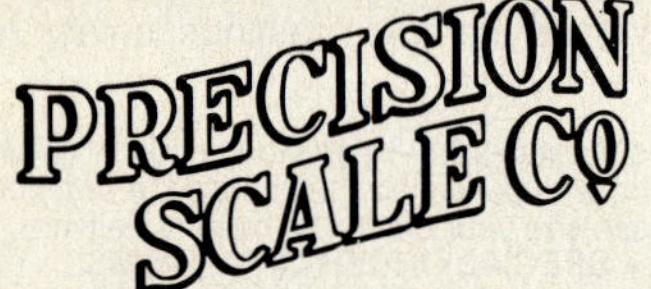

PRECISION SCALE CO.

HO SCALE (1/87)

All Precision Scale Company parts are brass castings, unless noted. Illustrations are not to scale.

+ (PLUS SIGN) = SPECIAL ORDER ONLY ITEMS

RUNNING BOARDS (continued)

.020" THICK

Raised Diamond
5 x 7" O Scale
585-48258
14.75

Raised Grid
5 x 7" O Scale
585-48259
14.75

.012" THICK

Raised Diamond
5 x 7" HO Scale
585-48260
14.75

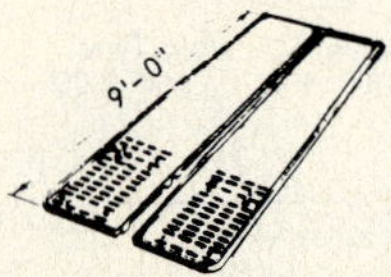

585-31084 Vanderbilt Tender, R&L +   pair 3.00
585-31710 Plastic   pair 1.75

HOn3 Modern C-16
585-31627   pkg(2 pcs) 3.75

Plastic
585-31628   pkg(2 pcs) 2.00

HOn3 Modern C-16
585-31623   pkg(3 pcs) 3.50
Plastic
585-31624 +   pkg(2 pcs) 2.00

(not illustrated)

585-31417 L&R Original C-16   each 3.00
585-31625 HOn3 Modern C-16, No Perforations +   pkg(2 pcs) 3.50
585-31626 Plastic +   pkg(2 pcs) 2.00
585-31621 Plain C-16 Modern   pkg(3 pcs) 3.50
585-31622 Plastic   each 2.00

BRASS WIRE SCREEN

Fine mesh screen is often useful where expanded metal is too large or the wrong texture. Try it for spark arrestors on logging locos or screen doors on buildings. Any mesh 4 x 6".

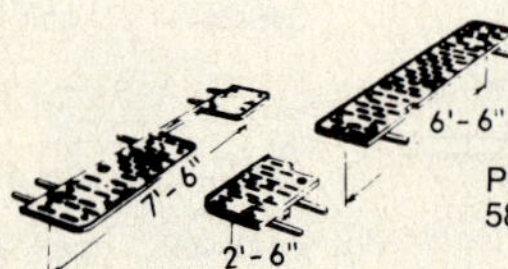

70 Mesh
585-48262 5.15

60 Mesh
585-48117 5.15

80 Mesh
585-48118 5.15

(not illustrated)
585-48119 100 Mesh   5.15

ETCHED PLANKING

6 styles of wood sheathing for use on brass models. Suitable for car sides and floors, building siding and flooring, and such things as fences, packing crates, etc. Can be used in all scales. All planking 5 x 7" and .020" thick. Dimensions are given in HO inches, except where noted.

4" Planking Grained
585-48245 + 14.75

6" Planking O Scale
585-48246 14.75

3" Planking
585-48247 + 14.75

6" Planking Grained
585-48248 14.75

12" Planking w/Grain
585-48249 14.75

12" Planking w/Grain
585-48250 14.75

 Inspection Lights, Brass
585-39071   pkg(4) 2.25

Plastic
585-39072   pkg(6) 1.50

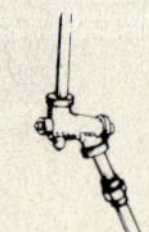 Pyle National Lights
585-3924   pkg(4) 2.50

Plastic
585-3925 +   pkg(4) 1.50

SANDERS

Valves D&RGW K-28/36
585-3083
pair 1.75

Vilco, Small
585-3414
pkg(16) 4.00

SANDERS (continued)

C-Class D&RGW
585-3191
pair 1.75

King Type D&RGW K-Series
585-3177
pair 1.75

Air, R&L
585-31469
pair 2.25

Leach
585-3198
pkg(2) 2.25

Covers, B&O T-31/32, E-2/6, S-1-1a
585-3596
pkg(4) 2.75

Viloco FL-317 Style, Cab Forward
585-3270
pkg(4) 2.50

Viloco
585-3377
pair 2.25

(not illustrated) SP Type, Small
585-3434   pair 2.00
585-3368 C&S   pair 2.25
D&RGW w/Pipes
585-3348 +   2.00

SCREENS, SHUTTERS, LOUVERS

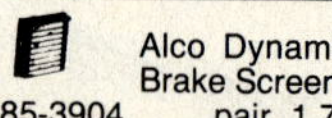

Alco Dynamic Brake Screens
585-3904   pair 1.75
Plastic
585-3905   pkg(2) 1.50

Alco Rear Gravity Shutter Intakes
585-3906   pair 1.75
Plastic
585-3907   pair 1.50

Alco Access Door Louvers
585-3908   pkg(8) 2.00
Plastic
585-3909   pkg(8) 1.50

Rear Radiator, Alco
585-3918   pair 2.75
Plastic
585-3919   pair 1.50

Alco Turbo Charger Exhaust Vents
585-3916   pair 2.00
Plastic
585-3917   pair 1.50

SEATS

Bench Type w/Storage Box Modern Steam Cab
585-3190
pair 2.75

Cab, Modified
585-3413
pair 2.25

Box Type with Backs, SP, UP Common Standard
585-3228
pair 3.00

K-37 Cab
585-3046
pair 2.75

Diesel Cab Auxillary
585-39092   2.25
585-39091 Engineer Cab ea 2.00

Cab Interior Folding
585-3489 +   pr 1.75

SHUT OFF VALVES

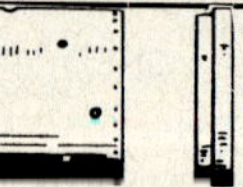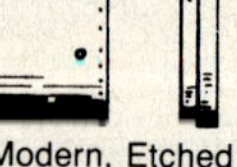

Main Stream Dome
585-3386   ea 1.75

SP Vandy Tender Water
585-31838   each 2.75

Tender, Oil Supply
585-3421   pr 2.75

SMOKEBOXES & FRONTS

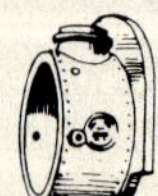

C-16 Modern, Etched Brass, Drilled with Adaptor Ring
585-31422   4.00

Wabash
585-31424 ea 4.00
Plastic
585-31676   2.00

HOn3 C-16 Intermediate
585-31421 3.50

with Stack Base Plastic
585-31674 1.75

Adaptor Ring for #31422
585-31423   each 1.50

with Front Plate for Saddle Tank
585-31420   each 3.50

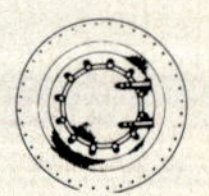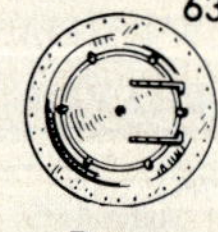

63"

54"

78" Diameter B&O Q-4
585-3072   3.00
Plastic
585-31641
each 1.75

52" C-16 Original & Intermediate
585-31426   3.50
Plastic
585-31679
each 1.50

Betsy
585-31431
each 3.50
Plastic
585-31678
each 1.75

Southern Pacific
585-31429
each 3.50
Plastic
585-31677
each 1.50

HO SCALE (1/87)

All Precision Scale Company parts are brass castings, unless noted. Illustrations are not to scale.

We have worked closely with this manufacturer to provide accurate availability information at the time this catalog was published. Items listed in *blue ink* may not be available at all times. Please see your dealer for current delivery information   + (PLUS SIGN) = SPECIAL ORDER ONLY ITEMS.

SMOKEBOXES & FRONTS (continued)

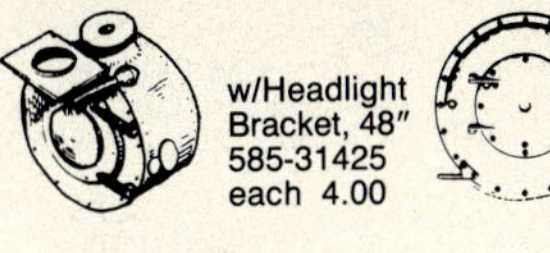
w/Headlight Bracket, 48″
585-31425
each 4.00

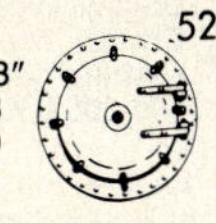
Wabash 63″
585-31433
each 3.50

52″ Plastic
585-31680
each 1.50

Short w/Stackbase
585-31419 +   3.50

Modern C-16
585-31428   3.50

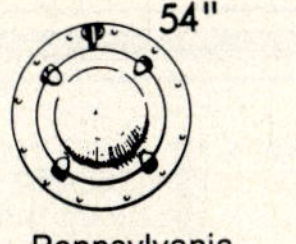
54″
Pennsylvania
585-31430
each 3.50

Plastic
585-31682
each 1.50

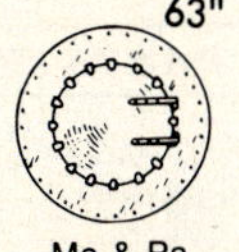
63″
Ma & Pa
585-31432
each 3.50

Plastic
585-31681
each 1.75

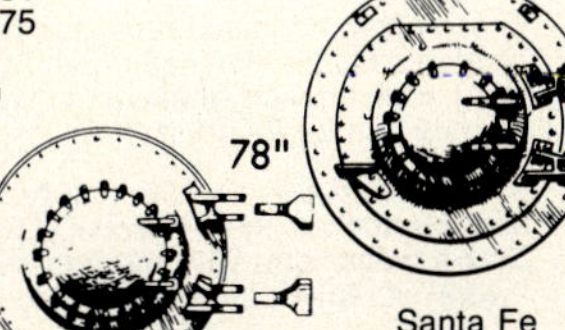
108″
C&O for Articulated Loco
585-31436   3.75

Plastic
585-32134   2.25

96″
NYC Niagara
585-31434 +
each 3.75

78″
w/Working Hinges
585-31437
each 3.50

99″
Santa Fe
585-31435   3.75

Plastic
585-31683
each 2.00

(not illustrated)
585-3015   Dog   pkg(6) 1.75
585-31761 Door Clamps, Plastic   pkg(12) 1.75

SMOKE & EXHAUST STACKS

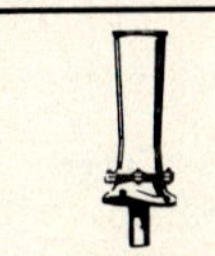

Small Tapered, with Base
585-31447
each 2.50

Double Tapered, with Base
585-31449
each 2.75

Tapered with Base, Wabash
585-31727
each 2.50

Double Taper with Base
585-31448
each 2.50

Straight, Old Style
585-31446
each 2.50

Straight w/Cap
585-31451
each 2.50

D&RGW Stack with Base K-36/37
585-3013
each 2.25

Straight w/Cap
585-31450
each 2.25

D&RGW Stack with Base K-27/28
585-3131
each 2.50

Modern Low Type
585-31452
each 2.50

Cabbage Stack
585-3088
each 3.50

D&RGW Diamond
585-3108
each 2.75

Wood Burning Climax
585-3003
each 3.00

7'5″ Congdon and Base
585-3539
each 4.50

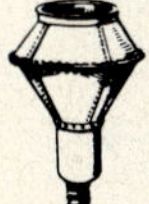

Diamond w/Screw Plug
585-31444
each 3.50

Plastic
585-31684
each 1.75

Logging
585-3591
each 3.00

Modified Straight, w/Cinder Catcher
585-31000
each 2.25

Ridgeway Bear Trap Cinder Catcher
585-3526
each 5.50

SMOKE & EXHAUST STACKS (continued)

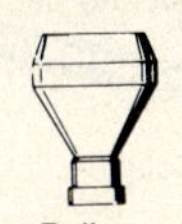
Balloon
585-31445
each 2.25

Ridgeway "Bear Trap" with Shoot Cinder Catcher
585-3455   4.00
Use stock #3131

Diamond, Short
585-31443
each 2.75

Stack Base Only
585-31454
each 1.75

D&RGW for K-28 Modern
585-3402 +
each 2.50

Texas & Pacific
585-3595 +
each 2.50

Modern
585-31453
each 2.75

D&RGW Stack Base
585-3097
each 1.75

SP AC-9
585-3548 +
each 1.75

Small, Early Diamond
585-3598
each 2.50

Western Maryland Shay
585-31821
each 2.50

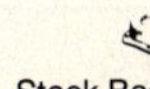
Early SP, 0-6-0/2-6-0 & Atlantics
585-31817
each 2.50

SP AC-4 to 12, Cab Forward
585-3547
each 1.75

Spark Arrestor, Fits Over #3131
585-3522
each 1.75

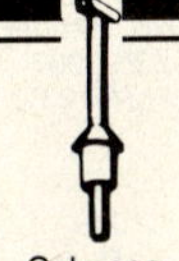
Stack Base, Shay Westside Lumber
585-3121
each 1.75

Auxiliary Base HOn3
585-3581
each 1.50

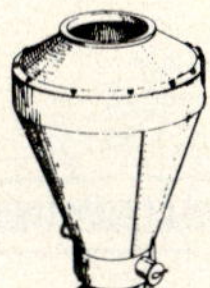
Radley Hunter
585-3516
each 3.50

(not illustrated)
585-39089 Alco   each 1.75
585-39111 Early   pkg(2) 2.00
585-3407   SP Deflector   each 2.50
585-31816 SP, Small, Late   each 2.75
585-3580   7'6″ High, Radley Hunter   each 3.25
585-3599   Large, Early, Diamond   each 2.50
585-3597   Gerlinger Early, Mushroom   ea 2.75

SMOKE JACKS

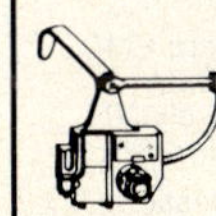

Coach Short
585-31458
pair 1.50

Coach Tall
585-31457
pair 1.50

Caboose
585-31455
each 1.75

Caboose
585-31456
each 1.50

SPEED CONTROL ACTUATORS, INDICATORS & RECORDERS

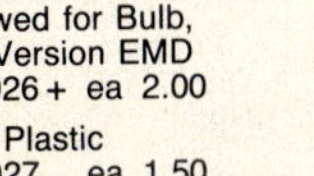
Speed Indicator, Hollowed for Bulb, Late Version EMD
585-3926 + ea 2.00

Plastic
585-3927   ea 1.50

Loco Valve Pilot Cambox w/Bracket
585-3499   ea 2.25

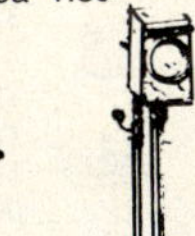
Speed Recorder CP Railway
585-3235
each 2.50

Speed Recorder w/Pick-up & Bracket Pennsy Q-2 Lead Truck
585-3540   ea 2.75

Speed Recorder Loco Valve Pilot Cab Mount
585-3498   ea 2.50
use with #3499

PRECISION SCALE Co.

HO SCALE (1/87)

All Precision Scale Company parts are brass castings, unless noted. Illustrations are not to scale.

We have worked closely with this manufacturer to provide accurate availability information at the time this catalog was published. Items listed in *blue ink* may not be available at all times. Please see your dealer for current delivery information   + (PLUS SIGN) = SPECIAL ORDER ONLY ITEMS.

SPRINGS

Springs for trucks and draft gear. Some are O Scale springs, but may be used for HO Scale.

For 14 Wheel Tender
585-31438
pkg(10) 2.75

Coil, Tender Truck
585-168
pkg(10) 2.25

Flex-Coupling
585-48244   each 1.75
for 3/32" shaft

Loco
585-31577
pkg(4) 3.00

Loco
585-31439
pkg(4) 3.25

Loco, Plastic
585-31440
pkg(4) 1.75

Loco, Plastic
585-31578   pkg(4) 2.25

D&RGW Driver
585-3167   pkg(8) 2.75

Truck, DG
585-31441
pkg(12) 2.00

Bolster
585-350
pkg(12) 2.00

Kingpin
585-160
pkg(6) 2.50

Journal Oversize
585-8054
pkg(4) 1.50

Truck
585-352
pkg(12) 2.25

Driver, Large
585-382
pkg(12) 2.50

585-356
pkg(12) 2.00

Driver, Small
585-381
pkg(12) 2.50

Journal Undersize
585-44
pkg(4) 1.75

STACKS — DIESEL EXHAUST

Stack Base w/Lift Rings, EMD
585-3979   3.00
585-3980 Plastic   2.00

Late EMD Hood Mount
585-3977   2.25
585-3978 Plastic   1.50

Tall Alco
585-39022
each 2.25

Short
585-39023
each 2.25

for GP-7
585-39024
each 1.50

STEPS

Loco Boiler "Down" Mount
585-3208
pkg(4) 2.00

Loco Boiler "Up" Mount
585-3207
pkg(4) 2.00

Boiler "Up" Small
585-3301
pkg(6) 2.00
Plastic
585-32034   pkg(7) 1.50

Boiler Modern Cast Steel
585-3452
pkg(4) 1.75

Cab, C-16 Original
585-31147
pair 1.75

Shay
585-3125
pair 2.25

Running Board
585-31460
pair 1.75

Tender
585-31461
pkg(4) 4.00

Tender, C-16 Intermediate
585-31465
pkg(4) 1.75
Plastic
585-31705 +
pkg(6) 1.50

C-16 Modern Tender
585-31466
pkg(4) 1.75
Plastic
585-31706
pkg(6) 1.50

EMD GP-7 & GP-9
585-39017
pair 2.00
Plastic
585-39018
pair 1.75

Modern EMD Drop
585-39020
pair 2.00
Plastic
585-39021
pair 1.50

Wabash
585-31463
pair 3.50

Tender
585-31462
pkg(4) 3.50

Tender Tank
585-31464
pkg(4) 2.50

Alco
585-3949   pkg(4) 2.50
Plastic
585-3950   pkg(4) 1.75
4 Short, 2 Long
585-31467   pkg(6) 2.25

(not illustrated)
585-31002 Passenger Car, End Mount   pkg(4) 1.75
585-33188 Wide, Harriman   pkg(4) 3.00
585-33189 Narrow, Harriman   pkg(4) 2.75
585-33192 Corner, Harriman   pkg(4) 2.75
585-33239 Pullman Passenger   pkg(4) 4.25

STOKERS

Duplex Type w/Elevators, Stoker Control, Pressure Gauge, Piping, Overfire Jets & Control Valves
585-3059 Kit   6.75

End Detail for Back of Locomotive
585-3220   1.75

(not illustrated)
585-31995 Engine, Simplex +   each 2.25
585-3766 Duplex Stoker, D-1 +   each 11.00

SWITCH MACHINE PARTS

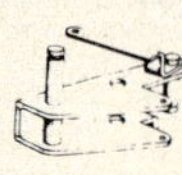

Dual Contact w/Silver Contact Points
585-253   3.00
for #250 KTM

Bell Crank & Pivot
585-422
each 1.75
for #250 KTM

Cam Spring
585-252
each 1.50
for #250 KTM

TENDERS & PARTS

These photo engraved brass tender parts are for the modeler who likes to scratch-build his own equipment. Supplied "in the flat", they require trimming, forming, and whatever drilling, etc. is necessary. Castings for these tenders can be found in these pages.

If you have never tried forming brass, try this: Heat the brass with a torch until it is dull red, then let it cool. It will be dead soft and can be easily formed over a wood form with the fingers. Brass tends to harden again as you "work" it, so you may be able to anneal it more than once.

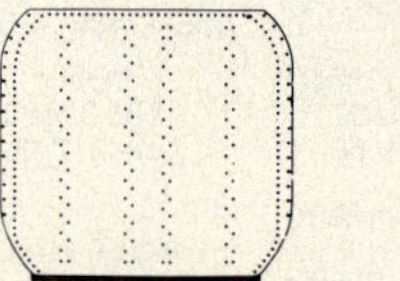

Rear End, Alco
585-31490   2.75
for #1700

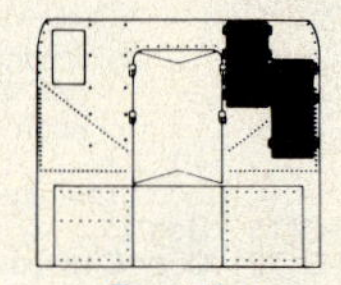

Front End
585-31489   2.00
for #1700

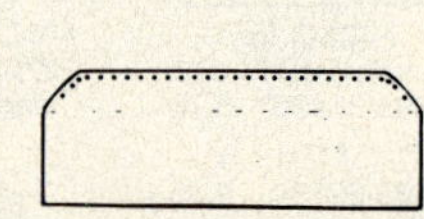

Coal Bunker Front
585-31492   1.75
for #1700

(not illustrated)
585-3656 Shay Bunker HOn3 Tender +   16.00

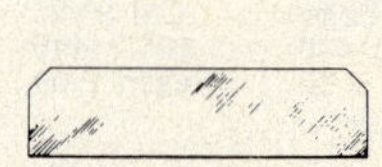

Front Bulkhead, Coal Bunker
585-31486 +   1.50

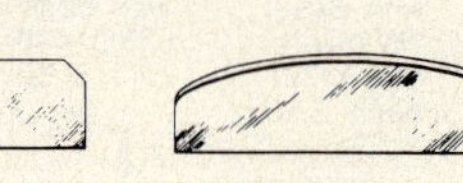

Rear Bulkhead, Coal Bunker
585-31485   1.50

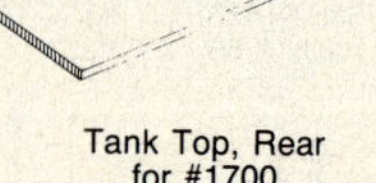

Tank Top, Rear for #1700
585-31494   2.25

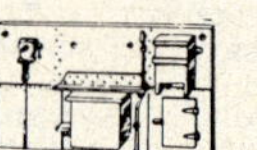

Oil Tank Front
585-31510   2.50
Plastic
585-31708   ea 1.75

Vanderbilt Oil Tank Top
585-31509   4.00
Plastic
585-31707   ea 2.00

Tank Front
585-31511 +   ea 1.75

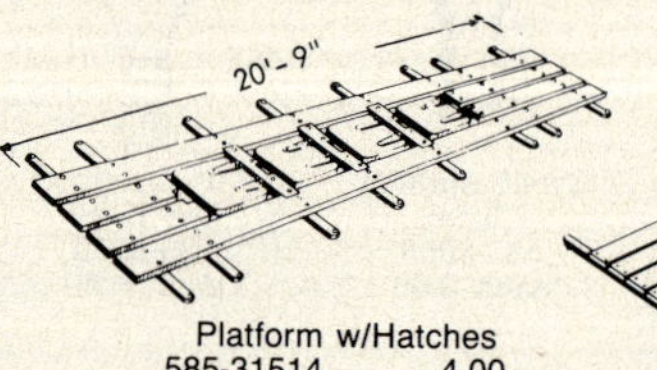

Platform w/Hatches
585-31514   4.00
Plastic
585-31709 +   1.75

HOn3 Platform with Manhole Covers for SP Wagon Top Tender
585-31518   each 7.50

Etched Side Boards Coal Bunker
585-31484   pair 1.50

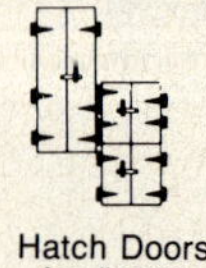

Hatch Doors for #1700
585-31502   pr 1.50

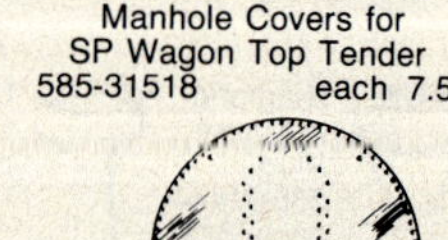

HOn3 End SP
585-31505   pair 2.25

PRECISION SCALE Co.

HO SCALE (1/87)

All Precision Scale Company parts are brass castings, unless noted. Illustrations are not to scale.

We have worked closely with this manufacturer to provide accurate availability information at the time this catalog was published. Items listed in *blue ink* may not be available at all times. Please see your dealer for current delivery information   + (PLUS SIGN) = SPECIAL ORDER ONLY ITEMS.

TENDERS & PARTS (continued)

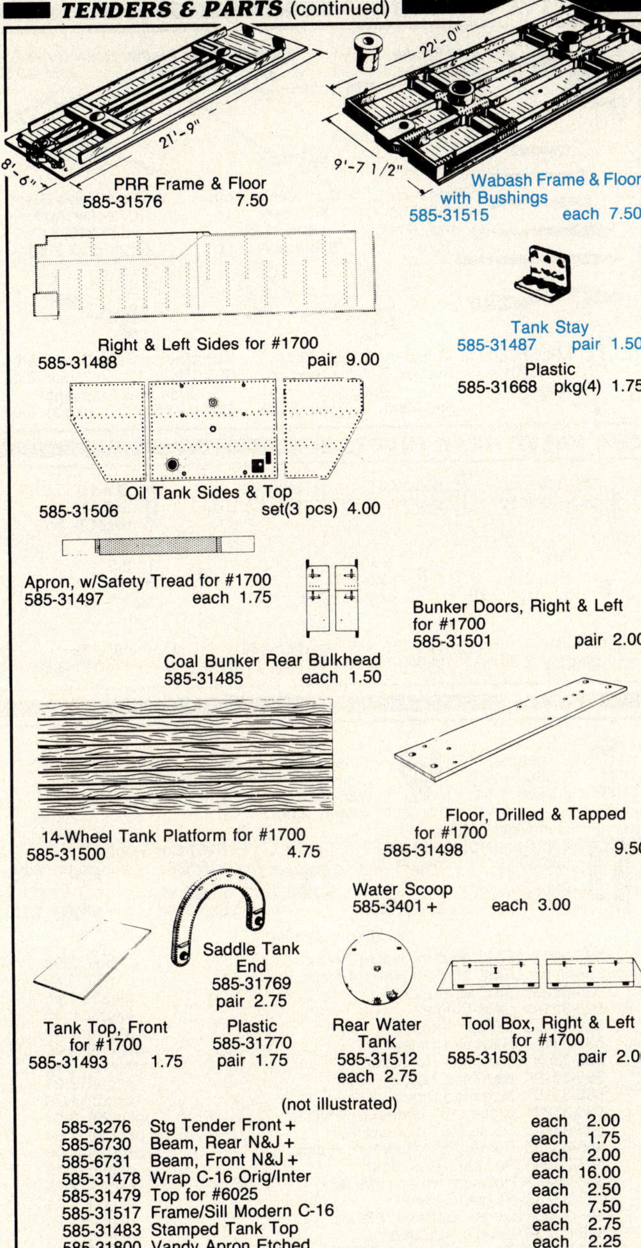

PRR Frame & Floor
585-31576   7.50

Wabash Frame & Floor with Bushings
585-31515   each 7.50

Tank Stay
585-31487   pair 1.50

Plastic
585-31668   pkg(4) 1.75

Right & Left Sides for #1700
585-31488   pair 9.00

Oil Tank Sides & Top
585-31506   set(3 pcs) 4.00

Apron, w/Safety Tread for #1700
585-31497   each 1.75

Bunker Doors, Right & Left for #1700
585-31501   pair 2.00

Coal Bunker Rear Bulkhead
585-31485   each 1.50

14-Wheel Tank Platform for #1700
585-31500   4.75

Floor, Drilled & Tapped for #1700
585-31498   9.50

Water Scoop
585-3401 +   each 3.00

Saddle Tank End
585-31769
pair 2.75

Tank Top, Front for #1700
585-31493   1.75

Plastic
585-31770
pair 1.75

Rear Water Tank
585-31512
each 2.75

Tool Box, Right & Left for #1700
585-31503   pair 2.00

(not illustrated)

585-3276	Stg Tender Front +	each	2.00
585-6730	Beam, Rear N&J +	each	1.75
585-6731	Beam, Front N&J +	each	2.00
585-31478	Wrap C-16 Orig/Inter	each	16.00
585-31479	Top for #6025	each	2.50
585-31517	Frame/Sill Modern C-16	each	7.50
585-31483	Stamped Tank Top	each	2.75
585-31800	Vandy Apron Etched	each	2.25

THROTTLES

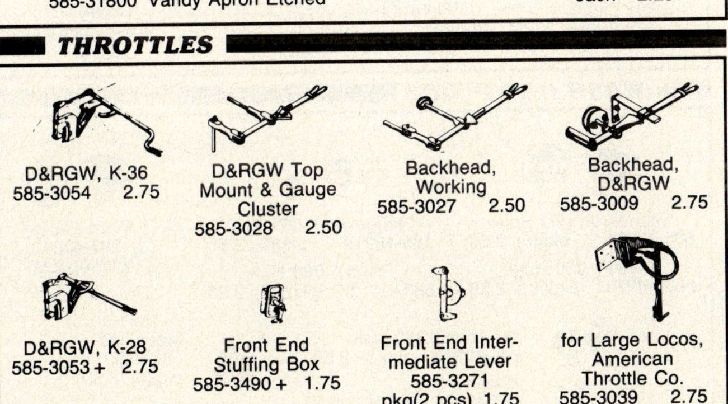

D&RGW, K-36
585-3054   2.75

D&RGW Top Mount & Gauge Cluster
585-3028   2.50

Backhead, Working
585-3027   2.50

Backhead, D&RGW
585-3009   2.75

D&RGW, K-28
585-3053 +   2.75

Front End Stuffing Box
585-3490 +   1.75

Front End Intermediate Lever
585-3271
pkg(2 pcs) 1.75

for Large Locos, American Throttle Co.
585-3039   2.75

THROTTLES (continued)

Overhead
585-3411 +
ea 2.75

Front End
585-3444 +
pkg(2) 1.50

General Purpose Backhead
585-3062
each 2.50

Chamber's Backhead, Large Loco
585-3058
each 2.75

Top Mount with Lamp & Gauges, D&RGW
585-3310   2.75

Overhead, SP Cab Forward
585-3225
2.75

Overhead, American Style
585-3180
2.75

Front End
585-3243
set 2.75

Front End Intermediate Lever, Cab Forward
585-3385   1.75

Front End w/Intermediate Lever, Baldwin
585-3311   pkg(2 pcs) 2.25

TOOL BOXES

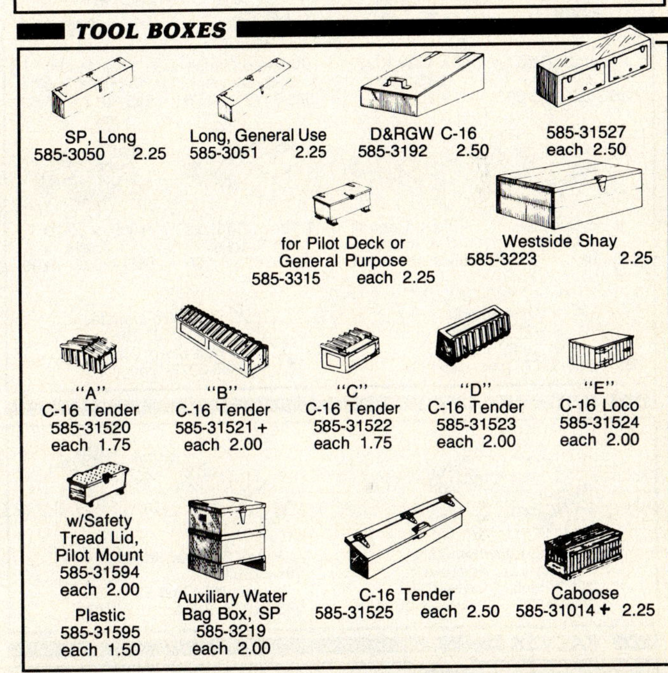

SP, Long
585-3050   2.25

Long, General Use
585-3051   2.25

D&RGW C-16
585-3192   2.50

585-31527
each 2.50

for Pilot Deck or General Purpose
585-3315   each 2.25

Westside Shay
585-3223   2.25

"A" C-16 Tender
585-31520
each 1.75

"B" C-16 Tender
585-31521 +
each 2.00

"C" C-16 Tender
585-31522
each 1.75

"D" C-16 Tender
585-31523
each 2.00

"E" C-16 Loco
585-31524
each 2.00

w/Safety Tread Lid, Pilot Mount
585-31594
each 2.00

Plastic
585-31595
each 1.50

Auxiliary Water Bag Box, SP
585-3219
each 2.00

C-16 Tender
585-31525   each 2.50

Caboose
585-31014 + 2.25

TRACKSIDE DETAILS

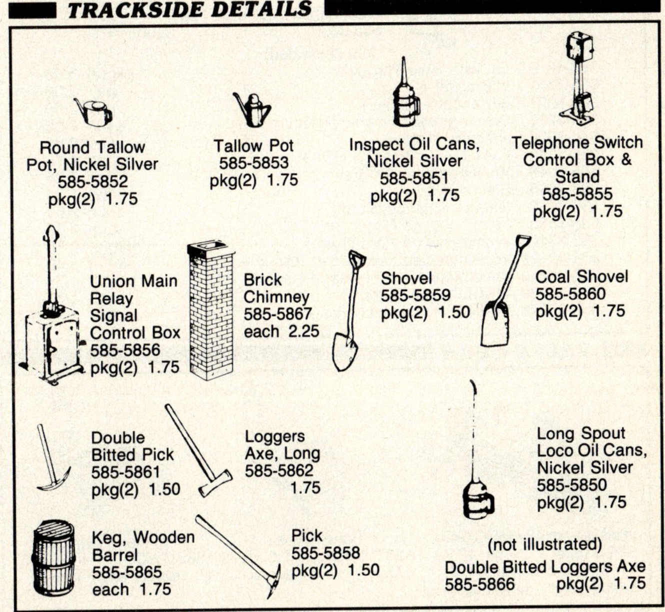

Round Tallow Pot, Nickel Silver
585-5852
pkg(2) 1.75

Tallow Pot
585-5853
pkg(2) 1.75

Inspect Oil Cans, Nickel Silver
585-5851
pkg(2) 1.75

Telephone Switch Control Box & Stand
585-5855
pkg(2) 1.75

Union Main Relay Signal Control Box
585-5856
pkg(2) 1.75

Brick Chimney
585-5867
each 2.25

Shovel
585-5859
pkg(2) 1.50

Coal Shovel
585-5860
pkg(2) 1.75

Double Bitted Pick
585-5861
pkg(2) 1.50

Loggers Axe, Long
585-5862
1.75

Long Spout Loco Oil Cans, Nickel Silver
585-5850
pkg(2) 1.75

Keg, Wooden Barrel
585-5865
each 1.75

Pick
585-5858
pkg(2) 1.50

(not illustrated)
Double Bitted Loggers Axe
585-5866   pkg(2) 1.75

PRECISION SCALE CO.

HO SCALE (1/87)

All Precision Scale Company parts are brass castings, unless noted. Illustrations are not to scale.

We have worked closely with this manufacturer to provide accurate availability information at the time this catalog was published. Items listed in *blue ink* may not be available at all times. Please see your dealer for current delivery information + (PLUS SIGN) = SPECIAL ORDER ONLY ITEMS.

TRACTION PARTS

Anti-Climber
585-31562
each 2.00

Trolley Pole Bushing, Delrin
585-31566
pkg(4) 2.00

Pilot Traction
585-31392   each 2.75

(not illustrated)

585-39012	Motor Access Cover, Brass	2.75
585-39013	Motor Access Cover, Plastic	2.00
585-48243	Coil Spring, Trolley	pkg(12) 2.75

TURRETS

Fountain Type D&RGW
585-3020 +   3.25

D&RGW K-28
585-3098
each 2.75

Standard Gauge Locomotives
585-3118   2.75

Top Mount D&RGW K-37
585-3017 +   3.50

K-36 Outside Top Mount
585-3081   2.75

4-Valve Control, Cab Interior
585-3518   3.00

6 Turret Controls on Bracket
585-3341   3.00

4-Valve 50-70 T Shays
585-3284   3.00

Valve Handle 5-1/2″ Diameter with Long Stem
585-3277 pair 1.75

Valve Handle, 3-15/16″ Dia with Short Stem
585-3278 pair 1.75

UNDERFRAME

HOn3 Caboose C&S 4-Wheel w/Pedestals & 26″ Wheels, 9″ Wheelbase
585-31569   each 9.00

HOn3 Box Car, Plastic
585-31567   2.50
Use #654 End Sill
585-31032 Brass   9.75

VALVES

Westinghouse Double Feed
585-3330   2.50

(not illustrated)

585-48197	GL with Hole Through	pkg(3) 3.00
585-3231	w/Bracket +	pair 2.00
585-3321	w/Hancock Elbow +	pair 2.00
585-3236	Westinghouse Double Pressure Feed +	each 2.25
585-3326	w/Nathan Elbow	pair 2.00
585-3340	Cylinder C-18/19/21, HOn3	pair 1.75
585-3446	Westinghouse Air Brake	pair 2.25
585-3513	Elesco Inlet +	pkg(2) 1.75
585-3550	Nathan Balance Starter +	each 2.00
585-3563	Westinghouse Reservoir	each 2.00
585-33198	Westinghouse Passenger +	pkg(2) 2.50
585-33199	Westinghouse Passenger, Plastic +	pkg(4) 2.50
585-33200	Westinghouse Universal, Plastic +	pkg(2) 1.75
585-33270	WABLO Passenger	each 1.75
585-33271	WABLO Passenger, Plastic +	pair 1.75

VALVE GEAR

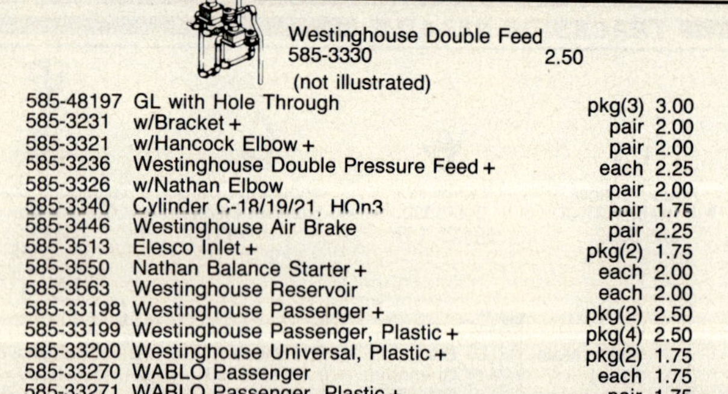

Walschaerts, for MDC 0-6-0
585-31528   kit 12.75
Use with 6 cylinder, cyliner block not included.

Baker Type 1
585-31529   kit 15.25
Use on passenger locos.

Baker Type 2
585-31530   kit 15.25
Use on freight locos.

VALVE GEAR PARTS

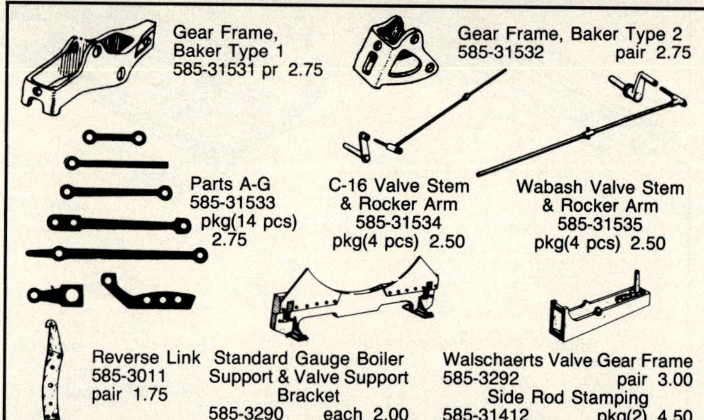

Gear Frame, Baker Type 1
585-31531 pr 2.75

Gear Frame, Baker Type 2
585-31532   pair 2.75

Parts A-G
585-31533
pkg(14 pcs)
2.75

C-16 Valve Stem & Rocker Arm
585-31534
pkg(4 pcs) 2.50

Wabash Valve Stem & Rocker Arm
585-31535
pkg(4 pcs) 2.50

Reverse Link
585-3011
pair 1.75

Standard Gauge Boiler Support & Valve Support Bracket
585-3290   each 2.00

Walschaerts Valve Gear Frame
585-3292   pair 3.00
Side Rod Stamping
585-31412   pkg(2) 4.50

VALVE GEAR RIVETS

585-140
pkg(12) 3.50

585-141
pkg(12) 3.50

585-142
pkg(12) 3.50

.9 × 3.0
585-316
pkg(12) 2.75

.9 × 1.5
585-313
pkg(12) 2.75

.9 × 2.0
585-314
pkg(12) 2.75

.9 × 2.5
585-315
pkg(12) 2.75

585-318
pkg(12) 2.75

585-137
pkg(12) 3.50

585-138
pkg(12) 3.50

585-139
pkg(12) 3.50

VENTS

Breather
585-31459
each 1.50

Coach Roof D&RGW
585-3268
pkg(4) 2.00

Coach
585-31570
pkg(12) 2.25

Cab Side, EMD & 2nd Generation Diesels
585-3993   pkg(8) 3.50
Plastic
585-3994   pkg(8) 2.25

EMD Cab Roof
585-3981   pkg(4) 2.25
Plastic
585-3982   pkg(4) 1.50

(not illustrated)

585-3983	EMD Modern Hood, Brass	pair 2.00
585-3984	EMD Modern Hood, Plastic	pair 1.50
585-39088	Alco Mushroom	pkg(3) 1.75
585-33182	Gold Dinner	pkg(3) 2.50
585-33183	w/Wind Vane	pkg(3) 2.50
585-33186	Harriman Utility	pkg(10) 3.00
585-33187	Harriman Recessed	pkg(10) 2.75
585-33190	Harriman Toilet	pkg(4) 2.25
585-33191	Harriman Stove	pkg(2) 1.75
585-33201	Globe (15″ diameter), Plastic	pkg(20) 3.00
585-33202	Dome (15″ diameter) +	pkg(10) 2.50
585-33203	Dome (15″ diameter), Plastic	pkg(20) 3.00
585-33235	Pullman Passenger	pkg(4) 2.75
585-33253	Pullman, w/Fan, Plastic	pkg(4) 1.75
585-33236	Single, Garland	pkg(6) 2.75
585-33256	Single, Garland, Plastic	pkg(4) 1.75
585-33237	Double, Garland	pkg(6) 2.75
585-33254	Double, Garland, Plastic	pkg(4) 1.75
585-33238	Triple, Garland	pkg(6) 3.00
585-33255	Triple, Garland, Plastic	pkg(4) 1.75

WASH OUT PLUGS

Standard, .080 Hole
585-48201   pkg(6) 2.50
Plastic .080 Hole
585-48273   pkg(12) 2.25

Flangeless, .060 Hole
585-48214   pkg(6) 2.50
Plastic .060 Hole
585-48275   pkg(12) 2.25

Wide Flange
585-48202
pkg(6) 2.50

w/Flange, .060 Hole
585-48213   pkg(6) 2.50
Plastic
585-48274   pkg(12) 2.25

Machined
585-4833
pkg(6) 2.50

PRECISION SCALE Co

HO SCALE
All Precision Scale Company parts are brass castings, unless noted. Illustrations are not to scale.

■ WATER GLASSES ■

585-3019 sight Type	each	2.50
585-3112 Water Gauge	each	2.50

■ WATER VALVES ■

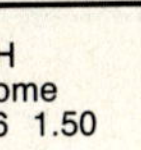

585-31519 Tender	pair 1.75	585-3029	D&RGW Tender	pair	2.00
585-31703 Plastic	pkg(4) 1.50		(not illustrated)		
		585-3267	Westinghouse, Cab	each	2.00

■ WHISTLES ■

Wabsh RH Mount, Dome
585-31346 1.50

Pennsy Style
585-3512 1.75

Nathan Chime, Fireman's Side Mount
585-3137 2.25

Top Mount, Early American Steam & Gauge Co
585-3105 2.00

Right Mount Nathan Chime, Engineer's Side Mount
585-3136 2.25

Nathan 5-Chime with Up Lever
585-3156 2.00

Actuator D&RGW Cab
585-3265 2.00

Chime Whistle Kit
585-31344 each 1.50

4-Chime Type
585-31345 each 1.75

Side Mount, Nathan with Valve
585-3113 1.75

Top Mount Baldwin 0-6-0
585-3104 2.00

Nathan Chime
585-3100 2.25

Caboose Handrail Mount with Bracket
585-31762 pair 2.00

Saturated Steam with Access Box, D&RGW M-64
585-3138 + 2.50

Saturated Steam Type On Steam Line
585-3378 2.75

Old Style
585-31604 ea 1.75

Plastic
585-31658 pr 1.50

Modern 5-Chime
585-3140 2.00

5-Chime Nathan Type Side Mount, Up-Lever
585-31824 2.25

CiBolo CroSSinG

HO SCALE
(1/87)

■ PLYWOOD SHEETS ■

231-1010
pkg(12) 1.79
1/2 x 1"

■ ROOF VENTS ■

Vents are cast in white metal.

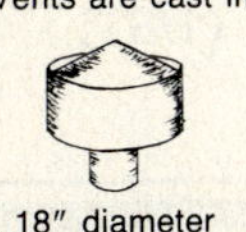
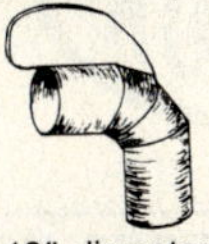

18" diameter
231-240
pkg(5) 1.79

18" diameter
231-244
pkg(3) 1.79
wind vane elbow, mouth into wind

18" diameter
231-243
pkg(3) 1.79
wind vane elbow, mouth downwind

18" diameter
231-242
pkg(4) 1.79
stacked cones

12" diameter
231-241
pkg(5) 1.79

TICHY TRAIN GROUP

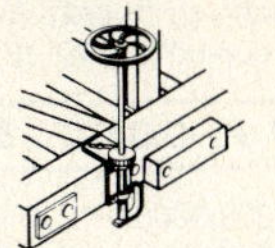

HO SCALE
(1/87)
Precision injection molded impact grade styrene parts.

■ BRAKE DETAILS ■

Brake Wheel & Bracket
293-3003   pkg(4) 1.50
For 1895 to 1920 era flat and gondola cars. Cored for .018 and .020 wire.

293-3005 KC West Brake		2.50
293-3013 AB Brake Set		2.50
293-3034 Split K Brake System		2.50

■ DOORS ■

293-3017 6' Wood Door with Tracks	pair	2.50
293-3018 6' Steel Door with Tracks	pair	2.50

■ GRAB IRONS ■

293-3015 18" Wire Drop	pkg(100)	3.00
293-3021 18" Straight	pkg(100)	3.00
293-3028 Roof Corner	pkg(100)	3.00
293-3053 Wire Straight 24" **NEW**		3.00
293-3054 Curved Wire Caboose **NEW**		3.00

■ MISCELLANEOUS ■

293-3006 Stake Pockets	pkg(32)	1.50
293-3019 U.S.R.A. SS Underframe Kit, Freight Car		3.95
293-3023 Wood Ice Platform	pkg(4)	2.50
293-3029 40' Wood Roofwalk (plastic)		2.00
293-3030 R-40 PFE Reefer Underframe		3.95
293-3033 Freight Car Ladders (assorted)		2.50
293-8001 Open Grate Platform		3.00
293-8002 Safety Cage Ladder/Staircase		3.00
293-8003 Coal Chute		3.00
293-8004 Coal Shed		9.50
293-8005 Hoist House and Sand House		9.50
293-3037 Eyebolts	pkg(80)	3.00
293-7012 100,000 gal. Steel Water Tank		29.50
293-3048 40' Steel Roof Walk		2.00
293-3055 Steeldoor Youngstown 6 x 9 **NEW**		3.00

(not illustrated)

293-8008 Coaling Tower Lift Mechanism		20.00
293-8009 Wood Door	pkg(3)	1.50
293-8010 6 Lite Windows	pkg(6)	1.50
293-8011 Brackets	pkg(8)	1.50
293-8012 Retaining Wall	pkg(3)	1.50
293-8013 Pipe Railings	pkg(4)	1.50

Water Column
293-8006 4.95

Jib Crane
293-8007 5.95

■ STEEL CAR ENDS ■

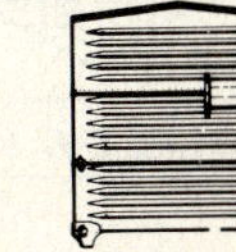

Youngstown Pressed
293-3001   pkg(2) 2.50
For USRA 40 ton Double Sheathed Freight Cars. End has separate order board and Facia strip.

(not illustrated)

293-3020 Youngstown Pressed Single Sheathed Freight Car Ends	pkg(2)	2.50
293-3031 USRA Rebuilt End w/Top Rib		2.50
293-3032 USRA Rebuilt End less Top Rib		2.50

■ STIRRUP STEPS ■

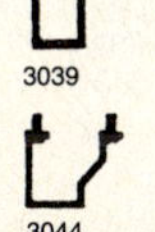
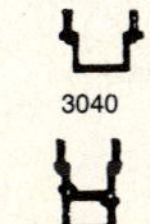

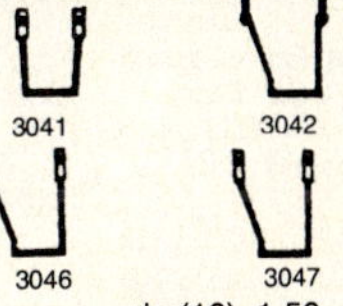

3038 3039 3040 3041 3042
3043 3044 3045 3046 3047

293-3038 Straight Side Mount	pkg(10)	1.50
293-3039 Straight Bottom Mount	pkg(10)	1.50
293-3040 Short Straight Bottom Mount	pkg(10)	1.50
293-3041 Slant Side Mount	pkg(10)	1.50
293-3042 Angled Offset Bottom Mount	pkg(10)	1.50
293-3043 Double Offset Bottom Mount	pkg(10)	1.50
293-3044 Stepped Offset Bottom Mount	pkg(10)	1.50
293-3045 Straight Double Step Side Mount	pkg(10)	1.50
293-3046 Angled Side/Bottom Mount	pkg(10)	1.50
293-3047 Angled Offset Side Mount	pkg(10)	1.50

■ TANK CAR DETAILS ■

293-3007 Tank Car Detail Set		4.95
293-3011 Tank Car Frame		3.95

Q-CAR COMPANY

HO SCALE (1/87)

Parts are cast in white metal, unless noted. Illustrations are not to scale.

CEILING FANS

608-8017	BMT Standard **(By Special Order Only.)**	pkg(6) 3.15
608-8018	IND **(By Special Order Only.)**	pkg(5) 2.90

FLOORS — NEW

608-8005	IND. R4 Metal floor w/motor adaptor	6.90
608-8006	PCC Metal floor	6.90
608-8007	BMT Standard floor w/motor adaptor plate	7.25

INTERIOR SETS

608-8200	BMT Standard	8.20
608-8201	IND R1 (Seats only) **(By Special Order Only.)**	6.35
608-8202	CRT 4000 (Seats only)	6.35
608-8203	Brooklyn PCC (Seats only)	6.70

OVERHEAD WIRE

608-118	Phos Bronze (.018 x 100')	6.45

TROLLEY PARTS

Line Pole Caps Universal Style
608-8022 pkg(12) 3.00

CP27 GE Compressor
608-8027 pkg(3) 1.65

Fuse Box w/Mount
608-8026 pkg(3) .75
(By Special Order Only.)

Wood Meter Box
608-8024 pkg(3) 1.25

Reverser Remote Operated
608-8025 pkg(3) 1.25

15 x 36" Riveted Tank
608-8029 pkg(3) 1.25

MU Control Box (CSL)
608-8023 pkg(3) 2.25

Resistor Bank
608-8030 pkg(3) 1.45

Westinghouse Resistor Bank
608-8016 pkg(3) 1.90

TROLLEY & SUBWAY SEATS/BENCHES

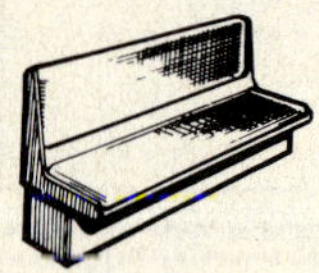

Long Rattan Bench w/Solid Base
608-8011 pkg(6) 2.25

Flop Over Rattan Seat w/Pedestal Base
608-8010 pkg(12) 3.60

PCC/Bus
608-8020 pkg(12) 3.15

IND Double-Sided Short Rattan
608-8019 pkg(6) 2.50

Rattan bench-short
608-8012 pkg(6) 1.60

Long Double-Sided Rattan w/Solid Base
608-8015 pkg(6) 2.50

Short Double-Sided Rattan w/Solid Base
608-8014 pkg(6) 2.50

Single Rattan w/Solid Base
608-8013 pkg(12) 1.90

PCC Motorman's
608-8021 pkg(6) 1.90

MISCELLANEOUS

Brake Cylinder
608-8028 pkg(3) .85

(not illustrated)

608-1	O&HO Illustrated Catalog	11.95
608-2	HO Illustrated Catalog	1.15
608-21	CSL Decal Set	1.75

BRASS CAR SIDES

HO SCALE (1/87)

CAR ENDS

Lead alloy ends for PS/ACF lightweight flat-top cars. Designed for use with brass sides and basic body kit. Included in kit 173-101 (Passenger section).

173-200 Streamlined Car Ends 3.50

BAGGAGE-MAIL DOORS — NEW

Etched brass.

3' 2-Window
173-300
pair 3.75

5' 3-Window
173-301
pair 3.75

HO SCALE (1/87)

Molded plastic structure detail parts.

DOORS

Overhead, 10 x 12'
699-4 pkg(2) 1.25

Hinged Freight, 10 x 9'
699-5 pkg(2) 1.25

699-4   699-5

CON-COR

HO SCALE (1/87)

MISCELLANEOUS

223-70	Buddman Roof Regular	pkg(2) 6.95
223-72	Buddman Roof Dome Regular	pkg(2) 6.95
223-73	Con-Cor Standard Roof (For scratch-building.)	pkg(2) 6.95
223-74	Passenger Car Truck Pin	pkg(8) 1.25

Finishing Touches — SELLEY

HO SCALE (1/87)

Details are unpainted metal castings.
Illustrations are not to scale.

CANS & DRUMS

Milk Cans
675-154
pkg(12) 1.65

Oil Drums
675-151
pkg(12) 1.65

CARTS & TRUCKS

4-Wheel Baggage Truck
675-144   each 1.95

2-Wheel Baggage Truck
675-145   each 1.25

Baggage Cart
675-143   each 1.75

Industrial Trailer
675-148   pkg(2) .95

Hand Truck
675-142   each .95

Stake Trailer
675-149   each 1.20

CRATES, BUCKETS & BARRELS

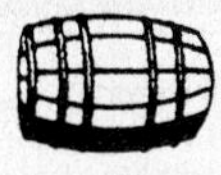

Buckets
675-298
pkg(3) .95

Packing Cases
675-153
pkg(12) 1.65

Beer Kegs
675-299
pkg(12) 1.50

Flour Barrels
675-152
pkg(12) 1.65

(not illustrated)

675-184 Trash Boxes   pkg(2) .95

INTERIORS

Stove, Hod, Shovel
675-646   1.10

Pump & Tub
675-166   .95

675-419 Country Store Set   3.95
Includes: figures, scale, pot belly stove,
pail & shovel, dolly, 2 chairs, barrel,
hatchet and assorted cases.

LUGGAGE

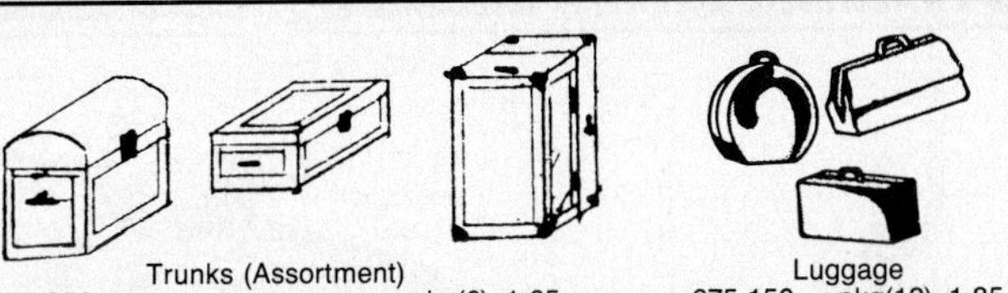

Trunks (Assortment)
675-656   pkg(6) 1.65

Luggage
675-150 pkg(12) 1.85

MAILBOXES

675-173 Letter Boxes   pkg(4) 1.25
675-174 Package Mail Boxes   pkg(3) 1.25
675-235 Rural Mail Boxes   pkg(4) 1.25
675-641 Mail Crane   each 1.50

MISCELLANEOUS

Barricade
675-230   each 1.25

Fire Hose on Rack
675-595   ea .80

Transformer-large
675-257   ea 2.50

MISCELLANEOUS (cont)

Giant Transformer
675-510   ea 3.50

Transformers
675-637   pkg(6) 1.50

Compressor Kit
675-659   ea 1.75

(not illustrated)

675-113 Parking Meters   pkg(12) 1.25
675-172 Fire Alarm Boxes   pkg(4) 1.25
675-180 Fire Hydrants   pkg(12) 1.65
675-283 Hand Car Kit   each 2.75
675-608 Go Devil Kit   each 6.95
675-673 Rowboat   .95
675-679 Vending Machine   1.50
Includes ice, candy, gum and newspaper machines.

PASSENGER CAR WEIGHTS

Flat, cast metal weights for improved rolling performance.

675-703 1/2 oz Athearn   pkg(4) 1.50
675-704 1/2 oz   pkg(4) 1.50
675-705 3/4 oz   pkg(3) 1.50
675-706 1-1/4 oz   pkg(2) 1.50
675-707 1 oz   pkg(2) 1.50

TOOLS

Wheelbarrows
675-1391
pkg(2) .95

Mower & Roller
675-290   each 1.25

Tools (Set of 5)
675-140   1.00

Step Ladder
675-605 ea 1.10

(not illustrated)

675-141 Scales   pkg(2) .95

POLA
Imported from Germany
by WALTHERS

HO SCALE (1/87)

INTERIOR DETAILS

Interior Furniture
578-460   5.99

SCHOOL YARD DETAILS

Playground Equipment
578-461   6.49

Sequoia SCALE MODELS

HO SCALE (1/87)

All items are cast in white metal unless noted. Illustrations are not to scale.

We have worked closely with this manufacturer to provide accurate availability information at the time this catalog was published. Items listed in *blue ink* may not be available at all times. Please see your dealer for current delivery information.

BUMPER & WHEEL STOPS

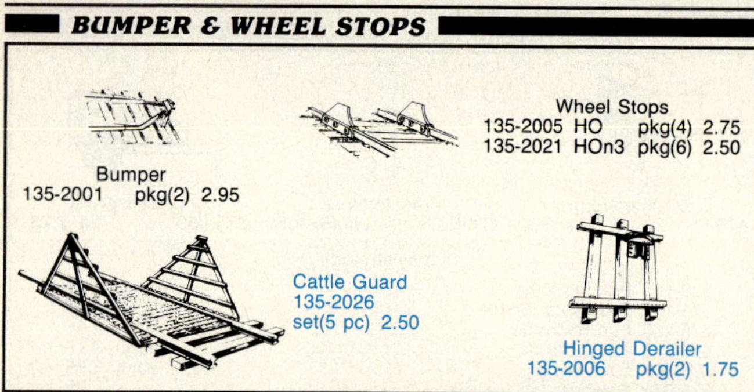

Wheel Stops
135-2005 HO   pkg(4) 2.75
135-2021 HOn3 pkg(6) 2.50

Bumper
135-2001   pkg(2) 2.95

Cattle Guard
135-2026
set(5 pc) 2.50

Hinged Derailer
135-2006   pkg(2) 1.75

CANS & KEGS

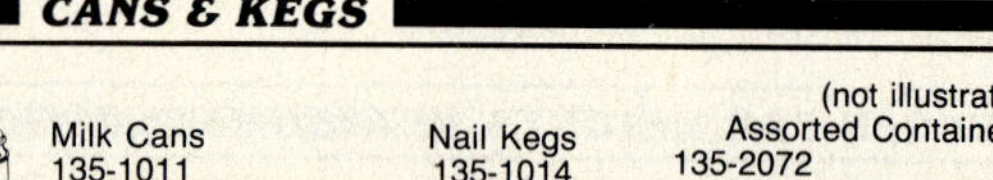

Milk Cans
135-1011
pkg(8) 1.75

Nail Kegs
135-1014
pkg(10) 1.75

(not illustrated)
Assorted Containers, Small
135-2072   pkg(9) 1.75
Garbage Cans
135-2068   pkg(4) 2.25

CHIMNEY & SMOKE STACK

Chimney
135-1007
each 1.75

(not illustrated)
135-2070 Brick Chimney, Small   pkg(2) 1.75
135-2073 Smoke Jack   pkg(2) 1.75

CORBEL & SUPPORTS

■ LTD QTY ■

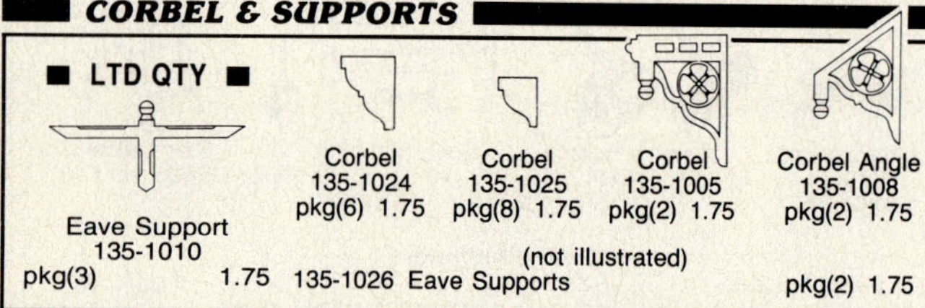

Eave Support
135-1010
pkg(3)   1.75

Corbel
135-1024
pkg(6) 1.75

Corbel
135-1025
pkg(8) 1.75

Corbel
135-1005
pkg(2) 1.75

Corbel Angle
135-1008
pkg(2) 1.75

(not illustrated)
135-1026 Eave Supports   pkg(2) 1.75

DOORS

w/Transom
135-1004
pkg(2) 1.75

Single
135-1020
pkg(2) 1.75

Victorian
135-1015
pkg(2) 1.75

Double
135-1019
pkg(2) 1.75

Door
135-1017
pkg(2) 1.75

LOCO DETAILS

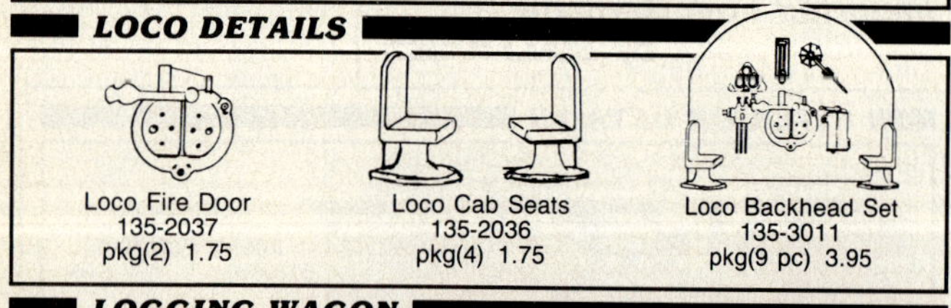

Loco Fire Door
135-2037
pkg(2) 1.75

Loco Cab Seats
135-2036
pkg(4) 1.75

Loco Backhead Set
135-3011
pkg(9 pc) 3.95

LOGGING WAGON

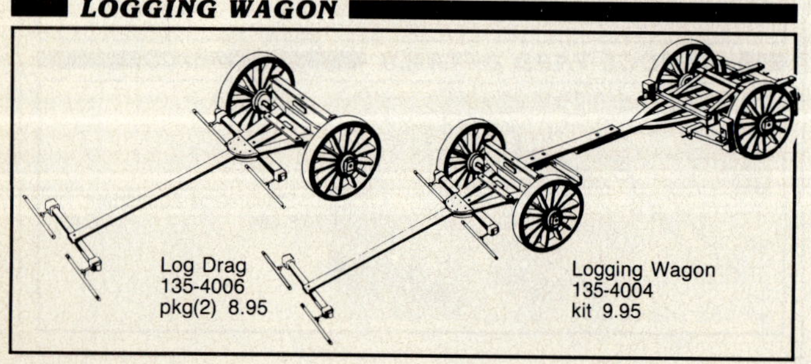

Log Drag
135-4006
pkg(2) 8.95

Logging Wagon
135-4004
kit 9.95

MARKER JEWELS

Extra small.
135-5002 Red   pkg(12) 1.50
135-5003 Amber pkg(12) 1.50

135-5004 Green pkg(12) 1.50
135-5005 Clear pkg(12) 1.50

MISCELLANEOUS

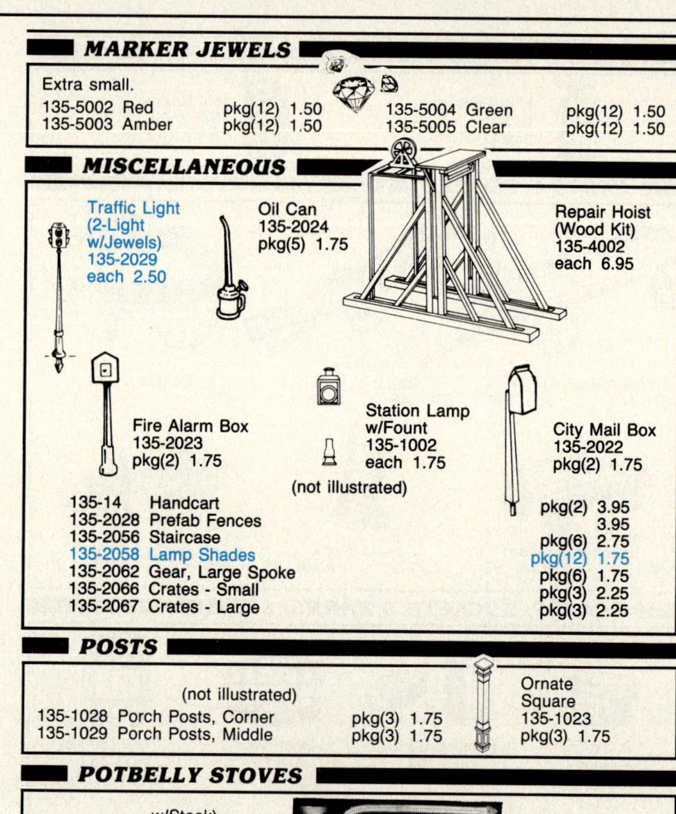

Traffic Light
(2-Light
w/Jewels)
135-2029
each 2.50

Oil Can
135-2024
pkg(5) 1.75

Repair Hoist
(Wood Kit)
135-4002
each 6.95

Fire Alarm Box
135-2023
pkg(2) 1.75

Station Lamp
w/Fount
135-1002
each 1.75

(not illustrated)

City Mail Box
135-2022
pkg(2) 1.75

135-14   Handcart   pkg(2) 3.95
135-2028 Prefab Fences   3.95
135-2056 Staircase   pkg(6) 2.75
135-2058 Lamp Shades   pkg(12) 1.75
135-2062 Gear, Large Spoke   pkg(6) 1.75
135-2066 Crates - Small   pkg(3) 2.25
135-2067 Crates - Large   pkg(3) 2.25

POSTS

(not illustrated)
135-1028 Porch Posts, Corner   pkg(3) 1.75
135-1029 Porch Posts, Middle   pkg(3) 1.75

Ornate
Square
135-1023
pkg(3) 1.75

POTBELLY STOVES

w/Stack)
135-2061 pkg(2) 2.25

RAILING

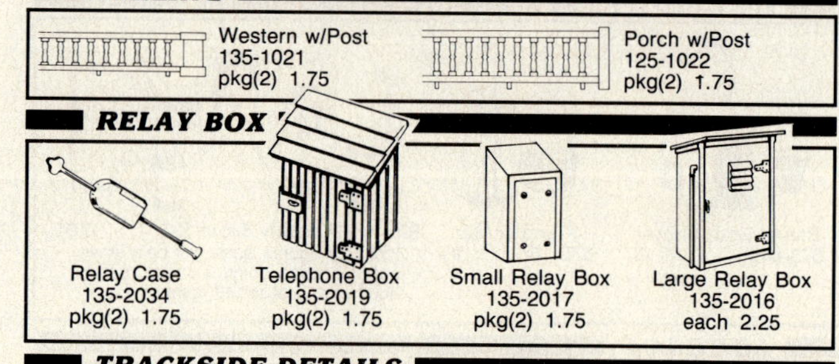

Western w/Post
135-1021
pkg(2) 1.75

Porch w/Post
125-1022
pkg(2) 1.75

RELAY BOX

Relay Case
135-2034
pkg(2) 1.75

Telephone Box
135-2019
pkg(2) 1.75

Small Relay Box
135-2017
pkg(2) 1.75

Large Relay Box
135-2016
each 2.25

TRACKSIDE DETAILS

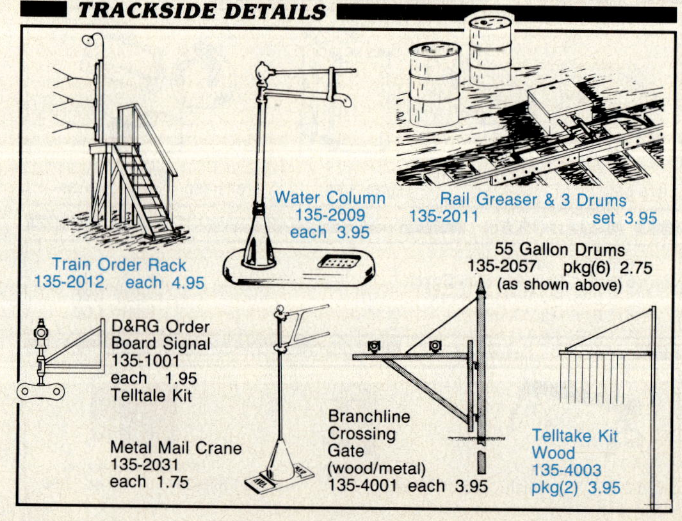

Water Column
135-2009
each 3.95

Rail Greaser & 3 Drums
135-2011
set 3.95

55 Gallon Drums
135-2057   pkg(6) 2.75
(as shown above)

Train Order Rack
135-2012   each 4.95

D&RG Order
Board Signal
135-1001
each 1.95
Telltale Kit

Metal Mail Crane
135-2031
each 1.75

Branchline
Crossing
Gate
(wood/metal)
135-4001 each 3.95

Telltake Kit
Wood
135-4003
pkg(2) 3.95

Sequoia SCALE MODELS

HO SCALE

All items are cast in white metal unless noted. Illustrations are not to scale.

■ WHEELS ■

Wagon Wheels, Large
135-2039   pkg(2) 1.75
Wagon Wheels, Small
135-2038   pkg(2) 1.75

Sheffield Wheels
135-1012 18″   pkg(4) 1.75
135-1013 15″   pkg(4) 1.75

■ WINDOWS ■

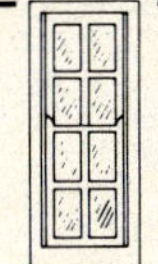

8-Pane
135-1003
pkg(3) 1.75

Window
135-1018
pkg(3) 1.75

Victorian
135-1016
pkg(3) 1.75

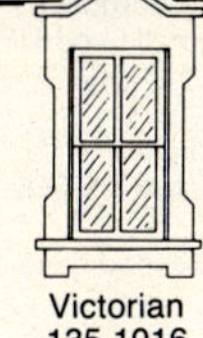

Bay Window
(3 piece assembly)
135-1009 each 2.25

(not illustrated)
135-1027 Four Pane Windows   pkg(3) 1.75

Pikestuff

HO SCALE (1/87)

All metal castings.

■ STEP PILOT ■

541-132 2-8-2	5.00
541-133 4-6-2	5.00

STEWART HOBBIES, INC.

HO SCALE (1/87)

All parts are plastic except where noted.

■ RS-3 ■

691-1075 PH-1B Undecorated Shell	10.00
includes handrails	
691-1076 Frame, metal	2.55
691-1077 Fuel Tank	1.20
691-2075 PH-2A Undecorated Shell	10.00
includes handrails	
691-3075 PH-3 Undecorated Shell	10.00
includes handrails	

■ AS-16/AS-616 ■

691-4075 Undecorated Shell	8.00
body, cab & deck only	
691-4076 Handrail Set	(6 pieces) 2.00
691-4077 Coupler Liftbars	pr 1.00
691-4078 Air Tanks	pr 1.00
691-4079 Bell	1.00
691-4080 Horn	1.00
691-4081 Frame, metal	3.00

■ U25B ■

691-7049 Windows/Lens Set	3.00
691-7075 Shell, Undecorated	15.00
691-7076 Handrail Set	(8 pieces) 3.00
691-7077 Horn, 3-Chime	1.00
691-7078 Screen Set	(6 pieces) 6.00
691-7079 Ladder	1.00
691-7080 Brakewheel	1.00
691-7081 Airtanks	pair 2.00
691-7082 Frame	5.00

Scale Scenics

Division of CIRCUITRON

HO SCALE

Easy-to-build white metal kits unless noted. Illustrations are not to scale.

■ CONSTRUCTION DETAILS ■

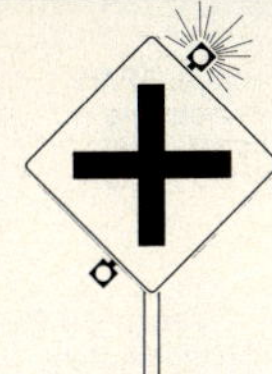

Flashing Highway Sign Kit
652-1520   14.95
Includes materials and circuit to construct one operational diamond shaped highway warning sign with dual alternating yellow flashing lamps.

Flashing Barricade Kit
652-1501   each 7.95
Prepainted orange and white sign, wire 1 x 1″ circuit board and yellow LED. Makes one operating and five dummy units.

Mutiple Flashing Barricade Kit
652-1505   19.95
Includes circuit and enough materials to construct 5 operational Flashing Barricades.

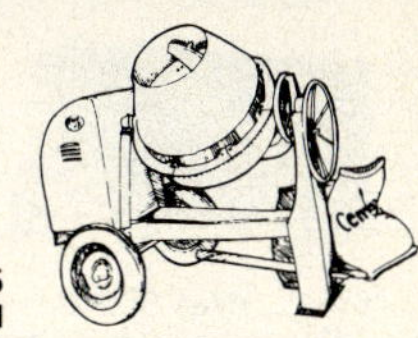

Cement Mixer
652-3502
each 6.95

■ ENGINES & MOTORS ■

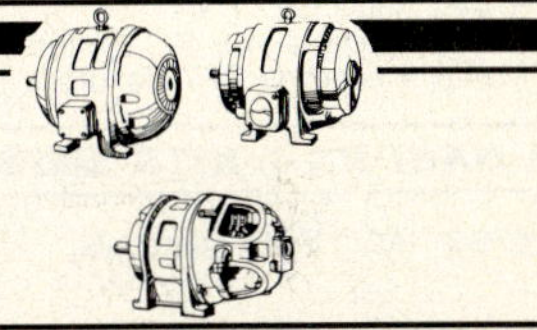

Industrial Electric Motors
652-3512
each 4.50

■ FORK LIFT & CONVEYER ■

2-Wheel Belt Conveyor
652-3508
each 8.95

Fork Lift Truck
652-3515
each 6.95

■ MISCELLANEOUS ■

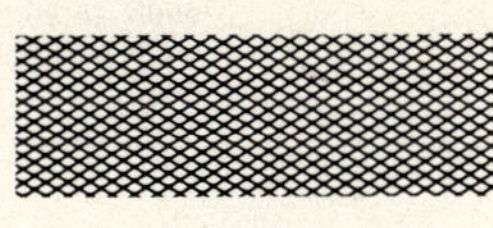

3 x 6″ Aluminum Micro-Mesh
652-3500   3.95

3 x 6″ Brass Micro-Mesh
652-3501
each 4.50

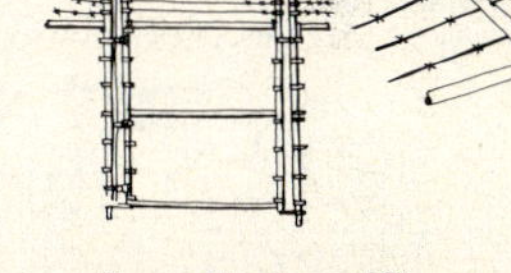

Fence Hardware Kit
652-3504   each 6.95
Posts are 12 foot lengths and can be cut. Less Micro-Mesh fence material and barbed wire.

(not illustrated)
652-1504 Flat Wire, Nickel Silver   (5 ft) 2.50
Measures .010 x .030″ may be used for strapping.

652-2001 Gear Assortment   each 3.95
Used for scratch-building machinery or junk on your layout. May include heavy machinery parts.

■ STOP SIGNS ■   NEW

Post mounted, scale sized sign kit includes preassembled electronic flasher circuit. 9 volt DC operation. May be battery powered, or Circuitron PS-3 to power from powerpack. Circuit can flash up to 3 additional signs.

652-1525 w/Red Flashing Light		kit 14.95
652-1526 w/Red Flashing Light		preassembled 22.95
652-1528 Stop Sign		kit 6.95
652-1529 Stop Sign		preassembled 12.95

SMOKEY VALLEY RAILROAD PRODUCTS

HO SCALE (1/87)

Loco Conversion and Dress Up kits.

B UNIT CONVERSION KITS

676-1 GP9B   each 19.95
Kit consists of 2 sides and 1 top casting from white metal, complete handrail set of .015" wire and can be used to make SD9 unit.

676-2 Atlas SD24B   each 19.95
Kit features all metal parts, including prototype handrails and handrail stanchions.

GE Utility Cabs/ B30-7A1 "B" 676-73   each 6.95
shown with 676-72 (GE High Short Hood/Dash-7)

676-82 Atlas GP7 Handrails	each 15.95
676-86 Bachmann 8-40C Handrails	each 15.95
676-87 Railpower CF7 Handrails	each 15.95

HANDRAIL KITS

676-3 Atlas SD24 Handrails   each 15.95

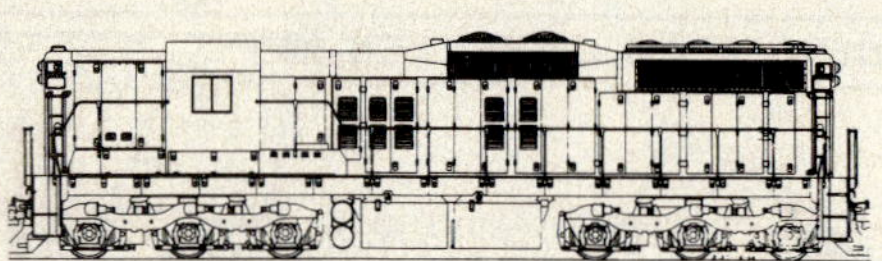

676-4 Athearn SD9	each 15.95
676-5 Atlas GP38 & GP40	each 15.95
676-6 Bachmann GP30	each 15.95
676-8 Cary SW1500	each 15.95
676-9 AHM SD40	each 15.95
676-10 Atlas SD35	each 15.95
676-11 AHM GP18/Tyco GP20	each 15.95
676-12 Bachmann GP40	each 15.95
676-23 Handrail Kit	each 15.95

Brass kit fits Cary and Athearn SW1500 and Athearn SW1000 engines.

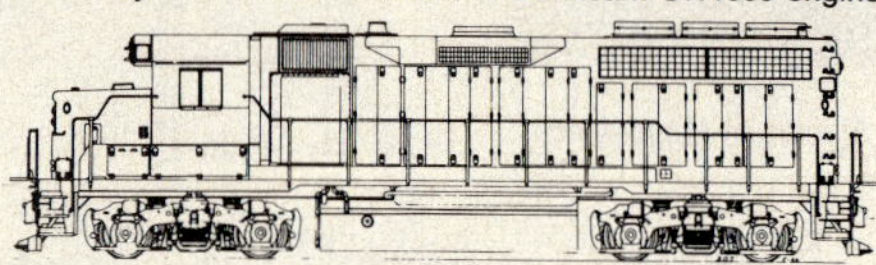

676-13 FM H-24-66 Athearn Trainmaster Handrails   each 15.95

676-14 GE "U" Boat   each 15.95
Will fit Bachmann U36B, Athearn units with B trucks and has .015" wire handrails.

676-15 GE "U" Boats   each 15.95
Fits Athearn GE units with C trucks

676-16 GE BQ23-7   each 15.95
Will fit Bachmann BQ23-7 and has .015" wire handrails.

676-17 Alco Switcher   each 15.95
Will fit Cary S-2&4 and the AHM S-4, but has new prototype stanchions (more than Cary stampings) and formed .015" wire handrails.

676-18 AHM Alco Road Switcher   each 15.95
676-19 SD40-2 SD40-2T   each 15.95
Will fit T&D SD40-2, SD40-2T and Athearn SD40-2, .015" wire handrails.

676-20 Athearn GP50		each 15.95
676-21 SD50, SD60		each 15.95
676-31 Atlas-Stewart RS3		each 15.95
676-42 Athearn SD45 and SDP40		each 15.95
676-43 Front Range GP9 "B" Unit		each 19.95
676-44 Atlas RS-1		each 15.95
676-45 Atlas RS11 and RSD12		each 16.95
676-200 8-40 CW	*NEW*	each 15.95
676-210 SD60M	*NEW*	each 15.95
676-211 GP60M	*NEW*	each 15.95

END BRACKETS

676-109 Alco Late Road Switcher	pkg(4) 7.95
676-111 Alco Early Road Switcher & All Yard Switchers	pkg(2) 4.95

END SILLS

676-65 GP-15 Deck Side Sills	each 2.95
676-66 EMD Large Anticlimb & End Sill	each 2.95
676-67 GP50 Anticlimb & End Sill	each 2.95
676-69 EMD Small Anticlimb & End Sill	each 2.95

HANDRAIL STANCHIONS

676-47 C-32-8 GE Locomotive		each 15.95
Includes handrails and stanchions.		
676-30 GP 38-2/40-2, Athearn		each 15.95
676-41 Concor MP		pkg(15) 15.95
676-101 Old GP9 & SD9		pkg(28) 11.95
Fits GP9, 18 and 20; SD9 18 and 24.		
676-103 Modern GP		pkg(28) 11.95
Also fits SD second generation diesels.		
676-104 Modern SD		pkg(37) 11.95
676-105 EMD GP30		pkg(28) 11.95
676-106 FM Trainmaster		pkg(30) 11.95
676-107 Alco Yard		pkg(16) 7.95
676-108 Alco Road Switchers (Old)		pkg(22) 7.95
676-110 GE "U" Boats		pkg(30) 11.95
676-113 GE C32-8		pkg(36) 11.95
676-117 Alco RS11 and RSD12		each 5.95
676-132 Alco RS-1		each 7.95
676-135 SD60		pkg(59) 11.95
676-205 EMD	*NEW*	pkg(28) 5.95

MISCELLANEOUS

676-97 GE C-32-8 Anti-Climber	each 2.95
676-98 EMD Battery Box Doors	pkg(8) 2.95
For GP "B" units.	
676-102 Handrail Tees	pkg(8) 3.95

GP15-1 PARTS

BODY SHELLS

Unpainted body shell kits are detailed to match specific prototypes. Kits are less cabs, but are designed to use the Cannon & Co or Athearn Dash-2 cab, sold separately. Includes assembly instructions.

676-48 MP, Phase Two	each 19.95
676-49 MP, Phase One	each 19.95
676-50 Conrail	each 19.95
676-51 Frisco	each 19.95
676-52 Chicago & North Western	each 20.95

HANDRAIL KITS

Kits include wire handrails and brass stanchions, designed to fit specific GP15-1 body shells.

676-53 MP Phase I/C&NW	each 15.95
676-54 MP Phase II/Frisco	each 15.95
676-55 Conrail	each 15.95

MISCELLANEOUS

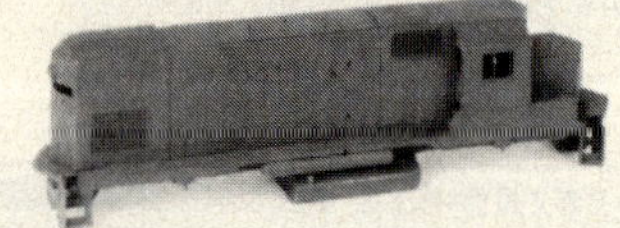

Frame 676-56   each 10.95
One-piece metal casting, fits all versions of GP15-1 body shell.

676-58 EMD EP/SD 80" Short Nose	each 6.95
676-59 EMD EP/SD 86" Short Nose	each 6.95
676-62 Fuel Tank	each 4.95
Plastic parts for use with #56.	
676-65 Deck Sidesills	each 2.95
676-68 Railpower GE 8-40B Handrails	each 15.95
676-70 Deck Steps	each 2.95
676-71 Front & Rear Top — Long Hood	each 2.95
676-72 GE HI Short Hood/Dash-7	each 6.95

676-290 Radiator Grills   *NEW* pkg(2) 2.95

Loco Truck 2-Axle (powered) 676-250   16.00 each
NEW

Trackside Parts

HO SCALE (1/87)

Parts are cast in white metal unless noted. Illustrations are not to scale.

We have worked closely with this manufacturer to provide accurate availability information at the time this catalog was published. Items listed in *blue ink* may not be available at all times. Please see your dealer for current delivery information.

AIR HORNS

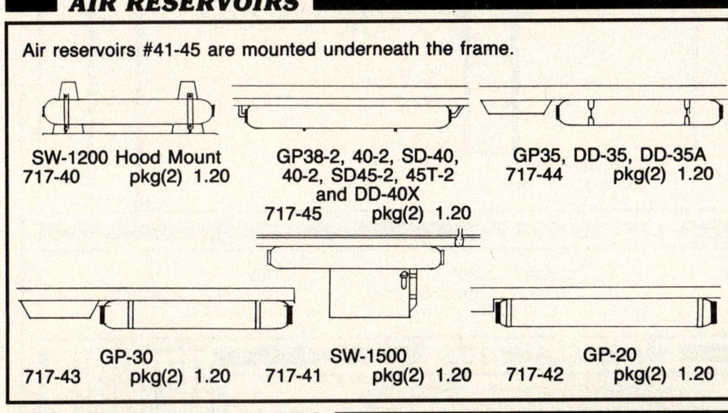

FA's & PA's Alco S-1
717-1   pkg(2) 1.25

RS's & Industrial Switchers, Alco S-2
717-2   pkg(2) 1.25

Handcock 4700
717-4700   pkg(2) 1.50

AIR RESERVOIRS

Air reservoirs #41-45 are mounted underneath the frame.

SW-1200 Hood Mount
717-40   pkg(2) 1.20

GP38-2, 40-2, SD-40, 40-2, SD45-2, 45T-2 and DD-40X
717-45   pkg(2) 1.20

GP35, DD-35, DD-35A
717-44   pkg(2) 1.20

GP-30
717-43   pkg(2) 1.20

SW-1500
717-41   pkg(2) 1.20

GP-20
717-42   pkg(2) 1.20

BRAKE CYLINDERS

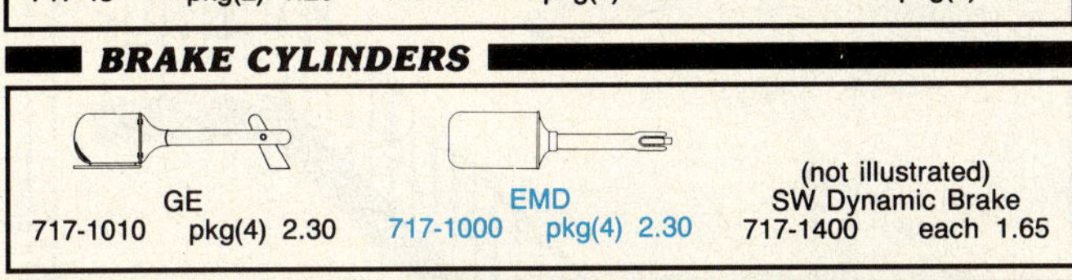

GE
717-1010   pkg(4) 2.30

EMD
717-1000   pkg(4) 2.30

(not illustrated)
SW Dynamic Brake
717-1400   each 1.65

DITCH LIGHTS

Ditch lights will accept MV Product lens (516-200).

GP & SW
717-1600
pkg(4) 1.25

Caboose
717-1500
pkg(4) 1.25

EXHAUST STACK & SILENCERS

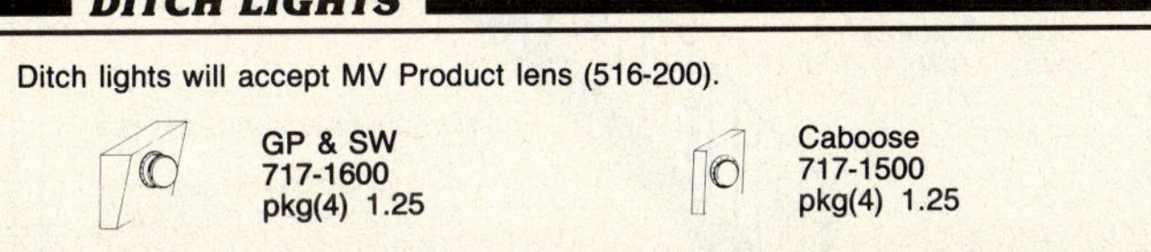

EMD Repower Stack
717-30   each 1.50

EMD MP15 Silencer, High
717-31   each 1.50

EMD MP15 Silencer, Low
717-32   each 1.50

(not illustrated)
717-1202 Alco RS Standard Stack   pkg(2) 1.30
717-1203 Alco RS Modified Stack   pkg(2) 1.30
717-1204 Steam Generator Stack   pkg(2) 1.30

MISCELLANEOUS

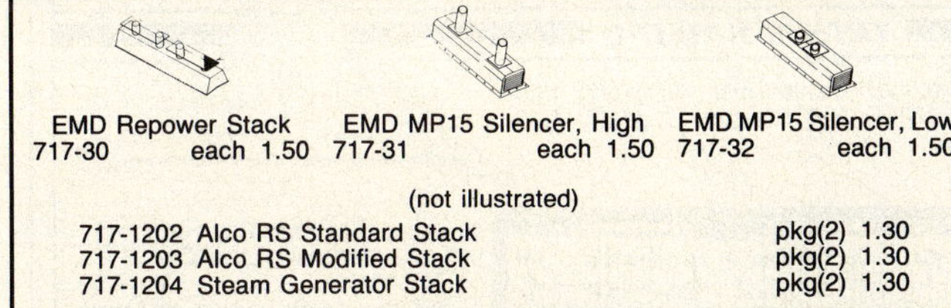

Steam Generator Details
717-70 pkg(2) 1.00

Cement Battery Cellar
717-186 pkg(3) 1.20

Grade Crossing Bell w/Cement Battery Cellar
717-188
each 1.50

Axle Bushing, Bronze
717-1136   pkg(12) 1.95
1/4" leaded common bronze. ID .096, length .125, flange thickness .026 – .032, flange diameter 1/4", body diameter of 5/32" with chamfer on the flange end of the bushing.

(not illustrated)
Alco Winterization Duct
717-80   each 1.55

PHONE BOXES

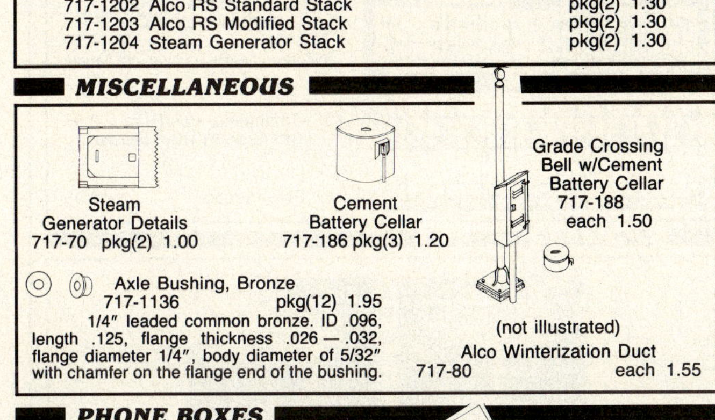

Wood
717-160
pkg(3) 1.10

Wood Terminal
717-161
pkg(3) 1.10

PHONE BOXES (continued)

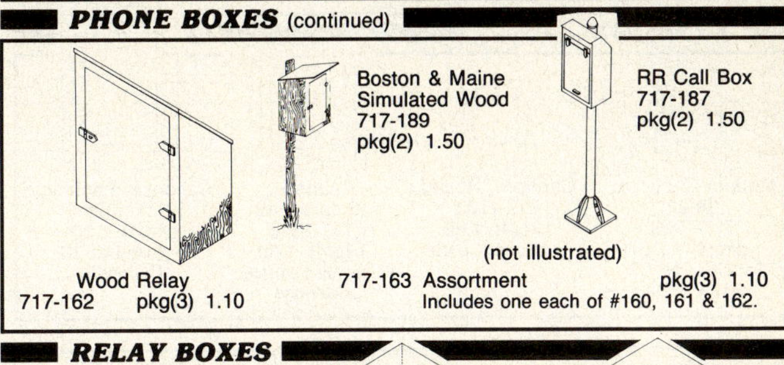

Boston & Maine Simulated Wood
717-189
pkg(2) 1.50

RR Call Box
717-187
pkg(2) 1.50

Wood Relay
717-162   pkg(3) 1.10

(not illustrated)
717-163 Assortment   pkg(3) 1.10
Includes one each of #160, 161 & 162.

RELAY BOXES

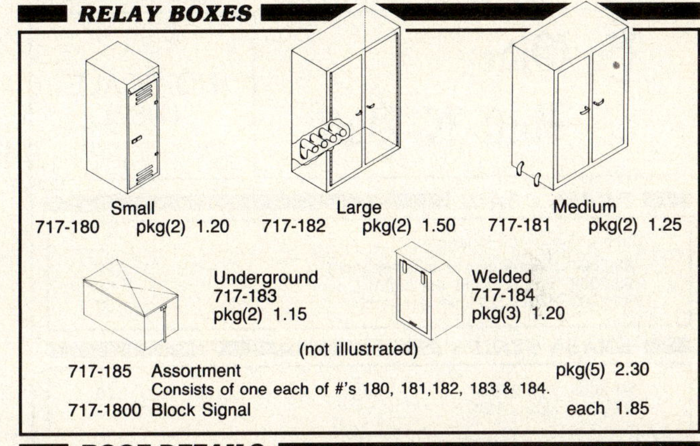

Small
717-180   pkg(2) 1.20

Large
717-182   pkg(2) 1.50

Medium
717-181   pkg(2) 1.25

Underground
717-183
pkg(2) 1.15

Welded
717-184
pkg(2) 1.20

(not illustrated)
717-185   Assortment   pkg(5) 2.30
Consists of one each of #'s 180, 181, 182, 183 & 184.
717-1800 Block Signal   each 1.85

ROOF DETAILS

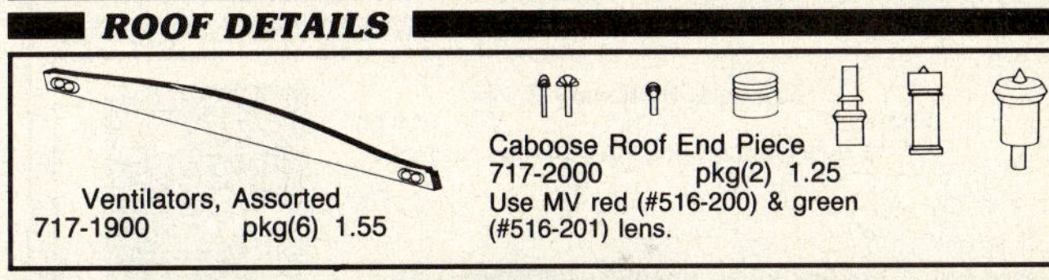

Ventilators, Assorted
717-1900   pkg(6) 1.55

Caboose Roof End Piece
717-2000   pkg(2) 1.25
Use MV red (#516-200) & green (#516-201) lens.

SMOKE JACKS

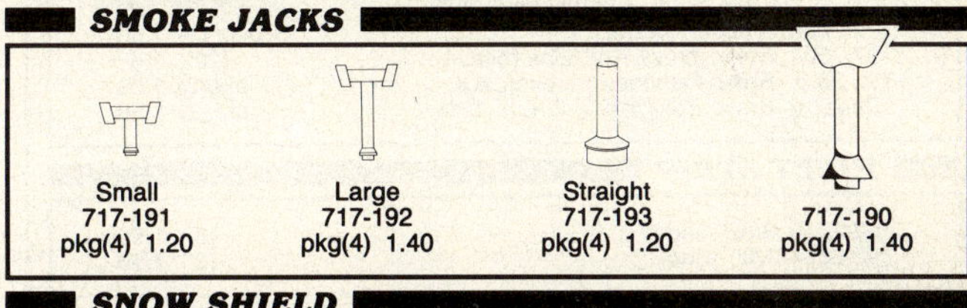

Small
717-191
pkg(4) 1.20

Large
717-192
pkg(4) 1.40

Straight
717-193
pkg(4) 1.20

717-190
pkg(4) 1.40

SNOW SHIELD

717-60 EMD Style (for GP38-40)   pkg(2) 1.20
717-61 CN and CP   pkg(2) 1.20

SPARK ARRESTORS

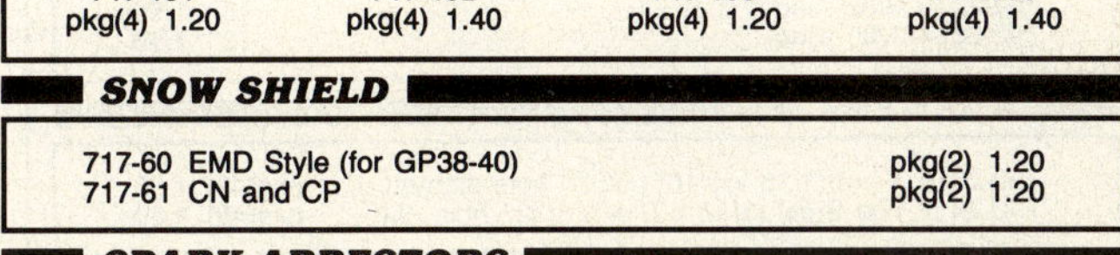

EMD-SW
717-1200 pkg(2) 1.50
For CN, CV, CP, GT, etc

EMD-GP
717-1201   pkg(2) 1.50
For CN, CV, CP, GT, etc.

TANKS

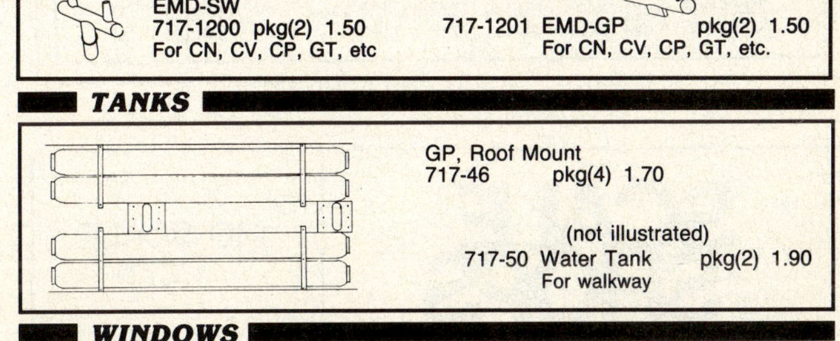

GP, Roof Mount
717-46   pkg(4) 1.70

(not illustrated)
717-50 Water Tank   pkg(2) 1.90
For walkway

WINDOWS

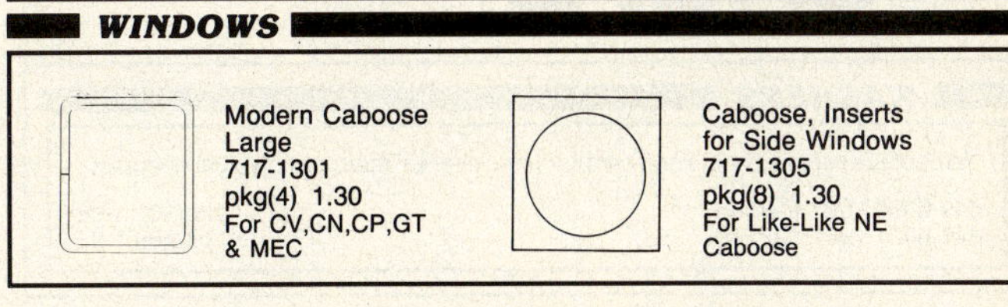

Modern Caboose Large
717-1301
pkg(4) 1.30
For CV, CN, CP, GT & MEC

Caboose, Inserts for Side Windows
717-1305
pkg(8) 1.30
For Like-Like NE Caboose

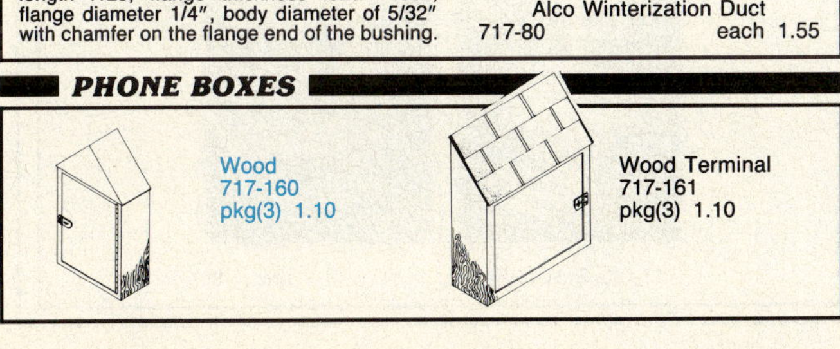

Trackside Parts

HO SCALE (1/87)

WINDOWS (continued)

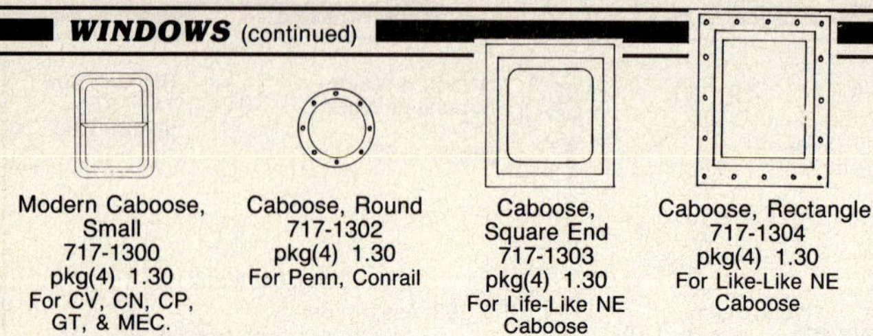

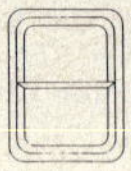

Modern Caboose, Small
717-1300
pkg(4) 1.30
For CV, CN, CP, GT, & MEC.

Caboose, Round
717-1302
pkg(4) 1.30
For Penn, Conrail

Caboose, Square End
717-1303
pkg(4) 1.30
For Life-Like NE Caboose

Caboose, Rectangle
717-1304
pkg(4) 1.30
For Like-Like NE Caboose

Ye Olde Huff-N-Puff

HO SCALE (1/87)

BRASS CHAIN

Each chain is 10″ in length.

792-2001	Extra-Fine (36 links per inch)	1.50
792-2002	Fine (27 links per inch)	1.50
792-2003	Heavy (20 links per inch)	1.50

BRASS STRIPS

792-2008	.005 x 3/32″	(6′) 1.50
792-2009	.005 x 1/8″	(6′) 1.50

MISCELLANEOUS

Horizontal Stationary Boiler
792-1027   11.00
Fine detail and includes many metal castings.

(not illustrated)

792-2000	Wooden Barrels	pkg(12) 1.50
792-2004	Nylon Truss Rod Line (black)	(20′) 1.50
792-2005	Brass Caboose Smoke Jack	pkg(2) 1.50
792-2016	Brass Bar (3/32 x 3/32 x 12″)	pkg(2) 1.50

RIVET STRIP

792-2013	3/32″ wide	(3′) 1.50
792-2014	1/8″ wide	(3′) 1.50

WASHERS

792-2010	Fibre (1/16 x 5/16″, 5/32″ hole diameter)	pkg(48) 1.50
792-2011	Flat Steel (3/32 x 7/16″, 5/32″ hole dia)	pkg(48) 1.50

WINDOWS

792-2006	Cast Nylon Frames (13/32 x 1/2″)	pkg(5) 1.50
792-2007	Cast Nylon Frames (7/32 x 1/2″)	pkg(5) 1.50

SCALE SHOPS

HO SCALE 1/87)

WASHERS

"Wobble-Stoppers" help keep cars running level for more prototypical operation.

649-6020	1/8″ Curved	pkg(10) 1.98
649-6021	1/4″ Curved	pkg(8) 1.98

TAURUS PRODUCTS

HO SCALE (1/87)

CHIMNEY & SMOKE JACK

Smokejack
707-502
pkg(4) 1.25

Brick Chimney
707-501
pkg(2) 1.25

LADDERS

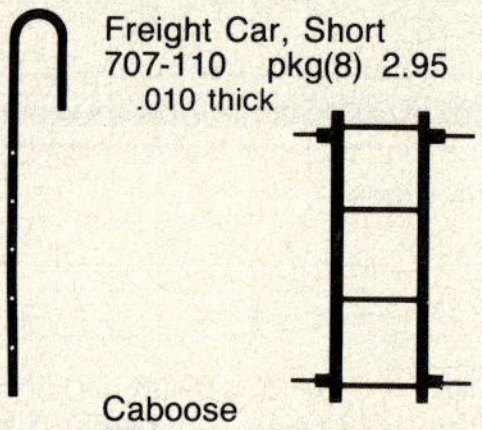

Freight Car, Short
707-110   pkg(8) 2.95
.010 thick

Freight Car, Long
707-109   pkg(4) 2.95
.010 thick. Includes instructions to adapt to cars using 5, 6 or 7 rung ladders.

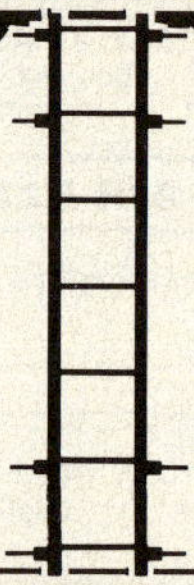

Caboose
707-101   pair 3.95

LIFT RINGS

Large Eye Bolt
707-112   pkg(36) 2.00
0.10 thick

Tiny
707-111   pkg(48) 2.00
0.10 thick

MISCELLANEOUS

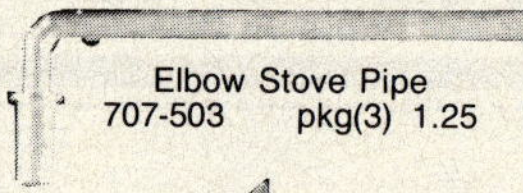

Elbow Stove Pipe
707-503   pkg(3) 1.25

Eave Supports
707-506   pkg(4) 1.25

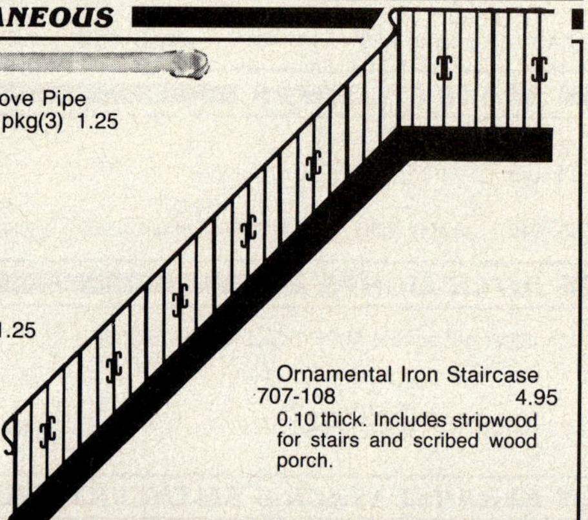

Ornamental Iron Staircase
707-108   4.95
0.10 thick. Includes stripwood for stairs and scribed wood porch.

TRIM & RAILING

707-507 Gable Small   pkg(2) 1.25
707-508 Gable Large   pkg(2) 1.50

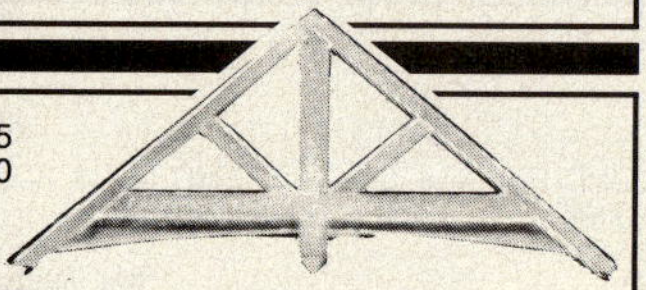

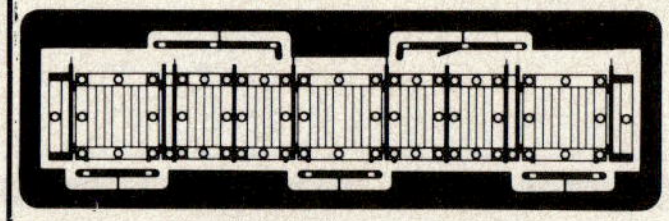

Platform Railings for Observation Cars
707-104   kit 2.50
includes brake stanchion and handle

707-107 Ornamental Iron Roof   2.95
.010 thick, 84 HO Scale feet

707-113 Gingerbread   4.95

TROLLEY FENDER

707-103 Eclipse Kit   pair 6.95

TRAIN STATION PRODUCTS
DIVISION OF QUALITY-WRIGHT CORPORATION

HO SCALE (1/87)
NEW

These detailed plastic parts can be combined with other manufacturers' products to create customized or superdetailed cars and locomotives. Basic instructions for assembly and installation are included.

CONVERSION KITS

732-32	RS3 "Hammerhead"	7.95
732-33	RS2	8.95
732-46	Athearn Adapt	4.95

DIAPHRAGMS

732-400	Amfleet	pkg(2) 2.95
732-401	Amfleet	pkg(6) 7.95

For Amfleet, Metroliner, Superliner, & some Heritage passenger cars. Fits Con-Cor, Bachmann, Walthers, & other passenger cars.

732-403	Union Pacific Style	pkg(2) 2.95
732-404	Union Pacific Style	pkg(6) 7.95

For use on Con-Cor AHM, Rivarossi, Athearn, brass and other passenger cars. Diaphragms come with end gates, support bars and leaf springs.

732-405	Tubular Style	pkg(2) 2.95

For use on Con-Cor AHM, Rivarossi, Athearn, brass and other passenger cars.

SIDEFRAMES

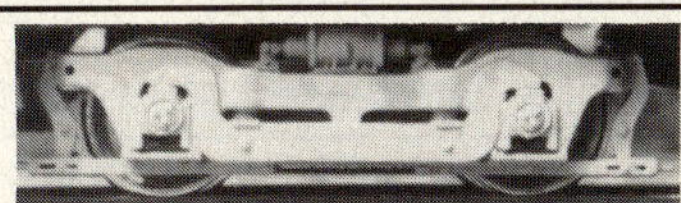

732-24	AAR Switcher w/Roller Bearings - Athearn	pkg(4) 8.95
732-77	GE GSC Dash 7 - Athearn	8.95

732-78	GE GSC Dash 8 - Athearn	8.95
732-79	GE GSC Dash 8 - Bachmann	8.95
732-83	GE AD Dash 7 - Athearn	8.95
732-84	GE AD Dash 8 - Athearn	8.95
732-85	GE AD Dash 8 - Bachmann	8.95
732-90	EMD Blomberg "M" Phase 2 - Athearn	8.95

732-99	EMD Flex-i-coil "C" w/low mounted brake cylinders	8.95
732-112	F-B2 Phase 1	8.95
732-114	FM C-Liner - Athearn	pkg(4) 8.95

732-119	Alco Blunt Switcher - Athearn	8.95
732-120	EMD Flex-i-coil "B" Switcher - Athearn	8.95

732-121	GE F-B2 Phase II - Athearn	8.95

732-137	EMD SD60 HTC w/roller bearing journals - Athearn	8.95

MISCELLANEOUS DETAIL PARTS

732-25	Canadian Safety Cab	10.95
732-57	EMD SD60M North American Safety Wide Cab	9.95
732-60	EMD Short Nose CP Rail 102" long	5.95
732-61	EMD Short Nose UP Snoot 115" long	5.95
732-63	Rear Battery Compartment Doors & Hand Brake	4.95

732-64	EMD Short Nose KCS Snoot 123" long	6.95
732-72	GE Hi Short Hood Dash 7	6.95
732-74	EMD SD60M North American Safety Wide Cab UP Phase II, BN, & Soo Line	9.95
732-75	GE Dynamic Brake Box for the C-36-7	4.95
732-76	GE Dynamic Brake Box for the B-30-7A1 "B" Unit	4.95
732-88	EMD GP60 Phase II Dynamic Brake Box Fits Athearn GP50	8.95
732-89	EMD GP60M North American Safety Wide Cab Fits Athearn GP50	9.95
732-93	Dynamic Brake & Steam Generator for Alco RS3 "Hammerhead"	2.95
732-116	Radiators and Air Intake Grills SD50-2	pkg(2) 4.95
732-118	Pilots for Bowser H-16-44	pkg(2) 3.25
732-131	Brake Cylinders for Diesel Trucks	pkg(16) 3.95
732-133	"40" Series Radiator Grills For GP40 & SD40 and some GP40-2 & SD40-2 Units	pkg(4) 3.95
732-134	EMD Louvers For early GP, SD, and F Units	pkg(48) 3.95
732-136	GE Truck Shock Absorbers	pkg(8) 3.95

732-138	GP9 Grills	2.95

Fit Life-Like's Proto 2000 Gp 18 and will convert the GP18 into a GP9.

732-139	48" Fan w/rotating blade	pkg(1) 2.95
732-140	48" Fan w/rotating blade	pkg(3) 7.95
732-141	52" Fan w/rotating blade	pkg(1) 2.95
732-402	Passenger Car Truck Mounting Screws	pkg(12) 4.95

For attaching pass, car trucks to Con-Cor, AHM, or Rivarossi Passenger Cars. Non-magnetic, Stainless Steel Screws.

732-408	End Door Gates Passenger Car	2.95

This scratch-built service station sees plenty of traffic on Gerry Gilliland's module. A scene from Faller provides the background while vehicles from Alloy Forms and Wiking complete the realistic touches. *Models and Photo by Gerry Gilliland*

Wabash Valley

HO SCALE (1/87)

Parts are metal detail castings. Illustrations are not to scale.

BODY BOLSTERS

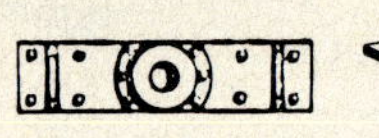

772-1118 pkg(2) 1.25

Heavy Duty Riveted Steel
772-1064 pkg(2) 1.25

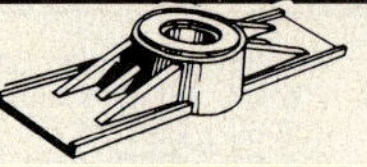

Heavy Duty Cast Steel
772-1136 pkg(2) 1.25

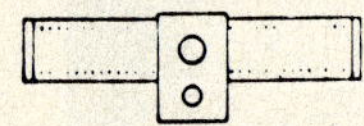

772-1113 pkg(2) 1.25

772-1119 pkg(2) 1.25

Span
772-1034 pkg(2) 1.25

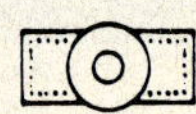

772-1161 pkg(2) 1.25

Standard Freight
772-1137 pkg(2) 1.25

Standard Wood Beam
772-1218 pkg(2) 1.25

(not illustrated)

772-1259 pkg(2) 1.00   772-1297 pkg(2) 1.25   772-1396 pkg(2) 1.25

BOILER FRONTS

With lugs and hinges.

(not illustrated)
772-1451 Brake Wheel pkg(4) 1.25

772-1345 16 mm pkg(2) 1.25
772-1353 25 mm each 1.25
772-1359 21 mm each 1.25

BRAKESTANDS

Peacock
772-1438
pkg(4) 1.25

Locomotive
772-1440
pkg(4) 1.25
(By Special Order Only.)

MU/Motor Car
772-1441
pkg(4) 1.25

BRAKEWHEELS

Standard
772-1430 pkg(4) 1.25

Old Time
772-1431 pkg(4) 1.25

Control Wheel
772-1032 pkg(4) 1.25

Superior w/Housing
772-1435 pkg(2) 1.25

Equipco w/Housing
772-1436 pkg(2) 1.25

Miner w/Housing
772-1434 pkg(2) 1.25

END SILLS

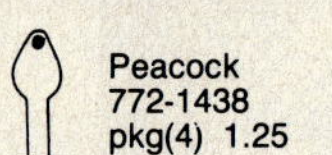

Convertible Gondola
772-1022 pkg(2) 1.25

Riveted
772-1120 pkg(2) 1.25

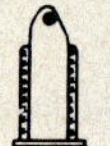

Freight
772-1025 pkg(2) 1.25

Narrow (circa 1880)
772-1001 pkg(2) 1.25

Pennsy Semi-Well Flat
772-1084 pkg(2) 1.25

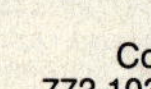

Wood
772-1179 pkg(2) 1.25

772-1176 pkg(2) 1.25

772-1180 pkg(2) 1.25

Loco Tender
772-1085 pkg(2) 1.25

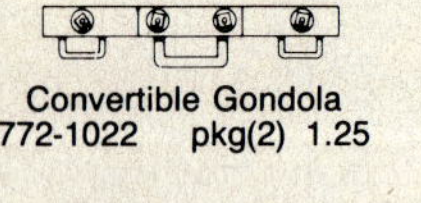

772-1174 pkg(2) 1.25

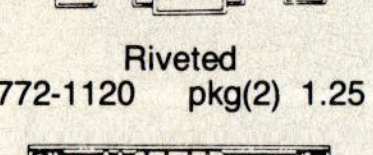

772-1172 pkg(2) 1.50

Depressed Center Flat
772-1094 pkg(2) 1.25

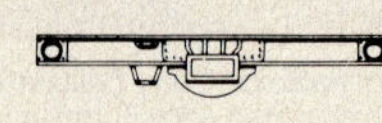

772-1177
pkg(2)
1.25

END SILLS (continued)

Alco Diesel Loco
772-1322
pkg(2) 1.25

(not illustrated)

772-1057 pkg(2) 1.25
772-1207 Wood pkg(2) 1.25
772-1221 pkg(2) 1.25

HATCHES

772-1334 **(By Special Order Only.)** pkg(4) 1.25

HINGE STRIP

772-1040 Reefer pkg(12) 1.25

HOPPER DOORS

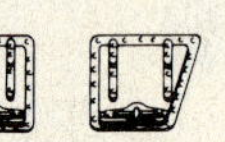

772-1131 pkg(4) 1.25

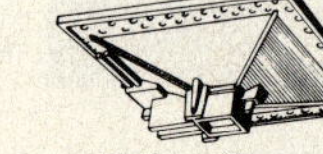

Bottom Covered
772-1096 pkg(2) 1.75

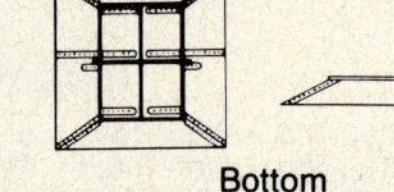

Bottom
772-1002 each 1.25

HOUSINGS

772-1437 Klassing pkg(4) 1.25
772-1446 Ajax, Side Mount pkg(4) 1.25

1437

1446

MISCELLANEOUS

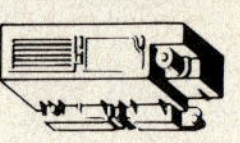

Passenger Car
Air Conditioner
772-1031 each 1.25

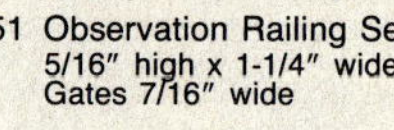

772-1251 Observation Railing Set 1.50
5/16" high x 1-1/4" wide
Gates 7/16" wide

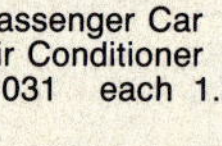

Brake Levers
772-1095 pkg(8) 1.25

772-1300 Generator Control Valve each 1.25

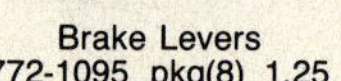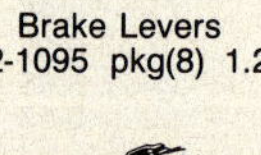

Turnbuckle
772-1073 pkg(12) 1.25

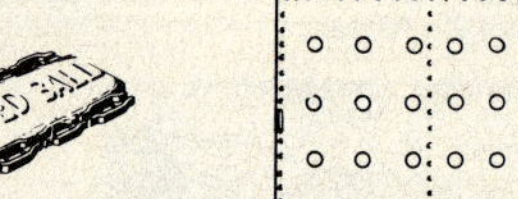

Flat Car
Steel Center
Floor
772-1312
each 1.25

Queenposts & Pedestal
772-1157 pkg(2) 1.25

Alco Vent Set
772-1499 each 1.75

(not illustrated)

772-628 Whistle Post pkg(2) 1.25
772-629 Whistle Post pkg(2) 1.25
772-678 Whistle Post, Round Top pkg(2) 1.25
772-1000 Semi Trailer Floor, Flat each 5.25
(By Special Order Only.)
772-1090 Tank Car Placards pkg(4) 1.25
(By Special Order Only.)
772-1105 Battery Box Lid pkg(2) 1.00
772-1128 Tank Car Ends 6' 6" Diameter pkg(2) 1.25
772-1129 Semi Trailer Roof each 4.25
(By Special Order Only.)
772-1167 Battleship Gondola pkg(2) 1.50
772-1230 Flanger Plow pkg(2) 2.25
772-1323 Heater Stack for RS3 each 1.25
772-1542 Roofwalk Support each 1.50
(By Special Order Only.)

Wabash Valley

HO SCALE (1/87)

PEDESTAL BARS

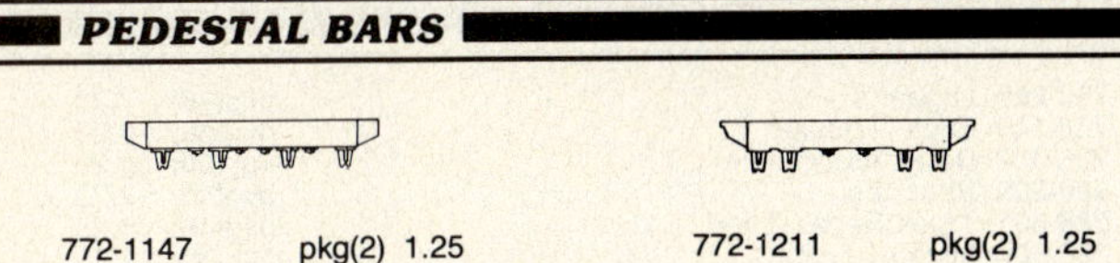

772-1147   pkg(2) 1.25   772-1211   pkg(2) 1.25

STEPS

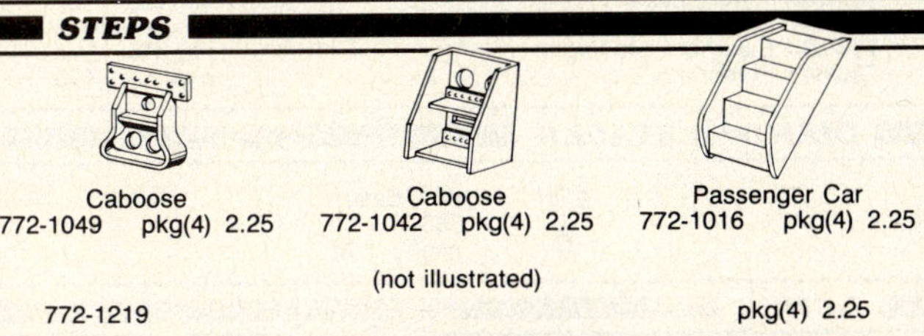

Caboose
772-1049   pkg(4) 2.25

Caboose
772-1042   pkg(4) 2.25

Passenger Car
772-1016   pkg(4) 2.25

(not illustrated)

772-1219   pkg(4) 2.25

TOOL BOXES

772-1220   pkg(2) 1.25

Truss Rod Unit, Short, L&R
772-1086 pkg(2) 1.25
(By Special Order Only.)

Long
772-1121   pkg(2) 1.25

UNDERFRAMES

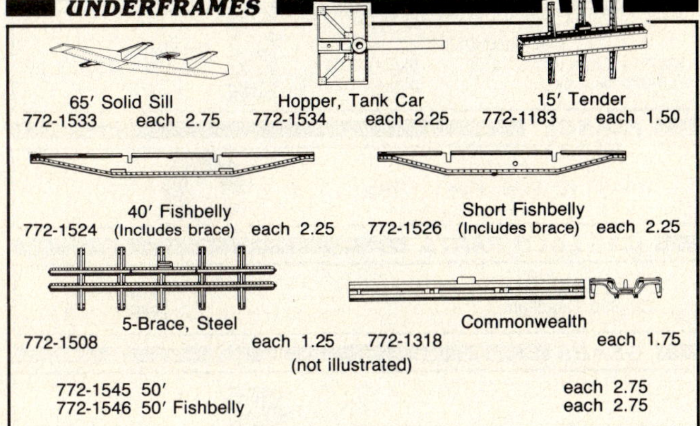

65' Solid Sill
772-1533   each 2.75

Hopper, Tank Car
772-1534   each 2.25

15' Tender
772-1183   each 1.50

40' Fishbelly
772-1524   (Includes brace)   each 2.25

Short Fishbelly
772-1526   (Includes brace)   each 2.25

5-Brace, Steel
772-1508   each 1.25

Commonwealth
772-1318   each 1.75
(not illustrated)

772-1545 50'   each 2.75
772-1546 50' Fishbelly   each 2.75

HO SCALE (1/87)

MODEL RAILROAD PRODUCTS
(Division of Tomar Inc.)

Parts are lost wax brass castings unless noted. Illustrations are not to scale.

ANTENNA MAST

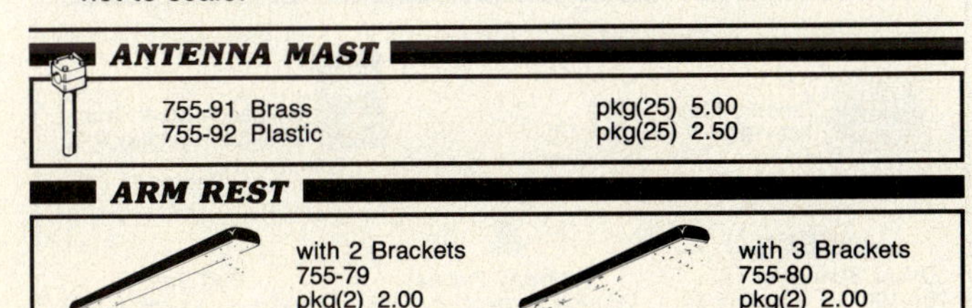

755-91 Brass   pkg(25) 5.00
755-92 Plastic   pkg(25) 2.50

ARM REST

with 2 Brackets
755-79
pkg(2) 2.00

with 3 Brackets
755-80
pkg(2) 2.00

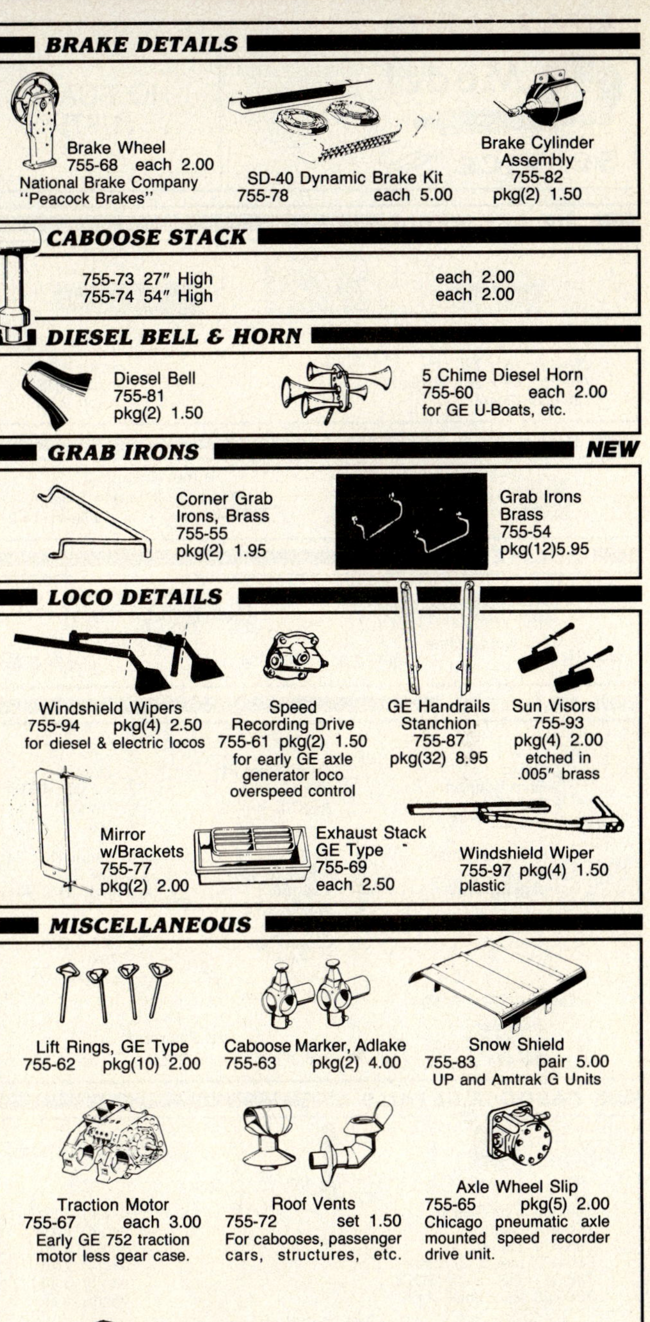

BRAKE DETAILS

Brake Wheel
755-68   each 2.00
National Brake Company
"Peacock Brakes"

SD-40 Dynamic Brake Kit
755-78   each 5.00

Brake Cylinder
Assembly
755-82
pkg(2) 1.50

CABOOSE STACK

755-73 27" High   each 2.00
755-74 54" High   each 2.00

DIESEL BELL & HORN

Diesel Bell
755-81
pkg(2) 1.50

5 Chime Diesel Horn
755-60   each 2.00
for GE U-Boats, etc.

GRAB IRONS   *NEW*

Corner Grab
Irons, Brass
755-55
pkg(2) 1.95

Grab Irons
Brass
755-54
pkg(12) 5.95

LOCO DETAILS

Windshield Wipers
755-94   pkg(4) 2.50
for diesel & electric locos

Speed
Recording Drive
755-61 pkg(2) 1.50
for early GE axle
generator loco
overspeed control

GE Handrails
Stanchion
755-87
pkg(32) 8.95

Sun Visors
755-93
pkg(4) 2.00
etched in
.005" brass

Mirror
w/Brackets
755-77
pkg(2) 2.00

Exhaust Stack
GE Type
755-69
each 2.50

Windshield Wiper
755-97 pkg(4) 1.50
plastic

MISCELLANEOUS

Lift Rings, GE Type
755-62   pkg(10) 2.00

Caboose Marker, Adlake
755-63   pkg(2) 4.00

Snow Shield
755-83   pair 5.00
UP and Amtrak G Units

Traction Motor
755-67   each 3.00
Early GE 752 traction
motor less gear case.

Roof Vents
755-72   set 1.50
For cabooses, passenger
cars, structures, etc.

Axle Wheel Slip
755-65   pkg(5) 2.00
Chicago pneumatic axle
mounted speed recorder
drive unit.

Brass Bell
w/Bracket
755-98
NEW
pkg(2) 2.25

Snow Plow
Brass
755-99
NEW
each 4.95

PYLE GYRALITE

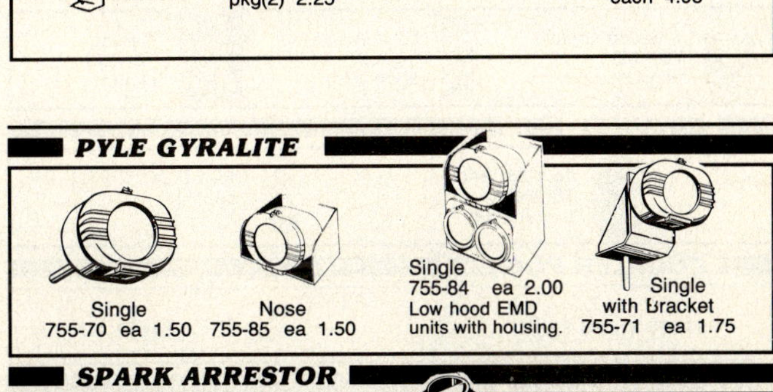

Single
755-70 ea 1.50

Nose
755-85 ea 1.50

Single
755-84   ea 2.00
Low hood EMD
units with housing.

Single
with Bracket
755-71   ea 1.75

SPARK ARRESTOR

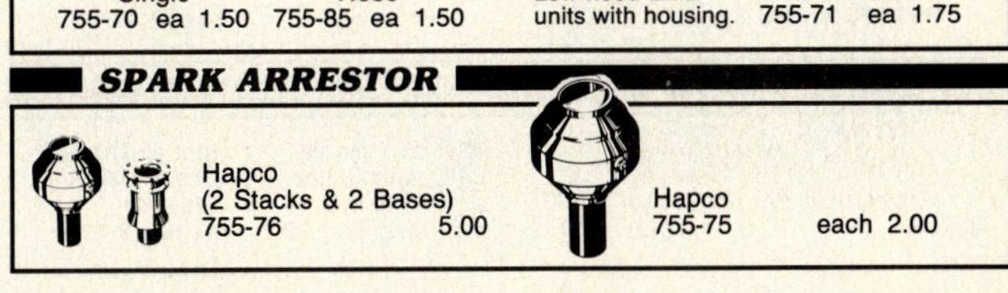

Hapco
(2 Stacks & 2 Bases)
755-76   5.00

Hapco
755-75   each 2.00

WALKER Model service

HO SCALE (1/87)

All items are cast in white metal, a lead-in-antimony alloy (should not be used in mechanical situations). Gears, frogs, main rods, etc., should be used for scenic effect only. Illustrations are not to scale.

■ AIR RESERVOIR

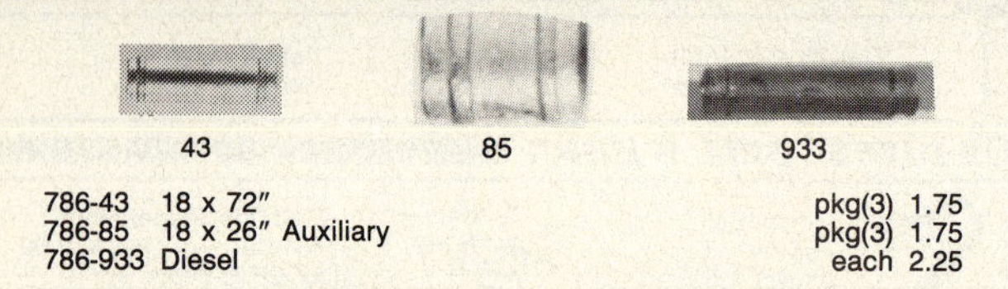

43	85	933

786-43	18 x 72″	pkg(3) 1.75
786-85	18 x 26″ Auxiliary	pkg(3) 1.75
786-933	Diesel	each 2.25

■ BEARINGS

Jib Crane Top
786-308
pkg(4) 1.50

(not illustrated)
Pivot (for 6″ shaft) 1 Bolt
786-248   pkg(6) 1.75

■ BOLSTERS

Riveted Steel   8′ x 9″ Steel
786-725   pkg(4) 2.20   786-534   pkg(8) 2.75

■ BRACKETS

Depot
Roof Support
786-219
pkg(12) 2.75

Depot Roof #1
786-1
pkg(12) 2.75

Strap
9 x 96″ 4-Bolt
786-232
pkg(12) 2.50

90° Steel Strap
786-322
pkg(12) 2.50

9x 60″
5-Bolt Strap
786-160
pkg(8) 1.75

Beam 16 x 24″
786-301
pkg(12) 2.00

Steam Pipe
3″ Pipe
786-97
pkg(12) 2.20

90° 6-Bolt
786-15
pkg(4) 1.75

Eave Set
(for SOO Depot)
786-434 pkg(20) 3.20

(not illustrated)
786-378 84 Piece Strap   set 10.20

■ CABOOSE DETAILS

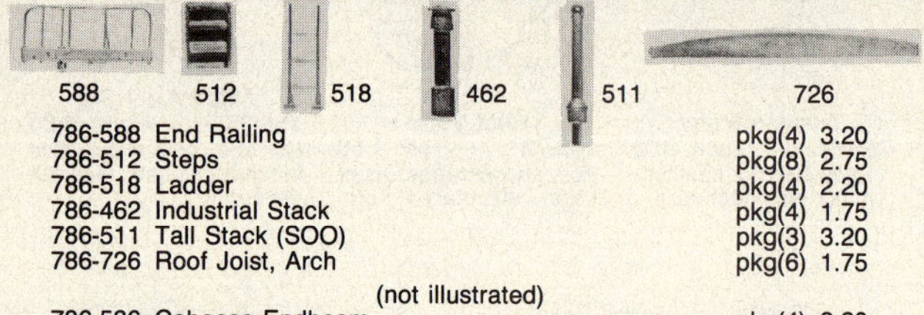

588	512	518	462	511	726

786-588	End Railing	pkg(4) 3.20
786-512	Steps	pkg(8) 2.75
786-518	Ladder	pkg(4) 2.20
786-462	Industrial Stack	pkg(4) 1.75
786-511	Tall Stack (SOO)	pkg(3) 3.20
786-726	Roof Joist, Arch	pkg(6) 1.75

(not illustrated)

786-536	Caboose Endbeam	pkg(4) 2.20
786-647	Hardware	(32 pcs) 5.75

■ CANS

5 Gallon Grease
786-646
pkg(12) 2.00

Old Milk Can
786-602
pkg(8) 2.20

Garbage
786-645
pkg(6) 1.75

■ CHIMNEY

16 x 33′ Brick
786-545
pkg(6) 2.00

Stove Pipe
786-370
pkg(6) 1.75

■ COUPLER POCKET

786-923 Link & Pin   pkg(4) 1.75

■ CRANE PARTS

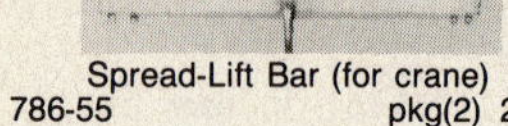 

Spread-Lift Bar (for crane)
786-55   pkg(2) 2.00

20″ Hook
with Pulley
786-110
pkg(2) 1.75

(not illustrated)
Crane Boom
786-879
pkg(2) 2.75

■ DETAIL SETS

786-268	Logger's	pkg(36)	7.20
786-148	Engine House	pkg(55)	9.20
786-422	Detail Assortment	pkg(100)	16.20
786-800	Structure	pkg(40)	7.20
786-801	Truck Repair Shed	pkg(48)	8.25
786-802	Modern Truck	pkg(30)	7.25
786-803	1940 Truck	pkg(30)	7.25
786-804	1920 Truck	pkg(30)	7.25
786-336	External Plumbing	pkg(12)	2.75
786-643	Platform	pkg(36)	8.20

■ DIAMOND STACKS

With Base
786-37
pkg(2) 1.75

■ DOMES

Steam, Fluted
786-608   each 2.00

Baldwin, Steam
786-210 pkg(2) 2.00
48″ diameter

Baldwin, Sand
786-208 pkg(2) 2.00
36″ diameter

Sand, Fluted
786-607   each 2.00

■ DOORS

(not illustrated)

786-924	Freight, 7′3″ x 9′	pkg(4) 2.00
786-925	Shanty	pkg(4) 1.75

Residence
786-620 pkg(4) 1.75

■ FLANGE

786-484 12″ Steam Pipe   pkg(12) 1.75

■ GAS LOCO PARTS

786-822	Cab Step	pkg(6) 1.75
786-830	Headlight	pkg(4) 1.75

■ GEARS

(not illustrated)

786-823	2 x 16″	pkg(8) 1.75
786-902	24 x 3″	pkg(6) 2.00
786-501	Set	pkg(36) 6.20

5 x 30″
Hollow Ground
786-459
pkg(8) 1.75

6 x 36″
w/Center Pin
786-456
pkg(8) 1.75

■ INDUSTRIAL ROLLERS

786-279 84″   pkg(6) 2.00

■ LOGGER PARTS

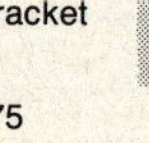 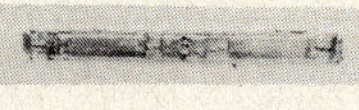   

Bunk w/Bracket
Wood
786-168
pkg(6) 2.75

Roller
12 x 48″
786-193 +
pkg(12) 2.50

Bunk w/Bracket
Steel
786-169
pkg(6) 2.75

36″ Bunk
Bracket Extender
786-247
pkg(12) 2.00

■ MISCELLANEOUS

Electric Motor, 440V
786-190   pkg(3) 1.75

55 Gallon Steel Drums
786-432 pkg(8) 2.50

Driver Spring for Loco
786-100 pkg(8) 2.50

Highway Pylons
786-427 pkg(12) 1.75

Bird Bath
786-59 pkg(3) 1.50

WALKER Model service

HO SCALE (1/87)

All items are cast in white metal, a lead-in-antimony alloy (should not be used in mechanical situations). Gears, frogs, main rods, etc., should be used for scenic effect only. Illustrations are not to scale.

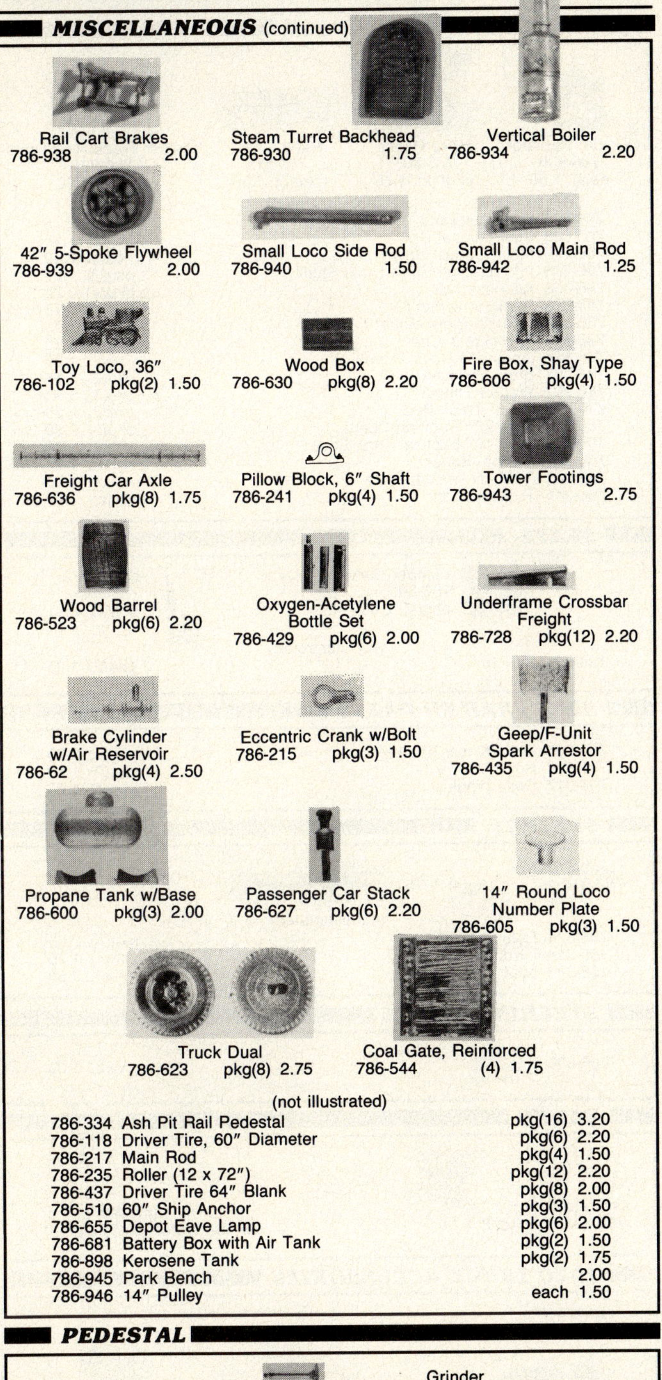

■ MISCELLANEOUS (continued)

Rail Cart Brakes 786-938 2.00	Steam Turret Backhead 786-930 1.75	Vertical Boiler 786-934 2.20
42″ 5-Spoke Flywheel 786-939 2.00	Small Loco Side Rod 786-940 1.50	Small Loco Main Rod 786-942 1.25
Toy Loco, 36″ 786-102 pkg(2) 1.50	Wood Box 786-630 pkg(8) 2.20	Fire Box, Shay Type 786-606 pkg(4) 1.50
Freight Car Axle 786-636 pkg(8) 1.75	Pillow Block, 6″ Shaft 786-241 pkg(4) 1.50	Tower Footings 786-943 2.75
Wood Barrel 786-523 pkg(6) 2.20	Oxygen-Acetylene Bottle Set 786-429 pkg(6) 2.00	Underframe Crossbar Freight 786-728 pkg(12) 2.20
Brake Cylinder w/Air Reservoir 786-62 pkg(4) 2.50	Eccentric Crank w/Bolt 786-215 pkg(3) 1.50	Geep/F-Unit Spark Arrestor 786-435 pkg(4) 1.50
Propane Tank w/Base 786-600 pkg(3) 2.00	Passenger Car Stack 786-627 pkg(6) 2.20	14″ Round Loco Number Plate 786-605 pkg(3) 1.50
Truck Dual 786-623 pkg(8) 2.75	Coal Gate, Reinforced 786-544 (4) 1.75	

(not illustrated)

786-334	Ash Pit Rail Pedestal	pkg(16) 3.20
786-118	Driver Tire, 60″ Diameter	pkg(6) 2.20
786-217	Main Rod	pkg(4) 1.50
786-235	Roller (12 x 72″)	pkg(12) 2.20
786-437	Driver Tire 64″ Blank	pkg(8) 2.00
786-510	60″ Ship Anchor	pkg(3) 1.50
786-655	Depot Eave Lamp	pkg(6) 2.00
786-681	Battery Box with Air Tank	pkg(2) 1.50
786-898	Kerosene Tank	pkg(2) 1.75
786-945	Park Bench	2.00
786-946	14″ Pulley	each 1.50

■ PEDESTAL

Grinder 786-642 pkg(2) 1.75

■ PULLEYS

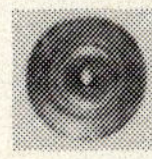 Flat Belt 786-76 pkg(4) 1.75	28″ Cable 786-81 pkg(6) 1.50	 Spoked Strap 786-349 pkg(6) 2.00

(not illustrated)

786-817	Pulley with Frame	pkg(4) 1.75
786-883	Pulleys with Brackets	pkg(4) 2.50
786-377	Pulley Set	pkg(36) 5.20

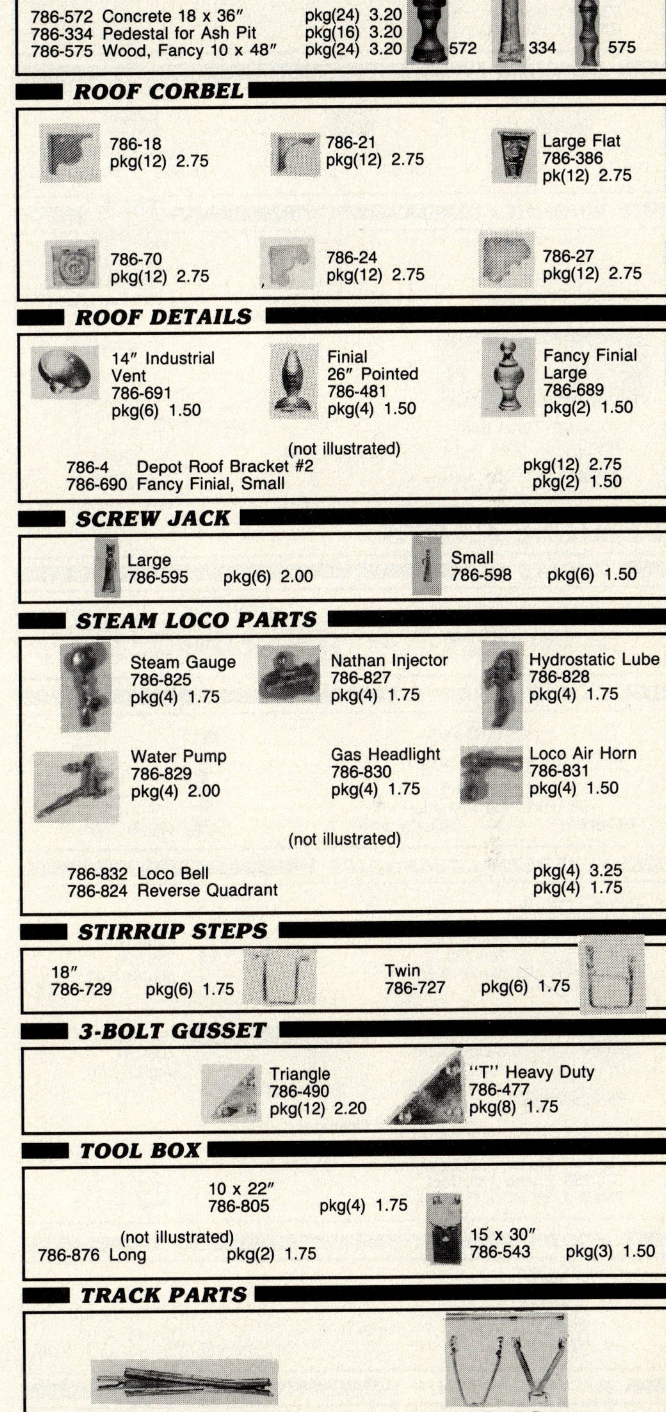

■ RAIL

786-572	Concrete 18 x 36″	pkg(24) 3.20
786-334	Pedestal for Ash Pit	pkg(16) 3.20
786-575	Wood, Fancy 10 x 48″	pkg(24) 3.20

572   334   575

■ ROOF CORBEL

786-18 pkg(12) 2.75	786-21 pkg(12) 2.75	Large Flat 786-386 pk(12) 2.75
786-70 pkg(12) 2.75	786-24 pkg(12) 2.75	786-27 pkg(12) 2.75

■ ROOF DETAILS

14″ Industrial Vent 786-691 pkg(6) 1.50	Finial 26″ Pointed 786-481 pkg(4) 1.50	Fancy Finial Large 786-689 pkg(2) 1.50

(not illustrated)

786-4	Depot Roof Bracket #2	pkg(12) 2.75
786-690	Fancy Finial, Small	pkg(2) 1.50

■ SCREW JACK

Large 786-595 pkg(6) 2.00	Small 786-598 pkg(6) 1.50

■ STEAM LOCO PARTS

Steam Gauge 786-825 pkg(4) 1.75	Nathan Injector 786-827 pkg(4) 1.75	Hydrostatic Lube 786-828 pkg(4) 1.75
Water Pump 786-829 pkg(4) 2.00	Gas Headlight 786-830 pkg(4) 1.75	Loco Air Horn 786-831 pkg(4) 1.50

(not illustrated)

786-832	Loco Bell	pkg(4) 3.25
786-824	Reverse Quadrant	pkg(4) 1.75

■ STIRRUP STEPS

18″ 786-729 pkg(6) 1.75	Twin 786-727 pkg(6) 1.75

■ 3-BOLT GUSSET

Triangle 786-490 pkg(12) 2.20	"T" Heavy Duty 786-477 pkg(8) 1.75

■ TOOL BOX

10 x 22″ 786-805 pkg(4) 1.75	15 x 30″ 786-543 pkg(3) 1.50

(not illustrated)

786-876 Long pkg(2) 1.75

■ TRACK PARTS

Rail Frog, Code 100, Scenic 786-325 pkg(4) 2.50	Hayes Track Bumper 786-200 pkg(2) 2.50

■ VENTS

786-95 12″ Roof pkg(6) 1.50

WALKER Model service

HO SCALE (1/87)

All items are cast in white metal, a lead-in-antimony alloy (should not be used in mechanical situations). Gears, frogs, main rods, etc., should be used for scenic effect only. Illustrations are not to scale.

WEIGHTS

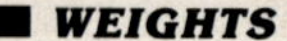

786-811	Box Car, 1.5oz	pkg(2)	1.74
786-812	House Car	pkg(10)	6.25

WINCHES

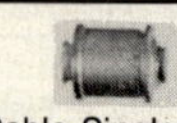

Cable Single Drum
786-73   pkg(4) 1.75

Heavy Duty Cable
786-547   pkg(4) 1.75

Heavy Duty Rope
786-504   pkg(3) 1.75

WINDOWS

28 x 30" Single Pane
786-229   pkg(8) 2.00

24 x 54" Two Pane
786-471   pkg(8) 1.50

48 x 76" Four Pane
786-582   pkg(6) 2.20

10' x 42" Three Pane
786-931   each 2.75

40 x 64" Two Pane
786-270   pkg(4) 1.75
(not illustrated)

786-926 3'6" x 5' 4-Pane   pkg(8) 2.20

VEHICLE PARTS

ENGINE

(not illustrated)
Tractor with Axle
786-895   pkg(8) 1.75

Cummins
786-648
each 2.00

EXHAUST PARTS

786-675 Stack   pkg(4) 1.50

(not illustrated)
Exhaust Pipe w/Muffler
786-886   pkg(2) 1.75

Twin Stacks with Cap
786-718
pkg(2) 1.75

FLATBED ACCESSORIES

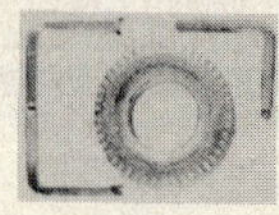
Spare Tire
786-733
pkg(6) 2.50

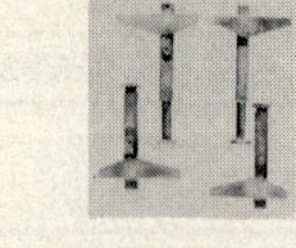
Land Gear
786-730
pkg(4) 2.00

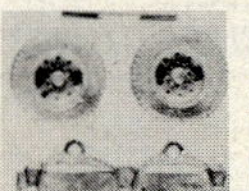
Trailer Dual Suspension
786-732
pkg(10) 3.25

Rear Bumper
786-731
pkg(2) 1.50

(not illustrated)

786-735	Trailer Single Suspension	pkg(4)	1.50
786-736	Trailer Dual Suspension	pkg(4)	1.75
786-758	Frame with Deck	pkg(14)	7.25
786-759	32' Semi Frame w/Deck	pkg(14)	7.25

HOODS

Mack Truck
786-821   pkg(2) 1.75

(not illustrated)
Transtar 4200
786-722   each 2.20

MISCELLANEOUS

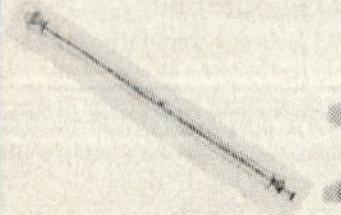

Drive Shaft, Long
786-724
pkg(2) 1.50

Timber Braces
786-810
pkg(8) 2.75

Clearance Light
786-698
pkg(12) 1.75

Transtar 4200 Door
786-694
pkg(4) 1.75

MISCELLANEOUS (continued)

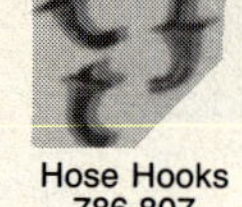

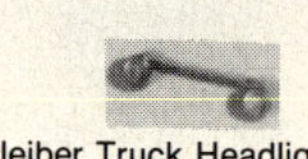

Kleiber Radiator
786-936
each 1.50

Hose Hooks
786-807
pkg(12) 1.75

Hand Crank
786-813
pkg(6) 1.50

Kleiber Truck Headlights
786-806
pkg(3) 1.50
(not illustrated)

786-654	24" Fuel Tank	pkg(6)	2.75
786-683	International Grill	pkg(2)	1.75
786-684	Main Frame, Long	each	2.00
786-723	International Short Drive Shaft	pkg(2)	1.50
786-808	Air Reservoir	pkg(4)	2.20
786-888	Radiator w/Fan		1.75
786-889	License Plate Mount	pkg(4)	1.50
786-891	Sprocket & Chain	pkg(2)	1.50
786-894	Jib Crane Deck Mount	each	1.75
786-897	Steel Pedestal	pkg(2)	1.75
786-901	Wagon Tongue	pkg(3)	1.75
786-914	9 x 6' Truck Bed	pkg(2)	2.20
786-917	12 x 96" Running Board	pkg(8)	2.20
786-918	30 x 48" Eliptical Tank Ends	pkg(4)	1.75
786-921	Journal Boxes	pkg(12)	2.20
786-941	Radiator w/Headlights	each	1.50
786-944	Transmission	each	1.75

SEATS

Lumber Carrier
786-809
pkg(4) 2.00

Cab
786-695
pkg(4) 1.50

(not illustrated)

786-881 Bench   pkg(2) 1.75

SEMI TRAILER PARTS

786-905	Dolly-Wheel Brackets	pkg(4)	1.75
786-907	Rear Axle	pkg(2)	1.50
786-912	Dolly Wheels	pkg(4)	1.50

SPRINGS

Lumber Carrier
786-814   pkg(4) 1.75

(not illustrated)

786-678	Rear	pkg(4)	2.00
786-814	Lumber Carrier	pkg(4)	1.75
786-896	Leaf	each	2.00

STEERING WHEEL

786-890   pkg(2) 1.50

TANKS

Hydraulic
786-815   pkg(3) 2.00

(not illustrated)
786-898 Kerosene pkg(2) 1.75

1920 TRUCK ACCESSORIES

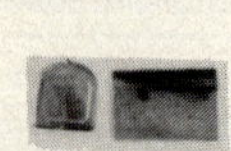

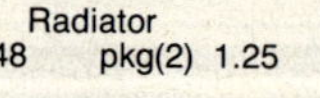

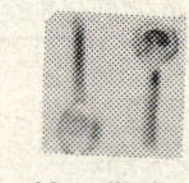

Hood with Radiator
786-755   pkg(2) 1.50

Radiator
786-748   pkg(2) 1.25

Headlights
786-756   pkg(6) 1.50

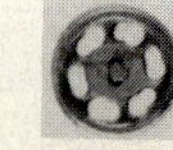

Front Tire
786-752   pkg(6) 2.75

Rear Dual Tires
786-753   pkg(6) 3.00

Spare Tire
786-741   pkg(6) 2.00

WALKER Model service

HO SCALE (1/87)

All items are cast in white metal, a lead-in-antimony alloy (should not be used in mechanical situations). Gears, frogs, main rods, etc., should be used for scenic effect only. Illustrations are not to scale.

◼ 1920 TRUCK ACCESSORIES (continued)

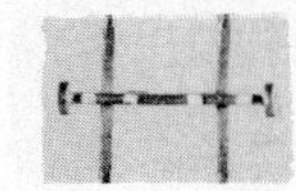

Cab Assembly	Steering Wheel	Rear Drive Shaft
786-749　pkg(7) 4.75	786-757　pkg(6) 1.50	786-750　pkg(2) 1.75

(not illustrated)

786-751	Frame with Fender	each 2.75
786-754	Front Spring with Axle	pkg(2) 1.50
786-761	Tires	pkg(4) 2.75

◼ 1940 TRUCK ACCESSORIES

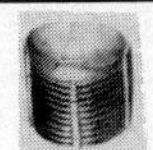

Spare Tire	Rear Tire	Radiator	Cab Seat	Rear Axle
786-740	786-742	786-744	786-745	786-746
pkg(4) 2.00	pkg(4) 2.00	pkg(2) 1.75	pkg(2) 1.50	pkg(2) 1.50

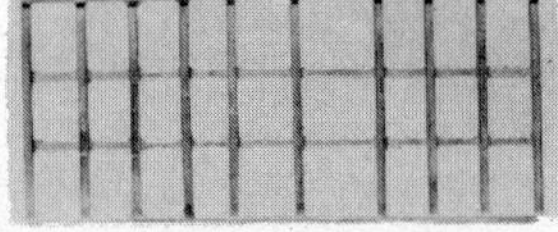

(not illustrated)

786-762	Front Tire	pkg(4) 2.20
786-743	Truck Tire Set	pkg(8) 2.50

Flatbed Frame	
786-747	pkg(2) 1.25

◼ TRUCK BODIES

786-4040	Flatbed w/17′2″ Deck	each 4.20
786-4041	Stakebed w/17′2″ Deck	each 5.20
786-4046	Log Trailer	each 5.20
786-4049	Flatbed w/Detail, 17′	each 6.20
786-4051	Flatbed w/Detail, 13′	each 6.20
786-4052	Stakebed, 13′	each 6.20
786-4053	Tank	each 5.20
786-4056	Sand	each 5.20
786-4058	Produce	each 5.20
786-4059	Dump	each 8.20
786-4060	Cement Mixer	each 9.20
786-4061	Kerosene Tank	each 9.20
786-4062	Light Delivery	each 4.20

◼ TRUCK TIRES

(not illustrated)

786-875	Wood Rim	pkg(4) 2.00
786-882	1910	pkg(4) 1.75
786-887	Steel	pkg(4) 1.75

Spare	Front
786-621	786-625
pkg(4) 2.00	pkg(4) 2.20

◼ WHEELS & ACCESSORIES

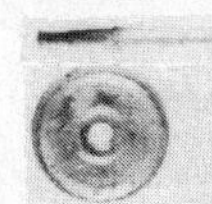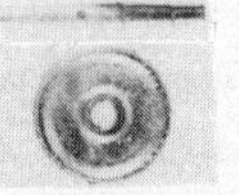

Power Axle w/Divider	Axle, Front	Axle Set
786-679　pkg(2) 1.50	786-687 pkg(2) 2.75	786-615　pkg(12) 2.50

(not illustrated)

786-593	Spare Tire, Car	pkg(6) 1.75
786-637	Wheel Axles, Scenic	pkg(18) 3.50
786-638	Wheel Axles, Scenic	pkg(36) 6.20
786-639	Wheel Axles, Scenic	pkg(54) 8.20
786-676	5th Wheel Assembly	pkg(2) 1.75
786-893	Wheel Rail Cart	pkg(8) 2.00
786-900	Truck 5th Wheel Teen era	pkg(2) 1.75
786-913	Kleiber Axle Set (front and rear)	pkg(4) 1.75

◼ NOW AVAILABLE

786-46	Diamond Stack (no base)	pkg(2) 1.50
786-67	Roof Corbel #6	pkg(12) 2.75
786-135	Roof Corbel #2 Large	pkg(12) 3.00
786-137	Roof Vent 16″ #2	pkg(6) 1.75
786-219	Roof Support Bracket	pkg(12) 2.75
786-226	Inside Corner Bracket 32″	pkg(12) 2.75
786-247	Log Bunk Extender 36″	pkg(12) 2.00
786-527	Brake Lever w/Clevis	pkg(6) 1.75
786-535	Concrete Pedestal	pkg(8) 2.75
786-641	Gas Station Details	(40 pieces set) 9.20
786-650	Truck Twin Rear Axel w/Duel	each 4.20
786-651	Truck Steering Wheel	pkg(4) 1.25
786-669	Shay Running Board	pkg(2) 1.25
786-677	Truck Spring Front	pkg(4) 1.75
786-680	Power Axle w/Odivider	pkg(2) 1.50
786-686	Truck Bumper	pkg(4) 1.50
786-688	Truck Airhorn	pkg(4) 1.50
786-696	Bench Grinder	pkg(4) 1.50
786-697	Wheels Fine Scale	pkg(12) 2.20
786-699	Deck Plate Diamond Pattern	pkg(2) 1.50
786-719	Air Cleaner	pkg(2) 1.50
786-720	T-Star Cab Assembly	each 5.20
786-721	T-Star-2 Cab Assembly	each 6.20
786-734	Flat Bed Trailer, Single Suspension	pkg(8) 2.50
786-816	14″ Rail-Cart Wheels	pkg(8) 2.00
786-826	Water Glass	pkg(4) 1.75
786-834	Whistle Single Chime	pkg(4) 1.75
786-874	Siphon Hose Locomotive	pkg(2) 1.75
786-878	Gas Loco Fuel Tank	pkg(4) 2.00
786-880	Gas Loco Cab Door	pkg(4) 2.75
786-884	Flywheel	pkg(2) 1.75
786-885	Truck Tire Solid Rubber	pkg(4) 1.75
786-892	Gas Loco Brake Cylinder	pkg(4) 1.75
786-899	Truck Rear Axle	pkg(2) 1.75
786-903	Bearings 9″ x 9″	pkg(6) 2.00
786-904	Road-Roller Break Levers	pkg(6) 2.00
786-906	Semi Trailer Rear Doors	pkg(3) 2.00
786-908	Semi Trailer Body Brace	pkg(12) 2.20
786-909	Semi Trailer RR Brake Cylinder	pkg(4) 1.75
786-910	Truck Brake Pipe Assembly	pkg(4) 1.75
786-911	Kleiber Cab Roof	pkg(2) 1.50
786-915	Truck Cab Steps	pkg(8) 2.20
786-916	Truck Spring Set	pkg(10) 2.20
786-919	Flatbed Semi	pkg(4) 2.00
786-927	6′9 x 7′4 Ind Window 4 Pane	pkg(6) 2.20
786-928	6′9 x 10′ Ind Window 6 Pane	pkg(6) 2.50
786-929	Vertical Steam Cylinder & Rod	each 1.75
786-932	Truck Bench Seat	each 2.00
786-937	2 Cylinder Steam Mech.	each 2.00
786-999	Weight f/ATH Impack Car	pkg(15) 2.14

NOCH

HO (1/87)

Imported from Germany *by WALTHERS*

Noch parts are made of appropriately colored plastic with molded and painted details.

◼ MISCELLANEOUS

Buffer Stop
528-5867
pkg(4)
9.99

Machine Tools
528-1104
5.99

(not illustrated)

528-6016	Wire Fasteners	pkg(10) 6.99
528-5868	Coal/Scrap Load Cargo	9.99

WESTERFIELD — GOLDEN AGE LINE

HO SCALE (1/87)

Parts are urethane castings unless noted. Illustrations are not to scale.

BRASS GRAB IRONS

783-1197 18" Drop	pkg(50)	2.00
783-1198 18" Straight	pkg(50)	2.00
(not illustrated)		
783-1183 23" Straight	pkg(50)	2.00
783-1196 End Walk	pkg(24)	2.00

DOORS

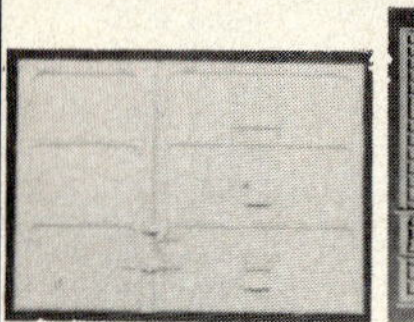
10' Creco 1-1/2 Dr
783-3012
pair 2.00

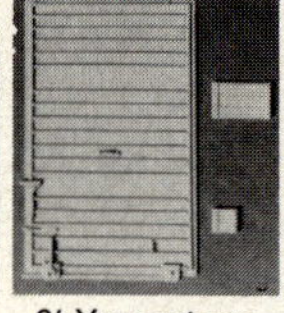
6' Youngstown
5-6-5 Panel
783-2863
pair 2.00

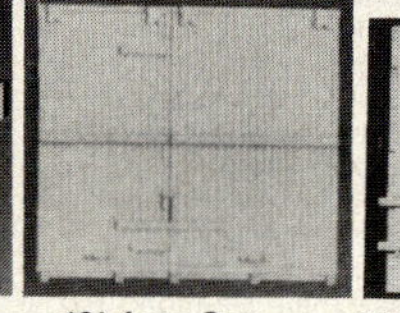
10' Auto Car
Door-and-a-Half
783-1915
pair 2.00

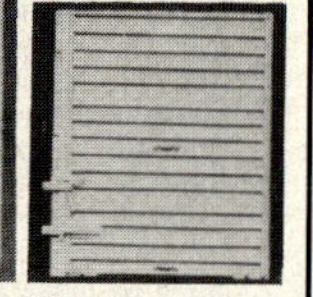
6' Youngstown
4-5-4 Panel
783-2913
pair 1.50

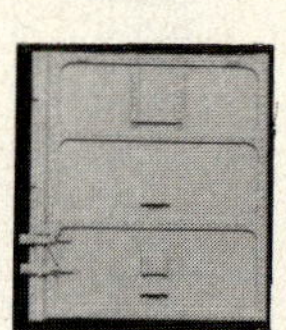
6' Creco
783-2912
pair 1.50

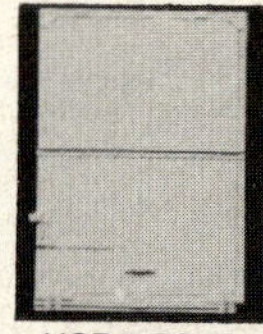
USRA SS Box
783-3332
pair 1.50

6' AT&SF
Steel Plate
783-3612   pair 1.50

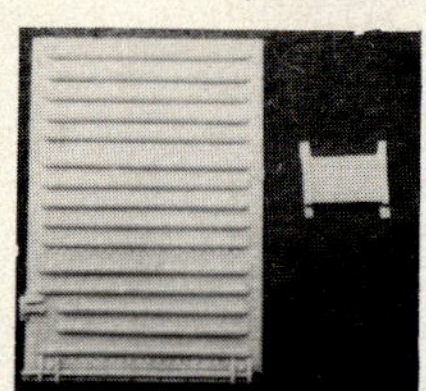
6' AT&SF
5-5-5 Corrugated
783-3613
pair 1.50

END SILL

■ LTD QTY AVAILABLE ■
Pennsylvania, circa 1900
783-1320   pair 1.50

Wood, Short
783-3926   pair 1.50

ICE HATCH DETAIL SET

Detail Set
(includes hatch cover top & bottom,
hold-up, false interior, hatch plug)
783-6024   *NEW* pkg(4) 3.50

Detail Set
(includes hatch cover, hold-up, self-
locking frame, false interior, hatch plug)
783-6724   *NEW* pkg(4) 3.50

LADDERS

Reefer Ladders,
5 and 6 rung
783-6690 2.00
pkg(5)
NEW

FREIGHT CAR ENDS

7-8 Corrugated for
SS Box Cars
783-3615   pair 2.50

USRA DS Box Car
783-3822   pair 2.50

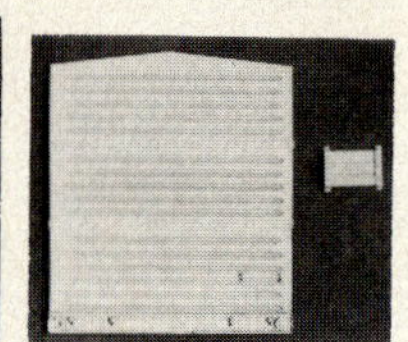
Murphy, 3-Panel
783-1990   pair 2.50

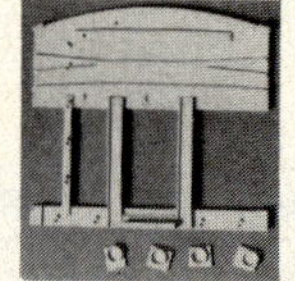
C&O Dreadnaught
Hopper w/Details
783-2164   pair 2.50

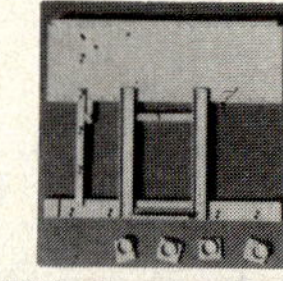
NYC Hopper w/Details
783-2166   pair 2.50

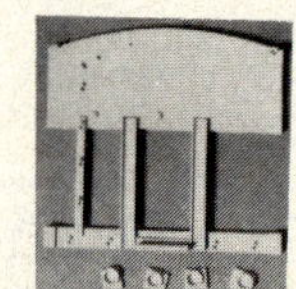
C&O Radial Hopper
w/Details
783-2162   pair 2.50

T-Brace for Truss Rod Car
783-4117   pair 2.50

BxY/Z Steel Reinforced
Wood
783-4023   pair 2.50

NEW
End, dreadnaught for
box car
783-4712   2.50

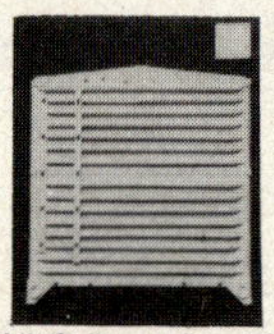
NYC Steel Box Car
783-2917   pair 2.50

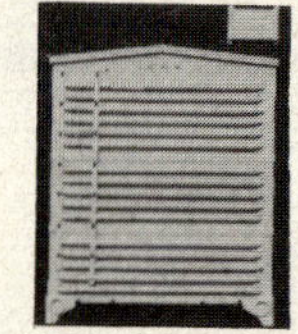
USRA SS Box Car
783-3333   pair 2.50

GN Box Car
783-2862   pair 2.50

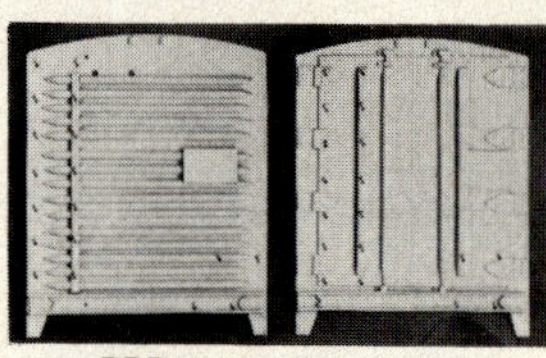
PRR A 50-4 Auto Car
783-1112   pair 2.50

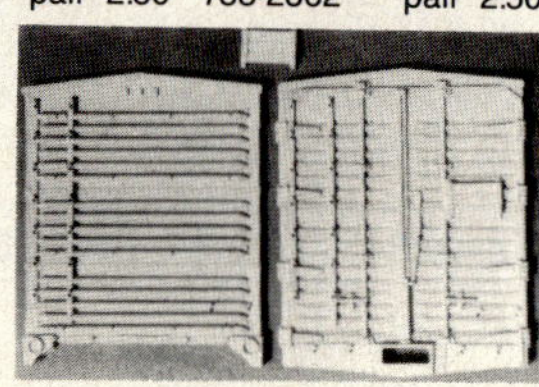
GN Auto Car
783-2812   pair 2.50

MISCELLANEOUS

Queen post, short
783-3922   pair 1.50

Wine Door Lock Set
783-1171   pkg(4) 1.50
injection molded

Bolster
Early Bettendorf
783-5325
pair 2.00

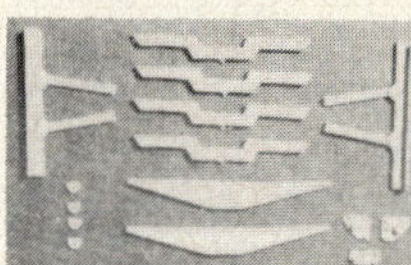
Hopper Detail Set
783-2190   set 2.00
Includes end peaks,
slope sheet support
struts and enterprise
door locks.

POLING POCKET

783-2290 Truss Rod Car	pkg(4)	1.50
783-2139 Hopper	pkg(4)	1.50

2290   2139

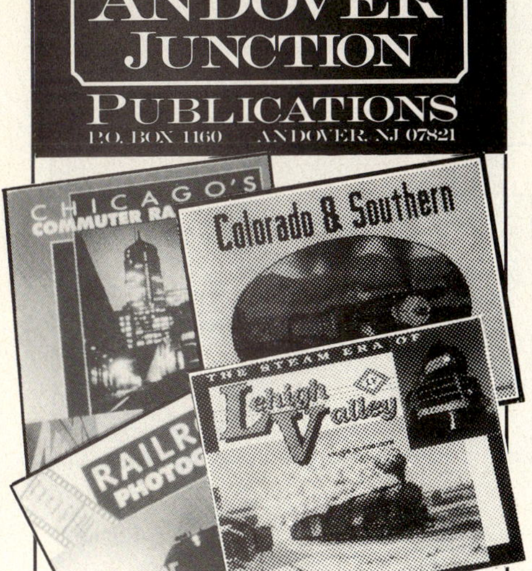

REMEMBER THE ROCK
133-101   13.95
Memories of Rock Island's diesel era in Iowa and Illinois. Softcover, 89 black and white photos, 11 x 8-1/2".

COLORADO & SOUTHERN
133-103   13.95
Standard gauge operations during the last years of steam. Softcover, 66 pages, 8-1/2 x 11".

KATY DIESELS TO THE GULF
133-105   39.95
Numerous photos and detailed text offer an insight into the operations and equipment of the Katy, from its lean years with repowered FA1's and AS-16's, to emergence as a major line in the 1980's and merger with the Union Pacific. Softcover, album size format, 108 pages, 10-3/4 x 12".

STEAM ERA OF LEHIGH VALLEY
133-107   29.95
A look back at the Lehigh Valley, from its distinctive steam to early diesels. Includes chapters on the early beginnings of the railroad, freight and passenger equipment, steam operations, the diesel invasion, shop facilities and more. Hundreds of black-and-white photos. Hardcover, album size format, 112 pages, 11-1/2 x 9-1/2".

BURLINGTON NORTHERN: A 21 YEAR SALUTE
133-108   59.95
Invaluable reference documenting the reign of the Burlington Northern, from the beginnings of the Great Northern, Burlington Route, Northern Pacific and Spokane, Portland & Seattle to the giant BN system of today. Hardcover, maps, hundreds of color photos, 192 pages.

CHICAGO'S COMMUTER RAILROADS: A GUIDE TO THE METRA SYSTEM
133-109   24.95

RAILROAD PHOTOGRAPHY: HOW TO SHOOT LIKE THE PROS
133-110   **NEW** 24.95
What you need to know to take pictures of your favorite railroad. Includes tips from well-known railroad photographers. Sections on specialties, like night shots, video and model railroad photography. Soft cover, many full color photos, 8-1/2 x 11".

LAKE MICHIGAN RAILROAD CAR FERRIES
133-111   **NEW** 24.95

■■ LTD QUANTITIES AVAILABLE ■■
CHESAPEAKE & OHIO
133-104   13.95
Early diesels in service on the Chesapeake & Ohio. Softcover.

BRAWA

Imported from Germany by WALTHERS

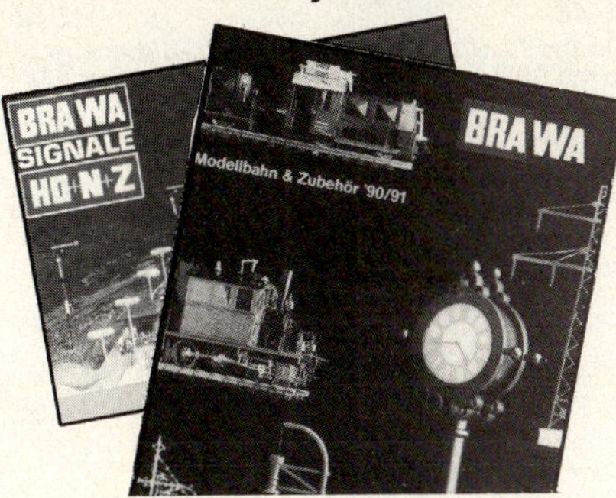

1990-91 HO, N&Z CATALOG
186-10   7.49
Color photos throughout full Brawa line of miniatures. Softcover, 86 pages, 8-1/4 x 11-3/4".

SIGNAL MANUAL
186-29   22.99
Signal manual tells model railroaders all they need to know about setting up, wiring and operating signals. Many illustrations and circuit diagrams. 85 pages, 11-3/4 x 18-1/4".

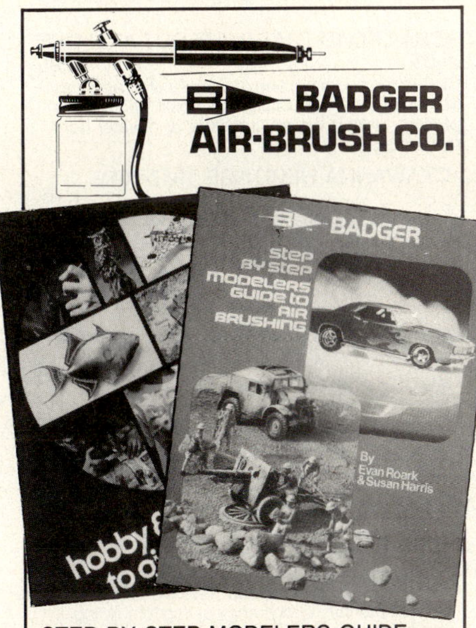

STEP BY STEP MODELERS GUIDE TO AIR-BRUSHING
165-505   8.95
Covers painting models, figures and dioramas. Also includes techniques from shadowing to properly mixing paint. Over 180 color photos, 32 pages, 8-1/2 x 11".

HOBBY & CRAFT GUIDE TO AIR-BRUSHING
165-500   5.95
Includes sections on preparation for painting, mixing paint, cleaning and maintenance. Over 130 full color illustrations, 32 pages, 8-1/2 x 11".

How-to-do and what-to-do reference and layout books.

BEGINNERS GUIDE TO HO MODEL RAILROADING
150-9   3.95
Construction tips and hints on the use of Atlas Snap-Track, plus information on how to assemble and wire 12 different layouts. 44 pages.

"CUSTOM-LINE" LAYOUTS FOR HO SCALE RAILROADS
150-11   **NEW** 4.95
Various phases of scale trackwork and layouts; plans for 11 layouts. Illustrated, 48 pages, 8-1/2 x 11".

THE COMPLETE ATLAS WIRING BOOK
150-12   **NEW** 4.95
This easy to follow reference book covers and simplifies almost every phase of HO Scale layout wiring. Diagrams, 56 pages, 8-1/2 x 11".

"CUSTOM-LINE" SIX RAILROADS YOU CAN BUILD
150-13   4.95
Detailed, step-by-step construction of six different layouts—including wiring & scenicking. Diagrams, illustrations, photos, 48 pages, 8-1/2 x 11".

"CUSTOM-LINE" KING SIZE PLAN BOOK: HO RAILROADS YOU CAN BUILD
150-14   6.95
Six railroad layouts with complete step-by-step instructions on construction, scenicking and wiring. Photos, plans, 36 pages, 18 x 11".

THE ALL NEW PARTS CATALOG
150-3   5.00
Includes all locomotive repair manuals, and currently available parts. 50 pages.

INTRODUCTION TO N SCALE MODEL RAILROADING
150-6   **NEW** 2.00
Nine layout options for table tops. Complete wiring instructions plus chapters on benchwork and tracklaying. 38 pages.

NINE N SCALE RAILROADS
150-7   4.95
Step by step instructions for benchwork, tracklaying, wiring and scenery. Illustrated with dozens of large photos. 50 pages.

433-8003 Basic for Beginners   1.00
          8th Edition
Loaded with useful tips and ideas on detailing, building and landscaping your layout.

Carstens
PUBLICATIONS, INC.

An assortment of railroad publications . . . plan books, electrical handbooks. Books are soft-cover unless noted.

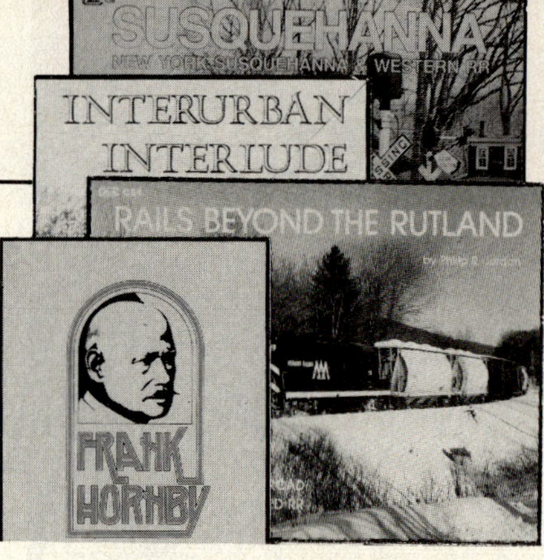

RAILROADS

CONNECTICUT COMPANY STREETCARS
205-82 **NEW** 21.95
Offers a brief historical overview, maps, photos and illustrations depicting operations in Hartford, New Haven, Norwich, New London, Derby, Waterbury, Bridgeport, and more. Over 150 photos and illustrations.

SUSQUEHANNA: NYS&W
205-80 15.95
New York, Susquehanna & Western from Erie Steam and railcars through RS1's to GP18's. Picturesque railroading in rural New Jersey. The pre-DO era. 98 pages, 11 x 8-1/2".

BALTIMORE & OHIO HERITAGE: 1945-1955
205-52 7.95
From 2-8-8-4's and 2-10-2's to 4-4-2's on the old Buffalo & Susquehanna. 48 pages. 11 x 8-1/2".

SLIM GAUGE CARS
205-72 19.95
This narrow gauge plan book includes virtually every popular type of narrow gauge freight car. Many photos in full color.

UPRR: THE OVERLAND ROUTE
205-60 12.95
Big power and long trains are a trade mark of this great American carrier. See it in the last great days of steam and the transition to diesel, and the famed passenger fleet. 11 x 8".

THE FINAL YEARS: NYO&W RY
205-61 15.95
Photo coverage of the New York Ontario & Western Ry's final 20 years of steam and diesel operation from Weehawken, New Jersey, to Otsego, New York, and Scranton, Pennsylvania. 100 pages, 11 x 8".

CUMBERLAND & PENNSYLVANIA
205-63 9.95
Western Maryland acquired the famous old C&P and in turn was absorbed by the Chessie. Photos of steam power and unusual gas-electrics operating in the Alleghenies. 11 x 8".

RAILS BEYOND THE RUTLAND
205-54 12.95
Contemporary operations of the Vermont Railway, Green Mountain Railroad and Clarendon & Pittsford are presented by Phil Jordan and Edwill Brown. Pictures of rail action in Vermont's green mountains, and a remembrance of Rutland steam

GRAND TRUNK HERITAGE
205-66 13.95
An enlarged edition of the original book, covers Grand Trunk steam in Maine, New Hampshire and Quebec. 64 pages.
(By Special Order Only.)

EXTRA SOUTH
205-53 21.95
Nostalgic look at southern steam railroading. Reprint of 1964 edition with expanded text and photos. 144 pages, 8-1/2 x 11".

LEHIGH & HUDSON RIVER VOL 2
205-56 8.95
Action in the diesel age is highlighted in this second of two volumes.

CHICAGO GREAT WESTERN
205-39 12.95
Philip P. Hastings' coverage of the CGW during its last decade as an independent operation before merging into the C&NW. Photos of early diesels and snow scenes. 2nd printing, 80 pages, 8 x 11".

LONG ISLAND ELECTRIC HERITAGE
205-50 7.95
Views of early Long Island electrification with Pennsy power and Gibbs subway-type cars. Rare photos, 8 x 11".

SEABOARD COAST LINE
205-46 15.95
Covers the time period from the ACL-SAL merger to the SBD 1982 image. Photos (some color), 80 pages, 8-1/2 x 11".

THE V&O STORY
205-47 19.95
Examines the philosophy, concepts and history behind W. Allen McClelland's mythical Virginia & Ohio super layout. Photos (some color), 100 pages, 8-1/2 x 11".

INTERURBAN INTERLUDE
205-76 14.95
A history of the North Jersey Rapid Transit Company. Hardcover, 92 pages, 8 x 11".
(By Special Order Only.)

EAST BROAD TOP
205-40 9.95
Photos, history and maps of the EBT from its first run in 1874 to its last run in 1956. 80 pages, 8-1/2 x 11."

C&O—SUPER POWER TO DIESELS
205-49 15.95
History of Chessie steam & diesels from World War II until the present. Photos, 128 pages.

COLORADO MEMORIES OF THE NARROW GAUGE CIRCLE
205-59 15.95
Photographs of the narrow gauge circle in Colorado during the period 1935 to 1960. Passenger trains as they were. 130 pages, 11 x 8".

THE RAILROAD THAT CAME OUT AT NIGHT
205-65 12.95
Covers railroading in and around Boston as it was from the time South Station was built through the present. Here is big city industrial and water front railroading.

LACKAWANNA HERITAGE 1947-1952
205-69 8.95
Covers the DL&W's final transition years before merger with Erie. Steam, diesel and electric operations on main line and branches. Milk trains. 8 x 11".

```
████ LIMITED QUANTITIES ████
         AVAILABLE
```
LEHIGH & NEW ENGLAND
205-81 **NEW** 13.95
Covers the road's turbulent history as a bridge road and major coal hauler. Photos, 80 pages.

MODELING

BRIDGE & TRESTLE HANDBOOK
205-79 **NEW** 18.95
Includes information about railroad bridges, from elementary bridge engineering to building the bridge that's right for your layout. Fourth edition, photos, 156 pages.

ELECTRICAL HANDBOOK FOR MODEL RAILROADERS, VOLUME I
205-21 7.95
Basic model railroad electric information for the beginner and advanced modeler. Diagrams and photos. 68 pages.

TRACK DESIGN 2
205-62 9.95
Selected model railroad layout designs to fit almost every space requirement with many practical do and don't hints. Adaptable to all scales and gauges. 76 pages.

COMPLETE LAYOUT PLANS (3rd Edition)
205-73 7.95
A track book for beginners and others who prefer sectional track whether in N, HO, TT, S or O. Nearly 150 designs, 186 piece track planning kit, 36 pages, 8 x 11".

ELECTRICAL HANDBOOK FOR MODEL RAILROADS, VOLUME 2 (Revised)
205-43 8.95
Some basics but primarily covers the more advanced aspects of the hobby, such as signaling. Photos, diagrams, 196 pages, 8-1/2 x 11".

DESIGN HANDBOOK FOR MODEL RAILROADERS
205-71 8.95
Paul Mallery explains how to design large and small model railroads. Terminals, yards, mainlines, mountains, cities, mistakes to avoid, and more. 66 pages, 8-1/4 x 11".

MODEL RR STRUCTURES FROM A to Z
205-48 12.95
Examines the art of creating structures from a wide variety of material and includes info on painting & weathering. 200 pages.

TRACTION PLANBOOK (2nd Edition)
205-16 9.95
Enlarged and revised. Packed with specially drawn traction plans. Photos, 98 pages, 8 x 11".

CIRCUS TRAINS, TRUCKS & MODELING
205-70 12.95
Model a railroad or truck circus with this historic and informative book. Includes photos of prototype equipment and operations, plus an up-to-date listing of available circus kits. 52 pages, 8-1/2 x 11".

MISCELLANEOUS

LIONEL STANDARD GAUGE ERA
205-13 4.00
Photos and text describing almost every major loco and car type made by Lionel in Standard Gauge 1906-1941. Invaluable reference for collectors, armchair buffs and dealers. 34 pages. 8-1/2 x 11".

TOY TRAINS OF YESTERYEAR
205-67 5.00
Collection of articles reprinted from ''Toy Trains Magazine'', covering early manufacturers, train sets and more. 52 pages, 8-1/4 x 11".

FRANK HORNBY
205-20002 3.95
The story of Frank Hornby; billed as ''The Boy Who Made $1,000,000.00 With A Toy''. Illustrations, hardcover, 141 pages, 3-3/4 x 5-3/4".

BASSETT-LOWKE CENTENNIAL BOOK
205-1004 12.00
Photos and information on Britain's famed Bassett-Lowke Works; reproductions of 13 famous B-L catalogs, numbered limited edition, hardcover (with case), 136 pages, 11 x 8".

ED CRIST, INC.

DOVER PUBLICATIONS

Historical railroad books and cut and assemble structure books.

All books are softcover and feature an 11 x 8-1/2" format to showcase dramatic photos.

RIO GRANDE SOUTHERN ALBUM
258-17   18.00

This full-color book will provide lots of modeling ideas for narrow gauge fans! These original photos by the late Philip Ronfor show the line as a working railroad and were taken on several fan trips in the late 40's and early 50's. Over 40 shots of equipment operating through spectacular mountain scenery, plus a map and timetable are included. 39 pages.

OLD DOMINION STEAM
258-23   12.95

This collection of photos illustrates the operations of the Chesapeake & Ohio in Virginia. Lots of heavy steam power, including the streamlined "Chessie" locos and the steam turbine versions are shown in action. A few early diesels are also seen. 64 pages.

MEMORIES OF ERIE
258-25   20.00

Covers the Erie in its entire length, from Chicago to Jersey City, covering all of the divisions and selected branches. The photos cover the period from the early 1930's up to the 1960 E-L merger. They include rare photos from the Depression years of long-gone trains as well as full coverage of the diesel era. One of America's premier railroads, gone now for thirty years, can be seen once again in all of its diversity and drama.

BUFFALO CREEK AND GAULEY
258-33   20.00

The Buffalo Creek & Gauley was a West Virginia shortline that labored in obscurity from its opening in 1905 to the end of the 1950's. As steam disappeared from the Class 1 railroads, the BC&G became a mecca for steam fans in the late 1950's and early 1960's. Heavy coal trains behind Consolidations worked the mainline, and Shay-powered logging trains worked the logging branch on the Lily Fork, while secondhand Mikado's hauled the unusual "gob pile" trains. Author Warden has covered the history of the BC&G from its earliest days through the railfan era and the last runs. A thorough history of the road is combined with exceptional photography to bring to life again one of the country's most fondly-remembered shortlines. 80 pages.

ROUTE OF THE ERIE LIMITED
258-82   9.95

All aboard the "Erie Limited" as it rolls on its 998 mile journey from Jersey City to Chicago. You'll travel behind a wide range of steam and diesel power, with photo stops at many of the major cities on the route. 48 pages.

TICKET TO SILVERTON
258-100   9.95

Best known as a tourist railroad today, the Silverton Branch of the Rio Grande was once a thriving railroad. This book looks at the history of the line and a primer on the narrow gauge highlights the lines of the Narrow Gauge Circle, including the Rio Grande Southern. "Hollywood on the Narrow Gauge" looks at many of the films made on the Silverton. 48 pages.

SEPTEMBER 15, 1830

England's Liverpool & Manchester Railway starts operations over its double track mainline, the first railroad specifically designed and built with this feature.

EARLY AMERICAN LOCOMOTIVES
241-22772   8.95

Historical (1804-1874), main-line (post,1870), special and foreign locomotive engravings from the late 19th Century. Illustration, 200 pages, 11-3/8 x 8-1/4".

ANTIQUE LOCOMOTIVES COLORING BOOK
241-23293   2.95

Coloring book of famous 19th and 20th Century American and European locomotives. 48 pages, 8-1/4 x 11".

TROLLEYS AND STREETCARS ON AMERICAN PICTURE POSTCARDS
241-23749   8.95

A unique and extensive collection of trolleys and streetcars as they appeared on American picture postcards. 191 illustrations (16 full color), 87 pages, 8-1/2 x 11".

A HISTORY OF THE AMERICAN LOCOMOTIVE: 1830-1880
241-23818   19.95

The American locomotive; its design and history from 1830-80. Scaled drawings, plans, photos, illustrations, 528 pages, 8-3/8 x 8".

THE GREAT CIRCUS PARADE IN PICTURES
241-26201   9.95

Contains 183 rare and unusual photographs and posters (10 in full color) of the great circus street parades so popular at the turn of the century. With captions. Soft cover, 127 pages, 8-3/8 x 9-1/4".

AMERICAN CIRCUS POSTERS
241-23693   9.95

Features reproductions of original posters from 1890 through 1940, highlights unusual acts, wild animals performers and more. Soft cover, 48 pages, 10-1/4 x 14-1/4".

THE LONG ISLAND RAILROAD IN EARLY PHOTOGRAPHS
241-26301   13.95

In this fascinating text-and-photo documentary, a noted railroad historian and expert on Long Island Railroad details the economic and social upheaval that followed as rapid, inexpensive railroad service ended the isolation of people, products, thought and culture on Long Island. Over 220 rare photographs capture not only significant milestones in history, but also offer a nostalgic glimpse of people and times long gone. Soft cover, 152 pages, 8-7/8 x 11-3/4".

CUT & ASSEMBLE STRUCTURES
HO buildings printed in full color on cardboard stock.

VICTORIAN HOUSES
241-23849   5.95

Four buildings, 32 pages, 12-1/4 x 9-1/4".

MAIN STREET
241-24473   5.95

Nine buildings of a typical American small town of the 1920s. 32 pages, 12-1/4 x 9-1/4".

EARLY NEW ENGLAND VILLAGE
241-23536   6.95

Twelve buildings. 48 pages, 12-1/4 x 9-1/4".

A WESTERN FRONTIER TOWN
241-23736   6.95

Ten buildings. 48 pages, 12-1/4 x 9-1/4".

OLD FASHIONED FARM
241-24589   5.95

Nine buildings. 12-1/4 x 9-1/4".

CASTLE
241-24663   6.95

Model of Caernarvon Castle in Wales.

EARLY AMERICAN SEAPORT
241-24754   5.95

Eleven buildings.

SEASIDE RESORT
241-25097   5.95

CIRCUS PARADE
241-24861   5.95

Includes band, horses, wild animals, wagons and more.

OLD TIME CAROUSEL
241-24992   6.95

OLD TIME TRAIN
241-25324   6.95

GREENFIELD VILLAGE
241-25635   5.95

HOUSE OF GABLES
241-26150   3.95

ARNOLD

Imported from Germany and marketed by **WALTHERS**

ARNOLD '93–'94 CATALOG ENGLISH EDITION
125-1593   8.49

Arnold, the pioneer of N Gauge, offers an enormous selection for European modeling. Discover top notch engine performance, self-cleaning rails and high technology. Prototype and modeling information included. Full color, 8-1/4 x 11-1/2".

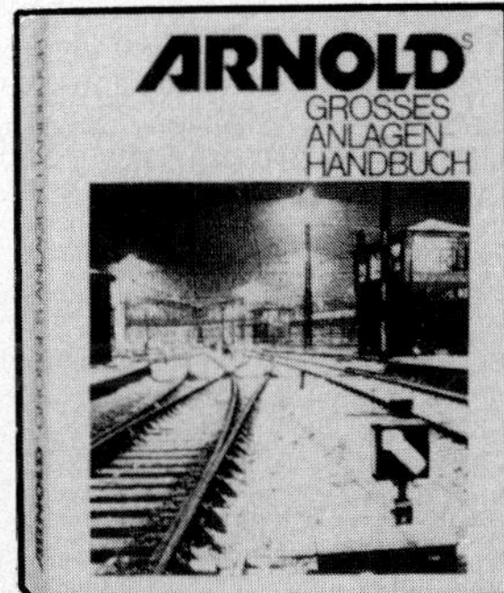

TRACK BOOK
125-36 German edition   68.49

Golden West Books

Nearly every phase of American railroading is represented: Steam, locos, diesels, logging and mining roads, interurbans and histories of the Santa Fe and the railroad caboose. All books are hardcover unless otherwise noted.

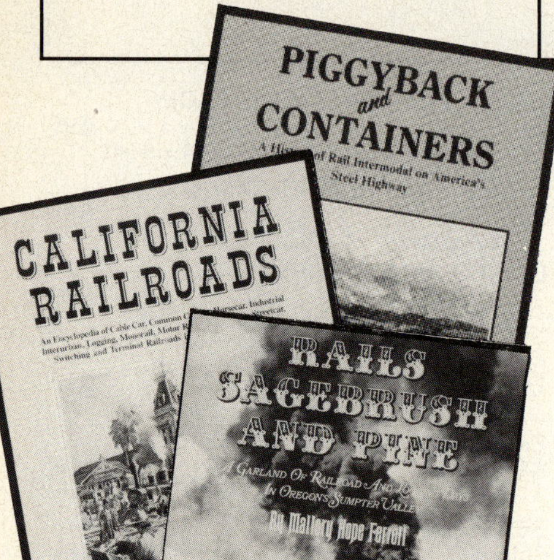

We have worked closely with this manufacturer to provide accurate availability information at the time this catalog was published. Items listed in *blue ink* may not be available at all times. Please see your dealer for current delivery information.

THE LOS ANGELES AND SALT LAKE RAILROAD COMPANY
290-81   54.95
Covers the 780 mile route between Salt Lake City and Los Angeles from the formation of the line to modern operations. Features locomotive ratings, complete steam loco roster, eight color plates, 20 maps and over 365 illustrations.

PIKE'S PEAK COG ROAD
290-32   36.95
Tells about the early railroad projections, problems of the line construction, operation of the cog road, the steam locomotives, today's modern diesel trains, snow fighting, the rolling stock and the workings of the rack system. Illustrated, 176 pages, 8-1/2 x 11″.

MOUNT LOWE: RAILWAY IN THE CLOUDS
290-51   39.95
Chronicles in word and picture the building of the great cable incline on a 62 percent grade, plus the grading construction of the narrow gauge line to Alpine Tavern, whose tracks followed the natural contour of the mountainside over 18 trestles and around 127 corners. Illustrated, 234 pages, 8-1/2 x 11″.

SUPER CHIEF: TRAIN OF THE STARS
290-83   39.95
On-the-spot narrative of the train's story. The first commercial passenger diesels for Super-1 of 1936, the custom made Super-2 with its red-nosed diesels, the test runs, the press preview trips, the train operation and personnel, the celebrities who rode the train, the dining car experience record and speed run. Illustrated, 256 pages, 6 x 9″.

THE BUDD RAIL-DIESEL CAR
290-84   57.95
Chronicles in word and picture, the history and development of the Budd Company's Rail-Diesel Car, better known as RDC. Included are an appendix, route map, model plans and roster by date built. Illustrations, 218 pages, 8-1/2 x 11″.

PIGGYBACK AND CONTAINERS: A HISTORY OF RAIL INTERMODAL ON AMERICA'S STEEL HIGHWAY
290-87   **NEW** 47.95
Describes the expansion of United Parcel Service. Features the container phenomenon, with its double-stack trains; also discusses the loading and unloading process. 205 illustrations, 192 pages, 8-1/2 x 11″.

CALIFORNIA RAILROADS
290-88   **NEW** 46.95
An encyclopedia of cable car, common carrier, horsecar, industrial, interurban, logging, monorail, motor road, short lines, streetcar, switching and terminal railroads in California (1851-1992), with an in-depth history of each. 228 illustrations, 200 pages, 8-1/2 x 11″.

RAILS, SAGEBRUSH & PINE
290-91   **NEW** 25.95
Railroad and logging days in Oregon's Sumpter Valley. Illustrated, 218 pages, 8-1/2 x 11″.

■■■ LIMITED QUANTITY ■■■

STREET RAILWAYS AND THE GROWTH OF LOS ANGELES
290-85   48.95
Tells the story of the horse, cable and electric lines, plus the men who played such an indispensable role in the growth of Los Angeles. Illustrated, 188 pages, 8-1/2 x 11″.

BEAUMONT HILL: SOUTHERN PACIFIC'S SOUTHERN CALIFORNIA GATEWAY
290-86   48.95
Covers beginnings in 1870's to the heavy double-stack trains of today. Learn about the operation of the line, the flash floods, the sandstorms and how the blistering heat affects day-to-day operations. 265 illustrations, 8 maps and 12 color plates. 174 pages, 8 1/2 x 11″.

THE RAILROAD CABOOSE
290-14   29.95
The 100 year history of the Railroad Caboose. Illustrated, 237 pages, 6 x 9″.

THE SOUTHERN PACIFIC OF MEXICO
290-76   39.95
An in-depth look at SP operations in Mexico. Over 330 illustrations. 9 maps and all-time roster. 168 pages, 8-1/2 x 11″.

THE TIME OF THE TROLLEY
290-78   42.95
A revised and updated version of the classic ''Time of the Trolley'' by William D. Middleton. 700 pages, over 700 illustrations. 8-1/2 x 11″.

TEHACHAPI
290-67   48.95
California's Tehachapi ''Loop'' where the rails of the SP and SF breast Tehachapi Pass. Illustrated, 278 pages, 8-1/2 x 11″.

THE GREAT YELLOW FLEET
290-90   45.95
Complete story of the refrigerator car from its origin to the current mechanical refrigerator cars and piggyback refrigerator trailers. Illustrations, specifications, 165 pages, 8-1/2 x 11″.

TRACTION CLASSICS: Volume 2
290-71   38.95
Features streamline high-speed cars, private cars, sleeping cars and parlor-observation cars which ran under overhead wire. 258 pages, 8-1/2 x 11″.

REDWOOD LUMBER INDUSTRY
290-65   17.50
The complete story of California's redwood lumber industry, from the days of the explorers to the present time. Illustrated, 218 pages, 8-1/2 x 11″.

BAJA CALIFORNIA RAILWAYS
290-79   29.95
A study of railroads and railroading south of the California border. Features an all-time roster of steam and diesel locomotives, maps and more than 225 illustrations. 350 pages, 5-1/2 x 8-1/2″.

WEEKEND CHIEF PUBLISHING

Weekend Chief covers a wide range of prototype railroading, with a special focus on operations in the eastern United States. Each book is loaded with photos, making them an ideal reference for the modeler or historian.

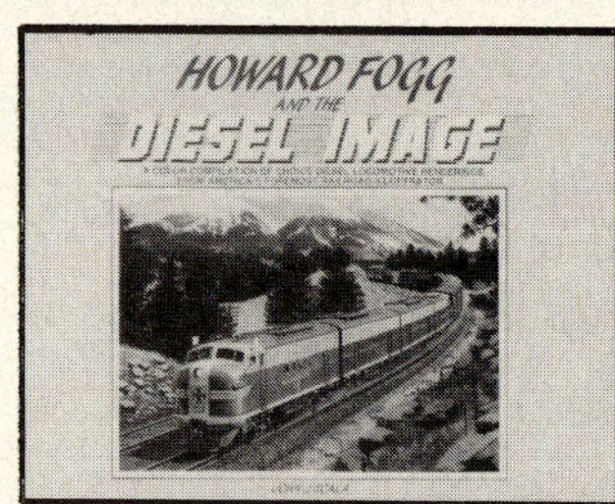

HOWARD FOGG AND THE DIESEL IMAGE
779-1   39.95
Showcases diesel locos prints by noted rail artist Howard Fogg. Prints are full-page, with caption information. Full-color, hardcover, 175 pages, indexed by railroad, 12 x 9″.

MAINLINE STEAM REVIVAL
779-4   39.95

GREAT DAYS CANADIAN STEAM
779-5 **(By Special Order Only.)**   29.95

LIRR EARLY PHOTOS
779-6   13.95

TRACTION YEARBOOK
779-103	1983	23.95
779-104	1984	23.95
779-105	1985	29.95
779-106	1986	34.95
779-107	1987 **(By Special Order Only.)**	39.95

THE COLORFUL PCC'S OF PITTSBURGH
779-108 **(By Special Order Only.)**   TBA

BROOKLYN'S WATERFRONT RAILWAYS
779-109   **NEW** 24.95
Brooklyn steam, diesel and electric's in color and black & white. Maps & brochures. Softcover, 64 pages.

DIESEL DEMONSTRATORS
779-110   **NEW** TBA

VICTORIAN RR STATION
779-1004 **(By Special Order Only.)**   39.95

kibri
Imported from Germany by WALTHERS

'93-'94 KIBRI CATALOG
405-99900   5.49

- More than 600 items listed
- Every page in color
- Separate sections for HO, N & Z
- 11 x 8-1/2″

CHARLES S. GREGG PUBLISHER

CLASSIC RAILROAD BOOK REPRINTS

TRAIN SHED CYCLOPEDIA

The Train Shed reprints contain the plans and photos from the various ''cyclopedias'' referred to in the listings. Excellent sources for reference on all types of cars and locos. No color information is given.

INDEX to TRAIN SHEDS 1 thru 42
310-874   2.95
Breakdown of which books contain what items.

1930 LOCOMOTIVE CYCLOPEDIA
(Total Reprint of Original)
310-943 hardcover, 1440 pages   49.95

TANK CARS 1922-1943
310-841 (TS 12) 80 pages   4.50

4-8-4's & OTHER HEAVY PASSENGER LOCOS 1927-1941
310-843 (TS 14) 70 pages   3.95

HEAVY TRACTION 1922-1941
310-844 (TS 15) 88 pages   4.95

FAMOUS PASSENGER TRAINS from the **1943 CAR BUILDERS CYCLOPEDIA**
310-845 (TS 16) 72 pages   3.95

BOX, STOCK & FLAT CARS from the **1943 CAR BUILDERS CYCLOPEDIA**
310-846 (TS 17) 72 pages   3.95

BUILDINGS & STRUCTURES of AMERICAN RAILROADS, 1893
310-848 (Part 3) (TS 19) 80 pages   4.50

DIESEL & GAS ELECTRIC LOCOMOTIVES 1925-1938 (with full color photos)
310-849 (TS 20) 80 pages   5.95

PASSENGER CARS from the **1943 CAR BUILDERS CYCLOPEDIA**
310-851 (TS 21) 80 pages   4.50

STEAM LOCOMOTIVES from the 1938 LOCOMOTIVE
310-852 (Part 1) (TS 22) 80 pages   4.50

STEAM LOCOMOTIVES & TENDERS from the 1938 LOCOMOTIVE CYCLOPEDIA
310-853 (Part 2) (TS 23) 80 pages   4.50

BUILDINGS & STRUCTURES of AMERICAN RAILROADS
310-854 (Part 4) (TS 24) 92 pages   4.95

ELECTRIC MOTOR CARS 1888-1928
310-855 (TS25) 80 pages   4.50

RAILWAY SERVICE CARS 1928-1943
310-856 (TS 26) 88 pages   4.95

SIGNALS & SIGNAL SYMBOLS
310-857 (TS 27) 32 pages   2.50

CARS, SCALES & GATES from the 1909 BUDA CATALOG
310-859 (TS 28) 80 pages   5.50
(160 full size pages reprinted as 80 pages from the original edition)

FREIGHT CARS, 1892 by William Voss
310-860 (TS 29) 80 pages   5.50

RAIL MOTOR CARS 1919-1928
310-861 (TS 30) 64 pages   4.50

LOCOMOTIVES, TENDERS & TRUCKS from the 1927 LOCOMOTIVE CYCLOPEDIA
310-862 (Part 1) (TS 31) 80 pages   5.50
310-863 (Part 2) (TS 32) 80 pages   5.50

BUILDINGS & STRUCTURES of AMERICAN RAILROADS, 1893
310-864 (Part 5) (TS 33) 72 pages   4.95
310-869 (Part 6) (TS 38) 72 pages   4.95

HAYS & other GEARED LOCOS from CATALOGS & CYCLOPEDIAS
310-865 (TS 34) 64 pages   4.50

INDUSTRIAL & FOREIGN LOCOS 1930
310-868 (TS 37) 72 pages   4.95

LOCOMOTIVE CABS & FITTINGS from the 1927 LOCOMOTIVE CYCLOPEDIA
310-871 (Part 1) (TS 40) 40 pages   3.00
310-872 (Part 2) (TS 41) 40 pages   3.00

DIESEL & OIL ELECTRICS from Westinghouse (1930) & Ingersoll-Rand (1936)
310-875 (TS 43) 64 pages   4.50

LOCOS from BALDWIN LOGGING LOCO CATALOG 1913 & LOCOMOTIVE STOKER CATALOG 1919
310-876 (TS 44) 64 pages   4.50

FLATS, GONDOLAS & HOPPERS from the 1931 CAR BUILDERS CYCLOPEDIA
310-878 (Part 1) (TS 46) 64 pages   4.50

LOCOS of the 40's & 50's (STEAM) from the 1941 LOCO CYCLOPEDIA & RAILWAY MECHANICAL ENGINEER. New Formula
310-877 (Part 1) (TS 45) 64 pages   4.50
310-879 (Part 2) (TS 47) 64 pages   4.50
310-881 (Part 3) (TS 49) 64 pages   4.50
310-882 (Part 4) (TS 50) 64 pages   4.50
310-883 (Part 5) (TS 51) 64 pages   4.50

HOPPERS, INDUSTRIALS, LETTERING from the 1931 CAR BUILDERS CYCLOPEDIA
310-880 (Part 2) (TS 48) 64 pages   4.50

BRIDGES & TRESTLES from VARIOUS RAILWAY ENGINEERING & MAINTENANCE CYCLOPEDIAS from 1921
310-889 (TS 54) 64 pages   4.50

LOCOS of the 40s & 50s (STEAM) from the 1942 LOCO CYC and RAILWAY MECHANICAL ENGINEER New Formula
310-891 (Part 6) (TS 56) 64 pages   4.50

LOCOS of the 40s & 50s (DIESEL) from the 1941 LOCO CYC and RAILWAY MECHANICAL ENGINEER New Formula
310-893 (Part 7) (TS 58) 64 pages   4.50

LOCOS of the 40s & 50s (DIESEL) from the 1941 LOCO CYC and RAILWAY MECHANICAL ENGINEER New Formula
310-895 (Part 8) (TS 60) 64 pages   4.50

THE 1925 CAR BUILDERS' CYCLOPEDIA Major Pages
310-896 (Part 1) (TS 61) 64 pages   4.50
310-897 (Part 2) (TS 62) 64 pages   4.50
310-898 (Part 3) (TS 63) 64 pages   4.50
310-900 (Part 4) (TS 65) 64 pages   4.50

LOCOS of the 40s & 50s NEW FORMULA (Still more DIESELS)
310-899 (Part 9) (TS 64) 64 pages   4.50

LOCOS of the 40s & 50s NEW FORMULA (Electrics and Turbines)
310-901 (Part 10) (TS 66) 64 pages   4.50

RAILWAY MECHANICAL ENGINEER Freight/Pass Cars, Shops/Terminals of the Late 40s-50s
310-908 Part 1 (TS 73) 64 pages   4.50

CAR BUILDER'S CYCLOPEDIA (1943) Cabooses-Freight Car Construction Details
310-910 (Part 4) (TS 75) 64 pages   4.50

CAR BUILDER'S CYCLOPEDIA (1925) Motor Passenger Cars/Construction Details
310-902 (Part 5) (TS 67) 64 pages   4.50

CAR BUILDERS CYCLOPEDIA (1925) Passenger Details, Trucks/Industrials
310-903 (Part 6) (TS 68) 64 pages   4.50

CAR BUILDERS CYCLOPEDIA (1943) Gondolas & Hoppers
310-905 (Part 2) (TS 70) 64 pages   4.50

CAR BUILDERS CYCLOPEDIA (1943) Hoppers, Tanks, Containers & Cabooses
310-906 (Part 3) (TS 71) 64 pages   4.50

CAR BUILDERS CYCLOPEDIA (1943) Freight Car Construction Details, Underframes and Brakes
310-912 (Part 5) (TS 77) 64 pages   4.50

FREIGHT & PASSENGER CARS, SHOPS & TERMINALS of the 40s and 50s
310-914 (Part 2) (TS 79) 64 pages   4.95

LOCOS of the 40s & 50s from the 1941 LOCO CYC & RAILWAY MECHANICAL ENGINEER
310-915 (Part 11) (TS 80) 64 pages   4.95

FREIGHT CAR CONSTRUCTION DETAILS, SAFETY APPLIANCES & TRUCKS from the 1943 CAR BUILDER'S CYCLOPEDIA
310-916 (Part 6) (TS 81) 64 pages   4.95

BOILERS from the 1919 LOCO CYCLOPEDIA
310-917 (Part 3) (TS 82) 64 pages   4.95

FREIGHT CAR CONSTRUCTION DETAILS, INDUSTRIAL & EXPORT CARS from the 1943 CAR BUILDERS CYCLOPEDIA
310-918 (Part 7) (TS 83) 64 pages   4.95

SMOKE BOXES & STOKERS from the 1919 LOCO CYCLOPEDIA
310-919 (Part 4) (TS 84) 64 pages   4.95
Full-size reprints of the entire contents of classic railroad originals. The books contain a wealth of technical details, accurate, authentic illustrations and comprehensive terminology. The Dictionaries also include a section of contemporary advertisements from manufacturers of parts and equipment.

FREIGHT & PASSENGER CARS, SHOPS & TERMINALS, in the 40s & 50s from the RAILWAY MECHANICAL ENGINEER
310-920 (Part 3) (TS 85) 64 pages   4.95

MOTOR CARS & PASSENGER CONSTRUCTION DETAILS, from the 1943 CAR BUILDERS CYCLOPEDIA
310-921 (Part 8) (TS 86) 64 pages   4.95

FRAMES, CYLINDERS & VALVE GEARS from the 1919 LOCO CYCLOPEDIA
310-922 (Part 5) (TS 87) 64 pages   4.95

CHARLES S. GREGG PUBLISHER

NOTE: Early TRAIN SHED CYCLOPEDIAS not listed are out of print and no longer available.

PASSENGER CONSTRUCTION DETAILS & INTERIOR FITTINGS from the 1943 CAR BUILDERS CYCLOPEDIA
310-923 (Part 9) (TS 88) 64 pages — 4.95

PISTONS THRU TRUCKS 1919
310-924 (Part 6) (TS 89) 64 pages — 4.95

CARS, SHOPS, TERMINALS of the 40s & 50s
310-925 (Part 4) (TS 90) — 4.95

■■■ LIMITED QUANTITIES ■■■ AVAILABLE

1931 FREIGHT CARS
310-827 (TS 3) 87 pages — 4.50

BUILDINGS & STRUCTURES OF AMERICAN RAILROADS (1893)
310-842 (PART 2) (TS13) 85 pages — 4.50

DICTIONARIES

LOCOMOTIVES selected from the 1916 LOCOMOTIVE DICTIONARY
310-847 (TS 18) 88 pages — 4.95

FREIGHT CARS from the 1919 CAR BUILDERS DICTIONARY
310-866 (Part 1) (TS 35) 80 pages — 5.50
310-867 (Part 2) (TS 36) 80 pages — 5.50

PASSENGER CARS from the 1919 CAR BUILDERS DICTIONARY
310-873 (TS 42) 32 pages — 3.00

STEAM LOCOMOTIVES from the 1919 LOCOMOTIVE DICTIONARY & CYCLOPEDIA
310-884 (Part 1) (TS 52) 64 pages — 4.50
310-885 (Part 2) (TS 53) 64 pages — 4.50

FREIGHT & PASSENGER CARS from the 1898 CAR BUILDERS DICTIONARY
310-890 (Part 1) (TS 55) 64 pages — 4.50
310-892 (Part 2) (TS 57) 64 pages — 4.50
310-894 (Part 3) (TS 59) 64 pages — 4.50

LOCOMOTIVE DICTIONARY 1912
310-904 (Part 1) (TS 69) 64 pages — 4.50
  Locomotive photos
310-907 (Part 2) (TS 72) 64 pages — 4.50
  Locomotive drawings & boilers
310-909 (Part 3) (TS 74) 64 pages — 4.50
  Smoke Boxes, Stokers, Valve Gears/Trucks
310-911 (Part 4) (TS 76) 64 pages — 4.50
  Cow Catchers, Cabs/Fittings plus Tenders
310-913 (Part 5) (TS 78) 64 pages — 4.50
  Electric Locomotives & Motor Cars.

U.S. WAR SERVICE LOCOMOTIVES from the 1919 LOCOMOTIVE DICTIONARY, AND WAR EQUIPMENT AND U.S. STANDARD CARS from the 1919 CAR BUILDERS' DICTIONARY
310-809 (TS 9) 88 pages — 4.50

MARCH 27, 1960

❉ Today ❉

IN RAILROAD HISTORY

The last regularly scheduled steam train in the United States makes its final run on the Grand Trunk Western.

CUSTOM RAILWAY SUPPLY

LIMITED EDITION Hand bound books

LENAHAN'S LOCOMOTIVE LEXICON, Volume 1
212-1003 — 9.50
Covers HO Scale steam and electric loco production from 1920 to 1970. Provides information on early brass industry plus origins of steam loco wheel arrangements and their names. Over 350 photos, softcover, 96 pages, 8-1/2 x 11".

LENAHAN'S LOCOMOTIVE LEXICON, Volume 2
212-1004 — 9.50
Provides a listing of all logging steamers, diesel and miscellaneous steam produced until 1970. Information on collecting HO and a look at early power drives. Photos.

GETTING MORE STEAM
212-1025 — 4.50
How-to-do book for improving the firing characteristics and efficiency of live steam locos. Illustrated, softbound, 36 pages, 5-1/2 x 8-1/2".

FIRING LOCOMOTIVES (Reprint)
212-1026 — 4.50
Firing Locomotives offers advice for getting maximum steam possible from coal burned for live steam locos. Softbound, 36 pages, 5-1/2 x 8-1/2".

LOCOMOTIVE WATER AND COALING STATIONS
212-1027 — 4.50
Reprint from PRACTICAL RAILROADING. 48 pages, 8-1/4 x 5-1/4".

ENGINE MODELERS' HANDBOOK
212-1029 — 4.75
Articles cover roundhouses and engine shops, tools, materials and methods used in plastic and metal modeling, methods for working with engine and structure detailing parts, both photo etched and cast, as well as track planning. Also included is a poster for the train collector and Custom Railway Supply's latest catalog of parts and videos. Some items in the catalog are not carried by wholesale or retail model railroad hobby suppliers.

See also: LOCOS, PASSENGER, TRACK, PARTS & VIDEO for additional CUSTOM RAILWAY SUPPLY items.

FALLER

Imported from Germany and marketed by WALTHERS

SCENIC MODELING MADE EASY
272-840 — 11.99
English text, introductory to scenic modeling. Covers initial considerations, tools & materials, first steps, mountain building, rock design, water, assembling structures, backgounds, laying track, ballasting, bridges & viaducts, winter landscaping, dioramas and electrical tips. Over 120 color illustrations, softcover, 35 pages, 8-1/4 x 11-1/2".

FALLER 1993-94 CATALOG
272-893 HO, N, and Z Scale — 8.99
• Separate sections for HO, N and Z
• Also includes a section of accessories & car system.

Z GAUGE MODELING
272-838 — 5.99
German text, lots of color photos and illustrated instructions. Softcover, 35 pages, 8-1/2 x 11".

DIORAMAS MADE EASY
272-843 German text — 17.49

We have worked closely with this manufacturer to provide accurate availability information at the time this catalog was published. Items listed in *blue ink* may not be available at all times. Please see your dealer for current delivery information.

Virnex Industries, Inc.

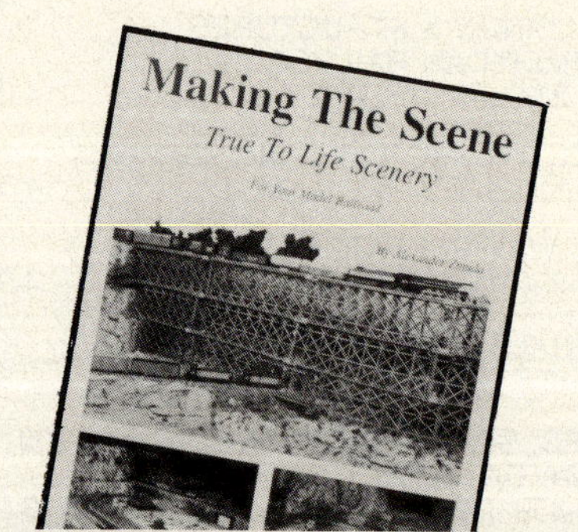

762-801 Making The Scene — 9.95
Includes chapters on track and trackwork, roadbed and ballasting, creating rivers and lakes, rockwork and more. Softcover, 74 pages.

HEIMBURGER HOUSE PUBLISHING

Heimburger House books cover an wide range of illustrated model and prototype railroad titles. Most books feature color covers and glossy enamel paper stock for the text. All books are softcover unless noted.

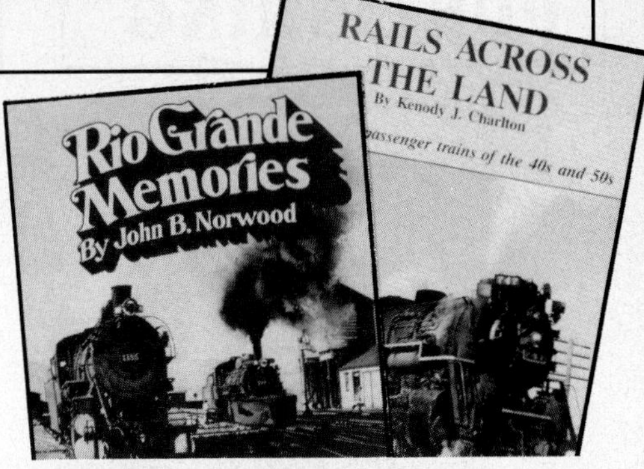

BUILDING AND OPERATING MODEL RAILROADS
030-1   9.95

Building & operations on 18 different S Scale model railroads. 18 diagrams, over 200 photos, 116 pages, 8-1/2 x 11".

S GAUGE LOCOMOTIVES & CARS
030-3   3.50

Techniques of model railroad rolling stock and loco construction. Emphasis on S Scale, but information is appropriate for all other scales. 40 pages, 8-1/2 x 11".

YOUR INTRODUCTION TO S GAUGE
030-5   6.95

In-depth descriptions of steam & diesel locomotives, freight & passenger cars, structures & other aspects of S Scale. Drawings, scale standards, 72 pages, 8-1/2 x 11".

Sn3 MODELING
030-6   11.95

A collection of articles, photos and plans of S Narrow Gauge model railroading, including color photos of Malcolm Furlow's Sn3 handiwork. 96 page, 8-1/2 x 11".

RIO GRANDE NARROW GAUGE
030-7   39.95

Features operations of the Rio Grande narrow gauge lines in southern Colorado and northern New Mexico. 275 illustrations, eight page color section, hardcover, 312 pages.

A.C. GILBERT'S HERITAGE
030-8   14.95

A collection of American Flyer articles and photos to help you learn more about the Gilbert Company. 164 pages, 8-1/2 x 11".

WABASH
030-9   39.95

History of the Wabash, as well as a dozen of its predecessor lines. Photos, roster, maps, timetables, hardcover, 320 pages, 8-1/2 x 11".

AMERICAN FLYER FEATURES
030-11   8.95

A collection of articles on AF collecting and operating. Many photos, some full color, 64 pages, 8-1/2 x 11".

FIDDLETOWN & COPPEROPOLIS
030-12   9.95

Covers the life and times of the mythical California railroad of Fiddletown & Copperopolis in the Sierra Nevada foothills. Depicted in cartoon form, this book features a map of the railroad. 144 pages, 9-1/2 x 6-1/4".

S GAUGE BUILDING AND REPAIR MANUAL
030-13   3.00

Contains how-to articles on building cars, locos, structures, trackwork and turnouts. Gives tips on trouble-shooting locos, painting, weathering and S Scale planning. 72 pages.

D&RGW NARROW GAUGE RECOLLECTIONS
030-14   39.95

John Norwood's personal account of 40 years service with the Rio Grande narrow gauge. A look at the daily operations, equipment and people of the area. Over 250 photos (some color), maps, timetables and a glossary of NG slang. Hardcover, 272 pages, 8-1/2 x 11".

ALONG THE EAST BROAD TOP
030-15 (By Special Order Only.)   39.95

Contains a detailed history of the Pennsylvania shortline, including station and car drawings. 350 photos, eight page color section, hardcover, 248 pages, 8-1/2 x 11".

AMERICAN FLYER INSTRUCTION BOOK
030-16 (By Special Order Only.)   4.95

Originally published in 1952 by A.C. Gilbert Co., includes instructions and suggestions on operating S Gauge, 2-rail trains and track tips. 14 track plans, layouts, 64 pages, 5-1/4 x 8-1/2".

RAILROADING WITH AMERICAN FLYER
030-17 (By Special Order Only.)   3.95

Hints for planning and operating 3-rail O Scale American Flyer layouts. Features 23 track plans and information on scenery, wiring, remote turnouts, crossing gates, block signals and testing for short circuits. 10 pages, 6-3/4 x 10-1/4".

LOGGING RAILROADS OF SOUTH CAROLINA
030-18   42.95

Details the hundreds of lumber railroads and shortlines that dotted South Carolina during the heyday of logging operations in the state. Hundreds of photos and dozens of drawings showing railroad lines, structures and track layouts. 175 black and white photos, 82 maps, hardcover, 8-1/2 x 11".

TRAINS OF AMERICA — Revised
030-19   43.95

Full color photo essay of dozens of American railroads, from late steam to early diesel. Photos arranged alphabetically by railroad name, and includes shortlines, class I railroads and regional rail lines. Features action, profile and detail shots with captions for each photo. Hardcover, 206 pages, 11 x 10".

VICTORY BRANCH RAILROAD OF VERMONT
030-20   8.95

Covers the 11 mile long railroad branch that ran between North Concord and Grancy, Vermont as part of the St. Johnsbury and Lake Champlain Railroad between 1883 and 1917. Approximately 20 black and white photos, 24 pages.

THE MAN WHO LIVES IN PARADISE: A.C. GILBERT'S AUTOBIOGRAPHY
030-22   24.95

Autobiography of A.C. Gilbert, founder of the A.C. Gilbert Company, maker of American Flyer trains and accessories. 8 pages of color photos, hardcover, approximately 400 pages.

COLLECTORS GUIDE TO AMERICAN TOY TRAINS
030-23   16.95

A complete reference to the U.S. toy train market. A chapter on terminology, information on pricing, identifying and locating pieces. Black and white photos, 234 pages, 7-1/2 x 9".

SOUVENIR EDITION OF S GAUGIAN
030-27   4.50

Magazine highlighting all the American Flyer S gauge trains made by Lionel from 1979-1989. Includes a detailed, handy reference list of items made. Color photos, 68 pages.

RAILS ACROSS THE LAND
030-24   39.95

Traces the railroad experiences of the author in the late 1940s and 1950s. Covers numerous railroads in the Midwest, West, East and South. The book recalls the fading majesty of time freights and quick-paced passenger trains throughout the US. Text accompanies 242 black and white and 14 color photographs, index, hardcover, 204 pages, 8-1/2 x 11".

RIO GRANDE MEMORIES
030-25   39.95

From Marshall Pass to the Royal Gorge War, from Cumbres Pass and Phantom Curve to the Dotsero Cut-Off, from wool loading on the Narrow Gauge to the *California Zephyr* and details of the *Silver Vista* viewing car, to first-hand accounts of numerous D&RGW people and events. Hundreds of black & white photos and an eight-page color photography section, index, hardcover, 192 pages, 8-1/2 x 11".

MILWAUKEE ROAD NARROW GAUGE
030-26   39.95

Describes the life and times of the three-foot narrow gauge line of the Chicago, Milwaukee and St Paul Railroad. Running 36 miles from Bellevue to Cascade, this colorful railroad linked the communities of Eastern Iowa with the outside world from 1877 until 1936. Hardcover, 270 pages, 8-1/2 x 11$_0$.

NORFOLK AND WESTERN COAL CAR EQUIPMENT
030-28   5.95

Covers the Norfolk & Western Railway coal hauling routes, rolling stock, and motive power and procedures during the mid-1940's. Gives a summary of the types of coal car equipment the N & W provided to its customers, along with specific car examples that give general arrangement drawings, specifications, car series number and a photograph of each car. 24 pages.

THE GILPIN GOLD TRAM
030-29   32.95

History, dates, stories, Gilpin rolling stock and motive power rosters, a list of mines served by the Gilpin, list of "Tramway Characters", proposed railroads of Gilpin and an index are included. Scale drawings of the different ore cars, Shays #2, 3 and 5, and caboose #400. Approximately 120 illustrations, hardcover, 116 pages.

WABASH STANDARD PLANS & REFERENCE
030-30   22.95

Features brief history of this 2,500-mile railroad that was eventually absorbed into the Norfolk & Western. Map of line; 55 standard plans such as trestles, markers, signs, milepost markings, spring switches, bulletin boards, crossings, telltales, telephone boxes, freight house skids, weights of rail, tie renewal references. Approximately 150 pages, 11 x 8-1/2".

COLORFUL EAST BROAD TOP
030-31   24.95

Defines the East's last original narrow gauge railroad in all of its glorious color during the 1950's. Features the major points of Railroad/Mining interest in Pennsylvania: Orbisonia, Rockhill Furnace, Mt Union, Robertsdale, Saltillo, Wray's Hill Tunnel and Sideling Hill Tunnel. Includes steam locos, freight & passenger cars, action trains, Orbisonia shops, timber transfer, mixed freights and more. Includes unpublished color photos, map and text. 88 pages, 11 x 8-1/2".

HEIMBURGER HOUSE PUBLISHING

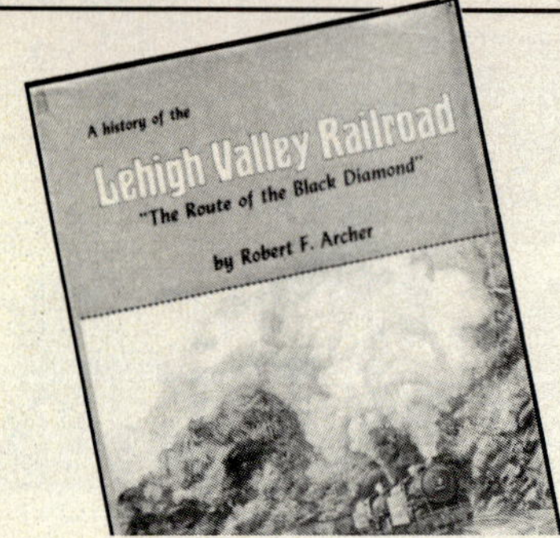

SPIRIT OF SOUTH SHORE
030-110 (By Special Order Only.) 22.95

This memorable look at the Chicago South Shore and South Bend Railroad's unique past and more recent history is told in more than 200 black and white photographs, a map of the line and a capsule history of the railroad. Hardcover

NARROW GAUGE IN THE ROCKIES
030-32 **NEW** 32.95

The story of the 3-foot cars and engines on which an entire generation of the Colorado frontier rode to golden destinies. Includes a matchless photograph album. With all the luxuries of overland travel, it is also the story of swaggering nabobs who peopled the rococo hotels and barrooms. An important contribution to the record of the old West. Hardcover, 290 illustrations, 8 x 11" trim size.

LEHIGH VALLEY RAILROAD
030-33 **NEW** TBA

A comprehensive history of the railroad, which was one of the major coal roads of the East. The Lehigh Valley was also a trunk line carrier with more than 1,000 locomotives, a steamship line, a fleet of express passenger trains, as well as part owner in the mining industry. Highlights the line's founding, expansion, prosperity, decline and dissolution. 655 photographs, maps, and drawings, 372 pages, 8-1/2 x 11".

H&M PRODUCTIONS

Softcover, 11 x 8-1/2" format.

JERSEY CITY WESTBOUND
91-1 29.95

Photographic study of Jersey Central Passenger Operations prior to the Adele plan.

FOUR GREAT DIVISIONS
91-50 36.95

Covers the New York Central's Hudson division. Erie Lackawanna's New York and Scranton Divisions & the Northern Pacific Burl. Northern Rocky Mt. Division.

BLUE DIESELS & BLACK DIAMONDS
91-200 29.95

Covers the operation of the West End of the Cumberland Division of the B&O.

CABINS, CRUMMIES & HACKS
91-100 Volume I 39.95

Comprehensive survey of the caboose. Full color.

91-101 Volume II 29.95

Covers the cabooses of the Old South. Full color.

91-102 Volume III 29.95

Covers the cabooses of the North & West plus Canada. Full color.

91-103 Volume IV 29.95

Covers the cabooses of the Southwest and Mexico. Full color.

CLASSIC FREIGHT CARS: THE SERIES
91-300 Volume I 19.95

Covers the wood & steel, 40' freight cars.

91-301 Volume II 23.95

Covers the 40' private and railroad owned tank cars.

91-302 Volume III 23.95

Railroad and private owner cars covering the whole United States. 160 color photos.

GOTHAM TURNSTILES
91-400 33.95

Covers the rapid transit of the New York Metropolitan area 1958-1968.

Tall timber makes for heavy loads, but this hard-working Shay is equal to the task. Dale Kuhn of Sheboygan, Wisconsin, photographed #10, which is a PFM brass import painted and decaled by Terry Piaskowski. Scenery products from Woodland Scenics and Highball were also used in the scene.
Photo by Dale Kuhn

Interurban Press

We have worked closely with this manufacturer to provide accurate availability information at the time this catalog was published. Items listed in *blue ink* may not be available at all times. Please see your dealer for current delivery information.

All books are softcover unless noted.

LIGHT RAIL TRANSIT ON THE WEST COAST
341-32   13.95

A great collection of facts and photos. Covering the return of streetcars to San Diego, Portland, Sacramento, San Jose and Los Angeles. 96 pages.

MONTEREY & PACIFIC GROVE STREET CAR ERA
341-112   16.95

From its start in 1890 as a financially successful horse-drawn California streetcar line, the Monterey & Pacific Grove Street Railway's expansion was rapid, and electricity replaced horses at an early date. 80 pages.

NORTH SHORE LINE MEMORIES
341-406   45.95

A fascinating narrative of day-to-day operations of this famous interurban, including interviews, archival records, newspaper clippings, and a motorman's diary. Hardcover, 288 pages.

SHAKER HEIGHTS RAPID TRANSIT
341-115   36.95

A detailed, illustrated history of this Cleveland, Ohio, interurban railroad. Hardcover, 144 pages.

LAST OF THE RED CARS
341-118   15.95

The Long Beach Line then and now. Recounts the history of the once-great L.A.-Long Beach line of the Pacific Electric Railway and continues to the emergence of the new Metro Blue Line. Softcover, 55 black & white, 28 color photos, 48 pages, 8-1/2 x 11".

BAEDEKER'S RAIL GUIDE TO EUROPE
341-16   16.95

Complete travel planner for Europe. Includes information about each country, facts and practical advice about using each country's rail system, station information, frequency of trains, and sample fares. Softcover, 221 color photos, maps, 330 pages, 5-1/2 x 11".

BRIDGE LINE BLUES: D&H
341-287   41.95

The D&H 1976-1986. Album format, hardcover, 120 pages, 10-1/2 x 8-1/2".

THE ART OF RAILROADING
341-12   6.95

Manual on how to run a railroad. Taken from the 1884 Railroad Gazette.

SAN DIEGO'S SOUTH BAY INTERURBANS
341-76   14.95

Operations of the San Diego and Southeastern Interurban Line are featured. Approximately 100 pages with maps and illustrations.

THE SHORT LINE DOODLEBUG: Volume III
341-77   32.95

Features the self-propelled cars that roamed rural America on the Short Lines. 210 photos, hardcover, 152 pages, 8-1/2 x 11".

ST. LOUIS CAR CO ALBUM
341-62   29.95

Album of official building photos from the St. Louis Car Company's collection. Photographs, some color, hardcover, 160 pages, 8 x 11".

RAIL VENTURES
341-14   12.95

The comprehensive planning guide to rail travel in the U.S., Canada and Mexico.

RAILROADS OF THE YOSEMITE VALLEY
341-255   29.95

A chronicle of four railroads (passenger and logging) that operated near Yosemite, California. 400 illustrations, hardcover, 206 pages, 8-1/2 x 11".

IRON MEN & COPPER WIRES: SOUTHERN CALIFORNIA EDISON CO.
341-278   11.95

The history of Southern California Edison Company; from hydro-electric power, to one of the largest U.S. electrical utilities. Photos, hardcover, 258 pages, 8-1/2 x 11".

SAN DIEGO & ARIZONA: THE IMPOSSIBLE RAILROAD
341-271   44.95

Traces the rise & fall of the SD&A, through its SP days to its present ownership. 326 photos, maps, hardcover, 224 pages, 8-1/2 x 11".

TRAILS BEGIN WHERE RAILS END
341-281   19.95

Every-day motoring adventures in the west and southwest. Black & white photos spanning 1900-1938, hardcover, 8-1/2 x 11".

THOSE MAGNIFICENT TRAINS
341-46   14.95

A collection of short stories on American railroading. 88 pages, all in full color.

CAJON—A PICTORIAL ALBUM
341-295   53.95

A brand-new array of photography from famous railfan locations, showcasing the work of over 40 top rail photographers! Hardcover, 184 pages, 119 color photos, 174 B&W photos, 8-1/2 x 11", with color dust jacket.

MODELING CAJON
341-273   13.95

Cajon Pass … Sullivan's Curve … Summit … double track and sidings. Author shows you how to do it. 72 pages, 120 photos and plans, 8-1/2 x 11".

RAILROADING IN THE ROCKIES A HALF CENTURY AGO
341-28   39.95

Take a 5,600-mile journey through Nevada, Utah, Colorado, New Mexico, and California in 1939, in search of steam and narrow gauge. Hardcover, 200 pages, over 300 photos, timetables, maps, and diagrams, 8-1/2 x 11".

RAILS THROUGH THE ORANGE GROVES: Volume I
341-288   31.95

Pioneering railroads of Orange County, California — including the Southern Pacific, Santa Fe and Pacific Electric. Hardcover, 150 black & white photos, 144 pages, 8-1/2 x 11".

RAILS THROUGH THE ORANGE GROVES: Volume 2
341-294   34.95

Brings the story up to the present day; along the way, we harken back to the days of the Orange Groves, all the time depending on railroads economic lifeline of the County. Hardcover, 144 pages, 8-1/2 x 11".

FROM RAILWAY TO FREEWAY
341-90   29.95

Pacific Electric and the Motor Coach. A detailed, lavishly illustrated account of the conversion of Pacific Electric's 1,000-mile interurban railway system to rubber-tired transport. Hardcover, 196 pages, maps, rosters, index, 8-1/2 x 11".

BOSTON & MAINE— Three Colorful Decades of New England Railroading
341-301   79.98

The first major all-color book about New England's favorite railroad. Begins with a descriptive memoir of the author's childhood years growing up near the railroad. Brief histories accompany each of the five major sections, each with a color map. Hardcover, 208 pages, 300 color photos, color system and division maps.

THE A—NORFOLK & WESTERN'S MERCEDES OF STEAM
341-296   44.95

History of the N&W's Roanoke Machine Works, later simply Roanoke Shops, and locomotive designs preceding and leading to the A, hardcover, 178 pages.

SAN DIEGO TROLLEY
341-114   25.95

Takes you through San Diego's transit yesterdays to the inception of the Trolley, with a detailed account of the obstacles that had to be overcome along the way.

UNION PACIFIC'S WEST
341-298   42.95

A guided tour of Union Pacific's West, from the banks of the Missouri River to the Pacific ports of Seattle, San Francisco, and Los Angeles. Hardcover, 192 pages, 17 black & white, 28 color photos, system map, color dust jacket.

Interurban Press

We have worked closely with this manufacturer to provide accurate availability information at the time this catalog was published. Items listed in *blue ink* may not be available at all times. Please see your dealer for current delivery information.

All books are softcover unless noted.

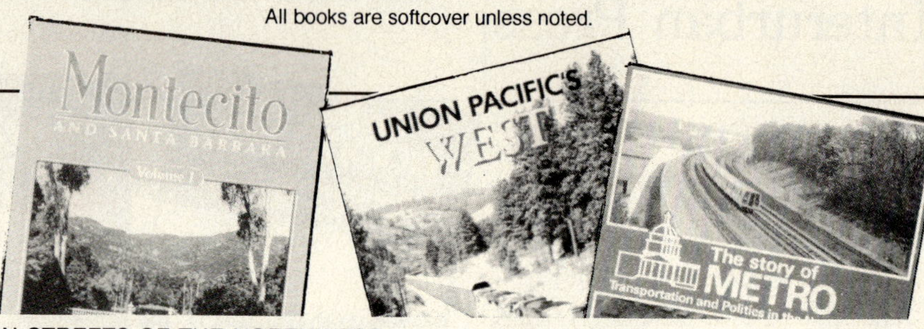

THE FEATHER RIVER ROUTE—PART ONE
341-291   42.95
This is the relationship between people and machines, and the battle they waged against nature and economic setbacks to keep trains running. Hardcover, 144 pages.

THE FEATHER RIVER ROUTE—PART TWO
341-303   47.95
A side trip to Bieber, then east to Salt Lake City. Hardcover, 168 pages, 340 B&W and 24 color photos, disposition rosters plus index for parts 1 and 2, 10-1/4 x 8-1/2".

MALLETS ON THE MENDOCINO COAST
341-275   21.95
Operating from 1861 until 1955, the Caspar Lumber Company's mill at Caspar was supplied with timber for 75 of those years by the company's own private railroad, which operated a fascinating array of motive power to bring in virgin redwood logs from the forest. 134 pages.

MORE CLASSIC TRAINS
341-404   85.95
First published in 1974, this monumental work, out of print for 16 years and a major collector's item, is back! Hardcover, 512 pages.

30 YEARS OVER DONNER
341-297   29.95
Learn what it takes to keep those trains running over a tough mountain route. Hardcover, 200 pages.

PINE ACROSS THE MOUNTAIN
341-299   44.95
The McCloud River Railroad story. Relates the ups and downs of this spectacularly located mountain shortline, from its construction as a log hauler to a diversified carrier. Hardcover, 224 pages.

HENRY HUNTINGTON & THE PACIFIC ELECTRIC
341-248   16.95
History of the PE and route list of the famed Los Angeles Red Car System. 200 illustrations, 112 pages, 8-1/2 x 11".

THE EARLY INTERURBAN NEWSLETTER
341-3   9.95
A tribute to Mr. Swett (founder of Interurban Press) plus an index to Interurban Specials published through 1978. 152 pages.

WHEN EASTERN MICHIGAN RODE THE RAILS: Volume II
341-105   39.95
This book takes an in-depth look at all forms of public transit in the Detroit—Port Huron Corridor. Hardcover, 232 pages, 350 photos.

THE STORY OF METRO
341-101   19.95
In the early 1960's Washington, D.C., lost its unique conduit streetcar system. After a decade of battles, Congress authorized the creation of Metro, a rail rapid transit system worthy of the nation's capital. 96 pages, 115 photos, 8-1/2 x 11".

MAIN STREETS OF THE NORTHWEST Volume I
341-285   19.95
Covering the spectacle of Northwest railroading from 1969 to 1988—including Oregon, Idaho and Western Montana, and featuring rail lines from UP and BN to short lines and regionals. Hardcover, 160 pages.

PACIFIC: 2472's FAMILY ALBUM
341-292   24.95
This is a pictorial of these famous 4-6-2s from their early development to the later years of steamlining, and from a roster of 146 locomotives system-wide to only three survivors today. 136 pages.

HETCH HETCHY AND ITS DAM RAILROAD
341-293   54.95
Problems existed with rights-of-way, water rights, funding, and opposition from the private water utility and conservationists as well. The major problem of just getting men and materials into the wild Sierra Nevada range had to be overcome by the building of a marvelous railroad. Hardcover, 298 pages, 456 illustrations.

THE 400 STORY
341-400   49.95
Here's the saga of high-stepping 4-6-2s, yellow-and-green streamliners as fast and fancy as any in the land, diesels and vacation crowds, the rise and fall of a midwest transport institution. 232 pages.

MONTECITO & SANTA BARBARA Volume II
341-300   49.95
Features the great estates which appeared as the area began shifting from a sleepy seaside town to a wealthy community. Includes an index for both volumes. Hardcover, 300 photos & maps, 312 pages.

INDIANA RAILROAD
341-770   55.00
A traction milestone of the 35 orange "high speed" cars which revolutionized trolley travel but failed to stem the tide of automobiles. Over 300 illustrations, hardcover, photos, timetables, promotional material, 224 pages.

SOUTHERN PACIFIC STEAM LOCOMOTIVE COMPENDIUM
341J31   47.95
Until this book came along, there was no single source of information on Southern Pacific's 4,200 steam locomotives. Hardcover, 426 pages, 298 illustrations.

TEXAS ELECTRIC ALBUM
341-1   13.95
Photo album of Dallas area interurbans; north-south Sherman-Dallas-Waco axis. 46 pages, 116 photos, maps, timetables, 8-1/2 x 11".

LIFE AND TIMES OF THE PE
341-10   9.98

TO SANTA FE/NARROW GAUGE
341-24   5.95

40 FEET BELOW
341-82   **NEW** 13.95
For half a century, Chicago possessed the best kept secret in the annals of railroad transportation: a system of more than 50 miles of tunnels beneath its famed loop, through which ran diminutive electric trains carrying merchandise, coal, cinders—even the U.S. Mail! Softcover, 80 pages.

MOUNTAIN MAINLINES OF THE WEST
341-38   12.95
A delightful and beautifully reproduced photo album of Western mountain railroading from the Colorado Railroad Museum. 64 pages, 67 photos, 9-1/2 x 8-1/2".

LOCOMOTIVES OF THE RIO GRANDE
341-40   11.95
A detailed locomotive roster of the Rio Grande system from 1871 to 1983. Takes the reader from the earliest narrow-gauge locomotives, through the Maffat Road power, to the big articulateds. 100 pages, 139 photos, 8-1/2 x 11".

THE RAILROAD STATIONS OF SAN DIEGO COUNTY
341-52   6.95
Excellent "then and now" views and histories of the railroad stations of an important Southern California area. Both railroad historians and Sunday afternoon explorers will find a wealth of information in this book. 56 pages, 42 photos, 6-1/2 x 10".

KALMBACH **BOOKS**®

All are softcover unless otherwise noted.

HOW-TO-DO-IT BOOKS

BASIC ELECTRONICS AND ELECTRICITY FOR MODEL RAILROADERS
400-12083　　　　　9.95

Up-to-date guide to the basics of electricity and how they apply to model railroading. Covers such topics as tools and safety, train control, blocking your layout, signals, lighting and sound, electrical testing, wiring the layout and more. 80 pages.

EASY-TO-BUILD ELECTRONIC PROJECTS FOR MODEL RAILROADERS
400-12081　　　　　9.95

All the info needed to build electronic devices, from switch machine power supplies to steam & diesel sound systems. 8-1/2 x 11".

THE ART OF THE DIORAMA
400-12080　　　　　7.95

"How to" design, build, paint and display box dioramas. 8-1/2 x 11".

ALL ABOARD: THE PRACTICAL GUIDE TO HO MODEL RAILROADING
400-12075　　　　　9.95

Step-by-step practical guide to HO Scale model railroading. Answers modelers questions about subjects from track planning to wiring to scenery construction. 88 pages, 8-1/4 x 11".

HOW TO BUILD SCALE MODELS
400-12107　　**NEW**　11.95

Learn special techniques for filling in seams, stretching sprue, detailing armour vehicles, painting natural metal finishes, simulating wood deck planking, painting faces of miniatures, modeling combat damage on military vehicles and more. Hundreds of color and black-and-white photos and illustrations, 104 pages.

HO NARROW GAUGE RAILROAD YOU CAN BUILD
400-12068　　　　　9.95

Malcom Furlow builds the HOn3 San Juan Central with step-by-step instructions on topics such as benchwork, scenery, structures and wiring. Color and black & white photos, 60 pages, 8-1/2 x 11".

BUILDING PLASTIC MODELS
400-12027　　　　　7.95

How-to-build plastic models from kit: aircraft, cars, trucks, motorcycles, military vehicles and ships. Photos and illustrations (some color), 68 pages.

TRACK PLANNING FOR REALISTIC OPERATION (Second Edition)
400-12004　　　　　9.95

Techniques and information needed to create the best continuing operation of your layout.

HO RAILROAD THAT GROWS
(Second Edition)
400-12015　　　　　6.95

An eight-stage construction plan book. Starts with simple 4 x 8' layout, developing into a two-level, two-train pike, complete with scenery.

THE ABC'S OF MODEL RAILROADING
400-12036　　　　　6.95

Answers to the questions beginning model railroaders ask most often. Topics as varied as scenery and signals, track and tools, painting and powerpacks. Illustrations, 70 pages.

CREATIVE MODEL RAILROAD DESIGN
400-12037　　　　　21.95

Provides creative ideas and solutions for layout problems. Addresses items such as, how to fit large scales into small spaces, design layouts based on prototype railroads. 123 pages, 8-1/4 x 11-1/4".

SCENERY FOR MODEL RAILROADS
400-12008　　　　　9.95

Describes professional ways to plan and build scenery with true realism, includes hard shell scenery and zip texturing.

N SCALE MODEL RAILROAD TRACK PLANS
400-12009　　　　　5.95

Current data on the major brands of N Scale track equipment and accessories. Contains 65 track plans with grid overprint and features simple layout plans for the beginner, as well as fullfledged layouts complete with scenery and structures.

SMALL RAILROADS YOU CAN BUILD
(Second Edition)
400-12013　　　　　5.95

Features four small railroad projects; each include a complete bill of material. 160 illustrations (some color).

HOW TO WIRE YOUR MODEL RAILROAD
400-12011　　　　　7.50

Easily understood drawings show step-by-step, fool-proof procedures in wiring.

101 TRACK PLANS FOR MODEL RAILROADERS
400-12012　　　　　6.95

Illustrates and describes methods of building scale model pikes, from small table to complete attic layouts. For all gauges.

TRACK PLANS FOR SECTIONAL TRACK
400-12010　　　　　4.95

Contains 144 easy-to-follow drawings for tinplate and HO sectional track layouts.

TRACK PLANNING IDEAS FROM MODEL RAILROADER
400-12050　　　　　12.95

58 imaginative and useful track plans selected from over 20 years of Model Railroader. Layouts small enough for apartments or big enough to fill an entire basement. 96 pages.

HOW TO BUILD DIORAMAS
400-12047　　　　　12.95

Sheperd Paine shows how to design and build dioramas from the ground up, explains weathering, covers figures and shadow box construction and even details model photography. 104 pages.

MODELING THE CLINCHFIELD IN N SCALE
400-12010　　　　　9.95

This popular reprint from 1979 includes how-to information and plans to construct the Clinchfield. Can be used to build any model railroad gauge or scale. Full-color track plans and layouts. 64 pages, 8-1/4 x 11-1/4".

HOW TO BUILD MODEL RAILROAD BENCHWORK
400-12041　　　　　6.95

Useful techniques, tips on roadbed construction and ballasting, and how benchwork and scenery can be combined effectively. Over 200 photos and illustrations, 56 pages.

HINTS AND TIPS FOR PLASTIC MODELING
400-12045　　　　　4.95

250 tips for all kinds of plastic modeling. Emphasis on modeling of aircraft; ships and armored vehicles are included. 48 pages.

BUILDING AN HO RAILROAD WITH PERSONALITY
400-12061　　　　　8.95

This book takes model railroaders step-by-step throught the construction of the 4 x 8' Jerome & Southwestern. Featured in Model Railroader in 1982-83.

18 TAILOR-MADE MODEL RAILROAD TRACK PLANS
400-12063　　　　　12.95

Custom-designed layouts by John Armstrong. Illustrated (some color), 80 pages, 8-1/2 x 11".

SCENERY TIPS & TECHNIQUES
400-12084　　　　　12.95

A collection of scenery articles from *Model Railroader* magazine. Covers all scales, new ideas and new materials. 116 pages, 8-1/4 x 11-1/4".

MODEL RAILROADING WITH JOHN ALLEN
400-12053　　　　　25.95

The legendary Gorre and Daphetid Railroad of the late John Allen inspired a generation of model railroaders, and continues to shape model railroading today. The 1981, Linn Westcott tribute to this master modeler is now, available as a softcover reprint of the original.

FUN WITH ELECTRIC TRAINS
400-12089　　　　　6.95

Includes information on buying an electric train and accessories, keeping your train running, laying track, wiring, constructing scenery and more. Illustrations.

BEGINNERS GUIDE TO TOY TRAIN COLLECTING AND OPERATING
400-12091　　　　　14.95

Start your own collection of toy trains, be able to add to your collection, and know how much to pay for a train. Explains how to restore toy trains and how to display them.

YOUR GUIDE TO EASY RAILROAD WIRING
400-12093　　　　　12.95

Easy-to-read book clearly explains the nuts and bolts of making trains run. Explains choosing a power pack, entire layout wiring, turnout control, trouble shooting and many others. 123 pages, 8-1/4 x 11-1/4".

KALMBACH ⓀBOOKS®

All are softcover unless otherwise noted.

BUILDING THE BURLINGTON NORTHERN IN N SCALE
400-12094   8.95

This guide is useful for building the Burlington Northern or any other road. The basic principles described can be applied to any layout, gauge or scale. Covers every step from choosing the stretch of track to be molded to erecting backdrops. 56 pages, 8-1/4 x 11-1/4″.

WALKAROUND MODEL RAILROAD TRACK PLANS
400-12097   12.95

Book is entirely devoted to the advanced control systems which make it possible for a model engineer to follow his trains ¢ to walk around with them. Contains 16 original, custom-designed layouts with the ideas behind them.

PAINTING AND FINISHING SCALE MODELS
400-12099   8.95

Explains how to paint your models, including how to effectively airbrush.

BEGINNERS GUIDE TO N SCALE
400-12021   11.95

Offers updated tips and techniques on every phase of N Scale modeling. Beginners learn how to: plan their pike, build benchwork, lay track, wire, and construct scenery. Plus, two N Scale layout projects are included. Color and black and white photos, 104 pages.

34 NEW ELECTRONIC PROJECTS FOR MODEL RAILROADERS
400-12057   10.95

Explains building electronic projects using up-to-date, readily available components. 225 photos, 80 pages, 8-1/4 x 11-1/4″.

A TREASURY OF MODEL RAILROAD PHOTOS
400-12095   16.95

Together four respected Model Railroad photographers have chronicled their work with over 100 examples of their craft. It introduces four creative approaches to Model Railroad photography and is explained in general lay terms. Over 100 color photos, 104 pages, 8-1/4 x 11-1/8″.

HOW TO OPERATE YOUR MODEL RAILROAD
400-12028   19.95

Explains how to run a model railroad equal to authentic railroad operation. 184 pages, 8-1/2 x 11″.

HOW TO BUILD REALISTIC MODEL RAILROAD SCENERY
400-12100   15.95

This guide uses a ''cookbook'' approach to creating workable scenery. Color and black and white photos, 130+ pages, 8-1/2 x 11 1/4″.

MODEL RAILROAD BRIDGES AND TRESTLES
400-12101   16.95

Includes 12 construction plans, prototype photos and over 20 sets of scale drawings. 152 pages, 8-1/2 x 11″.

SCALE MODELING TIPS AND TECHNIQUES
400-12102   5.95

Offers the most helpful hints from 10 years of *Fine Scale Modeler* magazine. 48 pages, 8-1/4 x 10-3/4″.

HO RAILROAD FROM START TO FINISH
400-12121   **NEW**   11.95

Beginner's book on the construction of the HO Scale Cripple Creek Central. Covers everything from benchwork to rolling stock, avoids projects requiring power tools and messy materials. 130 photos, 75 in color, 8-1/2 x 11″ format.

DETAILING TIPS & TECHNIQUES
400-12120   **NEW**   12.95

Covers topics such as modeling junk, a kite blowing in the wind, weeds, flowers, roadside signs, roof details and more. Practical advice on planning and building urban scenes, using mirrors, and time appropriate details. Includes five pages of full-color signs to cut out.

222 TIPS FOR BUILDING MODEL RAILROAD STRUCTURES
400-12115   **NEW**   9.95

When is it a good idea not to follow kit instructions? What's the best way to make barnacles? Includes answers to these, and hundreds of other questions.

CYCLOPEDIAS

MODEL RAILROADER CYCLOPEDIA, VOL 1: STEAM LOCOMOTIVES
400-1001   39.95

Tells what all the piping, springs and pumps are for. 127 HO Scale drawings, 700 photos, 272 pages.

MODEL RAILROADER CYCLOPEDIA, VOL 2: DIESEL LOCOMOTIVES
400-1033   27.95

Large-format pages of HO Scale plans and photos of North American diesel locomotives. Turbine locos are included, also a primer on diesel operation and components. Photos, illustrations, 160 pages, 14 x 11″.

RAILROADS

CONTEMPORARY DIESEL SPOTTER'S GUIDE
400-1042   18.95

Revised version features detailed information on diesel developments since 1972, including spotting features of new models, upgrades and rebuilds, leased units and how railroads select and use motive power. Illustrations, 336 pages.

SECOND DIESEL SPOTTER'S GUIDE
400-1026   24.95

Comprehensive catalog of American diesel practice through 1973. Specs and production data of all models. 548 photos, 5-1/2 x 8″.

■ **LIMITED QUANTITIES AVAILABLE** ■

KITBASHING HO MODEL RAILROAD STRUCTURES
400-12082   **NEW**   8.50

Compilation of articles from *Model Railroader* magazine, tips and techniques for working with plastics, plus painting and weathering hints. 76 pages.

PHOTOS AMERICA - SUPER RAILROADS
400-68056   17.95

PHOTOS TRAINS - YESTERYEAR
400-68057   17.95

MILWAUKEE ROAD REMEMBERED
400-1044   39.95

The glory years of the Milwaukee Road live on. A fresh look at the innovative operations and equipment of the line, from the midwest to the pacific coast. Hardcover, 200 photos (10 full-color) 186 pages.

AMERICAN SHORTLINE RAILWAY GUIDE
400-1047   18.95

Up-to-date reference book featuring over 400 shortline railways in the U.S. Includes histories and detailed locomotive roster. 4th edition. 241 pages, 8-1/4 x 5-1/2″.

HISTORICAL GUIDE TO NORTH AMERICAN RAILROADS
400-1037   24.95

A look at more than 160 railroads abandoned or merged since 1930. Includes histories, system maps and more. 360 pages.

TRAINWATCHERS GUIDE TO NORTH AMERICA, 2ND EDITION
400-1049   14.95

Significant facts, figures and features of over 140 railroads in the U.S., Canada and Mexico. Maps, photos, 220 pages, 8-1/2 x 5-1/2″.

THE SPIRIT OF RAILROADING
400-1046   44.95

A collection of new color photos from top railroad photographers capture both the spirit & substance of today's railroad scene. Hardcover. 196 pages. 8-1/2 x 11-1/2″.

SOUTHERN PACIFIC'S BLUE STREAK MERCHANDISE
400-1048   39.95

Author Frailey reveals how the line survived six decades from its beginnings during the Great Depression. Hardcover. 168 pages, 8-1/2 x 11-1/2″.

DIESEL LOCOMOTIVE ROSTER
400-1050   12.95

This compact guide is loaded with updated information on 30,000 locomotives. 192 pages, 8-1/2 x 5-1/2″.

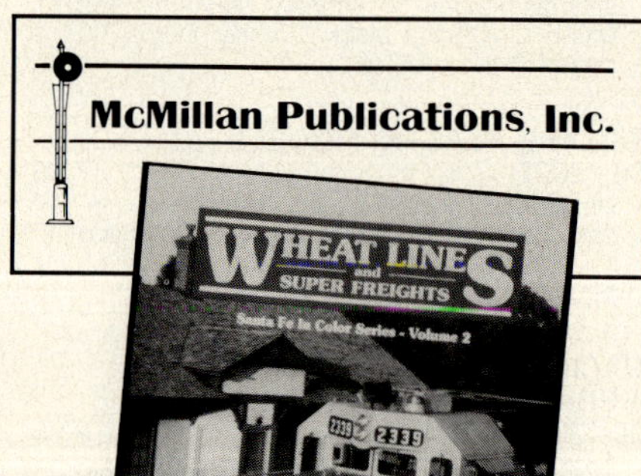

All McMillan Railroad books feature color photos, are hardcover and 8-1/2 x 11.″

HIGH GREEN TO MARCELINE
051-16   49.50

This book is Volume I of the ''Santa Fe in Color Series'', and will take you from Dearborn Street Station in Chicago to Argentine Yard in Kansas City, and all points in between. 191 pages.

WHEAT LINES & SUPER FREIGHTS
051-21   64.95

Second full-color book on modern AT&SF operations, with 440 photos from Oklahoma, Kansas and Colorado, 240 pages.

The color and action of historic railroading in the United States comes to life in this line of all-color hardcover books.

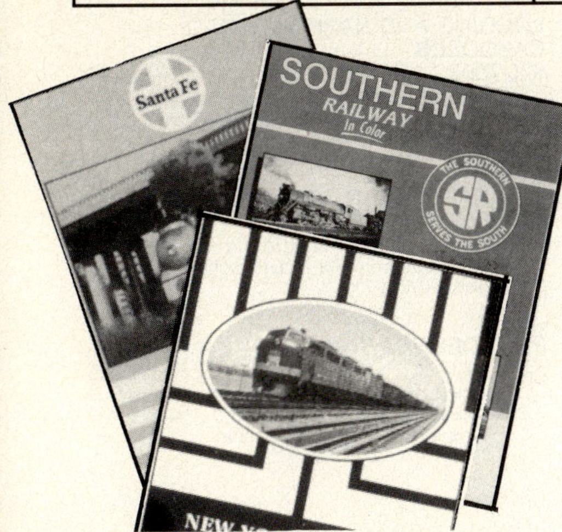

ERIE LACKAWANNA IN COLOR
484-5 Volume I: The West End   45.00
The Erie Lackawanna Railroad was created in the merger of the Erie and the Delaware Lackawanna and Western in 1960. Legendary for its colorful motive power and rolling stock; its valiant attempts to compete with bigger, stronger roads; and its fleet of large power, dominated by unique variations on EMD's SD45. Take a trip from Chicago to Meadville, PA.

ERIE LACKWANNA IN COLOR
484-122 Volume II: NY State   45.00
Continues the journey from west to east begun in Volume 1 showing the struggle of this railroad in the State of New York. Mainlines and branches are thoroughly documented in color.

PENNSY ELECTRIC YEARS
484-7   45.00
Delightful rendering of the story of the Pennsy electric locomotives. Author's first hand experience. 190 full color photos, 128 pages.

JERSEY CENTRAL LINES
484-9 Volume 1   45.00
This all-color book on the Central Railroad of New Jersey is primarily about the period of the mid-1960's. Approximately 200 photos, 128 pages.

JERSEY CENTRAL LINES
484-19 Volume 2   **NEW** 49.95
Highlights the period of Camelbacks, Mikados and tangerine & blue Baldwin babyfaces and F3s. Special emphasis is also given to the Pennsylvania Division. 128 pages.

TIDEWATER TRIANGLE
484-16   45.00
Travel trackside into Virginia and North Carolina for a look at the operations of the Seaboard, Atlantic Coast Line, Chesapeake & Ohio, Southern and Norfolk and Western in the 1960's. 160 pages.

ERIE RAILROAD IN COLOR
484-17   45.00
Your journey starts at the ferry slips of Jersey City and proceeds westward. Destination: Chicago, IL. Photographed in full color between World War II and 1960. 128 pages.

PENNSY DIESEL YEARS
484-24 Volume 1   45.00
With the introduction of the first cab units in 1947, the Pennsylvania acquired an impressive fleet of diesels. This book shows all types of switchers, freight units and and passenger power in color and in action, through the late 60's. A roster from December, 1960, when the road reached its peak ownership of 2,465 diesels is included. 160 pages.

PENNSY DIESEL YEARS
484-32 Volume 2   45.00
This companion volume features 20 additional photos of Pennsylvania diesels in action on ''The Standard Railroad of the World.'' A comprehensive roster of renumbered and second generation units from 1960 through 1968 is included. 128 pages.

PENNSY DIESEL YEARS
484-75 Volume 3   45.00
The diverse diesels of the mighty PRR: such oddities as the rubber-tired diesels, steam-diesel tandems, the unique RS3 ''hammerhead'', and the rare LS25 Lima transfer unit. Approximately 200 color photos.

PENNSY DIESEL YEARS
484-91 Volume 4   45.00
Travel aboard a Centipede-drawn excursion that starts out at the Harrisburg Station and ends in Detroit! 128 page full color.

PENNSY DIESEL YEARS
484-157 Volume 5   **NEW** 49.95
In 1955, the Pennsylvania reorganized itself into nine districts called the Lake, Northern, New York, Philadelphia, Chesapeake, Pittsburgh, Buckeye, Southwestern and Northwestern Regions. Takes you on a photographic tour of each of the regions, both before and after the realignment. Hundreds of photos, 128 pages.

NEW ENGLAND RAILS: 1948-1968
484-40   45.00
The railroad scene in New England changed dramatically between 1948 and 1968. Over 200 color photos show the many paint schemes appearing on diesel and electric power, plus a last look at vanishing steam. Some 12 different roads are represented. 128 pages.

WABASH IN COLOR
484-41   45.00
From Buffalo to Kansas City and Council Bluffs, the Wabash covered the heartland of the United States. It was the only railroad operating in both the East and West to straddle the Mississippi River. Over 180 color photos, 128 pages.

LEHIGH VALLEY IN COLOR
484-59 Volume 1   45.00
Racing along with priority freight or idling away the evening hours, the drama of diesel power on the Lehigh Valley comes to life in this book. Some 222 pages of color photos are featured, showing units in action from 1952 through 1976.

LEHIGH VALLEY IN COLOR
484-33 Volume 2   45.00
Sequel to *LEHIGH VALLEY In Color*. Special emphasis is given to PA-drawn passenger trains of the Valley and the early freight cabs. Rare diesels — FT and HH660 are shown along with extemely hard-to-find paint schemes: the prewar switcher scheme, the single FA painted in Tuscan, and Steam. 210 color photos, 128 pages.

NEW YORK CENTRAL LIGHTNING STRIPES
484-67 Volume 1   45.00
The years following 1945 were a time of change for the New York Central as the transition from steam to diesel power began. Over 200 color photos of steam, diesel and electric locos, representing all parts of the railroad from the midwest to Canada are highlighted. 128 pages.

NEW YORK CENTRAL LIGHTNING STRIPES
484-165 Volume 2   49.95
Takes you on an end-to-end tour of the NYC between 1946 and 1968, with special focus on diesel and electric power. 128 pages.

LACKAWANNA RAILROAD IN COLOR
484-83   45.00
The Delaware Lackawanna & Western Railroad during the post World War II years featuring the best of steam, electric and diesel operations. Approximately 200 color photos, 128 pages.

PRR GUIDE TO FREIGHT AND PASSENGER EQUIPMENT
484-76   45.00
Everything from baggage cars to business cars, cabins to coaches, wagontops to wire cars are portrayed. 325 color photos, 128 pages.

PENNSY STEAM YEARS
484-84 Volume 1   45.00
Pennsy steam from the forties and fifties. Visits to NJ sidelines, Philadelphia Terminal, Maryland, the Middle and Northern Divisions, Altoona, Ohio and west to see miniature A5 0-4-0's to giant duplex T1's! Color, 128 pages.

NEW YORK CENTRAL COLOR PHOTOGRAPHY OF ED NOWAK
484-92 Volume I   45.00
Taken during his tenure as photographer for the NYC, Ed Nowak details the whys and wherefors on some of his work during the period 1943-1968 shooting steam and diesel. Color, 128 pages.

NEW YORK CENTRAL COLOR PHOTOGRAPHY OF ED NOWAK
484-73 Volume II   49.95
Takes you behind the lens of NYC's official photographer as he visits New York City, the Hudson River Valley, Buffalo, Chicago and other hot spots during the 1940's, 50's and 60's. 128 pages.

DELAWARE & HUDSON IN COLOR
484-106 Volume 1   45.00
This ''Bridge Line'' between the East and New England is captured during its heyday, the period 1946 to 1968 in 185 color photos including 47 rare steam shots. 128 pages.

RIO GRANDE IN COLOR
484-114 Volume 1: Colorado   45.00
The Mainline through the Rockies, from the late steam, early diesel period. The Rio Grande operated steamers as well as FT's, PA's and strange Krauss Maffei units. 200 color photos, 128 pages.

A GOLDEN DECADE OF TRAINS: THE 1950's IN COLOR
484-608   45.00
Rail photographer Robert R. Malinoski displays color work from his journeys across the nation during the 1950s. Photos ranging from Maine to Florida, New Jersey to Wyoming during the era when steam was vanishing and the diesel just arriving. 128 pages.

SANTA FE IN COLOR 1940-1971
484-30 Vol 1: Chicago-Kansas City **NEW** 49.95
First in a four volume series. Shows Santa Fe steam at its best and at least one of every diesel class that the road had during this period. Features such rarities as ''The Blue Goose,'' E3's, Baldwin center-cabs, FT's in passenger service.

SANTA FE IN COLOR 1940-1971
484-130 Vol 2: KC-Albuquerque **NEW** 49.95
See rare DL109s in KC and then spend a day in 1946 as everything from 2-10-2s to FTs pass by. Watch as 2-10-4s help F7s thru Abo Canyon and E1s glide over Raton Pass.

SOUTHERN RAILWAY IN COLOR
484-203   **NEW** 49.95
Details the exciting period after WWII to the early Sixties. The last of steam is shown along with the pioneering green diesels that wrested control. Shows everything from FTs to PAs and Train Masters across the entire system. 128 pages.

N.J. International

Famous locomotive classes are featured in the *Classic Power Series*, which include data sheets and line drawings.

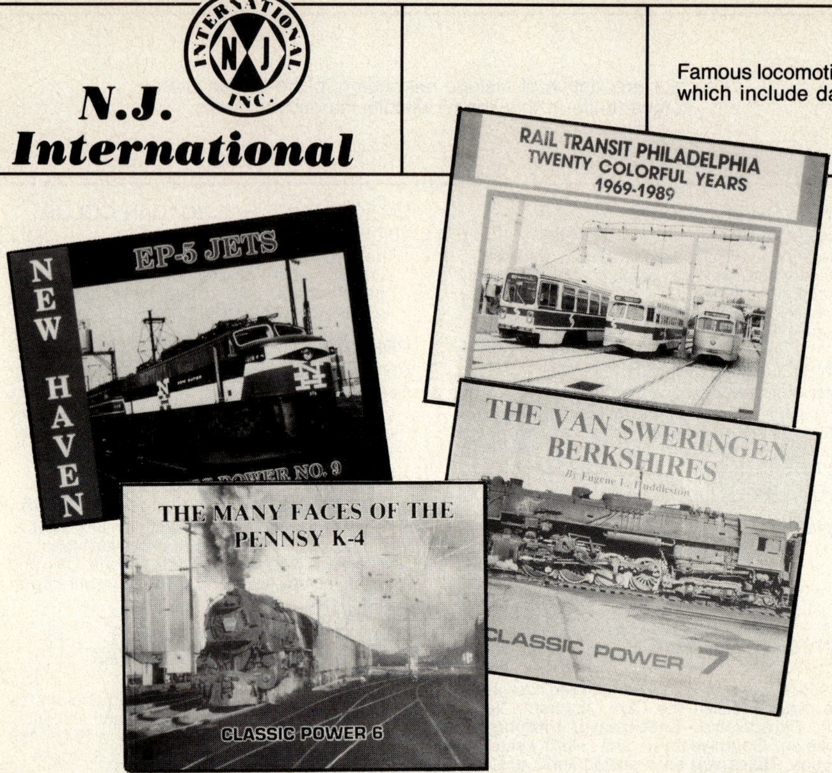

LOGGING AND NARROW GAUGE CABOOSES
525-7505   14.95
Contains detail drawings, photo coverage in color and black and white of 12 unique logging and NG cabooses.

PRR PASSENGER CAR PLAN BOOK
525-7503   19.95
Features 24 foldout HO plans and covers most Pennsy cars from the heavyweight era. 100 pages, 8-1/2 x 11″.

PHILADELPHIA TRANSIT   *NEW*   32.95
525-7613
Includes copies of books like "Philadelphia Traction: The PTC Era 1940-1968." This new volume features 156 color photos.

E-UNITS: AMERICAN PASSENGER TRAINS
525-7605   25.95
All color, 178 photos, full rosters, 72 pages.

PHILADELPHIA TRANSIT - TWENTY COLORFUL YEARS (1969-1989)
525-7608   19.95
All color, 125 photos, system and route maps, 56 pages.

ELECTRIC LOCO PLAN BOOK #1
525-7504   24.95
Detail drawings of 25 Electric Loco's, spanning America's Mainline Electric heritage. Full photo coverage of each, with technical specifications. NYC, PRR, NH, N&W, ITC, GN, Milw, B&M, GTW.

KANSAS CITY STREET CARS - REMEMBERED
525-7611   19.95
155 color and black and white photos covering all car types - PCC's, conventional cars, Birneys, Freight and work equipment. System maps and details. Softcover, 80 pages.

CLASSIC POWER SERIES

Famous locomotive classes. Data sheets and 23 x 35″ line drawings (packed separately)

#1 CHESAPEAKE & OHIO H-7 SERIES
525-7201   6.95
The H-7 was one of the first super powered compound steam engines; its success led to the development of a new generation of powerful steam engines. 54 pages, 11 x 8-1/2″

#5 THE PRR Q-2, 4-6-4-4
525-7205   17.95
The Q-2 was Pennsy's last duplex and saw service on hot shots in the late 40s. Detailed drawings.

#6 THE MANY FACES OF THE PENNSY K-4
525-7206   21.95
Study of the famous K-4, covering all variations on the K-4 theme. Features fold-out detail drawing and full color rendering, over 125 photos, 120 pages.

#7 THE VAN SWERINGEN BERKSHIRES
525-7207   19.95
Covers the development of the 2-8-4 steamers by the C&O, PM, NKP and Erie. Drawings plus a color rendering.

#8 PENNSY M1's
525-7208   24.95
Complete history of Pennsy's M-1 Class. Complete set of detail drawings and color rendering by Allen B. Chesley. 120 pages.

#9 NEW HAVEN EP-5 ELECTRICS
525-7209   29.95
A complete history of the revolutionary EP-5 electrics covering all aspects of their design, construction and operation.

DATA PACKAGES

CHESAPEAKE & OHIO H-7A
525-7401   1.75

CABOOSE DATA SERIES

CABOOSES OF THE PRR & LIRR
525-7502   14.95
Contains many scale drawings and color photos of the N, NC, ND, NG, A, B, N8, N6A, N6B, N52A, N52B, N22, N22A, ex IC, Cars, and other classes. Softcover, 60 pages.

CABOOSES OF THE NEW HAVEN & NEW YORK CENTRAL
525-7501   14.95
Contains 17 detail drawings of 6 New Haven and 11 NYC cabooses, along with photo coverage in color and black and white, and technical construction data.

MODELING HINT

HOW DO I PLAN MY LAYOUT?

That seems to be the $64 question every model railroader faces soon after he becomes interested in Model Railroading, usually before he really has discovered what the hobby is all about. Perhaps he starts out with a program of building locomotives or cars and is happy with a single section of straight track on which to test his models; or perhaps he is the type that wants his track laid first, before he acquires rolling stock or power; but in either case, the problem usually pops up before he is ready for it. Layouts don't come in kits, and if they did, he probably wouldn't find one to completely satisfy him anyway. You can learn the hard way if you want, but we feel you'll have more fun with less work if you listen to a few pointers first.

1. Don't try to do too much. You're going to learn as you go along — and there hasn't been a model railroader born who didn't have dozens of ideas for rebuilding or remodeling long before his first plan was off the drawing board onto the plywood.

2. Set your minimum radius as large as possible. This will enable you to operate a larger variety of equipment & won't create such a bind if you decide to add a 2nd track inside the basic pattern.

3. Try to design a layout that can be completed in "stages". This way you can have one section completed, scenicked and operating while you are working on the second.

4. Read as many of the "How To" books as possible. Learn from the experts. The list of suggested titles below are featured in the Book Section of this catalog.

NorthWest Short Line

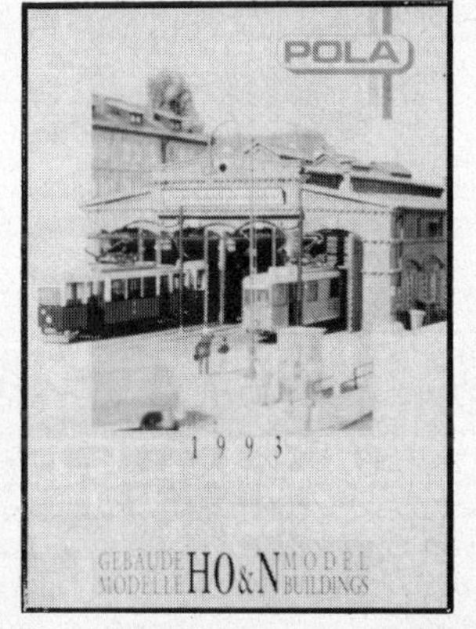

SAGAMI MOTOR SPECIFICATIONS AND USAGE INFORMATION BOOKLET
053-9 .50

LOGGING TO THE SALT CHUCK
053-5069 Hardcover 45.95
053-5169 Softcover 36.95

A photographic essay of over 100 years of Simpson Timber Co railroad logging history. 200 pages, over 200 historic photographs, specially researched maps showing locations of railroad grades for Western Mason County railroad loggers.

LOGGING RAILROADS IN SKAGIT COUNTY
053-5089 Hardcover 59.95
053-5189 Softcover 44.95

The first comprehensive history of all logging railroads in Skagit County, Washington. 308 pages, over 400 photographs brings the age of railroad logging back for the historian and the modeler with 22 maps showing logging camps locations and all logging railroads in Skagit County.

POLA

Imported from Germany by WALTHERS

578-1093 1993 HO/N Scale **NEW** 6.49
Catalog
115 full-color pages, 8-1/4 x 11-3/4".

JOIN THE NATIONAL MODEL RAILROAD ASSOCIATION

We all know that the NMRA developed the standards that make the interchange of model equipment possible, but so what? What has the NMRA got to offer this coming year that is worth 24 bucks to me?

1. More pleasure from the World's Finest Hobby. After all, whether you buy a book, an all-brass loco, a bag of loose parts, or a complete kit, you expect to get your money's worth of fun, pleasure, entertainment, relaxation or enjoyment out of the purchase. The NMRA costs less than one quality kit, a very small bag of parts, or a good book and will return many times that small cost in the fun of getting together, the relaxation of reading, the enjoyment of building and operating and the satisfaction of knowing what's going on.

2. Information. The monthly BULLETIN and, when published, a Special Edition BULLETIN that contains standards, recommended practices, NMRA constitution and by-laws. Each year, usually in June as part of the BULLETIN, there is a periodical index which catalogs the articles by subject and type that appeared in the major model railroad magazines during the previous year.

3. As a member, you may purchase the DATA PAK. These sheets can answer your questions on loco wheel arrangements, required double track clearance standards, or what a "Lamont" six-wheel truck looks like. Are you interested in illustrations of various heralds, or a classification of freight and passenger cars? Do you sometimes wonder what Narrow Gauge, turnout sizes and those various electrical terms mean? Answers to all these questions and thousands more will come to you with NMRA membership. If you know all these things already, why not join and help others?.

4. We think it makes good sense to belong to a group that does so many things. . .for so many people. . .all for fun!

Bruce Walthers

P.S. Use the application blank below.

MEMBERSHIP APPLICATION
NMRA, INC., 4121 Cromwell Rd. Chattanooga, TN 37421

I Enclose. . . . ☐ Check ☐ Money Order ☐ Charge

		Two Years	One Year
Regular (All benefits)		☐ $48.00	☐ $24.00
Sustaining, (All benefits-mandatory for Clubs, Groups & Business)		☐ $96.00	☐ $48.00
Family, (Per name, available to spouse or minor children of regular members)		☐ $10.00	☐ $ 5.00
Affilliate Membership			☐ $13.00
Youth Membership, (Under 20-date of birth required)			☐ $16.50

Life & Disabled Life Membership (Based on date of birth contact Home Office for details).

Annual Dues of of $24.00 includes $13.00 for subscription to the BULLETIN.

(U.S. FUNDS ONLY)

☐ NEW ☐ RENEWAL Date of Birth (Youth and Retired Life Only) _______________

Scale & Gauge _______________ Occupation (Optional) _______________

NAME _______________

STREET _______________

CITY _______________

STATE, ZIP _______________

Charge to: ☐ American Express ☐ VISA
☐ MasterCard Exp.Date

CARD NUMBER

Signature _______________

Price subject to change. Recommended by **WALTHERS**

R. ROBB LTD.

NARROW GAUGE PICTORIALS

Colorado narrow gauge equipment, from various roads, is featured in these softcover books. Each has a horizontal format and over 100 black and white photos.

PASSENGER CARS OF THE D&RGW
622-2   23.50
   Vol II, 191 pages, 11 x 8-1/2″

GONDOLAS, BOX CARS AND FLAT CARS OF THE D&RGW
622-3   23.50
   Vol III, 208 pages, 11 x 8-1/2″

D&RGW REFIGERATOR, STOCK AND TANK CARS
622-4   25.00
   Vol IV

MOTIVE POWER OF THE C&S
622-6   28.50
   Vol VI, 224 pages, 11 x 8-1/2″

WORK EQUIPMENT OF THE D&RGW
622-7   28.50
   Vol VII, 224 pages, 11 x 8-1/2″

C&S FREIGHT & PASSENGER CARS
622-8   29.00
   Vol VIII, 224 pages, 11 x 8-1/2″

RGS RICO TO DURANGO
622-9   22.00
   Vol IX, 160 pages

D&RGW NUMBERED WORK EQUIPMENT
622-10   **NEW** 27.50
   Vol X, 240 pages

Roco

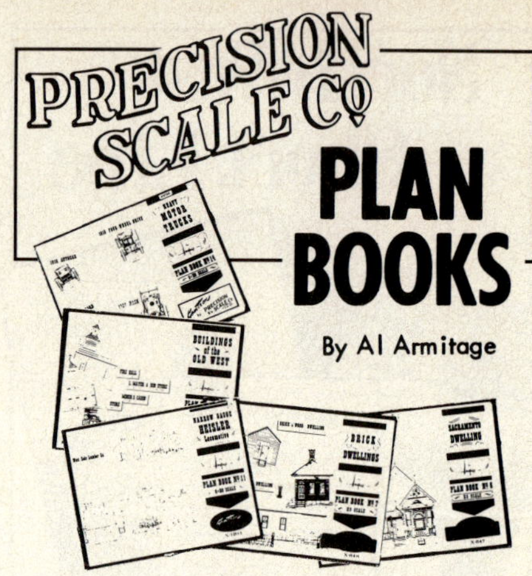

Imported from Austria by WALTHERS

ROCO-REPORTS

The ROCO-Reports are intended to contribute to more comprehensive information for all model railway hobbyists. The models and their prototypes will be extensively described and illustrated in the ROCO-Report. The reports also bring general railway background information, ''how-to-do'' advice and suggestions for conversions and rebuilding of models. Known model railway authors contribute to the report which is published at irregular intervals. Full color and in loose-leaf format. German text.

625-81001 #1	.99	625-81010 #10	.99
625-81002 #2	.99	625-81011 #11	.99
625-81003 #3	.99	625-81012 #12	.99
625-81004 #4	.99	625-81013 #13	.99
625-81005 #5	.99	625-81014 #14	1.99
625-81006 #6	.99	625-81015 #15	2.99
625-81007 #7	.99	625-81016 #16	1.99
625-81008 #8	.99	625-81017 #17	2.99
625-81009 #9	.99		

BERLIN CITY RAILWAY
625-84000   22.99
   Prototype history of the Berlin City Railway. 120 pages, 100 illustrations, German text.

GLASKATEN
625-84001   22.99
   In depth history of the Glaskaten locomotives and Bavarian coach models. German text.

40 YEARS OF DB
625-84002   22.99
   German text

ROCO LINE PLAN BOOK
625-81447 **(By Special Order Only.)** 32.99

ROCO LINE TRACK PLAN SHEET
625-81455   9.99

ROCO LINE TRACK SYSTEM
625-81457   .99

PRECISION SCALE CO.

PLAN BOOKS

By Al Armitage

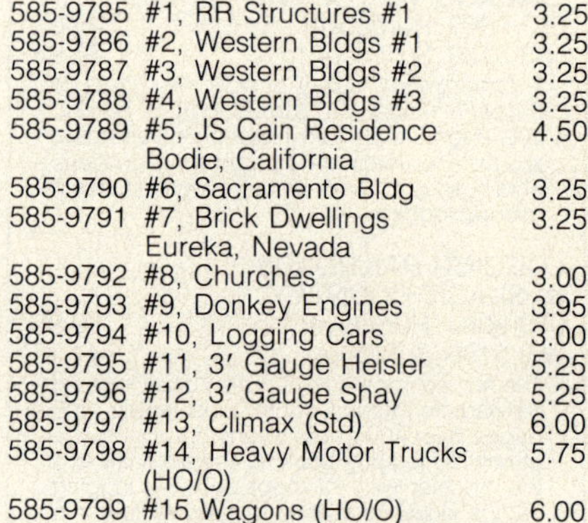

This series features scale drawings of a wide variety of authentic material carefully chosen for their adaptability to railroad modeling. Each plan includes photos of the prototype, pertinent data and a brief history of the subject. Some Plan Books contain several structures or pieces of equipment, while others are limited to one subject of complex nature. All books are loose-leaf, printed on one side only. . . ready for insertion in your own binder.

585-9785	#1, RR Structures #1	3.25
585-9786	#2, Western Bldgs #1	3.25
585-9787	#3, Western Bldgs #2	3.25
585-9788	#4, Western Bldgs #3	3.25
585-9789	#5, JS Cain Residence Bodie, California	4.50
585-9790	#6, Sacramento Bldg	3.25
585-9791	#7, Brick Dwellings Eureka, Nevada	3.25
585-9792	#8, Churches	3.00
585-9793	#9, Donkey Engines	3.95
585-9794	#10, Logging Cars	3.00
585-9795	#11, 3′ Gauge Heisler	5.25
585-9796	#12, 3′ Gauge Shay	5.25
585-9797	#13, Climax (Std)	6.00
585-9798	#14, Heavy Motor Trucks (HO/O)	5.75
585-9799	#15, Wagons (HO/O)	6.00

STYRENE FABRICATIONS
585-9784   4.50
   This fully illustrated reference handbook, by Al Armitage, explains simple techniques of constructing from styrene. Explains in detail the ''how, when and why'' to help beginners as well as advanced modelers. Loose-leaf form, 8-1/2 x 11″.

HO/HOn3 STEAM LOCO CATALOG
585-9740   TRA

NOVEMBER 7, 1885

Today IN RAILROAD HISTORY

Canadian Pacific rails from east and west are linked at Craigellachie, in Eagle Pass, British Columbia, completing the first railroad across Canada.

Quadrant Press, Inc.

All books feature black & white photos and are softcover unless noted.

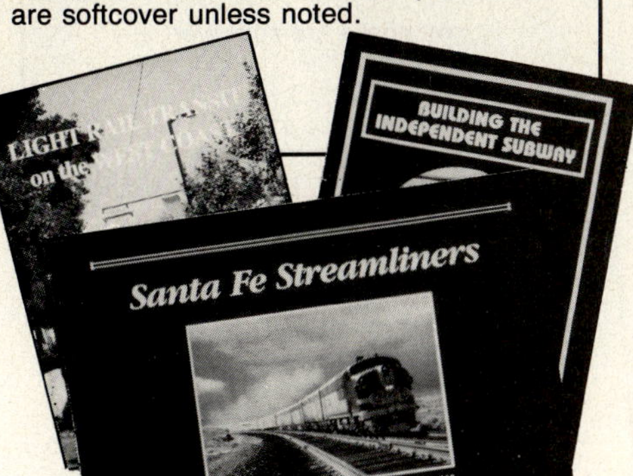

SANTA FE STREAMLINERS
069-41   17.95

Comprehensive survey of Santa Fe's famed streamliners, beginning with the inaugural run of the streamlined ''Super Chief'' in the 30's up to Amtrak's ''Southwest Limited''. Dozens of historic photos, 112 pages.

TOURING PITTSBURGH BY TROLLEY
069-5   14.95

A pictorial review of the extensive network of trolley lines operated by Pittsburgh Railways in the 50's and 60's. By Harold A. Smith. Color cover, 140 photos, 88 pages.

BUILDING THE INDEPENDENT SUBWAY
069-50   13.95

The story behind the subways of the Big Apple. Focusing on New York City's 15 year struggle to build its own subway system, the book includes information on construction, the 207th Street shops and subway rolling stock. Over 120 photos, 80 pages.

OCEAN LINERS OF THE WORLD
069-43   11.50

Covers transatlantic ships and principal liner routes around the globe since the end of WWII. 125 photos, 96 pages, 8-1/2 x 11".

ERIE LACKAWANNA EAST
069-12   9.95

Covers operations from the 1960 merger of the Erie and Lackawanna railroads, through 1975. Photos of most types of diesels then in service, plus a look at operations on various divisions. 146 black and white photos, 80 pages.

HOBOKEN'S LACKAWANNA TERMINAL
069-46   12.50

Covers the history and operation of the Lackawanna Railroad terminal, plus commuter trains and ferry service in Hoboken, New Jersey. 97 pages, 8-1/2 x 11".

NORFOLK & WESTERN STEAM
069-3   10.95

The story of the last years of steam power on the N&W. Action & builders photos, plans, diagrams, roster, index, 96 pages, 11 x 8-1/2".

ACROSS NEW YORK TROLLEY
069-13   5.95

A pictorial review of the Third Avenue railway streetcars in the 30s & 40s. Rare photos of trolleys taken against the New York background. 100 photos, 64 pages, 11 x 8-1/2".

TWILIGHT ON THE NARROW GAUGE
069-14   8.50

Reissued story of the Rio Grande of the 1950's. Photos, 64 pages, 11 x 8-1/2".

THE REMARKABLE GG-1
069-16   9.50

The famous Pennsy electrics from #4800, the first of the line, to the rededication of #4935 in May 1977. 110 photos, 72 pages, 11 x 8-1/2".

TRAINS OF NORTHERN NEW ENGLAND
069-17   8.95

40s & 50s, steam and diesel engines of the B&M, CV, RUT and MC. 120 photos, 96 pages.

LIGHT RAIL TRAINSIT ON THE WEST COAST
069-49   13.95

How, why and where the trolley car is returning to the West Coast in the form of light rail transit. Covers 6 cities from Portland, OR to San Diego, CA. By Harre Demoro and John Harder. 96 pages, 125 photos.

AMERICA'S WORKHORSE LOCOMOTIVE: THE 2-8-2
069-54   **NEW** 14.95

Contains a photo-history of the 2-8-2 steam locomotive. Almost 10,000 engines of this type were built from 1884 to 1949 for the railroads of North America. Features the work of many noted photographers. 160 photos, 80 pages, 8-1/2 x 11".

BERKSHIRE DAYS ON THE BOSTON & ALBANY
069-35   6.50

The steam locos of the B&A from 1925 to 1950, featuring the 2-8-4 Berkshire engines. 100 photos, 64 pages, 11 x 8-1/2".

RAILS TO SAN FRANCISCO BAY
069-51   **NEW** 15.95

A look at the years from 1900 to 1955 when the SP, WP, Santa Fe and several electric lines operated rail-maritime service in the San Francisco Bay area of California. 120 photos, 96 pages, 8-1/2 x 11".

THE STATEN ISLAND FERRY
069-37   9.95

New York City's last year-round public ferry operation. Information on boats, the people who ran them, and the Staten Island & New York Harbor. 120 photos, 96 pages, 8-1/2 x 11".

F-UNITS
069-39   11.95

The story of General Motor's F-Unit diesel from the initial model FT to the farewell model F9. 100 photos, 80 pages, 11 x 8-1/2".

THE VALLEY RAILROAD STORY
069-40   4.50

All about the Valley Railroad from its opening in 1871 as the Connecticut Valley Railroad through its slow decline as a New Haven branch line, to its modern-day development as one of the most popular steam tourist lines. 70 photos, 40 pages, 8-1/2 x 11".

BALTIMORE AND ITS STREET CARS
069-44   10.95

A nostalgic look at Baltimore and its environs in the immediate post WWII years. A pictorial revue. 170 photos, 96 pages, 8-1/2 x 11".

COMMUTER TRAINS TO GRAND CENTRAL TERMINAL
069-45   7.95

150 years of commuter train operation north and northeast of New York City. NYC and NH trains, steam, diesel and electric motivepower from the past; today's Metro-North Commuter Railroad in the present. 100 photos, 64 pages.

WALTHERS

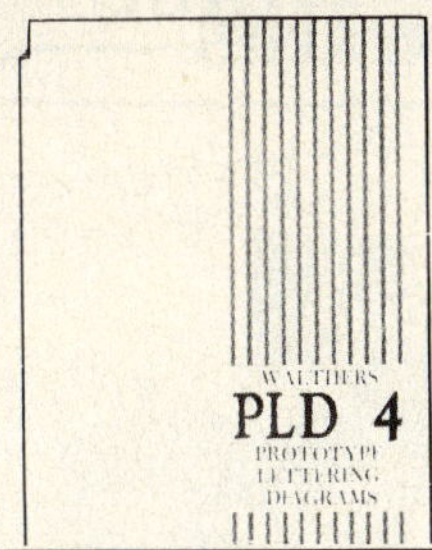

■ LIMITED QUANTITIES ■ AVAILABLE

RAILROAD BOOK

Shows the size, color and arrangement of lettering on railroad equipment of all types. Covers lettering for a given period.

PROTOTYPE LETTERING DIAGRAMS, #4 (Revised 1966)
949-614   3.98

(PLD4) Contains 300 diagrams of railroad lettering that was new during 1962 through 1966, including 60' center-flow hoppers, 86' and high-cube box cars, plus the latest in diesel loco, passenger, and freight car lettering. This book also includes an explanation of the new loading device, and other special markings found on cars, car doors and car ends. Indicates type of car and number series as well as placement of lettering. 76 pages, 6 x 9".

JUNE 30, 1831

❧ Today ❧
IN RAILROAD HISTORY

Troops are carried aboard a passenger train of the Baltimore & Ohio, marking the first use of railroads for the transport of military personnel in the United States.

VOLLMER

Imported from Germany and marketed by WALTHERS

VOLLMER '93–'94 CATALOG (HO, N & Z Scale)
770-9993   5.99

- 8-1/4 x 11-3/4"
- Separate sections for HO, N & Z Scale
- Full-Color
- Measurements for all buildings

RAILROAD AVENUE ENTERPRISES

All books are softcover.

THE ROUTE OF THE PHOEBE SNOW
615-12 **NEW** 24.95

A look at the Lackawanna Railroad in both the steam and diesel era plus electric operations in New Jersey. The entire railroad is portrayed with a large coverage of trains in New York State. 235 black and white photos, plus maps and timetable. Reprint, 192 pages.

"THE NORTHEAST RAILROAD SCENE" SERIES

615-1	Volume 2 The Lehigh & Hudson River	4.00
615-2	Volume 4 The Erie Lackawanna	6.50
615-3	Volume 5 The Jersey Central	6.00
615-4	Volume 6 The Penn Central	10.00

A series of photo essays on the last twenty years of the roads that eventually became Conrail. The 11 x 8-1/2″ books are between 56 and 88 pages long and feature illustrations and maps.

RAILROAD STATIONS OF NEW ENGLAND, VOLUME 1
615-5   7.95

Covers the variety of stations seen along the lines of one of New England's largest carriers with photos from yesterday and today. 72 pages, 190 photos, 8-1/2 x 11″.

LEHIGH VALLEY PASSENGER CARS
615-6   13.95

Features full-size HO Scale plans for Lehigh Valley passenger cars, redrafted from original railroad blueprints. 64 pages, 31 photos, maps, 11 x 17″.

26 MILES TO JERSEY CITY
615-7   8.95

A brief history of stations of the Central Railroad of New Jersey from 1970 to the present. 64 pages, 130 photos, floor plans, 8-1/2 x 11″.

ONE DAY, ONE CONDUCTOR
615-8   5.00

Pictorial ride with an NJ Transit (Conrail) conductor as he travels from Gladstone to Hoboken and Dover on the old Delaware Lackawanna & Western MU cars. 5-1/2 x 8-1/2″.

THE MORRISTOWN & ERIE RAILWAY
615-9   8.95

A look at one of the fastest growing New Jersey shortlines following its 1982 reorganization. 48 pages, 89 photos, maps, 11 x 8-1/2″.

THE HANDSOMEST TRAINS IN THE WORLD
615-10   15.95

The history of passenger service on the Lehigh Valley Railroad. The book contains over 150 photos plus maps and illustrations. Reprint, 120 pages.

ELECTRIC TRAINS TO READING TERMINAL
615-11   17.95

A complete history of each branch: the building of the electrification, how it works, how the cars were constructed and how they worked. This is a comprehensive work on the system from the planning in the 1920's to the trains of today. 112 pages.

TESTORS

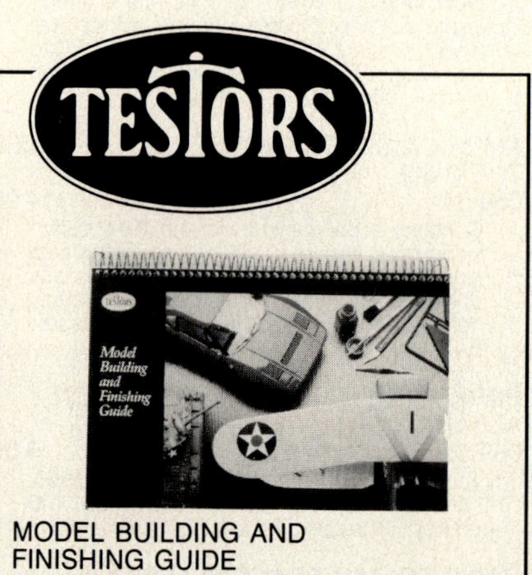

MODEL BUILDING AND FINISHING GUIDE
704-8820   8.95

An introduction to basic skills of modeling.

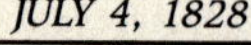

JULY 4, 1828
Today IN RAILROAD HISTORY

The first rail is laid to begin construction of the Baltimore & Ohio Railroad.

Cartoon courtesy of *Model Railroader* Magazine.

CHILTON BOOK COMPANY

All Chilton Books are Softcover.

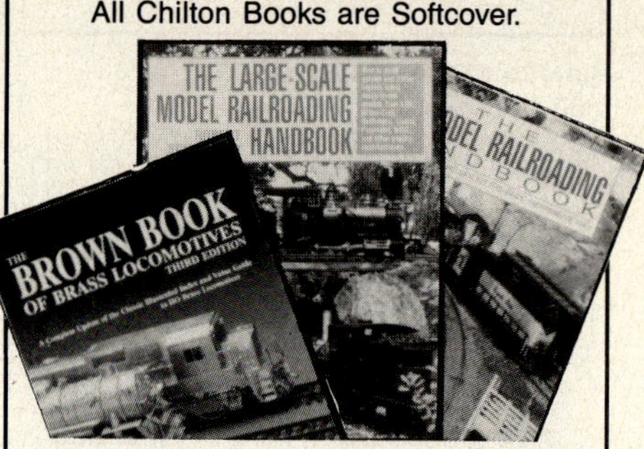

THE MODEL RAILROADING HANDBOOK VOLUME I
213-6168   15.95

Practical comprehensive guide to building locos and rolling stock, scenery, track, benchwork, wiring and how to create operating realism. 8 color photos, 240 pages, 11-3/8 x 8-5/8″.

THE LARGE SCALE MODEL RAILROADING HANDBOOK
213-8229   18.95

Hands on advice on track plans, rolling stock, scenery, buildings & accessories, locomotive maintenance and upgrading, outdoor garden railroads and more. Glossary, over 100 black & white and 16 color photos, 224 pages, 8-1/4 x 10-7/8″.

HO MODEL RAILROADING HANDBOOK (Revised)
213-8346   **NEW** 15.95

Photos and handy tips on all aspects of the HO Model Railroading hobby, such as track plans, rolling stock, scenery, locomotive maintenance and outdoor garden railways. 224 pages, 8-1/4 x 10-7/8″.

BROWN BOOK OF BRASS LOCOMOTIVES
213-8395   **NEW** 24.95

Previously unavailable for nearly a decade, this book contains comprehensive specs on brass HO models by locomotive type, importer, manufacturer and current market value. Also covers information on safe storage, questions about original boxes and painting & weathering. 352 pages, 7 x 10″.

X-ACTO

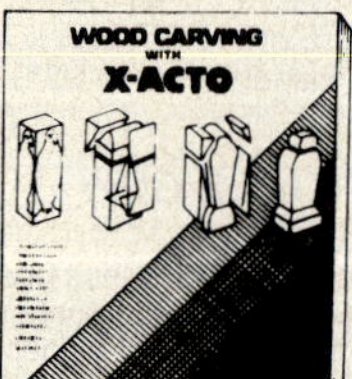

WOOD CARVING WITH X-ACTO
790-90001   10.95

Techniques of wood carving for beginners as well as craftsman. Fully illustrated, 128 pages, 6-1/2 x 8″.

Tarjany Publications

TRACKSIDE STRUCTURES (VOL 1)
706-100   7.95
Twelve scratchbuilding projects; the techniques to do them and helpful diagrams. Photos, 68 pages.

MODULAR RAILROADING
706-200   7.95
The art of module making from both the beginner and the advanced approach. Photos, plans, 66 pages, 8-1/2 x 11".

HOW TO DO IT BOOKS
Emphasis on the modification and super detailing of manufactured kits. A new issue available every three months.

MINIATURE RAILROADING QUARTERLY #1
706-501   9.75
How-to-Build a railroad of the twentieth century; including chapters on locos, trucks, buildings, suggested readings and more. 80 pages, 8-1/2 x 11".

PLAN PACKETS
Plan packets feature: One prototype structure or piece of railroad equipment, HO or O Scale drawings, photos of the prototype and a brief history of the subject, loose-leaf and printed on one side.

SP NARROW GAUGE GONDOLA
706-1   2.15

SP NARROW GAUGE BOX CAR
706-2   2.15

HANDCAR SHED
706-3   2.15

CHART OF SCALES

Model Railroading Scale	Proportion	Number of Inches to one Foot	Track Gauge Inches	Millimeters
1"	1:12	1	4.75	120.66
3/4"	1:16	3/4	3.521	89.69
17/32"	1:22.6	17/32	2.5	63.51
1/2"	1.24	1/2	2.5	63.51
No 1	1:32	3/8	1.75	44.46
O17	1:45.2	17/64	1.25	31.76
O	1:48	1/4	1.25	31.76
S	1:64	3/16	.875	22.23
OO	1:76.2	.157	.75	19.0
HO	1:87.1	.138	.65	16.5
TT	1:120	1/10	.471	11.97
N	1:160	.075	.354	9.0
Z	1:220	.054	.256	6.5
Narrow Gauge				
On3	1.48	1/4	.75	19.06
On2	1.48	1/4	.50	12.71
HOn3	1:87.1	.138	.413	10.50
HOn2	1:87.1	.138	.276	7.02

* Compiled from a STANDARD established by the National Model Railroad Association 1977, printed with permission.

SINGLE SHOT GALLERY

All books are softcover and 8-1/2 x 11".

SHAY INSTRUCTION SHEETS #2
671-8000   5.50
Reprint of 11 Class B Shay service bulletins, first issued by Lima in July of 1923. Covers proper servicing of trucks, gears and pinons, superheaters and other equipment. 32 pages.

B2 SHAY HANDBOOK
671-9501   10.50
This modelers handbook covers wood, coal and oil fired shay in their natural habitat. Illustrations, prototype drawings, 64 pages.

C3 SHAY MODELERS HANDBOOK
671-9506   **NEW** 12.50

THE LIMA SHAY CATALOG (1925)
671-9502   7.50
Reproduced Shay photos and documentation, much of it is "never been seen before" material. 32 pages.

INSTRUCTIONS FOR THE CARE OF THE SHAY LOCOMOTIVE
671-9507   5.50
Proper procedures for firing, care of boiler and other general information about the operation and specifications of Class B Shays. Period photographs and isometric drawings highlight this 32 page book.

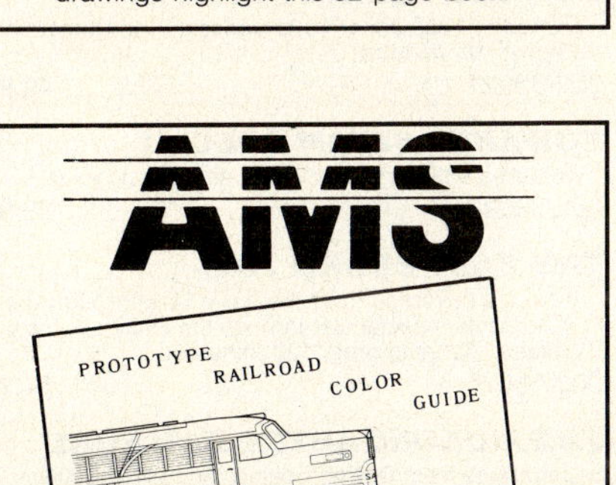

PROTOTYPE RAILROAD COLOR GUIDE
109-1982   7.99
A collection of information gathered from observation of prototype locos, articles and photos appearing in well known publications. Paint references to Floquil, Scalecoat and Accu-paint. Spiral, 35 pages, 8-1/2 x 5-1/2"

All books are paperback and 7 x 10".

BUILD YOUR OWN UNIVERSAL COMPUTER INTERFACE
714-3122   21.95
Tells how to interface your model railroad to any one of 105 personal computers. Includes circuits, parts updates and explanatory test. 217 black and white illustrations, 309 pages.

REAL LIFE SCENIC TECHNIQUES
714-2765   14.95
Expert how-to's for creating authentic scenic backdrops, mountains, tunnels, terrain, trees, foilage, fences and water. Color photos, 204 illustrations, 176 pages.

MODEL RAILROAD SCENERY AND DETAILING
714-3420   19.95
Helpful hints for finishing and superdetailing your layout. Chapters cover environment, tools, weathering, benchwork, lettering and more. Each chapter is illustrated with photos and reference charts for easy research. 353 pages.

SMALL SCALE MODEL RAILROADS
714-3518 **(By Special Order Only.)**   12.95
From initial planning to construction and finishing, new and experienced modelers will find lots of information in this book that defines many of the basic methods and terms used throughout the hobby. 206 pages.

Fine Scale Miniatures

NEW

THE FABULOUS FRANKLIN & SOUTH MANCHESTER RAILROAD
275-1 Volume 1   19.95
Features the layouts of two major cities, Manchester and Dovertown. A visual treat, from the towering 20-story buildings, down to the tiniest details, such as weeds growing in sidewalk cracks. Softcover, 82 color photos, 80 pages, 8-1/2 x 11".

 **GREEN FROG PRODUCTIONS**

VHS VIDEO TAPES

Travel back in time with these video tapes, covering railroad operations and history, from the 50's to the present.

MAINLINE RAILROAD

PREVIEWS
Features selections of Green Frog's most current videos, from Narrow Gauge steam to standard gauge contemporary action. 75 minutes.
302-1   Volume I   19.95

Short, selected scenes not found on Volume I (such as Illinois Central, GP-9's, Rails to Steel City, Illinois Hot Spots and NASA Railroad). 40 minutes.
302-2   Volume II   14.95

Combination of Volumes 1 & 2.
302-3   Volume III   **NEW** 29.95

THE NEW GEORGIA RAILROAD
This tape takes you on board and trackside to watch operations of former Florida East Coast 4-6-2 #750. An E8 in New Georgia Railroad colors is also highlighted. Color, 28 minutes with stereo sound.
302-53002   24.95

STEAM IN THE 1950'S
Period footage of big steam power from 11 different railroads, in the twilight years of the 1950's. Running time: 41 minutes. Revised.
302-53006   34.95

DIESELS '86 - THE VIDEO
Filmed in 1986, diesel power of nine different roads is shown in this 35 minute tape.
302-53007   29.95

RAILS BUFFALO
Video action of modern day railroading in and around Buffalo, New York. 60 minutes.
302-53040   39.95

RAILS CHICAGO
Switching and mainline running featuring 12 area roads in the "Windy City". Running time: 56 minutes. Revised.
302-53011   34.95

RAILS CANADA
Modern operations of Canadian National and Canadian Pacific. Running time: 25 minutes.
302-53012   24.95

WESTERN MARYLAND— END OF AN ERA
Original color films chronicling the final years of the Western Maryland. Running time: 70 minutes.
302-53010   49.95

MICHIGAN FAST FREIGHT
Railroad action in Michigan's lower peninsula, circa 1967. Running time: 54 minutes.
302-53009   49.95

DETROIT, TOLEDO & IRONTON TAPES
Historical footage traces the development of the line from the 1920's through 1983. Black and white and color, running time: 60 minutes.
302-53013   Volume I   49.95

The last years of DT&I operations, to integration and merger with the Grand Trunk Western. Running time: 60 minutes.
302-53014   Volume II   49.95

RAILS IN TRANSITION
Original footage by Jerry Carson, showcasing the changing face of railroading in the 1960's. Scenes from Frisco, Pennsy, Norfolk & Western, Gulf, Mobile & Ohio and more highlights this 60 minute tape, 90% of which is in color.
302-53016   Volume I   49.95

Features railroads such as: C&NW, South Shore, Katy, Milwaukee Road, Santa Fe, Chesapeake & Ohio, Baltimore & Ohio, TRRA and CB&Q. 40 minutes.
302-53039   Volume II   39.95

CANADIAN STEAM
Canadian National 4-4-0 and Canadian Pacific 4-8-4. 25 minutes.
302-53018   24.95

SANTA FE ODYSSEY
Steam and diesels of all kinds are seen in switching plus freight & passenger service, capturing almost 30 years of Santa Fe operations from Chicago to the West Coast. Color. Running time: 150 minutes. (2 tapes).
302-53019   Volume I   99.95

Features "newer" power of the '70's as the Santa Fe revitalizes its fleet for the 80's and 90's. Two tape set. Running time: 120 minutes.
302-53029   Volume II   79.95

Covers Santa Fe from the 1950's to the present. Filmed during the summer of 1991 features the SF Warbonnets as they work their way from Chicago to Kansas City. Two-tape set. 105 minutes.
302-53037   Volume III   64.95

RAILS TO STEEL CITY
This tape chronicles activity around the Pittsburgh area, and covers CSX, Conrail, Bessemer and Lake Erie, the PAT train operations, and Pittsburgh and Lake Erie. Color. Running time: 60 minutes.
302-53022   39.95

THE GP-9's
Sights and sounds of EMD's General Purpose diesels. Fast paced action on a railroad known as the Georgia Northeastern. Color with stereo sound. Running time: 70 minutes.
302-53023   39.95

THE ILLINOIS CENTRAL
Two tape set chronicles 37 years of the Illinois Central, from steam to diesel. Color with stereo sound. Running time: over 2 hours.
302-53024   79.95

ILLINOIS HOTSPOTS
Railroad action in the land of Lincoln. Color. Running time: 60 minutes.
302-53025   34.95

NASA RAILROAD
Take an in-depth look at a truly different railroad that moves rocket motors, rocket fuel, and a wide range of items with a fleet of special cars and colorful SW1500's in "The NASA Railroad". Also featured are great shots of shuttle launches, space shots and more. Color. Running time: 60 minutes.
302-53026   24.95

THE CALIFORNIA ZEPHYR
Filmed in 1965 aboard and trackside the California Zephyr. 60 minutes.
302-53027   49.95

SUWANEE STEAM SPECIAL
Features #1218 in the Florida sun. 60 minutes.
302-53028   29.95

THE EAST BROAD TOP
Includes coverage from the early 50's through the 70's. Winter spectacular through the lense of Emery Gulash. Running time: 120 minutes.
302-53031   54.95

THE MONONGAHELA RAILROAD
Unit trains from Detroit Edison, Somerset Railway, Wisconsin Electric and others. Motive power from the P&LE, C&NW, CSX, Detroit Edison, Conrail and the Monongahela's Super 7's. Filmed in Pennsylvania and Virginia hills. 60 minutes.
302-53032   39.95

ROCK ISLAND RAILROAD
Follow the history of the Rock Island with photography captured during the 1958 through the 1970's era. Color.
302-53033   49.95

UNION PACIFIC ODYSSEY
History. Running time: 120 minutes.
302-53034   79.95

WESTERN MARYLAND SCENIC RAILROAD
302-53038   16.95

NEW YORK CENTRAL ODYSSEY
Two-tape set features action of first-generation diesels, including Mohawks, Hudsons, E and F units, Alco hood units, GE's, Baldwins and more. 150 minutes.
302-53036   79.95

NARROW GAUGE

C&T IN '73
Features 16 mm photography of the Cumbres & Toltec during the fall of 1973. Color, 36 minutes with stereo sound.
302-53017   24.95

The following tapes are made from original films, shot by noted rail photographer Emery Gulash in the 1960's.

TWILIGHT OF THE RIO GRANDE
Scenes of the entire Denver & Rio Grande Western. Running time: 40 minutes.
302-53004   34.95

WORKTRAIN TO SILVERTON
Ride along with a work train of drop bottom gondolas on their way to Silverton. Running time: 23 minutes.
302-53005   19.95

SWITCHIN' ALONG THE RIO GRANDE
Switching and servicing operations at various stops. Running time: 22 minutes.
302-53008   19.95

THE CHAMA TURN
Action and operations over Cumbres. Running time: 60 minutes.
302-53003   49.95

COLORADO NARROW GAUGE PASSENGER CHASE
Filmed in 1965, features the last passenger run the Rocky Mountain Railroad Club took of the Rio Grande narrow gauge. Color. Running time: 45 minutes.
302-53020   39.95

ROTARY ON THE RIO GRANDE NARROW GAUGE
Follow the Cumbres & Toltec in 1975 and 1976 as they opened their line using the former Rio Grande rotary snow plow OM. Color. Running time: 70 minutes.
302-53021   49.95

BEST OF NARROW GAUGE
Rio Grande narrow-gauge action assembled from previously released footage by Emery Gulash. All material has been re-edited, including all-new narration and a number of new scenes. 62 minutes.
302-53035   39.95

RAILFAIR '91
Follow the Union Pacific Challenger and Northern as they double-head through the spectacular mountain scenery to Sacramento for Railfair '91. Includes complete coverage of the event, with up-close looks at engines and cars assembled from around the country. 60 minutes.
302-57000   24.95

GREEN FROG PRODUCTIONS

IN SEARCH OF NARROW GAUGE MIKADOS
Back country of Colorado, along the canyons and off the beaten path. Durango & Silverton and the Cumbres & Toltec from end to end. 70 min, color.
302-53054   **NEW** 39.95

VINTAGE STANDARD GAUGE

PENNSYLVANIA RAILROAD
From 1952 until the merger with the New York Central, this tape covers the end of steam and classic First Generation diesels.
302-53043   **NEW** 49.95

WABASH RAILROAD
From 1954 until the merger with the Norfolk & Western, this covers one of America's favorite railroads. First Generation diesels and plenty of passenger trains. 60 minutes.
302-53044   **NEW** 49.95

CHICAGO ODYSSEY
Action in and around Chicago in the 50's and 60's. Santa Fe, CB&Q, NP, GN, C&WI, North Shore, Grand Trunk, GM&O, IC, Monon, N&W, C&EI, C&O plus more. 2-1/2 hours.
302-53047   **NEW** 79.95

THE NICKEL PLATE
Steam & 1st Generation diesels in the 50's and 60's as well as the Akron Canton & Youngstown. 45 minutes.
302-53048   **NEW** 34.95

RIO GRANDE ODYSSEY
Fron the early 60's until the 80's, see Frist Generation Geeps, narrow gauge steam, and great freight and passenger train action as well. 2-1/2 hours.
302-53049   **NEW** 79.95

TRAVELIN' TRAINS
About hobos in the depression era, accompanied by blues music. 30 minutes.
302-53050   **NEW** 9.95

MODERN DAY RAILROADING

MARION HOT SPOTS
The train watching capitol of Ohio. More than 30 scheduled trains a day on CSX and Norfolk Southern. 60 minutes.
302-53045   **NEW** 34.95

EMPIRE BUILDER
Documentary about the Amtrak train from Chicago to Seattle. On train, in the cab, aerial shots, and interviews with crew members.
302-53046   Volume I   **NEW** 34.95

''Railfan'' oriented tape. Aerial shots, in cab scenes, runbys, train action.
302-53052   Volume II   **NEW** 19.95

THE TOLEDO, PEORIA & WESTERN
This tape was produced in a Civil War documentary fashion showing many classic old photos from the 1800's and early 1900's from the collection of Thomas Finson. 90 minutes.
302-53055   **NEW** 39.95

MAGNOLIA CUT-OFF OF THE CSX
Sweeping curves, tunnels, trestles, and lots of fall foliage serve as a back drop for GP-40's, GP 50's and rare U30-C's. 60 minutes. Color.
302-53056   **NEW** 39.95

COMMAND CONTROL
302-53057   **NEW** 39.95

STEAM IN THE 50's
302-53061   Volume II   **NEW** 24.95

UNION PACIFIC ODYSSEY
Starts where Volume I left off. More First Generation diesels, ''City'' trains, new Second Generation diesels, more Big Blows (turbines), the Centennial locomotives, and DD 35's. 120 minutes, Color.
302-53059   Vol. II   **NEW** 79.95

MODEL RAILROADING

MODELING YOUR FAVORITE RAILROAD - THE RIO GRANDE SOUTHERN
Tips and ideas for adapting prototype operations of the RGS to a model railroad. Running time: 45 minutes.
302-53001   29.95

CUSTOM RAILWAY SUPPLY

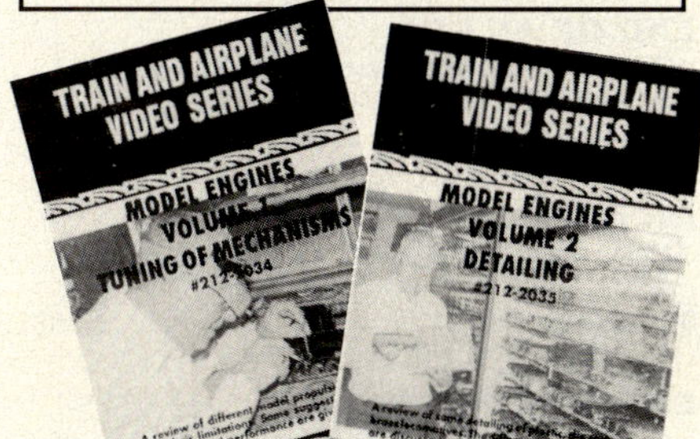

DENVER & RIO GRANDE A MOUNTAIN CLIMBER
Climb over the Rocky Mountains, through the Tennesse Pass, around Horseshoe Curve and more with trains, some using over 50,000 horsepower to carry massive loads of coal and general freight loads.
212-2001   34.95

SUNSET ON THE PENNSY
View seens of the ex-PRR properties such as Fort Wayne & The 59th Street engine house, 4 track Horse-Shoe curve and the ''race-track'' before the PRR type operations and ''fixed plant'' are eliminated by Conrail.
212-2002   34.95

CHICAGO RAILROADING, I, JUNCTIONS
Visit the massive and complex railroad junctions of Chicago in the 1970's when Chicago teamed with other trains. See the 21st Street Jct., and South Branch Bridge, St. Charles Air Line, Steam from La Salle Street Station across 16th Street Jct. and beyond.
212-2004   29.95

CHICAGO RAILROADING, II, PASSENGER & FREIGHT
Take a front end ride on the bustling trains of Chicago in the 1970's. Visit C&NW Station, C&NW RR, Soo RR and Milwaukee RR at Deval Jct., C&NW ''Scoots'', UP/C&NW E-2b converted to -503 commuter cab unit, ride the Milwaukee RR to Union Station and more.
212-2007   29.95

THE MODERN DESIGN STEAM LOCOMOTIVE
Construction and testing of the N&W RR class J 4-8-4 Steam locomotives and a glimpse at the similar operational efficiencies of the Y-6b articulated. Also railroading in Canada during the second world war.
212-2008   34.95

1951 N&W RR OPERATIONS
See how cars were loaded in 1951. Enjoy the sights of various locomotives used by the Norfolk and Western RR in their various 1951 operations. See engine construction, passenger and freight operations, right of way construction, following of car movements and cost charges before the use of computers, scenic runbys in the mountains, coal train marshaling yards and all the trimmings that go with around the clock movement of freight to its eventual destination. This is truly a window to the past of the steam railroading era.
212-2009   34.95

PAINTING BRASS LOCOMOTIVES
A very detailed step by step explanation of how the professional model painter works on a brass loco. For those learning the art of brass painting, this 2 hour video is a step by step tutorial that covers all facets from surprise patch-up jobs where the factory used instant glues, to the differences in using various air brush spraying pressures, to the differences in bottled air and various types of air compressors. This video can give the buyer of custom painting services or the collector a solid insight into the work one might expect from a professional job. VHS.
212-2032   **NEW** 34.95

KEITHLEY'S AND OTHER COLORADO RR MEMORIES
Scenes of the Midland Terminal in Manitou Springs, The Rio Grande Southern, 3' D&RGW of the 1940's to 1960's, D&RG at Silverton with sound, Yampa Valley Mail with Alco power, Cog RR last ride in steam as well as a ride in steam with sound from about 1980, Steam on the Denver to Pueblo Joint Line, Compressed air mine train ride, Great Western RR fan trip, CATS freight train ride with sound, Colorado & Wyoming RR shops tour, C&W Slag train dumping molten slag.
212-2003   **NEW** 29.95

MODEL ENGINES — TUNING OF MECHANISMS
Examines different model power systems and their limitations with suggestions for improving model performance. Both steam and diesel engines are featured.
212-2034   **NEW** 24.95

MODEL ENGINES — DETAILING
A review of detailing plastic, die-cast and brass locos using different methods and tools. Jim Lenahan demonstrates a variety of techniques, along with painting and decaling.
212-2035   **NEW** 24.95

Interurban Films

VHS VIDEO CASSETTES

A wide range of traction, mainline and documentary railroad subjects are offered in VHS format. All videos have sound narration and are black and white unless noted.

We have worked closely with this manufacturer to provide accurate availability information at the time this catalog was published. Items listed in *blue ink* may not be available at all times. Please see your dealer for current delivery information.

MAINLINE RAILROADS
COLOR VIDEOS

PACIFIC NORTHWEST HOLIDAY
Ride the "Olympian Hiawatha" Super Domeliner as it is propelled by diesel and electric power from Chicago to Seattle via some of the finest scenery anywhere! 41.45 minutes.

341-85251   39.95

MONON: SHE'S A HOOSIER LINE
Early black and white and rare color movie footage catches Monon steam in action, streamliners, 1947 Centennial celebration and more. Color and narration, featuring vintage Monon music. 57 minutes.

341-85521   39.95

THE STANDARD RAILROAD OF THE WORLD
125 years of the Pennsylvania Railroad—a video biography. You'll see steam, diesel, electric, even doodlebugs, Penn Station and Washington Union, the Broadway and Congressional limiteds and more. In color and black and white, with narration. 60 minutes.

341-85550   39.95

RIDE THE LAST OF THE BIG RED CARS
Al Fishel and friends photographed in color the L.A.-Long Beach line of the Pacific Electric shortly before it closed in 1961. Nicely done, with cab shots and runbys galore, 15 minutes.

341-70121   19.95

THE FIRST AUTOMATED RAILWAY
Solid GP9 power hauling mine trains is a rare enough sight, but in this General Railway Signal Company-produced film you'll see them running without crews. Color, sound, 17 minutes.

341-85511 VHS   19.95

MID CONTINENT STEAM STORY
A variety of small steam power including fan trip favorite, are shown in action on freight and passenger run-bys. Sound, color, 30 minutes.

341-85461 VHS   29.95

MILEPOST 100
In 1968, the Santa Fe Railway produced a film to commemorate its 100th anniversary, and the beginning of the railway's second century. Color, sound, 27 minutes.

341-85471 VHS   24.95

NARROW RAILS STILL SHINE
A Colorado-New Mexico Steamfest. The Durango & Silverton and the Cumbres & Toltec Scenic Railroad are still narrow-gauge, still in steam, still doing fine. Color, 30 minutes.

341-85361 VHS   39.95

STEAM DOWNUNDER
An Australian Rail Odyssey. Produced in black & white as "A Steam Train Passes," this video captures the mood of steam closing out a chapter in that country's railway history. 21.05 minutes.

341-85371 VHS   19.95

RIDING THE WHITE PASS & YUKON
Starting in the US (Alaska), and ending up in Canada (Yukon Territory), the WP&Y's narrow-gauge rails carried freight and passengers (mostly tourists) for half a century. Narrated, color, 13.25 minutes.

341-85381 VHS   19.95

STEAMUP IN BLUEGRASS COUNTRY
Kentucky was alive with short lines in the 1950s. Includes: Cadiz RR, Brimstone RR (Tenn.), Kentucky & Tennessee RR, Buffalo Creek & Gauley (WV), Meadow River, Morehead & North Fork—and the famous Illinois Central steam excursions of 1953-55. Color, 23 minutes.

341-85421 VHS   24.95

THE WATER LEVEL ROUTE
The New York Central ran its trains with style, dash and grace. Documentary stretching from the 1905 *Empire State Express* to the end of the *20th Century Limited* era. Color and black & white, 55 minutes.

341-85431 VHS   39.95

TRAINS OF TOMORROW
Documentary shows us England's IC-125, France's TGV, Japan's Bullet Train and other amazingly new rail developments. Color, 23.15 minutes.

341-85451 VHS   19.95

SLIM PRINCESS
The Espee's California narrow gauge ran from Keeler to Laws. 1954, color, 10 minutes.

341-80221 VHS   19.95

AMERICAN FREEDOM TRAIN
Resplendent in red, white and blue, #4449 tours America in 1977. This original film has now been expanded for video! Color, 30 minutes.

341-80241 VHS   29.95

AMERICAN RAILS AT MID-CENTURY
A look at 1950s steam and first generation diesel progress combines "Big Trains A-Rolling," "Mainline USA" and "225,000 Mile Proving Ground". Color, 62 minutes.

341-85321 VHS   39.95

END OF AN ERA
Baldwin steam locos working the tall timber of Washington. Color, 20 minutes.

341-81001 VHS   19.95

NICKEL PLATE STORY
Mainline action from 1948 tells the "Nickel Plate Story". Color, 20 minutes.

341-83301 VHS   19.95

EMPIRE ON PARADE
A look at Great Northern passenger, freight and streamliner service. Color, 40 minutes.

341-80601 VHS   39.95

GREAT AGE OF STEAM
Steam loco history from John Bull to the Big Boy. Color, 28 minutes.

341-85071 VHS   29.95

ONCE UPON THE WABASH
A 1950s look at The Bluebird streamliner. Color, 25 minutes.

341-85111 VHS   24.95

LOADED FOR WAR
AT&SF mobilizing for WWII. Color, 14 minutes.

341-80151 VHS   19.95

ILLINOIS TERMINAL
Features the big orange traction cars, the blue-and-silver streamliners, heavy trolley freight drags, PCC trains, and even the Alton-Grafton railbus. Color, 45 minutes.

341-71107   **NEW**   39.95

SAFE HIGHWAYS   **NEW**
341-75008   19.95

NEW YORK TRANSIT IN THE 1940s
341-75171   19.95

MAINLINE RAILROADS
BLACK & WHITE VIDEOS

GERALD M. BEST's 1927 STEAM ODYSSEY
Trip starts in Chicago and works east, along the New York Central's famed Water Level Route mainline. Shown are the Camelback steam locomotives of the New York, Ontario & Western and the Erie. Called "Mother Hubbards," you'll see them working through some beautiful New York State countryside. Also featured are the Chicago & North Western, Rock Island, New York Central, and Delaware, Lackawanna & Western. 20 minutes.

341-85531   19.95

NEW YORK CENTRAL COLLECTION
During the 1940s the New York Central produced a series of films designed to showcase the modern NYC system—spotlighting the mighty Hudson—Class Steam locomotives, as well as freight yards and signal systems. Sound, 63 minutes.

341-85491 VHS   39.95

PENNSYLVANIA COLLECTION
The Pennsylvania Railroad of the 1950s was a railroading show unlike anything else. With powerful duplex-drive T-1s, classic GG1 electrics and "next generation" cab-unit diesels. Sound, 69 minutes.

341-85501 VHS   39.95

WESTWARD HO!
A 1926 trip on the Northern Pacific. See the wonders of the Great Plains, the majesty of the mountains, glimpse wild buffalo, a 26-horse combine! Catch vignettes of the cities and towns of America 60 years ago. Black and white, 16.25 minutes.

341-85401 VHS   19.95

CALIFORNIA LIMITEDS
For devotees of the Southern Pacific and the Santa Fe. Back to the late 1920s and early 1930s for Best's own movie about the *Lark,* the *Daylight,* the *Grand Canyon Limited* and, yes—the *Santa Paula Local*! Best knew the great trains of that great era. Black and white, 33 minutes.

341-85411 VHS   39.95

■ **LTD QUANTITIES AVAILABLE** ■

PROGRESS ON RAILS
Tells how the new diesels cracked the steam bastion that was the Pennsy. You'll see how cab signals and ATC works, too. Black and white. 15 minutes.

341-83211 VHS   14.95

SAFE SWITCHING
Dos and Don'ts on the Great Northern. Originally entitled "Why Risk Your Life," this GN safety film is a graphic instruction on how to handle engines and cars in a busy freight yard (we think St. Paul). All action is from 40 years ago, and most of the power is steam. Black and white, 35.50 minutes.

341-85391 VHS   29.95

BIG POWER — NORFOLK & WESTERN
The A Class #1218 and J Class #611 are brought together on fan trips in 1987. Original footage from 1958 looks at these and other classes in action. 30 minutes.

341-85351 VHS   29.95

Interurban Films

VHS VIDEO CASSETTES

A wide range of traction, mainline and documentary railroad subjects are offered in VHS format. All videos have sound narration and are black and white unless noted.

MAINLINE RAILROADS
(continued)

WHEELS OF STEEL
In the cab and trackside following Pennsy GG1's. 14 minutes.
341-83221 VHS   19.95

TO MOUNT LOWE WITH LOVE
Ride through southern California's Rubio Canyon on narrow gauge electrics. 32 minutes.
341-70141 VHS   34.95

STEAM DAYLIGHT RIDES AGAIN
Return of SP #4449 to the Coast Route. 11 minutes.
341-80231 VHS   19.98

THE STEAM LOCOMOTIVE
A look at NYC steams in 1941. 20 minutes.
341-83131 VHS   19.95

THE GENERAL
A classic silent comedy, based on the Great Locomotive Chase. Written and directed by Buster Keaton. 76 minutes.
341-50131 VHS   29.95

SAN DIEGO AND ARIZONA
Rare 1920s footage of this mountain railroad, including Carrizo Gorge. 10 minutes.
341-80801 VHS   19.95

DOUBLEHEADIN' ON THE SIERRA
A 4-4-0 and 4-6-0 team up at Jamestown. 10 minutes.
341-85051 VHS   19.95

DAYLIGHTING THE PADRE TRAIL
Los Angeles to San Francisco behind streamlined steam in 1939. 20 minutes.
341-80211 VHS   19.95

FLIGHT OF THE CENTURY
1935 ride aboard 20th Century Ltd from Chicago to New York. 18 minutes.
341-83101 VHS   19.95

CLEAR TRACK AHEAD
Pennsy steam, including the T1 Duplex. 27 minutes.
341-83201 VHS   29.95

THE FREIGHT YARD
1946 NYC yard action and loco servicing. 19 minutes.
341-83111 VHS   19.95

TRACTION

COLOR VIDEOS

TROLLEYS OF BALTIMORE
We visit this great streetcar city in 1946, when green PCC's vied for track space with Red Rocket deck-roof cars, MU trains to Sparrow Point, yellow Peter Witts, rural runs and heavy city traction action. Color, 27 minutes.
341-71031 VHS   24.95

CHICAGO's 3 INTERURBANS
Midwest Traction Classics II, a color and black & white, visit to Insull's Big Three: North Shore, South Shore, and the Chicago, Aurora & Elgin, from Electroliners to Birneys. There's footage from every era, plus present-day action on the two survivors. Color, 30 minutes.
341-73011 VHS   29.95

ELECTRIC TRANSIT TODAY & TOMORROW
This tape combines three vintage documentary films produced by General Electric. The tape looks at rapid transit in the 40s and 50s, plus the proposed airport monorails ''of the future''. Color, 35 minutes.
341-71021 VHS   34.95

RIDING THE NO. 10
Ride on Milwaukee's last operating streetcar line. Color, 30 minutes.
341-72201 VHS   29.95

IT'S A BIG JOB
1947 film on operating Los Angeles trolleys. Color, 22 minutes.
341-70201 VHS   24.95

RIDE THE P.E. TO SAN BERNARDINO
A 1939 excursion on the Pacific Electric featuring two 1300 class steel combos. 8 minutes.
341-70111 VHS   19.95

DOWN MARKET STREET
Horse, steam and electric railways in 1905 San Francisco.
341-70401 VHS   14.95

BLACK & WHITE VIDEOS

COLUMBUS DELAWARE & MARION
A Great Ohio interurban, filmed in its closing days back in 1932. B&W, silent. 8 minutes.
341-75011 VHS   19.95

SPOTLIGHT ON ELECTRIC TRANSIT
Here is wonderful color action of the famed North Shore *Electroliners*, Pacific Electic on the Hollywood Freeway, plus rare footage of trackless trolleys. Includes footage of then existing systems in various cities, plus an in-depth look at the not-yet-built Bay Area Rapid Transit (BART) system. 39 minutes.
341-71061 VHS   29.95

90 YEARS OF CHICAGO TRACTION
In this video by Bill Warrick and Walther Keevil, you'll see a marvelous collection of vintage footage, spanning over 90 years! The Chicago Surface Lines and predecessors—including horse, cable, and electric railways—are covered from circa 1900 to the 1950s, 58 minutes.
341-73021 VHS   39.95

LAKE SHORE ELECTRIC
Filmed on the Ohio interurban between 1931 and 1938, following the line from Cleveland to Toledo. 14 minutes.
341-75041 VHS   19.95

SOUTH SHORE IN 1927
Sam Insull's personal inspection tour of the CSS&SB in 1927. Dubbed sound, 40 minutes.
341-72401 VHS   29.95

SOUTH SHORE STORY
A history of the ''Last Interurban'' from earliest days to modern operations. Some color. 30 minutes.
341-72411 VHS   29.95

STREAMLINING CHICAGO
Vintage tractioniana showing 1941 streetcar shoofly operation as the streets of Chicago are torn up. From the archives of Bill Warrick. 19 minutes.
341-72601 VHS   19.95

1945 ON THE NORTH SHORE LINE
Electroliners, freight, city cars and more in operation. 24 minutes.
341-72321 VHS   24.95

GETTING ABOUT
1934 film covering Detroit's streetcar system. 14 minutes.
341-75031 VHS   19.98

NEW YORK TRANSIT IN THE 1940s
Combines ''IRT Rapid Transit'' and ''Vanishing El.'' 20 minutes.
341-75171 VHS   19.98

THE RAILROAD VIDEO SERIES

Quarterly railroad video series on VHS. Stories span the world of diesel, steam, electric, freight and passenger railroading from around the US and Canada.

Volume 1, Tape 1
Compare Amtrak's GEP32's and EMD F40's on the ride from Chicago to Kansas city; explore SP's Oregon branchlines; rare EMD F-units in Northeast U.S., the last GE U28B's in Kentucky; fire up a steam engine and visit BN's last interlocking tower in Chicago. 87 minutes.
299-11   39.95

Volume 1, Tape 2
Conrail's iron-ore unloaders in Cleveland; Milwaukee Road's Montana electrification; Fairbanks Morse's last ''Junior Trainmaster'' diesel; UP3985 and AT & SF3751 in Kansas; President Bush's 1992 campaign train on the Wisconsin Central. 63 minutes.
299-12   39.95

Volume 1, Tape 3
Grand Canyon railway; five of the busiest crossings in Chicago; GE diesel lugging coal on the Monongahela Railway; commuter railroading on MARC; learn how a mechanic keeps C&NW diesels in top condition and see track being renewed on Midsouth Rail Corp. 60 minutes.
299-13   39.95

VHS VIDEO CASSETTES

From contemporary operations to the classic trains of yesteryear, and the excitement of railroading in Europe, you'll see a wide range of railroad action in these video cassettes. Each is in full-color with sound (unless noted).

PREVIEWS: VOLUME 3
Highlights include footage from: Best of 1988, 1989, 1990; Cumbres & Toltec Scenic's Rotary Snow Plow, Montana Rail Link, Napa Valley Wine Train, Horse Shoe Curve, Steam to St. Louis, Sacramento Railfair 1991 and more. 80 minutes.

561-3   19.95

CUMBRES & TOLTEC'S ROTARY SNOW PLOW
Steam action features the May blizzard of 1991, when this famous tourist line was cleared using steam rotary OY before operations could resume. 40 minutes.

561-194   24.95

STEAM TO SACRAMENTO
Catch the action and excitement as several steam locos make their way to Railfair '91. Follow the UP main as #844 and #3985 doublehead to California, and SP #4449 and #2472 team up for a run to Oakland and return. 60 minutes.

561-195 **(By Special Order Only.)**   29.95

SANTA FE'S ARIZONA MAINLINE
Stretching across the mountains and deserts of Arizona, the Santa Fe mainline is double-track, high-density railroading at its finest. This 80-minute color videotape features red and silver warbonnets with both Electro-Motive and General Electric engines in an exciting tour of Santa Fe's Arizona mainline.

561-196   39.95

WISCONSIN CENTRAL
90 minutes of regional railroading, showcasing the rare SDL39's and other motive power around the system.

561-197   39.95

HUNTINGTON STEAM CELEBRATION
Big time action from the 1991 NRHS convention in Huntington, WV. Featured is side-by-side running of the NKP 765 and Pere Marquette 1225 down a double-tracked mainline. 90 minutes.

561-198   Huntington Steam Celebration   29.95

View the 765 and 1225 as they pull a freight double-headed, and a huge 1218 as it travels from Cincinnati to Portsmouth, Ohio. 90 minutes.

561-199   Steam to Huntington   29.95

Two-volume set of Huntington steam, #'s 561-198 and 561-199.

561-200   Huntington Steam Set   49.95

RAILROADS OF MEXICO
Coverage begins at the border crossing town of Laredo, Texas. Union Pacific and Katy engines on lease in both freight and passenger service. 105 minutes.

561-202   Northern Mexico Rails   39.95

Take a ride through the mountains on the last narrow gauge line left in Mexico. 90 minutes.

561-203   Central Mexico Rails   39.95

Two-volume set of railroads of Mexico, #'s 561-202 and 561-203. **(By Special Order Only.)**

561-204   Mexico Rails — Volume 1 and 2   69.95

CANFOR'S ENGLEWOOD RAILWAY
An up-close visit to the Englewood Logging Division of Canadian Forest Products, Ltd., where logs move from forest to the sea on a 76-mile-long logging railway that is the backbone of a modern forest operation. 45 minutes.

561-205   24.95

CUMBRES & TOLTEC PASSENGER
Ride the longest and highest narrow gauge line in North America, aboard Cumbres & Toltec passenger trains. There's also a cab ride aboard one of the line's Mikado's, photo run-bys and spectacular mountain scenery. 75 minutes.

561-206   29.95

LTV MINING RAILROAD
Alco's, Baldwins and matched sets of F-Units are alive and well on the LTV Mining Railroad of Minnesota. Also covers the mine operations from start-to-finish, showing how taconite is mined, pelletized and shipped by rail to the ore dock. 60 minutes.

561-207   39.95

WESTERN MARYLAND'S SCENIC RAILROAD
Alco action abounds in this tape, covering equipment and operation of this museum line. The road's RS3, FPA-4 and RSD5 are resplendent in their Western Maryland "fireball" colors and are shown in operation through beautiful mountain scenery.

561-208   19.95

SANTA FE #3751 — RETURN TO STEAM
Northern #3751 is shown undergoing restoration, being tested on break-in runs and her magnificent return to excursion service. Plus, you're trackside to watch the 4-8-4 celebrate the 99th anniversary of ''The California Limited'', including the return trip through Cajon & Tehachapi with ''warbonnet'' FP45 helpers. 60 minutes.

561-209   29.95

CHATTANOOGA STEAM REUNION
561-210   24.95

LOGGING RAILROADS OF SIERRAS
561-212   24.95

TODAY'S CHICAGO RAILROADS
Nineteen different railroads are included in this tour of Chicago like Dolton, McCook and State Line Tower. Locomotives from the latest Santa Fe Warbonnets to time-worn Northwestern Geeps. 2 hours.

561-106   49.95

CALIFORNIA WESTERN RAILROAD
A look at a fascinating, well-maintained, and historic shortline, which treats you to cab rides and hi-railing ahead of the locomotives. 60 minutes.

561-192   39.95

SOUTHERN PACIFIC'S SHASTA DIVISION
Watch trains travel across the Redding trestle and then stop at Dunsmuir to add more power for the battle through Cantara Loop and up the stiff 2.1 degree grade through Azalea. 60 minutes.

561-193   39.95

VHS VIDEO CASSETTES

From contemporary operations to the classic trains of yesteryear, and the excitement of railroading in Europe, you'll see a wide range of railroad action in these video cassettes. Each is in full-color with sound (unless noted).

RAILS TO THE REDWOOD EMPIRE

A look at the pre-1950's steam era operations of the Northwestern Pacific. Shows steam and diesel action from a combination of vintage tapes, slides, photos and contemporary video footage. 76 minutes.

561-108   59.95

EASTERN KENTUCKY COAL LINES

See the CSX's Louisville & Nashville, Chesapeake & Ohio and Norfolk Southern's broad range of power units hauling ''black diamond'' out of the Appalachian terrain. Tunnels, high trestles and helpers on coal trains add to the interest on this visit to the coal fields of Eastern Kentucky. 75 minutes.

561-109   39.95

NAPA VALLEY WINE TRAIN

Ride in luxury behind an Alco FA4 as you enjoy the elegance of dining and a completely refurbished heavyweight passenger car. Take a trip through the scenic and wine grape growing region of Napa Valley, California. 30 minutes.

561-102 **(By Special Order Only.)**   19.95

CUMBRES & TOLTEC SCENIC FREIGHT TRAIN

Relive the glorious days of the Rio Grande freight train, battling its way up the 10,000 foot Cumbres Pass and winding its way over the longest narrow gauge railroad in America. Filmed in September, 1990. 1 hour.

561-103   29.95

THE MONTANA RAIL LINK

From locomotives to mountain scenery, ''Montana Rail Link'' is filled with modern railroading action. Both local freights and Burlington Northern hotshots are seen in action. 70 minutes.

561-681   39.95

UNION PACIFIC 3985 CHALLENGER

Watch the action of the 3985 at work as it handles each new assignment in a manner befitting a 1943 Alco superpower. It features the largest locomotive in the world, pulling freight and passenger trains from Cheyenne, Wyoming to Omaha, Nebraska. 60 min.

561-691   29.95

CASS SCENIC RAILROAD

Ride along in the cabs as the firemen work to keep the engines fueled with shovel after shovelful of coal. Watch as the intricate system of shafts, flywheels and gears are seen close up, straining to pull the trains up the 11% grades on the mountainside. 52 minutes.

561-671   29.95

BURLINGTON NORTHERN E-UNITS

View the triple-track BN Mainline and the afternoon ''Dinky Parade'' as train after train is scheduled. See curves, bridges and scenic stations along this line. Many meets are captured as the E-units speed ''along the race track''. 60 minutes.

561-701   39.95

KANSAS CITY SOUTHERN LINES

Witness the transition of paint schemes with white diesels and many in the new gray roll by. Tour the entire KCS system south from Kansas City through the Ozarks, over the Ouachita Mountains in Arkansas and on to Port Arthur, Texas. Every class of engine presently running on the KCS is seen in action. 80 minutes.

561-651   39.95

STEAM TO SAINT LOUIS

The most complete coverage available of the 1218, 844 and 819 mighty locomotives on their way to St Louis. 90 minutes.

561-661   29.95

THE COPPER CANYON— CHIHUAHUA PACIFICO RAILROAD

Ride the Chihuahua Pacifico over Mexico's Sierra Madre mountains through the Copper Canyon, one of the most rugged mountain passes in North America. 80 minutes.

561-641   39.95

THE MIGHTY STEAM SERIES

This series is a collection of tapes covering today's famous fantrip engines. Each features an individual steam locomotive revealing its own power.

CANADIAN STEAM

Highlights include a visit to SteamExpo in 1986, footage of the famous 1988 excursion featuring the Royal Hudson 6060 and 3716 on a run from Vancouver to Prince George and back. 30 minutes.

561-1106   19.95

COTTONBELT #819

Discover what #819 has to offer with its power and dramatic performance. 30 minutes.

561-1104   19.95

UNION PACIFIC #844

Ride aboard #844 as it teams up with #3985 and see events encountered on the trip to California. 30 minutes.

561-1102   19.95

NORFOLK & WESTERN #1218

Includes 1218 rambling on its home rails in Virginia, side-by-side run-bys with N&W 611, plus coverage of its trip to St. Louis for the 1990 National Railway Historical Society Convention. 30 minutes.

561-1105   19.95

UNION PACIFIC #3985

Check out the doubleheaded Union Pacific train with #844 as they venture from Cheyenne, Wyoming to Sacramento, California. 30 minutes.

561-1103   19.95

SP ''DAYLIGHT'' #4449

Engage in this escapade when #4449 departs Portland, Oregon in its journey to Sacramento, California. 30 minutes.

561-1101   19.95

VHS VIDEO CASSETTES

From contemporary operations to the classic trains of yesteryear, and the excitement of railroading in Europe, you'll see a wide range of railroad action in these video cassettes. Each is full-color with sound (unless noted).

ARKANSAS & MISSOURI
An in-depth look at a modern shortline, whose operations are 100% Alco! A fleet of C420's are seen in freight service, while a T6 works a switch run. A special trip by the road's RS-1 rounds out the action. 60 minutes.

561-221 **(By Special Order Only.)**   39.95

BAY AREA RAIL TRANSIT
Over 50 years of transit history in the San Francisco and Oakland, California, area are presented in this tape. Produced by Oakland TV station Channel 2, the tape includes prewar footage of many "lost" systems. Comparisons of facilities, equipment and operations of BART are presented by knowledgeable historians. You'll also see scenes of the Sacramento Northern, MUNI, Key System and others. 27 minutes.

561-501 **(By Special Order Only.)**   24.95

VINTAGE COLLECTION VOLUME ONE
Five classic black and white shorts are combined into a full-length historic feature: "Friendship Train" a special movie in the 1940's on the Southern Pacific, "Right-of-Way USA" with rare footage of troop trains, "Last Narrow Gauge Railroad" a 1950's newsreel on the Rio Grande's Durango-Silverton line, "Omaha - Rail Metropolis of the Plains" which chronicles operations in the famous railroad city, circa 1953, and "Magic Rails to Yesterday" with streetcar scenes of San Francisco before and after the 1906 earthquake, plus footage of the California Zephyr. Black and white, running time: 65 minutes.

561-511 **(By Special Order Only.)**   39.95

SAND PATCH GRADE
The famous grade is the stage for a look at CSX operations on the mainline from Baltimore to Chicago. Motive power from F units to SD50's are seen in an assortment of colorful paint schemes. Visits to the working interlocking towers at SA and Hyndman are also featured. 60 minutes.

561-521   39.95

TODAY'S ST. LOUIS RAILROADS
The St. Louis area ranks as the third busiest rail center in the nation, with 13 railroads serving the city! A variety of local hotspots are featured, where you'll see trains of the UP, CSX, BN, Conrail, Alton & Southern, IC, Gateway Western, Manufacturer's Junction, Norfolk Southern, TRRA, and more in action. 60 minutes.

561-531   39.95

SNOW ON THE RUN
The men and machinery of the Southern Pacific take on the fury of the winter of 1952 when 790" of snow fell at Donner Summit in the Sierra Nevada mountains. The tape shows Jordan spreaders, rotary plows, cab forwards and "black widow" F units in service. There's also coverage of the rescue of "The City of San Francisco" stopped in its tracks by a fierce blizzard. 20 minutes.

561-551   19.95

DESTINATIONS
Celebrate 125 years of railroading in New Zealand in this tape, which covers contemporary freight and passenger operations. Watch the last run of Dx series diesels, the new Class 30 electrics, the "Silver Fern" and more. You'll also meet many of the people, from dispatchers to track gangs, that keep the road moving every day. 50 minutes.

561-611 **(By Special Order Only.)**   24.95

RAILROADS & NATIONAL DEFENSE
You're part of the action as America's railroads gear up for the Korean War. Heavyweight Pullmans and coaches move troops, while freight trains roll trucks and tanks to seaports for shipment overseas. Scenes of new diesels pulling streamliners and steam in freight service are featured. 15 minutes.
(By Special Order Only.)

561-561   19.95

ON THE TRACK
Here's the story of the important role railroads play in everyday life. Shots of SP, NYC, PRR, MILW, NH, GN and more show how food, automobiles, clothing and other essentials are moved by train. 18 minutes.

561-581   19.95

ST. LOUIS STEAM CELEBRATION
In June of 1990, four of the nation's favorite restored steam locomotives visited the National Railway Historical Society Convention in St. Louis. Camera crews on board and following the trains covered the excursions pulled by Frisco #1522, Norfolk & Western #1218, Cotton Belt #819 and Union Pacific #844. 60 minutes.

561-541   29.95

STEAM ON PARADE
This 1988 visit to new Zealand showcases over 50 steam engines in a salute to the 125th anniversary of the country's railroads. Several restored locos were in operation for the Ferrymead 125 celebration and are shown on parade. The tape also uses historic footage shot from 1901 to 1967 to show different types of engines in action. 60 minutes.

561-601 **(By Special Order Only.)**   24.95

STEAM LIVES ON
Although steam has been retired from New Zealand Railways for 20 years, a pair of restored engines make a triumphal return to the mainline. A Ks945 from Paekakariki and a Ja 1250 from the Glenbrook Vintage Railway are doubleheaded for a fantrip. The tape also includes a pair of films: "Kb Country" featuring the country's biggest steam locos and "The Ride of the 480" a 1,000 kilometer journey of a tank engine under its own steam. 50 minutes.

561-621 **(By Special Order Only.)**   24.95

225,000 MILES PROVING GROUND
Named for the 225,000 miles of track in service in 1953 when the film was made, this documentary covers the switch from steam to diesel power taking place on many roads. Narrated by TV star Hugh Beaumont, the film shows many of the brand new F units, a UP gas turbine and Santa Fe "map" reefers. 40 minutes.

561-571 **(By Special Order Only.)**   19.95

LIFELINE OF THE NATION
Railroads played an essential role in moving men and machinery during World War II. This period film is filled with steam action and the few diesels shown are early models. 20 minutes.

561-591   19.95

Pentrex

VHS VIDEO CASSETTES

From contemporary operations to the classic trains of yesteryear, and the excitement of railroading in Europe, you'll see a wide range of railroad action in these video cassettes. Each is in full-color with sound (unless noted).

995 DAYS
The complete story of the construction of the British Columbia Railway's Tumbler Ridge electric line, the only 50 kilovolt operation in North America. 29 minutes.

561-331 **(By Special Order Only.)**   19.95

CANADIAN DOUBLEHEADER STEAM
Canada's largest steamers, #2860 from the Canadian Pacific and #6060 from Canadian National, doublehead a passenger special through British Columbia and Alberta. 60 minutes.

561-261   29.95

MILE 63.5
A derailment means trouble anytime, but this one took place in the dead of winter on the British Columbia Railway. You'll see the efforts and equipment required to rerail three diesels. 27 minutes.

561-341   19.95

DAYLINER ONE AND SNOW TRAIN
These travelogues, produced by the British Columbia Railway, take you on board the line's rail diesel cars for trips of the line and a look at their spectacular scenery. 37 minutes.

561-351 **(By Special Order Only.)**   19.95

UNCOMMON CARRIER
A general overview of the operations and equipment, including steam, diesel and electric power, on the British Columbia Railway. 21 minutes.

561-321 **(By Special Order Only.)**   19.95

"BEST OF" SERIES
Fantrips, inaugural runs of new motive power, special events and more from railroading history in the 80's are presented in this series.

BEST OF 1984
A collection of railroad events from 1984 are highlighted, including the Speeno rail grinder in the Mojave desert, Southern Pacific Olympic Special, Union Pacific on the Feather River and more. 90 minutes.

561-51 **(By Special Order Only.)**   39.95

BEST OF 1985
A look at railroad action from 1985 including: the new Southern Pacific red and yellow paint scheme, EMD SD60 demos on the Santa Fe, The Ringling Brothers circus train, 1985 National Motorcar Championship, Union Pacific Junior Oldtimers Special, McCloud River steam excursions and more. 2 hours.

561-61 **(By Special Order Only.)**   49.95

BEST OF 1986
A review of railroading in 1986 including: EMD GP60 demos on the Santa Fe, highlights of STEAMEXPO, movement of Santa Fe #3751, the Santa Fe Museum Special, Chicago & North Western inspection train in the west, a visit to the railroads of Chicago and more. 2 hours.

561-81 **(By Special Order Only.)**   49.95

BEST OF 1987
A review of action on the nation's railroads in 1987, including: National Railway Historical Society convention with Norfolk & Western #1218 and #611, SP and UP Super Bowl Specials, Susquehanna stack trains, California Operation Lifesaver Special and more. 2 hours.

561-201 **(By Special Order Only.)**   49.95

BEST OF 1988
The restoration of Cotton Belt #819, CSX F units in action, eastern Canadian railroading, railroads in Mexico and the Cumbres and Toltec Scenic Railway were among the highlights of 1988. 2 hours.

561-271 **(By Special Order Only.)**   49.95

BEST OF 1989
Exciting happenings in railroad history during 1989 included: Santa Fe's first two FP45's repainted in "Warbonnet" colors, Norfolk & Western #611 on the Rathole Division, Napa Valley Wine Train with Alco FPA4 power, CSX F units #118 and #119 on the New River Train, Trailer Train special run through Cajon Pass, Nickel Plate #765, and F units on the Western Allegheny. 2 hours.

561-251 **(By Special Order Only.)**   49.95

BEST OF 1990
From steam to diesel. Highlights include UP Silver Zone Pass, Blue Unit Circus Train, Green Bay & Western "Boat Train", SP's Siskiyou Line, Boone & Scenic Valley RR, Railroads of Omaha, Frisco 1522 & the Eisenhower Centennial. 2 hours.

561-105   49.95

BEST OF 1991
561-213   **NEW** 49.95

VHS VIDEO CASSETTES

From contemporary operations to the classic trains of yesteryear, and the excitement of railroading in Europe, you'll see a wide range of railroad action in these video cassettes. Each is in full-color with sound (unless noted).

DAYLIGHT TO THE FAIR
Follow Southern Pacific #4449, with a matching train of ''Daylight'' orange and red cars, as it travels from Portland to New Orleans for the World's Fair. 90 minutes.

561-11 **(By Special Order Only.)** 49.95

THE ALASKA RAILROAD
Spectacular scenery and F units highlight this tape, shot in 1984. Ride the cab of an F unit from Anchorage to Fairbanks and drive a car aboard the Whitier Shuttle for a terrific ride. Freight operations, including summer gravel trains and unloading of barges are also featured. 90 minutes.

561-21 49.95

BC RAIL
Travel by train through some of the most beautiful scenery in Canada, aboard the British Columbia Railway. Ride behind the Royal Hudson and aboard the Budd rail diesel car from North Vancouver to Prince George. Freight operations on several sub-divisions are also examined, including the Tumbler Ridge electrics and their coal loading operations. 90 minutes.

561-31 49.95

PRIVATE VARNISH ROUNDUP
Take a rare look inside many of the privately owned and restored rail cars in service today. Shot at the 1985 convention in Portland, Oregon, the tape also includes interviews with various car owners and guided tours of their cars. 60 minutes.

561-41 **(By Special Order Only.)** 39.95

STEAM EXPO
Over twenty steam locomotives were in operation for EXPO '86 held in Vancouver. This tape covers their arrival, the Grand Parade and a week of exhibitions. Interviews with operating crews are also included. PLUS, this tape covers the March, 1986, trip of Southern Pacific #4449 from Portland to Los Angeles for the filming of the Walt Disney movie, ''Tough Guys''. 90 minutes.

561-71 **(By Special Order Only.)** 49.95

DENVER & RIO GRANDE
Here's mountain railroading at its finest in all four seasons, on the Rio Grande from Salt Lake to Denver and beyond. Travel to Tennessee Pass, Royal Gorge, the Joint Line, Winter Park and more for a look at freight operations, Amtrak and the famed Ski Train. 90 minutes.

561-91 49.95

CAJON - TEHACHAPI
Visit southern California's most famous railroading landmarks for a look at fast-paced action on the Southern Pacific, Santa Fe and Union Pacific. Visit the ATSF Dispatcher's office in San Bernadino for a view of operations over Cajon, see helpers couple on at Victorville, and visit the Barstow hump yard. Includes a custom drawn area map. 90 minutes.

561-101 49.95

UNION PACIFIC 8444-1987
In September of 1987, famed UP steamer #8444 rolled out of the shops repainted in the classic two-tone gray color scheme. We follow the engine from Wyoming to Nebraska for fantrip service and back to Denver for an excursion over Sherman Hill. The engine is seen at speed, with both freight and passenger trains. 60 minutes.

561-181 **(By Special Order Only.)** 29.95

MISSOURI-KANSAS-TEXAS THE KATY
A last look at the day-to-day operations of the Katy in 1988, before the merger with the Union Pacific was finalized. Green and yellow units are seen in action through Texas, Oklahoma and Kansas. 60 minutes.

561-211 39.95

SIERRA PACIFIC LINES
The Pasadena Model Railroad Club operates this immense line. Occupying a 5,000 square foot room, the scale features a 1,750 foot mainline, which takes a train running at normal speed over an hour to travel. 60 minutes.

561-631 39.95

SACRAMENTO RAILFAIR 1991
A gathering of major steam locos can be seen as Sacramento, California, meets them from across the United States, Canada, Great Britain and beyond. Visits with all the attending locomotives, views of the museum grounds, and festivities. 60 minutes.

561-107 29.95

SANTA FE TRAINING
A look into the ins and outs of operations on your model railroad. Information on the communication radios, end of train devices, end of train markers and more. 33 minutes.

561-104 **(By Special Order Only.)** 19.95

THIS IS MY RAILROAD - STEAM
This promotional film, made by the Southern Pacific in 1947, shows what it takes to operate one of the nation's largest railroads. Filmed throughout the system, lots of steam power is shown in action. 60 minutes.

561-231 39.95

THIS IS MY RAILROAD - DIESEL
In 1950, ''This is My Railroad'' was updated with footage of the new diesels being delivered and placed in service on the Southern Pacific. 30 minutes.

561-241 **(By Special Order Only.)** 29.95

STEAM TO LOS ANGELES
Celebrate the 50th anniversary of the Los Angeles Union Passenger Depot with the Union Pacific and Southern Pacific as they roll out their fan trip favorites, #8444 and #4449. This tape also includes the spectacular side-by-side run over Cajon! Running time: 60 minutes.

561-411 29.95

WASHINGTON CENTENNIAL STEAM
Steam and snow produce a spectacular show as Southern Pacific #4449 rolls over the Burlington Northern and through the Cascade Tunnel. Filmed in February of 1989, the tape follows the travels of this train for Washington State's Centennial and Winter Games. You'll also see the Mount Ranier Scenic Railroad's 2-8-2 in action pulling trains. 60 minutes.

561-421 29.95

CHALLENGE FOR TOMORROW
Produced by the Santa Fe in the 1950's, this tape looks at the road's past with footage of classic steam, and the changes coming in the future, including shiny new ''warbonnet'' F and Alco PA units. 28 minutes.

561-451 **(By Special Order Only.)** 19.95

MICHIGAN ORE LINES
Operations of the Escanaba & Lake Superior, Lake Superior & Ishpeming and Chicago & North Western ore districts of upper Michigan are featured in this tape. See LS&I Alcos in action, along with the road's only U25C, an RS3 and go for a cab ride in an RSD-15. On the E&LS, you'll see Baldwins and the recently acquired SD9's in action. Finally, C&NW first generation power and the Escanaba ore docks are seen, along with ore drags pulled by modern units. 55 minutes.

561-441 19.95

SANTA FE SUPER CHIEF
Enjoy a first class look at the Santa Fe ''Super Chief'' as it travels from Chicago to Los Angeles in 1960. 10 minutes.

561-361 **(By Special Order Only.)** 14.95

THE NORTH SHORE LINE
For over 60 years, this high speed interurban connected Milwaukee and Chicago. This tape looks at the line's last 25 years of operations, along with the physical plant and equipment. 90 minutes.

561-431 **(By Special Order Only.)** 74.95

JOURNEY TO YESTERDAY
Originally produced to show how the movie 'Denver & Rio Grande'' was made, this historic film covers much of the Silverton branch. Footage of authentic passenger and freight trains, plus a ''behind-the-scenes'' look at how many of the movie shots were made highlight the tape. 30 minutes.

561-461 **(By Special Order Only.)** 19.95

TRANSPORTATION IN THE U.S.A.
Produced in 1948, this tape looks at all forms of transport, but concentrates on railroading. Most of the footage covers steam power on eastern roads. You'll also visit with C&O President Robert Young at home, at work and travelling on a business car. 18 minutes.

561-471 19.95

HORSESHOE CURVE
Horseshoe Curve has been a favorite with generations of railfans! Today, this central Pennsylvania landmark is home to Conrail, and some 40 to 60 trains thunder around the curve every day. You're trackside for all the action, from helper units running light to priority mail and pig trains fighting their way through the Allegheny Mountains. 75 minutes.

561-481 39.95

SACRAMENTO NORTHERN
Travel back to 1940, for a look at this thriving traction system which ran from the Bay Area to Chico, California. Lots of freight and passenger equipment is seen, along with helper operations, tunnel and bridge crossings, plus a car ferry equipped with overhead catenary! 50 minutes.

561-491 **(By Special Order Only.)** 44.95

VHS VIDEO CASSETTES

From contemporary operations to the classic trains of yesteryear, and the excitement of railroading in Europe, you'll see a wide range of railroad action in these video cassettes. Each is in full-color with sound (unless noted).

ACROSS MARIAS PASS

Combines spectacular scenery with the power and drama of mountain railroading in the 90's. Provides a first-hand look at Burlington Northern's transcontinental main line, set against beautiful autumn colors, as well as in the middle of winter. 90 minutes.

561-214 **NEW** 39.95

ACROSS DONNER SUMMIT

Takes you out to meet winter head-on in this historic area. The action includes flangers and spreaders at work, multiple helper freights and passenger trains battling their way across the line. 2 hours.

561-215 **NEW** 39.95

LAST OF THE GIANTS

Produced by the UP, this historic film shows development of steam power on the road from 4-6-0's to the Big Boys, through photos, animated diagrams and films. Footage of the 4-8-8-4's being serviced, rebuilt and running flat out over the road in spectacular western scenery. 25 minutes.

561-216 **NEW** 19.95

UNION PACIFIC'S FEATHER RIVER ROUTE

One of the most famous railroad landmarks in the United States is featured. Covering today's operations through the Feather River Canyon, you'll also visit the Keddie Wye, Williams Loop, Clio Trestle and other famous locations. 60 minutes.

561-217 **NEW** 39.95

PICKERING'S SUGAR PINE RAILROAD

A unique lood at the history of California's Pickering Lumber Corporation. Highlights include interviews with brothers Manny and Toom Marshall, who both worked for the line between 1920 and 1942. Rare photographs and movie footage show the various steamers, as well as mill equipment, in action. 62 minutes.

561-218 **NEW** 39.95

POWDER RIVER....BASIN COAL TRAINS

Watch Chicago & North Western and Burlington Northern motive power move heavy tonnage trains around the clock in the Powder River Basin of Wyoming. C&NW's new C40-8's are seen along with a mix of old and new power on the BN. You'll also ride in the cab of helpers pushing a 14,000-ton train up and over the mountain. 90 minutes.

561-219 **NEW** 39.95

MEXICO'S PACIFICO RAILROAD

Covers operations and equipment throughout the 1100-mile long FCP, from Guadalajara to the United States border. Along the way, numerous Alco locos, including the freshly painted PA #17 and former BC Rail units are seen in action. Also looks at the line's passenger service and tours the main shop.

561-220 **NEW** 39.95

SAN JOSE STEAM CELEBRATION

Plenty of steam action showing UP's famed #3985, plus SP's #4449 and #2472 making a variety of fantrips during the NRHS convention.

561-222 **NEW** 29.95

FORTY FEET BELOW

A fascinating tour of the Chicago freight tunnels, back in the days when tiny locomotives pulled trains of short, heavy cars through a maze of sharp curves and endless tunnels. Also includes 1992 footage of the flooded tunnels in Chicago's Loop. 30 minutes.

561-223 **NEW** 19.95

SAN DIEGO MODEL RAILROAD MUSEUM

Tour the largest indoor model railroad exhibit in the U.S. in this visit to the San Diego Model Railroad Museum. Features an O Scale, N Scale and two HO layouts, which feature operating segments, plus new areas under construction. 30 minutes.

561-224 **NEW** 19.95

SANTA FE STEAM EMPLOYEE SPECIAL

One of summer's biggest steam events is covered on the west end as 4-8-4 #3751 pulls the Santa Fe Employee Recognition Special. The big steamer is accompanied by three "Super Fleet" diesels, plus a string of stainless passenger cars, as it rolls through California, Arizona and New Mexico. 40 minutes.

561-225 **NEW** 14.95

NEW YORK, NEW HAVEN & HARTFORD

One of New England's favorite lines lives again in this new production, featuring equipment and action on the New Haven.

561-226 **NEW** 19.98

PACIFIC ELECTRIC SERIES

Roll along on the big red cars and save money when you purchase the two-volume set! (Both titles are also available separately.)

PACIFIC ELECTRIC — LOS ANGELES STREET CARS

561-9229 **NEW** pkg(2) 49.95

PACIFIC ELECTRIC — TWILIGHT YEARS

561-229 **NEW** 29.95

LOS ANGELES STREET CARS — THE FINAL YEARS

561-230 **NEW** 29.95

AMTRAK SERIES

High speed action abounds in three new tapes, featuring action on the Corridor from New York to Philadelphia, Philadelphia to Washington, DC, and a cab ride from Washington to Philadelphia. A money saving two-volume set (#9237) with the New York to Philadelphia and Philadelphia to DC tapes is available too.

NEW YORK TO PHILADELPHIA — PHILADELPHIA TO DC

561-9237 **NEW** pkg(2) 69.95

NEW YORK TO PHILADELPHIA

561-236 **NEW** 39.95

PHILADELPHIA TO DC

561-237 **NEW** 39.95

CAB RIDE DC TO PHILADELPHIA

561-238 **NEW** 29.95

ALONG THE HUDSON — AMTRAK TURBO TRAIN CAB RIDE

561-9227 **NEW** 49.95

ALONG THE HUDSON DIVISION

561-227 **NEW** 39.95

AMTRAK TURBO TRAIN CAB RIDE

561-228 **NEW** 19.95

SANTA FE MOJAVE MAINLINE

561-232 **NEW** 39.95

THE GREEN BAY ROUTE

561-233 **NEW** 39.95

ARIZONA SHORTLINE RAILROAD

561-234 **NEW** 39.95

SOUTHERN PACIFIC #2472

561-235 **NEW** 29.95

TODAY'S MAINE RAILROADS

A look at current operations in the Pine Tree States includes a number of old favorites and new regionals. Covers plenty of freight and passenger traffic, with a few motive power surprises! 105 minutes.

561-242 **NEW** 39.95

NEW GEORGIA STEAM EXCURSIONS

Join the fun as Atlanta & West Point #290 handles three different steam excursions through Alabama and Georgia. This restored Pacific is shown on her first outing, resplendent in fresh paint. There's also a 1992 trip over the original A&WP right-of-way, and an excursion from Atlanta to Macon. 80 minutes.

561-243 **NEW** 29.95

UP FEATHER RIVER ROTARY

When heavy snows slammed into the Feather River Canyon in January of 1993, the Union Pacific fought back with one of their rotary plows. You'll have a ringside seat for the action, with footage from the cab and trackside. Plus, Steve Lee, Manager of UP's Steam Operations, takes you on a tour through the cab of the plow, explaining its history and operation. 45 minutes.

561-244 **NEW** 29.95

TODAY'S NORTHWESTERN PACIFIC

Running 156 miles from Suisin City to Willits, the NWP has long been a favorite with train watchers. Shows a number of changes during the three years of filming along the line, as well as breathtaking scenery. 110 minutes.

561-245 **NEW** 39.95

McCLOUD RIVER RAILROAD

Travel back in time near California's Mount Shasta to watch the Baldwin diesel fleet. Covering the years from 1948 to 1955, the new Baldwins are shown double-headed over the switchback at Signal Butte. The Russell plow is also seen in action, and there's footage of the Burney Branch with steamer #25. 35 minutes.

561-246 **NEW** 29.95

STEAM ACROSS AMERICA

561-247 Volume I **NEW** 39.95
561-248 Volume II **NEW** 39.95
561-9247 Set (Vol I & II) **NEW** 59.95

SLOW TRAIN TO OLYMPIA

561-311 39.95

DECCAN

561-171 39.95

CLINCHFIELD CHALLENGE

561-240 29.95

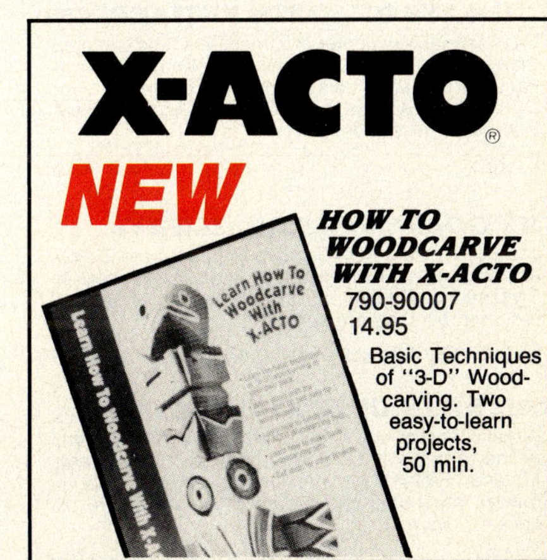

SALFORD CONSULTING, LTD

Imported from Great Britain by WALTHERS

VHS VIDEO CASSETTES

All items are ''Special Order Only''

Climb into the cab or relax in first class comfort as we travel across Europe by train with these video cassettes. Filmed on location throughout Europe, these tapes capture all the color and excitement of modern railway operations and equipment in many countries. History buffs will find plenty of steam and early motive power in action, too. All tapes are fully compatible with U.S. video equipment and are available in VHS format.

EUROPEAN DOCUMENTARIES

SWISS RAILWAY SPECTACULAR

A journey on the Swiss Railways from Geneva to Bern, showing a variety of international passenger traffic, various shortline operations and some steam action.

647-101   49.99

THE GOTTHARD ROUTE

Head through the Swiss Alps towards Italy on one of the most famous rail lines in Switzerland. This tape tells the story of the railroad today, from Basel to Chiasso. Lots of freight and international passenger traffic, plus connecting railroads are also seen. 60 minutes.

647-102   49.99

RAILWAYS OF THE RHINE

An incredible variety of railways and the magnificent scenery along the Rhine River are highlighted in this tape. You'll see it all, from the Swiss Oberalp narrow gauge, to private industrial operations, to first-class passenger trains. 60 minutes.

647-103   49.99

GLACIER EXPRESS ROUTE

This famous passenger train has delighted travelers since 1930 with it's breathtaking route through the Swiss Alps. You'll see the entire route along with other passenger and freight operations, plus some of the historic motive power once used on this line. 60 minutes.

647-104   49.99

RAILWAYS OF NORTH SWITZERLAND

From the railway center of Zurich, this tape explores many of the regional and mainline railways in Northeast Switzerland. Lots of colorful equipment, including rack railways, narrow gauge and the ''Orient Express'' are shown.

647-105   49.99

THE GOLDEN PASS RAILWAYS

Journey by train from Geneva to Lucerne to Zurich through some of the most spectacular scenery in Switzerland. Equipment and operations of several regional railroads are seen.

647-106 (By Special Order Only.)   49.99

RAILWAYS OF SCANDINAVIA

A documentary look at the operations and equipment of the railways of Denmark, Norway, Sweden and Finland. Freight and passenger service, visits to railway museums and steam preservation are all covered. 60 minutes.

647-107   49.99

IBERIAN RAIL TRAIL

Travel by train through Spain and Portugal, covering some of the less familiar routes to such locations as Barcelona and Madrid. 60 minutes.

647-108   49.99

THE RAILWAYS OF THE MOSEL(le)

This hour long documentary follows the railways along the Moselle River from Bussang in France to Koble in Germany. Capturing major events such as an international NATO exercise to the harvesting of grapes, this video takes a special riverside journey.

647-109   37.99

THE RAILWAY OF NORTHERN GERMANY

This video covers a wide variety of railways and trains throughout Germany. Scenes from Bebra, the arrival point for many refugee trains from the East to the industries of the West, are captured.

647-110   49.99

RHATISCHE BAHN

In 1989, the gauge Rhatische Bahn celebrated it's 100th birthday. Journey with the RhB through the mountains of Switzerland and across deep Alpine ravines. Tour with legendary passenger trains from the past and present, such as the Glacier, Bernina, Engadine and the famous Italian ''Penolina''. The video is one hour long with full commentary.

647-111   49.99

ALPINE EXPRESS

Alpine Express combines three of the world's greatest Alpine railway journeys, each of which starts from the high mountain resort of Kandersteg, deep in the heart of Switzerland. This one hour documentary has full commentary.

647-112 (By Special Order Only.)   49.99

PRIVATE SWISS RAILWAYS

See and experience the equipment and operation of all 25 private standard gauge lines operating in Switzerland. 60 minutes.

647-113   49.99

SCANDINAVIAN STEAM CENTRES

A visit to railway museums and preserved rail lines in Denmark, Norway, Sweden and Finland. 60 minutes.

647-114   49.99

150 YEARS OF EAST GERMAN RAILROADS

Commemorating 150 years of railroading on the lines that served East Germany, this tape provides complete coverage of the 47 trains taking part in the festivities, including lots of steam power. 45 minutes.

647-115   34.99

RAILWAYS OF ITALY

Travel the length and width of Italy by train, on both standard and narrow gauge lines. Lots of historic lines and equipment are featured, along with the latest Italian State Railways locos and trains.

647-116   49.99

AUSTRIAN RAILWAY VIDEO SPECTACULAR

From a ride on the world's oldest operating steam tramway to the latest electric and diesel power, you'll see a wide range of Austrian equipment in action. You'll enjoy spectacular scenery, (including some cab rides) along private and State railway lines, of both standard and narrow gauge operations. 60 minutes.

647-117   49.99

RAILWAYS OF SOUTHERN GERMANY

The Black Forest, Bavaria, Main and Rhine are among the stops on this rail tour of the southern part of Germany. The trip covers main routes, plus private railways. 60 minutes.

647-119   49.99

MALLARD 88

A restored ''Mallard'' class steam loco (originally used on the London North Eastern Railway) is seen in operation, running a variety of trips. Pacing from a helicopter, ground level shots and historic material from the National Railways Museum Archives tell the complete story of the engine.

647-403   34.99

EUROPEAN MAGAZINE PROGRAMMES

EUROPEAN VIDEO EXPERIENCE

These hour-long video magazines provide the latest news on European railroading. Each tape includes a visit to a major railway center, a locomotive profile, visits to various museums and steam operating sessions, plus coverage of special trains and other events.

647-301	Volume One	37.99
647-302	Volume Two	37.99
647-303	Volume Three	37.99
647-304	Volume Four	37.99
647-305	Volume Five	37.99
	(By Special Order Only.)	
647-306	Volume Six	37.99
647-307	Volume Seven	37.99
647-308	Volume Eight	37.99
647-309	Volume Nine	49.99

SALFORD CONSULTING, LTD
Imported from Great Britain by WALTHERS

VHS VIDEO CASSETTES
All items are "Special Order Only"

Climb into the cab or relax in first class comfort as we travel across Europe by train with these video cassettes. Filmed on location throughout Europe, these tapes capture all the color and excitement of modern railway operations and equipment in many countries. History buffs will find plenty of steam and early motive power in action, too. All tapes are fully compatible with U.S. video equipment and are available in VHS format.

CAB RIDES

GLACIER EXPRESS CAB RIDE
You're in the cab on the famous Glacier Express as it travels the Furka-Oberalp between Brig and Oberwald. You'll have a stunning view of the line from your seat in the new Hge4/4 electric loco, including several rack sections and a trip through a spiral tunnel! The tape has no narration, but place names are identified. 50 minutes.

647-201   34.99

GOTTHARD CAB RIDE
Ride the engineer's seat of a powerful Re4/4 11 electric loco as we make the run from Luzern to Bellinzona. Natural sound without narration makes this a truly realistic experience! 60 minutes.

647-202   34.99

RAILS TO SAINT GALLEN
This major railway center is served by several regional roads, which are seen in this tape. A ride on the meter gauge Appenzellerbahn, plus a modern Re4/4 of the Bodensee-Toggenburg Railway are just a few of the highlights.

647-203   34.99

RUSSIAN BORDER CAB RIDE
For the first time ever, an independent video service rides the cab of the Finnish State Railways train from Helsinki to the Russian border. Several passing trains are seen from the cab of the broad gauge loco and there's a look at the Russian State Railways electric. 60 minutes.

647-206   34.99

BAVARIAN CAB RIDE
You'll have the best seat aboard the German Federal Railways "Passau Express" in this tape, shot from the cab of the loco as the train rolls from Nuremberg to Wurzburg. 60 minutes.

647-207   37.99

SUPER PANORAMA EXPRESS

Ultra-modern equipment provides a panoramic view of the countryside on the Montreux-Oberland-Bernois Railway line. You'll ride in the highly desired front seats of the lead cab/coach from Zweisimen to Montreaux.

647-204   34.99

ARCTIC CAB RIDE
Cross the arctic circle aboard the Iron Ore Railway as it crosses the tundra of Lapland and Norway. You'll ride aboard a Swedish Rc electric on the run from Boden to Narvik, the most northerly railway station in Europe. 60 minutes.

647-205   34.99

THE BRITISH SCENE

SEVERN VALLEY ROUTE
39 minutes of 12 steam locomotives on passenger and freight trains. No commentary.

647-401   27.99

FFESTINIOG STEAM 125
Relive the 125th anniversary of the Ffestinog Railway in North Wales with a variety of steam powered fan-trips. Filmed during a weekend celebration in 1988, there's lots of action, plus a look at the history and development of the line. 60 minutes.

647-402   27.99

WATERCRESS' LINE GALA 1989
The Mid-Hants Railway, or Watercress Line as it's known, runs for ten miles through rural Hampshire. It's a hilly route with a mid point 400 feet higher than its Western terminus. Crowded trains on sharp gradients require large locomotives and no one runs big engines with greater style than the Watercress Line. 46 minutes with commentary.

647-405   27.99

STEAM IN WALES — VOLUME I

Explores four of the ever popular Welsh steam railways. The country is renowned for its narrow gauge systems, but the first visit is to a standard gauge railway at Llangollen. Here the might of Great Western steam power is used on a four mile line through the Valley of the Dee. A Manor Class locomotive is the main source of power, but there is diesel traction and horse drawn canal traffic as well.
60 minutes.

647-404   34.99

STEAM IN WALES — VOLUME II
647-406   37.99

TALYLLLN RAILWAY SOUVENIR
This Welsh mining line was one of the first to be preserved in Great Britain and is a favorite with narrow gauge fans world wide. The tape covers two special member's weekends, when the complete collection of historic steam and diesel locos were in operation. 45 minutes.

647-407   37.99

WATERCRESS RAILWAY SOUVENIR
Operating 10 miles of trackage in Hampshire, England, this tape covers two days of special operations in 1989 and 1990 when many of the line's historic steam locos were in operation. Among the highlights is the "Franklin D. Roosevelt," a U.S. Army 2-8-0 shown returning to service after a complete restoration. 45 minutes.

647-408   37.99

WELSH HIGHLAND RAILWAY SOUVENIR
Complete coverage of the 1990 "Transport Gala" provides a look at the collection of historic steam power. 45 minutes.

647-409   37.99

BLUEBELL RAILWAY SOUVENIR
"Branchline and Parade" days are covered in this commemorative tape, showing much of the collection of restored motive power and equipment in action on this preserved line. 45 minutes.

647-410   37.99

DUCHESS OF HAMILTON 1990
The complete restoration and return to service of one of Britain's most famous "Coronation" class Pacifics is showcased in this tape. Rebuilt in 1990, the loco has had a long and colorful career, including a visit to the 1939 New York World's Fair. 60 minutes.

647-118   49.99

SUPERIOR
PROMOTIONS, INC.

NEW

VIDEOS

THUNDER ON THE RAILS
Covers two of the west's best-known lines, the Virginia & Truckee and the Nevada Northern. Puts you in the cab of the big Baldwin steamers to see what railroading was like a century ago. 30 minutes.

662-4785   9.95

DAYLIGHT EXPRESS
Turn back time and ride through western scenery aboard the SP "Daylight." Coverage of this famous loco includes cameras in the cab and outside, showcasing scenery in the Cascade Mountains and across the trestle over the Sacramento River Gorge. 90 minutes.

662-378262   39.95

VIDEO PRODUCTIONS

From the Colorado narrow gauge to the rebirth of UP Challenger #3985, these video cassettes cover a wide range of historic and contemporary western railroad subjects. Cassettes are available in VHS. Beta are available directly through WB Video Productions.

SANTA FE'S NEW MEXICO MAIN

The desolute beauty of Santa Fe's New Mexico mainline comes alive in this newest offering. The program documents the Santa Fe Chicago-Los Angeles mainline as it descends from the high desert at Mountainair through rugged Abo Canyon to Belen. It's one of the nation's railfan hot spots. Narrated by Rege Cordic. Approximately 60 minutes.

798-39 VHS **(By Special Order Only.)**   39.95

SILVER RAILS & GOLDEN MEMORIES

A tribute to the 50th anniversary of the Rocky Mountain Railroad Club. Features original 16mm films from the collection of Irving August, made from 1952 to 1962. Highlights include Rio Grande narrow gauge, Colorado & Southern standard gauge, a Union Pacific 4-8-4, Great Western Railway action and more. 72 minutes, with narration and dubbed sound.

798-26 VHS **(By Special Order Only.)**   39.95

ASSAULT ON SNOW

See man and machine battle the elements as the Wyoming & Colorado shortline F Units buck drifts, and Union Pacific rotary snow plow #900080 works west of Laramie. Color and live sound. 52 minutes.

798-27 VHS **(By Special Order Only.)**   39.95

THE MILWAUKEE'S MIGHTY ELECTRICS

See the "Joe's" in action over Pipestone Pass and "Box Cabs" crossing the Columbia River. A steeple cab switches the South Butte Yard. (1965, 1968).

798-28 VHS   39.95

KINDIG'S DIESELS — PART 1

Richard H. Kindig is famous for his steam era photographs but in 1971 he began taking 16mm color movies of diesel powered trains (features films from 1971 and 1972).

BURLINGTON NORTHERN, AMTRAK, DENVER AND RIO GRANDE WESTERN. Dubbed sound.

798-29 VHS **(By Special Order Only.)**   39.95

AMERICA ON RAILS

Series begins in the thirties showing a cross section of America's railroads with an emphasis on Interurbans and Passenger Trains. Featured in this first program: The 6000 Mile Tour — In July, 1938; passenger trains, Southern Pacific steam and Interurbans. Color with some black & white. 32 minutes. **(By Special Order Only.)**

Section 1
798-30 VHS   29.95

Section 2
798-36 VHS   29.95

Section 3
798-37 VHS   29.95

TEHACHAPI — PART 1: SANTA FE

Noted for its active mainlines and spectacular scenery, the Tehachapi, California area has become a favorite with railfans the world over! This two-part series of tapes takes you trackside from Caliente, over Tehachapi and into the Mojave desert. Part one covers operations of the Santa Fe, including a pacing sequence south of the summit. This full color and sound tape runs 57 minutes.

798-20 VHS **(By Special Order Only.)**   39.95

TEHACHAPI —PART 2: SOUTHERN PACIFIC

The action continues on the Southern Pacific Lines, with a look at the unit "Tank Train" and #4449 with the 1984 "Daylight". This tape is also in full color, with sound, and runs 52 minutes.

798-21 VHS **(By Special Order Only.)**   39.95

THE RIO GRANDE TODAY

Operations on the modern Rio Grande are covered in this new video. Filmed between 1982 and 1986, the tape covers a wide range of trains and motive power. Highlights include the Zephyr behind F9's, the Ski Train and a snowplow train. Scenic locations including Moffat Tunnel, Tennessee Pass and more are seen. The full color cassette has sound and runs for two hours.

798-22 VHS **(By Special Order Only.)**   49.95

THE FIFTIES EXPRESS

America's railroads underwent revolutionary changes in the 1950's. This tape takes you trackside to see the newest diesels, electrics and steam locos in action. Some 15 different roads are featured on the cassette, which was compiled using original films from the collection of the Rocky Mountain Railroad Club. The color tape runs 52 minutes, with narration and dubbed sound.

798-23 VHS   39.95

ALLEGHENY RAILS — VOLUME I

Baltimore & Ohio steam comes to life on this tape compiled from the original 8mm films made by noted rail photographer William Price in 1953 and 1954. Featured locos include a 2-10-2, 2-8-8-4, 4-6-2, 2-8-2 and Alco FA filmed on the Pittsburgh Division over Sand Patch Grade and the Cumberland Division. Each scene is documented with historical information. Narration, musical background. 55 minutes.

798-24 VHS   39.95

ALLEGHENY RAILS — VOLUME II

Western Maryland trains of the mid 50's return to the mainline in the new "Allegheny Rails-Volume II: The Western Maryland". This tape is compiled from original 8mm films by noted rail photographer and historian William Price. Numerous locations including Salisbury Viaduct, Big Savage Tunnel, Black Fork Grade and more are featured. Locos seen in action include a 2-10-0, 4-6-6-4, 2-8-0, 4-6-2, 4-8-4, F7 and RS-2. Narration and musical background. 52 minutes.

798-25 VHS   39.95

EXCURSION TO THE THIRTIES

Reproduced from original films made from 1937 to 1941, this tape provides a rare look at pre-war narrow gauge operations on the C&S, D&RGW and RGS. Appropriate sound and narration have been added. 52 minutes, color and sound.

798-3 VHS **(By Special Order Only.)**   39.95

THE LAST STEAMERS OF THE C&S

Original footage from 1958-60 shows 2-10-2, 2-8-2, 2-8-0, rotary snow plow and more. 52 minutes, color with dubbed sound and narration.

798-19 VHS **(By Special Order Only.)**   39.95

A FORTIES MEMORY

A look at postwar mainline and narrow gauge railroading including ATSF, D&RGW, SP, RGS and others. A descriptive narrative and sound have been added to these original films. 24 minutes, color and sound.

798-10 VHS **(By Special Order Only.)**   34.95

Photo by William E. Botkin

CHALLENGER '82

A comprehensive study of #3985 from delivery in 1943 to restoration and fantrip service in 1982. Rare photos of the loco in the 50's. 55 min, color, sound.

798-2 VHS **(By Special Order Only.)**   39.95

SANTA FE'S RATON ROUTE

Features modern Santa Fe power against a panorama of the Old West filmed between 1989 and 1991. Includes Kansas City — El Paso freights, local coal drags, the red and silver F45 War Bonnets, Amtrak's Southwest Limited and more. 112 minutes, color narration, stereo sound.

798-42 VHS   49.95

Photo by William E. Botkin

UP "CHALLENGER" 3985

Covers the testing and operation of the famous 4-6-6-4 "Challenger" in 1981. The loco is seen on a special freight movement and pulling two fantrips, one doubleheaded with UP #8444. 55 minutes, color and sound.

798-1 VHS   39.95

RIO GRANDE NARROW GAUGE IN THE FIFTIES

Follow K-36 and K-27 Mikados in freight and passenger service through the Colorado narrow gauge country. The tape includes a tour of Silverton in 1950, plus a brief look at the San Juan Lumber Co and the Silver Bell Mine at Ophir. 58 minutes, color and sound.

798-4 VHS **(By Special Order Only.)**   39.95

WB VIDEO PRODUCTIONS

From the Colorado narrow gauge to the rebirth of UP Challenger #3985, these video cassettes cover a wide range of historic and contemporary western railroad subjects. Cassettes are available in VHS. Beta are available directly through WB Video Productions.

NARROW GAUGE VIDEO VIGNETTE

Large and small D&RGW narrow gauge locos are featured in this tape. 2-8-0 #346 is shown in steam, along with other equipment, at the Colorado Railroad Museum. K-36 #484 is shown pulling a special freight on July 6, 1979 along the Cumbres and Toltec Scenic Railway. 55 minutes, color and sound.

798-5   VHS **(By Special Order Only.)**   39.95

Photo by William E. Botkin

DIESELS WEST

Today's high-horsepower diesels are shown in action along the Union Pacific and Rio Grande. The tape includes footage of the Rio Grande Zephyr and a cab ride in the lead F9. Other highlights include a look at Alco locos in service on the Utah Railroad. 55 minutes, color and sound.

798-8   VHS **(By Special Order Only.)**   39.95

Photo by William E. Botkin

LEGEND OF THE RIO GRANDE ZEPHYR

The last privately owned and operated streamliner is shown on its final run, April 24, 1983. Footage from several years of Zephyr watching show earlier action in the Rockies, Moffat Tunnel and the Utah desert. 52 minutes, color and sound.

798-9   VHS **(By Special Order Only.)**   39.95

D&RGW NARROW GAUGE FREIGHT TRAINS

From films made in November and December of 1967, this tape follows freights behind K-37's #493 and 497. The locos are seen working at Alamosa, Bhama, Cembres Pass (including the covered wye), Durango and the Farmington Branch. 60 minutes, color, silent.

798-6   VHS **(By Special Order Only.)**   39.95

DOUBLE HEADER '83

On October 12 & 13, 1983 Peter-Built Locomotive Works sponsored a two-engine freight over the Cumbres & Toltec Scenic Railroad. All engines and cars were authentically lettered for the Rio Grande, effectively rolling back time to a train on this famous line of the 1940's. This is the sight and sound of that trip as two D&RGW K-36's battle the grade from Chama, New Mexico over Cumbres Pass to Sublette, Colorado and return. 28 minutes, color and sound.

798-16   VHS **(By Special Order Only.)**   24.95

D&RGW NARROW GAUGE STOCK TRAIN AND KOLOR KARAVAN

Filmed in October of 1966, the tape opens with coverage of #498 and #497 working stock cars and lumber from Chama to Alamosa and then through Cumbres Pass. The tape concludes with the last Kolor Karavan over the Alamosa to Durango to Silverton line. 62 minutes, color, silent.

798-7   VHS   39.95

STEAM OVER SHERMAN

Steam's last days on the Union Pacific. Big Boys, Challengers, early diesels and the turbine are all seen in service near Cheyenne, Wyoming. 54 minutes, color and dubbed sound.

798-11   VHS   39.95

RAILS ACROSS THE SUMMIT

This award-winning production takes you trackside, onboard and in the cab as Cumbres and Toltec Scenic Railway Mikado 483 heads for Cumbres Summit. Historic shots in black and white show a rotary in action and an old timer recounts a wreck at Cumbres. 28 minutes, color and sound.

798-12   VHS   24.95

DIESELS ON THE UP

A look at contemporary operations from Cheyenne to Dale Junction. Many trackside and pacing shots of 6900 series "Centennials". 60 minutes, color and sound.

798-13   VHS   39.95

DIESELS ON THE UP—THE SEQUEL

SD-40's, U30C's and DDA40X's do battle with a Wyoming blizzard on the New Line near Cheyenne. A cab ride in Centennial 6922 and shots of the San Francisco Zephyr in snow round out the tape. 60 minutes, color and sound

798-14   VHS   39.95

RIO GRANDE OF THE ROCKIES

Colorado mainline and narrow gauge D&RGW operations in the 50s. 2-8-8-2's, F9 helpers, The California Zephyr pulled by Alco PA's and a variety of narrow gauge steam highlights this production. 59 minutes, color (4 minutes B&W) and dubbed sound.

798-15   VHS **(By Special Order Only.)**   39.95

HEAVY FREIGHT AND UNION PACIFIC 3985

Union Pacific 3985 steamer pulling an eastbound heavy freight (143 cars, 7657 tons, 8900 feet long) between Cheyenne and North Platte, Nebraska, on 8-1-90. Also see Union Pacific 3985's freight run between Cheyenne and LeSalle, Colorado on 7-24-90. Approximately 60 minutes.

798-40   VHS **(By Special Order Only.)**   39.95

SNOWTRAIN: RIO GRANDE'S SKI SPECIAL

Filmed in 1984, follows former Zephyr F9's and heavyweight passenger cars from Denver to Winter Park. 28 minutes, color and sound.

798-17   VHS **(By Special Order Only.)**   34.95

THE SUGAR CANE TRAIN

Ride behind steam on the Lahaina—Kaanipall & Pacific, a 3' tourist line based on the sugar cane haulers of Hawaii. 17 minutes, color and sound.

798-18   VHS **(By Special Order Only.)**   24.95

RAILS ALONG THE ROCKIES

See trains of the Burlington Northern, Rio Grande and Santa Fe on Colorado's Joint Line. 60 minutes, live sound and narration.

798-31   VHS   39.95

SANTA FE SELIGMAN SUB

You'll see a variety of Santa Fe power as trains from California, Texas, and the Midwest thunder over the Arizona Divide between Winslow, Arizona, and Needles, California. 60 minutes.

798-33   VHS **(By Special Order Only.)**   39.95

A SALUTE TO SOLDIER SUMMIT

All trains on the Rio Grande's Utah Division have a common goal...to reach Soldier Summit. The western approach through the Wasateh Mountains is distinctively different from the eastern side which rises from a desert floor through rugged arid canyons. 60 minutes.

798-34   VHS **(By Special Order Only.)**   39.95

BLUE RIDGE STEAM

These original films of Norfolk and Western Steam in the late 1950's are from the collection of original films shot from 1955-1958 by Bill Price. The action takes place along the Blue Ridge Summit, the Christianburg grade and the Shenandoah Line. 82 minutes, musical background and narration.

798-35   VHS **(By Special Order Only.)**   39.95

UNION PACIFIC'S LAST STEAM GIANTS

It's the summer of 1958. At Cheyenne, Wyoming, Union Pacific's 4-8-8-4 BIG BOYS are being readied for their last months of service. See the UP's mighty mammoths of the Steam Age being prepared for the battle up Sherman Hill. Rekindle the memory of coal smoke, steam, and hot cylinder oil with this all-steam program. Color and dubbed sound. 24 minutes.

798-38   VHS   24.95

UNION PACIFIC SUPER CABS AND STEAM

The revolutionary new wide cab EMD SD60M's and GE Dash 8-40CW's are taking the lead up Sherman Hill these days. You'll see the Union Pacific Super Cabs EMD SD60M, GE Dash 8-40CW along with the Union Pacific 844 St Louis NRHS Convention enroute and the Union Pacific 3985 freight enroute River City round-up. Stereo, 88 minutes.

798-41   VHS   39.95

BAINBRIDGE

Sounds of steam and diesel locos in action are presented in these high quality recordings.

Chama Graphics

SONIC BOOMS

This superb recording features sounds of USAF F-16's and USA Blackhawk UH 6 helicopters. A ''must have'' for railfans and sound effect enthusiasts!

Compact Disc
167-62764   15.98

SONIC BOOMS - VOLUME II

Features fire department horns, steam loco #1218, narrow gauge railroading, U.S. Marine Corp Military exercise w/heavy artillery, Space Shuttle Atlantis launch and more!

167-62854   Compact Disc   15.98

SOUND OF TRAINS-VOLUME I

Sounds of railroading from Canada to the Colorado Rockies are featured, with recordings of Challenger #3985, VIA FP9's, Southern Pacific #4449, and Cumbres & Toltec Scenic narrow gauge steamers.

167-62704   Compact Disc   15.98
167-6270   Cassette Tape   8.98

SOUNDS OF TRAINS-VOLUME II

Fan trip locos are the stars in this recording! Hear trackside sounds of N&W 611 and 1218, Southern 4501, L&N 152 and the Southern FP7's.

167-62714   Compact Disc   15.98
167-6271   Cassette Tape   8.98

SOUND OF TRAINS - VOLUME III

Features #'s 2860, 6060, 3716 and 2860; trackside and aboard locomotives. Approx one hour.

167-62864   Compact Disc   15.98
167-6286   Cassette   8.98

SOUNDS OF TRAINS - VOLUME IV

Features action from NRHS 1990, St Louis, 1522, 819, 1218, 844/1522 double-headed. Also includes Challenger 800 class DH, No 765 and Blue Mt No 425. Approx one hour.

167-62874   Compact Disc   15.98
167-6287   Cassette   8.98

STEAM RAILROADING UNDER THUNDERING SKIES

Thunder on the rails and in the skies is captured in this superb recording! A Mikado 2-8-2 on side one, and a Prairie 2-6-2 on side two, are recorded working in rain and thunder.

167-6242   Cassette Tape   8.98

STEEL RAILS UNDER THUNDERING SKIES

The sounds of rain and thunder make these action recordings more dramatic! Steam locos from the Reader and Sierra shortlines, museum power from Steamtown and fantrip engines #4449 and #759 are featured.

167-62434   Compact Disc   15.98
167-62432   LP Record   8.98
(By Special Order Only.)
167-6243   Cassette Tape   8.98

THE POWER AND THE MAJESTY   *NEW*

The raw power of steam is captured in these two compact discs. Volume I features SP #4449 rolling through a thunderstorm, while Volume II combines vintage WWII aircraft, outdoor sounds and various steam power.

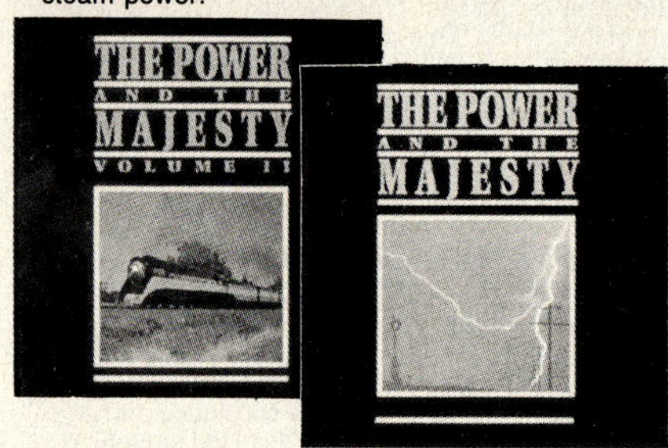

167-6291   Volume I   15.98
167-6292   Volume II   15.98

4449 PINNACLE!   *NEW*

This 2-tape/disc set captures the sounds of a Brooklyn Roundhouse, station arrivals at Portland and Berkeley, air brake application and the East Portland Corridor.

167-62954   Compact Disc   15.98
167-6295   Cassette   8.98

SONIC BOOMS 3   *NEW*

A collection of natural and man-made sound effects, this 3-disc set features the fury of a shuttle launch. Set also includes the trucks and sirens of a fire department response, a thunderstorm and a Southern Pacific #4449 locomotive.

167-62894   3-Disc Set   15.98

Chama Graphics

RAILROAD ART PRINTS

Featured in these full-color prints, from original paintings by Jim Finnell, are narrow gauge locos. Limited editions of each print are also available numbered and signed by the artist.

LAST TRAIN TO TUOLUMNE

208-106   Signed   11 x 17"   30.00
208-105   Standard   11 x 17"   25.00

SNOW TIME AT CHAMA

208-108   Signed   11 x 17"   35.00
208-107   Standard   11 x 17"   30.00
(By Special Order Only.)

DURANGO SUMMER #473

208-109   Signed   11 x 17"   40.00
208-110   Standard   11 x 17"   35.00

DENVER & RIO GRANDE WESTERN STEAMER #345

208-111   Standard   25.00

SAN JUAN #473   *NEW*

208-114   Signed   11 x 14"   40.00

SALIDA NIGHT #473   *NEW*

208-115   Signed   11 x 14"   40.00
208-116   San Juan/Salida Set   *NEW*   70.00

R.G.S. CENTENNIAL

208-112   Signed   18 x 24"   45.00
208-113   Standard   18 x 24"   40.00

COUNTRY TRAINS

Let the world know you're a railfan with this collection of signs and scenes that add humor and interest to any office, den or train room. Items are printed in full color except as noted.

WALL SIGNS

Printed in prototypical colors on heavy cardboard. 12 x 12" unless otherwise noted.

203-914	203-916	203-923
1.98	1.98	1.98

203-922	24 x 24" 203-918	203-932
1.98	1.98	1.98

You Want to Be A Model Railroader?
203-928   1.98

750 TRACKS
750 Tracks
203-917 (6 x 12") 1.98

12 x 18"
203-915
1.98

STOP · LOOK · LISTEN PROCEED WHEN TRAIN IS COMING
Stop, Look & Listen
203-919 (6 x 12") 1.98

ON THIS MODEL RAILROAD
12 x 18"
203-927
1.98

DON'T TOUCH DEM TRAINS

WARNING NEIGHBORHOOD RAILROAD HOBO WATCH

203-900	1.98	203-910	1.98

(not illustrated)

203-874	Temporary Parking Reserved for Model Railroader (12 x 18")	1.98
203-875	To the Trains (12 x 12")	1.98
203-933	Murphy's Law #1	1.98
203-934	Murphy's Rules #2 (12 x 12")	1.98
203-935	Murphy's Rules #3 (12 x 12")	1.98

LIMITED QUANTITIES AVAILABLE

203-937	Glossary of RR #1	1.98

ROADNAME SIGNS

All signs are heavy cardboard.

203-876	The Rock (7 x 12")	1.98
203-877	Delaware and Hudson (10 x 12")	1.98
203-878	Cotton Belt (11 x 11")	1.98

203-884	Lehigh Valley	1.98
203-885	Sandy River	1.98
203-888	Chicago & North Western	1.98
203-889	California Zephyr	1.98
203-892	Seaboard	1.98
203-893	Burlington Route (10 x 11")	1.98
203-894	Illinois Central (7 x 11")	1.98
203-895	Canadian Pacific	1.98
203-896	Canadian National (12-1/8 x 7-1/2")	1.98
203-897	Rock Island (11-1/4 x 8")	1.98
203-899	Milwaukee Road (12-1/2 x 8-1/2")	1.98
203-901	Boston & Maine	1.98
203-902	Atlantic Coast Line	1.98
203-903	Seaboard System	1.98
203-906	Virginian	1.98
203-907	Texas & Pacific	1.98
203-908	Norfolk & Western	1.98
203-909	Maine Central	1.98
203-911	Bangor Aroostook	1.98
203-926	Railway Express Agency	1.98
203-929	Nickel Plate Road	1.98
203-930	Missouri Kansas Texas (10 x 11")	1.98
203-931	Western Maryland	1.98
203-940	Conrail	1.98
203-941	Chessie System	1.98
203-942	Central of Georgia (8 x 12") NEW	1.98
203-943	Central of New York (12 x 12") NEW	1.98
203-944	Chesapeake & Ohio (12 x 12") NEW	1.98
203-945	Clinchfield (7 x 12") NEW	1.98
203-946	CSX (9 x 12") NEW	1.98
203-947	Frisco (6 x 12") NEW	1.98
203-948	Gulf, Mobile & Ohio (6 x 12") NEW	1.98
203-949	Kansas City Southern (12 x 12") NEW	1.98
203-950	Long Island (Dashing Dan) (12 x 12") NEW	1.98
203-951	Monon (12 x 12") NEW	1.98
203-952	New York, New Haven & Hartford (6 x 12") NEW	1.98
203-953	New York Central	1.98
203-954	New York Central Lines (5 x 12") NEW	1.98
203-955	New Haven (8 x 12")	1.98
203-956	Erie (12 x 12")	1.98
203-957	Norfolk Southern (Horse) (8 x 12") NEW	1.98
203-958	Reading (9-1/2 x 11")	1.98
203-959	Lackawanna Railroad (9 x 12")	1.98
203-960	Penn Central (5 x 12") NEW	1.98
203-961	Baltimore & Ohio (12 x 12")	1.98
203-963	Wabash (12 x 12") NEW	1.98
203-970	Missouri Pacific LNS (18 x 12")	1.98
203-971	Northern Pacific (10 x 11")	1.98
203-972	Soo Line	1.98
203-973	Western Pacific (12-1/8 x 12-1/8")	1.98
203-974	Amtrak (12-1/2 x 7")	1.98
203-975	Santa Fe (11-3/4 x 11-3/4")	1.98
203-976	Great Northern (11-3/4 x 11-3/4")	1.98
203-978	Southern Pacific (12-1/8 x 12-1/8")	1.98

203-979	SP Daylight (12 x 6")	1.98
203-981	Pennsylvania (12-1/8 x 12-1/8")	1.98
203-982	Rio Grande Southern	1.98
203-988	D&RGW (9 x 12")	1.98
203-990	Colorado & Southern (12 x 12")	1.98
203-991	Burlington Northern (12 x 8-3/4")	1.98
203-992	Union Pacific (12 x 12")	1.98
203-993	Lionel Trains	1.98
203-996	Southern	1.98
203-997	American Flyer Lines (5 x 12") NEW	1.98

LICENSE PLATE FRAMES

White plastic w/silkscreened blue lettering.

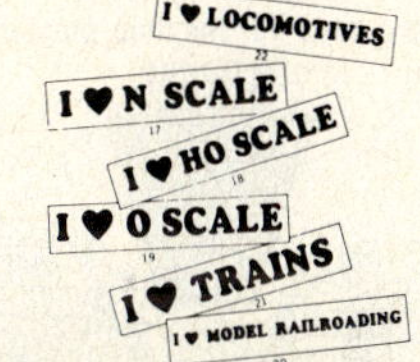

203-100	Get A Jolly Ride A Trolley	2.95
203-104	My Other Car Is A Pullman (By Special Order Only.)	2.35
203-109	I Love HO Scale (By Special Order Only.)	2.35
203-111	I (Love) Model Railroading	2.95
203-112	I (Love) Trains	2.95
203-114	Please Pray For My Husband He Is A Model Railroader	2.95
203-115	So the Car Smokes A Little, So Do Locomotives	2.95

BUMPER STICKERS

Silkscreen printed, red & black. 10 x 2"

203-17	I Love N Scale	.85
203-18	I Love HO Scale	.85
203-19	I Love O Scale	.85
203-20	I Love Model Railroading	.85
203-21	I Love Trains	.85
203-22	I Love Locomotives	.85
203-23	My Other Car is a Pullman (2 x 10")	.85
203-24	My Wife Says if I Buy One More Train She'll Leave Me. Gee, I'll Miss Her. (4 x 8") NEW	.85
203-25	Pray for Me, My Husband Chases Trains. (2 x 10") NEW	.85
203-26	I Love Live Steam (2 x 10") NEW	.85
203-27	I Love S Scale (2 x 10") NEW	.85
203-28	I'd Rather be on a Train (2 x 10") NEW	.85
203-29	No Smoking Unless You Are a Locomotive (2 x 10) NEW	.85
203-30	Pray for Me, My Wife Likes Trains (2 x 10") NEW	.85
203-34	Happiness is Being a Train Buff (2 x 12")	.85
203-36	Pass with Caution Model I'm a Model Railroader (2 x 12")	.85
203-37	Honk if you're a Model Railroader (2 x 10")	.85
203-38	Caution Railroader at Throttle (2 x 10")	.85
203-39	Railroaders Love to Couple Up (2 x 12")	.85

LOGOS

8 x 8" decal stickers

203-301	Atlantic Coast Line	1.89
203-302	Bangor and Aroostook	1.89
203-303	Boston and Maine	1.89
203-304	Burlington Northern	1.89

COUNTRY TRAINS

LOGOS (continued)

203-306	Chessie	1.89
203-307	Chicago and Northwestern	1.89
203-308	Conrail	1.89
203-309	Denver Rio Grande Western	1.89
203-311	Erie	1.89
203-312	Illinois Central	1.89
203-313	Lehigh Valley	1.89
203-315	Missouri Kansas Texas (M-K-T)	1.89
203-316	Missouri Pacific Lines	1.89
203-317	MoPac	1.89
203-318	Norfolk and Western	1.89
203-319	Penn Central	1.89
203-320	Reading Lines	1.89
203-321	Southern Route	1.89
203-322	Texas and Pacific	1.89
203-323	Virginian	1.89
203-324	Western Maryland	1.89
203-340	Great Northern	1.89
203-341	Santa Fe	1.89
203-342	Southern Pacific	1.89
203-343	Union Pacific	1.89
203-344	Western Pacific	1.89
203-345	Amtrak	1.89
203-346	D&RGW	1.89
203-347	Pennsylvania	1.89
203-348	Baltimore & Ohio	1.89
203-349	Milwaukee Road	1.89
203-350	Seaboard Air Line	1.89
203-351	Delaware & Hudson	1.89
203-353	Lionel	1.89
203-354	American Flyer Lines	1.89

DRUMHEADS

Printed on translucent 11 x 11" flexible plastic.

203-2400	California Zephyr	3.25
203-2401	Western Pacific	3.25
203-2402	SF, The Chief	3.25
203-2404	SF, Super Chief	3.25
203-2410	NP, North Coast Ltd	3.25
203-2411	GN, Empire Builder	3.25
203-2412	SF, El Capitan	3.25
203-2413	SF, KC Chief	3.25
203-2414	SF, Texas Chief	3.25
203-2417	UP, Overland (1920)	3.25
203-2419	PRR, Broadway Ltd	3.25
203-2425	Great Northern	3.25
203-2427	MILW, Olympia, Hiawatha	3.25
203-2434	NYC 20th Century	3.25
203-2437	NJC Blue Comet	*NEW* 3.25
203-2438	D&RGW Mainline	3.25
203-2440	MKT, The Texas Special	*NEW* 3.25
203-2441	DRGW, Royal George	*NEW* 3.25
203-2442	UP, Challenger	*NEW* 3.25

LARGE DRUMHEADS

Printed on translucent flexible plastic, approximately 17 x 12".

203-2501	Western Pacific	4.98
203-2506	UP City of SF	4.98
	(By Special Order Only.)	
203-2513	SF, KC Chief	4.98
203-2517	UP Overland Logo	4.98
203-2523	Southern Pacific	4.98
203-2525	Great Northern	4.98
203-2527	MILW, Olympia, Hiawatha	4.98
203-2536	SF Texas Chief	4.98

BELT BUCKLES

Cast metal belt buckles feature various railroad designs. Buckles have pewter finish, detailed engraving and a rugged brass clasp. Fits belts up to 1-3/4" wide.

Durango Highline
204-1045   5.98

C&O #614 Montage
204-1050   5.98

Broadway Limited
204-1088   5.98

U.P. Overland Route
204-1504   5.98

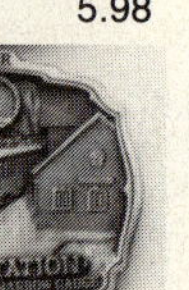

Durango Station
204-1467   5.98

Western Pacific F7
204-1089   5.98

New York Central E9
204-1502   5.98

California Zephyr
204-1511   5.98

Rio Grande Zephyr
204-1513   5.98

S.F. Super Chief
204-1172   5.98

American Type 4-4-0
204-1440   5.98

Georgetown Loop
204-1463   5.98

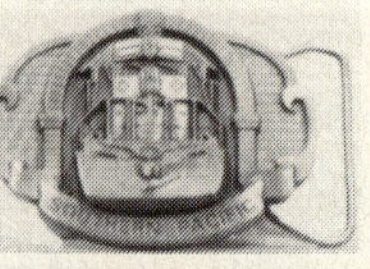

Southern Pacific
204-1474   5.98

Central of Georgia
204-1535   5.98

(not illustrated)
Lineman
204-1591 *NEW* 5.98

Mountain Pass
204-1564   5.98

CONWAY
INCENTIVES CORPORATION

NEW

T-SHIRTS

Walthers T-shirt   14.98
Black shirt with white and yellow locomotive design. 100% Cotton. Machine wash.

41-50 Small	41-56 X-Large
41-52 Medium	41-58 XX-Large
41-54 Large	

WHISTLES UNLIMITED **NEW**

WOOD TRAIN WHISTLES

753-10	Regular	4.95
753-20	Junior	4.50
753-30	Mini	4.00

AUGUST 8, 1829

Today
IN RAILROAD HISTORY

Operated by Horatio Allen, "Stourbridge Lion" makes first test run at Honesdale, Pennsylvania.

? ? ? ? ? ? ? ? ? ?

__________ is a pair of switches that allow trains to travel from one parellel track to the adjacent one on double-track system.

(Answer: Crossover)

CRESCENT STATION

(Formerly Mountain State Model Works)

Greeting & Note Cards

Pack contains six cards of same design with envelopes. Interior blank for personal message. Statement on back of card describes scene details (5-1/2 x 4-1/2")

513-505 Santa Arrives at   pkg(6)   2.95
Ives Station (O Scale model)

513-506 Great Northern S-2 pkg(6)   2.95
4-8-4 Loco

513-507 Manchester Loco   pkg(6)   2.95
Works Ad (1888)

DOVER PUBLICATIONS

POSTCARDS

Full-color, ready-to-mail, reproductions of early 1900s cards.

241-25320 Old Trolley   pkg(24) 3.95

PHIL DERRIG DESIGN

Authentic looking Railroad and product signs feature multi-color heavy stampings on a porcelain/enamel base. All signs are 8" diameter or square, unless noted.

RAILROAD SIGNS

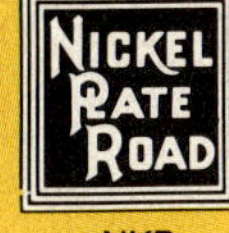

Santa Fe 234-200 12.95 — Western Pacific 234-201 12.95 — NKP 234-202 12.95 — Amtrak 234-223 12.95 — MoPac Eagle 234-224 12.95 — Monon 234-225 12.95

Erie 234-203 12.95 — UP Overland 234-204 12.95 — Chessie 234-205 12.95 12 x 8" — Norfolk & Western 234-226 — New York Central Pay Toilet 234-101 12.95 3-1/2 x 12" — (not illustrated) RR Crossing 234-232 12.95

Milwaukee Road 234-206 12.95 — Southern Pacific 234-207 12.95 — Great Northern RY 234-208 12.95 — Express Railway Agency 234-104 12.95 — Wells Fargo & Co. Express 234-105 12.95 — Santa Fe "The Chief" 234-102 NEW 12.95

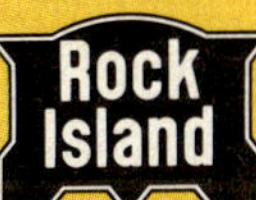

Northern Pacific 234-209 12.95 — Rock Island 234-210 12.95 (12 x 8") — Seaboard Railroad 234-211 12.95 — Finck's Overalls 234-109 13.95 (9 x 12") — Burlington Northern 234-103 NEW 12.95 — Maine Central 234-106 NEW 12.95

Chicago & North Western 234-212 12.95 — Illinois Central 234-213 12.95 — Pennsylvania 234-214 12.95 — Lionel Trains 234-218 12.95 — Boston & Maine 234-108 NEW 12.95

Missouri Kansas Texas 234-215 12.95 — Atlantic Coast Line 234-216 12.95 — Burlington Route 234-217 12.95 — Pacific Electric 234-227 12.95 — Telephone 234-110 12.95

Baltimore & Ohio 234-220 12.95 — Rio Grande 234-221 12.95 — Southern 234-222 12.95 — Wabash 234-229 12.95 — Reading 234-230 12.95 — Soo Line 234-231 12.95

Evda Slides

FULL COLOR 35mm SLIDE SETS

Not all items shown will be available at all times. May have to be backordered.

Full color, 35mm slides are available in sets of five or twenty.

+ (Plus Sign) = Special Order Only Items.

RAILROAD   set(5)

273-244	Illinois Central Steam	NEW	6.95
273-314	Lehigh Valley 1950-52	NEW	6.95
273-563	Chicago, Rock Island, and Pacific	NEW	6.95
273-568	Missouri Pacific 1979-83	NEW	6.95
273-569	Missouri Pacific in Missouri 1973-83	NEW	6.95
273-570	Missouri Pacific in St. Louis 1977-86	NEW	6.95
273-571	Norfolk and Western 1968-81	NEW	6.95
273-572	Pennsylvania 1964-81	NEW	6.95
273-574	St. Louis and San Francisco 1964-66	NEW	6.95
273-575	Terminal RR in St Louis 1953, 1976	NEW	6.95
273-576	Terminal RR in St Louis 1973-84	NEW	6.95
273-577	Union Pacific 1978-79	NEW	6.95
273-2024	St Louis & San Francisco RR 1976-78	NEW	24.95
273-201	Alco Diesels 1972-79		6.95
273-206	American Freedom in St Louis Set 1		6.95
273-209	Amtrak 1979		6.95
273-210	Amtrak Diesel & Electric Set 3		6.95
273-517	Amtrak 1981-83		6.95
273-208	Amtrak Turbos 1978-80 +		6.95
273-557	Amtrak Es 1973-80 +		6.95
273-558	Amtrak F40PH St Louis Area 1978-86 +		6.95
273-559	Amtrak SDP40F 1973-79		6.95
273-560	Amtrak/West 1977-83 +		6.95
273-376	AT&SF, Illinois Locations 1963-69		6.95
273-500	AT&SF, 1956-76		6.95
273-211	AT&SF, Cajon Pass		6.95
273-561	Baltimore & Ohio 1957-73 +		6.95

273-216	Bangor & Aroostook Diesel 1979	6.95
273-217	Bicentennial Shortline I 1976 +	6.95
273-219	Burlington Northern Diesel 1979 +	6.95
273-215	B&O Steam, Willard Ohio 9/57	6.95
273-221	Canadian Steam 1958 +	6.95
273-223	CB&Q Diesels 1968	6.95
273-518	CP, BC Rockies 1982	6.95
273-220	CP & CN Steam #1	6.95
273-377	Burlington 1962-73	6.95
273-501	CB&Q Steam	6.95
273-519	C&O Steam 1958-63	6.95

273-225	Chicago, Rock Island & Pacific 1971-80	6.95
273-224	Chicago, Rock Island & Pacific 1975-80 +	6.95
273-521	Chicago, Milwaukee & Pacific 1957-70	6.95
273-562	Chicago, Milwaukee & Pacific E&F 1964-78	6.95
273-573	PC/Amtrak Es 1971-76	6.95
273-523	Conrail 1976-1979	6.95
273-380	Conrail, Cleveland & St. Louis 1978-81	6.95

273-381	E-L, Binghamton NY 1972-76	6.95
273-239	E-L, Diesel Set 1 1970s	6.95
273-240	E-L, Diesel Set 2	6.95
273-564	E-L, 1969-75 +	6.95
273-227	D&H 1972-79	6.95

273-228	D&RGW Vintage Steam 1953	6.95
273-229	D&RGW Diesel 1979	6.95
273-382	Great Northern 1964-75	6.95
273-384	Gulf, Mobile & Ohio + 1971-1979	6.95
273-383	GM&O 1963-74	6.95
273-244	Illinois Central, Steam 1950-63	6.95
273-385	Illinois Terminal 1978-81	6.95
273-386	Lehigh Valley 1959, 1975	6.95
273-245	Louisville & Nashville, Steam 1953	6.95
273-565	Louisville & Nashville 1971-81 +	6.95

273-566	Manufacturers RR St Louis 1977-79 +	6.95
273-253	M-K-T 1967, Diesels	6.95
273-567	Missouri, Kansas, Texas 1961-80	6.95
273-250	Midwest Steam #1	6.95
273-379	MILW, Milwaukee Yards 1972-80	6.95
273-387	Mopac 1960-71	6.95
273-502	Monon, Lafayette Ind 1962 +	6.95
273-526	Muskingham RR 1968-1985	6.95
273-529	New Haven 1957, 1969	6.95
273-527	Norfolk & Western, Steam 1958	6.95
273-528	N&W 611, Decatur, IL, St. Louis, Moberley, MO 1983	6.95
273-257	NYC Diesels 1966-68	6.95
273-261	NYC Steam 1952-55	6.95
273-262	NYC Steam 1953	6.95
273-263	NP Steam 1953 +	6.95
273-555	Northern Pacific 1963	6.95
273-267	PRR Steam, Altoona 1950-56	6.95
273-268	PRR Steam 1956	6.95
273-388	PRR, Columbus Ohio 1961-62	6.95
273-389	PC, Chicago 1968 76 +	6.05
273-530	Penn Central E8's, Chicago 1971-1972 +	6.95
273-373	Railfair, Sacramento 5/81 Set 1	6.95
273-374	Railfair, Sacramento 5/81 Set 2 +	6.95
273-390	Soo Line 1966-81	6.95
273-281	SP Steam 1953	6.95

273-282	SP Classic Diesel	6.95
273-531	TP&W Diesels 1978	6.95
273-532	Union Pacific Steam 1950s	6.95
285-336	UP 1967-69 +	6.95
273-283	Union Pacific 1977-79	6.95
273-284	Union Pacific 1977-79	6.95

273-552	UP 8444, Missouri 1984	6.95
273-287	Wabash 1958-61	6.95
273-391	Wabash 1958-62	6.95
273-392	Western Maryland 1969-70	6.95
273-393	Western Pacific 1977-81 +	6.95
273-534	Western Pacific 1966-82 +	6.95

TROLLEY   set (5)

273-290	Altoona PA 1954 +		6.95
273-291	Atlantic City 1953 +		6.95
273-292	Baltimore 1954-61		6.95
273-536	Baltimore 1963		6.95
273-315	Montreal 1954-59 Set 1		6.95
273-316	Montreal 1954-59 Set 2 +		6.95
273-317	Montreal 1954-59 Set 3 +		6.95
273-303	Cincinnati 1948 +		6.95
273-304	Cincinnati 1948 +		6.95
273-305	Dallas 1948		6.95
273-541	EL Paso PCC Cars 1968 +		6.95
273-306	Hagertown/Frederick 1941-53		6.95
273-307	Hagertown/Frederick 1953-54		6.95
273-395	Illinois Terminal 1953-58 Set 1		6.95
273-310	IT PCC at Shaker Hts 1978-79 +		6.95
273-311	Johnstown 1958-60 +		6.95
273-312	Johnstown 1958-60 +		6.95
273-318	Newark, PSNJ 1950-53 +		6.95
273-544	Newark PCCs 1975 +		6.95
273-546	Omaha 1952		6.95
273-319	Ottawa 1958		6.95
273-322	Philadelphia 1953-56		6.95
273-325	Philadelphia, Red Arrow 1968-75		6.95
273-547	Philadelphia PCC Cars - Willow Grove Road 1957		6.95
273-326	Pittsburgh 1974-75		6.95
273-329	Rochester 1956		6.95
273-330	St Louis 1959-64 +		6.95

273-550	BART 1975	6.95
273-339	Scranton 1952-53 +	6.95
273-340	Shaker Heights PCC 1965-1975 +	6.95
273-341	Toronto, Witts and Air PCCs 1962, 1966 +	6.95
273-398	Twin Cities 1953 Set 1 +	6.95
273-342	Washington DC 1956-61	6.95
273-343	Washington DC 1948-56	6.95
273-344	West Penn 1950-52	6.95
273-504	Wilkes Barre 1946-58	6.95
273-421	St Joseph MO 1966 Set 2 +	6.95
273-429	Vancouver 1975	6.95

FOREIGN TROLLEY   set (5)

273-345	Graz, Austria +		6.95
273-346	Innsbruk, Austria +		6.95
273-354	Hershey, Cuba Interurban +	NEW	6.95
273-367	Mexico City 1973	NEW	6.95
273-371	Zurich 1972 +	NEW	6.95
273-399	Moscow 1972		6.95
273-438	Tramway Museum Crich England +	NEW	6.95
273-514	Hungary/Budapest +		6.95
273-349	Belgium, Brussels 1970		6.95
273-372	Belgrade, Serbia 1972 +		6.95
273-505	Denmark, Copenhagen 1962 +		6.95

Evda Slides

Not all items shown will be available at all times. May have to be backordered.

Full color, 35mm slides are available in sets of five or twenty.

+ (Plus Sign) = Special Order Only Items.

FOREIGN TROLLEY set(5) (continued)

273-506	Egypt, Alexandria	6.95
273-507	Egypt, Cairo 1/76	6.95
273-508	France, Marseilles, St Etienne & Strasburg	6.95
273-511	East & West Berlin, S/U-bahn 1962-67 +	6.95
273-512	East & West Berlin S/U-bahn 1962-67	6.95
273-352	Ghent, Belgium 1970-74	6.95
273-369	Glasgow, Scotland 1960-62 +	6.95
273-345	Graz, Austria	6.95
273-354	Hershey, Cuba Interurban1980 +	6.95
273-514	Hungary, Budapest +	6.95
273-346	Innsbruk, Austria +	6.95
273-399	Moscow 1972	6.95
273-400	Kiev, Leningrad 1972-76 +	6.95
273-515	Poland, Warsaw, Cracow, Gdansk & Posen +	6.95
273-516	Portugal & Spain +	6.95
273-365	Reutlingen +	6.95
273-499	Riga, Tallin & Irkutsk 1972-78	6.95
273-438	Tramway Museum, Crich, England 1969-70 +	6.95
273-371	Zurich, Switzerland 1972 +	6.95

BUS/TROLLEYBUS set(5)

273-413	Key System 1955 White/Mack/GM +	6.95
273-414	Las Vegas 1982 **NEW**	6.95
273-415	Montreal 1959 +	6.95
273-416	New York 1963-74	6.95
273-418	Portland 1978 +	6.95

273-419	Provincial Quebec & Quebec City 1959 +	6.95
273-425	San Francisco 1975 +	6.95
273-429	Vancouver 1975 +	6.95
273-432	Milwaukee 1979	6.95
273-437	Youngstown, OH 1958-59 +	6.95

■ LIMITED QUANTITIES AVAILABLE ■

273-408	Edmonton 1982 Set 1	6.95
273-436	Mexico City 1973	6.95

TRACTION & LIGHT RAIL set(20)
Full descriptive material included with sets.

273-2002	Calgary Light Rail 1982 +	24.95

273-2003	Chicago, North Shore & Milwaukee 1958-63	24.95
	includes electroliners, freight motors, Chicago EL and locos	
273-2023	Chicago EL 1970s (4000 and 6000's) +	24.95
273-2005	Illinois Terminal Interurbans 1953-58 +	24.95
273-2006	Los Angeles 1955-63 +	24.95
	old cars and 3 classes of PCC	
273-2007	Midwest 1947-1953 + (2 Indianapolis, 3 Memphis, 15 Detroit)	24.95
273-2011	Philly PTC 1955-65	24.95
273-2017	Shaker Heights 1975-83	24.95

273-2018	Toronto 1952-58 +	24.95
	includes Witts & air PCC's	
273-2020	Washington DC 1953-62 +	24.95
	mostly PCC's	
273-2021	Western 1946-1957 + (8 Kansas City PCC, 5 Denver, 3 Pacific Electric, 2 Key System, 1 Bamberger (Utah), 1 Portland)	24.95

RAIL TALK

Did you know that . . .

a **COUPLING PIN** was also called a: rivit, tack.

C M SHOPS, INC.
WHISTLE STOP MUGS
Full color, baked enamel ceramic mugs. Dishwasher safe.

each 4.95

RAILROAD HERALDS

012-9001	EL		012-9011	PRR
012-9002	CNJ			(Keystone)
012-9003	D&H		012-9012	PC
012-9004	L&HR		012-9013	Reading
012-9005	B&O		012-9014	Erie
012-9006	Family Line		012-9015	DL&W
012-9007	BN		012-9016	Santa Fe
012-9008	ICG		012-9017	Rio Grande
012-9009	L&NE		012-9018	Chessie
012-9010	C&NW (Employee Owned)		012-9019	NY,NH&H (Script)

C M SHOPS, INC.
WHISTLE STOP MUGS
Full color, baked enamel ceramic mugs. Dishwasher safe.

each 4.95

012-9020	C&NW	012-9093	B&LE
012-9021	The Rock	012-9094	Amtrak
012-9022	NYC	012-9095	Colorado Midland
012-9023	LV		
012-9024	Southern	012-9096	NS
012-9025	UP	012-9097	Alaska
012-9026	Erie Western	012-9098	Virginian
012-9027	CB&Q	012-9099	Texas-Mexican-Railway
012-9028	WP		
012-9029	MILW	012-9100	NJ Transit
012-9030	GN	012-9102	C&NW System
012-9031	WM	012-9103	C&O Kitten
012-9032	SAL	012-9104	Boston & Maine (McGinnis)
012-9033	P&W		
012-9034	RF&P	012-9105	CP Rail
012-9035	MP	012-9106	Erie Centennial
012-9036	B&M	012-9107	Great Northern (Big Sky Blue)
012-9037	SP		
012-9038	NYSW	012-9108	Minneapolis & St. Louis
012-9039	Frisco		
012-9040	NP	012-9109	Montana Rail Link
012-9041	PENN-RDG Seashore Lines	012-9110	Wisconsin Central
012-9042	NY-O&W		
012-9043	KCS	012-9111	Union Pacific "Overland"
012-9044	Ann Arbor		
012-9045	M-K-T(Katy)	012-9112	Trona
012-9046	C&O	012-9113	Toronto Hamilton & Buffalo
012-9047	MEC		
012-9048	DT&I		
012-9049	Conrail		
012-9050	N&W		

NEW	
012-9114	Monongahela
012-9115	British Columbia
012-9116	Belt Railway of Chicago
012-9117	Bangor & Aroostook (shield)

012-9051	Soo Line		
012-9052	CRIP-RI		
012-9053	GB&W		
012-9054	Rutland		
012-9055	Raritan River		
012-9056	Wabash		
012-9057	VTR		
012-9058	GM&O		
012-9059	IC		
012-9060	LI-Dash Dan		
012-9061	BAR		
012-9062	DM&IR		
012-9063	NKP		
012-9064	L&N		
012-9065	Soo-Modern		
012-9066	CN-Maple Leaf		
012-9067	SSW-Blue Streak		
012-9068	Clinchfield		
012-9069	New Haven (McGinnis)		
012-9070	P&LE		
012-9072	FEC		
012-9073	NYS&W-Susie Q		
012-9074	CGW		
012-9075	CIRR		
012-9076	SP&S		
012-9077	MN&S		
012-9078	ACL		
012-9079	CV-Old		
012-9080	GTW		
012-9081	CP-Old		
012-9082	Delaware Otsego		
012-9083	Seaboard		
012-9085	Morristown & Erie		
012-9086	C&IM		
012-9087	T&P		
012-9089	Appalachicola Northern		
012-9090	Central of Georgia		
012-9091	SCL		
012-9092	Monon		

F-UNITS

012-8001	O&W
012-8002	LV
012-8003	GN
012-8004	D&RGW
012-8005	C&NW
012-8006	GM&O
012-8007	SP
012-8008	L&N
012-8009	CN
012-8010	E-L
012-8011	Santa Fe
012-8012	NYC
012-8013	PRR
012-8014	Wabash
012-8015	UP

NEW	
012-8016	Pennsylvania PS
012-8017	Southern
012-8018	Santa Fe
012-8019	Erie
012-8020	Clinchfield
012-8021	Burlington Route
012-8022	Northern Pacific
012-8023	Frisco
012-8024	Western Pacific
012-8025	Canadian Pacific
012-8026	Baltimore & Ohio

ANNIVERSARY MUGS

012-9084	MR 50th
012-9088	NMRA 50th

GIL REID

ART PRINTS
All items are "Special Order Only"

The Great Trains of America Series
Gil Reid Railroad prints. Four color process. Each print has 19 x 13″ image printed on 22 x 16″ stock with clear border on all sides. Newer prints have a title printed in bottom margin. Interurban prints smaller size.

Emperors of the Road Series
4-color lithograph on heavy paper. Each print has a 22 x 15-1/4″ image printed on 25 x 19″ stock, with clear border on all sides. Title is printed in bottom margin. Separate insert gives history and details.

Emperors of the Road Series

NYC-Headquarters is Watching.
Road foreman joins 3005's crew
070-24   19.95

PRR-Hand Off at Harrisburg.
Two K4's take over Broadway Limited
070-26   19.95

NYC (Big Four) Oiling 'round.
Two boys visit 5382's engineer
070-25   19.95

The Great Trains of America Series

C&NW Ten-Wheeler Tradition. R1 1385 and SD45's at Butler, WI
070-27   9.95

NYC/PRR Race of the Century is east out of Englewood, Illinois
070-2   9.95

CUT-Queen City Quietude. 5 locos at Cincinnati engine terminal
070-3   9.95

PRR-No. 65 The American stays on time despite drifting snow
070-4   9.95

Almost Home-Late night arrival. Train lurches through switches
070-1   9.95

WAB, ICRR, C&A-Those Night Trains at St. Louis Union Station
070-6   9.95

UP Flagship-No. 27, the Overland Limited fights night snowstorm
070-7   9.95

CMSP&P-Roaring Through Rondout. Hiawatha sweeps north 100mph
070-8   9.95

CMS P&P-No. 5, Day Express Double-header slams through Brookfield
070-5   9.95

SAL-A Name Like a Cocktail. The Orange Blossom Special at speed
070-10   9.95

PRR-Pennsy's Finest. K4 5425 is smoking it up (fireman's side).
070-11   9.95

SP-Gray plus Orange and Red. Lark headed by Daylight 4-8-4
070-12   9.95

C&NW-Class D on the Run. 81″ drivered 4-4-2 takes a curve
070-9   9.95

NKP-Berkshire at Midnight. S-2 765's crew ready for a fast run
070-14   9.95

T&P-The Snuff Dipper. 2-10-2 tries lignite-fuel experiment
070-16   9.95

PRR-Pennsy Perfection. GG1 4895 passes MP54 owl car 569
070-18   9.95

GIL REID

ART PRINTS
All items are "Special Order Only"

Great Train Series (continued)

NYC-Centuries Pass at Night. J3a passes
Valley series observation car
070-13   9.95

ICRR-6.6 Miles from Destiny.
It's Casey Jones on No. 1 tonight!
070-19   9.95

CMSP&P-Happy Hiawatha Holiday.
Engine 1 leaves Milwaukee 1935
070-31   9.95

ERIE-No. 1, of Course. Loco 2942 heads
west with Erie Limited
070-17   9.95

PRR-Still on the Payroll 1935.
K2s rolls out of Richmond, IN
070-30   9.95

MISCELLANEOUS

The C.A.Reiss Coal Co. 1880-1980
070-290   29.95
Special edition of 500 prints commemorates the 100th anniversary of the Reiss Coal Company in 1980. Laker William A. Reiss and tugboat Green Bay shown at the company's Sheboygan dock. Under 100 signed and numbered prints left. 22 x 12-3/4" image printed on 26 x 17" stock.

NYC&HR-The Day Before 112.5 mph.
999 and the Empire State Express
070-28   9.95
NYC&HR-The Day Before 112.5 mph.
Numbered print signed by artist
070-280   35.00

The Competitors   **NEW** 9.95
070-32
A Milwaukee Road Twin Cities Time freight speeds under the CNW bridge. CNW Hotshot 488 Class H3002 goes over it.

INTERURBANS
These four Gil Reid interurban prints are four color process. 8-3/4 x 11-1/4" image printed on 12 x 15" stock.

CSS&SB in Chicago
Juice vs. Steam
070-21   9.95

C&LE Red Devil
Fast as a Plane
070-22   9.95

Yakima Valley
Niles car 100
070-23   9.95

CNS&M 763 with
diner passes 757
070-20   9.95

STEWART PRODUCTS

RECORD BOOKS

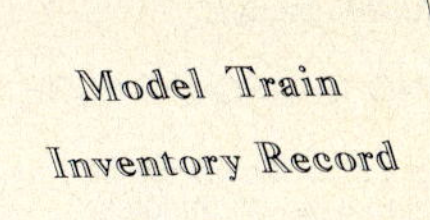

683-509 Model Train Inventory   7.95

(not illustrated)
683-508 Trainwatcher's Scratchpad 5.95

Gaus Enterprises

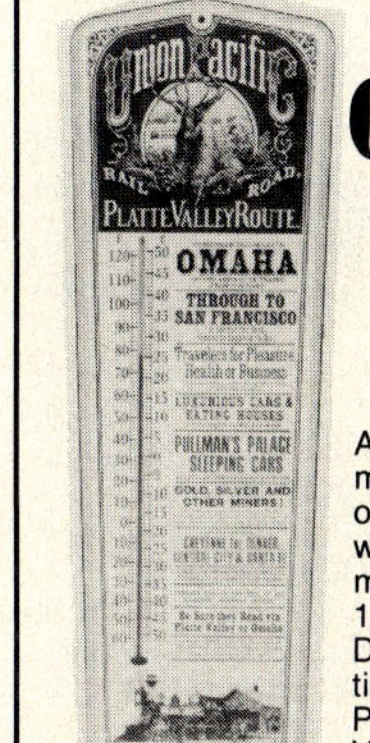

Antique Reproduction Thermometer is 24" high. Constructed of stamped metal (heavy duty), with an installed glass thermometer tube measuring 60° F to 120° F with Celsius equivalents. Decoration consists of promotion memorabilia for the Union Pacific Railroad — the Platte Valley Route.

297-100 UP Thermometer   21.98

Campbell Scale Models

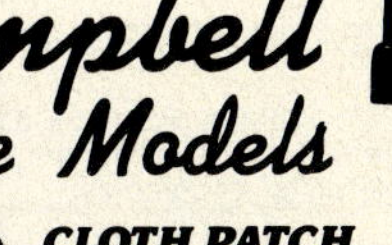

CLOTH PATCH
200-1 Patch   1.15
The Campbell Scotsman on a cloth patch, stitched as shown here (red, black and white). For your vest, hat or bib-overalls. Actual size is 2 x 3-1/4" oval.

JULY 24, 1848

❧ Today ❧
IN RAILROAD HISTORY

The locomotive "James Ferrier" makes its first run on the Montreal & Lachine Railway. This is the first loco imported into Canada from Great Britain.

GREEN FROG PRODUCTIONS

AUDIO TAPES

High quality Dolby cassette tapes of railroad sounds, digitally mastered and dubbed in real time for outstanding reproduction.

STEAM & DIESEL SOUNDS OF THE 1950's
302-54000   8.95
Nickel Plate Berkshires, Alco PA's, F3's and more. Playing time: 20 minutes.

THUNDERING NARROW GAUGE
302-54005   10.95
Outstanding action recordings of Colorado narrow gauge. Playing time: 38 minutes.

SOUNDS OF THE NEW GEORGIA RAILROAD
302-54006   8.95
Hear a former Florida East Coast 4-6-2 in action. Playing time: 20 minutes.

DIESELS '87
302-54108   11.95
The contemporary sounds of modern railroading, including a GP50, rebuilt GP7's and more. Playing time: 43 minutes.

STEAM AND DIESEL SOUNDS OF THE 1980'S
302-54110   11.95
A wide range of active and restored locos in service across America, including an Alco RS-1, 0-6-0, 4-8-4, GP7 and more. Playing time: 47 minutes.

DIESELS '86
302-54003   Volume I   8.95
302-54004   Volume II   8.95
Two volumes of diesels still operating in the late 80's. Each tape has a playing time of 20 minutes.

SOUNDS OF THE EAST BROAD TOP
302-54113   10.95
Steam power of the Pennsylvania narrow gauge line captured in stereo during 1988. Playing time: 36 minutes.

THE GP9's
302-54112   12.95
Original sounds of EMD's General Purpose diesel that changed the face of railroading forever. Playing time: 56 minutes.

STEAM SOLILOQUY
302-54114   12.95
Featuring 4-6-2's, 2-8-0's, 2-8-2's and more. Playing time: 60 minutes.

FIRST GENERATION DIESELS
302-54115   11.95
Features GP-7's, GP-9's, RS-1's, F-3's, F-7's, PA's and E-8's. Many locos are in tandem, some are running as single units. 44 minutes.

SOUNDS OF THE SILVERTON
302-54116   12.95

STEAM & DIESELS GEORGIA COMBO
302-54117   12.95

SOUNDS OF JOINT LINE
302-54118   12.95

SOUNDS OF THE 1218
302-54119   12.95
Captures the most powerful operating steam loco on a ferry trip and in service as an excursion trrain in Florida. 60 minutes.

BAR ROOM/STATION ANNOUNCEMENTS
302-55014   14.95

HARBOR SOUNDS
302-55015   12.95

REMEMBER STEAM — TRACKSIDE
302-55016   9.95

REMEMBER STEAM — TRAIN RIDE
302-55017   9.95

BACKGROUND SERIES

Basic background sounds designed to be played in the background of a layout with birds (daytime) and crickets (nighttime). Each tape is 60 minutes.

COUNTRY

302-55000	Daytime Steam	12.95
302-55001	Daytime Diesel Contemp	12.95
302-55002	Daytime Diesel 1st Generation	12.95
302-55003	Nighttime Steam	12.95
302-55004	Nighttime 1st Generation Diesel	12.95
302-55005	Nighttime Diesel Contemp	12.95

CITY

302-55006	Daytime Diesel 1st Generation	12.95
302-55007	Daytime Diesel Contemp	12.95
302-55008	Daytime Steam	12.95
302-55009	Nighttime Diesel 1st Generation	12.95
302-55010	Nighttime Diesel Contemp	12.95
302-55011	Nighttime Steam	12.95

NARROW GAUGE

302-55012	Daytime Steam	12.95
302-55013	Nighttime Steam	12.95

STAR HEADLIGHT & LANTERN CO.

RAILROAD LANTERN
A large polished reflector gives an evenly distributed bright spot, and the clear base picks up light in the base rings and legs, making the lantern appear brighter and larger from a distance. Requires one 6 volt lantern battery.

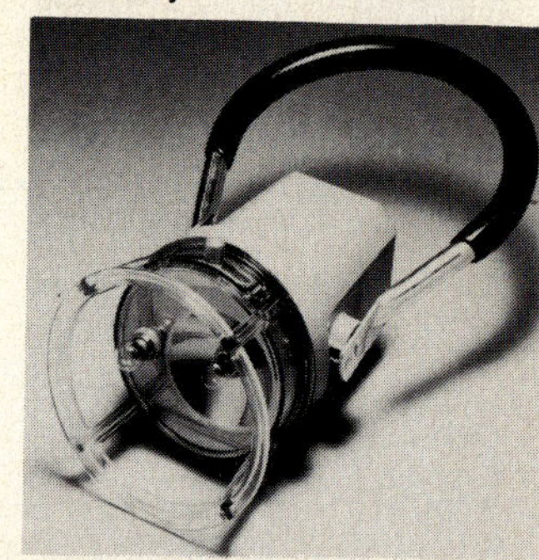

666-222   Starlite Railroad Lantern   42.19
Corrosion resistant Lexan with thick rubber handle. Base and case will not corrode, rust, dent or break, even at temperatures as low as -75° F.

With bells ringing and brakes squealing, one of the daily passenger trains makes a stop in the bustling city of Port Sendem. Train time is an important event for this city, which is served by a modified Dyna Models station. Downtown consists of buildings from Walthers Cornerstone Series® and Woodland Scenics, blended with several Instant Buildings© and Instant Horizon™ background scenes. Adding a splash of color are numerous decal signs from Micro Scale and Woodland Scenics dry transfers, which give each structure its own identity. A Jordan stagecoach offers hardier travelers a connection to the rail line, while several Preiser figures are on hand to watch the incoming train. Power is supplied by a Key Imports brass model, pulling a Balboa brass coach. The frontier town is the work of Fred Gill.
Models and Photo by Fred Gill

hobby helpers

RAILROAD CAPS

RAILROAD CAP — 7.95 each

Lightweight cloth cap & brim w/nylon mesh back.
One size fits all; adjustable plastic band.

HE WHO DIES WITH THE MOST TRAINS WIN$

099-701 Milwaukee Road
099-702 Milwaukee (Hiawatha)
099-703 Soo Line (Modern)
099-704 Soo Line (Old)
099-705 Milwaukee/Soo Line
099-706 New York Central
099-707 C&NW
099-708 Northern Pacific
099-709 Great Northern
099-710 Rock Island (Old)
099-711 Chessie

This Budd's for You!

099-712 Santa Fe
099-713 Frisco
099-714 Nickel Plate Road
099-715 Burlington Route
099-716 Pennsylvania (Keystone)
099-717 B&O (Capital)
099-718 Lionel Electric Trains
099-719 I'm an Alco-haulic
099-720 This Budd's For You
099-721 Not a Full Train
099-722 I Love Trains

OFFICIAL MODEL RAILROAD NITPICKER

099-723 I Love O Gauge
099-724 I Love HO Gauge
099-725 I'm an N-Thusiast
099-726 I'm a Model Railroad Widow
099-727 Norfolk & Western
099-728 Cotton Belt
099-729 Burlington Northern
099-730 Union Pacific
099-731 Southern Pacific, Modern
099-732 Southern Pacific
099-733 Amtrak

I ♥ TRAINS

NARROWMINDED & PROUD OF IT!

Not Pulling a Full Train!

099-734 Southern Railways
099-735 Rio Grande
099-736 SP&S Railway
099-737 Illinois Central Gulf
099-738 Canadian National
099-739 CB&Q Zephyr
099-740 Chicago Belt Railway
099-741 CMS&P
099-742 KC Southern (By Special Order Only.)
099-744 CNS&M, North Shore (By Special Order Only.)
099-746 Derailed
099-747 In Training
099-748 Narrow Minded & Proud of It
099-749 Official Railroad Nitpicker
099-750 Dies with Most Trains Wins

099-745 Headlights On—No One In
099-751 Dies with Most Lionel Wins
099-752 Ferroequinolist at Large
099-753 Caution! Railfan at Large
099-754 Model RRing is Contagious—Catch It!

099-755 Caution! Railfan with Camera
099-756 Construction—Enter at Own Risk
099-757 No One's On Board
099-758 Stops at All Hobby Shops
099-759 Still Plays with Trains
099-760 GM&O
099-761 Western Maryland
099-762 Chicago, Missouri & Western
099-763 Louisville & Nashville (Old)
099-764 M-K-T KATY (Old)
099-765 Wisconsin Central

Mountains in Minutes™
I.S.L.E. LABORATORIES

WALL SIGN

473-840 Beware of the Trains
Wall Sign/Plaque   9.98
Made of high density foam. 14 x 10".

WALTHERS

RAILROAD CAP
each 6.98

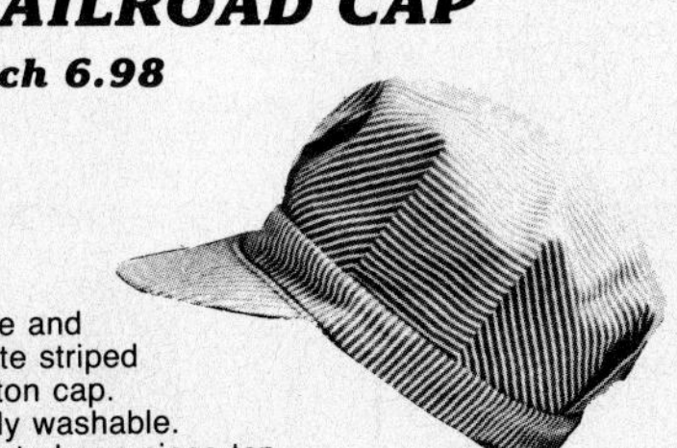

Blue and white striped cotton cap.
Fully washable.
Pleated one piece top.

407-775 Adjustable Cap   6.98

ATLAS
MODEL RAILROAD CO., INC.

ALL-AMERICAN LOCOMOTIVE PRINTS
Full color, 24 x 36".

150-352 Midwest Terminal   6.95
150-353 Union Pacific Fast Freight   6.95
150-354 Santa Fe "War Bonnet"   6.95
150-355 Mainline Action   6.95

MIL-SCALE Products

COMPUTERIZED RAILROAD TRIVIA GAME
Hundreds of questions and answers. For use w/Commodore 64 (disk drive). Computer keeps score and tracks playing times.

Rail-Triv
477-1120   18.95
for Commodore 64

This product is a special order item. When ordering, please request that your Dealer "Back Order" the item, or the order can not be processed. Please allow 2-3 weeks for delivery.

BACHMANN

160-17000 Caboose Lamp   129.95
4-wheel bobber caboose in G Scale with Santa Fe markings.
(By Special Order Only.)

ART PRINTS
All items are
"Special Order Only"

DUO-TONE PRINTS 12.95 each
Duo-tone color process prints, (printed in brown and black), representing both narrow and standard gauge and the 4-4-0 to the 2-8-8-4 locomotives. Printed on 15 x 20″ six point cover stock.

Included with each print is a description of each loco, a short informative statement on its wheel arrangement and its disposition.

413-2   Wildcat RR "2" 2-6-2

413-4   Clover Valley "4" 2-6-6-2T

413-29   Virginia & Truckee "29" 2-8-0

413-94   Western Pacific "94" 4-6-0

413-488   Rio Grande "488" 2-8-2

413-610   Texas & Pacific "610" 2-10-4

413-6060   Canadian National "6060" 4-8-2

413-765   Nickel Plate Road "765" 2-8-4

FULL-COLOR PRINT

413-2479   Southern Pacific #2479   40.00
18 x 22″ print of 8-10 engine No. 2479 at San Jose, California, in the 1930's. Image size 17 x 24″. Limited edition of 300 prints; signed and numbered by the artist.

413-2839   Southern "Royal Hudson"-"2839" 4-6-4

413-3025   Southern Pacific "3025" 4-4-2

413-3811   Southern Pacific "3811" 2-8-8-4

SIGNATURE SERIES

413-47300   The Winter San Juan Express "473"   65.00
Finished to a large poster format of 22 x 30″. Image area is 18 x 26″. Includes description of the loco and its history. Printed on museum-quality Buckeye Ltd. A "Limited Edition/Select Run" of 500 prints will be drawn off for cataloging, artist signature and date of signature.

Union Pacific #836
413-836   17.95

Southern Pacific #5011
413-5011   17.95

Union Pacific #2860
(13 x 16″)
413-2860   19.95

413-9039   Union Pacific #9039   29.95
(This print measures 18 x 14″.)

The Wabash Cannonball
413-700   17.95

ART PRINTS
All items are "Special Order Only"

Each print is trimmed, hand mounted, signed and numbered by the artist with a certificate 16 x 12″, ready to frame, and is accompanied by a data sheet pertaining to the history of the locomotive.

SIGNATURE SERIES (continued)

1801		2584
413-1801	Dixie Flyers	17.95
413-2584	The First High Steppin' Northern	17.95

2925		3000
413-2925	All the Way w/Santa Fe	17.95
413-3000	An Ageless High Stepper' SP	17.95

3003		3460
413-3003	The Northern Racers	17.95
413-3460	The Tallest High Stepper, SF	17.95

5200		5302
413-5200	The Hudson	17.95
413-5302	Royal Blue—and Fast, B&O	17.95

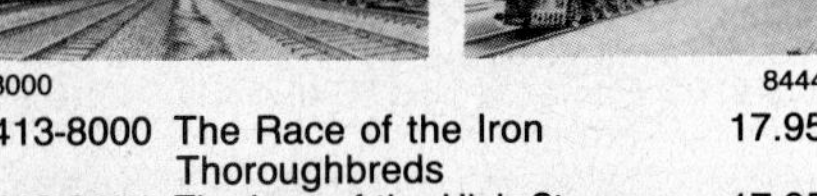

8000		8444
413-8000	The Race of the Iron Thoroughbreds	17.95
413-8444	The Last of the High Steppers	17.95

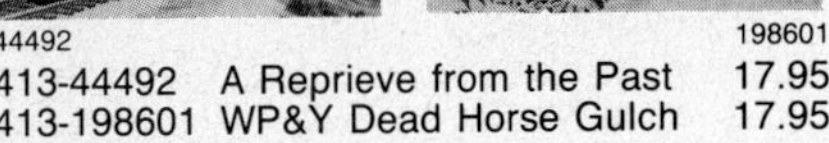

44492		198601
413-44492	A Reprieve from the Past	17.95
413-198601	WP&Y Dead Horse Gulch	17.95

198602		198603
413-198602	Pacific Coast Ry #106	17.95
413-198603	WSL Shay #9, Tuolomne	17.95

198604		198605
413-198604	Lake Tahoe's Railroad	17.95
413-198605	The Suntan Route	17.95

198606		198607
413-198606	RGS at Trout Lake	17.95
413-198607	Uintah Ry, Morro Castle	17.95

198608		198609
413-198608	Morenci Southern	17.95
413-198609	Sumpter Valley, Baker	17.95

198610		198611
413-198610	D&RGW at Chama	17.95
413-198611	SP Narrow Gauge from Keeler	17.95

199009		198612
413-199009	Chesapeake & Ohio #1309	19.95
413-198612	NCNG Bear River Bridge	17.95

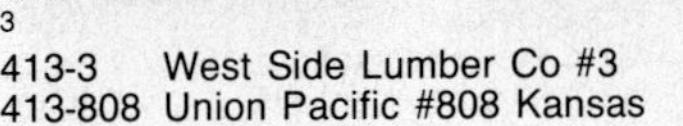

3		808
413-3	West Side Lumber Co #3	17.95
413-808	Union Pacific #808 Kansas	17.95

199001		199002
413-199001	New York Central's Niagra #5500	19.95
413-199002	Nickel Plate	19.95

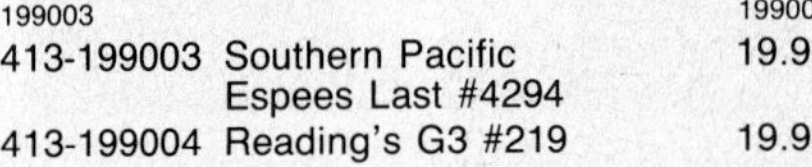

199003		199004
413-199003	Southern Pacific Espees Last #4294	19.95
413-199004	Reading's G3 #219	19.95

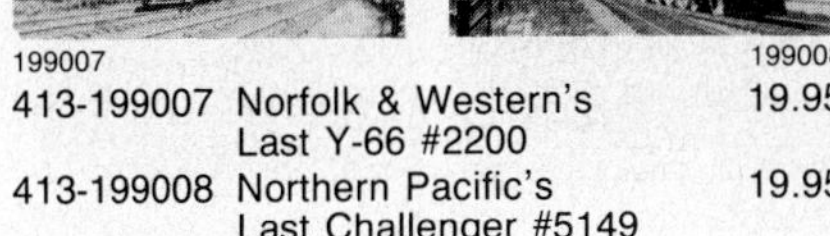
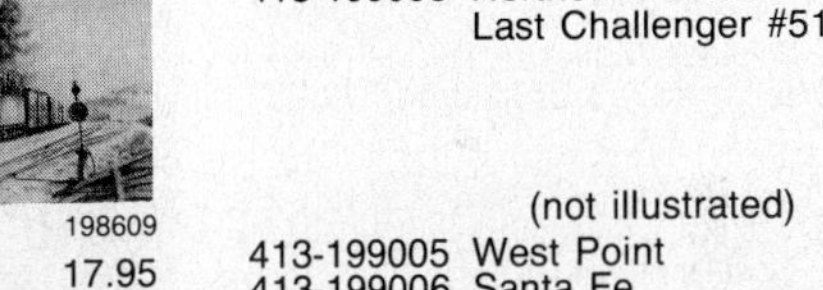
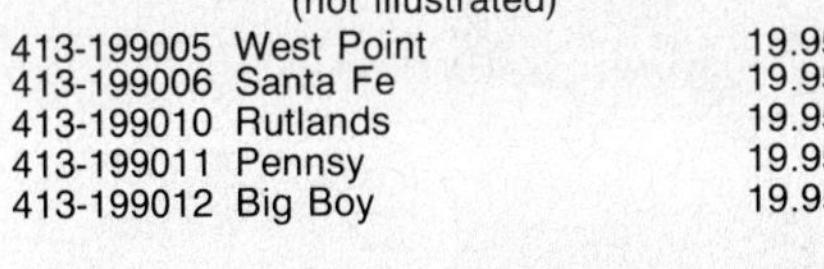

199007		199008
413-199007	Norfolk & Western's Last Y-66 #2200	19.95
413-199008	Northern Pacific's Last Challenger #5149	19.95

(not illustrated)

413-199005	West Point	19.95
413-199006	Santa Fe	19.95
413-199010	Rutlands	19.95
413-199011	Pennsy	19.95
413-199012	Big Boy	19.95

MIGHTY MALLET SIGNATURE SERIES (13 x 16″)

7		200
413-7	"Skookum" Deep River 2-4-4-2	19.95
413-200	Out of the Moffat Tunnel	19.95

208		800
413-208	Western Pacific, M-80 Class Mallets +	19.95
413-800	Virginian 800 Class Mallet	19.95

ART PRINTS
All items are
"Special Order Only"

Each print is trimmed, hand mounted, signed and numbered by the artist with a certificate 16 x 13", ready to frame, and is accompanied by a data sheet pertaining to the history of the locomotive.

MIGHTY MALLET SIGNATURE SERIES (13 x 16") (continued)

1218   1399
413-1218   Class "A" Number 1218   19.95
413-1399   Santa Fe Passenger Mallet   19.95

1601   1981
413-1601   Allegheny Barrels Toward Sunlight   19.95
413-1981   Great Northern #1981, 2-6-8-0   19.95

2601   3703
413-2601   Erie L-1 Class Mallet   19.95
413-3703   Rio Grande #3703 Challenger   19.95

4015   4294
413-4015   Union Pacific Big Boy   19.95
413-4294   Cab Forward   19.95

STREAMLINER SIGNATURE SERIES

100   118
413-100   Milwaukee #100   19.95
413-118   Reading #118   19.95

652   1026
413-652   Southern Pacific #652   19.95
413-1026   Frisco #1026   19.95

1380   1400
413-1380   Southern #1380   19.95
413-1400   NYH&H #1400   19.95

2102   2906
413-2102   Lehigh Valley #2102   19.95
413-2906   Union Pacific #2906 +   19.95

3768   4000
413-3768   Pennsylvania #3768   19.95
413-4000   C&NW #4000   19.95

5304   5450
413-5304   Baltimore & Ohio #5304   19.95
413-5450   NYC J3A #5450   19.95

MOUNTAIN CLASS SIGNATURE SERIES

179   1460
413-179   Western Pacific #179 FEC 414, MT44   19.95
413-1460   Saluda Mountain #1460   19.95

1607   3001
413-1607   Rio Grande #1607 + M-75 Heavyweight   19.95
413-3001   NYC Mowhawk #3001   19.95

4117   5594
413-4117   Hercules #4117 B&M   19.95
413-5594   F3 Class #5594 B&O   19.95

2523   4352
413-2523   Great Northern #2523 Fast Tracking   19.95
413-4352   San Joaquin SP #4352   19.95

6755   60603
413-6755   Pennsylvania #6755   19.95
413-60603   Bullet Nose Betty #6060 +   19.95

7002   1522
413-7002   Pony Express #7002 UP   19.95
413-1522   Frisco #1522 at Fork Valley   19.95

CALIFORNIA CLASSICS

9201   9202
413-9201   Pacific Coast "105" at Santa Maria   **NEW** 19.95
413-9202   Santa Fe "3450" at Fresno   **NEW** 19.95

9203   9204
413-9203   Southern Pacific "2921" at Capitola Trestle   **NEW** 19.95
413-9204   Southern Pacific "2479" at San Jose   **NEW** 19.95

ART PRINTS

Each print is trimmed, hand mounted, signed and numbered by the artist with a certificate 16 x 13,″ ready to frame, and is accompanied by a data sheet pertaining to the history of the locomotive. All items are Special Order only.

B L HOBBY PRODUCTS

FLASHER LAPEL PIN

Pin is a plastic HO Scale operating railroad crossing flasher that uses a 9v battery. Includes 10″ wires and printed circuit board, less battery.

Flasher Lapel Pin
183-580   19.95

CALIFORNIA CLASSICS (continued)

9205 — 9206

413-9205 Southern Pacific "2412" **NEW** 19.95
  at Milbrae
413-9206 Napa Valley Line "60" **NEW** 19.95

9207 — 9208

413-9207 Southern Pacific "4100" **NEW** 19.95
  at Niles Tower
413-9208 Southern Pacific "4402" **NEW** 19.95
  at Salinas

9209 — 9210

413-9209 Modesto & Empire **NEW** 19.95
  Traction "100"
413-9210 Western Pacific "94" **NEW** 19.95
  & SP "3025" at Altamont Pass

9211 — 9212

413-9211 Stockton Terminal & **NEW** 19.95
  Eastern "1"
413-9212 Santa Fe "3940" at Pinole **NEW** 19.95

CONTEMPORARY STEAM TRAINS

9213 — 9214

413-9213 Spokane, Portland & **NEW** 19.95
  Seattle "700"
413-9214 Sierra Railroad "3" **NEW** 19.95
  & "34"

9215 — 9216

413-9215 Cotton Belt "819" **NEW** 19.95
413-9216 NKP "765" vs Pere **NEW** 19.95
  Marquette "1225"

9217 — 9218

413-9217 Nevada Northern "40" **NEW** 19.95
413-9218 Southern Pacific "2472" **NEW** 19.95

9219 — 9220

413-9219 Cumbres & Toltec "488" **NEW** 19.95
413-9220 Atlantic & West **NEW** 19.95
  Point "290"

9221 — 9222

413-9221 Santa Fe "3731" **NEW** 19.95
413-9222 Norfolk & Western "611" **NEW** 19.95

9223 — 9224

413-9223 Union Pacific "3985" **NEW** 19.95
413-9224 Blue Mountain & **NEW** 19.95
  Reading "2102"

N.J. International

ENGINEER CAP

525-6620 Engineer Cap   4.99
Hickory striped, adjustable band.

One of Hoosic Junction's employers, and a steady customer for the Rutland, is the Proctor Scale Company. This handsome New England mill complex was created by kitbashing structures from Magnuson, along with a Heljan building. The tall smokestack is a plaster casting. Lou Sassi created this scene for his layout in Charlton, New York. *Models and Photo by Lou Sassi*

L & H RAILSONICS
EST. 1978

Steam Tracks
138-4085 Cassette   9.98
Featured locomotives include Norfolk & Southern 2-6-6-4 #1218, Southern Pacific 4-8-4 #4449, Nickel Plate 2-8-4 #765 plus engines from the Pennsy, Reading and Sierra.

Diesel Super Power Vol 1
138-4017 Cassette   9.98
Engines featured: EMD, SW-1500, GP-20, GP-30, GP-35, SD-40-2, SDP-40F, SD-45, SDP-45, SD-45T-2, F-45, DD-35 A & B, DD-40AX. G.E.:U23B, U25B. Alco: DL-640, DL-721.

Railroads featured: SP, UP, Amtrak, NYC, EL, CNW, CRIP, ATSF, D&H. Also features recordings at Donner Pass and Cajon Pass. Both runby and onboard recordings.

Accent on Steam Vol 2
138-4077 Cassette   9.98
Feature G&O #'s 46 and 43; Brazilian (EFDTC) #'s 308, 310, 406, 313; NKP #765; Reading 4-8-4 #2102; Cass Shay #4; South African Rwys Bethlehem Depot and 25NC class 4-8-4; and South African Garratt #59.

1st Generation Diesels Vol 2
138-4055 Cassette   9.98
Engines featured: EMD: F-3, F-7, F-9, FL-9, E-8, GP-7. Alco: PA-1, RS-2, RS-3, FM: H-10-44, H-12-44, Baldwin: S-12, RS-12.

Railroads featured: ATSF, NH, EL, NYC, Sierra, D&H, C&NW, Michigan Northern, SP, MILW, D&RGW (California Zephyr). Both runby and onboard recordings.

High Country Steam
138-4058 Cassette   9.98
Includes sequences of Cumbres & Toltec passenger trains, the "Great Freight '79" railfan special caught in a thunderstorm, steam rotary OM, and the days of common carrier freight operation. All new recordings made on D&RG Narrow Gauge in the 60's & 70's.

A Decade of Steam Vol 1
138-4067 Cassette   9.98
Locomotives featured: UP 3985 4-6-6-4, Southern 2716 2-8-4, SP 4449 4-8-4, Southern 610 2-10-4, Chessie 614 4-8-4, UP 8444 4-8-4, Reading 2102 4-8-4, Sierra 28-2-8-0, Sierra 34 2-8-2, Southern 2839 4-6-4.

Daylight 4449 Sounds
138-4078 Cassette   9.98
Sound of steam, recorded in Dolby stereo. 40 minutes of the World's Fair Daylight.

Steam Tracks, Vol 2
138-4095   Cassette   9.98
138-6095 Compact Disc (all digital, DDD) 15.98
Engines featured: CN 6060, CP (BCR) 2860 and 3716 "Alberta Bound", NKP 587, NS 611 and 1218, UP 8444, Grand Canyon Ry., SP 4449 on Cantara Loop, EBT. Digitally recorded and mastered, Chrome tape, Dolby Stereo. 53 minutes.

RAILROAD RECORDINGS

L&H Railsonics cassettes and compact discs are full stereo recordings.

Cassettes all utilize high quality 5-screw cassette shells, imported German tape. These stereo cassettes are compatible with all monophonic players.

Diesel Tracks-Big Engines and Heavy Rail
138-4096 Cassette   9.98
Engines featured: UP Williams Loop, BN SD-60's in the Columbia River Gorge, two NS freights on Old Fort Mtn., Santa Fe freights roaring across the desert at 70 mph and grinding up Tehachapi, One morning on Horsehoe Curve, Amtraks Zephyr at Blue Canyon and more. Lots of third generation power. Digitally recorded and mastered, Chrome tape, Dolby stereo, 60 minutes.

Northern Pacific Steam (Nostalgia Series)
138-7001 Cassette   11.98
Featured: Northern Pacific steam in actual service in the Pacific northwest as recorded by Elwin Purington. Simulated stereo.

The Sound of Steam (Nostalgia Series)
138-7002 Cassette   11.98
Featured: PRR K-4 Pacifics, RDGT-1's, CN 4-8-4's, CP 4-4-0 and 4-6-0, DM&IR 2-8-8-4's and much more. John Brigg's North Jersey recordings. Some simulated and some true stereo.

Modellers Sounds, Steam
138-3001 Cassette   9.98
Steam engine sounds pacing and on-board with long sequences of stack talk and whistling. Especially for model railroad background sounds.

First Generation Diesels Vol. 1
138-4010   9.98
Engines featured: The diesels that killed the steam locomotive on U.S. railroads. Features early EMD, ALCO and Baldwin road and switching power.

Steam Tracks #3 "Giants Meet"
138-4111   9.98
Engines featured: The engines that attended Railfair 1991, the 1991 and 1992 Conventions, and the 1990 Yakima steam meet. Hear the big engines working hard and running fast. Digitally recorded.

■ LIMITED QUANTITIES ■ AVAILABLE

A Decade of Steam Vol 3
138-4081 Cassette   9.98
Engines featured: NS 611, UP 3985 in Utah, NS 4501, NKP 765, Ex-PRR 1223 and 7002 on the Strasburg's run to Harrisburg, D&RGW Narrow Gauge.

Steams Sunset (Nostalgia Series)
138-7000 Cassette   11.98
Featured: Steam in actual service on the Canadian Prairies and in Mexico in the late 1950's and 1960's. Also SP 4460 "Last of Steam". Simulated stereo.

Opened cassettes and compact discs will be replaced if defective, but cannot be returned for credit or refund.

Virnex Industries, Inc.

RAILROAD DECALS

Full color railroad herald decals, 2-1/2″ to 3″ in size. (Illustrations are 1/3 actual size.)

RAILROAD DECALS   each 1.50

762-101	D&RGW	762-114	MILW
762-102	GN	762-115	Chessie
762-103	IHB	762-116	EJ&E
762-104	N&W	762-117	ICG
762-105	CSS&SB	762-118	CNS&M
762-106	CP	762-119	UP
762-107	CB&Q	762-120	NKP
762-108	MO-PAC	762-121	E-L
762-109	GM&O	762-122	RI
762-110	NYC	762-123	L&N
762-111	Frisco	762-124	BRC
762-112	C&NW	762-125	CV
762-113	PRR		

762-100 Assortment   pkg(25) 35.50
one each of #101-125

762-151	BN	762-164	NYO&W
762-152	GT	762-165	PC
762-153	Conrail	762-166	SCL
762-154	CN	762-167	SOU
762-155	AMTK	762-168	SP
762-156	ATSF	762-169	VTR
762-157	CP	762-170	WAB
762-158	The Rock	762-171	NP
762-159	FEC	762-172	Family Lines
762-160	GN (blue)	762-173	WP
762-161	KCS	762-174	ACL
762-162	MKT	762-175	SOO
762-163	MONON		

762-150 Assortment   pkg(25) 35.50
one each of #151-175

762-201	B&O	762-208	GB&W
762-202	C&O	762-209	GMRC
762-203	CNJ	762-210	MEC
762-204	C&EI	762-211	NS
762-205	CGW	762-212	RDG
762-206	Cotton Belt	762-213	MP Buzz
762-207	DT&I		Saw

MISCELLANEOUS DECALS

762-131 "I am a Railfan"   1.50
762-132 "Pray for Me — My husband   1.50
    collects trains"

HOT PAD

'Pray for Me — My Husband Collects Trains"
762-432   1.98
6 x 6″
White with red lettering

Mayfair Games

487-467

487-466

487-1450

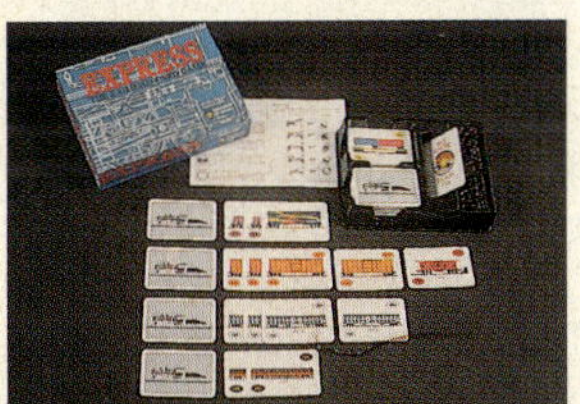

487-458

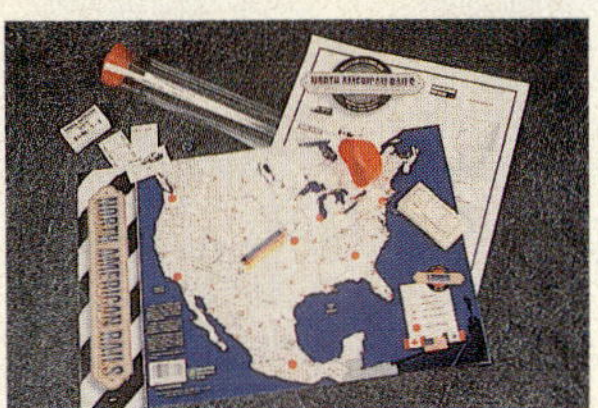

487-1451

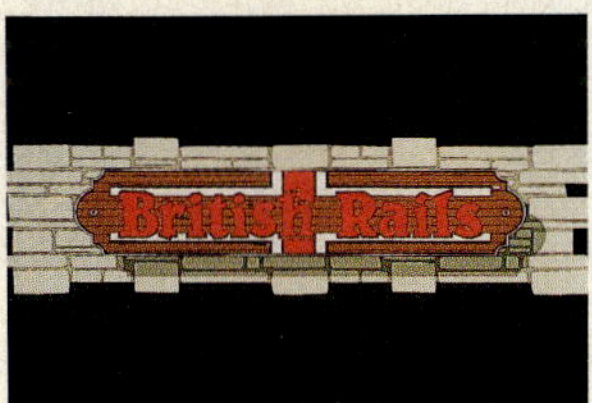

487-1452

487-550   "1835"   60.00

Game of railway building and share speculation set in Germany. In 1835, each player learns what it is like to be a shareholder in railroad companies and aims to be the wealthiest player at the end of the game. Players that become directors of companies can manipulate their railroads, making their companies stronger and themselves rich—two things that do not always coincide. For 3 to 7 players, ages 16 to adult.

487-450   Empire Builder   25.00

Empire Builder is as easy as connecting the dots, as players draw tracks in erasable crayon and operate a rail empire in an effort to accumulate the most money. Players create a new strategy and deliver a variety of goods across the continent. Players learn the locations of cities, states, mountains and rivers of the United States and southern Canada. For 2 to 6 players, ages 12 to adult.

487-457   Eurorails   40.00

Eurorails allows players to amass fortune and power by picking up commodities from cities that produce them and delivering them to cities that need them. Players use erasable crayons to lay track between major European cities and use the European Currency as money to purchase routes. For 2 to 6 players, ages 12 to adult.

487-1040   Empire Builder Miniatures   **NEW** 25.00

Players use lead miniatures that are based on famous trains from America's past. The Empire Builder Miniatures package includes four locos: the Big Boy, the J, the GP 30 and the Consolidated. Each is designed for use by players of Empire Builder and related games and/or as adult collectibles.

487-467 Iron Dragon   **NEW** 30.00

Fantasy and reality meet in this exciting offshoot of our popular game system. A must for any Empire fan looking for a new twist! The Iron Dragons cross a make-believe world, delivering treasures to those in need. Magical items make every game a new adventure through the unknown plains. Due to the resounding response of fans of all ages to this idea, this game will come in a deluxe boxed set.

487-458 Express   12.50

Building trains is an integral part of America's history. Now the tradition continues with Express, a unique card game for the 90's. Reminiscent of classic card games but including new play twists, Express is as easy to learn as rummy. Players start with a one-car train and build on their meld to maximize points and bonuses. For 2 to 6 players, ages 8 to adult.

487-466 Uncle Happy's Train   **NEW** 14.95

With this simplified version of the Empire Builder system, players use crayons to draw their railroad tracks across a wipe-off board of the United States, and transport goods such as teddy bears, computers and dolls. For 2-6 players, ages 6 to adult.

487-1450 Nippon Rails   **NEW** 25.00

Build rail lines across the four Japanese Islands of Hokkaido, Honshu, Shikoku, and Kyushyu. Deliver commodities such as electronics, sake and silk. But beware of snow storms, volcanic eruptions and your opponents strategy. Comes complete with wipe-off playing mat, crayons, tokens & complete instructions. For 2-6 players, ages 12 to adult.

487-1451 North American Rails   **NEW** 25.00
487-1452 British Rails   **NEW** 25.00

The following games, 1450, 1451, and 1452 come with an 18" clear tube, which allows the laminated map to double as the game board and outside packaging. The base of the tube is squared off to prevent rolling.

WALTHERS AND YOU

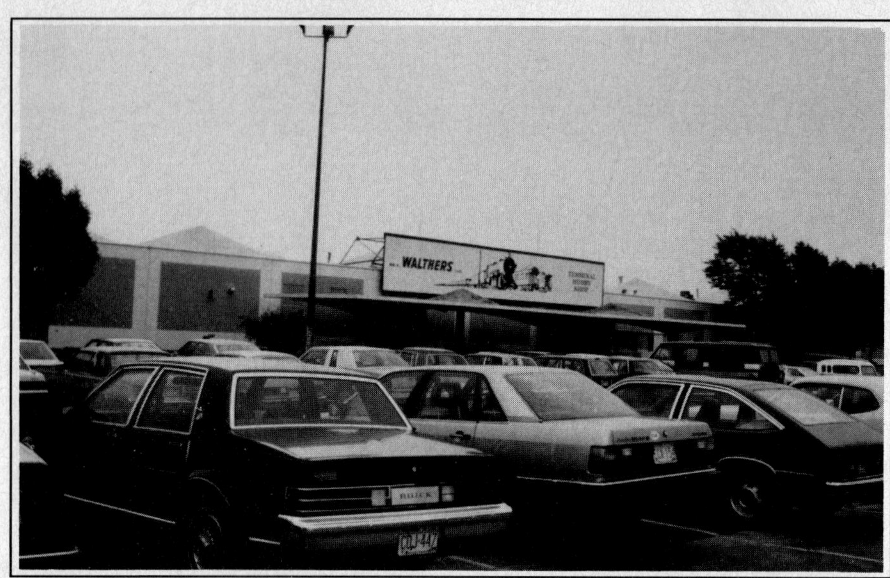

Walthers is a manufacturer and a wholesaler of Model Railroad equipment. Our company occupies 90,000 square feet of building space on 14 acres of land in a modern industrial park on the Northwest side of Milwaukee.

Walthers is both a manufacturer and a wholesaler of model railroad equipment. We manufacturer Walthers line of plastic passenger car and freight car kits and Instant Horizons. We are also wholesalers for the other manufacturers whose products are listed in our catalogs.

We are committed to enhancing your enjoyment of model railroading. We will try to answer your questions, and we will help you locate dealers in your area. As a manufacturer — wholesaler, we sell to dealers, supplying shops around the world. For a list of Participating Walthers Dealers near you, write to:

Walthers Dealer Services Dept.
P.O. Box 18676
Milwaukee, Wisconsin 53218

(A self-addressed, stamped envelope will be appreciated).

AVAILABILITY OF MERCHANDISE

We constantly strive to make this catalog an accurate representation of what is actually available in the model railroad marketplace. A new program, now being implemented with the help of our many suppliers, puts the emphasis on products which are currently in production. This means that the majority of products in this catalog are readily available or will be delivered shortly.

Items which have not been available for the last 12 months are printed in blue type. These products are not discontinued. Some items may be out of stock and subject to backorder. Unforeseen delays in production and/or delivery also affect the availability of some products. Items which have been discontinued by a manufacturer are subject to stock on hand.

All-in-all, most of the announced items are generally available, and we are doing our best to make sure that you can purchase the products you need as conveniently as possible.

BACKORDERS ARE NOT AUTOMATIC

Walthers operates an efficient Advance Reservation and Backorder service for Participating Dealers, but items are NOT automatically backordered. Backorders are entered only where dealers instruct us to backorder, and where there is a reasonable chance of delivery. Items not shipped may be cancelled instead of backordered. Confirmation of backorders is shown on dealer invoices.

The best way to tell what is available is to ask your dealer to look it up in SAS,™ the Stock Advisory Service on Microfiche. Your dealer should also confirm the backorder from his records.

An inside look at Walthers Creative Services Group, the department where the pages for the catalog originate.

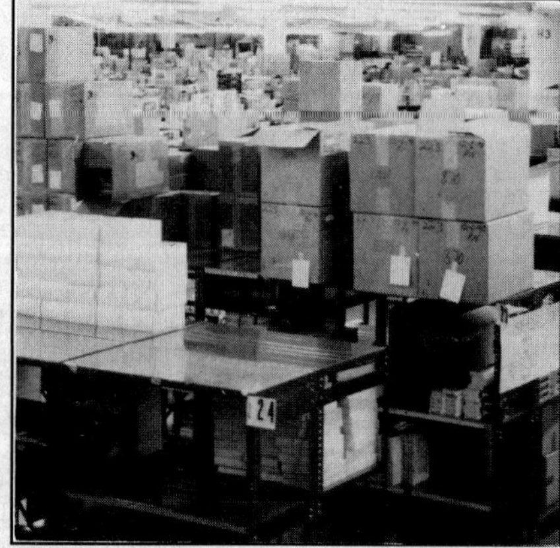

"As far as the eye can see" is a suitable description for the Walthers Warehouse. Here you see only a portion of the merchandise we stock.

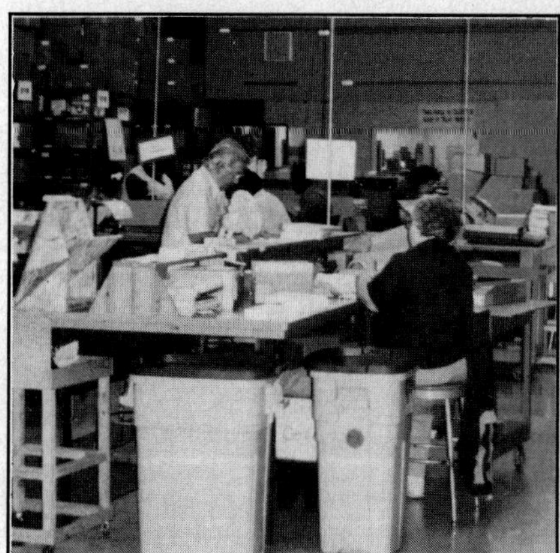

A view of Walthers employees, busy packing orders. Walthers merchandise is shipped to customers and dealers around the world.

PARTICIPATING WALTHERS DEALERS

In order to get the merchandise from "Walthers Inventory" to "your layout", we have established a network of "Participating Walthers Dealers" who have made a commitment to help you enjoy the hobby. These dealers are listed periodically in a published list, and are identified by a window emblem.

This emblem shown here along with an address where you can write for a list of Participating Walthers Dealers in your area.

The service programs described on this page are available to all Participating Dealers to help them provide you with more information and fast service.

PARTICIPATING DEALER SERVICES

*Participating Walthers Dealers are supported by special program of **INFORMATION** and **FAST SERVICE** to help you enjoy the Hobby of Model Railroading.*

STOCK ADVISORY SERVICE (SAS™)

Of course, it's important to be able to tell which items are available and which are on Advance Reservation (AR), Backorder (BO), etc. Now, through Walthers "SAS"™ service, your dealer can get this information, and can tell you which items are available, which are on backorder, which have been discontinued, and which are "not ready yet".

SAS™ is a michrofiche service developed by Walthers. "Stock Advisory Service" is available to Participating Walthers Dealers and is updated monthly.

The SAS™ microfiche contains details of: new items received in stock, projected delivery dates for items out of stock and the price changes which have occured since the catalog was published.

CRAFT TRAIN NEWS

Walthers publishes a monthly newsletter "Craft Train News," which is available from Walthers Dealers.

Craft Train News contains industry news, announcements of new products, detailed information on new arrivals, and interesting features and reports on what's going on in the hobby.

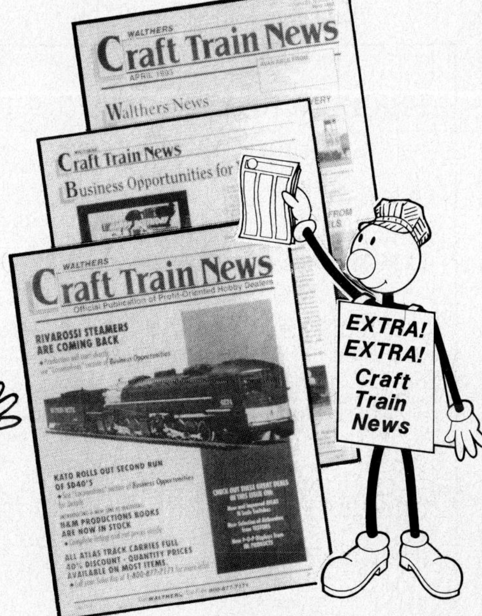

INSTANT INFORMATION WITH EXPRES II

An innovative computer system, known as EXPRES II, is now being field tested. This new system will make it easy for you to check product availability, place orders, check your backorder status and check your account.

EXPRES II will operate as an interactive system that will give you a direct connection to the Walthers computer. Being on-line will provide you instant, accurate information and you'll be in control at all times. The system is designed to be available when you need it most, day or night, to fit your schedule.

The new EXPRES II is being designed to work with your present PC and modem. Walthers will provide on-line documentation, a step-by-step user's manual and a complete communications software package. This material will be made available at no charge-we even pay for the phone calls!

During the current "break-in" period, we're fine tuning the system to make it as user friendly as possible. We're also getting feedback from Dealers like you, on how we can expand the capabilities of the system to best suit your needs.

For a list of the **Participating Walthers Dealers near you, write to:**

Walthers Consumer Services Dept.
P.O. Box 18676
Milwaukee, Wisconsin 53218

(A self-addressed, stamped envelope will be appreciated.)

NEW from **INTERNATIONAL HOBBY CORPORATION**

COUPLERS
348-220075 Heavyweight short/ (pair) 2.60
 for Rivarossi/IHC passenger cars.

348-222076 Smoothside long (pair) 2.60
 Corrugated Side/for Rivarossi/
 IHC passenger cars

NEW from **NEW ENGLAND RAIL SERVICE**

PASSENGER CARS
Injection molded styrene with a one piece carbody and separate roof.

70' STANDARD COMBINE
529-1001 New York Central TBA
529-1000 Undecorated TBA

NEW from **MODEL POWER**

PARTS
FURNITURE
490-550 Garage Sale 3.98

NEW from **CIBOLO CROSSINGS**

PARTS

ROOF VENTS

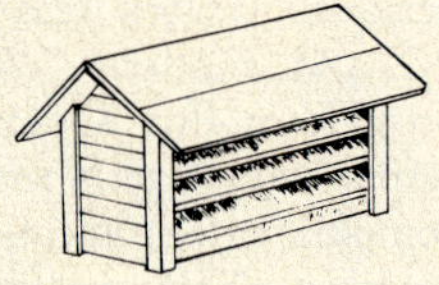

231-17 Slat Vent Kit 8.95
 9/16" x 1/8" 1.4 x 2.8 cm
 Makes up to five vents.

CORRECTION FOR

A-LINE

On page 801 in the PARTS SECTION, the following pictures were reversed. Shown below are the correct pictures and listings.

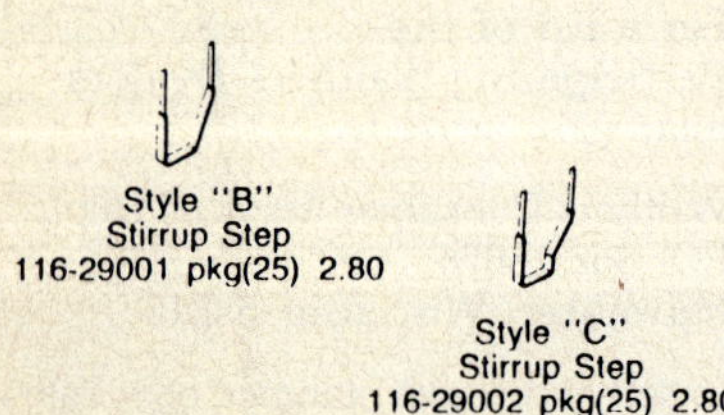

NEW from **CM SHOPS**

FREIGHT CARS
40' BOX CAR
012-102 Delaware & Hudson 7.95
012-104 AT&SF 7.95

50' SINGLE DOOR BOX CAR
012-107 Reading 8.50
012-109 Vermont 8.50
012-110 Family Lines (L&N) 8.50
012-112 MOPAC 8.50
012-116 Frisco 8.50
012-122 Bangor & Aroostook 8.50
012-131 Santa Fe 8.50
012-132 Penn Central 8.50
012-135 Ashley, Drew & Northern 8.50
012-136 Gulf, Mobile & Ohio 8.50
012-146 Seaboard Airline 8.50
012-152 Nacionales de Mexico 8.50
012-153 Western Maryland 8.50
012-155 Seaboard Coast Line 8.50
012-156 Illinois Central 8.50
012-164 Norfolk & Western 8.50
012-167 Maine Central 8.50
012-169 Union Pacific 8.50
012-172 Louisiana Midland 8.50
012-173 Clinchfield 8.50
012-175 Soo Line 8.50
012-178 Milwaukee Road 8.50
012-180 Rock Island 8.50

50' PLUG DOOR BOX CARS
012-125 Milwaukee Road 8.50
012-114 The Rock 8.50
012-144 Western Pacific 8.50
012-162 Napierville Junction 8.50
012-163 CNW (Employee Owned) 8.50
012-159 Erie Lackawanna 8.50
012-168 Missouri Pacific 8.50
012-170 Southern Pacific 8.50

50' COVERED GONDOLA
012-140 New Haven 8.50
012-185 Bessemer & Lake Erie 8.50
012-138 Chicago & North Western 8.50
012-150 Illinois Central 8.50

54' PS RIBSIDE COVERED HOPPER
012-199 CNW (green) 9.50
 (Employee Owned)

PRICE INCREASE
for **GYROS** items

TOOLS
SAW BLADES
321-92405 1 each of Thick pkg(2) 13.71
 and Thin

FIBER-DISK
321-93102 1" dia x 1/32," pkg(2) 2.80
 soft
321-93104 1-1/2" dia x 1/32," pkg(2) 3.47
 soft
321-93106 1-1/2" dia x a/32," pkg(2) 3.47
 hard
321-93108 2" dia x 1/32," pkg(2) 4.47
 hard
321-93109 2-1/2," hard 2.93

NEW from **A-WEST**

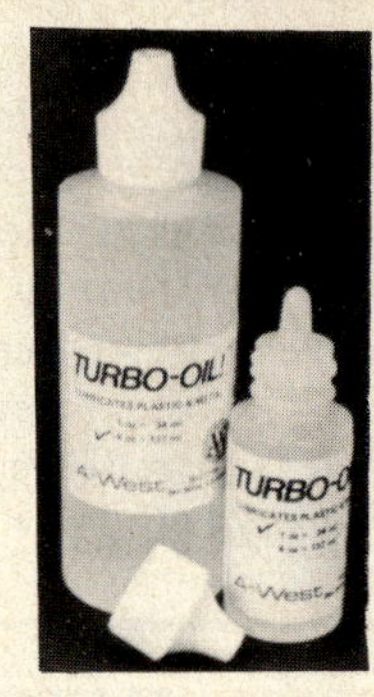

LUBRICANTS
TURBO OIL
Not a petroleum product. Fine for plastics and/or metal. Bottle is fitted with a plastic dropper applicator tip and overcap.

158-3 1 oz 2.50
158-14 4 oz w/needle tip 4.98

STAINLESS NEEDLEPOINT APPLICATOR BOTTLES
Use for solvent, flux, paint, oil, glue, ink, cement, contact cleaner, fuel, ceramic decor. Length 1" or 4" snaps into bottle neck. Includes 1 oz bottle, cap, label and cleaning wire.

w/1" Needle 2.29
w/4" Needle 3.39

1" Needle	4" Needle					
158-16	158-164	Blue	.016od	.008id	flow	1
158-20	158-204	Ylw	.020od	.010	flow	2
158-25	158-254	Red	.025od	.013	flow	3
158-35	158-354	Wht	.035od	.023	flow	8
158-50	158-504	Blk	.050od	.033	flow	17
158-65	158-654	Clr	.065od	.047	flow	35

G-GUN
Hi pressure syringe, apply grease, glue, goop, putty and latex/plaster molding material. Plastic tip cuts to any shape or size.

158-900 G-Gun 1/2 oz 1.98
158-901 Jr G-Gun pkg(2) 1.98

NEEDLE FILE SETS
321-1406 Economy 6 piece 6.80

5 1/2" FILES
Dealers: MUST order Dealer Packs of 12.
321-1460 1/2" Round each 1.20
 (By Special Order Only.)
321-1461 Knife each 1.20
321-1462 Round each 1.20
 (By Special Order Only.)
321-1463 Square each 1.20
 (By Special Order Only.)
321-1464 Triangle 1.20
321-1465 Equaling each 1.20
321-1466 Flat 1.20

DRILL ACCESSORIES
321-1285 Drill set #61-80 34.98

NEW from **SHERLINE PRODUCTS**

Allows the machinist to reset the handwheel to "zero" (or any desired setting) at any time during a machining operation.

RESETTABLE HANDWHEELS
677-3420	2″ Asmb, Inch	30.00
677-3430	2″ Asmb, Metric	30.00
677-3440	2-1/2″ Asmb, Inch	30.00
677-3450	2-1/2″ Asmb, Metric	30.00

OPTIONAL TAILSTOCK

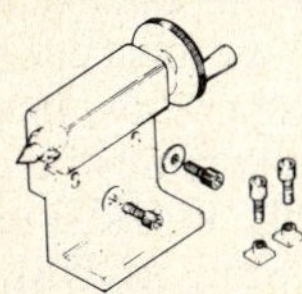

677-3702   50.00
For 4″ Rotary Table (#3700). With the table mounted vertically, an optional tailstock can be mounted to the mill table. It is used to support and stabilize the other end of long work held in a chuck or otherwise attached to the rotary table.

MILLING CONVERSION

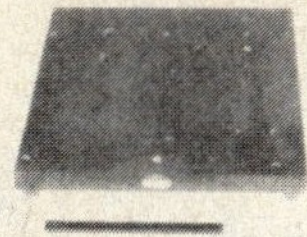

677-6100   Horizontal   120.00
Includes base and parts shown

Increase the size of work that can be machined with the addition of the Horizontal Milling Conversion. By allowing the vertical column to be mounted in various positions in relation to the table, and with the headstock and spindle rotated 90 degrees into the horizontal position, a tremendous variety of machining possibilities are opened up. Plus, the mill can remain mounted to the conversion base and still operate in its conventional vertical mode as well.

WOOD TOOL REST SET

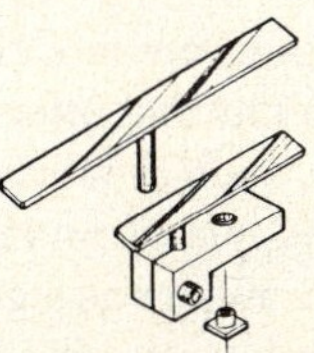

677-3038   50.00
Adjustable 3″ and 5″ rests are placed near the work and the cutting tool is rested on and moved across their surface to cut wood.

ADJUSTABLE LIVE CENTER

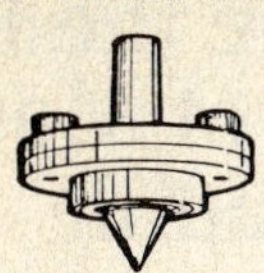

677-1201   50.00
Allows you to precisely position the center. The center is attached to one plate, while the shaft is part of another. Two slightly oversize holes in one side allow adjustment screws to be loosened, the center located and then locked down where you want it.

TAILSTOCK CHUCK HOLDER
671-1202   Adjustable   35.00 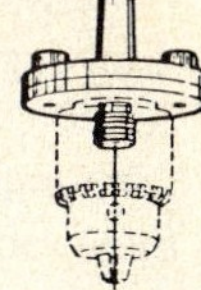
Holds a tailstock chuck in absolutely perfect alignment. Adjustment screws and split design allow perfect centering for the chuck.

TAILSTOCK CUSTOM TOOL HOLDER
671-1203   Adjustable   35.00 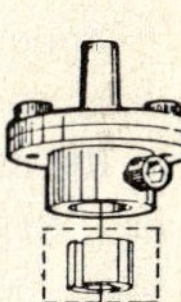
By making your own custom split collet with a 5/8″ outside diameter, this part can hold virtually any tool you wish to adapt to it.

NEW from
MARKET IDENTITY

Beautiful, cuddly, 10″ Teddy Bears — must be seen, touched and hugged to be believed. They arrive dressed in a railroad suit with Walthers logo on the front and also sporting a railroad cap.

TEDDY BEARS
497-10	Panda	(black/white)	19.99
497-20	Polar Bear	(white)	19.99
497-30	Grizzley	(dark brown)	19.99
497-40	Black w/Beige Ears, Nose & Feet		19.99
497-50	Golden	(suntan)	19.99
497-60	Beige	(cream)	19.99

Explore the Fascinating World of Model Railroading

Many people are familiar with train sets. They either owned one or wanted one — or knew someone who did. Grandfathers are familiar with the Lionel trains of the 30's and 40's, while the younger generation has been fascinated with the smaller sizes.

Many know that model railroading is an engaging hobby, and a rewarding activity. In its simplest sense, "running the trains" can be watching them race around a circle. More sophisticated hobbyists enjoy simulating the activity of real trains.

Model Railroading is a lasting hobby, because it can be as simple or as complex as the owner desires. Beginners find it easy to get started, while old timers keep their interest because there's always something new to do.

Model Railroading can be a social hobby too, and many people enjoy the hobby through clubs. Here, members from every profession and income level work side by side (And it takes another club member to tell who's who!) to recreate a railroad in miniature. Everybody can find a challenge and satisfaction in Model Railroading.

When in Milwaukee Stop in and See Us

You're invited "behind the scenes" for a fascinating look at how Walthers products are made, packaged and shipped to dealers around the world! Our tour guides will show you various departments, thousands of model railroad products in the warehouse, plus a variety of layouts. Tours are conducted Monday through Friday at 10:00, and 11:00 AM; and 12:30, 1:30, and 2:30 PM.

The Special Appeal of Craft Trains . . .

The hobby has a special appeal for those who enjoy making things with their hands. This is the world of Craft Trains.

What Are Craft Trains?

Craft Trains are model railroads built with kits that offer more challenge, such as fabricating parts from wood, plastic and metal, using detailed drawings as a guide.

Craft Trains offer the chance to make each model a little bit different than any other, regardless of the materials used.

Craft Trains can be as simple as assembling a model on the kitchen table, or as complicated as turning detailed parts on a lathe in a home workshop.

Surprisingly, for some people, Craft Trains have nothing to do with building a layout! For them, Craft Trains offer the fun of building a mantlepiece model, a diorama or a miniature building. It's the "making" that counts. And working with your hands sets Craft Trains apart.

It all starts with a simple kit and from then on, it's up to each individual to set his or her own pace, to develop their own interests and to express their personal preferences.

Model Railroading is an Art Form, Too

There is also a third involvement in the hobby — that of the artist. To us, an artist is a person who wants to express his individuality in a chosen medium: wood or canvas, stone or steel, music or theatre, wire or plaster. Each spokesman selects his own medium.

Many people believe that Craft Trains are a 3-dimensional art form, in which a miniature empire can come to life under the control of its human creator.

We feel Craft Trains are all of these. Our job at Walthers is to try to do our best!

The Crew

Answering Questions

We are always glad to answer questions about the products listed in our catalog. However, we must ask your cooperation, in view of the large volume of mail we handle. PLEASE include a #10 SELF ADDRESSED, STAMPED ENVELOPE with your request.

Ask Your Dealer to Get it from Walthers

Yes, your dealer can get anything in this catalog from us and we hope that you will encourage him to do so. This doesn't mean that he will be able to stock everything —but he CAN get fast shipment from our complete inventory of kits, parts and accessories.

If, however, you are unable to find a local source of supply and desire to order by mail, you may send your order to us and we will forward it to Terminal Hobby Shop for processing.

Your Guarantee — You're the Boss

If for any reason, you are not satisfied with Walthers merchandise, we will refund your money.

This is a world of change and improvement and we reserve the right to make improvements, and change designs and prices when necessary — without notice — but if you do not like the new design, prices, or improvements, we will refund your money.

We do ask that you return the merchandise to us (or your dealer) in saleable condition.

If any part is missing or defective, we will replace it — unless it happens to be so old that we are not making it any more, in which case, we will do our best to supply a substitute.